Blue type indicates global example

W9-AQK-983

ECONOMICS IN ACTION

1: Boy or Girl? It Depends on the Cost, 10 ■ Restoring Equilibrium on the Freeways, 17 ■ Adventures in Babysitting, 20

2: Rich Nation, Poor Nation, 39 ■ Economists, Beyond the Ivory Tower, 43

3: Beating the Traffic, 78 ■ Only Creatures Small and Pampered, 85 ■ The Price of Admission, 89 ■ NEW: The Cotton Panic and Crash of 2001, 95

4: When Money Isn't Enough, 110 ■ High Times Down on the Farm, 115 ■ NEW: Take the Keys, Please, 121 ■ A Great Leap—Backward, 124

5: NEW: Price Controls in Venezuela: "You Buy What They Have," 140 ■ NEW: The Rise and Fall of the Unpaid Intern, 146 ■ NEW: Crabbing, Quotas, and Saving Lives in Alaska, 152

6: Estimating Elasticities, 165 ■ Responding to Your Tuition Bill, 173 ■ Spending It, 177 ■ European Farm Surpluses, 180

7: Who Pays the FICA?, 193 ■ Taxing the Marlboro Man, 202 ■ Federal Tax Philosophy, 205 ■ The Top Marginal Income Tax Rate, 210

8: NEW: How Hong Kong Lost Its Shirts, 226 ■ Trade, Wages, and Land Prices in the Nineteenth Century, 233 ■ Trade Protection in the United States, 237 ■ Beefing Up Exports, 242

9: Farming in the Shadow of Suburbia, 254 ■ The Cost of a Life, 263 ■ A Billion Here, a Billion There..., 264 ■ "The Jingle Mail Blues," 269

10: Oysters versus Chicken, 284 ■ The Great Condiment Craze, 289 ■ Buying Your Way Out of Temptation, 294 ■ Mortgage Rates and Consumer Demand, 296

11: The Mythical Man-Month, 336 ■ NEW: Smart Grid Economics, 344 ■ There's No Business Like Snow Business, 350

12: NEW: Paid to Delay, 360 ■ NEW: Farmers Move Up Their Supply Curves, 371 ■ NEW: From Global Wine Glut to Shortage, 378

13: Newly Emerging Markets: A Diamond Monopolist's Best Friend, 392 ■ Shocked by the High Price of Electricity, 399 ■ NEW: Why Is Your Broadband So Slow? And Why Does It Cost So Much?, 406 ■ Sales, Factory Outlets, and Ghost Cities, 412

14: Is It an Oligopoly, or Not?, 421 ■ Bitter Chocolate?, 425 ■ The Rise and Fall and Rise of OPEC, 431 ■ The Price Wars of Christmas, 438

15: Any Color, So Long as It's Black, 449 ■ The Housing Bust and the Demise of the 6% Commission, 454 ■ NEW: The Perfume Industry: Leading Customers by the Nose, 459

16: NEW: How Much Does Your Electricity Really Cost?, 471 ■ Cap and Trade, 477 ■ The Impeccable Economic Logic of Early-Childhood Intervention Programs, 480 ■ The Microsoft Case, 483

17: From Mayhem to Renaissance, 492 ■ Old Man River, 498 ■ Saving the Oceans with ITQs, 502 ■ Blacked-Out Games, 504

18: Long-term Trends in Income Inequality in the United States, 519 ■ NEW: Programs and Poverty in the Great Recession, 524 ■ What Medicaid Does, 533 ■ French Family Values, 536

19: The Factor Distribution of Income in the United States, 545 ■ Help Wanted!, 555 ■ Marginal Productivity and the "1%", 562 ■ The Decline of the Summer Job, 568

20: Warranties, 588 ■ When Lloyd's Almost Llost It, 596 ■ Franchise Owners Try Harder, 600

BUSINESS CASES

1: How Priceline.com Revolutionized the Travel Industry, 21

2: Efficiency, Opportunity Cost, and the Logic of Lean Production at Boeing, 45

3: NEW: An Uber Way to Get a Ride, 97

4: StubHub Shows Up the Boss, 126

5: Medallion Financial: Cruising Right Along, 154

6: The Airline Industry: Fly Less, Charge More, 182

7: Amazon versus BarnesandNoble.com, 211

8: Li & Fung: From Guangzhou to You, 244

9: NEW: J. C. Penney's One-Price Strategy Upsets Its Customers, 271

10: Having a Happy Meal at McDonald's, 298

11: Kiva Systems' Robots versus Humans: The Challenge of Holiday Order Fulfillment, 351

12: Shopping Apps, Showrooming, and the Challenges Facing Brick-and-Mortar Retailers, 379

13: NEW: Amazon and Hachette Go to War, 414

14: Virgin Atlantic Blows the Whistle...or Blows It?, 440

15: Gillette versus Schick: A Case of Razor Burn?, 461

16: NEW: Are We Still Friends? A Tale of Facebook, MySpace, and Friendster, 485

17: Mauricedale Game Ranch and Hunting Endangered Animals to Save Them, 506

18: Welfare State Entrepreneurs, 538

19: NEW: Wages and Workers at Costco and Walmart, 569

20: The Agony of AIG, 602

See inside back cover for Chapters 21–34

ECONOMICS

ECONOMICS

FOURTH EDITION

Paul Krugman
Princeton University

Robin Wells

WORTH
PUBLISHERS

A Macmillan Education Imprint

Vice President, Editorial: Charles Linsmeier

Publisher: Shani Fisher

Marketing Manager: Tom Digiano

Marketing Assistant: Alex Kaufman

Executive Development Editor: Sharon Balbos

Consultant: Ryan Herzog

Executive Media Editor: Rachel Comerford

Media Editor: Lukia Kliossis

Editorial Assistant: Carlos Marin

Director of Editing, Design, and Media Production:
   Tracey Kuehn

Managing Editor: Lisa Kinne

Project Editor: Jeanine Furino

Senior Design Manager: Vicki Tomaselli

Cover Design: Brian Sheridan, Hothouse Designs, Inc.

Illustrations: TSI evolve, Network Graphics

Illustration Coordinator: Janice Donnola

Photo Editor: Cecilia Varas

Photo Researcher: Elyse Rieder

Production Managers: Barbara Anne Seixas,
   Stacey Alexander

Supplements Project Editor: Edgar Bonilla

Composition: TSI evolve

Printing and Binding: RR Donnelley

ISBN-13: 978-1-4641-4384-7

ISBN-10: 1-4641-4384-6

Library of Congress Control Number: 2015930273

Printed in the United States of America

Second printing

Worth Publishers
41 Madison Avenue
New York, NY 10010

www.worthpublishers.com

Cover Photos Credits

Central Photo: Lobby in the rush hour is made in the manner of blur and a blue tonality: *blurAZ/Shutterstock*

First Row (left to right): Female Korean factory worker: *Image Source/Getty Images;* Market food: *Izzy Schwartz/Getty Images;* High gas prices in Fremont, California: *Mpiotti/Getty Images*

Second Row: Red sports car: *Shutterstock;* View of smoking coal power plant: *iStockphoto/Thinkstock;* Lab technician using microscope: *Jim Arbogast/Getty Images*

Third Row: Lightbulbs in box: © *fStop/Alamy;* Market food: *Izzy Schwartz/Getty Images*

Fourth Row: Set of coloured flags of many nations of the world: © *FC_Italy/Alamy;* Stack of cargo containers at sunrise in an intermodal yard: *Shutterstock;* Depression era photo of man holding sign: *The Image Works*

Fifth Row: Stock market quotes from a computer screen: *Stephen VanHorn/Shutterstock;* Portrait of a college student on campus: *pkchai/Shutterstock;* Peaches: *Stockbyte/Photodisc*

Sixth Row: Rear view of people window shopping: *Thinkstock;* Power plant pipes: *Corbis;* Power lines: *Brand X Pictures;* Three students taking a test: © *Royalty-Free/Corbis;* Paper money: *Shutterstock*

Seventh Row: Woman from the Sacred Valley of the Incas: *hadynyah/Getty Images;* Paint buckets with various colored paint: *Shutterstock;* Close up of hands woman using her cell phone: *Shutterstock;* Paper money: *Shutterstock*

Eighth Row: Cows: *Stockbyte/Photodisc;* Wind turbine farm over sunset: *Ted Nad/Shutterstock;* Wall Street sign: *thinkstock;* Busy shopping street Center Gai Shibuya, Tokyo: *Tom Bonaventure/Photographer's Choice RF/Getty Images;* Paper money: *Shutterstock*

Ninth/Tenth Rows: Waiter in Panjim: *Steven Miric/Getty Images;* Group of friends carrying shopping bags on city street: *Monkey Business Images/Shutterstock;* Set of coloured flags of many nations of the world: © *FC_Italy/Alamy;* Soybean Field: *Fotokostic/Shutterstock;* Drilling rig workers: *Istockphoto;* Tropical fish and hard corals in the Red Sea, Egypt: *Vlad61/Shutterstock;* Modern train on platform: *Shutterstock*

Eleventh/Twelfth Rows: Paper money: *Shutterstock;* View of smoking coal power plant: *iStockphoto/Thinkstock;* Welder: *Tristan Savatier/Getty Images;* container ship: *EvrenKalinbacak/Shutterstock;* Market food: *Izzy Schwartz/Getty Images;* Modern train on platform: *Shutterstock*

Thirteenth Row: Printing U.S. dollar banknotes: *Thinkstock;* Stock market quotes from a computer screen: *Stephen VanHorn/Shutterstock*

To beginning students everywhere,
which we all were at one time.

Paul Krugman, recipient of the 2008 Nobel Memorial Prize in Economic Sciences, taught at Princeton University for 14 years and, as of June 2015, he will have joined the faculty of the Graduate Center of the City University of New York. In his new position, he is associated with the Luxembourg Income Study, which tracks and analyzes income inequality around the world. He received his BA from Yale and his PhD from MIT. Before Princeton, he taught at Yale, Stanford, and MIT. He also spent a year on the staff of the Council of Economic Advisers in 1982–1983. His research has included pathbreaking work on international trade, economic geography, and currency crises. In 1991,

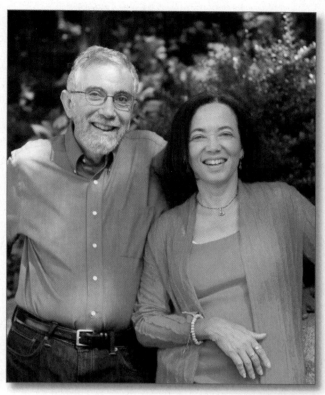

Ligaya Franklin

Krugman received the American Economic Association's John Bates Clark medal. In addition to his teaching and academic research, Krugman writes extensively for nontechnical audiences. He is a regular op-ed columnist for the *New York Times*. His best-selling trade books include *End This Depression Now!, The Return of Depression Economics and the Crisis of 2008,* a history of recent economic troubles and their implications for economic policy, and *The Conscience of a Liberal,* a study of the political economy of economic inequality and its relationship with political polarization from the Gilded Age to the present. His earlier books, *Peddling Prosperity* and *The Age of Diminished Expectations,* have become modern classics.

Robin Wells was a Lecturer and Researcher in Economics at Princeton University. She received her BA from the University of Chicago and her PhD from the University of California at Berkeley; she then did postdoctoral work at MIT. She has taught at the University of Michigan, the University of Southampton (United Kingdom), Stanford, and MIT.

BRIEF CONTENTS

Preface xxv

PART 1 What Is Economics?

Introduction The Ordinary Business of Life 1
Chapter 1 First Principles 5
Chapter 2 Economic Models: Trade-offs and Trade 25
Appendix Graphs in Economics 51

PART 2 Supply and Demand

Chapter 3 Supply and Demand 67
Chapter 4 Consumer and Producer Surplus 103
Chapter 5 Price Controls and Quotas: Meddling with Markets 131
Chapter 6 Elasticity 161

PART 3 Individuals and Markets

Chapter 7 Taxes 187
Chapter 8 International Trade 217

PART 4 Economics and Decision Making

Chapter 9 Decision Making by Individuals and Firms 249
Appendix Toward a Fuller Understanding of Present Value 277

PART 5 The Consumer

Chapter 10 The Rational Consumer 281
Appendix Consumer Preferences and Consumer Choice 303

PART 6 The Production Decision

Chapter 11 Behind the Supply Curve: Inputs and Costs 329
Chapter 12 Perfect Competition and the Supply Curve 357

PART 7 Market Structure: Beyond Perfect Competition

Chapter 13 Monopoly 385
Chapter 14 Oligopoly 419
Chapter 15 Monopolistic Competition and Product Differentiation 445

PART 8 Microeconomics and Public Policy

Chapter 16 Externalities 465
Chapter 17 Public Goods and Common Resources 489

Chapter 18 The Economics of the Welfare State 511

PART 9 Factor Markets and Risk

Chapter 19 Factor Markets and the Distribution of Income 543
Appendix Indifference Curve Analysis of Labor Supply 575
Chapter 20 Uncertainty, Risk, and Private Information 581

PART 10 Introduction to Macroeconomics

Chapter 21 Macroeconomics: The Big Picture 607
Chapter 22 GDP and the CPI: Tracking the Macroeconomy 629
Chapter 23 Unemployment and Inflation 655

PART 11 Long-Run Economic Growth

Chapter 24 Long-Run Economic Growth 683
Chapter 25 Savings, Investment Spending, and the Financial System 717

PART 12 Short-Run Economic Fluctuations

Chapter 26 Income and Expenditure 751
Appendix Deriving the Multiplier Algebraically 781
Chapter 27 Aggregate Demand and Aggregate Supply 783

PART 13 Stabilization Policy

Chapter 28 Fiscal Policy 819
Appendix Taxes and the Multiplier 851
Chapter 29 Money, Banking, and the Federal Reserve System 853
Chapter 30 Monetary Policy 889
Appendix Reconciling the Two Models of the Interest Rate 915
Chapter 31 Inflation, Disinflation, and Deflation 919
Chapter 32 Crises and Consequences 947

PART 14 Events and Ideas

Chapter 33 Macroeconomics: Events and Ideas 973

PART 15 The Open Economy

Chapter 34 Open-Economy Macroeconomics 997

Macroeconomic Data Tables M-1
Solutions to "Check Your Understanding" Questions S-1
Glossary G-1
Index I-1

CONTENTS

Preface xxv

PART 1 What Is Economics?

▶ INTRODUCTION The Ordinary
Business of Life 1

ANY GIVEN SUNDAY 1

The Invisible Hand 2

My Benefit, Your Cost 3

Good Times, Bad Times 3

Onward and Upward 4

An Engine for Discovery 4

▶ CHAPTER 1 First Principles 5

COMMON GROUND 5

Principles That Underlie Individual Choice:
The Core of Economics 6

   Principle #1: Choices Are Necessary Because
   Resources Are Scarce 6

   Principle #2: The True Cost of Something Is Its
   Opportunity Cost 7

   Principle #3: "How Much" Is a Decision at
   the Margin 8

   Principle #4: People Usually Respond to
   Incentives, Exploiting Opportunities to Make
   Themselves Better Off 9

FOR INQUIRING MINDS: Cashing In at School 10

ECONOMICS ➤ IN ACTION Boy or Girl? It Depends
                      on the Cost 10

Interaction: How Economies Work 12

   Principle #5: There Are Gains from Trade 12

   Principle #6: Markets Move Toward Equilibrium 13

FOR INQUIRING MINDS: Choosing Sides 14

   Principle #7: Resources Should Be Used Efficiently to
   Achieve Society's Goals 15

   Principle #8: Markets Usually Lead to Efficiency 16

   Principle #9: When Markets Don't Achieve Efficiency,
   Government Intervention Can Improve Society's
   Welfare 16

ECONOMICS ➤ IN ACTION Restoring Equilibrium on
                      the Freeways 17

Economy-Wide Interactions 18

   Principle #10: One Person's Spending Is Another
   Person's Income 18

   Principle #11: Overall Spending Sometimes Gets Out
   of Line with the Economy's Productive Capacity 19

   Principle #12: Government Policies Can Change
   Spending 19

ECONOMICS ➤ IN ACTION Adventures in Babysitting 20

BUSINESS CASE: How Priceline.com Revolutionized the Travel
              Industry 21

▶ CHAPTER 2 Economics Models:
Trade-offs and Trade 25

FROM KITTY HAWK TO DREAMLINER 25

Models in Economics: Some Important Examples 26

FOR INQUIRING MINDS: The Model That Ate the Economy 26

   Trade-offs: The Production Possibility Frontier 27

   Comparative Advantage and Gains from Trade 33

   Comparative Advantage and International Trade,
   in Reality 36

GLOBAL COMPARISON: Pajama Republics 37

   Transactions: The Circular-Flow Diagram 37

ECONOMICS ➤ IN ACTION Rich Nation, Poor Nation 39

Using Models 40

   Positive versus Normative Economics 40

   When and Why Economists Disagree 41

FOR INQUIRING MINDS: When Economists Agree 42

ECONOMICS ➤ IN ACTION Economists, Beyond the
                      Ivory Tower 43

BUSINESS CASE: Efficiency, Opportunity Cost, and
              the Logic of Lean Production 45

CHAPTER 2 APPENDIX Graphs in
Economics 51

Getting the Picture 51

Graphs, Variables, and Economic Models 51

How Graphs Work 51

   Two-Variable Graphs 51

   Curves on a Graph 53

A Key Concept: The Slope of a Curve 54

   The Slope of a Linear Curve 54

   Horizontal and Vertical Curves and Their Slopes 55

   The Slope of a Nonlinear Curve 56

   Calculating the Slope Along a Nonlinear Curve 56

   Maximum and Minimum Points 58

Calculating the Area Below or Above a Curve **59**
Graphs That Depict Numerical Information **60**
   Types of Numerical Graphs **60**
   Problems in Interpreting Numerical Graphs **62**

PART **2** Supply and Demand

▶ CHAPTER **3** Supply and Demand **67**

A NATURAL GAS BOOM **67**
Supply and Demand: A Model of a Competitive Market 68
The Demand Curve 69
   The Demand Schedule and the Demand Curve **69**
   Shifts of the Demand Curve **70**
GLOBAL COMPARISON: Pay More, Pump Less **71**
   Understanding Shifts of the Demand Curve **73**
ECONOMICS ➤ IN ACTION Beating the Traffic **78**
The Supply Curve 79
   The Supply Schedule and the Supply Curve **79**
   Shifts of the Supply Curve **80**
   Understanding Shifts of the Supply Curve **81**
ECONOMICS ➤ IN ACTION Only Creatures Small and Pampered **85**
Supply, Demand, and Equilibrium 86
   Finding the Equilibrium Price and Quantity **86**
   Why Do All Sales and Purchases in a Market Take Place at the Same Price? **87**
   Why Does the Market Price Fall If It Is Above the Equilibrium Price? **88**
   Why Does the Market Price Rise If It Is Below the Equilibrium Price? **88**
   Using Equilibrium to Describe Markets **89**
ECONOMICS ➤ IN ACTION The Price of Admission **89**
Changes in Supply and Demand 90
   What Happens When the Demand Curve Shifts **91**
   What Happens When the Supply Curve Shifts **92**
   Simultaneous Shifts of Supply and Demand Curves **93**
FOR INQUIRING MINDS: Tribulations on the Runway **94**
ECONOMICS ➤ IN ACTION The Cotton Panic and Crash of 2011 **95**
Competitive Markets—And Others 96
BUSINESS CASE: An Uber Way to Get a Ride **97**

▶ CHAPTER **4** Consumer and Producer Surplus **103**

MAKING GAINS BY THE BOOK **103**
Consumer Surplus and the Demand Curve 104
   Willingness to Pay and the Demand Curve **104**

   Willingness to Pay and Consumer Surplus **104**
   How Changing Prices Affect Consumer Surplus **107**
FOR INQUIRING MINDS: A Matter of Life and Death **110**
ECONOMICS ➤ IN ACTION When Money Isn't Enough **110**
Producer Surplus and the Supply Curve 111
   Cost and Producer Surplus **111**
   How Changing Prices Affect Producer Surplus **114**
ECONOMICS ➤ IN ACTION High Times Down on the Farm **115**
Consumer Surplus, Producer Surplus, and the Gains from Trade 116
   The Gains from Trade **116**
   The Efficiency of Markets **117**
   Equity and Efficiency **121**
ECONOMICS ➤ IN ACTION Take the Keys, Please **121**
A Market Economy 122
   Why Markets Typically Work So Well **123**
   A Few Words of Caution **124**
ECONOMICS ➤ IN ACTION A Great Leap—Backward **125**
BUSINESS CASE: StubHub Shows Up The Boss **126**

▶ CHAPTER **5** Price Controls and Quotas: Meddling with Markets **131**

BIG CITY, NOT-SO-BRIGHT IDEAS **131**
Why Governments Control Prices 132
Price Ceilings 132
   Modeling a Price Ceiling **133**
   How a Price Ceiling Causes Inefficiency **134**
FOR INQUIRING MINDS: Winners, Losers, and Rent Control **136**
FOR INQUIRING MINDS: Mumbai's Rent-Control Millionaires **138**
   So Why Are There Price Ceilings? **139**
ECONOMICS ➤ IN ACTION Price Controls in Venezuela: "You Buy What They Have" **140**
Price Floors 141
   How a Price Floor Causes Inefficiency **143**
GLOBAL COMPARISON: Check Out Our Low, Low Wages! **145**
   So Why Are There Price Floors? **146**
ECONOMICS ➤ IN ACTION The Rise and Fall of the Unpaid Intern **146**
Controlling Quantities 147
   The Anatomy of Quantity Controls **148**
   The Costs of Quantity Controls **151**
ECONOMICS ➤ IN ACTION Crabbing, Quotas, and Saving Lives in Alaska **152**
BUSINESS CASE: Medallion Financial: Cruising Right Along **154**

▶ **CHAPTER 6** Elasticity 161

TAKEN FOR A RIDE 161

Defining and Measuring Elasticity 162

Calculating the Price Elasticity of Demand 162

An Alternative Way to Calculate Elasticities:
The Midpoint Method **164**

ECONOMICS ➤ *IN ACTION* Estimating Elasticities **165**

Interpreting the Price Elasticity of Demand 166

How Elastic Is Elastic? **166**

Price Elasticity Along the Demand Curve **171**

What Factors Determine the Price Elasticity
of Demand? **172**

ECONOMICS ➤ *IN ACTION* Responding to Your Tuition
Bill **173**

Other Demand Elasticities 174

The Cross-Price Elasticity of Demand **174**

The Income Elasticity of Demand **175**

FOR INQUIRING MINDS: Will China Save the U.S
Farming Sector? **176**

GLOBAL COMPARISON: Food's Bite in World Budgets **176**

ECONOMICS ➤ *IN ACTION* Spending It **177**

The Price Elasticity of Supply 177

Measuring the Price Elasticity of Supply **178**

What Factors Determine the Price Elasticity of
Supply? **179**

ECONOMICS ➤ *IN ACTION* European Farm Surpluses **180**

An Elasticity Menagerie 181

BUSINESS CASE: The Airline Industry: Fly Less, Charge
More **182**

PART 3 Individuals and Markets

▶ **CHAPTER 7** Taxes 187

THE FOUNDING TAXERS 187

The Economics of Taxes: A Preliminary View 188

The Effect of an Excise Tax on Quantities and
Prices **188**

Price Elasticities and Tax Incidence **191**

ECONOMICS ➤ *IN ACTION* Who Pays the FICA? **193**

The Benefits and Costs of Taxation 194

The Revenue from an Excise Tax **194**

Tax Rates and Revenue **195**

FOR INQUIRING MINDS: French Tax Rates and *L'Arc Laffer* **197**

The Costs of Taxation **198**

Elasticities and the Deadweight Loss of a Tax **200**

ECONOMICS ➤ *IN ACTION* Taxing the Marlboro Man **202**

Tax Fairness and Tax Efficiency 203

Two Principles of Tax Fairness **203**

Equity versus Efficiency **204**

ECONOMICS ➤ *IN ACTION* Federal Tax Philosophy **205**

Understanding the Tax System 206

Tax Bases and Tax Structure **206**

Equity, Efficiency, and Progressive Taxation **207**

Taxes in the United States **208**

GLOBAL COMPARISON: You Think You Pay High Taxes? **209**

Different Taxes, Different Principles **209**

FOR INQUIRING MINDS: Taxing Income versus Taxing
Consumption **209**

ECONOMICS ➤ *IN ACTION* The Top Marginal Income Tax
Rate **210**

BUSINESS CASE: Amazon versus BarnesandNoble.com **211**

▶ **CHAPTER 8** International Trade 217

THE EVERYWHERE PHONE 217

Comparative Advantage and International Trade 218

Production Possibilities and Comparative
Advantage, Revisited **219**

The Gains from International Trade **221**

Comparative Advantage versus Absolute
Advantage **222**

GLOBAL COMPARISON: Productivity and Wages Around
the World **223**

Sources of Comparative Advantage **224**

FOR INQUIRING MINDS: Increasing Returns to Scale and
International Trade **226**

ECONOMICS ➤ *IN ACTION* How Hong Kong Lost
Its Shirts **226**

Supply, Demand, and International Trade 227

The Effects of Imports **228**

The Effects of Exports **230**

International Trade and Wages **232**

ECONOMICS ➤ *IN ACTION* Trade, Wages, and Land Prices
in the Nineteenth Century **233**

The Effects of Trade Protection 234

The Effects of a Tariff **234**

The Effects of an Import Quota **236**

ECONOMICS ➤ *IN ACTION* Trade Protection in the United
States **237**

The Political Economy of Trade Protection 238

Arguments for Trade Protection **238**

The Politics of Trade Protection **238**

International Trade Agreements and the World Trade
Organization **239**

FOR INQUIRING MINDS: Tires Under Pressure **240**

Challenges to Globalization **240**

ECONOMICS ➤ *IN ACTION* Beefing Up Exports **242**

BUSINESS CASE: Li & Fung: From Guangzhou to You **244**

PART 4 Economics and Decision Making

▶CHAPTER 9 Decision Making by Individuals and Firms 249

GOING BACK TO SCHOOL 249

Costs, Benefits, and Profits 250

Explicit versus Implicit Costs 250

Accounting Profit versus Economic Profit 251

Making "Either–Or" Decisions 253

FOR INQUIRING MINDS: A Tale of Two Invasions 253

ECONOMICS ➤ IN ACTION Farming in the Shadow of Suburbia 254

Making "How Much" Decisions: The Role of Marginal Analysis 255

Marginal Cost 256

Marginal Benefit 258

Marginal Analysis 259

GLOBAL COMPARISON: Portion Sizes 261

A Principle with Many Uses 262

ECONOMICS ➤ IN ACTION The Cost of a Life 263

Sunk Costs 263

ECONOMICS ➤ IN ACTION A Billion Here, a Billion There... 264

Behavioral Economics 265

Rational, but Human, Too 265

Irrationality: An Economist's View 266

FOR INQUIRING MINDS: In Praise of Hard Deadlines 267

Rational Models for Irrational People? 269

ECONOMICS ➤ IN ACTION "The Jingle Mail Blues" 269

BUSINESS CASE: J. C. Penney's One-Price Strategy Upsets Its Customers 271

CHAPTER 9 APPENDIX **Toward a Fuller Understanding of Present Value** 277

How to Calculate the Present Value of One-Year Projects 277

How to Calculate the Present Value of Multiyear Projects 278

How to Calculate the Present Value of Projects with Revenues and Costs 279

PART 5 The Consumer

▶CHAPTER 10 **The Rational Consumer** 281

A CLAM TOO FAR 281

Utility: Getting Satisfaction 282

Utility and Consumption 282

The Principle of Diminishing Marginal Utility 283

FOR INQUIRING MINDS: Is Marginal Utility Really Diminishing? 284

ECONOMICS ➤ IN ACTION Oysters versus Chicken 284

Budgets and Optimal Consumption 285

Budget Constraints and Budget Lines 285

Optimal Consumption Choice 287

FOR INQUIRING MINDS: Food for Thought on Budget Constraints 288

ECONOMICS ➤ IN ACTION The Great Condiment Craze 289

Spending the Marginal Dollar 290

Marginal Utility per Dollar 291

Optimal Consumption 292

ECONOMICS ➤ IN ACTION Buying Your Way Out of Temptation 294

From Utility to the Demand Curve 294

Marginal Utility, the Substitution Effect, and the Law of Demand 294

The Income Effect 295

ECONOMICS ➤ IN ACTION Mortgage Rates and Consumer Demand 296

BUSINESS CASE: Having a Happy Meal at McDonald's 298

CHAPTER 10 APPENDIX **Consumer Preferences and Consumer Choice** 303

Mapping the Utility Function 303

Indifference Curves 303

Properties of Indifference Curves 306

Indifference Curves and Consumer Choice 307

The Marginal Rate of Substitution 308

The Tangency Condition 311

The Slope of the Budget Line 312

Prices and the Marginal Rate of Substitution 313

Preferences and Choices 315

Using Indifference Curves: Substitutes and Complements 316

Perfect Substitutes 316

Perfect Complements 318

Less Extreme Cases 319

Prices, Income, and Demand 319

The Effects of a Price Increase **319**

Income and Consumption **320**

Income and Substitution Effects **323**

PART 6 The Production Decision

▶**CHAPTER 11 Behind the Supply Curve: Inputs and Costs**....................**329**

THE FARMER'S MARGIN **329**

The Production Function 330

Inputs and Output **330**

GLOBAL COMPARISON: Wheat Yields Around the World **332**

From the Production Function to Cost Curves **334**

ECONOMICS ➤ *IN ACTION* The Mythical Man-Month **336**

Two Key Concepts: Marginal Cost and Average Cost 337

Marginal Cost **337**

Average Total Cost **339**

Minimum Average Total Cost **342**

Does the Marginal Cost Curve Always Slope Upward? **343**

ECONOMICS ➤ *IN ACTION* Smart Grid Economics **344**

Short-Run versus Long-Run Costs 345

Returns to Scale **348**

Summing Up Costs: The Short and Long of It **349**

ECONOMICS ➤ *IN ACTION* There's No Business Like Snow Business **350**

BUSINESS CASE: Kiva Systems' Robots versus Humans: The Challenge of Holiday Order Fulfillment **351**

▶**CHAPTER 12 Perfect Competition and the Supply Curve**........**357**

DECK THE HALLS **357**

Perfect Competition 358

Defining Perfect Competition **358**

Two Necessary Conditions for Perfect Competition **358**

Free Entry and Exit **359**

FOR INQUIRING MINDS: What's a Standardized Product? **360**

ECONOMICS ➤ *IN ACTION* Paid to Delay **360**

Production and Profits 361

Using Marginal Analysis to Choose the Profit-Maximizing Quantity of Output **362**

When Is Production Profitable? **364**

The Short-Run Production Decision **367**

Changing Fixed Cost **370**

Summing Up: The Perfectly Competitive Firm's Profitability and Production Conditions **370**

ECONOMICS ➤ *IN ACTION* Farmers Move Up Their Supply Curves **371**

The Industry Supply Curve 372

The Short-Run Industry Supply Curve **372**

The Long-Run Industry Supply Curve **373**

The Cost of Production and Efficiency in Long-Run Equilibrium **377**

ECONOMICS ➤ *IN ACTION* From Global Wine Glut to Shortage **378**

BUSINESS CASE: Shopping Apps, Showrooming, and the Challenges Facing Brick-and-Mortar Retailers **379**

PART 7 Market Structure: Beyond Perfect Competition

▶**CHAPTER 13 Monopoly**....................**385**

EVERYBODY MUST GET STONES **385**

Types of Market Structure 386

The Meaning of Monopoly 387

Monopoly: Our First Departure from Perfect Competition **387**

What Monopolists Do **387**

Why Do Monopolies Exist? **389**

GLOBAL COMPARISON: The Price We Pay **391**

ECONOMICS ➤ *IN ACTION* Newly Emerging Markets: A Diamond Monopolist's Best Friend **392**

How a Monopolist Maximizes Profit 393

The Monopolist's Demand Curve and Marginal Revenue **393**

The Monopolist's Profit-Maximizing Output and Price **397**

Monopoly versus Perfect Competition **398**

Monopoly: The General Picture **398**

ECONOMICS ➤ *IN ACTION* Shocked by the High Price of Electricity **399**

Monopoly and Public Policy 400

Welfare Effects of Monopoly **401**

Preventing Monopoly **402**

Dealing with Natural Monopoly **402**

ECONOMICS ➤ *IN ACTION* Why Is Your Broadband So Slow? And Why Does It Cost So Much? **406**

Price Discrimination 407

The Logic of Price Discrimination **408**

Price Discrimination and Elasticity **409**

Perfect Price Discrimination **410**

ECONOMICS ➤ IN ACTION Sales, Factory Outlets, and Ghost Cities 412

BUSINESS CASE: Amazon and Hachette Go to War 414

▶CHAPTER 14 Oligopoly 419

CAUGHT IN THE ACT 419

The Prevalence of Oligopoly 420

ECONOMICS ➤ IN ACTION Is It an Oligopoly or Not? 421

Understanding Oligopoly 422

A Duopoly Example 422

Collusion and Competition 423

ECONOMICS ➤ IN ACTION Bitter Chocolate? 425

Games Oligopolists Play 426

The Prisoners' Dilemma 426

FOR INQUIRING MINDS: Prisoners of the Arms Race 429

Overcoming the Prisoners' Dilemma: Repeated Interaction and Tacit Collusion 429

ECONOMICS ➤ IN ACTION The Rise and Fall and Rise of OPEC 431

Oligopoly in Practice 433

The Legal Framework 433

GLOBAL COMPARISON: Contrasting Approaches to Antitrust Regulation 434

Tacit Collusion and Price Wars 435

Product Differentiation and Price Leadership 436

How Important Is Oligopoly? 437

ECONOMICS ➤ IN ACTION The Price Wars of Christmas 438

BUSINESS CASE: Virgin Atlantic Blows the Whistle … or Blows It? 440

▶CHAPTER 15 Monopolistic Competition and Product Differentiation 445

FAST-FOOD DIFFERENTIATION 445

The Meaning of Monopolistic Competition 446

Large Numbers 446

Differentiated Products 446

Free Entry and Exit in the Long Run 447

Product Differentiation 447

Differentiation by Style or Type 447

Differentiation by Location 448

Differentiation by Quality 448

ECONOMICS ➤ IN ACTION Any Color, So Long As It's Black 449

Understanding Monopolistic Competition 449

Monopolistic Competition in the Short Run 450

Monopolistic Competition in the Long Run 451

FOR INQUIRING MINDS: Hits and Flops 453

ECONOMICS ➤ IN ACTION The Housing Bust and the Demise of the 6% Commission 454

Monopolistic Competition versus Perfect Competition 455

Price, Marginal Cost, and Average Total Cost 455

Is Monopolistic Competition Inefficient? 456

Controversies About Product Differentiation 457

The Role of Advertising 457

Brand Names 458

ECONOMICS ➤ IN ACTION The Perfume Industry: Leading Consumers by the Nose 459

BUSINESS CASE: Gillette versus Schick: A Case of Razor Burn? 461

PART 8 Microeconomics and Public Policy

▶CHAPTER 16 Externalities 465

TROUBLE UNDERFOOT 465

External Costs and Benefits 466

FOR INQUIRING MINDS: Talking, Texting, and Driving 466

Pollution: An External Cost 467

The Socially Optimum Quantity of Pollution 467

Why a Market Economy Produces Too Much Pollution 468

Private Solutions to Externalities 469

ECONOMICS ➤ IN ACTION How Much Does Your Electricity Really Cost? 471

Policies Toward Pollution 472

Environmental Standards 472

Emissions Taxes 473

GLOBAL COMPARISON: Economic Growth and Greenhouse Gases in Six Countries 473

Tradable Emissions Permits 474

Comparing Environmental Policies with an Example 475

ECONOMICS ➤ IN ACTION Cap and Trade 477

Positive Externalities 478

Preserved Farmland: An External Benefit 479

Positive Externalities in Today's Economy 480

ECONOMICS ➤ IN ACTION The Impeccable Economic Logic of Early-Childhood Intervention Programs 480

Network Externalities 481

The External Benefits of a Network Externality 481

ECONOMICS ➤ IN ACTION The Microsoft Case 483

BUSINESS CASE: Are We Still Friends? A Tale of Facebook, MySpace, and Friendster 485

▶CHAPTER **17** Public Goods and
Common Resources...........489

THE GREAT STINK 489

Private Goods—and Others 490

Characteristics of Goods 490

Why Markets Can Supply Only Private Goods
Efficiently 491

ECONOMICS ➤ *IN ACTION* From Mayhem to
Renaissance 492

Public Goods 493

Providing Public Goods 493

How Much of a Public Good Should Be Provided? 494

FOR INQUIRING MINDS: Voting as a Public Good 496

GLOBAL COMPARISON: Voting as a Public Good: The Global
Perspective 496

Cost-Benefit Analysis 497

ECONOMICS ➤ *IN ACTION* Old Man River 498

Common Resources 499

The Problem of Overuse 499

FOR INQUIRING MINDS: When Fertile Farmland Turned
to Dust 501

The Efficient Use and Maintenance of a Common
Resource 501

ECONOMICS ➤ *IN ACTION* Saving the Oceans with
ITQs 502

Artificially Scarce Goods 503

ECONOMICS ➤ *IN ACTION* Blacked-Out Games 504

BUSINESS CASE: Mauricedale Game Ranch and Hunting
Endangered Animals to Save Them 506

▶CHAPTER **18** The Economics of
the Welfare State...................511

THE COMING OF OBAMACARE 511

Poverty, Inequality, and Public Policy 512

The Logic of the Welfare State 512

FOR INQUIRING MINDS: Justice and the Welfare State 513

The Problem of Poverty 513

GLOBAL COMPARISON: Redistribution and Inequality in Rich
Countries 515

Economic Inequality 517

Economic Insecurity 519

ECONOMICS ➤ *IN ACTION* Long-Term Trends in Income
Inequality in the United
States 519

The U.S. Welfare State 521

Means-Tested Programs 522

Social Security and Unemployment Insurance 523

The Effects of the Welfare State on Poverty and
Inequality 523

ECONOMICS ➤ *IN ACTION* Welfare State Programs and
Poverty Rates in the Great
Recession, 2007–2010 524

The Economics of Health Care 525

The Need for Health Insurance 525

FOR INQUIRING MINDS: A California Death Spiral 527

Government Health Insurance 527

The Problem of the Uninsured Before the Affordable
Care Act 528

Health Care in Other Countries 529

The Affordable Care Act 530

ECONOMICS ➤ *IN ACTION* What Medicaid Does 533

The Debate over the Welfare State 534

Problems with the Welfare State 534

The Politics of the Welfare State 535

FOR INQUIRING MINDS: "We Are the 99%!" 536

ECONOMICS ➤ *IN ACTION* French Family Values 536

BUSINESS CASE: Welfare State Entrepreneurs 538

PART **9** Factor Markets and Risk

▶CHAPTER **19** Factor Markets and
the Distribution of
Income...............................543

THE VALUE OF A DEGREE 543

The Economy's Factors of Production 544

The Factors of Production 544

Why Factor Prices Matter: The Allocation of
Resources 544

Factor Incomes and the Distribution of Income 544

FOR INQUIRING MINDS: The Factor Distribution of Income and
Social Change in the Industrial
Revolution 545

ECONOMICS ➤ *IN ACTION* The Factor Distribution
of Income in the United
States 545

Marginal Productivity and Factor Demand 546

Value of the Marginal Product 546

Value of the Marginal Product and Factor Demand 548

Shifts of the Factor Demand Curve 550

The Marginal Productivity Theory of Income
Distribution 551

The Markets for Land and Capital 553

The Marginal Productivity Theory of Income
Distribution 555

ECONOMICS ➤ *IN ACTION* Help Wanted! 555

**Is the Marginal Productivity Theory of Income
Distribution Really True?** 556

Wage Disparities in Practice 557

Marginal Productivity and Wage Inequality **558**

Market Power **559**

Efficiency Wages **560**

Discrimination **561**

FOR INQUIRING MINDS: How Labor Works the German Way **561**

So Does Marginal Productivity Theory Work? **562**

ECONOMICS ➤ IN ACTION Marginal Productivity and the "1%" **562**

The Supply of Labor 563

Work versus Leisure **563**

Wages and Labor Supply **564**

FOR INQUIRING MINDS: Why You Can't Find a Cab When It's Raining **566**

Shifts of the Labor Supply Curve **566**

GLOBAL COMPARISON: The Overworked American? **567**

ECONOMICS ➤ IN ACTION The Decline of the Summer Job **568**

BUSINESS CASE: Wages and Workers at Costco and Walmart **569**

CHAPTER 19 APPENDIX Indifference Curve Analysis of Labor Supply 575

The Time Allocation Budget Line 575

The Effect of a Higher Wage Rate 576

Indifference Curve Analysis 579

▶CHAPTER 20 Uncertainty, Risk, and Private Information 581

EXTREME WEATHER **581**

The Economics of Risk Aversion 582

Expectations and Uncertainty **582**

The Logic of Risk Aversion **583**

FOR INQUIRING MINDS: The Paradox of Gambling **587**

Paying to Avoid Risk **587**

ECONOMICS ➤ IN ACTION Warranties **588**

Buying, Selling, and Reducing Risk 588

Trading Risk **589**

Making Risk Disappear: The Power of Diversification **592**

FOR INQUIRING MINDS: Those Pesky Emotions **594**

The Limits of Diversification **595**

ECONOMICS ➤ IN ACTION When Lloyd's Almost Lost It **596**

Private Information: What You Don't Know Can Hurt You 596

Adverse Selection: The Economics of Lemons **597**

Moral Hazard **599**

ECONOMICS ➤ IN ACTION Franchise Owners Try Harder **600**

BUSINESS CASE: The Agony of AIG **602**

PART **10** Introduction to Macroeconomics

▶CHAPTER **21** Macroeconomics: The Big Picture.....................607

THE PAIN IN SPAIN **607**

The Nature of Macroeconomics 608

Macroeconomic Questions **608**

Macroeconomics: The Whole Is Greater Than the Sum of Its Parts **609**

Macroeconomics: Theory and Policy **609**

ECONOMICS ➤ IN ACTION Fending Off Depression **610**

The Business Cycle 611

Charting the Business Cycle **612**

The Pain of Recession **613**

FOR INQUIRING MINDS: Defining Recessions and Expansions **614**

Taming the Business Cycle **615**

GLOBAL COMPARISON: Slumps Across the Atlantic **615**

ECONOMICS ➤ IN ACTION Comparing Recessions **616**

Long-Run Economic Growth 616

FOR INQUIRING MINDS: When Did Long-Run Growth Start? **618**

ECONOMICS ➤ IN ACTION A Tale of Two Countries **618**

Inflation and Deflation 619

The Causes of Inflation and Deflation **619**

The Pain of Inflation and Deflation **620**

ECONOMICS ➤ IN ACTION A Fast (Food) Measure of Inflation **620**

International Imbalances 621

ECONOMICS ➤ IN ACTION Spain's Costly Surplus **622**

BUSINESS CASE: The Business Cycle and the Decline of Montgomery Ward **624**

▶CHAPTER **22** GDP and the CPI: Tracking the Macroeconomy...........629

THE NEW #2 **629**

The National Accounts 630

The Circular-Flow Diagram, Revisited and Expanded **630**

Gross Domestic Product **633**

Calculating GDP **634**

FOR INQUIRING MINDS: Our Imputed Lives **635**

FOR INQUIRING MINDS: Gross What? **638**

What GDP Tells Us **639**

ECONOMICS ➤ *IN ACTION* Creating the National
Accounts **639**

Real GDP: A Measure of Aggregate Output 640

Calculating Real GDP **640**

What Real GDP Doesn't Measure **641**

GLOBAL COMPARISON: GDP and the Meaning of Life **642**

ECONOMICS ➤ *IN ACTION* Miracle in Venezuela? **643**

Price Indexes and the Aggregate Price Level 643

Market Baskets and Price Indexes **644**

The Consumer Price Index **645**

Other Price Measures **646**

ECONOMICS ➤ *IN ACTION* Indexing to the CPI **647**

BUSINESS CASE: Getting a Jump on GDP **649**

▶ CHAPTER **23** Unemployment and
Inflation **655**

HITTING THE BRAKING POINT **655**

The Unemployment Rate 656

Defining and Measuring Unemployment **656**

The Significance of the Unemployment Rate **657**

Growth and Unemployment **659**

ECONOMICS ➤ *IN ACTION* Failure to Launch **661**

The Natural Rate of Unemployment 662

Job Creation and Job Destruction **662**

Frictional Unemployment **663**

Structural Unemployment **665**

The Natural Rate of Unemployment **667**

GLOBAL COMPARISON: Natural Unemployment Around the
OECD **668**

Changes in the Natural Rate of Unemployment **668**

ECONOMICS ➤ *IN ACTION* Structural Unemployment in
East Germany **670**

Inflation and Deflation 671

The Level of Prices Doesn't Matter . . . **671**

. . . But the Rate of Change of Prices Does **672**

Winners and Losers from Inflation **675**

Inflation Is Easy; Disinflation Is Hard **676**

ECONOMICS ➤ *IN ACTION* Israel's Experience with
Inflation **677**

BUSINESS CASE: Day Labor in the Information Age **678**

PART 11 Long-Run Economic Growth

▶ CHAPTER **24** Long-Run Economic
Growth **683**

AIRPOCALYPSE NOW **683**

Comparing Economies Across Time and Space 684

Real GDP per Capita **684**

Growth Rates **686**

ECONOMICS ➤ *IN ACTION* India Takes Off **687**

The Sources of Long-Run Growth 688

The Crucial Importance of Productivity **688**

Explaining Growth in Productivity **689**

Accounting for Growth: The Aggregate Production
Function **689**

What About Natural Resources? **693**

ECONOMICS ➤ *IN ACTION* Is the End of Economic Growth
in Sight? **694**

Why Growth Rates Differ 695

Explaining Differences in Growth Rates **696**

FOR INQUIRING MINDS: Inventing R&D **697**

GLOBAL COMPARISON: What's the Matter with Italy? **698**

The Role of Government in Promoting Economic
Growth **698**

FOR INQUIRING MINDS: The New Growth Theory **699**

ECONOMICS ➤ *IN ACTION* Why Did Britain Fall
Behind? **700**

Success, Disappointment, and Failure 701

East Asia's Miracle **702**

Latin America's Disappointment **703**

Africa's Troubles and Promise **703**

ECONOMICS ➤ *IN ACTION* Are Economies
Converging? **704**

Is World Growth Sustainable? 706

Natural Resources and Growth, Revisited **706**

Economic Growth and the Environment **708**

ECONOMICS ➤ *IN ACTION* The Cost of Limiting
Carbon **710**

BUSINESS CASE: How Boeing Got Better **712**

▶ CHAPTER **25** Savings, Investment
Spending, and the
Financial System **717**

FUNDS FOR FACEBOOK **717**

Matching Up Savings and Investment Spending 718

The Savings–Investment Spending Identity **718**

FOR INQUIRING MINDS: Who Enforces the Accounting? **721**

The Market for Loanable Funds **722**

FOR INQUIRING MINDS: Using Present Value **723**

ECONOMICS ➤ *IN ACTION* Sixty Years of U.S. Interest
Rates **730**

The Financial System 731

Three Tasks of a Financial System **732**

Types of Financial Assets **734**

Financial Intermediaries **735**

GLOBAL COMPARISON: Bonds Versus Banks **737**

ECONOMICS ➤ IN ACTION Banks and the South Korean Miracle **738**

Financial Fluctuations 739

The Demand for Stocks **739**

FOR INQUIRING MINDS: How Now, Dow Jones? **740**

The Demand for Other Assets **741**

Asset Price Expectations **741**

FOR INQUIRING MINDS: Behavioral Finance **742**

Asset Prices and Macroeconomics **743**

ECONOMICS ➤ IN ACTION The Great American Housing Bubble **744**

BUSINESS CASE: Grameen Bank: Banking Against Poverty **746**

PART 12 Short-Run Economic Fluctuations

▶ CHAPTER 26 Income and Expenditure **751**

FROM BOOM TO BUST **751**

The Multiplier: An Informal Introduction 752

ECONOMICS ➤ IN ACTION Sand State Slump **754**

Consumer Spending 755

Current Disposable Income and Consumer Spending **755**

Shifts of the Aggregate Consumption Function **758**

ECONOMICS ➤ IN ACTION Famous First Forecasting Failures **760**

Investment Spending 761

The Interest Rate and Investment Spending **762**

Expected Future Real GDP, Production Capacity, and Investment Spending **763**

Inventories and Unplanned Investment Spending **764**

ECONOMICS ➤ IN ACTION Interest Rates and the U.S. Housing Boom **765**

The Income–Expenditure Model 766

Planned Aggregate Spending and Real GDP **767**

Income–Expenditure Equilibrium **768**

The Multiplier Process and Inventory Adjustment **770**

ECONOMICS ➤ IN ACTION Inventories and the End of a Recession **773**

BUSINESS CASE: What's Good for America Is Good for GM **775**

CHAPTER 26 APPENDIX Deriving the Multiplier Algebraically **781**

▶ CHAPTER 27 Aggregate Demand and Aggregate Supply **783**

WHAT KIND OF SHOCK? **783**

Aggregate Demand 784

Why Is the Aggregate Demand Curve Downward Sloping? **785**

The Aggregate Demand Curve and the Income–Expenditure Model **786**

Shifts of the Aggregate Demand Curve **788**

Government Policies and Aggregate Demand **791**

ECONOMICS ➤ IN ACTION Moving Along the Aggregate Demand Curve, 1979–1980 **792**

Aggregate Supply 792

The Short-Run Aggregate Supply Curve **793**

FOR INQUIRING MINDS: What's Truly Flexible, What's Truly Sticky **794**

Shifts of the Short-Run Aggregate Supply Curve **795**

The Long-Run Aggregate Supply Curve **798**

From the Short Run to the Long Run **800**

ECONOMICS ➤ IN ACTION Sticky Wages in the Great Recession **801**

The AD–AS Model 802

Short-Run Macroeconomic Equilibrium **802**

Shifts of Aggregate Demand: Short-Run Effects **803**

Shifts of the SRAS Curve **804**

GLOBAL COMPARISON: Supply Shocks of the Twenty-first Century **806**

Long-Run Macroeconomic Equilibrium **806**

FOR INQUIRING MINDS: Where's the Deflation? **809**

ECONOMICS ➤ IN ACTION Supply Shocks Versus Demand Shocks in Practice **809**

Macroeconomic Policy 810

FOR INQUIRING MINDS: Keynes and the Long Run **811**

Policy in the Face of Demand Shocks **811**

Responding to Supply Shocks **812**

ECONOMICS ➤ IN ACTION Is Stabilization Policy Stabilizing? **812**

BUSINESS CASE: Slow Steaming **814**

PART 13 Stabilization Policy

▶ CHAPTER 28 Fiscal Policy **819**

HOW BIG IS BIG ENOUGH? **819**

Fiscal Policy: The Basics 820

Taxes, Purchases of Goods and Services, Government Transfers, and Borrowing **820**

The Government Budget and Total Spending **821**

Expansionary and Contractionary Fiscal Policy **822**

Can Expansionary Fiscal Policy Actually Work? **824**

A Cautionary Note: Lags in Fiscal Policy **825**

ECONOMICS ➤ *IN ACTION* What Was in the Recovery Act? **826**

Fiscal Policy and the Multiplier 827

Multiplier Effects of an Increase in Government Purchases of Goods and Services **827**

Multiplier Effects of Changes in Government Transfers and Taxes **828**

How Taxes Affect the Multiplier **829**

ECONOMICS ➤ *IN ACTION* Austerity and the Multiplier **830**

The Budget Balance 831

The Budget Balance as a Measure of Fiscal Policy **832**

The Business Cycle and the Cyclically Adjusted Budget Balance **832**

Should the Budget Be Balanced? **835**

ECONOMICS ➤ *IN ACTION* Europe's Search for a Fiscal Rule **835**

Long-Run Implications of Fiscal Policy 836

Deficits, Surpluses, and Debt **837**

GLOBAL COMPARISON: The American Way of Debt **838**

Problems Posed by Rising Government Debt **839**

Deficits and Debt in Practice **840**

FOR INQUIRING MINDS: What Happened to the Debt from World War II? **841**

Implicit Liabilities **841**

ECONOMICS ➤ *IN ACTION* Are We Greece? **843**

BUSINESS CASE: Here Comes the Sun **845**

CHAPTER 28 APPENDIX **Taxes and the Multiplier** **851**

▶ **CHAPTER 29 Money, Banking, and the Federal Reserve System** **853**

FUNNY MONEY **853**

The Meaning of Money 854

What Is Money? **854**

Roles of Money **855**

GLOBAL COMPARISON: The Big Moneys **855**

Types of Money **856**

Measuring the Money Supply **857**

FOR INQUIRING MINDS: What's with All the Currency? **858**

ECONOMICS ➤ *IN ACTION* The History of the Dollar **859**

The Monetary Role of Banks 860

What Banks Do **860**

The Problem of Bank Runs **861**

Bank Regulation **862**

ECONOMICS ➤ *IN ACTION* It's a Wonderful Banking System **863**

Determining the Money Supply 864

How Banks Create Money **864**

Reserves, Bank Deposits, and the Money Multiplier **866**

The Money Multiplier in Reality **867**

ECONOMICS ➤ *IN ACTION* Multiplying Money Down **868**

The Federal Reserve System 869

The Structure of the Fed **869**

What the Fed Does: Reserve Requirements and the Discount Rate **870**

Open-Market Operations **871**

FOR INQUIRING MINDS: Who Gets the Interest on the Fed's Assets? **873**

The European Central Bank **873**

ECONOMICS ➤ *IN ACTION* The Fed's Balance Sheet, Normal and Abnormal **874**

The Evolution of the American Banking System 875

The Crisis in American Banking in the Early Twentieth Century 875

Responding to Banking Crises: The Creation of the Federal Reserve **876**

The Savings and Loan Crisis of the 1980s **878**

Back to the Future: The Financial Crisis of 2008 **878**

ECONOMICS ➤ *IN ACTION* Regulation After the 2008 Crisis **881**

BUSINESS CASE: The Perfect Gift: Cash or a Gift Card? **883**

▶ **CHAPTER 30 Monetary Policy** **889**

THE MOST POWERFUL PERSON IN GOVERNMENT **889**

The Demand for Money 890

The Opportunity Cost of Holding Money **890**

The Money Demand Curve **892**

Shifts of the Money Demand Curve **893**

ECONOMICS ➤ *IN ACTION* A Yen for Cash **894**

Money and Interest Rates 895

The Equilibrium Interest Rate **895**

Two Models of Interest Rates? **897**

Monetary Policy and the Interest Rate **897**

Long-Term Interest Rates **899**

ECONOMICS ➤ *IN ACTION* The Fed Reverses Course **900**

Monetary Policy and Aggregate Demand 901

Expansionary and Contractionary Monetary Policy **901**

Monetary Policy in Practice **902**

The Taylor Rule Method of Setting Monetary Policy **903**

Inflation Targeting **903**

GLOBAL COMPARISON: Inflation Targets **904**

The Zero Lower Bound Problem **905**

ECONOMICS ➤ IN ACTION What the Fed Wants, the Fed Gets 905

Money, Output, and Prices in the Long Run 906
Short-Run and Long-Run Effects of an Increase in the Money Supply 906
Monetary Neutrality 908
Changes in the Money Supply and the Interest Rate in the Long Run 908

ECONOMICS ➤ IN ACTION International Evidence of Monetary Neutrality 909

BUSINESS CASE: PIMCO Bets on Cheap Money 911

CHAPTER 30 APPENDIX **Reconciling the Two Models of the Interest Rate** 915
The Interest Rate in the Short Run 915
The Interest Rate in the Long Run 916

▶ CHAPTER 31 **Inflation, Disinflation, and Deflation** 919

BRINGING A SUITCASE TO THE BANK 919
Money and Inflation 920
The Classical Model of Money and Prices 920
The Inflation Tax 922
The Logic of Hyperinflation 923

ECONOMICS ➤ IN ACTION Zimbabwe's Inflation 925

Moderate Inflation and Disinflation 925
The Output Gap and the Unemployment Rate 926

FOR INQUIRING MINDS: Okun's Law 928
The Short-Run Phillips Curve 928

FOR INQUIRING MINDS: The Aggregate Supply Curve and the Short-Run Phillips Curve 930
Inflation Expectations and the Short-Run Phillips Curve 931

ECONOMICS ➤ IN ACTION The Phillips Curve in the Great Recession 933

Inflation and Unemployment in the Long Run 934
The Long-Run Phillips Curve 934
The Natural Rate of Unemployment, Revisited 936
The Costs of Disinflation 936

GLOBAL COMPARISON: Disinflation Around the World 936

ECONOMICS ➤ IN ACTION The Great Disinflation of the 1980s 937

Deflation 938
Debt Deflation 938
Effects of Expected Deflation 939

ECONOMICS ➤ IN ACTION Is Europe Turning Japanese? 940

BUSINESS CASE: Licenses to Print Money 942

▶ CHAPTER 32 **Crises and Consequences** 947

FROM PURVEYOR OF DRY GOODS TO DESTROYER OF WORLDS 947
Banking: Benefits and Dangers 948
The Trade-off Between Rate of Return and Liquidity 948
The Purpose of Banking 949
Shadow Banks and the Re-emergence of Bank Runs 950

ECONOMICS ➤ IN ACTION The Day the Lights Went Out at Lehman 951

Banking Crises and Financial Panics 952
The Logic of Banking Crises 952
Historical Banking Crises: The Age of Panics 954
Modern Banking Crises Around the World 955

ECONOMICS ➤ IN ACTION Erin Go Broke 956

The Consequences of Banking Crises 957
Banking Crises, Recessions, and Recovery 957
Why Are Banking-Crisis Recessions So Bad? 958
Governments Step In 959

ECONOMICS ➤ IN ACTION Banks and the Great Depression 961

The 2008 Crisis and Its Aftermath 962
Severe Crisis, Slow Recovery 962
Aftershocks in Europe 963
The Stimulus–Austerity Debate 965
The Lesson of the Post-Crisis Slump 966

ECONOMICS ➤ IN ACTION If Only It Were the 1930s 966

Regulation in the Wake of the Crisis 967

ECONOMICS ➤ IN ACTION Bent Breaks the Buck 968

PART 14 Events and Ideas

▶ CHAPTER 33 **Macroeconomics: Events and Ideas** 973

A TALE OF TWO SLUMPS 973
Classical Macroeconomics 974
Money and the Price Level 974
The Business Cycle 974

ECONOMICS ➤ IN ACTION When Did the Business Cycle Begin? 974

The Great Depression and the Keynesian Revolution 975
Keynes's Theory 976

FOR INQUIRING MINDS: The Politics of Keynes 977
Policy to Fight Recessions 978

ECONOMICS ➤ *IN ACTION* The End of the Great
Depression **978**

Challenges to Keynesian Economics 979

The Revival of Monetary Policy **979**

Monetarism **980**

Limits to Macroeconomic Policy: Inflation and the
Natural Rate of Unemployment **983**

The Political Business Cycle **983**

ECONOMICS ➤ *IN ACTION* The Fed's Flirtation with
Monetarism **984**

**Rational Expectations, Real Business Cycles, and
New Classical Macroeconomics 984**

Rational Expectations **985**

Real Business Cycles **986**

FOR INQUIRING MINDS: Supply-Side Economics **986**

ECONOMICS ➤ *IN ACTION* The 1970s in Reverse **987**

**Consensus and Conflict in Modern
Macroeconomics 988**

Question 1: Is Expansionary Monetary Policy Helpful in
Fighting Recessions? **988**

Question 2: Is Expansionary Fiscal Policy Effective in
Fighting Recessions? **989**

Question 3: Can Monetary and/or Fiscal Policy Reduce
Unemployment in the Long Run? **989**

Question 4: Should Fiscal Policy Be Used in a
Discretionary Way? **989**

Question 5: Should Monetary Policy Be Used in a
Discretionary Way? **990**

Crises and Aftermath 990

ECONOMICS ➤ *IN ACTION* Lats of Luck **992**

PART 15 The Open Economy

➤**CHAPTER 34 Open-Economy
Macroeconomics**...............**997**

SWITZERLAND DOESN'T WANT YOUR MONEY **997**

Capital Flows and the Balance of Payments 998

Balance of Payments Accounts **998**

FOR INQUIRING MINDS: GDP, GNP, and the Current
Account **1000**

Modeling the Financial Account **1002**

GLOBAL COMPARISON: Big Surpluses **1003**

Underlying Determinants of International Capital
Flows **1005**

FOR INQUIRING MINDS: A Global Savings Glut? **1005**

Two-Way Capital Flows **1006**

ECONOMICS ➤ *IN ACTION* The Golden Age of Capital
Flows **1006**

The Role of the Exchange Rate 1007

Understanding Exchange Rates **1008**

The Equilibrium Exchange Rate **1008**

Inflation and Real Exchange Rates **1011**

Purchasing Power Parity **1013**

FOR INQUIRING MINDS: Burgernomics **1013**

ECONOMICS ➤ *IN ACTION* Low-Cost America **1014**

Exchange Rate Policy 1015

Exchange Rate Regimes **1016**

How Can an Exchange Rate Be Held Fixed? **1016**

The Exchange Rate Regime Dilemma **1018**

FOR INQUIRING MINDS: From Bretton Woods to the Euro **1018**

ECONOMICS ➤ *IN ACTION* China Pegs the Yuan **1019**

Exchange Rates and Macroeconomic Policy 1020

1. Devaluation and Revaluation of Fixed Exchange
Rates **1020**

2. Monetary Policy Under Floating Exchange
Rates **1021**

3. International Business Cycles **1022**

ECONOMICS ➤ *IN ACTION* The Little Currency That
Could **1023**

BUSINESS CASE: A Yen for Japanese Cars **1025**

Macroeconomic Data Tables   M-1
Solutions to "Check Your Understanding" Questions   S-1
Glossary   G-1
Index   I-1

PREFACE

The Importance of a Narrative Approach

More than a decade ago, when Robin and I began writing the first edition of this textbook, we had many small ideas: particular aspects of economics that we believed weren't covered the right way in existing textbooks. But we also had one big idea: the belief that an economics textbook could and should be built around narratives, that it should never lose sight of the fact that economics is, in the end, a set of stories about what people do.

Many of the stories economists tell take the form of models—for whatever else they are, economic models are stories about how the world works. But we believed that students' understanding of and appreciation for models would be greatly enhanced if they were presented, as much as possible, in the context of stories about the real world, stories that both illustrate economic concepts and touch on the concerns we all face as individuals living in a world shaped by economic forces.

Those stories have been integrated into every edition, including this one. Once again, you'll find them in the openers, in special features like Economics in Action, For Inquiring Minds, Global Comparison, and in our business cases. We have been gratified by the reception this storytelling approach has received and in this edition of *Economics* we continue to expand the book's appeal by including many new stories on a broad range of topics, and by updating and revising others. Specifically, there are 13 new opening stories, 27 new Economics in Actions, and 8 new business cases. As always, a significant number of the features that aren't completely new have been updated.

We remain extremely fortunate in our reviewers, who have put in an immense amount of work helping us to make this book even better. And we are also deeply thankful to the users who have given us feedback, telling us what works and, even more important, what doesn't.

Despite the many changes in this new edition, we've tried to keep the spirit the same. This is a book about economics as the study of what people do and how they interact, a study very much informed by real-world experience.

The Fourth Edition: What's New

Robin and I have been extremely gratified by the success of the first three editions of *Economics*, which has made it one of the best-selling economics textbooks. Yet we are aware that success can have its dangers. Given the book's wide acceptance, it might be tempting for an author to do less in the next revision. In fact, it might be downright rational. However, we believe we have resisted that temptation in this latest edition. Following is an overview of the changes we've made.

Big Changes in the First Half of the Book (Chapters 1–20 on Microeconomics) . . .

Many new examples and stories focusing on environmental concerns, new technology, and policy debates

After touring college campuses and observing anti-fracking signs everywhere, we were impressed by how much students really do want to participate in the big economic issues of the day. However, we can also note how much today's students are attached to their energy-hungry devices, from smartphones to tablets to computers to personal dorm fridges. Hence one of the aims of this edition is to both acknowledge students' idealism as well as to help inform them about the realities of resource scarcity and the need to make choices.

To that end we have made fracking and its effects on the market for natural gas the subject of the opening story for Chapter 3, on supply and demand. However, we have been careful not to take sides in the debate over fracking—while highlighting how it has dramatically lowered the price of energy, like natural gas, we alert students to the environmental concerns it raises in Chapter 16 on externalities.

These are just two of the many new examples and stories we have introduced in the fourth edition with the aim of thoroughly freshening up the new edition and keeping it current and relevant. We have paid particular attention to how changes in technology are transforming the economic landscape. For example, we discuss the rise of Uber to illustrate market equilibrium, the use of Smart Grid technology to show the importance of measuring cost, and how the advent of "showrooming" and shopping Apps moves the market for consumer goods closer to one of perfect competition. We have also chosen stories and examples on topics close to the lives of today's students, like the Economics in Action, "The Rise and Fall of the Unpaid Intern," in Chapter 5 on price controls and quotas.

We have also chosen topics that illustrate important policy debates, such as the introduction of the Affordable Care Act, the regulatory questions raised by the fight between Amazon and Hachette Books, and the environmental trade-offs of coal-fired versus natural-gas-fired power plants. And as always, we pay great attention to integrating an international perspective, in our Global Comparison feature, but also in the many globally oriented applications and stories. All global examples are highlighted with the following icon:

A listing of opening stories,
Economics in Actions, For Inquiring Minds,
Global Comparisons, and business cases can be
found inside the front and back covers
and on the facing pages.

A major revision of Chapter 16, Externalities

We believe environmental concerns are one of the most pressing issues today and are a good means of sparking students' interests in economics.

The focus on the economics and environmental effects of fracking that begins in Chapter 3 on supply and demand continues in Chapter 16 on externalities where we've added a new opening story ("Trouble Underfoot") to illustrate the concept of a negative externality, using the environmental debate over contaminated groundwater from fracking. Following in that same vein, and in order to sharpen students' appreciation of environmental trade-offs, we include a new Economics in Action, "How Much Does Your Electricity Really Cost?" that compares the social cost of different types of power generation.

Pedagogical changes to the chapter include an improved discussion of the costs and benefits of pollution and a much simplified analysis of the Coase theorem.

There is also a completely revised and updated section on network externalities, along with a new business case tracing the rise of Facebook and the fall of MySpace to show network externalities in action.

New coverage of the Affordable Care Act and other improvements in Chapter 18, The Economics of the Welfare State

This chapter is a unique feature of our book that has become even more relevant since first introduced in the second edition. For one thing, the major provisions of the Affordable Care Act, aka Obamacare, went into effect at the beginning of 2014; this is the biggest expansion of the U.S. welfare state since the creation of Medicare in the 1960s. We examine the economics behind the act, and discuss the early, relatively favorable returns of its performance.

Meanwhile, the Great Recession and its aftermath have been a major test of the ability of welfare-state programs to cushion Americans from hardship; we discuss new research showing a dramatic effect from food stamps and other programs in limiting the rise in poverty.

In addition, the chapter continues to offer a comprehensive look at the U.S. welfare state and its philosophical origins, along with a close look at how programs in the United States compare to those in other countries.

Despite the many changes and updates, our goal for the chapter is the same: to motivate students to think more deeply about economic trade-offs, social welfare, and the political process.

. . . And Big Changes in the Second Half of the Book (Chapters 21–34 on Macroeconomics)

This revision fully incorporates recent events

The first edition of this textbook was published at a time of calm in the U.S. and world economies. In fact, at the time (in 2005), many economists believed that the so-called Great Moderation, an era of relative stability that began in the mid-1980s, would continue indefinitely. We chose, nonetheless, to put recessions and the policies governments use to fight them front and center, believing that the business cycle is still the core issue in macroeconomics. And subsequent events have both validated that decision and provided plenty of material to incorporate in each new edition. We also believe that hard times in the world economy have, perversely, greatly improved our ability to teach macroeconomics. We can now vividly illustrate that macroeconomics does make sense of the world and that it really matters.

The financial crisis of 2008 is slowly receding in the rearview mirror, but the aftershocks continue to reverberate, and most of the big changes since the third edition reflect those aftershocks. We have, of course, updated virtually every data-based figure and table in these chapters, but beyond that, we have updated or replaced many of the real-world narratives that provide context for the analytical content, and which we believe make this book special.

This doesn't mean that we have torn up the basic analysis of previous editions. On the contrary, one little-appreciated aspect of world economic developments since the crisis is how well basic macroeconomic models have worked in tracking, for example, the effects of fiscal policy and monetary expansion. As a result, we make extensive use of recent events to illustrate macroeconomic principles and concepts in a way that wouldn't have been possible in a more stable world.

This incorporation of recent developments literally begins at the start, in the first chapter: Chapter 21, "Macroeconomics: The Big Picture." Previously, we began by depicting mass unemployment in the 1930s; now we begin with a new chapter-opening story about mass unemployment in today's Spain ("The Pain in Spain").

Depression-type conditions are no longer something that happened long ago; as we show in Chapter 23, "Unemployment and Inflation," they're happening right now to young Europeans who are a lot like our students. And as we also show, even in America, college graduates have faced years of tough times and many students' families and friends will have experienced the pain of protracted unemployment firsthand, so that we believe that the analysis has gained extra relevance.

Later on, we use recent data to demonstrate the validity of a number of key concepts. For example, macroeconomists talk about sticky wages that may not fall even in the face of unemployment; as we show in Chapter 27, "Aggregate Demand and Aggregate Supply," in recent years that stickiness has been dramatically illustrated by a surge in the number of workers whose wages don't change at all from year to year. Similarly, we don't need to appeal to events decades ago to support the concept of a short-run trade-off between unemployment and inflation as we show in Chapter 31, "Inflation, Disinflation, Deflation." You can see that trade-off clearly by looking across advanced countries and seeing that where unemployment has risen, inflation has fallen the most.

Another example of how recent events have allowed us to look at macroeconomic concepts in a new way is the effect of fiscal policy. This used to be a very difficult topic to teach in a way that seemed real, because large discretionary changes in government spending hardly ever happened. That's no longer true. The U.S. stimulus program of 2009–2010 gave substance to the concept of expansionary fiscal policy that we illustrated in the third edition. But now, in the fourth edition, we have even more real-world experience. As we discuss in Chapter 28, "Fiscal Policy," since 2010 many but not all countries have imposed drastic fiscal austerity,

and—as we discuss in the new Economics in Action, "Austerity and the Multiplier"—international comparisons between countries with varying degrees of austerity make the discussion of fiscal impacts much more concrete and accessible. Meanwhile, long-run fiscal issues—including concerns about solvency—have also become a lot less abstract. We see this in another new Economics in Action: "Are We Greece?", which nobody would have considered writing a few years ago.

What about the analysis of crises themselves? We already had a crisis chapter in the third edition, but it's now possible to say much more. Chapter 32, "Crises and Consequences," extends the story to cover the many aftershocks of the 2008 crisis, especially the successive waves of turmoil that have swept Europe. It also includes a discussion of Dodd-Frank financial reform, which is now a crucial part of the economic scene.

And there's more. For example, when we discuss open-economy macroeconomics in Chapter 34, we can illustrate the difference between fixed and floating exchange rates by comparing experiences around the European periphery, where Iceland and Latvia have followed dramatically different paths. One new Economics in Action illustrates how Latvia has taken on outsize significance in the debate over fiscal policy, serving as an example of successful austerity ("Lats of Luck"). Another looks at the advantages that Iceland, a country with its own currency, has had over euro-using countries, like Greece, when workers' wages needed to be cut during tough economic times ("The Little Currency That Could").

And the revision extends beyond post-crisis analysis

But we don't want to convey the sense that all the changes in this edition reflect the aftermath of the financial crisis. We have also added a lot of new material in Chapter 24 on long-run growth, ranging from the all-too-visible effects of rapid growth on air quality in Beijing (in the opening story, "Airpocalypse Now"), to the disturbing collapse of productivity growth in Italy (in a new Global Comparison, "What's the Matter with Italy"). Progress in air travel has helped illustrate one of our favorite themes, the often inconspicuous nature of progress. Today's jets look a lot like the jets of the 1960s, but they're vastly more efficient, as we discuss in the new Chapter 9 business case, "How Boeing Got Better."

We continue to address environmental concerns in the second half of the book, with two new applications in the chapter on growth. In a new Economics in Action we examine the financial costs and environmental benefits of limiting carbon ("The Cost of Limiting Carbon"). A new business case illustrates how stimulus spending on concentrated thermal solar power plants has led to job creation and environmental benefits ("Here Comes the Sun").

We also address the challenges facing the Fed Chair Janet Yellen in a new opening story, "The Most Powerful Person in Government" in Chapter 30 on monetary policy; explore why U.S. companies issue a lot more bonds than their European counterparts in a new Global Comparison, "Bonds Versus Banks" in Chapter 25 on the financial system; and look at the impact that adopting the euro has had on Spain's national account balance in a new Economics in Action, "Spain's Costly Surplus," in Chapter 21 on macroeconomic measurement.

A New Online Feature: Work It Out Tutorials

This new feature ties together our textbook and the accompanying online course materials to offer students interactive assistance with solving one key problem in every chapter. Available in LaunchPad, the new Work It Out feature includes an online tutorial that guides students through each step of the problem-solving process. There are also choice-specific feedback and video explanations, providing interactive assistance tailored to each student's needs. Students can use the Work It Outs, along with the other offerings in LaunchPad, to independently test their comprehension of concepts, build their math and graphing skills, and prepare for class and exams.

Scan here for a sample Work It Out problem.

http://qrs.ly/px49xiv

Advantages of This Book

Our basic approach to textbook writing is the same as it was in the first edition:

- **Chapters build intuition through realistic examples.** In every chapter, we use real-world examples, stories, applications, and case studies to teach the core concepts and motivate student learning. The best way to introduce concepts and reinforce them is through real-world examples; students simply relate more easily to them.

- **Pedagogical features reinforce learning.** We've crafted a genuinely helpful set of features that are described in the following Walkthrough, "Tools for Learning."

- **Chapters are accessible and entertaining.** We use a fluid and friendly writing style to make concepts accessible and, whenever possible, we use examples that are familiar to students.

- **Although easy to understand, the book also prepares students for further coursework.** There's no need to choose between two unappealing alternatives: a textbook that is "easy to teach" but leaves major gaps in students' understanding, or a textbook that is "hard to teach" but adequately prepares students for future coursework. We offer the best of both worlds.

Every chapter is structured around a common set of features that help students learn while keeping them engaged.

Supply and Demand

▶ **What You Will Learn in This Chapter**

■ What a **competitive market** is and how it is described by the **supply and demand model**

■ What the **demand curve** and the **supply curve** are

■ The difference between **movements along a curve** and **shifts of a curve**

■ How the supply and demand curves determine a market's **equilibrium price** and **equilibrium quantity**

■ In the case of a **shortage** or **surplus**, how price moves the market back to equilibrium

A NATURAL GAS BOOM

The adoption of new drilling technologies lead to cheaper natural gas and vigorous protests.

> **Chapter Overviews** offer students a helpful preview of the key concepts they will learn about in the chapter.

... VIVID ... speech ... ew York ...ent was greeted by more than 500 chanting and sign-toting supporters and opponents. Why the ruckus? Because upstate New York is a key battleground over the adoption of a relatively new method of producing energy supplies. *Hydraulic fracturing,* or *fracking,* is a method of extracting natural gas (and to a lesser extent, oil) from deposits trapped between layers of shale rock thousands of feet underground using—using powerful jets of chemical-laden water to release the gas. While it has been known for almost a century that the United States contains vast deposits of natural gas within these shale formations, they lay untapped because drilling for them was considered too difficult.

Until recently, that is. A few decades ago, new drilling technologies were developed that made it possible to reach these deeply embedded deposits. But what finally pushed energy companies to invest in and adopt these new extraction technologies was the high price of natural gas over the last decade. What a...unted for these high natural prices a quadrupling

from 2002 to 2006? There were two principal factors—one reflecting the demand for natural gas, the other the supply of natural gas.

First, the demand side. In 2002, the U.S. economy was mired in recession; with economic activity low and job losses high, people and businesses cut back their energy consumption. For example, to save money, homeowners turned down their thermostats in winter and turned them up in the summer. But by 2006, the U.S. economy came roaring back, and natural gas consumption rose. Second, the supply side. In 2005, Hurricane Katrina devastated the American Gulf Coast, site of most of the country's natural gas production at the time. So by 2006 the demand for natural gas had surged while the supply of natural gas had been severely curtailed. As a result, in 2006 natural gas prices peaked at around $14 per thousand cubic feet, up from around $2 in 2002.

Fast-forward to 2013: natural gas prices once again fell to $2 per thousand cubic feet. But this time it wasn't a slow economy that was the principal explanation, it was the use of the new technologies. "Boom," "supply shock," and

"game changer" was how energy experts described the impact of these technologies on oil and natural gas production and prices. To illustrate, the United States produced 8.13 trillion cubic feet of natural gas from shale deposits in 2012, nearly doubling the total from 2010. That total increased again in 2013, to 9.35 trillion cubic feet of natural gas, making the U.S. the world's largest producer of both oil and natural gas—overtaking both Russia and Saudia Arabia.

The benefits of much lower natural gas prices have not only led to lower heating costs for American consumers, they have also cascaded through American industries, particularly power generation and transportation. Electricity-generating power plants are switching from coal to natural gas, and mass-transit vehicles are switching from gasoline to natural gas. (You can even buy an inexpensive kit to convert your car from gasoline to natural gas.) The effect has been so significant that many European manufacturers, paying four times more for gas than their U.S. rivals, have been forced to relocate plants to American soil to survive. In addition, the revived U.S. natural gas industry has directly created tens of thousands of new jobs.

67

> **Opening Stories** Each chapter begins with a compelling story that is often integrated throughout the rest of the chapter. Many of the stories in this edition are new, including the one shown here.

Economics in Action cases conclude every major text section. This much-lauded feature lets students immediately apply concepts they've read about to real phenomena.

AND DEMAND

ECONOMICS ▶ in Action

Beating the Traffic

Cities can reduce traffic congestion by raising the price of driving.

All big cities have traffic problems, and many local authorities to discourage driving in the crowded city center. If we think of a
the city center as a good that people consume, we can use t
of demand to analyze anti-traffic policies.

One common strategy is to reduce the demand for auto trips by
prices of substitutes. Many metropolitan areas subsidize bus and
hoping to lure commuters out of their cars. An alternative is to rai
complements: several major U.S. cities impose high taxes on comme
garages and impose short time limits on parking meters, both to
and to discourage people from driving into the city.

A few major cities—including Singapore, London, Oslo, Stockholm, and
Milan—have been willing to adopt a direct and politically controversial approach:
reducing congestion by raising the price of driving. Under "congestion pricing"
(or "congestion charging" in the United Kingdom), a charge is imposed on cars
entering the city center during business hours. Drivers buy passes, which are then
debited electronically as they drive by monitoring stations. Compliance is monitored with automatic cameras that photograph license plates.

In 2012, Moscow adopted a modest charge for parking in certain areas in an
attempt to reduce its traffic jams, considered the worst of all major cities. After
the approximately $1.60 charge was applied, city officials estimated that Moscow
traffic decreased by 4%.

The current daily cost of driving in London ranges from £9 to £12 (about $14
to $19). And drivers who don't pay and are caught pay a fine of £120 (about $192)
for each transgression.

Not surprisingly, studies have shown that after the implementation of congestion pricing, traffic does indeed decrease. In the 1990s, London had some of the
worst traffic in Europe. The introduction of its congestion charge in 2003 immediately reduced traffic in the city center by about 15%, with overall traffic falling
by 21% between 2002 and 2006. And there has been increased use of substitutes,
such as public transportation, bicycles, motorbikes, and ride-sharing. From 2001
to 2011, bike trips in London increased by 79%, and bus usage was up by 30%.

In the United States, the U.S. Department of Transportation has implemented
pilot programs to study congestion pricing. For example, in 2012 Los Angeles
County imposed a congestion charge on an 11-mile stretch of highway in central
Los Angeles. Drivers pay up to $1.40 per mile, the amount depending upon traffic
congestion, with a money-back guarantee that their average speed w
below 45 miles per hour. While some drivers were understandably a
charge, others were more philosophical. One driver felt that the toll wa
to escape what often turned into a crawling 45-minute drive, saying, "
you're in a hurry to get home. You got to pay the price. If not, get stuc

Global Stamps identify which boxes, cases, and applications are global in focus.

Check Your Understanding questions allow students to immediately test their understanding of a section. Solutions appear at the back of the book.

Check Your Understanding   3-1

1. Explain whether each of the following events represents (i) a *shift o*
   curve or (ii) a *movement along* the demand curve.
   a. A store owner finds that customers are willing to pay more for
      rainy days.
   b. When Circus Cruise Lines offered reduced prices for summer
      Caribbean, their number of bookings increased sharply.
   c. People buy more long-stem roses the week of Valentine's Day, ev
      prices are higher than at other times during the year.
   d. A sharp rise in the price of gasoline leads many commuters to join carpools in
      order to reduce their gasoline purchases.

Solutions appear at back of book.

▼ Quick Review

- The **supply and demand model** is a model of a **competitive market**—one in which there are many buyers and sellers of the same good or service.

- The **demand schedule** shows how the **quantity demanded** changes as the price changes. A **demand curve** illustrates this relationship.

- The **law of demand** asserts that a higher price reduces the quantity demanded. Thus, demand curves normally slope downward.

- An increase in demand leads to a rightward **shift of the demand curve**: the quantity demanded rises for any given price. A decrease in demand leads to a leftward shift: the quantity demanded falls for any given price. A change in price results in a change in the quantity demanded and a **movement along the demand curve**.

- The five main factors that can shift the demand curve are changes in (1) the price of a related good, such as a **substitute** or a **complement**, (2) income, (3) tastes, (4) expectations, and (5) the number of consumers.

- The market demand curve is the horizontal sum of the **individual demand curves** of all consumers in the market.

Quick Reviews offer students a short, bulleted summary of key concepts in the section to aid understanding.

FOR INQUIRING MINDS | Tribulations on the Runway

You probably don't spend much time worrying about the trials and tribulations of fashion models. Most of them don't lead glamorous lives; in fact, except for a lucky few, life as a fashion model today can be very trying and not very lucrative. And it's all because of supply and demand.

Consider the case of Bianca Gomez, a willowy 18-year-old from Los Angeles, with green eyes, honey-colored hair, and flawless skin, whose experience was detailed in a *Wall Street Journal* article. Bianca began modeling while still in high school, earning about $30,000 in modeling fees during her senior year. Having attracted the interest of some top designers in New York, she moved there after graduation, hoping to land jobs in leading fashion houses and photoshoots for leading fashion magazines.

But once in New York, Bianca entered the global market for fashion models. And it wasn't very pretty. Due

by a rightward shift of the supply curve in the market for fashion models, which would by itself tend to lower the price paid to models.

And that wasn't the only change in the market. Unfortunately for Bianca and others like her, the tastes of many of those who hire models have changed as well. Fashion magazines have come to prefer using celebrities such as Beyoncé on their pages rather than anonymous models, believing that their readers connect better with a familiar face. This amounts to a leftward shift of the demand curve for models—again reducing the equilibrium price paid to them.

This was borne out in Bianca's experiences. After paying her rent, her transportation, all her modeling expenses, and 20% of her earnings to her modeling agency (which markets her to prospective clients and books her

For Inquiring Minds boxes apply economic concepts to real-world events in unexpected and sometimes surprising ways, generating a sense of the power and breadth of economics. The feature furthers the book's goal of helping students build intuition with real-world examples.

GLOBAL COMPARISON | Pay More, Pump Less

For a real-world illustration of the law of demand, consider how gasoline consumption varies according to the prices consumers pay at the pump. Because of high taxes, gasoline and diesel fuel are more than twice as expensive in most European countries and in many East Asian countries than in the United States. According to the law of demand, this should lead Europeans to buy less gasoline than Americans—and they do. As you can see from the figure, per person, Europeans consume less than half as much fuel as Americans, mainly because they drive smaller cars with better mileage.

Prices aren't the only factor affecting fuel consumption, but they're probably the main cause of the difference between European and American fuel consumption per person.

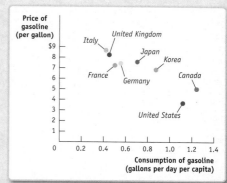

Source: World Development Indicators and U.S. Energy Information Administration, 2013.

Global Comparison boxes use real data from several countries and colorful graphs to illustrate how and why countries reach different economic outcomes. The boxes give students an international perspective that will expand their understanding of economics.

PITFALLS

WHICH CURVE IS IT, ANYWAY?
When the price of some good or service changes, in general, we can say that this reflects a change in either supply or demand. But it is easy to get confused about which one. A helpful clue is the direction of change in the quantity. If the quantity sold changes in the *same* direction as the price—for example, if both the price and the quantity rise—this suggests that the demand curve has shifted. If the price and the quantity move in *opposite* directions, the likely cause is a shift of the supply curve.

Pitfalls boxes clarify concepts that are easily misunderstood by students new to economics.

Summary Tables serve as a helpful study aid for readers. Many incorporate visuals to help students grasp important economic concepts.

TABLE 3-2 Factors That Shift Supply

When this happens . . .	. . . supply increases	But when this happens . . .	. . . supply decreases
When the price of an input falls . . .	. . . supply of the good increases.	When the price of an input rises . . .	. . . supply of the good decreases.
When the price [of a substitute] in [production] falls . . .	. . . supply of the original good increases.	When the price of a substitute in production rises . . .	. . . supply of the original good decreases.

Business Cases

close each chapter, applying key economic principles to real-life business situations in both American and international companies. Each case concludes with critical thinking questions.

BUSINESS CASE

An Uber Way to Get a Ride

In a densely populated city like New York City, finding a taxi is a relatively easy task on most days—stand on a corner, put out your arm and, usually, before long an available cab stops to pick you up. And even before you step into the car you will know approximately how much it will cost to get to your destination, because taxi meter rates are set by city regulators and posted for riders.

But at times it is not so easy to find a taxi—on rainy days, during rush hour, and at crowded locations where many people are looking for a taxi at the same time. At such times, you could wait a very long while before finding an available cab. As you wait, you will probably notice empty taxis passing you by—drivers who have quit working for the day and are headed home or back to the garage. There will be drivers who might stop, but then won't pick you up because they find your destination inconvenient. Moreover, there are times when it is simply impossible to hail a taxi—for example, during a snowstorm or on New Year's Eve when the demand for taxis far exceeds the supply.

In 2009 two young entrepreneurs, Garrett Camp and Travis Kalanick, founded Uber, a company that they believe offers a better way to get a ride. Using a smartphone app, Uber serves as a clearinghouse connecting people who want a ride to drivers with cars who are registered with Uber. Confirm your location using the Uber app and you'll be shown the available cars in your vicinity. Tap "book" and you receive a text saying your car—typically a spotless Lincoln Town Car—is on its way. At the end of your trip, fare plus tip are automatically deducted from your credit card. As of 2014 Uber operates in 70 cities around the world and booked more than $1 billion in rides in 2013.

Given that Uber provides personalized service and better quality cars, their fares are somewhat higher than regular taxi fares *during normal driving days*—a situation that customers seem happy with. However, the qualification *during normal driving hours* is an important one because at other times Uber's rates fluctuate. When a lot of people are looking for a car—such as during a snowstorm or on New Year's Eve—Uber uses what it calls *surge pricing*, setting the rate higher until everyone who wants a car at the going price can get one. So during a recent New York snowstorm, rides cost up to 8.25 times the standard price. Enraged, some of Uber's customers have accused them of price gouging.

But according to Kalanick, the algorithm that Uber uses to determine the surge price is set to leave as few people as possible without a ride, and he's just doing what is necessary to keep customers happy. As he explains, "We do not own cars nor do we employ drivers. Higher prices are required in order to get cars on the road and keep them on the road during the busiest times." This explanation was confirmed by one Uber driver who said, "If I don't have anything to do and see a surge price, I get out there."

QUESTIONS FOR THOUGHT

1. Before Uber, how were prices set in the market for rides in New York City? Was it a competitive market?
2. What accounts for the fact that during good weather there are typically

---

WORK IT OUT

 Macmillan Education **LaunchPad**

For interactive, step-by-step help in solving the following problem, visit LaunchPad by using the URL on the back cover of this book.

19. The accompanying table gives the annual U.S. demand and supply schedules for pickup trucks.

Price of truck	Quantity of trucks demanded (millions)	Quantity of trucks supplied (millions)
$20,000	20	14
25,000	18	15
30,000	16	16
35,000	14	17
40,000	12	18

a. Plot the demand and supply curves using these schedules. Indicate the equilibrium price and quantity on your diagram.

b. Suppose the tires used on pickup trucks are found to be defective. What would you expect to happen in the market for pickup trucks? Show this on your diagram.

c Suppose that the U.S. Department of Transportation imposes costly regulations on manufacturers that cause them to reduce supply by one-third at any given price. Calculate and plot the new supply schedule and indicate the new equilibrium price and quantity on your diagram.

NEW! Work It Out

appears in all end-of-chapter problem sets, offering students online tutorials that guide them step by step through solving key problems. Available in LaunchPad.

PROBLEMS

1. A survey indicated that chocolate is the most popular flavor of ice cream in America. For each of the following, indicate the possible effects on demand, supply, or both as well as equilibrium price and quantity of chocolate ice cream.

b. The market for St. Louis Rams cotton T-shirts
Case 1: The Rams win the Super Bowl.
Case 2: The price of cotton increases.

c. The market for bagels

End-of-Chapter Reviews include a brief but complete summary of key concepts, a list of key terms, and a comprehensive, high-quality set of end-of-chapter Problems.

SUMMARY

1. The **supply and demand model** illustrates how a **competitive market**, one with many buyers and sellers, none of whom can influence the market price, w...

2. The **de...**

ing supply, they mean **shifts of the supply curve**—a change in the quantity supplied at any given price. An increase in supply causes a rightward shift of the sup-...

KEY TERMS

Competitive market, p. 68	Substitutes, p. 74	Movement along the supply curve, p. 80
Supply and demand model, p. 68	Complements, p. 74	Input, p. 82
Demand schedule, p. 69	Normal good, p. 74	Individual supply curve, p. 83
Quantity demanded, p. 69	Inferior good, p. 74	Equilibrium price, p. 86
Demand curve, p. 69	Individual demand curve, p. 76	

Organization of This Book: What's Core, What's Optional

To help with planning your course, following is a list of what we view as core chapters and those that could be considered optional, along with a brief description of the coverage in each chapter.

Core	Optional
	Introduction: The Ordinary Business of Life Initiates students into the study of economics with basic terms and explains the difference between microeconomics and macroeconomics.
1. First Principles Outlines 12 principles underlying the study of economics: principles of individual choice, interaction between individuals, and economy-wide interaction.	
2. Economic Models: Trade-offs and Trade Employs two economic models—the production possibilities frontier and comparative advantage—as an introduction to gains from trade and international comparisons.	**Chapter 2 Appendix: Graphs in Economics** Offers a comprehensive review of graphing and math skills for students who would find a refresher helpful and to prepare them for better economic literacy.
3. Supply and Demand Covers the essentials of supply, demand, market equilibrium, surplus, and shortage.	
4. Consumer and Producer Surplus Introduces students to market efficiency, the ways markets fail, the role of prices as signals, and property rights.	
5. Price Controls and Quotas: Meddling with Markets Covers market interventions and their consequences: price and quantity controls, inefficiency, and deadweight loss.	
6. Elasticity Introduces the various elasticity measures and explains how to calculate and interpret them, including price, cross-price and income elasticity of demand, and price elasticity of supply.	
7. Taxes Covers basic tax analysis along with a review of the burden of taxation and considerations of equity versus efficiency. The structure of taxation, tax policy, and public spending are also introduced.	
	8. International Trade Here we trace the sources of comparative advantage, consider tariffs and quotas, and explore the politics of trade protection. The chapter includes coverage on the controversy over imports from low-wage countries.
9. Decision Making by Individuals and Firms Microeconomics is a science of how to make decisions. The chapter focuses on marginal analysis ("either–or" and "how much" decisions) and the concept of sunk cost; it also includes a section on behavioral economics, showing the limitations of rational thought.	**Chapter 9 Appendix: Toward a Fuller Understanding of Present Value** Expands on the coverage of present value in the chapter.
10. The Rational Consumer Provides a complete treatment of consumer behavior for instructors who don't cover indifference curves, including the budget line, optimal consumption choice, diminishing marginal utility, and substitution effects.	**Chapter 10 Appendix: Consumer Preferences and Consumer Choice** Offers more detailed treatment for those who wish to cover indifference curves.
11. Behind the Supply Curve: Inputs and Costs Develops the production function and the various cost measures of the firm, including discussion of the difference between average cost and marginal cost.	

Core	Optional

Core

12. Perfect Competition and the Supply Curve
Explains the output decision of the perfectly competitive firm, its entry/exit decision, the industry supply curve, and the equilibrium of a perfectly competitive market.

13. Monopoly
A complete treatment of monopoly, including topics such as price discrimination and the welfare effects of monopoly.

14. Oligopoly
This chapter focuses on defining the concept of oligopoly along with basic game theory in both a one-shot and repeated game context. Coverage of the kinked demand curve now appears online.

15. Monopolistic Competition and Product Differentiation
The chapter emphasizes instances in which students encounter monopolistic competition, covering the entry/exit decision, efficiency considerations, and advertising.

16. Externalities
Significantly revised and updated in the new edition, the chapter covers negative externalities and solutions to them, such as Coasian private trades, emissions taxes, and a system of tradable permits. Also examined are positive externalities, technological spillovers, and network externalities.

17. Public Goods and Common Resources
Explains how to classify goods into four categories (private goods, common resources, public goods, and artificially scarce goods) based on excludability and rivalry in consumption, in the process clarifying why some goods but not others can be efficiently managed by markets.

21. Macroeconomics: The Big Picture
Introduces the big ideas of macroeconomics with an overview of recessions and expansions, employment and unemployment, long-run growth, inflation versus deflation, and the open economy.

22. GDP and the CPI: Tracking the Macroeconomy
Explains how the numbers macroeconomists use are calculated and why, including the basics of national income accounting and price indexes.

Optional

18. The Economics of the Welfare State
Significantly revised and updated, this chapter provides a comprehensive overview of the welfare state as well as its philosophical foundations. Examined in the chapter are health care economics (including new coverage of the Affordable Care Act), the problem of poverty, and the issue of income inequality.

19. Factor Markets and the Distribution of Income and Appendix: Indifference Curve Analysis of Labor Supply
Covers the efficiency-wage model of the labor market as well as the influence of education, discrimination, and market power. The appendix examines the labor-leisure trade-off and the backward bending labor supply curve.

20. Uncertainty, Risk, and Private Information
This unique, applied chapter explains attitudes toward risk, examines the benefits and limits of diversification, and considers private information, adverse selection, and moral hazard.

Core	Optional

23. Unemployment and Inflation
Covers the measurement of unemployment, the reasons why positive employment exists even in booms, and the problems posed by inflation.

24. Long-Run Economic Growth
Emphasizes an international perspective—economic growth is about the world as a whole—and explains why some countries have been more successful than others.

25. Savings, Investment Spending, and the Financial System
Introduces students to financial markets and institutions, loanable funds and the determination of interest rates. Includes coverage of present value.

26. Income and Expenditure
Addresses the determinants of consumer and investment spending, introduces the famous 45-degree diagram, and explains the logic of the multiplier.

Chapter 26 Appendix: Deriving the Multiplier Algebraically
A rigorous and mathematical approach to deriving the multiplier.

27. Aggregate Demand and Aggregate Supply
Provides the traditional focus on aggregate price level using the traditional approach to AD-AS. It also covers the ability of the economy to recover in the long run.

28. Fiscal Policy
Provides an analysis of the role of discretionary fiscal policy, automatic stabilizers, and long-run issues of debt and solvency.

Chapter 28 Appendix: Taxes and the Multiplier
A rigorous derivation of the roles of taxes in reducing the size of the multiplier and acting as an automatic stabilizer.

29. Money, Banking, and the Federal Reserve System
Covers the roles of money, the ways in which banks create money, and the structure and the role of the Federal Reserve and other central banks.

30. Monetary Policy
Covers the role of Federal Reserve policy in driving interest rates and aggregate demand. It includes a section bridging the short and long run by showing how interest rates set in the short run reflect the supply and demand of savings in the long run.

Chapter 30 Appendix: Reconciling the Two Models of the Interest Rate
This appendix explains why the loanable funds model (long-run discussions) and the liquidity preference approach (short-run discussions) are both valuable approaches.

31. Inflation, Disinflation, and Deflation
Covers the causes and consequences of inflation, the large cost deflation imposes on the economy, and the danger that disinflation leads the economy into a liquidity trap.

32. Crises and Consequences
Provides an up-to-date look at the recent financial crisis, starting with the Lehman Brothers collapse, integrating coverage about the dangers posed by banking, shadow banking, asset bubbles, and financial contagion.

33. Macroeconomics: Events and Ideas
Provides a unique overview of the history of macroeconomic thought, set in the context of changing policy concerns, and the current state of macroeconomic debates.

34. Open-Economy Macroeconomics
Analyzes special issues raised for macroeconomics in an open economy: a weak dollar, foreign accumulation of dollar reserves, and debates surrounding the euro.

Resources for Students and Instructors

www.macmillanhighered.com/launchpad/krugmanwellsecon4

Our new course space, LaunchPad combines an interactive e-Book with high-quality multimedia content and ready-made assessment options, including LearningCurve adaptive quizzing. Pre-built, curated units are easy to assign or adapt with your own material, such as readings, videos, quizzes, discussion groups, and more. LaunchPad also provides access to a gradebook that provides a clear window on performance for your whole class, for individual students, and for individual assignments.

For Students

LearningCurve is an adaptive quizzing engine that automatically adjusts questions to the student's mastery level. With LearningCurve activities, each student follows a unique path to understanding the material. The more questions a student answers correctly, the more difficult the questions become. Each question is written specifically for the text and is linked to the relevant e-Book section. LearningCurve also provides a personal study plan for students as well as complete metrics for instructors. Proven to raise student performance, LearningCurve serves as an ideal formative assessment and learning tool. For detailed information, visit http://learningcurveworks.com.

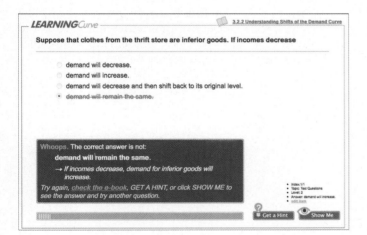

NEW Work It Out Tutorials New to this edition, these tutorials guide students through the process of applying economic analysis and math skills to solve the final problem in each chapter. Choice-specific feedback and video explanations provide students with interactive assistance for each step of the problem.

Economics in Action Based on the feature from the text, these real-life applications are accompanied by assessment and links to additional data.

Living Graphs Based on figures from the text, Living Graphs are animated and interactive graphs that first demonstrate a concept to students and then ask them to manipulate the graph or answer questions to check understanding.

Interactive Tutorials These interactive modules are designed to teach students key principles and concepts through example problems, animated graphs, and interactive activities.

For Instructors

Graphing Questions As a further question bank for instructors building assignments and tests, the electronically gradable graphing problems utilize our own robust graphing engine. In these problems, students will be asked to draw their response to a question, and the software will automatically grade that response. Graphing questions are tagged to appropriate textbook sections and range in difficulty level and skill.

Test Bank The Test Bank, coordinated by Doris Bennett, Jacksonville State University, provides a wide range of questions appropriate for assessing your students' comprehension, interpretation, analysis, and synthesis skills. The Test Bank offers multiple-choice, true/false, and short-answer questions designed for comprehensive coverage of the text concepts. Questions are categorized according to difficulty level (easy, moderate, and difficult) and skill descriptor (definitional, concept-based, critical thinking, and analytical thinking) and are tagged to their appropriate textbook section.

End-of-Chapter Problems The end-of-chapter problems from the text have been converted to a multiple-choice format with answer-specific feedback. These problems can be assigned in homework assignments or quizzes.

Practice and Graded Homework Assignments Each LaunchPad unit contains prebuilt assignments, providing instructors with a curated set of multiple-choice and graphing questions that can be easily assigned for practice or graded assessment.

Instructor's Resource Manual The Instructor's Resource Manual, revised by Nora Underwood, University of Central Florida, is a resource meant to provide materials and tips to enhance the classroom experience as it provides chapter objectives, chapter outlines, and teaching tips and ideas.

Solutions Manual Prepared by the authors of the text, the Solutions Manual contains detailed solutions to all of the end-of-chapter problems from the textbook.

Solutions to business case study Questions for Thought are also provided.

Interactive Presentation Slides This set of Interactive Presentation slides, designed by Solina Lindahl, CalPoly San Luis Obispo, is available as an alternative to traditional lecture outline slides. The slides are brief, interactive, and visually interesting to keep students' attention in class. They offer instructors the following:

- Additional graphics and animations to demonstrate key concepts
- Many additional (and interesting) real-world examples
- Hyperlinks to other relevant outside sources, including links to videos, that provide even more helpful real-world examples to illustrate key concepts
- Opportunities to incorporate active learning in your classroom

Additional Online Offerings

Aplia Worth/Aplia courses are all available with digital textbooks, interactive assignments, and detailed feedback. For a preview of Aplia materials and to learn more, visit www.aplia.com/worth.

www.saplinglearning.com

Sapling Learning provides the most effective interactive homework and instruction that improves student-learning outcomes for the problem-solving disciplines.

Acknowledgments

We are indebted to the following reviewers, class testers, focus group participants, and other consultants for their suggestions and advice on previous editions.

Carlos Aguilar,
El Paso Community College

Giuliana Campanelli Andreopoulos,
William Patterson University

Seemi Ahmad,
Dutchess Community College

Terence Alexander,
Iowa State University

Morris Altman,
University of Saskatchewan

Farhad Ameen,
*State University of New York,
Westchester Community College*

Dean Baim,
Pepperdine University

Christopher P. Ball,
Quinnipiac University

David Barber,
Quinnipiac College

Janis Barry-Figuero,
Fordham University at Lincoln Center

Sue Bartlett,
University of South Florida

Hamid Bastin,
Shippensburg University

Scott Beaulier,
Mercer University

David Bernotas,
University of Georgia

Marc Bilodeau,
Indiana University and Purdue University, Indianapolis

Kelly Blanchard,
Purdue University

Michael Bonnal,
University of Tennessee, Chattanooga

Milicia Bookman,
Saint Joseph's University

Anne Bresnock,
California State Polytechnic University, Pomona

Douglas M. Brown,
Georgetown University

Joseph Calhoun,
Florida State University

Colleen Callahan,
American University

Charles Campbell,
Mississippi State University

Douglas Campbell,
University of Memphis

Randall Campbell,
Mississippi State University

Kevin Carlson,
University of Massachusetts, Boston

Joel Carton,
Florida International University

Andrew Cassey,
Washington State University

Shirley Cassing,
University of Pittsburgh

Sewin Chan,
New York University

Mitchell M. Charkiewicz,
Central Connecticut State University

Joni S. Charles,
Texas State University, San Marcos

Adhip Chaudhuri,
Georgetown University

Sanjukta Chaudhuri,
University of Wisconsin, Eau Claire

Eric Chiang,
Florida Atlantic University

Hayley H. Chouinard,
Washington State University

Abdur Chowdhury,
Marquette University

Kenny Christianson,
Binghamton University

Lisa Citron,
Cascadia Community College

Steven L. Cobb,
University of North Texas

Barbara Z. Connolly,
Westchester Community College

Stephen Conroy,
University of San Diego

Thomas E. Cooper,
Georgetown University

Cesar Corredor,
Texas A&M University and University of Texas, Tyler

Chad Cotti,
University of Wisconsin, Oshkosh

Jim F. Couch,
University of Northern Alabama

Maria DaCosta,
University of Wisconsin, Eau Claire

Daniel Daly,
Regis University

H. Evren Damar,
Pacific Lutheran University

James P. D'Angelo,
University of Cincinnati

Antony Davies,
Duquesne University

Greg Delemeester,
Marietta College

Patrick Dolenc,
Keene State College

Christine Doyle-Burke,
Framingham State College

Ding Du,
South Dakota State University

Jerry Dunn,
Southwestern Oklahoma State University

Robert R. Dunn,
Washington and Jefferson College

Ann Eike,
University of Kentucky

Harold Elder,
University of Alabama

Tisha L. N. Emerson,
Baylor University

Hadi Salehi Esfahani,
University of Illinois

William Feipel,
Illinois Central College

Rudy Fichtenbaum,
Wright State University

David W. Findlay,
Colby College

Mary Flannery,
University of California, Santa Cruz

Sherman Folland,
Oakland University

Robert Francis,
Shoreline Community College

Amanda Freeman,
Kansas State University

Shelby Frost,
Georgia State University

Frank Gallant,
George Fox University

Robert Gazzale,
Williams College

Satyajit Ghosh,
University of Scranton

Robert Godby,
University of Wyoming

Fidel Gonzalez,
Sam Houston State University

Michael G. Goode,
Central Piedmont Community College

Douglas E. Goodman,
University of Puget Sound

Marvin Gordon,
University of Illinois at Chicago

Kathryn Graddy,
Brandeis University

Alan Gummerson,
Florida International University

Eran Guse,
West Virginia University

Alan Day Haight,
State University of New York, Cortland

Mehdi Haririan,
Bloomsburg University

Clyde A. Haulman,
College of William and Mary

Richard R. Hawkins,
University of West Florida

Mickey A. Hepner,
University of Central Oklahoma

Michael Hilmer,
San Diego State University

Tia Hilmer,
San Diego State University

Jane Himarios,
University of Texas, Arlington

Jim Holcomb,
University of Texas, El Paso

Don Holley,
Boise State University

Alexander Holmes,
University of Oklahoma

Julie Holzner,
Los Angeles City College

Robert N. Horn,
James Madison University

Scott Houser,
Colorado School of Mines

Steven Husted,
University of Pittsburgh

Hiro Ito,
Portland State University

Mike Javanmard,
Rio Hondo Community College

Jonatan Jelen,
The City College of New York

Robert T. Jerome,
James Madison University

Shirley Johnson-Lans,
Vassar College

David Kalist,
Shippensburg University

Lillian Kamal,
Northwestern University

Roger T. Kaufman,
Smith College

Elizabeth Sawyer Kelly,
University of Wisconsin, Madison

Herb Kessel,
St. Michael's College

Rehim Kilic,
Georgia Institute of Technology

Grace Kim,
University of Michigan, Dearborn

Miles Kimball,
University of Michigan

Michael Kimmitt,
University of Hawaii, Manoa

Robert Kling,
Colorado State University

Colin Knapp,
University of Florida

Sherrie Kossoudji,
University of Michigan

Stephan Kroll,
Colorado State University

Charles Kroncke,
College of Mount Saint Joseph

Reuben Kyle,
Middle Tennessee State University (retired)

Katherine Lande-Schmeiser,
University of Minnesota, Twin Cities

Vicky Langston,
Columbus State University

Richard B. Le,
Cosumnes River College

Yu-Feng Lee,
New Mexico State University

David Lehr,
Longwood College

Mary Jane Lenon,
Providence College

Mary H. Lesser,
Iona College

Solina Lindahl,
California Polytechnic Institute, San Luis Obispo

Haiyong Liu,
East Carolina University

Jane S. Lopus,
California State University, East Bay

María José Luengo-Prado,
Northeastern University

Volodymyr Lugovskyy,
Indiana University

Rotua Lumbantobing,
North Carolina State University

Ed Lyell,
Adams State College

John Marangos,
Colorado State University

Ralph D. May,
Southwestern Oklahoma State University

Mark E. McBride,
Miami University (Ohio)

Wayne McCaffery,
University of Wisconsin, Madison

Larry McRae,
Appalachian State University

Mary Ruth J. McRae,
Appalachian State University

Ellen E. Meade,
American University

Meghan Millea,
Mississippi State University

Norman C. Miller,
Miami University (Ohio)

Michael Mogavero,
University of Notre Dame

Khan A. Mohabbat,
Northern Illinois University

Myra L. Moore,
University of Georgia

Jay Morris,
Champlain College in Burlington

Akira Motomura,
Stonehill College

Gary Murphy,
Case Western Reserve University

Kevin J. Murphy,
Oakland University

Robert Murphy,
Boston College

Ranganath Murthy,
Bucknell University

Anna Musatti,
Columbia University

Christopher Mushrush,
Illinois State University

Anthony Myatt,
University of New Brunswick, Canada

ABM Nasir,
North Carolina Central University

Gerardo Nebbia,
El Camino College

Pattabiraman Neelakantan,
East Stroudsburg University

Randy A. Nelson,
Colby College

Charles Newton,
Houston Community College

Daniel X. Nguyen,
Purdue University

Pamela Nickless,
University of North Carolina, Asheville

Dmitri Nizovtsev,
Washburn University

Nick Noble,
Miami University (Ohio)

Thomas A. Odegaard,
Baylor University

Constantin Oglobin,
Georgia Southern University

Charles C. Okeke,
College of Southern Nevada

Terry Olson,
Truman State University

Una Okonkwo Osili,
Indiana University and Purdue University, Indianapolis

Maxwell Oteng,
University of California, Davis

P. Marcelo Oviedo,
Iowa State University

Jeff Owen,
Gustavus Adolphus College

Orgul Demet Ozturk,
University of South Carolina

James Palmieri,
Simpson College

Walter G. Park,
American University

Elliott Parker,
University of Nevada, Reno

Michael Perelman,
California State University, Chico

Nathan Perry,
Utah State University

Brian Peterson,
Central College

Dean Peterson,
Seattle University

Ken Peterson,
Furman University

Paul Pieper,
University of Illinois at Chicago

Dennis L. Placone,
Clemson University

Michael Polcen,
Northern Virginia Community College

Linnea Polgreen,
University of Iowa

Raymond A. Polchow,
Zane State College

Eileen Rabach,
Santa Monica College

Matthew Rafferty,
Quinnipiac University

Jaishankar Raman,
Valparaiso University

Margaret Ray,
Mary Washington College

Helen Roberts,
University of Illinois at Chicago

Jeffrey Rubin,
Rutgers University, New Brunswick

Rose M. Rubin,
University of Memphis

Lynda Rush,
California State Polytechnic University, Pomona

Michael Ryan,
Western Michigan University

Sara Saderion,
Houston Community College

Djavad Salehi-Isfahani,
Virginia Tech

Jesse A. Schwartz,
Kennesaw State University

Chad Settle,
University of Tulsa

Steve Shapiro,
University of North Florida

Robert L. Shoffner III,
Central Piedmont Community College

Joseph Sicilian,
University of Kansas

Judy Smrha,
Baker University

John Solow,
University of Iowa

John Somers,
Portland Community College

Stephen Stageberg,
University of Mary Washington

Monty Stanford,
DeVry University

Rebecca Stein,
University of Pennsylvania

William K. Tabb,
Queens College, City University of New York (retired)

Sarinda Taengnoi,
University of Wisconsin, Oshkosh

Henry Terrell,
University of Maryland

Rebecca Achée Thornton,
University of Houston

Michael Toma,
Armstrong Atlantic State University

Brian Trinque,
University of Texas, Austin

Boone A. Turchi,
University of North Carolina, Chapel Hill

Nora Underwood,
University of Central Florida

J. S. Uppal,
State University of New York, Albany

John Vahaly,
University of Louisville

Jose J. Vazquez-Cognet,
University of Illinois, Urbana–Champaign

Daniel Vazzana,
Georgetown College

Roger H. von Haefen,
North Carolina State University

Andreas Waldkirch,
Colby College

Christopher Waller,
University of Notre Dame

Gregory Wassall,
Northeastern University

Robert Whaples,
Wake Forest University

Thomas White,
Assumption College

Jennifer P. Wissink,
Cornell University

Mark Witte,
Northwestern University

Kristen M. Wolfe,
St. Johns River Community College

Larry Wolfenbarger,
Macon State College

Louise B. Wolitz,
University of Texas, Austin

Gavin Wright,
Stanford University

Bill Yang,
Georgia Southern University

Jason Zimmerman,
South Dakota State University

Our deep appreciation and heartfelt thanks to the following reviewers, whose input helped us shape this fourth edition.

Innocentus Alhamis,
Southern New Hampshire University

Becca Arnold,
San Diego Mesa College

Dean Baim,
Pepperdine University

Jeremy Baker,
Owens Community College

Jim Barbour,
Elon University

Richard Beil,
Auburn University

Joydeep Bhattacharya,
Iowa State University

Joanne Blankenship,
State Fair Community College

Emma Bojinova,
Canisius College

Milica Bookman,
Saint John's University

Ralph Bradburd,
Williams College

Mark Brandly,
Ferris State University

Douglas Campbell,
University of Memphis

Semih Cekin,
Texas Tech University

Timothy Classen,
Loyola University Chicago

Maryanne Clifford,
Eastern Connecticut State University

Attila Cseh,
Valdosta State University

Sean D'Evelyn,
Loyola Marymount University

Ronald Dieter,
Iowa State University

Christina Edmundson,
North Idaho College

Hossein Eftekari,
University of Wisconsin-River Falls

Mark Evans,
California State University-Bakersfield

Cynthia Foreman,
Clark College

Bruce Gervais,
California State University-Sacramento

Stuart Glosser,
University of Wisconsin at Whitewater

Julie Gonzalez,
University of California-Santa Cruz

Robert Harris,
Indiana University and Purdue University, Indianapolis

Hadley Hartman,
Santa Fe College

Ryan Herzog,
Gonzaga University

Scott Houser,
Colorado School of Mines

Steven Husted,
University of Pittsburgh

Ali Jalili,
New England College

Carl Jensen,
Seton Hall University

Donn Johnson,
Quinnipiac University

Elizabeth Sawyer Kelly,
University of Wisconsin, Madison

Farida Khan,
University of Wisconsin-Parkside

Ara Khanjian,
Ventura College

Janet Koscianski,
Shippensburg University

Sherrie Kossoudji,
University of Michigan

Stephan Kroll,
Colorado State University

Liaoliao Li,
Kutztown University

Solina Lindahl,
California Polytechnic State University

Haiyong Liu,
East Carolina University

Fernando Lozano,
Claremont McKenna College

Martin Ma,
Washington State University

Stephen Marks,
Claremont McKenna College

Mark McBride,
Miami University

Ashley Miller,
Mount Holyoke College

Myra Moore,
University of Georgia

Kevin Murphy,
Oakland University

Steven Nafziger,
Williams College

Kathryn Nantz,
Fairfield University

Gerald Nyambane,
Davenport University

Fola Odebunmi,
Cypress College

Tomi Odegaard,
University of Nevada-Reno

Tomi Ovaska,
Youngstown State University

Tim Payne,
Shoreline College

Sonia Pereira,
Barnard College, Columbia University

David Pieper,
City College of San Francisco

Paul Pieper,
University of Illinois at Chicago

Arthur Raymond,
Muhlenberg College

Greg Rose,
Sacramento City College

Matt Rutledge,
Boston College

Martin Sabo,
Community College of Denver

Mikael Sandberg,
University of Florida

Michael Sattinger,
University at Albany

Duncan Sattler,
Wilbur Wright College

Lucie Schmidt,
Williams College

Zamira Simkins,
University of Wisconsin-Superior

Ralph Sonenshine,
American University

Daniel Talley,
Dakota State University

Kerry Tan,
Loyola University, Maryland

Julianne Treme,
University of North Carolina at Wilmington

Nora Underwood,
University of Central Florida

Lee Van Scyoc,
University of Wisconsin, Oshkosh

Mark Witte,
Northwestern University

Jadrian Wooten,
Pennsylvania State University

A special thanks must go to Ryan Herzog, Gonzaga University, for all of his hard work and many contributions to this edition. Ryan's role began in the manuscript stage as data researcher, continued into pages with accuracy reviewing, and has now extended to the text's media, with his expertly prepared Work It Out items. This is the first time we've had the opportunity to work with Ryan, and we count ourselves extremely fortunate to have found him (thank you, Charles Linsmeier, for that). Ryan has quickly become an indispensable and tireless advisor to everyone involved in the revision. Many thanks, as well, to Annie Voy, for her consulting work with Ryan on chapters like "Externalities." Ryan's efforts were also supported by accuracy checkers Dixie Dalton, Southside Virginia Community College, and Janet Koscianski, Shippensburg University. Dixie and Janet began their accuracy work on the third edition of our Economics in Modules text. They are both very good at what they do, and we are so happy that they were able to continue their work with us on the fourth edition of this text. Thanks to Marilyn Freedman, as well, for her contributions.

We must also thank the many people at Worth Publishers for their contributions: vice president, editorial, Charles Linsmeier, who ably oversaw the revision and contributed throughout; Shani Fisher, our new publisher, with whom we look forward to working on this and upcoming editions; Craig Bleyer, our original publisher at Worth and now national sales director, who always puts so much effort into making each edition a success; and Sharon Balbos, executive development editor on each of our editions, for her continued dedication and professionalism while working on our chapters.

We have had an incredible production and design team on this book, people whose hard work, creativity, dedication, and patience continue to amaze us. Once again, you have outdone yourselves. Thank you all: Tracey Kuehn, Lisa Kinne, and Jeanine Furino, for producing this book; Vicki Tomaselli for the beautiful interior design and cover; Diana Blume for her assistance with design and art preparation; Deb Heimann, for her thoughtful copyedit; Barbara Seixas and Stacey Alexander, who have worked magic with the project schedule; Cecilia Varas and Elyse Rieder for photo research and the many beautiful, new images you see in this edition; Edgar Bonilla for coordinating all the production of the supplemental materials; Mary Walsh and Bruce Kaplan for their ongoing assistance; and Carlos Marin for preparing the manuscript for production.

Many thanks to Lukia Kliossis and Rachel Comerford for devising and coordinating the impressive collection of online resources for students and instructors that accompany our book. Thanks to the incredible team of writers and coordinators who worked with Lukia; we are forever grateful for your tireless efforts.

Thanks to Tom Digiano, marketing manager, for his enthusiastic and tireless advocacy of this book; to Tom Acox, digital solutions director, who once worked on this text as an editorial assistant and now, from his new perch, offers an array of creative suggestions for our book, its website, and media.

And lastly, to all of you who have introduced our books to your students and colleagues, and who continue to shape our experience as textbook authors, we welcome and encourage your feedback, formal or informal, as we look forward to future revisions.

Please send your comments to

wortheconomics@macmillan.com

Paul Krugman   Robin Wells

ECONOMICS

Introduction: The Ordinary Business of Life

ANY GIVEN SUNDAY

Flickr Editorial/Getty Images

Delivering the goods: the market economy in action.

IT'S SUNDAY AFTERNOON IN THE spring of 2014, and Route 1 in central New Jersey is a busy place. Thousands of people crowd the shopping malls that line the road for 20 miles, all the way from Trenton to New Brunswick. Most of the shoppers are cheerful—and why not? The stores in those malls offer an extraordinary range of choice; you can buy everything from the latest tablet and fashions to caramel macchiattos.

There are probably 100,000 distinct items available along that stretch of road. And most of these items are not luxury goods that only the rich can afford; they are products that millions of Americans can and do purchase every day.

The scene along Route 1 on this spring day is, of course, perfectly ordinary—very much like the scene along hundreds of other stretches of road, all across America, that same afternoon. And the discipline of economics is mainly concerned with ordinary things. As the great nineteenth-century economist Alfred Marshall put it, economics is "a study of mankind in the ordinary business of life."

What can economics say about this "ordinary business"? Quite a lot, it turns out. What we'll see in this book is that even familiar scenes of economic life pose some very important questions—questions that economics can help answer. Among these questions are:

- How does our economic system work? That is, how does it manage to deliver the goods?

- When and why does our economic system go astray, leading people into counterproductive behavior?

- Why are there ups and downs in the economy? That is, why does the economy sometimes have a "bad year"?

- Finally, why is the long run mainly a story of ups rather than downs? That is, why has America, along with other advanced nations, become so much richer over time?

Let's take a look at these questions and offer a brief preview of what you will learn in this book.

The Invisible Hand

That ordinary scene in central New Jersey would not have looked at all ordinary to an American from colonial times—say, one of the patriots who helped George Washington win the Battle of Trenton in 1776. At the time, Trenton was a small village, and farms lined the route of Washington's epic night march from Trenton to Princeton—a march that took him right past the future site of the giant Quakerbridge shopping mall.

Imagine that you could transport an American from the colonial period forward in time to our own era. (Isn't that the plot of a movie? Several, actually.) What would this time-traveler find amazing?

Surely the most amazing thing would be the sheer prosperity of modern America—the range of goods and services that ordinary families can afford. Looking at all that wealth, our transplanted colonial would wonder, "How can I get some of that?" Or perhaps he would ask himself, "How can my society get some of that?"

The answer is that to get this kind of prosperity, you need a well-functioning system for coordinating productive activities—the activities that create the goods and services people want and get them to the people who want them. That kind of system is what we mean when we talk about the **economy.** And **economics** is the social science that studies the production, distribution, and consumption of goods and services.

An economy succeeds to the extent that it, literally, delivers the goods. A time-traveler from the eighteenth century—or even from 1950—would be amazed at how many goods and services the modern American economy delivers and at how many people can afford them. Compared with any past economy and with all but a few other countries today, America has an incredibly high standard of living.

So our economy must be doing something right, and the time-traveler might want to compliment the person in charge. But guess what? There isn't anyone in charge. The United States has a **market economy,** in which production and consumption are the result of decentralized decisions by many firms and individuals. There is no central authority telling people what to produce or where to ship it. Each individual producer makes what he or she thinks will be most profitable; each consumer buys what he or she chooses.

The alternative to a market economy is a *command economy,* in which there *is* a central authority making decisions about production and consumption. Command economies have been tried, most notably in the former Soviet Union between 1917 and 1991. But they didn't work very well. Producers in the Soviet Union routinely found themselves unable to produce because they did not have crucial raw materials, or they succeeded in producing but then found that nobody wanted their products. Consumers were often unable to find necessary items—command economies are famous for long lines at shops.

Market economies, however, are able to coordinate even highly complex activities and to reliably provide consumers with the goods and services they want. Indeed, people quite casually trust their lives to the market system: residents of any major city would starve in days if the unplanned yet somehow orderly actions of thousands of businesses did not deliver a steady supply of food. Surprisingly, the unplanned "chaos" of a market economy turns out to be far more orderly than the "planning" of a command economy.

In 1776, in a famous passage in his book *The Wealth of Nations,* the pioneering Scottish economist Adam Smith wrote about how individuals, in pursuing their own interests, often end up serving the interests of society as a whole. Of a businessman whose pursuit of profit makes the nation wealthier, Smith wrote: "[H]e intends only his own gain, and he is in this, as in many other cases, led by an invisible hand to promote an end which was no part of his intention." Ever since, economists have used the term **invisible hand** to refer to the way a market economy manages to harness the power of self-interest for the good of society.

An **economy** is a system for coordinating society's productive activities.

Economics is the social science that studies the production, distribution, and consumption of goods and services.

A **market economy** is an economy in which decisions about production and consumption are made by individual producers and consumers.

The **invisible hand** refers to the way in which the individual pursuit of self-interest can lead to good results for society as a whole.

The study of how individuals make decisions and how these decisions interact is called **microeconomics.** One of the key themes in microeconomics is the validity of Adam Smith's insight: individuals pursuing their own interests often do promote the interests of society as a whole.

So part of the answer to our time-traveler's question—"How can my society achieve the kind of prosperity you take for granted?"—is that his society should learn to appreciate the virtues of a market economy and the power of the invisible hand.

But the invisible hand isn't always our friend. It's also important to understand when and why the individual pursuit of self-interest can lead to counterproductive behavior.

My Benefit, Your Cost

One thing that our time-traveler would not admire about modern Route 1 is the traffic. In fact, although most things have gotten better in America over time, traffic congestion has gotten a lot worse.

When traffic is congested, each driver is imposing a cost on all the other drivers on the road—he is literally getting in their way (and they are getting in his way). This cost can be substantial: in major metropolitan areas, each time someone drives to work, instead of taking public transportation or working at home, he can easily impose $15 or more in hidden costs on other drivers. Yet when deciding whether or not to drive, commuters have no incentive to take the costs they impose on others into account.

Traffic congestion is a familiar example of a much broader problem: sometimes the individual pursuit of one's own interest, instead of promoting the interests of society as a whole, can actually make society worse off. When this happens, it is known as **market failure.** Other important examples of market failure involve air and water pollution as well as the overexploitation of natural resources such as fish and forests.

The good news, as you will learn as you use this book to study microeconomics, is that economic analysis can be used to diagnose cases of market failure. And often, economic analysis can also be used to devise solutions for the problem.

Good Times, Bad Times

Route 1 was bustling on that day in 2014. But if you'd visited the malls in 2008, the scene wouldn't have been quite as cheerful. That's because New Jersey's economy, along with that of the United States as a whole, was depressed in 2008: in early 2007, businesses began laying off workers in large numbers, and employment didn't start bouncing back until the summer of 2009.

Such troubled periods are a regular feature of modern economies. The fact is that the economy does not always run smoothly: it experiences fluctuations, a series of ups and downs. By middle age, a typical American will have experienced three or four downs, known as **recessions.** (The U.S. economy experienced serious recessions beginning in 1973, 1981, 1990, 2001, and 2007.) During a severe recession, millions of workers may be laid off.

Like market failure, recessions are a fact of life; but also like market failure, they are a problem for which economic analysis offers some solutions. Recessions are one of the main concerns of the branch of economics known as **macroeconomics,** which is concerned with

Microeconomics is the branch of economics that studies how people make decisions and how these decisions interact.

When the individual pursuit of self-interest leads to bad results for society as a whole, there is **market failure.**

A **recession** is a downturn in the economy.

Macroeconomics is the branch of economics that is concerned with overall ups and downs in the economy.

"Remember, an economic boom is usually followed by an economic kaboom."

Economic growth is the growing ability of the economy to produce goods and services.

the overall ups and downs of the economy. If you study macroeconomics, you will learn how economists explain recessions and how government policies can be used to minimize the damage from economic fluctuations.

Despite the occasional recession, however, over the long run the story of the U.S. economy contains many more ups than downs. And that long-run ascent is the subject of our final question.

Onward and Upward

At the beginning of the twentieth century, most Americans lived under conditions that we would now think of as extreme poverty. Only 10% of homes had flush toilets, only 8% had central heating, only 2% had electricity, and almost nobody had a car, let alone a washing machine or air conditioning.

Such comparisons are a stark reminder of how much our lives have been changed by **economic growth,** the growing ability of the economy to produce goods and services. Why does the economy grow over time? And why does economic growth occur faster in some times and places than in others? These are key questions for economics because economic growth is a good thing, as those shoppers on Route 1 can attest, and most of us want more of it.

An Engine for Discovery

We hope we have convinced you that the "ordinary business of life" is really quite extraordinary, if you stop to think about it, and that it can lead us to ask some very interesting and important questions.

In this book, we will describe the answers economists have given to these questions. But this book, like economics as a whole, isn't a list of answers: it's an introduction to a discipline, a way to address questions like those we have just asked. Or as Alfred Marshall, who described economics as a study of the "ordinary business of life," put it: "Economics . . . is not a body of concrete truth, but an engine for the discovery of concrete truth."

So let's turn the key and start the ignition.

KEY TERMS

Economy, p. 2
Economics, p. 2
Market economy, p. 2
Invisible hand, p. 2
Microeconomics, p. 3
Market failure, p. 3
Recession, p. 3
Macroeconomics, p. 3
Economic growth, p. 4

First Principles

> ○ **What You Will Learn in This Chapter**
>
> ■ A set of principles for understanding the economics of how individuals make choices
>
> ■ A set of principles for understanding how economies work through the interaction of individual choices
>
> ■ A set of principles for understanding economy-wide interactions

Audrey Rudakov/Bloomberg via Getty Images

COMMON GROUND

One must choose.

THE ANNUAL MEETING OF THE American Economic Association draws thousands of economists, young and old, famous and obscure. There are booksellers, business meetings, and quite a few job interviews. But mainly the economists gather to talk and listen. During the busiest times, 60 or more presentations may be taking place simultaneously, on questions that range from financial market crises to who does the cooking in two-earner families.

What do these people have in common? An expert on financial markets probably knows very little about the economics of housework, and vice versa. Yet an economist who wanders into the wrong seminar and ends up listening to presentations on some unfamiliar topic is nonetheless likely to hear much that is familiar. The reason is that all economic analysis is based on a set of common principles that apply to many different issues.

Some of these principles involve *individual choice*—for economics is, first of all, about the choices that individuals make. Do you save your money and take the bus or do you buy a car? Do you keep your old smartphone or upgrade to a new one? These decisions involve *making a choice* from among a limited number of alternatives—limited because no one can have everything that he or she wants. Every question in economics at its most basic level involves individuals making choices.

But to understand how an economy works, you need to understand more than how individuals make choices. None of us are Robinson Crusoe, alone on an island. We must make decisions in an environment that is shaped by the decisions of others.

Indeed, in a modern economy even the simplest decisions you make—say, what to have for breakfast—are shaped by the decisions of thousands of other people, from the banana grower in Costa Rica who decided to grow the fruit you

eat to the farmer in Iowa who provided the corn in your cornflakes.

Because each of us in a market economy depends on so many others—and they, in turn, depend on us—our choices interact. So although all economics at a basic level is about individual choice, in order to understand how market economies behave we must also understand *economic interaction*—how my choices affect your choices, and vice versa.

Many important economic interactions can be understood by looking at the markets for individual goods, like the market for corn. But an economy as a whole has ups and downs, and we therefore need to understand economy-wide interactions as well as the more limited interactions that occur in individual markets.

In this chapter, we will look at twelve basic principles of economics—four principles involving individual choice, five involving the way individual choices interact, and three more involving economy-wide interactions.

Principles That Underlie Individual Choice: The Core of Economics

Every economic issue involves, at its most basic level, **individual choice**—decisions by an individual about what to do and what not to do. In fact, you might say that it isn't economics if it isn't about choice.

Step into a big store like a Walmart or Target. There are thousands of different products available, and it is extremely unlikely that you—or anyone else—could afford to buy everything you might want to have. And anyway, there's only so much space in your dorm room or apartment. So will you buy another bookcase or a mini-refrigerator? Given limitations on your budget and your living space, you must choose which products to buy and which to leave on the shelf.

The fact that those products are on the shelf in the first place involves choice—the store manager chose to put them there, and the manufacturers of the products chose to produce them. All economic activities involve individual choice.

Four economic principles underlie the economics of individual choice, as shown in Table 1-1. We'll now examine each of these principles in more detail.

TABLE **1-1**	The Principles of Individual Choice
1. People must make choices because resources are scarce.	
2. The opportunity cost of an item—what you must give up in order to get it—is its true cost.	
3. "How much" decisions require making trade-offs at the margin: comparing the costs and benefits of doing a little bit more of an activity versus doing a little bit less.	
4. People usually respond to incentives, exploiting opportunities to make themselves better off.	

Principle #1: Choices Are Necessary Because Resources Are Scarce

You can't always get what you want. Everyone would like to have a beautiful house in a great location (and have help with the housecleaning), a new car or two, and a nice vacation in a fancy hotel. But even in a rich country like the United States, not many families can afford all that. So they must make choices—whether to go to Disney World this year or buy a better car, whether to make do with a small backyard or accept a longer commute in order to live where land is cheaper.

Limited income isn't the only thing that keeps people from having everything they want. Time is also in limited supply: there are only 24 hours in a day. And because the time we have is limited, choosing to spend time on one activity also means choosing not to spend time on a different activity—studying for an exam means forgoing a night spent watching a movie. Indeed, many people are so limited by the number of hours in the day that they are willing to trade money for time. For example, convenience stores normally charge higher prices than a regular supermarket. But they fulfill a valuable role by catering to time-pressured customers who would rather pay more than travel farther to the supermarket.

This leads us to our first principle of individual choice:

> ### People must make choices because resources are scarce.

A **resource** is anything that can be used to produce something else. Lists of the economy's resources usually begin with land, labor (the time of workers), capital (machinery, buildings, and other man-made productive assets), and human capital (the educational achievements and skills of workers). A resource is **scarce** when there's not enough of the resource available to satisfy all the ways a society wants to use it.

There are many scarce resources. These include natural resources that come from the physical environment, such as minerals, lumber, and petroleum. There is also a limited quantity of human resources, such as labor, skill, and intelligence. And in a growing world economy with a rapidly increasing human population, even clean air and water have become scarce resources.

Just as individuals must make choices, the scarcity of resources means that society as a whole must make choices. One way a society makes choices is by

Individual choice is the decision by an individual of what to do, which necessarily involves a decision of what not to do.

A **resource** is anything that can be used to produce something else.

Resources are **scarce**—not enough of the resources are available to satisfy all the various ways a society wants to use them.

allowing them to emerge as the result of many individual choices, which is what usually happens in a market economy. For example, Americans as a group have only so many hours in a week: how many of those hours will they spend going to supermarkets to get lower prices, rather than saving time by shopping at convenience stores? The answer is the sum of individual decisions: each of the millions of individuals in the economy makes his or her own choice about where to shop, and the overall choice is simply the sum of those individual decisions.

But for various reasons, there are some decisions that a society decides are best not left to individual choice. For example, the authors live in an area that until recently was mainly farmland but is now being rapidly built up. Most local residents feel that the community would be a more pleasant place to live if some of the land was left undeveloped. But no individual has an incentive to keep his or her land as open space, rather than sell it to a developer. So a trend has emerged in many communities across the United States of local governments purchasing undeveloped land and preserving it as open space.

We'll see in later chapters why decisions about how to use scarce resources are often best left to individuals but sometimes should be made at a higher, community-wide, level.

Resources are scarce.

Principle #2: The True Cost of Something Is Its Opportunity Cost

It is the last term before you graduate, and your class schedule allows you to take only one elective. There are two, however, that you would really like to take: Intro to Computer Graphics and History of Jazz.

Suppose you decide to take the History of Jazz course. What's the cost of that decision? It is the fact that you can't take the computer graphics class, your next best alternative choice. Economists call that kind of cost—what you must give up in order to get an item you want—the **opportunity cost** of that item. This leads us to our second principle of individual choice:

> *The opportunity cost of an item—what you must give up in order to get it—is its true cost.*

So the opportunity cost of taking the History of Jazz class is the benefit you would have derived from the Intro to Computer Graphics class.

The concept of opportunity cost is crucial to understanding individual choice because, in the end, all costs are opportunity costs. That's because every choice you make means forgoing some other alternative.

Sometimes critics claim that economists are concerned only with costs and benefits that can be measured in dollars and cents. But that is not true. Much economic analysis involves cases like our elective course example, where it costs no extra tuition to take one elective course—that is, there is no direct monetary cost. Nonetheless, the elective you choose has an opportunity cost—the other desirable elective course that you must forgo because your limited time permits taking only one. More specifically, the opportunity cost of a choice is what you forgo by not choosing your next best alternative.

You might think that opportunity cost is an add-on—that is, something *additional* to the monetary cost of an item. Suppose that an elective class costs additional tuition of $750; now there is a monetary cost to taking History of Jazz. Is the opportunity cost of taking that course something separate from that monetary cost?

Well, consider two cases. First, suppose that taking Intro to Computer Graphics also costs $750. In this case, you would have to spend that $750 no matter which class you take. So what you give up to take the History of Jazz class is still the computer graphics class, period—you would have to spend that $750

The real cost of an item is its **opportunity cost:** what you must give up in order to get it.

Mark Zuckerberg understood the concept of opportunity cost.

AP Photo/Jeff Chiu

either way. But suppose there isn't any fee for the computer graphics class. In that case, what you give up to take the jazz class is the benefit from the computer graphics class *plus* the benefit you could have gained from spending the $750 on other things.

Either way, the real cost of taking your preferred class is what you must give up to get it. As you expand the set of decisions that underlie each choice—whether to take an elective or not, whether to finish this term or not, whether to drop out or not—you'll realize that all costs are ultimately opportunity costs.

Sometimes the money you have to pay for something is a good indication of its opportunity cost. But many times it is not.

One very important example of how poorly monetary cost can indicate opportunity cost is the cost of attending college. Tuition and housing are major monetary expenses for most students; but even if these things were free, attending college would still be an expensive proposition because most college students, if they were not in college, would have a job. That is, by going to college, students *forgo* the income they could have earned if they had worked instead. This means that the opportunity cost of attending college is what you pay for tuition and housing plus the forgone income you would have earned in a job.

It's easy to see that the opportunity cost of going to college is especially high for people who could be earning a lot during what would otherwise have been their college years. That is why star athletes like LeBron James and entrepreneurs like Mark Zuckerberg, founder of Facebook, often skip or drop out of college.

Principle #3: "How Much" Is a Decision at the Margin

Some important decisions involve an "either–or" choice—for example, you decide either to go to college or to begin working; you decide either to take economics or to take something else. But other important decisions involve "how much" choices—for example, if you are taking both economics and chemistry this semester, you must decide how much time to spend studying for each. When it comes to understanding "how much" decisions, economics has an important insight to offer: "how much" is a decision made at the margin.

Suppose you are taking both economics and chemistry. And suppose you are a pre-med student, so your grade in chemistry matters more to you than your grade in economics. Does that therefore imply that you should spend *all* your study time on chemistry and wing it on the economics exam? Probably not; even if you think your chemistry grade is more important, you should put some effort into studying economics.

Spending more time studying chemistry involves a benefit (a higher expected grade in that course) and a cost (you could have spent that time doing something else, such as studying to get a higher grade in economics). That is, your decision involves a **trade-off**—a comparison of costs and benefits.

How do you decide this kind of "how much" question? The typical answer is that you make the decision a bit at a time, by asking how you should spend the next hour. Say both exams are on the same day, and the night before you spend time reviewing your notes for both courses. At 6:00 P.M., you decide that it's a good idea to spend at least an hour on each course. At 8:00 P.M., you decide you'd better spend another hour on each course. At 10:00 P.M., you are getting tired and figure you have one more hour to study before bed—chemistry or economics? If you are pre-med, it's likely to be chemistry; if you are pre-MBA, it's likely to be economics.

Note how you've made the decision to allocate your time: at each point the question is whether or not to spend *one more hour* on either course. And in deciding whether to spend another hour studying for chemistry, you weigh the costs (an hour forgone of studying for economics or an hour forgone of sleeping) versus the benefits (a likely increase in your chemistry grade). As long as the benefit of studying chemistry for one more hour outweighs the cost, you should choose to study for that additional hour.

You make a **trade-off** when you compare the costs with the benefits of doing something.

Decisions of this type—whether to do a bit more or a bit less of an activity, like what to do with your next hour, your next dollar, and so on—are **marginal decisions.** This brings us to our third principle of individual choice:

> *"How much" decisions require making trade-offs at the margin: comparing the costs and benefits of doing a little bit more of an activity versus doing a little bit less.*

The study of such decisions is known as **marginal analysis.** Many of the questions that we face in economics—as well as in real life—involve marginal analysis: How many workers should I hire in my shop? At what mileage should I change the oil in my car? What is an acceptable rate of negative side effects from a new medicine? Marginal analysis plays a central role in economics because it is the key to deciding "how much" of an activity to do.

Principle #4: People Usually Respond to Incentives, Exploiting Opportunities to Make Themselves Better Off

One day, while listening to the morning financial news, the authors heard a great tip about how to park cheaply in Manhattan. Garages in the Wall Street area charge as much as $30 per day. But according to this news report, some people had found a better way: instead of parking in a garage, they had their oil changed at the Manhattan Jiffy Lube, where it costs $19.95 to change your oil—and they keep your car all day!

It's a great story, but unfortunately it turned out not to be true—in fact, there is no Jiffy Lube in Manhattan. But if there were, you can be sure there would be a lot of oil changes there. Why? Because when people are offered opportunities to make themselves better off, they normally take them—and if they could find a way to park their car all day for $19.95 rather than $30, they would.

In this example economists say that people are responding to an **incentive**—an opportunity to make themselves better off. We can now state our fourth principle of individual choice:

> *People usually respond to incentives, exploiting opportunities to make themselves better off.*

When you try to predict how individuals will behave in an economic situation, it is a very good bet that they will respond to incentives—that is, exploit opportunities to make themselves better off. Furthermore, individuals will *continue* to exploit these opportunities until they have been fully exhausted. If there really were a Manhattan Jiffy Lube and an oil change really were a cheap way to park your car, we can safely predict that before long the waiting list for oil changes would be weeks, if not months.

In fact, the principle that people will exploit opportunities to make themselves better off is the basis of *all* predictions by economists about individual behavior. If the earnings of those who get MBAs soar while the earnings of those who get law degrees decline, we can expect more students to go to business school and fewer to go to law school. If the price of gasoline rises and stays high for an extended period of time, we can expect people to buy smaller cars with higher gas mileage—making themselves better off in the presence of higher gas prices by driving more fuel-efficient cars.

One last point: economists tend to be skeptical of any attempt to change people's behavior that *doesn't* change their incentives. For example, a plan that calls on manufacturers to reduce pollution voluntarily probably won't be effective because it hasn't changed manufacturers' incentives. In contrast, a plan that gives them a financial reward to reduce pollution is a lot more likely to work because it has changed their incentives.

Decisions about whether to do a bit more or a bit less of an activity are **marginal decisions.** The study of such decisions is known as **marginal analysis.**

An **incentive** is anything that offers rewards to people who change their behavior.

FOR INQUIRING MINDS | Cashing In At School

The true reward for learning is, of course, the learning itself. Many students, however, struggle with their motivation to study and work hard. Teachers and policy makers have been particularly challenged to help students from disadvantaged backgrounds, who often have poor school attendance, high dropout rates, and low standardized test scores.

Two studies, a 2009 study by Harvard economist Roland Fryer Jr. and a 2011 study by University of Chicago economist Steve Levitt along with others, found that monetary incentives—cash rewards—could improve students' academic performance in schools in economically disadvantaged areas. How cash incentives work, however, is both surprising and predictable.

In the Fryer study, research was conducted in four different school districts, employing a different set of incentives and a different measure of performance in each. In New York, students were paid according to their scores on standardized tests; in Chicago, they were paid according to their grades; in Washington, D.C., they were paid according to attendance and good behavior as well as their grades; in Dallas, second-graders were paid each time they read a book.

Fryer evaluated the results by comparing the performance of students who were in the program to other students in the same school who were not.

In New York, the program had no perceptible effect on test scores. In Chicago, students in the program got better grades and attended class more. In Washington, the program boosted

the outcomes of the kids who are normally the hardest to reach, those with serious behavioral problems, raising their test scores by an amount equivalent to attending five extra months of school.

The most dramatic results occurred in Dallas, where students significantly boosted their reading-comprehension test scores; results continued into the next year, after the cash rewards had ended.

So what explains the various results?

To motivate students with cash rewards, Fryer found that students had to believe that they could have a significant effect on the performance measure. So in Chicago, Washington, and Dallas—where students had a significant amount of control over outcomes such as grades, attendance, behavior, and the number of books read—the program produced significant results.

But because New York students had little idea how to affect their score on a standardized test, the prospect of a reward had little influence on their behavior. Also, the timing of the reward matters: a $1 reward has more effect on behavior if performance is measured at shorter intervals and the reward is delivered soon after.

The Levitt study, involving 7,000 students in the Chicago area, confirmed these results: monetary incentives lead to an increase in standardized test scores equivalent to five or six months of studying for the test. In addition, the Levitt survey found that offering more money ($20) resulted in significantly higher scores than offering less ($10).

Cash incentives have been shown to improve student performance.

And, like Fryer, Levitt and his co-authors found that delaying the reward to a month after the test had no impact on scores.

These two experiments reveal critical insights about how to motivate behavior with incentives. How incentives are designed is very important: the relationship between effort and outcome, as well as the speed of reward, matters a lot. Moreover, the design of incentives may depend quite a lot on the characteristics of the people you are trying to motivate: what motivates a student from an economically privileged background may not motivate a student from an economically disadvantaged one.

Fryer's insights give teachers and policy makers an important new tool for helping disadvantaged students succeed in school. ■

So are we ready to do economics? Not yet—because most of the interesting things that happen in the economy are the result not merely of individual choices but of the way in which individual choices interact.

Boy or Girl? It Depends on the Cost

One fact about China is indisputable: it's a big country with lots of people. As of 2012, the population of China was 1,354,040,000. That's right: over *one billion three hundred and fifty million*.

In 1978, the government of China introduced the "one-child policy" to address the economic and demographic challenges presented by China's large population. China was very, very poor in 1978, and its leaders worried that the country could not afford to adequately educate and care for its growing population. The average Chinese woman in the 1970s was giving birth to more than five children during her lifetime. So the government restricted most couples, particularly those in urban areas, to one child, imposing penalties on those who defied the mandate. As a result, by 2011 the average number of births for a woman in China was only 1.6.

But the one-child policy had an unfortunate unintended consequence. Because China is an overwhelmingly rural country and sons can perform the manual labor of farming, families had a strong preference for sons over daughters. In addition, tradition dictates that brides become part of their husbands' families and that sons take care of their elderly parents. As a result of the one-child policy, China soon had too many "unwanted girls." Some were given up for adoption abroad, but many simply "disappeared" during the first year of life, the victims of neglect and mistreatment.

India, another highly rural poor country with high demographic pressures, also has a significant problem with "disappearing girls." In 1990, Amartya Sen, an Indian-born British economist who would go on to win the Nobel Prize in 1998, estimated that there were up to 100 million "missing women" in Asia. (The exact figure is in dispute, but it is clear that Sen identified a real and pervasive problem.)

Demographers have recently noted a distinct turn of events in China, which is quickly urbanizing. In all but one of the provinces with urban centers, the gender imbalance between boys and girls peaked in 1995 and has steadily fallen toward the biologically natural ratio since then.

Many believe that the source of the change is China's strong economic growth and increasing urbanization. As people move to cities to take advantage of job growth there, they don't need sons to work the fields. Moreover, land prices in Chinese cities are skyrocketing, making the custom of parents buying an apartment for a son before he can marry unaffordable for many.

To be sure, sons are still preferred in the rural areas. But as a sure mark of how times have changed, websites have popped up advising couples on how to have a girl rather than a boy.

The cost of China's "one-child policy" was a generation of "disappeared" daughters—a phenomenon that itself is disappearing as economic conditions change.

Check Your Understanding 1-1

1. Explain how each of the following situations illustrates one of the four principles of individual choice.
   a. You are on your third trip to a restaurant's all-you-can-eat dessert buffet and are feeling very full. Although it would cost you no additional money, you forgo a slice of coconut cream pie but have a slice of chocolate cake.
   b. Even if there were more resources in the world, there would still be scarcity.
   c. Different teaching assistants teach several Economics 101 tutorials. Those taught by the teaching assistants with the best reputations fill up quickly, with spaces left unfilled in the ones taught by assistants with poor reputations.
   d. To decide how many hours per week to exercise, you compare the health benefits of one more hour of exercise to the effect on your grades of one fewer hour spent studying.

2. You make $45,000 per year at your current job with Whiz Kids Consultants. You are considering a job offer from Brainiacs, Inc., that will pay you $50,000 per year. Which of the following are elements of the opportunity cost of accepting the new job at Brainiacs, Inc.?
   a. The increased time spent commuting to your new job
   b. The $45,000 salary from your old job
   c. The more spacious office at your new job

Solutions appear at back of book.

Quick Review

• All economic activities involve **individual choice.**

• People must make choices because **resources** are **scarce.**

• The real cost of something is its **opportunity cost**—what you must give up to get it. All costs are opportunity costs. Monetary costs are sometimes a good indicator of opportunity costs, but not always.

• Many choices involve not *whether* to do something but *how much* of it to do. "How much" choices call for making a **trade-off** at the margin. The study of **marginal decisions** is known as **marginal analysis.**

• Because people usually exploit opportunities to make themselves better off, **incentives** can change people's behavior.

Interaction: How Economies Work

As we learned in the Introduction, an economy is a system for coordinating the productive activities of many people. In a market economy like we live in, coordination takes place without any coordinator: each individual makes his or her own choices.

Yet those choices are by no means independent of one another: each individual's opportunities, and hence choices, depend to a large extent on the choices made by other people. So to understand how a market economy behaves, we have to examine this **interaction** in which my choices affect your choices, and vice versa.

When studying economic interaction, we quickly learn that the end result of individual choices may be quite different from what any one individual intends. For example, over the past century farmers in the United States have eagerly adopted new farming techniques and crop strains that have reduced their costs and increased their yields. Clearly, it's in the interest of each farmer to keep up with the latest farming techniques.

But the end result of each farmer trying to increase his or her own income has actually been to drive many farmers out of business. Because American farmers have been so successful at producing larger yields, agricultural prices have steadily fallen. These falling prices have reduced the incomes of many farmers, and as a result fewer people find farming worth doing. That is, an individual farmer who plants a better variety of corn is better off; but when many farmers plant a better variety of corn, the result may be to make farmers as a group worse off.

A farmer who plants a new, more productive corn variety doesn't just grow more corn. Such a farmer also affects the market for corn through the increased yields attained, with consequences that will be felt by other farmers, consumers, and beyond.

Just as there are four economic principles that underlie individual choice, there are five principles underlying the economics of interaction. These principles are summarized in Table 1-2 and we will now examine each of them more closely.

TABLE 1-2	The Principles of the Interaction of Individual Choices
5. There are gains from trade.	
6. Because people respond to incentives, markets move toward equilibrium.	
7. Resources should be used as efficiently as possible to achieve society's goals.	
8. Because people usually exploit gains from trade, markets usually lead to efficiency.	
9. When markets don't achieve efficiency, government intervention can improve society's welfare.	

Principle #5: There Are Gains from Trade

Why do the choices I make interact with the choices you make? A family could try to take care of all its own needs—growing its own food, sewing its own clothing, providing itself with entertainment, writing its own economics textbooks. But trying to live that way would be very hard.

The key to a much better standard of living for everyone is **trade,** in which people divide tasks among themselves and each person provides a good or service that other people want in return for different goods and services that he or she wants.

The reason we have an economy, not many self-sufficient individuals, is that there are **gains from trade:** by dividing tasks and trading, two people (or 6 billion people) can each get more of what they want than they could get by being self-sufficient. This leads us to our fifth principle:

> *There are gains from trade.*

Gains from trade arise from this division of tasks, which economists call **specialization**—a situation in which different people each engage in a different task, specializing in those tasks that they are good at performing. The advantages of specialization, and the resulting gains from trade, were the starting point for Adam Smith's 1776 book *The Wealth of Nations*, which many regard as the beginning of economics as a discipline.

Interaction of choices—my choices affect your choices, and vice versa—is a feature of most economic situations. The results of this interaction are often quite different from what the individuals intend.

In a market economy, individuals engage in **trade:** they provide goods and services to others and receive goods and services in return.

There are **gains from trade:** people can get more of what they want through trade than they could if they tried to be self-sufficient. This increase in output is due to **specialization:** each person specializes in the task that he or she is good at performing.

Smith's book begins with a description of an eighteenth-century pin factory where, rather than each of the 10 workers making a pin from start to finish, each worker specialized in one of the many steps in pin-making:

> One man draws out the wire, another straights it, a third cuts it, a fourth points it, a fifth grinds it at the top for receiving the head; to make the head requires two or three distinct operations; to put it on, is a particular business, to whiten the pins is another; it is even a trade by itself to put them into the paper; and the important business of making a pin is, in this manner, divided into about eighteen distinct operations. . . . Those ten persons, therefore, could make among them upwards of forty-eight thousand pins in a day. But if they had all wrought separately and independently, and without any of them having been educated to this particular business, they certainly could not each of them have made twenty, perhaps not one pin a day. . . .

"I hunt and she gathers—otherwise we couldn't make ends meet."

The same principle applies when we look at how people divide tasks among themselves and trade in an economy. *The economy, as a whole, can produce more when each person specializes in a task and trades with others.*

The benefits of specialization are the reason a person typically chooses only one career. It takes many years of study and experience to become a doctor or to become a commercial airline pilot. Many doctors might well have had the potential to become excellent pilots, and vice versa; but it is very unlikely that anyone who decided to pursue both careers would be as good a pilot or as good a doctor as someone who decided at the beginning to specialize in that field. So it is to everyone's advantage that individuals specialize in their career choices.

Markets are what allow a doctor and a pilot to specialize in their own fields. Because markets for commercial flights and for doctors' services exist, a doctor is assured that she can find a flight and a pilot is assured that he can find a doctor. As long as individuals know that they can find the goods and services they want in the market, they are willing to forgo self-sufficiency and to specialize. But what assures people that markets will deliver what they want? The answer to that question leads us to our second principle of how individual choices interact.

Principle #6: Markets Move Toward Equilibrium

It's a busy afternoon at the supermarket; there are long lines at the checkout counters. Then one of the previously closed cash registers opens. What happens? The first thing, of course, is a rush to that register. After a couple of minutes, however, things will have settled down; shoppers will have rearranged themselves so that the line at the newly opened register is about the same length as the lines at all the other registers.

How do we know that? We know from our fourth principle that people will exploit opportunities to make themselves better off. This means that people will rush to the newly opened register in order to save time standing in line. And things will settle down when shoppers can no longer improve their position by switching lines—that is, when the opportunities to make themselves better off have all been exploited.

A story about supermarket checkout lines may seem to have little to do with how individual choices interact, but in fact it illustrates an important principle. A situation in which individuals cannot make themselves better off by doing something different—the situation in which all the checkout lines are the same length—is what economists call an **equilibrium.** An economic situation is in equilibrium when no individual would be better off doing something different.

An economic situation is in **equilibrium** when no individual would be better off doing something different.

FOR INQUIRING MINDS | Choosing Sides

Why do people in America drive on the right side of the road? Of course, it's the law. But long before it was the law, it was an equilibrium.

Before there were formal traffic laws, there were informal "rules of the road," practices that everyone expected everyone else to follow. These rules included an understanding that people would normally keep to one side of the road. In some places, such as England, the rule was to keep to the left; in others, such as France, it was to keep to the right.

Why would some places choose the right and others, the left? That's not completely clear, although it may have depended on the dominant form of traffic. Men riding horses and carrying swords on their left hip preferred to ride on the left (think about getting on or off the horse, and you'll see why). On the other hand, right-handed people walking

but leading horses apparently preferred to walk on the right.

In any case, once a rule of the road was established, there were strong incentives for each individual to stay on the "usual" side of the road: those who didn't would keep colliding with oncoming traffic.

So once established, the rule of the road would be self-enforcing—that is, it would be an equilibrium. Nowadays, of course, which side you drive on is determined by law; some countries have even changed sides. In 2009, the island nation of Samoa switched from right to left to conform with the left-side driving in other South Pacific countries.

But what about pedestrians? There are no laws—but there are informal rules. In the United States, urban pedestrians normally keep to the right. But if you should happen to visit a country where people drive on the left, watch out: people who drive on the left

Before traffic laws, the rule of the road was an equilibrium.

also typically walk on the left. So when in a foreign country, do as the locals do. You won't be arrested if you walk on the right, but you will be worse off than if you accept the equilibrium and walk on the left. ∎

Recall the story about the mythical Jiffy Lube, where it was supposedly cheaper to leave your car for an oil change than to pay for parking. If the opportunity had really existed and people were still paying $30 to park in garages, the situation would *not* have been an equilibrium. And that should have been a giveaway that the story couldn't be true. In reality, people would have seized an opportunity to park cheaply, just as they seize opportunities to save time at the checkout line. And in so doing they would have eliminated the opportunity! Either it would have become very hard to get an appointment for an oil change or the price of a lube job would have increased to the point that it was no longer an attractive option (unless you really needed a lube job). This brings us to our sixth principle:

Because people respond to incentives, markets move toward equilibrium.

As we will see, markets usually reach equilibrium via changes in prices, which rise or fall until no opportunities for individuals to make themselves better off remain.

The concept of equilibrium is extremely helpful in understanding economic interactions because it provides a way of cutting through the sometimes complex details of those interactions. To understand what happens when a new line is opened at a supermarket, you don't need to worry about exactly how shoppers rearrange themselves, who moves ahead of whom, which register just opened, and so on. What you need to know is that any time there is a change, the situation will move to an equilibrium.

The fact that markets move toward equilibrium is why we can depend on them to work in a predictable way. In fact, we can trust markets to supply us with the essentials of life. For example, people who live in big cities can be sure that the supermarket shelves will always be fully stocked. Why? Because if some merchants who distribute food *didn't* make deliveries, a big profit opportunity would be created for any merchant who did—and there would be a rush to supply food, just like the rush to a newly opened cash register.

So the market ensures that food will always be available for city dwellers. And, returning to our fifth principle, this allows city dwellers to be city dwellers—to specialize in doing city jobs rather than living on farms and growing their own food.

A market economy, as we have seen, allows people to achieve gains from trade. But how do we know how well such an economy is doing? The next principle gives us a standard to use in evaluating an economy's performance.

Principle #7: Resources Should Be Used Efficiently to Achieve Society's Goals

Suppose you are taking a course in which the classroom is too small for the number of students—many people are forced to stand or sit on the floor—despite the fact that large, empty classrooms are available nearby. You would say, correctly, that this is no way to run a college. Economists would call this an *inefficient* use of resources. But if an inefficient use of resources is undesirable, just what does it mean to use resources *efficiently*?

You might imagine that the efficient use of resources has something to do with money, maybe that it is measured in dollars-and-cents terms. But in economics, as in life, money is only a means to other ends. The measure that economists really care about is not money but people's happiness or welfare. Economists say that *an economy's resources are used efficiently when they are used in a way that has fully exploited all opportunities to make everyone better off*. To put it another way, an economy is **efficient** if it takes all opportunities to make some people better off without making other people worse off.

In our classroom example, there clearly was a way to make everyone better off— moving the class to a larger room would make people in the class better off without hurting anyone else in the college. Assigning the course to the smaller classroom was an inefficient use of the college's resources, whereas assigning the course to the larger classroom would have been an efficient use of the college's resources.

When an economy is efficient, it is producing the maximum gains from trade possible given the resources available. Why? Because there is no way to rearrange how resources are used in a way that can make everyone better off. When an economy is efficient, one person can be made better off by rearranging how resources are used *only* by making someone else worse off.

In our classroom example, if all larger classrooms were already occupied, the college would have been run in an efficient way: your class could be made better off by moving to a larger classroom only by making people in the larger classroom worse off by making them move to a smaller classroom.

We can now state our seventh principle:

> *Resources should be used as efficiently as possible to achieve society's goals.*

Should economic policy makers always strive to achieve economic efficiency? Well, not quite, because efficiency is only a means to achieving society's goals. Sometimes efficiency may conflict with a goal that society has deemed worthwhile to achieve. For example, in most societies, people also care about issues of fairness, or **equity.** And there is typically a trade-off between equity and efficiency: policies that promote equity often come at a cost of decreased efficiency in the economy, and vice versa.

To see this, consider the case of disabled-designated parking spaces in public parking lots. Many people have difficulty walking due to age or disability, so it seems only fair to assign closer parking spaces specifically for their use. You may have noticed, however, that a certain amount of inefficiency is involved. To make sure that there is always a parking space available should a disabled person want one, there are typically more such spaces available than there are disabled people who want one. As a result, desirable parking spaces are unused. (And the temptation for nondisabled people to use them is so great that we must be dissuaded by fear of getting a ticket.)

So, short of hiring parking valets to allocate spaces, there is a conflict between *equity*, making life "fairer" for disabled people, and *efficiency*, making sure that

An economy is **efficient** if it takes all opportunities to make some people better off without making other people worse off.

Equity means that everyone gets his or her fair share. Since people can disagree about what's "fair," equity isn't as well defined a concept as efficiency.

Sometimes equity trumps efficiency.

all opportunities to make people better off have been fully exploited by never letting close-in parking spaces go unused.

Exactly how far policy makers should go in promoting equity over efficiency is a difficult question that goes to the heart of the political process. As such, it is not a question that economists can answer. What is important for economists, however, is always to seek to use the economy's resources as efficiently as possible in the pursuit of society's goals, whatever those goals may be.

Principle #8: Markets Usually Lead to Efficiency

No branch of the U.S. government is entrusted with ensuring the general economic efficiency of our market economy—we don't have agents who go around making sure that brain surgeons aren't plowing fields or that Minnesota farmers aren't trying to grow oranges. The government doesn't need to enforce the efficient use of resources, because in most cases the invisible hand does the job.

The incentives built into a market economy ensure that resources are usually put to good use and that opportunities to make people better off are not wasted. If a college were known for its habit of crowding students into small classrooms while large classrooms went unused, it would soon find its enrollment dropping, putting the jobs of its administrators at risk. The "market" for college students would respond in a way that induced administrators to run the college efficiently.

A detailed explanation of why markets are usually very good at making sure that resources are used well will have to wait until we have studied how markets actually work. But the most basic reason is that in a market economy, in which individuals are free to choose what to consume and what to produce, people normally take opportunities for mutual gain—that is, gains from trade.

If there is a way in which some people can be made better off, people will usually be able to take advantage of that opportunity. And that is exactly what defines efficiency: all the opportunities to make some people better off without making other people worse off have been exploited. This gives rise to our eighth principle:

> *Because people usually exploit gains from trade, markets usually lead to efficiency.*

However, there are exceptions to this principle that markets are generally efficient. In cases of *market failure*, the individual pursuit of self-interest found in markets makes society worse off—that is, the market outcome is inefficient. And, as we will see in examining the next principle, when markets fail, government intervention can help. But short of instances of market failure, the general rule is that markets are a remarkably good way of organizing an economy.

Principle #9: When Markets Don't Achieve Efficiency, Government Intervention Can Improve Society's Welfare

Let's recall from the Introduction the nature of the market failure caused by traffic congestion—a commuter driving to work has no incentive to take into account the cost that his or her action inflicts on other drivers in the form of increased traffic congestion.

There are several possible remedies to this situation; examples include charging road tolls, subsidizing the cost of public transportation, and taxing sales of gasoline to individual drivers. All these remedies work by changing the incentives of would-be drivers, motivating them to drive less and use alternative transportation. But they also share another feature: each relies on government intervention in the market. This brings us to our ninth principle:

> *When markets don't achieve efficiency, government intervention can improve society's welfare.*

That is, when markets go wrong, an appropriately designed government policy can sometimes move society closer to an efficient outcome by changing how society's resources are used.

An important branch of economics is devoted to studying why markets fail and what policies should be adopted to improve social welfare. We will study these problems and their remedies in depth in later chapters, but, briefly, there are three principal ways in which they fail:

- Individual actions have side effects that are not properly taken into account by the market. An example is an action that causes pollution.

- One party prevents mutually beneficial trades from occurring in an attempt to capture a greater share of resources for itself. An example is a drug company that prices a drug higher than the cost of producing it, making it unaffordable for some people who would benefit from it.

- Some goods, by their very nature, are unsuited for efficient management by markets. An example of such a good is air traffic control.

An important part of your education in economics is learning to identify not just when markets work but also when they don't work, and to judge what government policies are appropriate in each situation.

ECONOMICS ▶ *in Action*

Restoring Equilibrium on the Freeways

When a powerful earthquake struck the Los Angeles area back in 1994, it caused several freeway bridges to collapse and thereby disrupted the normal commuting routes of hundreds of thousands of drivers. The events that followed offer a particularly clear example of interdependent decision making—in this case, the decisions of commuters about how to get to work.

In the immediate aftermath of the earthquake, there was great concern about the impact on traffic, since motorists would now have to crowd onto alternative routes or detour around the blockages by using city streets. Public officials and news programs warned commuters to expect massive delays and urged them to avoid unnecessary travel, reschedule their work to commute before or after the rush, or use mass transit.

These warnings were unexpectedly effective. In fact, so many people heeded them that in the first few days following the quake, those who maintained their regular commuting routine actually found the drive to and from work faster than before.

Of course, this situation could not last. As word spread that traffic was relatively light, people abandoned their less convenient new commuting methods and reverted to their cars—and traffic got steadily worse. Within a few weeks

Witness equilibrium in action on a Los Angeles freeway.

after the quake, serious traffic jams had appeared. After a few more weeks, however, the situation stabilized: the reality of worse-than-usual congestion discouraged enough drivers to prevent the nightmare of citywide gridlock from materializing. Los Angeles traffic, in short, had settled into a new equilibrium, in which each commuter was making the best choice he or she could, given what everyone else was doing.

This was not, by the way, the end of the story: fears that traffic would strangle the city led local authorities to repair the roads with record speed. Within only 18 months after the quake, all the freeways were back to normal, ready for the next one.

Check Your Understanding   1-2

1. Explain how each of the following situations illustrates one of the five principles of interaction.
    a. Using eBay any student who wants to sell a used textbook for at least $30 is able to sell it to someone who is willing to pay $30.
    b. At a college tutoring co-op, students can arrange to provide tutoring in subjects they are good in (like economics) in return for receiving tutoring in subjects they are poor in (like philosophy).
    c. The local municipality imposes a law that requires bars and nightclubs near residential areas to keep their noise levels below a certain threshold.
    d. To provide better care for low-income patients, the local municipality has decided to close some underutilized neighborhood clinics and shift funds to the main hospital.
    e. On eBay books of a given title with approximately the same level of wear and tear sell for about the same price.
2. Which of the following describes an equilibrium situation? Which does not? Explain your answer.
    a. The restaurants across the street from the university dining hall serve better-tasting and cheaper meals than those served at the university dining hall. The vast majority of students continue to eat at the dining hall.
    b. You currently take the subway to work. Although taking the bus is cheaper, the ride takes longer. So you are willing to pay the higher subway fare in order to save time.

Solutions appear at back of book.

Economy-Wide Interactions

As mentioned in the Introduction, the economy as a whole has its ups and downs. For example, business in America's shopping malls was depressed in 2008, because the economy was in a recession. While the economy had begun to recover in 2009, the effects of the downturn were still being felt—not until May 2014 did the number of Americans employed recover to its pre-recession level.

To understand recessions and recoveries, we need to understand economy-wide interactions, and understanding the big picture of the economy requires three more economic principles, which are summarized in Table 1-3.

TABLE 1-3	The Principles of Economy-Wide Interactions
10. One person's spending is another person's income.	
11. Overall spending sometimes gets out of line with the economy's productive capacity.	
12. Government policies can change spending.	

Principle #10: One Person's Spending Is Another Person's Income

Between 2005 and 2011, home construction in America plunged more than 60% because builders found it increasingly hard to make sales. At first the damage was mainly limited to the construction industry. But over time the slump spread into just about every part of the economy, with consumer spending falling across the board.

But why should a fall in home construction mean empty stores in the shopping malls? After all, malls are places where families, not builders, do their shopping.

The answer is that lower spending on construction led to lower incomes throughout the economy; people who had been employed either directly in construction, producing goods and services builders need (like wallboard), or in producing goods and services new homeowners need (like new furniture), either lost their jobs or were forced to take pay cuts. And as incomes fell, so did spending by consumers. This example illustrates our tenth principle:

> *One person's spending is another person's income.*

In a market economy, people make a living selling things—including their labor—to other people. If some group in the economy decides, for whatever reason, to spend more, the income of other groups will rise. If some group decides to spend less, the income of other groups will fall.

Because one person's spending is another person's income, a chain reaction of changes in spending behavior tends to have repercussions that spread through the economy. For example, a cut in business investment spending, like the one that happened in 2008, leads to reduced family incomes; families respond by reducing consumer spending; this leads to another round of income cuts; and so on. These repercussions play an important role in our understanding of recessions and recoveries.

Principle #11: Overall Spending Sometimes Gets Out of Line with the Economy's Productive Capacity

Macroeconomics emerged as a separate branch of economics in the 1930s, when a collapse of consumer and business spending, a crisis in the banking industry, and other factors led to a plunge in overall spending. This plunge in spending, in turn, led to a period of very high unemployment known as the Great Depression.

The lesson economists learned from the troubles of the 1930s is that overall spending—the amount of goods and services that consumers and businesses want to buy—sometimes doesn't match the amount of goods and services the economy is capable of producing. In the 1930s, spending fell far short of what was needed to keep American workers employed, and the result was a severe economic slump. In fact, shortfalls in spending are responsible for most, though not all, recessions.

It's also possible for overall spending to be too high. In that case, the economy experiences *inflation*, a rise in prices throughout the economy. This rise in prices occurs because when the amount that people want to buy outstrips the supply, producers can raise their prices and still find willing customers. Taking account of both shortfalls in spending and excesses in spending brings us to our eleventh principle:

> *Overall spending sometimes gets out of line with the economy's productive capacity.*

Principle #12: Government Policies Can Change Spending

Overall spending sometimes gets out of line with the economy's productive capacity. But can anything be done about that? Yes—which leads to our twelfth and last principle:

> *Government policies can change spending.*

In fact, government policies can dramatically affect spending.

For one thing, the government itself does a lot of spending on everything from military equipment to education—and it can choose to do more or less. The government can also vary how much it collects from the public in taxes, which in turn affects how much income consumers and businesses have left to spend. And the government's control of the quantity of money in circulation, it turns out, gives it another powerful tool with which to affect total spending. Government spending, taxes, and control of money are the tools of *macro-economic policy*.

Modern governments deploy these macroeconomic policy tools in an effort to manage overall spending in the economy, trying to steer it between the perils of recession and inflation. These efforts aren't always successful—recessions still happen, and so do periods of inflation. But it's widely believed that aggressive efforts to sustain spending in 2008 and 2009 helped prevent the financial crisis of 2008 from turning into a full-blown depression.

As participants in a babysitting co-op soon discovered, fewer nights out made everyone worse off.

ECONOMICS ▶ *in Action*

Adventures in Babysitting

The website, myarmyonesource.com, which offers advice to army families, suggests that parents join a babysitting cooperative—an arrangement that is common in many walks of life. In a babysitting cooperative, a number of parents exchange babysitting services rather than hire someone to babysit. But how do these organizations make sure that all members do their fair share of the work?

As myarmyonesource.com explained, "Instead of money, most co-ops exchange tickets or points. When you need a sitter, you call a friend on the list, and you pay them with tickets. You earn tickets by babysitting other children within the co-op." In other words, a babysitting co-op is a miniature economy in which people buy and sell babysitting services. And it happens to be a type of economy that can have macroeconomic problems.

A famous article titled "Monetary Theory and the Great Capitol Hill Babysitting Co-Op Crisis" described the troubles of a babysitting cooperative that issued too few tickets. Bear in mind that, on average, people in a babysitting co-op want to have a reserve of tickets stashed away in case they need to go out several times before they can replenish their stash by doing some more babysitting.

In this case, because there weren't that many tickets out there to begin with, most parents were anxious to add to their reserves by babysitting but reluctant to run them down by going out. But one parent's decision to go out was another's chance to babysit, so it became difficult to earn tickets. Knowing this, parents became even more reluctant to use their reserves except on special occasions.

In short, the co-op had fallen into a recession. Recessions in the larger, non-babysitting economy are a bit more complicated than this, but the troubles of the Capitol Hill babysitting co-op demonstrate two of our three principles of economy-wide interactions. One person's spending is another person's income: opportunities to babysit arose only to the extent that other people went out.

An economy can also suffer from too little spending: when not enough people were willing to go out, everyone was frustrated at the lack of babysitting opportunities.

And what about government policies to change spending? Actually, the Capitol Hill co-op did that, too. Eventually, it solved its problem by handing out more tickets, and with increased reserves, people were willing to go out more.

▼ Quick Review

- In a market economy, one person's spending is another person's income. As a result, changes in spending behavior have repercussions that spread through the economy.

- Overall spending sometimes gets out of line with the economy's capacity to produce goods and services. When spending is too low, the result is a recession. When spending is too high, it causes inflation.

- Modern governments use macroeconomic policy tools to affect the overall level of spending in an effort to steer the economy between recession and inflation.

Check Your Understanding 1-3

1. Explain how each of the following examples illustrates one of the three principles of economy-wide interactions.
   a. The White House urged Congress to pass a package of temporary spending increases and tax cuts in early 2009, a time when employment was plunging and unemployment soaring.
   b. Oil companies are investing heavily in projects that will extract oil from the "oil sands" of Canada. In Edmonton, Alberta, near the projects, restaurants and other consumer businesses are booming.
   c. In the mid-2000s, Spain, which was experiencing a big housing boom, also had the highest inflation rate in Europe.

Solutions appear at back of book.

How Priceline.com Revolutionized the Travel Industry

I n 2001 and 2002, the travel industry was in deep trouble. After the terrorist attacks of September 11, 2001, many people simply stopped flying. As the economy went into a deep slump, airplanes sat empty on the tarmac and the airlines lost billions of dollars. When several major airlines spiraled toward bankruptcy, Congress passed a $15 billion aid package that was critical in stabilizing the airline industry.

This was also a particularly difficult time for Priceline.com, the online travel service. Just four years after its founding, Priceline.com was in danger of going under. The change in the company's fortunes had been dramatic.

In 1999, one year after Priceline.com was formed, investors were so impressed by its potential for revolutionizing the travel industry that they valued the company at $9 billion dollars. But by 2002 investors had taken a decidedly dimmer view of the company, reducing its valuation by 95% to only $425 million.

To make matters worse, Priceline.com was losing several million dollars a year. Yet the company managed to survive and thrive; in 2014 it was valued by investors at over $63 billion.

So exactly how did Priceline.com bring such dramatic change to the travel industry? And what has allowed it to survive and prosper as a company in the face of dire economic conditions?

Priceline.com's success lies in its ability to spot exploitable opportunities for itself and its customers. The company understood that when a plane departs with empty seats or a hotel has empty beds, it bears a cost—the revenue that would have been earned if that seat or bed had been filled. And although some travelers like the security of booking their flights and hotels well in advance and are willing to pay for that, others are quite happy to wait until the last minute, risking not getting the flight or hotel they want but enjoying a lower price.

Customers specify the price they are willing to pay for a given trip or hotel location, and then Priceline.com presents them with a list of options from airlines or hotels that are willing to accept that price, with the price typically declining as the date of the trip nears.

By bringing airlines and hotels with unsold capacity together with travelers who are willing to sacrifice some of their preferences for a lower price, Priceline.com made everyone better off—including itself, since it charged a small commission for each trade it facilitated.

Priceline.com was also quick on its feet when it saw its market challenged by newcomers Expedia and Orbitz. In response, it aggressively moved more of its business toward hotel bookings and into Europe, where the online travel industry was still quite small. Its network was particularly valuable in the European hotel market, with many more small hotels compared to the U.S. market, which is dominated by nationwide chains. The efforts paid off, and by 2003 Priceline.com had turned its first profit.

Priceline.com now operates within a network of more than 295,000 hotels in over 190 countries. As of 2013, its revenues had grown well over 20% in each of the previous five years, even growing 34% during the 2008 recession.

Clearly, the travel industry will never be the same again.

QUESTION FOR THOUGHT

1. Explain how each of the twelve principles of economics is illustrated in this case study.

SUMMARY

1. All economic analysis is based on a set of basic principles that apply to three levels of economic activity. First, we study how individuals make choices; second, we study how these choices interact; and third, we study how the economy functions overall.

2. Everyone has to make choices about what to do and what *not* to do. **Individual choice** is the basis of economics—if it doesn't involve choice, it isn't economics.

3. The reason choices must be made is that **resources**—anything that can be used to produce something else—are **scarce.** Individuals are limited in their choices by money and time; economies are limited by their supplies of human and natural resources.

4. Because you must choose among limited alternatives, the true cost of anything is what you must give up to get it—all costs are **opportunity costs.**

5. Many economic decisions involve questions not of "whether" but of "how much"—how much to spend on some good, how much to produce, and so on. Such decisions must be made by performing a **trade-off** *at the margin*—by comparing the costs and benefits of doing a bit more or a bit less. Decisions of this type are called **marginal decisions,** and the study of them, **marginal analysis,** plays a central role in economics.

6. The study of how people *should* make decisions is also a good way to understand actual behavior. Individuals usually respond to **incentives**—exploiting opportunities to make themselves better off.

7. The next level of economic analysis is the study of **interaction**—how my choices depend on your choices, and vice versa. When individuals interact, the end result may be different from what anyone intends.

8. Individuals interact because there are **gains from trade:** by engaging in the **trade** of goods and services with one another, the members of an economy can all be made better off. **Specialization**—each person specializes in the task he or she is good at—is the source of gains from trade.

9. Because individuals usually respond to incentives, markets normally move toward **equilibrium**—a situation in which no individual can make himself or herself better off by taking a different action.

10. An economy is **efficient** if all opportunities to make some people better off without making other people worse off are taken. Resources should be used as efficiently as possible to achieve society's goals. But efficiency is not the sole way to evaluate an economy: **equity,** or fairness, is also desirable, and there is often a trade-off between equity and efficiency.

11. Markets usually lead to efficiency, with some well-defined exceptions.

12. When markets fail and do not achieve efficiency, government intervention can improve society's welfare.

13. Because people in a market economy earn income by selling things, including their own labor, one person's spending is another person's income. As a result, changes in spending behavior can spread throughout the economy.

14. Overall spending in the economy can get out of line with the economy's productive capacity. Spending below the economy's productive capacity leads to a recession; spending in excess of the economy's productive capacity leads to inflation.

15. Governments have the ability to strongly affect overall spending, an ability they use in an effort to steer the economy between recession and inflation.

KEY TERMS

Individual choice, p. 6
Resource, p. 6
Scarce, p. 6
Opportunity cost, p. 7
Trade-off, p. 8

Marginal decisions, p. 9
Marginal analysis, p. 9
Incentive, p. 9
Interaction, p. 12
Trade, p. 12

Gains from trade, p. 12
Specialization, p. 12
Equilibrium, p. 13
Efficient, p. 15
Equity, p. 15

PROBLEMS

1. In each of the following situations, identify which of the twelve principles is at work.

   a. You choose to shop at the local discount store rather than paying a higher price for the same merchandise at the local department store.

   b. On your spring break trip, your budget is limited to $35 a day.

   c. The student union provides a website on which departing students can sell items such as used books, appliances, and furniture rather than give them away to their roommates as they formerly did.

   d. After a hurricane did extensive damage to homes on the island of St. Crispin, homeowners wanted to purchase many more building materials and hire many more workers than were available on the island. As a result, prices for goods and services rose dramatically across the board.

   e. You buy a used textbook from your roommate. Your roommate uses the money to buy songs from iTunes.

   f. You decide how many cups of coffee to have when studying the night before an exam by considering how much more work you can do by having another cup versus how jittery it will make you feel.

   g. There is limited lab space available to do the project required in Chemistry 101. The lab supervisor assigns lab time to each student based on when that student is able to come.

   h. You realize that you can graduate a semester early by forgoing a semester of study abroad.

   i. At the student union, there is a bulletin board on which people advertise used items for sale, such as bicycles. Once you have adjusted for differences in quality, all the bikes sell for about the same price.

   j. You are better at performing lab experiments, and your lab partner is better at writing lab reports. So the two of you agree that you will do all the experiments and she will write up all the reports.

   k. State governments mandate that it is illegal to drive without passing a driving exam.

   l. Your parents' after-tax income has increased because of a tax cut passed by Congress. They therefore increase your allowance, which you spend on a spring break vacation.

2. Describe some of the opportunity costs when you decide to do the following.

   a. Attend college instead of taking a job

   b. Watch a movie instead of studying for an exam

   c. Ride the bus instead of driving your car

3. Liza needs to buy a textbook for the next economics class. The price at the college bookstore is $65. One online site offers it for $55 and another site, for $57. All prices include sales tax. The accompanying table indicates the typical shipping and handling charges for the textbook ordered online.

Shipping method	Delivery time	Charge
Standard shipping	3–7 days	$3.99
Second-day air	2 business days	8.98
Next-day air	1 business day	13.98

   a. What is the opportunity cost of buying online instead of at the bookstore? Note that if you buy the book online, you must wait to get it.

   b. Show the relevant choices for this student. What determines which of these options the student will choose?

4. Use the concept of opportunity cost to explain the following.

   a. More people choose to get graduate degrees when the job market is poor.

   b. More people choose to do their own home repairs when the economy is slow and hourly wages are down.

   c. There are more parks in suburban than in urban areas.

   d. Convenience stores, which have higher prices than supermarkets, cater to busy people.

   e. Fewer students enroll in classes that meet before 10:00 A.M.

5. In the following examples, state how you would use the principle of marginal analysis to make a decision.

   a. Deciding how many days to wait before doing your laundry

   b. Deciding how much library research to do before writing your term paper

   c. Deciding how many bags of chips to eat

   d. Deciding how many lectures of a class to skip

6. This morning you made the following individual choices: you bought a bagel and coffee at the local café, you drove to school in your car during rush hour, and you typed your roommate's term paper because you are a fast typist—in return for which she will do your laundry for a month. For each of these actions, describe how your individual choices interacted with the individual choices made by others. Were other people left better off or worse off by your choices in each case?

7. The Hatfield family lives on the east side of the Hatatoochie River, and the McCoy family lives on the west side. Each family's diet consists of fried chicken and corn-on-the-cob, and each is self-sufficient, raising their own chickens and growing their own corn. Explain the conditions under which each of the following would be true.

a. The two families are made better off when the Hatfields specialize in raising chickens, the McCoys specialize in growing corn, and the two families trade.

b. The two families are made better off when the McCoys specialize in raising chickens, the Hatfields specialize in growing corn, and the two families trade.

8. Which of the following situations describes an equilibrium? Which does not? If the situation does not describe an equilibrium, what would an equilibrium look like?

a. Many people regularly commute from the suburbs to downtown Pleasantville. Due to traffic congestion, the trip takes 30 minutes when you travel by highway but only 15 minutes when you go by side streets.

b. At the intersection of Main and Broadway are two gas stations. One station charges $3.00 per gallon for regular gas and the other charges $2.85 per gallon. Customers can get service immediately at the first station but must wait in a long line at the second.

c. Every student enrolled in Economics 101 must also attend a weekly tutorial. This year there are two sections offered: section A and section B, which meet at the same time in adjoining classrooms and are taught by equally competent instructors. Section A is overcrowded, with people sitting on the floor and often unable to see what is written on the board at the front of the room. Section B has many empty seats.

9. In each of the following cases, explain whether you think the situation is efficient or not. If it is not efficient, why not? What actions would make the situation efficient?

a. Electricity is included in the rent at your dorm. Some residents in your dorm leave lights, computers, and appliances on when they are not in their rooms.

b. Although they cost the same amount to prepare, the cafeteria in your dorm consistently provides too many dishes that diners don't like, such as tofu casserole, and too few dishes that diners do like, such as roast turkey with dressing.

c. The enrollment for a particular course exceeds the spaces available. Some students who need to take this course to complete their major are unable to get a space even though others who are taking it as an elective do get a space.

10. Discuss the efficiency and equity implications of each of the following policies. How would you go about balancing the concerns of equity and efficiency in these areas?

a. The government pays the full tuition for every college student to study whatever subject he or she wishes.

b. When people lose their jobs, the government provides unemployment benefits until they find new ones.

11. Governments often adopt certain policies in order to promote desired behavior among their citizens. For each of the following policies, determine what the incentive is and what behavior the government wishes to promote. In each case, why do you think that the government might wish to change people's behavior, rather than allow their actions to be solely determined by individual choice?

a. A tax of $5 per pack is imposed on cigarettes.

b. The government pays parents $100 when their child is vaccinated for measles.

c. The government pays college students to tutor children from low-income families.

d. The government imposes a tax on the amount of air pollution that a company discharges.

12. In each of the following situations, explain how government intervention could improve society's welfare by changing people's incentives. In what sense is the market going wrong?

a. Pollution from auto emissions has reached unhealthy levels.

b. Everyone in Woodville would be better off if streetlights were installed in the town. But no individual resident is willing to pay for installation of a streetlight in front of his or her house because it is impossible to recoup the cost by charging other residents for the benefit they receive from it.

13. In 2010, Tim Geithner, Treasury secretary at the time, published an article defending the administration's policies. In it he said, "The recession that began in late 2007 was extraordinarily severe. But the actions we took at its height to stimulate the economy helped arrest the free fall, preventing an even deeper collapse and putting the economy on the road to recovery." Which two of the three principles of economy-wide interaction are at work in this statement?

14. In August 2007, a sharp downturn in the U.S. housing market reduced the income of many who worked in the home construction industry. A *Wall Street Journal* news article reported that Walmart's wire-transfer business was likely to suffer because many construction workers are Hispanics who regularly send part of their wages back to relatives in their home countries via Walmart. With this information, use one of the principles of economy-wide interaction to trace a chain of links that explains how reduced spending for U.S. home purchases is likely to affect the performance of the Mexican economy.

15. In 2012, Hurricane Sandy caused massive destruction to the northeast United States. Tens of thousands of people lost their homes and possessions. Even those who weren't directly affected by the destruction were hurt because businesses failed or contracted and jobs dried up. Using one of the principles of economy-wide interaction, explain how government intervention can help in this situation.

16. During the Great Depression, food was left to rot in the fields or fields that had once been actively cultivated were left fallow. Use one of the principles of economy-wide interaction to explain how this could have occurred.

Economic Models:
Trade-offs and Trade

▶ **What You Will Learn
in This Chapter**

■ Why **models**—simplified
representations of reality—play a
crucial role in economics

■ Two simple but important
models: the **production
possibility frontier** and
comparative advantage

■ The **circular-flow diagram,** a
schematic representation of the
economy

■ The difference between **positive
economics,** which analyzes
how the economy works, and
normative economics, which
prescribes economic policy

■ When economists agree and
why they sometimes disagree

FROM KITTY HAWK TO DREAMLINER

UPI/Alan Marts/Boeing/Landov

The Wright brothers' model made modern airplanes, including the Dreamliner, possible.

In DECEMBER 2009, BOEING'S NEW-est jet, the 787 Dreamliner, took its first three-hour test flight. It was a historic moment: the Dreamliner was the result of an aerodynamic revolution—a super efficient airplane designed to cut airline operating costs and the first to use superlight composite materials.

To ensure that the Dreamliner was sufficiently lightweight and aerodynam-ic, it underwent over 15,000 hours of wind tunnel tests—tests that resulted in subtle design changes that improved its performance, making it 20% more fuel efficient and 20% less pollutant emitting than existing passenger jets.

The first flight of the Dreamliner was a spectacular advance from the 1903 maiden voyage of the Wright Flyer, the first successful powered airplane, in Kitty Hawk, North Carolina. Yet the

Boeing engineers—and all aeronautic engineers—owe an enormous debt to the Wright Flyer's inventors, Wilbur and Orville Wright.

What made the Wrights truly visionary was their invention of the wind tunnel, an apparatus that let them experiment with many different designs for wings and control surfaces. Doing experiments with a miniature airplane, inside a wind tun-nel the size of a shipping crate, gave the Wright brothers the knowledge that would make heavier-than-air flight possible.

Neither a miniature airplane inside a packing crate nor a miniature model of the Dreamliner inside Boeing's state-of-the-art Transonic Wind Tunnel is the same thing as an actual aircraft in flight. But it is a very useful *model* of a flying plane—a simplified representation of the real thing that can be used to answer crucial ques-

tions, such as how much lift a given wing shape will generate at a given airspeed.

Needless to say, testing an airplane design in a wind tunnel is cheaper and safer than building a full-scale version and hoping it will fly. More generally, models play a crucial role in almost all sci-entific research—economics very much included.

In fact, you could say that economic theory consists mainly of a collection of models, a series of simplified representa-tions of economic reality that allow us to understand a variety of economic issues.

In this chapter, we'll look at two economic models that are crucially important in their own right and also illustrate why such models are so useful. We'll conclude with a look at how economists actually use models in their work.

A **model** is a simplified representation of a real situation that is used to better understand real-life situations.

Models in Economics: Some Important Examples

A **model** is any simplified representation of reality that is used to better understand real-life situations. But how do we create a simplified representation of an economic situation?

One possibility—an economist's equivalent of a wind tunnel—is to find or create a real but simplified economy. For example, economists interested in the economic role of money have studied the system of exchange that developed in World War II prison camps, in which cigarettes became a universally accepted form of payment even among prisoners who didn't smoke.

Another possibility is to simulate the workings of the economy on a computer. For example, when changes in tax law are proposed, government officials use *tax models*—large mathematical computer programs—to assess how the proposed changes would affect different types of people.

Models are important because their simplicity allows economists to focus on the effects of only one change at a time. That is, they allow us to hold everything else constant and study how one change affects the overall economic outcome.

FOR INQUIRING MINDS | The Model That Ate the Economy

A model is just a model, right? So how much damage can it do? Economists probably would have answered that question quite differently before the financial meltdown of 2008–2009 than after it. The financial crisis continues to reverberate today—a testament to why economic models are so important. For an economic model—a *bad* economic model, it turns out—played a significant role in the origins of the crisis.

"The model that ate the economy" originated in finance theory, the branch of economics that seeks to understand what assets like stocks and bonds are

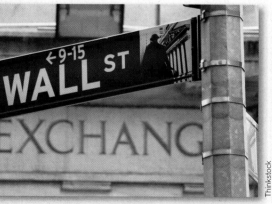

A model that underestimated the risks of investing in MBSs had dire consequences for financial firms on Wall Street and for the global economy.

worth. Financial theorists often get hired (at very high salaries, mind you) to devise complex mathematical models to help investment companies decide what assets to buy and sell and at what price.

The trouble began with an asset known as an MBS, which is short for mortgage-backed security. The owner of an MBS is entitled to a stream of earnings based on the payments made by thousands of people on their home loans. But an MBS carries with it a potential problem: those homeowners can stop paying their mortgages, inflicting losses on the owner of the MBS. So investors wanted to know how risky an MBS was—that is, how likely it was to lose money.

In 2000, a Wall Street financial theorist announced that he had solved the problem by adopting a huge mathematical simplification. With it, he devised a simple model for estimating the risk of an MBS. Financial firms loved the model because it opened up a huge and extraordinarily profitable market for them in the selling of MBSs to investors. Using the model, financial firms were able to package and sell billions of dollars in MBSs, generating billions in profits for themselves.

Or investors *thought* they had calculated the risk of losing money on an MBS. Some financial experts—particularly Darrell Duffie, a Stanford

University finance professor—warned from the sidelines that the estimates of risk calculated by this simple model were just plain wrong. He, and other critics, said that in the search for simplicity, the model seriously underestimated the risk of losing money on an MBS.

The warnings fell on deaf ears—no doubt because financial firms were making so much money. Billions of dollars worth of MBSs were sold to investors in the United States and abroad. In 2008–2009, the problems critics warned about exploded in catastrophic fashion.

Over the previous decade, American home prices had risen too high, and mortgages had been extended to many who were unable to pay. As home prices fell to earth, millions of homeowners didn't pay their mortgages. With losses mounting for MBS investors, it became all too clear that the model had indeed underestimated the risks.

When investors and financial institutions around the world realized the extent of their losses, the worldwide economy ground to an abrupt halt.

People lost their homes, companies went bankrupt, and unemployment surged. The recovery over the past six years has been achingly slow, and it wasn't until 2014 that the number of employed Americans returned to pre-recession levels. ■

So an important assumption when building economic models is the **other things equal assumption,** which means that all other relevant factors remain unchanged.

But you can't always find or create a small-scale version of the whole economy, and a computer program is only as good as the data it uses. (Programmers have a saying: "garbage in, garbage out.") For many purposes, the most effective form of economic modeling is the construction of "thought experiments": simplified, hypothetical versions of real-life situations.

In Chapter 1 we illustrated the concept of equilibrium with the example of how customers at a supermarket would rearrange themselves when a new cash register opens. Though we didn't say it, this was an example of a simple model—an imaginary supermarket, in which many details were ignored. (What were customers buying? Never mind.) This simple model can be used to answer a "what if" question: what if another cash register were opened?

As the cash register story showed, it is often possible to describe and analyze a useful economic model in plain English. However, because much of economics involves changes in quantities—in the price of a product, the number of units produced, or the number of workers employed in its production—economists often find that using some mathematics helps clarify an issue. In particular, a numerical example, a simple equation, or—especially—a graph can be key to understanding an economic concept.

Whatever form it takes, a good economic model can be a tremendous aid to understanding. The best way to grasp this point is to consider some simple but important economic models and what they tell us.

- First, we will look at the *production possibility frontier,* a model that helps economists think about the trade-offs every economy faces.

- We then turn to *comparative advantage,* a model that clarifies the principle of gains from trade—trade both between individuals and between countries.

- We will also examine the *circular-flow diagram,* a schematic representation that helps us understand how flows of money, goods, and services are channeled through the economy.

In discussing these models, we make considerable use of graphs to represent mathematical relationships. Graphs play an important role throughout this book. If you are already familiar with how graphs are used, you can skip the appendix to this chapter, which provides a brief introduction to the use of graphs in economics. If not, this would be a good time to turn to it.

Trade-offs: The Production Possibility Frontier

The first principle of economics introduced in Chapter 1 is that resources are scarce and that, as a result, any economy—whether it's an isolated group of a few dozen hunter-gatherers or the 6 billion people making up the twenty-first-century global economy—faces trade-offs. No matter how lightweight the Boeing Dreamliner is, no matter how efficient Boeing's assembly line, producing Dreamliners means using resources that therefore can't be used to produce something else.

To think about the trade-offs that face any economy, economists often use the model known as the **production possibility frontier.** The idea behind this model is to improve our understanding of trade-offs by considering a simplified economy that produces only two goods. This simplification enables us to show the trade-off graphically.

Suppose, for a moment, that the United States was a one-company economy, with Boeing its sole employer and aircraft its only product. But there would still be a choice of what kinds of aircraft to produce—say, Dreamliners versus small commuter jets.

The **other things equal assumption** means that all other relevant factors remain unchanged.

The **production possibility frontier** illustrates the trade-offs facing an economy that produces only two goods. It shows the maximum quantity of one good that can be produced for any given quantity produced of the other.

Figure 2-1 shows a hypothetical production possibility frontier representing the trade-off this one-company economy would face. The frontier—the line in the diagram—shows the maximum quantity of small jets that Boeing can produce per year *given* the quantity of Dreamliners it produces per year, and vice versa. That is, it answers questions of the form, "What is the maximum quantity of small jets that Boeing can produce in a year if it also produces 9 (or 15, or 30) Dreamliners that year?"

There is a crucial distinction between points *inside* or *on* the production possibility frontier (the shaded area) and *outside* the frontier. If a production point lies inside or on the frontier—like point *C*, at which Boeing produces 20 small jets and 9 Dreamliners in a year—it is feasible. After all, the frontier tells us that if Boeing produces 20 small jets, it could also produce a maximum of 15 Dreamliners that year, so it could certainly make 9 Dreamliners.

However, a production point that lies outside the frontier—such as the hypothetical production point *D*, where Boeing produces 40 small jets and 30 Dreamliners—isn't feasible. Boeing can produce 40 small jets and no Dreamliners, *or* it can produce 30 Dreamliners and no small jets, but it can't do both.

In Figure 2-1 the production possibility frontier intersects the horizontal axis at 40 small jets. This means that if Boeing dedicated all its production capacity to making small jets, it could produce 40 small jets per year but could produce no Dreamliners. The production possibility frontier intersects the vertical axis at 30 Dreamliners. This means that if B oeing dedicated all its production capacity to making Dreamliners, it could produce 30 Dreamliners per year but no small jets.

The figure also shows less extreme trade-offs. For example, if Boeing's managers decide to make 20 small jets this year, they can produce at most 15 Dreamliners; this production choice is illustrated by point *A*. And if Boeing's managers decide to produce 28 small jets, they can make at most 9 Dreamliners, as shown by point *B*.

Thinking in terms of a production possibility frontier simplifies the complexities of reality. The real-world U.S. economy produces millions of different goods. Even Boeing can produce more than two different types of planes. Yet it's important to realize that even in its simplicity, this stripped-down model gives us important insights about the real world.

By simplifying reality, the production possibility frontier helps us understand some aspects of the real economy better than we could without the model: efficiency, opportunity cost, and economic growth.

FIGURE 2-1   **The Production Possibility Frontier**

The production possibility frontier illustrates the trade-offs Boeing faces in producing Dreamliners and small jets. It shows the maximum quantity of one good that can be produced given the quantity of the other good produced. Here, the maximum quantity of Dreamliners manufactured per year depends on the quantity of small jets manufactured that year, and vice versa. Boeing's feasible production is shown by the area *inside* or *on* the curve. Production at point *C* is feasible but not efficient. Points *A* and *B* are feasible and efficient in production, but point *D* is not feasible.

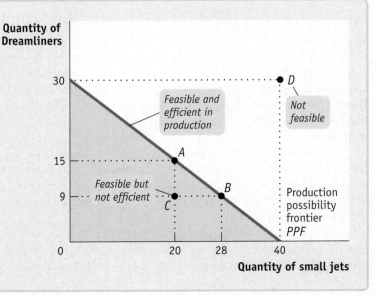

Efficiency First of all, the production possibility frontier is a good way to illustrate the general economic concept of *efficiency*. Recall from Chapter 1 that an economy is efficient if there are no missed opportunities—there is no way to make some people better off without making other people worse off.

One key element of efficiency is that there are no missed opportunities in production—there is no way to produce more of one good without producing less of other goods. As long as Boeing operates on its production possibility frontier, its production is efficient. At point *A*, 15 Dreamliners are the maximum quantity feasible given that Boeing has also committed to producing 20 small jets; at point *B*, 9 Dreamliners are the maximum number that can be made given the choice to produce 28 small jets; and so on.

But suppose for some reason that Boeing was operating at point *C*, making 20 small jets and 9 Dreamliners. In this case, it would not be operating efficiently and would therefore be *inefficient*: it could be producing more of both planes.

Although we have used an example of the production choices of a one-firm, two-good economy to illustrate efficiency and inefficiency, these concepts also carry over to the real economy, which contains many firms and produces many goods. If the economy as a whole could not produce more of any one good without producing less of something else—that is, if it is on its production possibility frontier—then we say that the economy is *efficient in production*.

If, however, the economy could produce more of some things without producing less of others—which typically means that it could produce more of everything—then it is inefficient in production. For example, an economy in which large numbers of workers are involuntarily unemployed is clearly inefficient in production. And that's a bad thing, because the economy could be producing more useful goods and services.

Although the production possibility frontier helps clarify what it means for an economy to be efficient in production, it's important to understand that efficiency in production is only *part* of what's required for the economy as a whole to be efficient. Efficiency also requires that the economy allocate its resources so that consumers are as well off as possible. If an economy does this, we say that it is *efficient in allocation*.

Our imaginary one-company economy is efficient if it (1) produces as many small jets as it can given the production of Dreamliners, and (2) if it produces the mix of small and large planes that people want to consume.

To see why efficiency in allocation is as important as efficiency in production, notice that points *A* and *B* in Figure 2-1 both represent situations in which the economy is efficient in production, because in each case it can't produce more of one good without producing less of the other. But these two situations may not be equally desirable from society's point of view. Suppose that society prefers to have more small jets and fewer Dreamliners than at point *A*; say, it prefers to have 28 small jets and 9 Dreamliners, corresponding to point *B*. In this case, point *A* is inefficient in allocation from the point of view of the economy as a whole because it would rather have Boeing produce at point *B* rather than at point *A*.

This example shows that efficiency for the economy as a whole requires *both* efficiency in production and efficiency in allocation: to be efficient, an economy must produce as much of each good as it can given the production of other goods, and it must also produce the mix of goods that people want to consume. And it must also deliver those goods to the right people: an economy that gives small jets to international airlines and Dreamliners to commuter airlines serving small rural airports is inefficient, too.

In the real world, command economies, such as the former Soviet Union, are notorious for inefficiency in allocation. For example, it was common for consumers to find stores well stocked with items few people wanted but lacking such basics as soap and toilet paper.

Opportunity Cost The production possibility frontier is also useful as a reminder of the fundamental point that the true cost of any good isn't the money it costs to buy, but what must be given up in order to get that good—the *opportunity cost*. If, for example, Boeing decides to change its production from point *A* to point *B*, it will produce 8 more small jets but 6 fewer Dreamliners. So the opportunity cost of 8 small jets is 6 Dreamliners—the 6 Dreamliners that must be forgone in order to produce 8 more small jets. This means that each small jet has an opportunity cost of ⁶/₈ = ¾ of a Dreamliner.

Is the opportunity cost of an extra small jet in terms of Dreamliners always the same, no matter how many small jets and Dreamliners are currently produced? In the example illustrated by Figure 2-1, the answer is yes. If Boeing increases its production of small jets from 28 to 40, the number of Dreamliners it produces falls from 9 to zero. So Boeing's opportunity cost per additional small jet is ⁹/₁₂ = ¾ of a Dreamliner, the same as it was when Boeing went from 20 small jets produced to 28.

However, the fact that in this example the opportunity cost of a small jet in terms of a Dreamliner is always the same is a result of an assumption we've made, an assumption that's reflected in how Figure 2-1 is drawn. Specifically, whenever we assume that the opportunity cost of an additional unit of a good doesn't change regardless of the output mix, the production possibility frontier is a straight line.

Moreover, as you might have already guessed, the slope of a straight-line production possibility frontier is equal to the opportunity cost—specifically, the opportunity cost for the good measured on the horizontal axis in terms of the good measured on the vertical axis. In Figure 2-1, the production possibility frontier has a *constant slope* of –¾, implying that Boeing faces a *constant opportunity cost* for 1 small jet equal to ¾ of a Dreamliner. (A review of how to calculate the slope of a straight line is found in this chapter's appendix.) This is the simplest case, but the production possibility frontier model can also be used to examine situations in which opportunity costs change as the mix of output changes.

Figure 2-2 illustrates a different assumption, a case in which Boeing faces *increasing opportunity cost*. Here, the more small jets it produces, the more costly it is to produce yet another small jet in terms of forgone production of a Dreamliner. And the same holds true in reverse: the more Dreamliners Boeing produces, the more costly it is to produce yet another Dreamliner in terms of forgone production of small jets. For example, to go from producing zero small jets to producing 20, Boeing has to forgo producing 5 Dreamliners. That is, the opportunity cost of those 20 small jets is 5 Dreamliners. But to increase its production

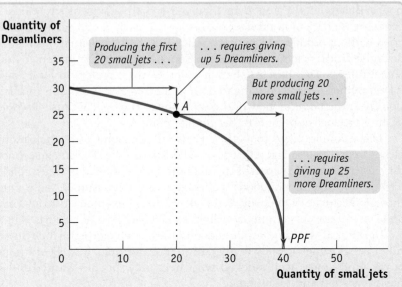

FIGURE **2-2**   **Increasing Opportunity Cost**

The bowed-out shape of the production possibility frontier reflects increasing opportunity cost. In this example, to produce the first 20 small jets, Boeing must forgo producing 5 Dreamliners. But to produce an additional 20 small jets, Boeing must forgo manufacturing 25 more Dreamliners.

of small jets to 40—that is, to produce an additional 20 small jets—it must forgo producing 25 more Dreamliners, a much higher opportunity cost. As you can see in Figure 2-2, when opportunity costs are increasing rather than constant, the production possibility frontier is a bowed-out curve rather than a straight line.

Although it's often useful to work with the simple assumption that the production possibility frontier is a straight line, economists believe that in reality opportunity costs are typically increasing. When only a small amount of a good is produced, the opportunity cost of producing that good is relatively low because the economy needs to use only those resources that are especially well suited for its production.

For example, if an economy grows only a small amount of corn, that corn can be grown in places where the soil and climate are perfect for corn-growing but less suitable for growing anything else, like wheat. So growing that corn involves giving up only a small amount of potential wheat output. Once the economy grows a lot of corn, however, land that is well suited for wheat but isn't so great for corn must be used to produce corn anyway. As a result, the additional corn production involves sacrificing considerably more wheat production. In other words, as more of a good is produced, its opportunity cost typically rises because well-suited inputs are used up and less adaptable inputs must be used instead.

Economic Growth Finally, the production possibility frontier helps us understand what it means to talk about *economic growth*. In the Introduction, we defined the concept of economic growth as *the growing ability of the economy to produce goods and services.* As we saw, economic growth is one of the fundamental features of the real economy. But are we really justified in saying that the economy has grown over time? After all, although the U.S. economy produces more of many things than it did a century ago, it produces less of other things—for example, horse-drawn carriages. Production of many goods, in other words, is actually down. So how can we say for sure that the economy as a whole has grown?

The answer is illustrated in Figure 2-3, where we have drawn two hypothetical production possibility frontiers for the economy. In them we have assumed once again that everyone in the economy works for Boeing and, consequently, the economy produces only two goods, Dreamliners and small jets. Notice how the two curves are nested, with the one labeled "Original *PPF*" lying completely inside the one labeled "New *PPF*." Now we can see graphically what we mean by economic growth of the economy: economic growth means an *expansion of the economy's production possibilities;* that is, the economy *can* produce more of everything.

FIGURE 2-3   **Economic Growth**

Economic growth results in an *outward shift* of the production possibility frontier because production possibilities are expanded. The economy can now produce more of everything. For example, if production is initially at point *A* (25 Dreamliners and 20 small jets), economic growth means that the economy could move to point *E* (30 Dreamliners and 25 small jets).

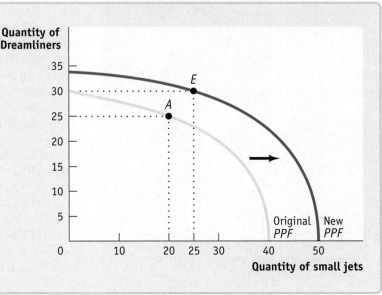

Factors of production are resources used to produce goods and services.

Technology is the technical means for producing goods and services.

For example, if the economy initially produces at point *A* (25 Dreamliners and 20 small jets), economic growth means that the economy could move to point *E* (30 Dreamliners and 25 small jets). *E* lies outside the original frontier; so in the production possibility frontier model, growth is shown as an outward shift of the frontier.

What can lead the production possibility frontier to shift outward? There are basically two sources of economic growth. One is an increase in the economy's **factors of production,** the resources used to produce goods and services. Economists usually use the term *factor of production* to refer to a resource that is not used up in production. For example, in traditional airplane manufacture workers used riveting machines to connect metal sheets when constructing a plane's fuselage; the workers and the riveters are factors of production, but the rivets and the sheet metal are not. Once a fuselage is made, a worker and riveter can be used to make another fuselage, but the sheet metal and rivets used to make one fuselage cannot be used to make another.

Broadly speaking, the main factors of production are the resources land, labor, physical capital, and human capital. Land is a resource supplied by nature; labor is the economy's pool of workers; physical capital refers to created resources such as machines and buildings; and human capital refers to the educational achievements and skills of the labor force, which enhance its productivity. Of course, each of these is really a category rather than a single factor: land in North Dakota is quite different from land in Florida.

To see how adding to an economy's factors of production leads to economic growth, suppose that Boeing builds another construction hangar that allows it to increase the number of planes—small jets or Dreamliners or both—it can produce in a year. The new construction hangar is a factor of production, a resource Boeing can use to increase its yearly output. We can't say how many more planes of each type Boeing will produce; that's a management decision that will depend on, among other things, customer demand. But we can say that Boeing's production possibility frontier has shifted outward because it can now produce more small jets without reducing the number of Dreamliners it makes, or it can make more Dreamliners without reducing the number of small jets produced.

The other source of economic growth is progress in **technology,** the technical means for the production of goods and services. Composite materials had been used in some parts of aircraft before the Boeing Dreamliner was developed. But Boeing engineers realized that there were large additional advantages to building a whole plane out of composites. The plane would be lighter, stronger, and have better aerodynamics than a plane built in the traditional way. It would therefore have longer range, be able to carry more people, and use less fuel, in addition to being able to maintain higher cabin pressure. So in a real sense Boeing's innovation—a whole plane built out of composites—was a way to do more with any given amount of resources, pushing out the production possibility frontier.

Because improved jet technology has pushed out the production possibility frontier, it has made it possible for the economy to produce more of everything, not just jets and air travel. Over the past 30 years, the biggest technological advances have taken place in information technology, not in construction or food services. Yet Americans have chosen to buy bigger houses and eat out more than they used to because the economy's growth has made it possible to do so.

The four factors of production: land, labor, physical capital, and human capital.

The production possibility frontier is a very simplified model of an economy. Yet it teaches us important lessons about real-life economies. It gives us our first clear sense of what constitutes economic efficiency, it illustrates the concept of opportunity cost, and it makes clear what economic growth is all about.

Comparative Advantage and Gains from Trade

Among the twelve principles of economics described in Chapter 1 was the principle of *gains from trade*—the mutual gains that individuals can achieve by specializing in doing different things and trading with one another. Our second illustration of an economic model is a particularly useful model of gains from trade—trade based on *comparative advantage*.

One of the most important insights in all of economics is that there are gains from trade—that it makes sense to produce the things you're especially good at producing and to buy from other people the things you aren't as good at producing. This would be true even if you could produce everything for yourself: even if a brilliant brain surgeon *could* repair her own dripping faucet, it's probably a better idea for her to call in a professional plumber.

How can we model the gains from trade? Let's stay with our aircraft example and once again imagine that the United States is a one-company economy where everyone works for Boeing, producing airplanes. Let's now assume, however, that the United States has the ability to trade with Brazil—another one-company economy where everyone works for the Brazilian aircraft company Embraer, which is, in the real world, a successful producer of small commuter jets. (If you fly from one major U.S. city to another, your plane is likely to be a Boeing, but if you fly into a small city, the odds are good that your plane will be an Embraer.)

In our example, the only two goods produced are large jets and small jets. Both countries could produce both kinds of jets. But as we'll see in a moment, they can gain by producing different things and trading with each other. For the purposes of this example, let's return to the simpler case of straight-line production possibility frontiers. America's production possibilities are represented by the production possibility frontier in panel (a) of Figure 2-4, which is similar to the production possibility

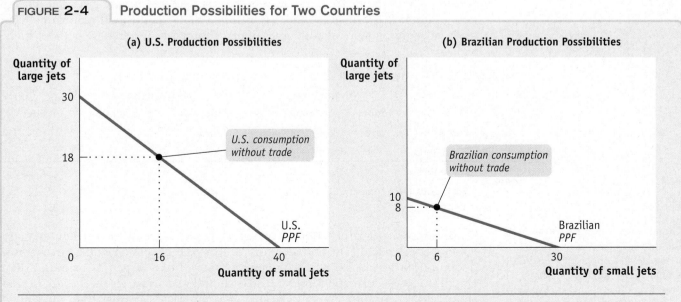

FIGURE 2-4   Production Possibilities for Two Countries

(a) U.S. Production Possibilities

Quantity of large jets

U.S. consumption without trade

U.S. PPF

Quantity of small jets

(b) Brazilian Production Possibilities

Quantity of large jets

Brazilian consumption without trade

Brazilian PPF

Quantity of small jets

Here, both the United States and Brazil have a constant opportunity cost of small jets, illustrated by a straight-line production possibility frontier. For the United States, each small jet has an opportunity cost of ¾ of a large jet. Brazil has an opportunity cost of a small jet equal to ⅓ of a large jet.

frontier in Figure 2-1. According to this diagram, the United States can produce 40 small jets if it makes no large jets and can manufacture 30 large jets if it produces no small jets. Recall that this means that the slope of the U.S. production possibility frontier is −¾: its opportunity cost of 1 small jet is ¾ of a large jet.

Panel (b) of Figure 2-4 shows Brazil's production possibilities. Like the United States, Brazil's production possibility frontier is a straight line, implying a constant opportunity cost of a small jet in terms of large jets. Brazil's production possibility frontier has a constant slope of −⅓. Brazil can't produce as much of anything as the United States can: at most it can produce 30 small jets or 10 large jets. But it is relatively better at manufacturing small jets than the United States; whereas the United States sacrifices ¾ of a large jet per small jet produced, for Brazil the opportunity cost of a small jet is only ⅓ of a large jet. Table 2-1 summarizes the two countries' opportunity costs of small jets and large jets.

TABLE 2-1	U.S. and Brazilian Opportunity Costs of Small Jets and Large Jets			
	U.S. Opportunity Cost		**Brazilian Opportunity Cost**	
One small jet	¾ large jet	>	⅓ large jet	
One large jet	4/3 small jets	<	3 small jets	

Now, the United States and Brazil could each choose to make their own large and small jets, not trading any airplanes and consuming only what each produced within its own country. (A country "consumes" an airplane when it is owned by a domestic resident.) Let's suppose that the two countries start out this way and make the consumption choices shown in Figure 2-4: in the absence of trade, the United States produces and consumes 16 small jets and 18 large jets per year, while Brazil produces and consumes 6 small jets and 8 large jets per year.

But is this the best the two countries can do? No, it isn't. Given that the two producers—and therefore the two countries—have different opportunity costs, the United States and Brazil can strike a deal that makes both of them better off.

Table 2-2 shows how such a deal works: the United States specializes in the production of large jets, manufacturing 30 per year, and sells 10 to Brazil. Meanwhile, Brazil specializes in the production of small jets, producing 30 per year, and sells 20 to the United States. The result is shown in Figure 2-5. The United States now consumes more of both small jets and large jets than before: instead of 16 small jets and 18 large jets, it now consumes 20 small jets and 20 large jets. Brazil also consumes more, going from 6 small jets and 8 large jets to 10 small jets and 10 large jets. As Table 2-2 also shows, both the United States and Brazil reap gains from trade, consuming more of both types of plane than they would have without trade.

TABLE 2-2	How the United States and Brazil Gain from Trade					
		Without Trade		**With Trade**		**Gains from Trade**
		Production	Consumption	Production	Consumption	
United States	Large jets	18	18	30	20	+2
	Small jets	16	16	0	20	+4
Brazil	Large jets	8	8	0	10	+2
	Small jets	6	6	30	10	+4

A country has a **comparative advantage** in producing a good or service if its opportunity cost of producing the good or service is lower than other countries'. Likewise, an individual has a comparative advantage in producing a good or service if his or her opportunity cost of producing the good or service is lower than for other people.

Both countries are better off when they each specialize in what they are good at and trade. It's a good idea for the United States to specialize in the production of large jets because its opportunity cost of a large jet is smaller than Brazil's: 4/3 < 3. Correspondingly, Brazil should specialize in the production of small jets because its opportunity cost of a small jet is smaller than the United States: ⅓ < ¾.

What we would say in this case is that the United States has a comparative advantage in the production of large jets and Brazil has a comparative advantage in the production of small jets. A country has a **comparative advantage** in

FIGURE **2-5**   Comparative Advantage and Gains from Trade

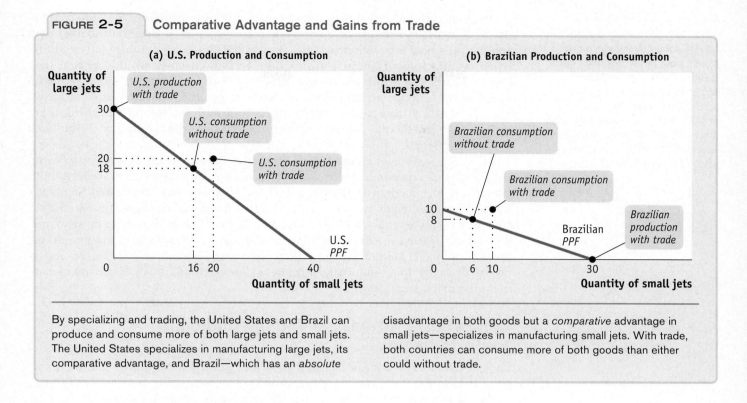

By specializing and trading, the United States and Brazil can produce and consume more of both large jets and small jets. The United States specializes in manufacturing large jets, its comparative advantage, and Brazil—which has an *absolute* disadvantage in both goods but a *comparative* advantage in small jets—specializes in manufacturing small jets. With trade, both countries can consume more of both goods than either could without trade.

producing something if the opportunity cost of that production is lower for that country than for other countries. The same concept applies to firms and people: a firm or an individual has a comparative advantage in producing something if its, his, or her opportunity cost of production is lower than for others.

One point of clarification before we proceed further. You may have wondered why the United States traded 10 large jets to Brazil in return for 20 small jets. Why not some other deal, like trading 10 large jets for 12 small jets? The answer to that question has two parts. First, there may indeed be other trades that the United States and Brazil might agree to. Second, there are some deals that we can safely rule out— one like 10 large jets for 10 small jets.

To understand why, reexamine Table 2-1 and consider the United States first. Without trading with Brazil, the U.S. opportunity cost of a small jet is ¾ of a large jet. So it's clear that the United States will not accept any trade that requires it to give up more than ¾ of a large jet for a small jet. Trading 10 jets in return for 12 small jets would require the United States to pay an opportunity cost of $^{10}/_{12} = {}^5/_6$ of a large jet for a small jet. Because $^5/_6 >$ than ¾, this is a deal that the United States would reject. Similarly, Brazil won't accept a trade that gives it less than ⅓ of a large jet for a small jet.

The point to remember is that the United States and Brazil will be willing to trade only if the "price" of the good each country obtains in the trade is less than its own opportunity cost of producing the good domestically. Moreover, this is a general statement that is true whenever two parties—countries, firms, or individuals—trade voluntarily.

While our story clearly simplifies reality, it teaches us some very important lessons that apply to the real economy, too.

First, the model provides a clear illustration of the gains from trade: through specialization and trade, both countries produce more and consume more than if they were self-sufficient.

Second, the model demonstrates a very important point that is often overlooked in real-world arguments: each country has a comparative advantage in producing something. This applies to firms and people as well: *everyone has a comparative advantage in something, and everyone has a comparative disadvantage in something.*

A country has an **absolute advantage** in producing a good or service if the country can produce more output per worker than other countries. Likewise, an individual has an absolute advantage in producing a good or service if he or she is better at producing it than other people. Having an absolute advantage is not the same thing as having a comparative advantage.

Crucially, in our example it doesn't matter if, as is probably the case in real life, U.S. workers are just as good as or even better than Brazilian workers at producing small jets. Suppose that the United States is actually better than Brazil at all kinds of aircraft production. In that case, we would say that the United States has an **absolute advantage** in both large-jet and small-jet production: in an hour, an American worker can produce more of either a large jet or a small jet than a Brazilian worker. You might be tempted to think that in that case the United States has nothing to gain from trading with the less productive Brazil.

But we've just seen that the United States can indeed benefit from trading with Brazil because *comparative, not absolute, advantage is the basis for mutual gain.* It doesn't matter whether it takes Brazil more resources than the United States to make a small jet; what matters for trade is that for Brazil the opportunity cost of a small jet is lower than the U.S. opportunity cost. So Brazil, despite its absolute disadvantage, even in small jets, has a comparative advantage in the manufacture of small jets. Meanwhile the United States, which can use its resources most productively by manufacturing large jets, has a comparative *dis*advantage in manufacturing small jets.

Comparative Advantage and International Trade, in Reality

Look at the label on a manufactured good sold in the United States, and there's a good chance you will find that it was produced in some other country—in China, or Japan, or even in Canada, eh? On the other side, many U.S. industries sell a large fraction of their output overseas. (This is particularly true of agriculture, high technology, and entertainment.)

Should all this international exchange of goods and services be celebrated, or is it cause for concern? Politicians and the public often question the desirability of international trade, arguing that the nation should produce goods for itself rather than buying them from foreigners. Industries around the world demand protection from foreign competition: Japanese farmers want to keep out American rice, American steelworkers want to keep out European steel. And these demands are often supported by public opinion.

Economists, however, have a very positive view of international trade. Why? Because they view it in terms of comparative advantage. As we learned from our example of U.S. large jets and Brazilian small jets, international trade benefits both countries. Each country can consume more than if it didn't trade and remained self-sufficient. Moreover, these mutual gains don't depend on each country being better than other countries at producing one kind of good. Even if one country has, say, higher output per worker in both industries—that is, even

PITFALLS

MISUNDERSTANDING COMPARATIVE ADVANTAGE

Students do it, pundits do it, and politicians do it all the time: they confuse *comparative advantage* with *absolute* advantage. For example, back in the 1980s, when the U.S. economy seemed to be lagging behind that of Japan, one often heard commentators warn that if we didn't improve our productivity, we would soon have no comparative advantage in anything.

What those commentators meant was that we would have no *absolute* advantage in anything—that there might come a time

when the Japanese were better at everything than we were. (It didn't turn out that way, but that's another story.) And they had the idea that in that case we would no longer be able to benefit from trade with Japan.

But just as Brazil, in our example, was able to benefit from trade with the United States (and vice versa) despite the fact that the United States was better at manufacturing both large and small jets, in real life nations can still gain from trade even if they are less productive in all industries than the countries they trade with.

Pajama Republics

In April 2013, a terrible industrial disaster made world headlines: in Bangladesh, a building housing five clothing factories collapsed, killing more than a thousand garment workers trapped inside. Attention soon focused on the substandard working conditions in those factories, as well as the many violations of building codes and safety procedures—including those required by Bangladeshi law—that set the stage for the tragedy.

While the story provoked a justified outcry, it also highlighted the remarkable rise of Bangladesh's clothing industry, which has become a major player in world markets—second only to China in total exports—and a desperately needed source of income and employment in a very poor country.

It's not that Bangladesh has especially high productivity in clothing manufacturing. In fact, recent estimates by the consulting firm McKinsey and Company suggest that it's about a quarter less productive than China. Rather, it has even lower productivity in other industries, giving it a comparative advantage in clothing manufacturing. This is typical in poor countries, which often rely heavily on clothing exports during the early phases of their economic development. An official from one such country once joked, "We are not a banana republic—we are a pajama republic."

The figure plots the per capita income of several such "pajama republics" (the total income of the country divided by the size of the population) against the share of total exports accounted for by clothing; per capita income is measured as a percentage of the U.S. level in order to give you a sense of just how poor these countries are. As you can see, they are very poor indeed—and the poorer they are, the more they depend on clothing exports.

It's worth pointing out, by the way, that relying on clothing exports is by no means necessarily a bad thing, despite tragedies like the Bangladesh factory disaster. Indeed, Bangladesh, although still desperately poor, is more than twice as rich as it was two decades ago, when it began its dramatic rise as a clothing exporter. (Also see the upcoming Economics in Action on Bangladesh.)

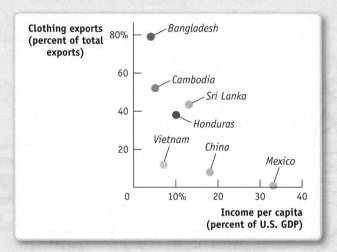

Source: WTO.

if one country has an absolute advantage in both industries—there are still gains from trade. The upcoming Global Comparison, which explains the pattern of clothing production in the global economy, illustrates just this point.

Transactions: The Circular-Flow Diagram

The model economies that we've studied so far—each containing only one firm—are a huge simplification. We've also greatly simplified trade between the United States and Brazil, assuming that they engage only in the simplest of economic transactions, **barter,** in which one party directly trades a good or service for another good or service without using money. In a modern economy, simple barter is rare: usually people trade goods or services for money—pieces of colored paper with no inherent value—and then trade those pieces of colored paper for the goods or services they want. That is, they sell goods or services and buy other goods or services.

And they both sell and buy a lot of different things. The U.S. economy is a vastly complex entity, with more than a hundred million workers employed by millions of companies, producing millions of different goods and services. Yet you can learn some very important things about the economy by considering the simple graphic shown in Figure 2-6, the **circular-flow diagram.** This diagram represents the transactions that take place in an economy by two kinds of flows around a circle: flows of physical things such as goods, services, labor, or raw materials in one direction, and flows of money that pay for these physical things in the opposite direction. In this case the physical flows are shown in yellow, the money flows in green.

Trade takes the form of **barter** when people directly exchange goods or services that they have for goods or services that they want.

The **circular-flow diagram** represents the transactions in an economy by flows around a circle.

FIGURE **2-6** The Circular-Flow Diagram

This diagram represents the flows of money and of goods and services in the economy. In the markets for goods and services, households purchase goods and services from firms, generating a flow of money to the firms and a flow of goods and services to the households. The money flows back to households as firms purchase factors of production from the households in factor markets.

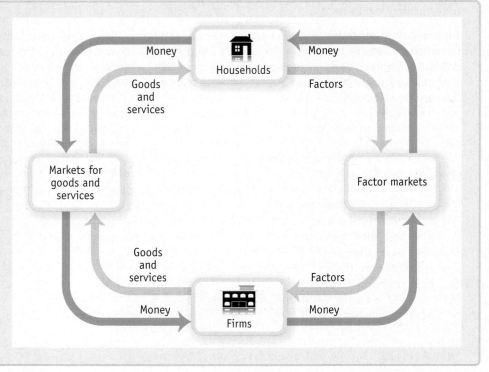

The simplest circular-flow diagram illustrates an economy that contains only two kinds of inhabitants: **households** and **firms.** A household consists of either an individual or a group of people (usually, but not necessarily, a family) that share their income. A firm is an organization that produces goods and services for sale—and that employs members of households.

As you can see in Figure 2-6, there are two kinds of markets in this simple economy. On one side (here the left side) there are **markets for goods and services** in which households buy the goods and services they want from firms. This produces a flow of goods and services to households and a return flow of money to firms.

On the right side, there are **factor markets** in which firms buy the resources they need to produce goods and services. Recall from earlier that the main factors of production are land, labor, physical capital, and human capital.

The factor market most of us know best is the labor market, in which workers sell their services. In addition, we can think of households as owning and selling the other factors of production to firms. For example, when a firm buys physical capital in the form of machines, the payment ultimately goes to the households that own the machine-making firm. In this case, the transactions are occurring in the *capital market,* the market in which capital is bought and sold. As we'll examine in detail later, factor markets ultimately determine an economy's **income distribution,** how the total income created in an economy is allocated between less skilled workers, highly skilled workers, and the owners of capital and land.

The circular-flow diagram ignores a number of real-world complications in the interests of simplicity. A few examples:

• In the real world, the distinction between firms and households isn't always that clear-cut. Consider a small, family-run business—a farm, a shop, a small hotel. Is this a firm or a household? A more complete picture would include a separate box for family businesses.

• Many of the sales firms make are not to households but to other firms; for example, steel companies sell mainly to other companies such as auto manufacturers, not to households. A more complete picture would include these flows of goods, services, and money within the business sector.

A **household** is a person or a group of people that share their income.

A **firm** is an organization that produces goods and services for sale.

Firms sell goods and services that they produce to households in **markets for goods and services.**

Firms buy the resources they need to produce goods and services in **factor markets.**

An economy's **income distribution** is the way in which total income is divided among the owners of the various factors of production.

- The figure doesn't show the government, which in the real world diverts quite a lot of money out of the circular flow in the form of taxes but also injects a lot of money back into the flow in the form of spending.

Figure 2-6, in other words, is by no means a complete picture either of all the types of inhabitants of the real economy or of all the flows of money and physical items that take place among these inhabitants.

Despite its simplicity, the circular-flow diagram is a very useful aid to thinking about the economy.

ECONOMICS ▶ *in Action*

Rich Nation, Poor Nation

Try taking off your clothes—at a suitable time and in a suitable place, of course—and taking a look at the labels inside that say where they were made. It's a very good bet that much, if not most, of your clothing was manufactured overseas, in a country that is much poorer than the United States—say, in El Salvador, Sri Lanka, or Bangladesh.

Why are these countries so much poorer than we are? The immediate reason is that their economies are much less *productive*—firms in these countries are just not able to produce as much from a given quantity of resources as comparable firms in the United States or other wealthy countries. Why countries differ so much in productivity is a deep question—indeed, one of the main questions that preoccupy economists. But in any case, the difference in productivity is a fact.

But if the economies of these countries are so much less productive than ours, how is it that they make so much of our clothing? Why don't we do it for ourselves?

Although less productive than American workers, Bangladeshi workers have a comparative advantage in clothing production.

The answer is "comparative advantage." Just about every industry in Bangladesh is much less productive than the corresponding industry in the United States. But the productivity difference between rich and poor countries varies across goods; it is very large in the production of sophisticated goods like aircraft but not that large in the production of simpler goods like clothing. So Bangladesh's position with regard to clothing production is like Embraer's position with respect to producing small jets: it's not as good at it as Boeing, but it's the thing Embraer does comparatively well.

Bangladesh, though it is at an absolute disadvantage compared with the United States in almost everything, has a comparative advantage in clothing production. This means that both the United States and Bangladesh are able to consume more because they specialize in producing different things, with Bangladesh supplying our clothing and the United States supplying Bangladesh with more sophisticated goods.

Check Your Understanding   2-1

1. True or false? Explain your answer.
   a. An increase in the amount of resources available to Boeing for use in producing Dreamliners and small jets does not change its production possibility frontier.
   b. A technological change that allows Boeing to build more small jets for any amount of Dreamliners built results in a change in its production possibility frontier.
   c. The production possibility frontier is useful because it illustrates how much of one good an economy must give up to get more of another good regardless of whether resources are being used efficiently.
2. In Italy, an automobile can be produced by 8 workers in one day and a washing machine by 3 workers in one day. In the United States, an automobile can be produced by 6 workers in one day and a washing machine by 2 workers in one day.

▼ Quick Review

- Most economic **models** are "thought experiments" or simplified representations of reality that rely on the **other things equal assumption.**

- The **production possibility frontier** model illustrates the concepts of efficiency, opportunity cost, and economic growth.

- Every person and every country has a **comparative advantage** in something, giving rise to gains from trade. Comparative advantage is often confused with **absolute advantage.**

- In the simplest economies people **barter** rather than transact with money. The **circular-flow diagram** illustrates transactions within the economy as flows of goods and services, **factors of production,** and money between **households** and **firms.** These transactions occur in **markets for goods and services** and **factor markets.** Ultimately, factor markets determine the economy's **income distribution.**

a. Which country has an absolute advantage in the production of automobiles? In washing machines?

b. Which country has a comparative advantage in the production of washing machines? In automobiles?

c. What pattern of specialization results in the greatest gains from trade between the two countries?

3. Using the numbers from Table 2-1, explain why the United States and Brazil are willing to engage in a trade of 10 large jets for 15 small jets.

4. Use the circular-flow diagram to explain how an increase in the amount of money spent by households results in an increase in the number of jobs in the economy. Describe in words what the circular-flow diagram predicts.

Solutions appear at back of book.

Using Models

Economics, we have now learned, is mainly a matter of creating models that draw on a set of basic principles but add some more specific assumptions that allow the modeler to apply those principles to a particular situation. But what do economists actually *do* with their models?

Positive versus Normative Economics

Imagine that you are an economic adviser to the governor of your state. What kinds of questions might the governor ask you to answer?

Well, here are three possible questions:

1. How much revenue will the tolls on the state turnpike yield next year?

2. How much would that revenue increase if the toll were raised from $1 to $1.50?

3. Should the toll be raised, bearing in mind that a toll increase will reduce traffic and air pollution near the road but will impose some financial hardship on frequent commuters?

There is a big difference between the first two questions and the third one. The first two are questions about facts. Your forecast of next year's toll collection will be proved right or wrong when the numbers actually come in. Your estimate of the impact of a change in the toll is a little harder to check—revenue depends on other factors besides the toll, and it may be hard to disentangle the causes of any change in revenue. Still, in principle there is only one right answer.

But the question of whether tolls should be raised may not have a "right" answer—two people who agree on the effects of a higher toll could still disagree about whether raising the toll is a good idea. For example, someone who lives near the turnpike but doesn't commute on it will care a lot about noise and air pollution but not so much about commuting costs. A regular commuter who doesn't live near the turnpike will have the opposite priorities.

This example highlights a key distinction between two roles of economic analysis. Analysis that tries to answer questions about the way the world works, which have definite right and wrong answers, is known as **positive economics.** In contrast, analysis that involves saying how the world *should* work is known as **normative economics.** To put it another way, positive economics is about description; normative economics is about prescription.

Positive economics occupies most of the time and effort of the economics profession. And models play a crucial role in almost all positive economics. As we mentioned earlier, the U.S. government uses a computer model to assess proposed changes in national tax policy, and many state governments have similar models to assess the effects of their own tax policy.

Positive economics is the branch of economic analysis that describes the way the economy actually works.

Normative economics makes prescriptions about the way the economy should work.

It's worth noting that there is a subtle but important difference between the first and second questions we imagined the governor asking. Question 1 asked for a simple prediction about next year's revenue—a **forecast.** Question 2 was a "what if" question, asking how revenue would change if the tax law were changed. Economists are often called upon to answer both types of questions, but models are especially useful for answering "what if" questions.

A **forecast** is a simple prediction of the future.

The answers to such questions often serve as a guide to policy, but they are still predictions, not prescriptions. That is, they tell you what will happen if a policy were changed; they don't tell you whether or not that result is good.

Suppose your economic model tells you that the governor's proposed increase in highway tolls will raise property values in communities near the road but will hurt people who must use the turnpike to get to work. Does that make this proposed toll increase a good idea or a bad one? It depends on whom you ask. As we've just seen, someone who is very concerned with the communities near the road will support the increase, but someone who is very concerned with the welfare of drivers will feel differently. That's a value judgment—it's not a question of economic analysis.

Still, economists often do engage in normative economics and give policy advice. How can they do this when there may be no "right" answer?

One answer is that economists are also citizens, and we all have our opinions. But economic analysis can often be used to show that some policies are clearly better than others, regardless of anyone's opinions.

Suppose that policies A and B achieve the same goal, but policy A makes everyone better off than policy B—or at least makes some people better off without making other people worse off. Then A is clearly more efficient than B. That's not a value judgment: we're talking about how best to achieve a goal, not about the goal itself.

For example, two different policies have been used to help low-income families obtain housing: rent control, which limits the rents landlords are allowed to charge, and rent subsidies, which provide families with additional money to pay rent. Almost all economists agree that subsidies are the more efficient policy. And so the great majority of economists, whatever their personal politics, favor subsidies over rent control.

When policies can be clearly ranked in this way, then economists generally agree. But it is no secret that economists sometimes disagree.

When and Why Economists Disagree

Economists have a reputation for arguing with each other. Where does this reputation come from, and is it justified?

One important answer is that media coverage tends to exaggerate the real differences in views among economists. If nearly all economists agree on an issue—for example, the proposition that rent controls lead to housing shortages—reporters and editors are likely to conclude that it's not a story worth covering, leaving the professional consensus unreported. But an issue on which prominent economists take opposing sides—for example, whether cutting taxes right now would help the economy—makes a news story worth reporting. So you hear much more about the areas of disagreement within economics than you do about the large areas of agreement.

It is also worth remembering that economics is, unavoidably, often tied up in politics. On a number of issues powerful interest groups know what opinions they want to hear; they therefore have an incentive to find and promote economists who profess those opinions, giving these economists a prominence and visibility out of proportion to their support among their colleagues.

While the appearance of disagreement among economists exceeds the reality, it remains true that economists often *do* disagree about important things. For example, some well respected economists argue

FOR INQUIRING MINDS | When Economists Agree

"If all the economists in the world were laid end to end, they still couldn't reach a conclusion." So goes one popular economist joke. But do economists really disagree that much?

Not according to an ongoing survey being conducted by the Booth School of Business at the University of Chicago. The Booth School assembled a panel of 41 economists, all with exemplary professional reputations, representing a mix of regions, schools, and political affiliations, and officially known as the Economic Experts Panel of Chicago Booth's Initiative on Global Markets. Four of these economists are pictured here (clockwise from top left): Amy Finkelstein of MIT, Hilary Hoynes of UC Berkeley, Emmanuel Saez also of Berkeley, and Abhjit Banerjee of Princeton.

Roughly once every two weeks these economists are polled on a question of current policy or political interest—often it is a question on which there are bitter divides among politicians or the general public.

So what do we learn from the survey? That there is much more agreement among economists than rumor would

have it, even on supposedly controversial topics. For example, 80% of the panel agreed that the American Recovery and Reconstruction Act of 2009—the so-called Obama stimulus—led to higher growth and employment, although there was more division about whether the plan was worth its cost.

Roughly the same percentage—82%—disagreed with the proposition that rent control increases the supply of quality, affordable housing.

In the first case, by the way, the panel of economists overwhelmingly agreed with a position widely considered liberal in American politics, while in the second case they agreed with a position widely considered politically conservative.

Were there areas of substantial disagreement among the economists? Yes, but they tended to involve untested economic policies. There was, for example, an almost even split over whether new Federal Reserve tactics aimed at boosting the economy would work.

Perhaps even more surprising than the relative lack of disagreement among economists was the relative absence of

clear ideological patterns when they did disagree. Economists known to be liberals did have slightly different positions, on average, from those known to be conservatives, but the differences weren't nearly as large as those among the general public.

So is the stereotype of the quarreling economists a myth? Not entirely: economists do disagree quite a lot on some issues, especially in macroeconomics. But there is a large area of common ground. ■

vehemently that the U.S. government should replace the income tax with a *value-added tax* (a national sales tax, which is the main source of government revenue in many European countries). Other equally respected economists disagree. Why this difference of opinion?

One important source of differences lies in values: as in any diverse group of individuals, reasonable people can differ. In comparison to an income tax, a value-added tax typically falls more heavily on people of modest means. So an economist who values a society with more social and income equality for its own sake will tend to oppose a value-added tax. An economist with different values will be less likely to oppose it.

A second important source of differences arises from economic modeling. Because economists base their conclusions on models, which are simplified representations of reality, two economists can legitimately disagree about which simplifications are appropriate—and therefore arrive at different conclusions.

Suppose that the U.S. government were considering introducing a value-added tax. Economist A may rely on a model that focuses on the administrative costs of tax systems—that is, the costs of monitoring, processing papers, collecting the tax, and so on. This economist might then point to the well-known high costs of administering a value-added tax and argue against the change. But economist B may think that the right way to approach the question is to ignore the administrative costs and focus on how the proposed law would change savings behavior. This economist might point to studies suggesting that value-added taxes promote higher consumer saving, a desirable result.

Because the economists have used different models—that is, made different simplifying assumptions—they arrive at different conclusions. And so the two economists may find themselves on different sides of the issue.

In most cases such disputes are eventually resolved by the accumulation of evidence showing which of the various models proposed by economists does a better job of fitting the facts. However, in economics, as in any science, it can take a long time before research settles important disputes—decades, in some cases. And since the economy is always changing, in ways that make old models invalid or raise new policy questions, there are always new issues on which economists disagree. The policy maker must then decide which economist to believe.

The important point is that economic analysis is a method, not a set of conclusions.

ECONOMICS ▶ *in Action*

Economists, Beyond the Ivory Tower

Many economists are mainly engaged in teaching and research. But quite a few economists have a more direct hand in events.

As described earlier in this chapter (For Inquiring Minds, "The Model That Ate the Economy"), one specific branch of economics, finance theory, plays an important role for financial firms on Wall Street—not always to good effect. But pricing assets is by no means the only useful function economists serve in the business world. Businesses need forecasts of the future demand for their products, predictions of future raw-material prices, assessments of their future financing needs, and more; for all of these purposes, economic analysis is essential.

Some of the economists employed in the business world work directly for the institutions that need their input. Top financial firms like Goldman Sachs and Morgan Stanley, in particular, maintain high-quality economics groups, which produce analyses of forces and events likely to affect financial markets. Other economists are employed by consulting firms like Macro Advisers, which sells analysis and advice to a wide range of other businesses.

Last but not least, economists participate extensively in government. According to the Bureau of Labor Statistics, government agencies employ about half of the professional economists in the United States. This shouldn't be surprising: one of the most important functions of government is to make economic policy, and almost every government policy decision must take economic effects into consideration. So governments around the world employ economists in a variety of roles.

In the U.S. government, a key role is played by the Council of Economic Advisers, whose sole purpose is to advise the president on economic matters. Unlike most government employees, most economists at the Council aren't long-time civil servants; instead, they are mainly professors on leave for one or two years from their universities. Many of the nation's best-known economists have served at the Council of Economic Advisers at some point in their careers.

Economists also play an important role in many other parts of the government, from the Department of Commerce to the Labor Department. Economists dominate the staff of the Federal Reserve, a government agency that controls the economy's money supply and oversees banks. And economists play an especially important role in two international organizations headquartered in Washington, D.C.: the International Monetary Fund, which provides advice and loans to countries experiencing economic difficulties, and the World Bank, which provides advice and loans to promote long-term economic development.

In the past, it wasn't that easy to track what all these economists working on practical affairs were up to. These days, however, there are very lively online discussions of economic prospects and policy. See, for example, the home page of the International Monetary Fund (www.imf.org), a business-

▼ Quick Review

- **Positive economics**—the focus of most economic research—is the analysis of the way the world works, in which there are definite right and wrong answers. It often involves making **forecasts.** But in **normative economics,** which makes prescriptions about how things ought to be, there are often no right answers and only value judgments.

- Economists do disagree—though not as much as legend has it—for two main reasons. One, they may disagree about which simplifications to make in a model. Two, economists may disagree—like everyone else—about values.

oriented site like economy.com, and the blogs of individual economists, like Mark Thoma (economistsview.typepad.com) or, yes, our own blog, which is among the Technorati top 100 blogs, at krugman.blogs.nytimes.com.

Check Your Understanding 2-2

1. Which of the following statements is a positive statement? Which is a normative statement?
   a. Society should take measures to prevent people from engaging in dangerous personal behavior.
   b. People who engage in dangerous personal behavior impose higher costs on society through higher medical costs.

2. True or false? Explain your answer.
   a. Policy choice A and policy choice B attempt to achieve the same social goal. Policy choice A, however, results in a much less efficient use of resources than policy choice B. Therefore, economists are more likely to agree on choosing policy choice B.
   b. When two economists disagree on the desirability of a policy, it's typically because one of them has made a mistake.
   c. Policy makers can always use economics to figure out which goals a society should try to achieve.

Solutions appear at back of book.

BUSINESS CASE | Efficiency, Opportunity Cost and the Logic of Lean Production

In the summer and fall of 2010, workers were rearranging the furniture in Boeing's final assembly plant in Everett, Washington, in preparation for the production of the Boeing 767. It was a difficult and time-consuming process, however, because the items of "furniture"—Boeing's assembly equipment—weighed on the order of 200 tons each. It was a necessary part of setting up a production system based on "lean manufacturing," also called "just-in-time" production.

Echo/Getty Images

Lean manufacturing, pioneered by Toyota Motors of Japan, is based on the practice of having parts arrive on the factory floor just as they are needed for production. This reduces the amount of parts Boeing holds in inventory as well as the amount of the factory floor needed for production—in this case, reducing the square footage required for manufacture of the 767 by 40%.

Boeing had adopted lean manufacturing in 1999 in the manufacture of the 737, the most popular commercial airplane. By 2005, after constant refinement, Boeing had achieved a 50% reduction in the time it takes to produce a plane and a nearly 60% reduction in parts inventory. An important feature is a continuously moving assembly line, moving products from one assembly team to the next at a steady pace and eliminating the need for workers to wander across the factory floor from task to task or in search of tools and parts.

Toyota's lean production techniques have been the most widely adopted, revolutionizing manufacturing worldwide. In simple terms, lean production is focused on organization and communication. Workers and parts are organized so as to ensure a smooth and consistent workflow that minimizes wasted effort and materials. Lean production is also designed to be highly responsive to changes in the desired mix of output—for example, quickly producing more sedans and fewer minivans according to changes in customer demand.

Toyota's lean production methods were so successful that they transformed the global auto industry and severely threatened once-dominant American automakers. Until the 1980s, the "Big Three"—Chrysler, Ford, and General Motors—dominated the American auto industry, with virtually no foreign-made cars sold in the United States. In the 1980s, however, Toyotas became increasingly popular in the United States due to their high quality and relatively low price—so popular that the Big Three eventually prevailed upon the U.S. government to protect them by restricting the sale of Japanese autos in the U.S. Over time, Toyota responded by building assembly plants in the United States, bringing along its lean production techniques, which then spread throughout American manufacturing.

QUESTIONS FOR THOUGHT

1. What is the opportunity cost associated with having a worker wander across the factory floor from task to task or in search of tools and parts?

2. Explain how lean manufacturing improves the economy's efficiency in allocation.

3. Before lean manufacturing innovations, Japan mostly sold consumer electronics to the United States. How did lean manufacturing innovations alter Japan's comparative advantage vis-à-vis the United States?

4. Predict how the shift in the location of Toyota's production from Japan to the United States is likely to alter the pattern of comparative advantage in automaking between the two countries.

SUMMARY

1. Almost all economics is based on **models,** "thought experiments" or simplified versions of reality, many of which use mathematical tools such as graphs. An important assumption in economic models is the **other things equal assumption,** which allows analysis of the effect of a change in one factor by holding all other relevant factors unchanged.

2. One important economic model is the **production possibility frontier.** It illustrates *opportunity cost* (showing how much less of one good can be produced if more of the other good is produced); *efficiency* (an economy is efficient in production if it produces on the production possibility frontier and efficient in allocation if it produces the mix of goods and services that people want to consume); and *economic growth* (an outward shift of the production possibility frontier). There are two basic sources of growth: an increase in **factors of production**—resources such as land, labor, capital, and human capital, inputs that are not used up in production—and improved **technology.**

3. Another important model is **comparative advantage,** which explains the source of gains from trade between individuals and countries. Everyone has a comparative advantage in something—some good or service in which that person has a lower opportunity cost than everyone else. But it is often confused with **absolute advantage,** an ability to produce a particular good or service better than anyone else. This confusion leads some to erroneously conclude that there are no gains from trade between people or countries.

4. In the simplest economies people **barter**—trade goods and services for one another—rather than trade them for money, as in a modern economy. The **circular-flow diagram** represents transactions within the economy as flows of goods, services, and money between **households** and **firms.** These transactions occur in **markets for goods and services** and **factor markets,** markets for **factors of production**—land, labor, physical capital, and human capital. It is useful in understanding how spending, production, employment, income, and growth are related in the economy. Ultimately, factor markets determine the economy's **income distribution,** how an economy's total income is allocated to the owners of the factors of production.

5. Economists use economic models for both **positive economics,** which describes how the economy works, and for **normative economics,** which prescribes how the economy *should* work. Positive economics often involves making **forecasts.** Economists can determine correct answers for positive questions but typically not for normative questions, which involve value judgments. The exceptions are when policies designed to achieve a certain objective can be clearly ranked in terms of efficiency.

6. There are two main reasons economists disagree. One, they may disagree about which simplifications to make in a model. Two, economists may disagree—like everyone else—about values.

KEY TERMS

Model, p. 26
Other things equal assumption, p. 27
Production possibility frontier, p. 27
Factors of production, p. 32
Technology, p. 32
Comparative advantage, p. 34

Absolute advantage, p. 36
Barter, p. 37
Circular-flow diagram, p. 37
Household, p. 38
Firm, p. 38
Markets for goods and services, p. 38

Factor markets, p. 38
Income distribution, p. 38
Positive economics, p. 40
Normative economics, p. 40
Forecast, p. 41

PROBLEMS

1. Two important industries on the island of Bermuda are fishing and tourism. According to data from the Food and Agriculture Organization of the United Nations and the Bermuda Department of Statistics, in 2009 the 306 registered fishermen in Bermuda caught 387 metric tons of marine fish. And the 2,719 people employed by hotels produced 554,400 hotel stays (measured by the number of visitor arrivals). Suppose that this production point is efficient in production. Assume also that the opportunity cost of 1 additional metric ton of fish

is 2,000 hotel stays and that this opportunity cost is constant (the opportunity cost does not change).

a. If all 306 registered fishermen were to be employed by hotels (in addition to the 2,719 people already working in hotels), how many hotel stays could Bermuda produce?

b. If all 2,719 hotel employees were to become fishermen (in addition to the 306 fishermen already working in the fishing industry), how many metric tons of fish could Bermuda produce?

c. Draw a production possibility frontier for Bermuda, with fish on the horizontal axis and hotel stays on the vertical axis, and label Bermuda's actual production point for the year 2009.

2. According to data from the U.S. Department of Agriculture's National Agricultural Statistics Service, 124 million acres of land in the United States were used for wheat or corn farming in a recent year. Of those 124 million acres, farmers used 50 million acres to grow 2.158 billion bushels of wheat and 74 million acres to grow 11.807 billion bushels of corn. Suppose that U.S. wheat and corn farming is efficient in production. At that production point, the opportunity cost of producing 1 additional bushel of wheat is 1.7 fewer bushels of corn. However, because farmers have increasing opportunity costs, additional bushels of wheat have an opportunity cost greater than 1.7 bushels of corn. For each of the following production points, decide whether that production point is (i) feasible and efficient in production, (ii) feasible but not efficient in production, (iii) not feasible, or (iv) unclear as to whether or not it is feasible.

   a. Farmers use 40 million acres of land to produce 1.8 billion bushels of wheat, and they use 60 million acres of land to produce 9 billion bushels of corn. The remaining 24 million acres are left unused.

   b. From their original production point, farmers transfer 40 million acres of land from corn to wheat production. They now produce 3.158 billion bushels of wheat and 10.107 bushels of corn.

   c. Farmers reduce their production of wheat to 2 billion bushels and increase their production of corn to 12.044 billion bushels. Along the production possibility frontier, the opportunity cost of going from 11.807 billion bushels of corn to 12.044 billion bushels of corn is 0.666 bushel of wheat per bushel of corn.

3. In the ancient country of Roma, only two goods, spaghetti and meatballs, are produced. There are two tribes in Roma, the Tivoli and the Frivoli. By themselves, the Tivoli each month can produce either 30 pounds of spaghetti and no meatballs, or 50 pounds of meatballs and no spaghetti, or any combination in between. The Frivoli, by themselves, each month can produce 40 pounds of spaghetti and no meatballs, or 30 pounds of meatballs and no spaghetti, or any combination in between.

   a. Assume that all production possibility frontiers are straight lines. Draw one diagram showing the monthly production possibility frontier for the Tivoli and another showing the monthly production possibility frontier for the Frivoli. Show how you calculated them.

   b. Which tribe has the comparative advantage in spaghetti production? In meatball production?

   In A.D. 100 the Frivoli discover a new technique for making meatballs that doubles the quantity of meatballs they can produce each month.

   c. Draw the new monthly production possibility frontier for the Frivoli.

   d. After the innovation, which tribe now has an absolute advantage in producing meatballs? In producing spaghetti? Which has the comparative advantage in meatball production? In spaghetti production?

4. One July, the United States sold aircraft worth $1 billion to China and bought aircraft worth only $19,000 from China. During the same month, however, the United States bought $83 million worth of men's trousers, slacks, and jeans from China but sold only $8,000 worth of trousers, slacks, and jeans to China. Using what you have learned about how trade is determined by comparative advantage, answer the following questions.

   a. Which country has the comparative advantage in aircraft production? In production of trousers, slacks, and jeans?

   b. Can you determine which country has the absolute advantage in aircraft production? In production of trousers, slacks, and jeans?

5. Peter Pundit, an economics reporter, states that the European Union (EU) is increasing its productivity very rapidly in all industries. He claims that this productivity advance is so rapid that output from the EU in these industries will soon exceed that of the United States and, as a result, the United States will no longer benefit from trade with the EU.

   a. Do you think Peter Pundit is correct or not? If not, what do you think is the source of his mistake?

   b. If the EU and the United States continue to trade, what do you think will characterize the goods that the EU sells to the United States and the goods that the United States sells to the EU?

6. You are in charge of allocating residents to your dormitory's baseball and basketball teams. You are down to the last four people, two of whom must be allocated to baseball and two to basketball. The accompanying table gives each person's batting average and free-throw average.

Name	Batting average	Free-throw average
Kelley	70%	60%
Jackie	50%	50%
Curt	10%	30%
Gerry	80%	70%

   a. Explain how you would use the concept of comparative advantage to allocate the players. Begin by establishing each player's opportunity cost of free throws in terms of batting average.

   b. Why is it likely that the other basketball players will be unhappy about this arrangement but the other baseball players will be satisfied? Nonetheless, why would an economist say that this is an efficient way to allocate players for your dormitory's sports teams?

7. The inhabitants of the fictional economy of Atlantis use money in the form of cowry shells. Draw a circular-flow diagram showing households and firms. Firms produce potatoes and fish, and households buy potatoes and fish. Households also provide the land and labor to firms. Identify where in the flows of cowry shells or physical things (goods and services, or resources) each of the following impacts would occur. Describe how this impact spreads around the circle.

    a. A devastating hurricane floods many of the potato fields.

    b. A very productive fishing season yields a very large number of fish caught.

    c. The inhabitants of Atlantis discover Shakira and spend several days a month at dancing festivals.

8. An economist might say that colleges and universities "produce" education, using faculty members and students as inputs. According to this line of reasoning, education is then "consumed" by households. Construct a circular-flow diagram to represent the sector of the economy devoted to college education: colleges and universities represent firms, and households both consume education and provide faculty and students to universities. What are the relevant markets in this diagram? What is being bought and sold in each direction? What would happen in the diagram if the government decided to subsidize 50% of all college students' tuition?

9. Your dormitory roommate plays loud music most of the time; you, however, would prefer more peace and quiet. You suggest that she buy some earphones. She responds that although she would be happy to use earphones, she has many other things that she would prefer to spend her money on right now. You discuss this situation with a friend who is an economics major. The following exchange takes place:

    He: How much would it cost to buy earphones?

    You: $15.

    He: How much do you value having some peace and quiet for the rest of the semester?

    You: $30.

    He: It is efficient for you to buy the earphones and give them to your roommate. You gain more than you lose; the benefit exceeds the cost. You should do that.

    You: It just isn't fair that I have to pay for the earphones when I'm not the one making the noise.

    a. Which parts of this conversation contain positive statements and which parts contain normative statements?

    b. Construct an argument supporting your viewpoint that your roommate should be the one to change her behavior. Similarly, construct an argument from the viewpoint of your roommate that you should be the one to buy the earphones. If your dormitory has a policy that gives residents the unlimited right to play music, whose argument is likely to win? If your dormitory has a rule that a person must stop playing music whenever a roommate complains, whose argument is likely to win?

10. A representative of the American clothing industry recently made the following statement: "Workers in Asia often work in sweatshop conditions earning only pennies an hour. American workers are more productive and as a result earn higher wages. In order to preserve the dignity of the American workplace, the government should enact legislation banning imports of low-wage Asian clothing."

    a. Which parts of this quote are positive statements? Which parts are normative statements?

    b. Is the policy that is being advocated consistent with the preceding statements about the wages and productivities of American and Asian workers?

    c. Would such a policy make some Americans better off without making any other Americans worse off? That is, would this policy be efficient from the viewpoint of all Americans?

    d. Would low-wage Asian workers benefit from or be hurt by such a policy?

11. Are the following statements true or false? Explain your answers.

    a. "When people must pay higher taxes on their wage earnings, it reduces their incentive to work" is a positive statement.

    b. "We should lower taxes to encourage more work" is a positive statement.

    c. Economics cannot always be used to completely decide what society ought to do.

    d. "The system of public education in this country generates greater benefits to society than the cost of running the system" is a normative statement.

    e. All disagreements among economists are generated by the media.

12. Evaluate the following statement: "It is easier to build an economic model that accurately reflects events that have already occurred than to build an economic model to forecast future events." Do you think this is true or not? Why? What does this imply about the difficulties of building good economic models?

13. Economists who work for the government are often called on to make policy recommendations. Why do you think it is important for the public to be able to differentiate normative statements from positive statements in these recommendations?

14. The mayor of Gotham City, worried about a potential epidemic of deadly influenza this winter, asks an economic adviser the following series of questions. Determine whether a question requires the economic adviser to make a positive assessment or a normative assessment.

    a. How much vaccine will be in stock in the city by the end of November?

    b. If we offer to pay 10% more per dose to the pharmaceutical companies providing the vaccines, will they provide additional doses?

    c. If there is a shortage of vaccine in the city, whom should we vaccinate first—the elderly or the very young? (Assume that a person from one group has an equal likelihood of dying from influenza as a person from the other group.)

d. If the city charges $25 per shot, how many people will pay?

e. If the city charges $25 per shot, it will make a profit of $10 per shot, money that can go to pay for inoculating poor people. Should the city engage in such a scheme?

15. Assess the following statement: "If economists just had enough data, they could solve all policy questions in a way that maximizes the social good. There would be no need for divisive political debates, such as whether the government should provide free medical care for all."

WORK IT OUT   Macmillan Education LaunchPad

For interactive, step-by-step help in solving the following problem, visit LaunchPad by using the URL on the back cover of this book.

16. Atlantis is a small, isolated island in the South Atlantic. The inhabitants grow potatoes and catch fish. The accompanying table shows the maximum annual output combinations of potatoes and fish that can be produced. Obviously, given their limited resources and available technology, as they use more of their resources for potato production, there are fewer resources available for catching fish.

Maximum annual output options	Quantity of potatoes (pounds)	Quantity of fish (pounds)
A	1,000	0
B	800	300
C	600	500
D	400	600
E	200	650
F	0	675

a. Draw a production possibility frontier with potatoes on the horizontal axis and fish on the vertical axis illustrating these options, showing points *A–F*.

b. Can Atlantis produce 500 pounds of fish and 800 pounds of potatoes? Explain. Where would this point lie relative to the production possibility frontier?

c. What is the opportunity cost of increasing the annual output of potatoes from 600 to 800 pounds?

d. What is the opportunity cost of increasing the annual output of potatoes from 200 to 400 pounds?

e. Can you explain why the answers to parts c and d are not the same? What does this imply about the slope of the production possibility frontier?

Graphs in Economics

Getting the Picture

Whether you're reading about economics in the *Wall Street Journal* or in your economics textbook, you will see many graphs. Visual images can make it much easier to understand verbal descriptions, numerical information, or ideas. In economics, graphs are the type of visual image used to facilitate understanding. To fully understand the ideas and information being discussed, you need to be familiar with how to interpret and construct these visual aids. This appendix explains how to do this.

Graphs, Variables, and Economic Models

One reason to attend college is that a bachelor's degree provides access to higher-paying jobs. Additional degrees, such as MBAs or law degrees, increase earnings even more. If you were to read an article about the relationship between educational attainment and income, you would probably see a graph showing the income levels for workers with different amounts of education. And this graph would depict the idea that, in general, more education increases income.

This graph, like most of those in economics, would depict the relationship between two economic variables. A **variable** is a quantity that can take on more than one value, such as the number of years of education a person has, the price of a can of soda, or a household's income.

As you learned in this chapter, economic analysis relies heavily on *models*, simplified descriptions of real situations. Most economic models describe the relationship between two variables, simplified by holding constant other variables that may affect the relationship.

For example, an economic model might describe the relationship between the price of a can of soda and the number of cans of soda that consumers will buy, assuming that everything else affecting consumers' purchases of soda stays constant. This type of model can be described mathematically or verbally, but illustrating the relationship in a graph makes it easier to understand, as you'll see next.

How Graphs Work

Most graphs in economics are based on a grid built around two perpendicular lines that show the values of two variables, helping you visualize the relationship between them. So a first step in understanding the use of such graphs is to see how this system works.

Two-Variable Graphs

Figure 2A-1 shows a typical two-variable graph. It illustrates the data in the accompanying table on outside temperature and the number of sodas a typical vendor can expect to sell at a baseball stadium during one game. The first column shows the values of outside temperature (the first variable) and the second column shows the values of the number of sodas sold (the second variable). Five combinations or pairs of the two variables are shown, each denoted by *A* through *E* in the third column.

Now let's turn to graphing the data in this table. In any two-variable graph, one variable is called the *x*-variable and the other is called the *y*-variable. Here

A quantity that can take on more than one value is called a **variable.**

FIGURE **2A-1**   Plotting Points on a Two-Variable Graph

The data from the table are plotted where outside temperature (the independent variable) is measured along the horizontal axis and number of sodas sold (the dependent variable) is measured along the vertical axis. Each of the five combinations of temperature and sodas sold is represented by a point: *A, B, C, D,* and *E.* Each point in the graph is identified by a pair of values. For example, point *C* corresponds to the pair (40, 30)—an outside temperature of 40°F (the value of the *x*-variable) and 30 sodas sold (the value of the *y*-variable).

The line along which values of the *x*-variable are measured is called the **horizontal axis** or ***x*-axis.** The line along which values of the *y*-variable are measured is called the **vertical axis** or ***y*-axis.** The point where the axes of a two-variable graph meet is the **origin.**

A **causal relationship** exists between two variables when the value taken by one variable directly influences or determines the value taken by the other variable. In a causal relationship, the determining variable is called the **independent variable;** the variable it determines is called the **dependent variable.**

we have made outside temperature the *x*-variable and number of sodas sold the *y*-variable. The solid horizontal line in the graph is called the **horizontal axis** or ***x*-axis,** and values of the *x*-variable—outside temperature—are measured along it. Similarly, the solid vertical line in the graph is called the **vertical axis** or ***y*-axis,** and values of the *y*-variable—number of sodas sold—are measured along it.

At the **origin,** the point where the two axes meet, each variable is equal to zero. As you move rightward from the origin along the *x*-axis, values of the *x*-variable are positive and increasing. As you move up from the origin along the *y*-axis, values of the *y*-variable are positive and increasing.

You can plot each of the five points *A* through *E* on this graph by using a pair of numbers—the values that the *x*-variable and the *y*-variable take on for a given point. In Figure 2A-1, at point *C,* the *x*-variable takes on the value 40 and the *y*-variable takes on the value 30. You plot point *C* by drawing a line straight up from 40 on the *x*-axis and a horizontal line across from 30 on the *y*-axis. We write point *C* as (40, 30). We write the origin as (0, 0).

Looking at point *A* and point *B* in Figure 2A-1, you can see that when one of the variables for a point has a value of zero, it will lie on one of the axes. If the value of the *x*-variable is zero, the point will lie on the vertical axis, like point *A.* If the value of the *y*-variable is zero, the point will lie on the horizontal axis, like point *B.*

Most graphs that depict relationships between two economic variables represent a **causal relationship,** a relationship in which the value taken by one variable directly influences or determines the value taken by the other variable. In a causal relationship, the determining variable is called the **independent variable;** the variable it determines is called the **dependent variable.** In our example of soda sales, the outside temperature is the independent variable. It directly influences the number of sodas that are sold, the dependent variable in this case.

By convention, we put the independent variable on the horizontal axis and the dependent variable on the vertical axis. Figure 2A-1 is constructed consistent with this convention; the independent variable (outside temperature) is on the horizontal axis and the dependent variable (number of sodas sold) is on the vertical axis.

An important exception to this convention is in graphs showing the economic relationship between the price of a product and quantity of the product: although price is generally the independent variable that determines quantity, it is always measured on the vertical axis.

> A **curve** is a line on a graph that depicts a relationship between two variables. It may be either a straight line or a curved line. If the curve is a straight line, the variables have a **linear relationship.** If the curve is not a straight line, the variables have a **nonlinear relationship.**

Curves on a Graph

Panel (a) of Figure 2A-2 contains some of the same information as Figure 2A-1, with a line drawn through the points *B, C, D,* and *E.* Such a line on a graph is called a **curve,** regardless of whether it is a straight line or a curved line. If the curve that shows the relationship between two variables is a straight line, or linear, the variables have a **linear relationship.** When the curve is not a straight line, or nonlinear, the variables have a **nonlinear relationship.**

A point on a curve indicates the value of the *y*-variable for a specific value of the *x*-variable. For example, point *D* indicates that at a temperature of 60°F, a vendor can expect to sell 50 sodas. The shape and orientation of a curve reveal

FIGURE 2A-2 | **Drawing Curves**

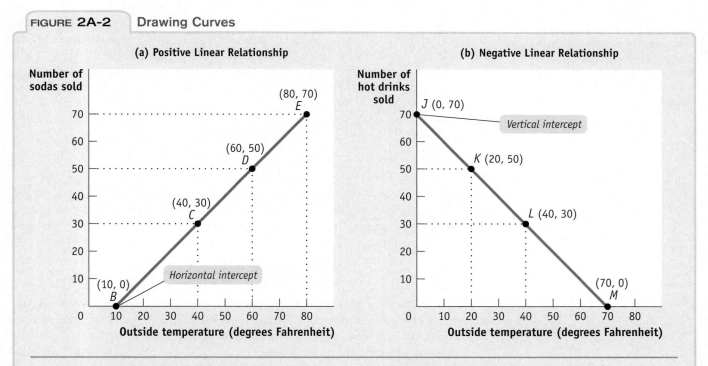

The curve in panel (a) illustrates the relationship between the two variables, outside temperature and number of sodas sold. The two variables have a positive linear relationship: positive because the curve has an upward tilt, and linear because it is a straight line. It implies that an increase in the *x*-variable (outside temperature) leads to an increase in the *y*-variable (number of sodas sold). The curve in panel (b) is also a straight line, but it tilts downward. The two variables here, outside temperature

and number of hot drinks sold, have a negative linear relationship: an increase in the *x*-variable (outside temperature) leads to a decrease in the *y*-variable (number of hot drinks sold). The curve in panel (a) has a horizontal intercept at point *B,* where it hits the horizontal axis. The curve in panel (b) has a vertical intercept at point *J,* where it hits the vertical axis, and a horizontal intercept at point *M,* where it hits the horizontal axis.

Two variables have a **positive relationship** when an increase in the value of one variable is associated with an increase in the value of the other variable. It is illustrated by a curve that slopes upward from left to right.

Two variables have a **negative relationship** when an increase in the value of one variable is associated with a decrease in the value of the other variable. It is illustrated by a curve that slopes downward from left to right.

The **horizontal intercept** of a curve is the point at which it hits the horizontal axis; it indicates the value of the x-variable when the value of the y-variable is zero.

The **vertical intercept** of a curve is the point at which it hits the vertical axis; it shows the value of the y-variable when the value of the x-variable is zero.

The **slope** of a line or curve is a measure of how steep it is. The slope of a line is measured by "rise over run"—the change in the y-variable between two points on the line divided by the change in the x-variable between those same two points.

the general nature of the relationship between the two variables. The upward tilt of the curve in panel (a) of Figure 2A-2 means that vendors can expect to sell more sodas at higher outside temperatures.

When variables are related this way—that is, when an increase in one variable is associated with an increase in the other variable—the variables are said to have a **positive relationship.** It is illustrated by a curve that slopes upward from left to right. Because this curve is also linear, the relationship between outside temperature and number of sodas sold illustrated by the curve in panel (a) of Figure 2A-2 is a positive linear relationship.

When an increase in one variable is associated with a decrease in the other variable, the two variables are said to have a **negative relationship.** It is illustrated by a curve that slopes downward from left to right, like the curve in panel (b) of Figure 2A-2. Because this curve is also linear, the relationship it depicts is a negative linear relationship. Two variables that might have such a relationship are the outside temperature and the number of hot drinks a vendor can expect to sell at a baseball stadium.

Return for a moment to the curve in panel (a) of Figure 2A-2 and you can see that it hits the horizontal axis at point B. This point, known as the **horizontal intercept,** shows the value of the x-variable when the value of the y-variable is zero. In panel (b) of Figure 2A-2, the curve hits the vertical axis at point J. This point, called the **vertical intercept,** indicates the value of the y-variable when the value of the x-variable is zero.

A Key Concept: The Slope of a Curve

The **slope** of a curve is a measure of how steep it is and indicates how sensitive the y-variable is to a change in the x-variable. In our example of outside temperature and the number of cans of soda a vendor can expect to sell, the slope of the curve would indicate how many more cans of soda the vendor could expect to sell with each 1 degree increase in temperature. Interpreted this way, the slope gives meaningful information. Even without numbers for x and y, it is possible to arrive at important conclusions about the relationship between the two variables by examining the slope of a curve at various points.

The Slope of a Linear Curve

Along a linear curve the slope, or steepness, is measured by dividing the "rise" between two points on the curve by the "run" between those same two points. The rise is the amount that y changes, and the run is the amount that x changes. Here is the formula:

$$\frac{\text{Change in } y}{\text{Change in } x} = \frac{\Delta y}{\Delta x} = \text{Slope}$$

In the formula, the symbol Δ (the Greek uppercase delta) stands for "change in." When a variable increases, the change in that variable is positive; when a variable decreases, the change in that variable is negative.

The slope of a curve is positive when the rise (the change in the y-variable) has the same sign as the run (the change in the x-variable). That's because when two numbers have the same sign, the ratio of those two numbers is positive. The curve in panel (a) of Figure 2A-2 has a positive slope: along the curve, both the y-variable and the x-variable increase.

The slope of a curve is negative when the rise and the run have different signs. That's because when two numbers have different signs, the ratio of those two numbers is negative. The curve in panel (b) of Figure 2A-2 has a negative slope: along the curve, an increase in the x-variable is associated with a decrease in the y-variable.

Figure 2A-3 illustrates how to calculate the slope of a linear curve. Let's focus first on panel (a). From point A to point B the value of the y-variable changes from

FIGURE **2A-3**   Calculating the Scope

Panels (a) and (b) show two linear curves. Between points A and B on the curve in panel (a), the change in y (the rise) is -5 and the change in x (the run) is 10. So the slope from A to B is $\frac{\Delta y}{\Delta x} = \frac{-5}{10} = -\frac{1}{2} = -0.5$, where the negative sign indicates that the curve is downward sloping. In panel (b), the curve has a slope from A to B of $\frac{\Delta y}{\Delta x} = \frac{10}{2} = 5$. The slope from C to D is $\frac{\Delta y}{\Delta x} = \frac{20}{4} = 5$.

The slope is positive, indicating that the curve is upward sloping. Furthermore, the slope between A and B is the same as the slope between C and D, making this a linear curve. The slope of a linear curve is constant: it is the same regardless of where it is measured along the curve.

25 to 20 and the value of the x-variable changes from 10 to 20. So the slope of the line between these two points is:

$$\frac{\text{Change in } y}{\text{Change in } x} = \frac{\Delta y}{\Delta x} = \frac{-5}{10} = -\frac{1}{2} = -0.5$$

Because a straight line is equally steep at all points, the slope of a straight line is the same at all points. In other words, a straight line has a constant slope. You can check this by calculating the slope of the linear curve between points A and B and between points C and D in panel (b) of Figure 2A-3.

Between A and B: $\dfrac{\Delta y}{\Delta x} = \dfrac{10}{2} = 5$

Between C and D: $\dfrac{\Delta y}{\Delta x} = \dfrac{20}{4} = 5$

Horizontal and Vertical Curves and Their Slopes

When a curve is horizontal, the value of the y-variable along that curve never changes—it is constant. Everywhere along the curve, the change in y is zero. Now, zero divided by any number is zero. So, regardless of the value of the change in x, the slope of a horizontal curve is always zero.

If a curve is vertical, the value of the x-variable along the curve never changes—it is constant. Everywhere along the curve, the change in x is zero. This means that the slope of a vertical curve is a ratio with zero in the denominator. A ratio with zero in the denominator is equal to infinity—that is, an infinitely large number. So the slope of a vertical curve is equal to infinity.

A **nonlinear curve** is one in which the slope is not the same between every pair of points.

The **absolute value** of a negative number is the value of the negative number without the minus sign.

A vertical or a horizontal curve has a special implication: it means that the *x*-variable and the *y*-variable are unrelated. Two variables are unrelated when a change in one variable (the independent variable) has no effect on the other variable (the dependent variable). Or to put it a slightly different way, two variables are unrelated when the dependent variable is constant regardless of the value of the independent variable. If, as is usual, the *y*-variable is the dependent variable, the curve is horizontal. If the dependent variable is the *x*-variable, the curve is vertical.

The Slope of a Nonlinear Curve

A **nonlinear curve** is one in which the slope changes as you move along it. Panels (a), (b), (c), and (d) of Figure 2A-4 show various nonlinear curves. Panels (a) and (b) show nonlinear curves whose slopes change as you move along them, but the slopes always remain positive. Although both curves tilt upward, the curve in panel (a) gets steeper as you move from left to right in contrast to the curve in panel (b), which gets flatter.

A curve that is upward sloping and gets steeper, as in panel (a), is said to have *positive increasing* slope. A curve that is upward sloping but gets flatter, as in panel (b), is said to have *positive decreasing* slope.

When we calculate the slope along these nonlinear curves, we obtain different values for the slope at different points. How the slope changes along the curve determines the curve's shape. For example, in panel (a) of Figure 2A-4, the slope of the curve is a positive number that steadily increases as you move from left to right, whereas in panel (b), the slope is a positive number that steadily decreases.

The slopes of the curves in panels (c) and (d) are negative numbers. Economists often prefer to express a negative number as its **absolute value,** which is the value of the negative number without the minus sign. In general, we denote the absolute value of a number by two parallel bars around the number; for example, the absolute value of −4 is written as |−4| = 4.

In panel (c), the absolute value of the slope steadily increases as you move from left to right. The curve therefore has *negative increasing* slope. And in panel (d), the absolute value of the slope of the curve steadily decreases along the curve. This curve therefore has *negative decreasing* slope.

Calculating the Slope Along a Nonlinear Curve

We've just seen that along a nonlinear curve, the value of the slope depends on where you are on that curve. So how do you calculate the slope of a nonlinear curve? We will focus on two methods: the *arc method* and the *point method*.

The Arc Method of Calculating the Slope An arc of a curve is some piece or segment of that curve. For example, panel (a) of Figure 2A-4 shows an arc consisting of the segment of the curve between points A and B. To calculate the slope along a nonlinear curve using the arc method, you draw a straight line between the two end-points of the arc. The slope of that straight line is a measure of the average slope of the curve between those two end-points.

You can see from panel (a) of Figure 2A-4 that the straight line drawn between points *A* and *B* increases along the *x*-axis from 6 to 10 (so that Δ*x* = 4) as it increases along the *y*-axis from 10 to 20 (so that Δ*y* = 10). Therefore the slope of the straight line connecting points *A* and *B* is:

$$\frac{\Delta y}{\Delta x} = \frac{10}{4} = 2.5$$

This means that the average slope of the curve between points *A* and *B* is 2.5.

FIGURE 2A-4 | Nonlinear Curves

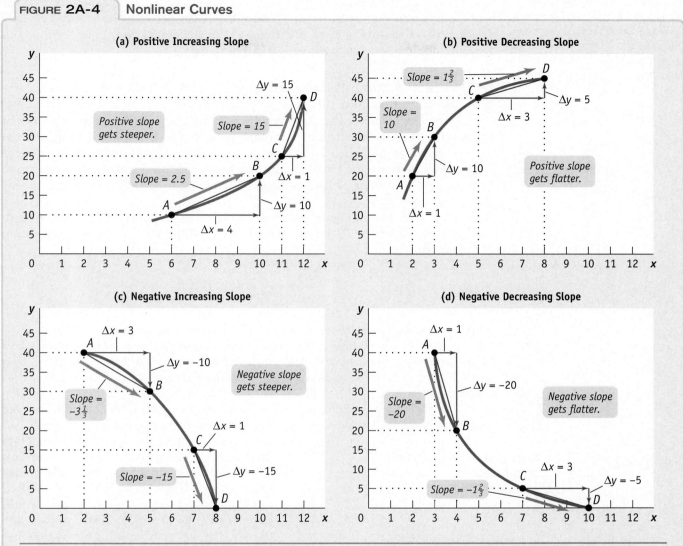

In panel (a) the slope of the curve from A to B is $\frac{y}{x} = \frac{10}{4} = 2.5$, and from C to D it is $\frac{\Delta y}{\Delta x} = \frac{15}{1} = 15$. The slope is positive and increasing; the curve gets steeper as you move to the right. In panel (b) the slope of the curve from A to B is $\frac{\Delta y}{\Delta x} = \frac{10}{1} = 10$, and from C to D it is $\frac{\Delta y}{\Delta x} = \frac{5}{3} = 1\frac{2}{3}$. The slope is positive and decreasing; the curve gets flatter as you move to the right. In panel (c) the slope from A to B is $\frac{\Delta y}{\Delta x} = \frac{-10}{3} = -3\frac{1}{3}$, and from C to D it is $\frac{\Delta y}{\Delta x} = \frac{-15}{1} = -15$. The slope is negative and increasing; the

curve gets steeper as you move to the right. And in panel (d) the slope from A to B is $\frac{\Delta y}{\Delta x} = \frac{-20}{1} = -20$, and from C to D it is $\frac{\Delta y}{\Delta x} = \frac{-5}{3} = -1\frac{2}{3}$. The slope is negative and decreasing; the curve gets flatter as you move to the right. The slope in each case has been calculated by using the arc method—that is, by drawing a straight line connecting two points along a curve. The average slope between those two points is equal to the slope of the straight line between those two points.

Now consider the arc on the same curve between points C and D. A straight line drawn through these two points increases along the x-axis from 11 to 12 ($\Delta x = 1$) as it increases along the y-axis from 25 to 40 ($\Delta y = 15$). So the average slope between points C and D is:

$$\frac{\Delta y}{\Delta x} = \frac{15}{1} = 15$$

A **tangent line** is a straight line that just touches, or is tangent to, a nonlinear curve at a particular point. The slope of the tangent line is equal to the slope of the nonlinear curve at that point.

Therefore the average slope between points C and D is larger than the average slope between points A and B. These calculations verify what we have already observed—that this upward-tilted curve gets steeper as you move from left to right and therefore has positive increasing slope.

The Point Method of Calculating the Slope The point method calculates the slope of a nonlinear curve at a specific point on that curve. Figure 2A-5 illustrates how to calculate the slope at point B on the curve. First, we draw a straight line that just touches the curve at point B. Such a line is called a **tangent line:** the fact that it just touches the curve at point B and does not touch the curve at any other point on the curve means that the straight line is *tangent* to the curve at point B. The slope of this tangent line is equal to the slope of the nonlinear curve at point B.

You can see from Figure 2A-5 how the slope of the tangent line is calculated: from point A to point C, the change in y is 15 and the change in x is 5, generating a slope of:

$$\frac{\Delta y}{\Delta x} = \frac{15}{5} = 3$$

By the point method, the slope of the curve at point B is equal to 3.

A natural question to ask at this point is how to determine which method to use—the arc method or the point method—in calculating the slope of a nonlinear curve. The answer depends on the curve itself and the data used to construct it.

You use the arc method when you don't have enough information to be able to draw a smooth curve. For example, suppose that in panel (a) of Figure 2A-4 you have only the data represented by points A, C, and D and don't have the data represented by point B or any of the rest of the curve. Clearly, then, you can't use the point method to calculate the slope at point B; you would have to use the arc method to approximate the slope of the curve in this area by drawing a straight line between points A and C.

But if you have sufficient data to draw the smooth curve shown in panel (a) of Figure 2A-4, then you could use the point method to calculate the slope at point B—and at every other point along the curve as well.

Maximum and Minimum Points

The slope of a nonlinear curve can change from positive to negative or vice versa. When the slope of a curve changes from positive to negative, it creates what is called a *maximum* point of the curve. When the slope of a curve changes from negative to positive, it creates a *minimum* point.

Panel (a) of Figure 2A-6 illustrates a curve in which the slope changes from positive to negative as you move from left to right. When x is between 0 and 50, the slope of the curve is positive. At x equal to 50, the curve attains

FIGURE **2A-5**   Calculating the Slope Using the Point Method

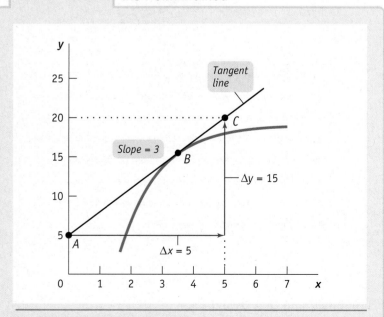

Here a tangent line has been drawn, a line that just touches the curve at point B. The slope of this line is equal to the slope of the curve at point B. The slope of the tangent line, measuring from A to C, is

$\frac{\Delta y}{\Delta x} = \frac{15}{5} = 3$.

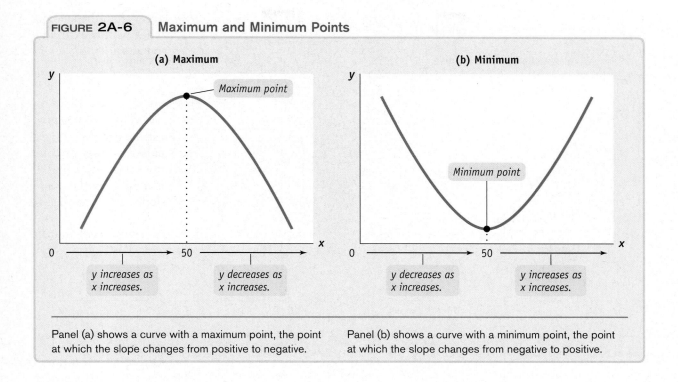

FIGURE **2A-6** Maximum and Minimum Points

(a) Maximum

Maximum point

y increases as x increases. *y decreases as x increases.*

(b) Minimum

Minimum point

y decreases as x increases. *y increases as x increases.*

Panel (a) shows a curve with a maximum point, the point at which the slope changes from positive to negative.

Panel (b) shows a curve with a minimum point, the point at which the slope changes from negative to positive.

its highest point—the largest value of *y* along the curve. This point is called the **maximum** of the curve. When *x* exceeds 50, the slope becomes negative as the curve turns downward. Many important curves in economics, such as the curve that represents how the profit of a firm changes as it produces more output, are hill-shaped like this.

In contrast, the curve shown in panel (b) of Figure 2A-6 is U-shaped: it has a slope that changes from negative to positive. At *x* equal to 50, the curve reaches its lowest point—the smallest value of *y* along the curve. This point is called the **minimum** of the curve. Various important curves in economics, such as the curve that represents how per-unit the costs of some firms change as output increases, are U-shaped like this.

A nonlinear curve may have a **maximum** point, the highest point along the curve. At the maximum, the slope of the curve changes from positive to negative.

A nonlinear curve may have a **minimum** point, the lowest point along the curve. At the minimum, the slope of the curve changes from negative to positive.

Calculating the Area Below or Above a Curve

Sometimes it is useful to be able to measure the size of the area below or above a curve. For the sake of simplicity, we'll only calculate the area below or above a linear curve.

How large is the shaded area below the linear curve in panel (a) of Figure 2A-7? First note that this area has the shape of a right triangle. A right triangle is a triangle that has two sides that make a right angle with each other. We will refer to one of these sides as the *height* of the triangle and the other side as the *base* of the triangle. For our purposes, it doesn't matter which of these two sides we refer to as the base and which as the height.

Calculating the area of a right triangle is straightforward: multiply the height of the triangle by the base of the triangle, and divide the result by 2. The height of the triangle in panel (a) of Figure 2A-7 is 10 − 4 = 6. And the base of the triangle is 3 − 0 = 3. So the area of that triangle is

$$\frac{6 \times 3}{2} = 9$$

FIGURE 2A-7 Calculating the Area Below and Above a Linear Curve

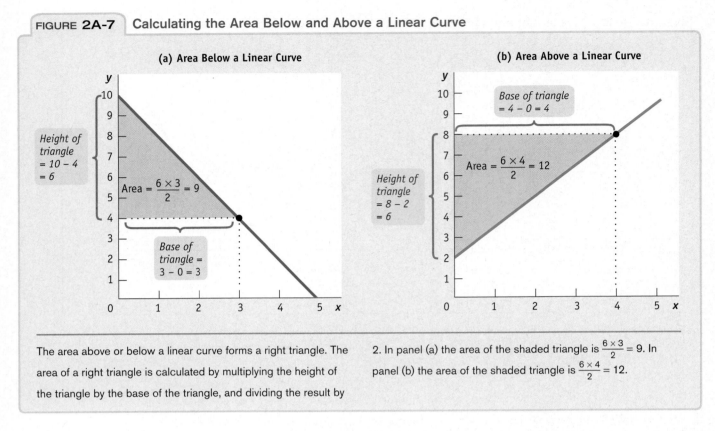

(a) Area Below a Linear Curve

Height of triangle = 10 – 4 = 6

Area = $\frac{6 \times 3}{2}$ = 9

Base of triangle = 3 – 0 = 3

(b) Area Above a Linear Curve

Base of triangle = 4 – 0 = 4

Area = $\frac{6 \times 4}{2}$ = 12

Height of triangle = 8 – 2 = 6

The area above or below a linear curve forms a right triangle. The area of a right triangle is calculated by multiplying the height of the triangle by the base of the triangle, and dividing the result by

2. In panel (a) the area of the shaded triangle is $\frac{6 \times 3}{2}$ = 9. In panel (b) the area of the shaded triangle is $\frac{6 \times 4}{2}$ = 12.

A **time-series graph** has dates on the horizontal axis and values of a variable that occurred on those dates on the vertical axis.

How about the shaded area above the linear curve in panel (b) of Figure 2A-7? We can use the same formula to calculate the area of this right triangle. The height of the triangle is 8 – 2 = 6. And the base of the triangle is 4 – 0 = 4. So the area of that triangle is

$$\frac{6 \times 4}{2} = 12$$

Graphs That Depict Numerical Information

Graphs can also be used as a convenient way to summarize and display data without assuming some underlying causal relationship. Graphs that simply display numerical information are called *numerical graphs*. Here we will consider four types of numerical graphs: *time-series graphs, scatter diagrams, pie charts,* and *bar graphs.* These are widely used to display real, empirical data about different economic variables because they often help economists and policy makers identify patterns or trends in the economy. But as we will also see, you must be aware of both the usefulness and the limitations of numerical graphs to avoid misinterpreting them or drawing unwarranted conclusions from them.

Types of Numerical Graphs

You have probably seen graphs that show what has happened over time to economic variables such as the unemployment rate or stock prices. A **time-series graph** has successive dates on the horizontal axis and the values of a variable that occurred on those dates on the vertical axis.

For example, Figure 2A-8 shows real gross domestic product (GDP) per capita—a rough measure of a country's standard of living—in the United States from 1947 to 2013. A line connecting the points that correspond to real GDP per capita for each calendar quarter during those years gives a clear idea of the overall trend in the standard of living over these years.

Figure 2A-9 is an example of a different kind of numerical graph. It represents information from a sample of 181 countries on the standard of living, again measured by GDP per capita, and the amount of carbon emissions per capita, a measure of environmental pollution. Each point here indicates an average resident's standard of living and his or her annual carbon emissions for a given country.

The points lying in the upper right of the graph, which show combinations of a high standard of living and high carbon emissions, represent economically advanced countries such as the United States. (The country with the highest carbon emissions, at the top of the graph, is Qatar.) Points lying in the bottom left of the graph, which show combinations of a low standard of living and low carbon emissions, represent economically less advanced countries such as Afghanistan and Sierra Leone.

The pattern of points indicates that there is a positive relationship between living standard and carbon emissions per capita: on the whole, people create more pollution in countries with a higher standard of living.

This type of graph is called a **scatter diagram,** in which each point corresponds to an actual observation of the *x*-variable and the *y*-variable. In scatter diagrams, a curve is typically fitted to the scatter of points; that is, a curve is drawn that approximates as closely as possible the general relationship between

FIGURE 2A-8   Time-Series Graph

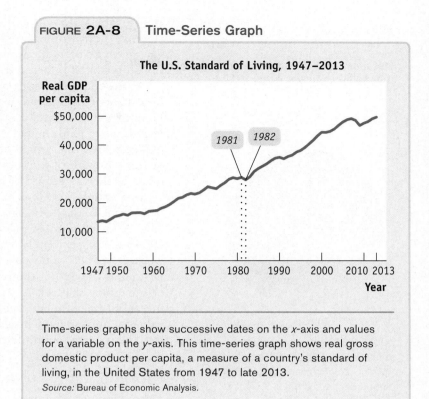

Time-series graphs show successive dates on the *x*-axis and values for a variable on the *y*-axis. This time-series graph shows real gross domestic product per capita, a measure of a country's standard of living, in the United States from 1947 to late 2013.
Source: Bureau of Economic Analysis.

A **scatter diagram** shows points that correspond to actual observations of the *x*- and *y*-variables. A curve is usually fitted to the scatter of points.

FIGURE 2A-9   Scatter Diagram

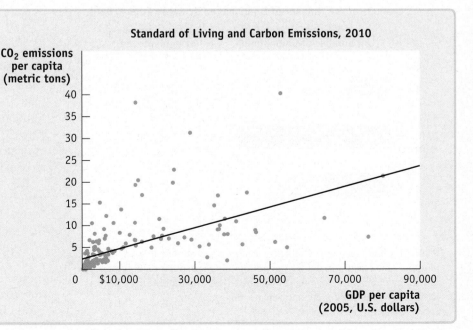

In a scatter diagram, each point represents the corresponding values of the *x*- and *y*-variables for a given observation. Here, each point indicates the GDP per capita and the amount of carbon emissions per capita for a given country for a sample of 181 countries. The upward-sloping fitted line here is the best approximation of the general relationship between the two variables.
Source: World Bank.

FIGURE **2A-10** | Pie Chart

Education Levels of Workers Paid at or Below Minimum Wage, 2012

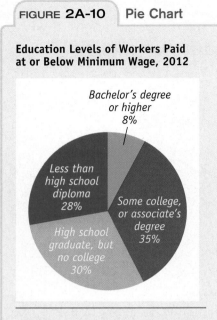

A pie chart shows the percentages of a total amount that can be attributed to various components. This pie chart shows the percentages of workers with given education levels who were paid at or below the federal minimum wage in 2012.

Source: Bureau of Labor Statistics.

the variables. As you can see, the fitted line in Figure 2A-9 is upward sloping, indicating the underlying positive relationship between the two variables. Scatter diagrams are often used to show how a general relationship can be inferred from a set of data.

A **pie chart** shows the share of a total amount that is accounted for by various components, usually expressed in percentages. For example, Figure 2A-10 is a pie chart that depicts the education levels of workers who in 2012 were paid the federal minimum wage or less. As you can see, the majority of workers paid at or below the minimum wage had no college degree. Only 8% of workers who were paid at or below the minimum wage had a bachelor's degree or higher.

Bar graphs use bars of various heights or lengths to indicate values of a variable. In the bar graph in Figure 2A-11, the bars show the percent change in the number of unemployed workers in the United States from 2009 to 2010, separately for White, Black or African-American, and Asian workers. Exact values of the variable that is being measured may be written at the end of the bar, as in this figure. For instance, the number of unemployed Black or African-American workers in the United States increased by 9.4% between 2009 and 2010. But even without the precise values, comparing the heights or lengths of the bars can give useful insight into the relative magnitudes of the different values of the variable.

Problems in Interpreting Numerical Graphs

Although we've explained that graphs are visual images that make ideas or information easier to understand, graphs can be constructed (intentionally or unintentionally) in ways that are misleading and can lead to inaccurate conclusions. This section raises some issues to be aware of when you are interpreting graphs.

Features of Construction Before drawing any conclusions about what a numerical graph implies, pay close attention to the scale, or size of increments, shown on the axes. Small increments tend to visually exaggerate changes in the variables, whereas large increments tend to visually diminish them. So the scale used in construction of a graph can influence your interpretation of the significance of the changes it illustrates—perhaps in an unwarranted way.

Take, for example, Figure 2A-12, which shows real GDP per capita in the United States from 1981 to 1982 using increments of $500. You can see that real GDP per capita fell from $28,936 to $27,839. A decrease, sure, but is it as enormous as the scale chosen for the vertical axis makes it seem?

If you go back and reexamine Figure 2A-8, which shows real GDP per capita in the United States from 1947 to 2013, you can see that this would be a misguided conclusion. Figure 2A-8 includes the same data shown in Figure 2A-12, but it is constructed with a scale having increments of $10,000 rather than $500. From it you can see that the fall in real GDP per capita from 1981 to 1982 was, in fact, relatively insignificant.

FIGURE **2A-11** | Bar Graph

A bar graph measures a variable by using bars of various heights or lengths. This bar graph shows the percent change in the number of unemployed workers between 2009 and 2010, separately for White, Black or African-American, and Asian workers.

Source: Bureau of Labor Statistics.

FIGURE **2A-12**   Interpreting Graphs: The Effect of Scale

Some of the same data for the years 1981 and 1982 used in Figure 2A-8 are represented here, except that here they are shown using increments of $500 rather than increments of $10,000. As a result of this change in scale, changes in the standard of living look much larger in this figure compared to Figure 2A-8.

Source: Bureau of Economic Analysis

The U.S. Standard of Living, 1981–1982

In fact, the story of real GDP per capita—a measure of the standard of living—in the United States is mostly a story of ups, not downs. This comparison shows that if you are not careful to factor in the choice of scale in interpreting a graph, you can arrive at very different, and possibly misguided, conclusions.

Related to the choice of scale is the use of *truncation* in constructing a graph. An axis is **truncated** when part of the range is omitted. This is indicated by two slashes (//) in the axis near the origin. You can see that the vertical axis of Figure 2A-12 has been truncated—some of the range of values from 0 to $27,000 has been omitted and a // appears in the axis. Truncation saves space in the presentation of a graph and allows smaller increments to be used in constructing it. As a result, changes in the variable depicted on a graph that has been truncated appear larger compared to a graph that has not been truncated and that uses larger increments.

You must also consider exactly what a graph is illustrating. For example, in Figure 2A-11, you should recognize that what is being shown are *percent* changes in the number of unemployed, not *numerical* changes. The unemployment rate for Black or African-American workers increased by the highest percentage, 9.4% in this example. If you were to confuse numerical changes with percent changes, you would erroneously conclude that the greatest number of newly unemployed workers were Black or African-American.

In fact, a correct interpretation of Figure 2A-11 shows that the greatest number of newly unemployed workers were White: the total number of unemployed White workers grew by 268,000, which is greater than the increase in the number of unemployed Black or African-American workers, which is 246,000 in this example. Although there was a higher percentage increase in the number of unemployed Black or African-American workers, the actual number of unemployed Black or African-American workers in the United States in 2009 was smaller than the number of unemployed White workers, leading to a smaller number of newly unemployed Black or African-American workers than White workers.

Omitted Variables From a scatter diagram that shows two variables moving either positively or negatively in relation to each other, it is easy to conclude that there is a causal relationship. But relationships between two variables are not always due to direct cause and effect. Quite possibly an observed relationship between two variables is due to the *unobserved* effect of a third variable on each of the other two variables.

A **pie chart** shows how some total is divided among its components, usually expressed in percentages.

A **bar graph** uses bars of varying height or length to show the comparative sizes of different observations of a variable.

An axis is **truncated** when some of the values on the axis are omitted, usually to save space.

An **omitted variable** is an unobserved variable that, through its influence on other variables, creates the erroneous appearance of a direct causal relationship among those variables.

The error of **reverse causality** is committed when the true direction of causality between two variables is reversed.

An unobserved variable that, through its influence on other variables, creates the erroneous appearance of a direct causal relationship among those variables is called an **omitted variable.** For example, in New England, a greater amount of snowfall during a given week will typically cause people to buy more snow shovels. It will also cause people to buy more de-icer fluid. But if you omitted the influence of the snowfall and simply plotted the number of snow shovels sold versus the number of bottles of de-icer fluid sold, you would produce a scatter diagram that showed an upward tilt in the pattern of points, indicating a positive relationship between snow shovels sold and de-icer fluid sold.

To attribute a causal relationship between these two variables, however, is misguided; more snow shovels sold do not cause more de-icer fluid to be sold, or vice versa. They move together because they are both influenced by a third, determining, variable—the weekly snowfall, which is the omitted variable in this case.

So before assuming that a pattern in a scatter diagram implies a cause-and-effect relationship, it is important to consider whether the pattern is instead the result of an omitted variable. Or to put it succinctly: correlation is not causation.

Reverse Causality Even when you are confident that there is no omitted variable and that there is a causal relationship between two variables shown in a numerical graph, you must also be careful that you don't make the mistake of **reverse causality**—coming to an erroneous conclusion about which is the dependent and which is the independent variable by reversing the true direction of causality between the two variables.

For example, imagine a scatter diagram that depicts the grade point averages (GPAs) of 20 of your classmates on one axis and the number of hours that each classmate spends studying on the other. A line fitted between the points will probably have a positive slope, showing a positive relationship between GPA and hours of studying. We could reasonably infer that hours spent studying is the independent variable and that GPA is the dependent variable. But you could make the error of reverse causality: you could infer that a high GPA causes a student to study more, whereas a low GPA causes a student to study less.

As you've just seen, it is important to understand how graphs can mislead or be interpreted incorrectly. Policy decisions, business decisions, and political arguments are often based on interpretation of the types of numerical graphs we've just discussed. Problems of misleading features of construction, omitted variables, and reverse causality can lead to important and undesirable consequences.

PROBLEMS

1. Study the four accompanying diagrams. Consider the following statements and indicate which diagram matches each statement. Which variable would appear on the horizontal and which on the vertical axis? In each of these statements, is the slope positive, negative, zero, or infinity?

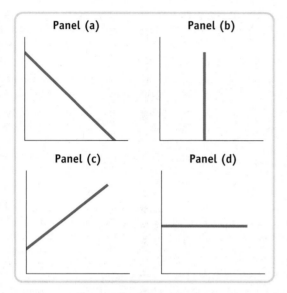

a. If the price of movies increases, fewer consumers go to see movies.

b. More experienced workers typically have higher incomes than less experienced workers.

c. Whatever the temperature outside, Americans consume the same number of hot dogs per day.

d. Consumers buy more frozen yogurt when the price of ice cream goes up.

e. Research finds no relationship between the number of diet books purchased and the number of pounds lost by the average dieter.

f. Regardless of its price, Americans buy the same quantity of salt.

2. During the Reagan administration, economist Arthur Laffer argued in favor of lowering income tax rates in order to increase tax revenues. Like most economists, he believed that at tax rates above a certain level, tax revenue would fall because high taxes would discourage some people from working and that people would refuse to work at all if they received no income after paying taxes. This relationship between tax rates and tax revenue is graphically summarized in what is widely known as the Laffer curve. Plot the Laffer curve relationship assuming that it has the shape of a nonlinear curve. The following questions will help you construct the graph.

a. Which is the independent variable? Which is the dependent variable? On which axis do you therefore measure the income tax rate? On which axis do you measure income tax revenue?

b. What would tax revenue be at a 0% income tax rate?

c. The maximum possible income tax rate is 100%. What would tax revenue be at a 100% income tax rate?

d. Estimates now show that the maximum point on the Laffer curve is (approximately) at a tax rate of 80%. For tax rates less than 80%, how would you describe the relationship between the tax rate and tax revenue, and how is this relationship reflected in the slope? For tax rates higher than 80%, how would you describe the relationship between the tax rate and tax revenue, and how is this relationship reflected in the slope?

3. In the accompanying figures, the numbers on the axes have been lost. All you know is that the units shown on the vertical axis are the same as the units on the horizontal axis.

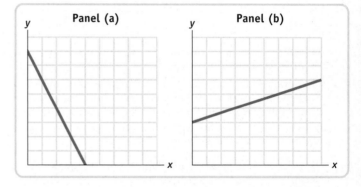

a. In panel (a), what is the slope of the line? Show that the slope is constant along the line.

b. In panel (b), what is the slope of the line? Show that the slope is constant along the line.

4. Answer each of the following questions by drawing a schematic diagram.

a. Taking measurements of the slope of a curve at three points farther and farther to the right along the horizontal axis, the slope of the curve changes from −0.3, to −0.8, to −2.5, measured by the point method. Draw a schematic diagram of this curve. How would you describe the relationship illustrated in your diagram?

b. Taking measurements of the slope of a curve at five points farther and farther to the right along the horizontal axis, the slope of the curve changes from 1.5, to 0.5, to 0, to −0.5, to −1.5, measured by the point method. Draw a schematic diagram of this curve. Does it have a maximum or a minimum?

5. For each of the accompanying diagrams, calculate the area of the shaded right triangle.

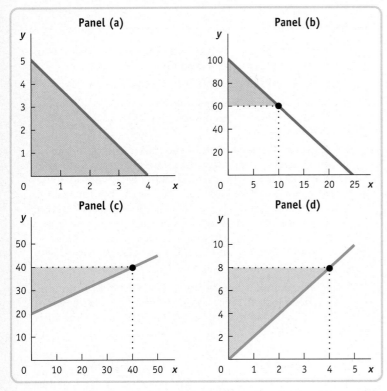

Panel (a)

Panel (b)

Panel (c)

Panel (d)

6. The base of a right triangle is 10, and its area is 20. What is the height of this right triangle?

7. The accompanying table shows the relationship between workers' hours of work per week and their hourly wage rate. Apart from the fact that they receive a different hourly wage rate and work different hours, these five workers are otherwise identical.

Name	Quantity of labor (hours per week)	Wage rate (per hour)
Athena	30	$15
Boris	35	30
Curt	37	45
Diego	36	60
Emily	32	75

a. Which variable is the independent variable? Which is the dependent variable?

b. Draw a scatter diagram illustrating this relationship. Draw a (nonlinear) curve that connects the points. Put the hourly wage rate on the vertical axis.

c. As the wage rate increases from $15 to $30, how does the number of hours worked respond according to the relationship depicted here? What is the average slope of the curve between Athena's and Boris's data points using the arc method?

d. As the wage rate increases from $60 to $75, how does the number of hours worked respond according to the relationship depicted here? What is the average slope of the curve between Diego's and Emily's data points using the arc method?

8. An insurance company has found that the severity of property damage in a fire is positively related to the number of firefighters arriving at the scene.

a. Draw a diagram that depicts this finding with number of firefighters on the horizontal axis and amount of property damage on the vertical axis. What is the argument made by this diagram? Suppose you reverse what is measured on the two axes. What is the argument made then?

b. Should the insurance company ask the city to send fewer firefighters to any fire in order to reduce its payouts to policy holders?

9. This table illustrates annual salaries and income tax owed by five individuals. Despite receiving different and owing salaries and owe different amounts of income tax, these five individuals are otherwise identical.

Name	Annual salary	Annual income tax owed
Susan	$22,000	$3,304
Eduardo	63,000	14,317
John	3,000	454
Camila	94,000	23,927
Peter	37,000	7,020

a. If you were to plot these points on a graph, what would be the average slope of the curve between the points for Eduardo's and Camila's salaries and taxes using the arc method? How would you interpret this value for slope?

b. What is the average slope of the curve between the points for John's and Susan's salaries and taxes using the arc method? How would you interpret that value for slope?

c. What happens to the slope as salary increases? What does this relationship imply about how the level of income taxes affects a person's incentive to earn a higher salary?

WORK IT OUT

For interactive, step-by-step help in solving the following problem, visit LaunchPad by using the URL on the back cover of this book.

10. Studies have found a relationship between a country's yearly rate of economic growth and the yearly rate of increase in airborne pollutants. It is believed that a higher rate of economic growth allows a country's residents to have more cars and travel more, thereby releasing more airborne pollutants.

a. Which variable is the independent variable? Which is the dependent variable?

b. Suppose that in the country of Sudland, when the yearly rate of economic growth fell from 3.0% to 1.5%, the yearly rate of increase in airborne pollutants fell from 6% to 5%. What is the average slope of a nonlinear curve between these points using the arc method?

c. Assume that when the yearly rate of economic growth rose from 3.5% to 4.5%, the yearly rate of increase in airborne pollutants rose from 5.5% to 7.5%. What is the average slope of a nonlinear curve between these two points using the arc method?

d. How would you describe the relationship between the two variables here?

Supply and Demand

▶ **What You Will Learn in This Chapter**

■ What a **competitive market** is and how it is described by the **supply and demand model**

■ What the **demand curve** and the **supply curve** are

■ The difference between **movements along a curve** and **shifts of a curve**

■ How the supply and demand curves determine a market's **equilibrium price** and **equilibrium quantity**

■ In the case of a **shortage** or **surplus**, how price moves the market back to equilibrium

A NATURAL GAS BOOM

The adoption of new drilling technologies lead to cheaper natural gas and vigorous protests.

PRESIDENT OBAMA GOT A VIVID illustration of American free speech in action while touring upstate New York on August 23, 2013. The president was greeted by more than 500 chanting and sign-toting supporters and opponents. Why the ruckus? Because upstate New York is a key battleground over the adoption of a relatively new method of producing energy supplies. *Hydraulic fracturing,* or *fracking,* is a method of extracting natural gas (and to a lesser extent, oil) from deposits trapped between layers of shale rock thousands of feet underground using—using powerful jets of chemical-laden water to release the gas. While it has been known for almost a century that the United States contains vast deposits of natural gas within these shale formations, they lay untapped because drilling for them was considered too difficult.

Until recently, that is. A few decades ago, new drilling technologies were developed that made it possible to reach these deeply embedded deposits. But what finally pushed energy companies to invest in and adopt these new extraction technologies was the high price of natural gas over the last decade. What accounted for these high natural gas prices—a quadrupling

from 2002 to 2006? There were two principal factors—one reflecting the demand for natural gas, the other the supply of natural gas.

First, the demand side. In 2002, the U.S. economy was mired in recession; with economic activity low and job losses high, people and businesses cut back their energy consumption. For example, to save money, homeowners turned down their thermostats in winter and turned them up in the summer. But by 2006, the U.S. economy came roaring back, and natural gas consumption rose. Second, the supply side. In 2005, Hurricane Katrina devastated the American Gulf Coast, site of most of the country's natural gas production at the time. So by 2006 the demand for natural gas had surged while the supply of natural gas had been severely curtailed. As a result, in 2006 natural gas prices peaked at around $14 per thousand cubic feet, up from around $2 in 2002.

Fast-forward to 2013: natural gas prices once again fell to $2 per thousand cubic feet. But this time it wasn't a slow economy that was the principal explanation, it was the use of the new technologies. "Boom," "supply shock," and

"game changer" was how energy experts described the impact of these technologies on oil and natural gas production and prices. To illustrate, the United States produced 8.13 trillion cubic feet of natural gas from shale deposits in 2012, nearly doubling the total from 2010. That total increased again in 2013, to 9.35 trillion cubic feet of natural gas, making the U.S. the world's largest producer of both oil and natural gas—overtaking both Russia and Saudia Arabia.

The benefits of much lower natural gas prices have not only led to lower heating costs for American consumers, they have also cascaded through American industries, particularly power generation and transportation. Electricity-generating power plants are switching from coal to natural gas, and mass-transit vehicles are switching from gasoline to natural gas. (You can even buy an inexpensive kit to convert your car from gasoline to natural gas.) The effect has been so significant that many European manufacturers, paying four times more for gas than their U.S. rivals, have been forced to relocate plants to American soil to survive. In addition, the revived U.S. natural gas industry has directly created tens of thousands of new jobs.

Yet the benefits of natural gas have been accompanied by deep reservations and controversy over the environmental effects of fracking. While there are clear environmental benefits from the shift by consumers and industries to natural gas (which burns cleaner than the other, heavily polluting fossil fuels, gasoline and coal), fracking has sparked another set of environmental worries. One is the potential for contamination of local groundwater by chemicals used in fracking. Another is that cheap natural gas may discourage the adoption of more expensive renewable energy sources like solar and wind power, furthering our dependence upon fossil fuel.

So it was the face-off between these interests—pro-fracking and anti-fracking—

that confronted President Obama that August day. While we, the authors, do not espouse one side or the other (believing that science as well as economics should provide guidance about the best course to follow), we will use the recent history of the U.S. natural gas industry to help illustrate important economic concepts such as supply and demand, price effects, firms' costs, international trade, pollution, and government regulation, among others. We discuss all of these topics in future chapters; we also revisit the fracking debate, particularly in Chapter 16, where we will learn about the economics of energy and environmental concerns.

But for this chapter we will stick to the topic of supply and demand. How,

exactly, does the high price of natural gas nearly a decade ago translate into today's switch to vehicles powered by natural gas? The short answer is that it's a matter of supply and demand. But what does that mean? Many people use "supply and demand" as a sort of catchphrase to mean "the laws of the marketplace at work." To economists, however, the concept of supply and demand has a precise meaning: it is a *model of how a market behaves* that is extremely useful for understanding many—but not all—markets.

In this chapter, we lay out the pieces that make up the *supply and demand model,* put them together, and show how this model can be used.

Supply and Demand: A Model of a Competitive Market

Natural gas sellers and natural gas buyers constitute a market—a group of producers and consumers who exchange a good or service for payment. In this chapter, we'll focus on a particular type of market known as a *competitive market*. A **competitive market** is a market in which there are many buyers and sellers of the same good or service. More precisely, the key feature of a competitive market is that no individual's actions have a noticeable effect on the price at which the good or service is sold. It's important to understand, however, that this is not an accurate description of every market.

For example, it's not an accurate description of the market for cola beverages. That's because in this market, Coca-Cola and Pepsi account for such a large proportion of total sales that they are able to influence the price at which cola beverages are bought and sold. But it is an accurate description of the market for natural gas. The global marketplace for natural gas is so huge that even the biggest U.S. driller for natural gas—Exxon Mobil—accounts for such a small share of total global transactions that it is unable to influence the price at which natural gas is bought and sold.

It's a little hard to explain why competitive markets are different from other markets until we've seen how a competitive market works. So let's take a rain check—we'll return to that issue at the end of this chapter. For now, let's just say that it's easier to model competitive markets than other markets. When taking an exam, it's always a good strategy to begin by answering the easier questions. In this book, we're going to do the same thing. So we will start with competitive markets.

When a market is competitive, its behavior is well described by the **supply and demand model.** Because many markets are competitive, the supply and demand model is a very useful one indeed.

There are five key elements in this model:

- The *demand curve*
- The *supply curve*

A **competitive market** is a market in which there are many buyers and sellers of the same good or service, none of whom can influence the price at which the good or service is sold.

The **supply and demand model** is a model of how a competitive market behaves.

- The set of factors that cause the demand curve to shift and the set of factors that cause the supply curve to shift
- The *market equilibrium*, which includes the *equilibrium price* and *equilibrium quantity*
- The way the market equilibrium changes when the supply curve or demand curve shifts

To understand the supply and demand model, we will examine each of these elements.

The Demand Curve

How much natural gas will American consumers want to buy in a given year? You might at first think that we can answer this question by adding up the amounts each American household and business consumes in that year. But that's not enough to answer the question, because how much natural gas Americans want to buy depends upon the price of natural gas.

When the price of natural gas falls, as it did from 2006 to 2013, consumers will generally respond to the lower price by using more natural gas—for example, by turning up their thermostats to keep their houses warmer in the winter or switching to vehicles powered by natural gas. In general, the amount of natural gas, or of any good or service that people want to buy, depends upon the price. The higher the price, the less of the good or service people want to purchase; alternatively, the lower the price, the more they want to purchase.

So the answer to the question "How many units of natural gas do consumers want to buy?" depends on the price of a unit of natural gas. If you don't yet know what the price will be, you can start by making a table of how many units of natural gas people would want to buy at a number of different prices. Such a table is known as a *demand schedule*. This, in turn, can be used to draw a *demand curve*, which is one of the key elements of the supply and demand model.

The Demand Schedule and the Demand Curve

A **demand schedule** is a table showing how much of a good or service consumers will want to buy at different prices. At the right of Figure 3-1, we show a hypothetical demand schedule for natural gas. It's expressed in BTUs (British thermal units), a commonly used measure of quantity of natural gas. It's a hypothetical demand schedule—it doesn't use actual data on American demand for natural gas.

According to the table, if a BTU of natural gas costs $3, consumers around the world will want to purchase 10 trillion BTUs of natural gas over the course of a year. If the price is $3.25 per BTU, they will want to buy only 8.9 trillion BTUs; if the price is only $2.75 per BTU, they will want to buy 11.5 trillion BTUs. The higher the price, the fewer BTUs of natural gas consumers will want to purchase. So, as the price rises, the **quantity demanded** of natural gas—the actual amount consumers are willing to buy at some specific price—falls.

The graph in Figure 3-1 is a visual representation of the information in the table. (You might want to review the discussion of graphs in economics in the appendix to Chapter 2.) The vertical axis shows the price of a BTU of natural gas and the horizontal axis shows the quantity of natural gas in trillions of BTUs. Each point on the graph corresponds to one of the entries in the table. The curve that connects these points is a **demand curve.** A demand curve is a graphical representation of the demand schedule, another way of showing the relationship between the quantity demanded and price.

Note that the demand curve shown in Figure 3-1 slopes downward. This reflects the inverse relationship between price and the quantity demanded: a higher price reduces the quantity demanded, and a lower price increases the quantity

A **demand schedule** shows how much of a good or service consumers will want to buy at different prices.

The **quantity demanded** is the actual amount of a good or service consumers are willing to buy at some specific price.

A **demand curve** is a graphical representation of the demand schedule. It shows the relationship between quantity demanded and price.

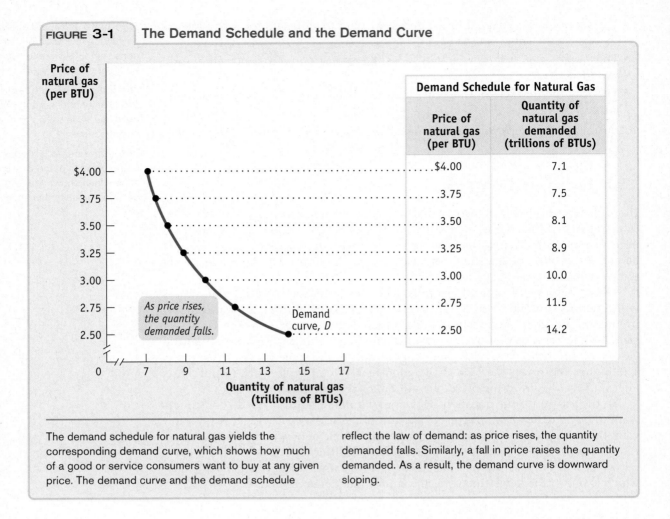

FIGURE **3-1** The Demand Schedule and the Demand Curve

As price rises, the quantity demanded falls.

Demand curve, D

Demand Schedule for Natural Gas	
Price of natural gas (per BTU)	Quantity of natural gas demanded (trillions of BTUs)
$4.00	7.1
3.75	7.5
3.50	8.1
3.25	8.9
3.00	10.0
2.75	11.5
2.50	14.2

The demand schedule for natural gas yields the corresponding demand curve, which shows how much of a good or service consumers want to buy at any given price. The demand curve and the demand schedule reflect the law of demand: as price rises, the quantity demanded falls. Similarly, a fall in price raises the quantity demanded. As a result, the demand curve is downward sloping.

demanded. We can see this from the demand curve in Figure 3-1. As price falls, we move down the demand curve and quantity demanded increases. And as price increases, we move up the demand curve and quantity demanded falls.

In the real world, demand curves almost always *do* slope downward. (The exceptions are so rare that for practical purposes we can ignore them.) Generally, the proposition that a higher price for a good, *other things equal*, leads people to demand a smaller quantity of that good is so reliable that economists are willing to call it a "law"—the **law of demand.**

Shifts of the Demand Curve

Although natural gas prices in 2006 were higher than they had been in 2002, U.S. consumption of natural gas was higher in 2006. How can we reconcile this fact with the law of demand, which says that a higher price reduces the quantity demanded, other things equal?

The answer lies in the crucial phrase *other things equal*. In this case, other things weren't equal: the U.S. economy had changed between 2002 and 2006 in ways that increased the amount of natural gas demanded at any given price. For one thing, the U.S. economy was much stronger in 2006 than in 2002. Figure 3-2 illustrates this phenomenon using the demand schedule and demand curve for natural gas. (As before, the numbers in Figure 3-2 are hypothetical.)

The table in Figure 3-2 shows two demand schedules. The first is the demand schedule for 2002, the same as shown in Figure 3-1. The second is the demand

The **law of demand** says that a higher price for a good or service, other things equal, leads people to demand a smaller quantity of that good or service.

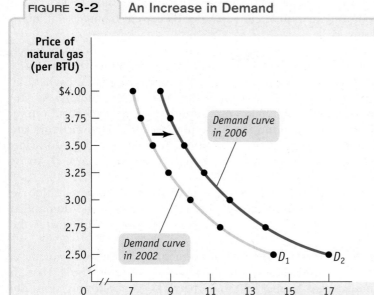

FIGURE **3-2**   An Increase in Demand

Demand Schedules for Natural Gas		
Price of natural gas (per BTU)	Quantity of natural gas demanded (trillions of BTUs)	
	in 2002	in 2006
$4.00	7.1	8.5
3.75	7.5	9.0
3.50	8.1	9.7
3.25	8.9	10.7
3.00	10.0	12.0
2.75	11.5	13.8
2.50	14.2	17.0

A strong economy is one factor that increases the demand for natural gas—a rise in the quantity demanded at any given price. This is represented by the two demand schedules—one showing the demand in 2002 when the economy was weak, the other showing the demand in 2006, when the economy was strong—and their corresponding demand curves. The increase in demand shifts the demand curve to the right.

schedule for 2006. It differs from the 2002 schedule because of the stronger U.S. economy, leading to an increase in the quantity of natural gas demanded at any given price. So at each price the 2006 schedule shows a larger quantity demanded than the 2002 schedule. For example, the quantity of natural gas consumers

GLOBAL COMPARISION   Pay More, Pump Less

For a real-world illustration of the law of demand, consider how gasoline consumption varies according to the prices consumers pay at the pump. Because of high taxes, gasoline and diesel fuel are more than twice as expensive in most European countries and in many East Asian countries than in the United States. According to the law of demand, this should lead Europeans to buy less gasoline than Americans—and they do. As you can see from the figure, per person, Europeans consume less than half as much fuel as Americans, mainly because they drive smaller cars with better mileage.

Prices aren't the only factor affecting fuel consumption, but they're probably the main cause of the difference between European and American fuel consumption per person.

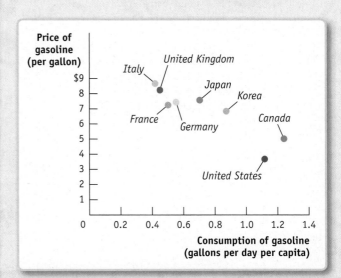

Source: World Development Indicators and U.S. Energy Information Administration, 2013.

A **shift of the demand curve** is a change in the quantity demanded at any given price, represented by the shift of the original demand curve to a new position, denoted by a new demand curve.

A **movement along the demand curve** is a change in the quantity demanded of a good arising from a change in the good's price.

wanted to buy at a price of $3 per BTU increased from 10 trillion to 12 trillion BTUs per year; the quantity demanded at $3.25 per BTU went from 8.9 trillion to 10.7 trillion, and so on.

What is clear from this example is that the changes that occurred between 2002 and 2006 generated a *new* demand schedule, one in which the quantity demanded was greater at any given price than in the original demand schedule. The two curves in Figure 3-2 show the same information graphically. As you can see, the demand schedule for 2006 corresponds to a new demand curve, D_2, that is to the right of the demand schedule for 2002, D_1. This **shift of the demand curve** shows the change in the quantity demanded at any given price, represented by the change in position of the original demand curve D_1 to its new location at D_2.

It's crucial to make the distinction between such shifts of the demand curve and **movements along the demand curve,** changes in the quantity demanded of a good arising from a change in that good's price. Figure 3-3 illustrates the difference.

The movement from point A to point B is a movement along the demand curve: the quantity demanded rises due to a fall in price as you move down D_1. Here, a fall in the price of natural gas from $3.50 to $3 per BTU generates a rise in the quantity demanded from 8.1 trillion to 10 trillion BTUs per year. But the quantity demanded can also rise when the price is unchanged if there is an *increase in demand*—a rightward shift of the demand curve. This is illustrated in Figure 3-3 by the shift of the demand curve from D_1 to D_2. Holding the price constant at $3.50 per BTU, the quantity demanded rises from 8.1 trillion BTUs at point A on D_1 to 9.7 trillion BTUs at point C on D_2.

When economists say "the demand for X increased" or "the demand for Y decreased," they mean that the demand curve for X or Y shifted—not that the quantity demanded rose or fell because of a change in the price.

FIGURE 3-3 | Movement Along the Demand Curve versus Shift of the Demand Curve

The rise in quantity demanded when going from point A to point B reflects a movement along the demand curve: it is the result of a fall in the price of the good. The rise in quantity demanded when going from point A to point C reflects a shift of the demand curve: it is the result of a rise in the quantity demanded at any given price.

PITFALLS

DEMAND VERSUS QUANTITY DEMANDED

When economists say "an increase in demand," they mean a rightward shift of the demand curve, and when they say "a decrease in demand," they mean a leftward shift of the demand curve—that is, when they're being careful. In ordinary speech most people, including professional economists, use the word *demand* casually. For example, an economist might say "the demand for air travel has doubled over the past 15 years, partly because of falling airfares" when he or she really means that the *quantity demanded* has doubled.

It's OK to be a bit sloppy in ordinary conversation. But when you're doing economic analysis, it's important to make the distinction between changes in the quantity demanded, which involve movements along a demand curve, and shifts of the demand curve (See Figure 3-3 for an illustration). Sometimes students end up writing something like this: "If demand increases, the price will go up, but that will lead to a fall in demand, which pushes the price down . . ." and then go around in circles. If you make a clear distinction between changes in *demand,* which mean shifts of the demand curve, and changes in *quantity demanded,* which means movement along the demand curve, you can avoid a lot of confusion.

Understanding Shifts of the Demand Curve

Figure 3-4 illustrates the two basic ways in which demand curves can shift. When economists talk about an "increase in demand," they mean a *rightward* shift of the demand curve: at any given price, consumers demand a larger quantity of the good or service than before. This is shown by the rightward shift of the original demand curve D_1 to D_2. And when economists talk about a "decrease in demand," they mean a *leftward* shift of the demand curve: at any given price, consumers demand a smaller quantity of the good or service than before. This is shown by the leftward shift of the original demand curve D_1 to D_3.

What caused the demand curve for natural gas to shift? As we mentioned earlier, the reason was the stronger U.S. economy in 2006 compared to 2002. If you think about it, you can come up with other factors that would be likely to shift the demand curve for natural gas. For example, suppose that the price of heating oil rises. This will induce some consumers, who heat their homes and businesses in winter with heating oil, to switch to natural gas instead, increasing the demand for natural gas.

FIGURE 3-4 | Shifts of the Demand Curve

Any event that increases demand shifts the demand curve to the right, reflecting a rise in the quantity demanded at any given price. Any event that decreases demand shifts the demand curve to the left, reflecting a fall in the quantity demanded at any given price.

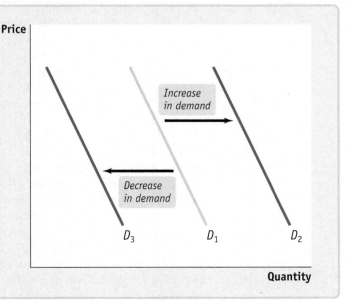

Two goods are **substitutes** if a rise in the price of one of the goods leads to an increase in the demand for the other good.

Two goods are **complements** if a rise in the price of one good leads to a decrease in the demand for the other good.

When a rise in income increases the demand for a good—the normal case—it is a **normal good.**

When a rise in income decreases the demand for a good, it is an **inferior good.**

Economists believe that there are five principal factors that shift the demand curve for a good or service:

- Changes in the prices of related goods or services
- Changes in income
- Changes in tastes
- Changes in expectations
- Changes in the number of consumers

Although this is not an exhaustive list, it contains the five most important factors that can shift demand curves. So when we say that the quantity of a good or service demanded falls as its price rises, *other things equal*, we are in fact stating that the factors that shift demand are remaining unchanged. Let's now explore, in more detail, how those factors shift the demand curve.

Changes in the Prices of Related Goods or Services Heating oil is what economists call a *substitute* for natural gas. A pair of goods are **substitutes** if a rise in the price of one good (heating oil) makes consumers more likely to buy the other good (natural gas). Substitutes are usually goods that in some way serve a similar function: coffee and tea, muffins and doughnuts, train rides and air flights. A rise in the price of the alternative good induces some consumers to purchase the original good *instead* of it, shifting demand for the original good to the right.

But sometimes a rise in the price of one good makes consumers *less* willing to buy another good. Such pairs of goods are known as **complements.** Complements are usually goods that in some sense are consumed together: computers and software, cappuccinos and cookies, cars and gasoline. Because consumers like to consume a good and its complement together, a change in the price of one of the goods will affect the demand for its complement. In particular, when the price of one good rises, the demand for its complement decreases, shifting the demand curve for the complement to the left. So, for example, when the price of gasoline began to rise in 2009 from under $3 per gallon to close to $4 per gallon in 2011, the demand for gas-guzzling cars fell.

Changes in Income Why did the stronger economy in 2006 lead to an increase in the demand for natural gas compared to the demand during the weak economy of 2002? Because with the stronger economy, Americans had more income, making them more likely to purchase more of *most* goods and services at any given price. For example, with a higher income you are likely to keep your house warmer in the winter than if your income is low.

And, the demand for natural gas, a major source of fuel for electricity-generating power plants, is tied to the demand for other goods and services. For example, businesses must consume power in order to provide goods and services to households. So when the economy is strong and household incomes are high, businesses will consume more electricity and, indirectly, more natural gas.

Why do we say that people are likely to purchase more of "most goods," not "all goods"? Most goods are **normal goods**—the demand for them increases when consumer income rises. However, the demand for some products falls when income rises. Goods for which demand decreases when income rises are known as **inferior goods.** Usually an inferior good is one that is considered less desirable than more expensive alternatives—such as a bus ride versus a taxi ride. When they can afford to, people stop buying an inferior good and switch their consumption to the preferred, more expensive alternative. So when a good is inferior, a rise in income shifts the demand curve to the left. And, not surprisingly, a fall in income shifts the demand curve to the right.

One example of the distinction between normal and inferior goods that has drawn considerable attention in the business press is the difference between so-called casual-dining restaurants such as Applebee's or Olive Garden and fast-food chains such as McDonald's and KFC. When their incomes rise, Americans tend to eat out more at casual-dining restaurants. However, some of this increased dining out comes at the expense of fast-food venues—to some extent, people visit McDonald's less once they can afford to move upscale. So casual dining is a normal good, whereas fast-food consumption appears to be an inferior good.

Changes in Tastes Why do people want what they want? Fortunately, we don't need to answer that question—we just need to acknowledge that people have certain preferences, or tastes, that determine what they choose to consume and that these tastes can change. Economists usually lump together changes in demand due to fads, beliefs, cultural shifts, and so on under the heading of changes in tastes or preferences.

For example, once upon a time men wore hats. Up until around World War II, a respectable man wasn't fully dressed unless he wore a dignified hat along with his suit. But the returning GIs adopted a more informal style, perhaps due to the rigors of the war. And President Eisenhower, who had been supreme commander of Allied Forces before becoming president, often went hatless. After World War II, it was clear that the demand curve for hats had shifted leftward, reflecting a decrease in the demand for hats.

Economists have relatively little to say about the forces that influence consumers' tastes. (Although marketers and advertisers have plenty to say about them!) However, a change in tastes has a predictable impact on demand. When tastes change in favor of a good, more people want to buy it at any given price, so the demand curve shifts to the right. When tastes change against a good, fewer people want to buy it at any given price, so the demand curve shifts to the left.

Changes in Expectations When consumers have some choice about when to make a purchase, current demand for a good is often affected by expectations about its future price. For example, savvy shoppers often wait for seasonal sales—say, buying next year's holiday gifts during the post-holiday markdowns. In this case, expectations of a future drop in price lead to a decrease in demand today. Alternatively, expectations of a future rise in price are likely to cause an increase in demand today.

For example, the fall in gas prices in recent years to around $2 per BTU has spurred more consumers to switch to natural gas from other fuel types than when natural gas fell to $2 per BTU in 2002. But why are consumers more willing to switch now? Because in 2002, consumers didn't expect the fall in the price of natural gas to last—and they were right.

In 2002, natural gas prices fell because of the weak economy. That situation changed in 2006 when the economy came roaring back and the price of natural gas rose dramatically. In contrast, consumers have come to expect that the more recent fall in the price of natural gas will not be temporary because it is based on a permanent change: the ability to tap much larger deposits of natural gas.

Expected changes in future income can also lead to changes in demand: if you expect your income to rise in the future, you will typically borrow today and increase your demand for certain goods; if you expect your income to fall in the future, you are likely to save today and reduce your demand for some goods.

Changes in the Number of Consumers Another factor that can cause a change in demand is a change in the number of consumers of a good or service. For example, population growth in the United States eventually leads to higher demand for natural gas as more homes and businesses need to be heated in the winter and cooled in the summer.

An **individual demand curve** illustrates the relationship between quantity demanded and price for an individual consumer.

Let's introduce a new concept: the **individual demand curve,** which shows the relationship between quantity demanded and price for an individual consumer. For example, suppose that the Gonzalez family is a consumer of natural gas for heating and cooling their home. Panel (a) of Figure 3-5 shows how many BTUs of natural gas they will buy per year at any given price. The Gonzalez family's individual demand curve is $D_{Gonzalez}$.

The *market demand curve* shows how the combined quantity demanded by all consumers depends on the market price of the good. (Most of the time when economists refer to the demand curve they mean the market demand curve.) The market demand curve is the *horizontal sum* of the individual demand curves of all consumers in that market. To see what we mean by the term *horizontal sum*, assume for a moment that there are only two consumers of natural gas, the Gonzalez family and the Murray family. The Murray family consumes natural gas to fuel their natural gas–powered car. The Murray family's individual demand curve, D_{Murray}, is shown in panel (b). Panel (c) shows the market demand curve. At any given price, the quantity demanded by the market is the sum of the quantities demanded by the Gonzalez family and the Murray family. For example, at a price of $5 per BTU, the Gonzalez family demands 30 BTUs of natural gas per year and the Murray family demands 20 BTUs per year. So the quantity demanded by the market is 50 BTUs per year, as seen on the market demand curve, D_{Market}.

Clearly, the quantity demanded by the market at any given price is larger with the Murray family present than it would be if the Gonzalez family were the only consumer. The quantity demanded at any given price would be even larger if we added a third consumer, then a fourth, and so on. So an increase in the number of consumers leads to an increase in demand.

For a review of the factors that shift demand, see Table 3-1.

FIGURE 3-5   Individual Demand Curves and the Market Demand Curve

The Gonzalez family and the Murray family are the only two consumers of natural gas in the market. Panel (a) shows the Gonzalez family's individual demand curve: the number of BTUs they will buy per year at any given price. Panel (b) shows the Murray family's individual demand curve. Given that the Gonzalez family and the Murray family are the only two consumers, the *market demand* curve, which shows the quantity of BTUs demanded by all consumers at any given price, is shown in panel (c). The market demand curve is the *horizontal sum* of the individual demand curves of all consumers. In this case, at any given price, the quantity demanded by the market is the sum of the quantities demanded by the Gonzalez family and the Murray family.

TABLE 3-1 Factors That Shift Demand

When this happens . . .	. . . demand increases	But when this happens . . .	. . . demand decreases
When the price of a substitute rises . . .	. . . demand for the original good increases.	When the price of a substitute falls . . .	. . . demand for the original good decreases.
When the price of a complement falls . . .	. . . demand for the original good increases.	When the price of a complement rises . . .	. . . demand for the original good decreases.
When income rises . . .	. . . demand for a normal good increases.	When income falls . . .	. . . demand for a normal good decreases.
When income falls . . .	. . . demand for an inferior good increases.	When income rises . . .	. . . demand for an inferior good decreases.
When tastes change in favor of a good . . .	. . . demand for the good increases.	When tastes change against a good . . .	. . . demand for the good decreases.
When the price is expected to rise in the future . . .	. . . demand for the good increases today.	When the price is expected to fall in the future . . .	. . . demand for the good decreases today.
When the number of consumers rises . . .	. . . market demand for the good increases.	When the number of consumers falls . . .	. . . market demand for the good decreases.

Cities can reduce traffic congestion by raising the price of driving.

▼ Quick Review

• The **supply and demand model** is a model of a **competitive market**—one in which there are many buyers and sellers of the same good or service.

• The **demand schedule** shows how the **quantity demanded** changes as the price changes. A **demand curve** illustrates this relationship.

• The **law of demand** asserts that a higher price reduces the quantity demanded. Thus, demand curves normally slope downward.

• An increase in demand leads to a rightward **shift of the demand curve:** the quantity demanded rises for any given price. A decrease in demand leads to a leftward shift: the quantity demanded falls for any given price. A change in price results in a change in the quantity demanded and a **movement along the demand curve.**

• The five main factors that can shift the demand curve are changes in (1) the price of a related good, such as a **substitute** or a **complement,** (2) income, (3) tastes, (4) expectations, and (5) the number of consumers.

• The market demand curve is the horizontal sum of the **individual demand curves** of all consumers in the market.

ECONOMICS ▶ in Action

Beating the Traffic

All big cities have traffic problems, and many local authorities try to discourage driving in the crowded city center. If we think of an auto trip to the city center as a good that people consume, we can use the economics of demand to analyze anti-traffic policies.

One common strategy is to reduce the demand for auto trips by lowering the prices of substitutes. Many metropolitan areas subsidize bus and rail service, hoping to lure commuters out of their cars. An alternative is to raise the price of complements: several major U.S. cities impose high taxes on commercial parking garages and impose short time limits on parking meters, both to raise revenue and to discourage people from driving into the city.

A few major cities—including Singapore, London, Oslo, Stockholm, and Milan—have been willing to adopt a direct and politically controversial approach: reducing congestion by raising the price of driving. Under "congestion pricing" (or "congestion charging" in the United Kingdom), a charge is imposed on cars entering the city center during business hours. Drivers buy passes, which are then debited electronically as they drive by monitoring stations. Compliance is monitored with automatic cameras that photograph license plates.

In 2012, Moscow adopted a modest charge for parking in certain areas in an attempt to reduce its traffic jams, considered the worst of all major cities. After the approximately $1.60 charge was applied, city officials estimated that Moscow traffic decreased by 4%.

The current daily cost of driving in London ranges from £9 to £12 (about $14 to $19). And drivers who don't pay and are caught pay a fine of £120 (about $192) for each transgression.

Not surprisingly, studies have shown that after the implementation of congestion pricing, traffic does indeed decrease. In the 1990s, London had some of the worst traffic in Europe. The introduction of its congestion charge in 2003 immediately reduced traffic in the city center by about 15%, with overall traffic falling by 21% between 2002 and 2006. And there has been increased use of substitutes, such as public transportation, bicycles, motorbikes, and ride-sharing. From 2001 to 2011, bike trips in London increased by 79%, and bus usage was up by 30%.

In the United States, the U.S. Department of Transportation has implemented pilot programs to study congestion pricing. For example, in 2012 Los Angeles County imposed a congestion charge on an 11-mile stretch of highway in central Los Angeles. Drivers pay up to $1.40 per mile, the amount depending upon traffic congestion, with a money-back guarantee that their average speed will never drop below 45 miles per hour. While some drivers were understandably annoyed at the charge, others were more philosophical. One driver felt that the toll was a fair price to escape what often turned into a crawling 45-minute drive, saying, "It's worth it if you're in a hurry to get home. You got to pay the price. If not, get stuck in traffic."

Check Your Understanding   3-1

1. Explain whether each of the following events represents (i) a *shift of* the demand curve or (ii) a *movement along* the demand curve.
   a. A store owner finds that customers are willing to pay more for umbrellas on rainy days.
   b. When Circus Cruise Lines offered reduced prices for summer cruises in the Caribbean, their number of bookings increased sharply.
   c. People buy more long-stem roses the week of Valentine's Day, even though the prices are higher than at other times during the year.
   d. A sharp rise in the price of gasoline leads many commuters to join carpools in order to reduce their gasoline purchases.

Solutions appear at back of book.

The Supply Curve

Some deposits of natural gas are easier to tap than others. Before the widespread use of fracking, drillers would limit their natural gas wells to deposits that lay in easily reached pools beneath the earth. How much natural gas they would tap from existing wells, and how extensively they searched for new deposits and drilled new wells, depended on the price they expected to get for the natural gas. The higher the price they expected, the more they would tap existing wells as well as drill and tap new wells.

So just as the quantity of natural gas that consumers want to buy depends upon the price they have to pay, the quantity that producers of natural gas, or of any good or service, are willing to produce and sell—the **quantity supplied**—depends upon the price they are offered.

The **quantity supplied** is the actual amount of a good or service people are willing to sell at some specific price.

A **supply schedule** shows how much of a good or service would be supplied at different prices.

A **supply curve** shows the relationship between quantity supplied and price.

The Supply Schedule and the Supply Curve

The table in Figure 3-6 shows how the quantity of natural gas made available varies with the price—that is, it shows a hypothetical **supply schedule** for natural gas.

A supply schedule works the same way as the demand schedule shown in Figure 3-1: in this case, the table shows the number of BTUs of natural gas producers are willing to sell at different prices. At a price of $2.50 per BTU, producers are willing to sell only 8 trillion BTUs of natural gas per year. At $2.75 per BTU, they're willing to sell 9.1 trillion BTUs. At $3, they're willing to sell 10 trillion BTUs, and so on.

In the same way that a demand schedule can be represented graphically by a demand curve, a supply schedule can be represented by a **supply curve,** as shown in Figure 3-6. Each point on the curve represents an entry from the table.

FIGURE 3-6   The Supply Schedule and the Supply Curve

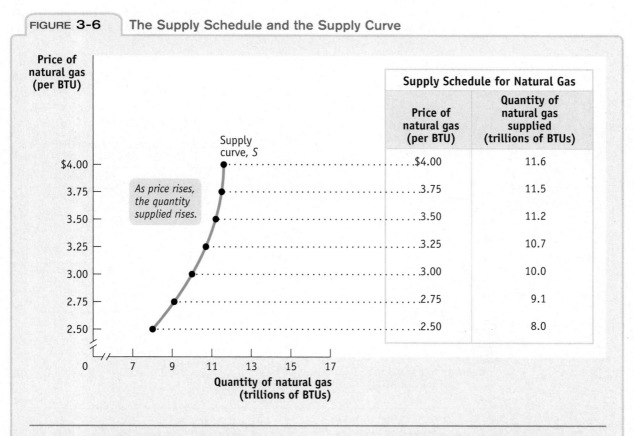

Supply Schedule for Natural Gas	
Price of natural gas (per BTU)	Quantity of natural gas supplied (trillions of BTUs)
$4.00	11.6
3.75	11.5
3.50	11.2
3.25	10.7
3.00	10.0
2.75	9.1
2.50	8.0

The supply schedule for natural gas is plotted to yield the corresponding supply curve, which shows how much of a good producers are willing to sell at any given price.

The supply curve and the supply schedule reflect the fact that supply curves are usually upward sloping: the quantity supplied rises when the price rises.

A **shift of the supply curve** is a change in the quantity supplied of a good or service at any given price. It is represented by the change of the original supply curve to a new position, denoted by a new supply curve.

A **movement along the supply curve** is a change in the quantity supplied of a good arising from a change in the good's price.

Suppose that the price of natural gas rises from $3 to $3.25; we can see that the quantity of natural gas producers are willing to sell rises from 10 trillion to 10.7 trillion BTUs. This is the normal situation for a supply curve, that a higher price leads to a higher quantity supplied. So just as demand curves normally slope downward, supply curves normally slope upward: the higher the price being offered, the more of any good or service producers will be willing to sell.

Shifts of the Supply Curve

As we described in the opening story, innovations in the technology of drilling natural gas deposits have recently led to a huge increase in U.S. production of natural gas—a 30% increase in daily production from 2005 through 2014. Figure 3-7 illustrates these events in terms of the supply schedule and the supply curve for natural gas. The table in Figure 3-7 shows two supply schedules. The schedule before improved natural gas–drilling technology was adopted is the same one as in Figure 3-6. The second schedule shows the supply of natural gas *after* the improved technology was adopted.

Just as a change in demand schedules leads to a shift of the demand curve, a change in supply schedules leads to a **shift of the supply curve**—a change in the quantity supplied at any given price. This is shown in Figure 3-7 by the shift of the supply curve before the adoption of new natural gas–drilling technology, S_1, to its new position after the adoption of new natural gas–drilling technology, S_2. Notice that S_2 lies to the right of S_1, a reflection of the fact that quantity supplied rises at any given price.

As in the analysis of demand, it's crucial to draw a distinction between such shifts of the supply curve and **movements along the supply curve**—changes in the quantity supplied arising from a change in price. We can see this difference in Figure 3-8. The movement from point A to point B is a movement along the supply curve: the quantity supplied rises along S_1 due to a rise in price. Here, a rise in price from $3 to $3.50 leads to a rise in the quantity supplied from 10 trillion to 11.2 trillion BTUs of natural gas. But the quantity supplied can also rise when

---

FIGURE 3-7 | **An Increase in Supply**

Supply Schedules for Natural Gas		
Price of natural gas (per BTU)	Quantity of natural gas supplied (trillions of BTUs)	
	Before new technology	After new technology
$4.00	11.6	13.9
3.75	11.5	13.8
3.50	11.2	13.4
3.25	10.7	12.8
3.00	10.0	12.0
2.75	9.1	10.9
2.50	8.0	9.6

The adoption of improved natural gas–drilling technology generated an increase in supply—a rise in the quantity supplied at any given price. This event is represented by the two supply schedules—one showing supply before the new technology was adopted, the other showing supply after the new technology was adopted—and their corresponding supply curves. The increase in supply shifts the supply curve to the right.

FIGURE 3-8   Movement Along the Supply Curve versus Shift of the Supply Curve

The increase in quantity supplied when going from point *A* to point *B* reflects a movement along the supply curve: it is the result of a rise in the price of the good. The increase in quantity supplied when going from point *A* to point *C* reflects a shift of the supply curve: it is the result of an increase in the quantity supplied at any given price.

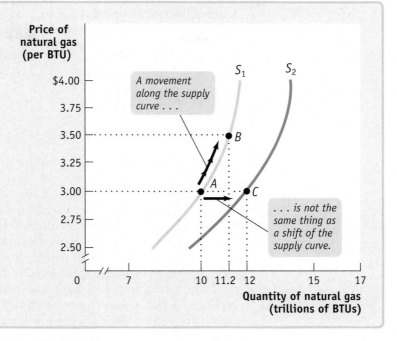

the price is unchanged if there is an increase in supply—a rightward shift of the supply curve. This is shown by the rightward shift of the supply curve from S_1 to S_2. Holding the price constant at $3, the quantity supplied rises from 10 trillion BTUs at point *A* on S_1 to 12 billion pounds at point *C* on S_2.

Understanding Shifts of the Supply Curve

Figure 3-9 illustrates the two basic ways in which supply curves can shift. When economists talk about an "increase in supply," they mean a *rightward* shift of the supply curve: at any given price, producers supply a larger quantity of the good than before. This is shown in Figure 3-9 by the rightward shift of the original supply curve S_1 to S_2. And when economists talk about a "decrease in supply," they mean

FIGURE 3-9   Shifts of the Supply Curve

Any event that increases supply shifts the supply curve to the right, reflecting a rise in the quantity supplied at any given price. Any event that decreases supply shifts the supply curve to the left, reflecting a fall in the quantity supplied at any given price.

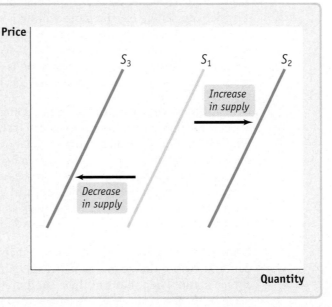

An **input** is a good or service that is used to produce another good or service.

a *leftward* shift of the supply curve: at any given price, producers supply a smaller quantity of the good than before. This is represented by the leftward shift of S_1 to S_3.

Economists believe that shifts of the supply curve for a good or service are mainly the result of five factors (though, as with demand, there are other possible causes):

- Changes in input prices
- Changes in the prices of related goods or services
- Changes in technology
- Changes in expectations
- Changes in the number of producers

Changes in Input Prices To produce output, you need inputs. For example, to make vanilla ice cream, you need vanilla beans, cream, sugar, and so on. An **input** is any good or service that is used to produce another good or service. Inputs, like outputs, have prices. And an increase in the price of an input makes the production of the final good more costly for those who produce and sell it. So producers are less willing to supply the final good at any given price, and the supply curve shifts to the left. That is, supply decreases. For example, fuel is a major cost for airlines. When oil prices surged in 2007–2008, airlines began cutting back on their flight schedules and some went out of business.

Similarly, a fall in the price of an input makes the production of the final good less costly for sellers. They are more willing to supply the good at any given price, and the supply curve shifts to the right. That is, supply increases.

Changes in the Prices of Related Goods or Services A single producer often produces a mix of goods rather than a single product. For example, an oil refinery produces gasoline from crude oil, but it also produces heating oil and other products from the same raw material. When a producer sells several products, the quantity of any one good it is willing to supply at any given price depends on the prices of its other co-produced goods.

This effect can run in either direction. An oil refiner will supply less gasoline at any given price when the price of heating oil rises, shifting the supply curve for gasoline to the left. But it will supply more gasoline at any given price when the price of heating oil falls, shifting the supply curve for gasoline to the right. This means that gasoline and other co-produced oil products are *substitutes in production* for refiners.

In contrast, due to the nature of the production process, other goods can be *complements in production*. For example, producers of natural gas often find that natural gas wells also produce oil as a by-product of extraction. The higher the price at which a driller can sell its oil, the more willing it will be to drill natural gas wells and the more natural gas it will supply at any given price. In other words, higher oil prices lead to more natural gas supplied at any given price because oil and natural gas can be tapped simultaneously. As a result, oil is a complement in the production of natural gas. The reverse is also true: natural gas is a complement in the production of oil.

Changes in Technology As the opening story illustrates, changes in technology affect the supply curve. Improvements in technology enable producers to spend less on inputs (in this case, drilling equipment, labor, land purchases, and so on), yet still produce the same amount of output. When a better technology becomes available, reducing the cost of production, supply increases and the supply curve shifts to the right.

Improved technology enabled natural gas producers to more than double output in less than two years. Technology is also the main reason that natural gas has remained relatively cheap, even as demand has grown.

Changes in Expectations Just as changes in expectations can shift the demand curve, they can also shift the supply curve. When suppliers have some choice about when they put their good up for sale, changes in the expected future price of the good can lead a supplier to supply less or more of the good today.

For example, consider the fact that gasoline and other oil products are often stored for significant periods of time at oil refineries before being sold to consumers. In fact, storage is normally part of producers' business strategy. Knowing that the demand for gasoline peaks in the summer, oil refiners normally store some of their gasoline produced during the spring for summer sale. Similarly, knowing that the demand for heating oil peaks in the winter, they normally store some of their heating oil produced during the fall for winter sale.

In each case, there's a decision to be made between selling the product now versus storing it for later sale. Which choice a producer makes depends on a comparison of the current price versus the expected future price. This example illustrates how changes in expectations can alter supply: an increase in the anticipated future price of a good or service reduces supply today, a leftward shift of the supply curve. But a fall in the anticipated future price increases supply today, a rightward shift of the supply curve.

Changes in the Number of Producers Just as changes in the number of consumers affect the demand curve, changes in the number of producers affect the supply curve. Let's examine the **individual supply curve,** by looking at panel (a) in Figure 3-10. The individual supply curve shows the relationship between quantity supplied and price for an individual producer. For example, suppose that Louisiana Drillers is a natural gas producer and that panel (a) of Figure 3-10 shows the quantity of BTUs it will supply per year at any given price. Then $S_{Louisiana}$ is its individual supply curve.

The *market supply curve* shows how the combined total quantity supplied by all individual producers in the market depends on the market price of that good. Just as the market demand curve is the horizontal sum of the individual demand curves of all consumers, the market supply curve is the horizontal sum of the individual supply curves of all producers. Assume for a moment that there are only two natural gas producers, Louisiana Drillers and Allegheny Natural Gas. Allegheny's individual supply curve is shown in panel (b). Panel (c) shows the market supply curve. At any given price, the quantity supplied to the market is the sum of the quantities supplied by

An **individual supply curve** illustrates the relationship between quantity supplied and price for an individual producer.

FIGURE 3-10 The Individual Supply Curve and the Market Supply Curve

Panel (a) shows the individual supply curve for Louisiana Drillers, $S_{Louisiana}$, the quantity it will sell at any given price. Panel (b) shows the individual supply curve for Allegheny Natural Gas, $S_{Allegheny}$. The market supply curve, which shows the quantity of natural gas supplied by all producers at any given price is shown in panel (c). The market supply curve is the horizontal sum of the individual supply curves of all producers.

Louisiana Drillers and Allegheny Natural Gas. For example at a price of around $2 per BTU, Louisiana Drillers supplies 200,000 BTUs and Allegheny Natural Gas supplies 100,000 BTUs per year, making the quantity supplied to the market 300,000 BTUs.

Clearly, the quantity supplied to the market at any given price is larger when Allegheny Natural Gas is also a producer than it would be if Louisiana Drillers were the only supplier. The quantity supplied at a given price would be even larger if we added a third producer, then a fourth, and so on. So an increase in the number of producers leads to an increase in supply and a rightward shift of the supply curve.

For a review of the factors that shift supply, see Table 3-2.

TABLE 3-2   Factors That Shift Supply

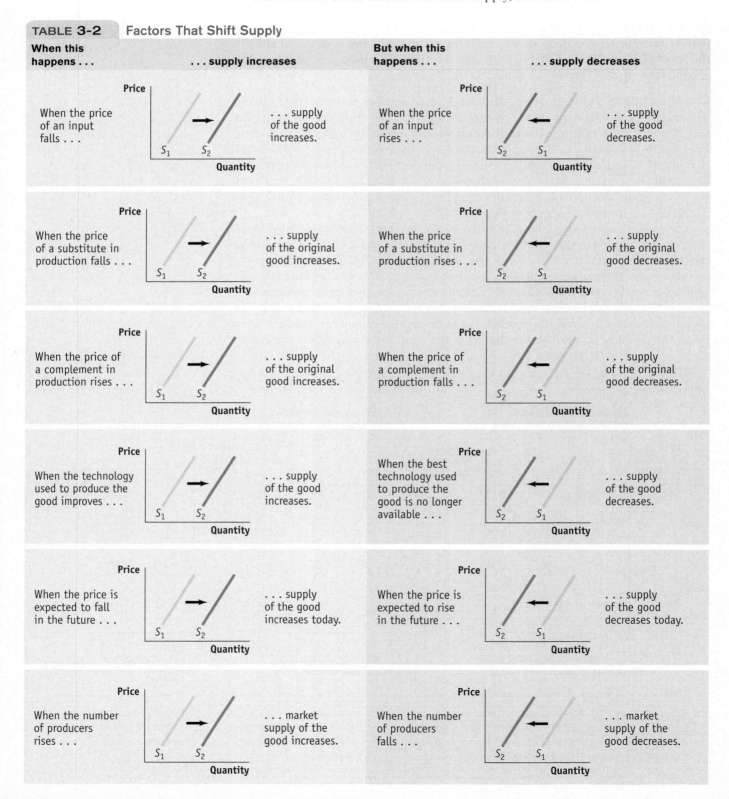

ECONOMICS ▶ *in Action*

Only Creatures Small and Pampered

Back in the 1970s, British television featured a popular show titled *All Creatures Great and Small*. It chronicled the real life of James Herriot, a country veterinarian who tended to cows, pigs, sheep, horses, and the occasional house pet, often under arduous conditions, in rural England during the 1930s. The show made it clear that in those days the local vet was a critical member of farming communities, saving valuable farm animals and helping farmers survive financially. And it was also clear that Mr. Herriot considered his life's work well spent.

But that was then and this is now. According to an article in the *New York Times*, the United States has experienced a severe decline in the number of farm veterinarians over the past 25 years. The source of the problem is competition. As the number of household pets has increased and the incomes of pet owners have grown, the demand for pet veterinarians has increased sharply. As a result, vets are being drawn away from the business of caring for farm animals into the more lucrative business of caring for pets. As one vet stated, she began her career caring for farm animals but changed her mind after "doing a C-section on a cow and it's 50 bucks. Do a C-section on a Chihuahua and you get $300. It's the money. I hate to say that."

Higher spending on pets means fewer veterinarians are available to tend to farm animals.

How can we translate this into supply and demand curves? Farm veterinary services and pet veterinary services are like gasoline and fuel oil: they're related goods that are substitutes in production. A veterinarian typically specializes in one type of practice or the other, and that decision often depends on the going price for the service. America's growing pet population, combined with the increased willingness of doting owners to spend on their companions' care, has driven up the price of pet veterinary services. As a result, fewer and fewer veterinarians have gone into farm animal practice. So the supply curve of farm veterinarians has shifted leftward—fewer farm veterinarians are offering their services at any given price.

In the end, farmers understand that it is all a matter of dollars and cents; they get fewer veterinarians because they are unwilling to pay more. As one farmer, who had recently lost an expensive cow due to the unavailability of a veterinarian, stated, "The fact that there's nothing you can do, you accept it as a business expense now. You didn't used to. If you have livestock, sooner or later you're going to have deadstock." (Although we should note that this farmer could have chosen to pay more for a vet who would have then saved his cow.)

Check Your Understanding   3-2

1. Explain whether each of the following events represents (i) a *shift of* the supply curve or (ii) a *movement along* the supply curve.
   a. More homeowners put their houses up for sale during a real estate boom that causes house prices to rise.
   b. Many strawberry farmers open temporary roadside stands during harvest season, even though prices are usually low at that time.
   c. Immediately after the school year begins, fast-food chains must raise wages, which represent the price of labor, to attract workers.
   d. Many construction workers temporarily move to areas that have suffered hurricane damage, lured by higher wages.
   e. Since new technologies have made it possible to build larger cruise ships (which are cheaper to run per passenger), Caribbean cruise lines offer more cabins, at lower prices, than before.

Solutions appear at back of book.

A competitive market is in equilibrium when price has moved to a level at which the quantity of a good or service demanded equals the quantity of that good or service supplied. The price at which this takes place is the **equilibrium price,** also referred to as the **market-clearing price.** The quantity of the good or service bought and sold at that price is the **equilibrium quantity.**

Supply, Demand, and Equilibrium

We have now covered the first three key elements in the supply and demand model: the demand curve, the supply curve, and the set of factors that shift each curve. The next step is to put these elements together to show how they can be used to predict the actual price at which the good is bought and sold, as well as the actual quantity transacted.

What determines the price at which a good or service is bought and sold? What determines the quantity transacted of the good or service? In Chapter 1 we learned the general principle that *markets move toward equilibrium,* a situation in which no individual would be better off taking a different action. In the case of a competitive market, we can be more specific: a competitive market is in equilibrium when the price has moved to a level at which the quantity of a good demanded equals the quantity of that good supplied. At that price, no individual seller could make herself better off by offering to sell either more or less of the good and no individual buyer could make himself better off by offering to buy more or less of the good. In other words, at the market equilibrium, price has moved to a level that exactly matches the quantity demanded by consumers to the quantity supplied by sellers.

The price that matches the quantity supplied and the quantity demanded is the **equilibrium price;** the quantity bought and sold at that price is the **equilibrium quantity.** The equilibrium price is also known as the **market-clearing price:** it is the price that "clears the market" by ensuring that every buyer willing to pay that price finds a seller willing to sell at that price, and vice versa. So how do we find the equilibrium price and quantity?

Finding the Equilibrium Price and Quantity

The easiest way to determine the equilibrium price and quantity in a market is by putting the supply curve and the demand curve on the same diagram. Since the supply curve shows the quantity supplied at any given price and the demand curve shows the quantity demanded at any given price, the price at which the two curves cross is the equilibrium price: the price at which quantity supplied equals quantity demanded.

Figure 3-11 combines the demand curve from Figure 3-1 and the supply curve from Figure 3-6. They *intersect* at point *E,* which is the equilibrium of this market; $3 is the equilibrium price and 10 trillion BTUs is the equilibrium quantity.

Let's confirm that point *E* fits our definition of equilibrium. At a price of $3 per BTU, natural gas producers are willing to sell 10 trillion BTUs a year and natural gas consumers want to buy 10 trillion BTUs a year. So at the price of $3 per BTU, the quantity of natural gas supplied equals the quantity demanded. Notice that at any other price the market would not clear: every willing buyer

PITFALLS

BOUGHT AND SOLD?
We have been talking about the price at which a good or service is bought *and* sold, as if the two were the same. But shouldn't we make a distinction between the price received by sellers and the price paid by buyers? In principle, yes; but it is helpful at this point to sacrifice a bit of realism in the interest of simplicity—by assuming away the difference between the prices received by sellers and those paid by buyers.

In reality, there is often a middleman—someone who brings buyers and sellers together. The middleman buys from suppliers, then sells to consumers at a markup. For example, natural gas brokers buy natural gas from drillers, and then sell the natural gas to gas companies who distribute it to households and firms. The drillers generally receive less than the gas companies pay per BTU of gas. But no mystery there: that

difference is how natural gas brokers make a living.

In many markets, however, the difference between the buying and selling price is quite small. So it's not a bad approximation to think of the price paid by buyers as being the *same* as the price received by sellers. And that is what we assume in this chapter.

FIGURE **3-11** Market Equilibrium

FIGURE **3-11** Market Equilibrium

Market equilibrium occurs at point *E*, where the supply curve and the demand curve intersect. In equilibrium, the quantity demanded is equal to the quantity supplied. In this market, the equilibrium price is $3 per BTU and the equilibrium quantity is 10 trillion BTUs per year.

would not be able to find a willing seller, or vice versa. More specifically, if the price were more than $3, the quantity supplied would exceed the quantity demanded; if the price were less than $3, the quantity demanded would exceed the quantity supplied.

The model of supply and demand, then, predicts that given the demand and supply curves shown in Figure 3-11, 10 trillion BTUs would change hands at a price of $3 per BTU. But how can we be sure that the market will arrive at the equilibrium price? We begin by answering three simple questions:

1. Why do all sales and purchases in a market take place at the same price?
2. Why does the market price fall if it is above the equilibrium price?
3. Why does the market price rise if it is below the equilibrium price?

Why Do All Sales and Purchases in a Market Take Place at the Same Price?

There are some markets where the same good can sell for many different prices, depending on who is selling or who is buying. For example, have you ever bought a souvenir in a "tourist trap" and then seen the same item on sale somewhere else (perhaps even in the shop next door) for a lower price? Because tourists don't know which shops offer the best deals and don't have time for comparison shopping, sellers in tourist areas can charge different prices for the same good.

But in any market where the buyers and sellers have both been around for some time, sales and purchases tend to converge at a generally uniform price, so we can safely talk about *the* market price. It's easy to see why. Suppose a seller offered a potential buyer a price noticeably above what the buyer knew other people to be paying. The buyer would clearly be better off shopping elsewhere—unless the seller were prepared to offer a better deal.

Conversely, a seller would not be willing to sell for significantly less than the amount he knew most buyers were paying; he would be better off waiting to get a

| FIGURE **3-12** | Price Above Its Equilibrium Level Creates a Surplus |

The market price of $3.50 is above the equilibrium price of $3. This creates a surplus: at a price of $3.50, producers would like to sell 11.2 trillion BTUs but consumers want to buy only 8.1 trillion BTUs, so there is a surplus of 3.1 trillion BTUs. This surplus will push the price down until it reaches the equilibrium price of $3.

more reasonable customer. So in any well-established, ongoing market, all sellers receive and all buyers pay approximately the same price. This is what we call the *market price.*

Why Does the Market Price Fall If It Is Above the Equilibrium Price?

Suppose the supply and demand curves are as shown in Figure 3-11 but the market price is above the equilibrium level of $3—say, $3.50. This situation is illustrated in Figure 3-12. Why can't the price stay there?

As the figure shows, at a price of $3.50 there would be more BTUs of natural gas available than consumers wanted to buy: 11.2 trillion BTUs versus 8.1 trillion BTUs. The difference of 3.1 trillion BTUs is the **surplus**—also known as the *excess supply*—of natural gas at $3.50.

This surplus means that some natural gas producers are frustrated: at the current price, they cannot find consumers who want to buy their natural gas. The surplus offers an incentive for those frustrated would-be sellers to offer a lower price in order to poach business from other producers and entice more consumers to buy. The result of this price cutting will be to push the prevailing price down until it reaches the equilibrium price. So the price of a good will fall whenever there is a surplus—that is, whenever the market price is above its equilibrium level.

Why Does the Market Price Rise If It Is Below the Equilibrium Price?

Now suppose the price is below its equilibrium level—say, at $2.75 per BTU, as shown in Figure 3-13. In this case, the quantity demanded, 11.5 trillion BTUs, exceeds the quantity supplied, 9.1 trillion BTUs, implying that there are would-be buyers who cannot find natural gas: there is a **shortage,** also known as an *excess demand,* of 2.4 trillion BTUs.

There is a **surplus** of a good or service when the quantity supplied exceeds the quantity demanded. Surpluses occur when the price is above its equilibrium level.

There is a **shortage** of a good or service when the quantity demanded exceeds the quantity supplied. Shortages occur when the price is below its equilibrium level.

FIGURE **3-13**   Price Below Its Equilibrium Level Creates a Shortage

The market price of $2.75 is below the equilibrium price of $3. This creates a shortage: consumers want to buy 11.5 trillion BTUs, but only 9.1 trillion BTUs are for sale, so there is a shortage of 2.4 trillion BTUs. This shortage will push the price up until it reaches the equilibrium price of $3.

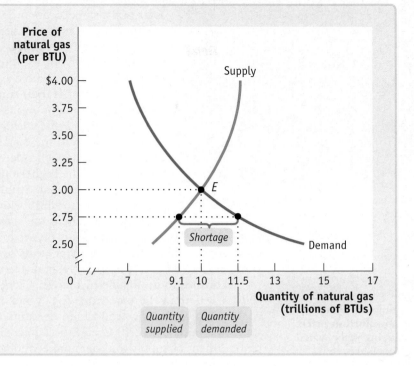

When there is a shortage, there are frustrated would-be buyers—people who want to purchase natural gas but cannot find willing sellers at the current price. In this situation, either buyers will offer more than the prevailing price or sellers will realize that they can charge higher prices. Either way, the result is to drive up the prevailing price. This bidding up of prices happens whenever there are shortages—and there will be shortages whenever the price is below its equilibrium level. So the market price will always rise if it is below the equilibrium level.

Using Equilibrium to Describe Markets

We have now seen that a market tends to have a single price, the equilibrium price. If the market price is above the equilibrium level, the ensuing surplus leads buyers and sellers to take actions that lower the price. And if the market price is below the equilibrium level, the ensuing shortage leads buyers and sellers to take actions that raise the price. So the market price always *moves toward* the equilibrium price, the price at which there is neither surplus nor shortage.

ECONOMICS ▶ *in Action*

The Price of Admission

The market equilibrium, so the theory goes, is pretty egalitarian because the equilibrium price applies to everyone. That is, all buyers pay the same price—the equilibrium price—and all sellers receive that same price. But is this realistic?

The market for concert tickets is an example that seems to contradict the theory—there's one price at the box office, and there's another price (typically much higher) for the same event online where people who already have tickets resell them, such as

The competitive market model determines the price you pay for concert tickets.

StubHub.com or eBay. For example, compare the box office price for a Drake concert in Miami, Florida, to the StubHub.com price for seats in the same location: $88.50 versus $155.

Puzzling as this may seem, there is no contradiction once we take opportunity costs and tastes into account. For major events, buying tickets from the box office means waiting in very long lines. Ticket buyers who use online resellers have decided that the opportunity cost of their time is too high to spend waiting in line. And tickets for major events being sold at face value by online box offices often sell out within minutes. In this case, some people who want to go to the concert badly but have missed out on the opportunity to buy cheaper tickets from the online box office are willing to pay the higher online reseller price.

Not only that—at StubHub.com, you can see that markets really do move to equilibrium. You'll notice that the prices quoted by different sellers for seats close to one another are also very close: $184.99 versus $185 for seats on the main floor of the Drake concert. As the competitive market model predicts, units of the same good end up selling for the same price. And prices move in response to demand and supply.

According to an article in the *New York Times,* tickets on StubHub.com can sell for less than the face value for events with little appeal, but prices can sky-rocket for events that are in high demand. (The article quotes a price of $3,530 for a Madonna concert.) Even StubHub.com's chief executive says his site is "the embodiment of supply-and-demand economics."

So the theory of competitive markets isn't just speculation. If you want to experience it for yourself, try buying tickets to a concert.

▼ Quick Review

• Price in a competitive market moves to the **equilibrium price,** or **market-clearing price,** where the quantity supplied is equal to the quantity demanded. This quantity is the **equilibrium quantity.**

• All sales and purchases in a market take place at the same price. If the price is above its equilibrium level, there is a **surplus** that drives the price down to the equilibrium level. If the price is below its equilibrium level, there is a **shortage** that drives the price up to the equilibrium level.

Check Your Understanding   3-3

1. In the following three situations, the market is initially in equilibrium. Explain the changes in either supply or demand that result from each event. After each event described below, does a surplus or shortage exist at the original equilibrium price? What will happen to the equilibrium price as a result?
   a. 2013 was a very good year for California wine-grape growers, who produced a bumper crop.
   b. After a hurricane, Florida hoteliers often find that many people cancel their upcoming vacations, leaving them with empty hotel rooms.
   c. After a heavy snowfall, many people want to buy second-hand snowblowers at the local tool shop.

Solutions appear at back of book.

Changes in Supply and Demand

The huge fall in the price of natural gas from $14 to $2 per BTU from 2006 to 2013 may have come as a surprise to consumers, but to suppliers it was no surprise at all. Suppliers knew that advances in drilling technology had opened up vast reserves of natural gas that had been too costly to tap in the past. And, predictably, an increase in supply reduces the equilibrium price.

The adoption of improved drilling technology is an example of an event that shifted the supply curve for a good without having an effect on the demand curve. There are many such events. There are also events that shift the demand curve without shifting the supply curve. For example, a medical report that chocolate is good for you increases the demand for chocolate but does not affect the supply. Events often shift either the supply curve or the demand curve, but not both; it is therefore useful to ask what happens in each case.

We have seen that when a curve shifts, the equilibrium price and quantity change. We will now concentrate on exactly how the shift of a curve alters the equilibrium price and quantity.

What Happens When the Demand Curve Shifts

Heating oil and natural gas are substitutes: if the price of heating oil rises, the demand for natural gas will increase, and if the price of heating oil falls, the demand for natural gas will decrease. But how does the price of heating oil affect the *market equilibrium* for natural gas?

Figure 3-14 shows the effect of a rise in the price of heating oil on the market for natural gas. The rise in the price of heating oil increases the demand for natural gas. Point E_1 shows the equilibrium corresponding to the original demand curve, with P_1 the equilibrium price and Q_1 the equilibrium quantity bought and sold.

An increase in demand is indicated by a *rightward* shift of the demand curve from D_1 to D_2. At the original market price P_1, this market is no longer in equilibrium: a shortage occurs because the quantity demanded exceeds the quantity supplied. So the price of natural gas rises and generates an increase in the quantity supplied, an upward *movement along the supply curve*. A new equilibrium is established at point E_2, with a higher equilibrium price, P_2, and higher equilibrium quantity, Q_2. This sequence of events reflects a general principle: *When demand for a good or service increases, the equilibrium price and the equilibrium quantity of the good or service both rise.*

What would happen in the reverse case, a fall in the price of heating oil? A fall in the price of heating oil reduces the demand for natural gas, shifting the demand curve to the *left*. At the original price, a surplus occurs as quantity supplied exceeds quantity demanded. The price falls and leads to a decrease in the quantity supplied, resulting in a lower equilibrium price and a lower equilibrium quantity. This illustrates another general principle: *When demand for a good or service decreases, the equilibrium price and the equilibrium quantity of the good or service both fall.*

FIGURE 3-14   **Equilibrium and Shifts of the Demand Curve**

The original equilibrium in the market for natural gas is at E_1, at the intersection of the supply curve and the original demand curve, D_1. A rise in the price of heating oil, a substitute, shifts the demand curve rightward to D_2. A shortage exists at the original price, P_1, causing both the price and quantity supplied to rise, a movement along the supply curve. A new equilibrium is reached at E_2, with a higher equilibrium price, P_2, and a higher equilibrium quantity, Q_2. When demand for a good or service increases, the equilibrium price and the equilibrium quantity of the good or service both rise.

To summarize how a market responds to a change in demand: *An increase in demand leads to a rise in both the equilibrium price and the equilibrium quantity. A decrease in demand leads to a fall in both the equilibrium price and the equilibrium quantity.*

What Happens When the Supply Curve Shifts

For most goods and services, it is a bit easier to predict changes in supply than changes in demand. Physical factors that affect supply, like weather or the availability of inputs, are easier to get a handle on than the fickle tastes that affect demand. Still, with supply as with demand, what we can best predict are the *effects* of shifts of the supply curve.

As we mentioned in the opening story, improved drilling technology significantly increased the supply of natural gas from 2006 onward. Figure 3-15 shows how this shift affected the market equilibrium. The original equilibrium is at E_1, the point of intersection of the original supply curve, S_1, with an equilibrium price P_1 and equilibrium quantity Q_1. As a result of the improved technology, supply increases and S_1 shifts *rightward* to S_2. At the original price P_1, a surplus of natural gas now exists and the market is no longer in equilibrium. The surplus causes a fall in price and an increase in the quantity demanded, a downward movement along the demand curve. The new equilibrium is at E_2, with an equilibrium price P_2 and an equilibrium quantity Q_2. In the new equilibrium E_2, the price is lower and the equilibrium quantity is higher than before. This can be stated as a general principle: *When supply of a good or service increases, the equilibrium price of the good or service falls and the equilibrium quantity of the good or service rises.*

What happens to the market when supply falls? A fall in supply leads to a *leftward* shift of the supply curve. At the original price a shortage now exists; as a result, the equilibrium price rises and the quantity demanded falls. This describes what happened to the market for natural gas after Hurricane Katrina damaged natural gas production in the Gulf of Mexico in 2006. We can formulate a general principle: *When supply of a good or service decreases, the equilibrium price of the good or service rises and the equilibrium quantity of the good or service falls.*

PITFALLS

WHICH CURVE IS IT, ANYWAY?
When the price of some good or service changes, in general, we can say that this reflects a change in either supply or demand. But it is easy to get confused about which one. A helpful clue is the direction of change in the quantity. If the quantity sold changes in the *same* direction as the price—for example, if both the price and the quantity rise—this suggests that the demand curve has shifted. If the price and the quantity move in *opposite* directions, the likely cause is a shift of the supply curve.

FIGURE 3-15 **Equilibrium and Shifts of the Supply Curve**

The original equilibrium in the market is at E_1. Improved technology causes an increase in the supply of natural gas and shifts the supply curve rightward from S_1 to S_2. A new equilibrium is established at E_2, with a lower equilibrium price, P_2, and a higher equilibrium quantity, Q_2.

To summarize how a market responds to a change in supply: *An increase in supply leads to a fall in the equilibrium price and a rise in the equilibrium quantity. A decrease in supply leads to a rise in the equilibrium price and a fall in the equilibrium quantity.*

Simultaneous Shifts of Supply and Demand Curves

Finally, it sometimes happens that events shift *both* the demand and supply curves at the same time. This is not unusual; in real life, supply curves and demand curves for many goods and services shift quite often because the economic environment continually changes. Figure 3-16 illustrates two examples of simultaneous shifts. In both panels there is an increase in supply—that is, a rightward shift of the supply curve from S_1 to S_2—representing, for example, adoption of an improved drilling technology. Notice that the rightward shift in panel (a) is larger than the one in panel (b): we can suppose that panel (a) represents a small, incremental change in technology while panel (b) represents a big advance in technology. Both panels show a decrease in demand—that is, a leftward shift from D_1 to D_2. Also notice that the leftward shift in panel (a) is relatively larger than the one in panel (b): we can suppose that panel (a) reflects the effect on demand of a deep recession in the overall economy, while panel (b) reflects the effect of a mild winter.

In both cases the equilibrium price falls from P_1 to P_2 as the equilibrium moves from E_1 to E_2. But what happens to the equilibrium quantity, the quantity of natural gas bought and sold? In panel (a) the decrease in demand is large relative to the increase in supply, and the equilibrium quantity falls as a result. In panel (b) the increase in supply is large relative to the decrease in demand, and the equilibrium quantity rises as a result. That is, when demand decreases and supply increases, the actual quantity bought and sold can go either way depending on *how much* the demand and supply curves have shifted.

FIGURE 3-16   Simultaneous Shifts of the Demand and Supply Curves

In panel (a) there is a simultaneous leftward shift of the demand curve and a rightward shift of the supply curve. Here the decrease in demand is relatively larger than the increase in supply, so the equilibrium quantity falls as the equilibrium price also falls. In panel (b) there is also a simultaneous leftward shift of the demand curve and rightward shift of the supply curve. Here the increase in supply is large relative to the decrease in demand, so the equilibrium quantity rises as the equilibrium price falls.

FOR INQUIRING MINDS | Tribulations on the Runway

You probably don't spend much time worrying about the trials and tribulations of fashion models. Most of them don't lead glamorous lives; in fact, except for a lucky few, life as a fashion model today can be very trying and not very lucrative. And it's all because of supply and demand.

Consider the case of Bianca Gomez, a willowy 18-year-old from Los Angeles, with green eyes, honey-colored hair, and flawless skin, whose experience was detailed in a *Wall Street Journal* article. Bianca began modeling while still in high school, earning about $30,000 in modeling fees during her senior year. Having attracted the interest of some top designers in New York, she moved there after graduation, hoping to land jobs in leading fashion houses and photoshoots for leading fashion magazines.

But once in New York, Bianca entered the global market for fashion models. And it wasn't very pretty. Due to the ease of transmitting photos electronically and the relatively low cost of international travel, top fashion centers such as New York and Milan, Italy, are deluged each year with thousands of beautiful young women from all over the world, eagerly trying to make it as models. Although Russians, other Eastern Europeans, and Brazilians are particular-

The global market for fashion models is not at all pretty.

ly numerous, some hail from places such as Kazakhstan and Mozambique.

Returning to our (less glamorous) economic model of supply and demand, the influx of aspiring fashion models from around the world can be represented

by a rightward shift of the supply curve in the market for fashion models, which would by itself tend to lower the price paid to models.

And that wasn't the only change in the market. Unfortunately for Bianca and others like her, the tastes of many of those who hire models have changed as well. Fashion magazines have come to prefer using celebrities such as Beyoncé on their pages rather than anonymous models, believing that their readers connect better with a familiar face. This amounts to a leftward shift of the demand curve for models—again reducing the equilibrium price paid to them.

This was borne out in Bianca's experiences. After paying her rent, her transportation, all her modeling expenses, and 20% of her earnings to her modeling agency (which markets her to prospective clients and books her jobs), Bianca found that she was barely breaking even. Sometimes she even had to dip into savings from her high school years. To save money, she ate macaroni and hot dogs; she traveled to auditions, often four or five in one day, by subway. As the *Wall Street Journal* reported, Bianca was seriously considering quitting modeling altogether. ∎

In general, when supply and demand shift in opposite directions, we can't predict what the ultimate effect will be on the quantity bought and sold. What we can say is that a curve that shifts a disproportionately greater distance than the other curve will have a disproportionately greater effect on the quantity bought and sold. That said, we can make the following prediction about the outcome when the supply and demand curves shift in opposite directions:

- When demand decreases and supply increases, the equilibrium price falls but the change in the equilibrium quantity is ambiguous.

- When demand increases and supply decreases, the equilibrium price rises but the change in the equilibrium quantity is ambiguous.

But suppose that the demand and supply curves shift in the same direction. This is what has happened in recent years in the United States, as the economy has made a gradual recovery from the recession of 2008, resulting in an increase in both demand and supply. Can we safely make any predictions about the changes in price and quantity? In this situation, the change in quantity bought and sold can be predicted, but the change in price is ambiguous. The two possible outcomes when the supply and demand curves shift in the same direction (which you should check for yourself) are as follows:

- When both demand and supply increase, the equilibrium quantity rises but the change in equilibrium price is ambiguous.

- When both demand and supply decrease, the equilibrium quantity falls but the change in equilibrium price is ambiguous.

ECONOMICS ▶ in Action

The Cotton Panic and Crash of 2011

When fear of a future price increase strikes a large enough number of consumers, it can become a self-fulfilling prophecy. Much to the dismay of owners of cotton textile mills, this is exactly what happened in early 2011, when a huge surge in the price of raw cotton peaked, followed by an equally spectacular fall. In situations like these, consumers become their own worst enemy, engaging in what is called *panic buying*: rushing to purchase more of a good because its price has gone up, which precipitates only a further price rise and more panic buying. So how did cotton buyers find themselves in this predicament in 2011? And what finally got them out of it?

The process had, in fact, been started by real events that occurred years earlier. By 2010, demand for cotton had rebounded sharply from lows set during the global financial crisis of 2006–2007. In addition, greater demand for cotton clothing in countries with rapidly growing middle classes, like China, added to the increased demand for cotton. This had the effect of shifting the demand curve rightward.

FIGURE 3-17 Cotton Prices in the United States, 1999–2013

The price for raw cotton spiked in the United States in 2011.

Source: USDA.

At the same time there were significant supply reductions to the worldwide market for cotton. India, the second largest exporter of cotton (an *exporter* is a seller of a good to foreign buyers), had imposed restrictions on the sale of its cotton abroad in order to aid its own textile mills. And Pakistan, China, and Australia, which were big growers of cotton, experienced widespread flooding that significantly reduced their cotton crops. The Indian export restrictions and the floods in cotton-producing areas had the effect of shifting the supply curve leftward.

So, as shown in Figure 3-17, while cotton had traded at between $0.35 and $0.60 per pound from 2000 to 2010, it surged to more than $2.40 per pound in early 2011—up more than 200% in one year. As high prices for cotton sparked panic buying, the demand curve shifted further rightward, further feeding the buying frenzy.

Yet by the end of 2011, cotton prices had plummeted to $0.86 per pound. What happened? A number of things, illustrating the forces of supply and demand. First, demand fell as clothing manufacturers, unwilling to pass on huge price increases to their customers, shifted to less expensive fabrics like polyester. Second, supply increased as farmers planted more acreage of cotton in hopes of garnering high prices. As the effects of supply and demand became obvious, buyers stopped panicking and cotton prices finally fell back down to earth.

Check Your Understanding 3-4

1. In each of the following examples, determine (i) the market in question; (ii) whether a shift in demand or supply occurred, the direction of the shift, and what induced the shift; and (iii) the effect of the shift on the equilibrium price and the equilibrium quantity.
   a. As the price of gasoline fell in the United States during the 1990s, more people bought large cars.
   b. As technological innovation has lowered the cost of recycling used paper, fresh paper made from recycled stock is used more frequently.
   c. When a local cable company offers cheaper on-demand films, local movie theaters have more unfilled seats.

▼ Quick Review

• Changes in the equilibrium price and quantity in a market result from shifts of the supply curve, the demand curve, or both.

• An increase in demand increases both the equilibrium price and the equilibrium quantity. A decrease in demand decreases both the equilibrium price and the equilibrium quantity.

• An increase in supply drives the equilibrium price down but increases the equilibrium quantity. A decrease in supply raises the equilibrium price but reduces the equilibrium quantity.

• Often fluctuations in markets involve shifts of both the supply and demand curves. When they shift in the same direction, the change in equilibrium quantity is predictable but the change in equilibrium price is not. When they shift in opposite directions, the change in equilibrium price is predictable but the change in equilibrium quantity is not. When there are simultaneous shifts of the demand and supply curves, the curve that shifts the greater distance has a greater effect on the change in equilibrium price and quantity.

2. When a new, faster computer chip is introduced, demand for computers using the older, slower chips decreases. Simultaneously, computer makers increase their production of computers containing the old chips in order to clear out their stocks of old chips.

Draw two diagrams of the market for computers containing the old chips:

a. one in which the equilibrium quantity falls in response to these events and

b. one in which the equilibrium quantity rises.

c. What happens to the equilibrium price in each diagram?

Solutions appear at back of book.

Competitive Markets—And Others

Early in this chapter, we defined a competitive market and explained that the supply and demand framework is a model of competitive markets. But we took a rain check on the question of why it matters whether or not a market is competitive. Now that we've seen how the supply and demand model works, we can offer some explanation.

To understand why competitive markets are different from other markets, compare the problems facing two individuals: a wheat farmer who must decide whether to grow more wheat and the president of a giant aluminum company—say, Alcoa—who must decide whether to produce more aluminum.

For the wheat farmer, the question is simply whether the extra wheat can be sold at a price high enough to justify the extra production cost. The farmer need not worry about whether producing more wheat will affect the price of the wheat he or she was already planning to grow. That's because the wheat market is competitive. There are thousands of wheat farmers, and no one farmer's decision will have any impact on the market price.

For the Alcoa executive, things are not that simple because the aluminum market is *not* competitive. There are only a few big producers, including Alcoa, and each of them is well aware that its actions *do* have a noticeable impact on the market price. This adds a whole new level of complexity to the decisions producers have to make. Alcoa can't decide whether or not to produce more aluminum just by asking whether the additional product will sell for more than it costs to make. The company also has to ask whether producing more aluminum will drive down the market price and reduce its *profit*, its net gain from producing and selling its output.

When a market is competitive, individuals can base decisions on less complicated analyses than those used in a noncompetitive market. This in turn means that it's easier for economists to build a model of a competitive market than of a noncompetitive market.

Don't take this to mean that economic analysis has nothing to say about noncompetitive markets. On the contrary, economists can offer some very important insights into how other kinds of markets work. But those insights require other models, which we will learn about later on.

An Uber Way to Get a Ride

Mark Avery/Zuma Wire/Alamy

In a densely populated city like New York City, finding a taxi is a relatively easy task on most days—stand on a corner, put out your arm and, usually, before long an available cab stops to pick you up. And even before you step into the car you will know approximately how much it will cost to get to your destination, because taxi meter rates are set by city regulators and posted for riders.

But at times it is not so easy to find a taxi—on rainy days, during rush hour, and at crowded locations where many people are looking for a taxi at the same time. At such times, you could wait a very long while before finding an available cab. As you wait, you will probably notice empty taxis passing you by—drivers who have quit working for the day and are headed home or back to the garage. There will be drivers who might stop, but then won't pick you up because they find your destination inconvenient. Moreover, there are times when it is simply impossible to hail a taxi—for example, during a snowstorm or on New Year's Eve when the demand for taxis far exceeds the supply.

In 2009 two young entrepreneurs, Garrett Camp and Travis Kalanick, founded Uber, a company that they believe offers a better way to get a ride. Using a smartphone app, Uber serves as a clearinghouse connecting people who want a ride to drivers with cars who are registered with Uber. Confirm your location using the Uber app and you'll be shown the available cars in your vicinity. Tap "book" and you receive a text saying your car—typically a spotless Lincoln Town Car—is on its way. At the end of your trip, fare plus tip are automatically deducted from your credit card. As of 2014 Uber operates in 70 cities around the world and booked more than $1 billion in rides in 2013.

Given that Uber provides personalized service and better quality cars, their fares are somewhat higher than regular taxi fares *during normal driving days*—a situation that customers seem happy with. However, the qualification *during normal driving hours* is an important one because at other times Uber's rates fluctuate. When a lot of people are looking for a car—such as during a snowstorm or on New Year's Eve—Uber uses what it calls *surge pricing*, setting the rate higher until everyone who wants a car at the going price can get one. So during a recent New York snowstorm, rides cost up to 8.25 times the standard price. Enraged, some of Uber's customers have accused them of price gouging.

But according to Kalanick, the algorithm that Uber uses to determine the surge price is set to leave as few people as possible without a ride, and he's just doing what is necessary to keep customers happy. As he explains, "We do not own cars nor do we employ drivers. Higher prices are required in order to get cars on the road and keep them on the road during the busiest times." This explanation was confirmed by one Uber driver who said, "If I don't have anything to do and see a surge price, I get out there."

QUESTIONS FOR THOUGHT

1. Before Uber, how were prices set in the market for rides in New York City? Was it a competitive market?

2. What accounts for the fact that during good weather there are typically enough taxis for everyone who wants one, but during snowstorms there typically aren't enough?

3. How does Uber's surge pricing solve the problem described in the previous question? Assess Kalanick's claim that the price is set to leave as few people possible without a ride.

SUMMARY

1. The **supply and demand model** illustrates how a **competitive market,** one with many buyers and sellers, none of whom can influence the market price, works.

2. The **demand schedule** shows the **quantity demanded** at each price and is represented graphically by a **demand curve.** The **law of demand** says that demand curves slope downward; that is, a higher price for a good or service leads people to demand a smaller quantity, other things equal.

3. A **movement along the demand curve** occurs when a price change leads to a change in the quantity demanded. When economists talk of increasing or decreasing demand, they mean **shifts of the demand curve—**a change in the quantity demanded at any given price. An increase in demand causes a rightward shift of the demand curve. A decrease in demand causes a leftward shift.

4. There are five main factors that shift the demand curve:
   - A change in the prices of related goods or services, such as **substitutes** or **complements**
   - A change in income: when income rises, the demand for **normal goods** increases and the demand for **inferior goods** decreases
   - A change in tastes
   - A change in expectations
   - A change in the number of consumers

5. The market demand curve for a good or service is the horizontal sum of the **individual demand curves** of all consumers in the market.

6. The **supply schedule** shows the **quantity supplied** at each price and is represented graphically by a **supply curve.** Supply curves usually slope upward.

7. A **movement along the supply curve** occurs when a price change leads to a change in the quantity supplied. When economists talk of increasing or decreasing supply, they mean **shifts of the supply curve—**a change in the quantity supplied at any given price. An increase in supply causes a rightward shift of the supply curve. A decrease in supply causes a leftward shift.

8. There are five main factors that shift the supply curve:
   - A change in **input** prices
   - A change in the prices of related goods and services
   - A change in technology
   - A change in expectations
   - A change in the number of producers

9. The market supply curve for a good or service is the horizontal sum of the **individual supply curves** of all producers in the market.

10. The supply and demand model is based on the principle that the price in a market moves to its **equilibrium price,** or **market-clearing price,** the price at which the quantity demanded is equal to the quantity supplied. This quantity is the **equilibrium quantity.** When the price is above its market-clearing level, there is a **surplus** that pushes the price down. When the price is below its market-clearing level, there is a **shortage** that pushes the price up.

11. An increase in demand increases both the equilibrium price and the equilibrium quantity; a decrease in demand has the opposite effect. An increase in supply reduces the equilibrium price and increases the equilibrium quantity; a decrease in supply has the opposite effect.

12. Shifts of the demand curve and the supply curve can happen simultaneously. When they shift in opposite directions, the change in equilibrium price is predictable but the change in equilibrium quantity is not. When they shift in the same direction, the change in equilibrium quantity is predictable but the change in equilibrium price is not. In general, the curve that shifts the greater distance has a greater effect on the changes in equilibrium price and quantity.

KEY TERMS

Competitive market, p. 68
Supply and demand model, p. 68
Demand schedule, p. 69
Quantity demanded, p. 69
Demand curve, p. 69
Law of demand, p. 70
Shift of the demand curve, p. 72
Movement along the demand curve, p. 72

Substitutes, p. 74
Complements, p. 74
Normal good, p. 74
Inferior good, p. 74
Individual demand curve, p. 76
Quantity supplied, p. 79
Supply schedule, p. 79
Supply curve, p. 79
Shift of the supply curve, p. 80

Movement along the supply curve, p. 80
Input, p. 82
Individual supply curve, p. 83
Equilibrium price, p. 86
Equilibrium quantity, p. 86
Market-clearing price, p. 86
Surplus, p. 88
Shortage, p. 88

PROBLEMS

1. A survey indicated that chocolate is the most popular flavor of ice cream in America. For each of the following, indicate the possible effects on demand, supply, or both as well as equilibrium price and quantity of chocolate ice cream.

   a. A severe drought in the Midwest causes dairy farmers to reduce the number of milk-producing cattle in their herds by a third. These dairy farmers supply cream that is used to manufacture chocolate ice cream.

   b. A new report by the American Medical Association reveals that chocolate does, in fact, have significant health benefits.

   c. The discovery of cheaper synthetic vanilla flavoring lowers the price of vanilla ice cream.

   d. New technology for mixing and freezing ice cream lowers manufacturers' costs of producing chocolate ice cream.

2. In a supply and demand diagram, draw the shift of the demand curve for hamburgers in your hometown due to the following events. In each case, show the effect on equilibrium price and quantity.

   a. The price of tacos increases.

   b. All hamburger sellers raise the price of their french fries.

   c. Income falls in town. Assume that hamburgers are a normal good for most people.

   d. Income falls in town. Assume that hamburgers are an inferior good for most people.

   e. Hot dog stands cut the price of hot dogs.

3. The market for many goods changes in predictable ways according to the time of year, in response to events such as holidays, vacation times, seasonal changes in production, and so on. Using supply and demand, explain the change in price in each of the following cases. Note that supply and demand may shift simultaneously.

   a. Lobster prices usually fall during the summer peak lobster harvest season, despite the fact that people like to eat lobster during the summer more than at any other time of year.

   b. The price of a Christmas tree is lower after Christmas than before but fewer trees are sold.

   c. The price of a round-trip ticket to Paris on Air France falls by more than $200 after the end of school vacation in September. This happens despite the fact that generally worsening weather increases the cost of operating flights to Paris, and Air France therefore reduces the number of flights to Paris at any given price.

4. Show in a diagram the effect on the demand curve, the supply curve, the equilibrium price, and the equilibrium quantity of each of the following events.

   a. The market for newspapers in your town
   Case 1: The salaries of journalists go up.
   Case 2: There is a big news event in your town, which is reported in the newspapers.

   b. The market for St. Louis Rams cotton T-shirts
   Case 1: The Rams win the Super Bowl.
   Case 2: The price of cotton increases.

   c. The market for bagels
   Case 1: People realize how fattening bagels are.
   Case 2: People have less time to make themselves a cooked breakfast.

   d. The market for the Krugman and Wells economics textbook
   Case 1: Your professor makes it required reading for all of his or her students.
   Case 2: Printing costs for textbooks are lowered by the use of synthetic paper.

5. Let's assume that each person in the United States consumes an average of 37 gallons of soft drinks (nondiet) at an average price of $2 per gallon and that the U.S. population is 294 million. At a price of $1.50 per gallon, each individual consumer would demand 50 gallons of soft drinks. From this information about the individual demand schedule, calculate the market demand schedule for soft drinks for the prices of $1.50 and $2 per gallon.

6. Suppose that the supply schedule of Maine lobsters is as follows:

Price of lobster (per pound)	Quantity of lobster supplied (pounds)
$25	800
20	700
15	600
10	500
5	400

Suppose that Maine lobsters can be sold only in the United States. The U.S. demand schedule for Maine lobsters is as follows:

Price of lobster (per pound)	Quantity of lobster demanded (pounds)
$25	200
20	400
15	600
10	800
5	1,000

   a. Draw the demand curve and the supply curve for Maine lobsters. What are the equilibrium price and quantity of lobsters?

Now suppose that Maine lobsters can be sold in France. The French demand schedule for Maine lobsters is as follows:

Price of lobster (per pound)	Quantity of lobster supplied (pounds)
$25	100
20	300
15	500
10	700
5	900

b. What is the demand schedule for Maine lobsters now that French consumers can also buy them? Draw a supply and demand diagram that illustrates the new equilibrium price and quantity of lobsters. What will happen to the price at which fishermen can sell lobster? What will happen to the price paid by U.S. consumers? What will happen to the quantity consumed by U.S. consumers?

7. Find the flaws in reasoning in the following statements, paying particular attention to the distinction between shifts of and movements along the supply and demand curves. Draw a diagram to illustrate what actually happens in each situation.

a. "A technological innovation that lowers the cost of producing a good might seem at first to result in a reduction in the price of the good to consumers. But a fall in price will increase demand for the good, and higher demand will send the price up again. It is not certain, therefore, that an innovation will really reduce price in the end."

b. "A study shows that eating a clove of garlic a day can help prevent heart disease, causing many consumers to demand more garlic. This increase in demand results in a rise in the price of garlic. Consumers, seeing that the price of garlic has gone up, reduce their demand for garlic. This causes the demand for garlic to decrease and the price of garlic to fall. Therefore, the ultimate effect of the study on the price of garlic is uncertain."

8. The following table shows a demand schedule for a normal good.

Price	Quantity demanded
$23	70
21	90
19	110
17	130

a. Do you think that the increase in quantity demanded (say, from 90 to 110 in the table) when price decreases (from $21 to $19) is due to a rise in consumers' income? Explain clearly (and briefly) why or why not.

b. Now suppose that the good is an inferior good. Would the demand schedule still be valid for an inferior good?

c. Lastly, assume you do not know whether the good is normal or inferior. Devise an experiment that would allow you to determine which one it was. Explain.

9. In recent years, the number of car producers in China has increased rapidly. In fact, China now has more car brands than the United States. In addition, car sales have climbed every year and automakers have increased their output at even faster rates, causing fierce competition and a decline in prices. At the same time, Chinese consumers' incomes have risen. Assume that cars are a normal good. Draw a diagram of the supply and demand curves for cars in China to explain what has happened in the Chinese car market.

10. Aaron Hank is a star hitter for the Bay City baseball team. He is close to breaking the major league record for home runs hit during one season, and it is widely anticipated that in the next game he will break that record. As a result, tickets for the team's next game have been a hot commodity. But today it is announced that, due to a knee injury, he will not in fact play in the team's next game. Assume that season ticket-holders are able to resell their tickets if they wish. Use supply and demand diagrams to explain your answers to parts a and b.

a. Show the case in which this announcement results in a lower equilibrium price and a lower equilibrium quantity than before the announcement.

b. Show the case in which this announcement results in a lower equilibrium price and a higher equilibrium quantity than before the announcement.

c. What accounts for whether case a or case b occurs?

d. Suppose that a scalper had secretly learned before the announcement that Aaron Hank would not play in the next game. What actions do you think he would take?

11. Fans of rock and rock stars often bemoan the high price of concert tickets. One superstar has argued that it isn't worth hundreds, even thousands, of dollars to hear him and his band play. Let's assume this star sold out arenas around the country at an average ticket price of $75.

a. How would you evaluate the argument that ticket prices are too high?

b. Suppose that due to this star's protests, ticket prices were lowered to $50. In what sense is this price too low? Draw a diagram using supply and demand curves to support your argument.

c. Suppose the rock superstar really wanted to bring down ticket prices. Since he and his band control the supply of their services, what do you recommend they do? Explain using a supply and demand diagram.

d. Suppose the band's next album was a total dud. Do you think they would still have to worry about ticket prices being too high? Why or why not? Draw a supply and demand diagram to support your argument.

e. Suppose the group announced their next tour was going to be their last. What effect would this likely have on the demand for and price of tickets? Illustrate with a supply and demand diagram.

12. After several years of decline, the market for handmade acoustic guitars is making a comeback. These guitars are usually made in small workshops employing relatively few highly skilled luthiers. Assess the impact on the equilibrium price and quantity of handmade acoustic guitars as a result of each of the following events. In your answers indicate which curve(s) shift(s) and in which direction.

a. Environmentalists succeed in having the use of Brazilian rosewood banned in the United States, forcing luthiers to seek out alternative, more costly woods.

b. A foreign producer reengineers the guitar-making process and floods the market with identical guitars.

c. Music featuring handmade acoustic guitars makes a comeback as audiences tire of heavy metal and alternative rock music.

d. The country goes into a deep recession and the income of the average American falls sharply.

13. *Demand twisters:* Sketch and explain the demand relationship in each of the following statements.

a. I would never buy a Miley Cyrus album! You couldn't even give me one for nothing.

b. I generally buy a bit more coffee as the price falls. But once the price falls to $2 per pound, I'll buy out the entire stock of the supermarket.

c. I spend more on orange juice even as the price rises. (Does this mean that I must be violating the law of demand?)

d. Due to a tuition rise, most students at a college find themselves with less disposable income. Almost all of them eat more frequently at the school cafeteria and less often at restaurants, even though prices at the cafeteria have risen, too. (This one requires that you draw both the demand and the supply curves for school cafeteria meals.)

14. Will Shakespeare is a struggling playwright in sixteenth-century London. As the price he receives for writing a play increases, he is willing to write more plays. For the following situations, use a diagram to illustrate how each event affects the equilibrium price and quantity in the market for Shakespeare's plays.

a. The playwright Christopher Marlowe, Shakespeare's chief rival, is killed in a bar brawl.

b. The bubonic plague, a deadly infectious disease, breaks out in London.

c. To celebrate the defeat of the Spanish Armada, Queen Elizabeth declares several weeks of festivities, which involves commissioning new plays.

15. This year, the small town of Middling experiences a sudden doubling of the birth rate. After three years, the birth rate returns to normal. Use a diagram to illustrate the effect of these events on the following.

a. The market for an hour of babysitting services in Middling this year

b. The market for an hour of babysitting services 14 years into the future, after the birth rate has returned to normal, by which time children born today are old enough to work as babysitters

c. The market for an hour of babysitting services 30 years into the future, when children born today are likely to be having children of their own

16. Use a diagram to illustrate how each of the following events affects the equilibrium price and quantity of pizza.

a. The price of mozzarella cheese rises.

b. The health hazards of hamburgers are widely publicized.

c. The price of tomato sauce falls.

d. The incomes of consumers rise and pizza is an inferior good.

e. Consumers expect the price of pizza to fall next week.

17. Although he was a prolific artist, Pablo Picasso painted only 1,000 canvases during his "Blue Period." Picasso is now dead, and all of his Blue Period works are currently on display in museums and private galleries throughout Europe and the United States.

a. Draw a supply curve for Picasso Blue Period works. Why is this supply curve different from ones you have seen?

b. Given the supply curve from part a, the price of a Picasso Blue Period work will be entirely dependent on what factor(s)? Draw a diagram showing how the equilibrium price of such a work is determined.

c. Suppose rich art collectors decide that it is essential to acquire Picasso Blue Period art for their collections. Show the impact of this on the market for these paintings.

18. Draw the appropriate curve in each of the following cases. Is it like or unlike the curves you have seen so far? Explain.

a. The demand for cardiac bypass surgery, given that the government pays the full cost for any patient

b. The demand for elective cosmetic plastic surgery, given that the patient pays the full cost

c. The supply of reproductions of Rembrandt paintings

WORK IT OUT

Macmillan Education LaunchPad

For interactive, step-by-step help in solving the following problem, visit LaunchPad by using the URL on the back cover of this book.

19. The accompanying table gives the annual U.S. demand and supply schedules for pickup trucks.

Price of truck	Quantity of trucks demanded (millions)	Quantity of trucks supplied (millions)
$20,000	20	14
25,000	18	15
30,000	16	16
35,000	14	17
40,000	12	18

a. Plot the demand and supply curves using these schedules. Indicate the equilibrium price and quantity on your diagram.

b. Suppose the tires used on pickup trucks are found to be defective. What would you expect to happen in the market for pickup trucks? Show this on your diagram.

c Suppose that the U.S. Department of Transportation imposes costly regulations on manufacturers that cause them to reduce supply by one-third at any given price. Calculate and plot the new supply schedule and indicate the new equilibrium price and quantity on your diagram.

Consumer and Producer Surplus

▶ What You Will Learn
in This Chapter

■ What **consumer surplus** is and
its relationship to the demand
curve

■ What **producer surplus** is and
its relationship to the supply curve

■ What **total surplus** is and how it
can be used both to measure the
gains from trade and to illustrate
why markets work so well

■ Why **property rights** and prices
as **economic signals** are critical
to smooth functioning of a market

■ Why markets typically lead to
efficient outcomes despite the
fact that they sometimes fail

MAKING GAINS BY THE BOOK

How much am I willing to pay for that used textbook?

There is a lively market in second-hand college textbooks. At the end of each term, some students who took a course decide that the money they can make by selling their used books is worth more to them than keeping the books. And some students who are taking the course next term prefer to buy a somewhat battered but less expensive used textbook rather than buy at full price.

Textbook publishers and authors are not happy about these transactions because they cut into sales of new books. But both the students who sell used books and those who buy them clearly benefit from the existence of second-hand textbook markets. That is why many college bookstores create them, buying used textbooks and selling them alongside the new books. And it is why there are several websites, such as Amazon.com and Half.com, devoted exclusively to the buying and selling of second-hand textbooks.

But can we put a number on what used textbook buyers and sellers gain from these transactions? Can we answer the question, "How much do the buyers and sellers of textbooks gain from the existence of the used-book market?"

Yes, we can. In this chapter we will see how to measure benefits, such as those to buyers of used textbooks, from being able to purchase a good—known as *consumer surplus*. And we will see that there is a corresponding measure, *producer surplus*, of the benefits sellers receive from being able to sell a good.

The concepts of consumer surplus and producer surplus are extremely useful for analyzing a wide variety of economic issues. They let us calculate how much benefit producers and consumers receive from the existence of a market. They also allow us to calculate how the welfare of consumers and producers is affected by changes in market prices. Such calculations play a crucial role in evaluating many economic policies.

What information do we need to calculate consumer and producer surplus? Surprisingly, all we need are the demand and supply curves for a good. That is, the supply and demand model isn't just a model of how a competitive market works—it's also a model of how much consumers and producers gain from participating in that market.

So our first step will be to learn how consumer and producer surplus can be derived from the demand and supply curves. We will then see how these concepts can be applied to actual economic issues.

Consumer Surplus and the Demand Curve

The market in used textbooks is a big business in terms of dollars and cents—several billion dollars each year. More importantly for us, it is a convenient starting point for developing the concepts of consumer and producer surplus. We'll use the concepts of consumer and producer surplus to understand exactly how buyers and sellers benefit from a competitive market and how big those benefits are. In addition, these concepts play important roles in analyzing what happens when competitive markets don't work well or there is interference in the market.

So let's begin by looking at the market for used textbooks, starting with the buyers. The key point, as we'll see in a minute, is that the demand curve is derived from their tastes or preferences—and that those same preferences also determine how much they gain from the opportunity to buy used books.

Willingness to Pay and the Demand Curve

A used book is not as good as a new book—it will be battered and coffee-stained, may include someone else's highlighting, and may not be completely up to date. How much this bothers you depends on your preferences. Some potential buyers would prefer to buy the used book even if it is only slightly cheaper than a new one; others would buy the used book only if it is considerably cheaper.

Let's define a potential buyer's **willingness to pay** as the maximum price at which he or she would buy a good, in this case a used textbook. An individual won't buy the good if it costs more than this amount but is eager to do so if it costs less. If the price is just equal to an individual's willingness to pay, he or she is indifferent between buying and not buying. For the sake of simplicity, we'll assume that the individual buys the good in this case.

The table in Figure 4-1 shows five potential buyers of a used book that costs $100 new, listed in order of their willingness to pay. At one extreme is Aleisha, who will buy a second-hand book even if the price is as high as $59. Brad is less willing to have a used book and will buy one only if the price is $45 or less. Claudia is willing to pay only $35 and Darren, only $25. And Edwina, who really doesn't like the idea of a used book, will buy one only if it costs no more than $10.

How many of these five students will actually buy a used book? It depends on the price. If the price of a used book is $55, only Aleisha buys one; if the price is $40, Aleisha and Brad both buy used books, and so on. So the information in the table can be used to construct the *demand schedule* for used textbooks.

As we saw in Chapter 3, we can use this demand schedule to derive the market demand curve shown in Figure 4-1. Because we are considering only a small number of consumers, this curve doesn't look like the smooth demand curves of Chapter 3, where markets contained hundreds or thousands of consumers. Instead, this demand curve is step-shaped, with alternating horizontal and vertical segments. Each horizontal segment—each step—corresponds to one potential buyer's willingness to pay.

However, we'll see shortly that for the analysis of consumer surplus it doesn't matter whether the demand curve is step-shaped, as in this figure, or whether there are many consumers, making the curve smooth.

Willingness to Pay and Consumer Surplus

Suppose that the campus bookstore makes used textbooks available at a price of $30. In that case Aleisha, Brad, and Claudia will buy books. Do they gain from their purchases, and if so, how much?

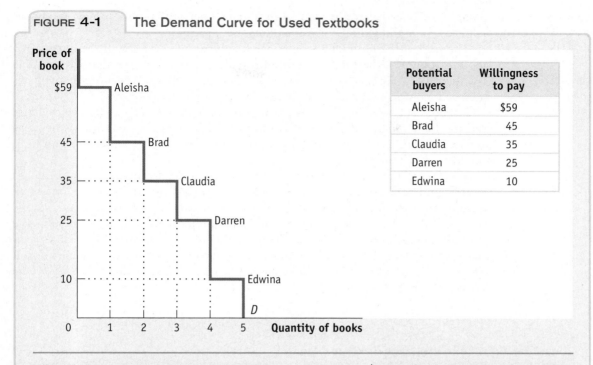

FIGURE 4-1   The Demand Curve for Used Textbooks

Potential buyers	Willingness to pay
Aleisha	$59
Brad	45
Claudia	35
Darren	25
Edwina	10

With only five potential consumers in this market, the demand curve is step-shaped. Each step represents one consumer, and its height indicates that consumer's willingness to pay—the maximum price at which he or she will buy a used textbook—as indicated in the table. Aleisha has the highest willingness to pay at $59, Brad has the next highest at $45, and so on down to Edwina with the lowest willingness to pay at $10. At a price of $59, the quantity demanded is one (Aleisha); at a price of $45, the quantity demanded is two (Aleisha and Brad); and so on until you reach a price of $10, at which all five students are willing to purchase a used textbook.

The answer, shown in Table 4-1, is that each student who purchases a book does achieve a net gain but that the amount of the gain differs among students.

Aleisha would have been willing to pay $59, so her net gain is $59 − $30 = $29. Brad would have been willing to pay $45, so his net gain is $45 − $30 = $15. Claudia would have been willing to pay $35, so her net gain is $35 − $30 = $5. Darren and Edwina, however, won't be willing to buy a used book at a price of $30, so they neither gain nor lose.

The net gain that a buyer achieves from the purchase of a good is called that buyer's **individual consumer surplus.** What we learn from this example is that

Individual consumer surplus is the net gain to an individual buyer from the purchase of a good. It is equal to the difference between the buyer's willingness to pay and the price paid.

TABLE 4-1   Consumer Surplus If Price of Used Textbook = $30

Potential buyer	Willingness to pay	Price paid	Individual consumer surplus = Willingness to pay − Price paid
Aleisha	$59	$30	$29
Brad	45	30	15
Claudia	35	30	5
Darren	25	—	—
Edwina	10	—	—
All buyers			**Total consumer surplus = $49**

Total consumer surplus is the sum of the individual consumer surpluses of all the buyers of a good in a market.

The term **consumer surplus** is often used to refer both to individual and to total consumer surplus.

whenever a buyer pays a price less than his or her willingness to pay, the buyer achieves some individual consumer surplus.

The sum of the individual consumer surpluses achieved by all the buyers of a good is known as the **total consumer surplus** achieved in the market. In Table 4-1, the total consumer surplus is the sum of the individual consumer surpluses achieved by Aleisha, Brad, and Claudia: $29 + $15 + $5 = $49.

Economists often use the term **consumer surplus** to refer to both individual and total consumer surplus. We will follow this practice; it will always be clear in context whether we are referring to the consumer surplus achieved by an individual or by all buyers.

Total consumer surplus can be represented graphically. Figure 4-2 reproduces the demand curve from Figure 4-1. Each step in that demand curve is one book wide and represents one consumer. For example, the height of Aleisha's step is $59, her willingness to pay. This step forms the top of a rectangle, with $30—the price she actually pays for a book—forming the bottom. The area of Aleisha's rectangle, ($59 – $30) × 1 = $29, is her consumer surplus from purchasing one book at $30. So the individual consumer surplus Aleisha gains is the *area of the dark blue rectangle* shown in Figure 4-2.

FIGURE 4-2 Consumer Surplus in the Used-Textbook Market

At a price of $30, Aleisha, Brad, and Claudia each buy a book but Darren and Edwina do not. Aleisha, Brad, and Claudia receive individual consumer surpluses equal to the difference between their willingness to pay and the price, illustrated by the areas of the shaded rectangles. Both Darren and Edwina have a willingness to pay less than $30, so they are unwilling to buy a book in this market; they receive zero consumer surplus. The total consumer surplus is given by the entire shaded area—the sum of the individual consumer surpluses of Aleisha, Brad, and Claudia—equal to $29 + $15 + $5 = $49.

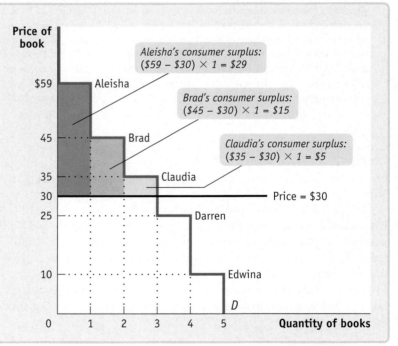

In addition to Aleisha, Brad and Claudia will also each buy a book when the price is $30. Like Aleisha, they benefit from their purchases, though not as much, because they each have a lower willingness to pay. Figure 4-2 also shows the consumer surplus gained by Brad and Claudia; again, this can be measured by the areas of the appropriate rectangles. Darren and Edwina, because they do not buy books at a price of $30, receive no consumer surplus.

The total consumer surplus achieved in this market is just the sum of the individual consumer surpluses received by Aleisha, Brad, and Claudia. So total consumer surplus is equal to the combined area of the three rectangles—

the entire shaded area in Figure 4-2. Another way to say this is that total consumer surplus is equal to the area below the demand curve but above the price.

Figure 4-2 illustrates the following general principle: *The total consumer surplus generated by purchases of a good at a given price is equal to the area below the demand curve but above that price.* The same principle applies regardless of the number of consumers.

When we consider large markets, this graphical representation of consumer surplus becomes extremely helpful. Consider, for example, the sales of iPads to millions of potential buyers. Each potential buyer has a maximum price that he or she is willing to pay. With so many potential buyers, the demand curve will be smooth, like the one shown in Figure 4-3.

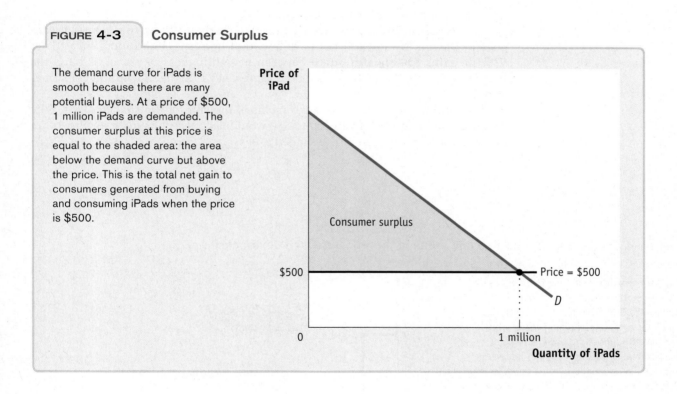

FIGURE 4-3   Consumer Surplus

The demand curve for iPads is smooth because there are many potential buyers. At a price of $500, 1 million iPads are demanded. The consumer surplus at this price is equal to the shaded area: the area below the demand curve but above the price. This is the total net gain to consumers generated from buying and consuming iPads when the price is $500.

Suppose that at a price of $500, a total of 1 million iPads are purchased. How much do consumers gain from being able to buy those 1 million iPads? We could answer that question by calculating the individual consumer surplus of each buyer and then adding these numbers up to arrive at a total. But it is much easier just to look at Figure 4-3 and use the fact that total consumer surplus is equal to the shaded area. As in our original example, consumer surplus is equal to the area below the demand curve but above the price. (To refresh your memory on how to calculate the area of a right triangle, see the appendix to Chapter 2.)

How Changing Prices Affect Consumer Surplus

It is often important to know how much consumer surplus *changes* when the price changes. For example, we may want to know how much consumers are hurt if a flood in cotton-growing areas of Pakistan drives up cotton prices or how much consumers gain if the introduction of fish farming makes salmon steaks less expensive. The same approach we have used to derive consumer surplus can be used to answer questions about how changes in prices affect consumers.

Let's return to the example of the market for used textbooks. Suppose that the bookstore decided to sell used textbooks for $20 instead of $30. How much would this fall in price increase consumer surplus?

The answer is illustrated in Figure 4-4. As shown in the figure, there are two parts to the increase in consumer surplus. The first part, shaded dark blue, is the gain of those who would have bought books even at the higher price of $30. Each of the students who would have bought books at $30—Aleisha, Brad, and Claudia—now pays $10 less, and therefore each gains $10 in consumer surplus from the fall in price to $20. So the dark blue area represents the $10 × 3 = $30 increase in consumer surplus to those three buyers.

The second part, shaded light blue, is the gain to those who would not have bought a book at $30 but are willing to pay more than $20. In this case that gain goes to Darren, who would not have bought a book at $30 but does buy one at $20. He gains $5—the difference between his willingness to pay of $25 and the new price of $20. So the light blue area represents a further $5 gain in consumer surplus.

The total increase in consumer surplus is the sum of the shaded areas, $35. Likewise, a rise in price from $20 to $30 would decrease consumer surplus by an amount equal to the sum of the shaded areas.

FIGURE 4-4 Consumer Surplus and a Fall in the Price of Used Textbooks

There are two parts to the increase in consumer surplus generated by a fall in price from $30 to $20. The first is given by the dark blue rectangle: each person who would have bought at the original price of $30—Aleisha, Brad, and Claudia—receives an increase in consumer surplus equal to the total reduction in price, $10. So the area of the dark blue rectangle corresponds to an amount equal to 3 × $10 = $30. The second part is given by the light blue area: the increase in consumer surplus for those who would not have bought at the original price of $30 but who buy at the new price of $20—namely, Darren. Darren's willingness to pay is $25, so he now receives consumer surplus of $5. The total increase in consumer surplus is (3 × $10) + $5 = $35, represented by the sum of the shaded areas. Likewise, a rise in price from $20 to $30 would decrease consumer surplus by $35, the amount corresponding to the sum of the shaded areas.

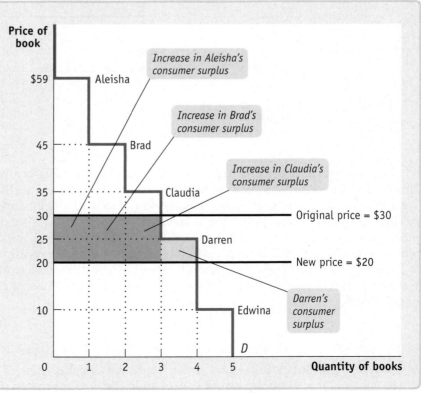

Figure 4-4 illustrates that when the price of a good falls, the area under the demand curve but above the price—which we have seen is equal to total consumer surplus—increases. Figure 4-5 shows the same result for the case of a smooth demand curve, the demand for iPads. Here we assume that the price of iPads falls from $2,000 to $500, leading to an increase in the quantity demanded from 200,000 to 1 million units.

As in the used-textbook example, we divide the gain in consumer surplus into two parts. The dark blue rectangle in Figure 4-5 corresponds to the dark blue area in Figure 4-4: it is the gain to the 200,000 people who would have bought iPads even at the higher price of $2,000. As a result of the price reduction, each receives additional surplus of $1,500. The light blue triangle in Figure 4-5 corresponds to the light blue area in Figure 4-4: it is the gain to people who would not have bought the good at the higher price but are willing to do so at a price of $500. For example, the light blue triangle includes the gain to someone who would have been willing to pay $1,000 for an iPad and therefore gains $500 in consumer surplus when it is possible to buy an iPad for only $500.

As before, the total gain in consumer surplus is the sum of the shaded areas: the increase in the area under the demand curve but above the price.

What would happen if the price of a good were to rise instead of fall? We would do the same analysis in reverse. Suppose, for example, that for some reason the price of iPads rises from $500 to $2,000. This would lead to a fall in consumer surplus, equal to the sum of the shaded areas in Figure 4-5. This loss consists of two parts. The dark blue rectangle represents the loss to consumers who would still buy an iPad, even at a price of $2,000. The light blue triangle represents the loss to consumers who decide not to buy an iPad at the higher price.

FIGURE 4-5 | **A Fall in the Price Increases Consumer Surplus**

A fall in the price of an iPad from $2,000 to $500 leads to an increase in the quantity demanded and an increase in consumer surplus. The change in total consumer surplus is given by the sum of the shaded areas: the total area below the demand curve and between the old and new prices. Here, the dark blue area represents the increase in consumer surplus for the 200,000 consumers who would have bought an iPad at the original price of $2,000; they each receive an increase in consumer surplus of $1,500. The light blue area represents the increase in consumer surplus for those willing to buy at a price equal to or greater than $500 but less than $2,000. Similarly, a rise in the price of an iPad from $500 to $2,000 generates a decrease in consumer surplus equal to the sum of the two shaded areas.

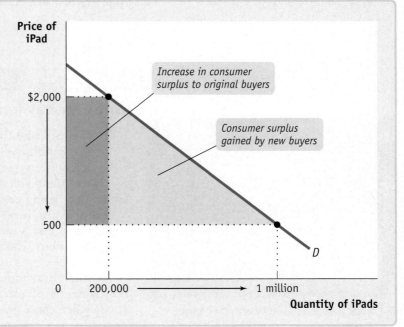

FOR INQUIRING MINDS | A Matter of Life and Death

In 2013, more than 6,500 Americans died because of a shortage of organs for transplant. As of 2014, more than 122,000 were wait-listed. And as you can see from the accompanying figure, the gap between the number of available organs and the number of organs actually donated continues to grow each year. (The difference you see between the number of living donors and the number of actual transplants is accounted for by organs transplanted from deceased patients.)

Since the number of those who need an organ far exceeds availability, what is the best way to allocate the available organs? A market isn't feasible. And for understandable reasons, the sale of human body parts is illegal in this country. So the task for establishing a protocol for these situations has fallen to the nonprofit group United Network for Organ Sharing (UNOS).

Kidney transplants, the most common type of organ transplant, were the focus of attention when UNOS decided to reformulate its protocol for allocating organs to transplant recipients. Under previous guidelines, a donated kidney would go to the person who had been waiting the longest. According to this system, an available kidney would go to a 75-year-old who

has been waiting for 2 years instead of to a 25-year-old who has been waiting for 6 months, even though the 25-year-old is likely to live longer and benefit from the transplanted organ for a longer period of time.

To address this issue, in 2013 UNOS adopted a new set of guidelines based

Organ Donors, Transplants, and Waitlist, 1989-2013

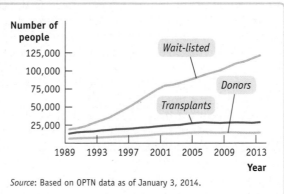

Source: Based on OPTN data as of January 3, 2014.

on a concept it calls "net survival benefit." Kidneys are ranked according to how long they are likely to last; similarly, recipients are ranked according to how long they are likely to live once receiving a transplanted kidney. Then, under the new guidelines, a kidney is matched to the recipient expected to achieve the greatest survival time from that kidney. In other

words, a kidney expected to last many decades will be allocated to a relatively younger person, while older recipients will receive kidneys expected to last a fewer number of years.

By matching the expected life span of a kidney to the expected life span of the recipient following the transplant, the new UNOS guideline tries to avert situations in which (1) a recipient outlives the transplanted kidney, requiring yet another transplant and reducing the number of kidneys available to others; or (2) a kidney significantly outlives its recipient, thereby wasting years of kidney function that could have benefited someone else.

So what does all this have to do with consumer surplus? As you may have guessed, the UNOS concept of "net survival benefit" is a lot like individual consumer surplus—the individual consumer surplus generated from getting a new kidney. In essence, UNOS has devised a system that allocates a kidney according to who gets the greatest individual consumer surplus. This way, the UNOS guidelines attempt to maximize the total consumer surplus from the available pool of kidneys. In terms of results, then, the kidney allocation system under the new UNOS guidelines operates a lot like a competitive market. ■

ECONOMICS ▶ in Action

When Money Isn't Enough

The key insight we get from the concept of consumer surplus is that purchases yield a net benefit to the consumer because the consumer typically pays a price less than his or her willingness to pay for the good. Another way to say this is that the right to buy a good at the going price is a valuable thing in itself.

Most of the time we don't think about the value associated with the right to buy a good. In a market economy, we take it for granted that we can buy whatever we want, as long as we are willing to pay the market price.

But that hasn't always been true. For example, during World War II the demands of wartime production created shortages of consumer goods when these goods were sold at prewar prices. Rather than allow prices to rise, government officials in many countries created a system of rationing. To buy sugar, meat, coffee, gasoline, and many other

For those who purchased WWII ration coupons illegally, the right to consumer surplus had a steep price.

goods, you not only had to pay cash; you also had to present stamps or coupons from books issued to each family by the government. These pieces of paper, which represented the right to buy goods at the government-regulated price, quickly became valuable commodities in themselves.

As a result, illegal markets in meat stamps and gasoline coupons sprang into existence. Moreover, criminals began stealing coupons and even counterfeiting stamps.

The funny thing was that even if you had bought a gasoline coupon on the illegal market, you still had to pay to purchase gasoline. So what you were buying on the illegal market was not the good but the right to buy the good at the government-regulated price. That is, people who bought ration coupons on the illegal market were paying for the right to get some consumer surplus.

Check Your Understanding   4-1

1. Consider the market for cheese-stuffed jalapeno peppers. There are two consumers, Casey and Josey, and their willingness to pay for each pepper is given in the accompanying table. (Neither is willing to consume more than 4 peppers at any price.) Use the table (i) to construct the demand schedule for peppers for prices of $0.00, $0.10, and so on, up to $0.90, and (ii) to calculate the total consumer surplus when the price of a pepper is $0.40.

Quantity of peppers	Casey's willingness to pay	Josey's willingness to pay
1st pepper	$0.90	$0.80
2nd pepper	0.70	0.60
3rd pepper	0.50	0.40
4th pepper	0.30	0.30

Solutions appear at back of book.

Producer Surplus and the Supply Curve

Just as some buyers of a good would have been willing to pay more for their purchase than the price they actually pay, some sellers of a good would have been willing to sell it for less than the price they actually receive. So just as there are consumers who receive consumer surplus from buying in a market, there are producers who receive producer surplus from selling in a market.

Cost and Producer Surplus

Consider a group of students who are potential sellers of used textbooks. Because they have different preferences, the various potential sellers differ in the price at which they are willing to sell their books. The table in Figure 4-6 shows the prices at which several different students would be willing to sell. Andrew is willing to sell the book as long as he can get at least $5; Betty won't sell unless she can get at least $15; Carlos, unless he can get $25; Donna, unless she can get $35; Engelbert, unless he can get $45.

The lowest price at which a potential seller is willing to sell has a special name in economics: it is called the seller's **cost.** So Andrew's cost is $5, Betty's is $15, and so on.

Using the term *cost*, which people normally associate with the monetary cost of producing a good, may sound a little strange when applied to sellers of used textbooks. The students don't have to manufacture the books, so it doesn't cost the student who sells a used textbook anything to make that book available for sale, does it?

Yes, it does. A student who sells a book won't have it later, as part of his or her personal collection. So there is an *opportunity* cost to selling a textbook, even

A seller's **cost** is the lowest price at which he or she is willing to sell a good.

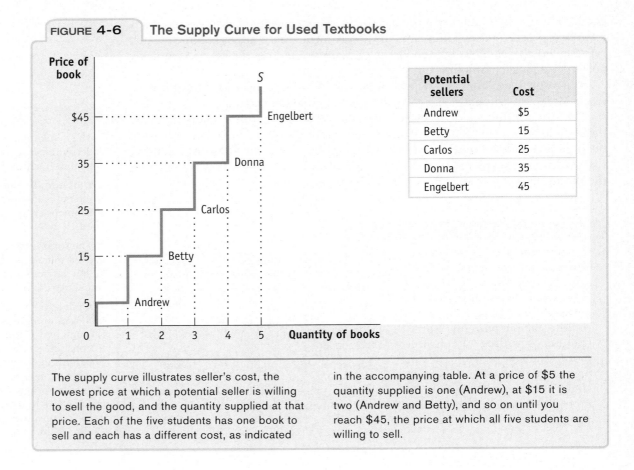

FIGURE **4-6** The Supply Curve for Used Textbooks

Potential sellers	Cost
Andrew	$5
Betty	15
Carlos	25
Donna	35
Engelbert	45

The supply curve illustrates seller's cost, the lowest price at which a potential seller is willing to sell the good, and the quantity supplied at that price. Each of the five students has one book to sell and each has a different cost, as indicated in the accompanying table. At a price of $5 the quantity supplied is one (Andrew), at $15 it is two (Andrew and Betty), and so on until you reach $45, the price at which all five students are willing to sell.

if the owner has completed the course for which it was required. And remember that one of the basic principles of economics is that the true measure of the cost of doing something is always its opportunity cost. That is, the real cost of something is what you must give up to get it.

So it is good economics to talk of the minimum price at which someone will sell a good as the "cost" of selling that good, even if he or she doesn't spend any money to make the good available for sale. Of course, in most real-world markets the sellers are also those who produce the good and therefore *do* spend money to make it available for sale. In this case, the cost of making the good available for sale includes monetary costs, but it may also include other opportunity costs.

Getting back to the example, suppose that Andrew sells his book for $30. Clearly he has gained from the transaction: he would have been willing to sell for only $5, so he has gained $25. This net gain, the difference between the price he actually gets and his cost—the minimum price at which he would have been willing to sell—is known as his **individual producer surplus.**

Just as we derived the demand curve from the willingness to pay of different consumers, we can derive the supply curve from the cost of different producers. The step-shaped curve in Figure 4-6 shows the supply curve implied by the costs shown in the accompanying table. At a price less than $5, none of the students are willing to sell; at a price between $5 and $15, only Andrew is willing to sell, and so on.

As in the case of consumer surplus, we can add the individual producer surpluses of sellers to calculate the **total producer surplus,** the total net gain to all sellers in the market. Economists use the term **producer surplus** to refer to either individual or total producer surplus. Table 4-2 shows the net

Individual producer surplus is the net gain to an individual seller from selling a good. It is equal to the difference between the price received and the seller's cost.

Total producer surplus is the sum of the individual producer surpluses of all the sellers of a good in a market.

Economists use the term **producer surplus** to refer both to individual and to total producer surplus.

TABLE 4-2   Producer Surplus When the Price of a Used Textbook = $30

Potential seller	Cost	Price received	Individual producer surplus = Price received – Cost
Andrew	$5	$30	$25
Betty	15	30	15
Carlos	25	30	5
Donna	35	—	—
Engelbert	45	—	—
All sellers			**Total producer surplus = $45**

gain to each of the students who would sell a used book at a price of $30: $25 for Andrew, $15 for Betty, and $5 for Carlos. The total producer surplus is $25 + $15 + $5 = $45.

As with consumer surplus, the producer surplus gained by those who sell books can be represented graphically. Figure 4-7 reproduces the supply curve from Figure 4-6. Each step in that supply curve is one book wide and represents one seller. The height of Andrew's step is $5, his cost. This forms the bottom of a rectangle, with $30, the price he actually receives for his book, forming the top. The area of this rectangle, ($30 − $5) × 1 = $25, is his producer surplus. So the producer surplus Andrew gains from selling his book is the *area of the red rectangle* shown in the figure.

Let's assume that the campus bookstore is willing to buy all the used copies of this book that students are willing to sell at a price of $30. Then, in addition to Andrew, Betty and Carlos will also sell their books. They will also benefit from their sales, though not as much as Andrew, because they have higher costs. Andrew, as we have seen, gains $25. Betty gains a smaller amount: since her cost is $15, she gains only $15. Carlos gains even less, only $5.

FIGURE 4-7   Producer Surplus in the Used-Textbook Market

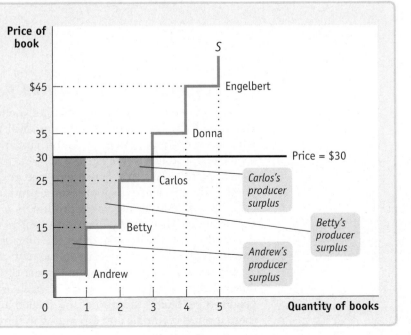

At a price of $30, Andrew, Betty, and Carlos each sell a book but Donna and Engelbert do not. Andrew, Betty, and Carlos get individual producer surpluses equal to the difference between the price and their cost, illustrated here by the shaded rectangles. Donna and Engelbert each have a cost that is greater than the price of $30, so they are unwilling to sell a book and so receive zero producer surplus. The total producer surplus is given by the entire shaded area, the sum of the individual producer surpluses of Andrew, Betty, and Carlos, equal to $25 + $15 + $5 = $45.

Again, as with consumer surplus, we have a general rule for determining the total producer surplus from sales of a good: *The total producer surplus from sales of a good at a given price is the area above the supply curve but below that price.*

This rule applies both to examples like the one shown in Figure 4-7, where there are a small number of producers and a step-shaped supply curve, and to more realistic examples, where there are many producers and the supply curve is smooth.

Consider, for example, the supply of wheat. Figure 4-8 shows how producer surplus depends on the price per bushel. Suppose that, as shown in the figure, the price is $5 per bushel and farmers supply 1 million bushels. What is the benefit to the farmers from selling their wheat at a price of $5? Their producer surplus is equal to the shaded area in the figure—the area above the supply curve but below the price of $5 per bushel.

FIGURE 4-8 | Producer Surplus

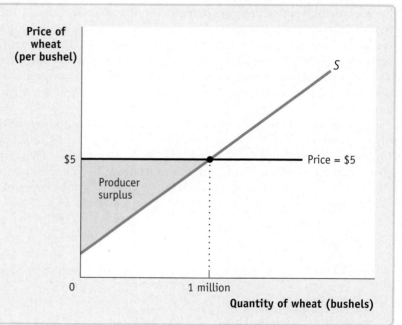

Here is the supply curve for wheat. At a price of $5 per bushel, farmers supply 1 million bushels. The producer surplus at this price is equal to the shaded area: the area above the supply curve but below the price. This is the total gain to producers—farmers in this case—from supplying their product when the price is $5.

How Changing Prices Affect Producer Surplus

As with the case of consumer surplus, a change in price alters producer surplus. But the effects are opposite. While a fall in price increases consumer surplus, it reduces producer surplus. And a rise in price reduces consumer surplus but increases producer surplus.

To see this, let's first consider a rise in the price of the good. Producers of the good will experience an increase in producer surplus, though not all producers gain the same amount. Some producers would have produced the good even at the original price; they will gain the entire price increase on every unit they produce. Other producers will enter the market because of the higher price; they will gain only the difference between the new price and their cost.

Figure 4-9 is the supply counterpart of Figure 4-5. It shows the effect on producer surplus of a rise in the price of wheat from $5 to $7 per bushel. The increase in producer surplus is the sum of the shaded areas, which consists of two parts. First, there is a red rectangle corresponding to the gains to those farmers who would have supplied wheat even at the original $5 price. Second, there is an additional pink

FIGURE **4-9**   A Rise in the Price Increases Producer Surplus

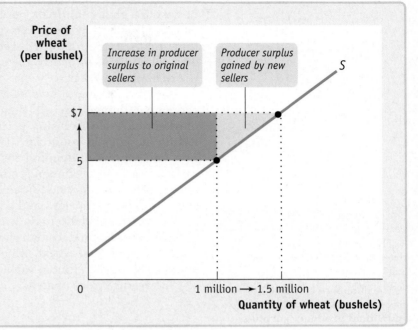

A rise in the price of wheat from $5 to $7 leads to an increase in the quantity supplied and an increase in producer surplus. The change in total producer surplus is given by the sum of the shaded areas: the total area above the supply curve but between the old and new prices. The red area represents the gain to the farmers who would have supplied 1 million bushels at the original price of $5; they each receive an increase in producer surplus of $2 for each of those bushels. The triangular pink area represents the increase in producer surplus achieved by the farmers who supply the additional 500,000 bushels because of the higher price. Similarly, a fall in the price of wheat from $7 to $5 generates a reduction in producer surplus equal to the sum of the shaded areas.

triangle that corresponds to the gains to those farmers who would not have supplied wheat at the original price but are drawn into the market by the higher price.

If the price were to fall from $7 to $5 per bushel, the story would run in reverse. The sum of the shaded areas would now be the decline in producer surplus, the decrease in the area above the supply curve but below the price. The loss would consist of two parts, the loss to farmers who would still grow wheat at a price of $5 (the red rectangle) and the loss to farmers who cease to grow wheat because of the lower price (the pink triangle).

ECONOMICS ▶ in Action

High Times Down on the Farm

The average value of an acre of Iowa farmland hit a record high of $8,716 in 2013, an increase of 5% from the previous year. This followed three years in a row in which prices had increased by more than 15%. Figure 4-10 shows the explosive increase in the price of Iowa farmland from 2009 to 2013. And there was no mystery as to why: it was all about the high prices being paid for corn, wheat, and soybeans. From 2009 to 2013, the price of corn had jumped by 75%, soybeans by 45%, and wheat by 40%.

Why were Iowa farm products commanding such high prices? There are three main reasons: ethanol, rising incomes in countries like China, and poor weather in other foodstuff-producing countries like Australia and Ukraine.

Ethanol—a product made from corn and the same kind of alcohol that's in beer and

FIGURE **4-10**   The Price of Iowa Farmland, 1950–2013

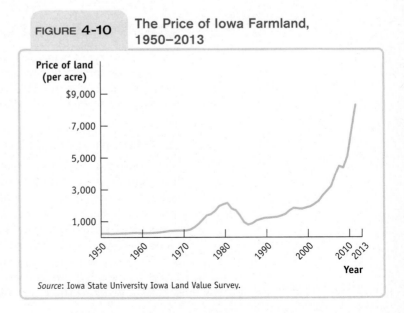

Source: Iowa State University Iowa Land Value Survey.

other alcoholic drinks—can also fuel automobiles. And in recent years government policy, at both the federal and state levels, has encouraged the use of gasoline that contains a percentage of ethanol. There are a couple of reasons for this policy, including some benefits in fighting air pollution and the hope that using ethanol will reduce U.S. dependence on imported oil. Since ethanol comes from corn, the shift to ethanol fuel has led to an increase in the demand for corn.

But Iowa farmers have also benefited greatly from events in the global economy. Changes in the demand for and supply of foodstuffs in world markets have led to rising prices for American corn, wheat, and soybeans. Rising incomes in countries like China have led to increased food consumption and increased demand for these foodstuffs. Simultaneously, very bad weather in food-producing countries like Australia has led to a fall in supply. Predictably, increased demand coupled with reduced supply has led to a surge in foodstuff prices and a windfall for Iowa farmers.

What does this have to do with the price of land? A person who buys a farm in Iowa buys the producer surplus generated by that farm. And higher prices for corn, soybeans, and wheat, which raise the producer surplus of Iowa farmers, make Iowa farmland more valuable. According to an Iowa State University survey, the average price of an acre of Iowa farmland has surged 383% in 10 years.

Check Your Understanding   4-2

1. Consider again the market for cheese-stuffed jalapeno peppers. There are two producers, Cara and Jamie, and their costs of producing each pepper are given in the accompanying table. (Neither is willing to produce more than 4 peppers at any price.) a. Use the

Quantity of peppers	Cara's cost	Jamie's cost
1st pepper	$0.10	$0.30
2nd pepper	0.10	0.50
3rd pepper	0.40	0.70
4th pepper	0.60	0.90

accompanying table to construct the supply schedule for peppers for prices of $0.00, $0.10, and so on, up to $0.90. b. Then, calculate the total producer surplus when the price of a pepper is $0.70.

Solutions appear at back of book.

Consumer Surplus, Producer Surplus, and the Gains from Trade

One of the 12 core principles of economics we introduced in Chapter 1 is that markets are a remarkably effective way to organize economic activity: they generally make society as well off as possible given the available resources. The concepts of consumer surplus and producer surplus can help us deepen our understanding of why this is so.

The Gains from Trade

Let's return to the market in used textbooks but now consider a much bigger market—say, one at a large state university. There are many potential buyers and sellers, so the market is competitive. Let's line up incoming students who are potential buyers of a book in order of their willingness to pay, so that the entering student with the highest willingness to pay is potential buyer number 1, the student with the next highest willingness to pay is number 2, and so on. Then we can use their willingness to pay to derive a demand curve like the one in Figure 4-11.

Similarly, we can line up outgoing students, who are potential sellers of the book, in order of their cost—starting with the student with the lowest cost, then

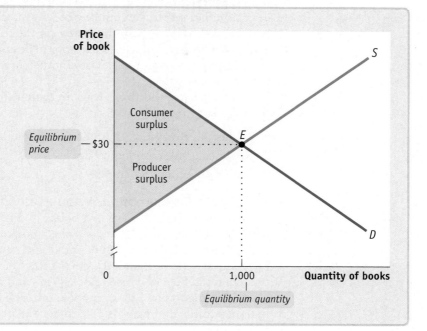

FIGURE 4-11   Total Surplus

In the market for used textbooks, the equilibrium price is $30 and the equilibrium quantity is 1,000 books. Consumer surplus is given by the blue area, the area below the demand curve but above the price. Producer surplus is given by the red area, the area above the supply curve but below the price. The sum of the blue and the red areas is total surplus, the total benefit to society from the production and consumption of the good.

the student with the next lowest cost, and so on—to derive a supply curve like the one shown in the same figure.

As we have drawn the curves, the market reaches equilibrium at a price of $30 per book, and 1,000 books are bought and sold at that price. The two shaded triangles show the consumer surplus (blue) and the producer surplus (red) generated by this market. The sum of consumer and producer surplus is known as the **total surplus** generated in a market.

The striking thing about this picture is that both consumers and producers gain—that is, both consumers and producers are better off because there is a market in this good. But this should come as no surprise—it illustrates another core principle of economics: *There are gains from trade.* These gains from trade are the reason everyone is better off participating in a market economy than they would be if each individual tried to be self-sufficient.

But are we as well off as we could be? This brings us to the question of the efficiency of markets.

The Efficiency of Markets

Markets produce gains from trade, but in Chapter 1 we made an even bigger claim: that markets are usually *efficient*. That is, we claimed that once the market has produced its gains from trade, there is no way to make some people better off without making other people worse off, except under some well-defined conditions.

The analysis of consumer and producer surplus helps us understand why markets are usually efficient. To gain more intuition into why this is so, consider the fact that market equilibrium is just *one* way of deciding who consumes the good and who sells the good. There are other possible ways of making that decision.

Consider, for example, the case of kidney transplants, discussed earlier in For Inquiring Minds, in which a decision must be made about who receives one. It is not possible to use a market to decide because in this situation, human organs are involved. Instead, in the past, kidneys were allocated according to a recipient's wait time—a very inefficient method. It has since been replaced with a new system created by the United Network for Organ Sharing, or UNOS, based on "net

The **total surplus** generated in a market is the total net gain to consumers and producers from trading in the market. It is the sum of the producer and the consumer surplus.

survival benefit," a concept an awful lot like consumer surplus that, although not a market system, succeeds in reproducing the efficiency of one.

To further our understanding of why markets usually work so well, imagine a committee charged with improving on the market equilibrium by deciding who gets and who gives up a used textbook. The committee's ultimate goal is to bypass the market outcome and devise another arrangement, one that would produce higher total surplus.

Let's consider the three ways in which the committee might try to increase the total surplus:

1. Reallocate consumption among consumers
2. Reallocate sales among sellers
3. Change the quantity traded

Reallocate Consumption Among Consumers The committee might try to increase total surplus by selling books to different consumers. Figure 4-12 shows why this will result in lower surplus compared to the market equilibrium outcome. Here we have smooth demand and supply curves because there are many buyers and sellers. Points *A* and *B* show the positions on the demand curve of two potential buyers of used books, Ana and Bob. As we can see from the figure, Ana is willing to pay $35 for a book, but Bob is willing to pay only $25. Since the market equilibrium price is $30, under the market outcome Ana buys a book and Bob does not.

Now suppose the committee reallocates consumption. This would mean taking the book away from Ana and giving it to Bob. Since the book is worth $35 to Ana but only $25 to Bob, this change *reduces total consumer surplus* by $35 − $25 = $10. Moreover, this result doesn't depend on which two students we pick. Every student who buys a book at the market equilibrium has a willingness to pay of $30 or more, and every student who doesn't buy a book has a willingness to pay of less than $30.

So reallocating the good among consumers always means taking a book away from a student who values it more and giving it to one who values it less. This necessarily reduces total consumer surplus.

FIGURE 4-12 | **Reallocating Consumption Lowers Consumer Surplus**

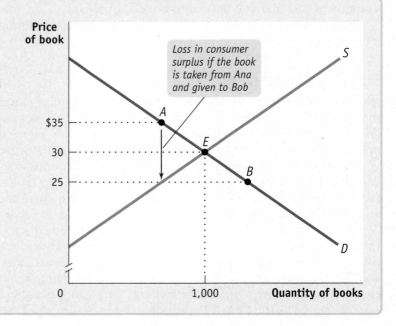

Ana (point *A*) has a willingness to pay of $35. Bob (point *B*) has a willingness to pay of only $25. At the market equilibrium price of $30, Ana purchases a book but Bob does not. If we rearrange consumption by taking a book from Ana and giving it to Bob, consumer surplus declines by $10 and, as a result, total surplus declines by $10.

Reallocate Sales Among Sellers The committee might try to increase total surplus by altering who sells their books, taking sales away from sellers who would have sold their books at the market equilibrium and instead compelling those who would not have sold their books at the market equilibrium to sell them.

Figure 4-13 shows why this will result in lower surplus. Here points X and Y show the positions on the supply curve of Xavier, who has a cost of $25, and Yvonne, who has a cost of $35. At the equilibrium market price of $30, Xavier would sell his book but Yvonne would not sell hers. If the committee reallocated sales, forcing Xavier to keep his book and Yvonne to sell hers, total producer surplus would be reduced by $35 − $25 = $10.

Again, it doesn't matter which two students we choose. Any student who sells a book at the market equilibrium has a lower cost than any student who keeps a book. So reallocating sales among sellers necessarily increases total cost and reduces total producer surplus.

Change the Quantity Traded The committee might try to increase total surplus by compelling students to trade either more books or fewer books than the market equilibrium quantity.

Figure 4-14 shows why this will result in lower surplus. It shows all four students: potential buyers Ana and Bob, and potential sellers Xavier and Yvonne. To reduce sales, the committee will have to prevent a transaction that would have occurred in the market equilibrium—that is, prevent Xavier from selling to Ana. Since Ana is willing to pay $35 and Xavier's cost is $25, preventing this transaction reduces total surplus by $35 − $25 = $10.

Once again, this result doesn't depend on which two students we pick: any student who would have sold the book at the market equilibrium has a cost of $30 or less, and any student who would have purchased the book at the market equilibrium has a willingness to pay of $30 or more. So preventing any sale that would have occurred in the market equilibrium necessarily reduces total surplus.

FIGURE 4-13   Reallocating Sales Lowers Producer Surplus

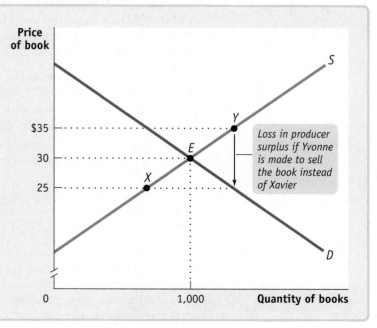

Yvonne (point Y) has a cost of $35, $10 more than Xavier (point X), who has a cost of $25. At the market equilibrium price of $30, Xavier sells a book but Yvonne does not. If we rearrange sales by preventing Xavier from selling his book and compelling Yvonne to sell hers, producer surplus declines by $10 and, as a result, total surplus declines by $10.

FIGURE 4-14 Changing the Quantity Lowers Total Surplus

If Xavier (point *X*) were prevented from selling his book to someone like Ana (point *A*), total surplus would fall by $10, the difference between Ana's willingness to pay ($35) and Xavier's cost ($25). This means that total surplus falls whenever fewer than 1,000 books—the equilibrium quantity—are transacted. Likewise, if Yvonne (point *Y*) were compelled to sell her book to someone like Bob (point *B*), total surplus would also fall by $10, the difference between Yvonne's cost ($35) and Bob's willingness to pay ($25). This means that total surplus falls whenever more than 1,000 books are transacted. These two examples show that at market equilibrium, all mutually beneficial transactions—and only mutually beneficial transactions—occur.

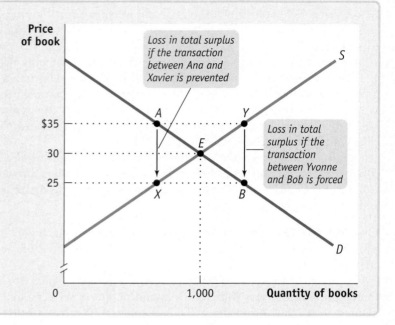

Finally, the committee might try to increase sales by forcing Yvonne, who would not have sold her book at the market equilibrium, to sell it to someone like Bob, who would not have bought a book at the market equilibrium. Because Yvonne's cost is $35, but Bob is only willing to pay $25, this transaction reduces total surplus by $10. And once again it doesn't matter which two students we pick—anyone who wouldn't have bought the book has a willingness to pay of less than $30, and anyone who wouldn't have sold has a cost of more than $30.

The key point to remember is that once this market is in equilibrium, there is no way to increase the gains from trade. Any other outcome reduces total surplus. (This is why the United Network for Organ Sharing, or UNOS, is trying, with its new guidelines based on "net survival benefit," to reproduce the allocation of donated kidneys that would occur if there were a competitive market for the organs.) We can summarize our results by stating that an efficient market performs four important functions:

1. It allocates consumption of the good to the potential buyers who most value it, as indicated by the fact that they have the highest willingness to pay.

2. It allocates sales to the potential sellers who most value the right to sell the good, as indicated by the fact that they have the lowest cost.

3. It ensures that every consumer who makes a purchase values the good more than every seller who makes a sale, so that all transactions are mutually beneficial.

4. It ensures that every potential buyer who doesn't make a purchase values the good less than every potential seller who doesn't make a sale, so that no mutually beneficial transactions are missed.

As a result of these four functions, *any way of allocating the good other than the market equilibrium outcome lowers total surplus.*

There are three caveats, however. First, although a market may be efficient, it isn't necessarily *fair*. In fact, fairness, or *equity*, is often in conflict with efficiency. We'll discuss this next.

The second caveat is that markets sometimes *fail*. As we mentioned in Chapter 1, under some well-defined conditions, markets can fail to deliver efficiency. When this occurs, markets no longer maximize total surplus. We provide a brief overview of why markets fail at the end of this chapter, reserving a more detailed analysis for later chapters.

Third, even when the market equilibrium maximizes total surplus, this does not mean that it results in the best outcome for every *individual* consumer and producer. Other things equal, each buyer would like to pay a lower price and each seller would like to receive a higher price. So if the government were to intervene in the market—say, by lowering the price below the equilibrium price to make consumers happy or by raising the price above the equilibrium price to make producers happy—the outcome would no longer be efficient. Although some people would be happier, total surplus would be lower.

Equity and Efficiency

For many patients who need kidney transplants, the new UNOS guidelines, covered earlier, were unwelcome news. Unsurprisingly, those who have been waiting years for a transplant have found the guidelines, which give precedence to younger patients, . . . well . . . unfair. And the guidelines raise other questions about fairness: Why limit potential transplant recipients to Americans? Why include younger patients with other chronic diseases? Why not give precedence to those who have made recognized contributions to society? And so on.

Efficiency is about the best way to achieve a goal, like extending the life spans of kidney transplant recipients.

The point is that efficiency is about *how to achieve goals, not what those goals should be.* For example, UNOS decided that its goal is to maximize the life span of kidney recipients. Some might have argued for a different goal, and efficiency does not address which goal is the best. *What efficiency does address is the best way to achieve a goal once it has been determined*—in this case, using the UNOS concept of "net survival benefit."

It's easy to get carried away with the idea that markets are always right and that economic policies that interfere with efficiency are bad. But that would be misguided because there is another factor to consider: society cares about equity, or what's "fair."

As we discussed in Chapter 1, there is often a trade-off between equity and efficiency: policies that promote equity often come at the cost of decreased efficiency, and policies that promote efficiency often result in decreased equity. So it's important to realize that a society's choice to sacrifice some efficiency for the sake of equity, however it defines equity, is a valid one. And it's important to understand that fairness, unlike efficiency, can be very hard to define. Fairness is a concept about which well-intentioned people often disagree.

ECONOMICS ▶ in Action

Take The Keys, Please

"Airbnb was really born from a math problem," said its co-founder, Joe Gebbia. "We quit our jobs to be entrepreneurs, and the landlord raised our rent beyond our means. And so we had a math problem to solve. It just so happened that that coming weekend, a design conference came to San Francisco that just wiped out the hotels in the city. We connected the dots. We had extra space in our apartment. So thus was born the air bed-and-breakfast."

From that bout of desperation-induced ingenuity sprang a company that now connects more than half a million listings in more than 34,000 cities

Owners use marketplaces like AirBnb to turn unused resources into cash.

and 192 countries available for shortterm rentals. Airbnb is the most famous and successful purveyor in what is now often called "the sharing economy": companies that provide a marketplace in which people can share the use of goods. And there are many others: Relay-Rides and Getaround let you rent cars from their owners, Boatbound facilitates boat rentals, Desktime office space, ParkAtMyHouse parking spaces. SnapGoods allows people to borrow consumer goods like power tools from others in their neighborhood or social network.

What's motivating all this sharing? Well, it isn't an outbreak of altruism—it's plain dollars and cents. If there are unused resources sitting around, why not make money by renting them to someone else? As Judith Chevalier, a Yale School of Management economist, says, "These companies let you wring a little bit of value out of . . . goods that are just sitting there." And generating a bit more surplus from your possessions leads to a more efficient use of those resources. Why now? Clearly, because of the ease by which people can be matched online. As a result, says Arun Sundararajan, a professor at the NYU Stern School of Business, "That makes it possible for people to rethink the way they consume."

Quick Review

- **Total surplus** measures the gains from trade in a market.

- Markets are efficient except under some well-defined conditions. We can demonstrate the efficiency of a market by considering what happens to total surplus if we start from the equilibrium and reallocate consumption, reallocate sales, or change the quantity traded. Any outcome other than the market equilibrium reduces total surplus, which means that the market equilibrium is efficient.

- Because society cares about equity, government intervention in a market that reduces efficiency while increasing equity can be justified.

Check Your Understanding 4-3

1. Using the tables in Check Your Understanding 4-1 and 4-2, find the equilibrium price and quantity in the market for cheese-stuffed jalapeno peppers. What is total surplus in the equilibrium in this market, and who receives it?

2. Show how each of the following three actions reduces total surplus:

   a. Having Josey consume one fewer pepper, and Casey one more pepper, than in the market equilibrium

   b. Having Cara produce one fewer pepper, and Jamie one more pepper, than in the market equilibrium

   c. Having Josey consume one fewer pepper, and Cara produce one fewer pepper, than in the market equilibrium

3. Suppose UNOS decides to further alter its guidelines for the allocation of donated kidneys, no longer relying solely on the concept of "net survival benefit" but also giving preference to patients with small children. If "total surplus" in this case is defined to be the total life span of kidney recipients, is this new guideline likely to reduce, increase, or leave total surplus unchanged? How might you justify this new guideline?

Solutions appear at back of book.

A Market Economy

As we learned earlier, in a market economy decisions about production and consumption are made via markets. In fact, the economy as a whole is made up of many *interrelated markets*. Up until now, to learn how markets work, we've been examining a single market—the market for used textbooks. But in reality, consumers and producers do not make decisions in isolated markets. For example, a student's decision in the market for used textbooks might be affected by how much interest must be paid on a student loan; thus, the decision in the used textbook market would be influenced by what is going on in the market for money.

We know that an efficient market equilibrium maximizes total surplus—the gains to buyers and sellers in that market. Is there a comparable result for an economy as a whole, an economy composed of a vast number of individual markets? The answer is yes, but with qualifications.

When each and every market in the economy maximizes total surplus, then the economy as a whole is efficient. This is a very important result: just as it is impossible to make someone better off without making other people worse off in a single market when it is efficient, the same is true when each and every market in that economy is efficient. However, it is important to realize that this is a *theoretical* result: it is virtually impossible to find an economy in which every market is efficient.

For now, let's examine why markets and market economies typically work so well. Once we understand why, we can then briefly address why markets sometimes get it wrong.

Why Markets Typically Work So Well

Economists have written volumes about why markets are an effective way to organize an economy. In the end, well-functioning markets owe their effectiveness to two powerful features: *property rights* and the role of prices as *economic signals*.

By **property rights** we mean a system in which valuable items in the economy have specific owners who can dispose of them as they choose. In a system of property rights, by purchasing a good you receive "ownership rights": the right to use and dispose of the good as you see fit. Property rights are what make the mutually beneficial transactions in the used-textbook market, or any market, possible.

To see why property rights are crucial, imagine that students do not have full property rights in their textbooks and are prohibited from reselling them when the semester ends. This restriction on property rights would prevent many mutually beneficial transactions. Some students would be stuck with textbooks they will never reread when they would be much happier receiving some cash instead. Other students would be forced to pay full price for brand-new books when they would be happier getting slightly battered copies at a lower price.

Once a system of well-defined property rights is in place, the second necessary feature of well-functioning markets—prices as economic signals—can operate. An **economic signal** is any piece of information that helps people and businesses make better economic decisions. For example, business forecasters say that sales of cardboard boxes are a good early indicator of changes in industrial production: if businesses are buying lots of cardboard boxes, you can be sure that they will soon increase their production.

But prices are far and away the most important signals in a market economy, because they convey essential information about other people's costs and their willingness to pay. If the equilibrium price of used books is $30, this in effect tells everyone both that there are consumers willing to pay $30 and up and that there are potential sellers with a cost of $30 or less. The signal given by the market price ensures that total surplus is maximized by telling people whether to buy books, sell books, or do nothing at all.

Each potential seller with a cost of $30 or less learns from the market price that it's a good idea to sell her book; if she has a higher cost, it's a good idea to keep it. Likewise, each consumer willing to pay $30 or more learns from the market price that it's a good idea to buy a book; if he is unwilling to pay $30, then it's a good idea not to buy a book.

This example shows that the market price "signals" to consumers with a willingness to pay equal to or more than the market price that they should buy the good, just as it signals to producers with a cost equal to or less than the market price that they should sell the good. And since, in equilibrium, the quantity demanded equals the quantity supplied, all willing consumers will find willing sellers.

Property rights are the rights of owners of valuable items, whether resources or goods, to dispose of those items as they choose.

An **economic signal** is any piece of information that helps people make better economic decisions.

Price is the most important economic signal in a market economy.

A market or an economy is **inefficient** if there are missed opportunities: some people could be made better off without making other people worse off.

Market failure occurs when a market fails to be efficient.

Prices can sometimes fail as economic signals. Sometimes a price is not an accurate indicator of how desirable a good is. When there is uncertainty about the quality of a good, price alone may not be an accurate indicator of the value of the good. For example, you can't infer from the price alone whether a used car is good or a "lemon." In fact, a well-known problem in economics is "the market for lemons," a market in which prices don't work well as economic signals.

A Few Words of Caution

As we've seen, markets are an amazingly effective way to organize economic activity. But as we've noted, markets can sometimes get it wrong. We first learned about this in Chapter 1 in our fifth principle of interaction: *When markets don't achieve efficiency, government intervention can improve society's welfare.*

When markets are **inefficient,** there are missed opportunities—ways in which production or consumption can be rearranged that would make some people better off without making other people worse off. In other words, there are gains from trade that go unrealized: total surplus could be increased. And when a market or markets are inefficient, the economy in which they are embedded is also inefficient.

Markets can be rendered inefficient for a number of reasons. Two of the most important are a lack of property rights and inaccuracy of prices as economic signals. When a market is inefficient, we have what is known as **market failure.** We will examine various types of market failure in later chapters. For now, let's review the three main ways in which markets sometimes fall short of efficiency.

1. Markets can fail when, in an attempt to capture more surplus, one party prevents mutually beneficial trades from occurring. This situation arises, for instance, when a market contains only a single seller of a good, known as a *monopolist.* In this case, the assumption we have relied on in supply and demand analysis—that no individual buyer or seller can have a noticeable effect on the market price—is no longer valid; the monopolist can determine the market price. As we'll see in Chapter 13, this gives rise to inefficiency as a monopolist manipulates the market price in order to increase profits, thereby preventing mutually beneficial trades from occurring.

2. Actions of individuals sometimes have side effects on the welfare of others that markets don't take into account. In economics, these side effects are known as *externalities,* and the best-known example is pollution. We can think of the problem of pollution as a problem of incomplete property rights; for example, existing property rights don't guarantee a right to ownership of clean air. We'll see in Chapter 16 that pollution and other externalities also give rise to inefficiency.

3. Markets for some goods fail because these goods, by their very nature, are unsuited for efficient management by markets. In Chapter 20, we will analyze goods that fall into this category because of problems of *private information*—information about a good that some people possess but others don't. For example, the seller of a used car that is a "lemon" may have information that is unknown to potential buyers.

In Chapter 17, we will encounter other types of goods that fall into the category of being unsuited for efficient management by markets—*public goods, common resources,* and *artificially scarce goods.* Markets for these goods fail because of problems in limiting people's access to and consumption of the good; examples are fish in the sea and trees in the Amazonian rain forest. In these instances, markets generally fail due to incomplete property rights.

But even with these limitations, it's remarkable how well markets work at maximizing the gains from trade.

ECONOMICS ▶ in Action

A Great Leap—Backward

Economies in which a central planner, rather than markets, makes consumption and production decisions are known as *planned economies*. Russia (formerly part of the U.S.S.R.), many Eastern European countries, and several Southeast Asian countries once had planned economies, and countries such as India and Brazil once had significant parts of their economies under central planning. China still does today.

Planned economies are notorious for their inefficiency, and what is probably the most compelling example of that is the so-called Great Leap Forward, an ambitious economic plan instituted in China during the late 1950s by its leader Mao Zedong. Its intention was to speed up the country's industrialization. Key to this plan was a shift from urban to rural manufacturing: farming villages were supposed to start producing heavy industrial goods such as steel.

Unfortunately, the plan backfired. Diverting farmers from their usual work led to a sharp fall in food production. Meanwhile, because raw materials for steel, such as coal and iron ore, were sent to ill-equipped and inexperienced rural producers rather than to urban factories, industrial output declined as well. The plan, in short, led to a fall in the production of everything in China.

Because China was a very poor country to start with, the results were catastrophic. The famine that followed is estimated to have reduced China's population by as much as 30 million.

China has recently moved closer to a free-market system, allowing for greater economic growth, increased wealth, and the emergence of a middle class. But some aspects of central planning remain, largely in the allocation of financial capital and other inputs to politically connected businesses. As a result, significant inefficiencies persist. Many economists have commented that these inefficiencies must be addressed if China is to sustain its rapid growth and Chinese consumers are to enjoy the efficient level of consumer surplus.

Although some aspects of central planning remain, China's economy has moved closer to a free-market system.

Check Your Understanding   4-4

1. In some states that are rich in natural resources, such as oil, the law separates the right to above-ground use of the land from the right to drill below ground (called "mineral rights"). Someone who owns both the above-ground rights and the mineral rights can sell the two rights separately. Explain how this division of the property rights enhances efficiency compared to a situation in which the two rights must always be sold together.

2. Suppose that in the market for used textbooks the equilibrium price is $30, but it is mistakenly announced that the equilibrium price is $300. How does this affect the efficiency of the market? Be specific.

3. What is wrong with the following statement? "Markets are always the best way to organize economic activity. Any policies that interfere with markets reduce society's welfare."

Solutions appear at back of book.

▼ Quick Review

- In a market economy, markets are interrelated. When each and every market in an economy is efficient, the economy as a whole is efficient. But in the real world, some markets in a market economy will almost certainly fail to be efficient.

- A system of **property rights** and the operation of prices as **economic signals** are two key factors that enable a market to be efficient. But under conditions in which property rights are incomplete or prices give inaccurate economic signals, markets can fail.

- Under certain conditions, **market failure** occurs and the market is **inefficient**: gains from trade are unrealized. The three principal ways in which markets fail are the prevention of mutually beneficial transactions caused by one party's attempt to capture more surplus, side effects that aren't properly accounted for, and problems in the nature of the goods themselves.

StubHub Shows Up The Boss

Splash News/Newscom

Back in 1965, long before Ticketmaster, StubHub, and TicketsNow, legendary rock music promoter Bill Graham noticed that mass parties erupted wherever local rock groups played. Graham realized that fans would pay for the experience of the concert, in addition to paying for a recording of the music. He went on to create the business of rock concert promoting—booking and managing multicity tours for bands and selling lots of tickets. Those tickets were carefully rationed, a single purchaser allowed to buy only a limited number. Fans would line up at box offices, sometimes camping out the night before for popular bands.

Wanting to maintain the aura of the 1960s that made rock concerts accessible to all their fans, many top bands choose to price their tickets below the market equilibrium level. For example, in 2012 Bruce Springsteen sold tickets at his concerts in New Jersey (his home state and home to his most ardent fans) for between $68 and $98. Tickets for Springsteen concerts could have sold for far more: economists Alan Krueger and Marie Connolly analyzed a 2002 Springsteen concert for which every ticket sold for $75 and concluded that The Boss forfeited about $4 million by not charging the market price, about $280. He likely forfeited much more surplus in 2012 as ticket prices soared to over $6,000 online at various resale sites.

So what was The Boss thinking? Cheap tickets can ensure that a concert sells out, making it a better experience for both band and audience. But it is believed that other factors are at work—that cheap tickets are a way for a band to reward fans' loyalty as well as a means to seem more "authentic" and less commercial. As Bruce Springsteen has said, "In some fashion, I help people hold on to their own humanity—if I'm doing my job right."

But the rise of the internet has complicated matters. Now, rather than queue for tickets at the venue, fans buy tickets online, either from a direct seller like Ticketmaster (which obtains tickets directly from the concert producer) or a reseller like StubHub or TicketsNow. Resellers (otherwise known as scalpers) can—and do—make lots of money by scooping up large numbers of tickets at the box office price and reselling them at the market price. StubHub currently dominates what has become a $5 billion resale market for tickets.

This practice has infuriated fans as well as bands. But resellers have cast the issue as one of the freedom to dispose of one's ticket as one chooses. Since ticket reselling comes under the purview of state laws, the two sides have been lobbying furiously to get an advantage. And as of 2014, there is a hodgepodge of state laws governing ticket reselling. Many states, such as Alaska, impose no restrictions on reselling. In contrast, Michigan forbids ticket reselling without permission from the event's sponsor. In general, the trend at the state level has been to allow ticket reselling as long as consumers are adequately protected against fraud.

QUESTIONS FOR THOUGHT

1. Use the concepts of consumer surplus and producer surplus to analyze the exchange between The Boss and his fans. Draw a diagram to illustrate.

2. Explain how the rise of the internet has disrupted this exchange.

3. Draw a diagram to show the effect of resellers on the allocation of consumer surplus and producer surplus in the market for concert tickets. What are the implications of the internet for all such exchanges?

SUMMARY

1. The **willingness to pay** of each individual consumer determines the demand curve. When price is less than or equal to the willingness to pay, the potential consumer purchases the good. The difference between willingness to pay and price is the net gain to the consumer, the **individual consumer surplus.**

2. **Total consumer surplus** in a market, the sum of all individual consumer surpluses in a market, is equal to the area below the market demand curve but above the price. A rise in the price of a good reduces consumer surplus; a fall in the price increases consumer surplus. The term **consumer surplus** is often used to refer to both individual and total consumer surplus.

3. The **cost** of each potential producer, the lowest price at which he or she is willing to supply a unit of a particular good, determines the supply curve. If the price of a good is above a producer's cost, a sale generates a net gain to the producer, known as the **individual producer surplus.**

4. **Total producer surplus** in a market, the sum of the individual producer surpluses in a market, is equal to the area above the market supply curve but below the price. A rise in the price of a good increases producer surplus; a fall in the price reduces producer surplus. The term **producer surplus** is often used to refer to both individual and total producer surplus.

5. **Total surplus,** the total gain to society from the production and consumption of a good, is the sum of consumer and producer surplus.

6. Usually markets are efficient and achieve the maximum total surplus. Any possible reallocation of consumption or sales, or a change in the quantity bought and sold, reduces total surplus. However, society also cares about equity. So government intervention in a market that reduces efficiency but increases equity can be a valid choice by society.

7. An economy composed of efficient markets is also efficient, although this is virtually impossible to achieve in reality. The keys to the efficiency of a market economy are **property rights** and the operation of prices as **economic signals.** Under certain conditions, **market failure** occurs, making a market **inefficient.** Three principal sources of market failure are attempts to capture more surplus that create inefficiencies, side effects of some transactions, and problems in the nature of the good.

KEY TERMS

Willingness to pay, p. 104
Individual consumer surplus, p. 105
Total consumer surplus, p. 106
Consumer surplus, p. 106
Cost, p. 111

Individual producer surplus, p. 112
Total producer surplus, p. 112
Producer surplus, p. 112
Total surplus, p. 117
Property rights, p. 123

Economic signal, p. 123
Inefficient, p. 124
Market failure, p. 124

PROBLEMS

1. Determine the amount of consumer surplus generated in each of the following situations.

   a. Leon goes to the clothing store to buy a new T-shirt, for which he is willing to pay up to $10. He picks out one he likes with a price tag of exactly $10. When he is paying for it, he learns that the T-shirt has been discounted by 50%.

   b. Alberto goes to the music store hoping to find a used copy of *Nirvana's Nevermind* for up to $30. The store has one copy of the record selling for $30, which he purchases.

   c. After soccer practice, Stacey is willing to pay $2 for a bottle of mineral water. The 7-Eleven sells mineral water for $2.25 per bottle, so she declines to purchase it.

2. Determine the amount of producer surplus generated in each of the following situations.

   a. Gordon lists his old Lionel electric trains on eBay. He sets a minimum acceptable price, known as his reserve price, of $75. After five days of bidding, the final high bid is exactly $75. He accepts the bid.

   b. So-Hee advertises her car for sale in the used-car section of the student newspaper for $2,000, but she is willing to sell the car for any price higher than $1,500. The best offer she gets is $1,200, which she declines.

   c. Sanjay likes his job so much that he would be willing to do it for free. However, his annual salary is $80,000.

3. There are six potential consumers of computer games, each willing to buy only one game. Consumer 1 is willing to pay $40 for a computer game, consumer 2 is willing to pay $35, consumer 3 is willing to pay $30, consumer 4 is willing to pay $25, consumer 5 is willing to pay $20, and consumer 6 is willing to pay $15.

   a. Suppose the market price is $29. What is the total consumer surplus?

   b. The market price decreases to $19. What is the total consumer surplus now?

   c. When the price falls from $29 to $19, how much does each consumer's individual consumer surplus change? How does total consumer surplus change?

4. a. In an auction, potential buyers compete for a good by submitting bids. Adam Galinsky, a social psychologist at Northwestern University, compared eBay auctions in which the same good was sold. He found that, on average, the larger the number of bidders, the higher the sales price. For example, in two auctions of identical iPods, the one with the larger number of bidders brought a higher selling price. According to Galinsky, this explains why smart sellers on eBay set absurdly low opening prices (the lowest price that the seller will accept), such as 1 cent for a new iPod. Use the concepts of consumer and producer surplus to explain Galinsky's reasoning.

   b. You are considering selling your vintage 1969 convertible Volkswagen Beetle. If the car is in good condition, it is worth a lot; if it is in poor condition, it is useful only as scrap. Assume that your car is in excellent condition but that it costs a potential buyer $500 for an inspection to learn the car's condition. Use what you learned in part a to explain whether or not you should pay for an inspection and share the results with all interested buyers.

5. Assume that due to an increase in demand, the average domestic airline fare increased from $319.85 in the fourth quarter of 2013 to $328.12 in the first quarter of 2014, an increase of $8.27. The number of passenger tickets sold in the fourth quarter of 2013 was 151.4 million. Over the same period, the airlines' costs remained roughly the same: the price of jet fuel averaged around $2 per gallon in both quarters, and airline pilots' salaries remained roughly the same, averaging $117,060 per year in 2013).

   Can you determine precisely by how much producer surplus has increased as a result of the $8.27 increase in the average fare? If you cannot be precise, can you determine whether it will be less than, or more than, a specific amount?

6. The accompanying table shows the supply and demand schedules for used copies of the third edition of this textbook. The supply schedule is derived from offers at Amazon.com. The demand schedule is hypothetical.

Price of book	Quantity of books demanded	Quantity of books supplied
$55	50	0
60	35	1
65	25	3
70	17	3
75	14	6
80	12	9
85	10	10
90	8	18
95	6	22
100	4	31
105	2	37
110	0	42

   a. Calculate consumer and producer surplus at the equilibrium in this market.

   b. Now the fourth edition of this textbook becomes available. As a result, the willingness to pay of each potential buyer for a second-hand copy of the third edition falls by $20. In a table, show the new demand schedule and again calculate consumer and producer surplus at the new equilibrium.

7. On Thursday nights, a local restaurant has a pasta special. Ari likes the restaurant's pasta, and his willingness to pay for each serving is shown in the accompanying table.

Quantity of pasta (servings)	Willingness to pay for pasta (per serving)
1	$10
2	8
3	6
4	4
5	2
6	0

   a. If the price of a serving of pasta is $4, how many servings will Ari buy? How much consumer surplus does he receive?

   b. The following week, Ari is back at the restaurant again, but now the price of a serving of pasta is $6. By how much does his consumer surplus decrease compared to the previous week?

c. One week later, he goes to the restaurant again. He discovers that the restaurant is offering an "all-you-can-eat" special for $25. How much pasta will Ari eat, and how much consumer surplus does he receive now?

d. Suppose you own the restaurant and Ari is a typical customer. What is the highest price you can charge for the "all-you-can-eat" special and still attract customers?

8. You are the manager of Fun World, a small amusement park. The accompanying diagram shows the demand curve of a typical customer at Fun World.

a. Suppose that the price of each ride is $5. At that price, how much consumer surplus does an individual consumer get? (Recall that the area of a right triangle is 1/2 × the height of the triangle × the base of the triangle.)

b. Suppose that Fun World considers charging an admission fee, even though it maintains the price of each ride at $5. What is the maximum admission fee it could charge? (Assume that all potential customers have enough money to pay the fee.)

c. Suppose that Fun World lowered the price of each ride to zero. How much consumer surplus does an individual consumer get? What is the maximum admission fee Fun World could charge?

9. The accompanying diagram illustrates a taxi driver's individual supply curve (assume that each taxi ride is the same distance).

a. Suppose the city sets the price of taxi rides at $4 per ride, and at $4 the taxi driver is able to sell as many taxi rides as he desires. What is this taxi driver's producer surplus? (Recall that the area of a right triangle is 1/2 × the height of the triangle × the base of the triangle.)

b. Suppose that the city keeps the price of a taxi ride set at $4, but it decides to charge taxi drivers a "licensing fee." What is the maximum licensing fee the city could extract from this taxi driver?

c. Suppose that the city allowed the price of taxi rides to increase to $8 per ride. Again assume that, at this price, the taxi driver sells as many rides as he is willing to offer. How much producer surplus does an individual taxi driver now get? What is the maximum licensing fee the city could charge this taxi driver?

10. In 2010, a New York district judge ruled in a copyright infringement lawsuit against the popular file-sharing website LimeWire and in favor of the 13 major record companies that had brought the lawsuit. The record companies, including Sony, Virgin, and Warner Brothers, had alleged that the file-sharing service encourages users to make illegal copies of copyrighted material. Allowing internet users to obtain music for free limits the record companies' right to dispose of the music as they choose; in particular, it limits their right to give access to their music only to those who have paid for it. In other words, it limits the record companies' property rights.

a. If everyone obtained music and video content for free from websites such as LimeWire, instead of paying the record companies, what would the record companies' producer surplus be from music sales? What are the implications for record companies' incentive to produce music content in the future?

b. If the record companies had lost the lawsuit and music could be freely downloaded from the internet, what do you think would happen to mutually beneficial transactions (the producing and buying of music) in the future?

WORK IT OUT

For interactive, step-by-step help in solving the following problem, visit LaunchPad by using the URL on the back cover of this book.

11. Hollywood screenwriters negotiate a new agreement with movie producers stipulating that they will receive 10% of the revenue from every video rental of a movie they authored. They have no such agreement for movies shown on on-demand television.

a. When the new writers' agreement comes into effect, what will happen in the market for video rentals—that is, will supply or demand shift, and how? As a result, how will consumer surplus in the market for video rentals change? Illustrate with a diagram. Do you think the writers' agreement will be popular with consumers who rent videos?

b. Consumers consider video rentals and on-demand movies substitutable to some extent. When the new writers' agreement comes into effect, what will happen in the market for on-demand movies—that is, will supply or demand shift, and how? As a result, how will producer surplus in the market for on-demand movies change? Illustrate with a diagram. Do you think the writers' agreement will be popular with cable television companies that show on-demand movies?

Price Controls and Quotas: Meddling with Markets

⏵ **What You Will Learn in This Chapter**

▪ The meaning of **price controls** and **quantity controls,** two kinds of government intervention in markets

▪ How price and quantity controls create problems and can make a market inefficient

▪ What **deadweight loss** is

▪ Why the predictable side effects of intervention in markets often lead economists to be skeptical of its usefulness

▪ Who benefits and who loses from market interventions, and why they are used despite their well-known problems

BIG CITY, NOT-SO-BRIGHT IDEAS

©UpperCut Images/Alamy

New York City: an empty taxi is hard to find.

NEW YORK CITY IS A PLACE where you can find almost anything—that is, anything, except a taxicab when you need one or a decent apartment at a rent you can afford. You might think that New York's notorious shortages of cabs and apartments are the inevitable price of big-city living. However, they are largely the product of government policies—specifically, of government policies that have, one way or another, tried to prevail over the market forces of supply and demand.

In Chapter 3, we learned the principle that a market moves to equilibrium—that the market price rises or falls to the level at which the quantity of a good that people are willing to supply is equal to the quantity that other people demand.

But sometimes governments try to defy that principle. Whenever a government tries to dictate either a market price or a market quantity that's different from the equilibrium price or quantity, the market strikes back in predictable ways. Our ability to predict what will happen when governments try to defy supply and demand shows the power and usefulness of supply and demand analysis itself.

The shortages of apartments and taxicabs in New York are two examples that illuminate what happens when the logic of the market is defied.

New York's housing shortage is the result of *rent control,* a law that prevents landlords from raising rents except when specifically given permission. Rent control was introduced during World War II to protect the interests of tenants, and it still remains in force. Many other American cities have had rent control at one time or another, but with the notable exceptions of New York and San Francisco, these controls have largely been done away with.

Similarly, New York's limited supply of taxis is the result of a licensing system introduced in the 1930s. New York taxi licenses are known as "medallions," and only taxis with medallions are allowed to pick up passengers. Although this system was originally intended to protect the interests of both drivers and customers, it has generated a shortage of taxis in the city. The number of medallions remained fixed for nearly 60 years, with no significant increase until 2004 and only a trickle since.

In this chapter, we begin by examining what happens when governments try to control prices in a competitive market, keeping the price in a market either below its equilibrium level—a *price ceiling* such as rent control—or above it—a *price floor* such as the minimum wage paid to workers in many countries. We then turn to schemes such as taxi medallions that attempt to dictate the quantity of a good bought and sold.

Price controls are legal restrictions on how high or low a market price may go. They can take two forms: a **price ceiling,** a maximum price sellers are allowed to charge for a good or service, or a **price floor,** a minimum price buyers are required to pay for a good or service.

Why Governments Control Prices

You learned in Chapter 3 that a market moves to equilibrium—that is, the market price moves to the level at which the quantity supplied equals the quantity demanded. But this equilibrium price does not necessarily please either buyers or sellers.

After all, buyers would always like to pay less if they could, and sometimes they can make a strong moral or political case that they should pay lower prices. For example, what if the equilibrium between supply and demand for apartments in a major city leads to rental rates that an average working person can't afford? In that case, a government might well be under pressure to impose limits on the rents landlords can charge.

Sellers, however, would always like to get more money for what they sell, and sometimes they can make a strong moral or political case that they should receive higher prices. For example, consider the labor market: the price for an hour of a worker's time is the wage rate. What if the equilibrium between supply and demand for less skilled workers leads to wage rates that yield an income below the poverty level? In that case, a government might well be pressured to require employers to pay a rate no lower than some specified minimum wage.

In other words, there is often a strong political demand for governments to intervene in markets. And powerful interests can make a compelling case that a market intervention favoring them is "fair." When a government intervenes to regulate prices, we say that it imposes **price controls.** These controls typically take the form either of an upper limit, a **price ceiling,** or a lower limit, a **price floor.**

Unfortunately, it's not that easy to tell a market what to do. As we will now see, when a government tries to legislate prices—whether it legislates them down by imposing a price ceiling or up by imposing a price floor—there are certain predictable and unpleasant side effects.

We make an important assumption in this chapter: the markets in question are efficient before price controls are imposed. But markets can sometimes be inefficient—for example, a market dominated by a monopolist, a single seller that has the power to influence the market price. When markets are inefficient, price controls don't necessarily cause problems and can potentially move the market closer to efficiency.

In practice, however, price controls are often imposed on efficient markets—like the New York apartment market. And so the analysis in this chapter applies to many important real-world situations.

Price Ceilings

Aside from rent control, there are not many price ceilings in the United States today. But at times they have been widespread. Price ceilings are typically imposed during crises—wars, harvest failures, natural disasters—because these events often lead to sudden price increases that hurt many people but produce big gains for a lucky few.

The U.S. government imposed ceilings on many prices during World War II: the war sharply increased demand for raw materials, such as aluminum and steel, and price controls prevented those with access to these raw materials from earning huge profits. Price controls on oil were imposed in 1973, when an embargo by Arab oil-exporting countries seemed likely to generate huge profits for U.S. oil companies. Price controls were instituted again in 2012 by New York and New Jersey authorities in the aftermath of Hurricane Sandy, as gas shortages led to rampant price-gouging.

Rent control in New York is, believe it or not, a legacy of World War II: it was imposed because wartime production produced an economic boom, which increased demand for apartments at a time when the labor and raw materials that might have been used to build them were being used to win the war instead. Although most price controls were removed soon after the war ended, New York's rent limits were retained and gradually extended to buildings not previously covered, leading to some very strange situations.

You can rent a one-bedroom apartment in Manhattan on fairly short notice— if you are able and willing to pay several thousand dollars a month and live in a less desirable area. Yet some people pay only a small fraction of this for comparable apartments, and others pay hardly more for bigger apartments in better locations.

Aside from producing great deals for some renters, however, what are the broader consequences of New York's rent-control system? To answer this question, we turn to the model we developed in Chapter 3: the supply and demand model.

Modeling a Price Ceiling

To see what can go wrong when a government imposes a price ceiling on an efficient market, consider Figure 5-1, which shows a simplified model of the market for apartments in New York. For the sake of simplicity, we imagine that all apartments are exactly the same and so would rent for the same price in an unregulated market.

The table in Figure 5-1 shows the demand and supply schedules; the demand and supply curves are shown on the left. We show the quantity of apartments on the horizontal axis and the monthly rent per apartment on the vertical axis. You can see that in an unregulated market the equilibrium would be at point E: 2 million apartments would be rented for $1,000 each per month.

Now suppose that the government imposes a price ceiling, limiting rents to a price below the equilibrium price—say, no more than $800.

FIGURE 5-1   The Market for Apartments in the Absence of Price Controls

Monthly rent (per apartment)	Quantity of apartments (millions)	
	Quantity demanded	Quantity supplied
$1,400	1.6	2.4
1,300	1.7	2.3
1,200	1.8	2.2
1,100	1.9	2.1
1,000	2.0	2.0
900	2.1	1.9
800	2.2	1.8
700	2.3	1.7
600	2.4	1.6

Without government intervention, the market for apartments reaches equilibrium at point E with a market rent of $1,000 per month and 2 million apartments rented.

FIGURE **5-2**   The Effects of a Price Ceiling

The black horizontal line represents the government-imposed price ceiling on rents of $800 per month. This price ceiling reduces the quantity of apartments supplied to 1.8 million, point *A*, and increases the quantity demanded to 2.2 million, point *B*. This creates a persistent shortage of 400,000 units: 400,000 people who want apartments at the legal rent of $800 but cannot get them.

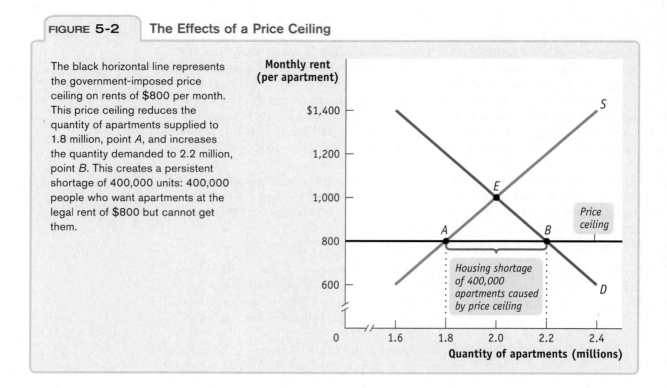

Figure 5-2 shows the effect of the price ceiling, represented by the line at $800. At the enforced rental rate of $800, landlords have less incentive to offer apartments, so they won't be willing to supply as many as they would at the equilibrium rate of $1,000. They will choose point *A* on the supply curve, offering only 1.8 million apartments for rent, 200,000 fewer than in the unregulated market.

At the same time, more people will want to rent apartments at a price of $800 than at the equilibrium price of $1,000; as shown at point *B* on the demand curve, at a monthly rent of $800 the quantity of apartments demanded rises to 2.2 million, 200,000 more than in the unregulated market and 400,000 more than are actually available at the price of $800. So there is now a persistent shortage of rental housing: at that price, 400,000 more people want to rent than are able to find apartments.

Do price ceilings always cause shortages? No. If a price ceiling is set above the equilibrium price, it won't have any effect. Suppose that the equilibrium rental rate on apartments is $1,000 per month and the city government sets a ceiling of $1,200. Who cares? In this case, the price ceiling won't be *binding*—it won't actually constrain market behavior—and it will have no effect.

How a Price Ceiling Causes Inefficiency

The housing shortage shown in Figure 5-2 is not merely annoying: like any shortage induced by price controls, it can be seriously harmful because it leads to inefficiency. In other words, there are gains from trade that go unrealized.

Rent control, like all price ceilings, creates inefficiency in at least four distinct ways.

1. It reduces the quantity of apartments rented below the efficient level.

2. It typically leads to inefficient allocation of apartments among would-be renters.

3. It leads to wasted time and effort as people search for apartments.

4. It leads landlords to maintain apartments in inefficiently low quality or condition.

In addition to inefficiency, price ceilings give rise to illegal behavior as people try to circumvent them. We'll now look at each of these inefficiencies caused by price ceilings.

Inefficiently Low Quantity In Chapter 4 we learned that the market equilibrium of an efficient market leads to the "right" quantity of a good or service being bought and sold—that is, the quantity that maximizes the sum of producer and consumer surplus. Because rent controls reduce the number of apartments supplied, they reduce the number of apartments rented, too.

Figure 5-3 shows the implications for total surplus. Recall that total surplus is the sum of the area above the supply curve and below the demand curve. If the only effect of rent control was to reduce the number of apartments available, it would cause a loss of surplus equal to the area of the shaded triangle in the figure.

The area represented by that triangle has a special name in economics, **deadweight loss:** the lost surplus associated with the transactions that no longer occur due to the market intervention. In this example, the deadweight loss is the lost surplus associated with the apartment rentals that no longer occur due to the price ceiling, a loss that is experienced by both disappointed renters and frustrated landlords. Economists often call triangles like the one in Figure 5-3 a *deadweight-loss triangle.*

Deadweight loss is a key concept in economics, one that we will encounter whenever an action or a policy leads to a reduction in the quantity transacted below the efficient market equilibrium quantity. It is important to realize that deadweight loss is a *loss to society*—it is a reduction in total surplus, a loss in surplus that accrues to no one as a gain. It is not the same as a loss in surplus to one person that then accrues as a gain to someone else, what an economist would call a *transfer* of surplus from one person to another. For an example of how a price ceiling can create deadweight loss as well as a transfer of surplus between renters and landlords, see the upcoming For Inquiring Minds.

Deadweight loss is not the only type of inefficiency that arises from a price ceiling. The types of inefficiency created by rent control go beyond reducing the quantity of apartments available. These additional inefficiencies—inefficient allocation to consumers, wasted resources, and inefficiently low quality—lead to a loss of surplus over and above the deadweight loss.

> **Deadweight loss** is the loss in total surplus that occurs whenever an action or a policy reduces the quantity transacted below the efficient market equilibrium quantity.

FIGURE **5-3**   **A Price Ceiling Causes Inefficiently Low Quantity**

A price ceiling reduces the quantity supplied below the market equilibrium quantity, leading to a deadweight loss. The area of the shaded triangle corresponds to the amount of total surplus lost due to the inefficiently low quantity transacted.

FOR INQUIRING MINDS | Winners, Losers, and Rent Control

Price controls create winners and losers: some people benefit from the policy but others are made worse off.

In New York City, some of the biggest beneficiaries of rent control are affluent tenants who have lived for decades in choice apartments that would now command very high rents. These winners include celebrities like actor Al Pacino and the singer and songwriter Cyndi Lauper. Similarly, in 2014, there were stories in the news citing the cases of rent-controlled tenants who also own million-dollar-plus properties in places like Palm Beach or Geneva. Ironically, in cases like these, the losers are the working-class renters the system was intended to help.

We can use the concepts of consumer and producer surplus, which you learned about in Chapter 4, to graphically evaluate the winners and the losers from rent control. Panel (a) of Figure 5-4 shows the consumer surplus and producer surplus

in the equilibrium of the unregulated market for apartments—before rent control. Recall that the consumer surplus, represented by the area below the demand curve and above the price, is the total net gain to consumers in the market equilibrium. Likewise, producer surplus, represented by the area above the supply curve and below the price, is the total net gain to producers in the market equilibrium.

Panel (b) of this figure shows the consumer and producer surplus in the market after the price ceiling of $800 has been imposed. As you can see, for consumers who can still obtain apartments under rent control, consumer surplus has increased. These renters are clearly winners: they obtain an apartment at $800, paying $200 less than the unregulated market price. These people receive a direct transfer of surplus from landlords in the form of lower rent. But not all renters win: there are fewer apartments to rent now

than if the market had remained unregulated, making it hard, if not impossible, for some to find a place to call home.

Without direct calculation of the surpluses gained and lost, it is generally unclear whether renters as a whole are made better or worse off by rent control. What we can say is that the greater the deadweight loss—the larger the reduction in the quantity of apartments rented—the more likely it is that renters as a whole lose.

However, we can say unambiguously that landlords are worse off: producer surplus has clearly decreased. Landlords who continue to rent out their apartments get $200 a month less in rent, and others withdraw their apartments from the market altogether. The deadweight-loss triangle, shaded yellow in panel (b), represents the value lost to both renters and landlords from rentals that essentially vanish thanks to rent control.

FIGURE **5-4**   Winners and Losers from Rent Control

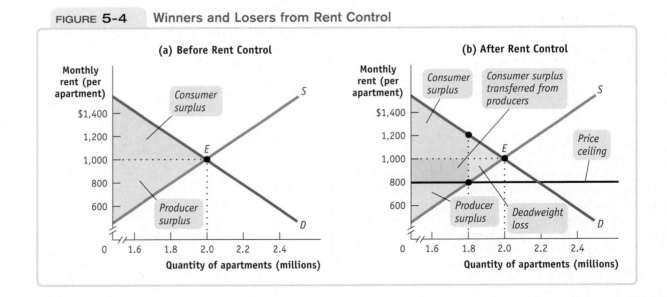

Inefficient Allocation to Consumers Rent control doesn't just lead to too few apartments being available. It can also lead to misallocation of the apartments that are available: people who badly need a place to live may not be able to find an apartment, but some apartments may be occupied by people with much less urgent needs.

In the case shown in Figure 5-2, 2.2 million people would like to rent an apartment at $800 per month, but only 1.8 million apartments are available. Of those 2.2 million who are seeking an apartment, some want one badly and are willing to pay a high price to get it. Others have a less urgent need and are only willing to pay a low price, perhaps because they have alternative housing.

An efficient allocation of apartments would reflect these differences: people who really want an apartment will get one and people who aren't all that anxious to find an apartment won't. In an inefficient distribution of apartments, the opposite will happen: some people who are not especially anxious to find an apartment will get one and others who are very anxious to find an apartment won't.

Because people usually get apartments through luck or personal connections under rent control, it generally results in an **inefficient allocation to consumers** of the few apartments available.

To see the inefficiency involved, consider the plight of the Lees, a family with young children who have no alternative housing and would be willing to pay up to $1,500 for an apartment—but are unable to find one. Also consider George, a retiree who lives most of the year in Florida but still has a lease on the New York apartment he moved into 40 years ago. George pays $800 per month for this apartment, but if the rent were even slightly more—say, $850—he would give it up and stay with his children when he visits New York.

This allocation of apartments—George has one and the Lees do not—is a missed opportunity: there is a way to make the Lees and George both better off at no additional cost. The Lees would be happy to pay George, say, $1,200 a month to sublease his apartment, which he would happily accept since the apartment is worth no more than $849 a month to him. George would prefer the money he gets from the Lees to keeping his apartment; the Lees would prefer to have the apartment rather than the money. So both would be made better off by this transaction—and nobody else would be made worse off.

Generally, if people who really want apartments could sublease them from people who are less eager to live there, both those who gain apartments and those who trade their occupancy for money would be better off. However, subletting is illegal under rent control because it would occur at prices above the price ceiling.

The fact that subletting is illegal doesn't mean it never happens. In fact, chasing down illegal subletting is a major business for New York private investigators. An article in the *New York Times* described how private investigators use hidden cameras and other tricks to prove that the legal tenants in rent-controlled apartments actually live somewhere else, and have sublet their apartments at two or three times the controlled rent.

This subletting is a kind of illegal activity, which we will discuss shortly. For now, just note that landlords and legal agencies actively discourage the practice. As a result, the problem of inefficient allocation of apartments remains.

Wasted Resources Another reason a price ceiling causes inefficiency is that it leads to **wasted resources:** people expend money, effort, and time to cope with the shortages caused by the price ceiling. Back in 1979, U.S. price controls on gasoline led to shortages that forced millions of Americans to wait on lines at gas stations for hours each week. The opportunity cost of the time spent in gas lines—the wages not earned, the leisure time not enjoyed—constituted wasted resources from the point of view of consumers and of the economy as a whole.

Because of rent control, the Lees will spend all their spare time for several months searching for an apartment, time they would rather have spent working or in family activities. That is, there is an opportunity cost to the Lees' prolonged search for an apartment—the leisure or income they had to forgo.

Price ceilings often lead to inefficiency in the form of **inefficient allocation to consumers:** some people who want the good badly and are willing to pay a high price don't get it, and some who care relatively little about the good and are only willing to pay a low price do get it.

Price ceilings typically lead to inefficiency in the form of **wasted resources:** people expend money, effort, and time to cope with the shortages caused by the price ceiling.

Price ceilings often lead to inefficiency in that the goods being offered are of **inefficiently low quality:** sellers offer low-quality goods at a low price even though buyers would prefer a higher quality at a higher price.

If the market for apartments worked freely, the Lees would quickly find an apartment at the equilibrium rent of $1,000, leaving them time to earn more or to enjoy themselves—an outcome that would make them better off without making anyone else worse off. Again, rent control creates missed opportunities.

Inefficiently Low Quality Yet another way a price ceiling creates inefficiency is by causing goods to be of inefficiently low quality. **Inefficiently low quality** means that sellers offer low-quality goods at a low price even though buyers would rather have higher quality and would be willing to pay a higher price for it.

Again, consider rent control. Landlords have no incentive to provide better conditions because they cannot raise rents to cover their repair costs but are able to find tenants easily. In many cases, tenants would be willing to pay much more for improved conditions than it would cost for the landlord to provide them—for example, the upgrade of an antiquated electrical system that cannot safely run air conditioners or computers. But any additional payment for such improvements would be legally considered a rent increase, which is prohibited.

FOR INQUIRING MINDS | Mumbai's Rent-Control Millionaires

Just how costly is rent control for landlords? In Mumbai, India, the answer is very high indeed. It is so high that thousands of rent-controlled tenants have become millionaires upon vacating their apartments.

In Mumbai, a magnet for a rapidly expanding number of high-income Indians, property prices rose by almost 70% in four years, from 2009 to 2013. According to real estate developer Pujit Agarwal, the highly desirable area of South Mumbai, hugging the Arabian Sea, is home to about 500 severely dilapidated stone structures which, once redeveloped, would be worth about $40 billion. But landlords and real estate developers have to address the fact that those dilapidated structures are occupied by rent-controlled tenants.

Take the case of Mea Kadwani, age 78, who had been living since he was a toddler in the same 2,600-square-foot apartment where he paid just $20 a month in an area where rents typically top $2,000 per month. His unit was so dilapidated that his roof collapsed. But he stayed put, which turned out to be a profitable decision: after three years of negotiations with the landlord, he was paid $2.5 million to vacate the apartment. As Agarwal says, "For generations, most tenants were living a hand-to-mouth existence, barely making two ends

meet. Now, with redevelopment, these tenants have become multimillionaires overnight as capital values of the properties they occupied soared." According to him, it is still a good deal for landlords, as newly constructed five-bedroom apartments are selling for $12.5 million.

But not all rent-controlled tenants agree to leave. In one famous story, three

In Mumbai, soaring property values have made multimillionaires of some, although many more Indians live in slums.

people were killed when four floors of a rent-controlled apartment building collapsed. Despite demands by the city to vacate the damaged building, 58 tenants camped out, refusing to go even though they were locked out of their apartments, and were subjects of a police raid.

Rent control began in Mumbai in 1947 to address a crucial shortage of housing caused by a flood of refugees fleeing conflict between Hindus and Muslims. Clearly intended as a temporary measure, it was so popular politically that it has been extended 20 times and now applies to about 60% of the buildings in the city's center. Tenants pass apartments on to heirs or sell the right to occupy to others. Landlords, who often are paying more in taxes and upkeep than they receive in rents, suffer financially and sometimes simply abandon their properties.

So although it's a world away, the dynamics of rent control in Mumbai are similar to those in New York where many rent-controlled tenants have also extracted tens of thousands of dollars from landlords eager to redevelop their properties (although the situation in Mumbai has been much more extreme).

So common is the experience in New York and other cities that it was the subject of a *Law and Order* episode in which a landlord is investigated for the murder of a rent-controlled tenant who had been blocking the lucrative sale of the building. Fortunately, we were unable to find evidence to suggest that this episode was based on a true story. ■

Indeed, rent-controlled apartments are notoriously badly maintained, rarely painted, subject to frequent electrical and plumbing problems, sometimes even hazardous to inhabit. As one former manager of Manhattan buildings described: "At unregulated apartments we'd do most things that the tenants requested. But on the rent-regulated units, we did absolutely only what the law required. . . . We had a perverse incentive to make those tenants unhappy."

This whole situation is a missed opportunity—some tenants would be happy to pay for better conditions, and landlords would be happy to provide them for payment. But such an exchange would occur only if the market were allowed to operate freely.

Black Markets In addition to these four inefficiencies there is a final aspect of price ceilings: the incentive they provide for illegal activities, specifically the emergence of **black markets.** We have already described one kind of black market activity—illegal subletting by tenants. But it does not stop there. Clearly, there is a temptation for a landlord to say to a potential tenant, "Look, you can have the place if you slip me an extra few hundred in cash each month"—and for the tenant to agree if he or she is one of those people who would be willing to pay much more than the maximum legal rent.

What's wrong with black markets? In general, it's a bad thing if people break any law, because it encourages disrespect for the law in general. Worse yet, in this case illegal activity worsens the position of those who are honest. If the Lees are scrupulous about upholding the rent-control law but other people—who may need an apartment less than the Lees—are willing to bribe landlords, the Lees may never find an apartment.

> A **black market** is a market in which goods or services are bought and sold illegally—either because it is illegal to sell them at all or because the prices charged are legally prohibited by a price ceiling.

So Why Are There Price Ceilings?

We have seen three common results of price ceilings:

- A persistent shortage of the good
- Inefficiency arising from this persistent shortage in the form of inefficiently low quantity (deadweight loss), inefficient allocation of the good to consumers, resources wasted in searching for the good, and the inefficiently low quality of the good offered for sale
- The emergence of illegal, black market activity

Given these unpleasant consequences of price ceilings, why do governments still sometimes impose them? Why does rent control, in particular, persist in New York?

One answer is that although price ceilings may have adverse effects, they do benefit some people. In practice, New York's rent-control rules—which are more complex than our simple model—hurt most residents but give a small minority of renters much cheaper housing than they would get in an unregulated market. And those who benefit from the controls are typically better organized and more vocal than those who are harmed by them.

Also, when price ceilings have been in effect for a long time, buyers may not have a realistic idea of what would happen without them. In our previous example, the rental rate in an unregulated market (Figure 5-1) would be only 25% higher than in the regulated market (Figure 5-2): $1,000 instead of $800. But how would renters know that? Indeed, they might have heard about black market transactions at much higher prices—the Lees or some other family paying George $1,200 or more—and would not realize that these black market prices are much higher than the price that would prevail in a fully unregulated market.

A last answer is that government officials often do not understand supply and demand analysis! It is a great mistake to suppose that economic policies in the real world are always sensible or well informed.

ECONOMICS ▶ *in Action*

Price Controls in Venezuela: "You Buy What They Have"

By all accounts, Venezuela is a rich country—one of the world's top oil producers in a time of high energy prices. But in late 2013, the chronic lack of basic items—toilet paper, rice, coffee, corn, flour, milk, meat—had hit a nerve. "Empty shelves and no one to explain why a rich country has no food. It's unacceptable," said Jesús López, a 90-year-old farmer.

The origins of Venezuela's food shortages can be traced to the policies put in place by former Venezuelan president Hugo Chávez and continued by his successor, Nicolás Maduro. Chávez came to power in 1998 on a platform denouncing the country's economic elite and promising policies that favored the poor and working class, including price controls on basic foodstuffs. These price controls led to shortages that began in 2003 and became severe by 2006. Prices were set so low that farmers reduced production. For example, Venezuela was a coffee exporter until 2009 when it was forced to import large amounts of coffee to make up for a steep fall in production. Venezuela now imports more than 70% of its food.

In addition, generous government programs for the poor and working class led to higher demand. The combination of price controls and higher demand led to sharply rising prices for goods that weren't subject to price controls or that were bought on the black market. The result was a big increase in the demand for price-controlled goods.

Worse yet, a sharp decline in the value of the Venezuelan currency made foreign imports more expensive. And it increased the incentives for smuggling: when goods are available at the government-mandated price, Venezuelans buy them and then resell across the border in Colombia, where a bottle of milk is worth seven or eight times more. Not surprisingly, fresh milk and butter are rarely seen in Venezuelan markets.

Venezuelans, queuing for hours to purchase goods at state-run stores, often come away empty handed. Or, as one shopper, Katherine Huga, said, "Whatever I can get. You buy what they have." While items can often be found on the black market at much higher prices, Chávez's price-control policies have disproportionately hurt the lower- and middle-income consumers he sought to help. One shopper in a low-income area who waited in line for hours said, "It fills me with rage to have to spend the one free day I have wasting my time for a bag of rice. I end up paying more at the resellers. In the end, all these price controls proved useless."

Venezuela's food shortages offer a lesson in why price ceilings, however well intentioned, are usually never a good idea.

▼ Quick Review

• **Price controls** take the form of either legal maximum prices—**price ceilings**—or legal minimum prices—**price floors.**

• A price ceiling below the equilibrium price benefits successful buyers but causes predictable adverse effects such as persistent shortages, which lead to four types of inefficiencies: **deadweight loss, inefficient allocation to consumers, wasted resources,** and **inefficiently low quality.**

• A deadweight loss is a loss of total surplus that occurs whenever a policy or action reduces the quantity transacted below the efficient market equilibrium level.

• Price ceilings also lead to **black markets,** as buyers and sellers attempt to evade the price controls.

Check Your Understanding   5-1

1. On game days, homeowners near Middletown University's stadium used to rent parking spaces in their driveways to fans at a going rate of $11. A new town ordinance now sets a maximum parking fee of $7. Use the accompanying supply and demand diagram to explain how each of the following corresponds to a price-ceiling concept.

   a. Some homeowners now think it's not worth the hassle to rent out spaces.

   b. Some fans who used to carpool to the game now drive alone.

   c. Some fans can't find parking and leave without seeing the game.

Explain how each of the following adverse effects arises from the price ceiling.

   d. Some fans now arrive several hours early to find parking.

   e. Friends of homeowners near the stadium regularly attend games, even if they aren't big fans. But some serious fans have given up because of the parking situation.

f. Some homeowners rent spaces for more than $7 but pretend that the buyers are nonpaying friends or family.

2. True or false? Explain your answer. A price ceiling below the equilibrium price of an otherwise efficient market does the following:

   a. Increases quantity supplied

   b. Makes some people who want to consume the good worse off

   c. Makes all producers worse off

3. Which of the following create deadweight loss? Which do not and are simply a transfer of surplus from one person to another? Explain your answer.

   a. You have been evicted from your rent-controlled apartment after the landlord discovered your pet boa constrictor. The apartment is quickly rented to someone else at the same price. You and the new renter do not necessarily have the same willingness to pay for the apartment.

   b. In a contest, you won a ticket to a jazz concert. But you can't go to the concert because of an exam, and the terms of the contest do not allow you to sell the ticket or give it to someone else. Would your answer to this question change if you could not sell the ticket but could give it to someone else?

   c. Your school's dean of students, who is a proponent of a low-fat diet, decrees that ice cream can no longer be served on campus.

   d. Your ice-cream cone falls on the ground and your dog eats it. (Take the liberty of counting your dog as a member of society, and assume that, if he could, your dog would be willing to pay the same amount for the ice-cream cone as you.)

Solutions appear at back of book.

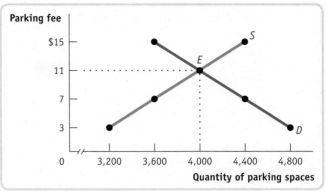

Price Floors

Sometimes governments intervene to push market prices up instead of down. *Price floors* have been widely legislated for agricultural products, such as wheat and milk, as a way to support the incomes of farmers. Historically, there were also price floors—legally mandated minimum prices—on such services as trucking and air travel, although these were phased out by the U.S. government in the 1970s.

If you have ever worked in a fast-food restaurant, you are likely to have encountered a price floor: governments in the United States and many other countries maintain a lower limit on the hourly wage rate of a worker's labor; that is, a floor on the price of labor called the **minimum wage.**

Just like price ceilings, price floors are intended to help some people but generate predictable and undesirable side effects. Figure 5-5 shows hypothetical supply and demand curves for butter. Left to itself, the market would move to equilibrium at point *E*, with 10 million pounds of butter bought and sold at a price of $1 per pound.

Now suppose that the government, in order to help dairy farmers, imposes a price floor on butter of $1.20 per pound. Its effects are shown in Figure 5-6, where the line at $1.20 represents the price floor. At a price of $1.20 per pound, producers would want to supply 12 million pounds (point *B* on the supply curve) but consumers would want to buy only 9 million pounds (point *A* on the demand curve). So the price floor leads to a persistent surplus of 3 million pounds of butter.

Does a price floor always lead to an unwanted surplus? No. Just as in the case of a price ceiling, the floor may not be binding—that is, it may be irrelevant. If the equilibrium price of butter is $1 per pound but the floor is set at only $0.80, the floor has no effect.

But suppose that a price floor is binding: what happens to the unwanted surplus? The answer depends on government policy. In the case of agricultural

> The **minimum wage** is a legal floor on the wage rate, which is the market price of labor.

FIGURE 5-5 The Market for Butter in the Absence of Government Controls

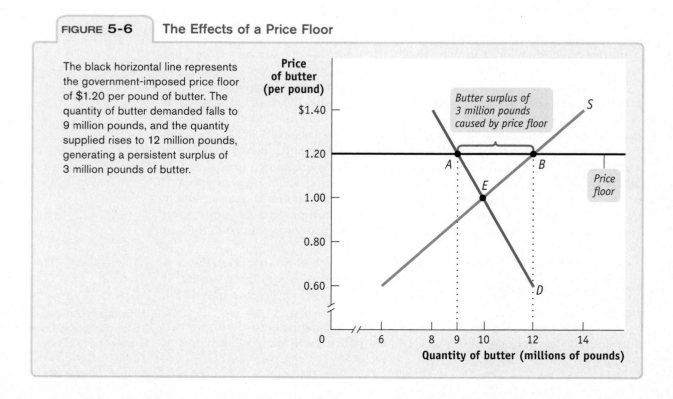

Price of butter (per pound)	Quantity of butter (millions of pounds)	
	Quantity demanded	Quantity supplied
$1.40	8.0	14.0
1.30	8.5	13.0
1.20	9.0	12.0
1.10	9.5	11.0
1.00	10.0	10.0
0.90	10.5	9.0
0.80	11.0	8.0
0.70	11.5	7.0
0.60	12.0	6.0

Without government intervention, the market for butter reaches equilibrium at a price of $1 per pound with 10 million pounds of butter bought and sold.

price floors, governments buy up unwanted surplus. As a result, the U.S. government has at times found itself warehousing thousands of tons of butter, cheese, and other farm products. (The European Commission, which administers price floors for a number of European countries, once found itself the

FIGURE 5-6 The Effects of a Price Floor

The black horizontal line represents the government-imposed price floor of $1.20 per pound of butter. The quantity of butter demanded falls to 9 million pounds, and the quantity supplied rises to 12 million pounds, generating a persistent surplus of 3 million pounds of butter.

owner of a so-called butter mountain, equal in weight to the entire population of Austria.) The government then has to find a way to dispose of these unwanted goods.

Some countries pay exporters to sell products at a loss overseas; this is standard procedure for the European Union. The United States gives surplus food away to citizens in need as well as to schools, which use the products in school lunches. In some cases, governments have actually destroyed the surplus production.

When the government is not prepared to purchase the unwanted surplus, a price floor means that would-be sellers cannot find buyers. This is what happens when there is a price floor on the wage rate paid for an hour of labor, the minimum wage: when the minimum wage is above the equilibrium wage rate, some people who are willing to work—that is, sell labor—cannot find buyers—that is, employers—willing to give them jobs.

How a Price Floor Causes Inefficiency

The persistent surplus that results from a price floor creates missed opportunities— inefficiencies—that resemble those created by the shortage that results from a price ceiling. Like a price ceiling, a price floor creates inefficiency in at least four ways:

1. It creates deadweight loss by reducing the quantity transacted to below the efficient level.
2. It leads to an inefficient allocation of sales among sellers.
3. It leads to a waste of resources.
4. It leads to sellers providing an inefficiently high-quality level.

In addition to inefficiency, like a price ceiling, a price floor leads to illegal behavior as people break the law to sell below the legal price.

Inefficiently Low Quantity Because a price floor raises the price of a good to consumers, it reduces the quantity of that good demanded; because sellers can't sell more units of a good than buyers are willing to buy, a price floor reduces the quantity of a good bought and sold below the market equilibrium quantity and leads to a deadweight loss. Notice that this is the *same* effect as a price ceiling. You might be tempted to think that a price floor and a price ceiling have opposite effects, but both have the effect of reducing the quantity of a good bought and sold (as you can see in the accompanying Pitfalls).

Since the equilibrium of an efficient market maximizes the sum of consumer and producer surplus, a price floor that reduces the quantity below the equilibrium quantity reduces total surplus. Figure 5-7 shows the implications for total surplus of a price floor on the price of butter. Total surplus is the sum of the area above the supply curve and below the demand curve. By reducing the quantity of butter sold, a price floor causes a deadweight loss equal to the area of the shaded triangle in the figure. As in the case of a price ceiling, however, deadweight loss is only one of the forms of inefficiency that the price control creates.

PITFALLS

CEILINGS, FLOORS, AND QUANTITIES
A price ceiling pushes the price of a good *down*. A price floor pushes the price of a good *up*. So it's easy to assume that the effects of a price floor are the opposite of the effects of a price ceiling. In particular, if a price ceiling reduces the quantity of a good bought

and sold, doesn't a price floor increase the quantity?

No, it doesn't. In fact, both floors and ceilings reduce the quantity bought and sold. Why? When the quantity of a good supplied isn't equal to the quantity demanded, the actual quantity sold is determined by the "short side" of the market—whichever quantity is less. If

sellers don't want to sell as much as buyers want to buy, it's the sellers who determine the actual quantity sold, because buyers can't force unwilling sellers to sell. If buyers don't want to buy as much as sellers want to sell, it's the buyers who determine the actual quantity sold, because sellers can't force unwilling buyers to buy.

FIGURE **5-7** A Price Floor Causes Inefficiently Low Quantity

A price floor reduces the quantity demanded below the market equilibrium quantity and leads to a deadweight loss.

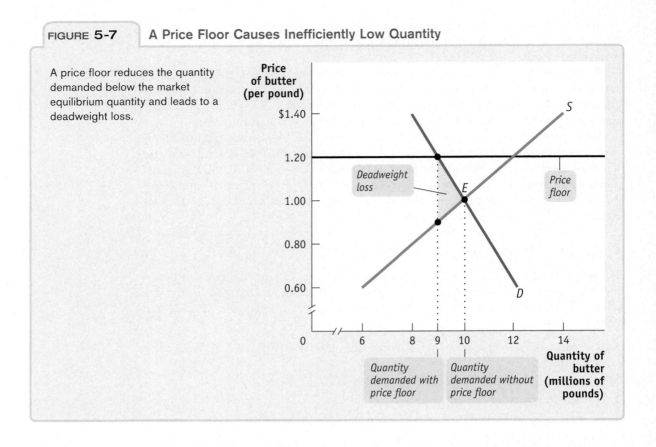

Inefficient Allocation of Sales Among Sellers Like a price ceiling, a price floor can lead to *inefficient allocation*—in this case, an **inefficient allocation of sales among sellers:** sellers who are willing to sell at the lowest price are unable to make sales, while sales go to sellers who are only willing to sell at a higher price.

One illustration of the inefficient allocation of selling opportunities caused by a price floor is the problem of unemployment and the black market for labor among the young in many European countries—notably France, Spain, Italy, and Greece. In these countries, a high minimum wage has led to a two-tier labor system, composed of the fortunate who have good jobs in the formal labor market that pay at least the minimum wage, and the rest who are locked out without any prospect of ever finding a good job. Either unemployed or underemployed in dead-end jobs in the black market for labor, the unlucky ones are disproportionately young, from the ages of 18 to early 30s. Although eager for good jobs in the formal sector and willing to accept less than the minimum wage—that is, willing to sell their labor for a lower price—it is illegal for employers to pay them less than the minimum wage. The inefficiency of unemployment and underemployment is compounded as a generation of young people is unable to get adequate job training, develop careers, and save for their future. These young people are also more likely to engage in crime. And many of these countries have seen their best and brightest young people emigrate, leading to a permanent reduction in the future performance of their economies.

Wasted Resources Also like a price ceiling, a price floor generates inefficiency by *wasting resources*. The most graphic examples involve government purchases of the unwanted surpluses of agricultural products caused by price floors. The surplus production is sometimes destroyed, which is pure waste; in other cases, the stored produce goes, as officials euphemistically put it, "out of condition" and must be thrown away.

Price floors also lead to wasted time and effort. Consider the minimum wage. Would-be workers who spend many hours searching for jobs, or waiting in line in the hope of getting jobs, play the same role in the case of price floors as hapless families searching for apartments in the case of price ceilings.

Price floors can lead to **inefficient allocation of sales among sellers:** sellers who are willing to sell at the lowest price are unable to make sales while sales go to sellers who are only willing to sell at a higher price.

Inefficiently High Quality Again like price ceilings, price floors lead to inefficiency in the quality of goods produced.

We saw that when there is a price ceiling, suppliers produce products that are of inefficiently low quality: buyers prefer higher-quality products and are willing to pay for them, but sellers refuse to improve the quality of their products because the price ceiling prevents their being compensated for doing so. This same logic applies to price floors, but in reverse: suppliers offer goods of **inefficiently high quality.**

How can this be? Isn't high quality a good thing? Yes, but only if it is worth the cost. Suppose that suppliers spend a lot to make goods of very high quality but that this quality isn't worth much to consumers, who would rather receive the money spent on that quality in the form of a lower price. This represents a missed opportunity: suppliers and buyers could make a mutually beneficial deal in which buyers got goods of lower quality for a much lower price.

A good example of the inefficiency of excessive quality comes from the days when transatlantic airfares were set artificially high by international treaty. Forbidden to compete for customers by offering lower ticket prices, airlines instead offered expensive services, like lavish in-flight meals that went largely uneaten. At one point the regulators tried to restrict this practice by defining maximum service standards—for example, that snack service should consist of no more than a sandwich. One airline then introduced what it called a "Scandinavian Sandwich," a towering affair that forced the convening of another conference to define *sandwich*. All of this was wasteful, especially considering that what passengers really wanted was less food and lower airfares.

Since the deregulation of U.S. airlines in the 1970s, American passengers have experienced a large decrease in ticket prices accompanied by a decrease in the quality of in-flight service—smaller seats, lower-quality food, and so on. Everyone complains about the service—but thanks to lower fares, the number of people flying on U.S. carriers has grown from 130 billion passenger miles when deregulation began to approximately 900 billion in 2014.

Illegal Activity In addition to the four inefficiencies we analyzed, like price ceilings, price floors provide incentives for illegal activity. For example, in countries where the minimum wage is far above the equilibrium wage rate, workers desperate for jobs sometimes agree to work off the books for employers who conceal their employment from the government—or bribe the government

Price floors often lead to inefficiency in that goods of **inefficiently high quality** are offered: sellers offer high-quality goods at a high price, even though buyers would prefer a lower quality at a lower price.

GLOBAL COMPARISION **Check Out Our Low, Low Wages!**

The minimum wage rate in the United States, as you can see in this graph, is actually quite low compared with that in other rich countries. Since minimum wages are set in national currency—the British minimum wage is set in British pounds, the French minimum wage is set in euros, and so on—the comparison depends on the exchange rate on any given day. As of 2013, Australia had a minimum wage over twice as high as the U.S. rate, with France, Canada, and Ireland not far behind. You can see one effect of this difference in the supermarket checkout line. In the United States there is usually someone to bag your groceries—someone typically paid the minimum wage or at best slightly more. In Europe, where hiring a bagger is a lot more expensive, you're almost always expected to do the bagging yourself.

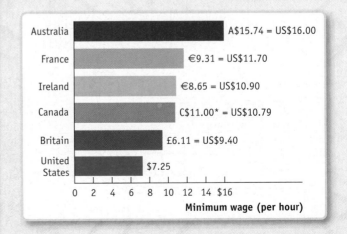

Source: Organization for Economic Cooperation and Development (OECD).
*The Canadian minimum wage varies by province from C$9.95 to C$11.00.

inspectors. This practice, known in Europe as "black labor," is especially common in Southern European countries such as Italy and Spain.

So Why Are There Price Floors?

To sum up, a price floor creates various negative side effects:

- A persistent surplus of the good
- Inefficiency arising from the persistent surplus in the form of inefficiently low quantity (deadweight loss), inefficient allocation of sales among sellers, wasted resources, and an inefficiently high level of quality offered by suppliers
- The temptation to engage in illegal activity, particularly bribery and corruption of government officials

So why do governments impose price floors when they have so many negative side effects? The reasons are similar to those for imposing price ceilings. Government officials often disregard warnings about the consequences of price floors either because they believe that the relevant market is poorly described by the supply and demand model or, more often, because they do not understand the model. Above all, just as price ceilings are often imposed because they benefit some influential buyers of a good, price floors are often imposed because they benefit some influential sellers.

ECONOMICS ▶ in Action

The Rise and Fall of the Unpaid Intern

The best-known example of a price floor is the minimum wage. Most economists believe, however, that the minimum wage has relatively little effect on the overall job market in the United States, mainly because the floor is set so low. In 1964, the U.S. minimum wage was 53% of the average wage of blue-collar production workers; by 2013, it had fallen to about 37%. However, there is one sector of the U.S. job market where it appears that the minimum wage can indeed be binding: the market for interns.

Internships are temporary work positions typically reserved for younger workers still in college or recent graduates. The sluggish U.S. economy of recent years has produced poor job prospects for workers 20 to 24 years old. The unemployment rate for this age group was almost 12% at the start of 2014. One result of this has been a rise in the availability of internships, which look increasingly appealing to enthusiastic young workers unable to find well-paid permanent jobs.

Internships fall into two broad categories: paid interns, who are formally hired as temporary workers, and must be paid at least the minimum wage, and unpaid interns, who perform tasks but are not legally designated employees and aren't covered by minimum wage laws. Because internships offer the promise of valuable work experience and credentials that can later prove very valuable, young workers are often willing to accept them at a low wage or even no wage. According to Robert Shindell, an executive at the consulting firm Intern Bridge, more than a million American students a year do internships; a fifth of those positions pay zero and provide no course credits.

Not surprisingly, some companies are tempted to use unpaid interns to perform work that in reality has little or no educational value but that directly benefits the company.

To guard against such practices, the Department of Labor (DOL), the federal agency that monitors compliance with mini-

"We have an opening for a part-time upaid intern, which could lead to a full-time unpaid internship."

mum wage laws, issued several criteria in 2010 to help companies determine whether their unpaid internships are legally exempt from minimum wage requirements. Among them are: (1) Is the experience primarily for the benefit of the intern and not the employer? (2) Is the internship comparable to training offered by an educational environment? and (3) Is there no displacement of a regular employee by the intern? If the answer to such questions is yes, then the DOL considers the internship to be a form of education that is exempt from minimum wage laws. However, if the answer to any of the questions is no, then the DOL may determine that the unpaid internship violates minimum wage laws, in which case, the position must either be converted into a paid internship that pays at least the minimum wage or be eliminated.

In 2012 and 2013, a spate of lawsuits brought by former unpaid interns claiming they were cheated out of wages brought the matter to public attention. In 2013, the movie company Fox Searchlight Pictures was found guilty of breaking federal minimum wage laws for employing two interns at zero pay. A common thread in these complaints is that interns were assigned "grunt work" that had no educational value—such as tracking lost cell phones. In some cases, unpaid interns complained that they were given the work of full-salaried employees.

As a result, many lawyers who advise companies on labor laws have been advising companies to either pay their interns minimum wage or shut down their internships. While some have axed their programs altogether, others—such as Fox Searchlight and NBC News—have converted their unpaid internships to paid ones. Some observers worry that the end of the unpaid internships means that programs that once offered valuable training will be lost. But as one lawyer commented, "The law says that when you work, you have to get paid [at least the minimum wage]."

Check Your Understanding 5-2

1. The state legislature mandates a price floor for gasoline of P_F per gallon. Assess the following statements and illustrate your answer using the figure provided.
   a. Proponents of the law claim it will increase the income of gas station owners. Opponents claim it will hurt gas station owners because they will lose customers.
   b. Proponents claim consumers will be better off because gas stations will provide better service. Opponents claim consumers will be generally worse off because they prefer to buy gas at cheaper prices.
   c. Proponents claim that they are helping gas station owners without hurting anyone else. Opponents claim that consumers are hurt and will end up doing things like buying gas in a nearby state or on the black market.

   Solutions appear at back of book.

Controlling Quantities

In the 1930s, New York City instituted a system of licensing for taxicabs: only taxis with a "medallion" were allowed to pick up passengers. Because this system was intended to assure quality, medallion owners were supposed to maintain certain standards, including safety and cleanliness. A total of 11,787 medallions were issued, with taxi owners paying $10 for each medallion.

In 1995, there were still only 11,787 licensed taxicabs in New York, even though the city had meanwhile become the financial capital of the world, a place where hundreds of thousands of people in a hurry tried to hail a cab every day. An additional 400 medallions were issued in 1995, and after several rounds of

A **quantity control,** or **quota,** is an upper limit on the quantity of some good that can be bought or sold. The total amount of the good that can be legally transacted is the **quota limit.**

A **license** gives its owner the right to supply a good.

The **demand price** of a given quantity is the price at which consumers will demand that quantity.

sales of additional medallions, today there are 15,000 medallions. The result of this restriction is that a New York city taxi medallion is a very valuable item: if you want to to operate a tax in the city, you must lease a medallion from someone else or buy one, with a current price today of over a million dollars.

It turns out that this story is not unique; other cities introduced similar medallion systems in the 1930s and, like New York, have issued few new medallions since. In San Francisco and Boston, as in New York, taxi medallions trade for seven-figure prices.

A taxi medallion system is a form of **quantity control,** or **quota,** by which the government regulates the quantity of a good that can be bought and sold rather than the price at which it is transacted. It is another way that government intervenes in markets along with price ceilings and price floors. The total amount of the good that can be transacted under the quantity control is called the **quota limit.** Typically, the government limits quantity in a market by issuing **licenses;** only people with a license can legally supply the good.

A taxi medallion is just such a license. The government of New York City limits the number of taxi rides that can be sold by limiting the number of taxis to only those who hold medallions. There are many other cases of quantity controls, ranging from limits on how much foreign currency (for instance, British pounds or Mexican pesos) people are allowed to buy to the quantity of clams New Jersey fishing boats are allowed to catch.

In the real world, quantity controls set an upper limit on the quantity of a good that can be transacted. Some attempts to control quantities are undertaken for good economic reasons, some for bad ones. In many cases, as we will see, quantity controls introduced to address a temporary problem become politically hard to remove later because the beneficiaries don't want them abolished, even after the original reason for their existence is long gone. But whatever the reasons for such controls, they have certain predictable—and usually undesirable—economic consequences.

The Anatomy of Quantity Controls

To understand why a New York taxi medallion is worth so much money, we consider a simplified version of the market for taxi rides, shown in Figure 5-8. Just as we assumed in the analysis of rent control that all apartments are the same, we now suppose that all taxi rides are the same—ignoring the real-world complication that some taxi rides are longer, and so more expensive, than others.

The table in the figure shows supply and demand schedules. The equilibrium—indicated by point *E* in the figure and by the shaded entries in the table—is a fare of $5 per ride, with 10 million rides taken per year. (You'll see in a minute why we present the equilibrium this way.)

The New York medallion system limits the number of taxis, but each taxi driver can offer as many rides as he or she can manage. (Now you know why New York taxi drivers are so aggressive!) To simplify our analysis, however, we will assume that a medallion system limits the number of taxi rides that can legally be given to 8 million per year.

Until now, we have derived the demand curve by answering questions of the form: "How many taxi rides will passengers want to take if the price is $5 per ride?" But it is possible to reverse the question and ask instead: "At what price will consumers want to buy 10 million rides per year?" The price at which consumers want to buy a given quantity—in this case, 10 million rides at $5 per ride—is the **demand price** of that quantity. You can see from the demand schedule in Figure 5-8 that the demand price of 6 million rides is $7 per ride, the demand price of 7 million rides is $6.50 per ride, and so on.

Similarly, the supply curve represents the answer to questions of the form: "How many taxi rides would taxi drivers supply at a price of $5 each?" But we

FIGURE **5-8**   The Market for Taxi Rides in the Absence of Government Controls

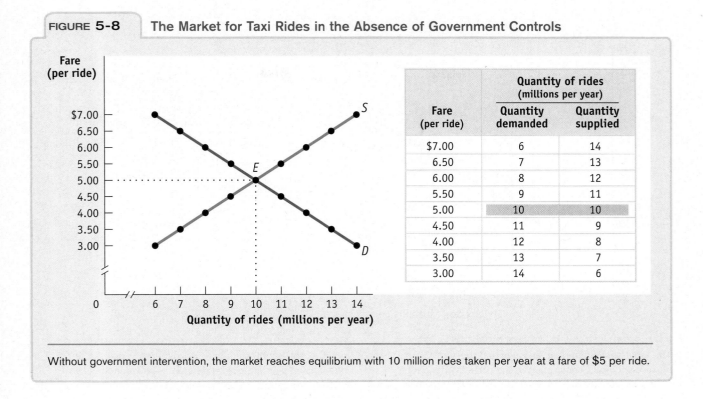

Fare (per ride)	Quantity of rides (millions per year)	
	Quantity demanded	Quantity supplied
$7.00	6	14
6.50	7	13
6.00	8	12
5.50	9	11
5.00	10	10
4.50	11	9
4.00	12	8
3.50	13	7
3.00	14	6

Without government intervention, the market reaches equilibrium with 10 million rides taken per year at a fare of $5 per ride.

can also reverse this question to ask: "At what price will suppliers be willing to supply 10 million rides per year?" The price at which suppliers will supply a given quantity—in this case, 10 million rides at $5 per ride—is the **supply price** of that quantity. We can see from the supply schedule in Figure 5-8 that the supply price of 6 million rides is $3 per ride, the supply price of 7 million rides is $3.50 per ride, and so on.

The **supply price** of a given quantity is the price at which producers will supply that quantity.

Now we are ready to analyze a quota. We have assumed that the city government limits the quantity of taxi rides to 8 million per year. Medallions, each of which carries the right to provide a certain number of taxi rides per year, are made available to selected people in such a way that a total of 8 million rides will be provided. Medallion-holders may then either drive their own taxis or rent their medallions to others for a fee.

Figure 5-9 shows the resulting market for taxi rides, with the black vertical line at 8 million rides per year representing the quota limit. Because the quantity of rides is limited to 8 million, consumers must be at point *A* on the demand curve, corresponding to the shaded entry in the demand schedule: the demand price of 8 million rides is $6 per ride. Meanwhile, taxi drivers must be at point *B* on the supply curve, corresponding to the shaded entry in the supply schedule: the supply price of 8 million rides is $4 per ride.

But how can the price received by taxi drivers be $4 when the price paid by taxi riders is $6? The answer is that in addition to the market in taxi rides, there is also a market in medallions. Medallion-holders may not always want to drive their taxis: they may be ill or on vacation. Those who do not want to drive their own taxis will sell the right to use the medallion to someone else.

So we need to consider two sets of transactions here, and so two prices: (1) the transactions in taxi rides and the price at which these will occur, and (2) the transactions in medallions and the price at which these will occur. It turns out that since we are looking at two markets, the $4 and $6 prices will both be right.

FIGURE 5-9   Effect of a Quota on the Market for Taxi Rides

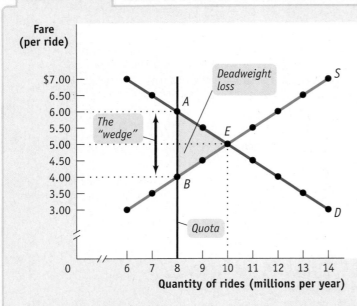

Fare (per ride)	Quantity of rides (millions per year)	
	Quantity demanded	Quantity supplied
$7.00	6	14
6.50	7	13
6.00	8	12
5.50	9	11
5.00	10	10
4.50	11	9
4.00	12	8
3.50	13	7
3.00	14	6

The table shows the demand price and the supply price corresponding to each quantity: the price at which that quantity would be demanded and supplied, respectively. The city government imposes a quota of 8 million rides by selling licenses for only 8 million rides, represented by the black vertical line. The price paid by consumers rises to $6 per ride, the demand price of 8 million rides, shown by point *A*. The supply price of 8 million rides is only $4 per ride, shown by point *B*. The difference between these two prices is the quota rent per ride, the earnings that accrue to the owner of a license. The quota rent drives a wedge between the demand price and the supply price. And since the quota discourages mutually beneficial transactions, it creates a deadweight loss equal to the shaded triangle.

A quantity control, or quota, drives a **wedge** between the demand price and the supply price of a good; that is, the price paid by buyers ends up being higher than that received by sellers.

The difference between the demand and supply price at the quota limit is the **quota rent,** the earnings that accrue to the license-holder from ownership of the right to sell the good. It is equal to the market price of the license when the licenses are traded.

To see how this all works, consider two imaginary New York taxi drivers, Sunil and Harriet. Sunil has a medallion but can't use it because he's recovering from a severely sprained wrist. So he's looking to rent his medallion out to someone else. Harriet doesn't have a medallion but would like to rent one. Furthermore, at any point in time there are many other people like Harriet who would like to rent a medallion. Suppose Sunil agrees to rent his medallion to Harriet. To make things simple, assume that any driver can give only one ride per day and that Sunil is renting his medallion to Harriet for one day. What rental price will they agree on?

To answer this question, we need to look at the transactions from the viewpoints of both drivers. Once she has the medallion, Harriet knows she can make $6 per day—the demand price of a ride under the quota. And she is willing to rent the medallion only if she makes at least $4 per day—the supply price of a ride under the quota. So Sunil cannot demand a rent of more than $2—the difference between $6 and $4. And if Harriet offered Sunil less than $2—say, $1.50—there would be other eager drivers willing to offer him more, up to $2. So, in order to get the medallion, Harriet must offer Sunil at least $2. Since the rent can be no more than $2 and no less than $2, it must be exactly $2.

It is no coincidence that $2 is exactly the difference between $6, the demand price of 8 million rides, and $4, the supply price of 8 million rides. In every case in which the supply of a good is legally restricted, there is a **wedge** between the demand price of the quantity transacted and the supply price of the quantity transacted.

This wedge, illustrated by the double-headed arrow in Figure 5-9, has a special name: the **quota rent.** It is the earnings that accrue to the license-holder from ownership of a valuable commodity, the license. In the case of Sunil and Harriet, the quota rent of $2 goes to Sunil because he owns the license, and the remaining $4 from the total fare of $6 goes to Harriet.

So Figure 5-9 also illustrates the quota rent in the market for New York taxi rides. The quota limits the quantity of rides to 8 million per year, a quantity at which the demand price of $6 exceeds the supply price of $4. The wedge between these two prices, $2, is the quota rent that results from the restrictions placed on the quantity of taxi rides in this market.

But wait a second. What if Sunil doesn't rent out his medallion? What if he uses it himself? Doesn't this mean that he gets a price of $6? No, not really. Even if Sunil doesn't rent out his medallion, he could have rented it out, which means that the medallion has an *opportunity cost* of $2: if Sunil decides to use his own medallion and drive his own taxi rather than renting his medallion to Harriet, the $2 represents his opportunity cost of not renting out his medallion. That is, the $2 quota rent is now the rental income he forgoes by driving his own taxi.

In effect, Sunil is in two businesses—the taxi-driving business and the medallion-renting business. He makes $4 per ride from driving his taxi and $2 per ride from renting out his medallion. It doesn't make any difference that in this particular case he has rented his medallion to himself!

So regardless of whether the medallion owner uses the medallion himself or herself, or rents it to others, it is a valuable asset. And this is represented in the going price for a New York City taxi medallion: in 2013, New York City taxi medallions sold for $1 to $1.2 million. According to Simon Greenbaum, a broker of New York taxi medallions, an owner of a medallion who leases it to a driver can expect to earn about $2,500 per month, or a 3% return—an attractive rate of return compared to other investments.

Notice, by the way, that quotas—like price ceilings and price floors—don't always have a real effect. If the quota were set at 12 million rides—that is, above the equilibrium quantity in an unregulated market—it would have no effect because it would not be binding.

The Costs of Quantity Controls

Like price controls, quantity controls can have some predictable and undesirable side effects. The first is the by-now-familiar problem of inefficiency due to missed opportunities: quantity controls create deadweight loss by preventing mutually beneficial transactions from occurring, transactions that would benefit both buyers and sellers. Looking back at Figure 5-9, you can see that starting at the quota limit of 8 million rides, New Yorkers would be willing to pay at least $5.50 per ride when 9 million rides are offered, 1 million more than the quota, and that taxi drivers would be willing to provide those rides as long as they got at least $4.50 per ride. These are rides that would have taken place if there were no quota limit.

The same is true for the next 1 million rides: New Yorkers would be willing to pay at least $5 per ride when the quantity of rides is increased from 9 to 10 million, and taxi drivers would be willing to provide those rides as long as they got at least $5 per ride. Again, these rides would have occurred without the quota limit.

Only when the market has reached the unregulated market equilibrium quantity of 10 million rides are there no "missed-opportunity rides." The quota limit of 8 million rides has caused 2 million "missed-opportunity rides."

Generally, *as long as the demand price of a given quantity exceeds the supply price, there is a deadweight loss.* A buyer would be willing to buy the good at a price that the seller would be willing to accept, but such a transaction does not occur because it is forbidden by the quota. The deadweight loss arising from the 2 million in missed-opportunity rides is represented by the shaded triangle in Figure 5-9.

And because there are transactions that people would like to make but are not allowed to, quantity controls generate an incentive to evade them or even to break the law. New York's taxi industry again provides clear examples. Taxi regulation applies only to those drivers who are hailed by passengers on the street. A car service that makes prearranged pickups does not need a medallion. As a result, such hired cars provide much of the service that might otherwise be provided by taxis, as in other cities. In addition, there are substantial numbers of unlicensed cabs that simply defy the law by picking up passengers without a medallion. Because these cabs are illegal, their drivers are completely unregulated, and they generate a disproportionately large share of traffic accidents in New York City.

In fact, in 2004 the hardships caused by the limited number of New York taxis led city leaders to authorize an increase in the number of licensed taxis by 900. The city auctioned off an additional 2,000 medallions in 2013, bringing the total number up to the current 15,000 medallions—a move that certainly cheered New York riders.

But those who already owned medallions were less happy with the increase; they understood that adding new taxis would reduce or eliminate the shortage of taxis. As a result, taxi drivers anticipated a decline in their revenues because they would no longer always be assured of finding willing customers. And, in turn, the value of a medallion would fall. So to placate the medallion owners, city officials also raised taxi fares: by 25% in 2004, by a smaller percentage in 2006, and again by about 17% in 2012. Although taxis are now easier to find, a ride now costs more—and that price increase slightly diminished the newfound cheer of New York taxi riders.

In sum, quantity controls typically create the following undesirable side effects:

- Deadweight loss because some mutually beneficial transactions don't occur

- Incentives for illegal activities

ECONOMICS ▶ *in Action*

Crabbing, Quotas, and Saving Lives in Alaska

Alaskan king and snow crab are considered delicacies worldwide. And crab fishing is one of the most important industries in the Alaskan economy. So many were justifiably concerned when, in 1983, the annual crab catch fell by 90% due to overfishing. In response, marine biologists set a *total catch quota system,* which limited the amount of crab that could be harvested annually in order to allow the crab population to return to a healthy, sustainable level.

Notice, by the way, that the Alaskan crab quota is an example of a quota that was justified by broader economic and environmental considerations—unlike the New York taxicab quota, which has long since lost any economic rationale. Another important difference is that, unlike New York taxicab medallions, owners of Alaskan crab boats did not have the ability to buy or sell individual quotas. So although depleted crab stocks eventually recovered with the total catch quota system in place, there was another, unintended and deadly consequence.

The Alaskan crabbing season is fairly short, running roughly from October to January, and it can be further shortened by bad weather. By the 1990s, Alaskan crab fishermen were engaging in "fishing derbies," made famous by the Discovery Channel's *Deadliest Catch.* To stay within the quota limit when the crabbing season began, boat crews rushed to fish for crab in dangerous, icy, rough water, straining to harvest in a few days a haul that could be worth several hundred thousand dollars. As a result, boats often became overloaded and capsized. Crews were pushed too hard, with many fatalities from hypothermia or drowning.

According to federal statistics, at the time Alaskan crab fishing was among the most dangerous of jobs, with an average of 7.3 deaths a year, about 80 times the fatality rate for an average worker. And after the brief harvest, the market for crab was flooded with supply, lowering the prices fishermen received.

In 2006 fishery regulators instituted another quota system called *quota share*—aimed at protecting crabbers as well as Alaska's crabs. Under individual quota share, each boat received a quota to fill during the three month season. Moreover, the individual quotas could be sold or leased. These changes transformed the industry as owners of bigger boats bought the individual quotas of smaller boats, shrinking the number of crabbing boats dramatically: from over 250 a few years earlier to about 60 in 2012. Bigger boats are much less likely to capsize, improving crew safety.

In addition, by extending the fishing season, the quota-share system boosted the crab population and crab prices. In 2004, under the old system, the quota was reached in just 3 days, while in 2010 in took 20 days. With more time to fish, fishermen could make sure that juvenile and female crabs were returned to sea rather than harvested. And with a longer fishing season, the catch comes to the market more gradually, eliminating the downward plunge in prices when supply hits the market. In 2011, snow crab sold for close to $7 per pound, up from close to $3 per pound in 2005.

The quota-share system protects Alaska's crab population and saves the lives of crabbers.

Predictably, an Alaskan crab fisherman earns more money under the quota-share system than under the total catch quota system. As one observer said in 2012, "The information we have on crabbers' income is anecdotal, but crewmen we surveyed said they're making about $100,000 a year and captains twice that. That's a lot more than a few years ago."

Check Your Understanding   5-3

1. Suppose that the supply and demand for taxi rides is given by Figure 5-8 but the quota is set at 6 million rides instead of 8 million. Find the following and indicate them on Figure 5-8.
   a. The price of a ride
   b. The quota rent
   c. The deadweight loss
   d. Suppose the quota limit on taxi rides is increased to 9 million. What happens to the quota rent? To the deadweight loss?
2. Assume that the quota limit is 8 million rides. Suppose demand decreases due to a decline in tourism. What is the smallest parallel leftward shift in demand that would result in the quota no longer having an effect on the market? Illustrate your answer using Figure 5-8.

Solutions appear at back of book.

Medallion Financial: Cruising Right Along

The Photo Works

Back in 1937, before New York City froze its number of taxi medallions, Andrew Murstein's immigrant grandfather bought his first one for $10. Over time, the grandfather accumulated 500 medallions, which he rented to other drivers. Those 500 taxi medallions became the foundation for Medallion Financial: the company that would eventually pass to Andrew, its current president.

With a market value of $385 million in late 2013, Medallion Financial has shifted its major line of business from renting out medallions to financing the purchase of new ones, lending money to those who want to buy a medallion but don't have the sizable amount of cash required to do so. Murstein believes that he is helping people who, like his Polish immigrant grandfather, want to buy a piece of the American dream.

Andrew Murstein carefully watches the value of a New York City taxi medallion: the more one costs, the more demand there is for loans from Medallion Financial, and the more interest the company makes on the loan. A loan from Medallion Financial is secured by the value of the medallion itself. If the borrower is unable to repay the loan, Medallion Financial takes possession of his or her medallion and resells it to offset the cost of the loan default. As of 2013, the value of a medallion has risen faster than stocks, oil, and gold. Over the past two decades, from 1990 through 2013, the value of a medallion rose 720%, compared to 500% for an index of stocks.

But medallion prices can fluctuate dramatically, threatening profits. During periods of a very strong economy, such as in 1999 and 2001, the price of New York taxi medallions fell as drivers found jobs in other sectors. When the New York economy tanked in the aftermath of 9/11, the price of a medallion fell to $180,000, its lowest level in 12 years. In 2004, medallion owners were concerned about the impending sale by the New York City Taxi and Limousine Commission of an additional 900 medallions. As Peter Hernandez, a worried New York cabdriver who financed his medallion with a loan from Medallion Financial, said at the time: "If they pump new taxis into the industry, it devalues my medallion. It devalues my daily income, too."

Yet Murstein has always been optimistic that medallions would hold their value. He believed that a 25% fare increase would offset potential losses in their value caused by the sale of new medallions. In addition, more medallions would mean more loans for his company.

As of 2013, Murstein's optimism had been justified. Because of the financial crisis of 2007–2009, many New York companies cut back the limousine services they ordinarily provided to their employees, forcing them to take taxis instead. As a result, the price of a medallion has nearly doubled, from $550,000 in 2008 to more than a million dollars in 2013. And investors have noticed the value in Medallion Financial's line of business: from November 2010 through November 2013, shares of Medallion Financial rose 120%.

QUESTIONS FOR THOUGHT

1. How does Medallion Financial benefit from the restriction on the number of New York taxi medallions?

2. What will be the effect on Medallion Financial if New York companies resume widespread use of limousine services for their employees? What is the economic motivation that prompts companies to offer this perk to their employees? (Note that it is very difficult and expensive to own a personal car in New York City.)

3. Predict the effect on Medallion Financial's business if New York City eliminates restrictions on the number of taxis. That is, if the quota is removed.

SUMMARY

1. Even when a market is efficient, governments often intervene to pursue greater fairness or to please a powerful interest group. Interventions can take the form of **price controls** or quantity controls, both of which generate predictable and undesirable side effects consisting of various forms of inefficiency and illegal activity.

2. A **price ceiling,** a maximum market price below the equilibrium price, benefits successful buyers but creates persistent shortages. Because the price is maintained below the equilibrium price, the quantity demanded is increased and the quantity supplied is decreased compared to the equilibrium quantity. This leads to predictable problems: inefficiencies in the form of **deadweight loss** from inefficiently low quantity, **inefficient allocation to consumers, wasted resources,** and **inefficiently low quality.** It also encourages illegal activity as people turn to **black markets** to get the good. Because of these problems, price ceilings have generally lost favor as an economic policy tool. But some governments continue to impose them either because they don't understand the effects or because the price ceilings benefit some influential group.

3. A **price floor,** a minimum market price above the equilibrium price, benefits successful sellers but creates persistent surplus. Because the price is maintained above the equilibrium price, the quantity demanded is decreased and the quantity supplied is increased compared to the equilibrium quantity. This leads to predictable problems: inefficiencies in the form of deadweight loss from inefficiently low quantity, **inefficient allocation of sales among sellers,** wasted resources, and **inefficiently high quality.** It also encourages illegal activity and black markets. The most well known kind of price floor is the **minimum wage,** but price floors are also commonly applied to agricultural products.

4. **Quantity controls,** or **quotas,** limit the quantity of a good that can be bought or sold. The quantity allowed for sale is the **quota limit.** The government issues **licenses** to individuals, the right to sell a given quantity of the good. The owner of a license earns a **quota rent,** earnings that accrue from ownership of the right to sell the good. It is equal to the difference between the **demand price** at the quota limit, what consumers are willing to pay for that quantity, and the **supply price** at the quota limit, what suppliers are willing to accept for that quantity. Economists say that a quota drives a **wedge** between the demand price and the supply price; this wedge is equal to the quota rent. Quantity controls lead to deadweight loss in addition to encouraging illegal activity.

KEY TERMS

Price controls, p. 132
Price ceiling, p. 132
Price floor, p. 132
Deadweight loss, p. 135
Inefficient allocation to consumers, p. 137
Wasted resources, p. 137

Inefficiently low quality, p. 138
Black market, p. 139
Minimum wage, p. 141
Inefficient allocation of sales among sellers, p. 144
Inefficiently high quality, p. 145
Quantity control, p. 148

Quota, p. 148
Quota limit, p. 148
License, p. 148
Demand price, p. 148
Supply price, p. 149
Wedge, p. 150
Quota rent, p. 150

PROBLEMS

1. In order to ingratiate himself with voters, the mayor of Gotham City decides to lower the price of taxi rides. Assume, for simplicity, that all taxi rides are the same distance and therefore cost the same. The accompanying table shows the demand and supply schedules for taxi rides.

	Quantity of rides (millions per year)	
Fare (per ride)	Quantity demanded	Quantity supplied
$7.00	10	12
6.50	11	11
6.00	12	10
5.50	13	9
5.00	14	8
4.50	15	7

a. Assume that there are no restrictions on the number of taxi rides that can be supplied (there is no medallion system). Find the equilibrium price and quantity.

b. Suppose that the mayor sets a price ceiling at $5.50. How large is the shortage of rides? Illustrate with a diagram. Who loses and who benefits from this policy?

c. Suppose that the stock market crashes and, as a result, people in Gotham City are poorer. This reduces the quantity of taxi rides demanded by 6 million rides per year at any given price. What effect will the mayor's new policy have now? Illustrate with a diagram.

d. Suppose that the stock market rises and the demand for taxi rides returns to normal (that is, returns to the demand schedule given in the table). The mayor now decides to ingratiate himself with taxi drivers. He announces a policy in which operating licenses are given to existing taxi drivers; the number of licenses is restricted such that only 10 million rides per year can be given. Illustrate the effect of this policy on the market, and indicate the resulting price and quantity transacted. What is the quota rent per ride?

2. In the late eighteenth century, the price of bread in New York City was controlled, set at a predetermined price above the market price.

a. Draw a diagram showing the effect of the policy. Did the policy act as a price ceiling or a price floor?

b. What kinds of inefficiencies were likely to have arisen when the controlled price of bread was above the market price? Explain in detail.

One year during this period, a poor wheat harvest caused a leftward shift in the supply of bread and therefore an increase in its market price. New York bakers found that the controlled price of bread in New York was below the market price.

c. Draw a diagram showing the effect of the price control on the market for bread during this one-year period. Did the policy act as a price ceiling or a price floor?

d. What kinds of inefficiencies do you think occurred during this period? Explain in detail.

3. The U.S. Department of Agriculture (USDA) administers the price floor for butter, which the 2008 Farm Bill set at $1.05 per pound. At that price, according to data from the USDA, the quantity of butter supplied in 2010 was 1.7 billion pounds, and the quantity demanded was 1.6 billion pounds. To support the price of butter at the price floor, the USDA therefore had to buy up 100 million pounds of butter. The accompanying diagram shows supply and demand curves illustrating the market for butter.

a. In the absence of a price floor, how much consumer surplus is created? How much producer surplus? What is the total surplus?

b. With the price floor at $1.05 per pound of butter, consumers buy 1.6 billion pounds of butter. How much consumer surplus is created now?

c. With the price floor at $1.05 per pound of butter, producers sell 1.7 billion pounds of butter (some to consumers and some to the USDA). How much producer surplus is created now?

d. How much money does the USDA spend on buying up surplus butter?

e. Taxes must be collected to pay for the purchases of surplus butter by the USDA. As a result, total surplus (producer plus consumer) is reduced by the amount the USDA spent on buying surplus butter. Using your answers for parts b–d, what is the total surplus when there is a price floor? How does this compare to the total surplus without a price floor from part a?

4. The accompanying table shows hypothetical demand and supply schedules for milk per year. The U.S. government decides that the incomes of dairy farmers should be maintained at a level that allows the traditional family dairy farm to survive. So it implements a price floor of $1 per pint by buying surplus milk until the market price is $1 per pint.

Price of milk (per pint)	Quantity of milk (millions of pints per year)	
	Quantity demanded	Quantity supplied
$1.20	550	850
1.10	600	800
1.00	650	750
0.90	700	700
0.80	750	650

a. In a diagram, show the deadweight loss from the inefficiently low quantity bought and sold.

b. How much surplus milk will be produced as a result of this policy?

c. What will be the cost to the government of this policy?

d. Since milk is an important source of protein and calcium, the government decides to provide the surplus milk it purchases to elementary schools at a price of only $0.60 per pint. Assume that schools will buy any amount of milk available at this low price. But parents now reduce their purchases of milk at any price by 50 million pints per year because they know their children are getting milk at school. How much will the dairy program now cost the government?

e. Explain how inefficiencies in the form of inefficient allocation to sellers and wasted resources arise from this policy.

5. European governments tend to make greater use of price controls than does the U.S. government. For example, the French government sets minimum starting yearly wages for new hires who have completed *le bac*, certification roughly equivalent to a high school diploma. The demand schedule for new hires with *le bac* and the supply schedule for similarly credentialed new job seekers are given in the accompanying table. The price here—given in euros, the currency used in France—is the same as the yearly wage.

Wage (per year)	Quantity demanded (new job offers per year)	Quantity supplied (new job seekers per year)
€45,000	200,000	325,000
40,000	220,000	320,000
35,000	250,000	310,000
30,000	290,000	290,000
25,000	370,000	200,000

a. In the absence of government interference, what are the equilibrium wage and number of graduates hired per year? Illustrate with a diagram. Will there be anyone seeking a job at the equilibrium wage who is unable to find one—that is, will there be anyone who is involuntarily unemployed?

b. Suppose the French government sets a minimum yearly wage of €35,000. Is there any involuntary unemployment at this wage? If so, how much? Illustrate with a diagram. What if the minimum wage is set at €40,000? Also illustrate with a diagram.

c. Given your answer to part b and the information in the table, what do you think is the relationship between the level of involuntary unemployment and the level of the minimum wage? Who benefits from such a policy? Who loses? What is the missed opportunity here?

6. In many European countries high minimum wages have led to high levels of unemployment and underemployment, and a two-tier labor system. In the formal labor market, workers have good jobs that pay at least the minimum wage. In the informal, or black market for labor, workers have poor jobs and receive less than the minimum wage.

a. Draw a demand and supply diagram showing the effect of the imposition of a minimum wage on the overall market for labor, with wage on the vertical axis and hours of labor on the horizontal axis. Your supply curve should represent the hours of labor offered by workers according to the wage, and the demand curve represents the hours of labor demanded by employers according to the wage. On your diagram show the deadweight loss from the imposition of a minimum wage. What type of shortage is created? Illustrate on your diagram the size of the shortage.

b. Assume that the imposition of the high minimum wage causes a contraction in the economy so that employers in the formal sector cut their production and their demand for workers. Illustrate the effect of this on the overall market for labor. What happens to the size of the deadweight loss? The shortage? Illustrate with a diagram.

c. Assume that the workers who cannot get a job paying at least the minimum wage move into the informal labor market where there is no minimum wage. What happens to the size of the informal market for labor as a result of the economic contraction? What happens to the equilibrium wage in the informal labor market? Illustrate with a supply and demand diagram for the informal market.

7. For the last 80 years the U.S. government has used price supports to provide income assistance to American farmers. To implement these price supports, at times the government has used price floors, which it maintains by buying up the surplus farm products. At other times, it has used target prices, a policy by which the government gives the farmer an amount equal to the difference between the market price and the target price for each unit sold. Consider the market for corn depicted in the accompanying diagram.

a. If the government sets a price floor of $5 per bushel, how many bushels of corn are produced? How many are purchased by consumers? By the government? How much does the program cost the government? How much revenue do corn farmers receive?

b. Suppose the government sets a target price of $5 per bushel for any quantity supplied up to 1,000 bushels. How many bushels of corn are purchased by consumers and at what price? By the government? How much does the program cost the government? How much revenue do corn farmers receive?

c. Which of these programs (in parts a and b) costs corn consumers more? Which program costs the government more? Explain.

d. Is one of these policies less inefficient than the other? Explain.

8. The waters off the North Atlantic coast were once teeming with fish. But because of overfishing by the commercial fishing industry, the stocks of fish became seriously depleted. In 1991, the National Marine Fishery Service of the U.S. government implemented a quota to allow fish stocks to recover. The quota limited the amount of swordfish caught per year by all U.S.-licensed fishing boats to 7 million pounds. As soon as the U.S. fishing fleet had met the quota limit, the swordfish catch was closed down for the rest of the year. The accompanying table gives the hypothetical demand and supply schedules for swordfish caught in the United States per year.

Price of swordfish (per pound)	Quantity of swordfish (millions of pounds per year)	
	Quantity demanded	Quantity supplied
$20	6	15
18	7	13
16	8	11
14	9	9
12	10	7

a. Use a diagram to show the effect of the quota on the market for swordfish in 1991. In your diagram, illustrate the deadweight loss from inefficiently low quantity.

b. How do you think fishermen will change how they fish in response to this policy?

9. In Maine, you must have a license to harvest lobster commercially; these licenses are issued yearly. The state of Maine is concerned about the dwindling supplies of lobsters found off its coast. The state fishery department has decided to place a yearly quota of 80,000 pounds of lobsters harvested in all Maine waters. It has also decided to give licenses this year only to those fishermen who had licenses last year. The accompanying diagram shows the demand and supply curves for Maine lobsters.

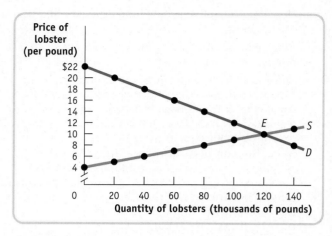

a. In the absence of government restrictions, what are the equilibrium price and quantity?

b. What is the *demand price* at which consumers wish to purchase 80,000 pounds of lobsters?

c. What is the *supply price* at which suppliers are willing to supply 80,000 pounds of lobsters?

d. What is the *quota rent* per pound of lobster when 80,000 pounds are sold? Illustrate the quota rent and the deadweight loss on the diagram.

e. Explain a transaction that benefits both buyer and seller but is prevented by the quota restriction.

10. The Venezuelan government has imposed a price ceiling on the retail price of roasted coffee beans. The accompanying diagram shows the market for coffee beans. In the absence of price controls, the equilibrium is at point *E*, with an equilibrium price of P_E and an equilibrium quantity bought and sold of Q_E.

a. Show the consumer and producer surplus before the introduction of the price ceiling.

After the introduction of the price ceiling, the price falls to P_C and the quantity bought and sold falls to Q_C.

b. Show the consumer surplus after the introduction of the price ceiling (assuming that the consumers with the highest willingness to pay get to buy the available coffee beans; that is, assuming that there is no inefficient allocation to consumers).

c. Show the producer surplus after the introduction of the price ceiling (assuming that the producers with the lowest cost get to sell their coffee beans; that is, assuming that there is no inefficient allocation of sales among producers).

d. Using the diagram, show how much of what was producer surplus before the introduction of the price ceiling has been transferred to consumers as a result of the price ceiling.

e. Using the diagram, show how much of what was total surplus before the introduction of the price ceiling has been lost. That is, how great is the dead-weight loss?

11. The accompanying diagram shows data from the U.S. Bureau of Labor Statistics on the average price of an airline ticket in the United States from 1975 until 1985, adjusted to eliminate the effect of *inflation* (the general increase in the prices of all goods over time). In 1978, the United States Airline Deregulation Act removed the price floor on airline fares, and it also allowed the airlines greater flexibility to offer new routes.

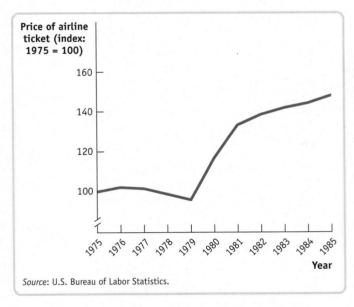

Source: U.S. Bureau of Labor Statistics.

a. Looking at the data on airline ticket prices in the diagram, do you think the price floor that existed before 1978 was binding or nonbinding? That is, do you think it was set above or below the equilibrium price? Draw a supply and demand diagram, showing where the price floor that existed before 1978 was in relation to the equilibrium price.

b. Most economists agree that the average airline ticket price per mile traveled actually *fell* as a result of the Airline Deregulation Act. How might you reconcile that view with what you see in the diagram?

12. Many college students attempt to land internships before graduation to burnish their resumes, gain experience in a chosen field, or try out possible careers. The hope shared by all of these prospective interns is that they will find internships that pay more than typical summer jobs, such as waiting tables or flipping burgers.

a. With wage measured on the vertical axis and number of hours of work on the horizontal axis, draw a supply and demand diagram for the market for interns in which the minimum wage is non-binding at the market equilibrium.

b. Assume that a market downturn reduces the demand for interns by employers. However, many students are willing and eager to work in unpaid internships. As a result, the new market equilibrium wage is equal to zero. Draw another supply and demand diagram to illustrate this new market equilibrium. As in Figure 5-7, include a shaded triangle that represents the deadweight loss from the minimum wage. Using the diagram, explain your findings.

WORK IT OUT

For interactive, step-by-step help in solving the following problem, visit *LaunchPad* by using the URL on the back cover of this book.

13. Suppose it is decided that rent control in New York City will be abolished and that market rents will now prevail. Assume that all rental units are identical and so are offered at the same rent. To address the plight of residents who may be unable to pay the market rent, an income supplement will be paid to all low-income households equal to the difference between the old controlled rent and the new market rent.

a. Use a diagram to show the effect on the rental market of the elimination of rent control. What will happen to the quality and quantity of rental housing supplied?

b. Use a second diagram to show the additional effect of the income-supplement policy on the market. What effect does it have on the market rent and quantity of rental housing supplied in comparison to your answers to part a?

c. Are tenants better or worse off as a result of these policies? Are landlords better or worse off? Is society as a whole better or worse off?

d. From a political standpoint, why do you think cities have been more likely to resort to rent control rather than a policy of income supplements to help low-income people pay for housing?

Elasticity

> ## ◐ What You Will Learn in This Chapter

- Why economists use **elasticity** to measure responsiveness to changes in prices or incomes

- Why the **price elasticity of demand, the income elasticity of demand,** and the **cross-price elasticity of demand** are important indicators of consumer behavior in response to changes in prices and income

- Why the **price elasticity of supply** is an important indicator of producer behavior in response to changes in price

- What factors influence the size of these various elasticities

TAKEN FOR A RIDE

Scott Kochsiek/iStockphoto/Getty Images

The demand for ambulance rides to the hospital is relatively unresponsive to the price.

I F YOU ARE EXPERIENCING A TRUE emergency, you aren't likely to quibble about the price of an ambulance ride to the nearest emergency room. But what if it isn't an emergency? Take the case of Kira Millas, who doesn't even know who called an ambulance after she swam into the side of a swimming pool, breaking three teeth. Shaken, she accepted the ambulance ride to a local hospital, 15 minutes away. A week later, she received the bill: $1,772.42. Stunned, she said: "We only drove nine miles and it was a non-life-threatening injury. I needed absolutely no emergency treatment."

Kira's experience is by no means exceptional. Although ambulances are often requested by a bystander or by 911 dispatchers, it is the patient who receives the bill. Undoubtedly, in a true medical emergency, a patient feels fortunate that an ambulance is available. But even in nonemergency cases, like Kira's, many patients often feel obliged to get into the ambulance once it arrives. And just like Kira, they are uninformed about the cost

of the ride to the hospital. (With luck, they have recovered by the time they receive the bill!) And while many people have health insurance that will cover some or all of the cost of the ambulance service, the patient is ultimately responsible for paying the rest.

An estimated 40 million ambulance trips, at a cost of $14 billion, are provided each year by nonprofit entities such as local fire departments and by for-profit companies each year in the United States. Sensing profit-making opportunities, in recent years for-profit companies have significantly expanded their operations, often taking over from nonprofit operators. And big investors are betting that ambulance services will generate significant profits: two private ambulance providers were recently bought by investors, one for $3 billion and another for $438 million.

Charges for an ambulance ride vary wildly across the country, from several hundred dollars to tens of thousands of dollars. The price may depend on many

things other than the patient's medical needs, from the level of skill of the ambulance team onboard to the distance traveled, or in some cases whether a friend or relative rides along (which can add hundreds of dollars to the cost). While it's impossible to know the total amount that Americans are paying for ambulance services, Medicare, the federally administered health insurance program for Americans age 65 and older, has seen its spending on ambulance services explode, from $2 billion a year in 2002 to nearly $6 billion in 2013.

What accounts for the extreme variation in the cost of ambulance services? How are these services able to charge thousands of dollars, regardless of whether an ambulance is actually needed? Or to charge for an ambulance equipped with heart resuscitation capabilities when the patient has only a broken leg? The answer to these questions is *price unresponsiveness:* in the heat of the moment, many consumers—particularly those with true emergencies—are *unresponsive* to the price of an ambulance. Ambulance operators judge correctly that a significant number of patients won't ask "How much is this ride to the emergency room going to cost?" before getting onboard. In other words, a large increase in the price of an ambulance ride leaves the quantity demanded by a significant number of consumers relatively unchanged.

Let's consider a very different scenario. Suppose that the maker of a par-

ticular brand of breakfast cereal decided to charge 10 times the original price. It would be extremely difficult, if not impossible, to find consumers willing to pay the much higher price. In other words, consumers of breakfast cereal are much more responsive to price than the consumers of ambulance rides.

But how do we define *responsiveness*? Economists measure responsiveness of consumers to price with a par-

ticular number, called the *price elasticity of demand*. In this chapter we will show how the price elasticity of demand is calculated and why it is the best measure of how the quantity demanded responds to changes in price. We will then see that the price elasticity of demand is only one of a family of related concepts, including the *income elasticity of demand, cross-price elasticity of demand*, and the *price elasticity of supply*.

Defining and Measuring Elasticity

In order for investors to know whether they can earn significant profits in the ambulance business, they need to know the *price elasticity of demand* for ambulance rides. With this information, investors can accurately predict whether or not a significant rise in the price of an ambulance ride results in an increase in revenue.

Calculating the Price Elasticity of Demand

Figure 6-1 shows a hypothetical demand curve for an ambulance ride. At a price of $200 per ride, consumers would demand 10 million rides per year (point *A*); at a price of $210 per ride, consumers would demand 9.9 million rides per year (point *B*).

Figure 6-1, then, tells us the change in the quantity demanded for a particular change in the price. But how can we turn this into a measure of price responsiveness? The answer is to calculate the *price elasticity of demand*.

The **price elasticity of demand** is the ratio of the *percent change in quantity demanded* to the *percent change in price* as we move along the demand curve. As we'll see later in this chapter, the reason economists use percent changes is to obtain a measure that doesn't depend on the units in which a good is measured (say, a 1-mile ambulance trip versus a 10-mile ambulance trip). But before we get to that, let's look at how elasticity is calculated.

To calculate the price elasticity of demand, we first calculate the *percent change in the quantity demanded* and the corresponding *percent change in the price* as we move along the demand curve. These are defined as follows:

$$\textbf{(6-1)} \quad \% \text{ change in quantity demanded} = \frac{\text{Change in quantity demanded}}{\text{Initial quantity demanded}} \times 100$$

and

$$\textbf{(6-2)} \quad \% \text{ change in price} = \frac{\text{Change in price}}{\text{Initial price}} \times 100$$

In Figure 6-1, we see that when the price rises from $200 to $210, the quantity demanded falls from 10 million to 9.9 million rides, yielding a change in the quantity demanded of 0.1 million rides. So the percent change in the quantity demanded is

$$\% \text{ change in quantity demanded} = \frac{-0.1 \text{ million rides}}{10 \text{ million rides}} \times 100 = -1\%$$

The **price elasticity of demand** is the ratio of the percent change in the quantity demanded to the percent change in the price as we move along the demand curve.

The initial price is $200 and the change in the price is $10, so the percent change in price is

$$\% \text{ change in price} = \frac{\$10}{\$200} \times 100 = 5\%$$

FIGURE 6-1   The Demand for Ambulance Rides

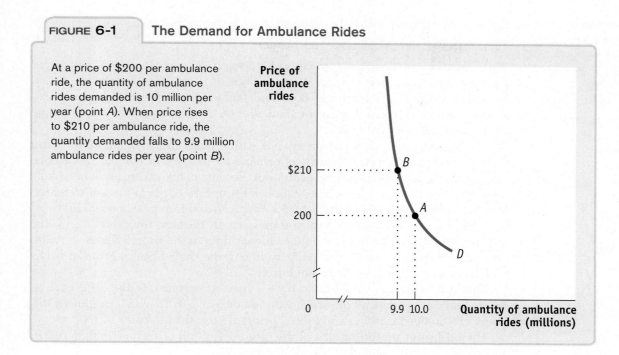

At a price of $200 per ambulance ride, the quantity of ambulance rides demanded is 10 million per year (point *A*). When price rises to $210 per ambulance ride, the quantity demanded falls to 9.9 million ambulance rides per year (point *B*).

To calculate the price elasticity of demand, we find the ratio of the percent change in the quantity demanded to the percent change in the price:

(6-3) Price elasticity of demand $= \dfrac{\%\ \text{change in quantity demanded}}{\%\ \text{change in price}}$

In Figure 6-1, the price elasticity of demand is therefore

$$\text{Price elasticity of demand} = \frac{1\%}{5\%} = 0.2$$

Notice that the minus sign that appeared in the calculation of the percent change in the quantity demanded has been dropped when we calculate this last equation, the price elasticity of demand. Why have we done this? The *law of demand* says that demand curves are downward sloping, so price and quantity demanded always move in opposite directions. In other words, a positive percent change in price (a rise in price) leads to a negative percent change in the quantity demanded; a negative percent change in price (a fall in price) leads to a positive percent change in the quantity demanded. This means that the price elasticity of demand is, in strictly mathematical terms, a negative number.

However, it is inconvenient to repeatedly write a minus sign. So when economists talk about the price elasticity of demand, they usually drop the minus sign and report the *absolute value* of the price elasticity of demand. In this case, for example, economists would usually say "the price elasticity of demand is 0.2," taking it for granted that you understand they mean *minus* 0.2. We follow this convention here.

The larger the price elasticity of demand, the more responsive the quantity demanded is to the price. When the price elasticity of demand is large—when consumers change their quantity demanded by a large percentage compared to the percent change in the price—economists say that demand is highly elastic.

As we'll see shortly, a price elasticity of 0.2 indicates a small response of quantity demanded to price. That is, the quantity demanded will fall by a relatively small amount when price rises. This is what economists call *inelastic* demand. And inelastic demand is exactly what enables an ambulance operator to increase the total amount earned by raising the price of an ambulance ride.

An Alternative Way to Calculate Elasticities: The Midpoint Method

Price elasticity of demand compares the *percent change in quantity demanded* with the *percent change in price*. When we look at some other elasticities, which we will do shortly, we'll learn why it is important to focus on percent changes. But at this point we need to discuss a technical issue that arises when you calculate percent changes in variables.

The best way to understand the issue is with a real example. Suppose you were trying to estimate the price elasticity of demand for gasoline by comparing gasoline prices and consumption in different countries. Because of high taxes, gasoline usually costs about three times as much per gallon in Europe as it does in the United States. So what is the percent difference between American and European gas prices?

Well, it depends on which way you measure it. Because the price of gasoline in Europe is approximately three times higher than in the United States, it is 200 percent higher. Because the price of gasoline in the United States is one-third as high as in Europe, it is 66.7 percent lower.

This is a nuisance: we'd like to have a percent measure of the difference in prices that doesn't depend on which way you measure it. To avoid computing different elasticities for rising and falling prices we use the *midpoint method*.

The **midpoint method** replaces the usual definition of the percent change in a variable, X, with a slightly different definition:

$$\textbf{(6-4)} \quad \% \text{ change in } X = \frac{\text{Change in } X}{\text{Average value of } X} \times 100$$

where the average value of X is defined as

$$\text{Average value of } X = \frac{\text{Starting value of } X + \text{Final value of } X}{2}$$

When calculating the price elasticity of demand using the midpoint method, both the percent change in the price and the percent change in the quantity demanded are found using this method. To see how this method works, suppose you have the following data for some good:

	Price	Quantity demanded
Situation A	$0.90	1,100
Situation B	$1.10	900

To calculate the percent change in quantity going from situation A to situation B, we compare the change in the quantity demanded—a fall of 200 units—with the *average* of the quantity demanded in the two situations. So we calculate

$$\% \text{ change in quantity demanded} = \frac{-200}{(1{,}100 + 900)/2} \times 100 = \frac{-200}{1{,}000} \times 100 = -20\%$$

In the same way, we calculate

$$\% \text{ change in price} = \frac{\$0.20}{(\$0.90 + \$1.10)/2} \times 100 = \frac{\$0.20}{\$1.00} \times 100 = 20\%$$

So in this case we would calculate the price elasticity of demand to be

$$\text{Price elasticity of demand} = \frac{\% \text{ change in quantity demanded}}{\% \text{ change in price}} = \frac{20\%}{20\%} = 1$$

again dropping the minus sign.

The important point is that we would get the same result, a price elasticity of demand of 1, whether we go up the demand curve from situation A to situation B or down from situation B to situation A.

To arrive at a more general formula for price elasticity of demand, suppose that we have data for two points on a demand curve. At point 1 the quantity demanded and price are (Q_1, P_1); at point 2 they are (Q_2, P_2). Then the formula for calculating the price elasticity of demand is:

(6-5) Price elasticity of demand $= \dfrac{\dfrac{Q_2 - Q_1}{(Q_1 + Q_2)/2}}{\dfrac{P_2 - P_1}{(P_1 + P_2)/2}}$

As before, when finding a price elasticity of demand calculated by the midpoint method, we drop the minus sign and use the absolute value.

ECONOMICS ▶ *in Action*

Estimating Elasticities

You might think it's easy to estimate price elasticities of demand from real-world data: just compare percent changes in prices with percent changes in quantities demanded. Unfortunately, it's rarely that simple because changes in price aren't the only thing affecting changes in the quantity demanded: other factors—such as changes in income, changes in tastes, and changes in the prices of other goods—shift the demand curve, thereby changing the quantity demanded at any given price.

To estimate price elasticities of demand, economists must use careful statistical analysis to separate the influence of the change in price, holding other things equal.

Economists have estimated price elasticities of demand for a number of goods and services. Table 6-1 summarizes some of these and shows a wide range of price elasticities. There are some goods, like gasoline for which demand hardly responds at all to changes in the price. There are other goods, such as airline travel for leisure, or Coke and Pepsi, for which the quantity demanded is very sensitive to the price.

Notice that Table 6-1 is divided into two parts: inelastic and elastic demand. We'll explain the significance of that division in the next section.

TABLE **6-1**	Some Estimated Price Elasticities of Demand
Good	**Price elasticity of demand**
Inelastic demand	
Gasoline (short-run)	0.09
Gasonline (long-run)	0.24
Airline travel (business)	0.80
Soda	0.80
College (in-state tuition)	0.87
Elastic demand	
Housing	1.2
College (out-of-state tuition)	1.2
Airline travel (leisure)	1.5
Coke/Pepsi	3.3

Check Your Understanding 6-1

1. The price of strawberries falls from $1.50 to $1.00 per carton and the quantity demanded goes from 100,000 to 200,000 cartons. Use the midpoint method to find the price elasticity of demand.

2. At the present level of consumption, 4,000 movie tickets, and at the current price, $5 per ticket, the price elasticity of demand for movie tickets is 1. Using the midpoint method, calculate the percentage by which the owners of movie theaters must reduce price in order to sell 5,000 tickets.

3. The price elasticity of demand for ice-cream sandwiches is 1.2 at the current price of $0.50 per sandwich and the current consumption level of 100,000 sandwiches. Calculate the change in the quantity demanded when price rises by $0.05. Use Equations 6-1 and 6-2 to calculate percent changes and Equation 6-3 to relate price elasticity of demand to the percent changes.

Solutions appear at back of book.

▼ **Quick Review**

The **price elasticity of demand** is equal to the percent change in the quantity demanded divided by the percent change in the price as you move along the demand curve, and dropping any minus sign.

In practice, percent changes are best measured using the **midpoint method,** in which the percent changes are calculated using the average of starting and final values.

Demand is **perfectly inelastic** when the quantity demanded does not respond at all to changes in the price. When demand is perfectly inelastic, the demand curve is a vertical line.

Interpreting the Price Elasticity of Demand

In a true emergency, a patient is unlikely to question the price of the ambulance ride to the hospital. But even in a nonemergency, like Kira's broken teeth, patients are often unlikely to respond to an increase in the price of an ambulance by reducing their demand because they are unaware of the cost. As a result, investors in private ambulance companies see profit-making opportunities in delivering ambulance services, because the price elasticity of demand is small. But what does that mean? How low does a price elasticity have to be for us to classify it as low? How big does it have to be for us to consider it high? And what determines whether the price elasticity of demand is high or low anyway?

To answer these questions, we need to look more deeply at the price elasticity of demand.

How Elastic Is Elastic?

As a first step toward classifying price elasticities of demand, let's look at the extreme cases.

First, consider the demand for a good when people pay no attention to the price—say, snake anti-venom. Suppose that consumers will buy 1,000 doses of anti-venom per year regardless of the price. In this case, the demand curve for anti-venom would look like the curve shown in panel (a) of Figure 6-2: it would be a vertical line at 1,000 doses of anti-venom. Since the percent change in the quantity demanded is zero for *any* change in the price, the price elasticity of demand in this case is zero. The case of a zero price elasticity of demand is known as **perfectly inelastic demand.**

FIGURE **6-2**   Two Extreme Cases of Price Elasticity of Demand

Panel (a) shows a perfectly inelastic demand curve, which is a vertical line. The quantity of snake anti-venom demanded is always 1,000 doses, regardless of price. As a result, the price elasticity of demand is zero—the quantity demanded is unaffected by the price. Panel (b) shows a perfectly elastic demand curve, which is a horizontal line. At a price of $5, consumers will buy any quantity of pink tennis balls, but they will buy none at a price above $5. If the price falls below $5, they will buy an extremely large number of pink tennis balls and none of any other color.

The opposite extreme occurs when even a tiny rise in the price will cause the quantity demanded to drop to zero or even a tiny fall in the price will cause the quantity demanded to get extremely large.

Panel (b) of Figure 6-2 shows the case of pink tennis balls; we suppose that tennis players really don't care what color their balls are and that other colors, such as neon green and vivid yellow, are available at $5 per dozen balls. In this case, consumers will buy no pink balls if they cost more than $5 per dozen but will buy only pink balls if they cost less than $5. The demand curve will therefore be a horizontal line at a price of $5 per dozen balls. As you move back and forth along this line, there is a change in the quantity demanded but no change in the price. Roughly speaking, when you divide a number by zero, you get infinity, denoted by the symbol ∞. So a horizontal demand curve implies an infinite price elasticity of demand. When the price elasticity of demand is infinite, economists say that demand is **perfectly elastic.**

The price elasticity of demand for the vast majority of goods is somewhere between these two extreme cases. Economists use one main criterion for classifying these intermediate cases: they ask whether the price elasticity of demand is greater or less than 1. When the price elasticity of demand is greater than 1, economists say that demand is **elastic.** When the price elasticity of demand is less than 1, they say that demand is **inelastic.** The borderline case is **unit-elastic demand,** where the price elasticity of demand is—surprise—exactly 1.

To see why a price elasticity of demand equal to 1 is a useful dividing line, let's consider a hypothetical example: a toll bridge operated by the state highway department. Other things equal, the number of drivers who use the bridge depends on the toll, the price the highway department charges for crossing the bridge: the higher the toll, the fewer the drivers who use the bridge.

Figure 6-3 shows three hypothetical demand curves—one in which demand is unit-elastic, one in which it is inelastic, and one in which it is elastic. In each case, point A shows the quantity demanded if the toll is $0.90 and point B shows the quantity demanded if the toll is $1.10. An increase in the toll from $0.90 to $1.10 is an increase of 20% if we use the midpoint method to calculate percent changes.

Panel (a) shows what happens when the toll is raised from $0.90 to $1.10 and the demand curve is unit-elastic. Here the 20% price rise leads to a fall in the quantity of cars using the bridge each day from 1,100 to 900, which is a 20% decline (again using the midpoint method). So the price elasticity of demand is 20%/20% = 1.

Panel (b) shows a case of inelastic demand when the toll is raised from $0.90 to $1.10. The same 20% price rise reduces the quantity demanded from 1,050 to 950. That's only a 10% decline, so in this case the price elasticity of demand is 10%/20% = 0.5.

Panel (c) shows a case of elastic demand when the toll is raised from $0.90 to $1.10. The 20% price increase causes the quantity demanded to fall from 1,200 to 800—a 40% decline, so the price elasticity of demand is 40%/20% = 2.

Why does it matter whether demand is unit-elastic, inelastic, or elastic? Because this classification predicts how changes in the price of a good will affect the *total revenue* earned by producers from the sale of that good. In many real-life situations, it is crucial to know how price changes affect total revenue. **Total revenue** is defined as the total value of sales of a good or service, equal to the price multiplied by the quantity sold.

(6-6) Total revenue = Price × Quantity sold

Total revenue has a useful graphical representation that can help us understand why knowing the price elasticity of demand is crucial when we ask whether

Demand is **perfectly elastic** when any price increase will cause the quantity demanded to drop to zero. When demand is perfectly elastic, the demand curve is a horizontal line.

Demand is **elastic** if the price elasticity of demand is greater than 1, **inelastic** if the price elasticity of demand is less than 1, and **unit-elastic** if the price elasticity of demand is exactly 1.

The **total revenue** is the total value of sales of a good or service. It is equal to the price multiplied by the quantity sold.

FIGURE **6-3** Unit-Elastic Demand, Inelastic Demand, and Elastic Demand

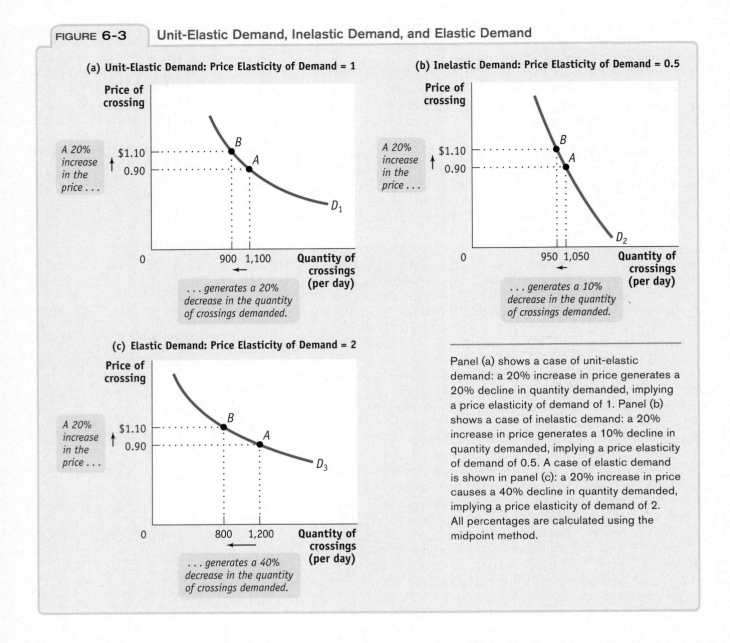

(a) Unit-Elastic Demand: Price Elasticity of Demand = 1

Price of crossing

A 20% increase in the price . . .

$1.10

0.90

B

A

D_1

0   900 1,100   Quantity of crossings (per day)

. . . generates a 20% decrease in the quantity of crossings demanded.

(b) Inelastic Demand: Price Elasticity of Demand = 0.5

Price of crossing

A 20% increase in the price . . .

$1.10

0.90

B

A

D_2

0   950 1,050   Quantity of crossings (per day)

. . . generates a 10% decrease in the quantity of crossings demanded.

(c) Elastic Demand: Price Elasticity of Demand = 2

Price of crossing

A 20% increase in the price . . .

$1.10

0.90

B

A

D_3

0   800   1,200   Quantity of crossings (per day)

. . . generates a 40% decrease in the quantity of crossings demanded.

Panel (a) shows a case of unit-elastic demand: a 20% increase in price generates a 20% decline in quantity demanded, implying a price elasticity of demand of 1. Panel (b) shows a case of inelastic demand: a 20% increase in price generates a 10% decline in quantity demanded, implying a price elasticity of demand of 0.5. A case of elastic demand is shown in panel (c): a 20% increase in price causes a 40% decline in quantity demanded, implying a price elasticity of demand of 2. All percentages are calculated using the midpoint method.

a price rise will increase or reduce total revenue. Panel (a) of Figure 6-4 shows the same demand curve as panel (a) of Figure 6-3. We see that 1,100 drivers will use the bridge if the toll is $0.90. So the total revenue at a price of $0.90 is $0.90 × 1,100 = $990. This value is equal to the area of the green rectangle, which is drawn with the bottom left corner at the point (0, 0) and the top right corner at (1,100, 0.90). In general, the total revenue at any given price is equal to the area of a rectangle whose height is the price and whose width is the quantity demanded at that price.

To get an idea of why total revenue is important, consider the following scenario. Suppose that the toll on the bridge is currently $0.90 but that the highway department must raise extra money for road repairs. One way to do this is to raise the toll on the bridge. But this plan might backfire, since a higher toll will reduce the number of drivers who use the bridge. And if traffic on the bridge dropped a lot, a higher toll would actually reduce total revenue instead of increasing it. So it's important for the highway department to know how drivers will respond to a toll increase.

FIGURE **6-4**   Total Revenue

(a) Total Revenue

Price of crossing

$0.90

Total revenue = price x quantity = $990

0   1,100   **Quantity of crossings (per day)**

D

(b) Effect of a Price Increase on Total Revenue

Price of crossing

Price effect of price increase: higher price for each unit sold

Quantity effect of price increase: fewer units sold

$1.10

0.90

C

B   A

D

0   900 1,100   **Quantity of crossings (per day)**

The green rectangle in panel (a) shows the total revenue generated from 1,100 drivers who each pay a toll of $0.90. Panel (b) shows how total revenue is affected when the price increases from $0.90 to $1.10. Due to the quantity effect, total revenue falls by area A. Due to the price effect, total revenue increases by the area C. In general, the overall effect can go either way, depending on the price elasticity of demand.

We can see graphically how the toll increase affects total bridge revenue by examining panel (b) of Figure 6-4. At a toll of $0.90, total revenue is given by the sum of the areas A and B. After the toll is raised to $1.10, total revenue is given by the sum of areas B and C. So when the toll is raised, revenue represented by area A is lost but revenue represented by area C is gained.

These two areas have important interpretations. Area C represents the revenue gain that comes from the additional $0.20 paid by drivers who continue to use the bridge. That is, the 900 who continue to use the bridge contribute an additional $0.20 × 900 = $180 per day to total revenue, represented by area C. But 200 drivers who would have used the bridge at a price of $0.90 no longer do so, generating a loss to total revenue of $0.90 × 200 = $180 per day, represented by area A. (In this particular example, because demand is unit-elastic—the same as in panel (a) of Figure 6-3—the rise in the toll has no effect on total revenue; areas A and C are the same size.)

Except in the rare case of a good with perfectly elastic or perfectly inelastic demand, when a seller raises the price of a good, two countervailing effects are present:

- *A price effect:* After a price increase, each unit sold sells at a higher price, which tends to raise revenue.

- *A quantity effect:* After a price increase, fewer units are sold, which tends to lower revenue.

But then, you may ask, what is the ultimate net effect on total revenue: does it go up or down? The answer is that, in general, the effect on total revenue can go either way—a price rise may either increase total revenue or lower it. If the price effect, which tends to raise total revenue, is the stronger of the two effects, then total revenue goes up. If the quantity effect, which tends to reduce total revenue,

The highway department uses the price elasticity of demand to calculate the change in revenue from higher tolls.

is the stronger, then total revenue goes down. And if the strengths of the two effects are exactly equal—as in our toll bridge example, where a $180 gain offsets a $180 loss—total revenue is unchanged by the price increase.

The price elasticity of demand tells us what happens to total revenue when price changes: its size determines which effect—the price effect or the quantity effect—is stronger. Specifically:

- If demand for a good is *unit-elastic* (the price elasticity of demand is 1), an increase in price does not change total revenue. In this case, the quantity effect and the price effect exactly offset each other.

- If demand for a good is *inelastic* (the price elasticity of demand is less than 1), a higher price increases total revenue. In this case, the quantity effect is weaker than the price effect.

- If demand for a good is *elastic* (the price elasticity of demand is greater than 1), an increase in price reduces total revenue. In this case, the quantity effect is stronger than the price effect.

Table 6-2 shows how the effect of a price increase on total revenue depends on the price elasticity of demand, using the same data as in Figure 6-3. An increase in the price from $0.90 to $1.10 leaves total revenue unchanged at $990 when demand is unit-elastic. When demand is inelastic, the quantity effect is dominated by the price effect; the same price increase leads to an increase in total revenue from $945 to $1,045. And when demand is elastic, the quantity effect dominates the price effect; the price increase leads to a decline in total revenue from $1,080 to $880.

The price elasticity of demand also predicts the effect of a *fall* in price on total revenue. When the price falls, the same two countervailing effects are present, but they work in the opposite directions as compared to the case of a price rise. There is the price effect of a lower price per unit sold, which tends to lower revenue. This is countered by the quantity effect of more units sold, which tends to raise revenue. Which effect dominates depends on the price elasticity. Here is a quick summary:

- When demand is *unit-elastic,* the two effects exactly balance; so a fall in price has no effect on total revenue.

- When demand is *inelastic,* the quantity effect is dominated by the price effect; so a fall in price reduces total revenue.

- When demand is *elastic,* the quantity effect dominates the price effect; so a fall in price increases total revenue.

TABLE 6-2   Price Elasticity of Demand and Total Revenue

	Price of toll = $0.90	Price of toll = $1.10
Unit-elastic demand (price elasticity of demand = 1)		
Quantity demanded	1,100	900
Total revenue	$990	$990
Inelastic demand (price elasticity of demand = 0.5)		
Quantity demanded	1,050	950
Total revenue	$945	$1,045
Elastic demand (price elasticity of demand = 2)		
Quantity demanded	1,200	800
Total revenue	$1,080	$880

Price Elasticity Along the Demand Curve

Suppose an economist says that "the price elasticity of demand for coffee is 0.25." What he or she means is that *at the current price* the elasticity is 0.25. In the previous discussion of the toll bridge, what we were really describing was the elasticity *at the toll price* of $0.90. Why this qualification? Because for the vast majority of demand curves, the price elasticity of demand at one point along the curve is different from the price elasticity of demand at other points along the same curve.

To see this, consider the table in Figure 6-5, which shows a hypothetical demand schedule. It also shows in the last column the total revenue generated at each price and quantity combination in the demand schedule. The upper panel of the graph in Figure 6-5 shows the corresponding demand curve. The lower panel illustrates the same data on total revenue: the height of a bar at each quantity demanded—which corresponds to a particular price—measures the total revenue generated at that price.

In Figure 6-5, you can see that when the price is low, raising the price increases total revenue: starting at a price of $1, raising the price to $2 increases total revenue from $9 to $16. This means that when the price is low, demand is

FIGURE 6-5   The Price Elasticity of Demand Changes Along the Demand Curve

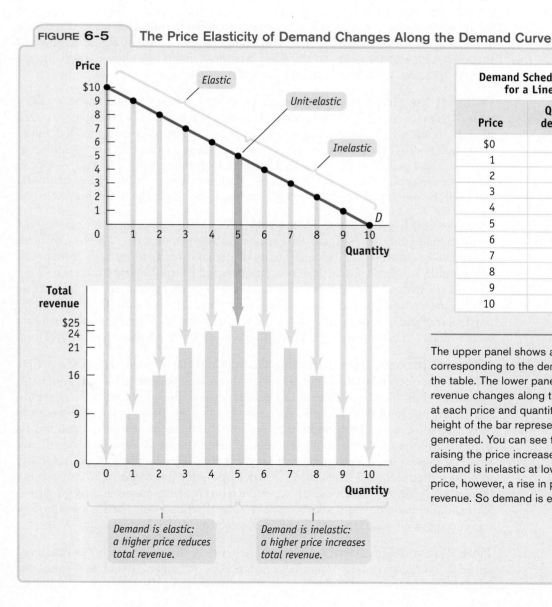

Demand Schedule and Total Revenue for a Linear Demand Curve		
Price	Quantity demanded	Total revenue
$0	10	$0
1	9	9
2	8	16
3	7	21
4	6	24
5	5	25
6	4	24
7	3	21
8	2	16
9	1	9
10	0	0

The upper panel shows a demand curve corresponding to the demand schedule in the table. The lower panel shows how total revenue changes along that demand curve: at each price and quantity combination, the height of the bar represents the total revenue generated. You can see that at a low price, raising the price increases total revenue. So demand is inelastic at low prices. At a high price, however, a rise in price reduces total revenue. So demand is elastic at high prices.

Demand is elastic: a higher price reduces total revenue.

Demand is inelastic: a higher price increases total revenue.

inelastic. Moreover, you can see that demand is inelastic on the entire section of the demand curve from a price of $0 to a price of $5.

When the price is high, however, raising it further reduces total revenue: starting at a price of $8, raising the price to $9 reduces total revenue, from $16 to $9. This means that when the price is high, demand is elastic. Furthermore, you can see that demand is elastic over the section of the demand curve from a price of $5 to $10.

For the vast majority of goods, the price elasticity of demand changes along the demand curve. So whenever you measure a good's elasticity, you are really measuring it at a particular point or section of the good's demand curve.

What Factors Determine the Price Elasticity of Demand?

Investors in private ambulance companies believe that the price elasticity of demand for an ambulance ride is low for two important reasons. First, in many if not most cases, an ambulance ride is a medical necessity. Second, in an emergency there really is no substitute for the standard of care that an ambulance provides. And even among ambulances there are typically no substitutes because in any given geographical area there is usually only one ambulance provider. (The exceptions are very densely populated areas, but even in those locations an ambulance dispatcher is unlikely to give you a choice of ambulance providers with an accompanying price list.)

In general there are four main factors that determine elasticity: whether a good is a necessity or luxury, the availability of close substitutes, the share of income a consumer spends on the good, and how much time has elapsed since a change in price. We'll briefly examine each of these factors.

Whether the Good Is a Necessity or a Luxury As our opening story illustrates, the price elasticity of demand tends to be low if a good is something you must have, like a life-saving ambulance ride to the hospital. The price elasticity of demand tends to be high if the good is a luxury—something you can easily live without. For example, most people would consider a 110 inch high-definition TV a luxury—nice to have, but something they can live without. Therefore, the price elasticity of demand for it will be much higher than for a life-saving ambulance ride to the hospital.

The Availability of Close Substitutes As we just noted, the price elasticity of demand tends to be low if there are no close substitutes or if they are very difficult to obtain. In contrast, the price elasticity of demand tends to be high if there are other readily available goods that consumers regard as similar and would be willing to consume instead. For example, most consumers believe that there are fairly close substitutes to their favorite brand of breakfast cereal. As a result, if the maker of a particular brand of breakfast cereal raised the price significantly, that maker is likely to lose much—if not all—of its sales to other brands for which the price has not risen.

Share of Income Spent on the Good Consider a good that some people consume frequently, such as gasoline—say, for a long commute to and from work every day. For these consumers, spending on gasoline will typically absorb a significant share of their income. As a result, when the price of gasoline goes up, these consumers are likely to be very responsive to the price change and have a higher elasticity of demand. Why? Because when the good absorbs a significant share of these consumers' income, it is worth their time and effort to find a way to reduce their demand when the price goes up—such as switching to car-pooling instead of driving alone. In contrast, people who consume gasoline infrequently— for example, people who walk to work or take the bus—will have a low share of income spent on gasoline and therefore a lower elasticity of demand.

Time Elapsed Since Price Change In general, the price elasticity of demand tends to increase as consumers have more time to adjust. This means that the long-run price elasticity of demand is often higher than the short-run elasticity.

A good illustration is the changes in Americans' behavior over the past decade in response to higher gasoline prices. In 1998, a gallon of gasoline was only about $1. Over the years, however, gasoline prices steadily rose, so that by 2014 a gallon of gas cost from $3.50 to $4.00 in much of the United States. Over time, however, people changed their habits and choices in ways that enabled them to gradually reduce their gasoline consumption. In a recent survey, 53% of responders said they had made major life changes in order to cope with higher gas prices—changes such as driving less, getting a more fuel-efficient car, and using other modes of transportation like buses or bicycles. Some even moved to a more convenient location to save gas. These changes are reflected in the data on American gasoline consumption: the trend line of consumption fluctuated until about 2003,

CARLSON©2006 Milwaukee Journal Sentinel. Reprinted with permission of UNIVERSAL UCLICK.

then took a nosedive. So by 2013, Americans were purchasing 30 million gallons of gasoline a day on average, less than half of the 64 million they purchased in 2003. This confirms that the long-run price elasticity of demand for gasoline was indeed much larger than the short-run elasticity.

ECONOMICS ▶ *in Action*

Responding to Your Tuition Bill

College costs more than ever—and not just because of inflation. Tuition has been rising faster than the overall cost of living for years. But does rising tuition keep people from going to college? Two studies found that the answer depends on the type of college. Both studies assessed how responsive the decision to go to college is to a change in tuition.

A 1988 study found that a 3% increase in tuition led to an approximately 2% fall in the number of students enrolled at four-year institutions, giving a price elasticity of demand of 0.67 (2%/3%). In the case of two-year institutions, the study found a significantly higher response: a 3% increase in tuition led to a 2.7% fall in enrollments, giving a price elasticity of demand of 0.9. In other words, the enrollment decision for students at two-year colleges was significantly more responsive to price than for students at four-year colleges. The result: students at two-year colleges are more likely to forgo getting a degree because of tuition costs than students at four-year colleges.

A 1999 study confirmed this pattern. In comparison to four-year colleges, it found that two-year college enrollment rates were significantly more responsive to changes in state financial aid (a decline in aid leading to a decline in enrollments), a predictable effect given these students' greater sensitivity to the cost of tuition. Another piece of evidence suggests that students at two-year colleges are more likely to be paying their own way and making a trade-off between attending college versus working: the study found that enrollments at two-year colleges are much more responsive to changes in the unemployment rate (an increase in the unemployment rate leading to an increase in enrollments) than enrollments at four-year colleges. So is the cost of tuition a barrier to getting a college degree in the United States? Yes, but more so for students at two-year colleges than for students at four-year colleges.

Wavebreakmedia/Shutterstock

Students at two-year schools are more responsive to the price of tuition than students at four-year schools.

In response to decreased state funding, many public colleges and universities have been experimenting with changes to their tuition schedule in order to increase revenue. A 2012 study found that in-state college freshmen were significantly more responsive to the cost of tuition than freshmen from out-of-state. In-state freshmen were found to have a measured elasticity of demand of 1.8; the elasticity of demand for out-of state freshmen was statistically insignificant (that is, virtually zero). Perhaps out-of-state applicants are less price sensitive because they have higher incomes.

Not surprisingly, many public colleges and universities have found that raising the tuition for enrollments of out-of-state students has boosted revenues.

Check Your Understanding 6-2

1. For each case, choose the condition that characterizes demand: elastic demand, inelastic demand, or unit-elastic demand.
   a. Total revenue decreases when price increases.
   b. The additional revenue generated by an increase in quantity sold is exactly offset by revenue lost from the fall in price received per unit.
   c. Total revenue falls when output increases.
   d. Producers in an industry find they can increase their total revenues by coordinating a reduction in industry output.

2. For the following goods, what is the elasticity of demand? Explain. What is the shape of the demand curve?
   a. Demand for a blood transfusion by an accident victim
   b. Demand by students for green erasers

Solutions appear at back of book.

Other Demand Elasticities

The quantity of a good demanded depends not only on the price of that good but also on other variables. In particular, demand curves shift because of changes in the prices of related goods and changes in consumers' incomes. It is often important to have a measure of these other effects, and the best measures are—you guessed it—elasticities. Specifically, we can best measure how the demand for a good is affected by prices of other goods using a measure called the *cross-price elasticity of demand*, and we can best measure how demand is affected by changes in income using the *income elasticity of demand*.

The Cross-Price Elasticity of Demand

In Chapter 3 you learned that the demand for a good is often affected by the prices of other, related goods—goods that are substitutes or complements. There you saw that a change in the price of a related good shifts the demand curve of the original good, reflecting a change in the quantity demanded at any given price. The strength of such a "cross" effect on demand can be measured by the **cross-price elasticity of demand,** defined as the ratio of the percent change in the quantity demanded of one good to the percent change in the price of the other.

(6-7) Cross-price elasticity of demand between goods A and B

$$= \frac{\% \text{ change in quantity of A demanded}}{\% \text{ change in price of B}}$$

The **cross-price elasticity of demand** between two goods measures the effect of the change in one good's price on the quantity demanded of the other good. It is equal to the percent change in the quantity demanded of one good divided by the percent change in the other good's price.

When two goods are substitutes, like hot dogs and hamburgers, the cross-price elasticity of demand is positive: a rise in the price of hot dogs increases the demand for hamburgers—that is, it causes a rightward shift of the demand curve for hamburgers. If the goods are close substitutes, the cross-price elasticity will be positive and large; if they are not close substitutes, the cross-price elasticity will be positive and small. So when the cross-price elasticity of demand is positive, its size is a measure of how closely substitutable the two goods are, with a higher number meaning the goods are closer substitutes.

When two goods are complements, like hot dogs and hot dog buns, the cross-price elasticity is negative: a rise in the price of hot dogs decreases the demand for hot dog buns—that is, it causes a leftward shift of the demand curve for hot dog buns. As with substitutes, the size of the cross-price elasticity of demand between two complements tells us how strongly complementary they are: if the cross-price elasticity is only slightly below zero, they are weak complements; if it is very negative, they are strong complements.

Note that in the case of the cross-price elasticity of demand, the sign (plus or minus) is very important: it tells us whether the two goods are complements or substitutes. So we cannot drop the minus sign as we did for the price elasticity of demand.

Our discussion of the cross-price elasticity of demand is a useful place to return to a point we made earlier: elasticity is a *unit-free* measure—that is, it doesn't depend on the units in which goods are measured.

To see the potential problem, suppose someone told you that "if the price of hot dog buns rises by $0.30, Americans will buy 10 million fewer hot dogs this year." If you've ever bought hot dog buns, you'll immediately wonder: is that a $0.30 increase in the price *per bun*, or is it a $0.30 increase in the price *per package*? Buns are usually sold in packages of eight. It makes a big difference what units we are talking about! However, if someone says that the cross-price elasticity of demand between buns and hot dogs is −0.3, it doesn't matter whether buns are sold individually or by the package. So elasticity is defined as a ratio of percent changes, as a way of making sure that confusion over units doesn't arise.

The Income Elasticity of Demand

The **income elasticity of demand** is a measure of how much the demand for a good is affected by changes in consumers' incomes. It allows us to determine whether a good is a normal or inferior good as well as to measure how intensely the demand for the good responds to changes in income.

(6-8) Income elasticity of demand $= \dfrac{\% \text{ change in quantity demanded}}{\% \text{ change in income}}$

Just as the cross-price elasticity of demand between two goods can be either positive or negative, depending on whether the goods are substitutes or complements, the income elasticity of demand for a good can also be either positive or negative. Recall from Chapter 3 that goods can be either *normal goods,* for which demand increases when income rises, or *inferior goods,* for which demand decreases when income rises. These definitions relate directly to the sign of the income elasticity of demand:

- When the income elasticity of demand is positive, the good is a normal good. In this case, the quantity demanded at any given price increases as income increases.

- When the income elasticity of demand is negative, the good is an inferior good. In this case, the quantity demanded at any given price decreases as income increases.

Economists often use estimates of the income elasticity of demand to predict which industries will grow most rapidly as the incomes of consumers grow over time. In doing this, they often find it useful to make a further distinction among normal goods, identifying which are *income-elastic* and which are *income-inelastic.*

The **income elasticity of demand** is the percent change in the quantity of a good demanded when a consumer's income changes divided by the percent change in the consumer's income.

FOR INQUIRING MINDS | Will China Save the U.S. Farming Sector

In the days of the Founding Fathers, the great majority of Americans lived on farms. As recently as the 1940s, one American in six—or approximately 17%—still did. But in the most recent U.S. Department of Agriculture census taken in 2012, the number of American farmers was estimated to be around 0.67% of the total population. Why do so few people now live and work on farms in the United States? There are two main reasons, both involving elasticities.

First, the income elasticity of demand for food is much less than 1—it is income-inelastic. As consumers grow richer, other things equal, spending on food rises less than income. As a result, as the U.S. economy has grown, the share of income it spends on food—and therefore the share of total U.S. income earned by farmers—has fallen.

Second, the demand for food is price-inelastic. This is important because technological advances in American agriculture have steadily raised yields over time and led to a

long-term trend of lower U.S. food prices for most of the past century and a half. The combination of price inelas-

Why do so few Americans work on farms?

ticity and falling prices led to falling total revenue for farmers. That's right: progress in farming has been good for American consumers but bad for American farmers.

The combination of these effects explains the long-term relative decline of farming in the United States. The low income elasticity of demand for food ensures that the income of farmers grows more slowly than the economy as a whole. And the combination of rapid technological progress in farming with price-inelastic demand for foodstuffs reinforces this effect, further reducing the growth of farm income.

That is, up until now. Starting in the mid-2000s, increased demand for foodstuffs from rapidly growing developing countries like China has pushed up the prices of agricultural products around the world. And American farmers have benefited, with U.S. farm income rising nearly 90% from 2009 to 2013. Eventually, as the growth in developing countries tapers off and agricultural innovation continues to progress, it's likely that the agricultural sector will resume its downward trend. But for now and for the foreseeable future, American farmers are enjoying the sector's revival. ∎

The demand for a good is **income-elastic** if the income elasticity of demand for that good is greater than 1.

The demand for a good is **income-inelastic** if the income elasticity of demand for that good is positive but less than 1.

The demand for a good is **income-elastic** if the income elasticity of demand for that good is greater than 1. When income rises, the demand for income-elastic goods rises *faster* than income. Luxury goods such as second homes and international travel tend to be income-elastic. The demand for a good is **income-inelastic** if the income elasticity of demand for that good is positive but less than 1. When income rises, the demand for income-inelastic goods rises, but more slowly than income. Necessities such as food and clothing tend to be income-inelastic.

GLOBAL COMPARISION | Food's Bite in World Budgets

If the income elasticity of demand for food is less than 1, we would expect to find that people in poor countries spend a larger share of their income on food than people in rich countries. And that's exactly what the data show. In this graph, we compare per capita income—a country's total income, divided by the population—with the share of income that is spent on food. (To make the graph a manageable size, per capita income is measured as a percentage of U.S. per capita income.)

In very poor countries, like Pakistan, people spend a large percent of their income on food. In middle-income countries, like Israel and Mexico, the share of spending that goes to food is much lower. And it's even lower in rich countries like the United States.

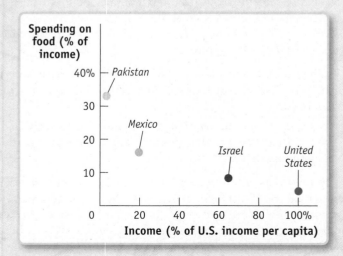

Source: U.S. Department of Agriculture and IMF *World Economic Outlook.*

ECONOMICS ▶ in Action

Spending It

The U.S. Bureau of Labor Statistics carries out extensive surveys of how families spend their incomes. This is not just a matter of intellectual curiosity. Quite a few government benefit programs involve some adjustment for changes in the cost of living; to estimate those changes, the government must know how people spend their money. But an additional payoff to these surveys is data on the income elasticity of demand for various goods.

What stands out from these studies? The classic result is that the income elasticity of demand for "food eaten at home" is considerably less than 1: as a family's income rises, the share of its income spent on food consumed at home falls. Correspondingly, the lower a family's income, the higher the share of income spent on food consumed at home.

In poor countries, many families spend more than half their income on food consumed at home. Although the income elasticity of demand for "food eaten at home" is estimated at less than 0.5 in the United States, the income elasticity of demand for "food eaten away from home" (restaurant meals) is estimated to be much higher—close to 1.

Judging from the activity at this busy McDonald's, incomes are rising in Vietnam.

Families with higher incomes eat out more often and at fancier places. In 1950, about 19% of U.S. income was spent on food consumed at home, a number that has dropped to 6.1% in 2012. But over the same time period, the share of U.S. income spent on food consumed away from home has stayed constant at 5%. In fact, a sure sign of rising income levels in developing countries is the arrival of fast-food restaurants that cater to newly affluent customers. For example, McDonald's can now be found in Hanoi, Jakarta, and Mumbai.

There is one clear example of an inferior good found in the surveys: rental housing. Families with higher income actually spend less on rent than families with lower income, because they are much more likely to own their own homes. And the category identified as "other housing"—which basically means second homes—is highly income-elastic. Only higher-income families can afford a luxury like a vacation home, so "other housing" has an income elasticity of demand greater than 1.

Check Your Understanding 6-3

1. After Chelsea's income increased from $12,000 to $18,000 a year, her purchases of album downloads increased from 10 to 40 downloads a year. Calculate Chelsea's income elasticity of demand for albums using the midpoint method.

2. Expensive restaurant meals are income-elastic goods for most people, including Sanjay. Suppose his income falls by 10% this year. What can you predict about the change in Sanjay's consumption of expensive restaurant meals?

3. As the price of margarine rises by 20%, a manufacturer of baked goods increases its quantity of butter demanded by 5%. Calculate the cross-price elasticity of demand between butter and margarine. Are butter and margarine substitutes or complements for this manufacturer?

Solutions appear at back of book.

▼ **Quick Review**

- Goods are substitutes when the **cross-price elasticity of demand** is positive. Goods are complements when the cross-price elasticity of demand is negative.

- Inferior goods have a negative **income elasticity of demand.** Most goods are normal goods, which have a positive income elasticity of demand.

- Normal goods may be either **income-elastic,** with an income elasticity of demand greater than 1, or **income-inelastic,** with an income elasticity of demand that is positive but less than 1.

The Price Elasticity of Supply

A fundamental characteristic of any market for ambulance services, no matter where it is located, is limited supply. For example, it would have been much harder to charge Kira Mills $1,772.42 for a 15-minute ride to the hospital if there

The **price elasticity of supply** is a measure of the responsiveness of the quantity of a good supplied to the price of that good. It is the ratio of the percent change in the quantity supplied to the percent change in the price as we move along the supply curve.

had been many ambulance providers cruising nearby and offering a lower price. But there are good economic reasons why are not: who among those experiencing a true health emergency would trust their health and safety to a "low-price" ambulance? And who would want to be a supplier, paying the expense of providing quality ambulance services, without being able to charge high prices to recoup costs? Not surprisingly, then, in most locations there is only one ambulance provider available, as we have seen.

In sum, a critical element in the ability of ambulance providers to charge high prices is limited supply: a low responsiveness in the quantity of output supplied to the higher prices charged for an ambulance ride. To measure the response of ambulance providers to price changes, we need a measure parallel to the price elasticity of demand—the *price elasticity of supply*, as we'll see next.

Measuring the Price Elasticity of Supply

The **price elasticity of supply** is defined the same way as the price elasticity of demand (although there is no minus sign to be eliminated here):

(6-9) Price elasticity of supply $= \dfrac{\% \text{ change in quantity supplied}}{\% \text{ change in price}}$

The only difference is that now we consider movements along the supply curve rather than movements along the demand curve.

Suppose that the price of tomatoes rises by 10%. If the quantity of tomatoes supplied also increases by 10% in response, the price elasticity of supply of tomatoes is 1 (10%/10%) and supply is unit-elastic. If the quantity supplied increases by 5%, the price elasticity of supply is 0.5 and supply is inelastic; if the quantity increases by 20%, the price elasticity of supply is 2 and supply is elastic.

As in the case of demand, the extreme values of the price elasticity of supply have a simple graphical representation. Panel (a) of Figure 6-6 shows the supply of

FIGURE 6-6   Two Extreme Cases of Price Elasticity of Supply

Panel (a) shows a perfectly inelastic supply curve, which is a vertical line. The price elasticity of supply is zero: the quantity supplied is always the same, regardless of price. Panel (b) shows a perfectly elastic supply curve, which is a horizontal line. At a price of $12, producers will supply any quantity, but they will supply none at a price below $12. If price rises above $12, they will supply an extremely large quantity.

cell phone frequencies, the portion of the radio spectrum that is suitable for sending and receiving cell phone signals. Governments own the right to sell the use of this part of the radio spectrum to cell phone operators inside their borders. But governments can't increase or decrease the number of cell phone frequencies that they have to offer—for technical reasons, the quantity of frequencies suitable for cell phone operation is a fixed quantity.

So the supply curve for cell phone frequencies is a vertical line, which we have assumed is set at the quantity of 100 frequencies. As you move up and down that curve, the change in the quantity supplied by the government is zero, whatever the change in price. So panel (a) illustrates a case in which the price elasticity of supply is zero. This is a case of **perfectly inelastic supply.**

Panel (b) shows the supply curve for pizza. We suppose that it costs $12 to produce a pizza, including all opportunity costs. At any price below $12, it would be unprofitable to produce pizza and all the pizza parlors in America would go out of business. Alternatively, there are many producers who could operate pizza parlors if they were profitable. The ingredients—flour, tomatoes, cheese—are plentiful. And if necessary, more tomatoes could be grown, more milk could be produced to make mozzarella, and so on. So any price above $12 would elicit an extremely large quantity of pizzas supplied. The implied supply curve is therefore a horizontal line at $12.

Since even a tiny increase in the price would lead to a huge increase in the quantity supplied, the price elasticity of supply would be more or less infinite. This is a case of **perfectly elastic supply.**

As our cell phone frequencies and pizza examples suggest, real-world instances of both perfectly inelastic and perfectly elastic supply are easy to find—much easier than their counterparts in demand.

What Factors Determine the Price Elasticity of Supply?

Our examples tell us the main determinant of the price elasticity of supply: the availability of inputs. In addition, as with the price elasticity of demand, time may also play a role in the price elasticity of supply. Here we briefly summarize the two factors.

The Availability of Inputs The price elasticity of supply tends to be large when inputs are readily available and can be shifted into and out of production at a relatively low cost. It tends to be small when inputs are difficult to obtain—and can be shifted into and out of production only at a relatively high cost. In the case of ambulance services, the high cost of providing quality ambulance services is the crucial element in keeping the elasticity of supply very low.

Time The price elasticity of supply tends to grow larger as producers have more time to respond to a price change. This means that the long-run price elasticity of supply is often higher than the short-run elasticity.

The price elasticity of the supply of pizza is very high because the inputs needed to expand the industry are readily available. The price elasticity of cell phone frequencies is zero because an essential input—the radio spectrum—cannot be increased at all.

Many industries are like pizza production and have large price elasticities of supply: they can be readily expanded because they don't require any special or unique resources. In contrast, the price elasticity of supply is usually substantially less than perfectly elastic for goods that involve limited natural resources: minerals like gold or copper, agricultural products like coffee that flourish only on certain types of land, and renewable resources like ocean fish that can only be exploited up to a point without destroying the resource.

There is **perfectly inelastic supply** when the price elasticity of supply is zero, so that changes in the price of the good have no effect on the quantity supplied. A perfectly inelastic supply curve is a vertical line.

There is **perfectly elastic supply** when even a tiny increase or reduction in the price will lead to very large changes in the quantity supplied, so that the price elasticity of supply is infinite. A perfectly elastic supply curve is a horizontal line.

But given enough time, producers are often able to significantly change the amount they produce in response to a price change, even when production involves a limited natural resource or a very costly input. Agricultural markets provide a good example. When American farmers receive much higher prices for a given commodity, like wheat (because of a drought in a big wheat-producing country like Australia), in the next planting season they are likely to switch their acreage planted from other crops to wheat.

For this reason, economists often make a distinction between the short-run elasticity of supply, usually referring to a few weeks or months, and the long-run elasticity of supply, usually referring to several years. In most industries, the long-run elasticity of supply is larger than the short-run elasticity.

ECONOMICS ▶ *in Action*

European Farm Surpluses

One of the policies we analyzed in Chapter 5 was the imposition of a *price floor*, a lower limit below which price of a good could not fall. We saw that price floors are often used by governments to support the incomes of farmers but create large unwanted surpluses of farm products. The most dramatic example of this is found in the European Union, where price floors have created a "butter mountain," a "wine lake," and so on.

Were European politicians unaware that their price floors would create huge surpluses? They probably knew that surpluses would arise but underestimated the price elasticity of agricultural supply. In fact, when the agricultural price supports were put in place, many analysts thought they were unlikely to lead to big increases in production. After all, European countries are densely populated and there is little new land available for cultivation.

What the analysts failed to realize, however, was how much farm production could expand by adding other resources, especially fertilizer and pesticides, which were readily available. So although European farm acreage didn't increase much in response to the imposition of price floors, European farm production did!

▼ Quick Review

• The **price elasticity of supply** is the percent change in the quantity supplied divided by the percent change in the price.

• Under **perfectly inelastic supply,** the quantity supplied is completely unresponsive to price and the supply curve is a vertical line. Under **perfectly elastic supply,** the supply curve is horizontal at some specific price. If the price falls below that level, the quantity supplied is zero. If the price rises above that level, the quantity supplied is extremely large.

• The price elasticity of supply depends on the availability of inputs, the ease of shifting inputs into and out of alternative uses, and the period of time that has elapsed since the price change.

Check Your Understanding 6-4

1. Using the midpoint method, calculate the price elasticity of supply for web-design services when the price per hour rises from $100 to $150 and the number of hours transacted increases from 300,000 to 500,000. Is supply elastic, inelastic, or unit-elastic?

2. True or false? If the demand for milk rose, then, in the long run, milk-drinkers would be better off if supply were elastic rather than inelastic.

3. True or false? Long-run price elasticities of supply are generally larger than short-run price elasticities of supply. As a result, the short-run supply curves are generally flatter than the long-run supply curves.

4. True or false? When supply is perfectly elastic, changes in demand have no effect on price.

Solutions appear at back of book.

An Elasticity Menagerie

We've just run through quite a few different elasticities. Keeping them all straight can be a challenge. So in Table 6-3 we provide a summary of all the elasticities we have discussed and their implications.

TABLE 6-3   An Elasticity Menagerie

Price elasticity of demand $= \dfrac{\% \text{ change in quantity demanded}}{\% \text{ change in price}}$ (dropping the minus sign)	
0	**Perfectly inelastic:** price has no effect on quantity demanded (vertical demand curve).
Between 0 and 1	**Inelastic:** a rise in price increases total revenue.
Exactly 1	**Unit-elastic:** changes in price have no effect on total revenue.
Greater than 1, less than ∞	**Elastic:** a rise in price reduces total revenue.
∞	**Perfectly elastic:** any rise in price causes quantity demanded to fall to 0. Any fall in price leads to an infinite quantity demanded (horizontal demand curve).
Cross-price elasticity of demand $= \dfrac{\% \text{ change in quantity of } \textit{one good} \text{ demanded}}{\% \text{ change in price of } \textit{another good}}$	
Negative	**Complements:** quantity demanded of one good falls when the price of another rises.
Positive	**Substitutes:** quantity demanded of one good rises when the price of another rises.
Income elasticity of demand $= \dfrac{\% \text{ change in quantity demanded}}{\% \text{ change in income}}$	
Negative	**Inferior good:** quantity demanded falls when income rises.
Positive, less than 1	**Normal good, income-inelastic:** quantity demanded rises when income rises, but not as rapidly as income.
Greater than 1	**Normal good, income-elastic:** quantity demanded rises when income rises, and more rapidly than income.
Price elasticity of supply $= \dfrac{\% \text{ change in quantity supplied}}{\% \text{ change in price}}$	
0	**Perfectly inelastic:** price has no effect on quantity supplied (vertical supply curve).
Greater than 0, less than ∞	ordinary upward-sloping supply curve.
∞	**Perfectly elastic:** any fall in price causes quantity supplied to fall to 0. Any rise in price elicits an infinite quantity supplied (horizontal supply curve).

The Airline Industry: Fly Less, Charge More

June Lloyd/Getty Images

The airline industry is forecast to earn nearly $20 billion in profits in 2014, up from nearly $12 billion in 2013. But in 2008, the industry was teetering on the edge of disaster. According to the International Air Transport Association, the industry lost $11 billion that year. However, by 2009, despite the fact that the economy was still extremely weak and airline traffic was still well below normal, profitability began to rebound. And by 2010, despite continued economic weakness, the airline industry had definitely recovered, achieving an $8.9 billion profit that year.

How did the airline industry achieve such a dramatic turnaround? Simple: fly less and charge more. In 2011, fares were 8% higher than they had been the previous year and 17% higher compared to 2009. Flights were more crowded than they had been in decades, with fewer than one in five seats empty on domestic flights. And that trend continues today.

In addition to cutting back on the number of flights—particularly money-losing ones—airlines began to vary ticket prices based on time of departure and when the ticket was purchased. For example, the cheapest day to fly is Wednesday, with Friday and Saturday the most expensive days to travel. The first flight of the morning (the one that requires you to get up at 4 a.m.) is cheaper than later flights. And the cheapest time to buy a ticket is Tuesday at 3 p.m. Eastern Standard Time, with tickets purchased over the weekend carrying the highest prices.

It doesn't stop there. As every beleaguered traveler knows, airlines have tacked on a wide variety of new fees and increased old ones—fees for food, blankets, baggage, even the right to board first or choose your seat in advance. Airlines have also become more inventive at imposing fees that are hard for travelers to track in advance—such as imposing a "holiday surcharge" while claiming that fares have not increased for the holiday. In 2007, airlines collected negligible amounts in fees, but by 2009 the amount had risen to $3.8 billion. By 2013 that number had exploded to $27 billion, a 611% increase from 2009.

But industry analysts question whether airlines can manage to maintain their currently high levels of profitability. In the past, as travel demand picked up, airlines increased capacity—added seats—too quickly, leading to falling airfares. "The wild card is always capacity discipline," says an airline industry researcher. "All it takes is one carrier to begin to add capacity aggressively, and then we follow and we undo all the good work that's been done."

QUESTIONS FOR THOUGHT

1. How would you describe the price elasticity of demand for airline flights given the information in this case? Explain.

2. Using the concept of elasticity, explain why airlines would create such great variations in the price of a ticket depending on when it is purchased and the day and time the flight departs. Assume that some people are willing to spend time shopping for deals as well as fly at inconvenient times, but others are not.

3. Using the concept of elasticity, explain why airlines have imposed fees on things such as checked bags. Why might they try to hide or disguise fees?

4. Use an elasticity concept to explain under what conditions the airline industry will be able to maintain its high profitability in the future. Explain.

SUMMARY

1. Many economic questions depend on the size of consumer or producer responses to changes in prices or other variables. *Elasticity* is a general measure of responsiveness that can be used to answer such questions.

2. The **price elasticity of demand**—the percent change in the quantity demanded divided by the percent change in the price (dropping the minus sign)—is a measure of the responsiveness of the quantity demanded to changes in the price. In practical calculations, it is usually best to use the **midpoint method,** which calculates percent changes in prices and quantities based on the average of starting and final values.

3. The responsiveness of the quantity demanded to price can range from **perfectly inelastic demand,** where the quantity demanded is unaffected by the price, to **perfectly elastic demand,** where there is a unique price at which consumers will buy as much or as little as they are offered. When demand is perfectly inelastic, the demand curve is a vertical line; when it is perfectly elastic, the demand curve is a horizontal line.

4. The price elasticity of demand is classified according to whether it is more or less than 1. If it is greater than 1, demand is **elastic;** if it is less than 1, demand is **inelastic;** if it is exactly 1, demand is **unit-elastic.** This classification determines how **total revenue,** the total value of sales, changes when the price changes. If demand is elastic, total revenue falls when the price increases and rises when the price decreases. If demand is inelastic, total revenue rises when the price increases and falls when the price decreases. If demand is unit-elastic, total revenue is unchanged by a change in price.

5. The price elasticity of demand depends on whether there are close substitutes for the good in question, whether the good is a necessity or a luxury, the share of income spent on the good, and the length of time that has elapsed since the price change.

6. The **cross-price elasticity of demand** measures the effect of a change in one good's price on the quantity demanded of another good. The cross-price elasticity of demand can be positive, in which case the goods are substitutes, or negative, in which case they are complements.

7. The **income elasticity of demand** is the percent change in the quantity of a good demanded when a consumer's income changes divided by the percent change in income. The income elasticity of demand indicates how intensely the demand for a good responds to changes in income. It can be negative; in that case the good is an inferior good. Goods with positive income elasticities of demand are normal goods. If the income elasticity is greater than 1, a good is **income-elastic;** if it is positive and less than 1, the good is **income-inelastic.**

8. The **price elasticity of supply** is the percent change in the quantity of a good supplied divided by the percent change in the price. If the quantity supplied does not change at all, we have an instance of **perfectly inelastic supply;** the supply curve is a vertical line. If the quantity supplied is zero below some price but infinite above that price, we have an instance of **perfectly elastic supply;** the supply curve is a horizontal line.

9. The price elasticity of supply depends on the availability of resources to expand production and on time. It is higher when inputs are available at relatively low cost and the longer the time elapsed since the price change.

KEY TERMS

Price elasticity of demand, p. 162
Midpoint method, p. 164
Perfectly inelastic demand, p. 166
Perfectly elastic demand, p. 167
Elastic demand, p. 167
Inelastic demand, p. 167
Unit-elastic demand, p. 167
Total revenue, p. 167
Cross-price elasticity of demand, p. 174
Income elasticity of demand, p. 175
Income-elastic demand, p. 176
Income-inelastic demand, p. 176
Price elasticity of supply, p. 178
Perfectly inelastic supply, p. 179
Perfectly elastic supply, p. 179

PROBLEMS

1. Do you think the price elasticity of demand for Ford sport-utility vehicles (SUVs) will increase, decrease, or remain the same when each of the following events occurs? Explain your answer.

   a. Other car manufacturers, such as General Motors, decide to make and sell SUVs.

   b. SUVs produced in foreign countries are banned from the American market.

   c. Due to ad campaigns, Americans believe that SUVs are much safer than ordinary passenger cars.

   d. The time period over which you measure the elasticity lengthens. During that longer time, new models such as four-wheel-drive cargo vans appear.

2. In the United States, 2013 was a bad year for growing wheat. And as wheat supply decreased, the price of wheat rose dramatically, leading to a lower quantity demanded (a movement along the demand curve). The accompanying table describes what happened to prices and the quantity of wheat demanded.

	2012	2013
Quantity demanded (bushels)	2.2 billion	2.0 billion
Average price (per bushel)	$3.42	$4.26

a. Using the midpoint method, calculate the price elasticity of demand for winter wheat.

b. What is the total revenue for U.S. wheat farmers in 2012 and 2013?

c. Did the bad harvest increase or decrease the total revenue of U.S. wheat farmers? How could you have predicted this from your answer to part a?

3. The accompanying table gives part of the supply schedule for personal computers in the United States.

Price of computer	Quantity of computers supplied
$1,100	12,000
900	8,000

a. Calculate the price elasticity of supply when the price increases from $900 to $1,100 using the midpoint method. Is it elastic, inelastic or unit-elastic?

b. Suppose firms produce 1,000 more computers at any given price due to improved technology. As price increases from $900 to $1,100, is the price elasticity of supply now greater than, less than, or the same as it was in part a?

c. Suppose a longer time period under consideration means that the quantity supplied at any given price is 20% higher than the figures given in the table. As price increases from $900 to $1,100, is the price elasticity of supply now greater than, less than, or the same as it was in part a?

4. The accompanying table lists the cross-price elasticities of demand for several goods, where the percent quantity change is measured for the first good of the pair, and the percent price change is measured for the second good.

Good	Cross-price elasticities of demand
Air-conditioning units and kilowatts of electricity	−0.34
Coke and Pepsi	+0.63
High-fuel-consuming sport-utility vehicles (SUVs) and gasoline	−0.28
McDonald's burgers and Burger King burgers	+0.82
Butter and margarine	+1.54

a. Explain the sign of each of the cross-price elasticities. What does it imply about the relationship between the two goods in question?

b. Compare the absolute values of the cross-price elasticities and explain their magnitudes. For example, why is the cross-price elasticity of McDonald's burgers and Burger King burgers less than the cross-price elasticity of butter and margarine?

c. Use the information in the table to calculate how a 5% increase in the price of Pepsi affects the quantity of Coke demanded.

d. Use the information in the table to calculate how a 10% decrease in the price of gasoline affects the quantity of SUVs demanded.

5. What can you conclude about the price elasticity of demand in each of the following statements?

a. "The pizza delivery business in this town is very competitive. I'd lose half my customers if I raised the price by as little as 10%."

b. "I owned both of the two Jerry Garcia autographed lithographs in existence. I sold one on eBay for a high price. But when I sold the second one, the price dropped by 80%."

c. "My economics professor has chosen to use the Krugman/Wells textbook for this class. I have no choice but to buy this book."

d. "I always spend a total of exactly $10 per week on coffee."

6. Take a linear demand curve like that shown in Figure 6-5, where the range of prices for which demand is elastic and inelastic is labeled. In each of the following scenarios, the supply curve shifts. Show along which portion of the demand curve (that is, the elastic or the inelastic portion) the supply curve must have shifted in order to generate the event described. In each case, show on the diagram the quantity effect and the price effect.

a. Recent attempts by the Colombian army to stop the flow of illegal drugs into the United States have actually benefited drug dealers.

b. New construction increased the number of seats in the football stadium and resulted in greater total revenue from box-office ticket sales.

c. A fall in input prices has led to higher output of Porsches. But total revenue for the Porsche Company has declined as a result.

7. The accompanying table shows the price and yearly quantity sold of souvenir T-shirts in the town of Crystal Lake according to the average income of the tourists visiting.

Price of T-shirt	Quantity of T-shirts demanded when average tourist income is $20,000	Quantity of T-shirts demanded when average tourist income is $30,000
$4	3,000	5,000
5	2,400	4,200
6	1,600	3,000
7	800	1,800

a. Using the midpoint method, calculate the price elasticity of demand when the price of a T-shirt rises from $5 to $6 and the average tourist income is $20,000. Also calculate it when the average tourist income is $30,000.

b. Using the midpoint method, calculate the income elasticity of demand when the price of a T-shirt is $4 and the average tourist income increases from $20,000 to $30,000. Also calculate it when the price is $7.

8. A recent study determined the following elasticities for Volkswagen Beetles:

Price elasticity of demand = 2
Income elasticity of demand = 1.5

The supply of Beetles is elastic. Based on this information, are the following statements true or false? Explain your reasoning.

a. A 10% increase in the price of a Beetle will reduce the quantity demanded by 20%.

b. An increase in consumer income will increase the price and quantity of Beetles sold.

9. In each of the following cases, do you think the price elasticity of supply is (i) perfectly elastic; (ii) perfectly inelastic; (iii) elastic, but not perfectly elastic; or (iv) inelastic, but not perfectly inelastic? Explain using a diagram.

a. An increase in demand this summer for luxury cruises leads to a huge jump in the sales price of a cabin on the *Queen Mary 2*.

b. The price of a kilowatt of electricity is the same during periods of high electricity demand as during periods of low electricity demand.

c. Fewer people want to fly during February than during any other month. The airlines cancel about 10% of their flights as ticket prices fall about 20% during this month.

d. Owners of vacation homes in Maine rent them out during the summer. Due to the soft economy this year, a 30% decline in the price of a vacation rental leads more than half of homeowners to occupy their vacation homes themselves during the summer.

10. Use an elasticity concept to explain each of the following observations.

a. During economic booms, the number of new personal care businesses, such as gyms and tanning salons, is proportionately greater than the number of other new businesses, such as grocery stores.

b. Cement is the primary building material in Mexico. After new technology makes cement cheaper to produce, the supply curve for the Mexican cement industry becomes relatively flatter.

c. Some goods that were once considered luxuries, like a telephone, are now considered virtual necessities. As a result, the demand curve for telephone services has become steeper over time.

d. Consumers in a less developed country like Guatemala spend proportionately more of their income on equipment for producing things at home, like sewing machines, than consumers in a more developed country like Canada.

11. Taiwan is a major world supplier of semiconductor chips. A recent earthquake severely damaged the production facilities of Taiwanese chip-producing companies, sharply reducing the amount of chips they could produce.

a. Assume that the total revenue of a typical non-Taiwanese chip manufacturer rises due to these events. In terms of an elasticity, what must be true for this to happen? Illustrate the change in total revenue with a diagram, indicating the price effect and the quantity effect of the Taiwan earthquake on this company's total revenue.

b. Now assume that the total revenue of a typical non-Taiwanese chip manufacturer falls due to these events. In terms of an elasticity, what must be true for this to happen? Illustrate the change in total revenue with a diagram, indicating the price effect and the quantity effect of the Taiwan earthquake on this company's total revenue.

12. There is a debate about whether sterile hypodermic needles should be passed out free of charge in cities with high drug use. Proponents argue that doing so will reduce the incidence of diseases, such as HIV/AIDS, that are often spread by needle sharing among drug users. Opponents believe that doing so will encourage more drug use by reducing the risks of this behavior. As an economist asked to assess the policy, you must know the following: (i) how responsive the spread of diseases like HIV/AIDS is to the price of sterile needles and (ii) how responsive drug use is to the price of sterile needles. Assuming that you know these two things, use the concepts of price elasticity of demand for sterile needles and the cross-price elasticity between drugs and sterile needles to answer the following questions.

a. In what circumstances do you believe this is a beneficial policy?

b. In what circumstances do you believe this is a bad policy?

13. Worldwide, the average coffee grower has increased the amount of acreage under cultivation over the past few years. The result has been that the average coffee plantation produces significantly more coffee than it did 10 to 20 years ago. Unfortunately for the growers, however, this has also been a period in which their total revenues have plunged. In terms of an elasticity, what must be true for these events to have occurred? Illustrate these events with a diagram, indicating the quantity effect and the price effect that gave rise to these events.

14. A recent report by the U.S. Centers for Disease Control and Prevention (CDC), published in the CDC's *Morbidity and Mortality Weekly Report,* studied the effect of an increase in the price of beer on the incidence of new cases of sexually transmitted disease in young adults. In particular, the researchers analyzed the responsiveness of gonorrhea cases to a tax-induced increase in the price of beer. The report concluded that "the . . . analysis suggested that a beer tax increase of $0.20 per six-pack could reduce overall gonorrhea rates by 8.9%." Assume that a six-pack costs $5.90 before the price increase. Use the midpoint method to determine the percent increase in the price of a six-pack, and then calculate the cross-price elasticity of demand between beer and incidence of gonorrhea. According to your estimate of this cross-price elasticity of demand, are beer and gonorrhea complements or substitutes?

15. The U.S. government is considering reducing the amount of carbon dioxide that firms are allowed to produce by issuing a limited number of tradable allowances for carbon dioxide (CO_2) emissions. In an April 25, 2007, report, the U.S. Congressional Budget Office (CBO) argues that "most of the cost of meeting a cap on CO_2 emissions would be borne by consumers, who would face persistently higher prices for products such as electricity and gasoline . . . poorer households would bear a larger burden relative to their income than wealthier households would." What assumption about one of the elasticities you learned about in this chapter has to be true for poorer households to be disproportionately affected?

16. According to data from the U.S. Department of Energy, sales of the fuel-efficient Toyota Prius hybrid fell from 158,574 vehicles sold in 2008 to 139,682 in 2009. Over the same period, according to data from the U.S. Energy Information Administration, the average price of regular gasoline fell from $3.27 to $2.35 per gallon. Using the midpoint method, calculate the cross-price elasticity of demand between Toyota Prii (the official plural of "Prius" is "Prii") and regular gasoline. According to your estimate of the cross-price elasticity, are the two goods complements or substitutes? Does your answer make sense?

17. Nile.com, the online bookseller, wants to increase its total revenue. One strategy is to offer a 10% discount on every book it sells. Nile.com knows that its customers can be divided into two distinct groups according to their likely responses to the discount. The accompanying table shows how the two groups respond to the discount.

	Group A (sales per week)	Group B (sales per week)
Volume of sales before the 10% discount	1.55 million	1.50 million
Volume of sales after the 10% discount	1.65 million	1.70 million

a. Using the midpoint method, calculate the price elasticities of demand for group A and group B.

b. Explain how the discount will affect total revenue from each group.

c. Suppose Nile.com knows which group each customer belongs to when he or she logs on and can choose whether or not to offer the 10% discount. If Nile.com wants to increase its total revenue, should discounts be offered to group A or to group B, to neither group, or to both groups?

Taxes

▶ What You Will Learn in This Chapter

■ **The effects of taxes on supply and demand**

■ **What determines who really bears the burden of a tax**

■ **The costs and benefits of taxes, and why taxes impose a cost that is greater than the tax revenue they raise**

■ **The difference between progressive and regressive taxes and the trade-off between tax equity and tax efficiency**

■ **The structure of the U.S. tax system**

THE FOUNDING TAXERS

The Granger Collection, New York

George Washington's 1791 tax on distillers, imposed to raise much needed government revenue, was widely viewed as unfair and sparked a rebellion.

IN 1794, LONG-STANDING grievances boiled over, and outraged farmers banded together in widespread revolt. Officials responded with deadly force: shots were fired, and several people killed, before government forces finally prevailed.

It wouldn't be surprising if you mistook this as an episode from the French Revolution. But, in fact, it occurred in western Pennsylvania—an event that severely shook the early American nation, and its first president, George Washington. Although the Whiskey Rebellion was eventually suppressed, it permanently reshaped American politics.

So what was the fighting about? Taxes. Facing a large debt after the War of Independence and unable to raise taxes any higher on imported goods, the Washington administration, at the suggestion of Treasury Secretary Alexander Hamiton, enacted a tax on whiskey distillers in 1791. Whiskey was a popular drink at the time, so such a tax could raise a lot of revenue. Meantime, a tax would encourage more "upstanding behavior" on the part of the young country's hard-drinking citizenry.

Yet the way the tax was applied was perceived as deeply unfair. Distillers could either pay a flat amount or pay by the gallon. Large distillers could afford the flat amount, but small distillers

could not and paid by the gallon. As a result, the small distillers—farmers who distilled whiskey to supplement their income—paid a higher proportion of their earnings in tax than large distillers.

Moreover, in the frontier of western Pennsylvania, cash was commonly hard to acquire and whiskey was often used as payment in transactions. By discouraging small distillers from producing whiskey, the tax left the local economy with less income and fewer means to buy and sell others goods.

Although the rebellion against the whiskey tax was eventually put down, the political party that supported the tax—the Federalist Party of Alexander Hamilton—never fully recovered its popularity. The Whiskey Rebellion paved the way for the emergence of a new political party: Thomas Jefferson's Republican Party, which repealed the tax in 1800.

There are two main morals to this story. One, taxes are necessary: all governments need money to function. Without taxes, governments could not provide the

services we want, from national defense to public parks. But taxes have a cost that normally exceeds the money actually paid to the government. That's because taxes distort incentives to engage in mutually beneficial transactions.

And that leads us to the second moral: making tax policy isn't easy—in fact, if you are a politician, it can be dangerous to your professional health. But the story also illustrates some crucial issues in tax policy—issues that economic models help clarify.

One principle used for guiding tax policy is efficiency: taxes should be designed to distort incentives as little as possible. But efficiency is not the only concern when designing tax rates. As the Washington administration learned from the Whiskey Rebellion, it's also important that a tax be seen as fair. Tax policy always involves striking a balance between the pursuit of efficiency and the pursuit of perceived fairness.

In this chapter, we will look at how taxes affect efficiency and fairness as well as raise revenue for the government.

An **excise tax** is a tax on sales of a good or service.

The Economics of Taxes: A Preliminary View

To understand the economics of taxes, it's helpful to look at a simple type of tax known as an **excise tax**—a tax charged on each unit of a good or service that is sold. Most tax revenue in the United States comes from other kinds of taxes, which we'll describe later in the chapter. But excise taxes are common. For example, there are excise taxes on gasoline, cigarettes, and foreign-made trucks, and many local governments impose excise taxes on services such as hotel room rentals. The lessons we'll learn from studying excise taxes apply to other, more complex taxes as well.

The Effect of an Excise Tax on Quantities and Prices

Suppose that the supply and demand for hotel rooms in the city of Potterville are as shown in Figure 7-1. We'll make the simplifying assumption that all hotel rooms are the same. In the absence of taxes, the equilibrium price of a room is $80 per night and the equilibrium quantity of hotel rooms rented is 10,000 per night.

Now suppose that Potterville's government imposes an excise tax of $40 per night on hotel rooms—that is, every time a room is rented for the night, the owner of the hotel must pay the city $40. For example, if a customer pays $80, $40 is collected as a tax, leaving the hotel owner with only $40. As a result, hotel owners are less willing to supply rooms at any given price.

What does this imply about the supply curve for hotel rooms in Potterville? To answer this question, we must compare the incentives of hotel owners *pre*-tax (before the tax is levied) to their incentives *post*-tax (after the tax is levied).

From Figure 7-1 we know that pre-tax, hotel owners are willing to supply 5,000 rooms per night at a price of $60 per room. But after the $40 tax per room is levied, they are willing to supply the same amount, 5,000 rooms, only if they receive $100 per room—$60 for themselves plus $40 paid to the city as tax. In

---

FIGURE 7-1   The Supply and Demand for Hotel Rooms in Potterville

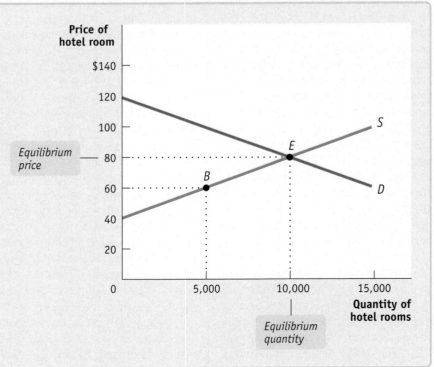

In the absence of taxes, the equilibrium price of hotel rooms is $80 a night, and the equilibrium number of rooms rented is 10,000 per night, as shown by point *E*. The supply curve, *S*, shows the quantity supplied at any given price, pre-tax. At a price of $60 a night, hotel owners are willing to supply 5,000 rooms, point *B*. But post-tax, hotel owners are willing to supply the same quantity only at a price of $100: $60 for themselves plus $40 paid to the city as tax.

other words, in order for hotel owners to be willing to supply the same quantity post-tax as they would have pre-tax, they must receive an additional $40 per room, the amount of the tax.

This implies that the post-tax supply curve shifts up by the amount of the tax compared to the pre-tax supply curve. At every quantity supplied, the supply price—the price that producers must receive to produce a given quantity—has increased by $40.

The upward shift of the supply curve caused by the tax is shown in Figure 7-2, where S_1 is the pre-tax supply curve and S_2 is the post-tax supply curve. As you can see, as a result of the tax the market equilibrium moves from E, at the equilibrium price of $80 per room and 10,000 rooms rented each night, to A, at a market price of $100 per room and only 5,000 rooms rented each night. A is, of course, on both the demand curve D and the new supply curve S_2.

Although, $100 is the demand price of 5,000 rooms, hotel owners receive only $60 of that price because they must pay $40 of it in tax. From the point of view of hotel owners, it is as if they were on their original supply curve at point B.

Let's check this again. How do we know that 5,000 rooms will be supplied at a price of $100? Because the price net of tax is $60, and according to the original supply curve, 5,000 rooms will be supplied at a price of $60, as shown by point B in Figure 7-2.

Does this look familiar? It should. In Chapter 5 we described the effects of a quota on sales: a quota *drives a wedge* between the price paid by consumers and the price received by producers. An excise tax does the same thing. As a result of this wedge, consumers pay more and producers receive less.

In our example, consumers—people who rent hotel rooms—end up paying $100 a night, $20 more than the pre-tax price of $80. At the same time, producers— the hotel owners—receive a price net of tax of $60 per room, $20 less than the pre-tax price. In addition, the tax creates missed opportunities: 5,000 potential consumers who would have rented hotel rooms—those willing to pay $80 but not $100 per night—are discouraged from doing so. Correspondingly, 5,000 rooms that would have been made available by hotel owners when they receive $80 are

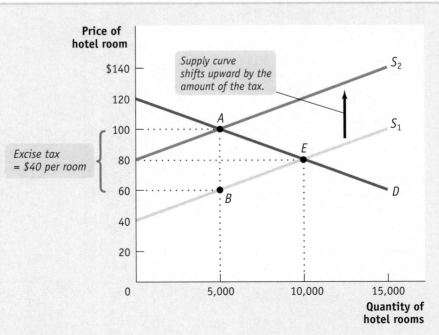

FIGURE 7-2   An Excise Tax Imposed on Hotel Owners

A $40 per room tax imposed on hotel owners shifts the supply curve from S_1 to S_2, an upward shift of $40. The equilibrium price of hotel rooms rises from $80 to $100 a night, and the equilibrium quantity of rooms rented falls from 10,000 to 5,000. Although hotel owners pay the tax, they actually bear only half the burden: the price they receive net of tax falls only $20, from $80 to $60. Guests who rent rooms bear the other half of the burden, because the price they pay rises by $20, from $80 to $100.

The **incidence** of a tax is a measure of who really pays it.

not offered when they receive only $60. Like a quota, this tax leads to inefficiency by distorting incentives and creating missed opportunities for mutually beneficial transactions.

It's important to recognize that as we've described it, Potterville's hotel tax is a tax on the hotel owners, not their guests—it's a tax on the producers, not the consumers. Yet the price received by producers, net of tax, falls by only $20, half the amount of the tax, and the price paid by consumers rises by $20. In effect, half the tax is being paid by consumers.

What would happen if the city levied a tax on consumers instead of producers? That is, suppose that instead of requiring hotel owners to pay $40 a night for each room they rent, the city required hotel *guests* to pay $40 for each night they stayed in a hotel. The answer is shown in Figure 7-3. If a hotel guest must pay a tax of $40 per night, then the price for a room paid by that guest must be reduced by $40 in order for the quantity of hotel rooms demanded post-tax to be the same as that demanded pre-tax. So the demand curve shifts *downward*, from D_1 to D_2, by the amount of the tax.

At every quantity demanded, the demand price—the price that consumers must be offered to demand a given quantity—has fallen by $40. This shifts the equilibrium from E to B, where the market price of hotel rooms is $60 and 5,000 hotel rooms are bought and sold. In effect, hotel guests pay $100 when you include the tax. So from the point of view of guests, it is as if they were on their original demand curve at point A.

If you compare Figures 7-2 and 7-3, you will immediately notice that they show equivalent outcomes. In both cases consumers pay $100, producers receive $60, and 5,000 hotel rooms are bought and sold. *In fact, it doesn't matter who officially pays the tax—the outcome is the same.*

This insight illustrates a general principle of the economics of taxation: the **incidence** of a tax—who really bears the burden of the tax—is typically not a question you can answer by asking who writes the check to the government. In this particular case, a $40 tax on hotel rooms is reflected in a $20 increase in the price paid by consumers and a $20 decrease in the price received by producers.

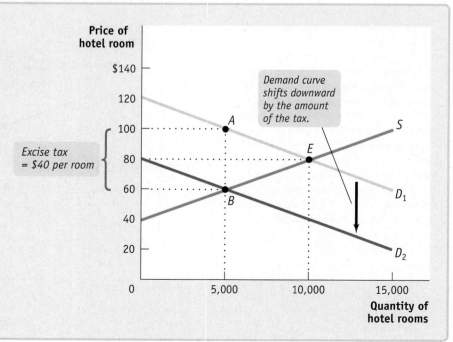

FIGURE 7-3 An Excise Tax Imposed on Hotel Guests

A $40 per room tax imposed on hotel guests shifts the demand curve from D_1 to D_2, a downward shift of $40. The equilibrium price of hotel rooms falls from $80 to $60 a night, and the quantity of rooms rented falls from 10,000 to 5,000. Although in this case the tax is officially paid by consumers, while in Figure 7-2 the tax was paid by producers, the outcome is the same: after taxes, hotel owners receive $60 per room but guests pay $100. This illustrates a general principle: *The incidence of an excise tax doesn't depend on whether consumers or producers officially pay the tax.*

Here, regardless of whether the tax is levied on consumers or producers, the incidence of the tax is evenly split between them.

Price Elasticities and Tax Incidence

We've just learned that the incidence of an excise tax doesn't depend on who officially pays it. In the example shown in Figures 7-1 through 7-3, a tax on hotel rooms falls equally on consumers and producers, no matter who the tax is levied on.

But it's important to note that this 50–50 split between consumers and producers is a result of our assumptions in this example. In the real world, the incidence of an excise tax usually falls unevenly between consumers and producers, as one group bears more of the burden than the other.

What determines how the burden of an excise tax is allocated between consumers and producers? The answer depends on the shapes of the supply and the demand curves. *More specifically, the incidence of an excise tax depends on the price elasticity of supply and the price elasticity of demand.* We can see this by looking first at a case in which consumers pay most of an excise tax, then at a case in which producers pay most of the tax.

When an Excise Tax Is Paid Mainly by Consumers Figure 7-4 shows an excise tax that falls mainly on consumers: an excise tax on gasoline, which we set at $1 per gallon. (There really is a federal excise tax on gasoline, though it is actually only about $0.18 per gallon in the United States. In addition, states impose excise taxes between $0.17 and $0.53 per gallon.) According to Figure 7-4, in the absence of the tax, gasoline would sell for $2 per gallon.

Two key assumptions are reflected in the shapes of the supply and demand curves in Figure 7-4. First, the price elasticity of demand for gasoline is assumed to be very low, so the demand curve is relatively steep. Recall that a low price elasticity of demand means that the quantity demanded changes little in response to a change in price—a feature of a steep demand curve. Second, the price elasticity of supply of gasoline is assumed to be very high, so the supply curve is relatively flat. A high price elasticity of supply means that the quantity supplied changes a lot in response to a change in price—a feature of a relatively flat supply curve.

We have learned that an excise tax drives a wedge, equal to the size of the tax, between the price paid by consumers and the price received by producers. This

FIGURE 7-4   **An Excise Tax Paid Mainly by Consumers**

The relatively steep demand curve here reflects a low price elasticity of demand for gasoline. The relatively flat supply curve reflects a high price elasticity of supply. The pre-tax price of a gallon of gasoline is $2.00, and a tax of $1.00 per gallon is imposed. The price paid by consumers rises by $0.95 to $2.95, reflecting the fact that most of the burden of the tax falls on consumers. Only a small portion of the tax is borne by producers: the price they receive falls by only $0.05 to $1.95.

wedge drives the price paid by consumers up and the price received by producers down. But as we can see from Figure 7-4, in this case those two effects are very unequal in size. The price received by producers falls only slightly, from $2.00 to $1.95, but the price paid by consumers rises by a lot, from $2.00 to $2.95. In this case consumers bear the greater share of the tax burden.

This example illustrates another general principle of taxation: *When the price elasticity of demand is low and the price elasticity of supply is high, the burden of an excise tax falls mainly on consumers.* Why? A low price elasticity of demand means that consumers have few substitutes and so little alternative to buying higher-priced gasoline. In contrast, a high price elasticity of supply results from the fact that producers have many production substitutes for their gasoline (that is, other uses for the crude oil from which gasoline is refined).

This gives producers much greater flexibility in refusing to accept lower prices for their gasoline. And, not surprisingly, the party with the least flexibility—in this case, consumers—gets stuck paying most of the tax. This is a good description of how the burden of the most significant excise taxes actually collected in the United States today, such as those on cigarettes and alcoholic beverages, is allocated between consumers and producers.

When an Excise Tax Is Paid Mainly by Producers Figure 7-5 shows an example of an excise tax paid mainly by producers, a $5.00 per day tax on downtown parking in a small city. In the absence of the tax, the market equilibrium price of parking is $6.00 per day.

We've assumed in this case that the price elasticity of supply is very low because the lots used for parking have very few alternative uses. This makes the supply curve for parking spaces relatively steep. The price elasticity of demand, however, is assumed to be high: substitutes are readily available as consumers can easily switch from the downtown spaces to other parking spaces a few minutes' walk from downtown, spaces that are not subject to the tax. This makes the demand curve relatively flat.

The tax drives a wedge between the price paid by consumers and the price received by producers. In this example, however, the tax causes the price paid by consumers to rise only slightly, from $6.00 to $6.50, but causes the price received by producers to fall a lot, from $6.00 to $1.50. In the end, consumers bear only $0.50 of the $5.00 tax burden, with producers bearing the remaining $4.50.

FIGURE 7-5 An Excise Tax Paid Mainly by Producers

The relatively flat demand curve here reflects a high price elasticity of demand for downtown parking, and the relatively steep supply curve results from a low price elasticity of supply. The pre-tax price of a daily parking space is $6.00 and a tax of $5.00 is imposed. The price received by producers falls a lot, to $1.50, reflecting the fact that they bear most of the tax burden. The price paid by consumers rises a small amount, $0.50, to $6.50, so they bear very little of the burden.

Again, this example illustrates a general principle: *When the price elasticity of demand is high and the price elasticity of supply is low, the burden of an excise tax falls mainly on producers.* A real-world example is a tax on purchases of existing houses. Before the collapse of the housing market that began in 2007, house prices in many American cities and towns had risen significantly, as well-off outsiders moved into desirable locations and purchased homes from the less-well-off original occupants.

Some of these towns have imposed taxes on house sales intended to extract money from the new arrivals. But this ignores the fact that the price elasticity of demand for houses in a particular town is often high, because potential buyers can choose to move to other towns. Furthermore, the price elasticity of supply is often low because most sellers must sell their houses due to job transfers or to provide funds for their retirement. So taxes on home purchases are actually paid mainly by the less well-off sellers—not, as town officials imagine, by wealthy buyers.

Putting It All Together We've just seen that when the price elasticity of supply is high and the price elasticity of demand is low, an excise tax falls mainly on consumers. And when the price elasticity of supply is low and the price elasticity of demand is high, an excise tax falls mainly on producers. This leads us to the general rule: *When the price elasticity of demand is higher than the price elasticity of supply, an excise tax falls mainly on producers. When the price elasticity of supply is higher than the price elasticity of demand, an excise tax falls mainly on consumers.*

So elasticity—not who officially pays the tax—determines the incidence of an excise tax.

ECONOMICS ▶ *in Action*

Who Pays the FICA?

Anyone who works for an employer receives a paycheck that itemizes not only the wages paid but also the money deducted from the paycheck for various taxes. For most people, one of the big deductions is *FICA*, also known as the payroll tax. FICA, which stands for the Federal Insurance Contributions Act, pays for the Social Security and Medicare systems, federal social insurance programs that provide income and medical care to retired and disabled Americans.

In 2014, most American workers paid 7.65% of their earnings in FICA. But this is literally only the half of it: each employer is required to pay an amount equal to the contributions of its employees.

How should we think about FICA? Is it really shared equally by workers and employers? We can use our previous analysis to answer that question because FICA is like an excise tax—a tax on the sale and purchase of labor. Half of it is a tax levied on the sellers—that is, workers. The other half is a tax levied on the buyers—that is, employers.

But we already know that the incidence of a tax does not really depend on who actually makes out the check. Almost all economists agree that FICA is a tax actually paid by workers, not by their employers. The reason for this conclusion lies in a comparison of the price elasticities of the supply of labor by households and the demand for labor by firms.

Evidence indicates that the price elasticity of demand for labor is quite high, at least 3. That is, an increase in average wages of 1% would lead to at least a 3% decline in the number of hours of work demanded by employers. Labor economists believe, however, that the price elasticity of supply of labor is very low. The reason is that although a fall in

Contrary to widely held beliefs, for 70% of Americans it's the FICA, not the income tax, that takes the biggest bite from their paychecks.

the wage rate reduces the incentive to work more hours, it also makes people poorer and less able to afford leisure time.

The strength of this second effect is shown in the data: the number of hours people are willing to work falls very little—if at all—when the wage per hour goes down.

Our general rule of tax incidence says that when the price elasticity of demand is much higher than the price elasticity of supply, the burden of an excise tax falls mainly on the suppliers. So the FICA falls mainly on the suppliers of labor, that is, workers—even though on paper half the tax is paid by employers. In other words, the FICA is largely borne by workers in the form of lower wages, rather than by employers in the form of lower profits.

This conclusion tells us something important about the American tax system: the FICA, rather than the much-maligned income tax, is the main tax burden on most families. For most workers, FICA is 15.3% of all wages and salaries up to $117,000 per year (note that 7.65% + 7.65% = 15.3%). That is, the great majority of workers in the United States pay 15.3% of their wages in FICA. Only a minority of American families pay more than 15% of their income in income tax. In fact, according to estimates by the Congressional Budget Office, for more than 70% of families FICA is Uncle Sam's main bite out of their income.

Quick Review

- An **excise tax** drives a wedge between the price paid by consumers and that received by producers, leading to a fall in the quantity transacted. It creates inefficiency by distorting incentives and creating missed opportunities.

- The **incidence** of an excise tax doesn't depend on who the tax is officially levied on. Rather, it depends on the price elasticities of demand and of supply.

- The higher the price elasticity of supply and the lower the price elasticity of demand, the heavier the burden of an excise tax on consumers. The lower the price elasticity of supply and the higher the price elasticity of demand, the heavier the burden on producers.

Check Your Understanding 7-1

1. Consider the market for butter, shown in the accompanying figure. The government imposes an excise tax of $0.30 per pound of butter. What is the price paid by consumers post-tax? What is the price received by producers post-tax? What is the quantity of butter transacted? How is the incidence of the tax allocated between consumers and producers? Show this on the figure.

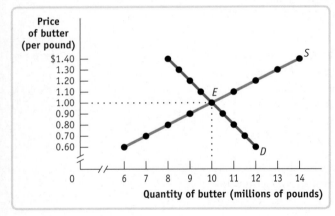

2. The demand for economics textbooks is very inelastic, but the supply is somewhat elastic. What does this imply about the incidence of an excise tax? Illustrate with a diagram.

3. True or false? When a substitute for a good is readily available to consumers, but it is difficult for producers to adjust the quantity of the good produced, then the burden of a tax on the good falls more heavily on producers.

4. The supply of bottled spring water is very inelastic, but the demand for it is somewhat elastic. What does this imply about the incidence of a tax? Illustrate with a diagram.

5. True or false? Other things equal, consumers would prefer to face a less elastic supply curve for a good or service when an excise tax is imposed.

Solutions appear at back of book.

"What taxes would you like to see imposed on other people?"

The Benefits and Costs of Taxation

When a government is considering whether to impose a tax or how to design a tax system, it has to weigh the benefits of a tax against its costs. We don't usually think of a tax as something that provides benefits, but governments need money to provide things people want, such as national defense and health care for those unable to afford it. The benefit of a tax is the revenue it raises for the government to pay for these services. Unfortunately, this benefit comes at a cost—a cost that is normally greater than the amount consumers and producers pay. Let's look first at what determines how much money a tax raises, then at the costs a tax imposes.

The Revenue from an Excise Tax

How much revenue does the government collect from an excise tax? In our hotel tax example, the revenue is equal to the area of the shaded rectangle in Figure 7-6.

FIGURE 7-6   The Revenue from an Excise Tax

The revenue from a $40 excise tax on hotel rooms is $200,000, equal to the tax rate, $40—the size of the wedge that the tax drives between the supply price and the demand price—multiplied by the number of rooms rented, 5,000. This is equal to the area of the shaded rectangle.

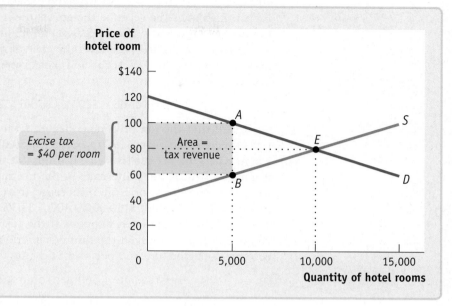

To see why this area represents the revenue collected by a $40 tax on hotel rooms, notice that the height of the rectangle is $40, equal to the tax per room. It is also, as we've seen, the size of the wedge that the tax drives between the supply price (the price received by producers) and the demand price (the price paid by consumers). Meanwhile, the width of the rectangle is 5,000 rooms, equal to the equilibrium quantity of rooms given the $40 tax. With that information, we can make the following calculations.

The tax revenue collected is:

$$\text{Tax revenue} = \$40 \text{ per room} \times 5{,}000 \text{ rooms} = \$200{,}000$$

The area of the shaded rectangle is:

$$\text{Area} = \text{Height} \times \text{Width} = \$40 \text{ per room} \times 5{,}000 \text{ rooms} = \$200{,}000$$

or

$$\text{Tax revenue} = \text{Area of shaded rectangle}$$

This is a general principle: *The revenue collected by an excise tax is equal to the area of the rectangle whose height is the tax wedge between the supply and demand curves and whose width is the quantity transacted under the tax.*

Tax Rates and Revenue

In Figure 7-6, $40 per room is the *tax rate* on hotel rooms. A **tax rate** is the amount of tax levied per unit of whatever is being taxed. Sometimes tax rates are defined in terms of dollar amounts per unit of a good or service; for example, $2.46 per pack of cigarettes sold. In other cases, they are defined as a percentage of the price; for example, the payroll tax is 15.3% of a worker's earnings up to $117,000.

There's obviously a relationship between tax rates and revenue. That relationship is not, however, one-for-one. In general, doubling the excise tax rate on a good or service won't double the amount of revenue collected, because the tax increase will reduce the quantity of the good or service transacted. And the relationship between the level of the tax and the amount of revenue collected may not even be positive: in some cases raising the tax rate actually *reduces* the amount of revenue the government collects.

A **tax rate** is the amount of tax people are required to pay per unit of whatever is being taxed.

We can illustrate these points using our hotel room example. Figure 7-6 showed the revenue the government collects from a $40 tax on hotel rooms. Figure 7-7 shows the revenue the government would collect from two alternative tax rates—a lower tax of only $20 per room and a higher tax of $60 per room.

Panel (a) of Figure 7-7 shows the case of a $20 tax, equal to half the tax rate illustrated in Figure 7-6. At this lower tax rate, 7,500 rooms are rented, generating tax revenue of:

Tax revenue = $20 per room × 7,500 rooms = $150,000

Recall that the tax revenue collected from a $40 tax rate is $200,000. So the revenue collected from a $20 tax rate, $150,000, is only 75% of the amount collected when the tax rate is twice as high ($150,000/$200,000 × 100 = 75%). To put it another way, a 100% increase in the tax rate from $20 to $40 per room leads to only a one-third, or 33.3%, increase in revenue, from $150,000 to $200,000 (($200,000 − $150,000)/$150,000 × 100 = 33.3%).

Panel (b) depicts what happens if the tax rate is raised from $40 to $60 per room, leading to a fall in the number of rooms rented from 5,000 to 2,500. The revenue collected at a $60 per room tax rate is:

Tax revenue = $60 per room × 2,500 rooms = $150,000

This is also *less* than the revenue collected by a $40 per room tax. So raising the tax rate from $40 to $60 actually reduces revenue. More precisely, in this case raising the tax rate by 50% (($60 − $40)/$40 × 100 = 50%) lowers the tax revenue by 25% (($150,000 − $200,000)/$200,000 × 100 = −25%). Why did this happen? Because the fall in tax revenue caused by the reduction in the number of rooms

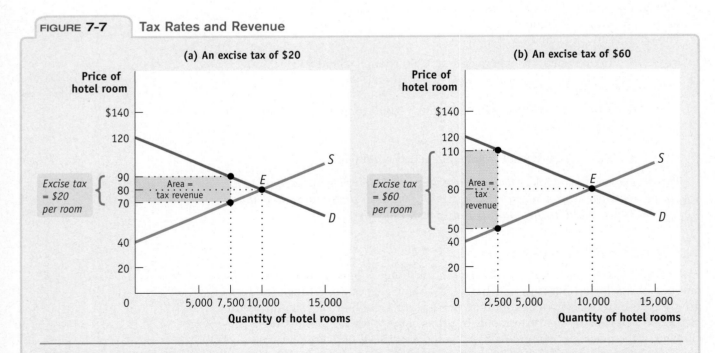

FIGURE **7-7**   **Tax Rates and Revenue**

In general, doubling the excise tax rate on a good or service won't double the amount of revenue collected, because the tax increase will reduce the quantity of the good or service bought and sold. And the relationship between the level of the tax and the amount of revenue collected may not even be positive. Panel (a) shows the revenue raised by a tax rate of $20 per room, only half the tax rate in Figure 7-6. The tax revenue raised, equal to the area of the shaded rectangle, is $150,000. That is 75% of $200,000, the revenue raised by a $40 tax rate. Panel (b) shows that the revenue raised by a $60 tax rate is also $150,000. So raising the tax rate from $40 to $60 actually reduces tax revenue.

rented more than offset the increase in the tax revenue caused by the rise in the tax rate. In other words, setting a tax rate so high that it deters a significant number of transactions will likely lead to a fall in tax revenue.

One way to think about the revenue effect of increasing an excise tax is that the tax increase affects tax revenue in two ways. On one side, the tax increase means that the government raises more revenue for each unit of the good sold, which other things equal would lead to a rise in tax revenue. On the other side, the tax increase reduces the quantity of sales, which other things equal would lead to a fall in tax revenue. The end result depends both on the price elasticities of supply and demand and on the initial level of the tax.

If the price elasticities of both supply and demand are low, the tax increase won't reduce the quantity of the good sold very much, so tax revenue will definitely rise. If the price elasticities are high, the result is less certain; if they are high enough, the tax reduces the quantity sold so much that tax revenue falls. Also, if the initial tax rate is low, the government doesn't lose much revenue from the decline in the quantity of the good sold, so the tax increase will definitely increase tax revenue. If the initial tax rate is high, the result is again less certain. Tax revenue is likely to fall or rise very little from a tax increase only in cases where the price elasticities are high and there is already a high tax rate.

The possibility that a higher tax rate can reduce tax revenue, and the corresponding possibility that cutting taxes can increase tax revenue, is a basic principle of taxation that policy makers take into account when setting tax rates. That is, when considering a tax created for the purpose of raising revenue (in contrast to taxes created to discourage undesirable behavior, known as "sin taxes"), a well-informed policy maker won't impose a tax rate so high that cutting the tax would increase revenue.

In the real world, however, policy makers aren't always well informed, but they usually aren't complete fools either. That's why it's very hard to find real-world examples in which raising a tax reduced revenue or cutting a tax increased revenue. Nonetheless, the theoretical possibility that a tax reduction increases tax revenue has played an important role in the folklore of American politics. As explained in For Inquiring Minds, an economist who sketched on a napkin the figure of a revenue-increasing income tax reduction had a significant impact on the economic policies adopted in the United States in the 1980s.

FOR INQUIRING MINDS | French Tax Rates and *L'Arc Laffer*

One afternoon in 1974, the American economist Arthur Laffer drew on a napkin a diagram that came to be known as the "Laffer curve." According to this diagram, raising tax rates initially increases tax revenue, but beyond a certain level a continued rise in tax rates causes tax revenues to fall as people forgo economic activity. Correspondingly, a reduction in tax rates from that threshold results in an increase in economic activity as more people are willing to undertake economic transactions.

Although not a new idea, Laffer's diagram captured the American political debate at the time. In 1981, newly elected President Ronald Reagan enacted tax cuts with the promise that they would

pay for themselves—that is, that the tax cuts would increase economic activity so much that the federal government's revenue would not fall.

Very few economists now believe that Reagan's tax cuts actually increased government revenue because, on the whole, American tax rates were simply not high enough to provide a significant deterrent to economic activity. Yet there is a theoretical case that the Laffer curve does exist at high tax rate levels. And the case of the French tax hike appears to present a real-world illustration.

A 1997 change to the French tax law significantly raised taxes on wealthy French citizens. Moreover, unlike in the United States, it is relatively easy for a

French person to move to a neighboring country, such as Belgium or Switzerland, with much lower taxes on the wealthy. As a result, according to one estimate, by 2013, 200 to 250 billion euros in assets—around $275 to $350 billion—had been moved out of France by those who had left France to escape the higher tax rates.

The matter exploded in a public fracas between French president, Francois Hollande, and France's most celebrated actor, Gerard Depardieu, when Hollande announced a 75% tax rate on high earning French to breach a huge government deficit. Hollande was eventually forced to back down, but not before Depardieu had moved just a few miles over the French border into Belgium. ■

The Costs of Taxation

What is the cost of a tax? You might be inclined to answer that it is the money taxpayers pay to the government. In other words, you might believe that the cost of a tax is the tax revenue collected. But suppose the government uses the tax revenue to provide services that taxpayers want. Or suppose that the government simply hands the tax revenue back to taxpayers. Would we say in those cases that the tax didn't actually cost anything?

No—because a tax, like a quota, prevents mutually beneficial transactions from occurring. Consider Figure 7-6 once more. Here, with a $40 tax on hotel rooms, guests pay $100 per room but hotel owners receive only $60 per room. Because of the wedge created by the tax, we know that some transactions don't occur that would have occurred without the tax.

For example, we know from the supply and demand curves that there are some potential guests who would be willing to pay up to $90 per night and some hotel owners who would be willing to supply rooms if they received at least $70 per night. If these two sets of people were allowed to trade with each other without the tax, they would engage in mutually beneficial transactions—hotel rooms would be rented.

But such deals would be illegal, because the $40 tax would not be paid. In our example, 5,000 potential hotel room rentals that would have occurred in the absence of the tax, to the mutual benefit of guests and hotel owners, do not take place because of the tax.

So an excise tax imposes costs over and above the tax revenue collected in the form of inefficiency, which occurs because the tax discourages mutually beneficial transactions. As we learned in Chapter 5, the cost to society of this kind of inefficiency—the value of the forgone mutually beneficial transactions—is called the deadweight loss. While all real-world taxes impose some deadweight loss, a badly designed tax imposes a larger deadweight loss than a well-designed one.

To measure the deadweight loss from a tax, we turn to the concepts of producer and consumer surplus. Figure 7-8 shows the effects of an excise tax on consumer and producer surplus. In the absence of the tax, the equilibrium is at E and the equilibrium price and quantity are P_E and Q_E, respectively. An excise tax drives a wedge equal to the amount of the tax between the price received by producers and the price paid by consumers, reducing the quantity sold. In this

---

FIGURE 7-8   A Tax Reduces Consumer and Producer Surplus

Before the tax, the equilibrium price and quantity are P_E and Q_E, respectively. After an excise tax of T per unit is imposed, the price to consumers rises to P_C and consumer surplus falls by the sum of the dark blue rectangle, labeled A, and the light blue triangle, labeled B. The tax also causes the price to producers to fall to P_P; producer surplus falls by the sum of the dark red rectangle, labeled C, and the pink triangle, labeled F. The government receives revenue from the tax equal to $Q(T) \times T$, which is given by the sum of the areas A and C. Areas B and F represent the losses to consumer and producer surplus that are not collected by the government as revenue. They are the deadweight loss to society of the tax.

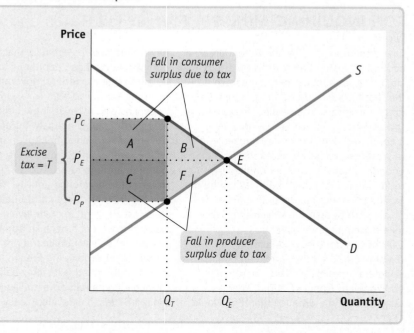

case, where the tax is T dollars per unit, the quantity sold falls to Q_T. The price paid by consumers rises to P_C, the demand price of the reduced quantity, Q_T, and the price received by producers falls to P_P, the supply price of that quantity. The difference between these prices, $P_C - P_P$, is equal to the excise tax, T.

Using the concepts of producer and consumer surplus, we can show exactly how much surplus producers and consumers lose as a result of the tax. From Figure 5-4 we learned that a fall in the price of a good generates a gain in consumer surplus that is equal to the sum of the areas of a rectangle and a triangle. Similarly, a price increase causes a loss to consumers that is represented by the sum of the areas of a rectangle and a triangle. So it's not surprising that in the case of an excise tax, the rise in the price paid by consumers causes a loss equal to the sum of the areas of a rectangle and a triangle: the dark blue rectangle labeled A and the area of the light blue triangle labeled B in Figure 7-8.

Meanwhile, the fall in the price received by producers leads to a fall in producer surplus. This, too, is equal to the sum of the areas of a rectangle and a triangle. The loss in producer surplus is the sum of the areas of the dark red rectangle labeled C and the pink triangle labeled F in Figure 7-8.

Of course, although consumers and producers are hurt by the tax, the government gains revenue. The revenue the government collects is equal to the tax per unit sold, T, multiplied by the quantity sold, Q_T. This revenue is equal to the area of a rectangle Q_T wide and T high. And we already have that rectangle in the figure: it is the sum of rectangles A and C. So the government gains part of what consumers and producers lose from an excise tax.

But a portion of the loss to producers and consumers from the tax is not offset by a gain to the government—specifically, the two triangles B and F. The deadweight loss caused by the tax is equal to the combined area of these two triangles. It represents the total surplus lost to society because of the tax—that is, the amount of surplus that would have been generated by transactions that now do not take place because of the tax.

Figure 7-9 is a version of Figure 7-8 that leaves out rectangles A (the surplus shifted from consumers to the government) and C (the surplus shifted from producers to the government) and shows only the deadweight loss, here drawn as a triangle shaded yellow. The base of that triangle is equal to the tax wedge, T; the height of the triangle is equal to the reduction in the quantity transacted due to

---

FIGURE 7-9   The Deadweight Loss of a Tax

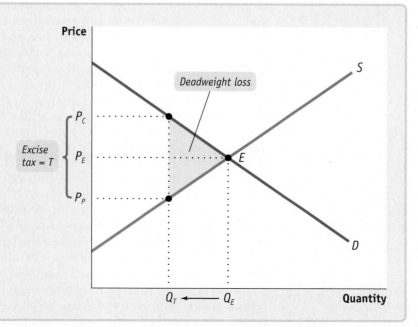

A tax leads to a deadweight loss because it creates inefficiency: some mutually beneficial transactions never take place because of the tax—namely, the transactions $Q_E - Q_T$. The yellow area here represents the value of the deadweight loss: it is the total surplus that would have been gained from the $Q_E - Q_T$ transactions. If the tax had not discouraged transactions—had the number of transactions remained at Q_E because of either perfectly inelastic supply or perfectly inelastic demand—no deadweight loss would have been incurred.

The **administrative costs** of a tax are the resources used for its collection, for the method of payment, and for any attempts to evade the tax.

the tax, $Q_E - Q_T$. Clearly, the larger the tax wedge and the larger the reduction in the quantity transacted, the greater the inefficiency from the tax.

But also note an important, contrasting point: if the excise tax somehow *didn't* reduce the quantity bought and sold in this market—if Q_T remained equal to Q_E after the tax was levied—the yellow triangle would disappear and the deadweight loss from the tax would be zero. This observation is simply the flip-side of the principle found earlier in the chapter: a tax causes inefficiency because it discourages mutually beneficial transactions between buyers and sellers. So if a tax does not discourage transactions, which would be true if either supply or demand were perfectly inelastic, it causes no deadweight loss. In this case, the tax simply shifts surplus straight from consumers and producers to the government.

Using a triangle to measure deadweight loss is a technique used in many economic applications. For example, triangles are used to measure the deadweight loss produced by types of taxes other than excise taxes. They are also used to measure the deadweight loss produced by monopoly, another kind of market distortion. And deadweight-loss triangles are often used to evaluate the benefits and costs of public policies besides taxation—such as whether to impose stricter safety standards on a product.

In considering the total amount of inefficiency caused by a tax, we must also take into account something not shown in Figure 7-9: the resources actually used by the government to collect the tax, and by taxpayers to pay it, over and above the amount of the tax. These lost resources are called the **administrative costs** of the tax. The most familiar administrative cost of the U.S. tax system is the time individuals spend filling out their income tax forms or the money they pay for tax return preparation services like those provided by H&R Block and companies like it. (The latter is considered an inefficiency from the point of view of society because resources spent on return preparation could be used for other, non-tax-related purposes.)

Included in the administrative costs that taxpayers incur are resources used to evade the tax, both legally and illegally. The costs of operating the Internal Revenue Service, the arm of the federal government tasked with collecting the federal income tax, are actually quite small in comparison to the administrative costs paid by taxpayers.

So the total inefficiency caused by a tax is the sum of its deadweight loss and its administrative costs. The general rule for economic policy is that, other things equal, a tax system should be designed to minimize the total inefficiency it imposes on society. In practice, other considerations also apply (as the Washington administration learned during the Whiskey Rebellion), but this principle nonetheless gives valuable guidance. Administrative costs are usually well known, more or less determined by the current technology of collecting taxes (for example, filing paper returns versus filing electronically). But how can we predict the size of the deadweight loss associated with a given tax? Not surprisingly, as in our analysis of the incidence of a tax, the price elasticities of supply and demand play crucial roles in making such a prediction.

Elasticities and the Deadweight Loss of a Tax

We know that the deadweight loss from an excise tax arises because it prevents some mutually beneficial transactions from occurring. In particular, the producer and consumer surplus that is forgone because of these missing transactions is equal to the size of the deadweight loss itself. This means that the larger the number of transactions that are prevented by the tax, the larger the deadweight loss.

This fact gives us an important clue in understanding the relationship between elasticity and the size of the deadweight loss from a tax. Recall that when demand or supply is elastic, the quantity demanded or the quantity supplied is relatively responsive to changes in the price. So a tax imposed on a good for which either demand or supply, or both, is elastic will cause a relatively large decrease in the

Society ultimately pays the administrative costs of taxes.

quantity transacted and a relatively large deadweight loss. And when we say that demand or supply is inelastic, we mean that the quantity demanded or the quantity supplied is relatively unresponsive to changes in the price.

As a result, a tax imposed when demand or supply, or both, is inelastic will cause a relatively small decrease in the quantity transacted and a relatively small deadweight loss.

The four panels of Figure 7-10 illustrate the positive relationship between a good's price elasticity of either demand or supply and the deadweight loss from taxing that good. Each panel represents the same amount of tax imposed but on a different good; the size of the deadweight loss is given by the area of the shaded

FIGURE 7-10 **Deadweight Loss and Elasticities**

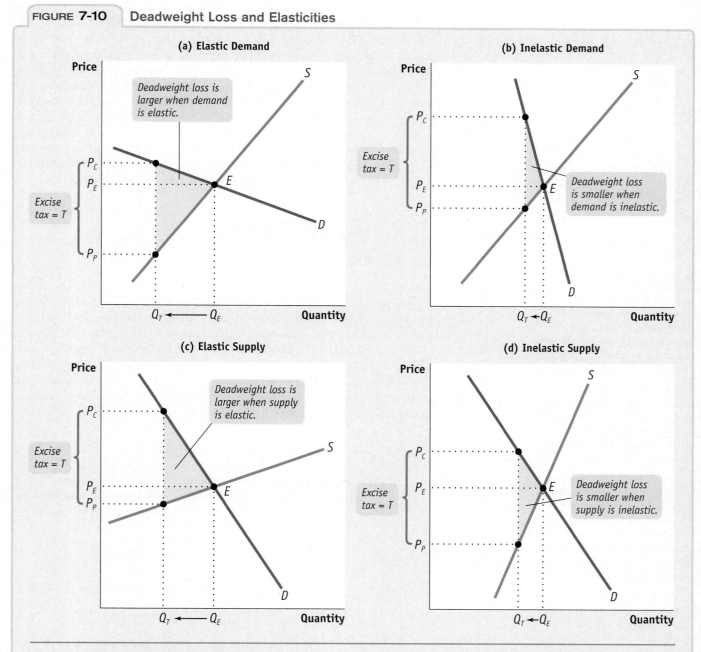

Demand is elastic in panel (a) and inelastic in panel (b), but the supply curves are the same. Supply is elastic in panel (c) and inelastic in panel (d), but the demand curves are the same. The deadweight losses are larger in panels (a) and (c) than in panels (b) and (d) because the greater the price elasticity of demand or supply, the greater the tax-induced fall in the quantity transacted. In contrast, the lower the price elasticity of demand or supply, the smaller the tax-induced fall in the quantity transacted and the smaller the deadweight loss.

triangle. In panel (a), the deadweight-loss triangle is large because demand for this good is relatively elastic—a large number of transactions fail to occur because of the tax. In panel (b), the same supply curve is drawn as in panel (a), but demand for this good is relatively inelastic; as a result, the triangle is small because only a small number of transactions are forgone. Likewise, panels (c) and (d) contain the same demand curve but different supply curves. In panel (c), an elastic supply curve gives rise to a large deadweight-loss triangle, but in panel (d) an inelastic supply curve gives rise to a small deadweight-loss triangle.

The implication of this result is clear: if you want to minimize the efficiency costs of taxation, you should choose to tax only those goods for which demand or supply, or both, is relatively inelastic. For such goods, a tax has little effect on behavior because behavior is relatively unresponsive to changes in the price. In the extreme case in which demand is perfectly inelastic (a vertical demand curve), the quantity demanded is unchanged by the imposition of the tax. As a result, the tax imposes no deadweight loss. Similarly, if supply is perfectly inelastic (a vertical supply curve), the quantity supplied is unchanged by the tax and there is also no deadweight loss.

So if the goal in choosing whom to tax is to minimize deadweight loss, then taxes should be imposed on goods and services that have the most inelastic response—that is, goods and services for which consumers or producers will change their behavior the least in response to the tax. (Unless they have a tendency to revolt, of course.) And this lesson carries a flip-side: using a tax to purposely decrease the amount of a harmful activity, such as underage drinking, will have the most impact when that activity is elastically demanded or supplied.

ECONOMICS ▶ in Action

Taxing the Marlboro Man

One of the most important excise taxes in the United States is the tax on cigarettes. The federal government imposes a tax of $1.01 a pack; state governments impose taxes that range from $0.17 cents a pack in Missouri to $4.35 a pack in New York; and many cities impose further taxes. In general, tax rates on cigarettes have increased over time, because more and more governments have seen them not just as a source of revenue but as a way to discourage smoking. But the rise in cigarette taxes has not been gradual. Usually, once a state government decides to raise cigarette taxes, it raises them a lot—which provides economists with useful data on what happens when there is a big tax increase.

TABLE 7-1		Results of Increases in Cigarette Taxes			
State	**Year**	**Increase in tax (per pack)**	**New state tax (per pack)**	**Change in quantity transacted**	**Change in tax revenue**
Mississippi	2009	$0.50	$0.68	−22.8%	188.3%
Hawaii	2009	0.60	2.60	−11.3	14.5
New Mexico	2010	0.75	1.66	−7.8	67.5
Florida	2010	1.00	2.00	−27.8	193.2
Washington	2010	1.00	3.03	−20.5	17.0

Source: Orzechowski & Walker, Tax Burden on Tobacco. U.S. Alcohol and Tobacco Tax and Trade Bureau.

Table 7-1 shows the results of big increases in cigarette taxes. In each case, sales fell, just as our analysis predicts. Although it's theoretically possible for tax revenue to fall after such a large tax increase, in reality tax revenue rose in each case. That's because cigarettes have a low price elasticity of demand.

▼ Quick Review

- An excise tax generates tax revenue equal to the **tax rate** times the number of units of the good or service transacted but reduces consumer and producer surplus.

- The government tax revenue collected is less than the loss in total surplus because the tax creates inefficiency by discouraging some mutually beneficial transactions.

- The difference between the tax revenue from an excise tax and the reduction in total surplus is the deadweight loss from the tax. The total amount of inefficiency resulting from a tax is equal to the deadweight loss plus the **administrative costs** of the tax.

- The larger the number of transactions prevented by a tax, the larger the deadweight loss. As a result, taxes on goods with a greater price elasticity of supply or demand, or both, generate higher deadweight losses. There is no deadweight loss when the number of transactions is unchanged by the tax.

Check Your Understanding   7-2

1. The accompanying table shows five consumers' willingness to pay for one can of diet soda each as well as five producers' costs of selling one can of diet soda each. Each consumer buys at most one can of soda; each producer sells at most one can of soda. The government asks your advice about the effects of an excise tax of $0.40 per can of diet soda. Assume that there are no administrative costs from the tax.

Consumer	Willingness to pay	Producer	Cost
Ana	$0.70	Zhang	$0.10
Bernice	0.60	Yves	0.20
Chizuko	0.50	Xavier	0.30
Dagmar	0.40	Walter	0.40
Ella	0.30	Vern	0.50

   a. Without the excise tax, what is the equilibrium price and the equilibrium quantity of soda transacted?

   b. The excise tax raises the price paid by consumers post-tax to $0.60 and lowers the price received by producers post-tax to $0.20. With the excise tax, what is the quantity of soda transacted?

   c. Without the excise tax, how much individual consumer surplus does each of the consumers gain? How much with the tax? How much total consumer surplus is lost as a result of the tax?

   d. Without the excise tax, how much individual producer surplus does each of the producers gain? How much with the tax? How much total producer surplus is lost as a result of the tax?

   e. How much government revenue does the excise tax create?

   f. What is the deadweight loss from the imposition of this excise tax?

2. In each of the following cases, focus on the price elasticity of demand and use a diagram to illustrate the likely size—small or large—of the deadweight loss resulting from a tax. Explain your reasoning.

   a. Gasoline

   b. Milk chocolate bars

Solutions appear at back of book.

Tax Fairness and Tax Efficiency

We've just seen how economic analysis can be used to determine the inefficiency caused by a tax. It's clear that, other things equal, policy makers should choose a tax that creates less inefficiency over a tax that creates more. But that guideline still leaves policy makers with wide discretion in choosing what to tax and, consequently, who bears the burden of the tax. How should they exercise this discretion?

One answer is that policy makers should make the tax system fair. But what exactly does fairness mean? Moreover, however you define fairness, how should policy makers balance considerations of fairness versus considerations of efficiency?

Two Principles of Tax Fairness

Fairness, like beauty, is often in the eyes of the beholder. When it comes to taxes, however, most debates about fairness rely on one of two principles of tax fairness: the *benefits principle* and the *ability-to-pay principle*.

According to the **benefits principle** of tax fairness, those who benefit from public spending should bear the burden of the tax that pays for that spending. For example, those who benefit from a road should pay for that road's upkeep, those who fly on airplanes should pay for air traffic control, and so on. The benefits principle is the basis for some parts of the U.S. tax system. For example, revenue from the federal tax on gasoline is specifically reserved for the maintenance and improvement of federal roads, including the Interstate Highway System. In this way motorists who benefit from the highway system also pay for it.

The benefits principle is attractive from an economic point of view because it matches well with one of the major justifications for public spending—the

According to the **benefits principle** of tax fairness, those who benefit from public spending should bear the burden of the tax that pays for that spending.

According to the **ability-to-pay principle** of tax fairness, those with greater ability to pay a tax should pay more tax.

A **lump-sum tax** is the same for everyone, regardless of any actions people take.

In a well-designed tax system, there is a **trade-off between equity and efficiency:** the system can be made more efficient only by making it less fair, and vice versa.

theory of *public goods,* which will be covered in Chapter 17. This theory explains why government action is sometimes needed to provide people with goods that markets alone would not provide, goods like national defense. If that's the role of government, it seems natural to charge each person in proportion to the benefits he or she gets from those goods.

Practical considerations, however, make it impossible to base the entire tax system on the benefits principle. It would be too cumbersome to have a specific tax for each of the many distinct programs that the government offers. Also, attempts to base taxes on the benefits principle often conflict with the other major principle of tax fairness: the **ability-to-pay principle,** according to which those with greater ability to pay a tax should pay more.

The ability-to-pay principle is usually interpreted to mean that high-income individuals should pay more in taxes than low-income individuals. Often the ability-to-pay principle is used to argue not only that high-income individuals should pay more taxes but also that they should pay a higher *percentage* of their income in taxes. We'll consider the issue of how taxes vary as a percentage of income later.

The Whiskey Rebellion described at the beginning of this chapter was basically a protest against the failure of the whiskey tax to take the ability-to-pay principle into account. In fact, the tax made small distillers—farmers of modest means—pay a higher proportion of their income than large, relatively well-off distillers. It's not surprising that farmers were upset that the new tax completely disregarded the ability-to-pay principle.

Equity versus Efficiency

Under the whiskey tax, the flat amount of tax paid by large distillers (in contrast to the per-gallon tax paid by small distillers) was an example of a **lump-sum tax,** a tax that is the same regardless of any actions people take. In this case, the large distillers paid the same amount of tax regardless of how many gallons they produced. Lump-sum taxes are widely perceived to be much less fair than a tax that is proportional to the amount of the transaction. And this was true in the Whiskey Rebellion: although the small farmers were unhappy to pay a proportional tax, it was still less than they would have owed with the lump-sum tax, which would have imposed an even more unfair burden on them.

But the per-gallon whiskey tax definitely distorted incentives to engage in mutually beneficial transactions and created deadweight loss. Because of the tax, some farmers would have reduced how much whiskey they distilled, with some forgoing distilling altogether. The result, surely, was a lower production of whiskey and less income earned by farmers because of the tax.

In contrast, a lump-sum tax does not distort incentives. Because under a lump-sum tax people have to pay the same amount of tax regardless of their actions, it does not lead them to change their actions and therefore causes no deadweight loss. So lump-sum taxes, although unfair, are better than other taxes at promoting economic efficiency.

A tax system can be made fairer by moving it in the direction of the benefits principle or the ability-to-pay principle. But this will come at a cost because the tax system will now tax people more heavily based on their actions, increasing the amount of deadweight loss. This observation reflects a general principle that we learned in Chapter 1: there is often a trade-off between equity and efficiency. Here, unless a tax system is badly designed, it can be made fairer only by sacrificing efficiency. Conversely, it can be made more efficient only by making it less fair. This means that there is normally a **trade-off between equity and efficiency** in the design of a tax system.

It's important to understand that economic analysis cannot say how much weight a tax system should give to equity and how much to efficiency. That choice is a value judgment, one we make through the political process.

ECONOMICS ▶ in Action

Federal Tax Philosophy

What is the principle underlying the federal tax system? (By federal, we mean taxes collected by the federal government, as opposed to the taxes collected by state and local governments.) The answer is that it depends on the tax.

The best-known federal tax, accounting for about half of all federal revenue, is the income tax. The structure of the income tax reflects the ability-to-pay principle: families with low incomes pay little or no income tax. In fact, some families pay negative income tax: a program known as the Earned Income Tax Credit "tops up," or adds to, the earnings of low-wage workers. Meanwhile, those with high incomes not only pay a lot of income tax but also must pay a larger share of their income in income taxes than the average family.

The second most important federal tax, FICA, also known as the payroll tax, is set up very differently. It was originally introduced in 1935 to pay for Social Security, a program that guarantees retirement income to qualifying older Americans and also provides benefits to workers who become disabled and to family members of workers who die. (Part of the payroll tax is now also used to pay for Medicare, a program that pays most medical bills of older Americans.) The Social Security system was set up to resemble a private insurance program: people pay into the system during their working years, then receive benefits based on their payments. And the tax more or less reflects the benefits principle: because the benefits of Social Security are mainly intended to assist lower- and middle-income people, and don't increase substantially for the rich, the Social Security tax is levied only on incomes up to a maximum level—$117,000 in 2014. (The Medicare portion of the payroll tax has no upper limit.) As a result, a high-income family doesn't pay much more in payroll taxes than a middle-income family.

Every year, Americans use the 1040 form to calculate the amount of federal taxes that they owe . . .

. . . and the vast majority of Americans submit those forms online.

Table 7-2 illustrates the difference in the two taxes, using data from a Congressional Budget Office study. The study divided American families into quintiles: the bottom quintile is the poorest 20% of families, the second quintile is the next poorest 20%, and so on. The second column shows the share of total U.S. pre-tax income received by each quintile. The third column shows the share of total federal income tax collected that is paid by each quintile.

As you can see, low-income families actually paid negative income tax through the Earned Income Tax Credit program. Even middle-income families paid a substantially smaller share of total income tax collected than their share of total income. In contrast, the fifth or top quintile, the richest 20% of families, paid a much higher share of total federal income tax collected compared with their share of total income. The fourth column shows the share of total payroll tax collected that is paid by each quintile, and the results

TABLE 7-2	Share of Pre-Tax Income, Federal Income Tax, and Payroll Tax, by Quintile in 2010		
Income group	Percent of total pre-tax income received	Percent of total federal income tax paid	Percent of total payroll tax paid
Bottom quintile	5.1%	−6.2%	5.6%
Second quintile	9.6	−2.9	9.8
Third quintile	14.2	2.9	15.4
Fourth quintile	20.4	13.3	23.9
Top quintile	51.9	92.9	45.1

Source: Congressional Budget Office.

are very different: the share of total payroll tax paid by the top quintile is substantially less than their share of total income.

Check Your Understanding   7-3

1. Assess each of the following taxes in terms of the benefits principle versus the ability-to-pay principle. What, if any, actions are distorted by the tax? Assume for simplicity in each case that the purchaser of the good bears 100% of the burden of the tax.
   a. A federal tax of $500 for each new car purchased that finances highway safety programs
   b. A local tax of 20% on hotel rooms that finances local government expenditures
   c. A local tax of 1% on the assessed value of homes that finances local schools
   d. A 1% sales tax on food that pays for government food safety regulation and inspection programs

   Solutions appear at back of book.

Understanding the Tax System

An excise tax is the easiest tax to analyze, making it a good vehicle for understanding the general principles of tax analysis. However, in the United States today, excise taxes are actually a relatively minor source of government revenue. In this section, we develop a framework for understanding more general forms of taxation and look at some of the major taxes used in the United States.

Tax Bases and Tax Structure

Every tax consists of two pieces: a *base* and a *structure*. The **tax base** is the measure or value that determines how much tax an individual or firm pays. It is usually a monetary measure, like income or property value. The **tax structure** specifies how the tax depends on the tax base. It is usually expressed in percentage terms; for example, homeowners in some areas might pay yearly property taxes equal to 2% of the value of their homes.

Some important taxes and their tax bases are as follows:

- **Income tax:** a tax that depends on the income of an individual or family from wages and investments

- **Payroll tax:** a tax that depends on the earnings an employer pays to an employee

- **Sales tax:** a tax that depends on the value of goods sold (also known as an excise tax)

- **Profits tax:** a tax that depends on a firm's profits

- **Property tax:** a tax that depends on the value of property, such as the value of a home

- **Wealth tax:** a tax that depends on an individual's wealth

Once the tax base has been defined, the next question is how the tax depends on the base. The simplest tax structure is a **proportional tax,** also sometimes called a *flat tax*, which is the same percentage of the base regardless of the taxpayer's income or wealth. For example, a property tax that is set at 2% of the value of the property, whether the property is worth $10,000 or $10,000,000, is a proportional tax. Many taxes, however, are not proportional. Instead, different people pay different percentages, usually because the tax law tries to take account of either the benefits principle or the ability-to-pay principle.

Because taxes are ultimately paid out of income, economists classify taxes according to how they vary with the income of individuals. A tax that rises *more* than in proportion to income, so that high-income taxpayers pay a larger percentage of their income than low-income taxpayers, is a **progressive tax.** A tax that rises *less* than in proportion to income, so that higher-income taxpayers pay a smaller percentage of their income than low-income taxpayers, is a **regressive tax.** A proportional tax on income would be neither progressive nor regressive.

The U.S. tax system contains a mixture of progressive and regressive taxes, though it is somewhat progressive overall.

Equity, Efficiency, and Progressive Taxation

Most, though not all, people view a progressive tax system as fairer than a regressive system. The reason is the ability-to-pay principle: a high-income family that pays 35% of its income in taxes is still left with a lot more money than a low-income family that pays only 15% in taxes. But attempts to make taxes strongly progressive run up against the trade-off between equity and efficiency.

To see why, consider a hypothetical example, illustrated in Table 7-3. We assume that there are two kinds of people in the nation of Taxmania: half of the population earns $40,000 a year and half earns $80,000, so the average income is $60,000 a year. We also assume that the Taxmanian government needs to collect one-fourth of that income—$15,000 a year per person—in taxes.

One way to raise this revenue would be through a proportional tax that takes one-fourth of everyone's income. The results of this proportional tax are shown in the second column of Table 7-3: after taxes, lower-income Taxmanians would be left with an income of $30,000 a year and higher-income Taxmanians, $60,000.

> A **progressive tax** takes a larger share of the income of high-income taxpayers than of low-income taxpayers.
>
> A **regressive tax** takes a smaller share of the income of high-income taxpayers than of low-income taxpayers.
>
> The **marginal tax rate** is the percentage of an increase in income that is taxed away.

TABLE **7-3**	Proportional versus Progressive Taxes in Taxmania	
Pre-tax income	After-tax income with proportional taxation	After-tax income with progressive taxation
$40,000	$30,000	$40,000
$80,000	$60,000	$50,000

Even this system might have some negative effects on incentives. Suppose, for example, that finishing college improves a Taxmanian's chance of getting a higher-paying job. Some people who would invest time and effort in going to college in hopes of raising their income from $40,000 to $80,000, a $40,000 gain, might not bother if the potential gain is only $30,000, the after-tax difference in pay between a lower-paying and higher-paying job.

But a strongly progressive tax system could create a much bigger incentive problem. Suppose that the Taxmanian government decided to exempt the poorer half of the population from all taxes but still wanted to raise the same amount of revenue. To do this, it would have to collect $30,000 from each individual earning $80,000 a year. As the third column of Table 7-3 shows, people earning $80,000 would then be left with income after taxes of $50,000—only $10,000 more than the after-tax income of people earning half as much. This would greatly reduce the incentive for people to invest time and effort to raise their earnings.

The point here is that any income tax system will tax away part of the gain an individual gets by moving up the income scale, reducing the incentive to earn more. But a progressive tax takes away a larger share of the gain than a proportional tax, creating a more adverse effect on incentives. In comparing the incentive effects of tax systems, economists often focus on the **marginal tax rate:** the percentage of an increase in income that is taxed away. In this example, the marginal tax rate on income above $40,000 is 25% with proportional taxation but 75% with progressive taxation.

Our hypothetical example is much more extreme than the reality of progressive taxation in the modern United States—although, as the upcoming Economics in Action explains, in previous years the marginal tax rates paid by high earners were very high indeed. However, these have moderated over time as concerns arose about the severe incentive effects of extremely progressive taxes. In short, the ability-to-pay principle pushes governments toward a highly progressive tax system, but efficiency considerations push them the other way.

Taxes in the United States

Table 7-4 shows the revenue raised by major taxes in the United States in 2013. Some of the taxes are collected by the federal government and the others by state and local governments.

TABLE 7-4 Major Taxes in the United States, 2013

Federal taxes ($ billion)		State and local taxes ($ billion)	
Income	$1,312.1	Income	$334.3
Payroll	1,106.0	Sales	498.1
Profits	338.9	Profits	91.7
		Property	444.6

Source: Bureau of Economic Analysis.

There is a major tax corresponding to five of the six tax bases we identified earlier. There are income taxes, payroll taxes, sales taxes, profits taxes, and property taxes, all of which play an important role in the overall tax system. The only item missing is a wealth tax. In fact, the United States does have a wealth tax, the *estate tax*, which depends on the value of someone's estate after he or she dies. But at the time of writing, the current law phases out the estate tax over a few years, and in any case it raises much less money than the taxes shown in the table.

In addition to the taxes shown, state and local governments collect substantial revenue from other sources as varied as driver's license fees and sewer charges. These fees and charges are an important part of the tax burden but very difficult to summarize or analyze.

Are the taxes in Table 7-4 progressive or regressive? It depends on the tax. The personal income tax is strongly progressive. The payroll tax, which, except for the Medicare portion, is paid only on earnings up to $117,000 is somewhat regressive. Sales taxes are generally regressive, because higher-income families save more of their income and thus spend a smaller share of it on taxable goods than do lower-income families. In addition, there are other taxes principally levied at the state and local level that are typically quite regressive: it costs the same amount to renew a driver's license no matter what your income is.

Overall, the taxes collected by the federal government are quite progressive. The second column of Table 7-5 shows estimates of the average federal tax rate paid by families at different levels of income earned in 2013. These estimates don't count just the money families pay directly. They also attempt to estimate the incidence of taxes directly paid by businesses, like the tax on corporate profits, which ultimately falls on individual shareholders. The table shows that the federal tax system is indeed progressive, with low-income families paying a relatively small share of their income in federal taxes and high-income families paying a greater share of their income.

TABLE 7-5 Federal, State, and Local Taxes as a Percentage of Income, by Income Category, 2013

Income group	Federal	State and local	Total
Bottom quintile	6.4%	12.4%	18.8%
Second quintile	10.9	11.6	22.5
Third quintile	15.4	11.2	26.6
Fourth quintile	18.8	11.0	29.8
Next 10%	20.4	11.0	31.4
Next 5%	21.4	10.6	32.0
Next 4%	22.0	10.2	32.2
Top 1%	24.3	8.7	33.0
Average	19.7	10.5	30.1

Source: Institute on Taxation and Economic Policy.

Since 2000, the federal government has cut income taxes for most families. The largest cuts, both as a share of income and as a share of federal taxes collected, have gone to families with high incomes. As a result, the federal system is less progressive (at the time of writing) than it was in 2000 because the share of income paid by high-income families has fallen relative to the share paid by middle- and low-income families. And it will become even less progressive over the next few years, as some delayed pieces of the post-2000 tax cut legislation take effect. However, even after those changes, the federal tax system will remain progressive.

As the third column of Table 7-5 shows, however, taxes at the state and local levels are generally regressive. That's because the sales tax, the largest source of revenue for most states, is somewhat regressive, and other items, such as vehicle licensing fees, are strongly regressive.

In sum, the U.S. tax system is somewhat progressive, with the richest fifth of the population paying a somewhat higher share of income in taxes than families in the middle and the poorest fifth paying considerably less.

Yet there are important differences within the American tax system: the federal income tax is more progressive than the payroll tax, which can be seen from Table 7-5. And federal taxation is more progressive than state and local taxation.

You Think You Pay High Taxes?

Everyone, everywhere complains about taxes. But citizens of the United States actually have less to complain about than citizens of most other wealthy countries.

To assess the overall level of taxes, economists usually calculate taxes as a share of *gross domestic product*—the total value of goods and services produced in a country. By this measure, as you can see in the accompanying figure, in 2013, U.S. taxes were near the bottom of the scale. Even our neighbor Canada has significantly higher taxes. Tax rates in Europe, where governments need a lot of revenue to pay for extensive benefits such as guaranteed health care and generous unemployment benefits, are 50% to 100% higher than in the United States.

Taxes (percent of GDP)

Country	Taxes (percent of GDP)
United States	24.3%
Korea	26.8%
Canada	30.7%
Israel	31.5%
Britain	35.2%
Sweden	44.3%
France	45.2%

Source: OECD.

Different Taxes, Different Principles

Why are some taxes progressive but others regressive? Can't the government make up its mind?

There are two main reasons for the mixture of regressive and progressive taxes in the U.S. system: the difference between levels of government and the fact that different taxes are based on different principles.

State and especially local governments generally do not make much effort to apply the ability-to-pay principle. This is largely because they are subject to *tax competition:* a state or local government that imposes high taxes on people with high incomes faces the prospect that those people may move to other locations where taxes are lower. This is much less of a concern at the national level, although a handful of very rich people have given up their U.S. citizenship to avoid paying U.S. taxes.

Although the federal government is in a better position than state or local governments to apply principles of fairness, it applies different principles to different taxes. We saw an example of this in the preceding Economics in Action. The most important tax, the federal income tax, is strongly progressive, reflecting the ability-to-pay principle. But the second most important tax, the federal payroll tax, or FICA, is somewhat regressive, because most of

FOR INQUIRING MINDS | Taxing Income versus Taxing Consumption

The U.S. government taxes people mainly on the money they *make*, not on the money they spend on consumption. Yet most tax experts argue that this policy badly distorts incentives. Someone who earns income and then invests that income for the future gets taxed twice: once on the original sum and again on any earnings made from the investment.

So a system that taxes income rather than consumption discourages people from saving and investing, instead

providing an incentive to spend their income today. And encouraging savings and investing is an important policy goal for two reasons. First, empirical evidence shows that Americans tend to save too little for retirement and health care expenses in their later years. Second, savings and investment both contribute to economic growth.

Moving from a system that taxes income to one that taxes consumption would solve this problem. In fact,

the governments of many countries get much of their revenue from a value-added tax, or VAT, which acts like a national sales tax. In some countries VAT rates are very high; in Sweden, for example, the rate is 25%.

The United States does not have a value-added tax for two main reasons. One is that it is difficult, though not impossible, to make a consumption tax progressive. The other is that a VAT typically has very high administrative costs. ∎

it is linked to specific programs—Social Security and Medicare—and, reflecting the benefits principle, is levied more or less in proportion to the benefits received from these programs.

ECONOMICS ▶ *in Action*

The Top Marginal Income Tax Rate

FIGURE 7-11   The Top Marginal Tax

Source: The Internal Revenue Service.

The amount of money an American owes in federal income taxes is found by applying marginal tax rates on successively higher "brackets" of income. For example, in 2013 a single person paid 10% on the first $8,925 of taxable income (that is, income after subtracting exemptions and deductions); 15% on the next $27,325; and so on up to a top rate of 39.6% on his or her income, if any, over $400,000. Relatively few people (less than 1% of taxpayers) have incomes high enough to pay the top marginal rate. In fact, more than 75% of Americans pay no income tax or they fall into either the 10% or 15% bracket. But the top marginal income tax rate is often viewed as a useful indicator of the progressivity of the tax system, because it shows just how high a tax rate the U.S. government is willing to impose on the very affluent.

Figure 7-11 shows the top marginal income tax rate from 1913, when the U.S. government first imposed an income tax, to 2013. The first big increase in the top marginal rate came during World War I (1914) and was reversed after the war ended (1918). After that, the figure is dominated by two big changes: a huge increase in the top marginal rate during the administration of Franklin Roosevelt (1933–1945) and a sharp reduction during the administration of Ronald Reagan (1981–1989). By comparison, recent changes have been relatively small potatoes.

▼ Quick Review

• Every tax consists of a **tax base** and a **tax structure.**

• Among the types of taxes are **income taxes, payroll taxes, sales taxes, profits taxes, property taxes,** and **wealth taxes.**

• Tax systems are classified as being **proportional, progressive,** or **regressive.**

• Progressive taxes are often justified by the ability-to-pay principle. But strongly progressive taxes lead to high **marginal tax rates,** which create major incentive problems.

• The United States has a mixture of progressive and regressive taxes. However, the overall structure of taxes is progressive.

Check Your Understanding   7-4

1. An income tax taxes 1% of the first $10,000 of income and 2% on all income above $10,000.
   a. What is the marginal tax rate for someone with income of $5,000? How much total tax does this person pay? How much is this as a percentage of his or her income?
   b. What is the marginal tax rate for someone with income of $20,000? How much total tax does this person pay? How much is this as a percentage of his or her income?
   c. Is this income tax proportional, progressive, or regressive?

2. When comparing households at different income levels, economists find that consumption spending grows more slowly than income. Assume that when income grows by 50%, from $10,000 to $15,000, consumption grows by 25%, from $8,000 to $10,000. Compare the percent of income paid in taxes by a family with $15,000 in income to that paid by a family with $10,000 in income under a 1% tax on consumption purchases. Is this a proportional, progressive, or regressive tax?

3. True or false? Explain your answers.
   a. Payroll taxes do not affect a person's incentive to take a job because they are paid by employers.
   b. A lump-sum tax is a proportional tax because it is the same amount for each person.

Solutions appear at back of book.

Amazon versus BarnesandNoble.com

In 2014, comparison shoppers in about half of the United States found that the final price of a book on Amazon was cheaper than on its competitor, BarnesandNoble.com. Why? It's simply a matter of taxes—or, more specifically, in which states BarnesandNoble.com is compelled to collect state sales tax on customer orders while Amazon is not. This difference arises as a result of interstate tax law. Sales tax is levied on transactions of most nonessential goods and services in 45 states, with an average sales tax bite of about 8% of the purchase price.

According to the law, online retailers without a physical presence in a given state can sell products without collecting sales tax. (Customers are supposed to report the transaction and pay the sales tax, which they—not surprisingly—fail to do.) In order to exploit this advantage, Amazon has historically maintained a physical presence in only five states. As a result, it collects sales tax only from customers in those states, including Washington state, home to its corporate headquarters. And Amazon has taken extreme measures to avoid collecting sales tax in other states, for example, forbidding employees to work or even send e-mails while in those states. In 2011 it terminated a joint advertising program with 25,000 California affiliate sellers in response to tougher sales tax collection laws in that state.

In contrast, the bricks-and-mortar book retailer, Barnes and Noble, the parent company of BarnesandNoble.com, has physical bookstores in every state. As a result, BarnesandNoble.com must collect sales tax on all of its online orders. This confers a significant advantage to Amazon, as the following example shows. The final price of *A Deadly Indifference*, by Marshall Jevons, shipped to California, is $20.69 if bought on Amazon versus $22.14 from BarnesandNoble.com. The $1.45 difference comes from the 7.5% California sales tax assessed on the BarnesandNoble.com sale (see Table 7-6).

Joshua Lott/Bloomberg via Getty Images

TABLE 7-6	Comparison Shopping for *A Deadly Indifference* by Marshall Jevons	
	Amazon	BarnesandNoble.com
Price of book	$20.69	$20.69
California sales tax (7.5%)	0	$1.45
Shipping fee	$3.99	$3.99
Final price	$20.69	$22.14

As reported in the *Wall Street Journal*, interviews and company documents show that Amazon believes that its avoidance of sales tax collection has been crucial to its success in becoming the dominant retailer of books in the United States. Estimates are that Amazon would have lost as much as $653 million in sales in 2011, or 1.4% of its annual revenue, if it had been forced to collect sales tax.

Since 2012, however, after vigorous pressure from state authorities, Amazon's ability to avoid collecting sales tax has been greatly curtailed. As of 2014 the number of states it collects sales taxes in has risen from 5 to 19. It's part of a new strategy by Amazon, to build warehouses in the states in which it collects sales taxes, reasoning that faster delivery will keep customers loyal despite having to pay sales tax. Yet, it's not hard to understand the view from BarnesandNoble.com that being forced to collect sales tax when Amazon is not deeply hurt its business.

QUESTIONS FOR THOUGHT

1. What effect do you think the difference in state sales tax collection has on Amazon's sales versus BarnesandNoble.com's sales?

2. Suppose sales tax is collected on all online book sales. From the evidence in this case, what do you think is the incidence of the tax between seller and buyer? What does this imply about the elasticity of supply of books by book retailers? (*Hint:* Compare the pre-tax prices of the book.)

3. How did Amazon's tax strategy distort its business behavior? What measures would eliminate these distortions?

SUMMARY

1. **Excise taxes**—taxes on the purchase or sale of a good—raise the price paid by consumers and reduce the price received by producers, driving a wedge between the two. The **incidence** of the tax—how the burden of the tax is divided between consumers and producers—does not depend on who officially pays the tax.

2. The incidence of an excise tax depends on the price elasticities of supply and demand. If the price elasticity of demand is higher than the price elasticity of supply, the tax falls mainly on producers; if the price elasticity of supply is higher than the price elasticity of demand, the tax falls mainly on consumers.

3. The tax revenue generated by a tax depends on the **tax rate** and on the number of taxed units transacted. Excise taxes cause inefficiency in the form of deadweight loss because they discourage some mutually beneficial transactions. Taxes also impose **administrative costs:** resources used to collect the tax, to pay it (over and above the amount of the tax), and to evade it.

4. An excise tax generates revenue for the government but lowers total surplus. The loss in total surplus exceeds the tax revenue, resulting in a deadweight loss to society. This deadweight loss is represented by a triangle, the area of which equals the value of the transactions discouraged by the tax. The greater the elasticity of demand or supply, or both, the larger the deadweight loss from a tax. If either demand or supply is perfectly inelastic, there is no deadweight loss from a tax.

5. An efficient tax minimizes both the sum of the deadweight loss due to distorted incentives and the administrative costs of the tax. However, tax fairness, or tax equity, is also a goal of tax policy.

6. There are two major principles of tax fairness, the **benefits principle** and the **ability-to-pay principle.** The most efficient tax, a **lump-sum tax,** does not distort incentives but performs badly in terms of fairness. The fairest taxes in terms of the ability-to-pay principle, however, distort incentives the most and perform badly on efficiency grounds. So in a well-designed tax system, there is a **trade-off between equity and efficiency.**

7. Every tax consists of a **tax base,** which defines what is taxed, and a **tax structure,** which specifies how the tax depends on the tax base. Different tax bases give rise to different taxes—the **income tax, payroll tax, sales tax, profits tax, property tax,** and **wealth tax.** A **proportional tax** is the same percentage of the tax base for all taxpayers.

8. A tax is **progressive** if higher-income people pay a higher percentage of their income in taxes than lower-income people and **regressive** if they pay a lower percentage. Progressive taxes are often justified by the ability-to-pay principle. However, a highly progressive tax system significantly distorts incentives because it leads to a high **marginal tax rate,** the percentage of an increase in income that is taxed away, on high earners. The U.S. tax system is progressive overall, although it contains a mixture of progressive and regressive taxes.

KEY TERMS

Excise tax, p. 188
Incidence, p. 190
Tax rate, p. 195
Administrative costs, p. 200
Benefits principle, p. 203
Ability-to-pay principle, p. 204
Lump-sum tax, p. 204

Trade-off between equity and
  efficiency, p. 204
Tax base, p. 206
Tax structure, p. 206
Income tax, p. 206
Payroll tax, p. 206
Sales tax, p. 206

Profits tax, p. 206
Property tax, p. 206
Wealth tax, p. 206
Proportional tax, p. 206
Progressive tax, p. 207
Regressive tax, p. 207
Marginal tax rate, p. 207

PROBLEMS

1. The United States imposes an excise tax on the sale of domestic airline tickets. Let's assume that in 2013 the total excise tax was $6.10 per airline ticket (consisting of the $3.60 flight segment tax plus the $2.50 September 11 fee). According to data from the Bureau of Transportation Statistics, in 2013, 643 million passengers traveled on domestic airline trips at an average price of $380 per trip. The accompanying table shows the supply and demand schedules for airline trips. The quantity demanded at the average price of $380 is actual data; the rest is hypothetical.

Price of trip	Quantity of trips demanded (millions)	Quantity of trips supplied (millions)
$380.02	642	699
380.00	643	698
378.00	693	693
373.90	793	643
373.82	913	642

a. What is the government tax revenue in 2013 from the excise tax?

b. On January 1, 2014, the total excise tax increased to $6.20 per ticket. What is the quantity of tickets transacted now? What is the average ticket price now? What is the 2014 government tax revenue?

c. Does this increase in the excise tax increase or decrease government tax revenue?

2. The U.S. government would like to help the American auto industry compete against foreign automakers that sell trucks in the United States. It can do this by imposing an excise tax on each foreign truck sold in the United States. The hypothetical pre-tax demand and supply schedules for imported trucks are given in the accompanying table.

Price of imported truck	Quantity of imported trucks (thousands)	
	Quantity demanded	Quantity supplied
$32,000	100	400
31,000	200	350
30,000	300	300
29,000	400	250
28,000	500	200
27,000	600	150

a. In the absence of government interference, what is the equilibrium price of an imported truck? The equilibrium quantity? Illustrate with a diagram.

b. Assume that the government imposes an excise tax of $3,000 per imported truck. Illustrate the effect of this excise tax in your diagram from part a. How many imported trucks are now purchased and at what price? How much does the foreign automaker receive per truck?

c. Calculate the government revenue raised by the excise tax in part b. Illustrate it on your diagram.

d. How does the excise tax on imported trucks benefit American automakers? Whom does it hurt? How does inefficiency arise from this government policy?

3. In 1990, the United States began to levy a tax on sales of luxury cars. For simplicity, assume that the tax was an excise tax of $6,000 per car. The accompanying figure shows hypothetical demand and supply curves for luxury cars.

a. Under the tax, what is the price paid by consumers? What is the price received by producers? What is the government tax revenue from the excise tax?

Over time, the tax on luxury automobiles was slowly phased out (and completely eliminated in 2002). Suppose that the excise tax falls from $6,000 per car to $4,500 per car.

b. After the reduction in the excise tax from $6,000 to $4,500 per car, what is the price paid by consumers? What is the price received by producers? What is tax revenue now?

c. Compare the tax revenue created by the taxes in parts a and b. What accounts for the change in tax revenue from the reduction in the excise tax?

4. All states impose excise taxes on gasoline. According to data from the Federal Highway Administration, the state of California imposes an excise tax of $0.40 per gallon of gasoline. In 2013, gasoline sales in California totaled 18.4 billion gallons. What was California's tax revenue from the gasoline excise tax? If California doubled the excise tax, would tax revenue double? Why or why not?

5. In the United States, each state government can impose its own excise tax on the sale of cigarettes. Suppose that in the state of North Texarkana, the state government imposes a tax of $2.00 per pack sold within the state. In contrast, the neighboring state of South Texarkana imposes no excise tax on cigarettes. Assume that in both states the pre-tax price of a pack of cigarettes is $1.00. Assume that the total cost to a resident of North Texarkana to smuggle a pack of cigarettes from South Texarkana is $1.85 per pack. (This includes the cost of time, gasoline, and so on.) Assume that the supply curve for cigarettes is neither perfectly elastic nor perfectly inelastic.

a. Draw a diagram of the supply and demand curves for cigarettes in North Texarkana showing a situation in which it makes economic sense for a North Texarkanan to smuggle a pack of cigarettes from South Texarkana to North Texarkana. Explain your diagram.

b. Draw a corresponding diagram showing a situation in which it does not make economic sense for a North Texarkanan to smuggle a pack of cigarettes from South Texarkana to North Texarkana. Explain your diagram.

c. Suppose the demand for cigarettes in North Texarkana is perfectly inelastic. How high could the cost of smuggling a pack of cigarettes go until a North Texarkanan no longer found it profitable to smuggle?

d. Still assume that demand for cigarettes in North Texarkana is perfectly inelastic and that all smokers in North Texarkana are smuggling their cigarettes at a cost of $1.85 per pack, so no tax is paid. Is there any inefficiency in this situation? If so, how much per pack? Suppose chip-embedded cigarette packaging makes it impossible to smuggle cigarettes across the state border. Is there any inefficiency in this situation? If so, how much per pack?

6. In each of the following cases involving taxes, explain: (i) whether the incidence of the tax falls more heavily on consumers or producers, (ii) why government revenue raised from the tax is not a good indicator of the true cost of the tax, and (iii) how deadweight loss arises as a result of the tax.

a. The government imposes an excise tax on the sale of all college textbooks. Before the tax was imposed, 1 million textbooks were sold every year at a price of $50. After the tax is imposed, 600,000 books are sold yearly; students pay $55 per book, $30 of which publishers receive.

b. The government imposes an excise tax on the sale of all airline tickets. Before the tax was imposed, 3 million airline tickets were sold every year at a price of $500. After the tax is imposed, 1.5 million tickets are sold yearly; travelers pay $550 per ticket, $450 of which the airlines receive.

c. The government imposes an excise tax on the sale of all toothbrushes. Before the tax, 2 million toothbrushes were sold every year at a price of $1.50. After the tax is imposed, 800,000 toothbrushes are sold every year; consumers pay $2 per toothbrush, $1.25 of which producers receive.

7. The accompanying diagram shows the market for cigarettes. The current equilibrium price per pack is $4, and every day 40 million packs of cigarettes are sold. In order to recover some of the health care costs associated with smoking, the government imposes a tax of $2 per pack. This will raise the equilibrium price to $5 per pack and reduce the equilibrium quantity to 30 million packs.

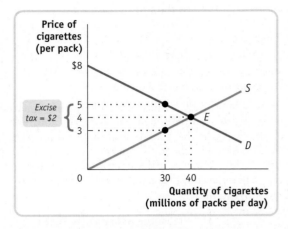

The economist working for the tobacco lobby claims that this tax will reduce consumer surplus for smokers by $40 million per day, since 40 million packs now cost $1 more per pack. The economist working for the lobby for sufferers of second-hand smoke argues that this is an enormous overestimate and that the reduction in consumer surplus will be only $30 million per day, since after the imposition of the tax only 30 million packs of cigarettes will be bought and each of these packs will now cost $1 more. They are both wrong. Why?

8. Consider the original market for pizza in Collegetown, illustrated in the accompanying table. Collegetown officials decide to impose an excise tax on pizza of $4 per pizza.

Price of pizza	Quantity of pizza demanded	Quantity of pizza supplied
$10	0	6
9	1	5
8	2	4
7	3	3
6	4	2
5	5	1
4	6	0
3	7	0
2	8	0
1	9	0

a. What is the quantity of pizza bought and sold after the imposition of the tax? What is the price paid by consumers? What is the price received by producers?

b. Calculate the consumer surplus and the producer surplus after the imposition of the tax. By how much has the imposition of the tax reduced consumer surplus? By how much has it reduced producer surplus?

c. How much tax revenue does Collegetown earn from this tax?

d. Calculate the deadweight loss from this tax.

9. The state needs to raise money, and the governor has a choice of imposing an excise tax of the same amount on one of two previously untaxed goods: the state can tax sales of either restaurant meals or gasoline. Both the demand for and the supply of restaurant meals are more elastic than the demand for and the supply of gasoline. If the governor wants to minimize the deadweight loss caused by the tax, which good should be taxed? For each good, draw a diagram that illustrates the deadweight loss from taxation.

10. Assume that the demand for gasoline is inelastic and supply is relatively elastic. The government imposes a sales tax on gasoline. The tax revenue is used to fund research into clean fuel alternatives to gasoline, which will improve the air we all breathe.

    a. Who bears more of the burden of this tax, consumers or producers? Show in a diagram who bears how much of the burden.

    b. Is this tax based on the benefits principle or the ability-to-pay principle? Explain.

11. Assess the following four tax policies in terms of the benefits principle versus the ability-to-pay principle.

    a. A tax on gasoline that finances maintenance of state roads

    b. An 8% tax on imported goods valued in excess of $800 per household brought in on passenger flights

    c. Airline-flight landing fees that pay for air traffic control

    d. A reduction in the amount of income tax paid based on the number of dependent children in the household.

12. You are advising the government on how to pay for national defense. There are two proposals for a tax system to fund national defense. Under both proposals, the tax base is an individual's income. Under proposal A, all citizens pay exactly the same lump-sum tax, regardless of income. Under proposal B, individuals with higher incomes pay a greater proportion of their income in taxes.

    a. Is the tax in proposal A progressive, proportional, or regressive? What about the tax in proposal B?

    b. Is the tax in proposal A based on the ability-to-pay principle or on the benefits principle? What about the tax in proposal B?

    c. In terms of efficiency, which tax is better? Explain.

13. Each of the following tax proposals has income as the tax base. In each case, calculate the marginal tax rate for each level of income. Then calculate the percentage of income paid in taxes for an individual with a pre-tax income of $5,000 and for an individual with a pre-tax income of $40,000. Classify the tax as being proportional, progressive, or regressive. (*Hint:* You can calculate the marginal tax rate as the percentage of an additional $1 in income that is taxed away.)

    a. All income is taxed at 20%.

    b. All income up to $10,000 is tax-free. All income above $10,000 is taxed at a constant rate of 20%.

    c. All income between $0 and $10,000 is taxed at 10%. All income between $10,000 and $20,000 is taxed at 20%. All income higher than $20,000 is taxed at 30%.

    d. Each individual who earns more than $10,000 pays a lump-sum tax of $10,000. If the individual's income is less than $10,000, that individual pays in taxes exactly what his or her income is.

    e. Of the four tax policies, which is likely to cause the worst incentive problems? Explain.

14. In Transylvania the basic income tax system is fairly simple. The first 40,000 sylvers (the official currency of Transylvania) earned each year are free of income tax. Any additional income is taxed at a rate of 25%. In addition, every individual pays a social security tax, which is calculated as follows: all income up to 80,000 sylvers is taxed at an additional 20%, but there is no additional social security tax on income above 80,000 sylvers.

    a. Calculate the marginal tax rates (including income tax and social security tax) for Transylvanians with the following levels of income: 20,000 sylvers, 40,000 sylvers, and 80,000 sylvers. (*Hint:* You can calculate the marginal tax rate as the percentage of an additional 1 sylver in income that is taxed away.)

    b. Is the income tax in Transylvania progressive, regressive, or proportional? Is the social security tax progressive, regressive, or proportional?

    c. Which income group's incentives are most adversely affected by the combined income and social security tax systems?

WORK IT OUT

For interactive, step-by-step help in solving the following problem, visit LaunchPad by using the URL on the back cover of this book.

15. You work for the Council of Economic Advisers, providing economic advice to the White House. The president wants to overhaul the income tax system and asks your advice. Suppose that the current income tax system consists of a proportional tax of 10% on all income and that there is one person in the country who earns $110 million; everyone else earns less than $100 million. The president proposes a tax cut targeted at the very rich so that the new tax system would consist of a proportional tax of 10% on all income up to $100 million and a marginal tax rate of 0% (no tax) on income above $100 million. You are asked to evaluate this tax proposal.

    a. For incomes of $100 million or less, is this proposed tax system progressive, regressive, or proportional? For incomes of more than $100 million? Explain.

    b. Would this tax system create more or less tax revenue, other things equal? Is this tax system more or less efficient than the current tax system? Explain.

International Trade

▶ **What You Will Learn in This Chapter**

■ **How comparative advantage leads to mutually beneficial international trade**

■ **The sources of international comparative advantage**

■ **Who gains and who loses from international trade, and why the gains exceed the losses**

■ **How tariffs and import quotas cause inefficiency and reduce total surplus**

■ **Why governments often engage in trade protection and how international trade agreements counteract this**

THE EVERYWHERE PHONE

The production and consumption of smartphones are examples of today's hyperglobal world with its soaring levels of international trade.

"WE FELL IN LOVE WHEN I was nineteen / Now we're staring at a screen." These lyrics, from Arcade Fire's 2013 hit song "Reflektor," describe an era in which everyone does indeed seem to be staring at the screen of a smartphone. Apple introduced its first iPhone in 2007, and since then the iPhone and its competitors have become ubiquitous.

They're everywhere—but where do smartphones come from? If you answered "America," because Apple is an American company, you're mostly wrong: Apple develops products, but outsources nearly all manufacturing of those products to other companies, mainly overseas. But it's not really right to say "China" either, even though that's where iPhones are assembled. You see, assembly—the last phase of iPhone production, in which the pieces are put together in the familiar metal-and-glass case—only accounts for a small fraction of the phone's value.

In fact, a study of the iPhone 4 estimated that of the average factory price of $229 per phone, only around $10 stayed in the Chinese economy. A substantially larger amount went to Korean manufacturers, who supplied the display and memory chips. There were also substantial outlays for raw materials, sourced all over the world. And the biggest share of the price—more than half—consisted of Apple's profit margin, which was largely a reward for research, development, and design.

So where do iPhones come from? Lots of places. And the case of the iPhone isn't unusual: the car you drive, the clothing you wear, even the food you eat are generally the end products of complex "supply chains" that span the globe.

Has this always been true? Yes and no. Large-scale international trade isn't new. By the early twentieth century, middle-class residents of London already ate bread made from Canadian wheat and beef from the Argentine Pampas, while wearing clothing woven from Australian wool and Egyptian cotton. In recent decades, however, new technologies for transportation and communication have interacted with pro-trade policies to produce an era of *hyperglobalization* in which international trade has soared thanks to complex chains of production like the one that puts an iPhone in front of your nose. As a result, now, more than ever before, we must have a full picture of international trade to understand how national economies work.

This chapter examines the economics of international trade. We start from the model of comparative advantage, which, as we saw in Chapter 2, explains why there are gains from international trade. We will briefly recap that model here, then turn to a more detailed examination of the causes and consequences of globalization.

Goods and services purchased from other countries are **imports;** goods and services sold to other countries are **exports.**

Globalization is the phenomenon of growing economic linkages among countries.

Hyperglobalization is the phenomenon of extremely high levels of international trade.

Comparative Advantage and International Trade

The United States buys smartphones—and many other goods and services—from other countries. At the same time, it sells many goods and services to other countries. Goods and services purchased from abroad are **imports;** goods and services sold abroad are **exports.**

As illustrated by the opening story, imports and exports have taken on an increasingly important role in the U.S. economy. Over the last 50 years, both imports into and exports from the United States have grown faster than the U.S. economy. Panel (a) of Figure 8-1 shows how the values of U.S. imports and exports have grown as a percentage of gross domestic product (GDP). Panel (b) shows imports and exports as a percentage of GDP for a number of countries. It shows that foreign trade is significantly more important for many other countries than it is for the United States. (Japan is the exception.)

Foreign trade isn't the only way countries interact economically. In the modern world, investors from one country often invest funds in another nation; many companies are multinational, with subsidiaries operating in several countries; and a growing number of individuals work in a country different from the one in which they were born. The growth of all these forms of economic linkages among countries is often called **globalization.** And as we saw in the opening story, certain sectors of the economy are characterized by extremely high levels of international trade. This **hyperglobalization** is often the result of supply chains of production that span the globe, in which each stage of a good's production takes place in a different country—all made possible by advances in communication and transportation technology. (We analyze a real-life example in this chapter's business case.)

| FIGURE **8-1** | The Growing Importance of International Trade |

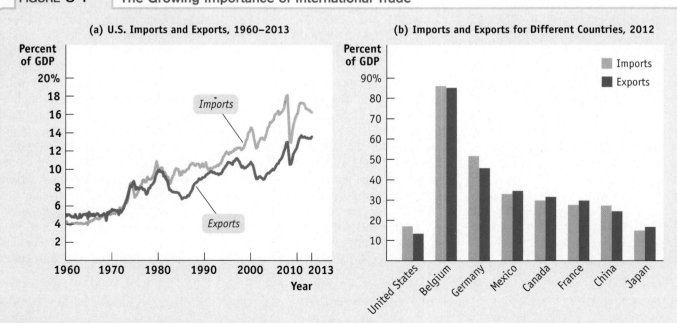

Panel (a) illustrates the fact that over the past 50 years, the United States has exported a steadily growing share of its GDP to other countries and imported a growing share of what it consumes. Panel (b) demonstrates that international trade is significantly more important to many other countries than it is to the United States, with the exception of Japan.

Sources: Bureau of Economic Analysis [panel (a)] and World Development Indicators [panel (b)].

In this chapter, however, we'll focus mainly on international trade. To understand why international trade occurs and why economists believe it is beneficial to the economy, we will first review the concept of comparative advantage.

Production Possibilities and Comparative Advantage, Revisited

To produce phones, any country must use resources—land, labor, capital, and so on—that could have been used to produce other things. The potential production of other goods a country must forgo to produce a phone is the opportunity cost of that phone.

In some cases, it's easy to see why the opportunity cost of producing a good is especially low in a given country. Consider, for example, shrimp—much of which now comes from seafood farms in Vietnam and Thailand. It's a lot easier to produce shrimp in Vietnam, where the climate is nearly ideal and there's plenty of coastal land suitable for shellfish farming, than it is in the United States.

Conversely, other goods are not produced as easily in Vietnam as in the United States. For example, Vietnam doesn't have the base of skilled workers and technological know-how that makes the United States so good at producing many high-technology goods. So the opportunity cost of a ton of shrimp, in terms of other goods such as aircraft, is much less in Vietnam than it is in the United States.

The opportunity cost of assembling smartphones in China is lower, giving it a comparative advantage.

In other cases, matters are a bit less obvious. It's as easy to assemble smartphones in the United States as it is in China, and Chinese electronics workers are, if anything, less efficient than their U.S. counterparts. But Chinese workers are a lot less productive than U.S. workers in other areas, such as automobile and chemical production. This means that diverting a Chinese worker into assembling phones reduces output of other goods less than diverting a U.S. worker into assembling phones. That is, the opportunity cost of assembling phones in China is less than it is in the United States.

Notice that we said the opportunity cost of *assembling* phones. As we've seen, most of the value of a "Chinese made" phone actually comes from other countries. For the sake of exposition, however, let's ignore that complication and consider a hypothetical case in which China makes phones from scratch.

So we say that China has a comparative advantage in producing smartphones. Let's repeat the definition of comparative advantage from Chapter 2: *A country has a comparative advantage in producing a good or service if the opportunity cost of producing the good or service is lower for that country than for other countries.*

Figure 8-2 provides a hypothetical numerical example of comparative advantage in international trade. We assume that only two goods are produced and consumed, phones and Ford trucks, and that there are only two countries in the world, the United States and China. The figure shows hypothetical production possibility frontiers for the United States and China.

As in Chapter 2, we simplify the model by assuming that the production possibility frontiers are straight lines, as shown in Figure 2-1, rather than the more realistic bowed-out shape shown in Figure 2-2. The straight-line shape implies that the opportunity cost of a phone in terms of trucks in each country is constant—it does not depend on how many units of each good the country produces. The analysis of international trade under the assumption that opportunity costs are constant, which makes production possibility frontiers straight lines, is known as the **Ricardian model of international trade,** named after the English economist David Ricardo, who introduced this analysis in the early nineteenth century.

In Figure 8-2 we show a situation in which the United States can produce 100,000 trucks if it produces no phones, or 100 million phones if it produces

The **Ricardian model of international trade** analyzes international trade under the assumption that opportunity costs are constant.

FIGURE **8-2** Comparative Advantage and the Production Possibility Frontier

The U.S. opportunity cost of 1 million phones in terms of trucks is 1,000: for every 1 million phones, 1,000 trucks must be forgone. The Chinese opportunity cost of 1 million phones in terms of trucks is 250 for every additional 1 million phones, only 250 trucks must be forgone. As a result, the United States has a comparative advantage in truck production, and China has a comparative advantage in phone production. In autarky, each country is forced to consume only what it produces: 50,000 trucks and 50 million phones for the United States; 25,000 trucks and 100 million phones for China.

Autarky is a situation in which a country does not trade with other countries.

no trucks. Thus, the slope of the U.S. production possibility frontier, or *PPF*, is −100,000/100 = −1,000. That is, to produce an additional million phones, the United States must forgo the production of 1,000 trucks.

Similarly, China can produce 50,000 trucks if it produces no phones or 200 million phones if it produces no trucks. Thus, the slope of China's *PPF* is −50,000/200 = −250. That is, to produce an additional million phones, China must forgo the production of 250 trucks.

Economists use the term **autarky** to refer to a situation in which a country does not trade with other countries. We assume that in autarky the United States chooses to produce and consume 50 million phones and 50,000 trucks. We also assume that in autarky China produces 100 million phones and 25,000 trucks.

The trade-offs facing the two countries when they don't trade are summarized in Table 8-1. As you can see, the United States has a comparative advantage in the production of trucks because it has a lower opportunity cost in terms of phones than China has: producing a truck costs the United States only 1,000 phones, while it costs China 4,000 phones. Correspondingly, China has a comparative advantage in phone production: 1 million phones costs only 250 trucks, while it costs the United States 1,000 trucks.

As we learned in Chapter 2, each country can do better by engaging in trade than it could by not trading. A country can accomplish this by specializing in the production of the good in which it has a comparative advantage and exporting that good, while importing the good in which it has a comparative disadvantage.

Let's see how this works.

TABLE **8-1**	U.S. and Chinese Opportunity Costs of Phones and Trucks			
	U.S. Opportunity Cost		**Chinese Opportunity Cost**	
1 million phones	1,000 trucks	>	250 trucks	
1 truck	1,000 phones	<	4,000 phones	

FIGURE **8-3**   The Gains from International Trade

Trade increases world production of both goods, allowing both countries to consume more. Here, each country specializes its production as a result of trade: the United States concentrates on producing trucks, and China concentrates on producing phones. Total world production of both goods rises, which means that it is possible for both countries to consume more of both goods.

The Gains from International Trade

Figure 8-3 illustrates how both countries can gain from specialization and trade, by showing a hypothetical rearrangement of production and consumption that allows *each* country to consume more of *both* goods. Again, panel (a) represents the United States and panel (b) represents China. In each panel we indicate again the autarky production and consumption assumed in Figure 8-2.

Once trade becomes possible, however, everything changes. With trade, each country can move to producing only the good in which it has a comparative advantage—trucks for the United States and phones for China. Because the world production of both goods is now higher than in autarky, trade makes it possible for each country to consume more of both goods.

Table 8-2 sums up the changes as a result of trade and shows why both countries can gain. The left part of the table shows the autarky situation, before trade, in which each country must produce the goods it consumes. The right part of the table shows what happens as a result of trade. After trade, the United States specializes in the production of trucks, producing 100,000 trucks and no phones; China specializes in the production of phones, producing 200 million phones and no trucks.

TABLE **8-2**   How the United States and China Gain from Trade

		In Autarky		With Trade		
		Production	Consumption	Production	Consumption	Gains from trade
United States	Million phones	50	50	0	75	+25
	Trucks	50,000	50,000	100,000	62,500	+12,500
China	Million phones	100	100	200	125	+25
	Trucks	25,000	25,000	0	37,500	+12,500

The result is a rise in total world production of both goods. As you can see in the Table 8-2 column at far right showing consumption with trade, the United States is able to consume both more trucks and more phones than before, even though it no longer produces phones, because it can import phones from China. China can also consume more of both goods, even though it no longer produces trucks, because it can import trucks from the United States.

The key to this mutual gain is the fact that trade liberates both countries from self-sufficiency—from the need to produce the same mixes of goods they consume. Because each country can concentrate on producing the good in which it has a comparative advantage, total world production rises, making a higher standard of living possible in both nations.

In this example we have simply assumed the post-trade consumption bundles of the two countries. In fact, the consumption choices of a country reflect both the preferences of its residents and the *relative prices*—the prices of one good in terms of another in international markets. Although we have not explicitly given the price of trucks in terms of phones, that price is implicit in our example: China sells the United States the 75 million phones the U.S. consumes in return for the 37,500 trucks China consumes, so 1 million phones are traded for 500 trucks. This tells us that the price of a truck on world markets must be equal to the price of 2,000 phones in our example.

One requirement that the relative price must satisfy is that no country pays a relative price greater than its opportunity cost of obtaining the good in autarky. That is, the United States won't pay more than 1,000 trucks for one million phones from China, and China won't pay more than 4,000 phones for each truck from the United States. Once this requirement is satisfied, the actual relative price in international trade is determined by supply and demand—and we'll turn to supply and demand in international trade in the next section. However, first let's look more deeply into the nature of the gains from trade.

Comparative Advantage versus Absolute Advantage

It's easy to accept the idea that Vietnam and Thailand have a comparative advantage in shrimp production: they have a tropical climate that's better suited to shrimp farming than that of the United States (even along the Gulf Coast), and they have a lot of usable coastal area. So the United States imports shrimp from Vietnam and Thailand. In other cases, however, it may be harder to understand why we import certain goods from abroad.

The tropical climates of Vietnam and Thailand give them a comparative advantage in shrimp production.

U.S. imports of phones from China are a case in point. There's nothing about China's climate or resources that makes it especially good at assembling electronic devices. In fact, it almost surely would take fewer hours of labor to assemble a smartphone or a tablet in the United States than in China.

Why, then, do we buy phones assembled in China? Because the gains from trade depend on *comparative advantage*, not absolute advantage. Yes, it would take less labor to assemble a phone in the United States than in China. That is, the productivity of Chinese electronics workers is less than that of their U.S. counterparts. But what determines comparative advantage is not the amount of resources used to produce a good but the opportunity cost of that good—here, the quantity of other goods forgone in order to produce a phone. And the opportunity cost of phones is lower in China than in the United States.

Here's how it works: Chinese workers have low productivity compared with U.S. workers in the electronics industry. But Chinese workers have even lower productivity compared with U.S. workers in other industries. Because Chinese labor productivity in industries other than electronics is relatively very low, producing a phone in China, even though it takes a lot of labor, does not require forgoing the production of large quantities of other goods.

In the United States, the opposite is true: very high productivity in other industries (such as automobiles) means that assembling electronic products in the United States, even though it doesn't require much labor, requires sacrificing lots of other goods. So the opportunity cost of producing electronics is less in China than in the United States. Despite its lower labor productivity, China has a comparative advantage in the production of many consumer electronics, although the United States has an absolute advantage.

The source of China's comparative advantage in consumer electronics is reflected in global markets by the wages Chinese workers are paid. That's because a country's wage rates, in general, reflect its labor productivity. In countries where labor is highly productive in many industries, employers are willing to pay high wages to attract workers, so competition among employers leads to an overall high wage rate. In countries where labor is less productive, competition for workers is less intense and wage rates are correspondingly lower.

As the accompanying Global Comparison shows, there is indeed a strong relationship between overall levels of productivity and wage rates around the world. Because China has generally low productivity, it has a relatively low wage rate. Low wages, in turn, give China a cost advantage in producing goods where its productivity is only moderately low, like consumer electronics. As a result, it's cheaper to produce these goods in China than in the United States.

The kind of trade that takes place between low-wage, low-productivity economies like China and high-wage, high-productivity economies like the United States gives rise to two common misperceptions. One, the *pauper labor fallacy*, is the belief that when a country with high wages imports goods produced by workers who are paid low wages, this must hurt the standard of living of workers

GLOBAL COMPARISION | Productivity and Wages Around the World

Is it true that both the pauper labor argument and the sweatshop labor argument are fallacies? Yes, it is. The real explanation for low wages in poor countries is low overall productivity.

The graph shows estimates of labor productivity, measured by the value of output (GDP) per worker, and wages, measured by the hourly compensation of the average worker, for several countries in 2012. Both productivity and wages are expressed as percentages of U.S. productivity and wages; for example, productivity and wages in Japan were 70% and 101%, respectively, of their U.S. levels. You can see the strong positive relationship between productivity and wages. The relationship isn't perfect. For example, Norway has higher wages than its productivity might lead you to expect. But simple comparisons of wages give a misleading sense of labor costs in poor countries: their low wage advantage is mostly offset by low productivity.

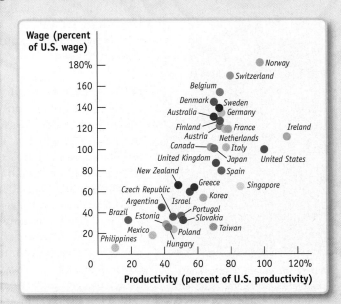

Sources: The Conference Board; Penn World Table 8.0.

in the importing country. The other, the *sweatshop labor fallacy*, is the belief that trade must be bad for workers in poor exporting countries because those workers are paid very low wages by our standards.

Both fallacies miss the nature of gains from trade: it's to the advantage of both countries if the poorer, lower-wage country exports goods in which it has a comparative advantage, even if its cost advantage in these goods depends on low wages. That is, both countries are able to achieve a higher standard of living through trade.

It's particularly important to understand that buying a good made by someone who is paid much lower wages than most U.S. workers doesn't necessarily imply that you're taking advantage of that person. It depends on the alternatives. Because workers in poor countries have low productivity across the board, they are offered low wages whether they produce goods exported to America or goods sold in local markets. A job that looks terrible by rich-country standards can be a step up for someone in a poor country.

International trade that depends on low-wage exports can nonetheless raise the exporting country's standard of living. This is especially true of very-low-wage nations. For example, Bangladesh and similar countries would be much poorer than they are—their citizens might even be starving—if they weren't able to export goods such as clothing based on their low wage rates.

Sources of Comparative Advantage

International trade is driven by comparative advantage, but where does comparative advantage come from? Economists who study international trade have found three main sources of comparative advantage: international differences in *climate*, international differences in *factor endowments*, and international differences in *technology*.

Differences in Climate One key reason the opportunity cost of producing shrimp in Vietnam and Thailand is less than in the United States is that shrimp need warm water—Vietnam has plenty of that, but America doesn't. In general, differences in climate play a significant role in international trade. Tropical countries export tropical products like coffee, sugar, bananas, and shrimp. Countries in the temperate zones export crops like wheat and corn. Some trade is even driven by the difference in seasons between the northern and southern hemispheres: winter deliveries of Chilean grapes and New Zealand apples have become commonplace in U.S. and European supermarkets.

Differences in Factor Endowments Canada is a major exporter of forest products—lumber and products derived from lumber, like pulp and paper—to the United States. These exports don't reflect the special skill of Canadian lumberjacks. Canada has a comparative advantage in forest products because its forested area is much greater compared to the size of its labor force than the ratio of forestland to the labor force in the United States.

Forestland, like labor and capital, is a *factor of production*: an input used to produce goods and services. (Recall from Chapter 2 that the factors of production are land, labor, physical capital, and human capital.) Due to history and geography, the mix of available factors of production differs among countries, providing an important source of comparative advantage. The relationship between comparative advantage and factor availability is found in an influential model of international trade, the *Heckscher–Ohlin model*, developed by two Swedish economists in the first half of the twentieth century.

A greater endowment of forestland gives Canada a comparative advantage in forest products.

Johner Images/Alamy

Two key concepts in the model are *factor abundance* and *factor intensity.* Factor abundance refers to how large a country's supply of a factor is relative to its supply of other factors. Factor intensity refers to the fact that producers use different ratios of factors of production in the production of different goods. For example, oil refineries use much more capital per worker than clothing factories. Economists use the term **factor intensity** to describe this difference among goods: oil refining is capital-intensive, because it tends to use a high ratio of capital to labor, but phone production is labor-intensive, because it tends to use a high ratio of labor to capital.

According to the **Heckscher–Ohlin model,** *a country that has an abundant supply of a factor of production will have a comparative advantage in goods whose production is intensive in that factor.* So a country that has a relative abundance of capital will have a comparative advantage in capital-intensive industries such as oil refining, but a country that has a relative abundance of labor will have a comparative advantage in labor-intensive industries such as phone production.

The basic intuition behind this result is simple and based on opportunity cost. The opportunity cost of a given factor—the value that the factor would generate in alternative uses—is low for a country when it is relatively abundant in that factor. Relative to the United States, China has an abundance of low-skilled labor. As a result, the opportunity cost of the production of low-skilled, labor-intensive goods is lower in China than in the United States.

The most dramatic example of the validity of the Heckscher–Ohlin model is world trade in clothing. Clothing production is a labor-intensive activity: it doesn't take much physical capital, nor does it require a lot of human capital in the form of highly educated workers. So you would expect labor-abundant countries such as China and Bangladesh to have a comparative advantage in clothing production. And they do.

The fact that international trade is the result of differences in factor endowments helps explain another fact: international specialization of production is often *incomplete.* That is, a country often maintains some domestic production of a good that it imports. A good example of this is the United States and oil. Saudi Arabia exports oil to the United States because Saudi Arabia has an abundant supply of oil relative to its other factors of production; the United States exports medical devices to Saudi Arabia because it has an abundant supply of expertise in medical technology relative to its other factors of production. But the United States also produces some oil domestically because the size of its domestic oil reserves in Texas and Alaska (and now, increasingly, its oil shale reserves elsewhere) makes it economical to do so.

In our supply and demand analysis in the next section, we'll consider incomplete specialization by a country to be the norm. We should emphasize, however, that the fact that countries often incompletely specialize does not in any way change the conclusion that there are gains from trade.

Differences in Technology In the 1970s and 1980s, Japan became by far the world's largest exporter of automobiles, selling large numbers to the United States and the rest of the world. Japan's comparative advantage in automobiles wasn't the result of climate. Nor can it easily be attributed to differences in factor endowments: aside from a scarcity of land, Japan's mix of available factors is quite similar to that in other advanced countries. Instead, Japan's comparative advantage in automobiles was based on the superior production techniques developed by its manufacturers, which allowed them to produce more cars with a given amount of labor and capital than their American or European counterparts.

The **factor intensity** of production of a good is a measure of which factor is used in relatively greater quantities than other factors in production.

According to the **Heckscher–Ohlin model,** a country has a comparative advantage in a good whose production is intensive in the factors that are abundantly available in that country.

FOR INQUIRING MINDS

Increasing Returns to Scale and International Trade

Most analyses of international trade focuses on how differences between countries—differences in climate, factor endowments, and technology—create national comparative advantage. However, economists have also pointed out another reason for international trade: the role of *increasing returns to scale.*

Production of a good is characterized by increasing returns to scale if the productivity of labor and other resources used in production rise with the quantity of output. For example, in an industry characterized by increasing returns to scale, increasing output by 10% might require only 8% more labor and 9% more raw materials. Examples of industries with increasing returns to scale include auto manufacturing, oil refining, and the production of jumbo jets, all of which require large outlays of capital. Increasing returns to scale (sometimes

also called economies of scale) can give rise to monopoly, a situation in which an industry is composed of only one producer, because it gives large firms a cost advantage over small ones.

But increasing returns to scale can also give rise to international trade. The logic runs as follows: if production of a good is characterized by increasing returns to scale, it makes sense to concentrate production in only a few locations, so each location has a high level of output. But that also means production occurs in only a few countries that export the good to other countries. A commonly cited example is the North American auto industry: although both the United States and Canada produce automobiles and their components, each particular model or component tends to be produced in only one of the two countries and exported to the other. Increasing returns to scale probably play

Thinkstock

Returns to scale in the auto industry leads to international trade in autos and auto parts.

a large role in the trade in manufactured goods between advanced countries, which is about 25% of the total value of world trade. ∎

Japan's comparative advantage in automobiles was a case of comparative advantage caused by differences in technology—the techniques used in production.

The causes of differences in technology are somewhat mysterious. Sometimes they seem to be based on knowledge accumulated through experience—for example, Switzerland's comparative advantage in watches reflects a long tradition of watchmaking. Sometimes they are the result of a set of innovations that for some reason occur in one country but not in others. Technological advantage, however, is often transitory. As we discussed in the Chapter 2 Business Case, by adopting lean production, American auto manufacturers have now closed much of the gap in productivity with their Japanese competitors. In addition, Europe's aircraft industry has closed a similar gap with the U.S. aircraft industry. At any given point in time, however, differences in technology are a major source of comparative advantage.

ECONOMICS ▶ in Action

How Hong Kong Lost Its Shirts

Jennifer Thermes/Getty Images

The rise of Hong Kong was one of the most improbable-sounding economic success stories of the twentieth century. When a communist regime took over China in 1949, Hong Kong—which was still at that point a British colony—became in effect a city without a hinterland, largely cut off from economic relations with the territory just over the border. Since Hong Kong had until that point made a living largely by serving as a point of entry into China, you might have expected the city to languish. Instead, however, Hong Kong prospered, to such an extent that today the city—now returned to China, but governed as a special autonomous region—has a GDP per capita comparable to that of the United States.

During much of its ascent, Hong Kong's rise rested, above all, on its clothing industry. In 1980 Hong Kong's garment and textile sectors employed almost 450,000 workers, close to 20% of total employment. These workers overwhelmingly made apparel—shirts, trousers, dresses, and more—for export, especially to the United States.

Since then, however, the Hong Kong clothing industry has fallen sharply in size—in fact, it has almost disappeared. So, too, have Hong Kong's apparel exports. Figure 8-4 shows Hong Kong's share of U.S. apparel imports since 1989, along with the share of a relative newcomer to the industry, Bangladesh. As you can see, Hong Kong has more or less dropped off the chart, while Bangladesh's share has risen significantly in recent years.

Why did Hong Kong lose its comparative advantage in making shirts, pants, and so on? It wasn't because the city's garment workers became less productive. Instead, it was because the city got better at other things. Apparel production is a labor-intensive, relatively low-tech industry; comparative advantage in that industry has historically always rested with poor, labor-abundant economies. Hong Kong no longer fits that description; Bangladesh does. Hong Kong's garment industry was a victim of the city's success.

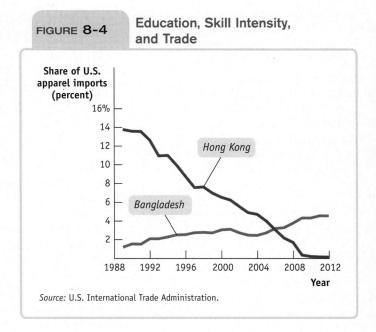

FIGURE 8-4   Education, Skill Intensity, and Trade

Source: U.S. International Trade Administration.

Check Your Understanding   8-1

1. In the United States, the opportunity cost of 1 ton of corn is 50 bicycles. In China, the opportunity cost of 1 bicycle is 0.01 ton of corn.
   a. Determine the pattern of comparative advantage.
   b. In autarky, the United States can produce 200,000 bicycles if no corn is produced, and China can produce 3,000 tons of corn if no bicycles are produced. Draw each country's production possibility frontier assuming constant opportunity cost, with tons of corn on the vertical axis and bicycles on the horizontal axis.
   c. With trade, each country specializes its production. The United States consumes 1,000 tons of corn and 200,000 bicycles; China consumes 3,000 tons of corn and 100,000 bicycles. Indicate the production and consumption points on your diagrams, and use them to explain the gains from trade.
2. Explain the following patterns of trade using the Heckscher–Ohlin model.
   a. France exports wine to the United States, and the United States exports movies to France.
   b. Brazil exports shoes to the United States, and the United States exports shoe-making machinery to Brazil.

Solutions appear at back of book.

Supply, Demand, and International Trade

Simple models of comparative advantage are helpful for understanding the fundamental causes of international trade. However, to analyze the effects of international trade at a more detailed level and to understand trade policy, it helps to return to the supply and demand model. We'll start by looking at the effects of imports on domestic producers and consumers, then turn to the effects of exports.

The **domestic demand curve** shows how the quantity of a good demanded by domestic consumers depends on the price of that good.

The **domestic supply curve** shows how the quantity of a good supplied by domestic producers depends on the price of that good.

The **world price** of a good is the price at which that good can be bought or sold abroad.

The Effects of Imports

Figure 8-5 shows the U.S. market for phones, ignoring international trade for a moment. It introduces a few new concepts: the *domestic demand curve,* the *domestic supply curve,* and the domestic or autarky price.

The **domestic demand curve** shows how the quantity of a good demanded by residents of a country depends on the price of that good. Why "domestic"? Because people living in other countries may demand the good, too. Once we introduce international trade, we need to distinguish between purchases of a good by domestic consumers and purchases by foreign consumers. So the domestic demand curve reflects only the demand of residents of our own country.

Similarly, the **domestic supply curve** shows how the quantity of a good supplied by producers inside our own country depends on the price of that good. Once we introduce international trade, we need to distinguish between the supply of domestic producers and foreign supply—supply brought in from abroad.

In autarky, with no international trade in phones, the equilibrium in this market would be determined by the intersection of the domestic demand and domestic supply curves, point A. The equilibrium price of phones would be P_A, and the equilibrium quantity of phones produced and consumed would be Q_A. As always, both consumers and producers gain from the existence of the domestic market. In autarky, consumer surplus would be equal to the area of the blue-shaded triangle in Figure 8-5. Producer surplus would be equal to the area of the red-shaded triangle. And total surplus would be equal to the sum of these two shaded triangles.

Now let's imagine opening up this market to imports. To do this, we must make an assumption about the supply of imports. The simplest assumption, which we will adopt here, is that unlimited quantities of phones can be purchased from abroad at a fixed price, known as the world price of phones. Figure 8-6 shows a situation in which the **world price** of a phone, P_W, is lower than the price of a phone that would prevail in the domestic market in autarky, P_A.

FIGURE 8-5 Consumer and Producer Surplus in Autarky

In the absence of trade, the domestic price is P_A, the autarky price at which the domestic supply curve and the domestic demand curve intersect. The quantity produced and consumed domestically is Q_A. Consumer surplus is represented by the blue-shaded area, and producer surplus is represented by the red-shaded area.

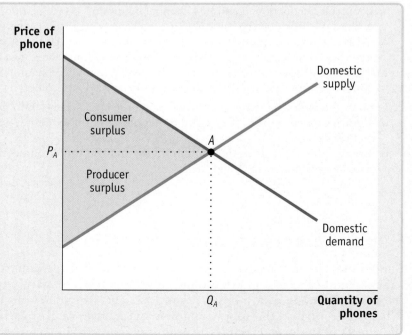

Given that the world price is below the domestic price of a phone, it is profitable for importers to buy phones abroad and resell them domestically. The imported phones increase the supply of phones in the domestic market, driving down the domestic market price. Phones will continue to be imported until the domestic price falls to a level equal to the world price.

The result is shown in Figure 8-6. Because of imports, the domestic price of a phone falls from P_A to P_W. The quantity of phones demanded by domestic consumers rises from Q_A to Q_D, and the quantity supplied by domestic producers falls from Q_A to Q_S. The difference between the domestic quantity demanded and the domestic quantity supplied, $Q_D - Q_S$, is filled by imports.

Now let's turn to the effects of imports on consumer surplus and producer surplus. Because imports of phones lead to a fall in their domestic price, consumer surplus rises and producer surplus falls. Figure 8-7 shows how this works. We label four areas: *W, X, Y,* and *Z.* The autarky consumer surplus we identified in Figure 8-5 corresponds to *W,* and the autarky producer surplus corresponds to the sum of *X* and *Y.* The fall in the domestic price to the world price leads to an increase in consumer surplus; it increases by *X* and *Z,* so consumer surplus now equals the sum of *W, X,* and *Z.* At the same time, producers lose *X* in surplus, so producer surplus now equals only *Y.*

The table in Figure 8-7 summarizes the changes in consumer and producer surplus when the phone market is opened to imports. Consumers gain surplus equal to the areas *X* + *Z.* Producers lose surplus equal to *X.* So the sum of producer and consumer surplus—the total surplus generated in the phone market—increases by *Z.* As a result of trade, consumers gain and producers lose, but the gain to consumers exceeds the loss to producers. This is an important result. We have just shown that opening up a market to imports leads to a net gain in total surplus, which is what we should have expected given the proposition that there are gains from international trade.

FIGURE **8-6**   The Domestic Market with Imports

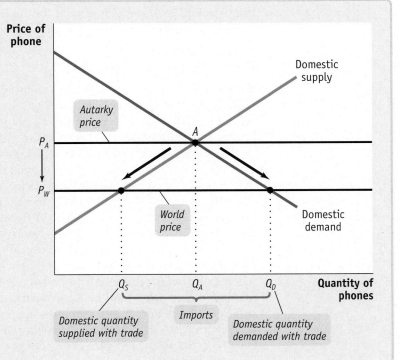

Here the world price of phones, P_W, is below the autarky price, P_A. When the economy is opened to international trade, imports enter the domestic market, and the domestic price falls from the autarky price, P_A, to the world price, P_W. As the price falls, the domestic quantity demanded rises from Q_A to Q_D and the domestic quantity supplied falls from Q_A to Q_S. The difference between domestic quantity demanded and domestic quantity supplied at P_W, the quantity $Q_D - Q_S$, is filled by imports.

FIGURE **8-7** The Effects of Imports on Surplus

	Changes in surplus	
	Gain	Loss
Consumer surplus	$X + Z$	
Producer surplus		$-X$
Change in total surplus	**+ Z**	

When the domestic price falls to P_W as a result of international trade, consumers gain additional surplus (areas $X + Z$) and producers lose surplus (area X). Because the gains to consumers outweigh the losses to producers, there is an increase in the total surplus in the economy as a whole (area Z).

However, we have also learned that although the country as a whole gains, some groups—in this case, domestic producers of phones—lose as a result of international trade. As we'll see shortly, the fact that international trade typically creates losers as well as winners is crucial for understanding the politics of trade policy.

We turn next to the case in which a country exports a good.

The Effects of Exports

Figure 8-8 shows the effects on a country when it exports a good, in this case trucks. For this example, we assume that unlimited quantities of trucks can be sold abroad at a given world price, P_W, which is higher than the price that would prevail in the domestic market in autarky, P_A.

The higher world price makes it profitable for exporters to buy trucks domestically and sell them overseas. The purchases of domestic trucks drive the domestic price up until it is equal to the world price. As a result, the quantity demanded by domestic consumers falls from Q_A to Q_D and the quantity supplied by domestic producers rises from Q_A to Q_S. This difference between domestic production and domestic consumption, $Q_S - Q_D$, is exported.

Like imports, exports lead to an overall gain in total surplus for the exporting country but also create losers as well as winners. Figure 8-9 shows the effects of truck exports on producer and consumer surplus. In the absence of trade, the price of each truck would be P_A. Consumer surplus in the absence of trade is the sum of areas W and X, and producer surplus is area Y. As a result of trade, price rises from P_A to P_W, consumer surplus falls to W, and producer surplus rises to $Y + X + Z$. So producers gain $X + Z$, consumers lose X, and, as shown in the table accompanying the figure, the economy as a whole gains total surplus in the amount of Z.

FIGURE 8-8   The Domestic Market with Exports

Here the world price, P_W, is greater than the autarky price, P_A. When the economy is opened to international trade, some of the domestic supply is now exported. The domestic price rises from the autarky price, P_A, to the world price, P_W. As the price rises, the domestic quantity demanded falls from Q_A to Q_D and the domestic quantity supplied rises from Q_A to Q_S. The portion of domestic production that is not consumed domestically, $Q_S - Q_D$, is exported.

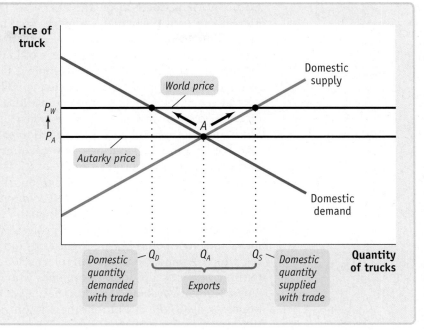

We have learned, then, that imports of a particular good hurt domestic producers of that good but help domestic consumers, whereas exports of a particular good hurt domestic consumers of that good but help domestic producers. In each case, the gains are larger than the losses.

FIGURE 8-9   The Effects of Exports on Surplus

	Changes in surplus	
	Gain	Loss
Consumer surplus		– X
Producer surplus	X + Z	
Change in total surplus	**+ Z**	

When the domestic price rises to P_W as a result of trade, producers gain additional surplus (areas $X + Z$) but consumers lose surplus (area X). Because the gains to producers outweigh the losses to consumers, there is an increase in the total surplus in the economy as a whole (area Z).

International Trade and Wages

So far we have focused on the effects of international trade on producers and consumers in a particular industry. For many purposes this is a very helpful approach. However, producers and consumers are not the only parts of society affected by trade—so are the owners of factors of production. In particular, the owners of labor, land, and capital employed in producing goods that are exported, or goods that compete with imported goods, can be deeply affected by trade.

Moreover, the effects of trade aren't limited to just those industries that export or compete with imports because *factors of production can often move between industries*. So now we turn our attention to the long-run effects of international trade on income distribution—how a country's total income is allocated among its various factors of production.

To begin our analysis, consider the position of Maria, an accountant at West Coast Phone Production, Inc. If the economy is opened up to imports of phones from China, the domestic phone industry will contract, and it will hire fewer accountants. But accounting is a profession with employment opportunities in many industries, and Maria might well find a better job in the automobile industry, which expands as a result of international trade. So it may not be appropriate to think of her as a producer of phones who is hurt by competition from imported parts. Rather, we should think of her as an accountant who is affected by phone imports only to the extent that these imports change the wages of accountants in the economy as a whole.

The wage rate of accountants is a *factor price*—the price employers have to pay for the services of a factor of production. One key question about international trade is how it affects factor prices—not just narrowly defined factors of production like accountants, but broadly defined factors such as capital, unskilled labor, and college-educated labor.

Earlier in this chapter we described the Heckscher–Ohlin model of trade, which states that comparative advantage is determined by a country's factor endowment. This model also suggests how international trade affects factor prices in a country: compared to autarky, international trade tends to raise the prices of factors that are abundantly available and reduce the prices of factors that are scarce.

We won't work this out in detail, but the idea is simple. The prices of factors of production, like the prices of goods and services, are determined by supply and demand. If international trade increases the demand for a factor of production, that factor's price will rise; if international trade reduces the demand for a factor of production, that factor's price will fall.

Now think of a country's industries as consisting of two kinds: **exporting industries,** which produce goods and services that are sold abroad, and **import-competing industries,** which produce goods and services that are also imported from abroad. Compared with autarky, international trade leads to higher production in exporting industries and lower production in import-competing industries. This indirectly increases the demand for factors used by exporting industries and decreases the demand for factors used by import-competing industries.

In addition, the Heckscher–Ohlin model says that a country tends to export goods that are intensive in its abundant factors and to import goods that are intensive in its scarce factors. *So international trade tends to increase the demand for factors that are abundant in our country compared with other countries, and to decrease the demand for factors that are scarce in our country compared with other countries. As a result, the prices of abundant factors tend to rise, and the prices of scarce factors tend to fall as international trade grows.*

In other words, international trade tends to redistribute income toward a country's abundant factors and away from its less abundant factors.

Exporting industries produce goods and services that are sold abroad.

Import-competing industries produce goods and services that are also imported.

U.S. exports tend to be human-capital-intensive (such as high-tech design and Hollywood movies) while U.S. imports tend to be unskilled-labor-intensive (such as phone assembly and clothing production). This suggests that the effect of international trade on the U.S. factor markets is to raise the wage rate of highly educated American workers and reduce the wage rate of unskilled American workers.

This effect has been a source of much concern in recent years. Wage inequality—the gap between the wages of high-paid and low-paid workers—has increased substantially over the last 30 years. Some economists believe that growing international trade is an important factor in that trend. If international trade has the effects predicted by the Heckscher–Ohlin model, its growth raises the wages of highly educated American workers, who already have relatively high wages, and lowers the wages of less educated American workers, who already have relatively low wages. But keep in mind another phenomenon: trade reduces the income inequality between countries as poor countries improve their standard of living by exporting to rich countries.

How important are these effects? In some historical episodes, the impacts of international trade on factor prices have been very large. As we explain in the following Economics in Action, the opening of transatlantic trade in the late nineteenth century had a large negative impact on land rents in Europe, hurting landowners but helping workers and owners of capital.

The effects of trade on wages in the United States have generated considerable controversy in recent years. Most economists who have studied the issue agree that growing imports of labor-intensive products from newly industrializing economies, and the export of high-technology goods in return, have helped cause a widening wage gap between highly educated and less educated workers in this country. However, most economists believe that it is only one of several forces explaining the growth in American wage inequality.

ECONOMICS ▶ in Action

TRADE, WAGES, AND LAND PRICES IN THE NINETEENTH CENTURY

Beginning around 1870, there was an explosive growth of world trade in agricultural products, based largely on the steam engine. Steam-powered ships could cross the ocean much more quickly and reliably than sailing ships. Until about 1860, steamships had higher costs than sailing ships, but after that costs dropped sharply. At the same time, steam-powered rail transport made it possible to bring grain and other bulk goods cheaply from the interior to ports. The result was that land-abundant countries—the United States, Canada, Argentina, and Australia—began shipping large quantities of agricultural goods to the densely populated, land-scarce countries of Europe.

This opening up of international trade led to higher prices of agricultural products, such as wheat, in exporting countries and a decline in their prices in importing countries. Notably, the difference between wheat prices in the midwestern United States and England plunged.

International trade redistributes income toward a country's abundant factors and away from its less abundant factors.

An economy has **free trade** when the government does not attempt either to reduce or to increase the levels of exports and imports that occur naturally as a result of supply and demand.

Policies that limit imports are known as **trade protection** or simply as **protection.**

A **tariff** is a tax levied on imports.

The change in agricultural prices created winners and losers on both sides of the Atlantic as factor prices adjusted. In England, land prices fell by half compared with average wages; landowners found their purchasing power sharply reduced, but workers benefited from cheaper food. In the United States, the reverse happened: land prices doubled compared with wages. Landowners did very well, but workers found the purchasing power of their wages dented by rising food prices.

Check Your Understanding 8-2

1. Due to a strike by truckers, trade in food between the United States and Mexico is halted. In autarky, the price of Mexican grapes is lower than that of U.S. grapes. Using a diagram of the U.S. domestic demand curve and the U.S. domestic supply curve for grapes, explain the effect of the strike on the following.
   a. U.S. grape consumers' surplus
   b. U.S. grape producers' surplus
   c. U.S. total surplus
2. What effect do you think the strike will have on Mexican grape producers? Mexican grape pickers? Mexican grape consumers? U.S. grape pickers?

Solutions appear at back of book.

The Effects of Trade Protection

Ever since David Ricardo laid out the principle of comparative advantage in the early nineteenth century, most economists have advocated **free trade.** That is, they have argued that government policy should not attempt either to reduce or to increase the levels of exports and imports that occur naturally as a result of supply and demand.

Despite the free-trade arguments of economists, however, many governments use taxes and other restrictions to limit imports. Less frequently, governments offer subsidies to encourage exports. Policies that limit imports, usually with the goal of protecting domestic producers in import-competing industries from foreign competition, are known as **trade protection** or simply as **protection.**

Let's look at the two most common protectionist policies, *tariffs* and *import quotas,* then turn to the reasons governments follow these policies.

The Effects of a Tariff

A **tariff** is a form of excise tax, one that is levied only on sales of imported goods. For example, the U.S. government could declare that anyone bringing in phones must pay a tariff of $100 per unit. In the distant past, tariffs were an important source of government revenue because they were relatively easy to collect. But in the modern world, tariffs are usually intended to discourage imports and protect import-competing domestic producers rather than as a source of government revenue.

The tariff raises both the price received by domestic producers and the price paid by domestic consumers. Suppose, for example, that our country imports phones, and a phone costs $200 on the world market. As we saw earlier, under free trade the domestic price would also be $200. But if a tariff of $100 per unit is imposed, the domestic price will rise to $300, because it won't be profitable to import phones unless the price in the domestic market is high enough to compensate importers for the cost of paying the tariff.

Figure 8-10 illustrates the effects of a tariff on imports of phones. As before, we assume that P_W is the world price of a phone. Before the tariff is imposed, imports have driven the domestic price down to P_W, so that pre-tariff domestic production is Q_S, pre-tariff domestic consumption is Q_D, and pre-tariff imports are $Q_D - Q_S$.

FIGURE **8-10** The Effect of a Tariff

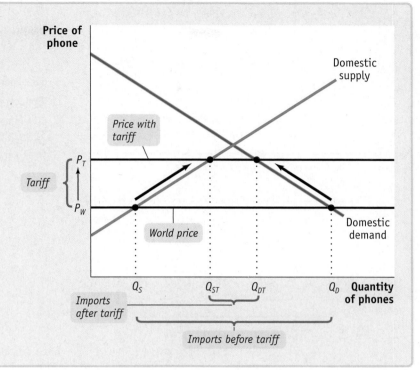

A tariff raises the domestic price of the good from P_W to P_T. The domestic quantity demanded shrinks from Q_D to Q_{DT}, and the domestic quantity supplied increases from Q_S to Q_{ST}. As a result, imports—which had been $Q_D - Q_S$ before the tariff was imposed—shrink to $Q_{DT} - Q_{ST}$ after the tariff is imposed.

Now suppose that the government imposes a tariff on each phone imported. As a consequence, it is no longer profitable to import phones unless the domestic price received by the importer is greater than or equal to the world price plus the tariff. So the domestic price rises to P_T, which is equal to the world price, P_W, plus the tariff. Domestic production rises to Q_{ST}, domestic consumption falls to Q_{DT}, and imports fall to $Q_{DT} - Q_{ST}$.

A tariff, then, raises domestic prices, leading to increased domestic production and reduced domestic consumption compared to the situation under free trade. Figure 8-11 shows the effects on surplus. There are three effects:

1. The higher domestic price increases producer surplus, a gain equal to area *A*.
2. The higher domestic price reduces consumer surplus, a reduction equal to the sum of areas *A, B, C,* and *D.*
3. The tariff yields revenue to the government. How much revenue? The government collects the tariff—which, remember, is equal to the difference between P_T and P_W on each of the $Q_{DT} - Q_{ST}$ units imported. So total revenue is $(P_T - P_W) \times (Q_{DT} - Q_{ST})$. This is equal to area *C.*

The welfare effects of a tariff are summarized in the table in Figure 8-11. Producers gain, consumers lose, and the government gains. But consumer losses are greater than the sum of producer and government gains, leading to a net reduction in total surplus equal to areas *B + D.*

An excise tax creates inefficiency, or deadweight loss, because it prevents mutually beneficial trades from occurring. The same is true of a tariff, where the deadweight loss imposed on society is equal to the loss in total surplus represented by areas *B + D.*

Tariffs generate deadweight losses because they create inefficiencies in two ways:

1. Some mutually beneficial trades go unexploited: some consumers who are willing to pay more than the world price, P_W, do not purchase the good, even though P_W is the true cost of a unit of the good to the economy. The cost of this inefficiency is represented in Figure 8-11 by area *D.*

FIGURE **8-11** A Tariff Reduces Total Surplus

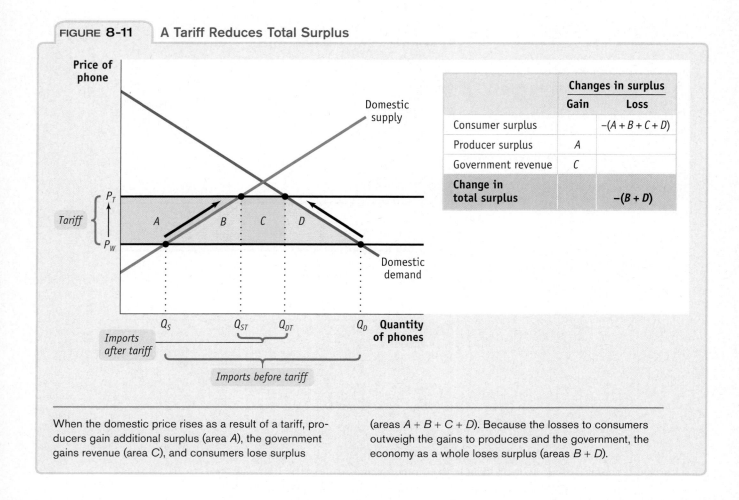

	Changes in surplus	
	Gain	**Loss**
Consumer surplus		$-(A + B + C + D)$
Producer surplus	A	
Government revenue	C	
Change in total surplus		$-(B + D)$

When the domestic price rises as a result of a tariff, producers gain additional surplus (area A), the government gains revenue (area C), and consumers lose surplus (areas $A + B + C + D$). Because the losses to consumers outweigh the gains to producers and the government, the economy as a whole loses surplus (areas $B + D$).

2. The economy's resources are wasted on inefficient production: some producers whose cost exceeds P_W produce the good, even though an additional unit of the good can be purchased abroad for P_W. The cost of this inefficiency is represented in Figure 8-11 by area B.

The Effects of an Import Quota

An **import quota,** another form of trade protection, is a legal limit on the quantity of a good that can be imported. For example, a U.S. import quota on Chinese phones might limit the quantity imported each year to 50 million units. Import quotas are usually administered through licenses: a number of licenses are issued, each giving the license-holder the right to import a limited quantity of the good each year.

A quota on sales has the same effect as an excise tax, with one difference: the money that would otherwise have accrued to the government as tax revenue under an excise tax becomes license-holders' revenue under a quota—also known as quota rents. (*Quota rent* was defined in Chapter 5.) Similarly, an import quota has the same effect as a tariff, with one difference: the money that would otherwise have been government revenue becomes quota rents to license-holders. Look again at Figure 8-11. An import quota that limits imports to $Q_{DT} - Q_{ST}$ will raise the domestic price of phones by the same amount as the tariff we considered previously. That is, it will raise the domestic price from P_W to P_T. However, area C will now represent quota rents rather than government revenue.

Who receives import licenses and so collects the quota rents? In the case of U.S. import protection, the answer may surprise you: the most important import licenses—mainly for clothing, and to a lesser extent for sugar—are granted to foreign governments.

An **import quota** is a legal limit on the quantity of a good that can be imported.

Because the quota rents for most U.S. import quotas go to foreigners, the cost to the nation of such quotas is larger than that of a comparable tariff (a tariff that leads to the same level of imports). In Figure 8-11 the net loss to the United States from such an import quota would be equal to areas $B + C + D$, the difference between consumer losses and producer gains.

ECONOMICS ▶ in Action

Trade Protection in The United States

The United States today generally follows a policy of free trade, both in comparison with other countries and in comparison with its own history. Most imports are subject to either no tariff or to a low tariff. So what are the major exceptions to this rule?

Most of the remaining protection involves agricultural products. Topping the list is ethanol, which in the United States is mainly produced from corn and used as an ingredient in motor fuel. Most imported ethanol is subject to a fairly high tariff, but some countries are allowed to sell a limited amount of ethanol in the United States, at high prices, without paying the tariff. Dairy products also receive substantial import protection, again through a combination of tariffs and quotas.

Until a few years ago, clothing and textiles were also strongly protected from import competition, thanks to an elaborate system of import quotas. However, this system was phased out in 2005 as part of a trade agreement reached a decade earlier. Some clothing imports are still subject to relatively high tariffs, but protection in the clothing industry is a shadow of what it used to be.

The most important thing to know about current U.S. trade protection is how limited it really is, and how little cost it imposes on the economy. Every two years the U.S. International Trade Commission, a government agency, produces estimates of the impact of "significant trade restrictions" on U.S. welfare. As Figure 8-12 shows, over the past two decades both average tariff levels and the cost of trade restrictions as a share of national income, which weren't all that big to begin with, have fallen sharply.

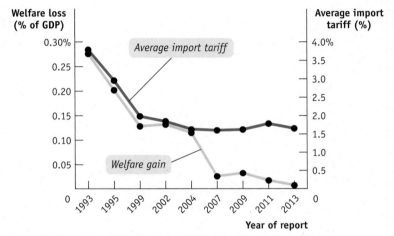

FIGURE 8-12   Tariff Rates and Estimated Welfare Losses, 1993–2013

Sources: U.S. International Trade Commission (2013), Federal Reserve Bank of St. Louis; and World Development Indicators.

▼ Quick Review

- Most economists advocate **free trade,** although many governments engage in **trade protection** of import-competing industries. The two most common protectionist policies are tariffs and import quotas. In rare instances, governments subsidize exporting industries.

- A **tariff** is a tax on imports. It raises the domestic price above the world price, leading to a fall in trade and domestic consumption and a rise in domestic production. Domestic producers and the government gain, but domestic consumer losses more than offset this gain, leading to deadweight loss.

- An **import quota** is a legal quantity limit on imports. Its effect is like that of a tariff, except that revenues—the quota rents—accrue to the license holder, not to the domestic government.

Check Your Understanding   8-3

1. Suppose the world price of butter is $0.50 per pound and the domestic price in autarky is $1.00 per pound. Use a diagram similar to Figure 8-10 to show the following.
   a. If there is free trade, domestic butter producers want the government to impose a tariff of no less than $0.50 per pound. Compare the outcome with a tariff of $0.25 per pound.
   b. What happens if a tariff greater than $0.50 per pound is imposed?

2. Suppose the government imposes an import quota rather than a tariff on butter. What quota limit would generate the same quantity of imports as a tariff of $0.50 per pound?

Solutions appear at back of book.

The Political Economy of Trade Protection

We have seen that international trade produces mutual benefits to the countries that engage in it. We have also seen that tariffs and import quotas, although they produce winners as well as losers, reduce total surplus. Yet many countries continue to impose tariffs and import quotas as well as to enact other protectionist measures.

To understand why trade protection takes place, we will first look at some common justifications for protection. Then we will look at the politics of trade protection. Finally, we will look at an important feature of trade protection in today's world: tariffs and import quotas are the subject of international negotiation and are policed by international organizations.

Arguments for Trade Protection

Advocates for tariffs and import quotas offer a variety of arguments. Three common arguments are *national security, job creation,* and the *infant industry argument.*

The national security argument is based on the proposition that overseas sources of goods are vulnerable to disruption in times of international conflict; therefore, a country should protect domestic suppliers of crucial goods with the aim to be self-sufficient in those goods. In the 1960s, the United States—which had begun to import oil as domestic oil reserves ran low—had an import quota on oil, justified on national security grounds. Some people have argued that we should again have policies to discourage imports of oil, especially from the Middle East.

The job creation argument points to the additional jobs created in import-competing industries as a result of trade protection. Economists argue that these jobs are offset by the jobs lost elsewhere, such as industries that use imported inputs and now face higher input costs. But noneconomists don't always find this argument persuasive.

Finally, the infant industry argument, often raised in newly industrializing countries, holds that new industries require a temporary period of trade protection to get established. For example, in the 1950s many countries in Latin America imposed tariffs and import quotas on manufactured goods, in an effort to switch from their traditional role as exporters of raw materials to a new status as industrial countries.

In theory, the argument for infant industry protection can be compelling, particularly in high-tech industries that increase a country's overall skill level. Reality, however, is more complicated: it is most often industries that are politically influential that gain protection. In addition, governments tend to be poor predictors of the best emerging technologies. Finally, it is often very difficult to wean an industry from protection when it should be mature enough to stand on its own.

The Politics of Trade Protection

In reality, much trade protection has little to do with the arguments just described. Instead, it reflects the political influence of import-competing producers.

We've seen that a tariff or import quota leads to gains for import-competing producers and losses for consumers. Producers, however, usually have much more influence over trade policy decisions. The producers who compete with imports of a particular good are usually a smaller, more cohesive group than the consumers of that good.

An example is trade protection for sugar: the United States has an import quota on sugar, which on average leads to a domestic price about twice the world price. This quota is difficult to rationalize in terms of any economic argument. However, consumers rarely complain about the quota because they are unaware that it exists: because no individual consumer buys large amounts of sugar, the cost of the quota is only a few dollars per family each year, not enough to attract notice. But there are only a few thousand sugar growers in the United States. They are very aware of the benefits they receive from the quota and make sure that their representatives in Congress are also aware of their interest in the matter.

Given these political realities, it may seem surprising that trade is as free as it is. For example, the United States has low tariffs, and its import quotas are mainly confined to clothing and a few agricultural products. It would be nice to say that the main reason trade protection is so limited is that economists have convinced governments of the virtues of free trade. A more important reason, however, is the role of *international trade agreements*.

International Trade Agreements and the World Trade Organization

When a country engages in trade protection, it hurts two groups. We've already emphasized the adverse effect on domestic consumers, but protection also hurts foreign export industries. This means that countries care about one anothers' trade policies: the Canadian lumber industry, for example, has a strong interest in keeping U.S. tariffs on forest products low.

Because countries care about one anothers' trade policies, they enter into **international trade agreements:** treaties in which a country promises to engage in less trade protection against the exports of another country in return for a promise by the other country to do the same for its own exports. Most world trade is now governed by such agreements.

Some international trade agreements involve just two countries or a small group of countries. The United States, Canada, and Mexico are joined together by the **North American Free Trade Agreement,** or **NAFTA.** This agreement was signed in 1993, and by 2008 it had removed all barriers to trade among the three nations.

In Europe, 28 nations are part of an even more comprehensive agreement, the **European Union,** or **EU.** In NAFTA, the member countries set their own tariff rates against imports from other nonmember countries. The EU, however, is a customs union: tariffs are levied at the same rate on goods from outside the EU entering the union.

There are also global trade agreements covering most of the world. Such global agreements are overseen by the **World Trade Organization,** or **WTO,** an international organization composed of member countries, which plays two roles. First, it provides the framework for the massively complex negotiations involved in a major international trade agreement (the full text of the last major agreement, approved in 1994, was 24,000 pages long). Second, the WTO resolves disputes between its members. These disputes typically arise when one country claims that another country's policies violate its previous agreements. Currently, the WTO has 160 member countries, accounting for the bulk of world trade.

Here are two examples that illustrate the WTO's role. First, in 1992 a trade dispute broke out over the European Union's import restrictions on bananas, which gave preference to producers in former European colonies over producers from Central America. In 1999 the WTO ruled that these restrictions were in violation of international trade rules. The United States took the side of the Central American countries, and the dispute became a major source of trade conflict between the European Union and the United States, known as the "banana wars." In 2012, twenty years after the dispute began, the European Union finally changed its import regulations to abide by the WTO ruling.

A more recent example is the dispute between the United States and Brazil over American subsidies to its cotton farmers. These subsidies, in the amount of $3 billion to $4 billion a year, are illegal under WTO rules. Brazil argues

International trade agreements are treaties in which a country promises to engage in less trade protection against the exports of other countries in return for a promise by other countries to do the same for its own exports.

The **North American Free Trade Agreement,** or **NAFTA,** is a a trade agreement among the United States, Canada, and Mexico.

The **European Union,** or **EU,** is a customs union among 28 European nations.

The **World Trade Organization,** or **WTO,** oversees international trade agreements and rules on disputes between countries over those agreements.

FOR INQUIRING MINDS | Tires Under Pressure

In September 2009 the U.S. government imposed steep tariffs on imports of tires from China. The tariffs were imposed for three years: 35% in the first year, 30% in the second, and 25% in the third.

The tariffs were a response to union complaints about the effects of surging Chinese tire exports: between 2004 and 2008, U.S. imports of automobile tires from China had gone from 15 million to 46 million, and labor groups warned that this was costing American jobs. The unions wanted an import quota, but getting the tariff was still a political vic-tory for organized labor. But wasn't the tariff a violation of WTO rules? No, said the Obama administration. When China joined the WTO in 2001, it agreed to what is known, in trade policy jargon, as a "safeguard mechanism": import-ing countries were granted the right to impose temporary limits on Chinese exports in the event of an import surge. Despite this agreement, the government of China protested the U.S. action and appealed to the WTO to rule the tariff illegal. But in December 2010 the WTO came down on America's side, ruling that the Obama administration had been within its rights.

You shouldn't be too cynical about this failure to achieve complete free trade in tires. World trade negotiations have always been based on the principle that half a loaf is better than none, that it's better to have an agreement that allows politically sensitive industries to retain some protection than to insist on free-trade purity. In spite of such actions as the tire tariff, world trade is, on the whole, remarkably free, and freer in many ways than it was just a few years ago. ■

that they artificially reduce the price of American cotton on world markets and hurt Brazilian cotton farmers. In 2005 the WTO ruled against the United States and in favor of Brazil, and the United States responded by cutting some export subsidies on cotton. However, in 2007 the WTO ruled that the United States had not done enough to fully comply, such as eliminating government loans to cotton farmers. After Brazil threatened, in turn, to impose import tariffs on U.S.-manufactured goods, in 2010 the two sides agreed to a framework for the solution to the cotton dispute.

Both Vietnam and Thailand are members of the WTO. Yet the United States has, on and off, imposed tariffs on shrimp imports from these countries. The reason this is possible is that WTO rules do allow trade protection under certain circumstances. One circumstance is where the foreign competition is "unfair" under certain technical criteria. Trade protection is also allowed as a temporary measure when a sudden surge of imports threatens to disrupt a domestic indus-try. The response to Chinese tire exports, described in the accompanying For Inquiring Minds, is an important recent example.

The WTO is sometimes, with great exaggeration, described as a world govern-ment. In fact, it has no army, no police, and no direct enforcement power. The grain of truth in that description is that when a country joins the WTO, it agrees to accept the organization's judgments—and these judgments apply not only to tariffs and import quotas but also to domestic policies that the organization con-siders trade protection disguised under another name. So in joining the WTO a country does give up some of its sovereignty.

Challenges to Globalization

The forward march of globalization over the past century is generally consid-ered a major political and economic success. Economists and policy makers alike have viewed growing world trade, in particular, as a good thing. We would be remiss, however, if we failed to acknowledge that many people are having second thoughts about globalization. To a large extent, these second thoughts reflect two concerns shared by many economists: worries about the effects of globalization on inequality and worries that new developments, in particular the growth in *offshore outsourcing,* are increasing economic insecurity.

Globalization and Inequality We've already mentioned the implications of international trade for factor prices, such as wages: when wealthy countries like the United States export skill-intensive products like aircraft while import-ing labor-intensive products like clothing, they can expect to see the wage gap between more educated and less educated domestic workers widen. Forty years ago, this wasn't a significant concern, because most of the goods wealthy coun-tries imported from poorer countries were raw materials or goods where com-parative advantage depended on climate. Today, however, many manufactured goods are imported from relatively poor countries, with a potentially much larger effect on the distribution of income.

Trade with China, in particular, raises concerns among labor groups try-ing to maintain wage levels in rich countries. Although China has experienced spectacular economic growth since the economic reforms that began in the late 1970s, it remains a poor, low-wage country: wages in Chinese manufacturing are estimated to be only about 5% of U.S. wages. Meanwhile, imports from China have soared. In 1983 less than 1% of U.S. imports came from China; by 2013, the figure was more than 16%. There's not much question that these surging imports from China put at least some downward pressure on the wages of less educated American workers.

Outsourcing Chinese exports to the United States overwhelmingly consist of labor-intensive manufactured goods. However, some U.S. workers have recently found themselves facing a new form of international competition. *Outsourcing,* in which a company hires another company to perform some task, such as run-ning the corporate computer system, is a long-standing business practice. Until recently, however, outsourcing was normally done locally, with a company hiring another company in the same city or country.

Now, modern telecommunications increasingly make it possible to engage in **offshore outsourcing,** in which businesses hire people in another country to perform various tasks. The classic example is call centers: the person answering the phone when you call a company's 1-800 help line may well be in India, which has taken the lead in attracting offshore outsourcing. Offshore outsourcing has also spread to fields such as software design and even health care: the radiolo-gist examining your X-rays, like the person giving you computer help, may be on another continent.

Although offshore outsourcing has come as a shock to some U.S. workers, such as programmers whose jobs have been out-sourced to India, it's still relatively small compared with more traditional trade. Some economists have warned, however, that millions or even tens of millions of workers who have never thought they could face foreign competition for their jobs may face unpleasant surprises in the not-too-distant future.

Concerns about income distribution and outsourcing, as we've said, are shared by many economists. There is also, however, widespread opposition to globalization in general, particularly among college students. In 1999, an attempt to start a major round of trade negotiations failed in part because the WTO meeting, in Seattle, was disrupted by anti-globalization demonstrators. However, the more important reason for its failure was disagreement among the countries represented. Another round of negotiations that began in 2001 in Doha, Qatar, and is therefore referred to as the "Doha development round." By 2008 it had stalled, mainly due to disagreements over agricultural trade rules. As of 2014 there was little sign of progress although the round was still being officially negotiated.

What motivates the antiglobalization movement? To some extent it's the sweat-shop labor fallacy: it's easy to get outraged about the low wages paid to the person

Offshore outsourcing takes place when businesses hire people in another country to perform various tasks.

Offshore outsourcing has the potential to disrupt the job prospects of millions of U.S. workers.

Terry Vine/Getty Images

who made your shirt, and harder to appreciate how much worse off that person would be if denied the opportunity to sell goods in rich countries' markets. It's also true, however, that the movement represents a backlash against supporters of globalization who have oversold its benefits. Countries in Latin America, in particular, were promised that reducing their tariff rates would produce an economic takeoff; instead, they have experienced disappointing results. Some groups, such as poor farmers facing new competition from imported food, ended up worse off.

Do these new challenges to globalization undermine the argument that international trade is a good thing? The great majority of economists would argue that the gains from reducing trade protection still exceed the losses. However, it has become more important than before to make sure that the gains from international trade are widely spread. And the politics of international trade are becoming increasingly difficult as the extent of trade has grown.

ECONOMICS ▶ *in Action*

Beefing Up Exports

The 2010 trade agreement between South Korea and the United States was the most important free-trade deal since NAFTA and a boon for the U.S. beef industry.

Kyodo via AP Images

In December 2010, negotiators from the United States and South Korea reached final agreement on a free-trade deal that would phase out many of the tariffs and other restrictions on trade between the two nations. The deal also involved changes in a variety of business regulations that were expected to make it easier for U.S. companies to operate in South Korea. This was, literally, a fairly big deal: South Korea's economy is comparable in size to Mexico's, so this was the most important free-trade agreement that the United States had been party to since NAFTA.

What made this deal possible? Estimates by the U.S. International Trade Commission found that the deal would raise average American incomes, although modestly: the commission put the gains at around one-tenth of one percent. Not bad when you consider the fact that South Korea, despite its relatively large economy, is still only America's seventh-most-important trading partner.

These overall gains played little role in the politics of the deal, however, which hinged on losses and gains for particular U.S. constituencies. Some opposition to the deal came from labor, especially from autoworkers, who feared that eliminating the 8% U.S. tariff on imports of Korean automobiles would lead to job losses. But there were also interest groups in America that badly wanted the deal, most notably the beef industry: Koreans are big beefeaters, yet American access to that market was limited by a 38% Korean tariff.

And the Obama administration definitely wanted a deal, in part for reasons unrelated to economics: South Korea is an important U.S. ally, and military tensions with North Korea were ratcheting up even as the final negotiations were taking place. So a trade deal was viewed in part as a symbol of U.S.–South Korean cooperation. Even labor unions weren't as opposed as they might have been; the administration's imposition of tariffs on Chinese tires, just described in For Inquiring Minds, was seen as a demonstration that it was prepared to defend labor interests.

It also helped that South Korea—unlike Mexico when NAFTA was signed—is both a fairly high-wage country and not right on the U.S. border, which meant less concern about massive shifts of manufacturing. In the end, the balance of interests was just favorable enough to make the deal politically possible. The deal went into effect on March 15, 2012.

Check Your Understanding   8-4

1. In 2002 the United States imposed tariffs on steel imports, which are an input in a large number and variety of U.S. industries. Explain why political lobbying to eliminate these tariffs is more likely to be effective than political lobbying to eliminate tariffs on consumer goods such as sugar or clothing.

2. Over the years, the WTO has increasingly found itself adjudicating trade disputes that involve not just tariffs or quota restrictions but also restrictions based on quality, health, and environmental considerations. Why do you think this has occurred? What method would you, as a WTO official, use to decide whether a quality, health, or environmental restriction is in violation of a free-trade agreement?

Solutions appear at back of book.

▼ Quick Review

- The three major justifications for trade protection are national security, job creation, and protection of infant industries.

- Despite the deadweight losses, import protections are often imposed because groups representing import-competing industries are more influential than groups of consumers.

- To further trade liberalization, countries engage in **international trade agreements.** Some agreements are among a small number of countries, such as the **North American Free Trade Agreement (NAFTA)** and the **European Union (EU).** The **World Trade Organization (WTO)** seeks to negotiate global trade agreements and referee trade disputes between members.

- Resistance to globalization has emerged in response to a surge in imports from relatively poor countries and the **offshore outsourcing** of many jobs that had been considered safe from foreign competition.

Li & Fung: From Guangzhou to You

It's a very good bet that as you read this, you're wearing something manufactured in Asia. And if you are, it's also a good bet that the Hong Kong company Li & Fung was involved in getting your garment designed, produced, and shipped to your local store. From Levi's to The Limited to Walmart, Li & Fung is a critical conduit from factories around the world to the shopping mall nearest you.

Jerome Favre/Bloomberg via Getty Images

The company was founded in 1906 in Guangzhou, China. According to Victor Fung, the company's chairman, his grandfather's "value added" was that he spoke English, allowing him to serve as an interpreter in business deals between Chinese and foreigners. When Mao's Communist Party seized control in mainland China, the company moved to Hong Kong. There, as Hong Kong's market economy took off during the 1960s and 1970s, Li & Fung grew as an export broker, bringing together Hong Kong manufacturers and foreign buyers.

The real transformation of the company came, however, as Asian economies grew and changed. Hong Kong's rapid growth led to rising wages, making Li & Fung increasingly uncompetitive in garments, its main business. So the company reinvented itself: rather than being a simple broker, it became a "supply chain manager." Not only would it allocate production of a good to a manufacturer, it would also break production down, allocate production of the inputs, and then allocate final assembly of the good among its 12,000+ suppliers around the globe. Sometimes production would be done in sophisticated economies like those of Hong Kong or even Japan, where wages are high but so is quality and productivity; sometimes it would be done in less advanced locations like mainland China or Thailand, where labor is less productive but cheaper.

For example, suppose you own a U.S. retail chain and want to sell garment-washed blue jeans. Rather than simply arrange for production of the jeans, Li & Fung will work with you on their design, providing you with the latest production and style information, like what materials and colors are hot. After the design has been finalized, Li & Fung will arrange for the creation of a prototype, find the most cost-effective way to manufacture it, and then place an order on your behalf. Through Li & Fung, the yarn might be made in Korea and dyed in Taiwan, and the jeans sewn in Thailand or mainland China. And because production is taking place in so many locations, Li & Fung provides transport logistics as well as quality control.

Li & Fung has been enormously successful. In 2012 the company had a market value of approximately $11.5 billion and business turnover of over $20 billion, with offices and distribution centers in more than 40 countries. Year after year, it has regularly doubled or tripled its profits.

QUESTIONS FOR THOUGHT

1. Why do you think it was profitable for Li & Fung to go beyond brokering exports to becoming a supply chain manager, breaking down the production process and sourcing the inputs from various suppliers across many countries?

2. What principle do you think underlies Li & Fung's decisions on how to allocate production of a good's inputs and its final assembly among various countries?

3. Why do you think a retailer prefers to have Li & Fung arrange international production of its jeans rather than purchase them directly from a jeans manufacturer in mainland China?

4. What is the source of Li & Fung's success? Is it based on human capital, on ownership of a natural resource, or on ownership of capital?

SUMMARY

1. International trade is of growing importance to the United States and of even greater importance to most other countries. International trade, like trade among individuals, arises from comparative advantage: the opportunity cost of producing an additional unit of a good is lower in some countries than in others. Goods and services purchased from abroad are **imports;** those sold abroad are **exports.** Foreign trade, like other economic linkages between countries, has been growing rapidly, a phenomenon called **globalization. Hyperglobalization,** the phenomenon of extremely high levels of international trade, has occurred as advances in communication and transportation technology have allowed supply chains of production to span the globe.

2. The **Ricardian model of international trade** assumes that opportunity costs are constant. It shows that there are gains from trade: two countries are better off with trade than in **autarky.**

3. In practice, comparative advantage reflects differences between countries in climate, factor endowments, and technology. The **Heckscher–Ohlin model** shows how differences in factor endowments determine comparative advantage: goods differ in **factor intensity,** and countries tend to export goods that are intensive in the factors they have in abundance.

4. The **domestic demand curve** and the **domestic supply curve** determine the price of a good in autarky. When international trade occurs, the domestic price is driven to equality with the **world price,** the price at which the good is bought and sold abroad.

5. If the world price is below the autarky price, a good is imported. This leads to an increase in consumer surplus, a fall in producer surplus, and a gain in total surplus. If the world price is above the autarky price, a good is exported. This leads to an increase in producer surplus, a fall in consumer surplus, and a gain in total surplus.

6. International trade leads to expansion in **exporting industries** and contraction in **import-competing industries.** This raises the domestic demand for abundant factors of production, reduces the demand for scarce factors, and so affects factor prices, such as wages.

7. Most economists advocate **free trade,** but in practice many governments engage in **trade protection.** The two most common forms of **protection** are tariffs and quotas. In rare occasions, export industries are subsidized.

8. A **tariff** is a tax levied on imports. It raises the domestic price above the world price, hurting consumers, benefiting domestic producers, and generating government revenue. As a result, total surplus falls. An **import quota** is a legal limit on the quantity of a good that can be imported. It has the same effects as a tariff, except that the revenue goes not to the government but to those who receive import licenses.

9. Although several popular arguments have been made in favor of trade protection, in practice the main reason for protection is probably political: import-competing industries are well organized and well informed about how they gain from trade protection, while consumers are unaware of the costs they pay. Still, U.S. trade is fairly free, mainly because of the role of **international trade agreements,** in which countries agree to reduce trade protection against one anothers' exports. The **North American Free Trade Agreement (NAFTA)** and the **European Union (EU)** cover a small number of countries. In contrast, the **World Trade Organization (WTO)** covers a much larger number of countries, accounting for the bulk of world trade. It oversees trade negotiations and adjudicates disputes among its members.

10. In the past few years, many concerns have been raised about the effects of globalization. One issue is the increase in income inequality due to the surge in imports from relatively poor countries over the past 20 years. Another concern is the increase in **offshore outsourcing,** as many jobs that were once considered safe from foreign competition have been moved abroad.

KEY TERMS

Imports, p. 218
Exports, p. 218
Globalization, p. 218
Hyperglobalization, p. 218
Ricardian model of international trade, p. 219
Autarky, p. 220
Factor intensity, p. 225
Heckscher–Ohlin model, p. 225

Domestic demand curve, p. 228
Domestic supply curve, p. 228
World price, p. 228
Exporting industries, p. 232
Import-competing industries, p. 232
Free trade, p. 234
Trade protection, p. 234
Protection, p. 234
Tariff, p. 234

Import quota, p. 236
International trade agreements, p. 239
North American Free Trade Agreement (NAFTA), p. 239
European Union (EU), p. 239
World Trade Organization (WTO), p. 239
Offshore outsourcing, p. 241

PROBLEMS

1. Both Canada and the United States produce lumber and footballs with constant opportunity costs. The United States can produce either 10 tons of lumber and no footballs, or 1,000 footballs and no lumber, or any combination in between. Canada can produce either 8 tons of lumber and no footballs, or 400 footballs and no lumber, or any combination in between.

   a. Draw the U.S. and Canadian production possibility frontiers in two separate diagrams, with footballs on the horizontal axis and lumber on the vertical axis.

   b. In autarky, if the United States wants to consume 500 footballs, how much lumber can it consume at most? Label this point *A* in your diagram. Similarly, if Canada wants to consume 1 ton of lumber, how many footballs can it consume in autarky? Label this point *C* in your diagram.

   c. Which country has the absolute advantage in lumber production?

   d. Which country has the comparative advantage in lumber production?

   Suppose each country specializes in the good in which it has the comparative advantage, and there is trade.

   e. How many footballs does the United States produce? How much lumber does Canada produce?

   f. Is it possible for the United States to consume 500 footballs and 7 tons of lumber? Label this point *B* in your diagram. Is it possible for Canada at the same time to consume 500 footballs and 1 ton of lumber? Label this point *D* in your diagram.

2. For each of the following trade relationships, explain the likely source of the comparative advantage of each of the exporting countries.

   a. The United States exports software to Venezuela, and Venezuela exports oil to the United States.

   b. The United States exports airplanes to China, and China exports clothing to the United States.

   c. The United States exports wheat to Colombia, and Colombia exports coffee to the United States.

3. The U.S. Census Bureau keeps statistics on U.S. imports and exports on its website. The following steps will take you to the foreign trade statistics. Use them to answer the questions below.

   i. Go to the U.S. Census Bureau's website at www.census.gov

   ii. Under the heading "Topics" select "Business" and then select "International Trade" under the section "Data by Sector" in the left menu bar

   iii. At the top of the page, select the tab "Data"

   iv. In the left menu bar, select "Country/Product Trade"

   v. Under the heading "North American Industry Classification System (NAICS)-Based," select "NAICS web application"

   vi. In the drop-down menu "3-digit and 6-digit NAICS by country," select the product category you are interested in, and hit "Go"

   vii. In the drop-down menu "Select 6-digit NAICS," select the good or service you are interested in, and hit "Go"

   viii. In the drop-down menus that allow you to select a month and year, select "December" and "2013," and hit "Go"

   ix. The right side of the table now shows the import and export statistics for the entire year 2013. For the questions below on U.S. imports, use the column for "Consumption Imports, Customs Value Basis."

   a. Look up data for U.S. imports of hats and caps: in step (vi), select "(315) Apparel & Accessories" and in step (vii), select "(315220) Men's and Boys' Cut and Sew Apparel." From which country do we import the most apparel? Which of the three sources of comparative advantage (climate, factor endowments, and technology) accounts for that country's comparative advantage in apparel production?

   b. Look up data for U.S. imports of grapes: in step (vi), select "(111) Agricultural Products" and in step (vii), select "(111332) Grapes." From which country do we import the most grapes? Which of the three sources of comparative advantage (climate, factor endowments, and technology) accounts for that country's comparative advantage in grape production?

   c. Look up data for U.S. imports of food product machinery: in step (vi), select "(333) Machinery, Except Electrical" and in step (vii), select "333241 Food Product Machinery." From which country do we import the most food product machinery? Which of the three sources of comparative advantage (climate, factor endowments, and technology) accounts for that country's comparative advantage in food product machinery?

4. Since 2000, the value of U.S. imports of men's and boy's apparel from China has more than tripled. What prediction does the Heckscher-Ohlin model make about the wages received by labor in China?

5. Shoes are labor-intensive and satellites are capital-intensive to produce. The United States has abundant capital. China has abundant labor. According to the Heckscher–Ohlin model, which good will China export? Which good will the United States export? In the United States, what will happen to the price of labor (the wage) and to the price of capital?

6. Before the North American Free Trade Agreement (NAFTA) gradually eliminated import tariffs on goods, the autarky price of tomatoes in Mexico was below the world price and in the United States was above the world price. Similarly, the autarky price of poultry in Mexico was above the world price and in the United States was below the world price. Draw diagrams with domestic supply and demand curves for each country and each of the two goods. As a result of NAFTA, the United States now imports tomatoes from Mexico and the United States now exports poultry to Mexico. How would you expect the following groups to be affected?

a. Mexican and U.S. consumers of tomatoes. Illustrate the effect on consumer surplus in your diagram.

b. Mexican and U.S. producers of tomatoes. Illustrate the effect on producer surplus in your diagram.

c. Mexican and U.S. tomato workers.

d. Mexican and U.S. consumers of poultry. Illustrate the effect on consumer surplus in your diagram.

e. Mexican and U.S. producers of poultry. Illustrate the effect on producer surplus in your diagram.

f. Mexican and U.S. poultry workers.

7. The accompanying table indicates the U.S. domestic demand schedule and domestic supply schedule for commercial jet airplanes. Suppose that the world price of a commercial jet airplane is $100 million.

Price of jet (millions)	Quantity of jets demanded	Quantity of jets supplied
$120	100	1,000
110	150	900
100	200	800
90	250	700
80	300	600
70	350	500
60	400	400
50	450	300
40	500	200

a. In autarky, how many commercial jet airplanes does the United States produce, and at what price are they bought and sold?

b. With trade, what will the price for commercial jet airplanes be? Will the United States import or export airplanes? How many?

8. The accompanying table shows the U.S. domestic demand schedule and domestic supply schedule for oranges. Suppose that the world price of oranges is $0.30 per orange.

Price of orange	Quantity of oranges demanded (thousands)	Quantity of oranges supplied (thousands)
$1.00	2	11
0.90	4	10
0.80	6	9
0.70	8	8
0.60	10	7
0.50	12	6
0.40	14	5
0.30	16	4
0.20	18	3

a. Draw the U.S. domestic supply curve and domestic demand curve.

b. With free trade, how many oranges will the United States import or export?

Suppose that the U.S. government imposes a tariff on oranges of $0.20 per orange.

c. How many oranges will the United States import or export after introduction of the tariff?

d. In your diagram, shade the gain or loss to the economy as a whole from the introduction of this tariff.

9. The U.S. domestic demand schedule and domestic supply schedule for oranges was given in Problem 10. Suppose that the world price of oranges is $0.30. The United States introduces an import quota of 3,000 oranges and assigns the quota rents to foreign orange exporters.

a. Draw the domestic demand and supply curves.

b. What will the domestic price of oranges be after introduction of the quota?

c. What is the value of the quota rents that foreign exporters of oranges receive?

10. The accompanying diagram illustrates the U.S. domestic demand curve and domestic supply curve for beef.

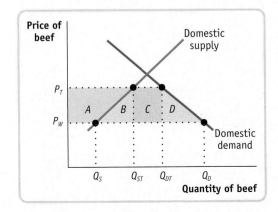

The world price of beef is P_W. The United States currently imposes an import tariff on beef, so the price of beef is P_T. Congress decides to eliminate the tariff. In terms of the areas marked in the diagram, answer the following questions.

a. With the elimination of the tariff what is the gain/ loss in consumer surplus?

b. With the elimination of the tariff what is the gain/ loss in producer surplus?

c. With the elimination of the tariff what is the gain/ loss to the government?

d. With the elimination of the tariff what is the gain/ loss to the economy as a whole?

11. As the United States has opened up to trade, it has lost many of its low-skill manufacturing jobs, but it has gained jobs in high-skill industries, such as the software industry. Explain whether the United States as a whole has been made better off by trade.

12. The United States is highly protective of its agricultural industry, imposing import tariffs, and sometimes quotas, on imports of agricultural goods. This chapter presented three arguments for trade protection. For each argument, discuss whether it is a valid justification for trade protection of U.S. agricultural products.

13. In World Trade Organization (WTO) negotiations, if a country agrees to reduce trade barriers (tariffs or quotas), it usually refers to this as a *concession* to other countries. Do you think that this terminology is appropriate?

14. Producers in import-competing industries often make the following argument: "Other countries have an advantage in production of certain goods purely because workers abroad are paid lower wages. In fact, American workers are much more productive than foreign workers. So import-competing industries need to be protected." Is this a valid argument? Explain your answer.

WORK IT OUT

For interactive, step-by-step help in solving the following problem, visit LaunchPad by using the URL on the back cover of this book.

15. Assume Saudi Arabia and the United States face the production possibilities for oil and cars shown in the accompanying table.

Saudi Arabia		United States	
Quantity of oil (millions of barrels)	Quantity of cars (millions)	Quantity of oil (millions of barrels)	Quantity of cars (millions)
0	4	0	10.0
200	3	100	7.5
400	2	200	5.0
600	1	300	2.5
800	0	400	0

a. What is the opportunity cost of producing a car in Saudi Arabia? In the United States? What is the opportunity cost of producing a barrel of oil in Saudi Arabia? In the United States?

b. Which country has the comparative advantage in producing oil? In producing cars?

c. Suppose that in autarky, Saudi Arabia produces 200 million barrels of oil and 3 million cars; similarly, that the United States produces 300 million barrels of oil and 2.5 million cars. Without trade, can Saudi Arabia produce more oil *and* more cars? Without trade, can the United States produce more oil *and* more cars?

Suppose now that each country specializes in the good in which it has the comparative advantage, and the two countries trade. Also assume that for each country the value of imports must equal the value of exports.

d. What is the total quantity of oil produced? What is the total quantity of cars produced?

e. Is it possible for Saudi Arabia to consume 400 million barrels of oil and 5 million cars and for the United States to consume 400 million barrels of oil and 5 million cars?

f. Suppose that, in fact, Saudi Arabia consumes 300 million barrels of oil and 4 million cars and the United States consumes 500 million barrels of oil and 6 million cars. How many barrels of oil does the United States import? How many cars does the United States export? Suppose a car costs $10,000 on the world market. How much, then, does a barrel of oil cost on the world market?

Decision Making by Individuals and Firms

CHAPTER

▶ What You Will Learn in This Chapter

- Why good decision making begins with accurately defining costs and benefits

- The importance of **implicit and explicit costs** in decision making

- How **accounting profit** and **economic profit** differ, and why economic profit is the correct basis for decisions

- Why there are three different types of economic decisions: "either–or," "how much," and those involving **sunk costs**

- The principles of decision making that correspond to each type of economic decision

- Why people sometimes behave in irrational yet predictable ways

- How to make decisions involving time (in this chapter's appendix)

GOING BACK TO SCHOOL

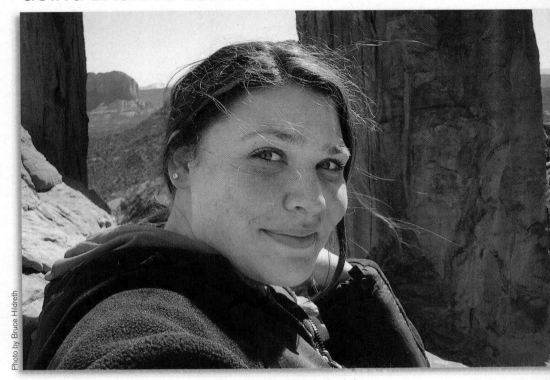

Photo by Bruce Hildreth

Grad school or job? Ashley Hildreth had to make that decision.

I N THE SPRING OF 2010, ASHLEY Hildreth, a class of 2008 journalism major at the University of Oregon, was deeply frustrated. After working for 18 months in what she described as a "dead-end, part-time job" in the food industry, she decided to apply to a master's degree program in teaching.

In explaining her decision, she pointed to the many job applications she submitted without a single call back for an interview. What she hoped for was an entry-level opportunity in advertising and marketing or an administrative position with a nonprofit. What she got instead was silence or gentle rejections. After considering her options, she decided to apply for graduate school.

Hildreth was far from alone in her decision. In the spring of 2010, because of a poor job market, colleges and universities across the country were reporting a record number of applications.

Applications soared not just for bachelor and associate degree programs. As Hildreth's story illustrates, they also soared for graduate and continuing education programs of all sorts.

Whatever the state of the job market, however, every year millions of people—just like you—face a choice about work versus continued schooling: should I continue another year (or semester, or quarter) in school, or should I get a job? That is, they are making a decision.

This chapter is about the economics of making decisions: how to make a decision that results in the best possible economic outcome. Economists have formulated principles of decision making that lead to the best possible—often called "optimal"—outcome, regardless of whether the decision maker is a consumer or a producer.

We'll start by examining three different types of economic decisions, each

with a corresponding principle, or method, of decision making that leads to the best possible economic outcome. In this chapter, we'll see why economists consider decision making to be the very essence of microeconomics.

Despite the fact that people *should* use the principles of economic decision making to achieve the best possible economic outcome, they sometimes fail to do so. In other words, people are not always rational when making decisions.

For example, a shopper in pursuit of a bargain may knowingly spend more on gasoline than he or she saves. Yet economists have also discovered that people are frequently *irrational in predictable ways*. In this chapter, we'll learn about these tendencies when we discuss *behavioral economics*, the branch of economics that studies predictably irrational economic behavior.

An **explicit cost** is a cost that requires an outlay of money.

An **implicit cost** does not require an outlay of money. It is measured by the value, in dollar terms, of benefits that are forgone.

Costs, Benefits, and Profits

In making any type of decision, it's critical to define the costs and benefits of that decision accurately. If you don't know the costs and benefits, it is nearly impossible to make a good decision. So that is where we begin.

An important first step is to recognize the role of *opportunity cost*, a concept we first encountered in Chapter 1, where we learned that opportunity costs arise because *resources are scarce*. Because resources are scarce, the true cost of anything is what you must give up to get it—its opportunity cost.

Whether you decide to continue in school for another year or leave to find a job, each choice has costs and benefits. Because your time—a resource—is scarce, you cannot be both a full-time student and a full-time worker. If you choose to be a full-time student, the opportunity cost of that choice is the income you would have earned at a full-time job. And there may be additional opportunity costs, such as the value of the experience you would have gained by working.

When making decisions, it is crucial to think in terms of opportunity cost, because the opportunity cost of an action is often considerably more than the cost of any outlays of money.

Economists use the concepts of *explicit costs* and *implicit costs* to compare the relationship between opportunity costs and monetary outlays. We'll discuss these two concepts first. Then we'll define the concepts of *accounting profit* and *economic profit*, which are *ways of measuring whether the benefit of an action is greater than the cost*. Armed with these concepts for assessing costs and benefits, we will be in a position to consider our first principle of economic decision making: how to make "either–or" decisions.

Always think in terms of opportunity cost when making decisions.

Explicit versus Implicit Costs

Suppose that, after graduating from college, you have two options: to go to school for an additional year to get an advanced degree or to take a job immediately. You would like to enroll in the extra year in school but are concerned about the cost.

What exactly is the cost of that additional year of school? Here is where it is important to remember the concept of opportunity cost: the cost of the year spent getting an advanced degree includes what you forgo by not taking a job for that year. The opportunity cost of an additional year of school, like any cost, can be broken into two parts: the *explicit* cost of the year's schooling and the *implicit* cost.

An **explicit cost** is a cost that requires an outlay of money. For example, the explicit cost of the additional year of schooling includes tuition. An **implicit cost,** though, does not involve an outlay of money. Instead, it is measured by the value, in dollar terms, of the benefits that are forgone. For example, the implicit cost of the year spent in school includes the income you would have earned if you had taken a job instead.

A common mistake, both in economic analysis and in life—whether individual or business—is to ignore implicit costs and focus exclusively on explicit costs. But often the implicit cost of an activity is quite substantial—indeed, sometimes it is much larger than the explicit cost.

Table 9-1 gives a breakdown of hypothetical explicit and implicit costs

TABLE **9-1**	Opportunity Cost of an Additional Year of School		
Explicit cost		**Implicit cost**	
Tuition	$7,000	Forgone salary	$35,000
Books and supplies	1,000		
Computer	1,500		
Total explicit cost	9,500	**Total implicit cost**	35,000
Total opportunity cost = Total explicit cost + Total implicit cost = $44,500			

associated with spending an additional year in school instead of taking a job. The explicit cost consists of tuition, books, supplies, and a computer for doing assignments—all of which require you to spend money. The implicit cost is the salary you would have earned if you had taken a job instead. As you can see, the total opportunity cost of attending an additional year of schooling is $44,500, the sum of the total implicit cost—$35,000 in forgone salary, and the total explicit cost—$9,500 in outlays on tuition, supplies, and computer. Because the implicit cost is more than three times as much as the explicit cost, ignoring the implicit cost would lead to a seriously misguided decision. This example illustrates a general principle: *the opportunity cost of any activity is equal to its explicit cost plus its implicit cost.*

A slightly different way of looking at the implicit cost in this example can deepen our understanding of opportunity cost. The forgone salary is the cost of using your own resources—your time—in going to school rather than working. The use of your time for more schooling, despite the fact that you don't have to spend any money on it, is still costly to you. This illustrates an important aspect of opportunity cost: in considering the cost of an activity, you should include the cost of using any of your own resources for that activity. You can calculate the cost of using your own resources by determining what they would have earned in their next best use.

Understanding the role of opportunity costs makes clear the reason for the surge in school applications in 2010: a rotten job market. Starting in 2009, the U.S. job market deteriorated sharply as the economy entered a severe recession. By 2010, the job market was still quite weak; although job openings had begun to reappear, a relatively high proportion of those openings were for jobs with low wages and no benefits. As a result, the opportunity cost of another year of schooling had declined significantly, making spending another year at school a much more attractive choice than when the job market was strong.

> **Accounting profit** is equal to revenue minus explicit cost.

Accounting Profit versus Economic Profit

Let's return to Ashley Hildreth and assume that she faces the choice of either completing a two-year full-time graduate program in teaching or spending those two years working in her original field of advertising. We'll also assume that in order to be certified as a teacher, she must complete the entire two years of the graduate program. Which choice should she make?

To get started, let's consider what Ashley gains by getting the teaching degree—what we might call her *revenue* from the teaching degree. Once she has completed her teaching degree two years from now, she will receive earnings from her degree valued today at $600,000 over the rest of her lifetime. In contrast, if she doesn't get the degree and stays in advertising, two years from now her future lifetime earnings will be valued today at $500,000. The cost of the tuition for her teaching degree program is $40,000, which she pays for with a student loan that costs her $4,000 in interest.

At this point, what she should do might seem obvious: if she chooses the teaching degree, she gets a lifetime increase in the value of her earnings of $600,000 – $500,000 = $100,000, and she pays $40,000 in tuition plus $4,000 in interest. Doesn't that mean she makes a profit of $100,000 – $40,000 – $4,000 = $56,000 by getting her teaching degree? This $56,000 is Ashley's **accounting profit** from obtaining her teaching degree: her revenue minus her explicit cost. In this example her explicit cost of getting the degree is $44,000, the amount of her tuition plus student loan interest.

"I've done the numbers, and I will marry you."

Economic profit is equal to revenue minus the opportunity cost of resources used. It is usually less than the accounting profit.

Capital is the total value of assets owned by an individual or firm—physical assets plus financial assets.

Although accounting profit is a useful measure, it would be misleading for Ashley to use it alone in making her decision. To make the right decision, the one that leads to the best possible economic outcome for her, she needs to calculate her **economic profit**—the revenue she receives from the teaching degree minus her opportunity cost of staying in school (which is equal to her explicit cost *plus* her implicit cost). In general, the economic profit of a given project will be less than the accounting profit because there are almost always implicit costs in addition to explicit costs.

When economists use the term *profit*, they are referring to *economic* profit, not *accounting* profit. This will be our convention in the rest of the book: when we use the term *profit*, we mean economic profit.

How does Ashley's economic profit from staying in school differ from her accounting profit? We've already encountered one source of the difference: her two years of forgone job earnings. This is an implicit cost of going to school full time for two years. We assume that the value today of Ashley's forgone earnings for the two years is $57,000.

Once we factor in Ashley's implicit costs and calculate her economic profit, we see that she is better off not getting a teaching degree. You can see this in Table 9-2: her economic profit from getting the teaching degree is –$1,000. In other words, she incurs an *economic*

TABLE 9-2	Ashley's Economic Profit from Acquiring Teaching Degree
Value of increase in lifetime earnings	$100,000
Explicit cost:	
Tuition	–40,000
Interest paid on student loan	– 4,000
Accounting Profit	**56,000**
Implicit cost:	
Value of income forgone during 2 years spent in school	–57,000
Economic Profit	**–1,000**

loss of $1,000 if she gets the degree. Clearly, she is better off sticking to advertising and going to work now.

Let's consider a slightly different scenario to make sure that the concepts of opportunity costs and economic profit are well understood. Let's suppose that Ashley does not have to take out $40,000 in student loans to pay her tuition. Instead, she can pay for it with an inheritance from her grandmother. As a result, she doesn't have to pay $4,000 in interest. In this case, her accounting profit is $60,000 rather than $56,000. Would the right decision now be for her to get the teaching degree? Wouldn't the economic profit of the degree now be $60,000 – $57,000 = $3,000?

The answer is no, because in this scenario Ashley is using her own *capital* to finance her education, and the use of that capital has an opportunity cost even when she owns it.

Capital is the total value of the assets of an individual or a firm. An individual's capital usually consists of cash in the bank, stocks, bonds, and the ownership value of real estate such as a house. In the case of a business, capital also includes its equipment, its tools, and its inventory of unsold goods and used parts. (Economists like to distinguish between *financial assets,* such as cash, stocks, and bonds, and *physical assets,* such as buildings, equipment, tools, and inventory.)

The point is that even if Ashley owns the $40,000, using it to pay tuition incurs an opportunity cost—what she forgoes in the next best use of that $40,000. If she hadn't used the money to pay her tuition, her next best use of the money would have been to deposit it in a bank to earn interest.

To keep things simple, let's assume that she earns $4,000 on that $40,000 once it is deposited in a bank. Now, rather than pay $4,000 in explicit costs in the form of student loan interest, Ashley pays $4,000 in implicit costs from the forgone interest she could have earned.

This $4,000 in forgone interest earnings is what economists call the **implicit cost of capital**—the income the owner of the capital could have earned if the capital had been employed in its next best alternative use. The net effect is that it makes no difference whether Ashley finances her tuition with a student loan or by using her own funds. This comparison reinforces how carefully you must keep track of opportunity costs when making a decision.

Making "Either–Or" Decisions

An "either–or" decision is one in which you must choose between two activities. That's in contrast to a "how much" decision, which requires you to choose how much of a given activity to undertake. For example, Ashley faced an "either–or" decision: to spend two years in graduate school to obtain a teaching degree, or to work. In contrast, a "how much" decision would be deciding how many hours to study or how many hours to work at a job. Table 9-3 contrasts a variety of "either–or" and "how much" decisions.

In making economic decisions, as we have already emphasized, it is vitally important to calculate opportunity costs correctly. The best way to make an "either–or" decision, the method that leads to the best possible economic outcome, is the straightforward **principle of "either–or" decision making.** According to this principle, *when making an "either–or" choice between two activities, choose the one with the positive economic profit.*

Let's examine Ashley's dilemma from a different angle to understand how this principle works. If she continues with advertising and goes to work immediately, the value today of her total lifetime earnings is $57,000 (the value today of her earnings over the next two years) + $500,000 (the value today of her total lifetime earnings thereafter) = $557,000. If she gets her teaching degree instead and works as a teacher, the value today of her total lifetime earnings is $600,000 (value today of her lifetime earnings after two years in school) – $40,000 (tuition) – $4,000 (interest payments) = $556,000. The economic profit from continuing in advertising versus becoming a teacher is $557,000 – $556,000 = $1,000.

> The **implicit cost of capital** is the opportunity cost of the use of one's own capital—the income earned if the capital had been employed in its next best alternative use.
>
> According to the **principle of "either–or" decision making,** when faced with an "either–or" choice between two activities, choose the one with the positive economic profit.

TABLE 9-3   "How Much" versus "Either–Or" Decisions

"Either–or" decisions	"How much" decisions
Tide or Cheer?	How many days before you do your laundry?
Buy a car or not?	How many miles do you go before an oil change in your car?
An order of nachos or a sandwich?	How many jalapenos on your nachos?
Run your own business or work for someone else?	How many workers should you hire in your company?
Prescribe drug A or drug B for your patients?	How much should a patient take of a drug that generates side effects?
Graduate school or not?	How many hours to study?

FOR INQUIRING MINDS | A Tale of Two Invasions

ON JUNE 6, 1944, ALLIED SOLDIERS stormed the beaches of Normandy, beginning the liberation of France from German rule. Long before the assault, however, Allied generals had to make a crucial decision: where would the soldiers land?

They had to make an "either–or" decision. Either the invasion force could cross the English Channel at its narrowest point, Calais—which was what the Germans expected—or it could try to surprise the Germans by landing farther west, in Normandy. Since men and land-

ing craft were in limited supply, the Allies could not do both. In fact, they chose to rely on surprise. The German defenses in Normandy were too weak to stop the landings, and the Allies went on to liberate France and win the war.

Thirty years earlier, at the beginning of World War I, German generals had to make a different kind of decision. They, too, planned to invade France, in this case via land, and had decided to mount that invasion through Belgium. The decision they had to make was not an "either–or" but a "how much"

decision: how much of their army should be allocated to the invasion force, and enough: the defending French army stopped it 30 miles from Paris. Most military historians believe that by allocating too few men to the attack, von Moltke cost Germany the war. ("How much" decisions are discussed in detail in the next section.)

So Allied generals made the right "either–or" decision in 1944; German generals made the wrong "how much" decision in 1914. The rest is history. ■

WHY ARE THERE ONLY TWO CHOICES?

In "either–or" decision making, we have assumed that there are only two activities to choose from. But, what if, instead of just two alternatives, there are three or more? Does the principle of "either–or" decision making still apply?

Yes, it does. That's because any choice between three (or more) alternatives can always be boiled down to a series of choices between two alternatives. Here's an illustration using three alternative activities: A, B, or C. (Remember that this is an "either–or" decision: you can choose only one of the three alternatives.)

Let's say you begin by considering A versus B: in this comparison, A has a positive economic profit but B yields an economic loss. At this point, you should discard B as a viable choice because A will always be superior to B. The next step is to compare A to C: in this comparison, C has a positive economic profit but A yields an economic loss. You can now discard A because C will always be superior to A. You are now done: since A is better than B, and C is better than A, C is the correct choice.

So the right choice for Ashley is to begin work in advertising immediately, which gives her an economic profit of $1,000, rather than become a teacher, which would give her an economic profit of –$1,000. In other words, by becoming a teacher she loses the $1,000 economic profit she would have gained by working in advertising immediately.

In making "either–or" decisions, mistakes most commonly arise when people or businesses use their own assets in projects rather than rent or borrow assets. That's because they fail to account for the implicit cost of using self-owned capital. In contrast, when they rent or borrow assets, these rental or borrowing costs show up as explicit costs. If, for example, a restaurant owns its equipment and tools, it would have to compute its implicit cost of capital by calculating how much the equipment could be sold for and how much could be earned by using those funds in the next best alternative project.

In addition, businesses run by the owner (an *entrepreneur*) often fail to calculate the opportunity cost of the owner's time in running the business. In that way, small businesses often underestimate their opportunity costs and overestimate their economic profit of staying in business.

Are we implying that the hundreds of thousands who have chosen to go back to school rather than find work in recent years are misguided? Not necessarily. As we mentioned before, the poor job market has greatly diminished the opportunity cost of forgone wages for many students, making continuing their education the optimal choice for them.

The following Economics in Action illustrates just how important it is in real life to understand the difference between accounting profit and economic profit.

ECONOMICS ▶ in Action

Farming in the Shadow of Suburbia

Beyond the sprawling suburbs, most of New England is covered by dense forest. But this is not the forest primeval: if you hike through the woods, you encounter many stone walls, relics of the region's agricultural past when stone walls enclosed fields and pastures. In 1880, more than half of New England's land was farmed; by 2013, the amount was down to 10%.

The remaining farms of New England are mainly located close to large metropolitan areas. There farmers get high prices for their produce from city dwellers who are willing to pay a premium for locally grown, extremely fresh fruits and vegetables.

But now even these farms are under economic pressure caused by a rise in the implicit cost of farming close to a metropolitan area. As metropolitan areas have expanded during the last two decades, farmers increasingly ask themselves whether they could do better by selling their land to property developers.

In 2013, the average value of an acre of farmland in the United States as a whole was $2,900; in Rhode Island, the most densely populated of the New England states, the average was $11,800. The Federal Reserve Bank of Boston has noted that "high land prices put intense pressure on the region's farms to generate incomes that are substantial enough to justify keeping the land in agriculture."

The important point is that the pressure is intense even if the farmer owns the land because the land is a form of capital used to run the business. So maintaining the land as a farm instead of selling it to a developer constitutes a large implicit cost of capital.

A fact provided by the U.S. Department of Agriculture (USDA) helps us put a dollar figure on the portion of the implicit cost of capital due to development pressure

In densely populated areas, working farms incur a large implicit cost of capital.

for some Rhode Island farms. In 2004, a USDA program designed to prevent development of Rhode Island farmland by paying owners for the "development rights" to their land paid an average of $4,949 per acre for those rights alone. By 2013, the amount had risen to more than $11,800.

About two-thirds of New England's farms remaining in business earn very little money. They are maintained as "rural residences" by people with other sources of income—not because operating them is an optimal choice, but more out of a personal commitment and the satisfaction these people derive from farm life. Although many businesses have important implicit costs, they can also have important benefits to their owners that go beyond the revenue earned.

Check Your Understanding 9-1

1. Karma and Don run a furniture-refinishing business from their home. Which of the following represent an explicit cost of the business and which represent an implicit cost?
   a. Supplies such as paint stripper, varnish, polish, sandpaper, and so on
   b. Basement space that has been converted into a workroom
   c. Wages paid to a part-time helper
   d. A van that they inherited and use only for transporting furniture
   e. The job at a larger furniture restorer that Karma gave up in order to run the business

2. Assume that Ashley has a third alternative to consider: entering a two-year apprenticeship program for skilled machinists that would, upon completion, make her a licensed machinist. During the apprenticeship, she earns a reduced salary of $15,000 per year. At the end of the apprenticeship, the value of her lifetime earnings is $725,000. What is Ashley's best career choice?

3. Suppose you have three alternatives—A, B, and C—and you can undertake only one of them. In comparing A versus B, you find that B has an economic profit and A yields an economic loss. But in comparing A versus C, you find that C has an economic profit and A yields an economic loss. How do you decide what to do?

Solutions appear at back of book.

Making "How Much" Decisions: The Role of Marginal Analysis

Although many decisions in economics are "either–or," many others are "how much." Not many people will give up their cars if the price of gasoline goes up, but many people will drive less. How much less? A rise in corn prices won't necessarily persuade a lot of people to take up farming for the first time, but it will persuade farmers who were already growing corn to plant more. How much more?

Recall from our principles of microeconomics that "how much" is a decision at the margin. So to understand "how much" decisions, we will use an approach known as *marginal analysis*. Marginal analysis involves comparing the benefit of doing a little bit more of some activity with the cost of doing a little bit more of that activity. The benefit of doing a little bit more of something is what economists call its *marginal benefit*, and the cost of doing a little bit more of something is what they call its *marginal cost*.

Why is this called "marginal" analysis? A margin is an edge; what you do in marginal analysis is push out the edge a bit and see whether that is a good move. We will study marginal analysis by considering a hypothetical decision of how many years of school to complete. We'll consider the case of Alex, who studies computer programming and design. Since there are many computer languages, app design methods, and graphics programs that can be learned one year at a time, each year Alex can decide whether to continue his studies or not.

Unlike Ashley, who faced an "either–or" decision of whether to get a teaching degree, Alex faces a "how much" decision of how many years to study computer programming and design. For example, he could study one more year, or five more years, or any number of years in between. We'll begin our analysis of Alex's decision problem by defining Alex's *marginal cost* of another year of study.

Marginal Cost

We'll assume that each additional year of schooling costs Alex $10,000 in explicit costs—tuition, interest on a student loan, and so on. In addition to the explicit costs, he also has an implicit cost—the income forgone by spending one more year in school.

Unlike Alex's explicit costs, which are constant (that is, the same each year), Alex's implicit cost changes each year. That's because each year he spends in school leaves him better trained than the year before; and the better trained he is, the higher the salary he can command. Consequently, the income he forgoes by not working rises each additional year he stays in school. In other words, the greater the number of years Alex has already spent in school, the higher his implicit cost of another year of school.

Table 9-4 contains the data on how Alex's cost of an additional year of schooling changes as he completes more years. The second column shows how his total cost of schooling changes as the number of years he has completed increases. For example, Alex's first year has a total cost of $30,000: $10,000 in explicit costs of tuition and the like as well as $20,000 in forgone salary.

The second column also shows that the total cost of attending two years is $70,000: $30,000 for his first year plus $40,000 for his second year. During his second year in school, his explicit costs have stayed the same ($10,000) but his implicit cost of forgone salary has gone up to $30,000. That's because he's a more valuable worker with one year of schooling under his belt than with no schooling.

TABLE 9-4	Alex's Marginal Cost of Additional Years in School	
Quantity of schooling (years)	Total cost	Marginal cost
0	$0	
		$30,000
1	30,000	
		40,000
2	70,000	
		60,000
3	130,000	
		90,000
4	220,000	
		130,000
5	350,000	

Likewise, the total cost of three years of schooling is $130,000: $30,000 in explicit cost for three years of tuition plus $100,000 in implicit cost of three years of forgone salary. The total cost of attending four years is $220,000, and $350,000 for five years.

The change in Alex's total cost of schooling when he goes to school an additional year is his *marginal cost* of the one-year increase in years of schooling. In general, the **marginal cost** of producing a good or service (in this case, producing one's own education) is the additional cost incurred by producing one more unit of that good or service. The arrows, which zigzag between the total costs in the second column and the marginal costs in the third column, are there to help you to see how marginal cost is calculated from total cost. Similarly, total cost can be calculated from marginal cost: the total cost of a given quantity is the sum of the marginal costs of that quantity and of all of the previous ones. So the total cost of three years of schooling is $30,000 + $40,000 + $60,000 = $130,000; that is, the marginal cost of year 1 plus the marginal cost of year 2 plus the marginal cost of year 3.

As already mentioned, the third column of Table 9-4 shows Alex's marginal costs of more years of schooling, which have a clear pattern: they are increasing. They go from $30,000, to $40,000, to $60,000, to $90,000, and finally to $130,000 for the fifth year of schooling. That's because each year of schooling would make Alex a more valuable and highly paid employee if he were to work. As a result, for-

The **marginal cost** of producing a good or service is the additional cost incurred by producing one more unit of that good or service.

going a job becomes much more costly as he becomes more educated. This is an example of what economists call **increasing marginal cost,** which occurs when each unit of a good costs more to produce than the previous unit.

Figure 9-1 shows the **marginal cost curve,** a graphical representation of Alex's marginal costs. The height of each shaded bar corresponds to the marginal cost of a given year of schooling. The red line connecting the dots at the midpoint of the top of each bar is Alex's marginal cost curve. Alex has an upward-sloping marginal cost curve because he has increasing marginal cost of additional years of schooling.

Although increasing marginal cost is a frequent phenomenon in real life, it's not the only possibility. **Constant marginal cost** occurs when the cost of producing an additional unit is the same as the cost of producing the previous unit. Plant nurseries, for example, typically have constant marginal cost—the cost of growing one more plant is the same, regardless of how many plants have already been produced. With constant marginal cost, the marginal cost curve is a horizontal line.

There can also be **decreasing marginal cost,** which occurs when marginal cost falls as the number of units produced increases. With decreasing marginal cost, the marginal cost line is downward sloping. Decreasing marginal cost is often due to *learning effects* in production: for complicated tasks, such as assembling a new model of a car, workers are often slow and mistake-prone when assembling the earliest units, making for higher marginal cost on those units. But as workers gain experience, assembly time and the rate of mistakes fall, generating lower marginal cost for later units. As a result, overall production has decreasing marginal cost.

Finally, for the production of some goods and services the shape of the marginal cost curve changes as the number of units produced increases. For example, auto production is likely to have decreasing marginal costs for the first batch of cars produced as workers iron out kinks and mistakes in production. Then production has constant marginal costs for the next batch of cars as workers settle into a predictable pace.

But at some point, as workers produce more cars, marginal cost begins to increase as they run out of factory floor space and the auto company incurs costly overtime wages. This gives rise to what we call a "swoosh"-shaped marginal cost curve—a topic we discuss in Chapter 11. For now, we'll stick to the simpler example of an increasing marginal cost curve.

Production of a good or service has **increasing marginal cost** when each additional unit costs more to produce than the previous one.

The **marginal cost curve** shows how the cost of producing one more unit depends on the quantity that has already been produced.

Production of a good or service has **constant marginal cost** when each additional unit costs the same to produce as the previous one.

Production of a good or service has **decreasing marginal cost** when each additional unit costs less to produce than the previous one.

FIGURE 9-1   Marginal Cost

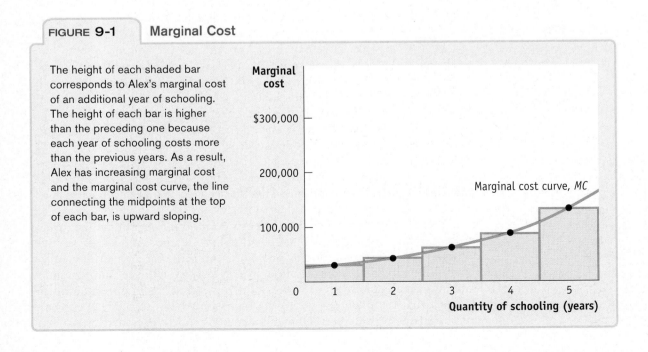

The height of each shaded bar corresponds to Alex's marginal cost of an additional year of schooling. The height of each bar is higher than the preceding one because each year of schooling costs more than the previous years. As a result, Alex has increasing marginal cost and the marginal cost curve, the line connecting the midpoints at the top of each bar, is upward sloping.

PITFALLS

TOTAL COST VERSUS MARGINAL COST

It can be easy to conclude that marginal cost and total cost must always move in the same direction. That is, if total cost is rising, then marginal cost must also be rising. Or if marginal cost is falling, then total cost must be falling as well. But the following example shows that this conclusion is wrong.

Let's consider the example of auto production, which, as we mentioned earlier, is likely to involve learning effects. Suppose that for the first batch of cars of a new model, each car costs $10,000 to assemble. As workers gain experience with the new model, they become better at production. As a result, the per-car cost

of assembly falls to $8,000 for the second batch. For the third batch, the per-car assembly cost falls again to $6,500 as workers continue to gain expertise. For the fourth batch, the per-car cost of assembly falls to $5,000 and remains constant for the rest of the production run.

In this example, marginal cost is *decreasing* over batches one through four, falling from $10,000 to $5,000. However, it's important to note that total cost is still *increasing* over the entire production run because marginal cost is greater than zero.

To see this point, assume that each batch consists of 100 cars. Then the total cost of producing the first batch is 100 × $10,000 = $1,000,000. The total cost of

producing the first and second batch of cars is $1,000,000 + (100 × $8,000) = $1,800,000. Likewise, the total cost of producing the first, second, and third batch is $1,800,000 + (100 × $6,500) = $2,450,000, and so on. As you can see, although marginal cost is decreasing over the first few batches of cars, total cost is increasing over the same batches.

This shows us that totals and marginals can sometimes move in opposite directions. So it is wrong to assert that they always move in the same direction. What we can assert is that *total cost increases whenever marginal cost is positive,* regardless of whether marginal cost is increasing or decreasing.

Marginal Benefit

Alex benefits from higher lifetime earnings as he completes more years of school. Exactly how much he benefits is shown in Table 9-5. Column 2 shows Alex's total benefit according to the number of years of school completed, expressed as the value of his lifetime earnings. The third column shows Alex's *marginal benefit* from an additional year of schooling. In general, the **marginal benefit** of producing a good or service is the additional benefit earned from producing one more unit.

As in Table 9-4, the data in the third column of Table 9-5 show a clear pattern. However, this time the numbers are decreasing rather than increasing. The first year of schooling gives Alex a $300,000 increase in the value of his lifetime earnings. The second year also gives him a positive return, but the size of that return has fallen to $150,000; the third year's return is also positive, but its size has fallen yet again to $90,000; and so on. In other words, the more years of school that Alex has already completed, the smaller the increase in the value of his lifetime earnings from attending one more year.

Alex's schooling decision has what economists call **decreasing marginal benefit:** each additional year of school yields a smaller benefit than the previous year. Or, to put it slightly differently, with decreasing marginal benefit, the benefit from producing one more unit of the good or service falls as the quantity already produced rises.

TABLE **9-5**	Alex's Marginal Benefit of Additional Years in School	
Quantity of schooling (years)	Total benefit	Marginal benefit
0	$0	
		$300,000
1	300,000	
		150,000
2	450,000	
		90,000
3	540,000	
		60,000
4	600,000	
		50,000
5	650,000	

The **marginal benefit** of a good or service is the additional benefit derived from producing one more unit of that good or service.

There is **decreasing marginal benefit** from an activity when each additional unit of the activity yields less benefit than the previous unit.

The **marginal benefit curve** shows how the benefit from producing one more unit depends on the quantity that has already been produced.

Just as marginal cost can be represented by a marginal cost curve, marginal benefit can be represented by a **marginal benefit curve,** shown in blue in Figure 9-2. Alex's marginal benefit curve slopes downward because he faces decreasing marginal benefit from additional years of schooling.

Not all goods or activities exhibit decreasing marginal benefit. In fact, there are many goods for which the marginal benefit of production is constant—that is, the additional benefit from producing one more unit is the same regardless of the number of units already produced. In later chapters, we will see that the shape of a firm's marginal benefit curve from producing output has important implications for how that firm behaves within its industry. We'll also see why constant marginal benefit is considered the norm for many important industries.

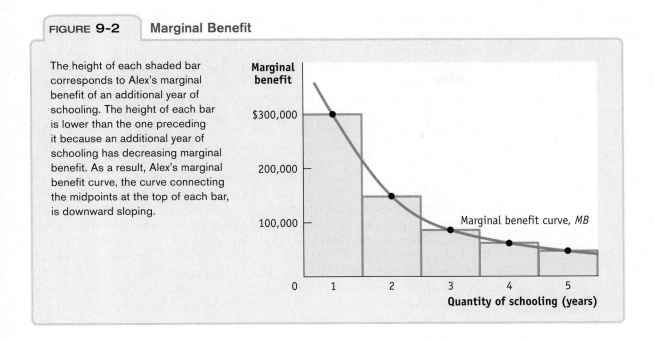

FIGURE **9-2**   Marginal Benefit

The height of each shaded bar corresponds to Alex's marginal benefit of an additional year of schooling. The height of each bar is lower than the one preceding it because an additional year of schooling has decreasing marginal benefit. As a result, Alex's marginal benefit curve, the curve connecting the midpoints at the top of each bar, is downward sloping.

Now we are ready to see how the concepts of marginal benefit and marginal cost are brought together to answer the question of how many years of additional schooling Alex should undertake.

Marginal Analysis

Table 9-6 shows the marginal cost and marginal benefit numbers from Tables 9-4 and 9-5. It also adds an additional column: the additional profit to Alex from staying in school one more year, equal to the difference between the marginal benefit and the marginal cost of that additional year in school. (Remember that it is Alex's economic profit that we care about, not his accounting profit.) We can now use Table 9-6 to determine how many additional years of schooling Alex should undertake in order to maximize his total profit.

First, imagine that Alex chooses not to attend any additional years of school. We can see from column 4 that this is a mistake if Alex wants to achieve the highest total profit from his schooling—the sum of the additional profits generated by another year of schooling. If he attends one additional year of school, he increases the value of his lifetime earnings by $270,000, the profit from the first additional year attended.

Now, let's consider whether Alex should attend the second year of school. The additional profit from the second year is $110,000, so Alex should attend the second year as well. What about the third year? The additional profit from that year is $30,000; so, yes, Alex should attend the third year as well.

What about a fourth year? In this case, the additional profit is negative: it is −$30,000. Alex loses $30,000 of the value of his lifetime earnings if he attends the fourth year. Clearly, Alex is worse off by attending the fourth additional year rather than taking a job. And the same is true for the fifth year as well: it has a negative additional profit of −$80,000.

TABLE **9-6**	Alex's Profit from Additional Years of Schooling		
Quantity of schooling (years)	Marginal benefit	Marginal cost	Additional profit
0			
	$300,000	$30,000	$270,000
1			
	150,000	40,000	110,000
2			
	90,000	60,000	30,000
3			
	60,000	90,000	−30,000
4			
	50,000	130,000	−80,000
5			

The **optimal quantity** is the quantity that generates the highest possible total profit.

What have we learned? That Alex should attend three additional years of school and stop at that point. Although the first, second, and third years of additional schooling increase the value of his lifetime earnings, the fourth and fifth years diminish it. So three years of additional schooling lead to the quantity that generates the maximum possible total profit. It is what economists call the **optimal quantity**—the quantity that generates the maximum possible total profit.

Figure 9-3 shows how the optimal quantity can be determined graphically. Alex's marginal benefit and marginal cost curves are shown together. If Alex chooses fewer than three additional years (that is, years 0, 1, or 2), he will choose a level of schooling at which his marginal benefit curve lies *above* his marginal cost curve. He can make himself better off by staying in school.

If instead he chooses more than three additional years (years 4 or 5), he will choose a level of schooling at which his marginal benefit curve lies *below* his marginal cost curve. He can make himself better off by choosing not to attend the additional year of school and taking a job instead.

The table in Figure 9-3 confirms our result. The second column repeats information from Table 9-6, showing Alex's marginal benefit minus marginal cost—the additional profit per additional year of schooling. The third column shows Alex's total profit for different years of schooling. The total profit, for each possible year of schooling is simply the sum of numbers in the second column up to and including that year.

For example, Alex's profit from additional years of schooling is $270,000 for the first year and $110,000 for the second year. So the total profit for two additional years of schooling is $270,000 + $110,000 = $380,000. Similarly, the total profit for three additional years is $270,000 + $110,000 + $30,000 = $410,000. Our claim that three years is the optimal quantity for Alex is confirmed by the data in the table in Figure 9-3: at three years of additional schooling, Alex reaps the greatest total profit, $410,000.

FIGURE 9-3   **Alex's Optimal Quantity of Years of Schooling**

The optimal quantity is the quantity that generates the highest possible total profit. It is the quantity at which marginal benefit is greater than or equal to marginal cost. Equivalently, it is the quantity at which the marginal benefit and marginal cost curves intersect. Here, they intersect at 3 additional years of schooling. The table confirms that 3 is indeed the optimal quantity: it leads to the maximum total profit of $410,000.

Alex's decision problem illustrates how you go about finding the optimal quantity when the choice involves a small number of quantities. (In this example, one through five years.) With small quantities, the rule for choosing the optimal quantity is: *increase the quantity as long as the marginal benefit from one more unit is greater than the marginal cost, but stop before the marginal benefit becomes less than the marginal cost.*

In contrast, when a "how much" decision involves relatively large quantities, the rule for choosing the optimal quantity simplifies to this: *The optimal quantity is the quantity at which marginal benefit is equal to marginal cost.*

To see why this is so, consider the example of a farmer who finds that her optimal quantity of wheat produced is 5,000 bushels. Typically, she will find that in going from 4,999 to 5,000 bushels, her marginal benefit is only very slightly greater than her marginal cost—that is, the difference between marginal benefit and marginal cost is close to zero. Similarly, in going from 5,000 to 5,001 bushels, her marginal cost is only very slightly greater than her marginal benefit—again, the difference between marginal cost and marginal benefit is very close to zero.

So a simple rule for her in choosing the optimal quantity of wheat is to produce the quantity at which the difference between marginal benefit and marginal cost is approximately zero—that is, the quantity at which marginal benefit equals marginal cost.

Now we are ready to state the general rule for choosing the optimal quantity—one that applies for decisions involving either small quantities or large quantities. This general rule is known as the **profit-maximizing principle of marginal analysis:** *When making a profit-maximizing "how much" decision, the optimal quantity is the largest quantity at which marginal benefit is greater than or equal to marginal cost.*

According to the **profit-maximizing principle of marginal analysis,** when faced with a profit-maximizing "how much" decision, the optimal quantity is the largest quantity at which the marginal benefit is greater than or equal to marginal cost.

GLOBAL COMPARISION | Portion Sizes

Health experts call it the "French Paradox." If you think French food is fattening, you're right: the French diet is, on average, higher in fat than the American diet. Yet the French themselves are considerably thinner than we are: in 2012, 15% of French adults were classified as obese, compared with 34.9% of Americans.

What's the secret? It seems that the French simply eat less, largely because they eat smaller portions. This chart compares average portion sizes at food establishments in Paris and Philadelphia. In four cases, researchers looked at portions served by the same chain; in the other cases, they looked at comparable establishments, such as local pizza parlors. In every case but one, U.S. portions were bigger, often much bigger.

Why are American portions so big? Because food is cheaper in the United States. At the margin, it makes sense for restaurants to offer big portions, since the additional cost of the larger portion is relatively small. As a news article notes: "So while it may cost a restaurant a few pennies to offer 25% more French fries, it can raise its prices much more than a few cents." Larger portions, then, lead to higher checks at U.S. restaurants. And if you have ever wondered why dieting seems to be a uniquely American obsession, the

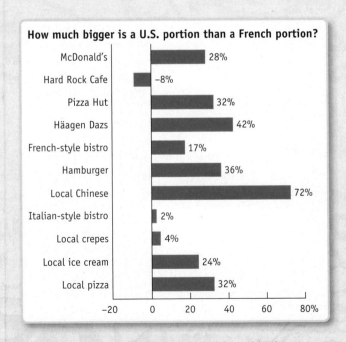

principle of marginal analysis can help provide the answer: it's to counteract the effects of our larger portion sizes.

Source: Paul Rozin, Kimberly Kabnick, Erin Pete, Claude Fischler, and Christy Shields, "The Ecology of Eating," *Psychological Science* 14 (September 2003): 450–454.

MUDDLED AT THE MARGIN

The idea of setting marginal benefit equal to marginal cost sometimes confuses people. Aren't we trying to maximize the *difference* between benefits and costs? Yes. And don't we wipe out our gains by setting benefits and costs equal to each other? Yes. But that is not what we are doing. Rather, what we are doing is setting *marginal*, not *total*, benefit and cost equal to each other.

Once again, the point is to maximize the total profit from an activity. If the marginal benefit from the activity is greater than the marginal cost, doing a bit more will increase that gain. If the marginal benefit is less than the marginal cost, doing a bit less will increase the total profit. So only when the *marginal* benefit and *marginal* cost are equal is the difference between *total* benefit and *total* cost at a maximum.

Graphically, the optimal quantity is the quantity of an activity at which the marginal benefit curve intersects the marginal cost curve. For example, in Figure 9-3 the marginal benefit and marginal cost curves cross each other at three years—that is, marginal benefit equals marginal cost at the choice of three additional years of schooling, which we have already seen is Alex's optimal quantity.

A straightforward application of marginal analysis explains why so many people went back to school in 2009 through 2011: in the depressed job market, the marginal cost of another year of school fell because the opportunity cost of forgone wages had fallen.

A straightforward application of marginal analysis can also explain many facts, such as why restaurant portion sizes in the United States are typically larger than those in other countries (as was just discussed in the Global Comparison).

A Principle with Many Uses

The profit-maximizing principle of marginal analysis can be applied to just about any "how much" decision in which you want to maximize the total profit for an activity. It is equally applicable to production decisions, consumption decisions, and policy decisions. Furthermore, decisions where the benefits and costs are not expressed in dollars and cents can also be made using marginal analysis (as long as benefits and costs can be measured in some type of common units). Table 9-7 includes three examples of decisions that are suitable for marginal analysis.

A Preview: How Consumption Decisions Are Different We've established that marginal analysis is an extraordinarily useful tool. It is used in "how much" decisions that are applied to both consumption choices and to profit maximization. Producers use it to make optimal production decisions at the margin and individuals use it to make optimal consumption decisions at the margin. But consumption decisions differ in form from production decisions. Why the difference? Because when individuals make choices, they face a limited amount of income. As a result, when they choose more of one good to consume (say, new clothes), they must choose less of another good (say, restaurant dinners).

In contrast, decisions that involve maximizing profit by producing a good or service—such as years of education or tons of wheat—are not affected by income limitations. For example, in Alex's case, he is not limited by income

---

TABLE 9-7 Making Decisions Using Marginal Analysis

The "how much" decision to be made	Applying marginal analysis	Arriving at the optimal quantity
The retailer PalMart must decide on the size of the new store it is constructing in Beijing.	PalMart must compare the marginal benefit of enlarging the store by 1 square foot (the value of the additional sales it makes from that additional square foot of floor space) to the marginal cost (the cost of constructing and maintaining the additional square foot).	The optimal store size for PalMart is the largest size at which marginal benefit is greater than or equal to marginal cost.
A physician must decide whether or not to increase the dosage of a drug in light of possible side effects.	The physician must consider the marginal cost, in terms of side effects, of increasing the dosage of a drug versus the marginal benefit of improving health by increasing the dosage.	The optimal dosage level is the largest level at which the marginal benefit of disease amelioration is greater than or equal to the marginal cost of side effects.
A farmer must decide how much fertilizer to apply.	More fertilizer increases crop yield but also costs more.	The optimal amount of fertilizer is the largest quantity at which the marginal benefit of higher crop yield is greater than or equal to the marginal cost of purchasing and applying more fertilizer.

because he can always borrow to pay for another year of school. In the next chapter we will see how consumption decisions differ from—yet are similar to—production decisions.

ECONOMICS ▶ in Action

The Cost of a Life

What's the marginal benefit to society of saving a human life? You might be tempted to answer that human life is infinitely precious. But in the real world, resources are scarce, so we must decide how much to spend on saving lives since we cannot spend infinite amounts. After all, we could surely reduce highway deaths by dropping the speed limit on interstates to 40 miles per hour, but the cost of a lower speed limit—in time and money—is more than most people are willing to pay.

Generally, people are reluctant to talk in a straightforward way about comparing the marginal cost of a life saved with the marginal benefit—it sounds too callous. Sometimes, however, the question becomes unavoidable.

For example, the cost of saving a life became an object of intense discussion in the United Kingdom after a horrible train crash near London's Paddington Station killed 31 people. There were accusations that the British government was spending too little on rail safety. However, the government estimated that improving rail safety would cost an additional $4.5 million per life saved. But if that amount was worth spending—that is, if the estimated marginal benefit of saving a life exceeded $4.5 million—then the implication was that the British government was spending far too little on traffic safety.

In contrast, the estimated marginal cost per life saved through highway improvements was only $1.5 million, making it a much better deal than saving lives through greater rail safety.

Check Your Understanding   9-2

1. For each of the "how much" decisions listed in Table 9-3, describe the nature of the marginal cost and of the marginal benefit.

2. Suppose that Alex's school charges a fixed fee of $70,000 for four years of schooling. If Alex drops out before he finishes those four years, he still has to pay the $70,000. Alex's total cost for different years of schooling is now given by the data in the accompanying table. Assume that Alex's total benefit and marginal benefit remain as reported in Table 9–5.

    Use this information to calculate (i) Alex's new marginal cost, (ii) his new profit, and (iii) his new optimal years of schooling. What kind of marginal cost does Alex now have—constant, increasing, or decreasing?

Quantity of schooling (years)	Total cost
0	$0
1	90,000
2	120,000
3	170,000
4	250,000
5	370,000

Solutions appear at back of book.

Sunk Costs

When making decisions, knowing what to ignore can be as important as what to include. Although we have devoted much attention in this chapter to costs that are important to take into account when making a decision, some costs should be ignored when doing so. We will now focus on the kinds of costs that people should ignore when making decisions—what economists call *sunk costs*—and why they should be ignored.

A **sunk cost** is a cost that has already been incurred and is nonrecoverable. A sunk cost should be ignored in decisions about future actions.

The $250 already spent on brake pads is irrelevant because it is a sunk cost.

To gain some intuition, consider the following scenario. You own a car that is a few years old, and you have just replaced the brake pads at a cost of $250. But then you find out that the entire brake system is defective and also must be replaced. This will cost you an additional $1,500. Alternatively, you could sell the car and buy another of comparable quality, but with no brake defects, by spending an additional $1,600. What should you do: fix your old car, or sell it and buy another?

Some might say that you should take the latter option. After all, this line of reasoning goes, if you repair your car, you will end up having spent $1,750: $1,500 for the brake system and $250 for the brake pads. If instead you sell your old car and buy another, you would spend only $1,600.

But this reasoning, although it sounds plausible, is wrong. It is wrong because it ignores the fact that you have *already* spent $250 on brake pads, and that $250 cannot be recovered. Therefore, it should be ignored and should have no effect on your decision whether or not to repair your car and keep it.

From a rational viewpoint, the real cost at this time of repairing and keeping your car is $1,500, not $1,750. So the correct decision is to repair your car and keep it rather than spend $1,600 on a new car.

In this example, the $250 that has already been spent and cannot be recovered is what economists call a **sunk cost.** Sunk costs should be ignored in making decisions about future actions because they have no influence on their actual costs and benefits. It's like the old saying, "There's no use crying over spilled milk": once something can't be recovered, it is irrelevant in making decisions about what to do in the future.

It is often psychologically hard to ignore sunk costs. And if, in fact, you haven't yet incurred the costs, then you should take them into consideration. That is, if you had known at the beginning that it would cost $1,750 to repair your car, then the right choice at that time would have been to buy a new car for $1,600. But once you have already paid the $250 for brake pads, you should no longer include it in your decision making about your next actions. It may be hard to accept that "bygones are bygones," but it is the right way to make a decision.

ECONOMICS ▶ *in Action*

A Billion Here, a Billion There . . .

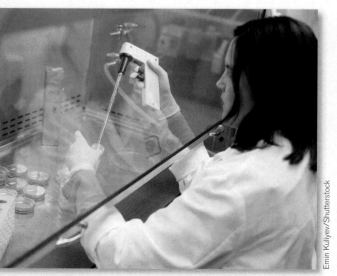

The biotech industry has been built on the premise that sunk costs don't matter.

If there is any industry that exemplifies the principle that sunk costs don't matter, it has to be the biotech industry. Biotech firms use cutting-edge bioengineering techniques to combat disease. But according to Arthur Levinson, chairman of Genentech, one of the largest and most successful biotech firms, biotechnology has been "one of the biggest money-losing industries in the history of mankind." He estimates that the industry has lost nearly $100 billion since 1976 (yes, that's "billion"). Of 241 publicly held American biotech firms, only 28 were profitable in 2012.

However, this is not a tale of incompetence, because the problem lies in the nature of the science. It takes about seven to eight years, on average, to develop and bring a new drug to the market. Moreover, there is a huge failure rate along the way, as only one in five drugs tested on humans ever makes it to market.

The company Xoma is a case in point: it has suffered setbacks on several drugs addressing diseases as varied as acne and complications from organ transplants. Since 1981, it has never earned a profit on one of its own drugs and has burned through nearly $1.1 billion dollars. Why does Xoma keep going? And, more importantly, why are investors willing to keep providing it with more money? It's because Xoma possesses a very promising technology and because shrewd investors understand the principle of sunk costs.

Check Your Understanding   9-3

1. You have decided to go into the ice-cream business and have bought a used ice-cream truck for $8,000. Now you are reconsidering. What is your sunk cost in the following scenarios?
   a. The truck cannot be resold.
   b. The truck can be resold, but only at a 50% discount.

2. You have gone through two years of medical school but are suddenly wondering whether you wouldn't be happier as a musician. Which of the following statements are potentially valid arguments and which are not?
   a. "I can't give up now, after all the time and money I've put in."
   b. "If I had thought about it from the beginning, I never would have gone to med school, so I should give it up now."
   c. "I wasted two years, but never mind—let's start from here."
   d. "My parents would kill me if I stopped now." (*Hint:* We're discussing your decision-making ability, not your parents'.)

Solutions appear at back of book.

Behavioral Economics

Most economic models assume that people make choices based on achieving the best possible economic outcome for themselves. Human behavior, however, is often not so simple. Rather than acting like economic computing machines, people often make choices that fall short—sometimes far short—of the greatest possible economic outcome, or payoff.

Why people sometimes make less-than-perfect choices is the subject of *behavioral economics*, a branch of economics that combines economic modeling with insights from human psychology. Behavioral economics grew out of economists' and psychologists' attempts to understand how people actually make—instead of theoretically make—economic choices.

It's well documented that people consistently engage in *irrational* behavior, choosing an option that leaves them worse off than other available options. Yet, as we'll soon learn, sometimes it's entirely *rational* for people to make a choice that is different from the one that generates the highest possible profit for themselves. For example, Ashley may decide to earn a teaching degree because she enjoys teaching more than advertising, even though the profit from the teaching degree is less than that from continuing with advertising.

The study of irrational economic behavior was largely pioneered by Daniel Kahneman and Amos Tversky. Kahneman won the 2002 Nobel Prize in economics for his work integrating insights from the psychology of human judgment and decision making into economics. Their work and the insights of others into why people often behave irrationally are having a significant influence on how economists analyze financial markets, labor markets, and other economic concerns.

Rational, but Human, Too

If you are **rational,** you will choose the available option that leads to the outcome you most prefer. But is the outcome you most prefer always the same as the one that gives you the best possible economic payoff? No. It can be entirely rational to choose an option that gives you a worse economic payoff because you care about

A **rational** decision maker chooses the available option that leads to the outcome he or she most prefers.

A decision maker operating with **bounded rationality** makes a choice that is close to but not exactly the one that leads to the best possible economic outcome.

Risk aversion is the willingness to sacrifice some economic payoff in order to avoid a potential loss.

An **irrational** decision maker chooses an option that leaves him or her worse off than choosing another available option.

something other than the size of the economic payoff. There are three principal reasons why people might prefer a worse economic payoff: concerns about fairness, bounded rationality, and risk aversion.

Concerns About Fairness In social situations, people often care about fairness as well as about the economic payoff to themselves. For example, no law requires you to tip a waiter or waitress. But concern for fairness leads most people to leave a tip (unless they've had outrageously bad service) because a tip is seen as fair compensation for good service according to society's norms. Tippers are reducing their own economic payoff in order to be fair to waiters and waitresses. A related behavior is gift-giving: if you care about another person's welfare, it's rational for you to lower your own economic payoff in order to give that person a gift.

Bounded Rationality Being an economic computing machine—choosing the option that gives you the best economic payoff—can require a fair amount of work: sizing up the options, computing the opportunity costs, calculating the marginal amounts, and so on. The mental effort required has its own opportunity cost. This realization led economists to the concept of **bounded rationality**— making a choice that is close to but not exactly the one that leads to the highest possible profit because the effort of finding the best payoff is too costly. In other words, bounded rationality is the "good enough" method of decision making.

Retailers are particularly good at exploiting their customers' tendency to engage in bounded rationality. For example, pricing items in units ending in 99¢ takes advantage of shoppers' tendency to interpret an item that costs, say, $2.99 as significantly cheaper than one that costs $3.00. Bounded rationality leads them to give more weight to the $2 part of the price (the first number they see) than the 99¢ part. And retailers also make use of shoppers' tendency to engage in what social scientists call *anchoring*, making decisions according to some perceived benchmark or reference point. For example, retailers attempt to influence shoppers' belief about whether they are getting a good deal by showing both the full price (the anchor) and the discounted price.

Risk Aversion Because life is uncertain and the future unknown, sometimes a choice comes with significant risk. Although you may receive a high payoff if things turn out well, the possibility also exists that things may turn out badly and leave you worse off.

So even if you think a choice will give you the best payoff of all your available options, you may forgo it because you find the possibility that things could turn out badly too, well, risky. This is called **risk aversion**—the willingness to sacrifice some potential economic payoff in order to avoid a potential loss. (We'll discuss risk in detail in Chapter 20.) Because risk makes most people uncomfortable, it's rational for them to give up some potential economic gain in order to avoid it. In fact, if it weren't for risk aversion, there would be no such thing as insurance.

Irrationality: An Economist's View

Sometimes, though, instead of being rational, people are **irrational**—they make choices that leave them worse off in terms of economic payoff *and* other considerations like fairness than if they had chosen another available option. Is there anything systematic that economists and psychologists can say about economically irrational behavior? Yes, because most people are irrational in predictable ways. People's irrational behavior *typically* stems from six mistakes they make when thinking about economic decisions. The mistakes are listed in Table 9-8, and we will discuss each in turn.

Misperceptions of Opportunity Costs As we discussed at the beginning of this chapter, people tend to ignore nonmonetary opportunity costs—opportunity costs that don't involve an outlay of cash. Likewise, a misperception of what exactly constitutes an opportunity cost (and what does not) is at the root of the tendency to count sunk costs in one's decision making. In this case, someone takes an opportunity cost into account when none actually exists.

Overconfidence It's a function of ego: we tend to think we know more than we actually do. And even if alerted to how widespread overconfidence is, people tend to think that it's someone else's problem, not theirs. (Certainly not yours or mine!)

TABLE 9-8	The Six Common Mistakes in Economic Decision Making
1. Misperceiving opportunity costs	
2. Being overconfident	
3. Having unrealistic expectations about future behavior	
4. Counting dollars unequally	
5. Being loss-averse	
6. Having a bias toward the status quo	

For example, a 1994 study asked students to estimate how long it would take them to complete their thesis "if everything went as well as it possibly could" and "if everything went as poorly as it possibly could." The results: the typical student thought it would take him or her 33.9 days to finish, with an average estimate of 27.4 days if everything went well and 48.6 days if everything went poorly. In fact, the average time it took to complete a thesis was much longer, 55.5 days. Students were, on average, from 14% to 102% more confident than they should have been about the time it would take to complete their thesis.

As you can see in the following For Inquiring Minds, overconfidence can cause problems with meeting deadlines. But it can cause far more trouble by having a strong adverse effect on people's financial health. Overconfidence often persuades people that they are in better financial shape than they actually are. It can also lead to bad investment and spending decisions. For example, nonprofessional investors who engage in a lot of speculative investing—such as quickly buying and selling stocks—on average have significantly worse results than professional brokers because of their misguided faith in their ability to spot a winner. Similarly, overconfidence can lead people to make a large spending decision, such

FOR INQUIRING MINDS | In Praise of Hard Deadlines

Dan Ariely, a professor of psychology and behavioral economics, likes to do experiments with his students that help him explore the nature of irrationality. In his book *Predictably Irrational,* Ariely describes an experiment that gets to the heart of procrastination and ways to address it.

At the time, Ariely was teaching the same subject matter to three different classes, but he gave each class different assignment schedules. The grade in all three classes was based on three equally weighted papers.

Students in the first class were required to choose their own personal deadlines for submitting each paper. Once set, the deadlines could not be changed. Late papers would be penalized at the rate of 1% of the grade for each day late. Papers could be turned in early without penalty but also without any advantage, since Ariely would not grade papers until the end of the semester.

Students in the second class could turn in the three papers whenever they

wanted, with no preset deadlines, as long as it was before the end of the term. Again, there would be no benefit for early submission.

Students in the third class faced what Ariely called the "dictatorial treatment." He established three hard deadlines at the fourth, eighth, and twelfth weeks.

So which classes do you think achieved the best and the worst grades? As it turned out, the class with the least flexible deadlines—the one that received the dictatorial treatment—got the best grades. The class with complete flexibility got the worst grades. And the class that got to choose its deadlines performed in the middle.

Ariely learned two simple things about overconfidence from these results. First—no surprise—students tend to procrastinate. Second, hard, equally spaced deadlines are the best cure for procrastination.

But the biggest revelation came from the class that set its own deadlines. The

majority of those students spaced their deadlines far apart and got grades as good as those of the students under the dictatorial treatment. Some, however, did not space their deadlines far enough apart, and a few did not space them out at all. These last two groups did less well, putting the average of the entire class below the average of the class with the least flexibility. As Ariely notes, without well-spaced deadlines, students procrastinate and the quality of their work suffers.

This experiment provides two important insights:

1. People who acknowledge their tendency to procrastinate are more likely to use tools for committing to a path of action.

2. Providing those tools allows people to make themselves better off.

If you have a problem with procrastination, hard deadlines, as irksome as they may be, are truly for your own good. ∎

Mental accounting is the habit of mentally assigning dollars to different accounts so that some dollars are worth more than others.

Loss aversion is an oversensitivity to loss, leading to unwillingness to recognize a loss and move on.

The **status quo bias** is the tendency to avoid making a decision and sticking with the status quo.

A dollar is a dollar, whether it's in your wallet or on your credit card.

as buying a car, without doing research on the pros and cons, relying instead on anecdotal evidence. Even worse, people tend to remain overconfident because they remember their successes, and explain away or forget their failures.

Unrealistic Expectations About Future Behavior Another form of overconfidence is being overly optimistic about your future behavior: tomorrow you'll study, tomorrow you'll give up ice cream, tomorrow you'll spend less and save more, and so on. Of course, as we all know, when tomorrow arrives, it's still just as hard to study or give up something that you like as it is right now.

Strategies that keep a person on the straight-and-narrow over time are often, at their root, ways to deal with the problem of unrealistic expectations about one's future behavior. Examples are automatic payroll deduction savings plans, diet plans with prepackaged foods, and mandatory attendance at study groups. By providing a way for someone to commit today to an action tomorrow, such plans counteract the habit of pushing difficult actions off into the future.

Counting Dollars Unequally If you tend to spend more when you pay with a credit card than when you pay with cash, particularly if you tend to splurge, then you are very likely engaging in **mental accounting.** This is the habit of mentally assigning dollars to different accounts, making some dollars worth more than others.

By spending more with a credit card, you are in effect treating dollars in your wallet as more valuable than dollars on your credit card balance, although in reality they count equally in your budget.

Credit card overuse is the most recognizable form of mental accounting. However, there are other forms as well, such as splurging after receiving a windfall, like an unexpected inheritance, or overspending at sales, buying something that seemed like a great bargain that you later regretted. It's the failure to understand that, regardless of the form it comes in, a dollar is a dollar.

Loss Aversion **Loss aversion** is an oversensitivity to loss, leading to an unwillingness to recognize a loss and move on. In fact, in the lingo of the financial markets, "selling discipline"—being able and willing to quickly acknowledge when a stock you've bought is a loser and sell it—is a highly desirable trait to have.

Many investors, though, are reluctant to acknowledge that they've lost money on a stock and won't make it back. Although it's rational to sell the stock at that point and redeploy the remaining funds, most people find it so painful to admit a loss that they avoid selling for much longer than they should. According to Daniel Kahneman and Amos Tversky, most people feel the misery of losing $100 about twice as keenly as they feel the pleasure of gaining $100.

Loss aversion can help explain why sunk costs are so hard to ignore: ignoring a sunk cost means recognizing that the money you spent is unrecoverable and therefore lost.

Status Quo Bias Another irrational behavior is **status quo bias,** the tendency to avoid making a decision altogether. A well-known example is the way that employees make decisions about investing in their employer-directed retirement accounts, known as 401(k)s. With a 401(k), employees can, through payroll deductions, set aside part of their salary tax-free, a practice that saves a significant amount of money every year in taxes. Some companies operate on an opt-in basis: employees have to actively choose to participate in a 401(k). Other companies operate on an opt-out basis: employees are automatically enrolled in a 401(k) unless they choose to opt out.

If everyone behaved rationally, then the proportion of employees enrolled in 401(k) accounts at opt-in companies would be roughly equal to the proportion enrolled at opt-out companies. In other words, your decision about whether to participate in a 401(k) should be independent of the default choice at your company. But, in reality, when companies switch to automatic enrollment and an opt-out system, employee enrollment rises dramatically. Clearly, people tend to just go with the status quo.

Why do people exhibit status quo bias? Some claim it's a form of "decision paralysis": when given many options, people find it harder to make a decision. Others claim it's due to loss aversion and the fear of regret, to thinking that "if I do nothing, then I won't have to regret my choice." Irrational, yes. But not altogether surprising. However, rational people know that, in the end, the act of not making a choice is still a choice.

Rational Models for Irrational People?

So why do economists still use models based on rational behavior when people are at times manifestly irrational? For one thing, models based on rational behavior still provide robust predictions about how people behave in most markets. For example, the great majority of farmers will use less fertilizer when it becomes more expensive—a result consistent with rational behavior.

Another explanation is that sometimes market forces can compel people to behave more rationally over time. For example, if you are a small-business owner who persistently exaggerates your abilities or refuses to acknowledge that your favorite line of items is a loser, then sooner or later you will be out of business unless you learn to correct your mistakes. As a result, it is reasonable to assume that when people are disciplined for their mistakes, as happens in most markets, rationality will win out over time.

Finally, economists depend on the assumption of rationality for the simple but fundamental reason that it makes modeling so much simpler. Remember that models are built on generalizations, and it's much harder to extrapolate from messy, irrational behavior. Even behavioral economists, in their research, search for *predictably* irrational behavior in an attempt to build better models of how people behave. Clearly, there is an ongoing dialogue between behavioral economists and the rest of the economics profession, and economics itself has been irrevocably changed by it.

ECONOMICS ▶ in Action

"The Jingle Mail Blues"

It's called jingle mail—when a homeowner seals the keys to his or her house in an envelope and leaves them with the bank that holds the mortgage on the house. (A mortgage is a loan taken out to buy a house.) By leaving the keys with the bank, the homeowner is walking away not only from the house but also from the obligation to continue paying the mortgage. And to their great consternation, banks have been flooded with jingle mail.

To default on a mortgage—that is, to walk away from one's obligation to repay the loan and lose the house to the bank in the process—used to be a fairly rare phenomenon. For decades, continually rising home values made homeownership a good investment for the typical household. In recent years, though, an entirely different phenomenon—called "strategic default"—has appeared. In a strategic default, a homeowner who is financially capable of paying the mortgage instead chooses not to, voluntarily walking away. Strategic defaults account for a significant proportion of jingle mail; in September 2010, they accounted for 36% of all

"Officer, that couple is walking away from their mortgage!"

foreclosures, up from 26 percent in 2009. And there is little indication that number will change dramatically: through 2013, 20% of all mortgages remained underwater with another 20% of homeowners barely above water.

What happened? After decades of huge increases, house prices began a precipitous fall in 2008, known as the Great American Housing Bust. Prices dropped so much that a significant proportion of homeowners found their homes "underwater"—they owed more on their homes than the homes were worth. And with house prices projected to stay depressed for several years, possibly a decade, there appeared to be little chance that an underwater house would recover its value enough in the foreseeable future to move "abovewater."

Many homeowners suffered a major loss. They lost their down payment, money spent on repairs and renovation, moving expenses, and so on. And because they were paying a mortgage that was greater than the house was now worth, they found they could rent a comparable dwelling for less than their monthly mortgage payments. In the words of a Florida resident, who paid $215,000 for an apartment in Miami where similar units were now selling for $90,000, "There is no financial sense in staying."

Realizing their losses were sunk costs, underwater homeowners walked away. Perhaps they hadn't made the best economic decision when purchasing their houses, but in leaving them showed impeccable economic logic.

▼ Quick Review

- Behavioral economics combines economic modeling with insights from human psychology.

- **Rational** behavior leads to the outcome a person most prefers. **Bounded rationality, risk aversion,** and concerns about fairness are reasons why people might prefer outcomes with worse economic payoffs.

- **Irrational** behavior occurs because of misperceptions of opportunity costs, overconfidence, **mental accounting,** and unrealistic expectations about the future. **Loss aversion** and **status quo bias** can also lead to choices that leave people worse off than they would be if they chose another available option.

Check Your Understanding 9-4

1. Which of the types of irrational behavior are suggested by the following events?
   a. Although the housing market has fallen and Jenny wants to move, she refuses to sell her house for any amount less than what she paid for it.
   b. Dan worked more overtime hours last week than he had expected. Although he is strapped for cash, he spends his unexpected overtime earnings on a weekend getaway rather than trying to pay down his student loan.
   c. Carol has just started her first job and deliberately decided to opt out of the company's savings plan. Her reasoning is that she is very young and there is plenty of time in the future to start saving. Why not enjoy life now?
   d. Jeremy's company requires employees to download and fill out a form if they want to participate in the company-sponsored savings plan. One year after starting the job, Jeremy had still not submitted the form needed to participate in the plan.

2. How would you determine whether a decision you made was rational or irrational?

Solutions appear at back of book.

J. C. Penney's One-Price Strategy Upsets Its Customers

In early 2013, the department store chain J. C. Penney unceremoniously dumped its recently hired chief executive, Ron Johnson. The action followed a disastrous 2012 for the company, in which sales dropped 25% to $13 billion. And it was a humbling defeat for Mr. Johnson's strategy of "everyday" low prices, implemented in early 2012.

A year before the one-price strategy was put into effect, the company held numerous sales, 590 of them in fact, and almost three-quarters of its goods were marked down 50% or more. Yet customers weren't actually paying less. The chain would just raise the prices of merchandise on the racks and then discount prices during the promotions. But why play an expensive game that is costly for the company and an illusion for customers?

So the new strategy seemed like a no-brainer for J. C. Penney. Rather than continue to promote sales and offer coupons, customers were now assured a low price at all times, regardless of the season and without clipping coupons.

The company reaped benefits from the strategy in the form of cost-savings from more accurate inventory and profit projections, from more consistent revenues, and by eliminating the need for manual labor to continually change prices. As John T. Gourville, a marketing professor at Harvard Business School, noted, a one-price pricing strategy "makes the operations side of things much easier. You don't have the whiplash effects of selling, say, a ton of Diet Coke one week and virtually none the next week."

But, there were problems with this pricing strategy as well. Just how low the prices were wasn't clear. "Trust us," was the message J. C. Penney communicated to its shoppers, "We will give you a fair deal." In addition, unlike Walmart, Penney did not offer to match competitors' prices, and it could not depend on making up for tiny per-item profits with a high volume of regular customers. Unlike Costco, it would not make money from annual membership fees. And a one-price strategy doesn't draw customers in during seasonal high-intensity shopping times, like Black Friday, when the holiday shopping season officially starts.

Mr. Johnson's strategy clearly alienated Tracie Fobes, who runs Penny Pinchin' Mom, a blog about couponing strategies, who said, ". . . seeing that something is marked down 20% off, then being able to hand over the coupon to save, it just entices me."

So with Johnson's departure, J. C. Penney backtracked and began offering coupons and weekly sales again. And the store assistants went back to work, marking items up in order to then immediately mark them down.

QUESTIONS FOR THOUGHT

1. Give an example of a type of rational decision making illustrated by this case and explain your choice.

2. Give an example of a type of irrational decision making illustrated by this case and explain your choice.

3. What purpose does Walmart's price-match guarantee serve? What do you predict would happen if it dropped this policy? Would you predict its competitors—say, the local supermarket or K-Mart—would adopt the same policy?

SUMMARY

1. All economic decisions involve the allocation of scarce resources. Some decisions are "either–or" decisions, in which the question is whether or not to do something. Other decisions are "how much" decisions, in which the question is how much of a resource to put into a given activity.

2. The cost of using a resource for a particular activity is the opportunity cost of that resource. Some opportunity costs are **explicit costs;** they involve a direct outlay of money. Other opportunity costs, however, are **implicit costs;** they involve no outlay of money but are measured by the dollar value of the benefits that are forgone. Both explicit and implicit costs should be taken into account in making decisions. Many decisions involve the use of **capital** and time, for both individuals and firms. So they should base decisions on **economic profit,** which takes into account implicit costs such as the opportunity cost of time and the **implicit cost of capital.** Making decisions based on **accounting profit** can be misleading. It is often considerably larger than the economic profit because it includes only explicit costs and not implicit costs.

3. According to the **principle of "either–or" decision making,** when faced with an "either–or" choice between two activities, one should choose the activity with the positive economic profit.

4. A "how much" decision is made using marginal analysis, which involves comparing the benefit to the cost of doing an additional unit of an activity. The **marginal cost** of producing a good or service is the additional cost incurred by producing one more unit of that good or service. The **marginal benefit** of producing a good or service is the additional benefit earned by producing one more unit. The **marginal cost curve** is the graphical illustration of marginal cost, and the **marginal benefit curve** is the graphical illustration of marginal benefit.

5. In the case of **constant marginal cost,** each additional unit costs the same amount to produce as the previous unit. However, marginal cost and marginal benefit typically depend on how much of the activity has already been done. With **increasing marginal cost,** each unit costs more to produce than the previous unit and is represented by an upward-sloping marginal cost curve. With **decreasing marginal cost,** each unit costs less to produce than the previous unit, leading to a downward-sloping marginal cost curve. In the case of **decreasing marginal benefit,** each additional unit produces a smaller benefit than the unit before.

6. The **optimal quantity** is the quantity that generates the highest possible total profit. According to the **profit-maximizing principle of marginal analysis,** the optimal quantity is the quantity at which marginal benefit is greater than or equal to marginal cost. It is the quantity at which the marginal cost curve and the marginal benefit curve intersect.

7. A cost that has already been incurred and that is nonrecoverable is a **sunk cost.** Sunk costs should be ignored in decisions about future actions because they have no effect on future benefits and costs.

8. With **rational** behavior, individuals will choose the available option that leads to the outcome they most prefer. **Bounded rationality** occurs because the effort needed to find the best economic payoff is costly. **Risk aversion** causes individuals to sacrifice some economic payoff in order to avoid a potential loss. People might also prefer outcomes with worse economic payoffs because they are concerned about fairness.

9. An **irrational** choice leaves someone worse off than if they had chosen another available option. It takes the form of misperceptions of opportunity cost; overconfidence; unrealistic expectations about future behavior; **mental accounting,** in which dollars are valued unequally; **loss aversion,** an oversensitivity to loss; and **status quo bias,** avoiding a decision by sticking with the status quo.

KEY TERMS

Explicit cost, p. 250
Implicit cost, p. 250
Accounting profit, p. 251
Economic profit, p. 252
Capital, p. 252
Implicit cost of capital, p. 253
Principle of "either–or" decision making, p. 253
Marginal cost, p. 256
Increasing marginal cost, p. 257

Marginal cost curve, p. 257
Constant marginal cost, p. 257
Decreasing marginal cost, p. 257
Marginal benefit, p. 258
Decreasing marginal benefit, p. 258
Marginal benefit curve, p. 258
Optimal quantity, p. 260
Profit-maximizing principle of marginal analysis, p. 261

Sunk cost, p. 264
Rational, p. 265
Bounded rationality, p. 266
Risk aversion, p. 266
Irrational, p. 266
Mental accounting, p. 268
Loss aversion. p. 268
Status quo bias, p. 268

PROBLEMS

1. Jackie owns and operates a website design business. To keep up with new technology, she spends $5,000 per year upgrading her computer equipment. She runs the business out of a room in her home. If she didn't use the room as her business office, she could rent it out for $2,000 per year. Jackie knows that if she didn't run her own business, she could return to her previous job at a large software company that would pay her a salary of $60,000 per year. Jackie has no other expenses.

   a. How much total revenue does Jackie need to make in order to break even in the eyes of her accountant? That is, how much total revenue would give Jackie an accounting profit of just zero?

   b. How much total revenue does Jackie need to make in order for her to want to remain self-employed? That is, how much total revenue would give Jackie an economic profit of just zero?

2. You own and operate a bike store. Each year, you receive revenue of $200,000 from your bike sales, and it costs you $100,000 to obtain the bikes. In addition, you pay $20,000 for electricity, taxes, and other expenses per year. Instead of running the bike store, you could become an accountant and receive a yearly salary of $40,000. A large clothing retail chain wants to expand and offers to rent the store from you for $50,000 per year. How do you explain to your friends that despite making a profit, it is too costly for you to continue running your store?

3. Suppose you have just paid a nonrefundable fee of $1,000 for your meal plan for this academic term. This allows you to eat dinner in the cafeteria every evening.

   a. You are offered a part-time job in a restaurant where you can eat for free each evening. Your parents say that you should eat dinner in the cafeteria anyway, since you have already paid for those meals. Are your parents right? Explain why or why not.

   b. You are offered a part-time job in a different restaurant where, rather than being able to eat for free, you receive only a large discount on your meals. Each meal there will cost you $2; if you eat there each evening this semester, it will add up to $200. Your roommate says that you should eat in the restaurant since it costs less than the $1,000 that you paid for the meal plan. Is your roommate right? Explain why or why not.

4. You have bought a $10 ticket in advance for the college soccer game, a ticket that cannot be resold. You know that going to the soccer game will give you a benefit equal to $20. After you have bought the ticket, you hear that there will be a professional baseball post-season game at the same time. Tickets to the baseball game cost $20, and you know that going to the baseball game will give you a benefit equal to $35. You tell your friends the following: "If I had known about the baseball game before buying the ticket to the soccer game, I would have gone to the baseball game instead. But now that I already have the ticket to the soccer game, it's better for me to just go to the soccer game." Are you making the correct decision? Justify your answer by calculating the benefits and costs of your decision.

5. Amy, Bill, and Carla all mow lawns for money. Each of them operates a different lawn mower. The accompanying table shows the total cost to Amy, Bill, and Carla of mowing lawns.

Quantity of lawns mowed	Amy's total cost	Bill's total cost	Carla's total cost
0	$0	$0	$0
1	20	10	2
2	35	20	7
3	45	30	17
4	50	40	32
5	52	50	52
6	53	60	82

   a. Calculate Amy's, Bill's, and Carla's marginal costs, and draw each of their marginal cost curves.

   b. Who has increasing marginal cost, who has decreasing marginal cost, and who has constant marginal cost?

6. You are the manager of a gym, and you have to decide how many customers to admit each hour. Assume that each customer stays exactly one hour. Customers are costly to admit because they inflict wear and tear on the exercise equipment. Moreover, each additional customer generates more wear and tear than the customer before. As a result, the gym faces increasing marginal cost. The accompanying table shows the marginal costs associated with each number of customers per hour.

Quantity of customers per hour	Marginal cost of customer
0	
	$14.00
1	
	14.50
2	
	15.00
3	
	15.50
4	
	16.00
5	
	16.50
6	
	17.00
7	

   a. Suppose that each customer pays $15.25 for a one-hour workout. Use the profit-maximizing principle of marginal analysis to find the optimal number of customers that you should admit per hour.

b. You increase the price of a one-hour workout to $16.25. What is the optimal number of customers per hour that you should admit now?

7. Georgia and Lauren are economics students who go to a karate class together. Both have to choose how many classes to go to per week. Each class costs $20. The accompanying table shows Georgia's and Lauren's estimates of the marginal benefit that each of them gets from each class per week.

Quantity of classes	Lauren's marginal benefit of each class	Georgia's marginal benefit of each class
0		
	$23	$28
1		
	19	22
2		
	14	15
3		
	8	7
4		

a. Use marginal analysis to find Lauren's optimal number of karate classes per week. Explain your answer.

b. Use marginal analysis to find Georgia's optimal number of karate classes per week. Explain your answer.

8. The Centers for Disease Control and Prevention (CDC) recommended against vaccinating the whole population against the smallpox virus because the vaccination has undesirable, and sometimes fatal, side effects. Suppose the accompanying table gives the data that are available about the effects of a smallpox vaccination program.

Percent of population vaccinated	Deaths due to smallpox	Deaths due to vaccination side effects
0%	200	0
10	180	4
20	160	10
30	140	18
40	120	33
50	100	50
60	80	74

a. Calculate the marginal benefit (in terms of lives saved) and the marginal cost (in terms of lives lost) of each 10% increment of smallpox vaccination. Calculate the net increase in human lives for each 10% increment in population vaccinated.

b. Using marginal analysis, determine the optimal percentage of the population that should be vaccinated.

9. Patty delivers pizza using her own car, and she is paid according to the number of pizzas she delivers. The accompanying table shows Patty's total benefit and total cost when she works a specific number of hours.

Quantity of hours worked	Total benefit	Total cost
0	$0	$0
1	30	10
2	55	21
3	75	34
4	90	50
5	100	70

a. Use marginal analysis to determine Patty's optimal number of hours worked.

b. Calculate the total profit to Patty from working 0 hours, 1 hour, 2 hours, and so on. Now suppose Patty chooses to work for 1 hour. Compare her total profit from working for 1 hour with her total profit from working the optimal number of hours. How much would she lose by working for only 1 hour?

10. Assume De Beers is the sole producer of diamonds. When it wants to sell more diamonds, it must lower its price in order to induce shoppers to buy more. Furthermore, each additional diamond that is produced costs more than the previous one due to the difficulty of mining for diamonds. De Beers's total benefit schedule is given in the accompanying table, along with its total cost schedule.

Quantity of diamonds	Total benefit	Total cost
0	$0	$0
1	1,000	50
2	1,900	100
3	2,700	200
4	3,400	400
5	4,000	800
6	4,500	1,500
7	4,900	2,500
8	5,200	3,800

a. Draw the marginal cost curve and the marginal benefit curve and, from your diagram, graphically derive the optimal quantity of diamonds to produce.

b. Calculate the total profit to De Beers from producing each quantity of diamonds. Which quantity gives De Beers the highest total profit?

11. In each of the following examples, explain whether the decision is rational or irrational. Describe the type of behavior exhibited.

a. Kookie's best friend likes to give her gift cards that Kookie can use at her favorite stores. Kookie, however, often forgets to use the cards before their expiration date or loses them. Kookie, though, is careful with her own cash.

b. In 2010, the Panera Bread company opened a store in Clayton, Missouri, that allowed customers to pay any amount they like for their orders; instead of prices, the store listed suggested donations based on the cost of the goods. All profits went to a charitable foundation set up by Panera. In 2011, the store was pleased with the success of the program.

c. Rick has just gotten his teaching degree and has two job offers. One job, replacing a teacher who has gone on leave, will last only two years. It is at a prestigious high school, and he will be paid $35,000 per year. He thinks he will probably be able to find another good job in the area after the two years are up but isn't sure. The other job, also at a high school, pays $25,000 per year and is virtually guaranteed for five years; after those five years, he will be evaluated for a permanent teaching position at the school. About 75% of the teachers who start at the school are hired for permanent positions. Rick takes the five-year position at $25,000 per year.

d. Kimora has planned a trip to Florida during spring break in March. She has several school projects due after her return. Rather than do them in February, she figures she can take her books with her to Florida and complete her projects there.

e. Sahir overpaid when buying a used car that has turned out to be a lemon. He could sell it for parts, but instead he lets it sit in his garage and deteriorate.

f. Barry considers himself an excellent investor in stocks. He selects new stocks by finding ones with characteristics similar to those of his previous winning stocks. He chocks up losing trades to ups and downs in the macroeconomy.

12. You have been hired as a consultant by a company to develop the company's retirement plan, taking into account different types of predictably irrational behavior commonly displayed by employees. State at least two types of irrational behavior employees might display with regard to the retirement plan and the steps you would take to forestall such behavior.

WORK IT OUT

For interactive, step-by-step help in solving the following problem, visit LaunchPad by using the URL on the back cover of this book.

13. Hiro owns and operates a small business that provides economic consulting services. During the year he spends $57,000 on travel to clients and other expenses. In addition, he owns a computer that he uses for business. If he didn't use the computer, he could sell it and earn yearly interest of $100 on the money created through this sale. Hiro's total revenue for the year is $100,000. Instead of working as a consultant for the year, he could teach economics at a small local college and make a salary of $50,000.

   a. What is Hiro's accounting profit?

   b. What is Hiro's economic profit?

   c. Should Hiro continue working as a consultant, or should he teach economics instead?

How to Make Decisions Involving Time: Understanding Present Value

As we learned in Chapter 9, the basic rule to follow when deciding whether or not to undertake a project is to compare the benefits of the project with its costs—explicit as well as implicit—and choose the course of action with the higher economic profit.

But many economic decisions involve choices in which the benefits and the costs arrive at different times, making comparisons between those choices more difficult. Ashley's decision, whether to go back to school and get an advanced degree or to get a job, is one of those types of comparisons. If she chooses to get an advanced degree, the costs—forgone wages, tuition, and books—are incurred immediately, while the benefits—higher earnings—are reaped in the future. In other cases, the benefits of a project come earlier than the costs, such as taking out a loan to pay for a vacation that must be repaid in the future. So how should we make decisions when time is a factor?

The economically correct way is to use a concept called *present value*. Using present value calculations allows you to convert costs and/or benefits that arrive in the future into a value today. This way, we can always compare projects that occur over time by comparing their values today. You might wonder why you didn't see present value calculations when we analyzed Ashley's decision in Chapter 9. The fact is that present value was used, but implicitly. For example, statements like "she will receive earnings from her degree valued today at $600,000 over the rest of her lifetime" mean that the future benefits had already been converted into a value today—that value being $600,000.

Now let's see exactly how present value works.

How to Calculate the Present Value of a One-Year Project

Suppose that you will graduate exactly one year from today and you will need $1,000 to rent your first apartment. In order to have $1,000 one year from now, how much do you need today? It's not $1,000, and the reason why has to do with the *interest rate*. The **interest rate,** which we will denote by r, is the price charged a borrower for borrowing money expressed as a percentage of the amount borrowed. And let's use X to denote the amount you need today in order to have $1,000 one year from now. If you put X in the bank today and earn an interest rate r on it, then after one year the bank will pay you $X \times (1 + r)$. If the amount paid to you by the bank one year from now is $1,000, then the amount you need to deposit with the bank today is given by the following equation:

(9A-1) $X \times (1 + r) = \$1,000$

You can apply some basic algebra to find that:

(9A-2) $X = \$1,000/(1 + r)$

When someone borrows money for a year, the **interest rate** is the price, calculated as a percentage of the amount borrowed, charged by the lender.

The **present value** of X is the amount of money needed today in order to receive X at a future date given the interest rate.

So the amount you need today to be assured of having $1,000 one year from now, X, is equal to $1,000 divided by $(1 + r)$. Notice that the value of X depends on the interest rate, r, which is always greater than zero. This fact implies that X is *always less than $1,000*. For example, if $r = 5\%$ (that is, $r = 0.05$), then $X = \$1,000/1.05 = \$952.38$. In other words, $952.38 is the value today of receiving $1,000 one year from now given an interest rate of 5%.

Now we can define the **present value** of X: it is the amount of money needed today in order to receive X in the future given the interest rate. In this example, $952.38 if the present value of $1,000 today given an interest rate of 5%.

The concept of present value is very useful when making decisions that require paying upfront costs now for benefits that arrive in the future. Say you had two options, A and B: the choice of taking a one-year job that pays $10,000 immediately (option A) or taking a one-year course that costs $1,000 now but allows you to earn a one-time payment of $12,000 one year from now (option B). Which one should you take?

On the one hand, the present value of option A is simply $10,000 because you receive its payoff immediately. On the other hand, the present value of option B, with an interest rate of 5%, is:

(9A-3) $\$12,000/1.05 - \$1,000 = \$11,429 - \$1,000 = \$10,429$

Since the present value of option B ($10,429) is greater than the present value of option A ($10,000), you should choose option B.

This example illustrates a general principle: when evaluating choices where the costs and/or benefits arrive over time, make your choice by converting the payoffs into their present values and choose the one with the highest present value. Next we will see how to use present value when projects have a time span of more than one year.

How to Calculate the Present Value of Multiyear Projects

Let's represent the value of $1 to be received two years from now as $X_{2\text{yrs}}$. If you lend out $X_{2\text{yrs}}$ today for two years, you will receive:

(9A-4) $X_{2\text{yrs}} \times (1 + r)$ at the end of one year

which you then reinvest to receive:

(9A-5) $X_{2\text{yrs}} \times (1 + r) \times (1 + r) = X_{2\text{yrs}} \times (1 + r)^2$ at the end of two years

From Equation 9A-5 we can calculate how much you would have to lend today in order to receive $1 two years from now:

(9A-6) $X_{2\text{yrs}} (1 + r)^2 = \$1$

To solve for $X_{2\text{yrs}}$, divide both sides of Equation 9A-6 by $(1 + r)^2$ to arrive at:

(9A-7) $X_{2\text{yrs}} = \$1/(1 + r)^2$

For example, if $r = 0.10$, then $X_{2\text{yrs}} = \$1/(1.10)^2 = \$1/1.21 = \$0.83$.

Equation 9A-7 points the way toward the general expression for present value, where $1 is paid after N years. It is

(9A-8) $X_{N\text{yrs}} = \$1/(1 + r)^N$

In other words, the present value of $1 to be received N years from now is equal to $$1/(1 + r)^N$.

How to Calculate the Present Value of Projects with Revenues and Costs

Now let's suppose you have to choose which one of three projects to undertake. Project A gives you an immediate payoff of $100. Project B costs you $10 now and pays $115 a year from now. Project C gives you an immediate payoff of $119 but requires you to pay $20 a year from now. We will assume that $r = 0.10$.

In order to compare these three projects, you must evaluate costs and revenues that are expended or realized at different times. It is here, of course, that the concept of present value is extremely handy: by using present value to convert any dollars realized in the future into today's value, you can factor out differences in time. Once differences in time are factored out, you can compare the three projects by calculating each one's *net present value*, the present value of current and future revenues minus the present value of current and future costs. The best project to undertake is the one with the highest net present value.

Table 9A-1 shows how to calculate the net present value of each of the three projects. The second and third columns show how many dollars are realized and when they are realized; costs are indicated by a minus sign. The fourth column shows the equations used to convert the flows of dollars into their present value, and the fifth column shows the actual amounts of the total net present value for each of the three projects.

TABLE 9A-1   The Net Present Value of Three Hypothetical Projects

Project	Dollars realized today	Dollars realized one year from today	Present value formula	Net present value given $r = 0.10$
A	$100	—	$100	$100.00
B	−$10	$115	−$10 + $115/(1 + r)	$94.55
C	$119	−$20	$119 − $20/(1 + r)	$100.82

For instance, to calculate the net present value of project B, you need to calculate the present value of $115 received one year from now. The present value of $1 received one year from now is $$1/(1 + r)$. So the present value of $115 received one year from now is $115 \times $1/(1 + r) = $115/(1 + r)$. The net present value of project B is the present value of current and future revenues minus the present value of current and future costs: $−$10 + $115/(1 + r)$.

From the fifth column, we can immediately see that, at an interest rate of 10%, project C is the best project. It has the highest net present value, $100.82, which is higher than the net present value of project A ($100) and much higher than the net present value of project B ($94.55).

This example shows how important the concept of present value is. If we had failed to use the present value calculations and had instead simply added up the revenues and costs, we would have been misled into believing that project B was the best project and C was the worst one.

KEY TERMS

Interest rate, p. 277
Present value, p. 278

PROBLEMS

1. Suppose that a major city's main thoroughfare, which is also an interstate highway, will be completely closed to traffic for two years, from January 2014 to December 2015, for reconstruction at a cost of $535 million. If the construction company were to keep the highway open for traffic during construction, the highway reconstruction project would take much longer and be more expensive. Suppose that construction would take four years if the highway were kept open, at a total cost of $800 million. The state department of transportation had to make its decision in 2013, one year before the start of construction (so that the first payment was one year away). So the department of transportation had the following choices:

   (i) Close the highway during construction, at an annual cost of $267.5 million per year for two years.

   (ii) Keep the highway open during construction, at an annual cost of $200 million per year for four years.

   a. Suppose the interest rate is 10%. Calculate the present value of the costs incurred under each plan. Which reconstruction plan is less expensive?

   b. Now suppose the interest rate is 80%. Calculate the present value of the costs incurred under each plan. Which reconstruction plan is now less expensive?

2. You have won the state lottery. There are two ways in which you can receive your prize. You can either have $1 million in cash now, or you can have $1.2 million that is paid out as follows: $300,000 now, $300,000 in one year's time, $300,000 in two years' time, and $300,000 in three years' time. The interest rate is 20%. How would you prefer to receive your prize?

3. The drug company Pfizer is considering whether to invest in the development of a new cancer drug. Development will require an initial investment of $10 million now; beginning one year from now, the drug will generate annual profits of $4 million for three years.

   a. If the interest rate is 12%, should Pfizer invest in the development of the new drug? Why or why not?

   b. If the interest rate is 8%, should Pfizer invest in the development of the new drug? Why or why not?

The Rational Consumer

THE ABSOLUTE LAST BITE

craftvision/Getty Images

When is more of a good thing too much?

RESTAURANTS OCCASIONALLY offer "all-you-can-eat" specials to entice customers: all-you-can-eat salad bars, all-you-can-eat breakfast buffets, and all-you-can-eat fried-clam dinners.

But how can a restaurant owner who offers such a special be sure he won't be eaten out of business? If he charges $12.99 for an all-you-can-eat clam dinner, what prevents his average customer from wolfing down $30 worth of clams?

The answer is that even though every once in a while you see someone really take advantage of the offer—heaping a plate high with 30 or 40 fried clams—it's a rare occurrence. And even those of us who like fried clams shudder a bit at the sight. Five or even 10 fried clams can be a treat, but 30 clams is ridiculous. Anyone who pays for an all-you-can-eat

meal wants to make the most of it, but a sensible person knows when one more bite would be one bite too many.

Notice that last sentence. We said that customers in a restaurant want to "make the most" of their meal; that sounds as if they are trying to maximize something. And we also said that they will stop when consuming one more bite would be a mistake; they are making a marginal decision.

But it is a marginal decision that also involves a person's tastes. While economists can't say much about where tastes come from, they can say a lot about how a rational individual uses marginal analysis to satisfy his or her tastes. And that is in fact the way that economists think about consumer choice. They work with a model of a *rational consumer*—a consumer who knows what he or she

wants and makes the most of the available opportunities.

In this chapter, we will show how to analyze the decisions of a rational consumer. We will begin by showing how the concept of *utility*—a measure of consumer satisfaction—allows us to think about rational consumer choice.

We will then look at how *budget constraints* determine what a consumer can afford to buy and how marginal analysis can be used to determine the consumption choice that maximizes utility.

Finally, we will see how this analysis can be used to understand the law of demand and why the demand curve slopes downward.

For those interested in a more detailed treatment of consumer behavior and coverage of indifference curves, see the appendix that follows this chapter.

The **utility** of a consumer is a measure of the satisfaction the consumer derives from consumption of goods and services.

An individual's **consumption bundle** is the collection of all the goods and services consumed by that individual.

An individual's **utility function** gives the total utility generated by his or her consumption bundle.

A **util** is a unit of utility.

Utility: Getting Satisfaction

When analyzing consumer behavior, we're talking about people trying to get satisfaction—that is, about subjective feelings. Yet there is no simple way to measure subjective feelings. How much satisfaction do I get from my third fried clam? Is it less or more than yours? Does it even make sense to ask the question?

Luckily, we don't need to make comparisons between your feelings and mine. All that is required to analyze consumer behavior is to suppose that each individual is trying to maximize some personal measure of the satisfaction gained from consumption of goods and services. That measure is known as the consumer's **utility,** a concept we use to understand behavior but don't expect to measure in practice. Nonetheless, we'll see that the assumption that consumers maximize utility helps us think clearly about consumer choice.

Utility and Consumption

An individual's utility depends on everything that individual consumes, from apples to Ziploc bags. The set of all the goods and services an individual consumes is known as the individual's **consumption bundle.** The relationship between an individual's consumption bundle and the total amount of utility it generates for that individual is known as the **utility function.** The utility function is a personal matter; two people with different tastes will have different utility functions. Someone who actually likes to consume 40 fried clams in a sitting must have a utility function that looks different from that of someone who would rather stop at 5 clams.

So we can think of consumers as using consumption to "produce" utility, much in the same way as in later chapters we will think of producers as using inputs to produce output. However, it's obvious that people do not have a little computer in their heads that calculates the utility generated by their consumption choices. Nonetheless, people must make choices, and they usually base them on at least a rough attempt to decide which choice will give them greater satisfaction. I can have either soup or salad with my dinner. Which will I enjoy more? I can go to Disney World this year or save the money toward buying a new car. Which will make me happier?

The concept of a utility function is just a way of representing the fact that when people consume, they take into account their preferences and tastes in a more or less rational way.

How do we measure utility? For the sake of simplicity, it is useful to suppose that we can measure utility in hypothetical units called—what else?—**utils.**

Figure 10-1 illustrates a utility function. It shows the total utility that Cassie, who likes fried clams, gets from an all-you-can-eat clam dinner. We suppose that her consumption bundle consists of a side of coleslaw, which comes with the meal, plus a number of clams to be determined. The table that accompanies the figure shows how Cassie's total utility depends on the number of clams; the curve in panel (a) of the figure shows that same information graphically.

Cassie's utility function slopes upward over most of the range shown, but it gets flatter as the number of clams consumed increases. And in this example it eventually turns downward. According to the information in the table in Figure 10-1, nine clams is a clam too many. Adding that additional clam actually makes Cassie worse off: it would lower her total utility. If she's rational, of course, Cassie will realize that and not consume the ninth clam.

So when Cassie chooses how many clams to consume, she will make this decision by considering the *change* in her total utility from consuming one more clam. This illustrates the general point: to maximize *total* utility, consumers must focus on *marginal* utility.

FIGURE **10-1**   Cassie's Total Utility and Marginal Utility

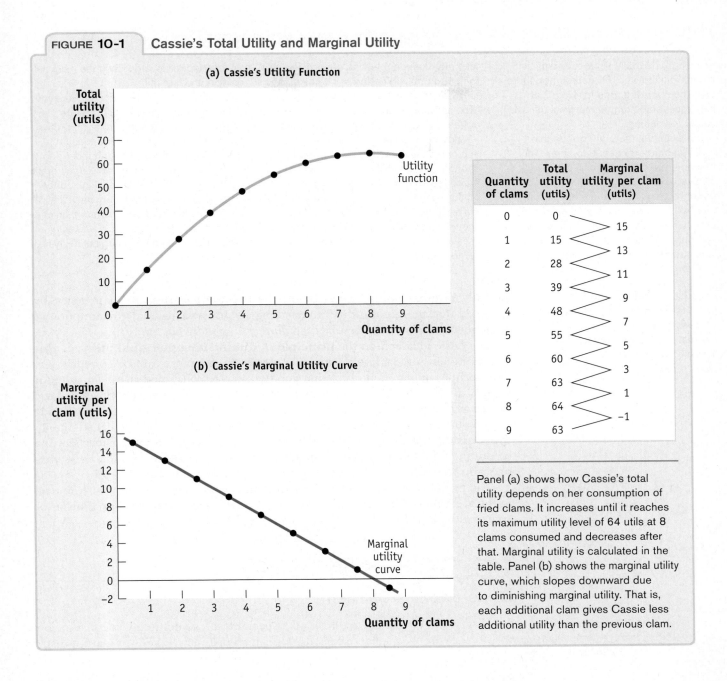

(a) Cassie's Utility Function

(b) Cassie's Marginal Utility Curve

Quantity of clams	Total utility (utils)	Marginal utility per clam (utils)
0	0	
		15
1	15	
		13
2	28	
		11
3	39	
		9
4	48	
		7
5	55	
		5
6	60	
		3
7	63	
		1
8	64	
		−1
9	63	

Panel (a) shows how Cassie's total utility depends on her consumption of fried clams. It increases until it reaches its maximum utility level of 64 utils at 8 clams consumed and decreases after that. Marginal utility is calculated in the table. Panel (b) shows the marginal utility curve, which slopes downward due to diminishing marginal utility. That is, each additional clam gives Cassie less additional utility than the previous clam.

The Principle of Diminishing Marginal Utility

In addition to showing how Cassie's total utility depends on the number of clams she consumes, the table in Figure 10-1 also shows the **marginal utility** generated by consuming each additional clam—that is, the *change* in total utility from consuming one additional clam. Panel (b) shows the implied **marginal utility curve.** Following our practice in Chapter 9 with the marginal benefit curve, the marginal utility curve is constructed by plotting points at the midpoint of the unit intervals.

The marginal utility curve slopes downward: each successive clam adds less to total utility than the previous clam. This is reflected in the table: marginal utility falls from a high of 15 utils for the first clam consumed to −1 for the ninth clam consumed. The fact that the ninth clam has negative marginal utility means that consuming it actually reduces total utility. (Restaurants that offer all-you-can-eat meals depend on the proposition that you can have too much of a good thing.)

The **marginal utility** of a good or service is the change in total utility generated by consuming one additional unit of that good or service. The **marginal utility curve** shows how marginal utility depends on the quantity of a good or service consumed.

FOR INQUIRING MINDS | Is Marginal Utility Really Diminishing?

Are all goods really subject to diminishing marginal utility? Of course not; there are a number of goods for which, at least over some range, marginal utility is surely *increasing*.

For example, there are goods that require some experience to enjoy. The first time you do it, downhill skiing involves a lot more fear than enjoyment—or so they say: the authors have never tried it! It only becomes a pleasurable activity if you do it enough to become reasonably competent. And even some less strenuous forms of consumption take practice; people who are not accustomed to drinking coffee say it has a bitter taste and can't understand its appeal. (The authors, on the other hand, regard coffee as one of the basic food groups.)

Another example would be goods that only deliver positive utility if you buy enough. The great Victorian economist Alfred Marshall, who more or less invented the supply and demand model, gave the example of wallpaper: buying only enough to do half a room is worse than useless. If you need two rolls of wallpaper to finish a room, the marginal utility of the second roll is larger than the marginal utility of the first roll.

So why does it make sense to assume diminishing marginal utility? For one thing, most goods don't suffer from these qualifications: nobody needs to learn to like ice cream. Also, although most people don't ski and some people don't drink coffee, those who do ski or drink coffee do enough of it that the marginal utility of one more ski run or one more cup is less than that of the last. So *in the relevant range* of consumption, marginal utility is still diminishing. ■

According to the **principle of diminishing marginal utility,** each successive unit of a good or service consumed adds less to total utility than the previous unit.

Not all marginal utility curves eventually become negative. But it is generally accepted that marginal utility curves do slope downward—that consumption of most goods and services is subject to *diminishing marginal utility.*

The basic idea behind the **principle of diminishing marginal utility** is that the additional satisfaction a consumer gets from one more unit of a good or service declines as the amount of that good or service consumed rises. Or, to put it slightly differently, the more of a good or service you consume, the closer you are to being satiated—reaching a point at which an additional unit of the good adds nothing to your satisfaction. For someone who almost never gets to eat a banana, the occasional banana is a marvelous treat. (This was the case in Eastern Europe before the fall of communism, when bananas were very hard to find.) For someone who eats them all the time, a banana is just, well, a banana.

The principle of diminishing marginal utility isn't always true. But it is true in the great majority of cases, enough to serve as a foundation for our analysis of consumer behavior.

ECONOMICS ▶ *in Action*

Oysters versus Chicken

How much utility would you get from eating one more oyster?

I s a particular food a special treat, something you consume on special occasions? Or is it an ordinary, take-it-or-leave-it dish? The answer depends a lot on how much of that food people normally consume, which determines how much utility they get *at the margin* from having a bit more.

Consider chicken. Modern Americans eat a lot of chicken, so much that they regard it as nothing special. Yet this was not always the case. Traditionally chicken was a luxury dish because chickens were expensive to raise. Restaurant menus from two centuries ago show chicken dishes as the most expensive items listed. As recently as 1928, Herbert Hoover ran for president on the slogan "A chicken in every pot," a promise to voters of great prosperity if he was elected.

What changed the status of chicken was the emergence of new, technologically advanced methods for raising and processing the birds. These methods made chicken abundant, cheap, and also—thanks to the principle of diminishing marginal utility—nothing to get excited about.

SARYMSAKOV ANDREY/Shutterstock

The reverse evolution took place for oysters. Not everyone likes oysters or, for that matter, has ever tried them—they are definitely not ordinary food. But they are regarded as a delicacy by some; at restaurants that serve them, an oyster appetizer often costs more than the main course.

Yet oysters were once very cheap and abundant—and were regarded as poverty food. In *The Pickwick Papers* by Charles Dickens, published in the 1830s, the author remarks that "poverty and oysters always seem to go together."

What changed? Pollution, which destroyed many oyster beds, greatly reduced the supply, while human population growth greatly increased the demand. As a result, thanks to the principle of diminishing marginal utility, oysters went from being a common food, regarded as nothing special, to being a highly prized luxury good.

Check Your Understanding   10-1

1. Explain why a rational consumer who has diminishing marginal utility for a good would not consume an additional unit when it generates negative marginal utility, even when that unit is free.

2. Marta drinks three cups of coffee a day, for which she has diminishing marginal utility. Which of her three cups generates the greatest increase in total utility? Which generates the least?

3. In each of the following cases, determine if the consumer experiences diminishing marginal utility. Explain your answer.
   a. The more Mabel exercises, the more she enjoys each additional visit to the gym.
   b. Although Mei's classical music collection is huge, her enjoyment from buying another album has not changed as her collection has grown.
   c. When Dexter was a struggling student, his enjoyment from a good restaurant meal was greater than now, when he has them more frequently.

Solutions appear at back of book.

Budgets and Optimal Consumption

The principle of diminishing marginal utility explains why most people eventually reach a limit, even at an all-you-can-eat buffet where the cost of another clam is measured only in future indigestion. Under ordinary circumstances, however, it costs some additional resources to consume more of a good, and consumers must take that cost into account when making choices.

What do we mean by cost? As always, the fundamental measure of cost is *opportunity cost*. Because the amount of money a consumer can spend is limited, a decision to consume more of one good is also a decision to consume less of some other good.

Budget Constraints and Budget Lines

Consider Sammy, whose appetite is exclusively for clams and potatoes (there's no accounting for tastes). He has a weekly income of $20 and since, given his appetite, more of either good is better than less, he spends all of it on clams and potatoes. We will assume that clams cost $4 per pound and potatoes cost $2 per pound. What are his possible choices?

Whatever Sammy chooses, we know that the cost of his consumption bundle cannot exceed his income, the amount of money he has to spend. That is,

(10-1) Expenditure on clams + Expenditure on potatoes ≤ Total income

Consumers always have limited income, which constrains how much they can consume. So the requirement illustrated by Equation 10-1—that a consumer

A **budget constraint** requires that the cost of a consumer's consumption bundle be no more than the consumer's income.

A consumer's **consumption possibilities** is the set of all consumption bundles that can be consumed given the consumer's income and prevailing prices.

A consumer's **budget line** shows the consumption bundles available to a consumer who spends all of his or her income.

must choose a consumption bundle that costs no more than his or her income—is known as the consumer's **budget constraint.** It's a simple way of saying that a consumer can't spend more than the total amount of income available to him or her. In other words, consumption bundles are affordable when they obey the budget constraint. We call the set of all of Sammy's affordable consumption bundles his **consumption possibilities.** In general, whether or not a particular consumption bundle is included in a consumer's consumption possibilities depends on the consumer's income and the prices of goods and services.

Figure 10-2 shows Sammy's consumption possibilities. The quantity of clams in his consumption bundle is measured on the horizontal axis and the quantity of potatoes on the vertical axis. The downward-sloping line connecting points A through F shows which consumption bundles are affordable and which are not. Every bundle on or inside this line (the shaded area) is affordable; every bundle outside this line is unaffordable.

As an example of one of the points, let's look at point C, representing 2 pounds of clams and 6 pounds of potatoes, and check whether it satisfies Sammy's budget constraint. The cost of bundle C is 6 pounds of potatoes × $2 per pound + 2 pounds of clams × $4 per pound = $12 + $8 = $20. So bundle C does indeed satisfy Sammy's budget constraint: it costs no more than his weekly income of $20. In fact, bundle C costs exactly as much as Sammy's income. By doing the arithmetic, you can check that all the other points lying on the downward-sloping line are also bundles at which Sammy spends all of his income.

The downward-sloping line has a special name, the **budget line.** It shows all the consumption bundles available to Sammy when he spends all of his income.

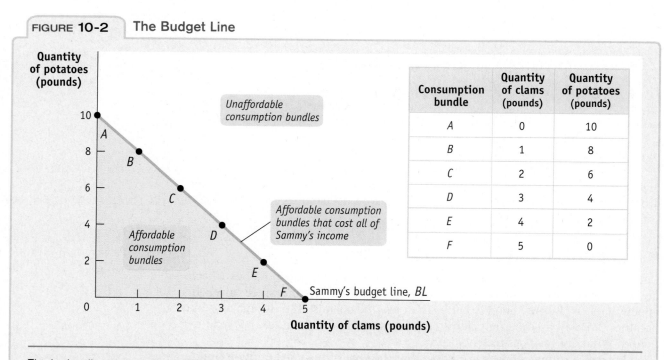

FIGURE 10-2   The Budget Line

Consumption bundle	Quantity of clams (pounds)	Quantity of potatoes (pounds)
A	0	10
B	1	8
C	2	6
D	3	4
E	4	2
F	5	0

The *budget line* represents the consumption bundles available to Sammy when he spends all of his income. Also, it is the boundary between the set of affordable consumption bundles (the *consumption possibilities*) and unaffordable ones. Given that clams cost $4 per pound and potatoes cost $2 per pound, if Sammy spends all of his income on clams (bundle F), he can purchase 5 pounds of clams. If he spends all of his income on potatoes (bundle A), he can purchase 10 pounds of potatoes.

It's downward sloping because when Sammy is consuming all of his income, say consuming at point A on the budget line, then in order to consume more clams he must consume fewer potatoes—that is, he must move to a point like *B*. In other words, when Sammy chooses a consumption bundle that is on his budget line, the opportunity cost of consuming more clams is consuming fewer potatoes, and vice versa. As Figure 10-2 indicates, any consumption bundle that lies above the budget line is unaffordable.

Do we need to consider the other bundles in Sammy's consumption possibilities, the ones that lie *within* the shaded region in Figure 10-2 bounded by the budget line? The answer is, for all practical situations, no: as long as Sammy continues to get positive marginal utility from consuming either good (in other words, Sammy doesn't get *satiated*)—and he doesn't get any utility from saving income rather than spending it, then he will always choose to consume a bundle that lies on his budget line and not within the shaded area.

Given his $20 per week budget, which point on his budget line will Sammy choose?

A consumer's **optimal consumption bundle** is the consumption bundle that maximizes the consumer's total utility given his or her budget constraint.

Optimal Consumption Choice

Because Sammy has a budget constraint, which means that he will consume a consumption bundle on the budget line, a choice to consume a given quantity of clams also determines his potato consumption, and vice versa. We want to find the consumption bundle—the point on the budget line—that maximizes Sammy's total utility. This bundle is Sammy's **optimal consumption bundle,** the consumption bundle that maximizes his total utility given the budget constraint.

Table 10-1 shows how much utility Sammy gets from different levels of consumption of clams and potatoes, respectively. According to the table, Sammy has a healthy appetite; the more of either good he consumes, the higher his utility.

But because he has a limited budget, he must make a trade-off: the more pounds of clams he consumes, the fewer pounds of potatoes, and vice versa. That is, he must choose a point on his budget line.

TABLE 10-1   Sammy's Utility from Clam and Potato Consumption

Utility from clam consumption		Utility from potato consumption	
Quantity of clams (pounds)	Utility from clams (utils)	Quantity of potatoes (pounds)	Utility from potatoes (utils)
0	0	0	0
1	15	1	11.5
2	25	2	21.4
3	31	3	29.8
4	34	4	36.8
5	36	5	42.5
		6	47.0
		7	50.5
		8	53.2
		9	55.2
		10	56.7

Table 10-2 shows how his total utility varies for the different consumption bundles along his budget line. Each of six possible consumption bundles, *A* through *F* from Figure 10-2, is given in the first column. The second column shows the level of clam consumption corresponding to each choice. The third column shows the utility Sammy gets from consuming those clams. The fourth column shows the quantity of potatoes Sammy can afford *given* the level of clam consumption; this quantity goes down as his clam consumption goes up, because he is sliding down the budget line. The fifth column shows the utility he gets from consuming those potatoes. And the final column shows his *total utility*. In this example, Sammy's total utility is the sum of the utility he gets from clams and the utility he gets from potatoes.

TABLE 10-2   Sammy's Budget and Total Utility

Consumption bundle	Quantity of clams (pounds)	Utility from clams (utils)	Quantity of potatoes (pounds)	Utility from potatoes (utils)	Total utility (utils)
A	0	0	10	56.7	56.7
B	1	15	8	53.2	68.2
C	2	25	6	47.0	72.0
D	3	31	4	36.8	67.8
E	4	34	2	21.4	55.4
F	5	36	0	0	36.0

Figure 10-3 gives a visual representation of the data shown in Table 10-2. Panel (a) shows Sammy's budget line, to remind us that when he decides to consume more clams he is also deciding to consume fewer potatoes. Panel (b) then shows how his total utility depends on that choice. The horizontal axis in panel (b) has two sets of labels: it shows both the quantity of clams, increasing from left to right, and the quantity of potatoes, increasing from right to left.

The reason we can use the same axis to represent consumption of both goods is, of course, the budget line: the more pounds of clams Sammy consumes, the fewer pounds of potatoes he can afford, and vice versa.

Clearly, the consumption bundle that makes the best of the trade-off between clam consumption and potato consumption, the optimal consumption bundle, is the one that maximizes Sammy's total utility. That is, Sammy's optimal consumption bundle puts him at the highest point of the total utility curve.

As always, we can find the highest point of the curve by direct observation. We can see from Figure 10-3 that Sammy's total utility is maximized at point *C*—that his optimal consumption bundle contains 2 pounds of clams and 6 pounds of potatoes. But we know that we usually gain more insight into "how much" problems when we use marginal analysis. So in the next section we turn to representing and solving the optimal consumption choice problem with marginal analysis.

FOR INQUIRING MINDS | Food for Thought on Budget Constraints

Budget constraints aren't just about money. In fact, there are many other budget constraints affecting our lives. You face a budget constraint if you have a limited amount of closet space for your clothes. All of us face a budget constraint on time: there are only so many hours in the day.

And people trying to lose weight on the Weight Watchers plan face a budget constraint on the foods they eat.

The Weight Watchers plan assigns each food a certain number of points. A 4-ounce scoop of premium ice cream is 8 points, a slice of cheese pizza with a medium crust is 7 points, and a cup of grapes is zero points. You are allowed a maximum number of points each day but are free to choose which foods you eat.

In other words, a dieter on the Weight Watchers plan is just like a consumer choosing a consumption bundle: points are the equivalent of prices, and the overall point limit is the equivalent of total income. ■

FIGURE **10-3**   Optimal Consumption Bundle

Panel (a) shows Sammy's budget line and his six possible consumption bundles. Panel (b) shows how his total utility is affected by his consumption bundle, which must lie on his budget line. The quantity of clams is measured from left to right on the horizontal axis, and the quantity of potatoes is measured from right to left. His total utility is maximized at bundle C, the highest point on his utility function, where he consumes 2 pounds of clams and 6 pounds of potatoes. This is Sammy's *optimal consumption bundle.*

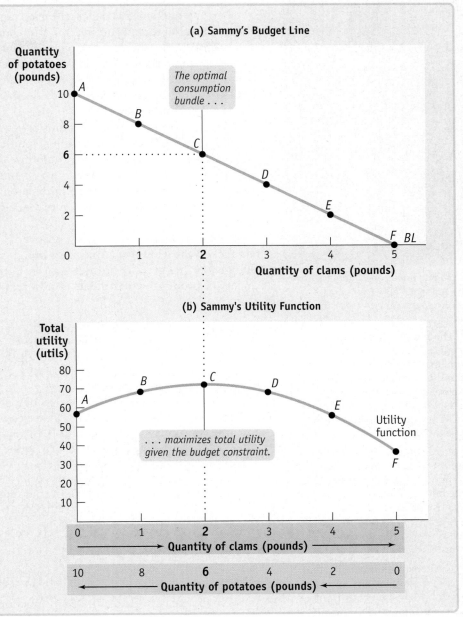

ECONOMICS ▶ in Action

The Great Condiment Craze

Those of us of a certain age remember when the only kind of mustard available in American grocery stores was a runny, fluorescent yellow concoction packaged in plastic squeeze bottles. Ditto for ketchup and mayonnaise—what little selection there was, tasted the same. As for salsa—wasn't that some sort of dance step?

No longer. Americans have developed an intense liking for condiments—in a dizzying array of varieties. Who wants plain mustard when you can get mustard flavored with roasted garlic, apricot, or even bourbon/molasses? Likewise, would you like saffron and garlic mayonnaise or sriracha mayonnaise on your

Changing tastes and budgets drove the American condiment craze.

club sandwich? And sales of salsa in the United States have long since overtaken ketchup sales.

So what happened? Tastes changed and budgets changed. Spurred by the severe recession that began in 2007, more budget-minded consumers ate at home. But having been exposed to gourmet cooking and ethnic cuisine, they sought ways to spice up their home cooking. Unsurprisingly, then, the onset of the recession coincided with an increase of condiment sales of 5.6% in 2008 and 6.2% in 2009. By 2012, U.S. condiment sales reached $9.7 billion, and have been forecast to reach $10.7 billion by 2017.

The explosion of varieties stems from the fact that it's fairly easy to make bottled condiments. This enables smaller companies to experiment with exotic flavors, finding the ones that appeal to consumers' increasingly sophisticated tastes. Eventually, the flavors that attract a significant following are picked up by the larger companies such as Kraft. As one industry analyst put it, "People want cheaper, more specialized gourmet products. It's like fashion."

As the economy has slowly recovered in recent years, restaurant dining has picked up. However, American home cooking appears to have been forever changed by the great condiment craze. Consumers continue to purchase a wide variety of premium condiments to add zest to their home-cooked meals.

▼ Quick Review

• The **budget constraint** requires that a consumer's total expenditure be no more than his or her income. The set of consumption bundles that satisfy the budget constraint is the consumer's **consumption possibilities.**

• A consumer who spends all of his or her income chooses a point on his or her **budget line.** The budget line slopes downward because on the budget line a consumer must consume less of one good in order to consume more of another.

• The consumption choice that maximizes total utility given the consumer's budget constraint is the **optimal consumption bundle.** It must lie on the consumer's budget line.

Check Your Understanding 10-2

1. In the following two examples, find all the consumption bundles that lie on the consumer's budget line. Illustrate these consumption possibilities in a diagram and draw the budget line through them.
   a. The consumption bundle consists of movie tickets and buckets of popcorn. The price of each ticket is $10.00, the price of each bucket of popcorn is $5.00, and the consumer's income is $20.00. In your diagram, put movie tickets on the vertical axis and buckets of popcorn on the horizontal axis.
   b. The consumption bundle consists of underwear and socks. The price of each pair of underwear is $4.00, the price of each pair of socks is $2.00, and the consumer's income is $12.00. In your diagram, put pairs of socks on the vertical axis and pairs of underwear on the horizontal axis.

Solutions appear at back of book.

Spending the Marginal Dollar

As we've just seen, we can find Sammy's optimal consumption choice by finding the total utility he receives from each consumption bundle on his budget line and then choosing the bundle at which total utility is maximized. But we can use marginal analysis instead, turning Sammy's problem of finding his optimal consumption choice into a "how much" problem.

How do we do this? By thinking about choosing an optimal consumption bundle as a problem of *how much to spend on each good.* That is, to find the optimal consumption bundle with marginal analysis, we ask whether Sammy can make himself better off by spending a little bit more of his income on clams and less on potatoes, or by doing the opposite—spending a little bit more on potatoes and less on clams. In other words, the marginal decision is a question of how to *spend the marginal dollar*—how to allocate an additional dollar between clams and potatoes in a way that maximizes utility.

Our first step in applying marginal analysis is to ask if Sammy is made better off by spending an additional dollar on either good; and if so, by how much is he better off. To answer this question we must calculate the **marginal utility per dollar** spent on either clams or potatoes—how much additional utility Sammy gets from spending an additional dollar on either good.

The **marginal utility per dollar** spent on a good or service is the additional utility from spending one more dollar on that good or service.

Marginal Utility per Dollar

We've already introduced the concept of marginal utility, the additional utility a consumer gets from consuming one more unit of a good or service; now let's see how this concept can be used to derive the related measure of marginal utility per dollar.

Table 10-3 shows how to calculate the marginal utility per dollar spent on clams and potatoes, respectively.

In panel (a) of the table, the first column shows different possible amounts of clam consumption. The second column shows the utility Sammy derives from each amount of clam consumption; the third column then shows the marginal utility, the increase in utility Sammy gets from consuming an additional pound of clams. Panel (b) provides the same information for potatoes. The next step is to derive marginal utility *per dollar* for each good. To do this, we must divide the marginal utility of the good by its price in dollars.

To see why we must divide by the price, compare the third and fourth columns of panel (a). Consider what happens if Sammy increases his clam consumption from 2 pounds to 3 pounds. As we can see, this increase in clam consumption raises his total utility by 6 utils. But he must spend $4 for that additional pound, so the increase in his utility per additional dollar spent on clams is 6 utils/$4 = 1.5 utils per dollar.

Similarly, if he increases his clam consumption from 3 pounds to 4 pounds, his marginal utility is 3 utils but his marginal utility per dollar is 3 utils/$4 = 0.75 util per dollar. Notice that because of diminishing marginal utility, Sammy's marginal utility per pound of clams falls as the quantity of clams he consumes rises. As a result, his marginal utility per dollar spent on clams also falls as the quantity of clams he consumes rises.

So the last column of panel (a) shows how Sammy's marginal utility per dollar spent on clams depends on the quantity of clams he consumes. Similarly, the last column of panel (b) shows how his marginal utility per dollar spent on potatoes depends on the quantity of potatoes he consumes. Again, marginal utility per

TABLE 10-3   Sammy's Marginal Utility per Dollar

(a) Clams (price of clams = $4 per pound)				(b) Potatoes (price of potatoes = $2 per pound)			
Quantity of clams (pounds)	Utility from clams (utils)	Marginal utility per pound of clams (utils)	Marginal utility per dollar (utils)	Quantity of potatoes (pounds)	Utility from potatoes (utils)	Marginal utility per pound of potatoes (utils)	Marginal utility per dollar (utils)
0	0			0	0		
		15	3.75			11.5	5.75
1	15			1	11.5		
		10	2.50			9.9	4.95
2	25			2	21.4		
		6	1.50			8.4	4.20
3	31			3	29.8		
		3	0.75			7.0	3.50
4	34			4	36.8		
		2	0.50			5.7	2.85
5	36			5	42.5		
						4.5	2.25
				6	47.0		
						3.5	1.75
				7	50.5		
						2.7	1.35
				8	53.2		
						2.0	1.00
				9	55.2		
						1.5	0.75
				10	56.7		

dollar spent on each good declines as the quantity of that good consumed rises, because of diminishing marginal utility.

We will use the symbols MU_C and MU_P to represent the marginal utility per pound of clams and potatoes, respectively. And we will use the symbols P_C and P_P to represent the price of clams (per pound) and the price of potatoes (per pound). Then the marginal utility per dollar spent on clams is MU_C/P_C and the marginal utility per dollar spent on potatoes is MU_P/P_P. In general, the additional utility generated from an additional dollar spent on a good is equal to:

(10-2) Marginal utility per dollar spent on a good
= Marginal utility of one unit of the good/Price of one unit of the good
= MU_{Good}/P_{Good}

Now let's see how this concept helps us derive a consumer's optimal consumption using marginal analysis.

Optimal Consumption

Let's consider Figure 10-4. As in Figure 10-3, we can measure both the quantity of clams and the quantity of potatoes on the horizontal axis due to the budget constraint. Along the horizontal axis of Figure 10-4—also as in Figure 10-3—the quantity of clams increases as you move from left to right, and the quantity of potatoes increases as you move from right to left. The curve labeled MU_C/P_C in Figure 10-4 shows Sammy's marginal utility per dollar spent on clams as derived in Table 10-3. Likewise, the curve labeled MU_P/P_P shows his marginal utility per dollar spent on potatoes. Notice that the two curves, MU_C/P_C and MU_P/P_P, cross at the optimal consumption bundle, point C, consisting of 2 pounds of clams and 6 pounds of potatoes.

Moreover, Figure 10-4 illustrates an important feature of Sammy's optimal consumption bundle: when Sammy consumes 2 pounds of clams and 6 pounds of potatoes, his marginal utility per dollar spent is the same, 2, for both goods. That is, at the optimal consumption bundle $MU_C/P_C = MU_P/P_P = 2$.

This isn't an accident. Consider another one of Sammy's possible consumption bundles—say, B in Figure 10-3, at which he consumes 1 pound of clams and 8 pounds of potatoes. The marginal utility per dollar spent on each good is shown by points B_C and B_P in Figure 10-4. At that consumption bundle, Sammy's marginal utility per dollar spent on clams would be approximately 3,

PITFALLS

THE RIGHT MARGINAL COMPARISON Marginal analysis solves "how much" decisions by weighing costs and benefits at the margin: the *benefit* of doing a little bit more versus the *cost* of doing a little bit more. However, as we noted in Chapter 9, the form of the marginal analysis can differ, depending upon whether you are making a production decision that maximizes profits or a consumption decision that maximizes utility. Let's review that difference again to make sure that it's clearly understood.

In Chapter 9, Alex's decision was a production decision because the problem he faced was maximizing the profit from years of schooling. The optimal

quantity of years that maximized his profit was found using marginal analysis: at the optimal quantity, the marginal benefit of another year of schooling was equal to its marginal cost. Alex did not face a budget constraint because he could always borrow to finance another year of school.

But if you were to extend the way we solved Alex's production problem to Sammy's consumption problem without any change in form, you might be tempted to say that Sammy's optimal consumption bundle is the one at which the marginal utility of clams is equal to the marginal utility of potatoes, or that the marginal utility of clams was equal to the

price of clams. But both those statements would be wrong because they don't properly account for the budget constraint and the fact that consuming more of one good requires consuming less of another.

In a consumption decision, your objective is to maximize the utility that your limited budget can deliver. And the right way to find the optimal consumption bundle is to set the *marginal utility per dollar* equal for each good in the consumption bundle. When this condition is satisfied, the "bang per buck" is the same across all the goods and services you consume. Only then is there no way to rearrange your consumption and get more utility from your budget.

FIGURE 10-4 | Marginal Utility per Dollar

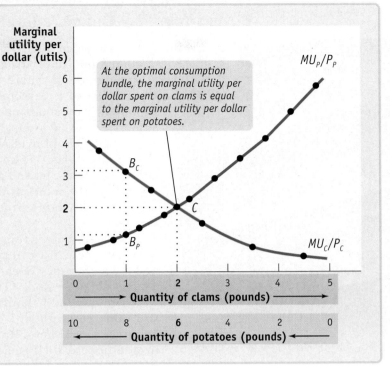

Sammy's optimal consumption bundle is at point *C*, where his marginal utility per dollar spent on clams, MU_C/P_C, is equal to his marginal utility per dollar spent on potatoes, MU_P/P_P. This illustrates the *utility-maximizing principle of marginal analysis:* at the optimal consumption bundle, the marginal utility per dollar spent on each good and service is the same. At any other consumption bundle on Sammy's budget line, such as bundle *B* in Figure 10-3, represented here by points B_C and B_P, consumption is not optimal: Sammy can increase his utility at no additional cost by reallocating his spending.

At the optimal consumption bundle, the marginal utility per dollar spent on clams is equal to the marginal utility per dollar spent on potatoes.

but his marginal utility per dollar spent on potatoes would be only approximately 1. This shows that he has made a mistake: he is consuming too many potatoes and not enough clams.

How do we know this? If Sammy's marginal utility per dollar spent on clams is higher than his marginal utility per dollar spent on potatoes, he has a simple way to make himself better off while staying within his budget: spend $1 less on potatoes and $1 more on clams. We can illustrate this with points B_C and B_P in Figure 10-4. By spending an additional dollar on clams, he gains the amount of utility given by B_C, about 3 utils. By spending $1 less on potatoes, he loses the amount of utility given by B_P, only about 1 util.

Because his marginal utility per dollar spent is higher for clams than for potatoes, reallocating his spending toward clams and away from potatoes would increase his total utility. But if his marginal utility per dollar spent on potatoes is higher, he can increase his utility by spending less on clams and more on potatoes. So if Sammy has in fact chosen his optimal consumption bundle, his marginal utility per dollar spent on clams and potatoes must be equal.

This is a general principle, which we call the **utility-maximizing principle of marginal analysis:** when a consumer maximizes utility in the face of a budget constraint, the marginal utility per dollar spent on each good or service in the consumption bundle is the same. That is, for any two goods *C* and *P* the optimal consumption rule says that at the optimal consumption bundle:

(10-3) $\dfrac{MU_C}{P_C} = \dfrac{MU_P}{P_P}$

It's easiest to understand this rule using examples in which the consumption bundle contains only two goods, but it applies no matter how many goods or services a consumer buys: in the optimal consumption bundle, the marginal utilities per dollar spent for each and every good or service in that bundle are equal.

According to the **utility-maximizing principle of marginal analysis,** the marginal utility per dollar spent must be the same for all goods and services in the optimal consumption bundle.

ECONOMICS ▶ *in Action*

Buying Your Way Out of Temptation

For many consumers, paying extra for portion control is worth it.

It might seem odd to pay more to get less. But snack food companies have discovered that consumers are indeed willing to pay more for smaller portions, and exploiting this trend is a recipe for success. A company executive explained why small packages are popular—they help consumers eat less without having to count calories themselves. "The irony," said David Adelman, a food industry analyst, "is if you take Wheat Thins or Goldfish, buy a large-size box, count out the items and put them in a Ziploc bag, you'd have essentially the same product." He estimates that snack packs are about 20% more profitable for snack makers than larger packages.

It's clear that in this case consumers are making a calculation: the extra utility gained from not having to worry about whether they've eaten too much is worth the extra cost. As one shopper said, "They're pretty expensive, but they're worth it. It's individually packaged for the amount I need, so I don't go overboard." So it's clear that consumers aren't being irrational here. Rather, they're being entirely rational: in addition to their snack, they're buying a little hand-to-mouth restraint.

▼ Quick Review

• According to the **utility-maximizing principle of marginal analysis,** the **marginal utility per dollar**—the marginal utility of a good divided by its price—is the same for all goods in the optimal consumption bundle.

• Whenever marginal utility per dollar is higher for one good than for another good, the consumer should spend $1 more on the good with the higher marginal utility per dollar and $1 less on the other. By doing this the consumer will move closer to his or her optimal consumption bundle.

Check Your Understanding | 10-3

1. In Table 10-3 you can see that marginal utility per dollar spent on clams and marginal utility per dollar spent on potatoes are equal when Sammy increases his consumption of clams from 3 pounds to 4 pounds and his consumption of potatoes from 9 pounds to 10 pounds. Explain why this is not Sammy's optimal consumption bundle. Illustrate your answer using the budget line in Figure 10-3.

2. Explain what is faulty about the following statement, using data from Table 10-3: "In order to maximize utility, Sammy should consume the bundle that gives him the maximum marginal utility per dollar for each good."

Solutions appear at back of book.

From Utility to the Demand Curve

We have now analyzed the optimal consumption choice of a consumer with a given amount of income who faces one particular set of prices—in our Sammy example, $20 of income per week, $4 per pound of clams, and $2 per pound of potatoes.

But the main reason for studying consumer behavior is to go behind the market demand curve—to explain how the utility-maximizing behavior of individual consumers leads to the downward slope of the market demand curve.

Marginal Utility, the Substitution Effect, and the Law of Demand

Suppose that the price of fried clams, P_C, rises. The price increase doesn't change the marginal utility a consumer gets from an additional pound of clams, MU_C, at any given level of clam consumption. However, it does reduce the marginal utility *per dollar spent* on fried clams, MU_C/P_C. And the decrease in marginal utility per dollar spent on clams gives the consumer an incentive to consume fewer clams when the price of clams rises.

To see why, recall the utility-maximizing principle of marginal analysis: a utility-maximizing consumer chooses a consumption bundle for which the marginal utility per dollar spent on all goods is the same. If the marginal utility per dollar spent on clams falls because the price of clams rises, the consumer can increase his or her utility by purchasing fewer clams and more of other goods.

The opposite happens if the price of clams falls. In that case the marginal utility per dollar spent on clams, MU_C/P_C, increases at any given level of clam consumption. As a result, a consumer can increase her utility by purchasing more clams and less of other goods when the price of clams falls.

So when the price of a good increases, an individual will normally consume less of that good and more of other goods. Correspondingly, when the price of a good decreases, an individual will normally consume more of that good and less of other goods. This explains why the individual demand curve, which relates an individual's consumption of a good to the price of that good, normally slopes downward—that is, it obeys the law of demand. And since—as we learned in Chapter 3—the market demand curve is the horizontal sum of all the individual demand curves of consumers, it, too, will slope downward.

An alternative way to think about why demand curves slope downward is to focus on opportunity costs. When the price of clams decreases, an individual doesn't have to give up as many units of other goods in order to buy one more unit of clams. So consuming clams becomes more attractive. Conversely, when the price of a good increases, consuming that good becomes a less attractive use of resources, and the consumer buys less.

This effect of a price change on the quantity consumed is always present. It is known as the **substitution effect**—the change in the quantity consumed as the consumer substitutes other goods that are now relatively cheaper in place of the good that has become relatively more expensive. When a good absorbs only a small share of the consumer's spending, the substitution effect is essentially the complete explanation of why the individual demand curve of that consumer slopes downward. And, by implication, when a good absorbs only a small share of the typical consumer's spending, the substitution effect is essentially the sole explanation of why the market demand curve slopes downward.

However, some goods, such as housing, absorb a large share of a typical consumer's spending. For such goods, the story behind the individual demand curve and the market demand curve becomes slightly more complicated.

The Income Effect

For the vast majority of goods, the substitution effect is pretty much the entire story behind the slopes of the individual and market demand curves. There are, however, some goods, like food or housing, that account for a substantial share of many consumers' spending. In such cases another effect, called the *income effect*, also comes into play.

Consider the case of a family that spends half its income on rental housing. Now suppose that the price of housing increases everywhere. This will have a substitution effect on the family's demand: other things equal, the family will have an incentive to consume less housing—say, by moving to a smaller apartment—and more of other goods. But the family will also, in a real sense, be made poorer by that higher housing price—its income will buy less housing than before.

The amount of income adjusted to reflect its true purchasing power is often termed "real income," in contrast to "money income" or "nominal income," which has not been adjusted. And this reduction in a consumer's real income will have an additional effect, beyond the substitution effect, on the family's consumption bundle, including its consumption of housing.

The change in the quantity of a good consumed that results from a change in the overall purchasing power of the consumer due to a change in the price of that good is known as the **income effect** of the price change. In this case, a change

The **substitution effect** of a change in the price of a good is the change in the quantity of that good consumed as the consumer substitutes other goods that are now relatively cheaper in place of the good that has become relatively more expensive.

The **income effect** of a change in the price of a good is the change in the quantity of that good consumed that results from a change in the consumer's purchasing power due to the change in the price of the good.

A **Giffen good** is a hypothetical inferior good for which the income effect outweighs the substitution effect and the demand curve slopes upward.

in the price of a good effectively changes a consumer's income because it alters the consumer's purchasing power. Along with the substitution effect, the income effect is another means by which changes in prices alter consumption choices.

It's possible to give more precise definitions of the substitution effect and the income effect of a price change, and we do this in the appendix to this chapter. For most purposes, however, there are only two things you need to know about the distinction between these two effects.

First, for the great majority of goods and services, the income effect is not important and has no significant effect on individual consumption. So most market demand curves slope downward solely because of the substitution effect—end of story.

Second, when it matters at all, the income effect usually reinforces the substitution effect. That is, when the price of a good that absorbs a substantial share of income rises, consumers of that good become a bit poorer because their purchasing power falls. As we learned in Chapter 3, the vast majority of goods are *normal goods,* goods for which demand decreases when income falls. So this effective reduction in income leads to a reduction in the quantity demanded and reinforces the substitution effect.

However, in the case of an *inferior good,* a good for which demand increases when income falls, the income and substitution effects work in opposite directions. Although the substitution effect tends to produce a decrease in the quantity of any good demanded as its price increases, in the case of an inferior good the income effect of a price increase tends to produce an *increase* in the quantity demanded.

As a result, there are hypothetical cases involving inferior goods in which the distinction between income and substitution effects is important. The most extreme example of this distinction is a **Giffen good,** a good that has an upward-sloping demand curve.

The classic story used to describe a Giffen good harks back to nineteenth-century Ireland, when it was a desperately poor country and a large portion of a typical household's diet consisted of potatoes. *Other things equal,* an increase in the price of potatoes would have led people to reduce their demand for potatoes. But other things were not equal: for the nineteenth-century Irish, a higher price of potatoes would have left them poorer and increased their demand for potatoes because potatoes were an inferior good.

If the income effect of a price increase outweighs the substitution effect—as was conjectured for potatoes in nineteenth-century Ireland—a rise in price leads to an increase in the quantity demanded. As a result, the demand curve slopes upward and the law of demand does not hold.

In theory, Giffen goods can exist; but they have never been validated in any real situation, nineteenth-century Ireland included. So as a practical matter, it's not a subject we need to worry about when discussing the demand for most goods. Typically, income effects are important only for a very limited number of goods.

ECONOMICS ▶ in Action

Mortgage Rates and Consumer Demand

Most people buy houses with mortgages—loans backed by the value of the house. The interest rates on such mortgages change over time; for example, from 2000 through 2003 interest rates fell by 3.3% and remained at record low levels through 2008. The decline in interest rates was a primary factor in the housing bubble that occurred over the same time period. When mortgage rates fall, the cost of housing falls for millions of people—even people who have mortgages at high interest rates are often able to "refinance" them at lower rates. The large fall in interest rates corresponded with a large increase in homeownership rates through the United States. The percentage of American households who owned their home increased from 67.1% in 2000 to a historical high of 69.2% in 2004. Homeownership rates remained well above 68% until the housing market collapsed in 2007.

It's not surprising that the demand for housing goes up when mortgage rates go down. Economists have noticed, however, that the demand for many other goods also rises when mortgage rates fall. Some of these goods are items connected with new or bigger houses, such as furniture. But people also buy new cars, eat more meals in restaurants, and take more vacations. Why?

The answer illustrates the distinction between substitution and income effects. When housing becomes cheaper, there is a *substitution effect:* people have an incentive to substitute housing or other goods in their consumption bundle. But housing also happens to be a good that absorbs a large part of consumer spending, with many families spending a quarter or more of their income on mortgage payments. So when the price of housing falls, people are in effect richer—there is a significant *income effect.*

Demand for housing goes up when mortgage rates go down. But so does the demand for exotic vacations.

The increase in the quantity of housing demanded when mortgage rates fall is the result of both effects: housing becomes a better buy compared with other consumer goods, and people also buy more and bigger houses because they feel richer. From 2000 through 2007 the average size of a new American home grew by nearly 250 square feet. And because they feel richer, people also buy more of all other normal goods, such as cars, restaurant meals, and vacations. Over the same time period there was a 20% increase in airplane departures, and Americans spent an additional 35% on eating out and entertainment.

Check Your Understanding   10-4

1. In each of the following cases, state whether the income effect, the substitution effect, or both are significant. In which cases do they move in the same direction? In opposite directions? Why?
   a. Orange juice represents a small share of Clare's spending. She buys more lemonade and less orange juice when the price of orange juice goes up. She does not change her spending on other goods.
   b. Apartment rents have risen dramatically this year. Since rent absorbs a major part of her income, Delia moves to a smaller apartment. Assume that rental housing is a normal good.
   c. The cost of a semester-long meal ticket at the student cafeteria rises, representing a significant increase in living costs. Assume that cafeteria meals are an inferior good.

2. In the example described in Question 1c, how would you determine whether or not cafeteria meals are a Giffen good?

Solutions appear at back of book.

Having a Happy Meal at McDonald's

In 2013, McDonald's agreed to stop featuring and promoting soda as a beverage option for its Happy Meals. It was the latest step in McDonald's efforts to make its standard child's Happy Meal more healthful. For example, in 2011 McDonald's changed its standard Happy Meal to include a quarter cup of apple slices and fewer french fries, and removed its caramel sauce, thereby lowering the salt, sugar, fat, and calorie content. To be sure, healthier options had always been available: a parent could ask for fruit or milk instead of fries or soda. But most people opted for the standard meal by default. According to restaurant analyst Peter Saleh, "This is good publicity, and if you sell more Happy Meals, you're selling more Big Macs to the parents."

The changes are meant to help offset long-standing criticism of the company for the lack of nutritional balance in its menu and address concerns over the growing epidemic of childhood obesity. Critics contend that at around 600 calories, Happy Meals are still too calorie rich for small children. Long-time observers say that more than just countering its critics, McDonald's is trying to hold onto a loyal customer base: Happy Meals accounted for an estimated 10% of its annual sales, or close to $9 billion in 2013. And although its rivals, such as Burger King and Wendy's, followed McDonald's lead by offering healthier kids' meals, McDonald's consistently sells more kids' meals than the competition.

McDonald's has, in fact, been amazingly successful at keeping its customers happy even in a tough environment. In 2009, at the lowest point of the recession that began in 2007, sales at full-service restaurants fell more than 6% but stayed about the same at fast-food outlets. These restaurants kept their sales up by offering discounts and promotions as well as $1 menus and cheap combination meals. Same-store sales at McDonald's have stayed approximately level during the downturn.

However, many fast-food chains, such as Burger King, Jack in the Box, and Carl Jr.'s, saw their sales fall during the recession years. They cut back their advertising spending as the much larger McDonald's increased its spending and its market share. McDonald's has also aggressively expanded its menus—from the healthier Happy Meals to the "McCafé" line of espresso drinks, smoothies, and exotically flavored wraps.

Observers are divided as to whether McDonald's is earnestly attempting to get its customers to eat healthier food or is just engaging in advertising spin. One unknown is how customers will react: as one commenter said, "Salt may be bad for you, but it tastes great. . . . You can't demand that McDonald's or Burger King stop selling hamburgers and fries." In the same vein, one franchise owner noted, "Expect customers to try the apples and then revert to asking for fries."

Michael Neelon/Alamy

QUESTIONS FOR THOUGHT

1. Give an example of a normal good and an inferior good mentioned in this case. Cite examples of substitution effects and income effects from the case.

2. To induce fast-food customers to eat more healthful meals, what alternatives are there to bans? Do you think these alternatives would work? Why or why not?

3. What do you think accounts for McDonald's success? Relate this to concepts discussed in the chapter.

SUMMARY

1. Consumers maximize a measure of satisfaction called **utility.** Each consumer has a **utility function** that determines the level of total utility generated by his or her **consumption bundle,** the goods and services that are consumed. We measure utility in hypothetical units called **utils.**

2. A good's or service's **marginal utility** is the additional utility generated by consuming one more unit of the good or service. We usually assume that the **principle of diminishing marginal utility** holds: consumption of another unit of a good or service yields less additional utility than the previous unit. As a result, the **marginal utility curve** slopes downward.

3. A **budget constraint** limits a consumer's spending to no more than his or her income. It defines the consumer's **consumption possibilities,** the set of all affordable consumption bundles. A consumer who spends all of his or her income will choose a consumption bundle on the **budget line.** An individual chooses the consumption bundle that maximizes total utility, the **optimal consumption bundle.**

4. We use marginal analysis to find the optimal consumption bundle by analyzing how to allocate the marginal dollar. According to the **utility-maximizing principle of marginal analysis,** at the optimal consumption bundle the **marginal utility per dollar** spent on each good and service—the marginal utility of a good divided by its price—is the same.

5. Changes in the price of a good affect the quantity consumed in two possible ways: the **substitution effect** and the **income effect.** Most goods absorb only a small share of a consumer's spending; for these goods, only the substitution effect—buying less of the good that has become relatively more expensive and more of goods that are now relatively cheaper—is significant. It causes the individual and the market demand curves to slope downward. When a good absorbs a large fraction of spending, the income effect is also significant: an increase in a good's price makes a consumer poorer, but a decrease in price makes a consumer richer. This change in purchasing power makes consumers demand less or more of a good, depending on whether the good is normal or inferior. For normal goods, the substitution and income effects reinforce each other. For inferior goods, however, they work in opposite directions. The demand curve of a **Giffen good** slopes upward because it is an inferior good in which the income effect outweighs the substitution effect. However, data have never confirmed the existence of a Giffen good.

KEY TERMS

Utility, p. 282
Consumption bundle, p. 282
Utility function, p. 282
Util, p. 282
Marginal utility, p. 283
Marginal utility curve, p. 283

Principle of diminishing marginal utility, p. 284
Budget constraint, p. 286
Consumption possibilities, p. 286
Budget line, p. 286
Optimal consumption bundle, p. 287

Marginal utility per dollar, p. 290
Utility-maximizing principle of marginal analysis, p. 293
Substitution effect, p. 295
Income effect, p. 295
Giffen good, p. 296

PROBLEMS

1. For each of the following situations, decide whether Al has diminishing marginal utility. Explain.

   a. The more economics classes Al takes, the more he enjoys the subject. And the more classes he takes, the easier each one gets, making him enjoy each additional class even more than the one before.

   b. Al likes loud music. In fact, according to him, "the louder, the better." Each time he turns the volume up a notch, he adds 5 utils to his total utility.

   c. Al enjoys watching reruns of the old sitcom *Friends*. He claims that these episodes are always funny, but he does admit that the more he sees an episode, the less funny it gets.

   d. Al loves toasted marshmallows. The more he eats, however, the fuller he gets and the less he enjoys each additional marshmallow. And there is a point at which he becomes satiated: beyond that point, more marshmallows actually make him feel worse rather than better.

2. Use the concept of marginal utility to explain the following: Newspaper vending machines are designed so that once you have paid for one paper, you could take more than one paper at a time. But soda vending machines, once you have paid for one soda, dispense only one soda at a time.

3. Bruno can spend his income on two different goods: Beyoncé MP3s and notebooks for his class notes. For each of the following three situations, decide if the given consumption bundle is within Bruno's consumption possibilities. Then decide if it lies on the budget line or not.

   a. MP3s cost $2 each, and notebooks cost $3 each. Bruno has income of $60. He is considering a consumption bundle containing 15 MP3s and 10 notebooks.

   b. MP3s cost $2 each, and notebooks cost $5 each. Bruno has income of $110. He is considering a consumption bundle containing 20 MP3s and 10 notebooks.

   c. MP3s cost $3 each, and notebooks cost $10 each. Bruno has income of $50. He is considering a consumption bundle containing 10 MP3s and 3 notebooks.

4. Bruno, the consumer in Problem 3, is best friends with Bernie, who shares his love for notebooks and Beyoncé MP3s. The accompanying table shows Bernie's utilities from notebooks and Beyoncé MP3s.

Quantity of Notebooks	Utility from Notebooks (utils)	Quantity of MP3s	Utility from MP3s (utils)
0	0	0	0
1	32	2	28
2	60	4	52
3	84	6	72
4	104	8	96
5	120	10	108

The price of a notebook is $4, the price of an MP3 is $2, and Bernie has $20 of income to spend.

   a. Which consumption bundles of notebooks and MP3s can Bernie consume if he spends all his income? Illustrate Bernie's budget line with a diagram, putting MP3s on the horizontal axis and notebooks on the vertical axis.

   b. Calculate the marginal utility of each notebook and the marginal utility of each MP3. Then calculate the marginal utility per dollar spent on notebooks and the marginal utility per dollar spent on MP3s.

   c. Draw a diagram like Figure 10-4 in which both the marginal utility per dollar spent on notebooks and the marginal utility per dollar spent on MP3s are illustrated. Using this diagram and the utility-maximizing principle of marginal analysis, predict which bundle—from all the bundles on his budget line—Bernie will choose.

5. For each of the following situations, decide whether the bundle Lakshani is considering is optimal or not. If it is not optimal, how could Lakshani improve her overall level of utility? That is, determine which good she should spend more on and which good should she spend less on.

   a. Lakshani has $200 to spend on sneakers and sweaters. Sneakers cost $50 per pair, and sweaters cost $20 each. She is thinking about buying 2 pairs of sneakers and 5 sweaters. She tells her friend that the additional utility she would get from the second pair of sneakers is the same as the additional utility she would get from the fifth sweater.

   b. Lakshani has $5 to spend on pens and pencils. Each pen costs $0.50 and each pencil costs $0.10. She is thinking about buying 6 pens and 20 pencils. The last pen would add five times as much to her total utility as the last pencil.

   c. Lakshani has $50 per season to spend on tickets to football games and tickets to soccer games. Each football ticket costs $10 and each soccer ticket costs $5. She is thinking about buying 3 football tickets and 2 soccer tickets. Her marginal utility from the third football ticket is twice as much as her marginal utility from the second soccer ticket.

6. Cal "Cool" Cooper has $200 to spend on cell phones and sunglasses.

   a. Each cell phone costs $100 and each pair of sunglasses costs $50. Which bundles lie on Cal's budget line? Draw a diagram like Figure 10-4 in which both the marginal utility per dollar spent on cell phones and the marginal utility per dollar spent on sunglasses are illustrated. Use this diagram and the optimal consumption rule to decide how Cal should allocate his money. That is, from all the bundles on his budget line, which bundle will Cal choose? The accompanying table gives his utility of cell phones and sunglasses.

Quantity of cell phones	Utility from cell phones (utils)	Quantity of sunglasses (pairs)	Utility from sunglasses (utils)
0	0	0	0
1	400	2	600
2	700	4	700

   b. The price of cell phones falls to $50 each, but the price of sunglasses remains at $50 per pair. Which bundles lie on Cal's budget line? Draw a diagram like Figure 10-4 in which both the marginal utility per dollar spent on cell phones and the marginal utility per dollar spent on sunglasses are illustrated.

Use this diagram and the utility-maximizing principle of marginal analysis to decide how Cal should allocate his money. That is, from all the bundles on his budget line, which bundle will Cal choose? The accompanying table gives his utility of cell phones and sunglasses.

Quantity of cell phones	Utility from cell phones (utils)	Quantity of sunglasses (pairs)	Utility from sunglasses (utils)
0	0	0	0
1	400	1	325
2	700	2	600
3	900	3	825
4	1,000	4	700

c. How does Cal's consumption of cell phones change as the price of cell phones falls? In words, describe the income effect and the substitution effect of this fall in the price of cell phones, assuming that cell phones are a normal good.

7. Damien Matthews is a busy actor. He allocates his free time to watching movies and working out at the gym. The accompanying table shows his utility from the number of times per week he watches a movie or goes to the gym.

Quantity of gym visits per week	Utility from gym visits (utils)	Quantity of movies per week	Utility from movies (utils)
1	100	1	60
2	180	2	110
3	240	3	150
4	280	4	180
5	310	5	190
6	330	6	195
7	340	7	197

Damien has 14 hours per week to spend on watching movies and going to the gym. Each movie takes 2 hours and each gym visit takes 2 hours. (Hint: Damien's free time is analogous to income he can spend. The hours needed for each activity are analogous to the price of that activity.)

a. Which bundles of gym visits and movies can Damien consume per week if he spends all his time either going to the gym or watching movies? Draw Damien's budget line in a diagram with gym visits on the horizontal axis and movies on the vertical axis.

b. Calculate the marginal utility of each gym visit and the marginal utility of each movie. Then calculate the marginal utility per hour spent at the gym and the marginal utility per hour spent watching movies.

c. Draw a diagram like Figure 10-4 in which both the marginal utility per hour spent at the gym and the marginal utility per hour spent watching movies are illustrated. Use this diagram and the utility-maximizing principle of marginal analysis to decide how Damien should allocate his time.

8. Anna Jenniferson is an actress who currently spends several hours each week watching movies and going to the gym. On the set of a new movie she meets Damien, the consumer in Problem 7. She tells him that she likes watching movies much more than going to the gym. In fact, she says that if she had to give up seeing 1 movie, she would need to go to the gym twice to make up for the loss in utility from not seeing the movie. A movie takes 2 hours, and a gym visit also lasts 2 hours. Damien tells Anna that she is not watching enough movies. Is he right?

9. Sven is a poor student who covers most of his dietary needs by eating cheap breakfast cereal, since it contains most of the important vitamins. As the price of cereal increases, he decides to buy even less of other foods and even more breakfast cereal to maintain his intake of important nutrients. This makes breakfast cereal a Giffen good for Sven. Describe in words the substitution effect and the income effect from this increase in the price of cereal. In which direction does each effect move, and why? What does this imply for the slope of Sven's demand curve for cereal?

10. In each of the following situations, describe the substitution effect and, if it is significant, the income effect. In which direction does each of these effects move? Why?

a. Ed spends a large portion of his income on his children's education. Because tuition fees rise, one of his children has to withdraw from college.

b. Homer spends much of his monthly income on home mortgage payments. The interest on his adjustable-rate mortgage falls, lowering his mortgage payments, and Homer decides to move to a larger house.

c. Pam thinks that Spam is an inferior good. Yet as the price of Spam rises, she decides to buy less of it.

11. Restaurant meals and housing (measured in the number of rooms) are the only two goods that Neha buys. She has income of $1,000. Initially, she buys a consumption bundle such that she spends exactly half her income on restaurant meals and the other half of her income on housing. Then her income increases by 50%, but the price of restaurant meals increases by 100% (it doubles). The price of housing remains the same. After these changes, if she wanted to, could Neha still buy the same consumption bundle as before?

12. Scott finds that the higher the price of orange juice, the more money he spends on orange juice. Does that mean that Scott has discovered a Giffen good?

13 Margo's marginal utility of one dance lesson is 100 utils per lesson. Her marginal utility of a new pair of dance shoes is 300 utils per pair. The price of a dance lesson is $50 per lesson. She currently spends all her income, and she buys her optimal consumption bundle. What is the price of a pair of dance shoes?

14. According to data from the U.S. Department of Energy, the average retail price of regular gasoline rose from $1.16 in 1990 to $3.24 in 2012, a 180% increase.

a. Other things equal, describe the effect of this price increase on the quantity of gasoline demanded. In your explanation, make use of the utility-maximizing principle of marginal analysis and describe income and substitution effects.

In fact, however, other things were not equal. Over the same time period, the prices of other goods and services rose as well. According to data from the Bureau of Labor Statistics, the overall price of a bundle of goods and services consumed by an average consumer rose by 75%.

b. Taking into account the rise in the price of gasoline and in overall prices, other things equal, describe the effect on the quantity of gasoline demanded.

However, this is not the end of the story. Between 1990 and 2012, the typical consumer's nominal income increased, too: the U.S. Census Bureau reports that U.S. median household nominal income rose from $29,943 in 1990 to $51,017 in 2012, an increase of 70%.

c. Taking into account the rise in the price of gasoline, in overall prices, and in consumers' incomes, describe the effect on the quantity of gasoline demanded.

WORK IT OUT Macmillan Education LaunchPad

For interactive, step-by-step help in solving the following problem, visit LaunchPad by using the URL on the back cover of this book.

15. Brenda likes to have bagels and coffee for breakfast. The accompanying table shows Brenda's total utility from various consumption bundles of bagels and coffee.

Consumption bundle		Total utility (utils)
Quantity of bagels	Quantity of coffee (cups)	
0	0	0
0	2	28
0	4	40
1	2	48
1	3	54
2	0	28
2	2	56
3	1	54
3	2	62
4	0	40
4	2	66

Suppose Brenda knows she will consume 2 cups of coffee for sure. However, she can choose to consume different quantities of bagels: she can choose either 0, 1, 2, 3, or 4 bagels.

a. Calculate Brenda's marginal utility from bagels as she goes from consuming 0 bagel to 1 bagel, from 1 bagel to 2 bagels, from 2 bagels to 3 bagels, and from 3 bagels to 4 bagels.

b. Draw Brenda's marginal utility curve of bagels. Does Brenda have diminishing marginal utility of bagels? Explain.

c. Brenda has $8 of income to spend on bagels and coffee. Bagels cost $2 each, and coffee costs $2 per cup. Which bundles are on Brenda's budget line? For each of these bundles, calculate the level of utility (in utils) that Brenda enjoys. Which bundle is her optimal bundle?

d. The price of bagels increases to $4, but the price of coffee remains at $2 per cup. Which bundles are now on Brenda's budget line? For each bundle, calculate Brenda's level of utility (in utils). Which bundle is her optimal bundle?

e. What do your answers to parts a and b imply about the slope of Brenda's demand curve for bagels? Describe the substitution effect and the income effect of this increase in the price of bagels, assuming that bagels are a normal good.

Consumer Preferences and Consumer Choice

Different people have different preferences. But even given an individual's preferences, there may be different consumption bundles that yield the same total utility. This insight leads to the concept of *indifference curves,* a useful way to represent individual preferences. In this appendix, we will look closely at indifference curves.

Using indifference curves to analyze consumer behavior will serve us in three ways. First, indifference curves show how diminishing marginal utility determines the tradeoff a consumer makes between consuming more of one good and less of another. Second, they provide a framework for a more in-depth analysis of income and substitution effects—how changes in price and income alter the optimal consumption bundle. Lastly, indifference curves allow us to illustrate differences in tastes between two people, and how those differences in tastes lead to different optimal consumption bundles. Indifference curves, then, allow us to get a deeper understanding of what it means to be a rational consumer.

Mapping the Utility Function

In Chapter 10 we introduced the concept of a utility function, which determines a consumer's total utility given his or her consumption bundle. In Figure 10-1 we saw how Cassie's total utility changed as we changed the quantity of fried clams consumed, holding fixed the quantities of other items in her bundle. That is, in Figure 10-1 we showed how total utility changed as consumption of only *one* good changed. But we also learned in Chapter 10, from our example of Sammy, that finding the optimal consumption bundle involves the problem of how to allocate the last dollar spent between *two* goods, clams and potatoes. In this appendix we will extend the analysis by learning how to express total utility as a function of consumption of two goods. In this way we will deepen our understanding of the trade-off involved when choosing the optimal consumption bundle and of how the optimal consumption bundle itself changes in response to changes in the prices of goods. In order to do that, we now turn to a different way of representing a consumer's utility function, based on the concept of *indifference curves.*

Indifference Curves

Ingrid is a consumer who buys only two goods: housing, measured in the number of rooms, and restaurant meals. How can we represent her utility function in a way that takes account of her consumption of both goods?

One way is to draw a three-dimensional picture. Figure 10A-1 shows a three-dimensional "utility hill." The distance along the horizontal axis measures the quantity of housing Ingrid consumes in terms of numbers of rooms; the distance along the vertical axis measures the number of restaurant meals she consumes. The altitude or height of the hill at each point is indicated by a contour line, along which the height of the hill is constant. For example, point *A*, which corresponds to a consumption bundle of 3 rooms and 30 restaurant meals, lies on the contour line labeled 450. So the total utility Ingrid receives from consuming 3 rooms and 30 restaurant meals is 450 utils.

A three-dimensional picture like Figure 10A-1 helps us think about the relationship between consumption bundles and total utility. But anyone who has ever

The three-dimensional hill shows how Ingrid's total utility depends on her consumption of housing and restaurant meals. Point A corresponds to consumption of 3 rooms and 30 restaurant meals. That consumption bundle yields Ingrid 450 utils, corresponding to the height of the hill at point A. The lines running around the hill are contour lines, along which the height is constant. Every point on a given contour line generates the same level of utility. So point B, corresponding to 6 rooms and 15 restaurant meals, generates the same level of utility as point A, 450 utils, since they lie on the same contour line.

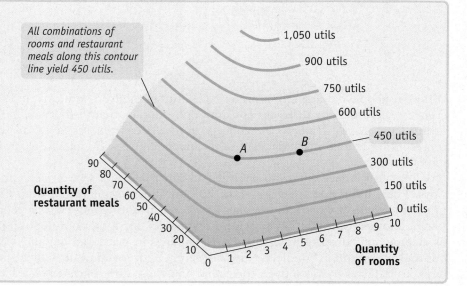

used a topographical map to plan a hiking trip knows that it is possible to represent a three-dimensional surface in only two dimensions. A topographical map doesn't offer a three-dimensional view of the terrain; instead, it conveys information about altitude solely through the use of contour lines.

The same principle can be applied to representing the utility function. In Figure 10A-2, Ingrid's consumption of rooms is measured on the horizontal axis and her consumption of restaurant meals on the vertical axis. The curve here corresponds to the contour line in Figure 10A-1, drawn at a total utility of 450 utils. This curve shows all the consumption bundles that yield a total utility of 450 utils. One point on that contour line is A, a consumption bundle consisting of 3 rooms and 30 restaurant meals. Another point on that contour line is B, a consumption

FIGURE **10A-2**   An Indifference Curve

An indifference curve is a contour line along which total utility is constant. In this case, we show all the consumption bundles that yield Ingrid 450 utils. Consumption bundle A, consisting of 3 rooms and 30 restaurant meals, yields the same total utility as bundle B, consisting of 6 rooms and 15 restaurant meals. That is, Ingrid is indifferent between bundle A and bundle B.

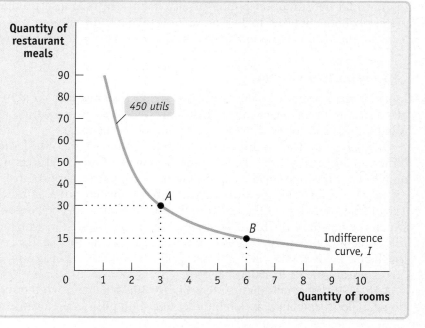

bundle consisting of 6 rooms but only 15 restaurant meals. Because *B* lies on the same contour line, it yields Ingrid the same total utility—450 utils—as *A*. We say that Ingrid is *indifferent* between *A* and *B*: because bundles *A* and *B* yield the same total utility level, Ingrid is equally well off with either bundle.

A contour line that maps consumption bundles yielding the same amount of total utility is known as an **indifference curve.** An individual is always indifferent between any two bundles that lie on the same indifference curve. For a given consumer, there is an indifference curve corresponding to each possible level of total utility. For example, the indifference curve in Figure 10A-2 shows consumption bundles that yield Ingrid 450 utils; different indifference curves would show consumption bundles that yield Ingrid 400 utils, 500 utils, and so on.

A collection of indifference curves that represents a given consumer's entire utility function, with each indifference curve corresponding to a different level of total utility, is known as an **indifference curve map.** Figure 10A-3 shows three indifference curves—I_1, I_2, and I_3—from Ingrid's indifference curve map, as well as several consumption bundles, *A*, *B*, *C*, and *D*. The accompanying table lists each bundle, its composition of rooms and restaurant meals, and the total utility it yields. Because bundles *A* and *B* generate the same number of utils, 450, they lie on the same indifference curve, I_2. Although Ingrid is indifferent between *A* and *B*, she is certainly not indifferent between *A* and *C*: as you can see from the table, *C* generates only 391 utils, a lower total utility than *A* or *B*. So Ingrid prefers consumption bundles *A* and *B* to bundle *C*. This is represented by the fact that *C* is on indifference curve I_1, and I_1 lies below I_2. Bundle *D*, though, generates 519 utils, a higher total utility than *A* and *B*. It is on I_3, an indifference curve that lies above I_2. Clearly, Ingrid prefers *D* to either *A* or *B*. And, even more strongly, she prefers *D* to *C*.

An **indifference curve** is a line that shows all the consumption bundles that yield the same amount of total utility for an individual.

The entire utility function of an individual can be represented by an **indifference curve map,** a collection of indifference curves in which each curve corresponds to a different total utility level.

FIGURE 10A-3   An Indifference Curve Map

Consumption bundle	Quantity of rooms	Quantity of meals	Total utility (utils)
A	3	30	450
B	6	15	450
C	5	10	391
D	4	45	519

The utility function can be represented in greater detail by increasing the number of indifference curves drawn, each corresponding to a different level of total utility. In this figure bundle C lies on an indifference curve corresponding to a total utility of 391 utils. As in Figure 10A-2, bundles A and B lie on an indifference curve corresponding to a total utility of 450 utils. Bundle D lies on an indifference curve corresponding to a total utility of 519 utils. Ingrid prefers any bundle on I_2 to any bundle on I_1, and she prefers any bundle on I_3 to any bundle on I_2.

Properties of Indifference Curves

No two individuals have the same indifference curve map because no two individuals have the same preferences. But economists believe that, regardless of the person, every indifference curve map has two general properties. These are illustrated in panel (a) of Figure 10A-4:

- *Indifference curves never cross.* Suppose that we tried to draw an indifference curve map like the one depicted in the left diagram in panel (a), in which two indifference curves cross at *A*. What is the total utility at *A*? Is it 100 utils or

---

FIGURE 10A-4 | **Properties of Indifference Curves**

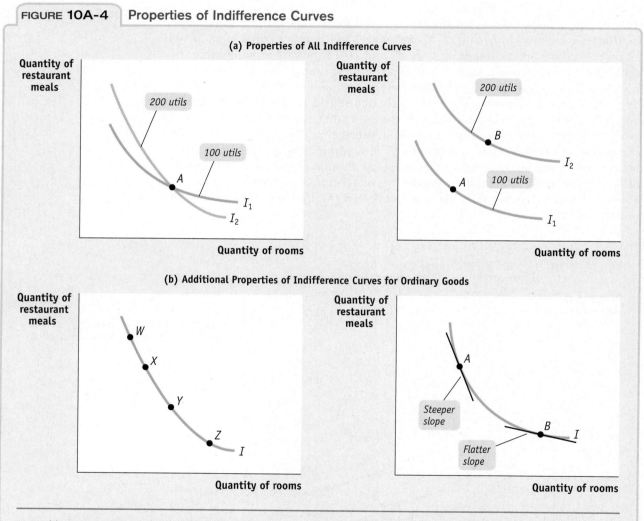

(a) Properties of All Indifference Curves

(b) Additional Properties of Indifference Curves for Ordinary Goods

Panel (a) represents two general properties that all indifference curve maps share. The left diagram shows why indifference curves cannot cross: if they did, a consumption bundle such as *A* would yield both 100 and 200 utils, a contradiction. The right diagram of panel (a) shows that indifference curves that are farther out yield higher total utility: bundle *B*, which contains more of both goods than bundle *A*, yields higher total utility. Panel (b) depicts two additional properties of indifference curves

for ordinary goods. The left diagram of panel (b) shows that indifference curves slope downward: as you move down the curve from bundle *W* to bundle *Z*, consumption of rooms increases. To keep total utility constant, this must be offset by a reduction in quantity of restaurant meals. The right diagram of panel (b) shows a convex-shaped indifference curve. The slope of the indifference curve gets flatter as you move down the curve to the right, a feature arising from diminishing marginal utility.

200 utils? Indifference curves cannot cross because each consumption bundle must correspond to a unique total utility level—not, as shown at *A*, two different total utility levels.

- *The farther out an indifference curve lies—the farther it is from the origin—the higher the level of total utility it indicates.* The reason, illustrated in the right diagram in panel (a), is that we assume that more is better—we consider only the consumption bundles for which the consumer is not satiated. Bundle *B*, on the outer indifference curve, contains more of both goods than bundle *A* on the inner indifference curve. So *B*, because it generates a higher total utility level (200 utils), lies on a higher indifference curve than *A*.

  Furthermore, economists believe that, for most goods, consumers' indifference curve maps also have two additional properties. They are illustrated in panel (b) of Figure 10A-4:

- *Indifference curves slope downward.* Here, too, the reason is that more is better. The left diagram in panel (b) shows four consumption bundles on the same indifference curve: *W*, *X*, *Y*, and *Z*. By definition, these consumption bundles yield the same level of total utility. But as you move along the curve to the right, from *W* to *Z*, the quantity of rooms consumed increases. The only way a person can consume more rooms without gaining utility is by giving up some restaurant meals. So the indifference curve must slope downward.

- *Indifference curves have a convex shape.* The right diagram in panel (b) shows that the slope of each indifference curve changes as you move down the curve to the right: the curve gets flatter. If you move up an indifference curve to the left, the curve gets steeper. So the indifference curve is steeper at *A* than it is at *B*. When this occurs, we say that an indifference curve has a *convex* shape—it is bowed-in toward the origin. This feature arises from diminishing marginal utility, a principle we discussed in Chapter 10. Recall that when a consumer has diminishing marginal utility, consumption of another unit of a good generates a smaller increase in total utility than the previous unit consumed. In the next section, we will examine in detail how diminishing marginal utility gives rise to convex-shaped indifference curves.

Goods that satisfy all four properties of indifference curve maps are called *ordinary goods*. The vast majority of goods in any consumer's utility function fall into this category. In the next section, we will define ordinary goods and see the key role that diminishing marginal utility plays for them.

Indifference Curves and Consumer Choice

At the beginning of the last section, we used indifference curves to represent the preferences of Ingrid, whose consumption bundles consist of rooms and restaurant meals. Our next step is to show how to use Ingrid's indifference curve map to find her utility-maximizing consumption bundle given her budget constraint, the fact that she must choose a consumption bundle that costs no more than her total income.

It's important to understand how our analysis here relates to what we did in Chapter 10. We are not offering a new theory of consumer behavior in this appendix—just as in Chapter 10, consumers are assumed to maximize total utility. In particular, we know that consumers will follow the *optimal consumption rule* from Chapter 10: the optimal consumption bundle lies on the budget line, and the marginal utility per dollar is the same for every good in the bundle.

But as we'll see shortly, we can derive this optimal consumer behavior in a somewhat different way—a way that yields deeper insights into consumer choice.

The Marginal Rate of Substitution

The first element of our approach is a new concept, the *marginal rate of substitution*. The essence of this concept is illustrated in Figure 10A-5.

Recall from the last section that for most goods, consumers' indifference curves are downward sloping and convex. Figure 10A-5 shows such an indifference curve. The points labeled *V*, *W*, *X*, *Y*, and *Z* all lie on this indifference curve—that is, they represent consumption bundles that yield Ingrid the same level of total utility. The table accompanying the figure shows the components of each of the bundles. As we move along the indifference curve from *V* to *Z*, Ingrid's consumption of housing steadily increases from 2 rooms to 6 rooms, her consumption of restaurant meals steadily decreases from 30 meals to 10 meals, and her total utility is kept constant. As we move down the indifference curve, then, Ingrid is trading more of one good in place of less of the other, with the *terms* of that trade-off—the ratio of additional rooms consumed to restaurant meals sacrificed—chosen to keep her total utility constant.

Notice that the quantity of restaurant meals that Ingrid is willing to give up in return for an additional room changes along the indifference curve. As we move from *V* to *W*, housing consumption rises from 2 to 3 rooms and restaurant meal consumption falls from 30 to 20—a trade-off of 10 restaurant meals for 1 additional room. But as we move from *Y* to *Z*, housing consumption rises from 5 to 6 rooms and restaurant meal consumption falls from 12 to 10, a trade-off of only 2 restaurant meals for an additional room.

To put it in terms of slopes, the slope of the indifference curve between *V* and *W* is −10: the change in restaurant meal consumption, −10, divided by the change in housing consumption, 1. Similarly, the slope of the indifference curve between *Y* and *Z* is −2.

FIGURE **10A-5**   **The Changing Slope of an Indifference Curve**

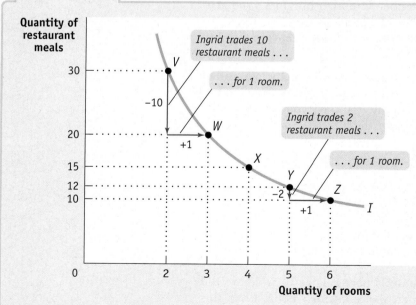

Consumption bundle	Quantity of rooms	Quantity of restaurant meals
V	2	30
W	3	20
X	4	15
Y	5	12
Z	6	10

This indifference curve is downward sloping and convex, implying that restaurant meals and rooms are ordinary goods for Ingrid. As Ingrid moves down her indifference curve from *V* to *Z*, she trades reduced consumption of restaurant meals for increased consumption of housing. However, the terms of that trade-off change. As she moves from *V* to *W*, she is willing to give up 10 restaurant meals in return for 1 more room. As her consumption of rooms rises and her consumption of restaurant meals falls, she is willing to give up fewer restaurant meals in return for each additional room. The flattening of the slope as you move from left to right arises from diminishing marginal utility.

So the indifference curve gets flatter as we move down it to the right—that is, it has a convex shape, one of the four properties of an indifference curve for ordinary goods.

Why does the trade-off change in this way? Let's think about it intuitively, then work through it more carefully. When Ingrid moves down her indifference curve, whether from V to W or from Y to Z, she gains utility from her additional consumption of housing but loses an equal amount of utility from her reduced consumption of restaurant meals. But at each step, the initial position from which Ingrid begins is different. At V, Ingrid consumes only a small quantity of rooms; because of diminishing marginal utility, her marginal utility per room at that point is high. At V, then, an additional room adds a lot to Ingrid's total utility. But at V she already consumes a large quantity of restaurant meals, so her marginal utility of restaurant meals is low at that point. This means that it takes a large reduction in her quantity of restaurant meals consumed to offset the increased utility she gets from the extra room of housing.

At Y, in contrast, Ingrid consumes a much larger quantity of rooms and a much smaller quantity of restaurant meals than at V. This means that an additional room adds fewer utils, and a restaurant meal forgone costs more utils, than at V. So Ingrid is willing to give up fewer restaurant meals in return for another room of housing at Y (where she gives up 2 meals for 1 room) than she is at V (where she gives up 10 meals for 1 room).

Now let's express the same idea—that the trade-off Ingrid is willing to make depends on where she is starting from—by using a little math. We do this by examining how the slope of the indifference curve changes as we move down it. Moving down the indifference curve—reducing restaurant meal consumption and increasing housing consumption—will produce two opposing effects on Ingrid's total utility: lower restaurant meal consumption will reduce her total utility, but higher housing consumption will raise her total utility. And since we are moving down the indifference curve, these two effects must exactly cancel out:

Along the indifference curve:
(10A-1) (Change in total utility due to lower restaurant meal consumption) + (Change in total utility due to higher housing consumption) = 0

or, rearranging terms,

Along the indifference curve:
(10A-2) –(Change in total utility due to lower restaurant meal consumption) = (Change in total utility due to higher housing consumption)

Let's now focus on what happens as we move only a short distance down the indifference curve, trading off a small increase in housing consumption in place of a small decrease in restaurant meal consumption. Following our notation from Chapter 10, let's use MU_R and MU_M to represent the marginal utility of rooms and restaurant meals, respectively, and ΔQ_R and ΔQ_M to represent the changes in room and meal consumption, respectively. In general, the change in total utility caused by a small change in consumption of a good is equal to the change in consumption multiplied by the *marginal utility* of that good. This means that we can calculate the change in Ingrid's total utility generated by a change in her consumption bundle using the following equations:

(10A-3) Change in total utility due to a change in restaurant meal consumption = $MU_M \times \Delta Q_M$

and

(10A-4) Change in total utility due to a change in housing consumption = $MU_R \times \Delta Q_R$

The **marginal rate of substitution,** or **MRS,** of good R in place of good M is equal to MU_R/MU_M, the ratio of the marginal utility of R to the marginal utility of M.

The principle of **diminishing marginal rate of substitution** states that the more of good R a person consumes in proportion to good M, the less M he or she is willing to substitute for another unit of R.

So we can write Equation 10A-2 in symbols as:

(10A-5) *Along the indifference curve:* $-MU_M \times \Delta Q_M = MU_R \times \Delta Q_R$

Note that the left-hand side of Equation 10A-5 has a minus sign; it represents the loss in total utility from decreased restaurant meal consumption. This must equal the gain in total utility from increased room consumption, represented by the right-hand side of the equation.

What we want to know is how this translates into the slope of the indifference curve. To find the slope, we divide both sides of Equation 10A-5 by ΔQ_R, and again by $-MU_M$, in order to get the ΔQ_M, ΔQ_R terms on one side and the MU_R, MU_M terms on the other. This results in:

(10A-6) *Along the indifference curve:* $\dfrac{\Delta Q_M}{\Delta Q_R} = -\dfrac{MU_R}{MU_M}$

The left-hand side of Equation 10A-6 is the slope of the indifference curve; it is the rate at which Ingrid is willing to trade rooms (the good on the horizontal axis) in place of restaurant meals (the good on the vertical axis) without changing her total utility level. The right-hand side of Equation 10A-6 is minus the ratio of the marginal utility of rooms to the marginal utility of restaurant meals—that is, the ratio of what she gains from one more room to what she gains from one more meal.

Putting all this together, we see that Equation 10A-6 shows that, along the indifference curve, the quantity of restaurant meals Ingrid is willing to give up in return for a room, $\Delta Q_M/\Delta Q_R$, is exactly equal to minus the ratio of the marginal utility of a room to that of a meal, $-MU_R/MU_M$. Only when this condition is met will her total utility level remain constant as she consumes more rooms and fewer restaurant meals.

Economists have a special name for the ratio of the marginal utilities found in the right-hand side of Equation 10A-6: it is called the **marginal rate of substitution,** or **MRS,** of rooms (the good on the horizontal axis) in place of restaurant meals (the good on the vertical axis). That's because as we slide down Ingrid's indifference curve, we are substituting more rooms in place of fewer restaurant meals in her consumption bundle. As we'll see shortly, the marginal rate of substitution plays an important role in finding the optimal consumption bundle.

Recall that indifference curves get flatter as you move down them to the right. The reason, as we've just discussed, is diminishing marginal utility: as Ingrid consumes more housing and fewer restaurant meals, her marginal utility from housing falls and her marginal utility from restaurant meals rises. So her marginal rate of substitution, which is equal to minus the slope of her indifference curve, falls as she moves down the indifference curve.

The flattening of indifference curves as you slide down them to the right—which reflects the same logic as the principle of diminishing marginal utility—is known as the principle of **diminishing marginal rate of substitution.** It says that an individual who consumes only a little bit of good A and a lot of good B will be willing to trade off a lot of B in return for one more unit of A; an individual who already consumes a lot of A and not much B will be less willing to make that trade-off.

We can illustrate this point by referring back to Figure 10A-5. At point V, a bundle with a high proportion of restaurant meals to rooms, Ingrid is willing to forgo 10 restaurant meals in return for 1 room. But at point Y, a bundle with a low proportion of restaurant meals to rooms, she is willing to forgo only 2 restaurant meals in return for 1 room.

From this example we can see that, in Ingrid's utility function, rooms and restaurant meals possess the two additional properties that characterize ordinary goods. Ingrid requires additional rooms to compensate her for the loss of a meal, and vice versa; so her indifference curves for these two goods slope downward. And her indifference curves are convex: the slope of her indifference curve—*minus* the marginal rate of substitution—becomes flatter as we move down it. In fact, an indifference curve is convex only when it has diminishing marginal rate of substitution—these two conditions are equivalent.

With this information, we can define **ordinary goods,** which account for the great majority of goods in any consumer's utility function. A pair of goods are ordinary goods in a consumer's utility function if they possess two properties: the consumer requires more of one good to compensate for less of the other, and the consumer experiences a diminishing marginal rate of substitution when substituting one good in place of the other.

Next we will see how to determine Ingrid's optimal consumption bundle using indifference curves.

> Two goods, *R* and *M*, are **ordinary goods** in a consumer's utility function when (1) the consumer requires additional units of *R* to compensate for less *M*, and vice versa; and (2) the consumer experiences a diminishing marginal rate of substitution when substituting one good in place of another.

The Tangency Condition

Now let's put some of Ingrid's indifference curves on the same diagram as her budget line, to illustrate an alternative way of representing her optimal consumption choice. Figure 10A-6 shows Ingrid's budget line, *BL*, when her income is $2,400 per month, housing costs $150 per room each month, and restaurant meals cost $30 each. What is her optimal consumption bundle?

To answer this question, we show several of Ingrid's indifference curves: I_1, I_2, and I_3. Ingrid would like to achieve the total utility level represented by I_3, the highest of the three curves, but she cannot afford to because she is constrained by her income: no consumption bundle on her budget line yields that much total utility. But she shouldn't settle for the level of total utility generated by *B*, which lies on I_1: there are other bundles on her budget line, such as *A*, that clearly yield higher total utility than *B*.

In fact, *A*—a consumption bundle consisting of 8 rooms and 40 restaurant meals per month—is Ingrid's optimal consumption choice. The reason is that *A* lies on the highest indifference curve Ingrid can reach given her income.

FIGURE 10A-6   The Optimal Consumption Bundle

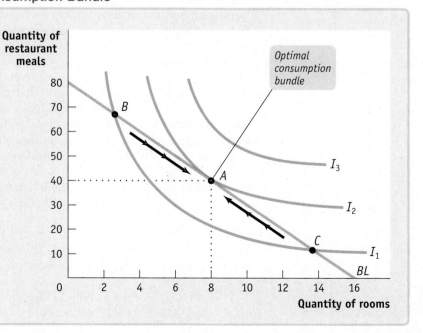

The budget line, *BL*, shows Ingrid's possible consumption bundles given an income of $2,400 per month, when rooms cost $150 per month and restaurant meals cost $30 each. I_1, I_2, and I_3 are indifference curves. Consumption bundles such as *B* and *C* are not optimal because Ingrid can move to a higher indifference curve. The optimal consumption bundle is *A*, where the budget line is just tangent to the highest possible indifference curve.

The **tangency condition** between the indifference curve and the budget line holds when the indifference curve and the budget line just touch. This condition determines the optimal consumption bundle when the indifference curves have the typical convex shape.

At the optimal consumption bundle *A*, Ingrid's budget line *just touches* the relevant indifference curve—the budget line is *tangent* to the indifference curve. This **tangency condition** between the indifference curve and the budget line applies to the optimal consumption bundle when the indifference curves have the typical convex shape: *at the optimal consumption bundle, the budget line just touches—is tangent to—the indifference curve.*

To see why, let's look more closely at how we know that a consumption bundle that *doesn't* satisfy the tangency condition can't be optimal. Reexamining Figure 10A-6, we can see that the consumption bundles *B* and *C* are both affordable because they lie on the budget line. However, neither is optimal. Both of them lie on the indifference curve I_1, which cuts through the budget line at both points. But because I_1 cuts through the budget line, Ingrid can do better: she can move down the budget line from *B* or up the budget line from *C*, as indicated by the arrows. In each case, this allows her to get onto a higher indifference curve, I_2, which increases her total utility.

Ingrid cannot, however, do any better than I_2: any other indifference curve either cuts through her budget line or doesn't touch it at all. And the bundle that allows her to achieve I_2 is, of course, her optimal consumption bundle.

The Slope of the Budget Line

Figure 10A-6 shows us how to use a graph of the budget line and the indifference curves to find the optimal consumption bundle, the bundle at which the budget line and the indifference curve are tangent. But rather than rely on drawing graphs, we can determine the optimal consumption bundle by using a bit of math. As you can see from Figure 10A-6, at *A*, the optimal consumption bundle, the budget line and the indifference curve have the same slope. Why? Because two curves can only touch each other if they have the same slope at their point of tangency. Otherwise, they would cross each other somewhere. And we know that if we are on an indifference curve that crosses the budget line (like I_1 in Figure 10A-6), we can't be on the indifference curve that contains the optimal consumption bundle (like I_2).

So we can use information about the slopes of the budget line and the indifference curve to find the optimal consumption bundle. To do that, we must first analyze the slope of the budget line, a fairly straightforward task. We know that Ingrid will get the highest possible utility by spending all of her income and consuming a bundle on her budget line. So we can represent Ingrid's budget line, the consumption bundles available to her when she spends all of her income, with the equation:

(10A-7) $(Q_R \times P_R) + (Q_M \times P_M) = N$

where *N* stands for Ingrid's income. To find the slope of the budget line, we divide its vertical intercept (where the budget line hits the vertical axis) by its horizontal intercept (where it hits the horizontal axis). The vertical intercept is the point at which Ingrid spends all her income on restaurant meals and none on housing (that is, $Q_R = 0$). In that case the number of restaurant meals she consumes is:

(10A-8) $Q_M = N/P_M = \$2,400/(\$30 \text{ per meal}) = 80 \text{ meals}$
= Vertical intercept of budget line

At the other extreme, Ingrid spends all her income on housing and none on restaurant meals (so that $Q_M = 0$). This means that at the horizontal intercept of the budget line, the number of rooms she consumes is:

(10A-9) $Q_R = N/P_R = \$2,400/(\$150 \text{ per room}) = 16 \text{ rooms}$
= Horizontal intercept of budget line

Now we have the information needed to find the slope of the budget line. It is:

(10A-10) Slope of budget line = –(Vertical intercept)/(Horizontal intercept)

$$= -\frac{\frac{N}{P_M}}{\frac{N}{P_R}} = -\left(\frac{P_R}{P_M}\right)$$

Notice the minus sign in Equation 10A-10; it's there because the budget line slopes downward. The quantity P_R/P_M is known as the **relative price** of rooms in terms of restaurant meals, to distinguish it from an ordinary price in terms of dollars. In this example it is equal to $150/$30 = 5. Because buying one more room requires Ingrid to give up P_R/P_M quantity of restaurant meals, or 5 meals, we can interpret the relative price P_R/P_M as the rate at which a room trades for restaurant meals in the market; it is the price—in terms of restaurant meals—Ingrid has to "pay" to get one more room.

Looking at this another way, the slope of the budget line—minus the relative price—tells us the opportunity cost of each good in terms of the other. The relative price illustrates the opportunity cost to an individual of consuming one more unit of one good in terms of how much of the other good in his or her consumption bundle must be forgone. This opportunity cost arises from the consumer's limited resources—his or her limited budget. It's useful to note that Equations 10A-8, 10A-9, and 10A-10 give us all the information we need about what happens to the budget line when relative price or income changes. From Equations 10A-8 and 10A-9 we can see that a change in income, N, leads to a parallel shift of the budget line: both the vertical and horizontal intercepts will shift. That is, how far out the budget line is from the origin depends on the consumer's income. If a consumer's income rises, the budget line moves outward. If the consumer's income shrinks, the budget line shifts inward. In each case, the slope of the budget line stays the same because the relative price of one good in terms of the other does not change.

In contrast, a change in the relative price P_R/P_M will lead to a change in the slope of the budget line. We'll analyze these changes in the budget line and how the optimal consumption bundle changes when the relative price changes or when income changes in greater detail later in the appendix.

Prices and the Marginal Rate of Substitution

Now we're ready to bring together the slope of the budget line and the slope of the indifference curve to find the optimal consumption bundle. From Equation 10A-6, we know that the slope of the indifference curve at any point is equal to minus the marginal rate of substitution:

(10A-11) Slope of indifference curve $= -\dfrac{MU_R}{MU_M}$

As we've already noted, at the optimal consumption bundle the slope of the budget line and the slope of the indifference curve are equal. We can write this formally by putting Equations 10A-10 and 10A-11 together, which gives us the **relative price rule** for finding the optimal consumption bundle:

(10A-12) *At the optimal consumption bundle:* $-\dfrac{MU_R}{MU_M} = -\dfrac{P_R}{P_M}$

or $\dfrac{MU_R}{MU_M} = \dfrac{P_R}{P_M}$

That is, at the optimal consumption bundle, the marginal rate of substitution between any two goods is equal to the ratio of their prices. Or to put it in a more intuitive way, at Ingrid's optimal consumption bundle, the rate at which she would trade a room in exchange for having fewer restaurant meals along her indifference curve, MU_R/MU_M, is equal to the rate at which rooms are traded for restaurant meals in the market, P_R/P_M.

What would happen if this equality did not hold? We can see by examining Figure 10A-7. There, at point B, the slope of the indifference curve, $-MU_R/MU_M$, is greater in absolute value than the slope of the budget line, $-P_R/P_M$. This means that, at B, Ingrid values an additional room in place of meals *more* than it costs her to buy an additional room and forgo some meals. As a result, Ingrid would be better off moving down her budget line toward A, consuming more rooms and fewer restaurant meals—and because of that, B could not have been her optimal bundle! Likewise, at C, the slope of Ingrid's indifference curve is less than the slope of the budget line. The implication is that, at C, Ingrid values additional meals in place of a room *more* than it costs her to buy additional meals and forgo a room. Again, Ingrid would be better off moving along her budget line—consuming more restaurant meals and fewer rooms—until she reaches A, her optimal consumption bundle.

But suppose that we do the following transformation to the last term of Equation 10A-12: divide both sides by P_R and multiply both by MU_M. Then the relative price rule becomes (from Chapter 10, Equation 10-3):

(10A-13) *Optimal consumption rule:* $\dfrac{MU_R}{P_R} = \dfrac{MU_M}{P_M}$

So using either the optimal consumption rule (from Chapter 10) or the relative price rule (from this appendix), we find the same optimal consumption bundle.

FIGURE 10A-7 | **Understanding the Relative Price Rule**

The *relative price* of rooms in terms of restaurant meals is equal to minus the slope of the budget line. The *marginal rate of substitution* of rooms in place of restaurant meals is equal to minus the slope of the indifference curve. The *relative price rule* says that at the optimal consumption bundle, the marginal rate of substitution must equal the relative price. This point can be demonstrated by considering what happens when the marginal rate of substitution is not equal to the relative price. At consumption bundle B, the marginal rate of substitution is larger than the relative price; Ingrid can increase her total utility by moving down her budget line, *BL*. At C, the marginal rate of substitution is smaller than the relative price, and Ingrid can increase her total utility by moving up the budget line. Only at A, where the relative price rule holds, is her total utility maximized given her budget constraint.

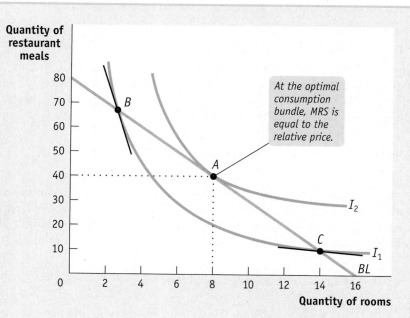

Preferences and Choices

Now that we have seen how to represent the optimal consumption choice in an indifference curve diagram, we can turn briefly to the relationship between consumer preferences and consumer choices.

When we say that two consumers have different preferences, we mean that they have different utility functions. This in turn means that they will have indifference curve maps with different shapes. And those different maps will translate into different consumption choices, even among consumers with the same income and who face the same prices.

To see this, suppose that Ingrid's friend Lars also consumes only housing and restaurant meals. However, Lars has a stronger preference for restaurant meals and a weaker preference for housing. This difference in preferences is shown in Figure 10A-8, which shows *two* sets of indifference curves: panel (a) shows Ingrid's preferences and panel (b) shows Lars's preferences. Note the difference in their shapes.

FIGURE 10A-8   Differences in Preferences

Ingrid and Lars have different preferences, reflected in the different shapes of their indifference curve maps. So they will choose different consumption bundles even when they have the same possible choices. Both of them have an income of $2,400 per month and face prices of $30 per meal and $150 per room. Panel (a) shows Ingrid's consumption choice: 8 rooms and 40 restaurant meals. Panel (b) shows Lars's choice: even though he has the same budget line, he consumes fewer rooms and more restaurant meals.

(a) Ingrid's Preferences and Her Optimal Consumption Bundle

(b) Lars's Preferences and His Optimal Consumption Bundle

Suppose, as before, that rooms cost $150 per month and restaurant meals cost $30. Let's also assume that both Ingrid and Lars have incomes of $2,400 per month, giving them identical budget lines. Nonetheless, because they have different preferences, they will make different consumption choices, as shown in Figure 10A-8. Ingrid will choose 8 rooms and 40 restaurant meals; Lars will choose 4 rooms and 60 restaurant meals.

Using Indifference Curves: Substitutes and Complements

Now that we've seen how to analyze consumer choice using indifference curves, we can get some payoffs from our new technique. First up is a new insight into the distinction between *substitutes* and *complements*.

Back in Chapter 3, we pointed out that the price of one good often affects the demand for another but that the direction of this effect can go either way: a rise in the price of tea increases the demand for coffee, but a rise in the price of cream reduces the demand for coffee. Tea and coffee are substitutes; cream and coffee are complements.

But what determines whether two goods are substitutes or complements? It depends on the shape of a consumer's indifference curves. This relationship can be illustrated with two extreme cases: the cases of *perfect substitutes* and *perfect complements*.

Perfect Substitutes

Consider Cokie, who likes cookies. She isn't particular: it doesn't matter to her whether she has 3 peanut butter cookies and 7 chocolate chip cookies, or vice versa. What would her indifference curves between peanut butter and chocolate chip cookies look like?

The answer is that they would be straight lines like I_1 and I_2 in Figure 10A-9. For example, I_1 shows that any combination of peanut butter cookies and chocolate chip cookies that adds up to 10 cookies yields Cokie the same utility.

FIGURE 10A-9   Perfect Substitutes

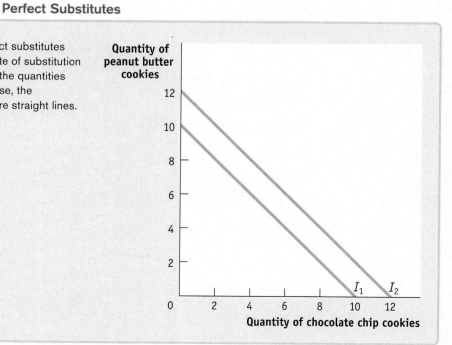

Two goods are perfect substitutes when the marginal rate of substitution does not depend on the quantities consumed. In that case, the indifference curves are straight lines.

A consumer whose indifference curves are straight lines is always willing to substitute the same amount of one good in place of one unit of the other, regardless of how much of either good he or she consumes. Cokie, for example, is always willing to accept one less peanut butter cookie in exchange for one more chocolate chip cookie, making her marginal rate of substitution *constant*.

When indifference curves are straight lines, we say that goods are **perfect substitutes.** When two goods are perfect substitutes, there is only one relative price at which consumers will be willing to purchase both goods; a slightly higher or lower relative price will cause consumers to buy only one of the two goods.

Figure 10A-10 illustrates this point. The indifference curves are the same as those in Figure 10A-9, but now we include Cokie's budget line, *BL*. In each panel we assume that Cokie has $12 to spend. In panel (a) we assume that chocolate chip cookies cost $1.20 and peanut butter cookies cost $1.00. Cokie's optimal consumption bundle is then at point *A*: she buys 12 peanut butter cookies and no chocolate chip cookies. In panel (b) the situation is reversed: chocolate chip cookies cost $1.00 and peanut butter cookies cost $1.20. In this case, her optimal consumption is at point *B*, where she consumes only chocolate chip cookies.

Why does such a small change in the price cause Cokie to switch all her consumption from one good to the other? Because her marginal rate of substitution is constant and therefore doesn't depend on the composition of her consumption bundle. If the relative price of chocolate chip cookies is more than the marginal rate of substitution of chocolate chip cookies in place of peanut butter cookies, she buys only peanut butter cookies; if it is less, she buys only chocolate chip.

Two goods are **perfect substitutes** if the marginal rate of substitution of one good in place of the other good is constant, regardless of how much of each an individual consumes.

FIGURE **10A-10**   Consumer Choice Between Perfect Substitutes

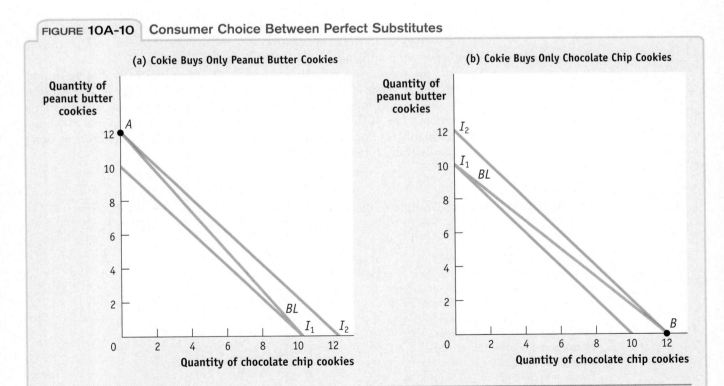

When two goods are perfect substitutes, small price changes lead to large changes in the consumption bundle. In panel (a), the relative price of chocolate chip cookies is slightly higher than the marginal rate of substitution of chocolate chip cookies in place of peanut butter cookies; this is enough to induce Cokie to choose consumption bundle *A*, which consists entirely of peanut butter cookies. In panel (b), the relative price of chocolate chip cookies is slightly lower than the marginal rate of substitution of chocolate chip cookies in place of peanut butter cookies; this induces Cokie to choose bundle *B*, consisting entirely of chocolate chip cookies.

Two goods are **perfect complements** when a consumer wants to consume the goods in the same ratio regardless of their relative price.

And if the relative price of chocolate chip cookies is equal to the marginal rate of substitution, Cokie can maximize her utility by buying any bundle on her budget line. That is, she will be equally happy with any combination of chocolate chip cookies and peanut butter cookies that she can afford. As a result, in this case we cannot predict which particular bundle she will choose among all the bundles that lie on her budget line.

Perfect Complements

The case of perfect substitutes represents one extreme form of consumer preferences; the case of perfect complements represents the other. Goods are **perfect complements** when a consumer wants to consume two goods in the same ratio, regardless of their relative price.

Suppose that Aaron likes cookies and milk—but only together. An extra cookie without an extra glass of milk yields no additional utility; neither does an extra glass of milk without another cookie. In this case, his indifference curves will form right angles, as shown in Figure 10A-11.

To see why, consider the three bundles labeled A, B, and C. At B, on I_4, Aaron consumes 4 cookies and 4 glasses of milk. At A, he consumes 4 cookies and 5 glasses of milk; but the extra glass of milk adds nothing to his utility. So A is on the same indifference curve as B, I_4. Similarly, at C he consumes 5 cookies and 4 glasses of milk, but this yields the same total utility as 4 cookies and 4 glasses of milk. So C is also on the same indifference curve, I_4.

Also shown in Figure 10A-11 is a budget line that would allow Aaron to choose bundle B. The important point is that the slope of the budget line has no effect on his relative consumption of cookies and milk. This means that he will always consume the two goods in the same proportions regardless of prices—which makes the goods perfect complements.

You may be wondering what happened to the marginal rate of substitution in Figure 10A-11. That is, exactly what is Aaron's marginal rate of substitution between cookies and milk, given that he is unwilling to make any substitutions between them? The answer is that in the case of perfect complements, the marginal rate of substitution is *undefined* because an individual's preferences don't allow *any* substitution between goods.

FIGURE **10A-11** | Perfect Complements

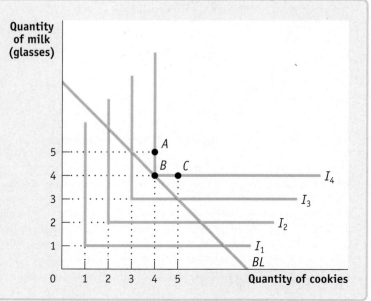

When two goods are perfect complements, a consumer wants to consume the goods in the same ratio regardless of their relative price. Indifference curves take the form of right angles. In this case, Aaron will choose to consume 4 glasses of milk and 4 cookies (bundle B) regardless of the slope of the budget line passing through B. The reason is that neither an additional glass of milk without an additional cookie (bundle A) nor an additional cookie without an additional glass of milk (bundle C) adds to his total utility.

Less Extreme Cases

There are real-world examples of pairs of goods that are very close to being perfect substitutes. For example, the list of ingredients on a package of Bisquick pancake mix says that it contains "soybean and/or cottonseed oil": the producer uses which-ever is cheaper, since consumers can't tell the difference. There are other pairs of goods that are very close to being perfect complements—for example, cars and tires.

In most cases, however, the possibilities for substitution lie somewhere between these extremes. In some cases it isn't easy to be sure whether goods are substitutes or complements.

Prices, Income, and Demand

Let's return now to Ingrid's consumption choices. In the situation we've considered, her income was $2,400 per month, housing cost $150 per room, and restaurant meals cost $30 each. Her optimal consumption bundle, as seen in Figure 10A-7, contained 8 rooms and 40 restaurant meals.

Let's now ask how her consumption choice would change if either the rent per room or her income changed. As we'll see, we can put these pieces together to deepen our understanding of consumer demand.

The Effects of a Price Increase

Suppose that for some reason there is a sharp increase in housing prices. Ingrid must now pay $600 per room instead of $150. Meanwhile, the price of restaurant meals and her income remain unchanged. How does this change affect her consumption choices?

When the price of rooms rises, the relative price of rooms in terms of restaurant meals rises; as a result, Ingrid's budget line changes (for the worse—but we'll get to that). She responds to that change by choosing a new consumption bundle.

Figure 10A-12 shows Ingrid's original (BL_1) and new (BL_2) budget lines—again, under the assumption that her income remains constant at $2,400 per month. With housing costing $150 per room and a restaurant meal costing $30, her budget line, BL_1, intersected the horizontal axis at 16 rooms and the vertical axis at 80 restaurant meals. After the price of a room rises to $600 per room, the budget line, BL_2, still hits

---

FIGURE 10A-12 | Effects of a Price Increase on the Budget Line

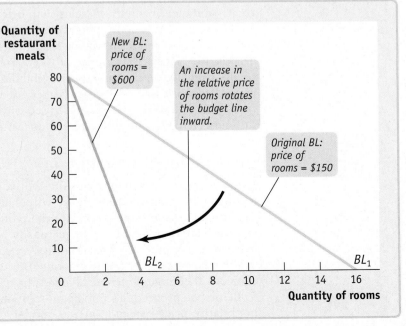

An increase in the price of rooms, holding the price of restaurant meals constant, increases the relative price of rooms in terms of restaurant meals. As a result, Ingrid's original budget line, BL_1, rotates inward to BL_2. Her maximum possible purchase of restaurant meals is unchanged, but her maximum possible purchase of rooms is reduced.

FIGURE 10A-13 Responding to a Price Increase

Ingrid responds to the higher relative price of rooms by choosing a new consumption bundle with fewer rooms and more restaurant meals. Her new optimal consumption bundle, *C*, contains 1 room instead of 8 and 60 restaurant meals instead of 40.

the vertical axis at 80 restaurant meals, but it hits the horizontal axis at only 4 rooms. That's because we know from Equation (10A-9) that the new horizontal intercept of the budget line is now $2,400/$600 = 4. Her budget line has rotated inward and become steeper, reflecting the new, higher relative price of a room in terms of restaurant meals.

Figure 10A-13 shows how Ingrid responds to her new circumstances. Her original optimal consumption bundle consists of 8 rooms and 40 meals. After her budget line rotates in response to the change in relative price, she finds her new optimal consumption bundle by choosing the point on BL_2 that brings her to as high an indifference curve as possible. At the new optimal consumption bundle, she consumes fewer rooms and more restaurant meals than before: 1 room and 60 restaurant meals.

Why does Ingrid's consumption of rooms fall? Part—but only part—of the reason is that the rise in the price of rooms reduces her purchasing power, making her poorer. That is, the higher relative price of rooms rotates her budget line inward toward the origin, reducing her consumption possibilities and putting her on a lower indifference curve. In a sense, when she faces a higher price of housing, it's as if her income declined.

To understand this effect, and to see why it isn't the whole story, let's consider a different change in Ingrid's circumstances: a change in her income.

Income and Consumption

In Chapter 3 we learned about the individual demand curve, which shows how a consumer's consumption choice will change as the price of one good changes, holding income and the prices of other goods constant. That is, movement along the individual demand curve primarily shows the substitution effect, as we learned in Chapter 10—how quantity consumed changes in response to changes in the *relative price* of the two goods. But we can also ask how the consumption choice will change if *income* changes, holding relative price constant.

Before we proceed, it's important to understand how a change in income, holding relative price constant, affects the budget line. Suppose that Ingrid's income

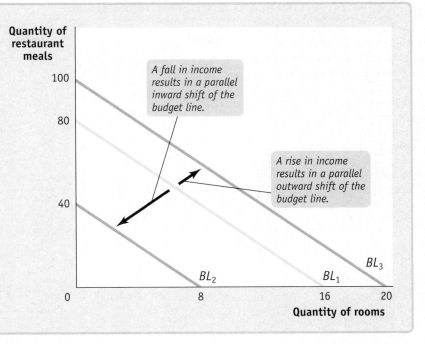

FIGURE 10A-14 | Effect of a Change in Income on the Budget Line

When relative prices are held constant, the budget line shifts parallel in response to changes in income. For example, if Ingrid's income falls from $2,400 to $1,200, she is clearly worse off: her budget line shifts inward from BL_1 to its new position at BL_2. In contrast, if Ingrid's income rises from $2,400 to $3,000, she is clearly better off: her budget line shifts outward from BL_1 to its new position at BL_3.

A fall in income results in a parallel inward shift of the budget line.

A rise in income results in a parallel outward shift of the budget line.

fell from $2,400 to $1,200 and we hold prices constant at $150 per room and $30 per restaurant meal. As a result, the maximum number of rooms she can afford drops from 16 to 8, and the maximum number of restaurant meals drops from 80 to 40. In other words, Ingrid's consumption possibilities have shrunk, as shown by the parallel inward shift of the budget line in Figure 10A-14 from BL_1 to BL_2. It's a parallel shift because the slope of the budget line—the relative price—remains unchanged when income changes. Alternatively, suppose Ingrid's income rises from $2,400 to $3,000. She can now afford a maximum of 20 rooms or 100 meals, leading to a *parallel outward shift* of the budget line—the shift from BL_1 to BL_3 in Figure 10A-14. In this case, Ingrid's consumption possibilities have expanded.

Now we are ready to consider how Ingrid responds to a direct change in income—that is, a change in her income level holding relative price constant. Figure 10A-15 compares Ingrid's budget line and optimal consumption choice at an income of $2,400 per month ($BL_1$) with her budget line and optimal consumption choice at an income of $1,200 per month ($BL_2$), keeping prices constant at $150 per room and $30 per restaurant meal. Point *A* is Ingrid's optimal consumption bundle at an income of $2,400, and point *B* is her optimal consumption bundle at an income of $1,200. In each case, her optimal consumption bundle is given by the point at which the budget line is tangent to the indifference curve. As you can see, at the lower income her budget line shifts inward compared to her budget line at the higher income but maintains the same slope because relative price has not changed.

This means that she must reduce her consumption of either housing or restaurant meals, or both. As a result, she is at a lower level of total utility, represented by a lower indifference curve.

As it turns out, Ingrid chooses to consume less of both goods when her income falls: as her income goes from $2,400 to $1,200, her consumption of housing falls from 8 to 4 rooms and her consumption of restaurant meals falls from 40 to 20. This is because in her utility function both goods are *normal goods,* as defined in Chapter 3: goods for which demand increases when income rises and for which demand decreases when income falls.

Although most goods are normal goods, we also pointed out in Chapter 3 that some goods are *inferior goods,* goods for which demand moves in the opposite

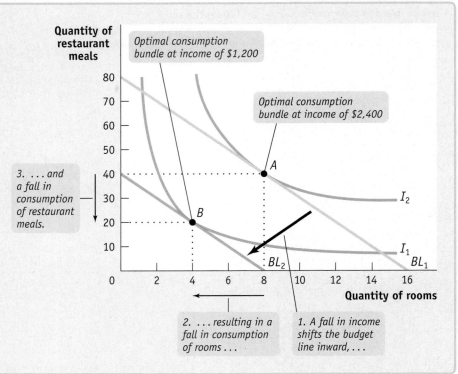

FIGURE **10A-15**   Income and Consumption: Normal Goods

At a monthly income of $2,400, Ingrid chooses bundle *A*, consisting of 8 rooms and 40 restaurant meals. When relative price remains unchanged, a fall in income shifts her budget line inward to BL_2. At a monthly income of $1,200, she chooses bundle *B*, consisting of 4 rooms and 20 restaurant meals. Since Ingrid's consumption of both restaurant meals and rooms falls when her income falls, both goods are normal goods.

direction to the change in income: demand decreases when income rises, and demand increases when income falls. An example might be second-hand furniture. Whether a good is an inferior good depends on the consumer's indifference curve map. Figure 10A-16 illustrates such a case, where second-hand furniture

FIGURE **10A-16**   Income and Consumption: An Inferior Good

When Ingrid's income falls from $2,400 to $1,200, her optimal consumption bundle changes from *D* to *E*. Her consumption of second-hand furniture increases, implying that second-hand furniture is an inferior good. In contrast, her consumption of restaurant meals falls, implying that restaurant meals are a normal good.

is measured on the horizontal axis and restaurant meals are measured on the vertical axis. Note that when Ingrid's income falls from $2,400 ($BL_1$) to $1,200 ($BL_2$), and her optimal consumption bundle goes from D to E, her consumption of second-hand furniture increases—implying that second-hand furniture is an inferior good. Simultaneously, her consumption of restaurant meals decreases—implying that restaurant meals are a normal good.

Income and Substitution Effects

Now that we have examined the effects of a change in income, we can return to the issue of a change in price—and show in a more specific way that the effect of a higher price on demand has an income component.

Figure 10A-17 shows, once again, Ingrid's original (BL_1) and new (BL_2) budget lines and consumption choices with a monthly income of $2,400. At a housing price of $150 per room, Ingrid chooses the consumption bundle at A; at a housing price of $600 per room, she chooses the consumption bundle at C.

Let's notice again what happens to Ingrid's budget line after the increase in the price of housing. It continues to hit the vertical axis at 80 restaurant meals; that is, if Ingrid were to spend all her income on restaurant meals, the increase in the price of housing would not affect her. But the new budget line hits the horizontal axis at only 4 rooms. So the budget line has rotated, *shifting inward* and *becoming steeper*, as a consequence of the rise in the relative price of rooms.

We already know what happens: Ingrid's consumption of housing falls from 8 rooms to 1 room. But the figure suggests that there are *two* reasons for the fall in Ingrid's housing consumption. One reason she consumes fewer rooms is that, because of the higher relative price of rooms, the opportunity cost of a room measured in restaurant meals—the quantity of restaurant meals she must give up to consume an additional room—has increased. This change in opportunity cost, which is reflected in the steeper slope of the budget line, gives her an incentive to substitute restaurant meals in place of rooms in her consumption.

FIGURE 10A-17 | **Income and Substitution Effects**

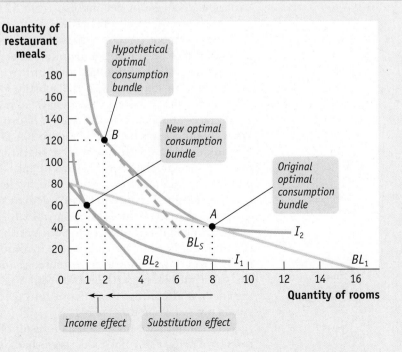

The movement from Ingrid's original optimal consumption bundle when the price of rooms is $150, A, to her new optimal consumption bundle when the price of rooms is $600, C, can be decomposed into two parts. The movement from A to B—the movement along the original indifference curve, I_2, as relative price changes—is the pure substitution effect. It captures how her consumption would change if she were given a hypothetical increase in income that just compensates her for the increase in the price of rooms so that her total utility is unchanged. The movement from B to C, the change in consumption when we remove that hypothetical income compensation, is the income effect of the price increase—how her consumption changes as a result of the fall in her purchasing power.

But the other reason Ingrid consumes fewer rooms after their price increases is that the rise in the price of rooms makes her *poorer*. True, her money income hasn't changed. But she must pay more for rooms, and as a result her budget line has rotated inward. So she cannot reach the same level of total utility as before, meaning that her real income has fallen. That is why she ends up on a lower indifference curve.

In the real world, these effects—an increase in the price of a good raises its opportunity cost and also makes consumers poorer—usually go together. But in our imagination we can separate them. In Chapter 10 we introduced the distinction between the *substitution effect* of a price change (the change in consumption that arises from the substitution of the good that is now relatively cheaper in place of the good that is now relatively more expensive) and the *income effect* (the change in consumption caused by the change in purchasing power arising from a price change). Now we can show these two effects more clearly.

To isolate the substitution effect, let's temporarily change the story about why Ingrid faces an increase in rent: it's not that housing has become more expensive, it's the fact that she has moved from Cincinnati to San Jose, where rents are higher. But let's consider a hypothetical scenario—let's suppose momentarily that she earns more in San Jose and that the higher income is just enough to *compensate* her for the higher price of housing, so that her total utility is exactly the same as before.

Figure 10A-17 shows her situation before and after the move. The bundle labeled *A* represents Ingrid's original consumption choice: 8 rooms and 40 restaurant meals. When she moves to San Jose, she faces a higher price of housing, so her budget line becomes steeper. But we have just assumed that her move increases her income by just enough to compensate for the higher price of housing—that is, just enough to let her reach the original indifference curve. So her new *hypothetical* optimal consumption bundle is at *B*, where the steeper dashed hypothetical budget line (BL_S) is just tangent to the original indifference curve (I_2). By assuming that we have compensated Ingrid for the loss in purchasing power due to the increase in the price of housing, we isolate the *pure substitution effect* of the change in relative price on her consumption.

At *B*, Ingrid's consumption bundle contains 2 rooms and 120 restaurant meals. This costs $4,800 (2 rooms at $600 each, and 120 meals at $30 each). So if Ingrid faces an increase in the price of housing from $150 to $600 per room, but also experiences a rise in her income from $2,400 to $4,800 per month, she ends up with the same level of total utility.

The movement from *A* to *B* is the pure substitution effect of the price change. It is the effect on Ingrid's consumption choice when we change the relative price of housing while keeping her total utility constant.

Now that we have isolated the substitution effect, we can bring back the income effect of the price change. That's easy: we just go back to the original story, in which Ingrid faces an increase in the price of housing *without* any rise in income. We already know that this leads her to *C* in Figure 10A-17. But we can think of the move from *A* to *C* as taking place in two steps. First, Ingrid moves from *A* to *B*, the substitution effect of the change in relative price. Then we take away the extra income needed to keep her on the original indifference curve, causing her to move to *C*. The movement from *B* to *C* is the additional change in Ingrid's demand that results because the increase in housing prices actually reduces her utility. So this is the income effect of the price change.

We can use Figure 10A-17 to confirm that rooms are a normal good in Ingrid's preferences. For normal goods, the income effect and the substitution effect work in the same direction: a price increase induces a fall in quantity consumed by the substitution effect (the move from *A* to *B*) and a fall in quantity consumed by the income effect (the move from *B* to *C*). That's why demand curves for normal goods always slope downward.

What would have happened as a result of the increase in the price of housing if, instead of being a normal good, rooms had been an inferior good for Ingrid? First, the movement from *A* to *B* depicted in Figure 10A-17, the substitution effect, would remain unchanged. But an income change causes quantity consumed to move in the opposite direction for an inferior good. So the movement from *B* to *C* shown in Figure 10A-17, the income effect for a normal good, would no longer hold. Instead, the income effect for an inferior good would cause Ingrid's quantity of rooms consumed to *increase* from *B*—say, to a bundle consisting of 3 rooms and 20 restaurant meals.

In the end, the demand curves for inferior goods normally slope downward: if Ingrid consumes 3 rooms after the increase in the price of housing, it is still 5 fewer rooms than she consumed before. So although the income effect moves in the opposite direction of the substitution effect in the case of an inferior good, in this example the substitution effect is stronger than the income effect.

But what if there existed a type of inferior good in which the income effect is so strong that it dominates the substitution effect? Would a demand curve for that good then slope upward—that is, would quantity demanded increase when price increases? The answer is yes: you have encountered such a good already—it is called a *Giffen good,* and it was described in Chapter 10. As we noted there, Giffen goods are rare creatures, but they cannot be ruled out.

Is the distinction between income and substitution effects important in practice? For analyzing the demand for goods, the answer is that it usually isn't that important. However, in Chapter 19 we'll discuss how individuals make decisions about how much of their labor to supply to employers. In that case income and substitution effects work in opposite directions, and the distinction between them becomes crucial.

PROBLEMS

1. For each of the following situations, draw a diagram containing three of Isabella's indifference curves.

   a. For Isabella, cars and tires are perfect complements, but in a ratio of 1:4; that is, for each car, Isabella wants exactly four tires. Be sure to label and number the axes of your diagram. Place tires on the horizontal axis and cars on the vertical axis.

   b. Isabella gets utility only from her caffeine intake. She can consume Valley Dew or cola, and Valley Dew contains twice as much caffeine as cola. Be sure to label and number the axes of your diagram. Place cola on the horizontal axis and Valley Dew on the vertical axis.

   c. Isabella gets utility from consuming two goods: leisure time and income. Both have diminishing marginal utility. Be sure to label the axes of your diagram. Place leisure on the horizontal axis and income on the vertical axis.

   d. Isabella can consume two goods: skis and bindings. For each ski she wants exactly one binding. Be sure to label and number the axes of your diagram. Place bindings on the horizontal axis and skis on the vertical axis.

   e. Isabella gets utility from consuming soda. But she gets no utility from consuming water: any more, or any less, water leaves her total utility level unchanged. Be sure to label the axes of your diagram. Place water on the horizontal axis and soda on the vertical axis.

2. Use the four properties of indifference curves for ordinary goods illustrated in Figure 10A-4 to answer the following questions.

   a. Can you rank the following two bundles? If so, which property of indifference curves helps you rank them?

   Bundle *A:* 2 movie tickets and 3 cafeteria meals

   Bundle *B:* 4 movie tickets and 8 cafeteria meals

   b. Can you rank the following two bundles? If so, which property of indifference curves helps you rank them?

   Bundle *A:* 2 movie tickets and 3 cafeteria meals

   Bundle *B:* 4 movie tickets and 3 cafeteria meals

   c. Can you rank the following two bundles? If so, which property of indifference curves helps you rank them?

   Bundle *A:* 12 videos and 4 bags of chips

   Bundle *B:* 5 videos and 10 bags of chips

   d. Suppose you are indifferent between the following two bundles:

   Bundle *A:* 10 breakfasts and 4 dinners

   Bundle *B:* 4 breakfasts and 10 dinners

   Now compare bundle *A* and the following bundle:

   Bundle *C:* 7 breakfasts and 7 dinners

   Can you rank bundle *A* and bundle *C*? If so, which property of indifference curves helps you rank them? (*Hint:* It may help if you draw this, placing dinners on the horizontal axis and breakfasts on the vertical axis. And remember that breakfasts and dinners are ordinary goods.)

3. The four properties of indifference curves for ordinary goods illustrated in Figure 10A-4 rule out certain indifference curves. Determine whether those general

properties allow each of the following indifference curves. If not, state which of the general principles rules out the curves.

a.

b.

c.

d.

4. Restaurant meals and housing (measured by the number of rooms) are the only two goods that Neha can buy. She has income of $1,000, and the price of each room is $100. The relative price of 1 room in terms of restaurant meals is 5. How many restaurant meals can she buy if she spends all her money on them?

5. Answer the following questions based on two assumptions: (1) Inflation increases the prices of all goods by 20%. (2) Ina's income increases from $50,000 to $55,000.

   a. Has Ina's budget line become steeper, less steep, or equally as steep?

   b. Has Ina's budget line shifted outward, inward, or not at all?

6. Kory has an income of $50, which she can spend on two goods: music albums and cups of hot chocolate. Both are normal goods for her. Each album costs $10, and each cup of hot chocolate costs $2. For each of the following situations, decide whether this is Kory's optimal consumption bundle. If not, what should Kory do to achieve her optimal consumption bundle?

   a. Kory is considering buying 4 albums and 5 cups of hot chocolate. At that bundle, her marginal rate of substitution of albums in place of hot chocolate is 1; that is, she would be willing to forgo only 1 cup of hot chocolate to acquire 1 album.

   b. Kory is considering buying 2 albums and 15 cups of hot chocolate. Kory's marginal utility of the second album is 25, and her marginal utility of the fifteenth cup of hot chocolate is 5.

   c. Kory is considering buying 1 album and 10 cups of hot chocolate. At that bundle, her marginal rate of substitution of albums in place of hot chocolate is 5; that is, she would be just willing to exchange 5 cups of hot chocolate for 1 album.

7. Raul has 4 Cal Ripken and 2 Nolan Ryan baseball cards. The prices of these baseball cards are $24 for Cal and $12 for Nolan. Raul, however, would be willing to exchange 1 Cal card for 1 Nolan card.

   a. What is Raul's marginal rate of substitution of Cal Ripken in place of Nolan Ryan baseball cards?

   b. Can Raul buy and sell baseball cards to make himself better off? How?

   c. Suppose Raul has traded baseball cards and after trading still has some of each kind of card. Also, he now no longer wants to make any more trades. What is his marginal rate of substitution of Cal Ripken in place of Nolan Ryan cards now?

8. Ralph and Lauren are talking about how much they like going to the gym and how much they like eating out at their favorite restaurant and they regularly do some of each. A session at the gym costs the same as a meal at the restaurant. Ralph says that, for his current consumption of gym sessions and restaurant meals, he values 1 more meal twice as much as he values 1 more session at the gym. Lauren is studying economics, and

she tells him that his current consumption bundle cannot be optimal.

   a. Is Lauren right? Why or why not? Draw a diagram of Ralph's budget line and the indifference curve that he is on by making his current consumption choice. Place restaurant meals on the horizontal axis and gym sessions on the vertical axis.

   b. How should Ralph adjust his consumption so that it is optimal? Illustrate an optimal choice in your diagram.

9. Sabine can't tell the difference between Coke and Pepsi—the two taste exactly the same to her.

   a. What is Sabine's marginal rate of substitution of Coke in place of Pepsi?

   b. Draw a few of Sabine's indifference curves for Coke and Pepsi. Place Coke on the horizontal axis and Pepsi on the vertical axis.

   c. Sabine has $6 to spend on cola this week. Coke costs $1.50 per six-pack and Pepsi costs $1.00. Draw Sabine's budget line for Coke and Pepsi on the same diagram.

   d. What is Sabine's optimal consumption bundle? Show this on your diagram.

   e. If the price of Coke and Pepsi is the same, what combination of Coke and Pepsi will Sabine buy?

10. For Norma, both nachos and salsa are normal goods. They are also ordinary goods for Norma. The price of nachos rises, but the price of salsa remains unchanged.

   a. Can you determine definitively whether she consumes more or fewer nachos? Explain with a diagram, placing nachos on the horizontal axis and salsa on the vertical axis.

   b. Can you determine definitively whether she consumes more or less salsa? Explain with a diagram, placing nachos on the horizontal axis and salsa on the vertical axis.

11. Gus spends his income on gas for his car and food. The government raises the tax on gas, thereby raising the price of gas. But the government also lowers the income tax, thereby increasing Gus's income. And this rise in income is just enough to place Gus on the same indifference curve as the one he was on before the price of gas rose. Will Gus buy more, less, or the same amount of gas as before these changes? Illustrate your answer with a diagram, placing gas on the horizontal axis and food on the vertical axis.

12. Pam spends her money on bread and Spam, and her indifference curves obey the four properties of indifference curves for ordinary goods. Suppose that, for Pam, Spam is an inferior, but not a Giffen, good; bread is a normal good. Bread costs $2 per loaf, and Spam costs $2 per can. Pam has $20 to spend.

   a. Draw a diagram of Pam's budget line, placing Spam on the horizontal axis and bread on the vertical axis. Suppose her optimal consumption bundle is 4 cans

of Spam and 6 loaves of bread. Illustrate that bundle and draw the indifference curve on which it lies.

   b. The price of Spam falls to $1; the price of bread remains the same. Pam now buys 7 loaves of bread and 6 cans of Spam. Illustrate her new budget line and new optimal consumption bundle in your diagram. Also draw the indifference curve on which this bundle lies.

   c. In your diagram, show the income and substitution effects from this fall in the price of Spam. Remember that Spam is an inferior good for Pam.

13. Katya commutes to work. She can either use public transport or her own car. Her indifference curves obey the four properties of indifference curves for ordinary goods.

   a. Draw Katya's budget line with car travel on the vertical axis and public transport on the horizontal axis. Suppose that Katya consumes some of both goods. Draw an indifference curve that helps you illustrate her optimal consumption bundle.

   b. Now the price of public transport falls. Draw Katya's new budget line.

   c. For Katya, public transport is an inferior, but not a Giffen, good. Draw an indifference curve that illustrates her optimal consumption bundle after the price of public transport has fallen. Is Katya consuming more or less public transport?

   d. Show the income and substitution effects from this fall in the price of public transport.

14. For Crandall, cheese cubes and crackers are perfect complements: he wants to consume exactly 1 cheese cube with each cracker. He has $2.40 to spend on cheese and crackers. One cheese cube costs 20 cents, and 1 cracker costs 10 cents. Draw a diagram, with crackers on the horizontal axis and cheese cubes on the vertical axis, to answer the following questions.

   a. Which bundle will Crandall consume?

   b. The price of crackers rises to 20 cents. How many cheese cubes and how many crackers will Crandall consume?

   c. Show the income and substitution effects from this price rise.

15. Carmen consumes nothing but cafeteria meals and music albums. Her indifference curves exhibit the four general properties of indifference curves. Cafeteria meals cost $5 each, and albums cost $10. Carmen has $50 to spend.

   a. Draw Carmen's budget line and an indifference curve that illustrates her optimal consumption bundle. Place cafeteria meals on the horizontal axis and albums on the vertical axis. You do not have enough information to know the specific tangency point, so choose one arbitrarily.

   b. Now Carmen's income rises to $100. Draw her new budget line on the same diagram, as well as an indifference curve that illustrates her optimal consumption bundle. Assume that cafeteria meals are an inferior good.

c. Can you draw an indifference curve showing that cafeteria meals and albums are both inferior goods?

16. The Japanese Ministry of Internal Affairs and Communications collects data on the prices of goods and services in the Ku-area of Tokyo, as well as data on the average Japanese household's monthly income. The accompanying table shows some of this data. (¥ denotes the Japanese currency the yen.)

Year	Price of eggs (per pack of 10)	Price of tuna (per 100- gram portion)	Average monthly income
2003	¥187	¥392	¥524,810
2005	231	390	524,585

a. For each of the two years for which you have data, what is the maximum number of packs of eggs that an average Japanese household could have consumed each month? The maximum number of 100-gram portions of tuna? In one diagram, draw the average Japanese household's budget line in 2003 and in 2005. Place the quantity of eggs on the *y*-axis and the quantity of tuna on the *x*-axis.

b. Calculate the relative price of eggs in terms of tuna for each year. Use the relative price rule to determine how the average household's consumption of eggs and tuna would have changed between 2003 and 2005.

WORK IT OUT

For interactive, step-by-step help in solving the following problem, visit LaunchPad by using the URL on the back cover of this book.

17. Tyrone is a utility maximizer. His income is $100, which he can spend on cafeteria meals and on notepads. Each meal costs $5, and each notepad costs $2. At these prices Tyrone chooses to buy 16 cafeteria meals and 10 notepads.

a. Draw a diagram that shows Tyrone's choice using an indifference curve and his budget line, placing notepads on the vertical axis and cafeteria meals on the horizontal axis. Label the indifference curve I_1 and the budget line BL_1.

b. The price of notepads falls to $1; the price of cafeteria meals remains the same. On the same diagram, draw Tyrone's budget line with the new prices and label it BL_H.

c. Lastly, Tyrone's income falls to $90. On the same diagram, draw his budget line with this income and the new prices and label it BL_2. Is he worse off, better off, or equally as well off with these new prices and lower income than compared to the original prices and higher income? (*Hint:* Determine whether Tyrone can afford to buy his original consumption bundle of 16 meals and 10 notepads with the lower income and new prices.) Illustrate your answer using an indifference curve and label it I_2.

d. Give an intuitive explanation of your answer to part c.

Behind the Supply Curve: Inputs and Costs

WORLD VIEW

THE FARMER'S MARGIN

> ► **What You Will Learn in This Chapter**
>
> ■ The importance of the firm's **production function,** the relationship between quantity of inputs and quantity of output
>
> ■ Why production is often subject to **diminishing returns to inputs**
>
> ■ The various types of costs a firm faces and how they generate the firm's marginal and average cost curves
>
> ■ Why a firm's costs may differ in the **short run** versus the **long run**
>
> ■ How the firm's technology of production can generate **increasing returns to scale**

©Terrance Klassen/AgeFotostock

How intensively an acre of land is worked—a decision at the margin—depends on the price of wheat a farmer faces.

"OBEAUTIFUL FOR SPACIOUS skies, for amber waves of grain." So begins the song "America the Beautiful." And those amber waves of grain are for real: though farmers are now only a small minority of America's population, our agricultural industry is immensely productive and feeds much of the world.

If you look at agricultural statistics, however, something may seem a bit surprising: when it comes to yield per acre, U.S. farmers are often nowhere near the top. For example, farmers in Western European countries grow about three times as much wheat per acre as their U.S. counterparts. Are the Europeans better at growing wheat than we are?

No: European farmers are very skillful, but no more so than Americans. They produce more wheat per acre because they employ more inputs—more fertilizer

and, especially, more labor—per acre. Of course, this means that European farmers have higher costs than their American counterparts. But because of government policies, European farmers receive a much higher price for their wheat than American farmers. This gives them an incentive to use more inputs and to expend more effort at the margin to increase the crop yield per acre.

Notice our use of the phrase "at the margin." Like most decisions that involve a comparison of benefits and costs, decisions about inputs and production involve a comparison of marginal quantities—the marginal cost versus the marginal benefit of producing a bit more from each acre.

In Chapter 9 we considered the case of Alex, who had to choose the number of years of schooling that maximized his profit from schooling. There we used the

profit-maximizing principle of marginal analysis to find the optimal quantity of years of schooling. In this chapter, we will encounter producers who have to make similar "how much" decisions: choosing the quantity of output produced to maximize profit.

Here and in Chapter 12, we will show how marginal analysis can be used to understand these output decisions—decisions that lie behind the supply curve. The first step in this analysis is to show how the relationship between a firm's inputs and its output—its *production function*—determines its *cost curves,* the relationship between cost and quantity of output produced. That is what we do in this chapter. In Chapter 12, we will use our understanding of the firm's cost curves to derive the individual and the market supply curves.

A **production function** is the relationship between the quantity of inputs a firm uses and the quantity of output it produces.

A **fixed input** is an input whose quantity is fixed for a period of time and cannot be varied.

A **variable input** is an input whose quantity the firm can vary at any time.

The **long run** is the time period in which all inputs can be varied.

The **short run** is the time period in which at least one input is fixed.

The **total product curve** shows how the quantity of output depends on the quantity of the variable input, for a given quantity of the fixed input.

The Production Function

A *firm* is an organization that produces goods or services for sale. To do this, it must transform inputs into output. The quantity of output a firm produces depends on the quantity of inputs; this relationship is known as the firm's **production function.** As we'll see, a firm's production function underlies its *cost curves.* As a first step, let's look at the characteristics of a hypothetical production function.

Inputs and Output

To understand the concept of a production function, let's consider a farm that we assume, for the sake of simplicity, produces only one output, wheat, and uses only two inputs, land and labor. This particular farm is owned by a couple named George and Martha. They hire workers to do the actual physical labor on the farm. Moreover, we will assume that all potential workers are of the same quality—they are all equally knowledgeable and capable of performing farmwork.

George and Martha's farm sits on 10 acres of land; no more acres are available to them, and they are currently unable to either increase or decrease the size of their farm by selling, buying, or leasing acreage. Land here is what economists call a **fixed input**—an input whose quantity is fixed for a period of time and cannot be varied. George and Martha are, however, free to decide how many workers to hire. The labor provided by these workers is called a **variable input**—an input whose quantity the firm can vary at any time.

In reality, whether or not the quantity of an input is really fixed depends on the time horizon. In the **long run** that is, given that a long enough period of time has elapsed—firms can adjust the quantity of any input. For example, in the long run, George and Martha can vary the amount of land they farm by buying or selling land. So there are no fixed inputs in the long run. In contrast, the **short run** is defined as the time period during which at least one input is fixed. Later in this chapter, we'll look more carefully at the distinction between the short run and the long run. But for now, we will restrict our attention to the short run and assume that at least one input is fixed.

George and Martha know that the quantity of wheat they produce depends on the number of workers they hire. Using modern farming techniques, one worker can cultivate the 10-acre farm, albeit not very intensively. When an additional worker is added, the land is divided equally among all the workers: each worker has 5 acres to cultivate when 2 workers are employed, each cultivates $3\frac{1}{3}$ acres when 3 are employed, and so on. So as additional workers are employed, the 10 acres of land are cultivated more intensively and more bushels of wheat are produced.

The relationship between the quantity of labor and the quantity of output, for a given amount of the fixed input, constitutes the farm's production function. The production function for George and Martha's farm, where land is the fixed input and labor is a variable input, is shown in the first two columns of the table in Figure 11-1; the diagram there shows the same information graphically. The curve in Figure 11-1 shows how the quantity of output depends on the quantity of the variable input, for a given quantity of the fixed input; it is called the farm's **total product curve.**

The physical quantity of output, bushels of wheat, is measured on the vertical axis; the quantity of the variable input, labor (that is, the number of workers employed), is measured on the horizontal axis. The total product curve here slopes upward, reflecting the fact that more bushels of wheat are produced as more workers are employed.

FIGURE 11-1   Production Function and Total Product Curve for George and Martha's Farm

Quantity of labor L (workers)	Quantity of wheat Q (bushels)	Marginal product of labor $MPL = \Delta Q/\Delta L$ (bushels per worker)
0	0	
		19
1	19	
		17
2	36	
		15
3	51	
		13
4	64	
		11
5	75	
		9
6	84	
		7
7	91	
		5
8	96	

The table shows the production function, the relationship between the quantity of the variable input (labor, measured in number of workers) and the quantity of output (wheat, measured in bushels) for a given quantity of the fixed input. It also calculates the marginal product of labor on George and Martha's farm. The total product curve shows the production function graphically. It slopes upward because more wheat is produced as more workers are employed. It also becomes flatter because the marginal product of labor declines as more and more workers are employed.

Although the total product curve in Figure 11-1 slopes upward along its entire length, the slope isn't constant: as you move up the curve to the right, it flattens out. To understand why the slope changes, look at the third column of the table in Figure 11-1, which shows the *change in the quantity of output* that is generated by adding one more worker. This is called the *marginal product* of labor, or *MPL:* the additional quantity of output from using one more unit of labor (where one unit of labor is equal to one worker). In general, the **marginal product** of an input is the additional quantity of output that is produced by using one more unit of that input.

In this example, we have data on changes in output at intervals of 1 worker. Sometimes data aren't available in increments of 1 unit—for example, you might have information only on the quantity of output when there are 40 workers and when there are 50 workers. In this case, we use the following equation to calculate the marginal product of labor:

(11-1) $\begin{array}{l} \text{Marginal} \\ \text{product} \\ \text{of labor} \end{array} = \begin{array}{l} \text{Change in quantity of} \\ \text{output produced by one} \\ \text{additional unit of labor} \end{array} = \dfrac{\text{Change in quantity of output}}{\text{Change in quantity of labor}}$

or

$$MPL = \frac{\Delta Q}{\Delta L}$$

In this equation, Δ, the Greek uppercase delta, represents the change in a variable.

Now we can explain the significance of the slope of the total product curve: it is equal to the marginal product of labor. The slope of a line is equal to "rise"

The **marginal product** of an input is the additional quantity of output that is produced by using one more unit of that input.

GLOBAL COMPARISION | **Wheat Yields Around the World**

Wheat yields differ substantially around the world. The disparity between France and the United States that you see in this graph is particularly striking, given that they are both wealthy countries with comparable agricultural technology. Yet the reason for that disparity is straightforward: differing government policies. In the United States, farmers receive payments from the government to supplement their incomes, but European farmers benefit from price floors. Since European farmers get higher prices for their output than American farmers, they employ more variable inputs and produce significantly higher yields.

Interestingly, in poor countries like Uganda and Ethiopia, foreign aid can lead to significantly depressed yields. Foreign aid from wealthy countries has often taken the form of surplus food, which depresses local market prices, severely hurting the local agriculture that poor countries normally depend on. Charitable organizations like OXFAM have asked wealthy food-producing countries to modify their aid policies—principally, to give aid in cash rather than in food products except in the case of acute food shortages—to avoid this problem.

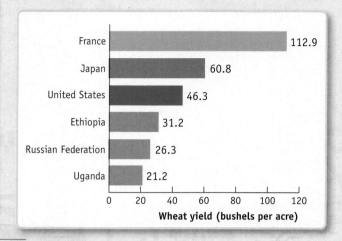

Source: Food and Agriculture Organization of the United Nations. Data are from 2012.

over "run" (see the appendix to Chapter 2). This implies that the slope of the total product curve is the change in the quantity of output (the "rise", ΔQ) divided by the change in the quantity of labor (the "run", ΔL). And this, as we can see from Equation 11-1, is simply the marginal product of labor. So in Figure 11-1, the fact that the marginal product of the first worker is 19 also means that the slope of the total product curve in going from 0 to 1 worker is 19. Similarly, the slope of the total product curve in going from 1 to 2 workers is the same as the marginal product of the second worker, 17, and so on.

In this example, the marginal product of labor steadily declines as more workers are hired—that is, each successive worker adds less to output than the previous worker. So as employment increases, the total product curve gets flatter.

Figure 11-2 shows how the marginal product of labor depends on the number of workers employed on the farm. The marginal product of labor, *MPL*, is measured on the vertical axis in units of physical output—bushels of wheat—produced per additional worker, and the number of workers employed is measured on the horizontal axis. You can see from the table in Figure 11-1 that if 5 workers are employed instead of 4, output rises from 64 to 75 bushels; in this case the marginal product of labor is 11 bushels—the same number found in Figure 11-2. To indicate that 11 bushels is the marginal product when employment rises from 4 to 5, we place the point corresponding to that information halfway between 4 and 5 workers.

There are **diminishing returns to an input** when an increase in the quantity of that input, holding the levels of all other inputs fixed, leads to a decline in the marginal product of that input.

In this example the marginal product of labor falls as the number of workers increases. That is, there are *diminishing returns to labor* on George and Martha's farm. In general, there are **diminishing returns to an input** when an increase in the quantity of that input, holding the quantity of all other inputs fixed, reduces that input's marginal product. Due to diminishing returns to labor, the *MPL* curve is negatively sloped.

FIGURE 11-2   Marginal Product of Labor Curve for George and Martha's Farm

The marginal product of labor curve plots each worker's marginal product, the increase in the quantity of output generated by each additional worker. The change in the quantity of output is measured on the vertical axis and the number of workers employed on the horizontal axis. The first worker employed generates an increase in output of 19 bushels, the second worker generates an increase of 17 bushels, and so on. The curve slopes downward due to diminishing returns to labor.

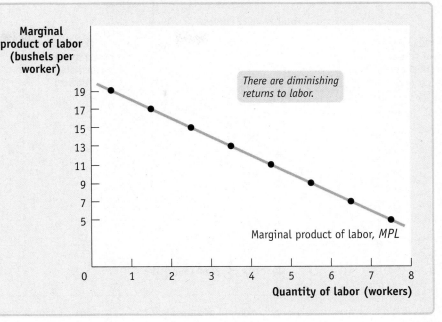

To grasp why diminishing returns can occur, think about what happens as George and Martha add more and more workers without increasing the number of acres of land. As the number of workers increases, the land is farmed more intensively and the number of bushels produced increases. But each additional worker is working with a smaller share of the 10 acres—the fixed input—than the previous worker. As a result, the additional worker cannot produce as much output as the previous worker. So it's not surprising that the marginal product of the additional worker falls.

The crucial point to emphasize about diminishing returns is that, like many propositions in economics, it is an "other things equal" proposition: each successive unit of an input will raise production by less than the last *if the quantity of all other inputs is held fixed.*

What would happen if the levels of other inputs were allowed to change? You can see the answer illustrated in Figure 11-3. Panel (a) shows two total product curves, TP_{10} and TP_{20}. TP_{10} is the farm's total product curve when its total area is 10 acres (the same curve as in Figure 11-1). TP_{20} is the total product curve when the farm has increased to 20 acres. Except when 0 workers are employed, TP_{20} lies everywhere above TP_{10} because with more acres available, any given number of workers produces more output. Panel (b) shows the corresponding marginal product of labor curves. MPL_{10} is the marginal product of labor curve given 10 acres to cultivate (the same curve as in Figure 11-2), and MPL_{20} is the marginal product of labor curve given 20 acres.

Both curves slope downward because, in each case, the amount of land is fixed, albeit at different levels. But MPL_{20} lies everywhere above MPL_{10}, reflecting the fact that the marginal product of the same worker is higher when he or she has more of the fixed input to work with.

Figure 11-3 demonstrates a general result: the position of the total product curve of a given input depends on the quantities of other inputs. If you change the quantity of the other inputs, both the total product curve and the marginal product curve of the remaining input will shift.

FIGURE 11-3 | Total Product, Marginal Product, and the Fixed Input

(a) Total Product Curves

(b) Marginal Product Curves

This figure shows how the quantity of output and the marginal product of labor depend on the level of the fixed input. Panel (a) shows two total product curves for George and Martha's farm, TP_{10} when their farm is 10 acres and TP_{20} when it is 20 acres. With more land, each worker can produce more wheat. So an increase in the fixed input shifts the total product curve up from TP_{10} to TP_{20}. This implies that the marginal product of each worker is higher when the farm is 20 acres than when it is 10 acres. Panel (b) shows the marginal product of labor curves. The increase in acreage also shifts the marginal product of labor curve up from MPL_{10} to MPL_{20}. Note that both marginal product of labor curves still slope downward due to diminishing returns to labor.

From the Production Function to Cost Curves

Once George and Martha know their production function, they know the relationship between inputs of labor and land and output of wheat. But if they want to maximize their profits, they need to translate this knowledge into information about the relationship between the quantity of output and cost. Let's see how they can do this.

To translate information about a firm's production function into information about its costs, we need to know how much the firm must pay for its inputs. We will assume that George and Martha face either an explicit or an implicit cost of $400 for the use of the land. As we learned in Chapter 9, it is irrelevant whether George and Martha must rent the ten acres of land for $400 from someone else or whether they own the land themselves and forgo earning $400 from renting it to someone else. Either way, they pay an opportunity cost of $400 by using the land to grow wheat. Moreover, since the land is a fixed input, the $400 George and Martha pay for it is a **fixed cost,** denoted by *FC*—a cost that does not depend on the quantity of output produced (in the short run). In business, fixed cost is often referred to as "overhead cost."

We also assume that George and Martha must pay each worker $200. Using their production function, George and Martha know that the number of workers they must hire depends on the amount of wheat they intend to produce. So the cost of labor, which is equal to the number of workers multiplied by $200, is a **variable cost,** denoted by *VC*—a cost that depends on the quantity of output produced. It is variable because in order to produce more they have to employ more units of input. Adding the fixed cost and the variable cost of a given quantity of output gives the **total cost,** or *TC*, of that quantity of output. We can express the relationship among fixed cost, variable cost, and total cost as an equation:

A **fixed cost** is a cost that does not depend on the quantity of output produced. It is the cost of the fixed input.

A **variable cost** is a cost that depends on the quantity of output produced. It is the cost of the variable input.

The **total cost** of producing a given quantity of output is the sum of the fixed cost and the variable cost of producing that quantity of output.

(11-2) Total cost = Fixed cost + Variable cost

or

$$TC = FC + VC$$

The table in Figure 11-4 shows how total cost is calculated for George and Martha's farm. The second column shows the number of workers employed, L. The third column shows the corresponding level of output, Q, taken from the table in Figure 11-1. The fourth column shows the variable cost, VC, equal to the number of workers multiplied by $200, the cost per worker. The fifth column shows the fixed cost, FC, which is $400 regardless of how many workers are employed. The sixth column shows the total cost of output, TC, which is the variable cost plus the fixed cost.

The first column labels each row of the table with a letter, from A to I. These labels will be helpful in understanding our next step: drawing the **total cost curve,** a curve that shows how total cost depends on the quantity of output.

George and Martha's total cost curve is shown in the diagram in Figure 11-4, where the horizontal axis measures the quantity of output in bushels of wheat and the vertical axis measures total cost in dollars. Each point on the curve corresponds to one row of the table in Figure 11-4. For example, point A shows

The **total cost curve** shows how total cost depends on the quantity of output.

FIGURE 11-4   Total Cost Curve for George and Martha's Farm

The table shows the variable cost, fixed cost, and total cost for various output quantities on George and Martha's 10-acre farm. The total cost curve shows how total cost (measured on the vertical axis) depends on the quantity of output (measured on the horizontal axis). The labeled points on the curve correspond to the rows of the table. The total cost curve slopes upward because the number of workers employed, and hence total cost, increases as the quantity of output increases. The curve gets steeper as output increases due to diminishing returns to labor.

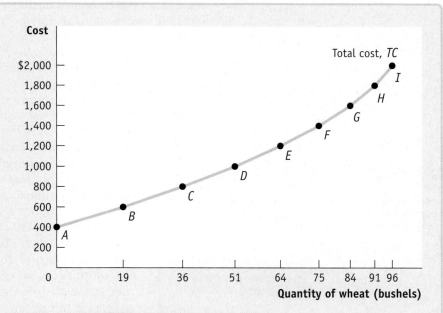

Point on graph	Quantity of labor L (workers)	Quantity of wheat Q (bushels)	Variable cost VC	Fixed cost FC	Total cost TC = FC + VC
A	0	0	$0	$400	$400
B	1	19	200	400	600
C	2	36	400	400	800
D	3	51	600	400	1,000
E	4	64	800	400	1,200
F	5	75	1,000	400	1,400
G	6	84	1,200	400	1,600
H	7	91	1,400	400	1,800
I	8	96	1,600	400	2,000

the situation when 0 workers are employed: output is 0, and total cost is equal to fixed cost, $400. Similarly, point *B* shows the situation when 1 worker is employed: output is 19 bushels, and total cost is $600, equal to the sum of $400 in fixed cost and $200 in variable cost.

Like the total product curve, the total cost curve slopes upward: due to the variable cost, the more output produced, the higher the farm's total cost. But unlike the total product curve, which gets flatter as employment rises, the total cost curve gets *steeper*. That is, the slope of the total cost curve is greater as the amount of output produced increases. As we will soon see, the steepening of the total cost curve is also due to diminishing returns to the variable input. Before we can understand this, we must first look at the relationships among several useful measures of cost.

ECONOMICS ▶ *in Action*

The Mythical Man-Month

The concept of diminishing returns to an input was first formulated by economists during the late eighteenth century. These economists, notably including Thomas Malthus, drew their inspiration from agricultural examples. However, the idea of diminishing returns to an input applies with equal force to the most modern of economic activities—such as, say, the design of software. In 1975 Frederick P. Brooks Jr., a project manager at IBM during the days when it dominated the computer business, published a book titled *The Mythical Man-Month* that soon became a classic—so much so that a special anniversary edition was published 20 years later.

The chapter that gave its title to the book is basically about diminishing returns to labor in the writing of software. Brooks observed that multiplying the number of programmers assigned to a project did not produce a proportionate reduction in the time it took to get the program written. A project that could be done by 1 programmer in 12 months could *not* be done by 12 programmers in 1 month—hence the "mythical man-month." It is the false notion that the number of lines of programming code produced was proportional to the number of code writers employed. In fact, above a certain number, adding another programmer on a project actually *increased* the time to completion.

The argument of *The Mythical Man-Month* is summarized in Figure 11-5. The upper part of the figure shows how the quantity of the project's output, as measured by the number of lines of code produced per month, varies with the number of programmers. Each additional programmer accomplishes less than the previous one, and beyond a certain point an additional programmer is actually counterproductive. The lower part of the figure shows the marginal product of each successive programmer, which falls as more programmers are employed and eventually becomes negative.

In other words, programming is subject to diminishing returns so severe that at some point more programmers actually have negative marginal product. The source of the diminishing returns lies in the nature of the production function for a programming project: each programmer must coordinate his or her work with that of all the other programmers on the project, leading each person to spend more time communicating with others as the number of

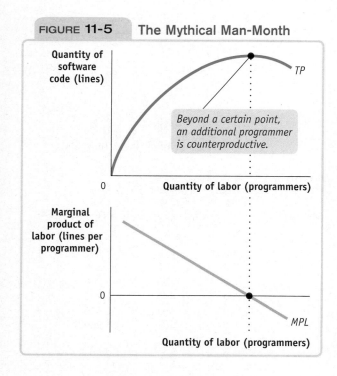

FIGURE 11-5 The Mythical Man-Month

Quantity of software code (lines)

Beyond a certain point, an additional programmer is counterproductive.

TP

0 Quantity of labor (programmers)

Marginal product of labor (lines per programmer)

0

MPL

Quantity of labor (programmers)

programmers increases. In other words, other things equal, there are diminishing returns to labor. It is likely, however, that if fixed inputs devoted to programming projects are increased—say, installing a faster and more accurate programming bug-detection system—the problem of diminishing returns for additional programmers can be mitigated.

A reviewer of the reissued edition of *The Mythical Man-Month* summarized the reasons for these diminishing returns: "There is an inescapable overhead to yoking up programmers in parallel. The members of the team must 'waste time' attending meetings, drafting project plans, exchanging e-mail, negotiating interfaces, enduring performance reviews, and so on. . . . At Microsoft, there will be at least one team member that just designs T-shirts for the rest of the team to wear."

Check Your Understanding   11-1

1. Bernie's ice-making company produces ice cubes using a 10-ton machine and electricity. The quantity of output, measured in terms of pounds of ice, is given in the accompanying table.
   a. What is the fixed input? What is the variable input?
   b. Construct a table showing the marginal product of the variable input. Does it show diminishing returns?
   c. Suppose a 50% increase in the size of the fixed input increases output by 100% for any given amount of the variable input. What is the fixed input now? Construct a table showing the quantity of output and marginal product in this case.

Quantity of electricity (kilowatts)	Quantity of ice (pounds)
0	0
1	1,000
2	1,800
3	2,400
4	2,800

Solutions appear at back of book.

Two Key Concepts: Marginal Cost and Average Cost

We've just learned how to derive a firm's total cost curve from its production function. Our next step is to take a deeper look at total cost by deriving two extremely useful measures: *marginal cost* and *average cost*. As we'll see, these two measures of the cost of production have a somewhat surprising relationship to each other. Moreover, they will prove to be vitally important in Chapter 12, where we will use them to analyze the firm's output decision and the market supply curve.

Marginal Cost

We defined marginal cost in Chapter 9: it is the change in total cost generated by producing one more unit of output. We've already seen that the marginal product of an input is easiest to calculate if data on output are available in increments of one unit of that input. Similarly, marginal cost is easiest to calculate if data on total cost are available in increments of one unit of output. When the data come in less convenient increments, it's still possible to calculate marginal cost. But for the sake of simplicity, let's work with an example in which the data come in convenient one-unit increments.

Selena's Gourmet Salsas produces bottled salsa and Table 11-1 shows how its costs per day depend on the number of cases of salsa it produces per day. The firm has fixed cost of $108 per day, shown in the second column, which represents the daily cost of its food-preparation equipment. The third column shows the variable cost, and the fourth column shows the total cost. Panel (a) of Figure 11-6 plots the total cost curve. Like the total cost curve for George and Martha's farm in Figure 11-4, this curve slopes upward, getting steeper as you move up it to the right.

The significance of the slope of the total cost curve is shown by the fifth column of Table 11-1, which calculates *marginal cost:* the additional cost of each additional unit. The general formula for marginal cost is:

$$\textbf{(11-3) } \text{Marginal cost} = \frac{\text{Change in total cost generated by one additional unit of output}}{} = \frac{\text{Change in total cost}}{\text{Change in quantity of output}}$$

or

$$MC = \frac{\Delta TC}{\Delta Q}$$

As in the case of marginal product, marginal cost is equal to "rise" (the increase in total cost) divided by "run" (the increase in the quantity of output). So just as marginal product is equal to the slope of the total product curve, marginal cost is equal to the slope of the total cost curve.

Now we can understand why the total cost curve gets steeper as we move up it to the right: as you can see in Table 11-1, marginal cost at Selena's Gourmet Salsas rises as output increases. Panel (b) of Figure 11-6 shows the marginal cost curve corresponding to the data in Table 11-1. Notice that, as in Figure 11-2, we plot the marginal cost for increasing output from 0 to 1 case of salsa halfway between 0 and 1, the marginal cost for increasing output from 1 to 2 cases of salsa halfway between 1 and 2, and so on.

Why does the marginal cost curve slope upward? Because there are diminishing returns to inputs in this example. As output increases, the marginal product of the variable input declines. This implies that more and more of the variable input must be used to produce each additional unit of output as the amount of output already produced rises. And since each unit of the variable input must be paid for, the additional cost per additional unit of output also rises.

TABLE 11-1 Costs at Selena's Gourmet Salsas

Quantity of salsa Q (cases)	Fixed cost FC	Variable cost VC	Total cost TC = FC + VC	Marginal cost of case MC = $\Delta TC/\Delta Q$
0	$108	$0	$108	
				$12
1	108	12	120	
				36
2	108	48	156	
				60
3	108	108	216	
				84
4	108	192	300	
				108
5	108	300	408	
				132
6	108	432	540	
				156
7	108	588	696	
				180
8	108	768	876	
				204
9	108	972	1,080	
				228
10	108	1,200	1,308	

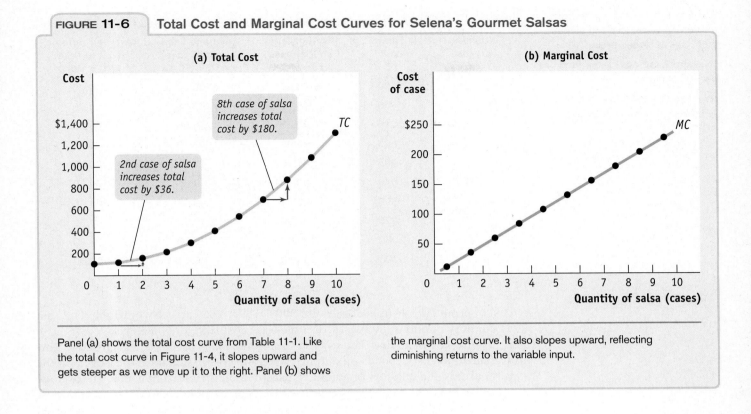

FIGURE **11-6** Total Cost and Marginal Cost Curves for Selena's Gourmet Salsas

Panel (a) shows the total cost curve from Table 11-1. Like the total cost curve in Figure 11-4, it slopes upward and gets steeper as we move up it to the right. Panel (b) shows the marginal cost curve. It also slopes upward, reflecting diminishing returns to the variable input.

In addition, recall that the flattening of the total product curve is also due to diminishing returns: the marginal product of an input falls as more of that input is used if the quantities of other inputs are fixed. The flattening of the total product curve as output increases and the steepening of the total cost curve as output increases are just flip-sides of the same phenomenon. That is, as output increases, the marginal cost of output also increases because the marginal product of the variable input decreases.

We will return to marginal cost in Chapter 12, when we consider the firm's profit-maximizing output decision. Our next step is to introduce another measure of cost: *average cost*.

Average Total Cost

In addition to total cost and marginal cost, it's useful to calculate another measure, **average total cost,** often simply called **average cost.** The average total cost is total cost divided by the quantity of output produced; that is, it is equal to total cost per unit of output. If we let ATC denote average total cost, the equation looks like this:

(11-4) $ATC = \dfrac{\text{Total cost}}{\text{Quantity of output}} = \dfrac{TC}{Q}$

Average total cost is important because it tells the producer how much the *average* or *typical* unit of output costs to produce. Marginal cost, meanwhile, tells the producer how much *one more* unit of output costs to produce. Although they may look very similar, these two measures of cost typically differ. And confusion between them is a major source of error in economics, both in the classroom and in real life, as illustrated by the upcoming Economics in Action.

Table 11-2 uses data from Selena's Gourmet Salsas to calculate average total cost. For example, the total cost of producing 4 cases of salsa is $300, consisting of $108 in fixed cost and $192 in variable cost (from Table 11-1). So the average total

Average total cost, often referred to simply as **average cost,** is total cost divided by quantity of output produced.

A **U-shaped average total cost curve** falls at low levels of output, then rises at higher levels.

Average fixed cost is the fixed cost per unit of output.

Average variable cost is the variable cost per unit of output.

TABLE 11-2 Average Costs for Selena's Gourmet Salsas

Quantity of salsa Q (cases)	Total cost TC	Average total cost of case ATC = TC/Q	Average fixed cost of case AFC = FC/Q	Average variable cost of case AVC = VC/Q
1	$120	$120.00	$108.00	$12.00
2	156	78.00	54.00	24.00
3	216	72.00	36.00	36.00
4	300	75.00	27.00	48.00
5	408	81.60	21.60	60.00
6	540	90.00	18.00	72.00
7	696	99.43	15.43	84.00
8	876	109.50	13.50	96.00
9	1,080	120.00	12.00	108.00
10	1,308	130.80	10.80	120.00

cost of producing 4 cases of salsa is $300/4 = $75. You can see from Table 11-2 that as quantity of output increases, average total cost first falls, then rises.

Figure 11-7 plots that data to yield the *average total cost curve,* which shows how average total cost depends on output. As before, cost in dollars is measured on the vertical axis and quantity of output is measured on the horizontal axis. The average total cost curve has a distinctive U shape that corresponds to how average total cost first falls and then rises as output increases. Economists believe that such **U-shaped average total cost curves** are the norm for producers in many industries.

To help our understanding of why the average total cost curve is U-shaped, Table 11-2 breaks average total cost into its two underlying components, *average fixed cost* and *average variable cost.* **Average fixed cost,** or *AFC,* is fixed cost divided by the quantity of output, also known as the fixed cost per unit of output. For example, if Selena's Gourmet Salsas produces 4 cases of salsa, average fixed cost is $108/4 = $27 per case. **Average variable cost,** or *AVC,* is variable cost divided by the quantity of

FIGURE 11-7 Average Total Cost Curve for Selena's Gourmet Salsas

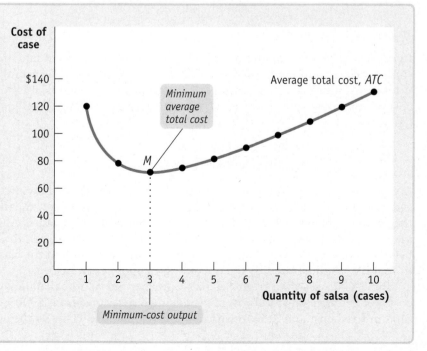

The average total cost curve at Selena's Gourmet Salsas is U-shaped. At low levels of output, average total cost falls because the "spreading effect" of falling average fixed cost dominates the "diminishing returns effect" of rising average variable cost. At higher levels of output, the opposite is true and average total cost rises. At point *M,* corresponding to an output of three cases of salsa per day, average total cost is at its minimum level, the minimum average total cost.

output, also known as variable cost per unit of output. At an output of 4 cases, average variable cost is $192/4 = $48 per case. Writing these in the form of equations:

$$(11\text{-}5)\ AFC = \frac{\text{Fixed cost}}{\text{Quantity of output}} = \frac{FC}{Q}$$

$$AVC = \frac{\text{Variable cost}}{\text{Quantity of output}} = \frac{VC}{Q}$$

Average total cost is the sum of average fixed cost and average variable cost. It has a U shape because these components move in opposite directions as output rises.

Average fixed cost falls as more output is produced because the numerator (the fixed cost) is a fixed number but the denominator (the quantity of output) increases as more is produced. Another way to think about this relationship is that, as more output is produced, the fixed cost is spread over more units of output; the end result is that the fixed cost *per unit of output*—the average fixed cost—falls. You can see this effect in the fourth column of Table 11-2: average fixed cost drops continuously as output increases.

Average variable cost, however, rises as output increases. As we've seen, this reflects diminishing returns to the variable input: each additional unit of output incurs more variable cost to produce than the previous unit. So variable cost rises at a faster rate than the quantity of output increases.

So increasing output has two opposing effects on average total cost—the "spreading effect" and the "diminishing returns effect":

- *The spreading effect.* The larger the output, the greater the quantity of output over which fixed cost is spread, leading to lower average fixed cost.
- *The diminishing returns effect.* The larger the output, the greater the amount of variable input required to produce additional units, leading to higher average variable cost.

At low levels of output, the spreading effect is very powerful because even small increases in output cause large reductions in average fixed cost. So at low levels of output, the spreading effect dominates the diminishing returns effect and causes the average total cost curve to slope downward. But when output is large, average fixed cost is already quite small, so increasing output further has only a very small spreading effect.

Diminishing returns, however, usually grow increasingly important as output rises. As a result, when output is large, the diminishing returns effect dominates the spreading effect, causing the average total cost curve to slope upward. At the bottom of the U-shaped average total cost curve, point *M* in Figure 11-7, the two effects exactly balance each other. At this point average total cost is at its minimum level, the minimum average total cost.

Figure 11-8 brings together in a single picture four members of the family of cost curves that we have derived from the total cost curve for Selena's Gourmet Salsas: the marginal cost curve (*MC*), the average total cost curve (*ATC*), the average variable cost curve (*AVC*), and the average fixed cost curve (*AFC*). All are based on the information in Tables 11-1 and 11-2. As before, cost is measured on the vertical axis and the quantity of output is measured on the horizontal axis.

Let's take a moment to note some features of the various cost curves. First of all, marginal cost slopes upward—the result of diminishing returns that make an additional unit of output more costly to produce than the one before. Average variable cost also slopes upward—again, due to diminishing returns—but is flatter than the marginal cost curve. This is because the higher cost of an additional unit of output is averaged across all units, not just the additional units, in the average variable cost measure. Meanwhile, average fixed cost slopes downward because of the spreading effect.

Finally, notice that the marginal cost curve intersects the average total cost curve from below, crossing it at its lowest point, point *M* in Figure 11-8. This last feature is our next subject of study.

FIGURE **11-8** Marginal Cost and Average Cost Curves for Selena's Gourmet Salsas

Here we have the family of cost curves for Selena's Gourmet Salsas: the marginal cost curve (*MC*), the average total cost curve (*ATC*), the average variable cost curve (*AVC*), and the average fixed cost curve (*AFC*). Note that the average total cost curve is U-shaped and the marginal cost curve crosses the average total cost curve at the bottom of the U, point *M*, corresponding to the minimum average total cost from Table 11-2 and Figure 11-7.

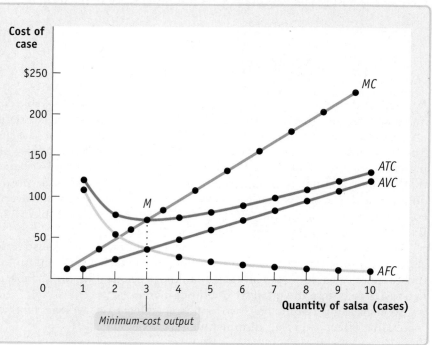

The **minimum-cost output** is the quantity of output at which average total cost is lowest—the bottom of the U-shaped average total cost curve.

Minimum Average Total Cost

For a U-shaped average total cost curve, average total cost is at its minimum level at the bottom of the U. Economists call the quantity of output that corresponds to the minimum average total cost the **minimum-cost output.** In the case of Selena's Gourmet Salsas, the minimum-cost output is three cases of salsa per day.

In Figure 11-8, the bottom of the U is at the level of output at which the marginal cost curve crosses the average total cost curve from below. Is this an accident? No—it reflects three general principles that are always true about a firm's marginal cost and average total cost curves:

1. At the minimum-cost output, average total cost *is equal to* marginal cost.
2. At output less than the minimum-cost output, marginal cost *is less than* average total cost and average total cost is falling.
3. At output greater than the minimum-cost output, marginal cost *is greater than* average total cost and average total cost is rising.

To understand these principles, think about how your grade in one course—say, a 3.0 in physics—affects your overall grade point average. If your GPA before receiving that grade was more than 3.0, the new grade lowers your average.

Similarly, if marginal cost—the cost of producing one more unit—is less than average total cost, producing that extra unit lowers average total cost. This is shown in Figure 11-9 by the movement from A_1 to A_2. In this case, the marginal cost of producing an additional unit of output is low, as indicated by the point MC_L on the marginal cost curve. When the cost of producing the next unit of output is less than average total cost, increasing production reduces average total cost. So any quantity of output at which marginal cost is less than average total cost must be on the downward-sloping segment of the U.

But if your grade in physics is more than the average of your previous grades, this new grade raises your GPA. Similarly, if marginal cost is greater than average total cost, producing that extra unit raises average total cost. This is illustrated by the movement from B_1 to B_2 in Figure 11-9, where the marginal cost, MC_H, is

FIGURE **11-9**   The Relationship Between the Average Total Cost and the Marginal Cost Curves

To see why the marginal cost curve (*MC*) must cut through the average total cost curve at the minimum average total cost (point *M*), corresponding to the minimum-cost output, we look at what happens if marginal cost is different from average total cost. If marginal cost is *less* than average total cost, an increase in output must reduce average total cost, as in the movement from A_1 to A_2. If marginal cost is *greater* than average total cost, an increase in output must increase average total cost, as in the movement from B_1 to B_2.

Cost of unit

If marginal cost is above average total cost, average total cost is rising.

If marginal cost is below average total cost, average total cost is falling.

Quantity

higher than average total cost. So any quantity of output at which marginal cost is greater than average total cost must be on the upward-sloping segment of the U.

Finally, if a new grade is exactly equal to your previous GPA, the additional grade neither raises nor lowers that average—it stays the same. This corresponds to point *M* in Figure 11-9: when marginal cost equals average total cost, we must be at the bottom of the U, because only at that point is average total cost neither falling nor rising.

Does the Marginal Cost Curve Always Slope Upward?

Up to this point, we have emphasized the importance of diminishing returns, which lead to a marginal product curve that always slopes downward and a marginal cost curve that always slopes upward. In practice, however, economists believe that marginal cost curves often slope *downward* as a firm increases its production from zero up to some low level, sloping upward only at higher levels of production: they look like the curve *MC* in Figure 11-10.

This initial downward slope occurs because a firm often finds that, when it starts with only a very small number of workers, employing more workers and expanding output allows its workers to specialize in various tasks. This, in turn, lowers the firm's marginal cost as it expands output. For example, one individual producing salsa would have to perform all the tasks involved: selecting and preparing the ingredients, mixing the salsa, bottling and labeling it, packing it into cases, and so on. As more workers are employed, they can divide the tasks, with each worker specializing in one or a few aspects of salsa-making.

This specialization leads to *increasing returns* to the hiring of additional workers and results in a marginal cost curve that initially slopes downward. But once there are enough workers to have completely exhausted the benefits of further specialization, diminishing returns to labor set in and the marginal cost curve changes direction and slopes upward. So typical marginal cost curves actually have the "swoosh" shape shown by *MC* in Figure 11-10. For the same reason, average variable cost curves typically look like *AVC* in Figure 11-10: they are U-shaped rather than strictly upward sloping.

However, as Figure 11-10 also shows, the key features we saw from the example of Selena's Gourmet Salsas remain true: the average total cost curve is U-shaped, and the marginal cost curve passes through the point of minimum average total cost.

FIGURE **11-10** | More Realistic Cost Curves

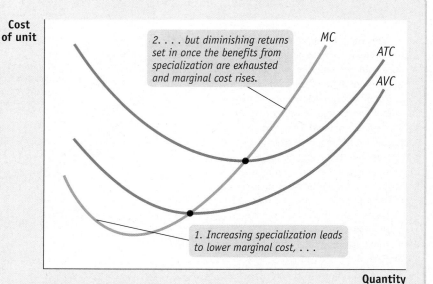

A realistic marginal cost curve has a "swoosh" shape. Starting from a very low output level, marginal cost often falls as the firm increases output. That's because hiring additional workers allows greater specialization of their tasks and leads to increasing returns. Once specialization is achieved, however, diminishing returns to additional workers set in and marginal cost rises. The corresponding average variable cost curve is now U-shaped, like the average total cost curve.

Cost of unit

2. . . . but diminishing returns set in once the benefits from specialization are exhausted and marginal cost rises.

MC

ATC

AVC

1. Increasing specialization leads to lower marginal cost, . . .

Quantity

ECONOMICS ▶ *in Action*

Smart Grid Economics

If you are a night owl who likes to listen to music, write term papers, or do laundry in the middle of the night, your local electricity grid would like to thank you. Why? Because you are using electricity when it is least costly to generate.

The problem is that energy cannot be stored efficiently on a large scale. So power plant operators maintain both the main power stations that are designed to run continuously, as well as smaller power plants that operate only during periods of peak demand—such as during daytime working hours or periods of extreme outside temperatures.

These smaller power plants are more expensive to operate, incurring higher marginal cost per kilowatt generated than the average cost of generating a kilowatt (that is, cost averaged over kilowatts generated by the large and small plants). According to the U.S. Government Accountability Office, it can cost up to 10 times more to generate electricity during a summer afternoon (when air conditioners are running at maximum capacity) compared to nighttime.

But consumers typically aren't aware that the marginal cost of electricity varies over the course of a day or according to the weather. Instead, consumers see prices on their electricity bills based on the average cost of electricity generation. As a result, electricity demand is inefficient—too high during high marginal cost periods and too low during low marginal cost periods. In the end, consumers end up paying more than they should for their electricity, as utility companies must eventually raise their prices to cover production costs.

To solve this inefficiency, utility companies, appliance manufacturers, and the federal government are working together to develop SMART Grid technologies—that help consumers adjust their usage according to the true marginal cost of a kilowatt in real time. "Smart" meters have been developed for home use, which allow the price to the consumer to vary according to the true mar-

With SMART Grid technology, consumers save money by basing their demand for electricity on marginal cost rather than average cost.

ginal cost—which the consumer can see. And appliances such as dishwashers, refrigerators, dryers, and hot water heaters have been developed to run when electricity rates are lowest.

Studies have consistently shown that when consumers see the real marginal cost fluctuations and are asked to pay accordingly, they scale back their consumption during peak demand times. Clearly, SMART Grid technologies are just an application of smart economics.

Check Your Understanding   11-2

1. Alicia's Apple Pies is a roadside business. Alicia must pay $9.00 in rent each day. In addition, it costs her $1.00 to produce the first pie of the day, and each subsequent pie costs 50% more to produce than the one before. For example, the second pie costs $1.00 × 1.5 = $1.50 to produce, and so on.
   a. Calculate Alicia's marginal cost, variable cost, average total cost, average variable cost, and average fixed cost as her daily pie output rises from 0 to 6. (*Hint:* The variable cost of two pies is just the marginal cost of the first pie, plus the marginal cost of the second, and so on.)
   b. Indicate the range of pies for which the spreading effect dominates and the range for which the diminishing returns effect dominates.
   c. What is Alicia's minimum-cost output? Explain why making one more pie lowers Alicia's average total cost when output is lower than the minimum-cost output. Similarly, explain why making one more pie raises Alicia's average total cost when output is greater than the minimum-cost output.

Solutions appear at back of book.

Short-Run versus Long-Run Costs

Up to this point, we have treated fixed cost as completely outside the control of a firm because we have focused on the short run. But as we noted earlier, all inputs are variable in the long run: this means that in the long run fixed cost may also be varied. *In the long run, in other words, a firm's fixed cost becomes a variable it can choose.* For example, given time, Selena's Gourmet Salsas can acquire additional food-preparation equipment or dispose of some of its existing equipment. In this section, we will examine how a firm's costs behave in the short run and in the long run. We will also see that the firm will choose its fixed cost in the long run based on the level of output it expects to produce.

Let's begin by supposing that Selena's Gourmet Salsas is considering whether to acquire additional food-preparation equipment. Acquiring additional machinery will affect its total cost in two ways. First, the firm will have to either rent or buy the additional equipment; either way, that will mean higher fixed cost in the short run. Second, if the workers have more equipment, they will be more productive: fewer workers will be needed to produce any given output, so variable cost for any given output level will be reduced.

The table in Figure 11-11 shows how acquiring an additional machine affects costs. In our original example, we assumed that Selena's Gourmet Salsas had a fixed cost of $108. The left half of the table shows variable cost as well as total cost and average total cost assuming a fixed cost of $108. The average total cost curve for this level of fixed cost is given by ATC_1 in Figure 11-11. Let's compare that to a situation in which the firm buys additional food-preparation equipment, doubling its fixed cost to $216 but reducing its variable cost at any given level of output. The right half of the table shows the firm's variable cost, total cost, and average total cost with this higher level of fixed cost. The average total cost curve corresponding to $216 in fixed cost is given by ATC_2 in Figure 11-11.

From the figure you can see that when output is small, 4 cases of salsa per day or fewer, average total cost is smaller when Selena forgoes the additional equipment

FIGURE **11-11**   Choosing the Level of Fixed Cost for Selena's Gourmet Salsas

For any given level of output, there is a tradeoff: a choice between lower fixed cost and higher variable cost, or higher fixed cost and lower variable cost. ATC_1 is the average total cost curve corresponding to a fixed cost of $108; it leads to lower fixed cost and higher variable cost. ATC_2 is the average total cost curve corresponding to a higher fixed cost of $216 but lower variable cost. At low output levels, at 4 or fewer cases of salsa per day, ATC_1 lies below ATC_2: average total cost is lower with only $108 in fixed cost. But as output goes up, average total cost is lower with the higher amount of fixed cost, $216: at more than 4 cases of salsa per day, ATC_2 lies below ATC_1.

	Low fixed cost (FC = $108)			High fixed cost (FC = $216)		
Quantity of salsa (cases)	High variable cost	Total cost	Average total cost of case ATC_1	Low variable cost	Total cost	Average total cost of case ATC_2
1	$12	$120	$120.00	$6	$222	$222.00
2	48	156	78.00	24	240	120.00
3	108	216	72.00	54	270	90.00
4	192	300	75.00	96	312	78.00
5	300	408	81.60	150	366	73.20
6	432	540	90.00	216	432	72.00
7	588	696	99.43	294	510	72.86
8	768	876	109.50	384	600	75.00
9	972	1,080	120.00	486	702	78.00
10	1,200	1,308	130.80	600	816	81.60

and maintains the lower fixed cost of $108: ATC_1 lies below ATC_2. For example, at 3 cases per day, average total cost is $72 without the additional machinery and $90 with the additional machinery. But as output increases beyond 4 cases per day, the firm's average total cost is lower if it acquires the additional equipment, raising its fixed cost to $216. For example, at 9 cases of salsa per day, average total cost is $120 when fixed cost is $108 but only $78 when fixed cost is $216.

Why does average total cost change like this when fixed cost increases? When output is low, the increase in fixed cost from the additional equipment outweighs the reduction in variable cost from higher worker productivity—that is, there are too few units of output over which to spread the additional fixed cost. So if Selena plans to produce 4 or fewer cases per day, she would be better off choosing the lower level of fixed cost, $108, to achieve a lower average total cost of production. When planned output is high, however, she should acquire the additional machinery.

In general, for each output level there is some choice of fixed cost that minimizes the firm's average total cost for that output level. So when the firm has a desired output level that it expects to maintain over time, it should choose the level of fixed cost optimal for that level—that is, the level of fixed cost that minimizes its average total cost.

Now that we are studying a situation in which fixed cost can change, we need to take time into account when discussing average total cost. All of the average total cost curves we have considered until now are defined for a given level of fixed cost—that is, they are defined for the short run, the period of time over which fixed cost doesn't vary. To reinforce that distinction, for the rest of this chapter we will refer to these average total cost curves as "short-run average total cost curves."

For most firms, it is realistic to assume that there are many possible choices of fixed cost, not just two. The implication: for such a firm, many possible short-run average total cost curves will exist, each corresponding to a different choice of fixed cost and so giving rise to what is called a firm's "family" of short-run average total cost curves.

At any given point in time, a firm will find itself on one of its short-run cost curves, the one corresponding to its current level of fixed cost; a change in output will cause it to move along that curve. If the firm expects that change in output level to be long-standing, then it is likely that the firm's current level of fixed cost is no longer optimal. Given sufficient time, it will want to adjust its fixed cost to a new level that minimizes average total cost for its new output level. For example, if Selena had been producing 2 cases of salsa per day with a fixed cost of $108 but found herself increasing her output to 8 cases per day for the foreseeable future, then in the long run she should purchase more equipment and increase her fixed cost to a level that minimizes average total cost at the 8-cases-per-day output level.

Suppose we do a thought experiment and calculate the lowest possible average total cost that can be achieved for each output level if the firm were to choose its fixed cost for each output level. Economists have given this thought experiment a name: the *long-run average total cost curve*. Specifically, the **long-run average total cost curve,** or *LRATC*, is the relationship between output and average total cost when fixed cost has been chosen to minimize average total cost *for each level of output*. If there are many possible choices of fixed cost, the long-run average total cost curve will have the familiar, smooth U shape, as shown by *LRATC* in Figure 11-12.

We can now draw the distinction between the short run and the long run more fully. In the long run, when a producer has had time to choose the fixed cost appropriate for its desired level of output, that producer will be at some point on the long-run average total cost curve. But if the output level is altered, the firm will no longer be on its long-run average total cost curve and will instead be moving along its current short-run average total cost curve. It will not be on its long-run average total cost curve again until it readjusts its fixed cost for its new output level.

Figure 11-12 illustrates this point. The curve ATC_3 shows short-run average total cost if Selena has chosen the level of fixed cost that minimizes average total cost at an output of 3 cases of salsa per day. This is confirmed by the fact that at 3 cases per day, ATC_3 touches *LRATC*, the long-run average total cost curve. Similarly, ATC_6 shows short-run average total cost if Selena has chosen the level of fixed cost that minimizes average total cost if her output is 6 cases per day. It touches *LRATC* at 6 cases per day. And ATC_9 shows short-run average total cost if Selena has chosen the level of fixed cost that minimizes average total cost if her output is 9 cases per day. It touches *LRATC* at 9 cases per day.

Suppose that Selena initially chose to be on ATC_6. If she actually produces 6 cases of salsa per day, her firm will be at point C on both its short-run and long-run average total cost curves. Suppose, however, that Selena ends up producing only 3 cases of salsa per day. In the short run, her average total cost is indicated by point B on ATC_6; it is no longer on *LRATC*. If Selena had known that she would be producing only 3 cases per day, she would have been

The **long-run average total cost curve** shows the relationship between output and average total cost when fixed cost has been chosen to minimize average total cost for each level of output.

To understand how firms operate over time, be sure to distinguish between short-run and long-run average total costs.

FIGURE **11-12** | Short-Run and Long-Run Average Total Cost Curves

Short-run and long-run average total cost curves differ because a firm can choose its fixed cost in the long run. If Selena has chosen the level of fixed cost that minimizes short-run average total cost at an output of 6 cases, and actually produces 6 cases, then she will be at point *C* on *LRATC* and *ATC*₆. But if she produces only 3 cases, she will move to point *B*. If she expects to produce only 3 cases for a long time, in the long run she will reduce her fixed cost and move to point *A* on *ATC*₃. Likewise, if she produces 9 cases (putting her at point *Y*) and expects to continue this for a long time, she will increase her fixed cost in the long run and move to point *X* on *ATC*₉.

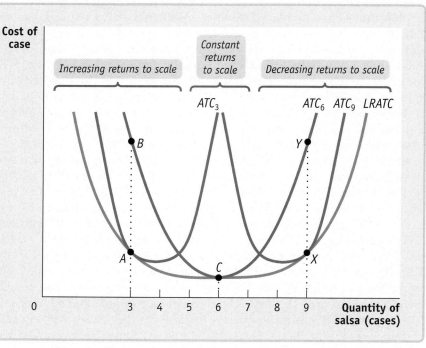

better off choosing a lower level of fixed cost, the one corresponding to ATC_3, thereby achieving a lower average total cost. She could do this, for example, by selling her production plant and purchasing a smaller one. Then her firm would have found itself at point *A* on the long-run average total cost curve, which lies below point *B*.

Suppose, conversely, that Selena ends up producing 9 cases per day even though she initially chose to be on ATC_6. In the short run her average total cost is indicated by point *Y* on ATC_6. But she would be better off purchasing more equipment and incurring a higher fixed cost in order to reduce her variable cost and move to ATC_9. This would allow her to reach point *X* on the long-run average total cost curve, which lies below *Y*.

The distinction between short-run and long-run average total costs is extremely important in making sense of how real firms operate over time. A company that has to increase output suddenly to meet a surge in demand will typically find that in the short run its average total cost rises sharply because it is hard to get extra production out of existing facilities. But given time to build new factories or add machinery, short-run average total cost falls.

Returns to Scale

What determines the shape of the long-run average total cost curve? The answer is that *scale*, the size of a firm's operations, is often an important determinant of its long-run average total cost of production. Firms that experience scale effects in production find that their long-run average total cost changes substantially depending on the quantity of output they produce. There are **increasing returns to scale** (also known as *economies of scale*) when long-run average total cost declines as output increases.

As you can see in Figure 11-12, Selena's Gourmet Salsas experiences increasing returns to scale over output levels ranging from 0 up to 5 cases of salsa per day—the output levels over which the long-run average total cost curve is declining. In contrast, there are **decreasing returns to scale** (also known as *diseconomies of scale*) when long-run average total cost increases as output increases. For Selena's Gourmet Salsas, decreasing returns to scale occur at output levels greater than 7 cases, the output levels over which its long-run average total cost curve is rising.

There are **increasing returns to scale** when long-run average total cost declines as output increases.

There are **decreasing returns to scale** when long-run average total cost increases as output increases.

There is also a third possible relationship between long-run average total cost and scale: firms experience **constant returns to scale** when long-run average total cost is constant as output increases. In this case, the firm's long-run average total cost curve is horizontal over the output levels for which there are constant returns to scale. As you see in Figure 11-12, Selena's Gourmet Salsas has constant returns to scale when it produces anywhere from 5 to 7 cases of salsa per day.

What explains these scale effects in production? The answer ultimately lies in the firm's technology of production. Increasing returns often arise from the increased *specialization* that larger output levels allow—a larger scale of operation means that individual workers can limit themselves to more specialized tasks, becoming more skilled and efficient at doing them.

Another source of increasing returns is very large initial setup cost; in some industries—such as auto manufacturing, electricity generating, or petroleum refining—incurring a high fixed cost in the form of plant and equipment is necessary to produce any output.

A third source of increasing returns, found in certain high-tech industries such as software development, is that the value of a good or service to an individual increases when a large number of others own or use the same good or service (known as *network externalities* and covered in Chapter 16). As we'll see in Chapter 13, where we study monopoly, increasing returns have very important implications for how firms and industries interact and behave.

Decreasing returns—the opposite scenario—typically arise in large firms due to problems of coordination and communication: as the firm grows in size, it becomes ever more difficult and so more costly to communicate and to organize its activities. Although increasing returns induce firms to get larger, decreasing returns tend to limit their size. And when there are constant returns to scale, scale has no effect on a firm's long-run average total cost: it is the same regardless of whether the firm produces 1 unit or 100,000 units.

> There are **constant returns to scale** when long-run average total cost is constant as output increases.

Summing Up Costs: The Short and Long of It

If a firm is to make the best decisions about how much to produce, it has to understand how its costs relate to the quantity of output it chooses to produce. Table 11-3 provides a quick summary of the concepts and measures of cost you have learned about.

TABLE 11-3   Concepts and Measures of Cost

	Measurement	Definition	Mathematical term
Short run	Fixed cost	Cost that does not depend on the quantity of output produced	FC
	Average fixed cost	Fixed cost per unit of output	$AFC = FC/Q$
Short run and long run	Variable cost	Cost that depends on the quantity of output produced	VC
	Average variable cost	Variable cost per unit of output	$AVC = VC/Q$
	Total cost	The sum of fixed cost (short run) and variable cost	$TC = FC$ (short run) $+ VC$
	Average total cost (average cost)	Total cost per unit of output	$ATC = TC/Q$
	Marginal cost	The change in total cost generated by producing one more unit of output	$MC = \Delta TC/\Delta Q$
Long run	Long-run average total cost	Average total cost when fixed cost has been chosen to minimize average total cost for each level of output	$LRATC$

Cities with higher average annual snow-fall maintain larger snowplow fleets.

ECONOMICS ▶ *in Action*

There's No Business Like Snow Business

Anyone who has lived both in a snowy city, like Chicago, and in a city that only occasionally experiences significant snowfall, like Washington, D.C., is aware of the differences in total cost that arise from making different choices about fixed cost.

In Washington, even a minor snowfall—say, an inch or two overnight—is enough to create chaos during the next morning's commute. The same snowfall in Chicago has hardly any effect at all. The reason is not that Washingtonians are wimps and Chicagoans are made of sterner stuff; it is that Washington, where it rarely snows, has only a fraction as many snowplows and other snowclearing equipment as cities where heavy snow is a fact of life.

In this sense Washington and Chicago are like two producers who expect to produce different levels of output, where the "output" is snow removal. Washington, which rarely has significant snow, has chosen a low level of fixed cost in the form of snow-clearing equipment. This makes sense under normal circumstances but leaves the city unprepared when major snow does fall. Chicago, which knows that it will face lots of snow, chooses to accept the higher fixed cost that leaves it in a position to respond effectively.

▼ Quick Review

- In the long run, firms choose fixed cost according to expected output. Higher fixed cost reduces average total cost when output is high. Lower fixed cost reduces average total cost when output is low.

- There are many possible short-run average total cost curves, each corresponding to a different level of fixed cost. The **long-run average total cost curve, *LRATC*,** shows average total cost over the long run, when the firm has chosen fixed cost to minimize average total cost for each level of output.

- A firm that has fully adjusted its fixed cost for its output level will operate at a point that lies on both its current short-run and long-run average total cost curves. A change in output moves the firm along its current short-run average total cost curve. Once it has readjusted its fixed cost, the firm will operate on a new short-run average total cost curve and on the long-run average total cost curve.

- Scale effects arise from the technology of production. **Increasing returns to scale** tend to make firms larger. **Decreasing returns to scale** tend to limit their size. With **constant returns to scale,** scale has no effect.

Check Your Understanding 11-3

1. The accompanying table shows three possible combinations of fixed cost and average variable cost. Average variable cost is constant in this example (it does not vary with the quantity of output produced).
   a. For each of the three choices, calculate the average total cost of producing 12,000, 22,000, and 30,000 units. For each of these quantities, which choice results in the lowest average total cost?
   b. Suppose that the firm, which has historically produced 12,000 units, experiences a sharp, permanent increase in demand that leads it to produce 22,000 units. Explain how its average total cost will change in the short run and in the long run.

Choice	Fixed cost	Average variable cost
1	$8,000	$1.00
2	12,000	0.75
3	24,000	0.25

   c. Explain what the firm should do instead if it believes the change in demand is temporary.

2. In each of the following cases, explain what kind of scale effects you think the firm will experience and why.
   a. A telemarketing firm in which employees make sales calls using computers and telephones
   b. An interior design firm in which design projects are based on the expertise of the firm's owner
   c. A diamond-mining company

3. Draw a graph like Figure 11-12 and insert a short-run average total cost curve corresponding to a long-run output choice of 5 cases of salsa per day. Use the graph to show why Selena should change her fixed cost if she expects to produce only 4 cases per day for a long period of time.

Solutions appear at back of book.

Kiva Systems' Robots versus Humans:
The Challenge of Holiday Order Fulfillment

For those who like to procrastinate when it comes to holiday shopping, the rise of e-commerce has been a welcome phenomenon. In 2103 Amazon.com boasted that customers living in 12 cities in the United States could receive same-day delivery for orders placed on the day before Christmas.

E-commerce retailers like Amazon.com and CrateandBarrel.com can see their sales quadruple for the holidays. With advances in order fulfillment technology that get customers' orders to them quickly, e-commerce sellers have been able to capture an ever-greater share of sales from brick-and-mortar retailers. Holiday sales at e-commerce sites grew by over 10% from 2012 to 2013.

Beth Hail/Bloomberg via Getty Images

Behind these technological advances, however, lies an intense debate: people versus robots. Amazon.com has relied on a large staff of temporary human workers to get it through the previous holiday seasons, often quadrupling its staff and operating 24 hours a day. In contrast, CrateandBarrel.com only doubled its workforce, thanks to a cadre of orange robots that allows each worker to do the work of six people.

But Amazon.com is set to increase its robotic work force in the future. In May 2012, Amazon.com bought Kiva Systems, the leader in order fulfillment robotics, for $775 million, with the hope of tailoring Kiva's systems to fit Amazon.com's warehouse and fulfillment needs.

Although many retailers—Staples, Gap, Saks Fifth Avenue, and Walgreens, for example—also use Kiva equipment, installation of a robotic system can be expensive, with some costing as much as $20 million. Yet hiring workers has a cost, too: during the 2013 holiday season, before it had installed an extensive robotic system, Amazon.com hired some 70,000 temporary workers at its 94 distribution centers around the United States.

As one industry analyst noted, an obstacle to the purchase of a robotic system for many e-commerce retailers is that it often doesn't make economic sense: it's too expensive to buy sufficient robots for the busiest time of the year because they would be idle at other times. Before Amazon.com's purchase, Kiva was testing a program to rent out its robots seasonally so that retailers could "hire" enough robots to handle their holiday orders just as Amazon.com used to hire more humans.

QUESTIONS FOR THOUGHT

1. Assume that a firm can sell a robot, but that the sale takes time and the firm is likely to get less than what it paid. Other things equal, which system, human-based or robotic, will have a higher fixed cost? Which will have a higher variable cost? Explain.

2. Predict the pattern of off-holiday sales versus holiday sales that would induce a retailer to keep a human-based system. Predict the pattern that would induce a retailer to move to a robotic system.

3. How would a "robot-for-hire" program affect your answer to Question 2? Explain.

SUMMARY

1. The relationship between inputs and output is a producer's **production function**. In the **short run,** the quantity of a **fixed input** cannot be varied but the quantity of a **variable input** can. In the **long run,** the quantities of all inputs can be varied. For a given amount of the fixed input, the **total product curve** shows how the quantity of output changes as the quantity of the variable input changes. We may also calculate the **marginal product** of an input, the increase in output from using one more unit of that input.

2. There are **diminishing returns to an input** when its marginal product declines as more of the input is used, holding the quantity of all other inputs fixed.

3. **Total cost,** represented by the **total cost curve,** is equal to the sum of **fixed cost,** which does not depend on output, and **variable cost,** which does depend on output. Due to diminishing returns, marginal cost, the increase in total cost generated by producing one more unit of output, normally increases as output increases.

4. **Average total cost** (also known as **average cost**), total cost divided by quantity of output, is the cost of the average unit of output, and marginal cost is the cost of one more unit produced. Economists believe that **U-shaped average total cost curves** are typical, because average total cost consists of two parts: **average fixed cost,** which falls when output increases (the spreading effect), and **average variable cost,** which rises with output (the diminishing returns effect).

5. When average total cost is U-shaped, the bottom of the U is the level of output at which average total cost is minimized, the point of **minimum-cost output.** This is also the point at which the marginal cost curve crosses the average total cost curve from below. Due to gains from specialization, the marginal cost curve may slope downward initially before sloping upward, giving it a "swoosh" shape.

6. In the long run, a producer can change its fixed input and its level of fixed cost. By accepting higher fixed cost, a firm can lower its variable cost for any given output level, and vice versa. The **long-run average total cost curve** shows the relationship between output and average total cost when fixed cost has been chosen to minimize average total cost at each level of output. A firm moves along its short-run average total cost curve as it changes the quantity of output, and it returns to a point on both its short-run and long-run average total cost curves once it has adjusted fixed cost to its new output level.

7. As output increases, there are **increasing returns to scale** if long-run average total cost declines; **decreasing returns to scale** if it increases; and **constant returns to scale** if it remains constant. Scale effects depend on the technology of production.

KEY TERMS

Production function, p. 330
Fixed input, p. 330
Variable input, p. 330
Long run, p. 330
Short run, p. 330
Total product curve, p. 330
Marginal product, p. 331
Diminishing returns to an input, p. 332

Fixed cost, p. 334
Variable cost, p. 334
Total cost, p. 334
Total cost curve, p. 335
Average total cost, p. 339
Average cost, p. 339
U-shaped average total cost curve, p. 340
Average fixed cost, p. 340

Average variable cost, p. 340
Minimum-cost output, p. 342
Long-run average total cost curve, p. 347
Increasing returns to scale, p. 348
Decreasing returns to scale, p. 348
Constant returns to scale, p. 349

PROBLEMS

1. Changes in the price of key commodities have a significant impact on a company's bottom line. For virtually all companies, the price of energy is a substantial portion of their costs. In addition, many industries—such as those that produce beef, chicken, high-fructose corn syrup and ethanol—are highly dependent on the price of corn. In particular, corn has seen a significant increase in price.

   a. Explain how the cost of energy can be both a fixed cost and a variable cost for a company.

   b. Suppose energy is a fixed cost and energy prices rise. What happens to the company's average total cost curve? What happens to its marginal cost curve? Illustrate your answer with a diagram.

   c. Explain why the cost of corn is a variable cost but not a fixed cost for an ethanol producer.

   d. When the cost of corn goes up, what happens to the average total cost curve of an ethanol producer? What happens to its marginal cost curve? Illustrate your answer with a diagram.

2. Marty's Frozen Yogurt is a small shop that sells cups of frozen yogurt in a university town. Marty owns three frozen-yogurt machines. His other inputs are refrigerators, frozen-yogurt mix, cups, sprinkle toppings, and, of course, workers. He estimates that his daily production function when he varies the number of workers employed (and at the same time, of course, yogurt mix, cups, and so on) is as shown in the accompanying table.

Quantity of labor (workers)	Quantity of frozen yogurt (cups)
0	0
1	110
2	200
3	270
4	300
5	320
6	330

a. What are the fixed inputs and variable inputs in the production of cups of frozen yogurt?

b. Draw the total product curve. Put the quantity of labor on the horizontal axis and the quantity of frozen yogurt on the vertical axis.

c. What is the marginal product of the first worker? The second worker? The third worker? Why does marginal product decline as the number of workers increases?

3. The production function for Marty's Frozen Yogurt is given in Problem 2. Marty pays each of his workers $80 per day. The cost of his other variable inputs is $0.50 per cup of yogurt. His fixed cost is $100 per day.

a. What is Marty's variable cost and total cost when he produces 110 cups of yogurt? 200 cups? Calculate variable and total cost for every level of output given in Problem 2.

b. Draw Marty's variable cost curve. On the same diagram, draw his total cost curve.

c. What is the marginal cost per cup for the first 110 cups of yogurt? For the next 90 cups? Calculate the marginal cost for all remaining levels of output.

4. The production function for Marty's Frozen Yogurt is given in Problem 2. The costs are given in Problem 3.

a. For each of the given levels of output, calculate the average fixed cost (AFC), average variable cost (AVC), and average total cost (ATC) per cup of frozen yogurt.

b. On one diagram, draw the AFC, AVC, and ATC curves.

c. What principle explains why the AFC declines as output increases? What principle explains why the AVC increases as output increases? Explain your answers.

d. How many cups of frozen yogurt are produced when average total cost is minimized?

5. Labor costs represent a large percentage of total costs for many firms. According to data from the Bureau of Labor Statistics, U.S. labor costs were up 0.8% in 2013, compared to 2012.

a. When labor costs increase, what happens to average total cost and marginal cost? Consider a case in which labor costs are only variable costs and a case in which they are both variable and fixed costs.

An increase in labor productivity means each worker can produce more output. Recent data on productivity show that labor productivity in the U.S. nonfarm business sector grew by 1.7% between 1970 and 1999, by 2.6% between 2000 and 2009, and by 1.1% between 2010 and 2013.

b. When productivity growth is positive, what happens to the total product curve and the marginal product of labor curve? Illustrate your answer with a diagram.

c. When productivity growth is positive, what happens to the marginal cost curve and the average total cost curve? Illustrate your answer with a diagram.

d. If labor costs are rising over time on average, why would a company want to adopt equipment and methods that increase labor productivity?

6. Magnificent Blooms is a florist specializing in floral arrangements for weddings, graduations, and other events. Magnificent Blooms has a fixed cost associated with space and equipment of $100 per day. Each worker is paid $50 per day. The daily production function for Magnificent Blooms is shown in the accompanying table.

Quantity of labor (workers)	Quantity of floral arrangements
0	0
1	5
2	9
3	12
4	14
5	15

a. Calculate the marginal product of each worker. What principle explains why the marginal product per worker declines as the number of workers employed increases?

b. Calculate the marginal cost of each level of output. What principle explains why the marginal cost per floral arrangement increases as the number of arrangements increases?

7. You have the information shown in the accompanying table about a firm's costs. Complete the missing data.

Quantity of output	TC	MC	ATC	AVC
0	$20		—	—
		$20		
1	?		?	?
		10		
2	?		?	?
		16		
3	?		?	?
		20		
4	?		?	?
		24		
5	?		?	?

8. Evaluate each of the following statements. If a statement is true, explain why; if it is false, identify the mistake and try to correct it.

a. A decreasing marginal product tells us that marginal cost must be rising.

b. An increase in fixed cost increases the minimum-cost output.

c. An increase in fixed cost increases marginal cost.

d. When marginal cost is above average total cost, average total cost must be falling.

9. Mark and Jeff operate a small company that produces souvenir footballs. Their fixed cost is $2,000 per month. They can hire workers for $1,000 per worker per month. Their monthly production function for footballs is as given in the accompanying table.

Quantity of labor (workers)	Quantity of footballs
0	0
1	300
2	800
3	1,200
4	1,400
5	1,500

a. For each quantity of labor, calculate average variable cost (*AVC*), average fixed cost (*AFC*), average total cost (*ATC*), and marginal cost (*MC*).

b. On one diagram, draw the *AVC*, *ATC*, and *MC* curves.

c. At what level of output is Mark and Jeff's average total cost minimized?

10. You produce widgets. Currently you produce four widgets at a total cost of $40.

a. What is your average total cost?

b. Suppose you could produce one more (the fifth) widget at a marginal cost of $5. If you do produce that fifth widget, what will your average total cost be? Has your average total cost increased or decreased? Why?

c. Suppose instead that you could produce one more (the fifth) widget at a marginal cost of $20. If you do produce that fifth widget, what will your average total cost be? Has your average total cost increased or decreased? Why?

11. In your economics class, each homework problem set is graded on the basis of a maximum score of 100. You have completed 9 out of 10 of the problem sets for the term, and your current average grade is 88. What range of grades for your 10th problem set will raise your overall average? What range will lower your overall average? Explain your answer.

12. Don owns a small concrete-mixing company. His fixed cost is the cost of the concrete-batching machinery and his mixer trucks. His variable cost is the cost of the sand, gravel, and other inputs for producing concrete; the gas and maintenance for the machinery and trucks; and his workers. He is trying to decide how many mixer trucks to purchase. He has estimated the costs shown in the accompanying table based on estimates of the number of orders his company will receive per week.

Quantity of trucks	FC	VC 20 orders	VC 40 orders	VC 60 orders
2	$6,000	$2,000	$5,000	$12,000
3	7,000	1,800	3,800	10,800
4	8,000	1,200	3,600	8,400

a. For each level of fixed cost, calculate Don's total cost for producing 20, 40, and 60 orders per week.

b. If Don is producing 20 orders per week, how many trucks should he purchase and what will his average total cost be? Answer the same questions for 40 and 60 orders per week.

13. Consider Don's concrete-mixing business described in Problem 12. Assume that Don purchased 3 trucks, expecting to produce 40 orders per week.

a. Suppose that, in the short run, business declines to 20 orders per week. What is Don's average total cost per order in the short run? What will his average total cost per order in the short run be if his business booms to 60 orders per week?

b. What is Don's long-run average total cost for 20 orders per week? Explain why his short-run average total cost of producing 20 orders per week when the number of trucks is fixed at 3 is greater than his long-run average total cost of producing 20 orders per week.

c. Draw Don's long-run average total cost curve. Draw his short-run average total cost curve if he owns 3 trucks.

14. True or false? Explain your reasoning.

a. The short-run average total cost can never be less than the long-run average total cost.

b. The short-run average variable cost can never be less than the long-run average total cost.

c. In the long run, choosing a higher level of fixed cost shifts the long-run average total cost curve upward.

15. Wolfsburg Wagon (WW) is a small automaker. The accompanying table shows WW's long-run average total cost.

Quantity of cars	LRATC of car
1	$30,000
2	20,000
3	15,000
4	12,000
5	12,000
6	12,000
7	14,000
8	18,000

a. For which levels of output does WW experience increasing returns to scale?

b. For which levels of output does WW experience decreasing returns to scale?

c. For which levels of output does WW experience constant returns to scale?

For interactive, step-by-step help in solving the following problem, visit LaunchPad by using the URL on the back cover of this book.

16. The accompanying table shows a car manufacturer's total cost of producing cars.

Quantity of cars	TC
0	$500,000
1	540,000
2	560,000
3	570,000
4	590,000
5	620,000
6	660,000
7	720,000
8	800,000
9	920,000
10	1,100,000

a. What is this manufacturer's fixed cost?

b. For each level of output, calculate the variable cost (VC). For each level of output except zero output, calculate the average variable cost (AVC), average total cost (ATC), and average fixed cost (AFC). What is the minimum-cost output?

c. For each level of output, calculate this manufacturer's marginal cost (MC).

d. On one diagram, draw the manufacturer's AVC, ATC, and MC curves.

Perfect Competition and the Supply Curve

What You Will Learn in This Chapter

- **What a perfectly competitive market is and the characteristics of a perfectly competitive industry**

- **How a price-taking producer determines its profit-maximizing quantity of output**

- **How to assess whether or not a producer is profitable and why an unprofitable producer may continue to operate in the short run**

- **Why industries behave differently in the short run and the long run**

- **What determines the industry supply curve in both the short run and the long run**

DECK THE HALLS

Stockbyte/Exactostock/Superstock

Whether it's Christmas trees or smartphones, how a good is produced determines its cost of production.

ONE SURE SIGN THAT it's the holiday season is the sudden appearance of Christmas tree sellers, who set up shop in vacant lots, parking lots, and garden centers all across the country. Until the 1950s, virtually all Christmas trees were obtained by individuals going to local forests to cut down their own. However, by the 1950s increased demand from population growth and diminished supply from the loss of forests created a market opportunity. Seeing an ability to profit by growing and selling Christmas trees, farmers responded. So rather than venturing into the forest to cut your own tree, you now have a wide range of sizes and varieties of trees to choose from—and they are available close to home. In 2013, nearly 25 million farmed trees were sold in the United States for a total of over $1 billion.

Note that the supply of Christmas trees is relatively price inelastic for two reasons: it takes time to acquire land for planting,

and it takes time for the trees to grow. However, these limits apply only in the short run. Over time, farms that are already in operation can increase their capacity and new tree farmers can enter the business. And, over time, the trees will mature and be ready to harvest. So the increase in the quantity supplied in response to an increase in price will be much larger in the long run than in the short run.

Where does the supply curve come from? Why is there a difference between the short-run and the long-run supply curve? In this chapter we will use our understanding of costs, developed in Chapter 11, as the basis for an analysis of the supply curve. As we'll see, this will require that we understand the behavior both of individual firms and of an entire industry, composed of these many individual firms.

Our analysis in this chapter assumes that the industry in question is character-

ized by *perfect competition*. We begin by explaining the concept of perfect competition, providing a brief introduction to the conditions that give rise to a perfectly competitive industry. We then show how a producer under perfect competition decides how much to produce. Finally, we use the cost curves of the individual producers to derive the *industry supply curve* under perfect competition.

By analyzing the way a competitive industry evolves over time, we will come to understand the distinction between the short-run and long-run effects of changes in demand on a competitive industry—such as, for example, the effect of America's preference for readily available trees for the holidays on the Christmas tree farming industry. We will conclude with a deeper discussion of the conditions necessary for an industry to be perfectly competitive.

A **price-taking producer** is a producer whose actions have no effect on the market price of the good or service it sells.

A **price-taking consumer** is a consumer whose actions have no effect on the market price of the good or service he or she buys.

A **perfectly competitive market** is a market in which all market participants are price-takers.

A **perfectly competitive industry** is an industry in which producers are price-takers.

Perfect Competition

Suppose that Yves and Zoe are neighboring farmers, both of whom grow Christmas trees. Both sell their output to the same set of Christmas tree consumers so, in a real sense, Yves and Zoe compete with each other.

Does this mean that Yves should try to stop Zoe from growing Christmas trees or that Yves and Zoe should form an agreement to grow less? Almost certainly not: there are thousands of Christmas tree farmers, and Yves and Zoe are competing with all those other growers as well as with each other. Because so many farmers sell Christmas trees, if any one of them produced more or less, there would be no measurable effect on market prices.

When people talk about business competition, the image they often have in mind is a situation in which two or three rival firms are intensely struggling for advantage. But economists know that when an industry consists of a few main competitors, it's actually a sign that competition is fairly limited. As the example of Christmas trees suggests, when there is enough competition, it doesn't even make sense to identify your rivals: there are so many competitors that you cannot single out any one of them as a rival.

We can put it another way: Yves and Zoe are **price-taking producers.** A producer is a price-taker when its actions cannot affect the market price of the good or service it sells. As a result, a price-taking producer considers the market price as given. When there is enough competition—when competition is what economists call "perfect"—then every producer is a price-taker.

And there is a similar definition for consumers: a **price-taking consumer** is a consumer who cannot influence the market price of the good or service by his or her actions. That is, the market price is unaffected by how much or how little of the good the consumer buys.

Defining Perfect Competition

In a **perfectly competitive market,** all market participants, both consumers and producers, are price-takers. That is, neither consumption decisions by individual consumers nor production decisions by individual producers affect the market price of the good.

The supply and demand model, which we introduced in Chapter 3 and have used repeatedly since then, is a model of a perfectly competitive market. It depends fundamentally on the assumption that no individual buyer or seller of a good, such as coffee beans or Christmas trees, believes that it is possible to affect the price at which he or she can buy or sell the good.

As a general rule, consumers are indeed price-takers. Instances in which consumers are able to affect the prices they pay are rare. It is, however, quite common for producers to have a significant ability to affect the prices they receive, a phenomenon we'll address in the next chapter. So the model of perfect competition is appropriate for some but not all markets. An industry in which producers are price-takers is called a **perfectly competitive industry.** Clearly, some industries aren't perfectly competitive; in later chapters we'll learn how to analyze industries that don't fit the perfectly competitive model.

Under what circumstances will all producers be price-takers? In the next section we will find that there are two necessary conditions for a perfectly competitive industry and that a third condition is often present as well.

Two Necessary Conditions for Perfect Competition

The markets for major grains, like wheat and corn, are perfectly competitive: individual wheat and corn farmers, as well as individual buyers of wheat and corn, take market prices as given. In contrast, the markets for some of the food items made from these grains—in particular, breakfast cereals—are by no means perfectly competitive. There is intense competition among cereal brands, but not *perfect* competition. To understand the difference between the market for wheat and the market for shredded wheat cereal is to understand the importance of the two necessary conditions for perfect competition.

First, for an industry to be perfectly competitive, it must contain many produc-ers, none of whom have a large **market share.** A producer's market share is the fraction of the total industry output accounted for by that producer's output. The distribution of market share constitutes a major difference between the grain industry and the breakfast cereal industry. There are thousands of wheat farm-ers, none of whom account for more than a tiny fraction of total wheat sales.

The breakfast cereal industry, however, is dominated by four producers: Kellogg's, General Mills, Post Foods, and the Quaker Oats Company. Kellogg's alone accounts for about one-third of all cereal sales. Kellogg's executives know that if they try to sell more cornflakes, they are likely to drive down the market price of cornflakes. That is, they know that their actions influence market prices, simply because they are such a large part of the market that changes in their pro-duction will significantly affect the overall quantity supplied. It makes sense to assume that producers are price-takers only when an industry does *not* contain any large producers like Kellogg's.

Second, an industry can be perfectly competitive only if consumers regard the products of all producers as equivalent. This clearly isn't true in the breakfast cereal market: consumers don't consider Cap'n Crunch to be a good substitute for Wheaties. As a result, the maker of Wheaties has some ability to increase its price without fear that it will lose all its customers to the maker of Cap'n Crunch.

Contrast this with the case of a **standardized product,** which is a product that consumers regard as the same good even when it comes from different producers, sometimes known as a **commodity.** Because wheat is a standardized product, consumers regard the output of one wheat producer as a perfect substi-tute for that of another producer. Consequently, one farmer cannot increase the price for his or her wheat without losing all sales to other wheat farmers. *So the second necessary condition for a competitive industry is that the industry output is a standardized product* (see the upcoming For Inquiring Minds).

Free Entry and Exit

All perfectly competitive industries have many producers with small market shares, producing a standardized product. Most perfectly competitive industries are also characterized by one more feature: it is easy for new firms to enter the industry or for firms that are currently in the industry to leave. That is, no obstacles in the form of government regulations or limited access to key resources prevent new producers from entering the market. And no additional costs are associated with shutting down a company and leaving the industry.

Economists refer to the arrival of new firms into an industry as *entry;* they refer to the departure of firms from an industry as *exit.* When there are no obstacles to entry into or exit from an industry, we say that the industry has **free entry and exit.**

Free entry and exit is not strictly necessary for perfect competition. In Chapter 5 we described the case of Alaskan crab fishing, where regulations place a quota on the amount of Alaskan crab that can be caught during a season, so entry is limited to established boat owners that have been given quotas. Despite this, there are enough boats operating that the crab fisherman are price-takers. But free entry and exit is a key factor in most competitive industries. It ensures that the number of producers in an industry can adjust to changing market conditions. And, in particular, it ensures that producers in an industry cannot act to keep new firms out.

To sum up, then, perfect competition depends on two necessary condi-tions. First, the industry must contain many producers, each having a small

A producer's **market share** is the fraction of the total industry output accounted for by that producer's output.

A good is a **standardized product,** also known as a **commodity,** when consumers regard the products of different producers as the same good.

An industry has **free entry and exit** when new producers can easily enter into an industry and existing producers can easily leave that industry.

FOR INQUIRING MINDS | What's a Standardized Product?

A perfectly competitive industry must produce a standardized product. But is it enough for the products of different firms actually to be the same? No: people must also *think* that they are the same. And producers often go to great lengths to convince consumers that they have a distinctive, or *differentiated*, product, even when they don't.

Consider, for example, champagne—not the superexpensive premium champagnes but the more ordinary stuff. Most people cannot tell the difference between champagne actually produced in the Champagne region of France, where the product originated, and similar products from Spain or California. But the French government has sought and obtained legal protection for the winemakers of Champagne,

In the end, only *kimchi* eaters can tell you if there is truly a difference between Korean-produced *kimchi* and the Japanese-produced variety.

ensuring that around the world only bubbly wine from that region can be called champagne. If it's from some-place else, all the seller can do is say

that it was produced using the *méthode Champenoise*. This creates a differentiation in the minds of consumers and lets the champagne producers of Champagne charge higher prices.

Similarly, Korean producers of *kimchi*, the spicy fermented cabbage that is the Korean national side dish, are doing their best to convince consumers that the same product packaged by Japanese firms is just not the real thing. The purpose is, of course, to ensure higher prices for Korean *kimchi*.

So is an industry perfectly competitive if it sells products that are indistinguishable except in name but that consumers, for whatever reason, don't think are standardized? No. When it comes to defining the nature of competition, the consumer is always right. ■

market share. Second, the industry must produce a standardized product. In addition, perfectly competitive industries are normally characterized by free entry and exit.

How does an industry that meets these three criteria behave? As a first step toward answering that question, let's look at how an individual producer in a perfectly competitive industry maximizes profit.

ECONOMICS ▶ in Action

Paid to Delay

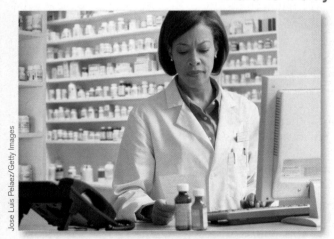

Patents allow drug makers to have a legal monopoly on new medications for 20 years.

Sometimes it is possible to see an industry become perfectly competitive. In fact, it happens frequently in the case of pharmaceuticals when the patent on a popular drug expires.

When a company develops a new drug, it is usually able to receive a patent, which gives it a *legal monopoly*—the exclusive right to sell the drug—for 20 years from the date of filing. Legally, no one else can sell that drug without the patent owner's permission.

When the patent expires, the market is open for other companies to sell their own versions of the drug, known collectively as *generics*. Generics are standardized products, much like aspirin, and are often sold by many producers. On average, a generic drug costs about 15% of the price of the equivalent patent-protected drug and quickly causes the patent-protected drug to lose up to 90% of its market share.

Not surprisingly, the makers of patent-protected drugs are eager to forestall the entry of generic competitors and have tried a variety of strategies. One especially successful tactic, called "pay-to-delay," is an agreement between the original drug maker and a potential generic competitor to delay the introduction of the generic drug for a specific period of time in return for compensation. As a result, the original drug maker continues to charge high prices and reap high profits. These agreements have been fiercely contested by government regulators, who view them as anti-competitive practices that hurt consumers. According to the Federal Trade Commission, the federal agency tasked with implementing antitrust law (laws regulating monopolies), between 2005 and 2013 pay-for-delay deals cost consumers $3.5 billion annually.

The defenders of pay-for-delay agreements argue that the deals are not anti-competitive and that they allow generics to come to market without their makers having to face the threat of costly patent litigation battles. In 2013 the Supreme Court ruled that pay-for-delay deals could in fact be anti-competitive, thus giving the Federal Trade Commission the green light to challenge the deals on a case-by-case basis.

Check Your Understanding 12-1

1. In each of the following situations, do you think the industry described will be perfectly competitive or not? Explain your answer.
   a. There are two producers of aluminum in the world, a good sold in many places.
   b. The price of natural gas is determined by global supply and demand. A small share of that global supply is produced by a handful of companies located in the North Sea.
   c. Dozens of designers sell high-fashion clothes. Each designer has a distinctive style and a loyal clientele.
   d. There are many baseball teams in the United States, one or two in each major city and each selling tickets to its hometown events.

Solutions appear at back of book.

Production and Profits

Consider Noelle, who runs a Christmas tree farm. Suppose that the market price of Christmas trees is $18 per tree and that Noelle is a price-taker—she can sell as many as she likes at that price. Then we can use the data in Table 12-1 to find her profit-maximizing level of output by direct calculation.

The first column shows the quantity of output in number of trees, and the second column shows Noelle's total revenue from her output: the market value of trees she produced. Total revenue, TR, is equal to the market price multiplied by the quantity of output:

(12-1) $TR = P \times Q$

In this example, total revenue is equal to $18 per tree times the quantity of output in trees.

The third column of Table 12-1 shows Noelle's total cost. The fourth column shows her profit, equal to total revenue minus total cost:

(12-2) Profit = $TR - TC$

TABLE 12-1 Profit for Noelle's Farm When Market Price Is $18

Quantity of trees Q	Total revenue TR	Total cost TC	Profit TR − TC
0	$0	$140	−$140
10	180	300	−120
20	360	360	0
30	540	440	100
40	720	560	160
50	900	720	180
60	1,080	920	160
70	1,260	1,160	100

As indicated by the numbers in the table, profit is maximized at an output of 50 trees, where profit is equal to $180. But we can gain more insight into the profit-maximizing choice of output by viewing it as a problem of marginal analysis, a task we'll do next.

Marginal revenue is the change in total revenue generated by an additional unit of output.

According to the **optimal output rule,** profit is maximized by producing the quantity of output at which the marginal revenue of the last unit produced is equal to its marginal cost.

According to the **price-taking firm's optimal output rule,** a price-taking firm's profit is maximized by producing the quantity of output at which the market price is equal to the marginal cost of the last unit produced.

Using Marginal Analysis to Choose the Profit-Maximizing Quantity of Output

Recall from Chapter 9 the *profit-maximizing principle of marginal analysis:* the optimal amount of an activity is the level at which marginal benefit is equal to marginal cost. To apply this principle, consider the effect on a producer's profit of increasing output by one unit. The marginal benefit of that unit is the additional revenue generated by selling it; this measure has a name—it is called the **marginal revenue** of that unit of output. The general formula for marginal revenue is:

$$\text{(12-3)} \quad \text{Marginal revenue} = \frac{\text{Change in total revenue generated by one additional unit of output}}{} = \frac{\text{Change in total revenue}}{\text{Change in quantity of output}}$$

or

$$MR = \Delta TR/\Delta Q$$

So Noelle maximizes her profit by producing trees up to the point at which the marginal revenue is equal to marginal cost. We can summarize this as the producer's **optimal output rule:** profit is maximized by producing the quantity at which the marginal revenue of the last unit produced is equal to its marginal cost. That is, $MR = MC$ at the optimal quantity of output.

We can learn how to apply the optimal output rule with the help of Table 12-2, which provides various short-run cost measures for Noelle's farm. The second column contains the farm's variable cost, and the third column shows its total cost of output based on the assumption that the farm incurs a fixed cost of $140. The fourth column shows marginal cost. Notice that, in this example, the marginal cost initially falls as output rises but then begins to increase. This gives the marginal cost curve the "swoosh" shape described in the Selena's Gourmet Salsas example in Chapter 11. Shortly it will become clear that this shape has important implications for short-run production decisions.

The fifth column contains the farm's marginal revenue, which has an important feature: Noelle's marginal revenue equal to price is constant at $18 for every output level. The sixth and final column shows the calculation of the net gain per tree, which is equal to marginal revenue minus marginal cost—or, equivalently in this case, market price minus marginal cost. As you can see, it is positive for the 10th through 50th trees; producing each of these trees raises Noelle's profit. For the 60th through 70th trees, however, net gain is negative: producing them would decrease, not increase, profit. (You can verify this by examining Table 12-1.) So a quantity of 50 trees is Noelle's profit-maximizing output; it is the level of output at which marginal cost is equal to the market price, $18.

This example, in fact, illustrates another general rule derived from marginal analysis—the **price-taking firm's optimal output rule,** which says that a price-taking firm's profit is maximized by producing the quantity of output at which the market price is equal to the marginal cost of the last unit produced. That is,

TABLE 12-2 Short-Run Costs for Noelle's Farm

Quantity of trees Q	Variable cost VC	Total cost TC	Marginal cost of tree MC = ΔTC/ΔQ	Marginal revenue of tree MR	Net gain of tree = MR − MC
0	$0	$140			
			$16	$18	$2
10	160	300			
			6	18	12
20	220	360			
			8	18	10
30	300	440			
			12	18	6
40	420	560			
			16	18	2
50	580	720			
			20	18	−2
60	780	920			
			24	18	−6
70	1,020	1,160			

P = MC at the price-taking firm's optimal quantity of output. In fact, the price-taking firm's optimal output rule is just an application of the optimal output rule to the particular case of a price-taking firm. Why? Because *in the case of a price-taking firm, marginal revenue is equal to the market price.*

A price-taking firm cannot influence the market price by its actions. It always takes the market price as given because it cannot lower the market price by selling more or raise the market price by selling less. So, for a price-taking firm, the additional revenue generated by producing one more unit is always the market price. We will need to keep this fact in mind in future chapters, where we will learn that marginal revenue is not equal to the market price if the industry is not perfectly competitive. As a result, firms are not price-takers when an industry is not perfectly competitive.

For the remainder of this chapter, we will assume that the industry in question is like Christmas tree farming, perfectly competitive. Figure 12-1 shows that Noelle's profit-maximizing quantity of output is, indeed, the number of trees at which the marginal cost of production is equal to price. The figure shows the marginal cost curve, *MC*, drawn from the data in the fourth column of Table 12-2. As in Chapter 9, we plot the marginal cost of increasing output from 10 to 20 trees halfway between 10 and 20, and so on. The horizontal line at $18 is Noelle's **marginal revenue curve.**

Note that whenever a firm is a price-taker, its marginal revenue curve is a horizontal line at the market price: it can sell as much as it likes at the market price. Regardless of whether it sells more or less, the market price is unaffected. *In effect, the individual firm faces a horizontal, perfectly elastic demand curve for its output—an individual demand curve for its output that is equivalent to its marginal revenue curve.* The marginal cost curve crosses the marginal revenue curve at point *E* where *MC = MR*. Sure enough, the quantity of output at *E* is 50 trees.

Does this mean that the price-taking firm's production decision can be entirely summed up as "produce up to the point where the marginal cost of production is equal to the price"? No, not quite. Before applying the profit-maximizing principle of marginal analysis to determine how much to produce, a potential producer must as a

The **marginal revenue curve** shows how marginal revenue varies as output varies.

FIGURE 12-1   The Price-Taking Firm's Profit-Maximizing Quantity of Output

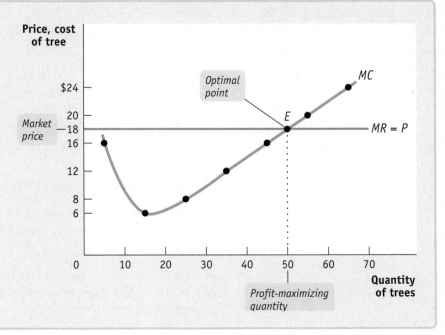

At the profit-maximizing quantity of output, the market price is equal to marginal cost. It is located at the point where the marginal cost curve crosses the marginal revenue curve, which is a horizontal line at the market price. Here, the profit-maximizing point is at an output of 50 trees, the output quantity at point *E*.

first step answer an "either–or" question: should it produce at all? If the answer to that question is yes, it then proceeds to the second step—a "how much" decision: maximizing profit by choosing the quantity of output at which marginal cost is equal to price.

To understand why the first step in the production decision involves an "either–or" question, we need to ask how we determine whether it is profitable or unprofitable to produce at all.

When Is Production Profitable?

Recall from Chapter 9 that a firm's decision whether or not to stay in a given business depends on its *economic profit*—the measure of profit based on the opportunity cost of resources used in the business. To put it a slightly different way: in the calculation of economic profit, a firm's total cost incorporates the implicit cost—the benefits forgone in the next best use of the firm's resources—as well as the explicit cost in the form of actual cash outlays.

In contrast, *accounting profit* is profit calculated using only the explicit costs incurred by the firm. This means that economic profit incorporates the opportunity cost of resources owned by the firm and used in the production of output, while accounting profit does not.

A firm may make positive accounting profit while making zero or even negative economic profit. It's important to understand clearly that a firm's decision to produce or not, to stay in business or to close down permanently, should be based on economic profit, not accounting profit.

So we will assume, as we always do, that the cost numbers given in Tables 12-1 and 12-2 include all costs, implicit as well as explicit, and that the profit numbers in Table 12-1 are therefore economic profit. So what determines whether Noelle's farm earns a profit or generates a loss? The answer is that, *given the farm's cost curves, whether or not it is profitable depends on the market price of trees—specifically, whether the market price is more or less than the farm's minimum average total cost.*

In Table 12-3 we calculate short-run average variable cost and short-run average total cost for Noelle's farm. These are short-run values because we take fixed cost as given. (We'll turn to the effects of changing fixed cost shortly.) The short-run average total cost curve, *ATC*, is shown in Figure 12-2, along with the marginal cost curve, *MC*, from Figure 12-1. As you can see, average total cost is minimized at point *C*, corresponding to an output of 40 trees—the *minimum-cost output*—and an average total cost of $14 per tree.

To see how these curves can be used to decide whether production is profitable or unprofitable, recall that profit is equal to total revenue minus total cost, $TR - TC$. This means:

- If the firm produces a quantity at which $TR > TC$, the firm is profitable.
- If the firm produces a quantity at which $TR = TC$, the firm breaks even.
- If the firm produces a quantity at which $TR < TC$, the firm incurs a loss.

We can also express this idea in terms of revenue and cost per unit of output. If we divide profit by the number of units of output, *Q*, we obtain the following expression for profit per unit of output:

(12-4) Profit/$Q = TR/Q - TC/Q$

TABLE 12-3 Short-Run Average Costs for Noelle's Farm

Quantity of trees Q	Variable cost VC	Total cost TC	Short-run average variable cost of tree AVC = VC/Q	Short-run average total cost of tree ATC = TC/Q
10	$160.00	$300.00	$16.00	$30.00
20	220.00	360.00	11.00	18.00
30	300.00	440.00	10.00	14.67
40	420.00	560.00	10.50	14.00
50	580.00	720.00	11.60	14.40
60	780.00	920.00	13.00	15.33
70	1,020.00	1,160.00	14.57	16.57

FIGURE 12-2   Costs and Production in the Short Run

This figure shows the marginal cost curve, *MC*, and the short-run average total cost curve, *ATC*. When the market price is $14, output will be 40 trees (the minimum-cost output), represented by point *C*. The price of $14, equal to the firm's minimum average total cost, is the firm's *break-even price*.

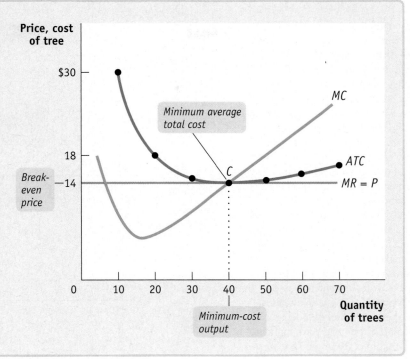

TR/Q is average revenue, which is the market price. *TC/Q* is average total cost. So a firm is profitable if the market price for its product is more than the average total cost of the quantity the firm produces; a firm loses money if the market price is less than average total cost of the quantity the firm produces. This means:

- If the firm produces a quantity at which $P > ATC$, the firm is profitable.
- If the firm produces a quantity at which $P = ATC$, the firm breaks even.
- If the firm produces a quantity at which $P < ATC$, the firm incurs a loss.

Figure 12-3 illustrates this result, showing how the market price determines whether a firm is profitable. It also shows how profits are depicted graphically. Each panel shows the marginal cost curve, *MC*, and the short-run average total cost curve, *ATC*. Average total cost is minimized at point *C*. Panel (a) shows the case we have already analyzed, in which the market price of trees is $18 per tree. Panel (b) shows the case in which the market price of trees is lower, $10 per tree.

In panel (a), we see that at a price of $18 per tree the profit-maximizing quantity of output is 50 trees, indicated by point *E*, where the marginal cost curve, *MC*, intersects the marginal revenue curve—which for a price-taking firm is a horizontal line at the market price. At that quantity of output, average total cost is $14.40 per tree, indicated by point *Z*. Since the price per tree exceeds average total cost per tree, Noelle's farm is profitable.

Noelle's total profit when the market price is $18 is represented by the area of the shaded rectangle in panel (a). To see why, notice that total profit can be expressed in terms of profit per unit:

(12-5) Profit $= TR - TC = (TR/Q - TC/Q) \times Q$

or, equivalently,

Profit $= (P - ATC) \times Q$

FIGURE **12-3**   Profitability and the Market Price

In panel (a) the market price is $18. The farm is profitable because price exceeds minimum average total cost, the break-even price, $14. The farm's optimal output choice is indicated by point E, corresponding to an output of 50 trees. The average total cost of producing 50 trees is indicated by point Z on the ATC curve, corresponding to an amount of $14.40. The vertical distance between E and Z corresponds to the farm's per-unit profit, $18.00 − $14.40 = $3.60. Total profit is given by the area of the shaded rectangle, 50 × $3.60 = $180.00. In panel (b) the market price is $10; the farm is unprofitable because the price falls below the minimum average total cost, $14. The farm's optimal output choice when producing is indicated by point A, corresponding to an output of 30 trees. The farm's per-unit loss, $14.67 − $10.00 = $4.67, is represented by the vertical distance between A and Y. The farm's total loss is represented by the shaded rectangle, 30 × $4.67 = $140.00 (adjusted for rounding error).

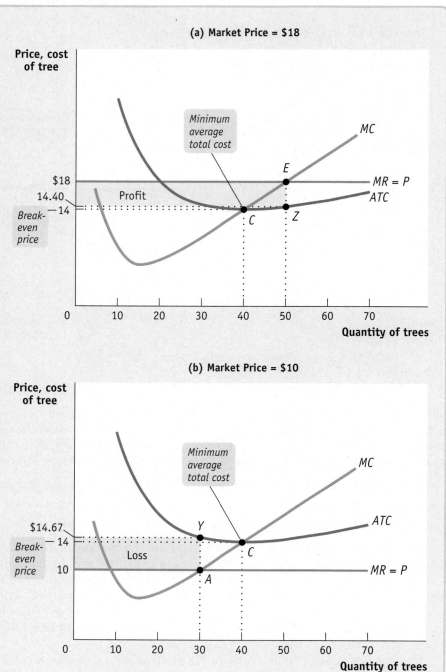

since P is equal to TR/Q and ATC is equal to TC/Q. The height of the shaded rectangle in panel (a) corresponds to the vertical distance between points E and Z. It is equal to P − ATC = $18.00 − $14.40 = $3.60 per tree. The shaded rectangle has a width equal to the output: Q = 50 trees. So the area of that rectangle is equal to Noelle's profit: 50 trees × $3.60 profit per tree = $180—the same number we calculated in Table 12-1.

What about the situation illustrated in panel (b)? Here the market price of trees is $10 per tree. Setting price equal to marginal cost leads to a profit-maximizing output of 30 trees, indicated by point A. At this output, Noelle has an average total cost of $14.67 per tree, indicated by point *Y.* At the profit-maximizing output quantity—30 trees—average total cost exceeds the market price. This means that Noelle's farm generates a loss, not a profit.

How much does she lose by producing when the market price is $10? On each tree she loses $ATC - P = \$14.67 - \$10.00 = \$4.67$, an amount corresponding to the vertical distance between points *A* and *Y.* And she would produce 30 trees, which corresponds to the width of the shaded rectangle. So the total value of the losses is $\$4.67 \times 30 = \$140.00$ (adjusted for rounding error), an amount that corresponds to the area of the shaded rectangle in panel (b).

But how does a producer know, in general, whether or not its business will be profitable? It turns out that the crucial test lies in a comparison of the market price to the producer's *minimum average total cost*. On Noelle's farm, minimum average total cost, which is equal to $14, occurs at an output quantity of 40 trees, indicated by point *C.*

Whenever the market price exceeds minimum average total cost, the producer can find some output level for which the average total cost is less than the market price. In other words, the producer can find a level of output at which the firm makes a profit. So Noelle's farm will be profitable whenever the market price exceeds $14. And she will achieve the highest possible profit by producing the quantity at which marginal cost equals the market price.

Conversely, if the market price is less than minimum average total cost, there is no output level at which price exceeds average total cost. As a result, the firm will be unprofitable at any quantity of output. As we saw, at a price of $10—an amount less than minimum average total cost—Noelle did indeed lose money. By producing the quantity at which marginal cost equals the market price, Noelle did the best she could, but the best that she could do was a loss of $140. Any other quantity would have increased the size of her loss.

The minimum average total cost of a price-taking firm is called its **break-even price,** the price at which it earns zero profit. (Recall that's *economic profit*.) A firm will earn positive profit when the market price is above the break-even price, and it will suffer losses when the market price is below the break-even price. Noelle's break-even price of $14 is the price at point *C* in Figures 12-2 and 12-3.

So the rule for determining whether a producer of a good is profitable depends on a comparison of the market price of the good to the producer's break-even price—its minimum average total cost:

* Whenever the market price exceeds minimum average total cost, the producer is profitable.
* Whenever the market price equals minimum average total cost, the producer breaks even.
* Whenever the market price is less than minimum average total cost, the producer is unprofitable.

The Short-Run Production Decision

You might be tempted to say that if a firm is unprofitable because the market price is below its minimum average total cost, it shouldn't produce any output. In the short run, however, this conclusion isn't right.

In the short run, sometimes the firm should produce even if price falls below minimum average total cost. The reason is that total cost includes *fixed cost*—cost that does not depend on the amount of output produced and can only be altered in the long run.

In the short run, fixed cost must still be paid, regardless of whether or not a firm produces. For example, if Noelle rents a refrigerated truck for the year, she has to pay the rent on the truck regardless of whether she produces any trees. *Since it cannot be changed in the short run, her fixed cost is irrelevant to her decision about whether to produce or shut down in the short run.*

The **break-even price** of a price-taking firm is the market price at which it earns zero profit.

A firm will cease production in the short run if the market price falls below the **shut-down price,** which is equal to minimum average variable cost.

Although fixed cost should play no role in the decision about whether to produce in the short run, other costs—variable costs—do matter. An example of variable costs is the wages of workers who must be hired to help with planting and harvesting. Variable costs can be saved by *not* producing; so they should play a role in determining whether or not to produce in the short run.

Let's turn to Figure 12-4: it shows both the short-run average total cost curve, *ATC,* and the short-run average variable cost curve, *AVC,* drawn from the information in Table 12-3. Recall that the difference between the two curves—the vertical distance between them—represents average fixed cost, the fixed cost per unit of output, *FC/Q.*

Because the marginal cost curve has a "swoosh" shape—falling at first before rising—the short-run average variable cost curve is U-shaped: the initial fall in marginal cost causes average variable cost to fall as well, before rising marginal cost eventually pulls it up again. The short-run average variable cost curve reaches its minimum value of $10 at point *A,* at an output of 30 trees.

We are now prepared to fully analyze the optimal production decision in the short run. We need to consider two cases:

1. When the market price is below minimum average *variable* cost
2. When the market price is greater than or equal to minimum average *variable* cost

When the market price is below minimum average variable cost, the price the firm receives per unit is not covering its variable cost per unit. A firm in this situation should cease production immediately. Why? Because there is no level of output at which the firm's total revenue covers its variable costs—the costs it can avoid by not operating.

In this case the firm maximizes its profits by not producing at all—by, in effect, minimizing its losses. It will still incur a fixed cost in the short run, but it will no longer incur any variable cost. This means that the minimum average variable cost is equal to the **shut-down price,** the price at which the firm ceases production in the short run. In the example of Noelle's tree farm, she will cease production in the short run by laying off workers and halting all planting and harvesting of trees.

FIGURE 12-4 | The Short-Run Individual Supply Curve

When the market price equals or exceeds Noelle's *shut-down price* of $10, the minimum average variable cost indicated by point *A,* she will produce the output quantity at which marginal cost is equal to price. So at any price equal to or above the minimum average *variable* cost, the short-run individual supply curve is the firm's marginal cost curve; this corresponds to the upward-sloping segment of the individual supply curve. When market price falls below minimum average variable cost, the firm ceases operation in the short run. This corresponds to the vertical segment of the individual supply curve along the vertical axis.

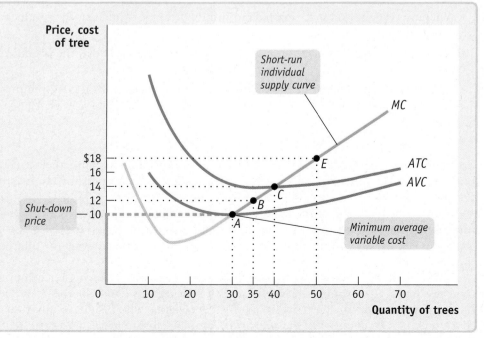

When price is greater than minimum average variable cost, however, the firm should produce in the short run. In this case, the firm maximizes profit—or minimizes loss—by choosing the output quantity at which its marginal cost is equal to the market price. For example, if the market price of each tree is $18, Noelle should produce at point *E* in Figure 12-4, corresponding to an output of 50 trees. Note that point *C* in Figure 12-4 corresponds to the farm's break-even price of $14 per tree. Since *E* lies above *C*, Noelle's farm will be profitable; she will generate a per-tree profit of $18.00 − $14.40 = $3.60 when the market price is $18.

But what if the market price lies between the shut-down price and the break-even price—that is, between minimum average *variable* cost and minimum average *total* cost? In the case of Noelle's farm, this corresponds to prices anywhere between $10 and $14—say, a market price of $12. At $12, Noelle's farm is not profitable; since the market price is below minimum average total cost, the farm is losing the difference between price and average total cost per unit produced.

Yet even if it isn't covering its total cost per unit, it is covering its variable cost per unit and some—but not all—of the fixed cost per unit. If a firm in this situation shuts down, it would incur no variable cost but would incur the *full* fixed cost. As a result, shutting down generates an even greater loss than continuing to operate.

This means that whenever price lies between minimum average total cost and minimum average variable cost, the firm is better off producing some output in the short run. The reason is that by producing, it can cover its variable cost per unit and at least some of its fixed cost, even though it is incurring a loss. In this case, the firm maximizes profit—that is, minimizes loss—by choosing the quantity of output at which its marginal cost is equal to the market price. So if Noelle faces a market price of $12 per tree, her profit-maximizing output is given by point *B* in Figure 12-4, corresponding to an output of 35 trees.

It's worth noting that the decision to produce when the firm is covering its variable costs but not all of its fixed cost is similar to the decision to ignore *sunk costs*. You may recall from Chapter 9 that a sunk cost is a cost that has already been incurred and cannot be recouped; and because it cannot be changed, it should have no effect on any current decision.

In the short-run production decision, fixed cost is, in effect, like a sunk cost—it has been spent, and it can't be recovered in the short run. This comparison also illustrates why variable cost does indeed matter in the short run: it can be avoided by not producing.

And what happens if market price is exactly equal to the shut-down price, minimum average variable cost? In this instance, the firm is indifferent between producing 30 units or 0 units. As we'll see shortly, this is an important point when looking at the behavior of an industry as a whole. For the sake of clarity, we'll assume that the firm, although indifferent, does indeed produce output when price is equal to the shut-down price.

Putting everything together, we can now draw the **short-run individual supply curve** of Noelle's farm, the red line in Figure 12-4; it shows how the profit-maximizing quantity of output in the short run depends on the price. As you can see, the curve is in two segments. The upward-sloping red segment starting at point *A* shows the short-run profit-maximizing output when market price is equal to or above the shut-down price of $10 per tree.

As long as the market price is equal to or above the shut-down price, Noelle produces the quantity of output at which marginal cost is equal to the market price. That is, at market prices equal to or above the shut-down price, the firm's short-run supply curve corresponds to its marginal cost curve. But at any market price below minimum average variable cost—in this case, $10 per tree—the firm shuts down and output drops to zero in the short run. This corresponds to the vertical segment of the curve that lies on top of the vertical axis.

Do firms really shut down temporarily without going out of business? Yes. In fact, in some businesses temporary shut-downs are routine. The most common

The **short-run individual supply curve** shows how an individual producer's profit-maximizing output quantity depends on the market price, taking fixed cost as given.

examples are industries in which demand is highly seasonal, like outdoor amusement parks in climates with cold winters. Such parks would have to offer very low prices to entice customers during the colder months—prices so low that the owners would not cover their variable costs (principally wages and electricity). The wiser choice economically is to shut down until warm weather brings enough customers who are willing to pay a higher price.

Changing Fixed Cost

Although fixed cost cannot be altered in the short run, in the long run firms can acquire or get rid of machines, buildings, and so on. As we learned in Chapter 11, in the long run the level of fixed cost is a matter of choice. There we saw that a firm will choose the level of fixed cost that minimizes the average total cost for its desired output quantity. Now we will focus on an even bigger question facing a firm when choosing its fixed cost: whether to incur *any* fixed cost at all by remaining in its current business.

istockphoto

Buying or selling equipment allows a firm to change its fixed cost.

In the long run, a producer can always eliminate fixed cost by selling off its plant and equipment. If it does so, of course, it can't ever produce—it has exited the industry. In contrast, a potential producer can take on some fixed cost by acquiring machines and other resources, which puts it in a position to produce—it can enter the industry. In most perfectly competitive industries the set of producers, although fixed in the short run, changes in the long run as firms enter or exit the industry.

Consider Noelle's farm once again. In order to simplify our analysis, we will sidestep the problem of choosing among several possible levels of fixed cost. Instead, we will assume from now on that Noelle has only one possible choice of fixed cost if she operates, the amount of $140, Noelle's minimum average total cost, that was the basis for the calculations in Tables 12-1, 12-2, and 12-3. (With this assumption, Noelle's short-run average total cost curve and long-run average total cost curve are one and the same.) Alternatively, she can choose a fixed cost of zero if she exits the industry.

Suppose that the market price of trees is consistently less than $14 over an extended period of time. In that case, Noelle never fully covers her fixed cost: her business runs at a persistent loss. In the long run, then, she can do better by closing her business and leaving the industry. In other words, *in the long run* firms will exit an industry if the market price is consistently less than their break-even price—their minimum average total cost.

Conversely, suppose that the price of Christmas trees is consistently above the break-even price, $14, for an extended period of time. Because her farm is profitable, Noelle will remain in the industry and continue producing.

But things won't stop there. The Christmas tree industry meets the criterion of *free entry*: there are many potential tree producers because the necessary inputs are easy to obtain. And the cost curves of those potential producers are likely to be similar to those of Noelle, since the technology used by other producers is likely to be very similar to that used by Noelle. If the price is high enough to generate profits for existing producers, it will also attract some of these potential producers into the industry. So *in the long run* a price in excess of $14 should lead to entry: new producers will come into the Christmas tree industry.

As we will see next, exit and entry lead to an important distinction between the *short-run industry supply curve* and the *long-run industry supply curve*.

Summing Up: The Perfectly Competitive Firm's Profitability and Production Conditions

In this chapter, we've studied where the supply curve for a perfectly competitive, price-taking firm comes from. Every perfectly competitive firm makes its production decisions by maximizing profit, and these decisions determine the supply curve. Table 12-4 summarizes the perfectly competitive firm's profitability and production conditions. It also relates them to entry into and exit from the industry.

TABLE 12-4	Summary of the Perfectly Competitive Firm's Profitability and Production Conditions
Profitability condition (minimum *ATC* = break-even price)	**Result**
P > minimum ATC	Firm profitable. Entry into industry in the long run.
P = minimum ATC	Firm breaks even. No entry into or exit from industry in the long run.
P < minimum ATC	Firm unprofitable. Exit from industry in the long run.
Production condition (minimum *AVC* = shut-down price)	**Result**
P > minimum AVC	Firm produces in the short run. If P < minimum ATC, firm covers variable cost and some but not all of fixed cost. If P > minimum ATC, firm covers all variable cost and fixed cost.
P = minimum AVC	Firm indifferent between producing in the short run or not. Just covers variable cost.
P < minimum AVC	Firm shuts down in the short run. Does not cover variable cost.

ECONOMICS ▶ in Action

Farmers Move Up Their Supply Curves

To reduce gasoline consumption, Congress mandated that increasing amounts of biofuel, mostly corn-based ethanol, be added to the American fuel supply—from 4 billion gallons of ethanol in 2006 to 14 billion gallons in 2013. The unsurprising result of this mandate was that the demand for corn skyrocketed, along with its price. In 2012, farmers received an average price per bushel of about $7 to $8, compared to less than $2 in 2005. Being the smart profit-maximizers that they are, American farmers responded by planting more corn and less of other crops such as cotton. By 2013, U.S. farmers had delivered five straight years of increase in acreage planted in corn.

If this sounds like a sure way to make a profit, think again. Corn farmers were taking a considerable gamble in planting more corn as their costs went up. Consider the cost of fertilizer, an important input. Corn requires more fertilizer than other crops, and with more farmers planting corn, the increased demand for fertilizer led to a price increase. In 2006 and 2007, fertilizer prices surged to five times their 2005 level; by 2013 prices were still twice as high.

The pull of higher corn prices also lifted farmland prices to record levels—levels so high that by 2013 there was talk of a bubble in farmland prices. Remember that even if a farmer owns land outright, that farmer still incurs an opportunity cost when planting rather than leasing the land or selling it to someone else. In 2013, the average price of an acre of farmland was up almost 300% over the past decade, with the price of some land increasing by as much as 1,000%.

Despite the risk and increase in costs, what corn farmers did made complete economic sense. By planting more corn, each farmer moved up his or her individual supply curve. And because the individual supply curve is the marginal cost curve, each farmer's costs also went up because of the need to use more inputs that are now more expensive to obtain.

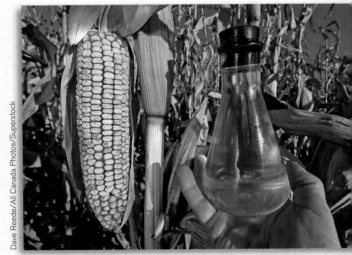

Although farmers were taking a big gamble by cutting the size of their other crops to plant more corn, their decision made good economic sense.

Dave Reede/All Canada Photos/Superstock

▼ Quick Review

- A producer chooses output according to the **optimal output rule.** For a price-taking firm, **marginal revenue** is equal to price and it chooses output according to the **price-taking firm's optimal output rule** $P = MC$.

- A firm is profitable whenever price exceeds its **break-even price,** equal to its minimum average total cost. Below that price it is unprofitable. It breaks even when price is equal to its break-even price.

- Fixed cost is irrelevant to the firm's optimal short-run production decision. When price exceeds its **shut-down price,** minimum average variable cost, the price-taking firm produces the quantity of output at which marginal cost equals price. When price is lower than its shut-down price, it ceases production in the short run. This defines the firm's **short-run individual supply curve.**

- Over time, fixed cost matters. If price consistently falls below minimum average total cost, a firm will exit the industry. If price exceeds minimum average total cost, the firm is profitable and will remain in the industry; other firms will enter the industry in the long run.

So the moral of the story is that farmers will increase their corn acreage until the marginal cost of producing corn is approximately equal to the market price of corn—which shouldn't come as a surprise, because corn production satisfies all the requirements of a perfectly competitive industry.

Check Your Understanding 12-2

1. Draw a short-run diagram showing a U-shaped average total cost curve, a U-shaped average variable cost curve, and a "swoosh"-shaped marginal cost curve. On it, indicate the range of output and the range of price for which the following actions are optimal.
   a. The firm shuts down immediately.
   b. The firm operates in the short run despite sustaining a loss.
   c. The firm operates while making a profit.

2. The state of Maine has a very active lobster industry, which harvests lobsters during the summer months. During the rest of the year, lobsters can be obtained from other parts of the world but at a much higher price. Maine is also full of "lobster shacks," roadside restaurants serving lobster dishes that are open only during the summer. Explain why it is optimal for lobster shacks to operate only during the summer.

Solutions appear at back of book.

The Industry Supply Curve

Why will an increase in the demand for Christmas trees lead to a large price increase at first but a much smaller increase in the long run? The answer lies in the behavior of the **industry supply curve**—the relationship between the price and the total output of an industry as a whole. The industry supply curve is what we referred to in earlier chapters as *the* supply curve or the market supply curve. But here we take some extra care to distinguish between the *individual supply curve* of a single firm and the supply curve of the industry as a whole.

As you might guess from the previous section, the industry supply curve must be analyzed in somewhat different ways for the short run and the long run. Let's start with the short run.

The Short-Run Industry Supply Curve

Recall that in the short run the number of producers in an industry is fixed—there is no entry or exit. And you may also remember from Chapter 3 that the market supply curve is the horizontal sum of the individual supply curves of all producers—you find it by summing the total output across all suppliers at every given price. We will do that exercise here under the assumption that all the producers are alike—an assumption that makes the derivation particularly simple. So let's assume that there are 100 Christmas tree farms, each with the same costs as Noelle's farm.

Each of these 100 farms will have an individual short-run supply curve like the one in Figure 12-4. At a price below $10, no farms will produce. At a price of $10 or more, each farm will produce the quantity of output at which its marginal cost is equal to the market price. As you can see from Figure 12-4, this will lead each farm to produce 40 trees if the price is $14 per tree, 50 trees if the price is $18, and so on. So if there are 100 tree farms and the price of Christmas trees is $18 per tree, the industry as a whole will produce 5,000 trees, corresponding to 100 farms × 50 trees per farm, and so on. The result is the **short-run industry supply curve,** shown as S in Figure 12-5. This curve shows the quantity that producers will supply at each price, *taking the number of producers as given.*

The demand curve D in Figure 12-5 crosses the short-run industry supply curve at E_{MKT}, corresponding to a price of $18 and a quantity of 5,000 trees. Point E_{MKT}

The **industry supply curve** shows the relationship between the price of a good and the total output of the industry as a whole.

The **short-run industry supply curve** shows how the quantity supplied by an industry depends on the market price given a fixed number of producers.

FIGURE **12-5** │ The Short-Run Market Equilibrium

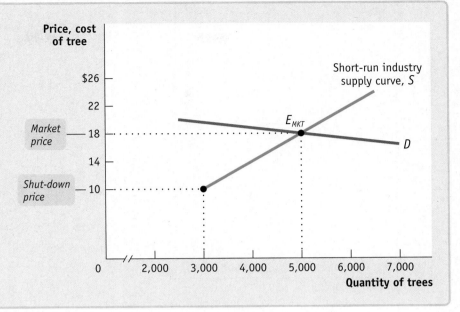

The short-run industry supply curve, *S*, is the industry supply curve taking the number of producers—here, 100—as given. It is generated by adding together the individual supply curves of the 100 producers. Below the shut-down price of $10, no producer wants to produce in the short run. Above $10, the short-run industry supply curve slopes upward, as each producer increases output as price increases. It intersects the demand curve, *D*, at point E_{MKT}, the point of short-run market equilibrium, corresponding to a market price of $18 and a quantity of 5,000 trees.

is a **short-run market equilibrium:** the quantity supplied equals the quantity demanded, taking the number of producers as given. But the long run may look quite different, because in the long run farms may enter or exit the industry.

> There is a **short-run market equilibrium** when the quantity supplied equals the quantity demanded, taking the number of producers as given.

The Long-Run Industry Supply Curve

Suppose that in addition to the 100 farms currently in the Christmas tree business, there are many other potential producers. Suppose also that each of these potential producers would have the same cost curves as existing producers like Noelle if it entered the industry.

When will additional producers enter the industry? Whenever existing producers are making a profit—that is, whenever the market price is above the break-even price of $14 per tree, the minimum average total cost of production. For example, at a price of $18 per tree, new firms will enter the industry.

What will happen as additional producers enter the industry? Clearly, the quantity supplied at any given price will increase. The short-run industry supply curve will shift to the right. This will, in turn, alter the market equilibrium and result in a lower market price. Existing firms will respond to the lower market price by reducing their output, but the total industry output will increase because of the larger number of firms in the industry.

Figure 12-6 illustrates the effects of this chain of events on an existing firm and on the market; panel (a) shows how the market responds to entry, and panel (b) shows how an individual existing firm responds to entry. (Note that these two graphs have been rescaled in comparison to Figures 12-4 and 12-5 to better illustrate how profit changes in response to price.) In panel (a), S_1 is the initial short-run industry supply curve, based on the existence of 100 producers. The initial short-run market equilibrium is at E_{MKT}, with an equilibrium market price of $18 and a quantity of 5,000 trees. At this price existing producers are profitable, which is reflected in panel (b): an existing firm makes a total profit represented by the green-shaded rectangle labeled *A* when market price is $18.

These profits will induce new producers to enter the industry, shifting the short-run industry supply curve to the right. For example, the short-run industry supply curve when the number of producers has increased to 167 is S_2.

FIGURE **12-6** The Long-Run Market Equilibrium

Point E_{MKT} of panel (a) shows the initial short-run market equilibrium. Each of the 100 existing producers makes an economic profit, illustrated in panel (b) by the green rectangle labeled *A*, the profit of an existing firm. Profits induce entry by additional producers, shifting the short-run industry supply curve outward from S_1 to S_2 in panel (a), resulting in a new short-run equilibrium at point D_{MKT}, at a lower market price of $16 and higher industry output. Existing firms reduce output

and profit falls to the area given by the striped rectangle labeled *B* in panel (b). Entry continues to shift out the short-run industry supply curve, as price falls and industry output increases yet again. Entry of new firms ceases at point C_{MKT} on supply curve S_3 in panel (a). Here market price is equal to the break-even price; existing producers make zero economic profits, and there is no incentive for entry or exit. So C_{MKT} is also a long-run market equilibrium.

Corresponding to this supply curve is a new short-run market equilibrium labeled D_{MKT}, with a market price of $16 and a quantity of 7,500 trees. At $16, each firm produces 45 trees, so that industry output is $167 \times 45 = 7,500$ trees (rounded).

From panel (b) you can see the effect of the entry of 67 new producers on an existing firm: the fall in price causes it to reduce its output, and its profit falls to the area represented by the striped rectangle labeled *B*.

Although diminished, the profit of existing firms at D_{MKT} means that entry will continue and the number of firms will continue to rise. If the number of producers rises to 250, the short-run industry supply curve shifts out again to S_3, and the market equilibrium is at C_{MKT}, with a quantity supplied and demanded of 10,000 trees and a market price of $14 per tree.

Like E_{MKT} and D_{MKT}, C_{MKT} is a short-run equilibrium. But it is also something more. Because the price of $14 is each firm's break-even price, an existing producer makes zero economic profit—neither a profit nor a loss, earning only the opportunity cost of the resources used in production—when producing its profit-maximizing output of 40 trees. At this price there is no incentive either for potential producers to enter or for existing producers to exit the industry. So C_{MKT} corresponds to a **long-run market equilibrium**—a situation in which the quantity supplied equals the quantity demanded given that sufficient time has elapsed for producers to either enter or exit the industry. In a long-run market equilibrium, all existing and potential producers have fully adjusted to their optimal long-run choices; as a result, no producer has an incentive to either enter or exit the industry.

A market is in **long-run market equilibrium** when the quantity supplied equals the quantity demanded, given that sufficient time has elapsed for entry into and exit from the industry to occur.

To explore further the significance of the difference between short-run and long-run equilibrium, consider the effect of an increase in demand on an industry with free entry that is initially in long-run equilibrium. Panel (b) in Figure 12-7 shows the market adjustment; panels (a) and (c) show how an existing individual firm behaves during the process.

In panel (b) of Figure 12-7, D_1 is the initial demand curve and S_1 is the initial short-run industry supply curve. Their intersection at point X_{MKT} is both a short-run and a long-run market equilibrium because the equilibrium price of $14 leads to zero economic profit—and therefore neither entry nor exit. It corresponds to point X in panel (a), where an individual existing firm is operating at the minimum of its average total cost curve.

Now suppose that the demand curve shifts out for some reason to D_2. As shown in panel (b), in the short run, industry output moves along the short-run industry supply curve S_1 to the new short-run market equilibrium at Y_{MKT}, the intersection of S_1 and D_2. The market price rises to $18 per tree, and industry output increases from Q_X to Q_Y. This corresponds to an existing firm's movement from X to Y in panel (a) as the firm increases its output in response to the rise in the market price.

But we know that Y_{MKT} is not a long-run equilibrium, because $18 is higher than minimum average total cost, so existing producers are making economic profits. This will lead additional firms to enter the industry.

FIGURE 12-7   The Effect of an Increase in Demand in the Short Run and the Long Run

Panel (b) shows how an industry adjusts in the short and long run to an increase in demand; panels (a) and (c) show the corresponding adjustments by an existing firm. Initially the market is at point X_{MKT} in panel (b), a short-run and long-run equilibrium at a price of $14 and industry output of Q_X. An existing firm makes zero economic profit, operating at point X in panel (a) at minimum average total cost. Demand increases as D_1 shifts rightward to D_2 in panel (b), raising the market price to $18. Existing firms increase their output, and industry output moves along the short-run industry supply curve S_1 to a short-run equilibrium at Y_{MKT}. Correspondingly, the existing firm in panel (a) moves from point X to point Y. But at a price of $18 existing firms are profitable. As shown in panel (b), in the long

run new entrants arrive and the short-run industry supply curve shifts rightward, from S_1 to S_2. There is a new equilibrium at point Z_{MKT}, at a lower price of $14 and higher industry output of Q_Z. An existing firm responds by moving from Y to Z in panel (c), returning to its initial output level and zero economic profit. Production by new entrants accounts for the total increase in industry output, $Q_Z - Q_X$. Like X_{MKT}, Z_{MKT} is also a short-run and long-run equilibrium: with existing firms earning zero economic profit, there is no incentive for any firms to enter or exit the industry. The horizontal line passing through X_{MKT} and Z_{MKT}, LRS, is the long-run industry supply curve: at the break-even price of $14, producers will produce any amount that consumers demand in the long run.

The **long-run industry supply curve** shows how the quantity supplied responds to the price once producers have had time to enter or exit the industry.

Over time entry will cause the short-run industry supply curve to shift to the right. In the long run, the short-run industry supply curve will have shifted out to S_2, and the equilibrium will be at Z_{MKT}—with the price falling back to $14 per tree and industry output increasing yet again, from Q_Y to Q_Z. Like X_{MKT} before the increase in demand, Z_{MKT} is both a short-run and a long-run market equilibrium.

The effect of entry on an existing firm is illustrated in panel (c), in the movement from Y to Z along the firm's individual supply curve. The firm reduces its output in response to the fall in the market price, ultimately arriving back at its original output quantity, corresponding to the minimum of its average total cost curve. In fact, every firm that is now in the industry—the initial set of firms and the new entrants—will operate at the minimum of its average total cost curve, at point Z. This means that the entire increase in industry output, from Q_X to Q_Z, comes from production by new entrants.

The line *LRS* that passes through X_{MKT} and Z_{MKT} in panel (b) is the **long-run industry supply curve.** It shows how the quantity supplied by an industry responds to the price given that producers have had time to enter or exit the industry.

In this particular case, the long-run industry supply curve is horizontal at $14. In other words, in this industry supply is *perfectly elastic* in the long run: given time to enter or exit, producers will supply any quantity that consumers demand at a price of $14. Perfectly elastic long-run supply is actually a good assumption for many industries. In this case we speak of there being *constant costs across the industry*: each firm, regardless of whether it is an incumbent or a new entrant, faces the same cost structure (that is, they each have the same cost curves). Industries that satisfy this condition are industries in which there is a perfectly elastic supply of inputs—industries like agriculture or bakeries.

In other industries, however, even the long-run industry supply curve slopes upward. The usual reason for this is that producers must use some input that is in limited supply (that is, inelastically supplied). As the industry expands, the price of that input is driven up. Consequently, later entrants in the industry find that they have a higher cost structure than early entrants. An example is beachfront resort hotels, which must compete for a limited quantity of prime beachfront property. Industries that behave like this are said to have *increasing costs across the industry*.

It is possible for the long-run industry supply curve to slope downward. This can occur when an industry faces increasing returns to scale, in which average costs fall as output rises. Notice we said that the *industry* faces increasing returns. However, when increasing returns apply at the level of the individual firm, the industry usually ends up dominated by a small number of firms (an *oligopoly*) or a single firm (a *monopoly*).

In some cases, the advantages of large scale for an entire industry accrue to all firms in that industry. For example, the costs of new technologies such as solar panels tend to fall as the industry grows because that growth leads to improved knowledge, a larger pool of workers with the right skills, and so on.

Regardless of whether the long-run industry supply curve is horizontal or upward sloping or even downward sloping, the long-run price elasticity of supply is *higher* than the short-run price elasticity whenever there is free entry and exit. As shown in Figure 12-8, the long-run industry supply curve is always flatter than the short-run industry supply curve. The reason is entry and exit: a high price caused by an increase in demand attracts entry by new producers, resulting in a rise in industry output and an eventual fall in price; a low price caused by a decrease in demand induces existing firms to exit, leading to a fall in industry output and an eventual increase in price.

The distinction between the short-run industry supply curve and the long-run industry supply curve is very important in practice. We often see a sequence of events like that shown in Figure 12-7: an increase in demand initially leads to a large price increase, but prices return to their initial level once new firms have entered the industry. Or we see the sequence in reverse: a fall in demand reduces prices in the short run, but they return to their initial level as producers exit the industry.

FIGURE 12-8   Comparing the Short-Run and Long-Run Industry Supply Curves

The long-run industry supply curve may slope upward, but it is always flatter—more elastic—than the short-run industry supply curve. This is because of entry and exit: a higher price attracts new entrants in the long run, resulting in a rise in industry output and a fall in price; a lower price induces existing producers to exit in the long run, generating a fall in industry output and an eventual rise in price.

The long-run industry supply curve is always flatter—more elastic—than the short-run industry supply curve.

The Cost of Production and Efficiency in Long-Run Equilibrium

Our analysis leads us to three conclusions about the cost of production and efficiency in the long-run equilibrium of a perfectly competitive industry. These results will be important in our discussion in Chapter 13 of how monopoly gives rise to inefficiency.

First, in a perfectly competitive industry in equilibrium, the value of marginal cost is the same for all firms. That's because all firms produce the quantity of output at which marginal cost equals the market price, and as price-takers they all face the same market price.

Second, in a perfectly competitive industry with free entry and exit, each firm will have zero economic profit in long-run equilibrium. Each firm produces the quantity of output that minimizes its average total cost—corresponding to point Z in panel (c) of Figure 12-7. So the total cost of production of the industry's output is minimized in a perfectly competitive industry.

The exception is an industry with increasing costs across the industry. Given a sufficiently high market price, early entrants make positive economic profits, but the last entrants do not as the market price falls. Costs are minimized for later entrants, as the industry reaches long-run equilibrium, but not necessarily for the early ones.

The third and final conclusion is that the long-run market equilibrium of a perfectly competitive industry is efficient: no mutually beneficial transactions go unexploited. To understand this, we need to recall a fundamental requirement for efficiency: all consumers who have a willingness to pay greater than or equal to sellers' costs actually get the good. We also learned that when a market is efficient (except under certain, well-defined conditions), the market price matches all consumers with a willingness to pay greater than or equal to the market price to all sellers who have a cost of producing the good less than or equal to the market price.

So in the long-run equilibrium of a perfectly competitive industry, production is efficient: costs are minimized and no resources are wasted. In addition, the allocation of goods to consumers is efficient: every consumer willing to pay the cost of producing a unit of the good gets it. Indeed, no mutually beneficial transaction is left unexploited. Moreover, this condition tends to persist over time as the environment changes: the force of competition makes producers responsive to changes in consumers' desires and to changes in technology.

PITFALLS

ECONOMIC PROFIT, AGAIN
Some readers may wonder why a firm would want to enter an industry if the market price is only slightly greater than the break-even price. Wouldn't a firm prefer to go into another business that yields a higher profit?

The answer is that here, as always, when we calculate cost, we mean *opportunity cost*—that is, cost that includes the return a firm could get by using its resources elsewhere. And so the profit that we calculate is *economic profit;* if the market price is above the break-even level, no matter how slightly, the firm can earn more in this industry than they could elsewhere.

ECONOMICS ▶ in Action

From Global Wine Glut to Shortage

A wine shortage may soon become a wine glut as growers respond by planting more vineyards.

If you were a wine producer still in business in 2012, you were probably breathing a big sigh of relief. Why? Because that is when the global wine market went from glut to shortage. This was a big change from the years 2004 to 2010, when the wine industry battled with an oversupply of product and plunging prices, driven first by a series of large global harvests and then by declining demand due to the global recession of 2008. After years of losses, many wine producers finally decided to exit the industry.

By 2012, wine production capacity was down significantly in Europe, South America, Africa, and Australia, and inventories were at their lowest point in over a decade. Moreover, 2012 was a year of bad weather for wine producers. And that same year, American wine consumption started growing again, while China's wine consumption was surging, quadrupling over the previous five years. So combine a significant drop in capacity, a weather-induced fall in supply, and an increase in demand and—*voilà!*—a wine shortage appears.

But as industry analysts noted, many vintners are cheering. The lack of production in other parts of the world and surging demand in China have opened opportunities for expansion. As the CEO of Washington State's Chateau Ste. Michelle winery, Ted Bessler, commented, "Right now, we have about 50,000 acres in the state. I can foresee that we could have as much as 150,000 or more."

Hold onto your wine glasses—the present shortage could turn into a glut once again.

▼ Quick Review

• The **industry supply curve** corresponds to the supply curve of earlier chapters. In the short run, the time period over which the number of producers is fixed, the **short-run market equilibrium** is given by the intersection of the **short-run industry supply curve** and the demand curve. In the long run, the time period over which producers can enter or exit the industry, the **long-run market equilibrium** is given by the intersection of the **long-run industry supply curve** and the demand curve. In the long-run market equilibrium, no producer has an incentive to enter or exit the industry.

• The long-run industry supply curve is often horizontal, although it may slope upward when a necessary input is in limited supply. It is always more elastic than the short-run industry supply curve.

• In the long-run market equilibrium of a perfectly competitive industry, each firm produces at the same marginal cost, which is equal to the market price, and the total cost of production of the industry's output is minimized. It is also efficient.

Check Your Understanding   12-3

1. Which of the following events will induce firms to enter an industry? Which will induce firms to exit? When will entry or exit cease? Explain your answer.
   a. A technological advance lowers the fixed cost of production of every firm in the industry.
   b. The wages paid to workers in the industry go up for an extended period of time.
   c. A permanent change in consumer tastes increases demand for the good.
   d. The price of a key input rises due to a long-term shortage of that input.

2. Assume that the egg industry is perfectly competitive and is in long-run equilibrium with a perfectly elastic long-run industry supply curve. Health concerns about cholesterol then lead to a decrease in demand. Construct a figure similar to Figure 12-7, showing the short-run behavior of the industry and how long-run equilibrium is reestablished.

Solutions appear at back of book.

Shopping Apps, Showrooming, and the Challenges Facing Brick-and-Mortar Retailers

I n a Sunnyvale, California Best Buy, Tri Trang found the perfect gift for his girlfriend, a $184.85 Garmin GPS. Before mobile shopping apps appeared, he would have purchased it there. Instead, Trang whipped out his smartphone to do a price comparison. Finding the same item on Amazon.com for $106.75 with free shipping, he bought it from Amazon on the spot.

For brick-and-mortar retailers like Best Buy, customers who "showroom"—examine the merchandise in-store and then buy it on-line—threaten their very survival. The explosive growth of shopping apps that allow you to immediately compare prices and make a purchase (TheFind), give you access to thousands of coupons (Coupons.com), and alert you to discount sales at nearby stores (SaleSorter), has struck terror in the corporate offices of traditional retailers.

Before shopping apps, a traditional retailer could lure customers into its store with enticing specials and reasonably expect them to buy more profitable items with prompting from a salesperson. But those days are fast disappearing. The consulting firm Accenture found that 73% of customers with mobile devices preferred to shop with their phones rather than talk to a salesperson. In just four years, from 2010 to 2014, the use of mobile coupons has quadrupled from 12.3 million to 53.2 million.

But brick-and-mortar retailers are now fighting back. To combat showrooming, Target stocks products that manufacturers have slightly modified for them alone. Like other retailers, Target has been building its online presence, quadrupling the number of items on its website, sending coupons and discount alerts to customers' mobile phones, and offering loyalty rewards. Walmart now offers free in-store delivery for online purchases so customers can avoid shipping charges. And Staples will give you a discount on a new printer if you trade in your old one.

However, traditional retailers know that their survival rests on pricing. While prices on their websites tend to be lower than in the stores, these retailers are still struggling to compete with online sellers like Amazon.com. A recent study showed Amazon.com's prices were about 9% lower than Walmart.com's and 14% lower than Target.com's. Best Buys now offers to match online prices for its best customers.

It's clearly a race for survival. As one analyst said, "Only a couple of retailers can play the lowest-price game. This is going to accelerate the demise of retailers who do not have either competitive pricing or standout store experience."

QUESTIONS FOR THOUGHT

1. From the evidence in the case, what can you infer about whether or not the retail market for electronics satisfied the conditions for perfect competition before the advent of mobile-device comparison price shopping? What was the most important impediment to competition?

2. What effect is the introduction of mobile shopping apps having on competition in the retail market for electronics? On the profitability of brick-and-mortar retailers like Best Buy? What, on average, will be the effect on the consumer surplus of purchasers of these items?

3. Why are some retailers responding by having manufacturers make exclusive versions of products for them? Is this trend likely to increase or diminish?

The Photo Works

SUMMARY

1. In a **perfectly competitive market** all producers are **price-taking producers** and all consumers are **price-taking consumers**—no one's actions can influence the market price. Consumers are normally price-takers, but producers often are not. In a **perfectly competitive industry,** all producers are price-takers.

2. There are two necessary conditions for a perfectly competitive industry: there are many producers, none of whom have a large **market share,** and the industry produces a **standardized product** or **commodity**—goods that consumers regard as equivalent. A third condition is often satisfied as well: **free entry and exit** into and from the industry.

3. A producer chooses output according to the **optimal output rule:** produce the quantity at which **marginal revenue** equals marginal cost. For a price-taking firm, marginal revenue is equal to price and its **marginal revenue curve** is a horizontal line at the market price. It chooses output according to the **price-taking firm's optimal output rule:** produce the quantity at which price equals marginal cost. However, a firm that produces the optimal quantity may not be profitable.

4. A firm is profitable if total revenue exceeds total cost or, equivalently, if the market price exceeds its **break-even price**—minimum average total cost. If market price exceeds the break-even price, the firm is profitable; if it is less, the firm is unprofitable; if it is equal, the firm breaks even. When profitable, the firm's per-unit profit is $P - ATC$; when unprofitable, its per-unit loss is $ATC - P$.

5. Fixed cost is irrelevant to the firm's optimal short-run production decision, which depends on its **shut-down price**—its minimum average variable cost—and the market price. When the market price is equal to or exceeds the shut-down price, the firm produces the output quantity where marginal cost equals the market price. When the market price falls below the shut-down price, the firm ceases production in the short run. This generates the firm's **short-run individual supply curve.**

6. Fixed cost matters over time. If the market price is below minimum average total cost for an extended period of time, firms will exit the industry in the long run. If above, existing firms are profitable and new firms will enter the industry in the long run.

7. The **industry supply curve** depends on the time period. The **short-run industry supply curve** is the industry supply curve given that the number of firms is fixed. The **short-run market equilibrium** is given by the intersection of the short-run industry supply curve and the demand curve.

8. The **long-run industry supply curve** is the industry supply curve given sufficient time for entry into and exit from the industry. In the **long-run market equilibrium**—given by the intersection of the long-run industry supply curve and the demand curve—no producer has an incentive to enter or exit. The long-run industry supply curve is often horizontal. It may slope upward if there is limited supply of an input, resulting in increasing costs across the industry. It may even slope downward, the case of decreasing costs across the industry. But it is always more elastic than the short-run industry supply curve.

9. In the long-run market equilibrium of a competitive industry, profit maximization leads each firm to produce at the same marginal cost, which is equal to market price. Free entry and exit means that each firm earns zero economic profit—producing the output corresponding to its minimum average total cost. So the total cost of production of an industry's output is minimized. The outcome is efficient because every consumer with a willingness to pay greater than or equal to marginal cost gets the good.

KEY TERMS

Price-taking producer, p. 358
Price-taking consumer, p. 358
Perfectly competitive market, p. 358
Perfectly competitive industry, p. 358
Market share, p. 359
Standardized product, p. 359
Commodity, p. 359

Free entry and exit, p. 359
Marginal revenue, p. 362
Optimal output rule, p. 362
Price-taking firm's optimal output rule, p. 362
Marginal revenue curve, p. 363
Break-even price, p. 367

Shut-down price, p. 368
Short-run individual supply curve, p. 369
Industry supply curve, p. 372
Short-run industry supply curve, p. 372
Short-run market equilibrium, p. 373
Long-run market equilibrium, p. 374
Long-run industry supply curve, p. 376

PROBLEMS

1. For each of the following, is the business a price-taking producer? Explain your answers.

  a. A cappuccino café in a university town where there are dozens of very similar cappuccino cafés

  b. The makers of Pepsi-Cola

  c. One of many sellers of zucchini at a local farmers' market

2. For each of the following, is the industry perfectly competitive? Referring to market share, standardization of the product, and/or free entry and exit, explain your answers.

  a. Aspirin

  b. Alicia Keys concerts

  c. SUVs

3. Bob produces Blu-ray movies for sale, which requires a building and a machine that copies the original movie onto a Blu-ray. Bob rents a building for $30,000 per month and rents a machine for $20,000 a month. Those are his fixed costs. His variable cost per month is given in the accompanying table.

Quantity of Blu-rays	VC
0	$0
1,000	5,000
2,000	8,000
3,000	9,000
4,000	14,000
5,000	20,000
6,000	33,000
7,000	49,000
8,000	72,000
9,000	99,000
10,000	150,000

  a. Calculate Bob's average variable cost, average total cost, and marginal cost for each quantity of output.

  b. There is free entry into the industry, and anyone who enters will face the same costs as Bob. Suppose that currently the price of a Blu-ray is $25. What will Bob's profit be? Is this a long-run equilibrium? If not, what will the price of Blu-ray movies be in the long run?

4. Consider Bob's Blu-ray company described in Problem 4. Assume that Blu-ray production is a perfectly competitive industry. For each of the following questions, explain your answers.

  a. What is Bob's break-even price? What is his shut-down price?

  b. Suppose the price of a Blu-ray is $2. What should Bob do in the short run?

  c. Suppose the price of a Blu-ray is $7. What is the profit-maximizing quantity of Blu-rays that Bob

should produce? What will his total profit be? Will he produce or shut down in the short run? Will he stay in the industry or exit in the long run?

  d. Suppose instead that the price of Blu-rays is $20. Now what is the profit-maximizing quantity of Blu-rays that Bob should produce? What will his total profit be now? Will he produce or shut down in the short run? Will he stay in the industry or exit in the long run?

5. Consider again Bob's Blu-ray company described in Problem 4.

  a. Draw Bob's marginal cost curve.

  b. Over what range of prices will Bob produce no Blu-rays in the short run?

  c. Draw Bob's individual supply curve. In your graph, plot the price range from $0 to $60 in increments of $10.

6. a. A profit-maximizing business incurs an economic loss of $10,000 per year. Its fixed cost is $15,000 per year. Should it produce or shut down in the short run? Should it stay in the industry or exit in the long run?

  b. Suppose instead that this business has a fixed cost of $6,000 per year. Should it produce or shut down in the short run? Should it stay in the industry or exit in the long run?

7. The first sushi restaurant opens in town. Initially people are very cautious about eating tiny portions of raw fish, as this is a town where large portions of grilled meat have always been popular. Soon, however, an influential health report warns consumers against grilled meat and suggests that they increase their consumption of fish, especially raw fish. The sushi restaurant becomes very popular and its profit increases.

  a. What will happen to the short-run profit of the sushi restaurant? What will happen to the number of sushi restaurants in town in the long run? Will the first sushi restaurant be able to sustain its short-run profit over the long run? Explain your answers.

  b. Local steakhouses suffer from the popularity of sushi and start incurring losses. What will happen to the number of steakhouses in town in the long run? Explain your answer.

8. A perfectly competitive firm has the following short-run total cost:

Quantity	TC
0	$5
1	10
2	13
3	18
4	25
5	34
6	45

Market demand for the firm's product is given by the following market demand schedule:

Price	Quantity demanded
$12	300
10	500
8	800
6	1,200
4	1,800

a. Calculate this firm's marginal cost and, for all output levels except zero, the firm's average variable cost and average total cost.

b. There are 100 firms in this industry that all have costs identical to those of this firm. Draw the short-run industry supply curve. In the same diagram, draw the market demand curve.

c. What is the market price, and how much profit will each firm make?

9. A new vaccine against a deadly disease has just been discovered. Presently, 55 people die from the disease each year. The new vaccine will save lives, but it is not completely safe. Some recipients of the shots will die from adverse reactions. The projected effects of the inoculation are given in the accompanying table:

Percent of population inoculated	Total deaths due to disease	Total deaths due to inoculation	Marginal benefit of inoculation	Marginal cost of inoculation	"Profit" of inoculation
0	55	0			
10	45	0	—	—	—
20	36	1	—	—	—
30	28	3	—	—	—
40	21	6	—	—	—
50	15	10	—	—	—
60	10	15	—	—	—
70	6	20	—	—	—
80	3	25	—	—	—
90	1	30	—	—	—
100	0	35	—	—	—

a. What are the interpretations of "marginal benefit" and "marginal cost" here? Calculate marginal benefit and marginal cost per each 10% increase in the rate of inoculation. Write your answers in the table.

b. What proportion of the population should optimally be inoculated?

c. What is the interpretation of "profit" here? Calculate the profit for all levels of inoculation.

10. Evaluate each of the following statements. If a statement is true, explain why; if it is false, identify the mistake and try to correct it.

a. A profit-maximizing firm in a perfectly competitive industry should select the output level at which the difference between the market price and marginal cost is greatest.

b. An increase in fixed cost lowers the profit-maximizing quantity of output produced in the short run.

11. The production of agricultural products like wheat is one of the few examples of a perfectly competitive industry. In this question, we analyze results from a study released by the U.S. Department of Agriculture about wheat production in the United States back in 2013.

a. The average variable cost per acre planted with wheat was $127 per acre. Assuming a yield of 44 bushels per acre, calculate the average variable cost per bushel of wheat.

b. The average price of wheat received by a farmer in 2013 was $7.58 per bushel. Do you think the average farm would have exited the industry in the short run? Explain.

c. With a yield of 44 bushels of wheat per acre, the average total cost per farm was $4.80 per bushel. The harvested acreage for rye (a type of wheat) in the United States increased from 242,000 in 2010 to 306,000 in 2013. Using the information on prices and costs here and in parts a and b, explain why this might have happened.

d. Using the above information, what do you think will happen to wheat production and prices after 2013?

12. The accompanying table presents prices for washing and ironing a man's shirt taken from a survey of California dry cleaners.

Dry Cleaner	City	Price
A-1 Cleaners	Santa Barbara	$1.50
Regal Cleaners	Santa Barbara	1.95
St. Paul Cleaners	Santa Barbara	1.95
Zip Kleen Dry Cleaners	Santa Barbara	1.95
Effie the Tailor	Santa Barbara	2.00
Magnolia Too	Goleta	2.00
Master Cleaners	Santa Barbara	2.00
Santa Barbara Cleaners	Goleta	2.00
Sunny Cleaners	Santa Barbara	2.00
Casitas Cleaners	Carpinteria	2.10
Rockwell Cleaners	Carpinteria	2.10
Norvelle Bass Cleaners	Santa Barbara	2.15
Ablitt's Fine Cleaners	Santa Barbara	2.25
California Cleaners	Goleta	2.25
Justo the Tailor	Santa Barbara	2.25
Pressed 4 Time	Goleta	2.50
King's Cleaners	Goleta	2.50

a. What is the average price per shirt washed and ironed in Goleta? In Santa Barbara?

b. Draw typical marginal cost and average total cost curves for California Cleaners in Goleta, assuming it is a perfectly competitive firm but is making a profit on each shirt in the short run. Mark the short-run equilibrium point and shade the area that corresponds to the profit made by the dry cleaner.

c. Assume $2.25 is the short-run equilibrium price in Goleta. Draw a typical short-run demand and supply curve for the market. Label the equilibrium point.

d. Observing profits in the Goleta area, another dry cleaning service, Diamond Cleaners, enters the market. It charges $1.95 per shirt. What is the new average price of washing and ironing a shirt in Goleta? Illustrate the effect of entry on the average Goleta price by a shift of the short-run supply curve, the demand curve, or both.

e. Assume that California Cleaners now charges the new average price and just breaks even (that is, makes zero economic profit) at this price. Show the likely effect of the entry on your diagram in part b.

f. If the dry cleaning industry is perfectly competitive, what does the average difference in price between Goleta and Santa Barbara imply about costs in the two areas?

For interactive, step-by-step help in solving the following problem, visit LaunchPad by using the URL on the back cover of this book.

13. Kate's Katering provides catered meals, and the catered meals industry is perfectly competitive. Kate's machinery costs $100 per day and is the only fixed input. Her variable cost consists of the wages paid to the cooks and the food ingredients. The variable cost per day associated with each level of output is given in the accompanying table.

Quantity of meals	VC
0	0
10	200
20	300
30	480
40	700
50	1,000

a. Calculate the total cost, the average variable cost, the average total cost, and the marginal cost for each quantity of output.

b. What is the break-even price and quantity? What is the shut-down price and quantity?

c. Suppose that the price at which Kate can sell catered meals is $21 per meal. In the short run, will Kate earn a profit? In the short run, should she produce or shut down?

d. Suppose that the price at which Kate can sell catered meals is $17 per meal. In the short run, will Kate earn a profit? In the short run, should she produce or shut down?

e. Suppose that the price at which Kate can sell catered meals is $13 per meal. In the short run, will Kate earn a profit? In the short run, should she produce or shut down?

Monopoly

▶ What You Will Learn in This Chapter

■ The significance of **monopoly**, where a single **monopolist** is the only producer of a good

■ How a monopolist determines its profit-maximizing output and price

■ The difference between monopoly and perfect competition, and the effects of that difference on society's welfare

■ How policy makers address the problems posed by monopoly

■ What **price discrimination** is, and why it is so prevalent when producers have **market power**

EVERYBODY MUST GET STONES

Corbis

"Got stones?"

A FEW YEARS AGO DE BEERS, the world's main supplier of diamonds, ran an ad urging men to buy their wives diamond jewelry. "She married you for richer, for poorer," read the ad. "Let her know how it's going."

Crass? Yes. Effective? No question. For generations diamonds have been a symbol of luxury, valued not only for their appearance but also for their rarity. Diamonds were famously idolized in song by Marilyn Monroe in the film "Gentlemen Prefer Blondes," where we learn that whether "square-cut or pear shaped," diamonds are "a girl's best friend."

But geologists will tell you that diamonds aren't all that rare. In fact, according to the *Dow Jones-Irwin Guide to Fine Gems and Jewelry,* diamonds are "more common than any other gem-quality colored stone. They only seem rarer . . ."

Why do diamonds seem rarer than other gems? Part of the answer is a brilliant marketing campaign. (We'll talk more about marketing and product differentiation in Chapter 15.) But mainly diamonds seem rare because De Beers *makes* them rare: the company controls most of the world's diamond mines and limits the quantity of diamonds supplied to the market.

Up to now we have concentrated exclusively on perfectly competitive markets—markets in which the producers are perfect competitors. But De Beers isn't like the producers we've studied so far: it is a *monopolist,* the sole (or almost sole) producer of a good. Monopolists behave differently from producers in perfectly competitive industries: whereas perfect competitors take the price at which they can sell their output as given, monopolists know that their actions affect market prices and take that effect into account when deciding how much to produce. Before we begin our analysis, let's step back and look at *monopoly* and perfect competition as parts of a broader system for classifying markets.

Perfect competition and monopoly are particular types of *market structure.* They are particular categories in a system economists use to classify markets and industries according to two main dimensions. This chapter begins with a brief overview of types of market structure. It will help us here and in subsequent chapters to understand on a deeper level why markets differ and why producers in those markets behave quite differently.

Types of Market Structure

In the real world, there is a mind-boggling array of different markets. We observe widely different behavior patterns by producers across markets: In some markets producers are extremely competitive; in others, they seem somehow to coordinate their actions to avoid competing with one another; and, as we have just described, some markets are monopolies in which there is no competition at all.

In order to develop principles and make predictions about markets and how producers will behave in them, economists have developed four principal models of market structure: *perfect competition, monopoly, oligopoly,* and *monopolistic competition.* This system of market structures is based on two dimensions:

- The number of producers in the market (one, few, or many)
- Whether the goods offered are identical or *differentiated*

Differentiated goods are goods that are different but considered somewhat substitutable by consumers (think Coke versus Pepsi).

Figure 13-1 provides a simple visual summary of the types of market structure classified according to the two dimensions. In *monopoly,* a single producer sells a single, undifferentiated product. In *oligopoly,* a few producers—more than one but not a large number—sell products that may be either identical or differentiated. In *monopolistic competition,* many producers each sell a differentiated product (think of producers of economics textbooks). And finally, as we know, in *perfect competition* many producers each sell an identical product.

You might wonder what determines the number of firms in a market: whether there is one (monopoly), a few (oligopoly), or many (perfect competition and monopolistic competition). We won't answer that question here because it will be covered in detail later in this chapter and in Chapters 14 and 15, which analyze oligopoly and monopolistic competition.

We will just briefly note that in the long run it depends on whether there are conditions that make it difficult for new firms to enter the market, such as control of necessary resources or inputs, increasing returns to scale in production, technological superiority, a network externality, or government regulations. When these conditions are present, industries tend to be monopolies or oligopolies; when they are not present, industries tend to be perfectly competitive or monopolistically competitive.

FIGURE **13-1** Types of Market Structure

The behavior of any given firm and the market it occupies are analyzed using one of four models of market structure—monopoly, oligopoly, perfect competition, or monopolistic competition. This system for categorizing market structure is based on two dimensions: (1) whether products are differentiated or identical, and (2) the number of producers in the industry—one, a few, or many.

How many producers are there?	Are products differentiated?	
	No	Yes
One	Monopoly	Not applicable
Few	Oligopoly	
Many	Perfect competition	Monopolistic competition

You might also wonder why some markets have differentiated products but others have identical ones. The answer is that it depends on the nature of the good and consumers' preferences. Some goods—soft drinks, economics textbooks, breakfast cereals—can readily be made into different varieties in the eyes and tastes of consumers. Other goods—hammers, for example—are much less easy to differentiate.

Although this chapter is devoted to monopoly, important aspects of monopoly carry over to oligopoly and monopolistic competition. In the next section, we will define monopoly and review the conditions that make it possible. These same conditions, in less extreme form, also give rise to oligopoly. We then show how a monopolist can increase profit by limiting the quantity supplied to a market—behavior that also occurs in oligopoly and monopolistic competition.

As we'll see, this kind of behavior is good for the producer but bad for consumers; it also causes inefficiency. An important topic of study will be the ways in which public policy tries to limit the damage. Finally, we turn to one of the surprising effects of monopoly—one that is very often present in oligopoly and monopolistic competition as well: the fact that different consumers often pay different prices for the same good.

> A **monopolist** is a firm that is the only producer of a good that has no close substitutes. An industry controlled by a monopolist is known as a **monopoly.**

The Meaning of Monopoly

The De Beers monopoly of South Africa was created in the 1880s by Cecil Rhodes, a British businessman. By 1880 mines in South Africa already dominated the world's supply of diamonds. There were, however, many mining companies, all competing with each other. During the 1880s Rhodes bought the great majority of those mines and consolidated them into a single company, De Beers. By 1889 De Beers controlled almost all of the world's diamond production.

De Beers, in other words, became a **monopolist.** A producer is a monopolist if it is the sole supplier of a good that has no close substitutes. When a firm is a monopolist, the industry is a **monopoly.**

Monopoly: Our First Departure from Perfect Competition

As we saw in Chapter 12, the supply and demand model of a market is not universally valid. Instead, it's a model of perfect competition, which is only one of several different types of market structure. We learned that a market will be perfectly competitive only if there are many producers, all of whom produce the same good. Monopoly is the most extreme departure from perfect competition.

In practice, true monopolies are hard to find in the modern American economy, partly because of legal obstacles. A contemporary entrepreneur who tried to consolidate all the firms in an industry the way that Rhodes did would soon find himself in court, accused of breaking *antitrust* laws, which are intended to prevent monopolies from emerging. Oligopoly, a market structure in which there is a small number of large producers, is much more common. In fact, most of the goods you buy, from autos to airline tickets, are supplied by oligopolies, which we will examine in detail in the next chapter.

Monopolies do, however, play an important role in some sectors of the economy, such as pharmaceuticals. Furthermore, our analysis of monopoly will provide a foundation for our later analysis of other departures from perfect competition, such as oligopoly and monopolistic competition.

What Monopolists Do

Why did Rhodes want to consolidate South African diamond producers into a single company? What difference did it make to the world diamond market?

Market power is the ability of a firm to raise prices.

Figure 13-2 offers a preliminary view of the effects of monopoly. It shows an industry in which the supply curve under perfect competition intersects the demand curve at C, leading to the price P_C and the output Q_C.

Suppose that this industry is consolidated into a monopoly. The monopolist *moves up the demand curve* by reducing quantity supplied to a point like M, at which the quantity produced, Q_M, is lower, and the price, P_M, is higher than under perfect competition.

The ability of a monopolist to raise its price above the competitive level by reducing output is known as **market power.** And market power is what monopoly is all about. A wheat farmer who is one of 100,000 wheat farmers has no market power: he or she must sell wheat at the going market price. Your local water utility company, though, does have market power: it can raise prices and still keep many (though not all) of its customers, because they have nowhere else to go. In short, it's a monopolist.

The reason a monopolist reduces output and raises price compared to the perfectly competitive industry levels is to increase profit. Cecil Rhodes consolidated the diamond producers into De Beers because he realized that the whole would be worth more than the sum of its parts—the monopoly would generate more profit than the sum of the profits of the individual competitive firms. As we saw in Chapter 12, under perfect competition economic profits normally vanish in the long run as competitors enter the market. Under monopoly the profits don't go away—a monopolist is able to continue earning economic profits in the long run.

In fact, monopolists are not the only types of firms that possess market power. In the next chapter we will study *oligopolists,* firms that can have market power as well. Under certain conditions, oligopolists can earn positive economic profits in the long run by restricting output like monopolists do.

But why don't profits get competed away? What allows monopolists to be monopolists?

FIGURE 13-2 **What a Monopolist Does**

Under perfect competition, the price and quantity are determined by supply and demand. Here, the competitive equilibrium is at C, where the price is P_C and the quantity is Q_C. A monopolist reduces the quantity supplied to Q_M and moves up the demand curve from C to M, raising the price to P_M.

2. ...and raises price.

1. Compared to perfect competition, a monopolist reduces output ...

Why Do Monopolies Exist?

A monopolist making profits will not go unnoticed by others. (Recall that this is "economic profit," revenue over and above the opportunity costs of the firm's resources.) But won't other firms crash the party, grab a piece of the action, and drive down prices and profits in the long run? For a profitable monopoly to persist, something must keep others from going into the same business; that "something" is known as a **barrier to entry.** There are five principal types of barriers to entry: control of a scarce resource or input, increasing returns to scale, technological superiority, a network externality, and a government-created barrier to entry.

1. Control of a Scarce Resource or Input
A monopolist that controls a resource or input crucial to an industry can prevent other firms from entering its market. Cecil Rhodes created the De Beers monopoly by establishing control over the mines that produced the great bulk of the world's diamonds.

2. Increasing Returns to Scale
Many Americans have natural gas piped into their homes, for cooking and heating. Invariably, the local gas company is a monopolist. But why don't rival companies compete to provide gas?

In the early nineteenth century, when the gas industry was just starting up, companies did compete for local customers. But this competition didn't last long; soon local gas supply became a monopoly in almost every town because of the large fixed costs involved in providing a town with gas lines. The cost of laying gas lines didn't depend on how much gas a company sold, so a firm with a larger volume of sales had a cost advantage: because it was able to spread the fixed costs over a larger volume, it had lower average total costs than smaller firms.

Local gas supply is an industry in which average total cost falls as output increases. As we learned in Chapter 11, this phenomenon is called *increasing returns to scale*. There we learned that when average total cost falls as output increases, firms tend to grow larger. In an industry characterized by increasing returns to scale, larger companies are more profitable and drive out smaller ones. For the same reason, established companies have a cost advantage over any potential entrant—a potent barrier to entry. So increasing returns to scale can both give rise to and sustain monopoly.

A monopoly created and sustained by increasing returns to scale is called a **natural monopoly.** The defining characteristic of a natural monopoly is that it possesses increasing returns to scale over the range of output that is relevant for the industry. This is illustrated in Figure 13-3, showing the firm's average total cost curve and the market demand curve, *D*. Here we can see that the natural monopolist's *ATC* curve declines over the output levels at which price is greater than or equal to average total cost.

So the natural monopolist has increasing returns to scale over the entire range of output for which any firm would want to remain in the industry—the range of output at which the firm would at least break even in the long run. The source of this condition is large fixed costs: when large fixed costs are required to operate, a given quantity of output is produced at lower average total cost by one large firm than by two or more smaller firms.

The most visible natural monopolies in the modern economy are local utilities—water, gas, and sometimes electricity. As we'll see, natural monopolies pose a special challenge to public policy.

3. Technological Superiority
A firm that maintains a consistent technological advantage over potential competitors can establish itself as a monopolist. For example, from the 1970s through the 1990s the chip manufacturer Intel was able to maintain a consistent advantage over potential competitors in both the design and production of microprocessors, the chips that run computers. But technological superiority is typically not a barrier to entry over the longer term: over time competitors will invest in upgrading their technology to match that of the

To earn economic profits, a monopolist must be protected by a **barrier to entry**—something that prevents other firms from entering the industry.

A **natural monopoly** exists when increasing returns to scale provide a large cost advantage to a single firm that produces all of an industry's output.

FIGURE **13-3** Increasing Returns to Scale Create Natural Monopoly

A natural monopoly can arise when fixed costs required to operate are very high. When this occurs, the firm's *ATC* curve declines over the range of output at which price is greater than or equal to average total cost. This gives the firm increasing returns to scale over the entire range of output at which the firm would at least break even in the long run. As a result, a given quantity of output is produced more cheaply by one large firm than by two or more smaller firms.

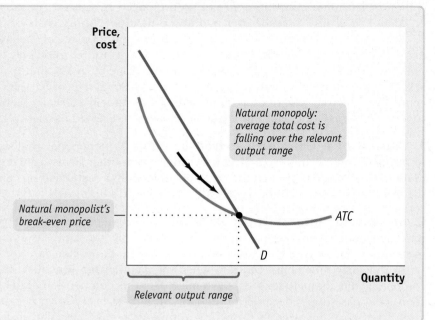

technology leader. In fact, Intel has found its technological superiority eroded by a competitor, Advanced Micro Devices (also known as AMD), which now produces chips approximately as fast and as powerful as Intel chips.

We should note, however, that in certain high-tech industries, technological superiority is not a guarantee of success against competitors because of *network externalities*.

4. Network Externality If you were the only person in the world with an internet connection, what would that connection be worth to you? The answer, of course, is nothing. Your internet connection is valuable only because other people are also connected. And, in general, the more people who are connected, the more valuable your connection is. This phenomenon, whereby the value of a good or service to an individual is greater when many others use the same good or service, is called a **network externality**—its value derives from enabling its users to participate in a network of other users.

The earliest form of network externalities arose in transportation, where the value of a road or airport increased as the number of people who had access to it rose. But network externalities are especially prevalent in the technology and communications sectors of the economy.

The classic case is computer operating systems. Worldwide, most personal computers run on Microsoft Windows. Although many believe that Apple has a superior operating system, the wider use of Windows in the early days of personal computers attracted more software development and technical support, giving it a lasting dominance.

When a network externality exists, the firm with the largest network of customers using its product has an advantage in attracting new customers, one that may allow it to become a monopolist. At a minimum, the dominant firm can charge a higher price and so earn higher profits than competitors. Moreover, a network externality gives an advantage to the firm with the "deepest pockets." Companies with the most money on hand can sell the most goods at a loss with the expectation that doing so will give them the largest customer base.

A **network externality** exists when the value of a good or service to an individual is greater when many other people use the good or service as well.

5. Government-Created Barrier In 1998 the pharmaceutical company Merck introduced Propecia, a drug effective against baldness. Despite the fact that Propecia was very profitable and other drug companies had the know-how to produce it, no other firms challenged Merck's monopoly. That's because the U.S. government had given Merck the sole legal right to produce the drug in the United States. Propecia is an example of a monopoly protected by government-created barriers.

The most important legally created monopolies today arise from *patents* and *copyrights*. A **patent** gives an inventor the sole right to make, use, or sell that invention for a period that in most countries lasts between 16 and 20 years. Patents are given to the creators of new products, such as drugs or devices. Similarly, a **copyright** gives the creator of a literary or artistic work the sole rights to profit from that work, usually for a period equal to the creator's lifetime plus 70 years.

The justification for patents and copyrights is a matter of incentives. If inventors are not protected by patents, they would gain little reward from their efforts: as soon as a valuable invention was made public, others would copy it and sell products based on it. And if inventors could not expect to profit from their inventions, then there would be no incentive to incur the costs of invention in the first place. Likewise for the creators of literary or artistic works. So the law gives a temporary monopoly that encourages invention and creation by imposing temporary property rights.

A **patent** gives an inventor a temporary monopoly in the use or sale of an invention.

A **copyright** gives the creator of a literary or artistic work sole rights to profit from that work.

GLOBAL COMPARISION | The Price We Pay

Although providing cheap patent-protected drugs to patients in poor countries is a new phenomenon, charging different prices to consumers in different countries is not: it's an example of price discrimination.

A monopolist will maximize profits by charging a higher price in the country with a lower price elasticity (the rich country) and a lower price in the country with a higher price elasticity (the poor country). Interestingly, however, drug prices can differ substantially even among countries with comparable income levels. How do we explain this?

The answer is differences in regulation.

This graph compares the prices paid by residents of different countries for Nasonex, a drug commonly prescribed for nasal allergies. It shows that Americans pay much more than residents of other countries, even wealthy countries like Switzerland. As you can see, Swiss residents pay approximately one-third of what Americans pay, and the British pay about one-tenth.

And this is not an exceptional comparison. For Nexium, a drug commonly prescribed for indigestion, the Swiss price is again approximately one-third the American price, while the British price is about one-seventh. And for Lipitor, commonly prescribed for high cholesterol, the American price is three times as high as the British price.

The reason? Governments in these other countries regulate drug prices more actively than the U.S. government does, helping to keep drug prices affordable for their citizens.

To save money, it's not surprising that Americans travel to Canada and Mexico to purchase their drugs, or buy them from abroad over the internet.

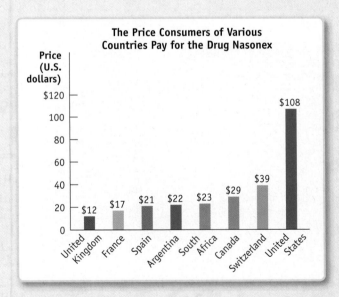

The Price Consumers of Various Countries Pay for the Drug Nasonex

Price (U.S. dollars)

United Kingdom $12; France $17; Spain $21; Argentina $22; South Africa $23; Canada $29; Switzerland $39; United States $108

Yet, American drug-makers contend that higher drug prices are necessary to cover the the high cost of research and development, which can run into the tens of millions of dollars over several years for successful drugs. Critics of the drug companies counter that American drug prices are in excess of what is needed for a socially desirable level of drug innovation. Instead, they say that drug companies are too often focused on developing drugs that generate high profits rather than those that improve health or save lives.

What's indisputable is that some level of profit is necessary to fund innovation.

Source: International Federation of Health Plans, 2012 Comparative Price Report.

Patents and copyrights are temporary because the law strikes a compromise. The higher price for the good that holds while the legal protection is in effect compensates inventors for the cost of invention; conversely, the lower price that results once the legal protection lapses and competition emerges benefits consumers and increases economic efficiency.

Because the duration of the temporary monopoly cannot be tailored to specific cases, this system is imperfect and leads to some missed opportunities. In some cases there can be significant welfare issues. For example, the violation of American drug patents by pharmaceutical companies in poor countries has been a major source of controversy, pitting the needs of poor patients who cannot afford retail drug prices against the interests of drug manufacturers that have incurred high research costs to discover these drugs.

To solve this problem, some American drug companies and poor countries have negotiated deals in which the patents are honored but the American companies sell their drugs at deeply discounted prices. (This is an example of *price discrimination*, which we'll learn more about shortly.)

ECONOMICS ▶ *in Action*

Newly Emerging Markets: A Diamond Monopolist's Best Friend

When Cecil Rhodes created the De Beers monopoly, it was a particularly opportune moment. The new diamond mines in South Africa dwarfed all previous sources, so almost all of the world's diamond production was concentrated in a few square miles.

An increase in demand for diamonds in emerging markets has led to increased depletion of the world's diamond mines and higher prices.

Until recently, De Beers was able to extend its control of resources even as new mines opened. De Beers either bought out new producers or entered into agreements with local governments that controlled some of the new mines, effectively making them part of the De Beers monopoly.

The most remarkable of these was an agreement with the former Soviet Union, which ensured that Russian diamonds would be marketed through De Beers, preserving its ability to control retail prices. De Beers also went so far as to stockpile a year's supply of diamonds in its London vaults so that when demand dropped, newly mined stones would be stored rather than sold, restricting retail supply until demand and prices recovered.

De Beers's peak market share reached almost 90% in the late 1980s but has been declining ever since. In 2013, decades-long litigation between De Beers and the U.S. government was finally settled with De Beers agreeing to stop attempting to monopolize the market for diamonds and to stop fixing the price of polished diamonds. De Beers has also lost control of supply as several independent companies have begun mining for diamonds in other African countries, as well as in Russia and Canada. In addition, high-quality, inexpensive synthetic diamonds have become an alternative to real gems, eating into De Beers's profit. So does this mean an end to high diamond prices and De Beers's high profits?

Not really. Although De Beers' is no longer the largest producer of rough diamonds, it still earns the highest revenue of any producer. Although supply and demand determine the outcome of today's diamond market much more than De Beers's actions, it and other diamond producers are highly profitable. There is still severely limited supply, as old mines have become depleted and new sources of diamonds have been difficult to find. At the same time consumers from rapidly growing economies like China and India have significantly boosted diamond demand. As a result, prices for polished diamonds have risen over 6% every year since 2008, when the global financial crisis precipitated a sharp fall in diamond prices.

In the end, although a diamond monopoly may not be forever, a greatly restricted supply along with rising demand from rapidly growing economies may be almost as profitable.

Check Your Understanding 13-1

1. Currently, Texas Tea Oil Co. is the only local supplier of home heating oil in Frigid, Alaska. This winter residents were shocked that the price of a gallon of heating oil had doubled and believed that they were the victims of market power. Explain which of the following pieces of evidence support or contradict that conclusion.
   a. There is a national shortage of heating oil, and Texas Tea could procure only a limited amount.
   b. Last year, Texas Tea and several other competing local oil-supply firms merged into a single firm.
   c. The cost to Texas Tea of purchasing heating oil from refineries has gone up significantly.
   d. Recently, some nonlocal firms have begun to offer heating oil to Texas Tea's regular customers at a price much lower than Texas Tea's.
   e. Texas Tea has acquired an exclusive government license to draw oil from the only heating oil pipeline in the state.

2. Suppose the government is considering extending the length of a patent from 20 years to 30 years. How would this change each of the following?
   a. The incentive to invent new products
   b. The length of time during which consumers have to pay higher prices

3. Explain the nature of the network externality in each of the following cases.
   a. A new type of credit card, called Passport
   b. A new type of car engine, which runs on solar cells
   c. A website for trading locally provided goods and services

Solutions appear at back of book.

How a Monopolist Maximizes Profit

As we've suggested, once Cecil Rhodes consolidated the competing diamond producers of South Africa into a single company, the industry's behavior changed: the quantity supplied fell and the market price rose. In this section, we will learn how a monopolist increases its profit by reducing output. And we will see the crucial role that market demand plays in leading a monopolist to behave differently from a perfectly competitive industry. (Remember that profit here is economic profit, not accounting profit.)

The Monopolist's Demand Curve and Marginal Revenue

In Chapter 12 we derived the firm's optimal output rule: a profit-maximizing firm produces the quantity of output at which the marginal cost of producing the last unit of output equals marginal revenue—the change in total revenue generated by that last unit of output. That is, $MR = MC$ at the profit-maximizing quantity of output.

Although the optimal output rule holds for all firms, we will see shortly that its application leads to different profit-maximizing output levels for a monopolist compared to a firm in a perfectly competitive industry—that is, a price-taking firm. The source of that difference lies in the comparison of the demand curve faced by a monopolist to the demand curve faced by an individual perfectly competitive firm.

▼ **Quick Review**

• In a **monopoly,** a single firm uses its **market power** to charge higher prices and produce less output than a competitive industry, generating profits in the short and long run.

• Profits will not persist in the long run unless there is a **barrier to entry** such as control of natural resources, increasing returns to scale, technological superiority, network externalities, or legal restrictions imposed by governments.

• A **natural monopoly** arises when average total cost is declining over the output range relevant for the industry. This creates a barrier to entry because an established monopolist has lower average total cost than an entrant.

• In certain technology and communications sectors of the economy, a **network externality** enables a firm with the largest number of customers to become a **monopolist.**

• **Patents** and **copyrights,** government-created barriers, are a source of temporary monopoly that attempt to balance the need for higher prices as compensation to an inventor for the cost of invention against the increase in consumer surplus from lower prices and greater efficiency.

In addition to the optimal output rule, we also learned that even though the market demand curve always slopes downward, each of the firms that make up a perfectly competitive industry faces a *perfectly elastic* demand curve that is horizontal at the market price, like D_C in panel (a) of Figure 13-4. Any attempt by an individual firm in a perfectly competitive industry to charge more than the going market price will cause it to lose all its sales. It can, however, sell as much as it likes at the market price.

As we saw in Chapter 12, the marginal revenue of a perfectly competitive producer is simply the market price. As a result, the price-taking firm's optimal output rule is to produce the output level at which the marginal cost of the last unit produced is equal to the market price.

A monopolist, in contrast, is the sole supplier of its good. So its demand curve is simply the market demand curve, which slopes downward, like D_M in panel (b) of Figure 13-4. This downward slope creates a "wedge" between the price of the good and the marginal revenue of the good—the change in revenue generated by producing one more unit.

Table 13-1 shows this wedge between price and marginal revenue for a monopolist, by calculating the monopolist's total revenue and marginal revenue schedules from its demand schedule.

The first two columns of Table 13-1 show a hypothetical demand schedule for De Beers diamonds. For the sake of simplicity, we assume that all diamonds are exactly alike. And to make the arithmetic easy, we suppose that the number of diamonds sold is far smaller than is actually the case. For instance, at a price of $500 per diamond, we assume that only 10 diamonds are sold. The demand curve implied by this schedule is shown in panel (a) of Figure 13-5.

The third column of Table 13-1 shows De Beers's total revenue from selling each quantity of diamonds—the price per diamond multiplied by the number of

FIGURE 13-4 **Comparing the Demand Curves of a Perfectly Competitive Producer and a Monopolist**

(a) Demand Curve of an Individual Perfectly Competitive Producer

(b) Demand Curve of a Monopolist

Because an individual perfectly competitive producer cannot affect the market price of a good, it faces the horizontal demand curve D_C, as shown in panel (a), allowing it to sell as much as it wants at the market price. A monopolist, though, can affect the price.

Because it is the sole supplier in the industry, it faces the market demand curve D_M, as shown in panel (b). To sell more output, it must lower the price; by reducing output, it raises the price.

diamonds sold. The last column calculates marginal revenue, the change in total revenue from producing and selling another diamond.

Clearly, after the 1st diamond, the marginal revenue a monopolist receives from selling one more unit is less than the price at which that unit is sold. For example, if De Beers sells 10 diamonds, the price at which the 10th diamond is sold is $500. But the marginal revenue—the change in total revenue in going from 9 to 10 diamonds—is only $50.

Why is the marginal revenue from that 10th diamond less than the price? It is less than the price because an increase in production by a monopolist has two opposing effects on revenue:

- A *quantity effect.* One more unit is sold, increasing total revenue by the price at which the unit is sold.

- A *price effect.* In order to sell the last unit, the monopolist must cut the market price on *all* units sold. This decreases total revenue.

The quantity effect and the price effect when the monopolist goes from selling 9 diamonds to 10 diamonds are illustrated by the two shaded areas in panel (a) of Figure 13-5. Increasing diamond sales from 9 to 10 means moving down the demand curve from *A* to *B*, reducing the price per diamond from $550 to $500. The green-shaded area represents the quantity effect: De Beers sells the 10th diamond at a price of $500. This is offset, however, by the price effect, represented by the yellow-shaded area. In order to sell that 10th diamond, De Beers must reduce the price on all its diamonds from $550 to $500. So it loses 9 × $50 = $450 in revenue, the yellow-shaded area. As point *C* indicates, the total effect on revenue of selling one more diamond—the marginal revenue—derived from an increase in diamond sales from 9 to 10 is only $50.

Point *C* lies on the monopolist's marginal revenue curve, labeled *MR* in panel (a) of Figure 13-5 and taken from the last column of Table 13-1. The crucial point about the monopolist's marginal revenue curve is that it is always *below* the demand curve. That's because of the price effect: a monopolist's marginal revenue from selling an additional unit is always less than the price the monopolist receives for the previous unit. It is the price effect that creates the wedge between the monopolist's marginal revenue curve and the demand curve: in order to sell an additional diamond, De Beers must cut the market price on all units sold.

In fact, this wedge exists for any firm that possesses market power, such as an oligopolist as well as a monopolist. Having market power means that the firm faces a downward-sloping demand curve. As a result, there will always be a price effect from an increase in its output. So for a firm with market power, the marginal revenue curve always lies below its demand curve.

Take a moment to compare the monopolist's marginal revenue curve with the marginal revenue curve for a perfectly competitive firm, one without market power. For such a firm there is no price effect from an increase in output: its marginal revenue curve is simply its horizontal demand curve. So for a perfectly competitive firm, market price and marginal revenue are always equal.

To emphasize how the quantity and price effects offset each other for a firm with market power, De Beers's total revenue curve is shown in panel (b) of Figure 13-5.

TABLE 13-1 Demand, Total Revenue, and Marginal Revenue for the De Beers Monopoly

Price of diamond P	Quantity of diamonds Q	Total revenue $TR = P \times Q$	Marginal revenue $MR = \Delta TR/\Delta Q$
$1,000	0	$0	
			$950
950	1	950	
			850
900	2	1,800	
			750
850	3	2,550	
			650
800	4	3,200	
			550
750	5	3,750	
			450
700	6	4,200	
			350
650	7	4,550	
			250
600	8	4,800	
			150
550	9	4,950	
			50
500	10	5,000	
			−50
450	11	4,950	
			−150
400	12	4,800	
			−250
350	13	4,550	
			−350
300	14	4,200	
			−450
250	15	3,750	
			−550
200	16	3,200	
			−650
150	17	2,550	
			−750
100	18	1,800	
			−850
50	19	950	
			−950
0	20	0	

FIGURE **13-5** | A Monopolist's Demand, Total Revenue, and Marginal Revenue Curves

Panel (a) shows the monopolist's demand and marginal revenue curves for diamonds from Table 13-1. The marginal revenue curve lies below the demand curve. To see why, consider point *A* on the demand curve, where 9 diamonds are sold at $550 each, generating total revenue of $4,950. To sell a 10th diamond, the price on all 10 diamonds must be cut to $500, as shown by point B. As a result, total revenue increases by the green area (the quantity effect: +$500) but decreases by the yellow area (the price effect: −$450). So the marginal revenue from the 10th diamond is $50 (the difference between the green and yellow areas), which is much lower than its price, $500. Panel (b) shows the monopolist's total revenue curve for diamonds. As output goes from 0 to 10 diamonds, total revenue increases. It reaches its maximum at 10 diamonds—the level at which marginal revenue is equal to 0—and declines thereafter. The quantity effect dominates the price effect when total revenue is rising; the price effect dominates the quantity effect when total revenue is falling.

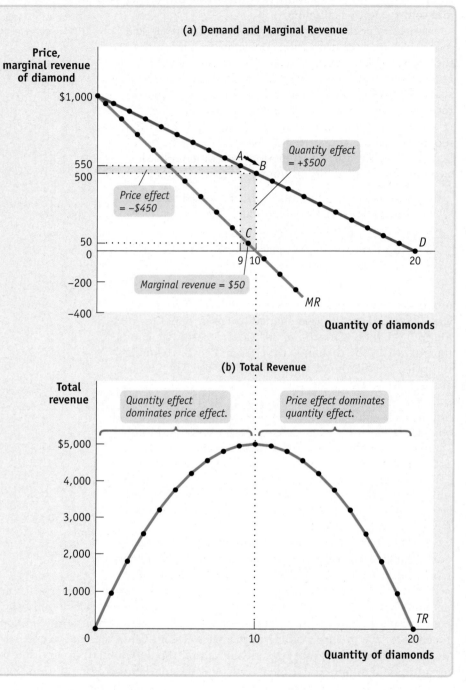

(a) Demand and Marginal Revenue

(b) Total Revenue

Notice that it is hill-shaped: as output rises from 0 to 10 diamonds, total revenue increases. This reflects the fact that at *low levels of output, the quantity effect is stronger than the price effect:* as the monopolist sells more, it has to lower the price on only very few units, so the price effect is small. As output rises beyond 10 diamonds, total revenue actually falls. This reflects the fact that *at high levels of output, the price effect is stronger than the quantity effect:* as the monopolist sells more, it now has to lower the price on many units of output, making the price effect very large.

Correspondingly, the marginal revenue curve lies below zero at output levels above 10 diamonds. For example, an increase in diamond production from 11 to

12 yields only $400 for the 12th diamond, simultaneously reducing the revenue from diamonds 1 through 11 by $550. As a result, the marginal revenue of the 12th diamond is –$150.

The Monopolist's Profit-Maximizing Output and Price

To complete the story of how a monopolist maximizes profit, we now bring in the monopolist's marginal cost. Let's assume that there is no fixed cost of production; we'll also assume that the marginal cost of producing an additional diamond is constant at $200, no matter how many diamonds De Beers produces. Then marginal cost will always equal average total cost, and the marginal cost curve (and the average total cost curve) is a horizontal line at $200, as shown in Figure 13-6.

To maximize profit, the monopolist compares marginal cost with marginal revenue. If marginal revenue exceeds marginal cost, De Beers increases profit by producing more; if marginal revenue is less than marginal cost, De Beers increases profit by producing less. So the monopolist maximizes its profit by using the optimal output rule:

(13-1) $MR = MC$ at the monopolist's profit-maximizing quantity of output

The monopolist's optimal point is shown in Figure 13-6. At A, the marginal cost curve, MC, crosses the marginal revenue curve, MR. The corresponding output level, 8 diamonds, is the monopolist's profit-maximizing quantity of output, Q_M. The price at which consumers demand 8 diamonds is $600, so the monopolist's

FIGURE 13-6   The Monopolist's Profit-Maximizing Output and Price

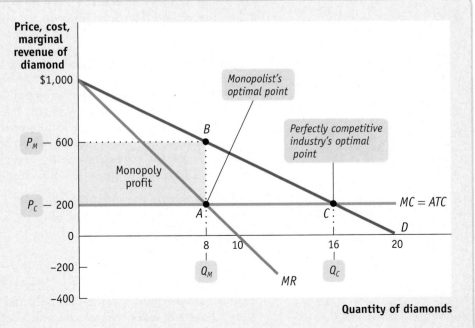

This figure shows the demand, marginal revenue, and marginal cost curves. Marginal cost per diamond is constant at $200, so the marginal cost curve is horizontal at $200. According to the optimal output rule, the profit-maximizing quantity of output for the monopolist is at $MR = MC$, shown by point A, where the marginal cost and marginal revenue curves cross at an output of 8 diamonds. The price De Beers can charge per diamond is found by going to the point on the demand curve directly above point A, which is point B here—a price of $600 per diamond. It makes a profit of $400 × 8 = $3,200. A perfectly competitive industry produces the output level at which $P = MC$, given by point C, where the demand curve and marginal cost curves cross. So a competitive industry produces 16 diamonds, sells at a price of $200, and makes zero profit.

price, P_M, is \$600—corresponding to point B. The average total cost of producing each diamond is \$200, so the monopolist earns a profit of \$600 − \$200 = \$400 per diamond, and total profit is 8 × \$400 = \$3,200, as indicated by the shaded area.

Monopoly versus Perfect Competition

When Cecil Rhodes consolidated many independent diamond producers into De Beers, he converted a perfectly competitive industry into a monopoly. We can now use our analysis to see the effects of such a consolidation.

Let's look again at Figure 13-6 and ask how this same market would work if, instead of being a monopoly, the industry were perfectly competitive. We will continue to assume that there is no fixed cost and that marginal cost is constant, so average total cost and marginal cost are equal.

If the diamond industry consists of many perfectly competitive firms, each of those producers takes the market price as given. That is, each producer acts as if its marginal revenue is equal to the market price. So each firm within the industry uses the price-taking firm's optimal output rule:

(13-2) $P = MC$ at the perfectly competitive firm's profit-maximizing quantity of output

In Figure 13-6, this would correspond to producing at C, where the price per diamond, P_C, is \$200, equal to the marginal cost of production. So the profit-maximizing output of an industry under perfect competition, Q_C, is 16 diamonds.

But does the perfectly competitive industry earn any profits at C? No: the price of \$200 is equal to the average total cost per diamond. So there are no economic profits for this industry when it produces at the perfectly competitive output level.

We've already seen that once the industry is consolidated into a monopoly, the result is very different. The monopolist's calculation of marginal revenue takes the price effect into account, so that marginal revenue is less than the price. That is,

(13-3) $P > MR = MC$ at the monopolist's profit-maximizing quantity of output

As we've already seen, the monopolist produces less than the competitive industry—8 diamonds rather than 16. The price under monopoly is \$600, compared with only \$200 under perfect competition. The monopolist earns a positive profit, but the competitive industry does not.

So, just as we suggested earlier, we see that compared with a competitive industry, a monopolist does the following:

• Produces a smaller quantity: $Q_M < Q_C$
• Charges a higher price: $P_M > P_C$
• Earns a profit

Monopoly: The General Picture

Figure 13-6 involved specific numbers and assumed that marginal cost was constant, that there was no fixed cost, and, therefore, that the average total cost curve was a horizontal line. Figure 13-7 shows a more general picture of monopoly in action: D is the market demand curve; MR, the marginal revenue curve; MC, the marginal cost curve; and ATC, the average total cost curve. Here we return to the usual assumption that the marginal cost curve has a "swoosh" shape and the average total cost curve is U-shaped.

Applying the optimal output rule, we see that the profit-maximizing level of output is the output at which marginal revenue equals marginal cost, indicated by point A. The profit-maximizing quantity of output is Q_M, and the price charged by the monopolist is P_M. At the profit-maximizing level of output, the monopolist's average total cost is ATC_M, shown by point C.

Recalling how we calculated profit in Equation 12-5, profit is equal to the difference between total revenue and total cost. So we have:

(13-4) $\begin{aligned}\text{Profit} &= TR - TC \\ &= (P_M \times Q_M) - (ATC_M \times Q_M) \\ &= (P_M - ATC_M) \times Q_M\end{aligned}$

Profit is equal to the area of the shaded rectangle in Figure 13-7, with a height of $P_M - ATC_M$ and a width of Q_M.

In Chapter 12 we learned that a perfectly competitive industry can have profits in the *short run but not in the long run*. In the short run, price can exceed average total cost, allowing a perfectly competitive firm to make a profit. But we also know that this cannot persist.

In the long run, any profit in a perfectly competitive industry will be competed away as new firms enter the market. In contrast, barriers to entry allow a monopolist to make profits in *both the short run and the long run.*

FIGURE 13-7   The Monopolist's Profit

In this case, the marginal cost curve has a "swoosh" shape and the average total cost curve is U-shaped. The monopolist maximizes profit by producing the level of output at which $MR = MC$, given by point A, generating quantity Q_M. It finds its monopoly price, P_M, from the point on the demand curve directly above point A, point B here. The average total cost of Q_M is shown by point C. Profit is given by the area of the shaded rectangle.

ECONOMICS ▶ in Action

Shocked by the High Price of Electricity

Historically, electric utilities were recognized as natural monopolies. A utility serviced a defined geographical area, owning the plants that generated electricity as well as the transmission lines that delivered it to retail customers. The rates charged customers were regulated by the government, set at a level to cover the utility's cost of operation plus a modest return on capital to its shareholders.

Beginning in the late 1990s, however, there was a move toward deregulation, based on the belief that competition would result in lower retail electricity prices Competition was introduced at two junctures in the channel from power generation to retail customers: (1) distributors would compete to sell electricity to retail customers, and (2) power generators would compete to supply power to the distributors.

That was the theory, at least. By 2014, only 16 states had instituted some form of electricity deregulation, while 7 had started but then suspended deregulation, leaving 27 states to continue with a regulated monopoly electricity provider. Why did so few states actually follow through on electricity deregulation?

Although some electric utilities were deregulated in the 1990s, currently there's a trend toward reregulating them.

One major obstacle to lowering electricity prices through deregulation is the lack of choice in power generators, the bulk of which still entail large up-front fixed costs. As a result, in many markets there is only one power generator. Although consumers appear to have a choice in their electricity distributor, the choice is illusory, as everyone must get their electricity from the same source in the end.

In fact, deregulation can make consumers worse off when there is only one power generator. That's because deregulation allows the power generator to engage in market manipulation—intentionally reducing the amount of power supplied to distributors in order to drive up prices. The most shocking case occurred during the California energy crisis of 2000–2001 that brought black-outs and billions of dollars in electricity surcharges to homes and businesses. On audiotapes later acquired by regulators, workers could be heard discussing plans to shut down power plants during times of peak energy demand, joking about how they were "stealing" more than $1 million a day from California.

Another problem is that without prices set by regulators, producers aren't guaranteed a profitable rate of return on new power plants. As a result, in states with deregulation, capacity has failed to keep up with growing demand. For example, Texas, a deregulated state, has experienced massive blackouts due to insufficient capacity, and in New Jersey and Maryland, regulators have inter-vened to compel producers to build more power plants.

Lastly, consumers in deregulated states have been subject to big spikes in their electricity bills, often paying much more than consumers in regulated states. So, angry customers and exasperated regulators have prompted many states to shift into reverse, with Illinois, Montana, and Virginia moving to regulate their indus-tries. California and Montana have gone so far as to mandate that their electric-ity distributors reacquire power plants that were sold off during deregulation. In addition, regulators have been on the prowl, fining utilities in Texas, New York, and Illinois for market manipulation.

Check Your Understanding 13-2

1. Use the accompanying total revenue schedule of Emerald, Inc., a monopoly producer of 10-carat emeralds, to calculate the answers to parts a–d. Then answer part e.
   a. The demand schedule
   b. The marginal revenue schedule
   c. The quantity effect component of marginal revenue per output level
   d. The price effect component of marginal revenue per output level
   e. What additional information is needed to determine Emerald, Inc.'s profit-maximizing output?

Quantity of emeralds demanded	Total revenue
1	$100
2	186
3	252
4	280
5	250

2. Use Figure 13-6 to show what happens to the following when the marginal cost of diamond production rises from $200 to $400.
   a. Marginal cost curve
   b. Profit-maximizing price and quantity
   c. Profit of the monopolist
   d. Perfectly competitive industry profits

Solutions appear at back of book.

Monopoly and Public Policy

It's good to be a monopolist, but it's not so good to be a monopolist's customer. A monopolist, by reducing output and raising prices, benefits at the expense of con-sumers. But buyers and sellers always have conflicting interests. Is the conflict of interest under monopoly any different than it is under perfect competition?

The answer is yes, because monopoly is a source of inefficiency: the losses to consumers from monopoly behavior are larger than the gains to the monopolist. Because monopoly leads to net losses for the economy, governments often try either to prevent the emergence of monopolies or to limit their effects. In this section, we will see why monopoly leads to inefficiency and examine the policies governments adopt in an attempt to prevent this inefficiency.

Welfare Effects of Monopoly

By restricting output below the level at which marginal cost is equal to the market price, a monopolist increases its profit but hurts consumers. To assess whether this is a net benefit or loss to society, we must compare the monopolist's gain in profit to the loss in consumer surplus. And what we learn is that the loss in consumer surplus is larger than the monopolist's gain. Monopoly causes a net loss for society.

To see why, let's return to the case where the marginal cost curve is horizontal, as shown in the two panels of Figure 13-8. Here the marginal cost curve is MC, the demand curve is D, and, in panel (b), the marginal revenue curve is MR.

Panel (a) shows what happens if this industry is perfectly competitive. Equilibrium output is Q_C; the price of the good, P_C, is equal to marginal cost, and marginal cost is also equal to average total cost because there is no fixed cost and marginal cost is constant. Each firm is earning exactly its average total cost per unit of output, so there is no profit and no producer surplus in this equilibrium.

The consumer surplus generated by the market is equal to the area of the blue-shaded triangle CS_C shown in panel (a). Since there is no producer surplus when the industry is perfectly competitive, CS_C also represents the total surplus.

Panel (b) shows the results for the same market, but this time assuming that the industry is a monopoly. The monopolist produces the level of output Q_M, at which marginal cost is equal to marginal revenue, and it charges the price P_M. The industry now earns profit—which is also the producer surplus—equal to the area of the green rectangle, PS_M. Note that this profit is surplus captured from consumers as consumer surplus shrinks to the area of the blue triangle, CS_M.

FIGURE 13-8 **Monopoly Causes Inefficiency**

Panel (a) depicts a perfectly competitive industry: output is Q_C, and market price, P_C, is equal to MC. Since price is exactly equal to each producer's average total cost of production per unit, there is no profit and no producer surplus. So total surplus is equal to consumer surplus, the entire shaded area. Panel (b) depicts the industry under monopoly: the monopolist decreases output to Q_M and charges P_M. Consumer surplus (blue area) has shrunk: a portion of it has been captured as profit (green area), and a portion of it has been lost to deadweight loss (yellow area), the value of mutually beneficial transactions that do not occur because of monopoly behavior. As a result, total surplus falls.

By comparing panels (a) and (b), we see that in addition to the redistribution of surplus from consumers to the monopolist, another important change has occurred: the sum of profit and consumer surplus—total surplus—is *smaller* under monopoly than under perfect competition. That is, the sum of CS_M and PS_M in panel (b) is less than the area CS_C in panel (a). In Chapter 7, we analyzed how taxes generated *deadweight loss* to society. Here we show that monopoly creates a deadweight loss to society equal to the area of the yellow triangle, *DL*. So monopoly produces a net loss for society.

This net loss arises because some mutually beneficial transactions do not occur. There are people for whom an additional unit of the good is worth more than the marginal cost of producing it but who don't consume it because they are not willing to pay P_M.

If you recall our discussion of the deadweight loss from taxes you will notice that the deadweight loss from monopoly looks quite similar. Indeed, by driving a wedge between price and marginal cost, monopoly acts much like a tax on consumers and produces the same kind of inefficiency.

So monopoly hurts the welfare of society as a whole and is a source of market failure. Is there anything government policy can do about it?

Preventing Monopoly

Policy toward monopoly depends crucially on whether or not the industry in question is a natural monopoly, one in which increasing returns to scale ensure that a bigger producer has lower average total cost. If the industry is not a natural monopoly, the best policy is to prevent monopoly from arising or break it up if it already exists. Let's focus on that case first, then turn to the more difficult problem of dealing with natural monopoly.

The De Beers monopoly on diamonds didn't have to happen. Diamond production is not a natural monopoly: the industry's costs would be no higher if it consisted of a number of independent, competing producers (as is the case, for example, in gold production).

So if the South African government had been worried about how a monopoly would have affected consumers, it could have blocked Cecil Rhodes in his drive to dominate the industry or broken up his monopoly after the fact. Today, governments often try to prevent monopolies from forming and break up existing ones.

De Beers is a rather unique case. For complicated historical reasons, it was allowed to remain a monopoly. But over the last century, most similar monopolies have been broken up. The most celebrated example in the United States is Standard Oil, founded by John D. Rockefeller in 1870. By 1878 Standard Oil controlled almost all U.S. oil refining; but in 1911 a court order broke the company into a number of smaller units, including the companies that later became Exxon and Mobil (and more recently merged to become ExxonMobil).

The government policies used to prevent or eliminate monopolies are known as *antitrust policies*, which we will discuss in the next chapter.

Dealing with Natural Monopoly

Breaking up a monopoly that isn't natural is clearly a good idea: the gains to consumers outweigh the loss to the producer. But it's not so clear whether a natural monopoly, one in which a large producer has lower average total costs than small producers, should be broken up, because this would raise average total cost. For example, a town government that tried to prevent a single company from dominating local gas supply—which, as we've discussed, is almost surely a natural monopoly—would raise the cost of providing gas to its residents.

Yet even in the case of a natural monopoly, a profit-maximizing monopolist acts in a way that causes inefficiency—it charges consumers a price that is higher than marginal cost and, by doing so, prevents some potentially beneficial transactions. Also, it can seem unfair that a firm that has managed to establish a monopoly position earns a large profit at the expense of consumers.

What can public policy do about this? There are two common answers.

1. Public Ownership In many countries, the preferred answer to the problem of natural monopoly has been **public ownership.** Instead of allowing a private monopolist to control an industry, the government establishes a public agency to provide the good and protect consumers' interests. In Britain, for example, telephone service was provided by the state-owned British Telecom before 1984, and airline travel was provided by the state-owned British Airways before 1987. (These companies still exist, but they have been privatized, competing with other firms in their respective industries.)

There are some examples of public ownership in the United States. Passenger rail service is provided by the public company Amtrak; regular mail delivery is provided by the U.S. Postal Service; some cities, including Los Angeles, have publicly owned electric power companies.

The advantage of public ownership, in principle, is that a publicly owned natural monopoly can set prices based on the criterion of efficiency rather than profit maximization. In a perfectly competitive industry, profit-maximizing behavior is efficient, because producers produce the quantity at which price is equal to marginal cost; that is why there is no economic argument for public ownership of, say, wheat farms.

Experience suggests, however, that public ownership as a solution to the problem of natural monopoly often works badly in practice. One reason is that publicly owned firms are often less eager than private companies to keep costs down or offer high-quality products. Another is that publicly owned companies all too often end up serving political interests—providing contracts or jobs to people with the right connections. For example, Amtrak has notoriously provided train service at a loss to destinations that attract few passengers—but that are located in the districts of influential members of Congress.

Amtrak, a public company, has provided train service, at a loss, to destinations that attract few passengers.

2. Regulation In the United States, the more common answer has been to leave the industry in private hands but subject it to regulation. In particular, most local utilities like electricity, land line telephone service, natural gas, and so on are covered by **price regulation** that limits the prices they can charge.

We saw in Chapter 5 that imposing a *price ceiling* on a competitive industry is a recipe for shortages, black markets, and other nasty side effects. Doesn't imposing a limit on the price that, say, a local gas company can charge have the same effects?

Not necessarily: a price ceiling on a monopolist need not create a shortage—in the absence of a price ceiling, a monopolist would charge a price that is higher than its marginal cost of production. So even if forced to charge a lower price—as long as that price is above *MC* and the monopolist at least breaks even on total output—the monopolist still has an incentive to produce the quantity demanded at that price.

Figure 13-9 shows an example of price regulation of a natural monopoly—a highly simplified version of a local gas company. The company faces a demand curve *D*, with an associated marginal revenue curve *MR*. For simplicity, we assume that the firm's total costs consist of two parts: a fixed cost and variable costs that are incurred at a constant proportion to output. So marginal cost is constant in this case, and the marginal cost curve (which here is also the average variable cost curve) is the horizontal line *MC*.

The average total cost curve is the downward-sloping curve *ATC*; it slopes downward because the higher the output, the lower the average fixed cost (the

In **public ownership** of a monopoly, the good is supplied by the government or by a firm owned by the government.

Price regulation limits the price that a monopolist is allowed to charge.

FIGURE **13-9** Unregulated and Regulated Natural Monopoly

(a) Total Surplus with an Unregulated Natural Monopolist

(b) Total Surplus with a Regulated Natural Monopolist

This figure shows the case of a natural monopolist. In panel (a), if the monopolist is allowed to charge P_M, it makes a profit, shown by the green area; consumer surplus is shown by the blue area. If it is regulated and must charge the lower price P_R, output increases from Q_M to Q_R and consumer surplus increases. Panel (b) shows what happens when the monopolist must charge a price equal to average total cost, the price P_R^*. Output expands to Q_R^*, and consumer surplus is now the entire blue area. The monopolist makes zero profit. This is the greatest total surplus possible when the monopolist is allowed to at least break even, making P_R^* the best regulated price.

fixed cost per unit of output). Because average total cost slopes downward over the range of output relevant for market demand, this is a natural monopoly.

Panel (a) illustrates a case of natural monopoly without regulation. The unregulated natural monopolist chooses the monopoly output Q_M and charges the price P_M. Since the monopolist receives a price greater than its average total cost, it earns a profit. This profit is exactly equal to the producer surplus in this market, represented by the green-shaded rectangle. Consumer surplus is given by the blue-shaded triangle.

Now suppose that regulators impose a price ceiling on local gas deliveries—one that falls below the monopoly price P_M but above ATC, say, at P_R in panel (a). At that price the quantity demanded is Q_R.

Does the company have an incentive to produce that quantity? Yes. If the price at which the monopolist can sell its product is fixed by regulators, the firm's output no longer affects the market price—so it ignores the MR curve and is willing to expand output to meet the quantity demanded as long as the price it receives for the next unit is greater than marginal cost and the monopolist at least breaks even on total output. So with price regulation, the monopolist produces more, at a lower price.

Of course, the monopolist will not be willing to produce at all if the imposed price means producing at a loss. That is, the price ceiling has to be set high enough to allow the firm to cover its average total cost. Panel (b) shows a situation in which regulators have pushed the price down as far as possible, at the level where the average total cost curve crosses the demand curve.

At any lower price the firm loses money. The price here, P_R^*, is the best regulated price: the monopolist is just willing to operate and produces Q_R^*, the quantity demanded at that price. Consumers and society gain as a result.

The welfare effects of this regulation can be seen by comparing the shaded areas in the two panels of Figure 13-9. Consumer surplus is increased by the regulation, with the gains coming from two sources. First, profits are eliminated and added instead to consumer surplus. Second, the larger output and lower price lead to an overall welfare gain—an increase in total surplus. In fact, panel (b) illustrates the largest total surplus possible.

This all looks terrific: consumers are better off, profits are eliminated, and overall welfare increases. Unfortunately, things are rarely that easy in practice. The main problem is that regulators don't have the information required to set the price exactly at the level at which the demand curve crosses the average total cost curve. Sometimes they set it too low, creating shortages; at other times they set it too high. Also, regulated monopolies, like publicly owned firms, tend to exaggerate their costs to regulators and to provide inferior quality to consumers.

Sometimes the cure is worse than the disease. Some economists have argued that the best solution, even in the case of natural monopoly, may be to live with it. The case for doing nothing is that attempts to control monopoly will, one way or another, do more harm than good—for example, by the politicization of pricing, which leads to shortages, or by the creation of opportunities for political corruption.

The upcoming Economics in Action describes the case of broadband, a natural monopoly that has been alternately regulated and deregulated as politicians change their minds about the appropriate policy.

Monopsony Is it possible for the buyer and not the seller to have market power? Put another way, is it possible to have a market in which there is only one buyer but many sellers, so that the buyer can use its power to capture surplus from the sellers? The answer is yes, and that market is called a **monopsony.**

> A **monopsony** exists when there is only one buyer of a good. A **monopsonist** is a firm that is the sole buyer in a market.

Like a monopolist, a **monopsonist** will distort the competitive market outcome in order to capture more of the surplus, except that the monopsonist will do this through quantity purchased and price paid for goods rather than through quantity sold and price charged for goods.

Monopsony, although it does exist, is rarer than monopoly. The classic example is a single employer in a small town—say, the local factory—that is purchasing labor services from workers. Recall that a monopolist, realizing that it can affect the price at which its goods are sold, reduces output in order to get a higher price and increase its profits. A monopsonist does much the same thing. But with a twist: realizing that it can affect the wage it pays its employees by moving down the labor supply curve, it reduces the number of employees hired to pay a lower wage and increase its profits.

Just as a monopolist creates a deadweight loss by producing too little of the output, a monopsonist creates a deadweight loss by hiring too few workers (and thereby producing too little output as well).

Monopsony seems to occur most frequently in markets in which workers have a specialized skill, and there is only one employer who hires based on that skill. For example, physicians have often complained that in some parts of the country where most patients are insured by one or two insurance companies, the companies act as monopsonists in setting the reimbursements rates they pay for medical procedures.

And in 2014, when the two largest cable providers, Time Warner Cable and Comcast, announced their intention to merge, questions of monopoly *and* monopsony arose: monopoly, because the combined company would cover 30 million subscribers, an overwhelming proportion of Americans with cable access; and monopsony because the combined company would be virtually the only purchaser of programming by companies that produce shows for broadcast. At the time of writing, whether the FCC will allow the merger was an open question.

So although monopsony may be rare, it can be an important phenomenon.

What to Do About Monopoly? As our discussion has made clear, managing monopoly (and monopsony) can be tricky because trade-offs are often present. For example, in the case of drug monopolies, how can the prices consumers pay for existing drugs be reduced if the profits from those sales fund research and development of new drugs?

In the case of a regulated natural monopoly like power generation, how can power producers invest in cost-saving technology and new production capacity if they receive regulated returns and are therefore insulated from market forces? And on the flip side, when the electricity industry is deregulated, how can regulators assure that consumers are not gouged through market manipulation?

Economists and policy makers have struggled with these questions for decades because the best answer is often found through trial and error—as we've seen through the various attempts at electricity deregulation.

And there is always the danger of what is called *regulatory capture:* because vast sums of money are at stake, regulators can be unduly influenced by the companies they are supposed to oversee.

Perhaps, in dealing with monopolies, the best answer is for economists and policy makers to remain vigilant and admit that sometimes midcourse policy corrections are needed.

Why Is Your Broadband So Slow? And Why Does It Cost So Much?

Consider this: In the United States, high-speed broadband access costs nearly three times as much as in the United Kingdom and France, and more than five times as much as in South Korea. According to a report by the Organization for Economic Cooperation and Development (OECD), the United States ranked 30th out of 33 countries, with a price of $0 per month ($200 per month once if phone, TV, and some premium channels were included). Figure 13-10 compares the average download speed and prices across select countries. In South Korea, the average download speed is 75 Mbps and costs less than $20 per month. Whereas, in the United States, the average download speed is under 20 Mbps and costs nearly $90 per month.

Why do we pay so much? Many observers conclude that the United States has been especially bad at regulating the cable companies that provide broadband to more than two-thirds of Americans. And cable service has the characteristics of a natural monopoly because running a cable to individual houses entails large fixed costs. So in the early days of cable, prices were regulated by local governments.

However, a decade ago Congress deregulated high-speed internet access. The industry then consolidated, with two big companies, Time Warner and Comcast, purchasing smaller, local monopolies. As a result, American cable consumers face companies with significant monopoly power and little oversight. It should come as no surprise, then, that consumers also face yearly price hikes: from 1995 to 2012, the average price of a basic cable subscription increased at an annual rate of more than 6%. In 2012, that was four times the rate of inflation. In the few locations where there are competing cable companies, bills are typically 15% lower and service is better.

But how did broadband consumers in other countries escape that same fate, given that cable

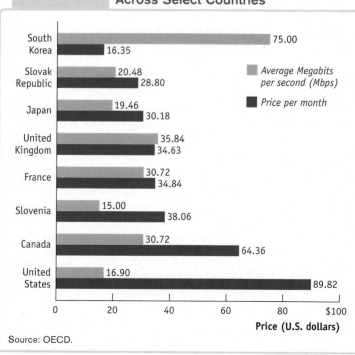

FIGURE **13-10**   Comparing Broadband Speed and Price Across Select Countries

Source: OECD.

is a natural monopoly? Regulators there imposed a *common carriage rule* on their industries, stipulating that cable companies must rent their cable capacity to internet service providers, who then compete to deliver internet access to consumers.

Without such a rule, the vast majority of Americans—around 70%—have only one cable provider and thus only one source of high-speed internet access. However, supporters of the American system counter that cable-provider profits fund improvements in infrastructure, such as in 4G and fiber optic networks, where Europe is lagging behind.

Check Your Understanding 13-3

1. What policy should the government adopt in the following cases? Explain.
   a. Internet service in Anytown, Ohio, is provided by cable. Customers feel they are being overcharged, but the cable company claims it must charge prices that let it recover the costs of laying cable.
   b. The only two airlines that currently fly to Alaska need government approval to merge. Other airlines wish to fly to Alaska but need government-allocated landing slots to do so.
2. True or false? Explain your answer.
   a. Society's welfare is lower under monopoly because some consumer surplus is transformed into profit for the monopolist.
   b. A monopolist causes inefficiency because there are consumers who are willing to pay a price greater than or equal to marginal cost but less than the monopoly price.
3. Suppose a monopolist mistakenly believes that its marginal revenue is always equal to the market price. Assuming constant marginal cost and no fixed cost, draw a diagram comparing the level of profit, consumer surplus, total surplus, and deadweight loss for this misguided monopolist compared to a smart monopolist.

Solutions appear at back of book.

Price Discrimination

Up to this point, we have considered only the case of a **single-price monopolist,** one that charges all consumers the same price. As the term suggests, not all monopolists do this. In fact, many if not most monopolists find that they can increase their profits by charging different customers different prices for the same good: they engage in **price discrimination.**

The most striking example of price discrimination most of us encounter regularly involves airline tickets. Although there are a number of airlines, most routes in the United States are serviced by only one or two carriers, which, as a result, have market power and can set prices. So any regular airline passenger quickly becomes aware that the question "How much will it cost me to fly there?" rarely has a simple answer.

If you are willing to buy a nonrefundable ticket a month in advance and happen to purchase the ticket on Tuesday or Wednesday evening, the round trip may cost only $150—or less if you are a senior citizen or a student. But if you have to go on a business trip tomorrow, which happens to be Tuesday, and come back on Wednesday, the same round trip might cost $550. Yet the business traveler and the visiting grandparent receive the same product—the same cramped seat, the same awful food (if indeed any food is served).

You might object that airlines are not usually monopolists—that in most flight markets the airline industry is an oligopoly. In fact, price discrimination takes place under oligopoly and monopolistic competition as well as monopoly. But it doesn't happen under perfect competition. And once we've seen why monopolists sometimes price-discriminate, we'll be in a good position to understand why it happens in oligopoly and monopolistic competition, too.

Quick Review
- By reducing output and raising price above marginal cost, a monopolist captures some of the consumer surplus as profit and causes deadweight loss. To avoid deadweight loss, government policy attempts to curtail monopoly behavior.
- When monopolies are "created" rather than natural, governments should act to prevent them from forming and break up existing ones.
- Natural monopoly poses a harder policy problem. One answer is **public ownership,** but publicly owned companies are often poorly run.
- A common response in the United States is **price regulation.** A price ceiling imposed on a monopolist does not create shortages as long as it is not set too low.
- There always remains the option of doing nothing; monopoly is a bad thing, but the cure may be worse than the disease.
- A **monopsony,** when there is only one buyer of a good, also results in deadweight loss. The **monopsonist** can affect the price of the good it buys: it captures surplus from sellers by reducing how much it purchases and thereby lowers the price.

A **single-price monopolist** offers its product to all consumers at the same price.

Sellers engage in **price discrimination** when they charge different prices to different consumers for the same good.

The Logic of Price Discrimination

To get a preliminary view of why price discrimination might be more profitable than charging all consumers the same price, imagine that Air Sunshine offers the only nonstop flights between Bismarck, North Dakota, and Ft. Lauderdale, Florida. Assume that there are no capacity problems—the airline can fly as many planes as the number of passengers warrants. Also assume that there is no fixed cost. The marginal cost to the airline of providing a seat is $125, however many passengers it carries.

Further assume that the airline knows there are two kinds of potential passengers. First, there are business travelers, 2,000 of whom want to travel between the destinations each week. Second, there are students, 2,000 of whom also want to travel each week.

Will potential passengers take the flight? It depends on the price. The business travelers, it turns out, really need to fly; they will take the plane as long as the price is no more than $550. Since they are flying purely for business, we assume that cutting the price below $550 will not lead to any increase in business travel. The students, however, have less money and more time; if the price goes above $150, they will take the bus. The implied demand curve is shown in Figure 13-11.

So what should the airline do? If it has to charge everyone the same price, its options are limited. It could charge $550; that way it would get as much as possible out of the business travelers but lose the student market. Or it could charge only $150; that way it would get both types of travelers but would make significantly less money from sales to business travelers.

We can quickly calculate the profits from each of these alternatives. If the airline charged $550, it would sell 2,000 tickets to the business travelers, earning total revenue of 2,000 × $550 = $1.1 million and incurring costs of 2,000 × $125 = $250,000; so its profit would be $850,000, illustrated by the shaded area *B* in Figure 13-11. If the airline charged only $150, it would sell 4,000 tickets, receiving revenue of 4,000 × $150 = $600,000 and incurring costs of 4,000 × $125 = $500,000; so its profit would be $100,000. If the airline must charge everyone the same price, charging the higher price and forgoing sales to students is clearly more profitable.

FIGURE **13-11** | Two Types of Airline Customers

Air Sunshine has two types of customers, business travelers willing to pay at most $550 per ticket and students willing to pay at most $150 per ticket. There are 2,000 of each kind of customer. Air Sunshine has constant marginal cost of $125 per seat. If Air Sunshine could charge these two types of customers different prices, it would maximize its profit by charging business travelers $550 and students $150 per ticket. It would capture all of the consumer surplus as profit.

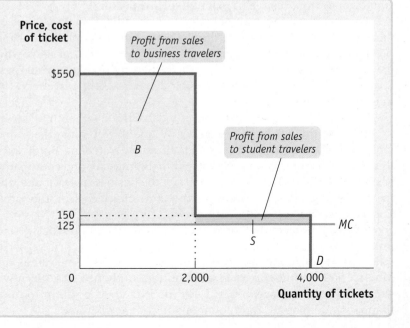

What the airline would really like to do, however, is charge the business travelers the full $550 but offer $150 tickets to the students. That's a lot less than the price paid by business travelers, but it's still above marginal cost; so if the airline could sell those extra 2,000 tickets to students, it would make an additional $50,000 in profit. That is, it would make a profit equal to the areas *B* plus *S* in Figure 13-11.

It would be more realistic to suppose that there is some "give" in the demand of each group: at a price below $550, there would be some increase in business travel; and at a price above $150, some students would still purchase tickets. But this, it turns out, does not do away with the argument for price discrimination.

The important point is that the two groups of consumers differ in their *sensitivity to price*—that a high price has a larger effect in discouraging purchases by students than by business travelers. As long as different groups of customers respond differently to the price, a monopolist will find that it can capture more consumer surplus and increase its profit by charging them different prices.

Price Discrimination and Elasticity

A more realistic description of the demand that airlines face would not specify particular prices at which different types of travelers would choose to fly. Instead, it would distinguish between the groups on the basis of their sensitivity to the price—their price elasticity of demand.

Suppose that a company sells its product to two easily identifiable groups of people—business travelers and students. It just so happens that business travelers are very insensitive to the price: there is a certain amount of the product they just have to have whatever the price, but they cannot be persuaded to buy much more than that no matter how cheap it is. Students, though, are more flexible: offer a good enough price and they will buy quite a lot, but raise the price too high and they will switch to something else. What should the company do?

The answer is the one already suggested by our simplified example: the company should charge business travelers, with their low price elasticity of demand, a higher price than it charges students, with their high price elasticity of demand.

The actual situation of the airlines is very much like this hypothetical example. Business travelers typically place a high priority on being at the right place at the right time and are not very sensitive to the price. But nonbusiness travelers are fairly sensitive to the price: faced with a high price, they might take the bus, drive to another airport to get a lower fare, or skip the trip altogether.

So why doesn't an airline simply announce different prices for business and nonbusiness customers? First, this would probably be illegal (U.S. law places some limits on the ability of companies to practice open price discrimination). Second, even if it were legal, it would be a hard policy to enforce: business travelers might be willing to wear casual clothing and claim they were visiting family in Ft. Lauderdale in order to save $400.

So what the airlines do—quite successfully—is impose rules that indirectly have the effect of charging business and nonbusiness travelers different fares. Business travelers usually travel during the week and want to be home on the weekend; so the round-trip fare is much higher if you don't stay over a Saturday night. The requirement of a weekend stay for a cheap ticket effectively separates business from nonbusiness travelers.

Similarly, business travelers often visit several cities in succession rather than make a simple round trip; so round-trip fares are much lower than twice the one-way fare. Many business trips are scheduled on short notice; so fares are much lower if you book far in advance. Fares are also lower if you purchase a last-minute ticket, taking your chances on whether you actually get a seat—business travelers have to make it to that meeting; people visiting their relatives don't.

On many airline routes, the fare you pay depends on the type of traveler you are.

Perfect price discrimination takes place when a monopolist charges each consumer his or her willingness to pay—the maximum that the consumer is willing to pay.

Because customers must show their ID at check-in, airlines make sure there are no resales of tickets between the two groups that would undermine their ability to price-discriminate—students can't buy cheap tickets and resell them to business travelers. Look at the rules that govern ticket-pricing, and you will see an ingenious implementation of profit-maximizing price discrimination.

Perfect Price Discrimination

Let's return to the example of business travelers and students traveling between Bismarck and Ft. Lauderdale, illustrated in Figure 13-11, and ask what would happen if the airline could distinguish between the two groups of customers in order to charge each a different price.

Clearly, the airline would charge each group its willingness to pay—that is, as we learned in Chapter 4, the maximum that each group is willing to pay. For business travelers, the willingness to pay is $550; for students, it is $150. As we have assumed, the marginal cost is $125 and does not depend on output, making the marginal cost curve a horizontal line. As we noted earlier, we can easily determine the airline's profit: it is the sum of the areas of the rectangle B and the rectangle S.

In this case, the consumers do not get any consumer surplus! The entire surplus is captured by the monopolist in the form of profit. When a monopolist is able to capture the entire surplus in this way, we say that it achieves **perfect price discrimination.**

In general, the greater the number of different prices a monopolist is able to charge, the closer it can get to perfect price discrimination. Figure 13-12 shows a monopolist facing a downward-sloping demand curve, a monopolist who we assume is able to charge different prices to different groups of consumers, with the consumers who are willing to pay the most being charged the most.

In panel (a) the monopolist charges two different prices; in panel (b) the monopolist charges three different prices. Two things are apparent:

- The greater the number of prices the monopolist charges, the lower the lowest price—that is, some consumers will pay prices that approach marginal cost.
- The greater the number of prices the monopolist charges, the more money it extracts from consumers.

With a very large number of different prices, the picture would look like panel (c), a case of perfect price discrimination. Here, consumers least willing to buy the good pay marginal cost, and the entire consumer surplus is extracted as profit.

Both our airline example and the example in Figure 13-12 can be used to make another point: a monopolist that can engage in perfect price discrimination doesn't cause any inefficiency! The reason is that the source of inefficiency is eliminated: all potential consumers who are willing to purchase the good at a price equal to or above marginal cost are able to do so. The perfectly price-discriminating monopolist manages to "scoop up" all consumers by offering some of them lower prices than it charges others.

Perfect price discrimination is almost never possible in practice. At a fundamental level, the inability to achieve perfect price discrimination is a problem of prices as economic signals, a phenomenon we noted in Chapter 4.

When prices work as economic signals, they convey the information needed to ensure that all mutually beneficial transactions will indeed occur: the market price signals the seller's cost, and a consumer signals willingness to pay by purchasing the good whenever that willingness to pay is at least as high as the market price.

The problem in reality, however, is that prices are often not perfect signals: a consumer's true willingness to pay can be disguised, as by a business traveler who claims to be a student when buying a ticket in order to obtain a

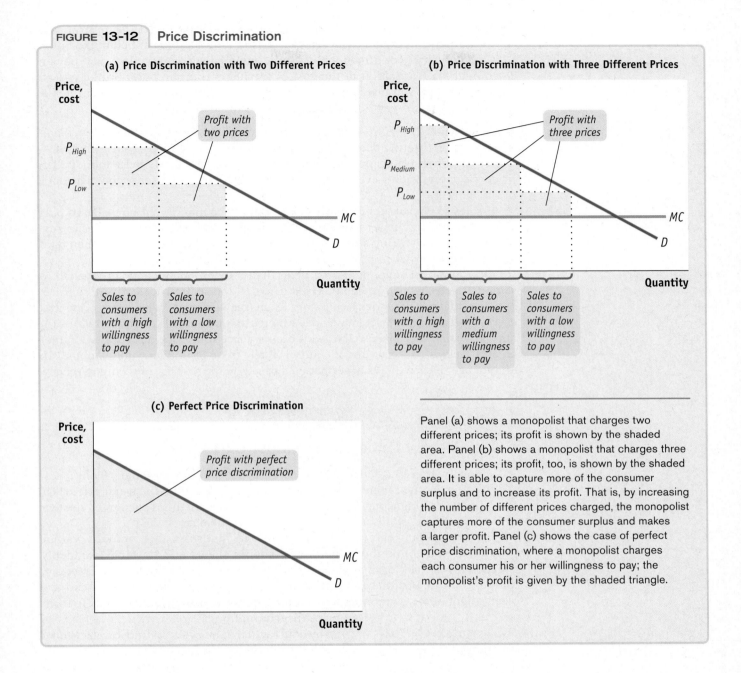

FIGURE 13-12 Price Discrimination

(a) Price Discrimination with Two Different Prices

(b) Price Discrimination with Three Different Prices

(c) Perfect Price Discrimination

Panel (a) shows a monopolist that charges two different prices; its profit is shown by the shaded area. Panel (b) shows a monopolist that charges three different prices; its profit, too, is shown by the shaded area. It is able to capture more of the consumer surplus and to increase its profit. That is, by increasing the number of different prices charged, the monopolist captures more of the consumer surplus and makes a larger profit. Panel (c) shows the case of perfect price discrimination, where a monopolist charges each consumer his or her willingness to pay; the monopolist's profit is given by the shaded triangle.

lower fare. When such disguises work, a monopolist cannot achieve perfect price discrimination.

However, monopolists do try to move in the direction of perfect price discrimination through a variety of pricing strategies. Common techniques for price discrimination include the following:

- *Advance purchase restrictions.* Prices are lower for those who purchase well in advance (or in some cases for those who purchase at the last minute). This separates those who are likely to shop for better prices from those who won't.

- *Volume discounts.* Often the price is lower if you buy a large quantity. For a consumer who plans to consume a lot of a good, the cost of the last unit—the marginal cost to the consumer—is considerably less than the average price. This separates those who plan to buy a lot and so are likely to be more sensitive to price from those who don't.

- *Two-part tariffs.* With a two-part tariff, a customer pays a flat fee upfront and then a per-unit fee on each item purchased. So in a discount club like Sam's Club (which is not a monopolist but a monopolistic competitor), you pay an annual fee in addition to the cost of the items you purchase. So the cost of the first item you buy is in effect much higher than that of subsequent items, making the two-part tariff behave like a volume discount.

Our discussion also helps explain why government policies on monopoly typically focus on preventing deadweight losses, not preventing price discrimination—unless it causes serious issues of equity. Compared to a single-price monopolist, price discrimination—even when it is not perfect—can increase the efficiency of the market.

If sales to consumers formerly priced out of the market but now able to purchase the good at a lower price generate enough surplus to offset the loss in surplus to those now facing a higher price and no longer buying the good, then total surplus increases when price discrimination is introduced.

An example of this might be a drug that is disproportionately prescribed to senior citizens, who are often on fixed incomes and so are very sensitive to price. A policy that allows a drug company to charge senior citizens a low price and everyone else a high price may indeed increase total surplus compared to a situation in which everyone is charged the same price. But price discrimination that creates serious concerns about equity is likely to be prohibited—for example, an ambulance service that charges patients based on the severity of their emergency.

ECONOMICS ▶ *in Action*

Sales, Factory Outlets, and Ghost Cities

Have you ever wondered why department stores occasionally hold sales, offering their merchandise for considerably less than the usual prices? Or why, driving along America's highways, you sometimes encounter clusters of "factory outlet" stores a few hours away from the nearest city?

These familiar features of the economic landscape are actually rather peculiar if you think about them: why should sheets and towels be suddenly cheaper for a week each winter, or raincoats be offered for less in Freeport, Maine, than in Boston? In each case the answer is that the sellers—who are often oligopolists or monopolistic competitors—are engaged in a subtle form of price discrimination.

Why hold regular sales of sheets and towels? Stores are aware that some consumers buy these goods only when they discover that they need them; they are not likely to put a lot of effort into searching for the best price and so have a relatively low price elasticity of demand. So the store wants to charge high prices for customers who come in on an ordinary day.

But shoppers who plan ahead, looking for the lowest price, will wait until there is a sale. By scheduling such sales only now and then, the store is in effect able to price-discriminate between high-elasticity and low-elasticity customers.

An outlet store serves the same purpose: by offering merchandise for low prices, but only at a considerable distance away, a seller is able to establish a separate market for those customers who are willing to make the effort to search out lower prices—and who therefore have a relatively high price elasticity of demand.

Periodic sales allow stores to price-discriminate between their high-elasticity and low-elasticity customers.

Finally, let's return to airline tickets to mention one of the truly odd features of their prices. Often a flight from one major destination to another—say, from Chicago to Los Angeles—is cheaper than a much shorter flight to a smaller city—say, from Chicago to Salt Lake City. Again, the reason is a difference in the price elasticity of demand: customers have a choice of many airlines between Chicago and Los Angeles, so the demand for any one flight is quite elastic; customers have very little choice in flights to a small city, so the demand is much less elastic.

But often there is a flight between two major destinations that makes a stop along the way—say, a flight from Chicago to Los Angeles with a stop in Salt Lake City. In these cases, it is sometimes cheaper to fly to the more distant city than to the city that is a stop along the way. For example, it may be cheaper to purchase a ticket to Los Angeles and get off in Salt Lake City than to purchase a ticket to Salt Lake City! It sounds ridiculous but makes perfect sense given the logic of monopoly pricing.

So why don't passengers simply buy a ticket from Chicago to Los Angeles, but get off at Salt Lake City? Well, some do—but the airlines, understandably, make it difficult for customers to find out about such "ghost cities." In addition, the airline will not allow you to check baggage only part of the way if you have a ticket for the final destination. And airlines refuse to honor tickets for return flights when a passenger has not completed all the legs of the outbound flight. All these restrictions are meant to enforce the separation of markets necessary to allow price discrimination.

Check Your Understanding   13-4

1. True or false? Explain your answer.
   a. A single-price monopolist sells to some customers that a price-discriminating monopolist refuses to.
   b. A price-discriminating monopolist creates more inefficiency than a single-price monopolist because it captures more of the consumer surplus.
   c. Under price discrimination, a customer with highly elastic demand will pay a lower price than a customer with inelastic demand.

2. Which of the following are cases of price discrimination and which are not? In the cases of price discrimination, identify the consumers with high and those with low price elasticity of demand.
   a. Damaged merchandise is marked down.
   b. Restaurants have senior citizen discounts.
   c. Food manufacturers place discount coupons for their merchandise in newspapers.
   d. Airline tickets cost more during the summer peak flying season.

Solutions appear at back of book.

▼ **Quick Review**

• Not every monopolist is a **single-price monopolist.** Many monopolists, as well as oligopolists and monopolistic competitors, engage in **price discrimination.**

• Price discrimination is profitable when consumers differ in their sensitivity to the price. A monopolist charges higher prices to low-elasticity consumers and lower prices to high-elasticity ones.

• A monopolist able to charge each consumer his or her willingness to pay for the good achieves **perfect price discrimination** and does not cause inefficiency because all mutually beneficial transactions are exploited.

Amazon and Hachette Go to War

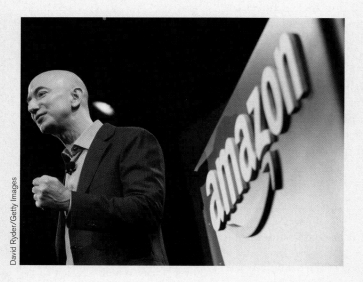

David Ryder/Getty Images

In May 2014, all-out war broke out between Amazon, the third largest U.S. book retailer, and Hachette, the fourth largest book publisher. Suddenly Amazon took weeks to deliver Hachette publications (paper and e-books), including best-sellers from authors like Stephen Colbert, Dan Brown, and J.D. Salinger, meanwhile offering shoppers suggestions for non-Hachette books as alternatives. In addition, pre-order options for forthcoming Hachette books—including one by J.K. Rowling of Harry Potter fame—disappeared from Amazon's website along with many other Hachette books. These same books were readily available, often at lower prices, at rival book retailers, such as barnesandnoble.com.

All publishers pay retailers a share of sales prices. What set off hostilities in this case was Amazon's demand that Hachette raise Amazon's share from 30 to 50%. This was a familiar story: Amazon has demanded ever-larger percentages during yearly contract negotiations. Since it won't carry a publisher's books without an agreement, protracted disagreement and the resulting loss of sales are disastrous for publishers. This time, however, Hachette refused to give in and went public with Amazon's demands.

Amazon claimed that the publisher could pay more out of its profit margin —around 75% on e-books, 60% on paperbacks, and 40% on hardcovers. Indeed, Amazon openly admitted that its long-term objective was to displace publishers altogether, and deal directly with authors itself. And it received support from some authors who had been rejected by traditional publishers but succeeded by selling directly to readers via Amazon. But publishers countered that Amazon's calculations ignored the costs of editing, marketing, advertising, and at times supporting struggling writers until they became successful. Amazon, they claimed, would eventually destroy the book industry.

Meanwhile, Amazon had other problems: in July 2014 it announced that it lost $800 million in the previous quarter because profits from sales were not paying for its vast warehouse and delivery system. In its 20 years of existence Amazon has never made a profit, and investors were growing impatient. As one industry analyst commented, "Skepticism is increasing. It's hard to have $20 billion in revenue and not make any money. It's a real feat."

As this book went to press, Amazon was in a public relations battle with Authors United, a group of over 900 best-selling authors who protested that "..no bookseller should block the sale of books or otherwise prevent or discourage customers from ordering or receiving the books they want." A leader of that group, Douglas Preston, a best-selling Hachette author of thrillers, has seen sales of his books drop by over 60% since the conflict began. Speaking of the comfortable lifestyle that his successful writing supports, Preston observed that if Amazon should decide not to sell his books at all, "All this goes away."

QUESTIONS FOR THOUGHT

1. What is the source of surplus in this industry? Who generates it? How is it divided among the various agents (author, publisher, and retailer)?

2. What are the various sources of market power here? What is at risk for the various parties?

SUMMARY

1. There are four main types of market structure based on the number of firms in the industry and product differentiation: perfect competition, monopoly, oligopoly, and monopolistic competition.

2. A **monopolist** is a producer who is the sole supplier of a good without close substitutes. An industry controlled by a monopolist is a **monopoly.**

3. The key difference between a monopoly and a perfectly competitive industry is that a single perfectly competitive firm faces a horizontal demand curve but a monopolist faces a downward-sloping demand curve. This gives the monopolist **market power,** the ability to raise the market price by reducing output compared to a perfectly competitive firm.

4. To persist, a monopoly must be protected by a **barrier to entry.** This can take the form of control of a natural resource or input, increasing returns to scale that give rise to **natural monopoly,** technological superiority, a **network externality,** or government rules that prevent entry by other firms, such as **patents** or **copyrights.**

5. The marginal revenue of a monopolist is composed of a quantity effect (the price received from the additional unit) and a price effect (the reduction in the price at which all units are sold). Because of the price effect, a monopolist's marginal revenue is always less than the market price, and the marginal revenue curve lies below the demand curve.

6. At the monopolist's profit-maximizing output level, marginal cost equals marginal revenue, which is less than market price. At the perfectly competitive firm's profit-maximizing output level, marginal cost equals the market price. So in comparison to perfectly competitive industries, monopolies produce less, charge higher prices, and earn profits in both the short run and the long run.

7. A monopoly creates deadweight losses by charging a price above marginal cost: the loss in consumer surplus exceeds the monopolist's profit. Thus monopolies are a source of market failure and should be prevented or broken up, except in the case of natural monopolies. **Monopsony,** an industry in which there is only one buyer of a good, is more rare than cases of monopoly. The **monopsonist** can affect the price of the good it buys: it captures surplus from sellers by reducing how much it purchases and thereby lowers the price. It creates deadweight loss by reducing the level of the good transacted to inefficiently low levels.

8. Natural monopolies can still cause deadweight losses. To limit these losses, governments sometimes impose **public ownership** and at other times impose **price regulation.** A price ceiling on a monopolist, as opposed to a perfectly competitive industry, need not cause shortages and can increase total surplus.

9. Not all monopolists are **single-price monopolists.** Monopolists, as well as oligopolists and monopolistic competitors, often engage in **price discrimination** to make higher profits, using various techniques to differentiate consumers based on their sensitivity to price and charging those with less elastic demand higher prices. A monopolist that achieves **perfect price discrimination** charges each consumer a price equal to his or her willingness to pay and captures the total surplus in the market. Although perfect price discrimination creates no inefficiency, it is practically impossible to implement.

KEY TERMS

Monopolist, p. 387
Monopoly, p. 387
Market power, p. 388
Barrier to entry, p. 389
Natural monopoly, p. 389

Network externality, p. 390
Patent, p. 391
Copyright, p. 391
Public ownership, p. 403
Price regulation, p. 403

Monopsony, p. 405
Monopsonist, p. 405
Single-price monopolist, p. 407
Price discrimination, p. 407
Perfect price discrimination, p. 410

PROBLEMS

1. Each of the following firms possesses market power. Explain its source.
   a. Merck, the producer of the patented cholesterol-lowering drug Zetia
   b. WaterWorks, a provider of piped water
   c. Chiquita, a supplier of bananas and owner of most banana plantations
   d. The Walt Disney Company, the creators of Mickey Mouse

2. Skyscraper City has a subway system, for which a one-way fare is $1.50. There is pressure on the mayor to reduce the fare by one-third, to $1.00. The mayor is dismayed, thinking that this will mean Skyscraper City is losing one-third of its revenue from sales of subway tickets. The mayor's economic adviser reminds her that she is focusing only on the price effect and ignoring the quantity effect. Explain why the mayor's estimate of a one-third loss of revenue is likely to be an overestimate. Illustrate with a diagram.

3. Bob, Bill, Ben, and Brad Baxter have just made a documentary movie about their basketball team. They are thinking about making the movie available for download on the internet, and they can act as a single-price monopolist if they choose to. Each time the movie is downloaded, their internet service provider charges them a fee of $4. The Baxter brothers are arguing about which price to charge customers per download. The accompanying table shows the demand schedule for their film.

Price of download	Quantity of downloads demanded
$10	0
8	1
6	3
4	6
2	10
0	15

a. Calculate the total revenue and the marginal revenue per download.

b. Bob is proud of the film and wants as many people as possible to down load it. Which price would he choose? How many downloads would be sold?

c. Bill wants as much total revenue as possible. Which price would he choose? How many downloads would be sold?

d. Ben wants to maximize profit. Which price would he choose? How many downloads would be sold?

e. Brad wants to charge the efficient price. Which price would he choose? How many downloads would be sold?

4. Jimmy's room overlooks a major league baseball stadium. He decides to rent a telescope for $50.00 a week and charge his friends to use it to peep at the games for 30 seconds. He can act as a single-price monopolist for renting out "peeps." For each person who takes a 30-second peep, it costs Jimmy $0.20 to clean the eyepiece. This table shows the information Jimmy has gathered about the weekly demand for the service.

Price of peep	Quantity of peeps demanded
$1.20	0
1.00	100
0.90	150
0.80	200
0.70	250
0.60	300
0.50	350
0.40	400
0.30	450
0.20	500
0.10	550

a. For each price in the table, calculate the total revenue from selling peeps and the marginal revenue per peep.

b. At what quantity will Jimmy's profit be maximized? What price will he charge? What will his total profit be?

c. Jimmy's landlady complains about all visitors and tells him to stop selling peeps. But, if he pays her $0.20 for every peep he sells, she won't complain. What effect does the $0.20-per-peep bribe have on Jimmy's marginal cost per peep? What is the new profit-maximizing quantity of peeps? What effect does the $0.20-per-peep bribe have on Jimmy's total profit?

5. Suppose that De Beers is a single-price monopolist in the diamond market. De Beers has five potential customers: Raquel, Jackie, Joan, Mia, and Sophia. Each of these customers will buy at most one diamond—and only if the price is just equal to, or lower than, her willingness to pay. Raquel's willingness to pay is $400; Jackie's, $300; Joan's, $200; Mia's, $100; and Sophia's, $0. De Beers's marginal cost per diamond is $100. The result is a demand schedule for diamonds as follows:

Price of diamond	Quantity of diamonds demanded
$500	0
400	1
300	2
200	3
100	4
0	5

a. Calculate De Beers's total revenue and its marginal revenue. From your calculation, draw the demand curve and the marginal revenue curve.

b. Explain why De Beers faces a downward-sloping demand curve and why the marginal revenue from an additional diamond sale is less than the price of the diamond.

c. Suppose De Beers currently charges $200 for its diamonds. If it lowers the price to $100, how large is the price effect? How large is the quantity effect?

d. Add the marginal cost curve to your diagram from part a and determine which quantity maximizes De Beers's profit and which price De Beers will charge.

6. Use the demand schedule for diamonds given in Problem 5. The marginal cost of producing diamonds is constant at $100. There is no fixed cost.

a. If De Beers charges the monopoly price, how large is the individual consumer surplus that each buyer experiences? Calculate total consumer surplus by summing the individual consumer surpluses. How large is producer surplus?

Suppose that upstart Russian and Asian producers enter the market and it becomes perfectly competitive.

b. What is the perfectly competitive price? What quantity will be sold in this perfectly competitive market?

c. At the competitive price and quantity, how large is the consumer surplus that each buyer experiences? How large is total consumer surplus? How large is producer surplus?

d. Compare your answer to part c to your answer to part a. How large is the deadweight loss associated with monopoly in this case?

7. Use the demand schedule for diamonds given in Problem 5. De Beers is a monopolist, but it can now price-discriminate perfectly among all five of its potential customers. De Beers's marginal cost is constant at $100. There is no fixed cost.

a. If De Beers can price-discriminate perfectly, to which customers will it sell diamonds and at what prices?

b. How large is each individual consumer surplus? How large is total consumer surplus? Calculate producer surplus by summing the producer surplus generated by each sale.

8. Download Records decides to release an album by the group Mary and the Little Lamb. It produces the album with no fixed cost, but the total cost of creating a digital album and paying Mary her royalty is $6 per album. Download Records can act as a single-price monopolist. Its marketing division finds that the demand schedule for the album is as shown in the accompanying table.

Price of album	Quantity of albums demanded
$22	0
20	1,000
18	2,000
16	3,000
14	4,000
12	5,000
10	6,000
8	7,000

a. Calculate the total revenue and the marginal revenue per album.

b. The marginal cost of producing each album is constant at $6. To maximize profit, what level of output should Download Records choose, and which price should it charge for each album?

c. Mary renegotiates her contract and will be paid a higher royalty per album. So the marginal cost rises to be constant at $14. To maximize profit, what level of output should Download Records now choose, and which price should it charge for each album?

9. This diagram illustrates your local electricity company's natural monopoly. It shows the demand curve for kilowatt-hours (kWh) of electricity, the company's marginal revenue (*MR*) curve, its marginal cost (*MC*) curve, and its average total cost (*ATC*) curve. The government wants to regulate the monopolist by imposing a price ceiling.

a. If the government does not regulate this monopolist, which price will it charge? Illustrate the inefficiency this creates by shading the deadweight loss from monopoly.

b. If the government imposes a price ceiling equal to the marginal cost, $0.30, will the monopolist make profits or lose money? Shade the area of profit (or loss) for the monopolist. If the government does impose this price ceiling, do you think the firm will continue to produce in the long run?

c. If the government imposes a price ceiling of $0.50, will the monopolist make a profit, lose money, or break even?

10. The Collegetown movie theater serves 900 students and 100 professors in town. Each student's willingness to pay for a movie ticket is $5. Each professor's willingness to pay is $10. Each will buy only one ticket. The movie theater's marginal cost per ticket is constant at $3, and there is no fixed cost.

a. Suppose the movie theater cannot price-discriminate and charges both students and professors the same price per ticket. If the movie theater charges $5, who will buy tickets and what will the movie theater's profit be? How large is consumer surplus?

b. If the movie theater charges $10, who will buy movie tickets and what will the movie theater's profit be? How large is consumer surplus?

c. Assume the movie theater can price-discriminate between students and professors by requiring students to show their student ID, charging students $5 and professors $10, how much profit will the movie theater make? How large is consumer surplus?

11. A monopolist knows that in order to expand the quantity of output it produces from 8 to 9 units it must lower the price of its output from $2 to $1. Calculate the quantity effect and the price effect. Use these results to calculate the monopolist's marginal revenue of producing the 9th unit. The marginal cost of producing the 9th unit is positive. Is it a good idea for the monopolist to produce the 9th unit?

12. In the United States, the Federal Trade Commission (FTC) is charged with promoting competition and challenging mergers that would likely lead to higher prices. Several years ago, Staples and Office Depot, two of the largest office supply superstores, announced their agreement to merge.

a. Some critics of the merger argued that, in many parts of the country, a merger between the two companies would create a monopoly in the office supply superstore market. Based on the FTC's argument and its mission to challenge mergers that would likely lead to higher prices, do you think it allowed the merger?

b. Staples and Office Depot argued that, while in some parts of the country they might create a monopoly in the office supply superstore market, the FTC should consider the larger market for all office supplies, which includes many smaller stores that sell office supplies (such as grocery stores and other retailers). In that market, Staples and Office Depot would face competition from many other, smaller stores. If the market for all office supplies is the relevant market that the FTC should consider, would it make the FTC more or less likely to allow the merger?

13. Prior to the late 1990s, the same company that generated your electricity also distributed it to you over high-voltage lines. Since then, 16 states and the District of Columbia have begun separating the generation from the distribution of electricity, allowing competition between electricity generators and between electricity distributors.

a. Assume that the market for electricity distribution was and remains a natural monopoly. Use a graph to illustrate the market for electricity distribution if the government sets price equal to average total cost.

b. Assume that deregulation of electricity generation creates a perfectly competitive market. Also assume that electricity generation does not exhibit the characteristics of a natural monopoly. Use a graph to illustrate the cost curves in the long-run equilibrium for an individual firm in this industry.

14. Explain the following situations.

a. In Europe, many cell phone service providers give away for free what would otherwise be very expensive cell phones when a service contract is purchased. Why might a company want to do that?

b. In the United Kingdom, the country's antitrust authority prohibited the cell phone service provider Vodaphone from offering a plan that gave customers free calls to other Vodaphone customers. Why might Vodaphone have wanted to offer these calls for free? Why might a government want to step in and ban this practice? Why might it not be a good idea for a government to interfere in this way?

15. The 2014 announcement that Time Warner Cable and Comcast intended to merge prompted questions of monopoly because the combined company would supply cable access to an overwhelming majority of Americans. It also raised questions of monopsony since the combined company would be virtually the only purchaser of programming for broadcast shows. Assume the merger occurs: in each of the following, determine whether it is evidence of monopoly, monopsony, or neither.

a. The monthly cable fee for consumers increases significantly more than the increase in the cost of producing and delivering programs over cable.

b. Companies that advertise on cable TV find that they must pay higher rates for advertising.

c. Companies that produce broadcast shows find they must produce more shows for the same amount they were paid before.

d. Consumers find that there are more shows available for the same monthly cable fee.

16. Walmart is the world's largest retailer. As a consequence, it has sufficient bargaining power to push its suppliers to lower their prices so it can honor its slogan of "Always Low Prices" for its customers.

a. Is Walmart acting like a monopolist or monopsonist when purchasing goods from suppliers? Explain.

b. How does Walmart affect the consumer surplus of its customers? The producer surplus of its suppliers?

c. Over time, what is likely to happen to the quality of products produced by Walmart suppliers?

WORK IT OUT

For interactive, step-by-step help in solving the following problem, visit LaunchPad by using the URL on the back cover of this book.

17. Consider an industry with the demand curve (*D*) and marginal cost curve (*MC*) shown in the accompanying diagram. There is no fixed cost. If the industry is a single-price monopoly, the monopolist's marginal revenue curve would be *MR*. Answer the following questions by naming the appropriate points or areas.

a. If the industry is perfectly competitive, what will be the total quantity produced? At what price?

b. Which area reflects consumer surplus under perfect competition?

c. If the industry is a single-price monopoly, what quantity will the monopolist produce? Which price will it charge?

d. Which area reflects the single-price monopolist's profit?

e. Which area reflects consumer surplus under single-price monopoly?

f. Which area reflects the deadweight loss to society from single-price monopoly?

g. If the monopolist can price-discriminate perfectly, what quantity will the perfectly price-discriminating monopolist produce?

Oligopoly

▶ **What You Will Learn
in This Chapter**

▪ **The meaning of oligopoly, and
why it occurs**

▪ **Why oligopolists have an
incentive to act in ways that
reduce their combined profit,
and why they can benefit from
collusion**

▪ **How our understanding of
oligopoly can be enhanced by
using game theory, especially
the concept of the prisoners'
dilemma**

▪ **How repeated interactions
among oligopolists can help them
achieve tacit collusion**

▪ **How oligopoly works in practice,
under the legal constraints of
antitrust policy**

CAUGHT IN THE ACT

Bryan Smith/Zuma Press

The law catches up with a colluding oligopolist.

THE AGRICULTURAL PRODUCTS company Archer Daniels Midland (also known as ADM) has often described itself as "supermarket to the world." Its name is familiar to many Americans not only because of its important role in the economy but also because of its advertising and sponsorship of public television programs. But on October 25, 1993, ADM itself was on camera.

On that day executives from ADM and its Japanese competitor Ajinomoto met at the Marriott Hotel in Irvine, California, to discuss the market for lysine, an additive used in animal feed. (How is lysine produced? It's excreted by genetically engineered bacteria.) In this and subsequent meetings, the two companies joined with several other competitors to set targets for the market price of lysine, behavior called *price-fixing*. Each company agreed to limit its production in order to achieve those targets. Agreeing

on specific limits would be their biggest challenge—or so they thought.

What the participants in the meeting didn't know was that they had a bigger problem: the FBI had bugged the room and was filming them with a hidden camera.

What the companies were doing was illegal. To understand why it was illegal and why the companies were doing it anyway, we need to examine the issues posed by industries that are neither perfectly competitive nor purely monopolistic.

In this chapter we focus on *oligopoly*, a type of market structure in which there are only a few producers. As we'll see, oligopoly is a very important reality—much more important, in fact, than monopoly and arguably more typical of modern economies than perfect competition.

Although much that we have learned about both perfect competition and

monopoly is relevant to oligopoly, oligopoly also raises some entirely new issues. Among other things, firms in an oligopoly are often tempted to engage in the kind of behavior that got ADM, Ajinomoto, and other lysine producers into trouble with the law. Over the past few years, there have been numerous investigations and some convictions for price-fixing in a variety of industries, from insurance to elevators to computer chips. For example, in 2012, the European Union, which has laws similar to those in the United States, fined six electronics companies $1.92 billion (yes, that's billion) for price-fixing of television components.

We will begin by examining what oligopoly is and why it is so important. Then we'll turn to the behavior of oligopolistic industries. Finally, we'll look at *antitrust policy,* which is primarily concerned with trying to keep oligopolies "well behaved."

An **oligopoly** is an industry with only a small number of producers. A producer in such an industry is known as an **oligopolist.**

When no one firm has a monopoly, but producers nonetheless realize that they can affect market prices, an industry is characterized by **imperfect competition.**

The Prevalence of Oligopoly

At the time of that elaborately bugged meeting, no one company controlled the world lysine industry, but there were only a few major producers. An industry with only a few sellers is known as an **oligopoly;** a firm in such an industry is known as an **oligopolist.**

Oligopolists obviously compete with one another for sales. But neither ADM nor Ajinomoto were like a firm in a perfectly competitive industry, which takes the price at which it can sell its product as given. Each of these firms knew that its decision about how much to produce would affect the market price. That is, like monopolists, each of the firms had some *market power.* So the competition in this industry wasn't "perfect."

Economists refer to a situation in which firms compete but also possess market power—which enables them to affect market prices—as **imperfect competition.** As we saw in Chapter 13, there are actually two important forms of imperfect competition: oligopoly and *monopolistic competition.* Of these, oligopoly is probably the more important in practice.

Although lysine is a multibillion-dollar business, it is not exactly a product familiar to most consumers. However, many familiar goods and services are supplied by only a few competing sellers, which means the industries in question are oligopolies. For example, most air routes are served by only two or three airlines: in recent years, regularly scheduled shuttle service between New York and either Boston or Washington, D.C., has been provided only by Delta and US Airways. Four firms—Kellogg, General Mills, Post, and Quaker—control 85% of the breakfast cereal market. Three firms—Apple, HTC, and Samsung—control 65% of the smartphone market. Most cola beverages are sold by Coke and Pepsi. This list could go on for many pages.

It's important to realize that an oligopoly isn't necessarily made up of large firms. What matters isn't size per se; the question is how many competitors there are. When a small town has only two grocery stores, grocery service there is just as much an oligopoly as air shuttle service between New York and Washington.

Why are oligopolies so prevalent? Essentially, oligopoly is the result of the same factors that sometimes produce monopoly, but in somewhat weaker form. Probably the most important source of oligopoly is the existence of *increasing returns to scale,* which give bigger producers a cost advantage over smaller ones. When these effects are very strong, they lead to monopoly; when they are not that strong, they lead to an industry with a small number of firms.

For example, larger grocery stores typically have lower costs than smaller ones. But the advantages of large scale taper off once grocery stores are reasonably large, which is why two or three stores often survive in small towns.

If oligopoly is so common, why has most of this book focused on competition in industries where the number of sellers is very large? And why did we study monopoly, which is relatively uncommon, first? The answer has two parts.

First, much of what we learn from the study of perfectly competitive markets—about costs, entry and exit, and efficiency—remains valid despite the fact that many industries are not perfectly competitive. Second, the analysis of oligopoly turns out to present some puzzles for which there are no easy solutions. It is almost always a good idea—in exams and in life in general—first to deal with the questions you can answer, then to puzzle over the harder ones. We have simply followed the same strategy, developing the relatively clear-cut theories of perfect competition and monopoly first, and only then turning to the puzzles presented by oligopoly.

ECONOMICS ▶ *in Action*

Is It an Oligopoly or Not?

In practice, it is not always easy to determine an industry's market structure just by looking at the number of sellers. Many oligopolistic industries contain a number of small "niche" producers, which don't really compete with the major players. For example, the U.S. airline industry includes a number of regional airlines like New Mexico Airlines, which flies propeller planes between Albuquerque and Carlsbad, New Mexico; if you count these carriers, the U.S. airline industry contains nearly a hundred sellers, which doesn't sound like competition among a small group. But there are only a handful of national competitors like American and United, and on many routes, as we've seen, there are only two or three competitors.

To get a better picture of market structure, economists often use a measure called the *Herfindahl–Hirschman Index*, or HHI. The HHI for an industry is the square of each firm's market share summed over the firms in the industry. (In Chapter 12 you learned that *market share* is the percentage of sales in the market accounted for by that firm.) For example, if an industry contains only three firms and their market shares are 60%, 25%, and 15%, then the HHI for the industry is:

$$HHI = 60^2 + 25^2 + 15^2 = 4,450$$

By squaring each market share, the HHI calculation produces numbers that are much larger when a larger share of an industry output is dominated by fewer firms. So it's a better measure of just how concentrated the industry is. This is confirmed by the data in Table 14-1. Here, the indexes for industries dominated by a small number of firms, like the personal computer operating systems industry or the wide-body aircraft industry, are many times larger than the index for the retail grocery industry, which has numerous firms of approximately equal size.

The HHI is used by the U.S. Justice Department and the Federal Trade Commission, which have the job of enforcing *antitrust policy,* a topic we'll investigate in more detail later in this chapter. Their mission is to try to ensure that there is adequate competition in an industry by prosecuting price-fixing, breaking up economically inefficient monopolies, and disallowing mergers between firms when it's believed that the merger will reduce competition.

According to Justice Department guidelines, an HHI below 1,500 indicates a strongly competitive market, between 1,500 and 2,500 indicates a somewhat competitive market, and over 2,500 indicates an oligopoly. In an industry with an HHI over 1,500, a merger that results in a significant increase in the HHI will receive special scrutiny and is likely to be disallowed.

However, defining an industry can be tricky. In 2007, Whole Foods and Wild Oats, two purveyors of high-end organic foods, proposed a merger. The Justice Department disallowed it, claiming it would substantially reduce competition and define the industry as consisting of only natural food groceries.

However, this ruling was appealed to a federal court, which found the merger allowable since regular supermarkets now carried organic foods as well, arguing that they would provide sufficient competition after the merger. Yet, in 2011, the

TABLE **14-1**		The HHI for Some Oligopolistic Industries
Industry	**HHI**	**Largest firms**
PC microprocessor	6,190	Intel, AMD
Aircraft	5,008	Boeing, Airbus
Operating systems	4,809	Windows, MacOS, Linux
Smartphone O.S.	4,326	Android, Apple
Warehouse stores	3,730	Costco, Sam's Club
Game consoles	3,706	Nintendo, Xbox, Playstation
Cell phone carriers	2,768	Verizon, AT&T, Sprint, T-Mobile
Tablets	2,306	Apple, Samsung, Amazon ASUS
Diamonds	2,029	De Beers, Alrosa, Rio Tinto
Automobiles	1,131	GM, Ford, Toyota, Chrysler, Honda, Nissan

Sources: www.cpubenchmark.net; thomsonreuters.com; www.statista.com; Neilson; Reuters; Forbes; Edmunds Auto.

Justice Department disallowed the merger between cell-phone carriers AT&T and T-Mobile, in a case in which the relevant industry was much clearer.

Check Your Understanding 14-1

1. Explain why each of the following industries is an oligopoly, not a perfectly competitive industry.
   a. The world oil industry, where a few countries near the Persian Gulf control much of the world's oil reserves
   b. The microprocessor industry, where two firms, Intel and its bitter rival AMD, dominate the technology
   c. The wide-body passenger jet industry, composed of the American firm Boeing and the European firm Airbus, where production is characterized by extremely large fixed cost
2. The accompanying table shows the market shares for search engines in 2013.
   a. Calculate the HHI in this industry.
   b. If Yahoo! and Bing were to merge, what would the HHI be?

Search engine	Market share
Google	67%
Bing	18
Yahoo!	11
Ask	3
AOL	1

Solutions appear at back of book.

Understanding Oligopoly

How much will a firm produce? Up to this point, we have always answered: the quantity that maximizes its profit. Together with its cost curves, the assumption that a firm maximizes profit is enough to determine its output when it is a perfect competitor or a monopolist.

When it comes to oligopoly, however, we run into some difficulties. Indeed, economists often describe the behavior of oligopolistic firms as a "puzzle."

A Duopoly Example

An oligopoly consisting of only two firms is a **duopoly.** Each firm is known as a **duopolist.**

Let's begin looking at the puzzle of oligopoly with the simplest version, an industry in which there are only two producing firms—a **duopoly**—and each is known as a **duopolist.**

Going back to our opening story, imagine that ADM and Ajinomoto are the only two producers of lysine. To make things even simpler, suppose that once a company has incurred the fixed cost needed to produce lysine, the marginal cost of producing another pound is zero. So the companies are concerned only with the revenue they receive from sales.

Table 14-2 shows a hypothetical demand schedule for lysine and the total revenue of the industry at each price–quantity combination.

If this were a perfectly competitive industry, each firm would have an incentive to produce more as long as the market price was above marginal cost. Since the marginal cost is assumed to be zero, this would mean that at equilibrium lysine would be provided free. Firms would produce until price equals zero, yielding a total output of 120 million pounds and zero revenue for both firms.

TABLE 14-2 Deman Schedule for Lysine

Price of lysine (per pound)	Quantity of lysine demanded (millions of pounds)	Total revenue (millions)
$12	0	$0
11	10	110
10	20	200
9	30	270
8	40	320
7	50	350
6	60	360
5	70	350
4	80	320
3	90	270
2	100	200
1	110	110
0	120	0

However, surely the firms would not be that stupid. With only two firms in the industry, each would realize that by producing more, it drives down the market price. So each firm would, like a monopolist, realize that profits would be higher if it and its rival limited their production.

So how much will the two firms produce?

One possibility is that the two companies will engage in **collusion**—they will cooperate to raise their joint profits. The strongest form of collusion is a **cartel,** an arrangement between producers that determines how much each is allowed to produce. The world's most famous cartel is the Organization of Petroleum Exporting Countries (OPEC), described in an Economics in Action later in the chapter.

As its name indicates, OPEC is actually an agreement among governments rather than firms. There's a reason this most famous of cartels is an agreement among governments: cartels among firms are illegal in the United States and many other jurisdictions. But let's ignore the law for a moment (which is, of course, what ADM and Ajinomoto did in real life—to their own detriment).

So suppose that ADM and Ajinomoto were to form a cartel and that this cartel decided to act as if it were a monopolist, maximizing total industry profits. It's obvious from Table 14-2 that in order to maximize the combined profits of the firms, this cartel should set total industry output at 60 million pounds of lysine, which would sell at a price of $6 per pound, leading to revenue of $360 million, the maximum possible.

Then the only question would be how much of that 60 million pounds each firm gets to produce. A "fair" solution might be for each firm to produce 30 million pounds with revenues for each firm of $180 million.

But even if the two firms agreed on such a deal, they might have a problem: each of the firms would have an incentive to break its word and produce more than the agreed-upon quantity.

Collusion and Competition

Suppose that the presidents of ADM and Ajinomoto were to agree that each would produce 30 million pounds of lysine over the next year. Both would understand that this plan maximizes their combined profits. And both would have an incentive to cheat.

To see why, consider what would happen if Ajinomoto honored its agreement, producing only 30 million pounds, but ADM ignored its promise and produced 40 million pounds. This increase in total output would drive the price down from $6 to $5 per pound, the price at which 70 million pounds are demanded. The industry's total revenue would fall from $360 million ($6 × 60 million pounds) to $350 million ($5 × 70 million pounds). However, ADM's revenue would *rise,* from $180 million to $200 million. Since we are assuming a marginal cost of zero, this would mean a $20 million increase in ADM's profits.

But Ajinomoto's president might make exactly the same calculation. And if both firms were to produce 40 million pounds of lysine, the price would drop to $4 per pound. So each firm's profits would fall, from $180 million to $160 million.

Why do individual firms have an incentive to produce more than the quantity that maximizes their joint profits? Because neither firm has as strong an incentive to limit its output as a true monopolist would.

Let's go back for a minute to the theory of monopoly. We know that a profit-maximizing monopolist sets marginal cost (which in this case is zero) equal to marginal revenue. But what is marginal revenue? Recall that producing an additional unit of a good has two effects:

Sellers engage in **collusion** when they cooperate to raise their joint profits. A **cartel** is an agreement among several producers to obey output restrictions in order to increase their joint profits.

When firms ignore the effects of their actions on each others' profits, they engage in **noncooperative behavior.**

1. A positive *quantity* effect: one more unit is sold, increasing total revenue by the price at which that unit is sold.
2. A negative *price* effect: in order to sell one more unit, the monopolist must cut the market price on *all* units sold.

The negative price effect is the reason marginal revenue for a monopolist is less than the market price. In the case of oligopoly, when considering the effect of increasing production, a firm is concerned only with the price effect on its *own* units of output, not those of its fellow oligopolists. Both ADM and Ajinomoto suffer a negative price effect if ADM decides to produce extra lysine and so drives down the price. But ADM cares only about the negative price effect on the units it produces, not about the loss to Ajinomoto.

This tells us that an individual firm in an oligopolistic industry faces a smaller price effect from an additional unit of output than does a monopolist; therefore, the marginal revenue that such a firm calculates is higher. So it will seem to be profitable for any one company in an oligopoly to increase production, even if that increase reduces the profits of the industry as a whole. But if everyone thinks that way, the result is that everyone earns a lower profit!

Until now, we have been able to analyze producer behavior by asking what a producer should do to maximize profits. But even if ADM and Ajinomoto are both trying to maximize profits, what does this predict about their behavior? Will they engage in collusion, reaching and holding to an agreement that maximizes their combined profits? Or will they engage in **noncooperative behavior,** with each firm acting in its own self-interest, even though this has the effect of driving down everyone's profits? Both strategies sound like profit maximization. Which will actually describe their behavior?

Now you see why oligopoly presents a puzzle: there are only a small number of players, making collusion a real possibility. If there were dozens or hundreds of firms, it would be safe to assume they would behave noncooperatively. Yet when there are only a handful of firms in an industry, it's hard to determine whether collusion will actually materialize.

Since collusion is ultimately more profitable than noncooperative behavior, firms have an incentive to collude if they can. One way to do so is to formalize it—sign an agreement (maybe even make a legal contract) or establish some financial incentives for the companies to set their prices high. But in the United States and many other nations, you can't do that—at least not legally. Companies cannot make a legal contract to keep prices high: not only is the contract unenforceable, but writing it is a one-way ticket to jail. Neither can they sign an informal "gentlemen's agreement," which lacks the force of law but perhaps rests on threats of retaliation—that's illegal, too.

In fact, executives from rival companies rarely meet without lawyers present, who make sure that the conversation does not stray into inappropriate territory. Even hinting at how nice it would be if prices were higher can bring you an unwelcome interview with the Justice Department or the Federal Trade Commission.

For example, in 2003 the Justice Department launched a price-fixing case against Monsanto and other large producers of genetically modified seed. The Justice Department was alerted by a series of meetings held between Monsanto and Pioneer Hi-Bred International, two companies that account for 60% of the U.S. market in maize and soybean seed. The two companies, parties to a licensing agreement involving genetically modified seed, claimed that no illegal discussions of price-fixing occurred in those meetings. But the fact that the two firms discussed prices as part of the licensing agreement was enough to trigger action by the Justice Department.

Sometimes, as we've seen, oligopolistic firms just ignore the rules. But more often they find ways to achieve collusion without a formal agreement, as we'll soon see.

ECONOMICS ▶ *in Action*

Bitter Chocolate?

The lysine price-fixing cartel prosecution is an especially memorable case because investigators had indisputable evidence of collusion in the form of recorded conversations. However, without solid evidence, the prosecution of price-fixing can be a tricky business, made clear by the different outcomes of Canadian and American investigations into price-fixing in the chocolate industry in 2013 and 2014.

Prompted by disclosures by Cadbury Canada of its collusion with the other three major Canadian chocolate makers—Hershey Canada, Nestlé Canada, and Mars Canada, Canadian regulators began an investigation into price-fixing in the Canadian chocolate market in 2007. In the case, Cadbury Canada received immunity from prosecution. While Hershey Canada eventually pleaded guilty and paid a nearly $4 million fine, Nestlé Canada and Mars Canada refused to settle. In the ensuing court proceedings, 13 Cadbury Canada executives voluntarily provided information about contacts with the other companies, including a 2005 episode in which a Nestlé Canada executive handed over a brown envelope containing details about a forthcoming price hike to a Cadbury Canada employee. And, according to affidavits filed in court, top executives of Hershey Canada, Nestlé Canada, and Mars Canada met secretly to set prices. In 2013, after protracted litigation, all four producers agreed to settle, paying a fine of more than $23 million to be distributed among consumers.

Are chocolate makers engaging in price-fixing?

However, prosecutions south of the border were much less successful. Many of the largest U.S. grocery stores and snack retailers were convinced that they, too, had been the victims of collusion. So in 2010, one of those stores, SUPERVALU, filed a lawsuit against the American divisions of the big four chocolate makers. In contrast to Canada, where the big four controlled a little less than 50% of the market, in the United States they controlled over 75%. SUPERVALU claimed that the American divisions of the big four had been fixing prices since 2002, regularly increasing prices by mid-single to double-digit amounts within a few days of one another.

Indeed, the price of chocolate candy had been soaring in the United States, climbing by 17% from 2008 to 2010, far in excess of the rate of inflation. Chocolate makers defended their actions, contending that they were simply passing on the higher costs of cocoa beans, dairy products, and sugar. And, as antitrust experts have pointed out, price collusion is often very difficult to prove because it is not illegal for producers to raise their prices at the same time. To prove collusion, there must be proof in the form of conversations or written agreements.

In March 2014 an American judge threw out the charges of collusion, stating that there was no evidence that executives at the big four chocolate producers were aware of the anti-competitive behavior of their colleagues in Canada, and that closely timed price increases were not sufficient proof of collusion. Federal Judge Christopher Conner concluded that the defendants engaged in "rational, competitive behavior" when they increased prices to counter anticipated cost increases. The case was a bitter reversal for American chocolate consumers who had hoped that they could soon enjoy their candy fix at lower prices.

▼ Quick Review

• Some of the key issues in oligopoly can be understood by looking at the simplest case, a **duopoly**—an industry containing only two firms, called **duopolists.**

• By acting as if they were a single monopolist, oligopolists can maximize their combined profits. So there is an incentive to form a **cartel.**

• However, each firm has an incentive to cheat—to produce more than it is supposed to under the cartel agreement. So there are two principal outcomes: successful **collusion** or behaving **noncooperatively** by cheating.

Check Your Understanding 14-2

1. Which of the following factors increase the likelihood that an oligopolist will collude with other firms in the industry? The likelihood that an oligopolist will act noncooperatively and raise output? Explain your answers.
   a. The firm's initial market share is small. (*Hint:* Think about the price effect.)
   b. The firm has a cost advantage over its rivals.

When a firm's decision significantly affects the profits of other firms in the industry, the firms are in a situation of **interdependence.**

The study of behavior in situations of interdependence is known as **game theory.**

The reward received by a player in a game, such as the profit earned by an oligopolist, is that player's **payoff.**

A **payoff matrix** shows how the payoff to each of the participants in a two-player game depends on the actions of both. Such a matrix helps us analyze situations of interdependence.

c. The firm's customers face additional costs when they switch from the use of one firm's product to another firm's product.

d. The oligopolist has a lot of unused production capacity but knows that its rivals are operating at their maximum production capacity and cannot increase the amount they produce.

Solutions appear at back of book.

Games Oligopolists Play

In our duopoly example and in real life, each oligopolistic firm realizes both that its profit depends on what its competitor does and that its competitor's profit depends on what it does. That is, the two firms are in a situation of **interdependence,** where each firm's decision significantly affects the profit of the other firm (or firms, in the case of more than two).

In effect, the two firms are playing a "game" in which the profit of each player depends not only on its own actions but on those of the other player (or players). In order to understand more fully how oligopolists behave, economists, along with mathematicians, developed the area of study of such games, known as **game theory.** It has many applications, not just to economics but also to military strategy, politics, and other social sciences.

Let's see how game theory helps us understand oligopoly.

The Prisoners' Dilemma

Game theory deals with any situation in which the reward to any one player—the **payoff**—depends not only on his or her own actions but also on those of other players in the game. In the case of oligopolistic firms, the payoff is simply the firm's profit.

When there are only two players, as in a duopoly, the interdependence between the players can be represented with a **payoff matrix** like that shown in Figure 14-1.

FIGURE 14-1   A Payoff Matrix

Two firms, ADM and Ajinomoto, must decide how much lysine to produce. The profits of the two firms are *interdependent:* each firm's profit depends not only on its own decision but also on the other's decision. Each row represents an action by ADM, each column, one by Ajinomoto. Both firms will be better off if they both choose the lower output, but it is in each firm's individual interest to choose the higher output.

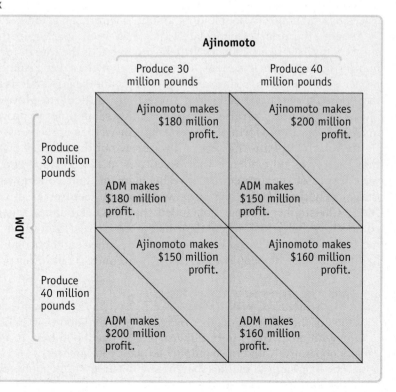

Each row corresponds to an action by one player (in this case, ADM); each column corresponds to an action by the other (in this case, Ajinomoto). For simplicity, let's assume that ADM can pick only one of two alternatives: produce 30 million pounds of lysine or produce 40 million pounds. Ajinomoto has the same pair of choices.

The matrix contains four boxes, each divided by a diagonal line. Each box shows the payoff to the two firms that results from a pair of choices; the number below the diagonal shows ADM's profits, the number above the diagonal shows Ajinomoto's profits.

These payoffs show what we concluded from our earlier analysis: the combined profit of the two firms is maximized if they each produce 30 million pounds. Either firm can, however, increase its own profits by producing 40 million pounds while the other produces only 30 million pounds. But if both produce the larger quantity, both will have lower profits than if they had both held their output down.

The particular situation shown here is a version of a famous—and seemingly paradoxical—case of interdependence that appears in many contexts. Known as the **prisoners' dilemma,** it is a type of game in which the payoff matrix implies the following:

- Each player has an incentive, regardless of what the other player does, to cheat—to take an action that benefits it at the other's expense.

- When both players cheat, both are worse off than they would have been if neither had cheated.

The original illustration of the prisoners' dilemma occurred in a fictional story about two accomplices in crime—let's call them Thelma and Louise—who have been caught by the police. The police have enough evidence to put them behind bars for 5 years. They also know that the pair have committed a more serious crime, one that carries a 20-year sentence; unfortunately, they don't have enough evidence to convict the women on that charge. To do so, they would need each of the prisoners to implicate the other in the second crime.

So the police put the miscreants in separate cells and say the following to each: "Here's the deal: if neither of you confesses, you know that we'll send you to jail for 5 years. If you confess and implicate your partner, and she doesn't do the same, we'll reduce your sentence from 5 years to 2. But if your partner confesses and you don't, you'll get the maximum 20 years. And if both of you confess, we'll give you both 15 years."

Figure 14-2 shows the payoffs that face the prisoners, depending on the decision of each to remain silent or to confess. (Usually the payoff matrix reflects the players' payoffs, and higher payoffs are better than lower payoffs. This case is an exception: a higher number of years in prison is bad, not good!) Let's assume that the prisoners have no way to communicate and that they have not sworn an oath not to harm each other or anything of that sort. So each acts in her own self-interest. What will they do?

The answer is clear: both will confess. Look at it first from Thelma's point of view: she is better off confessing, regardless of what Louise does. If Louise doesn't confess, Thelma's confession reduces her own sentence from 5 years to 2. If Louise *does* confess, Thelma's confession reduces her sentence from 20 to 15 years. Either way, it's clearly in Thelma's interest to confess. And because she faces the same incentives, it's clearly in Louise's interest to confess, too. To confess in this situation is a type of action that economists call a *dominant strategy.* An action is a **dominant strategy** when it is the player's best action regardless of the action taken by the other player.

It's important to note that not all games have a dominant strategy—it depends on the structure of payoffs in the game. But in the case of Thelma and Louise, it is clearly in the interest of the police to structure the payoffs so that confessing is

Prisoners' dilemma is a game based on two premises: (1) Each player has an incentive to choose an action that benefits itself at the other player's expense (2) When both players act in this way, both are worse off than if they had acted cooperatively.

An action is a **dominant strategy** when it is a player's best action regardless of the action taken by the other player.

FIGURE 14-2 The Prisoners' Dilemma

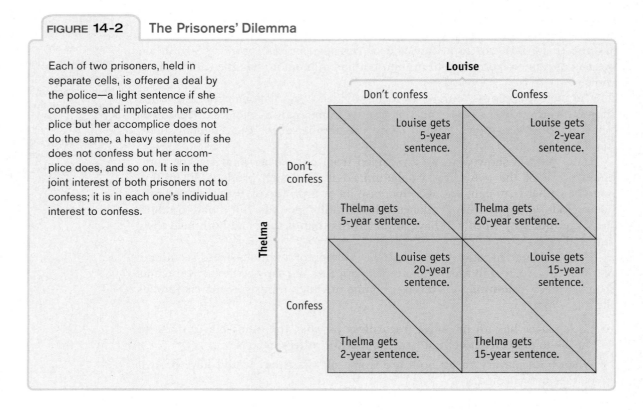

Each of two prisoners, held in separate cells, is offered a deal by the police—a light sentence if she confesses and implicates her accomplice but her accomplice does not do the same, a heavy sentence if she does not confess but her accomplice does, and so on. It is in the joint interest of both prisoners not to confess; it is in each one's individual interest to confess.

A **Nash equilibrium,** also known as a **noncooperative equilibrium,** results when each player in a game chooses the action that maximizes his or her payoff given the actions of other players, ignoring the effects of his or her action on the payoffs received by those other players.

PITFALLS

PLAYING FAIR IN THE PRISONERS' DILEMMA

One common reaction to the prisoners' dilemma is to assert that it isn't really rational for either prisoner to confess. Thelma wouldn't confess because she'd be afraid Louise would beat her up, or Thelma would feel guilty because Louise wouldn't do that to her.

But this kind of answer is, well, cheating—it amounts to changing the payoffs in the payoff matrix. To understand the dilemma, you have to play fair and imagine prisoners who care *only* about the length of their sentences.

Luckily, when it comes to oligopoly, it's a lot easier to believe that the firms care only about their profits. There is no indication that anyone at ADM felt either fear of or affection for Ajinomoto, or vice versa; it was strictly about business.

a dominant strategy for each person. So as long as the two prisoners have no way to make an enforceable agreement that neither will confess (something they can't do if they can't communicate, and the police certainly won't allow them to do so because the police want to compel each one to confess), Thelma and Louise will each act in a way that hurts the other.

So if each prisoner acts rationally in her own interest, both will confess. Yet if neither of them had confessed, both would have received a much lighter sentence! In a prisoners' dilemma, each player has a clear incentive to act in a way that hurts the other player—but when both make that choice, it leaves both of them worse off.

When Thelma and Louise both confess, they reach an *equilibrium* of the game. We have used the concept of equilibrium many times; it is an outcome in which no individual or firm has any incentive to change his or her action.

In game theory, this kind of equilibrium, in which each player takes the action that is best for her given the actions taken by other players, and vice versa, is known as a **Nash equilibrium,** after the mathematician and Nobel laureate John Nash. (Nash's life was chronicled in the best-selling biography *A Beautiful Mind,* which was made into a movie.) Because the players in a Nash equilibrium do not take into account the effect of their actions on others, this is also known as a **noncooperative equilibrium.**

Now look back at Figure 14-1: ADM and Ajinomoto are in the same situation as Thelma and Louise. Each firm is better off producing the higher output, regardless of what the other firm does. Yet if both produce 40 million pounds, both are worse off than if they had followed their agreement and produced only 30 million pounds. In both cases, then, the pursuit of individual self-interest—the effort to maximize profits or to minimize jail time—has the perverse effect of hurting both players.

Prisoners' dilemmas appear in many situations. The upcoming For Inquiring Minds describes an example from the days of the Cold War. Clearly, the players in any prisoners' dilemma would be better off if they

FOR INQUIRING MINDS | Prisoners of the Arms Race

Between World War II and the late 1980s, the United States and the Soviet Union were locked in a seemingly endless struggle that never broke out into open war. During this Cold War, both countries spent huge sums on arms, sums that were a significant drain on the U.S. economy and eventually proved a crippling burden for the Soviet Union, whose underlying economic base was much weaker. Yet neither country was ever able to achieve a decisive military advantage.

As many have pointed out, both nations would have been better off if they had both spent less on arms. Yet the arms race continued for 40 years.

Why? As political scientists were quick to notice, one way to explain the arms race was to suppose that the two countries were locked in a classic prisoners' dilemma. Each government would have liked to achieve decisive military superiority, and each feared military inferiority. But both would have preferred a stalemate with low military spending to one with high spending.

Caught in the prisoners' dilemma: heavy military spending hastened the collapse of the Soviet Union.

However, each government rationally chose to engage in high spending. If its rival did not spend heavily, its own high spending would lead to military superiority; not spending heavily would lead to inferiority if the other government continued its arms buildup. So the countries were trapped.

The answer to this trap could have been an agreement not to spend as much; indeed, the two sides tried repeatedly to negotiate limits on certain weapons. But these agreements weren't very effective. In the end the issue was resolved as heavy military spending hastened the collapse of the Soviet Union in 1991.

Unfortunately, the logic of an arms race did not disappear. A nuclear arms race developed between Pakistan and India, two neighboring countries with a history of mutual antagonism. In 1998 both countries confirmed the unrelenting logic of the prisoners' dilemma by publicly testing nuclear weapons in a tit-for-tat sequence.

However, by 2013 a glimmer of hope emerged, as the prime ministers of these South Asian nuclear rivals began a series of meetings aimed at making "a new beginning." ■

had some way of enforcing cooperative behavior—if Thelma and Louise had both sworn to a code of silence or if ADM and Ajinomoto had signed an enforceable agreement not to produce more than 30 million pounds of lysine.

But in the United States an agreement setting the output levels of two oligopolists isn't just unenforceable, it's illegal. So it seems that a noncooperative equilibrium is the only possible outcome. Or is it?

Overcoming the Prisoners' Dilemma: Repeated Interaction and Tacit Collusion

Thelma and Louise in their cells are playing what is known as a *one-shot* game—that is, they play the game with each other only once. They get to choose once and for all whether to confess or hang tough, and that's it. However, most of the games that oligopolists play aren't one-shot; instead, they expect to play the game repeatedly with the same rivals. An oligopolist usually expects to be in business for many years, and it knows that its decision today about whether to cheat is likely to affect the way other firms treat it in the future. So a smart oligopolist doesn't just decide what to do based on the effect on profit in the short run. Instead, it engages in **strategic behavior,** taking account of the effects of the action it chooses today on the future actions of other players in the game. And under some conditions oligopolists that behave strategically can manage to behave as if they had a formal agreement to collude.

Suppose that ADM and Ajinomoto expect to be in the lysine business for many years and therefore expect to play the game of cheat versus collude shown in Figure 14-1 many times. Would they really betray each other time and again?

Probably not. Suppose that ADM considers two strategies. In one strategy it always cheats, producing 40 million pounds of lysine each year, regardless of

A firm engages in **strategic behavior** when it attempts to influence the future behavior of other firms.

A strategy of **tit for tat** involves playing cooperatively at first, then doing whatever the other player did in the previous period.

what Ajinomoto does. In the other strategy, it starts with good behavior, producing only 30 million pounds in the first year, and watches to see what its rival does. If Ajinomoto also keeps its production down, ADM will stay cooperative, producing 30 million pounds again for the next year. But if Ajinomoto produces 40 million pounds, ADM will take the gloves off and also produce 40 million pounds the next year. This latter strategy—start by behaving cooperatively, but thereafter do whatever the other player did in the previous period—is generally known as **tit for tat.**

Tit for tat is a form of strategic behavior, which we have just defined as behavior intended to influence the future actions of other players. Tit for tat offers a reward to the other player for cooperative behavior—if you behave cooperatively, so will I. It also provides a punishment for cheating—if you cheat, don't expect me to be nice in the future.

The payoff to ADM of each of these strategies would depend on which strategy Ajinomoto chooses. Consider the four possibilities, shown in Figure 14-3:

1. If ADM plays tit for tat and so does Ajinomoto, both firms will make a profit of $180 million each year.
2. If ADM plays always cheat but Ajinomoto plays tit for tat, ADM makes a profit of $200 million the first year but only $160 million per year thereafter.
3. If ADM plays tit for tat but Ajinomoto plays always cheat, ADM makes a profit of only $150 million in the first year but $160 million per year thereafter.
4. If ADM plays always cheat and Ajinomoto does the same, both firms will make a profit of $160 million each year.

Which strategy is better? In the first year, ADM does better playing always cheat, whatever its rival's strategy: it assures itself that it will get either $200 million or $160 million (which of the two payoffs it actually receives depends on whether Ajinomoto plays tit for tat or always cheat). This is better than what it

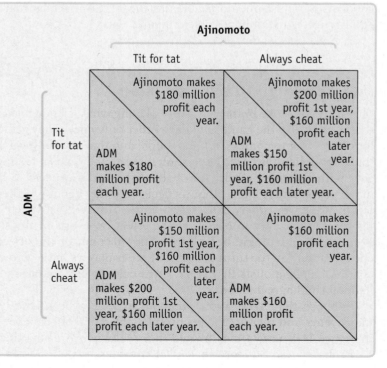

FIGURE **14-3**   How Repeated Interaction Can Support Collusion

A strategy of tit for tat involves playing cooperatively at first, then following the other player's move. This rewards good behavior and punishes bad behavior. If the other player cheats, playing tit for tat will lead to only a short-term loss in comparison to playing always cheat. But if the other player plays tit for tat, also playing tit for tat leads to a long-term gain. So a firm that expects other firms to play tit for tat may well choose to do the same, leading to successful tacit collusion.

would get in the first year if it played tit for tat: either $180 million or $150 million. But by the second year, a strategy of always cheat gains ADM only $160 million per year for the second and all subsequent years, regardless of Ajinomoto's actions.

Over time, the total amount gained by ADM by playing always cheat is less than the amount it would gain by playing tit for tat: for the second and all subsequent years, it would never get any less than $160 million and would get as much as $180 million if Ajinomoto played tit for tat as well. Which strategy, always cheat or tit for tat, is more profitable depends on two things: how many years ADM expects to play the game and what strategy its rival follows.

If ADM expects the lysine business to end in the near future, it is in effect playing a one-shot game. So it might as well cheat and grab what it can. Even if ADM expects to remain in the lysine business for many years (therefore to find itself repeatedly playing this game with Ajinomoto) and, for some reason, expects Ajinomoto always to cheat, it should also always cheat. That is, ADM should follow the old rule "Do unto others before they do unto you."

But if ADM expects to be in the business for a long time and thinks Ajinomoto is likely to play tit for tat, it will make more profits over the long run by playing tit for tat, too. It could have made some extra short-term profits by cheating at the beginning, but this would provoke Ajinomoto into cheating, too, and would, in the end, mean lower profits.

The lesson of this story is that when oligopolists expect to compete with one another over an extended period of time, each individual firm will often conclude that it is in its own best interest to be helpful to the other firms in the industry. So it will restrict its output in a way that raises the profits of the other firms, expecting them to return the favor. Despite the fact that firms have no way of making an enforceable agreement to limit output and raise prices (and are in legal jeopardy if they even discuss prices), they manage to act "as if" they had such an agreement. When this happens, we say that firms engage in **tacit collusion.**

> When firms limit production and raise prices in a way that raises one anothers' profits, even though they have not made any formal agreement, they are engaged in **tacit collusion.**

ECONOMICS ▶ in Action

The Rise and Fall and Rise of OPEC

Call it the cartel that does not need to meet in secret. The Organization of Petroleum Exporting Countries, usually referred to as OPEC, includes 12 national governments (Algeria, Angola, Ecuador, Iran, Iraq, Kuwait, Libya, Nigeria, Qatar, Saudi Arabia, the United Arab Emirates, and Venezuela), and it controls 40% of the world's oil exports and 80% of its proven reserves. Two other oil-exporting countries, Norway and Mexico, are not formally part of the cartel but act as if they were. (Russia, also an important oil exporter, has not yet become part of the club.)

Unlike corporations, which are often legally prohibited by governments from reaching agreements about production and prices, national governments can talk about whatever they feel like. OPEC members routinely meet to try to set targets for production.

It is in OPEC's interest to keep oil prices high and output low.

These nations are not particularly friendly with one another. Indeed, OPEC members Iraq and Iran fought a spectacularly bloody war with each other in the 1980s. And, in 1990, Iraq invaded another member, Kuwait. (A mainly American force based in yet another OPEC member, Saudi Arabia, drove the Iraqis out of Kuwait.)

FIGURE **14-4**

Crude Oil Prices, 1949–2013 (in Constant 2012 Dollars)

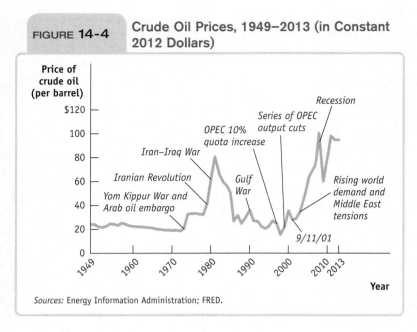

Sources: Energy Information Administration; FRED.

Yet the members of OPEC are effectively players in a game with repeated interactions. In any given year it is in their combined interest to keep output low and prices high. But it is also in the interest of any one producer to cheat and produce more than the agreed-upon quota—unless that producer believes that his actions will bring future retaliation.

So how successful is the cartel? Well, it's had its ups and downs. Analysts have estimated that of 12 announced quota reductions, OPEC was able to successfully defend its price floor 80% of the time.

Figure 14-4 shows the price of oil in constant dollars (that is, the value of a barrel of oil in terms of other goods) since 1949. OPEC first demonstrated its muscle in 1974: in the aftermath of a war in the Middle East, several OPEC producers limited their output—and they liked the results so much that they decided to continue the practice. Following a second wave of turmoil in the aftermath of Iran's 1979 revolution, prices shot still higher.

By the mid-1980s, however, there was a growing glut of oil on world markets, and cheating by cash-short OPEC members became widespread. The result, in 1985, was that producers who had tried to play by the rules—especially Saudi Arabia, the largest producer—got fed up, and collusion collapsed.

The cartel started acting effectively at the end of the 1990s, thanks largely to the efforts of Mexico's oil minister, who orchestrated output reductions, and Saudi Arabia's assumption of the role of "swing producer." As the key decision maker and the largest OPEC producer by far, Saudi Arabia allowed other members to produce as much as they could, and then adjusted its own output to meet the overall limit, thereby easing friction among members. These actions helped raise the price of oil from less than $10 per barrel in 1998 to a range of $20 to $30 per barrel in 2003.

Since 2008, OPEC has experienced the steepest roller-coaster ride of oil prices in its history. By 2008, prices had soared to over $145 per barrel. But at the end of 2008, one year into the recession of 2007–2009, prices dropped sharply to $32 per barrel. In response, Saudi Arabia cut its output by 20%, as other members reduced their output by 5%. By early 2009, prices began to rebound. Political instability in several member countries caused prices to skyrocket in 2011, as Saudi Arabia increased its output to prevent a global oil shortage.

More recently, as Iraq and Iran have signaled their intention to raise output, as the United States produces increasing amounts of oil from its shale formations, and as oil production from Brazil and Canada increases, some OPEC watchers are predicting that the cartel's future cohesion may very well be in jeopardy.

▼ **Quick Review**

• Economists use **game theory** to study firms' behavior when there is **interdependence** between their **payoffs**. The game can be represented with a **payoff matrix**. Depending on the payoffs, a player may or may not have a **dominant strategy**.

• When each firm has an incentive to cheat, but both are worse off if both cheat, the situation is known as a **prisoners' dilemma**.

• Players who don't take their interdependence into account arrive at a **Nash**, or **noncooperative, equilibrium**. But if a game is played repeatedly, players may engage in **strategic behavior**, sacrificing short-run profit to influence future behavior.

• In repeated prisoners' dilemma games, **tit for tat** is often a good strategy, leading to successful **tacit collusion**.

Check Your Understanding 14-3

1. Find the Nash (noncooperative) equilibrium actions for the following payoff matrix. Which actions maximize the total payoff of Nikita and Margaret? Why is it unlikely that they will choose those actions without some communication?

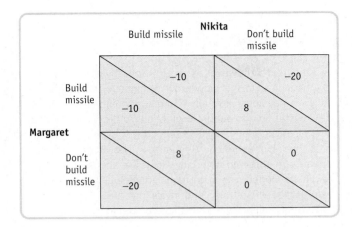

2. Which of the following factors make it more likely that oligopolists will play noncooperatively? Which make it more likely that they will engage in tacit collusion? Explain.

   a. Each oligopolist expects several new firms to enter the market in the future.

   b. It is very difficult for a firm to detect whether another firm has raised output.

   c. The firms have coexisted while maintaining high prices for a long time.

Solutions appear at back of book.

Oligopoly in Practice

In an earlier Economics in Action, we described how the four leading chocolate companies in Canada were allegedly colluding to raise prices for many years. Collusion is not, fortunately, the norm. But how do oligopolies usually work in practice? The answer depends both on the legal framework that limits what firms can do and on the underlying ability of firms in a given industry to cooperate without formal agreements.

The Legal Framework

To understand oligopoly pricing in practice, we must be familiar with the legal constraints under which oligopolistic firms operate. In the United States, oligopoly first became an issue during the second half of the nineteenth century, when the growth of railroads—themselves an oligopolistic industry—created a national market for many goods.

Large firms producing oil, steel, and many other products soon emerged. The industrialists quickly realized that profits would be higher if they could limit price competition. So, many industries formed cartels—that is, they signed formal agreements to limit production and raise prices. Until 1890, when the first federal legislation against such cartels was passed, this was perfectly legal.

However, although these cartels were legal, they weren't legally *enforceable*—members of a cartel couldn't ask the courts to force a firm that was violating its agreement to reduce its production. And firms often did violate their agreements, for the reason already suggested by our duopoly example: there is always a temptation for each firm in a cartel to produce more than it is supposed to.

In 1881 clever lawyers at John D. Rockefeller's Standard Oil Company came up with a solution—the so-called trust. In a trust, shareholders of all the major companies in an industry placed their shares in the hands of a board of trustees who controlled the companies. This, in effect, merged the companies into a single firm that could then engage in monopoly pricing. In this way, the Standard Oil Trust established what was essentially a monopoly of the oil industry, and it was soon followed by trusts in sugar, whiskey, lead, cottonseed oil, and linseed oil.

GLOBAL COMPARISION | Contrasting Approaches to Antitrust Regulation

In the European Union, a competition commission enforces competition and antitrust regulation for the 28 member nations. The commission has the authority to block mergers, force companies to sell subsidiaries, and impose heavy fines if it determines that companies have acted unfairly to inhibit competition.

Although companies are able to dispute charges at a hearing once a complaint has been issued, if the commission feels that its own case is convincing, it rules against the firm and levies a penalty. Companies that believe they have been unfairly treated have only limited recourse. Critics complain that the commission acts as prosecutor, judge, and jury.

In contrast, charges of unfair competition in the United States must be made in court, where lawyers for the Federal Trade Commission have to present their evidence to independent judges. Companies employ legions of highly trained and highly paid lawyers to counter the government's case. For U.S. regulators, there is no guarantee of success. In fact, judges in many cases have found in favor of companies and against the regulators. Moreover, companies can appeal unfavorable decisions, so reaching a final verdict can take several years.

Companies, not surprisingly, prefer the American system. The accompanying figure further shows why. In recent years, on average, fines for unfair competition have been higher in the European Union than in the United States.

Observers, however, criticize both systems for their inadequacies. In the slow-moving, litigious, and expensive American system, consumers and rival companies may wait a very long time to secure protection. And companies often prevail, raising questions about how well consumers are protected. But some charge that the EU system gives inadequate protection to companies that are accused. This is a particular concern in high-tech industries, where network externalities are strong and rivals can use complaints of unfair competition to hobble their competitors.

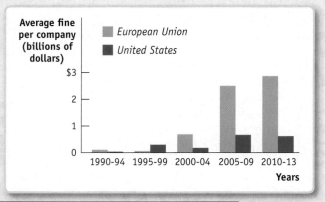

Sources: European Commission, Department of Justice Workload Statistics; PACIFIC Exchange Rate Service at University of British Columbia.

Antitrust policy consists of efforts undertaken by the government to prevent oligopolistic industries from becoming or behaving like monopolies.

"Frankly, I'm dubious about amalgamated smelting and refining pleading innocent to their anti-trust violation due to insanity."

Eventually there was a public backlash, driven partly by concern about the economic effects of the trust movement, partly by fear that the owners of the trusts were simply becoming too powerful. The result was the Sherman Antitrust Act of 1890, which was intended both to prevent the creation of more monopolies and to break up existing ones. At first this law went largely unenforced. But over the decades that followed, the federal government became increasingly committed to making it difficult for oligopolistic industries either to become monopolies or to behave like them. Such efforts are known to this day as **antitrust policy.**

One of the most striking early actions of antitrust policy was the breakup of Standard Oil in 1911. (Its components formed the nuclei of many of today's large oil companies—Standard Oil of New Jersey became Exxon, Standard Oil of New York became Mobil, and so on.) In the 1980s a long-running case led to the breakup of Bell Telephone, which once had a monopoly of both local and long-distance phone service in the United States. As we mentioned earlier, the Justice Department reviews proposed mergers between companies in the same industry and will bar mergers that it believes will reduce competition.

Among advanced countries, the United States is unique in its long tradition of antitrust policy. Until recently, other advanced countries did not have policies against price-fixing, and some had even supported the creation of cartels, believing that it would help their own firms against foreign rivals. But the situation has changed radically over the past 30 years, as the European Union (EU)—a supranational body tasked with enforcing antitrust policy for its member countries—has moved toward U.S. practices. Today, EU and U.S. regulators often target the same firms because price-fixing has "gone global" as international trade has expanded.

During the early 1990s, the United States instituted an amnesty program in which a price-fixer receives a much-reduced penalty if it informs on its co-conspirators. In addition, Congress increased the maximum fines levied upon conviction. These two new policies clearly made informing on your cartel partners a dominant strategy, and it has paid off as executives from Belgium, Britain, Canada, France, Germany, Italy, Mexico, the Netherlands, South Korea, and Switzerland, as well as from the United States, have been convicted in U.S. courts of cartel crimes. As one lawyer commented, "you get a race to the courthouse" as each conspirator seeks to be the first to come clean.

Life has gotten much tougher over the past few years if you want to operate a cartel. So what's an oligopolist to do?

Tacit Collusion and Price Wars

If a real industry were as simple as our lysine example, it probably wouldn't be necessary for the company presidents to meet or do anything that could land them in jail. Both firms would realize that it was in their mutual interest to restrict output to 30 million pounds each and that any short-term gains to either firm from producing more would be much less than the later losses as the other firm retaliated. So even without any explicit agreement, the firms would probably achieve the tacit collusion needed to maximize their combined profits.

Real industries are nowhere near that simple. Nonetheless, in most oligopolistic industries, most of the time, the sellers do appear to succeed in keeping prices above their noncooperative level. Tacit collusion, in other words, is the normal state of oligopoly.

Although tacit collusion is common, it rarely allows an industry to push prices all the way up to their monopoly level; collusion is usually far from perfect. As we discuss next, there are four factors that make it hard for an industry to coordinate on high prices.

Less Concentration In a less concentrated industry, the typical firm will have a smaller market share than in a more concentrated industry. This tilts firms toward noncooperative behavior because when a smaller firm cheats and increases its output, it gains for itself all of the profit from the higher output. And if its rivals retaliate by increasing their output, the firm's losses are limited because of its relatively modest market share. A less concentrated industry is often an indication that there are low barriers to entry.

Complex Products and Pricing Schemes In our lysine example the two firms produce only one product. In reality, however, oligopolists often sell thousands or even tens of thousands of different products. Under these circumstances, keeping track of what other firms are producing and the prices they are charging is difficult. This makes it hard to determine whether a firm is cheating on the tacit agreement.

Differences in Interests In the lysine example, a tacit agreement for the firms to split the market equally is a natural outcome, probably acceptable to both firms. In real industries, however, firms often differ both in their perceptions about what is fair and in their real interests.

For example, suppose that Ajinomoto was a long-established lysine producer and ADM a more recent entrant to the industry. Ajinomoto might feel that it deserved to continue producing more than ADM, but ADM might feel that it was entitled to 50% of the business. (A disagreement along these lines was one of the contentious issues in those meetings the FBI was filming.)

Alternatively, suppose that ADM's marginal costs were lower than Ajinomoto's. Even if they could agree on market shares, they would then disagree about the profit-maximizing level of output.

A **price war** occurs when tacit collusion breaks down and prices collapse.

Product differentiation is an attempt by a firm to convince buyers that its product is different from the products of other firms in the industry.

Bargaining Power of Buyers Often oligopolists sell not to individual consumers but to large buyers—other industrial enterprises, nationwide chains of stores, and so on. These large buyers are in a position to bargain for lower prices from the oligopolists: they can ask for a discount from an oligopolist and warn that they will go to a competitor if they don't get it. An important reason large retailers like Walmart are able to offer lower prices to customers than small retailers is precisely their ability to use their size to extract lower prices from their suppliers.

These difficulties in enforcing tacit collusion have sometimes led companies to defy the law and create illegal cartels. We've already examined the cases of the lysine industry and the chocolate industry. An older, classic example was the U.S. electrical equipment conspiracy of the 1950s, which led to the prosecution of and jail sentences for some executives. The industry was one in which tacit collusion was especially difficult because of the reasons just mentioned.

- There were many firms—40 companies were indicted.
- They produced a very complex array of products, often more or less custom-built for particular clients.
- They differed greatly in size, from giants like General Electric to family firms with only a few dozen employees.
- The customers in many cases were large buyers like electrical utilities, which would normally try to force suppliers to compete for their business.

Tacit collusion just didn't seem practical—so executives met secretly and illegally to decide who would bid what price for which contract.

Because tacit collusion is often hard to achieve, most oligopolies charge prices that are well below what the same industry would charge if it were controlled by a monopolist—or what they would charge if they were able to collude explicitly. In addition, sometimes collusion breaks down and there is a **price war.** A price war sometimes involves simply a collapse of prices to their noncooperative level. Sometimes they even go *below* that level, as sellers try to put each other out of business or at least punish what they regard as cheating.

Meetings between rival firms are likely to trigger an antitrust investigation, so firms try to engage in tacit collusion.

Martin Barraud/Getty Images

Product Differentiation and Price Leadership

Lysine is lysine: there was no question in anyone's mind that ADM and Ajinomoto were producing the same good and that consumers would make their decision about which company's lysine to buy based on the price.

In many oligopolies, however, firms produce products that consumers regard as similar but not identical. A $10 difference in the price won't make many customers switch from a Ford to a Chrysler, or vice versa. Sometimes the differences between products are real, like differences between Froot Loops and Wheaties; sometimes, like differences between brands of vodka (which is supposed to be tasteless), they exist mainly in the minds of consumers. Either way, the effect is to reduce the intensity of competition among the firms: consumers will not all rush to buy whichever product is cheapest.

As you might imagine, oligopolists welcome the extra market power that comes when consumers think that their product is different from that of competitors. So in many oligopolistic industries, firms make considerable efforts to create the perception that their product is different—that is, they engage in **product differentiation.**

A firm that tries to differentiate its product may do so by altering what it actually produces, adding "extras," or choosing a different design. It may also use advertising and marketing campaigns to create a differentiation in the minds of consumers, even though its product is more or less identical to the products of rivals.

A classic case of how products may be perceived as different even when they are really pretty much the same is over-the-counter medication. For many years there were only three widely sold pain relievers—aspirin, ibuprofen, and acetaminophen. Yet these generic pain relievers were marketed under a number of brand names, each brand using a marketing campaign implying some special superiority (one classic slogan was "contains the pain reliever doctors recommend most"—that is, aspirin).

Whatever the nature of product differentiation, oligopolists producing differentiated products often reach a tacit understanding not to compete on price. For example, during the years when the great majority of cars sold in the United States were produced by the Big Three auto companies (General Motors, Ford, and Chrysler), there was an unwritten rule that none of the three companies would try to gain market share by making its cars noticeably cheaper than those of the other two.

But then who would decide on the overall price of cars? The answer was normally General Motors: as the biggest of the three, it would announce its prices for the year first, and the other companies would match it. This pattern of behavior, in which one company tacitly sets prices for the industry as a whole, is known as **price leadership.**

Interestingly, firms that have a tacit agreement not to compete on price often engage in vigorous **nonprice competition**—adding new features to their products, spending large sums on ads that proclaim the inferiority of their rivals' offerings, and so on.

Perhaps the best way to understand the mix of cooperation and competition in such industries is with a political analogy. During the long Cold War between the United States and the Soviet Union, the two countries engaged in intense rivalry for global influence. They not only provided financial and military aid to their allies; they sometimes supported forces trying to overthrow governments allied with their rival (as the Soviet Union did in Vietnam in the 1960s and early 1970s, and as the United States did in Afghanistan from 1979 until the collapse of the Soviet Union in 1991). They even sent their own soldiers to support allied governments against rebels (as the United States did in Vietnam and the Soviet Union did in Afghanistan). But they did not get into direct military confrontations with each other; open warfare between the two superpowers was regarded by both as too dangerous—and tacitly avoided.

Price wars aren't as serious as shooting wars, but the principle is the same.

How Important Is Oligopoly?

We have seen that, across industries, oligopoly is far more common than either perfect competition or monopoly. When we try to analyze oligopoly, the economist's usual way of thinking—asking how self-interested individuals would behave, then analyzing their interaction—does not work as well as we might hope because we do not know whether rival firms will engage in noncooperative behavior or manage to engage in some kind of collusion.

Given the prevalence of oligopoly, then, is the analysis we developed in earlier chapters, which was based on perfect competition, still useful?

The conclusion of the great majority of economists is yes. For one thing, important parts of the economy are fairly well described by perfect competition. And even though many industries are oligopolistic, in many cases the limits to collusion keep prices relatively close to marginal costs—in other words, the industry behaves "almost" as if it were perfectly competitive.

In **price leadership,** one firm sets its price first, and other firms then follow.

Firms that have a tacit understanding not to compete on price often engage in intense **nonprice competition,** using advertising and other means to try to increase their sales.

It is also true that predictions from supply and demand analysis are often valid for oligopolies. For example, in Chapter 5 we saw that price controls will produce shortages. Strictly speaking, this conclusion is certain only for perfectly competitive industries. But in the 1970s, when the U.S. government imposed price controls on the definitely oligopolistic oil industry, the result was indeed to produce shortages and lines at the gas pumps.

So how important is it to take account of oligopoly? Most economists adopt a pragmatic approach. As we have seen in this chapter, the analysis of oligopoly is far more difficult and messy than that of perfect competition; so in situations where they do not expect the complications associated with oligopoly to be crucial, economists prefer to adopt the working assumption of perfectly competitive markets. They always keep in mind the possibility that oligopoly might be important; they recognize that there are important issues, from antitrust policies to price wars, where trying to understand oligopolistic behavior is crucial.

We will follow the same approach in the chapters that follow.

ECONOMICS ▶ in Action

The Price Wars of Christmas

Over the last decade, the toy aisles of American retailers have been the scene of cutthroat competition. The 2011 Christmas shopping season saw Elmo at the center of a price-slashing competition when Target priced the latest Elmo doll at 89 cents less than Walmart (for those with a coupon), and $6 less than Toys "R" Us. The competition has been so extreme that three toy retailers—KB Toys, FAO Schwarz, and Zany Brainy—have been forced into bankruptcy since 2003. Due to aggressive price-cutting by Walmart, the market share of Toys "R" Us has fallen from first to second.

What is happening? The turmoil can be traced back to trouble in the toy industry itself as well as to changes in toy retailing. Every year for several years now, overall toy sales have fallen a few percentage points as children increasingly turn to video games and the internet.

The result is much like a story of tacit collusion sustained by repeated interaction run in reverse: because the overall industry has been in a state of decline and there are new entrants, the future payoff from collusion is shrinking. The predictable outcome is a price war.

Since retailers depend on holiday sales for nearly half of their annual sales, the holidays are a time of particularly intense price-cutting. Traditionally, the biggest shopping day of the year has been "Black Friday," the day after Thanksgiving. But in an effort to expand sales and undercut rivals, retailers begin their price-cutting earlier in the fall, typically in early November, well before Thanksgiving.

And with each passing year, the holiday price-war competition becomes more intense. In 2013, Amazon slashed its toy prices 16% in early November, followed by Walmart, Target, and Best Buy who also slashed prices. In addition, five of the eight major toy retailers offered to match their competitors' prices during the holiday season. According to Brian Sozzi, head of a retail research firm, "Amazon launched deals before the holiday that forced the others to follow. This wave

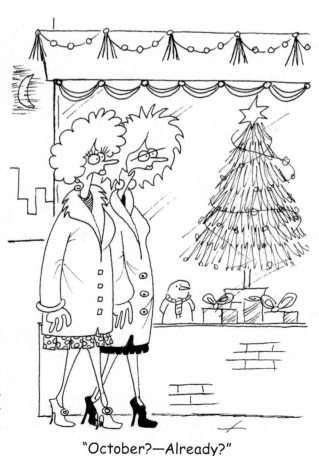

"October?—Already?"

is happening before promotions are supposed to happen. . . . things are looking kind of irrational."

With toy retailers forced to cut prices to keep pace with their rivals or lose sales, we have a phenomenon known as "creeping Christmas": the price wars of Christmas arrive earlier each year.

Check Your Understanding   14-4

1. Which of the following factors are likely to support the conclusion that there is tacit collusion in this industry? Which are not? Explain.
   a. For many years the price in the industry has changed infrequently, and all the firms in the industry charge the same price. The largest firm publishes a catalog containing a "suggested" retail price. Changes in price coincide with changes in the catalog.
   b. There has been considerable variation in the market shares of the firms in the industry over time.
   c. Firms in the industry build into their products unnecessary features that make it hard for consumers to switch from one company's products to another company's products.
   d. Firms meet yearly to discuss their annual sales forecasts.
   e. Firms tend to adjust their prices upward at the same times.

Solutions appear at back of book.

Virgin Atlantic Blows the Whistle . . . or Blows It?

The United Kingdom is home to two long-haul airline carriers (carriers that fly between continents): British Airways and its rival, Virgin Atlantic. Although British Airways is the dominant company, with a market share generally between 50% and 100% on routes between London and various American cities, Virgin has been a tenacious competitor.

The rivalry between the two has ranged from relatively peaceable to openly hostile over the years. In the 1990s, British Airways lost a court case alleging it had engaged in "dirty tricks" to drive Virgin out of business. In April 2010, however, British Airways may well have wondered if the tables had been turned.

AP Photo/Alastair Grant

It all began in mid-July 2004, when oil prices were rising. British prosecutors alleged that the two airlines had plotted to levy fuel surcharges on passengers. For the next two years, according to the prosecutors, the rivals had established a cartel through which they coordinated increases in surcharges. British Airways first introduced a £5 ($8.25) surcharge on long-haul flights when a barrel of oil traded at about $38. It increased the surcharge six times, so that by 2006, when oil was trading at about $69 a barrel, the surcharge was £70 ($115). At the same time, Virgin Atlantic also levied a £70 fee. These surcharges increased within days of each other.

Eventually, three Virgin executives decided to blow the whistle in exchange for immunity from prosecution. British Airways immediately suspended its executives under suspicion and paid fines of nearly $500 million to U.S. and U.K. authorities. And in 2010 four British Airways executives were prosecuted by British authorities for their alleged role in the conspiracy.

The lawyers for the executives argued that although the two airlines had swapped information, this was not proof of a criminal conspiracy. In fact, they argued, Virgin was so fearful of American regulators that it had admitted to criminal behavior before confirming that it had indeed committed an offense. One of the defense lawyers, Clare Montgomery, argued that because U.S. laws against anti-competitive behavior are much tougher than those in the United Kingdom, companies may be compelled to blow the whistle to avoid investigation. "It's a race," she said. "If you don't get to them and confess first, you can't get immunity. The only way to protect yourself is to go to the authorities, even if you haven't [done anything]." The result was that the Virgin executives were given immunity in both the United States and the United Kingdom, but the British Airways executives were subject to prosecution (and possible multiyear jail terms) in both countries.

In late 2011 the case came to a shocking end for Virgin Atlantic and U.K. authorities. Citing e-mails that Virgin was forced to turn over by the court, the judge found insufficient evidence that there was ever a conspiracy between the two airlines. The court was incensed enough to threaten to rescind the immunity granted to the three Virgin executives.

QUESTIONS FOR THOUGHT

1. Explain why Virgin Atlantic and British Airlines might collude in response to increased oil prices. Was the market conducive to collusion or not?

2. How would you determine whether illegal behavior actually occurred? What might explain these events other than illegal behavior?

3. Explain the dilemma facing the two airlines as well as their individual executives.

SUMMARY

1. Many industries are **oligopolies:** there are only a few sellers. In particular, a **duopoly** has only two sellers. Oligopolies exist for more or less the same reasons that monopolies exist, but in weaker form. They are characterized by **imperfect competition:** firms compete but possess market power.

2. Predicting the behavior of **oligopolists** poses something of a puzzle. The firms in an oligopoly could maximize their combined profits by acting as a **cartel,** setting output levels for each firm as if they were a single monopolist; to the extent that firms manage to do this, they engage in **collusion.** But each individual firm has an incentive to produce more than it would in such an arrangement—to engage in **non-cooperative behavior.**

3. The situation of **interdependence,** in which each firm's profit depends noticeably on what other firms do, is the subject of **game theory.** In the case of a game with two players, the **payoff** of each player depends both on its own actions and on the actions of the other; this interdependence can be represented as a **payoff matrix.** Depending on the structure of payoffs in the payoff matrix, a player may have a **dominant strategy**—an action that is always the best regardless of the other player's actions.

4. **Duopolists** face a particular type of game known as a **prisoners' dilemma;** if each acts independently in its own interest, the resulting **Nash equilibrium** or **noncooperative equilibrium** will be bad for both. However, firms that expect to play a game repeatedly tend to engage in **strategic behavior,** trying to influence each other's future actions. A particular strategy that seems to work well in maintaining **tactic collusion** is **tit for tat.**

5. In order to limit the ability of oligopolists to collude and act like monopolists, most governments pursue an **antitrust policy** designed to make collusion more difficult. In practice, however, tacit collusion is widespread.

6. A variety of factors make tacit collusion difficult: large numbers of firms, complex products and pricing, differences in interests, and bargaining power of buyers. When tacit collusion breaks down, there is a **price war.** Oligopolists try to avoid price wars in various ways, such as through **product differentiation** and through **price leadership,** in which one firm sets prices for the industry. Another is through **nonprice competition,** like advertising.

KEY TERMS

Oligopoly, p. 420
Oligopolist, p. 420
Imperfect competition, p. 420
Duopoly, p. 422
Duopolist, p. 422
Collusion, p. 423
Cartel, p. 423
Noncooperative behavior, p. 424

Interdependence, p. 426
Game theory, p. 426
Payoff, p. 426
Payoff matrix, p. 426
Prisoners' dilemma, p. 427
Dominant strategy, p. 427
Nash equilibrium, p. 428
Noncooperative equilibrium, p. 428

Strategic behavior, p. 429
Tit for tat, p. 430
Tacit collusion, p. 431
Antitrust policy, p. 434
Price war, p. 436
Product differentiation, p. 436
Price leadership, p. 437
Nonprice competition, p. 437

PROBLEMS

1. The accompanying table presents market share data for the U.S. breakfast cereal market.

Company	Market Share
Kellogg	28%
General Mills	28
PepsiCo (Quaker Oats)	14
Kraft	13
Private Label	11
Other	6

Source: Advertising Age.

a. Use the data provided to calculate the Herfindahl–Hirschman Index (HHI) for the market.

b. Based on this HHI, what type of market structure is the U.S. breakfast cereal market?

2. The accompanying table shows the demand schedule for vitamin D. Suppose that the marginal cost of producing vitamin D is zero.

Price of vitamin D (per ton)	Quantity of vitamin D demanded (tons)
$8	0
7	10
6	20
5	30
4	40
3	50
2	60
1	70

a. Assume that BASF is the only producer of vitamin D and acts as a monopolist. It currently produces 40 tons of vitamin D at $4 per ton. If BASF were to produce 10 more tons, what would be the price effect for BASF? What would be the quantity effect? Would BASF have an incentive to produce those 10 additional tons?

b. Now assume that Roche enters the market by also producing vitamin D and the market is now a duopoly. BASF and Roche agree to produce 40 tons of vitamin D in total, 20 tons each. BASF cannot be punished for deviating from the agreement with Roche. If BASF, on its own, were to deviate from that agreement and produce 10 more tons, what would be the price effect for BASF? What would be the quantity effect for BASF? Would BASF have an incentive to produce those 10 additional tons?

3. The market for olive oil in New York City is controlled by two families, the Sopranos and the Contraltos. Both families will ruthlessly eliminate any other family that attempts to enter the New York City olive oil market. The marginal cost of producing olive oil is constant and equal to $40 per gallon. There is no fixed cost. The accompanying table gives the market demand schedule for olive oil.

Price of olive oil (per gallon)	Quantity of olive oil demanded (gallons)
$100	1,000
90	1,500
80	2,000
70	2,500
60	3,000
50	3,500
40	4,000
30	4,500
20	5,000
10	5,500

a. Suppose the Sopranos and the Contraltos form a cartel. For each of the quantities given in the table, calculate the total revenue for their cartel and the marginal revenue for each additional gallon. How

many gallons of olive oil would the cartel sell in total and at what price? The two families share the market equally (each produces half of the total output of the cartel). How much profit does each family make?

b. Uncle Junior, the head of the Soprano family, breaks the agreement and sells 500 more gallons of olive oil than under the cartel agreement. Assuming the Contraltos maintain the agreement, how does this affect the price for olive oil and the profit earned by each family?

c. Anthony Contralto, the head of the Contralto family, decides to punish Uncle Junior by increasing his sales by 500 gallons as well. How much profit does each family earn now?

4. In France, the market for bottled water is controlled by two large firms, Perrier and Evian. Each firm has a fixed cost of €1 million and a constant marginal cost of €2 per liter of bottled water (€1 = 1 euro). The following table gives the market demand schedule for bottled water in France.

Price of bottled water (per liter)	Quantity of bottled water demanded (millions of liters)
€10	0
9	1
8	2
7	3
6	4
5	5
4	6
3	7
2	8
1	9

a. Suppose the two firms form a cartel and act as a monopolist. Calculate marginal revenue for the cartel. What will the monopoly price and output be? Assuming the firms divide the output evenly, how much will each produce and what will each firm's profit be?

b. Now suppose Perrier decides to increase production by 1 million liters. Evian doesn't change its production. What will the new market price and output be? What is Perrier's profit? What is Evian's profit?

c. What if Perrier increases production by 3 million liters? Evian doesn't change its production. What would its output and profit be relative to those in part b?

d. What do your results tell you about the likelihood of cheating on such agreements?

5. To preserve the North Atlantic fish stocks, it is decided that only two fishing fleets, one from the United States and the other from the European Union (EU), can fish in those waters. Suppose that this fisheries agreement breaks down, so that the fleets behave noncooperatively. Assume that the United States and the EU each can send out either one or two fleets. The more fleets in the area, the more fish they catch in total but the lower the catch of each fleet. The accompanying matrix shows the profit (in dollars) per week earned by each side.

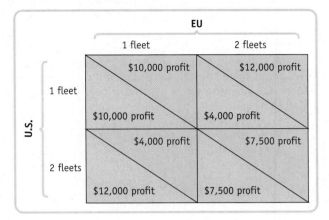

a. What is the noncooperative Nash equilibrium? Will each side choose to send out one or two fleets?

b. Suppose that the fish stocks are being depleted. Each region considers the future and comes to a tit-for-tat agreement whereby each side will send only one fleet out as long as the other does the same. If either of them breaks the agreement and sends out a second fleet, the other will also send out two and will continue to do so until its competitor sends out only one fleet. If both play this tit-for-tat strategy, how much profit will each make every week?

6. Untied and Air "R" Us are the only two airlines operating flights between Collegeville and Bigtown. That is, they operate in a duopoly. Each airline can charge either a high price or a low price for a ticket. The accompanying matrix shows their payoffs, in profits per seat (in dollars), for any choice that the two airlines can make.

a. Suppose the two airlines play a one-shot game—that is, they interact only once and never again. What will be the Nash (noncooperative) equilibrium in this one-shot game?

b. Now suppose the two airlines play this game twice. And suppose each airline can play one of two strategies: it can play either always charge the low price or tit for tat—that is, it starts off charging the high price in the first period, and then in the second period it does whatever the other airline did in the previous period. Write down the payoffs to Untied from the following four possibilities:

   i. Untied plays always charge the low price when Air "R" Us also plays always charge the low price.

   ii. Untied plays always charge the low price when Air "R" Us plays tit for tat.

   iii. Untied plays tit for tat when Air "R" Us plays always charge the low price.

   iv. Untied plays tit for tat when Air "R" Us also plays tit for tat.

7. Suppose that Coke and Pepsi are the only two producers of cola drinks, making them duopolists. Both companies have zero marginal cost and a fixed cost of $100,000.

a. Assume first that consumers regard Coke and Pepsi as perfect substitutes. Currently both are sold for $0.20 per can, and at that price each company sells 4 million cans per day.

   i. How large is Pepsi's profit?

   ii. If Pepsi were to raise its price to $0.30 per can, and Coke does not respond, what would happen to Pepsi's profit?

b. Now suppose that each company advertises to differentiate its product from the other company's. As a result of advertising, Pepsi realizes that if it raises or lowers its price, it will sell less or more of its product, as shown by the demand schedule in the accompanying table.

Price of Pepsi (per can)	Quantity of Pepsi demanded (millions of cans)
$0.10	5
0.20	4
0.30	3
0.40	2
0.50	1

If Pepsi now were to raise its price to $0.30 per can, what would happen to its profit?

c. Comparing your answer to part a(i) and to part b, what is the maximum amount Pepsi would be willing to spend on advertising?

8. Philip Morris and R.J. Reynolds spend huge sums of money each year to advertise their tobacco products in an attempt to steal customers from each other. Suppose each year Philip Morris and R.J. Reynolds have to decide whether or not they want to spend money on advertising. If neither firm advertises, each will earn a profit of $2 million. If they both advertise, each will earn a profit of $1.5 million. If one firm advertises and the other does not, the firm that advertises will earn a profit of $2.8 million and the other firm will earn $1 million.

a. Use a payoff matrix to depict this problem.

b. Suppose Philip Morris and R.J. Reynolds can write an enforceable contract about what they will do. What is the cooperative solution to this game?

c. What is the Nash equilibrium without an enforceable contract? Explain why this is the likely outcome.

9. Over the last 40 years the Organization of Petroleum Exporting Countries (OPEC) has had varied success in forming and maintaining its cartel agreements. Explain how the following factors may contribute to the difficulty of forming and/or maintaining its price and output agreements.

a. New oil fields are discovered and increased drilling is undertaken in the Gulf of Mexico and the North Sea by nonmembers of OPEC.

b. Crude oil is a product that is differentiated by sulfur content: it costs less to refine low-sulfur crude oil into gasoline. Different OPEC countries possess oil reserves of different sulfur content.

c. Cars powered by hydrogen are developed.

10. Suppose you are an economist working for the Antitrust Division of the Department of Justice. In each of the following cases you are given the task of determining whether the behavior warrants an antitrust investigation for possible illegal acts or is just an example of undesirable, but not illegal, tacit collusion. Explain your reasoning.

a. Two companies dominate the industry for industrial lasers. Several people sit on the boards of directors of both companies.

b. Three banks dominate the market for banking in a given state. Their profits have been going up recently as they add new fees for customer transactions. Advertising among the banks is fierce, and new branches are springing up in many locations.

c. The two oil companies that produce most of the petroleum for the western half of the United States have decided to forgo building their own pipelines and to share a common pipeline, the only means of transporting petroleum products to that market.

d. The two major companies that dominate the market for herbal supplements have each created a subsidiary that sells the same product as the parent company in large quantities but with a generic name.

e. The two largest credit card companies, Passport and OmniCard, have required all retailers who accept their cards to agree to limit their use of rival credit cards.

For interactive, step-by-step help in solving the following problem, visit LaunchPad by using the URL on the back cover of this book.

11. Let's revisit the fisheries agreement introduced in Problem 5 stating that to preserve the North Atlantic fish stocks, only two fishing fleets, one from the United States and the other from the European Union (EU), can fish in those waters. The accompanying table shows the market demand schedule per week for fish from these waters. The only costs are fixed costs, so fishing fleets maximize profit by maximizing revenue.

Price of fish (per pound)	Quantity of fish demanded (pounds)
$17	1,800
16	2,000
15	2,100
14	2,200
12	2,300

a. If both fishing fleets collude, what is the revenue-maximizing output for the North Atlantic fishery? What price will a pound of fish sell for?

b. If both fishing fleets collude and share the output equally, what is the revenue to the EU fleet? To the U.S. fleet?

c. Suppose the EU fleet cheats by expanding its own catch by 100 pounds per week. The U.S. fleet doesn't change its catch. What is the revenue to the U.S. fleet? To the EU fleet?

d. In retaliation for the cheating by the EU fleet, the U.S. fleet also expands its catch by 100 pounds per week. What is the revenue to the U.S. fleet? To the EU fleet?

Monopolistic Competition and Product Differentiation

▶ **What You Will Learn in This Chapter**

■ The meaning of **monopolistic competition**

■ Why oligopolists and monopolistically competitive firms differentiate their products

■ How prices and profits are determined in monopolistic competition in the short run and the long run

■ Why monopolistic competition poses a trade-off between lower prices and greater product diversity

■ The economic significance of advertising and **brand names**

FAST-FOOD DIFFERENTIATION

Competing for your tastebuds.

A BEST-SELLING BOOK TITLED *Fast Food Nation* offered a fascinating if rather negative report on the burgers, pizza, tacos, and fried chicken that make up so much of the modern American diet. According to the book, all fast-food chains produce and deliver their food in pretty much the same way. In particular, a lot of the taste of fast food—whatever kind of fast food it is—comes from food additives manufactured in New Jersey.

But each fast-food provider goes to great lengths to convince you that it has something special to offer. As a sign of how well McDonald's carefully cultivates its image, everyone recognizes the McDonald's slogan—"I'm lovin'it!"—and knows what a Big Mac or a Quarter Pounder is. Its rivals Burger King and Wendy's emphasize their cooking techniques—Burger King with its "flame-broiled patties" and Wendy's with its "hot and juicy made-to-order old-fashioned hamburger"—to make consumers believe that their burgers are better tasting. A few years back Wendy's went so far as to mount an advertising claim with a little old lady yelling "Where's the beef?" to highlight its somewhat bigger burgers (compared to those at McDonald's).

So how would you describe the fast-food industry? On the one side, it clearly isn't a monopoly. When you go to a fast-food court, you have a choice among vendors, and there is real competition between the different burger outlets and between the burgers and the fried chicken. On the other side, in a way each vendor *does* possess some aspects of a monopoly: at one point McDonald's had the slogan "Nobody does it like McDonald's." That was literally true—though McDonald's competitors would claim that they did it *better*. In any case, the point is that each fast-food provider offers a product that is *differentiated* from its rivals' products.

In the fast-food industry, many firms compete to satisfy more or less the same demand—the desire of consumers for something tasty but quick. But each firm offers to satisfy that demand with a distinctive, differentiated product—products that consumers typically view as close but not perfect substitutes.

When there are many firms offering competing, differentiated products, as there are in the fast-food industry, economists say that the industry is characterized by *monopolistic competition*. This is the fourth and final market structure that we will discuss, after perfect competition, monopoly, and oligopoly.

We'll start by defining monopolistic competition more carefully and explaining its characteristic features. Then we'll explore how firms differentiate their products; this will allow us to analyze how monopolistic competition works. The chapter concludes with a discussion of some ongoing controversies about product differentiation—in particular, the question of why advertising is effective.

Monopolistic competition is a market structure in which there are many competing producers in an industry, each producer sells a differentiated product, and there is free entry into and exit from the industry in the long run.

The Meaning of Monopolistic Competition

Leo manages the Wonderful Wok stand in the food court of a big shopping mall. He offers the only Chinese food there, but there are more than a dozen alternatives, from Bodacious Burgers to Pizza Paradise. When deciding what to charge for a meal, Leo knows that he must take those alternatives into account: even people who normally prefer stir-fry won't order a $15 lunch from Leo when they can get a burger, fries, and drink for $4.

But Leo also knows that he won't lose all his business even if his lunches cost a bit more than the alternatives. Chinese food isn't the same thing as burgers or pizza. Some people will really be in the mood for Chinese that day, and they will buy from Leo even if they could dine more cheaply on burgers. Of course, the reverse is also true: even if Chinese is a bit cheaper, some people will choose burgers instead. In other words, Leo does have some market power: he has *some* ability to set his own price.

So how would you describe Leo's situation? He definitely isn't a price-taker, so he isn't in a situation of perfect competition. But you wouldn't exactly call him a monopolist, either. Although he's the only seller of Chinese food in that food court, he does face competition from other food vendors.

Yet it would also be wrong to call him an oligopolist. Oligopoly, remember, involves competition among a small number of interdependent firms in an industry protected by some—albeit limited—barriers to entry and whose profits are highly interdependent. Because their profits are highly interdependent, oligopolists have an incentive to collude, tacitly or explicitly. But in Leo's case there are *lots* of vendors in the shopping mall, too many to make tacit collusion feasible.

Economists describe Leo's situation as one of **monopolistic competition.** Monopolistic competition is particularly common in service industries like restaurants and gas stations, but it also exists in some manufacturing industries. It involves three conditions: large numbers of competing producers, differentiated products, and free entry into and exit from the industry in the long run.

In a monopolistically competitive industry, each producer has some ability to set the price of her differentiated product. But exactly how high she can set it is limited by the competition she faces from other existing and potential producers that produce close, but not identical, products.

Large Numbers

In a monopolistically competitive industry, there are many producers. Such an industry does not look either like a monopoly, where the firm faces no competition, or an oligopoly, where each firm has only a few rivals. Instead, each seller has many competitors. For example, there are many vendors in a big food court, many gas stations along a major highway, and many hotels at a popular beach resort.

Differentiated Products

In a monopolistically competitive industry, each producer has a product that consumers view as somewhat distinct from the products of competing firms; at the same time, though, consumers see these competing products as close substitutes. If Leo's food court contained 15 vendors selling exactly the same kind and quality of food, there would be perfect competition: any seller who tried to charge a higher price would have no customers. But suppose that Wonderful Wok is the only Chinese food vendor, Bodacious Burgers is the only hamburger stand, and so on. The result of this differentiation is that each seller has some ability to set his own price: each producer has some—albeit limited—market power.

Free Entry and Exit in the Long Run

In monopolistically competitive industries, new producers, with their own distinct products, can enter the industry freely in the long run. For example, other food vendors would open outlets in the food court if they thought it would be profitable to do so. In addition, firms will exit the industry if they find they are not covering their costs in the long run.

Monopolistic competition, then, differs from the three market structures we have examined so far. It's not the same as perfect competition: firms have some power to set prices. It's not pure monopoly: firms face some competition. And it's not the same as oligopoly: because there are many firms and free entry, the potential for collusion so important in oligopoly no longer exists.

We'll see in a moment how prices, output, and the number of products available are determined in monopolistically competitive industries. But first, let's look a little more closely at what it means to have differentiated products.

Product Differentiation

We pointed out in Chapter 14 that product differentiation often plays an important role in oligopolistic industries. In such industries, product differentiation reduces the intensity of competition between firms when tacit collusion cannot be achieved. Product differentiation plays an even more crucial role in monopolistically competitive industries. Because tacit collusion is virtually impossible when there are many producers, product differentiation is the only way monopolistically competitive firms can acquire some market power.

How do firms in the same industry—such as fast-food vendors, gas stations, or chocolate makers—differentiate their products? Sometimes the difference is mainly in the minds of consumers rather than in the products themselves. We'll discuss the role of advertising and the importance of brand names in achieving this kind of product differentiation later in the chapter. But, in general, firms differentiate their products by—surprise!—actually making them different.

The key to product differentiation is that consumers have different preferences and are willing to pay somewhat more to satisfy those preferences. Each producer can carve out a market niche by producing something that caters to the particular preferences of some group of consumers better than the products of other firms.

There are three important forms of product differentiation: differentiation by style or type, differentiation by location, and differentiation by quality.

Differentiation by Style or Type

The sellers in Leo's food court offer different types of fast food: hamburgers, pizza, Chinese food, Mexican food, and so on. Each consumer arrives at the food court with some preference for one or another of these offerings. This preference may depend on the consumer's mood, her diet, or what she has already eaten that day. These preferences will not make consumers indifferent to price: if Wonderful Wok were to charge $15 for an egg roll, everybody would go to Bodacious Burgers or Pizza Paradise instead. But some people will choose a more expensive meal if that type of food is closer to their preference. So the products of the different vendors are substitutes, but they aren't *perfect* substitutes—they are *imperfect substitutes*.

Vendors in a food court aren't the only sellers that differentiate their offerings by type. Clothing stores concentrate on women's or men's clothes, on business or casual clothes, on trendy or classic styles, and so on. Auto manufacturers offer sedans, minivans, sport-utility vehicles, and sports cars, each type aimed at drivers with different needs and tastes.

Books offer yet another example of differentiation by type and style. Mysteries are differentiated from romances; among mysteries, we can differentiate among hard-boiled detective stories, whodunits, and police procedurals. And no two writers of hard-boiled detective stories are exactly alike: Raymond Chandler and Sue Grafton each have their devoted fans.

In fact, product differentiation is characteristic of most consumer goods. As long as people differ in their tastes, producers find it possible and profitable to produce a range of varieties.

Differentiation by Location

Gas stations along a road offer differentiated products. True, the gas may be exactly the same. But the location of the stations is different, and location matters to consumers: it's more convenient to stop for gas near your home, near your workplace, or near wherever you are when the gas gauge gets low.

In fact, many monopolistically competitive industries supply goods differentiated by location. This is especially true in service industries, from dry cleaners to hairdressers, where customers often choose the seller who is closest rather than cheapest.

Differentiation by Quality

Do you have a craving for chocolate? How much are you willing to spend on it? You see, there's chocolate and then there's chocolate: although ordinary chocolate may not be very expensive, gourmet chocolate can cost several dollars per bite.

With chocolate, as with many goods, there is a range of possible qualities. You can get a usable bicycle for less than $100; you can get a much fancier bicycle for 10 times as much. It all depends on how much the additional quality matters to you and how much you will miss the other things you could have purchased with that money.

Because consumers vary in what they are willing to pay for higher quality, producers can differentiate their products by quality—some offering lower-quality, inexpensive products and others offering higher-quality products at a higher price.

Product differentiation, then, can take several forms. Whatever form it takes, however, there are two important features of industries with differentiated products: *competition among sellers* and *value in diversity*.

Competition among sellers means that even though sellers of differentiated products are not offering identical goods, they are to some extent competing for a limited market. If more businesses enter the market, each will find that it sells less quantity at any given price. For example, if a new gas station opens along a road, each of the existing gas stations will sell a bit less.

Value in diversity refers to the gain to consumers from the proliferation of differentiated products. A food court with eight vendors makes consumers happier than one with only six vendors, even if the prices are the same, because some customers will get a meal that is closer to what they had in mind. A road on which there is a gas station every two miles is more convenient for motorists than a road where gas stations are five miles apart.

When a product is available in many different qualities, fewer people are forced to pay for more quality than they need or to settle for lower quality than they want. There are, in other words, benefits to consumers from a greater diversity of available products.

As we'll see next, competition among the sellers of differentiated products is the key to understanding how monopolistic competition works.

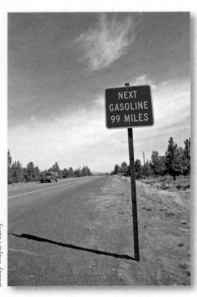

For industries that differentiate by location, proximity is everything.

Buddy Mays/Alamy

ECONOMICS ▶ *in Action*

Any Color, So Long as It's Black

The early history of the auto industry offers a classic illustration of the power of product differentiation.

The modern automobile industry was created by Henry Ford, who first introduced assembly-line production. This technique made it possible for him to offer the famous Model T at a far lower price than anyone else was charging for a car; by 1920, Ford dominated the automobile business.

Ford's strategy was to offer just one style of car, which maximized his economies of scale in production but made no concessions to differences in consumers' tastes. He supposedly declared that customers could get the Model T in "any color, so long as it's black."

This strategy was challenged by Alfred P. Sloan, who had merged a number of smaller automobile companies into General Motors. Sloan's strategy was to offer a range of car types, differentiated by quality and price. Chevrolets were basic cars that directly challenged the Model T, Buicks were bigger and more expensive, and so on up to Cadillacs. And you could get each model in several different colors.

By the 1930s the verdict was clear: customers preferred a range of styles, and General Motors, not Ford, became the dominant auto manufacturer for the rest of the twentieth century.

Ford's Model T in basic black.

Science and Society/Superstock

Check Your Understanding   15-1

1. Each of the following goods and services is a differentiated product. Which are differentiated as a result of monopolistic competition and which are not? Explain your answers.
   a. Ladders
   b. Soft drinks
   c. Department stores
   d. Steel
2. You must determine which of two types of market structure better describes an industry, but you are allowed to ask only one question about the industry. What question should you ask to determine if an industry is:
   a. Perfectly competitive or monopolistically competitive?
   b. A monopoly or monopolistically competitive?

Solutions appear at back of book.

▼ Quick Review

• In **monopolistic competition** there are many competing producers, each with a differentiated product, and free entry and exit in the long run.

• Product differentiation can occur in oligopolies that fail to achieve tacit collusion as well as in monopolistic competition. It takes three main forms: by style or type, by location, or by quality. The products of competing sellers are considered imperfect substitutes.

• Producers compete for the same market, so entry by more producers reduces the quantity each existing producer sells at any given price. In addition, consumers gain from the increased diversity of products.

Understanding Monopolistic Competition

Suppose an industry is monopolistically competitive: it consists of many producers, all competing for the same consumers but offering differentiated products. How does such an industry behave?

As the term *monopolistic competition* suggests, this market structure combines some features typical of monopoly with others typical of perfect competition. Because each firm is offering a distinct product, it is in a way like a monopolist: it faces a downward-sloping demand curve and has some market power—the ability within limits to determine the price of its product. However, unlike a pure monopolist, a monopolistically competitive firm does face competition: the amount of its product it can sell depends on the prices and products offered by other firms in the industry.

The same, of course, is true of an oligopoly. In a monopolistically competitive industry, however, there are *many* producers, as opposed to the small number that defines an oligopoly. This means that the "puzzle" of oligopoly—will firms collude or will they behave noncooperatively?—does not arise in the case of monopolistically competitive industries. True, if all the gas stations or all the restaurants in a town could agree—explicitly or tacitly—to raise prices, it would be in their mutual interest to do so.

But such collusion is virtually impossible when the number of firms is large and, by implication, there are no barriers to entry. So in situations of monopolistic competition, we can safely assume that firms behave noncooperatively and ignore the potential for collusion.

Monopolistic Competition in the Short Run

We introduced the distinction between short-run and long-run equilibrium back in Chapter 12. The short-run equilibrium of an industry takes the number of firms as given. The long-run equilibrium, by contrast, is reached only after enough time has elapsed for firms to enter or exit the industry. To analyze monopolistic competition, we focus first on the short run and then on how an industry moves from the short run to the long run.

Panels (a) and (b) of Figure 15-1 show two possible situations that a typical firm in a monopolistically competitive industry might face in the short run. In each case, the firm looks like any monopolist: it faces a downward-sloping demand curve, which implies a downward-sloping marginal revenue curve.

FIGURE 15-1 | The Monopolistically Competitive Firm in the Short Run

The firm in panel (a) can be profitable for some output quantities: the quantities for which its average total cost curve, *ATC*, lies below its demand curve, D_P. The profit-maximizing output quantity is Q_P, the output at which marginal revenue, MR_P, is equal to marginal cost, *MC*. The firm charges price P_P and earns a profit, represented by the area of the green-shaded rectangle. The firm in panel (b), however, can never

be profitable because its average total cost curve lies above its demand curve, D_U, for every output quantity. The best that it can do if it produces at all is to produce quantity Q_U and charge price P_U. This generates a loss, indicated by the area of the yellow-shaded rectangle. Any other output quantity results in a greater loss.

We assume that every firm has an upward-sloping marginal cost curve but that it also faces some fixed costs, so that its average total cost curve is U-shaped. This assumption doesn't matter in the short run, but, as we'll see shortly, it is crucial to understanding the long-run equilibrium.

In each case the firm, in order to maximize profit, sets marginal revenue equal to marginal cost. So how do these two figures differ? In panel (a) the firm is profitable; in panel (b) it is unprofitable. (Recall that we are referring always to economic profit, not accounting profit—that is, a profit given that all factors of production are earning their opportunity costs.)

In panel (a) the firm faces the demand curve D_P and the marginal revenue curve MR_P. It produces the profit-maximizing output Q_P, the quantity at which marginal revenue is equal to marginal cost, and sells it at the price P_P. This price is above the average total cost at this output, ATC_P. The firm's profit is indicated by the area of the shaded rectangle.

In panel (b) the firm faces the demand curve D_U and the marginal revenue curve MR_U. It chooses the quantity Q_U at which marginal revenue is equal to marginal cost. However, in this case the price P_U is *below* the average total cost ATC_U; so at this quantity the firm loses money. Its loss is equal to the area of the shaded rectangle. Since Q_U is the profit-maximizing quantity—which means, in this case, the loss-minimizing quantity—there is no way for a firm in this situation to make a profit. We can confirm this by noting that at *any* quantity of output, the average total cost curve in panel (b) lies above the demand curve D_U. Because $ATC > P$ at all quantities of output, this firm always suffers a loss.

As this comparison suggests, the key to whether a firm with market power is profitable or unprofitable in the short run lies in the relationship between its demand curve and its average total cost curve. In panel (a) the demand curve D_P crosses the average total cost curve, meaning that some of the demand curve lies above the average total cost curve. So there are some price–quantity combinations available at which price is higher than average total cost, indicating that the firm can choose a quantity at which it makes positive profit.

In panel (b), by contrast, the demand curve D_U does not cross the average total cost curve—it always lies below it. So the price corresponding to each quantity demanded is always less than the average total cost of producing that quantity. There is no quantity at which the firm can avoid losing money.

These figures, showing firms facing downward-sloping demand curves and their associated marginal revenue curves, look just like ordinary monopoly analysis. The "competition" aspect of monopolistic competition comes into play, however, when we move from the short run to the long run.

Monopolistic Competition in the Long Run

Obviously, an industry in which existing firms are losing money, like the one in panel (b) of Figure 15-1, is not in long-run equilibrium. When existing firms are losing money, some firms will *exit* the industry. The industry will not be in long-run equilibrium until the persistent losses have been eliminated by the exit of some firms.

It may be less obvious that an industry in which existing firms are earning profits, like the one in panel (a) of Figure 15-1, is also not in long-run equilibrium. Given that there is *free entry* into the industry, persistent profits earned by the existing firms will lead to the entry of additional producers. The industry will not be in long-run equilibrium until the persistent profits have been eliminated by the entry of new producers.

How will entry or exit by other firms affect the profits of a typical existing firm? Because the differentiated products offered by firms in a monopolistically competitive industry compete for the same set of customers, entry or exit by other firms will affect the demand curve facing every existing producer. If new gas stations open along a highway, each of the existing gas stations will no longer be

In the long run, a monopolistically competitive industry ends up in **zero-profit equilibrium:** each firm makes zero profit at its profit-maximizing quantity.

able to sell as much gas as before at any given price. So, as illustrated in panel (a) of Figure 15-2, entry of additional producers into a monopolistically competitive industry will lead to a *leftward* shift of the demand curve and the marginal revenue curve facing a typical existing producer.

Conversely, suppose that some of the gas stations along the highway close. Then each of the remaining stations will be able to sell more gasoline at any given price. So, as illustrated in panel (b), exit of firms from an industry will lead to a *rightward* shift of the demand curve and marginal revenue curve facing a typical remaining producer.

The industry will be in long-run equilibrium when there is neither entry nor exit. This will occur only when every firm earns zero profit. So in the long run, a monopolistically competitive industry will end up in **zero-profit equilibrium,** in which firms just manage to cover their costs at their profit-maximizing output quantities.

We have seen that a firm facing a downward-sloping demand curve will earn positive profits if any part of that demand curve lies above its average total cost curve; it will incur a loss if its demand curve lies everywhere below its average total cost curve. So in zero-profit equilibrium, the firm must be in a borderline position between these two cases; its demand curve must just touch its average total cost curve. That is, it must be just *tangent* to it at the firm's profit-maximizing output quantity—the output quantity at which marginal revenue equals marginal cost.

If this is not the case, the firm operating at its profit-maximizing quantity will find itself making either a profit or loss, as illustrated in the panels of Figure 15-1. But we also know that free entry and exit means that this cannot be a long-run equilibrium. Why? In the case of a profit, new firms will enter the industry, shifting the demand curve of every existing firm leftward until all profits are

---

FIGURE **15-2** Entry and Exit Shift Existing Firm's Demand Curve and Marginal Revenue Curve

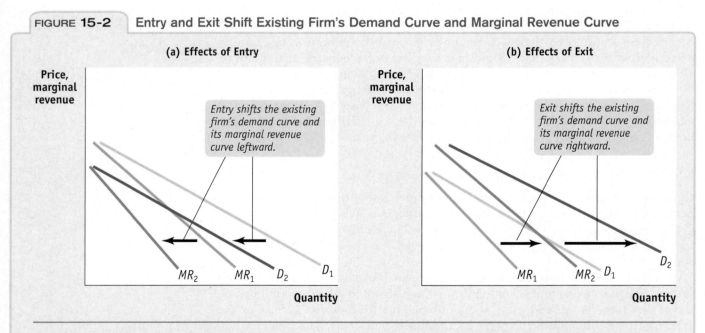

(a) Effects of Entry

(b) Effects of Exit

Entry will occur in the long run when existing firms are profitable. In panel (a), entry causes each existing firm's demand curve and marginal revenue curve to shift to the left. The firm receives a lower price for every unit it sells, and its profit falls. Entry will cease when firms make zero profit. Exit will occur in the long run when existing firms are unprofitable. In panel (b), exit from the industry shifts each remaining firm's demand curve and marginal revenue curve to the right. The firm receives a higher price for every unit it sells, and profit rises. Exit will cease when the remaining firms make zero profit.

FOR INQUIRING MINDS | Hits and Flops

On the face of it, the movie business seems to meet the criteria for monopolistic competition. Movies compete for the same consumers; each movie is different from the others; new companies can and do enter the business. But where's the zero-profit equilibrium? After all, some movies are enormously profitable.

The key is to realize that for every successful blockbuster, there are several flops—and that the movie studios don't know in advance which will be which. And by the time it becomes

clear that a movie will be a flop, it's too late to cancel it.

The difference between movie-making and the type of monopolistic competition we model in this chapter is that the fixed costs of making a movie are also *sunk costs*—once they've been incurred, they can't be recovered.

Yet there is still, in a way, a zero-profit equilibrium. If movies on average were highly profitable, more studios would enter the industry and more movies would be made. If movies on average lost money, fewer movies would be made.

In fact, as you might expect, the movie industry on average earns just about enough to cover the cost of production—that is, it earns roughly zero economic profit.

This kind of situation—in which firms earn zero profit on average but have a mixture of highly profitable hits and money-losing flops—can be found in other industries characterized by high up-front sunk costs. A notable example is the pharmaceutical industry, where many research projects lead nowhere but a few lead to highly profitable drugs. ∎

extinguished. In the case of a loss, some existing firms will exit and so shift the demand curve of every remaining firm to the right until all losses are extinguished. All entry and exit ceases only when every existing firm makes zero profit at its profit-maximizing quantity of output.

Figure 15-3 shows a typical monopolistically competitive firm in such a zero-profit equilibrium. The firm produces Q_{MC}, the output at which $MR_{MC} = MC$, and charges price P_{MC}. At this price and quantity, represented by point Z, the demand curve is just tangent to its average total cost curve. The firm earns zero profit because price, P_{MC}, is equal to average total cost, ATC_{MC}.

The normal long-run condition of a monopolistically competitive industry, then, is that each producer is in the situation shown in Figure 15-3. Each producer acts like a monopolist, facing a downward-sloping demand curve and setting marginal cost equal to marginal revenue so as to maximize profits. But this is just enough to achieve zero economic profit. The producers in the industry are like monopolists without monopoly profits.

FIGURE 15-3 | The Long-Run Zero-Profit Equilibrium

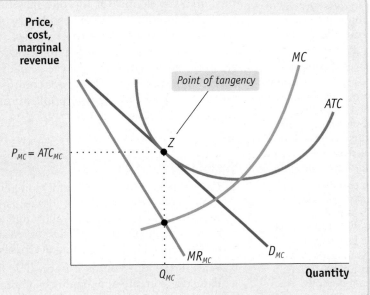

If existing firms are profitable, entry will occur and shift each existing firm's demand curve leftward. If existing firms are unprofitable, each remaining firm's demand curve shifts rightward as some firms exit the industry. Entry and exit will cease when every existing firm makes zero profit at its profit-maximizing quantity. So, in long-run zero-profit equilibrium, the demand curve of each firm is tangent to its average total cost curve at its profit-maximizing quantity: at the profit-maximizing quantity, Q_{MC}, price, P_{MC}, equals average total cost, ATC_{MC}. A monopolistically competitive firm is like a monopolist without monopoly profits.

ECONOMICS ▶ in Action

The Housing Bust and the Demise of the 6% Commission

The vast majority of home sales in the United States are transacted with the use of real estate agents. A homeowner looking to sell hires an agent, who lists the house for sale and shows it to interested buyers. Correspondingly, prospective home buyers hire their own agent to arrange inspections of available houses. Traditionally, agents were paid by the seller: a commission equal to 6% of the sales price of the house, which the seller's agent and the buyer's agent would split equally. If a house sold for $300,000, for example, the seller's agent and the buyer's agent each received $9,000 (equal to 3% of $300,000).

The real estate brokerage industry fits the model of monopolistic competition quite well: in any given local market, there are many real estate agents, all competing with one another, but the agents are differentiated by location and personality as well as by the type of home they sell (some focus on condominiums, others on very expensive homes, and so on). And the industry has free entry: it's relatively easy for someone to become a real estate agent (take a course and then pass a test to obtain a license).

But for a long time there was one feature that didn't fit the model of monopolistic competition: the fixed 6% commission that had not changed over time and was unaffected by the ups and downs of the housing market. How could this be? Why didn't new agents enter the market and drive the commission down to the zero-profit level?

One tactic used by agents was their control of the Multiple Listing Service, or MLS, which lists nearly all the homes for sale in a community. Traditionally, only sellers who agreed to the 6% commission were allowed to list homes on the MLS.

But protecting the 6% commission was always an iffy endeavor because any action by the brokerage industry to fix the commission rate at a given percentage would run afoul of antitrust laws. And by the early to mid-2000s, as the housing boom intensified, discount brokers had appeared on the scene. But traditional agents refused to work with them. So in 2005, the Justice Department sued the National Association of Realtors, the powerful trade group of agents.

Oversight by regulators and the housing market bust which began in 2006 hastened the demise of the non-negotiable 6% commission. With sellers forced to accept less for their houses than expected, pressure built for agents to accept less as well. In addition, the Internet and sites like Zillow.com and Redfin.com have made it much easier for homeowners to sell on their own or find a discount realtor who is willing to charge a much lower percentage. As a result, even full-service realtors regularly accept commissions less than 6%. As Steve Murray, the editor of a real estate trade publication said, "The standard 6 percent went out the window a long time ago."

▼ Quick Review

• Like a monopolist, each firm in a monopolistically competitive industry faces a downward-sloping demand curve and marginal revenue curve. In the short run, it may earn a profit or incur a loss at its profit-maximizing quantity.

• If the typical firm earns positive profit, new firms will enter the industry in the long run, shifting each existing firm's demand curve to the left. If the typical firm incurs a loss, some existing firms will exit the industry in the long run, shifting the demand curve of each remaining firm to the right.

• The long-run equilibrium of a monopolistically competitive industry is a **zero-profit equilibrium** in which firms just break even. The typical firm's demand curve is tangent to its average total cost curve at its profit-maximizing quantity.

Check Your Understanding 15-2

1. Currently a monopolistically competitive industry, composed of firms with U-shaped average total cost curves, is in long-run equilibrium. Describe how the industry adjusts, in both the short and long run, in each of the following situations.
   a. A technological change that increases fixed cost for every firm in the industry
   b. A technological change that decreases marginal cost for every firm in the industry

2. Why, in the long run, is it impossible for firms in a monopolistically competitive industry to create a monopoly by joining together to form a single firm?

Solutions appear at back of book.

Monopolistic Competition versus Perfect Competition

In a way, long-run equilibrium in a monopolistically competitive industry looks a lot like long-run equilibrium in a perfectly competitive industry. In both cases, there are many firms; in both cases, profits have been competed away; in both cases, the price received by every firm is equal to the average total cost of production.

However, the two versions of long-run equilibrium are different—in ways that are economically significant.

Price, Marginal Cost, and Average Total Cost

Figure 15-4 compares the long-run equilibrium of a typical firm in a perfectly competitive industry with that of a typical firm in a monopolistically competitive industry. Panel (a) shows a perfectly competitive firm facing a market price equal to its minimum average total cost; panel (b) reproduces Figure 15-3. Comparing the panels, we see two important differences.

First, in the case of the perfectly competitive firm shown in panel (a), the price, P_{PC}, received by the firm at the profit-maximizing quantity, Q_{PC}, is equal to the firm's marginal cost of production, MC_{PC}, at that quantity of output. By contrast, at the profit-maximizing quantity chosen by the monopolistically competitive firm in panel (b), Q_{MC}, the price, P_{MC}, is *higher* than the marginal cost of production, MC_{MC}.

FIGURE 15-4   Comparing Long-Run Equilibrium in Perfect Competition and Monopolistic Competition

Panel (a) shows the situation of the typical firm in long-run equilibrium in a perfectly competitive industry. The firm operates at the minimum-cost output Q_{PC}, sells at the competitive market price P_{PC}, and makes zero profit. It is indifferent to selling another unit of output because P_{PC} is equal to its marginal cost, MC_{PC}. Panel (b) shows the situation of the typical firm in long-run equilibrium in a monop-

olistically competitive industry. At Q_{MC} it makes zero profit because its price, P_{MC}, just equals average total cost, ATC_{MC}. At Q_{MC} the firm would like to sell another unit at price P_{MC} since P_{MC} exceeds marginal cost, MC_{MC}. But it is unwilling to lower price to make more sales. It therefore operates to the left of the minimum-cost output level and has excess capacity.

Firms in a monopolistically competitive industry have **excess capacity:** they produce less than the output at which average total cost is minimized.

This difference translates into a difference in the attitude of firms toward consumers. A wheat farmer, who can sell as much wheat as he likes at the going market price, would not get particularly excited if you offered to buy some more wheat at the market price. Since he has no desire to produce more at that price and can sell the wheat to someone else, you are not doing him a favor.

But if you decide to fill up your tank at Jamil's gas station rather than at Katy's, you are doing Jamil a favor. He is not willing to cut his price to get more customers—he's already made the best of that trade-off. But if he gets a few more customers than he expected at the *posted* price, that's good news: an additional sale at the posted price increases his revenue more than it increases his costs because the posted price exceeds marginal cost.

The fact that monopolistic competitors, unlike perfect competitors, want to sell more at the going price is crucial to understanding why they engage in activities like advertising that help increase sales.

The other difference between monopolistic competition and perfect competition that is visible in Figure 15-4 involves the position of each firm on its average total cost curve. In panel (a), the perfectly competitive firm produces at point Q_{PC}, at the bottom of the U-shaped *ATC* curve. That is, each firm produces the quantity at which average total cost is minimized—the *minimum-cost output*. As a consequence, the total cost of industry output is also minimized.

Under monopolistic competition, in panel (b), the firm produces at Q_{MC}, on the *downward-sloping* part of the U-shaped *ATC* curve: it produces less than the quantity that would minimize average total cost. This failure to produce enough to minimize average total cost is sometimes described as the **excess capacity** issue. The typical vendor in a food court or gas station along a road is not big enough to take maximum advantage of available cost savings. So the total cost of industry output is not minimized in the case of a monopolistically competitive industry.

Some people have argued that, because every monopolistic competitor has excess capacity, monopolistically competitive industries are inefficient. But the issue of efficiency under monopolistic competition turns out to be a subtle one that does not have a clear answer.

Is Monopolistic Competition Inefficient?

A monopolistic competitor, like a monopolist, charges a price that is above marginal cost. As a result, some people who are willing to pay at least as much for an egg roll at Wonderful Wok as it costs to produce it are deterred from doing so. In monopolistic competition, some mutually beneficial transactions go unexploited.

Furthermore, it is often argued that monopolistic competition is subject to a further kind of inefficiency: that the excess capacity of every monopolistic competitor implies *wasteful duplication* because monopolistically competitive industries offer too many varieties. According to this argument, it would be better if there were only two or three vendors in the food court, not six or seven. If there were fewer vendors, they would each have lower average total costs and so could offer food more cheaply.

Is this argument against monopolistic competition right—that it lowers total surplus by causing inefficiency? Not necessarily. It's true that if there were fewer gas stations along a highway, each gas station would sell more gasoline and so would have lower costs per gallon. But there is a drawback: motorists would be inconvenienced because gas stations would be farther apart. The point is that the diversity of products offered in a monopolistically competitive industry is beneficial to consumers. So the higher price consumers pay because of excess capacity is offset to some extent by the value they receive from greater diversity.

There is, in other words, a trade-off: more producers means higher average total costs but also greater product diversity. Does a monopolistically competitive industry arrive at the socially optimal point on this trade-off? Probably not—but it is hard to say whether there are too many firms or too few! Most economists now believe that duplication of effort and excess capacity in monopolistically competitive industries are not important issues in practice.

Check Your Understanding 15-3

1. True or false? Explain your answers.
   a. Like a firm in a perfectly competitive industry, a firm in a monopolistically competitive industry is willing to sell a good at any price that equals or exceeds marginal cost.
   b. Suppose there is a monopolistically competitive industry in long-run equilibrium that possesses excess capacity. All the firms in the industry would be better off if they merged into a single firm and produced a single product, but whether consumers are made better off by this is ambiguous.
   c. Fads and fashions are more likely to arise in monopolistic competition or oligopoly than in monopoly or perfect competition.

Solutions appear at back of book.

> **▼ Quick Review**
>
> • In the long-run equilibrium of a monopolistically competitive industry, there are many firms, each earning zero profit.
>
> • Price exceeds marginal cost, so some mutually beneficial trades are unexploited.
>
> • Monopolistically competitive firms have **excess capacity** because they do not minimize average total cost. But it is not clear that this is actually a source of inefficiency since consumers gain from product diversity.

Controversies About Product Differentiation

Up to this point, we have assumed that products are differentiated in a way that corresponds to some real desire of consumers. There is real convenience in having a gas station in your neighborhood; Chinese food and Mexican food are really different from each other.

In the real world, however, some instances of product differentiation can seem puzzling if you think about them. What is the real difference between Crest and Colgate toothpaste? Between Energizer and Duracell batteries? Or a Marriott and a Hilton hotel room? Most people would be hard-pressed to answer any of these questions. Yet the producers of these goods make considerable efforts to convince consumers that their products are different from and better than those of their competitors.

No discussion of product differentiation is complete without spending at least a bit of time on the two related issues—and puzzles—of *advertising* and *brand names*.

The Role of Advertising

Wheat farmers don't advertise their wares on TV, but car dealers do. That's not because farmers are shy and car dealers are outgoing; it's because advertising is worthwhile only in industries in which firms have at least some market power.

The purpose of advertisements is to convince people to buy more of a seller's product at the going price. A perfectly competitive firm, which can sell as much as it likes at the going market price, has no incentive to spend money convincing consumers to buy more. Only a firm that has some market power, and that therefore charges a price above marginal cost, can gain from advertising. Industries that are more or less perfectly competitive, like the milk industry, do advertise—but these ads are sponsored by an association on behalf of the industry as a whole, not on behalf of the milk that comes from the cows on a particular farm.

Given that advertising "works," it's not hard to see why firms with market power would spend money on it. But the big question about advertising is *why* it works. A related question is whether advertising is, from society's point of view, a waste of resources.

Not all advertising poses a puzzle. Much of it is straightforward: it's a way for sellers to inform potential buyers about what they have to offer (or, occasionally, for buyers to inform potential sellers about what they want). Nor is there

"The active ingredient is marketing."

much controversy about the economic usefulness of ads that provide information: the real estate ad that declares "sunny, charming, 2 br, 1 ba, a/c" tells you things you need to know (even if a few euphemisms are involved—"charming," of course, means "small").

But what information is being conveyed when a TV actress proclaims the virtues of one or another toothpaste or a sports hero declares that some company's batteries are better than those inside that pink mechanical rabbit? Surely nobody believes that the sports star is an expert on batteries—or that he chose the company that he personally believes makes the best batteries, as opposed to the company that offered to pay him the most. Yet companies believe, with good reason, that money spent on such promotions increases their sales—and that they would be in big trouble if they stopped advertising but their competitors continued to do so.

Why are consumers influenced by ads that do not really provide any information about the product? One answer is that consumers are not as rational as economists typically assume. Perhaps consumers' judgments, or even their tastes, can be influenced by things that economists think ought to be irrelevant, such as which company has hired the most charismatic celebrity to endorse its product. And there is surely some truth to this. As we learned in Chapter 9, consumer rationality is a useful working assumption; it is not an absolute truth.

However, another answer is that consumer response to advertising is not entirely irrational because ads can serve as indirect "signals" in a world where consumers don't have good information about products. Suppose, to take a common example, that you need to avail yourself of some local service that you don't use regularly—body work on your car, say, or furniture moving. You visit YellowPages.com, where you see a number of small listings and several large display, or featured, ads. You know that those display ads are large because the firms paid extra for them; still, it may be quite rational to call one of the firms with a big display ad. After all, the big ad probably means that it's a relatively large, successful company—otherwise, the company wouldn't have found it worth spending the money for the larger ad.

The same principle may partly explain why ads feature celebrities. You don't really believe that the supermodel prefers that watch; but the fact that the watch manufacturer is willing and able to pay her fee tells you that it is a major company that is likely to stand behind its product. According to this reasoning, an expensive advertisement serves to establish the quality of a firm's products in the eyes of consumers.

The possibility that it is rational for consumers to respond to advertising also has some bearing on the question of whether advertising is a waste of resources. If ads only work by manipulating the weak-minded, the $545 billion U.S. businesses are projected to spend in 2014 will have been an economic waste—except to the extent that ads sometimes provide entertainment. To the extent that advertising conveys important information, however, it is an economically productive activity after all.

Brand Names

You've been driving all day, and you decide that it's time to find a place to sleep. On your right, you see a sign for the Bates Motel; on your left, you see a sign for a Motel 6, or a Best Western, or some other national chain. Which one do you choose?

Unless they were familiar with the area, most people would head for the chain. In fact, most motels in the United States are members of major chains; the same is true of most fast-food restaurants and many, if not most, stores in shopping malls.

Motel chains and fast-food restaurants are only one aspect of a broader phenomenon: the role of **brand names,** names owned by particular companies that differentiate their products in the minds of consumers. In many cases, a company's brand name is the most important asset it possesses: clearly, McDonald's is worth far more than the sum of the deep-fat fryers and hamburger grills the company owns.

In fact, companies often go to considerable lengths to defend their brand names, suing anyone else who uses them without permission. You may talk about blowing your nose on a kleenex or xeroxing a document, but unless the product in question comes from Kleenex or Xerox, legally the seller must describe it as a facial tissue or a photocopier.

As with advertising, with which they are closely linked, the social usefulness of brand names is a source of dispute. Does the preference of consumers for known brands reflect consumer irrationality? Or do brand names convey real information? That is, do brand names create unnecessary market power, or do they serve a real purpose?

As in the case of advertising, the answer is probably some of both. On one side, brand names often do create unjustified market power. Many consumers will pay more for brand-name goods in the supermarket even though consumer experts assure us that the cheaper store brands are equally good. Similarly, many common medicines, like aspirin, are cheaper—with no loss of quality—in their generic form.

On the other side, for many products the brand name does convey information. A traveler arriving in a strange town can be sure of what awaits in a Holiday Inn or a McDonald's; a tired and hungry traveler may find this preferable to trying an independent hotel or restaurant that might be better—but might be worse.

In addition, brand names offer some assurance that the seller is engaged in repeated interaction with its customers and so has a reputation to protect. If a traveler eats a bad meal at a restaurant in a tourist trap and vows never to eat there again, the restaurant owner may not care, since the chance is small that the traveler will be in the same area again in the future. But if that traveler eats a bad meal at McDonald's and vows never to eat at a McDonald's again, that matters to the company. This gives McDonald's an incentive to provide consistent quality, thereby assuring travelers that quality controls are in place.

> A **brand name** is a name owned by a particular firm that distinguishes its products from those of other firms.

ECONOMICS ▶ *in Action*

The Perfume Industry: Leading Consumers by the Nose

The perfume industry has remarkably few barriers to entry: to make a fragrance, it is easy to purchase ingredients, mix them, and bottle the result. Even if you don't think you have a very good "nose," consultants are readily available to help you create something special (or even copy someone else's fragrance). So how is it possible that a successful perfume can generate a profit rate of almost 100%? Why don't rivals enter and compete away those profits?

A clue to the answer is that the most successful perfumes these days are heavily promoted by celebrities. Beyoncé, Britney Spears, Christina Aguilera, and Katy Perry all have perfumes that are marketed by them. Jennifer Lopez has eight! In fact, the cost of producing what is in the bottle is minuscule compared to the total cost of selling a successful perfume—only about 3% of the production cost and less than 1% of the retail price. The remaining 97% of the production cost goes into packaging, marketing, and advertising.

In the perfume industry, it's packaging and advertising that generate profits.

The extravagant bottles that modern perfumes come in—some shaped like spaceships or encrusted with rhinestones—incur a cost of four to six times the cost of the perfume inside. Top bottle designers earn well over $100,000 for a single design. Add onto that the cost of advertising, in-store employees who spritz and hawk, and commissions to salespeople. Finally, include the cost of celebrity endorsements that run into the millions of dollars. For example, Jennifer Lopez reportedly has earned more than $30 million dollars on her fragrances. Moreover, in comparison to older fragrances that have been around for decades like Chanel or Dior, modern fragrances are made with much cheaper synthetic ingredients. So while a scent like Chanel would last 24 hours, modern fragrances last only a few hours at best.

As one celebrated "nose," Roja Dora, commented, "Studies show that people will say that a particular perfume is one of their favorites, but in a blind test they hate it. The trouble is that most people buy scent for their ego, after seeing an image in an advert and wanting to identify themselves in a certain way."

So here's a metaphysical question: even if perfume buyers really hate a fragrance in a blind test, but advertising convinces them that it smells wonderful, who are we to say that they are wrong to buy it? Isn't the attractiveness of a scent in the mind of the beholder?

▼ **Quick Review**

• In industries with product differentiation, firms advertise in order to increase the demand for their products.

• Advertising is not a waste of resources when it gives consumers useful information about products.

• Advertising that simply touts a product is harder to explain. Either consumers are irrational, or expensive advertising communicates that the firm's products are of high quality.

• Some firms create **brand names.** As with advertising, the economic value of brand names can be ambiguous. They convey real information when they assure consumers of the quality of a product.

Check Your Understanding 15-4

1. In which of the following cases is advertising likely to be economically useful? Economically wasteful? Explain your answer.
   a. Advertisements on the benefits of aspirin
   b. Advertisements for Bayer aspirin
   c. Advertisements on the benefits of drinking orange juice
   d. Advertisements for Tropicana orange juice
   e. Advertisements that state how long a plumber or an electrician has been in business

2. Some industry analysts have stated that a successful brand name is like a barrier to entry. Explain the reasoning behind this statement.

Solutions appear at back of book.

BUSINESS CASE

Gillette versus Schick: A Case of Razor Burn?

In early 2010, Schick introduced the Hydro system, its latest and most advanced razor, two months before Gillette introduced a new upgrade to its Fusion ProGlide line. According to reports at the time, Schick and Gillette would jointly spend over $250 million in advertising for the two systems. It was another round in a century-long rivalry between the razor makers. Despite the rivalry, the razor business has been a profitable one; it is one of the priciest and highest profit margin sectors of nonfood packaged goods.

Schick and Gillette clearly hoped that the sophistication and features of their new shavers would appeal to customers. Hydro came with a lubricating gel dispenser and blade guards for smoother shaving, and a five-blade version came with a trimming blade. The Hydro was priced below comparable versions of Gillette's razors, including the Pro-Glide, which was going to be priced at 10 to 15 percent above the existing Fusion line.

This was not the first instance of a competitive razor launch. Back in 2003, Gillette and Schick went head-to-head when Gillette introduced its Mach 3 Turbo (an upgrade to its existing Mach 3), which delivered battery-powered pulses that Gillette said caused hair follicles to stand up, facilitating a closer shave. In 2003 Schick introduced the Quattro, the world's first four-blade razor, which it called "unlike any other razor." More recently, the companies introduced yet another new line of razors in 2014, Gillette with its new Fusion Pro-Glide with FlexBall™ Technology, and Schick with the new Hydro 5.

Gillette is by far the larger company of the two, capturing 70% of the U.S. razor market in 2013. Although Schick has only about 12% of the market, many analysts believe it is the leader in innovation. According to William Peoriello, an analyst at investment bank Morgan Stanley, "the roster of new razors from Schick is forcing Gillette to change the pace of its new product launches and appears likely to give Gillette its strongest competition ever."

Many customers, though, have become exasperated with both companies' offerings. In 2012 a small startup, the Dollar Shave Club (DSC), challenged the two giants by producing a video—that soon went viral—in which its founder, Michael Dubin, asks, "Do you like spending $20 a month on brand-name razors?" For $3 to $9 a month, including shipping, the DSC delivers to its customers less expensive razors from China and South Korea.

While Gillette and Schick publicly claimed they were not worried, others are not so sure that they shouldn't be. As one Wall Street market analyst said, "There's clearly almost a backlash among shavers, among razor users, about the price of a man's razor."

QUESTIONS FOR THOUGHT

1. What explains the complexity of today's razors and the pace of innovation in their features?

2. Why is the razor business so profitable? What explains the size of the advertising budgets of Schick and Gillette?

3. What explains the popularity of the Dollar Shave Club? What dilemma do Schick and Gillette face in their decisions about whether to maintain their older, simpler razor models? What does this indicate about the welfare value of the innovation in razors?

SUMMARY

1. **Monopolistic competition** is a market structure in which there are many competing producers, each producing a differentiated product, and there is free entry and exit in the long run. Product differentiation takes three main forms: by style or type, by location, or by quality. Products of competing sellers are considered imperfect substitutes, and each firm has its own downward-sloping demand curve and marginal revenue curve.

2. Short-run profits will attract entry of new firms in the long run. This reduces the quantity each existing producer sells at any given price and shifts its demand curve to the left. Short-run losses will induce exit by some firms in the long run. This shifts the demand curve of each remaining firm to the right.

3. In the long run, a monopolistically competitive industry is in **zero-profit equilibrium:** at its profit-maximizing quantity, the demand curve for each existing firm is tangent to its average total cost curve. There are zero profits in the industry and no entry or exit.

4. In long-run equilibrium, firms in a monopolistically competitive industry sell at a price greater than marginal cost. They also have **excess capacity** because they produce less than the minimum-cost output; as a result, they have higher costs than firms in a perfectly competitive industry. Whether or not monopolistic competition is inefficient is ambiguous because consumers value the diversity of products that it creates.

5. A monopolistically competitive firm will always prefer to make an additional sale at the going price, so it will engage in advertising to increase demand for its product and enhance its market power. Advertising and **brand names** that provide useful information to consumers are economically valuable. But they are economically wasteful when their only purpose is to create market power. In reality, advertising and brand names are likely to be some of both: economically valuable and economically wasteful.

KEY TERMS

Monopolistic competition, p. 446
Zero-profit equilibrium, p. 452

Excess capacity, p. 456

Brand name, p. 459

PROBLEMS

1. Use the three conditions for monopolistic competition discussed in the chapter to decide which of the following firms are likely to be operating as monopolistic competitors. If they are not monopolistically competitive firms, are they monopolists, oligopolists, or perfectly competitive firms?
   a. A local band that plays for weddings, parties, and so on
   b. Minute Maid, a producer of individual-serving juice boxes
   c. Your local dry cleaner
   d. A farmer who produces soybeans

2. You are thinking of setting up a coffee shop. The market structure for coffee shops is monopolistic competition. There are three Starbucks shops and two other coffee shops very much like Starbucks in your town already. In order for you to have some degree of market power, you may want to differentiate your coffee shop. Thinking about the three different ways in which products can be differentiated, explain how you would decide whether you should copy Starbucks or whether you should sell coffee in a completely different way.

3. The market structure of the local gas station industry is monopolistic competition. Suppose that currently each gas station incurs a loss. Draw a diagram for a typical gas station to show this short-run situation. Then, in a separate diagram, show what will happen to the typical gas station in the long run. Explain your reasoning.

4. The local hairdresser industry has the market structure of monopolistic competition. Your hairdresser boasts that he is making a profit and that if he continues to do so, he will be able to retire in five years. Use a diagram to illustrate your hairdresser's current situation. Do you expect this to last? In a separate diagram, draw what you expect to happen in the long run. Explain your reasoning.

5. Magnificent Blooms is a florist in a monopolistically competitive industry. It is a successful operation, producing the quantity that minimizes its average total cost and making a profit. The owner also says that at its current level of output, its marginal cost is above marginal revenue. Illustrate the current situation of Magnificent Blooms in a diagram. Answer the following questions by illustrating with a diagram.

a. In the short run, could Magnificent Blooms increase its profit?

b. In the long run, could Magnificent Blooms increase its profit?

6. "In the long run, there is no difference between monopolistic competition and perfect competition." Discuss whether this statement is true, false, or ambiguous with respect to the following criteria.

   a. The price charged to consumers

   b. The average total cost of production

   c. The efficiency of the market outcome

   d. The typical firm's profit in the long run

7. "In both the short run and in the long run, the typical firm in monopolistic competition and a monopolist each make a profit." Do you agree with this statement? Explain your reasoning.

8. The market for clothes has the structure of monopolistic competition. What impact will fewer firms in this industry have on you as a consumer? Address the following issues.

   a. Variety of clothes

   b. Differences in quality of service

   c. Price

9. For each of the following situations, decide whether advertising is directly informative about the product or simply an indirect signal of its quality. Explain your reasoning.

   a. Football great, Peyton Manning, drives a Buick in a TV commercial and claims that he prefers it to any other car.

   b. A Craigslist ad states, "For sale: 1999 Honda Civic, 160,000 miles, new transmission."

   c. McDonald's spends millions of dollars on an advertising campaign that proclaims: "I'm lovin' it."

   d. Subway advertises one of its sandwiches by claiming that it contains 6 grams of fat and fewer than 300 calories.

10. In each of the following cases, explain how the advertisement functions as a signal to a potential buyer. Explain what information the buyer lacks that is being supplied by the advertisement and how the information supplied by the advertisement is likely to affect the buyer's willingness to buy the good.

   a. "Looking for work. Excellent references from previous employers available."

   b. "Electronic equipment for sale. All merchandise carries a one-year, no-questions-asked warranty."

   c. "Car for sale by original owner. All repair and maintenance records available."

11. The accompanying table shows the Herfindahl–Hirschman Index (HHI) for the restaurant, cereal, movie, and laundry detergent industries as well as the advertising expenditures of the top 10 firms in each industry. Use the information in the table to answer the following questions.

Industry	HHI	Advertising expenditures (millions)
Restaurants	179	$1,784
Cereal	2,098	732
Movie studios	918	3,324
Laundry detergent	2,068	132

   a. Which market structure—oligopoly or monopolistic competition—best characterizes each of the industries?

   b. Based on your answer to part a, which type of market structure has higher advertising expenditures? Use the characteristics of each market structure to explain why this relationship might exist.

12. McDonald's spends millions of dollars each year on legal protection of its brand name, thereby preventing any unauthorized use of it. Explain what information this conveys to you as a consumer about the quality of McDonald's products.

WORK IT OUT Macmillan Education

For interactive, step-by-step help in solving the following problem, visit LaunchPad by using the URL on the back cover of this book.

13. The restaurant business in town is a monopolistically competitive industry in long-run equilibrium. One restaurant owner asks for your advice. She tells you that, each night, not all tables in her restaurant are full. She also tells you that she would attract more customers if she lowered the prices on her menu and that doing so would lower her average total cost. Should she lower her prices? Draw a diagram showing the demand curve, marginal revenue curve, marginal cost curve, and average total cost curve for this restaurant to explain your advice. Show in your diagram what would happen to the restaurant owner's profit if she were to lower the price so that she sells at the minimum-cost output.

Externalities

▶ **What You Will Learn in This Chapter**

■ What **externalities** are and why they can lead to inefficiency and government intervention in the market

■ How **negative, positive, and network externalities** differ

■ The importance of the **Coase theorem,** which explains how private individuals can sometimes remedy externalities

■ Why some government policies to deal with externalities, like **emissions taxes, tradable emissions permits,** or **Pigouvian subsidies,** are efficient and others, like **environmental standards,** are not

■ What makes network externalities an important feature of high-tech industries

TROUBLE UNDERFOOT

Does pollution from fracking for natural gas endanger underground sources of drinking water? If so, how should society make the trade-off?

IN JUNE 2013, RESEARCHERS AT Duke University published a paper with an unassuming title, "Increased stray gas abundance in a subset of drinking water wells near Marcellus shale gas extraction." Yet the effects of that publication were anything but restrained. While its results are not definitive, the paper presented evidence that fracking—the extraction of natural gas by fracturing underground shale deposits with chemical-laden pressurized jets of water—at the Marcellus gas field in Pennsylvania contaminated underground drinking water supplies with ethane and propane. The paper provided support to some critics of fracking who claim that it poses an intolerable pollution threat to drinking water supplies. The Duke paper has helped fuel an increasingly polarized debate over the costs and benefits of fracking.

You may recall our discussion of fracking in Chapter 3, where we learned that fracking has dramatically reduced the cost of energy in the United States, leading to lower heating bills for home-owners and lower production costs for suppliers. And fracking has the potential to significantly reduce air pollution as consumers and industries move from dirtier-burning gasoline and coal to cleaner-burning natural gas. However, as we anticipated in Chapter 3, the environmental benefits of cleaner air from cheaper natural gas have been challenged by the specter of polluted drinking water from fracking. A key question in assessing the trade-off is the role of government: should regulators do more to protect groundwater supplies? Would more regulatory oversight of how fracking wells are drilled reduce groundwater contamination? What amount of contamination would regulators find acceptable? And how would they enforce it?

The dilemma posed by fracking is just one example of the dilemmas that are caused by *externalities*. An externality occurs when individuals impose costs or deliver benefits to others, but don't have an economic incentive to take those costs or benefits into account when making decisions. We briefly noted the concept of externalities in Chapters 1 and 4. There we stated that one of the principal sources of market failure is actions that create *side effects* that are not properly taken into account—that is, actions that create externalities. In this chapter we'll examine the economics of externalities, seeing how they can get in the way of market efficiency and lead to market failure, why they provide a reason for government intervention in markets, and how economic analysis can be used to guide government policy.

Externalities arise from the side effects of actions. First, we'll study the case of pollution, which generates a *negative externality*—a side effect that imposes costs on others. Whenever a side effect can be directly observed and quantified, it can be regulated: by imposing direct controls on it, taxing it, or subsidizing it. As we will see, government intervention in this case should be aimed directly at moving the market to the right quantity of the side effect.

An **external cost** is an uncompensated cost that an individual or firm imposes on others.

An **external benefit** is a benefit that an individual or firm confers on others without receiving compensation.

External costs and benefits are known as **externalities.** External costs are **negative externalities,** and external benefits are **positive externalities.**

External Costs and Benefits

The environmental costs of pollution are the best known and most important example of an **external cost**—an uncompensated cost that an individual or firm imposes on others. In a modern economy there are many examples of an external cost that an individual or firm imposes on others. A very familiar one is the external cost of traffic congestion: an individual who chooses to drive during rush hour increases congestion and has no incentive to take into account the inconvenience inflicted on other drivers. Another familiar example is the cost created by people who text while driving, increasing the risk of accidents that will harm others as well as themselves (see the upcoming For Inquiring Minds).

Pollution leads to an external cost because in the absence of government intervention those who decide how much pollution to create have no incentive to take into account the costs of pollution that they impose on others. In the case of air pollution from a coal-fired power plant, the power company has no incentive to take into account the health costs imposed upon people who breathe dirty air. Instead, the company's incentives are determined by the private monetary costs and benefits of generating power, such as the price of coal, the price earned for a kilowatt of energy, and so on.

We'll see later in this chapter that there are also important examples of **external benefits,** benefits that individuals or firms confer on others without receiving compensation. For example, when you get a flu shot, you are less likely to pass on the flu virus to your roommates. Yet you alone incur the monetary cost of the vaccination and the painful jab. Businesses that develop new technologies also generate external benefits, because their ideas often contribute to innovation by other firms.

External costs and benefits are jointly known as **externalities,** with external costs called **negative externalities** and external benefits called **positive externalities.** Externalities can lead to private decisions—that is, decisions by individuals or firms—that are not optimal for society as a whole. Let's take a closer look at why.

FOR INQUIRING MINDS | Talking, Texting, and Driving

Why is that person in the car in front of us driving so erratically? Is the driver drunk? No, the driver is talking on the phone or texting.

Traffic safety experts take the risks posed by driving while using a cell phone very seriously: A recent study found a six-fold increase in accidents caused by this type of driving while distracted. And in 2012, the National Safety Council estimated that nearly 250,000, or one in four traffic accidents, was attributed to the use of cell phones while driving.

One estimate suggests that talking while driving may be responsible for 3,000 or more traffic deaths each year. And using hands-free, voice-activated devices to make a call doesn't seem to help much because the main danger is distraction. As one traffic consultant put it, "It's not where your eyes are; it's where your head is."

The National Safety Council urges people not to use cell-phones while driving. Most states have some restrictions on cell-phone use while driving. But in response to a growing number of accidents, several states have banned cell-phone use behind the wheel altogether. In 43 states and the District of Columbia, it is illegal to text and drive. Cell-phone use while driving is illegal in many other countries as well, including Japan and Israel.

Why not leave the decision up to the driver? Because the risk posed by driving while using a cell phone isn't just a risk to the driver; it's also a safety risk to others—to a driver's passengers, pedestrians, and people in other cars. Even if you decide that the benefit to you of using your cell phone while driving is worth the cost, you aren't taking into account the cost

Using a cell phone while driving makes you a danger to others as well as yourself.

to other people. Driving while using a cell phone, in other words, generates a serious—and sometimes fatal—negative externality. ■

Pollution: An External Cost

Pollution is a bad thing. Yet most pollution is a side effect of activities that provide us with good things: our air is polluted by power plants generating the electricity that lights our cities, and our rivers are damaged by fertilizer runoff from farms that grow our food. And groundwater contamination may occur from fracking, which also produces cleaner-burning fuel. Why shouldn't we accept a certain amount of pollution as the cost of a good life?

Actually, we do. Even highly committed environmentalists don't think that we can or should completely eliminate pollution—even an environmentally conscious society would accept *some* pollution as the cost of producing useful goods and services. What environmentalists argue is that unless there is a strong and effective environmental policy, our society will generate *too much* pollution—too much of a bad thing. And the great majority of economists agree.

To see why, we need a framework that lets us think about how much pollution a society *should* have. We'll then be able to see why a market economy, left to itself, will produce more pollution than it should. We'll start by adopting the simplest framework to study the problem—assuming that the amount of pollution emitted by a polluter is directly observable and controllable.

The Socially Optimal Quantity of Pollution

How much pollution should society allow? We learned in Chapter 9 that "how much" decisions always involve comparing the marginal benefit from an additional unit of something with the marginal cost of that additional unit. The same is true of pollution.

The **marginal social cost of pollution** is the additional cost imposed on society as a whole by an additional unit of pollution.

For example, sulfur dioxide from coal-fired power plants mixes with rainwater to form acid rain, which damages fisheries, crops, and forests, while groundwater contamination, which may be a side effect of fracking, damages health. Typically, the marginal social cost of pollution is increasing—each additional unit of pollution emitted causes a greater level of damage than the unit before. That's because nature can often safely handle low levels of pollution but is increasingly harmed as pollution reaches higher levels.

The **marginal social benefit of pollution** is the benefit to society from an additional unit of pollution. This may seem like a confusing concept—how can there be any benefit to society from pollution? The answer lies in the understanding that pollution can be reduced—but at a cost. For example, air pollution from coal-fired power plants can be reduced by using more-expensive coal and expensive scrubbing technology; contamination of drinking water due to fracking can be limited with more-expensive drilling techniques; wastewater contamination of rivers and oceans can be reduced by building water treatment facilities.

All these methods of reducing pollution have an opportunity cost. That is, avoiding pollution requires using scarce resources that could have been employed to produce other goods and services. So the marginal social benefit of pollution is the goods and services that could be had by society if it tolerated another unit of pollution.

Comparisons between the pollution levels tolerated in rich and poor countries illustrate the importance of the level of the marginal social benefit of pollution in deciding how much pollution a society wishes to tolerate. Because poor countries have a higher opportunity cost of resources spent on reducing pollution than richer countries, they tolerate higher levels of pollution. For example, the World Health Organization has estimated that 3.5 million people in poor countries die prematurely from breathing polluted indoor air caused by burning dirty fuels like wood, dung, and coal to heat and cook—a situation that residents of rich countries can afford to avoid.

Using hypothetical numbers, Figure 16-1 shows how we can determine the **socially optimal quantity of pollution**—the quantity of pollution society would choose if all the social costs and benefits were fully accounted for. The upward-sloping

The **marginal social cost of pollution** is the additional cost imposed on society as a whole by an additional unit of pollution.

The **marginal social benefit of pollution** is the additional gain to society as a whole from an additional unit of pollution.

The **socially optimal quantity of pollution** is the quantity of pollution that society would choose if all the costs and benefits of pollution were fully accounted for.

FIGURE **16-1**   The Socially Optimal Quantity of Pollution

Pollution yields both costs and benefits. Here the curve *MSC* shows how the marginal cost to society as a whole from emitting one more unit of pollution emissions depends on the quantity of emissions. The *MSC* curve is upward sloping, so the marginal social cost increases as pollution increases. The curve *MSB* shows how the marginal benefit to society as a whole of emitting an additional unit of pollution emissions depends on the quantity of pollution emissions. The *MSB* curve is downward sloping, so the marginal social benefit falls as pollution increases. The socially optimal quantity of pollution is Q_{OPT}; at that quantity, the marginal social benefit of pollution is equal to the marginal social cost, corresponding to $200.

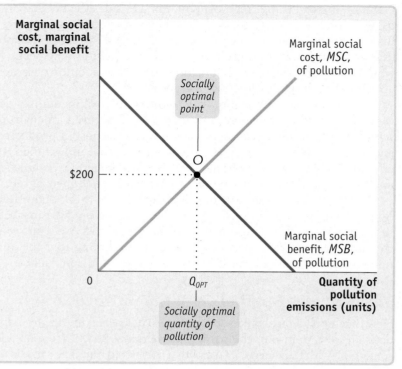

marginal social cost curve, *MSC*, shows how the marginal cost to society of an additional unit of pollution varies with the quantity of pollution. As we mentioned, marginal social cost of pollution is typically increasing, as another unit of pollution causes more harm than prior units. The marginal social benefit curve, *MSB*, is downward sloping. At high levels of pollution, the cost of achieving a reduction in pollution is fairly small. However, as pollution levels drop, it becomes progressively more costly to engineer a further fall in pollution as more expensive techniques must be used, so the *MSB* is higher at lower levels of pollution..

The socially optimal quantity of pollution in this example isn't zero. It's Q_{OPT}, the quantity corresponding to point *O*, where *MSB* crosses *MSC*. At Q_{OPT}, the marginal social benefit from an additional unit of pollution and its marginal social cost are equalized at $200.

But will a market economy, left to itself, arrive at the socially optimal quantity of pollution? No, it won't.

Why a Market Economy Produces Too Much Pollution

While pollution yields both benefits and costs to society, in a market economy without government intervention too much pollution will be produced. In that case it is polluters alone— owners of power plants or gas-drilling companies, for example—who decide how much pollution is created. And they have no incentive to take into account the cost that pollution inflicts on others.

Figure 16-2 shows the result of this asymmetry between who reaps the benefits and who pays the costs. In a market economy without government intervention, since polluters are the only ones making the decisions, only the benefits of pollution are taken into account when choosing how much pollution to produce. So instead of producing the socially optimal quantity, Q_{OPT}, the market economy will generate the amount Q_{MKT}. At Q_{MKT}, the marginal social benefit of an additional unit of pollution is zero, while the marginal social cost of an additional unit is much higher—$400.

Why? Well, take a moment to consider what the polluter would do if he found himself emitting Q_{OPT} of pollution. Remember that the *MSB* curve represents

FIGURE 16-2   Why a Market Economy Produces Too Much Pollution

In the absence of government intervention, the quantity of pollution will be Q_{MKT}, the level at which the marginal social benefit of pollution is zero. This is an inefficiently high quantity of pollution: the marginal social cost, $400, greatly exceeds the marginal social benefit, $0. An optimal Pigouvian tax* of $200, the value of the marginal social cost of pollution when it equals the marginal social benefit of pollution, can move the market to the socially optimal quantity of pollution, Q_{OPT}.

Pigouvian taxes will be covered in the next section on pollution policy.

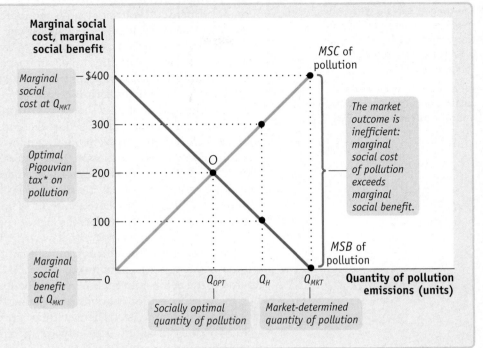

the resources made available by tolerating one more unit of pollution. The polluter would notice that if he increases his emission of pollution by moving down the *MSB* curve from Q_{OPT} to Q_H, he would gain $200 − $100 = $100. That gain of $100 comes from using less-expensive but higher-emission production techniques. Remember, he suffers none of the costs of doing this—only others do. However, it won't stop there. At Q_H, he notices that if he increases his emissions from Q_H to Q_{MKT}, he would gain another $100 as he moves down the *MSB* curve yet again. This would be achieved by using even cheaper and higher-emission production techniques. He will stop at Q_{MKT} because at this emission level the marginal social benefit of a unit of pollution is zero. That is, at Q_{MKT} he gains nothing by using yet cheaper and dirtier production techniques and emitting more pollution.

The market outcome, Q_{MKT}, is inefficient. Recall that an outcome is inefficient if someone could be made better off without someone else being made worse off. At an inefficient outcome, a mutually beneficial trade is being missed. At Q_{MKT}, the benefit accruing to the polluter of the last unit of pollution is very low—virtually zero. But the cost imposed on society of that last unit of pollution is quite high—$400. So by reducing the quantity of pollution at Q_{MKT} by one unit, the total social cost of pollution falls by $400 but the total social benefit falls by virtually zero.

So total surplus rises by approximately $400 if the quantity of pollution at Q_{MKT} is reduced by one unit. At Q_{MKT}, society would be willing to pay the polluter up to $400 not to emit the last unit of pollution, and the polluter would be willing to accept their offer since that last unit gains him virtually nothing. But because there is no means in this market economy for this transaction to take place, an inefficient outcome occurs.

Private Solutions to Externalities

As we've just seen, externalities in a market economy cause inefficiency: there is a mutually beneficial trade that is being missed. So can the private sector solve

According to the **Coase theorem,** even in the presence of externalities an economy can always reach an efficient solution as long as **transaction costs**—the costs to individuals of making a deal—are sufficiently low.

When individuals take external costs or benefits into account, they **internalize the externality.**

the problem of externalities without government intervention? Will individuals be able to make that deal on their own?

In an influential 1960 article, the economist and Nobel laureate Ronald Coase pointed out that in an ideal world the private sector could indeed solve the problem of inefficiency caused by externalities. According to the **Coase theorem,** even in the presence of externalities an economy can always reach an efficient solution provided that the costs of making a deal are sufficiently low. The costs of making a deal are known as **transaction costs.**

For an illustration of how the Coase theorem might work, consider the case of groundwater contamination caused by drilling. There are two ways a private transaction can address this problem. First, landowners whose groundwater is at risk of contamination can pay drillers to use more-expensive, less-polluting technology. Second, the drilling companies can pay landowners the value of damage to their groundwater sources—say, by buying their properties outright so that the landowners move. If drillers legally have the right to pollute, then the first outcome is more likely. If drillers don't legally have the right to pollute, then the second is more likely.

What Coase argued is that, either way, if transaction costs are sufficiently low, then drillers and landowners can make a mutually beneficial deal. Regardless of how the transaction is structured, the social cost of the pollution is taken into account in decision making. When individuals take externalities into account when making decisions, economists say that they **internalize the externality.** In that case the outcome is efficient without government intervention.

So why don't private parties always internalize externalities? The problem is transaction costs in one form or another that prevent an efficient outcome. Here is a sample:

- *The high cost of communication.* Suppose a power plant emits pollution that covers a wide area. The cost of communicating with the many people affected will be very high.
- *The high cost of making legally binding and timely agreements.* What if some landowners band together and pay a driller to reduce groundwater pollution. It can be very expensive to make an effective agreement, requiring lawyers, groundwater tests, engineers, and others. And there is no guarantee that the negotiations will go smoothly or quickly: some landowners may refuse to pay even if their groundwater is protected, while the drillers may hold out for a better deal.

To be sure, there are examples in the real world in which private parties internalize the externalities. Take the case of private communities that set rules for appearances—no cars on blocks in the driveway!—and behavior—no loud parties at midnight! These rules internalize the externality that one homeowner's lack of upkeep or rowdy behavior has on the market value of a neighbor's house. But for major externalities like widespread pollution, it is necessary to look for government solutions because transaction costs are just too high to achieve an efficient private outcome.

In some cases, people do find ways to reduce transaction costs, allowing them to internalize externalities. For example, a house with a junk-filled yard and peeling paint imposes a negative externality on the neighboring houses, diminishing their value in the eyes of potential home buyers. So, many people live in private communities that set rules for home maintenance and behavior, making bargaining between neighbors unnecessary. But in many other cases, transaction costs are too high to make it possible to deal with externalities through private action. For example, tens of millions of people are adversely affected by acid rain. It would be prohibitively expensive to try to make a deal among all those people and all those power companies.

When transaction costs prevent the private sector from dealing with externalities, it is time to look for government solutions. We turn to public policy in the next section.

ECONOMICS ▶ *in Action*

How Much Does Your Electricity Really Cost?

In 2011, three leading economists, Nicholas Z. Muller, Robert Mendelsohn, and William Nordhaus, published a paper drawn from the results of an ambitious study that estimated the external cost of pollution generated by 10,000 pollution sources in the United States, broken down by industry. In it they model the costs to society of emissions of six major pollutants: sulfur dioxide, nitrogen oxides, volatile organic compounds, ammonia, fine particulate matter, and coarse particulate matter. The costs took a variety of forms, from harmful effects on health to reduced agricultural yields. In the case of the electricity-generating sector, the authors also included the cost to society from carbon dioxide emissions—one of many greenhouse gases, the pollution that causes climate change. For each industry a total external cost of pollution, or TEC, was calculated and then compared to the total value to society, or TVC, created by that industry.

What is the social cost of carbon?

An industry with a TEC/TVC ratio greater than 1 indicates that the external cost of pollution exceeds the value created. In other words, a ratio greater than 1 means that a marginal reduction in both industry output and its ensuing pollution increases total social welfare. But as the authors of the study emphasize, this doesn't mean that the industry should be shut down. Rather, it means that the current level of pollution emitted is too high. A contentious issue in any model of the external cost of greenhouse gases—commonly known as SCC, the social cost of carbon—is exactly what price to assign to it. That's because the negative effects of climate change fall most heavily on future generations.

So how do you value today the cost imposed on those not yet born? A difficult question, for sure. Economists address this puzzle by using a range of estimates for SCC. For example, in November 2013, the Environmental Protection Agency, or EPA, the federal agency tasked with protecting the environment, published estimates ranging from $12 to $116 and settled on a cost of $37 per metric ton of carbon dioxide.

Using a relatively conservative estimate of $27 for SCC, Muller, Mendelsohn, and Nordhaus compare the TEC/TVC ratio and the TEC per kilowatt-hour produced for two types of electricity generation—coal-fired plants and natural gas–fired plants.

	TEC/TVC	TEC/ kilowatt-hour
Coal	2.83	$0.039
Natural gas	1.30	0.005

As you can see, both modes of electricity generation are under-regulated: with TEC/TVC ratios greater than 1, society would benefit from a reduction in their emissions. And although both emit greenhouse gases, the TEC per kilowatt-hour generated with natural gas is nearly one-eighth the cost of one generated with coal. That's because natural gas burns cleaner than coal and produces less-toxic pollutants. With the average kilowatt-hour in the United States costing a little over $0.11 in 2013, a conservative estimate of the external cost of that kilowatt hour is one-third of the retail price when generated by coal, and one-twentieth when generated by natural gas.

In response to growing concerns about carbon emissions, in early 2014 the EPA issued rules that limited the amount of carbon emitted by newly constructed coal-fired and natural gas–fired plants. The rules are unlikely to hinder the construction of new natural gas–fired plants because the latest technology meets the standard. Under the new rules, however, new coal-fired plants cannot be built unless they use carbon-capture and storage technology, which captures 20% to 40% of their carbon emissions and stores them underground. While coal

▼ Quick Review

• External costs and benefits are known as **externalities.** Pollution is an example of an **external cost,** or **negative externality;** in contrast, some activities can give rise to **external benefits,** or **positive externalities.**

• There are costs as well as benefits to reducing pollution, so the optimal quantity of pollution isn't zero. Instead, the **socially optimal quantity of pollution** is the quantity at which the **marginal social cost of pollution** is equal to the **marginal social benefit of pollution.**

• Left to itself, a market economy will typically generate an inefficiently high level of pollution because polluters have no incentive to take into account the costs they impose on others.

• According to the **Coase theorem,** the private sector can sometimes resolve externalities on its own: if **transaction costs** aren't too high, individuals can reach a deal to **internalize the externality.** When transaction costs are too high, government intervention may be warranted.

advocates argue that the new rules will effectively stop construction of new coal-fired plants, market forces have increasingly tilted toward natural gas over coal as the use of fracking has made the cost of natural gas plummet.

Check Your Understanding 16-1

1. Wastewater runoff from large poultry farms adversely affects their neighbors. Explain the following:
   a. The nature of the external cost imposed
   b. The outcome in the absence of government intervention or a private deal
   c. The socially optimal outcome

2. According to Yasmin, any student who borrows a book from the university library and fails to return it on time imposes a negative externality on other students. She claims that rather than charging a modest fine for late returns, the library should charge a huge fine so that borrowers will never return a book late. Is Yasmin's economic reasoning correct?

Solutions appear at back of book.

Policies Toward Pollution

Before 1970, there were no rules governing the amount of sulfur dioxide that coal-burning power plants in the United States could emit. When sulfur dioxide is emitted into the air, it mixes with water and produces sulfuric acid, which falls to earth as acid rain. Acid rain is as acidic as lemon juice and has killed fish in lakes over a wide swath of the northeastern United States, damaged trees and crops, and in time even began to dissolve limestone buildings.

In 1970, Congress adopted the Clean Air Act, which set rules forcing power plants to reduce their emissions. And it worked—the acidity of rainfall declined significantly. Economists, however, argued that a more flexible system of rules that exploits the effectiveness of markets could reduce pollution at a lower cost. In 1990 this theory was put into effect with a modified version of the Clean Air Act. And guess what? The economists were right!

In this section we'll look at the policies governments use to deal with pollution and at how economic analysis has been used to improve those policies.

Environmental Standards

The most serious external costs in the modern world are surely those associated with actions that damage the environment—air pollution, water pollution, habitat destruction, and so on. Protection of the environment has become a major role of government in all advanced nations. In the United States, the Environmental Protection Agency is the principal enforcer of environmental policies at the national level, supported by the actions of state and local governments.

How does a country protect its environment? At present the main policy tools are **environmental standards,** rules that protect the environment by specifying actions by producers and consumers. A familiar example is the law that requires almost all vehicles to have catalytic converters, which reduce the emission of chemicals that can cause smog and lead to health problems. Other rules require communities to treat their sewage or factories to avoid or limit certain kinds of pollution. And as we just saw in the Economics in Action, environmental standards were put in place in 2014, compelling new coal- and gas-fired power plants to adopt cleaner-burning technologies.

Environmental standards came into widespread use in the 1960s and 1970s, and they have had considerable success in reducing pollution. For example, since the United States passed the Clean Air Act in 1970, overall emission of pollutants into the

Environmental standards are rules that protect the environment by specifying actions by producers and consumers.

air has fallen by more than a third, even though the population has grown by a third and the size of the economy has more than doubled. Even in Los Angeles, still famous for its smog, the air has improved dramatically: in 1976 ozone levels in the South Coast Air Basin exceeded federal standards on 194 days; in 2013, on only 5 days.

> An **emissions tax** is a tax that depends on the amount of pollution a firm produces.

Emissions Taxes

Another way to deal with pollution directly is to charge polluters an **emissions tax.** Emissions taxes are taxes that depend on the amount of pollution a firm emits. As we learned in Chapter 7, a tax imposed on an activity will reduce the

GLOBAL COMPARISION | Economic Growth and Greenhouse Gases in Six Countries

At first glance, a comparison of the per capita greenhouse gas emissions of various countries, shown in panel (a) of this graph, suggests that Australia, Canada, and the United States are the worst offenders. The average American is responsible for 16.1 tonnes of greenhouse gas emissions (measured in CO_2 equivalents)—the pollution that causes climate change—compared to only 3.9 tonnes for the average Uzbek, 6.7 tonnes for the average Chinese, and 1.8 tonnes for the average Indian. (A tonne, also called a metric ton, equals 1.10 ton.)

Such a conclusion, however, ignores an important factor in determining the level of a country's greenhouse gas emissions: its gross domestic product, or GDP—the total value of a country's domestic output. Output typically cannot be produced without more energy, and more energy usage typically results in more pollution. In fact, some have argued that criticizing a country's level of greenhouse gases without taking account of its level of economic development is misguided. It would be equivalent to faulting a country for being at a more advanced stage of economic development.

A more meaningful way to compare pollution across countries is to measure emissions per $1 million of a country's GDP, as shown in panel (b). On this basis, the United

States, Canada, and Australia are now "green" countries, but China, India, and Uzbekistan are not. What explains the reversal once GDP is accounted for? The answer: both economics and government behavior.

First, there is the issue of economics. Countries that are poor and have begun to industrialize, such as China and Uzbekistan, often view money spent to reduce pollution as better spent on other things. From their perspective, they are still too poor to afford as clean an environment as wealthy advanced countries. They claim that to impose a wealthy country's environmental standards on them would jeopardize their economic growth.

Second, there is the issue of government behavior—or more precisely, whether or not a government possesses the tools necessary to effectively control pollution. China is a good illustration of this problem. The Chinese government lacks sufficient regulatory power to enforce its own environmental rules, promote energy conservation, or encourage pollution reduction. To produce $1 of GDP, China spends three times the world average on energy—far more than Indonesia, for example, which is also a poor country. The case of China illustrates just how important government intervention is in improving society's welfare in the presence of externalities.

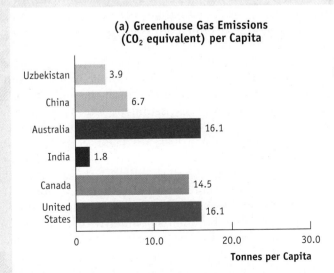

(a) Greenhouse Gas Emissions (CO_2 equivalent) per Capita

Country	Tonnes per Capita
Uzbekistan	3.9
China	6.7
Australia	16.1
India	1.8
Canada	14.5
United States	16.1

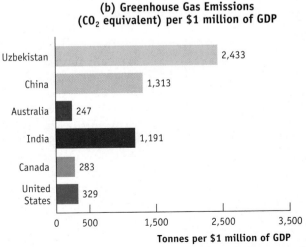

(b) Greenhouse Gas Emissions (CO_2 equivalent) per $1 million of GDP

Country	Tonnes per $1 million of GDP
Uzbekistan	2,433
China	1,313
Australia	247
India	1,191
Canada	283
United States	329

Sources: Global Carbon Atlas; IMF—World Economic Outlook.

Taxes designed to reduce external costs are known as **Pigouvian taxes.**

Tradable emissions permits are licenses to emit limited quantities of pollutants that can be bought and sold by polluters.

level of that activity. Looking again at Figure 16-2, we can find the amount of tax on emissions that moves the market to the socially optiimal point. At Q_{OPT}, the socially optimal quantity of pollution, the marginal social benefit and marginal social cost of an additional unit of pollution is equal at $200. But in the absence of government intervention, polluters will push pollution up to the quantity Q_{MKT}, at which marginal social benefit is zero.

It's now easy to see how an emissions tax can solve the problem. If polluters are required to pay a tax of $200 per unit of pollution, they now face a marginal cost of $200 per unit and have an incentive to reduce their emissions to Q_{OPT}, the socially optimal quantity. This illustrates a general result: an emissions tax equal to the marginal social cost at the socially optimal quantity of pollution induces polluters to internalize the externality—to take into account the true cost to society of their actions.

The term *emissions* tax may convey the misleading impression that taxes are a solution to only one kind of external cost, pollution. In fact, taxes can be used to discourage any activity that generates negative externalities, such as driving (which inflicts environmental damage greater than the cost of producing gasoline) or smoking (which inflicts health costs on society far greater than the cost of making a cigarette). In general, taxes designed to reduce external costs are known as **Pigouvian taxes,** after the economist A. C. Pigou, who emphasized their usefulness in his classic 1920 book, *The Economics of Welfare.* In our example, the optimal Pigouvian tax is $200. As you can see from Figure 16-2, this corresponds to the marginal social cost of pollution at the optimal output quantity Q_{OPT}.

Are there any problems with emissions taxes? The main concern is that in practice government officials usually aren't sure how high the tax should be set. If they set it too low, there won't be sufficient reduction in pollution; if they set it too high, emissions will be reduced by more than is efficient. This uncertainty around the optimal level of the emissions tax can't be eliminated, but the nature of the risks can be changed by using an alternative policy, issuing tradable emissions permits.

Tradable Emissions Permits

Tradable emissions permits are licenses to emit limited quantities of pollutants that can be bought and sold by polluters. Tradable emissions permits work in practice much like the tradable quotas discussed in a Chapter 5 Economics in Action in which regulators created a system of tradable licenses to fish for crabs. The tradable licenses resulted in an efficient way to allocate the right to fish as boat-owners with the safest and lowest cost of operation purchase the rights of owners with less safe, higher cost boats. Although tradable emissions permits involve trading a "bad" like pollution instead of a "good" like crab, both systems work to allocate an activity efficiently because the permits, like licenses, are *tradable.*

Here's why this system works in the case of pollution. Firms that pollute typically have different costs of reducing pollution—for example, it will be more costly for plants using older technology to reduce pollution than plants using newer technology. Regulators begin the system by issuing polluters with permits to pollute based on some formula—say, for example, equal to 50% of a given firm's historical level of emissions. Firms then have the right to trade permits among themselves. Under this system, a market in permits to pollute will emerge. Polluters who place a higher value on the right to pollute—those with older technology—will purchase permits from polluters who place a lower value on the right to pollute—those with newer technology. As a result, a polluter with a higher value for a unit of emissions will pollute more than a polluter with a lower value.

In the end, those with the lowest cost of reducing pollution will reduce their pollution the most, while those with the highest cost of reducing pollution will reduce their pollution the least. The total effect is to allocate pollution reduction efficiently—that is, in the least costly way.

Just like emissions taxes, tradable emissions permits provide polluters with an incentive to take the marginal social cost of pollution into account. To see why, suppose that the market price of a permit to emit one unit of pollution is $200. Every polluter now has an incentive to limit its emissions to the point where its marginal benefit of one unit of pollution is $200. Why?

If the marginal benefit of one more unit of pollution is greater than $200 then it is cheaper to pollute more than to pollute less. In that case the polluter will buy a permit and emit another unit. And if the marginal benefit of one more unit of pollution is less than $200, then it is cheaper to reduce pollution than to pollute more. In that scenario the polluter will reduce pollution rather than buy the $200 permit.

From this example we can see how an emissions permit leads to the same outcome as an emissions tax when they are the same amount: a polluter who pays $200 for the right to emit one unit faces the same incentives as a polluter who faces an emissions tax of $200 per unit. And it's equally true for polluters that have received more permits from regulators than they plan to use: by not emitting one unit of pollution, a polluter frees up a permit that it can sell for $200. In other words, the opportunity cost of a unit of pollution to this firm is $200, regardless of whether it is used.

Recall that when using emissions taxes to arrive at the optimal level of pollution, the problem arises of finding the right amount of the tax: if the tax is too low, too much pollution is emitted; if the tax is too high, too little pollution is emitted (in other words, too many resources are spent reducing pollution). A similar problem with tradable emissions permits is getting the quantity of permits right, which is much like the flip-side of getting the level of the tax right.

Because it is difficult to determine the optimal quantity of pollution, regulators can find themselves either issuing too many permits, so that there is insufficient pollution reduction, or issuing too few, so that there is too much pollution reduction.

In the case of sulfur dioxide pollution, the U.S. government first relied on environmental standards, but then turned to a system of tradable emissions permits. Currently the largest emissions permit trading system is the European Union system for controlling emissions of carbon dioxide.

Comparing Environmental Policies with an Example

Figure 16-3 shows a hypothetical industry consisting of only two plants, plant A and plant B. We'll assume that plant A uses newer technology, giving it a lower cost of pollution reduction, while plant B uses older technology and has a higher cost of pollution reduction. Reflecting this difference, plant A's marginal benefit of pollution curve, MB_A, lies below plant B's marginal benefit of pollution curve, MB_B. Because it is more costly for plant B to reduce its pollution at any output quantity, an additional unit of pollution is worth more to plant B than to plant A.

In the absence of government action, we know that polluters will pollute until the marginal social benefit of a unit of pollution is equal to zero. As a result, without government intervention each plant will pollute until its own marginal benefit of pollution is equal to zero. This corresponds to an emissions quantity of 600 units for each plant—the quantities of pollution at which MB_A and MB_B are equal to zero. So although plant A and plant B have different costs of pollution reduction, they will each choose to emit the same amount of pollution.

Now suppose that regulators decide that the overall pollution from this industry should be cut in half, from 1,200 units to 600 units. Panel (a) of Figure 16-3 shows this might be achieved with an environmental standard that requires each plant to cut its emissions in half, from 600 to 300 units. The standard has the desired effect of reducing overall emissions from 1,200 to 600 units but accomplishes it inefficiently.

FIGURE **16-3** Comparing Environmental Policies

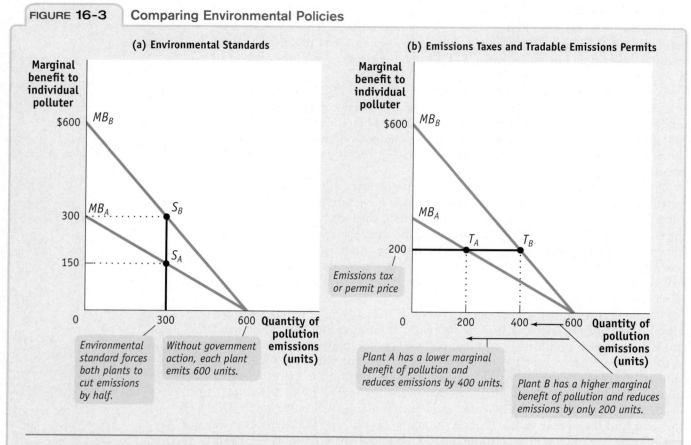

In both panels, MB_A shows the marginal benefit of pollution to plant A and MB_B shows the marginal benefit of pollution to plant B. In the absence of government intervention, each plant would emit 600 units. However, the cost of reducing emissions is lower for plant A, as shown by the fact that MB_A lies below MB_B. Panel (a) shows the result of an environmental standard that requires both plants to cut emissions in half; this

is inefficient, because it leaves the marginal benefit of pollution higher for plant B than for plant A. Panel (b) shows that an emissions tax as well as a system of tradable permits achieves the same quantity of overall pollution efficiently. Faced with either an emissions tax of $200 per unit, or a market price of a permit of $200 per unit, each plant reduces pollution to the point where its marginal benefit is $200.

As you can see from panel (a), the environmental standard leads plant A to produce at point S_A, where its marginal benefit of pollution is $150, but plant B produces at point S_B, where its marginal benefit of pollution is twice as high, $300.

This difference in marginal benefits between the two plants tells us that the same quantity of pollution can be achieved at lower total cost by allowing plant B to pollute more than 300 units but inducing plant A to pollute less. In fact, the efficient way to reduce pollution is to ensure that at the industry-wide outcome, the marginal benefit of pollution is the same for all plants. When each plant values a unit of pollution equally, there is no way to rearrange pollution reduction among the various plants that achieves the optimal quantity of pollution at a lower total cost.

We can see from panel (b) how an emissions tax achieves exactly that result. Suppose both plant A and plant B pay an emissions tax of $200 per unit, so that the marginal cost of an additional unit of emissions to each plant is now $200 rather than zero. As a result, plant A produces at T_A and plant B produces at T_B. So plant A reduces its pollution more than it would under an inflexible environmental standard, cutting its emissions from 600 to 200 units; meanwhile, plant B reduces its pollution less, going from 600 to 400 units.

In the end, total pollution—600 units—is the same as under the environmental standard, but total surplus is higher. That's because the reduction in pollution has been achieved efficiently, allocating most of the reduction to plant A, the plant that can reduce emissions at lower cost. (Remember that producer surplus is the area below the supply curve and above the price line. So there is more total producer surplus in Panel (b) than in Panel (a).)

Panel (b) also illustrates why a system of tradable emissions permits also achieves an efficient allocation of pollution among the two plants. Assume that in the market for permits, the market price of a permit is $200 and each plant has 300 permits to start the system. Plant B, with the higher cost of pollution reduction, will buy 200 permits from Plant A, enough to allow it to emit 400 units. Correspondingly, Plant A, with the lower cost, will sell 200 of its permits to Plant B and emit only 200 units. Provided that the market price of a permit is the same as the optimal emissions tax, the two systems arrive at the same outcome.

ECONOMICS ▶ in Action

Cap and Trade

The tradable emissions permit systems for both acid rain in the United States and greenhouse gases in the European Union are examples of *cap and trade systems:* the government sets a *cap* (a maximum amount of pollutant that can be emitted), issues tradable emissions permits, and enforces a yearly rule that a polluter must hold a number of permits equal to the amount of pollutant emitted. The goal is to set the cap low enough to generate environmental benefits, while giving polluters flexibility in meeting environmental standards and motivating them to adopt new technologies that will lower the cost of reducing pollution.

In 1994 the United States began a cap and trade system for the sulfur dioxide emissions that cause acid rain by issuing permits to power plants based on their historical consumption of coal. Thanks to the system, air pollutants in the United States decreased by more than 40% from 1990 to 2008, and by 2012 acid rain levels dropped to approximately 70% of their 1980 levels. Economists who have analyzed the sulfur dioxide cap and trade system point to another reason for its success: it would have been a lot more expensive—80% more to be exact—to reduce emissions by this much using a non-market-based regulatory policy.

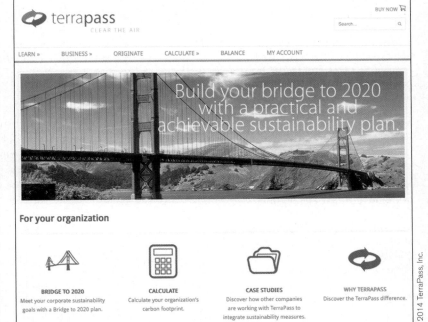

Companies like Terrapass help individuals and companies manage their carbon emissions.

The EU cap and trade scheme, begun in 2005 and covering all 28 member nations of the European Union, is the world's only mandatory trading system for greenhouse gases. Other countries, like Australia and New Zealand, have adopted less comprehensive schemes.

According to the World Bank, the worldwide market for greenhouse gases—also called *carbon trading*—has grown rapidly, from $11 billion in permits traded in 2005 to $56 billion in 2013. In response to rising anger and frustration over unhealthy pollution levels, in 2012 China ordered seven of its provinces to make preparations for local cap and trade markets to begin in 2014. China, the world's largest carbon emitter—it burns almost as much coal as the rest of the world's countries combined—is presently considering a national cap and trade system.

Yet cap and trade systems are not silver bullets for the world's pollution problems. Although they are appropriate for pollution that's geographically dispersed, like sulfur dioxide and greenhouse gases, they don't work for pollution that's localized, like groundwater contamination. And there must be vigilant monitoring of compliance for the system to work. Finally, the amount of total reduction in pollution depends on the level of the cap, a critical issue illustrated by the troubles of the EU cap and trade scheme.

EU regulators, under industry pressure, allowed too many permits to be handed out when the system was created. By the spring of 2013 the price of a permit for a ton of greenhouse gas had fallen to 2.75 euros (about $3.70), less than a tenth of what experts believe is necessary to induce companies to switch to cleaner fuels like natural gas. The price of a permit was too low to alter polluters' incentives and, not surprisingly, coal use in Europe boomed in 2012. Alarmed European Union legislators voted in the summer of 2013 to reduce the number of permits issued in future years in the hope of increasing the current price of a permit. There is evidence the reduction in permits has already altered polluters' incentives. As of mid-2014, pollution throughout the EU is projected to drop by 4.4% as the price of a permit has more than doubled to 5.71 euros (about $7.34).

Check Your Understanding 16-2

1. Some opponents of tradable emissions permits object to them on the grounds that polluters that sell their permits benefit monetarily from their contribution to polluting the environment. Assess this argument.

2. Explain the following.
   a. Why an emissions tax smaller than or greater than the marginal social cost at Q_{OPT} leads to a smaller total surplus compared to the total surplus generated if the emissions tax had been set optimally
   b. Why a system of tradable emissions permits that sets the total quantity of allowable pollution higher or lower than Q_{OPT} leads to a smaller total surplus compared to the total surplus generated if the number of permits had been set optimally.

Solutions appear at back of book.

Positive Externalities

New Jersey is the most densely populated state in the country, lying along the northeastern corridor, an area of almost continuous development stretching from Washington, D.C., to Boston. Yet a drive through New Jersey reveals a surprising feature: acre upon acre of farmland, growing everything from corn to pumpkins to the famous Jersey tomatoes. This situation is no accident: starting in 1961, New Jerseyans have voted in a series of measures that subsidize farmers to permanently preserve their farmland rather than sell it to developers. By 2013, the Green Acres Program, administered by the state, had preserved over 640,000 acres of open space.

Why have New Jersey citizens voted to raise their own taxes to subsidize the preservation of farmland? Because they believe that preserved farmland in an already heavily developed state provides external benefits, such as natural beauty, access to fresh food, and the conservation of wild bird populations. In addition, preservation alleviates the external costs that come with more development, such as pressure on roads, water supplies, and municipal services—and, inevitably, more pollution.

In this section we'll explore the topics of external benefits and positive externalities. They are, in many ways, the mirror images of external costs and negative externalities. Left to its own, the market will produce too little of a good (in this case, preserved New Jersey farmland) that confers external benefits on others. But society as a whole is better off when policies are adopted that increase the supply of such a good.

Preserved Farmland: An External Benefit

Preserved farmland yields both benefits and costs to society. In the absence of government intervention, the farmer who wants to sell his land incurs all the costs of preservation—namely, the forgone profit to be made from selling the farmland to a developer. But the benefits of preserved farmland accrue not to the farmer but to neighboring residents, who have no right to influence how the farmland is disposed of.

Figure 16-4 illustrates society's problem. The marginal social cost of preserved farmland, shown by the *MSC* curve, is the additional cost imposed on society by an additional acre of such farmland. This represents the forgone profits that would have accrued to farmers if they had sold their land to developers. The line is upward sloping because when very few acres are preserved and there is plenty of land available for development, the profit that could be made from selling an acre to a developer is small. But as the number of preserved acres increases and few are left for development, the amount a developer is willing to pay for them, and therefore the forgone profit, increases as well.

The *MSB* curve represents the marginal social benefit of preserved farmland. It is the additional benefit that accrues to society—in this case, the farmer's neighbors—when an additional acre of farmland is preserved. The curve is downward sloping because as more farmland is preserved, the benefit to society of preserving another acre falls.

As Figure 16-4 shows, the socially optimal point, *O*, occurs when the marginal social cost and the marginal social benefit are equalized—here, at a price of $10,000 per acre. At the socially optimal point, Q_{OPT} acres of farmland are preserved.

The market alone will not provide Q_{OPT} acres of preserved farmland. Instead, in the market outcome no acres will be preserved; the level of preserved farmland, Q_{MKT}, is equal to zero. That's because farmers will set the marginal social cost of preservation—their forgone profits—at zero and sell all their acres to developers.

FIGURE 16 -4 **Why a Market Economy Preserves Too Little Farmland**

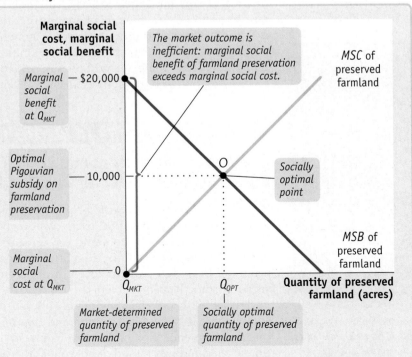

Without government intervention, the quantity of preserved farmland will be zero, the level at which the marginal social cost of preservation is zero. This is an inefficiently low quantity of preserved farmland: the marginal social benefit is $20,000, but the marginal social cost is zero. An optimal Pigouvian subsidy of $10,000, the value of the marginal social benefit of preservation when it equals the marginal social cost, can move the market to the socially optimal level of preservation, Q_{OPT}.

The market outcome is inefficient: marginal social benefit of farmland preservation exceeds marginal social cost.

MSC of preserved farmland

Marginal social cost, marginal social benefit

Marginal — $20,000
social
benefit
at Q_{MKT}

Optimal
Pigouvian
subsidy on — 10,000
farmland
preservation

O

Socially
optimal
point

MSB of preserved farmland

Marginal
social
cost at Q_{MKT} — 0

Q_{MKT} Q_{OPT}

Quantity of preserved farmland (acres)

Market-determined
quantity of preserved
farmland

Socially optimal
quantity of preserved
farmland

A **Pigouvian subsidy** is a payment designed to encourage activities that yield external benefits.

A **technology spillover** is an external benefit that results when knowledge spreads among individuals and firms.

Because farmers bear the entire cost of preservation but gain none of the benefits, an inefficiently low quantity of acres will be preserved in the market outcome.

This is clearly inefficient because at zero acres preserved, the marginal social benefit of preserving an acre of farmland is $20,000. So how can the economy be induced to produce Q_{OPT} acres of preserved farmland, the socially optimal level? The answer is a **Pigouvian subsidy:** a payment designed to encourage activities that yield external benefits. The optimal Pigouvian subsidy, as shown in Figure 16-4, is equal to the marginal social benefit of preserved farmland at the socially optimal level, Q_{OPT}—that is, $10,000 per acre.

So New Jersey voters are indeed implementing the right policy to raise their social welfare—taxing themselves in order to provide subsidies for farmland preservation.

Positive Externalities in Today's Economy

In the overall U.S. economy, the most important single source of external benefits is the creation of knowledge. In high-tech industries such as semiconductors, software design, green technology, and bioengineering, innovations by one firm are quickly emulated and improved upon by rival firms. Such spreading of knowledge across individuals and firms is known as a **technology spillover.** In today's economy, the greatest sources of technology spillovers are major universities and research institutes.

In technologically advanced countries such as the United States, Japan, the United Kingdom, Germany, France, and Israel, there is an ongoing exchange of people and ideas among private industries, major universities, and research institutes located in close proximity. The dynamic interplay that occurs in these *research clusters* spurs innovation and competition, theoretical advances, and practical applications.

One of the best known and most successful research clusters is the Research Triangle in North Carolina, anchored by Duke University and the University of North Carolina, several other universities and hospitals, and companies such as IBM, Pfizer, and Qualcomm. Ultimately, these areas of technology spillover increase the economy's productivity and raise living standards.

But research clusters don't appear out of thin air. Except in a few instances in which firms have funded basic research on a long-term basis, research clusters have grown up around major universities. And like farmland preservation in New Jersey, major universities and their research activities are subsidized by government. In fact, government policy makers in advanced countries have long understood that the external benefits generated by knowledge, stemming from basic education to high-tech research, are key to the economy's growth over time.

ECONOMICS ▶ in Action

The Impeccable Economic Logic of Early-Childhood Intervention Programs

One of the most vexing problems facing any society is how to break what researchers call the "cycle of poverty": children who grow up in disadvantaged socioeconomic circumstances are far more likely to remain trapped in poverty as adults, even after we account for differences in ability. They are more likely to be unemployed or underemployed, to engage in crime, and to suffer chronic health problems.

Early-childhood intervention has offered some hope of breaking the cycle. A study by the RAND Corporation found that high-quality early-childhood programs that focus on education and health care lead to significant social, intellectual, and financial advantages for kids who would otherwise be at risk of dropping out of high

Early-childhood intervention programs focusing on education and health offer many external benefits to society.

fatihhoca/istockphoto/Getty Images

school and of engaging in criminal behavior. Children in programs like Head Start were less likely to engage in such destructive behaviors and more likely to end up with a job and to earn a high salary later in life.

Another study by researchers at the University of Pittsburgh looked at early-childhood intervention programs from a dollars-and-cents perspective, finding from $4 to $7 in benefits for every $1 spent on early-childhood intervention programs, while a Rand study put the figure as high as $17 per $1 spent. The Pittsburgh study also pointed to one program whose participants, by age 20, were 26% more likely to have finished high school, 35% less likely to have been charged in juvenile court, and 40% less likely to have repeated a grade compared to individuals of similar socioeconomic background who did not attend preschool.

The observed external benefits to society of these programs are so large that the Brookings Institution predicts that providing high-quality preschool education to every American child would result in an increase in GDP, the total value of a country's domestic output, by almost 2%, representing over 3 million more jobs.

Check Your Understanding   16-3

1. In 2013, the U.S. Department of Education spent almost $36 billion on college student aid. Explain why this can be an optimal policy to encourage the creation of knowledge.

2. In each of the following cases, determine whether an external cost or an external benefit is imposed and what an appropriate policy response would be.
   a. Trees planted in urban areas improve air quality and lower summer temperatures.
   b. Water-saving toilets reduce the need to pump water from rivers and aquifers. The cost of a gallon of water to homeowners is virtually zero.
   c. Old computer monitors contain toxic materials that pollute the environment when improperly disposed of.

   Solutions appear at back of book.

> ### ▼ Quick Review
>
> • When there are positive externalities, or external benefits, a market economy, left to itself, will typically produce too little of the good or activity. The socially optimal quantity of the good or activity can be achieved by an optimal **Pigouvian subsidy.**
>
> • The most important example of external benefits in the economy is the creation of knowledge through **technology spillover.**

Network Externalities

In Chapter 13 we explained that a *network externality* exists when the value of a good or service is greater when a large number of other people also use the good or service. Although network externalities are common in technology-driven and communication-driven sectors of the economy, the phenomenon is considerably more widespread than that. Consider the case of a car. You might not think that the value of having a car depends on how many others also have cars, but in the early days of car consumerism it certainly did. That's because when very few cars existed, service stations and repair shops were few and far between, and local governments had little or no incentive to upgrade their roads so that they were car-worthy. However, as more people purchased cars, service stations and repair shops sprang up and roads were improved. As a result, owning a car became even more valuable.

What a network externality shares with positive and negative externalities is an external effect: one person's actions affect the payoff to another person's actions. Network externalities play a key role both in the economy and in a number of regulatory policy controversies.

The External Benefits of a Network Externality

We can now deepen our understanding of network externalities by noting that a network externality involves an external benefit: one person's adoption of a good or

A good is subject to **positive feedback** when success breeds greater success and failure breeds further failure.

service extends an external benefit to another person who also adopts that good or service. As a result, the marginal benefit of the good or service to any one person depends on the number of other people who also use it.

Although the most common network externalities involve methods of communication—the internet, cell phones, social media, and so on—they are also frequently present in transportation. For example, the value to a traveler of a given airport increases as more travelers use that airport as well, making more airlines and more destinations available from it. A marketplace website like eBay is more valuable to use, either to buy or to sell, the greater the number of other people also using that site. Similarly, many of us value banking with a particular bank because of the number of ATMs it has, and it will have more ATMs the larger its customer base.

The classic case of network externalities in the high-tech industry arises from computer operating systems. Most personal computers around the world run on Windows by Microsoft rather than on Apple's competing system. In 2013, 18.8 new PCs that run Windows were sold for every Apple Mac sold. Why does Windows dominate personal computers? There are two channels, both involving network externalities. First, a direct effect: it is easier for a Windows user to get help and advice from other Windows users. Second, an indirect effect: Window's early dominance attracted more software developers, so more programs were developed to run on Windows than on a competing system. (This second effect has largely vanished now, but it was important early on in making PCs dominant.)

Today, social media websites are perhaps the best illustration of a network externality at work, a subject we'll address in this chapter's business case.

When a network externality arises from the use of a good or service, it leads to **positive feedback,** also known as a *bandwagon effect:* if large numbers of people use it, other people become more likely to use it too. And if fewer people use the good or service, others become less likely to use it as well. This leads to a chicken-versus-egg-problem: if one person's value of the good depends on whether another person also uses the good, how do you get anyone to buy the good in the first place? Not surprisingly, producers of goods and services with network externalities are aware of this problem. They understand that of two competing products, the one with the largest network—not necessarily the one that's the better product—will win in the end. The product with the larger network will continue to grow and dominate the market, while its rival will shrink and eventually disappear.

Everyone wants to join the network that everyone else joins.

An important way to gain an advantage at the early stages of a market with network externalities is to sell the product cheaply, perhaps at a loss, in order to increase the size of the network of users. For example, Skype, the internet calling company, allows free calls from one Skype member to another Skype member via the internet. This builds Skype's network of users, who will then pay for using Skype to call a non-Skype contact or place a call to a landline phone. And as we explain in the following Economics in Action, the fact that all web browsers—including Internet Explorer, Chrome, and Firefox—are free to download is a legacy of Microsoft's early strategy of providing Internet Explorer free on its computers in order to buttress its Windows operating system dominance.

Network externalities present special challenges for antitrust regulators because the antitrust laws do not, strictly speaking, forbid monopoly. Rather, they only prohibit *monopolization*—efforts to create a monopoly. If you just happen to end up ruling an industry, that's OK, but if you take actions designed to drive out competition, that's not OK. So we could argue that monopolies in goods with network externalities, because they occur naturally, should not pose legal problems.

Unfortunately, it isn't that simple. Firms investing in new technologies are clearly trying to establish monopoly positions. Furthermore, in the face of positive feedback, firms have an incentive to engage in aggressive strategies to push their goods in order to increase their network size and tip the market in their favor. So what is the dividing line between legal and illegal actions? In the Microsoft antitrust case, described next, reasonable economists and legal experts disagreed sharply about whether the company had broken the law.

ECONOMICS ▶ *in Action*

The Microsoft Case

In 2011, a consent decree between Microsoft and a federal court prohibiting certain business practices expired, marking the end of an era for the company. Beginning in 1998, the federal Justice Department as well as 20 states and the District of Columbia sued Microsoft, alleging predatory practices against competitors to protect the monopoly position held by its Windows operating system. At the time, Microsoft was by any reasonable definition a monopoly, as just about all personal computers in the late 1990s ran Windows. And the key feature supporting this dominance was a network externality: people used Windows because other people used Windows.

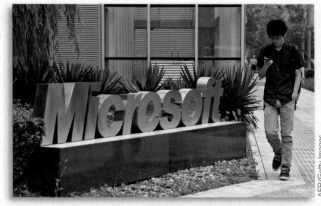

The Microsoft case was a good example of the pros and cons raised by goods with network externalities.

Despite urging by some economists, the Justice Department did not challenge the Windows monopoly itself, as most experts agreed that monopoly was the natural outcome of an industry with network externalities. What Justice Department lawyers did claim, however, was that Microsoft had used the monopoly position of its Windows operating system to give its other products an unfair advantage over competitors.

For example, by bundling Internet Explorer free as part of Windows, it was alleged that Microsoft had given itself an unfair advantage over rival web browser Netscape, because it prevented Netscape from charging customers for its use. The Justice Department argued that this was harmful because it discouraged innovation: potential software innovators were unwilling to invest large sums out of fear that Microsoft would bundle an equivalent software with Windows free. Microsoft, in contrast, argued that by setting the precedent that companies would be punished for success, the government was the real opponent of innovation.

After many years of legal wrangling, the consent decree was signed in 2002, which barred Microsoft from excluding rivals from its computers and forced the company to make Windows seamlessly interoperable with non-Microsoft software. This eliminated any advantage Microsoft had through free bundling of its own programs into the Windows package.

Although the case against Microsoft consumed many tens of millions of dollars in legal costs and is considered one of the most significant antitrust cases of its generation, its long-term effects are hotly debated. Some say that the case essentially had no effect, as the cutting edge of technology moved into mobile devices like smartphones and tablets, leaving Microsoft and its PC-centered business behind. Others argue that, although the case may not have dampened overall innovation as Microsoft claimed, it changed the culture of Microsoft itself, making it more cautious and therefore unable to explore and capitalize on new technological trends.

Two effects, however, are beyond dispute. Because of Microsoft's example, products with network externalities are often priced at a loss or even at zero—as

▼ Quick Review

● *Network externalities* arise when the value of a good increases when a large number of other people also use the good. They are prevalent in communications, transportation, and high-technology industries.

● Goods with network externalities exhibit **positive feedback:** success breeds further success, and failure breeds further failure. The good with the largest network eventually dominates the market, and rival goods disappear. As a result, in early stages of the market, firms have an incentive to take aggressive actions, such as lowering price below production cost, to enlarge the size of their good's network.

● Goods with network externalities pose special problems for anti-trust regulators because they tend toward monopoly. It can be difficult to distinguish what is a natural growth of the network and what is an illegal monopolization effort by the producer.

in the case of today's web browsers, Chrome, Firefox, and Internet Explorer, which are all available free. Second, rival high-tech companies now routinely charge one another with predatory behavior that exploits a network externality advantage—as in Microsoft's recent charges against Google for its advantage in the search engine market.

Check Your Understanding 16-4

1. For each of the following goods, explain the nature of the network externality present.
   a. Appliances using a particular voltage, such as 110 volts versus 220 volts
   b. 8½-by-11-inch paper versus 8-by-12½-inch paper

2. Suppose there are two competing companies in an industry that has a network externality. Explain why it is likely that the company able to sustain the largest initial losses will eventually dominate the market.

Solutions appear at back of book.

Are We Still Friends? A Tale of Facebook, MySpace, and Friendster

There was a big shake-out in the world of social media websites in 2011. That year Facebook was in the midst of negotiating a half-billion dollar investment, MySpace was preparing to fire nearly half its staff, and Friendster was transformed from a failed social media website to an online gaming website. The irony of these events is that Friendster and MySpace started before Facebook—Friendster in 2002, MySpace in 2003, and Facebook in 2004. Yet, by 2011 Friendster was in complete collapse and MySpace was in steep decline.

By 2013, MySpace's registered users fell by a third, to 36 million, compared to 54 million in 2011. As the former president of MTV Networks, Michael J. Wolf, commented, "MySpace was like a big party, and then the party moved on. Facebook has become much more of a utility and communications vehicle." MySpace became difficult to navigate and cluttered with pop-up ads of dubious value selling things like weight-loss products, while Facebook offered a simple, Google-like interface. One Myspace user who defected to Facebook said it became "amateurish" and "boorish." She said, "Every time I logged on it was just messages from bands I barely heard of. Facebook allows you to actually connect with real people, rather than bands or celebrities."

Friendster's demise began in 2009 when a change of interface and technical problems upset users while Facebook was on the rise. As one expert noted, Friendster imploded in a systematic way: first less-connected users left, lowering the benefits of staying to more-connected users, until the cascade of departures unraveled the site.

The events of 2011 were not what industry insiders had expected. In 2005, the newspaper conglomerate News Corporation bought MySpace for $580 million. Until April 2008, the number of MySpace users consistently exceeded the number of Facebook users. After the acquisition, News Corporation announced an ambitious revenue target of $1 billion. But to meet these goals, ads were accepted that made the site slow, buggy, and difficult to use. By 2011 MySpace was losing money and News Corporation sold it for $35 million, a 94% loss over 6 years.

Chris Wolfe, a founder of MySpace, tried to explain the reversals: "The paradox in business is, 'When do you focus on growth, and when do you focus on money? We focused on money and Facebook focused on growing the user base and user experience.'" In contrast to MySpace, Facebook refused to be acquired by a larger company, allowing it to ignore revenue goals. That is, until 2012 when Facebook began a push to open its website to ads, provoking a backlash among users. Some observers have warned that Facebook could go the way of Friendster, as it has experienced a dramatic decline among younger users, who have switched to competitors like Snapchat, Instagram, Tumblr, and Twitter. Stay logged on, somewhere, for the outcome.

QUESTIONS FOR THOUGHT

1. Describe the nature of the externality in social media websites.

2. Assume that there are two competing social media websites. Explain why it is likely that one will come to dominate. Explain why the decline of a site is likely to be swift, with a cascade of departures.

3. Explain the nature of the problem that undermined MySpace relative to Facebook. Is it unique to MySpace or common to all social media sites?

SUMMARY

1. When pollution can be directly observed and controlled, government policies should be geared directly to producing the **socially optimal quantity of pollution,** the quantity at which the **marginal social cost of pollution** is equal to the **marginal social benefit of pollution.** In the absence of government intervention, a market produces too much pollution because polluters take only their benefit from polluting into account, not the costs imposed on others.

2. The costs to society of pollution are an example of an **external cost;** in some cases, however, economic activities yield **external benefits.** External costs and benefits are jointly known as **externalities,** with external costs called **negative externalities** and external benefits called **positive externalities.**

3. According to the **Coase theorem,** individuals can find a way to **internalize the externality,** making government intervention unnecessary, as long as **transaction costs**—the costs of making a deal—are sufficiently low. However, in many cases transaction costs are too high to permit such deals.

4. Governments often deal with pollution by imposing **environmental standards,** a method, economists argue, that is usually an inefficient way to reduce pollution. Two efficient (cost-minimizing) methods for reducing pollution are **emissions taxes,** a form of **Pigouvian tax,** and **tradable emissions permits.** The

optimal Pigouvian tax on pollution is equal to its marginal social cost at the socially optimal quantity of pollution. These methods also provide incentives for the creation and adoption of production technologies that cause less pollution.

5. When a good or activity yields external benefits, or positive externalities, such as **technology spillovers,** then an optimal **Pigouvian subsidy** to producers moves the market to the socially optimal quantity of production.

6. Communications, transportation, and high-technology goods are frequently subject to *network externalities,* which arise when the value of the good to an individual is greater when a large number of people use the good. Such goods are likely to be subject to **positive feedback:** if large numbers of people buy the good, other people are more likely to buy it, too. So success breeds greater success and failure breeds failure: the good with the larger network will eventually dominate, and rival goods will disappear. As a result, producers have an incentive to take aggressive action in the early stages of the market to increase the size of their network. Markets with network externalities tend to be monopolies. They are especially challenging for antitrust regulators because it can be hard to differentiate between the natural progression of the network externality and illegal monopolization efforts by producers.

KEY TERMS

External cost, p. 466
External benefit, p. 466
Externalities, p. 466
Negative externalities, p. 466
Positive externalities, p. 466
Marginal social cost of pollution, p. 467

Marginal social benefit of pollution, p. 467
Socially optimal quantity of pollution, p. 467
Coase theorem, p. 470
Transaction costs, p. 470
Internalize the externality, p. 470

Environmental standards, p. 472
Emissions tax, p. 473
Pigouvian tax, p. 474
Tradable emissions permits, p. 474
Pigouvian subsidy, p. 480
Technology spillover, p. 480
Positive feedback, p. 482

PROBLEMS

1. What type of externality (positive or negative) is present in each of the following examples? Is the marginal social benefit of the activity greater than or equal to the marginal benefit to the individual? Is the marginal social cost of the activity greater than or equal to the marginal cost to the individual? Without intervention, will there be too little or too much (relative to what would be socially optimal) of this activity?

   a. Mr. Chau plants lots of colorful flowers in his front yard.

   b. Your next-door neighbor likes to build bonfires in his backyard, and sparks often drift onto your house.

   c. Maija, who lives next to an apple orchard, decides to keep bees to produce honey.

   d. Justine buys a large SUV that consumes a lot of gasoline.

2. Many dairy farmers in California are adopting a new technology that allows them to produce their own electricity from methane gas captured from animal waste.

(One cow can produce up to 2 kilowatts a day.) This practice reduces the amount of methane gas released into the atmosphere. In addition to reducing their own utility bills, the farmers are allowed to sell any electricity they produce at favorable rates.

a. Explain how the ability to earn money from capturing and transforming methane gas behaves like a Pigouvian tax on methane gas pollution and can lead dairy farmers to emit the efficient amount of methane gas pollution.

b. Suppose some dairy farmers have lower costs of transforming methane into electricity than others. Explain how this system of capturing and selling methane gas leads to an efficient allocation of emissions reduction among farmers.

3. Voluntary environmental programs were extremely popular in the United States, Europe, and Japan in the 1990s. Part of their popularity stems from the fact that these programs do not require legislative authority, which is often hard to obtain. The 33/50 program started by the Environmental Protection Agency (EPA) is an example of such a program. With this program, the EPA attempted to reduce industrial emissions of 17 toxic chemicals by providing information on relatively inexpensive methods of pollution control. Companies were asked to voluntarily commit to reducing emissions from their 1988 levels by 33% by 1992 and by 50% by 1995. The program actually met its second target by 1994.

a. As in Figure 16-3, draw marginal benefit curves for pollution generated by two plants, A and B, in 1988. Assume that without government intervention, each plant emits the same amount of pollution, but that at all levels of pollution less than this amount, plant A's marginal benefit of polluting is less than that of plant B. Label the vertical axis "Marginal benefit to individual polluter" and the horizontal axis "Quantity of pollution emissions." Mark the quantity of pollution each plant produces without government action.

b. Do you expect the total quantity of pollution before the program was put in place to have been less than or more than the optimal quantity of pollution? Why?

c. Suppose the plants whose marginal benefit curves you depicted in part a were participants in the 33/50 program. In a replica of your graph from part a, mark targeted levels of pollution in 1995 for the two plants. Which plant was required to reduce emissions more? Was this solution necessarily efficient?

d. What kind of environmental policy does the 33/50 program most closely resemble? What is the main shortcoming of such a policy? Compare it to two other types of environmental policies discussed in this chapter.

4. According to a report from the U.S. Census Bureau, "the average [lifetime] earnings of a full-time, year round worker with a high school education are about $1.2 million compared with $2.1 million for a college graduate." This indicates that there is a considerable benefit to a graduate from investing in his or her own education. Tuition at most state universities covers only about two-thirds to three-quarters of the cost, so the state applies a Pigouvian subsidy to college education.

If a Pigouvian subsidy is appropriate, is the externality created by a college education a positive or a negative externality? What does this imply about the differences between the costs and benefits to students compared to social costs and benefits? What are some reasons for the differences?

5. The city of Falls Church, Virginia, subsidizes the planting of trees in homeowners' front yards when they are within 15 feet of the street.

a. Using concepts in the chapter, explain why a municipality would subsidize planting trees on private property, but near the street.

b. Draw a diagram similar to Figure 16-4 that shows the marginal social benefit, the marginal social cost, and the optimal Pigouvian subsidy on planting trees.

6. Fishing for sablefish has been so intensive that sablefish were threatened with extinction. After several years of banning such fishing, the government is now proposing to introduce tradable vouchers, each of which entitles its holder to a catch of a certain size. Explain how uncontrolled fishing generates a negative externality and how the voucher scheme may overcome the inefficiency created by this externality.

7. The two dry-cleaning companies in Collegetown, College Cleaners and Big Green Cleaners, are a major source of air pollution. Together they currently produce 350 units of air pollution, which the town wants to reduce to 200 units. The accompanying table shows the current pollution level produced by each company and each company's marginal cost of reducing its pollution. The marginal cost is constant.

Companies	Initial pollution level (units)	Marginal cost of reducing pollution (per unit)
College Cleaners	230	$5
Big Green Cleaners	120	$2

a. Suppose that Collegetown passes an environmental standards law that limits each company to 100 units of pollution. What would be the total cost to the two companies of each reducing its pollution emissions to 100 units?

Suppose instead that Collegetown issues 100 pollution vouchers to each company, each entitling the company to one unit of pollution, and that these vouchers can be traded.

b. How much is each pollution voucher worth to College Cleaners? To Big Green Cleaners? (That is, how much would each company, at most, be willing to pay for one more voucher?)

c. Who will sell vouchers and who will buy them? How many vouchers will be traded?

d. What is the total cost to the two companies of the pollution controls under this voucher system?

8. a. EAuction and EMarketplace are two competing internet auction sites, where buyers and sellers transact goods. Each auction site earns money by charging sellers for listing their goods. EAuction has decided to eliminate fees for the first transaction for sellers that are new to its site. Explain why this is likely to be a good strategy for EAuction in its competition with EMarketplace.

b. EMarketplace complained to the Justice Department that EAuction's practice of eliminating fees for new sellers was anti-competitive and would lead to monopolization of the internet auction industry. Is EMarketplace correct? How should the Justice Department respond?

c. EAuction stopped its practice of eliminating fees for new sellers. But since it provided much better technical service than its rival, EMarketplace, buyers and sellers came to prefer EAuction. Eventually, EMarketplace closed down, leaving EAuction as a monopolist. Should the Justice Department intervene to break EAuction into two companies? Explain.

d. EAuction is now a monopolist in the internet auction industry. It also owns a site that handles payments over the internet, called PayForIt. It is competing with another internet payment site, called PayBuddy. EAuction has now stipulated that any transaction on its auction site must use PayForIt, rather than PayBuddy, for the payment. Should the Justice Department intervene? Explain.

9. Which of the following are characterized by network externalities? Which are not? Explain.

a. The choice between installing 110-volt electrical current in structures rather than 220-volt

b. The choice between purchasing a Toyota versus a Ford

c. The choice of a printer, where each printer requires its own specific type of ink cartridge

d. The choice of whether to purchase an iPod Touch or an iPod Nano.

WORK IT OUT

For interactive, step-by-step help in solving the following problem, visit LaunchPad by using the URL on the back cover of this book.

10. The loud music coming from the sorority next to your dorm is a negative externality that can be directly quantified. The accompanying table shows the marginal social benefit and the marginal social cost per decibel (dB, a measure of volume) of music.

Volume of music (dB)	Marginal social benefit of dB	Marginal social cost of dB
90		
	$36	$0
91		
	30	2
92		
	24	4
93		
	18	6
94		
	12	8
95		
	6	10
96		
	0	12
97		

a. Draw the marginal social benefit curve and the marginal social cost curve. Use your diagram to determine the socially optimal volume of music.

b. Only the members of the sorority benefit from the music, and they bear none of the cost. Which volume of music will they choose?

c. The college imposes a Pigouvian tax of $3 per decibel of music played. From your diagram, determine the volume of music the sorority will now choose.

Public Goods and Common Resources

▶ What You Will Learn in This Chapter

■ A way to classify goods that predicts whether or not a good is a **private good**—a good that can be efficiently provided by markets

■ What **public goods** are, and why markets fail to supply them

■ What **common resources** are, and why they are overused

■ What **artificially scarce goods** are, and why they are underconsumed

■ How government intervention in the production and consumption of these types of goods can make society better off

■ Why finding the right level of government intervention is often difficult

THE GREAT STINK

London's River Thames then . . .

. . . and the same river now, thanks to government intervention.

BY THE MIDDLE OF THE NINE-teenth century, London had become the world's largest city, with close to 2.5 million inhabitants. Unfortunately, all those people produced a lot of waste—and there was no place for it to go except into the Thames, the river flowing through the city. Nobody with a working nose could ignore the results. And the river didn't just smell bad— it carried dangerous waterborne diseases like cholera and typhoid. London neighborhoods close to the Thames had death rates from cholera more than six times greater than the neighborhoods farthest away. And the great majority of Londoners drew their drinking water from the Thames.

What the city needed, said reformers, was a sewage system to carry waste away from the river. Yet no private individual was willing to build such a system, and influential people were opposed to the idea that the government should take responsibility for the problem.

But the hot summer of 1858 brought what came to be known as the Great Stink, which was so bad that one health journal reported "men struck down with the stench." Even the privileged and powerful suffered: Parliament met in a building next to the river. After unsuccessful efforts to stop the smell by covering the windows with chemical-soaked curtains, Parliament finally approved a plan for an immense system of sewers and pumping stations to direct sewage away from the city.

The system, opened in 1865, brought dramatic improvement in the city's quality of life; cholera and typhoid epidemics, which had been regular occurrences, completely disappeared. The Thames was turned from the filthiest to the cleanest metropolitan river in the world, and the sewage system's principal engineer, Sir Joseph Bazalgette, was lauded as having "saved more lives than any single Victorian public official." It was estimated at the time that his sewer system added 20 years to the life span of the average Londoner.

The story of the Great Stink and the policy response that followed illustrate two important reasons for government intervention in the economy. London's new sewage system was a clear example of a *public good*—a good that benefits many people, whether or not they have paid for it, and whose benefits to any one individual do not depend on how many others also benefit. As we will see, public goods differ in important ways from the *private goods* we have studied so far—and these differences mean that public goods cannot be efficiently supplied by the market.

In addition, clean water in the Thames is an example of a *common resource*, a good that many people can consume whether or not they have paid for it but whose consumption by each person reduces the amount available to others. Such goods tend to be overused by individuals in a market system unless the government takes action.

In earlier chapters, we saw that markets sometimes fail to deliver efficient levels of production and consumption of a good or activity. We saw how inefficiency can arise from market power, which allows monopolists and colluding oligopolists to charge prices that are higher than marginal cost, thereby preventing mutually beneficial transactions from occurring. We also saw how inefficiency can arise from positive and negative externalities, which cause a divergence between the costs and benefits of an individual's or industry's actions and the costs and benefits of those actions borne by society as a whole.

In this chapter, we will take a somewhat different approach to the question of why markets sometimes fail. Here we focus on how *the characteristics of goods often determine whether markets can deliver them efficiently.* When goods have the "wrong" characteristics, the resulting market failures resemble those associated with externalities or market power. This alternative way of looking at sources of inefficiency deepens our understanding of why markets sometimes don't work well and how government can take actions that increase society's welfare.

Private Goods—and Others

What's the difference between installing a new bathroom in a house and building a municipal sewage system? What's the difference between growing wheat and fishing in the open ocean?

These aren't trick questions. In each case there is a basic difference in the characteristics of the goods involved. Bathroom fixtures and wheat have the characteristics necessary to allow markets to work efficiently. Public sewage systems and fish in the sea do not.

Let's look at these crucial characteristics and why they matter.

Characteristics of Goods

A good is **excludable** if the supplier of that good can prevent people who do not pay from consuming it.

A good is **rival in consumption** if the same unit of the good cannot be consumed by more than one person at the same time.

A good that is both excludable and rival in consumption is a **private good.**

When a good is **nonexcludable,** the supplier cannot prevent consumption by people who do not pay for it.

A good is **nonrival in consumption** if more than one person can consume the same unit of the good at the same time.

Goods like bathroom fixtures or wheat have two characteristics that, as we'll soon see, are essential if a good is to be efficiently provided by a market economy.

- They are **excludable:** suppliers of the good can prevent people who don't pay from consuming it.

- They are **rival in consumption:** the same unit of the good cannot be consumed by more than one person at the same time.

When a good is both excludable and rival in consumption, it is called a **private good.** Wheat is an example of a private good. It is *excludable*: the farmer can sell a bushel to one consumer without having to provide wheat to everyone in the county. And it is *rival in consumption*: if I eat bread baked with a farmer's wheat, that wheat cannot be consumed by someone else.

But not all goods possess these two characteristics. Some goods are **nonexcludable**—the supplier cannot prevent consumption of the good by people who do not pay for it. Fire protection is one example: a fire department that puts out fires before they spread protects the whole city, not just people who have made contributions to the Firemen's Benevolent Association. An improved environment is another: the city of London couldn't have ended the Great Stink for some residents while leaving the river Thames foul for others.

Nor are all goods rival in consumption. Goods are **nonrival in consumption** if more than one person can consume the same unit of the good at the same time. TV shows are nonrival in consumption: your decision to watch a show does not prevent other people from watching the same show.

Because goods can be either excludable or nonexcludable, rival or nonrival in consumption, there are four types of goods, illustrated by the matrix in Figure 17-1:

FIGURE 17-1   Four Types of Goods

	Rival in consumption	Nonrival in consumption
Excludable	**Private goods** • Wheat • Bathroom fixtures	**Artificially scarce goods** • On-demand movies • Computer software
Non-excludable	**Common resources** • Clean water • Biodiversity	**Public goods** • Public sanitation • National defense

There are four types of goods. The type of a good depends on (1) whether or not it is excludable—whether a producer can prevent someone from consuming it; and (2) whether or not it is rival in consumption—whether it is impossible for the same unit of a good to be consumed by more than one person at the same time.

- *Private goods,* which are excludable and rival in consumption, like wheat
- *Public goods,* which are nonexcludable and nonrival in consumption, like a public sewer system
- *Common resources,* which are nonexcludable but rival in consumption, like clean water in a river
- *Artificially scarce goods,* which are excludable but nonrival in consumption, like on-demand movies on Netflix

There are, of course, many other characteristics that distinguish between types of goods—necessities versus luxuries, normal versus inferior, and so on. Why focus on whether goods are excludable and rival in consumption?

Why Markets Can Supply Only Private Goods Efficiently

As we learned in earlier chapters, markets are typically the best means for a society to deliver goods and services to its members; that is, markets are efficient except in the case of the well-defined problems of market power, externalities, or other instances of market failure. But there is yet another condition that must be met, one rooted in the nature of the good itself: markets cannot supply goods and services efficiently unless they are private goods—excludable and rival in consumption.

To see why excludability is crucial, suppose that a farmer had only two choices: either produce no wheat or provide a bushel of wheat to every resident of the county who wants it, whether or not that resident pays for it. It seems unlikely that anyone would grow wheat under those conditions.

Yet the operator of a municipal sewage system faces pretty much the same problem as our hypothetical farmer. A sewage system makes the whole city cleaner and healthier—but that benefit accrues to all the city's residents, whether or not they pay the system operator. That's why no private entrepreneur came forward with a plan to end London's Great Stink.

The general point is that if a good is nonexcludable, self-interested consumers won't be willing to pay for it—they will take a "free ride" on anyone who *does* pay. So there is a **free-rider problem.** Examples of the free-rider problem are familiar from daily life. One example you may have encountered happens when students are required to do a group project. There is often a tendency for some group members to shirk, relying on others in the group to get the work done. The shirkers *free-ride* on someone else's effort.

Because of the free-rider problem, the forces of self-interest alone do not lead to an efficient level of production for a nonexcludable good. Even though consumers would benefit from increased production of the good, no one individual is willing to pay for more, and so no producer is willing to supply it. The result is that nonexcludable goods suffer from *inefficiently low production* in a market economy. In fact, in the face of the free-rider problem, self-interest may not ensure that any amount of the good—let alone the efficient quantity—is produced.

Goods that are excludable and nonrival in consumption, like on-demand movies, suffer from a different kind of inefficiency. As long as a good is excludable, it is possible to earn a profit by making it available only to those who pay. Therefore, producers are willing to supply an excludable good. But the marginal cost of letting an additional viewer watch an on-demand movie is zero because it is nonrival in consumption. So the efficient price to the consumer is also zero—or, to put it another way, individuals should watch movies up to the point where their marginal benefit is zero.

But if Netflix actually charges viewers $4 for on-demand movies, viewers will consume the good only up to the point where their marginal

Goods that are nonexcludable suffer from the **free-rider problem:** many individuals are unwilling to pay for their own consumption and instead will take a "free ride" on anyone who does pay.

PITFALLS

MARGINAL COST OF WHAT EXACTLY?
In the case of a good that is nonrival in consumption, it's easy to confuse the marginal cost of *producing* a unit of the good with the marginal cost of *allowing* a unit of the good *to be consumed*. For example, Netflix incurs a marginal cost in making an on-demand movie available to its subscribers that is equal to the cost of the resources it uses to produce and broadcast that movie. However, *once that movie is being broadcast*, no marginal cost is incurred by letting an additional family watch it. In other words, no costly resources are "used up" when one more family consumes a movie that has already been produced and is being broadcast.

This complication does not arise, however, when a good is rival in consumption. In that case, the resources used to produce a unit of the good are "used up" by a person's consumption of it—they are no longer available to satisfy someone else's consumption. So when a good is rival in consumption, the marginal cost to society of allowing an individual to consume a unit is equal to the resource cost of producing that unit—that is, equal to the marginal cost of producing it.

benefit is $4. When consumers must pay a price greater than zero for a good that is nonrival in consumption, the price they pay is higher than the marginal cost of allowing them to consume that good, which is zero. So in a market economy goods that are nonrival in consumption suffer from *inefficiently low consumption.*

Now we can see why private goods are the only goods that can be efficiently produced and consumed in a competitive market. (That is, a private good will be efficiently produced and consumed in a market free of market power, externalities, or other instances of market failure.) Because private goods are excludable, producers can charge for them and so have an incentive to produce them. And because they are also rival in consumption, it is efficient for consumers to pay a positive price—a price equal to the marginal cost of production. If one or both of these characteristics are lacking, a market economy will not lead to efficient production and consumption of the good.

Fortunately for the market system, most goods are private goods. Food, clothing, shelter, and most other desirable things in life are excludable and rival in consumption, so markets can provide us with most things. Yet there are crucial goods that don't meet these criteria—and in most cases, that means that the government must step in.

ECONOMICS ▶ *in Action*

From Mayhem to Renaissance

Life during the European Middle Ages—from approximately 1100 to 1500—was difficult and dangerous, with high rates of violent crime, banditry, and war casualties. According to researchers, murder rates in Europe in 1200 were 30 to 40 per 100,000 people. But by 1500 the rate had been halved to around 20 per 100,000; today, it is less than 1 per 100,000. What accounts for the sharp decrease in mayhem over the last 900 years?

Think public goods, as the history of medieval Italian city-states illustrates.

Starting around the year 900 in Venice and 1100 in other city-states like Milan and Florence, citizens began to organize and create institutions for protection. In Venice, citizens built a defensive fleet to battle the pirates and other marauders who regularly attacked them. Other city-states built strong defensive walls to encircle their cities and also paid defensive militias. Institutions were created to maintain law and order: cadres of guards, watchmen, and magistrates were hired; courthouses and jails were built.

As a result, trade, commerce, and banking were able to flourish, as well as literacy, numeracy, and the arts. By 1300, the leading cities of Venice, Milan, and Florence had each grown to over 100,000 people. As resources and the standard of living increased, the rate of violent deaths diminished.

For example, the Republic of Venice was known as *La Serenissima*—the Most Serene One—because of its enlightened governance, overseen by a council of leading citizens. Owing to its stability, diplomatic prowess, and prodigious fleet of vessels, Venice became enormously wealthy in the fifteenth and sixteenth centuries.

Also through stability, high literacy, and numeracy, Florence became the banking center of Italy. During the fifteenth century it was ruled by the Medici, an immensely wealthy banking family. And it was the patronage of the Medici to artists such as Leonardo da Vinci and Michelangelo that ushered in the Renaissance.

So Western Europe was able to move from mayhem to Renaissance through the creation of public goods like good gov-

The emergence of institutions to maintain law and order—public goods—allowed for a move away from the war and brutality that marked the Middle Ages and toward a new era.

ernance and defense—goods that benefited everyone and could not be diminished by any one person's use.

Check Your Understanding   17-1

1. Classify each of the following goods according to whether they are excludable and whether they are rival in consumption. What kind of good is each?
   a. Use of a public space such as a park
   b. A cheese burrito
   c. Information from a website that is password-protected
   d. Publicly announced information on the path of an incoming hurricane
2. Which of the goods in Question 1 will be provided by a competitive market? Which will not be? Explain your answer.

Solutions appear at back of book.

Public Goods

A **public good** is the exact opposite of a private good: it is a good that is both nonexcludable and nonrival in consumption. A public sewer system is an example of a public good: you can't keep a river clean without making it clean for everyone who lives near its banks, and my protection from great stinks does not come at my neighbor's expense.

Here are some other examples of public goods:

• *Disease prevention.* When doctors act to stamp out the beginnings of an epidemic before it can spread, they protect people around the world.

• *National defense.* A strong military protects all citizens.

• *Scientific research.* More knowledge benefits everyone.

Because these goods are nonexcludable, they suffer from the free-rider problem, so no private firm would be willing to produce them. And because they are nonrival in consumption, it would be inefficient to charge people for consuming them. As a result, society must find nonmarket methods for providing these goods.

Providing Public Goods

Public goods are provided through a variety of means. The government doesn't always get involved—in many cases a nongovernmental solution has been found for the free-rider problem. But these solutions are usually imperfect in some way.

Some public goods are supplied through voluntary contributions. For example, private donations support a considerable amount of scientific research. But private donations are insufficient to finance huge, socially important projects like basic medical research.

Some public goods are supplied by self-interested individuals or firms because those who produce them are able to make money in an indirect way. The classic example is broadcast television, which in the United States is supported entirely by advertising. The downside of such indirect funding is that it skews the nature and quantity of the public goods that are supplied, as well as imposing additional costs on consumers. TV stations show the programs that yield the most advertising revenue (that is, programs best suited for selling prescription drugs, weight-loss remedies, antihistamines, and the like to the segment of the population that buys them), which are not necessarily the programs people most want to see. And viewers must also endure many commercials.

Some potentially public goods are deliberately made excludable and therefore subject to charge, like on-demand movies. In the United Kingdom, where most

A **public good** is both nonexcludable and nonrival in consumption.

On the prowl: a British TV detection van at work.

television programming is paid for by a yearly license fee assessed on every television owner (£145.50, or about $245 in 2014), television viewing is made artificially excludable by the use of "television detection vans" that roam neighborhoods in an attempt to detect televisions in nonlicensed households and fine them. However, as noted earlier, when suppliers charge a price greater than zero for a nonrival good, consumers will consume an inefficiently low quantity of that good.

In small communities, a high level of social encouragement or pressure can be brought to bear on people to contribute money or time to provide the efficient level of a public good. Volunteer fire departments, which depend both on the volunteered services of the firefighters themselves and on contributions from local residents, are a good example. But as communities grow larger and more anonymous, social pressure is increasingly difficult to apply, compelling larger towns and cities to tax residents to provide salaried firefighters for fire protection services.

As this last example suggests, when these other solutions fail, it is up to the government to provide public goods. Indeed, the most important public goods—national defense, the legal system, disease control, fire protection in large cities, and so on—are provided by government and paid for by taxes. Economic theory tells us that the provision of public goods is one of the crucial roles of government.

How Much of a Public Good Should Be Provided?

In some cases, provision of a public good is an "either–or" decision: London would either have a sewage system—or not. But in most cases, governments must decide not only whether to provide a public good but also *how much* of that public good to provide. For example, street cleaning is a public good—but how often should the streets be cleaned? Once a month? Twice a month? Every other day?

Imagine a city in which there are only two residents, Ted and Alice. Assume that the public good in question is street cleaning and that Ted and Alice truthfully tell the government how much they value a unit of the public good, where a unit is equal to one street cleaning per month. Specifically, each of them tells the government *his or her willingness to pay for another unit of the public good supplied*—an amount that corresponds to that *individual's marginal benefit* of another unit of the public good.

Using this information plus information on the cost of providing the good, the government can use marginal analysis to find the efficient level of providing the public good: the level at which the *marginal social benefit* of the public good is equal to the marginal cost of producing it. Recall from Chapter 16 that the marginal social benefit of a good is the benefit that accrues to society as a whole from the consumption of one additional unit of the good.

But what is the marginal social benefit of another unit of a public good—a unit that generates utility for *all* consumers, not just one consumer, because it is nonexcludable and nonrival in consumption? This question leads us to an important principle: *In the special case of a public good, the marginal social benefit of a unit of the good is equal to the sum of the individual marginal benefits that are enjoyed by all consumers of that unit.* Or to consider it from a slightly different angle, if a consumer could be compelled to pay for a unit before consuming it (the good is made excludable), then the marginal social benefit of a unit is equal to the *sum* of each consumer's willingness to pay for that unit. Using this principle, the marginal social benefit of an additional street cleaning per month is equal to Ted's individual marginal benefit from that additional cleaning *plus* Alice's individual marginal benefit.

Why? Because a public good is nonrival in consumption—Ted's benefit from a cleaner street does not diminish Alice's benefit from that same clean street, and vice versa. Because

We all benefit when someone else does the cleaning up.

people can all simultaneously consume the same unit of a public good, the marginal social benefit of an additional unit of that good is the *sum* of the individual marginal benefits of all who enjoy the public good. And the efficient quantity of a public good is the quantity at which the marginal social benefit is equal to the marginal cost of providing it.

Figure 17-2 illustrates the efficient provision of a public good, showing three marginal benefit curves. Panel (a) shows Ted's individual marginal benefit curve from street cleaning, MB_T: he would be willing to pay $25 for the city to clean its streets once a month, an additional $18 to have it done a second time, and so on. Panel (b) shows Alice's individual marginal benefit curve from street

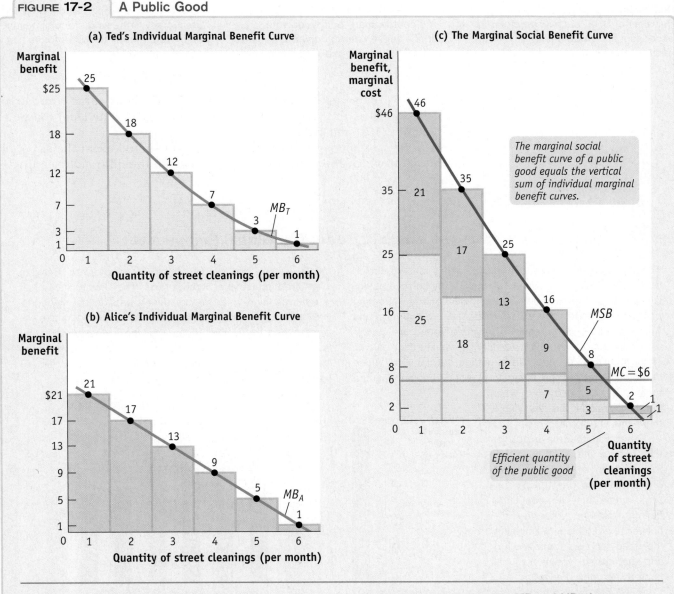

FIGURE 17-2 A Public Good

(a) Ted's Individual Marginal Benefit Curve

(b) Alice's Individual Marginal Benefit Curve

(c) The Marginal Social Benefit Curve

The marginal social benefit curve of a public good equals the vertical sum of individual marginal benefit curves.

Panel (a) shows Ted's individual marginal benefit curve of street cleanings per month, MB_T, and panel (b) shows Alice's individual marginal benefit curve, MB_A. Panel (c) shows the marginal social benefit of the public good, equal to the sum of the individual marginal benefits to all consumers (in this case, Ted and Alice). The marginal social benefit curve, MSB, is the vertical sum of the individual marginal benefit curves MB_T and MB_A. At a constant marginal cost of $6, there should be 5 street cleanings per month, because the marginal social benefit of going from 4 to 5 cleanings is $8 ($3 for Ted plus $5 for Alice), but the marginal social benefit of going from 5 to 6 cleanings is only $2.

FOR INQUIRING MINDS | Voting as a Public Good

It's a sad fact that many Americans who are eligible to vote don't bother to. As a result, their interests tend to be ignored by politicians. But what's even sadder is that this self-defeating behavior may be completely rational.

As the economist Mancur Olson pointed out in a famous book titled *The Logic of Collective Action,* voting is a public good, one that suffers from severe free-rider problems.

Imagine that you are one of a million people who would stand to gain the equivalent of $100 each if some plan is passed in a statewide referendum—say, a plan to improve public schools. And

suppose that the opportunity cost of the time it would take you to vote is $10. Will you be sure to go to the polls and vote for the referendum? If you are rational, the answer is no because it is very unlikely that your vote will decide the issue, either way. If the measure passes, you benefit, even if you didn't bother to vote—the benefits are nonexcludable. If the measure doesn't pass, your vote would not have changed the outcome. By not voting and free-riding on those who do vote you save $10.

Of course, many people do vote out of a sense of civic duty. But because political action is a public good, in gen-

eral people devote too little effort to defending their own interests.

The result, Olson pointed out, is that when a large group of people share a common political interest, they are likely to exert too little effort promoting their cause and so will be ignored. Conversely, small, well-organized interest groups that act on issues narrowly targeted in their favor tend to have disproportionate power.

Is this a reason to distrust democracy? Winston Churchill said it best: "Democracy is the worst form of government, except for all the other forms that have been tried." ∎

cleaning, MB_A. Panel (c) shows the marginal social benefit curve from street cleaning, *MSB:* it is the vertical sum of Ted's and Alice's individual marginal benefit curves, MB_T and MB_A.

To maximize society's welfare, the government should clean the street up to the level at which the marginal social benefit of an additional cleaning is

GLOBAL COMPARISION | Voting as a Public Good: The Global Perspective

Despite the fact that it can be an entirely rational choice not to vote, many countries consistently achieve astonishingly high turnout rates in their elections by adopting policies that encourage voting. In Belgium, Singapore, and Australia, voting is compulsory; eligible voters are penalized if they fail to do their civic duty by casting their ballots. These penalties are effective at getting out the vote. When Venezuela dropped its mandatory voting requirement, the turnout rate dropped 30%; when the Netherlands did the same, there was a 20% drop-off.

Other countries have policies that reduce the cost of voting; for example, declaring election day a work holiday (giving citizens ample time to cast their ballots), allowing voter registration on election day (eliminating the need for advance planning), and permitting voting by mail (increasing convenience).

This figure shows turnout rates in several countries, measured as the percentage of eligible voters who cast ballots, averaged over elections held between 1945 and

2013. As you can see, Australia, Singapore, and Belgium have the highest voter turnout rates. The United States has a relatively high voter turnout during presidential elections. However, turnout drops significantly in nonpresidential elections, when the United States has the lowest turnout rate among advanced countries. In general, the past four decades have seen a decline in voter turnout rates in the major democracies, most dramatically among the youngest voters.

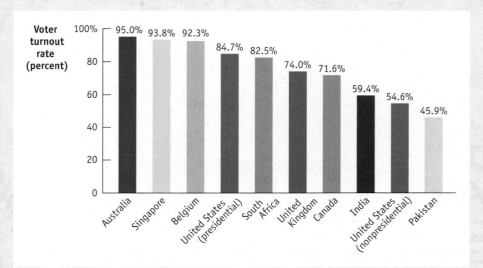

Source: International Institute for Democracy and Electoral Assistance.

no longer greater than the marginal cost. Suppose that the marginal cost of street cleaning is $6 per cleaning. Then the city should clean its streets 5 times per month, because the marginal social benefit of going from 4 to 5 cleanings is $8, but going from 5 to 6 cleanings would yield a marginal social benefit of only $2.

Figure 17-2 can help reinforce our understanding of why we cannot rely on individual self-interest to yield provision of an efficient quantity of public goods. Suppose that the city did one fewer street cleaning than the efficient quantity and that either Ted or Alice was asked to pay for the last cleaning. Neither one would be willing to pay for it! Ted would personally gain only the equivalent of $3 in utility from adding one more street cleaning—so he wouldn't be willing to pay the $6 marginal cost of another cleaning. Alice would personally gain the equivalent of $5 in utility—so she wouldn't be willing to pay either.

The point is that the marginal social benefit of one more unit of a public good is always greater than the individual marginal benefit to any one individual. That is why no individual is willing to pay for the efficient quantity of the good.

Does this description of the public-good problem, in which the marginal social benefit of an additional unit of the public good is greater than any individual's marginal benefit, sound a bit familiar? It should: we encountered a somewhat similar situation in our discussion of *positive externalities*. Remember that in the case of a positive externality, the marginal social benefit accruing to all consumers of another unit of the good is greater than the price that the producer receives for that unit; as a result, the market produces too little of the good.

In the case of a public good, the individual marginal benefit of a consumer plays the same role as the price received by the producer in the case of positive externalities: both cases create insufficient incentive to provide an efficient amount of the good.

The problem of providing public goods is very similar to the problem of dealing with positive externalities; in both cases there is a market failure that calls for government intervention. One basic rationale for the existence of government is that it provides a way for citizens to tax themselves in order to provide public goods—particularly a vital public good like national defense.

Of course, if society really consisted of only two individuals, they would probably manage to strike a deal to provide the good. But imagine a city with a million residents, each of whose individual marginal benefit from provision of the good is only a tiny fraction of the marginal social benefit. It would be impossible for people to reach a voluntary agreement to pay for the efficient level of street cleaning—the potential for free-riding makes it too difficult to make and enforce an agreement among so many people. But they could and would vote to tax themselves to pay for a citywide sanitation department.

Cost-Benefit Analysis

How do governments decide in practice how much of a public good to provide? Sometimes policy makers just guess—or do whatever they think will get them reelected. However, responsible governments try to estimate and compare both the social benefits and the social costs of providing a public good, a process known as **cost-benefit analysis.**

It's straightforward to estimate the cost of supplying a public good. Estimating the benefit is harder. In fact, it is a very difficult problem.

Now you might wonder why governments can't figure out the marginal social benefit of a public good just by asking people their willingness to pay for it (their individual marginal benefit). But it turns out that it's hard to get an honest answer.

This is not a problem with private goods: we can determine how much an individual is willing to pay for one more unit of a private good by looking at his

Cost-benefit analysis is the estimation and comparison of the social costs and social benefits of providing a public good.

or her actual choices. But because people don't actually pay for public goods, the question of willingness to pay is always hypothetical.

Worse yet, it's a question that people have an incentive not to answer truthfully. People naturally want more rather than less. Because they cannot be made to pay for whatever quantity of the public good they use, people are apt to overstate their true feelings when asked how much they desire a public good. For example, if street cleaning were scheduled according to the stated wishes of homeowners alone, the streets would be cleaned every day—an inefficient level of provision.

So governments must be aware that they cannot simply rely on the public's statements when deciding how much of a public good to provide—if they do, they are likely to provide too much. In contrast, as For Inquiring Minds in the preceding section explains, relying on the public to indicate how much of the public good they want through voting has problems as well—and is likely to lead to too little of the public good being provided.

ECONOMICS ▶ in Action

Old Man River

It just keeps rolling along—but now and then it decides to roll in a different direction. In fact, the Mississippi River changes its course every few hundred years. Sediment carried downstream gradually clogs the river's route to the sea, and eventually the river breaches its banks and opens a new channel. Over the millennia, the mouth of the Mississippi has swung back and forth along an arc some 200 miles wide.

So when is the Mississippi due to change course again? Oh, about 45 years ago.

The Mississippi currently runs to the sea past New Orleans; but by 1950 it was apparent that the river was about to shift course, taking a new route to the sea. If the Army Corps of Engineers hadn't gotten involved, the shift would probably have happened by 1970.

A shift in the Mississippi would have severely damaged the Louisiana economy. A major industrial area would have lost good access to the ocean, and salt water would have contaminated much of its water supply. So the Army Corps of Engineers has kept the Mississippi in its place with a huge complex of dams, walls, and gates known as the Old River Control Structure. At times the amount of water released by this control structure is five times the flow at Niagara Falls.

The Old River Control Structure is a dramatic example of a public good. No individual would have had an incentive to build it, yet it protects many billions of dollars' worth of private property. The history of the Army Corps of Engineers, which handles water-control projects across the United States, illustrates a persistent problem associated with government provision of public goods: everyone wants a project that benefits his or her own property—if other people are going to pay for it. So there is a systematic tendency for potential beneficiaries of Corps projects to overstate the benefits. And the Corps has become notorious for undertaking expensive projects that cannot be justified with any reasonable cost-benefit analysis.

The flip-side of the problem of overfunding of public projects is chronic underfunding. A tragic illustration of this problem was the devastation of New Orleans by Hurricane Katrina in 2005.

Although it was well understood from the time of its founding that New Orleans was at risk for severe flooding because it sits below sea level, very little was done to shore up the crucial system of levees and pumps that protects the city. More than 50 years of inadequate funding for construction and maintenance,

The Old River Control Structure discharges water from the Mississippi into the Atchafalaya River to help keep the Mississippi on course.

Jim Wark/Air Photo

coupled with inadequate supervision, left the system weakened and unable to cope with the onslaught from Katrina. The catastrophe was compounded by the failure of local and state government to develop an evacuation plan in the event of a hurricane. In the end, because of this neglect of a public good, 1,464 people in and around New Orleans lost their lives and the city suffered economic losses totaling billions of dollars.

Check Your Understanding 17-2

1. The town of Centreville, population 16, has two types of residents, Homebodies and Revelers. Using the accompanying table, the town must decide how much to spend on its New Year's Eve party. No individual resident expects to directly bear the cost of the party.
   a. Suppose there are 10 Homebodies and 6 Revelers. Determine the marginal social benefit schedule of money spent on the party. What is the efficient level of spending?
   b. Suppose there are 6 Homebodies and 10 Revelers. How do your answers to part a change? Explain.

Money spent on party	Individual marginal benefit of additional $1 spent on party	
	Homebody	Reveler
$0		
	$0.05	$0.13
1		
	0.04	0.11
2		
	0.03	0.09
3		
	0.02	0.07
4		

   c. Suppose that the individual marginal benefit schedules are known but no one knows the true proportion of Homebodies versus Revelers. Individuals are asked their preferences. What is the likely outcome if each person assumes that others will pay for any additional amount of the public good? Why is it likely to result in an inefficiently high level of spending? Explain.

Solutions appear at back of book.

Common Resources

A **common resource** is a good that is nonexcludable but is rival in consumption. An example is the stock of fish in a limited fishing area, like the fisheries off the coast of New England. Traditionally, anyone who had a boat could go out to sea and catch fish—fish in the sea were a nonexcludable good. Yet because the total number of fish is limited, the fish that one person catches are no longer available to be caught by someone else. So fish in the sea are rival in consumption.

Other examples of common resources are clean air and water as well as the diversity of animal and plant species on the planet (biodiversity). In each of these cases the fact that the good, though rival in consumption, is nonexcludable poses a serious problem.

The Problem of Overuse

Because common resources are nonexcludable, individuals cannot be charged for their use. Yet because they are rival in consumption, an individual who uses a unit depletes the resource by making that unit unavailable to others. As a result, a common resource is subject to **overuse**: an individual will continue to use it until his or her marginal benefit of its use is equal to his or her own individual marginal cost, ignoring the cost that this action inflicts on society as a whole. As we will see shortly, the problem of overuse of a common resource is similar to a problem we studied in Chapter 16: the problem of a good that generates a negative externality, such as ground-water contamination from fracking.

A **common resource** is nonexcludable and rival in consumption: you can't stop me from consuming the good, and more consumption by me means less of the good available for you.

Common resources left to the market suffer from **overuse**: individuals ignore the fact that their use depletes the amount of the resource remaining for others.

FIGURE **17-3**   A Common Resource

The supply curve S, which shows the marginal cost of production of the fishing industry, is composed of the individual supply curves of the individual fishermen. But each fisherman's individual marginal cost does not include the cost that his or her actions impose on others: the depletion of the common resource. As a result, the marginal social cost curve, *MSC*, lies above the supply curve; in an unregulated market, the quantity of the common resource used, Q_{MKT}, exceeds the efficient quantity of use, Q_{OPT}.

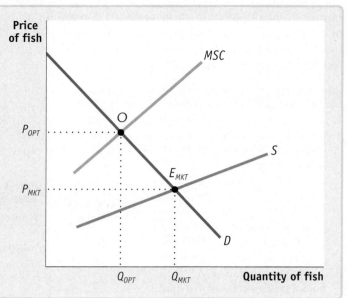

Fishing is a classic example of a common resource. In heavily fished waters, my fishing imposes a cost on others by reducing the fish population and making it harder for others to catch fish. But I have no personal incentive to take this cost into account, since I cannot be charged for fishing. As a result, from society's point of view, I catch too many fish.

Traffic congestion is another example of overuse of a common resource. A major highway during rush hour can accommodate only a certain number of vehicles per hour. If I decide to drive to work alone rather than carpool or work at home, I make the commute of many other people a bit longer; but I have no incentive to take these consequences into account.

In the case of a common resource, the *marginal social cost* of my use of that resource is higher than my *individual marginal cost,* the cost to me of using an additional unit of the good.

Figure 17-3 illustrates the point. It shows the demand curve for fish, which measures the marginal benefit of fish—the benefit to consumers when an additional unit of fish is caught and consumed. It also shows the supply curve for fish, which measures the marginal cost of production of the fishing industry. We know from Chapter 12 that the industry supply curve is the horizontal sum of each individual fisherman's supply curve—equivalent to his or her individual marginal cost curve. The fishing industry supplies the quantity where its marginal cost is equal to the price, the quantity Q_{MKT}.

But the efficient outcome is to catch the quantity Q_{OPT}, the quantity of output that equates the marginal benefit to the marginal social cost, not to the fishing industry's marginal cost of production. The market outcome results in overuse of the common resource.

As we noted, there is a close parallel between the problem of managing a common resource and the problem posed by negative externalities. In the case of an activity that generates a negative externality, the marginal social cost of production is greater than the industry's marginal cost of production, the difference being the marginal external cost imposed on society. Here, the loss to society arising from a fisherman's depletion of the common resource plays the same role as the external cost plays when there is a negative externality. In fact, many negative externalities (such as pollution) can be thought of as involving common resources (such as clean air).

FOR INQUIRING MINDS | When Fertile Farmland Turned to Dust

Ashley Yost's grandfather sank a well deep underneath his prime Kansas farmland and struck a source of water so bountiful that he could pump 1,600 gallons to the surface every minute. Now fifty years later, his grandson is having trouble getting just 300 gallons of water per minute. And that water is so contaminated by sediment that tens of thousands of dollars worth of pumping equipment has been destroyed. As Mr. Yost ruefully remarked, "That's prime land. I've raised 294 bushels of corn an acre before…. Now, it's over." In west-central Kansas, the problem is widespread. Wells in up to a fifth of the irrigated farmland have already gone dry. In the Texas Panhandle, many farms have been abandoned and rural communities hollowed out as once highly productive farmland returns to prairie.

This is the sad consequence of mismanagement of a remarkable common resource, the Ogallala Aquifer, one of the world's largest underground reservoirs of water. It stretches across portions of eight Great Plains states and underlies approximately 174,000 square miles, supplying drinking water for millions of people. The water in the Ogallala Aquifer

The depletion of the Ogallala Aquifer, one of the world's largest underground reservoirs, was the result of mismanagement of a common resource.

was deposited 2 to 6 million years ago when the Great Plains region was geologically active. As you might guess, water that was deposited millions of years ago cannot be replenished quickly. For the many parts of the Ogallala that are now dry, it would take over 100,000 years of rainfall to fill them back up.

How did this happen? The decimation of the Ogallala began in the 1950s with the large scale irrigation of Plains farmland with groundwater. The virtually unrestricted pumping of groundwater turned

millions of acres of the semi-arid Great Plains into one of the world's most productive areas for the cultivation of wheat, corn, and other crops. However, as a common resource, farmers had no interest in conserving the Ogallala's water. As a result even the most arid areas, like the Texas Panhandle, were coaxed into growing water-thirsty crops like corn.

While some areas in the northern Plains states still have enough groundwater for approximately 200 years, farmers and residents of the southern Plains know that the days of endless water supplies have ended, as much of the Ogallala Aquifer has been pumped to dangerously low levels.

Some farmers have given up all together, while others have switched to less thirsty crops or to livestock farming. Towns, industries, and recreation activities have all been affected. In Kansas, the state legislature has adopted a new set of water use regulations to encourage conservation, but, at the time of writing it is too early to determine their effectiveness. What we do know is that the days of ignoring a common resource like the Ogallala are over. ■

Steve Liss/The LIFE Images Collection/Getty Images

The Efficient Use and Maintenance of a Common Resource

Because common resources pose problems similar to those created by negative externalities, the solutions are also similar. To ensure efficient use of a common resource, society must find a way of getting individual users of the resource to take into account the costs they impose on other users. This is basically the same principle as that of getting individuals to internalize a negative externality that arises from their actions.

There are three fundamental ways to induce people who use common resources to internalize the costs they impose on others.

- Tax or otherwise regulate the use of the common resource

- Create a system of tradable licenses for the right to use the common resource

- Make the common resource excludable and assign property rights to some individuals

Like activities that generate negative externalities, use of a common resource can be reduced to the efficient quantity by imposing a Pigouvian tax. For example, some countries have imposed "congestion charges" on those who drive during rush hour, in effect charging them for use of the common resource of city streets. Likewise, visitors to national parks must pay a fee, and the number of visitors to any one park is restricted.

A second way to correct the problem of overuse is to create a system of tradable licenses for the use of the common resource much like the systems designed to address negative externalities. The policy maker issues the number of licenses that corresponds to the efficient level of use of the good. Making the licenses tradable ensures that the right to use the good is allocated efficiently—that is, those who end up using the good (those willing to pay the most for a license) are those who gain the most from its use.

But when it comes to common resources, often the most natural solution is simply to assign property rights. At a fundamental level, common resources are subject to overuse because *nobody owns them*. The essence of ownership of a good—the *property right* over the good—is that you can limit who can and cannot use the good as well as how much of it can be used.

When a good is nonexcludable, in a very real sense no one owns it because a property right cannot be enforced—and consequently no one has an incentive to use it efficiently. So one way to correct the problem of overuse is to make the good excludable and assign property rights over it to someone. The good now has an owner who has an incentive to protect the value of the good—to use it efficiently rather than overuse it.

As the following Economics in Action shows, a system of tradable licenses, called individual transferable quotas or ITQs, has been a successful strategy in some fisheries.

ECONOMICS ▶ *in Action*

Saving the Oceans with ITQs

The world's oceans are in serious trouble. According to a study by the International Program on the State of the Oceans, there is an imminent risk of widespread extinctions of multiple species of fish. In Europe, 30% of the fish stocks are in danger of collapse. In the North Sea, 93% of cod are fished before they can breed. And bluefin tuna, a favorite in Japanese sushi, are in danger of imminent extinction.

Not surprisingly, the principal culprit is overfishing. The decline of fishing stocks has worsened as fishermen trawl in deeper waters with their very large nets to catch the remaining fish, unintentionally killing many other marine animals in the process.

The fishing industry is in crisis, too, as fishermen's incomes decline and they are compelled to fish for longer periods of time and in more dangerous waters in order to make a living.

But, individual transferable quotas, or ITQs, may provide a solution to both crises. Under an ITQ scheme, a fisherman receives a license entitling him to catch an annual quota within a given fishing ground. The ITQ is given for a long period of time, sometimes indefinitely. Because it is transferable, the owner can sell or lease it.

Researchers who analyzed 121 established ITQ schemes around the world concluded that ITQs can help reverse the collapse of fisheries because each ITQ holder now has a financial interest in the long-term maintenance of his particular fishery.

ITQ schemes (also called catch-share schemes) are common in New Zealand, Australia, Iceland, and increasingly in the United States and Canada. (The quota share program for Alaska crab fishing that we analyzed in Chapter 5 is an example of an American ITQ.) The Alaskan halibut fishery is one example of a successful ITQ scheme. When it was implemented, the annual fishing season had shrunk from four months to two or three days, resulting in dangerous races by

Will ITQs help save the North Sea's cod?

Vlada Z./Shutterstock

the boats. Now the season lasts nearly eight months. Steve Gaines, Director of the Marine Science Institute at the University of California at Santa Barbara says, "Halibut fishermen were barely squeaking by—but now the fishery is insanely profitable."

Quick Review

- A **common resource** is rival in consumption but nonexcludable.
- The problem with common resources is **overuse**: a user depletes the amount of the common resource available to others but does not take this cost into account when deciding how much to use the common resource.
- Like negative externalities, a common resource can be efficiently managed by Pigouvian taxes, by the creation of a system of tradable licenses for its use, or by making it excludable and assigning property rights.

Artificially Scarce Goods

An **artificially scarce good** is a good that is excludable but nonrival in consumption. As we've already seen, on-demand movies are a familiar example. The marginal cost to society of allowing an individual to watch the movie is zero, because one person's viewing doesn't interfere with other people's viewing. Yet Netflix and companies like it prevent an individual from seeing an on-demand movie if he or she hasn't paid. Goods like computer software or MP3s, which are valued for the information they embody (and are sometimes called "information goods"), are also artificially scarce.

As we've already seen, markets will supply artificially scarce goods: because they are excludable, the producers can charge people for consuming them.

But artificially scarce goods are nonrival in consumption, which means that the marginal cost of an individual's consumption is zero. So the price that the supplier of an artificially scarce good charges exceeds marginal cost. Because the efficient price is equal to the marginal cost of zero, the good is "artificially scarce," and consumption of the good is inefficiently low. However, unless the producer can somehow earn revenue for producing and selling the good, he or she will be unwilling to produce at all—an outcome that leaves society even worse off than it would otherwise be with positive but inefficiently low consumption.

Figure 17-4 illustrates the loss in total surplus caused by artificial scarcity. The demand curve shows the quantity of on-demand movies watched at any given price. The marginal cost of allowing an additional person to watch the movie is zero, so the efficient quantity of movies viewed is Q_{OPT}. Netflix charges a positive price, in this case \$4, to unscramble the signal, and as a result only Q_{MKT} on-demand movies will be watched. This leads to a deadweight loss equal to the area of the shaded triangle.

Does this look familiar? Like the problems that arise with public goods and common resources, the problem created by artificially scarce goods is similar to the problem of *natural monopoly*. A natural monopoly, you will recall, is an industry in which average total cost is above marginal cost for the relevant output range. In order to be willing to produce output, the producer must charge a price at least as high as average total cost—that is, a price above marginal cost. But a price above marginal cost leads to inefficiently low consumption.

An **artificially scarce good** is excludable but nonrival in consumption.

FIGURE **17-4**   An Artificially Scarce Good

An artificially scarce good is excludable and nonrival in consumption. It is made artificially scarce because producers charge a positive price, but the marginal cost of allowing one more person to consume the good is zero. In this example, the market price of an on-demand movie is $4 and the quantity demanded at that price is Q_{MKT}. But the efficient level of consumption is Q_{OPT}, the quantity demanded when the price is zero. The efficient quantity, Q_{OPT}, exceeds the quantity demanded in an unregulated market, Q_{MKT}. The shaded area represents the loss in total surplus from charging a price of $4.

ECONOMICS ▶ in Action

Blacked-Out Games

It was the first weekend of 2014 and the Green Bay Packers were hosting the San Francisco 49ers in the wild-card round of the National Football League playoffs. This was a very big game and football fans in Green Bay Wisconsin, known for their passionate devotion to their team, were shocked when a few days prior to the game, reports surfaced that the game was not sold out (a rare occurrence for such a popular team). Imagine a game that is being nationally televised by one of the major networks but Packer fans would flip to the local channel that is an affiliate of that network and instead of the game, would see some other show with a message scrolling across the bottom of the screen that the game has been blacked out in their area.

What the message wouldn't say, but that Packer's fans understood quite well, was that this blackout was at the insistence of the team's owners, who didn't want people who might have paid for tickets staying home and watching the game on TV instead. Often games that fail to sell out their stadium tickets are blacked out in local broadcast markets.

So the good in question—watching the game on TV—was made artificially scarce. Because the game was being broadcast anyway, no scarce resources would have been used to make it available in its immediate locality as well. But it wasn't available—which meant a loss in welfare to those who would have watched the game on TV but were not willing to pay the price, in time and money, to go to the stadium.

Sometimes, though, accommodations are made in specific situations. In this case, enough Packers' fans rallied in sub-zero temperatures that the NFL changed its policy, allowing football fans in the area to watch the game in real time in the warmth of their homes.

Check Your Understanding   17-4

1. Xena is a software program produced by Xenoid. Each year Xenoid produces an upgrade that costs $300,000 to produce. It costs nothing to allow customers to download it from the company's website. The demand schedule for the upgrade is shown in the accompanying table.

   a. What is the efficient price to a consumer of this upgrade? Explain your answer.

   b. What is the lowest price at which Xenoid is willing to produce and sell the upgrade? Draw the demand curve and show the loss of total surplus that occurs when Xenoid charges this price compared to the efficient price.

Solutions appear at back of book.

Price of upgrade	Quantity of upgrades demanded
$180	1,700
150	2,000
120	2,300
90	2,600
0	3,500

Mauricedale Game Ranch and Hunting Endangered Animals to Save Them

Artur Tiutenko/Shutterstock

John Hume's Mauricedale ranch occupies 16,000 square miles in the hot, scrubby grasslands of South Africa. There Hume raises endangered species, such as rhinos, and nonendangered species, such as Cape buffalo, antelopes, hippos, giraffes, zebras, and ostriches. From revenues of around $2.5 million per year, the ranch earns a small profit, with 20% of the revenues coming from trophy hunting and 80% from selling live animals.

Although he entered this business to earn a profit, Hume sees himself as a conservator of these animals and this land. And he is convinced that to protect rhinos, some amount of legalized hunting of them is necessary. The story of one of Hume's male rhinos, named "65," illustrates his point. Hume and his staff knew that 65 was a problem: too old to breed, he was belligerent enough to kill younger male rhinos. He was part of what wildlife conservationists call the "surplus male problem," a male whose presence inhibits the growth of the herd.

Eventually, Hume obtained permission for the hunting of 65 from CITES (Convention on International Trade in Endangered Species) that regulates the trade and legalized hunting of endangered species. A wealthy hunter paid Hume $150,000, and the troublesome 65 was quickly dispatched.

Conservationist ranchers like Hume, who advocate regulated hunting of wildlife, point to the experience of Kenya to buttress their case. In 1977, Kenya banned the trophy hunting or ranching of wildlife. Since then, Kenya has lost 60% to 70% of its large wildlife through poaching or conversion of habitat to agriculture. Its herd of black rhinos, once numbered at 20,000, now stands at about 540, surviving only in protected areas. In contrast, since regulated hunting of the less endangered white buffalo began in South Africa in 1968, its numbers have risen from 1,800 to 19,400.

Many conservationists now agree that the key to recovery for a number of endangered species is legalized hunting on well-regulated game ranches that are actively engaged in breeding and maintaining the animals. As Dr. Rosie Cooney, head of the International Union for the Conservation of Nature, the world's oldest and largest conservation group, recently said, "I'm afraid it would be nice to be able to recommend alternative approaches for conservation that don't involve killing animals....[but] we view trophy hunting as playing an important and generally effective role in conservation."

However, legalized hunting is a very controversial policy, strongly opposed by some wildlife advocates. Because establishing a ranch like Mauricedale requires a huge capital investment, many are concerned that smaller, fly-by-night ranches will engage in "canned hunts" with drugged or sick animals obtained elsewhere. And there is a fear that the high prices paid for trophy hunts will make ranchers too eager to cull their herds.

QUESTIONS FOR THOUGHT

1. Using the concepts you learned in this chapter, explain the economic incentives behind the huge losses in Kenyan wildlife.

2. Compare the economic incentives facing John Hume with those facing a Kenyan rancher.

3. What regulations should be imposed on a rancher who sells opportunities to trophy hunt? Relate these to the concepts in the chapter.

SUMMARY

1. Goods may be classified according to whether or not they are **excludable** and whether or not they are **rival in consumption.**

2. Free markets can deliver efficient levels of production and consumption for **private goods,** which are both excludable and rival in consumption. When goods are nonexcludable or nonrival in consumption, or both, free markets cannot achieve efficient outcomes.

3. When goods are **nonexcludable,** there is a **free-rider problem:** some consumers will not pay for the good, consuming what others have paid for and leading to inefficiently low production. When goods are **nonrival in consumption,** they should be free, and any positive price leads to inefficiently low consumption.

4. A **public good** is nonexcludable and nonrival in consumption. In most cases a public good must be supplied by the government. The marginal social benefit of a public good is equal to the sum of the individual marginal benefits to each consumer. The efficient quantity of a public good is the quantity at which marginal social benefit equals the marginal cost of providing the good. Like a positive externality, marginal social benefit is greater than any one individual's marginal benefit, so no individual is willing to provide the efficient quantity.

5. One rationale for the presence of government is that it allows citizens to tax themselves in order to provide public goods. Governments use **cost-benefit analysis** to determine the efficient provision of a public good. Such analysis is difficult, however, because individuals have an incentive to overstate the good's value to them.

6. A **common resource** is rival in consumption but nonexcludable. It is subject to **overuse,** because an individual does not take into account the fact that his or her use depletes the amount available for others. This is similar to the problem of a negative externality: the marginal social cost of an individual's use of a common resource is always higher than his or her individual marginal cost. Pigouvian taxes, the creation of a system of tradable licenses, or the assignment of property rights are possible solutions.

7. **Artificially scarce goods** are excludable but nonrival in consumption. Because no marginal cost arises from allowing another individual to consume the good, the efficient price is zero. A positive price compensates the producer for the cost of production but leads to inefficiently low consumption. The problem of an artificially scarce good is similar to that of a natural monopoly.

KEY TERMS

Excludable, p. 490
Rival in consumption, p. 490
Private good, p. 490
Nonexcludable, p. 490

Nonrival in consumption, p. 490
Free-rider problem, p. 491
Public good, p. 493
Cost-benefit analysis, p. 497

Common resource, p. 499
Overuse, p. 499
Artificially scarce good, p. 503

PROBLEMS

1. The government is involved in providing many goods and services. For each of the goods or services listed, determine whether it is rival or nonrival in consumption and whether it is excludable or nonexcludable. What type of good is it? Without government involvement, would the quantity provided be efficient, inefficiently low, or inefficiently high?

   a. Street signs

   b. Amtrak rail service

   c. Regulations limiting pollution

   d. A congested interstate highway without tolls

   e. A lighthouse on the coast

2. An economist gives the following advice to a museum director: "You should introduce 'peak pricing.' At times when the museum has few visitors, you should admit visitors for free. And at times when the museum has many visitors, you should charge a higher admission fee."

   a. When the museum is quiet, is it rival or nonrival in consumption? Is it excludable or nonexcludable? What type of good is the museum at those times? What would be the efficient price to charge visitors during that time, and why?

   b. When the museum is busy, is it rival or nonrival in consumption? Is it excludable or nonexcludable? What type of good is the museum at those times? What would be the efficient price to charge visitors during that time, and why?

3. In many planned communities, various aspects of community living are subject to regulation by a homeowners' association. These rules can regulate house

architecture; require snow removal from sidewalks; exclude outdoor equipment, such as backyard swimming pools; require appropriate conduct in shared spaces such as the community clubhouse; and so on. Suppose there has been some conflict in one such community because some homeowners feel that some of the regulations mentioned above are overly intrusive. You have been called in to mediate. Using what you have learned about public goods and common resources, how would you decide what types of regulations are warranted and what types are not?

4. The accompanying table shows Tanisha's and Ari's individual marginal benefit of different amounts of street cleanings per month. Suppose that the marginal cost of street cleanings is constant at $9 each.

Quantity of street cleanings per month	Tanisha's individual marginal benefit	Ari's individual marginal benefit
0		
	$10	$8
1		
	6	4
2		
	2	1
3		

a. If Tanisha had to pay for street cleaning on her own, how many street cleanings would there be?

b. Calculate the marginal social benefit of street cleaning. What is the optimal number of street cleanings?

c. Consider the optimal number of street cleanings. The last street cleaning of that number costs $9. Is Tanisha willing to pay for that last cleaning on her own? Is Ari willing to pay for that last cleaning on his own?

5. Anyone with a radio receiver can listen to public radio, which is funded largely by donations.

a. Is public radio excludable or nonexcludable? Is it rival in consumption or nonrival? What type of good is it?

b. Should the government support public radio? Explain your reasoning.

c. In order to finance itself, public radio decides to transmit only to satellite radios, for which users have to pay a fee. What type of good is public radio then? Will the quantity of radio listening be efficient? Why or why not?

6. Your economics professor assigns a group project for the course. Describe the free-rider problem that can lead to a suboptimal outcome for your group. To combat this problem, the instructor asks you to evaluate the contribution of your peers in a confidential report. Will this evaluation have the desired effects?

7. The village of Upper Bigglesworth has a village "commons," a piece of land on which each villager, by law, is free to graze his or her cows. Use of the commons is measured in units of the number of cows grazing on it. Assume that the marginal private cost curve of cow-grazing on the commons is upward sloping (say due to more time spent herding). There is also a marginal social cost curve of cow-grazing on the commons: each additional cow grazed means less grass available for others, and the damage done by overgrazing of the commons increases as the number of cows grazing increases. Finally, assume that the private benefit to the villagers of each additional cow grazing on the commons declines as more cows graze, since each additional cow has less grass to eat than the previous one.

a. Is the commons excludable or nonexcludable? Is it rival in consumption or nonrival? What kind of good is the commons?

b. Draw a diagram showing the marginal social cost, marginal private cost, and the marginal private benefit of cow-grazing on the commons, with the quantity of cows that graze on the commons on the horizontal axis. How does the quantity of cows grazing in the absence of government intervention compare to the efficient quantity? Show both in your diagram.

c. The villagers hire you to tell them how to achieve an efficient use of the commons. You tell them that there are three possibilities: a Pigouvian tax, the assignment of property rights over the commons, and a system of tradable licenses for the right to graze a cow. Explain how each one of these options would lead to an efficient use of the commons. In the assignment of property rights, assume that one person is assigned the rights to the commons and the rights to all the cows. Draw a diagram that shows the Pigouvian tax.

8. Prior to 2003, the city of London was often one big parking lot. Traffic jams were common, and it could take hours to travel a couple of miles. Each additional commuter contributed to the congestion, which can be measured by the total number of cars on London roads. Although each commuter suffered by spending valuable time in traffic, none of them paid for the inconvenience they caused others. The total cost of travel includes the opportunity cost of time spent in traffic and any fees levied by London authorities.

a. Draw a graph illustrating the overuse of London roads, assuming that there is no fee to enter London in a vehicle and that roads are a common resource. Put the cost of travel on the vertical axis and the quantity of cars on the horizontal axis. Draw typical demand, individual marginal cost (MC), and marginal social cost (MSC) curves and label the equilibrium point. (*Hint:* The marginal cost takes into account the opportunity cost of spending time on the road for individual drivers but not the inconvenience they cause to others.)

b. In February 2003, the city of London began charging a £5 congestion fee on all vehicles traveling in central London. Illustrate the effects of this congestion charge on your graph and label the new equilibrium point. Assume the new equilibrium point is not optimally set (that is, assume that the £5 charge is too low relative to what would be efficient).

c. The congestion fee was raised to £9 in January 2011. Illustrate the new equilibrium point on your graph, assuming the new charge is now optimally set.

9. The accompanying table shows six consumers' willingness to pay (his or her individual marginal benefit) for one MP3 file copy of a Jay-Z album. The marginal cost of making the file accessible to one additional consumer is constant, at zero.

Consumer	Individual marginal benefit
Adriana	$2
Bhagesh	15
Chizuko	1
Denzel	10
Emma	5
Frank	4

a. What would be the efficient price to charge for a download of the file?

b. All six consumers are able to download the file for free from a file-sharing service, Pantster. Which consumers will download the file? What will be the total consumer surplus to those consumers?

c. Pantster is shut down for copyright law infringement. In order to download the file, consumers now have to pay $4.99 at a commercial music site. Which consumers will download the file? What will be the total consumer surplus to those consumers? How much producer surplus accrues to the commercial music site? What is the total surplus? What is the deadweight loss from the new pricing policy?

10. Butchart Gardens is a very large garden in Victoria, British Columbia, renowned for its beautiful plants. It is so large that it could hold many times more visitors than currently visit it. The garden charges an admission fee of approximately $30. At this price, 1,000 people visit the garden each day. If admission were free, 2,000 people would visit each day.

a. Are visits to Butchart Gardens excludable or nonexcludable? Are they rival in consumption or nonrival? What type of good is it?

b. In a diagram, illustrate the demand curve for visits to Butchart Gardens. Indicate the situation when Butchart Gardens charges an admission fee of $30. Also indicate the situation when Butchart Gardens charges no admission fee.

c. Illustrate the deadweight loss from charging a $30 admission fee. Explain why charging a $30 admission fee is inefficient.

11. Software has historically been an artificially scarce good—it is nonrival because the cost of replication is negligible once the investment to write the code is made, but software companies make it excludable by charging for user licenses. But then open-source software emerged, most of which is free to download and can be modified and maintained by anyone.

a. Discuss the free-rider problem that might exist in the development of open-source software. What effect might this have on quality? Why does this problem not exist for proprietary software, such as the products of a company like Microsoft or Adobe?

b. Some argue that open-source software serves an unsatisfied market demand that proprietary software ignores. Draw a typical diagram that illustrates how proprietary software may be underproduced. Put the price and marginal cost of software on the vertical axis and the quantity of software on the horizontal axis. Draw a typical demand curve and a marginal cost curve (MC) that is always equal to zero. Assume that the software company charges a positive price, P, for the software. Label the equilibrium point and the efficient point.

12. In developing a vaccine for the SARS virus, a pharmaceutical company incurs a very high fixed cost. The marginal cost of delivering the vaccine to patients, however, is negligible (consider it to be equal to zero). The pharmaceutical company holds the exclusive patent to the vaccine. You are a regulator who must decide what price the pharmaceutical company is allowed to charge.

a. Draw a diagram that shows the price for the vaccine that would arise if the company is unregulated, and label it P_M. What is the efficient price for the vaccine? Show the deadweight loss that arises from the price P_M.

b. On another diagram, show the lowest price that the regulator can enforce that would still induce the pharmaceutical company to develop the vaccine. Label it P^*. Show the deadweight loss that arises from this price. How does it compare to the deadweight loss that arises from the price P_M?

c. Suppose you have accurate information about the pharmaceutical company's fixed cost. How could you use price regulation of the pharmaceutical company, combined with a subsidy to the company, to have the efficient quantity of the vaccine provided at the lowest cost to the government?

WORK IT OUT

For interactive, step-by-step help in solving the following problem, visit LaunchPad by using the URL on the back cover of this book.

13. A residential community has 100 residents who are concerned about security. The accompanying table gives the total cost of hiring a 24-hour security service as well as each individual resident's total benefit.

Quantity of security guards	Total cost	Total individual benefit to each resident
0	$0	$0
1	150	10
2	300	16
3	450	18
4	600	19

a. Explain why the security service is a public good for the residents of the community.

b. Calculate the marginal cost, the individual marginal benefit for each resident, and the marginal social benefit.

c. If an individual resident were to decide about hiring and paying for security guards on his or her own, how many guards would that resident hire?

d. If the residents act together, how many security guards will they hire?

The Economics of the Welfare State

▶ **What You Will Learn in This Chapter**

■ What the **welfare state** is and the rationale for it

■ What defines poverty, what causes poverty, and the consequences of poverty

■ How income inequality in America has changed over time

■ How programs like **Social Security** affect poverty and income inequality

■ The special concerns presented by health insurance

■ Why there are political differences and debate over the size of the welfare state

THE COMING OF OBAMACARE

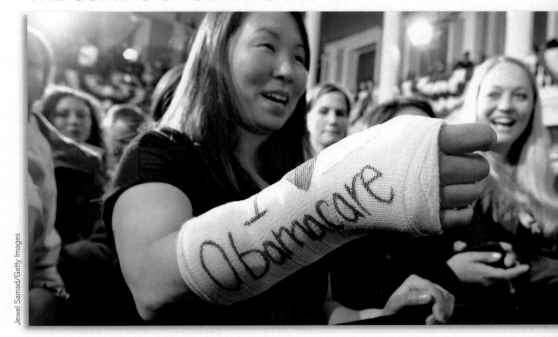

Jewel Samad/Getty Images

Implementation of the Affordable Care Act, ACA, in 2014 was a major expansion of the U.S. welfare state.

ON JANUARY 1, 2014, LOU Vincent finally got health insurance.

Vincent, a resident of Ohio, had Type II diabetes, and as a result no insurance company was willing to offer him a policy, leaving him uninsured for 10 years. "We got 30 denial letters," his wife told a reporter. So what changed at the beginning of 2014? A major new government program, the Patient Protection and Affordable Care Act—often referred to as the Affordable Care Act, the ACA, or "Obamacare"—went into effect.

Tens of millions of Americans receive health insurance directly from the government, mainly from Medicare (which covers those 65 and older) and Medicaid (which covers the poor and near-poor, and which was expanded under the ACA). Obamacare works differently, because it's run through private insurance companies that are subject to extensive regulation, which among other things prevents them from either denying coverage or charging extra to subscribers like Vincent, who have preexisting health problems.

And that's not all. In addition to regulating insurers, the ACA imposes new rules on the public: U.S. citizens and permanent residents are required to purchase insurance that meets cer-tain minimum standards. To keep policies affordable for lower-income families, the law provides substantial subsidies. And to help pay for these subsidies, the law imposed new taxes, mainly on high incomes.

Overall, Obamacare was a substantial expansion of the government's role in the economy. Specifically, it marked a major expansion of the *welfare state*, the collection of government programs designed to limit economic insecurity and/or reduce economic inequality.

There is intense political dispute about the appropriate size and role of the welfare state. Indeed, you can argue that this dispute is what politics is mainly about, with liberals seeking to expand the welfare state's reach and conservatives seeking to scale it back. The creation of Obamacare, the biggest expansion of the U.S. welfare state since the 1960s, was a big victory for liberals—and was therefore met with intense criticism from the other side of the political spectrum. There were, for example, bitter complaints over the cancellation of insurance policies that didn't meet the new standards, compelling some individuals to upgrade to more comprehensive policies.

Opinions about Obamacare, not surprisingly, are deeply divided. In contemporary America, politicians often disagree about how much help financially troubled families should receive to pay for health care, housing, food, and other necessities, but there is a broad political consensus that troubled families should receive some help. And they do. Even conservatives generally accept a fairly extensive welfare state as a fact of life. Governments of all wealthy nations play a large role in everything from health care, to retirement, to aid to the poor and jobless.

We start this chapter by discussing the rationale for welfare state programs. Then we look at the two main programs operating in the United States: *income support programs,* of which Social Security is by far the largest, and *health care programs,* dominated by Medicare and Medicaid, but with the Affordable Care Act in line to play a growing role.

The **welfare state** is the collection of government programs designed to alleviate economic hardship.

A **government transfer** is a government payment to an individual or a family.

A **poverty program** is a government program designed to aid the poor.

A **social insurance program** is a government program designed to provide protection against unpredictable financial distress.

Poverty, Inequality, and Public Policy

During World War II, a British clergyman gave a speech in which he contrasted the "warfare state" of Nazi Germany, dedicated to conquest, with Britain's "welfare state," dedicated to serving the welfare of its people. Since then, the term **welfare state** has come to refer to the collection of government programs that are designed to alleviate economic hardship. A large share of the government spending of all wealthy countries consists of **government transfers—** payments by the government to individuals and families—that provide financial aid to the poor, assistance to unemployed workers, guaranteed income for the elderly, and assistance in paying medical bills for those with large health care expenses.

The Logic of the Welfare State

There are three major economic rationales for the creation of the welfare state. We'll turn now to a discussion of each.

1. Alleviating Income Inequality Suppose that the Taylor family, which has an income of only $15,000 a year, were to receive a government check for $1,500. This check might allow the Taylors to afford a better place to live, eat a more nutritious diet, or in other ways significantly improve their quality of life. Also suppose that the Fisher family, which has an income of $300,000 a year, were to face an extra tax of $1,500. This probably wouldn't make much difference to their quality of life: at worst, they might have to give up a few minor luxuries.

This hypothetical exchange illustrates the first major rationale for the welfare state: *alleviating income inequality*. Because a marginal dollar is worth more to a poor person than a rich one, modest transfers from the rich to the poor will do the rich little harm but benefit the poor a lot. So, according to this argument, a government that plays Robin Hood, taking from the rich to give to the poor, does more good than harm. Programs that are designed to aid the poor are known as **poverty programs.**

2. Alleviating Economic Insecurity The second major rationale for the welfare state is *alleviating economic insecurity*. Imagine ten families, each of which can expect an income next year of $50,000 if nothing goes wrong. But suppose the odds are that something *will* go wrong for one of the families, although nobody knows which one. For example, suppose each of the families has a one in ten chance of experiencing a sharp drop in income because one family member is laid off or incurs large medical bills. And assume that this event will produce severe hardship for the family—a family member will have to drop out of school or the family will lose its home.

Now suppose there's a government program that provides aid to families in distress, paying for that aid by taxing families that are having a good year. Arguably, this program will make all the families better off, because even families that don't currently receive aid from the program might need it at some point in the future. Each family will therefore feel safer knowing that the government stands ready to help when disaster strikes. Programs designed to provide protection against unpredictable financial distress are known as **social insurance programs.**

These two rationales for the welfare state, alleviating income inequality and alleviating economic insecurity, are closely related to the *ability-to-pay principle* we learned about in Chapter 7. Recall how the ability-to-pay principle is used to justify progressive taxation: it says that people with low incomes, for whom an additional dollar makes a big difference to economic well-being, should pay a smaller fraction of their income in taxes than people with higher incomes, for

FOR INQUIRING MINDS | JUSTICE AND THE WELFARE STATE

In 1971 the philosopher John Rawls published *A Theory of Justice*, the most famous attempt to date to develop a theory of economic fairness. He asked readers to imagine deciding economic and social policies behind a "veil of ignorance" about their own identity. That is, suppose you knew you would be a human being but did not know whether you would be rich or poor, healthy or sick, and so on. Rawls argued that the policies that would emerge if people had to make decisions behind the veil of ignorance define what we mean by economic justice. It's sort of a generalized

version of the Golden Rule: do unto others as you would have them do unto you if you were in their place.

Rawls further argued that people behind the veil of ignorance would choose policies that placed a high value on the well-being of the worst-off members of society: after all, each of us might be one of those unlucky individuals. As a result, Rawlsian theory is often used as an argument for a generous welfare state.

Three years after Rawls published his book, another philosopher, Robert Nozick, published *Anarchy, State, and Utopia*, which is often considered the

libertarian response. Nozick argued that justice is a matter of rights, not results, and that the government has no right to force people with high incomes to support others with lower incomes. He argued for a minimal government that enforces the law and provides security—the "night watchman state"—and against the welfare state programs that account for so much government spending.

Philosophers, of course, don't run the world. But real-world political debate often contains arguments that are clearly based upon either a Rawls-type or a Nozick-type position. ■

whom an additional dollar makes much less difference. The same principle suggests that those with very low incomes should actually get money back from the tax system.

3. Reducing Poverty and Providing Access to Health Care The third and final major rationale for the welfare state involves the *social benefits of poverty reduction and access to health care*, especially when applied to children of poor households. Researchers have documented that such children, on average, suffer lifelong disadvantage. Even after adjusting for ability, children from economically disadvantaged backgrounds are more likely to be underemployed or unemployed, engage in crime, and to suffer chronic health problems—all of which impose significant social costs. So, according to the evidence, programs that help to alleviate poverty and provide access to health care generate external benefits to society.

More broadly, as the following For Inquiring Minds explains, some political philosophers argue that principles of social justice demand that society take care of the poor and unlucky. Others disagree, arguing that welfare state programs go beyond the proper role of government. To an important extent, the difference between those two philosophical positions defines what we mean in politics by "liberalism" and "conservatism."

But before we get carried away, it's important to realize that things aren't quite that cut and dried. Even conservatives who believe in limited government typically support some welfare state programs. And even economists who support the goals of the welfare state are concerned about the effects of large-scale aid to the poor and unlucky on their incentives to work and save. Like taxes, welfare state programs can create substantial deadweight losses, so their true economic costs can be considerably larger than the direct monetary cost.

We'll turn to the costs and benefits of the welfare state later in this chapter. First, however, let's examine the problems the welfare state is supposed to address.

The Problem of Poverty

For at least the past 75 years, every U.S. president has promised to do his best to reduce poverty. In 1964 President Lyndon Johnson went so far as to declare a "war on poverty," creating a number of new programs to aid the poor. Anti-poverty

The **poverty threshold** is the annual income below which a family is officially considered poor.

The **poverty rate** is the percentage of the population living below the poverty threshold.

programs account for a significant part of the U.S. welfare state, although social insurance programs are an even larger part.

But what, exactly, do we mean by poverty? Any definition is somewhat arbitrary. Since 1965, however, the U.S. government has maintained an official definition of the **poverty threshold,** a minimum annual income that is considered adequate to purchase the necessities of life. Families whose incomes fall below the poverty threshold are considered poor.

The official poverty threshold depends on the size and composition of a family. In 2014 the poverty threshold for an adult living alone was $11,670; for a household consisting of two adults and two children, it was $23,850.

Trends in Poverty Contrary to popular misconceptions, although the official poverty threshold is adjusted each year to reflect changes in the cost of living, it has not been adjusted upward over time to reflect the long-term rise in the standard of living of the average American family. As a result, as the economy grows and becomes more prosperous, and as average incomes rise, you might expect the percentage of the population living below the poverty threshold to steadily decline.

Somewhat surprisingly, however, this hasn't happened. The orange line in Figure 18-1 shows the official U.S. **poverty rate**—the percentage of the population living below the poverty threshold—from 1967 to 2012. As you can see, since 1967 the poverty rate—which fell steeply during the early 1960s—has fluctuated up and down, with no clear trend. In 2012, the poverty rate was higher than it was in 1967, but had fallen to 14.5 in 2013, the average rate in the 1970s.

But have we really made no progress at all in reducing poverty since the 1960s? Researchers both inside and outside the government have identified a number of limitations to the official poverty measure, of which the most important is that the definition of income doesn't actually include many forms of government aid. For example, it excludes the monetary value of food stamps. In response to criticisms leveled at the limitations, the U.S. Census Bureau has begun releasing a Supplemental Poverty Measure that includes these sources of income while deducting certain expenses. For this reason, experts consider this measure to be more accurate. The burgundy line in Figure 18-1 shows how this measure has changed over time. It shows more progress than the standard measure, but still

FIGURE 18-1   Trends in the U.S. Poverty Rate, 1967–2012

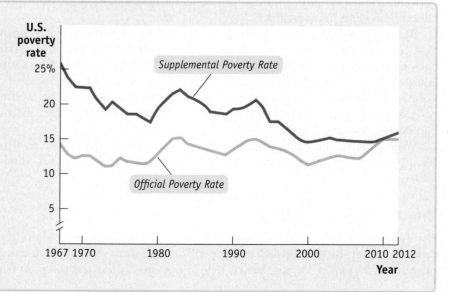

The official poverty rate has shown no clear trend since the late 1960s. However, an alternative measure, known as the supplemental poverty rate or SPM, which most experts consider to be more accurate, has declined modestly.

Source: U.S. Census Bureau; Fox, Liana, et al., NBER Report No. w19789.

surprisingly little considering that GDP—a measure of the total output of the economy—has grown 230% since 1970.

Who Are the Poor? Many Americans probably hold a stereotyped image of poverty: an African-American or Hispanic family with no husband present and the female head of the household unemployed at least part of the time. This picture isn't completely off-base: poverty is disproportionately high among African-Americans and Hispanics as well as among female-headed households. But a majority of the poor don't fit the stereotype.

In 2013, 45.3 million Americans were in poverty—14.5% of the population, or slightly more than one in seven persons. And 27% of the poor were African-American, substantially exceeding their share of the overall population (only about 13% of the population is African-American). Hispanics were also more likely than the average American to be poor, with a poverty rate of 23.5%. But there was also widespread poverty among non-Hispanic Whites, who made up more than half the ranks of the poor.

There is also a correlation between family makeup and poverty. Female-headed families with no husband present had a very high poverty rate: 30.6%. Married couples were much less likely to be poor, with a poverty rate of only 5.8%; still, about 38% of the poor were in married families with both spouses present.

What really stands out in the data, however, is the association between poverty and inadequate employment. Adults who work full time are very unlikely to be poor: only 2.7% of full-time workers were poor in 2013. Many industries, particularly in the retail and service sectors, now rely primarily on part-time workers. Part-time work typically lacks benefits such as health plans, paid vacation days, and retirement benefits, and it also usually pays a lower hourly wage than comparable full-time work. As a result, many of the poor are members of what analysts call the *working poor:* workers whose incomes fall at or below the poverty threshold.

What Causes Poverty? Poverty is often blamed on lack of education, and educational attainment clearly has a strong positive effect on income level—those with more education earn, on average, higher incomes than those with less education. For example, in 1979 the average hourly wage of men with a college degree was 38% higher than that of men with only a high school diploma; by 2013, the "college premium" had increased to 82%.

Lack of proficiency in English is also a barrier to higher income. For example, Mexican-born male workers in the United States—two-thirds of whom have not graduated from high school and many of whom have poor English skills— earn less than half of what native-born men earn.

And it's important not to overlook the role of racial and gender discrimination; although less pervasive today than 50 years ago, discrimination still erects formidable barriers to advancement for many Americans. Non-Whites earn less and are less likely to be employed than Whites with comparable levels of education. Studies find that African-American males suffer persistent discrimination by employers in favor of Whites, African-American women, and Hispanic immigrants. Women earn lower incomes than men with similar qualifications.

The United States has a high poverty rate compared to other rich countries.

In addition, one important source of poverty that should not be overlooked is bad luck. Many families find themselves impoverished when a wage-earner loses a job or a family member falls seriously ill.

Consequences of Poverty The consequences of poverty are often severe, particularly for children. In 2013, 19.9% of children in the United States lived in poverty. Poverty is often associated with lack of access to health care, which can lead to further health problems that erode the ability to attend school and work later in life. Affordable housing is also frequently a problem, leading poor families to move often, disrupting school and work schedules. Recent medical studies have shown that children raised in severe poverty tend to suffer from lifelong learning disabilities. As a result, American children growing up in or near poverty don't have an equal chance at the starting line: they tend to be at a disadvantage throughout their lives. Even talented children who come from poor families are unlikely to finish college.

TABLE 18-1	Percent of Eighth-Graders Finishing College, 1988	
Parents' socioeconomic status	**Mathematics test score in bottom quartile**	**Mathematics test score in top quartile**
Parents in bottom quartile	3%	29%
Parents in top quartile	30	74

Source: National Center for Education Statistics, *The Condition of Education 2003*, p. 47.

Table 18-1 shows the results of a long-term survey conducted by the U.S. Department of Education, which tracked a group of students who were in eighth grade in 1988. That year, the students took a mathematics test that the study used as an indicator of their innate ability; the study also identified students by the socioeconomic status of their families, a measure that took into account their parents' income and employment.

As you can see, the results were disturbing: among students who were in the highest-scoring 25% on the test, but whose parents were of low status, only 29% finished college. By contrast, the equally talented children of high-status parents

GLOBAL COMPARISON | Income, Redistribution, and Inequality in Rich Countries

Spend some time traveling around the United States, then spend some more time traveling around Sweden and Denmark. You'll almost surely come away with the impression that Scandinavia has substantially less income inequality than America, that the rich aren't as rich and the poor aren't as poor. And the numbers confirm this impression: Gini coefficients, a number that summarizes a country's level of income inequality, for Sweden and Denmark, and indeed for most of Western Europe, are substantially lower than in the United States. But why?

The answer, to a large extent, is the role of government, which, in the United States, plays a significant role in redistributing income away from those with the highest incomes to those who earn the least. But European nations have substantially bigger welfare states than we do, and do a lot more income redistribution.

The accompanying figure shows two measures of the Gini coefficient for a number of rich countries. A country with a perfectly equal income distribution—one in which every household had the same income—would have a Gini coefficient of zero. At the other extreme, in which all of a country's income goes to one household, would have a Gini coefficient of 1. For each country, the purple bar shows the actual Gini, a measure of the observed inequality in income before taxes and transfers are made. The orange bars show what each country's Gini would be after taxes and transfers are made. It turns out that the inequality of market incomes in Denmark and Sweden is comparable to that in the United States—their much lower observed inequality is the result of their bigger welfare states.

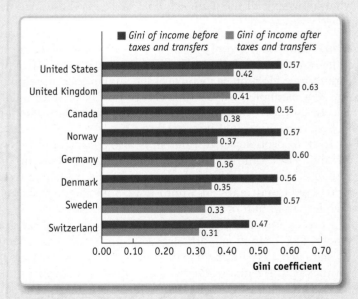

There are some caveats to this conclusion. On one side, the data probably don't do a very good job of tracking very high incomes, which are probably a bigger factor in the United States than elsewhere. On the other side, European welfare states may indirectly increase measured income inequality through their effects on incentives. Still, the data strongly suggest that differences in inequality among rich countries largely reflect different policies rather than differences in the underlying economic situation. We'll have more to say about Gini coefficients shortly.

Source: Luxembourg Income Study.

had a 74% chance of finishing college—and children of high-status parents had a 30% chance of finishing college even if they had low test scores. What this tells us is that poverty is, to an important degree, self-perpetuating: the children of the poor start at such a disadvantage relative to other Americans that it's very hard for them to achieve a better life.

Economic Inequality

The United States is a rich country. In 2007, before the recession hit, the average U.S. household had an income (in 2012 prices) of $74,869, far exceeding the poverty threshold. Even after a devastating recession followed by a sluggish recovery, average household income in 2013 was $72,641. How is it possible, then, that so many Americans still live in poverty? The answer is that income is unequally distributed, with many households earning much less than the average and others earning much more.

Table 18-2 shows the distribution of pre-tax income—income before federal income taxes are paid—among U.S. families in 2013, as estimated by the Census Bureau. Households are grouped into *quintiles*, each containing 20%, or one-fifth, of the population. The first, or bottom, quintile contains households whose income put them below the 20th percentile in income, the second quintile contains households whose income put them between the 20th and 40th percentiles, and so on.

TABLE **18-2**	U.S. Income Distribution in 2013		
Income group	**Income range**	**Average income**	**Percent of total income**
Bottom quintile	Less than $20,900	$11,657	3.2%
Second quintile	$20,900 to $40,187	30,127	8.3
Third quintile	$40,187 to $65,501	51,933	14.4
Fourth quintile	$65,501 to $105,910	83,291	23.0
Top quintile	More than $105,910	184,548	51.0
Top 5%	More than $196,000	322,674	22.2
Mean income = $72,641		**Median income = $51,939**	

Source: U.S. Census Bureau.

For each group, Table 18-2 shows three numbers. The second column shows the income ranges that define the group. For example, in 2013, the bottom quintile consisted of households with annual incomes of less than $20,900, the next quintile of households had incomes between $20,900 and $40,187, and so on. The third column shows the average income in each group, ranging from $11,657 for the bottom fifth to $322,674 for the top 5%. The fourth column shows the percentage of total U.S. income received by each group.

Mean versus Median Household Income At the bottom of Table 18-2 are two useful numbers for thinking about the incomes of American households. **Mean household income,** also called average household income, is the total income of all U.S. households divided by the number of households. **Median household income** is the income of a household in the exact middle of the income distribution— the level of income at which half of all households have lower income and half have higher income. It's very important to realize that these two numbers do not measure the same thing.

Economists often illustrate the difference by asking people first to imagine a room containing several dozen more or less ordinary wage-earners, then to think about what happens to the mean and median incomes of the people in the room if a Wall Street tycoon, some of whom earn more than a billion dollars a year, walks in. The mean income soars, because the tycoon's income pulls up the average, but median income hardly rises at all.

This example helps explain why economists generally regard median income as a better guide to the economic status of typical American families than mean income: mean income is strongly affected by the incomes of a relatively small number of very-high-income Americans, who are not representative of the population as a whole; median income is not.

What we learn from Table 18-2 is that income in the United States is quite unequally distributed. The average income of the poorest fifth of families is less

Mean household income is the average income across all households.

Median household income is the income of the household lying at the exact middle of the income distribution.

The **Gini coefficient** is a number that summarizes a country's level of income inequality based on how unequally income is distributed across quintiles.

than a quarter of the average income of families in the middle, and the richest fifth have an average income more than three times that of families in the middle. The incomes of the richest fifth of the population are, on average, about 15 times as high as those of the poorest fifth. In fact, the distribution of income in America has become more unequal since 1980, rising to a level that has made it a significant political issue. The upcoming Economics in Action discusses long-term trends in U.S. income inequality, which declined in the 1930s and 1940s, was stable for more than 30 years after World War II, but began rising again in the late 1970s.

The Gini Coefficient It's often convenient to have a single number that summarizes a country's level of income inequality. The **Gini coefficient,** the most widely used measure of inequality, is based on how disparately income is distributed across the quintiles (as we learned in the preceding Global Comparison). A country with a perfectly equal distribution of income—that is, one in which the bottom 20% of the population received 20% of the income, the bottom 40% of the population received 40% of the income, and so on—would have a Gini coefficient of 0. At the other extreme, the highest possible value for the Gini coefficient is 1—the level it would attain if all a country's income went to just one person.

One way to get a sense of what Gini coefficients mean in practice is to look at international comparisons. Figure 18-2 shows recent estimates of the Gini coefficient for many of the world's countries. Aside from a few countries in Africa, the highest levels of income inequality are found in Latin America, especially Colombia; countries with a high degree of inequality have Gini coefficients close to 0.6. The most equal distributions of income are in Europe, especially in Scandinavia; countries with very equal income distributions, such as Sweden, have Gini coefficients around 0.25. Compared to other wealthy countries, as of 2012 the United States, with a Gini coefficient of 0.47, has unusually high inequality, though it isn't as unequal as in Latin America.

How serious an issue is income inequality? In a direct sense, high income inequality means that some people don't share in a nation's overall prosperity. As we've seen, rising inequality explains how it's possible that the U.S. poverty rate has failed to fall for the past 40 years even though the country as a whole has become considerably richer. Also, extreme inequality, as found in Latin America,

FIGURE 18-2 Income Inequality Around the World The highest levels of income inequality are found in Africa and Latin America. The most equal distributions of income are in Europe, especially in Scandinavia. Compared to other wealthy countries, the United States, with a Gini coefficient of 0.42, has unusually high inequality.

Sources: World Bank, *World Development Indicators* 2010. Luxembourg Income Study.

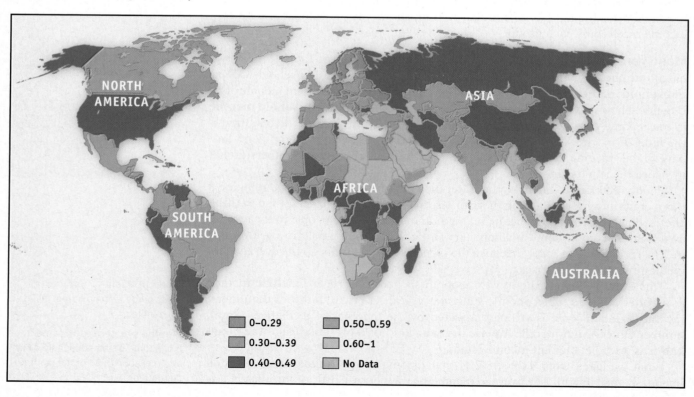

0–0.29		0.50–0.59	
0.30–0.39		0.60–1	
0.40–0.49		No Data	

is often associated with political instability because of tension between a wealthy minority and the rest of the population.

It's important to realize, however, that the data shown in Table 18-2 overstate the true degree of inequality in America, for several reasons. One is that the data represent a snapshot for a single year, whereas the incomes of many individual families fluctuate over time. That is, many of those near the bottom in any given year are having an unusually bad year and many of those at the top are having an unusually good one. Over time, their incomes will revert to a more normal level. So a table showing average incomes within quintiles over a longer period, such as a decade, would not show as much inequality.

Furthermore, a family's income tends to vary over its life cycle: most people earn considerably less in their early working years than they will later in life, then experience a considerable drop in income when they retire. Consequently, the numbers in Table 18-2, which combine young workers, mature workers, and retirees, show more inequality than would a table that compares families of similar ages.

Despite these qualifications, there is a considerable amount of genuine inequality in the United States. In fact, inequality not only persists for long periods of time for individuals, it extends across generations. The children of poor parents are much more likely to be poor than the children of affluent parents, and vice versa—a correlation that is even stronger in the United States than in other rich countries. Moreover, the fact that families' incomes fluctuate from year to year isn't entirely good news. Measures of inequality in a given year *do* overstate true inequality. But those year-to-year fluctuations are part of a problem that worries even affluent families—economic insecurity.

Economic Insecurity

As we stated earlier, although the rationale for the welfare state rests in part on the social benefits of reducing poverty and inequality, it also rests in part on the benefits of reducing economic insecurity, which afflicts even relatively well-off families.

One form economic insecurity takes is the risk of a sudden loss of income, which usually happens when a family member loses a job and either spends an extended period without work or is forced to take a new job that pays considerably less. In a given year, according to recent estimates, about one in six American families will see their income cut in half from the previous year. Related estimates show that the percentage of people who find themselves below the poverty threshold for at least one year over the course of a decade is several times higher than the percentage of people below the poverty threshold in any given year.

Even if a family doesn't face a loss in income, it can face a surge in expenses. Until implementation of the Affordable Care Act in 2014, the most common reason for such surges was a medical problem that required expensive treatment, such as heart disease or cancer. In fact, in 2013 it was estimated that 60 percent of the personal bankruptcies of Americans were due to medical expenses. The rise in medical-bill bankruptcies—up nearly 50 percent from 46 percent in 2001, and on up to 62 percent in 2007—was a major source of support for the passage of the ACA.

ECONOMICS ▶ *in Action*

Long-term Trends in Income Inequality in the United States

Does inequality tend to rise, fall, or stay the same over time? The answer is yes—all three. Over the course of the past century, the United States has gone through periods characterized by all three trends: an era of falling

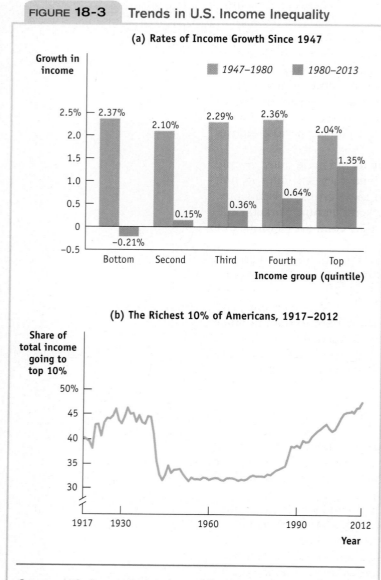

FIGURE **18-3** Trends in U.S. Income Inequality

(a) Rates of Income Growth Since 1947

(b) The Richest 10% of Americans, 1917–2012

Sources: U.S. Census Bureau (panel (a)). Emmanuel Saez, "Striking It Richer: The Evolution of Top Incomes in the United States," University of California, Berkeley, discussion paper, 2008 (updated 2013) (panel (b)).

inequality during the 1930s and 1940s, an era of stable inequality for about 35 years after World War II, and an era of rising inequality over the past 30 years.

Detailed U.S. data on income by quintiles, as shown in Table 18-2, are only available starting in 1947. Panel (a) of Figure 18-3 shows the annual rate of growth of income, adjusted for inflation, for each quintile over two periods: from 1947 to 1980, and from 1980 to 2013. There's a clear difference between the two periods. In the first period, income within each group grew at about the same rate—that is, there wasn't much change in the inequality of income, just growing incomes across the board.

After 1980, however, incomes grew much more quickly at the top than in the middle, and more quickly in the middle than at the bottom. So inequality has increased substantially since 1980. Overall, inflation-adjusted income for families in the top quintile rose 55% between 1980 and 2013, while actually falling slightly for families in the bottom quintile.

Although detailed data on income distribution aren't available before 1947, economists have instead used other information like income tax data to estimate the share of income going to the top 10% of the population all the way back to 1917. Panel (b) of Figure 18-3 shows this measure from 1917 to 2012. These data, like the more detailed data available since 1947, show that American inequality was more or less stable between 1947 and the late 1970s but has risen substantially since.

The longer-term data also show, however, that the relatively equal distribution of 1947 was something new. In the late nineteenth century, often referred to as the Gilded Age, American income was very unequally distributed. This high level of inequality persisted into the 1930s. But inequality declined sharply between the late 1930s and the end of World War II. In a famous paper, Claudia Goldin and Robert Margo, two economic historians, dubbed this narrowing of income inequality "the Great Compression."

The Great Compression roughly coincided with World War II, a period during which the U.S. government imposed special controls on wages and prices. Evidence indicates that these controls were applied in ways that reduced inequality—for example, it was much easier for employers to get approval to increase the wages of their lowest-paid employees than to increase executive salaries. What remains puzzling is that the equality imposed by wartime controls lasted for decades after those controls were lifted in 1946.

Since the 1970s, as we've already seen, inequality has increased substantially. In fact, pre-tax income appears to be as unequally distributed in America today as it was in the 1920s, prompting many commentators to describe the current state of the nation as a new Gilded Age—albeit one in which the effects of inequality are moderated by taxes and the existence of the welfare state.

There is intense debate among economists about the causes of this widening inequality. The most popular explanation is rapid technological change, which has increased the demand for highly skilled or talented workers more rapidly than the demand for other workers, leading to a rise in the wage gap between the highly skilled and other workers. Growing international trade may also have contributed by allowing the United States to import labor-intensive products from low-wage countries rather than making them domestically, reducing the demand for less skilled American workers and depressing their wages. Rising immigration may be yet another source. On average, immigrants have lower education levels than native-born workers and increase the supply of low-skilled labor while depressing low-skilled wages.

All these explanations, however, fail to account for one key feature: much of the rise in inequality doesn't reflect a rising gap between highly educated workers and those with less education but rather growing differences among highly educated workers themselves. For example, schoolteachers and top business executives have similarly high levels of education, but executive paychecks have risen dramatically and teachers' salaries have not. For some reason, a few "superstars"—a group that includes literal superstars in the entertainment world but also such groups as Wall Street traders and top corporate executives—now earn much higher incomes than was the case a generation ago. It's still unclear what caused the change.

Check Your Understanding   18-1

1. Indicate whether each of the following programs is a poverty program or a social insurance program.
   a. A pension guarantee program, which provides pensions for retirees if they have lost their employment-based pension due to their employer's bankruptcy
   b. The federal program known as SCHIP, which provides health care for children in families that are above the poverty threshold but still have relatively low income
   c. The Section 8 housing program, which provides housing subsidies for low-income households
   d. The federal flood program, which provides financial help to communities hit by major floods

2. Recall that the poverty threshold is not adjusted to reflect changes in the standard of living. As a result, is the poverty threshold a relative or an absolute measure of poverty? That is, does it define poverty according to how poor someone is relative to others or according to some fixed measure that doesn't change over time? Explain.

3. The accompanying table gives the distribution of income for a very small economy.
   a. What is the mean income? What is the median income? Which measure is more representative of the income of the average person in the economy? Why?
   b. What income range defines the first quintile? The third quintile?

	Income
Sephora	$39,000
Kelly	17,500
Raul	900,000
Vijay	15,000
Oskar	28,000

4. Which of the following statements more accurately reflects the principal source of rising inequality in the United States today?
   a. The salary of the manager of the local branch of Sunrise Bank has risen relative to the salary of the neighborhood gas station attendant.
   b. The salary of the CEO of Sunrise Bank has risen relative to the salary of the local branch bank manager, although the two have similar education levels.

Solutions appear at back of book.

The U.S. Welfare State

In 2013 the U.S. welfare state consisted of three huge programs (Social Security, Medicare, and Medicaid); several other fairly big programs, including Temporary Assistance for Needy Families, food stamps, and the Earned Income Tax Credit; and a number of smaller programs. The Affordable Care Act will eventually become a large program, although not as big as the "big three." Table 18-3 shows

TABLE **18-3**	Major U.S. Welfare State Programs, 2013	
	Monetary transfers	**In-kind**
Means-tested	Temporary Assistance for Needy Families: $22 billion	Food stamps: $83 billion
	Supplemental Security Income: $56 billion	Medicaid: $265 billion
	Earned Income Tax Credit: $57 billion	
Not means-tested	Social Security: $813 billion	Medicare: $591 billion
	Unemployment insurance: $72 billion	

A **means-tested** program is a program available only to individuals or families whose incomes fall below a certain level.

An **in-kind benefit** is a benefit given in the form of goods or services.

A **negative income tax** is a program that supplements the income of low-income working families.

one useful way to categorize the programs existing in 2013, along with the amount spent on each listed program. (The Affordable Care Act was implemented in 2014 so data was not available at time of writing.)

First, the table distinguishes between programs that are **means-tested** and those that are not. In means-tested programs, benefits are available only to families or individuals whose income and/or wealth falls below some minimum. Basically, means-tested programs are poverty programs designed to help only those with low incomes. By contrast, non-means-tested programs provide their benefits to everyone, although, as we'll see, they tend in practice to reduce income inequality.

Second, the table distinguishes between programs that provide monetary transfers that beneficiaries can spend as they choose and those that provide **in-kind benefits,** which are given in the form of goods or services rather than money. As the numbers suggest, in-kind benefits are dominated by Medicare and Medicaid, which pay for health care. We'll discuss health care in the next section of this chapter. For now, let's examine the other major programs.

Means-Tested Programs

When people use the term *welfare,* they're often referring to monetary aid to poor families. The main source of such monetary aid in the United States is Temporary Assistance for Needy Families, or TANF. This program does not aid everyone who is poor; it is available only to poor families with children and only for a limited period of time.

TANF was introduced in the 1990s to replace a highly controversial program known as Aid to Families with Dependent Children, or AFDC. The older program was widely accused of creating perverse incentives for the poor, including encouraging family breakup. Partly as a result of the change in programs, the benefits of modern "welfare" are considerably less generous than those available a generation ago, once the data are adjusted for inflation. Also, TANF contains time limits, so welfare recipients—even single parents—must eventually seek work. As you can see from Table 18-3, TANF is a relatively small part of the modern U.S. welfare state.

Other means-tested programs, though more expensive, are less controversial. The Supplemental Security Income program aids disabled Americans who are unable to work and have no other source of income. The food stamp program or SNAP—officially the Supplemental Nutrition Assistance Program, since it now provides debit cards rather than stamps—helps low-income families and individuals, who can use those debit cards to buy food staples but not other items.

Finally, economists use the term **negative income tax** for a program that supplements the earnings of low-income working families. The United States has a program known as the Earned Income Tax Credit (EITC), which provides additional income to millions of workers. It has become more generous as traditional welfare has become less generous. Only workers who earn income are eligible for the EITC; over a certain range of incomes, the more a worker earns, the higher the amount of EITC received. That is, the EITC acts

One of every seven Americans receives food stamps, officially known as SNAP.

as a negative income tax for low-wage workers. In 2013, married couples with two children earning less than $13,430 per year received EITC payments equal to 40% of their earnings. (Payments were slightly lower for single-parent families or workers without children.) The EITC is phased out at higher incomes. As of 2013, the payment ceased at an income of $43,038 for married couples with two children.

Social Security and Unemployment Insurance

Social Security, the largest program in the U.S. welfare state, is a non-means-tested program that guarantees retirement income to qualifying older Americans. It also provides benefits to workers who become disabled and "survivor benefits" to family members of workers who die.

Social Security is supported by a dedicated tax on wages: the Social Security portion of the payroll tax, which was described in Chapter 7, pays for Social Security benefits. The benefits workers receive on retirement depend on their taxable earnings during their working years: the more you earn up to the maximum amount subject to Social Security taxes ($113,700 in 2013), the more you receive in retirement. Benefits are not, however, strictly proportional to earnings. Instead, they're determined by a formula that gives high earners more than low earners, but with a sliding scale that makes the program relatively more generous for low earners.

Because most seniors don't receive pensions from their former employers and most don't own enough assets to provide them with a living, Social Security benefits are an enormously important source of income for them. Fully 60% of Americans 65 and older rely on Social Security for more than half their income, and 20% have no income at all except for Social Security.

President Franklin D. Roosevelt signed the Social Security Act in 1935, creating the modern welfare state.

Unemployment insurance, although normally a much smaller amount of government transfers than Social Security, is another key social insurance program. It provides workers who lose their jobs with about 35% of their previous salary until they find a new job or until 26 weeks have passed. (Benefits were temporarily extended in response to the severe recession of 2007–2009, with some unemployed workers supported as long as 99 weeks.) Unemployment insurance is financed by a tax on employers; outlays for unemployment insurance were still unusually high in 2013, due to a high national unemployment rate. Like Social Security, unemployment insurance is not means-tested.

The Effects of the Welfare State on Poverty and Inequality

Because the people who receive government transfers tend to be different from those who are taxed to pay for those transfers, the U.S. welfare state has the effect of redistributing income from some people to others. Government statisticians have put considerable effort into calculating the effects of this redistribution, which makes a big difference to poverty rates and a somewhat smaller difference to overall inequality. A caveat: such reports calculate only the *direct* effect of taxes and transfers, without taking into account changes in behavior that the taxes and transfers might cause. For example, they don't try to estimate how many older Americans who are now retired would still be working if they weren't receiving Social Security checks. As a result, the estimates are only a partial indicator of the true effects of the welfare state. Nonetheless, the results are striking.

Table 18-4 shows how a number of government programs affected the poverty rate, as measured by the Supplemental Poverty Measure, for the population as a whole and for different age groups in 2012. For each program it shows the amount, in percentage points, by which that group's poverty rate was reduced by the

TABLE 18-4 Effects of Government Programs on Reducing the Rate of Poverty, 2012

	All People	Children	Nonelderly Adults	65 Years and Older
Social Security	8.56%	1.97%	4.08%	39.86%
Refundable Tax Credits	3.02	6.66	2.25	0.20
SNAP (Food Stamps)	1.62	3.01	1.27	0.76
Unemployment insurance	0.79	0.82	0.88	0.31
Supplemental Security Income	1.07	0.84	1.12	1.21
Housing Subsidies	0.91	1.39	0.66	1.12
School lunch	0.38	0.91	0.25	0.03
Temporary Assistance for Needy Families	0.21	0.46	0.14	0.05
WIC	0.13	0.29	0.09	0.00

Source: Council of Economic Advisers.

TABLE 18-5 Effects of Taxes and Transfers on Income Distribution, 2007

Quintiles	Share of aggregate income without taxes and transfers	Share of aggregate income with taxes and transfers
Bottom quintile	2.5%	5.1%
Second quintile	7.3	9.2
Third quintile	12.2	14.0
Fourth quintile	19.0	19.9
81st–99th percentiles	38.6	35.6
Top 1 percent	21.3	17.1

Source: Congressional Budget Office.

program. For example, it says that without Social Security, the poverty rate among older Americans would have been almost 40 percentage points higher than it was.

Table 18-5 shows a Congressional Budget Office estimate of the effect of taxes and transfers on the share of aggregate income going to each quintile of the income distribution in 2007 (the latest available date).

The effect of government programs was to increase the share of income going to the poorest 80% of the population, especially the share going to the poorest 20%, while reducing the share of income going to the richest 20%.

ECONOMICS ▶ in Action

Welfare State Programs and Poverty Rates in the Great Recession, 2007-2010

In 2007 the U.S. economy entered a deep downturn, the worst since the 1930s. Recovery officially began in 2009, but it was slow and disappointing. As of 2013 both average and median family income, adjusted for inflation, were still well below their 2007 levels.

Given this poor economic performance, you might have expected to see a sharp rise in poverty, and the official poverty rate did in fact move up, as you can see in Figure 18-1. But while the Great Recession and its aftermath certainly hurt many American families, the country never seemed as desperate as it did during the Great Depression, or even during the last big slump, in 1981–1982. And sure enough, the Supplemental Poverty Measure, which most experts consider a better measure of economic hardship, rose only slightly. Why?

The main answer, it turns out, was antipoverty programs, which automatically expanded during the slump and were further reinforced by legislation that temporarily expanded food stamps and other forms of aid. Figure 18-4 shows an estimate of how much

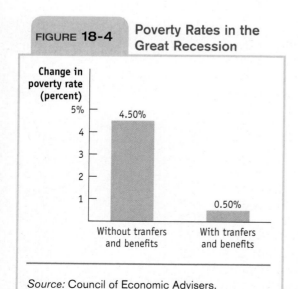

FIGURE 18-4 Poverty Rates in the Great Recession

Source: Council of Economic Advisers.

the poverty rate would have risen between 2007 and 2010 in the absence of welfare state programs, compared with how much it actually rose. Without transfers and benefits the poverty rate would have risen by 4.50%; but with transfers and benefits it rose only 0.50%. The U.S. welfare state didn't prevent the slump, or stop many people from losing their jobs and some from losing their houses. But it did strikingly limit the rise in poverty.

Check Your Understanding   **18-2**

1. Explain how the negative income tax avoids the disincentive to work that characterizes poverty programs that simply give benefits based on low income.

2. According to Table 18-4, what effect does the U.S. welfare state have on the overall poverty rate? On the poverty rate for those aged 65 and over?

Solutions appear at back of book.

The Economics of Health Care

A large part of the welfare state, in both the United States and other wealthy countries, is devoted to paying for health care. In most wealthy countries, the government pays between 70% and 80% of all medical costs. The private sector plays a larger role in the U.S. health care system. Yet even in America, as of 2013 the government pays almost half of all health care costs; furthermore, it indirectly subsidizes private health insurance through the federal tax code.

Figure 18-5 shows who paid for U.S. health care in 2012. Only 14% of health care consumption spending (that is, all spending on health care except investment in health care buildings and facilities) was expenses "out of pocket"—that is, paid directly by individuals. Most health care spending, 77%, was paid for by some kind of insurance. Of this 77%, considerably less than half was private insurance; the rest was some kind of government insurance, mainly Medicare and Medicaid. To understand why, we need to examine the special economics of health care.

The Need for Health Insurance

In 2012, U.S. personal health care expenses were $8,915 per person—17.2% of gross domestic product. This did not, however, mean that the typical American spent nearly $9,000 on medical treatment. In fact, in any given year half the population incurs only minor medical expenses. But a small percentage of the population faces huge medical bills, with 10% of the population typically accounting for almost two-thirds of medical costs.

Is it possible to predict who will have high medical costs? To a limited extent, yes: there are broad patterns to illness. For example, the elderly are more likely to need expensive surgery and/or drugs than the young. But the fact is that anyone can suddenly find himself or herself needing very expensive medical treatment, costing many thousands of dollars in a very short time—far beyond what most families can easily afford. Yet nobody wants to be unable to afford such treatment if it becomes necessary.

Private Health Insurance Market economies have an answer to this problem: health insurance. Under **private health insurance,** each member of a large pool of individuals agrees to pay a fixed amount annually (called a *premium*)

▼ Quick Review

• **Means-tested** programs are designed to reduce poverty, but non-means-tested programs do so as well. Programs are classified according to whether they provide monetary or **in-kind benefits.**

• "Welfare," now known as TANF, is far less generous today than a generation ago due to concerns about its effect on incentives to work and family breakup. The **negative income tax** addresses these concerns: it supplements the incomes of only low-income working families.

• Social Security, the largest program in the U.S. welfare state, is a non-means-tested program that provides retirement income for the elderly. It provides a significant share of the income of most elderly Americans. Unemployment insurance is also a key social insurance program that is not means-tested.

• Overall, the American welfare state is redistributive. It increases the share of income going to the poorest 80% while reducing the share going to the richest 20%.

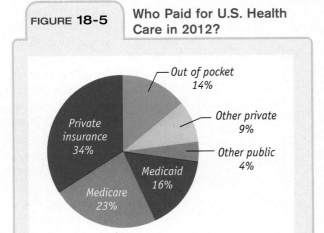

FIGURE 18-5   Who Paid for U.S. Health Care in 2012?

In the United States in 2012, insurance paid for 77% of health care consumption costs: the sum of 34% (private insurance), 23% (Medicare), 16% (Medicaid), and 4% (other public). The percentage paid for by private insurance, 34%, was a uniquely high number among advanced countries. Even so, substantially more U.S. health care was paid for by Medicare, Medicaid, and other government programs than by other means.

Source: Department of Health and Human Services Centers for Medicare and Medicaid Services.

Under **private health insurance,** each member of a large pool of individuals pays a fixed amount annually to a private company that agrees to pay most of the medical expenses of the pool's members.

into a common fund that is managed by a private company, which then pays most of the medical expenses of the pool's members. Although members must pay fees even in years in which they don't have large medical expenses, they benefit from the reduction in risk: if they do turn out to have high medical costs, the pool will take care of those expenses.

There are, however, inherent problems with the market for private health insurance. These problems arise from the fact that medical expenses, although basically unpredictable, aren't *completely* unpredictable. That is, people often have some idea whether or not they are likely to face large medical bills over the next few years. This creates a serious problem for private health insurance companies.

Suppose that an insurance company offers a "one-size-fits-all" health care policy, under which customers pay an annual premium equal to the average American's annual medical expenses, plus a bit more to cover the company's operating expenses and a normal rate of profit. In return, the insurance company pays the policyholder's medical bills, whatever they are.

If all potential customers had an equal risk of incurring high medical expenses for the year, this might be a workable business proposition. In reality, however, people often have very different risks of facing high medical expenses—and, crucially, they often know this ahead of time. This reality would quickly undermine any attempt by an insurance company to offer one-size-fits-all health insurance. The policy would be a bad deal for healthy people, who don't face a significant risk of high medical bills: on average, they would pay much more in insurance premiums than the cost of their actual medical bills. But it would be a very good deal for people with chronic, costly conditions, who would on average pay less in premiums than the cost of their care.

As a result, some healthy people are likely to take their chances and go without insurance. This would make the insurance company's average customer less healthy than the average American. This raises the medical bills the company will have to pay and raises the company's costs per customer. That is, the insurance company would face a problem called *adverse selection*, which is discussed in detail in Chapter 20. Because of adverse selection, a company that offers health insurance to everyone at a price reflecting average medical costs of the general population, and that gives people the freedom to decline coverage, would find itself losing a lot of money.

The insurance company could respond by charging more—raising its premium to reflect the higher-than-average medical bills of its customers. But this would drive off even more healthy people, leaving the company with an even sicker, higher-cost clientele, forcing it to raise the premium even more, driving off even more healthy people, and so on. This phenomenon is known as the *adverse selection death spiral*, which ultimately leads the health insurance company to fail.

This description of the problems with health insurance might lead you to believe that private health insurance can't work. In fact, however, most Americans are covered by private health insurance. Insurance companies are able, to some extent, to overcome the problem of adverse selection two ways: by carefully *screening* people who apply for coverage and through employment-based health insurance. With screening, people who are likely to have high medical expenses are charged higher-than-average premiums—or in many cases, insurance companies refuse to cover them at all. The problem that screening creates is that those people who need health insurance the most are more likely to be denied coverage or charged an unaffordable price. This is yet another reason behind the support for passage of the ACA, which expanded coverage to everyone regardless of their health history. The next section explains how employment-based health insurance, a unique feature of the American workplace, also allows private health insurance to work.

Employment-Based Health Insurance One way insurers have overcome adverse selection is by selling insurance indirectly, to peoples' employers rather than to individuals. The big advantage of *employment-based health insurance*—

FOR INQUIRING MINDS | A California Death Spiral

Early in 2006, 116,000 workers at more than 6,000 California small businesses received health coverage from PacAdvantage, a "purchasing pool" that offered employees at member businesses a choice of insurance plans. The idea behind PacAdvantage, which was founded in 1992, was that by banding together, employees of small businesses could get better deals on health insurance.

But only a few months later, in August 2006, PacAdvantage announced that it was closing up shop because it could no longer find insurance companies willing to offer plans to its members.

What happened? It was the adverse selection death spiral. PacAdvantage offered the same policies to everyone, regardless of their prior health history. But employees didn't have to get insurance from PacAdvantage—they were free, if they chose, to opt out and buy insurance on their own. And sure enough, healthy workers started to find that they could get lower rates by buying insurance directly for themselves. As a result, PacAdvantage began to lose healthy clients, leaving behind an increasingly sick—and expensive—pool of customers. Premiums had to go up, driving out even more healthy workers, and eventually the whole plan had to shut down. ∎

insurance that a company provides to its employees—is that these employees are likely to contain a representative mix of healthy and less healthy people, rather than a group of people who want insurance because they expect to pay high medical bills. This is especially true if the employer is a large company with thousands or tens of thousands of workers. Employers require their employees to participate in the company health insurance plan because allowing employees to opt out (which healthier ones will be tempted to do) raises the cost of providing insurance for everyone else.

There's another reason employment-based insurance is widespread in the United States: it gets special, favorable tax treatment. Workers pay taxes on their paychecks, but workers who receive health insurance from their employers don't pay taxes on the value of the benefit. So employment-based health insurance is, in effect, subsidized by the U.S. tax system. Economists estimate the value of this subsidy at about $150 billion each year.

In spite of this subsidy, however, many working Americans don't receive employment-based health insurance. Those who aren't covered include most older Americans, because relatively few employers offer workers insurance that continues after they retire; the many workers whose employers don't offer coverage (especially part-time workers); and the unemployed.

Government Health Insurance

Table 18-6 shows the breakdown of health insurance coverage across the U.S. population in 2013. A majority of Americans, nearly 170 million people, received health insurance through their employers. The majority of those who didn't have private insurance were covered by two government programs, Medicare and Medicaid. (The numbers don't add up because some people have more than one form of coverage. For example, many recipients of Medicare also have supplemental coverage either through Medicaid or private policies.)

Medicare, financed by payroll taxes, is available to all Americans 65 and older, regardless of their income and wealth. It began in 1966 as a program to cover the cost of hospitalization but has since been expanded to cover a number of other medical expenses. You can get an idea of how much difference Medicare makes to the finances of elderly Americans by comparing the median income per person of Americans 65 and older—$21,238—with average annual Medicare payments per recipient, which were more than $10,000 in 2013. As with health care spending in general, however, the average can be misleading: in a given year, about 7% of Medicare recipients account for 50% of the costs.

TABLE 18-6	Number of Americans Covered by Health Insurance, 2013 (millions)
Covered by private health insurance	**201.1**
Employment-based	169.0
Direct purchase	34.5
Covered by government	**107.6**
Medicaid	54.1
Medicare	49.0
Military health care	14.1
Not covered	**42.0**

Source: U.S. Census Bureau.

Frank Cotham, The New Yorker Colletction/The Cartoon Bank

"For me, crime pays for what Medicare doesn't cover."

At the beginning of 2006, there was a major expansion of Medicare to cover the cost of prescription drugs. At the time Medicare was created, drugs played a relatively minor role in medicine and were rarely a major expense for patients. Today, however, many health problems, especially among the elderly, are treated with expensive drugs that must be taken for years on end, placing severe strains on some people's finances. As a result, a new Medicare program, known as Part D, was created to help pay these expenses.

Unlike Medicare, Medicaid is a means-tested program, paid for with federal and state government revenues. There's no simple way to summarize the criteria for eligibility because it is partly paid for by state governments and each state sets its own rules. Of the nearly 51 million Americans covered by Medicaid in 2013, 26 million were children under 18 and many of the rest were parents of children under 18. Most of the cost of Medicaid, however, is accounted for by a small number of older Americans, especially those needing long-term care.

Nearly 14 million Americans receive health insurance as a consequence of military service. Unlike Medicare and Medicaid, which pay medical bills but don't deliver health care directly, the Veterans Health Administration, which has more than 8 million clients, runs hospitals and clinics around the country.

The U.S. health care system, then, offers a mix of private insurance, mainly from employers, and public insurance of various forms. Most Americans have health insurance either from private insurance companies or through various forms of government insurance. Yet in 2012, before the implementation of the Affordable Care Act, almost 48 million, or 15.4% of the population, had no health insurance at all. What accounted for the high number of uninsured? And why was it such a severe problem that it spurred the passage of the Affordable Care Act?

The Problem of the Uninsured Before the Affordable Care Act

Before the passage of the ACA, the Kaiser Family Foundation, an independent nonpartisan group that studies health care issues, offered a succinct summary of who was uninsured in America: "The uninsured are largely low-income adult workers for whom coverage is unaffordable or unavailable." The reason the uninsured were primarily adults is that Medicaid, supplemented by SCHIP (which provides health care for children in families that are above the poverty threshold but still have relatively low income), covers many, though not all, low-income children but is much less likely to provide coverage to adults, especially if they didn't have children.

Low-income workers tended to be uninsured for two reasons: they were less likely than workers with higher income to have jobs that provided health insurance benefits, and they were less likely to be able to afford to directly purchase health insurance themselves. Finally, before the ACA, insurance companies frequently refused to cover people, regardless of their income, if they had a preexisting medical condition or something in their medical history suggesting that they were likely to need expensive medical treatment at some future date. As a result, a significant number of Americans with incomes that most would consider middle class could not get insurance.

It's important to realize that lack of insurance was not simply due to poverty. Before the ACA, most of the uninsured had incomes above the poverty threshold, and 35% had incomes more than twice the poverty threshold. We should also note that some of the uninsured were people who could afford insurance but preferred to save money and take their chances.

Like poverty, lack of health insurance has severe consequences, both medical and financial. On the medical side, the uninsured frequently have limited access to health care. Figure 18-6 summarizes some of the common problems associated with access to care, all of which are much worse for the uninsured than for the insured. On the monetary side, those who are uninsured often face serious financial problems when illness strikes. In many cases those without insurance are five times more likely than those with health insurance to be contacted by collection agencies, deplete their savings paying for medical expenses, or not pay altogether.

Health Care in Other Countries

Health care is one area in which the United States is very different from other wealthy countries, including both European nations and Canada. In fact, we're distinctive in three ways. First, we rely much more on private health insurance than any other wealthy country. Second, we spend much more on health care per person. Third, we were the only wealthy nation in which large numbers of people lacked health insurance until the ACA started to change that.

Table 18-7 compares the United States with three other wealthy countries: Canada, France, and Britain. The United States is the only one of the four countries that relies on private health insurance to cover most people; as a result, it's the only one in which private spending on health care is (slightly) larger than public spending on health care. (This will not change under the ACA as most health insurance will continue to be provided by private insurers.)

Canada has a **single-payer system:** a health care system in which the government acts as the principal payer of medical bills funded through taxes. For comparison, Medicare is essentially a single-payer system for older Americans—and the Canadian system is, in fact, called Medicare. The British system is like the American Veterans Health Administration, extended to everyone: a government agency, the British National Health Service, employs health care workers and runs hospitals and clinics that are available free of charge to the public. France is somewhere in between the Canadian and British systems. In France, the government acts as a single-payer, providing health insurance to everyone, and French citizens can receive treatment from private doctors and hospitals. But they also have the choice of receiving care from a sizable health care system run directly by the French government.

Canada, Britain, and France provide health insurance to all their citizens; the United States does not. Yet all three spend much less on health care per person than we do. Many Americans assume this must mean that foreign health care is inferior in quality. But many health care experts disagree with the claim that the health care systems of other wealthy countries deliver poor-quality

FIGURE 18-6 Barriers to Receiving Health Care, 2012

The figure shows that the uninsured face significantly greater barriers to receiving health care than the insured. Compared to the insured, a much higher proportion of the uninsured needed care but either did not receive it or postponed it.
Source: The Henry J Kaiser Family Foundation, *The Uninsured: A Primer.*

TABLE 18-7 Health Care Systems in Advanced Countries, 2012

	Government share of health care spending	Health care spending per capita (US$, purchasing power parity)	Life expectancy (total population at birth, years)	Infant mortality (deaths per 1,000 live births)
United States	47.6%	$8,745	78.7	6.0
Canada	70.1	4,603	81.2	4.7
France	77.4	4,288	82.6	3.4
Britain	84.0	3,289	81.5	4.1

Source: OECD.

A **single-payer system** is a health care system in which the government is the principal payer of medical bills funded through taxes.

care. As they point out, Britain, Canada, and France generally match or exceed the United States in terms of many measures of health care provision, such as the number of doctors, nurses, and hospital beds per 100,000 people. It's true that U.S. medical care includes more advanced technology in some areas and many more expensive surgical procedures. U.S. patients also have shorter waiting times for elective surgery than patients in Canada or Britain. France, however, also has very short waiting times.

Surveys of patients seem to suggest that there are no significant differences in the quality of care received by patients in Canada, Europe, and the United States. And as Table 18-7 shows, the United States does considerably worse than other advanced countries in terms of basic measures such as life expectancy and infant mortality, although our poor performance on these measures may have causes other than the quality of medical care—notably our relatively high levels of poverty and income inequality.

So why does the United States spend so much more on health care than other wealthy countries? Some of the disparity is the result of higher doctors' salaries, but most studies suggest that this is a secondary factor. One possibility is that Americans are getting better care than their counterparts abroad, but in ways that don't show up in either surveys of patient experiences or statistics on health performance.

However, the most likely explanation is that the U.S. system suffers from serious inefficiencies that other countries manage to avoid. Critics of the U.S. system emphasize the fact that our system's reliance on private insurance companies makes it highly fragmented, as individual insurance companies each expend resources on overhead and on such activities as marketing and trying to identify and weed out high-risk patients, leads to high operating costs. On average, the operating costs of private health insurers consume 14% of the premiums clients pay, leaving only 86% to spend on providing health care.

By contrast, Medicare spends only 3% of its funds on operating costs, leaving 97% to spend on health care. A study by the McKinsey Global Institute found that the United States spends almost six times as much per person on health care administration as other wealthy countries. Americans also pay higher prices for prescription drugs because, in other countries, government agencies bargain with pharmaceutical companies to get lower drug prices.

The Affordable Care Act

However one rates the past performance of the U.S. health care system, by 2009 it was clearly in trouble, on two fronts.

First, a growing number of working-age Americans were uninsured. Coverage of children improved between 1999 and 2009, largely thanks to an expansion of a

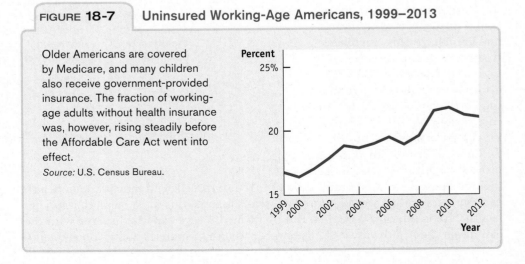

FIGURE **18-7**   Uninsured Working-Age Americans, 1999–2013

Older Americans are covered by Medicare, and many children also receive government-provided insurance. The fraction of working-age adults without health insurance was, however, rising steadily before the Affordable Care Act went into effect.
Source: U.S. Census Bureau.

government program associated with Medicaid, the Children's Health Insurance Program, and seniors were covered by Medicare. But as Figure 18-7 shows, the percentage of working age Americans (considered to be those between the ages of 18 and 64) without insurance was on a clear upward trend even before the severe economic downturn of 2007–2009.

Lying behind the growing number of uninsured, in turn, were sharply rising premiums for health insurance, reflecting rapid growth in overall health care costs. Figure 18-8 shows overall U.S. spending on health care as a percentage of GDP, a measure of the nation's total income, since the 1960s. As you can see, health spending has tripled as a share of income since 1965; this increase in spending explains why health insurance has become more expensive. Similar trends can be observed in other countries.

Why was health spending rising? The consensus of health experts is that it's a result of medical progress. As medical science progresses, conditions that could not be treated in the past become treatable—but often only at great expense. Both private insurers and government programs feel compelled to cover the new procedures—but this means higher costs, which either have to be passed on in the form of higher insurance premiums or require larger commitments of taxpayer funds.

The combination of a rising number of uninsured and rising costs led to many calls for health care reform in the United States. And so in 2010 Congress passed the Affordable Care Act (ACA) which took full effect in 2014. It was the largest expansion of the American welfare state since the creation of Medicare and Medicaid in 1965. It had two major objectives: covering the uninsured and cost control. Let's look at each in turn.

Covering the Uninsured   On the coverage side, the ACA closely follows a model that has been successfully used in Massachusetts since 2006 (introduced under Republican governor at the time, Mitt Romney). To understand the logic of both the Massachusetts plan and the ACA, consider the problem facing one major category of uninsured Americans: the many people who seek coverage in the individual insurance market but are turned down because they have preexisting medical conditions, which insurance companies fear could lead to large future expenses. (Insurance companies were known to deny coverage for even minor ailments, like allergies or a rash you had in college.) How could insurance be made available to such people?

One answer would be regulations requiring that insurance companies offer the same policies to everyone, regardless of medical history—a rule known as

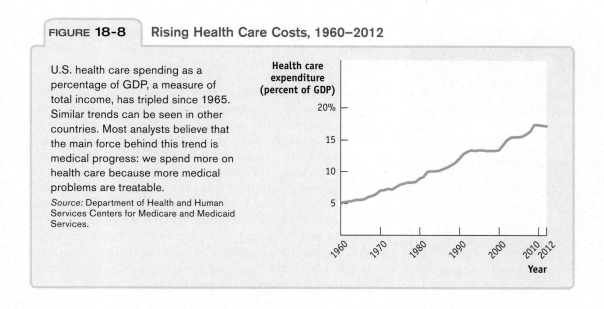

FIGURE **18-8**   **Rising Health Care Costs, 1960–2012**

U.S. health care spending as a percentage of GDP, a measure of total income, has tripled since 1965. Similar trends can be seen in other countries. Most analysts believe that the main force behind this trend is medical progress: we spend more on health care because more medical problems are treatable.

Source: Department of Health and Human Services Centers for Medicare and Medicaid Services.

"community rating." In fact, a number of states have such a rule. But community rating tends to lead to an adverse selection death spiral: Healthy individuals don't buy insurance until or unless they get sick, and because only people with health problems are getting coverage, insurance becomes very expensive.

To make community rating work, it's necessary to supplement it with other policies. Both the Massachusetts reform and the ACA add two key features. First is the requirement that everyone purchase health insurance—known as the *individual mandate*. This prevents an adverse selection death spiral. Second, government subsidies make the required insurance affordable for lower- and lower-middle income families.

It's important to realize that this system is like a three-legged stool: all three components must be present in order for it to work. Take away community rating, and those with preexisting conditions won't get coverage. Take away the individual mandate, and community rating will produce an adverse selection death spiral. And you can't require that people buy insurance without providing subsidies to those with lower incomes.

Will this arrangement, once fully implemented, succeed in covering more or less everyone? The Massachusetts precedent is encouraging on that front: by 2012, more than 96% of the state's residents had health insurance and virtually all children were covered. Since the ACA is very similar in structure, it ought to produce similar results.

Cost Control But will the ACA control costs? In itself, the expansion of coverage will raise health care spending, although not by as much as you might think. The uninsured are by and large relatively young, and the young have relatively low health care costs. (The elderly are already covered by Medicare.) The question is whether the reform can succeed in "bending the curve"—reducing the rate of growth of health costs over time.

The ACA's promise to control costs starts from the premise that the U.S. medical system, as currently constituted, has skewed incentives that waste resources. Because most care is paid for by insurance, neither doctors nor patients have an incentive to worry about costs. In fact, because health care providers are generally paid for each procedure they perform, there's a financial incentive to provide additional care—do more tests and, in some cases, perform more operations—even when there are little or no medical benefits.

The bill attempts to correct these skewed incentives in a variety of ways, from stricter oversight of reimbursements, to linking payments to a procedure's medical value, to paying health care providers for improved health outcomes rather than the number of procedures, and by limiting the tax deductibility of employment-based plans. Even supporters of the reform admit that nobody knows how well any one of these measures will work, but they point out that ACA incorporates virtually every idea for cost control that has been proposed by health care economists and that some of these ideas are likely to be highly successful.

The ACA's launch As you might gather, the ACA sets up an insurance system considerably more complex than other government programs like Medicare and Medicaid, which simply provide insurance directly. The ACA sets up special online marketplaces, the "exchanges," in which insurance companies offer policies from which individuals must choose. To figure out how much these policies really cost, it's necessary to calculate the subsidy you receive, which depends on your income as well as the premium. Making all of that work is a difficult programming problem. And sure enough, when healthcare.gov, the federally run online exchange, started up in October 2013, the system crashed repeatedly. For the next two months few people managed to sign up.

Once the bugs in the healthcare.gov website were fixed, millions of people signed up for healthcare coverage.

Mike Segar/Reuters/Landov

This was, however, a problem with the software, not the fundamental structure of the law, and by the beginning of 2014 it was largely solved. There was a huge surge of people signing up as the deadline for 2014 coverage approached, and by the time that deadline arrived more than 8 million people had signed up via the exchanges, while millions more had either purchased directly from insurers or been covered by an expansion of Medicaid.

How many of those signing up were newly insured? At first there were warnings that many of the policies being bought through the exchanges might simply be replacing existing coverage. By the summer of 2014, however, multiple independent surveys showed a sharp drop in the percentage of respondents without insurance. At this point it seems likely that the ACA will, indeed, manage to cover many though not all uninsured Americans. Whether it will also succeed in reducing the rate of cost growth remains to be seen, although by 2014 there were early signs that the rate of growth of health care costs was indeed falling.

ECONOMICS ▶ *in Action*

What Medicaid Does

Medicaid has been shown to make a big difference in the well-being of recipients.

Do social insurance programs actually help their beneficiaries? The answer isn't always as obvious as you might think. Take the example of Medicaid, which provides health insurance to low-income Americans. Some skeptics about the program's effectiveness have argued that in the absence of Medicaid, the poor would still find ways to get essential health care, and that there is no clear evidence that receiving Medicaid actually leads to better health.

Testing such assertions is tricky. You can't just compare people who are on Medicaid with people who aren't, since the program's beneficiaries differ in many ways from those who aren't on the program. And we don't normally get to do controlled experiments in which otherwise comparable groups receive different government benefits.

Once in a while, however, events provide the equivalent of a controlled experiment—and that's what happened with Medicaid. In 2008, the state of Oregon—which had sharply curtailed its Medicaid program because it lacked sufficient funds—found itself with enough money to put some but not all deserving recipients back on the program. To allocate the limited number of slots, the state used a lottery. And there you had it: in effect, a controlled experiment, in which researchers could compare a random sample of people receiving Medicaid with similar people who didn't win the lottery.

So what were the results? It turned out that Medicaid made a big difference. Those on Medicaid received

- 60% more mammograms
- 35% more outpatient care
- 30% more hospital care
- 20% more cholesterol checks

Medicaid recipients were also

- 70% more likely to have a consistent source of care
- 55% more likely to see the same doctor over time
- 45% more likely to have had a Pap test within the last year (for women)
- 40% less likely to need to borrow money or skip payment on other bills because of medical expenses
- 25% percent more likely to report themselves in "good" or "excellent" health

- 15% more likely to use prescription drugs
- 15% more likely to have had a blood test for high blood sugar or diabetes
- 10% percent less likely to screen positive for depression

In short, Medicaid led to major improvements in access to medical care and the well-being of those receiving it. So although there is a valid debate over the size of a state's Medicaid program because it costs taxpayers a significant amount of money, the Oregon results show that one criticism of Medicaid—the claim that it doesn't work at all—isn't valid.

Check Your Understanding 18-3

1. If you are enrolled in a four-year degree program, it is likely that you are required to enroll in a health insurance program run by your school unless you can show proof of existing insurance coverage..
   a. Explain how you and your parents benefit from this health insurance program even though, given your age, it is unlikely that you will need expensive medical treatment.
   b. Explain how your school's health insurance program avoids the adverse selection death spiral.
2. According to its critics, what accounts for the higher costs of the U.S. health care system compared to those of other wealthy countries?

Solutions appear at back of book.

The Debate over the Welfare State

The goals of the welfare state seem laudable: to help the poor, to protect against severe economic hardship and to ensure access to essential health care. But good intentions don't always make for good policy. There is an intense debate about how large the welfare state should be, a debate that partly reflects differences in philosophy but also reflects concern about the possibly counterproductive effects on incentives of welfare state programs. Disputes about the size of the welfare state are also one of the defining issues of modern American politics.

Problems with the Welfare State

There are two different arguments against the welfare state. One, which we described earlier in this chapter, is based on philosophical concerns about the proper role of government. As we learned, some political theorists believe that redistributing income is not a legitimate role of government. Rather, they believe that government's role should be limited to maintaining the rule of law, providing public goods, and managing externalities.

The more conventional argument against the welfare state involves the trade-off between efficiency and equity, an issue that we first encountered in Chapter 7. As we explained there, the *ability-to-pay-principle*—the argument that an extra dollar of income matters more to a less well-off individual than to a more well-off individual—implies that the tax system should be progressive, with high-income taxpayers paying a higher fraction of their income in taxes than those with lower incomes.

But this must be balanced against the efficiency costs of high marginal tax rates. Consider an extremely progressive tax system that imposes a marginal rate of 90% on very high incomes. The problem is that such a high marginal rate reduces the incentive to increase a family's income by working hard or making risky investments. As a result, an extremely progressive tax system tends to make society as a whole poorer, which could hurt even those the system was intended to benefit. That's why even economists who strongly favor progressive taxation don't support a return to the extremely progressive system that prevailed in the 1950s, when the top U.S. marginal income tax rate was more than 90%. So, the design of the tax system involves a trade-off between equity and efficiency.

A similar trade-off between equity and efficiency implies that there should be a limit to the size of the welfare state. A government that operates a large welfare state requires more revenue than one that restricts itself mainly to provision of public goods such as national defense. A large welfare state requires higher tax revenue and higher marginal tax rates than a smaller welfare state.

Table 18-8 shows "social expenditure," a measure that roughly corresponds to total welfare state spending, as a percentage of GDP in the United States, Britain, and France. It also compares this with an estimate of the marginal tax rate faced by an average single wage-earner, including payroll taxes paid by employers and state and local taxes. As you can see, France's large welfare state goes along with a high marginal rate of taxation. As the upcoming Economics in Action explains, some but not all economists believe that this high rate of taxation is a major reason the French work substantially fewer hours per year than Americans.

TABLE 18-8	Social Expenditure and Marginal Tax Rates	
	Social expenditure in 2012 (percent of GDP)	Marginal tax rate in 2009
United States	19.4%	43.6%
Britain	23.9	40.3
France	32.1	59.8

Source: OECD. Marginal tax rate is defined as a percentage of total labor costs.

One way to hold down the costs of the welfare state is to means-test benefits: make them available only to those who need them. But means-testing benefits creates a different kind of trade-off between equity and efficiency. Consider the following example: Suppose there is some means-tested benefit, worth $2,000 per year, that is available only to families with incomes of less than $20,000 per year. Now suppose that a family currently has an income of $19,500 but that one family member is deciding whether to take a new job that will raise the family's income to $20,500. Well, taking that job will actually make the family worse off, because it will gain $1,000 in earnings but lose the $2,000 government benefit.

This feature of means-tested benefits, which makes a family worse off if it earns more is known as a *notch*. It is a well-known problem with programs that aid the poor and behaves much like a high marginal tax rate on income. Most welfare state programs are designed to avoid a notch by setting a sliding scale for benefits. With a sliding scale, benefits diminish gradually as the recipient's income rises rather than come to an abrupt end.

Even so, the combined effects of the major means-tested programs shown in Table 18-3, plus additional means-tested programs, such as housing aid, that are offered by some state and local governments, are to create very high effective marginal tax rates. For example, one 2005 study found that a family consisting of two adults and two children that raised its income from $20,000 a year—just above the poverty threshold in 2005—to $35,000 would find almost all its increase in after-tax income offset by loss of benefits such as food stamps, the Earned Income Tax Credit, and Medicaid.

The Politics of the Welfare State

In 1791, in the early phase of the French Revolution, French citizens convened a congress, the Legislative Assembly, in which representatives were seated according to social class: the upper classes, who pretty much liked the way things were, sat on the right; commoners, who wanted big changes, sat on the left. Ever since, political commentators refer to politicians as being on the "right" (more conservative) or on the "left" (more liberal).

But what do modern politicians on the left and right disagree about? In the modern United States, they mainly disagree about the appropriate size of the welfare state. The debate over the Affordable Care Act was a case in point, with the vote on the bill breaking down entirely according to party lines—Democrats (on the left) in favor of the ACA and Republicans (on the right) opposed.

You might think that saying that political debate is really about just one thing—how big to make the welfare state—is a huge oversimplification. But political scientists have found that once you carefully rank members of Congress

FOR INQUIRING MINDS | "We Are the 99%!"

In the fall of 2011, Zuccotti Park, a small open space in Manhattan's financial district, was taken over by protestors, part of a movement known as "Occupy Wall Street." The protestors had a number of grievances, but the most pressing were their complaints about Wall Street and its perceived contribution to growing inequality in the United States. "We are the 99 percent!" became the movement's favored slogan, a reference to the large increase in share of income going to the top 1% of the American population. Wall Street, they charged, contributed to growing inequality by paying its bankers huge salaries and bonuses, while engaging in overly risky behavior that led to the housing boom and bust of 2007–2009 that decimated the economy. Was this a reasonable charge?

Those who found it unreasonable pointed to the contributions that Wall Street, and the American finance

industry in general, have made to the U.S. economy. Compared to other countries, the United States is a leader in financial services and innovation, generating billions annually in revenues, and attracting trillions of dollars of investment from abroad. High salaries on Wall Street, they contend, are simply the rewards for skill and hard work in the competitive market for talent on Wall Street.

What is incontrovertible, however, are the data that show that incomes in the finance industry have contributed to growing inequality in the United States. This is especially clear when you look not at the top percentile of the income distribution, but at an even smaller group, the top 0.1%—those with a median annual income of $5.6 million.

Although financial industry people are a minority (18%) within this income elite—consisting also of executives,

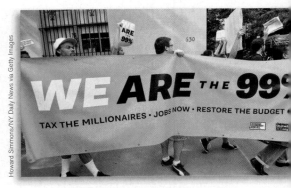

In 2011 growing income inequality prompted protests in the United States.

managers, lawyers, and others—they are greatly overrepresented since only about 6% of American workers are employed in finance. So, the protesters were making a valid point: Wall Street salaries are indeed one of the sources of the rapid rise in incomes at the top. ■

from right to left on past legislation, a congressperson's position in that ranking does a very good job of predicting his or her votes on future legislation.

The same studies that show a strong left–right spectrum in U.S. politics also show strong polarization between the major parties on this spectrum. Forty years ago, there was a substantial overlap between the parties: some Democrats were to the right of some Republicans, or, if you prefer, some Republicans were to the left of some Democrats. Today, however, the rightmost Democrats appear to be to the left of the leftmost Republicans. There's nothing necessarily wrong with this. Although it's common to decry "partisanship," it's hard to see why members of different political parties shouldn't have different views about policy.

Can economic analysis help resolve this political conflict? Only up to a point.

Some of the political controversy over the welfare state involves differences in opinion about the trade-offs we have just discussed: if you believe that the disincentive effects of generous benefits and high taxes are very large, you're likely to look less favorably on welfare state programs than if you believe they're fairly small. Economic analysis, by improving our knowledge of the facts, can help resolve some of these differences.

To an important extent, however, differences of opinion on the welfare state reflect differences in values and philosophy. And those are differences economics can't resolve.

ECONOMICS ▶ in Action

French Family Values

The United States has the smallest welfare state of any major advanced economy. France has one of the largest. As we've already described, France has much higher social spending than America as a percentage of total national income, and French citizens face much higher tax rates than Americans. One argument against a large welfare state is that it has negative effects on efficiency. Does French experience support this argument?

On the face of it, the answer would seem to be a clear yes. French GDP per capita—the total value of the economy's output, divided by the total population—is only about 75% of the U.S. level. This reflects the fact that the French work less: French workers and U.S. workers have almost exactly the same productivity per hour, but a smaller fraction of the French population is employed, and the average French employee works substantially fewer hours over the course of a year than his or her American counterpart. Some economists have argued that high tax rates in France explain this difference: the incentives to work are weaker in France than in the United States because the government takes away so much of what you earn from an additional hour of work.

A closer examination, however, reveals that the story is more complicated than that. The low level of employment in France is entirely the result of low rates of employment among the young and the old; about 80% of French residents of prime working age, 25–54, are employed, exactly the same

France guarantees health care for all its citizens—a benefit of having one of the largest welfare states in the world.

percentage as in the United States. So high tax rates don't seem to discourage the French from working in the prime of their lives. But only about 30% of 15- to 24-year-olds are employed in France, compared with more than half of 15- to 24-year-olds in the United States. And young people in France don't work in part because they don't have to: college education is generally free, and students receive financial support, so French students, unlike their American counterparts, rarely work while attending school. The French will tell you that that's a virtue of their system, not a problem.

Shorter working hours also reflect factors besides tax rates. French law requires employers to offer at least a month of vacation, but most U.S. workers get less than two weeks off. Here, too, the French will tell you that their policy is better than ours because it helps families spend time together.

The aspect of French policy even the French agree is a big problem is that their retirement system allows workers to collect generous pensions even if they retire very early. As a result, only 45% of French residents between the ages of 55 and 64 are employed, compared with more than 60% of Americans. The cost of supporting all those early retirees is a major burden on the French welfare state—and getting worse as the French population ages.

Check Your Understanding 18-4

1. Explain how each of the following policies creates a disincentive to work or undertake a risky investment.
   a. A high sales tax on consumer items
   b. The complete loss of a housing subsidy when yearly income rises above $25,000
2. Over the past 40 years, has the polarization in Congress increased, decreased, or stayed the same?

Solutions appear at back of book.

▼ Quick Review

• Intense debate on the size of the welfare state centers on philosophy and on equity-versus-efficiency concerns. The high marginal tax rates needed to finance an extensive welfare state can reduce the incentive to work. Holding down the cost of the welfare state by means-testing can also cause inefficiency through notches that create high effective marginal tax rates for benefit recipients.

• Politics is often depicted as an opposition between left and right; in the modern United States, that division mainly involves disagreement over the appropriate size of the welfare state.

Welfare State Entrepreneurs

"Wiggo Dalmo is a classic entrepreneurial type: the Working Class Kid Made Good." So began a profile in the January 2011 issue of *Inc.* magazine. Dalmo began as an industrial mechanic who worked for a large company, repairing mining equipment. Eventually, however, he decided to strike out on his own and start his own business. Momek, the company he founded, eventually grew into a $44 million, 150-employee operation that does a variety of contract work on oil rigs and in mines.

You can read stories like this all the time in U.S. business publications. What was unusual about this particular article is that Dalmo and his company aren't American, they're Norwegian—and Norway, like other Scandinavian countries, has a very generous welfare state, supported by high levels of taxation. So what does Dalmo think of that system? He approves, saying that Norway's tax system is "good and fair," and he thinks the system is good for business. In fact, the *Inc.* article was titled, "In Norway, Start-Ups Say Ja to Socialism."

Why? After all, the financial rewards for being a successful entrepreneur are more limited in a country like Norway, with its high taxes, than they are in the United States, with its lower taxes. But there are other considerations. For example, at least until the Affordable Care Act kicked in in January 2014, an American thinking of leaving a large company to start a new business needed to worry about whether he or she would be able to get health insurance, whereas a Norwegian in the same position was assured of health care regardless of employment. And the downside of failure is larger in the U.S. system, which offers minimal aid to the unemployed.

Still, is Wiggo Dalmo an exceptional case? Table 18-9 shows the nations with the highest level of entrepreneurial activity, according to a study financed by the U.S. Small Business Administration, which tried to quantify the level of entrepreneurial activity in different nations. The United States is at the top of the list, but so are several Scandinavian countries which have very high levels of taxation and extensive social insurance. (Norway, for example, is number 14.)

The moral is that when comparing how business friendly different welfare state systems really are, you have to think a bit past the obvious question of the level of taxes.

TABLE 18-9	The Top 10 Entrepreneurial Countries, 2014
Rank	**Country**
1	United States
2	Australia
3	Sweden
4	Denmark
5	Switzerland
6	Taiwan
7	Finland
8	Netherlands
9	United Kingdom
10	Singapore

Source: The Global Entrepreneurship and Development Index 2014, by Zoltan Acs, Laszlo Szerb and Erkko Autio.

QUESTIONS FOR THOUGHT

1. Why does Norway have to have higher taxes overall than the United States?

2. This case suggests that government-paid health care helps entrepreneurs. How does this relate to the arguments for social insurance in the text?

3. How would the incentives of people like Wiggo Dalmo be affected if Norwegian health care was means-tested instead of available to all?

Erika Larsen/Redux

SUMMARY

1. The **welfare state** absorbs a large share of government spending in all wealthy countries. **Government transfers** are the payments made by the government to individuals and families. **Poverty programs** alleviate income inequality by helping the poor; **social insurance programs** alleviate economic insecurity. Welfare state programs also deliver external benefits to society through poverty reduction and improved access to health care, particularly for children.

2. Despite the fact that the **poverty threshold** is adjusted according to the cost of living but not according to the standard of living, and that the average American income has risen substantially over the last 30 years, the **poverty rate,** the percentage of the population with an income below the poverty threshold, is no lower than it was 30 years ago. There are various causes of poverty: lack of education, the legacy of discrimination, and bad luck. The consequences of poverty are particularly harmful for children, resulting in more chronic disease, lower lifetime earnings, and higher rates of criminality.

3. **Median household income,** the income of a family at the center of the income distribution, is a better indicator of the income of the typical household than **mean household income** because it is not distorted by the inclusion of a small number of very wealthy households. The **Gini coefficient,** a number that summarizes a country's level of income inequality based on how unequally income is distributed across quintiles, is used to compare income inequality across countries.

4. Both **means-tested** and non-means-tested programs reduce poverty. The major **in-kind benefits** programs are Medicare and Medicaid, which pay for medical care. Due to concerns about the effects on incentives to work and on family cohesion, aid to poor families has become significantly less generous even as the **negative income tax** has become more generous. Social Security, the largest U.S. welfare state program,

has significantly reduced poverty among the elderly. Unemployment insurance is also a key social insurance program.

5. Health insurance satisfies an important need because most families cannot afford expensive medical treatment. **Private health insurance,** unless it is employment-based or carefully screens applicants, has the potential to fall into an adverse selection death spiral. Most Americans are covered by employment-based private health insurance; the majority of the remaining are covered by Medicare (a **single-payer system** for those 65 and over in which the government pays for most medical bills from tax revenue) or Medicaid (for those with low incomes).

6. Compared to other countries, the United States relies more heavily on private health insurance and has substantially higher health care costs per person without clearly providing better care. Health care costs are rising, largely due to advances in technology. The rising number of uninsured and the financial distress caused by lack of insurance prompted the passage in 2010 of the Affordable Care Act, or ACA. Its objective is to reduce the number of uninsured and reduce the rate of growth of health care costs.

7. Debates over the size of the welfare state are based on philosophical and equity-versus-efficiency considerations. Although high marginal tax rates to finance an extensive welfare state can reduce the incentive to work, means-testing of programs in order to reduce the cost of the welfare state can also reduce the incentive to work unless carefully designed to avoid notches.

8. Politicians on the left tend to favor a bigger welfare state and those on the right to oppose it. This left–right distinction is central to today's politics. America's two major political parties have become more polarized in recent decades, with a much clearer distinction than in the past about where their members stand on the left–right spectrum.

KEY TERMS

Welfare state, p. 512
Government transfer, p. 512
Poverty program, p. 512
Social insurance program, p. 512
Poverty threshold, p. 514

Poverty rate, p. 514
Mean household income, p. 517
Median household income, p. 517
Gini coefficient, p. 518
Means-tested, p. 522

In-kind benefit, p. 522
Negative income tax, p. 522
Private health insurance, p. 526
Single-payer system, p. 529

PROBLEMS

1. The accompanying table contains data on the U.S. economy for the years 1983 and 2013. The second column shows the poverty threshold. The third column shows the consumer price index (CPI), a measure of the overall level of prices. And the fourth column shows U.S. gross domestic product (GDP) per capita, a measure of the standard of living.

Year	Poverty threshold	CPI (1982–1984 = 100)	GDP per capita
1983	$5,180	99.6	$15,525
2013	11,490	233.0	53,086

Sources: U.S. Census Bureau; Bureau of Labor Statistics; Bureau of Economic Analysis.

a. By what factor has the poverty threshold increased from 1983 to 2013? That is, has it doubled, tripled, and so on?

b. By what factor has the CPI (a measure of the overall price level) increased from 1983 to 2013? That is, has it doubled, tripled, and so on?

c. By what factor has GDP per capita (a measure of the standard of living) increased from 1983 to 2013? That is, has it doubled, tripled, and so on?

d. What do your results tell you about how people officially classified as "poor" have done economically relative to other U.S. citizens?

2. In the city of Metropolis, there are 100 residents, each of whom lives until age 75. Residents of Metropolis have the following incomes over their lifetime: Through age 14, they earn nothing. From age 15 until age 29, they earn 200 metros (the currency of Metropolis) per year. From age 30 to age 49, they earn 400 metros. From age 50 to age 64, they earn 300 metros. Finally, at age 65 they retire and are paid a pension of 100 metros per year until they die at age 75. Each year, everyone consumes whatever their income is that year (that is, there is no saving and no borrowing). Currently, 20 residents are 10 years old, 20 residents are 20 years old, 20 residents are 40 years old, 20 residents are 60 years old, and 20 residents are 70 years old.

a. Study the income distribution among all residents of Metropolis. Split the population into quintiles according to their income. How much income does a resident in the lowest quintile have? In the second, third, fourth, and top quintiles? What share of total income of all residents goes to the residents in each quintile? Construct a table showing the share of total income that goes to each quintile. Does this income distribution show inequality?

b. Now look only at the 20 residents of Metropolis who are currently 40 years old, and study the income distribution among only those residents. Split those 20 residents into quintiles according to their income. How much income does a resident in the lowest quintile have? In the second, third, fourth, and top quintiles? What share of total income of all 40-year-olds goes to the residents in each quintile? Does this income distribution show inequality?

c. What is the relevance of these examples for assessing data on the distribution of income in any country?

3. The accompanying table presents data from the U.S. Census Bureau on median and mean income of male workers for the years 1972 and 2012. The income figures are adjusted to eliminate the effect of inflation.

Year	Median income	Mean income
	(in 2012 dollars)	
1972	$36,547	$42,383
2012	33,904	49,915

Source: U.S. Census Bureau.

a. By what percentage has median income changed over this period? By what percentage has mean income changed over this period?

b. Between 1972 and 2012, has the income distribution become less or more unequal? Explain.

4. There are 100 households in the economy of Equalor. Initially, 99 of them have an income of $10,000 each, and one household has an income of $1,010,000.

a. What is the median income in this economy? What is the mean income?

Through its poverty programs, the government of Equalor now redistributes income: it takes $990,000 away from the richest household and distributes it equally among the remaining 99 households.

b. What is the median income in this economy now? What is the mean income? Has the median income changed? Has the mean income changed? Which indicator (mean or median household income) is a better indicator of the typical Equalorian household's income? Explain.

5. The country of Marxland has the following income tax and social insurance system. Each citizen's income is taxed at an average tax rate of 100%. A social insurance system then provides transfers to each citizen such that each citizen's after-tax income is exactly equal. That is, each citizen gets (through a government transfer payment) an equal share of the income tax revenue. What is the incentive for one individual citizen to work and earn income? What will the total tax revenue in Marxland be? What will be the after-tax income (including the transfer payment) for each citizen? Do you think such a tax system that creates perfect equality will work?

6. The tax system in Taxilvania includes a negative income tax. For all incomes below $10,000, individuals pay an income tax of –40% (that is, they receive a payment of 40% of their income). For any income above the $10,000 threshold, the tax rate on that additional income is 10%. For the first three scenarios below, calculate the amount of income tax to be paid and after-tax income.

a. Lowani earns income of $8,000.

b. Midram earns income of $40,000.

c. Hi-Wan earns income of $100,000.

d. Can you find a notch in this tax system? That is, can you find a situation where earning more pre-tax income actually results in less after-tax income?

7. In the city of Notchingham, each worker is paid a wage rate of $10 per hour. Notchingham administers its own unemployment benefit, which is structured as follows: If you are unemployed (that is, if you do not work at all), you get unemployment benefits (a transfer from the government) of $50 per day. As soon as you work for only one hour, the unemployment benefit is completely withdrawn. That is, there is a notch in the benefit system.

a. How much income does an unemployed person have per day? How much daily income does an individual who works four hours per day have? How many hours do you need to work to earn just the same as if you were unemployed?

b. Will anyone ever accept a part-time job that requires working four hours per day, rather than being unemployed?

c. Suppose that Notchingham now changes the way in which the unemployment benefit is withdrawn. For each additional dollar an individual earns, $0.50 of the unemployment benefit is withdrawn. How much daily income does an individual who works four hours per day now have? Is there an incentive now to work four hours per day rather than being unemployed?

8. The accompanying table shows data on the total number of people in the United States and the number of all people who were uninsured, for selected years from 1999 to 2011. It also shows data on the total number of poor children in the United States—those under 18 and below the poverty threshold—and the number of poor children who were uninsured.

Year	Total people	Uninsured people	Total poor children	Uninsured poor children
		(millions)		
1999	276.8	38.8	12.3	3.8
2001	282.1	39.8	11.7	3.3
2003	288.3	43.4	12.9	3.3
2005	293.8	44.8	12.9	3.1
2007	299.1	45.7	13.3	3.1
2009	304.3	50.7	15.5	3.1
2011	308.8	48.6	16.1	3.0

Source: U.S. Census Bureau.

For each year, calculate the percentage of all people who were uninsured and the percentage of poor children who were uninsured. How have these percentages changed over time? What is a possible explanation for the change in the percentage of uninsured poor children?

9. The American National Election Studies conducts periodic research on the opinions of U.S. voters. The accompanying table shows the percentage of people, in selected years from 1952 to 2008, who agreed with the statement "There are important differences in what the Republicans and Democrats stand for."

Year	Agree with statement
1952	50%
1972	46
1992	60
2004	76
2008	78

Source: American National Election Studies.

What do these data say about the degree of partisanship in U.S. politics over time?

WORK IT OUT

For interactive, step-by-step help in solving the following problem, visit LaunchPad by using the URL on the back cover of this book.

10. In a private insurance market, there are two different kinds of people: some who are more likely to require expensive medical treatment and some who are less likely to require medical treatment and who, if they do, require less expensive treatment. One health insurance policy is offered, tailored to the average person's health care needs: the premium is equal to the average person's medical expenses (plus the insurer's expenses and normal profit).

a. Explain why such an insurance policy is unlikely to be feasible.

In an effort to avoid the adverse selection death spiral, a private health insurer offers two health insurance policies: one that is intended for those who are more likely to require expensive treatment (and therefore charges a higher premium) and one that is intended for those who are less likely to require treatment (and therefore charges a lower premium).

b. Could this system overcome the problem created by adverse selection?

c. How does the British National Health Service (NHS) avoid these problems?

Factor Markets and the Distribution of Income

◯ **What You Will Learn in This Chapter**

◼ How factors of production—resources like land, labor, **physical capital** and **human capital**—are traded in factor markets, determining the **factor distribution of income**

◼ How the demand for factors leads to the **marginal productivity theory of income distribution**

◼ About the sources of wage disparities and the role of discrimination

◼ How labor supply arises from a worker's decision about **time allocation**

THE VALUE OF A DEGREE

Monika Graff/The Image Works

If you have doubts about completing college, consider this: not getting a college degree will cost you about half a million dollars over your lifetime.

DOES HIGHER EDUCATION pay? Yes, it does: in the modern economy, employers are willing to pay a premium for workers with more education. And the size of that premium has increased a lot over the last few decades. In 2013, Americans with four-year college degrees made 98% more per hour on average than those without a degree. That percentage is up from 89% in 2008, 85% in 2003, and 64% in the early 1980s. In fact, according to David Autor, a professor of economics at MIT, the true cost of a college degree is approximately *negative* $500,000. That is, a college degree is cheaper than free. In other words, not getting a college degree will cost you about half a million dollars over your lifetime. That's roughly double what the negative cost was 30 years

ago. And because having a bachelor's degree is so valuable, more Americans than ever are getting one: in 2013, 34.5% of those aged 25 to 29 had at least a bachelor's degree, compared to 24.7% in 1995.

Who decided that the wages of workers with a four-year college degree would be so much more than for workers without one? The answer, of course, is that nobody decided it. Wage rates are prices, the prices of different kinds of labor; and they are decided, like other prices, by supply and demand.

Still, there is a qualitative difference between the wage rate of high school grads and the price of used textbooks: the wage rate isn't the price of a *good*, it's the price of a *factor of production*. And although markets for factors of production are in many ways similar to those

for goods, there are also some important differences.

In this chapter, we examine *factor markets*, the markets in which the factors of production such as labor, land, and capital are traded. Factor markets, like markets for goods and services, play a crucial role in the economy: they allocate productive resources to producers and help ensure that those resources are used efficiently.

This chapter begins by describing the major factors of production and the demand for factors of production, which leads to a crucial insight: the *marginal productivity theory of income distribution*. We then consider some challenges to the marginal productivity theory and examine the markets for capital and for land. The chapter concludes with a discussion of the supply of the most important factor, labor.

Physical capital—often referred to simply as "capital"—consists of manufactured productive resources such as equipment, buildings, tools, and machines.

Human capital is the improvement in labor created by education and knowledge that is embodied in the workforce.

The Economy's Factors of Production

You may recall that we defined a factor of production in Chapter 2 in the context of the circular-flow diagram: it is any resource that is used by firms to produce goods and services for consumption by households. Factors of production are bought and sold in *factor markets,* and the prices in factor markets are known as *factor prices.*

What are these factors of production, and why do factor prices matter?

The Factors of Production

As we learned in Chapter 2, economists divide factors of production into four principal classes: land, labor, physical capital, and human capital. Land is a resource provided by nature; labor is the work done by human beings.

In Chapter 9 we defined *capital:* it is the value of the assets that are used by a firm in producing its output. There are two broad types of capital. **Physical capital**—often referred to simply as "capital"—consists of manufactured resources such as equipment, buildings, tools, and machines.

In the modern economy, **human capital,** the improvement in labor created by education and knowledge, and embodied in the workforce, is at least equally significant. The importance of human capital has been greatly increased by the progress of technology, which has made a high level of technical sophistication essential to many jobs—one cause of the increased premium paid for workers with advanced degrees.

Why Factor Prices Matter: The Allocation of Resources

Factor markets and factor prices play a key role in one of the most important processes that must take place in any economy: the allocation of resources among producers.

Consider the example of Williston, North Dakota. Formerly a sleepy agricultural town, the population has more than doubled from 12,000 to 30,000 as Williston is the site of a boom in fracking for natural gas and oil. It is estimated that there are four drills every square mile.

What ensured that the oil field workers came to Williston? The factor market: the high demand for workers drove up wages. In the oil fields starting pay can easily exceed $100,000. People who can't work in the oil fields also move there, to do things that the oil workers don't have time to do—such as cook meals and do laundry. In other words, the markets for factors of production—oil field workers and cooks in this example—allocate the factors of production to where they are needed.

In this sense factor markets are similar to goods markets, which allocate goods among consumers. But there are two features that make factor markets special. Unlike in a goods market, demand in a factor market is what we call *derived demand.* That is, demand for the factor is derived from the firm's output choice. The second feature is that factor markets are where most of us get the largest shares of our income (government transfers being the next largest source of income in the economy).

Factor Incomes and the Distribution of Income

Most American families get most of their income in the form of wages and salaries—that is, they get their income by selling labor. Some people, however, get most of their income from physical capital: when you own stock in a company, what you really own is a share of that company's physical capital. And some people get much of their income from rents earned on land they own.

PITFALLS

WHAT IS A FACTOR, ANYWAY?

Imagine a business that produces shirts. The business will make use of workers and machines—that is, of labor and capital. But it will also use other inputs, such as electricity and cloth. Are all of these inputs factors of production? No: labor and capital are factors of production, but cloth and electricity are not.

The key distinction is that a factor of production earns income from the selling of its services over and over again but an input cannot. For example, a worker earns income over time from repeatedly selling his or her efforts; the owner of a machine earns income over time from repeatedly selling the use of that machine.

So a factor of production, such as labor and capital, represents an enduring source of income. An input like electricity or cloth, however, is used up in the production process. Once exhausted, it cannot be a source of future income for its owner.

FOR INQUIRING MINDS | **The Factor Distribution of Income and Social Change in the Industrial Revolution**

Have you read any novels by Jane Austen? How about Charles Dickens? If you've read both, you probably noticed that they seem to be describing quite different societies. Austen's novels, set in England around 1800, describe a world in which the leaders of society are landowning aristocrats. Dickens, writing about 50 years later, describes an England in which businessmen, especially factory owners, are in control.

This literary shift reflects a dramatic transformation in the factor distribution of income in England at the time. The Industrial Revolution,

By altering how people lived and worked, the Industrial Revolution led to huge economic and social changes.

which took place between the late eighteenth century and the middle of the nineteenth century, changed England from a mainly agricultural country, in which land earned a fairly substantial share of income, to an urbanized and industrial one, in which land rents were dwarfed by capital income. Estimates by the economist Nancy Stokey show that between 1780 and 1850 the share of national income represented by land fell from 20% to 9%, but the share represented by capital rose from 35% to 44%. That shift changed everything—even literature. ■

Obviously, then, the prices of factors of production have a major impact on how the economic "pie" is sliced among different groups. For example, a higher wage rate, other things equal, means that a larger proportion of the total income in the economy goes to people who derive their income from labor, and less goes to those who derive their income from capital or land. Economists refer to how the economic pie is sliced as the "distribution of income." Specifically, factor prices determine the **factor distribution of income**—how the total income of the economy is divided among labor, land, and capital.

As the following Economics in Action explains, the factor distribution of income in the United States has been quite stable over the past few decades. In other times and places, however, large changes have taken place in the factor distribution. One notable example: during the Industrial Revolution, the share of total income earned by English landowners fell sharply, while the share earned by English capital owners rose. As we just learned in the For Inquiring Minds, this shift had a profound effect on society.

ECONOMICS ▶ *in Action*

The Factor Distribution of Income in the United States

When we talk about the factor distribution of income, what are we talking about in practice?

In the United States, as in all advanced economies, payments to labor account for most of the economy's total income. Figure 19-1 shows the factor distribution of income in the United States in 2013: in that year, 66.3% of total income in the economy took the form of "compensation of employees"—a number that includes both wages and benefits such as health insurance. This number is somewhat low by historical standards (it was 72.1% in 1972 and 70.2% in 2007). It reflects the slow recovery after the

The **factor distribution of income** is the division of total income among labor, land, and capital.

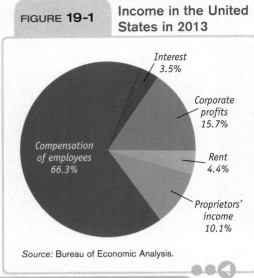

FIGURE **19-1**

Factor Distribution of Income in the United States in 2013

Interest 3.5%

Corporate profits 15.7%

Compensation of employees 66.3%

Rent 4.4%

Proprietors' income 10.1%

Source: Bureau of Economic Analysis.

▼ Quick Review

• Economists usually divide the economy's factors of production into four principal categories: labor, land, **physical capital,** and **human capital.**

• The demand for a factor is a derived demand. Factor prices, which are set in factor markets, determine the **factor distribution of income.** Labor receives the bulk—66% in 2013—of the income in the modern U.S. economy. Although the exact share is not directly measurable, much of what is called compensation of employees is a return to human capital.

Great Recession where unemployment and wages rates have yet to return to pre-recession levels.

However, measured wages and benefits don't capture the full income of "labor" because a significant fraction of total income in the United States (usually 7 to 10%) is "proprietors' income"—the earnings of people who own their own businesses. Part of that income should be considered wages these business owners pay themselves. So the true share of labor in the economy is probably a few percentage points higher than the reported "compensation of employees" share.

But much of what we call compensation of employees is really a return on human capital. A surgeon isn't just supplying the services of a pair of ordinary hands (at least the patient hopes not!): that individual is also supplying the result of many years and hundreds of thousands of dollars invested in training and experience. We can't directly measure what fraction of wages is really a payment for education and training, but many economists believe that human capital has become *the* most important factor of production in modern economies.

Check Your Understanding   19-1

1. Suppose that the government places price controls on the market for college professors, imposing a wage that is lower than the market wage. Describe the effect of this policy on the production of college degrees. What sectors of the economy do you think will be adversely affected by this policy? What sectors of the economy might benefit?

Solutions appear at back of book.

Marginal Productivity and Factor Demand

All economic decisions are about comparing costs and benefits—and usually about comparing marginal costs and marginal benefits. This goes both for a consumer, deciding whether to undertake another year of schooling, and for a producer, deciding whether to hire an additional worker.

Although there are some important exceptions, most factor markets in the modern American economy are perfectly competitive, meaning that buyers and sellers of a given factor are price-takers. And in a competitive labor market, it's clear how to define an employer's marginal cost of a worker: it is simply the worker's wage rate. But what is the marginal benefit of that worker? To answer that question, we return to a concept first introduced in Chapter 11: the production function, which relates inputs to output. And as in Chapter 12, we will assume throughout this chapter that all producers are price-takers in their output markets—that is, they operate in a perfectly competitive industry.

Value of the Marginal Product

Figure 19-2 reproduces Figures 11-1 and 11-2, which showed the production function for wheat on George and Martha's farm. Panel (a) uses the total product curve to show how total wheat production depends on the number of workers employed on the farm; panel (b) shows how the *marginal product* of labor, the increase in output from employing one more worker, depends on the number of workers employed. Table 19-1, which reproduces the table in Figure 11-1, shows the numbers behind the figure.

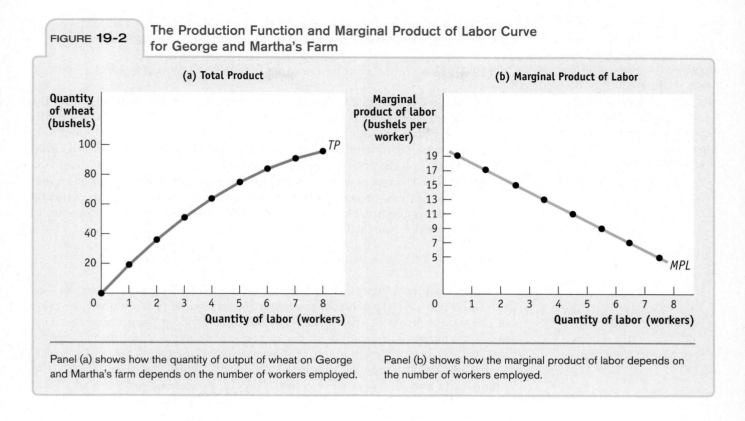

FIGURE 19-2 The Production Function and Marginal Product of Labor Curve for George and Martha's Farm

(a) Total Product

(b) Marginal Product of Labor

Panel (a) shows how the quantity of output of wheat on George and Martha's farm depends on the number of workers employed.

Panel (b) shows how the marginal product of labor depends on the number of workers employed.

Assume that George and Martha want to maximize their profit, that workers must be paid $200 each, and that wheat sells for $20 per bushel. What is their optimal number of workers? That is, how many workers should they employ to maximize profit?

In Chapters 11 and 12 we showed how to answer this question in several steps. In Chapter 11 we used information from the producer's production function to derive the firm's total cost and its marginal cost. And in Chapter 12 we derived the *price-taking firm's optimal output rule:* a price-taking firm's profit is maximized by producing the quantity of output at which the marginal cost of the last unit produced is equal to the market price. Having determined the optimal quantity of output, we can go back to the production function and find the optimal number of workers—it is simply the number of workers needed to produce the optimal quantity of output.

There is, however, another way to use marginal analysis to find the number of workers that maximizes a producer's profit. We can go directly to the question of what level of employment maximizes profit. This alternative approach is equivalent to the approach we outlined in the preceding paragraph—it's just a different way of looking at the same thing. But it gives us more insight into the demand for factors as opposed to the supply of goods.

To see how this alternative approach works, let's suppose that George and Martha are considering whether or not to employ an additional worker. The increase in *cost* from employing that additional worker is the wage rate, *W*. The *benefit* to George and Martha from employing that extra worker is the value of the extra output that worker can produce. What is this value? It is the marginal product of labor, *MPL*, multiplied by the price per unit of output, *P*. This amount—the

TABLE 19-1 Employment and Output for George and Martha's Farm

Quantity of labor L (workers)	Quantity of wheat Q (bushels)	Marginal product of labor $MPL = \dfrac{\Delta Q}{\Delta L}$ (bushels per worker)
0	0	
		19
1	19	
		17
2	36	
		15
3	51	
		13
4	64	
		11
5	75	
		9
6	84	
		7
7	91	
		5
8	96	

The **value of the marginal product** of a factor is the value of the additional output generated by employing one more unit of that factor.

The **value of the marginal product curve** of a factor shows how the value of the marginal product of that factor depends on the quantity of the factor employed.

extra value of output that is generated by employing one more unit of labor—is known as the **value of the marginal product** of labor, or *VMPL*:

(19-1) Value of the marginal product of labor = $VMPL = P \times MPL$

So should George and Martha hire that extra worker? The answer is yes if the value of the extra output is more than the cost of the worker—that is, if $VMPL > W$. Otherwise they shouldn't hire that worker.

So the decision to hire labor is a marginal decision, in which the marginal benefit to the producer from hiring an additional worker (*VMPL*) should be compared with the marginal cost to the producer (*W*). And as with any marginal decision, the optimal choice is where marginal benefit is just equal to marginal cost. That is, to maximize profit George and Martha will employ workers up to the point at which, for the last worker employed:

(19-2) $VMPL = W$ *at the profit-maximizing level of employment*

This rule doesn't apply only to labor; it applies to any factor of production. The value of the marginal product of any factor is its marginal product times the price of the good it produces. The general rule is that *a profit-maximizing price-taking producer employs each factor of production up to the point at which the value of the marginal product of the last unit of the factor employed is equal to that factor's price.*

It's important to realize that this rule doesn't conflict with our analysis in Chapters 11 and 12. There we saw that a profit-maximizing producer of a good chooses the level of output at which the price of that good is equal to the marginal cost of production. It's just a different way of looking at the same rule. If the level of output is chosen so that price equals marginal cost, then it is also true that at that output level the value of the marginal product of labor will equal the wage rate.

Now let's look more closely at why choosing the level of employment at which the value of the marginal product of the last worker employed is equal to the wage rate works—and at how it helps us understand factor demand.

Value of the Marginal Product and Factor Demand

Table 19-2 calculates the value of the marginal product of labor on George and Martha's farm, on the assumption that the price of wheat is $20 per bushel. In Figure 19-3 the horizontal axis shows the number of workers employed; the vertical axis measures the value of the marginal product of labor *and* the wage rate. The curve shown is the **value of the marginal product curve** of labor. This curve, like the marginal product of labor curve, slopes downward because of diminishing returns to labor in production. That is, the value of the marginal product of each worker is less than that of the preceding worker, because the marginal product of each worker is less than that of the preceding worker.

We have just seen that to maximize profit, George and Martha must hire workers up to the point at which the wage rate is equal to the value of the marginal product of the last worker employed. Let's use the example to see how this principle really works.

Assume that George and Martha currently employ 3 workers and that workers must be paid the market wage rate of $200. Should they employ an additional worker?

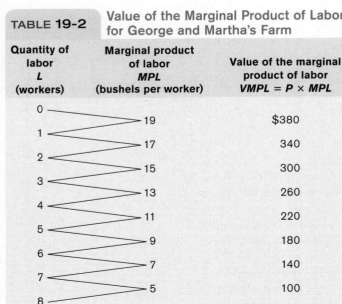

TABLE 19-2 Value of the Marginal Product of Labor for George and Martha's Farm

Quantity of labor L (workers)	Marginal product of labor MPL (bushels per worker)	Value of the marginal product of labor VMPL = P × MPL
0		
	19	$380
1		
	17	340
2		
	15	300
3		
	13	260
4		
	11	220
5		
	9	180
6		
	7	140
7		
	5	100
8		

FIGURE **19-3**   The Value of the Marginal Product Curve

This curve shows how the value of the marginal product of labor depends on the number of workers employed. It slopes downward because of diminishing returns to labor in production. To maximize profit, George and Martha choose the level of employment at which the value of the marginal product of labor is equal to the market wage rate. For example, at a wage rate of $200 the profit-maximizing level of employment is 5 workers, shown by point *A*. The value of the marginal product curve of a factor is the producer's individual demand curve for that factor.

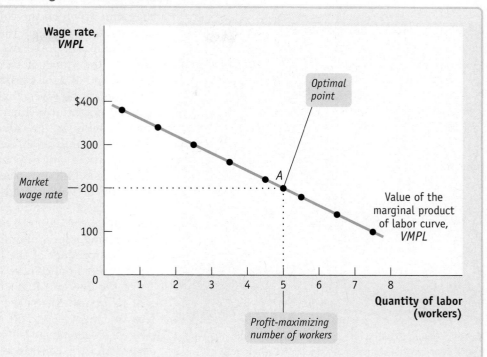

Looking at Table 19-2, we see that if George and Martha currently employ 3 workers, the value of the marginal product of an additional worker is $260. So if they employ an additional worker, they will increase the value of their production by $260 but increase their cost by only $200, yielding an increased profit of $60. In fact, a producer can always increase total profit by employing one more unit of a factor of production as long as the value of the marginal product produced by that unit exceeds its factor price.

Alternatively, suppose that George and Martha employ 8 workers. By reducing the number of workers to 7, they can save $200 in wages. In addition, the value of the marginal product of the last one, the 8th worker, was only $100. So, by reducing employment by one worker, they can increase profit by $200 − $100 = $100. In other words, a producer can always increase total profit by employing one less unit of a factor of production as long as the value of the marginal product produced by that unit is less than the factor price.

Using this method, we can see from Table 19-2 that the profit-maximizing employment level is 5 workers given a wage rate of $200. The value of the marginal product of the 5th worker is $220, so adding the 5th worker results in $20 of additional profit. But George and Martha should not hire more than 5 workers: the value of the marginal product of the 6th worker is only $180, $20 less than the cost of that worker. So, to maximize total profit, George and Martha should employ workers up to but not beyond the point at which the value of the marginal product of the last worker employed is equal to the wage rate.

Now look again at the value of the marginal product curve in Figure 19-3. To determine the profit-maximizing level of employment, we set the value of the marginal product of labor equal to the price of labor—a wage rate of $200 per worker. This means that the profit-maximizing level of employment is at point *A*, corresponding to an employment level of 5 workers. If the wage rate were higher than $200, we would simply move up the curve and reduce the number of workers employed; if the wage rate were lower than $200, we would move down the curve and increase the number of workers employed.

In this example, George and Martha have a small farm in which the potential employment level varies from 0 to 8 workers, and they hire workers up to the point at which the value of the marginal product of the last worker is greater than or equal to the wage rate. (To go beyond this point and hire workers for which the wage exceeds the value of the marginal product would reduce George and Martha's profit.)

Suppose, however, that the firm in question is large and has the potential of hiring many workers. When there are many employees, the value of the marginal product of labor falls only slightly when an additional worker is employed. As a result, there will be some worker whose value of the marginal product almost exactly equals the wage rate. (In keeping with the George and Martha example, this means that some worker generates a value of the marginal product of approximately $200.) In this case, the firm maximizes profit by choosing a level of employment at which the value of the marginal product of the last worker hired *equals* (to a very good approximation) the wage rate.

In the interest of simplicity, we will assume from now on that firms use this rule to determine the profit-maximizing level of employment. *This means that the value of the marginal product of labor curve is the individual producer's labor demand curve.* And, in general, a producer's value of the marginal product curve for any factor of production is that producer's individual demand curve for that factor of production.

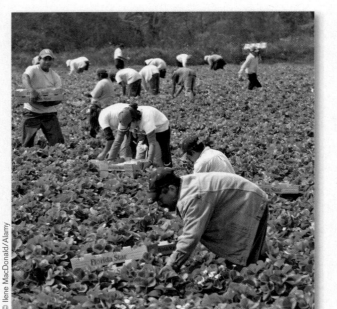

Firms continue to hire workers until the value of the marginal product of the last worker hired equals the wage rate.

Shifts of the Factor Demand Curve

As in the case of ordinary demand curves, it is important to distinguish between movements along the factor demand curve and shifts of the factor demand curve. What causes factor demand curves to shift? There are three main causes:

1. Changes in price of output
2. Changes in supply of other factors
3. Changes in technology

1. Changes in Price of Output Remember that factor demand is derived demand: if the price of the good that is produced with a factor changes, so will the value of the marginal product of the factor. That is, in the case of labor demand, if P changes, $VMPL = P \times MPL$ will change at any given level of employment.

Figure 19-4 illustrates the effects of changes in the price of wheat, assuming that $200 is the current wage rate. Panel (a) shows the effect of an *increase* in the price of wheat. This shifts the value of the marginal product of labor curve upward, because $VMPL$ rises at any given level of employment. If the wage rate remains unchanged at $200, the optimal point moves from point A to point B: the profit-maximizing level of employment rises.

Panel (b) shows the effect of a *decrease* in the price of wheat. This shifts the value of the marginal product of labor curve downward. If the wage rate remains unchanged at $200, the optimal point moves from point A to point C: the profit-maximizing level of employment falls.

2. Changes in Supply of Other Factors Suppose that George and Martha acquire more land to cultivate—say, by clearing a woodland on their property. Each worker now produces more wheat because each one has more land to work with. As a result, the marginal product of labor on the farm rises at any given level of employment. This has the same effect as an increase in the price of wheat,

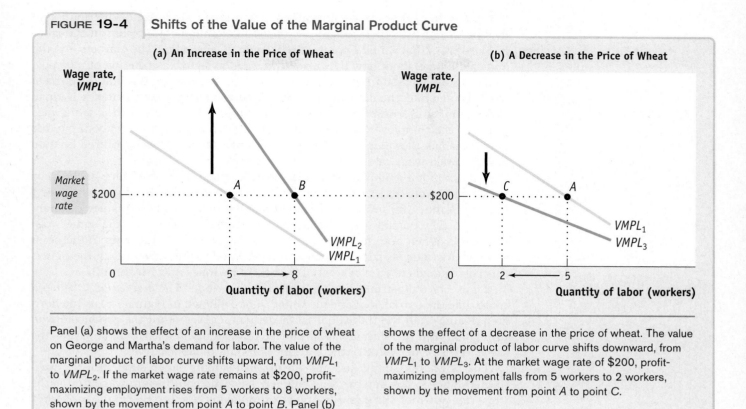

FIGURE **19-4** | Shifts of the Value of the Marginal Product Curve

(a) An Increase in the Price of Wheat

(b) A Decrease in the Price of Wheat

Panel (a) shows the effect of an increase in the price of wheat on George and Martha's demand for labor. The value of the marginal product of labor curve shifts upward, from $VMPL_1$ to $VMPL_2$. If the market wage rate remains at $200, profit-maximizing employment rises from 5 workers to 8 workers, shown by the movement from point *A* to point *B*. Panel (b)

shows the effect of a decrease in the price of wheat. The value of the marginal product of labor curve shifts downward, from $VMPL_1$ to $VMPL_3$. At the market wage rate of $200, profit-maximizing employment falls from 5 workers to 2 workers, shown by the movement from point *A* to point *C*.

which is illustrated in panel (a) of Figure 19-4: the value of the marginal product of labor curve shifts upward, and at any given wage rate the profit-maximizing level of employment rises.

In contrast, suppose George and Martha cultivate less land. This leads to a fall in the marginal product of labor at any given employment level. Each worker produces less wheat because each has less land to work with. As a result, the value of the marginal product of labor curve shifts downward—as in panel (b) of Figure 19-4—and the profit-maximizing level of employment falls.

3. Changes in Technology In general, the effect of technological progress on the demand for any given factor can go either way: improved technology can either increase or reduce the demand for a given factor of production.

How can technological progress reduce factor demand? Consider horses, which were once an important factor of production. The development of substitutes for horse power, such as automobiles and tractors, greatly reduced the demand for horses.

The usual effect of technological progress, however, is to increase the demand for a given factor by raising its productivity. So despite persistent fears that machinery would reduce the demand for labor, over the long run the U.S. economy has seen both large wage increases and large increases in employment. That's because technological progress has raised labor productivity, and as a result increased the demand for labor.

The Marginal Productivity Theory of Income Distribution

We've now seen that each perfectly competitive producer in a perfectly competitive factor market maximizes profit by hiring labor up to the point at which its value of the marginal product is equal to its price—in the case of labor, to the point where

$VMPL = W$. What does this tell us about labor's share in the factor distribution of income? To answer that question, we need to examine equilibrium in the labor market. From that vantage point we will go on to learn about the markets for land and capital and about how they also influence the factor distribution of income.

Let's start by assuming that the labor market is in equilibrium: at the current market wage rate, the number of workers that producers want to employ is equal to the number of workers willing to work. Thus, all employers pay the *same* wage rate, and *each* employer, whatever he or she is producing, employs labor up to the point at which the value of the marginal product of the last worker hired is equal to the market wage rate.

This situation is illustrated in Figure 19-5, which shows the value of the marginal product curves of two producers—Farmer Jones, who produces wheat, and Farmer Smith, who produces corn. Despite the fact that they produce different products, they compete for the same workers and so must pay the same wage rate, $200. When both farmers maximize profit, both hire labor up to the point at which its value of the marginal product is equal to the wage rate. In the figure, this corresponds to employment of 5 workers by Jones and 7 by Smith.

Figure 19-6 illustrates the labor market as a whole. The *market labor demand curve*, like the market demand curve for a good (shown in Figure 3-5), is the horizontal sum of all the individual labor demand curves of all the producers who hire labor. And recall that each producer's individual labor demand curve is the same as his or her value of the marginal product of labor curve.

For now, let's simply assume an upward-sloping labor supply curve; we'll discuss labor supply later in this chapter. Then the equilibrium wage rate is the wage rate at which the quantity of labor supplied is equal to the quantity of labor demanded. In Figure 19-6, this leads to an equilibrium wage rate of W^* and the corresponding equilibrium employment level of L^*. (The equilibrium wage rate is also known as the market wage rate.)

FIGURE 19-5 **All Producers Face the Same Wage Rate**

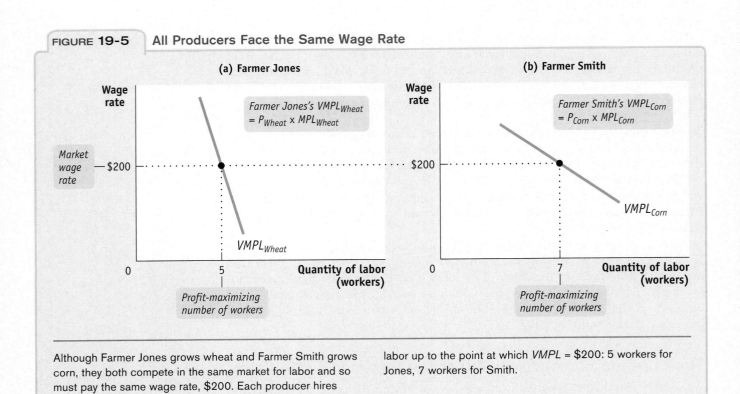

(a) Farmer Jones

Farmer Jones's $VMPL_{Wheat}$ = $P_{Wheat} \times MPL_{Wheat}$

$VMPL_{Wheat}$

Market wage rate — $200

Profit-maximizing number of workers

(b) Farmer Smith

Farmer Smith's $VMPL_{Corn}$ = $P_{Corn} \times MPL_{Corn}$

$VMPL_{Corn}$

$200

Profit-maximizing number of workers

Although Farmer Jones grows wheat and Farmer Smith grows corn, they both compete in the same market for labor and so must pay the same wage rate, $200. Each producer hires labor up to the point at which $VMPL$ = $200: 5 workers for Jones, 7 workers for Smith.

FIGURE **19-6**	Equilibrium in the Labor Market

The market labor demand curve is the horizontal sum of the individual labor demand curves of all producers. Here the equilibrium wage rate is W^*, the equilibrium employment level is L^*, and every producer hires labor up to the point at which $VMPL = W^*$. So labor is paid its equilibrium value of the marginal product, the value of the marginal product of the last worker hired in the labor market as a whole.

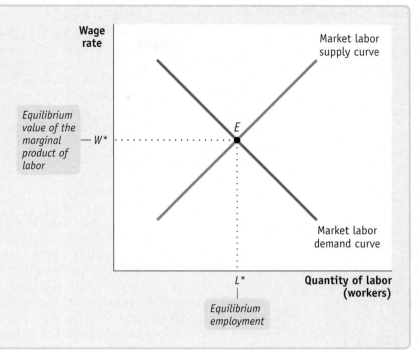

And as we showed in the examples of the farms of George and Martha and of Farmer Jones and Farmer Smith (where the equilibrium wage rate is $200), each farm hires labor up to the point at which the value of the marginal product of labor is equal to the equilibrium wage rate. Therefore, in equilibrium, the value of the marginal product of labor is the same for all employers. So the equilibrium (or market) wage rate is equal to the **equilibrium value of the marginal product** of labor—the additional value produced by the last unit of labor employed in the labor market as a whole. It doesn't matter where that additional unit is employed, since equilibrium $VMPL$ is the same for all producers.

What we have just learned, then, is that the market wage rate is equal to the equilibrium value of the marginal product of labor. And the same is true of each factor of production: in a perfectly competitive market economy, the market price of each factor is equal to its equilibrium value of the marginal product. Let's examine the markets for land and (physical) capital now. (From this point on, we'll refer to physical capital as simply "capital.")

> The **equilibrium value of the marginal product** of a factor is the additional value produced by the last unit of that factor employed in the factor market as a whole.

The Markets for Land and Capital

If we maintain the assumption that the markets for goods and services are perfectly competitive, the result that we derived for the labor market also applies to other factors of production. Suppose, for example, that a farmer is considering whether to rent an additional acre of land for the next year. He or she will compare the cost of renting that acre with the value of the additional output generated by employing an additional acre—the value of the marginal product of an acre of land. To maximize profit, the farmer must employ land up to the point at which the value of the marginal product of an acre of land is equal to the rental rate per acre.

What if the farmer already owns the land? We already saw the answer in Chapter 9, which dealt with economic decisions: even if you own land, there is an implicit cost—the opportunity cost—of using it for a given activity, because it could be used for something else, such as renting it out to other farmers at the

The **rental rate** of either land or capital is the cost, explicit or implicit, of using a unit of that asset for a given period of time.

market rental rate. So a profit-maximizing producer employs additional acres of land up to the point at which the cost of the last acre employed, explicit or implicit, is equal to the value of the marginal product of that acre.

The same is true for capital. The explicit or implicit cost of using a unit of land or capital for a set period of time is called its **rental rate.** In general, a unit of land or capital is employed up to the point at which that unit's value of the marginal product is equal to its rental rate over that time period. How are the rental rates for land and capital determined? By the equilibria in the land market and the capital market, of course. Figure 19-7 illustrates those outcomes.

Panel (a) shows the equilibrium in the market for land. Summing over the individual demand curves for land of all producers gives us the market demand curve for land. Due to diminishing returns, the demand curve slopes downward, like the demand curve for labor. As we have drawn it, the supply curve of land is relatively steep and therefore relatively inelastic. This reflects the fact that finding new supplies of land for production is typically difficult and expensive—for example, creating new farmland through expensive irrigation. The equilibrium rental rate for land, R^*_{Land}, and the equilibrium quantity of land employed in production, Q^*_{Land}, are given by the intersection of the two curves.

Panel (b) shows the equilibrium in the market for capital. In contrast to the supply curve for land, the supply curve for capital is relatively elastic. That's because the supply of capital is relatively responsive to price: capital is paid for with funds that come from the savings of investors, and the amount of savings that investors make available is relatively responsive to the rental rate for capital. The equilibrium rental rate for capital, $R^*_{Capital}$, and the equilibrium quantity of capital employed in production, $Q^*_{Capital}$, are given by the intersection of the two curves.

FIGURE 19-7 | **Equilibria in the Land and Capital Markets**

Panel (a) illustrates equilibrium in the market for land; panel (b) illustrates equilibrium in the market for capital. The supply curve for land is relatively steep, reflecting the high cost of increasing the quantity of productive land. The supply curve for capital, in contrast, is relatively flat, due to the relatively high responsiveness of savings to changes in the rental rate for capital. The equilibrium rental rates for land and capital, as well as the equilibrium quantities transacted, are given by the intersections of the demand and supply curves. In a competitive land market, each unit of land will be paid the equilibrium value of the marginal product of land, R^*_{Land}. Likewise, in a competitive capital market, each unit of capital will be paid the equilibrium value of the marginal product of capital, $R^*_{Capital}$.

The Marginal Productivity Theory of Income Distribution

So we have learned that when the markets for goods and services and the factor markets are perfectly competitive, a factor of production will be employed up to the point at which its value of the marginal product is equal to its market equilibrium price. That is, it will be paid its equilibrium value of the marginal product. What does this say about the factor distribution of income? It leads us to the **marginal productivity theory of income distribution,** which says that each factor is paid the value of the output generated by the last unit of that factor employed in the factor market as a whole—its equilibrium value of the marginal product.

To understand why the marginal productivity theory of income distribution is important, look back at Figure 19-1, which shows the factor distribution of income in the United States, and ask yourself this question: who or what decided that labor would get 66% of total U.S. income? Why not 90% or 50%?

The answer, according to the marginal productivity theory of income distribution, is that the division of income among the economy's factors of production isn't arbitrary: it is determined by each factor's marginal productivity at the economy's equilibrium. The wage rate earned by *all* workers in the economy is equal to the increase in the value of output generated by the last worker employed in the economy-wide labor market.

Here we have assumed that all workers are of the same ability. (Similarly, we've assumed that all units of land and capital are equally productive.) But in reality workers differ considerably in ability.

Rather than thinking of one labor market for all workers in the economy, we can instead think of different markets for different types of workers, where workers are of equivalent ability within each market. For example, the market for computer programmers is different from the market for pastry chefs.

In the market for computer programmers, all participants are assumed to have equal ability; likewise for the market for pastry chefs. In this scenario, the marginal productivity theory of income distribution still holds. That is, when the labor market for computer programmers is in equilibrium, the wage rate earned by all computer programmers is equal to the market's equilibrium value of the marginal product—the value of the marginal product of the last computer programmer hired in that market.

> According to the **marginal productivity theory of income distribution,** every factor of production is paid its equilibrium value of the marginal product.

ECONOMICS ▶ in Action

Help Wanted!

Hamill Manufacturing of Pennsylvania makes precision components for military helicopters and nuclear submarines. Their highly skilled senior machinists are well paid compared to other workers in manufacturing, earning nearly $70,000 in 2013, excluding benefits. Like most skilled machinists in the United States, Hamill's machinists are very productive: according to the U.S. Census Annual Survey of Manufacturers, in 2010 the average skilled machinist generated approximately $137,000 in value added.

But there is a $67,000 difference between the salary paid to Hamill machinists and the value added they generate. Does this mean that the marginal productivity theory of income distribution doesn't hold? Doesn't the theory imply that machinists should be paid $137,000, the average value added that each one generates?

The marginal productivity theory of income distribution holds for skilled machinists at Hamill Manufacturing.

The answer is no, for two reasons. First, the $137,000 figure is averaged over *all machinists currently employed.* The theory says that machinists will be paid the value of the marginal product of the *last machinist hired,* and due to diminishing returns to labor, that value will be lower than the average over all machinists currently employed. Second, a worker's equilibrium wage rate includes other costs, such as employee benefits, that have to be added to the $70,000 salary. The marginal productivity theory of income distribution says that workers are paid a wage rate, *including all benefits,* equal to the value of the marginal product.

You can see all these costs are present at Hamill. There the machinists have good benefits and job security, which add to their salary. Including these benefits, machinists' total compensation will be equal to the value of the marginal product of the last machinist employed.

In Hamill's case, there is yet another factor that explains the $67,000 gap: there are not enough machinists at the current wage rate. Although the company increased the number of employees from 85 in 2004 to 124 in 2013, they would like to hire more. Why doesn't Hamill raise its wages in order to attract more skilled machinists? The problem is that the work they do is so specialized that it is hard to hire from the outside, even when the company raises wages as an inducement. To address this problem, Hamill has spent a significant amount of money training each new hire, approximately $130,000 plus the cost of benefits per trainee. (Unfortunately, training new hires has left Hamill vulnerable to *poaching,* which occurs when other companies that haven't incurred the cost of training lure employees away by offering higher wages.) In the end, it does appear that the marginal productivity theory of income distribution holds.

Check Your Understanding 19-2

1. In the following cases, state the direction of the shift of the demand curve for labor and what will happen, other things equal, to the market equilibrium wage rate and quantity of labor employed as a result.
   a. Service industries, such as retailing and banking, experience an increase in demand. These industries use relatively more labor than nonservice industries.
   b. Due to overfishing, there is a fall in the amount of fish caught per day by commercial fishers; this decrease affects their demand for workers.
2. Explain the following statement: "When firms in different industries all compete for the same workers, then the value of the marginal product of the last worker hired will be equal across all firms regardless of whether they are in different industries."

Solutions appear at back of book.

Is the Marginal Productivity Theory of Income Distribution Really True?

Although the marginal productivity theory of income distribution is a well-established part of economic theory, closely linked to the analysis of markets in general, it is a source of some controversy. There are two main objections to it.

First, in the real world we see large disparities in income between factors of production that, in the eyes of some observers, should receive the same payment. Perhaps the most conspicuous examples in the United States are the large differences in the average wages between women and men and among various racial and ethnic groups. Do these wage differences really reflect differences in marginal productivity, or is something else going on?

Second, many people wrongly believe that the marginal productivity theory of income distribution gives a *moral* justification for the distribution of income, implying that the existing distribution is fair and appropriate. This misconception sometimes leads other people, who believe that the current distribution of income is unfair, to reject marginal productivity theory.

To address these controversies, we'll start by looking at income disparities across gender and ethnic groups. Then we'll ask what factors might account for these disparities and whether these explanations are consistent with the marginal productivity theory of income distribution.

Wage Disparities in Practice

Wage rates in the United States cover a very wide range. In 2013, hundreds of thousands of workers received the legal federal minimum of $7.25 per hour. At the other extreme, the chief executives of several companies were paid more than $100 million, which works out to $20,000 per hour even if they worked 100-hour weeks. Even leaving out these extremes, there is a huge range of wage rates. Are people really that different in their marginal productivities?

A particular source of concern is the existence of systematic wage differences across gender and ethnicity. Figure 19-8 compares annual median earnings in 2013 of workers age 25 or older classified by gender and ethnicity. As a group, White males had the highest earnings. Other data show that women (averaging across all ethnicities) earned only about 72% as much; African-American workers (male and female combined), only 68% as much; Hispanic workers (again, male and female combined), only 57% as much.

We are a nation founded on the belief that all men are created equal—and if the Constitution were rewritten today, we would say that *all people* are created equal. So why do they receive such unequal pay? Let's start with the marginal productivity explanations, then look at other influences.

FIGURE **19-8**   Median Earnings by Gender and Ethnicity, 2013

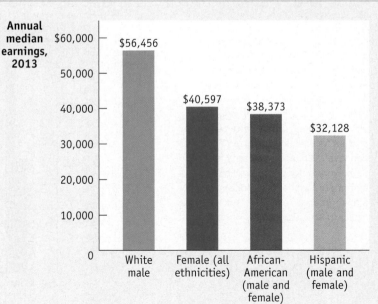

The U.S. labor market continues to show large differences across workers according to gender and ethnicity. Women are paid substantially less than men; African-American and Hispanic workers are paid substantially less than White male workers.
Source: U.S. Census Bureau.

Compensating differentials are wage differences across jobs that reflect the fact that some jobs are less pleasant than others.

Marginal Productivity and Wage Inequality

A large part of the observed inequality in wages can be explained by considerations that are consistent with the marginal productivity theory of income distribution. In particular, there are three well-understood sources of wage differences across occupations and individuals.

First is the existence of **compensating differentials**: across different types of jobs, wages are often higher or lower depending on how attractive or unattractive the job is. Workers with unpleasant or dangerous jobs demand a higher wage in comparison to workers with jobs that require the same skill and effort but lack the unpleasant or dangerous qualities. For example, truckers who haul hazardous loads are paid more than truckers who haul non-hazardous loads. But for any *given* job, the marginal productivity theory of income distribution generally holds true. For example, hazardous-load truckers are paid a wage equal to the equilibrium value of the marginal product of the last person employed in the labor market for hazardous-load truckers.

A second reason for wage inequality that is clearly consistent with marginal productivity theory is differences in talent. People differ in their abilities: a higher-ability person, by producing a better product that commands a higher price compared to a lower-ability person, generates a higher value of the marginal product. And these differences in the value of the marginal product translate into differences in earning potential. We all know that this is true in sports: practice is important, but 99.99% (at least) of the population just doesn't have what it takes to throw passes like Tom Brady or hit tennis balls like Roger Federer. The same is true, though less obvious, in other fields of endeavor.

A third and very important reason for wage differences is differences in the quantity of *human capital*. Recall that human capital—education and training—is at least as important in the modern economy as physical capital in the form of buildings and machines. Different people "embody" quite different quantities of human capital, and a person with a higher quantity of human capital typically generates a higher value of the marginal product by producing a product that commands a higher price. So differences in human capital account for substantial differences in wages. People with high levels of human capital, such as skilled surgeons or engineers, generally receive high wages. In 2013, surgeons earned an average of $233,150.

FIGURE **19-9** | Earnings Differentials by Education, Gender, and Ethnicity, 2013

It is clear that, regardless of gender or ethnicity, education pays: those with a high school diploma earn more than those without one, and those with a college degree earn substantially more than those with only a high school diploma. Other patterns are evident as well: for any given education level, White males earn more than every other group, and males earn more than females for any given ethnic group.

Source: U.S. Census Bureau.

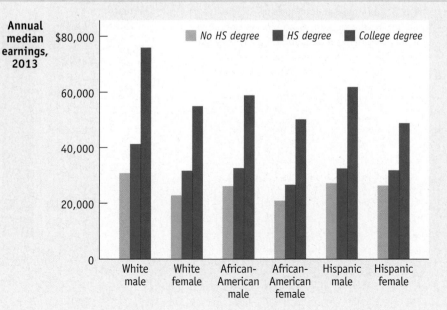

The most direct way to see the effect of human capital on wages is to look at the relationship between educational levels and earnings. Figure 19-9 shows earnings differentials by gender, ethnicity, and three educational levels for people age 25 or older in 2013. As you can see, regardless of gender or ethnicity, higher education is associated with higher median earnings. For example, in 2013 White females with 9 to 12 years of schooling but without a high school diploma had median earnings 28% less than those with a high school diploma and 65% less than those with a college degree—and similar patterns exist for the other five groups.

Because even now men typically have had more years of education than women and Whites more years than non-Whites, differences in level of education are part of the explanation for the earnings differences shown in Figure 19-8.

It's important to realize that formal education is not the only source of human capital; on-the-job-training and work experience also generate human capital. In fact, there are other factors that also influence wage differences. A good illustration of these factors is found in research on the *gender-wage gap*, the persistent difference in the earnings of men compared to women. In the U.S. labor market, researchers have found that the gender gap is largely explained by differences in:

- human capital (women tend to have lower levels of it)
- choice of occupation (women tend to choose occupations such as nursing and teaching in which they earn less)
- career interruptions (women move in and out of labor force more frequently)
- part-time status (women are more likely to work part-time instead of full-time)
- overtime status (women are less likely to work overtime)

For example, in a U.S. Department of Labor study using recent census data, the gender-wage gap fell from 20.4% to 5% once these five factors were accounted for. Moreover, over the past 30 years even the unadjusted gender-wage gap has fallen significantly, from 36.5% in 1979 to 16.5% in 2011, as women have begun to close in on men in terms of these five factors.

But it's also important to emphasize that earnings differences arising from these factors are not necessarily "fair." When women do most of the work caring for children, they will inevitably have more career interruptions or need to work part-time instead of full-time. Similarly, a society where non-White children typically receive a poor education because they live in underfunded school districts, then go on to earn low wages because they are poorly educated, may have labor markets that are well described by marginal productivity theory (and would be consistent with the earnings differentials across ethnic groups and between the genders shown in Figure 19-8). Yet many people would still consider the resulting distribution of income unfair.

Still, many observers think that actual wage differentials cannot be entirely explained by compensating differentials, differences in talent, differences in human capital, or differences in job status. They believe that market power, *efficiency wages,* and discrimination also play an important role. We will examine these forces next.

Market Power

The marginal productivity theory of income distribution is based on the assumption that factor markets are perfectly competitive. In such markets we can expect workers to be paid the equilibrium value of their marginal product, regardless of who they are. But how valid is this assumption?

We studied markets that are *not* perfectly competitive in Chapters 13, 14, and 15; now let's touch briefly on the ways in which labor markets may deviate from the competitive assumption.

One undoubted source of differences in wages between otherwise similar workers is the role of **unions**—organizations that try to raise wages and improve

Unions are organizations of workers that try to raise wages and improve working conditions for their members by bargaining collectively with employers.

According to the **efficiency-wage model,** some employers pay an above-equilibrium wage as an incentive for better performance.

working conditions for their members. Labor unions, when they are successful, replace one-on-one wage deals between workers and employers with collective bargaining, in which the employer must negotiate wages with union representatives. Without question, this leads to higher wages for those workers who are represented by unions. In 2013 the median weekly earnings of union members in the United States were $966, compared with $797 for workers not represented by unions—more than a 20% difference.

How much does collective action, either by workers or by employers, affect wages in the modern United States? Several decades ago, when around 30% of American workers were union members, unions probably had a significant upward effect on wages. Today, however, most economists think unions exert a fairly minor influence.

In 2013, less than 7% of the employees of private businesses were represented by unions. Just as workers can sometimes organize to extract higher wages than they would otherwise receive, employers can sometimes organize to pay *lower* wages than would result from competition. For example, health care workers— doctors, nurses, and so on—sometimes argue that health maintenance organizations (HMOs) are engaged in a collective effort to hold down their wages. Yet the sheer size of the U.S. labor market is enormous and the ease with which most workers can move in search of higher-paying jobs probably means that concerted efforts to hold wages below the unrestrained market equilibrium level rarely occur and even more rarely succeed.

Efficiency Wages

A second source of wage inequality is the phenomenon of *efficiency wages*—a type of incentive scheme used by employers to motivate workers to work hard and to reduce worker turnover. Suppose a worker performs a job that is extremely important but that the employer can observe how well the job is being performed only at infrequent intervals—say, serving as a caregiver for the employer's child. Then it often makes sense for the employer to pay more than the worker could earn in an alternative job—that is, more than the equilibrium wage. Why? Because earning a premium makes losing this job and having to take the alternative job quite costly for the worker.

So a worker who happens to be observed performing poorly and is therefore fired is now worse off for having to accept a lower-paying job. The threat of losing a job that pays a premium motivates the worker to perform well and avoid being fired. Likewise, paying a premium also reduces worker turnover—the frequency with which an employee leaves a job voluntarily. Despite the fact that it may take no more effort and skill to be a child's caregiver than to be an office worker, efficiency wages show why it often makes economic sense for a parent to pay a caregiver more than the equilibrium wage of an office worker.

The **efficiency-wage model** explains why we might observe wages offered above their equilibrium level. Like the price floors we studied in Chapter 5— and, in particular, much like the minimum wage—this phenomenon leads to a surplus of labor in labor markets that are characterized by the efficiency-wage model. This surplus of labor translates into unemployment—some workers are actively searching for a high-paying efficiency-wage job but are unable to get one, and other more fortunate but no more deserving workers are able to acquire one.

As a result, two workers with exactly the same profile—the same skills and same job history—may earn unequal wages: the worker who is lucky enough to get an efficiency-wage job earns more than the worker who gets a standard job (or who remains unemployed while searching for a higher-paying job).

Efficiency wages are a response to a type of market failure that arises when some employees are able to hide the fact that they don't always perform as well as they should. As a result, employers use nonequilibrium wages to motivate their employees, leading to an inefficient outcome.

Discrimination

It is a real and ugly fact that throughout history there has been discrimination against workers who are considered to be of the wrong race, ethnicity, gender, or other characteristics. How does this fit into our economic models?

The main insight economic analysis offers is that discrimination is *not* a natural consequence of market competition. On the contrary, market forces tend to work against discrimination. To see why, consider the incentives that would exist if social convention dictated that women be paid, say, 30% less than men with equivalent qualifications and experience. A company whose management was itself unbiased would then be able to reduce its costs by hiring women rather than men—and such companies would have an advantage over other companies that hired men despite their higher cost. The result would be to create an excess demand for female workers, which would tend to drive up their wages.

But if market competition works against discrimination, how is it that so much discrimination has taken place? The answer is twofold. First, when

FOR INQUIRING MINDS | How Labor Works the German Way

Germany is home to some of the finest manufacturing firms in the world. From the automotive sector to beer brewing, and from home appliances to chemical engineering and pharmaceuticals, German products are considered among the highest quality available. And unlike in the United States, blue-collar jobs—those that don't require college degrees—pay high enough wages that they are still prized. If you ask Germans what accounts for their ability to combine a highly successful manufacturing sector with well-paying blue-collar jobs, two overlapping institutions will top their lists: Germany's works councils system and their apprenticeship system.

Enshrined in the German constitution, works councils exist in every factory to encourage management and employees to work together on issues like work conditions, productivity, and wages, with the goal of discouraging costly conflict. Workers are given seats in supervisory or management organizations such as a company's board of directors. This collaborative environment, in turn, supports higher levels of unionization within German manufacturing. As a result,

German unions are more successful at raising the wages of their members.

But what allows German manufacturing to compete successfully while paying higher wages? One explanation is the German apprentice system. For example, in 2012, the average hourly wage of a German autoworker was $58.82 compared to $45.34 (at the high end) for an American autoworker, and $14.50 (at the low end) in newly opened automotive plants in the United States. Promoted and accredited by the German government, apprenticeship programs provide hands-on training to young workers in specific skills from automotive electronics to hairdressing. About 60% of German high school students train in an apprenticeship program, graduating with a formal certificate, and often landing a permanent job at the company where they were trained. As a result, the typical German manufacturing worker starts a job with higher levels of job-specific human capital than his or her American counterpart.

So integral is the apprenticeship system to the success of German manufacturing that German companies have

Thanks to the German apprenticeship system, young manufacturing workers start with higher levels of job-specific human capital than their American counterparts.

been replicating it at their plants in the United States. In South Carolina, where BMW and Tognum, a German engine maker, have recently located, apprenticeship programs have been created in partnership with local and state governments to assure that young workers are trained in the skills that the companies need. And, needless to say, the apprentices welcome such training and the well-paying jobs that it will bring. ■

labor markets don't work well, employers may have the ability to discriminate without hurting their profits. For example, market interferences (such as unions or minimum-wage laws) or market failures (such as efficiency wages) can lead to wages that are above their equilibrium levels. In these cases, there are more job applicants than there are jobs, leaving employers free to discriminate among applicants. In 2011, with unemployment over 9%, the Equal Employment Opportunity Commission, the federal agency tasked with investigating employment discrimination charges, reported that the complaints from workers and job-seekers had hit an all-time high, the most logged in the agency's 46-year history.

In research published in the *American Economic Review*, two economists, Marianne Bertrand and Sendhil Mullainathan, documented discrimination in hiring by sending fictitious résumés to prospective employers on a random basis. Applicants with "White-sounding" names such as Emily Walsh were 50% more likely to be contacted than applicants with "African-American-sounding" names such as Lakisha Washington. Also, applicants with White-sounding names and good credentials were much more likely to be contacted than those without such credentials. By contrast, potential employers seemed to ignore the credentials of applicants with African-American-sounding names.

Second, discrimination has sometimes been institutionalized in government policy. This institutionalization of discrimination has made it easier to maintain it against market pressure, and historically it is the form that discrimination has typically taken. For example, at one time in the United States, African-Americans were barred from attending "Whites-only" public schools and universities in many parts of the country and forced to attend inferior schools.

Although market competition tends to work against *current* discrimination, it is not a remedy for past discrimination, which typically has had an impact on the education and experience of its victims and thereby reduces their income.

So Does Marginal Productivity Theory Work?

The main conclusion you should draw from this discussion is that the marginal productivity theory of income distribution is not a perfect description of how factor incomes are determined but that it works pretty well. The deviations are important. But, by and large, in a modern economy with well-functioning labor markets, factors of production are paid the equilibrium value of the marginal product—the value of the marginal product of the last unit employed in the market as a whole.

It's important to emphasize, once again, that this does not mean that the factor distribution of income is morally justified.

ECONOMICS ▶ in Action

Marginal Productivity and the "1%"

In the fall of 2011, there were widespread public demonstrations in the United States and in a number of other countries against the growing inequality of personal income. U.S. protestors, known as the Occupy Wall Street movement, adopted the slogan "We are the 99%" to emphasize the fact that the incomes of the top 1% of the population had grown much faster than those of most Americans.

Indeed, just as the protest movement was gathering strength, the Congressional Budget Office released a study on income inequality. The CBO found that, between 1979 and 2010, the income of the average household headed by a worker with a high school degree fell by 2.9%, while the income of the average household headed by a worker with an advanced degree rose by 27.6%. But the average income of the top 1% of households had risen 177.5%.

Why have the richest Americans been pulling away from the rest? The short answer is that the causes are a source of considerable dispute and continuing research. One thing is clear, however: this aspect of growing inequality can't be explained simply in terms of the growing demand for highly educated labor. In this chapter's opening story, we pointed out that there has been a growing wage premium for workers with advanced degrees. Yet despite this growing premium, as Figure 19-10 shows, such workers have seen only a fraction of the gains going to the top 1%.

This does not prove that the top 1% aren't "earning" their incomes. It does show, however, that whatever the explanation for their huge gains, it's not education.

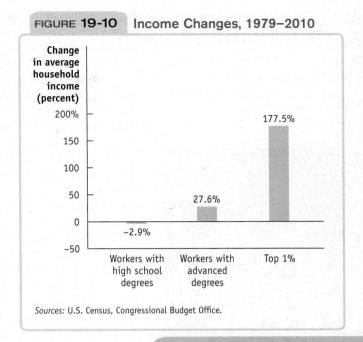

FIGURE 19-10   Income Changes, 1979–2010

Sources: U.S. Census, Congressional Budget Office.

Check Your Understanding   19-3

1. Assess each of the following statements. Do you think they are true, false, or ambiguous? Explain.
   a. The marginal productivity theory of income distribution is inconsistent with the presence of income disparities associated with gender, race, or ethnicity.
   b. Companies that engage in workplace discrimination but whose competitors do not are likely to have lower profits as a result of their actions.
   c. Workers who are paid less because they have less experience are not the victims of discrimination.

Solutions appear at back of book.

The Supply of Labor

Up to this point we have focused on the demand for factors, which determines the quantities demanded of labor, capital, or land by producers as a function of their factor prices. What about the supply of factors?

In this section we focus exclusively on the supply of labor. We do this for two reasons. First, in the modern U.S. economy, labor is the most important factor of production, accounting for most of factor income. Second, as we'll see, labor supply is the area in which factor markets look most different from markets for goods and services.

Work versus Leisure

In the labor market, the roles of firms and households are the reverse of what they are in markets for goods and services. A good such as wheat is supplied by firms and demanded by households; labor, though, is demanded by firms and supplied by households. How do people decide how much labor to supply?

As a practical matter, most people have limited control over their work hours: either you take a job that involves working a set number of hours per week, or you

▼ Quick Review

- Existing large disparities in wages both among individuals and across groups lead some to question the marginal productivity theory of income distribution.

- **Compensating differentials,** as well as differences in the values of the marginal products of workers that arise from differences in talent, job experience, job status, and human capital, account for some wage disparities.

- Market power, in the form of **unions** or collective action by employers, as well as the **efficiency-wage model,** in which employers pay an above-equilibrium wage to induce better performance, also explain how some wage disparities arise.

- Discrimination has historically been a major factor in wage disparities. Market competition tends to work against discrimination. But discrimination can leave a long-lasting legacy of diminished human capital acquisition.

Decisions about labor supply result from decisions about **time allocation:** how many hours to spend on different activities.

Leisure is time available for purposes other than earning money to buy marketed goods.

Every worker faces a trade-off between leisure and work.

don't get the job at all. To understand the logic of labor supply, however, it helps to put realism to one side for a bit and imagine an individual who can choose to work as many or as few hours as he or she likes.

Why wouldn't such an individual work as many hours as possible? Because workers are human beings, too, and have other uses for their time. An hour spent on the job is an hour not spent on other, presumably more pleasant, activities. So the decision about how much labor to supply involves making a decision about **time allocation**—how many hours to spend on different activities.

By working, people earn income that they can use to buy goods. The more hours an individual works, the more goods he or she can afford to buy. But this increased purchasing power comes at the expense of a reduction in **leisure,** the time spent not working. (Leisure doesn't necessarily mean time spent goofing off. It could mean time spent with one's family, pursuing hobbies, exercising, and so on.) And though purchased goods yield utility, so does leisure. Indeed, we can think of leisure itself as a normal good, which most people would like to consume more of as their incomes increase.

How does a rational individual decide how much leisure to consume? By making a marginal comparison, of course. In analyzing consumer choice, we asked how a utility-maximizing consumer uses a marginal *dollar.* In analyzing labor supply, we ask how an individual uses a marginal *hour.*

Consider Clive, an individual who likes both leisure and the goods money can buy. Suppose that his wage rate is $10 per hour. In deciding how many hours he wants to work, he must compare the marginal utility of an additional hour of leisure with the additional utility he gets from $10 worth of goods. If $10 worth of goods adds more to his total utility than an additional hour of leisure, he can increase his total utility by giving up an hour of leisure in order to work an additional hour. If an extra hour of leisure adds more to his total utility than $10 worth of goods, he can increase his total utility by working one fewer hour in order to gain an hour of leisure.

At Clive's optimal labor supply choice, then, his marginal utility of one hour of leisure is equal to the marginal utility he gets from the goods that his hourly wage can purchase. This is very similar to the *optimal consumption rule* we encountered in Chapter 10, except that it is a rule about time rather than money.

Our next step is to ask how Clive's decision about time allocation is affected when his wage rate changes.

Wages and Labor Supply

Suppose that Clive's wage rate doubles, from $10 to $20 per hour. How will he change his time allocation?

You could argue that Clive will work longer hours, because his incentive to work has increased: by giving up an hour of leisure, he can now gain twice as much money as before. But you could equally well argue that he will work less, because he doesn't need to work as many hours to generate the income to pay for the goods he wants.

As these opposing arguments suggest, the quantity of labor Clive supplies can either rise or fall when his wage rate rises. To understand why, let's recall the distinction between *substitution effects* and *income effects* that we learned in Chapter 10 and its appendix. We saw there that a price change affects consumer choice in two ways: by changing the opportunity cost of a good in terms of other goods (the substitution effect) and by making the consumer richer or poorer (the income effect).

Now think about how a rise in Clive's wage rate affects his demand for leisure. The opportunity cost of leisure—the amount of money he gives up by taking an hour off instead of working—rises. That substitution effect gives him an incentive, other things equal, to consume *less* leisure and work *longer* hours. Conversely, a higher wage rate makes Clive richer—and this income effect leads him, other things equal, to want to consume *more* leisure and work *fewer* hours, because leisure is a normal good.

So in the case of labor supply, the substitution effect and the income effect work in opposite directions. If the substitution effect is so powerful that it dominates the income effect, an increase in Clive's wage rate leads him to supply *more* hours of labor. If the income effect is so powerful that it dominates the substitution effect, an increase in the wage rate leads him to supply *fewer* hours of labor.

We see, then, that the **individual labor supply curve**—the relationship between the wage rate and the number of hours of labor supplied by an individual worker—does not necessarily slope upward. If the income effect dominates, a higher wage rate will reduce the quantity of labor supplied.

Figure 19-11 illustrates the two possibilities for labor supply. If the substitution effect dominates the income effect, the individual labor supply curve slopes upward; panel (a) shows an increase in the wage rate from $10 to $20 per hour leading to a *rise* in the number of hours worked from 40 to 50. However, if the income effect dominates, the quantity of labor supplied goes down when the wage rate increases. Panel (b) shows the same rise in the wage rate leading to a *fall* in the number of hours worked from 40 to 30. (Economists refer to an individual labor supply curve that contains both upward-sloping and downward-sloping segments as a "backward-bending labor supply curve"—a concept that we analyze in detail in this chapter's appendix.)

Is a negative response of the quantity of labor supplied to the wage rate a real possibility? Yes: many labor economists believe that income effects on the supply of labor may be somewhat stronger than substitution effects. The most compelling piece of evidence for this belief comes from Americans' increasing consumption of leisure over the past century. At the end of the nineteenth

The **individual labor supply curve** shows how the quantity of labor supplied by an individual depends on that individual's wage rate.

FIGURE **19-11**   The Individual Labor Supply Curve

When the substitution effect of a wage increase dominates the income effect, the individual labor supply curve slopes upward, as in panel (a). Here a rise in the wage rate from $10 to $20 per hour increases the number of hours worked from 40 to 50. But when the income effect of a wage increase dominates the substitution effect, the individual labor supply curve slopes downward, as in panel (b). Here the same rise in the wage rate reduces the number of hours worked from 40 to 30. The individual labor supply curve shows how the quantity of labor supplied by an individual depends on that individual's wage rate.

FOR INQUIRING MINDS | Why You Can't Find a Cab When It's Raining

Everyone says that you can't find a taxi in New York when you really need one—say, when it's raining. Could it be because everyone else is trying to get a taxi at the same time? According to a study published in the *Quarterly Journal of Economics*, it's more than that: cab drivers actually go home early when it's raining because they are buying more leisure with the higher hourly wage rate that the rain brings.

When it's raining, drivers get more fares and therefore earn more per hour. But it seems that the income effect of this higher wage rate outweighs the substitution effect.

This behavior led the authors of the study to question drivers' rationality. They point out that if taxi drivers thought in terms of the long run, they would realize that rainy days and nice days tend to average out and that their high earnings on a rainy day don't really affect their long-run income very much.

Indeed, experienced drivers (who have probably figured this out) are less likely than inexperienced drivers to go home early on a rainy day. But leaving such issues to one side, the study does seem to show clear evidence of a labor supply curve that slopes downward instead of upward, thanks to income effects.

These findings give us a deeper understanding of the economics behind the spectacular rise of Uber, the company that matches passengers with available drivers for hire via a smartphone app. The fact that taxi drivers tend to head home just when people really need a ride has provided an opportunity for Uber: by allowing its drivers to charge more when demand shifts outward (a practice called *surge pricing*), Uber puts more drivers on the road despite the income effects on taxi drivers' labor supply curves. ∎

century, wages adjusted for inflation were only about one-eighth what they are today; the typical workweek was 70 hours, and very few workers retired at age 65. Today the typical workweek is less than 40 hours, and most people retire at age 65 or earlier. So it seems that Americans have chosen to take advantage of higher wages in part by consuming more leisure.

Shifts of the Labor Supply Curve

Now that we have examined how income and substitution effects shape the individual labor supply curve, we can turn to the market labor supply curve. In any labor market, the market supply curve is the horizontal sum of the individual labor supply curves of all workers in that market. A change in any factor *other than the wage* that alters workers' willingness to supply labor causes a shift of the labor supply curve. A variety of factors can lead to such shifts, including changes in preferences and social norms, changes in population, changes in opportunities, and changes in wealth.

Changes in Preferences and Social Norms Changes in preferences and social norms can lead workers to increase or decrease their willingness to work at any given wage. A striking example of this phenomenon is the large increase in the number of employed women—particularly married employed women—that has occurred in the United States since the 1960s. Until that time, women who could afford to largely avoided working outside the home. Changes in preferences and norms in post–World War II America (helped along by the invention of labor-saving home appliances such as washing machines, increasing urbanization of the population, and higher female education levels) have induced large numbers of American women to join the workforce—a phenomenon often repeated in other countries that experience similar social and technological forces.

Changes in Population Changes in the population size generally lead to shifts of the labor supply curve. A larger population tends to shift the labor supply curve rightward as more workers are available at any given wage; a smaller population tends to shift the labor supply curve leftward. From 1990 to 2008, the U.S. labor force has grown approximately 1% per year, generated by immigration and a relatively high birth rate. As a result, from 1990 to 2008 the U.S. labor market had a rightward-shifting labor supply curve. However, while the population continued to grow after 2008, the size of the labor force began to shrink beginning

GLOBAL COMPARISION | The Overworked American?

Americans today may work less than they did a hundred years ago, but they still work more than workers in any other industrialized country.

This figure compares average annual hours worked in the United States with those worked in other industrialized countries. The differences result from a combination of Americans' longer workweeks and shorter vacations. For example, the great majority of full-time American workers put in at least 40 hours per week. Until recently, however, a government mandate limited most French workers to a 35-hour workweek; collective bargaining has achieved a similar reduction in the workweek for many German workers.

In 2013, American workers got, on average, eight paid vacation days, but 23% of American workers got none at all. In contrast, German workers are guaranteed six weeks of paid vacation a year. Also, American workers use fewer of the vacation days they are entitled to than do workers in other industrialized countries. A 2013 survey found that American workers used only 51% of the vacation days they are entitled to, compared to 90% in France.

Why do Americans work so much more than others? Unlike their counterparts in other industrialized countries,

Americans are not legally entitled to paid vacation days; as a result, the average American worker gets fewer of them.

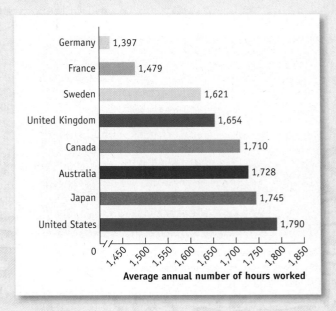

Average annual number of hours worked

Source: OECD.

in 2009 as workers, disillusioned by bad job prospects, left the labor force. As a result, since 2009 the U.S. labor supply curve has been shifting leftward.

Changes in Opportunities At one time, teaching was the only occupation considered suitable for well-educated women. However, as opportunities in other professions opened up to women starting in the 1960s, many women left teaching and potential female teachers chose other careers. This generated a leftward shift of the supply curve for teachers, reflecting a fall in the willingness to work at any given wage and forcing school districts to pay more to maintain an adequate teaching staff. These events illustrate a general result: when superior alternatives arise for workers in another labor market, the supply curve in the original labor market shifts leftward as workers move to the new opportunities. Similarly, when opportunities diminish in one labor market—say, layoffs in the manufacturing industry due to increased foreign competition—the supply in alternative labor markets increases as workers move to these other markets.

Changes in Wealth A person whose wealth increases will buy more normal goods, including leisure. So when a class of workers experiences a general rise in their wealth levels—say, due to a stock market boom—the income effect from the wealth increase will shift the labor supply curve associated with those workers leftward as workers consume more leisure and work less. Note that *the income effect caused by a change in wealth shifts the labor supply curve,* but *the income effect from a wage rate increase*—as we discussed in the case of the individual labor supply curve—*is a movement along the labor supply curve.* The following Economics in Action illustrates how such a change in the wealth levels of many families led to a shift of the market labor supply curve associated with their employable children.

ECONOMICS ▶ *in Action*

The Decline of the Summer Job

Come summertime, resort towns along the New Jersey shore find themselves facing a recurring annual problem: a serious shortage of lifeguards. Traditionally, lifeguard positions, together with many other seasonal jobs, had been filled mainly by high school and college students. But in recent years a combination of adverse shifts in supply and demand have severely diminished summer employment for young workers. In 1979, 71% of Americans between the ages of 16 and 19 were in the summer workforce. By 2007, that number was 50%, and by 2013 it had taken another sharp fall to around 43%.

A fall in supply is one explanation for the change. More students now feel that they should devote their summer to additional study rather than to work. An increase in household affluence over the past 20 years has also contributed to fewer teens taking jobs because they no longer feel pressured to contribute to household finances. In other words, the income effect has led to a reduced labor supply.

Another explanation is the substitution effect: increased competition from immigrants, who are now doing the jobs typically done by teens (like mowing lawns and delivering pizzas), has led to a decline in wages. So many teenagers have forgone summer work to consume leisure instead.

But it was the deep recession of 2007–2009 that contributed most to the severe fall in youth summer employment in the ensuing years. As of 2014, youth employment has not yet rebounded. Post-recession cutbacks in employment by private employers, as well as in local and state government programs that hire teens during the summer, have led to the lowest number of teens employed during the summer in decades. Thus a steep fall in demand, along with a long-run trend of falling supply, has led to the decline of what was once a summer tradition.

While some teenagers manage to find jobs, the current trend is toward a decline of the summer job due to a steep fall in demand and falling supply.

Radius Images/Alamy

▼ Quick Review

• The choice of how much labor to supply is a problem of **time allocation:** a choice between work and **leisure.**

• A rise in the wage rate causes both an income and a substitution effect on an individual's labor supply. The substitution effect of a higher wage rate induces more hours of work supplied, other things equal. This is countered by the income effect: higher income leads to a higher demand for leisure, a normal good. If the income effect dominates, a rise in the wage rate can actually cause the **individual labor supply curve** to slope the "wrong" way: downward.

• The market labor supply curve is the horizontal sum of the individual labor supply curves of all workers in that market. It shifts for four main reasons: changes in preferences and social norms, changes in population, changes in opportunities, and changes in wealth.

Check Your Understanding 19-4

1. Formerly, Clive was free to work as many or as few hours per week as he wanted. But a new law limits the maximum number of hours he can work per week to 35. Explain under what circumstances, if at all, he is made:
   a. Worse off
   b. Equally as well off
   c. Better off

2. Explain in terms of the income and substitution effects how a fall in Clive's wage rate can induce him to work more hours than before.

Solutions appear at back of book.

BUSINESS CASE

Wages and Workers at Costco and Walmart

I|n July 2013 President Barack Obama gave a much anticipated and widely discussed speech on the economy, arguing for policies that would raise wages and reduce income inequality. Along the way, he name-checked Costco, the giant retail chain, "which pays good wages and offers good benefits." Good wages compared to what? He didn't say it, but everyone understood that he was implicitly comparing Costco to an even bigger retail giant, Walmart, which famously pays so little that some of its workers qualify for food stamps and other poverty programs.

Indeed, that same year, a Bloomberg *BusinessWeek* story about Costco reported that it paid an average wage of $20.89 an hour, compared with $12.67 at Walmart, and provided much more generous health benefits too. Despite paying much higher wages, however, Costco has been substantially more profitable than Walmart in recent years. How is this possible?

Rob Crandall/Alamy

According to Costco executives, what they get in return for relatively high wages is a stable and highly productive workforce. Retail companies typically have high labor turnover—that is, workers frequently quit, and then new workers have to be trained—but turnover at Costco is relatively low. Costco workers also appear to have high morale, and deliver better customer service than their counterparts at other stores.

Would Walmart be more profitable if it paid like Costco? Skeptics argue that the retailers aren't completely comparable: Costco offers a narrower range of products and caters to a higher-income clientele. Still, Costco's success shows that paying the lowest possible wage isn't always the best business decision.

QUESTIONS FOR THOUGHT

1. Use the marginal productivity theory of income distribution to explain how companies like Walmart can pay workers so little that they fall below the poverty line.

2. How does the Costco story fit into our discussion of the reasons similar workers may end up being paid different wages?

3. President Obama, as his speech indicated, would like to encourage more companies to adopt a high-wage strategy. Other politicians would like to do the same. What are the possible positive and negative effects if this becomes official government policy?

SUMMARY

1. Just as there are markets for goods and services, there are markets for factors of production, including labor, land, and both **physical capital** and **human capital.** These markets determine the **factor distribution of income.**

2. Profit-maximizing price-taking producers will employ a factor up to the point at which its price is equal to its **value of the marginal product—** the marginal product of the factor multiplied by the price of the output it produces. The **value of the marginal product curve** is therefore the individual price-taking producer's demand curve for a factor.

3. The market demand curve for labor is the horizontal sum of the individual demand curves of producers in that market. It shifts for three main reasons: changes in output price, changes in the supply of other factors, and technological changes.

4. When a competitive labor market is in equilibrium, the market wage is equal to the **equilibrium value of the marginal product** of labor, the additional value produced by the last worker hired in the labor market as a whole. The same principle applies to other factors of production: the **rental rate** of land or capital is equal to the equilibrium value of the marginal products. This insight leads to the **marginal productivity theory of income distribution,** according to which each factor is paid the value of the marginal product of the last unit of that factor employed in the factor market as a whole.

5. Large disparities in wages raise questions about the validity of the marginal productivity theory of income distribution. Many disparities can be explained by **compensating differentials** and by differences in talent, job experience, job status, and human capital across workers. Market interference in the forms of **unions** and collective action by employers also creates wage disparities. The **efficiency-wage model,** which arises from a type of market failure, shows how wage disparities can result from employers' attempts to increase worker performance. Free markets tend to diminish discrimination, but discrimination remains a real source of wage disparity, especially through its effects on human capital acquisition. Discrimination is typically maintained either through problems in labor markets or (historically) through institutionalization in government policies.

6. Labor supply is the result of decisions about **time allocation,** where each worker faces a trade-off between **leisure** and work. An increase in the hourly wage rate tends to increase work hours via the substitution effect but to reduce work hours via the income effect. If the net result is that a worker increases the quantity of labor supplied in response to a higher wage, the **individual labor supply curve** slopes upward. If the net result is that a worker reduces work hours, the individual labor supply curve—unlike supply curves for goods and services—slopes downward.

7. The market labor supply curve is the horizontal sum of the individual labor supply curves of all workers in that market. It shifts for four main reasons: changes in preferences and social norms, changes in population, changes in opportunities, and changes in wealth.

KEY TERMS

Physical capital, p. 544
Human capital, p. 544
Factor distribution of income, p. 545
Value of the marginal product, p. 548
Value of the marginal product curve, p. 548

Equilibrium value of the marginal product, p. 553
Rental rate, p. 554
Marginal productivity theory of income distribution, p. 555
Compensating differentials, p. 558

Unions, p. 559
Efficiency-wage model, p. 560
Time allocation, p. 564
Leisure, p. 564
Individual labor supply curve, p. 565

PROBLEMS

1. In 2013, national income in the United States was $14,542.4 billion. In the same year, 137 million workers were employed, at an average wage, including benefits, of $64,667 per worker per year.

   a. How much compensation of employees was paid in the United States in 2013?

   b. Analyze the factor distribution of income. What percentage of national income was received in the form of compensation to employees in 2013?

   c. Suppose that a huge wave of corporate downsizing leads many terminated employees to open their own businesses. What is the effect on the factor distribution of income?

   d. Suppose the supply of labor rises due to an increase in the retirement age. What happens to the percentage of national income received in the form of compensation of employees?

2. Marty's Frozen Yogurt has the production function per day shown in the accompanying table. The equilibrium wage rate for a worker is $80 per day. Each cup of frozen yogurt sells for $2.

Quantity of labor (workers)	Quantity of frozen yogurt (cups)
0	0
1	110
2	200
3	270
4	300
5	320
6	330

   a. Calculate the marginal product of labor for each worker and the value of the marginal product of labor per worker.

   b. How many workers should Marty employ?

3. The production function for Patty's Pizza Parlor is given in the table in Problem 14. The price of pizza is $2, but the hourly wage rate rises from $10 to $15. Use a diagram to determine how Patty's demand for workers responds as a result of this wage rate increase.

4. Jameel runs a driver education school. The more driving instructors he hires, the more driving lessons he can sell. But because he owns a limited number of training automobiles, each additional driving instructor adds less to Jameel's output of driving lessons. The accompanying table shows Jameel's production function per day. Each driving lesson can be sold at $35 per hour.

Quantity of labor (driving instructors)	Quantity of driving lessons (hours)
0	0
1	8
2	15
3	21
4	26
5	30
6	33

Determine Jameel's labor demand schedule (his demand schedule for driving instructors) for each of the following daily wage rates for driving instructors: $160, $180, $200, $220, $240, and $260.

5. Dale and Dana work at a self-service gas station and convenience store. Dale opens up every day, and Dana arrives later to help stock the store. They are both paid the current market wage of $9.50 per hour. But Dale feels he should be paid much more because the revenue generated from the gas pumps he turns on every morning is much higher than the revenue generated by the items that Dana stocks. Assess this argument.

6. A *New York Times* article observed that the wage of farmworkers in Mexico was $11 an hour but the wage of immigrant Mexican farmworkers in California was $9 an hour.

a. Assume that the output sells for the same price in the two countries. Does this imply that the marginal product of labor of farmworkers is higher in Mexico or in California? Explain your answer, and illustrate with a diagram that shows the demand and supply curves for labor in the respective markets. In your diagram, assume that the quantity supplied of labor for any given wage rate is the same for Mexican farmworkers as it is for immigrant Mexican farmworkers in California.

b. Now suppose that farmwork in Mexico is more arduous and more dangerous than farmwork in California. As a result, the quantity supplied of labor for any given wage rate is not the same for Mexican farmworkers as it is for immigrant Mexican farmworkers in California. How does this change your answer to part a? What concept best accounts for the difference between wage rates for Mexican farmworkers and immigrant Mexican farmworkers in California?

c. Illustrate your answer to part b with a diagram. In this diagram, assume that the quantity of labor demanded for any given wage rate is the same for Mexican employers as it is for Californian employers.

7. Kendra is the owner of Wholesome Farms, a commercial dairy. Kendra employs labor, land, and capital. In her operations, Kendra can substitute between the amount of labor she employs and the amount of capital she employs. That is, to produce the same quantity of output she can use more labor and less capital; similarly, to produce the same quantity of output she can use less labor and more capital. Let w^* represent the annual cost of labor in the market, let r_L^* represent the annual cost of a unit of land in the market, and let r_K^* represent the annual cost of a unit of capital in the market.

a. Suppose that Kendra can maximize her profits by employing less labor and more capital than she is currently using but the same amount of land. What three conditions must now hold for Kendra's operations (involving her value of the marginal product of labor, land, and capital) for this to be true?

b. Kendra believes that she can increase her profits by renting and using more land. However, if she uses more land, she must use more of both labor and capital; if she uses less land, she can use less of both labor and capital. What three conditions must hold (involving her value of the marginal product of labor, land, and capital) for this to be true?

8. For each of the following situations in which similar workers are paid different wages, give the most likely explanation for these wage differences.

a. Test pilots for new jet aircraft earn higher wages than airline pilots.

b. College graduates usually have higher earnings in their first year on the job than workers without college degrees have in their first year on the job.

c. Full professors command higher salaries than assistant professors for teaching the same class.

d. Unionized workers are generally better paid than non-unionized workers.

9. Research consistently finds that despite nondiscrimination policies, African-American workers on average receive lower wages than White workers do. What are the possible reasons for this? Are these reasons consistent with marginal productivity theory?

10. Greta is an enthusiastic amateur gardener and spends a lot of her free time working in her yard. She also has a demanding and well-paid job as a freelance advertising consultant. Because the advertising business is going through a difficult time, the hourly consulting fee Greta can charge falls. Greta decides to spend more time gardening and less time consulting. Explain her decision in terms of income and substitution effects.

11. You are the governor's economic policy adviser. The governor wants to put in place policies that encourage employed people to work more hours at their jobs and that encourage unemployed people to find and take jobs. Assess each of the following policies in terms of reaching that goal. Explain your reasoning in terms of income and substitution effects, and indicate when the impact of the policy may be ambiguous.

a. The state income tax rate is lowered, which has the effect of increasing workers' after-tax wage rate.

b. The state income tax rate is increased, which has the effect of decreasing workers' after-tax wage rate.

c. The state property tax rate is increased, which reduces workers' after-tax income.

WORK IT OUT

For interactive, step-by-step help in solving the following problem, visit LaunchPad by using the URL on the back cover of this book.

12. Patty's Pizza Parlor has the production function per hour shown in the accompanying table. The hourly wage rate for each worker is $10. Each pizza sells for $2.

Quantity of labor (workers)	Quantity of pizza
0	0
1	9
2	15
3	19
4	22
5	24

a. Calculate the marginal product of labor for each worker and the value of the marginal product of labor per worker.

b. Draw the value of the marginal product of labor curve. Use your diagram to determine how many workers Patty should employ.

c. Now the price of pizza increases to $4. Calculate the value of the marginal product of labor per worker, and draw the new value of the marginal product of labor curve in your diagram. Use your diagram to determine how many workers Patty should employ now.

Now let's assume that Patty buys a new high-tech pizza oven that allows her workers to become twice as productive as before. That is, the first worker now produces 18 pizzas per hour instead of 9, and so on.

d. Calculate the new marginal product of labor and the new value of the marginal product of labor at the original price of $2 per pizza.

e. Use a diagram to determine how Patty's hiring decision responds to this increase in the productivity of her workforce.

Indifference Curve Analysis of Labor Supply

In the body of this chapter, we explained why the labor supply curve can slope downward instead of upward: the substitution effect of a higher wage rate, which provides an incentive to work longer hours, can be outweighed by the income effect of a higher wage rate, which may lead individuals to consume more leisure. In this appendix we show how this analysis can be carried out using the *indifference curves* introduced in the appendix to Chapter 10.

The Time Allocation Budget Line

Let's return to the example of Clive, who likes leisure but also likes having money to spend. We now assume that Clive has a total of 80 hours per week that he could spend either working or enjoying as leisure time. (The remaining hours in his week, we assume, are taken up with necessary activities, mainly sleeping.) Let's also assume, initially, that his hourly wage rate is $10.

His consumption possibilities are defined by the **time allocation budget line** in Figure 19A-1, a budget line that shows Clive's trade-offs between consumption of leisure and income. Hours of leisure per week are measured on the horizontal axis, and the money he earns from working is measured on the vertical axis.

The horizontal intercept, point X, is at 80 hours: if Clive didn't work at all, he would have 80 hours of leisure per week but would not earn any money. The vertical intercept, point Y, is at $800: if Clive worked all the time, he would earn $800 per week.

Why can we use a budget line to describe Clive's time allocation choice? The budget lines found in Chapter 10 and its appendix represent the trade-offs facing

> A **time allocation budget line** shows an individual's trade-off between consumption of leisure and the income that allows consumption of marketed goods.

FIGURE 19A-1 The Time Allocation Budget Line

Clive's time allocation budget line shows his trade-off between work, which pays a wage rate of $10 per hour, and leisure. At point X he allocates all his time, 80 hours, to leisure but has no income. At point Y he allocates all his time to work, earning $800, but consumes no leisure. His hourly wage rate of $10, the opportunity cost of an hour of leisure, is equal to minus the slope of the time allocation budget line. We have assumed that point A, at 40 hours of leisure and $400 in income, is Clive's optimal time allocation choice. It obeys the optimal time allocation rule: the additional utility Clive gets from one more hour of leisure must equal the additional utility he gets from the goods he can purchase with one hour's wages.

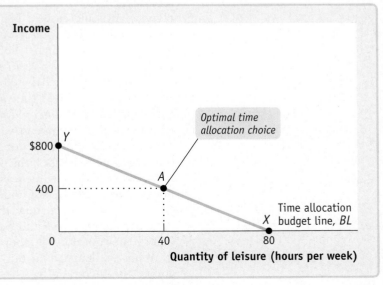

The **optimal time allocation rule** says that an individual should allocate time so that the marginal utility gained from the income earned from an additional hour worked is equal to the marginal utility of an additional hour of leisure.

consumers deciding how to allocate their income among different goods. Here, instead of asking how Clive allocates his income, we ask how he allocates his *time*. But the principles underlying the allocation of income and the allocation of time are the same: each involves allocating a fixed amount of a resource (80 hours of time in this case) with a constant trade-off (Clive must forgo $10 for each additional hour of leisure). So using a budget line is just as appropriate for time allocation as it is for income allocation.

As in the case of ordinary budget lines, opportunity cost plays a key role. The opportunity cost of an hour of leisure is what Clive must forgo by working one less hour—$10 in income. This opportunity cost is, of course, Clive's hourly wage rate and is equal to minus the slope of his time allocation budget line. You can verify this by noting that the slope is equal to minus the vertical intercept, point *Y*, divided by the horizontal intercept, point *X*—that is, –$800/(80 hours) = –$10 per hour.

To maximize his utility, Clive must choose the optimal point on the time allocation budget line in Figure 19A-1. In Chapter 10 we saw that a consumer who allocates spending to maximize utility finds the point on the budget line that satisfies the *utility-maximizing principle of marginal analysis:* the marginal utility per dollar spent on two goods must be equal. Although Clive's choice involves allocating time rather than money, the same principles apply.

Since Clive "spends" time rather than money, the counterpart of the utility-maximizing principle of marginal analysis is the **optimal time allocation rule:** the marginal utility Clive gets from the extra money earned from an additional hour spent working must equal the marginal utility of an additional hour of leisure.

The Effect of a Higher Wage Rate

Depending on his tastes, Clive's utility-maximizing choice of hours of leisure and income could lie anywhere on the time allocation budget line in Figure 19A-1. Let's assume that his optimal choice is point *A*, at which he consumes 40 hours of leisure and earns $400. Now we are ready to link the analysis of time allocation to labor supply.

When Clive chooses a point like *A* on his time allocation budget line, he is also choosing the quantity of labor he supplies to the labor market. By choosing to consume 40 of his 80 available hours as leisure, he has also chosen to supply the other 40 hours as labor.

Now suppose that Clive's wage rate doubles, from $10 to $20 per hour. The effect of this increase in his wage rate is shown in Figure 19A-2. His time allocation budget line rotates outward: the vertical intercept, which represents the amount he could earn if he devoted all 80 hours to work, shifts upward from point *Y* to point *Z*. As a result of the doubling of his wage, Clive would earn $1,600 instead of $800 if he devoted all 80 hours to working.

But how will Clive's time allocation actually change? As we saw in the chapter, this depends on the *income effect* and *substitution effect* that we learned about in Chapter 10 and its appendix.

The substitution effect of an increase in the wage rate works as follows. When the wage rate increases, the opportunity cost of an hour of leisure increases; this induces Clive to consume less leisure and work more hours—that is, to substitute hours of work in place of hours of leisure as the wage rate rises. If the substitution effect were the whole story, the individual labor supply curve would look like any ordinary supply curve and would always slope upward—a higher wage rate leads to a greater quantity of labor supplied.

What we learned in our analysis of demand was that for most consumer goods, the income effect isn't very important because most goods account for

FIGURE 19A-2   An Increase in the Wage Rate

The two panels show Clive's initial optimal choice, point A on BL_1, the time allocation budget line corresponding to a wage rate of $10. After his wage rate rises to $20, his budget line rotates out to the new budget line, BL_2: if he spends all his time working, the amount of money he earns rises from $800 to $1,600, reflected in the movement from point Y to point Z. This generates two opposing effects: the substitution effect pushes him to consume less leisure and to work more hours; the income effect pushes him to consume more leisure and to work fewer hours. Panel (a) shows the change in time allocation when the substitution effect is stronger: Clive's new optimal choice is point B, representing a decrease in hours of leisure to 30 hours and an increase in hours of labor to 50 hours. In this case the individual labor supply curve slopes upward. Panel (b) shows the change in time allocation when the income effect is stronger: point C is the new optimal choice, representing an increase in hours of leisure to 50 hours and a decrease in hours of labor to 30 hours. Now the individual labor supply curve slopes downward.

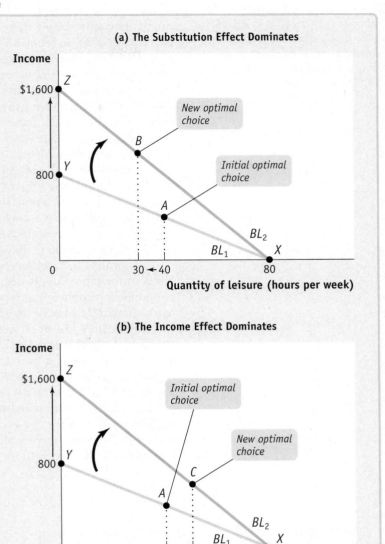

(a) The Substitution Effect Dominates

(b) The Income Effect Dominates

only a very small share of a consumer's spending. In addition, in the few cases of goods where the income effect is significant—for example, major purchases like housing—it usually reinforces the substitution effect: most goods are normal goods, so when a price increase makes a consumer poorer, he or she buys less of that good.

In the labor/leisure choice, however, the income effect takes on a new significance, for two reasons. First, most people get the great majority of their income from wages. This means that the income effect of a change in the wage rate is *not* small: an increase in the wage rate will generate a significant increase in income. Second, leisure is a normal good: when income rises, other things equal, people tend to consume more leisure and work fewer hours.

So the income effect of a higher wage rate tends to *reduce* the quantity of labor supplied, working in opposition to the substitution effect, which tends to *increase* the quantity of labor supplied. So the net effect of a higher wage rate on the quantity

A **backward-bending individual labor supply curve** is an individual labor supply curve that slopes upward at low to moderate wage rates and slopes downward at higher wage rates.

of labor Clive supplies could go either way—depending on his preferences, he might choose to supply more labor, or he might choose to supply less labor. The two panels of Figure 19A-2 illustrate these two outcomes. In each panel, point *A* represents Clive's initial consumption choice. Panel (a) shows the case in which Clive works more hours in response to a higher wage rate. An increase in the wage rate induces him to move from point *A* to point *B*, where he consumes less leisure than at *A* and therefore works more hours. Here the substitution effect prevails over the income effect. Panel (b) shows the case in which Clive works fewer hours in response to a higher wage rate. Here, he moves from point *A* to point *C*, where he consumes more leisure and works *fewer* hours than at *A*. Here the income effect prevails over the substitution effect.

When the income effect of a higher wage rate is stronger than the substitution effect, the individual labor supply curve, which shows how much labor an individual will supply at any given wage rate will have a segment that slopes the "wrong" way—downward: a higher wage rate leads to a smaller quantity of labor supplied. An example is the segment connecting points *B* and *C* in Figure 19A-3.

Economists believe that the substitution effect usually dominates the income effect in the labor supply decision when an individual's wage rate is low. An individual labor supply curve typically slopes upward for lower wage rates as people work more in response to rising wage rates. But they also believe that many individuals have stronger preferences for leisure and will choose to cut back the number of hours worked as their wage rate continues to rise. For these individuals, the income effect eventually dominates the substitution effect as the wage rate rises, leading their individual labor supply curves to change slope and to "bend backward" at high wage rates. An individual labor supply curve with this feature, called a **backward-bending individual labor supply curve,** is shown in Figure 19A-3. Although an *individual* labor supply curve may bend backward, *market* labor supply curves almost always slope upward over their entire range as higher wage rates draw more new workers into the labor market.

FIGURE 19A-3 | A Backward-Bending Individual Labor Supply Curve

At lower wage rates, the substitution effect dominates the income effect for this individual. This is illustrated by the movement along the individual labor supply curve from point *A* to point *B:* a rise in the wage rate from W_1 to W_2 leads the quantity of labor supplied to increase from L_1 to L_2. But at higher wage rates, the income effect dominates the substitution effect, shown by the movement from point *B* to point *C:* here, a rise in the wage rate from W_2 to W_3 leads the quantity of labor supplied to decrease from L_2 to L_3.

Indifference Curve Analysis

In the appendix to Chapter 10, we showed that consumer choice can be represented using the concept of *indifference curves*, which provide a "map" of consumer preferences. If you have covered the appendix, you may find it interesting to learn that indifference curves are also useful for addressing the issue of labor supply. In fact, this is one place where they are particularly helpful.

Using indifference curves, Figure 19A-4 shows how an increase in the wage rate can lead to a fall in the quantity of labor supplied. Point *A* is Clive's initial optimal choice, given an hourly wage rate of $10. It is the same as point *A* in Figure 19A-1; this time, however, we include an indifference curve to show that it is a point at which the budget line is tangent to the highest possible indifference curve.

Now consider the effect of a rise in the wage rate to $20. Imagine, for a moment, that at the same time Clive was offered a higher wage, he was told that he had to start repaying his student loan and that the good-news/bad-news combination left his utility unchanged. Then he would find himself at point *S:* on the same indifference curve as at *A*, but tangent to a steeper budget line, the dashed line *BL_S* in Figure 19A-4, which is parallel to *BL_2*. The move from point *A* to point *S* is the substitution effect of his wage increase: it leads him to consume less leisure and therefore supply more labor.

But now cancel the repayment on the student loan, and Clive is able to move to a higher indifference curve. His new optimum is at point *C*, which corresponds to *C* in panel (b) of Figure 19A-2. The move from point *S* to point *C* is the income effect of his wage increase. And we see that this income effect can outweigh the substitution effect: at *C* he consumes more leisure, and therefore supplies less labor, than he did at *A*.

FIGURE 19A-4   **Labor Supply Choice: The Indifference Curve Approach**

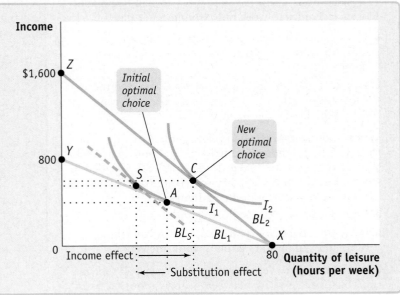

Point *A*, on *BL_1*, is Clive's initial optimal choice. After a wage rate increase, his income and utility level increase: his new time allocation budget line is *BL_2* and his new optimal choice is point *C*. This change can be decomposed into the substitution effect, the fall in the hours of leisure from point *A* to point *S*, and the income effect, the increase in the number of hours of leisure from point *S* to point *C*. As shown here, the income effect dominates the substitution effect: the net result of an increase in the wage rate is an increase in the hours of leisure consumed and a decrease in the hours of labor supplied.

PROBLEMS

1. Leandro has 16 hours per day that he can allocate to work or leisure. His job pays a wage rate of $20. Leandro decides to consume 8 hours of leisure. His indifference curves have the usual shape: they slope downward, they do not cross, and they have the characteristic convex shape.

   a. Draw Leandro's time allocation budget line for a typical day. Then illustrate the indifference curve at his optimal choice.

   Now Leandro's wage rate falls to $10.

   b. Draw Leandro's new budget line.

   c. Suppose that Leandro now works only 4 hours as a result of his reduced wage rate. Illustrate the indifference curve at his new optimal choice.

   d. Leandro's decision to work less as the wage rate falls is the result of a substitution effect and an income effect. In your diagram, show the income effect and the substitution effect from this reduced wage rate. Which effect is stronger?

2. Florence is a highly paid fashion consultant who earns $100 per hour. She has 16 hours per day that she can allocate to work or leisure, and she decides to work for 12 hours.

   a. Draw Florence's time allocation budget line for a typical day, and illustrate the indifference curve at her optimal choice.

   One of Florence's clients is featured on the front page of *Vague,* an influential fashion magazine. As a result, Florence's consulting fee now rises to $500 per hour. Florence decides to work only 10 hours per day.

   b. Draw Florence's new time allocation budget line, and illustrate the indifference curve at her optimal choice.

   c. In your diagram, show the income effect and the substitution effect from this increase in the wage rate. Which effect is stronger?

3. Wendy works at a fast-food restaurant. When her wage rate was $5 per hour, she worked 30 hours per week. When her wage rate rose to $6 per hour, she decided to work 40 hours. But when her wage rate rose further to $7, she decided to work only 35 hours.

   a. Draw Wendy's individual labor supply curve.

   b. Is Wendy's behavior irrational, or can you find a rational explanation? Explain your answer.

4. Over the past fifty years the average American's leisure time has increased by between 4 and 8 hours a week. some economists think that this increase is primarily driven by a rise in wage rates.

   a. Use the income and substitution effects to describe the labor supply for the average American. Which effect dominates?

   b. The study also finds an increase in female labor force participation—more women are choosing to hold jobs rather than exclusively perform household tasks. For the average woman who has newly entered the labor force, which effect dominates?

   c. Draw typical individual labor supply curves that illustrate your answers to part a and part b above.

WORK IT OUT

For interactive, step-by-step help in solving the following problem, visit LaunchPad by using the URL on the back cover of this book.

5. Tamara has 80 hours per week that she can allocate to work or leisure. Her job pays a wage rate of $20 per hour, but Tamara is being taxed on her income in the following way. On the first $400 that Tamara makes, she pays no tax. That is, for the first 20 hours she works, her net wage—what she takes home after taxes—is $20 per hour. On all income above $400, Tamara pays a 75% tax. That is, for all hours above the first 20 hours, her net wage rate is only $5 per hour. Tamara decides to work 30 hours. Her indifference curves have the usual shape.

   a. Draw Tamara's time allocation budget line for a typical week. Also illustrate the indifference curve at her optimal choice.

   The government changes the tax scheme. Now only the first $100 of income is tax-exempt. That is, for the first 5 hours she works, Tamara's net wage rate is $20 per hour. But the government reduces the tax rate on all other income to 50%. That is, for all hours above the first 5 hours, Tamara's net wage rate is now $10. After these changes, Tamara finds herself exactly equally as well off as before. That is, her new optimal choice is on the same indifference curve as her initial optimal choice.

   b. Draw Tamara's new time allocation budget line on the same diagram. Also illustrate her optimal choice. Bear in mind that she is equally as well off (on the same indifference curve) as before the tax changes occurred.

   c. Will Tamara work more or less than before the changes to the tax scheme? Why?

Uncertainty, Risk, and Private Information

What You Will Learn in This Chapter

- That **risk** is a key feature of the economy and that most people are **risk-averse**

- Why diminishing marginal utility makes people risk-averse and determines the **premium** they are willing to pay to reduce risk

- How risk can be traded—the risk-averse can pay others to assume part of their risk

- How exposure to risk can be reduced through **diversification** and **pooling**

- The special problems posed by **private information**—when some people know things that other people do not

EXTREME WEATHER

Uncertainty is an important feature of the real world as illustrated by the devastation wrought by Hurricane Sandy and the 2012 drought.

WHEN HURRICANE SANDY blasted onshore in New York and New Jersey in October 2012, residents and local governments were stunned but well prepared. They had, after all, been through Hurricane Irene just 14 months earlier. Irene resulted in 56 deaths and almost $16 billion in costs. But Sandy, a bigger category 2 storm, was even more devastating. It killed 160 people, destroyed homes and businesses, left over 8 million households without power for weeks, and led to shortages of essentials like clean water and gasoline. It even flooded the New York City subway system for the first time in 110 years. In total, Sandy inflicted $65 billion in damages on the U.S. economy.

But Hurricane Sandy was only one part of a pattern of extreme weather in the United States in 2011 and 2012. In August of 2012, Hurricane Isaac hit Louisiana, resulting in 7 deaths and more than $2 billion in damage. If that were not enough, record-breaking heat and drought throughout the lower 48 states led to widespread crop failures and wildfires, destroying entire communities. The estimated costs of the 2012 drought alone were $14 billion.

Moreover, these estimates of damages significantly understated the true cost of these weather events because many of the uninsured or underinsured (those with insurance insufficient to cover their losses) failed to report their losses.

Anyone who lives in an area subject to extreme weather knows that uncertainty is a feature of the real world. Up to this point, we have assumed that people make decisions with knowledge of exactly how the future will unfold. (The exception being health insurance decisions.) In reality, people often make economic decisions, such as whether to build a house in a coastal area, without full knowledge of future events. As the victims of these extreme weather events learned, making decisions when the future is uncertain carries with it the *risk of loss*.

It is often possible for individuals to use markets to reduce their risk. For example, hurricane victims who had insurance were able to receive some, if not complete, compensation for their losses. In fact, through insurance and other devices, the modern economy offers many ways for individuals to reduce their exposure to risk.

However, a market economy cannot always solve the problems created by

uncertainty. Markets do very well at coping with risk when two conditions hold: when risk can be reasonably well *diversified* and when the probability of loss is equally well known by everyone.

Over the past several years, the increase in extreme weather events has led many insurers to no longer rely on *diversification* for weather-related losses. As a result, they have sharply reduced coverage of such losses. Insurers no longer believe that profits from areas with good weather will offset losses from hurricane- and drought-prone areas.

But in practice, the second condition is often the more limiting one. Markets run into trouble when some people know things that others do not—a situation that involves what is called *private information*. We'll see that private information can cause inefficiency by preventing mutually beneficial transactions from occurring—especially in insurance markets.

In this chapter we'll examine why most people dislike risk. Then we'll explore how a market economy allows people to reduce risk at a price. Finally, we'll turn to the special problems created for markets by private information.

A **random variable** is a variable with an uncertain future value.

The **expected value** of a random variable is the weighted average of all possible values, where the weights on each possible value correspond to the probability of that value occurring.

A **state of the world** is a possible future event.

Risk is uncertainty about future outcomes. When the uncertainty is about monetary outcomes, it becomes **financial risk.**

The Economics of Risk Aversion

In general, people don't like risk and are willing to pay a price to avoid it. Just ask the U.S. insurance industry, which collects more than $1 trillion in premiums every year. But what exactly is risk? And why don't most people like it? To answer these questions, we need to look briefly at the concept of *expected value* and the meaning of uncertainty. Then we can turn to why people dislike *risk.*

Expectations and Uncertainty

The Lee family doesn't know how big its medical bills will be next year. If all goes well, it won't have any medical expenses at all. Let's assume that there's a 50% chance of that happening. But if family members require hospitalization or expensive drugs, they will face medical expenses of $10,000. Let's assume that there's also a 50% chance that these high medical expenses will materialize.

In this example—which is designed to illustrate a point, rather than to be realistic—the Lees' medical expenses for the coming year are a **random variable,** a variable that has an uncertain future value. No one can predict which of its possible values, or outcomes, a random variable will take. But that doesn't mean we can say nothing about the Lees' future medical expenses. On the contrary, an actuary (a person trained in evaluating uncertain future events) could calculate the **expected value** of expenses next year—the weighted average of all possible values, where the weights on each possible value correspond to the probability of that value occurring. In this example, the expected value of the Lees' medical expenses is $(0.5 \times \$0) + (0.5 \times \$10,000) = \$5,000$.

To derive the general formula for the expected value of a random variable, we imagine that there are a number of different **states of the world,** possible future events. Each state is associated with a different realized value—the value that actually occurs—of the random variable. You don't know which state of the world will actually occur, but you can assign probabilities, one for each state of the world.

Let's assume that P_1 is the probability of state 1, P_2 the probability of state 2, and so on. And you know the realized value of the random value in each state of the world: S_1 in state 1, S_2 in state 2, and so on. Let's also assume that there are N possible states. Then the expected value of a random variable is:

(20-1) *Expected value of a random variable*
$$EV = (P_1 \times S_1) + (P_2 \times S_2) + \ldots + (P_N \times S_N)$$

In the case of the Lee family, there are only two possible states of the world, each with a probability of 0.5.

Notice, however, that the Lee family doesn't actually expect to pay $5,000 in medical bills next year. That's because in this example there is no state of the world in which the family pays exactly $5,000. Either the family pays nothing, or it pays $10,000. So the Lees face considerable uncertainty about their future medical expenses.

But what if the Lee family can buy health insurance that will cover its medical expenses, whatever they turn out to be? Suppose, in particular, that the family can pay $5,000 up front in return for full coverage of whatever medical expenses actually arise during the coming year. Then the Lees' future medical expenses are no longer uncertain *for them:* in return for $5,000—an amount equal to the expected value of the medical expenses—the insurance company assumes all responsibility for paying those medical expenses. Would this be a good deal from the Lees' point of view?

Yes, it would—or at least most families would think so. Most people prefer, other things equal, to reduce **risk**—uncertainty about future outcomes. (We'll focus here on **financial risk,** in which the uncertainty is about monetary outcomes, as opposed to uncertainty about outcomes that can't be assigned a monetary value.) In fact, most people are willing to pay a substantial price to reduce their risk; that's why we have an insurance industry.

But before we study the market for insurance, we need to understand why people feel that risk is a bad thing, an attitude that economists call *risk aversion*. The source of risk aversion lies in a concept we first encountered in our analysis of consumer demand, back in Chapter 10: *diminishing marginal utility*.

The Logic of Risk Aversion

To understand how diminishing marginal utility gives rise to risk aversion, we need to look not only at the Lees' medical costs but also at how those costs affect the income the family has left after medical expenses. Let's assume the family knows that it will have an income of $30,000 next year. If the family has no medical expenses, it will be left with all of that income. If its medical expenses are $10,000, its income after medical expenses will be only $20,000. Since we have assumed that there is an equal chance of these two outcomes, the expected value of the Lees' income after medical expenses is (0.5 × $30,000) + (0.5 × $20,000) = $25,000. At times we will simply refer to this as expected income.

But as we'll now see, if the family's utility function has the shape typical of most families', its **expected utility**—the expected value of its total utility given uncertainty about future outcomes—is less than it would be if the family didn't face any risk and knew with certainty that its income after medical expenses would be $25,000.

To see why, we need to look at how total utility depends on income. Panel (a) of Figure 20-1 shows a hypothetical utility function for the Lee family, where total utility depends on income—the amount of money the Lees have available for consumption of goods and services (after they have paid any medical bills). The table within the figure shows how the family's total utility varies over the income range of $20,000 to $30,000. As usual, the utility function slopes upward, because more income leads to higher total utility. Notice as well that the curve gets flatter as we move up and to the right, which reflects diminishing marginal utility.

In Chapter 10 we applied the principle of diminishing marginal utility to individual goods and services: each successive unit of a good or service that a consumer purchases adds less to his or her total utility. The same principle applies to income used for consumption: each successive dollar of income adds less to total utility than the previous dollar. Panel (b) shows how marginal utility varies with income, confirming that marginal utility of income falls as income rises. As we'll see in a moment, diminishing marginal utility is the key to understanding the desire of individuals to reduce risk.

To analyze how a person's utility is affected by risk, economists start from the assumption that individuals facing uncertainty maximize their *expected* utility. We can use the data in Figure 20-1 to calculate the Lee family's expected utility. We'll first do the calculation assuming that the Lees have no insurance, and then we'll recalculate it assuming that they have purchased insurance.

Without insurance, if the Lees are lucky and don't incur any medical expenses, they will have an income of $30,000, generating total utility of 1,080 utils. But if they have no insurance and are unlucky, incurring $10,000 in medical expenses, they will have just $20,000 of their income to spend on consumption and total utility of only 920 utils. So *without insurance*, the family's expected utility is (0.5 × 1,080) + (0.5 × 920) = 1,000 utils.

Now let's suppose that an insurance company offers to pay whatever medical expenses the family incurs during the next year in return for a **premium**—a payment to the insurance company—of $5,000. Note that the amount of the premium in this case is equal to the expected value of the Lees' medical expenses—the expected value of their future claim against the policy. An insurance policy with this feature, for which the premium is equal to the expected value of the claim, has a special name—a **fair insurance policy.**

Expected utility is the expected value of an individual's total utility given uncertainty about future outcomes.

A **premium** is a payment to an insurance company in return for the insurance company's promise to pay a claim in certain states of the world.

A **fair insurance policy** is an insurance policy for which the premium is equal to the expected value of the claim.

FIGURE **20-1**   The Utility Function and Marginal Utility Curve of a Risk-Averse Family

(a) Total Utility

Income	Total utility (utils)
$20,000	920
21,000	945
22,000	968
23,000	989
24,000	1,008
25,000	1,025
26,000	1,040
27,000	1,053
28,000	1,064
29,000	1,073
30,000	1,080

(b) Marginal Utility

Panel (a) shows how the total utility of the Lee family depends on its income available for consumption (that is, its income after medical expenses). The curve slopes upward: more income leads to higher total utility. But it gets flatter as we move up it and to the right, reflecting diminishing marginal utility. Panel (b) reflects the negative relationship between income and marginal utility when there is risk aversion: the marginal utility from each additional $1,000 of income is lower the higher your income. So the marginal utility of income is higher when the family has high medical expenses (point S) than when it has low medical expenses (point H).

If the family purchases this fair insurance policy, the expected value of its income available for consumption is the *same* as it would be without insurance: $25,000—that is, $30,000 minus the $5,000 premium. But the family's risk has been eliminated: the family has an income available for consumption of $25,000 *for sure,* which means that it receives the utility level associated with an income of $25,000.

Reading from the table in Figure 20-1, we see that this utility level is 1,025 utils. Or to put it a slightly different way, their expected utility with insurance is $1 \times 1,025 = 1,025$ utils, because with insurance they will receive a utility of 1,025 utils with a probability of 1. And this is higher than the level of expected utility without insurance—only 1,000 utils. So by eliminating risk through the purchase of a fair insurance policy, the family increases its expected utility even though its expected income hasn't changed.

The calculations for this example are summarized in Table 20-1. This example shows that the Lees, like most people in real life, are **risk-averse:** they will choose to reduce the risk they face when the cost of that reduction leaves the expected

Risk-averse individuals will choose to reduce the risk they face when that reduction leaves the expected value of their income or wealth unchanged.

TABLE 20-1	The Effect of Fair Insurance on the Lee Family's Income Available for Consumption and Expected Utility			
	Income in different states of the world			
	$0 in medical expenses (0.5 probability)	**$10,000 in medical expenses (0.5 probability)**	**Expected value of income available for consumption**	**Expected utility**
Without insurance	$30,000	$20,000	(0.5 × $30,000) + (0.5 × $20,000) = $25,000	(0.5 × 1,080 utils) + (0.5 × 920 utils) = 1,000 utils
With fair insurance	$25,000	$25,000	(0.5 × $25,000) + (0.5 × $25,000) = $25,000	(0.5 × 1,025 utils) + (0.5 × 1,025 utils) = 1,025 utils

value of their income or wealth unchanged. So the Lees, like most people, will be willing to buy fair insurance.

You might think that this result depends on the specific numbers we have chosen. In fact, however, the proposition that purchase of a fair insurance policy increases expected utility depends on only one assumption: diminishing marginal utility. The reason is that *with diminishing marginal utility, a dollar gained when income is low adds more to utility than a dollar gained when income is high.*

That is, having an additional dollar matters more when you are facing hard times than when you are facing good times. And as we will shortly see, a fair insurance policy is desirable because it transfers a dollar from high-income states (where it is valued less) to low-income states (where it is valued more).

But first, let's see how diminishing marginal utility leads to risk aversion by examining expected utility more closely. In the case of the Lee family, there are two states of the world; let's call them H and S, for healthy and sick. In state H the family has no medical expenses; in state S it has $10,000 in medical expenses. Let's use the symbols U_H and U_S to represent the Lee family's total utility in each state. Then the family's expected utility is:

(20-2) Expected utility = (Probability of state H × Total utility in state H) +
(Probability of state S × Total utility in state S)
= $(0.5 \times U_H) + (0.5 \times U_S)$

The fair insurance policy *reduces* the family's income available for consumption in state H by $5,000, but it *increases* it in state S by the same amount. As we've just seen, we can use the utility function to directly calculate the effects of these changes on expected utility. But as we have also seen in many other contexts, we gain more insight into individual choice by focusing on *marginal* utility.

To use marginal utility to analyze the effects of fair insurance, let's imagine introducing the insurance a bit at a time, say in 5,000 small steps. At each of these steps, we reduce income in state H by $1 and simultaneously increase income in state S by $1. At each of these steps, total utility in state H falls by the marginal utility of income in that state but total utility in state S rises by the marginal utility of income in that state.

Now look again at panel (b) of Figure 20-1, which shows how marginal utility varies with income. Point S shows marginal utility when the Lee family's income is $20,000; point H shows marginal utility when income is $30,000. Clearly, marginal utility is higher when income after medical expenses is low. Because of diminishing marginal utility, an additional dollar of income adds more to total utility when the family has low income (point S) than when it has high income (point H).

This tells us that the gain in expected utility from increasing income in state S is larger than the loss in expected utility from reducing income in state H by the same amount. So at each step of the process of reducing risk, by transferring $1 of income from state H to state S, expected utility increases. This is the same as saying that the family is risk-averse; that is, risk aversion is a result of diminishing marginal utility.

Almost everyone is risk-averse, because almost everyone has diminishing marginal utility. But the degree of risk aversion varies among individuals—some people

A **risk-neutral** person is completely insensitive to risk.

are more risk-averse than others. To illustrate this point, Figure 20-2 compares two individuals, Danny and Mel. We suppose that each of them earns the same income now but is confronted with the possibility of earning either $1,000 more or $1,000 less.

Panel (a) of Figure 20-2 shows how each individual's total utility would be affected by the change in income. Danny would gain very few utils from a rise in income, which moves him from N to H_D, but lose a large number of utils from a fall in income, which moves him from N to L_D. That is, he is highly risk-averse. This is reflected in panel (b) by his steeply declining marginal utility curve.

Mel, though, as shown in panel (a), would gain almost as many utils from higher income, which moves him from N to H_M, as he would lose from lower income, which moves him from N to L_M. He is barely risk-averse at all. This is reflected in his marginal utility curve in panel (b), which is almost horizontal. So, other things equal, Danny will gain a lot more utility from insurance than Mel will. Someone who is completely insensitive to risk is called **risk-neutral.**

FIGURE **20-2** Differences in Risk Aversion

Danny and Mel have different utility functions. Danny is highly risk-averse: a gain of $1,000 in income, which moves him from N to H_D, adds only a few utils to his total utility, but a $1,000 fall in income, which moves him from N to L_D, reduces his total utility by a large number of utils. By contrast, Mel gains almost as many utils from a $1,000 rise in income (the movement from N to H_M) as he loses from a $1,000 fall in income (the movement from N to L_M). This difference—reflected in the differing slopes of the two men's marginal utility curves—means that Danny would be willing to pay much more than Mel for insurance.

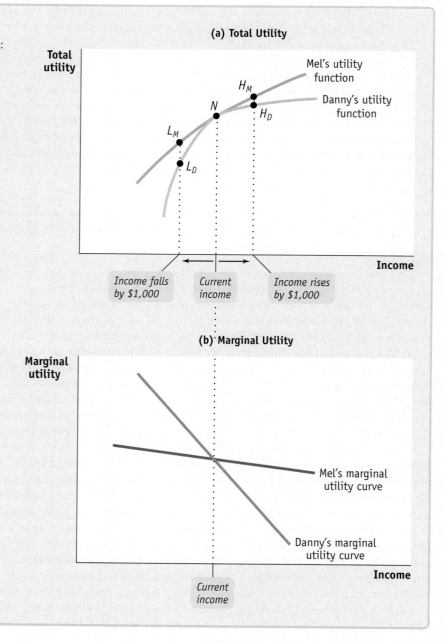

(a) Total Utility

(b) Marginal Utility

FOR INQUIRING MINDS | The Paradox of Gambling

If most people are risk-averse and risk-averse individuals won't take a fair gamble, how come Las Vegas, Atlantic City, and other places where gambling is legal do so much business?

After all, a casino doesn't even offer gamblers a fair gamble: all the games in any gambling facility are designed so that, on average, the casino makes money. So why would anyone play their games?

You might argue that the gambling industry caters to the minority of people who are actually the opposite of risk-averse: risk-loving. But a glance at the customers of Las Vegas hotels quickly refutes that

Are most gamblers risk takers or risk averse?

hypothesis: most of them aren't daredevils who also skydive and go snowboarding.

Instead, most of them are ordinary people who have health and life insurance and who wear seat belts. In other words, they are risk-averse like the rest of us.

So why do people gamble? Presumably because they enjoy the experience.

Also, gambling may be one of those areas where the assumption of rational behavior goes awry. Psychologists have concluded that gambling can be addictive in ways that are not that different from the addictive effects of drugs. Taking dangerous drugs is irrational; so is excessive gambling. Alas, both happen all the same. ∎

Individuals differ in risk aversion for two main reasons: differences in preferences and differences in initial income or wealth.

- *Differences in preferences.* Other things equal, people simply differ in how much their marginal utility is affected by their level of income. Someone whose marginal utility is relatively unresponsive to changes in income will be much less sensitive to risk. In contrast, someone whose marginal utility depends greatly on changes in income will be much more risk-averse.

- *Differences in initial income or wealth.* The possible loss of $1,000 makes a big difference to a family living below the poverty threshold; it makes very little difference to someone who earns $1 million a year. In general, people with whigh incomes or high wealth will be less risk-averse.

Differences in risk aversion have an important consequence: they affect how much an individual is willing to pay to avoid risk.

Paying to Avoid Risk

The risk-averse Lee family is clearly better off taking out a fair insurance policy—a policy that leaves their expected income unchanged but eliminates their risk. Unfortunately, real insurance policies are rarely fair: because insurance companies have to cover other costs, such as salaries for salespeople and actuaries, they charge more than they expect to pay in claims.

Will the Lee family still want to purchase an "unfair" insurance policy—one for which the premium is larger than the expected claim?

It depends on the size of the premium. Look again at Table 20-1. We know that without insurance expected utility is 1,000 utils and that insurance costing $5,000 raises expected utility to 1,025 utils. If the premium were $6,000, the Lees would be left with an income of $24,000, which, as you can see from Figure 20-1, would give them a total utility of 1,008 utils—which is still higher than their expected utility if they had no insurance at all. So the Lees would be willing to buy insurance with a $6,000 premium. But they wouldn't be willing to pay $7,000, which would reduce their income to $23,000 and their total utility to 989 utils.

This example shows that risk-averse individuals are willing to make deals that reduce their expected income but also reduce their risk: they are willing to pay a premium that exceeds their expected claim. The

PITFALLS

BEFORE THE FACT VERSUS AFTER THE FACT

Why is an insurance policy different from a doughnut?

No, it's not a riddle. Although the supply and demand for insurance behave like the supply and demand for any good or service, the payoff is very different. When you buy a doughnut, you know what you're going to get; when you buy insurance, by definition you *don't* know what you're going to get. If you bought car insurance and then didn't have an accident, you got nothing from the policy, except peace of mind, and might wish that you hadn't bothered. But if you did have an accident, you probably would be glad that you bought insurance that covered the cost.

This means we have to be careful in assessing the rationality of insurance purchases (or, for that matter, any decision made in the face of uncertainty). *After the fact*—after the uncertainty has been resolved—such decisions are almost always subject to second-guessing. But that doesn't mean that the decision was wrong *before the fact,* given the information available at the time.

One highly successful Wall Street investor told us that he never looks back—that as long as he believes he made the right decision given what he knew when he made it, he never reproaches himself if things turn out badly. That's the right attitude, and it almost surely contributes to his success.

more risk-averse they are, the higher the premium they are willing to pay. That willingness to pay is what makes the insurance industry possible. In contrast, a risk-neutral person is unwilling to pay at all to reduce his or her risk.

ECONOMICS ▶ in Action

Warranties

"Call me when you invent the warranty."

Many expensive consumer goods—electronic devices, major appliances, cars—come with some form of *warranty*. Typically, the manufacturer guarantees to repair or replace the item if something goes wrong with it during some specified period after purchase—usually six months or one year.

Why do manufacturers offer warranties? Part of the answer is that warranties *signal* to consumers that the goods are of high quality. But mainly warranties are a form of consumer insurance. For many people, the cost of repairing or replacing an expensive item like a refrigerator—or, worse yet, a car—would be a serious burden. If they were obliged to come up with the cash, their consumption of other goods would be restricted; as a result, their marginal utility of income would be higher than if they didn't have to pay for repairs.

So a warranty that covers the cost of repair or replacement increases the consumer's expected utility, even if the cost of the warranty is greater than the expected future claim paid by the manufacturer.

▼ Quick Review

- The **expected value** of a **random variable** is the weighted average of all possible values, where the weight corresponds to the probability of a given value occurring.

- Uncertainty about **states of the world** entails **risk**, or **financial risk** when there is an uncertain monetary outcome. When faced with uncertainty, consumers choose the option yielding the highest level of **expected utility.**

- Most people are **risk-averse:** they would be willing to purchase a **fair insurance policy** in which the premium is equal to the expected value of the claim.

- Risk aversion arises from diminishing marginal utility. Differences in preferences and in income or wealth lead to differences in risk aversion.

- Depending on the size of the **premium,** a risk-averse person may be willing to purchase an "unfair" insurance policy with a premium larger than the expected claim. The greater your risk aversion, the greater the premium you are willing to pay. A **risk-neutral** person is unwilling to pay any premium to avoid risk.

Check Your Understanding 20-1

1. Compare two families who own homes near the coast in Florida. Which family is likely to be more risk-averse—(i) a family with income of $2 million per year or (ii) a family with income of $60,000 per year? Would either family be willing to buy an "unfair" insurance policy to cover losses to their Florida home?

2. Karma's income next year is uncertain: there is a 60% probability she will make $22,000 and a 40% probability she will make $35,000. The accompanying table shows some income and utility levels for Karma.
   a. What is Karma's expected income? Her expected utility?
   b. What certain income level leaves her as well off as her uncertain income? What does this imply about Karma's attitudes toward risk? Explain.
   c. Would Karma be willing to pay some amount of money greater than zero for an insurance policy that guarantees her an income of $26,000? Explain.

Income	Total utility (utils)
$22,000	850
25,000	1,014
26,000	1,056
35,000	1,260

Solutions appear at back of book.

Buying, Selling, and Reducing Risk

Lloyd's of London is the oldest existing commercial insurance company, and it is an institution with an illustrious past. Originally formed in the eighteenth century to help merchants cope with the risks of commerce, it grew in the heyday of the British Empire into a mainstay of imperial trade.

The basic idea of Lloyd's was simple. In the eighteenth century, shipping goods via sailing vessels was risky: the chance that a ship would sink in a storm or be captured by pirates was fairly high. The merchant who owned the ship and its cargo could easily be ruined financially by such an event. Lloyd's matched ship-owners seeking insurance with wealthy investors who promised to compensate a merchant if his ship were lost. In return, the merchant paid the investor a fee in advance; if his ship *didn't* sink, the investor still kept the fee.

In effect, the merchant paid a price to relieve himself of risk. By matching people who wanted to purchase insurance with people who wanted to provide it, Lloyd's performed the functions of a market. The fact that British merchants could use Lloyd's to reduce their risk made many more people in Britain willing to undertake merchant trade.

Insurance companies have changed quite a lot from the early days of Lloyd's. They no longer consist of wealthy individuals deciding on insurance deals over port and boiled mutton. But asking why Lloyd's worked to the mutual benefit of merchants and investors is a good way to understand how the market economy as a whole "trades" and thereby transforms risk.

The insurance industry rests on two principles. The first is that trade in risk, like trade in any good or service, can produce mutual gains. In this case, the gains come when people who are less willing to bear risk transfer it to people who are more willing to bear it. The second is that some risk can be made to disappear through *diversification*. Let's consider each principle in turn.

Trading Risk

It may seem a bit strange to talk about "trading" risk. After all, risk is a bad thing—and aren't we supposed to be trading goods and services?

But people often trade away things they don't like to other people who dislike them less. Suppose you have just bought a house for $100,000, the average price for a house in your community. But you have now learned, to your horror, that the building next door is being turned into a nightclub. You want to sell the house immediately and are willing to accept $95,000 for it. But who will now be willing to buy it? The answer: a person who doesn't really mind late-night noise. Such a person might be willing to pay up to $100,000. So there is an opportunity here for a mutually beneficial deal—you are willing to sell for as little as $95,000, and the other person is willing to pay as much as $100,000, so any price in between will benefit both of you.

The key point is that the two parties have different sensitivities to noise, which enables those who most dislike noise, in effect, to pay other people to make their lives quieter. Trading risk works exactly the same way: people who want to reduce the risk they face can pay other people who are less sensitive to risk to take some of their risk away.

As we saw in the previous section, individual preferences account for some of the variations in people's attitudes toward risk, but differences in income and wealth are probably the principal reason behind different risk sensitivities. Lloyd's made money by matching wealthy investors who were more risk-tolerant with less wealthy and therefore more risk-averse shipowners.

Suppose, staying with our Lloyd's of London story, that a merchant whose ship went down would lose £1,000 and that there was a 10% chance of such a disaster. The expected loss in this case would be $0.10 \times £1,000 = £100$. But the merchant, whose whole livelihood was at stake, might have been willing to pay £150 to be compensated in the amount of £1,000 if the ship sank. Meanwhile, a wealthy investor for whom the loss of £1,000 was no big deal would have been willing to take this risk for a return only slightly better than the expected loss—say, £110. Clearly, there is room for a mutually beneficial deal here: the merchant pays something less than £150 and more than £110—say, £130—in return for compensation if the ship goes down. In effect, he has paid a less risk-averse individual to bear the burden of his risk. Everyone has been made better off by this transaction.

The funds that an insurer places at risk when providing insurance are called the insurer's **capital at risk.** In our example, the wealthy Lloyd's investor places

The funds that an insurer places at risk when providing insurance are called the insurer's **capital at risk.**

An **efficient allocation of risk** is an allocation of risk in which those who are most willing to bear risk are those who end up bearing it.

capital of £1,000 at risk in return for a premium of £130. In general, the amount of capital that potential insurers are willing to place at risk depends, other things equal, on the premium offered. If every ship is worth £1,000 and has a 10% chance of going down, nobody would offer insurance for less than a £100 premium, equal to the expected claim. In fact, only an investor who isn't risk-averse at all—that is, who is risk-neutral—would be willing to offer a policy at that price, because accepting a £100 premium would leave the insurer's expected income unchanged while increasing his or her risk.

Suppose there is one investor who is risk-neutral; but the next most willing investor is slightly risk-averse and insists on a £105 premium. The next investor, being somewhat more risk-averse, demands a premium of £110, and so on. By varying the premium and asking how many insurers would be willing to provide insurance at that premium, we can trace out a supply curve for insurance, as shown in Figure 20-3. As the premium increases as we move up the supply curve, more risk-averse investors are induced to provide coverage.

Meanwhile, potential buyers will consider their willingness to pay a given premium, defining the demand curve for insurance. In Figure 20-4, the highest premium that any shipowner is willing to pay is £200. Who's willing to pay this? The most risk-averse shipowner, of course. A slightly less risk-averse shipowner might be willing to pay £190, an even slightly less risk-averse shipowner is willing to pay £180, and so on.

Now imagine a market in which there are thousands of shipowners and potential insurers, so that the supply and demand curves for insurance are smooth lines. In this market, as in markets for ordinary goods and services, there will be an equilibrium price and quantity. Figure 20-5 illustrates such a market equilibrium at a premium of £130, with a total quantity of 5,000 policies bought and sold, representing a total capital at risk of £5,000,000.

Notice that in this market risk is transferred from the people who most want to get rid of it (the most risk-averse shipowners) to the people least bothered by risk (the least risk-averse investors). So just as markets for goods and services typically produce an efficient allocation of resources, markets for risk also typically lead to an **efficient allocation of risk**—an allocation

---

FIGURE **20-3** The Supply of Insurance

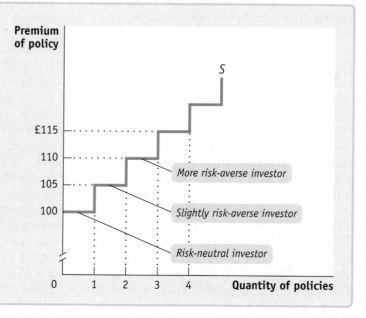

This is the supply of insurance policies to provide £1,000 in coverage to a merchant ship that has a 10% chance of being lost. Each investor has £1,000 of capital at risk. The lowest possible premium at which a policy is offered is £100, equal to the expected claim, and only a risk-neutral investor is willing to supply this policy. As the premium increases, investors who are more risk-averse are induced to supply policies to the market, increasing the quantity of policies supplied.

FIGURE 20-4   The Demand for Insurance

This is the demand for insurance policies for £1,000 in coverage of a merchant ship that has a 10% chance of being lost. In this example, the highest premium at which anyone demands a policy is £200, which only the most risk-averse shipowner will desire. As the premium falls, shipowners who are less risk-averse are induced to demand policies, increasing the quantity of policies demanded.

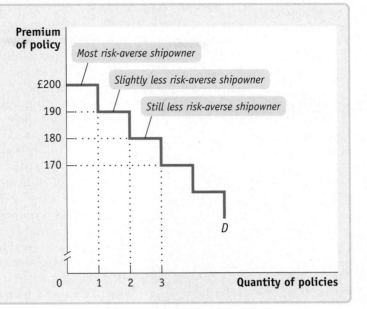

of risk in which those who are most willing to bear risk are those who end up bearing it. But as in the case of the markets for goods and services, there is an important qualification to this result: there are well-defined cases in which the market for risk fails to achieve efficiency. These arise from the presence of *private information,* which we will discuss in the next section.

The trading of risk between individuals who differ in their degree of risk aversion plays an extremely important role in the economy, but it is not the only way that markets can help people cope with risk. Under some circumstances, markets can perform a sort of magic trick: they can make some (though rarely all) of the risk that individuals face simply disappear.

FIGURE 20-5   The Insurance Market

Here we represent the hypothetical market for insuring a merchant ship, where each ship requires £1,000 in coverage. The demand curve is made up of shipowners who wish to buy insurance, and the supply curve is made up of wealthy investors who wish to supply insurance. In this example, at a premium of £200, only the most risk-averse shipowners will purchase insurance; at a premium of £100, only risk-neutral investors are willing to supply insurance. The equilibrium is at a premium of £130 with 5,000 policies bought and sold. In the absence of *private information,* (which we explain in the next section), the insurance market leads to an efficient allocation of risk.

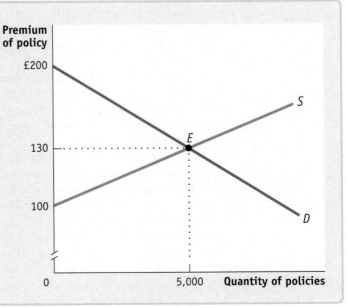

Two possible events are **independent events** if each of them is neither more nor less likely to happen if the other one happens.

Great Britain became a great maritime trading country because Lloyd's enabled investors and shipowners to trade risks.

Making Risk Disappear: The Power of Diversification

In the early days of Lloyd's, British merchant ships traversed the world, trading spices and silk from Asia, tobacco and rum from the New World, and textiles and wool from Britain, among other goods. Each of the many routes that British ships took had its own unique risks—pirates in the Caribbean, gales in the North Atlantic, typhoons in the Indian Ocean.

In the face of all these risks, how were merchants able to survive? One important way was by reducing their risks by not putting all their eggs in one basket: by sending different ships to different destinations, they could reduce the probability that all their ships would be lost. A strategy of investing in such a way as to reduce the probability of severe losses is known as *diversification*. As we'll now see, diversification can often make some of the economy's risk disappear.

Let's stay with our shipping example. It was all too likely that a pirate might seize a merchant ship in the Caribbean or that a typhoon might sink another ship in the Indian Ocean. But the key point here is that the various threats to shipping didn't have much to do with each other. So it was considerably less likely that a merchant who had one ship in the Caribbean and another ship in the Indian Ocean in a given year would lose them both, one to a pirate and the other to a typhoon. After all, there was no connection: the actions of cutthroats in the Caribbean had no influence on weather in the Indian Ocean, or vice versa.

Statisticians refer to such events—events that have no connection, so that one is no more likely to happen if the other does than if it does not—as **independent events.** Many unpredictable events are independent of each other. If you toss a coin twice, the probability that it will come up heads on the second toss is the same whether it came up heads or tails on the first toss. If your house burns down today, it does not affect the probability that my house will burn down the same day (unless we live next door to each other or employ the services of the same incompetent electrician).

There is a simple rule for calculating the probability that two independent events will both happen: multiply the probability that one event would happen on its own by the probability that the other event would happen on its own. If you toss a coin once, the probability that it will come up heads is 0.5; if you toss the coin twice, the probability that it will come up heads *both* times is $0.5 \times 0.5 = 0.25$.

But what did it matter to shipowners or Lloyd's investors that ship losses in the Caribbean and ship losses in the Indian Ocean were independent events? The answer is that by spreading their investments across different parts of the world, shipowners or Lloyd's investors could make some of the riskiness of the shipping business simply disappear.

Let's suppose that Joseph Moneypenny, Esq., is wealthy enough to outfit two ships—and let's ignore for a moment the possibility of insuring his ships. Should Mr. Moneypenny equip two ships for the Caribbean trade and send them off together? Or should he send one ship to Barbados and one to Calcutta?

Assume that both voyages will be equally profitable if successful, yielding £1,000 if the voyage is completed. Also assume that there is a 10% chance both that a ship sent to Barbados will run into a pirate and that a ship sent to Calcutta will be sunk by a typhoon. And if two ships travel to the same destination, we will assume that they share the same fate. So if Mr. Moneypenny were to send both his ships to either destination, he would face a probability of 10% of losing all his investment.

But if Mr. Moneypenny were instead to send one ship to Barbados and one to Calcutta, the probability that he would lose both of them would be only 0.1 × 0.1 = 0.01, or just 1%. As we will see shortly, his expected payoff would be the same—but the chance of losing it all would be much less. So by engaging in **diversification**—investing in several different things, where the possible losses are independent events—he could make some of his risk disappear.

Table 20-2 summarizes Mr. Moneypenny's options and their possible consequences. If he sends both ships to the same destination, he runs a 10% chance of losing them both. If he sends them to different destinations, there are three possible outcomes.

1. Both ships could arrive safely: because there is a 0.9 probability of either one making it, the probability that both will make it is 0.9 × 0.9 = 81%.

2. Both could be lost—but the probability of that happening is only 0.1 × 0.1 = 1%.

3. Only one ship can arrive. The probability that the first ship arrives and the second ship is lost is 0.9 × 0.1 = 9%. The probability that the first ship is lost but the second ship arrives is 0.1 × 0.9 = 9%. So the probability that only one ship makes it is 9% + 9% = 18%.

You might think that diversification is a strategy available only to those with a lot of money to begin with. Can Mr. Moneypenny diversify if he is able to afford only one ship? There are ways for even small investors to diversify. Even if Mr. Moneypenny is only wealthy enough to equip one ship, he can enter a partnership with another merchant. They can jointly outfit two ships, agreeing to share the profits equally, and then send those ships to different destinations. That way each faces less risk than if he equips one ship alone.

In the modern economy, diversification is made much easier for investors by the fact that they can easily buy shares in many companies by using the *stock market*. The owner of a **share** in a company is the owner of part of that company—typically a very small part, one-millionth or less. An individual who put all of his or her wealth in shares of a single company would lose all of that wealth if the company went bankrupt. But most investors hold shares in many companies, which makes the chance of losing all their investment very small.

In fact, Lloyd's of London wasn't just a way to trade risks; it was also a way for investors to diversify. To see how this worked, let's introduce Lady Penelope, a wealthy aristocrat, who decides to increase her income by placing £1,000 of her capital at risk via Lloyd's. She could use that capital to insure just one ship. But more typically she would enter a "syndicate," a group of investors, who would jointly insure a number of ships going to different destinations, agreeing to share the cost if any one of those ships went down. Because it would be much less likely for all the ships insured by the syndicate to sink than for any one of them to go down, Lady Penelope would be at much less risk of losing her entire capital.

> An individual can engage in **diversification** by investing in several different things, so that the possible losses are independent events.
>
> A **share** in a company is a partial ownership of that company.

TABLE 20-2 How Diversification Reduces Risk

(a) If both ships sent to the same destination

State	Probability	Payoff	Expected payoff
Both ships arrive	0.9 = 90%	£2,000	(0.9 × £2,000) + (0.1 × £0) = £1,800
Both ships lost	0.1 = 10%	0	

(b) If one ship sent east, one west

State	Probability	Payoff	Expected payoff
Both ships arrive	0.9 × 0.9 = 81%	£2,000	(0.81 × £2,000) + (0.01 × £0) + (0.18 × £1,000) = £1,800
Both ships lost	0.1 × 0.1 = 1%	0	
One ship arrives	(0.9 × 0.1) + (0.1 × 0.9) = 18%	1,000	

Pooling is a strong form of diversification in which an investor takes a small share of the risk in many independent events. This produces a payoff with very little total overall risk.

In some cases, an investor can make risk almost entirely disappear by taking a small share of the risk in many independent events. This strategy is known as **pooling.**

Consider the case of a health insurance company, which has millions of policyholders, with thousands of them requiring expensive treatment each year. The insurance company can't know whether any given individual will, say, require a heart bypass operation. But heart problems for two different individuals are pretty much independent events. And when there are many possible independent events, it is possible, using statistical analysis, to predict with great accuracy *how many* events of a given type will happen. For example, if you toss a coin 1,000 times, it will come up heads about 500 times—and it is very unlikely to be more than a percent or two off that figure.

So a company offering fire insurance can predict very accurately how many of its clients' homes will burn down in a given year; a company offering health insurance can predict very accurately how many of its clients will need heart surgery in a given year; a life insurance company can predict how many of its clients will . . . Well, you get the idea.

When an insurance company is able to take advantage of the predictability that comes from aggregating a large number of independent events, it is said to engage in *pooling of risks.* And this pooling often means that even though insurance companies protect people from risk, the owners of the insurance companies may not themselves face much risk.

Lloyd's of London wasn't just a way for wealthy individuals to get paid for taking on some of the risks of less wealthy merchants. It was also a vehicle for pooling some of those risks. The effect of that pooling was to shift the supply curve in Figure 20-5 rightward: to make investors willing to accept more risk, at a lower price, than would otherwise have been possible.

FOR INQUIRING MINDS | Those Pesky Emotions

For a small investor (someone investing less than several hundred thousand dollars), financial economists agree that the best strategy for investing in stocks is to buy an index fund.

Why index funds? Because they contain a wide range of stocks that reflect the overall market, they achieve diversification; and they have very low management fees. In addition, financial economists agree that it's a losing strategy to try to "time" the market: to buy when the stock market is low and sell when it's high. Instead, small investors should buy a fixed dollar amount of stocks and other financial assets every year, regardless of the state of the market.

Yet many, if not most, small investors don't follow this advice. Instead, they buy individual stocks or funds that charge high fees. They spend endless hours online chasing the latest hot tip or sifting through data trying to discern patterns in stocks' behavior. They try to time the market but

"Your mother called to remind you to diversify."

invariably buy when stocks are high and refuse to sell losers before they lose even more. And they fail to diversify, instead concentrating too much money in a few stocks they think are "winners."

So why are human beings so dense when it comes to investing? According to experts, the culprit is emotion. In his book *Your Money and Your Brain,* Jason Zweig states, "the brain is not an optimal tool

for making financial decisions." As he explains it, the problem is that the human brain evolved to detect and interpret simple patterns. (Is there a lion lurking in that bush?) As a consequence, "when it comes to investing, our incorrigible search for patterns leads us to assume that order exists where it often doesn't." In other words, investors fool themselves into believing that they've discovered a lucrative stock market pattern when, in fact, stock market behavior is largely random.

Not surprisingly, how people make financial decisions is a major topic of study in the area of behavioral economics, a branch of economics that studies why human beings often fail to behave rationally (as covered in Chapter 9).

So, what's the typical twenty-first-century investor to do? According to Mr. Zweig, there's hope: if you recognize the influence of your emotions, then you can tame them. ■

The Limits of Diversification

Diversification can reduce risk. In some cases it can eliminate it. But these cases are not typical, because there are important limits to diversification. We can see the most important reason for these limits by returning to Lloyd's one more time.

In Lloyd's early days, there was one important hazard facing British shipping other than pirates or storms: war. Between 1690 and 1815, Britain fought a series of wars, mainly with France (which, among other things, went to war with Britain in support of the American Revolution). Each time, France would sponsor "privateers"—basically pirates with official backing—to raid British shipping and thus indirectly damage Britain's war effort.

Whenever war broke out between Britain and France, losses of British merchant ships would increase. Unfortunately, merchants could not protect themselves against this eventuality by sending ships to different ports: the privateers would prey on British ships anywhere in the world. So the loss of a ship to French privateers in the Caribbean and the loss of another ship to French privateers in the Indian Ocean would *not* be independent events. It would be quite likely that they would happen in the same year.

When an event is more likely to occur if some other event occurs, these two events are said to be **positively correlated.** And like the risk of having a ship seized by French privateers, many financial risks are, alas, positively correlated.

Here are some of the positively correlated financial risks that investors in the modern world face:

- *Severe weather.* Within any given region of the United States, losses due to weather are definitely not independent events. When a hurricane hits Florida, a lot of Florida homes will suffer hurricane damage. To some extent, insurance companies can diversify away this risk by insuring homes in many states. But events like El Niño (a recurrent temperature anomaly in the Pacific Ocean that disrupts weather around the world) can cause simultaneous flooding across the United States. And as we mentioned in our opening story, over the past several years, there has been a significant increase in extreme weather.

- *Political events.* Modern governments do not, thankfully, license privateers—although submarines served much the same function during World War II. Even today, however, some kinds of political events—say, a war or revolution in a key raw-material-producing area—can damage business around the globe.

- *Business cycles.* The causes of *business cycles,* fluctuations in the output of the economy as a whole, are a subject for macroeconomics. What we can say here is that if one company suffers a decline in business because of a nationwide economic slump, many other companies will also suffer such declines. So these events will be positively correlated.

When events are positively correlated, the risks they pose cannot be diversified away. An investor can protect herself from the risk that any one company will do badly by investing in many companies; she cannot use the same technique to protect against an economic slump in which *all* companies do badly.

An insurance company can protect itself against the risk of losses from local flooding by insuring houses in many different places; but a global weather pattern that produces floods in many places will defeat this strategy. Not surprisingly, insurers pulled back from writing policies when it became clear that extreme weather patterns had become worse. They could no longer be confident that profits from policies written in good weather areas would be sufficient to compensate for losses incurred on policies in hurricane and drought prone areas.

So institutions like insurance companies and stock markets cannot make risk go away completely. There is always an irreducible core of risk that cannot be diversified. Markets for risk, however, do accomplish two things: First, they enable the economy to eliminate the risk that can be diversified. Second, they allocate the risk that remains to the people most willing to bear it.

Two events are **positively correlated** if each event is more likely to occur if the other event also occurs.

ECONOMICS ▶ in Action

When Lloyd's Almost Lost It

At the end of the 1980s, the venerable institution of Lloyd's found itself in severe trouble. Investors who had placed their capital at risk, believing that the risks were small and the return on their investments more or less assured, found themselves required to make large payments to satisfy enormous claims. A number of investors, including members of some very old aristocratic families, found themselves pushed into bankruptcy.

What happened? Part of the answer is that ambitious managers at Lloyd's had persuaded investors to take on risks that were much larger than the investors realized. (Or to put it a different way, the premiums the investors accepted were too small for the true level of risk contained in the policies.)

But the biggest single problem was that many of the events against which Lloyd's had become a major insurer were *not* independent. In the 1970s and 1980s, Lloyd's had become a major provider of corporate liability insurance in the United States: it protected American corporations against the possibility that they might be sued for selling defective or harmful products. Everyone expected such suits to be more or less independent events. Why should one company's legal problems have much to do with another's?

The answer turned out to lie in one word: asbestos. For decades, this fireproofing material had been used in many products, which meant that many companies were responsible for its use. Then it turned out that asbestos can cause severe damage to the lungs, especially in children. The result was a torrent of lawsuits by people who believed they were injured by asbestos and billions of dollars in damage awards—many of them ultimately paid by Lloyd's investors.

The overwhelming number of asbestos claims faced by Lloyd's make it clear that insurance companies cannot completely eliminate risk.

▼ Quick Review

• Insurance markets exist because there are gains from trade in risk. Except in the case of private information, they lead to an **efficient allocation of risk**: those who are most willing to bear risk place their **capital at risk** to cover the financial losses of those least willing to bear risk.

• When **independent events** are involved, a strategy of **diversification** can substantially reduce risk. Diversification is made easier by the existence of institutions like the stock market, in which people trade **shares** of companies. A form of diversification, relevant especially to insurance companies, is **pooling**.

• When events are **positively correlated,** there is a core of risk that cannot be eliminated, no matter how much individuals diversify.

Check Your Understanding 20-2

1. Explain how each of the following events would change the equilibrium premium and quantity of insurance in the market, indicating any shifts in the supply and demand curves.
   a. An increase in the number of ships traveling the same trade routes and so facing the same kinds of risks
   b. An increase in the number of trading routes, with the same number of ships traveling a greater variety of routes and so facing different kinds of risk
   c. An increase in the degree of risk aversion among the shipowners in the market
   d. An increase in the degree of risk aversion among the investors in the market
   e. An increase in the risk affecting the economy as a whole
   f. A fall in the wealth levels of investors in the market

Solutions appear at back of book.

Private Information: What You Don't Know Can Hurt You

Markets do very well at dealing with diversifiable risk and with risk due to uncertainty: situations in which nobody knows what is going to happen, whose house will be flooded, or who will get sick. However, markets have much more trouble with situations in which *some people know things that other people don't know*—situations of **private information.** As we will see, private information can distort economic decisions and sometimes prevent mutually beneficial economic transactions from taking place. (Sometimes economists use the term *asymmetric information* rather than *private information,* but they are equivalent.)

Why is some information private? The most important reason is that people generally know more about themselves than other people do. For example, you know whether or not you are a careful driver; but unless you have already been in several accidents, your auto insurance company does not. You are more likely to have a better estimate than your insurance company of whether or not you will need an expensive medical procedure. And if you are selling me your used car, you are more likely to be aware of any problems with it than I am.

But why should such differences in who knows what be a problem? It turns out that there are two distinct sources of trouble: *adverse selection,* which arises from having private information about the way things are, and *moral hazard,* which arises from having private information about what people do.

> **Private information** is information that some people have but others do not.

> **Adverse selection** occurs when an individual knows more about the way things are than other people do. Private information leads buyers to expect hidden problems in items offered for sale, leading to low prices and the best items being kept off the market.

Adverse Selection: The Economics of Lemons

Suppose that someone offers to sell you an almost brand-new car—purchased just three months ago, with only 2,000 miles on the odometer and no dents or scratches. Will you be willing to pay almost the same for it as for a car direct from the dealer?

Probably not, for one main reason: you cannot help but wonder why this car is being sold. Is it because the owner has discovered that something is wrong with it—that it is a "lemon"? Having driven the car for a while, the owner knows more about it than you do—and people are more likely to sell cars that give them trouble.

You might think that the fact that sellers of used cars know more about them than the buyers do represents an advantage to the sellers. But potential buyers know that potential sellers are likely to offer them lemons—they just don't know exactly which car is a lemon. For this reason, buyers will offer a lower price than they would if they had a guarantee of the car's quality. And this poor opinion of used cars tends to be self-reinforcing, precisely because it depresses the prices that buyers offer. Used cars sell at a significant discount because buyers expect a disproportionate share of those cars to be lemons.

Even a used car that is not a lemon would sell only at a large discount because buyers don't know whether it's a lemon or not. But potential sellers who have good cars are unwilling to sell them at a deep discount, except under exceptional circumstances. So good used cars are rarely offered for sale, and used cars that are offered for sale have a strong tendency to be lemons. (This is why people who have a compelling reason to sell a car, such as moving overseas, make a point of revealing that information to potential buyers—as if to say "This car is not a lemon!")

The end result, then, is not only that used cars sell for low prices and that there are a large number of used cars with hidden problems. Equally important, many potentially beneficial transactions—sales of good cars by people who would like to get rid of them to people who would like to buy them—end up being frustrated by the inability of potential sellers to convince potential buyers that their cars are actually worth the higher price being asked. So some mutually beneficial trades between those who want to sell used cars and those who want to buy them go unexploited.

Although economists sometimes refer to situations like this as the "lemons problem," the more formal name of the problem is **adverse selection.** The reason for the name is obvious: because the potential sellers know more about the quality of what they are selling than the potential buyers, they have an incentive to select the worst things to sell.

How do I know whether or not this used car is a lemon?

Adverse selection can be reduced through **screening:** using observable information about people to make inferences about their private information.

Adverse selection can be diminished by people **signaling** their private information through actions that credibly reveal what they know.

A long-term **reputation** allows an individual to reassure others that he or she isn't concealing adverse private information.

Adverse selection does not apply only to used cars. It is a problem for many parts of the economy—notably for insurance companies, and most notably for health insurance companies.

Suppose that a health insurance company were to offer a standard policy to everyone with the same premium. The premium would reflect the *average* risk of incurring a medical expense. But that would make the policy look very expensive to healthy people, who know that they are less likely than the average person to incur medical expenses. So healthy people would be less likely than less healthy people to buy the policy, leaving the health insurance company with exactly the customers it doesn't want: people with a higher-than-average risk of needing medical care, who would find the premium to be a good deal.

In order to cover its expected losses from this sicker customer pool, the health insurance company is compelled to raise premiums, driving away more of the remaining healthier customers, and so on. Because the insurance company can't determine who is healthy and who is not, it must charge everyone the same premium, thereby discouraging healthy people from purchasing policies and encouraging unhealthy people to buy policies.

As we discussed in Chapter 18, before the passage of the Affordable Care Act, adverse selection could lead to a phenomenon called an *adverse selection death spiral* as the market for health insurance collapsed: insurance companies refused to offer policies because there was no premium at which the company could cover its losses. Because of the severe adverse selection problems, governments in many advanced countries have assumed the role of providing health insurance to their citizens. In the United States, adverse selection in health insurance is avoided in two ways. First, U.S. government insurance programs, which provided almost half of the total payments for medical care in the United States in 2014, are financed by dedicated taxes which people cannot opt out of. Second, the ACA requires that everyone have health insurance, so healthy people cannot opt out of paying premiums.

However, adverse selection still exists in other insurance markets such as auto insurance. In general, people or firms faced with the problem of adverse selection follow one of several well-established strategies for dealing with it. One strategy is **screening:** using observable information to make inferences about private information. If you apply to purchase auto insurance, you'll find that the insurance company will ask about your driving record in an attempt to "screen out" unsafe drivers—people they will refuse to insure or will insure only at very high premiums.

Auto insurance companies provide a very good example of the use of statistics in screening to reduce adverse selection. They may not know whether you are a careful driver, but they have statistical data on the accident rates of people who resemble your profile—and use those data in setting premiums. A 19-year-old male who drives a sports car and has already had a fender-bender is likely to pay a much higher premium than a 40-year-old female who drives an SUV and has never had an accident.

In some cases, this may be unfair: some adolescent males are very careful drivers, and some women drive SUVs as if they were F-16's. But nobody can deny that the insurance companies are right on average.

Another strategy to counter the problems caused by adverse selection is for people who are good prospects to do something **signaling** their private information—taking some action that wouldn't be worth taking unless they were indeed good prospects. For example, reputable used-car dealers often offer warranties—promises to repair any problems with the cars they sell that arise within a given amount of time. This isn't just a way of insuring their customers against possible expenses; it's a way of credibly showing that they are not selling lemons. As a result, more sales occur and dealers can command higher prices for their used cars.

Finally, in the face of adverse selection, it can be very valuable to establish a good **reputation:** a used-car dealership will often advertise how long it has been in business to show that it has continued to satisfy its customers. As a result, new customers will be willing to purchase cars and to pay more for that dealer's cars.

Moral Hazard

In the late 1970s, New York and other major cities experienced an epidemic of suspicious fires that appeared to be deliberately set. Investigators eventually became aware of patterns in a number of the fires. Particular landlords who owned several buildings seemed to have an unusually large number of their buildings burn down. Although it was difficult to prove, police suspected that most of these fire-prone landlords were hiring professional arsonists to torch their own properties.

Why burn your own building? These buildings were typically in declining neighborhoods, where rising crime and middle-class flight had led to a decline in property values. But the insurance policies on the buildings were written to compensate owners based on historical property values, and so would pay the owner of a destroyed building more than the building was worth in the current market. For an unscrupulous landlord who knew the right people, this presented a profitable opportunity.

The arson epidemic became less severe during the 1980s, partly because insurance companies began making it difficult to overinsure properties, and partly because a boom in real estate values made many previously arson-threatened buildings worth more unburned.

The arson episodes make it clear that it is a bad idea for insurance companies to let customers insure buildings for more than their value—it gives the customers some destructive incentives. You might think, however, that the incentive problem would go away as long as the insurance is no more than 100% of the value of what is being insured.

But, unfortunately, anything close to 100% insurance still distorts incentives—it induces policyholders to behave differently than they would in the absence of insurance. The reason is that preventing fires requires effort and cost on the part of a building's owner. Fire alarms and sprinkler systems have to be kept in good repair, and fire safety rules have to be strictly enforced. All of this takes time and money that the owner may not find worth spending if the insurance policy will provide close to full compensation for any losses.

Of course, the insurance company could specify in the policy that it won't pay if basic safety precautions have not been taken. But it isn't always easy to tell how careful a building's owner has been—the owner knows, but the insurance company does not.

The point is that the building's owner has private information about his or her own actions, about whether he or she has really taken all appropriate precautions. As a result, the insurance company is likely to face more claims than if it were able to determine exactly how much effort a building owner exerts to prevent a loss. The problem of distorted incentives arises when an individual has private information about his or her own actions but someone else bears the costs of a lack of care or effort. This is known as **moral hazard.**

To deal with moral hazard, it is necessary to give individuals with private information some personal stake in what happens so they have a reason to exert effort even if others cannot verify that they have done so. Moral hazard is the reason salespeople in many stores receive a commission on sales: it's hard for managers to be sure how hard the salespeople are really working, and if they were paid only a straight salary, they would not have an incentive to exert effort to make those sales.

Insurance companies deal with moral hazard by requiring a **deductible:** they compensate for losses only above a certain amount, so that coverage is always less than 100%. The insurance on your car, for example, may pay for repairs only after the first $500 in loss. This means that a careless driver who gets into a fender-bender will end up paying $500 for repairs even if he is insured, which provides at least some incentive to be careful and reduces moral hazard.

Moral hazard occurs when an individual knows more about his or her own actions than other people do. This leads to a distortion of incentives to take care or to exert effort when someone else bears the costs of the lack of care or effort.

A **deductible** in an insurance policy is a sum that the insured individual must pay before being compensated for a claim.

In addition to reducing moral hazard, deductibles provide a partial solution to the problem of adverse selection. Your insurance premium often drops substantially if you are willing to accept a large deductible. This is an attractive option to people who know they are low-risk customers; it is less attractive to people who know they are high-risk—and so are likely to have an accident and end up paying the deductible. By offering a menu of policies with different premiums and deductibles, insurance companies can screen their customers, inducing them to sort themselves out on the basis of their private information.

As the example of deductibles suggests, moral hazard limits the ability of the economy to allocate risks efficiently. You generally can't get full (100%) insurance on your home or car, even though you would like to buy it, and you bear the risk of large deductibles, even though you would prefer not to. The following Economics in Action illustrates how in some cases moral hazard limits the ability of investors to diversify their investments.

ECONOMICS ▶ in Action

Franchise Owners Try Harder

When Americans go out for a quick meal, they often end up at one of the fast-food chains—McDonald's, Pizza Hut, Wendy's, and so on. Because these are large corporations, most customers probably imagine that the people who serve them are themselves employees of large corporations. But usually they aren't. Most fast-food restaurants—for example, 85% of McDonald's outlets—are franchises. That is, some individual has paid the parent company for the right to operate a restaurant selling its product; he or she may look like an arm of a giant company but is in fact a small-business owner.

Becoming a franchisee is not a guarantee of success. You must put up a large amount of money, both to buy the license and to set up the restaurant itself. For example, in 2014 it cost between $1.1 and $2.2 million to open a McDonald's franchise. And although McDonald's takes care that its franchises are not too close to each other, they often face stiff competition from rival chains and even from a few truly independent restaurants. Becoming a franchise owner, in other words, involves taking on a lot of risk.

But why should people be willing to take these risks? Didn't we just learn that it is better to diversify, to spread your wealth among many investments?

The logic of diversification would seem to say that it's better for someone with $1.7 million to invest in a wide range of stocks rather than put it all into one Taco Bell. This implies that Taco Bell would find it hard to attract franchisees: nobody would be willing to be a franchisee unless they expected to earn considerably more than they would as a simple hired manager with their wealth invested in a diversified portfolio of stocks. So wouldn't it be more profitable for Pizza Hut or Taco Bell simply to hire managers to run their restaurants?

It turns out that it isn't, because the success of a restaurant depends a lot on how hard the manager works, on the effort he or she puts into choosing the right employees, on keeping the place clean and attractive to customers, and so on. The problem is moral hazard: the manager knows whether he or she is really putting 100% into the job; but company headquarters, which bears the costs of a poorly run

Franchise owners face risk, which motivates them to work harder than salaried managers.

restaurant, does not. So a salaried manager, who gets paid even without doing everything possible to make the restaurant a success, does not have the incentive to do that extra bit—an incentive the owner does have because he or she has a substantial personal stake in the restaurant's success.

In other words, there is a moral hazard problem when a salaried manager runs a Pizza Hut, where the private information is how hard the manager works. Franchising solves this problem. A franchisee, whose wealth is tied up in the business and who stands to profit personally from its success, has every incentive to work extremely hard.

The result is that fast-food chains rely mainly on franchisees to operate their restaurants, even though the contracts with these owner-managers allow the franchisees on average to make much more than it would have cost the companies to employ store managers. The higher earnings of franchisees compensate them for the risk they accept, and the companies are compensated by higher sales that lead to higher license fees.

In addition, franchisees are forbidden by the licensing agreement with the company from reducing their risk by taking actions such as selling shares of the franchise to outside investors and using the proceeds to diversify. It's an illustration of the fact that moral hazard prevents the elimination of risk through diversification.

Check Your Understanding   20-3

1. Your car insurance premiums are lower if you have had no moving violations for several years. Explain how this feature tends to decrease the potential inefficiency caused by adverse selection.

2. A common feature of home construction contracts is that when it costs more to construct a building than was originally estimated, the contractor must absorb the additional cost. Explain how this feature reduces the problem of moral hazard but also forces the contractor to bear more risk than she would like.

3. True or false? Explain your answer, stating what concept analyzed in this chapter accounts for the feature.
   People with higher deductibles on their auto insurance:
   a. Generally drive more carefully
   b. Pay lower premiums
   c. Generally are wealthier

   Solutions appear at back of book.

> ### ▼ Quick Review
>
> • **Private information** can distort incentives and prevent mutually beneficial transactions from occurring. One source is **adverse selection:** sellers have private information about their goods and buyers offer low prices, leading the sellers of quality goods to drop out and leaving the market dominated by "lemons."
>
> • Adverse selection can be reduced by revealing private information through **screening** or **signaling,** or by cultivating a long-term **reputation.**
>
> • Another source of problems is **moral hazard.** In the case of insurance, it leads individuals to exert too little effort to prevent losses. This gives rise to features like **deductibles,** which limit the efficient allocation of risk.

AP Photo/Clive Gee

Aig (American International Group) was once the largest insurance company in the United States, known for insuring millions of homes and businesses and managing the pension plans of millions of workers.

But in September 2008, AIG was at the epicenter of the crisis sweeping global financial markets because major commercial and investment banks faced potentially devastating losses through their transactions with AIG. Fearful that a chaotic bankruptcy of AIG would panic the already distressed financial markets, the Federal Reserve stepped in and orchestrated a $182 billion corporate bailout of AIG, the largest in U.S. history. In return, American taxpayers became owners of nearly 80% of AIG. How did things go so wrong?

AIG's problems originated not in its main businesses—property insurance and pension management—but in its smaller Financial Products Division, which sold *credit-default swaps*, or CDS. A CDS is like an insurance policy for an investor who buys a bond. A bond is simply an IOU—a promise to repay on the part of the person or company that issued the bond. But any IOU carries the possibility that the borrower will default on the loan. So bond investors who wish to protect themselves against the risk of default purchases a CDS from a company like AIG. If the borrower defaults, bond investors collect an amount equal to their losses from the company that issued the CDS.

In the mid-2000s, Joseph Cassano, the head of AIG's Financial Products Division, sold hundreds of billions of dollars worth of CDSs to investors in mortgage-backed securities—bonds created by combining thousands of American home mortgages. Sales of CDSs made the Financial Products Division AIG's most profitable department. And there were virtually no costs involved because mortgage defaults were low and the Financial Products Division was located in London, meaning that AIG was not required to abide by U.S. insurance regulations to set aside capital to cover potential losses—despite the fact that AIG, the parent company, was headquartered in the United States. As Cassano stated in 2007, "It is hard for us . . . to even see a scenario within any kind of realm of reason that would see us losing $1 in any of those transactions." Cassano was so confident in his strategy and fearful of outside meddling that he prevented auditors from inspecting his books, leaving AIG's management and shareholders in the dark about the risks they faced.

Yet the hard-to-see scenario appeared in 2008 when the U.S. housing market crashed. As mortgage defaults surged, investors in mortgage-backed securities incurred huge losses and turned to AIG to collect. But with no capital to cover claims, AIG faced bankruptcy until the U.S. government stepped in.

Banks such as Goldman Sachs, had made huge profits by putting together low-quality mortgage-backed securities with high likelihoods of default and then insuring them with AIG. Despite an outcry, Goldman's claims were paid in full by the government because their transaction with AIG was entirely legal.

QUESTIONS FOR THOUGHT

1. Did AIG accurately assess the default risk that it insured? Why or why not?

2. What did AIG assume about the probabilities of defaults by different homeowners in the U.S. housing market? Were they wrong or right?

3. What are the examples of moral hazard in the case? For each example, explain who committed the moral hazard and against whom and identify the source of the private information.

4. Cite an example of adverse selection from the case. What was the source of the private information?

SUMMARY

1. The **expected value** of a **random variable** is the weighted average of all possible values, where the weight corresponds to the probability of a given value occurring.

2. **Risk** is uncertainty about future events or **states of the world.** It is **financial risk** when the uncertainty is about monetary outcomes.

3. Under uncertainty, people maximize **expected utility.** A **risk-averse** person will choose to reduce risk when that reduction leaves the expected value of his or her income or wealth uncha nged. A **fair insurance policy** has that feature: the **premium** is equal to the expected value of the claim. A **risk-neutral** person is completely insensitive to risk and therefore unwilling to pay any premium to avoid it.

4. Risk aversion arises from diminishing marginal utility: an additional dollar of income generates higher marginal utility in low-income states than in high-income states. A fair insurance policy increases a risk-averse person's utility because it transfers a dollar from a high-income state (a state when no loss occurs) to a low-income state (a state when a loss occurs).

5. Differences in preferences and income or wealth lead to differences in risk aversion. Depending on the size of the premium, a risk-averse person is willing to purchase "unfair" insurance, a policy for which the premium exceeds the expected value of the claim. The greater your risk aversion, the higher the premium you are willing to pay.

6. There are gains from trade in risk, leading to an **efficient allocation of risk:** those who are most willing to bear risk put their **capital at risk** to cover the losses of those least willing to bear risk.

7. Risk can also be reduced through **diversification,** investing in several different things that correspond to **independent events.** The stock market, where **shares** in companies are traded, offers one way to diversify. Insurance companies can engage in **pooling,** insuring many independent events so as to eliminate almost all risk. But when the underlying events are **positively correlated,** all risk cannot be diversified away.

8. **Private information** can cause inefficiency in the allocation of risk. One problem is **adverse selection,** private information about the way things are. It creates the "lemons problem" in used-car markets, where sellers of high-quality cars drop out of the market. Adverse selection can be limited in several ways—through **screening** of individuals, through the **signaling** that people use to reveal their private information, and through the building of a **reputation.**

9. A related problem is **moral hazard:** individuals have private information about their actions, which distorts their incentives to exert effort or care when someone else bears the costs of that lack of effort or care. It limits the ability of markets to allocate risk efficiently. Insurance companies try to limit moral hazard by imposing **deductibles,** placing more risk on the insured.

KEY TERMS

Random variable, p. 582
Expected value, p. 582
State of the world, p. 582
Risk, p. 582
Financial risk, p. 582
Expected utility, p. 583
Premium, p. 583
Fair insurance policy, p. 583

Risk-averse, p. 584
Risk-neutral, p. 586
Capital at risk, p. 589
Efficient allocation of risk, p. 590
Independent events, p. 592
Diversification, p. 593
Share, p. 593
Pooling, p. 594

Positively correlated, p. 595
Private information, p. 597
Adverse selection, p. 597
Screening, p. 598
Signaling, p. 598
Reputation, p. 598
Moral hazard, p. 599
Deductible, p. 599

PROBLEMS

1. For each of the following situations, calculate the expected value.

   a. Tanisha owns one share of IBM stock, which is currently trading at $80. There is a 50% chance that the share price will rise to $100 and a 50% chance that it will fall to $70. What is the expected value of the future share price?

   b. Sharon buys a ticket in a small lottery. There is a probability of 0.7 that she will win nothing, of 0.2 that she will win $10, and of 0.1 that she will win $50. What is the expected value of Sharon's winnings?

   c. Aaron is a farmer whose rice crop depends on the weather. If the weather is favorable, he will make a profit of $100. If the weather is unfavorable, he will make a profit of −$20 (that is, he will lose money). The weather forecast reports that the probability of weather being favorable is 0.9 and the probability of weather being unfavorable is 0.1. What is the expected value of Aaron's profit?

2. Vicky N. Vestor is considering investing some of her money in a startup company. She currently has income of $4,000, and she is considering investing $2,000 of that in the company. There is a 0.5 probability that the company will succeed and will pay out $8,000 to Vicky (her original investment of $2,000 plus $6,000 of the company's profits). And there is a 0.5 probability that the company will fail and Vicky will get nothing (and lose her investment). The accompanying table illustrates Vicky's utility function.

Income	Total utility (utils)
$0	0
1,000	50
2,000	85
3,000	115
4,000	140
5,000	163
6,000	183
7,000	200
8,000	215
9,000	229
10,000	241

   a. Calculate Vicky's marginal utility of income for each income level. Is Vicky risk-averse?

   b. Calculate the expected value of Vicky's income if she makes this investment.

   c. Calculate Vicky's expected utility from making the investment.

   d. What is Vicky's utility from not making the investment? Will Vicky therefore invest in the company?

3. Vicky N. Vestor's utility function was given in Problem 2. As in Problem 2, Vicky currently has income of $4,000. She is considering investing in a startup company, but the investment now costs $4,000 to make. If the company fails, Vicky will get nothing from the company. But if the company succeeds, she will get $10,000 from the company (her original investment of $4,000 plus $6,000 of the company's profits). Each event has a 0.5 probability of occurring. Will Vicky invest in the company?

4. You have $1,000 that you can invest. If you buy Ford stock, you face the following returns and probabilities from holding the stock for one year: with a probability of 0.2 you will get $1,500; with a probability of 0.4 you will get $1,100; and with a probability of 0.4 you will get $900. If you put the money into the bank, in one year's time you will get $1,100 for certain.

   a. What is the expected value of your earnings from investing in Ford stock?

   b. Suppose you are risk-averse. Can we say for sure whether you will invest in Ford stock or put your money into the bank?

5. Wilbur is an airline pilot who currently has income of $60,000. If he gets sick and loses his flight medical certificate, he loses his job and has only $10,000 income. His probability of staying healthy is 0.6, and his probability of getting sick is 0.4. Wilbur's utility function is given in the accompanying table.

Income	Total utility (utils)
$0	0
10,000	60
20,000	110
30,000	150
40,000	180
50,000	200
60,000	210

   a. What is the expected value of Wilbur's income?

   b. What is Wilbur's expected utility?

   Wilbur thinks about buying "loss-of-license" insurance that will compensate him if he loses his flight medical certificate.

   c. One insurance company offers Wilbur full compensation for his income loss (that is, the insurance company pays Wilbur $50,000 if he loses his flight medical certificate), and it charges a premium of $40,000. That is, regardless of whether he loses his flight medical certificate, Wilbur's income after insurance will be $20,000. What is Wilbur's utility? Will he buy the insurance?

   d. What is the highest premium Wilbur would just be willing to pay for full insurance (insurance that completely compensates him for the income loss)?

6. From 1990 to 2013, 1 in approximately every 277 cars produced in the United States was stolen. Beth owns a car worth $20,000 and is considering purchasing an insurance policy to protect herself from car theft. For the following questions, assume that the chance of car theft is the same in all regions and across all car models.

   a. What should the premium for a fair insurance policy have been in 2013 for a policy that replaces Beth's car if it is stolen?

   b. Suppose an insurance company charges 0.6% of the car's value for a policy that pays for replacing a stolen car. How much will the policy cost Beth?

   c. Will Beth purchase the insurance in part b if she is risk-neutral?

   d. Discuss a possible moral hazard problem facing Beth's insurance company if she purchases the insurance.

7. Hugh's income is currently $5,000. His utility function is shown in the accompanying table.

Income	Total utility (utils)
$0	0
1,000	100
2,000	140
3,000	166
4,000	185
5,000	200
6,000	212
7,000	222
8,000	230
9,000	236
10,000	240

   a. Calculate Hugh's marginal utility of income. What is his attitude toward risk?

   b. Hugh is thinking about gambling in a casino. With a probability of 0.5 he will lose $3,000, and with a probability of 0.5 he will win $5,000. What is the expected value of Hugh's income? What is Hugh's expected utility? Will he decide to gamble? (Suppose that he gets no extra utility from going to the casino.)

   c. Suppose that the "spread" (how much he can win versus how much he can lose) of the gamble narrows, so that with a probability of 0.5 Hugh will lose $1,000, and with a probability of 0.5 he will win $3,000. What is the expected value of Hugh's income? What is his expected utility? Is this gamble better for him than the gamble in part b? Will he decide to gamble?

8. Eva is risk-averse. Currently she has $50,000 to invest. She faces the following choice: she can invest in the stock of a dot-com company, or she can invest in IBM stock. If she invests in the dot-com company, then with probability 0.5 she will lose $30,000, but with probabil-

ity 0.5 she will gain $50,000. If she invests in IBM stock, then with probability 0.5 she will lose only $10,000, but with probability 0.5 she will gain only $30,000. Can you tell which investment she will prefer to make?

9. Suppose you have $1,000 that you can invest in Ted and Larry's Ice Cream Parlor and/or Ethel's House of Cocoa. The price of a share of stock in either company is $100. The fortunes of each company are closely linked to the weather. When it is warm, the value of Ted and Larry's stock rises to $150 but the value of Ethel's stock falls to $60. When it is cold, the value of Ethel's stock rises to $150 but the value of Ted and Larry's stock falls to $60. There is an equal chance of the weather being warm or cold.

   a. If you invest all your money in Ted and Larry's, what is your expected stock value? What if you invest all your money in Ethel's?

   b. Suppose you diversify and invest half of your $1,000 in each company. How much will your total stock be worth if the weather is warm? What if it is cold?

   c. Suppose you are risk-averse. Would you prefer to put all your money in Ted and Larry's, as in part a? Or would you prefer to diversify, as in part b? Explain your reasoning.

10. LifeStrategy Conservative Growth and Energy are two portfolios constructed and managed by the Vanguard Group of mutual funds, comprised of stocks of conservatively managed U.S. companies and stocks of U.S. energy companies. The accompanying table shows historical annualized return from the period 2004 to 2014, which suggest the expected value of the annual percentage returns associated with these portfolios.

Portfolio	Expected value of return (percent)
LifeStrategy Conservative Growth	5.88%
Energy	12.66

   a. Which portfolio would a risk-neutral investor prefer?

   b. Juan, a risk-averse investor, chooses to invest in the LifeStrategy Conservative Growth portfolio. What can be inferred about the risk of the two portfolios from Juan's choice of investment? Based on historical performance, would a risk-neutral investor ever choose LifeStrategy Conservative Growth?

   c. Juan is aware that diversification can reduce risk. He considers a portfolio in which half his investment is in conservatively managed companies and the other half in Energy companies. What is the expected value of the return for this combined portfolio? Would you expect this combined portfolio to be more risky or less risky than the LifeStrategy Conservative Growth portfolio? Why or why not?

11. You are considering buying a second-hand Volkswagen. From reading car magazines, you know that half of all Volkswagens have problems of some kind (they are "lemons") and the other half run just fine (they are "plums"). If you knew that you were getting a plum, you would be willing to pay $10,000 for it: this is how much a plum is worth to you. You would also be willing to buy a lemon, but only if its price was no more than $4,000: this is how much a lemon is worth to you. And someone who owns a plum would be willing to sell it at any price above $8,000. Someone who owns a lemon would be willing to sell it for any price above $2,000.

a. For now, suppose that you can immediately tell whether the car that you are being offered is a lemon or a plum. Suppose someone offers you a plum. Will there be trade?

Now suppose that the seller has private information about the car she is selling: the seller knows whether she has a lemon or a plum. But when the seller offers you a Volkswagen, you do not know whether it is a lemon or a plum. So this is a situation of adverse selection.

b. Since you do not know whether you are being offered a plum or a lemon, you base your decision on the expected value to you of a Volkswagen, assuming you are just as likely to buy a lemon as a plum. Calculate this expected value.

c. Suppose, from driving the car, the seller knows she has a plum. However, you don't know whether this particular car is a lemon or a plum, so the most you are willing to pay is your expected value. Will there be trade?

12. You own a company that produces chairs, and you are thinking about hiring one more employee. Each chair produced gives you revenue of $10. There are two potential employees, Fred Ast and Sylvia Low. Fred is a fast worker who produces ten chairs per day, creating revenue for you of $100. Fred knows that he is fast and so will work for you only if you pay him more than $80 per day. Sylvia is a slow worker who produces only five chairs per day, creating revenue for you of $50. Sylvia knows that she is slow and so will work for you if you pay her more than $40 per day. Although Sylvia knows she is slow and Fred knows he is fast, you do not know who is fast and who is slow. So this is a situation of adverse selection.

a. Since you do not know which type of worker you will get, you think about what the expected value of your revenue will be if you hire one of the two. What is that expected value?

b. Suppose you offered to pay a daily wage equal to the expected revenue you calculated in part a. Whom would you be able to hire: Fred, or Sylvia, or both, or neither?

c. If you know whether a worker is fast or slow, which one would you prefer to hire and why? Can you devise a compensation scheme to guarantee that you employ only the type of worker you prefer?

13. For each of the following situations, do the following: first describe whether it is a situation of moral hazard or of adverse selection. Then explain what inefficiency can arise from this situation and explain how the proposed solution reduces the inefficiency.

a. When you buy a second-hand car, you do not know whether it is a lemon (low quality) or a plum (high quality), but the seller knows. A solution is for sellers to offer a warranty with the car that pays for repair costs.

b. Some people are prone to see doctors unnecessarily for minor complaints like headaches, and

health maintenance organizations do not know how urgently you need a doctor. A solution is for insurees to have to make a co-payment of a certain dollar amount (for example, $10) each time they visit a health care provider. All insurees are risk-averse.

c. When airlines sell tickets, they do not know whether a buyer is a business traveler (who is willing to pay a lot for a seat) or a leisure traveler (who has a low willingness to pay). A solution for a profit-maximizing airline is to offer an expensive ticket that is very flexible (it allows date and route changes) and a cheap ticket that is very inflexible (it has to be booked in advance and cannot be changed).

d. A company does not know whether workers on an assembly line work hard or whether they slack off. A solution is to pay the workers "piece rates," that is, pay them according to how much they have produced each day. All workers are risk-averse, but the company is not risk-neutral.

e. When making a decision about hiring you, prospective employers do not know whether you are a productive or unproductive worker. A solution is for productive workers to provide potential employers with references from previous employers.

14. Kory owns a house that is worth $300,000. If the house burns down, she loses all $300,000. If the house does not burn down, she loses nothing. Her house burns down with a probability of 0.02. Kory is risk-averse.

a. What would a fair insurance policy cost?

b. Suppose an insurance company offers to insure her fully against the loss from the house burning down, at a premium of $1,500. Can you say for sure whether Kory will or will not take the insurance?

c. Suppose an insurance company offers to insure her fully against the loss from the house burning down, at a premium of $6,000. Can you say for sure whether Kory will or will not take the insurance?

d. Suppose that an insurance company offers to insure her fully against the loss from the house burning down, at a premium of $9,000. Can you say for sure whether Kory will or will not take the insurance?

WORK IT OUT

For interactive, step-by-step help in solving the following problem, visit LaunchPad by using the URL on the back cover of this book.

15. You have $1,000 that you can invest. If you buy General Motors stock, then, in one year's time: with a probability of 0.4 you will get $1,600; with a probability of 0.4 you will get $1,100; and with a probability of 0.2 you will get $800. If you put the money into the bank, in one year's time you will get $1,100 for certain.

a. What is the expected value of your earnings from investing in General Motors stock?

b. Suppose you prefer putting your money into the bank to investing it in General Motors stock. What does that tell us about your attitude to risk?

Macroeconomics: The Big Picture

▶ **What You Will Learn in This Chapter**

■ What makes **macroeconomics** different from **microeconomics**

■ What a **business cycle** is and why policy makers seek to diminish the severity of business cycles

■ How **long-run economic growth** determines a country's standard of living

■ The meaning of **inflation** and **deflation** and why **price stability** is preferred

■ The importance of **open-economy macroeconomics** and how economies interact through **trade deficits** and **trade surpluses**

THE PAIN IN SPAIN

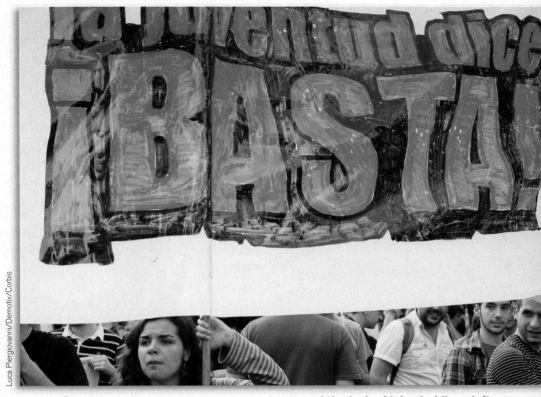

In 2011 Spanish students protest government cuts and the lack of jobs, holding aloft a banner that proclaimed, "The Youth say 'Enough'!"

Luca Piergiovanni/Demotix/Corbis

IN 2012 JAVIER DIAZ, A 25-YEAR-old Spanish college graduate, found himself where he never expected to be: unemployed and living at home. He went to college with the intention of becoming a teacher, but by the time he graduated, no one would offer him a job. And we mean *any* kind of job. Diaz was willing to work at McDonald's, but even that wasn't an option.

Was this lack of job prospects a reflection on Mr. Diaz's qualifications? Probably not. No matter who you were, finding a job in Spain in the year 2012 was tough indeed. Of Spaniards under the age of 25 seeking work, 57%—that's right, 57%—were unemployed. Having a college degree didn't help much: the unemployment rate among recent college graduates was 39%.

Yet it wasn't always like that. Five years earlier Mr. Diaz probably would have found it fairly easy to get a job that

made use of his education. In 2007–2008, however, much of the world economy, the United States included, plunged into a severe slump. The United States and some other countries began recovering from the slump in 2009, although the recovery was slow and painful. But as of 2012 Spain and a number of other European countries hadn't recovered at all—in fact, unemployment kept rising.

As bad as things were for the global economy after 2007, they could have been much worse. In fact, they were much worse during an epic global slump that began in 1929 and persisted until the beginning of World War II. It was a time of severe economic troubles known as the *Great Depression*. To emphasize that the troubles were the worst since the Great Depression, economists refer to the downturn that began in 2007 as the *Great Recession*.

Why wasn't the slump after 2007 as bad as the slump after 1929? There were many reasons, but one stands out: economists learned something about what to do from the earlier catastrophe. When the Great Depression struck, political leaders and their economic advisers literally had no idea what to do. Fortunately, during the Great Recession they did know what needed to be done, although not all of the good advice on offer was taken.

At the time of the Great Depression, *microeconomics*, which is concerned with the consumption and production decisions of individual consumers and producers and with the allocation of scarce resources among industries, was already a well-developed branch of economics. But *macroeconomics*, which focuses on the behavior of the economy as a whole, was still in its infancy.

What happened to much of the world during the Great Depression and during the Great Recession—and has happened in many other times and places, although rarely with the same severity—was a blow to the economy as a whole. During normal times, at any given moment there are always some industries laying off workers. For example, the number of independent record stores in America fell almost 30% between 2003 and 2007, as consumers turned to online purchases. But workers who lost their jobs at record stores had a good chance of finding new jobs elsewhere, because other industries were expanding even as record stores shut their doors. However, in Europe and America during the Great Recession, there were no expanding industries: everything was headed downward.

Macroeconomics came into its own as a branch of economics during the Great Depression. Economists realized that they needed to understand the nature of the catastrophe that had overtaken the United States and much of the rest of the world in order to extricate themselves, as well as to learn how to avoid such catastrophes in the future. To this day, the effort to understand economic slumps and find ways to prevent them is at the core of macroeconomics. Over time, however, macroeconomics has broadened its reach to encompass a number of other subjects, such as *long-run economic growth, inflation,* and *open-economy macroeconomics.*

This chapter offers an overview of macroeconomics. We start with a general description of the difference between macroeconomics and microeconomics, then briefly describe some of the field's major concerns.

The Nature of Macroeconomics

What makes macroeconomics different from microeconomics? The distinguishing feature of macroeconomics is that it focuses on the behavior of the economy as a whole.

Macroeconomic Questions

Table 21-1 lists some typical questions that involve economics. A microeconomic version of the question appears on the left paired with a similar macroeconomic question on the right. By comparing the questions, you can begin to get a sense of the difference between microeconomics and macroeconomics.

As these questions illustrate, microeconomics focuses on how decisions are made by individuals and firms and the consequences of those decisions. For example, we use microeconomics to determine how much it would cost a university or college to offer a new course, which includes the instructor's salary, the cost of class materials, and so on. The school can then decide whether or not to offer the course by weighing the costs and benefits.

TABLE 21-1   Microeconomic versus Macroeconomic Questions

Microeconomic Questions	Macroeconomic Questions
Should I go to business school or take a job right now?	How many people are employed in the economy as a whole this year?
What determines the salary offered by Citibank to Cherie Camajo, a new MBA?	What determines the overall salary levels paid to workers in a given year?
What determines the cost to a university or college of offering a new course?	What determines the overall level of prices in the economy as a whole?
What government policies should be adopted to make it easier for low-income students to attend college?	What government policies should be adopted to promote employment and growth in the economy as a whole?
What determines whether Citibank opens a new office in Shanghai?	What determines the overall trade in goods, services, and financial assets between the United States and the rest of the world?

Macroeconomics, in contrast, examines the *overall* behavior of the economy—how the actions of all the individuals and firms in the economy interact to produce a particular economy-wide level of economic performance. For example, macroeconomics is concerned with the general level of prices in the economy and how high or how low it is relative to the general level of prices last year, rather than with the price of one particular good or service.

You might imagine that macroeconomic questions can be answered simply by adding up microeconomic answers. For example, the model of supply and demand we introduced in Chapter 3 tells us how the equilibrium price of an individual good or service is determined in a competitive market. So you might think that applying supply and demand analysis to every good and service in the economy, then summing the results, is the way to understand the overall level of prices in the economy as a whole.

But that turns out not to be right: although basic concepts such as supply and demand are as essential to macroeconomics as they are to microeconomics, answering macroeconomic questions requires an additional set of tools and an expanded frame of reference.

Macroeconomics: The Whole Is Greater Than the Sum of Its Parts

If you occasionally drive on a highway, you probably know what a rubber-necking traffic jam is and why it is so annoying. Someone pulls over to the side of the road for something minor, such as changing a flat tire, and, pretty soon, a long traffic jam occurs as drivers slow down to take a look.

What makes it so annoying is that the length of the traffic jam is greatly out of proportion to the minor event that precipitated it. Because some drivers hit their brakes in order to rubber-neck, the drivers behind them must also hit their brakes, those behind them must do the same, and so on. The accumulation of all the individual hitting of brakes eventually leads to a long, wasteful traffic jam as each driver slows down a little bit more than the driver in front of him or her. In other words, each person's response leads to an amplified response by the next person.

Understanding a rubber-necking traffic jam gives us some insight into one very important way in which macroeconomics is different from microeconomics: many thousands or millions of individual actions compound upon one another to produce an outcome that isn't simply the sum of those individual actions.

Consider, for example, what macroeconomists call the *paradox of thrift:* when families and businesses are worried about the possibility of economic hard times, they prepare by cutting their spending. This reduction in spending depresses the economy as consumers spend less and businesses react by laying off workers. As a result, families and businesses may end up worse off than if they hadn't tried to act responsibly by cutting their spending.

This is a paradox because seemingly virtuous behavior—preparing for hard times by saving more—ends up harming everyone. And there is a flip-side to this story: when families and businesses are feeling optimistic about the future, they spend more today. This stimulates the economy, leading businesses to hire more workers, which further expands the economy. Seemingly profligate behavior leads to good times for all.

Or consider what happens when something causes the quantity of cash circulating through the economy to rise. An individual with more cash on hand is richer. But if everyone has more cash, the long-run effect is simply to push the overall level of prices higher, taking the purchasing power of the total amount of cash in circulation right back to where it was before.

A key insight of macroeconomics, then, is that the combined effect of individual decisions can have results that are very different from what any one individual intended, results that are sometimes perverse. The behavior of the macroeconomy is, indeed, greater than the sum of individual actions and market outcomes.

The behavior of the macroeconomy is greater than the sum of individual actions and market outcomes.

SFC/Shutterstock

Macroeconomics: Theory and Policy

To a much greater extent than microeconomists, macroeconomists are concerned with questions about *policy,* about what the government can do to make macroeconomic performance better. This policy focus was strongly shaped by history, in particular by the Great Depression of the 1930s.

In a **self-regulating economy,** problems such as unemployment are resolved without government intervention, through the working of the invisible hand.

According to **Keynesian economics,** economic slumps are caused by inadequate spending, and they can be mitigated by government intervention.

Monetary policy uses changes in the quantity of money to alter interest rates and affect overall spending.

Fiscal policy uses changes in government spending and taxes to affect overall spending.

Before the 1930s, economists tended to regard the economy as **self-regulating:** they believed that problems such as unemployment would be corrected through the working of the invisible hand and that government attempts to improve the economy's performance would be ineffective at best—and would probably make things worse.

The Great Depression changed all that. The sheer scale of the catastrophe, which left a quarter of the U.S. workforce without jobs and threatened the political stability of many countries—the Depression is widely believed to have been a major factor in the Nazi takeover of Germany—created a demand for action. It also led to a major effort on the part of economists to understand economic slumps and find ways to prevent them.

In 1936 the British economist John Maynard Keynes (pronounced "canes") published *The General Theory of Employment, Interest, and Money,* a book that transformed macroeconomics. According to **Keynesian economics,** a depressed economy is the result of inadequate spending. In addition, Keynes argued that government intervention can help a depressed economy through *monetary policy* and *fiscal policy.* **Monetary policy** uses changes in the quantity of money to alter interest rates, which in turn affect the level of overall spending. **Fiscal policy** uses changes in taxes and government spending to affect overall spending.

In general, Keynes established the idea that managing the economy is a government responsibility. Keynesian ideas continue to have a strong influence on both economic theory and public policy: in 2008 and 2009, Congress, the White House, and the Federal Reserve (a quasi-governmental agency that manages U.S. monetary policy) took steps to fend off an economic slump that were clearly Keynesian in spirit, as described in the following Economics in Action.

ECONOMICS ▶ *in Action*

Fending Off Depression

In 2008 the world economy experienced a severe financial crisis that was all too reminiscent of the early days of the Great Depression. Major banks teetered on the edge of collapse; world trade slumped. In the spring of 2009, the economic historians Barry Eichengreen and Kevin O'Rourke, reviewing the available data, pointed out that "globally we are tracking or even doing worse than the Great Depression."

But the worst did not, in the end, come to pass. Figure 21-1 shows one of Eichengreen and O'Rourke's measures of economic activity, world industrial production, during the Great Depression (the top line) and during the Great Recession (the bottom line). During the first year the two crises were indeed comparable. But fortunately, one year into the Great Recession, world production leveled off and turned around. In contrast, three years into the Great Depression world production continued to fall. Why the difference?

At least part of the answer is that policy makers responded

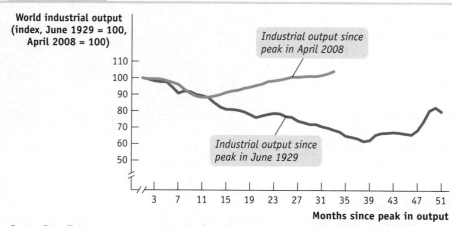

FIGURE 21-1 Measures of Economic Activity and World Industrial Production During the Great Depression and the Great Recession

Source: Barry Eichengreen and Kevin O'Rourke (2009), "A Tale of Two Depressions." © VoxEU.org; CPB Netherlands Bureau for Economic Policy Analysis World Trade Monitor.

very differently. During the Great Depression, it was widely argued that the slump should simply be allowed to run its course. Any attempt to mitigate the ongoing catastrophe, declared Joseph Schumpeter—the Austrian-born Harvard economist now famed for his work on innovation—would "leave the work of depression undone." In the early 1930s, some countries' monetary authorities actually raised interest rates in the face of the slump, while governments cut spending and raised taxes—actions that, as we'll see in later chapters, deepened the recession.

In the aftermath of the 2008 crisis, by contrast, interest rates were slashed, and a number of countries, the United States included, used temporary increases in spending and reductions in taxes in an attempt to sustain spending. Governments also moved to shore up their banks with loans, aid, and guarantees.

Many of these measures were controversial, to say the least. But most economists believe that by responding actively to the Great Recession—and doing so using the knowledge gained from the study of macroeconomics—governments helped avoid a global economic catastrophe.

Check Your Understanding   21-1

1. Which of the following questions involve microeconomics, and which involve macroeconomics? In each case, explain your answer.
   a. Why did consumers switch to smaller cars in 2008?
   b. Why did overall consumer spending slow down in 2008?
   c. Why did the standard of living rise more rapidly in the first generation after World War II than in the second?
   d. Why have starting salaries for students with geology degrees risen sharply of late?
   e. What determines the choice between rail and road transportation?
   f. Why did salmon get much cheaper between 1980 and 2000?
   g. Why did inflation fall in the 1990s?

2. In 2008, problems in the financial sector led to a drying up of credit around the country: home-buyers were unable to get mortgages, students were unable to get student loans, car-buyers were unable to get car loans, and so on.
   a. Explain how the drying up of credit can lead to compounding effects throughout the economy and result in an economic slump.
   b If you believe the economy is self-regulating, what would you advocate that policy makers do?
   c. If you believe in Keynesian economics, what would you advocate that policy makers do?

Solutions appear at back of book.

▼ Quick Review

- Microeconomics focuses on decision making by individuals and firms and the consequences of the decisions made. Macroeconomics focuses on the overall behavior of the economy.

- The combined effect of individual actions can have unintended consequences and lead to worse or better macroeconomic outcomes for everyone.

- Before the 1930s, economists tended to regard the economy as **self-regulating.** After the Great Depression, **Keynesian economics** provided the rationale for government intervention through **monetary policy** and **fiscal policy** to help a depressed economy.

The Business Cycle

The Great Depression was by far the worst economic crisis in U.S. history. But although the economy managed to avoid catastrophe for the rest of the twentieth century, it has experienced many ups and downs.

It's true that the ups have consistently been bigger than the downs: a chart of any of the major numbers used to track the U.S. economy shows a strong upward trend over time. For example, panel (a) of Figure 21-2 shows total U.S. private-sector employment (the total number of jobs offered by private businesses) measured along the left vertical axis, with the data from 1985 to 2014 given by the purple line. The graph also shows the index of industrial production (a measure of the total output of U.S. factories) measured along the right vertical axis, with the data from 1985 to 2014 given by the red line. Both private-sector employment and industrial production were much higher at the end of this period than at the beginning, and in most years both measures rose.

FIGURE **21-2** | U.S. Growth, Interrupted, 1985–2014

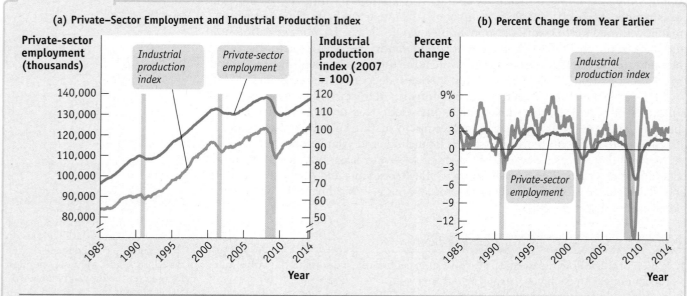

Panel (a) shows two important economic numbers, the industrial production index and total private-sector employment. Both numbers grew substantially from 1985 to 2014, but they didn't grow steadily. Instead, both suffered from three downturns associated with *recessions*, which are indicated by the shaded areas in the figure. Panel (b) emphasizes those downturns by showing the annual rate of change of industrial production and employment, that is, the percentage increase over the past year. The simultaneous downturns in both numbers during the three recessions are clear.

Source: Federal Reserve Bank of St. Louis.

But they didn't rise steadily. As you can see from the figure, there were three periods—in the early 1990s, in the early 2000s, and again beginning in late 2007—when both employment and industrial output stumbled. Panel (b) emphasizes these stumbles by showing the *rate of change* of employment and industrial production over the previous year. For example, the percent change in employment for December 2007 was 0.7, because employment in December 2007 was 0.7% higher than it had been in December 2006. The three big downturns stand out clearly. What's more, a detailed look at the data makes it clear that in each period the stumble wasn't confined to only a few industries: in each downturn, just about every sector of the U.S. economy cut back on production and on the number of people employed.

The economy's forward march, in other words, isn't smooth. And the uneven pace of the economy's progress, its ups and downs, is one of the main preoccupations of macroeconomics.

Charting the Business Cycle

Figure 21-3 shows a stylized representation of the way the economy evolves over time. The vertical axis shows either employment or an indicator of how much the economy is producing, such as industrial production or *real gross domestic product (real GDP)*, a measure of the economy's overall output that we'll learn about in the next chapter. As the data in Figure 21-2 suggest, these two measures tend to move together. Their common movement is the starting point for a major theme of macroeconomics: the economy's alternation between short-run downturns and upturns.

A broad-based downturn, in which output and employment fall in many industries, is called a **recession** (sometimes referred to as a *contraction*). Recessions, as

Recessions, or contractions, are periods of economic downturn when output and employment are falling.

Expansions, or recoveries, are periods of economic upturn when output and employment are rising.

The **business cycle** is the short-run alternation between recessions and expansions.

The point at which the economy turns from expansion to recession is a **business-cycle peak.**

The point at which the economy turns from recession to expansion is a **business-cycle trough.**

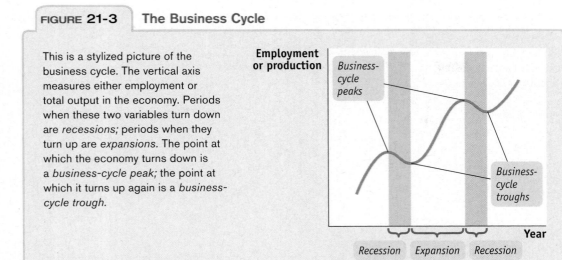

FIGURE 21-3   The Business Cycle

This is a stylized picture of the business cycle. The vertical axis measures either employment or total output in the economy. Periods when these two variables turn down are *recessions;* periods when they turn up are *expansions.* The point at which the economy turns down is a *business-cycle peak;* the point at which it turns up again is a *business-cycle trough.*

officially declared by the National Bureau of Economic Research, or NBER (discussed in the upcoming For Inquiring Minds), are indicated by the shaded areas in Figure 21-2. When the economy isn't in a recession, when most economic numbers are following their normal upward trend, the economy is said to be in an **expansion** (sometimes referred to as a *recovery*).

The alternation between recessions and expansions is known as the **business cycle.** The point in time at which the economy shifts from expansion to recession is known as a **business-cycle peak;** the point at which the economy shifts from recession to expansion is known as a **business-cycle trough.**

The business cycle is an enduring feature of the economy. Table 21-2 shows the official list of business-cycle peaks and troughs. As you can see, there have been recessions and expansions for at least the past 155 years. Whenever there is a prolonged expansion, as there was in the 1960s and again in the 1990s, books and articles come out proclaiming the end of the business cycle. Such proclamations have always proved wrong: the cycle always comes back. But why does it matter?

The Pain of Recession

Not many people complain about the business cycle when the economy is expanding. Recessions, however, create a great deal of pain.

The most important effect of a recession is its effect on the ability of workers to find and hold jobs. The most widely used indicator of conditions in the labor market is the *unemployment rate.* We'll explain how that rate is calculated in Chapter 23, but for now it's enough to say that a high unemployment rate tells us that jobs are scarce and a low unemployment rate tells us that jobs are easy to find.

Figure 21-4 shows the unemployment rate from 1988 to 2014. As you can see, the U.S. unemployment rate surged during and after each recession but eventually fell during periods of expansion.

TABLE 21-2   The History of the Business Cycle

Business-Cycle Peak	Business-Cycle Trough
no prior data available	December 1854
June 1857	December 1858
October 1860	June 1861
April 1865	December 1867
June 1869	December 1870
October 1873	March 1879
March 1882	May 1885
March 1887	April 1888
July 1890	May 1891
January 1893	June 1894
December 1895	June 1897
June 1899	December 1900
September 1902	August 1904
May 1907	June 1908
January 1910	January 1912
January 1913	December 1914
August 1918	March 1919
January 1920	July 1921
May 1923	July 1924
October 1926	November 1927
August 1929	March 1933
May 1937	June 1938
February 1945	October 1945
November 1948	October 1949
July 1953	May 1954
August 1957	April 1958
April 1960	February 1961
December 1969	November 1970
November 1973	March 1975
January 1980	July 1980
July 1981	November 1982
July 1990	March 1991
March 2001	November 2001
December 2007	June 2009

Source: National Bureau of Economic Research.

FIGURE 21-4   The U.S. Unemployment Rate, 1988–2014

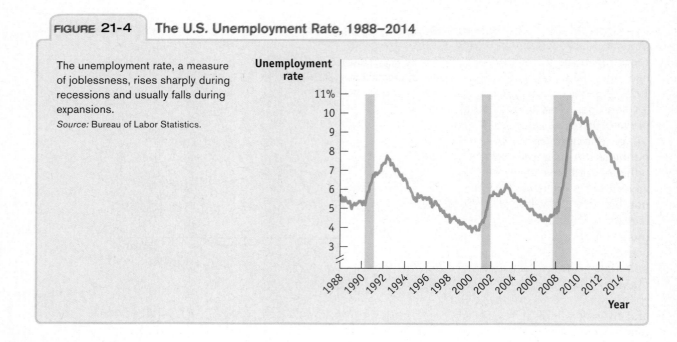

The unemployment rate, a measure of joblessness, rises sharply during recessions and usually falls during expansions.

Source: Bureau of Labor Statistics.

©Aaron Bacall/www.CartoonStock.com

"I can't move in with my parents. They moved in with my grandparents."

The rising unemployment rate in 2008 was a sign that a new recession might be under way, which was later confirmed by the NBER to have begun in December 2007.

Because recessions cause many people to lose their jobs and also make it hard to find new ones, recessions hurt the standard of living of many families. Recessions are usually associated with a rise in the number of people living below the poverty line, an increase in the number of people who lose their houses because they can't afford the mortgage payments, and a fall in the percentage of Americans with health insurance coverage.

You should not think, however, that workers are the only group that suffers during a recession. Recessions are also bad for firms: like employment and wages, profits suffer during recessions, with many small businesses failing.

All in all, then, recessions are bad for almost everyone. Can anything be done to reduce their frequency and severity?

FOR INQUIRING MINDS | Defining Recessions and Expansions

Some readers may be wondering exactly how recessions and expansions are defined. The answer is that there is no exact definition!

In many countries, economists adopt the rule that a recession is a period of at least two consecutive quarters (a quarter is three months) during which the total output of the economy shrinks. The two-consecutive-quarters requirement is designed to avoid classifying brief hiccups in the economy's performance, with no lasting significance, as recessions.

Sometimes, however, this definition seems too strict. For example, an economy that has three months of sharply declining output, then three months of slightly positive growth, then another three months of rapid decline, should surely be considered to have endured a nine-month recession.

In the United States, we try to avoid such misclassifications by assigning the task of determining when a recession begins and ends to an independent panel of experts at the National Bureau of Economic Research (NBER). This panel looks at a variety of economic indicators, with the main focus on employment and produc-

tion. But, ultimately, the panel makes a judgment call.

Sometimes this judgment is controversial. In fact, there is lingering controversy over the 2001 recession. According to the NBER, that recession began in March 2001 and ended in November 2001 when output began rising. Some critics argue, however, that the recession really began several months earlier, when industrial production began falling. Other critics argue that the recession didn't really end in 2001 because employment continued to fall and the job market remained weak for another year and a half. ■

Taming the Business Cycle

Modern macroeconomics largely came into being as a response to the worst recession in history—the 43-month downturn that began in 1929 and continued into 1933, ushering in the Great Depression. The havoc wreaked by the 1929–1933 recession spurred economists to search both for understanding and for solutions: they wanted to know how such things could happen and how to prevent them.

As we explained earlier in this chapter, the work of John Maynard Keynes, published during the Great Depression, suggested that monetary and fiscal policies could be used to mitigate the effects of recessions, and to this day governments turn to Keynesian policies when recession strikes. Later work, notably that of another great macroeconomist, Milton Friedman, led to a consensus that it's important to rein in booms as well as to fight slumps. So modern policy makers try to "smooth out" the business cycle. They haven't been completely successful, as a look back at Figure 21-2 makes clear. It's widely believed, however, that policy guided by macroeconomic analysis has helped make the economy more stable.

Although the business cycle is one of the main concerns of macroeconomics and historically played a crucial role in fostering the development of the field, macroeconomists are also concerned with other issues. We turn next to the question of long-run growth.

 GLOBAL COMPARISION | **Slumps Across the Atlantic**

This figure shows manufacturing production from 2007 to 2013 in two of the world's biggest economies: the United States and the Euro Area, the group of European countries that share a common currency, the euro. As you can see, both economies suffered a severe downturn in 2008–2009, probably because banks in both economies had made many bad loans, and failures on one side of the Atlantic helped create a crisis of confidence on the other side as well.

More or less simultaneous recessions in different countries are, in fact, quite common. But that doesn't mean that economies always or even usually move in lockstep. As you can see from the figure, both the Euro Area and the United States began to recover in mid-2009. In 2011, however, their paths diverged. The U.S. economy continued to recover steadily, although more slowly than most would have liked. The Euro Area, by contrast, entered a new recession in 2011, due to problems of excessive debt in some countries and a wrong turn in economic policy, discussed in Chapter 32.

What we learn from recent experience, then, is that the business cycle is to some extent an international

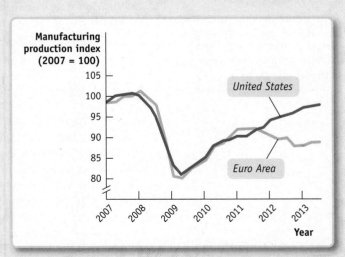

phenomenon. But individual countries can diverge from each other for a variety of reasons, including policy differences and differences in the underlying structure of their economies.

Source: Federal Reserve Bank of St. Louis.

ECONOMICS ▶ in Action

Comparing Recessions

The alternation of recessions and expansions seems to be an enduring feature of economic life. However, not all business cycles are created equal. In particular, some recessions have been much worse than others.

Let's compare the two most recent U.S. recessions: the 2001 recession and the Great Recession of 2007–2009. These recessions differed in duration: the first lasted only eight months, the second more than twice as long. Even more important, however, they differed greatly in depth.

In Figure 21-5 we compare the depth of the recessions by looking at what happened to industrial production over the months after the recession began. In each case, production is measured as a percentage of its level at the recession's start. Thus the line for the 2007–2009 recession shows that industrial production eventually fell to about 85% of its initial level.

Clearly, the 2007–2009 recession hit the economy vastly harder than the 2001 recession. Indeed, by comparison to many recessions, the 2001 slump was very mild.

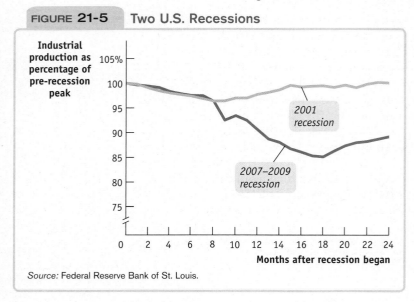

FIGURE 21-5 Two U.S. Recessions

Source: Federal Reserve Bank of St. Louis.

Of course, this was no consolation to the millions of American workers who lost their jobs, even in that mild recession.

Check Your Understanding   21-2

1. Why do we talk about business cycles for the economy as a whole, rather than just talking about the ups and downs of particular industries?

2. Describe who gets hurt in a recession, and how.

Solutions appear at back of book.

Long-Run Economic Growth

In 1955, Americans were delighted with the nation's prosperity. The economy was expanding, consumer goods that had been rationed during World War II were available for everyone to buy, and most Americans believed, rightly, that they were better off than the citizens of any other nation, past or present. Yet by today's standards, Americans were quite poor in 1955. Figure 21-6 shows the percentage of American homes equipped with a variety of appliances in 1905, 1955, and 2005: in 1955 only 37% of American homes contained washing machines and hardly anyone had air conditioning. And if we turn the clock back another half-century, to 1905, we find that life for many Americans was startlingly primitive by today's standards.

Why are the vast majority of Americans today able to afford conveniences that many Americans lacked in 1955? The answer is **long-run economic growth,** the sustained rise in the quantity of goods and services the economy produces. Figure 21-7 shows the growth between 1900 and 2013 in real GDP per capita, a measure of total output per person in the economy. The severe recession of 1929–1933 stands out, but business cycles between World War II and 2007 are almost invisible, dwarfed by the strong upward trend.

Part of the long-run increase in output is accounted for by the fact that we have a growing population and workforce. But the economy's overall production

Long-run economic growth is the sustained upward trend in the economy's output over time.

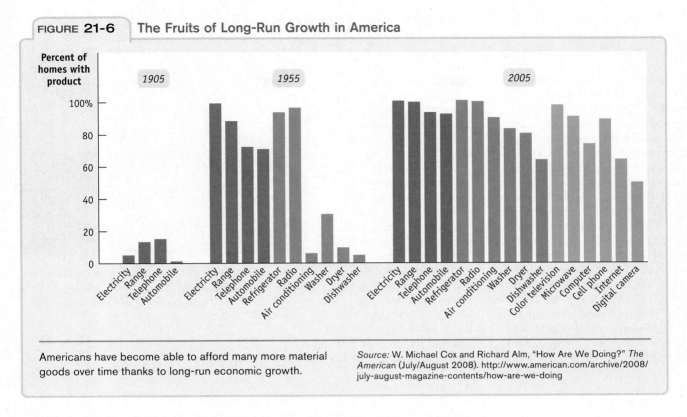

FIGURE 21-6 The Fruits of Long-Run Growth in America

Americans have become able to afford many more material goods over time thanks to long-run economic growth.

Source: W. Michael Cox and Richard Alm, "How Are We Doing?" *The American* (July/August 2008). http://www.american.com/archive/2008/july-august-magazine-contents/how-are-we-doing

has increased by much more than the population. On average, in 2013 the U.S. economy produced about $53,000 worth of goods and services per person, about twice as much as in 1972, about three times as much as in 1952, and about eight times as much as in 1900.

Long-run economic growth is fundamental to many of the most pressing economic questions today. Responses to key policy questions, like the country's ability to bear the future costs of government programs such as Social Security and Medicare, depend in part on how fast the U.S. economy grows over the next few decades.

More broadly, the public's sense that the country is making progress depends crucially on success in achieving long-run growth. When growth slows, as it did in the

FIGURE 21-7 American Growth, the Long View

Over the long run, growth in real GDP per capita in America has dwarfed the ups and downs of the business cycle. Except for the recession that began the Great Depression, recessions are almost invisible until 2007.

Sources: Angus Maddison, *Statistics on World Population, GDP, and Per Capita GDP, 1–2008 AD,* http://www.ggdc.net/MADDISON/oriindex.htm; Bureau of Economic Analysis; The Conference Board Total Economy Database™, January 2014.

FOR INQUIRING MINDS | When Did Long-Run Growth Start?

Today, the United States is a much richer country than it was in 1955; in 1955 it was much richer than it had been in 1905. But how did 1855 compare with 1805? Or 1755? How far back does long-run economic growth go?

The answer is that long-run growth is a relatively modern phenomenon. The U.S. economy was already growing steadily by the mid-nineteenth century—think railroads. But if you go back to the period before 1800, you find a world economy that grew extremely slowly by today's standards. Furthermore, the population grew almost as fast as the economy, so there was very little increase in output per person. According to the economic historian Angus Maddison, from the years 1000 to 1800, real aggregate output around the world grew less than 0.2% per year, with population rising at about the same rate.

Economic stagnation meant unchanging living standards. For example, information on prices and wages from sources such as monastery records shows that workers in England weren't significantly better off in the early eighteenth century than they had been five centuries earlier. And it's a good bet that they weren't much better off than Egyptian peasants in the age of the pharaohs. However, long-run economic growth has increased significantly since 1800. In the last 50 years or so, real GDP per capita has grown about 3.5% per year. ■

Economic stagnation and unchanging living standards prevailed for centuries until the Industrial Revolution in the mid-1800s ushered in a new era of wealth and sustained increases in living standards.

1970s, it can help feed a national mood of pessimism. In particular, *long-run growth per capita*—a sustained upward trend in output per person—is the key to higher wages and a rising standard of living. A major concern of macroeconomics—and the theme of Chapter 24—is trying to understand the forces behind long-run growth.

Long-run growth is an even more urgent concern in poorer, less developed countries. In these countries, which would like to achieve a higher standard of living, the question of how to accelerate long-run growth is the central concern of economic policy.

As we'll see, macroeconomists don't use the same models to think about long-run growth that they use to think about the business cycle. It's always important to keep both sets of models in mind, because what is good in the long run can be bad in the short run, and vice versa. For example, we've already mentioned the paradox of thrift: an attempt by households to increase their savings can cause a recession. But a higher level of savings, as we'll see in Chapter 25, plays a crucial role in encouraging long-run economic growth.

ECONOMICS ▶ *in Action*

A Tale of Two Countries

Many countries have experienced long-run growth, but not all have done equally well. One of the most informative contrasts is between Canada and Argentina, two countries that, at the beginning of the twentieth century, seemed to be in a good economic position.

From today's vantage point, it's surprising to realize that Canada and Argentina looked rather similar before World War I. Both were major exporters of agricultural products; both attracted large numbers of European immigrants; both also attracted large amounts of European investment, especially in the railroads that opened up their agricultural hinterlands. Economic historians believe that the average level of per capita income was about the same in the two countries as late as the 1930s.

After World War II, however, Argentina's economy performed poorly, largely due to political instability and bad macroeconomic policies. Argentina experienced several periods of extremely high inflation, during which the cost of living soared. Meanwhile, Canada made steady progress. Thanks to the fact that Canada has achieved sustained long-run growth since 1930, but Argentina has not, Canada's standard of living today is almost as high as that of the United States—and is about three times as high as Argentina's.

Check Your Understanding   21-3

1. Many poor countries have high rates of population growth. What does this imply about the long-run growth rates of overall output that they must achieve in order to generate a higher standard of living per person?

2. Argentina used to be as rich as Canada; now it's much poorer. Does this mean that Argentina is poorer than it was in the past? Explain.

Solutions appear at back of book.

Inflation and Deflation

In January 1980 the average production worker in the United States was paid $6.57 an hour. By January 2014, the average hourly earnings for such a worker had risen to $20.18 an hour. Three cheers for economic progress!

But wait. American workers were paid much more in 2014, but they also faced a much higher cost of living. In January 1980, a dozen eggs cost only about $0.88; by January 2014, that was up to $2.01. The price of a loaf of white bread went from about $0.50 to $1.37. And the price of a gallon of gasoline rose from just $1.13 to $3.38.

Figure 21-8 compares the percentage increase in hourly earnings between 1980 and 2014 with the increases in the prices of some standard items: the average worker's paycheck went farther in terms of some goods, but less far in terms of others. Overall, the rise in the cost of living wiped out many, if not all, of the wage gains of the typical American worker from 1980 to 2014. In other words, once inflation is taken into account, the living standard of the typical American worker barely rose from 1980 to the present.

The point is that between 1980 and 2014 the economy experienced substantial **inflation:** a rise in the overall level of prices. Understanding the causes of inflation and its opposite, **deflation**—a fall in the overall level of prices—is another main concern of macroeconomics.

The Causes of Inflation and Deflation

You might think that changes in the overall level of prices are just a matter of supply and demand. For example, higher gasoline prices reflect the higher price of crude

A rising overall level of prices is **inflation.**

A falling overall level of prices is **deflation.**

FIGURE 21-8   Rising Prices

Between 1980 and 2014, American workers' hourly earnings rose by 207%. But the prices of just about all the goods bought by workers also rose, some by more, some by less. Overall, the rising cost of living offset most of the rise in the average U.S. worker's wage.

Source: Bureau of Labor Statistics.

	Percent increase
Hourly earnings	207%
Eggs	128%
Roast coffee	57%
White bread	172%
Gasoline	204%

0   50   100   150   200   250%

Percent increase

The economy has **price stability** when the overall level of prices changes slowly or not at all.

oil, and higher crude oil prices reflect such factors as the exhaustion of major oil fields, growing demand from China and other emerging economies as more people grow rich enough to buy cars, and so on. Can't we just add up what happens in each of these markets to find out what happens to the overall level of prices?

The answer is no, we can't. Supply and demand can only explain why a particular good or service becomes more expensive *relative to other goods and services.* It can't explain why, for example, the price of chicken has risen over time in spite of the facts that chicken production has become more efficient (you don't want to know) and that chicken has become substantially cheaper compared to other goods.

What causes the overall level of prices to rise or fall? As we'll learn in Chapter 23, in the short run, movements in inflation are closely related to the business cycle. When the economy is depressed and jobs are hard to find, inflation tends to fall; when the economy is booming, inflation tends to rise. For example, prices of most goods and services fell sharply during the terrible recession of 1929–1933.

In the long run, by contrast, the overall level of prices is mainly determined by changes in the *money supply,* the total quantity of assets that can be readily used to make purchases. As we'll see in Chapter 31, *hyperinflation,* in which prices rise by thousands or hundreds of thousands of percent, invariably occurs when governments print money to pay a large part of their bills.

The Pain of Inflation and Deflation

Both inflation and deflation can pose problems for the economy. Here are two examples: inflation discourages people from holding onto cash, because cash loses value over time if the overall price level is rising. That is, the amount of goods and services you can buy with a given amount of cash falls. In extreme cases, people stop holding cash altogether and turn to barter. Deflation can cause the reverse problem. If the price level is falling, cash gains value over time. In other words, the amount of goods and services you can buy with a given amount of cash increases. So holding on to it can become more attractive than investing in new factories and other productive assets. This can deepen a recession.

We'll describe other costs of inflation and deflation in Chapters 23 and 31. For now, let's just note that, in general, economists regard **price stability**—in which the overall level of prices is changing, if at all, only slowly—as a desirable goal. Price stability is a goal that seemed far out of reach for much of the American economy during post–World War II period. However, beginning in the 1990s and continuing to the present, it has been achieved to the satisfaction of most macroeconomists.

ECONOMICS ▶ *in Action*

A Fast (Food) Measure of Inflation

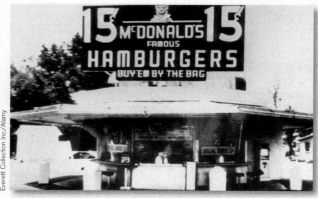

Everett Collection Inc./Alamy

Even though a burger costs 6 times more than it did in 1954 when McDonald's first opened, it's still a good bargain compared to other consumer goods.

The original McDonald's opened in 1954. It offered fast service—it was, indeed, the original fast-food restaurant. And it was also very inexpensive: hamburgers cost $0.15, $0.25 with fries. By 2014, a hamburger at a typical McDonald's cost more than six times as much, about $1.00. Has McDonald's lost touch with its fast-food roots? Have burgers become luxury cuisine?

No—in fact, compared with other consumer goods, a burger is a better bargain today than it was in 1954. Burger prices were about 6.5 times as high in 2013 as they were in 1954. But the consumer price index, the most widely used measure of the cost of living, was 8.5 times as high in 2013 as it was in 1954.

1. Which of these sound like inflation, which sound like deflation, and which are ambiguous?
    a. Gasoline prices are up 10%, food prices are down 20%, and the prices of most services are up 1–2%.
    b. Gas prices have doubled, food prices are up 50%, and most services seem to be up 5% or 10%.
    c. Gas prices haven't changed, food prices are way down, and services have gotten cheaper, too.

Solutions appear at back of book.

International Imbalances

The United States is an **open economy:** an economy that trades goods and services with other countries. There have been times when that trade was more or less balanced—when the United States sold about as much to the rest of the world as it bought. But this isn't one of those times.

In 2013, the United States ran a big **trade deficit**—that is, the value of the goods and services U.S. residents bought from the rest of the world was a lot larger than the value of the goods and services American producers sold to customers abroad. Meanwhile, some other countries were in the opposite position, selling much more to foreigners than they bought.

Figure 21-9 shows the exports and imports of goods for several important economies in 2013. As you can see, the United States imported much more than it exported, but Germany, China, and Saudi Arabia did the reverse: they each ran a **trade surplus.** A country runs a trade surplus when the value of the goods and services it buys from the rest of the world is smaller than the value of the goods and services it sells abroad. Was America's trade deficit a sign that something was wrong with our economy—that we weren't able to make things that people in other countries wanted to buy?

No, not really. Trade deficits and their opposite, trade surpluses, are macroeconomic phenomena. They're the result of situations in which the whole is very different from the sum of its parts. You might think that countries with highly productive workers or widely desired products and services to sell run trade surpluses but countries with unproductive workers or poor-quality products and

An **open economy** is an economy that trades goods and services with other countries.

A country runs a **trade deficit** when the value of goods and services bought from foreigners is more than the value of goods and services it sells to them. It runs a **trade surplus** when the value of goods and services bought from foreigners is less than the value of the goods and services it sells to them.

FIGURE 21-9   Unbalanced Trade

In 2013, the goods and services the United States bought from other countries were worth considerably more than the goods and services we sold abroad. Germany, China, and Saudi Arabia were in the reverse position. Trade deficits and trade surpluses reflect macroeconomic forces, especially differences in savings and investment spending.
Source: CIA World Factbook.

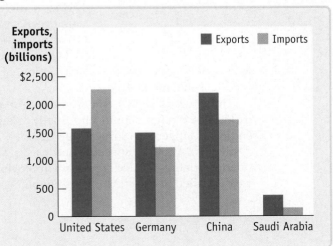

services run deficits. But the reality is that there's no simple relationship between the success of an economy and whether it runs trade surpluses or deficits.

Microeconomic analysis tells us why countries trade but not why they run trade surpluses or deficits. In Chapter 2 we learned that international trade is the result of comparative advantage: countries export goods they're relatively good at producing and import goods they're not as good at producing. That's why the United States exports wheat and imports coffee. One important thing the concept of comparative advantage doesn't explain, however, is why the value of a country's imports is sometimes much larger than the value of its exports, or vice versa.

So what does determine whether a country runs a trade surplus or a trade deficit? In Chapter 34 we'll learn the surprising answer: the determinants of the overall balance between exports and imports lie in decisions about savings and investment spending—spending on goods like machinery and factories that are in turn used to produce goods and services for consumers. Countries with high investment spending relative to savings run trade deficits; countries with low investment spending relative to savings run trade surpluses.

ECONOMICS ▶ *in Action*

Spain's Costly Surplus

n 1999 Spain took a momentous step: it gave up its national currency, the peseta, in order to adopt the euro, a shared currency intended to promote closer economic and political union among the nations of Europe. How did this affect Spain's international trade?

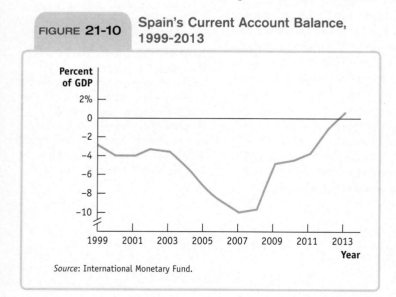

FIGURE **21-10**   Spain's Current Account Balance, 1999-2013

Source: International Monetary Fund.

Figure 21-10 shows Spain's current account balance—a broad definition of its trade balance—from 1999 to 2013, measured as a share of *gross domestic product*, the country's total production of goods and services. A negative current account balance, as shown here, means the country is running a trade deficit. As you can see, after Spain switched to the euro it began running large trade deficits, which at their peak were more than 10% of gross domestic product. After 2008, however, the trade deficit began shrinking rapidly, and by 2013 Spain was running a small surplus.

Did this mean that Spain's economy was doing badly in the mid-2000s, and better thereafter? Just the opposite. When Spain adopted the euro, foreign investors became highly optimistic about its prospects, and money poured into the country, fueling rapid economic expansion. At the heart of this expansion was a huge housing boom, led in particular by the construction of holiday homes along Spain's famed Mediterranean coast.

Unfortunately, this epic boom eventually turned into an epic bust, and the inflows of foreign capital into Spain dried up. One consequence was that Spain could no longer run large trade deficits, and by 2013 was forced into running a surplus. Another consequence was a severe recession, leading to very high unemployment—including the unemployment of Javier Diaz, the jobless graduate we described at the start of this chapter.

Check Your Understanding   21-5

1. Which of the following reflect comparative advantage, and which reflect macroeconomic forces?
   a. Thanks to the development of huge oil sands in the province of Alberta, Canada has become an exporter of oil and an importer of manufactured goods.
   b. Like many consumer goods, the Apple iPod is assembled in China, although many of the components are made in other countries.
   c. Since 2002, Germany has been running huge trade surpluses, exporting much more than it imports.
   d. The United States, which had roughly balanced trade in the early 1990s, began running large trade deficits later in the decade, as the technology boom took off.

Solutions appear at back of book.

▼ Quick Review

- Comparative advantage can explain why an **open economy** exports some goods and services and imports others, but it can't explain why a country imports more than it exports, or vice versa.

- **Trade deficits** and **trade surpluses** are macroeconomic phenomena, determined by decisions about investment spending and savings.

The Business Cycle and the Decline of Montgomery Ward

Before there was the internet, there was mail order, and for rural and small-town America, what that meant, above all, was the Montgomery Ward catalog. Starting in 1872, that catalog made it possible for families far from the big city to buy goods their local store wasn't likely to stock—everything from bicycles to pianos. In 1896 Sears, Roebuck and Co. introduced a competing catalog, and the two firms struggled for dominance right up to World War II. After that, however, Montgomery Ward fell far behind (it finally closed all its stores in 2000).

Why did Montgomery Ward falter? One key factor was that its management misjudged postwar prospects. The 1930s were a difficult time for retailers in general because of the catastrophic economic impact wrought by the Great Depression. Figure 21-11 shows an index of department store sales, which plunged after 1930 and hadn't fully recovered by 1940. Montgomery Ward coped with this tough environment by cutting back: it closed some of its stores, cut costs, and accumulated a large hoard of cash. This strategy served the company well, restoring profitability and putting it in a very strong financial position.

Unfortunately for the company, it made the mistake of returning to this strategy after World War II—and the postwar environment was nothing like the environment of the 1930s. Overall department store sales surged: by 1960 they were more than four times their level in 1940. Sears and other retailers expanded to meet this surge in demand, especially in the rapidly growing suburbs. But Montgomery Ward, expecting the 1930s to return, just sat on its cash; it didn't open any new stores until 1959. By failing to expand with the market, Montgomery Ward suffered what turned out to be an irretrievable loss of market share, reputation, and name recognition.

Nothing in business is forever. Eventually Sears too entered a long, slow decline. First it was overtaken by newer retailers like Walmart, whose "big box" stores didn't sell large appliances but generally sold other goods more cheaply than Sears, in part because Walmart used information technology to hold costs down. More recently, the rise of internet sales has hurt traditional retailers of all kinds. But Montgomery Ward's self-inflicted defeat in the years after World War II nonetheless shows how important it is for businesses to understand what is happening in the broader economic environment—that is, to take macroeconomics into account.

FIGURE 21-11 Department Store Sales Index, 1919–1946

U.S. Index (1935–1939 = 100)

Great Depression

Year

Source: National Bureau of Economic Research.

QUESTIONS FOR THOUGHT

1. What caused the steep decline in department store sales in the 1930s?

2. In terms of macroeconomics, what was the management of Montgomery Ward betting would happen after World War II?

3. Economists believe that improvements in our macroeconomic understanding over the course of the 1930s led to better policies thereafter. If this is true, how did better policies after World War II end up hurting Montgomery Ward?

SUMMARY

1. Macroeconomics is the study of the behavior of the economy as a whole, which can be different from the sum of its parts. Macroeconomics differs from microeconomics in the type of questions it tries to answer. Macroeconomics also has a strong policy focus: **Keynesian economics,** which emerged during the Great Depression, advocates the use of **monetary policy** and **fiscal policy** to fight economic slumps. Prior to the Great Depression, the economy was thought to be **self-regulating.**

2. One key concern of macroeconomics is the **business cycle,** the short-run alternation between **recessions,** periods of falling employment and output, and **expansions,** periods of rising employment and output. The point at which expansion turns to recession is a **business-cycle peak.** The point at which recession turns to expansion is a **business-cycle trough.**

3. Another key area of macroeconomic study is **long-run economic growth,** the sustained upward trend in the economy's output over time. Long-run economic growth is the force behind long-term increases in living standards and is important for financing some economic programs. It is especially important for poorer countries.

4. When the prices of most goods and services are rising, so that the overall level of prices is going up, the economy experiences **inflation.** When the overall level of prices is going down, the economy is experiencing **deflation.** In the short run, inflation and deflation are closely related to the business cycle. In the long run, prices tend to reflect changes in the overall quantity of money. Because both inflation and deflation can cause problems, economists and policy makers generally aim for **price stability.**

5. Although comparative advantage explains why **open economies** export some things and import others, macroeconomic analysis is needed to explain why countries run **trade surpluses** or **trade deficits.** The determinants of the overall balance between exports and imports lie in decisions about savings and investment spending.

KEY TERMS

Self-regulating economy, p. 610
Keynesian economics, p. 610
Monetary policy, p. 610
Fiscal policy, p. 610
Recession, p. 612
Expansion, p. 613

Business cycle, p. 613
Business-cycle peak, p. 613
Business-cycle trough, p. 613
Long-run economic growth, p. 616
Inflation, p. 619
Deflation, p. 619

Price stability, p. 620
Open economy, p. 621
Trade deficit, p. 621
Trade surplus, p. 621

PROBLEMS

1. Which of the following questions are relevant for the study of macroeconomics and which for microeconomics?

   a. How will Ms. Martin's tips change when a large manufacturing plant near the restaurant where she works closes?

   b. What will happen to spending by consumers when the economy enters a downturn?

   c. How will the price of oranges change when a late frost damages Florida's orange groves?

   d. How will wages at a manufacturing plant change when its workforce is unionized?

   e. What will happen to U.S. exports as the dollar becomes less expensive in terms of other currencies?

   f. What is the relationship between a nation's unemployment rate and its inflation rate?

2. When one person saves more, that person's wealth is increased, meaning that he or she can consume more in the future. But when everyone saves more, everyone's income falls, meaning that everyone must consume less today. Explain this seeming contradiction.

3. Before the Great Depression, the conventional wisdom among economists and policy makers was that the economy is largely self-regulating.

   a. Is this view consistent or inconsistent with Keynesian economics? Explain.

   b. What effect did the Great Depression have on conventional wisdom?

   c. Contrast the response of policy makers during the 2007–2009 recession to the actions of policy makers during the Great Depression. What would have been the likely outcome of the 2007–2009 recession if policy makers had responded in the same fashion as policy makers during the Great Depression?

4. How do economists in the United States determine when a recession begins and when it ends? How do other countries determine whether or not a recession is occurring?

5. The U.S. Department of Labor reports statistics on employment and earnings that are used as key indicators by many economists to gauge the health of the economy. Figure 21-4 in the text plots historical data on the unemployment rate each month. Noticeably, the numbers were high during the recessions in the early 1990s, in 2001, and in the aftermath of the Great Recession, 2008–2014.

   a. Locate the latest data on the national unemployment rate. (*Hint:* Go to the website of the Bureau of Labor Statistics, www.bls.gov, and locate the latest release of the Employment Situation.)

   b. Compare the current numbers with those during the early 1990s, 2001, and during 2008-2014, as well as with the periods of relatively high economic growth just before the recessions. Are the current numbers indicative of a recessionary trend?

6. In the 1990s there were some dramatic economic events that came to be known as the *Asian financial crisis*. A decade later similar events came to be known as the *global financial crisis*. The accompanying figure shows the growth rate of real GDP in the United States and Japan from 1995 to 2011. Using the graph, explain why the two sets of events are referred to this way.

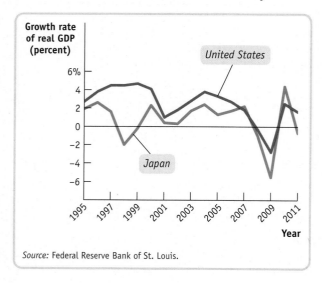

Source: Federal Reserve Bank of St. Louis.

7. a. What three measures of the economy tend to move together during the business cycle? Which way do they move during an upturn? During a downturn?

   b. Who in the economy is hurt during a recession? How?

   c. How did Milton Friedman alter the consensus that had developed in the aftermath of the Great Depression on how the economy should be managed? What is the current goal of policy makers in managing the economy?

8. Why do we consider a business-cycle expansion different from long-run economic growth? Why do we care about the size of the long-run growth rate of real GDP relative to the size of the growth rate of the population?

9. In 1798, Thomas Malthus's *Essay on the Principle of Population* was published. In it, he wrote: "Population, when unchecked, increases in a geometrical ratio. Subsistence increases only in an arithmetical ratio. . . . This implies a strong and constantly operating check on population from the difficulty of subsistence." Malthus was saying that the growth of the population is limited by the amount of food available to eat; people will live at the subsistence level forever. Why didn't Malthus's description apply to the world after 1800?

10. Each year, *The Economist* publishes data on the price of the Big Mac in different countries and exchange rates. The accompanying table shows some data from 2007 and 2014. Use this information to answer the following questions.

	2007		2014	
Country	**Price of Big Mac (in local currrency)**	**Price of Big Mac (in U.S. dollars)**	**Price of Big Mac (in local currency)**	**Price of Big Mac (in U.S. dollars)**
Argentina	peso8.25	$2.65	peso21.0	$2.57
Canada	C$3.63	$3.08	C$5.25	$5.64
Euro area	€2.94	$3.82	€3.68	$4.95
Japan	¥280	$2.31	¥370	$3.64
United States	$3.22	$3.22	$4.80	$4.80

   a. Where was it cheapest to buy a Big Mac in U.S. dollars in 2007?

   b. Where was it cheapest to buy a Big Mac in U.S. dollars in 2014?

   c. Using the increase in the local currency price of the Big Mac in each country to measure the percent change in the overall price level from 2007 to 2014, which nation experienced the most inflation? Did any of the nations experience deflation?

11. The accompanying figure illustrates the trade deficit of the United States since 1987. The United States has been consistently and, on the whole, increasingly importing more goods than it has been exporting. One of the countries it runs a trade deficit with is China. Which of the following statements are valid possible explanations of this fact? Explain.

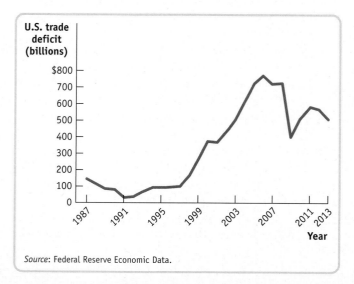

Source: Federal Reserve Economic Data.

a. Many products, such as televisions, that were formerly manufactured in the United States are now manufactured in China.

b. The wages of the average Chinese worker are far lower than the wages of the average American worker.

c. Investment spending in the United States is high relative to its level of savings.

WORK IT OUT

For interactive, step-by-step help in solving the following problem, visit LaunchPad by using the URL on the back cover of this book.

12. College tuition has risen significantly in the last few decades. From the 1981–1982 academic year to the 2011–2012 academic year, total tuition, room, and board paid by full-time undergraduate students went from $2,871 to $16,789 at public institutions and from $6,330 to $33,716 at private institutions. This is an average annual tuition increase of 6.1% at public institutions and 5.7% at private institutions. Over the same time, average personal income after taxes rose from $9,785 to $39,409 per year, which is an average annual rate of growth of personal income of 4.8%. Have these tuition increases made it more difficult for the average student to afford college tuition?

GDP and the CPI: Tracking the Macroeconomy

▶ **What You Will Learn in This Chapter**

■ How economists use aggregate measures to track the performance of the economy

■ What **gross domestic product,** or **GDP,** is and the three ways of calculating it

■ The difference between **real GDP** and **nominal GDP** and why real GDP is the appropriate measure of real economic activity

■ What a **price index** is and how it is used to calculate the **inflation rate**

THE NEW #2

Iain Masterton/Alamy

China has become an economic superpower, surpassing Japan.

"CHINA PASSES JAPAN AS Second-Largest Economy." That was the headline in the *New York Times* on August 15, 2010. Citing economic data suggesting that Japan's economy was weakening while China's was roaring ahead, the article predicted—correctly, as it turned out—that 2010 would mark the first year in which the surging Chinese economy finally overtook Japan's, taking second place to the United States on the world economic stage. "The milestone," wrote the *Times,* "though anticipated for some time, is the most striking evidence yet that China's ascendance is for real and that the rest of the world will have to reckon with a new economic superpower."

But what does it mean to say that China's economy is larger than Japan's? The two economies are, after all, producing very different mixes of goods. Despite its rapid advance, China is still

a fairly poor country whose greatest strength is in relatively low-tech production. Japan, by contrast, is very much a high-tech nation, and it dominates world output of some sophisticated goods, like electronic sensors for automobiles. That's why the 2011 earthquake in northeastern Japan, which put many factories out of action, temporarily caused major production disruptions for auto factories around the world.

So how can you compare the sizes of two economies when they aren't producing the same things?

The answer is that comparisons of national economies are based on the *value* of their production. When news reports declared that China's economy had overtaken Japan's, they meant that China's *gross domestic product,* or *GDP*—a measure of the overall value of goods and services produced—had surpassed Japan's GDP.

GDP is one of the most important measures used to track the macroeconomy—that is, to quantify movements in the overall level of output and prices. Measures like GDP and *price indexes* play an important role in formulating economic policy, since policy makers need to know what's going on, and anecdotes are no substitute for hard data. They're also important for business decisions—to such an extent that, as the business case at the end of the chapter illustrates, corporations and other players are willing to pay significant sums for early reads on what official economic measurements are likely to find.

In this chapter, we explain how macroeconomists measure key aspects of the economy. We first explore ways to measure the economy's total output and total income. We then turn to the problem of how to measure the level of prices and the change in prices in the economy.

The **national income and product accounts,** or **national accounts,** keep track of the flows of money between different sectors of the economy.

Consumer spending is household spending on goods and services.

A **stock** is a share in the ownership of a company held by a shareholder.

A **bond** is borrowing in the form of an IOU that pays interest.

Government transfers are payments by the government to individuals for which no good or service is provided in return.

Disposable income, equal to income plus government transfers minus taxes, is the total amount of household income available to spend on consumption and to save.

The National Accounts

Almost all countries calculate a set of numbers known as the *national income and product accounts.* In fact, the accuracy of a country's accounts is a remarkably reliable indicator of its state of economic development—in general, the more reliable the accounts, the more economically advanced the country. When international economic agencies seek to help a less developed country, typically the first order of business is to send a team of experts to audit and improve the country's accounts.

In the United States, these numbers are calculated by the Bureau of Economic Analysis, a division of the U.S. government's Department of Commerce. The **national income and product accounts,** often referred to simply as the **national accounts,** keep track of the spending of consumers, sales of producers, business investment spending, government purchases, and a variety of other flows of money between different sectors of the economy. Let's see how they work.

The Circular-Flow Diagram, Revisited and Expanded

To understand the principles behind the national accounts, it helps to look at Figure 22-1, a revised and expanded *circular-flow diagram* similar to the one we introduced in Chapter 2. Recall that in Figure 2-7 we showed the flows of money, goods and services, and factors of production through the economy. Here we restrict ourselves to flows of money but add extra elements that allow us to show the key concepts behind the national accounts. As in our original version of the circular-flow diagram, the underlying principle is that the inflow of money into each market or sector is equal to the outflow of money coming from that market or sector.

Figure 2-7 showed a simplified world containing only two kinds of "inhabitants," households and firms. And it illustrated the circular flow of money between households and firms, which remains visible in Figure 22-1. In the markets for goods and services, households engage in **consumer spending,** buying goods and services from domestic firms and from firms in the rest of the world.

Households also own factors of production—labor, land, physical capital, human capital, and financial capital. They sell the use of these factors of production to firms, receiving wages, profit, interest payments, and rent in return. Firms buy and pay households for the use of those factors of production in the factor markets. Most households derive the bulk of their income from wages earned by selling labor and human capital.

But households derive additional income from their indirect ownership of the physical capital used by firms, mainly in the form of **stocks,** shares in the ownership of a company, and from direct ownership of **bonds,** borrowing by firms in the form of an IOU that pays interest. So the income households receive from the factor markets includes profits distributed to shareholders known as *dividends,* and the interest payments on bonds held by bondholders. Finally, households receive rent in return for allowing firms to use land or structures that they own. So households receive income in the form of wages, profit, interest payments, and rent via factor markets.

In our original, simplified circular-flow diagram, households spent all the income they received via factor markets on goods and services. Figure 22-1, however, illustrates a more complicated but more realistic diagram. There we see two reasons why goods and services don't in fact absorb all of households' income.

First, households don't get to keep all the income they receive via the factor markets. They must pay part of their income to the government in the form of taxes, such as income taxes and sales taxes. In addition, some households receive **government transfers**—payments by the government to individuals for which no good or service is provided in return, such as Social Security benefits and unemployment insurance payments. The total income households have left after paying taxes and receiving government transfers is **disposable income.**

FIGURE **22-1**   An Expanded Circular-Flow Diagram: The Flows of Money Through the Economy

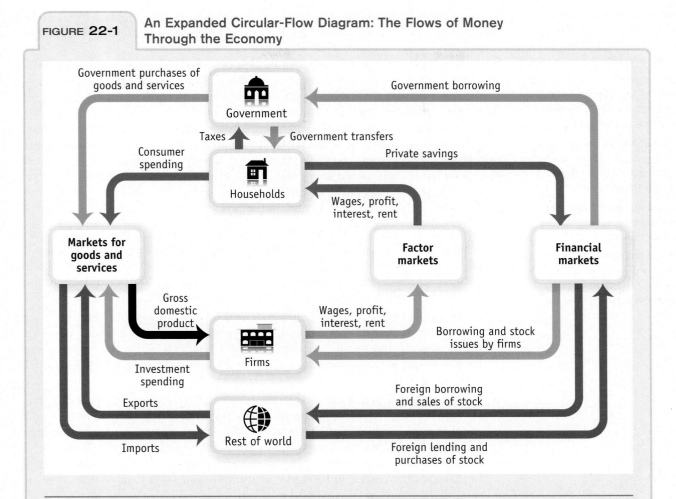

A circular flow of funds connects the four sectors of the economy—households, firms, government, and the rest of the world—via three types of markets: the factor markets, the markets for goods and services, and the *financial markets.* Funds flow from firms to households in the form of wages, profit, interest, and rent through the factor markets. After paying taxes to the government and receiving *government transfers,* households allocate the remaining income—*disposable income*—to private savings and consumer spending. Via the financial markets, *private savings* and funds from the rest of the world are channeled into investment spending by firms, government borrowing, foreign borrowing and lending, and foreign transactions of stocks. In turn, funds flow

from the government and households to firms to pay for purchases of goods and services. Finally, exports to the rest of the world generate a flow of funds into the economy and imports lead to a flow of funds out of the economy. If we add up consumer spending on goods and services, investment spending by firms, government purchases of goods and services, and exports, then subtract the value of imports, the total flow of funds represented by this calculation is total spending on final goods and services produced in the United States. Equivalently, it's the value of all the final goods and services produced in the United States—that is, the *gross domestic product* of the economy.

Second, households normally don't spend all of their disposable income on goods and services. Instead, a portion of their income is typically set aside as **private savings,** which goes into **financial markets** where individuals, banks, and other institutions buy and sell stocks and bonds as well as make loans. As Figure 22-1 shows, the financial markets also receive funds from the rest of the world and provide funds to the government, to firms, and to the rest of the world.

Before going further, we can use the box representing households to illustrate an important general feature of the circular-flow diagram: the total sum of flows of money out of a given box is equal to the total sum of flows of money into that box. It's simply a matter of accounting: what goes in must come out. So, for example, the total flow of money out of households—the sum of taxes paid,

Private savings, equal to disposable income minus consumer spending, is disposable income that is not spent on consumption.

The banking, stock, and bond markets, which channel private savings and foreign lending into investment spending, government borrowing, and foreign borrowing, are known as the **financial markets.**

Government borrowing is the total amount of funds borrowed by federal, state, and local governments in the financial markets.

Government purchases of goods and services are total expenditures on goods and services by federal, state, and local governments.

Goods and services sold to other countries are **exports.** Goods and services purchased from other countries are **imports.**

Inventories are stocks of goods and raw materials held to facilitate business operations.

Investment spending is spending on productive physical capital—such as machinery and construction of buildings—and on changes to inventories.

consumer spending, and private savings—must equal the total flow of money into households—the sum of wages, profits, interest payments, rent, and government transfers.

Now let's look at the other types of inhabitants we've added to the circular-flow diagram, including the government—all federal, state, and local governments—and the rest of the world. The government returns a portion of the money it collects from taxes to households in the form of government transfers. However, it uses much of its tax revenue, plus additional funds borrowed in the financial markets through **government borrowing,** to buy goods and services. **Government purchases of goods and services,** the total purchases by federal, state, and local governments, include everything from military spending on ammunition to your local public school's spending on chalk, erasers, and teacher salaries.

The rest of the world participates in the U.S. economy in three ways.

1. Some of the goods and services produced in the United States are sold to residents of other countries. For example, more than half of America's annual wheat and cotton crops are sold abroad. Goods and services sold to other countries are known as **exports.** Export sales lead to a flow of funds from the rest of the world into the United States to pay for them.

2. Some of the goods and services purchased by residents of the United States are produced abroad. For example, many consumer goods are now made in China. Goods and services purchased from residents of other countries are known as **imports.** Import purchases lead to a flow of funds out of the United States to pay for them.

3. Foreigners can participate in U.S. financial markets by making transactions. Foreign lending—lending by foreigners to borrowers in the United States, and purchases by foreigners of shares of stock in American companies—generates a flow of funds into the United States from the rest of the world. Conversely, foreign borrowing—borrowing by foreigners from U.S. lenders and purchases by Americans of stock in foreign companies—leads to a flow of funds out of the United States to the rest of the world.

Finally, let's go back to the markets for goods and services. In Chapter 2 we focused only on purchases of goods and services by households. We now see that there are other types of spending on goods and services, including government purchases, *investment spending* by firms, imports, and exports.

Notice that firms also buy goods and services in our expanded economy. For example, an automobile company that is building a new factory will buy investment goods—machinery like stamping presses and welding robots that are used to produce goods and services for consumers—from companies that manufacture these items. It will also accumulate an *inventory* of finished cars in preparation for shipment to dealers. **Inventories,** then, are stocks of goods and raw materials that firms hold to facilitate their operations. The national accounts count this **investment spending**—spending on productive physical capital, such as machinery and construction of buildings, and on changes to inventories—as part of total spending on goods and services.

You might ask why *changes* to inventories are included in investment spending—finished cars aren't, after all, used to produce more cars. Changes to inventories of finished goods are counted as investment spending because, like machinery, they change the ability of a firm to make future sales. So spending on additions to inventories is a form of investment spending by a firm. Conversely, a drawing-down of inventories is counted as a fall in investment spending because it leads to lower future sales.

It's also important to understand that investment spending includes spending on construction of any structure, regardless of whether it is an assembly plant or a new house. Why include construction of homes? Because, like a plant, a new house produces a future stream of output—housing services for its occupants.

Suppose we add up consumer spending on goods and services, investment spending, government purchases of goods and services, and the value of exports, then subtract the value of imports. This gives us a measure of the overall market value of the goods and services the economy produces. That measure has a name: it's a country's *gross domestic product*. But before we can formally define gross domestic product, or GDP, we have to examine an important distinction between classes of goods and services: the difference between *final goods and services* versus *intermediate goods and services*.

Gross Domestic Product

A consumer's purchase of a new car from a dealer is one example of a sale of **final goods and services:** goods and services sold to the final, or end, user. But an automobile manufacturer's purchase of steel from a steel foundry or glass from a glassmaker is an example of purchasing **intermediate goods and services:** goods and services that are inputs for production of final goods and services. In the case of intermediate goods and services, the purchaser—another firm—is *not* the final user.

Gross domestic product, or **GDP,** is the total value of all *final goods and services* produced in an economy during a given period, usually a year. In 2013 the GDP of the United States was $16,800 billion, or about $53,000 per person. If you are an economist trying to construct a country's national accounts, *one way to calculate GDP is to calculate it directly: survey firms and add up the total value of their production of final goods and services.* We'll explain in detail in the next section why intermediate goods, and some other types of goods as well, are not included in the calculation of GDP.

But adding up the total value of final goods and services produced isn't the only way of calculating GDP. There is another way, based on total spending on final goods and services. Since GDP is equal to the total value of final goods and services produced in the economy, it must also equal the flow of funds received by firms from sales in the goods and services market.

If you look again at the circular-flow diagram in Figure 22-1, you will see that the arrow going from markets for goods and services to firms is indeed labeled "Gross domestic product." According to our basic rule of accounting, flows out of any box are equal to flows into the box; so the flow of funds out of the markets for goods and services to firms is equal to the total flow of funds into the markets for goods and services from other sectors. And as you can see from Figure 22-1, the total flow of funds into the markets for goods and services is total or **aggregate spending** on domestically produced final goods and services—the sum of consumer spending, investment spending, government purchases of goods and services, and exports minus imports. *So a second way of calculating GDP is to add up aggregate spending on domestically produced final goods and services in the economy.*

And there is yet a third way of calculating GDP, based on total income earned in the economy. Firms, and the factors of production that they employ, are owned by households. So firms must ultimately pay out what they earn to households. The flow from firms to the factor markets is the factor income paid out by firms to households in the form of wages, profit, interest, and rent. Again, by accounting rules, the value of the flow of factor income from firms to households must be equal to the flow of money into firms from the markets for goods and services. And this last value, we know, is the total value of production in the economy—GDP.

Why is GDP equal to the total value of factor income paid by firms in the economy to households? Because each sale in the economy must accrue to someone as income—either as wages, profit, interest, or rent. *So a third way of calculating GDP is to sum the total factor income earned by households from firms in the economy.*

Final goods and services are goods and services sold to the final, or end, user.

Intermediate goods and services are goods and services—bought from one firm by another firm—that are inputs for production of final goods and services.

Gross domestic product, or **GDP,** is the total value of all final goods and services produced in the economy during a given year.

Aggregate spending, the sum of consumer spending, investment spending, government purchases of goods and services, and exports minus imports, is the total spending on domestically produced final goods and services in the economy.

"You wouldn't think there'd be much money in potatoes, chickens, and woodchopping, but it all adds up."

Calculating GDP

We've just explained that there are in fact three methods for calculating GDP:

1. adding up total value of all final goods and services produced
2. adding up spending on all domestically produced goods and services
3. adding up total factor income earned by households from firms in the economy

Government statisticians use all three methods. To illustrate how these three methods work, we will consider a hypothetical economy, shown in Figure 22-2. This economy consists of three firms—American Motors, Inc., which produces one car per year; American Steel, Inc., which produces the steel that goes into the car; and American Ore, Inc., which mines the iron ore that goes into the steel. So GDP is $21,500, the value of the one car per year the economy produces. Let's look at how the three different methods of calculating GDP yield the same result.

Measuring GDP as the Value of Production of Final Goods and Services The first method for calculating GDP is to add up the value of all the final goods and services produced in the economy—a calculation that excludes the value of intermediate goods and services. Why are intermediate goods and services excluded? After all, don't they represent a very large and valuable portion of the economy?

To understand why only final goods and services are included in GDP, look at the simplified economy described in Figure 22-2. Should we measure the GDP of this economy by adding up the total sales of the iron ore producer, the steel producer, and the auto producer? If we did, we would in effect be counting the value of the steel twice—once when it is sold by the steel plant to the auto plant, and again when the steel auto body is sold to a consumer as a finished car. And we

FIGURE **22-2**   Calculating GDP

In this hypothetical economy consisting of three firms, GDP can be calculated in three different ways: 1) measuring GDP as the value of production of final goods and services, by summing each firm's value added; 2) measuring GDP as aggregate spending on domestically produced final goods and services; and 3) measuring GDP as factor income earned by households from firms in the economy.

2. Aggregate spending on domestically produced final goods and services = $21,500

	American Ore, Inc.	American Steel, Inc.	American Motors, Inc.	Total factor income
Value of sales	$4,200 (ore)	$9,000 (steel)	$21,500 (car)	
Intermediate goods	0	4,200 (iron ore)	9,000 (steel)	
Wages	2,000	3,700	10,000	$15,700
Interest payments	1,000	600	1,000	2,600
Rent	200	300	500	1,000
Profit	1,000	200	1,000	2,200
Total expenditure by firm	4,200	9,000	21,500	
Value added per firm = Value of sales − Cost of intermediate goods	4,200	4,800	12,500	

3. Total payments to factors = $21,500

1. Value of production of final goods and services, sum of value added = $21,500

would be counting the value of the iron ore *three* times—once when it is mined and sold to the steel company, a second time when it is made into steel and sold to the auto producer, and a third time when the steel is made into a car and sold to the consumer.

So counting the full value of each producer's sales would cause us to count the same items several times and artificially inflate the calculation of GDP. For example, in Figure 22-2, the total value of all sales, intermediate and final, is $34,700: $21,500 from the sale of the car, plus $9,000 from the sale of the steel, plus $4,200 from the sale of the iron ore. Yet we know that GDP is only $21,500. The way we avoid double-counting is to count only each producer's **value added** in the calculation of GDP: the difference between the value of its sales and the value of the intermediate goods and services it purchases from other businesses.

That is, we subtract the cost of inputs—the intermediate goods—at each stage of the production process. In this case, the value added of the auto producer is the dollar value of the cars it manufactures *minus* the cost of the steel it buys, or $12,500. The value added of the steel producer is the dollar value of the steel it produces *minus* the cost of the ore it buys, or $4,800. Only the ore producer, which we have assumed doesn't buy any inputs, has value added equal to its total sales, $4,200. The sum of the three producers' value added is $21,500, equal to GDP.

Measuring GDP as Spending on Domestically Produced Final Goods and Services

Another way to calculate GDP is by adding up aggregate spending on domestically produced final goods and services. That is, GDP can be measured by the flow of funds into firms. Like the method that estimates GDP as the value of domestic production of final goods and services, this measurement must be carried out in a way that avoids double-counting.

In terms of our steel and auto example, we don't want to count both consumer spending on a car (represented in Figure 22-2 by $12,500, the sales price of the car) and the auto producer's spending on steel (represented in Figure 22-2 by $9,000, the price of a car's worth of steel). If we counted both, we would be counting the steel embodied in the car twice. We solve this problem by counting only the value of sales to *final buyers*, such as consumers, firms that purchase investment goods, the government, or foreign buyers. In other words, in order to avoid double-counting

Steel is an intermediate good because it is sold to other product manufacturers like automakers, and rarely to final buyers, such as consumers.

The **value added** of a producer is the value of its sales minus the value of its purchases of intermediate goods and services.

FOR INQUIRING MINDS | Our Imputed Lives

An old line says that when a person marries the household cook, GDP falls. And it's true: when someone provides services for pay, those services are counted as a part of GDP. But the services family members provide to each other are not. Some economists have produced alternative measures that try to "impute" the value of household work—that is, assign an estimate of what the market value of that work would have been if it had been paid for. But the standard measure of GDP doesn't contain that imputation.

GDP estimates do, however, include an imputation for the value of "owner-occupied housing." That is, if you buy the home you were formerly renting, GDP does not go down. It's true that

The value of the services that family members provide to each other is not counted as part of GDP.

because you no longer pay rent to your landlord, the landlord no longer sells a service to you—namely, use of the house or apartment. But the statisticians make an estimate of what you would have paid if you rented whatever you live in, whether it's an apartment or a house. For the purposes of the statistics, it's as if you were renting your dwelling from yourself.

If you think about it, this makes a lot of sense. In a home-owning country like the United States, the pleasure we derive from our houses is an important part of the standard of living. So to be accurate, estimates of GDP must take into account the value of housing that is occupied by owners as well as the value of rental housing. ■

of spending, we omit sales of inputs from one business to another when estimating GDP using spending data. You can see from Figure 22-2 that aggregate spending on final goods and services—the finished car—is $21,500.

As we've already pointed out, the national accounts *do* include investment spending by firms as a part of final spending. That is, an auto company's purchase of steel to make a car isn't considered a part of final spending, but the company's purchase of new machinery for its factory *is* considered a part of final spending. What's the difference? Steel is an input that is used up in production; machinery will last for a number of years. Since purchases of capital goods that will last for a considerable time aren't closely tied to current production, the national accounts consider such purchases a form of final sales.

In later chapters, we will make use of the proposition that GDP is equal to aggregate spending on domestically produced goods and services by final buyers. We will also develop models of how final buyers decide how much to spend. With that in mind, we'll now examine the types of spending that make up GDP.

Look again at the markets for goods and services in Figure 22-1, and you will see that one component of sales by firms is consumer spending. Let's denote consumer spending with the symbol C. Figure 22-1 also shows three other components of sales: sales of investment goods to other businesses, or investment spending, which we will denote by I; government purchases of goods and services, which we will denote by G; and sales to foreigners—that is, exports—which we will denote by X.

In reality, not all of this final spending goes toward domestically produced goods and services. We must take account of spending on imports, which we will denote by IM. Income spent on imports is income not spent on domestic goods and services—it is income that has "leaked" across national borders. So to accurately value domestic production using spending data, we must subtract out spending on imports to arrive at spending on domestically produced goods and services. Putting this all together gives us the following equation that breaks GDP down by the four sources of aggregate spending:

(22-1) $GDP = C + I + G + X - IM$

We'll be seeing a lot of Equation 22-1 in later chapters.

PITFALLS

GDP: WHAT'S IN AND WHAT'S OUT

It's easy to confuse what is included in and what is excluded from GDP. So let's stop here for a moment and make sure the distinction is clear. The most likely source of confusion is the difference between investment spending and spending on intermediate goods and services. Investment spending—spending on productive physical capital (including construction of residential and commercial structures), and changes to inventories—is included in GDP. But spending on intermediate goods and services is not.

Why the difference? Recall from Chapter 2 that we made a distinction between resources that are *used up* and those that are *not used up* in production. An input, like steel, is used up in production. An investment good, like a metal-stamping machine, is not. It will last for many years and will be used repeatedly

to make many cars. Since spending on productive physical capital—investment goods—and construction of structures is not directly tied to current output, economists consider such spending to be spending on final goods.

Spending on changes to inventories is considered a part of investment spending, so it is also included in GDP. Why? Because, like a machine, additional inventory is an investment in future sales. And when a good is released for sale from inventories, its value is subtracted from the value of inventories and so from GDP.

Used goods are not included in GDP because, as with inputs, to include them would be to double-count: counting them once when sold as new and again when sold as used.

Also, financial assets such as stocks and bonds are not included in GDP because they don't represent either the

production or the sale of final goods and services. Rather, a bond represents a promise to repay with interest, and a stock represents a proof of ownership. And for obvious reasons, foreign-produced goods and services are not included in calculations of GDP.

Here is a summary of what's included and not included in GDP:

Included

- Domestically produced final goods and services, including capital goods, new construction of structures, and changes to inventories

Not Included

- Intermediate goods and services
- Inputs
- Used goods
- Financial assets like stocks and bonds
- Foreign-produced goods and services

Measuring GDP as Factor Income Earned from Firms in the Economy A final way to calculate GDP is to add up all the income earned by factors of production from firms in the economy—the wages earned by labor; the interest paid to those who lend their savings to firms and the government; the rent earned by those who lease their land or structures to firms; and dividends, the profits paid to the shareholders, the owners of the firms' physical capital. This is a valid measure because the money firms earn by selling goods and services must go somewhere; whatever isn't paid as wages, interest, or rent is profit. Ultimately, profits are paid out to shareholders as dividends.

Figure 22-2 shows how this calculation works for our simplified economy. The numbers shaded in the column at far right show the total wages, interest, and rent paid by all these firms as well as their total profit. Summing up all of these items yields total factor income of $21,500—again, equal to GDP.

We won't emphasize factor income as much as the other two methods of calculating GDP. It's important to keep in mind, however, that all the money spent on domestically produced goods and services generates factor income to households—that is, there really is a circular flow.

The Components of GDP Now that we know how GDP is calculated in principle, let's see what it looks like in practice.

Figure 22-3 shows the first two methods of calculating GDP side by side. The height of each bar above the horizontal axis represents the GDP of the U.S. economy in 2013: $16,800 billion. Each bar is divided to show the breakdown of that total in terms of where the value was added and how the money was spent.

FIGURE 22-3   **U.S. GDP in 2013: Two Methods of Calculating GDP**

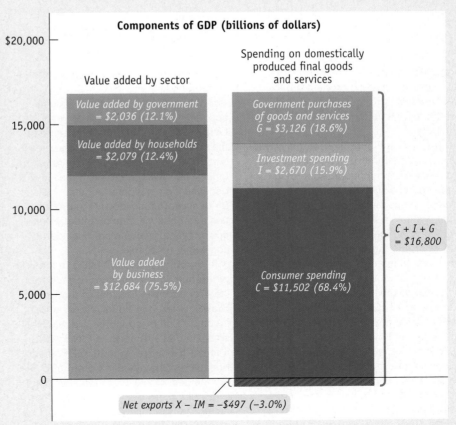

The two bars show two equivalent ways of calculating GDP. The height of each bar above the horizontal axis represents $16,800 billion, U.S. GDP in 2013. The left bar shows the breakdown of GDP according to the value added of each sector of the economy: government, households, and firms. The right bar shows the breakdown of GDP according to the four types of aggregate spending: $C + I + G + X - IM$. The right bar has a total length of $16,800 billion + $497 billion = $17,297 billion. The $497 billion, shown as the area extending below the horizontal axis, is the amount of total spending absorbed by net exports, which were negative in 2013. (Numbers don't add due to rounding.)

Source: Bureau of Economic Analysis.

Components of GDP (billions of dollars)

Value added by sector

Value added by government = $2,036 (12.1%)

Value added by households = $2,079 (12.4%)

Value added by business = $12,684 (75.5%)

Spending on domestically produced final goods and services

Government purchases of goods and services G = $3,126 (18.6%)

Investment spending I = $2,670 (15.9%)

Consumer spending C = $11,502 (68.4%)

$C + I + G = $16,800$

Net exports $X - IM = -$497 (−3.0%)$

Net exports are the difference between the value of exports and the value of imports.

In the left bar in Figure 22-3, we see the breakdown of GDP by value added according to sector, the first method of calculating GDP. Of the $16,800 billion, $12,684 billion consisted of value added by businesses. Another $2,079 billion of value added was added by households and institutions; a large part of that was the imputed services of owner-occupied housing, described in the earlier For Inquiring Minds "Our Imputed Lives." Finally, $2,036 billion consisted of value added by government, in the form of military, education, and other government services.

The right bar in Figure 22-3 corresponds to the second method of calculating GDP, showing the breakdown by the four types of aggregate spending. The total length of the right bar is longer than the total length of the left bar, a difference of $497 billion (which, as you can see, is the amount by which the right bar extends below the horizontal axis). That's because the total length of the right bar represents total spending in the economy, spending on both domestically produced and foreign-produced final goods and services. Within the bar, consumer spending (C), which is 68.4% of GDP, dominates overall spending.

But some of that spending was absorbed by foreign-produced goods and services. In 2013, **net exports,** the difference between the value of exports and the value of imports ($X - IM$ in Equation 22-1) was negative—the United States was a net importer of foreign goods and services. The 2013 value of $X - IM$ was −$497 billion, or −3.0% of GDP. Thus, a portion of the right bar extends below the horizontal axis by $497 billion to represent the amount of total spending that was absorbed by net imports and so did not lead to higher U.S. GDP. Investment spending (I) constituted 15.9% of GDP; government purchases of goods and services (G) constituted 18.6% of GDP.

FOR INQUIRING MINDS | Gross What?

Occasionally you may see references not to gross domestic product but to gross *national* product, or GNP. Is this just another name for the same thing? Not quite.

If you look at Figure 22-1 carefully, you may realize that there's a possibility that is missing from the figure. According to the figure, all factor income goes to domestic households. But what happens when profits are paid to foreigners who own stock in General Motors or Apple? And where do the profits earned by American companies operating overseas fit in?

To answer these questions, an alternative measure, GNP, was devised. GNP is defined as the total factor income earned by residents of a country. It *excludes* factor income earned by foreigners, like profits paid to foreign investors who own American stocks and payments to foreigners who work temporarily in the United States. And it *includes* factor income earned abroad by Americans, like the profits of Apple's European operations that accrue to Apple's American shareholders and the

wages of Americans who work abroad temporarily.

In the early days of national income accounting, economists usually used GNP rather than GDP as a measure of the economy's size—although the measures were generally very close to each other. They switched to GDP mainly because it's considered a better indicator of short-run movements in production and because data on international flows of factor income are considered somewhat unreliable.

In practice, it doesn't make much difference which measure is used for large economies like that of the United States, where the flows of net factor income to other countries are relatively small. In 2013, America's GNP was about 1.5% larger than its GDP, mainly because of the overseas profit of U.S. companies. However, for smaller countries, which are likely to be hosts to a number of foreign companies, GDP and GNP can diverge significantly. For example, much of Ireland's industry is owned by American corporations, whose profit must be deducted from

GNP, the value of output produced within a country's borders, typically differs from GDP, the value of output produced worldwide that is owned by a country's citizens and firms.

Ireland's GNP. In addition, Ireland has become a host to many temporary workers from poorer regions of Europe, whose wages must also be deducted from Ireland's GNP. As a result, in 2013 Ireland's GNP was only 86% of its GDP. ∎

What GDP Tells Us

Now we've seen the various ways that gross domestic product is calculated. But what does the measurement of GDP tell us?

The most important use of GDP is as a measure of the size of the economy, providing us a scale against which to measure the economic performance of other years or to compare the economic performance of other countries. For example, suppose you want to compare the economies of different nations. A natural approach is to compare their GDPs. In 2013, as we've seen, U.S. GDP was $16,800 billion, China's GDP was $9,181 billion, and the combined GDP of the 27 countries that make up the European Union was $17,371 billion. This comparison tells us that China, although it has the world's second-largest national economy, carries considerably less economic weight than does the United States. When taken in aggregate, Europe is America's equal or superior.

Still, one must be careful when using GDP numbers, especially when making comparisons over time. That's because part of the increase in the value of GDP over time represents increases in the *prices* of goods and services rather than an increase in output. For example, U.S. GDP was $8,608 billion in 1997 and had approximately doubled to $16,800 billion by 2013. But the U.S. economy didn't actually double in size over that period. To measure actual changes in aggregate output, we need a modified version of GDP that is adjusted for price changes, known as *real GDP*. We'll see next how real GDP is calculated.

ECONOMICS ▶ in Action

Creating the National Accounts

The national accounts, like modern macroeconomics, owe their creation to the Great Depression. As the economy plunged into depression, government officials found their ability to respond crippled not only by the lack of adequate economic theories but also by the lack of adequate information. All they had were scattered statistics: railroad freight car loadings, stock prices, and incomplete indexes of industrial production. They could only guess at what was happening to the economy as a whole.

In response to this perceived lack of information, the Department of Commerce commissioned Simon Kuznets, a young Russian-born economist, to develop a set of national income accounts. (Kuznets later won the Nobel Prize in economics for his work.) The first version of these accounts was presented to Congress in 1937 and in a research report titled *National Income, 1929–35.*

Kuznets's initial estimates fell short of the full modern set of accounts because they focused on income, not production. The push to complete the national accounts came during World War II, when policy makers were in even more need of comprehensive measures of the economy's performance. The federal government began issuing estimates of gross domestic product and gross national product in 1942.

In January 2000, in its publication *Survey of Current Business,* the Department of Commerce ran an article titled "GDP: One of the Great Inventions of the 20th Century." This may seem a bit over the top, but national income accounting, invented in the United States, has since become a tool of economic analysis and policy making around the world.

Check Your Understanding 22-1

1. Explain why the three methods of calculating GDP produce the same estimate of GDP.

2. What are the various sectors to which firms make sales? What are the various ways in which households are linked with other sectors of the economy?

3. Consider Figure 22-2 and suppose you mistakenly believed that total value added was $30,500, the sum of the sales price of a car and a car's worth of steel. What items would you be counting twice?

Solutions appear at back of book.

Aggregate output is the economy's total quantity of output of final goods and services.

Real GDP is the total value of all final goods and services produced in the economy during a given year, calculated using the prices of a selected base year.

Real GDP: A Measure of Aggregate Output

In this chapter's opening story, we described how China passed Japan as the world's second-largest economy in 2010. At the time, Japan's economy was weakening: during the second quarter of 2010, output declined by an annual rate of 6.3%. Oddly, however, GDP was up. In fact, Japan's GDP measured in yen, its national currency, rose by an annual rate of 4.8% during the quarter. How was that possible? The answer is that Japan was experiencing inflation at the time. As a result, the yen value of Japan's GDP rose although output actually fell.

The moral of this story is that the commonly cited GDP number is an interesting and useful statistic, one that provides a good way to compare the size of different economies, but it's not a good measure of the economy's growth over time. GDP can grow because the economy grows, but it can also grow simply because of inflation. Even if an economy's output doesn't change, GDP will go up if the prices of the goods and services the economy produces have increased. Likewise, GDP can fall either because the economy is producing less or because prices have fallen.

In order to accurately measure the economy's growth, we need a measure of **aggregate output:** the total quantity of final goods and services the economy produces. The measure that is used for this purpose is known as *real GDP*. By tracking real GDP over time, we avoid the problem of changes in prices distorting the value of changes in production of goods and services over time. Let's look first at how real GDP is calculated, then at what it means.

Calculating Real GDP

To understand how real GDP is calculated, imagine an economy in which only two goods, apples and oranges, are produced and in which both goods are sold only to final consumers. The outputs and prices of the two fruits for two consecutive years are shown in Table 22-1.

TABLE 22-1   Calculating GDP and Real GDP in a Simple Economy

	Year 1	Year 2
Quantity of apples (billions)	2,000	2,200
Price of apple	$0.25	$0.30
Quantity of oranges (billions)	1,000	1,200
Price of orange	$0.50	$0.70
GDP (billions of dollars)	$1,000	$1,500
Real GDP (billions of year 1 dollars)	$1,000	$1,150

The first thing we can say about these data is that the value of sales increased from year 1 to year 2. In the first year, the total value of sales was (2,000 billion × $0.25) + (1,000 billion × $0.50) = $1,000 billion; in the second it was (2,200 billion × $0.30) + (1,200 billion × $0.70) = $1,500 billion, which is 50% larger. But it is also clear from the table that this increase in the dollar value of GDP overstates the real growth in the economy. Although the quantities of both apples and oranges increased, the prices of both apples and oranges also rose. So part of the 50% increase in the dollar value of GDP from year 1 to year 2 simply reflects higher prices, not higher production of output.

To estimate the true increase in aggregate output produced, we have to ask the following question: how much would GDP have gone up if prices had *not* changed? To answer this question, we need to find the value of output in year 2 expressed in year 1 prices. In year 1 the price of apples was $0.25 each and the price of oranges $0.50 each. So year 2 output *at year 1 prices* is (2,200 billion × $0.25) + (1,200 billion × $0.50) = $1,150 billion. And output in year 1 at year 1 prices was $1,000 billion. So in this example GDP measured in year 1 prices rose 15%—from $1,000 billion to $1,150 billion.

Now we can define **real GDP:** it is the total value of final goods and services produced in the economy during a year, calculated as if prices had stayed constant at the level of some given base year. A real GDP number always comes with information about what the base year is.

A GDP number that has not been adjusted for changes in prices is calculated using the prices in the year in which the output is produced. Economists call this measure **nominal GDP,** GDP at current prices. If we had used nominal GDP to measure the true change in output from year 1 to year 2 in our apples and oranges example, we would have overstated the true growth in output: we would have claimed it to be 50%, when in fact it was only 15%. By comparing output in the two years using a common set of prices—the year 1 prices in this example—we are able to focus solely on changes in the quantity of output by eliminating the influence of changes in prices.

Table 22-2 shows a real-life version of our apples and oranges example. The second column shows nominal GDP in 2005, 2009, and 2013. The third column shows real GDP for each year in 2009 dollars. For 2009 the two numbers are the same. But real GDP in 2005 expressed in 2009 dollars was higher than nominal GDP in 2005, reflecting the fact that prices were in general higher in 2009 than in 2005. Real GDP in 2013 expressed in 2009 dollars, however, was less than nominal GDP in 2013 because prices in 2009 were lower than in 2013.

TABLE **22-2**	Nominal versus Real GDP in 2005, 2009, and 2013	
	Nominal GDP (billions of current dollars)	**Real GDP (billions of 2009 dollars)**
2005	$13,094	$14,234
2009	14,419	14,419
2013	16,768	15,710

You might have noticed that there is an alternative way to calculate real GDP using the data in Table 22-1. Why not measure it using the prices of year 2 rather than year 1 as the base-year prices? This procedure seems equally valid. According to that calculation, real GDP in year 1 at year 2 prices is (2,000 billion × $0.30) + (1,000 billion × $0.70) = $1,300 billion; real GDP in year 2 at year 2 prices is $1,500 billion, the same as nominal GDP in year 2. So using year 2 prices as the base year, the growth rate of real GDP is equal to ($1,500 billion – $1,300 billion)/$1,300 billion = 0.154, or 15.4%. This is slightly higher than the figure we got from the previous calculation, in which year 1 prices were the base-year prices. In that calculation, we found that real GDP increased by 15%. Neither answer, 15.4% versus 15%, is more "correct" than the other.

In reality, the government economists who put together the U.S. national accounts have adopted a method to measure the change in real GDP known as chain-linking, which uses the average between the GDP growth rate calculated using an early base year and the GDP growth rate calculated using a late base year. As a result, U.S. statistics on real GDP are always expressed in **chained dollars.**

What Real GDP Doesn't Measure

GDP, nominal or real, is a measure of a country's aggregate output. Other things equal, a country with a larger population will have higher GDP simply because there are more people working. So if we want to compare GDP across countries but want to eliminate the effect of differences in population size, we use the measure **GDP per capita**—GDP divided by the size of the population, equivalent to the average GDP per person.

Real GDP per capita can be a useful measure in some circumstances, such as in a comparison of labor productivity between countries. However, despite the fact that it is a rough measure of the average real output per person, real GDP per capita has well-known limitations as a measure of a country's living standards. Every once in a while economists are accused of believing that growth in real GDP per capita is the only thing that matters—that is, thinking that increasing real GDP per capita is a goal in itself. In fact, economists rarely make that mistake; the idea that economists care only about real GDP per capita is a sort of urban legend.

Let's take a moment to be clear about why a country's real GDP per capita is not a sufficient measure of human welfare in that country and why growth in real GDP per capita is not an appropriate policy goal in itself.

Nominal GDP is the value of all final goods and services produced in the economy during a given year, calculated using the prices current in the year in which the output is produced.

Chained dollars is the method of calculating changes in real GDP using the average between the growth rate calculated using an early base year and the growth rate calculated using a late base year.

GDP per capita is GDP divided by the size of the population; it is equivalent to the average GDP per person.

GLOBAL COMPARISION | GDP and the Meaning of Life

"I've been rich and I've been poor," the actress Mae West famously declared. "Believe me, rich is better." But is the same true for countries?

This figure shows two pieces of information for a number of countries: how rich they are, as measured by GDP per capita, and how people assess their well-being. Well-being was measured by a Gallup world survey that asked people to rate their lives at the current time and their expectations for the next five years. The graph shows the percentage of people who rated their well-being as "thriving." The figure seems to tell us three things:

1. *Rich is better.* Richer countries on average have higher well-being than poor countries.
2. *Money matters less as you grow richer.* As GDP rises, the average gain in life satisfaction gets smaller

and smaller. For example, the rise in GDP per capita from lower-income Italy to middle-income Belgium is about the same as from middle-income Belgium to the high-income United States. But the increase in life satisfaction is much greater going from Italy to Belgium compared to going from Belgium to the United States.

3. *Money isn't everything.* Israelis, though rich by world standards, are poorer than Americans—but they seem more satisfied with their lives. Japan is richer than most other nations, but by and large quite miserable.

These results are consistent with the observation that high GDP per capita makes it easier to achieve a good life but that countries aren't equally successful in taking advantage of that possibility.

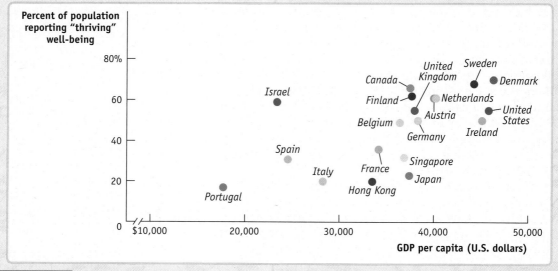

Source: Gallup; World Bank.

One way to think about this issue is to say that an increase in real GDP means an expansion in the economy's production possibility frontier. Because the economy has increased its productive capacity, society can achieve more things. But whether society actually makes good use of that increased potential to improve living standards is another matter. To put it in a slightly different way, your income may be higher this year than last year, but whether you use that higher income to improve your quality of life is your choice.

So let's say it again: real GDP per capita is a measure of an economy's average aggregate output per person—and so of what it *can* do. It is not a sufficient goal in itself because it doesn't address how a country uses that output to affect living standards. A country with a high GDP can afford to be healthy, to be well educated, and in general to have a good quality of life. But there is not a one-to-one match between GDP and the quality of life.

ECONOMICS ▶ *in Action*

Miracle in Venezuela?

The South American nation of Venezuela has a distinction that may surprise you: in recent years, it has had one of the world's fastest-growing nominal GDPs. Between 2000 and 2013, Venezuelan nominal GDP grew by an average of 29% each year—much faster than nominal GDP in the United States or even in booming economies like China.

So is Venezuela experiencing an economic miracle? No, it's just suffering from unusually high inflation. Figure 22-4 shows Venezuela's nominal and real GDP from 2000 to 2013, with real GDP measured in 1997 prices. Real GDP did grow over the period, but at an annual rate of only 3.2%. That's about twice the U.S. growth rate over the same period, but it is far short of China's 10% growth.

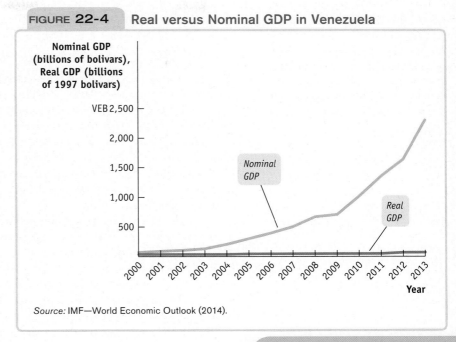

FIGURE **22-4**   Real versus Nominal GDP in Venezuela

Source: IMF—World Economic Outlook (2014).

Check Your Understanding   22-2

1. Assume there are only two goods in the economy, french fries and onion rings. In 2013, 1,000,000 servings of french fries were sold at $0.40 each and 800,000 servings of onion rings at $0.60 each. From 2013 to 2014, the price of french fries rose by 25% and the servings sold fell by 10%; the price of onion rings fell by 15% and the servings sold rose by 5%.
   a. Calculate nominal GDP in 2013 and 2014. Calculate real GDP in 2014 using 2013 prices.
   b. Why would an assessment of growth using nominal GDP be misguided?
2. From 2005 to 2010, the price of electronic equipment fell dramatically and the price of housing rose dramatically. What are the implications of this in deciding whether to use 2005 or 2010 as the base year in calculating 2013 real GDP?

Solutions appear at back of book.

▼ Quick Review

• To determine the actual growth in **aggregate output,** we calculate **real GDP** using prices from some given base year. In contrast, **nominal GDP** is the value of aggregate output calculated with current prices. U.S. statistics on real GDP are always expressed in **chained dollars.**

• Real **GDP per capita** is a measure of the average aggregate output per person. But it is not a sufficient measure of human welfare, nor is it an appropriate goal in itself, because it does not reflect important aspects of living standards within an economy.

Price Indexes and the Aggregate Price Level

In the spring and summer of 2011, Americans were facing sticker shock at the gas pump: the price of a gallon of regular gasoline had risen from an average of $1.61 at the end of December 2008 to close to $4. Many other prices were also up. Some prices, though, were heading down: some foods, like eggs, were coming down from a run-up in late 2010, and virtually anything involving electronics was getting cheaper as well. Yet practically everyone felt that the overall cost of living was rising. But how fast?

Clearly, there was a need for a single number summarizing what was happening to consumer prices. Just as macroeconomists find it useful to have a single number representing the overall level of output, they also find it useful to have

The **aggregate price level** is a measure of the overall level of prices in the economy.

A **market basket** is a hypothetical set of consumer purchases of goods and services.

A **price index** measures the cost of purchasing a given market basket in a given year, where that cost is normalized so that it is equal to 100 in the selected base year.

a single number representing the overall level of prices: the **aggregate price level.** Yet a huge variety of goods and services are produced and consumed in the economy. How can we summarize the prices of all these goods and services with a single number? The answer lies in the concept of a *price index*—a concept best introduced with an example.

Market Baskets and Price Indexes

Suppose that a frost in Florida destroys most of the citrus harvest. As a result, the price of an orange rises from $0.20 to $0.40, the price of a grapefruit rises from $0.60 to $1.00, and the price of a lemon rises from $0.25 to $0.45. How much has the price of citrus fruit increased?

One way to answer that question is to state three numbers—the changes in prices for oranges, grapefruit, and lemons. But this is a very cumbersome method. Rather than having to recite three numbers in an effort to track changes in the prices of citrus fruit, we would prefer to have some kind of overall measure of the *average* price change.

To measure average price changes for consumer goods and services, economists track changes in the cost of a typical consumer's *consumption bundle*—the typical basket of goods and services purchased before the price changes. A hypothetical consumption bundle, used to measure changes in the overall price level, is known as a **market basket.** Suppose that before the frost a typical consumer bought 200 oranges, 50 grapefruit, and 100 lemons over the course of a year, our market basket for this example.

Table 22-3 shows the pre-frost and post-frost cost of this market basket. Before the frost, it cost $95; after the frost, the same bundle of goods cost $175. Since $175/$95 = 1.842, the post-frost basket costs 1.842 times the cost of the pre-frost basket, a cost increase of 84.2%. In this example, the average price of citrus fruit has increased 84.2% since the base year as a result of the frost, where the base year is the initial year used in the measurement of the price change.

TABLE 22-3   Calculating the Cost of a Market Basket

	Pre-frost	Post-frost
Price of orange	$0.20	$0.40
Price of grapefruit	0.60	1.00
Price of lemon	0.25	0.45
Cost of market basket (200 oranges, 50 grapefruit, 100 lemons)	(200 × $0.20) + (50 × $0.60) + (100 × $0.25) = $95.00	(200 × $0.40) + (50 × $1.00) + (100 × $0.45) = $175.00

Economists use the same method to measure changes in the overall price level: they track changes in the cost of buying a given market basket. In addition, they perform another simplification in order to avoid having to keep track of the information that the market basket cost—for example, to avoid saying that the market basket costs $95 in 1997 dollars and $103 in 2001 dollars. They *normalize* the measure of the aggregate price level, which means that they set the cost of the market basket equal to 100 in the chosen base year. Working with a market basket and a base year, and after performing normalization, we obtain what is known as a **price index,** a normalized measure of the overall price level. It is always cited along with the year for which the aggregate price level is being measured and the base year. A price index can be calculated using the following formula:

$$\text{(22-2)} \quad \text{Price index in a given year} = \frac{\text{Cost of market basket in a given year}}{\text{Cost of market basket in base year}} \times 100$$

In our example, the citrus fruit market basket cost $95 in the base year, the year before the frost. So by Equation 22-2 we define the price index for citrus fruit as (cost of market basket in a given year/$95) × 100, yielding an index of 100 for the period before the frost and 184.2 after the frost. You should note that the price index for the base year always results in a price index equal to 100. This is because the price index in the base year is equal to: (cost of market basket in base year/cost of market basket in base year) × 100 = 100.

Thus, the price index makes it clear that the average price of citrus has risen 84.2% as a consequence of the frost. Because of its simplicity and intuitive appeal, the method we've just described is used to calculate a variety of price indexes to track average price changes among a variety of different groups of goods and services. For example, the *consumer price index*, which we'll discuss shortly, is the most widely used measure of the aggregate price level, the overall price level of final consumer goods and services across the economy.

Price indexes are also the basis for measuring inflation. The **inflation rate** is the annual percent change in an official price index. The inflation rate from year 1 to year 2 is calculated using the following formula, where we assume that year 1 and year 2 are consecutive years.

(22-3) Inflation rate = $\dfrac{\text{Price index in year 2} - \text{Price index in year 1}}{\text{Price index in year 1}} \times 100$

Typically, a news report that cites "the inflation rate" is referring to the annual percent change in the consumer price index.

> The **inflation rate** is the percent change per year in a price index—typically the consumer price index.
>
> The **consumer price index,** or **CPI,** measures the cost of the market basket of a typical urban American family.

The Consumer Price Index

The most widely used measure of prices in the United States is the **consumer price index** (often referred to simply as the **CPI**), which is intended to show how the cost of all purchases by a typical urban family has changed over time. It is calculated by surveying market prices for a market basket that is constructed to represent the consumption of a typical family of four living in a typical American city. The base period for the index is currently 1982–1984; that is, the index is calculated so that the average of consumer prices in 1982–1984 is 100.

The market basket used to calculate the CPI is far more complex than the three-fruit market basket we described above. In fact, to calculate the CPI, the Bureau of Labor Statistics sends its employees out to survey supermarkets, gas stations, hardware stores, and so on—some 23,000 retail outlets in 87 cities. Every month it tabulates about 80,000 prices, on everything from romaine lettuce to a medical check-up.

Figure 22-5 shows the weight of major categories in the consumer price index as of December 2010. For example, motor fuel, mainly gasoline, accounted for 5% of the CPI in December 2010. So when gas prices rose nearly 150%, from about $1.61 a gallon in late 2008 to $3.96 a gallon in May 2011, the effect was to increase the CPI by about 1.5 times 5%—that is, around 7.5%.

Figure 22-6 shows how the CPI has changed since measurement began in 1913. Since 1940, the CPI has risen steadily, although its annual percent increases in recent years have been much smaller than those of the 1970s and early 1980s. (A logarithmic scale is used so that equal percent changes in the CPI have the same slope.)

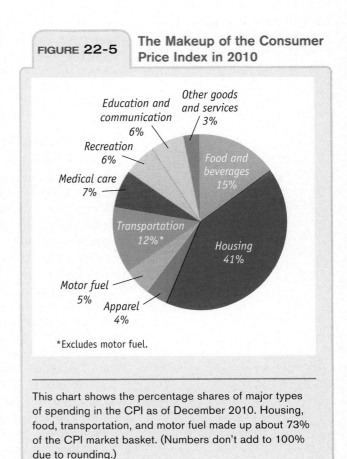

FIGURE 22-5   The Makeup of the Consumer Price Index in 2010

Education and communication 6%
Other goods and services 3%
Recreation 6%
Medical care 7%
Food and beverages 15%
Transportation 12%*
Motor fuel 5%
Apparel 4%
Housing 41%

*Excludes motor fuel.

This chart shows the percentage shares of major types of spending in the CPI as of December 2010. Housing, food, transportation, and motor fuel made up about 73% of the CPI market basket. (Numbers don't add to 100% due to rounding.)

Source: Bureau of Labor Statistics.

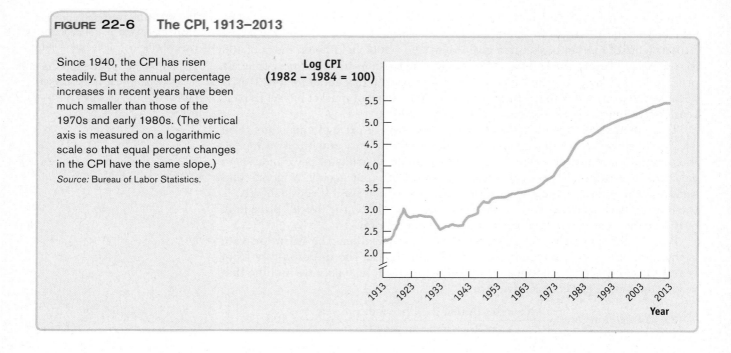

FIGURE 22-6 | The CPI, 1913–2013

Since 1940, the CPI has risen steadily. But the annual percentage increases in recent years have been much smaller than those of the 1970s and early 1980s. (The vertical axis is measured on a logarithmic scale so that equal percent changes in the CPI have the same slope.)
Source: Bureau of Labor Statistics.

The **producer price index,** or **PPI,** measures changes in the prices of goods purchased by producers.

The **GDP deflator** for a given year is 100 times the ratio of nominal GDP to real GDP in that year.

The United States is not the only country that calculates a consumer price index. In fact, nearly every country has one. As you might expect, the market baskets that make up these indexes differ quite a lot from country to country. In poor countries, where people must spend a high proportion of their income just to feed themselves, food makes up a large share of the price index. Among high-income countries, differences in consumption patterns lead to differences in the price indexes: the Japanese price index puts a larger weight on raw fish and a smaller weight on beef than ours does, and the French price index puts a larger weight on wine.

Other Price Measures

There are two other price measures that are also widely used to track economy-wide price changes. One is the **producer price index** (or **PPI,** which used to be known as the *wholesale price index*). As its name suggests, the producer price index measures the cost of a typical basket of goods and services—containing raw commodities such as steel, electricity, coal, and so on—purchased by producers. Because commodity producers are relatively quick to change prices when they perceive a change in overall demand for their goods, the PPI often responds to inflationary or deflationary pressures more quickly than the CPI. As a result, the PPI is often regarded as an "early warning signal" of changes in the inflation rate.

The other widely used price measure is the *GDP deflator*; it isn't exactly a price index, although it serves the same purpose. Recall how we distinguished between nominal GDP (GDP in current prices) and real GDP (GDP calculated using the prices of a base year). The **GDP deflator** for a given year is equal to 100 times the ratio of nominal GDP for that year to real GDP for that year. Since real GDP is currently expressed in 2005 dollars, the GDP deflator for 2005 is equal to 100. If nominal GDP doubles but real GDP does not change, the GDP deflator indicates that the aggregate price level doubled.

Perhaps the most important point about the different inflation rates generated by these three measures of prices is that they usually move closely together (although the producer price index tends to fluctuate more than either of the other two measures). Figure 22-7 shows the annual percent changes in the three indexes since 1930. By all three measures, the U.S. economy experienced defla-

| FIGURE **22-7** | The CPI, the PPI, and the GDP Deflator |

As the figure shows, the three different measures of inflation, the PPI (orange), the CPI (green), and the GDP deflator (purple), usually move closely together. Each reveals a drastic acceleration of inflation during the 1970s and a return to relative price stability in the 1990s. With the exception of a brief period of deflation in 2009, prices have remained stable from 2000 to 2013.

Sources: Bureau of Labor Statistics; Bureau of Economic Analysis.

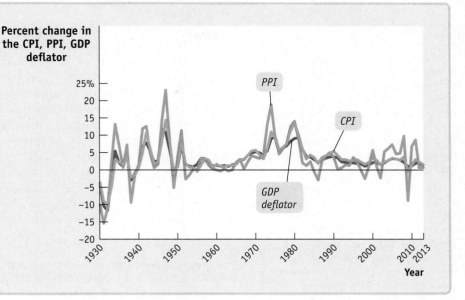

tion during the early years of the Great Depression, inflation during World War II, accelerating inflation during the 1970s, and a return to relative price stability in the 1990s. Notice, by the way, the dramatic ups and downs in producer prices from 2000 to 2013 on the graph; this reflects large swings in energy and food prices, which play a much bigger role in the PPI than they do in either the CPI or the GDP deflator.

ECONOMICS ▶ *in Action*

Indexing to the CPI

Although GDP is a very important number for shaping economic policy, official statistics on GDP don't have a direct effect on people's lives. The CPI, by contrast, has a direct and immediate impact on millions of Americans.

The reason is that many payments are tied, or "indexed," to the CPI—the amount paid rises or falls when the CPI rises or falls.

The practice of indexing payments to consumer prices goes back to the dawn of the United States as a nation. In 1780 the Massachusetts State Legislature recognized that the pay of its soldiers fighting the British needed to be increased because of inflation that occurred during the Revolutionary War. The legislature adopted a formula that made a soldier's pay proportional to the cost of a market basket, consisting of 5 bushels of corn, 68 4/7 pounds of beef, 10 pounds of sheep's wool, and 16 pounds of shoe leather.

Today, 54 million people receive payments from Social Security, a national retirement program that accounts for almost a quarter of current total federal spending—more than the defense budget. The amount of an individual's Social Security payment is determined by a formula that reflects his or her previous payments into the system as well as other factors. In addition, all Social Security payments are adjusted each year to offset any increase in consumer prices over the previous year. The CPI is used to calculate the official estimate of the inflation rate used to

A small change in the CPI has large consequences for those dependent on Social Security payments.

adjust these payments yearly. So every percentage point added to the official estimate of the rate of inflation adds 1% to the checks received by tens of millions of individuals.

Other government payments are also indexed to the CPI. In addition, income tax brackets, the bands of income levels that determine a taxpayer's income tax rate, are also indexed to the CPI. (An individual in a higher income bracket pays a higher income tax rate in a progressive tax system like ours.) Indexing also extends to the private sector, where many private contracts, including some wage settlements, contain cost-of-living allowances (called COLAs) that adjust payments in proportion to changes in the CPI.

Because the CPI plays such an important and direct role in people's lives, it's a politically sensitive number. The Bureau of Labor Statistics, which calculates the CPI, takes great care in collecting and interpreting price and consumption data. It uses a complex method in which households are surveyed to determine what they buy and where they shop, and a carefully selected sample of stores are surveyed to get representative prices.

Check Your Understanding 22-3

1. Consider Table 22-3 but suppose that the market basket is composed of 100 oranges, 50 grapefruit, and 200 lemons. How does this change the pre-frost and post-frost price indexes? Explain. Generalize your explanation to how the construction of the market basket affects the price index.

2. For each of the following events, how would an economist using a 10-year-old market basket create a bias in measuring the change in the cost of living today?
   a. A typical family owns more cars than it would have a decade ago. Over that time, the average price of a car has increased more than the average prices of other goods.
   b. Virtually no households had broadband internet access a decade ago. Now many households have it, and the price has regularly fallen each year.

3. The consumer price index in the United States (base period 1982–1984) was 226.229 in 2012 and 229.324 in 2013. Calculate the inflation rate from 2012 to 2013.

Solutions appear at back of book.

Getting a Jump on GDP

GDP matters. Investors and business leaders are always anxious to get the latest numbers. When the Bureau of Economic Analysis releases its first estimate of each quarter's GDP, normally on the 27th or 28th day of the month after the quarter ends, it's invariably a big news story.

In fact, many companies and other players in the economy are so eager to know what's happening to GDP that they don't want to wait for the official estimate. So a number of organizations produce numbers that can be used to predict what the official GDP number will say. Let's talk about two of those organizations, the economic consulting firm Macroeconomic Advisers and the nonprofit Institute of Supply Management.

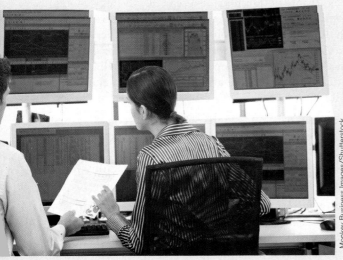

Monkey Business Images/Shutterstock

Macroeconomic Advisers takes a direct approach: it produces its own estimates of GDP based on raw data from the U.S. government. But whereas the Bureau of Economic Analysis estimates GDP only on a quarterly basis, Macroeconomic Advisers produces monthly estimates. This means that clients can, for example, look at the estimates for January and February and make a pretty good guess at what first-quarter GDP, which also includes March, will turn out to be. The monthly estimates are derived by looking at a number of monthly measures that track purchases, such as car and truck sales, new housing construction, and exports.

The Institute for Supply Management (ISM) takes a very different approach. It relies on monthly surveys of purchasing managers—that is, executives in charge of buying supplies—who are basically asked whether their companies are increasing or reducing production. (We say "basically" because the ISM asks a longer list of questions.)

Responses to the surveys are released in the form of indexes showing the percentage of companies that are expanding. Obviously, these indexes don't directly tell you what is happening to GDP. But historically, the ISM indexes have been strongly correlated with the rate of growth of GDP, and this historical relationship can be used to translate ISM data into "early warning" GDP estimates.

So if you just can't wait for those quarterly GDP numbers, you're not alone. The private sector has responded to demand, and you can get your data fix every month.

QUESTIONS FOR THOUGHT

1. Why do businesses care about GDP to such an extent that they want early estimates?

2. How do the methods of Macroeconomic Advisers and the Institute for Supply Management fit into the three different ways to calculate GDP?

3. If private firms are producing GDP estimates, why do we need the Bureau of Economic Analysis?

SUMMARY

1. Economists keep track of the flows of money between sectors with the **national income and product accounts,** or **national accounts.** Households earn income via the factor markets from wages, interest on **bonds,** profit accruing to owners of **stocks,** and rent on land and structures. In addition, they receive **government transfers** from the government. **Disposable income,** total household income minus taxes plus government transfers, is allocated to **consumer spending** (C) and **private savings.** Via the **financial markets,** private savings and foreign lending are channeled to **investment spending** (I), government borrowing, and foreign borrowing. **Government purchases of goods and services** (G) are paid for by tax revenues and any **government borrowing.** **Exports** (X) generate an inflow of funds into the country from the rest of the world, but **imports** (IM) lead to an outflow of funds to the rest of the world. Foreigners can also buy stocks and bonds in the U.S. financial markets.

2. **Gross domestic product,** or **GDP,** measures the value of all **final goods and services** produced in the economy. It does not include the value of **intermediate goods and services,** but it does include **inventories** and **net exports** (X − IM). It can be calculated in three ways: add up the **value added** by all producers; add up all spending on domestically produced final goods and services, leading to the equation GDP = C + I + G + X − IM, also known as **aggregate spending;** or add up all the income paid by domestic firms to factors of production. These three methods are equivalent because in the economy as a whole, total income paid by domestic firms to factors of production must equal total spending on domestically produced final goods and services.

3. **Real GDP** is the value of the final goods and services produced calculated using the prices of a selected base year. Except in the base year, real GDP is not the same as **nominal GDP,** the value of **aggregate output** calculated using current prices. Analysis of the growth rate of aggregate output must use real GDP because doing so eliminates any change in the value of aggregate output due solely to price changes. Real **GDP per capita** is a measure of average aggregate output per person but is not in itself an appropriate policy goal. U.S. statistics on real GDP are always expressed in **chained dollars.**

4. To measure the **aggregate price level,** economists calculate the cost of purchasing a **market basket.** A **price index** is the ratio of the current cost of that market basket to the cost in a selected base year, multiplied by 100.

5. The **inflation rate** is the yearly percent change in a price index, typically based on the **consumer price index,** or **CPI,** the most common measure of the aggregate price level. A similar index for goods and services purchased by firms is the **producer price index,** or **PPI.** Finally, economists also use the **GDP deflator,** which measures the price level by calculating the ratio of nominal GDP to real GDP times 100.

KEY TERMS

National income and product accounts (national accounts), p. 630
Consumer spending, p. 630
Stock, p. 630
Bond, p. 630
Government transfers, p. 630
Disposable income, p. 630
Private savings, p. 631
Financial markets, p. 631
Government borrowing, p. 632
Government purchases of goods and services, p. 632
Exports, p. 632
Imports, p. 632
Inventories, p. 632
Investment spending, p. 632
Final goods and services, p. 633
Intermediate goods and services, p. 633
Gross domestic product (GDP), p. 633
Aggregate spending, p. 633
Value added, p. 635
Net exports, p. 638
Aggregate output, p. 640
Real GDP, p. 640
Nominal GDP, p. 641
Chained dollars, p. 641
GDP per capita, p. 641
Aggregate price level, p. 644
Market basket, p. 644
Price index, p. 644
Inflation rate, p. 645
Consumer price index (CPI), p. 645
Producer price index (PPI), p. 646
GDP deflator, p. 646

PROBLEMS

1. At right is a simplified circular-flow diagram for the economy of Micronia. (Note that there is no investment in Micronia.)

   a. What is the value of GDP in Micronia?

   b. What is the value of net exports?

   c. What is the value of disposable income?

   d. Does the total flow of money out of households—the sum of taxes paid and consumer spending—equal the total flow of money into households?

   e. How does the government of Micronia finance its purchases of goods and services?

2. A more complex circular-flow diagram for the economy of Macronia is shown at right. (Note that Macronia has investment and financial markets.)

   a. What is the value of GDP in Macronia?

   b. What is the value of net exports?

   c. What is the value of disposable income?

   d. Does the total flow of money out of households—the sum of taxes paid, consumer spending, and private savings—equal the total flow of money into households?

   e. How does the government finance its spending?

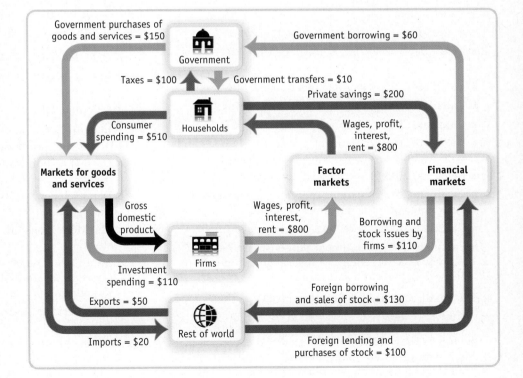

3. The components of GDP in the accompanying table were produced by the Bureau of Economic Analysis.

Category	Components of GDP in 2013 (billions of dollars)
Consumer spending	
Durable goods	$1,263.0
Nondurable goods	2,622.9
Services	7,615.7
Private investment spending	
Fixed investment spending	2,564.0
Nonresidential	2,047.1
Structures	456.4
Equipment and intellectual property products	1,590.7
Residential	516.9
Change in private inventories	106.1
Net exports	
Exports	2,259.9
Imports	2,757.2
Government purchases of goods and services and investment spending	
Federal	1,245.9
National defense	770.7
Nondefense	475.1
State and local	1,879.6

a. Calculate 2013 consumer spending.

b. Calculate 2013 private investment spending.

c. Calculate 2013 net exports.

d. Calculate 2013 government purchases of goods and services and government investment spending.

e. Calculate 2013 gross domestic product.

f. Calculate 2013 consumer spending on services as a percentage of total consumer spending.

g. Calculate 2013 exports as a percentage of imports.

h. Calculate 2013 government purchases on national defense as a percentage of federal government purchases of goods and services.

4. The small economy of Pizzania produces three goods (bread, cheese, and pizza), each produced by a separate company. The bread and cheese companies produce all the inputs they need to make bread and cheese, respectively. The pizza company uses the bread and cheese from the other companies to make its pizzas. All three companies employ labor to help produce their goods, and the difference between the value of goods sold and the sum of labor and input costs is the firm's profit.

The accompanying table summarizes the activities of the three companies when all the bread and cheese produced are sold to the pizza company as inputs in the production of pizzas.

	Bread company	Cheese company	Pizza company
Cost of inputs	$0	$0	$50 (bread)
			35 (cheese)
Wages	15	20	75
Value of output	50	35	200

a. Calculate GDP as the value added in production.

b. Calculate GDP as spending on final goods and services.

c. Calculate GDP as factor income.

5. In the economy of Pizzania (from Problem 4), bread and cheese produced are sold both to the pizza company for inputs in the production of pizzas and to consumers as final goods. The accompanying table summarizes the activities of the three companies.

	Bread company	Cheese company	Pizza company
Cost of inputs	$0	$0	$50 (bread)
			35 (cheese)
Wages	25	30	75
Value of output	100	60	200

a. Calculate GDP as the value added in production.

b. Calculate GDP as spending on final goods and services.

c. Calculate GDP as factor income.

6. Which of the following transactions will be included in GDP for the United States?

a. Coca-Cola builds a new bottling plant in the United States.

b. Delta sells one of its existing airplanes to Korean Air.

c. Ms. Moneybags buys an existing share of Disney stock.

d. A California winery produces a bottle of Chardonnay and sells it to a customer in Montreal, Canada.

e. An American buys a bottle of French perfume in Tulsa.

f. A book publisher produces too many copies of a new book; the books don't sell this year, so the publisher adds the surplus books to inventories.

7. The accompanying table shows data on nominal GDP (in billions of dollars), real GDP (in billions of 2005 dollars), and population (in thousands) of the United States in 1960, 1970, 1980, 1990, 2000, and 2010. The U.S. price level rose consistently over the period 1960–2010.

Year	Nominal GDP (billions of dollars)	Real GDP (billions of 2005 dollars)	Population (thousands)
1960	$526.4	$2,828.5	180,760
1970	1,038.5	4,266.3	205,089
1980	2,788.1	5,834.0	227,726
1990	5,800.5	8,027.1	250,181
2000	9,951.5	11,216.4	282,418
2010	14,526.5	13,088.0	310,106

a. Why is real GDP greater than nominal GDP for all years until 2000 and lower for 2010?

b. Calculate the percent change in real GDP from 1960 to 1970, 1970 to 1980, 1980 to 1990, 1990 to 2000, and 2000 to 2010. Which period had the highest growth rate?

c. Calculate real GDP per capita for each of the years in the table.

d. Calculate the percent change in real GDP per capita from 1960 to 1970, 1970 to 1980, 1980 to 1990, 1990 to 2000, and 2000 to 2010. Which period had the highest growth rate?

e. How do the percent change in real GDP and the percent change in real GDP per capita compare? Which is larger? Do we expect them to have this relationship?

8. Eastland College is concerned about the rising price of textbooks that students must purchase. To better identify the increase in the price of textbooks, the dean asks you, the Economics Department's star student, to create an index of textbook prices. The average student purchases three English, two math, and four economics textbooks per year. The prices of these books are given in the accompanying table.

	2012	2013	2014
English textbook	$100	$110	$114
Math textbook	140	144	148
Economics textbook	160	180	200

a. What is the percent change in the price of an English textbook from 2012 to 2014?

b. What is the percent change in the price of a math textbook from 2012 to 2014?

c. What is the percent change in the price of an economics textbook from 2012 to 2014?

d. Using 2013 as a base year, create a price index for these books for all years.

e. What is the percent change in the price index from 2012 to 2014?

9. The consumer price index, or CPI, measures the cost of living for a typical urban household by multiplying the price for each category of expenditure (housing, food, and so on) times a measure of the importance of that expenditure in the average consumer's market basket and summing over all categories. However, using data from the consumer price index, we can see that changes in the cost of living for different types of consumers can vary a great deal. Let's compare the cost of living for a hypothetical retired person and a hypothetical college student. Let's assume that the market basket of a retired person is allocated in the following way: 10% on housing, 15% on food, 5% on transportation, 60% on medical care, 0% on education, and 10% on recreation. The college student's market basket is allocated as follows: 5% on housing, 15% on food, 20% on transportation, 0% on medical care, 40% on education, and 20% on recreation. The accompanying table shows the March 2014 CPI for each of the relevant categories.

	CPI March 2014
Housing	228.7
Food	239.7
Transportation	219.3
Medical care	436.5
Education	229.1
Recreation	115.7

Calculate the overall CPI for the retired person and for the college student by multiplying the CPI for each of the categories by the relative importance of that category to the individual and then summing each of the categories. The CPI for all items in March 2014 was 235.6. How do your calculations for a CPI for the retired person and the college student compare to the overall CPI?

10. Go to the Bureau of Labor Statistics home page at www.bls.gov. Place the cursor over the "Economic Releases" tab and then click on "Major Economic Indicators" in the drop-down menu that appears. Once on the "Major Economic Indicators" page, click on "Consumer Price Index." On that page, under "Table of Contents," click on "Table 1: Consumer Price Index for All Urban Consumers." Using the "unadjusted" figures, determine what the CPI was for the previous month. How did it change from the previous month? How does the CPI compare to the same month one year ago?

11. The accompanying table provides the annual real GDP (in billions of 2009 dollars) and nominal GDP (in billions of dollars) for the United States.

	2009	2010	2011	2012	2013
Real GDP (billions of 2009 dollars)	14,417.9	14,779.4	15,052.4	15,470.7	15,761.3
Nominal GDP (billions of dollars)	14,417.9	14,958.3	15,533.8	16,244.6	16,799.7

a. Calculate the GDP deflator for each year.

b. Use the GDP deflator to calculate the inflation rate for all years except 2009.

12. The accompanying table contains two price indexes for the years 2011, 2012, and 2013: the GDP deflator and the CPI. For each price index, calculate the inflation rate from 2011 to 2012 and from 2012 to 2013.

Year	GDP deflator	CPI
2011	103.199	224.939
2012	105.002	229.594
2013	106.588	232.957

13. The cost of a college education in the United States is rising at a rate faster than inflation. The following table shows the average cost of a college education in the United States during the academic year that began in 2011 and the academic year that began in 2012 for public and private colleges. Assume the costs listed in the table are the only costs experienced by the various college students in a single year.

a. Calculate the cost of living for an average college student in each category for 2011 and 2012.

b. Calculate an inflation rate for each type of college student between 2011 and 2012.

For interactive, step-by-step help in solving the following problem, visit LaunchPad by using the URL on the back cover of this book.

14. The economy of Britannica produces three goods: computers, DVDs, and pizza. The accompanying table shows the prices and output of the three goods for the years 2012, 2013, and 2014.

	Computers		DVDs		Pizzas	
Year	Price	Quantity	Price	Quantity	Price	Quantity
2012	$900	10	$10	100	$15	2
2013	1,000	10.5	12	105	16	2
2014	1,050	12	14	110	17	3

a. What is the percent change in production of each of the goods from 2012 to 2013 and from 2013 to 2014?

b. What is the percent change in prices of each of the goods from 2012 to 2013 and from 2013 to 2014?

c. Calculate nominal GDP in Britannica for each of the three years. What is the percent change in nominal GDP from 2012 to 2013 and from 2013 to 2014?

d. Calculate real GDP in Britannica using 2012 prices for each of the three years. What is the percent change in real GDP from 2012 to 2013 and from 2013 to 2014?

	Cost of college education during academic year beginning 2011 (averages in 2011 dollars)			
	Tuition and fees	Room and board	Books and supplies	Other expenses
Two-year public college: commuter	$2,970	$5,552	$1,314	$2,988
Four-year public college: in-state, on-campus	7,731	8,831	1,232	3,203
Four-year public college: out-of-state, on-campus	20,823	8,831	1,232	3,203
Four-year private college: on-campus	27,949	9,853	1,238	2,378
	Cost of college education during academic year beginning 2012 (averages in 2012 dollars)			
	Tuition and fees	Room and board	Books and supplies	Other expenses
Two-year public college: commuter	$3,080	$5,817	$1,341	$3,040
Four-year public college: in-state, on-campus	8,805	9,183	1,243	3,253
Four-year public college: out-of-state, on-campus	21,706	9,183	1,243	3,253
Four-year private college: on-campus	29,115	10,181	1,243	2,423

Unemployment and Inflation

▶ **What You Will Learn in This Chapter**

■ How **unemployment** is measured and how the **unemployment rate** is calculated

■ The significance of the unemployment rate for the economy

■ The relationship between the unemployment rate and economic growth

■ The factors that determine the **natural rate of unemployment**

■ The economic costs of inflation

■ How inflation and deflation create winners and losers

■ Why policy makers try to maintain a stable rate of inflation

HITTING THE BRAKING POINT

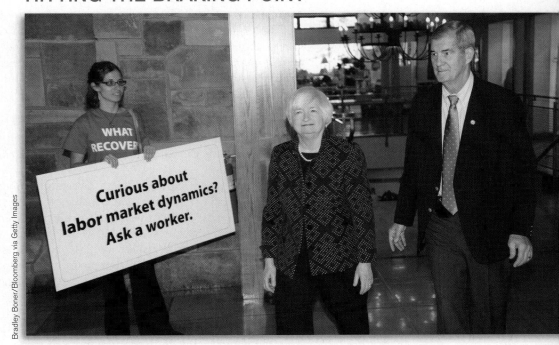

Bradley Boner/Bloomberg via Getty Images

As chair of the Federal Reserve, Janet Yellen balances the goals of low unemployment and price stability when deciding whether to give the economy more gas or hit the brakes.

Every August many of the world's most powerful financial officials and many influential economists gather in Jackson Hole, Wyoming, for a conference sponsored by the Federal Reserve Bank of Kansas City. Financial journalists come too, hoping to get clues about the future direction of policy. It's always an interesting scene—but in August 2014 it was even more interesting than usual.

What was different about that year's conclave? One answer was that the Federal Reserve's Board of Governors, which makes U.S. monetary policy, had a new chair—and Janet Yellen had already made history as the first woman to hold the position.

Beyond the historic first, however, there was a widespread sense that August that U.S. monetary policy might be approaching a critical moment. For almost six years the Fed's goal had been simple, if hard to accomplish: boost the U.S. economy out of a sustained

job drought that had kept unemployment high. By the summer of 2014, however, the unemployment rate had fallen much of the way back toward historically normal levels. At some point, almost everyone agreed, it would be time for the Fed to take its foot off the gas and hit the brakes instead, raising interest rates that had been close to zero for years. But when?

It was a fraught question. Some Fed officials—so-called hawks, always ready to pounce on any sign of inflation—warned that if the Fed waited too long to raise rates, inflation would shoot up to unacceptable levels. Others—so-called doves—warned that the economy was still fragile, and that raising rates too soon would risk condemning the economy to a further stretch of high unemployment. Ms. Yellen was, in general, part of the dovish camp. But even she warned that controlling inflation must eventually take priority over reducing unemployment. At that point the Fed would have to raise rates.

Only time would tell who was right about the timing. But the dispute highlighted the key concerns of macroeconomic policy. Unemployment and inflation are the two great evils of macroeconomics. So the two principal goals of macroeconomic policy are low unemployment and price stability, usually defined as a low but positive rate of inflation. Unfortunately, these goals sometimes seem to be in conflict with each other: economists often warn that policies intended to reduce unemployment run the risk of increasing inflation; conversely, policies intended to bring down inflation can raise unemployment.

We'll learn much more about the nature of the trade-off between low unemployment and low inflation and the policy dilemma it creates in later chapters. This chapter provides an overview of the basic facts about unemployment and inflation: how they're measured, how they affect consumers and firms, and how they change over time.

Employment is the number of people currently employed in the economy, either full time or part time.

Unemployment is the number of people who are actively looking for work but aren't currently employed.

The Unemployment Rate

The U.S. unemployment rate in October 2014 was 5.8%. That was a substantial improvement from the situation a few years earlier. In late 2009, after the Great Recession, unemployment peaked at 10%. But unemployment was still well above pre-recession levels; it was only 4.7% in November 2007.

Figure 23-1 shows the U.S. unemployment rate from 1948 to late 2014; as you can see, unemployment soared during the Great Recession of 2007–2009 and fell only slowly in the years that followed. What did the elevated unemployment rate mean, and why was it such a big factor in people's lives? To understand why policy makers pay so much attention to employment and unemployment, we need to understand how they are both defined and measured.

Defining and Measuring Unemployment

It's easy to define employment: you're employed if and only if you have a job. **Employment** is the total number of people currently employed, either full time or part time.

Unemployment, however, is a more subtle concept. Just because a person isn't working doesn't mean that we consider that person unemployed. For example, as of October 2014, there were 41.8 million retired workers in the United States receiving Social Security checks. Most of them were probably happy that they were no longer working, so we wouldn't consider someone who has settled into a comfortable, well-earned retirement to be unemployed. There were also 11 million disabled U.S. workers receiving benefits because they were unable to work. Again, although they weren't working, we wouldn't normally consider them to be unemployed.

The U.S. Census Bureau, the federal agency tasked with collecting data on unemployment, considers the unemployed to be those who are "jobless, looking for jobs, and available for work." Retired people don't count because they aren't looking for jobs; the disabled don't count because they aren't available for work. More specifically, an individual is considered unemployed if he or she doesn't currently have a job and has been actively seeking a job during the past four weeks. So **unemployment** is defined as the total number of people who are actively looking for work but aren't currently employed.

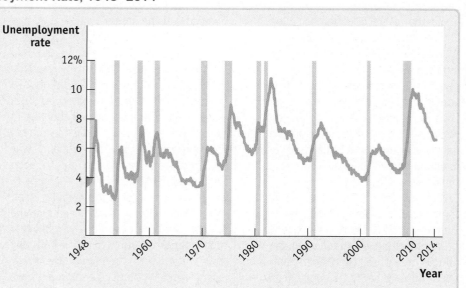

FIGURE **23-1**   The U.S. Unemployment Rate, 1948–2014

The unemployment rate has fluctuated widely over time. It always rises during recessions, which are shown by the shaded bars. It usually, but not always, falls during periods of economic expansion.

Sources: Bureau of Labor Statistics; National Bureau of Economic Research.

A country's **labor force** is the sum of employment and unemployment—that is, of people who are currently working and people who are currently looking for work, respectively. The **labor force participation rate,** defined as the percentage of the working-age population that is in the labor force, is calculated as follows:

(23-1) $\text{Labor force participation rate} = \dfrac{\text{Labor force}}{\text{Population age 16 and older}} \times 100$

The **unemployment rate,** defined as the percentage of the total number of people in the labor force who are unemployed, is calculated as follows:

(23-2) $\text{Unemployment rate} = \dfrac{\text{Number of unemployed workers}}{\text{Labor force}} \times 100$

To estimate the numbers that go into calculating the unemployment rate, the U.S. Census Bureau carries out a monthly survey called the Current Population Survey, which involves interviewing a random sample of 60,000 American families. People are asked whether they are currently employed. If they are not employed, they are asked whether they have been looking for a job during the past four weeks. The results are then scaled up, using estimates of the total population, to estimate the total number of employed and unemployed Americans.

The Significance of the Unemployment Rate

In general, the unemployment rate is a good indicator of how easy or difficult it is to find a job given the current state of the economy. When the unemployment rate is low, nearly everyone who wants a job can find one. In 2000, when the unemployment rate averaged just 4%, jobs were so abundant that employers spoke of a "mirror test" for getting a job: if you were breathing (therefore your breath would fog a mirror), you could find work. By contrast, in 2010, with the unemployment rate above 9% all year, it was very hard to find work. In fact, there were almost five times as many Americans seeking work as there were job openings.

Although the unemployment rate is a good indicator of current labor market conditions, it's not a literal measure of the percentage of people who want a job but can't find one. That's because in some ways the unemployment rate exaggerates the difficulty people have in finding jobs. But in other ways, the opposite is true—a low unemployment rate can conceal deep frustration over the lack of job opportunities.

How the Unemployment Rate Can Overstate the True Level of Unemployment If you are searching for work, it's normal to take at least a few weeks to find a suitable job. Yet a worker who is quite confident of finding a job, but has not yet accepted a position, is counted as unemployed. As a consequence, the unemployment rate never falls to zero, even in boom times when jobs are plentiful. Even in the buoyant labor market of 2000, when it was easy to find work, the unemployment rate was still 4%. Later in this chapter, we'll discuss in greater depth the reasons that measured unemployment persists even when jobs are abundant.

How the Unemployment Rate Can Understate the True Level of Unemployment Frequently, people who would like to work but aren't working still don't get counted as unemployed. In particular, an individual who has given up looking for a job for the time being because there are no jobs available—say, a laid-off steelworker in a deeply depressed steel town—isn't counted as unemployed because he or she has not been searching for a job during the previous four weeks. Individuals who want to work but have told government researchers that they aren't currently searching because they see little prospect of finding a

The **labor force** is equal to the sum of employment and unemployment.

The **labor force participation rate** is the percentage of the population aged 16 or older that is in the labor force.

The **unemployment rate** is the percentage of the total number of people in the labor force who are unemployed.

Discouraged workers are nonworking people who are capable of working but have given up looking for a job given the state of the job market.

Marginally attached workers would like to be employed and have looked for a job in the recent past but are not currently looking for work.

Underemployment is the number of people who work part time because they cannot find full-time jobs.

job given the state of the job market are called **discouraged workers.** Because it does not count discouraged workers, the measured unemployment rate may understate the percentage of people who want to work but are unable to find jobs.

Discouraged workers are part of a larger group—**marginally attached workers.** These are people who say they would like to have a job and have looked for work in the recent past but are not currently looking for work. They, too, are not included when calculating the unemployment rate. Finally, another category of workers who are frustrated in their ability to find work but aren't counted as unemployed are the **underemployed:** workers who would like to find full-time jobs but are currently working part time "for economic reasons"—that is, they can't find a full-time job. Again, they aren't counted in the unemployment rate.

The Bureau of Labor Statistics is the federal agency that calculates the official unemployment rate. It also calculates broader "measures of labor underutilization" that include the three categories of frustrated workers. Figure 23-2 shows what happens to the measured unemployment rate once discouraged workers, other marginally attached workers, and the underemployed are counted. The broadest measure of unemployment and underemployment, known as U-6, is the sum of these three measures plus the unemployed. It is substantially higher than the rate usually quoted by the news media. But U-6 and the unemployment rate move very much in parallel, so changes in the unemployment rate remain a good guide to what's happening in the overall labor market, including frustrated workers.

Finally, it's important to realize that the unemployment rate varies greatly among demographic groups. Other things equal, jobs are generally easier to find for more experienced workers and for workers during their "prime" working years, from ages 25 to 54. For younger workers, as well as workers nearing retirement age, jobs are typically harder to find, other things equal.

Figure 23-3 shows unemployment rates for different groups in 2007, when the overall unemployment rate was low by historical standards, in 2010, when the rate was high in the aftermath of the Great Recession, and in 2014, when it had come down much of, but not all, the way to pre-crisis levels. As you can see, the unemployment rate for African-American workers is consistently much higher than the national average; the unemployment rate for White teenagers (ages 16–19) is normally even higher; and the unemployment rate for African-American teenagers is higher still. (Bear in mind that a teenager isn't considered unemployed, even

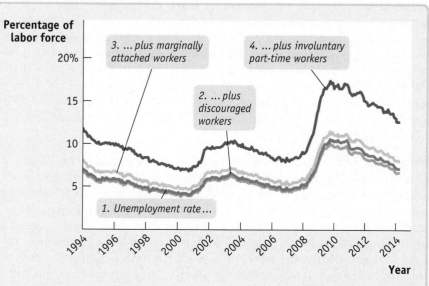

FIGURE **23-2** Alternative Measures of Unemployment, 1994–2014

The unemployment number usually quoted in the news media counts someone as unemployed only if he or she has been looking for work during the past four weeks. Broader measures also count discouraged workers, marginally attached workers, and the underemployed. These broader measures show a higher unemployment rate, but they move closely in parallel with the standard rate.

Source: Bureau of Labor Statistics.

FIGURE **23-3**   **Unemployment Rates of Different Groups in 2007, 2010, and 2014**

Unemployment rates vary greatly among different demographic groups. For example, although the overall unemployment rate in October 2014 was 5.8%, the unemployment rate among African-American teenagers was 28.1%. As a result, even during periods of low overall unemployment, unemployment remains a serious problem for some groups.

Source: Bureau of Labor Statistics.

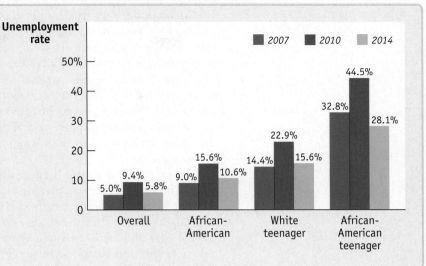

if he or she isn't working, unless that teenager is looking for work but can't find it.) So even at times when the overall unemployment rate is relatively low, jobs are hard to find for some groups.

So you should interpret the unemployment rate as an indicator of overall labor market conditions, not as an exact, literal measure of the percentage of people unable to find jobs. The unemployment rate is, however, a very good indicator: its ups and downs closely reflect economic changes that have a significant impact on people's lives. Let's turn now to the causes of these fluctuations.

Growth and Unemployment

Compared to Figure 23-1, Figure 23-4 shows the U.S. unemployment rate over a somewhat shorter period, the 35 years from 1979 through late 2014. The shaded bars represent periods of recession. As you can see, during every recession,

FIGURE **23-4**   **Unemployment and Recessions, 1979–2014**

This figure shows a close-up of the unemployment rate for the past three decades, with the shaded bars indicating recessions. It's clear that unemployment always rises during recessions and *usually* falls during expansions. But in both the early 1990s and the early 2000s, unemployment continued to rise for some time after the recession was officially declared over.

Sources: Bureau of Labor Statistics; National Bureau of Economic Research.

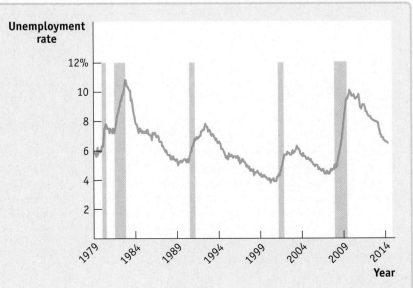

without exception, the unemployment rate rose. The severe recession of 2007–2009, like the earlier one of 1981–1982, led to a huge rise in unemployment.

Correspondingly, during periods of economic expansion the unemployment rate usually falls. The long economic expansion of the 1990s eventually brought the unemployment rate to 4.0%, and the expansion of the mid-2000s brought the rate down to 4.7%. However, it's important to recognize that *economic expansions aren't always periods of falling unemployment.* Look at the periods immediately following the recessions of 1990–1991 and 2001 in Figure 23-4. In each case the unemployment rate continued to rise for more than a year after the recession was officially over. The explanation in both cases is that although the economy was growing, it was not growing fast enough to reduce the unemployment rate.

Figure 23-5 is a scatter diagram showing U.S. data for the period from 1949 to 2013. The horizontal axis measures the annual rate of growth in real GDP—the percent by which each year's real GDP changed compared to the previous year's real GDP. (Notice that there were ten years in which growth was negative—that is, real GDP shrank.) The vertical axis measures the *change* in the unemployment rate over the previous year in percentage points—last year's unemployment rate minus this year's unemployment rate. Each dot represents the observed growth rate of real GDP and change in the unemployment rate for a given year. For example, in 2000 the average unemployment rate fell to 4.0% from 4.2% in 1999; this is shown as a value of –0.2 along the vertical axis for the year 2000. Over the same period, real GDP grew by 3.7%; this is the value shown along the horizontal axis for the year 2000.

FIGURE 23-5   **Growth and Changes in Unemployment, 1949–2013**

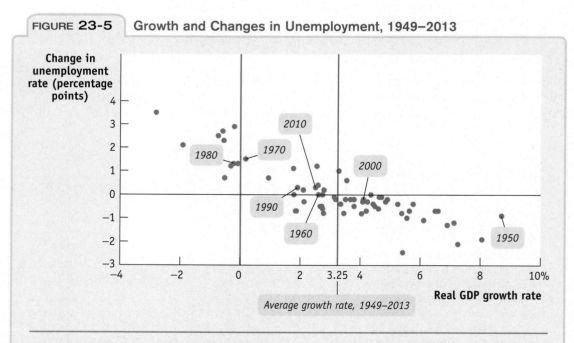

Each dot shows the growth rate of the economy and the change in the unemployment rate for a specific year between 1949 and 2013. For example, in 2000 the economy grew 3.7% and the unemployment rate fell 0.2 percentage points, from 4.2% to 4.0%. In general, the unemployment rate fell when growth was above its average rate of 3.25% a year and rose when growth was below average. Unemployment always rose when real GDP fell.

Sources: Bureau of Labor Statistics; Bureau of Economic Analysis.

The downward trend of the scatter diagram in Figure 23-5 shows that there is a generally strong negative relationship between growth in the economy and the rate of unemployment. Years of high growth in real GDP were also years in which the unemployment rate fell, and years of low or negative growth in real GDP were years in which the unemployment rate rose.

The green vertical line in Figure 23-5 at the value of 3.25% indicates the average growth rate of real GDP over the period from 1949 to 2013. Points lying to the right of the vertical line are years of above-average growth. In these years, the value on the vertical axis is usually negative, meaning that the unemployment rate fell. That is, years of above-average growth were usually years in which the unemployment rate was falling. Conversely, points lying to the left of the green vertical line were years of below-average growth. In these years, the value on the vertical axis is usually positive, meaning that the unemployment rate rose. That is, years of below-average growth were usually years in which the unemployment rate was rising.

A period in which real GDP is growing at a below-average rate and unemployment is rising is called a **jobless recovery** or a "growth recession." Since 1990, there have been three recessions, each of which was followed by a period of jobless recovery. But true recessions, periods when real GDP falls, are especially painful for workers. As illustrated by the points to the left of the purple vertical line in Figure 23-5 (representing years in which the real GDP growth rate is negative), falling real GDP is always associated with a rising rate of unemployment, causing a great deal of hardship to families.

> A **jobless recovery** is a period in which the real GDP growth rate is positive but the unemployment rate is still rising.

ECONOMICS ▶ in Action

Failure to Launch

In March 2010, when the U.S. job situation was near its worst, the *Harvard Law Record* published a brief note titled "Unemployed law student will work for $160K plus benefits." In a self-mocking tone, the author admitted to having graduated from Harvard Law School the previous year but not landing a job offer. "What mark on our résumé is so bad that it outweighs the crimson H?" the note asked.

The answer, of course, is that it wasn't about the résumé—it was about the economy. Times of high unemployment are especially hard on new graduates, who often find it hard to get any kind of full-time job.

How bad was it around the time that note was written? Figure 23-6 shows unemployment rates for two kinds of college graduates—all graduates 25 and older, and recent graduates in their 20s—for each year from 2007 to 2011. Even at its peak, in October 2009, the unemployment rate among older graduates was less than 5 percent. Among recent graduates, however, the rate peaked at 15.5 percent, and it was still well into double digits in late 2011. The U.S. labor market had a

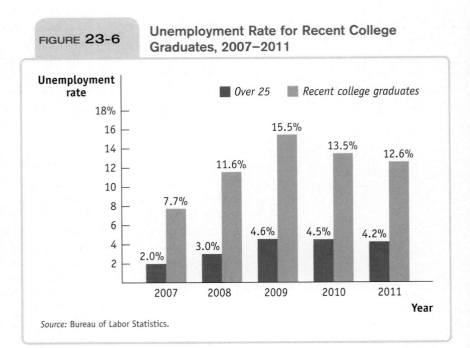

FIGURE 23-6   Unemployment Rate for Recent College Graduates, 2007–2011

Source: Bureau of Labor Statistics.

long way to go before being able to offer college graduates—and young people in general—the kinds of opportunities they deserved.

Check Your Understanding | **23-1**

1. Suppose that the advent of employment websites enables job-seekers to find suitable jobs more quickly. What effect will this have on the unemployment rate over time? Also suppose that these websites encourage job-seekers who had given up their searches to begin looking again. What effect will this have on the unemployment rate?

2. In which of the following cases is a worker counted as unemployed? Explain.
   a. Rosa, an older worker who has been laid off and who gave up looking for work months ago
   b. Anthony, a schoolteacher who is not working during his three-month summer break
   c. Grace, an investment banker who has been laid off and is currently searching for another position
   d. Sergio, a classically trained musician who can only find work playing for local parties
   e. Natasha, a graduate student who went back to school because jobs were scarce

3. Which of the following are consistent with the observed relationship between growth in real GDP and changes in the unemployment rate as shown in Figure 23-5? Which are not?
   a. A rise in the unemployment rate accompanies a fall in real GDP.
   b. An exceptionally strong business recovery is associated with a greater percentage of the labor force being employed.
   c. Negative real GDP growth is associated with a fall in the unemployment rate.

Solutions appear at back of book.

The Natural Rate of Unemployment

Fast economic growth tends to reduce the unemployment rate. So how low can the unemployment rate go? You might be tempted to say zero, but that isn't feasible. Over the past half-century, the national unemployment rate has never dropped below 2.9%.

How can there be so much unemployment even when many businesses are having a hard time finding workers? To answer this question, we need to examine the nature of labor markets and why they normally lead to substantial measured unemployment even when jobs are plentiful. Our starting point is the observation that even in the best of times, jobs are constantly being created and destroyed.

Job Creation and Job Destruction

Even during good times, most Americans know someone who has lost his or her job. In July 2007, the U.S. unemployment rate was only 4.7%, relatively low by historical standards. Yet in that month there were 4.5 million "job separations"—terminations of employment that occur because a worker is either fired or quits voluntarily.

There are many reasons for such job loss. One is structural change in the economy: industries rise and fall as new technologies emerge and consumers' tastes change. For example, employment in high-tech industries such as telecommunications surged in the late 1990s but slumped severely after 2000. However, structural change also brings the creation of new jobs: after 2000, the number of jobs in the American health care sector surged as new medical technologies and the aging of the population increased the demand for medical care. Poor management performance or bad luck at individual companies also leads to job loss for their employees. For example, in 2009 General Motors announced plans to eliminate 47,000 jobs after several years of lagging sales, even as Japanese companies such as Toyota were opening new plants in North America to meet growing demand for their cars.

Continual job creation and destruction are a feature of modern economies, making a naturally occurring amount of unemployment inevitable. Within this naturally occurring amount, there are two types of unemployment—*frictional* and *structural.*

"At this point, I'm just happy to still have a job"

Frictional Unemployment

When a worker loses a job involuntarily due to job destruction, he or she often doesn't take the first new job offered. For example, suppose a skilled programmer, laid off because her software company's product line was unsuccessful, sees a help-wanted ad for clerical work online. She might respond to the ad and get the job—but that would be foolish. Instead, she should take the time to look for a job that takes advantage of her skills and pays accordingly. In addition, individual workers are constantly leaving jobs voluntarily, typically for personal reasons—family moves, dissatisfaction, and better job prospects elsewhere.

Economists say that workers who spend time looking for employment are engaged in **job search.** If all workers and all jobs were alike, job search wouldn't be necessary; if information about jobs and workers was perfect, job search would be very quick. In practice, however, it's normal for a worker who loses a job, or a young worker seeking a first job, to spend at least a few weeks searching.

Frictional unemployment is unemployment due to the time workers spend in job search. A certain amount of frictional unemployment is inevitable due to the constant process of economic change. Thus even in 2007, a year of low unemployment, there were 62 million "job separations," in which workers left or lost their jobs. Total employment grew because these separations were more than offset by more than 63 million hires. Inevitably, some of the workers who left or lost their jobs spent at least some time unemployed, as did some of the workers newly entering the labor force.

Figure 23-7 shows the average monthly flows of workers among three states: employed, unemployed, and not in the labor force during 2007, a year of relatively

Workers who spend time looking for employment are engaged in **job search.**

Frictional unemployment is unemployment due to the time workers spend in job search.

FIGURE 23-7   Labor Market Flows in an Average Month in 2007

Even in 2007, a low-unemployment year, large numbers of workers moved into and out of both employment and unemployment each month. On average, each month in 2007, 1.781 million unemployed became employed, and 1.929 million employed became unemployed.
Source: Bureau of Labor Statistics.

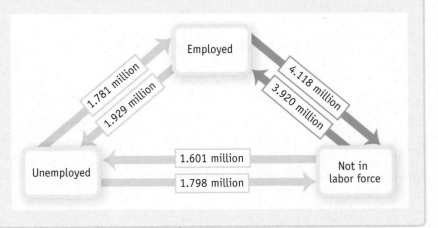

low unemployment. What the figure suggests is how much churning is constantly taking place in the labor market. An inevitable consequence of that churning is a significant number of workers who haven't yet found their next job—that is, frictional unemployment.

A limited amount of frictional unemployment is relatively harmless and may even be a good thing. The economy is more productive if workers take the time to find jobs that are well matched to their skills, and workers who are unemployed for a brief period while searching for the right job don't experience great hardship. In fact, when there is a low unemployment rate, periods of unemployment tend to be quite short, suggesting that much of the unemployment is frictional.

Figure 23-8 shows the composition of unemployment for all of 2007, when the unemployment rate was only 4.6%. Thirty-six percent of the unemployed had been unemployed for less than 5 weeks, and only 33% had been unemployed for 15 or more weeks. Only about one in six unemployed workers were considered to be "long-term unemployed"—unemployed for 27 or more weeks.

In periods of higher unemployment, however, workers tend to be jobless for longer periods of time, suggesting that a smaller share of unemployment is frictional. Figure 23-9 shows the fraction of the unemployed who had been out of work for six months or more from 2007 to mid-2014. It jumped to 45% after the Great Recession, and was still historically high five years after the recession officially ended.

FIGURE **23-8**   Distribution of the Unemployed by Duration of Unemployment, 2007

In years when the unemployment rate is low, most unemployed workers are unemployed for only a short period. In 2007, a year of low unemployment, 36% of the unemployed had been unemployed for less than 5 weeks and 67% for less than 15 weeks. The short duration of unemployment for most workers suggests that most unemployment in 2007 was frictional.

Source: Bureau of Labor Statistics.

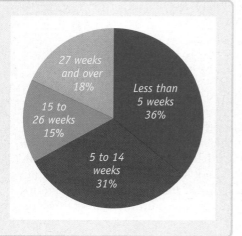

FIGURE **23-9**   Percentage of Unemployed U.S. Workers Who Had Been Unemployed for Six Months or Longer, 2007–2014

Before the Great Recession, relatively few U.S. workers had been unemployed for long periods. However, the percentage of long-term unemployed shot up after 2007, and remained high for a number of years.

Source: Bureau of Labor Statistics.

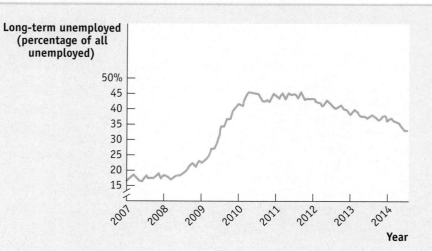

Structural Unemployment

Frictional unemployment exists even when the number of people seeking jobs is equal to the number of jobs being offered—that is, the existence of frictional unemployment doesn't mean that there is a surplus of labor. Sometimes, however, there is a *persistent surplus* of job-seekers in a particular labor market, even when the economy is at the peak of the business cycle. There may be more workers with a particular skill than there are jobs available using that skill, or there may be more workers in a particular geographic region than there are jobs available in that region. **Structural unemployment** is unemployment that results when there are more people seeking jobs in a particular labor market than there are jobs available at the current wage rate.

The supply and demand model tells us that the price of a good, service, or factor of production tends to move toward an equilibrium level that matches the quantity supplied with the quantity demanded. This is equally true, in general, of labor markets.

Figure 23-10 shows a typical market for labor. The labor demand curve indicates that when the price of labor—the wage rate—increases, employers demand less labor. The labor supply curve indicates that when the price of labor increases, more workers are willing to supply labor at the prevailing wage rate. These two forces coincide to lead to an equilibrium wage rate for any given type of labor in a particular location. That equilibrium wage rate is shown as W_E.

Even at the equilibrium wage rate W_E, there will still be some frictional unemployment. That's because there will always be some workers engaged in job search even when the number of jobs available is equal to the number of workers seeking jobs. But there wouldn't be any structural unemployment in this labor market. *Structural unemployment occurs when the wage rate is, for some reason, persistently above W_E.* Several factors can lead to a wage rate in excess of W_E, the most important being minimum wages, labor unions, *efficiency wages,* the side effects of government policies, and mismatches between employees and employers.

Minimum Wages A minimum wage is a government-mandated floor on the price of labor. In the United States, the national minimum wage in early 2014 was $7.25 an hour. A number of state and local governments also determine the minimum wage within their jurisdictions, typically for the purpose of setting it higher than the federal level. For example, the city of Seattle has set a minimum wage at $15 an hour. For many American workers, the minimum wage is irrelevant; the market equilibrium wage for these workers is well above the national price floor. But for less skilled workers, the minimum wage may be binding—it affects the wages that people are actually paid and can lead to structural unemployment in particular markets for labor. Other wealthy countries have higher minimum wages; for example, in 2014 the French minimum wage was 9.40 euros an hour, or around $12.40. In these countries, the range of workers for whom the minimum wage is binding is larger.

Figure 23-10 shows the effect of a binding minimum wage. In this market, there is a legal floor on wages, W_F, which is above the equilibrium wage rate, W_E. This leads to a persistent surplus in the labor market: the quantity of labor supplied, Q_S, is larger than the quantity demanded, Q_D. In other words, more people want to work than can find jobs at the minimum wage, leading to structural unemployment.

Given that minimum wages—that is, binding minimum wages—generally lead to structural unemployment, you might wonder why governments impose them. The rationale is to help ensure that people who work can earn enough income to afford at least a minimally comfortable lifestyle. However, this may come at a cost, because it may eliminate the opportunity to work for some workers who would have willingly worked for lower wages. As illustrated in Figure 23-10, not only are there more sellers of labor than there are buyers, but there are also fewer

In **structural unemployment,** more people are seeking jobs in a particular labor market than there are jobs available at the current wage rate, even when the economy is at the peak of the business cycle.

FIGURE **23-10** The Effect of a Minimum Wage on a Labor Market

When the government sets a minimum wage, W_F, that exceeds the market equilibrium wage rate in that market, W_E, the number of *workers* who would like to work at that minimum wage, Q_S, is greater than the number of workers demanded at that wage rate, Q_D. This surplus of labor is structural unemployment.

people working at a minimum wage (Q_D) than there would have been with no minimum wage at all (Q_E).

Although economists broadly agree that a high minimum wage has the employment-reducing effects shown in Figure 23-10, there is some question about whether this is a good description of how the U.S. minimum wage actually works. The minimum wage in the United States is quite low compared with that in other wealthy countries. For three decades, from the 1970s to the mid-2000s, the American minimum wage was so low that it was not binding for the vast majority of workers.

In addition, some researchers have produced evidence showing that increases in the minimum wage actually lead to higher employment when, as was the case in the United States at one time, the minimum wage is low compared to average wages. They argue that firms that employ low-skilled workers sometimes restrict their hiring in order to keep wages low and that, as a result, the minimum wage can sometimes be increased without any loss of jobs. Most economists, however, agree that a sufficiently high minimum wage *does* lead to structural unemployment.

Labor Unions The actions of *labor unions* can have effects similar to those of minimum wages, leading to structural unemployment. By bargaining collectively for all of a firm's workers, unions can often win higher wages from employers than workers would have obtained by bargaining individually. This process, known as *collective bargaining*, is intended to tip the scales of bargaining power more toward workers and away from employers. Labor unions exercise bargaining power by threatening firms with a *labor strike,* a collective refusal to work. The threat of a strike can have serious consequences for firms. In such cases, workers acting collectively can exercise more power than they could if acting individually.

Employers have acted to counter the bargaining power of unions by threatening and enforcing lockouts—periods in which union workers are locked out and rendered unemployed—while hiring replacement workers.

When workers have increased bargaining power, they tend to demand and receive higher wages. Unions also bargain over benefits, such as health care and pensions, which we can think of as additional wages. Indeed, economists who study the effects of unions on wages find that unionized workers earn higher wages and more generous benefits than non-union workers with similar skills. The result of these increased wages can be the same as the result of a minimum wage: labor unions push the wage that workers receive above the equilibrium wage. Consequently, there are more people willing to work at the wage being paid than there are jobs available. Like a binding minimum wage, this leads to structural unemployment. In the United States, however, due to a low level of unionization, the amount of unemployment generated by union demands is likely to be very small.

Efficiency Wages Actions by firms can contribute to structural unemployment. Firms may choose to pay **efficiency wages**—wages that employers set above the equilibrium wage rate as an incentive for their workers to perform better.

Employers may feel the need for such incentives for several reasons. For example, employers often have difficulty observing directly how hard an employee works. They can, however, elicit more work effort by paying above-market wages: employees receiving these higher wages are more likely to work harder to ensure that they aren't fired, which would cause them to lose their higher wages.

When many firms pay efficiency wages, the result is a pool of workers who want jobs but can't find them. So the use of efficiency wages by firms leads to structural unemployment.

Side Effects of Government Policies In addition, government policies designed to help workers who lose their jobs can lead to structural unemployment as an unintended side effect. Most economically advanced countries provide benefits to laid-off workers as a way to tide them over until they find a new job. In the United States, these benefits typically replace only a small fraction of a worker's income and expire after 26 weeks. (This was extended in some cases to 99 weeks during the period of high unemployment in 2009–2011). In other countries, particularly in Europe, benefits are more generous and last longer. The drawback to this generosity is that it reduces a worker's incentive to quickly find a new job. During the 1980s, it was often argued that unemployment benefits in some European countries were one of the causes of *Eurosclerosis,* persistently high unemployment that afflicts a number of European economies.

Mismatches Between Employees and Employers It takes time for workers and firms to adjust to shifts in the economy. The result can be a mismatch between what employees have to offer and what employers are looking for. A skills mismatch is one form; for example, in the aftermath of the housing bust of 2009, there were more construction workers looking for jobs than were available. Another form is geographic as in Michigan, which has had a long-standing surplus of workers after its auto industry declined. Until the mismatch is resolved through a big enough fall in wages of the surplus workers that induces retraining or relocation, there will be structural unemployment.

The Natural Rate of Unemployment

Because some frictional unemployment is inevitable and because many economies also suffer from structural unemployment, a certain amount of unemployment is normal, or "natural." Actual unemployment fluctuates around this normal level. The **natural rate of unemployment** is the normal unemployment rate around which the actual unemployment rate fluctuates. It is the rate of unemployment that arises from the effects of frictional plus structural unemployment. **Cyclical unemployment** is the deviation of the actual rate of unemployment from the natural rate; that is, it is the difference between the actual and natural rates of unemployment. As the name suggests, cyclical unemployment is the share of unemployment that arises from the downturns of the business cycle.

Efficiency wages are wages that employers set above the equilibrium wage rate as an incentive for better employee performance.

The **natural rate of unemployment** is the unemployment rate that arises from the effects of frictional plus structural unemployment.

Cyclical unemployment is the deviation of the actual rate of unemployment from the natural rate due to downturns in the business cycle.

GLOBAL COMPARISION | Natural Unemployment Around the OECD

The Organization for Economic Cooperation and Development (OECD) is an association of relatively wealthy countries in Europe and North America that also includes Japan, Korea, New Zealand, and Australia. Among other activities, the OECD makes estimates of the natural rate of unemployment. The figure shows these estimates for 2013. The population-weighted average across the OECD is given by the purple bar.

While the U.S. natural rate of unemployment at 6.1% is below the OECD average of 7.7%, those of many European

countries (including the major economies of Germany, Italy, and France) are above average. Many economists think that persistently high European unemployment rates are the result of government policies, such as high minimum wages and generous unemployment benefits, which discourage employers from offering jobs and discourage workers from accepting jobs, leading to high rates of structural unemployment.

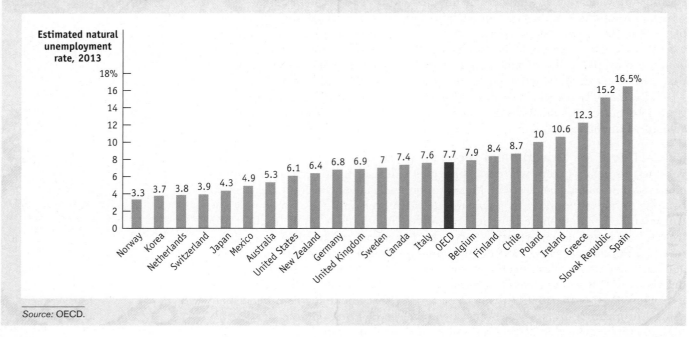

Source: OECD.

We'll see in Chapter 31 that an economy's natural rate of unemployment is a critical policy variable because a government cannot keep the unemployment rate persistently below the natural rate without leading to accelerating inflation.

We can summarize the relationships between the various types of unemployment as follows:

(23-3) Natural unemployment =
Frictional unemployment + Structural unemployment

(23-4) Actual unemployment =
Natural unemployment + Cyclical unemployment

Perhaps because of its name, people often imagine that the natural rate of unemployment is a constant that doesn't change over time and can't be affected by government policy. Neither proposition is true. Let's take a moment to stress two facts: the natural rate of unemployment changes over time, and it can be affected by government policies.

Changes in the Natural Rate of Unemployment

Private-sector economists and government agencies need estimates of the natural rate of unemployment both to make forecasts and to conduct policy analyses. Almost all these estimates show that the U.S. natural rate rises and falls over time. For example, the Congressional Budget Office, the independent agency that conducts budget and economic analyses for Congress, believes that the U.S. natural rate of unemployment was 5.3% in 1950, rose to 6.3% by the end of the 1970s, but has fallen to 5.2% at the end of 2014. European countries have experienced even larger swings in their natural rates of unemployment.

What causes the natural rate of unemployment to change? The most important factors are changes in labor force characteristics, changes in labor market institutions, and changes in government policies. Let's look briefly at each factor.

Changes in Labor Force Characteristics In 2007 the rate of unemployment in the United States was 4.6%. Young workers, however, had much higher unemployment rates: 15.7% for teenagers and 8.2% for workers aged 20 to 24. Workers aged 25 to 54 had an unemployment rate of only 3.7%.

In general, unemployment rates tend to be lower for experienced than for inexperienced workers. Because experienced workers tend to stay in a given job longer than do inexperienced ones, they have lower frictional unemployment. Also, because older workers are more likely than young workers to be family breadwinners, they have a stronger incentive to find and keep jobs.

One reason the natural rate of unemployment rose during the 1970s was a large rise in the number of new workers—children of the post–World War II baby boom entered the labor force, as did a rising percentage of married women. As Figure 23-11 shows, both the percentage of the labor force less than 25 years old and the percentage of women in the labor force grew rapidly in the 1970s. By the end of the 1990s, however, the share of women in the labor force had leveled off and the percentage of workers under 25 had fallen sharply. As a result, the labor force as a whole is more experienced today than it was in the 1970s, one likely reason that the natural rate of unemployment is lower today than in the 1970s.

Changes in Labor Market Institutions As we pointed out earlier, unions that negotiate wages above the equilibrium level can be a source of structural unemployment. Some economists believe that the high natural rate of unemployment in Europe, discussed in the Global Comparison, is caused, in part, by strong labor unions. In the United States, a sharp fall in union membership after 1980 may have been one reason the natural rate of unemployment fell between the 1970s and the 1990s.

FIGURE **23-11**   The Changing Makeup of the U.S. Labor Force, 1948–2014

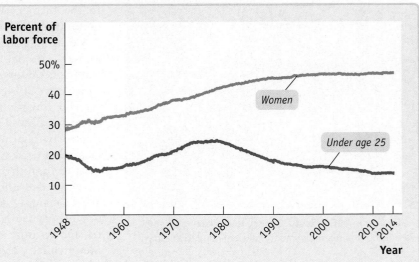

In the 1970s the percentage of women in the labor force rose rapidly, as did the percentage of those under age 25. These changes reflected the entry of large numbers of women into the paid labor force for the first time and the fact that baby boomers were reaching working age. The natural rate of unemployment may have risen because many of these workers were relatively inexperienced. Today, the labor force is much more experienced, which is one possible reason the natural rate has fallen since the 1970s.

Source: Bureau of Labor Statistics.

Other institutional changes may also be at work. For example, some labor economists believe that temporary employment agencies, which have proliferated in recent years, have reduced frictional unemployment by helping match workers to jobs. Furthermore, as discussed in the Business Case at the end of the chapter, websites such as Elance-oDesk may have reduced frictional unemployment.

Technological change, coupled with labor market institutions, can also affect the natural rate of unemployment. Technological change tends to increase the demand for skilled workers who are familiar with the relevant technology and reduce the demand for unskilled workers. Economic theory predicts that wages should increase for skilled workers and decrease for unskilled workers as technology advances. But if wages for unskilled workers cannot go down—say, due to a binding minimum wage—increased structural unemployment, and therefore a higher natural rate of unemployment, will result during periods of faster technological change.

Changes in Government Policies A high minimum wage can cause structural unemployment. Generous unemployment benefits can increase both structural and frictional unemployment. So government policies intended to help workers can have the undesirable side effect of raising the natural rate of unemployment.

Some government policies, however, may reduce the natural rate. Two examples are job training and employment subsidies. Job-training programs are supposed to provide unemployed workers with skills that widen the range of jobs they can perform. Employment subsidies are payments either to workers or to employers that provide a financial incentive to accept or offer jobs.

ECONOMICS ▶ *in Action*

Structural Unemployment in East Germany

I n one of the most dramatic events in world history, a spontaneous popular uprising in 1989 overthrew the communist dictatorship in East Germany. Citizens quickly tore down the wall that had divided Berlin, and in short order East and West Germany united into one democratic nation.

Then the trouble started.

After reunification, employment in East Germany plunged and the unemployment rate soared. This high unemployment rate has gradually come down, but remains well above the rate in the rest of Germany. In late 2014 the unemployment rate in what was formerly East Germany was more than 9%, compared with 5.6% in the former West Germany. Other parts of formerly communist Eastern Europe have done much better. For example, the Czech Republic, which was often cited along with East Germany as a relatively successful communist economy, had an unemployment rate of only 5.7% in October 2014. What went wrong in East Germany?

The answer is that, through nobody's fault, East Germany found itself suffering from severe structural unemployment. When Germany was reunified, it became clear that workers in East Germany were much less productive than their cousins in the west. Yet unions initially demanded and received wage rates equal to those in West Germany. These wage rates have been slow to come down because East German workers objected to being treated as inferior to their West German counterparts. Meanwhile, productivity in the former East Germany remains well below West German levels, in part because of decades of misguided investment under the former dictatorship. The result has been a persistently

After reunification in 1989, East Germany found itself suffering from severe structural unemployment that continues to this day.

Robert Wallis/Corbis

large mismatch between the number of workers demanded and the number of those seeking jobs, and persistently high structural unemployment in the former East Germany.

Check Your Understanding   23-2

1. Explain the following statements.
   a. Frictional unemployment is higher when the pace of technological advance quickens.
   b. Structural unemployment is higher when the pace of technological advance quickens.
   c. Frictional unemployment accounts for a larger share of total unemployment when the unemployment rate is low.

2. Why does collective bargaining have the same general effect on unemployment as a minimum wage? Illustrate your answer with a diagram.

3. Suppose that at the peak of the business cycle the United States dramatically increases benefits for unemployed workers. Explain what will happen to the natural rate of unemployment.

Solutions appear at back of book.

Inflation and Deflation

As we mentioned in the opening story, monetary officials are perennially divided between doves and hawks—between those who want to place a high priority on low unemployment and those who want to place a high priority on low inflation. It's easy to see why high unemployment is a problem. But why is inflation something to worry about? Why do policy makers even now get anxious when they see the inflation rate moving upward? The answer is that inflation can impose costs on the economy—but not in the way most people think.

The Level of Prices Doesn't Matter . . .

The most common complaint about inflation, an increase in the price level, is that it makes everyone poorer—after all, a given amount of money buys less. But inflation does not make everyone poorer. To see why, it's helpful to imagine what would happen if the United States did something other countries have done from time to time—replacing the dollar with a new currency.

An example of this kind of currency conversion happened in 2002, when France, like a number of other European countries, replaced its national currency, the franc, with the new pan-European currency, the euro. People turned in their franc coins and notes, and received euro coins and notes in exchange, at a rate of precisely 6.55957 francs per euro. At the same time, all contracts were restated in euros at the same rate of exchange. For example, if a French citizen had a home mortgage debt of 500,000 francs, this became a debt of 500,000/6.55957 = 76,224.51 euros. If a worker's contract specified that he or she should be paid 100 francs per hour, it became a contract specifying a wage of 100/6.55957 = 15.2449 euros per hour, and so on.

Inflation can distort consumers' incentives about what and when to buy.

You could imagine doing the same thing here, replacing the dollar with a "new dollar" at a rate of exchange of, say, 7 to 1. If you owed $140,000 on your home, that would become a debt of 20,000 new dollars. If you had a wage rate of $14 an hour, it would become 2 new dollars an hour, and so on. This would bring the overall U.S. price level back to about what it was in 1962, when John F. Kennedy was president.

The **real wage** is the wage rate divided by the price level.

Real income is income divided by the price level.

So would everyone be richer as a result because prices would be only one-seventh as high? Of course not. Prices would be lower, but so would wages and incomes in general. If you cut a worker's wage to one-seventh of its previous value, but also cut all prices to one-seventh of their previous level, the worker's **real wage**—the wage rate divided by the price level—hasn't changed. In fact, bringing the overall price level back to what it was during the Kennedy administration would have no effect on overall purchasing power because doing so would reduce income exactly as much as it reduced prices.

Conversely, the rise in prices that has actually taken place since the early 1960s hasn't made America poorer because it has also raised incomes by the same amount: **real incomes**—incomes divided by the price level—haven't been affected by the rise in overall prices.

The moral of this story is that the *level* of prices doesn't matter: the United States would be no richer than it is now if the overall level of prices was still as low as it was in 1961; conversely, the rise in prices over the past 50 years hasn't made us poorer.

. . . But the Rate of Change of Prices Does

The conclusion that the level of prices doesn't matter might seem to imply that the inflation rate doesn't matter either. But that's not true.

To see why, it's crucial to distinguish between the *level of prices* and the *inflation rate:* the percent increase in the overall level of prices per year. Recall from Chapter 22 that the inflation rate is defined as follows:

$$\text{Inflation rate} = \frac{\text{Price index in year 2} - \text{Price index in year 1}}{\text{Price index in year 1}} \times 100$$

Figure 23-12 highlights the difference between the price level and the inflation rate in the United States over the last half-century, with the price level measured

FIGURE **23-12**   The Price Level versus the Inflation Rate, 1960–2014

With the exception of 2009, over the past half-century the price level has continuously increased. But the *inflation rate*—the rate at which prices are rising—has had both ups and downs. And in 2009, the inflation rate briefly turned negative, a phenomenon called *deflation*.
Source: Bureau of Labor Statistics.

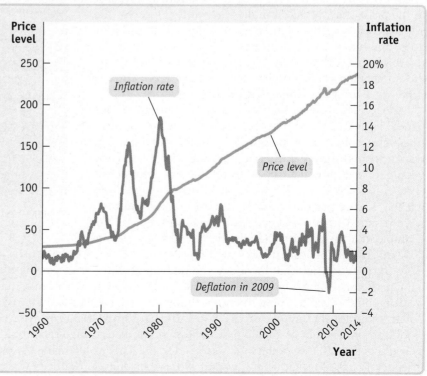

along the left vertical axis and the inflation rate measured along the right vertical axis. In the 2000s, the overall level of prices in America was much higher than it had been in 1960—but that, as we've learned, didn't matter. The inflation rate in the 2000s, however, was much lower than in the 1970s—and that almost certainly made the economy richer than it would have been if high inflation had continued.

Economists believe that high rates of inflation impose significant economic costs. The most important of these costs are *shoe-leather costs, menu costs,* and *unit-of-account costs.* We'll discuss each in turn.

Shoe-Leather Costs People hold money—cash in their wallets and bank deposits on which they can write checks—for convenience in making transactions. A high inflation rate, however, discourages people from holding money because the purchasing power of the cash in your wallet and the funds in your bank account steadily erode as the overall level of prices rises. This leads people to search for ways to reduce the amount of money they hold, often at considerable economic cost.

The upcoming Economics in Action describes how Israelis spent a lot of time at the bank during the periods of high inflation rates that afflicted Israel in 1984–1985. During the most famous of all inflations, the German *hyperinflation* of 1921–1923, merchants employed runners to take their cash to the bank many times a day to convert it into something that would hold its value, such as a stable foreign currency. In each case, in an effort to avoid having the purchasing power of their money eroded, people used up valuable resources, such as time for Israeli citizens and the labor of those German runners that could have been used productively elsewhere. During the German hyperinflation, so many banking transactions were taking place that the number of employees at German banks nearly quadrupled—from around 100,000 in 1913 to 375,000 in 1923.

More recently, Brazil experienced hyperinflation during the early 1990s; during that episode, the Brazilian banking sector grew so large that it accounted for 15% of GDP, more than twice the size of the financial sector in the United States measured as a share of GDP. The large increase in the Brazilian banking sector needed to cope with the consequences of inflation represented a loss of real resources to its society.

Increased costs of transactions caused by inflation are known as **shoe-leather costs,** an allusion to the wear and tear caused by the extra running around that takes place when people are trying to avoid holding money. Shoe-leather costs are substantial in economies with very high inflation, as anyone who has lived in such an economy—say, one suffering inflation of 100% or more per year—can attest. Most estimates suggest, however, that the shoe-leather costs of inflation at the rates seen in the United States—which in peacetime has never had inflation above 15%—are quite small.

Menu Costs In a modern economy, most of the things we buy have a listed price. There's a price listed under each item on a supermarket shelf, a price printed on the back of a book, and a price listed for each dish on a restaurant's menu. Changing a listed price has a real cost, called a **menu cost.** For example, to change prices in a supermarket requires sending clerks through the store to change the listed price under each item. In the face of inflation, of course, firms are forced to change prices more often than they would if the aggregate price level was more or less stable. This means higher costs for the economy as a whole.

In times of very high inflation, menu costs can be substantial. During the Brazilian inflation of the early 1990s, for instance, supermarket workers reportedly spent half of their time replacing old price stickers with new ones. When inflation is high, merchants may decide to stop listing prices in terms of the local currency and use either an artificial unit—in effect, measuring prices relative to one another—or a more stable currency, such as the U.S. dollar. This is exactly what the Israeli real estate market began doing in the mid-1980s: prices were

Shoe-leather costs are the increased costs of transactions caused by inflation.

The **menu cost** is the real cost of changing a listed price.

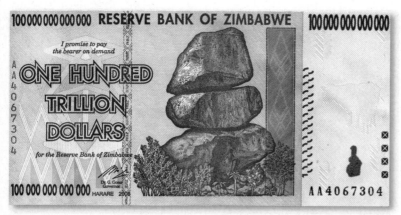

When one hundred trillion dollar bills are in circulation as they were in Zimbabwe, menu costs are substantial.

quoted in U.S. dollars, even though payment was made in Israeli shekels. And this is also what happened in Zimbabwe when, in May 2008, official estimates of the inflation rate reached 1,694,000%. By 2009, the government had suspended the Zimbabwean dollar, allowing Zimbabweans to buy and sell goods using foreign currencies.

Menu costs are also present in low-inflation economies, but they are not severe. In low-inflation economies, businesses might update their prices only sporadically—not daily or even more frequently, as is the case in high-inflation or hyperinflation economies. Also, with the growing popularity of online shopping, menu costs are becoming less and less important, since prices can be changed electronically and fewer merchants attach price stickers to merchandise.

Unit-of-Account Costs In the Middle Ages, contracts were often specified "in kind": a tenant might, for example, be obliged to provide his landlord with a certain number of cattle each year (the phrase *in kind* actually comes from an ancient word for *cattle*). This may have made sense at the time, but it would be an awkward way to conduct modern business. Instead, we state contracts in monetary terms: a renter owes a certain number of dollars per month, a company that issues a bond promises to pay the bondholder the dollar value of the bond when it comes due, and so on. We also tend to make our economic calculations in dollars: a family planning its budget, or a small business owner trying to figure out how well the business is doing, makes estimates of the amount of money coming in and going out.

This role of the dollar as a basis for contracts and calculation is called the *unit-of-account* role of money. It's an important aspect of the modern economy. Yet it's a role that can be degraded by inflation, which causes the purchasing power of a dollar to change over time—a dollar next year is worth less than a dollar this year. The effect, many economists argue, is to reduce the quality of economic decisions: the economy as a whole makes less efficient use of its resources because of the uncertainty caused by changes in the unit of account, the dollar. The **unit-of-account** costs of inflation are the costs arising from the way inflation makes money a less reliable unit of measurement.

Unit-of-account costs may be particularly important in the tax system because inflation can distort the measures of income on which taxes are collected. Here's an example: assume that the inflation rate is 10%, so the overall level of prices rises 10% each year. Suppose that a business buys an asset, such as a piece of land, for $100,000, then resells it a year later for $110,000. In a fundamental sense, the business didn't make a profit on the deal: in real terms, it got no more for the land than it paid for it. But U.S. tax law would say that the business made a capital gain of $10,000, and it would have to pay taxes on that phantom gain.

During the 1970s, when the United States had relatively high inflation, the distorting effects of inflation on the tax system were a serious problem. Some businesses were discouraged from productive investment spending because they found themselves paying taxes on phantom gains. Meanwhile, some unproductive investments became attractive because they led to phantom losses that reduced tax bills. When inflation fell in the 1980s—and tax rates were reduced—these problems became much less important.

Unit-of-account costs arise from the way inflation makes money a less reliable unit of measurement.

Winners and Losers from Inflation

As we've just learned, a high inflation rate imposes overall costs on the economy. In addition, inflation can produce winners and losers within the economy. The main reason inflation sometimes helps some people while hurting others is that economic transactions often involve contracts that extend over a period of time, such as loans, and these contracts are normally specified in nominal—that is, in dollar—terms.

In the case of a loan, the borrower receives a certain amount of funds at the beginning, and the loan contract specifies the *interest rate* on the loan and when it must be paid off. The **interest rate** is the return a lender receives for allowing borrowers the use of their savings for one year, calculated as a percentage of the amount borrowed.

But what that dollar is worth in real terms—that is, in terms of purchasing power—depends greatly on the rate of inflation over the intervening years of the loan. Economists summarize the effect of inflation on borrowers and lenders by distinguishing between the *nominal* interest rate and the *real* interest rate. The **nominal interest rate** is the interest rate in dollar terms—for example, the interest rate on a student loan. The **real interest rate** is the nominal interest rate minus the rate of inflation. For example, if a loan carries an interest rate of 8%, but there is 5% inflation, the real interest rate is 8% − 5% = 3%.

When a borrower and a lender enter into a loan contract, the contract is normally written in dollar terms—that is, the interest rate it specifies is a nominal interest rate. (And in later chapters, when we say the interest rate we will mean the nominal interest rate unless noted otherwise.) But each party to a loan contract has an expectation about the future rate of inflation and therefore an expectation about the real interest rate on the loan. If the actual inflation rate is *higher* than expected, borrowers gain at the expense of lenders: borrowers will repay their loans with funds that have a lower real value than had been expected. Conversely, if the inflation rate is *lower* than expected, lenders will gain at the expense of borrowers: borrowers must repay their loans with funds that have a higher real value than had been expected.

Historically, the fact that inflation creates winners and losers has sometimes been a major source of political controversy. In 1896 William Jennings Bryan electrified the Democratic presidential convention with a speech in which he declared, "You shall not crucify mankind on a cross of gold." What he was actually demanding was an inflationary policy. At the time, the U.S. dollar had a fixed value in terms of gold. Bryan wanted to abandon that gold standard and have the U.S. government print more money, which would have raised the level of prices. The reason he wanted inflation was to help farmers, many of whom were deeply in debt.

In modern America, home mortgages are the most important source of gains and losses from inflation. Americans who took out mortgages in the early 1970s quickly found their real payments reduced by higher-than-expected inflation: by 1983, the purchasing power of a dollar was only 45% of what it had been in 1973. Those who took out mortgages in the early 1990s were not so lucky, because the inflation rate fell to lower-than-expected levels in the following years: in 2003 the purchasing power of a dollar was 78% of what it had been in 1993.

Because gains for some and losses for others result from inflation that is either higher or lower than expected, yet another problem arises: uncertainty about the future inflation rate discourages people from entering into any form of long-term contract. This is an additional cost of high inflation, because high rates of inflation are usually unpredictable. In countries with high and uncertain inflation, long-term loans are rare, which makes it difficult in many cases to make long-term investments.

The **interest rate** on a loan is the price, calculated as a percentage of the amount borrowed, that lenders charge borrowers the use of their savings for one year.

The **nominal interest rate** is the interest rate expressed in dollar terms.

The **real interest rate** is the nominal interest rate minus the rate of inflation.

Disinflation is the process of bringing the inflation rate down.

One last point: unexpected *deflation*—a surprise fall in the price level—creates winners and losers, too. Between 1929 and 1933, as the U.S. economy plunged into the Great Depression, the consumer price index fell by 35%. This meant that debtors, including many farmers and homeowners, saw a sharp rise in the real value of their debts, which led to widespread bankruptcy and helped create a banking crisis, as lenders found their customers unable to pay back their loans. And as you can see in Figure 23-12, deflation occurred again in 2009, when the inflation rate fell to −2% at the trough of a deep recession. Like the Great Depression (but to a much lesser extent), the unexpected deflation of 2009 imposed heavy costs on debtors. We will discuss the effects of deflation in more detail in Chapter 31.

Inflation Is Easy; Disinflation Is Hard

There is not much evidence that a rise in the inflation rate from, say, 2% to 5% would do a great deal of harm to the economy. Still, policy makers generally move forcefully to bring inflation back down when it creeps above 2% or 3%. Why? Because experience shows that bringing the inflation rate down—a process called **disinflation**—is very difficult and costly once a higher rate of inflation has become well established in the economy.

Figure 23-13 shows what happened during two major episodes of disinflation in the United States, in the mid-1970s and in the early 1980s. The horizontal axis shows the unemployment rate. The vertical axis shows "core" inflation over the previous year, a measure that excludes volatile food and energy prices and is widely considered a better measure of underlying inflation than overall consumer prices. Each marker represents the inflation rate and the unemployment rate for one month. In each episode, unemployment and inflation followed a sort of clockwise spiral, with high inflation gradually falling in the face of an extended period of very high unemployment.

According to many economists, these periods of high unemployment that temporarily depressed the economy were necessary to reduce inflation that had become deeply embedded in the economy. The best way to avoid having to put the economy through a wringer to reduce inflation, however, is to avoid having a serious inflation problem in the first place. So policy makers respond forcefully to signs that inflation may be accelerating as a form of preventive medicine for the economy.

FIGURE **23-13** | The Cost of Disinflation

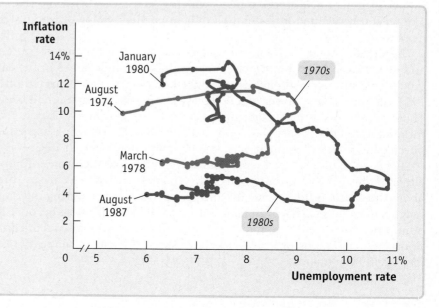

There were two major periods of disinflation in modern U.S. history, in the mid-1970s and the early 1980s. This figure shows the track of the unemployment rate and the "core" inflation rate, which excludes food and energy, during these two episodes. In each case bringing inflation down required a temporary but very large increase in the unemployment rate, demonstrating the high cost of disinflation.
Source: Bureau of Labor Statistics.

ECONOMICS ▶ in Action

Israel's Experience With Inflation

It's often hard to see the costs of inflation clearly because serious inflation problems are often associated with other problems that disrupt economic life, notably war or political instability (or both). In the mid-1980s, however, Israel experienced a "clean" inflation: there was no war, the government was stable, and there was order in the streets. Yet a series of policy errors led to very high inflation, with prices often rising more than 10% a month.

As it happens, one of the authors spent a month visiting at Tel Aviv University at the height of the inflation, so we can give a first-hand account of the effects.

First, the shoe-leather costs of inflation were substantial. At the time, Israelis spent a lot of time in lines at the bank, moving money in and out of accounts that provided high enough interest rates to offset inflation. People walked around with very little cash in their wallets; they had to go to the bank whenever they needed to make even a moderately large cash payment. Banks responded by opening a lot of branches, a costly business expense.

The shoe-leather costs of inflation in Israel: when the inflation rate hit 500% in 1985, people spent a lot of time in line at banks.

Second, although menu costs weren't that visible to a visitor, what you could see were the efforts businesses made to minimize them. For example, restaurant menus often didn't list prices. Instead, they listed numbers that you had to multiply by another number, written on a chalkboard and changed every day, to figure out the price of a dish.

Finally, it was hard to make decisions because prices changed so much and so often. It was a common experience to walk out of a store because prices were 25% higher than at one's usual shopping destination, only to discover that prices had just been increased 25% there, too.

Check Your Understanding   23-3

1. The widespread use of technology has revolutionized the banking industry, making it much easier for customers to access and manage their assets. Does this mean that the shoe-leather costs of inflation are higher or lower than they used to be?

2. Most people in the United States have grown accustomed to a modest inflation rate of around 2% to 3%. Who would gain and who would lose if inflation unexpectedly came to a complete stop over the next 15 or 20 years?

Solutions appear at back of book.

▼ Quick Review

- The **real wage** and **real income** are unaffected by the level of prices.

- Inflation, like unemployment, is a major concern of policy makers—so much so that in the past they have accepted high unemployment as the price of reducing inflation.

- While the overall level of prices is irrelevant, high rates of inflation impose real costs on the economy: **shoe-leather costs, menu costs,** and **unit-of-account costs.**

- The **interest rate** is the return a lender receives for use of his or her funds for a year. The **real interest rate** is equal to the **nominal interest rate** minus the inflation rate. As a result, unexpectedly high inflation helps borrowers and hurts lenders. With high and uncertain inflation, people will often avoid long-term investments.

- **Disinflation** is very costly, so policy makers try to avoid getting into situations of high inflation in the first place.

Day Labor in the Information Age

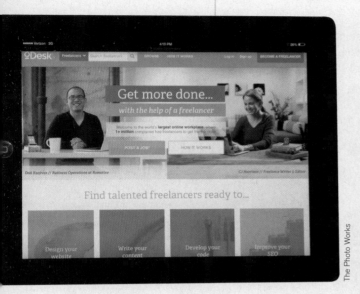

The Photo Works

By the usual measures, California-based Elance-oDesk is a pretty small business, with only 250 employees. But in mid-2014 it was supplying workers to 2.5 million businesses. Elance-oDesk could do that because it doesn't offer services directly; instead, it operates as an online marketplace, matching employers with freelance workers.

While most American workers consistently work for a single employer, temporary workers have always accounted for a significant portion of the labor force. On urban street corners across America, workers line up early each morning in the hope of getting day jobs in industries like construction where the need for workers fluctuates, sometimes unpredictably. For more skilled workers, there are temporary staffing agencies like Allegis Group that provide workers on a subcontracting basis, from a few days to months at a time. Figure 23-14 shows the share of temporary employment accounted for by these agencies in total employment. As you can see, in the late stages of the economic expansion in the 1990s and the 2000s, temporary employment soared as companies needed more workers but had difficulty hiring permanent employees in a tight labor market. Temporary employment then proceeded to plunge once demand for additional workers fell off.

FIGURE 23-14 The Rise in Temporary Employment, 1990–2014

Percent of total employment (y-axis): 2.5%, 2.0, 1.5, 1.0, 0.5

Year (x-axis): 1990, 1994, 1998, 2002, 2006, 2010, 2014

Source: Bureau of Labor Statistics.

At first glance, the rapid growth of temporary employment since the end of the 2007–2009 recession might seem to follow the same pattern. But this time companies were hiring temporary workers in a weak labor market. With more than three times as many Americans seeking work as there were job openings, companies shouldn't have had any trouble hiring. So why the surge in temp work?

One answer may be the way in which advances in technology have opened up a new breed of services. Manual laborers might still be lining up on street corners, but information technology workers and other professionals were increasingly finding temporary, freelance work through web-based services like the two companies Elance (e-commerce + freelance—get it?) and oDesk, which merged in 2014.

By 2014 Elance-oDesk was serving more than 8 million workers (three-quarters of them outside the United States), twice as many as in 2012. Growth like that indicates the economy may be undergoing a fundamental shift in the way work is structured, one in which temporary arrangements of convenience replace long-term commitment.

QUESTIONS FOR THOUGHT

1. Use the flows shown in Figure 23-7 to explain the role of temporary staffing in the economy.

2. What is the likely effect of improved matching of job-seekers and employers through online services listings on the unemployment rate?

3. What does the fact that temporary staffing fell sharply during the 2008–2009 surge in unemployment suggest about the nature of that surge?

SUMMARY

1. The twin goals of reducing inflation and unemployment are the main concerns of macroeconomic policy.

2. **Employment** is the number of people employed; **unemployment** is the number of people unemployed and actively looking for work. Their sum is equal to the **labor force,** and the **labor force participation rate** is the percentage of the population age 16 or older that is in the labor force.

3. The **unemployment rate,** the percentage of the labor force that is unemployed and actively looking for work, can both overstate and understate the true level of unemployment. It can overstate because it counts as unemployed those who are continuing to search for a job despite having been offered one. It can understate because it ignores frustrated workers, such as **discouraged workers, marginally attached workers,** and the **underemployed.** In addition, the unemployment rate varies greatly among different groups in the population; it is typically higher for younger workers and for workers near retirement age than for workers in their prime working years.

4. The unemployment rate is affected by the business cycle. The unemployment rate generally falls when the growth rate of real GDP is above average and generally increases when the growth rate of real GDP is below average. A **jobless recovery,** a period in which real GDP is growing but unemployment rises, often follows recessions.

5. Job creation and destruction, as well as voluntary job separations, lead to **job search** and **frictional unemployment.** In addition, a variety of factors such as minimum wages, unions, **efficiency wages,** government policies designed to help laid-off workers, and mismatch between employees and employers result in a situation in which there is a surplus of labor at the

market wage rate, creating **structural unemployment.** As a result, the **natural rate of unemployment,** the sum of frictional and structural unemployment, is well above zero, even when jobs are plentiful.

6. The actual unemployment rate is equal to the natural rate of unemployment, the share of unemployment that is independent of the business cycle, plus **cyclical unemployment,** the share of unemployment that depends on fluctuations in the business cycle.

7. The natural rate of unemployment changes over time, largely in response to changes in labor force characteristics, labor market institutions, and government policies.

8. Inflation does not, as many assume, make everyone poorer by raising the level of prices. That's because wages and incomes are adjusted to take into account a rising price level, leaving **real wages** and **real income** unaffected. However, a high inflation rate imposes overall costs on the economy: **shoe-leather costs, menu costs,** and **unit-of-account costs.**

9. Inflation can produce winners and losers within the economy, because long-term contracts are generally written in dollar terms. The **interest rate** specified in a loan is typically a **nominal interest rate,** which differs from the **real interest rate** due to inflation. A higher-than-expected inflation rate is good for borrowers and bad for lenders. A lower-than-expected inflation rate is good for lenders and bad for borrowers.

10. Many believe policies that depress the economy and produce high unemployment are necessary to reduce embedded inflation. Because **disinflation** is very costly, policy makers try to prevent inflation from becoming excessive in the first place.

KEY TERMS

Employment, p. 656
Unemployment, p. 656
Labor force, p. 657
Labor force participation rate, p. 657
Unemployment rate, p. 657
Discouraged workers, p. 658
Marginally attached workers, p. 658
Underemployment, p. 658

Jobless recovery, p. 661
Job search, p. 663
Frictional unemployment, p. 663
Structural unemployment, p. 665
Efficiency wages, p. 667
Natural rate of unemployment, p. 667
Cyclical unemployment, p. 667
Real wage, p. 672

Real income, p. 672
Shoe-leather costs, p. 673
Menu costs, p. 673
Unit-of-account costs, p. 674
Interest rate, p. 675
Nominal interest rate, p. 675
Real interest rate, p. 675
Disinflation, p. 676

PROBLEMS

1. Each month, usually on the first Friday of the month, the Bureau of Labor Statistics releases the Employment Situation Summary for the previous month. Go to www.bls.gov and find the latest report. On the Bureau of Labor Statistics home page, at the top of the page, select the "Subjects" tab, find "Unemployment," and select "National Unemployment Rate." You will find the Employment Situation Summary under "CPS News Releases" on the left-hand side of the page. How does the current unemployment rate compare to the rate one month earlier? How does the current unemployment rate compare to the rate one year earlier?

2. In general, how do changes in the unemployment rate vary with changes in real GDP? After several quarters of a severe recession, explain why we might observe a decrease in the official unemployment rate. Explain why we could see an increase in the official unemployment rate after several quarters of a strong expansion.

3. In each of the following situations, what type of unemployment is Melanie facing?

   a. After completing a complex programming project, Melanie is laid off. Her prospects for a new job requiring similar skills are good, and she has signed up with a programmer placement service. She has passed up offers for low-paying jobs.

   b. When Melanie and her co-workers refused to accept pay cuts, her employer outsourced their programming tasks to workers in another country. This phenomenon is occurring throughout the programming industry.

   c. Due to the current slump, Melanie has been laid off from her programming job. Her employer promises to rehire her when business picks up.

4. Part of the information released in the Employment Situation Summary concerns how long individuals have been unemployed. Go to www.bls.gov to find the latest report. Use the same technique as in Problem 1 to find the Employment Situation Summary. Near the end of the Employment Situation, click on Table A-12, titled "Unemployed persons by duration of unemployment." Use the seasonally adjusted numbers to answer the following questions.

   a. How many workers were unemployed less than 5 weeks? What percentage of all unemployed workers do these workers represent? How do these numbers compare to the previous month's data?

   b. How many workers were unemployed for 27 or more weeks? What percentage of all unemployed workers do these workers represent? How do these numbers compare to the previous month's data?

   c. How long has the average worker been unemployed (average duration, in weeks)? How does this compare to the average for the previous month's data?

   d. Comparing the latest month for which there are data with the previous month, has the problem of long-term unemployment improved or deteriorated?

5. A country's labor force is the sum of the number of employed and unemployed workers. The accompanying table provides data on the size of the labor force and the number of unemployed workers for different regions of the United States.

Region	Labor force (thousands)		Unemployed (thousands)	
	April 2013	April 2014	April 2013	April 2014
Northeast	28,407.2	28,288.9	2,174.4	1,781.3
South	56,787.8	57,016.4	4,089.9	3,363.8
Midwest	34,320.0	34,467.0	2,473.7	2,109.0
West	36,122.2	36,307.3	2,940.8	2,535.7

Source: Bureau of Labor Statistics.

   a. Calculate the number of workers employed in each of the regions in April 2013 and April 2014. Use your answers to calculate the change in the total number of workers employed between April 2013 and April 2014.

   b. For each region, calculate the growth in the labor force from April 2013 to April 2014.

   c. Compute unemployment rates in the different regions of the country in April 2013 and April 2014.

   d. What can you infer about the fall in unemployment rates over this period? Was it caused by a net gain in the number of jobs or by a large fall in the number of people seeking jobs?

6. In which of the following cases is it more likely for efficiency wages to exist? Why?

   a. Jane and her boss work as a team selling ice cream.

   b. Jane sells ice cream without any direct supervision by her boss.

   c. Jane speaks Korean and sells ice cream in a neighborhood in which Korean is the primary language. It is difficult to find another worker who speaks Korean.

7. How will the following changes affect the natural rate of unemployment?

   a. The government reduces the time during which an unemployed worker can receive unemployment benefits.

   b. More teenagers focus on their studies and do not look for jobs until after college.

   c. Greater access to the internet leads both potential employers and potential employees to use the internet to list and find jobs.

   d. Union membership declines.

8. With its tradition of a job for life for most citizens, Japan once had a much lower unemployment rate than that of the United States; from 1960 to 1995, the unemployment rate in Japan exceeded 3% only once. However, since the crash of its stock market in 1989 and slow economic growth in the 1990s, the job-for-life

system has broken down and unemployment rose to more than 5% in 2003.

a. Explain the likely effect of the breakdown of the job-for-life system in Japan on the Japanese natural rate of unemployment.

b. As the accompanying diagram shows, the rate of growth of real GDP picked up in Japan after 2001 and before the global economic crisis of 2007–2009. Explain the likely effect of this increase in real GDP growth on the unemployment rate. Was the likely cause of the change in the unemployment rate during this period a change in the natural rate of unemployment or a change in the cyclical unemployment rate?

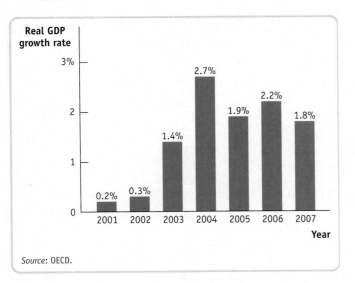

Source: OECD.

9. In the following examples, is inflation creating winners and losers at no net cost to the economy or is inflation imposing a net cost on the economy? If a net cost is being imposed, which type of cost is involved?

a. When inflation is expected to be high, workers get paid more frequently and make more trips to the bank.

b. Lanwei is reimbursed by her company for her work-related travel expenses. Sometimes, however, the company takes a long time to reimburse her. So when inflation is high, she is less willing to travel for her job.

c. Hector Homeowner has a mortgage with a fixed nominal 6% interest rate that he took out five years ago. Over the years, the inflation rate has crept up unexpectedly to its present level of 7%.

d. In response to unexpectedly high inflation, the manager of Cozy Cottages of Cape Cod must reprint and resend expensive color brochures correcting the price of rentals this season.

10. The accompanying diagram shows the interest rate on one-year loans and inflation during 1998–2013 in the economy of Albernia. When would one-year loans have been especially attractive and why?

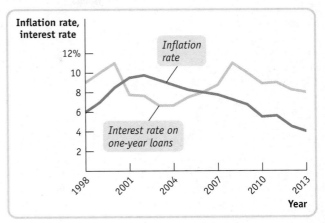

11. The accompanying table provides the inflation rate in the year 2000 and the average inflation rate over the period 2001–2013 for seven different countries.

Country	Inflation rate in 2000	Average inflation rate in 2001–2013
Brazil	7.06%	6.72%
China	0.4	2.34
France	1.83	1.86
Indonesia	3.77	7.56
Japan	−0.78	−0.23
Turkey	55.03	18.79
United States	3.37	2.43

Source: IMF.

a. Given the expected relationship between average inflation and menu costs, rank the countries in descending order of menu costs using average inflation over the period 2001–2013.

b. Rank the countries in order of inflation rates that most favored borrowers with ten-year loans that were taken out in 2000. Assume that the loans were agreed upon with the expectation that the inflation rate for 2001 to 2013 would be the same as the inflation rate in 2000.

c. Did borrowers who took out ten-year loans in Japan gain or lose overall versus lenders? Explain.

12. The accompanying diagram shows the inflation rate in the United Kingdom from 1980 to 2013.

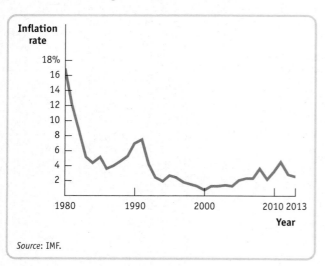

Source: IMF.

a. Between 1980 and 1985, policy makers in the United Kingdom worked to lower the inflation rate. What would you predict happened to unemployment between 1980 and 1985?

b. Policy makers in the United Kingdom react forcefully when the inflation rate rises above a target rate of 2%. Why would it be harmful if inflation rose from 2.6% (the level in 2013) to, say, a level of 5%?

WORK IT OUT

For interactive, step-by-step help in solving the following problem, visit LaunchPad by using the URL on the back cover of this book.

13. There is only one labor market in Profunctia. All workers have the same skills, and all firms hire workers with these skills. Use the accompanying diagram, which shows the supply of and demand for labor, to answer the following questions. Illustrate each answer with a diagram.

a. What is the equilibrium wage rate in Profunctia? At this wage rate, what are the level of employment, the size of the labor force, and the unemployment rate?

b. If the government of Profunctia sets a minimum wage equal to $12, what will be the level of employment, the size of the labor force, and the unemployment rate?

c. If unions bargain with the firms in Profunctia and set a wage rate equal to $14, what will be the level of employment, the size of the labor force, and the unemployment rate?

d. If the concern for retaining workers and encouraging high-quality work leads firms to set a wage rate equal to $16, what will be the level of employment, the size of the labor force, and the unemployment rate?

Long-Run Economic Growth

▶ What You Will Learn in This Chapter

■ Why long-run economic growth is measured as the increase in real GDP per capita, how real GDP per capita has changed over time, and how it varies across countries

■ Why **productivity** is the key to long-run economic growth and how productivity is driven by **physical capital, human capital,** and **technological progress**

■ The factors that explain why long-run growth rates differ so much among countries

■ How growth has varied among several important regions of the world and why the **convergence hypothesis** applies to economically advanced countries

■ The question of **sustainability** and the challenges to growth posed by scarcity of natural resources and environmental degradation

epa european pressphoto agency b.v./Alamy

Rapid, uncontrolled economic growth has resulted in much higher living standards in China but at the cost of very high levels of pollution.

On January 16, 2014, reported the *New York Times,* "Some residents of Beijing woke up with splitting headaches. A curtain of haze had fallen across the city of more than 20 million. It was the first 'airpocalypse' of the year in the Chinese capital and nearby provinces."

As the article suggested, severe air pollution—at levels that make the once-famous smog of Los Angeles (mostly gone now thanks to pollution regulations) seem mild by comparison—has become commonplace in China's cities. This is, it goes without saying, a bad thing, and must be dealt with. But it is a byproduct of a very good thing: China's extraordinary economic growth in the past few decades, which has raised literally hundreds of millions of people out of abject poverty. These newly enriched masses want what everyone wants if they can afford it: better food, better housing, and consumer goods—including, in many cases, cars. As recently as 1999 there were fewer than 15 million motor vehicles in China, barely 1 for every 100 people. By 2012 that number had risen to 240 million, and was still rising fast.

Unfortunately, the growth in China's car population has run ahead of its pollution controls. And the result, combined with the emissions of the country's burgeoning industry, is epochal smog.

Despite its troubling environmental problems, China has obviously made enormous economic strides over the past few decades. Indeed, its recent history is probably the world's most impressive example to date of long-run economic growth—a sustained increase in output per capita. Yet despite its impressive performance, China is currently playing catch-up with economically advanced countries like the United States and Japan. It's still a relatively poor country because these other nations began their own processes of long-run economic growth many decades ago—and in the case of the United States and European countries, more than a century ago.

Many economists have argued that long-run economic growth—why it happens and how to achieve it—is the single most important issue in macroeconomics. In this chapter, we present some facts about long-run growth, look at the factors that economists believe determine the pace at which long-run growth takes place, examine how government policies can help or hinder growth, and address questions about the environmental sustainability of long-run growth.

Comparing Economies Across Time and Space

Before we analyze the sources of long-run economic growth, it's useful to have a sense of just how much the U.S. economy has grown over time and how large the gaps are between wealthy countries like the United States and countries that have yet to achieve comparable growth. So let's take a look at the numbers.

Real GDP per Capita

The key statistic used to track economic growth is *real GDP per capita*—real GDP divided by the population size. We focus on GDP because, as we learned in Chapter 22, GDP measures the total value of an economy's production of final goods and services as well as the income earned in that economy in a given year. We use *real* GDP because we want to separate changes in the quantity of goods and services from the effects of a rising price level. We focus on real GDP *per capita* because we want to isolate the effect of changes in the population. For example, other things equal, an increase in the population lowers the standard of living for the average person—there are now more people to share a given amount of real GDP. An increase in real GDP that only matches an increase in population leaves the average standard of living unchanged.

Although we also learned in Chapter 22 that growth in real GDP per capita should not be a policy goal in and of itself, it does serve as a very useful summary measure of a country's economic progress over time. Figure 24-1 shows real GDP per capita for the United States, India, and China, measured in 1990 dollars, from 1900 to 2010. (We'll talk about India and China in a moment.) The vertical axis is drawn on a logarithmic scale so that equal percent changes in real GDP per capita across countries are the same size in the graph.

To give a sense of how much the U.S. economy grew during the last century, Table 24-1 shows real GDP per capita at selected years, expressed two ways: as a percentage of the 1900 level and as a percentage of the 2010 level. In 1920, the U.S. economy already produced 136% as much per person as it did in 1900. In 2010,

---

FIGURE 24-1 | Economic Growth in the United States, India, and China over the Past Century

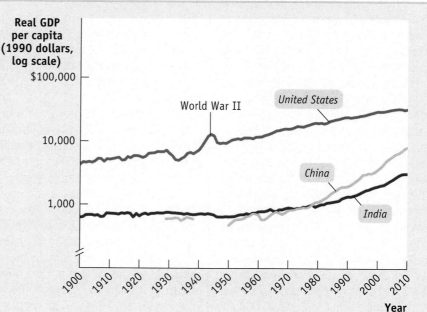

Real GDP per capita from 1900 to 2010, measured in 1990 dollars, is shown for the United States, India, and China. Equal percent changes in real GDP per capita are drawn the same size. As the steeper slopes of the lines representing China and India show, since 1980 India and China had a much higher growth rate than the United States. In 2000, China attained the standard of living achieved in the United States in 1900. In 2010, India was still poorer than the United States was in 1900. (The break in China data from 1940 to 1950 is due to war.)

Sources: Angus Maddison, *Statistics on World Population, GDP, and Per Capita GDP, 1–2008AD,* http://www.ggdc.net/maddison; The Conference Board Total Economy Database™, January 2014, http://www.conference-board.org/data/economydatabase/.

it produced 758% as much per person as it did in 1900, an almost eightfold increase. Alternatively, in 1900 the U.S. economy produced only 13% as much per person as it did in 2010.

The income of the typical family normally grows more or less in proportion to per capita income. For example, a 1% increase in real GDP per capita corresponds, roughly, to a 1% increase in the income of the median or typical family—a family at the center of the income distribution. In 2010, the median American household had an income of about $50,000. Since Table 24-1 tells us that real GDP per capita in 1900 was only 13% of its 2010 level, a typical family in 1900 probably had a purchasing power only 13% as large as the purchasing power of a typical family in 2010. That's around $6,850 in today's dollars, representing a standard of living that we would now consider severe poverty. Today's typical American family, if transported back to the United States of 1900, would feel quite a lot of deprivation.

Yet many people in the world have a standard of living equal to or lower than that of the United States at the beginning of the last century. That's the message about China and India in Figure 24-1: despite dramatic economic growth in China over the last three decades and the less dramatic acceleration of economic growth in India, China has only recently exceeded the standard of living that the United States enjoyed in the early twentieth century, while India is still poorer than the United States was at that time. And much of the world today is poorer than China or India.

You can get a sense of how poor much of the world remains by looking at Figure 24-2, a map of the world in which countries are classified according to their 2013 levels of GDP per capita, in U.S. dollars. As you can see, large parts of the world have very low incomes. Generally speaking, the countries of Europe and North America, as well as a few in the Pacific, have high incomes. The rest of the world, containing most of its population, is dominated by countries with GDP less than $5,000 per capita—and often much less. In fact, today about 50% of the world's people live in countries with a lower standard of living than the United States had a century ago.

TABLE 24-1 U.S. Real GDP per Capita

Year	Percentage of 1900 real GDP per capita	Percentage of 2010 real GDP per capita
1900	100%	13%
1920	136	18
1940	171	23
1980	454	60
2000	696	92
2010	758	100

Sources: Angus Maddison, *Statistics on World Population, GDP, and Per Capita GDP, 1–2008AD,* "The First Update of the Madison Project: Reestimating Growth Before 1820" http://www.ggdc.net/maddison; Bureau of Economic Analysis.

FIGURE 24-2 Incomes Around the World, 2013
Although the countries of Europe and North America—along with a few in the Pacific—have high incomes, much of the world is still very poor. Today, about 50% of the world's population lives in countries with a lower standard of living than the United States had a century ago.
Source: International Monetary Fund.

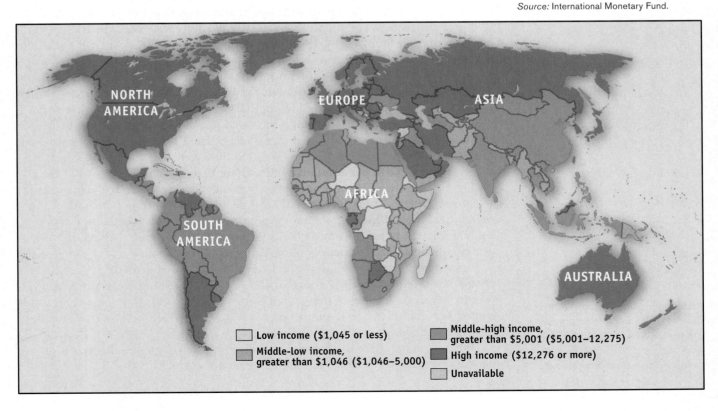

PITFALLS

CHANGE IN LEVELS VERSUS RATE OF CHANGE

When studying economic growth, it's vitally important to understand the difference between a change in level and a rate of change. When we say that real GDP "grew," we mean that the level of real GDP increased. For example, we might say that U.S. real GDP grew during 2013 by $297 billion.

If we knew the level of U.S. real GDP in 2012, we could also represent the amount of 2013 growth in terms of a rate of change. For example, if U.S. real GDP in 2012 had been $15,470 billion, then U.S. real GDP in 2013 would have been $15,470 billion + $297 billion = $15,767 billion. We could calculate the rate of change, or the growth rate, of U.S. real GDP during 2013 as: (($15,767 billion – $15,470 billion)/$15,470 billion) × 100 = $297 billion/$15,470 billion) × 100 = 1.92%. Statements about economic growth over a period of years almost always refer to changes in the growth rate.

When talking about growth or growth rates, economists often use phrases that appear to mix the two concepts and so can be confusing. For example, when we say that "U.S. growth fell during the 1970s," we are really saying that the U.S. growth rate of real GDP was lower in the 1970s in comparison to the 1960s. When we say that "growth accelerated during the early 1990s," we are saying that the growth rate increased year after year in the early 1990s—for example, going from 3% to 3.5% to 4%.

Growth Rates

How did the United States manage to produce over eight times as much per person in 2013 than in 1900? A little bit at a time. Long-run economic growth is normally a gradual process in which real GDP per capita grows at most a few percent per year. From 1900 to 2013, real GDP per capita in the United States increased an average of 1.9% each year.

To have a sense of the relationship between the annual growth rate of real GDP per capita and the long-run change in real GDP per capita, it's helpful to keep in mind the **Rule of 70,** a mathematical formula that tells us how long it takes real GDP per capita, or any other variable that grows gradually over time, to double. The approximate answer is:

$$\textbf{(24-1)} \quad \text{Number of years for variable to double} = \frac{70}{\text{Annual growth rate of variable}}$$

(Note that the Rule of 70 can only be applied to a positive growth rate.) So if real GDP per capita grows at 1% per year, it will take 70 years to double. If it grows at 2% per year, it will take only 35 years to double. In fact, U.S. real GDP per capita rose on average 1.9% per year over the last century.

Applying the Rule of 70 to this information implies that it should have taken 37 years for real GDP per capita to double; it would have taken 111 years—three periods of 37 years each—for U.S. real GDP per capita to double three times. That is, the Rule of 70 implies that over the course of 111 years, U.S. real GDP per capita should have increased by a factor of 2 × 2 × 2 = 8. And this does turn out to be a pretty good approximation of reality. Between 1899 and 2010—a period of 111 years—real GDP per capita rose just about eightfold.

Figure 24-3 shows the average annual rate of growth of real GDP per capita for selected countries from 1980 to 2013. Some countries were notable success stories: for example, China, though still quite poor, has made spectacular progress. India, although not matching China's performance, has also achieved impressive growth, as discussed in the following Economics in Action.

Some countries, though, have had very disappointing growth. Argentina was once considered a wealthy nation. In the early years of the twentieth century, it was in the same league as the United States and Canada. But since then it has lagged far behind more dynamic economies. And still others, like Zimbabwe, have slid backward.

What explains these differences in growth rates? To answer that question, we need to examine the sources of long-run economic growth.

According to the **Rule of 70,** the time it takes a variable that grows gradually over time to double is approximately 70 divided by that variable's annual growth rate.

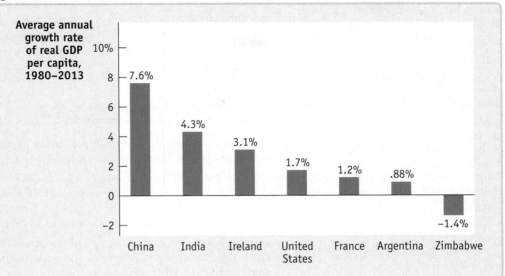

| FIGURE **24-3** | Comparing Recent Growth Rates |

The average annual rate of growth of real GDP per capita from 1980 to 2013 is shown here for selected countries. China and, to a lesser extent, India and Ireland achieved impressive growth. The United States and France had moderate growth. Once considered an economically advanced country, Argentina had more sluggish growth. Still others, such as Zimbabwe, slid backward.

Source: The Conference Board Total Economy Database™, January 2014, http://www.conference-board.org/data/economydatabase

ECONOMICS ▶ in Action

India Takes Off

India achieved independence from Great Britain in 1947, becoming the world's most populous democracy—a status it has maintained to this day. For more than three decades after independence, however, this happy political story was partly overshadowed by economic disappointment. Despite ambitious economic development plans, India's performance was consistently sluggish. In 1980, India's real GDP per capita was only about 50% higher than it had been in 1947. The gap between Indian living standards and those in wealthy countries like the United States had been growing rather than shrinking.

Since then, however, India has done much better. As Figure 24-3 shows, real GDP per capita has grown at an average rate of 4.3% a year, more than tripling between 1980 and 2013. India now has a large and rapidly growing middle class.

What went right in India after 1980? Many economists point to policy reforms. For decades after independence, India had a tightly controlled, highly regulated economy. Today, things are very different: a series of reforms opened the economy to international trade and freed up domestic competition. Some economists, however, argue that this can't be the main story because the big policy reforms weren't adopted until 1991, yet growth accelerated around 1980.

Regardless of the explanation, India's economic rise has transformed it into a major new economic power—and allowed hundreds of millions of people to have a much better life, better than their grandparents could have dreamed.

The big question now is whether this growth can continue. Skeptics argue that there are important bottlenecks in the Indian economy that may constrain

India's high rate of economic growth since 1980 has raised living standards and led to the emergence of a rapidly growing middle class.

future growth. They point in particular to the still low education level of much of India's population and inadequate infrastructure—that is, the poor quality and limited capacity of the country's roads, railroads, power supplies, and health and sanitation infrastructure. Pollution is a severe and growing problem as well. But India's economy has defied the skeptics for several decades and the hope is that it can continue doing so.

Check Your Understanding   24-1

1. Why do economists use real GDP per capita to measure economic progress rather than some other measure, such as nominal GDP per capita or real GDP?

2. Apply the Rule of 70 to the data in Figure 24-3 to determine how long it will take each of the countries listed there (except Zimbabwe) to double its real GDP per capita. Would India's real GDP per capita exceed that of the United States in the future if growth rates remain as shown in Figure 24-3? Why or why not?

3. Although China and India currently have growth rates much higher than the U.S. growth rate, the typical Chinese or Indian household is far poorer than the typical American household. Explain why.

Solutions appear at back of book.

The Sources of Long-Run Growth

Long-run economic growth depends almost entirely on one ingredient: rising *productivity*. However, a number of factors affect the growth of productivity. Let's look first at why productivity is the key ingredient and then examine what affects it.

The Crucial Importance of Productivity

Sustained economic growth occurs only when the amount of output produced by the average worker increases steadily. The term **labor productivity,** or **productivity** for short, is used to refer either to output per worker or, in some cases, to output per hour. (The number of hours worked by an average worker differs to some extent across countries, although this isn't an important factor in the difference between living standards in, say, India and the United States.) In this book we'll focus on output per worker. For the economy as a whole, productivity—output per worker—is simply real GDP divided by the number of people working.

You might wonder why we say that higher productivity is the only source of long-run growth. Can't an economy also increase its real GDP per capita by putting more of the population to work? The answer is, yes, but . . . . For short periods of time, an economy can experience a burst of growth in output per capita by putting a higher percentage of the population to work. That happened in the United States during World War II, when millions of women who previously worked only in the home entered the paid workforce. The percentage of adult civilians employed outside the home rose from 50% in 1941 to 58% in 1944, and you can see the resulting bump in real GDP per capita during those years in Figure 24-1.

Over the longer run, however, the rate of employment growth is never very different from the rate of population growth. Over the course of the twentieth century, for example, the population of the United States rose at an average rate of 1.3% per year and employment rose 1.5% per year. Real GDP per capita rose 1.9% per year; of that, 1.7%—that is, almost 90% of the total—was the result of rising productivity. In general, overall real GDP can grow because of population growth, but any large increase in real GDP *per capita* must be the result of increased output *per worker*. That is, it must be due to higher productivity.

So increased productivity is the key to long-run economic growth. But what leads to higher productivity?

Labor productivity, often referred to simply as **productivity,** is output per worker.

Explaining Growth in Productivity

There are three main reasons why the average U.S. worker today produces far more than his or her counterpart a century ago. First, the modern worker has far more *physical capital,* such as machinery and office space, to work with. Second, the modern worker is much better educated and so possesses much more *human capital.* Finally, modern firms have the advantage of a century's accumulation of technical advancements reflecting a great deal of *technological progress.*

Let's look at each of these factors in turn.

Increase in Physical Capital Economists define **physical capital** as manufactured resources such as buildings and machines. Physical capital makes workers more productive. For example, a worker operating a backhoe can dig a lot more feet of trench per day than one equipped only with a shovel.

The average U.S. private-sector worker today is backed up by more than $150,000 worth of physical capital—far more than a U.S. worker had 100 years ago and far more than the average worker in most other countries has today.

Increase in Human Capital It's not enough for a worker to have good equipment—he or she must also know what to do with it. **Human capital** refers to the improvement in labor created by the education and knowledge embodied in the workforce.

The human capital of the United States has increased dramatically over the past century. A century ago, although most Americans were able to read and write, very few had an extensive education. In 1910, only 13.5% of Americans over 25 had graduated from high school and only 3% had four-year college degrees. By 2010, the percentages were 87% and 30%, respectively. It would be impossible to run today's economy with a population as poorly educated as that of a century ago.

Analyses based on *growth accounting,* described later in this chapter, suggest that education—and its effect on productivity—is an even more important determinant of growth than increases in physical capital.

Technological Progress Probably the most important driver of productivity growth is **technological progress,** which is broadly defined as an advance in the technical means of the production of goods and services. We'll see shortly how economists measure the impact of technology on growth.

Workers today are able to produce more than those in the past, even with the same amount of physical and human capital, because technology has advanced over time. It's important to realize that economically important technological progress need not be flashy or rely on cutting-edge science. Historians have noted that past economic growth has been driven not only by major inventions, such as the railroad or the semiconductor chip, but also by thousands of modest innovations, such as the flat-bottomed paper bag, patented in 1870, which made packing groceries and many other goods much easier, and the Post-it® note, introduced in 1981, which has had surprisingly large benefits for office productivity. Experts attribute much of the productivity surge that took place in the United States late in the twentieth century to new technology adopted by service-producing companies like Walmart rather than to high-technology companies.

Accounting for Growth: The Aggregate Production Function

Productivity is higher, other things equal, when workers are equipped with more physical capital, more human capital, better technology, or any combination of the three. But can we put numbers to these effects? To do this, economists make use of estimates of the **aggregate production function,** which shows how productivity depends on the quantities of physical capital per worker and human capital per worker as well as the state of technology.

Physical capital consists of human-made resources such as buildings and machines.

Human capital is the improvement in labor created by the education and knowledge embodied in the workforce.

Technological progress is an advance in the technical means of the production of goods and services.

The **aggregate production function** is a hypothetical function that shows how productivity (real GDP per worker) depends on the quantities of physical capital per worker and human capital per worker as well as the state of technology.

An aggregate production function exhibits **diminishing returns to physical capital** when, holding the amount of human capital per worker and the state of technology fixed, each successive increase in the amount of physical capital per worker leads to a smaller increase in productivity.

In general, all three factors tend to rise over time, as workers are equipped with more machinery, receive more education, and benefit from technological advances. What the aggregate production function does is allow economists to disentangle the effects of these three factors on overall productivity.

An example of an aggregate production function applied to real data comes from a comparative study of Chinese and Indian economic growth by the economists Barry Bosworth and Susan Collins of the Brookings Institution. They used the following aggregate production function:

GDP per worker = $T \times$ (Physical capital per worker)$^{0.4} \times$ (Human capital per worker)$^{0.6}$

where T represented an estimate of the level of technology and they assumed that each year of education raises workers' human capital by 7%. Using this function, they tried to explain why China grew faster than India between 1978 and 2004. About half the difference, they found, was due to China's higher levels of investment spending, which raised its level of physical capital per worker faster than India's. The other half was due to faster Chinese technological progress.

In analyzing historical economic growth, economists have discovered a crucial fact about the estimated aggregate production function: it exhibits **diminishing returns to physical capital.** That is, when the amount of human capital per worker and the state of technology are held fixed, each successive increase in the amount of physical capital per worker leads to a smaller increase in productivity.

Figure 24-4 and the table to its right give a hypothetical example of how the level of physical capital per worker might affect the level of real GDP per worker, holding human capital per worker and the state of technology fixed. In this example, we measure the quantity of physical capital in dollars.

FIGURE **24-4**   **Physical Capital and Productivity**

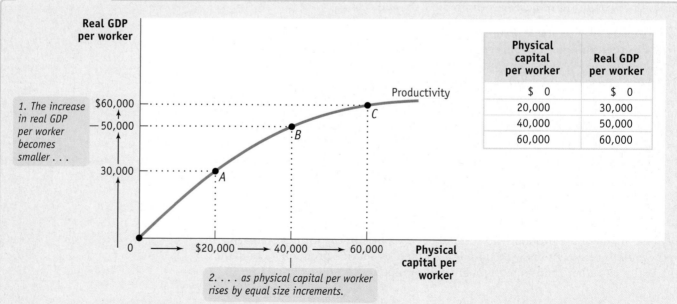

Physical capital per worker	Real GDP per worker
$ 0	$ 0
20,000	30,000
40,000	50,000
60,000	60,000

1. The increase in real GDP per worker becomes smaller . . .

2. . . . as physical capital per worker rises by equal size increments.

The aggregate production function shows how, in this case, holding human capital per worker and technology fixed, productivity increases as physical capital per worker rises. Other things equal, a greater quantity of physical capital per worker leads to higher real GDP per worker but is subject to diminishing returns: each successive addition to physical capital per worker produces a smaller increase in productivity. Starting at the origin, 0, a $20,000 increase in physical capital per worker leads to an increase in real GDP per worker of $30,000, indicated by point *A*. Starting from point *A*, another $20,000 increase in physical capital per worker leads to an increase in real GDP per worker but only of $20,000, indicated by point *B*. Finally, a third $20,000 increase in physical capital per worker leads to only a $10,000 increase in real GDP per worker, indicated by point *C*.

To see why the relationship between physical capital per worker and productivity exhibits diminishing returns, think about how having farm equipment affects the productivity of farmworkers. A little bit of equipment makes a big difference: a worker equipped with a tractor can do much more than a worker without one. And a worker using more expensive equipment will, other things equal, be more productive: a worker with a $40,000 tractor will normally be able to cultivate more farmland in a given amount of time than a worker with a $20,000 tractor because the more expensive machine will be more powerful, perform more tasks, or both.

But will a worker with a $40,000 tractor, holding human capital and technology constant, be twice as productive as a worker with a $20,000 tractor? Probably not: there's a huge difference between not having a tractor at all and having even an inexpensive tractor; there's much less difference between having an inexpensive tractor and having a better tractor. And we can be sure that a worker with a $200,000 tractor won't be 10 times as productive: a tractor can be improved only so much. Because the same is true of other kinds of equipment, the aggregate production function shows diminishing returns to physical capital.

Diminishing returns to physical capital imply a relationship between physical capital per worker and output per worker like the one shown in Figure 24-4. As the productivity curve for physical capital and the accompanying table illustrate, more physical capital per worker leads to more output per worker. But each $20,000 increment in physical capital per worker adds less to productivity.

As you can see from the table, there is a big payoff for the first $20,000 of physical capital: real GDP per worker rises by $30,000. The second $20,000 of physical capital also raises productivity, but not by as much: real GDP per worker goes up by only $20,000. The third $20,000 of physical capital raises real GDP per worker by only $10,000. By comparing points along the curve you can also see that as physical capital per worker rises, output per worker also rises—but at a diminishing rate. Going from the origin at 0 to point A, a $20,000 increase in physical capital per worker, leads to an increase of $30,000 in real GDP per worker. Going from point A to point B, a second $20,000 increase in physical capital per worker, leads to an increase of only $20,000 in real GDP per worker. And from point B to point C, a $20,000 increase in physical capital per worker, increased real GDP per worker by only $10,000.

It's important to realize that diminishing returns to physical capital is an "other things equal" phenomenon: additional amounts of physical capital are less productive *when the amount of human capital per worker and the technology are held fixed.* Diminishing returns may disappear if we increase the amount of human capital per worker, or improve the technology, or both at the same time the amount of physical capital per worker is increased.

For example, a worker with a $40,000 tractor who has also been trained in the most advanced cultivation techniques may in fact be more than twice as productive as a worker with only a $20,000 tractor and no additional human capital. But diminishing returns to any one input—regardless of whether it is physical capital, human capital, or number of workers—is a pervasive characteristic of production. Typical estimates suggest that in practice a 1% increase in the quantity of physical capital per worker increases output per worker by only one-third of 1%, or 0.33%.

In practice, all the factors contributing to higher productivity rise during the course of economic growth: both physical capital and human capital per worker increase, and technology advances as well. To disentangle the effects of these factors, economists use **growth accounting,** which estimates the contribution of each major factor in the aggregate production function to economic growth. For example, suppose the following are true:

- The amount of physical capital per worker grows 3% per year.
- According to estimates of the aggregate production function, each 1% rise in physical capital per worker, holding human capital and technology constant, raises output per worker by one-third of 1%, or 0.33%.

Growth accounting estimates the contribution of each major factor in the aggregate production function to economic growth.

PITFALLS

IT MAY BE DIMINISHED . . . BUT IT'S STILL POSITIVE

It's important to understand what diminishing returns to physical capital means and what it doesn't mean. As we've already explained, it's an "other things equal" statement: holding the amount of human capital per worker and the technology fixed, each successive increase in the amount of physical capital per worker results in a smaller increase in real GDP per worker. But this doesn't mean that real GDP per worker eventually falls as more and more physical capital is added. It's just that the *increase* in real GDP per worker gets smaller and smaller, albeit remaining at or above zero. So an increase in physical capital per worker will never reduce productivity. But due to diminishing returns, at some point increasing the amount of physical capital per worker no longer produces an economic payoff: at some point the increase in output is so small that it is not worth the cost of the additional physical capital.

In that case, we would estimate that growing physical capital per worker is responsible for 3% × 0.33 = 1 percentage point of productivity growth per year. A similar but more complex procedure is used to estimate the effects of growing human capital. The procedure is more complex because there aren't simple dollar measures of the quantity of human capital.

Growth accounting allows us to calculate the effects of greater physical and human capital on economic growth. But how can we estimate the effects of technological progress? We do so by estimating what is left over after the effects of physical and human capital have been taken into account. For example, let's imagine that there was no increase in human capital per worker so that we can focus on changes in physical capital and in technology.

In Figure 24-5, the lower curve shows the same hypothetical relationship between physical capital per worker and output per worker shown in Figure 24-4. Let's assume that this was the relationship given the technology available in 1940.

FIGURE 24-5 | Technological Progress and Productivity Growth

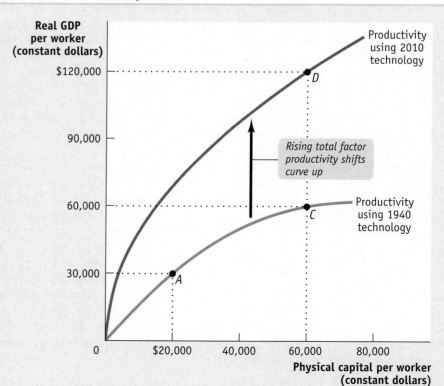

Technological progress raises productivity at any given level of physical capital per worker, and therefore shifts the aggregate production function upward. Here we hold human capital per worker fixed. We assume that the lower curve (the same curve as in Figure 24-4) reflects technology in 1940 and the upper curve reflects technology in 2010. Holding technology and human capital fixed, tripling physical capital per worker from $20,000 to $60,000 leads to a doubling of real GDP per worker, from $30,000 to $60,000. This is shown by the movement from point A to point C, reflecting an approximately 1% per year rise in real GDP per worker. In reality, technological progress raised productivity at any given level of physical capital—shown here by the upward shift of the curve— and the actual rise in real GDP per worker is shown by the movement from point A to point D. Real GDP per worker grew 2% per year, leading to a quadrupling during the period. The extra 1% in growth of real GDP per worker is due to higher total factor productivity.

The upper curve also shows a relationship between physical capital per worker and productivity, but this time given the technology available in 2010. (We've chosen a 70-year stretch to allow us to use the Rule of 70.) The 2010 curve is shifted up compared to the 1940 curve because technologies developed over the previous 70 years make it possible to produce more output for a given amount of physical capital per worker than was possible with the technology available in 1940. (Note that the two curves are measured in constant dollars.)

Total factor productivity is the amount of output that can be achieved with a given amount of factor inputs.

Let's assume that between 1940 and 2010 the amount of physical capital per worker rose from $20,000 to $60,000. If this increase in physical capital per worker had taken place without any technological progress, the economy would have moved from *A* to *C:* output per worker would have risen, but only from $30,000 to $60,000, or 1% per year (using the Rule of 70 tells us that a 1% growth rate over 70 years doubles output). In fact, however, the economy moved from *A* to *D:* output rose from $30,000 to $120,000, or 2% per year. There was an increase in both physical capital per worker and technological progress, which shifted the aggregate production function.

In this case, 50% of the annual 2% increase in productivity—that is, 1% in annual productivity growth—is due to higher **total factor productivity,** the amount of output that can be produced with a given amount of factor inputs. So when total factor productivity increases, the economy can produce more output with the same quantity of physical capital, human capital, and labor.

Most estimates find that increases in total factor productivity are central to a country's economic growth. We believe that observed increases in total factor productivity in fact measure the economic effects of technological progress. All of this implies that technological change is crucial to economic growth.

The Bureau of Labor Statistics estimates the growth rate of both labor productivity and total factor productivity for nonfarm business in the United States. According to the Bureau's estimates, over the period from 1948 to 2010 American labor productivity rose 2.3% per year. Only 49% of that rise is explained by increases in physical and human capital per worker; the rest is explained by rising total factor productivity—that is, by technological progress.

What About Natural Resources?

In our discussion so far, we haven't mentioned natural resources, which certainly have an effect on productivity. Other things equal, countries that are abundant in valuable natural resources, such as highly fertile land or rich mineral deposits, have higher real GDP per capita than less fortunate countries. The most obvious modern example is the Middle East, where enormous oil deposits have made a few sparsely populated countries very rich. For example, Kuwait has about the same level of real GDP per capita as Germany, but Kuwait's wealth is based on oil, not manufacturing, the source of Germany's high output per worker.

But other things are often not equal. In the modern world, natural resources are a much less important determinant of productivity than human or physical capital for the great majority of countries. For example, some nations with very high real GDP per capita, such as Japan, have very few natural resources. Some resource-rich nations, such as Nigeria (which has sizable oil deposits), are very poor.

Historically, natural resources played a much more prominent role in determining productivity. In the nineteenth century, the countries with the highest real GDP per capita were those abundant in rich farmland and mineral deposits: the United States, Canada, Argentina, and Australia. As a consequence, natural resources figured prominently in the development of economic thought.

In a famous book published in 1798, *An Essay on the Principle of Population,* the English economist Thomas Malthus made the fixed quantity of land in the world the basis of a pessimistic prediction about future productivity. As population grew, he pointed out, the amount of land per worker would decline. And this, other things equal, would cause productivity to fall.

His view, in fact, was that improvements in technology or increases in physical capital would lead only to temporary improvements in productivity because they would always be offset by the pressure of rising population and more workers on the supply of land. In the long run, he concluded, the great majority of people were condemned to living on the edge of starvation. Only then would death rates be high enough and birth rates low enough to prevent rapid population growth from outstripping productivity growth.

It hasn't turned out that way, although many historians believe that Malthus's prediction of falling or stagnant productivity was valid for much of human history. Population pressure probably did prevent large productivity increases until the eighteenth century. But in the time since Malthus wrote his book, any negative effects on productivity from population growth have been far outweighed by other, positive factors—advances in technology, increases in human and physical capital, and the opening up of enormous amounts of cultivable land in the New World.

It remains true, however, that we live on a finite planet, with limited supplies of resources such as oil and limited ability to absorb environmental damage. We address the concerns these limitations pose for economic growth in the final section of this chapter.

ECONOMICS ▶ *in Action*

Is the End of Economic Growth in Sight?

In 2012 Robert Gordon of Northwestern University, an influential macroeconomist and economic historian, created a stir with a paper suggesting that the best days of long-run economic growth are behind us. Technological innovation continues, of course. But Gordon made the case that the payoff from recent innovations will be limited, especially compared with the great innovations of the past.

Gordon made his case, in part, by contrasting recent innovations—which have mainly centered around information technology, from computers and smartphones to the internet—with the great innovations that took place in the late-nineteenth century. He argued that these late-nineteenth-century innovations, often described as the "Second Industrial Revolution," continued to drive growth for most of the twentieth century. According to Gordon, there were five big innovations:

1. Electricity
2. The internal combustion engine
3. Running water and central heating
4. Modern chemistry
5. Mass communication, movies, and telephones

How does the information technology revolution stack up against these changes? In Gordon's account, it's less important than any one of the five. As he likes to put it, which would you rather give up—the internet, or indoor plumbing?

Gordon also argues that the numbers bear him out. Figure 24-6 illustrates his argument. The blue and red lines show the historical rate of growth of real GDP per capita in the

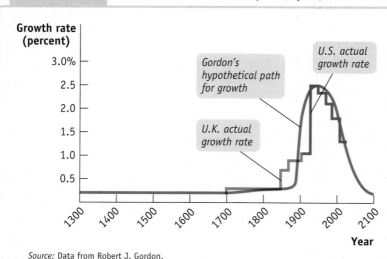

FIGURE **24-6** Is the End of Economic Growth Near? A Look at Growth of Real GDP per Capita, 1300–2100

Source: Data from Robert J. Gordon.

world's "technological leaders"—Britain (red) before 1906, the United States (blue) thereafter. The green line shows a "smoothed" version of this history, which Gordon sees as a huge but temporary hump, and then extrapolates this pattern forward. As he says, growth rates got higher and higher until around the 1950s, but have fallen since then—and he argues that they will keep on falling, and that growth will eventually come to a virtual halt.

Is Gordon right? The most persuasive counterargument says that we have only just begun to see the payoff of modern technologies. As a recent book by MIT's Eric Brynjolfsson and Andrew McAfee, *Race Against the Machine*, points out, in the past few years innovative technologies addressing a number of seemingly intractable problems have reached the state where they're either already on the market or ready to go—these include useful speech recognition, machine translation, self-driving vehicles, and more. So you can make the case that we are on the cusp of truly transformative technological change right now.

Who's right? As Yogi Berra said, "It's tough to make predictions, especially about the future." What's clear, however, is that both sides are asking the right question, because technology is, ultimately, the main driver of long-run economic growth.

Check Your Understanding	**24-2**

1. Predict the effect of each of the following events on the growth rate of productivity.
   a. The amounts of physical and human capital per worker are unchanged, but there is significant technological progress.
   b. The amount of physical capital per worker grows at a steady pace, but the level of human capital per worker and technology are unchanged.

2. Output in the economy of Erewhon has grown 3% per year over the past 30 years. The labor force has grown at 1% per year, and the quantity of physical capital has grown at 4% per year. The average education level hasn't changed. Estimates by economists say that each 1% increase in physical capital per worker, other things equal, raises productivity by 0.3%. (*Hint:* % change in (X/Y) = % change in X − % change in Y.)
   a. How fast has productivity in Erewhon grown?
   b. How fast has physical capital per worker grown?
   c. How much has growing physical capital per worker contributed to productivity growth? What percentage of productivity growth is that?
   d. How much has technological progress contributed to productivity growth? What percentage of productivity growth is that?

3. Multinomics, Inc., is a large company with many offices around the country. It has just adopted a new computer system that will affect virtually every function performed within the company. Why might a period of time pass before employees' productivity is improved by the new computer system? Why might there be a temporary decrease in employees' productivity?

Solutions appear at back of book.

Why Growth Rates Differ

In 1820, according to estimates by the economic historian Angus Maddison, Mexico had somewhat higher real GDP per capita than Japan. Today, Japan has higher real GDP per capita than most European nations and Mexico is a poor country, though by no means among the poorest. The difference? Over the long run—since 1820—real GDP per capita grew at 1.9% per year in Japan but at only 1.3% per year in Mexico.

As this example illustrates, even small differences in growth rates have large consequences over the long run. So why do growth rates differ across countries and across periods of time?

Explaining Differences in Growth Rates

As one might expect, economies with rapid growth tend to be economies that add physical capital, increase their human capital, or experience rapid technological progress. Striking economic success stories, like Japan in the 1950s and 1960s or China today, tend to be countries that do all three: rapidly add to their physical capital through high savings and investment spending, upgrade their educational level, and make fast technological progress. Evidence also points to the importance of government policies, property rights, political stability, and good governance in fostering the sources of growth.

Savings and Investment Spending One reason for differences in growth rates between countries is that some countries are increasing their stock of physical capital much more rapidly than others, through high rates of investment spending. In the 1960s, Japan was the fastest-growing major economy; it also spent a much higher share of its GDP on investment goods than did other major economies. Today, China is the fastest-growing major economy, and it similarly spends a very large share of its GDP on investment goods. In 2014, investment spending was 48% of China's GDP, compared with only 20% in the United States.

Where does the money for high investment spending come from? From savings. In the next chapter we'll analyze how financial markets channel savings into investment spending. For now, however, the key point is that investment spending must be paid for either out of savings from domestic households or by savings from foreign households—that is, an inflow of foreign capital.

Foreign capital has played an important role in the long-run economic growth of some countries, including the United States, which relied heavily on foreign funds during its early industrialization. For the most part, however, countries that invest a large share of their GDP are able to do so because they have high domestic savings. In fact, China in 2014 saved an even higher percentage of its GDP than it invested at home. The extra savings were invested abroad, largely in the United States.

One reason for differences in growth rates, then, is that countries add different amounts to their stocks of physical capital because they have different rates of savings and investment spending.

Education Just as countries differ substantially in the rate at which they add to their physical capital, there have been large differences in the rate at which countries add to their human capital through education.

A case in point is the comparison between Argentina and China. In both countries the average educational level has risen steadily over time, but it has risen much faster in China. Figure 24-7 shows the average years of education of adults in China, which we have highlighted as a spectacular example of long-run growth, and in Argentina, a country whose growth has been disappointing. Compared to China, sixty years ago, Argentina had a much more educated population, while many Chinese were still illiterate. Today, the average educational level in China is still slightly below that in Argentina—but that's mainly because there are still many elderly adults who never received basic education. In terms of secondary and tertiary education, China has outstripped once-rich Argentina.

Research and Development The advance of technology is a key force behind economic growth. What drives technological progress?

Scientific advances make new technologies possible. To take the most spectacular example in today's world, the semiconductor chip—which is the basis for all modern information technology—could not have been developed without the theory of quantum mechanics in physics.

But science alone is not enough: scientific knowledge must be translated into useful products and processes. And that often requires devoting a lot of resources

FIGURE **24-7** China's Students Are Catching Up

In both China and Argentina, the average educational level—measured by the number of years the average adult aged 25 or older has spent in school—has risen over time. Although China is still lagging behind Argentina, it is catching up—and China's success at adding human capital is one key to its spectacular long-run growth.

Source: Robert Barro and Jong-Wha Lee, "A New Data Set of Educational Attainment in the World, 1950–2010," NBER Working Paper No. 15902 (April 2010), http://www.barrolee.com.

to **research and development, or R&D,** spending to create new technologies and apply them to practical use.

Although some research and development is conducted by governments, much R&D is paid for by the private sector, as discussed below. The United States became the world's leading economy in large part because American businesses were among the first to make systematic research and development a part of their operations. The upcoming For Inquiring Minds describes how Thomas Edison created the first modern industrial research laboratory.

Developing new technology is one thing; applying it is another. There have often been notable differences in the pace at which different countries take advantage of new technologies. For example, as the following Global Comparison shows, since 2000, Italy has suffered a significant decline in its total factor productivity, while the United States and Germany have powered ahead. The sources of these national differences are the subject of a great deal of economic research.

> **Research and development,** or **R&D,** is spending to create and implement new technologies.

FOR INQUIRING MINDS | Inventing R&D

Thomas Edison is best known as the inventor of the lightbulb and the phonograph. But his biggest invention may surprise you: he invented research and development.

Before Edison's time, there had, of course, been many inventors. Some of them worked in teams. But in 1875 Edison created something new: his Menlo Park, New Jersey, laboratory. It employed 25 men full time to generate new products and processes for business. In other words, he did not set out to pursue a particular idea and then cash in. He created an organization whose purpose was to create new ideas year after year.

Edison's Menlo Park lab is now a museum. "To name a few of

Edison in his lab in 1888 with a work in progress: the phonograph.

the products that were developed in Menlo Park," says the museum's website, "we can list the following: the carbon button mouthpiece for the telephone, the phonograph, the incandescent lightbulb and the electrical distribution system, the electric train, ore separation, the Edison effect bulb, early experiments in wireless, the grasshopper telegraph, and improvements in telegraphic transmission."

You could say that before Edison's lab, technology just sort of happened: people came up with ideas, but businesses didn't plan to make continuous technological progress. Now R&D operations, often much bigger than Edison's original team, are standard practice throughout the business world. ∎

GLOBAL COMPARISION | What's the Matter with Italy?

In the preceding Economics in Action, we described the ongoing debate over the state of technological progress. Will information technology lead to sustained growth, or is it already past its prime? Nobody really knows. One thing does seem clear, however: some countries have been much more successful at making use of new technologies than others.

In the early stages of the information technology, or IT, revolution, it seemed that the United States was pulling ahead of Europe. That's less clear now: some European countries have moved forward rapidly in broadband, the wireless internet, and more. But one major European nation is clearly lagging on all fronts: Italy.

The accompanying figure shows estimates of total factor productivity growth since 2000 in three countries: the United States, Germany (Europe's largest economy), and Italy. The United States and Germany have been roughly keeping pace. But Italy seems, remarkably, to have actually been slipping backwards.

This may be, in part, a consequence of the continuing economic slump in Europe. But researchers studying Italian business argue that a variety of institutional factors, ranging from rigid labor markets to poor management, have prevented Italy

from taking advantage of the opportunities new technology has to offer.

It's a troubling picture, and one that surely should be addressed with a variety of economic reforms. Unfortunately, Italy's troubles aren't just economic: it also suffers from chronic political weakness, which has left successive governments with little ability to take strong action on any front.

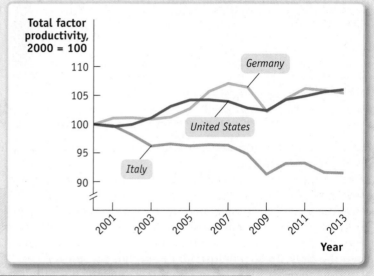

Source: The Conference Board Total Economy Database™, January 2014, http://www.conference-board.org/data/economydatabase/.

The Role of Government in Promoting Economic Growth

Governments can play an important role in promoting—or blocking—all three sources of long-term economic growth: physical capital, human capital, and technological progress. They can either affect growth directly through subsidies to factors that enhance growth, or by creating an environment that either fosters or hinders growth.

Government Policies Government policies can increase the economy's growth rate through four main channels.

1. GOVERNMENT SUBSIDIES TO INFRASTRUCTURE Governments play an important direct role in building **infrastructure:** roads, power lines, ports, information networks, and other large-scale physical capital projects that provide a foundation for economic activity. Although some infrastructure is provided by private companies, much of it is either provided by the government or requires a great deal of government regulation and support. Ireland is often cited as an example of the importance of government-provided infrastructure. After the government invested in an excellent telecommunications infrastructure in the 1980s, Ireland became a favored location for high-technology companies from abroad and its economy took off in the 1990s.

Poor infrastructure, such as a power grid that frequently fails and cuts off electricity, is a major obstacle to economic growth in many countries. To provide good infrastructure, an economy must not only be able to afford it, but it must also have the political discipline to maintain it.

Perhaps the most crucial infrastructure is something we, in an advanced country, rarely think about: basic public health measures in the form of a clean

Roads, power lines, ports, information networks, and other underpinnings for economic activity are known as **infrastructure.**

water supply and disease control. As we'll see in the next section, poor health infrastructure is a major obstacle to economic growth in poor countries, especially those in Africa.

2. GOVERNMENT SUBSIDIES TO EDUCATION In contrast to physical capital, which is mainly created by private investment spending, much of an economy's human capital is the result of government spending on education. Government pays for the great bulk of primary and secondary education. And it pays for a significant share of higher education: 75% of students attend public colleges and universities, and government significantly subsidizes research performed at private colleges and universities. As a result, differences in the rate at which countries add to their human capital largely reflect government policy. As we saw in Figure 24-7, educational levels in China are increasing much more rapidly than in Argentina. This isn't because China is richer than Argentina; until recently, China was, on average, poorer than Argentina. Instead, it reflects the fact that the Chinese government has made education of the population a high priority.

3. GOVERNMENT SUBSIDIES TO R&D Technological progress is largely the result of private initiative. But in the more advanced countries, important R&D is done by government agencies as well. For example, the internet grew out of a system, the Advanced Research Projects Agency Network (ARPANET), created by the U.S. Defense department, then extended to educational institutions by the National Science Foundation.

4. MAINTAINING A WELL-FUNCTIONING FINANCIAL SYSTEM Governments play an important indirect role in making high rates of private investment spending possible. Both the amount of savings and the ability of an economy to direct savings into productive investment spending depend on the economy's institutions, especially its financial system. In particular, a well-regulated and well-functioning financial system is very important for economic growth because in most countries it is the principal way in which savings are channeled into investment spending.

If a country's citizens trust their banks, they will place their savings in bank deposits, which the banks will then lend to their business customers. But if people don't trust their banks, they will hoard gold or foreign currency, keeping their

FOR INQUIRING MINDS | The New Growth Theory

Until the 1990s, economic models of technological progress assumed that what drove innovation was a mystery—unknown and unpredictable. In the words of economists, the sources of technological progress were *exogenous*—they were outside the models of economics and assumed to "just happen." Then, in a series of influential papers written in the 1980s and 1990s, Paul Romer founded what we now call "the New Growth Theory." In Romer's model, technological progress was explainable because it was in fact *endogenous*—the outcome of economic variables and incentives. And because technological progress was endogenous, policies could be adopted to foster its growth.

At any point in time, an economy has a stock of knowledge capital—the accumulated knowledge generated by past investments in research and development, education, and skill enhancement, as well as knowledge acquired from other economies. And that stock of knowledge capital is spread throughout the economy, so all firms benefit from it. According to the New Growth Theory, a rising stock of knowledge capital creates the foundation for further technological progress as innovation, shared by firms throughout the economy, makes further innovation possible. For example, touch-screen technology—developed in the 1970s and 1980s—became the basis for later developments such as smartphones and tablets.

Yet, as Romer pointed out, there is a severe wrinkle in this story: because knowledge is shared throughout the economy, it may be very difficult for an innovator to capture the rewards of his or her innovation as others exploit the innovation for their own interests. So in the New Growth Theory, government protection of intellectual property rights is critical to furthering technological progress. In addition, governments, institutions, and firms can enhance technological progress by subsidizing investments in education and research and development, which, in turn, can increase the stock of knowledge capital.

By giving us a better model of where technological progress comes from, the New Growth Theory makes clear how important the policies of government, institutions, and firms are in fostering it. ∎

savings in safe deposit boxes or under the mattress, where it cannot be turned into productive investment spending. As we'll discuss later, a well-functioning financial system requires appropriate government regulation to assure depositors that their funds are protected from loss.

Protection of Property Rights *Property rights* are the rights of owners of valuable items to dispose of those items as they choose. A subset, *intellectual property rights,* are the rights of an innovator to accrue the rewards of her innovation. The state of property rights generally, and intellectual property rights in particular, are important factors in explaining differences in growth rates across economies. Why? Because no one would bother to spend the effort and resources required to innovate if someone else could appropriate that innovation and capture the rewards. So, for innovation to flourish, intellectual property rights must receive protection.

Sometimes this is accomplished by the nature of the innovation: it may be too difficult or expensive to copy. But, generally, the government has to protect intellectual property rights. A *patent* is a government-created temporary monopoly given to an innovator for the use or sale of his or her innovation. It's a temporary rather than permanent monopoly because while it's in society's interests to give an innovator an incentive to invent, it's also in society's interests to eventually encourage competition.

Political Stability and Good Governance There's not much point in investing in a business if rioting mobs are likely to destroy it, or in saving your money if someone with political connections can steal it. Political stability and good governance (including the protection of property rights) are essential ingredients in fostering economic growth in the long run.

Long-run economic growth in successful economies, like that of the United States, has been possible because there are good laws, institutions that enforce those laws, and a stable political system that maintains those institutions. The law must say that your property is really yours so that someone else can't take it away. The courts and the police must be honest so that they can't be bribed to ignore the law. And the political system must be stable so that laws don't change capriciously.

Americans take these preconditions for granted, but they are by no means guaranteed. Aside from the disruption caused by war or revolution, many countries find that their economic growth suffers due to corruption among the government officials who should be enforcing the law. For example, until 1991 the Indian government imposed many bureaucratic restrictions on businesses, which often had to bribe government officials to get approval for even routine activities—a tax on business, in effect. Economists have argued that a reduction in this burden of corruption is one reason Indian growth has been much faster in recent years.

Even when the government isn't corrupt, excessive government intervention can be a brake on economic growth. If large parts of the economy are supported by government subsidies, protected from imports, subject to unnecessary monopolization, or otherwise insulated from competition, productivity tends to suffer because of a lack of incentives. As we'll see in the next section, excessive government intervention is one often-cited explanation for slow growth in Latin America.

ECONOMICS ▶ in Action

Why Did Britain Fall Behind?

I t's one of the classic questions in economic history: Why did Britain, the home of the Industrial Revolution, by far the world's leading economy for much of the nineteenth century, end up falling behind other nations at the start of a new century? It's not a tragic story: the British economy continued to grow, and it remained a rich country by international standards. Still, by the early twentieth century it was obvious that British industry was no longer at the cutting edge. Instead, the United States and Germany had come to supplant Britain as the new economic frontier. What happened?

That's not an easy question to answer. Robert Solow, an MIT economics professor and Nobel laureate who pioneered the theory of economic growth, once memorably declared that all efforts to explain Britain's lag end in "a blaze of amateur sociology." Indeed, among the reasons often given for the lag are such things as the excessive influence of the landed aristocracy, social barriers that prevented talented individuals from the wrong class from rising, and a cult of amateurism that was good enough for people running small family firms but not for the managers of large modern corporations.

There were, however, other factors in Britain's relative decline that were more easily measured. Of special importance was education. Britain was much slower than other industrial countries, the United States in particular, to establish universal basic education. Moreover, its universities, for all their ancient glories, remained too focused on preparing young gentlemen for their role in society; college education was for a long time restricted to a narrow segment of the population. And Britain was late in developing the close ties between academics and industry that did so much to drive the Second Industrial Revolution in both America and Germany. These barriers to education and skill acquisition placed Britain at a human capital disadvantage.

The good news for today's British residents is that most of these problems lie well in the past. Currently, young Britons are slightly more likely than their American counterparts to receive a college education. British real GDP per capita is still below U.S. levels, but it has made up part of the gap. And nobody walking around London today would consider it a backward-looking city.

Now catching up, Britain fell behind the United States and Germany largely due to barriers to education.

Check Your Understanding   24-3

1. Explain the link between a country's growth rate, its investment spending as a percent of GDP, and its domestic savings.

2. U.S. centers of academic biotechnology research have closer connections with private biotechnology companies than do their European counterparts. What effect might this have on the pace of creation and development of new drugs in the United States versus Europe?

3. During the 1990s in the former Soviet Union a lot of property was seized and controlled by those in power. How might this have affected the country's growth rate at that time? Explain.

Solutions appear at back of book.

Success, Disappointment, and Failure

As we've seen, rates of long-run economic growth differ quite a lot around the world. Now let's look at three regions of the world that have had quite different experiences with economic growth over the last few decades.

Figure 24-8 shows trends since 1960 in real GDP per capita in 2000 dollars for three countries: Argentina, Nigeria, and South Korea. (As in Figure 24-1, the vertical axis is drawn in logarithmic scale.) We have chosen these countries because each is a particularly striking example of what has happened in its region. South Korea's amazing rise is part of a broad "economic miracle" in East

don jon red/Alamy

▼ Quick Review

• Countries differ greatly in their growth rates of real GDP per capita due to differences in the rates at which they accumulate physical capital and human capital as well as differences in technological progress. A prime cause of differences in growth rates is differences in rates of domestic savings and investment spending as well as differences in education levels, and **research and development,** or **R&D,** levels. R&D largely drives technological progress.

• Government actions can promote or hinder the sources of long-term growth.

• Government policies that directly promote growth are subsidies to **infrastructure,** particularly public health infrastructure, subsidies to education, subsidies to R&D, and the maintenance of a well-functioning financial system.

• Governments improve the environment for growth by protecting property rights (particularly intellectual property rights through patents), by providing political stability, and through good governance. Poor governance includes corruption and excessive government intervention.

FIGURE **24-8** | **Success and Disappointment**

Real GDP per capita from 1960 to 2013, measured in 2000 dollars, is shown for Argentina, South Korea, and Nigeria, using a logarithmic scale. South Korea and some other East Asian countries have been highly successful at achieving economic growth. Argentina, like much of Latin America, has had several setbacks, slowing its growth. Nigeria's standard of living in 2013 was only barely higher than it had been in 1960, an experience shared by many African countries. Neither Argentina nor Nigeria exhibited much growth over the 50-year period, although both have had significantly higher growth in recent years.

Source: The Conference Board Total Economy Database™, January 2014, http://www.conference-board.org/data/economydatabase

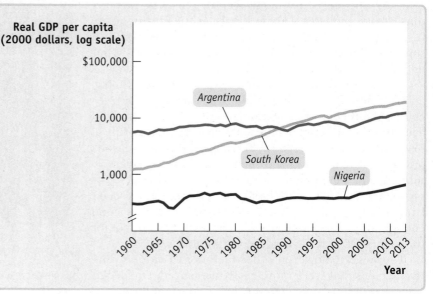

Asia. Argentina's slow progress, interrupted by repeated setbacks, is more or less typical of the disappointing growth that has characterized Latin America. And Nigeria's unhappy story until very recently—with little growth in real GDP until after 2000—was, unfortunately, an experience shared by many African countries.

East Asia's Miracle

In 1960 South Korea was a very poor country. In fact, in 1960 its real GDP per capita was lower than that of India today. But, as you can see from Figure 24-8, beginning in the early 1960s South Korea began an extremely rapid economic ascent: real GDP per capita grew about 7% per year for more than 30 years. Today South Korea, though still somewhat poorer than Europe or the United States, looks very much like an economically advanced country.

South Korea's economic growth is unprecedented in history: it took the country only 35 years to achieve growth that required centuries elsewhere. Yet South Korea is only part of a broader phenomenon, often referred to as the East Asian economic miracle. High growth rates first appeared in South Korea, Taiwan, Hong Kong, and Singapore but then spread across the region, most notably to China. Since 1975, the whole region has increased real GDP per capita by 6% per year, more than three times America's historical rate of growth.

How have the Asian countries achieved such high growth rates? The answer is that all of the sources of productivity growth have been firing on all cylinders. Very high savings rates, the percentage of GDP that is saved nationally in any given year, have allowed the countries to significantly increase the amount of physical capital per worker. Very good basic education has permitted a rapid improvement in human capital. And these countries have experienced substantial technological progress.

Why were such high rates of growth unheard of in the past? Most economic analysts think that East Asia's growth spurt was possible because of its *relative* backwardness. That is, by the time that East Asian economies began to move into the modern world, they could benefit from adopting the technological advances that had been generated in technologically advanced countries such as the United States.

In 1900, the United States could not have moved quickly to a modern level of productivity because much of the technology that powers the modern economy, from jet planes to computers, hadn't been invented yet. In 1970, South Korea probably still had lower labor productivity than the United States had in 1900, but it could rapidly upgrade its productivity by adopting technology that had been developed in the United States, Europe, and Japan over the previous century. This was aided by a huge investment in human capital through widespread schooling.

The East Asian experience demonstrates that economic growth can be especially fast in countries that are playing catch-up to other countries with higher GDP per capita. On this basis, many economists have suggested a general principle known as the **convergence hypothesis.** It says that differences in real GDP per capita among countries tend to narrow over time because countries that start with lower real GDP per capita tend to have higher growth rates. We'll look at the evidence on the convergence hypothesis in the upcoming Economics in Action.

Even before we get to that evidence, however, we can say right away that starting with a relatively low level of real GDP per capita is no guarantee of rapid growth, as the examples of Latin America and Africa both demonstrate.

According to the **convergence hypothesis,** international differences in real GDP per capita tend to narrow over time.

Latin America's Disappointment

In 1900, Latin America was not considered an economically backward region. Natural resources, including both minerals and cultivable land, were abundant. Some countries, notably Argentina, attracted millions of immigrants from Europe in search of a better life. Measures of real GDP per capita in Argentina, Uruguay, and southern Brazil were comparable to those in economically advanced countries.

Since about 1920, however, growth in Latin America has been disappointing. As Figure 24-8 shows in the case of Argentina, growth has been disappointing for many decades, until 2000 when it finally began to increase. The fact that South Korea is now much richer than Argentina would have seemed inconceivable a few generations ago.

Why did Latin America stagnate? Comparisons with East Asian success stories suggest several factors. The rates of savings and investment spending in Latin America have been much lower than in East Asia, partly as a result of irresponsible government policy that has eroded savings through high inflation, bank failures, and other disruptions. Education—especially broad basic education—has been underemphasized: even Latin American nations rich in natural resources often failed to channel that wealth into their educational systems. And political instability, leading to irresponsible economic policies, has taken a toll.

In the 1980s, many economists came to believe that Latin America was suffering from excessive government intervention in markets. They recommended opening the economies to imports, selling off government-owned companies, and, in general, freeing up individual initiative. The hope was that this would produce an East Asian–type economic surge.

So far, however, only one Latin American nation, Chile, has achieved sustained rapid growth. It now seems that pulling off an economic miracle is harder than it looks. Although, in recent years Brazil and Argentina have seen their growth rates increase significantly as they exported large amounts of commodities to the advanced countries and rapidly developing China.

Africa's Troubles and Promise

Africa south of the Sahara is home to about 780 million people, more than 2 1/2 times the population of the United States. On average, they are very poor, nowhere close to U.S. living standards 100 or even 200 years ago. And economic progress has been both slow and uneven, as the example of Nigeria, the most

Slow and uneven economic growth in sub-Saharan Africa has led to extreme and ongoing poverty for many of its people.

populous nation in the region, suggests. In fact, real GDP per capita in sub-Saharan Africa actually fell 13% from 1980 to 1994, although it has recovered since then. The consequence of this poor growth performance has been intense and continuing poverty.

This is a very disheartening story. What explains it?

Several factors are probably crucial. Perhaps first and foremost is the problem of political instability. In the years since 1975, large parts of Africa have experienced savage civil wars (often with outside powers backing rival sides) that have killed millions of people and made productive investment spending impossible. The threat of war and general anarchy has also inhibited other important preconditions for growth, such as education and provision of necessary infrastructure.

Property rights are also a major problem. The lack of legal safeguards means that property owners are often subject to extortion because of government corruption, making them averse to owning property or improving it. This is especially damaging in a country that is very poor.

While many economists see political instability and government corruption as the leading causes of underdevelopment in Africa, some—most notably Jeffrey Sachs of Columbia University and the United Nations—believe the opposite. They argue that Africa is politically unstable because Africa is poor. And Africa's poverty, they go on to claim, stems from its extremely unfavorable geographic conditions—much of the continent is landlocked, hot, infested with tropical diseases, and cursed with poor soil.

Sachs, along with economists from the World Health Organization, has highlighted the importance of health problems in Africa. In poor countries, worker productivity is often severely hampered by malnutrition and disease. In particular, tropical diseases such as malaria can only be controlled with an effective public health infrastructure, something that is lacking in much of Africa. At the time of writing, economists are studying certain regions of Africa to determine whether modest amounts of aid given directly to residents for the purposes of increasing crop yields, reducing malaria, and increasing school attendance can produce self-sustaining gains in living standards.

Although the example of African countries represents a warning that long-run economic growth cannot be taken for granted, there are some signs of hope. As we saw in Figure 24-8, Nigeria's per capita GDP, after decades of stagnation, turned upward after 2000, and it has achieved an average annual growth rate of 4.3% from 2008 through 2013.

The same is true for sub-Saharan African economies as a whole. In 2013, real GDP per capita growth rates averaged around 5.1% across sub-Saharan African countries, and they are projected to be over 6% in 2014. Rising prices for their exports are part of the reason for recent success, but there is growing optimism among development experts that a period of relative peace and better government is ushering in a new era for Africa's economies.

ECONOMICS ▶ *in Action*

Are Economies Converging?

In the 1950s, much of Europe seemed quaint and backward to American visitors, and Japan seemed very poor. Today, a visitor to Paris or Tokyo sees a city that looks about as rich as New York. Although real GDP per capita is still somewhat higher in the United States, the differences in the standards of living among the United States, Europe, and Japan are relatively small.

FIGURE 24-9   Do Economies Converge?

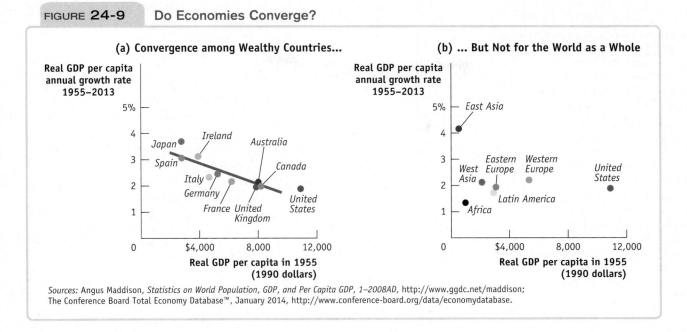

(a) Convergence among Wealthy Countries...

Real GDP per capita annual growth rate 1955–2013

(b) ... But Not for the World as a Whole

Real GDP per capita annual growth rate 1955–2013

Sources: Angus Maddison, *Statistics on World Population, GDP, and Per Capita GDP, 1–2008AD,* http://www.ggdc.net/maddison; The Conference Board Total Economy Database™, January 2014, http://www.conference-board.org/data/economydatabase.

Many economists have argued that this convergence in living standards is normal; the convergence hypothesis says that relatively poor countries should have higher rates of growth of real GDP per capita than relatively rich countries. And if we look at today's relatively well-off countries, the convergence hypothesis seems to be true.

Panel (a) of Figure 24-9 shows data for a number of today's wealthy economies measured in 1990 dollars. On the horizontal axis is real GDP per capita in 1955; on the vertical axis is the average annual growth rate of real GDP per capita from 1955 to 2013. There is a clear negative relationship as can be seen from the line fitted through the points. The United States was the richest country in this group in 1955 and had the slowest rate of growth. Japan and Spain were the poorest countries in 1955 and had the fastest rates of growth. These data suggest that the convergence hypothesis is true.

But economists who looked at similar data realized that these results depend on the countries selected. If you look at successful economies that have a high standard of living today, you find that real GDP per capita has converged. But looking across the world as a whole, including countries that remain poor, there is little evidence of convergence.

Panel (b) of Figure 24-9 illustrates this point using data for regions rather than individual countries (other than the United States). In 1955, East Asia and Africa were both very poor regions. Over the next 58 years, the East Asian regional economy grew quickly, as the convergence hypothesis would have predicted, but the African regional economy grew very slowly. In 1955, Western Europe had substantially higher real GDP per capita than Latin America. But, contrary to the convergence hypothesis, the Western European regional economy grew more quickly over the next 58 years, widening the gap between the regions.

So is the convergence hypothesis all wrong? No: economists still believe that countries with relatively low real GDP per capita tend to have higher rates of growth than countries with relatively high real GDP per capita, *other things equal.* But other things—education, infrastructure, rule of law, and so on—are often not equal. Statistical studies find that when you adjust for differences in these other factors, poorer countries do tend to have higher growth rates. This result is known as *conditional convergence.*

Because other factors differ, however, there is no clear tendency toward convergence in the world economy as a whole. Western Europe, North America, and parts of Asia are becoming more similar in real GDP per capita, but the gap between these regions and the rest of the world is growing.

Check Your Understanding   24-4

1. Some economists think the high rates of growth of productivity achieved by many Asian economies cannot be sustained. Why might they be right? What would have to happen for them to be wrong?

2. Consider Figure 24-9, panel (b). Based on the data there, which regions support the convergence hypothesis? Which do not? Explain.

3. Some economists think the best way to help African countries is for wealthier countries to provide more funds for basic infrastructure. Others think this policy will have no long-run effect unless African countries have the financial and political means to maintain this infrastructure. What policies would you suggest?

Solutions appear at back of book.

Is World Growth Sustainable?

Earlier in this chapter we described the views of Thomas Malthus, the early-nineteenth-century economist who warned that the pressure of population growth would tend to limit the standard of living. Malthus was right about the past: for around 58 centuries, from the origins of civilization until his own time, limited land supplies effectively prevented any large rise in real incomes per capita. Since then, however, technological progress and rapid accumulation of physical and human capital have allowed the world to defy Malthusian pessimism.

But will this always be the case? Some skeptics have expressed doubt about whether **sustainable long-run economic growth** is possible—whether it can continue in the face of the limited supply of natural resources and the impact of growth on the environment.

Natural Resources and Growth, Revisited

In 1972 a group of scientists called The Club of Rome made a big splash with a book titled *The Limits to Growth,* which argued that long-run economic growth wasn't sustainable due to limited supplies of nonrenewable resources such as oil and natural gas. These "neo-Malthusian" concerns at first seemed to be validated by a sharp rise in resource prices in the 1970s, then came to seem foolish when resource prices fell sharply in the 1980s. After 2005, however, resource prices rose sharply again, leading to renewed concern about resource limitations to growth.

Figure 24-10 shows the real price of oil—the price of oil adjusted for inflation in the rest of the economy. The rise, fall, and rise of concern about resource-based limits to growth have more or less followed the rise, fall, and rise of oil prices shown in the figure.

Differing views about the impact of limited natural resources on long-run economic growth turn on the answers to three questions:

• How large are the supplies of key natural resources?

• How effective will technology be at finding alternatives to natural resources?

• Can long-run economic growth continue in the face of resource scarcity?

It's mainly up to geologists to answer the first question. Unfortunately, there's wide disagreement among the experts, especially about the prospects for future oil production. Some analysts believe that there is enough untapped oil in the ground that world oil production can continue to rise for several decades. Others,

Sustainable long-run economic growth is long-run growth that can continue in the face of the limited supply of natural resources and the impact of growth on the environment.

FIGURE 24-10 The Real Price of Oil, 1949–2011

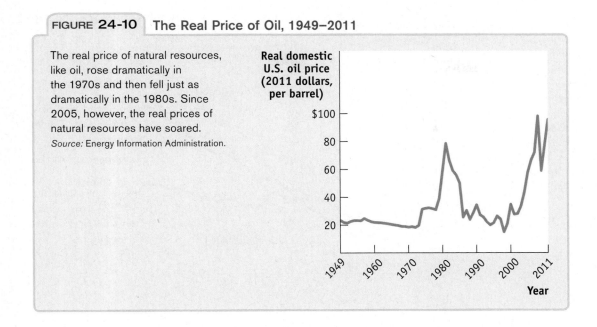

The real price of natural resources, like oil, rose dramatically in the 1970s and then fell just as dramatically in the 1980s. Since 2005, however, the real prices of natural resources have soared.

Source: Energy Information Administration.

including a number of oil company executives, believe that the growing difficulty of finding new oil fields will cause oil production to plateau—that is, stop growing and eventually begin a gradual decline—in the fairly near future. Some analysts believe that we have already reached that plateau.

The answer to the second question, whether there are alternatives to natural resources, has to come from engineers. There's no question that there are many alternatives to the natural resources currently being depleted, some of which are already being exploited. Indeed, since around 2005 there have been dramatic developments in energy production, with large amounts of previously unreachable oil and gas extracted through fracking, and with a huge decline in the cost of electricity generated by wind and especially solar power.

The third question, whether economies can continue to grow in the face of resource scarcity, is mainly a question for economists. And most, though not all, economists are optimistic: they believe that modern economies can find ways to work around limits on the supply of natural resources. One reason for this optimism is the fact that resource scarcity leads to high resource prices. These high prices in turn provide strong incentives to conserve the scarce resource and to find alternatives.

For example, after the sharp oil price increases of the 1970s, American consumers turned to smaller, more fuel-efficient cars, and U.S. industry also greatly intensified its efforts to reduce energy bills. The result is shown in Figure 24-11, which compares U.S. real GDP per capita and oil consumption before and after the 1970s energy crisis. In the United States before 1973 there seemed to be a more or less one-to-one relationship between economic growth and oil consumption. But after 1973 the U.S. economy continued to deliver growth in real GDP per capita even as it substantially reduced the use of oil.

This move toward conservation paused after 1990, as low real oil prices encouraged consumers to shift back to gas-greedy larger cars and SUVs. But a sharp rise in oil prices from 2005 to 2008, and again in 2010, encouraged renewed shifts toward oil conservation.

Given such responses to prices, economists generally tend to see resource scarcity as a problem that modern economies handle fairly well, and so not a fundamental limit to long-run economic growth. Environmental issues, however, pose a more difficult problem because dealing with them requires effective political action.

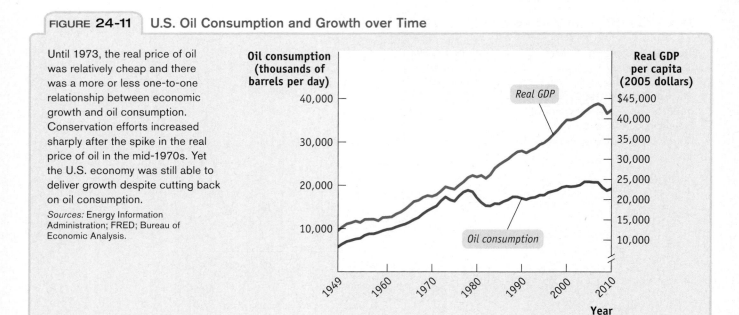

FIGURE **24-11** U.S. Oil Consumption and Growth over Time

Until 1973, the real price of oil was relatively cheap and there was a more or less one-to-one relationship between economic growth and oil consumption. Conservation efforts increased sharply after the spike in the real price of oil in the mid-1970s. Yet the U.S. economy was still able to deliver growth despite cutting back on oil consumption.

Sources: Energy Information Administration; FRED; Bureau of Economic Analysis.

Economic Growth and the Environment

Economic growth, other things equal, tends to increase the human impact on the environment. As we saw in this chapter's opening story, China's spectacular economic growth has also brought a spectacular increase in air pollution in that nation's cities.

It's important to realize, however, that other things aren't necessarily equal: countries can and do take action to protect their environments. In fact, air and water quality in today's advanced countries is generally much better than it was a few decades ago. London's famous "fog"—actually a form of air pollution, which killed 4,000 people during a two-week episode in 1952—is gone, thanks to regulations that virtually eliminated the use of coal heat. As noted in the chapter's opening story, the equally famous smog of Los Angeles is also largely gone, again thanks to pollution regulations.

Despite these past environmental success stories, there is widespread concern today about the environmental impacts of continuing economic growth, reflecting a change in the scale of the problem. Environmental success stories have mainly involved dealing with *local* impacts of economic growth, such as the effect of widespread car ownership on air quality in the Los Angeles basin. Today, however, we are faced with *global* environmental issues—the adverse impacts on the environment of the Earth as a whole by worldwide economic growth. The biggest of these issues involves the impact of fossil-fuel consumption on the world's climate.

Burning coal and oil releases carbon dioxide into the atmosphere. There is broad scientific consensus that rising levels of carbon dioxide and other gases are causing a greenhouse effect on the Earth, trapping more of the sun's energy and raising the planet's overall temperature. And rising temperatures may impose high human and economic costs: rising sea levels may flood coastal areas; changing climate may disrupt agriculture, especially in poor countries; and so on.

The problem of climate change is clearly linked to economic growth. Figure 24-12 shows carbon dioxide emissions from the United States, Europe, and China since 1980. Historically, the wealthy nations have been responsible for the bulk of these emissions because they have consumed far more energy per person than poorer countries. As China and other emerging economies have grown, however, they have begun to consume much more energy and emit much more carbon dioxide.

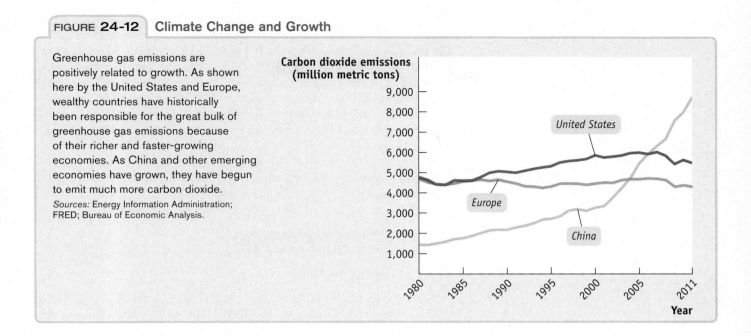

FIGURE **24-12**   Climate Change and Growth

Greenhouse gas emissions are positively related to growth. As shown here by the United States and Europe, wealthy countries have historically been responsible for the great bulk of greenhouse gas emissions because of their richer and faster-growing economies. As China and other emerging economies have grown, they have begun to emit much more carbon dioxide.

Sources: Energy Information Administration; FRED; Bureau of Economic Analysis.

Is it possible to continue long-run economic growth while curbing the emissions of greenhouse gases? The answer, according to most economists who have studied the issue, is yes. It should be possible to reduce greenhouse gas emissions in a wide variety of ways, ranging from the use of non-fossil-fuel energy sources such as wind, solar, and nuclear power; to preventive measures such as carbon sequestration (capturing the carbon dioxide from power plants and storing it); to simpler things like designing buildings so that they're easier to keep warm in winter and cool in summer. Such measures would impose costs on the economy, but the best available estimates suggest that even a large reduction in greenhouse gas emissions over the next few decades would only modestly dent the long-term rise in real GDP per capita.

The problem is how to make all of this happen. Unlike resource scarcity, environmental problems don't automatically provide incentives for changed behavior. Pollution is an example of a *negative externality,* a cost that individuals or firms impose on others without having to offer compensation. In the absence of government intervention, individuals and firms have no incentive to reduce negative externalities, which is why it took regulation to reduce air pollution in America's cities. And as Nicholas Stern, the author of an influential report on climate change, put it, greenhouse gas emissions are "the mother of all externalities."

So there is a broad consensus among economists—although there are some dissenters—that government action is needed to deal with climate change. There is also broad consensus that this action should take the form of market-based incentives, either in the form of a carbon tax—a tax per unit of carbon emitted—or a cap and trade system in which the total amount of emissions is capped, and producers must buy licenses to emit greenhouse gases. There is, however, considerable dispute about how much action is appropriate, reflecting both uncertainty about the costs and benefits and scientific uncertainty about the pace and extent of climate change.

There are also several aspects of the climate change problem that make it much more difficult to deal with than, say, smog in Beijing. One is the problem of taking the long view. The impact of greenhouse gas emissions on the climate is very gradual: carbon dioxide put into the atmosphere today won't have its full effect on the climate for several generations. As a result, there is the political problem of persuading voters to accept pain today in return for gains that will benefit their children, grandchildren, or even great-grandchildren.

There is also a difficult problem of international burden sharing. As Figure 24-12 shows, today's rich economies have historically been responsible for most greenhouse gas emissions, but newly emerging economies like China are responsible for most of the recent growth. Inevitably, rich countries are reluctant to pay the price of reducing emissions only to have their efforts frustrated by rapidly growing emissions from new players. On the other hand, countries like China, which are still relatively poor, consider it unfair that they should be expected to bear the burden of protecting an environment threatened by the past actions of rich nations.

The general moral of this story is that it is possible to reconcile long-run economic growth with environmental protection. The main question is one of getting political consensus around the necessary policies.

ECONOMICS ▶ *in Action*

The Cost of Limiting Carbon

Over the years several bills have been introduced in Congress that would greatly reduce U.S. emissions of greenhouse gases over the next few decades. By 2014, however, it was clear that given the depth of the U.S. political divide, such bills were unlikely to pass for the foreseeable future. However, the U.S. Environmental Protection Agency (EPA) is already required by the Clean Air Act to regulate pollutants that endanger public health, and in 2007 the Supreme Court ruled that carbon dioxide emissions meet that criterion.

So the EPA began a series of steps to limit carbon emissions. First, it set new fuel-efficiency standards that will reduce emissions from motor vehicles. Then it introduced rules limiting emissions from new power plants. Finally, in June 2014 it announced plans to limit emissions from existing power plants. This was a crucial step because coal-burning power plants account for a large part of carbon emissions, both in the United States and in the rest of the world.

But how would new rules affect the economy? A number of politicians and industry groups were quick to assert that the EPA rules would cripple economic growth. For the most part, however, economists disagreed. The EPA's own analysis suggested that by 2030 its rules would cost the U.S. economy about $9 billion in today's dollars each year—a trivial sum in an economy that produces $17 trillion of goods and services annually.

Still, the EPA's proposed rules would at best make a small dent in the problem of climate change. How much would a program that really deals with the problem cost? In April 2014 the U.N. International Panel on Climate Change (IPCC) estimated that global measures limiting the rise in temperatures to 2 degrees centigrade would impose gradually rising costs, reaching about 5% of output by the year 2100. The impact on the world's rate of economic growth would, however, be small—around 0.06 percentage points each year. The IPCC's numbers were more or less in line with other estimates; most independent studies have found that environmental protection need not greatly reduce growth.

The answer is blowing in the wind.

Shutterstock

Why this optimism? At a fundamental level, the key insight is that given the right incentives modern economies can find many ways to reduce emissions, ranging from the use of renewable energy sources (which have grown much cheaper in the past few years) to inducing consumers to choose goods with lower environmental impact. Economic growth and environmental damage don't have to go together.

Check Your Understanding 24-5

1. Are economists typically more concerned about the limits to growth imposed by environmental degradation or those imposed by resource scarcity? Explain, noting the role of negative externalities in your answer.

2. What is the link between greenhouse gas emissions and growth? What is the expected effect on growth from emissions reduction? Why is international burden sharing of greenhouse gas emissions reduction a contentious problem?

Solutions appear at back of book.

▼ Quick Review

• There's wide disagreement about whether it is possible to have **sustainable long-run economic growth.** However, economists generally believe that modern economies can find ways to alleviate limits to growth from natural resource scarcity through the price response that promotes conservation and the creation of alternatives.

• Overcoming the limits to growth arising from environmental degradation is more difficult because it requires effective government intervention. Limiting the emission of greenhouse gases would require only a modest reduction in the growth rate.

• There is broad consensus that government action to address climate change and greenhouse gases should be in the form of market-based incentives, like a carbon tax or a cap and trade system. It will also require rich and poor countries to come to some agreement on how the cost of emissions reductions will be shared.

How Boeing Got Better

When we think about innovation and technological progress, we tend to focus on the big, dramatic changes: cars replacing horses and buggies, electric lightbulbs replacing gaslights, computers replacing adding machines and typewriters. A lot of progress, however, is incremental and almost invisible to most people—yet such unglamorous change can have huge effects over time. Consider, for example, the progress of jet travel, as illustrated by the history of Boeing Corporation.

Chris Edwards/
Woodys Aero Images

The Boeing 707, introduced in 1957, was the first commercially successful jetliner, and for a number of years it ruled the skies. When the Beatles made their famous 1964 arrival in America, it was a 707 that brought them there. So what did the 707 look like? What's striking about it, from a modern perspective, is how ordinary it appears. Basically, it looks like a jet airliner. If you walked past one today, and nobody told you it was an antique, you probably wouldn't notice; 50-year old jets aren't nearly as different on the outside from their contemporary descendants as, say, a classic Cadillac—fins and all—is from a modern SUV.

Furthermore, the visible performance of modern jets, like the Boeing 777 or the even more advanced 787, isn't that much better than those of the old 707. They only fly slightly faster; once you take extra security procedures and air traffic delays into account, traveling from London to New York probably takes more time now than it did in 1964. It's nice to have a selection of movies (although there never does seem to be anything you want to watch), and business-class travelers now get flatbed seats that make sleeping easier. Still, all of this seems fairly marginal.

Yet Boeing's modern jets (and those of its main competitor, Airbus) are vastly more efficient than jets half a century ago—so much more efficient that average air fares, adjusted for inflation, are only about a third what they were in 1960. What changed?

The answer is, things passengers can't see. Most important, there has been a drastic improvement in fuel efficiency, with modern planes using less than a third as much fuel per passenger-mile than their ancestors. Behind this improvement, in turn, lie fundamental changes in engine design (high-bypass engines that direct most of their intake around the combustion chamber rather than through it), small but important improvements in aerodynamics, and the use of new materials to make airframes much lighter.

The moral is that the technological progress that drives growth is much broader and more powerful than meets the eye. Even when things look more or less the same, there is often enormous change beneath the surface.

QUESTIONS FOR THOUGHT

1. A modern jet airliner does pretty much the same thing as an airliner from the 1960s: it gets you there from here, in about the same time. Where's the technological progress?

2. Do scientific advances play any role in the progress we've described? Explain.

3. Some travelers complain that the flight experience has gone downhill. Does this refute the claim of technological progress?

SUMMARY

1. Growth is measured as changes in real GDP per capita in order to eliminate the effects of changes in the price level and changes in population size. Levels of real GDP per capita vary greatly around the world: more than half of the world's population lives in countries that are still poorer than the United States was in 1900. GDP per capita in the United States is about 8 times as high as it was in 1900.

2. Growth rates of real GDP per capita also vary widely. According to the **Rule of 70,** the number of years it takes for real GDP per capita to double is equal to 70 divided by the annual growth rate of real GDP per capita.

3. The key to long-run economic growth is rising **labor productivity,** or just **productivity,** which is output per worker. Increases in productivity arise from increases in **physical capital** per worker and **human capital** per worker as well as **technological progress.** The **aggregate production function** shows how real GDP per worker depends on these three factors. Other things equal, there are **diminishing returns to physical capital:** holding human capital per worker and technology fixed, each successive addition to physical capital per worker yields a smaller increase in productivity than the one before. Equivalently, more physical capital per worker results in a lower, but still positive, increase in productivity. **Growth accounting,** which estimates the contribution of each factor to a country's economic growth, has shown that rising **total factor productivity,** the amount of output produced from a given amount of factor inputs, is key to long-run growth. It is usually interpreted as the effect of technological progress. In contrast to earlier times, natural resources are a less significant source of productivity growth in most countries today.

4. The large differences in countries' growth rates are largely due to differences in their rates of accumulation of physical and human capital as well as differences in technological progress. Although inflows of foreign savings from abroad help, a prime factor is differences in domestic savings and investment spending rates, since most countries that have high investment spending in physical capital finance it by high domestic savings. Technological progress is largely a result of **research and development,** or **R&D.**

5. Governments can help or hinder growth. Government policies that directly foster growth are subsidies to **infrastructure,** particularly public health infrastructure, subsidies to education, subsidies to R&D, and maintenance of a well-functioning financial system that channels savings into investment spending, education, and R&D. Governments can enhance the environment for growth by protecting property rights (particularly intellectual property rights through patents), by being politically stable, and by providing good governance. Poor governance includes corruption and excessive government intervention.

6. The world economy contains examples of success and failure in the effort to achieve long-run economic growth. East Asian economies have done many things right and achieved very high growth rates. The low growth rates of Latin American and African economies over many years led economists to believe that the **convergence hypothesis,** the claim that differences in real GDP per capita across countries narrow over time, fits the data only when factors that affect growth, such as education, infrastructure, and favorable government policies and institutions, are held equal across countries. In recent years, there has been an uptick in growth among some Latin American and sub-Saharan African countries, largely due to a boom in commodity exports.

7. Economists generally believe that environmental degradation poses a greater challenge to **sustainable long-run economic growth** than does natural resource scarcity. Addressing environmental degradation requires effective governmental intervention, but the problem of natural resource scarcity is often well handled by the market price response.

8. The emission of greenhouse gases is clearly linked to growth, and limiting them will require some reduction in growth. However, the best available estimates suggest that a large reduction in emissions would require only a modest reduction in the growth rate.

9. There is broad consensus that government action to address climate change and greenhouse gases should be in the form of market-based incentives, like a carbon tax or a cap and trade system. It will also require rich and poor countries to come to some agreement on how the cost of emissions reductions will be shared.

KEY TERMS

Rule of 70, p. 686
Labor productivity, p. 688
Productivity, p. 688
Physical capital, p. 689
Human capital, p. 689
Technological progress, p. 689

Aggregate production function, p. 689
Diminishing returns to physical capital, p. 690
Growth accounting, p. 691
Total factor productivity, p. 693
Research and development (R&D), p. 697

Infrastructure, p. 698
Convergence hypothesis, p. 703
Sustainable long-run economic growth, p. 706

PROBLEMS

1. The accompanying table shows data from the Penn World Table, Version 8.0, for real GDP per capita in 2005 U.S. dollars for Argentina, Ghana, South Korea, and the United States for 1960, 1970, 1980, 1990, 2000, and 2011.

   a. Complete the table by expressing each year's real GDP per capita as a percentage of its 1960 and 2011 levels.

   b. How does the growth in living standards from 1960 to 2011 compare across these four nations? What might account for these differences?

	Argentina			Ghana			South Korea			United States		
Year	Real GDP per capita (2005 dollars)	Percentage of 1960 real GDP per capita	Percentage of 2011 real GDP per capita	Real GDP per capita (2005 dollars)	Percentage of 1960 real GDP per capita	Percentage of 2011 real GDP per capita	Real GDP per capita (2005 dollars)	Percentage of 1960 real GDP per capita	Percentage of 2011 real GDP per capita	Real GDP per capita (2005 dollars)	Percentage of 1960 real GDP per capita	Percentage of 2011 real GDP per capita
1960	$6,585	?	?	$1,557	?	?	$1,610	?	?	$15,136	?	?
1970	8,147	?	?	1,674	?	?	2,607	?	?	20,115	?	?
1980	8,938	?	?	1,418	?	?	5,161	?	?	25,221	?	?
1990	6,889	?	?	1,296	?	?	11,376	?	?	31,431	?	?
2000	9,208	?	?	1,530	?	?	20,016	?	?	39,498	?	?
2011	13,882	?	?	2,349	?	?	29,618	?	?	42,244	?	?

2. The accompanying table shows the average annual growth rate in real GDP per capita for Argentina, Ghana, and South Korea using data from the Penn World Table, Version 8.0, for the past few decades.

	Average annual growth rate of real GDP per capita		
Years	Argentina	Ghana	South Korea
1960–1970	2.15%	0.73%	4.94%
1970–1980	0.93	−1.64	7.07
1980–1990	−2.57	−0.90	8.22
1990–2000	3.40	1.67	5.81
2000–2010	7.92	3.16	3.67

   a. For each decade and for each country, use the Rule of 70 where possible to calculate how long it would take for that country's real GDP per capita to double.

   b. Suppose that the average annual growth rate that each country achieved over the period 2000–2010 continues indefinitely into the future. Starting from 2010, use the Rule of 70 to calculate, where possible, the year in which a country will have doubled its real GDP per capita.

3. The accompanying table provides approximate statistics on per capita income levels and growth rates for regions defined by income levels. According to the Rule of 70, starting in 2012 the high-income countries are projected to double their per capita GDP in approximately 78 years, in 2088. Throughout this question, assume constant growth rates for each of the regions that are equal to their average value between 2000 and 2012.

Region	Real GDP per capita (2012)	Average annual growth rate of real GDP per capita (2000–2012)
High-income countries	$31,372	1.1%
Middle-income countries	2,730	4.7
Low-income countries	422	3.2

Source: World Bank.

   a. Calculate the ratio of per capita GDP in 2012 of the following:

      i. Middle-income to high-income countries

      ii. Low-income to high-income countries

      iii. Low-income to middle-income countries

   b. Calculate the number of years it will take the low-income and middle-income countries to double their per capita GDP.

   c. Calculate the per capita GDP of each of the regions in 2076. (*Hint:* How many times does their per capita GDP double in 64 years, the number of years from 2012 to 2076?)

   d. Repeat part a with the projected per capita GDP in 2076.

   e. Compare your answers to parts a and d. Comment on the change in economic inequality between the regions.

4. The country of Androde is currently using Method 1 for its production function. By chance, scientists stumble onto a technological breakthrough that will enhance Androde's productivity. This technological breakthrough is reflected in another production function, Method 2. The accompanying table shows

combinations of physical capital per worker and output per worker for both methods, assuming that human capital per worker is fixed.

Method 1		Method 2	
Physical capital per worker	**Real GDP per worker**	**Physical capital per worker**	**Real GDP per worker**
0	0.00	0	0.00
50	35.36	50	70.71
100	50.00	100	100.00
150	61.24	150	122.47
200	70.71	200	141.42
250	79.06	250	158.11
300	86.60	300	173.21
350	93.54	350	187.08
400	100.00	400	200.00
450	106.07	450	212.13
500	111.80	500	223.61

a. Using the data in the accompanying table, draw the two production functions in one diagram. Androde's current amount of physical capital per worker is 100. In your figure, label that point A.

b. Starting from point A, over a period of 70 years, the amount of physical capital per worker in Androde rises to 400. Assuming Androde still uses Method 1, in your diagram, label the resulting point of production B. Using the Rule of 70, calculate by how many percent per year output per worker has grown.

c. Now assume that, starting from point A, over the same period of 70 years, the amount of physical capital per worker in Androde rises to 400, but that during that time period, Androde switches to Method 2. In your diagram, label the resulting point of production C. Using the Rule of 70, calculate by how many percent per year output per worker has grown now.

d. As the economy of Androde moves from point A to point C, what share of the annual productivity growth is due to higher total factor productivity?

5. The Bureau of Labor Statistics regularly releases the "Productivity and Costs" report for the previous month. Go to www.bls.gov and find the latest report. (On the Bureau of Labor Statistics home page, from the tab "Subjects," select the link to "Productivity: Labor Productivity & Costs"; then, from the heading "LPC News Releases," find the most recent "Productivity and Costs" report.) What were the percent changes in business and nonfarm business productivity for the previous quarter? How does the percent change in that quarter's productivity compare to the percent change from the same quarter a year ago?

6. What roles do physical capital, human capital, technology, and natural resources play in influencing long-run economic growth of aggregate output per capita?

7. How have U.S. policies and institutions influenced the country's long-run economic growth?

8. Over the next 100 years, real GDP per capita in Groland is expected to grow at an average annual rate of 2.0%. In Sloland, however, growth is expected to be somewhat slower, at an average annual growth rate of 1.5%. If both countries have a real GDP per capita today of $20,000, how will their real GDP per capita differ in 100 years? [*Hint:* A country that has a real GDP today of x and grows at y% per year will achieve a real GDP of $x \times (1 + (y/100))^z$ in z years. We assume that $0 \le y < 10$.]

9. The accompanying table shows data from the Penn World Table, Version 8.0, for real GDP per capita (2005 U.S. dollars) in France, Japan, the United Kingdom, and the United States in 1950 and 2011. Complete the table. Have these countries converged economically?

	1950		2011	
	Real GDP per capita (2005 dollars)	**Percentage of U.S. real GDP per capita**	**Real GDP per capita (2005 dollars)**	**Percentage of U.S. real GDP per capita**
France	$6,475	?	$29,476	?
Japan	2,329	?	31,587	?
United Kingdom	9,669	?	32,079	?
United States	15,136	?	42,244	?

10. The accompanying table shows data from the Penn World Table, Version 8.0, for real GDP per capita (2005 U.S. dollars) for Argentina, Ghana, South Korea, and the United States in 1960 and 2011. Complete the table. Have these countries converged economically?

	1960		2011	
	Real GDP per capita (2005 dollars)	**Percentage of U.S. real GDP per capita**	**Real GDP per capita (2005 dollars)**	**Percentage of U.S. real GDP per capita**
Argentina	$6,585	?	$13,882	?
Ghana	1,557	?	2,349	?
South Korea	1,610	?	29,618	?
United States	15,136	?	42,244	?

11. Why would you expect real GDP per capita in California and Pennsylvania to exhibit convergence but not in California and Baja California, a state of Mexico that borders the United States? What changes would allow California and Baja California to converge?

12. According to the *Oil & Gas Journal*, the proven oil reserves existing in the world in 2012 consisted of 1,525 billion barrels. In that year, the U.S. Energy Information Administration reported that the world daily oil production was 75.58 million barrels a day.

    a. At this rate, for how many years will the proven oil reserves last? Discuss the Malthusian view in the context of the number you just calculated.

    b. In order to do the calculations in part a, what did you assume about the total quantity of oil reserves over time? About oil prices over time? Are these assumptions consistent with the Malthusian view on resource limits?

    c. Discuss how market forces may affect the amount of time the proven oil reserves will last, assuming that no new oil reserves are discovered and that the demand curve for oil remains unchanged.

13. The accompanying table shows the annual growth rate for the years 2000–2011 in per capita emissions of carbon dioxide (CO_2) and the annual growth rate in real GDP per capita for selected countries.

Country	2000–2011 average annual growth rate of:	
	Real GDP per capita	CO_2 emissions per capita
Argentina	2.25%	2.95%
Bangladesh	4.16	6.52
Canada	1.10	−0.33
China	10.72	9.31
Germany	1.25	−1.20
Ireland	0.57	−0.96
Japan	0.59	−0.16
South Korea	3.74	3.06
Mexico	0.79	1.72
Nigeria	5.93	−0.55
Russia	5.08	1.61
South Africa	2.73	1.63
United Kingdom	1.05	−1.09
United States	0.74	−0.60

Sources: Energy Information Administration; The Conference Board.

a. Rank the countries in terms of their growth in CO_2 emissions, from highest to lowest. What five countries have the highest growth rate in emissions? What five countries have the lowest growth rate in emissions?

b. Now rank the countries in terms of their growth in real GDP per capita, from highest to lowest. What five countries have the highest growth rate? What five countries have the lowest growth rate?

c. Would you infer from your results that CO_2 emissions are linked to growth in output per capita?

d. Do high growth rates necessarily lead to high CO_2 emissions?

WORK IT OUT

For interactive, step-by-step help in solving the following problem, visit LaunchPad by using the URL on the back cover of this book.

14. You are hired as an economic consultant to the countries of Albernia and Brittania. Each country's current relationship between physical capital per worker and output per worker is given by the curve labeled "Productivity₁" in the accompanying diagram. Albernia is at point *A* and Brittania is at point *B*.

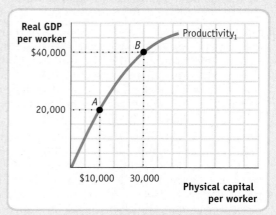

a. In the relationship depicted by the curve Productivity₁, what factors are held fixed? Do these countries experience diminishing returns to physical capital per worker?

b. Assuming that the amount of human capital per worker and the technology are held fixed in each country, can you recommend a policy to generate a doubling of real GDP per capita in Albernia?

c. How would your policy recommendation change if the amount of human capital per worker could be changed? Assume that an increase in human capital doubles the output per worker when physical capital per worker equals $10,000. Draw a curve on the diagram that represents this policy for Albernia.

Savings, Investment Spending, and the Financial System

▶ **What You Will Learn in This Chapter**

■ The relationship between savings and investment spending

■ Aspects of the **loanable funds market,** which show how savers are matched with borrowers

■ The purpose of the five principal types of **financial assets:** stocks, bonds, **loans,** real estate, and bank deposits

■ How **financial intermediaries** help investors achieve **diversification**

■ Some competing views of what determines asset prices and why asset market fluctuations can be a source of macroeconomic instability

FUNDS FOR FACEBOOK

AP Photo/The Bulletin, Andy Tullis

Facebook obtained millions of dollars in financing to pay for the physical capital it needed to expand.

"Facebook Is Hunting for More Money"—so read a 2009 headline in *Business Week,* which reported that the social networking site was seeking to borrow a $100 million credit line. Why would a wildly successful business like Facebook need to borrow money? Everyone knows Facebook. Founded in 2004, it has gone on to become arguably the biggest business success story of the twenty-first century—so far—with over 1 billion users worldwide reported to have Facebook pages. How did Facebook grow so big, so fast?

In large part, of course, the answer is that the company had a good idea. Personalized web pages providing information to friends and family turned out to be something many people really wanted. Equally important, since advertisers wanted access to the readers of those pages, Facebook could make a lot of money selling advertising space.

But having a good idea isn't enough to build a business. Entrepreneurs need funds: you have to spend money to make money. Although businesses like Facebook seem to exist solely in the virtual world of cyberspace, free of the worldly burdens of brick-and-mortar establishments, the truth is that running such businesses requires a lot of very real and expensive hardware. Like Google, Amazon, and other internet giants, Facebook maintains huge "server farms," arrays of linked computers that track and process all the information needed to provide the user experience.

So where did Facebook get the money to equip these server farms? Some of it came from investors who acquired shares in the business, but much of it was borrowed. As Facebook grew bigger, so did the amount it borrowed.

The ability of Facebook to raise large sums of money to finance its growth is, in its own way, as remarkable as the company's product. In effect, some young guy with a bright idea is able to lay his hands on hundreds of millions of dollars to build his business. It's an amazing story.

Yet this sort of thing is common in modern economies. The long-run growth we analyzed in the previous chapter depends crucially on a set of markets and institutions, collectively known as the *financial system,* that channels the funds of savers into productive investment spending. Without this system, businesses like Facebook would not be able to purchase much of the physical capital that is an important source of productivity growth. And savers would be forced to accept a lower return on their funds.

Historically, financial systems channeled funds into investment spending projects such as railroads and factories. Today, financial systems channel funds into new sources of growth such as green technology, social media, and investments in human capital. Without a well-functioning financial system, a country will suffer stunted economic growth.

In this chapter, we begin by focusing on the economy as a whole. We will examine the relationship between savings and investment spending. Next, we go behind this relationship and analyze the financial system, the means by which savings is transformed into investment spending. We'll see how the financial system works by creating assets, markets, and institutions that increase the welfare of both savers (those with funds to invest) and borrowers (those with investment spending projects to finance). Finally, we examine the behavior of financial markets and why they often resist economists' attempts at explanation.

According to the **savings–investment spending identity,** savings and investment spending are always equal for the economy as a whole.

Matching Up Savings and Investment Spending

We learned in the previous chapter that two of the essential ingredients in economic growth are increases in the economy's levels of *human capital* and *physical capital.* Human capital is largely provided by governments through public education. (In countries with a large private education sector, like the United States, private post-secondary education is also an important source of human capital.) But physical capital, with the exception of infrastructure, is mainly created through private investment spending—that is, spending by firms rather than by the government.

Who pays for private investment spending? In some cases it's the people or corporations that actually do the spending—for example, a family that owns a business might use its own savings to buy new equipment or a new building, or a corporation might reinvest some of its own profits to build a new factory. In the modern economy, however, individuals and firms that create physical capital often do it with other people's money—money that they borrow or raise by selling stock.

To understand how investment spending is financed, we need to look first at how savings and investment spending are related for the economy as a whole. Then we will examine how savings are allocated among investment spending projects.

The Savings–Investment Spending Identity

The most basic point to understand about savings and investment spending is that they are always equal. This is not a theory; it's a fact of accounting called the **savings–investment spending identity.**

To see why the savings–investment spending identity must be true, let's look again at the national income accounting that we learned in Chapter 22. Recall that GDP is equal to total spending on domestically produced final goods and services, and that we can write the following equation (which is the same as Equation 22-1):

(25-1) $GDP = C + I + G + X - IM$

where C is spending by consumers, I is investment spending, G is government purchases of goods and services, X is the value of exports to other countries, and IM is spending on imports from other countries.

The Savings–Investment Spending Identity in a Closed Economy

In a closed economy, there are no exports or imports. So $X = 0$ and $IM = 0$, which makes Equation 25-1 simpler. As we learned in Chapter 22, the overall income of this simplified economy would, by definition, equal total spending. Why? Recall one of the basic principles of economics from Chapter 1, that one person's spending is another person's income: the only way people can earn income is by selling something to someone else, and every dollar spent in the economy creates income for somebody. This is represented by Equation 25-2: on the left, GDP represents total income earned in the economy, and on the right, $C + I + G$ represents total spending in the economy:

(25-2) $GDP = C + I + G$
Total income = Total spending

Now, what can be done with income? It can either be spent on consumption—consumer spending (C) plus government purchases of goods and services (G)—or saved (S). So it must be true that:

(25-3) $GDP = C + G + S$
Total income = Consumption spending + Savings

where S is savings. Meanwhile, as Equation 25-2 tells us, total spending consists of either consumption spending ($C + G$) or investment spending (I):

(25-4)   GDP = $C + G + I$
         Total income = Consumption spending + Investment spending

Putting Equations 25-3 and 25-4 together, we get:

(25-5) $C + G + S = C + G + I$
         Consumption spending + savings = Consumption spending +
         Investment spending

Subtract consumption spending ($C + G$) from both sides, and we get:

(25-6) $S = I$
         Savings = Investment spending

As we said, then, it's a basic accounting fact that savings equals investment spending for the economy as a whole.

   Now, let's take a closer look at savings. Households are not the only parties that can save in an economy. In any given year, the government can save, too, if it collects more tax revenue than it spends. When this occurs, the difference is called a **budget surplus** and is equivalent to savings by government. If, alternatively, government spending exceeds tax revenue, there is a **budget deficit**—a negative budget surplus. In this case, we often say that the government is "dissaving": by spending more than its tax revenues, the government is engaged in the opposite of savings.

   We'll define the term **budget balance** to refer to both cases, with the understanding that the budget balance can be positive (a budget surplus) or negative (a budget deficit). The budget balance is defined as:

(25-7) $S_{Government} = T - G - TR$

Where T is the value of tax revenues and TR is the value of government transfers. The budget balance is equivalent to savings by government—if it's positive, the government is saving; if it's negative, the government is dissaving. **National savings,** which we just called savings, for short, is equal to the sum of the budget balance and private savings, where private savings is disposable income (income after taxes) minus consumption. It is given by:

(25-8) $S_{National} = S_{Government} + S_{Private}$

So Equations 25-6 and 25-8 tell us that, in a closed economy, the savings–investment spending identity has the following form:

(25-9) $S_{National} = I$
         National savings = Investment

The Savings–Investment Spending Identity in an Open Economy An
open economy is an economy in which goods and money can flow into and out of the country. This changes the savings–investment spending identity because savings need not be spent on investment spending projects in the same country in which the savings are generated. That's because the savings of people who live in any one country can be used to finance investment spending that takes place in other countries. So any given country can receive *inflows* of funds—foreign savings that finance investment spending in that country. Any given country can also generate *outflows* of funds—domestic savings that finance investment spending in another country.

   The net effect of international inflows and outflows of funds on the total savings available for investment spending in any given country is known as the **net capital inflow** into that country, equal to the total inflow of foreign funds minus the total outflow of domestic funds to other countries. Like the budget balance, a

The **budget surplus** is the difference between tax revenue and government spending when tax revenue exceeds government spending.

The **budget deficit** is the difference between tax revenue and government spending when government spending exceeds tax revenue.

The **budget balance** is the difference between tax revenue and government spending.

National savings, the sum of private savings and the budget balance, is the total amount of savings generated within the economy.

Net capital inflow is the total inflow of funds into a country minus the total outflow of funds out of a country.

net capital inflow can be negative—that is, more capital can flow out of a country than flows into it. In recent years, the United States has experienced a consistent positive net capital inflow from foreigners, who view our economy as an attractive place to put their savings. In 2013, for example, net capital inflows into the United States were $423 billion.

It's important to note that, from a national perspective, a dollar generated by national savings and a dollar generated by capital inflow are not equivalent. Yes, they can both finance the same dollar's worth of investment spending. But any dollar borrowed from a saver must eventually be repaid with interest. A dollar that comes from national savings is repaid with interest to someone domestically—either a private party or the government. But a dollar that comes as capital inflow must be repaid with interest to a foreigner. So a dollar of investment spending financed by a capital inflow comes at a higher *national* cost—the interest that must eventually be paid to a foreigner—than a dollar of investment spending financed by national savings.

The fact that a net capital inflow represents funds borrowed from foreigners is an important aspect of the savings–investment spending identity in an open economy. Consider an individual who spends more than his or her income; that person must borrow the difference from others. Similarly, a country that spends more on imports than it earns from exports must borrow the difference from foreigners. And that difference, the amount of funds borrowed from foreigners, is the country's net capital inflow. As we will explain at greater length in Chapter 34, this means that the net capital inflow into a country is equal to the difference between imports and exports:

(25-10)
$$NCI = IM - X$$
Net capital inflow = Imports − Exports

Rearranging Equation 25-1 we get:

(25-11) $I = (GDP - C - G) + (IM - X)$

Using Equations 25-3 and 25-9 we know that GDP − C − G is equal to National savings, so that:

(25-12) $I = S_{National} + (IM - X) = S_{National} + NCI$
Investment spending = National savings + Net capital inflow

So the application of the savings–investment spending identity to an economy that is open to inflows or outflows of capital means that investment spending is equal to savings, where savings is equal to national savings *plus* net capital inflow. That is, in an economy with a positive net capital inflow, some investment spending is funded by the savings of foreigners. And in an economy with a negative net capital inflow (that is, more capital is flowing out than flowing in), some portion of national savings is funding investment spending in other countries.

In the United States in 2013, investment spending totaled $3,244.3 billion. Private savings totaled $3,402 billion, offset by government savings of −$368 billion and supplemented by a net capital inflow of $423 billion. Notice that these numbers don't quite add up; because data collection isn't perfect, there is a "statistical discrepancy" of −$212 billion. But we know that this is an error in the data, not in the theory, because the savings–investment spending identity must hold in reality.

Figure 25-1 shows what the savings–investment spending identity looked like in 2013 for two of the world's major economies, those of the United States and Germany. To make the two economies easier to compare, we've measured savings and investment spending as percentages of GDP. In each panel the orange bars on the left show total investment spending and the multicolored bars on the right show the components of savings. U.S. investment spending was 19.4% of GDP, financed by a combination of private savings (22.5% of GDP) and positive

PITFALLS

THE DIFFERENT KINDS OF CAPITAL
It's important to understand clearly the three different kinds of capital: physical capital, human capital, and financial capital (as explained in the previous chapter):

1. *Physical capital* consists of manufactured resources such as buildings and machines.
2. *Human capital* is the improvement in the labor force generated by education and knowledge.
3. *Financial capital* is funds from savings that are available for investment spending. A country that has a positive net capital inflow is experiencing a flow of funds into the country from abroad that can be used for investment spending.

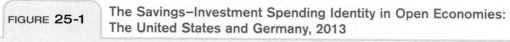

FIGURE **25-1**   The Savings–Investment Spending Identity in Open Economies: The United States and Germany, 2013

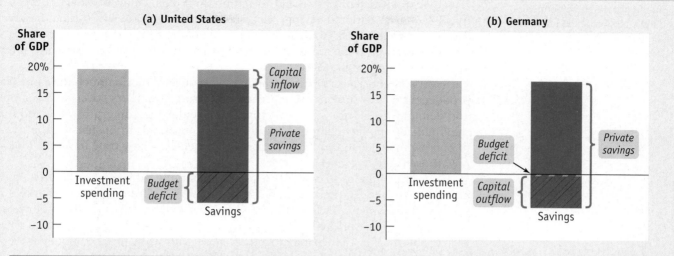

U.S. investment spending in 2013 (equal to 19.4% of GDP) was financed by a combination of private savings (22.5% of GDP) and a capital inflow (2.7% of GDP), which were partially offset by a government budget deficit (–5.8% of GDP). German investment spending in 2013 was slightly lower as a percentage of GDP (17.6%). It was financed by a higher level of private savings as a percentage of GDP (24%), which was offset by both a capital outflow (–6% of GDP) and a small government budget deficit (–0.4% of GDP).

Source: International Monetary Fund.

net capital inflow (2.7% of GDP) and partly offset by a government budget deficit (–5.8% of GDP). German investment spending was lower as a percentage of GDP, at 17.6%. It was financed by a higher level of private savings as a percentage of GDP (24%) and was offset by both a negative net capital inflow or capital outflow (–6% of GDP) and a small budget deficit (–0.4% of GDP).

The economy's savings finance its investment spending. But how are these funds that are available for investment spending allocated among various projects? That is, what determines which projects get financed (such as Facebook's server farms) and which don't (such as Microsoft's Courier tablet computer, an innovative concept that the software giant decided not to pursue)? We'll see shortly that funds get allocated to investment spending projects using a familiar method: by the market, via supply and demand.

FOR INQUIRING MINDS | Who Enforces the Accounting?

The savings–investment spending identity is a fact of accounting. By definition, savings equals investment spending for the economy as a whole. But who enforces the arithmetic? For example, what happens if the amount that businesses want to invest in capital equipment is less than the amount households want to save?

The short answer is that actual and *desired* investment spending aren't always equal. Suppose that households suddenly decide to save more by spending less—say, by putting off the purchase of new cars. The immediate

effect will be that unsold goods pile up—in this case, in the form of cars sitting in dealers' lots. And this increase in inventory counts as investment spending, albeit unintended. So the savings–investment spending identity still holds, because auto dealers end up engaging in more investment spending than they intended to. Similarly, if households suddenly decide to save less and spend more, inventories will drop—and this will be counted as *negative* investment spending.

A real-world example occurred in 2001. Savings and investment spending,

measured at an annual rate, both fell by $126 billion between the second and the fourth quarters of 2001. But on the investment spending side, $71 billion of that fall took the form of negative inventory investment spending. In particular, car dealers sold many of the vehicles that had been sitting on their lots.

Of course, businesses respond to changes in their inventories by changing their production. The inventory reduction in late 2001 prepared the ground for a spurt in output in early 2002. We'll examine the special role of inventories in economic fluctuations in Chapter 26. ■

The **loanable funds market** is a hypothetical market that illustrates the market outcome of the demand for funds generated by borrowers and the supply of funds provided by lenders.

The Market for Loanable Funds

For the economy as a whole, savings always equals investment spending. In a closed economy, savings is equal to national savings. In an open economy, savings is equal to national savings plus capital inflow. At any given time, however, savers, the people with funds to lend, are usually not the same as borrowers, the people who want to borrow to finance their investment spending. How are savers and borrowers brought together?

Savers and borrowers are matched up with one another in much the same way producers and consumers are matched up: through markets governed by supply and demand. In Figure 22-1, the expanded circular-flow diagram, we noted that the *financial markets* channel the savings of households to businesses that want to borrow in order to purchase capital equipment. It's now time to take a look at how those financial markets work.

To do this, it helps to consider a somewhat simplified version of reality. As we noted in Chapter 22, there are a large number of different financial markets in the financial system, such as the bond market and the stock market. However, economists often work with a simplified model in which they assume that there is just one market that brings together those who want to lend money (savers) and those who want to borrow (firms with investment spending projects). This hypothetical market is known as the **loanable funds market.** The price that is determined in the loanable funds market is the interest rate, denoted by *r*. As we noted in Chapter 23, loans typically specify a nominal interest rate. So although we call *r* "the interest rate," it is with the understanding that *r* is a nominal interest rate—an interest rate that is unadjusted for inflation.

We're not quite done simplifying things. There are, in reality, many different kinds of interest rates, because there are many different kinds of loans—short-term loans, long-term loans, loans made to corporate borrowers, loans made to governments, and so on. In the interest of simplicity, we'll ignore those differences and assume that there is only one type of loan.

OK, now we're ready to analyze how savings and investment get matched up.

The Demand for Loanable Funds Figure 25-2 illustrates a hypothetical demand curve for loanable funds, *D*, which slopes downward. On the horizontal axis we show the quantity of loanable funds demanded. On the vertical axis

---

FIGURE 25-2 | **The Demand for Loanable Funds**

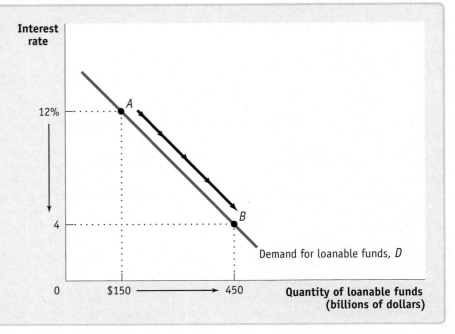

The demand curve for loanable funds slopes downward: the lower the interest rate, the greater the quantity of loanable funds demanded. Here, reducing the interest rate from 12% to 4% increases the quantity of loanable funds demanded from $150 billion to $450 billion.

Demand for loanable funds, *D*

we show the interest rate, which is the "price" of borrowing. But why does the demand curve for loanable funds slope downward?

To answer this question, consider what a firm is doing when it engages in investment spending—say, by buying new equipment. Investment spending means laying out money right now, expecting that this outlay will lead to higher profits at some point in the future. In fact, however, the promise of a dollar five or ten years from now is worth less than an actual dollar right now. So an investment is worth making only if it generates a future return that is *greater* than the monetary cost of making the investment today. How much greater?

To answer that, we need to take into account the *present value* of the future return the firm expects to get. You may recall that we introduced the concept of present value earlier in the book, in the Chapter 9 appendix. There you learned how present value can be applied to dollars earned multiple years in the future.

In present value calculations, we use the interest rate to determine how the value of a dollar in the future compares to the value of a dollar today. But the fact is that future dollars are worth less than a dollar today, and they are worth even less when the interest rate is higher.

> The **present value** of X is the amount of money needed today in order to receive X at a future date given the interest rate.

FOR INQUIRING MINDS | Using Present Value

An understanding of the concept of present value shows why the demand curve for loanable funds slopes downward. A simple way to grasp the essence of present value is to consider an example that illustrates the difference in value between having a sum of money today and having the same sum of money a year from now.

Suppose that exactly one year from today you will graduate, and you want to reward yourself by taking a trip that will cost $1,000. In order to have $1,000 a year from now, how much do you need today? It's not $1,000, and the reason why has to do with the interest rate. Let's call the amount you need today X. We'll use r to represent the interest rate you receive on funds deposited in the bank. If you put X into the bank today and earn interest rate r on it, then after one year, the bank will pay you $X \times (1 + r)$. If what the bank will pay you a year from now is equal to $1,000, then the amount you need today is

$$X \times (1 + r) = \$1,000$$

You can apply some basic algebra to find that

$$X = \$1,000/(1 + r)$$

Notice that the value of X depends on the interest rate r, which is always greater than 0. This fact implies that X is always *less than* $1,000. For example, if $r = 5\%$ (that is, $r = 0.05$), then $X = \$952.38$. In other words, having $952.38 today is equivalent to having $1,000 a year from now when the interest rate is 5%. That

When making financial decisions, individuals and firms must always keep in mind that having $1,000 today is worth more than having $1,000 a year from now.

is, $952.38 is the value of $1,000 today given an interest rate of 5%. Now we can define the **present value** of X: it is the amount of money needed today in order to receive X in the future given the interest rate. In this numerical example, $952.38 is the present value of $1,000 received one year from now given an interest rate of 5%.

The concept of present value also applies to decisions made by firms. Think about a firm that has two potential investment projects in mind, each of which will yield $1,000 a year from now. However, each project has different initial costs—say, one requires that

the firm borrow $900 right now and the other requires that the firm borrow $950. Which, if any, of these projects is worth borrowing money to finance and undertake?

The answer depends on the interest rate, which determines the present value of $1,000 a year from now. If the interest rate is 10%, the present value of $1,000 delivered a year from now is $909. In other words, at an interest rate of 10%, a $909 loan requires a repayment of $1,000 in a year's time. A loan less than $909 requires a repayment less than $1,000, while a loan of more than $909 requires a repayment of more than $1,000. So only the first project, which has an initial cost of less than $909, is profitable, because its return in a year's time is more than the amount of the loan repayment.

With an interest rate of 10%, the return on any project costing more than $909 is less than the amount the firm has to repay on its loan and is therefore unprofitable. If the interest rate is only 5%, however, the present value of $1,000 rises to $952. At this interest rate, both projects are profitable, because $952 exceeds both projects' initial cost. So a firm will borrow more and engage in more investment spending when the interest rate is lower.

Meanwhile, similar calculations will be taking place at other firms. So a lower interest rate will lead to higher investment spending in the economy as a whole: the demand curve for loanable funds slopes downward. ■

The intuition behind present value calculations is simple. The interest rate measures the opportunity cost of investment spending that results in a future return: instead of spending money on an investment spending project, a company could simply put the money into the bank and earn interest on it. And the higher the interest rate, the more attractive it is to simply put money into the bank and let it earn interest instead of investing it in an investment spending project.

In other words, the higher the interest rate, the higher the opportunity cost of investment spending. And, the higher the opportunity cost of investment spending, the lower the number of investment spending projects firms want to carry out, and therefore the lower the quantity of loanable funds demanded. It is this insight (discussed in the accompanying For Inquiring Minds) that explains why the demand curve for loanable funds is downward sloping.

When businesses engage in investment spending, they spend money right now in return for an expected payoff in the future. To evaluate whether a particular investment spending project is worth undertaking, a business must compare the present value of the future payoff with the current cost of that project. If the present value of the future payoff is greater than the current cost, a project is profitable and worth investing in. If the interest rate falls, then the present value of any given project rises, so more projects pass that test. If the interest rate rises, then the present value of any given project falls, and fewer projects pass that test.

So total investment spending, and hence the demand for loanable funds to finance that spending, is negatively related to the interest rate. Thus, the demand curve for loanable funds slopes downward. You can see this in Figure 25-2. When the interest rate falls from 12% to 4%, the quantity of loanable funds demanded rises from $150 billion (point A) to $450 billion (point B).

The Supply of Loanable Funds Figure 25-3 shows a hypothetical supply curve for loanable funds, S. Again, the interest rate plays the same role that the price plays in ordinary supply and demand analysis. But why is this curve upward sloping?

The answer is that loanable funds are supplied by savers, and savers incur an opportunity cost when they lend to a business: the funds could instead be spent on consumption—say, a nice vacation. Whether a given saver becomes a lender

FIGURE 25-3   The Supply of Loanable Funds

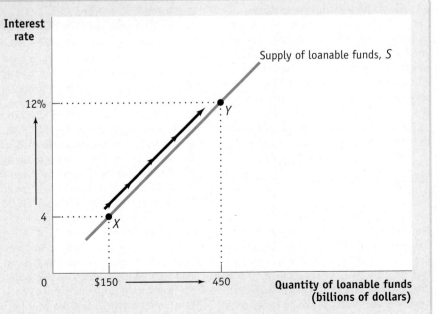

The supply curve for loanable funds slopes upward: the higher the interest rate, the greater the quantity of loanable funds supplied. Here, increasing the interest rate from 4% to 12% increases the quantity of loanable funds supplied from $150 billion to $450 billion.

by making funds available to borrowers depends on the interest rate received in return. By saving your money today and earning interest on it, you are rewarded with higher consumption in the future when the loan you made is repaid with interest. So it is a good assumption that more people are willing to forgo current consumption and make a loan to a borrower when the interest rate is higher.

As a result, our hypothetical supply curve of loanable funds slopes upward. In Figure 25-3, lenders will supply $150 billion to the loanable funds market at an interest rate of 4% (point X); if the interest rate rises to 12%, the quantity of loanable funds supplied will rise to $450 billion (point Y).

The Equilibrium Interest Rate The interest rate at which the quantity of loanable funds supplied equals the quantity of loanable funds demanded is called the **equilibrium interest rate.** As you can see in Figure 25-4, the equilibrium interest rate, r^*, and the total quantity of lending, Q^*, are determined by the intersection of the supply and demand curves, at point E. Here, the equilibrium interest rate is 8%, at which $300 billion is lent and borrowed. In this equilibrium, only investment spending projects that are profitable if the interest rate is 8% or higher are funded. Projects that would not be undertaken unless they are profitable only when the interest rate falls below 8% are not funded. Correspondingly, only lenders who are willing to accept an interest rate of 8% or less will have their offers to lend funds accepted; lenders who demand an interest rate higher than 8% do not have their offers to lend accepted.

Figure 25-4 shows how the market for loanable funds matches up desired savings with desired investment spending: in equilibrium, the quantity of funds that savers want to lend is equal to the quantity of funds that firms want to borrow. The figure also shows that this match-up is efficient, in two senses. First, the right investments get made: the investment spending projects that are actually financed have higher payoffs (in terms of present value) than those that do not get financed. Second, the right people do the saving and lending: the savers who actually lend funds are willing to lend for lower interest rates than those who do not.

The insight that the loanable funds market leads to an efficient use of savings, although drawn from a highly simplified model, has important implications for

The interest rate at which the quantity of loanable funds supplied equals the quantity of loanable funds demanded is the **equilibrium interest rate.**

FIGURE 25-4   Equilibrium in the Loanable Funds Market

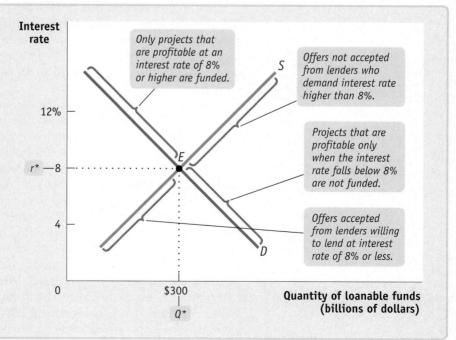

At the equilibrium interest rate, the quantity of loanable funds supplied equals the quantity of loanable funds demanded. Here, the equilibrium interest rate is 8%, with $300 billion of funds lent and borrowed. Lenders who demand an interest rate of 8% or lower have their offers of loans accepted; those who demand a higher interest rate do not. Projects that are profitable at an interest rate of 8% or higher are funded; those that are profitable only when the interest rate falls below 8% are not.

Only projects that are profitable at an interest rate of 8% or higher are funded.

Offers not accepted from lenders who demand interest rate higher than 8%.

Projects that are profitable only when the interest rate falls below 8% are not funded.

Offers accepted from lenders willing to lend at interest rate of 8% or less.

Crowding out occurs when a government budget deficit drives up the interest rate and leads to reduced investment spending.

real life. As we'll see shortly, it is the reason that a well-functioning financial system increases an economy's long-run economic growth rate.

Before we get to that, let's look at how the market for loanable funds responds to shifts of demand and supply. As in the standard model of supply and demand, where the equilibrium price changes in response to shifts of the demand or supply curves, here, the equilibrium interest rate changes when there are shifts of the demand curve for loanable funds, the supply curve for loanable funds, or both.

Shifts of the Demand for Loanable Funds Let's start by looking at the causes and effects of changes in demand.

The factors that can cause the demand curve for loanable funds to shift include the following:

1. *Changes in perceived business opportunities.* A change in beliefs about the payoff of investment spending can increase or reduce the amount of desired spending at any given interest rate. For example, during the 1990s there was great excitement over the business possibilities created by the internet, which had just begun to be widely used. As a result, businesses rushed to buy computer equipment, put fiber-optic cables in the ground, launch websites, and so on. This shifted the demand for loanable funds to the right. By 2001, the failure of many dot-com businesses had led to disillusionment with technology-related investment; this shifted the demand for loanable funds back to the left.

2. *Changes in government borrowing.* A government runs a budget deficit when, in a given year, it spends more than it receives. A government that runs budget deficits can be a major source of demand for loanable funds. As a result, changes in the government budget deficit can shift the demand curve for loanable funds. For example, between 2000 and 2003, as the U.S. federal government went from a budget surplus to a budget deficit, the government went from being a net saver that provided loanable funds to the market to being a net borrower, borrowing funds from the market. In 2000, net federal borrowing was *minus* $152 billion, as the federal government was paying off some of its preexisting debt. But by 2003, net federal borrowing was *plus* $469 billion because the government had to borrow large sums to pay its bills. This change in the federal budget position had the effect, other things equal, of shifting the demand curve for loanable funds to the right.

Figure 25-5 shows the effects of an increase in the demand for loanable funds. S is the supply of loanable funds, and D_1 is the initial demand curve. The initial equilibrium interest rate is r_1. An increase in the demand for loanable funds means that the quantity of funds demanded rises at any given interest rate, so the demand curve shifts rightward to D_2. As a result, the equilibrium interest rate rises to r_2.

The fact that an increase in the demand for loanable funds leads, other things equal, to a rise in the interest rate has one especially important implication: it tells us that increasing or persistent government budget deficits are cause for concern because an increase in the government's deficit shifts the demand curve for loanable funds to the right, which leads to a higher interest rate. If the interest rate rises, businesses will cut back on their investment spending.

So, other things equal, a rise in the government budget deficit tends to reduce overall investment spending. Economists call the negative effect of government budget deficits on investment spending **crowding out.** Concerns about crowding out are one key reason to worry about increasing or persistent budget deficits.

However, it's important to add a qualification here: crowding out may not occur if the economy is depressed. When the economy is operating far below full employment, government spending can lead to higher incomes, and these higher incomes lead to increased savings at any given interest rate. Higher savings allows the government to borrow without raising interest rates. Many

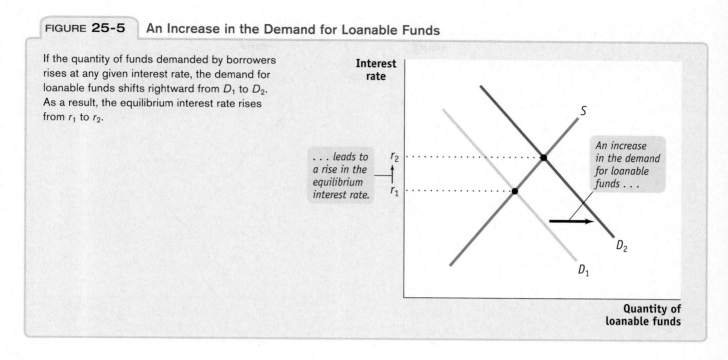

FIGURE 25-5   An Increase in the Demand for Loanable Funds

If the quantity of funds demanded by borrowers rises at any given interest rate, the demand for loanable funds shifts rightward from D_1 to D_2. As a result, the equilibrium interest rate rises from r_1 to r_2.

economists believe, for example, that the large budget deficits that the U.S. government ran from 2008 to 2013 in the face of a depressed economy caused little if any crowding out.

Shifts of the Supply of Loanable Funds Like the demand for loanable funds, the supply of loanable funds can shift. Among the factors that can cause the supply of loanable funds to shift are the following:

1. *Changes in private savings behavior.* A number of factors can cause the level of private savings to change at any given interest rate. For example, between 2000 and 2006 rising home prices in the United States made many homeowners feel richer, making them willing to spend more and save less. This had the effect of shifting the supply curve of loanable funds to the left.

2. *Changes in net capital inflows.* Capital flows into and out of a country can change as investors' perceptions of that country change. For example, Greece experienced large net capital inflows after the creation of the euro, Europe's common currency, in 1999, because investors believed that Greece's adoption of the euro as its currency had made it a safe place to put their funds. By 2009, however, worries about the Greek government's solvency (and the discovery that it had been understating its debt) led to a collapse in investor confidence, and the net inflow of funds dried up. The effect of shrinking capital inflows was to shift the supply curve in the Greek loanable funds market to the left.

   In the mid-2000s, the United States received large net capital inflows, with much of the money coming from China and the Middle East. Those inflows helped fuel a big increase in residential investment spending—newly constructed homes—from 2003 to 2006. As a result of the bursting of the U.S. housing bubble in 2006–2007 and the subsequent deep recession, those inflows began to trail off in 2008.

Figure 25-6 shows the effects of an increase in the supply of loanable funds. D is the demand for loanable funds, and S_1 is the initial supply curve. The initial equilibrium interest rate is r_1. An increase in the supply of loanable funds means that the quantity of funds supplied rises at any given interest rate, so the supply curve shifts rightward to S_2. As a result, the equilibrium interest rate falls to r_2.

FIGURE **25-6** An Increase in the Supply of Loanable Funds

If the quantity of funds supplied by lenders rises at any given interest rate, the supply of loanable funds shifts rightward from S_1 to S_2. As a result, the equilibrium interest rate falls from r_1 to r_2.

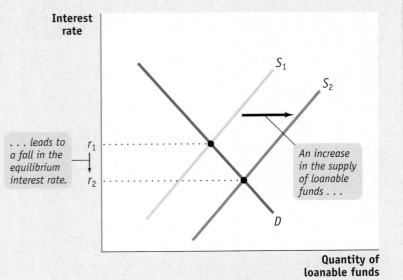

Inflation and Interest Rates Anything that shifts either the supply of loanable funds curve or the demand for loanable funds curve changes the interest rate. Historically, major changes in interest rates have been driven by many factors, including changes in government policy and technological innovations that created new investment opportunities.

However, arguably the most important factor affecting interest rates over time—the reason, for example, that interest rates today are much lower than they were in the late 1970s and early 1980s—is changing expectations about future inflation, which shift both the supply and the demand for loanable funds.

To understand the effect of expected future inflation on interest rates, recall our discussion in Chapter 23 of the way inflation creates winners and losers—for example, the way that higher than expected U.S. inflation in the 1970s and 1980s reduced the real value of homeowners' mortgages, which was good for the homeowners but bad for the banks. We also learned that economists summarize the effect of inflation on borrowers and lenders by distinguishing between the *nominal interest rate* and the *real interest rate*, where the difference is:

$$\text{Real interest rate} = \text{Nominal interest rate} - \text{Inflation rate}$$

The true cost of borrowing is the real interest rate, not the nominal interest rate. To see why, suppose a firm borrows $10,000 for one year at a 10% nominal interest rate. At the end of the year, it must repay $11,000—the amount borrowed plus the interest. But suppose that over the course of the year the average level of prices increases by 10%, so that the real interest rate is zero. Then the $11,000 repayment has the same purchasing power as the original $10,000 loan. In real terms, the borrower has received a zero-interest loan.

Similarly, the true payoff to lending is the real interest rate, not the nominal interest rate. Suppose that a bank makes a $10,000 loan for one year at a 10% nominal interest rate. At the end of the year, the bank receives an $11,000 repayment. But if the average level of prices rises by 10% per year, the purchasing power of the money the bank gets back is no more than that of the money it lent out. In real terms, the bank has made a zero-interest loan.

Now we can add an important detail to our analysis of the loanable funds market. Figures 25-5 and 25-6 are drawn with the vertical axis measuring the *nominal interest rate for a given expected future inflation rate*. Why do we use the nominal interest rate rather than the real interest rate? Because in the real world neither borrowers nor lenders know what the future inflation rate will be when they make a deal. Actual loan contracts therefore specify a nominal interest rate rather than a real interest rate. Because we are holding the expected future inflation rate fixed in Figures 25-5 and 25-6, however, changes in the nominal interest rate also lead to changes in the real interest rate.

The expectations of borrowers and lenders about future inflation rates are normally based on recent experience. In the late 1970s, after a decade of high inflation, borrowers and lenders expected future inflation to be high. By the late 1990s, after a decade of fairly low inflation, borrowers and lenders expected future inflation to be low. And these changing expectations about future inflation had a strong effect on the nominal interest rate, largely explaining why nominal interest rates were much lower in the early years of the twenty-first century than they were in the early 1980s.

Let's look at how changes in the expected future rate of inflation are reflected in the loanable funds model.

In Figure 25-7, the curves S_0 and D_0 show the supply and demand for loanable funds given that the expected future rate of inflation is 0%. In that case, equilibrium is at E_0, and the equilibrium nominal interest rate is 4%. Because expected future inflation is 0%, the equilibrium expected real interest rate over the life of the loan is also 4%.

Now suppose that the expected future inflation rate rises to 10%. The demand curve for loanable funds shifts upward to D_{10}: borrowers are now willing to borrow as much at a nominal interest rate of 14% as they were previously willing to borrow at 4%. That's because with a 10% inflation rate, a 14% nominal interest rate corresponds to a 4% real interest rate. Similarly, the supply curve of loanable funds shifts upward to S_{10}: lenders require a nominal interest rate of 14% to persuade them to lend as much as they would previously have lent at 4%. The new equilibrium is at E_{10}: the result of an expected future inflation rate of 10% is that the equilibrium nominal interest rate rises from 4% to 14%.

This situation can be summarized as a general principle, known as the **Fisher effect** (after the American economist Irving Fisher, who proposed it in 1930): *the expected real interest rate is unaffected by changes in expected future inflation.*

According to the **Fisher effect,** an increase in expected future inflation drives up the nominal interest rate, leaving the expected real interest rate unchanged.

FIGURE 25-7   The Fisher Effect

D_0 and S_0 are the demand and supply curves for loanable funds when the expected future inflation rate is 0%. At an expected inflation rate of 0%, the equilibrium nominal interest rate is 4%. An increase in expected future inflation pushes both the demand and supply curves upward by 1 percentage point for every percentage point increase in expected future inflation. D_{10} and S_{10} are the demand and supply curves for loanable funds when the expected future inflation rate is 10%. The 10 percentage point increase in expected future inflation raises the equilibrium nominal interest rate to 14%. The expected real interest rate remains at 4%, and the equilibrium quantity of loanable funds also remains unchanged.

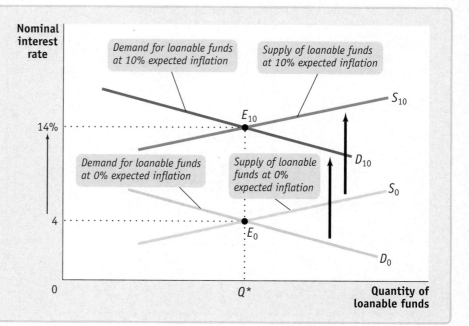

According to the Fisher effect, an increase in expected future inflation drives up the nominal interest rate, where each additional percentage point of expected future inflation drives up the nominal interest rate by 1 percentage point. The central point is that both lenders and borrowers base their decisions on the expected real interest rate. As a result, a change in the expected rate of inflation does not affect the equilibrium quantity of loanable funds or the expected real interest rate; all it affects is the equilibrium nominal interest rate.

ECONOMICS ▶ *in Action*

Sixty Years of U.S. Interest Rates

There have been some large movements in U.S. interest rates dating back to the 1950s. These movements clearly show how both changes in expected future inflation and changes in the expected return on investment spending move interest rates.

Panel (a) of Figure 25-8 illustrates the first effect. It shows the average interest rate on bonds issued by the U.S. government—specifically, bonds for which the government promises to repay the full amount after 10 years—from 1953 to early 2014, along with the rate of consumer price inflation over the same period. As you can see, the big story about interest rates is the way they soared in the 1970s, before coming back down in the 1980s. It's not hard to see why that happened: inflation shot up during the 1970s, leading to widespread expectations that high inflation would continue. And as we've seen, a higher expected inflation rate raises the equilibrium interest rate. As the inflation rate came down in the 1980s, so did expectations of future inflation, and this brought interest rates down as well.

Panel (b) illustrates the second effect: changes in the expected return on investment spending and interest rates, with a "close-up" of interest rates from 2002 to 2014. Notice the rise in interest rates during the middle years of the last decade, followed by a sharp drop. We know from other evidence (such as surveys of investor opinion) that the expected rate of inflation didn't change much over

FIGURE **25-8**   Changes in U.S. Interest Rates Over Time

Source: Federal Reserve Bank of St. Louis.

those years. What happened, instead, was the boom and bust in housing: interest rates rose as demand for housing soared, pushing the demand curve for loanable funds to the right, then fell as the housing boom collapsed, shifting the demand curve for loanable funds back to the left.

Throughout this whole process, total savings was equal to total investment spending, and the rise and fall of the interest rate played a key role in matching lenders with borrowers.

Check Your Understanding   25-1

1. Use a diagram of the loanable funds market to illustrate the effect of the following events on the equilibrium interest rate and investment spending.
   a. An economy is opened to international movements of capital, and a net capital inflow occurs.
   b. Retired people generally save less than working people at any interest rate. The proportion of retired people in the population goes up.

2. Explain what is wrong with the following statement: "Savings and investment spending may not be equal in the economy as a whole because when the interest rate rises, households will want to save more money than businesses will want to invest."

3. Suppose that expected inflation rises from 3% to 6%.
   a. How will the real interest rate be affected by this change?
   b. How will the nominal interest rate be affected by this change?
   c. What will happen to the equilibrium quantity of loanable funds?

   Solutions appear at back of book.

The Financial System

A well-functioning financial system that brought together the funds of investors and the ideas of brilliant nerds made the rise of Facebook possible. But to think that this is an exclusively modern phenomenon would be misguided. Financial markets raised the funds that were used to develop colonial markets in India, to build canals across Europe, and to finance the Napoleonic wars in the eighteenth and early nineteenth centuries. Capital inflows financed the early economic development of the United States, funding investment spending in mining, railroads, and canals. In fact, many of the principal features of financial markets and assets have been well understood in Europe and the United States since the eighteenth century. These features are no less relevant today. So let's begin by understanding exactly what is traded in financial markets.

Financial markets are where households invest their current savings and their accumulated savings, or **wealth,** by purchasing *financial assets.* A **financial asset** is a paper claim that entitles the buyer to future income from the seller. For example, when a saver lends funds to a company, the loan is a financial asset sold by the company that entitles the lender (the buyer of the financial asset) to future income from the company.

A household can also invest its current savings or wealth by purchasing a **physical asset,** a tangible object that can be used to generate future income such as a preexisting house or preexisting piece of equipment. It gives the owner the right to dispose of the object as he or she wishes (for example, rent it or sell it).

Recall that the purchase of a financial or physical asset is typically called investing. So if you purchase a preexisting piece of equipment—say, a used airliner—you are investing in a physical asset. In contrast, if you spend funds that *add* to the stock of physical capital in the economy—say, purchasing a newly manufactured airplane—you are engaging in investment spending. (See the Pitfalls on investment versus investment spending that appears earlier in the chapter.)

A household's **wealth** is the value of its accumulated savings.

A **financial asset** is a paper claim that entitles the buyer to future income from the seller.

A **physical asset** is a tangible object that can be used to generate future income.

A **liability** is a requirement to pay income in the future.

Transaction costs are the expenses of negotiating and executing a deal.

Financial risk is uncertainty about future outcomes that involve financial losses or gains.

If you get a loan from your local bank—say, to buy a new car—you and the bank are creating a financial asset: your loan. A *loan* is one important kind of financial asset in the real world, one that is owned by the lender—in this case, your local bank. In creating that loan, you and the bank are also creating a **liability,** a requirement to pay income in the future.

So although your loan is a financial asset from the bank's point of view, it is a liability from your point of view: a requirement that you repay the loan, including any interest. In addition to loans, there are three other important kinds of financial assets: stocks, bonds, and *bank deposits*. Because a financial asset is a claim to future income that someone has to pay, it is also someone else's liability. We'll explain in detail shortly who bears the liability for each type of financial asset.

These four types of financial assets—loans, stocks, bonds, and bank deposits—exist because the economy has developed a set of specialized markets, like the stock market and the bond market, and specialized institutions, like banks, that facilitate the flow of funds from lenders to borrowers. In Chapter 22, in the context of the circular-flow diagram, we defined the financial markets and institutions that make up the financial system.

A well-functioning financial system is a critical ingredient in achieving long-run growth because it encourages greater savings and investment spending. It also ensures that savings and investment spending are undertaken efficiently. To understand how this occurs, we first need to know what tasks the financial system needs to accomplish. Then we can see how the job gets done.

Three Tasks of a Financial System

Our earlier analysis of the loanable funds market ignored three important problems facing borrowers and lenders: *transaction costs, risk,* and the desire for *liquidity*. The three tasks of a financial system are to reduce these problems in a cost-effective way. Doing so enhances the efficiency of financial markets: it makes it more likely that lenders and borrowers will make mutually beneficial trades—trades that make society as a whole richer. We'll turn now to examining how financial assets are designed and how institutions are developed to cope with these problems.

Task 1: Reducing Transaction Costs The expenses of actually putting together and executing a deal are known as **transaction costs.** For example, arranging a loan requires spending time and money negotiating the terms of the deal, verifying the borrower's ability to pay, drawing up and executing legal documents, and so on. Suppose a large business decided that it wanted to raise $1 billion for investment spending. No individual would be willing to lend that much. And negotiating individual loans from thousands of different people, each willing to lend a modest amount, would impose very large total costs because each individual transaction would incur a cost. Total costs would be so large that the entire deal would probably be unprofitable for the business.

Fortunately, that's not necessary: when large businesses want to borrow money, they either go to a bank or sell bonds in the bond market. Obtaining a loan from a bank avoids large transaction costs because it involves only a single borrower and a single lender. We'll explain more about how bonds work in the next section. For now, it is enough to know that the principal reason there is a bond market is that it allows companies to borrow large sums of money without incurring large transaction costs.

Task 2: Reducing Risk Another problem that real-world borrowers and lenders face is **financial risk,** uncertainty about future outcomes that involve financial losses or gains. Financial risk, or simply risk, is a problem because the future is uncertain, containing the potential for losses as well as gains. For example, owning and driving a car entails the financial risk of a costly accident. Most people view potential losses and gains in an *asymmetrical* way: most people experience the loss in welfare from losing a given amount of money more intensely than they experience the increase in welfare from gaining the same amount of money.

A person who is more sensitive to a loss than to a gain of an equal dollar amount is called *risk-averse*. Most people are risk-averse, although to differing degrees. For example, people who are wealthy are typically less risk-averse than those who are not so well-off.

An individual can engage in **diversification** by investing in several different things so that the possible losses are independent events.

A well-functioning financial system helps people reduce their exposure to risk, which risk-averse people would like to do. Suppose the owner of a business expects to make a greater profit if she buys additional capital equipment, but she isn't completely sure that this will indeed happen. She could pay for the equipment by using her savings or selling her house. But if the profit is significantly less than expected, she will have lost her savings, or her house, or both. That is, she would be exposing herself to a lot of risk due to uncertainty about how well or poorly the business performs. (This is why business owners, who typically have a significant portion of their own personal wealth tied up in their businesses, are usually people who are more tolerant of risk than the average person.)

So, being risk-averse, this business owner wants to share the risk of purchasing new capital equipment with someone, even if that requires sharing some of the profit if all goes well. How can she do this? By selling shares of her company to other people and using the money she receives from selling shares, rather than money from the sale of her other assets, to finance the equipment purchase. By selling shares in her company, she reduces her personal losses if the profit is less than expected: she won't have lost her other assets. But if things go well, the shareholders earn a share of the profit as a return on their investment.

By selling a share of her business, the owner has achieved *diversification:* she has been able to invest in several things in a way that lowers her total risk. She has maintained her investment in her bank account, a financial asset; in ownership of her house, a physical asset; and in ownership of the unsold portion of her business, a financial asset. These investments are likely to carry some risk of their own; for example, her bank may fail or her house may burn down (though in the modern United States it is likely that she is partly protected against these risks by insurance).

But even in the absence of insurance, she is better off having maintained investments in these different assets because their different risks are *unrelated,* or *independent, events*. This means, for example, that her house is no more likely to burn down if her business does poorly and that her bank is no more likely to fail if her house burns down.

To put it another way, if one asset performs poorly, it is very likely that her other assets will be unaffected and, as a result, her total risk of loss has been reduced. But if she had invested all her wealth in her business, she would have faced the prospect of losing everything if the business had performed poorly. By engaging in **diversification**—investing in several assets with unrelated, or independent, risks—our business owner has lowered her total risk of loss.

The desire of individuals to reduce their total risk by engaging in diversification is why we have stocks and a stock market. In the next section on types of financial assets, we'll explain in more detail how certain features of the stock market increase the ability of individuals to manage and reduce risk.

Task 3: Providing Liquidity The financial system also exists to provide investors with *liquidity,* a concern that—like risk—arises because the future is uncertain. Suppose that, having made a loan, a lender suddenly finds himself in need of cash—say, to meet a medical emergency. Unfortunately, if that loan was made to a business that used it to buy new equipment, the business cannot repay the loan on short notice to satisfy the lender's need to recover his money. Knowing in advance that there is a danger of needing to get his money back before the term of the loan is up, our lender might be reluctant to lock up his money by lending it to a business.

An asset is **liquid** if it can be quickly converted into cash with relatively little loss of value.

An asset is **illiquid** if it cannot be quickly converted into cash with relatively little loss of value.

A **loan** is a lending agreement between an individual lender and an individual borrower.

A **default** occurs when a borrower fails to make payments as specified by the loan or bond contract.

A **loan-backed security** is an asset created by pooling individual loans and selling shares in that pool.

An asset is **liquid** if it can be quickly converted into cash with relatively little loss of value, **illiquid** if it cannot. As we'll see, stocks and bonds are a partial answer to the problem of liquidity. Banks provide an additional way for individuals to hold liquid assets and still finance illiquid investment spending projects.

To help lenders and borrowers make mutually beneficial deals, then, the economy needs ways to reduce transaction costs, to reduce and manage risk through diversification, and to provide liquidity. How does it achieve these tasks?

Types of Financial Assets

In the modern economy there are four main types of financial assets: *loans*, bonds, stocks, and *bank deposits*. In addition, financial innovation has allowed the creation of a wide range of *loan-backed securities*. Each asset serves a somewhat different purpose. We'll examine loans, bonds, stocks, and loan-backed securities now, reserving our discussion of bank deposits until the following section.

Loans A lending agreement made between an individual lender and an individual borrower is a **loan.** Most people encounter loans in the form of a student loan or a bank loan to finance the purchase of a car or a house. And small businesses usually use bank loans to buy new equipment.

The good aspect of loans is that a given loan is usually tailored to the needs of the borrower. Before a small business can get a loan, it usually has to discuss its business plans, its profits, and so on with the lender. This results in a loan that meets the borrower's needs and ability to pay.

The bad aspect of loans is that making a loan to an individual person or a business typically involves a lot of transaction costs, such as the cost of negotiating the terms of the loan, investigating the borrower's credit history and ability to repay, and so on. To minimize these costs, large borrowers such as major corporations and governments often take a more streamlined approach: they sell (or issue) bonds.

Bonds As we learned in Chapter 22, a bond is an IOU issued by the borrower. Normally, the seller of the bond promises to pay a fixed sum of interest each year and to repay the principal—the value stated on the face of the bond—to the owner of the bond on a particular date. So a bond is a financial asset from its owner's point of view and a liability from its issuer's point of view. A bond issuer sells a number of bonds with a given interest rate and maturity date to whoever is willing to buy them, a process that avoids costly negotiation of the terms of a loan with many individual lenders.

Bond purchasers can acquire information free of charge on the quality of the bond issuer, such as the bond issuer's credit history, from bond-rating agencies rather than having to incur the expense of investigating it themselves. A particular concern for investors is the possibility of **default,** the risk that the bond issuer will fail to make payments as specified by the bond contract. Once a bond's risk of default has been rated, it can be sold on the bond market as a more or less standardized product—a product with clearly defined terms and quality. In general, bonds with a higher default risk must pay a higher interest rate to attract investors.

Another important advantage of bonds is that they are easy to resell. This provides liquidity to bond purchasers. Indeed, a bond will often pass through many hands before it finally comes due. Loans, in contrast, are much more difficult to resell because, unlike bonds, they are not standardized: they differ in size, quality, terms, and so on. This makes them a lot less liquid than bonds.

Loan-Backed Securities Assets created by pooling individual loans and selling shares in that pool (a process called *securitization*) are called **loan-backed securities.** This type of asset has become extremely popular over the past two decades. While mortgage-backed securities—in which thousands of individual home mortgages are pooled and shares are sold to investors—are the best-known example, securitization has also been widely applied to student loans, credit card loans, and auto loans.

A **financial intermediary** is an institution that transforms the funds it gathers from many individuals into financial assets.

These loan-backed securities are traded on financial markets like bonds; they are preferred by investors because they provide more diversification and liquidity than individual loans. However, with so many loans packaged together, it can be difficult to assess the true quality of the asset. That difficulty came to haunt investors during the financial crisis of 2008, when the bursting of the housing bubble led to widespread defaults on mortgages and large losses for holders of "supposedly safe" mortgage-backed securities, pain that spread throughout the entire financial system.

Stocks As we learned in Chapter 22, a stock is a share in the ownership of a company. A share of stock is a financial asset from its owner's point of view and a liability from the company's point of view. Not all companies sell shares of their stock; "privately held" companies are owned by an individual or a few partners, who get to keep all of the company's profit. Most large companies, however, do sell stock. For example, Microsoft has nearly 8 billion shares outstanding; if you buy one of those shares, you are entitled to one-eleven billionth of the company's profit, as well as 1 of 11 billion votes on company decisions.

Why does Microsoft, historically a very profitable company, allow you to buy a share in its ownership? Why didn't Bill Gates and Paul Allen, the two founders of Microsoft, keep complete ownership for themselves and just sell bonds for their investment spending needs? The reason, as we have just learned, is risk: few individuals are risk-tolerant enough to face the risk involved in being the sole owner of a large company.

Reducing the risk that business owners face, however, is not the only way in which the existence of stocks improves society's welfare: it also improves the welfare of investors who buy stocks. Shareowners are able to enjoy the higher returns over time that stocks generally offer in comparison to bonds. Over the past century, stocks have typically yielded about 7% after adjusting for inflation; bonds have yielded only about 2%. But as investment companies warn you, "past performance is no guarantee of future results."

And there is a downside: owning the stock of a given company is riskier than owning a bond issued by the same company. Why? Loosely speaking, a bond is a promise while a stock is a hope: by law, a company must pay what it owes its lenders before it distributes any profit to its shareholders. And if the company should fail (that is, be unable to pay its interest obligations and declare bankruptcy), its physical and financial assets go to its bondholders—its lenders—while its shareholders generally receive nothing. So although a stock generally provides a higher return to an investor than a bond, it also carries higher risk.

But the financial system has devised ways to help investors as well as business owners simultaneously manage risk and enjoy somewhat higher returns. It does that through the services of institutions known as *financial intermediaries.*

Financial Intermediaries

A **financial intermediary** is an institution that transforms funds gathered from many individuals into financial assets. The most important types of financial intermediaries are *mutual funds, pension funds, life insurance companies,* and *banks.* About three-quarters of the financial assets Americans own are held through these intermediaries rather than directly.

Mutual Funds As we've explained, owning shares of a company entails accepting risk in return for a higher potential reward. But it should come as no surprise that stock investors can lower their total risk by engaging in diversification. By owning

A **mutual fund** is a financial intermediary that creates a stock portfolio and then resells shares of this portfolio to individual investors.

A **pension fund** is a type of mutual fund that holds assets in order to provide retirement income to its members.

a *diversified portfolio* of stocks—a group of stocks in which risks are unrelated to, or offset, one another—rather than concentrating investment in the shares of a single company or a group of related companies, investors can reduce their risk.

In addition, financial advisers, aware that most people are risk-averse, almost always advise their clients to diversify not only their stock portfolio but also their entire wealth by holding other assets in addition to stock—assets such as bonds, real estate, and cash. (And, for good measure, to have plenty of insurance in case of accidental losses!)

However, for individuals who don't have a large amount of money to invest— say, $1 million or more—building a diversified stock portfolio can incur high transaction costs (particularly fees paid to stockbrokers) because they are buying a few shares of a lot of companies. Fortunately for such investors, *mutual funds* help solve the problem of achieving diversification without high transaction costs.

A **mutual fund** is a financial intermediary that creates a stock portfolio by buying and holding shares in companies and then selling shares of the stock portfolio to individual investors. By buying these shares, investors with a relatively small amount of money to invest can indirectly hold a diversified portfolio, achieving a better return for any given level of risk than they could otherwise achieve. Table 25-1 shows an example of a diversified mutual fund, the Fidelity Spartan 500 Index Fund. It shows the percentage of investors' money invested in the stocks of the largest companies in the mutual fund's portfolio.

TABLE **25-1**	Fidelity Spartan 500 Index Fund, Top Holdings (as of November 2014)
Company	**Percent of mutual fund assets invested in a company**
Apple Inc.	3.4%
Exxon Mobil Corp.	2.3
Microsoft Corp.	1.8
S&P 500 Index Future	1.7
Johnson & Johnson	1.6
General Electric Co.	1.4
Berkshire Hathaway Inc.	1.3
Wells Fargo & Co.	1.3
Chevron Corp.	1.3
JPMorgan Chase & Co.	1.2

Source: Fidelity Investments.

Many mutual funds also perform market research on the companies they invest in. This is important because there are thousands of stock-issuing U.S. companies (not to mention foreign companies), each differing in terms of its likely profitability, dividend payments, and so on. It would be extremely time-consuming and costly for an individual investor to do adequate research on even a small number of companies. Mutual funds save transaction costs by doing this research for their customers.

The mutual fund industry represents a huge portion of the modern U.S. economy, not just of the U.S. financial system. In total, U.S. mutual funds had assets of $15 trillion at the end of 2013. In 2013, the largest mutual fund company was Fidelity, with almost $5 trillion in assets in September 2014.

We should mention, by the way, that mutual funds charge fees for their services. These fees are quite small for mutual funds that simply hold a diversified portfolio of stocks without trying to pick winners. But the fees charged by mutual funds that claim to have special expertise in investing your money can be quite high.

Pension Funds and Life Insurance Companies In addition to mutual funds, many Americans have holdings in **pension funds,** nonprofit institutions that collect the savings of their members and invest those funds in a wide variety of assets, providing their members with income when they retire. Although pension funds are subject to some special rules and receive special treatment for tax purposes, they function much like mutual funds. They invest in a diverse array of financial assets, allowing their members to achieve more cost-effective diversification and market research than they would be able to achieve individually. At the end of 2013, pension funds in the United States held more than $16 trillion in assets.

Americans also have substantial holdings in the policies of **life insurance companies,** which guarantee a payment to the policyholder's beneficiaries (typically, the family) when the policyholder dies. By enabling policyholders to cushion their beneficiaries from financial hardship arising from their death, life insurance companies also improve welfare by reducing risk.

Banks Recall the problem of liquidity: other things equal, people want assets that can be readily converted into cash. Bonds and stocks are much more liquid than physical assets or loans, yet the transaction cost of selling bonds or stocks to meet a sudden expense can be large. Furthermore, for many small and moderate-size companies, the cost of issuing bonds and stocks is too large given the modest amount of money they seek to raise. A *bank* is an institution that helps resolve the conflict between lenders' needs for liquidity and the financing needs of borrowers who don't want to use the stock or bond markets.

A bank works by first accepting funds from *depositors:* when you put your money in a bank, you are essentially becoming a lender by lending the bank your money. In return, you receive credit for a **bank deposit**—a claim on the bank, which is obliged to give you your cash if and when you demand it. So a bank deposit is a financial asset owned by the depositor and a liability of the bank that holds it.

> A **life insurance company** sells policies that guarantee a payment to a policyholder's beneficiaries when the policyholder dies.
>
> A **bank deposit** is a claim on a bank that obliges the bank to give the depositor his or her cash when demanded.

GLOBAL COMPARISION | Bonds Versus Banks

Suppose that a business wants to borrow funds to finance investment. There are actually two ways it could do this: It could sell bonds to investors, or it could get loans from banks. There are advantages and disadvantages to each strategy.

On the one hand, issuing bonds tends to be cheaper than borrowing from a bank, because it eliminates the middleman. Also, banks often place conditions on loans, restricting the borrower's freedom to conduct its business as it chooses. On the other hand, bank loans can be less risky than issuing bonds. If a borrower gets into difficulty, its bank will typically be supportive, offering them more time to repay if a good plan is in place to fix their problems. Bond holders, in contrast, are inflexible and can inflict deep costs on a company that misses its interest payments. So going with bonds means taking somewhat bigger risks for the sake of flexibility. Going with bank loans means reducing risk at the cost of less flexibility.

It's a tough choice—and interestingly, companies in the United States and their counterparts in Europe generally make different choices. The figure shows the value of corporate bonds outstanding in the United States and the European Union, in each case measured as a percentage of GDP. What you see is that U.S. companies issue a lot more bonds than their European counterparts. Correspondingly, European firms rely much more on bank borrowing.

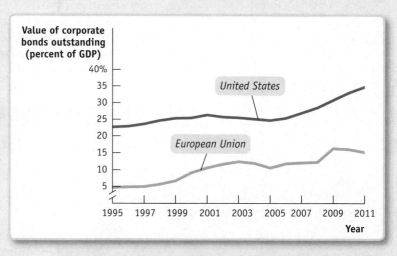

Why the difference? Generally, American companies are more inclined to take risks. Also, European households are more inclined than U.S. households to leave large sums in bank accounts. As a result, European banks have more money to lend than their American counterparts.

If you look at the figure, however, you'll notice something else: European companies are relying much more on bonds than in the past. In the wake of the financial crisis, troubled European banks have pulled back from lending, which has forced European companies to issue bonds to fill the financing gap. As the data show, the European financial system is becoming more like the U.S. system.

Sources: Bijlsma, Michiel J., and Gijsbert T.J. Zwart, "The Changing Landscape of Financial Markets in Europe, the United States and Japan," No. 2013/02, Bruegel Working Paper, 2013; Bank for International Settlements.

A **bank** is a financial intermediary that provides liquid assets in the form of bank deposits to lenders and uses those funds to finance the illiquid investment spending needs of borrowers.

A bank, however, keeps only a fraction of its customers' deposits in the form of ready cash. Most of its deposits are lent out to businesses, buyers of new homes, and other borrowers. These loans come with a long-term commitment by the bank to the borrower: as long as the borrower makes his or her payments on time, the loan cannot be recalled by the bank and converted into cash. So a bank enables those who wish to borrow for long lengths of time to use the funds of those who wish to lend but simultaneously want to maintain the ability to get their cash back on demand.

More formally, a **bank** is a financial intermediary that provides liquid financial assets in the form of deposits to lenders and uses their funds to finance the illiquid investment spending needs of borrowers. In essence, a bank is engaging in a kind of mismatch: lending for long periods of time while subject to the condition that its depositors could demand their funds back at any time. How can it manage that?

The bank counts on the fact that, on average, only a small fraction of its depositors will want their cash at the same time. On any given day, some people will make withdrawals and others will make new deposits; these will roughly cancel each other out. So the bank needs to keep only a limited amount of cash on hand to satisfy its depositors. In addition, if a bank becomes financially incapable of paying its depositors, individual bank deposits are guaranteed to depositors up to $250,000 by the Federal Deposit Insurance Corporation, or FDIC, a federal agency. This reduces the risk to a depositor of holding a bank deposit, in turn reducing the incentive to withdraw funds if concerns about the financial state of the bank should arise. So, under normal conditions, banks need hold only a fraction of their depositors' cash.

By reconciling the needs of savers for liquid assets with the needs of borrowers for long-term financing, banks play a key economic role. As the following Economics in Action explains, the creation of a well-functioning banking system was a key turning point in South Korea's economic success.

ECONOMICS ▶ *in Action*

Banks and the South Korean Miracle

South Korea's experience with banks shows how important a good financial system is to economic growth.

South Korea, now a very rich modern country, is one of the great success stories of economic growth. In the early 1960s, it was a very poor nation. Then it experienced spectacularly high rates of economic growth. And South Korean banks had a lot to do with it.

In the early 1960s, South Korea's banking system was a mess. Interest rates on deposits were set very low by government regulation at a time when the country was experiencing high inflation. So savers didn't want to put their money in a bank, fearing that much of their purchasing power would be eroded by rising prices. Instead, they engaged in current consumption by spending their money on goods and services or used their wealth to buy physical assets such as real estate and gold. Because savers refused to make bank deposits, businesses found it very hard to borrow money to finance investment spending.

In 1965 the South Korean government reformed the country's banks and increased interest rates to a level that was attractive to savers. Over the next five years the value of bank deposits increased sevenfold, and the national savings rate—the percentage of GDP going into national savings—more than doubled. The rejuvenated banking system made it possible for South Korean businesses to launch a great investment spending boom, a key element in the country's growth surge.

Many other factors besides banking were involved in South Korea's success, but the country's experience does show how important a good financial system is to economic growth.

Check Your Understanding   25-2

1. Rank the following assets in terms of (i) level of transaction costs, (ii) level of risk, (iii) level of liquidity.
   a. A bank deposit with a guaranteed interest rate
   b. A share of a highly diversified mutual fund, which can be quickly sold
   c. A share of the family business, which can be sold only if you find a buyer and all other family members agree to the sale
2. What relationship would you expect to find between the level of development of a country's financial system and its level of economic development? Explain in terms of the country's level of savings and level of investment spending.

Solutions appear at back of book.

Financial Fluctuations

We've learned that the financial system is an essential part of the economy; without stock markets, bond markets, and banks, long-run economic growth would be hard to achieve. Yet the news isn't entirely good: the financial system sometimes doesn't function well and instead is a source of instability in the short run.

In fact, the financial consequences of a sharp fall in housing prices became a major problem for economic policy makers starting in the summer of 2007. By the fall of 2008, it was clear that the U.S. economy faced a severe slump as it adjusted to the consequences of greatly reduced home values. And in 2014, the time of writing, the economy still hadn't fully recovered from the severe recession of 2007–2009. We could easily write a whole book on asset market fluctuations. In fact, many people have. Here, we briefly discuss the causes of asset price fluctuations.

The Demand for Stocks

Once a company issues shares of stock to investors, those shares can then be resold to other investors in the stock market. And these days, thanks to cable TV and the internet, you can easily spend all day watching stock market fluctuations—the movement up and down of the prices of individual stocks as well as summary measures of stock prices like the Dow Jones Industrial Average. These fluctuations reflect changes in supply and demand by investors. But what causes the supply and demand for stocks to shift?

Remember that stocks are financial assets: they are shares in the ownership of a company. Unlike a good or service, whose value to its owner comes from its consumption, the value of an asset comes from its ability to generate higher future consumption of goods or services.

A financial asset allows higher future consumption in two ways. First, many financial assets provide regular income to their owners in the form of interest payments or dividends. But many companies don't pay dividends; instead, they retain their earnings to finance future investment spending. Investors purchase non-dividend-paying stocks in the belief that they will earn income from selling the stock in the future at a profit, the second way of generating higher future income. Even in the cases of a bond or a dividend-paying stock, investors will not want to purchase an asset that they believe will sell for less in the future than today, because such an asset will reduce their wealth when they sell it.

FOR INQUIRING MINDS | How Now, Dow Jones?

Financial news reports often lead with the day's stock market action, as measured by changes in the Dow Jones Industrial Average, the S&P 500, and the NASDAQ. What are these numbers, and what do they tell us?

All three are stock market indices. Like the consumer price index, they are numbers constructed as a summary of average prices—in this case, prices of stocks. The Dow, created by the financial analysis company Dow Jones, is an index of the prices of stock in 30 leading companies, such as Microsoft, Walmart, and General Electric. The S&P 500 is an index of 500 companies, created by Standard and Poor's, another financial company. The NASDAQ is compiled by the National Association of Securities Dealers, which trades the stocks of smaller new companies, like the satellite radio company SiriusXM or the computer manufacturer Dell.

Because these indices contain different groups of stocks, they track somewhat different things. The Dow, because it

contains only 30 of the largest companies, tends to reflect the "old economy," traditional business powerhouses like Exxon Mobil. The NASDAQ is heavily influenced by technology stocks. The S&P 500, a broad measure, is in between.

Why are these indices important? Because the movement in an index gives investors a quick, snapshot view of how stocks from certain sectors of the economy are doing. As we'll soon explain, the price of a stock at a given point in time embodies investors' expectations about the future prospects of the underlying company. By implication, an index composed of stocks drawn from companies in a particular sector embodies investors' expectations of the future prospects of that sector of the economy.

The numbers tell the tale.

So a day on which the NASDAQ moves up but the Dow moves down implies that, on that day, prospects appear brighter for the high-tech sector than for the old-economy sector. The movement in the indices reflects the fact that investors are acting on their beliefs by selling stocks in the Dow and buying stocks in the NASDAQ. ■

So the value of a financial asset today depends on investors' beliefs about the future value or price of the asset. If investors believe that it will be worth more in the future, they will demand more of the asset today at any given price; consequently, today's equilibrium price of the asset will rise. Conversely, if investors believe the asset will be worth less in the future, they will demand less today at any given price; consequently, today's equilibrium price of the asset will fall. Today's stock prices will change according to changes in investors' expectations about future stock prices.

Suppose an event occurs that leads to a rise in the expected future price of a company's shares—say, for example, Apple announces that it forecasts higher than expected profitability due to torrential sales of the latest version of the iPhone. Demand for Apple shares will increase. At the same time, existing shareholders will be less willing to supply their shares to the market at any given price, leading to a decrease in the supply of Apple shares. And as we know, an increase in demand or a decrease in supply (or both) leads to a rise in price.

Alternatively, suppose that an event occurs that leads to a fall in the expected future price of a company's shares—say, Home Depot announces that it expects lower profitability because a slump in home sales has depressed the demand for home improvements. Demand for Home Depot shares will decrease. At the same time, supply will increase because existing shareholders will be more willing to supply their Home Depot shares to the market. Both changes lead to a fall in the stock price.

So stock prices are determined by the supply and demand for shares—which, in turn, depend on investors' expectations about the future stock price.

Stock prices are also affected by changes in the attractiveness of substitute assets, like bonds. As we learned early on, the demand for a particular good decreases when purchasing a substitute good becomes more attractive—say, due to a fall in its price. The same lesson holds true for stocks: when purchasing bonds becomes more attractive due to a rise in interest rates, stock prices will fall. And when purchasing bonds becomes less attractive due to a fall in interest rates, stock prices will rise.

The Demand for Other Assets

Everything we've just said about stocks applies to other assets as well, including physical assets. Consider the demand for commercial real estate—office buildings, shopping malls, and other structures that provide space for business activities. An investor who buys an office building does so for two reasons. First, because space in the building can be rented out, the owner of the building receives income in the form of rents. Second, the investor may expect the building to rise in value, meaning that it can be sold at a higher price at some future date.

As in the case of stocks, the demand for commercial real estate also depends on the attractiveness of substitute assets, especially bonds. When interest rates rise, the demand for commercial real estate decreases; when interest rates fall, the demand for commercial real estate increases.

Most Americans don't own commercial real estate. Only half of the population owns any stock, even indirectly through mutual funds, and for most of those people, stock ownership is well under $50,000. However, at the end of 2013 about 65% of American households owned another kind of asset: their own homes. What determines housing prices?

You might wonder whether home prices can be analyzed the same way we analyze stock prices or the price of commercial real estate. After all, stocks pay dividends, commercial real estate yields rents, but when a family lives in its own home, no money changes hands.

In economic terms, however, that doesn't matter very much. To a large extent, the benefit of owning your own home is the fact that you don't have to pay rent to someone else—or, to put it differently, it's as if you were paying rent to yourself. In fact, the U.S. government includes "implicit rent"—an estimate of the amount that homeowners, in effect, pay to themselves—in its estimates of GDP. The amount people are willing to pay for a house depends in part on the implicit rent they expect to receive from that house.

The demand for housing, like the demand for other assets, also depends on what people expect to happen to future prices: they're willing to pay more for a house if they believe they can sell it at a higher price sometime in the future. Last but not least, the demand for houses depends on interest rates: a rise in the interest rate increases the cost of a mortgage and leads to a decrease in housing demand; a fall in the interest rate reduces the cost of a mortgage and causes an increase in housing demand.

All asset prices, then, are determined by a similar set of factors. But we haven't yet fully answered the question of what determines asset prices because we haven't explained what determines investors' *expectations* about future asset prices.

Asset Price Expectations

There are two principal competing views about how asset price expectations are determined. One view, which comes from traditional economic analysis, emphasizes the rational reasons why expectations *should* change. The other, widely held by market participants and also supported by some economists, emphasizes the irrationality of market participants.

The Efficient Markets Hypothesis Suppose you were trying to assess what Home Depot's stock is really worth. To do this, you would look at the *fundamentals,* the underlying determinants of the company's future profits. These would

According to the **efficient markets hypothesis,** asset prices embody all publicly available information.

include factors like the changing shopping habits of the American public and the prospects for home remodeling. You would also want to compare the earnings you could expect to receive from Home Depot with the likely returns on other financial assets, such as bonds.

According to one view of asset prices, the value you would come up with after a careful study of this kind would, in fact, turn out to be the price at which Home Depot stock is already selling in the market. Why? Because all publicly available information about Home Depot's fundamentals is already embodied in its stock price. Any difference between the market price and the value suggested by a careful analysis of the underlying fundamentals indicates a profit opportunity to smart investors, who then sell Home Depot stock if it looks overpriced and buy it if it looks underpriced.

The **efficient markets hypothesis** is the general form of this view; it means that asset prices always embody all publicly available information. One implication of the efficient markets hypothesis is that at any point in time, stock prices are fairly valued: they reflect all currently available information about fundamentals. So they are neither overpriced nor underpriced.

FOR INQUIRING MINDS | Behavioral Finance

Individuals often make irrational—sometimes predictably irrational—choices that leave them worse off economically than would other, feasible alternatives. People also have a habit of repeating the same decision-making mistakes. This kind of behavior is the subject of *behavioral economics,* which includes the rapidly growing subfield of *behavioral finance,* the study of how investors in financial markets often make predictably irrational choices. In fact, the 2013 Nobel Prize in Economics was awarded to Yale professor Robert Shiller (along with two others), for his work showing how financial markets exhibit clear signs of irrationality.

Like most people, investors depart from rationality in systematic ways. In particular, they are prone to *overconfidence,* as in having a misguided faith that they are able to spot a winning stock; to *loss aversion,* being unwilling to sell an unprofitable asset and accept the loss; and to a *herd mentality,* buying an asset when its price has already been driven high and selling it when its price has already been driven low.

This irrational behavior raises an important question: can investors who *are* rational make a lot of money at the expense of those investors who aren't—for example, by buying a company's stock if irrational fears make it cheap?

The answer to this question is sometimes yes and sometimes no. Some professional investors have made huge profits by betting against irrational moves

in the market (buying when there is irrational selling and selling when there is irrational buying). For example, the billionaire hedge fund manager John Paulson made $4 billion by betting against subprime mortgages during the U.S. housing bubble of 2007–2008 because he understood that financial assets containing subprime mortgages were being sold at inflated prices.

But sometimes even a rational investor cannot profit from market irrationality. For example, a money manager has to obey customers' orders to buy or sell even when those actions are irrational. Likewise, it can be much safer for professional money managers to follow the herd: if they do that and their investments go badly, they have the career-saving excuse that no one foresaw a problem. But if they've gone against the herd and their investments go south, they are likely to be fired for making poor choices. So rational investors can even exacerbate the irrational moves in financial markets.

KAL/CartoonArts International / The New York Times Syndicate

Some observers of historical trends hypothesize that financial markets alternate between periods of complacency and forgetfulness, which breed bubbles as investors irrationally believe that prices can only go up, followed by a crash, which in turn leads investors to avoid financial markets altogether and renders asset prices irrationally cheap. Clearly, the events of the past decade, with its huge housing bubble followed by extreme turmoil in financial markets, have given researchers in the area of behavioral finance a lot of material to work with. ■

Another implication of the efficient markets hypothesis is that the prices of stocks and other assets should change only in response to new information about the underlying fundamentals. Since new information is by definition unpredictable—if it were predictable, it wouldn't be new information— movements in asset prices are also unpredictable. As a result, the movement of, say, stock prices will follow a **random walk**—the general term for the movement over time of an unpredictable variable.

The efficient markets hypothesis plays an important role in understanding how financial markets work. Most investment professionals and many economists, however, regard it as an oversimplification. Investors, they claim, aren't that rational.

A **random walk** is the movement over time of an unpredictable variable.

Irrational Markets? Many people who actually trade in the markets, such as individual investors and professional money managers, are skeptical of the efficient markets hypothesis. They believe that markets often behave irrationally and that a smart investor can engage in successful "market timing"—buying stocks when they are underpriced and selling them when they are overpriced.

Although economists are generally skeptical about claims that there are surefire ways to outsmart the market, many have also challenged the efficient markets hypothesis. It's important to understand, however, that finding particular examples where the market got it wrong does not disprove the efficient markets hypothesis. If the price of Home Depot stock plunges from $40 to $10 because of a sudden change in buying patterns, this doesn't mean that the market was inefficient in originally pricing the stock at $40. The fact that buying patterns were about to change wasn't publicly available information, so it wasn't embodied in the earlier stock price.

Serious challenges to the efficient markets hypothesis focus instead either on evidence of systematic misbehavior of market prices or on evidence that individual investors don't behave in the way the theory suggests. For example, some economists believe they have found strong evidence that stock prices fluctuate more than can be explained by news about fundamentals.

Others believe they have strong evidence that individual investors behave in systematically irrational ways. For example, people seem to expect that a stock that has risen in the past will keep on rising, even though the efficient markets hypothesis tells us there is no reason to expect this. The same appears to be true of other assets, especially housing: the great housing bubble, described in the Economics in Action that follows this section, arose in large part because home-buyers assumed that home prices would continue rising in the future.

Asset Prices and Macroeconomics

How should macroeconomists and policy makers deal with the fact that asset prices fluctuate a lot and that these fluctuations can have important economic effects? This question has become one of the major problems facing macroeconomic policy. On one side, policy makers are reluctant to assume that the market is wrong—that asset prices are either too high or too low. In part, this reflects the efficient markets hypothesis, which says that any information that is publicly available is already accounted for in asset prices. More generally, it's hard to make the case that government officials are better judges of appropriate prices than private investors who are putting their own money on the line.

On the other side, the past 20 years were marked by not one but two huge asset bubbles, each of which created major macroeconomic problems when it burst. In the late 1990s the prices of technology stocks, including but not limited to dot-com internet firms, soared to hard-to-justify heights. When the bubble burst, these stocks lost, on average, two-thirds of their value in a short time, helping to cause the 2001 recession and a period of high unemployment. A few years later there was a major bubble in housing prices. The collapse of this bubble in 2008 triggered a severe financial crisis followed by a deep recession, and the lingering effects of the crisis were still afflicting the U.S. economy years later.

These events have prompted much debate over whether and how to limit financial instability. We discuss financial regulation and the efforts to make it more effective in Chapter 29.

ECONOMICS ▶ *in Action*

The Great American Housing Bubble

Between 2000 and 2006, there was a huge increase in the price of houses in America. By the summer of 2006, home prices were well over twice as high as they had been in January 2000 in a number of major U.S. metropolitan areas, including Los Angeles, San Diego, San Francisco, Washington, Miami, Las Vegas, and New York. By 2004, as the increase in home prices accelerated, a number of economists (including the authors of this textbook) argued that this price increase was excessive—that it was a bubble, a rise in asset prices driven by unrealistic expectations about future prices.

It was certainly true that home prices rose much more than the cost of renting a comparable place to live. Panel (a) of Figure 25-9 compares a widely used index of U.S. housing prices with the U.S. government's index of the cost of renting, both shown as index numbers with January 2000 = 100. Home prices shot up, even though rental rates grew only gradually.

Yet there were also a number of economists who argued that the rise in housing prices was completely justified. They pointed, in particular, to the fact that interest rates were unusually low in the years of rapid price increases, and they argued that low interest rates combined with other factors, such as growing population, explained the surge in prices. Alan Greenspan, then chairman of the Federal Reserve, conceded in 2005 that there might be some "froth" in the markets but denied that there was any national bubble.

Unfortunately, it turned out that the skeptics were right. Greenspan himself would later concede that there had, in fact, been a huge national bubble. In 2006, as home prices began to level off, it became apparent that many buyers had

FIGURE 25-9   The Great American Housing Bubble

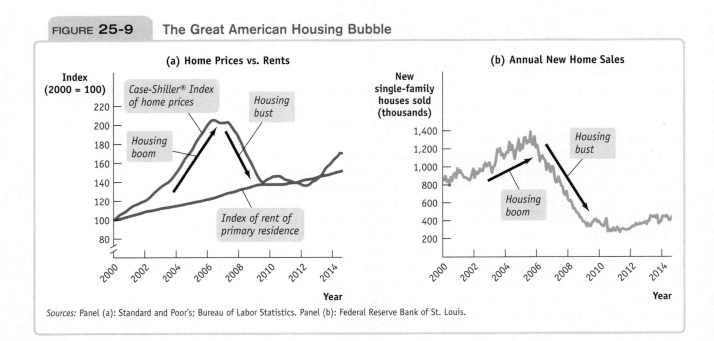

Sources: Panel (a): Standard and Poor's; Bureau of Labor Statistics. Panel (b): Federal Reserve Bank of St. Louis.

held unrealistic expectations about future prices. As home prices began to fall, expectations of future increases in home prices were revised downward, precipitating a sudden and dramatic collapse in prices. And with home prices falling, the demand for housing fell drastically, as illustrated by panel (b) of Figure 25-9.

The implosion in housing, in turn, created numerous economic difficulties, including severe stress on the banking system, which we will examine in Chapter 29.

Check Your Understanding   25-3

1. What is the likely effect of each of the following events on the stock price of a company? Explain your answers.
   a. The company announces that although profits are low this year, it has discovered a new line of business that will generate high profits next year.
   b. The company announces that although it had high profits this year, those profits will be less than had been previously announced.
   c. Other companies in the same industry announce that sales are unexpectedly slow this year.
   d. The company announces that it is on track to meet its previously forecast profit target.

2. Assess the following statement: "Although many investors may be irrational, it is unlikely that over time they will behave irrationally in exactly the same way—such as always buying stocks the day after the Dow has risen by 1%."

Solutions appear at back of book.

▼ **Quick Review**

• Financial market fluctuations can be a source of short-run macroeconomic instability.

• Asset prices are driven by supply and demand as well as by the desirability of competing assets like bonds. Supply and demand also reflect expectations about future asset prices. One view of expectations is the **efficient markets hypothesis,** which leads to the view that stock prices follow a **random walk.**

• Market participants and some economists question the efficient markets hypothesis. In practice, policy makers don't assume that they can outsmart the market, but they also don't assume that markets will always behave rationally.

Grameen Bank: Banking Against Poverty

EPA/LucusDolega/Newscom

An old joke says that a banker will only lend you money if you don't need it. So when Guadalupe Perez found it hard to pay the rent for her party decoration store in Queens, New York, as the recession hurt her business, she normally would have been forced to close her doors. Instead she was able to turn for help to Grameen America, obtaining a loan to tide her over. "It opened up a way for me to keep my business," she said. "It was a loan that I could pay little by little; I felt it was a good choice for me." And she returned to Grameen, borrowing several more times to expand her store and to invest in more inventory.

Grameen America is a subsidiary of Grameen Bank in Bangladesh, which pioneered the business of *microcredit,* providing small loans to poor individuals. It was created in the mid-1970s by Mohammed Yunus, a Bangladeshi economist with a PhD from Vanderbilt University. Regular banks require a borrower to have an established credit history and/or assets that are put up as collateral for the loan (and will be seized if the loan isn't repaid on time)—requirements that a poor person can rarely meet.

Instead, Grameen Bank relies on collective responsibility to ensure that its loans are repaid: each borrower is part of a five-member group that approves each other's loan and provides oversight. The group doesn't have any legal obligation to repay the loan, but in practice the group usually does take financial responsibility if a borrower gets into difficulties. If everyone in the group repays on time, each member is able to borrow a larger amount the next time.

Grameen operates in over 100 countries, from the United States to Uganda. The great majority of its customers are rural women seeking to escape poverty by starting small businesses. Since its inception it has lent over $10 billion dollars to well over eight million women.

Even in a rich country like the United States, micro-lending—defined as a loan less than $50,000—has become a booming business. Since 2008, when it was founded, through 2014, Grameen America has made nearly 100,000 loans and dispensed over $200 million. The company estimates that borrowers have increased their income by an average of $2,500 during a six-month loan cycle.

Although independent researchers admit it is hard to pin down exactly how much additional income is gained by virtue of micro-loans, what is clear from the research is that micro-lending gives people flexibility and added security, often preventing working people as well as entrepreneurs from falling deeper into poverty when experiencing a bad financial patch. Fittingly, in 2006 Yunus and Grameen received the Nobel Peace Prize for their contributions to development and poverty reduction.

QUESTIONS FOR THOUGHT

1. What market inefficiency is being exploited by Grameen Bank? What is the source of this inefficiency?

2. What tasks of a financial system does micro-lending perform?

3. What do you predict is the effect of Grameen Bank's lending on a community?

SUMMARY

1. Investment in physical capital is necessary for long-run economic growth. So in order for an economy to grow, it must channel savings into investment spending.

2. According to the **savings–investment spending identity,** savings and investment spending are always equal for the economy as a whole. The government is a source of savings when it runs a positive **budget balance,** also known as a **budget surplus;** it is a source of dissavings when it runs a negative budget balance, also known as a **budget deficit.** In a closed economy, savings is equal to **national savings,** the sum of private savings plus the budget balance. In an open economy, savings is equal to national savings plus **net capital inflow** of foreign savings. When a negative net capital inflow occurs, some portion of national savings is funding investment spending in other countries.

3. The hypothetical **loanable funds market** shows how loans from savers are allocated among borrowers with investment spending projects. At the **equilibrium interest rate** the quantity of loans demanded equals the quantity of loans offered. Only those investment projects with an expected return greater or equal to the equilibrium interest rate are funded. By showing how gains from trade between lenders and borrowers are maximized, the loanable funds market shows why a well-functioning financial system leads to greater long-run economic growth. Increasing or persistent government budget deficits can lead to **crowding out:** higher interest rates and reduced investment spending. Changes in perceived business opportunities and in government borrowing shift the demand curve for loanable funds; changes in private savings and capital inflows shift the supply curve.

4. In order to evaluate a project in which the return, X, is realized in the future, you must transform X into its **present value** using the interest rate, r. The present value of $1 received one year from now is $1 / (1 + r)$, the amount of money you must lend out today to have $1 one year from now. The present value of a given project rises as the interest rate falls and falls as the interest rate rises. This tells us that the demand curve for loanable funds is downward sloping.

5. Because neither borrowers nor lenders can know the future inflation rate, loans specify a nominal interest rate rather than a real interest rate. For a given expected future inflation rate, shifts of the demand and supply curves of loanable funds result in changes in the underlying real interest rate, leading to changes in the nominal interest rate. According to the **Fisher effect,** an increase in expected future inflation raises the nominal interest rate one-to-one so that the expected real interest rate remains unchanged.

6. Households invest their current savings or **wealth**— their accumulated savings—by purchasing assets. Assets come in the form of either a **financial asset,** a paper claim that entitles the buyer to future income from the seller, or a **physical asset,** a tangible object that can generate future income. A financial asset is also a **liability** from the point of view of its seller. There are four main types of financial assets: **loans,** bonds, stocks, and **bank deposits.** Each of them serves a different purpose in addressing the three fundamental tasks of a financial system: reducing **transaction costs**—the cost of making a deal; reducing **financial risk**—uncertainty about future outcomes that involves financial gains and losses; and providing **liquid** assets—assets that can be quickly converted into cash without much loss of value (in contrast to **illiquid** assets, which are not easily converted).

7. Although many small and moderate borrowers use bank loans to fund investment spending, larger companies typically issue bonds. Bonds with a higher risk of **default** must typically pay a higher interest rate. Business owners reduce their risk by selling stock. Although stocks usually generate a higher return than bonds, investors typically wish to reduce their risk by engaging in **diversification,** owning a wide range of assets whose returns are based on unrelated, or independent, events. Most people are risk-averse, more sensitive to a loss than to an equal-size gain. **Loan-backed securities,** a recent innovation, are assets created by pooling individual loans and selling shares of that pool to investors. Because they are more diversified and more liquid than individual loans, bonds are preferred by investors. It can be difficult, however, to assess a bond's quality.

8. **Financial intermediaries**—institutions such as **mutual funds, pension funds, life insurance companies,** and **banks**—are critical components of the financial system. Mutual funds and pension funds allow small investors to diversify, and life insurance companies reduce risk.

9. A bank allows individuals to hold liquid bank deposits that are then used to finance illiquid loans. Banks can perform this mismatch because on average only a small fraction of depositors withdraw their funds at any one time. A well-functioning banking sector is a key ingredient of long-run economic growth.

10. Asset market fluctuations can be a source of short-run macroeconomic instability. Asset prices are determined by supply and demand as well as by the desirability of competing assets, like bonds: when the interest rate rises, prices of stocks and physical assets such as real estate generally fall, and vice versa. Expectations drive the supply of and demand for assets: expectations of

higher future prices push today's asset prices higher, and expectations of lower future prices drive them lower. One view of how expectations are formed is the **efficient markets hypothesis,** which holds that the prices of assets embody all publicly available information. It implies that fluctuations are inherently unpredictable—they follow a **random walk.**

11. Many market participants and economists believe that, based on actual evidence, financial markets are not as rational as the efficient markets hypothesis claims. Such evidence includes the fact that stock price fluctuations are too great to be driven by fundamentals alone. Policy makers assume neither that markets always behave rationally nor that they can outsmart them.

KEY TERMS

Savings–investment spending identity, p. 718
Budget surplus, p. 719
Budget deficit, p. 719
Budget balance, p. 719
National savings, p. 719
Net capital inflow, p. 719
Loanable funds market, p. 722
Present value, p. 723
Equilibrium interest rate, p. 725
Crowding out, p. 726

Fisher effect, p. 729
Wealth, p. 731
Financial asset, p. 731
Physical asset, p. 731
Liability, p. 732
Transaction costs, p. 732
Financial risk, p. 732
Diversification, p. 733
Liquid, p. 734
Illiquid, p. 734
Loan, p. 734

Default, p. 734
Loan-backed securities, p. 734
Financial intermediary, p. 735
Mutual fund, p. 736
Pension fund, p. 736
Life insurance company, p. 737
Bank deposit, p. 737
Bank, p. 738
Efficient markets hypothesis, p. 742
Random walk, p. 743

PROBLEMS

1. Given the following information about the closed economy of Brittania, what is the level of investment spending and private savings, and what is the budget balance? What is the relationship among the three? Is national savings equal to investment spending? There are no government transfers.

   GDP = $1,000 million T = $50 million
   C = $850 million G = $100 million

2. Given the following information about the open economy of Regalia, what is the level of investment spending and private savings, and what are the budget balance and net capital inflow? What is the relationship among the four? There are no government transfers. (*Hint:* net capital inflow equals the value of imports *(IM)* minus the value of exports *(X)*.)

   GDP = $1,000 million G = $100 million
   C = $850 million X = $100 million
   T = $50 million IM = $125 million

3. The accompanying table shows the percentage of GDP accounted for by private savings, investment spending, and net capital inflow in the economies of Capsland and Marsalia. Capsland is currently experiencing a positive net capital inflow and Marsalia, a negative net capital outflow. What is the budget balance (as a percentage of GDP) in both countries? Are Capsland and Marsalia running a budget deficit or surplus?

	Capsland	Marsalia
Investment spending as a percentage of GDP	20%	20%
Private savings as a percentage of GDP	10	25
Net capital inflow as a percentage of GDP	5	–2

4. Assume the economy is open to capital inflows and outflows and therefore net capital inflow equals imports *(IM)* minus exports *(X)*. Answer each of the following questions.

   a. X = $125 million
   IM = $80 million
   Budget balance = –$200 million
   I = $350 million
   Calculate private savings.

   b. X = $85 million
   IM = $135 million
   Budget balance = $100 million
   Private savings = $250 million
   Calculate I.

   c. X = $60 million
   IM = $95 million
   Private savings = $325 million
   I = $300 million
   Calculate the budget balance.

   d. Private savings = $325 million
   I = $400 million
   Budget balance = $10 million
   Calculate $IM - X$.

5. The accompanying table, taken from the National Income and Product Accounts Tables, shows the various components of U.S. GDP in 2012 and 2013 in billions of dollars.

Year	Gross domestic product	Private consumption	Gross domestic investment	Government purchases of goods and services	Government savings (budget balance)	Net government taxes after transfers
	(billions of dollars)					
2012	$16,163.2	$11,083.1	$2,479.2	$2,549.7	−$1,311.7	?
2013	16,768.1	11,484.3	2,648.0	2,547.6	?	1,673.3

a. Complete the table by filling in the missing figures.

b. For each year, calculate taxes (after transfers) as a percentage of GDP.

c. For each year, calculate national savings and private savings.

6. The government is running a budget balance of zero when it decides to increase education spending by $200 billion and finance the spending by selling bonds. The accompanying diagram shows the market for loanable funds before the government sells the bonds. Assume that there are no capital inflows or outflows. How will the equilibrium interest rate and the equilibrium quantity of loanable funds change? Is there any crowding out in the market?

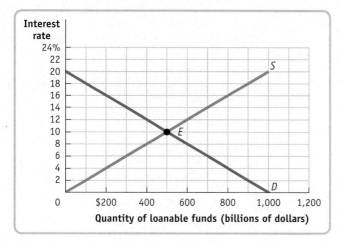

7. In 2014, Congress estimated that the cost of increasing support and expanding pre-kindergarten education and infant and toddler childcare would cost $28 billion. Since the U.S. government was running a budget deficit at the time, assume that the new pre-K funding was financed by government borrowing, which increases the demand for loanable funds without affecting supply. This question considers the likely effect of this government expenditure on the interest rate.

a. Draw typical demand (D_1) and supply (S_1) curves for loanable funds without the cost of the expanded pre-K programs accounted for. Label the vertical axis "Interest rate" and the horizontal axis "Quantity of loanable funds." Label the equilibrium point (E_1) and the equilibrium interest rate (r_1).

b. Now draw a new diagram with the cost of the expanded pre-K programs included in the analysis. Shift the demand curve in the appropriate direction. Label the new equilibrium point (E_2) and the new equilibrium interest rate (r_2).

c. How does the equilibrium interest rate change in response to government expenditure on the expanded pre-K programs? Explain.

8. Explain why equilibrium in the loanable funds market maximizes efficiency.

9. How would you respond to a friend who claims that the government should eliminate all purchases that are financed by borrowing because such borrowing crowds out private investment spending?

10. Boris Borrower and Lynn Lender agree that Lynn will lend Boris $10,000 and that Boris will repay the $10,000 with interest in one year. They agree to a nominal interest rate of 8%, reflecting a real interest rate of 3% on the loan and a commonly shared expected inflation rate of 5% over the next year.

a. If the inflation rate is actually 4% over the next year, how does that lower-than-expected inflation rate affect Boris and Lynn? Who is better off?

b. If the actual inflation rate is 7% over the next year, how does that affect Boris and Lynn? Who is better off?

11. Using the accompanying diagram, explain what will happen to the market for loanable funds when there is a fall of 2 percentage points in the expected future inflation rate. How will the change in the expected future inflation rate affect the equilibrium quantity of loanable funds?

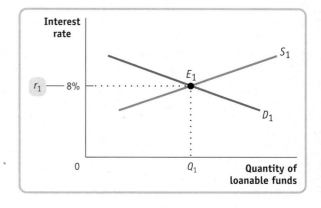

12. The accompanying diagram shows data for the interest rate on 10-year euro area government bonds and inflation rate for the euro area for 1996 through mid-2014, as reported by the European Central Bank. How would you describe the relationship between the two? How does the pattern compare to that of the United States in Figure 25-8?

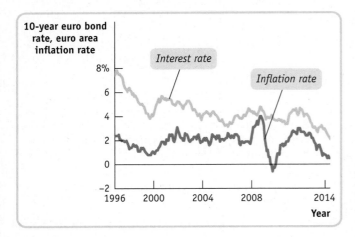

13. For each of the following, is it an example of investment spending, investing in financial assets, or investing in physical assets?

a. Rupert Moneybucks buys 100 shares of existing Coca-Cola stock.

b. Rhonda Moviestar spends $10 million to buy a mansion built in the 1970s.

c. Ronald Basketballstar spends $10 million to build a new mansion with a view of the Pacific Ocean.

d. Rawlings builds a new plant to make catcher's mitts.

e. Russia buys $100 million in U.S. government bonds.

14. Explain how a well-functioning financial system increases savings and investment spending, holding the budget balance and any capital flows fixed.

15. What are the important types of financial intermediaries in the U.S. economy? What are the primary assets of these intermediaries, and how do they facilitate investment spending and saving?

16. Explain the effect on a company's stock price today of each of the following events, other things held constant.

a. The interest rate on bonds falls.

b. Several companies in the same sector announce surprisingly higher sales.

c. A change in the tax law passed last year reduces this year's profit.

d. The company unexpectedly announces that due to an accounting error, it must amend last year's accounting statement and reduce last year's reported profit by $5 million. It also announces that this change has no implications for future profits.

17. Sallie Mae is a quasi-governmental agency that packages individual student loans into pools of loans and sells shares of these pools to investors as Sallie Mae bonds.

a. What is this process called? What effect will it have on investors compared to situations in which they could only buy and sell individual student loans?

b. What effect do you think Sallie Mae's actions will have on the ability of students to get loans?

c. Suppose that a very severe recession hits and, as a consequence, many graduating students cannot get jobs and default on their student loans. What effect will this have on Sallie Mae bonds? Why is it likely that investors now believe Sallie Mae bonds to be riskier than expected? What will be the effect on the availability of student loans?

WORK IT OUT

For interactive, step-by-step help in solving the following problem, visit LaunchPad by using the URL on the back cover of this book.

18. Use the market for loanable funds shown in the accompanying diagram to explain what happens to private savings, private investment spending, and the interest rate if each of the following events occur. Assume that there are no capital inflows or outflows.

a. The government reduces the size of its deficit to zero.

b. At any given interest rate, consumers decide to save more. Assume the budget balance is zero.

c. At any given interest rate, businesses become very optimistic about the future profitability of investment spending. Assume the budget balance is zero.

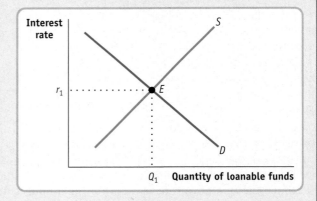

Income and Expenditure

▶ **What You Will Learn in This Chapter**

■ About the importance of the **multiplier,** a number summarizing how initial changes in spending lead to further changes

■ What the **aggregate consumption function** is

■ How **expected future income and aggregate wealth** affect consumer spending

■ The determinants of investment spending and the distinction between **planned investment spending** and **unplanned inventory investment**

■ How the **inventory adjustment process** moves the economy to a new equilibrium after a change in demand

■ Why investment spending is considered a **leading indicator** of the future state of the economy

FROM BOOM TO BUST

AP Photo/Chris O'Meara

The foreclosure tour business flourished in Ft. Myers after its housing market went from boom to bust.

Ft. Myers, Florida, was a boom town from 2003 to 2005. Jobs were plentiful: the unemployment rate in the Ft. Myers–Cape Coral metropolitan area was less than 3%. Shopping malls were humming, and new stores were opening everywhere.

But then the boom went bust. Jobs became scarce, and by the middle of 2010, the unemployment rate was above 13%. Stores had few customers, and many were closing. One new business was flourishing, however. As the local economy plunged, real estate agents began offering "foreclosure tours": visits to homes that had been seized by banks after the owners were unable to make mortgage payments—and were available at bargain prices.

What happened? Ft. Myers boomed from 2003 to 2005 because of a surge in home construction, fueled in part by speculators who bought houses not to live in, but to resell at much higher prices. Home construction gave jobs to construction workers, electricians, roofers, real estate agents, and others. These workers, in turn, spent money locally, creating jobs for school teachers, bus drivers, sales people, and more. These workers, in turn, also spent money locally, creating further expansion, and so on.

The boom turned into a bust when home construction suddenly came to a virtual halt. It turned out that speculation had been feeding on itself: people were buying houses as investments, then selling them to others who were also buying houses as investments, and prices rose to levels far beyond what people who actually wanted to live in houses were willing to pay. Eventually there was a "Wile E. Coyote moment"— named after the cartoon character who has a habit of running off the edge of cliffs but doesn't fall until he looks down and realizes that nothing is supporting him. In 2005 people looked down—and suddenly realized that home prices had lost touch with reality. And when they did, the housing market collapsed.

The local economy then collapsed, as the process that had created the earlier boom operated in reverse. The jobs created by home construction went away, leading to a fall in local spending, leading to a loss of other local jobs, leading to further declines in spending, and so on.

The boom and bust in Ft. Myers illustrates, on a small scale, the way booms and busts happen for the economy as a whole. The business cycle is often driven by ups or downs in investment spending—either residential investment spending (that is, home construction) or nonresidential investment spending (such as the construction of office buildings, factories, and shopping malls). Changes in investment spending, in turn, indirectly lead to changes in consumer spending, which magnify—or, as economists usually say, *multiply*—the effect of the investment spending changes on the economy as a whole.

In this chapter we'll study how this process works, showing how *multiplier* analysis helps us understand the business cycle. As a first step, we introduce the concept of the multiplier informally.

The Multiplier: An Informal Introduction

The story of the boom and bust in Ft. Myers involves a sort of chain reaction in which an initial rise or fall in aggregate spending leads to changes in income, which lead to further changes in aggregate spending, and so on. Let's examine that chain reaction more closely, this time thinking through the effects of changes in aggregate spending in the economy as a whole.

For the sake of this analysis, we'll make four simplifying assumptions that will have to be reconsidered in later chapters.

1. We assume that *producers are willing to supply additional output at a fixed price.* That is, if consumers or businesses buying investment goods decide to spend an additional $1 billion, that will translate into the production of $1 billion worth of additional goods and services without driving up the overall level of prices. As a result, *changes in aggregate spending translate into changes in aggregate output,* as measured by real GDP. As we'll learn in the next chapter, this assumption isn't too unrealistic in the short run, but it needs to be changed when we think about the long-run effects of changes in demand.

2. We take the interest rate as given.

3. We assume that there is no government spending and no taxes.

4. We assume that exports and imports are zero.

Given these simplifying assumptions, consider what happens if there is a change in investment spending. Specifically, imagine that for some reason home builders decide to spend an extra $100 billion on home construction over the next year.

The direct effect of this increase in investment spending will be to increase income and the value of aggregate output by the same amount. That's because each dollar spent on home construction translates into a dollar's worth of income for construction workers, suppliers of building materials, electricians, and so on. If the process stopped there, the increase in housing investment spending would raise overall income by exactly $100 billion.

But the process doesn't stop there. The increase in aggregate output leads to an increase in disposable income that flows to households in the form of profits and wages. The increase in households' disposable income leads to a rise in consumer spending, which, in turn, induces firms to increase output yet again. This generates another rise in disposable income, which leads to another round of consumer spending increases, and so on. So there are multiple rounds of increases in aggregate output.

How large is the total effect on aggregate output if we sum the effect from all these rounds of spending increases? To answer this question, we need to introduce the concept of the **marginal propensity to consume,** or *MPC:* the increase in consumer spending when disposable income rises by $1. When consumer spending changes because of a rise or fall in disposable income, *MPC* is the change in consumer spending divided by the change in disposable income:

$$\textbf{(26-1)} \quad MPC = \frac{\Delta \text{ Consumer spending}}{\Delta \text{ Disposable income}}$$

where the symbol Δ (delta) means "change in." For example, if consumer spending goes up by $6 billion when disposable income goes up by $10 billion, *MPC* is $6 billion/$10 billion = 0.6.

Because consumers normally spend part but not all of an additional dollar of disposable income, *MPC* is a number between 0 and 1. The additional disposable income that consumers don't spend is saved; the **marginal propensity to save,** or *MPS,* is the fraction of an additional dollar of disposable income that is saved. *MPS* is equal to $1 - MPC$.

The **marginal propensity to consume,** or *MPC,* is the increase in consumer spending when disposable income rises by $1.

The **marginal propensity to save,** or *MPS,* is the increase in household savings when disposable income rises by $1.

Because we assumed that there are no taxes and no international trade, each $1 increase in aggregate spending raises both real GDP and disposable income by $1. So the $100 billion increase in investment spending initially raises real GDP by $100 billion. This leads to a second-round increase in consumer spending, which raises real GDP by a further $MPC \times$ $100 billion. It is followed by a third-round increase in consumer spending of $MPC \times MPC \times$ $100 billion, and so on. After an infinite number of rounds, the total effect on real GDP is:

Increase in investment spending = $100 billion
+ Second-round increase in consumer spending = MPC × $100 billion
+ Third-round increase in consumer spending = MPC^2 × $100 billion
+ Fourth-round increase in consumer spending = MPC^3 × $100 billion
•
•
•

Total increase in real GDP = $(1 + MPC + MPC^2 + MPC^3 + \ldots) \times$ $100 billion

So the $100 billion increase in investment spending sets off a chain reaction in the economy. The net result of this chain reaction is that a $100 billion increase in investment spending leads to a change in real GDP that is a *multiple* of the size of that initial change in spending.

How large is this multiple? It's a mathematical fact that an infinite series of the form $1 + x + x^2 + x^3 + \ldots$, where x is between 0 and 1, is equal to $1/(1 - x)$. So the total effect of a $100 billion increase in investment spending, I, taking into account all the subsequent increases in consumer spending (and assuming no taxes and no international trade), is given by:

(26-2) Total increase in real GDP from a $100 billion rise in I

$$= \frac{1}{1 - MPC} \times \text{\$100 billion}$$

Let's consider a numerical example in which $MPC = 0.6$: each $1 in additional disposable income causes a $0.60 rise in consumer spending. In that case, a $100 billion increase in investment spending raises real GDP by $100 billion in the first round. The second-round increase in consumer spending raises real GDP by another 0.6 × $100 billion, or $60 billion. The third-round increase in consumer spending raises real GDP by another 0.6 × $60 billion, or $36 billion. Table 26-1 shows the successive stages of increases, where ". . ." means the process goes on an infinite number of times. In the end, real GDP rises by $250 billion as a consequence of the initial $100 billion rise in investment spending:

$$\frac{1}{1 - 0.6} \times \text{\$100 billion} = 2.5 \times \text{\$100 billion} = \text{\$250 billion}$$

TABLE **26-1**	Rounds of Increases in Real GDP When $MPC = 0.6$	
	Increase in real GDP (billions)	Total increase in real GDP (billions)
First round	$100	$100
Second round	60	160
Third round	36	196
Fourth round	21.6	217.6
…	…	…
Final round	0	250

Notice that even though there are an infinite number of rounds of expansion of real GDP, the total rise in real GDP is limited to $250 billion. The reason is that at each stage some of the rise in disposable income "leaks out" because it is saved. How much of an additional dollar of disposable income is saved depends on MPS, the marginal propensity to save.

We've described the effects of a change in investment spending, but the same analysis can be applied to any other change in aggregate spending. The important thing is to distinguish between the initial change in aggregate spending, before real GDP rises, and the additional change in aggregate spending caused by the change in real GDP as the chain reaction unfolds. For example, suppose that a boom in housing prices makes consumers feel richer and that, as a result,

An **autonomous change in aggregate spending** is an initial change in the desired level of spending by firms, households, or government at a given level of real GDP.

The **multiplier** is the ratio of the total change in real GDP caused by an autonomous change in aggregate spending to the size of that autonomous change.

they become willing to spend more at any given level of disposable income. This will lead to an initial rise in consumer spending, before real GDP rises. But it will also lead to second and later rounds of higher consumer spending as real GDP rises.

An initial rise or fall in aggregate spending at a given level of real GDP is called an **autonomous change in aggregate spending.** It's autonomous—which means "self-governing"—because it's the cause, not the result, of the chain reaction we've just described. Formally, the **multiplier** is the ratio of the total change in real GDP caused by an autonomous change in aggregate spending to the size of that autonomous change. If we let ΔAAS stand for autonomous change in aggregate spending and ΔY stand for the change in real GDP, then the multiplier is equal to $\Delta Y/\Delta AAS$. And we've already seen how to find the value of the multiplier. Assuming no taxes and no trade, the change in real GDP caused by an autonomous change in spending is:

$$(26\text{-}3) \quad \Delta Y = \frac{1}{1 - MPC} \times \Delta AAS$$

So the multiplier is:

$$(26\text{-}4) \quad \text{Multiplier} = \frac{\Delta Y}{\Delta AAS} = \frac{1}{1 - MPC}$$

Notice that the size of the multiplier depends on *MPC*. If the marginal propensity to consume is high, so is the multiplier. This is true because the size of *MPC* determines how large each round of expansion is compared with the previous round. To put it another way, the higher *MPC* is, the less disposable income "leaks out" into savings at each round of expansion.

In later chapters we'll use the concept of the multiplier to analyze the effects of fiscal and monetary policies. We'll also see that the formula for the multiplier changes when we introduce various complications, including taxes and foreign trade. First, however, we need to look more deeply at what determines consumer spending.

ECONOMICS ▶ in Action

Sand State Slump

Our opening story focused on the early 2000s boom and bust in a single region of Florida. But the Ft. Myers–Cape Coral metropolitan area wasn't alone: much of Florida was caught up in a similar cycle of housing boom followed by housing bust, and so were three other states: Arizona, California, and Nevada. And comparing the experience of the four boom-and-bust states—often referred to as the "sand states"—with that of the rest of the country provides a useful illustration of the multiplier at work.

Figure 26-1 presents some relevant employment numbers for the sand states and the non-sand states. The bars show the percent change in employment between two years: 2006, the height of the housing boom, and 2010, the bottom of the subsequent slump. We look at the change in two kinds of employment: construction employment, mainly driven by housing, and everything

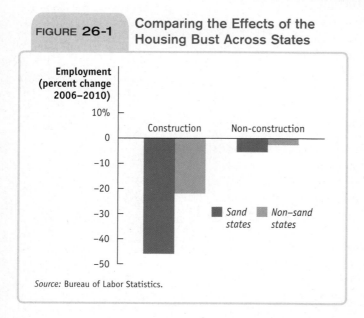

FIGURE **26-1** Comparing the Effects of the Housing Bust Across States

Employment (percent change 2006–2010)

Source: Bureau of Labor Statistics.

else. What we see immediately is that the sand states suffered a much deeper construction slump than the rest of the country. But sand-state suffering wasn't limited to construction jobs: non-construction employment also fell much more than in non-sand states.

Why did non-construction employment fall? Mainly because the collapse of construction in the sand states reduced incomes, leading to a fall in consumer spending on all kinds of goods and services, causing layoffs in everything from shopping malls to auto dealerships. That is, what we see in the sand-state slump is the multiplier in action.

Check Your Understanding   26-1

1. Explain why a decline in investment spending caused by a change in business expectations leads to a fall in consumer spending.

2. What is the multiplier if the marginal propensity to consume is 0.5? What is it if *MPC* is 0.8?

3. As a percentage of GDP, savings accounts for a larger share of the economy in the country of Scania compared to the country of Amerigo. Which country is likely to have the larger multiplier? Explain.

Solutions appear at back of book.

Consumer Spending

Should you splurge on a restaurant meal or save money by eating at home? Should you buy a new car and, if so, how expensive a model? Should you redo that bathroom or live with it for another year? In the real world, households are constantly confronted with such choices—not just about the consumption mix but also about how much to spend in total. These choices, in turn, have a powerful effect on the economy: consumer spending normally accounts for two-thirds of total spending on final goods and services. In particular, as we've just seen, the decision about how much of an additional dollar in income to spend—the marginal propensity to consume—determines the size of the multiplier, which determines the ultimate effect on the economy of autonomous changes in spending.

But what determines how much consumers spend?

Current Disposable Income and Consumer Spending

The most important factor affecting a family's consumer spending is its current disposable income—income after taxes are paid and government transfers are received. It's obvious from daily life that people with high disposable incomes on average drive more expensive cars, live in more expensive houses, and spend more on meals and clothing than people with lower disposable incomes. And the relationship between current disposable income and spending is clear in the data.

The Bureau of Labor Statistics (BLS) collects annual data on family income and spending. Families are grouped by levels of before-tax income, and after-tax income for each group is also reported. Since the income figures include transfers from the government, what the BLS calls a household's after-tax income is equivalent to its current disposable income.

Figure 26-2 is a scatter diagram illustrating the relationship between household current disposable income and household consumer spending for American households by income group in 2013. For example, point *A* shows that in 2013 the middle

During recessions, consumers tend to avoid higher-priced brand-name goods in favor of generics that cost less.

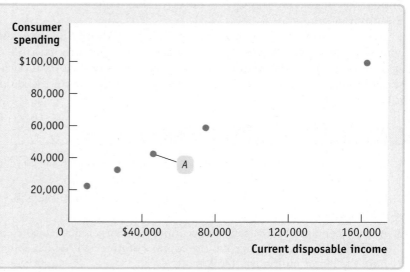

FIGURE 26-2 Current Disposable Income and Consumer Spending for American Households in 2013

For each income group of households, average current disposable income in 2012 is plotted versus average consumer spending in 2013. For example, the middle income group, with current disposable income of $40,187 to $65,501, is represented by point *A*, indicating a household average current disposable income of $45,826 and average household consumer spending of $42,495. The data clearly show a positive relationship between current disposable income and consumer spending: families with higher current disposable income have higher consumer spending.

Source: Bureau of Labor Statistics.

fifth of the population had an average current disposable income of $45,826 and average spending of $42,495. The pattern of the dots slopes upward from left to right, making it clear that households with higher current disposable income had higher consumer spending.

It's very useful to represent the relationship between an individual household's current disposable income and its consumer spending with an equation. The **consumption function** is an equation showing how an individual household's consumer spending varies with the household's current disposable income. The simplest version of a consumption function is a linear equation:

(26-5) $c = a + MPC \times yd$

where lowercase letters indicate variables measured for an individual household.

In this equation, c is individual household consumer spending and yd is individual household current disposable income. Recall that *MPC*, the marginal propensity to consume, is the amount by which consumer spending rises if current disposable income rises by $1. Finally, a is a constant term—individual household *autonomous consumer spending,* the amount of spending a household would do if it had zero disposable income. We assume that a is greater than zero because a household with zero disposable income is able to fund some consumption by borrowing or using its savings. Notice, by the way, that we're using y for income. That's standard practice in macroeconomics, even though *income* isn't actually spelled "yncome." The reason is that I is reserved for investment spending.

Recall that we expressed *MPC* as the ratio of a change in consumer spending to the change in current disposable income. We've rewritten it for an individual household as Equation 26-6:

(26-6) $MPC = \Delta c / \Delta yd$

Multiplying both sides of Equation 26-6 by Δyd, we get:

(26-7) $MPC \times \Delta yd = \Delta c$

The **consumption function** is an equation showing how an individual household's consumer spending varies with the household's current disposable income.

Equation 26-7 tells us that when yd goes up by $1, c goes up by $MPC \times$ $1.

Figure 26-3 shows what Equation 26-5 looks like graphically, plotting yd on the horizontal axis and c on the vertical axis. Individual household autonomous consumer spending, a, is the value of c when yd is zero—it is the vertical *intercept*

FIGURE 26-3   The Consumption Function

The consumption function relates a household's current disposable income to its consumer spending. The vertical intercept, a, is individual household autonomous consumer spending: the amount of a household's consumer spending if its current disposable income is zero. The slope of the consumption function line, cf, is the marginal propensity to consume, or MPC: of every additional $1 of current disposable income, $MPC \times \$1$ is spent.

of the consumption function, cf. MPC is the *slope* of the line, measured by rise over run. If current disposable income rises by Δyd, household consumer spending, c, rises by Δc. Since MPC is defined as $\Delta c / \Delta yd$, the slope of the consumption function is:

(26-8)   Slope of consumption function
   = Rise over run
   = $\Delta c / \Delta yd$
   = MPC

In reality, actual data never fit Equation 26-5 perfectly, but the fit can be pretty good. Figure 26-4 shows the data from Figure 26-2 again, together with a line drawn to fit the data as closely as possible. According to the data on households' consumer spending and current disposable income, the best estimate of a is $19,343 and of MPC is 0.50. So the consumption function fitted to the data is:

$$c = \$19{,}343 + 0.50 \times yd$$

FIGURE 26-4   A Consumption Function Fitted to Data

The data from Figure 26-2 are reproduced here, along with a line drawn to fit the data as closely as possible. For American households in 2013, the best estimate of the average household's autonomous consumer spending, a, is $19,343 and the best estimate of MPC is 0.50.

Source: Bureau of Labor Statistics.

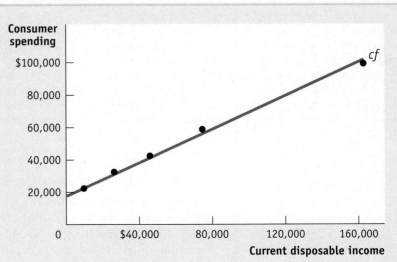

The **aggregate consumption function** is the relationship for the economy as a whole between aggregate current disposable income and aggregate consumer spending.

That is, the data suggest a marginal propensity to consume of approximately 0.50. This implies that the marginal propensity to save (*MPS*)—the amount of an additional $1 of disposable income that is saved—is approximately 0.50, and the multiplier is approximately 1/0.50 = 2.00.

It's important to realize that Figure 26-4 shows a *microeconomic* relationship between the current disposable income of individual households and their spending on goods and services. However, macroeconomists assume that a similar relationship holds *for the economy as a whole:* that there is a relationship, called the **aggregate consumption function,** between aggregate current disposable income and aggregate consumer spending. We'll assume that it has the same form as the household-level consumption function:

(26-9) $C = A + MPC \times YD$

Here, *C* is aggregate consumer spending (called just "consumer spending"); *YD* is aggregate current disposable income (called, for simplicity, just "disposable income"); and *A* is aggregate autonomous consumer spending, the amount of consumer spending when *YD* equals zero. This is the relationship represented in Figure 26-5 by *CF,* analogous to *cf* in Figure 26-3.

FIGURE 26-5 Shifts of the Aggregate Consumption Function

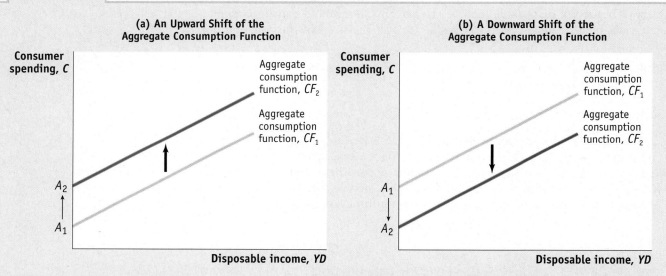

Panel (a) illustrates the effect of an increase in expected aggregate future disposable income. Consumers will spend more at every given level of aggregate current disposable income, *YD*. As a result, the initial aggregate consumption function *CF₁*, with aggregate autonomous consumer spending *A₁*, shifts up to a new position at *CF₂* and aggregate autonomous consumer spending *A₂*. An increase in aggregate wealth will also shift the aggregate consumption function up.

Panel (b), in contrast, illustrates the effect of a reduction in expected aggregate future disposable income. Consumers will spend less at every given level of aggregate current disposable income, *YD*. Consequently, the initial aggregate consumption function *CF₁*, with aggregate autonomous consumer spending *A₁*, shifts down to a new position at *CF₂* and aggregate autonomous consumer spending *A₂*. A reduction in aggregate wealth will have the same effect.

Shifts of the Aggregate Consumption Function

The aggregate consumption function shows the relationship between disposable income and consumer spending for the economy as a whole, other things equal. When things other than disposable income change, the aggregate consumption function shifts. There are two principal causes of shifts of the aggregate consumption function: changes in expected future disposable income and changes in aggregate wealth.

Changes in Expected Future Disposable Income Suppose you land a really good, well-paying job on graduating from college in May—but the job, and the paychecks, won't start until September. So your disposable income hasn't risen yet. Even so, it's likely that you will start spending more on final goods and services right away—maybe buying nicer work clothes than you originally planned—because you know that higher income is coming.

Conversely, suppose you have a good job but learn that the company is planning to downsize your division, raising the possibility that you may lose your job and have to take a lower-paying one somewhere else. Even though your disposable income hasn't gone down yet, you might well cut back on spending even while still employed, to save for a rainy day.

Both of these examples show how expectations about future disposable income can affect consumer spending. The two panels of Figure 26-5, which plot disposable income against consumer spending, show how changes in expected future disposable income affect the aggregate consumption function. In both panels, CF_1 is the initial aggregate consumption function. Panel (a) shows the effect of good news: information that leads consumers to expect higher disposable income in the future than they did before.

Consumers will now spend more at any given level of current disposable income, YD, corresponding to an increase in A, aggregate autonomous consumer spending, from A_1 to A_2. The effect is to shift the aggregate consumption function up, from CF_1 to CF_2. Panel (b) shows the effect of bad news: information that leads consumers to expect lower disposable income in the future than they did before. Consumers will now spend less at any given level of current disposable income, YD, corresponding to a fall in A from A_1 to A_2. The effect is to shift the aggregate consumption function down, from CF_1 to CF_2.

In a famous 1956 book, *A Theory of the Consumption Function*, Milton Friedman showed that taking the effects of expected future income into account explains an otherwise puzzling fact about consumer behavior. If we look at consumer spending during any given year, we find that people with high current income save a larger fraction of their income than those with low current income. (This is obvious from the data in Figure 26-4: people in the highest income group spend considerably less than their income; those in the lowest income group spend more than their income.) You might think this implies that the overall savings rate will rise as the economy grows and average current incomes rise; in fact, however, this hasn't happened.

Friedman pointed out that when we look at individual incomes in a given year, there are systematic differences between current and expected future income that create a positive relationship between current income and the savings rate. On one side, people with low current incomes are often having an unusually bad year. For example, they may be workers who have been laid off but will probably find new jobs eventually. They are people whose expected future income is higher than their current income, so it makes sense for them to have low or even negative savings. On the other side, people with high current incomes in a given year are often having an unusually good year. For example, they may have investments that happened to do extremely well. They are people whose expected future income is lower than their current income, so it makes sense for them to save most of their windfall.

When the economy grows, by contrast, current and expected future incomes rise together. Higher current income tends to lead to higher savings today, but higher expected future income tends to lead to less savings today. As a result, there's a weaker relationship between current income and the savings rate.

Friedman argued that consumer spending ultimately depends mainly on the income people expect to have over the long term rather than on their current income. This argument is known as the *permanent income hypothesis.*

Changes in Aggregate Wealth Imagine two individuals, Maria and Mark, both of whom expect to earn $30,000 this year. Suppose, however, that they have different histories. Maria has been working steadily for the past 10 years, owns her own home, and has $200,000 in the bank. Mark is the same age as Maria, but he has been in and out of work, hasn't managed to buy a house, and has very little in savings. In this case, Maria has something that Mark doesn't have: wealth. Even though they have the same disposable income, other things equal, you'd expect Maria to spend more on consumption than Mark. That is, *wealth* has an effect on consumer spending.

The effect of wealth on spending is emphasized by an influential economic model of how consumers make choices about spending versus saving called the *life-cycle hypothesis.* According to this hypothesis, consumers plan their spending over a life-time, not just in response to their current disposable income. As a result, people try to smooth their consumption over their lifetimes—they save some of their current disposable income during their years of peak earnings (typically occurring during a worker's 40s and 50s) and during their retirement live off the wealth they accumulated while working. We won't go into the details of this hypothesis but will simply point out that it implies an important role for wealth in determining consumer spending. For example, a middle-aged couple who have accumulated a lot of wealth—who have paid off the mortgage on their house and already own plenty of stocks and bonds—will, other things equal, spend more on goods and services than a couple who have the same current disposable income but still need to save for their retirement.

Because wealth affects household consumer spending, changes in wealth across the economy can shift the aggregate consumption function. A rise in aggregate wealth—say, because of a booming stock market—increases the vertical intercept A, aggregate autonomous consumer spending. This, in turn, shifts the aggregate consumption function up in the same way as does an expected increase in future disposable income. A decline in aggregate wealth—say, because of a fall in housing prices as occurred in 2008—reduces A and shifts the aggregate consumption function down.

ECONOMICS ▶ in Action

Famous First Forecasting Failures

The Great Depression created modern macroeconomics. It also gave birth to the modern field of *econometrics*—the use of statistical techniques to fit economic models to empirical data. The aggregate consumption function was one of the first things econometricians studied. And, sure enough, they quickly experienced one of the first major failures of economic forecasting: consumer spending after World War II was much higher than estimates of the aggregate consumption function based on prewar data would have predicted.

Figure 26-6 tells the story. Panel (a) shows aggregate data on disposable income and consumer spending from 1929 to 1941, measured in billions of 2005 dollars. A simple linear consumption function, CF_1, seems to fit the data very well. And many economists thought this relationship would continue to hold in the future. But panel (b) shows what actually happened in later years. The points in the circle at the left are the data from the Great Depression shown in panel (a). The points in the circle at the right are data from 1946 to 1960. (Data from 1942 to 1945 aren't included because rationing during World War II prevented consumers from spending normally.) The solid line in the figure, CF_1, is the consumption function fitted to 1929–1941 data. As you can see, post–World War II consumer spending was much higher than the relationship from the Depression years would have predicted. For example, in 1960 consumer spending was 13.5% higher than the level predicted by CF_1.

FIGURE **26-6**   Changes in the Aggregate Consumption Function Over Time

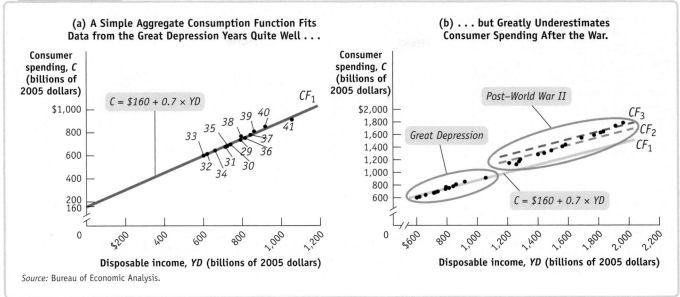

Source: Bureau of Economic Analysis.

Why was extrapolating from the earlier relationship so misleading? The answer is that from 1946 onward, both expected future disposable income and aggregate wealth were steadily rising. Consumers grew increasingly confident that the Great Depression wouldn't reemerge and that the post–World War II economic boom would continue. At the same time, wealth was steadily increasing. As indicated by the dashed lines in panel (b), CF_2 and CF_3, the increases in expected future disposable income and in aggregate wealth shifted the aggregate consumption function up a number of times.

In macroeconomics, failure—whether of economic policy or of economic prediction—often leads to intellectual progress. The embarrassing failure of early estimates of the aggregate consumption function to predict post–World War II consumer spending led to important progress in our understanding of consumer behavior.

> ### ▼ Quick Review
>
> • The **consumption function** shows the relationship between an individual household's current disposable income and its consumer spending.
>
> • The **aggregate consumption function** shows the relationship between disposable income and consumer spending across the economy. It can shift due to changes in expected future disposable income and changes in aggregate wealth.

Check Your Understanding   26-2

1. Suppose the economy consists of three people: Angelina, Felicia, and Marina. The table shows how their consumer spending varies as their current disposable income rises by $10,000.
   a. Derive each individual's consumption function, where *MPC* is calculated for a $10,000 change in current disposable income.
   b. Derive the aggregate consumption function.

Current disposable income	Consumer spending		
	Angelina	Felicia	Marina
$0	$8,000	$6,500	$7,250
10,000	12,000	14,500	14,250

2. Suppose that problems in the capital markets make consumers unable either to borrow or to put money aside for future use. What implication does this have for the effects of expected future disposable income on consumer spending?

Solutions appear at back of book.

Investment Spending

Although consumer spending is much larger than investment spending, booms and busts in investment spending tend to drive the business cycle. In fact, most recessions originate as a fall in investment spending. Figure 26-7 illustrates this point; it shows the annual percent change of investment spending and consumer

---

FIGURE **26-7** | Fluctuations in Investment Spending and Consumer Spending

The bars illustrate the annual percent change in investment spending and consumer spending during six recent recessions. As the lengths of the bars show, swings in investment spending were much larger in percentage terms than those in consumer spending. This pattern has led economists to believe that recessions typically originate as a slump in investment spending.

Source: Bureau of Economic Analysis.

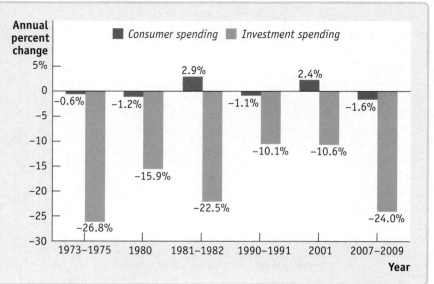

---

spending in the United States, measured in real terms, during six recessions from 1973 to 2009. As you can see, swings in investment spending are much more dramatic than those in consumer spending. In addition, due to the multiplier process, economists believe that declines in consumer spending are usually the result of a process that begins with a slump in investment spending. Soon we'll examine in more detail how a slump in investment spending generates a fall in consumer spending through the multiplier process.

Before we do that, however, let's analyze the factors that determine investment spending, which are somewhat different from those that determine consumer spending. The most important ones are the interest rate and expected future real GDP. We'll also revisit a fact that we noted in Chapter 25: the level of investment spending businesses *actually* carry out is sometimes not the same level as **planned investment spending,** the investment spending that firms *intend* to undertake during a given period. Planned investment spending depends on three principal factors: the interest rate, the expected future level of real GDP, and the current level of production capacity. First, we'll analyze the effect of the interest rate.

The Interest Rate and Investment Spending

Interest rates have their clearest effect on one particular form of investment spending: spending on residential construction—that is, on the construction of homes. The reason is straightforward: home builders only build houses they think they can sell, and houses are more affordable—and so more likely to sell—when the interest rate is low.

Consider a potential home-buying family that needs to borrow $150,000 to buy a house. At an interest rate of 7.5%, a 30-year home mortgage will mean payments of $1,048 per month. At an interest rate of 5.5%, those payments would be only $851 per month, making houses significantly more affordable. As described in the upcoming Economics in Action, interest rates actually did drop from roughly 7.5% to 5.5% between the late 1990s and 2003, helping set off the great housing boom described in this chapter's opening story.

Interest rates also affect other forms of investment spending. Firms with investment spending projects will only go ahead with a project if they expect a rate of return higher than the cost of the funds they would have to borrow to

Planned investment spending is the investment spending that businesses intend to undertake during a given period.

finance that project. As we saw in Chapter 25, if the interest rate rises, fewer projects will pass that test, and as a result investment spending will be lower.

You might think that the trade-off a firm faces is different if it can fund its investment project with its past profits rather than through borrowing. Past profits used to finance investment spending are called *retained earnings*. But even if a firm pays for investment spending out of retained earnings, the trade-off it must make in deciding whether or not to fund a project remains the same because it must take into account the opportunity cost of its funds. For example, instead of purchasing new equipment, the firm could lend out the funds and earn interest. The forgone interest earned is the opportunity cost of using retained earnings to fund an investment project.

So the trade-off the firm faces when comparing a project's rate of return to the market interest rate has not changed when it uses retained earnings rather than borrowed funds, which means that regardless of whether a firm funds investment spending through borrowing or retained earnings, a rise in the market interest rate makes any given investment project less profitable. Conversely, a fall in the interest rate makes some investment projects that were unprofitable before profitable at the now lower interest rate. So some projects that had been unfunded before will be funded now.

So planned investment spending—spending on investment projects that firms voluntarily decide whether or not to undertake—is negatively related to the interest rate. Other things equal, a higher interest rate leads to a lower level of planned investment spending.

Expected Future Real GDP, Production Capacity, and Investment Spending

Suppose a firm has enough capacity to continue to produce the amount it is currently selling but doesn't expect its sales to grow in the future. Then it will engage in investment spending only to replace existing equipment and structures that wear out or are rendered obsolete by new technologies. But if, instead, the firm expects its sales to grow rapidly in the future, it will find its existing production capacity insufficient for its future production needs. So the firm will undertake investment spending to meet those needs. This implies that, other things equal, firms will undertake more investment spending when they expect their sales to grow.

Now suppose that the firm currently has considerably more capacity than necessary to meet current production needs. Even if it expects sales to grow, it won't have to undertake investment spending for a while—not until the growth in sales catches up with its excess capacity. This illustrates the fact that, other things equal, the current level of productive capacity has a negative effect on investment spending: other things equal, the higher the current capacity, the lower is investment spending.

If we put together the effects on investment spending of growth in expected future sales and the size of current production capacity, we can see one situation in which we can be reasonably sure that firms will undertake high levels of investment spending: when they expect sales to grow rapidly. In that case, even excess production capacity will soon be used up, leading firms to resume investment spending.

What is an indicator of high expected growth of future sales? It's a high expected future growth rate of real GDP. A higher expected future growth rate of real GDP results in a higher level of planned investment spending, but a lower expected future growth rate of real GDP leads to lower planned investment spending. This relationship is summarized in a proposition known as the **accelerator principle.** As we explain in the upcoming Economics in Action, in 2006, when expectations of future real GDP growth turned negative, planned investment spending—and, in particular, residential investment spending—

According to the **accelerator principle,** a higher growth rate of real GDP leads to higher planned investment spending, but a lower growth rate of real GDP leads to lower planned investment spending.

Inventories are stocks of goods held to satisfy future sales.

Inventory investment is the value of the change in total inventories held in the economy during a given period.

Unplanned inventory investment occurs when actual sales are more or less than businesses expected, leading to unplanned changes in inventories.

Actual investment spending is the sum of planned investment spending and unplanned inventory investment.

plunged, accelerating the economy's slide into recession. Generally, the effects of the accelerator principle play an important role in *investment spending slumps,* periods of low investment spending.

Inventories and Unplanned Investment Spending

Most firms maintain **inventories,** stocks of goods held to satisfy future sales. Firms hold inventories so they can quickly satisfy buyers—a consumer can purchase an item off the shelf rather than waiting for it to be manufactured. In addition, businesses often hold inventories of their inputs to be sure they have a steady supply of necessary materials and spare parts. At the end of the second quarter of 2014, the overall value of inventories in the U.S. economy was estimated at $1.7 trillion, just over 10% of GDP.

As we explained in Chapter 22, a firm that increases its inventories is engaging in a form of investment spending. Suppose, for example, that the U.S. auto industry produces 800,000 cars per month but sells only 700,000. The remaining 100,000 cars are added to the inventory at auto company warehouses or car dealerships, ready to be sold in the future. **Inventory investment** is the value of the change in total inventories held in the economy during a given period. Unlike other forms of investment spending, inventory investment can actually be negative. If, for example, the auto industry reduces its inventory over the course of a month, we say that it has engaged in negative inventory investment.

To understand inventory investment, think about a manager stocking the canned goods section of a supermarket. The manager tries to keep the store fully stocked so that shoppers can almost always find what they're looking for. But the manager does not want the shelves too heavily stocked because shelf space is limited and products can spoil. Similar considerations apply to many firms and typically lead them to manage their inventories carefully.

However, sales fluctuate. And because firms cannot always accurately predict sales, they often find themselves holding more or less inventories than they had intended. These unintended swings in inventories due to unforeseen changes in sales are called **unplanned inventory investment.** They represent investment spending, positive or negative, that occurred but was unplanned.

So in any given period, **actual investment spending** is equal to planned investment spending plus unplanned inventory investment. If we let $I_{Unplanned}$ represent unplanned inventory investment, $I_{Planned}$ represent planned investment spending, and I represent actual investment spending, then the relationship among all three can be represented as:

$$\textbf{(26-10)} \quad I = I_{Unplanned} + I_{Planned}$$

To see how unplanned inventory investment can occur, let's continue to focus on the auto industry and make the following assumptions. First, let's assume that the industry must determine each month's production volume in advance, before it knows the volume of actual sales. Second, let's assume that it anticipates selling 800,000 cars next month and that it plans neither to add to nor subtract from existing inventories. In that case, it will produce 800,000 cars to match anticipated sales.

Now imagine that next month's actual sales are less than expected, only 700,000 cars. As a result, the value of 100,000 cars will be added to investment spending as unplanned inventory investment.

The auto industry will, of course, eventually adjust to this slowdown in sales and the resulting unplanned inventory investment. It is likely that it will cut next month's

In 2009, vehicles sat unsold on car dealership lots when the economy slumped and consumer spending plunged.

Fabrizio Costantini/The New York Times/Reduax

production volume in order to reduce inventories. In fact, economists who study macroeconomic variables in an attempt to determine the future path of the economy pay careful attention to changes in inventory levels. Rising inventories typically indicate positive unplanned inventory investment and a slowing economy, as sales are less than had been forecast. Falling inventories typically indicate negative unplanned inventory investment and a growing economy, as sales are greater than forecast. In the next section, we will see how production adjustments in response to fluctuations in sales and inventories ensure that the value of final goods and services actually produced is equal to desired purchases of those final goods and services.

ECONOMICS ▶ *in Action*

Interest Rates and the U.S. Housing Boom

The housing boom in the Ft. Myers metropolitan area, described at the beginning of this chapter, was part of a broader housing boom in the country as a whole. There is little question that this housing boom was caused, in the first instance, by low interest rates.

Figure 26-8 shows the interest rate on 30-year home mortgages—the traditional way to borrow money for a home purchase—and the number of housing starts, the number of homes for which construction is started per month, from 1995 to mid-2014, in the United States. Panel (a), which shows the mortgage rate, gives you an idea of how much interest rates fell. In the second half of the 1990s, mortgage rates generally fluctuated between 7% and 8%; by 2003, they were down to between 5% and 6%. These lower rates were largely the result of Federal Reserve policy: the Fed cut rates in response to the 2001 recession and continued cutting them into 2003 out of concern that the economy's recovery was too weak to generate sustained job growth.

FIGURE **26-8**   Interest Rates and the U.S. Housing Boom

Source: Federal Reserve Bank of St. Louis.

The low interest rates led to a large increase in residential investment spending, reflected in a surge of housing starts, shown in panel (b). This rise in investment spending drove an overall economic expansion, both through its direct effects and through the multiplier process.

- **Planned investment spending** is negatively related to the interest rate and positively related to expected future real GDP. According to the **accelerator principle,** there is a positive relationship between planned investment spending and the expected future growth rate of real GDP.

- Firms hold **inventories** to sell in the future. **Inventory investment,** a form of investment spending, can be positive or negative.

- When actual sales are more or less than expected, **unplanned inventory investment** occurs. **Actual investment spending** is equal to planned investment spending plus unplanned inventory investment.

Unfortunately, the housing boom eventually turned into too much of a good thing. By 2006, it was clear that the U.S. housing market was experiencing a bubble: people were buying housing based on unrealistic expectations about future price increases. When the bubble burst, housing—and the U.S. economy—took a fall. The fall was so severe that even when the Fed cut rates to near zero, and mortgage rates consequently dropped to below 5% beginning in 2009, housing starts merely stabilized. And the extremely low mortgage rates of 2013 led to a significant rise in housing starts in 2014, although they were still far below boom levels.

Check Your Understanding 26-3

1. For each event, explain whether planned investment spending or unplanned inventory investment will change and in what direction.
    a. An unexpected increase in consumer spending
    b. A sharp rise in the cost of business borrowing
    c. A sharp increase in the economy's growth rate of real GDP
    d. An unanticipated fall in sales

2. Historically, investment spending has experienced more extreme upward and downward swings than consumer spending. Why do you think this is so? (*Hint:* Consider the marginal propensity to consume and the accelerator principle.)

3. Consumer spending was sluggish in late 2007, and economists worried that an *inventory overhang*—a high level of unplanned inventory investment throughout the economy—would make it difficult for the economy to recover anytime soon. Explain why an inventory overhang might, like the existence of too much production capacity, depress current economic activity.

Solutions appear at back of book.

The Income–Expenditure Model

Earlier in this chapter, we described how autonomous changes in spending—such as a fall in investment spending when a housing bubble bursts—lead to a multistage process through the actions of the multiplier that magnifies the effect of these changes on real GDP. In this section, we will examine this multistage process more closely. We'll see that the multiple rounds of changes in real GDP are accomplished through changes in the amount of output produced by firms—changes that they make in response to changes in their inventories. We'll come to understand why inventories play a central role in macroeconomic models of the economy in the short run as well as why economists pay particular attention to the behavior of firms' inventories when trying to understand the likely future state of the economy.

Before we begin, let's quickly recap the assumptions underlying the multiplier process.

1. *Changes in overall spending lead to changes in aggregate output.* We assume that producers are willing to supply additional output at a fixed price level. As a result, changes in spending translate into changes in output rather than moves of the overall price level up or down. A fixed aggregate price level also implies that there is no difference between nominal GDP and real GDP. So we can use the two terms interchangeably in this chapter.

2. *The interest rate is fixed.* We'll take the interest rate as predetermined and unaffected by the factors we analyze in the model. As in the case of the aggregate price level, what we're really doing here is leaving the determinants of the interest rate outside the model. As we'll see, the model can still be used to study the effects of a change in the interest rate.

3. *Taxes, government transfers, and government purchases are all zero.*

4. *Exports and imports are both zero.*

In all subsequent chapters, we will drop the assumption that the aggregate price level is fixed. The Chapter 28 appendix addresses how taxes affect the multiplier process. We'll explain how the interest rate is determined in Chapter 30 and bring foreign trade back into the picture in Chapter 34.

Planned aggregate spending is the total amount of planned spending in the economy.

Planned Aggregate Spending and Real GDP

In an economy with no government and no foreign trade, there are only two sources of aggregate spending: consumer spending, C, and investment spending, I. And since we assume that there are no taxes or transfers, aggregate disposable income is equal to GDP (which, since the aggregate price level is fixed, is the same as real GDP): the total value of final sales of goods and services ultimately accrues to households as income. So in this highly simplified economy, there are two basic equations of national income accounting:

(26-11) $GDP = C + I$

(26-12) $YD = GDP$

As we learned earlier in this chapter, the aggregate consumption function shows the relationship between disposable income and consumer spending. Let's continue to assume that the aggregate consumption function is of the same form as in Equation 26-9:

(26-13) $C = A + MPC \times YD$

In our simplified model, we will also assume planned investment spending, $I_{Planned}$, is fixed.

We need one more concept before putting the model together: **planned aggregate spending,** the total amount of planned spending in the economy. Unlike firms, households don't take unintended actions like unplanned inventory investment. So planned aggregate spending is equal to the sum of consumer spending and planned investment spending. We denote planned aggregate spending by $AE_{Planned}$, so:

(26-14) $AE_{Planned} = C + I_{Planned}$

The level of planned aggregate spending in a given year depends on the level of real GDP in that year. To see why, let's look at a specific example, shown in Table 26-2. We assume that the aggregate consumption function is:

(26-15) $C = 300 + 0.6 \times YD$

Real GDP, YD, C, $I_{Planned}$, and $AE_{Planned}$ are all measured in billions of dollars, and we assume that the level of planned investment, $I_{Planned}$, is fixed at $500 billion per year. The first column shows possible levels of real GDP. The second column shows disposable income, YD, which in our simplified model is equal to real GDP. The third column shows consumer spending, C, equal to $300 billion plus 0.6 times disposable income, YD. The fourth column shows planned investment spending, $I_{Planned}$, which we have assumed is $500 billion regardless of the level of real GDP. Finally, the last column shows planned aggregate spending, $AE_{Planned}$, the sum of aggregate consumer spending, C, and planned investment spending, $I_{Planned}$. (To economize on notation, we'll assume that it is understood from now on that all the variables in Table 26-2 are measured in billions of dollars per year.) As you can see, a higher level of real GDP leads to a higher level of disposable income: every 500 increase in real GDP raises YD by 500, which in turn raises C by $500 \times 0.6 = 300$ and $AE_{Planned}$ by 300.

Figure 26-9 illustrates the information in Table 26-2 graphically. Real GDP is measured on the horizontal axis. CF is the aggregate consumption function; it shows how consumer spending depends on real GDP. $AE_{Planned}$, the planned

TABLE 26-2

Real GDP	YD	C	$I_{Planned}$	$AE_{Planned}$
		(billions of dollars)		
$0	$0	$300	$500	$800
500	500	600	500	1,100
1,000	1,000	900	500	1,400
1,500	1,500	1,200	500	1,700
2,000	2,000	1,500	500	2,000
2,500	2,500	1,800	500	2,300
3,000	3,000	2,100	500	2,600
3,500	3,500	2,400	500	2,900

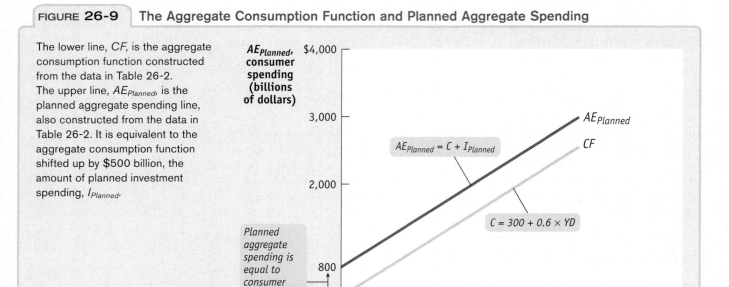

FIGURE **26-9** The Aggregate Consumption Function and Planned Aggregate Spending

The lower line, *CF*, is the aggregate consumption function constructed from the data in Table 26-2. The upper line, $AE_{Planned}$, is the planned aggregate spending line, also constructed from the data in Table 26-2. It is equivalent to the aggregate consumption function shifted up by $500 billion, the amount of planned investment spending, $I_{Planned}$.

aggregate spending line, corresponds to the aggregate consumption function shifted up by 500 (the amount of $I_{Planned}$). It shows how planned aggregate spending depends on real GDP. Both lines have a slope of 0.6, equal to *MPC*, the marginal propensity to consume.

But this isn't the end of the story. Table 26-2 reveals that real GDP equals planned aggregate spending, $AE_{Planned}$, only when the level of real GDP is at 2,000. Real GDP does not equal $AE_{Planned}$ at any other level. Is that possible? Didn't we learn in Chapter 22, with the circular-flow diagram, that total spending on final goods and services in the economy is equal to the total value of output of final goods and services? The answer is that for *brief* periods of time, planned aggregate spending can differ from real GDP because of the role of *unplanned* aggregate spending—$I_{Unplanned}$, unplanned inventory investment.

But as we'll see in the next section, the economy moves over time to a situation in which there is no unplanned inventory investment, a situation called *income–expenditure equilibrium*. And when the economy is in income–expenditure equilibrium, planned aggregate spending on final goods and services equals aggregate output.

Income–Expenditure Equilibrium

For all but one value of real GDP shown in Table 26-2, real GDP is either more or less than $AE_{Planned}$, the sum of consumer spending and *planned* investment spending. For example, when real GDP is 1,000, consumer spending, *C*, is 900 and planned investment spending is 500, making planned aggregate spending 1,400. This is 400 *more* than the corresponding level of real GDP. Now consider what happens when real GDP is 2,500; consumer spending, *C*, is 1,800 and planned investment spending is 500, making planned aggregate spending only 2,300, 200 *less* than real GDP.

As we've just explained, planned aggregate spending can be different from real GDP only if there is unplanned inventory investment, $I_{Unplanned}$, in the economy. Let's examine Table 26-3, which includes the numbers for real GDP and for planned aggregate spending from Table 26-2. It also includes the levels of unplanned inventory investment, $I_{Unplanned}$, that each combination of real GDP and planned aggregate spending implies. For example, if real GDP is 2,500, planned aggregate spending is only 2,300. This 200 excess of real GDP over $AE_{Planned}$ must consist of positive unplanned inventory investment. This can happen only if firms have overestimated sales and produced too much, leading to unintended additions to inventories. More generally, any level of real GDP in excess of 2,000 corresponds to a situation in which firms are producing more than consumers and other firms want to purchase, creating an unintended increase in inventories.

Conversely, a level of real GDP below 2,000 implies that planned aggregate spending is *greater* than real GDP. For example, when real GDP is 1,000, planned aggregate spending is much larger, at 1,400. The 400 excess of $AE_{Planned}$ over real GDP corresponds to negative unplanned inventory investment equal to −400. More generally, any level of real GDP below 2,000 implies that firms have underestimated sales, leading to a negative level of unplanned inventory investment in the economy.

By putting together Equations 26-10, 26-11, and 26-14, we can summarize the general relationships among real GDP, planned aggregate spending, and unplanned inventory investment as follows:

(26-16) $GDP = C + I$

$\qquad = C + I_{Planned} + I_{Unplanned}$

$\qquad = AE_{Planned} + I_{Unplanned}$

So whenever real GDP exceeds $AE_{Planned}$, $I_{Unplanned}$ is positive; whenever real GDP is less than $AE_{Planned}$, $I_{Unplanned}$ is negative.

But firms will act to correct their mistakes. We've assumed that they don't change their prices, but they *can* adjust their output. Specifically, they will reduce production if they have experienced an unintended rise in inventories or increase production if they have experienced an unintended fall in inventories. And these responses will eventually eliminate the unanticipated changes in inventories and move the economy to a point at which real GDP is equal to planned aggregate spending.

Staying with our example, if real GDP is 1,000, negative unplanned inventory investment will lead firms to increase production, leading to a rise in real GDP. In fact, this will happen whenever real GDP is less than 2,000—that is, whenever real GDP is less than planned aggregate spending. Conversely, if real GDP is 2,500, positive unplanned inventory investment will lead firms to reduce production, leading to a fall in real GDP. This will happen whenever real GDP is greater than planned aggregate spending.

The only situation in which firms won't have an incentive to change output in the next period is when aggregate output, measured by real GDP, is equal to planned aggregate spending in the current period, an outcome known as **income–expenditure equilibrium.** In Table 26-3, income–expenditure equilibrium is achieved when real GDP is 2,000, the only level of real GDP at which unplanned inventory investment is zero. From now on, we'll denote the real GDP level at which income–expenditure equilibrium occurs as Y^* and call it the **income–expenditure equilibrium GDP.**

Figure 26-10 illustrates the concept of income–expenditure equilibrium graphically. Real GDP is on the horizontal axis and planned aggregate spending, $AE_{Planned}$, is on the vertical axis. There are two lines in the figure. The solid line is the planned aggregate spending line. It shows how $AE_{Planned}$, equal to $C + I_{Planned}$, depends on real GDP; it has a slope of 0.6, equal to the marginal propensity to consume, *MPC*, and a vertical intercept equal to $A + I_{Planned}$ (300 + 500 = 800). The dashed line, which goes through the origin with a slope of 1 (often called a 45-degree line), shows all the possible points at which planned aggregate spending is equal to real GDP.

TABLE 26-3

Real GDP	$AE_{Planned}$	$I_{Unplanned}$
(billions of dollars)		
$0	$800	-$800
500	1,100	-600
1,000	1,400	-400
1,500	1,700	-200
2,000	2,000	0
2,500	2,300	200
3,000	2,600	400
3,500	2,900	600

The economy is in **income–expenditure equilibrium** when aggregate output, measured by real GDP, is equal to planned aggregate spending.

Income–expenditure equilibrium GDP is the level of real GDP at which real GDP equals planned aggregate spending.

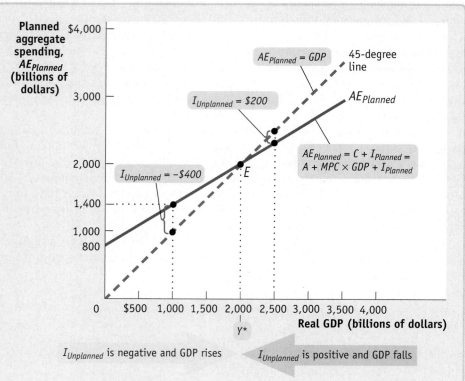

FIGURE **26-10** | Income–Expenditure Equilibrium

Income–expenditure equilibrium occurs at E, the point where the planned aggregate spending line, $AE_{Planned}$, crosses the 45-degree line. At E, the economy produces real GDP of $2,000 billion per year, the only point at which real GDP equals planned aggregate spending, $AE_{Planned}$, and unplanned inventory investment, $I_{Unplanned}$, is zero. This is the level of income–expenditure equilibrium GDP, Y^*. At any level of real GDP less than Y^*, $AE_{Planned}$ exceeds real GDP. As a result, unplanned inventory investment, $I_{Unplanned}$, is negative and firms respond by increasing production. At any level of real GDP greater than Y^*, real GDP exceeds $AE_{Planned}$. Unplanned inventory investment, $I_{Unplanned}$, is positive and firms respond by reducing production.

This line allows us to easily spot the point of income–expenditure equilibrium, which must lie on both the 45-degree line and the planned aggregate spending line. So the point of income–expenditure equilibrium is at E, where the two lines cross. And the income–expenditure equilibrium GDP, Y^*, is 2,000—the same outcome we derived in Table 26-3.

Now consider what happens if the economy isn't in income–expenditure equilibrium. We can see from Figure 26-10 that whenever real GDP is less than Y^*, the planned aggregate spending line lies above the 45-degree line and $AE_{Planned}$ exceeds real GDP. In this situation, $I_{Unplanned}$ is negative: as shown in the figure, at a real GDP of 1,000, $I_{Unplanned}$ is −400. As a consequence, real GDP will rise. In contrast, whenever real GDP is greater than Y^*, the planned aggregate expenditure line lies below the 45-degree line. Here, $I_{Unplanned}$ is positive: as shown, at a real GDP of 2,500, $I_{Unplanned}$ is 200. The unanticipated accumulation of inventory leads to a fall in real GDP.

The type of diagram shown in Figure 26-10, which identifies income–expenditure equilibrium as the point at which the planned aggregate spending line crosses the 45-degree line, has a special place in the history of economic thought. Known as the **Keynesian cross,** it was developed by Paul Samuelson, one of the greatest economists of the twentieth century (as well as a Nobel Prize winner), to explain the ideas of John Maynard Keynes, the founder of macroeconomics as we know it.

The Multiplier Process and Inventory Adjustment

The **Keynesian cross** diagram identifies income–expenditure equilibrium as the point where the planned aggregate spending line crosses the 45-degree line.

We've just learned about a very important feature of the macroeconomy: when planned spending by households and firms does not equal the current aggregate output by firms, this difference shows up in changes in inventories. The response of firms to those inventory changes moves real GDP over time to the point at which real GDP and planned aggregate spending are equal. That's why, as we mentioned earlier, changes in inventories are considered a leading indicator of future economic activity.

Now that we understand how real GDP moves to achieve income–expenditure equilibrium for a given level of planned aggregate spending, let's turn to understanding what happens when there is *a shift of the planned aggregate spending line*. How does the economy move from the initial point of income–expenditure equilibrium to a new point of income–expenditure equilibrium? And what are the possible sources of changes in planned aggregate spending?

In our simple model there are only two possible sources of a shift of the planned aggregate spending line: a change in planned investment spending, $I_{Planned}$, or a shift of the aggregate consumption function, CF. For example, a change in $I_{Planned}$ can occur because of a change in the interest rate. (Remember, we're assuming that the interest rate is fixed by factors that are outside the model. But we can still ask what happens when the interest rate changes.) A shift of the aggregate consumption function (that is, a change in its vertical intercept, A) can occur because of a change in aggregate wealth—say, due to a rise in house prices. When the planned aggregate spending line shifts—when there is a change in the level of planned aggregate spending at any given level of real GDP—there is an autonomous change in planned aggregate spending.

Recall from earlier in this chapter that an autonomous change in planned aggregate spending is a change in the desired level of spending by firms, households, and government at any given level of real GDP (although we've assumed away the government for the time being). How does an autonomous change in planned aggregate spending affect real GDP in income–expenditure equilibrium?

Table 26-4 and Figure 26-11 start from the same numerical example we used in Table 26-3 and Figure 26-10. They also show the effect of an autonomous increase in planned aggregate spending of 400—what happens when planned aggregate spending is 400 higher at each level of real GDP. Look first at Table 26-4. Before the autonomous increase in planned aggregate spending, the level of real GDP at which planned aggregate spending is equal to real GDP, Y^*, is 2,000. After the autonomous change, Y^* has risen to 3,000. The same result is visible in Figure 26-11. The initial income–expenditure equilibrium is at E_1, where Y_1^* is 2,000. The autonomous rise in planned aggregate spending shifts the planned aggregate spending line up, leading to a new income–expenditure equilibrium at E_2, where Y_2^* is 3,000.

The fact that the rise in income–expenditure equilibrium GDP, from 2,000 to 3,000, is much larger than the autonomous increase in aggregate spending, which is only 400, has a familiar explanation: the multiplier process. In the specific example we have just described, an autonomous increase in planned aggregate spending of 400 leads to an increase in Y^* from 2,000 to 3,000, a rise of 1,000. So the multiplier in this example is $1,000/400 = 2.5$.

We can examine in detail what underlies the multistage multiplier process by looking more closely at Figure 26-11. First, starting from E_1, the autonomous increase in planned aggregate spending leads to a gap between planned aggregate spending and real GDP. This is represented by the vertical distance between X, at 2,400, and E_1, at 2,000. This gap illustrates an unplanned fall in inventory investment: $I_{Unplanned} = -400$. Firms respond by increasing production, leading to a rise in real GDP from Y_1^*. The rise in real GDP translates into an increase in disposable income, YD. That's the first stage in the chain reaction. But it doesn't stop

TABLE 26-4

Real GDP	$AE_{Planned}$ before autonomous change	$AE_{Planned}$ after autonomous change
	(billions of dollars)	
$0	$800	$1,200
500	1,100	1,500
1,000	1,400	1,800
1,500	1,700	2,100
2,000	2,000	2,400
2,500	2,300	2,700
3,000	2,600	3,000
3,500	2,900	3,300
4,000	3,200	3,600

FIGURE 26-11 The Multiplier

This figure illustrates the change in Y^* caused by an autonomous increase in planned aggregate spending. The economy is initially at equilibrium point E_1 with an income–expenditure equilibrium GDP, Y_1^*, equal to 2,000. An autonomous increase in $AE_{Planned}$ of 400 shifts the planned aggregate spending line upward by 400. The economy is no longer in income–expenditure equilibrium: real GDP is equal to 2,000 but $AE_{Planned}$ is now 2,400, represented by point X. The vertical distance between the two planned aggregate spending lines, equal to 400, represents $I_{Unplanned} = -400$—the negative inventory investment that the economy now experiences. Firms respond by increasing production, and the economy eventually reaches a new income–expenditure equilibrium at E_2 with a higher level of income–expenditure equilibrium GDP, Y_2^*, equal to 3,000.

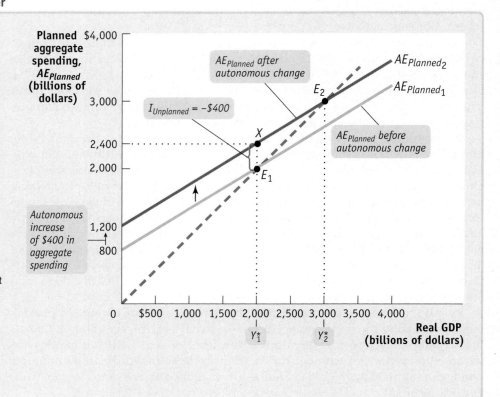

there—the increase in YD leads to a rise in consumer spending, C, which sets off a second-round rise in real GDP. This in turn leads to a further rise in disposable income and consumer spending, and so on. And we could play this process in reverse: an autonomous fall in aggregate spending will lead to a chain reaction of reductions in real GDP and consumer spending.

We can summarize these results in an equation, where $\Delta AAE_{Planned}$ represents the autonomous change in $AE_{Planned}$, and $\Delta Y^* = Y_2^* - Y_1^*$, the subsequent change in income–expenditure equilibrium GDP:

$$(26\text{-}17) \quad \Delta Y^* = \text{Multiplier} \times \Delta AAE_{Planned} = \frac{1}{1 - MPC} \times \Delta AAE_{Planned}$$

Recalling that the multiplier, $1/(1 - MPC)$, is greater than 1, Equation 26-17 tells us that the change in income–expenditure equilibrium GDP, ΔY^*, is several times as large as the autonomous change in planned aggregate spending, $\Delta AAE_{Planned}$. It also helps us recall an important point: because the marginal propensity to consume is less than 1, each increase in disposable income and each corresponding increase in consumer spending is smaller than in the previous round. That's because at each round some of the increase in disposable income leaks out into savings. As a result, although real GDP grows at each round, the increase in real GDP diminishes from each round to the next. At some point the increase in real GDP is negligible, and the economy converges to a new income–expenditure equilibrium GDP at Y_2^*.

The Paradox of Thrift You may recall that in Chapter 21 we mentioned the paradox of thrift to illustrate the fact that in macroeconomics the outcome of many individual actions can generate a result that is different from and worse than the simple sum of those individual actions. In the paradox of thrift, households and firms cut their spending in anticipation of future tough economic times. These actions depress the economy, leaving households and firms worse off than if they hadn't acted virtuously to prepare for tough times. It is called a paradox because what's usually "good" (saving to provide for your family in hard times) is "bad" (because it can make everyone worse off).

Using the multiplier, we can now see exactly how this scenario unfolds. Suppose that there is a slump in consumer spending or investment spending, or both, just like the slump in residential construction investment spending leading up to the 2007–2009 recession. This causes a fall in income–expenditure equilibrium GDP that is several times larger than the original fall in spending. The fall in real GDP leaves consumers and producers worse off than they would have been if they hadn't cut their spending.

Conversely, prodigal behavior is rewarded: if consumers or producers increase their spending, the resulting multiplier process makes the increase in income–expenditure equilibrium GDP several times larger than the original increase in spending. So prodigal spending makes consumers and producers better off than if they had been cautious spenders.

It's important to realize that our result that the multiplier is equal to $1/(1 - MPC)$ depends on the simplifying assumption that there are no taxes or transfers, so that disposable income is equal to real GDP. In the appendix to Chapter 28, we'll bring taxes into the picture, which makes the expression for the multiplier more complicated and the multiplier itself smaller. But the general principle we have just learned—an autonomous change in planned aggregate spending leads to a change in income–expenditure equilibrium GDP, both directly and through an induced change in consumer spending— remains valid.

Extravagant spending on the part of producers and consumers makes everyone better off thanks to the multiplier process.

As we noted earlier in this chapter, declines in planned investment spending are usually the major factor causing recessions, because historically they have been the most common source of autonomous reductions in aggregate spending. The tendency of the consumption function to shift upward over time, which we pointed out earlier in the Economics in Action, "Famous First Forecasting Failures," means that autonomous changes in both planned investment spending and consumer spending play important roles in expansions. But regardless of the source, there are multiplier effects in the economy that magnify the size of the initial change in aggregate spending.

ECONOMICS ▶ in Action

Inventories and the End of a Recession

A very clear example of the role of inventories in the multiplier process took place in late 2001, as that year's recession came to an end. The driving force behind the recession was a slump in business investment spending. It took several years before investment spending bounced back in the form of a housing boom. Still, the economy did start to recover in late 2001, largely because of an increase in consumer spending—especially on durable goods such as automobiles.

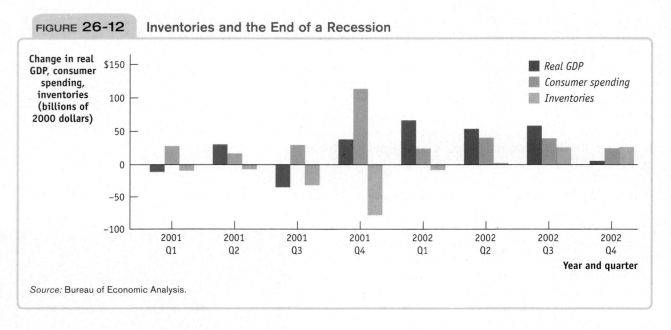

FIGURE **26-12**   Inventories and the End of a Recession

Change in real GDP, consumer spending, inventories (billions of 2000 dollars)

Legend: Real GDP, Consumer spending, Inventories

Year and quarter: 2001 Q1, 2001 Q2, 2001 Q3, 2001 Q4, 2002 Q1, 2002 Q2, 2002 Q3, 2002 Q4

Source: Bureau of Economic Analysis.

Initially, this increase in consumer spending caught manufacturers by surprise. Figure 26-12 shows changes in real GDP, real consumer spending, and real inventories in each quarter of 2001 and 2002. Notice the surge in consumer spending in the fourth quarter of 2001. It didn't lead to a lot of GDP growth because it was offset by a plunge in inventories. But in the first quarter of 2002 producers greatly increased their production, leading to a jump in real GDP.

Check Your Understanding 26-4

1. Although economists believe that recessions typically begin as slumps in investment spending, they also believe that consumer spending eventually slumps during a recession. Explain why.

2. **a.** Use a diagram like Figure 26-10 to show what happens when there is an autonomous fall in planned aggregate spending. Describe how the economy adjusts to a new income–expenditure equilibrium.
   b. Suppose Y^* is originally $500 billion, the autonomous reduction in planned aggregate spending is $300 million ($0.3 billion), and $MPC = 0.5$. Calculate Y^* after such a change.

Solutions appear at back of book.

▼ Quick Review

- The economy is in **income–expenditure equilibrium** when **planned aggregate spending** is equal to real GDP.

- At any output level greater than **income–expenditure equilibrium GDP,** real GDP exceeds planned aggregate spending and inventories are rising. At any lower output level, real GDP falls short of planned aggregate spending and inventories are falling.

- After an autonomous change in planned aggregate spending, the economy moves to a new income–expenditure equilibrium through the inventory adjustment process, as illustrated by the **Keynesian cross.** Because of the multiplier effect, the change in income–expenditure equilibrium GDP is a multiple of the autonomous change in aggregate spending.

What's Good for America Is Good for GM

Bill Pugliano/Stringer/Getty Images

In 2009, with the economy in a steep nose-dive, the U.S. government took many measures, some of which were highly controversial. Among the most controversial was the decision to use taxpayer's funds to bail out General Motors, which was teetering on the edge of bankruptcy. To keep the company afloat, the U.S. government gave it $49.5 billion in loans; these loans were then converted into stock, giving the government temporary ownership of 61% of the company.

General Motors—or GM, as it was often called in its heyday—was once an American icon, so dominant that in the 1950s the company's president, who had been nominated as Secretary of Defense, famously claimed that any conflict of interest was inconceivable: "I thought what was good for our country was good for General Motors, and vice versa."

By 2009 the fate of GM and the fate of America seemed less intertwined. Still, the case for the bailout rested crucially on the belief that GM's problems weren't entirely self-made, that the company was in trouble because the U.S. economy was in trouble, and that national recovery would make a big difference to the automaker's fortune too.

On the face of it, this interdependence wasn't entirely obvious: the 2007–2009 recession was driven by a housing bust and troubles in the banking sector, not by developments in the auto industry. But multiplier effects had indeed led to a plunge in auto sales, as shown in Figure 26-13. And sure enough, as the economy began to recover, auto sales made up most of their lost ground, with GM sharing in the industry's resurgence.

Did saving GM justify the bailout? The company's recovery meant that taxpayers got most of their money back—but not all of it. Recall that the government loan of almost $50 billion was converted into GM stock. Over time, the government sold off its stake for roughly $40 billion—leaving taxpayers with a $10 billion loss.

Defenders of the bailout nonetheless declared it a success, because it resuscitated the U.S. auto industry and saved many jobs, not just in the auto companies and their suppliers, but in the many businesses whose sales depend on the incomes of workers employed in the auto industry. In the summer of 2009 the unemployment rate in Michigan, still America's automotive heartland, rose above 14%—but it then began a rapid decline, falling to 7.4% by early 2014. Few would argue that the speedy recovery in employment in Michigan would have happened without the auto bailout.

In the end, GM bounced back because the U.S. economy as a whole recovered; what was good for America was indeed still good for General Motors. And what was good for General Motors was clearly good for Michigan—and maybe, arguably, for America as a whole.

FIGURE 26-13 U.S. Auto Sales, 2000–2013

Auto sales (millions)

Source: Federal Reserve Bank of St. Louis.

QUESTIONS FOR THOUGHT

1. Why did a national slump that began with housing affect companies like General Motors?

2. Why was it reasonable in June 2009 to predict that auto sales would improve in the near future?

3. How does this story about General Motors help explain how a slump in housing—a relatively small part of the U.S. economy—could produce such a deep national recession?

SUMMARY

1. An **autonomous change in aggregate spending** leads to a chain reaction in which the total change in real GDP is equal to the **multiplier** times the initial change in aggregate spending. The size of the multiplier, $1/(1 - MPC)$, depends on the **marginal propensity to consume, MPC,** the fraction of an additional dollar of disposable income spent on consumption. The larger the MPC, the larger the multiplier and the larger the change in real GDP for any given autonomous change in aggregate spending. The **marginal propensity to save, MPS,** is equal to $1 - MPC$.

2. The **consumption function** shows how an individual household's consumer spending is determined by its current disposable income. The **aggregate consumption function** shows the relationship for the entire economy. According to the life-cycle hypothesis, households try to smooth their consumption over their lifetimes. As a result, the aggregate consumption function shifts in response to changes in expected future disposable income and changes in aggregate wealth.

3. **Planned investment spending** depends negatively on the interest rate and on existing production capacity; it depends positively on expected future real GDP. The **accelerator principle** says that investment spending is greatly influenced by the expected growth rate of real GDP.

4. Firms hold **inventories** of goods so that they can satisfy consumer demand quickly. **Inventory investment** is positive when firms add to their inventories, negative when they reduce them. Often, however, changes in inventories are not a deliberate decision but the result of mistakes in forecasts about sales. The result is **unplanned inventory investment,** which can be either positive or negative. **Actual investment spending** is the sum of planned investment spending and unplanned inventory investment.

5. In **income–expenditure equilibrium, planned aggregate spending,** which in a simplified model with no government and no trade is the sum of consumer spending and planned investment spending, is equal to real GDP. At the **income–expenditure equilibrium GDP,** or Y^*, unplanned inventory investment is zero. When planned aggregate spending is larger than Y^*, unplanned inventory investment is negative; there is an unanticipated reduction in inventories and firms increase production. When planned aggregate spending is less than Y^*, unplanned inventory investment is positive; there is an unanticipated increase in inventories and firms reduce production. The **Keynesian cross** shows how the economy self-adjusts to income–expenditure equilibrium through inventory adjustments.

6. After an autonomous change in planned aggregate spending, the inventory adjustment process moves the economy to a new income–expenditure equilibrium. The change in income–expenditure equilibrium GDP arising from an autonomous change in spending is equal to $(1/(1 - MPC)) \times \Delta AAE_{Planned}$.

KEY TERMS

Marginal propensity to consume (*MPC*), p. 752
Marginal propensity to save (*MPS*), p. 752
Autonomous change in aggregate spending, p. 754
Multiplier, p. 754
Consumption function, p. 756

Aggregate consumption function, p. 758
Planned investment spending, p. 762
Accelerator principle, p. 763
Inventories, p. 764
Inventory investment, p. 764
Unplanned inventory investment, p. 764

Actual investment spending, p. 764
Planned aggregate spending, p. 767
Income–expenditure equilibrium, p. 769
Income–expenditure equilibrium GDP, p. 769
Keynesian cross, p. 770

PROBLEMS

1. Due to an increase in consumer wealth, there is a $40 billion autonomous increase in consumer spending in the economies of Westlandia and Eastlandia. Assuming that the aggregate price level is constant, the interest rate is fixed in both countries, and there are no taxes and no foreign trade, complete the accompanying tables to show the various rounds of increased spending that will occur in both economies if the marginal propensity to consume is 0.5 in Westlandia and 0.75 in Eastlandia. What do your results indicate about the relationship between the size of the marginal propensity to consume and the multiplier?

Westlandia

Rounds	Incremental change in GDP		Total change in GDP
1	$\Delta C =$ $40 billion		?
2	$MPC \times \Delta C =$	?	?
3	$MPC \times MPC \times \Delta C =$	?	?
4	$MPC \times MPC \times MPC \times \Delta C =$	?	?
...		...	...
Total change in GDP	$(1/(1 - MPC)) \times \Delta C =$		?

Eastlandia

Rounds	Incremental change in GDP		Total change in GDP
1	$\Delta C =$ $40 billion		?
2	$MPC \times \Delta C =$	?	?
3	$MPC \times MPC \times \Delta C =$	?	?
4	$MPC \times MPC \times MPC \times \Delta C =$	?	?
...		...	...
Total change in GDP	$(1/(1 - MPC)) \times \Delta C =$		?

2. Assuming that the aggregate price level is constant, the interest rate is fixed, and there are no taxes and no foreign trade, what will be the change in GDP if the following events occur?

a. There is an autonomous increase in consumer spending of $25 billion; the marginal propensity to consume is 2/3.

b. Firms reduce investment spending by $40 billion; the marginal propensity to consume is 0.8.

c. The government increases its purchases of military equipment by $60 billion; the marginal propensity to consume is 0.6.

3. Economists observed the only five residents of a very small economy and estimated each one's consumer spending at various levels of current disposable income. The accompanying table shows each resident's consumer spending at three income levels.

Individual consumer spending by	Individual current disposable income		
	$0	**$20,000**	**$40,000**
Andre	1,000	$15,000	29,000
Barbara	2,500	12,500	22,500
Casey	2,000	20,000	38,000
Declan	5,000	17,000	29,000
Elena	4,000	19,000	34,000

a. What is each resident's consumption function? What is the marginal propensity to consume for each resident?

b. What is the economy's aggregate consumption function? What is the marginal propensity to consume for the economy?

4. From 2009 to 2014, Eastlandia experienced large fluctuations in both aggregate consumer spending and disposable income, but wealth, the interest rate, and expected future disposable income did not change. The accompanying table shows the level of aggregate consumer spending and disposable income in millions of dollars for each of these years. Use this information to answer the following questions.

Year	Disposable income (millions of dollars)	Consumer spending (millions of dollars)
2009	$100	$180
2010	350	380
2011	300	340
2012	400	420
2013	375	400
2014	500	500

a. Plot the aggregate consumption function for Eastlandia.

b. What is the marginal propensity to consume? What is the marginal propensity to save?

c. What is the aggregate consumption function?

5. The Bureau of Economic Analysis reported that, in real terms, overall consumer spending increased by $66.2 billion during the second quarter of 2014.

a. If the marginal propensity to consume is 0.52, by how much will real GDP change in response?

b. If there are no other changes to autonomous spending other than the increase in consumer spending in part a, and unplanned inventory investment, $I_{Unplanned}$, decreased by $50 billion, what is the change in real GDP?

c. GDP at the end of the first quarter in 2014 was $16,014.1 billion. If GDP were to increase by the amount calculated in part b, what would be the percent increase in GDP?

6. During the early 2000s, the Case–Shiller U.S. Home Price Index, a measure of average home prices, rose continuously until it peaked in March 2006. From March 2006 to May 2009, the index lost 32% of its value. Meanwhile, the stock market experienced similar ups and downs. From March 2003 to October 2007, the Standard and Poor's 500 (S&P 500) stock index, a broad measure of stock market prices, almost doubled, from 800.73 to a high of 1,565.15. From that time until March 2009, the index fell by almost 60%, to a low of 676.53. How do you think the movements in home prices both influenced the growth in real GDP during the first half of the decade and added to the concern about maintaining consumer spending after the collapse in the housing market that began in 2006? To what extent did the movements in the stock market hurt or help consumer spending?

7. How will planned investment spending change as the following events occur?

a. The interest rate falls as a result of Federal Reserve policy.

b. The U.S. Environmental Protection Agency decrees that corporations must upgrade or replace their machinery in order to reduce their emissions of sulfur dioxide.

c. Baby boomers begin to retire in large numbers and reduce their savings, resulting in higher interest rates.

8. Explain how each of the following actions will affect the level of planned investment spending and unplanned inventory investment. Assume the economy is initially in income–expenditure equilibrium.

a. The Federal Reserve raises the interest rate.

b. There is a rise in the expected growth rate of real GDP.

c. A sizable inflow of foreign funds into the country lowers the interest rate.

9. In an economy with no government and no foreign sectors, autonomous consumer spending is $250 billion, planned investment spending is $350 billion, and the marginal propensity to consume is 2/3.

a. Plot the aggregate consumption function and planned aggregate spending.

b. What is unplanned inventory investment when real GDP equals $600 billion?

c. What is Y^*, income–expenditure equilibrium GDP?

d. What is the value of the multiplier?

e. If planned investment spending rises to $450 billion, what will be the new Y^*?

10. An economy has a marginal propensity to consume of 0.5, and Y^*, income–expenditure equilibrium GDP, equals $500 billion. Given an autonomous increase in

planned investment of $10 billion, show the rounds of increased spending that take place by completing the accompanying table. The first and second rows are filled in for you. In the first row, the increase of planned investment spending of $10 billion raises real GDP and YD by $10 billion, leading to an increase in consumer spending of $5 billion ($MPC \times$ change in disposable income) in row 2, raising real GDP and YD by a further $5 billion.

Rounds	Change in $I_{Planned}$ or C	Change in real GDP	Change in YD
	(billions of dollars)		
1	$\Delta I_{Planned}$ = $10.00	$10.00	$10.00
2	ΔC = $ 5.00	$ 5.00	$ 5.00
3	ΔC = ?	?	?
4	ΔC = ?	?	?
5	ΔC = ?	?	?
6	ΔC = ?	?	?
7	ΔC = ?	?	?
8	ΔC = ?	?	?
9	ΔC = ?	?	?
10	ΔC = ?	?	?

a. What is the total change in real GDP after the 10 rounds? What is the value of the multiplier? What would you expect the total change in Y^* to be based on the multiplier formula? How do your answers to the first and third questions compare?

b. Redo the table starting from round 2, assuming the marginal propensity to consume is 0.75. What is the total change in real GDP after 10 rounds? What is the value of the multiplier? As the marginal propensity to consume increases, what happens to the value of the multiplier?

11. Although the United States is one of the richest nations in the world, it is also the world's largest debtor nation. We often hear that the problem is the nation's low savings rate. Suppose policy makers attempt to rectify this by encouraging greater savings in the economy. What effect will their successful attempts have on real GDP?

12. The U.S. economy slowed significantly in early 2008, and policy makers were extremely concerned about growth. To boost the economy, Congress passed several relief packages (the Economic Stimulus Act of 2008 and the American Recovery and Reinvestment Act of 2009) that combined would deliver about $700 billion in government spending. Assume, for the sake of argument, that this spending was in the form of payments made directly to consumers. The objective was to boost the economy by increasing the disposable income of American consumers.

a. Calculate the initial change in aggregate consumer spending as a consequence of this policy measure if the marginal propensity to consume (MPC) in the United States is 0.5. Then calculate the resulting change in real GDP arising from the $700 billion in payments.

b. Illustrate the effect on real GDP with the use of a graph depicting the income–expenditure equilibrium. Label the vertical axis "Planned aggregate spending, $AE_{Planned}$" and the horizontal axis "Real GDP." Draw two planned aggregate expenditure curves ($AE_{Planned1}$ and $AE_{Planned2}$) and a 45-degree line to show the effect of the autonomous policy change on the equilibrium.

WORK IT OUT

For interactive, step-by-step help in solving the following problem, visit LaunchPad by using the URL on the back cover of this book.

13. a. The accompanying table shows gross domestic product (GDP), disposable income (YD), consumer spending (C), and planned investment spending ($I_{Planned}$) in an economy. Assume there is no government or foreign sector in this economy. Complete the table by calculating planned aggregate spending ($AE_{Planned}$) and unplanned inventory investment ($I_{Unplanned}$).

GDP	YD	C	$I_{Planned}$	$AE_{Planned}$	$I_{Unplanned}$
(billions of dollars)					
$0	$0	$100	$300	?	?
400	400	400	300	?	?
800	800	700	300	?	?
1,200	1,200	1,000	300	?	?
1,600	1,600	1,300	300	?	?
2,000	2,000	1,600	300	?	?
2,400	2,400	1,900	300	?	?
2,800	2,800	2,200	300	?	?
3,200	3,200	2,500	300	?	?

b. What is the aggregate consumption function?

c. What is Y^*, income–expenditure equilibrium GDP?

d. What is the value of the multiplier?

e. If planned investment spending falls to $200 billion, what will be the new Y^*?

f. If autonomous consumer spending rises to $200 billion, what will be the new Y^*?

Deriving the Multiplier Algebraically

This appendix shows how to derive the multiplier algebraically. First, recall that in this chapter planned aggregate spending, $AE_{Planned}$, is the sum of consumer spending, C, which is determined by the consumption function, and planned investment spending, $I_{Planned}$. That is, $AE_{Planned} = C + I_{Planned}$. Rewriting this equation to express all its terms fully, we have:

(26A-1) $AE_{Planned} = A + MPC \times YD + I_{Planned}$

Because there are no taxes or government transfers in this model, disposable income is equal to GDP, so Equation 26A-1 becomes:

(26A-2) $AE_{Planned} = A + MPC \times GDP + I_{Planned}$

The income–expenditure equilibrium GDP, Y^*, is equal to planned aggregate spending:

(26A-3) $Y^* = AE_{Planned}$
$$= A + MPC \times Y^* + I_{Planned}$$
in income–expenditure equilibrium

Just two more steps. Subtract $MPC \times Y^*$ from both sides of Equation 26A-3:

(26A-4) $Y^* - MPC \times Y^* = Y^* \times (1 - MPC) = A + I_{Planned}$

Finally, divide both sides by $(1 - MPC)$:

(26A-5) $Y^* = \dfrac{A + I_{Planned}}{1 - MPC}$

Equation 26A-5 tells us that a \$1 autonomous change in planned aggregate spending—a change in either A or $I_{Planned}$—causes a \$1/(1 – MPC) change in income–expenditure equilibrium GDP, Y^*. The multiplier in our simple model is therefore:

(26A-6) Multiplier = $1/(1 - MPC)$

PROBLEMS

1. Complete the following table by calculating the value of the multiplier and identifying the change in Y^* due to the change in autonomous spending. How does the value of the multiplier change with the marginal propensity to consume?

MPC	Value of multiplier	Change in spending	Change in Y^*
0.5	?	$\Delta C = +$ \$50 million	?
0.6	?	$\Delta I = -$ \$10 million	?
0.75	?	$\Delta C = -$ \$25 million	?
0.8	?	$\Delta I = +$ \$20 million	?
0.9	?	$\Delta C = -$ \$2.5 million	?

WORK IT OUT

For interactive, step-by-step help in solving the following problem, visit LaunchPad by using the URL on the back cover of this book.

2. In an economy without government purchases, transfers, or taxes, and without imports or exports, aggregate autonomous consumer spending is \$500 billion, planned investment spending is \$250 billion, and the marginal propensity to consume is 0.5.

    a. Write the expression for planned aggregate spending as in Equation 26A-1.

    b. Solve for Y^* algebraically.

    c. What is the value of the multiplier?

    d. How will Y^* change if autonomous consumer spending falls to \$450 billion?

Aggregate Demand and Aggregate Supply

▶ What You Will Learn in This Chapter

- How the **aggregate demand curve** illustrates the relationship between the aggregate price level and the quantity of aggregate output demanded in the economy

- How the **aggregate supply curve** illustrates the relationship between the aggregate price level and the quantity of aggregate output supplied in the economy

- Why the aggregate supply curve is different in the short run compared to the long run

- How the *AD–AS* model is used to analyze economic fluctuations

- How monetary policy and fiscal policy can stabilize the economy

WHAT KIND OF SHOCK?

United States government work

Jim West/Alamy

The Federal Open Market Committee, which decides whether to pump cash into the economy to fight unemployment or pull cash out of the economy to fight inflation, got its priorities wrong in 2008.

The Federal Open Market Committee, or FOMC, is the branch of the Federal Reserve System that sets U.S. monetary policy and arguably has much more power over the economy than anyone else—including the president. It held one of its regular meetings on September 16, 2008. That was, it turned out, a very important day. Simmering problems in the financial industry had just boiled over with the failure of the investment bank Lehman Brothers, and the U.S. economy, already in recession, was about to go into free fall. Not surprisingly, the officials around the table were worried.

But many committee members, it turns out, were worried about the wrong thing. When the committee released transcripts of its 2008 meetings—which it didn't do until 2014—we learned that during the summer of 2008 most of the people around the table were much more worried about inflation than they were about the financial crisis or the prospect of a sharp rise in unemployment from a crisis-caused recession—an attitude that persisted into September. In the

June and August 2008 meetings the word *inflation* came up more than ten times as often as the word *unemployment.* Even in that fateful September meeting, inflation mentions outnumbered unemployment mentions five to one.

Later events showed that this was a case of misplaced priorities, with important consequences. Why? Because the appropriate policy responses to soaring unemployment, on one side, and soaring inflation, on the other, are more or less opposite. If unemployment is the main problem, the Fed should be cutting interest rates in an attempt to boost spending; if inflation is the main problem, the Fed should be raising rates to cool things off. By focusing on inflation, which turned out not to be a problem at all during the

fall and summer of 2008, as opposed to unemployment, which was about to skyrocket, the committee was looking for trouble in all the wrong places.

How could the committee have had its priorities so wrong? Well, we know now that the big shock hitting the economy in 2008 was the financial crisis, which in turn led to plunging spending by businesses and consumers. For much of that year, however, the eyes of the Federal Reserve and, to be fair, many other observers were instead focused on a different shock: the soaring price of oil, which had jumped from $60 a barrel in the summer of 2007 to a peak of $145 a barrel in July 2008. And many members of the committee worried more about the effects of oil prices than they did about the gathering financial storm.

As we've just suggested, financial crises and soaring oil prices can both create devastating economic problems—but the problems they create are very different, and so is the appropriate policy response. A financial crisis hurts the economy by reducing spending—it's a *demand shock,* which raises unemployment while cutting inflation and possibly even leading to *deflation,* as it did during the worst slump in history, the economy's plunge from 1929 to 1933. And the appropriate policy in response to such a shock involves propping up spending, among other things by cutting interest rates.

A surge in the price of oil, however, does much of its damage by raising costs and discouraging production; it's a *supply shock.* Like negative demand shocks, adverse supply shocks cause the economy to shrink and unemployment to rise. But they also cause inflation—specifically, they cause the unpleasant combination of high inflation and high unemployment known as *stagflation,* which afflicted the U.S. economy during much of the 1970s (largely thanks to two spikes in the price of oil, in 1973 and again in 1979). And responding to stagflation is tricky: you might want to cut interest rates to defend employment, but on the other hand you might want to raise interest rates to fight inflation.

In the end, what the FOMC did in response to these conflicting stories about what ailed the economy was . . . nothing. It kept interest rates unchanged all through the summer and left them unchanged in September of 2008. Within a few weeks it became clear that demand, not supply, was the serious concern, at which point the Fed began a frantic effort to pull the economy out of its accelerating tailspin. But the perplexity of the Fed in 2008 tells us both that such decisions aren't always easy to understand and that we need a model of the economy that goes beyond the income–expenditure framework we developed in the last chapter.

We should mention, by the way, that the Fed's policy response to the financial crisis was, in the end, a partial success at best. With the Fed's help the economy did stabilize over the course of 2009, but the subsequent recovery was painfully slow. Even if the Fed had realized the true danger sooner, the economy probably would have still suffered a lot of damage. But its confusion in 2008 certainly didn't help.

In this chapter, we'll develop a model that goes beyond the income–expenditure model and shows us how to distinguish between different types of short-run economic fluctuations.

To develop this model, we'll proceed in three steps. First, we'll develop the concept of *aggregate demand.* Then we'll turn to the parallel concept of *aggregate supply.* Finally, we'll put them together in the *AD–AS model.*

Aggregate Demand

The Great Depression, the great majority of economists agree, was the result of a massive negative demand shock. What does that mean? In Chapter 3 we explained that when economists talk about a fall in the demand for a particular good or service, they're referring to a leftward shift of the demand curve. Similarly, when economists talk about a negative demand shock to the economy as a whole, they're referring to a leftward shift of the **aggregate demand curve,** a curve that shows the relationship between the aggregate price level and the quantity of aggregate output demanded by households, firms, the government, and the rest of the world.

Figure 27-1 shows what the aggregate demand curve may have looked like in 1933, at the end of the 1929–1933 recession. The horizontal axis shows the total quantity of domestic goods and services demanded, measured in 2009 dollars. We use real GDP to measure aggregate output and will often use the two terms interchangeably. The vertical axis shows the aggregate price level, measured by the GDP deflator. With these variables on the axes, we can draw a curve, *AD,* showing how much aggregate output would have been demanded at any given aggregate price level. Since *AD* is meant to illustrate aggregate demand in 1933, one point on the curve corresponds to actual data for 1933, when the aggregate price level was 7.3 and the total quantity of domestic final goods and services purchased was $778 billion in 2009 dollars.

As drawn in Figure 27-1, the aggregate demand curve is downward sloping, indicating a negative relationship between the aggregate price level and the quantity of aggregate output demanded. A higher aggregate price level, other things equal, reduces the quantity of aggregate output demanded; a lower aggregate price level, other things equal, increases the quantity of aggregate output demanded. According to Figure 27-1, if the price level in 1933 had been 4.2 instead of 7.3, the total quantity of domestic final goods and services demanded would have been $1,000 billion in 2009 dollars instead of $778 billion.

The **aggregate demand curve** shows the relationship between the aggregate price level and the quantity of aggregate output demanded by households, businesses, the government, and the rest of the world.

FIGURE 27-1   The Aggregate Demand Curve

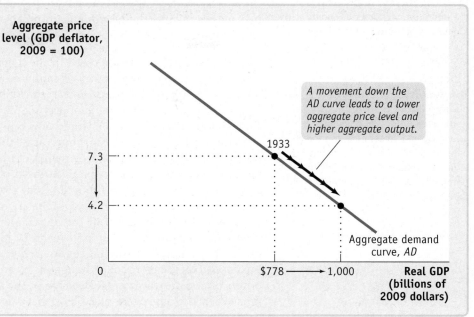

The aggregate demand curve shows the relationship between the aggregate price level and the quantity of aggregate output demanded. The curve is downward sloping due to the wealth effect of a change in the aggregate price level and the interest rate effect of a change in the aggregate price level. Corresponding to the actual 1933 data, here the total quantity of goods and services demanded at an aggregate price level of 7.3 is $778 billion in 2009 dollars. According to our hypothetical curve, however, if the aggregate price level had been only 4.2, the quantity of aggregate output demanded would have risen to $1,000 billion.

The first key question about the aggregate demand curve is: why should the curve be downward sloping?

Why Is the Aggregate Demand Curve Downward Sloping?

In Figure 27-1, the curve *AD* is downward sloping. Why? Recall the basic equation of national income accounting:

(27-1) $GDP = C + I + G + X - IM$

where C is consumer spending, I is investment spending, G is government purchases of goods and services, X is exports to other countries, and IM is imports. If we measure these variables in constant dollars—that is, in prices of a base year—then $C + I + G + X - IM$ is the quantity of domestically produced final goods and services demanded during a given period. G is decided by the government, but the other variables are private-sector decisions. To understand why the aggregate demand curve slopes downward, we need to understand why a rise in the aggregate price level reduces C, I, and $X - IM$.

You might think that the downward slope of the aggregate demand curve is a natural consequence of the *law of demand* we defined back in Chapter 3. That is, since the demand curve for any one good is downward sloping, isn't it natural that the demand curve for aggregate output is also downward sloping? This turns out, however, to be a misleading parallel. The demand curve for any individual good shows how the quantity demanded depends on the price of that good, *holding the prices of other goods and services constant*. The main reason the quantity of a good demanded falls when the price of that good rises—that is, the quantity of a good demanded falls as we move up the demand curve—is that people switch their consumption to other goods and services.

But when we consider movements up or down the aggregate demand curve, we're considering *a simultaneous change in the prices of all final goods and services*. Furthermore, changes in the composition of goods and services in consumer spending aren't relevant to the aggregate demand curve: if consumers decide to buy fewer clothes but more cars, this doesn't necessarily change the total quantity of final goods and services they demand.

The **wealth effect of a change in the aggregate price level** is the effect on consumer spending caused by the effect of a change in the aggregate price level on the purchasing power of consumers' assets.

The **interest rate effect of a change in the aggregate price level** is the effect on consumer spending and investment spending caused by the effect of a change in the aggregate price level on the purchasing power of consumers' and firms' money holdings.

Why, then, does a rise in the aggregate price level lead to a fall in the quantity of all domestically produced final goods and services demanded? There are two main reasons: the *wealth effect* and the *interest rate effect* of a change in the aggregate price level.

The Wealth Effect An increase in the aggregate price level, other things equal, reduces the purchasing power of many assets. Consider, for example, someone who has $5,000 in a bank account. If the aggregate price level were to rise by 25%, what used to cost $5,000 would now cost $6,250, and would no longer be affordable. And what used to cost $4,000 would now cost $5,000, so that the $5,000 in the bank account would now buy only as much as $4,000 would have bought previously. With the loss in purchasing power, the owner of that bank account would probably scale back his or her consumption plans. Millions of other people would respond the same way, leading to a fall in spending on final goods and services, because a rise in the aggregate price level reduces the purchasing power of everyone's bank account.

Correspondingly, a fall in the aggregate price level increases the purchasing power of consumers' assets and leads to more consumer demand. The **wealth effect of a change in the aggregate price level** is the effect on consumer spending caused by the effect of a change in the aggregate price level on the purchasing power of consumers' assets. Because of the wealth effect, consumer spending, *C*, falls when the aggregate price level rises, leading to a downward-sloping aggregate demand curve.

The Interest Rate Effect Economists use the term *money* in its narrowest sense to refer to cash and bank deposits on which people can write checks. People and firms hold money because it reduces the cost and inconvenience of making transactions. An increase in the aggregate price level, other things equal, reduces the purchasing power of a given amount of money holdings. To purchase the same basket of goods and services as before, people and firms now need to hold more money. So, in response to an increase in the aggregate price level, the public tries to increase its money holdings, either by borrowing more or by selling assets such as bonds. This reduces the funds available for lending to other borrowers and drives interest rates up.

In Chapter 25 we learned that a rise in the interest rate reduces investment spending because it makes the cost of borrowing higher. It also reduces consumer spending because households save more of their disposable income. So a rise in the aggregate price level depresses investment spending, *I*, and consumer spending, *C*, through its effect on the purchasing power of money holdings, an effect known as the **interest rate effect of a change in the aggregate price level.** This also leads to a downward-sloping aggregate demand curve.

We'll have a lot more to say about money and interest rates in Chapter 30 on monetary policy. We'll also see, in Chapter 34, which covers open-economy macroeconomics, that a higher interest rate indirectly tends to reduce exports (*X*) and increase imports (*IM*). For now, the important point is that the aggregate demand curve is downward sloping due to both the wealth effect and the interest rate effect of a change in the aggregate price level.

The Aggregate Demand Curve and the Income–Expenditure Model

In the preceding chapter we introduced the *income–expenditure model,* which shows how the economy arrives at *income–expenditure equilibrium.* Now we've introduced the aggregate demand curve, which relates the overall demand for goods and services to the overall price level. How do these concepts fit together?

Recall that one of the assumptions of the income–expenditure model is that the aggregate price level is fixed. We now drop that assumption. We can still use the income–expenditure model, however, to ask what aggregate spending would be *at any given aggregate price level,* which is precisely what the aggregate demand

---

Income–expenditure equilibrium occurs at the point where the curve $AE_{Planned}$, which shows real aggregate planned spending, crosses the 45-degree line. A fall in the aggregate price level causes the $AE_{Planned}$ curve to shift from $AE_{Planned_1}$ to $AE_{Planned_2}$, leading to a rise in income–expenditure equilibrium GDP from Y_1 to Y_2.

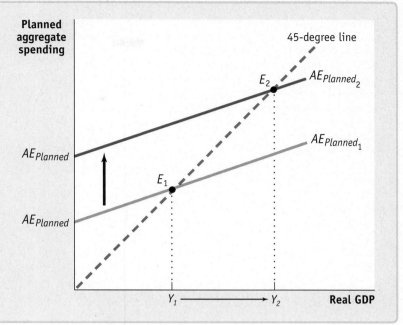

---

curve shows. So the AD curve is actually derived from the income–expenditure model. Economists sometimes say that the income–expenditure model is "embedded" in the AD–AS model.

Figure 27-2 shows, once again, how income–expenditure equilibrium is determined. Real GDP is on the horizontal axis; real planned aggregate spending is on the vertical axis. Other things equal, planned aggregate spending, equal to consumer spending plus planned investment spending, rises with real GDP. This is illustrated by the upward-sloping lines $AE_{Planned_1}$ and $AE_{Planned_2}$. Income–expenditure equilibrium, as we learned in Chapter 26, is at the point where the line representing planned aggregate spending crosses the 45-degree line. For example, if $AE_{Planned_1}$ is the relationship between real GDP and planned aggregate spending, then income–expenditure equilibrium is at point E_1, corresponding to a level of real GDP equal to Y_1.

We've just seen, however, that changes in the aggregate price level change the level of planned aggregate spending *at any given level of real GDP*. This means that when the aggregate price level changes, the $AE_{Planned}$ curve shifts. For example, suppose that the aggregate price level falls. As a result of both the wealth effect and the interest rate effect, the fall in the aggregate price level will lead to higher planned aggregate spending at any given level of real GDP. So the $AE_{Planned}$ curve will shift up, as illustrated in Figure 27-2 by the shift from $AE_{Planned_1}$ to $AE_{Planned_2}$. The increase in planned aggregate spending leads to a multiplier process that moves the income–expenditure equilibrium from point E_1 to point E_2, raising real GDP from Y_1 to Y_2.

Figure 27-3 shows how this result can be used to derive the aggregate demand curve. In Figure 27-3, we show a fall in the aggregate price level from P_1 to P_2. We saw in Figure 27-2 that a fall in the aggregate price level would lead to an upward shift of the $AE_{Planned}$ curve and hence a rise in real GDP. You can see this same result in Figure 27-3 as a movement along the AD curve: as the aggregate price level falls, real GDP rises from Y_1 to Y_2.

So the aggregate demand curve doesn't replace the income–expenditure model. Instead, it's a way to summarize what the income–expenditure model says about the effects of changes in the aggregate price level.

In practice, economists often use the income–expenditure model to analyze short-run economic fluctuations, even though strictly speaking it should be seen as a component of a more complete model. In the short run, in particular, this is usually a reasonable shortcut.

FIGURE **27-3** | The Income–Expenditure Model and the Aggregate Demand Curve

In Figure 27-2 we saw how a fall in the aggregate price level shifts the planned aggregate spending curve up, leading to a rise in real GDP. Here we show that same result as a movement along the aggregate demand curve. If the aggregate price level falls from P_1 to P_2, real GDP rises from Y_1 to Y_2. The AD curve is therefore downward sloping.

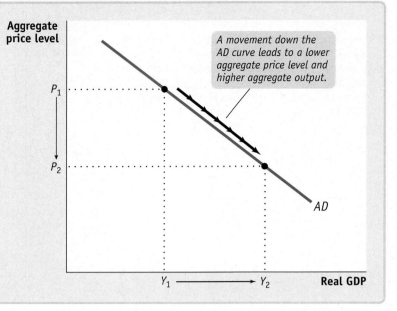

A movement down the AD curve leads to a lower aggregate price level and higher aggregate output.

Shifts of the Aggregate Demand Curve

In Chapter 3, where we introduced the analysis of supply and demand in the market for an individual good, we stressed the importance of the distinction between *movements along* the demand curve and *shifts of* the demand curve. The same distinction applies to the aggregate demand curve. Figure 27-1 shows a *movement along* the aggregate demand curve, a change in the aggregate quantity of goods and services demanded as the aggregate price level changes.

But there can also be *shifts of* the aggregate demand curve, changes in the quantity of goods and services demanded at any given price level, as shown in Figure 27-4. When we talk about an increase in aggregate demand, we mean a

FIGURE **27-4** | Shifts of the Aggregate Demand Curve

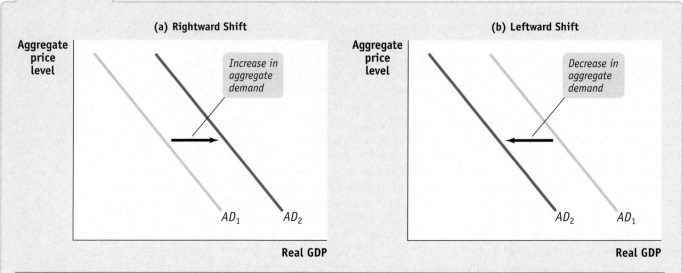

Panel (a) shows the effect of events that increase the quantity of aggregate output demanded at any given aggregate price level, such as improvements in business and consumer expectations or increased government spending. Such changes shift the aggregate demand curve to the right, from AD_1 to AD_2. Panel (b) shows the effect of events that decrease the quantity of aggregate output demanded at any given aggregate price level, such as a fall in wealth caused by a stock market decline. This shifts the aggregate demand curve leftward from AD_1 to AD_2.

shift of the aggregate demand curve to the right, as shown in panel (a) by the shift from AD_1 to AD_2. A rightward shift occurs when the quantity of aggregate output demanded increases at any given aggregate price level. A decrease in aggregate demand means that the *AD* curve shifts to the left, as in panel (b). A leftward shift implies that the quantity of aggregate output demanded falls at any given aggregate price level.

A number of factors can shift the aggregate demand curve. Among the most important factors are changes in expectations, changes in wealth, and the size of the existing stock of physical capital. In addition, both fiscal and monetary policy can shift the aggregate demand curve. All five factors set the multiplier process in motion. By causing an initial rise or fall in real GDP, they change disposable income, which leads to additional changes in aggregate spending, which lead to further changes in real GDP, and so on. For an overview of factors that shift the aggregate demand curve, see upcoming Table 27-1.

Changes in Expectations As explained in Chapter 26, both consumer spending and planned investment spending depend in part on people's expectations about the future. Consumers base their spending not only on the income they have now but also on the income they expect to have in the future. Firms base their planned investment spending not only on current conditions but also on the sales they expect to make in the future. As a result, changes in expectations can push consumer spending and planned investment spending up or down. If consumers and firms become more optimistic, aggregate spending rises; if they become more pessimistic, aggregate spending falls.

In fact, short-run economic forecasters pay careful attention to surveys of consumer and business sentiment. In particular, forecasters watch the Consumer Confidence Index, a monthly measure calculated by the Conference Board, and the Michigan Consumer Sentiment Index, a similar measure calculated by the University of Michigan.

Changes in Wealth Consumer spending depends in part on the value of household assets. When the real value of these assets rises, the purchasing power they embody also rises, leading to an increase in aggregate spending. For example, in the 1990s there was a significant rise in the stock market that increased aggregate demand. And when the real value of household assets falls—for example, because of a stock market crash—the purchasing power they embody is reduced and aggregate demand also falls. The stock market crash of 1929 was a significant factor leading to the Great Depression. Similarly, a sharp decline in real estate values was a major factor depressing consumer spending during the 2007–2009 recession.

Size of the Existing Stock of Physical Capital Firms engage in planned investment spending to add to their stock of physical capital. Their incentive to spend depends in part on how much physical capital they already have: the more they have, the less they will feel a need to add more, other things equal. The same applies to other types of investment spending—for example, if a large number of houses have been built in recent years, this will depress the demand for new houses and as a result also tend to reduce residential investment spending. In fact, that's part of the reason for the deep slump in residential investment spending that began

PITFALLS

CHANGES IN WEALTH: A MOVEMENT ALONG VERSUS A SHIFT OF THE AGGREGATE DEMAND CURVE
Earlier we explained that one reason the *AD* curve is downward sloping is the wealth effect of a change in the aggregate price level: a higher aggregate price level reduces the purchasing power of households' assets and leads to a fall in consumer spending, *C*. But we've just explained that changes in wealth lead to a shift of the *AD* curve. Aren't those two explanations contradictory? Which one is it—does a change in wealth move the economy along the *AD* curve or does it shift the *AD* curve? The answer is both: it depends on the *source* of the change in wealth. A movement along the *AD* curve occurs when a change in the aggregate price level changes the purchasing power of consumers' existing wealth (the real value of their assets). This is the *wealth effect of a change in the aggregate price level*—a change in the aggregate price level is the source of the change in wealth.

For example, a fall in the aggregate price level increases the purchasing power of consumers' assets and leads to a movement down the *AD* curve. In contrast, a change in wealth *independent of a change in the aggregate price level* shifts the *AD* curve. For example, a rise in the stock market or a rise in real estate values leads to an increase in the real value of consumers' assets at any given aggregate price level. In this case, the source of the change in wealth is a change in the values of assets without any change in the aggregate price level—that is, a change in asset values holding the prices of all final goods and services constant.

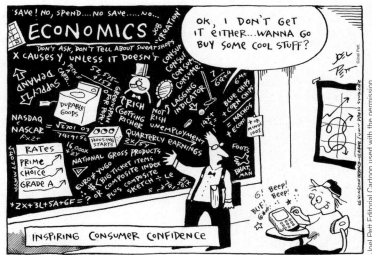

in 2006. The housing boom of the previous few years had created an oversupply of houses: by spring 2009, the inventory of unsold houses on the market was equal to more than 14 months of sales, and prices of new homes had fallen more than 25% from their peak. This gave the construction industry little incentive to build even more homes.

TABLE 27-1 Factors That Shift Aggregate Demand

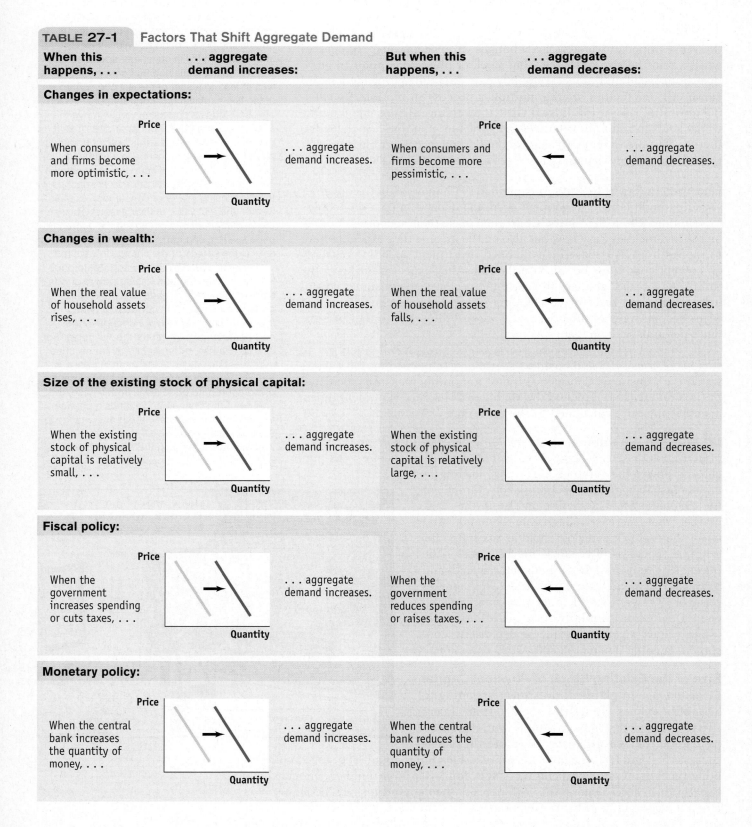

When this happens, . . .	. . . aggregate demand increases:		But when this happens, . . .	. . . aggregate demand decreases:	
Changes in expectations:					
When consumers and firms become more optimistic, . . .		. . . aggregate demand increases.	When consumers and firms become more pessimistic, . . .		. . . aggregate demand decreases.
Changes in wealth:					
When the real value of household assets rises, . . .		. . . aggregate demand increases.	When the real value of household assets falls, . . .		. . . aggregate demand decreases.
Size of the existing stock of physical capital:					
When the existing stock of physical capital is relatively small, . . .		. . . aggregate demand increases.	When the existing stock of physical capital is relatively large, . . .		. . . aggregate demand decreases.
Fiscal policy:					
When the government increases spending or cuts taxes, . . .		. . . aggregate demand increases.	When the government reduces spending or raises taxes, . . .		. . . aggregate demand decreases.
Monetary policy:					
When the central bank increases the quantity of money, . . .		. . . aggregate demand increases.	When the central bank reduces the quantity of money, . . .		. . . aggregate demand decreases.

Government Policies and Aggregate Demand

One of the key insights of macroeconomics is that the government can have a powerful influence on aggregate demand and that, in some circumstances, this influence can be used to improve economic performance.

The two main ways the government can influence the aggregate demand curve are through fiscal policy and monetary policy. We'll briefly discuss their influence on aggregate demand, leaving a full-length discussion for upcoming chapters.

Fiscal Policy As we learned in Chapter 21, fiscal policy is the use of either government spending—government purchases of final goods and services and government transfers—or tax policy to stabilize the economy. In practice, governments often respond to recessions by increasing spending, cutting taxes, or both. They often respond to inflation by reducing spending or increasing taxes.

The effect of government purchases of final goods and services, G, on the aggregate demand curve is *direct* because government purchases are themselves a component of aggregate demand. So an increase in government purchases shifts the aggregate demand curve to the right and a decrease shifts it to the left. History's most dramatic example of how increased government purchases affect aggregate demand was the effect of wartime government spending during World War II.

Because of the war, U.S. federal purchases surged 400%. This increase in purchases is usually credited with ending the Great Depression. In the 1990s Japan used large public works projects—such as government-financed construction of roads, bridges, and dams—in an effort to increase aggregate demand in the face of a slumping economy. Similarly, in 2009, in the wake of the Great Recession, the United States began spending more than $100 billion on infrastructure projects such as improving highways, bridges, public transportation, and more, to stimulate overall spending.

In contrast, changes in either tax rates or government transfers influence the economy *indirectly* through their effect on disposable income. A lower tax rate means that consumers get to keep more of what they earn, increasing their disposable income. An increase in government transfers also increases consumers' disposable income. In either case, this increases consumer spending and shifts the aggregate demand curve to the right. A higher tax rate or a reduction in transfers reduces the amount of disposable income received by consumers. This reduces consumer spending and shifts the aggregate demand curve to the left.

Monetary Policy We opened this chapter by talking about the problems faced by the FOMC, the branch of the Federal Reserve that controls monetary policy—the use of changes in the quantity of money or the interest rate to stabilize the economy. We've just discussed how a rise in the aggregate price level, by reducing the purchasing power of money holdings, causes a rise in the interest rate. That, in turn, reduces both investment spending and consumer spending.

But what happens if the quantity of money in the hands of households and firms changes? In modern economies, the quantity of money in circulation is largely determined by the decisions of a *central bank* created by the government. As we'll learn in Chapter 29, the Federal Reserve, the U.S. central bank, is a special institution that is neither exactly part of the government nor exactly a private institution. When the central bank increases the quantity of money in circulation, households and firms have more money, which they are willing to lend out. The effect is to drive the interest rate down at any given aggregate price level, leading to higher investment spending and higher consumer spending.

That is, increasing the quantity of money shifts the aggregate demand curve to the right. Reducing the quantity of money has the opposite effect: households and firms have less money holdings than before, leading them to borrow more and lend less. This raises the interest rate, reduces investment spending and consumer spending, and shifts the aggregate demand curve to the left.

ECONOMICS ▶ *in Action*

The interest rate effect of a rise in the aggregate price level leads to a drop in consumer and investment spending.

Moving Along the Aggregate Demand Curve, 1979–1980

When looking at data, it's often hard to distinguish between changes in spending that represent *movements along* the aggregate demand curve and *shifts of* the aggregate demand curve. One telling exception, however, is what happened right after the oil crisis of 1979, which we mentioned in this chapter's opening story. Faced with a sharp increase in the aggregate price level—the rate of consumer price inflation reached 14.8% in March of 1980—the Federal Reserve stuck to a policy of increasing the quantity of money slowly. The aggregate price level was rising steeply, but the quantity of money circulating in the economy was growing slowly. The net result was that the purchasing power of the quantity of money in circulation fell.

This led to an increase in the demand for borrowing and a surge in interest rates. The *prime rate,* which is the interest rate banks charge their best customers, climbed above 20%. High interest rates, in turn, caused both consumer spending and investment spending to fall: in 1980 purchases of durable consumer goods like cars fell by 5.3% and real investment spending fell by 8.9%.

In other words, in 1979–1980 the economy responded just as we'd expect if it were moving upward along the aggregate demand curve from right to left: due to the wealth effect and the interest rate effect of a change in the aggregate price level, the quantity of aggregate output demanded fell as the aggregate price level rose. This does not explain, of course, why the aggregate price level rose. But as we'll see in the upcoming section on the *AD–AS* model, the answer to that question lies in the behavior of the *short-run aggregate supply curve.*

▼ Quick Review

- The **aggregate demand curve** is downward sloping because of the **wealth effect of a change in the aggregate price level** and the **interest rate effect of a change in the aggregate price level.**

- The aggregate demand curve shows how income–expenditure equilibrium GDP changes when the aggregate price level changes.

- Changes in consumer spending caused by changes in wealth and expectations about the future shift the aggregate demand curve. Changes in investment spending caused by changes in expectations and by the size of the existing stock of physical capital also shift the aggregate demand curve.

- Fiscal policy affects aggregate demand directly through government purchases and indirectly through changes in taxes or government transfers. Monetary policy affects aggregate demand indirectly through changes in the interest rate.

Check Your Understanding   27-1

1. Determine the effect on aggregate demand of each of the following events. Explain whether it represents a movement along the aggregate demand curve (up or down) or a shift of the curve (leftward or rightward).
   a. A rise in the interest rate caused by a change in monetary policy
   b. A fall in the real value of money in the economy due to a higher aggregate price level
   c. News of a worse-than-expected job market next year
   d. A fall in tax rates
   e. A rise in the real value of assets in the economy due to a lower aggregate price level
   f. A rise in the real value of assets in the economy due to a surge in real estate values

   Solutions appear at back of book.

Aggregate Supply

Between 1929 and 1933, there was a sharp fall in aggregate demand—a reduction in the quantity of goods and services demanded at any given price level. One consequence of the economy-wide decline in demand was a fall in the prices of most goods and services. By 1933, the GDP deflator (one of the price indexes we defined in Chapter 22) was 26% below its 1929 level, and other indexes were down by similar amounts. A second consequence was a decline in the output of most goods and services: by 1933, real GDP was 27% below its 1929 level. A third consequence, closely tied to the fall in real GDP, was a surge in the unemployment rate from 3% to 25%.

The association between the plunge in real GDP and the plunge in prices wasn't an accident. Between 1929 and 1933, the U.S. economy was moving down its **aggregate supply curve,** which shows the relationship between the economy's aggregate price level (the overall price level of final goods and services in the economy) and the total quantity of final goods and services, or aggregate output, producers are willing to supply. (As you will recall, we use real GDP to measure aggregate output. So we'll often use the two terms interchangeably.) More specifically, between 1929 and 1933 the U.S. economy moved down its *short-run aggregate supply curve.*

The Short-Run Aggregate Supply Curve

The period from 1929 to 1933 demonstrated that there is a positive relationship in the short run between the aggregate price level and the quantity of aggregate output supplied. That is, a rise in the aggregate price level is associated with a rise in the quantity of aggregate output supplied, other things equal; a fall in the aggregate price level is associated with a fall in the quantity of aggregate output supplied, other things equal. To understand why this positive relationship exists, consider the most basic question facing a producer: is producing a unit of output profitable or not? Let's define profit per unit:

(27-2) Profit per unit of output =
Price per unit of output – Production cost per unit of output

Thus, the answer to the question depends on whether the price the producer receives for a unit of output is greater or less than the cost of producing that unit of output. At any given point in time, many of the costs producers face are fixed per unit of output and can't be changed for an extended period of time. Typically, the largest source of inflexible production cost is the wages paid to workers. *Wages* here refers to all forms of worker compensation, such as employer-paid health care and retirement benefits in addition to earnings.

Wages are typically an inflexible production cost because the dollar amount of any given wage paid, called the **nominal wage,** is often determined by contracts that were signed some time ago. And even when there are no formal contracts, there are often informal agreements between management and workers, making companies reluctant to change wages in response to economic conditions. For example, companies usually will not reduce wages during poor economic times—unless the downturn has been particularly long and severe—for fear of generating worker resentment. Correspondingly, they typically won't raise wages during better economic times—until they are at risk of losing workers to competitors—because they don't want to encourage workers to routinely demand higher wages.

As a result of both formal and informal agreements, then, the economy is characterized by **sticky wages:** nominal wages that are slow to fall even in the face of high unemployment and slow to rise even in the face of labor shortages. It's important to note, however, that nominal wages cannot be sticky forever: ultimately, formal contracts and informal agreements will be renegotiated to take into account changed economic circumstances. As the Pitfalls at the end of this section explains, how long it takes for nominal wages to become flexible is an integral component of what distinguishes the short run from the long run.

To understand how the fact that many costs are fixed in nominal terms gives rise to an upward-sloping short-run aggregate supply curve, it's helpful to know that prices are set somewhat differently in different kinds of markets. In *perfectly competitive markets,* producers take prices as given; in *imperfectly competitive markets,* producers have some ability to choose the prices they charge. In both kinds of markets, there is a short-run positive relationship between prices and output, but for slightly different reasons.

Let's start with the behavior of producers in perfectly competitive markets; remember, they take the price as given. Imagine that, for some reason, the aggregate price level falls, which means that the price received by the typical producer

The **aggregate supply curve** shows the relationship between the aggregate price level and the quantity of aggregate output supplied in the economy.

The **nominal wage** is the dollar amount of the wage paid.

Sticky wages are nominal wages that are slow to fall even in the face of high unemployment and slow to rise even in the face of labor shortages.

The **short-run aggregate supply curve** shows the relationship between the aggregate price level and the quantity of aggregate output supplied that exists in the short run, the time period when many production costs can be taken as fixed.

of a final good or service falls. Because many production costs are fixed in the short run, production cost per unit of output doesn't fall by the same proportion as the fall in the price of output. So the profit per unit of output declines, leading perfectly competitive producers to reduce the quantity supplied in the short run.

On the other hand, suppose that for some reason the aggregate price level rises. As a result, the typical producer receives a higher price for its final good or service. Again, many production costs are fixed in the short run, so production cost per unit of output doesn't rise by the same proportion as the rise in the price of a unit. And since the typical perfectly competitive producer takes the price as given, profit per unit of output rises and output increases.

Now consider an imperfectly competitive producer that is able to set its own price. If there is a rise in the demand for this producer's product, it will be able to sell more at any given price. Given stronger demand for its products, it will probably choose to increase its prices as well as its output, as a way of increasing profit per unit of output. In fact, industry analysts often talk about variations in an industry's "pricing power": when demand is strong, firms with pricing power are able to raise prices—and they do.

Conversely, if there is a fall in demand, firms will normally try to limit the fall in their sales by cutting prices.

Both the responses of firms in perfectly competitive industries and those of firms in imperfectly competitive industries lead to an upward-sloping relationship between aggregate output and the aggregate price level. The positive relationship between the aggregate price level and the quantity of aggregate output producers are willing to supply during the time period when many production costs, particularly nominal wages, can be taken as fixed is illustrated by the **short-run aggregate supply curve.** The positive relationship between the aggregate price level and aggregate output in the short run gives the short-run aggregate supply curve its upward slope.

Figure 27-5 shows a hypothetical short-run aggregate supply curve, *SRAS*, which matches actual U.S. data for 1929 and 1933. On the horizontal axis is aggregate output (or, equivalently, real GDP)—the total quantity of final goods and services supplied in the economy—measured in 2009 dollars. On the vertical axis is the aggregate price level as measured by the GDP deflator, with the value for the year 2009 equal to 100. In 1929, the aggregate price level was 9.9 and real GDP was $1,057 billion. In 1933, the aggregate price level was 7.3 and real GDP was only $778 billion. The movement down the *SRAS* curve corresponds to the deflation and fall in aggregate output experienced over those years.

FOR INQUIRING MINDS | What's Truly Flexible, What's Truly Sticky

Most macroeconomists agree that the basic picture shown in Figure 27-5 is correct: there is, other things equal, a positive short-run relationship between the aggregate price level and aggregate output. But many would argue that the details are a bit more complicated.

So far we've stressed a difference in the behavior of the aggregate price level and the behavior of nominal wages. That is, we've said that the aggregate price level is flexible but nominal wages are sticky in the short run. Although this assumption is a good way to explain why the short-run aggregate supply curve is upward sloping, empirical data on wages and prices don't wholly support a sharp distinction between flexible prices

of final goods and services and sticky nominal wages.

On one side, some nominal wages are in fact flexible even in the short run because some workers are not covered by a contract or informal agreement with their employers. Since some nominal wages are sticky but others are flexible, we observe that the *average nominal wage*—the nominal wage averaged over all workers in the economy—falls when there is a steep rise in unemployment. For example, nominal wages fell substantially in the early years of the Great Depression.

On the other side, some prices of final goods and services are sticky rather than flexible. For example, some

firms, particularly the makers of luxury or name-brand goods, are reluctant to cut prices even when demand falls. Instead they prefer to cut output even if their profit per unit hasn't declined.

These complications, as we've said, don't change the basic picture. When the aggregate price level falls, some producers cut output because the nominal wages they pay are sticky. And some producers don't cut their prices in the face of a falling aggregate price level, preferring instead to reduce their output. In both cases, the positive relationship between the aggregate price level and aggregate output is maintained. So, in the end, the short-run aggregate supply curve is still upward sloping. ■

The Short-Run Aggregate Supply Curve

The short-run aggregate supply curve shows the relationship between the aggregate price level and the quantity of aggregate output supplied in the short run, the period in which many production costs such as nominal wages are fixed. It is upward sloping because a higher aggregate price level leads to higher profit per unit of output and higher aggregate output given fixed nominal wages. Here we show numbers corresponding to the Great Depression, from 1929 to 1933: when deflation occurred and the aggregate price level fell from 9.9 (in 1929) to 7.3 (in 1933), firms responded by reducing the quantity of aggregate output supplied from $1,057 billion to $778 billion measured in 2009 dollars.

Shifts of the Short-Run Aggregate Supply Curve

Figure 27-5 shows a *movement along* the short-run aggregate supply curve, as the aggregate price level and aggregate output fell from 1929 to 1933. But there can also be *shifts of* the short-run aggregate supply curve, as shown in Figure 27-6. Panel (a) shows a *decrease in short-run aggregate supply*—a leftward shift of the short-run aggregate supply curve. Aggregate supply decreases when producers reduce the quantity of aggregate output they are willing to supply at any given aggregate price level. Panel (b) shows an *increase in short-run aggregate supply*—a rightward shift of the short-run aggregate supply curve. Aggregate supply increases when producers increase the quantity of aggregate output they are will-ing to supply at any given aggregate price level.

To understand why the short-run aggregate supply curve can shift, it's impor-tant to recall that producers make output decisions based on their profit per unit of output. The short-run aggregate supply curve illustrates the relationship between the aggregate price level and aggregate output: because some production costs are fixed in the short run, a change in the aggregate price level leads to a change in producers' profit per unit of output and, in turn, leads to a change in aggregate output. But other factors besides the aggregate price level can affect profit per unit and, in turn, aggregate output. It is changes in these other factors that will shift the short-run aggregate supply curve.

To develop some intuition, suppose that something happens that raises pro-duction costs—say, an increase in the price of oil. At any given price of output, a producer now earns a smaller profit per unit of output. As a result, producers reduce the quantity supplied at any given aggregate price level, and the short-run aggregate supply curve shifts to the left. If, in contrast, something happens that lowers production costs—say, a fall in the nominal wage—a producer now earns a higher profit per unit of output at any given price of output. This leads produc-ers to increase the quantity of aggregate output supplied at any given aggregate price level, and the short-run aggregate supply curve shifts to the right.

Now we'll discuss some of the important factors that affect producers' profit per unit and so can lead to shifts of the short-run aggregate supply curve.

FIGURE **27-6** Shifts of the Short-Run Aggregate Supply Curve

Panel (a) shows a decrease in short-run aggregate supply: the short-run aggregate supply curve shifts leftward from $SRAS_1$ to $SRAS_2$, and the quantity of aggregate output supplied at any given aggregate price level falls. Panel (b) shows an increase in short-run aggregate supply: the short-run aggregate supply curve shifts rightward from $SRAS_1$ to $SRAS_2$, and the quantity of aggregate output supplied at any given aggregate price level rises.

Changes in Commodity Prices In this chapter's opening story, we described how a surge in the price of oil caused problems for the U.S. economy in the 1970s and early in 2008. Oil is a commodity, a standardized input bought and sold in bulk quantities. An increase in the price of a commodity—oil—raised production costs across the economy and reduced the quantity of aggregate output supplied at any given aggregate price level, shifting the short-run aggregate supply curve to the left. Conversely, a decline in commodity prices reduces production costs, leading to an increase in the quantity supplied at any given aggregate price level and a rightward shift of the short-run aggregate supply curve.

Why isn't the influence of commodity prices already captured by the short-run aggregate supply curve? Because commodities—unlike, say, soft drinks—are not a final good, their prices are not included in the calculation of the aggregate price level. Further, commodities represent a significant cost of production to most suppliers, just like nominal wages do. So changes in commodity prices have large impacts on production costs. And in contrast to noncommodities, the prices of commodities can sometimes change drastically due to industry-specific shocks to supply—such as wars in the Middle East or rising Chinese demand that leaves less oil for the United States.

Changes in Nominal Wages At any given point in time, the dollar wages of many workers are fixed because they are set by contracts or informal agreements made in the past. Nominal wages can change, however, once enough time has passed for contracts and informal agreements to be renegotiated. Suppose, for example, that there is an economy-wide rise in the cost of health care insurance premiums paid by employers as part of employees' wages. From the employers' perspective, this is equivalent to a rise in nominal wages because it is an increase in employer-paid compensation. So this rise in nominal wages increases production costs and shifts the short-run aggregate supply curve to the left. Conversely, suppose there is an economy-wide fall in the cost of such premiums. This is equivalent to a fall in nominal wages from the point of view of employers; it reduces production costs and shifts the short-run aggregate supply curve to the right.

An important historical fact is that during the 1970s the surge in the price of oil had the indirect effect of also raising nominal wages. This "knock-on" effect occurred because many wage contracts included *cost-of-living allowances* that automatically raised the nominal wage when consumer prices increased. Through this channel, the surge in the price of oil—which led to an increase in overall consumer prices—ultimately caused a rise in nominal wages.

So the economy, in the end, experienced two leftward shifts of the aggregate supply curve: the first generated by the initial surge in the price of oil, the second generated by the induced increase in nominal wages. The negative effect on the economy of rising oil prices was greatly magnified through the cost-of-living allowances in wage contracts. Today, cost-of-living allowances in wage contracts are rare.

Changes in Productivity An increase in productivity means that a worker can produce more units of output with the same quantity of inputs. For example, the introduction of bar-code scanners in retail stores greatly increased the ability of a single worker to stock, inventory, and resupply store shelves. As a result, the cost to a store of "producing" a dollar of sales fell and profit rose. And, correspondingly, the quantity supplied increased. (Think of Walmart and the increase in the number of its stores as an increase in aggregate supply.) So a rise in productivity, whatever the source, increases producers' profits and shifts the short-run aggregate supply curve to the right.

Conversely, a fall in productivity—say, due to new regulations that require workers to spend more time filling out forms—reduces the number of units of output a worker can produce with the same quantity of inputs. Consequently, the cost per unit of output rises, profit falls, and quantity supplied falls. This shifts the short-run aggregate supply curve to the left.

For a summary of the factors that shift the short-run aggregate supply curve, see Table 27-2.

TABLE 27-2   Factors That Shift Aggregate Supply

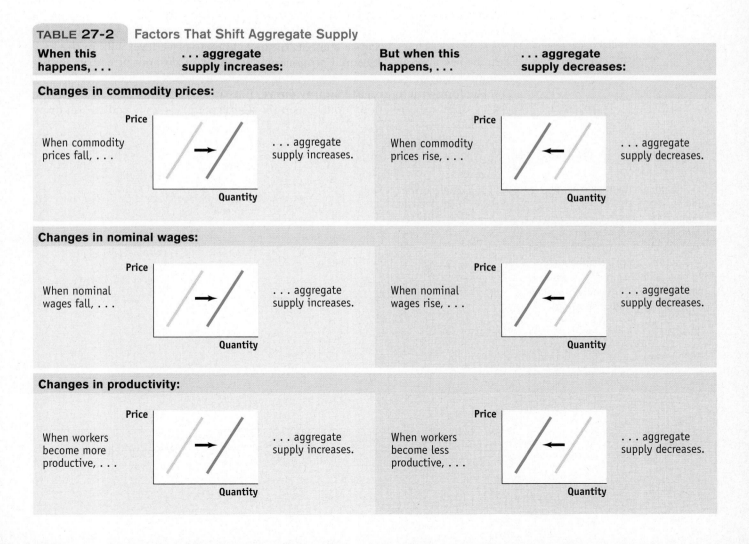

When this happens, . . .	. . . aggregate supply increases:	But when this happens, . . .	. . . aggregate supply decreases:
Changes in commodity prices:			
When commodity prices fall, . . .	. . . aggregate supply increases.	When commodity prices rise, . . .	. . . aggregate supply decreases.
Changes in nominal wages:			
When nominal wages fall, . . .	. . . aggregate supply increases.	When nominal wages rise, . . .	. . . aggregate supply decreases.
Changes in productivity:			
When workers become more productive, . . .	. . . aggregate supply increases.	When workers become less productive, . . .	. . . aggregate supply decreases.

The **long-run aggregate supply curve** shows the relationship between the aggregate price level and the quantity of aggregate output supplied that would exist if all prices, including nominal wages, were fully flexible.

The Long-Run Aggregate Supply Curve

We've just seen that in the short run a fall in the aggregate price level leads to a decline in the quantity of aggregate output supplied because nominal wages are sticky in the short run. But, as we mentioned earlier, contracts and informal agreements are renegotiated in the long run. So in the long run, nominal wages—like the aggregate price level—are flexible, not sticky. This fact greatly alters the long-run relationship between the aggregate price level and aggregate supply. In fact, in the long run the aggregate price level has *no* effect on the quantity of aggregate output supplied.

To see why, let's conduct a thought experiment. Imagine that you could wave a magic wand—or maybe a magic bar-code scanner—and cut *all prices* in the economy in half at the same time. By "all prices" we mean the prices of all inputs, including nominal wages, as well as the prices of final goods and services. What would happen to aggregate output, given that the aggregate price level has been halved and all input prices, including nominal wages, have been halved?

The answer is: nothing. Consider Equation 27-2 again: each producer would receive a lower price for its product, but costs would fall by the same proportion. As a result, every unit of output profitable to produce before the change in prices would still be profitable to produce after the change in prices. So a halving of *all* prices in the economy has no effect on the economy's aggregate output. In other words, changes in the aggregate price level now have no effect on the quantity of aggregate output supplied.

In reality, of course, no one can change all prices by the same proportion at the same time. But now, we'll consider the *long run, the period of time over which all prices are fully flexible.* In the long run, inflation or deflation has the same effect as someone changing all prices by the same proportion. *As a result, changes in the aggregate price level do not change the quantity of aggregate output supplied in the long run.* That's because changes in the aggregate price level will, in the long run, be accompanied by equal proportional changes in *all* input prices, including nominal wages.

The **long-run aggregate supply curve,** illustrated in Figure 27-7 by the curve *LRAS,* shows the relationship between the aggregate price level and the quantity

---

FIGURE 27-7 | The Long-Run Aggregate Supply Curve

The long-run aggregate supply curve shows the quantity of aggregate output supplied when all prices, including nominal wages, are flexible. It is vertical at potential output, Y_P, because in the long run a change in the aggregate price level has no effect on the quantity of aggregate output supplied.

of aggregate output supplied that would exist if all prices, including nominal wages, were fully flexible. The long-run aggregate supply curve is vertical because changes in the aggregate price level have *no* effect on aggregate output in the long run. At an aggregate price level of 15.0, the quantity of aggregate output supplied is $800 billion in 2009 dollars. If the aggregate price level falls by 50% to 7.5, the quantity of aggregate output supplied is unchanged in the long run at $800 billion in 2009 dollars.

It's important to understand not only that the *LRAS* curve is vertical but also that its position along the horizontal axis represents a significant measure. The horizontal intercept in Figure 27-7, where *LRAS* touches the horizontal axis ($800 billion in 2009 dollars), is the economy's **potential output,** Y_P: the level of real GDP the economy would produce if all prices, including nominal wages, were fully flexible.

In reality, the actual level of real GDP is almost always either above or below potential output. We'll see why later in this chapter, when we discuss the *AD–AS* model. Still, an economy's potential output is an important number because it defines the trend around which actual aggregate output fluctuates from year to year.

In the United States, the Congressional Budget Office, or CBO, estimates annual potential output for the purpose of federal budget analysis. In Figure 27-8, the CBO's estimates of U.S. potential output from 1990 to 2014 are represented by the orange line and the actual values of U.S. real GDP over the same period are represented by the blue line. Years shaded purple on the horizontal axis correspond to periods in which actual aggregate output fell short of potential output, years shaded green to periods in which actual aggregate output exceeded potential output.

Potential output is the level of real GDP the economy would produce if all prices, including nominal wages, were fully flexible.

FIGURE 27-8   Actual and Potential Output from 1990 to 2014

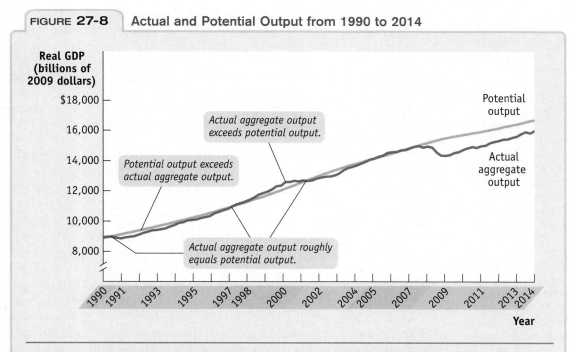

This figure shows the performance of actual and potential output in the United States from 1990 to 2014. The orange line shows estimates of U.S. potential output, produced by the Congressional Budget Office, and the blue line shows actual aggregate output. The purple-shaded years are periods in which actual aggregate output fell below potential output, and the green-shaded years are periods in which actual aggregate output exceeded potential output. As shown, significant shortfalls occurred in the recessions of the early 1990s and after 2000. Actual aggregate output was significantly above potential output in the boom of the late 1990s, and a huge shortfall occurred after the recession of 2007–2009.

Sources: Congressional Budget Office; Bureau of Economic Analysis.

As you can see, U.S. potential output has risen steadily over time—implying a series of rightward shifts of the *LRAS* curve. What has caused these rightward shifts? The answer lies in the factors related to long-run growth that we discussed in Chapter 24, such as increases in physical capital and human capital as well as technological progress. Over the long run, as the size of the labor force and the productivity of labor both rise, the level of real GDP that the economy is capable of producing also rises. Indeed, one way to think about long-run economic growth is that it is the growth in the economy's potential output. We generally think of the long-run aggregate supply curve as shifting to the right over time as an economy experiences long-run growth.

From the Short Run to the Long Run

As you can see in Figure 27-8, the economy normally produces more or less than potential output: actual aggregate output was below potential output in the early 1990s, above potential output in the late 1990s, below potential output for most of the 2000s, and significantly below potential output after the recession of 2007–2009. So the economy is normally on its short-run aggregate supply curve—but not on its long-run aggregate supply curve. So why is the long-run curve relevant? Does the economy ever move from the short run to the long run? And if so, how?

The first step to answering these questions is to understand that the economy is always in one of only two states with respect to the short-run and long-run aggregate supply curves. It can be on both curves simultaneously by being at a point where the curves cross (as in the few years in Figure 27-8 in which actual aggregate output and potential output roughly coincided). Or it can be on the short-run aggregate supply curve but not the long-run aggregate supply curve (as in the years in which actual aggregate output and potential output *did not* coincide). But that is not the end of the story. If the economy is on the short-run but not the long-run aggregate supply curve, the short-run aggregate supply curve will shift over time until the economy is at a point where both curves cross—a point where actual aggregate output is equal to potential output.

Figure 27-9 illustrates how this process works. In both panels *LRAS* is the long-run aggregate supply curve, $SRAS_1$ is the initial short-run aggregate supply curve, and the aggregate price level is at P_1. In panel (a) the economy starts at the initial production point, A_1, which corresponds to a quantity of aggregate output supplied, Y_1, that is higher than potential output, Y_P. Producing an aggregate output level (such as Y_1) that is higher than potential output (Y_P) is possible only because nominal wages haven't yet fully adjusted upward. Until this upward adjustment in nominal wages occurs, producers are earning high profits and producing a high level of output. But a level of aggregate output higher than potential output means a low level of unemployment. Because jobs are abundant and workers are scarce, nominal wages will rise over time, gradually shifting the short-run aggregate supply curve leftward. Eventually it will be in a new position, such as $SRAS_2$. (Later in this chapter, we'll show where the short-run aggregate supply curve ends up. As we'll see, that depends on the aggregate demand curve as well.)

In panel (b), the initial production point, A_1, corresponds to an aggregate output level, Y_1, that is lower than potential output, Y_P. Producing an aggregate output level (such as Y_1) that is lower than potential output (Y_P) is possible only because nominal wages haven't yet fully adjusted downward. Until this downward adjustment occurs, producers are earning low (or negative) profits and

PITFALLS

ARE WE THERE YET? WHAT THE LONG RUN REALLY MEANS

We've used the term *long run* in two different contexts. In an earlier chapter we focused on *long-run economic growth:* growth that takes place over decades. In this chapter we introduced the *long-run aggregate supply curve,* which depicts the economy's potential output: the level of aggregate output that the economy would produce if all prices, including nominal wages, were fully flexible. It might seem that we're using the same term, *long run,* for two different concepts. But we aren't: these two concepts are really the same thing.

Because the economy always tends to return to potential output in the long run, actual aggregate output *fluctuates around* potential output, rarely getting too far from it. As a result, the economy's rate of growth over long periods of time—say, decades—is very close to the rate of growth of potential output. And potential output growth is determined by the factors we analyzed in the chapter on long-run economic growth. So that means that the "long run" of long-run growth and the "long run" of the long-run aggregate supply curve coincide.

FIGURE **27-9**   From the Short Run to the Long Run

(a) Leftward Shift of the Short-Run
Aggregate Supply Curve

(b) Rightward Shift of the Short-Run
Aggregate Supply Curve

In panel (a), the initial short-run aggregate supply curve is $SRAS_1$. At the aggregate price level, P_1, the quantity of aggregate output supplied, Y_1, exceeds potential output, Y_P. Eventually, low unemployment will cause nominal wages to rise, leading to a leftward shift of the short-run aggregate supply curve from $SRAS_1$ to $SRAS_2$. In panel (b), the reverse happens: at the aggregate price level, P_1, the quantity of aggregate output supplied is less than potential output. High unemployment eventually leads to a fall in nominal wages over time and a rightward shift of the short-run aggregate supply curve.

producing a low level of output. An aggregate output level lower than potential output means high unemployment. Because workers are abundant and jobs are scarce, nominal wages will fall over time, shifting the short-run aggregate supply curve gradually to the right. Eventually it will be in a new position, such as $SRAS_2$.

We'll see shortly that these shifts of the short-run aggregate supply curve will return the economy to potential output in the long run.

ECONOMICS ▶ *in Action*

Sticky Wages in the Great Recession

We've asserted that the aggregate supply curve is upward-sloping in the short run mainly because of *sticky wages*—in particular, because employers are reluctant to cut nominal wages (and workers are unwilling to accept wage cuts) even when labor is in excess supply. But what is the evidence for wage stickiness?

The answer is that we can look at what happens to wages at times when we might have expected to see many workers facing wage cuts because similar workers are unemployed and would be willing to work for less. If wages are sticky, what we would expect to find at such times is that many workers' wages don't change at all: there's no reason for employers to give them a raise, but because wages are sticky, they don't face cuts either.

And that is exactly what you find during and after the Great Recession of 2007–2009. Mary Daly and Bart Hobijn, economists at the Federal Reserve Bank of San Francisco, looked at data on wage changes for a sample of workers.

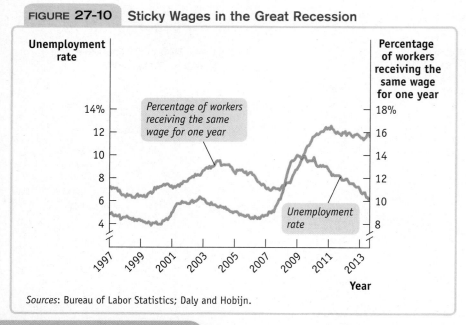

FIGURE **27-10** Sticky Wages in the Great Recession

Sources: Bureau of Labor Statistics; Daly and Hobijn.

Their findings are shown in Figure 27-10: as unemployment soared after 2007, so did the fraction of U.S. workers receiving the same wage as they did a year ago.

Similar results can be found in European nations facing high unemployment, such as Spain. The Great Recession provided strong confirmation that wages are indeed sticky.

When unemployment soared in the face of the economic slump following the 2008 financial crisis, you might have expected to see widespread wage cuts. But employers are reluctant to cut wages. So what we saw instead was a sharp rise in the number of workers whose wages were flat—neither rising nor falling.

▼ Quick Review

- The **aggregate supply curve** illustrates the relationship between the aggregate price level and the quantity of aggregate output supplied.

- The **short-run aggregate supply curve** is upward sloping: a higher aggregate price level leads to higher aggregate output given that **nominal wages** are **sticky.**

- Changes in commodity prices, nominal wages, and productivity shift the short-run aggregate supply curve.

- In the long run, all prices are flexible, and changes in the aggregate price level have no effect on aggregate output. The **long-run aggregate supply curve** is vertical at **potential output.**

- If actual aggregate output exceeds potential output, nominal wages eventually rise and the short-run aggregate supply curve shifts leftward. If potential output exceeds actual aggregate output, nominal wages eventually fall and the short-run aggregate supply curve shifts rightward.

Check Your Understanding 27-2

1. Determine the effect on short-run aggregate supply of each of the following events. Explain whether it represents a movement along the *SRAS* curve or a shift of the *SRAS* curve.
   a. A rise in the consumer price index (CPI) leads producers to increase output.
   b. A fall in the price of oil leads producers to increase output.
   c. A rise in legally mandated retirement benefits paid to workers leads producers to reduce output.

2. Suppose the economy is initially at potential output and the quantity of aggregate output supplied increases. What information would you need to determine whether this was due to a movement along the *SRAS* curve or a shift of the *LRAS* curve?

Solutions appear at back of book.

The *AD–AS* Model

From 1929 to 1933, the U.S. economy moved down the short-run aggregate supply curve as the aggregate price level fell. In contrast, from 1979 to 1980 the U.S. economy moved up the aggregate demand curve as the aggregate price level rose. In each case, the cause of the movement along the curve was a shift of the other curve. In 1929–1933, it was a leftward shift of the aggregate demand curve—a major fall in consumer spending. In 1979–1980, it was a leftward shift of the short-run aggregate supply curve—a dramatic fall in short-run aggregate supply caused by the oil price shock.

So to understand the behavior of the economy, we must put the aggregate supply curve and the aggregate demand curve together. The result is the *AD–AS* **model,** the basic model we use to understand economic fluctuations.

Short-Run Macroeconomic Equilibrium

We'll begin our analysis by focusing on the short run. Figure 27-11 shows the aggregate demand curve and the short-run aggregate supply curve on the same diagram. The point at which the *AD* and *SRAS* curves intersect, E_{SR}, is the **short-run macroeconomic equilibrium:** the point at which the quantity of aggregate

FIGURE 27-11   The *AD–AS* Model

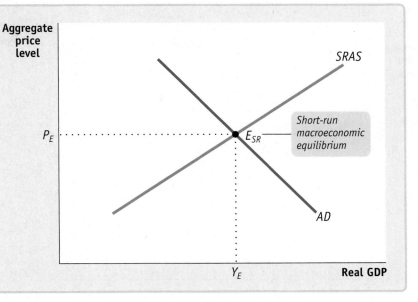

The *AD–AS* model combines the aggregate demand curve and the short-run aggregate supply curve. Their point of intersection, E_{SR}, is the point of short-run macroeconomic equilibrium where the quantity of aggregate output demanded is equal to the quantity of aggregate output supplied. P_E is the short-run equilibrium aggregate price level, and Y_E is the short-run equilibrium level of aggregate output.

output supplied is equal to the quantity demanded by domestic households, businesses, the government, and the rest of the world. The aggregate price level at E_{SR}, P_E, is the **short-run equilibrium aggregate price level.** The level of aggregate output at E_{SR}, Y_E, is the **short-run equilibrium aggregate output.**

In the supply and demand model of Chapter 3 we saw that a shortage of any individual good causes its market price to rise but a surplus of the good causes its market price to fall. These forces ensure that the market reaches equilibrium. The same logic applies to short-run macroeconomic equilibrium. If the aggregate price level is above its equilibrium level, the quantity of aggregate output supplied exceeds the quantity of aggregate output demanded. This leads to a fall in the aggregate price level and pushes it toward its equilibrium level.

If the aggregate price level is below its equilibrium level, the quantity of aggregate output supplied is less than the quantity of aggregate output demanded. This leads to a rise in the aggregate price level, again pushing it toward its equilibrium level. In the discussion that follows, we'll assume that the economy is always in short-run macroeconomic equilibrium.

We'll also make another important simplification based on the observation that in reality there is a long-term upward trend in both aggregate output and the aggregate price level. We'll assume that a fall in either variable really means a fall compared to the long-run trend. For example, if the aggregate price level normally rises 4% per year, a year in which the aggregate price level rises only 3% would count, for our purposes, as a 1% decline. In fact, since the Great Depression there have been very few years in which the aggregate price level of any major nation actually declined—Japan's period of deflation since 1995 is one of the few exceptions. We'll explain why in Chapter 31. There have, however, been many cases in which the aggregate price level fell relative to the long-run trend.

Short-run equilibrium aggregate output and the short-run equilibrium aggregate price level can change either because of shifts of the *AD* curve or because of shifts of the *SRAS* curve. Let's look at each case in turn.

Shifts of Aggregate Demand: Short-Run Effects

An event that shifts the aggregate demand curve, such as a change in expectations or wealth, the effect of the size of the existing stock of physical capital, or the use of fiscal or monetary policy, is known as a **demand shock.** The Great Depression

In the **AD–AS model,** the aggregate supply curve and the aggregate demand curve are used together to analyze economic fluctuations.

The economy is in **short-run macroeconomic equilibrium** when the quantity of aggregate output supplied is equal to the quantity demanded.

The **short-run equilibrium aggregate price level** is the aggregate price level in the short-run macroeconomic equilibrium.

Short-run equilibrium aggregate output is the quantity of aggregate output produced in the short-run macroeconomic equilibrium.

An event that shifts the aggregate demand curve is a **demand shock.**

FIGURE **27-12** | Demand Shocks

A demand shock shifts the aggregate demand curve, moving the aggregate price level and aggregate output in the same direction. In panel (a), a negative demand shock shifts the aggregate demand curve leftward from AD_1 to AD_2, reducing the aggregate price level from P_1 to P_2 and aggregate output from Y_1 to Y_2. In panel (b), a positive demand shock shifts the aggregate demand curve rightward, increasing the aggregate price level from P_1 to P_2 and aggregate output from Y_1 to Y_2.

was caused by a negative demand shock, the collapse of wealth and of business and consumer confidence that followed the stock market crash of 1929 and the banking crisis of 1930–1931.

The Depression was ended by a positive demand shock—the huge increase in government purchases during World War II. In 2008 the U.S. economy experienced another significant negative demand shock as the housing market turned from boom to bust, leading consumers and firms to scale back their spending.

Figure 27-12 shows the short-run effects of negative and positive demand shocks. A negative demand shock shifts the aggregate demand curve, AD, to the left, from AD_1 to AD_2, as shown in panel (a). The economy moves down along the $SRAS$ curve from E_1 to E_2, leading to lower short-run equilibrium aggregate output and a lower short-run equilibrium aggregate price level. A positive demand shock shifts the aggregate demand curve, AD, to the right, as shown in panel (b). Here, the economy moves up along the $SRAS$ curve, from E_1 to E_2. This leads to higher short-run equilibrium aggregate output and a higher short-run equilibrium aggregate price level. Demand shocks cause aggregate output and the aggregate price level to move in the same direction.

Shifts of the *SRAS* Curve

An event that shifts the short-run aggregate supply curve, such as a change in commodity prices, nominal wages, or productivity, is known as a **supply shock.** A *negative* supply shock raises production costs and reduces the quantity producers are willing to supply at any given aggregate price level, leading to a leftward shift of the short-run aggregate supply curve. The U.S. economy experienced severe negative supply shocks following disruptions to world oil supplies in 1973 and 1979. In contrast, a *positive* supply shock reduces production costs and increases the quantity supplied at any given aggregate price level, leading to a rightward shift of the short-run aggregate supply curve. The United States experienced a positive supply shock between 1995 and 2000, when the increasing use of the internet and other information technologies caused productivity growth to surge.

An event that shifts the short-run aggregate supply curve is a **supply shock.**

FIGURE **27-13**   Supply Shocks

(a) A Negative Supply Shock

A negative supply shock...

SRAS₂   SRAS₁

E_2

P_2

P_1

E_1

...leads to lower aggregate output and a higher aggregate price level.

AD

$Y_2 \leftarrow Y_1$ **Real GDP**

Aggregate price level

(b) A Positive Supply Shock

A positive supply shock...

SRAS₁   SRAS₂

E_1

P_1

P_2

E_2

...leads to higher aggregate output and a lower aggregate price level.

AD

$Y_1 \rightarrow Y_2$ **Real GDP**

Aggregate price level

A supply shock shifts the short-run aggregate supply curve, moving the aggregate price level and aggregate output in opposite directions. Panel (a) shows a negative supply shock, which shifts the short-run aggregate supply curve leftward and causes stagflation—lower aggregate output and a higher aggregate price level. Here the short-run aggregate supply curve shifts from $SRAS_1$ to $SRAS_2$, and the economy moves from E_1 to E_2. The aggregate price level rises from P_1 to P_2,

and aggregate output falls from Y_1 to Y_2. Panel (b) shows a positive supply shock, which shifts the short-run aggregate supply curve rightward, generating higher aggregate output and a lower aggregate price level. The short-run aggregate supply curve shifts from $SRAS_1$ to $SRAS_2$, and the economy moves from E_1 to E_2. The aggregate price level falls from P_1 to P_2, and aggregate output rises from Y_1 to Y_2.

The effects of a negative supply shock are shown in panel (a) of Figure 27-13. The initial equilibrium is at E_1, with aggregate price level P_1 and aggregate output Y_1. The disruption in the oil supply causes the short-run aggregate supply curve to shift to the left, from $SRAS_1$ to $SRAS_2$. As a consequence, aggregate output falls and the aggregate price level rises, an upward movement along the AD curve. At the new equilibrium, E_2, the short-run equilibrium aggregate price level, P_2, is higher, and the short-run equilibrium aggregate output level, Y_2, is lower than before.

The combination of inflation and falling aggregate output shown in panel (a) has a special name: **stagflation,** for "stagnation plus inflation." When an economy experiences stagflation, it's very unpleasant: falling aggregate output leads to rising unemployment, and people feel that their purchasing power is squeezed by rising prices. Stagflation in the 1970s led to a mood of national pessimism. It also, as we'll see shortly, poses a dilemma for policy makers.

A positive supply shock, shown in panel (b), has exactly the opposite effects. A rightward shift of the $SRAS$ curve from $SRAS_1$ to $SRAS_2$ results in a rise in aggregate output and a fall in the aggregate price level, a downward movement along the AD curve. The favorable supply shocks of the late 1990s led to a combination of full employment and declining inflation. That is, the aggregate price level fell compared with the long-run trend. This combination produced, for a time, a great wave of national optimism.

The distinctive feature of supply shocks, both negative and positive, is that, unlike demand shocks, they cause the aggregate price level and aggregate output to move in *opposite* directions.

There's another important contrast between supply shocks and demand shocks. As we've seen, monetary policy and fiscal policy enable the government to shift the AD curve, meaning that governments are in a position to create the

Stagflation is the combination of inflation and falling aggregate output.

GLOBAL COMPARISION | Supply Shocks of the Twenty-first Century

The price of oil and other raw materials has been highly unstable in recent years, with surging prices in 2007–2008, plunging prices in 2008–2009, and another surge starting in the second half of 2010. The reasons for these wild swings are somewhat controversial, but their macroeconomic implications are clear: much of the world has been subjected to a series of supply shocks. There was a negative shock in 2007–2008, a positive shock in 2008–2009, and another negative shock in 2010–2011.

You can see the effect of these shocks in the accompanying figure, which shows the rate of inflation, as measured by the percentage change in consumer prices over the previous year, in three large economies. Economic policies have been quite different in the United States, Germany (which shares a currency with many other European countries), and

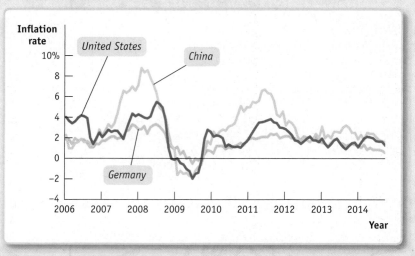

China. Yet in all three inflation rose sharply in 2007–2008, fell dramatically thereafter, and rose sharply again in 2011.

Source: Federal Reserve Bank of St. Louis.

kinds of shocks shown in Figure 27-12. It's much harder for governments to shift the *AS* curve. Are there good policy reasons to shift the *AD* curve? We'll turn to that question soon. First, however, let's look at the difference between short-run macroeconomic equilibrium and long-run macroeconomic equilibrium.

Long-Run Macroeconomic Equilibrium

Figure 27-14 combines the aggregate demand curve with both the short-run and long-run aggregate supply curves. The aggregate demand curve, *AD*, crosses the short-run aggregate supply curve, *SRAS*, at E_{LR}. Here we assume that enough time has elapsed that the economy is also on the long-run aggregate supply curve, *LRAS*. As a result, E_{LR} is at the intersection of all three curves—*SRAS*, *LRAS*, and *AD*. So short-run equilibrium aggregate output is equal to potential output, Y_P. Such a situation, in which the point of short-run macroeconomic equilibrium is on the long-run aggregate supply curve, is known as **long-run macroeconomic equilibrium.**

To see the significance of long-run macroeconomic equilibrium, let's consider what happens if a demand shock moves the economy away from long-run macroeconomic equilibrium. In Figure 27-15, we assume that the initial aggregate demand curve is AD_1 and the initial short-run aggregate supply curve is $SRAS_1$. So the initial macroeconomic equilibrium is at E_1, which lies on the long-run aggregate supply curve, *LRAS*. The economy, then, starts from a point of short-run and long-run macroeconomic equilibrium, and short-run equilibrium aggregate output equals potential output at Y_1.

Now suppose that for some reason—such as a sudden worsening of business and consumer expectations—aggregate demand falls and the aggregate demand curve shifts leftward to AD_2. This results in a lower equilibrium aggregate price level at P_2 and a lower equilibrium aggregate output level at Y_2 as the economy settles in the short run at E_2. The short-run effect of such a fall in aggregate demand is what the U.S. economy experienced in 1929–1933: a falling aggregate price level and falling aggregate output.

The economy is in **long-run macroeconomic equilibrium** when the point of short-run macroeconomic equilibrium is on the long-run aggregate supply curve.

There is a **recessionary gap** when aggregate output is below potential output.

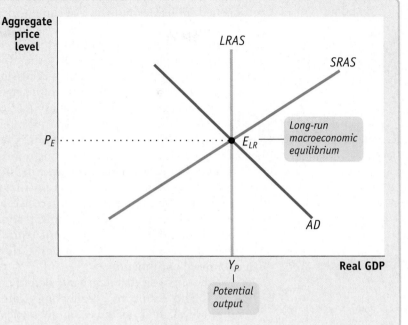

FIGURE **27-14**   Long-Run Macroeconomic Equilibrium

Here the point of short-run macroeconomic equilibrium also lies on the long-run aggregate supply curve, *LRAS*. As a result, short-run equilibrium aggregate output is equal to potential output, Y_P. The economy is in long-run macroeconomic equilibrium at E_{LR}.

Aggregate output in this new short-run equilibrium, E_2, is below potential output. When this happens, the economy faces a **recessionary gap.** A recessionary gap inflicts a great deal of pain because it corresponds to high unemployment.

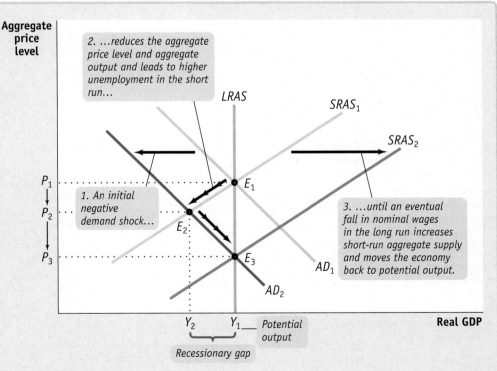

FIGURE **27-15**   Short-Run versus Long-Run Effects of a Negative Demand Shock

In the long run the economy is self-correcting: demand shocks have only a short-run effect on aggregate output. Starting at E_1, a negative demand shock shifts AD_1 leftward to AD_2. In the short run the economy moves to E_2 and a recessionary gap arises: the aggregate price level declines from P_1 to P_2, aggregate output declines from Y_1 to Y_2, and unemployment rises. But in the long run nominal wages fall in response to high unemployment at Y_2, and $SRAS_1$ shifts rightward to $SRAS_2$. Aggregate output rises from Y_2 to Y_1, and the aggregate price level declines again, from P_2 to P_3. Long-run macroeconomic equilibrium is eventually restored at E_3.

There is an **inflationary gap** when aggregate output is above potential output.

The large recessionary gap that had opened up in the United States by 1933 caused intense social and political turmoil. And the devastating recessionary gap that opened up in Germany at the same time played an important role in Hitler's rise to power.

But this isn't the end of the story. In the face of high unemployment, nominal wages eventually fall, as do any other sticky prices, ultimately leading producers to increase output. As a result, a recessionary gap causes the short-run aggregate supply curve to gradually shift to the right over time. This process continues until $SRAS_1$ reaches its new position at $SRAS_2$, bringing the economy to equilibrium at E_3, where AD_2, $SRAS_2$, and $LRAS$ all intersect. At E_3, the economy is back in long-run macroeconomic equilibrium; it is back at potential output Y_1 but at a lower aggregate price level, P_3, reflecting a long-run fall in the aggregate price level. In the end, the economy is *self-correcting* in the long run.

What if, instead, there was an increase in aggregate demand? The results are shown in Figure 27-16, where we again assume that the initial aggregate demand curve is AD_1 and the initial short-run aggregate supply curve is $SRAS_1$, so that the initial macroeconomic equilibrium, at E_1, lies on the long-run aggregate supply curve, $LRAS$. Initially, then, the economy is in long-run macroeconomic equilibrium.

Now suppose that aggregate demand rises, and the AD curve shifts rightward to AD_2. This results in a higher aggregate price level, at P_2, and a higher aggregate output level, at Y_2, as the economy settles in the short run at E_2. Aggregate output in this new short-run equilibrium is above potential output, and unemployment is low in order to produce this higher level of aggregate output. When this happens, the economy experiences an **inflationary gap.**

As in the case of a recessionary gap, this isn't the end of the story. In the face of low unemployment, nominal wages will rise, as will other sticky prices. An inflationary gap causes the short-run aggregate supply curve to shift gradually to the left as producers reduce output in the face of rising nominal wages. This process continues until $SRAS_1$ reaches its new position at $SRAS_2$, bringing the economy to

---

FIGURE 27-16 Short-Run versus Long-Run Effects of a Positive Demand Shock

Starting at E_1, a positive demand shock shifts AD_1 rightward to AD_2, and the economy moves to E_2 in the short run. This results in an inflationary gap as aggregate output rises from Y_1 to Y_2, the aggregate price level rises from P_1 to P_2, and unemployment falls to a low level. In the long run, $SRAS_1$ shifts leftward to $SRAS_2$ as nominal wages rise in response to low unemployment at Y_2. Aggregate output falls back to Y_1, the aggregate price level rises again to P_3, and the economy self-corrects as it returns to long-run macroeconomic equilibrium at E_3.

FOR INQUIRING MINDS | Where's the Deflation?

The *AD–AS* model says that either a negative demand shock or a positive supply shock should lead to a fall in the aggregate price level—that is, deflation. However, since 1949, an actual fall in the aggregate price level has been a rare occurrence in the United States. Similarly, most other countries have had little or no experience with deflation. Japan, which experienced sustained mild deflation in the late 1990s and the early part of the next decade, is the big (and much discussed) exception. What happened to deflation?

The basic answer is that since World War II economic fluctuations have largely taken place around a long-run inflationary trend. Before the war, it was common for prices to fall during recessions, but since then negative demand shocks have largely been reflected in a *decline in the rate of inflation* rather than an actual fall in prices. For example, the rate of consumer price inflation fell from more than 3% at the beginning of the 2001 recession to 1.1% a year later, but it never went below zero.

All of this changed during the recession of 2007–2009. The negative demand shock that followed the 2008 financial crisis was so severe that, for most of 2009, consumer prices in the United States indeed fell. But the deflationary period didn't last long: beginning in 2010, prices again rose, at a rate of between 1% and 4% per year. ■

equilibrium at E_3, where AD_2, $SRAS_2$, and $LRAS$ all intersect. At E_3, the economy is back in long-run macroeconomic equilibrium. It is back at potential output, but at a higher price level, P_3, reflecting a long-run rise in the aggregate price level. Again, the economy is self-correcting in the long run.

To summarize the analysis of how the economy responds to recessionary and inflationary gaps, we can focus on the **output gap,** the percentage difference between actual aggregate output and potential output. The output gap is calculated as follows:

(27-3) $\text{Output gap} = \dfrac{\text{Actual aggregate output} - \text{Potential output}}{\text{Potential output}} \times 100$

Our analysis says that the output gap always tends toward zero.

If there is a recessionary gap, so that the output gap is negative, nominal wages eventually fall, moving the economy back to potential output and bringing the output gap back to zero. If there is an inflationary gap, so that the output gap is positive, nominal wages eventually rise, also moving the economy back to potential output and again bringing the output gap back to zero. So in the long run the economy is **self-correcting:** shocks to aggregate demand affect aggregate output in the short run but not in the long run.

ECONOMICS ▶ *in Action*

Supply Shocks Versus Demand Shocks in Practice

How often do supply shocks and demand shocks, respectively, cause recessions? The verdict of most, though not all, macroeconomists is that recessions are mainly caused by demand shocks. But when a negative supply shock does happen, the resulting recession tends to be particularly severe.

Let's get specific. Officially there have been twelve recessions in the United States since World War II. However, two of these, in 1979–1980 and 1981–1982, are often treated as a single "double-dip" recession, bringing the total number down to eleven. Of these eleven recessions, only two—the recession of 1973–1975 and the double-dip recession of 1979–1982—showed the distinctive combination of falling aggregate output and a surge in the price level that we call stagflation. In each case, the cause of the supply shock was political turmoil in the Middle East—the Arab–Israeli war of 1973 and the Iranian revolution of 1979—that disrupted world oil supplies and sent oil prices skyrocketing. In fact, economists sometimes refer to the two slumps as "OPEC I" and "OPEC II," after the Organization of Petroleum Exporting Countries, the world oil cartel. A third

The **output gap** is the percentage difference between actual aggregate output and potential output.

The economy is **self-correcting** when shocks to aggregate demand affect aggregate output in the short run, but not the long run.

FIGURE **27-17** Negative Supply Shocks Are Relatively Rare but Nasty

Source: Bureau of Labor Statistics.

recession that began in 2007 and lasted until 2009 was at least partially exacerbated, if not at least partially caused, by a spike in oil prices.

So eight of eleven postwar recessions were purely the result of demand shocks, not supply shocks. The few supply-shock recessions, however, were the worst as measured by the unemployment rate. Figure 27-17 shows the U.S. unemployment rate since 1948, with the dates of the 1973 Arab–Israeli war and the 1979 Iranian revolution marked on the graph. Some of the highest unemployment rates since World War II came after these big negative supply shocks.

There's a reason the aftermath of a supply shock tends to be particularly severe for the economy: macroeconomic policy has a much harder time dealing with supply shocks than with demand shocks. Indeed, the reason the Federal Reserve was having a hard time in 2008, as described in the opening story, was the fact that in early 2008 the U.S. economy was in a recession partially caused by a supply shock (although it was also facing a demand shock). We'll see in a moment why supply shocks present such a problem.

Check Your Understanding **27-3**

1. Describe the short-run effects of each of the following shocks on the aggregate price level and on aggregate output.
   a. The government sharply increases the minimum wage, raising the wages of many workers.
   b. Solar energy firms launch a major program of investment spending.
   c. Congress raises taxes and cuts spending.
   d. Severe weather destroys crops around the world.

2. A rise in productivity increases potential output, but some worry that demand for the additional output will be insufficient even in the long run. How would you respond?

Solutions appear at back of book.

Macroeconomic Policy

We've just seen that the economy is self-correcting in the long run: it will eventually trend back to potential output. Most macroeconomists believe, however, that the process of self-correction typically takes a decade or more. In particular, if aggregate output is below potential output, the economy can suffer an extended period of depressed aggregate output and high unemployment before it returns to normal.

This belief is the background to one of the most famous quotations in economics: John Maynard Keynes's declaration, "In the long run we are all dead." We explain the context in which he made this remark in the accompanying For Inquiring Minds.

Economists usually interpret Keynes as having recommended that governments not wait for the economy to correct itself. Instead, it is argued by many economists, but not all, that the government should use monetary and fiscal policy to get the economy back to potential output in the aftermath of a shift of the aggregate demand curve. This is the rationale for an active **stabilization policy,** which is the use of government policy to reduce the severity of recessions and rein in excessively strong expansions.

FOR INQUIRING MINDS | Keynes and the Long Run

The British economist Sir John Maynard Keynes (1883–1946), probably more than any other single economist, created the modern field of macroeconomics. We'll look at his role, and the controversies that still swirl around some aspects of his thought, in a later chapter on macroeconomic events and ideas. But for now let's just look at his most famous quote.

In 1923 Keynes published *A Tract on Monetary Reform*, a small book on the economic problems of Europe after World War I. In it he decried the

Keynes focused the attention of economists of his day on the short run.

tendency of many of his colleagues to focus on how things work out in the long run—as in the long-run macroeconomic equilibrium we have just analyzed—while ignoring the often very painful and possibly disastrous things that can happen along the way. Here's a fuller version of the quote:

This long run is a misleading guide to current affairs. In the long run we are all dead. Economists set themselves too easy, too useless a task if in tempestuous seasons they can only tell us that when the storm is long past the sea is flat again. ■

Can stabilization policy improve the economy's performance? If we reexamine Figure 27-8, the answer certainly appears to be yes. Under active stabilization policy, the U.S. economy returned to potential output in 1996 after an approximately five-year recessionary gap. Likewise, in 2001 it also returned to potential output after an approximately four-year inflationary gap. These periods are much shorter than the decade or more that economists believe it would take for the economy to self-correct in the absence of active stabilization policy. However, as we'll see shortly, the ability to improve the economy's performance is not always guaranteed. It depends on the kinds of shocks the economy faces.

Policy in the Face of Demand Shocks

Imagine that the economy experiences a negative demand shock, like the one shown in Figure 27-15. As we've discussed in this chapter, monetary and fiscal policy shift the aggregate demand curve. If policy makers react quickly to the fall in aggregate demand, they can use monetary or fiscal policy to shift the aggregate demand curve back to the right. And if policy were able to perfectly anticipate shifts of the aggregate demand curve, it could short-circuit the whole process shown in Figure 27-15. Instead of going through a period of low aggregate output and falling prices, the government could manage the economy so that it would stay at E_1.

Why might a policy that short-circuits the adjustment shown in Figure 27-15 and maintains the economy at its original equilibrium be desirable? For two reasons. First, the temporary fall in aggregate output that would happen without policy intervention is a bad thing, particularly because such a decline is associated with high unemployment. Second, as we explained in Chapter 23, *price stability* is generally regarded as a desirable goal. So preventing deflation—a fall in the aggregate price level—is a good thing.

Does this mean that policy makers should always act to offset declines in aggregate demand? Not necessarily. As we'll see in later chapters, some policy measures to increase aggregate demand, especially those that increase budget deficits, may have long-term costs in terms of lower long-run growth. Furthermore, in the real world policy makers aren't perfectly informed, and the effects of their policies aren't perfectly predictable. This creates the danger that stabilization policy will do more harm than good; that is, attempts to stabilize the economy may end up creating more instability. We'll describe the long-running debate over macroeconomic policy in Chapter 33. Despite these qualifications,

Stabilization policy is the use of government policy to reduce the severity of recessions and rein in excessively strong expansions.

most economists believe that a good case can be made for using macroeconomic policy to offset major negative shocks to the *AD* curve.

Should policy makers also try to offset positive shocks to aggregate demand? It may not seem obvious that they should. After all, even though inflation may be a bad thing, isn't more output and lower unemployment a good thing? Not necessarily. Most economists now believe that any short-run gains from an inflationary gap must be paid back later. So policy makers today usually try to offset positive as well as negative demand shocks. For reasons we'll explain in Chapter 30, attempts to eliminate recessionary gaps and inflationary gaps usually rely on monetary rather than fiscal policy. In 2007 and 2008 the Federal Reserve sharply cut interest rates in an attempt to head off a rising recessionary gap; earlier in the decade, when the U.S. economy seemed headed for an inflationary gap, it raised interest rates to generate the opposite effect.

But how should macroeconomic policy respond to supply shocks?

Responding to Supply Shocks

We've now come full circle to the story that began this chapter. We can now explain why FOMC committee members dread stagflation.

Back in panel (a) of Figure 27-13 we showed the effects of a negative supply shock: in the short run such a shock leads to lower aggregate output but a higher aggregate price level. As we've noted, policy makers can respond to a negative *demand* shock by using monetary and fiscal policy to return aggregate demand to its original level. But what can or should they do about a negative *supply* shock?

In contrast to the aggregate demand curve, there are no easy policies that shift the short-run aggregate supply curve. That is, there is no government policy that can easily affect producers' profitability and so compensate for shifts of the short-run aggregate supply curve. So the policy response to a negative supply shock cannot aim to simply push the curve that shifted back to its original position.

And if you consider using monetary or fiscal policy to shift the aggregate demand curve in response to a supply shock, the right response isn't obvious. Two bad things are happening simultaneously: a fall in aggregate output, leading to a rise in unemployment, *and* a rise in the aggregate price level. Any policy that shifts the aggregate demand curve helps one problem only by making the other worse. If the government acts to increase aggregate demand and limit the rise in unemployment, it reduces the decline in output but causes even more inflation. If it acts to reduce aggregate demand, it curbs inflation but causes a further rise in unemployment.

It's a trade-off with no good answer. In the end, the United States and other economically advanced nations suffering from the supply shocks of the 1970s eventually chose to stabilize prices even at the cost of higher unemployment. But being an economic policy maker in the 1970s, or in early 2008, meant facing even harder choices than usual.

ECONOMICS ▶ *in Action*

Is Stabilization Policy Stabilizing?

We've described the theoretical rationale for stabilization policy as a way of responding to demand shocks. But does stabilization policy actually stabilize the economy? One way we might try to answer this question is to look at the long-term historical record. Before World War II, the U.S. government didn't really have a stabilization policy, largely because macroeconomics as we know it didn't exist, and there was no consensus about what to do. Since World War II, and especially since 1960, active stabilization policy has become standard practice.

So here's the question: has the economy actually become more stable since the government began trying to stabilize it? The answer is a qualified yes. It's qualified for two reasons. One is that data from the pre–World War II era are less reliable than more modern data. The other is that the severe and protracted slump that began in 2007 has shaken confidence in the effectiveness of government policy. Still, there seems to have been a reduction in the size of fluctuations.

Figure 27-18 shows the number of unemployed as a percentage of the nonfarm labor force since 1890. (We focus on nonfarm workers because farmers, though they often suffer economic hardship, are rarely reported as unemployed.) Even ignoring the huge spike in unemployment during the Great Depression, unemployment seems to have varied a lot more before World War II than after. It's also worth noticing that the peaks in postwar unemployment, in 1975, 1982, and to some extent in 2010 (as described in the Global Comparison earlier in the chapter), corresponded to major supply shocks—the kind of shock for which stabilization policy has no good answer.

It's possible that the greater stability of the economy reflects good luck rather than policy. But on the face of it, the evidence suggests that stabilization policy is indeed stabilizing.

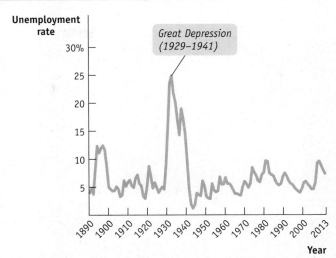

FIGURE **27-18**   **Has Stabilization Policy Been Stabilizing?**

Sources: Christina Romer, "Spurious Volatility in Historical Unemployment Data." *Jounal of Political Economy* 94, no. 1 (1986): 1–37(years 1890–1928); Bureau of Labor Statistics (years 1929–2014).

Check Your Understanding   27-4

1. Suppose someone says, "Using monetary or fiscal policy to pump up the economy is counterproductive—you get a brief high, but then you have the pain of inflation."
   a. Explain what this means in terms of the *AD–AS* model.
   b. Is this a valid argument against stabilization policy? Why or why not?

2. In 2008, in the aftermath of the collapse of the housing bubble and a sharp rise in the price of commodities, particularly oil, there was much internal disagreement within the Fed about how to respond, with some advocating lowering interest rates and others contending that this would set off a rise in inflation. Explain the reasoning behind each one of these views in terms of the *AD–AS* model.

Solutions appear at back of book.

▼ Quick Review

• **Stabilization policy** is the use of fiscal or monetary policy to offset demand shocks. There can be drawbacks, however. Such policies may lead to a long-term rise in the budget deficit and lower long-run growth because of crowding out. And, due to incorrect predictions, a misguided policy can increase economic instability.

• Negative supply shocks pose a policy dilemma because fighting the slump in aggregate output worsens inflation and fighting inflation worsens the slump.

Slow Steaming

The global economic slump of 2008–2009 took a toll on almost everyone. By 2011, however, the acute crisis was receding in the rearview mirror. Unemployment remained high in wealthy countries, but the world economy as a whole was growing fairly fast, and so were corporate profits.

One industry that wasn't doing well, however, was shipping. A 2012 report from the Boston Consulting Group declared that executives in the container-shipping industry—which moves the ubiquitous standard-sized boxes of cargo that are transferred between ships and trucks by the giant cranes visible at every major port—"would probably like to forget 2011." The world's largest shipping company, the Danish firm Maersk, saw its profits fall more than 30%, even though world trade was growing at a fairly rapid clip and it was carrying more cargo than it did the year before.

Why was 2011 a bad year to be in the shipping business? The answer is that while world trade and hence the overall demand for shipping were rising, there was a surge in oil prices. This was bad news for shippers, for whom the cost of fuel oil is a major expense. As you can see in Figure 27-19, profits temporarily increased immediately after the Great Recession when fuel costs were low. But that changed near the end of 2010, as the price of fuel started to rise. And in 2011, as fuel prices spiked at almost $700 per ton, profits fell by more than $1 billion.

One consequence of the oil price shock was a literal slowdown in world trade: shippers turned to "slow steaming," in which ships get somewhat better fuel economy by traveling more slowly, typically 17 knots rather than their usual 20. Some carriers even went to "super-slow" steaming, dropping their speed to 15 knots, although this damaged their engines.

© Peter Titmuss/Alamy

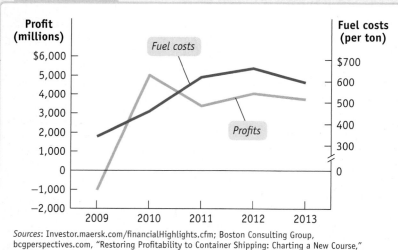

FIGURE 27-19   An Oil Price Shock in the Shipping Industry

Sources: Investor.maersk.com/financialHighlights.cfm; Boston Consulting Group, bcgperspectives.com, "Restoring Profitability to Container Shipping: Charting a New Course," October 10, 2012.

Maersk and other shippers did better in 2012, as oil prices receded somewhat. But the troubles of 2011 were a reminder that there is more than one way to get into economic trouble.

QUESTIONS FOR THOUGHT

1. How did Maersk's problem in 2011 relate to our analysis of the causes of recessions?

2. The Fed had to make a choice between fighting two evils in early 2008. How would that choice affect Maersk compared with, say, a company producing a service without expensive raw-material inputs, like health care?

3. In 2011, the world economy was holding up fairly well, but Europe was sliding back into recession. What do you think was happening to the business of intra-European transport (which mainly goes by truck, not ship)? Why?

SUMMARY

1. The **aggregate demand curve** shows the relationship between the aggregate price level and the quantity of aggregate output demanded.

2. The aggregate demand curve is downward sloping for two reasons. The first is the **wealth effect of a change in the aggregate price level**—a higher aggregate price level reduces the purchasing power of households' wealth and reduces consumer spending. The second is the **interest rate effect of a change in the aggregate price level**—a higher aggregate price level reduces the purchasing power of households' and firms' money holdings, leading to a rise in interest rates and a fall in investment spending and consumer spending.

3. The aggregate demand curve shifts because of changes in expectations, changes in wealth not due to changes in the aggregate price level, and the effect of the size of the existing stock of physical capital. Policy makers can use fiscal policy and monetary policy to shift the aggregate demand curve.

4. The **aggregate supply curve** shows the relationship between the aggregate price level and the quantity of aggregate output supplied.

5. The **short-run aggregate supply curve** is upward sloping because **nominal wages** are **sticky** in the short run: a higher aggregate price level leads to higher profit per unit of output and increased aggregate output in the short run.

6. Changes in commodity prices, nominal wages, and productivity lead to changes in producers' profits and shift the short-run aggregate supply curve.

7. In the long run, all prices, including nominal wages, are flexible and the economy produces at its **potential output.** If actual aggregate output exceeds potential output, nominal wages will eventually rise in response to low unemployment and aggregate output will fall. If potential output exceeds actual aggregate output, nominal wages will eventually fall in response to high unemployment and aggregate output will rise. So the **long-run aggregate supply curve** is vertical at potential output.

8. In the *AD–AS* **model,** the intersection of the short-run aggregate supply curve and the aggregate demand curve is the point of **short-run macroeconomic**

equilibrium. It determines the **short-run equilibrium aggregate price level** and the level of **short-run equilibrium aggregate output.**

9. Economic fluctuations occur because of a shift of the aggregate demand curve (a *demand shock*) or the short-run aggregate supply curve (a *supply shock*). A **demand shock** causes the aggregate price level and aggregate output to move in the same direction as the economy moves along the short-run aggregate supply curve. A **supply shock** causes them to move in opposite directions as the economy moves along the aggregate demand curve. A particularly nasty occurrence is **stagflation**—inflation and falling aggregate output—which is caused by a negative supply shock.

10. Demand shocks have only short-run effects on aggregate output because the economy is **self-correcting** in the long run. In a **recessionary gap,** an eventual fall in nominal wages moves the economy to **long-run macroeconomic equilibrium,** where aggregate output is equal to potential output. In an **inflationary gap,** an eventual rise in nominal wages moves the economy to long-run macroeconomic equilibrium. We can use the **output gap,** the percentage difference between actual aggregate output and potential output, to summarize how the economy responds to recessionary and inflationary gaps. Because the economy tends to be self-correcting in the long run, the output gap always tends toward zero.

11. The high cost—in terms of unemployment—of a recessionary gap and the future adverse consequences of an inflationary gap lead many economists to advocate active **stabilization policy:** using fiscal or monetary policy to offset demand shocks. There can be drawbacks, however, because such policies may contribute to a long-term rise in the budget deficit and crowding out of private investment, leading to lower long-run growth. Also, poorly timed policies can increase economic instability.

12. Negative supply shocks pose a policy dilemma: a policy that counteracts the fall in aggregate output by increasing aggregate demand will lead to higher inflation, but a policy that counteracts inflation by reducing aggregate demand will deepen the output slump.

KEY TERMS

Aggregate demand curve, p. 784
Wealth effect of a change in the aggregate price level, p. 786
Interest rate effect of a change in the aggregate price level, p. 786
Aggregate supply curve, p. 793

Nominal wage, p. 793
Sticky wages, p. 793
Short-run aggregate supply curve, p. 794
Long-run aggregate supply curve, p. 798

Potential output, p. 799
AD–AS model, p. 803
Short-run macroeconomic equilibrium, p. 803
Short-run equilibrium aggregate price level, p. 803

Short-run equilibrium aggregate
  output, p. 803
Demand shock, p. 803
Supply shock, p. 804

Stagflation, p. 805
Long-run macroeconomic equilibrium,
  p. 806
Recessionary gap, p. 806

Inflationary gap, p. 808
Output gap, p. 809
Self-correcting, p. 809
Stabilization policy, p. 811

PROBLEMS

1. A fall in the value of the dollar against other currencies makes U.S. final goods and services cheaper to foreigners even though the U.S. aggregate price level stays the same. As a result, foreigners demand more American aggregate output. Your study partner says that this represents a movement down the aggregate demand curve because foreigners are demanding more in response to a lower price. You, however, insist that this represents a rightward shift of the aggregate demand curve. Who is right? Explain.

2. Your study partner is confused by the upward-sloping short-run aggregate supply curve and the vertical long-run aggregate supply curve. How would you explain this?

3. Suppose that in Wageland all workers sign annual wage contracts each year on January 1. No matter what happens to prices of final goods and services during the year, all workers earn the wage specified in their annual contract. This year, prices of final goods and services fall unexpectedly after the contracts are signed. Answer the following questions using a diagram and assume that the economy starts at potential output.
   a. In the short run, how will the quantity of aggregate output supplied respond to the fall in prices?
   b. What will happen when firms and workers renegotiate their wages?

4. The economy is at point A in the accompanying diagram. Suppose that the aggregate price level rises from P_1 to P_2. How will aggregate supply adjust in the short run and in the long run to the increase in the aggregate price level? Illustrate with a diagram.

5. Suppose that all households hold all their wealth in assets that automatically rise in value when the aggregate price level rises (an example of this is what is called an "inflation-indexed bond"—a bond whose interest

rate, among other things, changes one-for-one with the inflation rate). What happens to the wealth effect of a change in the aggregate price level as a result of this allocation of assets? What happens to the slope of the aggregate demand curve? Will it still slope downward? Explain.

6. Suppose that the economy is currently at potential output. Also suppose that you are an economic policy maker and that a college economics student asks you to rank, if possible, your most preferred to least preferred type of shock: positive demand shock, negative demand shock, positive supply shock, negative supply shock. How would you rank them and why?

7. Explain whether the following government policies affect the aggregate demand curve or the short-run aggregate supply curve and how.
   a. The government reduces the minimum nominal wage.
   b. The government increases Temporary Assistance to Needy Families (TANF) payments, government transfers to families with dependent children.
   c. To reduce the budget deficit, the government announces that households will pay much higher taxes beginning next year.
   d. The government reduces military spending.

8. In Wageland, all workers sign an annual wage contract each year on January 1. In late January, a new computer operating system is introduced that increases labor productivity dramatically. Explain how Wageland will move from one short-run macroeconomic equilibrium to another. Illustrate with a diagram.

9. The Conference Board publishes the Consumer Confidence Index (CCI) every month based on a survey of 5,000 representative U.S. households. It is used by many economists to track the state of the economy. A press release by the Board on June 28, 2011, stated: "The Conference Board Consumer Confidence Index, which had declined in May, decreased again in June. The Index now stands at 58.5 (1985 = 100), down from 61.7 in May."
   a. As an economist, is this news encouraging for economic growth?
   b. Explain your answer to part a with the help of the AD–AS model. Draw a typical diagram showing two equilibrium points (E_1) and (E_2). Label the vertical axis "Aggregate price level" and the horizontal axis "Real GDP." Assume that all other major macroeconomic factors remain unchanged.

c. How should the government respond to this news? What are some policy measures that could be used to help neutralize the effect of falling consumer confidence?

10. There were two major shocks to the U.S. economy in 2007, leading to the severe recession of 2007–2009. One shock was related to oil prices; the other was the slump in the housing market. This question analyzes the effect of these two shocks on GDP using the *AD–AS* framework.

a. Draw typical aggregate demand and short-run aggregate supply curves. Label the horizontal axis "Real GDP" and the vertical axis "Aggregate price level." Label the equilibrium point E_1, the equilibrium quantity Y_1, and equilibrium price P_1.

b. Data taken from the Department of Energy indicate that the average price of crude oil in the world increased from $54.63 per barrel on January 5, 2007, to $92.93 on December 28, 2007. Would an increase in oil prices cause a demand shock or a supply shock? Redraw the diagram from part a to illustrate the effect of this shock by shifting the appropriate curve.

c. The Housing Price Index, published by the Office of Federal Housing Enterprise Oversight, calculates that U.S. home prices fell by an average of 3.0% in the 12 months between January 2007 and January 2008. Would the fall in home prices cause a supply shock or demand shock? Redraw the diagram from part b to illustrate the effect of this shock by shifting the appropriate curve. Label the new equilibrium point E_3, the equilibrium quantity Y_3, and equilibrium price P_3.

d. Compare the equilibrium points E_1 and E_3 in your diagram for part c. What was the effect of the two shocks on real GDP and the aggregate price level (increase, decrease, or indeterminate)?

11. Using aggregate demand, short-run aggregate supply, and long-run aggregate supply curves, explain the process by which each of the following economic events will move the economy from one long-run macroeconomic equilibrium to another. Illustrate with diagrams. In each case, what are the short-run and long-run effects on the aggregate price level and aggregate output?

a. There is a decrease in households' wealth due to a decline in the stock market.

b. The government lowers taxes, leaving households with more disposable income, with no corresponding reduction in government purchases.

12. Using aggregate demand, short-run aggregate supply, and long-run aggregate supply curves, explain the process by which each of the following government policies will move the economy from one long-run macroeconomic equilibrium to another. Illustrate with diagrams. In each case, what are the short-run and long-run effects on the aggregate price level and aggregate output?

a. There is an increase in taxes on households.

b. There is an increase in the quantity of money.

c. There is an increase in government spending.

13. The economy is in short-run macroeconomic equilibrium at point E_1 in the accompanying diagram. Based on the diagram, answer the following questions.

a. Is the economy facing an inflationary or a recessionary gap?

b. What policies can the government implement that might bring the economy back to long-run macroeconomic equilibrium? Illustrate with a diagram.

c. If the government did not intervene to close this gap, would the economy return to long-run macroeconomic equilibrium? Explain and illustrate with a diagram.

d. What are the advantages and disadvantages of the government implementing policies to close the gap?

14. In the accompanying diagram, the economy is in long-run macroeconomic equilibrium at point E_1 when an oil shock shifts the short-run aggregate supply curve to $SRAS_2$. Based on the diagram, answer the following questions.

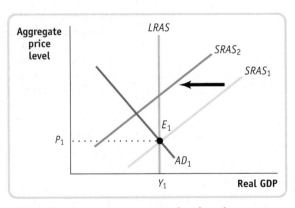

a. How do the aggregate price level and aggregate output change in the short run as a result of the oil shock? What is this phenomenon known as?

b. What fiscal or monetary policies can the government use to address the effects of the supply shock? Use a diagram that shows the effect of policies chosen to address the change in real GDP. Use another diagram to show the effect of policies chosen to address the change in the aggregate price level.

c. Why do supply shocks present a dilemma for government policy makers?

15. The late 1990s in the United States were characterized by substantial economic growth with low inflation; that is, real GDP increased with little, if any, increase in the aggregate price level. Explain this experience using aggregate demand and aggregate supply curves. Illustrate with a diagram.

WORK IT OUT

For interactive, step-by-step help in solving the following problem, visit LaunchPad by using the URL on the back cover of this book.

16. In each of the following cases, in the short run, determine whether the events cause a shift of a curve or a movement along a curve. Determine which curve is involved and the direction of the change.

a. As a result of an increase in the value of the dollar in relation to other currencies, American producers now pay less in dollar terms for foreign steel, a major commodity used in production.

b. An increase in the quantity of money by the Federal Reserve increases the quantity of money that people wish to lend, lowering interest rates.

c. Greater union activity leads to higher nominal wages.

d. A fall in the aggregate price level increases the purchasing power of households' and firms' money holdings. As a result, they borrow less and lend more.

Fiscal Policy

What You Will Learn in This Chapter

- What fiscal policy is and why it is an important tool in managing economic fluctuations

- Which policies constitute **expansionary fiscal policy** and which constitute **contractionary fiscal policy**

- Why fiscal policy has a multiplier effect and how this effect is influenced by **automatic stabilizers**

- Why governments calculate the cyclically **adjusted budget balance**

- Why a large **public debt** may be a cause for concern

- Why **implicit liabilities** of the government are also a cause for concern

HOW BIG IS BIG ENOUGH?

"WE'RE GONNA NEED A BIGGER BOAT."

On February 27, 2009, President Obama signed the American Recovery and Reinvestment Act, a $787 billion package of spending, aid, and tax cuts intended to help the struggling U.S. economy reverse a severe recession that began in December 2007. A week earlier, as the bill neared final passage in Congress, Obama hailed the measure: "It is the right size; it is the right scope. Broadly speaking it has the right priorities to create jobs that will jumpstart our economy and transform it for the twenty-first century."

Others weren't so sure. Some argued that the government should be cutting spending, not increasing it, at a time when American families were suffering. "It's time for government to tighten their belts and show the American people that we 'get' it," said John Boehner, the leader of Republicans in the House of Representatives. Some economic analysts warned that the stimulus bill, as the Recovery Act was commonly called, would drive up interest rates and increase the burden of national debt.

Others had the opposite complaint— that the stimulus was too small given the economy's troubles. For example, Joseph Stiglitz, the 2001 recipient of the Nobel Prize in economics, stated about the stimulus, "First of all that it was not enough should be pretty apparent from what I just said: it is trying to offset the deficiency in aggregate demand and it is just too small."

Nor did the passage of time resolve these disputes. True, some predictions were proved false. On one side, Obama's hope that the bill would "jumpstart" the economy fell short: although the recession officially ended in June 2009, unemployment remained high through 2011 and into 2012, by which time the stimulus had largely run its course. On the other side, the soaring interest rates predicted by stimulus opponents failed to materialize, as U.S. borrowing costs remained low by historical standards.

But the net effect of the stimulus remained controversial, with opponents arguing that it had failed to help the economy and defenders arguing that things would have been much worse without it.

Whatever the verdict—and this is one of those issues that economists and historians will probably be arguing about for decades to come—the Recovery Act of 2009 was a classic example of *fiscal policy*, the use of government spending and taxes to manage aggregate demand. In this chapter we'll see how fiscal policy fits into the models of economic fluctuations we studied in Chapters 26 and 27. We'll also see why budget deficits and government debt can be a problem and how short-run and long-run concerns can pull fiscal policy in different directions.

Fiscal Policy: The Basics

Let's begin with the obvious: modern governments in economically advanced countries spend a great deal of money and collect a lot in taxes. Figure 28-1 shows government spending and tax revenue as percentages of GDP for a selection of high-income countries in 2013. As you can see, the French government sector is relatively large, accounting for more than half of the French economy. The government of the United States plays a smaller role in the economy than those of Canada or most European countries. But that role is still sizable, with the government playing a major role in the U.S. economy. As a result, changes in the federal budget—changes in government spending or in taxation—can have large effects on the American economy.

| FIGURE 28-1 | Government Spending and Tax Revenue for Some High-Income Countries in 2013 |

Government spending and tax revenue are represented as a percentage of GDP. France has a particularly large government sector, representing more than half of its GDP. The U.S. government sector, although sizable, is smaller than those of Canada and most European countries.

Source: OECD.

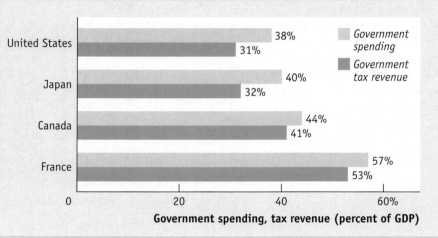

To analyze these effects, we begin by showing how taxes and government spending affect the economy's flow of income. Then we can see how changes in spending and tax policy affect aggregate demand.

Taxes, Purchases of Goods and Services, Government Transfers, and Borrowing

In Figure 22-1 we showed the circular flow of income and spending in the economy as a whole. One of the sectors represented in that figure was the government. Funds flow *into* the government in the form of taxes and government borrowing; funds flow *out* in the form of government purchases of goods and services and government transfers to households.

What kinds of taxes do Americans pay, and where does the money go? Figure 28-2 shows the composition of U.S. tax revenue in 2013. Taxes, of course, are required payments to the government. In the United States, taxes are collected at the national level by the federal government; at the state level by each state government; and at local levels by counties, cities, and towns. At the federal level, the taxes that generate the greatest revenue are income taxes on both personal income and corporate profits as well as *social insurance* taxes, which we'll explain shortly. At the state and local levels, the picture is more complex: these governments rely on a mix of sales taxes, property taxes, income taxes, and fees of various kinds.

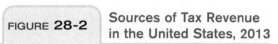

| FIGURE 28-2 | Sources of Tax Revenue in the United States, 2013 |

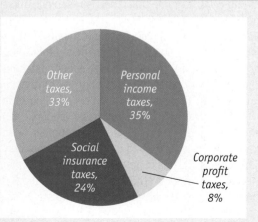

Personal income taxes, taxes on corporate profits, and social insurance taxes account for most government tax revenue. The rest is a mix of property taxes, sales taxes, and other sources of revenue.

Source: Bureau of Economic Analysis.

Overall, taxes on personal income and corporate profits accounted for 43% of total government revenue in 2013; social insurance taxes accounted for 24%; and a variety of other taxes, collected mainly at the state and local levels, accounted for the rest.

Figure 28-3 shows the composition of total U.S. government spending in 2013, which takes two broad forms. One form is purchases of goods and services. This includes everything from ammunition for the military to the salaries of public school teachers (who are treated in the national accounts as providers of a service—education). The big items here are national defense and education. The category "Other goods and services" consists mainly of state and local spending on a variety of services, from police and firefighters to highway construction and maintenance.

The other form of government spending is government transfers, which are payments by the government to households for which no good or service is provided in return. In the modern United States, as well as in Canada and Europe, government transfers represent a very large proportion of the budget. Most U.S. government spending on transfer payments is accounted for by three big programs:

- Social Security, which provides guaranteed income to older Americans, disabled Americans, and the surviving spouses and dependent children of deceased or retired beneficiaries

- Medicare, which covers much of the cost of health care for Americans over age 65

- Medicaid, which covers much of the cost of health care for Americans with low incomes

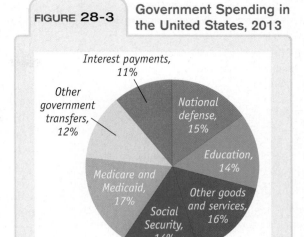

FIGURE 28-3 Government Spending in the United States, 2013

The two types of government spending are purchases of goods and services and government transfers. The big items in government purchases are national defense and education. The big items in government transfers are Social Security and the Medicare and Medicaid health care programs. (Percentages do not add to 100% due to rounding.)

Source: Bureau of Economic Analysis.

The term **social insurance** is used to describe government programs that are intended to protect families against economic hardship. These include Social Security, Medicare and Medicaid as well as smaller programs such as unemployment insurance and food stamps. And in 2014, the Affordable Care Act, or ACA, was implemented. Created to ensure that every American is covered by health insurance, the ACA works through a system of regulated private insurance markets, subsidies, and an expansion of Medicaid eligibility. In the United States, social insurance programs are largely paid for with special, dedicated taxes on wages—the social insurance taxes we mentioned earlier. (Except for the ACA, which relies mostly on private purchases of health insurance coverage.)

But how do tax policy and government spending affect the economy? The answer is that taxation and government spending have a strong effect on total aggregate spending in the economy.

The Government Budget and Total Spending

Let's recall the basic equation of national income accounting:

(28-1) $GDP = C + I + G + X - IM$

The left-hand side of this equation is GDP, the value of all final goods and services produced in the economy. The right-hand side is aggregate spending, total spending on final goods and services produced in the economy. It is the sum of consumer spending (C), investment spending (I), government purchases of goods and services (G), and the value of exports (X) minus the value of imports (IM). It includes all the sources of aggregate demand.

The government directly controls one of the variables on the right-hand side of Equation 28-1: government purchases of goods and services (G). But that's not the only effect fiscal policy has on aggregate spending in the economy. Through changes in taxes and transfers, it also influences consumer spending (C) and, in some cases, investment spending (I).

Social insurance programs are government programs intended to protect families against economic hardship.

Expansionary fiscal policy is fiscal policy that increases aggregate demand.

Contractionary fiscal policy is fiscal policy that reduces aggregate demand.

To see why the budget affects consumer spending, recall that *disposable income,* the total income households have available to spend, is equal to the total income they receive from wages, dividends, interest, and rent, *minus* taxes, *plus* government transfers. So either an increase in taxes or a reduction in government transfers *reduces* disposable income. And a fall in disposable income, other things equal, leads to a fall in consumer spending. Conversely, either a decrease in taxes or an increase in government transfers *increases* disposable income. And a rise in disposable income, other things equal, leads to a rise in consumer spending.

The government's ability to affect investment spending is a more complex story, which we won't discuss in detail. The important point is that the government taxes profits, and changes in the rules that determine how much a business owes can increase or reduce the incentive to spend on investment goods.

Because the government itself is one source of spending in the economy, and because taxes and transfers can affect spending by consumers and firms, the government can use changes in taxes or government spending to *shift the aggregate demand curve.* And as we saw in Chapter 27, there are sometimes good reasons to shift the aggregate demand curve.

In early 2009, as this chapter's opening story explained, the Obama administration believed it was crucial that the U.S. government act to increase aggregate demand—that is, to move the aggregate demand curve to the right of where it would otherwise be. The 2009 stimulus package was a classic example of *fiscal policy:* the use of taxes, government transfers, or government purchases of goods and services to stabilize the economy by shifting the aggregate demand curve.

Expansionary and Contractionary Fiscal Policy

Why would the government want to shift the aggregate demand curve? Because it wants to close either a recessionary gap, created when aggregate output falls below potential output, or an inflationary gap, created when aggregate output exceeds potential output.

Figure 28-4 shows the case of an economy facing a recessionary gap. *SRAS* is the short-run aggregate supply curve, *LRAS* is the long-run aggregate supply curve, and AD_1 is the initial aggregate demand curve. At the initial short-run macroeconomic equilibrium, E_1, aggregate output is Y_1, below potential output, Y_P. What the government would like to do is increase aggregate demand, shifting the aggregate demand curve rightward to AD_2. This would increase aggregate output, making it equal to potential output. Fiscal policy that increases aggregate demand, called **expansionary fiscal policy,** normally takes one of three forms:

- An increase in government purchases of goods and services
- A cut in taxes
- An increase in government transfers

The 2009 American Recovery and Reinvestment Act, or simply, the Recovery Act, was a combination of all three: a direct increase in federal spending and aid to state governments to help them maintain spending, tax cuts for most families, and increased aid to the unemployed.

Figure 28-5 shows the opposite case—an economy facing an inflationary gap. Again, *SRAS* is the short-run aggregate supply curve, *LRAS* is the long-run aggregate supply curve, and AD_1 is the initial aggregate demand curve. At the initial equilibrium, E_1, aggregate output is Y_1, above potential output, Y_P. As we'll explain in later chapters, policy makers often try to head off inflation by eliminating inflationary gaps. To eliminate the inflationary gap shown in Figure 28-5, fiscal policy must reduce aggregate demand and shift the aggregate demand curve leftward to AD_2. This reduces aggregate output and makes it equal to potential output. Fiscal

FIGURE 28-4   Expansionary Fiscal Policy Can Close a Recessionary Gap

The economy is in short-run macroeconomic equilibrium at E_1, where the aggregate demand curve, AD_1, intersects the SRAS curve. However, it is not in long-run macroeconomic equilibrium. At E_1, there is a recessionary gap of $Y_P - Y_1$. An expansionary fiscal policy—an increase in government purchases of goods and services, a reduction in taxes, or an increase in government transfers—shifts the aggregate demand curve rightward. It can close the recessionary gap by shifting AD_1 to AD_2, moving the economy to a new short-run macroeconomic equilibrium, E_2, which is also a long-run macroeconomic equilibrium.

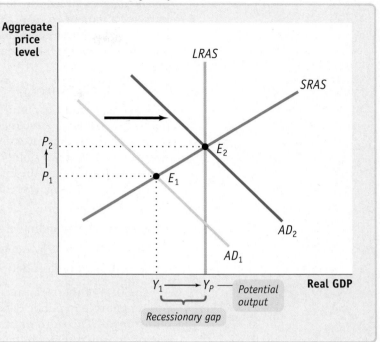

policy that reduces aggregate demand, called **contractionary fiscal policy,** is the opposite of expansionary fiscal policy. It is implemented in three possible ways:

1. A reduction in government purchases of goods and services
2. An increase in taxes
3. A reduction in government transfers

FIGURE 28-5   Contractionary Fiscal Policy Can Close an Inflationary Gap

The economy is in short-run macroeconomic equilibrium at E_1, where the aggregate demand curve, AD_1, intersects the SRAS curve. But it is not in long-run macroeconomic equilibrium. At E_1, there is an inflationary gap of $Y_1 - Y_P$. A contractionary fiscal policy—such as reduced government purchases of goods and services, an increase in taxes, or a reduction in government transfers—shifts the aggregate demand curve leftward. It closes the inflationary gap by shifting AD_1 to AD_2, moving the economy to a new short-run macroeconomic equilibrium, E_2, which is also a long-run macroeconomic equilibrium.

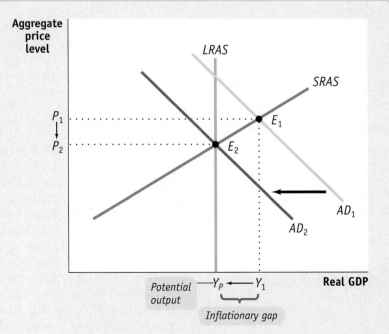

A classic example of contractionary fiscal policy occurred in 1968, when U.S. policy makers grew worried about rising inflation. President Lyndon Johnson imposed a temporary 10% surcharge on taxable income—everyone's income taxes were increased by 10%. He also tried to scale back government purchases of goods and services, which had risen dramatically because of the cost of the Vietnam War.

Can Expansionary Fiscal Policy Actually Work?

In practice, the use of fiscal policy—in particular, the use of expansionary fiscal policy in the face of a recessionary gap—is often controversial. We'll examine the origins of these controversies in detail in Chapter 33. But for now, let's quickly summarize the major points of the debate over expansionary fiscal policy, so we can understand when the critiques are justified and when they are not.

Broadly speaking, there are three arguments against the use of expansionary fiscal policy.

- Government spending always crowds out private spending
- Government borrowing always crowds out private investment spending
- Government budget deficits lead to reduced private spending

The first of these claims is wrong in principle, but it has nonetheless played a prominent role in public debates. The second is valid under some, but not all, circumstances. The third argument, although it raises some important issues, isn't a good reason to believe that expansionary fiscal policy doesn't work.

Claim 1: "Government Spending Always Crowds Out Private Spending"

Some claim that expansionary fiscal policy can never raise aggregate spending and therefore can never raise aggregate income, with reasons that go something like this: "Every dollar that the government spends is a dollar taken away from the private sector. So any rise in government spending must be offset by an equal fall in private spending." In other words, every dollar spent by the government *crowds out*, or displaces, a dollar of private spending.

So what's wrong with this view? The answer is that the statement is wrong because it assumes that resources in the economy are always fully employed and, as a result, the aggregate income earned in the economy is always a fixed sum—which isn't true. In reality, whether or not government spending crowds out private spending depends upon the state of the economy. In particular, when the economy is suffering from a recessionary gap, there are unemployed resources in the economy and output, and therefore income, is below its potential level. Expansionary fiscal policy during these periods puts unemployed resources to work and generates higher spending and higher income. Government spending crowds out private spending only when the economy is operating at full employment. So the argument that expansionary fiscal policy always crowds out private spending is wrong in principle.

Claim 2: "Government Borrowing Always Crowds Out Private Investment Spending"

In Chapter 25, we discussed the possibility that government borrowing uses funds that would have otherwise been used for private investment spending—that is, it crowds out private investment spending. So how valid is the argument that government borrowing always reduces private investment spending?

Much like Claim 1, Claim 2 is wrong because whether crowding out occurs depends upon whether the economy is depressed or not. If the economy is not depressed, then increased government borrowing, by increasing the demand for loanable funds, can raise interest rates and crowd out private investment spending. However, what if the economy is depressed? In that case, crowding out is much less likely. When the economy is at far less than full employment, a fiscal expansion will lead to higher incomes, which in turn leads to increased savings at any given interest rate. This larger pool of savings allows the government to borrow without driving up interest rates. The Recovery Act of 2009 was a case in point: despite high levels of government borrowing, U.S. interest rates stayed near historic lows. In the end, government borrowing crowds out private investment spending only when the economy is operating at full employment.

Claim 3: "Government Budget Deficits Lead to Reduced Private Spending" Other things equal, expansionary fiscal policy leads to a larger budget deficit and greater government debt. And higher debt will eventually require the government to raise taxes to pay it off. So, according to the third argument against expansionary fiscal policy, consumers, anticipating that they must pay higher taxes in the future to pay off today's government debt, will cut their spending today in order to save money. This argument, first made by nineteenth-century economist David Ricardo, is known as Ricardian equivalence. It is an argument often taken to imply that expansionary fiscal policy will have no effect on the economy because far-sighted consumers will undo any attempts at expansion by the government. (And will also undo any contractionary fiscal policy, for that matter.)

In reality, however, it's doubtful that consumers behave with such foresight and budgeting discipline. Most people, when provided with extra cash (generated by the fiscal expansion), will spend at least some of it. So even fiscal policy that takes the form of temporary tax cuts or transfers of cash to consumers probably does have an expansionary effect.

Moreover, it's possible to show that even with Ricardian equivalence, a temporary rise in government spending that involves direct purchases of goods and services—such as a program of road construction—would still lead to a boost in total spending in the near term. That's because even if consumers cut back their current spending in anticipation of higher future taxes, their reduced spending will take place over an extended period as consumers save over time to pay the future tax bill. Meanwhile, the additional government spending will be concentrated in the near future, when the economy needs it.

So although the effects emphasized by Ricardian equivalence may reduce the impact of fiscal expansion, the claim that it makes fiscal expansion completely ineffective is neither consistent with how consumers actually behave nor a reason to believe that increases in government spending have no effect. So, in the end, it's not a valid argument against expansionary fiscal policy.

In sum, then, the extent to which we should expect expansionary fiscal policy to work depends upon the circumstances. When the economy has a recessionary gap—as it did when the 2009 Recovery Act was passed—economics tells us that this is just the kind of situation in which expansionary fiscal policy helps the economy. However, when the economy is already at full employment, expansionary fiscal policy is the wrong policy and will lead to crowding out, an overheated economy, and higher inflation.

A Cautionary Note: Lags in Fiscal Policy

Looking back at Figures 28-4 and 28-5, it may seem obvious that the government should actively use fiscal policy—always adopting an expansionary fiscal policy when the economy faces a recessionary gap and always adopting a contractionary fiscal policy when the economy faces an inflationary gap. But many economists caution against an extremely active stabilization policy, arguing that a government that tries too hard to stabilize the economy—through either fiscal policy or monetary policy—can end up making the economy less stable.

We'll leave discussion of the warnings associated with monetary policy to Chapter 30. In the case of fiscal policy, one key reason for caution is that there are important *time lags* between when the policy is decided upon and when it is implemented. To understand the nature of these lags, think about what has to happen before the government increases spending to fight a recessionary gap. First, the government has to realize that the recessionary gap exists: economic data take time to collect and analyze, and recessions are often recognized only months after they have begun. Second, the government has to develop a spending plan, which can itself take months, particularly if politicians take time debating how the money should be spent and passing legislation. Finally, it takes time to spend money. For example, a road construction project begins with activities such as surveying that don't involve spending large sums. It may be quite some time before the big spending begins.

Because of these lags, an attempt to increase spending to fight a recessionary gap may take so long to get going that the economy has already recovered on its own. In fact, the recessionary gap may have turned into an inflationary gap by the time the fiscal policy takes effect. In that case, the fiscal policy will make things worse instead of better.

This doesn't mean that fiscal policy should never be actively used. In early 2009 there was good reason to believe that the slump facing the U.S. economy would be both deep and long and that a fiscal stimulus designed to arrive over the next year or two would almost surely push aggregate demand in the right direction. In fact, as we'll see later in this chapter, the 2009 stimulus arguably faded out too soon, leaving the economy still deeply depressed. But the problem of lags makes the actual use of both fiscal and monetary policy harder than you might think from a simple analysis like the one we have just given.

ECONOMICS ▶ in Action

What Was in the Recovery Act?

As we've just learned, fiscal stimulus can take three forms: increased government purchases of goods and services, increased transfer payments, and tax cuts. So what form did the Recovery Act take? The answer is that it's a bit complicated.

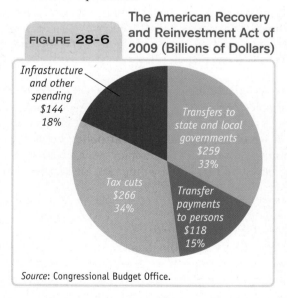

FIGURE 28-6

The American Recovery and Reinvestment Act of 2009 (Billions of Dollars)

Infrastructure and other spending $144 18%

Transfers to state and local governments $259 33%

Tax cuts $266 34%

Transfer payments to persons $118 15%

Source: Congressional Budget Office.

Figure 28-6 shows the composition of the budget impact of the Recovery Act, a measure that adds up the dollar value of tax cuts, transfer payments, and government spending. Here, the numbers are broken down into *four* categories, not three. "Infrastructure and other spending" means spending on roads, bridges, and schools as well as "nontraditional" infrastructure like research and development, all of which fall under government purchases of goods and services. "Tax cuts" are self-explanatory. "Transfer payments to persons" mostly took the form of expanded benefits for the unemployed. But a fourth category, "transfers to state and local governments," accounted for roughly a third of the funds. Why this fourth category?

Because America has multiple levels of government. The authors live in Princeton Township, which has its own budget, which is part of Mercer County, which has its own budget, which is part of the state of New Jersey, which has its own budget, which is part of the United States. One effect of the recession was a sharp drop in revenues at the state and local levels, which in turn forced these lower levels of government to cut spending. Federal aid—those transfers to state and local governments—was intended to mitigate these spending cuts.

Perhaps the most surprising aspect of the Recovery Act was how little direct federal spending on goods and services was involved. The great bulk of the program involved giving money to other people, one way or another, in the hope that they would spend it.

Check Your Understanding   28-1

1. In each of the following cases, determine whether the policy is an expansionary or contractionary fiscal policy.
   a. Several military bases around the country, which together employ tens of thousands of people, are closed.
   b. The number of weeks an unemployed person is eligible for unemployment benefits is increased.
   c. The federal tax on gasoline is increased.
2. Explain why federal disaster relief, which quickly disburses funds to victims of natural disasters such as hurricanes, floods, and large-scale crop failures, will stabilize the economy more effectively after a disaster than relief that must be legislated.
3. Is the following statement true or false? Explain. "When the government expands, the private sector shrinks; when the government shrinks, the private sector expands."

Solutions appear at back of book.

Fiscal Policy and the Multiplier

An expansionary fiscal policy, like the 2009 U.S. stimulus, pushes the aggregate demand curve to the right. A contractionary fiscal policy, like Lyndon Johnson's tax surcharge, pushes the aggregate demand curve to the left. For policy makers, however, knowing the direction of the shift isn't enough: they need estimates of *how much* a given policy will shift the aggregate demand curve. To get these estimates, they use the concept of the multiplier, which we learned about in Chapter 26.

Multiplier Effects of an Increase in Government Purchases of Goods and Services

Suppose that a government decides to spend $50 billion building bridges and roads. The government's purchases of goods and services will directly increase total spending on final goods and services by $50 billion. But as we learned in Chapter 26, there will also be an indirect effect: the government's purchases will start a chain reaction throughout the economy. The firms that produce the goods and services purchased by the government earn revenues that flow to households in the form of wages, profits, interest, and rent. This increase in disposable income leads to a rise in consumer spending. The rise in consumer spending, in turn, induces firms to increase output, leading to a further rise in disposable income, which leads to another round of consumer spending increases, and so on.

As we know, the *multiplier* is the ratio of the change in real GDP caused by an autonomous change in aggregate spending to the size of that autonomous change. An increase in government purchases of goods and services is a prime example of such an autonomous increase in aggregate spending.

In Chapter 26 we considered a simple case in which there are no taxes or international trade, so that any change in GDP accrues entirely to households. We also assumed that the aggregate price level is fixed, so that any increase in nominal GDP is also a rise in real GDP, and that the interest rate is fixed. In that case the multiplier is $1/(1 - MPC)$. Recall that *MPC* is the *marginal propensity to consume,* the fraction of an additional dollar in disposable income that is spent. For example, if the marginal propensity to consume is 0.5, the multiplier is $1/(1 - 0.5) = 1/0.5 = 2$. Given a multiplier of 2, a $50 billion increase in government purchases of goods and services would increase real GDP by $100 billion. Of that $100 billion, $50 billion is the initial effect from the increase in *G*, and the remaining $50 billion is the subsequent effect arising from the increase in consumer spending.

What happens if government purchases of goods and services are instead reduced? The math is exactly the same, except that there's a minus sign in front: if government purchases of goods and services fall by $50 billion and the marginal propensity to consume is 0.5, real GDP falls by $100 billion.

Multiplier Effects of Changes in Government Transfers and Taxes

Expansionary or contractionary fiscal policy need not take the form of changes in government purchases of goods and services. Governments can also change transfer payments or taxes. In general, however, a change in government transfers or taxes shifts the aggregate demand curve by *less* than an equal-sized change in government purchases, resulting in a smaller effect on real GDP.

To see why, imagine that instead of spending $50 billion on building bridges, the government simply hands out $50 billion in the form of government transfers. In this case, there is no direct effect on aggregate demand, as there was with government purchases of goods and services. Real GDP goes up only because households spend some of that $50 billion—and they probably won't spend it all.

Table 28-1 shows a hypothetical comparison of two expansionary fiscal policies assuming an *MPC* equal to 0.5 and a multiplier equal to 2: one in which the government directly purchases $50 billion in goods and services and one in which the government makes transfer payments instead, sending out $50 billion in checks to consumers. In each case there is a first-round effect on real GDP, either from purchases by the government or from purchases by the consumers who received the checks, followed by a series of additional rounds as rising real GDP raises disposable income.

However, the first-round effect of the transfer program is smaller; because we have assumed that the *MPC* is 0.5, only $25 billion of the $50 billion is spent, with the other $25 billion saved. And as a result, all the further rounds are smaller, too. In the end, the transfer payment increases real GDP by only $50 billion. In comparison, a $50 billion increase in government purchases produces a $100 billion increase in real GDP.

Overall, when expansionary fiscal policy takes the form of a rise in transfer payments, real GDP may rise by either more or less than the initial government outlay—that is, the multiplier may be either more or less than 1 depending upon the size of the *MPC*. In Table 28-1, with an *MPC* equal to 0.5, the multiplier is exactly 1: a $50 billion rise in transfer payments increases real GDP by $50 billion. If the *MPC* is less than 0.5, so that a smaller share of the initial transfer is spent, the multiplier on that transfer is *less* than 1. If a larger share of the initial transfer is spent, the multiplier is *more* than 1.

Ralf Hettler/Getty Images

Expansionary or contractionary fiscal policy will start a chain reaction throughout the economy.

TABLE **28-1**	Hypothetical Effects of a Fiscal Policy with Multiplier of 2	
Effect on real GDP	**$50 billion rise in government purchases of goods and services**	**$50 billion rise in government transfer payments**
First round	$50 billion	$25 billion
Second round	$25 billion	$12.5 billion
Third round	$12.5 billion	$6.25 billion
• • •	• • •	• • •
Eventual effect	$100 billion	$50 billion

A tax cut has an effect similar to the effect of a transfer. It increases disposable income, leading to a series of increases in consumer spending. But the overall effect is smaller than that of an equal-sized increase in government purchases of goods and services: the autonomous increase in aggregate spending is smaller because households save part of the amount of the tax cut.

We should also note that taxes introduce a further complication—they typically change the size of the multiplier. That's because in the real world governments rarely impose **lump-sum taxes,** in which the amount of tax a household owes is independent of its income. With lump-sum taxes there is no change in the multiplier. Instead, the great majority of tax revenue is raised via taxes that are not lump-sum, and so tax revenue depends upon the level of real GDP. As we'll discuss shortly, and analyze in detail in the appendix to this chapter, non-lump-sum taxes reduce the size of the multiplier.

In practice, economists often argue that the size of the multiplier determines *who* among the population should get tax cuts or increases in government transfers. For example, compare the effects of an increase in unemployment benefits with a cut in taxes on profits distributed to shareholders as dividends. Consumer surveys suggest that the average unemployed worker will spend a higher share of any increase in his or her disposable income than would the average recipient of dividend income. That is, people who are unemployed tend to have a higher *MPC* than people who own a lot of stocks because the latter tend to be wealthier and tend to save more of any increase in disposable income. If that's true, a dollar spent on unemployment benefits increases aggregate demand more than a dollar's worth of dividend tax cuts.

> **Lump-sum taxes** are taxes that don't depend on the taxpayer's income.

How Taxes Affect the Multiplier

When we introduced the analysis of the multiplier in Chapter 26, we simplified matters by assuming that a $1 increase in real GDP raises disposable income by $1. In fact, however, government taxes capture some part of the increase in real GDP that occurs in each round of the multiplier process, since most government taxes depend positively on real GDP. As a result, disposable income increases by considerably less than $1 once we include taxes in the model.

The increase in government tax revenue when real GDP rises isn't the result of a deliberate decision or action by the government. It's a consequence of the way the tax laws are written, which causes most sources of government revenue to increase *automatically* when real GDP goes up. For example, income tax receipts increase when real GDP rises because the amount each individual owes in taxes depends positively on his or her income, and households' taxable income rises when real GDP rises. Sales tax receipts increase when real GDP rises because people with more income spend more on goods and services. And corporate profit tax receipts increase when real GDP rises because profits increase when the economy expands.

The effect of these automatic increases in tax revenue is to reduce the size of the multiplier. Remember, the multiplier is the result of a chain reaction in which higher real GDP leads to higher disposable income, which leads to higher consumer spending, which leads to further increases in real GDP. The fact that the government siphons off some of any increase in real GDP means that at each stage of this process, the increase in consumer spending is smaller than it would be if taxes weren't part of the picture. The result is to reduce the multiplier. The appendix to this chapter shows how to derive the multiplier when taxes that depend positively on real GDP are taken into account.

Many macroeconomists believe it's a good thing that in real life taxes reduce the multiplier. In Chapter 27 we argued that most, though not all, recessions are the result of negative demand shocks. The same mechanism that causes tax

Automatic stabilizers are government spending and taxation rules that cause fiscal policy to be automatically expansionary when the economy contracts and automatically contractionary when the economy expands.

Discretionary fiscal policy is fiscal policy that is the result of deliberate actions by policy makers rather than rules.

revenue to increase when the economy expands causes it to decrease when the economy contracts. Since tax receipts decrease when real GDP falls, the effects of these negative demand shocks are smaller than they would be if there were no taxes. The decrease in tax revenue reduces the adverse effect of the initial fall in aggregate demand.

The automatic decrease in government tax revenue generated by a fall in real GDP—caused by a decrease in the amount of taxes households pay—acts like an automatic expansionary fiscal policy implemented in the face of a recession. Similarly, when the economy expands, the government finds itself automatically pursuing a contractionary fiscal policy—a tax increase. Government spending and taxation rules that cause fiscal policy to be automatically expansionary when the economy contracts and automatically contractionary when the economy expands, without requiring any deliberate action by policy makers, are called **automatic stabilizers.**

The rules that govern tax collection aren't the only automatic stabilizers, although they are the most important ones. Some types of government transfers also play a stabilizing role. For example, more people receive unemployment insurance when the economy is depressed than when it is booming. The same is true of Medicaid and food stamps. So transfer payments tend to rise when the economy is contracting and fall when the economy is expanding. Like changes in tax revenue, these automatic changes in transfers tend to reduce the size of the multiplier because the total change in disposable income that results from a given rise or fall in real GDP is smaller.

As in the case of government tax revenue, many macroeconomists believe that it's a good thing that government transfers reduce the multiplier. Expansionary and contractionary fiscal policies that are the result of automatic stabilizers are widely considered helpful to macroeconomic stabilization because they blunt the extremes of the business cycle.

But what about fiscal policy that *isn't* the result of automatic stabilizers? **Discretionary fiscal policy** is fiscal policy that is the direct result of deliberate actions by policy makers rather than automatic adjustment. For example, during a recession, the government may pass legislation that cuts taxes and increases government spending in order to stimulate the economy. In general, economists tend to support the use of discretionary fiscal policy only in special circumstances, such as an especially severe recession. We'll explain why, and describe the debates among macroeconomists on the appropriate role of fiscal policy, in Chapter 33.

The Works Progress Administration (known as WPA), a relief measure established during the Great Depression that put millions of unemployed Americans to work building bridges, roads, buildings, and parks, is a historical example of discretionary fiscal policy.

ECONOMICS ▶ *in Action*

Austerity and the Multiplier

We've explained the logic of the fiscal multiplier, but what empirical evidence do economists have about multiplier effects in practice? Until a few years ago, the answer would have been that we didn't have nearly as much evidence as we'd like.

The problem was that large changes in fiscal policy are fairly rare, and usually happen at the same time other things are taking place, making it hard to separate the effects of spending and taxes from those of other factors. For example, the U.S. drastically increased spending during World War II—but it also instituted rationing of many consumer goods, more or less banned construction of new houses, and so on. So the effects of the spending increase are hard to distinguish from the overall conversion from a peacetime to a war economy.

Recent events have, however, offered considerable new evidence. As we explain later in this chapter, after 2009 several European countries found themselves facing debt crises, so they were forced to turn to the rest of Europe for aid. A condition of this aid was *austerity*—sharp cuts in spending plus tax increases. (We will explain *austerity* more fully in Chapter 32.) By comparing the economic performance of countries that were forced into austerity with that of countries that weren't, we get a relatively clear view of the effects of changes in spending and taxes.

Figure 28-7 compares the amount of austerity imposed in a number of countries between 2009 and 2013 with the growth in their GDP over the same period. Austerity is measured by the change in the cyclically adjusted budget balance, defined later in this chapter. Greece—which was forced to impose severe spending cuts, and suffered a huge fall in output—stands out, but even without Greece there is a clear negative relationship. A line fitted through the scatterplot has a slope of –1.6. That is, the figure suggests that spending cuts and tax increases (we can't distinguish between them here) had an average multiplier of 1.6.

As you might expect, economists have offered a number of qualifications and caveats to this result, coming from the fact that this wasn't truly a controlled experiment. Overall, however, recent experience seems to support the notion that fiscal policy does indeed move GDP in the predicted direction, with a multiplier of more than 1.

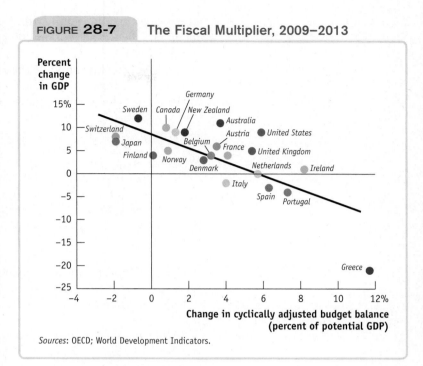

FIGURE 28-7 The Fiscal Multiplier, 2009–2013

Sources: OECD; World Development Indicators.

Check Your Understanding 28-2

1. Explain why a $500 million increase in government purchases of goods and services will generate a larger rise in real GDP than a $500 million increase in government transfers.

2. Explain why a $500 million reduction in government purchases of goods and services will generate a larger fall in real GDP than a $500 million reduction in government transfers.

3. The country of Boldovia has no unemployment insurance benefits and a tax system using only lump-sum taxes. The neighboring country of Moldovia has generous unemployment benefits and a tax system in which residents must pay a percentage of their income. Which country will experience greater variation in real GDP in response to demand shocks, positive and negative? Explain.

Solutions appear at back of book.

The Budget Balance

Headlines about the government's budget tend to focus on just one point: whether the government is running a surplus or a deficit and, in either case, how big. People usually think of surpluses as good: when the federal government ran a record surplus in 2000, many people regarded it as a cause for celebration.

> **▼ Quick Review**
>
> • The amount by which changes in government purchases raise real GDP is determined by the multiplier.
>
> • Changes in taxes and government transfers also move real GDP, but by less than equal-sized changes in government purchases.
>
> • Taxes reduce the size of the multiplier unless they are **lump-sum taxes.**
>
> • Taxes and some government transfers act as **automatic stabilizers** as tax revenue responds positively to changes in real GDP and some government transfers respond negatively to changes in real GDP. Many economists believe that it is a good thing that they reduce the size of the multiplier. In contrast, the use of **discretionary fiscal policy** is more controversial.

Conversely, people usually think of deficits as bad: when the U.S. federal government ran record deficits in 2009 and 2010, many people regarded it as a cause for concern.

How do surpluses and deficits fit into the analysis of fiscal policy? Are deficits ever a good thing and surpluses a bad thing? To answer those questions, let's look at the causes and consequences of surpluses and deficits.

The Budget Balance as a Measure of Fiscal Policy

What do we mean by surpluses and deficits? The budget balance, which we defined in Chapter 25, is the difference between the government's revenue, in the form of tax revenue, and its spending, both on goods and services and on government transfers, in a given year. That is, the budget balance—savings by government—is defined by Equation 28-2 (which is the same as Equation 25-7):

(28-2) $S_{Government} = T - G - TR$

where T is the value of tax revenues, G is government purchases of goods and services, and TR is the value of government transfers. As we learned in Chapter 25, a budget surplus is a positive budget balance and a budget deficit is a negative budget balance.

Other things equal, expansionary fiscal policies—increased government purchases of goods and services, higher government transfers, or lower taxes—reduce the budget balance for that year. That is, expansionary fiscal policies make a budget surplus smaller or a budget deficit bigger. Conversely, contractionary fiscal policies—reduced government purchases of goods and services, lower government transfers, or higher taxes—increase the budget balance for that year, making a budget surplus bigger or a budget deficit smaller.

You might think this means that changes in the budget balance can be used to measure fiscal policy. In fact, economists often do just that: they use changes in the budget balance as a "quick-and-dirty" way to assess whether current fiscal policy is expansionary or contractionary. But they always keep in mind two reasons this quick-and-dirty approach is sometimes misleading:

1. Two different changes in fiscal policy that have equal-sized effects on the budget balance may have quite unequal effects on the economy. As we have already seen, changes in government purchases of goods and services have a larger effect on real GDP than equal-sized changes in taxes and government transfers.

2. Often, changes in the budget balance are themselves the result, not the cause, of fluctuations in the economy.

To understand the second point, we need to examine the effects of the business cycle on the budget.

The Business Cycle and the Cyclically Adjusted Budget Balance

Historically there has been a strong relationship between the federal government's budget balance and the business cycle. The budget tends to move into deficit when the economy experiences a recession, but deficits tend to get smaller or even turn into surpluses when the economy is expanding. Figure 28-8 shows the federal budget deficit as a percentage of GDP from 1964 to 2013. Shaded areas indicate recessions; unshaded areas indicate expansions. As you can see, the federal budget deficit increased around the time of each recession and usually declined during expansions. In fact, in the late stages of the long expansion from 1991 to 2000, the deficit actually became negative—the budget deficit became a budget surplus.

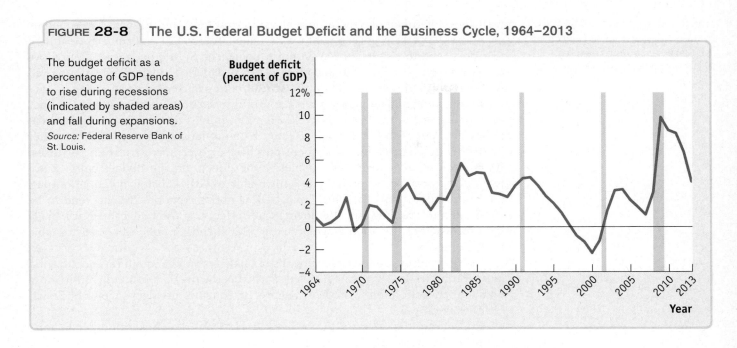

| FIGURE **28-8** | The U.S. Federal Budget Deficit and the Business Cycle, 1964–2013 |

The budget deficit as a percentage of GDP tends to rise during recessions (indicated by shaded areas) and fall during expansions.

Source: Federal Reserve Bank of St. Louis.

The relationship between the business cycle and the budget balance is even clearer if we compare the budget deficit as a percentage of GDP with the unemployment rate, as we do in Figure 28-9. The budget deficit almost always rises when the unemployment rate rises and falls when the unemployment rate falls.

Is this relationship between the business cycle and the budget balance evidence that policy makers engage in discretionary fiscal policy, using expansionary fiscal policy during recessions and contractionary fiscal policy during expansions? Not necessarily. To a large extent the relationship in Figure 28-9 reflects automatic stabilizers at work. As we saw earlier in the discussion of automatic stabilizers, government tax revenue tends to rise and some government

| FIGURE **28-9** | The U.S. Federal Budget Deficit and the Unemployment Rate, 1964–2013 |

There is a close relationship between the budget balance and the business cycle: a recession moves the budget balance toward deficit, but an expansion moves it toward surplus. Here, the unemployment rate serves as an indicator of the business cycle, and we should expect to see a higher unemployment rate associated with a higher budget deficit. This is confirmed by the figure: the budget deficit as a percentage of GDP moves closely in tandem with the unemployment rate.

Source: Federal Reserve Bank of St. Louis.

The **cyclically adjusted budget balance** is an estimate of what the budget balance would be if real GDP were exactly equal to potential output.

transfers, like unemployment benefit payments, tend to fall when the economy expands. Conversely, government tax revenue tends to fall and some government transfers tend to rise when the economy contracts. So the budget tends to move toward surplus during expansions and toward deficit during recessions even without any deliberate action on the part of policy makers.

In assessing budget policy, it's often useful to separate movements in the budget balance due to the business cycle from movements due to discretionary fiscal policy changes. The former are affected by automatic stabilizers and the latter by deliberate changes in government purchases, government transfers, or taxes. It's important to realize that business-cycle effects on the budget balance are temporary: both recessionary gaps (in which real GDP is below potential output) and inflationary gaps (in which real GDP is above potential output) tend to be eliminated in the long run. Removing their effects on the budget balance sheds light on whether the government's taxing and spending policies are sustainable in the long run.

In other words, do the government's tax policies yield enough revenue to fund its spending in the long run? As we'll learn shortly, this is a fundamentally more important question than whether the government runs a budget surplus or deficit in the current year.

To separate the effect of the business cycle from the effects of other factors, many governments produce an estimate of what the budget balance would be if there were neither a recessionary nor an inflationary gap. The **cyclically adjusted budget balance** is an estimate of what the budget balance would be if real GDP were exactly equal to potential output. It takes into account the extra tax revenue the government would collect and the transfers it would save if a recessionary gap were eliminated—or the revenue the government would lose and the extra transfers it would make if an inflationary gap were eliminated.

Figure 28-10 shows the actual budget deficit and the Congressional Budget Office estimate of the cyclically adjusted budget deficit, both as a percentage of GDP, from 1964 to 2014. As you can see, the cyclically adjusted budget deficit doesn't fluctuate as much as the actual budget deficit. In particular, large actual deficits, such as those of 1975, 1983, and 2009, are usually caused in part by a depressed economy.

FIGURE 28-10 | The Actual Budget Deficit Versus the Cyclically Adjusted Budget Deficit

The cyclically adjusted budget deficit is an estimate of what the budget deficit would be if the economy was at potential output. It fluctuates less than the actual budget deficit because years of large budget deficits also tend to be years when the economy has a large recessionary gap.

Sources: Congressional Budget Office; Bureau of Economic Analysis.

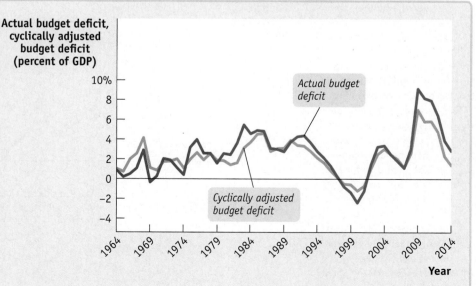

Should the Budget Be Balanced?

As we'll see in the next section, persistent budget deficits can cause problems for both the government and the economy. Yet politicians are always tempted to run deficits because this allows them to cater to voters by cutting taxes without cutting spending or by increasing spending without increasing taxes. As a result, there are occasional attempts by policy makers to force fiscal discipline by introducing legislation—even a constitutional amendment—forbidding the government from running budget deficits. This is usually stated as a requirement that the budget be "balanced"—that revenues at least equal spending each fiscal year. Would it be a good idea to require a balanced budget annually?

Most economists don't think so. They believe that the government should only balance its budget on average—that it should be allowed to run deficits in bad years, offset by surpluses in good years. They don't believe the government should be forced to run a balanced budget *every year* because this would undermine the role of taxes and transfers as automatic stabilizers.

As we learned earlier in this chapter, the tendency of tax revenue to fall and transfers to rise when the economy contracts helps to limit the size of recessions. But falling tax revenue and rising transfer payments generated by a downturn in the economy push the budget toward deficit. If constrained by a balanced-budget rule, the government would have to respond to this deficit with contractionary fiscal policies that would tend to deepen a recession.

Yet policy makers concerned about excessive deficits sometimes feel that rigid rules prohibiting—or at least setting an upper limit on—deficits are necessary. As the following Economics in Action explains, Europe has had a lot of trouble reconciling rules to enforce fiscal responsibility with the challenges of short-run fiscal policy.

ECONOMICS ▶ in Action

Europe's Search for a Fiscal Rule

In 1999 a group of European nations took a momentous step when they adopted a common currency, the euro, to replace their various national currencies, such as the French franc, the German mark, and the Italian lira. Along with the introduction of the euro came the creation of the European Central Bank, which sets monetary policy for the whole region.

As part of the agreement creating the new currency, governments of member countries signed on to the European "stability pact." This agreement required each government to keep its budget deficit—its actual deficit, not a cyclically adjusted number—below 3% of the country's GDP or face fines. The pact was intended to prevent irresponsible deficit spending arising from political pressure that might eventually undermine the new currency.

The stability pact, however, had a serious downside: in principle, it would force countries to slash spending and/or raise taxes whenever an economic downturn pushed their deficits above the critical level. This would turn fiscal policy into a force that worsens recessions instead of fighting them.

Nonetheless, the stability pact proved impossible to enforce: European nations, including France and even Germany, with its reputation for fiscal probity, simply ignored the rule during the 2001 recession and its aftermath.

In 2011 the Europeans tried again, this time against the background of a severe debt crisis. In the wake of the 2008 financial crisis, Greece, Ireland, Portugal, Spain, and Italy all lost the confidence of

Although several European nations have adopted a common currency—the euro—they struggle to establish effective fiscal policy.

investors, who were worried about their ability and/or willingness to repay all their debt—and the efforts of these nations to reduce their deficits seemed likely to push Europe back into recession. Yet a return to the old stability pact didn't seem to make sense. Among other things, it was clear that the stability pact's rule on the size of budget deficits would not have done much to prevent the crisis—in 2007 all of the problem debtors except Greece were running deficits under 3% of GDP, with Ireland and Spain actually running surpluses.

So the agreement reached in December 2011 was framed in terms of the "structural" budget balance, more or less corresponding to the cyclically adjusted budget balance as we defined it. According to the new rule, the structural budget balance of each country should be very nearly zero, with deficits not to exceed 0.5% of GDP. This seemed like a much better rule than the old stability pact.

Yet big problems remained. One was the question of how reliable were the estimates of the structural budget balances. Also, the new rule seemed to ban any use of discretionary fiscal policy, under any circumstances. By early 2015 it was clear that this fiscal straight-jacket was a problem: a weakening European economy clearly needed stimulus but the fiscal rule prohibited it.

Before patting themselves on the back over the superiority of their own fiscal rules, Americans should note that the United States has its own version of the original, flawed European stability pact. The federal government's budget acts as an automatic stabilizer, but 49 of the 50 states are required by their state constitutions to balance their budgets every year. When recession struck in 2008, most states were forced to—guess what?—slash spending and raise taxes in the face of a recession, exactly the wrong thing from a macroeconomic point of view.

> ### ▼ Quick Review
>
> • The budget deficit tends to rise during recessions and fall during expansions. This reflects the effect of the business cycle on the budget balance.
>
> • The **cyclically adjusted budget balance** is an estimate of what the budget balance would be if the economy were at potential output. It varies less than the actual budget deficit.
>
> • Most economists believe that governments should run budget deficits in bad years and budget surpluses in good years. A rule requiring a balanced budget would undermine the role of automatic stabilizers.

Check Your Understanding 28-3

1. Why is the cyclically adjusted budget balance a better measure of whether government policies are sustainable in the long run than the actual budget balance?

2. Explain why states required by their constitutions to balance their budgets are likely to experience more severe economic fluctuations than states not held to that requirement.

Solutions appear at back of book.

Long-Run Implications of Fiscal Policy

In 2009 the government of Greece ran into a financial wall. Like most other governments in Europe (and the U.S. government, too), the Greek government was running a large budget deficit, which meant that it needed to keep borrowing more funds, both to cover its expenses and to pay off existing loans as they came due. But governments, like companies or individuals, can only borrow if lenders believe there's a good chance they are willing or able to repay their debts. By 2009 most investors, having lost confidence in Greece's financial future, were no longer willing to lend to the Greek government. Those few who were willing to lend demanded very high interest rates to compensate them for the risk of loss.

Figure 28-11 compares interest rates on 10-year bonds issued by the governments of Greece and Germany. At the beginning of 2007, Greece could borrow at almost the same rate as Germany, widely considered a very safe borrower. By the end of 2011, however, Greece had to pay an interest rate around 10 times the rate Germany paid.

Why was Greece having these problems? Largely because investors had become deeply worried about the level of its debt (in part because it became clear that the Greek government had been using creative accounting to hide just how much debt it had already taken on). Government debt is, after all, a promise to

| FIGURE **28-11** | Greek and German Long-Term Interest Rates |

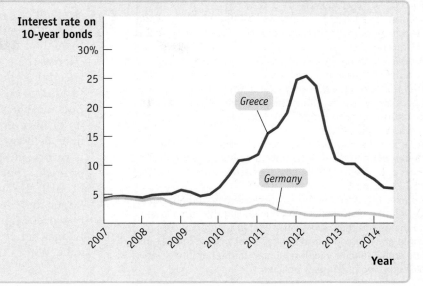

As late as 2008, the government of Greece could borrow at interest rates only slightly higher than those facing Germany, widely considered a very safe borrower. But in early 2009, as it became clear that both Greek debt and Greek deficits were larger than previously reported, investors lost confidence, sending Greek borrowing costs sky-high.

Sources: Federal Reserve Bank of St. Louis; OECD "Main Economic Indicators Complete Database."

make future payments to lenders. By 2009 it seemed likely that the Greek government had already promised more than it could possibly deliver.

The result was that Greece found itself unable to borrow more from private lenders; it received emergency loans from other European nations and the International Monetary Fund, but these loans came with the requirement that the Greek government make severe spending cuts, which wreaked havoc with its economy, imposed severe economic hardship on Greeks, and led to massive social unrest.

The good news is that by mid-2014 Greek borrowing costs had fallen sharply. In part this reflected a growing sense that Greece would stay the course on spending despite the huge suffering. It also, however, reflected the intervention of the European Central Bank, which assured investors that it would do "whatever it takes" to sustain the euro, Europe's common currency; this move was widely interpreted as a guarantee that, if necessary, it would step in to buy the bonds of Greece and other troubled debtors.

Despite this good news, however, the crisis in Greece and elsewhere made it clear that no discussion of fiscal policy is complete without taking into account the long-run implications of government budget surpluses and deficits, especially the implications for government debt. We now turn to those long-run implications.

Deficits, Surpluses, and Debt

When a family spends more than it earns over the course of a year, it has to raise the extra funds either by selling assets or by borrowing. And if a family borrows year after year, it will eventually end up with a lot of debt.

The same is true for governments. With a few exceptions, governments don't raise large sums by selling assets such as national parkland. Instead, when a government spends more than the tax revenue it receives—when it runs a budget deficit—it almost always borrows the extra funds. And governments that run persistent budget deficits end up with substantial debts.

To interpret the numbers that follow, you need to know a slightly peculiar feature of federal government accounting. For historical reasons, the U.S. government does not keep books by calendar years. Instead, budget totals are kept by **fiscal years,** which run from October 1 to September 30 and are labeled

A **fiscal year** runs from October 1 to September 30 and is labeled according to the calendar year in which it ends.

PITFALLS

DEFICITS VERSUS DEBT

One common mistake—it happens all the time in newspaper reports—is to confuse *deficits* with *debt.* Let's review the difference.

A *deficit* is the difference between the amount of money a government spends and the amount it receives in taxes over a given period—usually, though not always, a year. Deficit numbers always come with a statement about the time period to which they apply, as in "the U.S. budget deficit *in fiscal 2011* was $1.3 trillion."

A *debt* is the sum of money a government owes at a particular point in time. Debt numbers usually come with a specific date, as in "U.S. public debt *at the end of fiscal 2011* was $10.1 trillion."

Deficits and debt are linked, because government debt grows when governments run deficits. But they aren't the same thing, and they can even tell different stories. For example, Italy, which found itself in debt trouble in 2011, had a fairly small deficit by historical standards, but it had very high debt, a legacy of past policies.

by the calendar year in which they end. For example, fiscal 2014 began on October 1, 2013, and ended on September 30, 2014.

At the end of fiscal 2013, the U.S. federal government had total debt equal to $17.1 trillion. However, part of that debt represented special accounting rules specifying that the federal government as a whole owes funds to certain government programs, especially Social Security. We'll explain those rules shortly. For now, however, let's focus on **public debt:** government debt held by individuals and institutions outside the government. At the end of fiscal 2013, the federal government's public debt was "only" $12.0 trillion, or 72% of GDP. Federal public debt at the end of 2013 was larger than at the end of 2012 because the government ran a deficit in 2013: a government that runs persistent budget deficits will experience a rising level of public debt. Why is this a problem?

GLOBAL COMPARISION | The American Way of Debt

How does the public debt of the United States stack up internationally? In dollar terms, we're number one—but this isn't very informative, since the U.S. economy and so the government's tax base are much larger than those of any other nation. A more informative comparison is the ratio of public debt to GDP.

The figure shows the *net public debt* of a number of rich countries as a percentage of GDP at the end of 2013. Net public debt is government debt minus any assets governments may have—an adjustment that can make a big difference. What you see here is that the United States is more or less in the middle of the pack.

It may not surprise you that Greece heads the list, and most of the other high net debt countries are European nations that have been making headlines for their debt problems. Interestingly, however, Japan is also high on the list because it used massive public spending to prop up its economy in the 1990s. Investors, however, still consider Japan a reliable government, so its borrowing costs remain low despite high net debt.

In contrast to the other countries, Norway has a large *negative* net

public debt. What's going on in Norway? In a word, oil. Norway is the world's third-largest oil exporter, thanks to large offshore deposits in the North Sea. Instead of spending its oil revenues immediately, the government of Norway has used them to build up an investment fund for future needs following the lead of traditional oil producers like Saudi Arabia. As a result, Norway has huge stock of government assets rather than a large government debt.

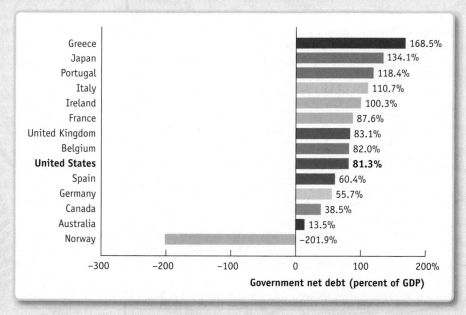

Source: International Monetary Fund.

Problems Posed by Rising Government Debt

There are two reasons to be concerned when a government runs persistent budget deficits. We described one reason in Chapter 25 where the concept of *crowding out* was defined: when the economy is at full employment and the government borrows funds in the financial markets, it is competing with firms that plan to borrow funds for investment spending. As a result, the government's borrowing may crowd out private investment spending, increasing interest rates and reducing the economy's long-run rate of growth.

But there's a second reason: today's deficits, by increasing the government's debt, place financial pressure on future budgets. The impact of current deficits on future budgets is straightforward. Like individuals, governments must pay their bills, including interest payments on their accumulated debt. When a government is deeply in debt, those interest payments can be substantial. In fiscal 2013, the U.S. federal government paid 1.3% of GDP—$221 billion—in interest on its debt. The more heavily indebted government of Italy paid interest of 5% of its GDP in 2013.

Other things equal, a government paying large sums in interest must raise more revenue from taxes or spend less than it would otherwise be able to afford— or it must borrow even more to cover the gap. And a government that borrows to pay interest on its outstanding debt pushes itself even deeper into debt. This process can eventually push a government to the point where lenders question its ability to repay. Like a consumer who has maxed out his or her credit cards, it will find that lenders are unwilling to lend any more funds. The result can be that the government defaults on its debt—it stops paying what it owes. Default is often followed by deep financial and economic turmoil.

Americans aren't used to the idea of government default, but such things do happen. In the 1990s Argentina, a relatively high-income developing country, was widely praised for its economic policies—and it was able to borrow large sums from foreign lenders. By 2001, however, Argentina's interest payments were spiraling out of control, and the country stopped paying the sums that were due. In the end, it reached a settlement with most of its lenders under which it paid less than a third of the amount originally due.

In 2010–2013 investors placed a fairly high probability on Argentine-type default by several European countries—namely, Greece, Ireland, and Portugal—and were seriously worried about Italy and Spain. Each one was forced to pay high interest rates on its debt by nervous lenders, exacerbating the risk of default.

Default creates havoc in a country's financial markets and badly shakes public confidence in both the government and the economy. Argentina's debt default was accompanied by a crisis in the country's banking system and a very severe recession. And even if a highly indebted government avoids default, a heavy debt burden typically forces it to slash spending or raise taxes, politically unpopular measures that can also damage the economy. In some cases, austerity measures intended to reassure lenders that the government can indeed pay end up depressing the economy so much that lender confidence continues to fall.

Some may ask: why can't a government that has trouble borrowing just print money to pay its bills? Yes, it can if it has its own currency (which the troubled European nations don't). But printing money to pay the government's bills can lead to another problem: inflation. In fact, budget problems are the main cause of very severe inflation. Governments do not want to find themselves in a position where the choice is between defaulting on their debts and inflating those debts away by printing money.

Public debt is government debt held by individuals and institutions outside the government.

The **debt–GDP ratio** is the government's debt as a percentage of GDP.

Concerns about the long-run effects of deficits need not rule out the use of expansionary fiscal policy to stimulate the economy when it is depressed. However, these concerns do mean that governments should try to offset budget deficits in bad years with budget surpluses in good years. In other words, governments should run a budget that is approximately balanced over time. Have they actually done so?

Deficits and Debt in Practice

Figure 28-12 shows the U.S. federal government's budget deficit and its debt evolved from 1940 to 2013. Panel (a) shows the federal deficit as a percentage of GDP. As you can see, the federal government ran huge deficits during World War II. It briefly ran surpluses after the war, but it has normally run deficits ever since, especially after 1980. This seems inconsistent with the advice that governments should offset deficits in bad times with surpluses in good times.

However, panel (b) of Figure 28-12 shows that for most of the period these persistent deficits didn't lead to runaway debt. To assess the ability of governments to pay their debt, we use the **debt–GDP ratio,** the government's debt as a percentage of GDP. We use this measure, rather than simply looking at the size of the debt, because GDP, which measures the size of the economy as a whole, is a good indicator of the potential taxes the government can collect. If the government's debt grows more slowly than GDP, the burden of paying that debt is actually falling compared with the government's potential tax revenue.

What we see from panel (b) is that although the federal debt grew in almost every year, the debt–GDP ratio fell for 30 years after the end of World War II. This shows that the debt–GDP ratio can fall, even when debt is rising, as long as GDP grows faster than debt. The upcoming For Inquiring Minds, which focuses on the large debt the U.S. government ran up during World War II, explains how growth and inflation sometimes allow a government that runs persistent budget deficits to nevertheless have a declining debt–GDP ratio.

FIGURE 28-12 | U.S. Federal Deficits and Debt

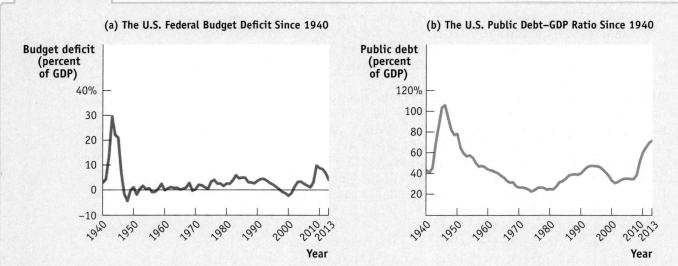

Panel (a) shows the U.S. federal budget deficit as a percentage of GDP from 1940 to 2013. The U.S. government ran huge deficits during World War II and has run smaller deficits ever since. Panel (b) shows the U.S. debt–GDP ratio. Comparing panels (a) and (b), you can see that in many years the debt–GDP ratio has declined in spite of government deficits. This seeming paradox reflects the fact that the debt–GDP ratio can fall, even when debt is rising, as long as GDP grows faster than debt.

Source: Office of Management and Budget.

FOR INQUIRING MINDS | What Happened to the Debt from World War II?

As you can see from Figure 28-12, the U.S. government paid for World War II by borrowing on a huge scale. By the war's end, the public debt was more than 100% of GDP, and many people worried about how it could ever be paid off.

The truth is that it never was paid off. In 1946 public debt was $242 billion; that

number dipped slightly in the next few years, as the United States ran postwar budget surpluses, but the government budget went back into deficit in 1950 with the start of the Korean War. By 1962 the public debt was back up to $248 billion.

But by that time nobody was worried about the fiscal health of the U.S.

government because the debt–GDP ratio had fallen by more than half. The reason? Vigorous economic growth, plus mild inflation, had led to a rapid rise in GDP. The experience was a clear lesson in the peculiar fact that modern governments can run deficits forever, as long as they aren't too large. ■

Still, a government that runs persistent *large* deficits will have a rising debt–GDP ratio when debt grows faster than GDP. In the aftermath of the financial crisis of 2008, the U.S. government began running deficits much larger than anything seen since World War II, and the debt–GDP ratio began rising sharply. Similar surges in the debt–GDP ratio could be seen in a number of other countries in 2008. Economists and policy makers agreed that this was not a sustainable trend, that governments would need to get their spending and revenues back in line.

But *when* to bring spending in line with revenue was a source of great disagreement. Some argued for fiscal tightening right away; others argued that this tightening should be postponed until the major economies had recovered from their slump.

Implicit Liabilities

Looking at Figure 28-12, you might be tempted to conclude that until the 2008 crisis struck, the U.S. federal budget was in fairly decent shape: the return to budget deficits after 2001 caused the debt–GDP ratio to rise a bit, but that ratio was still low compared with both historical experience and some other wealthy countries. In fact, however, experts on long-run budget issues view the situation of the United States (and other countries such as Japan and Italy) with alarm. The reason is the problem of *implicit liabilities*. **Implicit liabilities** are spending promises made by governments that are effectively a debt despite the fact that they are not included in the usual debt statistics.

The largest implicit liabilities of the U.S. government arise from two transfer programs that principally benefit older Americans: Social Security and Medicare. The third-largest implicit liability, Medicaid, benefits low-income families. In each of these cases, the government has promised to provide transfer payments to future as well as current beneficiaries. So these programs represent a future debt that must be honored, even though the debt does not currently show up in the usual statistics. Together, these three programs currently account for almost 40% of federal spending.

The implicit liabilities created by these transfer programs worry fiscal experts. Figure 28-13 shows why. It shows actual spending on Social Security and on Medicare, Medicaid, and CHIP (a program that provides health care coverage to uninsured children) as percentages of GDP from 2000 to 2013, together with Congressional Budget Office projections of spending through 2038. According to these projections, spending on Social Security will rise substantially over the next few decades and spending on the three health care programs will soar. Why?

In the case of Social Security, the answer is demography. Social Security is a "pay-as-you-go" system: current workers pay payroll taxes that fund the benefits of current retirees. So the ratio of the number of retirees drawing benefits to the number of workers paying into Social Security has a major impact on the system's finances.

Implicit liabilities are spending promises made by governments that are effectively a debt despite the fact that they are not included in the usual debt statistics.

FIGURE **28-13** Future Demands on the Federal Budget

This figure shows Congressional Budget Office projections of spending on social insurance programs as a share of GDP. Partly as a result of an aging population, but mainly because of rising health care costs, these programs are expected to become much more expensive over time, posing problems for the federal budget.
Source: Congressional Budget Office.

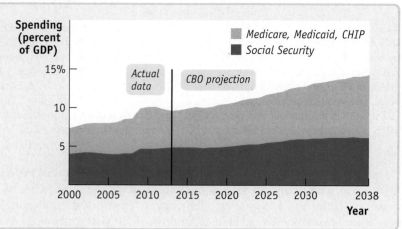

There was a huge surge in the U.S. birth rate between 1946 and 1964, the years of what is commonly called the *baby boom*. Most baby boomers are currently of working age—which means they are paying taxes, not collecting benefits. But some are starting to retire, and as more and more of them do so, they will stop earning taxable income and start collecting benefits.

As a result, the ratio of retirees receiving benefits to workers paying into the Social Security system will rise. In 2010 there were 34 retirees receiving benefits for every 100 workers paying into the system. By 2030, according to the Social Security Administration, that number will rise to 46; by 2050, it will rise to 48; and by 2080, that number will be 51. So as baby boomers move into retirement, benefit payments will continue to rise relative to the size of the economy.

The aging of the baby boomers, by itself, poses only a moderately sized long-run fiscal problem. The projected rise in Medicare and Medicaid spending is a much more serious concern. The main story behind projections of higher Medicare and Medicaid spending is the long-run tendency of health care spending to rise faster than overall spending, both for government-funded and for privately funded health care.

To some extent, the implicit liabilities of the U.S. government are already reflected in debt statistics. We mentioned earlier that the government had a total debt of $17 trillion at the end of fiscal 2013 but that only $12 trillion of that total was owed to the public. The main explanation for that discrepancy is that both Social Security and part of Medicare (the hospital insurance program) are supported by *dedicated taxes:* their expenses are paid out of special taxes on wages. At times, these dedicated taxes yield more revenue than is needed to pay current benefits.

In particular, since the mid-1980s the Social Security system has been taking in more revenue than it currently needs in order to prepare for the retirement of the baby boomers. This surplus in the Social Security system has been used to accumulate a *Social Security trust fund,* which was $2.8 trillion at the end of fiscal 2013.

The money in the trust fund is held in the form of U.S. government bonds, which are included in the $17 trillion in total debt. You could say that there's something funny about counting bonds in the Social Security trust fund as part of government debt. After all, these bonds are owed by one part of the government (the government outside the Social Security system) to another part of the government (the Social Security system itself). But the debt corresponds to a real, if implicit, liability: promises by the government to pay future retirement benefits.

So many economists argue that the gross debt of $17 trillion, the sum of public debt and government debt held by Social Security and other trust funds, is a more accurate indication of the government's fiscal health than the smaller amount owed to the public alone.

ECONOMICS ▶ *in Action*

Are We Greece?

In late 2009, Greece found itself in fiscal crisis, unable to borrow except at very high interest rates, and several other European countries soon found themselves in the same predicament. Meanwhile, the United States was also running large budget deficits and had debt that was high by historical standards. So was America at risk of turning into Greece?

Some influential people thought so, and many dire warnings were issued. For example, in 2010, Alan Greenspan, the former chairman of the Federal Reserve, published an editorial titled "U.S. Debt and the Greece Analogy," in which he warned that the United States could soon face soaring interest rates. In 2011, Erskine Bowles and Alan Simpson, co-chairmen of a presidential commission on the budget, warned that a fiscal crisis was likely within two years. And many others joined the chorus.

In fact, U.S. borrowing costs remained low into 2014, with no hint of a cutoff of lending. But was America just lucky?

Not according to a number of economists, especially the Belgian economist Paul De Grauwe, who began arguing in 2011 that the currency in which a country borrows makes a crucial difference. While the United States has a lot of government debt, it's in dollars; similarly, Britain's debt is in pounds, and Japan's debt is in yen. Greece, Spain, and Portugal, by contrast, no longer have their own currencies; their debts are in euros.

Why does this matter? As we've explained previously, even the United States can't always rely on printing money to cover its deficits, because doing so can lead to runaway inflation. But the ability to print dollars does mean that the U.S. government can't run out of cash. This, in turn, means that we're not vulnerable to fiscal panic, in which investors fear a sudden default and, by refusing to lend, cause the very default they fear. And De Grauwe argued that the woes of European debtors were largely driven by the risk of such a fiscal panic.

Figure 28-14 shows some evidence for De Grauwe's view. It compares net debt as a percentage of GDP with interest rates on government bonds for a number of countries in 2012, the worst year of the European debt crisis. The purple markers correspond to countries on the euro—that is, without their own currencies (the euro area)—while the green markers show countries with their own currencies. Among the euro nations there was a clear correlation between debt and borrowing costs, but not among the non-euro countries, including the United Kingdom and Japan as well as the United States.

In fact, as we've seen, even within the euro area, borrowing costs of high-debt countries dropped sharply after the European Central Bank promised to do "whatever it takes" by

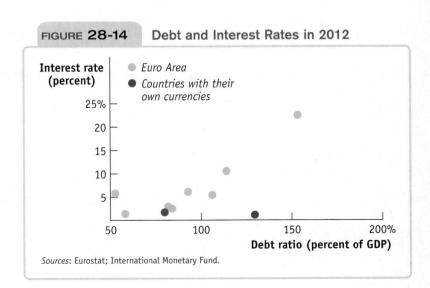

FIGURE 28-14   Debt and Interest Rates in 2012

Sources: Eurostat; International Monetary Fund.

providing cash to governments in trouble—offering further evidence that the risk of panic was a big factor in high interest rates. Removing that risk greatly calmed the situation.

In any case, by 2014, warnings that the United States was about to turn into Greece had mostly vanished. There are many risks facing America, but that doesn't seem to be anywhere near the top of the list.

Check Your Understanding   28-4

1. Explain how each of the following events would affect the public debt or implicit liabilities of the U.S. government, other things equal. Would the public debt or implicit liabilities be greater or smaller?
   a. A higher growth rate of real GDP
   b. Retirees live longer
   c. A decrease in tax revenue
   d. Government borrowing to pay interest on its current public debt

2. Suppose the economy is in a slump and the current public debt is quite large. Explain the trade-off of short-run versus long-run objectives that policy makers face when deciding whether or not to engage in deficit spending.

3. Explain how a policy of fiscal austerity can make it more likely that a government is unable to pay its debts.

Solutions appear at back of book.

Here Comes the Sun

Ralph Lauer/ZUMA Press/Corbis

The Solana power plant, which opened in 2013, covers 3 square miles of the Arizona desert in Gila Bend, about 70 miles from Phoenix. Whereas most solar installations rely on photovoltaic panels that convert light directly into electricity, Solana uses a system of mirrors to concentrate the sun's heat on black pipes, which convey that heat to tanks of molten salt. The heat in the salt is, in turn, used to generate electricity. The advantage of this arrangement is that the plant can keep generating power long after the sun has gone down, greatly enhancing its efficiency.

Solana is one of only a small number of concentrated thermal solar plants operating or under construction, and as Figure 28-15 shows, solar power has been rapidly rising in importance, with the amount of electricity generated by solar almost quadrupling between 2008 and 2013. There are a number of reasons for this sudden rise, but the Obama stimulus—which put substantial sums into the promotion of green energy—was a major factor. Solana, in particular, was built by the Spanish company Abengoa with the aid of a $1.45 billion federal loan guarantee; Abengoa also received $1.2 billion for a similar plant in the Mojave Desert.

While Solana is a good example of stimulus spending at work, it is also a good example of why such spending tends to be politically difficult. There were many protests over federal loans to a non-American firm, although Abengoa had the necessary technology, and the construction jobs created by the project were, of course, in the United States. Also, the long-term financial viability of solar power projects depends in part on whether government subsidies and other policies favoring renewable energy will continue, which isn't certain.

In terms of the goals of the stimulus, however, Solana seems to have done what it was supposed to: it generated jobs at a time when borrowing was cheap and many construction workers were unemployed.

FIGURE 28-15   The Solar Sunrise, 2005–2013

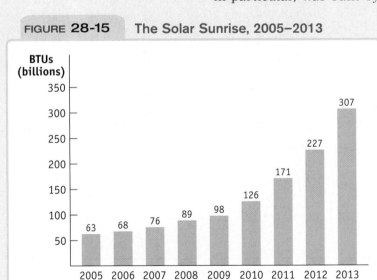

Source: U.S. Energy Information Administration.

QUESTIONS FOR THOUGHT

1. How did the political reaction to government funding for the Solana project differ from the reaction to more conventional government spending projects such as roads and schools? What does the case tell us about how to assess the value of a fiscal stimulus project?

2. In the chapter we talked about the problem of lags in discretionary fiscal policy. What does the Solana case tell us about this issue?

3. Is the depth of a recession a good or a bad time to undertake an energy project? Why or why not?

SUMMARY

1. The government plays a large role in the economy, collecting a large share of GDP in taxes and spending a large share both to purchase goods and services and to make transfer payments, largely for **social insurance.** *Fiscal policy* is the use of taxes, government transfers, or government purchases of goods and services to shift the aggregate demand curve.

2. Government purchases of goods and services directly affect aggregate demand, and changes in taxes and government transfers affect aggregate demand indirectly by changing households' disposable income. **Expansionary fiscal policy** shifts the aggregate demand curve rightward; **contractionary fiscal policy** shifts the aggregate demand curve leftward.

3. Only when the economy is at full employment is there potential for crowding out of private spending and private investment spending by expansionary fiscal policy. The argument that expansionary fiscal policy won't work because of Ricardian equivalence—that consumers will cut back spending today to offset expected future tax increases—appears to be untrue in practice. What is clearly true is that very active fiscal policy may make the economy less stable due to time lags in policy formulation and implementation.

4. Fiscal policy has a multiplier effect on the economy, the size of which depends on the fiscal policy. Except in the case of lump-sum taxes, taxes reduce the size of the multiplier. Expansionary fiscal policy leads to an increase in real GDP, and contractionary fiscal policy leads to a reduction in real GDP. Because part of any change in taxes or transfers is absorbed by savings in the first round of spending, changes in government purchases of goods and services have a more powerful effect on the economy than equal-sized changes in taxes or transfers.

5. Rules governing taxes—with the exception of **lump-sum taxes**—and some transfers act as **automatic stabilizers,** reducing the size of the multiplier and automatically reducing the size of fluctuations in the business cycle. In contrast, **discretionary fiscal policy** arises from deliberate actions by policy makers rather than from the business cycle.

6. Some of the fluctuations in the budget balance are due to the effects of the business cycle. In order to separate the effects of the business cycle from the effects of discretionary fiscal policy, governments estimate the **cyclically adjusted budget balance,** an estimate of the budget balance if the economy were at potential output.

7. U.S. government budget accounting is calculated on the basis of **fiscal years.** Persistent budget deficits have long-run consequences because they lead to an increase in **public debt.** This can be a problem for two reasons. Public debt may crowd out investment spending, which reduces long-run economic growth. And in extreme cases, rising debt may lead to government default, resulting in economic and financial turmoil.

8. A widely used measure of fiscal health is the **debt–GDP ratio.** This number can remain stable or fall even in the face of moderate budget deficits if GDP rises over time. However, a stable debt–GDP ratio may give a misleading impression that all is well because modern governments often have large **implicit liabilities.** The largest implicit liabilities of the U.S. government come from Social Security, Medicare, and Medicaid, the costs of which are increasing due to the aging of the population and rising medical costs.

KEY TERMS

Social insurance, p. 821
Expansionary fiscal policy, p. 822
Contractionary fiscal policy, p. 822
Lump-sum taxes, p. 829
Automatic stabilizers, p. 830
Discretionary fiscal policy, p. 830
Cyclically adjusted budget balance, p. 834
Fiscal year, p. 837
Public debt, p. 839
Debt–GDP ratio, p. 840
Implicit liabilities, p. 841

PROBLEMS

1. The accompanying diagram shows the current macroeconomic situation for the economy of Albernia. You have been hired as an economic consultant to help the economy move to potential output, Y_P.

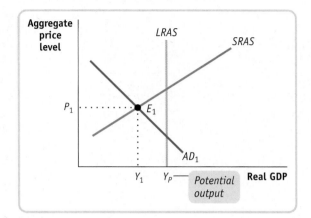

a. Is Albernia facing a recessionary or inflationary gap?

b. Which type of fiscal policy—expansionary or contractionary—would move the economy of Albernia to potential output, Y_P? What are some examples of such policies?

c. Illustrate the macroeconomic situation in Albernia with a diagram after the successful fiscal policy has been implemented.

2. The accompanying diagram shows the current macroeconomic situation for the economy of Brittania; real GDP is Y_1, and the aggregate price level is P_1. You have been hired as an economic consultant to help the economy move to potential output, Y_P.

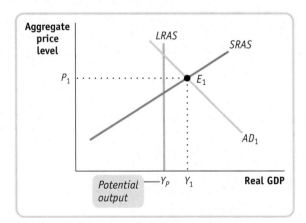

a. Is Brittania facing a recessionary or inflationary gap?

b. Which type of fiscal policy—expansionary or contractionary—would move the economy of Brittania to potential output, Y_P? What are some examples of such policies?

c. Illustrate the macroeconomic situation in Brittania with a diagram after the successful fiscal policy has been implemented.

3. An economy is in long-run macroeconomic equilibrium when each of the following aggregate demand shocks occurs. What kind of gap—inflationary or recessionary—will the economy face after the shock, and what type of fiscal policies would help move the economy back to potential output? How would your recommended fiscal policy shift the aggregate demand curve?

a. A stock market boom increases the value of stocks held by households.

b. Firms come to believe that a recession in the near future is likely.

c. Anticipating the possibility of war, the government increases its purchases of military equipment.

d. The quantity of money in the economy declines and interest rates increase.

4. During a 2008 interview, then German Finance Minister Peer Steinbrueck said, "We have to watch out that in Europe and beyond, nothing like a combination of downward economic [growth] and high inflation rates emerges—something that experts call stagflation." Such a situation can be depicted by the movement of the short-run aggregate supply curve from its original position, $SRAS_1$, to its new position, $SRAS_2$, with the new equilibrium point E_2 in the accompanying figure. In this question, we try to understand why stagflation is particularly hard to fix using fiscal policy.

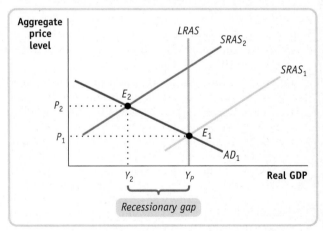

a. What would be the appropriate fiscal policy response to this situation if the primary concern of the government was to maintain economic growth? Illustrate the effect of the policy on the equilibrium point and the aggregate price level using the diagram.

b. What would be the appropriate fiscal policy response to this situation if the primary concern of the government was to maintain price stability? Illustrate the effect of the policy on the equilibrium point and the aggregate price level using the diagram.

c. Discuss the effectiveness of the policies in parts a and b in fighting stagflation.

5. Show why a $10 billion reduction in government purchases of goods and services will have a larger effect on real GDP than a $10 billion reduction in government transfers by completing the accompanying table for an economy with a marginal propensity to consume (*MPC*) of 0.6. The first and second rows of the table are filled in for you: on the left side of the table, in the first row, the $10 billion reduction in government purchases decreases real GDP and disposable income, *YD*, by $10 billion, leading to a reduction in consumer spending of $6 billion (*MPC* × change in disposable income) in row 2. However, on the right side of the table, the $10 billion reduction in transfers has no effect on real GDP in round 1 but does lower *YD* by $10 billion, resulting in a decrease in consumer spending of $6 billion in round 2.

	Decrease in G = −$10 billion			Decrease in TR = −$10 billion		
	Billions of dollars			**Billions of dollars**		
Rounds	**Change in G or C**	**Change in real GDP**	**Change in YD**	**Change in TR or C**	**Change in real GDP**	**Change in YD**
1	$\Delta G = -\$10.00$	−$10.00	−$10.00	$\Delta TR = -\$10.00$	$0.00	−$10.00
2	$\Delta C = -6.00$	−6.00	−6.00	$\Delta C = -6.00$	−6.00	−6.00
3	$\Delta C = ?$	?	?	$\Delta C = ?$	?	?
4	$\Delta C = ?$	?	?	$\Delta C = ?$	?	?
5	$\Delta C = ?$	?	?	$\Delta C = ?$	?	?
6	$\Delta C = ?$	?	?	$\Delta C = ?$	?	?
7	$\Delta C = ?$	?	?	$\Delta C = ?$	?	?
8	$\Delta C = ?$	?	?	$\Delta C = ?$	?	?
9	$\Delta C = ?$	?	?	$\Delta C = ?$	?	?
10	$\Delta C = ?$	?	?	$\Delta C = ?$	?	?

a. When government purchases decrease by $10 billion, what is the sum of the changes in real GDP after the 10 rounds?

b. When the government reduces transfers by $10 billion, what is the sum of the changes in real GDP after the 10 rounds?

c. Using the formula for the multiplier for changes in government purchases and for changes in transfers, calculate the total change in real GDP due to the $10 billion decrease in government purchases and the $10 billion reduction in transfers. What explains the difference? (*Hint:* The multiplier for government purchases of goods and services is $1/(1 - MPC)$. But since each $1 change in government transfers only leads to an initial change in real GDP of $MPC \times \$1$, the multiplier for government transfers is $MPC/(1 - MPC)$.)

6. In each of the following cases, either a recessionary or inflationary gap exists. Assume that the aggregate supply curve is horizontal, so that the change in real GDP arising from a shift of the aggregate demand curve equals the size of the shift of the curve. Calculate both the change in government purchases of goods and services and the change in government transfers necessary to close the gap.

a. Real GDP equals $100 billion, potential output equals $160 billion, and the marginal propensity to consume is 0.75.

b. Real GDP equals $250 billion, potential output equals $200 billion, and the marginal propensity to consume is 0.5.

c. Real GDP equals $180 billion, potential output equals $100 billion, and the marginal propensity to consume is 0.8.

7. Most macroeconomists believe it is a good thing that taxes act as automatic stabilizers and lower the size of the multiplier. However, a smaller multiplier means that the change in government purchases of goods and services, government transfers, or taxes needed to close an inflationary or recessionary gap is larger. How can you explain this apparent inconsistency?

8. The government's budget surplus in Macroland has risen consistently over the past five years. Two government policy makers disagree as to why this has happened. One argues that a rising budget surplus indicates a growing economy; the other argues that it shows that the government is using contractionary fiscal policy. Can you determine which policy maker is correct? If not, why not?

9. Figure 28-10 shows the actual budget deficit and the cyclically adjusted budget deficit as a percentage of GDP in the United States from 1970 to 2014. Assuming that potential output was unchanged, use this figure to determine which of the years from 1990 to 2013

the government used expansionary fiscal policy and in which years it used contractionary fiscal policy.

10. You are an economic adviser to a candidate for national office. She asks you for a summary of the economic consequences of a balanced-budget rule for the federal government and for your recommendation on whether she should support such a rule. How do you respond?

11. In 2014, the policy makers of the economy of Eastlandia projected the debt–GDP ratio and the ratio of the budget deficit to GDP for the economy for the next 10 years under different scenarios for growth in the government's deficit. Real GDP is currently $1,000 billion per year and is expected to grow by 3% per year, the public debt is $300 billion at the beginning of the year, and the deficit is $30 billion in 2014.

Year	Real GDP (billions of dollars)	Debt (billions of dollars)	Budget deficit (billions of dollars)	Debt (percent of real GDP)	Budget deficit (percent of real GDP)
2014	$1,000	$300	$30	?	?
2015	1,030	?	?	?	?
2016	1,061	?	?	?	?
2017	1,093	?	?	?	?
2018	1,126	?	?	?	?
2019	1,159	?	?	?	?
2020	1,194	?	?	?	?
2021	1,230	?	?	?	?
2022	1,267	?	?	?	?
2023	1,305	?	?	?	?
2024	1,344	?	?	?	?

a. Complete the accompanying table to show the debt–GDP ratio and the ratio of the budget deficit to GDP for the economy if the government's budget deficit remains constant at $30 billion over the next 10 years. (Remember that the government's debt will grow by the previous year's deficit.)

b. Redo the table to show the debt–GDP ratio and the ratio of the budget deficit to GDP for the economy if the government's budget deficit grows by 3% per year over the next 10 years.

c. Redo the table again to show the debt–GDP ratio and the ratio of the budget deficit to GDP for the economy if the government's budget deficit grows by 20% per year over the next 10 years.

d. What happens to the debt–GDP ratio and the ratio of the budget deficit to GDP for the economy over time under the three different scenarios?

12. Your study partner argues that the distinction between the government's budget deficit and debt is similar to the distinction between consumer savings and wealth. He also argues that if you have large budget deficits, you must have a large debt. In what ways is your study partner correct and in what ways is he incorrect?

13. In which of the following cases does the size of the government's debt and the size of the budget deficit indicate potential problems for the economy?
a. The government's debt is relatively low, but the government is running a large budget deficit as it builds a high-speed rail system to connect the major cities of the nation.
b. The government's debt is relatively high due to a recently ended deficit-financed war, but the government is now running only a small budget deficit.
c. The government's debt is relatively low, but the government is running a budget deficit to finance the interest payments on the debt.

14. How did or would the following affect the current public debt and implicit liabilities of the U.S. government?
a. In 2003, Congress passed and President Bush signed the Medicare Modernization Act, which provides seniors and individuals with disabilities with a prescription drug benefit. Some of the benefits under this law took effect immediately, but others will not begin until sometime in the future.
b. The age at which retired persons can receive full Social Security benefits is raised to age 70 for future retirees.
c. Social Security benefits for future retirees are limited to those with low incomes.
d. Because the cost of health care is increasing faster than the overall inflation rate, annual increases in Social Security benefits are increased by the annual increase in health care costs rather than the overall inflation rate.

15. Unlike households, governments are often able to sustain large debts. For example, in 2013, the U.S. government's total debt reached $17.3 trillion, approximately equal to 101.6% of GDP. At the time, according to the U.S. Treasury, the average interest rate paid by the government on its debt was 2.0%. However, running budget deficits becomes hard when very large debts are outstanding.
a. Calculate the dollar cost of the annual interest on the government's total debt assuming the interest rate and debt figures cited above.
b. If the government operates on a balanced budget before interest payments are taken into account, at what rate must GDP grow in order for the debt–GDP ratio to remain unchanged?

c. Calculate the total increase in national debt if the government incurs a deficit of $600 billion in 2014.

d. At what rate would GDP have to grow in order for the debt–GDP ratio to remain unchanged when the deficit in 2014 is $600 billion?

e. Why is the debt–GDP ratio the preferred measure of a country's debt rather than the dollar value of the debt? Why is it important for a government to keep this number under control?

WORK IT OUT

Macmillan Education **LaunchPad**

For interactive, step-by-step help in solving the following problem, visit LaunchPad by using the URL on the back cover of this book.

16. The accompanying table shows how consumers' marginal propensities to consume in a particular economy are related to their level of income.

Income range	Marginal propensity to consume
$0–$20,000	0.9
$20,001–$40,000	0.8
$40,001–$60,000	0.7
$60,001–$80,000	0.6
Above $80,000	0.5

a. Suppose the government engages in increased purchases of goods and services. For each of the income groups in the table, what is the value of the multiplier—that is, what is the "bang for the buck" from each dollar the government spends on government purchases of goods and services in each income group?

b. If the government needed to close a recessionary or inflationary gap, at which group should it primarily aim its fiscal policy of changes in government purchases of goods and services?

Taxes and the Multiplier

In the chapter, we described how taxes that depend positively on real GDP reduce the size of the multiplier and act as an automatic stabilizer for the economy. Let's look a little more closely at the mathematics of how this works.

Specifically, let's assume that the government "captures" a fraction t of any increase in real GDP in the form of taxes, where t, the tax rate, is a fraction between 0 and 1. And let's repeat the exercise we carried out in Chapter 26, where we consider the effects of a $100 billion increase in investment spending. The same analysis holds for *any* autonomous increase in aggregate spending—in particular, it is also true for increases in government purchases of goods and services.

The $100 billion increase in investment spending initially raises real GDP by $100 billion (the first round). In the absence of taxes, disposable income would rise by $100 billion. But because part of the rise in real GDP is collected in the form of taxes, disposable income only rises by $(1 - t) \times$ $100 billion. The second-round increase in consumer spending, which is equal to the marginal propensity to consume *(MPC)* multiplied by the rise in disposable income, is $(MPC \times (1 - t)) \times$ $100 billion. This leads to a third-round increase in consumer spending of $(MPC \times (1 - t)) \times (MPC \times (1 - t)) \times$ $100 billion, and so on. So the total effect on real GDP is

Increase in investment spending	$=$	$100 billion
+ Second-round increase in consumer spending	$= (MPC \times (1 - t))$	$\times$ $100 billion
+ Third-round increase in consumer spending	$= (MPC \times (1 - t))^2$	$\times$ $100 billion
+ Fourth-round increase in consumer spending	$= (MPC \times (1 - t))^3$	$\times$ $100 billion
$\bullet$		$\bullet$
$\bullet$		$\bullet$
$\bullet$		$\bullet$

$$\text{Total increase in real GDP} = [1 + (MPC \times (1 - t)) + (MPC \times (1 - t))^2 + (MPC \times (1 - t))^3 + \ldots] \times \$100 \text{ billion}$$

As we pointed out in Chapter 26, an infinite series of the form $1 + x + x^2 + \ldots$, with $0 < x < 1$, is equal to $1/(1 - x)$. In this example, $x = (MPC \times (1 - t))$. So the total effect of a $100 billion increase in investment spending, taking into account all the subsequent increases in consumer spending, is to raise real GDP by:

$$\frac{1}{1 - (MPC \times (1 - t))} \times \$100 \text{ billion}$$

When we calculated the multiplier assuming away the effect of taxes, we found that it was $1/(1 - MPC)$. But when we assume that a fraction t of any change in real GDP is collected in the form of taxes, the multiplier is:

$$\text{Multiplier} = \frac{1}{1 - (MPC \times (1 - t))}$$

This is always a smaller number than $1/(1 - MPC)$, and its size diminishes as t grows. Suppose, for example, that $MPC = 0.6$. In the absence of taxes, this implies a multiplier of $1/(1 - 0.6) = 1/0.4 = 2.5$. But now let's assume that $t = 1/3$, that is, that 1/3 of any increase in real GDP is collected by the government. Then the multiplier is:

$$\frac{1}{1 - (0.6 \times (1 - 1/3))} = \frac{1}{1 - (0.6 \times 2/3)} = \frac{1}{1 - 0.4} = \frac{1}{0.6} = 1.667$$

PROBLEMS

1. An economy has a marginal propensity to consume of 0.6, real GDP equals $500 billion, and the government collects 20% of GDP in taxes. If government purchases increase by $10 billion, show the rounds of increased spending that take place by completing the accompanying table. The first and second rows are filled in for you. In the first row, the increase in government purchases of $10 billion raises real GDP by $10 billion, taxes increase by $2 billion, and *YD* increases by $8 billion; in the second row, the increase in *YD* of $8 billion increases consumer spending by $4.80 billion (*MPC* × change in disposable income).

	Change in *G* or *C*	Change in real GDP	Change in taxes	Change in *YD*
Rounds		(billions of dollars)		
1	Δ*G* = $10.00	$10.00	$2.00	$8.00
2	Δ*C* = 4.80	4.80	0.96	3.84
3	Δ*C* = ?	?	?	?
4	Δ*C* = ?	?	?	?
5	Δ*C* = ?	?	?	?
6	Δ*C* = ?	?	?	?
7	Δ*C* = ?	?	?	?
8	Δ*C* = ?	?	?	?
9	Δ*C* = ?	?	?	?
10	Δ*C* = ?	?	?	?

a. What is the total change in real GDP after the 10 rounds? What is the value of the multiplier? What would you expect the total change in real GDP to be, based on the multiplier formula? How do your two answers compare?

b. Redo the accompanying table, assuming the marginal propensity to consume is 0.75 and the government collects 10% of the rise in real GDP in taxes. What is the total change in real GDP after 10 rounds? What is the value of the multiplier? How do your two answers compare?

WORK IT OUT

For interactive, step-by-step help in solving the following problem, visit LaunchPad by using the URL on the back cover of this book.

2. Calculate the change in government purchases of goods and services necessary to close the recessionary or inflationary gaps in the following cases. Assume that the short-run aggregate supply curve is horizontal, so that the change in real GDP arising from a shift of the aggregate demand curve equals the size of the shift of the curve.

a. Real GDP equals $100 billion, potential output equals $160 billion, the government collects 20% of any change in real GDP in the form of taxes, and the marginal propensity to consume is 0.75.

b. Real GDP equals $250 billion, potential output equals $200 billion, the government collects 10% of any change in real GDP in the form of taxes, and the marginal propensity to consume is 0.5.

c. Real GDP equals $180 billion, potential output equals $100 billion, the government collects 25% of any change in real GDP in the form of taxes, and the marginal propensity to consume is 0.8.

Money, Banking, and the Federal Reserve System

▶ **What You Will Learn in This Chapter**

■ The various roles **money** plays and the many forms it takes in the economy

■ How the actions of private banks and the Federal Reserve determine the **money supply**

■ How the Federal Reserve uses **open-market operations** to change the **monetary base**

FUNNY MONEY

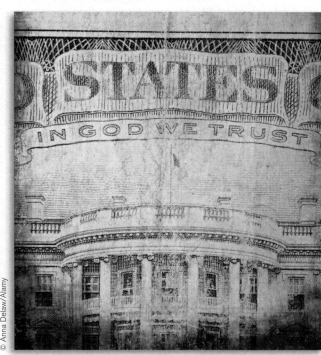

© Anna Delaw/Alamy

Money is the essential channel that links the various parts of the modern economy.

In 2013, police in Lima, Peru, were stunned when they arrested a 13-year-old boy carrying a sack filled with $700,000 in counterfeit U.S. dollars. The boy, along with several other children, worked for one of the many highly successful counterfeiting rings in Peru.

In recent years, Peru has become a major source for the production of counterfeit U.S. currency. Workers in these rings meticulously add decorative details to printed bills by hand, creating high-quality fakes that are very hard to detect.

The funny thing is that elaborately decorated pieces of paper have little or no intrinsic value. Indeed, a $100 bill printed with blue or orange ink wouldn't be worth the paper it was printed on.

But if the ink on that piece of paper is just the right shade of green, people will think that it's *money* and will accept it as payment for very real goods and services. Why? Because they believe, correctly, that they can do the same thing: exchange that piece of green paper for real goods and services.

In fact, here's a riddle: If a fake $100 bill from Peru enters the United States and is successfully exchanged for a good or service with nobody ever realizing it's fake, who gets hurt? Accepting a fake $100 bill isn't like buying a car that turns out to be a lemon or a meal that turns out to be inedible. As long as the bill's counterfeit nature remains undiscovered, it will pass from hand to hand just like a real $100 bill.

The answer to the riddle is that the actual victims of the counterfeiting are U.S. taxpayers because counterfeit dollars reduce the revenues available to pay for the operations of the U.S. government. Accordingly, the Secret Service diligently monitors the integrity of U.S. currency, promptly investigating any reports of counterfeit dollars.

The efforts of the Secret Service attest to the fact that money isn't like ordinary goods and services, and it certainly is not like a piece of colored paper. In this section we'll look at what money is, the role that it plays, the workings of a modern monetary system, and the institutions that sustain and regulate it, including the *Federal Reserve*.

Money is any asset that can easily be used to purchase goods and services.

Currency in circulation is cash held by the public.

Checkable bank deposits are bank accounts on which people can write checks.

The **money supply** is the total value of financial assets in the economy that are considered money.

The Meaning of Money

In everyday conversation, people often use the word *money* to mean "wealth." If you ask, "How much money does Mark Zuckerberg have?" the answer will be something like, "Oh, $30 billion or so, but who's counting?" That is, the number will include the value of the stocks, bonds, real estate, and other assets he owns.

But the economist's definition of money doesn't include all forms of wealth. The dollar bills in your wallet are money; other forms of wealth—such as cars, houses, and stock certificates—aren't money. What, according to economists, distinguishes money from other forms of wealth?

What Is Money?

Money is defined in terms of what it does: **money** is any asset that can easily be used to purchase goods and services. In Chapter 25 we defined an asset as *liquid* if it can easily be converted into cash. Money consists of cash itself, which is liquid by definition, as well as other assets that are highly liquid.

You can see the distinction between money and other assets by asking yourself how you pay for groceries. The person at the cash register will accept dollar bills in return for milk and frozen pizza—but he or she won't accept stock certificates or a collection of vintage baseball cards. If you want to convert stock certificates or vintage baseball cards into groceries, you have to sell them—trade them for money—and then use the money to buy groceries.

Of course, many stores allow you to write a check on your bank account in payment for goods (or to pay with a debit card that is linked to your bank account). Does that make your bank account money, even if you haven't converted it into cash? Yes. **Currency in circulation—** actual cash in the hands of the public—is considered money. So are **checkable bank deposits—**bank accounts on which people can write checks.

Without a liquid asset like money, making purchases would be much harder.

Are currency and checkable bank deposits the only assets that are considered money? It depends. As we'll see later, there are two widely used definitions of the **money supply,** the total value of financial assets in the economy that are considered money. The narrower definition considers only the most liquid assets to be money: currency in circulation, traveler's checks, and checkable bank deposits. The broader definition includes these three categories plus other assets that are "almost" checkable, such as savings account deposits that can be transferred into a checking account with a phone call or a mouse click. Both definitions of the money supply, however, make a distinction between those assets that can easily be used to purchase goods and services and those that can't.

Money plays a crucial role in generating *gains from trade* because it makes indirect exchange possible. Think of what happens when a cardiac surgeon buys a new refrigerator. The surgeon has valuable services to offer—namely, heart operations. The owner of the store has valuable goods to offer—refrigerators and other appliances. It would be extremely difficult for both parties if, instead of using money, they had to directly barter the goods and services they sell. In a barter system, a cardiac surgeon and an appliance store owner could trade only if the store owner happened to want a heart operation and the surgeon happened to want a new refrigerator.

This is known as the problem of finding a *double coincidence of wants:* in a barter system, two parties can trade only when each wants what the other has to offer. Money solves this problem: individuals can trade what they have to offer for money and trade money for what they want.

Because the ability to make transactions with money rather than relying on bartering makes it easier to achieve gains from trade, the existence of money increases welfare, even though money does not directly produce anything. As Adam Smith put it, money "may very properly be compared to a highway, which, while it circulates and carries to market all the grass and corn of the country, produces itself not a single pile of either."

Let's take a closer look at the roles money plays in the economy.

> A **medium of exchange** is an asset that individuals acquire for the purpose of trading goods and services rather than for their own consumption.

Roles of Money

Money plays three main roles in any modern economy: it is a *medium of exchange,* a *store of value,* and a *unit of account.*

1. Medium of Exchange Our cardiac surgeon/refrigerator example illustrates the role of money as a **medium of exchange**—an asset that individuals use to trade for goods and services rather than for consumption. People can't eat dollar bills; rather, they use dollar bills to trade for edible goods and their accompanying services.

In normal times, the official money of a given country—the dollar in the United States, the peso in Mexico, and so on—is also the medium of exchange in virtually all transactions in that country. During troubled economic times, however, other goods or assets often play that role instead. For example, during economic turmoil people often turn to other countries' moneys as the medium of exchange: U.S. dollars have played this role in troubled Latin American countries, as have euros in troubled Eastern European countries. In a famous example, cigarettes functioned as the medium of exchange in World War II prisoner-of-war camps: even nonsmokers traded goods and services for cigarettes because the cigarettes could in turn be easily traded for other items. During the extreme German inflation of 1923, goods such as eggs and lumps of coal became, briefly, mediums of exchange.

 GLOBAL COMPARISION | **The Big Moneys**

Americans tend to think of the dollar as the world's leading currency—and it does remain the currency most likely to be accepted in payment around the globe. But there are other important currencies, too. One simple measure of a currency's importance is the value of the quantity of that currency in circulation. This figure shows the value, in billions of dollars, of the quantity of four major currencies in circulation at the end of 2013. The dollar, it turns out, is only number 2, behind the euro. The euro's prominence isn't that surprising, since the combined economies of the countries using the euro, the eurozone, are about as big as the U.S. economy. And despite the fact that its economy is much smaller, Japan is closely behind the United States, largely because the Japanese make much more use of cash, as opposed to checks and credit cards, than either Europeans or

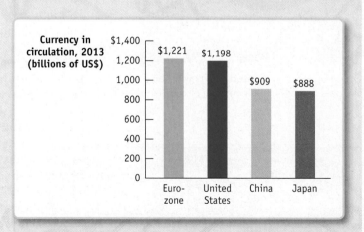

Americans. Finally, China, with its rapidly growing economy, is moving up the charts, and has now passed Japan.

Sources: Federal Reserve Bank of St. Louis; European Central Bank; Bank of Japan; The People's Bank of China.

A **store of value** is a means of holding purchasing power over time.

A **unit of account** is a measure used to set prices and make economic calculations.

Commodity money is a good used as a medium of exchange that has intrinsic value in other uses.

Commodity-backed money is a medium of exchange with no intrinsic value whose ultimate value is guaranteed by a promise that it can be converted into valuable goods.

2. Store of Value In order to act as a medium of exchange, money must also be a **store of value**—a means of holding purchasing power over time. To see why this is necessary, imagine trying to operate an economy in which ice-cream cones were the medium of exchange. Such an economy would quickly suffer from, well, monetary meltdown: your medium of exchange would often turn into a sticky puddle before you could use it to buy something else. (As we'll see in Chapter 31, one of the problems caused by high inflation is that, in effect, it causes the value of money to "melt.") Of course, money is by no means the only store of value. Any asset that holds its purchasing power over time is a store of value. So the store-of-value role is a necessary but not distinctive feature of money.

3. Unit of Account Finally, money normally serves as the **unit of account**—the commonly accepted measure individuals use to set prices and make economic calculations. To understand the importance of this role, consider a historical fact: during the Middle Ages, peasants typically were required to provide land-owners with goods and labor rather than money. A peasant might, for example, be required to work on the lord's land one day a week and hand over one-fifth of his harvest.

Today, rents, like other prices, are almost always specified in money terms. That makes things much clearer: imagine how hard it would be to decide which apartment to rent if modern landlords followed medieval practice. Suppose, for example, that Mr. Smith says he'll let you have a place if you clean his house twice a week and bring him a pound of steak every day, whereas Ms. Jones wants you to clean her house just once a week but wants four pounds of chicken every day. Who's offering the better deal? It's hard to say. If, instead, Smith wants $600 a month and Jones wants $700, the comparison is easy. In other words, without a commonly accepted measure, the terms of a transaction are harder to determine, making it more difficult to make transactions and achieve gains from trade.

Types of Money

In some form or another, money has been in use for thousands of years. For most of that period, people used **commodity money:** the medium of exchange was a good, normally gold or silver, that had intrinsic value in other uses. These alternative uses gave commodity money value independent of its role as a medium of exchange. For example, cigarettes, which served as money in World War II prisoner-of-war camps, were also valuable because many prisoners smoked. Gold was valuable because it was used for jewelry and ornamentation, aside from the fact that it was minted into coins.

For centuries, people used goods with value, like gold and silver, as a medium of exchange.

By 1776, the year in which the United States declared independence and Adam Smith published *The Wealth of Nations*, there was widespread use of paper money in addition to gold or silver coins. Unlike modern dollar bills, however, this paper money consisted of notes issued by private banks, which promised to exchange their notes for gold or silver coins on demand. So the paper currency that initially replaced commodity money was **commodity-backed money,** a medium of exchange with no intrinsic value whose ultimate value was guaranteed by a promise that it could always be converted into valuable goods on demand.

By issuing paper notes to be used instead of gold and silver coins, banks freed up valuable resources that had been used to function as money.

The big advantage of commodity-backed money over simple commodity money, like gold and silver coins, was that it tied up fewer valuable resources. Although a note-issuing bank still had to keep some gold and silver on hand, it had to keep only enough to satisfy demands for redemption of its notes. And it could rely on the fact that on a normal day only a fraction of its paper notes would be redeemed. So the bank needed to keep only a portion of the total value of its notes in circulation in the form of gold and silver in its vaults. It could lend out the remaining gold and silver to those who wished to use it. This allowed society to use the remaining gold and silver for other purposes, all with no loss in the ability to achieve gains from trade.

In a famous passage in *The Wealth of Nations,* Adam Smith described paper money as a "waggon-way through the air." Smith was making an analogy between money and an imaginary highway that did not absorb valuable land beneath it. An actual highway provides a useful service but at a cost: land that could be used to grow crops is instead paved over. If the highway could be built through the air, it wouldn't destroy useful land. As Smith understood, when banks replaced gold and silver money with paper notes, they accomplished a similar feat: they reduced the amount of real resources used by society to provide the functions of money.

At this point you may ask: why make any use at all of gold and silver in the monetary system, even to back paper money? In fact, today's monetary system goes even further than the system Smith admired, having eliminated any role for gold and silver. A U.S. dollar bill isn't commodity money, and it isn't even commodity-backed. Rather, its value arises entirely from the fact that it is generally accepted as a means of payment, a role that is ultimately decreed by the U.S. government. Money whose value derives entirely from its official status as a means of exchange is known as **fiat money** because it exists by government fiat, a historical term for a policy declared by a ruler.

Fiat money has two major advantages over commodity-backed money. First, it is even more of a "waggon-way through the air"—creating it doesn't use up any real resources beyond the paper it's printed on. Second, the supply of money can be adjusted based on the needs of the economy, instead of being determined by the amount of gold and silver prospectors happen to discover.

Fiat money, though, poses some risks. In this chapter's opening story, we described one such risk—counterfeiting. Counterfeiters usurp a privilege of the U.S. government, which has the sole legal right to print dollar bills. And the benefit that counterfeiters get by exchanging fake bills for real goods and services comes at the expense of the U.S. federal government, which covers a small but nontrivial part of its own expenses by issuing new currency to meet a growing demand for money.

The larger risk is that governments that can create money whenever they feel like it will be tempted to abuse the privilege. In Chapter 31 we'll learn how governments sometimes rely too heavily on printing money to pay their bills, leading to high inflation. In this chapter, however, we'll stay focused on the question of what money is and how it is managed.

Measuring the Money Supply

The Federal Reserve calculates the size of two **monetary aggregates,** overall measures of the money supply, which differ in how strictly money is defined. The two aggregates are known, rather cryptically, as M1 and M2. (There used to be a third aggregate named—you guessed it—M3, but in 2006 the Federal Reserve concluded that measuring it was no longer useful.)

M1, the narrowest definition, contains only currency in circulation (also known as cash), traveler's checks, and checkable bank deposits. M2 adds several other kinds of assets, often referred to as **near-moneys**—financial assets that aren't directly usable as a medium of exchange but can be readily converted into cash or checkable bank deposits, such as savings accounts. Examples are time

Fiat money is a medium of exchange whose value derives entirely from its official status as a means of payment.

A **monetary aggregate** is an overall measure of the money supply.

Near-moneys are financial assets that can't be directly used as a medium of exchange but can be readily converted into cash or checkable bank deposits.

PITFALLS

WHAT'S NOT IN THE MONEY SUPPLY
Are financial assets like stocks and bonds part of the money supply? No, not under any definition, because they're not liquid enough.

M1 consists, roughly speaking, of assets you can use to buy groceries: currency, traveler's checks, and checkable deposits (which work as long as your grocery store accepts either checks or debit cards). M2 is broader, because it includes things like savings accounts that can easily and quickly be converted into M1. Normally, for example, you can switch funds between your savings and checking accounts with a click of a mouse or a call to an automated phone service.

By contrast, converting a stock or a bond into cash requires selling the stock or bond—something that usually takes some time and also involves paying a broker's fee. That makes these assets much less liquid than bank deposits. So stocks and bonds, unlike bank deposits, aren't considered money.

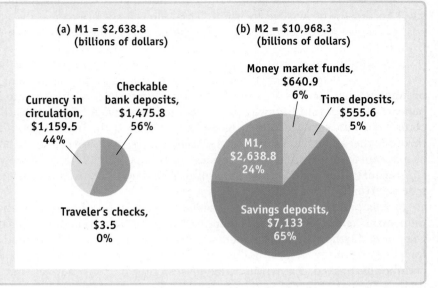

FIGURE **29-1** Monetary Aggregates, September 2013

The Federal Reserve uses two definitions of the money supply, M1 and M2. As panel (a) shows, more than half of M1 consists of checkable bank deposits with currency in circulation making up virtually all of the rest. M2, as panel (b) shows, has a much broader definition: it includes M1 plus a range of other deposits and deposit-like assets, making it almost five times as large.
Source: Federal Reserve Bank of St. Louis.

deposits such as small-denomination CDs, which aren't checkable but can be withdrawn at any time before their maturity date by paying a penalty. Because currency and checkable deposits are directly usable as a medium of exchange, M1 is the most liquid measure of money.

Figure 29-1 shows the actual composition of M1 and M2 in December 2013, in billions of dollars. M1 was valued at $2,639 billion, with about 44% accounted for by currency in circulation, almost all the rest accounted for by checkable bank deposits, and a tiny slice accounted for by traveler's checks. In turn, M1 made up 24% of M2, valued at $10,969 billion. M2 consists of M1 plus other types of assets: two types of bank deposits, known as savings deposits and time deposits, both of which are considered noncheckable, plus money market funds, which are mutual funds that invest only in liquid assets and bear a close resemblance to bank deposits. These near-moneys pay interest, although cash (currency in circulation) does not, and they typically pay higher interest rates than any offered on checkable bank deposits.

FOR INQUIRING MINDS | What's with All the Currency?

Alert readers may be a bit startled at one of the numbers in the money supply: more than $1 trillion of currency in circulation. That's over $3,000 in cash for every man, woman, and child in the United States. How many people do you know who carry $3,000 in their wallets? Not many. So where is all that cash?

Part of the answer is that it isn't in individuals' wallets—it's in cash registers. Businesses as well as individuals need to hold cash.

Economists believe that cash also plays an important role in transactions that people want to keep hidden. Small businesses and the self-employed sometimes prefer to be paid in cash so they can avoid paying taxes by hiding income from the Internal Revenue Service. Also, drug dealers and other criminals obviously don't want bank records of their dealings. In fact, some analysts have tried to infer the amount of illegal activity in the economy from the

total amount of cash holdings held by the public.

The most important reason for those huge currency holdings, however, is foreign use of dollars. The Federal Reserve estimates that 60% of U.S. currency is actually held outside the United States—largely in countries in which residents are so distrustful of their national currencies that the U.S. dollar has become a widely accepted medium of exchange. ■

ECONOMICS ▶ *in Action*

The History of the Dollar

U.S. dollar bills are pure fiat money: they have no intrinsic value, and they are not backed by anything that does. But American money wasn't always like that. In the early days of European settlement, the colonies that would become the United States used commodity money, partly consisting of gold and silver coins minted in Europe. But such coins were scarce on this side of the Atlantic, so the colonists relied on a variety of other forms of commodity money. For example, settlers in Virginia used tobacco as money and settlers in the Northeast used "wampum," a type of clamshell.

Later in American history, commodity-backed paper money came into wide-spread use. But this wasn't paper money as we now know it, issued by the U.S. government and bearing the signature of the Secretary of the Treasury. Before the Civil War, the U.S. government didn't issue any paper money. Instead, dollar bills were issued by private banks, which promised that their bills could be redeemed for silver coins on demand. These promises weren't always credible because banks sometimes failed, leaving holders of their bills with worthless pieces of paper. Understandably, people were reluctant to accept currency from any bank rumored to be in financial trouble. In this private money system, some dollars were less valuable than others.

A curious legacy of that time was notes issued by the Citizens' Bank of Louisiana, based in New Orleans, that became among the most widely used bank notes in the southern states. These notes were printed in English on one side and French on the other. (At the time, many people in New Orleans, originally a colony of France, spoke French.) Thus, the $10 bill read *Ten* on one side and *Dix,* the French word for "ten," on the other. These $10 bills became known as "dixies," probably the source of the nickname of the U.S. South.

The U.S. government began issuing official paper money, called "greenbacks," in 1862 as a way to pay for the ongoing Civil War. At first greenbacks had no fixed value in terms of commodities. After 1873, the U.S. government guaranteed the value of a dollar in terms of gold, effectively turning dollars into commodity-backed money.

In 1933, when President Franklin D. Roosevelt broke the link between dollars and gold, his own federal budget director—who feared that the public would lose confidence in the dollar if it wasn't ultimately backed by gold—declared ominously, "This will be the end of Western civilization." It wasn't. The link between the dollar and gold was restored a few years later, then dropped again—seemingly for good—in August 1971. Despite the warnings of doom, the U.S. dollar went on to become the world's most widely used currency. (Now it is the second-most widely used, after the euro.)

Win McNamee/Reuters/Corbis

Not until the Civil War did the U.S. government issue official paper money.

Check Your Understanding   29-1

1. Suppose you hold a gift card, good for certain products at participating stores. Is this gift card money? Why or why not?

2. Although most bank accounts pay some interest, depositors can get a higher interest rate by buying a certificate of deposit, or CD. The difference between a CD and a checking account is that the depositor pays a penalty for withdrawing the money before the CD comes due—a period of months or even years. Small CDs are counted in M2 but not in M1. Explain why they are not part of M1.

3. Explain why a system of commodity-backed money uses resources more efficiently than a system of commodity money.

Solutions appear at back of book.

Bank reserves are the currency banks hold in their vaults plus their deposits at the Federal Reserve.

A **T-account** is a tool for analyzing a business's financial position by showing, in a single table, the business's assets (on the left) and liabilities (on the right).

The Monetary Role of Banks

Roughly 40% of M1, the narrowest definition of the money supply, consists of currency in circulation—$1 bills, $5 bills, and so on. It's obvious where currency comes from: it's printed by the U.S. Treasury. But the rest of M1 consists of bank deposits, and deposits account for the great bulk of M2, the broader definition of the money supply. By either measure, then, bank deposits are a major component of the money supply. And this fact brings us to our next topic: the monetary role of banks.

What Banks Do

As we learned in Chapter 25, a bank is a *financial intermediary* that uses liquid assets in the form of bank deposits to finance the illiquid investments of borrowers. Banks can create liquidity because it isn't necessary for a bank to keep all of the funds deposited with it in the form of highly liquid assets. Except in the case of a *bank run*—which we'll get to shortly—all of a bank's depositors won't want to withdraw their funds at the same time. So a bank can provide its depositors with liquid assets yet still invest much of the depositors' funds in illiquid assets, such as mortgages and business loans.

Banks can't, however, lend out all the funds placed in their hands by depositors because they have to satisfy any depositor who wants to withdraw his or her funds. In order to meet these demands, a bank must keep substantial quantities of liquid assets on hand. In the modern U.S. banking system, these assets take the form either of currency in the bank's vault or deposits held in the bank's own account at the Federal Reserve. As we'll see shortly, the latter can be converted into currency more or less instantly. Currency in bank vaults and bank deposits held at the Federal Reserve are called **bank reserves.** Because bank reserves are in bank vaults and at the Federal Reserve, not held by the public, they are not part of currency in circulation.

To understand the role of banks in determining the money supply, we start by introducing a simple tool for analyzing a bank's financial position: a **T-account.** A business's T-account summarizes its financial position by showing, in a single table, the business's assets and liabilities, with assets on the left and liabilities on the right.

Figure 29-2 shows the T-account for a hypothetical business that *isn't* a bank—Samantha's Smoothies. According to Figure 29-2, Samantha's Smoothies owns a building worth $30,000 and has $15,000 worth of smoothie-making equipment. These are assets, so they're on the left side of the table. To finance its opening, the business borrowed $20,000 from a local bank. That's a liability, so the loan is on the right side of the table. By looking at the T-account, you can immediately see what Samantha's Smoothies owns and what it owes. Oh, and it's called a T-account because the lines in the table make a T-shape.

Samantha's Smoothies is an ordinary, nonbank business. Now let's look at the T-account for a hypothetical bank, First Street Bank, which is the repository of $1 million in bank deposits.

FIGURE 29-2 A T-Account for Samantha's Smoothies

A T-account summarizes a business's financial position. Its assets, in this case consisting of a building and some smoothie-making machinery, are on the left side. Its liabilities, consisting of the money it owes to a local bank, are on the right side.

Assets		Liabilities	
Building	$30,000	Loan from bank	$20,000
Smoothie-making machines	$15,000		

| FIGURE **29-3** | Assets and Liabilities of First Street Bank |

First Street Bank's assets consist of $1,200,000 in loans and $100,000 in reserves. Its liabilities consist of $1,000,000 in deposits—money owed to people who have placed funds in First Street's hands.

Assets		Liabilities	
Loans	$1,200,000	Deposits	$1,000,000
Reserves	$100,000		

Figure 29-3 shows First Street Bank's financial position. The loans First Street Bank has made are on the left side because they're assets: they represent funds that those who have borrowed from the bank are expected to repay. The bank's only other assets, in this simplified example, are its reserves, which, as we've learned, can take the form either of cash in the bank's vault or deposits at the Federal Reserve. On the right side we show the bank's liabilities, which in this example consist entirely of deposits made by customers at First Street Bank. These are liabilities because they represent funds that must ultimately be repaid to depositors.

Notice, by the way, that in this example First Street Bank's assets are larger than its liabilities. That's the way it's supposed to be! In fact, as we'll see shortly, banks are required by law to maintain assets larger by a specific percentage than their liabilities.

In this example, First Street Bank holds reserves equal to 10% of its customers' bank deposits. The fraction of bank deposits that a bank holds as reserves is its **reserve ratio.** In the modern American system, the Federal Reserve—which, among other things, regulates banks operating in the United States—sets a minimum required reserve ratio that banks are required to maintain. To understand why banks are regulated, let's consider a problem banks can face: bank runs.

The Problem of Bank Runs

A bank can lend out most of the funds deposited in its care because in normal times only a small fraction of its depositors want to withdraw their funds on any given day. But what would happen if, for some reason, all or at least a large fraction of its depositors did try to withdraw their funds during a short period of time, such as a couple of days?

If a significant share of its depositors demanded their money back at the same time, the bank wouldn't be able to raise enough cash to meet those demands. The reason is that banks convert most of their depositors' funds into loans made to borrowers; that's how banks earn revenue—by charging interest on loans.

Bank loans, however, are illiquid: they can't easily be converted into cash on short notice. To see why, imagine that First Street Bank has lent $100,000 to Drive-A-Peach Used Cars, a local dealership. To raise cash to meet demands for withdrawals, First Street Bank can sell its loan to Drive-A-Peach to someone else—another bank or an individual investor. But if First Street Bank tries to sell the loan quickly, potential buyers will be wary: they will suspect that First Street Bank wants to sell the loan because there is something wrong and the loan might not be repaid. As a result, First Street Bank can sell the loan quickly only by offering it for sale at a deep discount—say, a discount of 40%, for a sale price of $60,000.

The upshot is that if a significant number of First Street Bank's depositors suddenly decided to withdraw their funds, the bank's efforts to raise the necessary cash quickly would force it to sell off its assets very cheaply. Inevitably, this leads to a *bank failure:* the bank would be unable to pay off its depositors in full.

The **reserve ratio** is the fraction of bank deposits that a bank holds as reserves.

A **bank run** is a phenomenon in which many of a bank's depositors try to withdraw their funds due to fears of a bank failure.

Deposit insurance guarantees that a bank's depositors will be paid even if the bank can't come up with the funds, up to a maximum amount per account.

What might start this whole process? That is, what might lead First Street Bank's depositors to rush to pull their money out? A plausible answer is a spreading rumor that the bank is in financial trouble. Even if depositors aren't sure the rumor is true, they are likely to play it safe and get their money out while they still can. And it gets worse: a depositor who simply thinks that *other* depositors are going to panic and try to get their money out will realize that this could "break the bank." So he or she joins the rush. In other words, fear about a bank's financial condition can be a self-fulfilling prophecy: depositors who believe that other depositors will rush to the exit will rush to the exit themselves.

A **bank run** is a phenomenon in which many of a bank's depositors try to withdraw their funds due to fears of a bank failure. Moreover, bank runs aren't bad only for the bank in question and its depositors. Historically, they have often proved contagious, with a run on one bank leading to a loss of faith in other banks, causing additional bank runs.

The upcoming Economics in Action describes an actual case of just such a contagion, the wave of bank runs that swept across the United States in the early 1930s. In response to that experience and similar experiences in other countries, the United States and most other modern governments have established a system of bank regulations that protect depositors and prevent most bank runs. We'll encounter bank runs again in Chapter 32, which contains an in-depth analysis of financial crises and their aftermath.

Bank Regulation

Should you worry about losing money in the United States due to a bank run? No. After the banking crises of the 1930s, the United States and most other countries put into place a system designed to protect depositors and the economy as a whole against bank runs. This system has four main features: *deposit insurance, capital requirements, reserve requirements,* and, in addition, banks have access to the *discount window,* a source of cash when it's needed.

1. Deposit Insurance Almost all banks in the United States advertise themselves as a "member of the FDIC"—the Federal Deposit Insurance Corporation. As we learned in Chapter 25, the FDIC provides **deposit insurance,** a guarantee that depositors will be paid even if the bank can't come up with the funds, up to a maximum amount per account. The FDIC currently guarantees the first $250,000 per depositor, per insured bank.

It's important to realize that deposit insurance doesn't just protect depositors if a bank actually fails. The insurance also eliminates the main reason for bank runs: since depositors know their funds are safe even if a bank fails, they have no incentive to rush to pull them out because of a rumor that the bank is in trouble.

2. Capital Requirements Deposit insurance, although it protects the banking system against bank runs, creates a well-known incentive problem. Because depositors are protected from loss, they have no incentive to monitor their bank's financial health, allowing risky behavior by the bank to go undetected. At the same time, the owners of banks have an incentive to engage in overly risky investment behavior, such as making questionable loans at high interest rates. That's because if all goes well, the owners profit; if things go badly, the government covers the losses through federal deposit insurance.

To reduce the incentive for excessive risk taking, regulators require that the owners of banks hold substantially more assets than the value of bank deposits. That way, the bank will still have assets larger than its deposits even if some of its loans go bad, and losses will accrue against the bank owners' assets, not the government. The excess of a bank's assets over its bank deposits and other liabilities is called the *bank's capital*. For example, First Street Bank has capital of $300,000, equal to $300,000/($1,200,000 + $100,000) = 23% of the total value of its assets. In practice, banks' capital is required to equal at least 7% of the value of their assets.

3. Reserve Requirements Another regulation used to reduce the risk of bank runs is **reserve requirements,** rules set by the Federal Reserve that specify the minimum reserve ratio for banks. For example, in the United States, the minimum reserve ratio for checkable bank deposits is 10%.

4. The Discount Window One final protection against bank runs is the fact that the Federal Reserve, which we'll discuss more thoroughly later in this chapter, stands ready to lend money to banks in trouble, an arrangement known as the **discount window.** The ability to borrow money means a bank can avoid being forced to sell its assets at fire-sale prices in order to satisfy the demands of a sudden rush of depositors demanding cash. Instead, it can turn to the Fed and borrow the funds it needs to pay off depositors.

Reserve requirements are rules set by the Federal Reserve that determine the minimum reserve ratio for banks.

The **discount window** is an arrangement in which the Federal Reserve stands ready to lend money to banks in trouble.

ECONOMICS ▶ *in Action*

It's a Wonderful Banking System

Next Christmastime, it's a sure thing that at least one TV channel will show the 1946 film *It's a Wonderful Life*, featuring Jimmy Stewart as George Bailey, a small-town banker whose life is saved by an angel. The movie's climactic scene is a run on Bailey's bank, as fearful depositors rush to take their funds out.

When the movie was made, such scenes were still fresh in Americans' memories. There was a wave of bank runs in late 1930, a second wave in the spring of 1931, and a third wave in early 1933. By the end, more than a third of the nation's banks had failed. To bring the panic to an end, on March 6, 1933, the newly inaugurated president, Franklin Delano Roosevelt, declared a national "bank holiday," closing all banks for a week to give bank regulators time to close unhealthy banks and certify healthy ones.

Since then, regulation has protected the United States and other wealthy countries against most bank runs. In fact, the scene in *It's a Wonderful Life* was already out of date when the movie was made. But recent decades have seen several waves of bank runs in developing countries. For example, bank runs played a role in an economic crisis that swept Southeast Asia in 1997–1998 and in the severe economic crisis in Argentina that began in late 2001. And as explained in Chapter 32, a "panic" with strong resemblance to a wave of bank runs swept world financial markets in 2008.

In July 2008, panicky IndyMac depositors lined up to pull their money out of the troubled California bank.

Notice that we said *most bank runs*. There are some limits on deposit insurance; in particular, in the United States currently only the first $250,000 of an individual depositor's funds in an insured bank is covered. As a result, there can still be a run on a bank perceived as troubled. In fact, that's exactly what happened in July 2008 to IndyMac, a Pasadena-based lender that had made a large number of questionable home loans. As questions about IndyMac's financial soundness were raised, depositors began pulling out funds, forcing federal regulators to step in and close the bank. In Britain the limits on deposit insurance are much lower, which exposed the bank Northern Rock to a classic bank run that same year. Unlike in the bank runs of the 1930s, however, most depositors at both IndyMac and Northern Rock got all their funds back—and the panics at these banks didn't spread to other institutions.

Check Your Understanding 29-2

1. Suppose you are a depositor at First Street Bank. You hear a rumor that the bank has suffered serious losses on its loans. Every depositor knows that the rumor isn't true, but each thinks that most other depositors believe the rumor. Why, in the absence of deposit insurance, could this lead to a bank run? How does deposit insurance change the situation?

2. A con artist has a great idea: he'll open a bank without investing any capital and lend all the deposits at high interest rates to real estate developers. If the real estate market booms, the loans will be repaid and he'll make high profits. If the real estate market goes bust, the loans won't be repaid and the bank will fail—but he will not lose any of his own wealth. How would modern bank regulation frustrate his scheme?

Solutions appear at back of book.

Determining the Money Supply

Without banks, there would be no checkable deposits, so the quantity of currency in circulation would equal the money supply. In that case, the money supply would be solely determined by whoever controls government minting and printing presses. But banks do exist, and through their creation of checkable bank deposits they affect the money supply in two ways.

1. Banks remove some currency from circulation: dollar bills that are sitting in bank vaults, as opposed to sitting in people's wallets, aren't part of the money supply.

2. Much more importantly, banks create money by accepting deposits and making loans—that is, they make the money supply larger than just the value of currency in circulation.

Our next topic is how banks create money and what determines the amount of money they create.

How Banks Create Money

To see how banks create money, let's examine what happens when someone decides to deposit currency in a bank. Consider the example of Silas, a miser, who keeps a shoebox full of cash under his bed. Suppose Silas realizes that it would be safer, as well as more convenient, to deposit that cash in the bank and to use his debit card when shopping. Assume that he deposits $1,000 into a checkable account at First Street Bank. What effect will Silas's actions have on the money supply?

Panel (a) of Figure 29-4 shows the initial effect of his deposit. First Street Bank credits Silas with $1,000 in his account, so the economy's checkable bank deposits rise by $1,000. Meanwhile, Silas's cash goes into the vault, raising First Street's reserves by $1,000 as well.

This initial transaction has no effect on the money supply. Currency in circulation, part of the money supply, falls by $1,000; checkable bank deposits, also part of the money supply, rise by the same amount.

FIGURE 29-4   Effect on the Money Supply of Turning Cash into a Checkable Deposit at First Street Bank

(a) Initial Effect Before Bank Makes a New Loan

Assets		Liabilities	
Loans	No change	Checkable deposits	+$1,000
Reserves	+$1,000		

(b) Effect When Bank Makes a New Loan

Assets		Liabilities	
Loans	+$900	No change	
Reserves	−$900		

When Silas deposits $1,000 (which had been stashed under his bed) into a checkable bank account, there is initially no effect on the money supply: currency in circulation falls by $1,000, but checkable bank deposits rise by $1,000. The corresponding entries on the bank's T-account, depicted in panel (a), show deposits initially rising by $1,000 and the bank's reserves initially rising by $1,000. In the second stage, depicted in panel (b), the bank holds 10% of Silas's deposit ($100) as reserves and lends out the rest ($900) to Maya. As a result, its reserves fall by $900 and its loans increase by $900. Its liabilities, including Silas's $1,000 deposit, are unchanged. The money supply, the sum of checkable bank deposits and currency in circulation, has now increased by $900—the $900 now held by Maya.

But this is not the end of the story because First Street Bank can now lend out part of Silas's deposit. Assume that it holds 10% of Silas's deposit—$100—in reserves and lends the rest out in cash to Silas's neighbor, Maya. The effect of this second stage is shown in panel (b). First Street's deposits remain unchanged, and so does the value of its assets. But the composition of its assets changes: by making the loan, it reduces its reserves by $900, so that they are only $100 larger than they were before Silas made his deposit. In the place of the $900 reduction in reserves, the bank has acquired an IOU, its $900 cash loan to Maya.

So by putting $900 of Silas's cash back into circulation by lending it to Maya, First Street Bank has, in fact, increased the money supply. That is, the sum of currency in circulation and checkable bank deposits has risen by $900 compared to what it had been when Silas's cash was still under his bed. Although Silas is still the owner of $1,000, now in the form of a checkable deposit, Maya has the use of $900 in cash from her borrowings.

And this may not be the end of the story. Suppose that Maya uses her cash to buy a television and a DVD player from Acme Merchandise. What does Anne Acme, the store's owner, do with the cash? If she holds on to it, the money supply doesn't increase any further. But suppose she deposits the $900 into a checkable bank deposit—say, at Second Street Bank. Second Street Bank, in turn, will keep only part of that deposit in reserves, lending out the rest, creating still more money.

Assume that Second Street Bank, like First Street Bank, keeps 10% of any bank deposit in reserves and lends out the rest. Then it will keep $90 in reserves and lend out $810 of Anne's deposit to another borrower, further increasing the money supply.

Table 29-1 shows the process of money creation we have described so far. At first the money supply consists only of Silas's $1,000. After he deposits the cash into a checkable bank deposit

TABLE 29-1   How Banks Create Money

	Currency in circulation	Checkable bank deposits	Money supply
First stage: Silas keeps his cash under his bed.	$1,000	$0	$1,000
Second stage: Silas deposits cash in First Street Bank, which lends out $900 to Maya, who then pays it to Anne Acme.	900	1,000	1,900
Third stage: Anne Acme deposits $900 in Second Street Bank, which lends out $810 to another borrower.	810	1,900	2,710

Excess reserves are a bank's reserves over and above its required reserves.

and the bank makes a loan, the money supply rises to $1,900. After the second deposit and the second loan, the money supply rises to $2,710. And the process will, of course, continue from there. (Although we have considered the case in which Silas places his cash in a checkable bank deposit, the results would be the same if he put it into any type of near-money.)

This process of money creation may sound familiar. In Chapter 26 we described the *multiplier process:* an initial increase in real GDP leads to a rise in consumer spending, which leads to a further rise in real GDP, which leads to a further rise in consumer spending, and so on. What we have here is another kind of multiplier—the *money multiplier*. Next, we'll learn what determines the size of this multiplier.

Reserves, Bank Deposits, and the Money Multiplier

In tracing out the effect of Silas's deposit in Table 29-1, we assumed that the funds a bank lends out always end up being deposited either in the same bank or in another bank—so funds disbursed as loans come back to the banking system, even if not to the lending bank itself.

In reality, some of these loaned funds may be held by borrowers in their wallets and not deposited in a bank, meaning that some of the loaned amount "leaks" out of the banking system. Such leaks reduce the size of the money multiplier, just as leaks of real income into savings reduce the size of the real GDP multiplier. (Bear in mind, however, that the "leak" here comes from the fact that borrowers keep some of their funds in currency, rather than the fact that consumers save some of their income.)

But let's set that complication aside for a moment and consider how the money supply is determined in a "checkable-deposits-only" monetary system, where funds are always deposited in bank accounts and none are held in wallets as currency. That is, in our checkable-deposits-only monetary system, any and all funds borrowed from a bank are immediately deposited into a checkable bank account. We'll assume that banks are required to satisfy a minimum reserve ratio of 10% and that every bank lends out all of its **excess reserves,** reserves over and above the amount needed to satisfy the minimum reserve ratio.

Now suppose that for some reason a bank suddenly finds itself with $1,000 in excess reserves. What happens? The answer is that the bank will lend out that $1,000, which will end up as a checkable bank deposit somewhere in the banking system, launching a money multiplier process very similar to the process shown in Table 29-1.

"There's money in there that could be used for other purposes."

In the first stage, the bank lends out its excess reserves of $1,000, which becomes a checkable bank deposit somewhere. The bank that receives the $1,000 deposit keeps 10%, or $100, as reserves and lends out the remaining 90%, or $900, which again becomes a checkable bank deposit somewhere. The bank receiving this $900 deposit again keeps 10%, which is $90, as reserves and lends out the remaining $810. The bank receiving this $810 keeps $81 in reserves and lends out the remaining $729, and so on. As a result of this process, the total increase in checkable bank deposits is equal to a sum that looks like:

$$\$1,000 + \$900 + \$810 + \$729 + \ldots$$

We'll use the symbol *rr* for the reserve ratio. More generally, the total increase in checkable bank deposits that is generated when a bank lends out $1,000 in excess reserves is:

(29-1) Increase in checkable bank deposits from $1,000 in excess reserves =
$\$1,000 + (\$1,000 \times (1 - rr)) + (\$1,000 \times (1 - rr)^2) + (\$1,000 \times (1 - rr)^3) + \ldots$

As we saw in Chapter 26, an infinite series of this form can be simplified to:

(29-2) Increase in checkable bank deposits from $1,000 in excess reserves = $1,000/$rr$

Given a reserve ratio of 10%, or 0.1, a $1,000 increase in excess reserves will increase the total value of checkable bank deposits by $1,000/0.1 = $10,000. In fact, in a checkable-deposits-only monetary system, the total value of checkable bank deposits will be equal to the value of bank reserves divided by the reserve ratio. Or to put it a different way, if the reserve ratio is 10%, each $1 of reserves held by a bank supports $1/$rr$ = $1/0.1 = $10 of checkable bank deposits.

> The **monetary base** is the sum of currency in circulation and bank reserves.

The Money Multiplier in Reality

In reality, the determination of the money supply is more complicated than our simple model suggests because it depends not only on the ratio of reserves to bank deposits but also on the fraction of the money supply that individuals choose to hold in the form of currency. In fact, we already saw this in our example of Silas depositing the cash under his bed: when he chose to hold a checkable bank deposit instead of currency, he set in motion an increase in the money supply.

To define the money multiplier in practice, it's important to recognize that the Federal Reserve controls the *sum* of bank reserves and currency in circulation, called the *monetary base*, but it does not control the allocation of that sum between bank reserves and currency in circulation. Consider Silas and his deposit one more time: by taking the cash from under his bed and depositing it in a bank, he reduced the quantity of currency in circulation but increased bank reserves by an equal amount—leaving the *monetary base*, on net, unchanged. The **monetary base,** which is the quantity the monetary authorities control, is the sum of currency in circulation and reserves held by banks.

The monetary base is different from the money supply in two ways. First, bank reserves, which are part of the monetary base, aren't considered part of the money supply. A $1 bill in someone's wallet is considered money because it's available for an individual to spend, but a $1 bill held as bank reserves in a bank vault or deposited at the Federal Reserve isn't considered part of the money supply because it's not available for spending. Second, checkable bank deposits, which are part of the money supply because they are available for spending, aren't part of the monetary base.

Figure 29-5 shows the two concepts schematically. The circle on the left represents the monetary base, consisting of bank reserves plus currency in circulation.

FIGURE 29-5   The Monetary Base and the Money Supply

The monetary base is equal to bank reserves plus currency in circulation. It is different from the money supply, consisting mainly of checkable or near-checkable bank deposits plus currency in circulation. Each dollar of bank reserves backs several dollars of bank deposits, making the money supply larger than the monetary base.

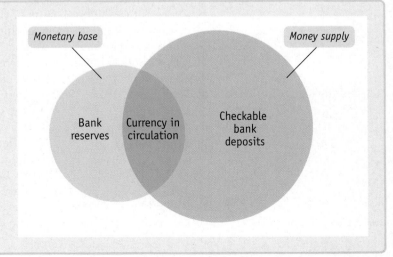

The **money multiplier** is the ratio of the money supply to the monetary base.

The circle on the right represents the money supply, consisting mainly of currency in circulation plus checkable or near-checkable bank deposits. As the figure indicates, currency in circulation is part of both the monetary base and the money supply. But bank reserves aren't part of the money supply, and checkable or near-checkable bank deposits aren't part of the monetary base. In practice, most of the monetary base actually consists of currency in circulation, which also makes up about half of the money supply.

Now we can formally define the **money multiplier:** it's the ratio of the money supply to the monetary base. Before the financial crisis of 2008, the money multiplier was about 1.6; after the crisis it fell to about 0.7. Even before the crisis it was a lot smaller than $1/0.1 = 10$, the money multiplier in a checkable-deposits-only system with a reserve ratio of 10% (the minimum required ratio for most checkable deposits in the United States). The reason the actual money multiplier was so small arises from the fact that people hold significant amounts of cash, and a dollar of currency in circulation, unlike a dollar in reserves, doesn't support multiple dollars of the money supply. In fact, before the crisis currency in circulation accounted for more than 90% of the monetary base. At the end of 2013, however, currency in circulation was less than a third of the monetary base. What had happened?

The answer is that the financial crisis created an abnormal situation. As explained later in this chapter, and at greater length in Chapter 32, a very abnormal situation developed after Lehman Brothers, a key financial institution, failed in September 2008. Banks, seeing few opportunities for safe, profitable lending, began parking large sums at the Federal Reserve in the form of deposits—deposits that counted as part of the monetary base. As a result, currency in circulation no longer dominated the monetary base, and thanks to all those deposits at the Fed the monetary base was actually larger than M1, with the money multiplier therefore less than 1.

ECONOMICS ▶ in Action

Multiplying Money Down

In our hypothetical example illustrating how banks create money, we described Silas the miser taking the currency from under his bed and turning it into a checkable bank deposit. This led to an increase in the money supply, as banks engaged in successive waves of lending backed by Silas's funds. It follows that if something happened to make Silas revert to old habits, taking his money out of the bank and putting it back under his bed, the result would be less lending and, ultimately, a decline in the money supply. That's exactly what happened as a result of the bank runs of the 1930s.

Table 29-2 shows what happened between 1929 and 1933, as bank failures shook the public's confidence in the banking system. The second column shows the public's holdings of currency. This increased sharply, as many Americans decided that money under the bed was safer than money in the bank after all. The third column shows the value of checkable bank deposits. This fell sharply, through the multiplier process we have just analyzed, when individuals pulled their cash out of banks. Loans also fell because banks that survived the waves of bank runs increased their excess reserves, just in case another wave began. The fourth column shows the value of M1, the first of the monetary aggregates we described earlier. It fell sharply because the total

TABLE **29-2**	The Effects of Bank Runs, 1929–1933		
	Currency in circulation	Checkable bank deposits	M1
	(billions of dollars)		
1929	$3.90	$22.74	$26.64
1933	5.09	14.82	19.91
Percent change	+31%	−35%	−25%

Source: U.S. Census Bureau (1975), *Historical Statistics of the United States.*

reduction in checkable or near-checkable bank deposits was much larger than the increase in currency in circulation.

Check Your Understanding   29-3

1. Assume that total reserves are equal to $200 and total checkable bank deposits are equal to $1,000. Also assume that the public does not hold any currency. Now suppose that the required reserve ratio falls from 20% to 10%. Trace out how this leads to an expansion in bank deposits.

2. Take the example of Silas depositing his $1,000 in cash into First Street Bank and assume that the required reserve ratio is 10%. But now assume that each time someone receives a bank loan, he or she keeps half the loan in cash. Trace out the resulting expansion in the money supply.

Solutions appear at back of book.

The Federal Reserve System

Who's in charge of ensuring that banks maintain enough reserves? Who decides how large the monetary base will be? The answer, in the United States, is an institution known as the Federal Reserve (or, informally, as "the Fed"). The Federal Reserve is a **central bank**—an institution that oversees and regulates the banking system and controls the monetary base. Other central banks include the Bank of England, the Bank of Japan, and the European Central Bank, or ECB. The ECB acts as a common central bank for 18 European countries: Austria, Belgium, Cyprus, Estonia, Finland, France, Germany, Greece, Ireland, Italy, Latvia, Luxembourg, Malta, the Netherlands, Portugal, Slovakia, Slovenia, and Spain. The world's oldest central bank, by the way, is Sweden's Sveriges Riksbank, which awards the Nobel Prize in economics.

The Structure of the Fed

The legal status of the Fed, which was created in 1913, is unusual: it is not exactly part of the U.S. government, but it is not really a private institution either. Strictly speaking, the Federal Reserve system consists of two parts: the Board of Governors and the 12 regional Federal Reserve Banks.

The Board of Governors, which oversees the entire system from its offices in Washington, D.C., is constituted like a government agency: its seven members are appointed by the president and must be approved by the Senate. However, they are appointed for 14-year terms, to insulate them from political pressure in their conduct of monetary policy. (Why this is a potential problem will become clear in the next chapter, when we discuss inflation.) Although the chair is appointed more frequently—every four years—it's traditional for chairs to be reappointed and serve much longer terms. For example, William McChesney Martin was chair of the Fed from 1951 until 1970. Alan Greenspan, appointed in 1987, served as the Fed's chair until 2006, and Ben Bernanke, Greenspan's successor, served until 2014.

The 12 Federal Reserve Banks each serve a region of the country, providing various banking and supervisory services. One of their jobs, for example, is to audit the books of private-sector banks to ensure their financial health. Each regional bank is run by a board of directors chosen from the local banking and business community. The Federal Reserve Bank of New York plays a special role: it carries out *open-market operations*, usually the main tool of monetary policy. Figure 29-6 shows the 12 Federal Reserve districts and the city in which each regional Federal Reserve Bank is located.

A **central bank** is an institution that oversees and regulates the banking system and controls the monetary base.

FIGURE 29-6
The Federal Reserve System
The Federal Reserve system consists
of the Board of Governors in
Washington, D.C., plus 12 regional
Federal Reserve Banks. This map
shows each of the 12 Federal Reserve
districts.

Source: Board of Governors of the Federal
Reserve System.

FIGURE **29-6**

The Federal Reserve System

The Federal Reserve system consists of the Board of Governors in Washington, D.C., plus 12 regional Federal Reserve Banks. This map shows each of the 12 Federal Reserve districts.

Source: Board of Governors of the Federal Reserve System.

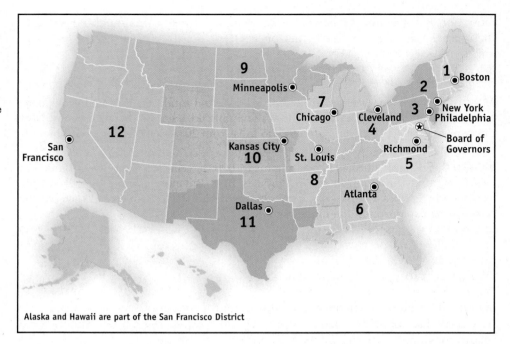

Alaska and Hawaii are part of the San Francisco District

Decisions about monetary policy are made by the Federal Open Market Committee, which consists of the Board of Governors plus five of the regional bank presidents. The president of the Federal Reserve Bank of New York is always on the committee, and the other four seats rotate among the 11 other regional bank presidents. The chairman of the Board of Governors normally also serves as the chairman of the Open Market Committee.

The effect of this complex structure is to create an institution that is ultimately accountable to the voting public because the Board of Governors is chosen by the president and confirmed by the Senate, all of whom are themselves elected officials. But the long terms served by board members, as well as the indirectness of their appointment process, largely insulate them from short-term political pressures.

What the Fed Does: Reserve Requirements and the Discount Rate

The Fed has three main policy tools at its disposal: *reserve requirements,* the *discount rate,* and, most importantly, *open-market operations.*

In our discussion of bank runs, we noted that the Fed sets a minimum reserve ratio requirement, currently equal to 10% for checkable bank deposits. Banks that fail to maintain at least the required reserve ratio on average over a two-week period face penalties.

What does a bank do if it looks as if it has insufficient reserves to meet the Fed's reserve requirement? Normally, it borrows additional reserves from other banks via the **federal funds market,** a financial market that allows banks that fall short of the reserve requirement to borrow reserves (usually just overnight) from banks that are holding excess reserves. The interest rate in this market is determined by supply and demand—but the supply and demand for bank reserves are both strongly affected by Federal Reserve actions. As we'll see in the next chapter, the **federal funds rate,** the interest rate at which funds are borrowed and lent in the federal funds market, plays a key role in modern monetary policy.

Alternatively, banks in need of reserves can borrow from the Fed itself via the *discount window.* The **discount rate** is the rate of interest the Fed charges on

The **federal funds market** allows banks that fall short of the reserve requirement to borrow funds from banks with excess reserves.

The **federal funds rate** is the interest rate determined in the federal funds market.

The **discount rate** is the rate of interest the Fed charges on loans to banks.

those loans. Normally, the discount rate is set 1 percentage point above the federal funds rate in order to discourage banks from turning to the Fed when they are in need of reserves. Beginning in the fall of 2007, however, the Fed reduced the spread between the federal funds rate and the discount rate as part of its response to an ongoing financial crisis, described in the upcoming Economics in Action. As a result, by the spring of 2008 the discount rate was only 0.25 percentage point above the federal funds rate. And in the summer of 2014 the discount rate was still only 0.65 percentage point above the federal funds rate.

In order to alter the money supply, the Fed can change reserve requirements, the discount rate, or both. If the Fed reduces reserve requirements, banks will lend a larger percentage of their deposits, leading to more loans and an increase in the money supply via the money multiplier. Alternatively, if the Fed increases reserve requirements, banks are forced to reduce their lending, leading to a fall in the money supply via the money multiplier.

If the Fed reduces the spread between the discount rate and the federal funds rate, the cost to banks of being short of reserves falls; banks respond by increasing their lending, and the money supply increases via the money multiplier. If the Fed increases the spread between the discount rate and the federal funds rate, bank lending falls—and so will the money supply via the money multiplier.

Under current practice, however, the Fed doesn't use changes in reserve requirements to actively manage the money supply. The last significant change in reserve requirements was in 1992. The Fed normally doesn't use the discount rate either, although, as we mentioned earlier, there was a temporary surge in lending through the discount window beginning in 2007 in response to a financial crisis. Ordinarily, monetary policy is conducted almost exclusively using the Fed's third policy tool: open-market operations.

> An **open-market operation** is a purchase or sale of government debt by the Fed.

Open-Market Operations

Like the banks it oversees, the Federal Reserve has assets and liabilities. The Fed's assets normally consist of holdings of debt issued by the U.S. government, mainly short-term U.S. government bonds with a maturity of less than one year, known as U.S. Treasury bills. Remember, the Fed isn't exactly part of the U.S. government, so U.S. Treasury bills held by the Fed are a liability of the government but an asset of the Fed. The Fed's liabilities consist of currency in circulation and bank reserves. Figure 29-7 summarizes the normal assets and liabilities of the Fed in the form of a T-account.

In an **open-market operation** the Federal Reserve buys or sells U.S. Treasury bills, normally through a transaction with *commercial banks*—banks that mainly make business loans, as opposed to home loans. The Fed never buys U.S. Treasury bills directly from the federal government. There's a good reason for this: when a central bank buys government debt directly from the government, it is lending directly to the government—in effect, the central bank is printing money to finance the government's budget deficit. As we'll see later in the book, this has historically been a formula for disastrously high levels of inflation.

FIGURE **29-7** **The Federal Reserve's Assets and Liabilities**

The Federal Reserve holds its assets mostly in short-term government bonds called U.S. Treasury bills. Its liabilities are the monetary base—currency in circulation plus bank reserves.

Assets	Liabilities
Government debt (Treasury bills)	Monetary base (currency in circulation + bank reserves)

The two panels of Figure 29-8 show the changes in the financial position of both the Fed and commercial banks that result from open-market operations. When the Fed buys U.S. Treasury bills from a commercial bank, it pays by crediting the bank's reserve account by an amount equal to the value of the Treasury bills. This is illustrated in panel (a): the Fed buys $100 million of U.S. Treasury bills from commercial banks, which increases the monetary base by $100 million because it increases bank reserves by $100 million. When the Fed sells U.S. Treasury bills to commercial banks, it debits the banks' accounts, reducing their reserves. This is shown in panel (b), where the Fed sells $100 million of U.S. Treasury bills. Here, bank reserves and the monetary base decrease.

You might wonder where the Fed gets the funds to purchase U.S. Treasury bills from banks. The answer is that it simply creates them with a stroke of the pen—or, more likely, a click of the mouse—that credits the banks' accounts with extra reserves. (The Fed prints money to pay for Treasury bills only when banks want the additional reserves in the form of currency.) Remember, the modern dollar is fiat money, which isn't backed by anything. So the Fed can create additional monetary base at its own discretion.

The change in bank reserves caused by an open-market operation doesn't directly affect the money supply. Instead, it starts the money multiplier in motion. After the $100 million increase in reserves shown in panel (a) of Figure 29-8, commercial banks would lend out their additional reserves, immediately increasing the money supply by $100 million. Some of those loans would be deposited back into the banking system, increasing reserves again and permitting a further round of loans, and so on, leading to a rise in the money supply. An open-market sale has the reverse effect: bank reserves fall, requiring banks to reduce their loans, leading to a fall in the money supply.

FIGURE **29-8**   Open-Market Operations by the Federal Reserve

(a) An Open-Market Purchase of $100 Million

Federal Reserve	Assets		Liabilities	
	Treasury bills	+$100 million	Monetary base	+$100 million

Commercial banks	Assets		Liabilities
	Treasury bills	−$100 million	No change
	Reserves	+$100 million	

(b) An Open-Market Sale of $100 Million

Federal Reserve	Assets		Liabilities	
	Treasury bills	−$100 million	Monetary base	−$100 million

Commercial banks	Assets		Liabilities
	Treasury bills	+$100 million	No change
	Reserves	−$100 million	

In panel (a), the Federal Reserve increases the monetary base by purchasing U.S. Treasury bills from private commercial banks in an open-market operation. Here, a $100 million purchase of U.S. Treasury bills by the Federal Reserve is paid for by a $100 million addition to private bank reserves, generating a $100 million increase in the monetary base. This will ultimately lead to an increase in the money supply via the money multiplier as banks lend out some of these new reserves. In panel (b), the Federal Reserve reduces the monetary base by selling U.S. Treasury bills to private commercial banks in an open-market operation. Here, a $100 million sale of U.S. Treasury bills leads to a $100 million reduction in private bank reserves, resulting in a $100 million decrease in the monetary base. This will ultimately lead to a fall in the money supply via the money multiplier as banks reduce their loans in response to a fall in their reserves.

FOR INQUIRING MINDS | Who Gets the Interest on the Fed's Assets?

As we've just learned, the Fed owns a lot of assets—Treasury bills—that it bought from commercial banks in exchange for monetary base in the form of credits to banks' reserve accounts. These assets pay interest. Yet the Fed's liabilities consist mainly of the monetary base, liabilities on which the Fed normally *doesn't* pay interest. So the Fed is, in effect, an institution that has the privilege of borrowing funds at a zero interest rate and lending them out at a positive interest rate. That sounds like a pretty profitable business. Who gets the profits?

The answer is, you do—or rather, U.S. taxpayers do. The Fed keeps some of the interest it receives to finance its

operations but turns most of it over to the U.S. Treasury. For example, in 2013 the total income of the Federal Reserve system was $79.5 billion, almost all in the form of interest on its assets, of which $77.7 billion was returned to the Treasury.

We can now finish the chapter's opening story—the impact of those forged dollars printed in Peru. When, say, a fake $20 bill enters circulation, it has the same economic effect as a real $20 bill printed by the U.S. government. That is, as long as nobody catches the forgery, the fake bill serves, for all practical purposes, as part of the monetary base.

Meanwhile, the Fed decides on the size of the monetary base based on economic considerations—in particular, the Fed normally doesn't let the monetary base get too large because that can cause higher inflation. So every fake $20 bill that enters circulation means that the Fed prints one less real $20 bill. When the Fed prints a $20 bill legally, however, it gets Treasury bills in return—and the interest on those bills helps pay for the U.S. government's expenses. So a counterfeit $20 bill reduces the amount of Treasury bills the Fed can acquire and thereby reduces the interest payments going to the Fed and the U.S. Treasury. Taxpayers, then, bear the real cost of counterfeiting. ■

Economists often say, loosely, that the Fed controls the money supply—checkable deposits plus currency in circulation. In fact, it controls only the monetary base—bank reserves plus currency in circulation. But by increasing or reducing the monetary base, the Fed can exert a powerful influence on both the money supply and interest rates. This influence is the basis of monetary policy, the subject of our next chapter.

The European Central Bank

As we noted earlier, the Fed is only one of a number of central banks around the world, and it's much younger than Sweden's Sveriges Riksbank and Britain's Bank of England. In general, other central banks operate in much the same way as the Fed. That's especially true of the only other central bank that rivals the Fed in terms of importance to the world economy: the European Central Bank.

The European Central Bank, known as the ECB, was created in January 1999 when 11 European nations abandoned their national currencies and adopted the euro as their common currency and placed their joint monetary policy in the ECB's hands. (Seven more countries have joined since 1999.) The ECB instantly became an extremely important institution: although no single European nation has an economy anywhere near as large as that of the United States, the combined economies of the eurozone, the group of countries that have adopted the euro as their currency, are roughly as big as the U.S. economy. As a result, the ECB and the Fed are the two giants of the monetary world.

Like the Fed, the ECB has a special status: it's not a private institution, but it's not exactly a government agency either. In fact, it can't be a government agency because there is no pan-European government! Luckily for puzzled Americans, there are strong analogies between European central banking and the Federal Reserve system.

First of all, the ECB, which is located in the German city of Frankfurt, isn't really the counterpart of the whole Federal Reserve system: it's the equivalent of the Board of Governors in Washington. The European counterparts of the regional Federal Reserve Banks are Europe's national central banks: the Bank of France, the Bank of Italy, and so on. Until 1999, each of these national banks was its country's equivalent to the Fed. For example, the Bank of France controlled the French monetary base.

Today these national banks, like regional Feds, provide various financial services to local banks and businesses and conduct open-market operations, but the making of monetary policy has moved upstream to the ECB. Still, the various European national central banks aren't small institutions: in total, they employ more than 50,000 people; in 2014, the ECB employed only around 2,000.

In the eurozone, each country chooses who runs its own national central bank. The ECB's Executive Board is the counterpart of the Fed's Board of Governors; its members are chosen by unanimous consent of the eurozone national governments. The counterpart of the Federal Open Market Committee is the ECB's Governing Council. Just as the Fed's Open Market Committee consists of the Board of Governors plus a rotating group of regional Fed presidents, the ECB's Governing Council consists of the Executive Board plus the heads of the national central banks.

Like the Fed, the ECB is ultimately answerable to voters, but given the fragmentation of political forces across national boundaries, it appears to be even more insulated than the Fed from short-term political pressures.

ECONOMICS ▶ *in Action*

The Fed's Balance Sheet, Normal and Abnormal

Figure 29-7 showed a simplified version of the Fed's balance sheet. Here, liabilities consisted entirely of the monetary base and assets consisted entirely of Treasury bills. This is an oversimplification because the Fed's operations are more complicated in reality and its balance sheet contains a number of additional things. But, in normal times, Figure 29-7 is a reasonable approximation: the monetary base typically accounts for 90% of the Fed's liabilities, and 90% of its assets are in the form of claims on the U.S. Treasury (as in Treasury bills).

But in late 2007 it became painfully clear that we were no longer in normal times. The source of the turmoil was the bursting of a huge housing bubble, described in Chapter 25, which led to massive losses for financial institutions that had made mortgage loans or held mortgage-related assets. This led to a widespread loss of confidence in the financial system.

As we'll describe in more detail in the next section, not only standard deposit-taking banks were in trouble, but also nondepository financial institutions—financial institutions that did not accept customer deposits. Because they carried a lot of debt, faced huge losses from the collapse of the housing bubble, and held illiquid assets, panic hit these "nonbank banks." Within hours the financial system was frozen as financial institutions experienced what were essentially bank runs.

For example, in 2008, many investors became worried about the health of Bear Stearns, a Wall Street nondepository financial institution that engaged in complex financial deals, buying and selling financial assets with borrowed funds. When confidence in Bear Stearns dried up, the firm found itself unable to raise the funds it needed to deliver on its end of these deals and it quickly spiraled into collapse.

The Fed sprang into action to contain what was becoming a meltdown across the entire financial sector. It greatly expanded its discount window—making huge loans to deposit-taking banks as well as nondepository financial institutions such as Wall Street financial firms. This gave financial institutions the liquidity that the financial market had now denied them. And as these firms took advantage of the ability to borrow cheaply from the Fed, they pledged their assets on hand as collateral—a motley collection of real estate loans, business loans, and so on.

Examining Figure 29-9, we see that starting in mid-2008, the Fed sharply reduced its holdings of traditional securities like Treasury bills, as its lending to financial institutions skyrocketed. "Lending to financial institutions" refers to discount window lending, but also loans the Fed made directly to firms like Bear Stearns. "Liquidity to key credit markets" covers purchases by the Fed of assets like corporate bonds, which was necessary to keep interest rates on loans to firms from soaring. Finally, "Federal agency debt" is the debt of Fannie Mae and Freddie Mac, the government-sponsored home mortgage agencies, which the Fed was also compelled to buy in order to prevent collapse in the mortgage market.

As the crisis subsided in late 2009, the Fed didn't return to its traditional asset holdings. Instead, it shifted into long-term Treasury bills and increased its purchases of Federal agency debt. The whole episode was very unusual—a major departure from the way in which the Fed normally conducts business, but one that it deemed necessary to stave off financial and economic collapse. It was also a graphic illustration of the fact that the Fed does much more than just determine the size of the monetary base.

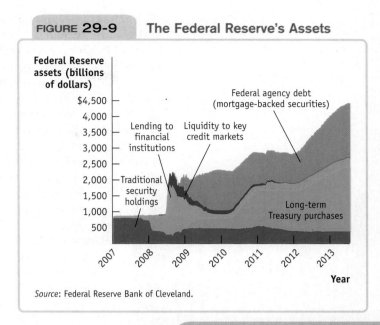

FIGURE 29-9   **The Federal Reserve's Assets**

Source: Federal Reserve Bank of Cleveland.

Check Your Understanding   29-4

1. Assume that any money lent by a bank is always deposited back in the banking system as a checkable deposit and that the reserve ratio is 10%. Trace out the effects of a $100 million open-market purchase of U.S. Treasury bills by the Fed on the value of checkable bank deposits. What is the size of the money multiplier?

Solution appears at back of book.

The Evolution of the American Banking System

Up to this point, we have been describing the U.S. banking system and how it works. To fully understand that system, however, it is helpful to understand how and why it was created—a story that is closely intertwined with the story of how and when things went wrong. The key elements of twenty-first-century U.S. banking weren't created out of thin air: efforts to change both the regulations that govern banking and the Federal Reserve system that began in 2008 have propelled financial reform to the forefront. This reform promises to continue reshaping the financial system well into future years.

The Crisis in American Banking in the Early Twentieth Century

The creation of the Federal Reserve system in 1913 marked the beginning of the modern era of American banking. From 1864 until 1913, American banking was dominated by a federally regulated system of national banks. They alone were allowed to issue currency, and the currency notes they issued were printed by the federal government with uniform size and design. How much currency a national bank could issue depended on its capital. Although this system was an improvement on the earlier period in which banks issued their own notes with no uniformity and virtually no regulation, the national banking regime still suffered numerous bank failures and major financial crises—at least one and often two per decade.

The main problem afflicting the system was that the money supply was not sufficiently responsive: it was difficult to shift currency around the country to respond quickly to local economic changes. (In particular, there was often a tug-of-war between New York City banks and rural banks for adequate amounts of currency.) Rumors that a bank had insufficient currency to satisfy demands for withdrawals would quickly lead to a bank run. A bank run would then spark a contagion, setting off runs at other nearby banks, sowing widespread panic and devastation in the local economy. In response, bankers in some locations pooled their resources to create local clearinghouses that would jointly guarantee a member's liabilities in the event of a panic, and some state governments began offering deposit insurance on their banks' deposits.

However, the cause of the Panic of 1907 was different from those of previous crises; in fact, its cause was eerily similar to the roots of the 2008 crisis. Ground zero of the 1907 panic was New York City, but the consequences devastated the entire country, leading to a deep four-year recession.

The crisis originated in institutions in New York known as trusts, bank-like institutions that accepted deposits but that were originally intended to manage only inheritances and estates for wealthy clients. Because these trusts were supposed to engage only in low-risk activities, they were less regulated, had lower reserve requirements, and had lower cash reserves than national banks.

However, as the American economy boomed during the first decade of the twentieth century, trusts began speculating in real estate and the stock market, areas of speculation forbidden to national banks. Less regulated than national banks, trusts were able to pay their depositors higher returns. Yet trusts took a free ride on national banks' reputation for soundness, with depositors considering them equally safe. As a result, trusts grew rapidly: by 1907, the total assets of trusts in New York City were as large as those of national banks. Meanwhile, the trusts declined to join the New York Clearinghouse, a consortium of New York City national banks that guaranteed one anothers' soundness; that would have required the trusts to hold higher cash reserves, reducing their profits.

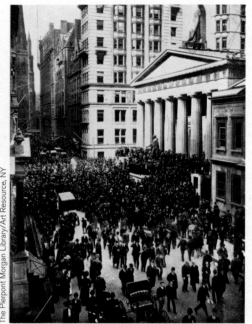

In both the Panic of 1907 and the financial crisis of 2008, large losses from risky speculation destabilized the banking system.

The Panic of 1907 began with the failure of the Knickerbocker Trust, a large New York City trust that failed when it suffered massive losses in unsuccessful stock market speculation. Quickly, other New York trusts came under pressure, and frightened depositors began queuing in long lines to withdraw their funds. The New York Clearinghouse declined to step in and lend to the trusts, and even healthy trusts came under serious assault. Within two days, a dozen major trusts had gone under. Credit markets froze, and the stock market fell dramatically as stock traders were unable to get credit to finance their trades and business confidence evaporated.

Fortunately, New York City's wealthiest man, the banker J. P. Morgan, quickly stepped in to stop the panic. Understanding that the crisis was spreading and would soon engulf healthy institutions, trusts and banks alike, he worked with other bankers, wealthy men such as John D. Rockefeller, and the U.S. Secretary of the Treasury to shore up the reserves of banks and trusts so they could withstand the onslaught of withdrawals. Once people were assured that they could withdraw their money, the panic ceased. Although the panic itself lasted little more than a week, it and the stock market collapse decimated the economy. A four-year recession ensued, with production falling 11% and unemployment rising from 3% to 8%.

Responding to Banking Crises: The Creation of the Federal Reserve

Concerns over the frequency of banking crises and the unprecedented role of J. P. Morgan in saving the financial system prompted the federal government to initiate banking reform. In 1913 the national banking system was eliminated and the Federal Reserve system was created as a way to compel all deposit-taking institutions to hold adequate reserves and to open their accounts to inspection by regulators. The Panic of 1907 convinced many that the time for centralized control of bank reserves had come. In addition, the Federal Reserve was given the sole right to issue currency in order to make the money supply sufficiently responsive to satisfy economic conditions around the country.

Although the new regime standardized and centralized the holding of bank reserves, it did not eliminate the potential for bank runs because banks' reserves were still less than the total value of their deposits. The potential for more bank runs became a reality during the Great Depression. Plunging commodity prices hit American farmers particularly hard, precipitating a series of bank runs in 1930, 1931, and 1933, each of which started at midwestern banks and then spread throughout the country.

After the failure of a particularly large bank in 1930, federal officials realized that the economy-wide effects compelled them to take a less hands-off approach and to intervene more vigorously. In 1932, the Reconstruction Finance Corporation (RFC) was established and given the authority to make loans to banks in order to stabilize the banking sector. Also, the Glass-Steagall Act of 1933, which created federal deposit insurance and increased the ability of banks to borrow from the Federal Reserve system, was passed. However, the beast had not yet been tamed. Banks became fearful of borrowing from the RFC because doing so signaled weakness to the public.

As we noted earlier, during the catastrophic bank run of 1933, the new president, Franklin Delano Roosevelt, was inaugurated. He immediately declared a "bank holiday," closing all banks until regulators could get a handle on the problem.

In March 1933, emergency measures were adopted that gave the RFC extraordinary powers to stabilize and restructure the banking industry by providing capital to banks through either loans or outright purchases of bank shares. With the new rules, regulators closed nonviable banks and recapitalized viable ones by allowing the RFC to buy preferred shares in banks (shares that gave the U.S. government more rights than regular shareholders) and by greatly expanding banks' ability to borrow from the Federal Reserve. By 1933, the RFC had invested over $16.2 billion (2010 dollars) in bank capital—one-third of the total capital of all banks in the United States at that time—and purchased shares in almost one-half of all banks. The RFC loaned more than $32.4 billion (2010 dollars) to banks during this period.

Economic historians uniformly agree that the banking crises of the early 1930s greatly exacerbated the severity of the Great Depression, rendering monetary policy ineffective as the banking sector broke down and currency, withdrawn from banks and stashed under beds, reduced the money supply.

Although the powerful actions of the RFC stabilized the banking industry, new legislation was needed to prevent future banking crises. The Glass-Steagall Act of 1933 separated banks into two categories, **commercial banks,** depository banks that accepted deposits and were covered by deposit insurance, and **investment banks,** which engaged in creating and trading financial assets such as stocks and corporate bonds but were not covered by deposit insurance because their activities were considered more risky.

Regulation Q prevented commercial banks from paying interest on checking accounts in the belief that this would promote unhealthy competition between banks. In addition, investment banks were much more lightly regulated than commercial banks. The most important measure for the prevention of bank runs, however, was the adoption of federal deposit insurance (with an original limit of $2,500 per deposit).

A **commercial bank** accepts deposits and is covered by deposit insurance.

An **investment bank** trades in financial assets and is not covered by deposit insurance.

Like FDR, President Obama, shown here meeting with economic advisers, was faced with a major financial crisis upon taking office.

Official White House Photo by Pete Souza

A **savings and loan (thrift)** is another type of deposit-taking bank, usually specialized in issuing home loans.

A financial institution engages in **leverage** when it finances its investments with borrowed funds.

These measures were clearly successful, and the United States enjoyed a long period of financial and banking stability. As memories of the bad old days dimmed, Depression-era bank regulations were lifted. In 1980, Regulation Q was eliminated; by 1999, the Glass-Steagall Act had been so weakened that offering services like trading financial assets was no longer off-limits to commercial banks.

The Savings and Loan Crisis of the 1980s

Along with banks, the banking industry also included **savings and loans** (also called S&Ls or **thrifts**), institutions designed to accept savings and turn them into long-term mortgages for home-buyers. S&Ls were covered by federal deposit insurance and were tightly regulated for safety. However, trouble hit in the 1970s, as high inflation led savers to withdraw their funds from low-interest-paying S&L accounts and put them into higher-interest-paying money market accounts. In addition, the high inflation rate severely eroded the value of the S&Ls' assets, the long-term mortgages they held on their books.

In order to improve S&Ls' competitive position vis-à-vis banks, Congress eased regulations to allow S&Ls to undertake much more risky investments in addition to long-term home mortgages. However, the new freedom did not bring with it increased oversight, leaving S&Ls with less oversight than banks. Not surprisingly, during the real estate boom of the 1970s and 1980s, S&Ls engaged in overly risky real estate lending. Also, corruption occurred as some S&L executives used their institutions as private piggy banks.

Unfortunately, during the late 1970s and early 1980s, political interference from Congress kept insolvent S&Ls open when a bank in a comparable situation would have been quickly shut down by bank regulators. By the early 1980s, a large number of S&Ls had failed. Because accounts were covered by federal deposit insurance, the liabilities of a failed S&L were now liabilities of the federal government, and depositors had to be paid from taxpayer funds. From 1986 through 1995, the federal government closed over 1,000 failed S&Ls, costing U.S. taxpayers over $124 billion.

In a classic case of shutting the barn door after the horse has escaped, in 1989 Congress put in place comprehensive oversight of S&L activities. It also empowered Fannie Mae and Freddie Mac to take over much of the home mortgage lending previously done by S&Ls. *Fannie Mae* and *Freddie Mac* are quasi-governmental agencies created during the Great Depression to make homeownership more affordable for low- and moderate-income households. It has been calculated that the S&L crisis helped cause a steep slowdown in the finance and real estate industries, leading to the recession of the early 1990s.

Back to the Future: The Financial Crisis of 2008

The financial crisis of 2008 shared features of previous crises. Like the Panic of 1907 and the S&L crisis, it involved institutions that were not as strictly regulated as deposit-taking banks, as well as excessive speculation. Like the crises of the early 1930s, it involved a U.S. government that was reluctant to take aggressive action until the scale of the devastation became clear.

In addition, by the late 1990s, advances in technology and financial innovation had created yet another systemic weakness that played a central role in 2008. The story of Long-Term Capital Management, or LTCM, highlights these problems.

Long-Term Capital (Mis)Management Created in 1994, LTCM was a hedge fund, a private investment partnership open only to wealthy individuals and institutions. Hedge funds are virtually unregulated, allowing them to make much riskier investments than mutual funds, which are open to the average investor. Using vast amounts of **leverage**—that is, borrowed money—in order to increase its returns, LTCM used sophisticated computer models to make money by taking advantage of small differences in asset prices in global financial markets to buy at a lower price and sell at a higher price. In one year, LTCM made a return as high as 40%.

LTCM was also heavily involved in derivatives, complex financial instruments that are constructed—derived—from the obligations of more basic financial assets. Derivatives are popular investment tools because they are cheaper to trade than basic financial assets and can be constructed to suit a buyer's or seller's particular needs. Yet their complexity can make it extremely hard to measure their value. LTCM believed that its computer models allowed it to accurately gauge the risk in the huge bets that it was undertaking in derivatives using borrowed money.

However, LTCM's computer models hadn't factored in a series of financial crises in Asia and in Russia during 1997 and 1998. Through its large borrowing, LTCM had become such a big player in global financial markets that attempts to sell its assets depressed the prices of what it was trying to sell. As the markets fell around the world and LTCM's panic-stricken investors demanded the return of their funds, LTCM's losses mounted as it tried to sell assets to satisfy those demands. Quickly, its operations collapsed because it could no longer borrow money and other parties refused to trade with it. Financial markets around the world froze in panic.

The Federal Reserve realized that allowing LTCM's remaining assets to be sold at panic-stricken prices presented a grave risk to the entire financial system through the **balance sheet effect:** as sales of assets by LTCM depressed asset prices all over the world, other firms would see the value of their balance sheets fall as assets held on these balance sheets declined in value. Moreover, falling asset prices meant the value of assets held by borrowers on their balance sheets would fall below a critical threshold, leading to a default on the terms of their credit contracts and forcing creditors to call in their loans. This in turn would lead to more sales of assets as borrowers tried to raise cash to repay their loans, more credit defaults, and more loans called in, creating a **vicious cycle of deleveraging.**

The Federal Reserve Bank of New York arranged a $3.625 billion bailout of LTCM in 1998, in which other private institutions took on shares of LTCM's assets and obligations, liquidated them in an orderly manner, and eventually turned a small profit. Quick action by the Federal Reserve Bank of New York prevented LTCM from sparking a contagion, yet virtually all of LTCM's investors were wiped out.

Subprime Lending and the Housing Bubble

After the LTCM crisis, U.S. financial markets stabilized. They remained more or less stable even as stock prices fell sharply from 2000 to 2002 and the U.S. economy went into recession. During the recovery from the 2001 recession, however, the seeds for another financial crisis were planted.

The story begins with low interest rates: by 2003, U.S. interest rates were at historically low levels, partly because of Federal Reserve policy and partly because of large inflows of capital from other countries, especially China. These low interest rates helped cause a boom in housing, which in turn led the U.S. economy out of recession. As housing boomed, however, financial institutions began taking on growing risks—risks that were not well understood.

Traditionally, people were only able to borrow money to buy homes if they could show that they had sufficient income to meet the mortgage payments. Home loans to people who don't meet the usual criteria for borrowing, called **subprime lending,** were only a minor part of overall lending. But in the booming housing market of 2003–2006, subprime lending started to seem like a safe bet. Since housing prices kept rising, borrowers who couldn't make their

The **balance sheet effect** is the reduction in a firm's net worth due to falling asset prices.

A **vicious cycle of deleveraging** takes place when asset sales to cover losses produce negative balance sheet effects on other firms and force creditors to call in their loans, forcing sales of more assets and causing further declines in asset prices.

Subprime lending is lending to home-buyers who don't meet the usual criteria for being able to afford their payments.

In **securitization,** a pool of loans is assembled and shares of that pool are sold to investors.

"Honey we're homeless."

mortgage payments could always pay off their mortgages, if necessary, by selling their homes. As a result, subprime lending exploded.

Who was making these subprime loans? For the most part, it wasn't traditional banks lending out depositors' money. Instead, most of the loans were made by "loan originators," who quickly sold mortgages to other investors. These sales were made possible by a process known as **securitization:** financial institutions assembled pools of loans and sold shares in the income from these pools. These shares were considered relatively safe investments, since it was considered unlikely that large numbers of home-buyers would default on their payments at the same time.

But that's exactly what happened. The housing boom turned out to be a bubble, and when home prices started falling in late 2006, many subprime borrowers were unable either to meet their mortgage payments or sell their houses for enough to pay off their mortgages. As a result, investors in securities backed by subprime mortgages started taking heavy losses. Many of the mortgage-backed assets were held by financial institutions, including banks and other institutions playing bank-like roles. Like the trusts that played a key role in the Panic of 1907, these "nonbank banks" were less regulated than commercial banks, which allowed them to offer higher returns to investors but left them extremely vulnerable in a crisis. Mortgage-related losses, in turn, led to a collapse of trust in the financial system.

Figure 29-10 shows one measure of this loss of trust: the TED spread, which is the difference between the interest rate on three-month loans that banks make to each other and the interest rate the federal government pays on three-month bonds. Since government bonds are considered extremely safe, the TED spread shows how much risk banks think they're taking on when lending to each other. Normally the spread is around a quarter of a percentage point, but it shot up in August 2007 and surged to an unprecedented 4.58 percentage points in October 2008, before returning to more normal levels in mid-2009.

Crisis and Response The collapse of trust in the financial system, combined with the large losses suffered by financial firms, led to a severe cycle of deleveraging and a credit crunch for the economy as a whole. Firms found it difficult to borrow, even for short-term operations; individuals found home loans unavailable and credit card limits reduced.

FIGURE 29-10 | The TED Spread

The TED spread is the difference between the interest rate at which banks lend to each other and the interest rate on U.S. government debt. It's widely used as a measure of financial stress. The TED spread soared as a result of the financial crisis of 2007–2008.

Sources: British Bankers' Association; Federal Reserve Bank of St. Louis.

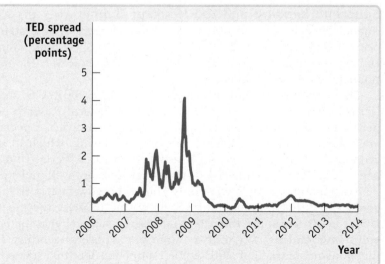

Overall, the negative economic effect of the financial crisis bore a distinct and troubling resemblance to the effects of the banking crisis of the early 1930s, which helped cause the Great Depression. Policy makers noticed the resemblance and tried to prevent a repeat performance. Beginning in August 2007, the Federal Reserve engaged in a series of efforts to provide cash to the financial system, lending funds to a widening range of institutions and buying private-sector debt. The Fed and the Treasury Department also stepped in to rescue individual firms that were deemed too crucial to be allowed to fail, such as the investment bank Bear Stearns and the insurance company AIG.

In September 2008, however, policy makers decided that one major investment bank, Lehman Brothers, could be allowed to fail. They quickly regretted the decision. Within days of Lehman's failure, widespread panic gripped the financial markets, as illustrated by the surge in the TED spread shown in Figure 29-10. In response to the intensified crisis, the U.S. government intervened further to support the financial system, as the U.S. Treasury began "injecting" capital into banks. Injecting capital, in practice, meant that the U.S. government would supply cash to banks in return for shares—in effect, partially nationalizing the financial system.

By the fall of 2010, the financial system appeared to be stabilized, and major institutions had repaid much of the money the federal government had injected during the crisis. It was generally expected that taxpayers would end up losing little if any money. However, the recovery of the banks was not matched by a successful turnaround for the overall economy: although the recession that began in December 2007 officially ended in June 2009, unemployment remained stubbornly high.

The Federal Reserve responded to this troubled situation with novel forms of open-market operations. Conventional open-market operations are limited to short-term government debt, but the Fed believed that this was no longer enough. It provided massive liquidity through discount window lending, as well as buying large quantities of other assets, mainly long-term government debt and debt of Fannie Mae and Freddie Mac, government-sponsored agencies that support home lending. This explains the surge in Fed assets after September 2008 visible in Figure 29-9.

Like earlier crises, the crisis of 2008 led to changes in banking regulation, most notably the Dodd-Frank financial regulatory reform bill enacted in 2010. We discuss that bill in the following Economics in Action.

ECONOMICS ▶ in Action

Regulation After the 2008 Crisis

In July 2010, President Obama signed the Wall Street Reform and Consumer Protection Act—generally known as Dodd-Frank, after its sponsors in the Senate and House, respectively—into law. It was the biggest financial reform enacted since the 1930s—not surprising given that the nation had just gone through the worst financial crisis since the 1930s. How did it change regulation?

For the most part, it left regulation of traditional deposit-taking banks more or less as it was. The main change these banks would face was the creation of a new agency, the Bureau of Consumer Financial Protection, whose mission was to protect borrowers from being exploited through seemingly attractive financial deals they didn't understand.

The major changes came in the regulation of financial institutions other than banks—institutions that, as the fall of Lehman Brothers showed, could trigger banking crises. The new law gave

The Wall Street Reform and Consumer Protection Act of 2010 was an attempt to extend the spirit of old-fashioned bank regulation to today's more complex financial system.

- The Federal Reserve system was created in response to the Panic of 1907.

- Widespread bank runs in the early 1930s resulted in greater bank regulation and the creation of federal deposit insurance. Banks were separated into two categories: **commercial** (covered by deposit insurance) and **investment** (not covered).

- In the **savings and loan (thrift)** crisis of the 1970s and 1980s, insufficiently regulated S&Ls incurred huge losses from risky speculation.

- During the mid-1990s, the hedge fund LTCM used huge amounts of **leverage** to speculate in global markets, incurred massive losses, and collapsed. In selling assets to cover its losses, LTCM caused **balance sheet effects** for firms around the world. To prevent a **vicious cycle of deleveraging,** the New York Fed coordinated a private bailout.

- In the mid-2000s, loans from **subprime lending** spread through the financial system via **securitization,** leading to a financial crisis. The Fed responded by injecting cash into financial institutions and buying private debt.

- In 2010, the Dodd-Frank bill revised financial regulation in an attempt to prevent repeats of the 2008 crisis.

a special government committee, the Financial Stability Oversight Council, the right to designate certain institutions as "systemically important" even if they weren't ordinary deposit-taking banks.

These systemically important institutions would be subjected to bank-style regulation, including relatively high capital requirements and limits on the kinds of risks they could take. In addition, the federal government would acquire "resolution authority," meaning the right to seize troubled financial institutions in much the same way that it routinely takes over troubled banks.

Beyond this, the law established new rules on the trading of derivatives, those complex financial instruments that sank LTCM and played an important role in the 2008 crisis as well: most derivatives would henceforth have to be bought and sold on exchanges, where everyone could observe their prices and the volume of transactions. The idea was to make the risks taken by financial institutions more transparent.

Overall, Dodd-Frank is probably best seen as an attempt to extend the spirit of old-fashioned bank regulation to the more complex financial system of the twenty-first century. Will it succeed in heading off future banking crises? Stay tuned.

Check Your Understanding 29-5

1. What are the similarities between the Panic of 1907, the S&L crisis, and the crisis of 2008?

2. Why did the creation of the Federal Reserve fail to prevent the bank runs of the Great Depression? What measures stopped the bank runs?

3. Describe the balance sheet effect. Describe the vicious cycle of deleveraging. Why is it necessary for the government to step in to halt a vicious cycle of deleveraging?

Solutions appear at back of book.

The Perfect Gift: Cash or a Gift Card?

It's always nice when someone shows his or her appreciation by giving you a gift. Over the past few years, more and more people have been showing their appreciation by giving gift cards, prepaid plastic cards issued by a retailer that can be redeemed for merchandise. The best-selling single item for more than 80% of the top 100 American retailers, says GiftCardUSA.com, is their gift cards.

What could be more simple and useful than allowing the recipient to choose what he or she wants? And isn't a gift card more personal than cash or a check?

Yet several websites are now making a profit from the fact that gift card recipients are often willing to sell their cards at a discount—sometimes at a fairly sizable discount—to turn them into cold, impersonal dollars and cents.

Cardpool.com is one such site. At the time of writing, it offers to pay cash to a seller of a Whole Foods gift card equivalent to 88% of the card's face value. For example, the seller of a card with a value of $100 would receive $88 in cash. But it offers cash equal to only 70% of a Gap card's face value. Cardpool.com profits by reselling the card at a premium over what it paid; for example, it buys a Whole Foods card for 88% of its face value and then resells it for 97% of its face value.

Many consumers will sell at a sizable discount to turn gift cards into cash. But retailers promote the use of gift cards over cash because much of the value of gift cards issued never gets used, a phenomenon known as *breakage*.

How does breakage occur? People lose cards. Or they spend only $47 of a $50 gift card, and never return to the store to spend that last $3. Also, retailers impose fees on the use of cards or make them subject to expiration dates, which customers forget about. And if a retailer goes out of business, the value of outstanding gift cards disappears with it.

In addition to breakage, retailers benefit when customers intent on using up the value of their gift card find that it is too difficult to spend exactly the amount of the card. Instead, they end up spending more than the card's face value, sometimes even more than they would have without the gift card.

Gift cards are so beneficial to retailers that instead of rewarding customer loyalty with rebate checks (once a common practice), they have switched to dispensing gift cards. As one commentator noted in explaining why retailers prefer gift cards to rebate checks, "Nobody neglects to spend cash."

However, the future may not be quite so profitable for gift card issuers. Hard economic times have made consumers more careful about spending down their cards. And legislation enacted in 2009 requires that cards remain valid for at least five years. As a result, breakage has fallen sharply, although it still amounts to more than $1 billion a year.

QUESTIONS FOR THOUGHT

1. Why are gift card owners willing to sell their cards for a cash amount less than their face value?

2. Why do gift cards for retailers like Walmart, Home Depot, and Whole Foods sell for a smaller discount than those for retailers like the Gap and Aeropostale?

3. Use your answer from Question 2 to explain why cash never "sells" at a discount.

4. Explain why retailers prefer to reward loyal customers with gift cards instead of rebate checks.

5. Recent legislation restricted retailers' ability to impose fees and expiration dates on their gift cards and mandated greater disclosure of their terms. Why do you think Congress enacted this legislation?

SUMMARY

1. **Money** is any asset that can easily be used to purchase goods and services. **Currency in circulation** and **checkable bank deposits** are both considered part of the **money supply.** Money plays three roles: it is a **medium of exchange** used for transactions, a **store of value** that holds purchasing power over time, and a **unit of account** in which prices are stated.

2. Over time, **commodity money,** which consists of goods possessing value aside from their role as money, such as gold and silver coins, was replaced by **commodity-backed money,** such as paper currency backed by gold. Today the dollar is pure **fiat money,** whose value derives solely from its official role.

3. The Federal Reserve calculates two measures of the money supply. M1 is the narrowest **monetary aggregate,** containing only currency in circulation, traveler's checks, and checkable bank deposits. M2 includes a wider range of assets called **near-moneys,** mainly other forms of bank deposits, that can easily be converted into checkable bank deposits.

4. Banks allow depositors immediate access to their funds, but they also lend out most of the funds deposited in their care. To meet demands for cash, they maintain **bank reserves** composed of both currency held in vaults and deposits at the Federal Reserve. The **reserve ratio** is the ratio of bank reserves to bank deposits. A **T-account** summarizes a bank's financial position, with loans and reserves counted as assets and deposits counted as liabilities.

5. Banks have sometimes been subject to **bank runs,** most notably in the early 1930s. To avert this danger, depositors are now protected by **deposit insurance,** bank owners face capital requirements that reduce the incentive to make overly risky loans with depositors' funds, and banks must satisfy **reserve requirements.**

6. When currency is deposited in a bank, it starts a multiplier process in which banks lend out **excess reserves,** leading to an increase in the money supply—so banks create money. If the entire money supply consisted of checkable bank deposits, the money supply would be equal to the value of reserves divided by the reserve ratio. In reality, much of the **monetary base** consists of currency in circulation, and the **money multiplier** is the ratio of the money supply to the monetary base.

7. The monetary base is controlled by the Federal Reserve, the **central bank** of the United States. The Fed regulates banks and sets reserve requirements. To meet those requirements, banks borrow and lend reserves in the **federal funds market** at the **federal funds rate.** Through the **discount window** facility, banks can borrow from the Fed at the **discount rate.**

8. **Open-market operations** by the Fed are the principal tool of monetary policy: the Fed can increase or reduce the monetary base by buying U.S. Treasury bills from banks or selling U.S. Treasury bills to banks.

9. In response to the Panic of 1907, the Fed was created to centralize the holding of reserves, inspect banks' books, and make the money supply sufficiently responsive to varying economic conditions.

10. The Great Depression sparked widespread bank runs in the early 1930s, which greatly worsened and lengthened it. Federal deposit insurance was created, and the government recapitalized banks by lending to them and by buying shares of banks. By 1933, banks had been separated into two categories: **commercial banks** (covered by deposit insurance) and **investment banks** (not covered). Public acceptance of deposit insurance finally stopped the bank runs of the Great Depression.

11. The **savings and loan (thrift)** crisis of the 1980s arose because insufficiently regulated S&Ls engaged in overly risky speculation and incurred huge losses. Depositors in failed S&Ls were compensated with taxpayer funds because they were covered by deposit insurance. The crisis caused steep losses in the financial and real estate sectors, resulting in a recession in the early 1990s.

12. During the mid-1990s, the hedge fund LTCM used huge amounts of **leverage** to speculate in global financial markets, incurred massive losses, and collapsed. LTCM was so large that, in selling assets to cover its losses, it caused **balance sheet effects** for firms around the world, leading to the prospect of a **vicious cycle of deleveraging.** As a result, credit markets around the world froze. The New York Fed coordinated a private bailout of LTCM and revived world credit markets.

13. **Subprime lending** during the U.S. housing bubble of the mid-2000s spread through the financial system via **securitization.** When the bubble burst, massive losses by banks and nonbank financial institutions led to widespread collapse in the financial system. To prevent another Great Depression, the Fed and the U.S. Treasury expanded lending to bank and nonbank institutions, provided capital through the purchase of bank shares, and purchased private debt. Because much of the crisis originated in nontraditional bank institutions, the crisis of 2008 indicated that a wider safety net and broader regulation are needed in the financial sector. The 2010 Dodd-Frank bill, the biggest financial reform since the 1930s, is an attempt to prevent another crisis.

KEY TERMS

Money, p. 854
Currency in circulation, p. 854
Checkable bank deposits, p. 854
Money supply, p. 854
Medium of exchange, p. 855
Store of value, p. 856
Unit of account, p. 856
Commodity money, p. 856
Commodity-backed money, p. 856
Fiat money, p. 857
Monetary aggregate, p. 857
Near-moneys, p. 857

Bank reserves, p. 860
T-account, p. 860
Reserve ratio, p. 861
Bank run, p. 862
Deposit insurance, p. 862
Reserve requirements, p. 863
Discount window, p. 863
Excess reserves, p. 866
Monetary base, p. 867
Money multiplier, p. 868
Central bank, p. 869
Federal funds market, p. 870

Federal funds rate, p. 870
Discount rate, p. 870
Open-market operation, p. 871
Commercial bank, p. 877
Investment bank, p. 877
Savings and loan (thrift), p. 878
Leverage, p. 878
Balance sheet effect, p. 879
Vicious cycle of deleveraging, p. 879
Subprime lending, p. 879
Securitization, p. 880

PROBLEMS

1. For each of the following transactions, what is the initial effect (increase or decrease) on M1? On M2?

　a. You sell a few shares of stock and put the proceeds into your savings account.

　b. You sell a few shares of stock and put the proceeds into your checking account.

　c. You transfer money from your savings account to your checking account.

　d. You discover $0.25 under the floor mat in your car and deposit it in your checking account.

　e. You discover $0.25 under the floor mat in your car and deposit it in your savings account.

2. There are three types of money: commodity money, commodity-backed money, and fiat money. Which type of money is used in each of the following situations?

　a. Bottles of rum were used to pay for goods in colonial Australia.

　b. Salt was used in many European countries as a medium of exchange.

　c. For a brief time, Germany used paper money (the "Rye Mark") that could be redeemed for a certain amount of rye, a type of grain.

　d. The town of Ithaca, New York, prints its own currency, the Ithaca HOURS, which can be used to purchase local goods and services.

3. The following table shows the components of M1 and M2 in billions of dollars for the month of December in the years 2003 to 2013 reported by the Federal Reserve Bank of St. Louis. Complete the table by calculating M1, M2, currency in circulation as a percentage of M1, and currency in circulation as a percentage of M2. What trends or patterns about M1, M2, currency in circulation as a percentage of M1, and currency in circulation as a percentage of M2 do you see? What might account for these trends?

Year	Currency in circulation	Traveler's checks	Checkable deposits	Savings deposits	Time deposits	Money market funds	M1	M2	Currency in circulation as a percentage of M1	Currency in circulation as a percentage of M2
2003	$662.5	$7.6	$635.9	$3,159.0	$818.1	$752.8	?	?	?	?
2004	697.8	7.5	670.6	3,506.5	828.4	677.6	?	?	?	?
2005	724.6	7.2	643.0	3,601.6	993.7	682.4	?	?	?	?
2006	750.2	6.7	610.6	3,691.8	1,206.0	776.6	?	?	?	?
2007	760.6	6.3	608.1	3,864.1	1,276.0	930.6	?	?	?	?
2008	816.2	5.5	782.0	4,085.6	1,457.6	1,021.6	?	?	?	?
2009	863.7	5.1	825.3	4,809.3	1,183.1	781.2	?	?	?	?
2010	918.7	4.7	912.7	5,329.6	927.9	675.7	?	?	?	?
2011	1,001.2	4.3	1,154.3	6,032.8	767.0	663.7	?	?	?	?
2012	1,090.0	3.8	1,353.5	6,687.5	633.0	642.0	?	?	?	?
2013	1,159.5	3.5	1,475.8	7,133.0	555.6	640.9	?	?	?	?

Source: Federal Reserve Bank of St. Louis.

4. Indicate whether each of the following is part of M1, M2, or neither:

   a. $95 on your campus meal card

   b. $0.55 in the change cup of your car

   c. $1,663 in your savings account

   d. $459 in your checking account

   e. 100 shares of stock worth $4,000

   f. A $1,000 line of credit on your Sears credit card

5. Tracy Williams deposits $500 that was in her sock drawer into a checking account at the local bank.

   a. How does the deposit initially change the T-account of the local bank? How does it change the money supply?

   b. If the bank maintains a reserve ratio of 10%, how will it respond to the new deposit?

   c. If every time the bank makes a loan, the loan results in a new checkable bank deposit in a different bank equal to the amount of the loan, by how much could the total money supply in the economy expand in response to Tracy's initial cash deposit of $500?

   d. If every time the bank makes a loan, the loan results in a new checkable bank deposit in a different bank equal to the amount of the loan and the bank maintains a reserve ratio of 5%, by how much could the money supply expand in response to Tracy's initial cash deposit of $500?

6. Ryan Cozzens withdraws $400 from his checking account at the local bank and keeps it in his wallet.

   a. How will the withdrawal change the T-account of the local bank and the money supply?

   b. If the bank maintains a reserve ratio of 10%, how will it respond to the withdrawal? Assume that the bank responds to insufficient reserves by reducing the amount of deposits it holds until its level of reserves satisfies its required reserve ratio. The bank reduces its deposits by calling in some of its loans, forcing borrowers to pay back these loans by taking cash from their checking deposits (at the same bank) to make repayment.

   c. If every time the bank decreases its loans, checkable bank deposits fall by the amount of the loan, by how much will the money supply in the economy contract in response to Ryan's withdrawal of $400?

   d. If every time the bank decreases its loans, checkable bank deposits fall by the amount of the loan and the bank maintains a reserve ratio of 20%, by how much will the money supply contract in response to a withdrawal of $400?

7. The government of Eastlandia uses measures of monetary aggregates similar to those used by the United States, and the central bank of Eastlandia imposes a required reserve ratio of 10%. Given the following information, answer the questions below.

   Bank deposits at the central bank = $200 million
   Currency held by public = $150 million
   Currency in bank vaults = $100 million

Checkable bank deposits = $500 million
Traveler's checks = $10 million

   a. What is M1?

   b. What is the monetary base?

   c. Are the commercial banks holding excess reserves?

   d. Can the commercial banks increase checkable bank deposits? If yes, by how much can checkable bank deposits increase?

8. In Westlandia, the public holds 50% of M1 in the form of currency, and the required reserve ratio is 20%. Estimate how much the money supply will increase in response to a new cash deposit of $500 by completing the accompanying table. (*Hint:* The first row shows that the bank must hold $100 in minimum reserves—20% of the $500 deposit—against this deposit, leaving $400 in excess reserves that can be loaned out. However, since the public wants to hold 50% of the loan in currency, only $400 × 0.5 = $200 of the loan will be deposited in round 2 from the loan granted in round 1.) How does your answer compare to an economy in which the total amount of the loan is deposited in the banking system and the public doesn't hold any of the loan in currency? What does this imply about the relationship between the public's desire for holding currency and the money multiplier?

Round	Deposits	Required reserves	Excess reserves	Loans	Held as currency
1	$500.00	$100.00	$400.00	$400.00	$200.00
2	200.00	?	?	?	?
3	?	?	?	?	?
4	?	?	?	?	?
5	?	?	?	?	?
6	?	?	?	?	?
7	?	?	?	?	?
8	?	?	?	?	?
9	?	?	?	?	?
Total after 10 rounds	?	?	?	?	?

9. What will happen to the money supply under the following circumstances in a checkable-deposits-only system?

   a. The required reserve ratio is 25%, and a depositor withdraws $700 from his checkable bank deposit.

   b. The required reserve ratio is 5%, and a depositor withdraws $700 from his checkable bank deposit.

   c. The required reserve ratio is 20%, and a customer deposits $750 to her checkable bank deposit.

   d. The required reserve ratio is 10%, and a customer deposits $600 to her checkable bank deposit.

10. Although the U.S. Federal Reserve doesn't use changes in reserve requirements to manage the money supply, the central bank of Albernia does. The commercial banks of Albernia have $100 million in reserves

and $1,000 million in checkable deposits; the initial required reserve ratio is 10%. The commercial banks follow a policy of holding no excess reserves. The public holds no currency, only checkable deposits in the banking system.

a. How will the money supply change if the required reserve ratio falls to 5%?

b. How will the money supply change if the required reserve ratio rises to 25%?

11. Using Figure 29-6, find the Federal Reserve district in which you live. Go to www.federalreserve.gov/bios/pres.htm and click on your district to identify the president of the Federal Reserve Bank in your district. Go to www.federalreserve.gov/fomc/ and determine if the president of the regional Federal Reserve bank in your district is currently a voting member of the Federal Open Market Committee (FOMC).

12. Show the changes to the T-accounts for the Federal Reserve and for commercial banks when the Federal Reserve sells $30 million in U.S. Treasury bills. If the public holds a fixed amount of currency (so that all new loans create an equal amount of checkable bank deposits in the banking system) and the minimum reserve ratio is 5%, by how much will checkable bank deposits in the commercial banks change? By how much will the money supply change? Show the final changes to the T-account for the commercial banks when the money supply changes by this amount.

13. The Congressional Research Service estimates that at least $45 million of counterfeit U.S. $100 notes produced by the North Korean government are in circulation.

a. Why do U.S. taxpayers lose because of North Korea's counterfeiting?

b. As of December 2014, the interest rate earned on one-year U.S. Treasury bills was 0.13%. At a 0.13% rate of interest, what is the amount of money U.S. taxpayers are losing per year because of these $45 million in counterfeit notes?

14. As shown in Figure 29-9, the portion of the Federal Reserve's assets made up of U.S. Treasury bills has declined since 2007. Go to www.federalreserve.gov. Under "Select Statistical Releases," click on "View All." Under the heading "Money Stock and Reserve Balances," click on "Factors Affecting Reserve Balances." Click on the date of the current release.

a. Under "Statement of Condition of Federal Reserve Bank," look in the "Total" column. What is the amount displayed next to "Total assets"? What is the amount displayed next to "U.S. Treasury securities"? What percentage of the Federal Reserve's total assets are currently made up of U.S. Treasury bills?

b. Do the Federal Reserve's assets consist primarily of U.S. Treasury securities, as they did in January 2007, the beginning of the graph in Figure 29-9, or does the Fed still own a large number of other assets, as it did in mid-2013, the end of the graph in Figure 29-9?

15. The accompanying figure shows new U.S. housing starts, in thousands of units per month, between January 1980 and January 2014. The graph shows a large drop in new housing starts in 1984–1991 and 2006–2009. New housing starts are related to the availability of mortgages.

a. What caused the drop in new housing starts in 1984–1991?

b. What caused the drop in new housing starts in 2006–2009?

c. How could better regulation of financial institutions have prevented these two instances?

Source: Federal Reserve Bank of St. Louis.

WORK IT OUT

For interactive, step-by-step help in solving the following problem, visit LaunchPad by using the URL on the back cover of this book.

16. Show the changes to the T-accounts for the Federal Reserve and for commercial banks when the Federal Reserve buys $50 million in U.S. Treasury bills. If the public holds a fixed amount of currency (so that all loans create an equal amount of deposits in the banking system), the minimum reserve ratio is 10%, and banks hold no excess reserves, by how much will deposits in the commercial banks change? By how much will the money supply change? Show the final changes to the T-account for commercial banks when the money supply changes by this amount.

Monetary Policy

▶ **What You Will Learn
in This Chapter**

■ What the **money demand curve** is

■ Why the **liquidity preference
model** determines the interest rate
in the short run

■ How the Federal Reserve
implements monetary policy, moving
the interest rate to affect aggregate
output

■ Why monetary policy is the main
tool for stabilizing the economy

■ How the behavior of the Federal
Reserve compares to that of other
central banks

■ Why economists believe in
monetary neutrality—that monetary
policy affects only the price level, not
aggregate output, in the long run

THE MOST POWERFUL PERSON IN GOVERNMENT

The chairmanship of the Federal
Reserve, currently held by Janet Yellen,
and previously by Ben Bernanke, is
arguably the most powerful position in
the U.S. government.

In 2014 Nicholas Lemann, a reporter for the *New Yorker,* visited the trading floor of the Federal Reserve Bank of New York. He found it oddly unimpressive—writing that the people at the desks "look like graduate students" and "dress business casual." Off the main floor were two small rooms. In one room five "serious-looking people" were buying "long-term U.S. government bonds amounting to thirty billion dollars every month." In the other, seven people were buying a slightly smaller amount of mortgage-backed securities—bonds backed by government-sponsored home loans. Lemann was bewildered by the lack of drama, asking "Can a spectacle so lacking in the indicia of importance— no pageantry, no emotions, not even any speaking—really be the beating heart of capitalism?"

The answer, basically, is yes. Lemann visited the New York Fed as part of his work on a profile of Janet Yellen, who had recently been appointed chairwoman of the Fed's Board of Governors. And that's a very important position indeed. As Lemann wrote, "There is an old saw

that the Fed chair is the most powerful person in government. In the aftermath of the financial crisis, that may actually be an understatement."

People sometimes say that the head of the Fed decides how much money to print. That's not quite true: for one thing, the Fed doesn't literally print money, and beyond that, monetary decisions are made by a committee rather than by one person. But as we learned in Chapter 29, the Federal Reserve can use open-market operations and other actions, such as changes in reserve requirements, to alter the money supply—and Janet Yellen has more influence over these actions than anyone else in America.

And these actions matter a lot. Roughly half of the recessions the United States has experienced since World War II can be attributed, at least in part, to the decisions of the Federal Reserve to tighten money to fight inflation. In a number of other cases, the Fed played a key role in fighting slumps and promoting recovery. The financial crisis of 2008 put the Fed at center stage. Its aggressive response to the crisis inspired both praise and condemnation.

In 2009 *Time* magazine declared Ben Bernanke, Janet Yellen's predecessor, "Person of the Year." The next year an open letter from a number of prominent Wall Street figures and economists accused him of "debasing" the dollar.

The power of the Fed chair comes from the ability of the Board of Governors to direct the actions of people like those working in those two small rooms in New York. For what the Fed does, mainly, is set *monetary policy.* Monetary policy in action isn't much to look at, but it's crucially important—for job creation, for price stability, and more—that it be done right.

In this chapter we'll learn how monetary policy works—how actions by the Federal Reserve can have a powerful effect on the economy. We'll start by looking at the *demand for money* from households and firms. Then we'll see how the Fed's ability to change the *supply of money* allows it to move interest rates in the short run and thereby affect real GDP. We'll look at U.S. monetary policy in practice and compare it to the monetary policy of other central banks. We'll conclude by examining monetary policy's long run effects.

The Demand for Money

In the previous chapter we learned about the various types of monetary aggregates: M1, the most commonly used definition of the money supply, consists of currency in circulation (cash), plus checkable bank deposits, plus traveler's checks; and M2, a broader definition of the money supply, consists of M1 plus deposits that can easily be transferred into checkable deposits. We also learned why people hold money—to make it easier to purchase goods and services. Now we'll go deeper, examining what determines how much money individuals and firms want to hold at any given time.

The Opportunity Cost of Holding Money

Most economic decisions involve trade-offs at the margin. That is, individuals decide how much of a good to consume by determining whether the benefit they'd gain from consuming a bit more of any given good is worth the cost. The same decision process is used when deciding how much money to hold.

There is a price to be paid for the convenience of holding money.

Individuals and firms find it useful to hold some of their assets in the form of money because of the convenience money provides: money can be used to make purchases directly, but other assets can't. But there is a price to be paid for that convenience: money normally yields a lower rate of return than nonmonetary assets.

As an example of how convenience makes it worth incurring some opportunity costs, consider the fact that even today—with the prevalence of credit cards, debit cards, and ATMs—people continue to keep cash in their wallets rather than leave the funds in an interest-bearing account. They do this because they don't want to have to go to an ATM to withdraw money every time they want to buy lunch from a place that doesn't accept credit cards or won't accept them for small amounts because of the processing fee. In other words, the convenience of keeping some cash in your wallet is more valuable than the interest you would earn by keeping that money in the bank.

Even holding money in a checking account involves a trade-off between convenience and earning interest. That's because you can earn a higher interest rate by putting your money in assets other than a checking account. For example, many banks offer certificates of deposit, or CDs, which pay a higher interest rate than ordinary bank accounts. But CDs also carry a penalty if you withdraw the funds before a certain amount of time—say, six months—has elapsed. An individual who keeps funds in a checking account is forgoing the higher interest rate those funds would have earned if placed in a CD in return for the convenience of having cash readily available when needed.

So making sense of the demand for money is about understanding how individuals and firms trade off the benefit of holding cash—that provides convenience but no interest—versus the benefit of holding interest-bearing non-monetary assets—that provide interest but not convenience. And that trade-off is affected by the interest rate. (As before, when we say *the interest rate* it is with the understanding that we mean a nominal interest rate—that is, it's unadjusted for inflation.) Next, we'll examine how that trade-off changed dramatically from June 2007 to June 2008, when there was a big fall in interest rates.

Table 30-1 illustrates the opportunity cost of holding money in a specific month, June 2007. The first row shows the interest rate on one-month certificates of deposit—that is, the interest rate individuals could get if they were willing to tie their funds up for one month. In June 2007, one-month CDs yielded 5.30%. The second row shows the interest rate on interest-bearing demand deposits (specifically, those included in M2, minus small time deposits). Funds in these accounts were more accessible than those in CDs, but the price of

TABLE 30-1	Selected Interest Rates, June 2007	
One-month certificates of deposit (CDs)		5.30%
Interest-bearing demand deposits		2.30%
Currency		0

Source: Federal Reserve Bank of St. Louis.

that convenience was a much lower interest rate, only 2.30%. Finally, the last row shows the interest rate on currency—cash in your wallet—which was, of course, zero.

Table 30-1 shows the opportunity cost of holding money at one point in time, but the opportunity cost of holding money changes when the overall level of interest rates changes. Specifically, when the overall level of interest rates falls, the opportunity cost of holding money falls, too.

Table 30-2 illustrates this point by showing how selected interest rates changed between June 2007 and June 2008, a period when the Federal Reserve was slashing rates in an (unsuccessful) effort to fight off a rapidly worsening recession. A comparison between interest rates in June 2007 and June 2008 illustrates what happens when the opportunity cost of holding money falls sharply. Between June 2007 and June 2008, the federal funds rate, which is the rate the Fed controls most directly, fell by 3.25 percentage points. The interest rate on one-month CDs fell almost as much, 2.8 percentage points. These interest rates are **short-term interest rates**—rates on financial assets that come due, or mature, within less than a year.

As short-term interest rates fell between June 2007 and June 2008, the interest rates on money didn't fall by the same amount. The interest rate on currency, of course, remained at zero. The interest rate paid on demand deposits did fall, but by much less than short-term interest rates. As a comparison of the two columns of Table 30-2 shows, the opportunity cost of holding money fell. The last two rows of Table 30-2 summarize this comparison: they give the differences between the interest rates on demand deposits and on currency and the interest rate on CDs.

These differences—the opportunity cost of holding money rather than interest-bearing assets—declined sharply between June 2007 and June 2008. This reflects a general result: *the higher the short-term interest rate, the higher the opportunity cost of holding money; the lower the short-term interest rate, the lower the opportunity cost of holding money.*

The fact that the federal funds rate in Table 30-2 and the interest rate on one-month CDs fell by almost the same percentage is not an accident: all short-term interest rates tend to move together, with rare exceptions. The reason short-term interest rates tend to move together is that CDs and other short-term assets (like one-month and three-month U.S. Treasury bills) are in effect competing for the same business. Any short-term asset that offers a lower-than-average interest rate will be sold by investors, who will move their wealth into a higher-yielding short-term asset. The selling of the asset, in turn, forces its interest rate up, because investors must be rewarded with a higher rate in order to induce them to buy it.

Conversely, investors will move their wealth into any short-term financial asset that offers an above-average interest rate. The purchase of the asset drives its interest rate down when sellers find they can lower the rate of return on the asset and still find willing buyers. So interest rates on short-term financial assets tend to be roughly the same because no asset will consistently offer a higher-than-average or a lower-than-average interest rate.

Table 30-2 contains only short-term interest rates. At any given moment, **long-term interest rates**—rates of interest on financial assets that mature, or come due, a number of years into the future—may be different from short-term interest rates. The difference between short-term and long-term interest rates is sometimes important as a practical matter.

Moreover, it's short-term rates rather than long-term rates that affect money demand, because the decision to hold money involves trading off the convenience of holding cash versus the payoff from holding assets that mature in the

Short-term interest rates are the interest rates on financial assets that mature within less than a year.

Long-term interest rates are interest rates on financial assets that mature a number of years in the future.

TABLE 30-2 Interest Rates and the Opportunity Cost of Holding Money

	June 2007	June 2008
Federal funds rate	5.25%	2.00%
One-month certificates of deposit (CDs)	5.30%	2.50%
Interest-bearing demand deposits	2.30%	1.24%
Currency	0	0
CDs minus interest-bearing demand deposits (percentage points)	**3.00**	**1.26**
CDs minus currency (percentage points)	**5.30**	**2.50**

Source: Federal Reserve Bank of St. Louis.

The **money demand curve** shows the relationship between the interest rate and the quantity of money demanded.

short term—a year or less. For the moment, however, let's ignore the distinction between short-term and long-term rates and assume that there is only one interest rate.

The Money Demand Curve

Because the overall level of interest rates affects the opportunity cost of holding money, the quantity of money individuals and firms want to hold is, other things equal, negatively related to the interest rate. In Figure 30-1, the horizontal axis shows the quantity of money demanded and the vertical axis shows the interest rate, r, which you can think of as a representative short-term interest rate such as the rate on one-month CDs. (As we discussed in Chapter 25, it is the nominal interest rate, not the real interest rate, that influences people's money allocation decisions. Hence, r in Figure 30-1 and all subsequent figures is the nominal interest rate.)

The relationship between the interest rate and the quantity of money demanded by the public is illustrated by the **money demand curve,** *MD*, in Figure 30-1. The money demand curve slopes downward because, other things equal, a higher interest rate increases the opportunity cost of holding money, leading the public to reduce the quantity of money it demands. For example, if the interest rate is very low—say, 1%—the interest forgone by holding money is relatively small. As a result, individuals and firms will tend to hold relatively large amounts of money to avoid the cost and nuisance of converting other assets into money when making purchases.

By contrast, if the interest rate is relatively high—say, 15%, a level it reached in the United States in the early 1980s—the opportunity cost of holding money is high. People will respond by keeping only small amounts in cash and deposits, converting assets into money only when needed.

You might ask why we draw the money demand curve with the interest rate—as opposed to rates of return on other assets, such as stocks or real estate—on the vertical axis. The answer is that for most people the relevant question in deciding how much money to hold is whether to put the funds in the form of other assets that can be turned fairly quickly and easily into money. Stocks don't fit that definition because there are significant transaction fees when you sell stock

FIGURE 30-1 The Money Demand Curve

The money demand curve illustrates the relationship between the interest rate and the quantity of money demanded. It slopes downward: a higher interest rate leads to a higher opportunity cost of holding money and reduces the quantity of money demanded. Correspondingly, a lower interest rate reduces the opportunity cost of holding money and increases the quantity of money demanded.

Interest rate, *r*

Money demand curve, *MD*

Quantity of money

(which is why stock market investors are advised not to buy and sell too often). Real estate doesn't fit the definition either because selling real estate involves even larger fees and can take a long time as well. So the relevant comparison is with assets that are "close to" money—fairly liquid assets like CDs. And as we've already seen, the interest rates on all these assets normally move closely together.

Shifts of the Money Demand Curve

A number of factors other than the interest rate affect the demand for money. When one of these factors changes, the money demand curve shifts. Figure 30-2 shows shifts of the money demand curve: an increase in the demand for money corresponds to a rightward shift of the MD curve, raising the quantity of money demanded at any given interest rate; a decrease in the demand for money corresponds to a leftward shift of the MD curve, reducing the quantity of money demanded at any given interest rate.

The most important factors causing the money demand curve to shift are changes in the aggregate price level, changes in real GDP, changes in credit markets and banking technology, and changes in institutions.

Changes in the Aggregate Price Level Americans keep a lot more cash in their wallets and funds in their checking accounts today than they did in the 1950s. One reason is that they have to if they want to be able to buy anything: almost everything costs more now than it did when you could get a burger, fries, and a drink at McDonald's for 45 cents and a gallon of gasoline for 29 cents. So, other things equal, higher prices increase the demand for money (a rightward shift of the MD curve), and lower prices decrease the demand for money (a leftward shift of the MD curve).

We can actually be more specific than this: other things equal, the demand for money is *proportional* to the price level. That is, if the aggregate price level rises by 20%, the quantity of money demanded at any given interest rate, such as r_1 in Figure 30-2, also rises by 20%—the movement from M_1 to M_2. Why? Because if the price of everything rises by 20%, it takes 20% more money to buy the same basket of goods and services. And if the aggregate price level falls by 20%, at any

FIGURE **30-2**   Increases and Decreases in the Demand for Money

The demand curve for money shifts when non-interest rate factors that affect the demand for money change. An increase in money demand shifts the money demand curve to the right, from MD_1 to MD_2, and the quantity of money demanded rises at any given interest rate. A decrease in money demand shifts the money demand curve to the left, from MD_1 to MD_3, and the quantity of money demanded falls at any given interest rate.

A decrease in money demand shifts the money demand curve to the left.

An increase in money demand shifts the money demand curve to the right.

given interest rate the quantity of money demanded falls by 20%—shown by the movement from M_1 to M_3 at the interest rate r_1. As we'll see later, the fact that money demand is proportional to the price level has important implications for the long-run effects of monetary policy.

Changes in Real GDP Households and firms hold money as a way to facilitate purchases of goods and services. The larger the quantity of goods and services they buy, the larger the quantity of money they will want to hold at any given interest rate. So an increase in real GDP—the total quantity of goods and services produced and sold in the economy—shifts the money demand curve rightward. A fall in real GDP shifts the money demand curve leftward.

Changes in Credit Markets and Banking Technology Credit cards are used everywhere in America today, but it wasn't always so. The first credit card that allowed customers to carry a balance from month to month (called a *revolving balance*) was issued in 1959. Before then, people had to either pay for purchases in cash or pay off their balance every month. The invention of revolving-balance credit cards allowed people to hold less money in order to fund their purchases and decreased the demand for money. In addition, changes in banking technology that made credit cards widely available and widely accepted magnified the effect, making it easier for people to make purchases without having to convert funds from their interest-bearing assets, further reducing the demand for money.

Changes in Institutions Changes in institutions can increase or decrease the demand for money. For example, until Regulation Q was eliminated in 1980, U.S. banks weren't allowed to offer interest on checking accounts. So the interest you would forgo by holding funds in a checking account instead of an interest-bearing asset made the opportunity cost of holding funds in checking accounts very high. When banking regulations changed, allowing banks to pay interest on checking account funds, the demand for money rose and shifted the money demand curve to the right.

ECONOMICS ▶ in Action

A Yen for Cash

Japan, say financial experts, is still a "cash society." Visitors from the United States or Europe are surprised at how little use the Japanese make of credit cards and how much cash they carry around in their wallets. Yet Japan is one of the most economically and technologically advanced countries, and superior to the United States in some areas such as transportation. So why do the citizens of this economic powerhouse still do business the way Americans and Europeans did a generation ago? The answer highlights the factors affecting the demand for money.

One reason the Japanese use cash so much is that their institutions never made the switch to heavy reliance on plastic. For complex reasons, Japan's retail sector is still dominated by small mom-and-pop stores, which are reluctant to invest in credit card technology. Japan's banks have also been slow about pushing transaction technology; visitors are often surprised to find that ATMs outside of major metropolitan areas close early in the evening rather than staying open all night.

But there's another reason the Japanese hold so much cash: there's little opportunity cost to doing so. Short-term interest rates in Japan have been below 1% since the mid-1990s. It also helps that

No matter what they are shopping for, Japanese consumers tend to pay with cash rather than plastic.

Akio Kon/Bloomberg via Getty Images

the Japanese crime rate is quite low, so you are unlikely to have your wallet stolen. So why not hold cash?

Check Your Understanding   30-1

1. Explain how each of the following would affect the quantity of money demanded. Does the change cause a movement along the money demand curve or a shift of the money demand curve?
   a. Short-term interest rates rise from 5% to 30%.
   b. All prices fall by 10%.
   c. New wireless technology automatically charges supermarket purchases to credit cards, eliminating the need to stop at the cash register.
   d. In order to avoid paying a sharp increase in taxes, residents of Laguria shift their assets into overseas bank accounts. These accounts are harder for tax authorities to trace but also harder for their owners to tap and convert funds into cash.

2. Which of the following will increase the opportunity cost of holding cash? Reduce it? Have no effect? Explain.
   a. Merchants charge a 1% fee on debit/credit card transactions for purchases of less than $50.
   b. To attract more deposits, banks raise the interest paid on six-month CDs.
   c. It's the holiday shopping season and retailers have temporarily slashed prices to unexpectedly low levels.
   d. The cost of food rises significantly.

Solutions appear at back of book.

Money and Interest Rates

The Federal Open Market Committee decided today to lower its target for the federal funds rate 75 basis points to 2¼ percent.

Recent information indicates that the outlook for economic activity has weakened further. Growth in consumer spending has slowed and labor markets have softened. Financial markets remain under considerable stress, and the tightening of credit conditions and the deepening of the housing contraction are likely to weigh on economic growth over the next few quarters.

So read the beginning of a press release from the Federal Reserve issued on March 18, 2008. (A basis point is equal to 0.01 percentage point. So the statement implies that the Fed lowered the target from 3% to 2.25%.) We learned about the federal funds rate in Chapter 29: it's the rate at which banks lend reserves to each other to meet the required reserve ratio. As the statement implies, at each of its eight-times-a-year meetings, a group called the Federal Open Market Committee sets a target value for the federal funds rate. It's then up to Fed officials to achieve that target. This is done by the Open Market Desk at the Federal Reserve Bank of New York, which buys and sells short-term U.S. government debt, known as Treasury bills, to achieve that target.

As we've already seen, other short-term interest rates, such as the rates on CDs, move with the federal funds rate. So when the Fed reduced its target for the federal funds rate from 3% to 2.25% in March 2008, many other short-term interest rates also fell by about three-quarters of a percentage point.

How does the Fed go about achieving a *target federal funds rate?* And more to the point, how is the Fed able to affect interest rates at all?

The Equilibrium Interest Rate

Recall that, for simplicity, we're assuming there is only one interest rate paid on nonmonetary financial assets, both in the short run and in the long run. To understand how the interest rate is determined, consider Figure 30-3, which

Equilibrium in the Money Market

The money supply curve, *MS*, is vertical at the money supply chosen by the Federal Reserve, $\overline{M}$. The money market is in equilibrium at the interest rate r_E; the quantity of money demanded by the public is equal to $\overline{M}$, the quantity of money supplied.

At a point such as *L*, the interest rate, r_L, is below r_E and the corresponding quantity of money demanded, M_L, exceeds the money supply, $\overline{M}$. In an attempt to shift their wealth out of nonmoney interest-bearing financial assets and raise their money holdings, investors drive the interest rate up to r_E. At a point such as *H*, the interest rate r_H exceeds r_E and the corresponding quantity of money demanded, M_H, is less than the money supply, $\overline{M}$. In an attempt to shift out of money holdings into nonmoney interest-bearing financial assets, investors drive the interest rate down to r_E.

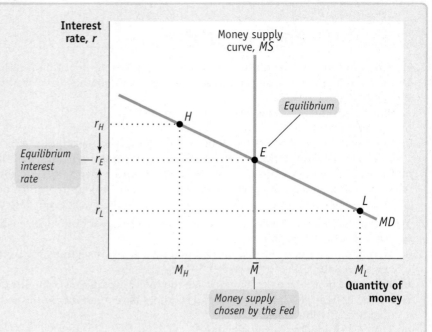

illustrates the **liquidity preference model of the interest rate;** this model says that the interest rate is determined by the supply and demand for money in the market for money. Figure 30-3 combines the money demand curve, *MD*, with the **money supply curve,** *MS*, which shows how the quantity of money supplied by the Federal Reserve varies with the interest rate.

In Chapter 29 we learned how the Federal Reserve can increase or decrease the money supply: it usually does this through *open-market operations*, buying or selling Treasury bills, but it can also lend via the *discount window* or change *reserve requirements*. Let's assume for simplicity that the Fed, using one or more of these methods, simply chooses the level of the money supply that it believes will achieve its interest rate target. Then the money supply curve is a vertical line, *MS* in Figure 30-3, with a horizontal intercept corresponding to the money supply chosen by the Fed, $\overline{M}$. The money market equilibrium is at *E*, where *MS* and *MD* cross. At this point the quantity of money demanded equals the money supply, $\overline{M}$, leading to an equilibrium interest rate of r_E.

To understand why r_E is the equilibrium interest rate, consider what happens if the money market is at a point like *L*, where the interest rate, r_L, is below r_E. At r_L the public wants to hold the quantity of money M_L, an amount larger than the actual money supply, $\overline{M}$. This means that at point *L*, the public wants to shift some of its wealth out of interest-bearing assets such as CDs into money.

This result has two implications. One is that the quantity of money demanded is *more* than the quantity of money supplied. The other is that the quantity of interest-bearing money assets demanded is less than the quantity supplied. So those trying to sell nonmoney assets will find that they have to offer a higher interest rate to attract buyers. As a result, the interest rate will be driven up from r_L until the public wants to hold the quantity of money that is actually available, $\overline{M}$. That is, the interest rate will rise until it is equal to r_E.

Now consider what happens if the money market is at a point such as *H* in Figure 30-3, where the interest rate r_H is above r_E. In that case the quantity of money demanded, M_H, is less than the quantity of money supplied, $\overline{M}$. Correspondingly, the quantity of interest-bearing nonmoney assets demanded is greater than the

According to the **liquidity preference model of the interest rate,** the interest rate is determined by the supply and demand for money.

The **money supply curve** shows how the quantity of money supplied varies with the interest rate.

quantity supplied. Those trying to sell interest-bearing nonmoney assets will find that they can offer a lower interest rate and still find willing buyers. This leads to a fall in the interest rate from r_H. It falls until the public wants to hold the quantity of money that is actually available, $\overline{M}$. Again, the interest rate will end up at r_E.

Two Models of Interest Rates?

You might have noticed that this is the second time we have discussed the determination of the interest rate. In Chapter 25 we studied the *loanable funds model* of the interest rate; according to that model, the interest rate is determined by the equalization of the supply of funds from lenders and the demand for funds by borrowers in the market for loanable funds. But here we have described a seemingly different model in which the interest rate is determined by the equalization of the supply and demand for money in the money market. Which of these models is correct?

The answer is both. We explain how the models are consistent with each other in the appendix to this chapter. For now, let's put the loanable funds model to one side and concentrate on the liquidity preference model of the interest rate. The most important insight from this model is that it shows us how monetary policy—actions by the Federal Reserve and other central banks—works.

Monetary Policy and the Interest Rate

Let's examine how the Federal Reserve can use changes in the money supply to change the interest rate. Figure 30-4 shows what happens when the Fed increases the money supply from $\overline{M}_1$ to $\overline{M}_2$. The economy is originally in equilibrium at E_1, with an equilibrium interest rate of r_1 and money supply, $\overline{M}_1$. An increase in the money supply by the Fed to $\overline{M}_2$ shifts the money supply curve to the right, from MS_1 to MS_2, and leads to a fall in the equilibrium interest rate to r_2. Why? Because r_2 is the only interest rate at which the public is willing to hold the quantity of money actually supplied, $\overline{M}_2$.

So an increase in the money supply drives the interest rate down. Similarly, a reduction in the money supply drives the interest rate up. By adjusting the money supply up or down, the Fed can set the interest rate.

FIGURE 30-4   **The Effect of an Increase in the Money Supply on the Interest Rate**

The Federal Reserve can lower the interest rate by increasing the money supply. Here, the equilibrium interest rate falls from r_1 to r_2 in response to an increase in the money supply from $\overline{M}_1$ to $\overline{M}_2$. In order to induce people to hold the larger quantity of money, the interest rate must fall from r_1 to r_2.

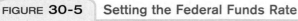

FIGURE **30-5** | Setting the Federal Funds Rate

The Federal Reserve sets a target for the federal funds rate and uses open-market operations to achieve that target. In both panels the target rate is r_T. In panel (a) the initial equilibrium interest rate, r_1, is above the target rate. The Fed increases the money supply by making an open-market purchase of Treasury bills, pushing the money supply curve rightward, from MS_1 to MS_2, and driving the interest rate down to r_T. In panel (b) the initial equilibrium interest rate, r_1, is below the target rate. The Fed reduces the money supply by making an open-market sale of Treasury bills, pushing the money supply curve leftward, from MS_1 to MS_2, and driving the interest rate up to r_T.

PITFALLS

THE TARGET VERSUS THE MARKET?

Over the years, the Federal Reserve has changed the way in which monetary policy is implemented. In the late 1970s and early 1980s, it set a target level for the money supply and altered the monetary base to achieve that target. Under this operating procedure, the federal funds rate fluctuated freely. Today the Fed uses the reverse procedure, setting a target for the federal funds rate and allowing the money supply to fluctuate as it pursues that target.

A common mistake is to imagine that these changes in the way the Federal Reserve operates alter the way the money market works. That is, you'll sometimes hear people say that the interest rate no longer reflects the supply and demand for money because the Fed sets the interest rate.

In fact, the money market works the same way as always: the interest rate is determined by the supply and demand for money. The only difference is that now the Fed adjusts the supply of money to achieve its target interest rate. It's important not to confuse a change in the Fed's operating procedure with a change in the way the economy works.

In practice, at each meeting the Federal Open Market Committee decides on the interest rate to prevail for the next six weeks, until its next meeting. The Fed sets a **target federal funds rate,** a desired level for the federal funds rate. This target is then enforced by the Open Market Desk of the Federal Reserve Bank of New York —in those two small rooms we mentioned in the opening story—which adjusts the money supply through the purchase and sale of Treasury bills until the actual federal funds rate equals the target rate. The other tools of monetary policy, lending through the discount window and changes in reserve requirements, aren't used on a regular basis (although the Fed used discount window lending in its efforts to address the 2008 financial crisis).

Figure 30-5 shows how this works. In both panels, r_T is the target federal funds rate. In panel (a), the initial money supply curve is MS_1 with money supply $\overline{M}_1$, and the equilibrium interest rate, r_1, is above the target rate. To lower the interest rate to r_T, the Fed makes an open-market purchase of Treasury bills. As we learned in Chapter 29, an open-market purchase of Treasury bills leads to an increase in the money supply via the money multiplier. This is illustrated in panel (a) by the rightward shift of the money supply curve from MS_1 to MS_2 and an increase in the money supply to $\overline{M}_2$. This drives the equilibrium interest rate down to the target rate, r_T.

Panel (b) shows the opposite case. Again, the initial money supply curve is MS_1 with money supply $\overline{M}_1$. But this time the equilibrium interest rate, r_1, is below the target federal funds rate, r_T. In this case, the Fed will make an open-market sale of Treasury bills, leading to a fall in the money supply to $\overline{M}_2$ via the money multiplier. The money supply curve shifts leftward from MS_1 to MS_2, driving the equilibrium interest rate up to the target federal funds rate, r_T.

The **target federal funds rate** is the Federal Reserve's desired federal funds rate.

Long-Term Interest Rates

Earlier in this chapter we mentioned that *long-term interest rates*—rates on bonds or loans that mature in several years—don't necessarily move with short-term interest rates. How is that possible, and what does it say about monetary policy?

Consider the case of Millie, who has already decided to place $10,000 in U.S. government bonds for the next two years. However, she hasn't decided whether to put the money in one-year bonds, at a 4% rate of interest, or two-year bonds, at a 5% rate of interest. If she buys the one-year bond, then in one year, Millie will receive the $10,000 she paid for the bond (the *principal*) plus interest earned. If instead she buys the two-year bond, Millie will have to wait until the end of the second year to receive her principal and her interest.

You might think that the two-year bonds are a clearly better deal—but they may not be. Suppose that Millie expects the rate of interest on one-year bonds to rise sharply next year. If she puts her funds in one-year bonds this year, she will be able to reinvest the money at a much higher rate next year. And this could give her a two-year rate of return that is higher than if she put her funds into the two-year bonds today. For example, if the rate of interest on one-year bonds rises from 4% this year to 8% next year, putting her funds in a one-year bond today and in another one-year bond a year from now will give her an annual rate of return over the next two years of about 6%, better than the 5% rate on two-year bonds.

The same considerations apply to all investors deciding between short-term and long-term bonds. If they expect short-term interest rates to rise, investors may buy short-term bonds even if long-term bonds bought today offer a higher interest rate today. If they expect short-term interest rates to fall, investors may buy long-term bonds even if short-term bonds bought today offer a higher interest rate today.

As the example suggests, long-term interest rates largely reflect the average expectation in the market about what's going to happen to short-term rates in the future. When long-term rates are higher than short-term rates, as they were in 2014, the market is signaling that it expects short-term rates to rise in the future.

This is not, however, the whole story: risk is also a factor. Return to the example of Millie, deciding whether to buy one-year or two-year bonds. Suppose that there is some chance she will need to cash in her investment after just one year—say, to meet an emergency medical bill. If she buys two-year bonds, she would have to sell those bonds to meet the unexpected expense. But what price will she get for those bonds? It depends on what has happened to interest rates in the rest of the economy. As we learned in Chapter 25, bond prices and interest rates move in opposite directions: if interest rates rise, bond prices fall, and vice versa.

This means that Millie will face extra risk if she buys two-year rather than one-year bonds, because if a year from now bond prices fall and she must sell her bonds in order to raise cash, she will lose money on the bonds. Owing to this risk factor, long-term interest rates are, on average, higher than short-term rates in order to compensate long-term bond purchasers for the higher risk they face (although this relationship is reversed when short-term rates are unusually high).

Advertising during the two world wars increased the demand for government long-term bonds from savers who might have been otherwise reluctant to tie up their funds for several years.

Flagg, James Montgomery, "I Want You for U.S. Army nearest recruiting station," 1917. Prints and Photographs Division

As we will see later in this chapter, the fact that long-term rates don't necessarily move with short-term rates is sometimes an important consideration for monetary policy.

ECONOMICS ▶ in Action

FIGURE **30-6**   The Fed Reverses Course

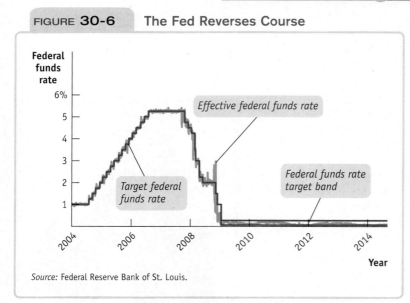

Source: Federal Reserve Bank of St. Louis.

The FED Reverses Course

We began this section with the Fed's announcement of March 18, 2008, that it was cutting its target interest rate. This particular action was part of a larger story: a dramatic reversal of Fed policy that began in September 2007.

Figure 30-6 shows two interest rates from the beginning of 2004 to mid-2014: the target federal funds rate, decided by the Federal Open Market Committee, and the effective, or actual, rate in the market. As you can see, the Fed raised its target rate in a series of steps from late 2004 until the middle of 2006. It did this to head off the possibility of an overheating economy and rising inflation (more on that later in this chapter). But the Fed dramatically reversed course beginning in September 2007, as falling housing prices triggered a growing financial crisis and ultimately a severe recession. And in December 2008, the Fed decided to allow the federal funds rate to move inside a target band between 0% and 0.25%. From then until the time of writing, the Fed funds rate was kept close to zero in response to a very weak economy and high unemployment.

Figure 30-6 also shows that the Fed doesn't always hit its target. There were a number of days, especially in 2008, when the effective federal funds rate was significantly above or below the target rate. But these episodes didn't last long, and overall the Fed got what it wanted, at least as far as short-term interest rates were concerned.

▼ Quick Review

• According to the **liquidity preference model of the interest rate,** the equilibrium interest rate is determined by the money demand curve and the **money supply curve.**

• The Federal Reserve can move the interest rate through open-market operations that shift the money supply curve. In practice, the Fed sets a **target federal funds rate** and uses open-market operations to achieve that target.

• Long-term interest rates reflect expectations about what's going to happen to short-term rates in the future. Because of risk, long-term interest rates tend to be higher than short-term rates.

Check Your Understanding   30-2

1. Assume that there is an increase in the demand for money at every interest rate. Using a diagram, show what effect this will have on the equilibrium interest rate for a given money supply.

2. Now assume that the Fed is following a policy of targeting the federal funds rate. What will the Fed do in the situation described in Question 1 to keep the federal funds rate unchanged? Illustrate with a diagram.

3. Frannie must decide whether to buy a one-year bond today and another one a year from now, or buy a two-year bond today. In which of the following scenarios is she better off taking the first action? The second action?
   a. This year, the interest on a one-year bond is 4%; next year, it will be 10%. The interest rate on a two-year bond is 5%.
   b. This year, the interest rate on a one-year bond is 4%; next year, it will be 1%. The interest rate on a two-year bond is 3%.

Solutions appear at back of book.

Monetary Policy and Aggregate Demand

In Chapter 28 we saw how fiscal policy can be used to stabilize the economy. Now we will see how monetary policy—changes in the money supply, and the interest rate—can play the same role.

Expansionary monetary policy is monetary policy that increases aggregate demand.

Expansionary and Contractionary Monetary Policy

In Chapter 27 we learned that monetary policy shifts the aggregate demand curve. We can now explain how that works: through the effect of monetary policy on the interest rate.

Figure 30-7 illustrates the process. Suppose, first, that the Federal Reserve wants to reduce interest rates, so it expands the money supply. As you can see in the top portion of the figure, a lower interest rate, in turn, will lead, other things equal, to more investment spending. This will in turn lead to higher consumer spending, through the multiplier process, and to an increase in aggregate output demanded. In the end, the total quantity of goods and services demanded at any given aggregate price level rises when the quantity of money increases, and the *AD* curve shifts to the right. Monetary policy that increases the demand for goods and services is known as **expansionary monetary policy.**

Suppose, alternatively, that the Federal Reserve wants to increase interest rates, so it contracts the money supply. You can see this process illustrated in the bottom portion of the diagram. Contraction of the money supply leads to a higher interest rate. The higher interest rate leads to lower investment spending, then to

"I told you the Fed should have tightened."

FIGURE 30-7   **Expansionary and Contractionary Monetary Policy**

EXPANSIONARY

| Increase money supply | → | Lower interest rate | → | Higher investment spending raises income | → | Higher consumer spending (via multiplier) | → | Increase in aggregate demand and *AD* curve shifts to the right |

Graph: Aggregate price level vs. Real GDP, with AD_1 shifting right to AD_2

CONTRACTIONARY

| Decrease money supply | → | Higher interest rate | → | Lower investment spending reduces income | → | Lower consumer spending (via multiplier) | → | Decrease in aggregate demand and *AD* curve shifts to the left |

Graph: Aggregate price level vs. Real GDP, with AD_1 shifting left to AD_2

The top portion shows what happens when the Fed adopts an expansionary monetary policy and increases the money supply. Interest rates fall, leading to higher investment spending, which raises income, which, in turn, raises consumer spending and shifts the *AD* curve to the right. The bottom portion shows what happens when the Fed adopts a contractionary monetary policy and reduces the money supply. Interest rates rise, leading to lower investment spending and a reduction in income. This lowers consumer spending and shifts the *AD* curve to the left.

Contractionary monetary policy is monetary policy that decreases aggregate demand.

lower consumer spending, and then to a decrease in aggregate output demanded. So the total quantity of goods and services demanded falls when the money supply is reduced, and the *AD* curve shifts to the left. Monetary policy that decreases the demand for goods and services is called **contractionary monetary policy.**

Monetary Policy in Practice

How does the Fed decide whether to use expansionary or contractionary monetary policy? And how does it decide how much is enough? In Chapter 21 we learned that policy makers try to fight recessions, as well as try to ensure *price stability:* low (though usually not zero) inflation. Actual monetary policy reflects a combination of these goals.

In general, the Federal Reserve and other central banks tend to engage in expansionary monetary policy when actual real GDP is below potential output. Panel (a) of Figure 30-8 shows the U.S. output gap, which we defined in Chapter 27 as the percentage difference between actual real GDP and potential output, versus the federal funds rate since 1985. (Recall that the output gap is positive when actual real GDP exceeds potential output.) As you can see, the Fed has tended to raise interest rates when the output gap is rising—that is, when the economy is developing an inflationary gap—and cut rates when the output gap is falling.

The big exception was the late 1990s, when the Fed left rates steady for several years even as the economy developed a positive output gap (which went along with a low unemployment rate). One reason the Fed was willing to keep interest rates low in the late 1990s was that inflation was low.

Panel (b) of Figure 30-8 compares the inflation rate, measured as the rate of change in consumer prices excluding food and energy, with the federal funds rate. You can see how low inflation during the mid-1990s, the early 2000s, and the late 2000s helped encourage loose monetary policy in the late 1990s, in 2002–2003, and again beginning in 2008.

FIGURE **30-8** | Tracking Monetary Policy Using the Output Gap and Inflation

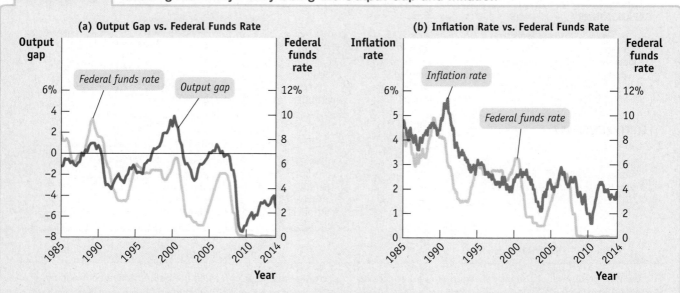

Panel (a) shows that the federal funds rate usually rises when the output gap is positive—that is, when actual real GDP is above potential output—and falls when the output gap is negative. Panel (b) illustrates that the federal funds rate tends to be high when inflation is high and low when inflation is low.
Source: Federal Reserve Bank of St. Louis.

The Taylor Rule Method of Setting Monetary Policy

In 1993 Stanford economist John Taylor suggested that monetary policy should follow a simple rule that takes into account concerns about both the business cycle and inflation. He also suggested that actual monetary policy often looks as if the Federal Reserve was, in fact, more or less following the proposed rule. A **Taylor rule for monetary policy** is a rule for setting interest rates that takes into account the inflation rate and the output gap or, in some cases, the unemployment rate.

A widely cited example of a Taylor rule is a relationship among Fed policy, inflation, and unemployment estimated by economists at the Federal Reserve Bank of San Francisco. These economists found that between 1988 and 2008 the Fed's behavior was well summarized by the following Taylor rule:

Federal funds rate = 2.07 + 1.28 × inflation rate – 1.95 × unemployment gap

where the inflation rate was measured by the change over the previous year in consumer prices excluding food and energy, and the unemployment gap was the difference between the actual unemployment rate and Congressional Budget Office estimates of the natural rate of unemployment.

Figure 30-9 compares the federal funds rate predicted by this rule with the actual federal funds rate from 1985 to mid-2014. As you can see, the Fed's decisions were quite close to those predicted by this particular Taylor rule from 1988 through the end of 2008. We'll talk about what happened after 2008 shortly.

Inflation Targeting

Until January 2012, the Fed did not explicitly commit itself to achieving a particular inflation rate. However, in January 2012, the Fed announced that it would set its policy to maintain an approximately 2% inflation rate per year. With that statement, the Fed joined a number of other central banks that have explicit inflation targets. So rather than using a Taylor rule to set monetary policy, they instead announce the inflation rate that they want to achieve—the *inflation*

> A **Taylor rule for monetary policy** is a rule that sets the federal funds rate according to the level of the inflation rate and either the output gap or the unemployment rate.

FIGURE 30-9 │ The Taylor Rule and the Federal Funds Rate

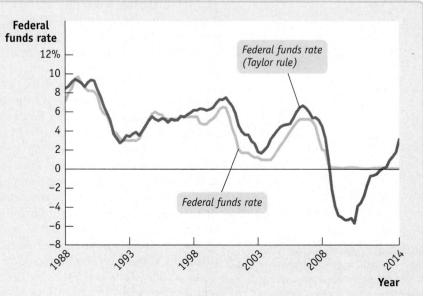

The purple line shows the federal funds rate predicted by the San Francisco Fed's version of the Taylor rule, which relates the interest rate to the inflation rate and the unemployment rate. The green line shows the actual federal funds rate. The actual rate tracked the predicted rate quite closely through the end of 2008. After that, however, the Taylor rule called for negative interest rates, which aren't possible.

Sources: Bureau of Labor Statistics; Congressional Budget Office; Federal Reserve Bank of St. Louis; Glenn D. Rudebusch, "The Fed's Monetary Policy Response to the Current Crisis," *FRBSF Economic Letter* #2009-17 (May 22, 2009).

GLOBAL COMPARISION | Inflation Targets

This figure shows the target inflation rates of six central banks that have adopted inflation targeting. The central bank of New Zealand introduced inflation targeting in 1990. Today it has an inflation target range of from 1% to 3%. The central banks of Canada and Sweden have the same target range but also specify 2% as the precise target. The central banks of Britain and Norway have specific targets for inflation, 2% and 2.5%, respectively. Neither states by how much they're prepared to miss those targets. Since 2012, the U.S. Federal Reserve also targets inflation at 2%.

In practice, these differences in detail don't seem to lead to any significant difference in results. New Zealand aims for the middle of its range, at 2% inflation; Britain, Norway, and the United States allow themselves considerable wiggle room around their target inflation rates.

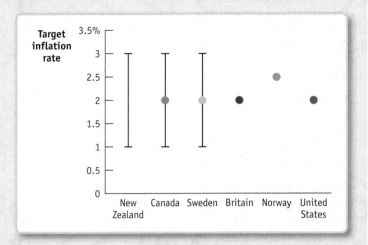

target—and set policy in an attempt to hit that target. This method of setting monetary policy, called **inflation targeting,** involves having the central bank announce the inflation rate it is trying to achieve and set policy in an attempt to hit that target. The central bank of New Zealand, which was the first country to adopt inflation targeting, specified a range for that target of 1% to 3%.

Other central banks commit themselves to achieving a specific number. For example, the Bank of England has committed to keeping inflation at 2%. In practice, there doesn't seem to be much difference between these versions: central banks with a target range for inflation seem to aim for the middle of that range, and central banks with a fixed target tend to give themselves considerable wiggle room.

One major difference between inflation targeting and the Taylor rule method is that inflation targeting is forward-looking rather than backward-looking. That is, the Taylor rule method adjusts monetary policy in response to *past* inflation, but inflation targeting is based on a forecast of future inflation.

Advocates of inflation targeting argue that it has two key advantages over a Taylor rule: *transparency* and *accountability*. First, economic uncertainty is reduced because the central bank's plan is transparent: the public knows the objective of an inflation-targeting central bank. Second, the central bank's success can be judged by seeing how closely actual inflation rates have matched the inflation target, making central bankers accountable.

Critics of inflation targeting argue that it's too restrictive because there are times when other concerns—like the stability of the financial system—should take priority over achieving any particular inflation rate. Indeed, in late 2007 and early 2008 the Fed cut interest rates much more than either a Taylor rule or inflation targeting would have dictated because it feared that turmoil in the financial markets would lead to a major recession. (In fact, it did.)

Many American macroeconomists have had positive things to say about inflation targeting—including Ben Bernanke (the previous chairman of the Fed). And in January 2012 the Fed declared that what it means by the "price stability" it seeks is 2% inflation, although there was no explicit commitment about when this inflation rate would be achieved.

Inflation targeting occurs when the central bank sets an explicit target for the inflation rate and sets monetary policy in order to hit that target.

The Zero Lower Bound Problem

As Figure 30-9 shows, a Taylor rule based on inflation and the unemployment rate does a good job of predicting Federal Reserve policy from 1988 through 2008. After that, however, things go awry, and for a simple reason: with very high unemployment and low inflation, the same Taylor rule called for an interest rate less than zero, which isn't possible.

Why aren't negative interest rates possible? Because people always have the alternative of holding cash, which offers a zero interest rate. Nobody would ever buy a bond yielding an interest rate less than zero because holding cash would be a better alternative.

The fact that interest rates can't go below zero—called the **zero lower bound for interest rates**—sets limits to the power of monetary policy. In 2009 and 2010, inflation was low and the economy was operating far below potential, so the Federal Reserve wanted to increase aggregate demand. Yet the normal way it does this—open-market purchases of short-term government debt to expand the money supply—had run out of room to operate because short-term interest rates were already at or near zero.

In November 2010 the Fed began an attempt to circumvent this problem, which went by the somewhat obscure name "quantitative easing." Instead of purchasing only short-term government debt, it began buying longer-term government debt—five-year or six-year bonds, rather than three-month Treasury bills. As we have already pointed out, long-term interest rates don't exactly follow short-term rates. At the time the Fed began this program, short-term rates were near zero, but rates on longer-term bonds were between 2% and 3%. The Fed hoped that direct purchases of these longer-term bonds would drive down interest rates on long-term debt, exerting an expansionary effect on the economy.

Later the Fed expanded the program further, also purchasing mortgage-backed securities, which normally offer somewhat higher rates than U.S. government debt. Here too the hope was that these rates could be driven down, with an expansionary effect on the economy. As with ordinary open-market operations, quantitative easing was undertaken by the Federal Reserve Bank of New York.

Was this policy effective? The Federal Reserve believes that it helped the economy. However, the pace of recovery remained disappointingly slow.

The **zero lower bound for interest rates** means that interest rates cannot fall below zero.

ECONOMICS ▶ in Action

What the FED Wants, the FED Gets

What's the evidence that the Fed can actually cause an economic contraction or expansion? You might think that finding such evidence is just a matter of looking at what happens to the economy when interest rates go up or down. But it turns out that there's a big problem with that approach: the Fed usually changes interest rates in an attempt to tame the business cycle, raising rates if the economy is expanding and reducing rates if the economy is slumping. So in the actual data, it often looks as if low interest rates go along with a weak economy and high rates go along with a strong economy.

In a famous 1994 paper titled "Monetary Policy Matters," the macroeconomists Christina Romer and David Romer solved this problem by focusing on episodes in which monetary policy wasn't a reaction to the business cycle. Specifically, they used minutes from the Federal Open Market Committee and other sources to identify episodes "in which the Federal Reserve in effect decided to attempt to create a recession to reduce inflation." As we'll learn in the next chapter, rather than just using monetary policy as a tool of macroeconomic stabilization, sometimes

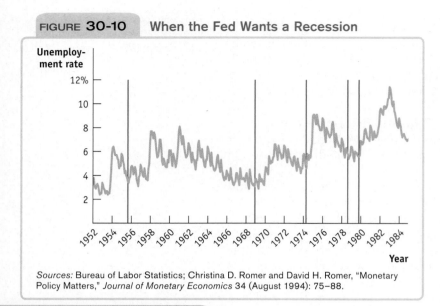

FIGURE **30-10** When the Fed Wants a Recession

Year

Sources: Bureau of Labor Statistics; Christina D. Romer and David H. Romer, "Monetary Policy Matters," *Journal of Monetary Economics* 34 (August 1994): 75–88.

it is used to eliminate *embedded inflation*—inflation that people believe will persist into the future. In such a case, the Fed needs to create a recessionary gap—not just eliminate an inflationary gap—to wring embedded inflation out of the economy.

Figure 30-10 shows the unemployment rate between 1952 and 1984 and also identifies five dates on which, according to Romer and Romer, the Fed decided that it wanted a recession (the vertical lines). In four out of the five cases, the decision to contract the economy was followed, after a modest lag, by a rise in the unemployment rate. On average, Romer and Romer found, the unemployment rate rises by 2 percentage points after the Fed decides that unemployment needs to go up.

So yes, the Fed gets what it wants.

▼ Quick Review

- The Federal Reserve can use **expansionary monetary policy** to increase aggregate demand and **contractionary monetary policy** to reduce aggregate demand. The Federal Reserve and other central banks generally try to tame the business cycle while keeping the inflation rate low but positive.

- Under a **Taylor rule for monetary policy,** the target federal funds rate rises when there is high inflation and either a positive output gap or very low unemployment; it falls when there is low or negative inflation and either a negative output gap or high unemployment.

- In contrast, some central banks set monetary policy by **inflation targeting,** a forward-looking policy rule, rather than by using the Taylor rule, a backward-looking policy rule. Although inflation targeting has the benefits of transparency and accountability, some think it is too restrictive. Until 2008, the Fed followed a loosely defined Taylor rule. Starting in early 2012, it began inflation targeting with a target of 2% per year.

- There is a **zero lower bound for interest rates**—they cannot fall below zero—that limits the power of monetary policy.

- Because it is subject to fewer lags than fiscal policy, monetary policy is the main tool for macroeconomic stabilization.

Check Your Understanding **30-3**

1. Suppose the economy is currently suffering from an output gap and the Federal Reserve uses an expansionary monetary policy to close that gap. Describe the short-run effect of this policy on the following.
   a. The money supply curve
   b. The equilibrium interest rate
   c. Investment spending
   d. Consumer spending
   e. Aggregate output

2. In setting monetary policy, which central bank—one that operates according to a Taylor rule or one that operates by inflation targeting—is likely to respond more directly to a financial crisis? Explain.

Solutions appear at back of book.

Money, Output, and Prices in the Long Run

Through its expansionary and contractionary effects, monetary policy is generally the policy tool of choice to help stabilize the economy. However, not all actions by central banks are productive. In particular, central banks sometimes print money not to fight a recessionary gap but to help the government pay its bills, an action that typically destabilizes the economy.

What happens when a change in the money supply pushes the economy away from, rather than toward, long-run equilibrium? In an earlier chapter we learned that the economy is self-correcting in the long run: a demand shock has only a temporary effect on aggregate output. If the demand shock is the result of a change in the money supply, we can make a stronger statement: in the long run, changes in the quantity of money affect the aggregate price level, but they do not change real aggregate output or the interest rate. To see why, let's look at what happens if the central bank permanently increases the money supply.

Short-Run and Long-Run Effects of an Increase in the Money Supply

To analyze the long-run effects of monetary policy, it's helpful to think of the central bank as choosing a target for the money supply rather than the interest

FIGURE 30-11   The Short-Run and Long-Run Effects of an Increase in the Money Supply

When the economy is already at potential output, an increase in the money supply generates a positive short-run effect, but no long-run effect, on real GDP.

Here, the economy begins at E_1, a point of short-run and long-run macroeconomic equilibrium. An increase in the money supply shifts the AD curve rightward, and the economy moves to a new short-run macroeconomic equilibrium at E_2 and a new real GDP of Y_2. But E_2 is not a long-run equilibrium: Y_2 exceeds potential output, Y_1, leading over time to an increase in nominal wages. In the long run, the increase in nominal wages shifts the short-run aggregate supply curve leftward, to a new position at $SRAS_2$.

The economy reaches a new short-run and long-run macroeconomic equilibrium at E_3 on the $LRAS$ curve, and output falls back to potential output, Y_1. When the economy is already at potential output, the only long-run effect of an increase in the money supply is an increase in the aggregate price level from P_1 to P_3.

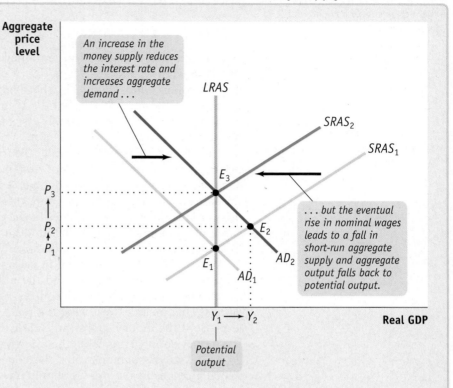

rate. In assessing the effects of an increase in the money supply, we return to the analysis of the long-run effects of an increase in aggregate demand, first introduced in Chapter 27.

Figure 30-11 shows the short-run and long-run effects of an increase in the money supply when the economy begins at potential output, Y_1. The initial short-run aggregate supply curve is $SRAS_1$, the long-run aggregate supply curve is $LRAS$, and the initial aggregate demand curve is AD_1. The economy's initial equilibrium is at E_1, a point of both short-run and long-run macroeconomic equilibrium because it is on both the short-run and the long-run aggregate supply curves. Real GDP is at potential output, Y_1.

Now suppose there is an increase in the money supply. Other things equal, an increase in the money supply reduces the interest rate, which increases investment spending, which leads to a further rise in consumer spending, and so on. So an increase in the money supply increases the quantity of goods and services demanded, shifting the AD curve rightward, to AD_2. In the short run, the economy moves to a new short-run macroeconomic equilibrium at E_2. The price level rises from P_1 to P_2, and real GDP rises from Y_1 to Y_2. That is, both the aggregate price level and aggregate output increase in the short run.

But the aggregate output level, Y_2, is above potential output. As a result, nominal wages will rise over time, causing the short-run aggregate supply curve to shift leftward. This process stops only when the $SRAS$ curve ends up at $SRAS_2$ and the economy ends up at point E_3, a point of both short-run and long-run macroeconomic equilibrium. The long-run effect of an increase in the money supply, then, is that the aggregate price level has increased from P_1 to P_3, but aggregate output is back at potential output, Y_1. In the long run, a monetary expansion raises the aggregate price level but has no effect on real GDP.

We won't describe the effects of a monetary contraction in detail, but the same logic applies. In the short run, a fall in the money supply leads to a fall in aggregate output as the economy moves down the short-run aggregate supply curve.

According to the concept of **monetary neutrality,** changes in the money supply have no real effects on the economy.

In the long run, however, the monetary contraction reduces only the aggregate price level, and real GDP returns to potential output.

Monetary Neutrality

How much does a change in the money supply change the aggregate price level in the long run? The answer is that a change in the money supply leads to an equal proportional change in the aggregate price level in the long run. For example, if the money supply falls 25%, the aggregate price level falls 25% in the long run; if the money supply rises 50%, the aggregate price level rises 50% in the long run.

How do we know this? Consider the following thought experiment: suppose all prices in the economy—prices of final goods and services and also factor prices, such as nominal wage rates—double. And suppose the money supply doubles at the same time. What difference does this make to the economy in real terms? The answer is none. All real variables in the economy—such as real GDP and the real value of the money supply (the amount of goods and services it can buy)—are unchanged. So there is no reason for anyone to behave any differently.

We can state this argument in reverse: if the economy starts out in long-run macroeconomic equilibrium and the money supply changes, restoring long-run macroeconomic equilibrium requires restoring all real values to their original values. This includes restoring the real value of the money supply to its original level. So if the money supply falls 25%, the aggregate price level must fall 25%; if the money supply rises 50%, the price level must rise 50%; and so on.

This analysis demonstrates the concept known as **monetary neutrality,** in which changes in the money supply have no real effects on the economy. In the long run, the only effect of an increase in the money supply is to raise the aggregate price level by an equal percentage. Economists argue that *money is neutral in the long run.*

This is, however, a good time to recall the dictum of John Maynard Keynes: "In the long run we are all dead." In the long run, changes in the money supply don't have any effect on real GDP, interest rates, or anything else except the price level. But it would be foolish to conclude from this that the Fed is irrelevant. Monetary policy does have powerful real effects on the economy in the short run, often making the difference between recession and expansion. And that matters a lot for society's welfare.

Changes in the Money Supply and the Interest Rate in the Long Run

In the short run, an increase in the money supply leads to a fall in the interest rate, and a decrease in the money supply leads to a rise in the interest rate. In the long run, however, changes in the money supply don't affect the interest rate.

Figure 30-12 shows why. It shows the money supply curve and the money demand curve before and after the Fed increases the money supply. We assume that the economy is initially at E_1, in long-run macroeconomic equilibrium at potential output, and with money supply $\overline{M}_1$. The initial equilibrium interest rate, determined by the intersection of the money demand curve MD_1 and the money supply curve MS_1, is r_1.

Now suppose the money supply increases from $\overline{M}_1$ to $\overline{M}_2$. In the short run, the economy moves from E_1 to E_2 and the interest rate falls from r_1 to r_2. Over time, however, the aggregate price level rises, and this raises money demand, shifting the money demand curve rightward from MD_1 to MD_2. The economy moves to a new long-run equilibrium at E_3, and the interest rate rises to its original level at r_1.

And it turns out that the long-run equilibrium interest rate is the original interest rate, r_1. We know this for two reasons. First, due to monetary neutrality, in the long run the aggregate price level rises by the same proportion as the money supply; so if the money supply rises by, say, 50%, the price level will also

FIGURE **30-12** The Long-Run Determination of the Interest Rate

In the short run, an increase in the money supply from $\overline{M}_1$ to $\overline{M}_2$ pushes the interest rate down from r_1 to r_2 and the economy moves to E_2, a short-run equilibrium. In the long run, however, the aggregate price level rises in proportion to the increase in the money supply, leading to an increase in money demand at any given interest rate in proportion to the increase in the aggregate price level, as shown by the shift from MD_1 to MD_2. The result is that the quantity of money demanded at any given interest rate rises by the same amount as the quantity of money supplied. The economy moves to long-run equilibrium at E_3 and the interest rate returns to r_1.

rise by 50%. Second, the demand for money is, other things equal, proportional to the aggregate price level.

So a 50% increase in the money supply raises the aggregate price level by 50%, which increases the quantity of money demanded at any given interest rate by 50%. As a result, the quantity of money demanded at the initial interest rate, r_1, rises exactly as much as the money supply—so that r_1 is still the equilibrium interest rate. In the long run, then, changes in the money supply do not affect the interest rate.

ECONOMICS ▶ *in Action*

International Evidence of Monetary Neutrality

These days monetary policy is quite similar among wealthy countries. Each major nation (or, in the case of the euro, the euro area) has a central bank that is insulated from political pressure. All of these central banks try to keep the aggregate price level roughly stable, which usually means inflation of at most 2% to 3% per year.

But if we look at a longer period and a wider group of countries, we see large differences in the growth of the money supply. Between 1970 and the present, the money supply rose only a few percent per year in some countries, such as Switzerland and the United States, but rose much more rapidly in some poorer countries, such as South Africa. These differences allow us to see whether it is really true that increases in the money supply lead, in the long run, to equal percent rises in the aggregate price level.

Figure 30-13 shows the annual percentage increases in the money supply and average annual increases in the

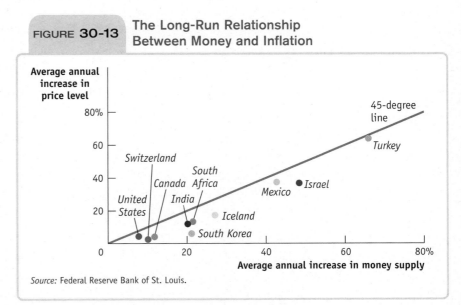

FIGURE **30-13** The Long-Run Relationship Between Money and Inflation

Source: Federal Reserve Bank of St. Louis.

aggregate price level—that is, the average rate of inflation—for a sample of countries during the period 1981–2013, with each point representing a country. If the relationship between increases in the money supply and changes in the aggregate price level were exact, the points would lie precisely on a 45-degree line.

In fact, the relationship isn't exact, because other factors besides money affect the aggregate price level. But the scatter of points clearly lies close to a 45-degree line, showing a more or less proportional relationship between money and the aggregate price level. That is, the data support the concept of monetary neutrality in the long run.

Check Your Understanding 30-4

1. Assume the central bank increases the quantity of money by 25%, even though the economy is initially in both short-run and long-run macroeconomic equilibrium. Describe the effects, in the short run and in the long run (giving numbers where possible), on the following.
   a. Aggregate output
   b. Aggregate price level
   c. Interest rate
2. Why does monetary policy affect the economy in the short run but not in the long run?

Solutions appear at back of book.

PIMCO Bets on Cheap Money

Pacific Investment Management Company, generally known as PIMCO, is one of the world's largest investment companies. Among other things, it runs PIMCO Total Return, the world's largest mutual fund. Bill Gross, who headed PIMCO from 1971 until 2014, was legendary for his ability to predict trends in financial markets, especially bond markets, where PIMCO does much of its investing.

In the fall of 2009, Gross decided to put more of PIMCO's assets into long-term U.S. government bonds. This amounted to a bet that long-term interest rates would fall. This bet was especially interesting because it was the opposite of the bet many other investors were making. For example, in November 2009 the investment bank Morgan Stanley told its clients to expect a sharp rise in long-term interest rates.

What lay behind PIMCO's bet? Gross explained the firm's thinking in his September 2009 commentary. He suggested that unemployment was likely to stay high and inflation low. "Global policy rates," he asserted—meaning the federal funds rate and its equivalents in Europe and elsewhere—"will remain low for extended periods of time."

PIMCO's view was in sharp contrast to those of other investors: Morgan Stanley expected long-term rates to rise in part because it expected the Fed to raise the federal funds rate in 2010.

Who was right? PIMCO, mostly. As Figure 30-14 shows, the federal funds rate stayed near zero, and long-term interest rates fell through much of 2010, although they rose somewhat very late in the year as investors became somewhat more optimistic about economic recovery. Morgan Stanley, which had bet on rising rates, actually apologized to investors for getting it so wrong.

Bill Gross's foresight, however, was a lot less accurate in 2011. Anticipating a significantly stronger U.S. economy by mid-2011 that would result in inflation, Gross bet heavily against U.S. government bonds early that year. But this time he was wrong, as weak growth continued. By late summer 2011, Gross realized his mistake as U.S. bonds rose in value and the value of his funds sank. He admitted to the *Wall Street Journal* that he had "lost sleep" over his bet, and called it a "mistake." It was a mistake from which he never fully recovered. Most observers agreed that the losses PIMCO suffered from Gross's bad bet in 2011 played a major rule in his departure in 2014.

FIGURE 30-14 The Federal Funds Rate and Long-Term Interest Rates, 2009–2011

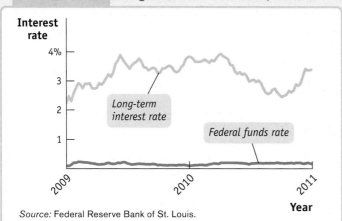

Source: Federal Reserve Bank of St. Louis.

QUESTIONS FOR THOUGHT

1. Why did PIMCO's view that unemployment would stay high and inflation low lead to a forecast that policy interest rates would remain low for an extended period?

2. Why would low policy rates suggest low long-term interest rates?

3. What might have caused long-term interest rates to rise in late 2010, even though the federal funds rate was still zero?

SUMMARY

1. The **money demand curve** arises from a trade-off between the opportunity cost of holding money and the liquidity that money provides. The opportunity cost of holding money depends on **short-term interest rates,** not **long-term interest rates.** Changes in the aggregate price level, real GDP, technology, and institutions shift the money demand curve.

2. According to the **liquidity preference model of the interest rate,** the interest rate is determined in the money market by the money demand curve and the **money supply curve.** The Federal Reserve can change the interest rate in the short run by shifting the money supply curve. In practice, the Fed uses open-market operations to achieve a **target federal funds rate,** which other short-term interest rates generally track. Although long-term interest rates don't necessarily move with short-term interest rates, they reflect expectations about what's going to happen to short-term rates in the future.

3. **Expansionary monetary policy** reduces the interest rate by increasing the money supply. This increases investment spending and consumer spending, which in turn increases aggregate demand and real GDP in the short run. **Contractionary monetary policy** raises the interest rate by reducing the money supply. This reduces investment spending and consumer spending, which in turn reduces aggregate demand and real GDP in the short run.

4. The Federal Reserve and other central banks try to stabilize the economy, limiting fluctuations of actual output around potential output, while also keeping inflation low but positive. Under a **Taylor rule for monetary policy,** the target federal funds rate rises when there is high inflation and either a positive output gap or very low unemployment; it falls when there is low or negative inflation and either a negative output gap or high unemployment. Some central banks (including the Fed as of January 2012) engage in **inflation targeting,** which is a forward-looking policy rule, whereas the Taylor rule method is a backward-looking policy rule. Because monetary policy is subject to fewer implementation lags than fiscal policy, it is the preferred policy tool for stabilizing the economy. Because interest rates cannot fall below zero—the **zero lower bound for interest rates**—the power of monetary policy is limited.

5. In the long run, changes in the money supply affect the aggregate price level but not real GDP or the interest rate. Data show that the concept of **monetary neutrality** holds: changes in the money supply have no real effect on the economy in the long run.

KEY TERMS

Short-term interest rates, p. 891
Long-term interest rates, p. 891
Money demand curve, p. 892
Liquidity preference model of the
   interest rate, p. 896

Money supply curve, p. 896
Target federal funds rate, p. 899
Expansionary monetary policy, p. 901
Contractionary monetary policy, p. 902
Taylor rule for monetary policy, p. 903

Inflation targeting, p. 904
Zero lower bound for interest rates,
   p. 905
Monetary neutrality, p. 908

PROBLEMS

1. Go to the FOMC page of the Federal Reserve Board's website (www.federalreserve.gov/FOMC/) to find the statement issued after the most recent FOMC meeting. (Click on "Meeting calendars and information" and then click on the most recent statement listed in the calendar.)
   a. What is the target federal funds rate?
   b. Is the target federal funds rate different from the target federal funds rate in the previous FOMC statement? If yes, by how much does it differ?
   c. Does the statement comment on current macroeconomic conditions in the United States? How does it describe the U.S. economy?

2. How will the following events affect the demand for money? In each case, specify whether there is a shift of the demand curve or a movement along the demand curve and its direction.
   a. There is a fall in the interest rate from 12% to 10%.
   b. Thanksgiving arrives and, with it, the beginning of the holiday shopping season.
   c. McDonald's and other fast-food restaurants begin to accept credit cards.
   d. The Fed engages in an open-market purchase of U.S. Treasury bills.

3. a. Go to www.treasurydirect.gov. Under "Individuals," go to "Treasury Securities & Programs." Click on "Treasury bills." Under "at a glance," click on "rates in recent auctions." What is the investment rate for the most recently issued 26-week T-bills?

b. Go to the website of your favorite bank. What is the interest rate for six-month CDs?

c. Why are the rates for six-month CDs higher than for 26-week Treasury bills?

4. Go to www.treasurydirect.gov. Under "Individuals," go to "Treasury Securities & Programs." Click on "Treasury notes." Under "at a glance," click on "rates in recent auctions." Use the list of Recent Note, Bond, and TIPS Auction Results to answer the following questions.

a. What are the interest rates on 2-year and 10-year notes?

b. How do the interest rates on the 2-year and 10-year notes relate to each other? Why is the interest rate on the 10-year note higher (or lower) than the interest rate on the 2-year note?

5. An economy is facing the recessionary gap shown in the accompanying diagram. To eliminate the gap, should the central bank use expansionary or contractionary monetary policy? How will the interest rate, investment spending, consumer spending, real GDP, and the aggregate price level change as monetary policy closes the recessionary gap?

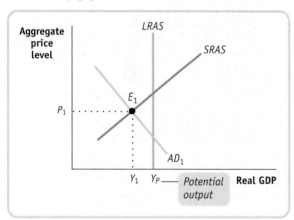

6. An economy is facing the inflationary gap shown in the accompanying diagram. To eliminate the gap, should the central bank use expansionary or contractionary monetary policy? How will the interest rate, investment spending, consumer spending, real GDP, and the aggregate price level change as monetary policy closes the inflationary gap?

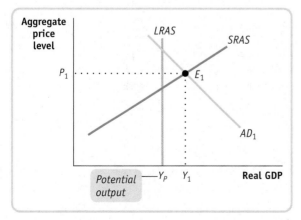

7. In the economy of Eastlandia, the money market is initially in equilibrium when the economy begins to slide into a recession.

a. Using the accompanying diagram, explain what will happen to the interest rate if the central bank of Eastlandia keeps the money supply constant at $\overline{M}_1$.

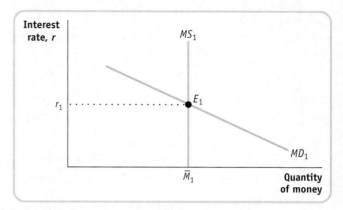

b. If the central bank is instead committed to maintaining an interest rate target of r_1, then as the economy slides into recession, how should the central bank react? Using your diagram from part a, demonstrate the central bank's reaction.

8. Suppose that the money market in Westlandia is initially in equilibrium and the central bank decides to decrease the money supply.

a. Using a diagram like the one in Problem 7, explain what will happen to the interest rate in the short run.

b. What will happen to the interest rate in the long run?

9. An economy is in long-run macroeconomic equilibrium with an unemployment rate of 5% when the government passes a law requiring the central bank to use monetary policy to lower the unemployment rate to 3% and keep it there. How could the central bank achieve this goal in the short run? What would happen in the long run? Illustrate with a diagram.

10. According to the European Central Bank website, the treaty establishing the European Community "makes clear that ensuring price stability is the most important contribution that monetary policy can make to achieve a favourable economic environment and a high level of employment." If price stability is the only goal of monetary policy, explain how monetary policy would be conducted during recessions. Analyze both the case of a recession that is the result of a demand shock and the case of a recession that is the result of a supply shock.

11. The effectiveness of monetary policy depends on how easy it is for changes in the money supply to change interest rates. By changing interest rates, monetary policy affects investment spending and the aggregate demand curve. The economies of Albernia and Brittania have very different money demand curves, as shown in the accompanying diagram. In which economy will changes in the money supply be a more effective policy tool? Why?

WORK IT OUT

For interactive, step-by-step help in solving the following problem, visit LaunchPad by using the URL on the back cover of this book.

13. Because of the economic slowdown associated with the 2007–2009 recession, the Federal Open Market Committee of the Federal Reserve, between September 18, 2007, and December 16, 2008, lowered the federal funds rate in a series of steps from a high of 5.25% to a rate between zero and 0.25%. The idea was to provide a boost to the economy by increasing aggregate demand.

   a. Use the liquidity preference model to explain how the Federal Open Market Committee lowers the interest rate in the short run. Draw a typical graph that illustrates the mechanism. Label the vertical axis "Interest rate" and the horizontal axis "Quantity of money." Your graph should show two interest rates, r_1 and r_2.

   b. Explain why the reduction in the interest rate causes aggregate demand to increase in the short run.

   c. Suppose that in 2015 the economy is at potential output but that this is somehow overlooked by the Fed, which continues its monetary expansion. Demonstrate the effect of the policy measure on the *AD* curve. Use the *LRAS* curve to show that the effect of this policy measure on the *AD* curve, other things equal, causes the aggregate price level to rise in the long run. Label the vertical axis "Aggregate price level" and the horizontal axis "Real GDP."

12. During the Great Depression, businesspeople in the United States were very pessimistic about the future of economic growth and reluctant to increase investment spending even when interest rates fell. How did this limit the potential for monetary policy to help alleviate the Depression?

Reconciling the Two Models of the Interest Rate

In the liquidity preference model of the interest rate developed in Chapter 30, at the equilibrium interest rate the quantity of money demanded equals the quantity of money supplied. Yet, in the loanable funds model of the interest rate developed in Chapter 25, the equilibrium interest rate matches the quantity of loanable funds supplied by savers with the quantity of loanable funds demanded for investment spending. Can these two models of the interest rate be reconciled? Yes, they can. We will do this in two steps, focusing first on the short run and then on the long run.

The Interest Rate in the Short Run

As explained in Chapter 30, a fall in the interest rate leads to a rise in investment spending, I, which then leads to a rise in both real GDP and consumer spending, C. The rise in real GDP doesn't lead only to a rise in consumer spending, however. It also leads to a rise in savings: at each stage of the multiplier process, part of the increase in disposable income is saved. How much do savings rise?

In Chapter 25 we introduced the *savings–investment spending identity:* total savings in the economy is always equal to investment spending. *This tells us that when a fall in the interest rate leads to higher investment spending, the resulting increase in real GDP generates exactly enough additional savings to match the rise in investment spending.* To put it another way, after a fall in the interest rate, the quantity of savings supplied rises exactly enough to match the quantity of savings demanded. Understanding this relationship is the key to reconciling the two models of the interest rate.

Figure 30A-1 illustrates how the two models of the interest rate are reconciled in the short run. Panel (a) shows the liquidity preference model of the interest rate where MS_1 and MD_1 are the initial supply and demand curves for money, and r_1, the initial equilibrium interest rate, equalizes the quantity of money supplied to the quantity of money demanded in the money market. Panel (b) shows the loanable funds model of the interest rate where S_1 is the initial supply curve, D is the demand curve for loanable funds, and r_1, the initial equilibrium interest rate, equalizes the quantity of loanable funds supplied to the quantity of loanable funds demanded in the market for loanable funds.

In Figure 30A-1 both the money market and the market for loanable funds are initially in equilibrium at E_1 with the same interest rate, r_1. You might think that this would only happen by accident, but in fact it will always be true. To see why, consider what happens in panel (a), the money market, when the Fed increases the money supply from $\overline{M}_1$ to $\overline{M}_2$, pushing the money supply curve rightward, to MS_2, reducing the equilibrium interest rate in the market to r_2, and moving the economy to a short-run equilibrium at E_2.

What happens in panel (b), the market for loanable funds? In the short run, the fall in the interest rate due to the increase in the money supply leads to a rise in real GDP, which generates a rise in savings through the multiplier process. This rise in savings shifts the supply curve for loanable funds rightward, from S_1 to S_2, moving the equilibrium in the loanable funds market from E_1 to E_2 and reducing the equilibrium interest rate in the loanable funds market. Since the

FIGURE **30A-1**   The Short-Run Determination of the Interest Rate

(a) The Liquidity Preference Model of the Interest Rate

In the short run, an increase in the money supply reduces the interest rate . . .

(b) The Loanable Funds Model of the Interest Rate

. . . which leads to a short-run increase in real GDP and an increase in the supply of loanable funds.

Panel (a) shows the liquidity preference model of the interest rate: the equilibrium interest rate matches the money supply to the quantity of money demanded. In the short run, the interest rate is determined in the money market, where an increase in the money supply, from $\bar{M}_1$ to $\bar{M}_2$, pushes the equilibrium interest rate down, from r_1 to r_2. Panel (b) shows the loanable funds model of the interest rate. The fall in the interest rate in the money market leads, through the multiplier effect, to an increase in real GDP and savings; to a rightward shift of the supply curve of loanable funds, from S_1 to S_2; and to a fall in the interest rate, from r_1 to r_2. As a result, the new equilibrium interest rate in the loanable funds market matches the new equilibrium interest rate in the money market at r_2.

rise in savings must exactly match the rise in investment spending, the equilibrium rate in the loanable funds market must fall to r_2, the same as the new equilibrium interest rate in the money market.

In the short run, then, the supply and demand for money determine the interest rate, and the loanable funds market follows the lead of the money market until the equilibrium interest rate in the loanable funds market is the same as the equilibrium interest rate in the money market.

Notice our use of the phrase "in the short run." Changes in aggregate demand affect aggregate output only in the short run. In the long run, aggregate output is equal to potential output. So our story about how a fall in the interest rate leads to a rise in aggregate output, which leads to a rise in savings, applies only to the short run.

In the long run, as we'll see next, the determination of the interest rate is quite different, because the roles of the two markets are reversed. In the long run, the loanable funds market determines the equilibrium interest rate, and it is the market for money that follows the lead of the loanable funds market.

The Interest Rate in the Long Run

In the short run an increase in the money supply leads to a fall in the interest rate, and a decrease in the money supply leads to a rise in the interest rate. In the long run, however, changes in the money supply don't affect the interest rate.

Figure 30A-2 shows why. As in Figure 30A-1, panel (a) shows the liquidity preference model of the interest rate and panel (b) shows the supply and demand for loanable funds. We assume that in both panels the economy is initially at E_1, in

FIGURE 30A-2 The Long-Run Determination of the Interest Rate

Panel (a) shows the liquidity preference model long-run adjustment to an increase in the money supply from $\overline{M}_1$ to $\overline{M}_2$; panel (b) shows the corresponding long-run adjustment in the loanable funds market. Both panels start from E_1, a long-run macroeconomic equilibrium at potential output and with interest rate r_1. As we discussed in Figure 30A-1, the increase in the money supply reduces the interest rate from r_1 to r_2, increases real GDP, and increases savings in the short run. This is shown in panel (a) and panel (b) as the movement from E_1 to E_2. In the long run, however, the increase in the money

supply raises wages and other nominal prices. This shifts the money demand curve in panel (a) from MD_1 to MD_2, leading to an increase in the interest rate from r_2 to r_1 as the economy moves from E_2 to E_3. The rise in the interest rate causes a fall in real GDP and a fall in savings, shifting the loanable funds supply curve back to S_1 from S_2 and moving the loanable funds market from E_2 back to E_1. In the long run, the equilibrium interest rate is determined by matching the supply and demand for loanable funds that arises when real GDP equals potential output.

long-run macroeconomic equilibrium at potential output with the money supply equal to $\overline{M}_1$. The demand curve for loanable funds is D, and the initial supply curve for loanable funds is S_1. The initial equilibrium interest rate in both markets is r_1.

Now suppose the money supply rises from $\overline{M}_1$ to $\overline{M}_2$. As in Figure 30A-1, this initially reduces the interest rate to r_2. According to the neutrality of money, in the long run the aggregate price level rises by the same proportion as the increase in the money supply. And we also know that a rise in the aggregate price level increases money demand by the same proportion. So in the long run the money demand curve shifts out to MD_2 as money demand responds to higher prices, and moving the equilibrium interest rate rises back to its original level, r_1.

Panel (b) of Figure 30A-2 shows what happens in the market for loanable funds. As before, an increase in the money supply leads to a short-run rise in real GDP, and this shifts the supply of loanable funds rightward from S_1 to S_2. In the long run, however, real GDP falls back to its original level as wages and other nominal prices rise. As a result, the supply of loanable funds, S, which initially shifted from S_1 to S_2, shifts back to S_1.

In the long run, then, changes in the money supply do not affect the interest rate. So what determines the interest rate in the long run, r_1, in Figure 30A-2? The answer is the supply and demand for loanable funds. More specifically, in the long run the equilibrium interest rate matches the supply and demand for loanable funds that arise at potential output.

PROBLEMS

1. Using a figure similar to Figure 30A-1, explain how the money market and the loanable funds market react to a reduction in the money supply in the short run.

WORK IT OUT

For interactive, step-by-step help in solving the following problem, visit LaunchPad by using the URL on the back cover of this book.

2. Contrast the short-run effects of an increase in the money supply on the interest rate to the long-run effects of an increase in the money supply on the interest rate. Which market determines the interest rate in the short run? Which market does so in the long run? What are the implications of your answers for the effectiveness of monetary policy in influencing real GDP in the short run and the long run?

Inflation, Disinflation, and Deflation

▶ **What You Will Learn in This Chapter**

■ Why efforts to collect an **inflation tax** by printing money can lead to high rates of inflation and hyperinflation

■ What the **Phillips curve** is and how it describes the short-run trade-off between inflation and unemployment

■ Why there is no long-run trade-off between inflation and unemployment

■ Why expansionary policies are limited due to the effects of expected inflation

■ Why even moderate levels of inflation can be hard to end

■ Why deflation is a problem for economic policy and leads policy makers to prefer a low but positive inflation rate

■ Why the nominal interest rate cannot go below the **zero bound** and the danger a **liquidity trap** poses

BRINGING A SUITCASE TO THE BANK

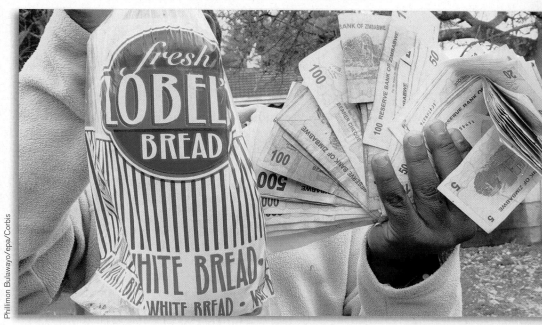

Phillimon Bulawayo/epa/Corbis

In 2008, the Zimbabwe dollar was so devalued by extreme inflation that this much currency was needed to pay for a single loaf of bread.

In 2008, the African nation of Zimbabwe achieved a dubious distinction: it exhibited one of the highest inflation rates ever recorded, peaking at around 500 billion percent. Although the government kept introducing ever-larger denominations of the Zimbabwe dollar—for example, in May 2008 it introduced a half-billion-dollar bill—it still took a lot of currency to pay for the necessities of life: a stack of Zimbabwean cash worth $100 U.S. dollars weighed about 40 pounds. Zimbabwean currency was worth so little that some people withdrawing funds from banks brought suitcases along in order to be able to walk away with enough cash to pay for ordinary living expenses. In the end, the Zimbabwe dollar lost all value—literally. By October 2008, the currency had more or less vanished from circulation, replaced by U.S. dollars and South African rands.

Zimbabwe's experience was shocking, but not unprecedented. In 1994 the inflation rate in Armenia hit 27,000%. In 1991 Nicaraguan inflation exceeded 60,000%. And Zimbabwe's experience was more or less matched by history's most famous example of extreme inflation, which took place in Germany in 1922–1923. Toward the end of the German hyperinflation, prices were rising 16% a *day,* which—through compounding—meant an increase of approximately 500 billion percent over the course of five months.

People became so reluctant to hold paper money, which lost value by the hour, that eggs and lumps of coal began to circulate as currency. German firms would pay their workers several times a day so that they could spend their earnings before they lost value (lending new meaning to the term *hourly wage*). Legend has it that men sitting down at a bar would order two beers at a time, out of fear that the price of a beer would rise before they could order a second round!

The United States has never experienced that kind of inflation. The worst U.S. inflation in modern times took place at the end of the 1970s, when consumer prices were rising at an annual rate of 13%. Yet inflation at even that rate was profoundly troubling to the American public, and the policies the Federal Reserve pursued in order to get U.S. inflation back down to an acceptable rate led to the deepest recession since the Great Depression.

What causes inflation to rise and fall? In this chapter, we'll look at the underlying reasons for inflation. We'll see that the underlying causes of very high inflation, the type of inflation suffered by Zimbabwe, are quite different from the causes of more moderate inflation. We'll also learn why *disinflation,* a reduction in the inflation rate, is often very difficult. Finally, we'll discuss the special problems associated with a falling price level, or deflation.

According to the **classical model of the price level,** the real quantity of money is always at its long-run equilibrium level.

Money and Inflation

As we'll soon see, moderate levels of inflation such as those experienced in the United States—even the double-digit inflation of the late 1970s—can have complex causes. But very high inflation is always associated with rapid increases in the money supply.

To understand why, we need to revisit the effect of changes in the money supply on the overall price level. Then we'll turn to the reasons governments sometimes increase the money supply very rapidly.

The Classical Model of Money and Prices

In Chapter 30 we learned that in the short run, an increase in the money supply increases real GDP by lowering the interest rate and stimulating investment spending and consumer spending. However, in the long run, as nominal wages and other sticky prices rise, real GDP falls back to its original level. So in the long run, an increase in the money supply does not change real GDP. Instead, other things equal, it leads to an equal percent rise in the overall price level; that is, the prices of all goods and services in the economy, including nominal wages and the prices of intermediate goods, rise by the same percentage as the money supply. And when the overall price level rises, the aggregate price level—the prices of all final goods and services—rises as well.

As a result, a change in the *nominal* money supply, M, leads in the long run to a change in the aggregate price level that leaves the *real* quantity of money, M/P, at its original level, with no long-run effect on aggregate demand or real GDP. For example, when Turkey dropped six zeros from its currency, the Turkish lira, in January 2005, Turkish real GDP did not change. The only thing that changed was the number of zeros in prices: instead of something costing 2,000,000 lira, it cost 2 lira.

This is, to repeat, what happens in the long run. When analyzing large changes in the aggregate price level, however, macroeconomists often find it useful to ignore the distinction between the short run and the long run. Instead, they work with a simplified model in which the effect of a change in the money supply on the aggregate price level takes place instantaneously rather than over a long period of time. You might be concerned about this assumption, given that in previous chapters we've emphasized the difference between the short run and the long run. However, for reasons we'll explain shortly, this is a reasonable assumption to make in the case of high inflation.

A simplified model in which the real quantity of money, M/P, is always at its long-run equilibrium level is known as the **classical model of the price level** because it was commonly used by "classical" economists who wrote before the work of John Maynard Keynes. To understand the classical model and why it is useful in the context of high inflation, let's revisit the *AD–AS* model and what it says about the effects of an increase in the money supply. (Unless otherwise noted, we will always be referring to changes in the *nominal* supply of money.)

Figure 31-1 reviews the effects of an increase in the money supply according to the *AD–AS* model. The economy starts at E_1, a point of short-run and long-run macroeconomic equilibrium. It lies at the intersection of the aggregate demand curve, AD_1, and the short-run aggregate supply curve, $SRAS_1$. It also lies on the long-run aggregate supply curve, *LRAS*. At E_1, the equilibrium aggregate price level is P_1.

Now suppose there is an increase in the money supply. This is an expansionary monetary policy, which shifts the aggregate demand curve to the right, to AD_2, and moves the economy to a new short-run macroeconomic equilibrium at E_2. Over time, however, nominal wages adjust upward in response to the rise in the aggregate price level, and the *SRAS* curve shifts to the left, to $SRAS_2$. The new long-run macroeconomic equilibrium is at E_3, and real GDP returns to its initial

FIGURE 31-1   The Classical Model of the Price Level

Starting at E_1, an increase in the money supply shifts the aggregate demand curve rightward, as shown by the movement from AD_1 to AD_2. There is a new short-run macroeconomic equilibrium at E_2 and a higher price level at P_2. In the long run, nominal wages adjust upward and push the $SRAS$ curve leftward to $SRAS_2$. The total percent increase in the price level from P_1 to P_3 is equal to the percent increase in the money supply. In the *classical model of the price level*, we ignore the transition period and think of the price level as rising to P_3 immediately. This is a good approximation under conditions of high inflation.

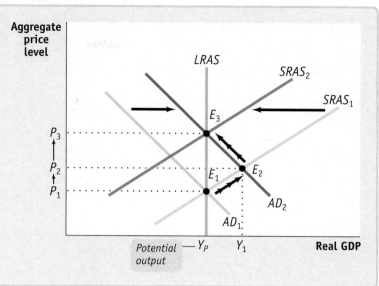

level. As we learned in Chapter 30, the long-run increase in the aggregate price level from P_1 to P_3 is proportional to the increase in the money supply. As a result, in the long run changes in the money supply have no effect on the real quantity of money, M/P, or on real GDP. In the long run, money—as we learned—is *neutral*.

The classical model of the price level ignores the short-run movement from E_1 to E_2, assuming that the economy moves directly from one long-run equilibrium to another long-run equilibrium. In other words, it assumes that the economy moves directly from E_1 to E_3 and that real GDP never changes in response to a change in the money supply. In effect, in the classical model the effects of money supply changes are analyzed as if the short-run as well as the long-run aggregate supply curves were vertical.

In reality, this is a poor assumption during periods of low inflation. With a low inflation rate, it may take a while for workers and firms to react to a monetary expansion by raising wages and prices. In this scenario, some nominal wages and the prices of some goods are sticky in the short run. As a result, under low inflation there is an upward-sloping $SRAS$ curve, and changes in the money supply can indeed change real GDP in the short run.

But what about periods of high inflation? In the face of high inflation, economists have observed that the short-run stickiness of nominal wages and prices tends to vanish. Workers and businesses, sensitized to inflation, are quick to raise their wages and prices in response to changes in the money supply. This implies that under high inflation, there is a quicker adjustment of wages and prices of intermediate goods than occurs in the case of low inflation. So the short-run aggregate supply curve shifts leftward more quickly, and there is a more rapid return to long-run equilibrium under high inflation. As a result, the classical model of the price level is much more likely to be a good approximation of reality for economies experiencing persistently high inflation.

The consequence of this rapid adjustment of all prices in the economy is that in countries with persistently high inflation, changes in the money supply are quickly translated into changes in the inflation rate. Let's look at Zimbabwe. Figure 31-2 shows the annual rate of growth in the money supply and the annual rate of change of consumer prices from 2003 through April 2008. As you can see, the surge in the growth rate of the money supply coincided closely with a roughly equal surge in the inflation rate. Note that to fit these very large percentage increases—several thousands of percent—onto the figure, we have drawn the

FIGURE **31-2** | Money Supply Growth and Inflation in Zimbabwe

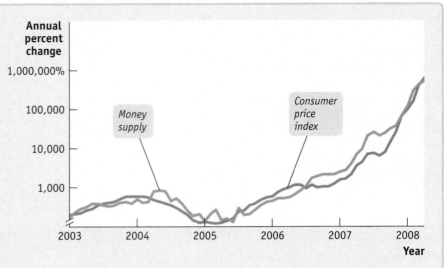

This figure, drawn on a logarithmic scale, shows the annual rates of change of the money supply and the price level in Zimbabwe from 2003 through April 2008. The surges in the money supply were quickly reflected in a roughly equal surge in the price level.

Source: International Monetary Fund.

vertical axis using a logarithmic scale that allows us to draw equal-size percent changes as the same size.

What leads a country to increase its money supply so much that the result is an inflation rate in the millions, or even billions, of percent?

The Inflation Tax

Modern economies use fiat money—pieces of paper that have no intrinsic value but are accepted as a medium of exchange. In the United States and most other wealthy countries, the decision about how many pieces of paper to issue is placed in the hands of a central bank that is somewhat independent of the political process. However, this independence can always be taken away if politicians decide to seize control of monetary policy.

So what is to prevent a government from paying for some of its expenses not by raising taxes or borrowing but simply by printing money? Nothing. In fact, governments, including the U.S. government, do it all the time. How can the U.S. government do this, given that the Federal Reserve issues money, not the U.S. Treasury? The answer is that the Treasury and the Federal Reserve work in concert. The Treasury issues debt to finance the government's purchases of goods and services, and the Fed *monetizes* the debt by creating money and buying the debt back from the public through open-market purchases of Treasury bills. In effect, the U.S. government can and does raise revenue by printing money.

For example, in August 2007, the U.S. monetary base—bank reserves plus currency in circulation—was $600 billion larger than it had been a year earlier. This occurred because, over the course of that year, the Federal Reserve had issued $20 billion in money or its electronic equivalent and put it into circulation through open-market operations. To put it another way, the Fed created money out of thin air and used it to buy

Nate Beeler © Cagel Cartoons

valuable government securities from the private sector. It's true that the U.S. government pays interest on debt owned by the Federal Reserve—but the Fed, by law, hands the interest payments it receives on government debt back to the Treasury, keeping only enough to fund its own operations. In effect, then, the Federal Reserve's actions enabled the government to pay off $600 billion in outstanding government debt by printing money.

An alternative way to look at this is to say that the right to print money is itself a source of revenue. Economists refer to the revenue generated by the government's right to print money as *seignorage,* an archaic term that goes back to the Middle Ages. It refers to the right to stamp gold and silver into coins, and charge a fee for doing so, that medieval lords—seigneurs, in France—reserved for themselves.

Seignorage normally accounts for only a tiny fraction (less than 1%) of the U.S. government's budget. Furthermore, concerns about seignorage don't have any influence on the Federal Reserve's decisions about how much money to print; the Fed is worried about inflation and unemployment, not revenue. But this hasn't always been true, even in America: both sides relied on seignorage to help cover budget deficits during the Civil War. And there have been many occasions in history when governments turned to their printing presses as a crucial source of revenue.

According to the usual scenario, a government finds itself running a large budget deficit—and lacks either the competence or the political will to eliminate this deficit by raising taxes or cutting spending. Furthermore, the government can't borrow to cover the gap because potential lenders won't extend loans given the fear that the government's weakness will continue and leave it unable to repay its debts.

In such a situation, governments end up printing money to cover the budget deficit. But by printing money to pay its bills, a government increases the quantity of money in circulation. And as we've just seen, increases in the money supply sooner or later translate into equally large increases in the aggregate price level. So printing money to cover a budget deficit leads to inflation.

Who ends up paying for the goods and services the government purchases with newly printed money? The people who currently hold money pay. They pay because inflation erodes the purchasing power of their money holdings. In other words, a government imposes an **inflation tax,** the reduction in the value of the money held by the public, by printing money to cover its budget deficit and creating inflation.

It's helpful to think about what this tax represents. If the inflation rate is 5%, then a year from now $1 will buy goods and services worth only $0.95 today. So a 5% inflation rate in effect imposes a tax rate of 5% on the value of all money held by the public.

But why would any government push the inflation tax to rates of hundreds or thousands of percent? We turn next to the logic of hyperinflation.

The Logic of Hyperinflation

Inflation imposes a tax on individuals who hold money. And, like most taxes, it will lead people to change their behavior. In particular, when inflation is high, people will try to avoid holding money and will instead substitute real goods as well as interest-bearing assets for money. In this chapter's opening story, we described how, during the German hyperinflation, people began using eggs or lumps of coal as a medium of exchange. They did this because lumps of coal maintained their real value over time, but money didn't. Indeed, during the peak of German hyperinflation, people often burned paper money, which was less valuable than wood.

Moreover, people don't just reduce their nominal money holdings—they reduce their *real* money holdings, cutting the amount of money

The **inflation tax** is the reduction in the value of money held by the public caused by inflation.

In the 1920s, hyperinflation made German currency worth so little that children made kites from banknotes.

they hold so much that it actually has less purchasing power than the amount of money they would hold if inflation were low. They do this by using the money to buy goods that last over time or assets that hold their value, like gold. Why? Because the more real money holdings they have, the greater the real amount of resources the government captures from them through the inflation tax.

We are now prepared to understand how countries can get themselves into situations of extreme inflation. High inflation arises when the government must print a large quantity of money, imposing a large inflation tax, to cover a large budget deficit.

Now, the seignorage collected by the government over a short period—say, one month—is equal to the change in the money supply over that period. Let's use M to represent the money supply and use the symbol Δ to mean "monthly change in." Then:

(31-1) Seignorage = ΔM

The money value of seignorage, however, isn't very informative by itself. After all, the whole point of inflation is that a given amount of money buys less and less over time. So it's more useful to look at *real* seignorage, the revenue created by printing money divided by the price level, P:

(31-2) Real seignorage = $\Delta M/P$

Equation 31-2 can be rewritten by dividing and multiplying by the current level of the money supply, M, giving us:

(31-3) Real seignorage = $(\Delta M/M) \times (M/P)$

or

Real seignorage = Rate of growth of the money supply × Real money supply

But as we've just explained, in the face of high inflation the public reduces the real amount of money it holds, so the far right-hand term in Equation 31-3, M/P, gets smaller. Suppose that the government needs to print enough money to pay for a given quantity of goods and services—that is, it needs to collect a given *real* amount of seignorage. Then, as the real money supply, M/P, falls as people hold smaller amounts of real money, the government has to respond by accelerating the rate of growth of the money supply, $\Delta M/M$. This will lead to an even higher rate of inflation. And people will respond to this new higher rate of inflation by reducing their real money holdings, M/P, yet again.

As the process becomes self-reinforcing, it can easily spiral out of control. Although the amount of real seignorage that the government must ultimately collect to pay off its deficit does not change, the inflation rate the government needs to impose to collect that amount rises. So the government is forced to increase the money supply more rapidly, leading to an even higher rate of inflation, and so on.

Here's an analogy: imagine a city government that tries to raise a lot of money with a special fee on taxi rides. The fee will raise the cost of taxi rides, and this will cause people to turn to easily available substitutes, such as walking or taking the bus. As taxi use declines, the government finds that its tax revenue declines, and it must impose a higher fee to raise the same amount of revenue as before. You can imagine the ensuing vicious circle: the government imposes fees on taxi rides, which leads to less taxi use, which causes the government to raise the fee on taxi rides, which leads to even less taxi use, and so on.

Substitute the real money supply for taxi rides and the inflation rate for the increase in the fee on taxi rides, and you have the story of hyperinflation. A race develops between the government printing presses and the public: the presses churn out money at a faster and faster rate to try to compensate for the fact that the public is reducing its real money holdings. At some point the inflation rate explodes into hyperinflation, and people are unwilling to hold any money at all (and resort to trading in eggs and lumps of coal). The government is then forced to abandon its use of the inflation tax and shut down the printing presses.

ECONOMICS ▶ in Action

Zimbabwe's Inflation

As we noted in this chapter's opening story, Zimbabwe offers a recent example of a country experiencing very high inflation. Figure 31-2 showed that surges in Zimbabwe's money supply growth were matched by almost simultaneous surges in its inflation rate. But looking at rates of change doesn't give a true feel for just how much prices went up.

Figure 31-3 shows Zimbabwe's consumer price index from January 2000 to July 2008, with the January 2000 level set equal to 100. As in Figure 31-2, we also use a logarithmic scale. Over the course of just over eight years, consumer prices rose by approximately 80 trillion percent.

Why did Zimbabwe's government pursue policies that led to runaway inflation? The reason boils down to political instability, which in turn had its roots in Zimbabwe's history. Until the 1970s, Zimbabwe had been ruled by its small white minority; even after the shift to majority rule, many of the country's farms remained in the hands of whites. Eventually Robert Mugabe, Zimbabwe's president, tried to solidify his position by seizing these farms and turning them over to his political supporters.

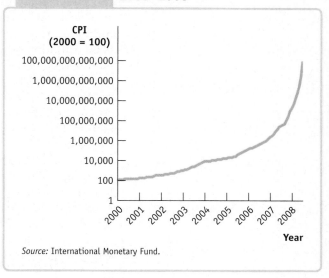

FIGURE **31-3**   Consumer Prices in Zimbabwe, 2000–2008

Source: International Monetary Fund.

But because this seizure disrupted production, the result was to undermine the country's economy and its tax base. It became impossible for the country's government to balance its budget either by raising taxes or by cutting spending. At the same time, the regime's instability left Zimbabwe unable to borrow money in world markets. Like many others before it, Zimbabwe's government turned to the printing press to cover the gap—leading to massive inflation.

Check Your Understanding   31-1

1. Suppose there is a large increase in the money supply in an economy that previously had low inflation. As a consequence, aggregate output expands in the short run. What does this say about situations in which the classical model of the price level applies?

2. Suppose that all wages and prices in an economy are indexed to inflation—that is, wages and prices are automatically adjusted to incorporate the latest inflation figures. Can there still be an inflation tax?

Solutions appear at back of book.

Moderate Inflation and Disinflation

The governments of wealthy, politically stable countries, like the United States and Britain, don't find themselves forced to print money to pay their bills. Yet over the past 40 years, both countries, along with a number of other nations, have experienced uncomfortable episodes of inflation. In the United States, the inflation rate peaked at 13% at the beginning of the 1980s. In Britain, the inflation rate reached 26% in 1975. Why did policy makers allow this to happen?

▼ Quick Review

• The **classical model of the price level** does not distinguish between the short and the long run. It explains how increases in the money supply feed directly into inflation. It is a good description of reality only for countries with persistently high inflation or hyperinflation.

• Governments sometimes print money to cover a budget deficit. The resulting loss in the value of money is called the **inflation tax.**

• A high inflation rate causes people to reduce their real money holdings, leading to the printing of more money and higher inflation in order to collect the inflation tax. This can cause a self-reinforcing spiral into hyperinflation.

The answer, in brief, is that in the short run, policies that produce a booming economy also tend to lead to higher inflation, and policies that reduce inflation tend to depress the economy. This creates both temptations and dilemmas for governments.

First, imagine yourself as a politician facing an election in a year or two, and suppose that inflation is fairly low at the moment. You might well be tempted to pursue expansionary policies that will push the unemployment rate down as a way to please voters, even if your economic advisers warn that this will eventually lead to higher inflation. You might also be tempted to find different economic advisers who will tell you not to worry: in politics, as in ordinary life, wishful thinking often prevails over realistic analysis.

Conversely, imagine yourself as a politician in an economy suffering from inflation. Your economic advisers will probably tell you that the only way to bring inflation down is to push the economy into a recession, which will lead to temporarily higher unemployment. Are you willing to pay that price? Maybe not.

This political asymmetry—inflationary policies often produce short-term political gains, but policies to bring inflation down carry short-term political costs—explains how countries with no need to impose an inflation tax sometimes end up with serious inflation problems. For example, that 26% rate of inflation in Britain was largely the result of the British government's decision in 1971 to pursue highly expansionary monetary and fiscal policies. Politicians disregarded warnings that these policies would be inflationary and were extremely reluctant to reverse course even when it became clear that the warnings had been correct.

But why do expansionary policies lead to inflation? To answer that question, we need to look first at the relationship between output and unemployment.

The Output Gap and the Unemployment Rate

In Chapter 27 we introduced the concept of *potential output,* the level of real GDP that the economy would produce once all prices had fully adjusted. Potential output typically grows steadily over time, reflecting long-run growth. However, as we learned from the aggregate demand–aggregate supply model, actual aggregate output fluctuates around potential output in the short run: a recessionary gap arises when actual aggregate output falls short of potential output; an inflationary gap arises when actual aggregate output exceeds potential output.

Recall from Chapter 27 that the percentage difference between the actual level of real GDP and potential output is called the *output gap.* A positive or negative output gap occurs when an economy is producing more than or less than what would be "expected" because all prices have not yet adjusted. And wages, as we've learned, are the prices in the labor market.

Meanwhile, we learned in Chapter 23 that the unemployment rate is composed of cyclical unemployment and natural unemployment, the portion of the unemployment rate unaffected by the business cycle. So there is a relationship between the unemployment rate and the output gap. This relationship is defined by two rules:

1. When actual aggregate output is equal to potential output, the actual unemployment rate is equal to the natural rate of unemployment.
2. When the output gap is positive (an inflationary gap), the unemployment rate is *below* the natural rate. When the output gap is negative (a recessionary gap), the unemployment rate is *above* the natural rate.

In other words, fluctuations of aggregate output around the long-run trend of potential output correspond to fluctuations of the unemployment rate around the natural rate.

This makes sense. When the economy is producing less than potential output— when the output gap is negative—it is not making full use of its productive resources. Among the resources that are not fully utilized is labor, the economy's most important resource. So we would expect a negative output gap to be associated with unusually high unemployment. Conversely, when the economy is producing more than potential output, it is temporarily using resources at higher-than-normal rates. With this positive output gap, we would expect to see lower-than-normal unemployment.

Figure 31-4 confirms this rule. Panel (a) shows the actual and natural rates of unemployment, as estimated by the Congressional Budget Office (CBO). Panel (b) shows two series. One is cyclical unemployment: the difference between the actual unemployment rate and the CBO estimate of the natural rate of unemployment, measured on the left. The other is the CBO estimate of the output gap, measured on the right. To make the relationship clearer, the output gap series is inverted—shown upside down—so that the line goes down if actual output rises above potential output and up if actual output falls below potential output.

As you can see, the two series move together quite closely, showing the strong relationship between the output gap and cyclical unemployment. Years of high cyclical unemployment, like 1982, 1992, or 2009, were also years of a strongly negative output gap. Years of low cyclical unemployment, like the late 1960s or 2000, were also years of a strongly positive output gap.

FIGURE **31-4**   Cyclical Unemployment and the Output Gap

Panel (a) shows the actual U.S. unemployment rate from 1949 through 2014, together with the Congressional Budget Office estimate of the natural rate of unemployment. The actual rate fluctuates around the natural rate, often for extended periods. Panel (b) shows cyclical unemployment—the difference between the actual unemployment rate and the natural rate of unemployment— and the output gap, also estimated by the CBO. The unemployment rate is measured on the left vertical axis, and the output gap is measured with an inverted scale on the right vertical axis. With an inverted scale, it moves in the same direction as the unemployment rate: when the output gap is positive, the actual unemployment rate is below its natural rate; when the output gap is negative, the actual unemployment rate is above its natural rate. The two series track one another closely, showing the strong relationship between the output gap and cyclical unemployment.

Sources: Federal Reserve Bank of St. Louis; Congressional Budget Office.

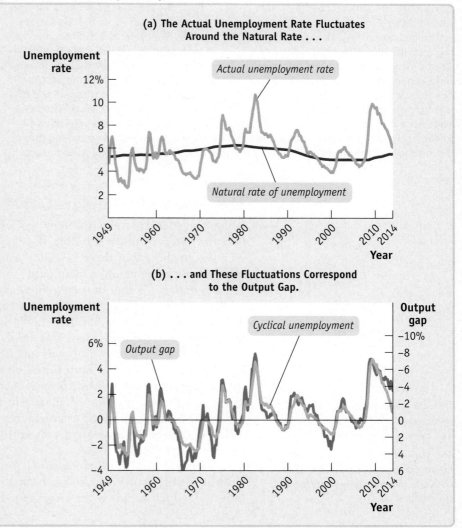

FOR INQUIRING MINDS | Okun's Law

Although cyclical unemployment and the output gap move together, cyclical unemployment seems to move *less* than the output gap. For example, the output gap reached −8% in 1982, but the cyclical unemployment rate reached only 4%. This observation is the basis of an important relationship originally discovered by Arthur Okun, John F. Kennedy's chief economic adviser.

Modern estimates of **Okun's law**—the negative relationship between the output gap and the unemployment rate—typically find that a rise in the output gap of 1 percentage point reduces the unemployment rate by about ½ of a percentage point.

For example, suppose that the natural rate of unemployment is 5.2% and that the economy is currently producing at only 98% of potential output. In that case, the output gap is −2%, and Okun's law predicts an unemployment rate of $5.2\% - \frac{1}{2} \times (-2\%) = 6.2\%$.

The fact that a 1% rise in output reduces the unemployment rate by only ½ of 1% may seem puzzling: you might have expected to see a one-to-one relationship between the output gap and unemployment. Doesn't a 1% rise in aggregate output require a 1% increase in employment? And shouldn't that take 1% off the unemployment rate?

The answer is no: there are several well-understood reasons why the relationship isn't one-to-one. For one thing, companies often meet changes in demand in part by changing the number of hours their existing employees work. For example, a company that experiences a sudden increase in demand for its products may cope by asking (or requiring) its workers to put in longer hours, rather than by hiring more workers. Conversely, a company that sees sales drop will often reduce workers' hours rather than lay off employees. This behavior dampens the effect of output fluctuations on the number of workers employed.

Also, the number of workers looking for jobs is affected by the availability of jobs. Suppose that the number of jobs falls by 1 million. Measured unemployment will rise by less than 1 million because some unemployed workers become discouraged and give up actively looking for work. (Recall from Chapter 23 that workers aren't counted as unemployed unless they are actively seeking work.) Conversely,

if the economy adds 1 million jobs, some people who haven't been actively looking for work will begin doing so. As a result, measured unemployment will fall by less than 1 million.

Finally, the rate of growth of labor productivity generally accelerates during booms and slows down or even turns negative during busts. The reasons for this phenomenon are the subject of some dispute among economists. The consequence, however, is that the effects of booms and busts on the unemployment rate are dampened. ■

Okun's law is the negative relationship between the output gap and cyclical unemployment.

The **short-run Phillips curve** is the negative short-run relationship between the unemployment rate and the inflation rate.

The Short-Run Phillips Curve

We've just seen that expansionary policies lead to a lower unemployment rate. Our next step in understanding the temptations and dilemmas facing governments is to show that there is a short-run trade-off between unemployment and inflation—lower unemployment tends to lead to higher inflation, and vice versa. The key concept is that of the *Phillips curve.*

The origins of this concept lie in a famous 1958 paper by the New Zealand–born economist A. W. H. Phillips. Looking at historical data for Britain, he found that when the unemployment rate was high, the wage rate tended to fall, and when the unemployment rate was low, the wage rate tended to rise. Using data from Britain, the United States, and elsewhere, other economists soon found a similar apparent relationship between the unemployment rate and the rate of inflation—that is, the rate of change in the aggregate price level. For example, Figure 31-5 shows the U.S. unemployment rate and the rate of consumer price inflation over each subsequent year from 1955 to 1968, with each dot representing one year's data.

Looking at evidence like Figure 31-5, many economists concluded that there is a negative short-run relationship between the unemployment rate and the inflation rate, which is called the **short-run Phillips curve,** or *SRPC.* (We'll explain

FIGURE **31-5** Unemployment and Inflation, 1955–1968

Each dot shows the average U.S. unemployment rate for one year and the percentage increase in the consumer price index over the subsequent year. Data like this lay behind the initial concept of the Phillips curve.

Source: Bureau of Labor Statistics.

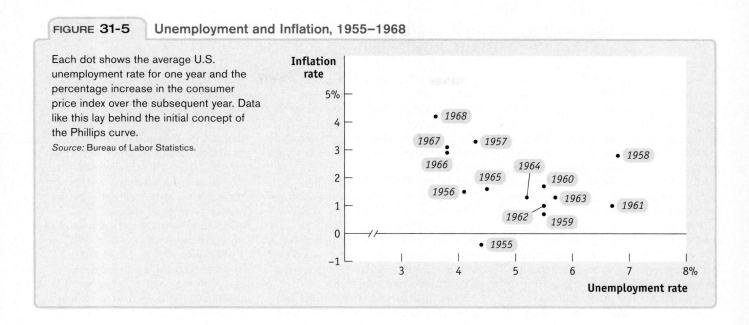

the difference between the short-run and the long-run Phillips curve soon.) Figure 31-6 shows a hypothetical short-run Phillips curve.

Early estimates of the short-run Phillips curve for the United States were very simple: they showed a negative relationship between the unemployment rate and the inflation rate, without taking account of any other variables. During the 1950s and 1960s, this simple approach seemed, for a while, to be adequate. And this simple relationship is clear in the data in Figure 31-5.

Even at the time, however, some economists argued that a more accurate short-run Phillips curve would include other factors. In Chapter 27 we discussed the effect of *supply shocks,* such as sudden changes in the price of oil, which shift the short-run aggregate supply curve. Such shocks also shift the short-run Phillips curve: surging oil prices were an important factor in the inflation of the 1970s and also played an important role in the acceleration of inflation in

FIGURE **31-6** The Short-Run Phillips Curve

The short-run Phillips curve, *SRPC,* slopes downward because the relationship between the unemployment rate and the inflation rate is negative.

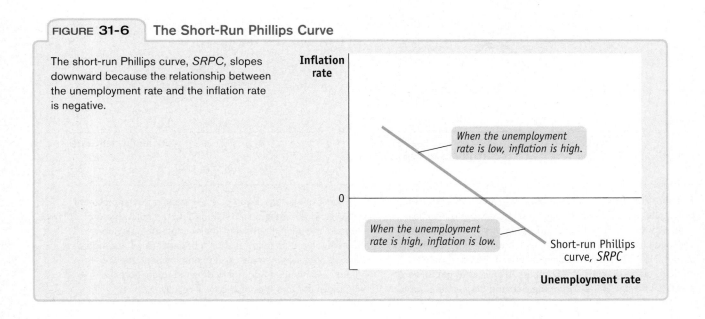

FOR INQUIRING MINDS | The Aggregate Supply Curve and the Short-Run Phillips Curve

In earlier chapters we made extensive use of the *AD–AS* model, in which the short-run aggregate supply curve—a relationship between real GDP and the aggregate price level—plays a central role. Now we've introduced the concept of the short-run Phillips curve, a relationship between the unemployment rate and the rate of inflation. How do these two concepts fit together?

We can get a partial answer to this question by looking at panel (a) of Figure 31-7, which shows how changes in the aggregate price level and the output gap depend on changes in aggregate demand. Assume that in year 1 the aggregate demand curve is AD_1, the long-run aggregate supply curve is *LRAS,* and the short-run aggregate supply curve is *SRAS.* The initial macroeconomic equilibrium is at E_1, where the price level is 100 and real GDP is $10 trillion. Notice that at E_1 real GDP is equal to potential output, so the output gap is zero.

Now consider two possible paths for the economy over the next year. One is that aggregate demand remains unchanged and the economy stays at E_1. The other is that aggregate demand shifts rightward to AD_2 and the economy moves to E_2.

At E_2, real GDP is $10.4 trillion, $0.4 trillion more than potential output— a 4% output gap. Meanwhile, at E_2 the aggregate price level is 102—a 2% increase. So panel (a) tells us that in this example, a zero output gap is associated with zero inflation and a 4% output gap is associated with 2% inflation.

Panel (b) shows what this implies for the relationship between unemployment and inflation. Assume that the natural rate of unemployment is 6% and that a rise of 1 percentage point in the output gap causes a fall of ½ percentage point in the unemployment rate per Okun's law, described in the previous For Inquiring Minds. In that case, the two cases shown in panel (a)—aggregate demand either

staying put or rising—correspond to the two points in panel (b). At E_1, the unemployment rate is 6% and the inflation rate is 0%. At E_2, the unemployment rate is 4%—because an output gap of 4% reduces the unemployment rate by 4% × 0.5 = 2% below its natural rate of 6%—and the inflation rate is 2%. So there is a negative relationship between unemployment and inflation.

So does the short-run aggregate supply curve say exactly the same thing as the short-run Phillips curve? Not quite. The short-run aggregate supply curve seems to imply a relationship between the *change* in the unemployment rate and the inflation rate, but the short-run Phillips curve shows a relationship between the *level* of the unemployment rate and the inflation rate. Reconciling these views completely would go beyond the scope of this book. The important point is that the short-run Phillips curve is a concept that is closely related, though not identical, to the short-run aggregate supply curve.

FIGURE **31-7**   The *AD–AS* Model and the Short-Run Phillips Curve

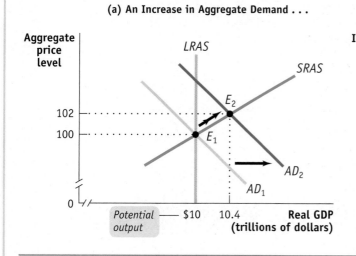

(a) An Increase in Aggregate Demand . . .

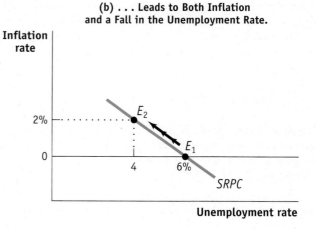

(b) . . . Leads to Both Inflation and a Fall in the Unemployment Rate.

The short-run Phillips curve is closely related to the short-run aggregate supply curve. In panel (a), the economy is initially in equilibrium at E_1, with the aggregate price level at 100 and aggregate output at $10 trillion, which we assume is potential output. Now consider two possibilities. If the aggregate demand curve remains at AD_1, there is an output gap of zero and 0% inflation. If the aggregate demand curve shifts out to AD_2, there is an output gap of 4%—reducing unemployment to 4%—and 2% inflation. Assuming that the natural rate of unemployment is 6%, the implications for unemployment and inflation are as follows, shown in panel (b): if aggregate demand does not increase, 6% unemployment and 0% inflation will result; if aggregate demand does increase, 4% unemployment and 2% inflation will result.

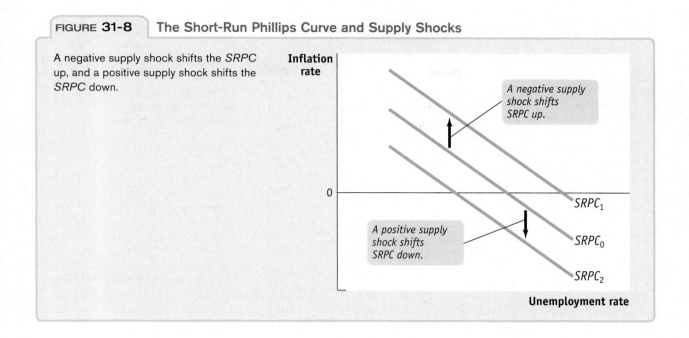

FIGURE **31-8**   The Short-Run Phillips Curve and Supply Shocks

A negative supply shock shifts the *SRPC* up, and a positive supply shock shifts the *SRPC* down.

A negative supply shock shifts SRPC up.

A positive supply shock shifts SRPC down.

Inflation rate

Unemployment rate

0

$SRPC_1$

$SRPC_0$

$SRPC_2$

2007–2008. In general, a negative supply shock shifts *SRPC* up as the inflation rate increases for every level of the unemployment rate, and a positive supply shock shifts it down as the inflation rate falls for every level of the unemployment rate. Both outcomes are shown in Figure 31-8.

But supply shocks are not the only factors that can change the inflation rate. In the early 1960s, Americans had little experience with inflation because inflation rates had been low for decades. But by the late 1960s, after inflation had been steadily increasing for a number of years, Americans had come to expect future inflation. In 1968, two economists—Milton Friedman of the University of Chicago and Edmund Phelps of Columbia University—independently set forth a crucial hypothesis: that expectations about future inflation directly affect the present inflation rate. Today most economists accept that the *expected inflation rate*—the rate of inflation that employers and workers expect in the near future—is the most important factor, other than the unemployment rate, affecting inflation.

Inflation Expectations and the Short-Run Phillips Curve

The expected rate of inflation is the rate of inflation that employers and workers expect in the near future. One of the crucial discoveries of modern macroeconomics is that changes in the expected rate of inflation affect the short-run trade-off between unemployment and inflation and shift the short-run Phillips curve.

Why do changes in expected inflation affect the short-run Phillips curve? Put yourself in the position of a worker and employer about to sign a contract setting the worker's wages over the next year. For a number of reasons, the wage rate they agree to will be higher if everyone expects high inflation (including rising wages) than if everyone expects prices to be stable. The worker will want a wage rate that takes into account future declines in the purchasing power of earnings. He or she will also want a wage rate that won't fall behind the wages of other workers. And the employer will be more willing to agree to a wage increase now if hiring workers later will be even more expensive. Also, rising prices will make paying a higher wage rate more affordable for the employer because the employer's output will sell for more.

For these reasons, an increase in expected inflation shifts the short-run Phillips curve upward: the actual rate of inflation at any given unemployment rate is higher when the expected inflation rate is higher. In fact, macroeconomists

FIGURE **31-9**   Expected Inflation and the Short-Run Phillips Curve

An increase in expected inflation shifts the short-run Phillips curve up. $SRPC_0$ is the initial short-run Phillips curve with an expected inflation rate of 0%; $SRPC_2$ is the short-run Phillips curve with an expected inflation rate of 2%. Each additional percentage point of expected inflation raises the actual inflation rate at any given unemployment rate by 1 percentage point.

SRPC shifts up by the amount of the increase in expected inflation.

believe that the relationship between changes in expected inflation and changes in actual inflation is one-to-one. That is, when the expected inflation rate increases, the actual inflation rate at any given unemployment rate will increase by the same amount. When the expected inflation rate falls, the actual inflation rate at any given level of unemployment will fall by the same amount.

Figure 31-9 shows how the expected rate of inflation affects the short-run Phillips curve. First, suppose that the expected rate of inflation is 0%. $SRPC_0$ is the short-run Phillips curve when the public expects 0% inflation. According to $SRPC_0$, the actual inflation rate will be 0% if the unemployment rate is 6%; it will be 2% if the unemployment rate is 4%.

Alternatively, suppose the expected rate of inflation is 2%. In that case, employers and workers will build this expectation into wages and prices: at any given unemployment rate, the actual inflation rate will be 2 percentage points higher than it would be if people expected 0% inflation. $SRPC_2$, which shows the Phillips curve when the expected inflation rate is 2%, is $SRPC_0$ shifted upward by 2 percentage points at every level of unemployment. According to $SRPC_2$, the actual inflation rate will be 2% if the unemployment rate is 6%; it will be 4% if the unemployment rate is 4%.

What determines the expected rate of inflation? In general, people base their expectations about inflation on experience. If the inflation rate has hovered around 0% in the last few years, people will expect it to be around 0% in the near future. But if the inflation rate has averaged around 5% lately, people will expect inflation to be around 5% in the near future.

Since expected inflation is an important part of the modern discussion about the short-run Phillips curve, you might wonder why it was not in the original formulation of the Phillips curve. The answer lies in history. Think back to what we said about the early 1960s: at that time, people were accustomed to low inflation rates and reasonably expected that future inflation rates would also be low. It was only after 1965 that persistent inflation became a fact of life. So only then did economists begin to argue that expected inflation should play an important role in price setting.

Sure enough, the seemingly clear relationship between inflation and unemployment fell apart after 1969. Figure 31-10 plots the track of U.S. unemployment and inflation rates from 1961 to 1990. As you can see, the track looks more like a tangled piece of yarn than like a smooth curve.

FIGURE 31-10   Unemployment and Inflation, 1961–1990

During the 1970s, the short-run Phillips curve relationship that seemed to hold during the 1950s and 1960s broke down as the U.S. economy experienced a combination of high unemployment and high inflation. Economists believe this was the result of both negative supply shocks and the cumulative effect of several years of higher than expected inflation. Inflation came down during the 1980s, and the 1990s were a time of both low unemployment and low inflation.

Source: Bureau of Labor Statistics.

Through much of the 1970s and early 1980s, the economy suffered from a combination of above-average unemployment rates coupled with inflation rates unprecedented in modern American history. This condition came to be known as *stagflation*—for stagnation combined with high inflation. In the late 1990s, by contrast, the economy was experiencing a blissful combination of low unemployment and low inflation. What explains these developments?

Part of the answer can be attributed to a series of negative supply shocks that the U.S. economy suffered during the 1970s. The price of oil, in particular, soared as wars and revolutions in the Middle East led to a reduction in oil supplies and as oil-exporting countries deliberately curbed production to drive up prices. Compounding the oil price shocks, there was also a slowdown in labor productivity growth. Both of these factors shifted the short-run Phillips curve upward. During the 1990s, by contrast, supply shocks were positive. Prices of oil and other raw materials were generally falling, and productivity growth accelerated. As a result, the short-run Phillips curve shifted downward.

Equally important, however, was the role of expected inflation. As mentioned earlier in the chapter, inflation accelerated during the 1960s. During the 1970s, the public came to expect high inflation, and this also shifted the short-run Phillips curve up. It took a sustained and costly effort during the 1980s to get inflation back down. The result, however, was that expected inflation was very low by the late 1990s, allowing actual inflation to be low even with low rates of unemployment.

ECONOMICS ▶ *in Action*

The Phillips Curve in the Great Recession

We have returned many times in the course of this book to the great global economic crisis that struck in 2008. This crisis caused a drastic rise in unemployment in many countries, especially in some (but not all) European nations, and unemployment remained high even years later. According to the logic of the Phillips curve, this surge in unemployment should have led to falling inflation, with the biggest declines in the worst-hit countries. And that is exactly what happened.

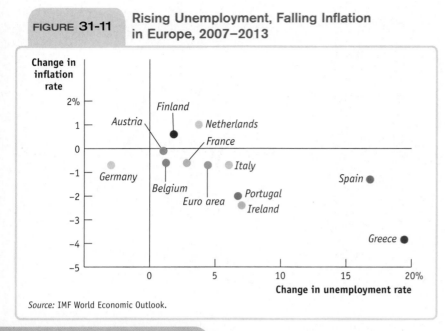

FIGURE **31-11** | Rising Unemployment, Falling Inflation in Europe, 2007–2013

Source: IMF World Economic Outlook.

Figure 31-11 shows how unemployment rates and inflation rates in a number of European economies changed between 2007, the eve of the Great Recession, and 2013. Unemployment rose in every country except Germany, soaring in Ireland and the troubled economies of southern Europe. Inflation fell in 9 out of 12 countries, falling much more than the average in those same troubled economies. The relationship between unemployment and inflation isn't exact—relationships in economics rarely are. But the data are consistent with the notion of a short-run trade-off between unemployment and inflation. Incidentally, researchers at the Federal Reserve have found a similar relationship between unemployment and inflation among major U.S. metropolitan areas, some of which were hit much harder by the housing bust than others.

• **Okun's law** describes the relationship between the output gap and cyclical unemployment.

• The **short-run Phillips curve** illustrates the negative relationship between unemployment and inflation.

• A negative supply shock shifts the short-run Phillips curve upward, but a positive supply shock shifts it downward.

• An increase in the expected rate of inflation pushes the short-run Phillips curve upward: each additional percentage point of expected inflation pushes the actual inflation rate at any given unemployment rate up by 1 percentage point.

• In the 1970s, a series of negative supply shocks and a slowdown in labor productivity growth led to *stagflation* and an upward shift in the short-run Phillips curve.

Check Your Understanding **31-2**

1. Explain how the short-run Phillips curve illustrates the negative relationship between cyclical unemployment and the actual inflation rate for a given level of the expected inflation rate.

2. Which way does the short-run Phillips curve move in response to a fall in commodities prices? To a surge in commodities prices? Explain.

Solutions appear at back of book.

Inflation and Unemployment in the Long Run

The short-run Phillips curve says that at any given point in time, there is a trade-off between unemployment and inflation. According to this view, policy makers have a choice: they can choose to accept the price of high inflation in order to achieve low unemployment. In fact, during the 1960s, many economists believed that this trade-off represented a real choice.

However, this view was greatly altered by the later recognition that expected inflation affects the short-run Phillips curve. In the short run, expectations often diverge from reality. In the long run, however, any consistent rate of inflation will be reflected in expectations. If inflation is consistently high, as it was in the 1970s, people will come to expect more of the same; if inflation is consistently low, as it has been in recent years, that, too, will become part of expectations.

So what does the trade-off between inflation and unemployment look like in the long run, when actual inflation is incorporated into expectations? Most macroeconomists believe that there is, in fact, no long-run trade-off. That is, it is not possible to achieve lower unemployment in the long run by accepting higher inflation. To see why, we need to introduce another concept: the *long-run Phillips curve.*

The Long-Run Phillips Curve

Figure 31-12 reproduces the two short-run Phillips curves from Figure 31-9, $SRPC_0$ and $SRPC_2$. It also adds an additional short-run Phillips curve, $SRPC_4$, representing a 4% expected rate of inflation. In a moment, we'll explain the significance of the vertical long-run Phillips curve, $LRPC$.

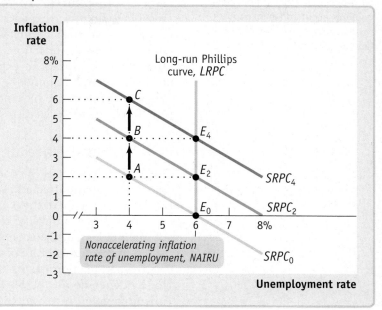

FIGURE 31-12 The NAIRU and the Long-Run Phillips Curve

$SRPC_0$ is the short-run Phillips curve when the expected inflation rate is 0%. At a 4% unemployment rate, the economy is at point A with an actual inflation rate of 2%. The higher inflation rate will be incorporated into expectations, and the $SRPC$ will shift upward to $SRPC_2$. If policy makers act to keep the unemployment rate at 4%, the economy will be at B and the actual inflation rate will rise to 4%. Inflationary expectations will be revised upward again, and $SRPC$ will shift to $SRPC_4$. At a 4% unemployment rate, the economy will be at C and the actual inflation rate will rise to 6%. Here, an unemployment rate of 6% is the NAIRU, or nonaccelerating inflation rate of unemployment. As long as unemployment is at the NAIRU, the actual inflation rate will match expectations and remain constant. An unemployment rate below 6% requires ever-accelerating inflation. The long-run Phillips curve, $LRPC$, which passes through E_0, E_2, and E_4, is vertical: no long-run trade-off between unemployment and inflation exists.

Suppose that the economy has, in the past, had a 0% inflation rate. In that case, the current short-run Phillips curve will be $SRPC_0$, reflecting a 0% expected inflation rate. If the unemployment rate is 6%, the actual inflation rate will be 0%.

Also suppose that policy makers decide to trade off lower unemployment for a higher rate of inflation. They use monetary policy, fiscal policy, or both to drive the unemployment rate down to 4%. This puts the economy at point A on $SRPC_0$, leading to an actual inflation rate of 2%.

Over time, the public will come to expect a 2% inflation rate. *This increase in inflationary expectations will shift the short-run Phillips curve upward* to $SRPC_2$. Now, when the unemployment rate is 6%, the actual inflation rate will be 2%. Given this new short-run Phillips curve, policies adopted to keep the unemployment rate at 4% will lead to a 4% actual inflation rate—point B on $SRPC_2$—rather than point A with a 2% actual inflation rate.

Eventually, the 4% actual inflation rate gets built into expectations about the future inflation rate, and the short-run Phillips curve shifts upward yet again to $SRPC_4$. To keep the unemployment rate at 4% would now require accepting a 6% actual inflation rate, point C on $SRPC_4$, and so on. In short, a persistent attempt to trade off lower unemployment for higher inflation leads to *accelerating* inflation over time.

To avoid accelerating inflation over time, the unemployment rate must be high enough that the actual rate of inflation matches the expected rate of inflation. This is the situation at E_0 on $SRPC_0$: when the expected inflation rate is 0% and the unemployment rate is 6%, the actual inflation rate is 0%. It is also the situation at E_2 on $SRPC_2$: when the expected inflation rate is 2% and the unemployment rate is 6%, the actual inflation rate is 2%. And it is the situation at E_4 on $SRPC_4$: when the expected inflation rate is 4% and the unemployment rate is 6%, the actual inflation rate is 4%. As we'll learn in Chapter 33, this relationship between accelerating inflation and the unemployment rate is known as the *natural rate hypothesis*.

The unemployment rate at which inflation does not change over time—6% in Figure 31-12—is known as the **nonaccelerating inflation rate of unemployment,** or **NAIRU** for short. Keeping the unemployment rate below the NAIRU leads to ever-accelerating inflation and cannot be maintained. Most macroeconomists believe that there is a NAIRU and that there is no long-run trade-off between unemployment and inflation.

The **nonaccelerating inflation rate of unemployment,** or **NAIRU,** is the unemployment rate at which inflation does not change over time.

The **long-run Phillips curve** shows the relationship between unemployment and inflation after expectations of inflation have had time to adjust to experience.

We can now explain the significance of the vertical line *LRPC*. It is the **long-run Phillips curve,** the relationship between unemployment and inflation in the long run, after expectations of inflation have had time to adjust to experience. It is vertical because any unemployment rate below the NAIRU leads to ever-accelerating inflation. In other words, the long-run Phillips curve shows that there are limits to expansionary policies, because an unemployment rate below the NAIRU cannot be maintained in the long run. Moreover, there is a corresponding point we have not yet emphasized: any unemployment rate above the NAIRU leads to decelerating inflation.

The Natural Rate of Unemployment, Revisited

Recall the concept of the natural rate of unemployment, the portion of the unemployment rate unaffected by the swings of the business cycle. Now we have introduced the concept of the *NAIRU*. How do these two concepts relate to each other?

The answer is that the NAIRU is another name for the natural rate. The level of unemployment the economy "needs" in order to avoid accelerating inflation is equal to the natural rate of unemployment.

In fact, economists estimate the natural rate of unemployment by looking for evidence about the NAIRU from the behavior of the inflation rate and the unemployment rate over the course of the business cycle. For example, the way major European countries learned, to their dismay, that their natural rates of unemployment were 9% or more was through unpleasant experience. In the late 1980s, and again in the late 1990s, European inflation began to accelerate as European unemployment rates, which had been above 9%, began to fall, approaching 8%.

In Figure 31-4 we cited Congressional Budget Office estimates of the U.S. natural rate of unemployment. The CBO has a model that predicts changes in the inflation rate based on the deviation of the actual unemployment rate from the natural rate. Given data on actual unemployment and inflation, this model can be used to deduce estimates of the natural rate—and that's where the CBO numbers come from. As of the final three months of 2014, the CBO estimate of the U.S. natural rate was 5.5%.

The Costs of Disinflation

Through experience, policy makers have found that bringing inflation down is a much harder task than increasing it. The reason is that once the public has come to expect continuing inflation, bringing inflation down is painful.

GLOBAL COMPARISION | **Disinflation Around the World**

The great disinflation of the 1980s wasn't unique to the United States. A number of other advanced countries also experienced high inflation during the 1970s, then brought inflation down during the 1980s at the cost of a severe recession. This figure shows the annual rate of inflation in Britain, Italy, and the United States from 1970 to 2013. All three nations experienced high inflation rates following the two oil price shocks of 1973 and 1979, with the U.S. inflation rate the least severe of the three. All three nations then weathered severe recessions in order to bring inflation down. Since the 1980s, inflation has remained low and stable in all wealthy nations.

Source: OECD.

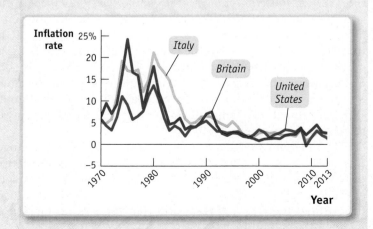

A persistent attempt to keep unemployment below the natural rate leads to accelerating inflation that becomes incorporated into expectations. To reduce inflationary expectations, policy makers need to run the process in reverse, adopting contractionary policies that keep the unemployment rate above the natural rate for an extended period of time. The process of bringing down inflation that has become embedded in expectations is known as *disinflation*, a concept we learned about in Chapter 23.

Disinflation can be very expensive. As the following Economics in Action documents, the U.S. retreat from high inflation at the beginning of the 1980s appears to have cost the equivalent of about 18% of a year's real GDP, the equivalent of roughly $2.6 trillion today. The justification for paying these costs is that they lead to a permanent gain. Although the economy does not recover the short-term production losses caused by disinflation, it no longer suffers from the costs associated with persistently high inflation. In fact, the United States, Britain, and other wealthy countries that experienced inflation in the 1970s eventually decided that the benefit of bringing inflation down was worth the required suffering—the large reduction in real GDP in the short term.

Some economists argue that the costs of disinflation can be reduced if policy makers explicitly state their determination to reduce inflation. A clearly announced, credible policy of disinflation, they contend, can reduce expectations of future inflation and so shift the short-run Phillips curve downward. Some economists believe that the clear determination of the Federal Reserve to combat the inflation of the 1970s was credible enough that the costs of disinflation, huge though they were, were lower than they might otherwise have been.

ECONOMICS ▶ in Action

The Great Disinflation of the 1980s

As we've mentioned several times in this chapter, the United States ended the 1970s with a high rate of inflation, at least by its own peacetime historical standards—13% in 1980. Part of this inflation was the result of one-time events, especially a world oil crisis. But expectations of future inflation at 10% or more per year appeared to be firmly embedded in the economy.

By the mid-1980s, however, inflation was running at about 4% per year. Panel (a) of Figure 31-13 shows the annual rate of change in the "core" consumer

FIGURE **31-13**   The Great Disinflation

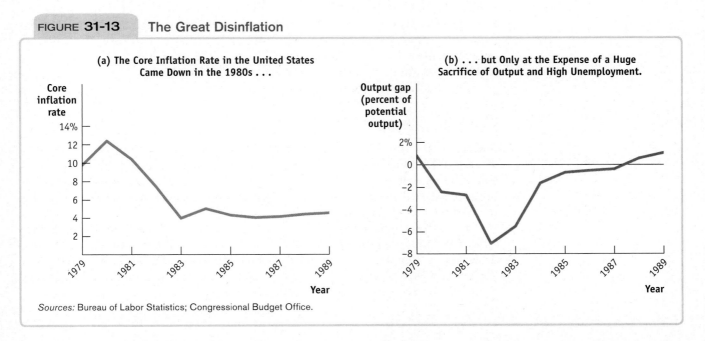

Sources: Bureau of Labor Statistics; Congressional Budget Office.

price index (CPI)—also called the *core inflation rate.* This index, which excludes volatile energy and food prices, is widely regarded as a better indicator of underlying inflation trends than the overall CPI. By this measure, inflation fell from about 12% at the end of the 1970s to about 4% by the mid-1980s.

How was this disinflation achieved? At great cost. Beginning in late 1979, the Federal Reserve imposed strongly contractionary monetary policies, which pushed the economy into its worst recession since the Great Depression. Panel (b) shows the Congressional Budget Office estimate of the U.S. output gap from 1979 to 1989: by 1982, actual output was 7% below potential output, corresponding to an unemployment rate of more than 9%. Aggregate output didn't get back to potential output until 1987.

Our analysis of the Phillips curve tells us that a temporary rise in unemployment, like that of the 1980s, is needed to break the cycle of inflationary expectations. Once expectations of inflation are reduced, the economy can return to the natural rate of unemployment at a lower inflation rate. And that's just what happened.

But the cost was huge. If you add up the output gap over 1980–1987, you find that the economy sacrificed approximately 18% of an average year's output over the period. If we had to do the same thing today, that would mean giving up roughly $2.6 trillion worth of goods and services.

Check Your Understanding   31-3

1. Why is there no long-run trade-off between unemployment and inflation?

2. British economists believe that the natural rate of unemployment in that country rose sharply during the 1970s, from around 3% to as much as 10%. During that period, Britain experienced a sharp acceleration of inflation, which for a time went above 20%. How might these facts be related?

3. Why is disinflation so costly for an economy? Are there ways to reduce these costs?

Solutions appear at back of book.

Deflation

Before World War II, *deflation*—a falling aggregate price level—was almost as common as inflation. (We introduced deflation in Chapter 21.) In fact, the U.S. consumer price index on the eve of World War II was 30% lower than it had been in 1920. After World War II, inflation became the norm in all countries. But in the 1990s, deflation reappeared in Japan and proved difficult to reverse. Concerns about potential deflation played a crucial role in U.S. monetary policy in the early 2000s and again in the aftermath of the 2008 financial crisis.

Why is deflation a problem? And why is it hard to end?

Debt Deflation

Deflation, like inflation, produces both winners and losers—but in the opposite direction. Due to the falling price level, a dollar in the future has a higher real value than a dollar today. So lenders, who are owed money, gain under deflation because the real value of borrowers' payments increases. Borrowers lose because the real burden of their debt rises.

In a famous analysis at the beginning of the Great Depression, Irving Fisher (who first analyzed the *Fisher effect* of expected inflation on interest rates, described in Chapter 25) claimed that the effects of deflation on borrowers and lenders can worsen an economic slump. Deflation, in effect, takes real resources away from borrowers and redistributes them to lenders.

Fisher argued that borrowers, who lose from deflation, are typically short of cash and will be forced to cut their spending sharply when their debt burden rises. Lenders, however, are unlikely to increase spending sharply when the values of the loans they own rise. The overall effect, said Fisher, is that deflation reduces aggregate demand, deepening an economic slump, which, in a vicious circle, may lead to further deflation. The effect of deflation in reducing aggregate demand, known as **debt deflation,** probably played a significant role in the Great Depression.

Effects of Expected Deflation

Like expected inflation, expected deflation affects the nominal interest rate. Look back at Figure 25-7, which demonstrated how expected inflation affects the equilibrium interest rate. In Figure 25-7, the equilibrium nominal interest rate is 4% if the expected inflation rate is 0%. Clearly, if the expected inflation rate is –3%—if the public expects deflation at 3% per year—the equilibrium nominal interest rate will be 1%.

But what would happen if the expected rate of inflation is –5%? Would the nominal interest rate fall to –1%, in which lenders are paying borrowers 1% on their debt? No. Nobody would lend money at a negative nominal rate of interest, because they could do better by simply holding cash. This illustrates what economists call the **zero bound** on the nominal interest rate: it cannot go below zero.

This zero bound can limit the effectiveness of monetary policy. Suppose the economy is depressed, with output below potential output and the unemployment rate above the natural rate. Normally the central bank can respond by cutting interest rates so as to increase aggregate demand. If the nominal interest rate is already zero, however, the central bank cannot push it down any further. Banks refuse to lend and consumers and firms refuse to spend because, with a negative inflation rate and a 0% nominal interest rate, holding cash yields a positive real return: with falling prices, a given amount of cash buys more over time. Any further increases in the monetary base will either be held in bank vaults or held as cash by individuals and firms, without being spent.

A situation in which conventional monetary policy to fight a slump—cutting interest rates—can't be used because nominal interest rates are up against the zero bound is known as a **liquidity trap.** A liquidity trap can occur whenever there is a sharp reduction in demand for loanable funds—which is exactly what happened during the Great Depression. Figure 31-14 shows the interest rate on

Debt deflation is the reduction in aggregate demand arising from the increase in the real burden of outstanding debt caused by deflation.

There is a **zero bound** on the nominal interest rate: it cannot go below zero.

The economy is in a **liquidity trap** when conventional monetary policy is ineffective, because nominal interest rates are up against the zero bound.

FIGURE 31-14 | **The Zero Bound in U.S. History**

This figure shows U.S. short-term interest rates, specifically the interest rate on three-month Treasury bills, from 1920 to 2014. As shown by the shaded area at left, for much of the 1930s, interest rates were very close to zero, leaving little room for expansionary monetary policy. After World War II, persistent inflation generally kept interest rates well above zero. However, in late 2008, in the wake of the housing bubble bursting and the financial crisis, the interest rate on three-month Treasury bills was again virtually zero.

Sources: National Bureau of Economic Research; Federal Reserve Bank of St. Louis.

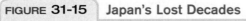

FIGURE **31-15** | Japan's Lost Decades

A prolonged economic slump in Japan led to deflation from the late 1990s on. The Bank of Japan responded by cutting interest rates—but eventually ran up against the zero bound.

Source: Federal Reserve Bank of St. Louis.

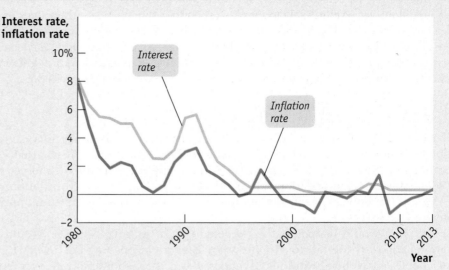

---

short-term U.S. government debt from 1920 to 2014. As you can see, from 1933 until World War II brought a full economic recovery, the U.S. economy was either close to or up against the zero bound. After World War II, when inflation became the norm around the world, the zero bound largely vanished as a problem, as the public came to expect inflation rather than deflation.

However, the recent history of the Japanese economy, shown in Figure 31-15, provides a modern illustration of the problem of deflation and the liquidity trap. Japan experienced a huge boom in the prices of both stocks and real estate in the late 1980s, then saw both bubbles burst. The result was a prolonged period of economic stagnation, the so-called Lost Decades, which gradually reduced the inflation rate and eventually led to persistent deflation.

In an effort to fight the weakness of the economy, the Bank of Japan—the equivalent of the Federal Reserve—repeatedly cut interest rates. Eventually, it arrived at the ZIRP: the *zero interest rate policy.* The call money rate, the equivalent of the U.S. federal funds rate, was literally set equal to zero. Because the economy was still depressed, it would have been desirable to cut interest rates even further. But that wasn't possible: Japan was up against the zero bound.

In the aftermath of the 2008 financial crisis, the world's most important central banks—the U.S. Federal Reserve and the European Central Bank—found themselves facing much the same problems the Bank of Japan had faced since the 1990s: the economies they were trying to manage remained depressed despite policy interest rates close to zero, and inflation was persistently below target. As of 2014, neither the United States nor the euro area was experiencing actual deflation, but as the following Economics in Action describes, Europe was getting alarmingly close.

ECONOMICS ▶ *in Action*

Is Europe Turning Japanese?

In the aftermath of the 2008 financial crisis, officials at the Federal Reserve were deeply worried about the possibility of "Japanification"—that is, they worried that, like Japan since the 1990s, the United States might find itself stuck in a deflationary trap. To avoid this possibility, they took some extraordinary measures, notably the large-scale purchases of assets—so-called "quantitative easing"—described in Chapter 30. By 2014, it seemed that the danger of deflation in the United States had at least somewhat receded.

But Europe was a different story. Where the U.S. recovery from the recession of 2007–2009 was steady, if disappointingly slow, the euro area, held back by debt crises, slid back into recession in late 2011. Growth resumed in 2013, but as you can see from panel (a) of Figure 31-16, it barely made a dent in high unemployment. And as panel (b) of Figure 31-16 shows, in 2013–2014 inflation began sliding below 1 percent, leading to worries that Europe was on track to replicate Japan's lost decades. While Europe was not yet experiencing actual deflation as of 2014, it was, as the International Monetary Fund put it, suffering from "lowflation"— inflation persistently below target—and this created many of the same problems. In particular, lower-than-expected inflation was worsening the problems of highly indebted nations, like Portugal, Spain, and Greece.

And like the Bank of Japan a number of years earlier, the European Central Bank was finding it hard to devise an effective answer to the slide toward deflation. In June 2014, it took the extraordinary step of reducing one of its key policy, rates, the interest rate it pays on deposits of private banks, to *minus* 0.1 percent— that is, it began actually charging banks a fee for holding their money. But even this didn't seem to be doing much to boost the economy.

FIGURE **31-16**   **Trouble in Europe, 2008–2014**

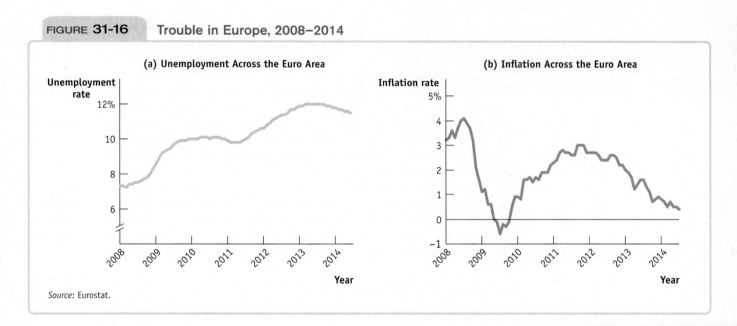

Source: Eurostat.

Check Your Understanding   31-4

1. Why won't anyone lend money at a negative nominal rate of interest? How can this pose problems for monetary policy?

Solution appears at back of book.

▼ **Quick Review**

• Unexpected deflation helps lenders and hurts borrowers. This can lead to **debt deflation,** which has a contractionary effect on aggregate demand.

• Deflation makes it more likely that interest rates will end up against the **zero bound.** When this happens, the economy is in a **liquidity trap,** and monetary policy is ineffective.

Licenses to Print Money

Epa European Pressphoto Agency b.v./Alamy

People sometimes talk about profitable companies as having a "license to print money." Well, the British firm De La Rue actually does. In 1930, De La Rue, printer of items such as postage stamps, expanded into the money-printing business, producing banknotes for the then-government of China. Today it is the largest manufacturer of banknotes, producing the currencies of about 150 countries, from the United Kingdom to Fiji.

De La Rue's business received some unexpected attention in 2011 when Muammar Gaddafi, the dictator who had ruled Libya from 1969 until 2011, was fighting to suppress a fierce popular uprising. To finance his efforts, he turned to seignorage, ordering around $1.5 billion worth of Libyan dinars printed. But Libyan banknotes weren't printed in Libya; they were printed in Britain at one of De La Rue's facilities. The British government, an enemy of the Gaddafi regime, seized the new banknotes before they could be flown to Libya, refusing to release them until Gaddafi had been overthrown.

Why do so many countries turn to private companies like De La Rue and its main rivals, the German firm Giesecke & Devrient and the French firm Oberthur, to print their currencies? The short answer is that printing money isn't as easy as it sounds—producing high-quality banknotes that are hard to counterfeit requires highly specialized equipment and expertise. This is particularly true now that many countries are turning to banknotes printed of polymer, which are more durable and harder to counterfeit than paper money. In 2014, De La Rue was chosen to produce the next generation of British banknotes, the first ones to be made of plastic.

Actually, De La Rue has had its own problems with quality control: a scandal erupted in 2010, when it emerged that one of its plants had been producing defective security paper and that employees had covered up the problems. Nonetheless, many countries will surely continue relying on expert private firms to produce their currencies.

QUESTIONS FOR THOUGHT

1. How can a government obtain revenue by printing money when someone else actually prints the money?

2. Why, exactly, would Gaddafi have resorted to the printing press in early 2011?

3. Were there risks to the Libyan economy in releasing those dinars to the new government?

SUMMARY

1. In analyzing high inflation, economists use the **classical model of the price level,** which says that changes in the money supply lead to proportional changes in the aggregate price level even in the short run.

2. Governments sometimes print money in order to finance budget deficits. When they do, they impose an **inflation tax,** generating tax revenue equal to the inflation rate times the money supply, on those who hold money. Revenue from the real inflation tax, the inflation rate times the real money supply, is the real value of resources captured by the government. In order to avoid paying the inflation tax, people reduce their real money holdings and force the government to increase inflation to capture the same amount of real inflation tax revenue. In some cases, this leads to a vicious circle of a shrinking real money supply and a rising rate of inflation, leading to hyperinflation and a fiscal crisis.

3. The output gap is the percentage difference between the actual level of real GDP and potential output. A positive output gap is associated with lower-than-normal unemployment; a negative output gap is associated with higher-than-normal unemployment. The relationship between the output gap and cyclical unemployment is described by **Okun's law.**

4. Countries that don't need to print money to cover government deficits can still stumble into moderate inflation, either because of political opportunism or because of wishful thinking.

5. At a given point in time, there is a downward-sloping relationship between unemployment and inflation known as the **short-run Phillips curve.** This curve is shifted by changes in the expected rate of inflation. The **long-run Phillips curve,** which shows the relationship between unemployment and inflation once expectations have had time to adjust, is vertical. It defines the **nonaccelerating inflation rate of unemployment,** or **NAIRU,** which is equal to the natural rate of unemployment. *Stagflation,* a combination of high unemployment and high inflation, reflects an upward shift of the short-run Phillips curve.

6. Once inflation has become embedded in expectations, getting inflation back down can be difficult because *disinflation* can be very costly, requiring the sacrifice of large amounts of aggregate output and imposing high levels of unemployment. However, policy makers in the United States and other wealthy countries were willing to pay that price of bringing down the high inflation of the 1970s.

7. Deflation poses several problems. It can lead to **debt deflation,** in which a rising real burden of outstanding debt intensifies an economic downturn. Also, interest rates are more likely to run up against the **zero bound** in an economy experiencing deflation. When this happens, the economy enters a **liquidity trap,** rendering conventional monetary policy ineffective.

KEY TERMS

Classical model of the price level, p. 920
Inflation tax, p. 923
Okun's law, p. 928
Short-run Phillips curve, p. 928
Nonaccelerating inflation rate of unemployment (NAIRU), p. 935
Long-run Phillips curve, p. 936
Debt deflation, p. 939
Zero bound, p. 939
Liquidity trap, p. 939

PROBLEMS

1. In the economy of Scottopia, policy makers want to lower the unemployment rate and raise real GDP by using monetary policy. Using the accompanying diagram, show why this policy will ultimately result in a higher aggregate price level but no change in real GDP.

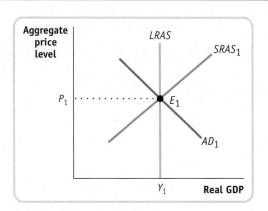

2. In the following examples, would the classical model of the price level be relevant?

   a. There is a great deal of unemployment in the economy and no history of inflation.

   b. The economy has just experienced five years of hyperinflation.

   c. Although the economy experienced inflation in the 10% to 20% range three years ago, prices have recently been stable and the unemployment rate has approximated the natural rate of unemployment.

3. The Federal Reserve regularly releases data on the U.S. monetary base. You can access that data at various websites, including the website for the Federal Reserve Bank of St. Louis. Go to http://research.stlouisfed.org/fred2/ and click on "Categories," then on "Money, Banking, & Finance," then on "Monetary Data," then on "Monetary Base," and then on "Monetary Base; Total" for the latest report. Then click on "View Data."

   a. The last two numbers in the column show the levels of the monetary base in the last year. How much did it change?

   b. How did this help in the government's efforts to finance its deficit?

   c. Why is it important for the central bank to be independent from the part of the government responsible for spending?

4. Answer the following questions about the (real) inflation tax, assuming that the price level starts at 1.

   a. Maria Moneybags keeps $1,000 in her sock drawer for a year. Over the year, the inflation rate is 10%. What is the real inflation tax paid by Maria for this year?

   b. Maria continues to keep the $1,000 in her drawer for a second year. What is the real value of this $1,000 at the beginning of the second year? Over the year, the inflation rate is again 10%. What is the real inflation tax paid by Maria for the second year?

   c. For a third year, Maria keeps the $1,000 in the drawer. What is the real value of this $1,000 at the beginning of the third year? Over the year, the inflation rate is again 10%. What is the real inflation tax paid by Maria for the third year?

   d. After three years, what is the cumulative real inflation tax paid?

   e. Redo parts a through d with an inflation rate of 25%. Why is hyperinflation such a problem?

5. The inflation tax is often used as a significant source of revenue in developing countries where the tax collection and reporting system is not well developed and tax evasion may be high.

   a. Use the numbers in the accompanying table to calculate the inflation tax in the United States and India (Rp = rupees).

	Inflation in 2013	Money supply in 2013 (billions)	Central government receipts in 2013 (billions)
India	9.48%	Rp19,118	Rp10,726
United States	1.46%	$2,832	$3,113

Sources: Bureau of Economic Analysis; Controller General of Accounts (India); Reserve Bank of India; International Monetary Fund; The World Bank.

   b. How large is the inflation tax for the two countries when calculated as a percentage of government receipts?

6. Concerned about the crowding-out effects of government borrowing on private investment spending, a candidate for president argues that the United States should just print money to cover the government's budget deficit. What are the advantages and disadvantages of such a plan?

7. The accompanying scatter diagram shows the relationship between the unemployment rate and the output gap in the United States from 1996 to 2013. Draw a straight line through the scatter of dots in the figure. Assume that this line represents Okun's law:

   Unemployment rate $= b - (m \times$ Output gap$)$
   where b is the vertical intercept and $-m$ is the slope

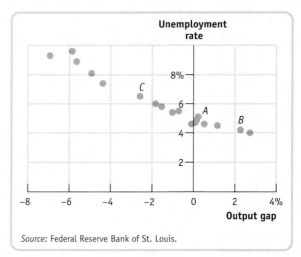

Source: Federal Reserve Bank of St. Louis.

What is the unemployment rate when aggregate output equals potential output? What would the unemployment rate be if the output gap were 2%? What if the output gap were −3%? What do these results tell us about the coefficient m in Okun's law?

8. After experiencing a recession for the past two years, the residents of Albernia were looking forward to a decrease in the unemployment rate. Yet after six months of strong positive economic growth, the unemployment rate has fallen only slightly below what it was at the end of the recession. How can you explain why the unemployment rate did not fall as much although the economy was experiencing strong economic growth?

9. a. Go to www.bls.gov. Click on link "Subjects"; on the left, under "Inflation & Prices," click on the link "Consumer Price Index." Scroll down to the section "CPI Tables," and find the link "Consumer Price Index Detailed Report, Tables Annual Averages 2009 (PDF)." What is the value of the percent change in the CPI from 2008 to 2009?

b. Now go to www.treasury.gov and click on "Resource Center." From there, click on "Data and Charts Center." Then click on "Interest Rate Statistics." In the scroll-down windows, select "Daily Treasury Bill Rates" and "2009." Examine the data in "4 Weeks Bank Discount." What is the maximum? The minimum? Then do the same for 2007. How do the data for 2009 and 2007 compare? How would you relate this to your answer in part (a)? From the data on Treasury bill interest rates, what would you infer about the level of the inflation rate in 2007 compared to 2009? (You can check your answer by going back to the www.bls.gov website to find the percent change in the CPI from 2006 to 2007.)

c. How would you characterize the change in the U.S. economy from 2007 to 2009?

10. The accompanying table provides data from the United States on the average annual rates of unemployment and inflation. Use the numbers to construct a scatter plot similar to Figure 31-5. Discuss why, in the short run, the unemployment rate rises when inflation falls.

Year	Unemployment rate	Inflation rate
2003	6.0	2.3
2004	5.5	2.7
2005	5.1	3.4
2006	4.6	3.2
2007	4.6	2.9
2008	5.8	3.8
2009	9.3	−0.3
2010	9.6	1.6
2011	8.9	3.1
2012	8.1	2.1
2013	7.2	1.5

Source: Bureau of Labor Statistics.

11. The economy of Brittania has been suffering from high inflation with an unemployment rate equal to its natural rate. Policy makers would like to disinflate the economy with the lowest economic cost possible. Assume that the state of the economy is not the result of a negative supply shock. How can they try to minimize the unemployment cost of disinflation? Is it possible for there to be no cost of disinflation?

12. Who are the winners and losers when a mortgage company lends $100,000 to the Miller family to buy a house worth $105,000 and during the first year prices unexpectedly fall by 10%? What would you expect to happen if the deflation continued over the next few years? How would continuing deflation affect borrowers and lenders throughout the economy as a whole?

WORK IT OUT Macmillan Education LaunchPad

For interactive, step-by-step help in solving the following problem, visit LaunchPad by using the URL on the back cover of this book.

13. Due to historical differences, countries often differ in how quickly a change in actual inflation is incorporated into a change in expected inflation. In a country such as Japan, which has had very little inflation in recent memory, it will take longer for a change in the actual inflation rate to be reflected in a corresponding change in the expected inflation rate. In contrast, in a country such as Zimbabwe, which has recently had very high inflation, a change in the actual inflation rate will immediately be reflected in a corresponding change in the expected inflation rate. What does this imply about the short-run and long-run Phillips curves in these two types of countries? What does this imply about the effectiveness of monetary and fiscal policy to reduce the unemployment rate?

Crises and Consequences

▶ **What You Will Learn
in This Chapter**

■ How depository banks and
shadow banks differ

■ Why, despite their differences,
both types of banks are subject to
bank runs

■ What happens during **financial
panics** and **banking crises**

■ Why the effects of panics and
crises on the economy are so
severe and long-lasting

■ How regulatory loopholes and
the rise of **shadow banking** led
to the financial crisis of 2008

■ How a new regulatory
framework seeks to avoid another
crisis

FROM PURVEYOR OF DRY GOODS TO DESTROYER OF WORLDS

Press Association via AP Images

**The collapse of Lehman Brothers, the once-venerable investment bank, set off a chain
of events that led to a worldwide financial panic.**

In 1844 Henry Lehman, a German immigrant, opened a dry goods store in Montgomery, Alabama. Over time, Lehman and his brothers, who followed him to America, branched out into cotton trading, then into a variety of financial activities. By 1850, Lehman Brothers was established on Wall Street; by 2008, thanks to its skill at trading financial assets, Lehman Brothers was one of the nation's top investment banks. Unlike commercial banks, investment banks trade in financial assets and don't accept deposits from customers.

But in September 2008, Lehman's luck ran out. The firm had invested heavily in subprime mortgages—loans to home-buyers with too little income or too few assets to qualify for standard mortgages. In the summer and fall of 2008, as the U.S. housing market plunge intensified and investments related to subprime mortgages lost much of their value, Lehman was hit hard.

Lehman had been borrowing heavily in the short-term credit market— often using overnight loans that must be repaid the next business day—to finance its ongoing operations and trading. As rumors began to spread about how heavily Lehman was exposed to the tanking housing market, its sources of credit dried up. On September 15, 2008, the firm declared bankruptcy, the largest bankruptcy to date in the United States. What happened would shock the world.

When Lehman fell, it set off a chain of events that came close to taking down the entire world financial system. Because Lehman had hidden the severity of its vulnerability, its failure came as a nasty surprise. Through securitization (a concept we defined in Chapter 29), financial institutions throughout the world were exposed to real estate loans that were quickly deteriorating in value as default rates on those loans rose.

Credit markets froze because those with funds to lend decided it was better to sit on the funds rather than lend them out and risk losing them to a borrower who might go under like Lehman had. Around the world, borrowers were hit by a global *credit crunch:* they either lost their access to credit or found themselves forced to pay drastically higher interest rates. Stocks plunged, and within weeks the Dow had fallen almost 3,000 points, more than a quarter of its value.

Nor were the consequences limited to financial markets. The U.S. economy was already in recession when Lehman fell, but the pace of the downturn accelerated drastically in the months that followed, resulting in the Great Recession, the worst slump in the U.S. economy since the Great Depression of the 1930s. By the time U.S. employment bottomed out in early 2010, more than 8 million jobs had been lost. Europe and Japan were also suffering their worst recessions since the 1930s, and world trade plunged even faster than it had in the first year of the Great Depression.

All of this came as a great shock because few people imagined that such events were possible in twenty-first-century America. Yet economists who knew their history quickly recognized what they were seeing: it was a modern version of a *financial panic,* a sudden and widespread disruption of financial markets. Financial panics were a regular feature of the U.S. financial system before World War II. As we discussed in Chapter 29, the financial panic that hit the United States in 2008 shared many features with the Panic of 1907, whose devastation prompted the creation of the Federal Reserve system. Financial panics almost always include a *banking crisis,* in which a significant portion of the banking sector ceases to function.

On reflection, the panic following Lehman's collapse was not unique, even in the modern world. The failure of Long-Term Capital Management in 1998 also precipitated a financial panic: global financial markets froze until the Federal Reserve rode to the rescue and coordinated a winding-down of the firm's operations. Because the Federal Reserve resolved the LTCM crisis quickly, its fall didn't result in a blow to the economy at large.

Financial panics and banking crises have happened fairly often, sometimes with disastrous effects on output and employment. Chile's 1981 banking crisis was followed by a 19% decline in real GDP per capita and a slump that lasted through most of the following decade. Finland's 1990 banking crisis was followed by a surge in the unemployment rate from 3.2% to 16.3%. Japan's banking crisis of the early 1990s led to more than a decade of economic stagnation.

In this chapter, we'll examine the causes and consequences of banking crises and financial panics, expanding on the discussion of this topic in Chapter 29. We'll begin by examining what makes banking vulnerable to a crisis and how this can mutate into a full-blown financial panic. Then we'll turn to the history of such crises and their aftermath, exploring why they are so destructive to the economy. Finally, we'll look at how governments have tried to limit the risks of financial crises.

Banking: Benefits and Dangers

As we learned in earlier chapters, banks perform an essential role in any modern economy. In Chapter 29 we defined commercial banks and savings and loans as financial intermediaries that provide liquid financial assets in the form of deposits to savers and use their funds to finance the illiquid investment-spending needs of borrowers. Deposit-taking banks perform the important functions of providing liquidity to savers and directly influencing the level of the money supply.

Lehman Brothers, however, was not a deposit-taking bank. Instead, it was an investment bank (also defined in Chapter 29)—in the business of speculative trading for its own profit and the profit of its investors. Yet Lehman got into trouble in much the same way that a deposit-taking bank does: it experienced a loss of confidence and something very much like a bank run—a phenomenon in which many of a bank's depositors try to withdraw their funds due to fears of a bank failure. Lehman was part of a larger category of institutions called shadow banks. *Shadow banking,* a term coined by the economist Paul McCulley of the giant bond fund PIMCO, is composed of a wide variety of types of financial firms: investment banks like Lehman, hedge funds like Long-Term Capital Management (LTCM), and money market funds. (As we will explain in more detail later, "shadow" refers to the fact that before the 2008 crisis these financial institutions were neither closely watched nor effectively regulated.)

Like deposit-taking banks, shadow banks are vulnerable to bank runs because they perform the same economic task: *maturity tranformation,* the transformation of short-term liabilities into long-term assets. From now on, we will use the term *depository banks* for banks that accept deposits (commercial banks and savings and loans) to better distinguish them from shadow banks (investment banks, hedge funds, and money market funds), which do not.

The Trade-off Between Rate of Return and Liquidity

Imagine that you live in a world without any banks. Further imagine that you have saved a substantial sum of money that you don't plan on spending anytime soon. What can you do with those funds?

One answer is that you could simply store the money—say, put it under your bed or in a safe. The money would always be there if you need it, but it would just sit there, not earning any interest.

Alternatively, you could lend the money out, say, to a growing business. This would have the great advantage of putting your money to work, both for you, since the loan would pay interest, and for the economy, since your funds would help pay for investment spending. There would, however, be a potential disadvantage: if you needed the money before the loan was paid off, you might not be able to recover it.

It's true that we asked you to assume that you had no plans for spending the money soon. But it's often impossible to predict when you will want or need to make cash outlays; for example, your car could break down or you could be offered an exciting opportunity to study abroad. Now, a loan is an asset, and there are ways to convert assets into cash. For example, you can try to sell the loan to someone else. But this can be difficult, especially if you need cash on short notice. So, in a world without banks, it's better to have some cash on hand when an unexpected financial need arises.

In other words, without banks, savers face a trade-off when deciding how much of their funds to lend out and how much to keep on hand in cash: a trade-off between liquidity, the ability to turn one's assets into cash on short notice, and the rate of return, in the form of interest or other payments received on one's assets. Without banks, people would make this trade-off by keeping a large fraction of their wealth idle, sitting in safes rather than helping pay for productive investment spending. Banking, however, changes that by allowing people ready access to their funds even while those funds are being used to make loans for productive purposes.

The Purpose of Banking

Banking, as we know it, emerged from a surprising place: it was originally a sideline business for medieval goldsmiths. By the nature of their business, goldsmiths needed vaults in which to store their gold. Over time, they realized that they could offer safekeeping services for their customers, too, because a wealthy person might prefer to leave his stash of gold and silver with a goldsmith rather than keep it at home, where thieves might snatch it.

Someone who deposited gold and silver with a goldsmith received a receipt that could be redeemed for those precious metals at any time. And a funny thing happened: people began paying for their purchases not by cashing in their receipts for gold and then paying with the gold, but simply by handing over their precious metal receipts to the seller. Thus, an early form of paper money was born.

Meanwhile, goldsmiths realized something else: even though they were obligated to return a customer's precious metals on demand, they didn't actually need to keep all of the treasure on their premises. After all, it was unlikely that all of their customers would want to lay hands on their gold and silver on the same day, especially if customers were using receipts as a means of payment. So a goldsmith could safely put some of his customers' wealth to work by lending it out to other businesses, keeping only enough on hand to pay off the few customers likely to demand their precious metals on short notice—plus some additional reserves in case of exceptional demand.

And so banking was born. In a more abstract form, depository banks today do the same thing those enterprising goldsmiths learned to do: they accept the savings of individuals, promising to return them on demand, but put most of those funds to work by

Banks make both savers and borrowers happy: savers get ready access to their cash and borrowers get funds to borrow.

Maturity transformation is the conversion of short-term liabilities into long-term assets.

A **shadow bank** is a nondepository financial institution that engages in maturity transformation.

taking advantage of the fact that not everyone will want access to those funds at the same time. A typical bank account lets you withdraw as much of your funds as you want, anytime you want—but the bank doesn't actually keep everyone's cash in its safe or even in a form that can be turned quickly into cash. Instead, the bank lends out most of the funds placed in its care, keeping limited reserves to meet day-to-day withdrawals. And because deposits can be put to use, banks don't charge you (or charge very little) for the privilege of keeping your savings safe. Depending on the type of account you have, they might even pay you interest on your deposits.

More generally, what depository banks do is borrow on a short-term basis from depositors (who can demand to be repaid at any time) and lend on a long-term basis to others (who cannot be forced to repay until the end date of their loan). This is what economists call **maturity transformation:** converting short-term liabilities (deposits in this case) into long-term assets (bank loans that earn interest). Shadow banks, such as Lehman Brothers, also engage in maturity transformation, but they do it in a way that doesn't involve taking deposits.

Instead of taking deposits, Lehman borrowed funds in the short-term credit markets and then invested those funds in longer-term speculative projects. Indeed, a **shadow bank** is any financial institution that does not accept deposits but does engage in maturity transformation—borrowing over the short term and lending or investing over the longer term. And just as bank depositors benefit from the liquidity and higher return that banking provides compared to sitting on their money, lenders to shadow banks like Lehman benefit from liquidity (their loans must be repaid quickly, often overnight) and higher return compared to other ways of investing their funds.

A generation ago, depository banks accounted for most banking. After about 1980, however, there was a steady rise in shadow banking. Shadow banking has grown in popularity because it is not subject to the regulations, such as capital requirements and reserve requirements, that are imposed on depository banking. So, like the unregulated trusts that set off the Panic of 1907, shadow banks can offer their customers a higher rate of return on their funds. As of July 2007, generally considered the start of the financial crisis that climaxed when Lehman fell in September 2008, the U.S. shadow banking sector was about 1.5 times larger, in terms of dollars, than the formal, deposit-taking banking sector.

As we pointed out in Chapter 29, things are not always simple in banking. There we learned why depository banks can be subject to bank runs. As the cases of Lehman and LTCM so spectacularly illustrate, the same vulnerability afflicts shadow banks. Next we explore why.

Shadow Banks and the Re-emergence of Bank Runs

Because a depository bank keeps on hand just a small fraction of its depositors' funds, a bank run typically results in a bank failure: the bank is unable to meet depositors' demands for their money and closes its doors. Ominously, bank runs can be self-fulfilling prophecies: although a bank may be in relatively good financial shape, if enough depositors believe it is in trouble and try to withdraw their money, their beliefs end up dooming the bank.

To prevent such occurrences, after the 1930s the United States (and most other countries) adopted wide-ranging banking regulation in the form of regular audits by the Federal Reserve, deposit insurance, capital requirements and reserve requirements, and provisions allowing troubled banks to borrow from the Fed's discount window.

Shadow banks, though, don't take deposits. So how can they be vulnerable to a bank run? The reason is that a shadow bank, like a depository bank, engages in maturity transformation: it borrows short term and lends or invests longer term. If a shadow bank's lenders suddenly decide one day that it's no longer safe to lend it money, the shadow bank can no longer fund its operations. Unless it can sell its assets immediately to raise cash, it will quickly fail. This is exactly what happened to Lehman.

Lehman borrowed funds in the overnight credit market (also known as the *repo* market), funds that it was required to repay the next business day, in order to fund its trading operations. So Lehman was on a very short leash: every day it had to be able to convince its creditors that it was a safe place to park their funds. And one day, that ability was no longer there. The same phenomenon happened at LTCM: the hedge fund was enormously leveraged (that is, it had borrowed huge amounts of money) also, like Lehman, to fund its trading operations. One day its credit simply dried up, in its case because creditors perceived that it had lost huge amounts of money during the Asian and Russian financial crises of 1997–1998.

Bank runs are destructive to everyone associated with a bank: its shareholders, its creditors, its depositors and loan customers, and its employees. But a bank run that spreads like a contagion is extraordinarily destructive, causing depositors at other banks to also lose faith, leading to a cascading sequence of bank failures and a banking crisis. This is what happened in the United States during the early 1930s as Americans in general rushed out of bank deposits—the total value of bank deposits fell by 35%—and started holding currency instead. Until 2008, it had never happened again in the United States. Our next topic is to explore how and why bank runs reappeared.

ECONOMICS ▶ *in Action*

The Day the Lights Went Out at Lehman

On Friday night, September 12, 2008, an urgent meeting was held in the New York Federal Reserve Bank's headquarters in lower Manhattan. Attending was the outgoing Bush Administration's Treasury Secretary, Hank Paulson, and then head of the New York Fed, Tim Geithner (later the Treasury Secretary in the Obama Administration), along with the heads of the country's largest investment banks. Lehman Brothers was rapidly imploding and Paulson called the meeting in the hope of pressing the investment bankers into a deal that would, like the LTCM bailout described in Chapter 29, avert a messy bankruptcy.

Since the forced sale of the nearly bankrupt investment bank Bear Stearns six months earlier to a healthier bank, Lehman had been under increasing pressure. Like Bear Stearns, Lehman had invested heavily in subprime mortgages and other assets tied to real estate. And when Bear Stearns fell as its creditors began calling in its loans and other banks refused to lend to it, many wondered if Lehman would fall next.

In July 2008, Lehman reported a $2.8 billion loss for the second quarter of 2008 (the months April–June), precipitating a 54% fall in its stock price. As its share price fell, Lehman's sources of credit began to dry up and its trading operations withered. CEO of Lehman, Richard Fuld, began a frantic search for a healthier bank to buy shares of Lehman and provide desperately needed funding. By early September 2008, Lehman's loss for the third quarter had risen to $3.9 billion. On September 9, JP Morgan Chase, a far healthier investment bank that had been Lehman's major source of financing for its trades, demanded $5 billion in cash as extra collateral or it would freeze Lehman's accounts and cut off its credit. Unable to come up with the cash, Lehman teetered on the edge of bankruptcy.

Was the refusal to bail out Lehman Brothers a catastrophic mistake?

In the September 12 meeting, Treasury Secretary Paulson urged the investment bankers to put together a package to purchase Lehman's bad assets. But, fearing for their own survival in an extremely turbulent market, they refused unless Paulson would give them a government guarantee on the value of Lehman's assets. The Treasury had made the Bear Stearns sale possible by arranging a huge loan from the New York Fed to its purchaser. This time, facing a backlash from Congress over "bailing out profligate bankers," Paulson refused to provide government help. And in the wee hours of Monday morning, September 15, 2008, Lehman went down, declaring the most expensive bankruptcy in history.

Yet, as Fuld had earlier warned Paulson, the failure of Lehman unleashed the furies. That same day the U.S. stock market fell 504 points, triggering an increase in bank borrowing costs and a run on money market funds and financial institutions around the world. By Tuesday, Paulson agreed to an $85 billion bailout of another major corporation, the foundering American International Group (AIG), at the time the world's largest insurer. Before the markets stabilized months later, the U.S. government made $250 billion of capital infusions to bolster major U.S. banks. Whether or not Paulson made a catastrophic mistake by not acting to save Lehman is a matter likely to be debated for years to come.

Check Your Understanding 32-1

1. Which of the following are examples of maturity transformations? Which are subject to a bank-run-like phenomenon in which fear of a failure becomes a self-fulfilling prophecy? Explain.
   a. You sell tickets to a lottery in which each ticket holder has a chance of winning a $10,000 jackpot.
   b. Dana borrows on her credit card to pay her living expenses while she takes a year-long course to upgrade her job skills. Without a better-paying job, she will not be able to pay her accumulated credit card balance.
   c. An investment partnership invests in office buildings. Partners invest their own funds and can redeem them only by selling their partnership share to someone else.
   d. The local student union savings bank offers checking accounts to students and invests those funds in student loans.

Solutions appear at back of book.

Banking Crises and Financial Panics

Bank failures are common: even in a good year, several U.S. banks typically go under for one reason or another. And shadow banks sometimes fail, too. **Banking crises**—episodes in which a large part of the depository banking sector or the shadow banking sector fails or threatens to fail—are relatively rare by comparison. Yet they do happen, often with severe negative effects on the broader economy. What would cause so many of these institutions to get into trouble at the same time? Let's take a look at the logic of banking crises, then review some of the historical experiences.

The Logic of Banking Crises

A **banking crisis** occurs when a large part of the depository banking sector or the shadow banking sector fails or threatens to fail.

When many banks—either depository banks or shadow banks—get into trouble at the same time, there are two possible explanations. First, many of them could have made similar mistakes, often due to an *asset bubble*. Second, there may be *financial contagion*, in which one institution's problems spread and create trouble for others.

Shared Mistakes In practice, banking crises usually owe their origins to many banks making the same mistake of investing in an *asset bubble*. In an **asset bubble,** the price of some kind of asset, such as housing, is pushed to an unreasonably high level by investors' expectations of further price gains. For a while, such bubbles can feed on themselves. A good example is the savings and loan crisis of the 1980s, when there was a huge boom in the construction of commercial real estate, especially office buildings. Many banks extended large loans to real estate developers, believing that the boom would continue indefinitely. By the late 1980s, it became clear that developers had gotten carried away, building far more office space than the country needed. Unable to rent out their space or forced to slash rents, a number of developers defaulted on their loans—and the result was a wave of bank failures.

A similar phenomenon occurred between 2002 and 2006, when rapidly rising housing prices led many people to borrow heavily to buy a house in the belief that prices would keep rising. This process accelerated as more buyers rushed into the market and pushed housing prices up even faster. Eventually the market runs out of new buyers and the bubble bursts. At this point asset prices fall; in some parts of the United States, housing prices fell by half between 2006 and 2009. This, in turn, undermines confidence in financial institutions that are exposed to losses due to falling asset prices. This loss of confidence, if it's sufficiently severe, can set in motion the kind of economy-wide vicious downward spiral that marks a financial contagion.

Financial Contagion In especially severe banking crises, a vicious downward spiral of **financial contagion** occurs among depository banks or shadow banks: each institution's failure worsens depositors' or lenders' fears and increases the odds that another bank will fail.

As already noted, one underlying cause of contagion arises from the logic of bank runs. In the case of depository banks, when one bank fails, depositors are likely to become nervous about others. Similarly in the case of shadow banks, when one fails, lenders in the short-term credit market become nervous about lending to others. The shadow banking sector, because it is largely unregulated, is especially prone to fear- and rumor-driven contagion.

There is also a second channel of contagion: asset markets and the vicious cycle of deleveraging, a phenomenon we learned about in Chapter 29. When a financial institution is under pressure to reduce debt and raise cash, it tries to sell assets. To sell assets quickly, though, it often has to sell them at a deep discount. The contagion comes from the fact that other financial institutions own similar assets, whose prices decline as a result of the "fire sale." This decline in asset prices hurts the other financial institutions' financial positions, too, leading their creditors to stop lending to them. This knock-on effect forces more financial institutions to sell assets, reinforcing the downward spiral of asset prices. This kind of downward spiral was clearly evident in the months immediately following Lehman's fall: prices of a wide variety of assets held by financial institutions, from corporate bonds to pools of student loans, plunged as everyone tried to sell assets and raise cash. Later, as the severity of the crisis abated, many of these assets saw at least a partial recovery in prices.

Combine an asset bubble with a huge, unregulated shadow-banking system and a vicious cycle of deleveraging and it is easy to see how a full-blown **financial panic**—a sudden and widespread disruption of financial markets that happens when people suddenly lose faith in the liquidity of financial institutions and markets—can arise, as happened in the U.S. economy in 2008. A financial panic almost always involves a banking crisis, either in the depository banking sector, or the shadow banking sector, or both.

Because banking provides much of the liquidity needed for trading financial assets like stocks and bonds, severe banking crises almost always lead to

In an **asset bubble,** the price of an asset is pushed to an unreasonably high level due to expectations of further price gains.

A **financial contagion** is a vicious downward spiral among depository banks or shadow banks: each bank's failure worsens fears and increases the likelihood that another bank will fail.

A **financial panic** is a sudden and widespread disruption of the financial markets that occurs when people suddenly lose faith in the liquidity of financial institutions and markets.

disruptions of the stock and bond markets. Disruptions of these markets, along with a headlong rush to sell assets and raise cash, lead to a vicious circle of deleveraging. As the panic unfolds, savers and investors come to believe that the safest place for their money is under their bed, and their hoarding of cash further deepens the distress.

So what can history tell us about banking crises and financial panics?

Historical Banking Crises: The Age of Panics

Between the Civil War and the Great Depression, the United States had a famously crisis-prone banking system. Even then, banks were regulated: most banking was carried out by "national banks" that were regulated by the federal government and subject to rules involving reserves and capital, of the kind described below. However, there was no system of guarantees for depositors. As a result, bank runs were common, and banking crises, also known at the time as panics, were fairly frequent.

Table 32-1 shows the dates of these nationwide banking crises and the number of banks that failed in each episode. Notice that the table is divided into two parts. The first part is devoted to the "national banking era," which preceded the 1913 creation of the Federal Reserve—which was supposed to put an end to such crises. It failed. The second part of the table is devoted to the epic waves of bank failures that took place in the early 1930s.

The events that sparked each of these panics differed. In the nineteenth century, there was a boom-and-bust cycle in railroad construction somewhat similar to the boom-and-bust cycle in office building construction during the 1980s. Like modern real estate companies, nineteenth-century railroad companies relied heavily on borrowed funds to finance their investment projects. And railroads, like office buildings, took a long time to build. This meant that there were repeated episodes of overbuilding: competing railroads would invest in expansion, only to find that collectively they had laid more track than the demand for rail transport warranted. When the overbuilding became apparent, business failures, debt defaults, and an overall banking crisis followed. The Panic of 1873 began when Jay Cooke and Co., a financial firm with a large stake in the railroad business, failed. The Panic of 1893 began with the failure of the overextended Philadelphia and Reading Railroad.

As we'll see later in this chapter, the major financial panics of the nineteenth and early twentieth centuries were followed by severe economic downturns. However, the banking crises of the early 1930s made previous crises seem minor by comparison. In four successive waves of bank runs from 1930 to 1932, about 40% of the banks in America failed. In the end, Franklin Delano Roosevelt declared a temporary closure of all banks—the so-called "bank holiday"—to put an end to the vicious circle. Meanwhile, the economy plunged, with real GDP shrinking by a third and a sharp fall in prices as well.

TABLE 32-1	Number of Bank Failures: National Banking Era and Great Depression		
National Banking era (1863–1912)		**Great Depression (1929–1941)**	
Panic dates	**Number of failures**	**Panic dates**	**Number of failures**
September 1873	101	November–December 1930	806
May 1884	42	April–August 1931	573
November 1890	18	September–October 1931	827
May–August 1893	503	June–July 1932	283
October–December 1907	73*	February–March 1933	Bank holiday (government-mandated temporary banking closure)

*This understates the scale of the 1907 crisis because it doesn't take into account the role of trusts.

There is still considerable controversy about the banking crisis of the early 1930s. In part, this controversy is about cause and effect: did the banking crisis cause the wider economic crisis, or vice versa? (No doubt causation ran in both directions, but the magnitude of these effects remains disputed.) There is also controversy about the extent to which the banking crisis could have been avoided. Milton Friedman and Anna Schwartz, in their famous study *A Monetary History of the United States,* argued that the Federal Reserve could and should have prevented the banking crisis—and that if it had, the Great Depression itself could also have been prevented. However, this view has been disputed by other economists.

In the United States, the experience of the 1930s led to banking reforms that prevented a replay for more than 70 years. Outside the United States, however, there were a number of major banking crises.

A typical scene outside a bank during the banking crises of the Great Depression.

Modern Banking Crises Around the World

Around the world, banking crises are relatively frequent events. However, the ways in which they occur differ according to the banking sector's particular institutional framework. According to a 2008 analysis by the International Monetary Fund, no fewer than 127 banking crises occurred around the world between 1970 and 2007. Most of these were in small, poor countries that lack the regulatory safeguards found in advanced countries. In poorer countries, banks generally get in trouble in much the same way: insufficient capital, poor accounting, too many loans and, often, corruption. But banks in advanced countries can also make the same mistakes—for example, there was the "Savings and Loans (S&L) crisis" in the United States during the 1980s (described in Chapter 29).

In more advanced countries, banking crises almost always occur as a consequence of an asset bubble—typically in real estate. Between 1985 and 1995, three advanced countries—Finland, Sweden, and Japan—experienced banking crises due to the bursting of a real estate bubble. Banks in the three countries lent heavily into a real estate bubble that their lending helped to inflate. Figure 32-1 shows real estate prices, adjusted for inflation, in Finland, Sweden, and Japan from 1985

| FIGURE **32-1** | Real Housing Prices in Three Banking Crises |

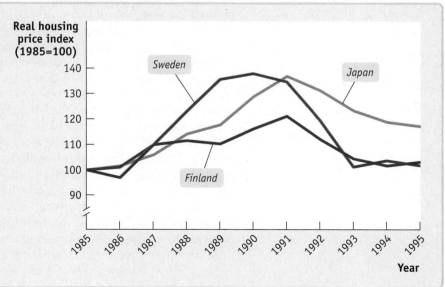

During the period 1985 to 1995, Finland, Sweden, and Japan each experienced a banking crisis due to a real estate bubble. Here you can see how real housing prices (housing prices adjusted for inflation) in each country rose dramatically and then fell sharply. The sharp fall in housing prices pushed a significant part of each country's banking sector into insolvency.

Sources: Bank of Finland; Statistics Sweden; Japan Real Estate Institute; Bank for International Settlements; OECD.

to 1995. As you can see, in each country a sharp rise was followed by a drastic fall, leading many borrowers to default on their real estate loans, pushing large parts of each country's banking system into insolvency.

In the United States, the fall of Lehman in September 2008 precipitated a banking crisis in the shadow banking sector that included financial contagion as well as financial panic, but left the depository banking sector largely unaffected. As we discussed in the opening story, the financial crisis of 2008 was devastating because of securitization, which had distributed subprime mortgage loans throughout the entire shadow banking sector both in the United States and abroad.

At the time of writing, shadow banking in the United States was still significantly smaller than it was before the crisis. Since 2008, investors have rediscovered the benefits of regulation, and the depository banking sector has grown at the expense of the shadow banking sector. However, shadow banking has certainly not gone away. China's shadow banking sector has grown at breakneck speed in the last few years, making it the third largest in the world as of 2014 and an area of great concern to Chinese leaders. In the next section, we will learn how troubles in the banking sector soon translate into troubles for the broader economy.

ECONOMICS ▶ *in Action*

Erin Go Broke

For much of the 1990s and 2000s, Ireland was celebrated as an economic success story: the "Celtic Tiger" was growing at a pace the rest of Europe could only envy. But the miracle came to an abrupt halt in 2008, as Ireland found itself facing a huge banking crisis.

Like the earlier banking crises in Finland, Sweden, and Japan, Ireland's crisis grew out of excessive optimism about real estate. Irish housing prices began rising in the 1990s, in part a result of the economy's strong growth. However, real estate developers began betting on ever-rising prices, and Irish banks were all too willing to lend these developers large amounts of money to back their speculations. Housing prices tripled between 1997 and 2007, home construction quadrupled over the same period, and total credit offered by banks rose far faster than in any other European nation. To raise the cash for their lending spree, Irish banks supplemented the funds of depositors by using large amounts of "wholesale" funding—short-term borrowing from other banks and private investors.

In 2007 the Irish real estate boom collapsed. Home prices started falling, and home sales collapsed. Many of the loans that Irish banks had made during the boom went into default. Now, so-called ghost estates, newly built housing developments full of unoccupied, crumbling homes, dot the Irish landscape. In 2008, the troubles of the Irish banks threatened to turn into a sort of bank run—not by depositors, but as in the cases of Lehman and Bear Stearns, by lenders who had provided the banks with short-term funding through the wholesale interbank lending market. And as in the case of the United States, government intervention was necessary to stabilize the situation: the Irish government stepped in and guaranteed repayment of all bank debt.

This created a new problem because it put Irish taxpayers on the hook for potentially huge bank losses. Until the crisis struck, Ireland appeared to be in good fiscal shape, with relatively low government debt and a budget surplus. The fallout from the banking crisis, however, led to serious questions about the solvency of the Irish government—whether it could raise the resources to meet its obligation to guarantee the repayment of all bank debt. As a result of these questions over the Irish government's solvency, it was forced to pay high interest rates on funds it raised in international bond markets.

As in most banking crises, Ireland experienced a severe recession. The Irish unemployment rate rose from less than 5% before the crisis to more than 15% in early 2012. It was still more than 11% at the time of writing.

It's also worth noting that Ireland's problems were part of a broader crisis affecting several European countries, notably Spain, Portugal, and Greece. We'll discuss this broader crisis later in the chapter.

Check Your Understanding   32-2

1. Regarding the Economics in Action "Erin Go Broke," identify the following:
   a. The asset bubble
   b. The channel of financial contagion
2. Again regarding "Erin Go Broke," why do you think the Irish government tried to stabilize the situation by guaranteeing the debts of the banks? Why was this a questionable policy?

Solutions appear at back of book.

The Consequences of Banking Crises

If banking crises affected only banks, they wouldn't be as serious a concern. But banking crises are almost always associated with recessions, and severe banking crises are associated with the worst economic slumps. Furthermore, history shows that recessions caused in part by banking crises inflict sustained economic damage, with economies taking years to recover.

Banking Crises, Recessions, and Recovery

A severe banking crisis is one in which a large fraction of the banking system either fails outright (that is, goes bankrupt) or suffers a major loss of confidence and must be bailed out by the government. Such crises almost invariably lead to deep recessions, which are usually followed by slow recoveries.

Figure 32-2 illustrates this phenomenon by tracking unemployment in the aftermath of three banking crises widely separated in space and time: the Panic of 1893, the Swedish banking crisis of 1991, and the American financial crisis of 2008 that spawned the Great Recession. In the figure, *t* represents the year of the crisis: 1893 for the United States, 1991 for Sweden. As the figure shows, these three crises, spanning over 100 years and continents apart, produced similarly

▼ **Quick Review**

• Although individual bank failures are common, a **banking crisis** is a rare event that typically will severely harm the broader economy.

• A banking crisis can occur because depository or shadow banks invest in an **asset bubble** or through **financial contagion,** set off by bank runs or by a vicious cycle of deleveraging. Largely unregulated, shadow banking is particularly vulnerable to contagion.

• In 2008, an asset bubble combined with a huge shadow banking sector and a vicious cycle of deleveraging created a **financial panic** and banking crisis, as savers cut their spending and investors hoarded their funds, sending the economy into a steep decline.

• Between the Civil War and the Great Depression, the United States suffered numerous banking crises and financial panics, each followed by a severe economic downturn. The banking reforms of the 1930s prevented another banking crisis until 2008.

• Banking crises usually occur in small, poor countries, although there have been banking crises in advanced countries as well. The fall of Lehman caused a banking crisis and a financial panic in the shadow banking sector, leading investors to shift back into the depository banking sector.

FIGURE 32-2   Unemployment Rates, Before and After Banking Crises

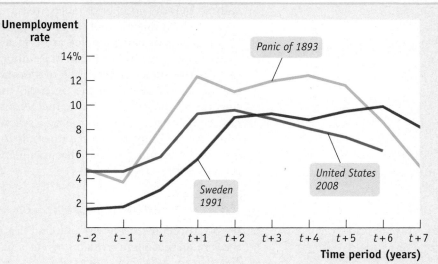

This figure tracks unemployment in the wake of three banking crises: the Panic of 1893, the Swedish banking crisis of 1991, and the American financial crisis of 2008. *t* represents the year of the crisis—1893 for the Panic of 1893, 1991 for the Swedish banking crisis, and 2008 for the American financial crisis of that year. *t* − 2 is the date two years before the crisis hit; *t* + 5 is the date five years after. In all three cases, the economy suffered severe damage from the banking crisis: unemployment shot up and came down only slowly and erratically. In all three cases, five years after the crisis the unemployment rate remained high compared to pre-crisis levels.

Sources: Christina D. Romer, "Spurious Volatility in Historical Unemployment Data," *Journal of Political Economy* 94, no. 1 (1986): 1–37; Eurostat; Bureau of Labor Statistics.

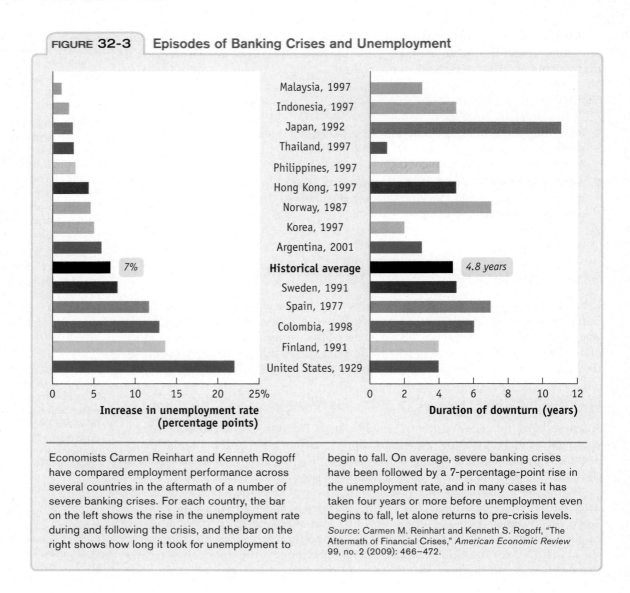

FIGURE 32-3 Episodes of Banking Crises and Unemployment

Economists Carmen Reinhart and Kenneth Rogoff have compared employment performance across several countries in the aftermath of a number of severe banking crises. For each country, the bar on the left shows the rise in the unemployment rate during and following the crisis, and the bar on the right shows how long it took for unemployment to begin to fall. On average, severe banking crises have been followed by a 7-percentage-point rise in the unemployment rate, and in many cases it has taken four years or more before unemployment even begins to fall, let alone returns to pre-crisis levels.

Source: Carmen M. Reinhart and Kenneth S. Rogoff, "The Aftermath of Financial Crises," *American Economic Review* 99, no. 2 (2009): 466–472.

devastating results: unemployment shot up and came down only slowly and erratically so that the number of jobless remained high by pre-crisis standards for many years. A third line shows U.S. unemployment in the aftermath of the 2008 crisis.

These historical examples are typical. Figure 32-3, taken from a widely cited study by the economists Carmen Reinhart and Kenneth Rogoff, compares employment performance in the wake of a number of severe banking crises. The bars on the left show the rise in the unemployment rate during and following the crisis; the bars on the right show the time it took before unemployment began to fall. The numbers are shocking: on average, severe banking crises have been followed by a 7-percentage-point rise in the unemployment rate, and in many cases it has taken four years or more before the unemployment rate even begins to fall, let alone returns to pre-crisis levels.

Why Are Banking-Crisis Recessions So Bad?

It's not difficult to see why banking crises normally lead to recessions. There are three main reasons: a *credit crunch* arising from reduced availability of credit, financial distress caused by a *debt overhang*, and the loss of monetary policy effectiveness.

1. *Credit crunch.* The disruption of the banking system typically leads to a reduction in the availability of credit, called a **credit crunch,** in which potential

In a **credit crunch,** potential borrowers either can't get credit at all or must pay very high interest rates.

borrowers either can't get credit at all or must pay very high interest rates. Unable to borrow or unwilling to pay higher interest rates, businesses and consumers cut back on spending, pushing the economy into a recession.

2. *Debt overhang.* A banking crisis typically pushes down the prices of many assets through a vicious circle of deleveraging, as distressed borrowers try to sell assets to raise cash, pushing down asset prices and causing further financial distress. As we have already seen, deleveraging is a factor in the spread of the crisis, lowering the value of the assets banks hold on their balance sheets and so undermining their solvency. It also creates problems for other players in the economy. To take an example all too familiar from recent events, falling housing prices can leave consumers substantially poorer, especially because they are still stuck with the debt they incurred to buy their homes. A banking crisis, then, tends to leave consumers and businesses with a **debt overhang:** high debt but diminished assets. Like a credit crunch, this also leads to a fall in spending and a recession as consumers and businesses cut back in order to reduce their debt and rebuild their assets.

3. *Loss of monetary policy effectiveness.* A key feature of banking-crisis recessions is that when they occur, monetary policy—the main tool of policy makers for fighting negative demand shocks caused by a fall in consumer and investment spending—loses much of its effectiveness. The ineffectiveness of monetary policy makes banking-crisis recessions especially severe and long-lasting.

> A **debt overhang** occurs when a vicious circle of deleveraging leaves a borrower with high debt but diminished assets.

Recall from Chapter 29 how the Fed normally responds to a recession: it engages in open-market operations, purchasing short-term government debt from banks. This leaves banks with excess reserves, which they lend out, leading to a fall in interest rates and causing an economic expansion through increased consumer and investment spending.

Under normal conditions, this policy response is highly effective. In the aftermath of a banking crisis, though, the whole process tends to break down. Banks, fearing runs by depositors or a loss of confidence by their creditors, tend to hold on to excess reserves rather than lend them out. Meanwhile, businesses and consumers, finding themselves in financial difficulty due to the plunge in asset prices, may be unwilling to borrow even if interest rates fall. As a result, even very low interest rates may not be enough to push the economy back to full employment.

In the previous chapter we described the problem of the economy's falling into a liquidity trap, when even pushing short-term interest rates to zero isn't enough. In fact, all the historical episodes in which the zero bound on interest rates became an important constraint on policy—the 1930s, Japan in the 1990s, and a number of countries after 2008—have occurred after a major banking crisis.

The inability of the usual tools of monetary policy to offset the macroeconomic devastation caused by banking crises is the major reason such crises produce deep, prolonged slumps. The obvious solution is to look for other policy tools. In fact, governments do typically take a variety of special steps when banks are in crisis.

Governments Step In

Before the Great Depression, policy makers often adopted a laissez-faire attitude toward banking crises, allowing banks to fail in the belief that market forces should be allowed to work. Since the catastrophe of the 1930s, though, almost all policy makers have believed that it's necessary to take steps to contain the damage from bank failures. In general, central banks and governments take three main kinds of action in an effort to limit the fallout from banking crises:

1. They act as the *lender of last resort.*
2. They offer guarantees to depositors and others with claims on banks.
3. In an extreme crisis, a central bank will step in and provide financing to private credit markets.

FIGURE **32-4** Total Borrowings of Depository Institutions from the Federal Reserve

Although commercial banks borrowed negligible amounts from the Fed before the crisis hit in 2008, in the months after Lehman's collapse their borrowing surged to $700 billion—an amount 14 times total bank reserves before the crisis.

Source: Federal Reserve Bank of St. Louis.

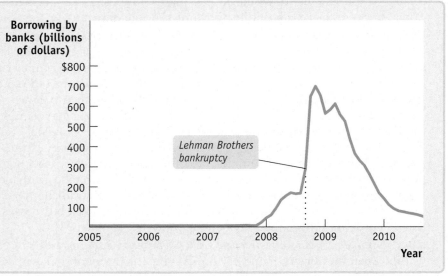

1. Lender of Last Resort An institution, usually a country's central bank, that provides funds to financial institutions when they are unable to borrow from the private credit markets is a **lender of last resort.** In particular, the central bank can provide cash to a bank that is facing a run by depositors but is fundamentally solvent, making it unnecessary for the bank to engage in fire sales of its assets to raise cash. This acts as a lifeline, working to prevent a loss of confidence in the bank's solvency from turning into a self-fulfilling prophecy.

Did the Federal Reserve act as a lender of last resort in the 2008 financial crisis? Very much so. Figure 32-4 shows borrowing by banks from the Fed between 2005 and 2010: commercial banks borrowed negligible amounts from the central bank before the crisis, but their borrowing rose to $700 billion in the months following Lehman's failure. To get a sense of how large this borrowing was, note that total bank reserves before the crisis were less than $50 billion— so these loans were 14 times the banks' initial reserves.

2. Government Guarantees There are limits, though, to how much a lender of last resort can accomplish: it can't restore confidence in a bank if there is good reason to believe the bank is fundamentally insolvent. If the public believes that the bank's assets aren't worth enough to cover its debts even if it doesn't have to sell these assets on short notice, a lender of last resort isn't going to help much. And in major banking crises there are often good reasons to believe that many banks are truly bankrupt.

As we have already learned, in such cases governments often step in to guarantee banks' liabilities. In 2007, a bank run hit the British bank, Northern Rock, ceasing only when the British government stepped in and guaranteed all deposits at the bank, regardless of size. Ireland's government eventually stepped in to guarantee repayment of not just deposits at all of the nation's banks, but all bank debts. Sweden did the same thing after its 1991 banking crisis.

When governments take on banks' risk, they often demand a quid pro quo; namely, they often take ownership of the banks they are rescuing—an action called *nationalization*. Northern Rock was nationalized in 2008. Sweden nationalized a significant part of its banking system in 1992. In the United States, the Federal Deposit Insurance Corporation routinely seizes banks that are no

A **lender of last resort** is an institution, usually a country's central bank, that provides funds to financial institutions when they are unable to borrow from the private credit markets.

longer solvent; it seized 140 banks in 2009. Ireland, however, chose not to seize any of the banks whose debts were guaranteed by taxpayers.

These government takeovers are almost always temporary. In general, modern governments want to save banks, not run them. So governments eventually *reprivatize* nationalized banks, selling them to private buyers, as soon as they believe they can.

3. Provider of Direct Financing As we learned in Chapter 29, during the depths of the 2008 financial crisis the Federal Reserve expanded its operations beyond the usual measures of open-market operations and lending to depository banks. It also began lending to shadow banks and buying commercial paper—short-term bonds issued by private companies—as well as buying the debt of Fannie Mae and Freddie Mac, the government-sponsored home mortgage agencies. In this way, the Fed provided credit to keep the economy afloat when private credit markets had dried up.

ECONOMICS ▶ *in Action*

Banks and the Great Depression

According to the official business-cycle chronology, the United States entered a recession in August 1929, two months before that year's famous stock market crash. Although the crash surely made the slump worse, through late 1930 it still seemed to be a more or less ordinary recession. Then the bank failures began. A majority of economists believe that the banking crisis is what turned a fairly severe but not catastrophic recession into the Great Depression.

How did the banking crisis hurt the wider economy? Largely by creating a credit crunch, in which businesses in particular either could not borrow or found themselves forced to pay sharply higher interest rates. Figure 32-5 shows one indicator of this credit crunch: the difference between the interest rates—known as the *spread*—at which businesses with good but not great credit could borrow and the borrowing costs of the federal government.

Baa corporate bonds are those that Moody's, the credit rating agency, considers "medium-grade obligations"—debts of companies that should be able to pay but aren't completely reliable. ("Baa" refers to the specific rating assigned to the bonds of such companies as DIRECTV or Time Warner Cable.) Until the banking crisis struck, Baa borrowers borrowed at interest rates only about 2 percentage points higher than the interest rates the government borrowed at, and this spread remained low until the summer of 1931. Then it surged, peaking at more than 7 percentage points in 1932. Bear in mind that this is just one indicator of the credit crunch: many would-be borrowers were completely shut out.

One striking fact about the banking crisis of the early 1930s is that the Federal Reserve, although it had the legal ability to act as a lender of last resort, largely failed to do so. Nothing like the surge in bank borrowing from the Fed that took place in 2007–2009 occurred. In fact, bank borrowing from the Fed throughout the 1930s banking crisis was at levels lower than those reached in 1928–1929.

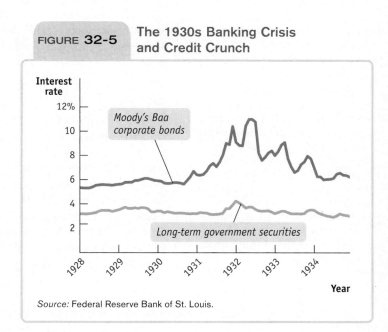

FIGURE **32-5** The 1930s Banking Crisis and Credit Crunch

Source: Federal Reserve Bank of St. Louis.

• Banking crises almost always result in recessions, with severe banking crises associated with the worst economic slumps. Historically, severe banking crises have resulted, on average, in a 7-percentage-point rise in the unemployment rate.

• Recessions caused by banking crises are especially severe because they involve a **credit crunch,** a vicious circle of deleveraging coupled with a **debt overhang,** leading households and businesses to cut spending, further deepening the downturn.

• Slumps induced by bank crises are so severe and prolonged because they make monetary policy ineffective: even though the central bank can lower interest rates, financially distressed households and businesses may still be unwilling to borrow and spend.

• Central banks and governments use two main types of policies to limit the damage from a banking crisis: acting as the **lender of last resort** and offering guarantees that the banks' liabilities will be repaid. In the aftermath of a bank rescue, governments sometimes nationalize the bank and then later reprivatize it. In an extreme crisis, the central bank will provide direct financing to private credit markets.

Meanwhile, neither the Fed nor the federal government did anything to rescue failing banks until 1933. So the early 1930s offer a clear example of a banking crisis that policy makers more or less allowed to take its course. It's not an experience anyone wants to repeat.

Check Your Understanding 32-3

1. Explain why the Federal Reserve was able to prevent the crisis of 2008 from turning into another Great Depression but was unable to prevent the surge in unemployment that occurred.

2. Explain why, in the aftermath of a severe banking crisis, a very low interest rate—even as low as 0%—may be unable to move the economy back to full employment.

Solutions appear at back of book.

The 2008 Crisis and Its Aftermath

As we've just seen, banking crises have typically been followed by major economic problems. How did the aftermath of the financial crisis of 2008 compare with this historical experience? The answer, unfortunately, is that history has proved a very good guide: once again, the economic damage from the financial crisis was both large and prolonged. And aftershocks from the crisis continue to shake the world economy today.

Severe Crisis, Slow Recovery

Figure 32-6 shows real GDP during the crisis and aftermath in the United States and the *eurozone*—the group of countries using the euro as a shared currency, which together form an economy roughly the same size as that of the United States. For both economies real GDP is shown as an index with the peak precrisis quarter—the last quarter of 2007 for the United States, the first quarter of 2008 for the eurozone—set equal to 100. What you can see is that the United States experienced a steep downturn followed by a relatively slow recovery, and Europe did even worse, sliding back into recession in 2011.

The severe slump and the slow recovery in the United States were very bad news for workers, since a healthy job market depends on an economy growing

---

FIGURE 32-6 | Crisis and Recovery in the United States and the Eurozone

In the aftermath of the 2008 financial crisis, aggregate output in the eurozone and in the United States fell dramatically. In the United States, output then began a sluggish but sustained recovery. Europe, however, slid back into recession in 2011.
Sources: Bureau of Economic Analysis; Eurostat.

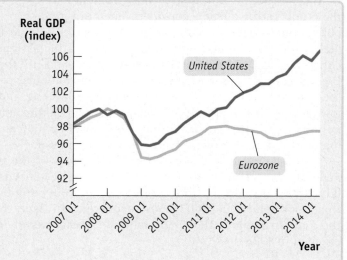

| FIGURE **32-7** | U.S. Unemployment in the Aftermath of the 2008 Crisis |

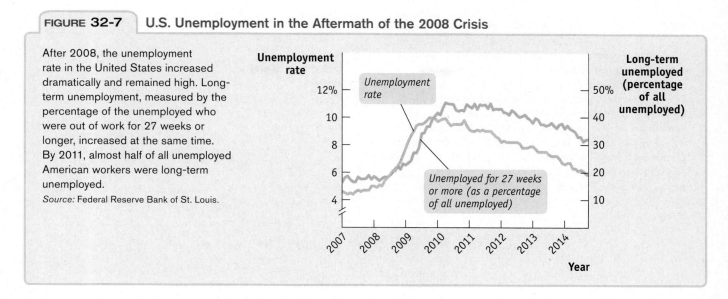

After 2008, the unemployment rate in the United States increased dramatically and remained high. Long-term unemployment, measured by the percentage of the unemployed who were out of work for 27 weeks or longer, increased at the same time. By 2011, almost half of all unemployed American workers were long-term unemployed.

Source: Federal Reserve Bank of St. Louis.

fast enough to accommodate both a growing workforce and rising productivity. Figure 32-7 shows two indicators of unemployment in the United States—the overall unemployment rate and the percentage of the unemployed who had been out of work 27 weeks or more. Both measures shot up during the crisis and remained very high years later, indicating a labor market in which it remained very hard to find a job.

This outcome was, sad to say, about what one should have expected given the severity of the initial financial shock and the historical experience with such shocks. Look back at Figure 32-2: compared with either the Panic of 1893 or the aftermath of the Swedish banking crisis of 1991, the U.S. experience after 2008, the Great Recession, has if anything been better. The United States, observed Kenneth Rogoff (whose work we cited earlier), has experienced a "garden variety severe financial crisis."

Aftershocks in Europe

One important factor bedeviling hopes for recovery was the emergence of special difficulties in several European nations—difficulties that repeatedly raised the specter of a second financial crisis.

The 2008 crisis was caused by problems with private debt, mainly home loans, which then triggered a crisis of confidence in banks. In 2011 and 2012, there were fears of a second crisis, this one arising from concerns about whether Southern European countries as well as Ireland could repay their burgeoning public debts.

Europe's troubles first surfaced in Greece, a country with a long history of fiscal irresponsibility. In late 2009 it was revealed that the previous Greek government had understated the size of the budget deficits and the amount of government debt. This prompted lenders to refuse further loans to Greece. To prevent a default on Greek public debt, other European countries provided emergency loans to the Greek government in return for harsh cuts to the Greek government budget. But these cuts depressed the Greek economy, and by late 2011 there was general agreement that Greece would be unable to pay back its public debt in full.

By itself, this was a manageable shock for the European economy since Greece accounts for less than 3% of European GDP. Unfortunately, foot-dragging and finger-pointing by European officials in confronting Greece's problems and the effects of the harsh budget cuts on the Greek economy spooked the markets for public debt of other European countries. So by the fall of 2011, the crisis had spread beyond the Greek borders, hitting two major European economies, Spain and Italy, which found themselves forced to pay much higher interest rates on their public debt.

FIGURE **32-8** | Interest Rate Spread Against German 10-Year Bonds

One indicator of investors' perceptions of the risk of government default is the spread of interest rates on government bonds between that country and a country that is perceived as a safe investment. The spread of the interest rates on 10-year government bonds for Italy and Spain, measured against the interest rate on German bonds, rose as investors' fears of default by Italy and Spain increased, then fell after the European Central Bank announced that it would, if necessary, buy national bonds to avert a cash crunch.

Sources: Federal Reserve Bank of St. Louis; OECD.

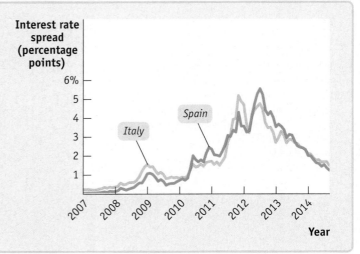

Figure 32-8 shows a measure of pressure on Italy and Spain during the 2008 and 2011 crises: the difference between interest rates on 10-year bonds issued by the governments of Spain and Italy, and the interest rate on German public debt, which most people consider a safe investment. Because all three countries use the same currency, the euro, these interest rates would all be the same if Italian and Spanish government debt were considered as safe as German government debt. The rise in the *spreads*—the differences between the interest rates on Spanish and Italian public debt versus the interest rate on German public debt—therefore indicated a growing perception of risk that the Spanish and Italian governments could not repay their debts in full. As you can see from Figure 32-8, the spreads were virtually zero in 2007, indicating investors felt that German, Spanish, and Italian public debt were equally risky. However, this changed in 2008 as the spreads began to rise.

Spain's fiscal problems were mainly fallout from the 2008 crisis. Before that crisis, Spain seemed to be in very good fiscal condition, with low debt and a budget surplus. However, Spain, like Ireland, had a huge housing bubble between 2000 and 2007. When the bubble burst, the Spanish economy fell into a deep slump, depressing tax receipts and causing large budget deficits. At the same time, there were worries that the Spanish government might eventually have to spend large amounts bailing out banks. As a result, investors began worrying about the solvency of the Spanish government and a possible default.

Italy's case was somewhat different. Italy has long had high levels of public debt as a percentage of GDP, but it has not run large deficits in recent years; as late as the spring of 2010 its fiscal position looked fairly stable. At that point, however, investors began to have doubts about the Italian government's solvency, in part because in the aftermath of the 2008 crisis the Italian economy was growing very slowly—too slowly, it was feared, to generate enough tax revenue to repay its public debt. These doubts drove up interest rates on Italian public debt, and this in turn created a vicious circle: higher interest payments, caused by fears about Italian government solvency, worsened Italy's fiscal position even further and pushed it closer to the edge.

Some economists argued that the problems of Spain and Italy were exacerbated by the fact that, having adopted the euro, their debts were in effect in a foreign currency. Why does this matter? Governments like those of the United States, Britain, or Japan, which borrow in their own currencies, can't run out of money—they can just print some more. True, this may have bad side effects, such as inflation; but a cash crunch, in which the government literally can't pay its debts, is ruled out. The governments of

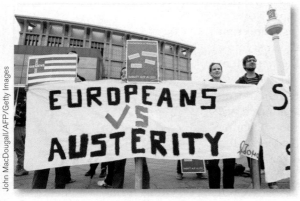

In recent years a public debt crisis in the eurozone followed by fiscal austerity has led to skyrocketing unemployment.

Spain and Italy, however, *can* run out of money—and bond investors, it was argued, worried that this made them vulnerable to something like a bank run, in which a loss of investor confidence produced a liquidity crisis—a lack of available cash—that forced them into default.

This argument gained a lot of credibility in 2012, when the European Central Bank declared that it would become a lender of last resort for the eurozone by buying directly the bonds of troubled governments in that area if necessary, greatly reducing the fears of a liquidity crisis for these governments. As you can see in Figure 32-8, spreads on Spanish and Italian debt fell sharply after the announcement. Although immediate fears of government defaults in the eurozone had been greatly eased, at the time of writing Europe's economic difficulties remain grave.

The Stimulus–Austerity Debate

The persistence of economic difficulties after the 2008 financial crisis led to fierce debates about appropriate policy responses. Broadly speaking, economists and policy makers were divided as to whether the situation called for more fiscal stimulus—expansionary fiscal measures such as more government spending and possibly tax cuts to promote spending and reduce unemployment—or for **fiscal austerity,** contractionary fiscal measures such as spending cuts and possibly tax increases to reduce budget deficits.

The proponents of more stimulus pointed to the continuing poor performance of major economies, arguing that the combination of high unemployment and relatively low inflation clearly pointed to the need for expansionary policies. And since monetary policy was limited by the zero bound (a concept we discussed in Chapter 31) for interest rates, stimulus proponents advocated expansionary fiscal policy to fill the gap.

The austerity camp took a very different view. Strongly influenced by the solvency troubles of Greece, they argued that the common source of all the problems were high levels of government deficits and debts. In their view, countries like the United States that continued to run large government deficits several years after the 2008 crisis were at risk of suffering a similar loss of investor confidence in their ability to repay their debts. Moreover, austerity advocates claimed that cuts in government spending would not actually be contractionary because they would improve investor confidence and keep interest rates on government debt low.

Each side of the debate argued that recent experience refuted the other side's claims. Austerity proponents argued that the persistence of high unemployment despite the fiscal stimulus programs adopted by the United States and other major economies in 2009 showed that stimulus doesn't work. Stimulus advocates argued that these programs were simply inadequate in size, pointing out that many economists had warned of their inadequacy from the start. Stimulus advocates further argued that warnings about the dangers of deficits were overblown, that far from rising, borrowing costs for Japan, the United States, and Britain—nations that, unlike the troubled European debtors, still had their own currencies with all the flexibility that implies—had fallen to record lows. And they dismissed claims that spending cuts would raise confidence as mainly fantasy.

By 2014, the intellectual debate seemed to have gone mostly against the advocates of austerity. Research at the International Monetary Fund and elsewhere seemed to support warnings that austerity policies depress output and employment, especially when there is little room for interest rates to fall. Interest rates in countries that borrow in their own currencies remained low despite years of high budget deficits—and as we saw in Figure 32-8, even eurozone governments with high levels of public debt saw their borrowing costs drop sharply once the European Central Bank moved to end fears of a cash crunch. The shift in the intellectual debate did not, however, lead to much change in actual economic policies.

Contractionary fiscal measures such as spending cuts and tax increases aimed at reducing budget deficits are known as **fiscal austerity.**

The Lesson of the Post-Crisis Slump

Almost all major economies had great difficulty dealing with the aftermath of the 2008 financial crisis—high unemployment, low growth and, for some, solvency concerns, and high interest rates on public debt.

Clearly, then, the best way to avoid the terrible problems that arise after a financial crisis is not to have a crisis in the first place. How can you do that? In part, one might hope, through better regulation of financial institutions. We turn next to attempts at regulatory reform.

ECONOMICS ▶ in Action

If Only It Were the 1930s

FIGURE **32-9** Real GDP in Europe, Pre-Crisis Peak = 100

Sources: Maddison Project; Eurostat.

In the United States, the aftermath of the 2008 financial crisis was terrible, but at least you can say that it was a lot better than what happened during the Great Depression, when real GDP fell by a third. In Europe, however, you can't even say that. Partly that's because the Great Depression wasn't as severe in Europe as it was in the United States. But it's also due to the fact that Europe has failed to stage a convincing recovery from the 2008 crisis, sliding back into recession in 2011. As a result, while the initial slump wasn't as deep as in the 1930s, by the time of writing Europe was actually doing worse than it did in the 1930s.

Figure 32-9 shows the painful comparison. The purple line shows real GDP in Western Europe from 1929 onwards, while the green line shows real GDP in the eurozone starting in 2008; in each case the pre-crisis peak is set to 100. The first year and a half of the two episodes were quite similar, and by the middle of 2009 Europe, like the United States, emerged from recession, causing everyone to breathe a sigh of relief. But while the initial plunge in Europe during the 1930s was followed by a strong and sustained recovery, this time around Europe's recovery sputtered out in 2011.

As a result, by late 2014 Europe was, incredibly, significantly behind where it was at this point in the 1930s, prompting the British economic historian Nicholas Crafts to publish a widely cited article with the title "The Eurozone: If Only It Were the 1930s."

We can attribute Europe's terrible performance since 2008 in part to policy mistakes and in part to the straitjacket created by the euro itself. However one apportions the blame, Europe's woes demonstrate the awesome damage financial crises can do.

▼ Quick Review

• Economic damage from the financial crisis of 2008 was both large and prolonged. Aftershocks from the crisis continue to shake the world economy.

• The world's two largest economies, the United States and the European Union, suffered severe downturns, shrinking more than 5%, followed by relatively slow recoveries. The severe slump and the slow recovery were very bad news for workers.

• The persistence of economic difficulties after the 2008 financial crisis led to severe solvency concerns for several European countries. A fierce debate erupted over whether fiscal stimulus or **fiscal austerity** was the right policy prescription, which the stimulus advocates appear to be winning.

Check Your Understanding 32-4

1. In November 2011, the government of France announced that it was reducing its forecast for economic growth in 2012. It was also reducing its estimates of tax revenue for 2012, since a weaker economy would mean smaller tax receipts. To offset the effect of lower revenue on the budget deficit, the government also announced a new package of tax increases and spending cuts. Which side of the stimulus–austerity debate was France taking?

Solutions appear at back of book.

Regulation in the Wake of the Crisis

By late 2009, interventions by governments and central banks around the world had restored calm to financial markets. However, huge damage had been done to the global economy. In much of the advanced world, countries suffered their deepest slumps since the 1930s. And all indications were that the typical pattern of slow recovery after a financial crisis would be repeated, with unemployment remaining high for years to come.

The banking crisis of 2008 demonstrated, all too clearly, that financial regulation is a continuing process—that regulations will and should change over time to keep up with a changing world. The dependence on very short-term loans, the lack of regulation, and being outside the lender-of-last-resort system made the shadow banking sector vulnerable to crises and panics. So what changes will the most recent crisis bring? One thing that became all too clear in the 2008 crisis was that the traditional scope of banking regulation was too narrow. Regulating only depository institutions was clearly inadequate in a world in which a large part of banking, properly understood, is undertaken by the shadow banking sector.

In the aftermath of the crisis, then, an overhaul of financial regulation was clearly needed. And in 2010 the U.S. Congress enacted a bill that represented an effort to respond to the events of the preceding years. Like most legislation, the Wall Street Reform and Consumer Protection Act—often referred to as the Dodd-Frank bill—is complex in its details. But it contains four main elements:

1. Consumer protection
2. Derivatives regulation
3. Regulation of shadow banks
4. Resolution authority over nonbank financial institutions that face bankruptcy

1. Consumer Protection One factor in the financial crisis was the fact that many borrowers accepted offers they didn't understand, such as mortgages that were easy to pay in the first two years but required sharply higher payments later on. In an effort to limit future abuses, the new law creates a special office, the Consumer Financial Protection Bureau, dedicated to policing financial industry practices and protecting borrowers.

2. Derivatives Regulation Another factor in the crisis was the proliferation of derivatives—complex financial instruments that were supposed to help spread risk but arguably simply concealed it. Under the new law, most derivatives have to be bought and sold in open, transparent markets, hopefully limiting the extent to which financial players can take on invisible risk.

3. Regulation of Shadow Banks A key element in the financial crisis, as we've seen, was the rise of institutions that didn't fit the conventional definition of a bank but played the role of banks and created the risk of a banking crisis. How can regulation be extended to such institutions? Dodd-Frank does not offer an explicit new definition of what it means to be a bank. Instead, it offers a sort of financial version of "you know it when you see it." Specifically, it gives a special panel the ability to designate financial institutions as "systemically important," meaning that their activities have the potential to create a banking crisis. Such institutions will be subject to bank-like regulation of their capital, their investments, and so on.

4. Resolution Authority The events of 2008 made it clear that governments would often feel the need to guarantee not only deposits but also a wide range of financial-institution debts in a crisis. Yet how can this be done without creating huge incentive problems, motivating financial institutions to undertake overly risky behavior in the knowledge that they will be bailed out by the government if they get into trouble?

Part of the answer is to empower the government to seize control of financial institutions that require a bailout, the way it already does with failing commercial banks and thrifts. This new power, known as resolution authority, should be viewed as solving a problem that seemed acute in early 2009, when several major financial institutions were teetering on the brink. Yet it wasn't clear whether Washington had the legal authority to orchestrate a rescue that was fair to taxpayers.

All this is now law in the United States, but two things remain unclear. (1) How will these regulations be worked into the international financial system? Will other nations adopt similar policies? If they do, how will conflicts among different national policies be resolved? (2) Will these regulations do the trick? Post-1930s bank regulation produced decades of stability, but will that happen again? Or will the new system fail in the face of a serious test?

Nobody knows the answers to these questions. We'll just have to wait and see.

ECONOMICS ▶ in Action

Bent Breaks the Buck

In September 2008, the $65 billion Reserve Primary Fund broke the buck after it was caught with bankrupt Lehman Brothers debt, leaving investors in a panic.

In 1970 a financial innovator named Bruce Bent introduced a new concept to American finance: the money market mutual fund. Most mutual funds offer ways for small investors to buy stocks: when you buy a share in a mutual fund like Fidelity or Vanguard, you are indirectly acquiring a diversified mix of stocks. Bent, however, created a mutual fund that invests only in short-term assets, such as Treasury bills and commercial paper issued by highly rated corporations, which carry a low risk of default. The idea was to give people a safe place to park their money, but one that offered a higher interest rate than a bank deposit. Many people eventually began seeing their investments in money market funds as equivalent to bank accounts, but better.

But money placed in money market funds was different from money deposited in a bank in one crucial dimension: money market funds weren't federally insured. And on September 16, 2008, the day after Lehman Brothers fell, it became known that one major money market fund had lost heavily on money placed with Lehman, to such an extent that it had "broken the buck"; that is, it no longer had enough assets to pay off all the people who had placed their money at its disposal. As a result, the fund had to suspend withdrawals; in effect, a "bank" had suddenly shut its doors.

And which fund was in this predicament? Reserve Primary Fund, controlled by none other than Bruce Bent. Panicked money market mutual fund customers pulled hundreds of billions of dollars out of money market funds over a two-day period.

The federal government stemmed the panic by instituting a temporary insurance scheme for money market funds, giving them the same protected status as bank deposits. But the money fund panic was an object lesson in the extent to which financial innovation had undermined the traditional bank safety net.

▼ Quick Review

- When the panic hit after Lehman's fall, governments and central banks around the world stepped in to fight the crisis and calm the markets. Most advanced economies experienced their worst slump since the 1930s.

- In 2010 Congress enacted the Dodd-Frank bill to remedy the regulatory oversights exposed by the crisis of 2007–2009. It created the Consumer Financial Protection Bureau to protect borrowers and consumers, implemented stricter regulation of derivatives, extended the reach of regulation to the shadow banking sector, and empowered the government to seize control of any financial institution requiring a bailout.

Check Your Understanding 32-5

1. Why does the use of short-term borrowing and being outside of the lender-of-last-resort system make shadow banks vulnerable to events similar to bank runs?

2. How do you think the crisis of 2008 would have been mitigated if there had been no shadow banking sector but only the formal depository banking sector?

3. Describe the incentive problem facing the U.S. government in responding to the 2007–2009 crisis with respect to the shadow banking sector. How did the Dodd-Frank bill attempt to address those incentive problems?

Solutions appear at back of book.

SUMMARY

1. Without banks, people would make the trade-off between liquidity and rate of return by holding a large fraction of their wealth in idle cash. Banks engage in **maturity transformation,** transforming short-term liabilities into long-term assets. Banking improves savers' welfare, allowing them immediate access to their funds as well as paying them interest on those funds.

2. **Shadow banks** have grown greatly since 1980. Largely unregulated, they can pay savers a higher rate of return than depository banks. Like depository banks, shadow banks engage in maturity transformation, depending on short-term borrowing to operate and investing in long-term assets. Therefore, shadow banks can also be subject to bank runs.

3. Although **banking crises** are rare, they typically inflict severe damage on the economy. They have two main sources: shared mistakes, such as investing in an **asset bubble,** and **financial contagion.** Contagion is spread through bank runs or via a vicious cycle of deleveraging. When unregulated, shadow banking is particularly vulnerable to contagion. In 2008, a **financial panic** hit the United States, arising from the combination of an asset bubble, a huge shadow banking sector, and a vicious cycle of deleveraging.

4. The United States has suffered numerous banking crises and financial panics, each followed by a severe downturn. The crisis of the 1930s spurred bank reform that prevented another crisis until 2008. Banking crises occur frequently throughout the world, mostly in small, poor countries. In the recent past, though, several advanced countries have had banking crises driven by real estate bubbles.

5. Severe banking crises almost invariably lead to deep and long recessions, with unemployment remaining high for several years after the crisis began. There are three main reasons why banking crises are so damaging to the economy: they result in a **credit crunch,** the vicious circle of deleveraging leads to a **debt overhang,** and monetary policy is rendered ineffective as the economy falls into a liquidity trap. As a result, households and businesses are either unable or unwilling to spend, deepening the downturn.

6. Unlike during the Great Depression, governments now step in to try to limit the damage from a banking crisis by acting as the **lender of last resort** and by guaranteeing the banks' liabilities. Sometimes, but not always, governments nationalize the banks and then later reprivatize them. In an extreme crisis, the central bank may directly finance commercial transactions.

7. Economic damage from the financial crisis of 2008 was large and prolonged. The world's two largest economies, the United States and the European Union, suffered severe downturns, shrinking more than 5%, followed by relatively slow recoveries. The persistence of economic difficulties after 2008 led to fierce debates about appropriate policy responses between economists and policy makers calling for more fiscal stimulus—more government spending and possibly tax cuts to promote spending and reduce unemployment—and those favoring **fiscal austerity—** spending cuts and possibly tax increases to reduce budget deficits.

8. The banking regulatory system put in place during the 1930s has eroded due to the rise of shadow banking. The dependence on short-term financing (repo), the lack of regulation, and being outside the lender-of-last-resort system makes the shadow banking sector vulnerable to a banking panic.

9. The crisis of 2008 began as the shadow banking sector suffered high losses when a real estate bubble burst. Despite the fact that governments and central banks around the world stepped in to fight the crisis and the downturn, most advanced countries experienced their worst slump since the 1930s. Persistently high unemployment is likely to endure for years to come.

10. In the aftermath of the crisis, the U.S. Congress enacted the Dodd-Frank bill in the hope of preventing a replay of the crisis. The main elements of the new reform are stronger consumer protection, greater regulation of derivatives, regulation of shadow banking, and resolution authority for a variety of financial institutions. We have yet to see whether these changes will be adequate or whether they will also be adopted by other countries.

KEY TERMS

Maturity transformation, p. 950
Shadow bank, p. 950
Banking crisis, p. 952
Asset bubble, p. 953
Financial contagion, p. 953
Financial panic, p. 953
Credit crunch, p. 958
Debt overhang, p. 959
Lender of last resort, p. 960
Fiscal austerity, p. 965

PROBLEMS

1. Which of the following are *not* examples of a vicious cycle of deleveraging? Explain.

   a. Your university decides to sell several commercial buildings in the middle of town in order to upgrade buildings on campus.

   b. A company decides to sell its large and valuable art collection because other asset prices on its balance sheet have fallen below a critical level, forcing creditors to call in their loans to the company because of provisions written into the original loan contract.

   c. A company decides to issue more stock in order to voluntarily pay off some of its debt.

   d. A shadow bank must sell its holdings of corporate bonds because falling asset prices have led to a default on the terms of its loans with some creditors.

2. In the following figure showing the Case–Shiller U.S. Home Price Index from 2000 to 2010, did housing prices peak before or after the financial crisis in the United States? Explain your answer.

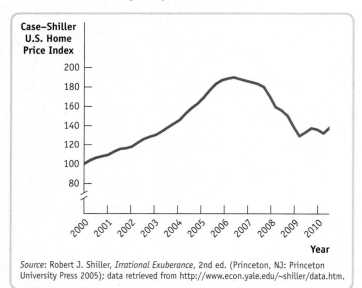

Source: Robert J. Shiller, *Irrational Exuberance*, 2nd ed. (Princeton, NJ: Princeton University Press 2005); data retrieved from http://www.econ.yale.edu/~shiller/data.htm.

3. Figure 32-2 tracks the unemployment rate in the years before and after the Panic of 1893 in the United States, the banking crisis of 1991 in Sweden, and the American financial crisis of 2008.

   a. In Figure 32-2, how many years after the Panic of 1893 did unemployment peak in the United States?

   b. In Figure 32-2, how many years after the banking crisis of 1991 did unemployment peak in Sweden?

   c. In Figure 32-2, how many years after the banking crisis of 2008 did unemployment peak in the United States?

4. In 2007–2009, the Federal Reserve, acting as a lender of last resort, stepped in to provide funds when private markets were unable to do so. The Fed also took over many banks. In 2007, it seized 3 banks; in 2008, it seized 25 banks; and in 2009, it seized 140 banks. Go to www.fdic.gov; under "Bank Closing Information," click on "Complete Failed Bank List." Then count the number of banks that the Federal Reserve has seized so far this year. Have bank failures decreased since the crisis in 2009?

5. During the financial crisis in October 2008, the federal government could borrow at a rate of 2.73% (the yield on five-year Treasury securities). During October 2008, though, Baa borrowers (corporate borrowers rated by Moody's as not being completely reliable) had to pay 8.88%.

   a. What was the difference in borrowing costs for these corporate borrowers and the federal government?

   b. Go to www.research.stlouisfed.org/fred2/categories/22. Click on the link for "Treasury Constant Maturity" and find the most recent interest rate on 10-year U.S. Treasury bonds. Then click back to the original web page on the link for "Corporate Bonds," then "Moody's," and find the rate for Baa corporate bonds. What is the current difference in borrowing costs between corporate borrowers and the U.S. government?

   c. Has this difference in borrowing costs increased or decreased since the height of the financial crisis in October of 2008? Why?

6. Go to www.federalreserve.gov and click on the tab "Banking Information & Regulation." Then select the links "Banking Data" followed by "Large Commercial Banks." Once there, choose the latest release of quarterly data.

   a. Which bank has the largest consolidated assets?

   b. Which bank has the largest domestic assets?

   c. What percent of U.S. GDP are the domestic assets of the bank listed in part b? (*Hint:* You can find U.S. GDP at http://research.stlouisfed.org/fred2/series/GDP?cid=106 using the links "Gross Domestic Product (GDP)" and then "Current-dollar and 'real' GDP.")

7. Go to www.fdic.gov and click on the tab "Industry Analysis" and then on the link "Research & Analysis." Select "The First Fifty Years: A History of the FDIC 1933–1983." Open Chapter 3, "Establishment of the FDIC," and scroll down to the section entitled "The Banking Crisis of 1933" and the section entitled "Federal Deposit Insurance Legislation." Read the section and then answer these questions.

   a. President Roosevelt was sworn in on March 4, 1933. What was one of his first official acts in response to the banking crisis?

   b. How many banks suspended operations during 1933?

   c. Who was the chief proponent of federal deposit insurance in Congress?

   d. How much coverage did the temporary fund for federal deposit insurance provide?

8. The U.S. Government Accountability Office (GAO) does research to support congressional decision making. After the Long-Term Capital Management (LTCM) crisis, the GAO produced a summary of the events of the crisis located at www.gao.gov/products/GGD-00-3. Read the summary and then answer the following questions.

   a. How much of its capital did LTCM lose in 1998?

   b. Why did the GAO conclude that LTCM was able to establish leveraged trading positions of a size that posed systemic risk to the banking system?

   c. What was the recommendation of the President's Working Group regarding the Securities and Exchange Commission (SEC) and the Commodity Futures Trading Commission (CFTC)?

9. Which of the following are examples of debt overhang? Which examples are likely to lead to a cutback in spending? Explain.

   a. Your uncle starts a restaurant, borrowing to fund his investment. The restaurant fails, and your uncle must shut down but still must pay his debt.

   b. Your parents take out a loan to buy a house. Your father is transferred to a new city, and now your parents must sell the house. The value of the house has gone up during the time your family has lived there.

   c. Your friend's parents take out a loan to buy her a condo to live in while she is at college. Meanwhile, the housing market plummets. By the time your friend leaves college, the condo is worth significantly less than the value of the loan.

   d. You finish college with an honors degree in a field with many good job prospects and with $25,000 in student loans that you must repay.

Macroeconomics: Events and Ideas

▶ **What You Will Learn in This Chapter**

■ Why classical macroeconomics was inadequate for the problems posed by the Great Depression

■ How Keynes and the experience of the Great Depression legitimized **macroeconomic policy activism**

■ What **monetarism** is and why monetarists claim there are limits to the use of **discretionary monetary policy**

■ How challenges led to a revision of **Keynesian economics** and the emergence of the **new classical macroeconomics**

■ Why the **Great Moderation consensus** was challenged by the 2008 financial crisis, leading to fierce debates among economists about the best use of fiscal and monetary policy during challenging economic times

A TALE OF TWO SLUMPS

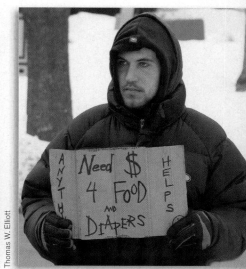

The problems of the Great Recession have been tackled using the macroeconomic tools that evolved from the experience of the Great Depression.

In November 2002, the Federal Reserve held a special conference to honor Milton Friedman on the occasion of his ninetieth birthday. Among those delivering tributes was Ben Bernanke, who had recently moved to the Fed from Princeton University and would later become the Fed's chairman. In his tribute, Bernanke surveyed Friedman's intellectual contributions, with particular focus on the argument made by Friedman and his collaborator Anna Schwartz that the Great Depression of the 1930s could have been avoided if only the Fed had done its job properly.

At the close of his talk, Bernanke directly addressed Friedman and Schwartz, who were sitting in the audience: "Let me end my talk by abusing slightly my status as an official representative of the Federal Reserve. I would like to say to Milton and Anna: Regarding the Great Depression. You're right, we did it. We're very sorry. But thanks to you, we won't do it again."

Today, in the aftermath of a devastating financial crisis that was followed by many years of high unemployment, those words ring somewhat hollow. Avoiding severe economic downturns, it turned out, wasn't as easy as Friedman, Schwartz, and Bernanke had believed. Yet, as bad as the Great Recession was, it was less devastating than the Great Depression. And it can be reasonably argued that some of the credit was due to the fact that macroeconomics had evolved greatly over the previous three generations. As a result, during the Great Recession policy makers knew more about the causes of depressions and how to fight them than they did during the Great Depression.

In this chapter we'll trace the development of macroeconomic ideas over the past 85 years. As we'll see, this development has been strongly influenced by economic events, from the Great Depression of the 1930s, to the stagflation of the 1970s, to the surprising period of economic stability achieved between 1985 and 2007. And as we'll also see, the process continues, as the economic difficulties of the Great Recession have spurred many macroeconomists to rethink what they thought they knew.

Classical Macroeconomics

The term *macroeconomics* appears to have been coined in 1933 by the Norwegian economist Ragnar Frisch. The date, during the worst year of the Great Depression, is no accident. Still, there were economists analyzing what we now consider macroeconomic issues—the behavior of the aggregate price level and aggregate output—before then.

Money and the Price Level

In Chapter 31, we described the *classical model of the price level.* According to the classical model, prices are flexible, making the aggregate supply curve vertical even in the short run. In this model, an increase in the money supply leads, other things equal, to an equal proportional rise in the aggregate price level, with no effect on aggregate output. As a result, increases in the money supply lead to inflation, and that's all. Before the 1930s, the classical model of the price level dominated economic thinking about the effects of monetary policy.

Did classical economists really believe that changes in the money supply affected only aggregate prices, without any effect on aggregate output? Probably not. Historians of economic thought argue that before 1930 most economists were aware that changes in the money supply affect aggregate output as well as aggregate prices in the short run—or, to use modern terms, they were aware that the short-run aggregate supply curve slopes upward. But they regarded such short-run effects as unimportant, stressing that it was the long run that mattered. It was this attitude that led John Maynard Keynes to scoff at the exclusive focus on the long run, in which, as he said, "we are all dead."

The Business Cycle

Despite their lack of interest in the short run, classical economists were aware that the economy did not grow smoothly. The American economist Wesley Mitchell pioneered the quantitative study of business cycles. In 1920 he founded the National Bureau of Economic Research, an independent, nonprofit organization that to this day has the official role of declaring the beginnings of recessions and expansions. Thanks to Mitchell's work, the *measurement* of business cycles was well advanced by 1930. But there was no widely accepted *theory* of what caused business cycles or what to do about them.

In the absence of any clear theory, conflicts arose among policy makers over how to respond to a recession. Some economists favored expansionary monetary and fiscal policies to fight a recession. Others believed that such policies would worsen the slump or merely postpone the inevitable. For example, in 1934 Harvard's Joseph Schumpeter, now famous for his early recognition of the importance of technological change, warned that any attempt to alleviate the Great Depression with expansionary monetary policy "would, in the end, lead to a collapse worse than the one it was called in to remedy." When the Great Depression hit, policy was paralyzed by this lack of consensus.

Necessity was, however, the mother of invention. As we'll explain next, the Great Depression provided a strong incentive for economists to develop theories that could serve as a guide to policy—and economists responded.

ECONOMICS ▶ *in Action*

When Did the Business Cycle Begin?

The official chronology of past U.S. business cycles maintained by the National Bureau of Economic Research goes back only to 1854. There are two reasons for this. First, the farther back in time you go, the less economic data are available. Second, business cycles, in the modern sense, may have not occurred in the United States before 1854.

In the first half of the nineteenth century the United States had an overwhelmingly rural, agricultural economy. Figure 33-1 shows estimates of the percentage of GDP derived from agriculture and the percentage derived from manufacturing and mining over the period from 1840 to 1900. From it you can see that in 1840 agriculture dwarfed manufacturing. It took until the 1880s for manufacturing to overtake agriculture in economic importance.

Why does the relative importance of the agricultural sector versus the manufacturing sector in the economy matter? It turns out that fluctuations in aggregate output in agricultural economies are very different from the business cycles we know today. That's because prices of agricultural goods tend to be highly flexible. As a result, the short-run aggregate supply curve of a mainly agricultural economy is probably close to vertical, so demand shocks don't cause output fluctuations. Instead, fluctuations in an agricultural economy are driven mainly by weather-induced effects on agricultural output. In contrast, the modern business cycle is, economists believe, largely caused by shifts in the aggregate demand curve.

The modern business cycle probably first appeared in Britain—home of the Industrial Revolution—which was already a largely industrial and urban society by 1820. The British recession of 1846–1847 had a particularly modern feel: it followed a bout of overoptimism in which aggregate demand was high thanks to heavy spending on an exciting new technology—railroads—then plunged as railway investors realized that they had overdone it.

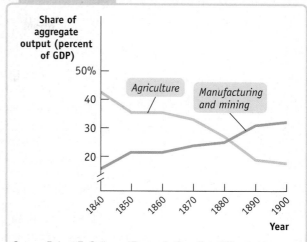

FIGURE 33-1 The Changing Character of the Nineteenth-Century Economy

Source: Robert E. Gallman, "Economic Growth and Structural Change in the Long Nineteenth Century," in Stanley L. Engerman and Robert E. Gallman, eds., *The Cambridge Economic History of the United States, vol. II: The Long Nineteenth Century* (Cambridge, UK: Cambridge University Press, 2000).

Check Your Understanding 33-1

1. When Ben Bernanke, in his tribute to Milton Friedman, said that "Regarding the Great Depression . . . we did it," he was referring to the fact that the Federal Reserve at the time did not pursue expansionary monetary policy. Why would a classical economist have thought that action by the Federal Reserve would not have made a difference in the length or depth of the Great Depression?

Solution appears at back of book.

▼ **Quick Review**

• Classical macroeconomists focused on the long-run effects of monetary policy on the aggregate price level, ignoring any short-run effects on aggregate output.

• By the time of the Great Depression, the measurement of business cycles was well advanced, but there was no widely accepted theory about why they happened.

The Great Depression and the Keynesian Revolution

The Great Depression demonstrated, once and for all, that economists cannot safely ignore the short run. Not only was the economic pain severe; it threatened to destabilize societies and political systems. In particular, the economic plunge helped Adolf Hitler rise to power in Germany, setting the stage for World War II.

The whole world wanted to know how this economic disaster could be happening and what should be done about it. But because there was no widely accepted theory of the business cycle, economists gave conflicting and often harmful advice. Some believed that only a huge change in the economic system—such as having the government take over much of private industry and replace markets with a command economy—could end the slump. Others argued that slumps were natural—even beneficial, helping to correct past excesses—and that nothing should be done.

Some economists, however, argued that slumps were destructive and should be cured. Moreover, they could be cured without compromising the market economy. The most compelling advocate for this view, the British economist John Maynard Keynes, compared the problems of the U.S. and British economies in 1930 to those of a car with a defective starter. Getting the economy running, he argued, would require only a modest repair, not a complete overhaul.

Nice metaphor. But what did he mean, specifically?

Keynes's Theory

In 1936 Keynes presented his analysis of the Great Depression—his explanation of what was wrong with the economy's starter—in a book titled *The General Theory of Employment, Interest, and Money*. In 1946 the great American economist and Nobel Prize winner Paul Samuelson wrote that "it is a badly written book, poorly organized. . . . Flashes of insight and intuition intersperse tedious algebra. . . . We find its analysis to be obvious and at the same time new. In short, it is a work of genius." Samuelson was correct on both counts: *The General Theory* isn't easy reading, yet it stands with Adam Smith's *The Wealth of Nations* as one of the most influential books on economics ever written.

As Samuelson's description indicates, Keynes's book offers a vast stew of ideas. *Keynesian economics* is principally based on two innovations. First, Keynes emphasized the importance of short-run effects of changes in aggregate demand on aggregate output, unlike the classicists who focused exclusively on the long-run determination of the aggregate price level. Until *The General Theory* appeared most economists had treated short-run macroeconomics as a minor issue, a view satirized by Keynes's famous remark that in the long run we are all dead. Keynes shifted the focus of attention of economists away from the unreachable long run to the world in which people actually live, one in which the short-run aggregate supply curve slopes upward and shifts in the aggregate demand curve affect aggregate output and employment as well as aggregate prices.

Figure 33-2 illustrates the difference between Keynesian and classical macroeconomics. Both panels of the figure show the short-run aggregate supply curve, *SRAS;* in both it is assumed that for some reason that demand falls and the aggregate demand curve shifts leftward from AD_1 to AD_2—say, for example, in response to a fall in stock market prices that leads households to reduce consumer spending.

FIGURE **33-2** | **Classical Versus Keynesian Macroeconomics**

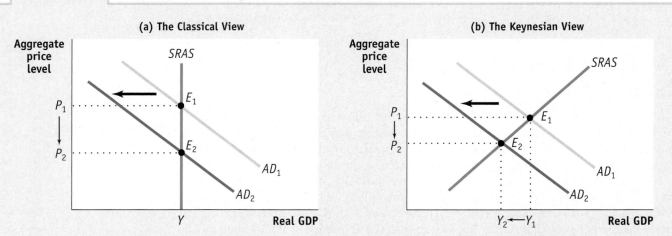

One important difference between classical and Keynesian economics involves the short-run aggregate supply curve. Panel (a) shows the classical view: the *SRAS* curve is vertical, so shifts in aggregate demand affect the aggregate price level but not aggregate output. Panel (b) shows the Keynesian view: in the short run the *SRAS* curve slopes upward, so shifts in aggregate demand affect aggregate output as well as aggregate prices.

Panel (a) shows the classical view: in it, the short-run aggregate supply curve is vertical. Therefore the fall in aggregate demand leads to a fall in the aggregate price level, from P_1 to P_2, but leaves aggregate output unchanged. Panel (b) shows the Keynesian view: in it, the short-run aggregate supply curve slopes upward. So a fall in aggregate demand leads to both a fall in the aggregate price level, from P_1 to P_2, and a fall in aggregate output, from Y_1 to Y_2.

As we've already explained, many classical macroeconomists would have agreed that panel (b) portrayed an accurate story in the short run—but they regarded the short run as unimportant. Keynes strongly disagreed, arguing that short-run economic problems caused great social distress and were in fact fixable. [Just to be clear, there isn't any diagram that looks like panel (b) of Figure 33-2 in Keynes's *General Theory*. But Keynes's discussion of aggregate supply, translated into modern terminology, clearly implies an upward-sloping *SRAS* curve.]

Keynes's second innovation concerned the question of what factors shifted the aggregate demand curve and caused business cycles. Classical economists attributed shifts in the demand curve almost exclusively to changes in the money supply. Keynes, by contrast, argued that other factors, especially changes in "animal spirits"—these days usually referred to with the bland term *business confidence*—are mainly responsible for business cycles. Before Keynes, economists argued that as long as the money supply stayed constant, changes in factors like business confidence would have no effect on either the aggregate price level or aggregate output. Keynes offered a very different picture in which, for example, pessimism about future profits can lead to a fall in investment spending, and this can cause a recession.

Keynesian economics, a view of the business cycle informed by these innovations, has penetrated deeply into the public consciousness, to the extent that many people who have never heard of Keynes, or have heard of him but think they disagree with his theory, use Keynesian ideas all the time. For example,

> **Keynesian economics** rests on two main tenets: changes in aggregate demand affect aggregate output, employment, and prices; and changes in business confidence cause the business cycle.

FOR INQUIRING MINDS | The Politics of Keynes

Some political commentators use the term *Keynesian economics* as a synonym for left-wing economics. Because Keynes offered a rationale for some kinds of government activism, these commentators have gone on to claim that he was a leftist of some kind, maybe even a socialist. But the truth is more complicated.

As we explained earlier, Keynesian ideas have actually been accepted among economists and policy makers across a broad range of the political spectrum. In 2004 the American president, George W. Bush, was a conservative, as was his top economist, N. Gregory Mankiw. But Mankiw is also a well-known promoter of Keynesian ideas. In fact, Keynes was no socialist—and not much of a leftist. At the time *The General Theory* was published, the Great Depression had convinced many intellectuals that socialism was the only solution to the economy's woes. They believed that the Great Depression was the final crisis of the capitalist economic

system and that only a government takeover of industry could save the economy. Keynes, in contrast, argued that socialism was not the answer. Instead, he

Some people consider Keynesian economics a synonym for left-wing economics. But this is misguided because in reality the ideas of John Maynard Keynes have been accepted across a broad sweep of the political spectrum.

said, all the capitalist market system needed was a narrow technical fix. In essence, his ideas were pro-capitalist and politically conservative.

What is true is that the rise of Keynesian economics in the 1940s, 1950s, and 1960s accompanied a general enlargement of the role of government in the economy, and those who favored a larger role for government tended to be enthusiastic Keynesians. Conversely, a swing of the pendulum back toward free-market policies in the 1970s and 1980s was accompanied by a series of challenges to Keynesian ideas, which we will describe later in this chapter.

Recent history shows that it is quite easy to find respected economists and policy makers who have conservative political preferences and who simultaneously respect Keynes's fundamental contributions to macroeconomics. And as we will learn shortly, it is equally possible to find those of a liberal bent who question some of Keynes's ideas. ■

Macroeconomic policy activism
is the use of monetary and fiscal
policy to smooth out the business
cycle.

suppose that a business commentator says something like this: "Businesses are holding back on investment spending because they're worried about low consumer demand, and that's why recovery has stalled." Whether the commentator knows it or not, that statement is pure Keynesian economics.

Keynes himself more or less predicted that someday people would make use of his ideas without knowing that they were "Keynesians." As he famously wrote in *The General Theory*, "Practical men, who believe themselves to be quite exempt from any intellectual influences, are usually the slaves of some defunct economist."

Policy to Fight Recessions

The greatest consequence of Keynes's work was that it legitimized **macroeconomic policy activism**—the use of monetary and fiscal policy to smooth out the business cycle.

It's true that some economists had called for macroeconomic activism before Keynes, in particular advocating monetary expansion to fight economic downturns. And some economists had even argued, as Keynes did, that temporary budget deficits were a good thing in times of recession. But macroeconomic policy activism at the time was considered deeply controversial and those who advocated it were fiercely attacked.

As a result, when some governments during the 1930s followed policies that we would now call Keynesian, they were carried out in a half-hearted way and were insufficient to turn the Great Depression around. In the United States, the administration of Franklin Roosevelt engaged in modest deficit spending in an effort to create jobs, actions which seemed to gain some traction in improving the economy. But, in 1937 Roosevelt gave in to advice from non-Keynesian economists who urged him to balance the federal budget and raise interest rates, even though the economy was still deeply depressed. The result was a renewed slump.

Over time, however, Keynesian ideas spread, and they were widely accepted among economists after World War II. There were, however, a series of challenges to those ideas, which led to a considerable shift in views even among those economists who continued to believe that Keynes was broadly right about the causes of recessions. In the upcoming section, we'll learn about those challenges and the schools, *new classical economics* and *new Keynesian economics,* that emerged.

ECONOMICS ▶ *in Action*

The End of the Great Depression

It would make a good story if Keynes's ideas had led to a change in economic policy that brought the Great Depression to an end. Unfortunately, that's not what happened. Yet, the way the Depression finally ended helped convince the economics profession that Keynes was basically right.

What economists learned from Keynes's work was that economic recovery requires aggressive fiscal expansion—deficit spending on a sufficiently large scale to create jobs and push up aggregate demand. And that happened in the United States not because of intentional economic policy, but as the result of a very large war that required an enormous amount of government spending, World War II. The overwhelming evidence that it was government expenditures for World War II that lifted the economy out of the Great Depression finally ended the debate over the validity of Keynes's views.

Figure 33-3 shows the U.S. unemployment rate and the federal budget deficit as a share of GDP from 1930 to 1947. As you can see, deficit spending during the 1930s was on a modest scale. In 1940, as the risk of war grew larger, the United States began a large military buildup, building tanks, planes, military bases and the like, moving the budget deep into deficit. After the attack on Pearl Harbor on December 7, 1941, the country began deficit spending on an enormous scale: in fiscal 1943, which began in July 1942, the deficit was 30% of GDP. Today that would be equivalent to a deficit of $5.1 trillion.

What was clear to economists and policy makers was that with this enormous surge in government spending the economy, mired in the Great Depression for well over a decade, finally recovered in a sustainable way. World War II wasn't intended as a Keynesian fiscal policy. And it is hard to believe that any event, short of a world war, would have compelled the U.S. government to spend so much money. Yet unintentional as it was, World War II spending demonstrated that expansionary fiscal policy can lift the economy out of a deep slump.

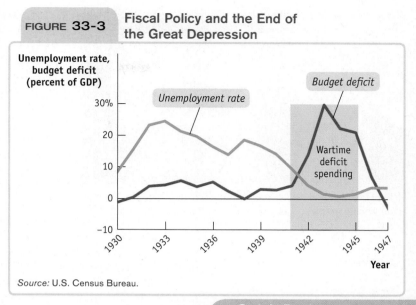

FIGURE 33-3   Fiscal Policy and the End of the Great Depression

Source: U.S. Census Bureau.

Check Your Understanding   33-2

1. In a press release from early 2012, the National Federation of Independent Business, which calculates the Small Business Optimism Index, stated "The Small Business Optimism Index rose just 0.1 points in January. . . . Historically, optimism remains at recession levels. While small business owners appeared less pessimistic about the outlook for business conditions and real sales growth, that optimism did not materialize in hiring or increased inventories plans." Would this statement seem familiar to a Keynesian economist? Which conclusion would a Keynesian economist draw for the need for public policy?

Solution appears at back of book.

Challenges to Keynesian Economics

Keynes's ideas fundamentally changed the way economists think about business cycles. They did not, however, go unquestioned. In the wake of the success of government expenditures in ending the Great Depression, Keynesian economics faced a new series of challenges. As a result, by the 1980s the consensus of macroeconomists retreated somewhat from the strong version of Keynesianism that prevailed in the 1950s. In particular, many economists began to suggest limits to the effectiveness of macroeconomic policy activism.

The Revival of Monetary Policy

Many macroeconomists agree with Keynes's view that during a depression monetary policy would be relatively ineffective. We met this phenomenon in Chapter 31 in what we called the *liquidity trap,* a situation in which monetary policy is ineffective because the interest rate is down against the zero bound. Remember that at the zero bound, interest rates cannot be pushed down any further to revive the economy, so expansionary monetary policy has no effect. In the 1930s, when Keynes wrote, interest rates were, in fact, very close to 0%.

When the era of near-0% interest rates came to an end after World War II and the economy had recovered, the pendulum had swung so far in favor of Keynesian economics that many economists continued to emphasize fiscal policy and downplay the usefulness of monetary policy. Eventually, however, the pendulum swung partly back as macroeconomists eventually reassessed the importance of monetary policy.

Milton Friedman and his co-author Anna Schwartz played a key role in convincing macroeconomists of the importance of monetary policy.

A key milestone in this reassessment was the 1963 publication of *A Monetary History of the United States, 1867–1960* by Milton Friedman, of the University of Chicago, and Anna Schwartz, of the National Bureau of Economic Research. Friedman and Schwartz showed that business cycles had historically been associated with fluctuations in the money supply. In particular, the money supply fell sharply during the onset of the Great Depression. As we mentioned in the opening story, Friedman and Schwartz persuaded many, though not all, economists that the Great Depression could have been avoided if the Federal Reserve had acted to prevent that monetary contraction by increasing the monetary base. They persuaded most economists that monetary policy should play a key role in economic management.

The revival of interest in monetary policy was significant because it suggested that the burden of managing the economy could be shifted away from fiscal policy—meaning that economic management could largely be taken out of the hands of politicians. This feature was attractive to many because fiscal policy necessarily involves political choices. If the government tries to stimulate the economy by cutting taxes, it must decide whose taxes will be cut. If it tries to stimulate the economy with government spending, it must decide what to spend the money on. As a result, management of the economy would often be bogged down by the political process if fiscal policy were the only tool available.

Monetary policy, in contrast, does not involve such political choices: when the central bank cuts interest rates to fight a recession, it cuts everyone's interest rate at the same time. So a shift from relying on fiscal policy to relying on monetary policy makes macroeconomics a more technical, less political undertaking. In fact, as we learned in Chapter 29, monetary policy in most major economies is set by an independent central bank that is insulated from the political process.

Monetarism

After the publication of *A Monetary History,* Milton Friedman led a movement that sought to eliminate all forms of macroeconomic policy activism—fiscal and monetary. Instead, he asserted that the best way to manage the economy was with non-activist or *nondiscretionary* monetary policy. **Monetarism** asserts that GDP will grow steadily if the money supply grows steadily. According to the monetarist policy prescription, the central bank should target a constant rate of growth of the money supply, such as 3% per year, and maintain that target regardless of any fluctuations in the economy.

It's important to realize that monetarism retained many Keynesian ideas. Like Keynes, Friedman asserted that the short run is important and that short-run changes in aggregate demand affect aggregate output as well as aggregate prices. Like Keynes, he argued that macroeconomic policy should have been much more expansionary during the Great Depression, even if he believed that only monetary policy was needed.

Monetarists argued, however, that in most cases activist macroeconomic policy to smooth out the business cycle actually makes things worse. In Chapter 28 we described how lags can cause problems for *discretionary fiscal policy.* For example, a government that tries to respond to recessions by increasing spending sometimes finds that by the time it realizes that a recession is underway, takes action, and gets results, the recession is over, and the spending increase feeds a boom instead of fighting a slump. According to monetarists, **discretionary monetary policy,** changes in the interest rate or the money supply by the central bank in order to stabilize the economy, faces similar problems and can easily make the economy less stable.

Monetarism asserts that GDP will grow steadily if the money supply grows steadily.

Discretionary monetary policy is the use of changes in the interest rate or the money supply to stabilize the economy.

FIGURE **33-4** | **Fiscal Policy with a Fixed Money Supply**

(a) The Increase in Aggregate Demand from an Expansionary Fiscal Policy Is Limited When the Money Supply Is Fixed...

(b) ...Because the Increase in Money Demand Drives up the Interest Rate, Crowding out Some Investment Spending.

In panel (a) an expansionary fiscal policy shifts the *AD* curve rightward, driving up both the aggregate price level and aggregate output. However, this leads to an increase in the demand for money. If the money supply is held fixed, as in panel (b), the increase in money demand drives up the interest rate, reducing investment spending and offsetting part of the fiscal expansion. So the shift of the *AD* curve is less than it would otherwise be: fiscal policy becomes less effective when the money supply is held fixed.

Friedman also argued that if the central bank followed his advice, adopting a non-activist monetary policy and refusing to change the money supply in response to fluctuations in the economy, fiscal policy would be much less effective than Keynesians believed due to *crowding out*—when government spending crowds out private investment spending. In Chapter 25 we analyzed how this can occur: government spending leads to deficits, which drive up interest rates and reduce investment spending. Friedman and others pointed out that if the money supply is held fixed while the government pursues an expansionary fiscal policy, crowding out will occur as the interest rate rises, limiting the effect of the fiscal expansion on aggregate demand.

Figure 33-4 illustrates this argument. Panel (a) shows aggregate output and the aggregate price level. AD_1 is the initial aggregate demand curve and *SRAS* is the short-run aggregate supply curve. At the initial equilibrium, E_1, the level of aggregate output is Y_1 and the aggregate price level is P_1. Panel (b) shows the money market. *MS* is the money supply curve and MD_1 is the initial money demand curve, so the initial interest rate is r_1.

Now suppose the government increases purchases of goods and services. We know that this will shift the *AD* curve rightward, as illustrated by the shift from AD_1 to AD_2, and that aggregate output will rise, from Y_1 to Y_2, and the aggregate price level will rise, from P_1 to P_2. Both the rise in aggregate output and the rise in the aggregate price level will, however, increase the demand for money, shifting the money demand curve rightward from MD_1 to MD_2. This drives up the equilibrium interest rate to r_2. Friedman's point was that this rise in the interest rate reduces investment spending, partially offsetting the initial rise in government spending. As a result, the rightward shift of the *AD* curve is smaller than the multiplier analysis in Chapter 28 indicated. And Friedman argued that with a constant rate of increase in the money supply, the multiplier is so small that there's not much point in using fiscal policy, even in a depressed economy.

A **monetary policy rule** is a formula that determines the central bank's actions.

The **velocity of money** is the ratio of nominal GDP to the money supply.

As we've already noted, Friedman didn't favor activist monetary policy either, arguing that the problems of time lags that limit the ability of discretionary fiscal policy to stabilize the economy also apply to discretionary monetary policy. Friedman's solution was to make monetary policy nondiscretionary, to put it on "autopilot." The central bank, he argued, should follow a **monetary policy rule,** a formula that determines its actions and leaves it relatively little discretion. During the 1960s and 1970s, most monetarists favored a monetary policy rule of slow, steady growth in the money supply.

Underlying this view was the concept of the **velocity of money,** the ratio of nominal GDP to the money supply. Velocity is a measure of the number of times the average dollar bill in the economy turns over per year between buyers and sellers (e.g., I tip the Starbucks barista a dollar, she uses it to buy lunch, and so on). This concept gives rise to the *velocity equation,* which relates nominal GDP to the money supply:

(33-1) $M \times V = P \times Y$

Where M is the money supply, V is velocity, P is the aggregate price level, and Y is real GDP.

Monetarists believed, with considerable historical justification, that the velocity of money, V, was stable in the short run and changes only slowly in the long run. As a result, they claimed, steady growth in M, the money supply, by the central bank would ensure steady growth in spending, and therefore in GDP.

Monetarism strongly influenced U.S. monetary policy in the late 1970s and early 1980s as the Fed tried to keep the rate of growth in the money supply constant. It quickly became clear, however, that this didn't ensure steady growth in the economy: the velocity of money wasn't stable enough for such a simple policy rule to work. Figure 33-5 shows how events eventually undermined the monetarists' view. The figure shows the velocity of money, as measured by the ratio of nominal GDP to M1, from 1960 through mid-2014. As you can see, until 1980 velocity followed a fairly smooth, seemingly predictable trend. After the Fed began to adopt monetarist ideas in the late 1970s and early 1980s, however, the velocity of money began moving erratically—probably due to financial market innovations such as the greater use of credit cards.

FIGURE 33-5 | The Velocity of Money

From 1960 to 1980, the velocity of money was stable, leading monetarists to believe that steady growth in the money supply would lead to a stable economy. After 1980, however, velocity began moving erratically, undermining the case for traditional monetarism. As a result, traditional monetarism fell out of favor.

Source: Federal Reserve Bank of St. Louis.

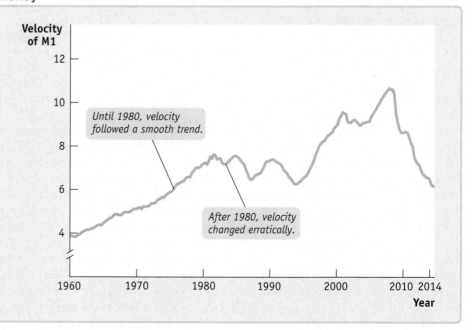

Consequently, traditional monetarists—those who believe that GDP will grow steadily if the money supply grows steadily—are hard to find among today's macroeconomists. As we'll see shortly, however, the concern that originally motivated the monetarists—that too much discretionary monetary policy can actually destabilize the economy—has become widely accepted.

Limits to Macroeconomic Policy: Inflation and the Natural Rate of Unemployment

The problem of time lags in the implementation of activist macroeconomic policy was not the only criticism leveled at Keynesian economics. Another serious concern arose over its effect on inflation. During the 1940s and 1950s, many Keynesian economists believed that expansionary fiscal policy could be used to achieve full employment on a permanent basis. By the 1960s, however, many economists realized that persistently expansionary policies could cause problems with inflation. Yet they still believed that governments could choose to keep unemployment low if they were willing to accept higher inflation.

In 1968, however, Milton Friedman and Edmund Phelps of Columbia University, working independently, argued that there isn't actually a long-run trade-off between unemployment and inflation. According to Friedman and Phelps's **natural rate hypothesis,** any attempt to keep unemployment below a minimum level would lead not just to inflation but to ever-rising inflation. We described the logic of this argument in Chapter 31; the important point to recognize here is that if true, the natural rate hypothesis implies that Keynesian policies can't accomplish as much as macroeconomists previously believed. Because the government can't keep unemployment below the natural rate, its task is not to keep unemployment low but to keep it *stable around the natural rate*—to prevent large fluctuations in unemployment above or below the natural rate.

And the natural rate hypothesis was, in fact, accepted by most economists after the 1970s. The Friedman–Phelps hypothesis made a strong prediction: that the apparent trade-off between unemployment and inflation would not survive an extended period of rising prices. Once inflation was embedded into the public's expectations, it would continue even in the face of high unemployment. Sure enough, that's exactly what happened in the 1970s. This accurate prediction was one of the triumphs of macroeconomic analysis. It convinced the great majority of economists that the natural rate hypothesis was correct, although some macroeconomists believe that at very low rates of inflation or deflation the hypothesis doesn't work.

The Political Business Cycle

One final challenge to Keynesian economics focused not on the validity of the economic analysis but on its political consequences. A number of economists and political scientists pointed out that activist macroeconomic policy lends itself to political manipulation.

Statistical evidence suggests that election results tend to be determined largely by the state of the economy in the months just before the election. In the United States, if the economy is growing rapidly and the unemployment rate is falling in the six months or so before Election Day, the incumbent party tends to be re-elected even if the economy performed poorly in the preceding three years. This creates an obvious temptation to abuse activist macroeconomic policy: pump up the economy in an election year, and pay the price in higher inflation and/or higher unemployment later. The consequence will be unnecessary instability in the economy, a **political business cycle** caused by the use of macroeconomic policy to serve political ends.

According to the **natural rate hypothesis,** because inflation is eventually embedded into expectations, to avoid accelerating inflation over time the unemployment rate must be high enough that the actual inflation rate equals the expected inflation rate.

A **political business cycle** results when politicians use macroeconomic policy to serve political ends.

Political manipulation in order to win votes is a danger of activist macroeconomic policy.

An often-cited example is the combination of expansionary fiscal and monetary policy that led to rapid growth in the U.S. economy just before the 1972 election and a sharp acceleration in inflation after the election. Kenneth Rogoff, a highly respected macroeconomist who served as chief economist at the International Monetary Fund, has proclaimed Richard Nixon, the president at the time, "the all-time hero of political business cycles."

As we've learned, one way to avoid a political business cycle is to place monetary policy in the hands of an independent central bank, insulated from political pressure. The political business cycle is also a reason to limit the use of discretionary fiscal policy to extreme circumstances like a liquidity trap.

ECONOMICS ▶ *in Action*

The Fed's Flirtation with Monetarism

In the late 1970s and early 1980s the Federal Reserve flirted with monetarism. For most of its prior existence, the Fed had targeted interest rates, adjusting its target based on the state of the economy. In the late 1970s, however, the Fed adopted a monetary policy rule and began announcing target ranges for several measures of the money supply. It also stopped setting targets for interest rates. Most people interpreted these changes as a strong move toward monetarism.

In 1982, however, the Fed turned its back on monetarism. Since 1982 the Fed has pursued a discretionary monetary policy, which has led to large swings in the money supply. At the end of the 1980s, the Fed returned to conducting monetary policy by setting target levels for the interest rate.

Why did the Fed flirt with monetarism, then abandon it? The turn to monetarism largely reflected the events of the 1970s, when a sharp rise in inflation broke the perceived trade-off between inflation and unemployment and discredited traditional Keynesianism. The accuracy of Friedman's prediction of a worsening trade-off between inflation and unemployment increased his prestige and that of his followers. As a result, policy makers adopted Friedman's proposals.

The turn away from monetarism also reflected events: as we saw in Figure 33-5, the velocity of money, which had followed a smooth trend before 1980, became erratic after 1980. This made monetarism seem like a much less good idea.

Check Your Understanding 33-3

1. Consider Figure 33-5.
   a. If the Federal Reserve had pursued a monetarist policy of a constant rate of growth in the money supply, what would have happened to output beginning in 2008 according to the velocity equation?
   b. In fact, the Federal Reserve accelerated the rate of growth in M1 rapidly beginning in 2008, partly in order to counteract a large increase in unemployment. Would a monetarist have agreed with this policy? What limits are there, according to a monetarist point of view, to changing the unemployment rate?
2. What are the limits of macroeconomic policy activism?

Solutions appear at back of book.

Rational Expectations, Real Business Cycles, and New Classical Macroeconomics

As we have seen, one key difference between classical economics and Keynesian economics is that classical economists believed that the short-run aggregate supply curve is vertical, while Keynesian economics claims that the aggregate supply curve slopes upward in the short run. A consequence of the upward-sloping demand curve is that demand shocks—shifts in the aggregate demand curve—cause fluctuations in aggregate output.

However, the challenges to Keynesian economics that arose in the 1950s and 1960s from monetarists and from natural rate theorists didn't rely on classical economics ideas. The challengers accepted an upward-sloping aggregate supply curve—that an increase in aggregate demand leads to a rise in aggregate output in the short run and that a decrease in aggregate demand leads to a fall in aggregate output in the short run. Instead, they argued that the policy medicine advocated by traditional Keynesians, activist macroeconomic policy, would worsen the very disease they were trying to cure—economic fluctuations.

In the 1970s and 1980s, the classical view that shifts in the aggregate demand curve affect only the aggregate price level, not aggregate output, was revived in an approach known as **new classical macroeconomics.** It evolved in two stages. First, some economists challenged traditional arguments about the slope of the short-run aggregate supply curve based on the concept of *rational expectations.* Second, some economists suggested that changes in productivity cause economic fluctuations, a view known as *real business cycle theory.*

Rational Expectations

In the 1970s a concept known as *rational expectations* had a powerful impact on macroeconomics. **Rational expectations,** originally introduced by John Muth in 1961, claims that individuals and firms make decisions optimally, using all available information.

For example, workers and employers bargaining over long-term wage contracts need to take account of the expected inflation rate over the life of that contract. Rational expectations says that in making estimates of future inflation, they won't just look at past rates of inflation; they will also take into account currently available information about monetary and fiscal policy. Suppose that prices didn't rise last year, but that the monetary and fiscal policies announced by policy makers have made it clear that there will be substantial inflation over the next few years. According to rational expectations, long-term wage contracts will be adjusted today to reflect this future inflation, even though prices haven't yet risen.

Adopting the premise of rational expectations can significantly alter beliefs about the effectiveness of activist macroeconomic policy. According to the original version of the natural rate hypothesis, a government attempt to persistently push the unemployment rate below the natural rate would work in the short run but will eventually fail because higher inflation will get built into expectations. According to rational expectations, we should remove the word *eventually* and replace it with *immediately:* if the government tries to lower unemployment today at the cost of higher inflation in the future, inflation will shoot up immediately without even a temporary fall in unemployment. So, under rational expectations, government intervention fails in the short run and the long run.

In the 1970s Robert Lucas of the University of Chicago, in a series of highly influential papers, used the logic of rational expectations to argue that monetary policy can change the level of output and unemployment only if it comes as a surprise to the public. Otherwise, attempts to lower unemployment will simply result in higher prices. According to Lucas's **rational expectations model** of the economy, monetary policy isn't useful in stabilizing the economy after all. In 1995 Lucas won the Nobel Prize in economics for this work, which remains widely admired. However, many—perhaps most—macroeconomists, especially those advising policy makers, now believe that his conclusions were overstated. The Federal Reserve certainly thinks that it can play a useful role in economic stabilization.

Why, in the view of many macroeconomists, doesn't Lucas's rational expectations model of macroeconomics accurately describe how the economy actually behaves? **New Keynesian economics,** a set of ideas that became influential in the 1990s, provides an explanation. It argues that market imperfections interact to make many prices in the economy temporarily sticky.

New classical macroeconomics is an approach to the business cycle that returns to the classical view that shifts in the aggregate demand curve affect only the aggregate price level, not aggregate output.

Rational expectations is the view that individuals and firms make decisions optimally, using all available information.

According to the **rational expectations model** of the economy, expected changes in monetary policy have no effect on unemployment and output and only affect the price level.

According to **new Keynesian economics,** market imperfections can lead to price stickiness for the economy as a whole.

Real business cycle theory claims that fluctuations in the rate of growth of total factor productivity cause the business cycle.

And with sticky prices, expected inflation can't rise quickly enough to offset activist macroeconomic policy.

For example, one new Keynesian argument points out that monopolists don't have to be too careful about setting prices exactly "right": if they set a price a bit too high, they'll lose some sales but make more profit on each sale; if they set the price too low, they'll reduce the profit per sale but sell more. As a result, even small costs to changing prices can lead to substantial price stickiness and make the economy as a whole behave in a Keynesian fashion.

Over time, new Keynesian ideas combined with actual experience have reduced the practical influence of the rational expectations concept. Nonetheless, the idea of rational expectations served as a useful caution for macroeconomists who had become excessively optimistic about their ability to manage the economy.

Real Business Cycles

In Chapter 24 we introduced the concept of *total factor productivity,* the amount of output that can be generated with a given level of factor inputs. Total factor productivity grows over time, but that growth isn't smooth. In the 1980s a number of economists argued that slowdowns in productivity growth, which they attributed to pauses in technological progress, are the main cause of recessions. **Real business cycle theory** claims that fluctuations in the rate of growth of total factor productivity cause the business cycle.

Believing that the aggregate supply curve is vertical, real business cycle theorists attribute the source of business cycles to shifts of the aggregate supply curve: a recession occurs because a slowdown in productivity growth shifts the aggregate supply curve leftward, and a recovery occurs because a pickup in productivity growth shifts the aggregate supply curve rightward. In the early days of real business cycle theory, the theory's proponents denied that changes

FOR INQUIRING MINDS | Supply-Side Economics

During the 1970s a group of economic writers began propounding a view of economic policy that came to be known as *supply-side economics.* The core of this view was the belief that reducing tax rates, and so increasing the incentives to work and invest, would have a powerful positive effect on the growth rate of potential output. The supply-siders urged the government to cut taxes without worrying about matching spending cuts: economic growth, they argued, would offset any negative effects from budget deficits.

Some supply-siders even argued that a cut in tax *rates* would have such a miraculous effect on economic growth that tax *revenues*—the total amount tax-payers pay to the government—would actually rise. That is, some supply-siders argued that the United States was on the wrong side of the *Laffer curve,* a hypothetical relationship between tax rates and total tax revenue that slopes upward at low tax rates but turns downward when tax rates are very high.

In the 1970s supply-side economics was enthusiastically supported by the

editors of the *Wall Street Journal* and other figures in the media, and it became popular with politicians. In 1980 Ronald Reagan made supply-side economics the basis of his presidential campaign.

Because supply-side economics emphasizes supply rather than demand, and because the supply-siders themselves are harshly critical of Keynesian economics, it might seem as if supply-side theory belongs in our discussion of new classical macroeconomics. But unlike rational expectations and real business cycle theory, supply-side economics is generally dismissed by economic researchers.

The main reason for this dismissal is lack of supporting evidence. Almost all economists agree that tax cuts increase incentives to work and invest. But attempts to estimate these incentive effects indicate that at current U.S. tax levels, the positive incentive effects

Although many have claimed that the Reagan tax cuts were pro-growth, data from the Congressional Budget Office and others show no sign of an acceleration in growth after the cuts were implemented.

aren't nearly strong enough to support the strong claims made by supply-siders. In particular, the supply-side doctrine implies that large tax cuts, such as those implemented by Ronald Reagan in the early 1980s, should sharply raise potential output. Yet estimates of potential output by the Congressional Budget Office and others show no sign of an acceleration in growth after the Reagan tax cuts. ∎

in aggregate demand—and, likewise, macroeconomic policy activism—had any effect on aggregate output.

This theory was strongly influential, reflected by the fact that two of the founders of real business cycle theory, Finn Kydland of Carnegie Mellon University and Edward Prescott of the Federal Reserve Bank of Minneapolis, won the 2004 Nobel Prize in economics. The current status of real business cycle theory, however, is somewhat similar to that of rational expectations. The theory is widely recognized as having made valuable contributions to our understanding of the economy, and it serves as a useful caution against too much emphasis on aggregate demand.

But many of the real business cycle theorists themselves now acknowledge that the actual economic data indicate that their models need an upward-sloping aggregate supply curve—and that this gives aggregate demand a potential role in determining aggregate output. And as we have seen, policy makers continue to strongly believe that aggregate demand policy has an important role to play in fighting recessions.

ECONOMICS ▶ in Action

The 1970s in Reverse

When economists talk about the natural rate hypothesis, they usually frame it in terms of what happens if the government tries to keep unemployment low. The hypothesis says that sustained low unemployment will lead to ever-rising inflation. That is why most economists took the experience of stagflation in the 1970s as strong evidence that the natural rate hypothesis was right. However, the same logic says that sustained *high* unemployment should lead to ever-*falling* inflation, and eventually to accelerating *deflation*. So the experience of the Great Recession and aftermath, with unemployment remaining very high for years, offered a test of this prediction.

As it turned out, the prediction wasn't very successful. Inflation in the United States has generally been somewhat lower since the Great Recession than it was before, but the United States never entered deflation. By 2014 prices were falling in some European countries with very high unemployment, but there was no sign of accelerating deflation.

The failure of deflation to materialize didn't come as a complete surprise, since some economists had long argued that the natural rate hypothesis breaks down at low inflation. However, that view became much more widespread after 2008 than it had been before—and it has an important implication. If high unemployment doesn't lead to ever-falling inflation, government policies to reduce unemployment may be effective even in the long run, as long as the unemployment target isn't too low. That is, an old-fashioned Keynesian view of macroeconomic policy, which says that it can permanently reduce unemployment even in the long run, may be right after all.

In that sense the era since the Great Recession has been the 1970s in reverse, with Keynesian views gaining strength in the light of experience.

Check Your Understanding 33-4

1. In late 2008, as it became clear that the United States was experiencing a recession, the Fed reduced its target for the federal funds rate to near zero, as part of a larger aggressively expansionary monetary policy stance (including what the Fed called *quantitative easing*). Most observers agreed that the Fed's aggressive monetary expansion helped reduce the length and severity of the Great Recession.
   a. What would rational expectations theorists say about this conclusion?
   b. What would real business cycle theorists say?

Solutions appear at back of book.

The **Great Moderation** is the period from 1985 to 2007 when the U.S. economy experienced relatively small fluctuations and low inflation.

The **Great Moderation consensus** combines a belief in monetary policy as the main tool of stabilization, with skepticism toward the use of fiscal policy, and an acknowledgement of the policy constraints imposed by the natural rate of unemployment and the political business cycle.

Consensus and Conflict in Modern Macroeconomics

The 1970s and the first half of the 1980s were a stormy period for the U.S. economy (and for other major economies, too). There was a severe recession in 1974–1975, then two back-to-back recessions in 1979–1982 that sent the unemployment rate to almost 11%. At the same time, the inflation rate soared into double digits—and then plunged. As we have seen, these events left a strong mark on macroeconomic thought.

After about 1985, however, the economy settled down. The recession of 1990–1991 was much milder than the 1974–1975 recession or the double-dip slump from 1979 to 1982, and the inflation rate generally stayed below 4%. The period of relative calm in the economy from 1985 to 2007 came to be known as the **Great Moderation.** And the calmness of the economy was to a large extent marked by a similar calm in macroeconomic policy discussion. In fact, it seemed that a broad consensus had emerged about several key macroeconomic issues.

The Great Moderation was, unfortunately, followed by the *Great Recession*, the severe and persistent slump that followed the 2008 financial crisis. We'll talk shortly about the policy disputes caused by the Great Recession. First, however, let's examine the apparent consensus that emerged during the Great Moderation, which we call the **Great Moderation consensus.** It combines a belief in monetary policy as the main tool of stabilization, with skepticism toward the use of fiscal policy, and an acknowledgement of the policy constraints imposed by the natural rate of unemployment and the political business cycle.

To understand where the Great Moderation consensus came from and what still remains in dispute, we'll look at how macroeconomists have changed their answers to five key questions about macroeconomic policy. The five questions and the various answers given by schools of macroeconomics over the decades are summarized in Table 33-1. (In the table, new classical economics is subsumed under classical economics, and new Keynesian economics is subsumed under the Great Moderation consensus.) Notice that classical macroeconomics said no to each question; basically, classical macroeconomists didn't think macroeconomic policy could accomplish very much. But let's go through the questions one by one.

TABLE 33-1 Five Key Questions About Macroeconomic Policy

	Classical macroeconomics	Keynesian macroeconomics	Monetarism	Great Moderation consensus
1. Is expansionary monetary policy helpful in fighting recessions?	No	Not very	Yes	Yes, except in special circumstances
2. Is expansionary fiscal policy effective in fighting recessions?	No	Yes	No	Yes
3. Can monetary and/or fiscal policy reduce unemployment in the long run?	No	Yes	No	No
4. Should fiscal policy be used in a discretionary way?	No	Yes	No	No, except possibly in special circumstances
5. Should monetary policy be used in a discretionary way?	No	Yes	No	Disputed

Question 1: Is Expansionary Monetary Policy Helpful in Fighting Recessions?

As we've seen, classical macroeconomists generally believed that expansionary monetary policy was ineffective or even harmful in fighting recessions. In the early years of Keynesian economics, macroeconomists weren't against monetary expansion during recessions, but they tended to believe that it was of doubtful effectiveness. Milton Friedman and his followers convinced economists that monetary policy is effective after all.

Nearly all macroeconomists now agree that monetary policy can be used to shift the aggregate demand curve and to reduce economic instability. The classical view that changes in the money supply affect only aggregate prices, not aggregate output, has few supporters today. The view held by early Keynesian economists—that changes in the money supply have little effect—has equally few supporters. Now it is generally agreed that monetary policy is ineffective only in the case of a liquidity trap.

Question 2: Is Expansionary Fiscal Policy Effective in Fighting Recessions?

Classical macroeconomists were, if anything, even more opposed to fiscal expansion than monetary expansion. Keynesian economists, on the other hand, gave fiscal policy a central role in fighting recessions. Monetarists argued that fiscal policy was ineffective if the money supply was held constant. But that strong view has become relatively rare.

Most macroeconomists now agree that fiscal policy, like monetary policy, can shift the aggregate demand curve. Most macroeconomists also agree that the government should not seek to balance the budget regardless of the state of the economy: they agree that the role of the budget as an automatic stabilizer helps keep the economy on an even keel.

Question 3: Can Monetary and/or Fiscal Policy Reduce Unemployment in the Long Run?

Classical macroeconomists didn't believe the government could do anything about unemployment. Some Keynesian economists moved to the opposite extreme, arguing that expansionary policies could be used to achieve a permanently low unemployment rate, perhaps at the cost of some inflation. Monetarists believed that unemployment could not be kept below the natural rate.

Almost all macroeconomists now accept the natural rate hypothesis. This hypothesis leads them to accept sharp limits to what monetary and fiscal policy can accomplish. Effective monetary and fiscal policy, most macroeconomists believe, can limit the size of fluctuations of the actual unemployment rate around the natural rate, but they can't be used to keep unemployment below the natural rate.

Question 4: Should Fiscal Policy Be Used in a Discretionary Way?

As we've already seen, views about the effectiveness of fiscal policy have gone back and forth, from rejection by classical macroeconomists, to a positive view by Keynesian economists, to a negative view once again by monetarists. Today most macroeconomists believe that tax cuts and spending increases are at least somewhat effective in increasing aggregate demand.

Many, but not all, macroeconomists, however, believe that *discretionary fiscal policy* is usually counterproductive, for the reasons discussed in Chapter 28: the lags in adjusting fiscal policy mean that, all too often, policies intended to fight a slump end up intensifying a boom.

As a result, the macroeconomic consensus gives monetary policy the lead role in economic stabilization. Some, but not all, economists believe that fiscal policy must be brought back into the mix under special circumstances, in particular when interest rates are at or near the zero lower bound and the economy is in a liquidity trap. As we'll see shortly, the proper role of fiscal policy became a huge point of contention after 2008.

Question 5: Should Monetary Policy Be Used in a Discretionary Way?

Classical macroeconomists didn't think that monetary policy should be used to fight recessions; Keynesian economists didn't oppose discretionary monetary policy, but they were skeptical about its effectiveness. Monetarists argued that discretionary monetary policy was doing more harm than good. Where are we today? This remains an area of dispute. Today, under the Great Moderation consensus, most macreconomists agree on these three points:

- Monetary policy should play the main role in stabilization policy.
- The central bank should be independent, insulated from political pressures, in order to avoid a political business cycle.
- Discretionary fiscal policy should be used sparingly, both because of policy lags and because of the risks of a political business cycle.

However, the Great Moderation was upended by events that posed very difficult questions—questions that were still being debated as this book went to press. We'll now examine what happened and why the ongoing debate is so fierce.

Crisis and Aftermath

The Great Recession shattered any sense among macroeconomists that they had entered a permanent era of agreement over key policy questions. Given the nature of the slump, however, this should not have come as a surprise. Why? Because the severity of the slump arguably made the policies that seemed to work during the Great Moderation inadequate.

Under the Great Moderation consensus, there had been broad agreement that the job of stabilizing the economy was best carried out by having the Federal Reserve and its counterparts abroad raise or lower interest rates as the economic situation warranted. But what should be done if the economy is deeply depressed, but the interest rates the Fed normally controls are already close to zero and can go no lower (that is, when the economy is in a liquidity trap)? Some economists called for the aggressive use of discretionary fiscal policy and/or unconventional monetary policies that might achieve results despite the zero lower bound. Others strongly opposed these measures, arguing either that they would be ineffective or that they would produce undesirable side effects.

The Debate over Fiscal Policy In 2009 a number of governments, including that of the United States, responded with expansionary fiscal policy, or "stimulus," generally taking the form of a mix of temporary spending measures and temporary tax cuts. From the start, however, these efforts were highly controversial.

Supporters of fiscal stimulus offered three main arguments for breaking with the normal presumption against discretionary fiscal policy:

1. They argued that discretionary fiscal expansion was needed because the usual tool for stabilizing the economy, monetary policy, could no longer be used now that interest rates were near zero.
2. They argued that one normal concern about expansionary fiscal policy—that deficit spending would drive up interest rates, crowding out private investment spending—was unlikely to be a problem in a depressed economy. Again, this was because interest rates were close to zero and likely to stay there as long as the economy was depressed.
3. Finally, they argued that another concern about discretionary fiscal policy—that it might take a long time to get going—was less of a concern than usual given the likelihood that the economy would be depressed for an extended period.

These arguments generally won the day in early 2009. However, opponents of fiscal stimulus raised two main objections:

1. They argued that households and firms would see any rise in government spending as a sign that tax burdens were likely to rise in the future, leading to a fall in private spending that would undo any positive effect. (This is the *Ricardian equivalence* argument that we encountered in Chapter 28.)

2. They also warned that spending programs might undermine investors' faith in the government's ability to repay its debts, leading to an increase in long-term interest rates despite loose monetary policy.

In fact, by 2010 a number of economists were arguing that the best way to boost the economy was actually to cut government spending, which they argued would increase private-sector confidence and lead to a rise in output and employment. This notion, often referred to as the doctrine of *expansionary austerity*, was especially popular in Europe, where it was supported by officials at the European Central Bank and became the official policy of the Cameron government in Britain, which took office in the spring of 2010.

As is often the case with major disputes in economics, the argument over fiscal policy went on for years, with some critics of fiscal policy still defending their position when this book went to press. It seems fair, however, to say that among economists a more or less Keynesian view of the effects of fiscal policy came to prevail. Careful statistical studies at the International Monetary Fund and elsewhere showed that austerity policies have historically been followed by contraction, not expansion. Recent experience, in which countries like Spain and Greece that were forced into severe austerity also experienced severe slumps, seemed to confirm that observation.

Furthermore, it was clear that those who had predicted a sharp rise in U.S. interest rates due to budget deficits, leading to conventional crowding out, had been wrong: U.S. long-term interest rates remained near record lows even during the years from 2009 to 2012, when the government ran very large deficits.

The Debate over Monetary Policy As we've learned, a central bank that wants to increase aggregate demand normally does this by buying short-term government debt, pushing short-term interest rates down and causing spending to rise. By the fall of 2008, however, this conventional form of monetary policy had already reached its limit because the relevant interest rates were close to zero. The question then became whether there were other things the Federal Reserve and other central banks could do.

In 2008–2009 and again in the fall of 2010, the Fed pursued one such alternative, known as *quantitative easing*, which involved buying assets other than short-term government debt, notably long-term debt whose interest rate was still significantly above zero. For example, in November 2010 the Fed began buying $600 billion worth of longer-term U.S. debt in a program generally referred to as "QE2" (quantitative easing 2). The idea was to drive down longer-term interest rates, which arguably matter more for private spending than short-term rates. In September 2011 the Fed announced another program, this time one that would involve selling shorter-term assets with interest rates already near zero and buying longer-term assets instead.

The policy of quantitative easing was controversial, facing criticisms both from those who believed that the Fed was doing too much and from those who believed it was doing too little. Those who believed that the Fed was doing too much were concerned about possible future inflation; they argued that the Fed would find its unconventional measures hard to reverse as the economy recovered and that the end result would be a much too expansionary monetary policy. Opponents of quantitative easing were not shy about making their views heard: in

The Fed's controversial QE2 program tested the limits of monetary policy and sharpened the debate over whether inflation or high unemployment was the greater danger.

October 2010 a Who's Who of conservative economists and major investors issued an open letter calling on Ben Bernanke to call off the policy, which they warned could lead to a "debased" dollar.

Critics from the other side argued that the Fed's actions were likely to be ineffective: long-term interest rates, they suggested, mainly reflected expectations about future short-term rates, and even large purchases of long-term bonds by the Fed would have little impact.

Many of those calling on the Fed for even more active policy advocated an official rise in the Fed's inflation target. Recall from Chapters 23 and 25 the distinction between the nominal interest rate, which is the number normally cited, and the *real* interest rate—the nominal rate minus expected inflation—which is what should matter for investment decisions. Advocates of a higher inflation target argued that by promising to raise prices over, say, the next 10 years by an annual average rate of 3% or 4%, the Fed could push the real interest rate down even though the nominal rate was up against the zero lower bound.

Such proposals, however, led to fierce disputes. Some economists pointed out that the Fed had fought hard to drive inflation expectations down and argued that changing course would undermine hard-won credibility. Others argued that given the enormous economic and human damage being done by high unemployment, it was time for extraordinary measures, and inflation-fighting could no longer be given first priority.

At the time of writing, these disputes were still raging, and it seemed unlikely that a new consensus about macroeconomic policy would emerge any time soon.

"I'll pause for a moment so you can let this information sink in."

ECONOMICS ▶ *in Action*

Lats of Luck

The Brookings Institution in Washington, DC, is one of the most influential U.S. think tanks, especially on economic issues. In particular, its twice-a-year Panel on Economic Activity, in which top academics present work on current concerns, is arguably the premier forum for debates over economic policy. Usually the issues under discussion are big themes: inflation, unemployment, financial stability. In the fall of 2013, however, one entire session was devoted to the economy of Latvia, a small nation on the eastern shore of the Baltic Sea.

Even some of the panelists were bemused, asking why Brookings was devoting so much time to a country with a population of just 2 million—less than that of Brooklyn. However, Latvia has taken on outsize significance in the debate over fiscal policy, because it has been widely held up as an example of successful austerity. The country has become such a touchstone that Olivier Blanchard—the chief economist of the International Monetary Fund, and one of the most influential macroeconomists in the world—was the lead author of the Latvia paper.

Figure 33-6, which shows Latvia's real GDP since 2005, helps explain both why the country is cited as a success story for austerity policies and why the extent of success was a subject of dispute. In the years before the

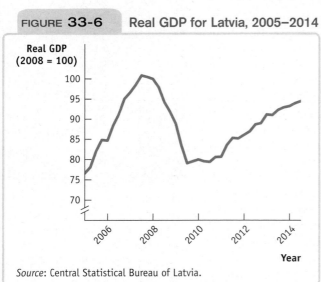

FIGURE 33-6   Real GDP for Latvia, 2005–2014

Real GDP (2008 = 100)

Source: Central Statistical Bureau of Latvia.

crisis Latvia was experiencing rapid growth, fueled by large inflows of capital. When these flows dried up, the country experienced a severe slump—comparable to the United States in the Great Depression. Many people drew parallels with Argentina's crisis in 2001, and expected Latvia to follow a similar path, devaluing its currency, the lats, and possibly defaulting on its debts.

Instead, however, the Latvian government kept the value of the lats fixed in terms of the euro, and adopted the euro itself in 2014. Meanwhile, it sharply cut spending in an attempt to shore up confidence. And as you can see in Figure 33-6, Latvia's economy eventually began to recover from its slump, which supporters of austerity claimed vindicated its policy. Critics, however, pointed out that as late as 2014 output was still below its pre-crisis level.

So whose case did Latvia support? Possibly neither. As both the authors and discussants of the Blanchard paper noted, Latvia is a relatively poor country—the poorest in the euro area—that has been able to grow quickly as it catches up technologically with the rest of Europe. So its experience may not tell us much about the choices facing other nations. But the very fact that so much attention was paid to a small, atypical country shows how intense the macroeconomic debate remains.

Check Your Understanding 33-5

1. Why did the Great Recession lead to the decline of the Great Moderation consensus? Given events, why is it predictable that a new consensus has not emerged?

Solution appears at back of book.

▼ Quick Review

• The **Great Moderation,** the period of relative economic calm from 1985 to 2007, produced the **Great Moderation consensus.**

• According to the Great Moderation consensus: monetary policy should be the main stabilization tool; to avoid a political business cycle, the central bank should be independent and fiscal policy should not be used, except possibly in exceptional circumstances such as a liquidity trap; and the natural rate of unemployment limits how much policy activism can reduce the unemployment rate.

• The Great Moderation consensus was severely challenged by the Great Recession. Active fiscal policy was revived given the ineffectiveness of monetary policy in the midst of a liquidity trap. Fiercely debated, fiscal stimulus in the United States failed to deliver a significant fall in unemployment. Critics cited this as evidence that fiscal policy doesn't work, while supporters countered that the size of the stimulus was too small. However, crowding out failed to materialize as critics had warned that it would.

• Monetary policy was also deeply controversial in the wake of the Great Recession, as the Fed pursued "quantitative easing" and other unconventional policies. Critics claimed the Fed was doing too much and too little, while some advocated the adoption of a higher inflation target to push the real interest rate down.

SUMMARY

1. Classical macroeconomics asserted that monetary policy affected only the aggregate price level, not aggregate output, and that the short run was unimportant. By the 1930s, measurement of business cycles was a well-established subject, but there was no widely accepted theory of business cycles.

2. **Keynesian economics** attributed the business cycle to shifts of the aggregate demand curve, often the result of changes in business confidence. Keynesian economics also offered a rationale for **macroeconomic policy activism.**

3. In the decades that followed Keynes's work, economists came to agree that monetary policy as well as fiscal policy is effective under certain conditions. **Monetarism,** a doctrine that called for a **monetary policy rule** as opposed to **discretionary monetary policy** and that argued—based on a belief that the **velocity of money** was stable—that GDP would grow steadily if the money supply grew steadily, was influential for a time but was eventually rejected by many macroeconomists.

4. The **natural rate hypothesis** became almost universally accepted, limiting the role of macroeconomic policy to stabilizing the economy rather than seeking a permanently lower unemployment rate. Fears of a **political business cycle** led to a consensus that monetary policy should be insulated from politics.

5. **Rational expectations** claims that individuals and firms make decisions using all available information. According to the **rational expectations model** of the economy, only unexpected changes in monetary policy affect aggregate output and employment; expected changes merely alter the price level. **Real business cycle theory** claims that changes in the rate of growth of total factor productivity are the main cause of business cycles. Both of these versions of **new classical macroeconomics** received wide attention and respect, but policy makers and many economists haven't accepted the conclusion that monetary and fiscal policy are ineffective in changing aggregate output.

6. **New Keynesian economics** argues that market imperfections can lead to price stickiness, so that changes in aggregate demand have effects on aggregate output after all.

7. The **Great Moderation** from 1985 to 2007 generated the **Great Moderation consensus:** belief in monetary policy as the main tool of stabilization; skepticism toward use of fiscal policy, except possibly in exceptional circumstances such as a liquidity trap; and acknowledgement of the policy constraints imposed by the natural rate of unemployment and the political business cycle. But the Great Moderation consensus was challenged by the post-2008 crisis events, as monetary policy lost its effectiveness in the midst of a liquidity trap. As a result, many advocated the use of fiscal policy to address the deep recession.

8. In 2009, a number of governments, including the United States, used fiscal stimulus to support their deeply depressed economies in the face of a liquidity trap. The use of fiscal policy remained highly controversial. In the United States, it failed to significantly reduce unemployment, with critics citing that as proof of its general ineffectiveness, while supporters argued the size of the stimulus was too small. Yet the crowding out predicted by its critics failed to occur.

9. Monetary policy was also hotly debated in the wake of the Great Recession, as the Fed pursued "quantitative easing" and other unconventional monetary policies to address the liquidity trap. Critics claimed the Fed was doing too much and would sacrifice its hard-won credibility as an inflation fighter. Others countered that the Fed was doing too little, yet others claimed the Fed's actions would have little impact. Some proposed the Fed adopt a higher inflation target to push the real interest rate down.

KEY TERMS

Keynesian economics, p. 977
Macroeconomic policy activism, p. 978
Monetarism, p. 980
Discretionary monetary policy, p. 980
Monetary policy rule, p. 982

Velocity of money, p. 982
Natural rate hypothesis, p. 983
Political business cycle, p. 983
New classical macroeconomics, p. 985
Rational expectations, p. 985

Rational expectations model, p. 985
New Keynesian economics, p. 985
Real business cycle theory, p. 986
Great Moderation, p. 988
Great Moderation consensus, p. 988

PROBLEMS

1. Since the crash of its stock market in 1989, the Japanese economy has seen little economic growth and some deflation. The accompanying table from the Organization for Economic Cooperation and Development (OECD) shows some key macroeconomic data for Japan for 1991 (a "normal" year) and 1995–2003.

   a. From the data, determine the type of policies Japan's policy makers undertook at that time to promote growth.

   b. We can safely consider a short-term interest rate that is less than 0.1% to effectively be a 0% interest rate. What is this situation called? What does it imply about the effectiveness of monetary policy? Of fiscal policy?

Year	Real GDP annual growth rate	Short-term interest rate	Government debt (percent of GDP)	Government budget deficit (percent of GDP)
1991	3.4%	7.38%	64.8%	−1.81%
1995	1.9	1.23	87.1	4.71
1996	3.4	0.59	93.9	5.07
1997	1.9	0.60	100.3	3.79
1998	−1.1	0.72	112.2	5.51
1999	0.1	0.25	125.7	7.23
2000	2.8	0.25	134.1	7.48
2001	0.4	0.12	142.3	6.13
2002	−0.3	0.06	149.3	7.88
2003	2.5	0.04	157.5	7.67

2. The National Bureau of Economic Research (NBER) maintains the official chronology of past U.S. business cycles. Go to its website at www.nber.org/cycles/cyclesmain.html to answer the following questions.

   a. How many business cycles have occurred since the end of World War II in 1945?

   b. What was the average duration of a business cycle when measured from the end of one expansion (its peak) to the end of the next? That is, what was the average duration of a business cycle in the period from 1945 to 2001?

   c. When was the last announcement by the NBER's Business Cycle Dating Committee, and what was it?

3. The fall of its military rival, the Soviet Union, in 1989 allowed the United States to significantly reduce its defense spending in subsequent years. Using the data in the following table from the Economic Report of the President, replicate Figure 33-3 for the 1990–2000 period. Given the strong economic growth in the United States during the late 1990s, why would a Keynesian see the reduction in defense spending during the 1990s as a good thing?

Year	Budget deficit (percent of GDP)	Unemployment rate
1990	3.9%	5.6%
1991	4.5	6.8
1992	4.7	7.5
1993	3.9	6.9
1994	2.9	6.1
1995	2.2	5.6
1996	1.4	5.4
1997	0.3	4.9
1998	−0.8	4.5
1999	−1.4	4.2
2000	−2.4	4.0

4. In the modern world, central banks are free to increase or reduce the money supply as they see fit. However, some people harken back to the "good old days" of the gold standard. Under the gold standard, the money supply could expand only when the amount of available gold increased.

   a. Under the gold standard, if the velocity of money were stable when the economy was expanding, what would have had to happen to keep prices stable?

   b. Why would modern macroeconomists consider the gold standard a bad idea?

5. The chapter explains that Kenneth Rogoff proclaimed Richard Nixon "the all-time hero of political business cycles." Using the upcoming table of data from the Economic Report of the President, explain why Nixon may have earned that title. (*Note:* Nixon entered office in January 1969 and was reelected in November 1972. He resigned in August 1974.)

Year	Government receipts (billions of dollars)	Government spending (billions of dollars)	Government budget balance (billions of dollars)	M1 growth	M2 growth	3-month Treasury bill rate
1969	$186.9	$183.6	$3.2	3.3%	3.7%	6.68%
1970	192.8	195.6	−2.8	5.1	6.6	6.46
1971	187.1	210.2	−23.0	6.5	13.4	4.35
1972	207.3	230.7	−23.4	9.2	13.0	4.07
1973	230.8	245.7	−14.9	5.5	6.6	7.04

6. The economy of Albernia is facing a recessionary gap, and the leader of that nation calls together five of its best economists representing the classical, Keynesian, monetarist, real business cycle, and Great Moderation consensus views of the macroeconomy. Explain what policies each economist would recommend and why.

7. Which of the following policy recommendations are consistent with the classical, Keynesian, monetarist, and/or Great Moderation consensus views of the macroeconomy?

   a. Since the long-run growth of GDP is 2%, the money supply should grow at 2%.

   b. Decrease government spending in order to decrease inflationary pressure.

   c. Increase the money supply in order to alleviate a recessionary gap.

   d. Always maintain a balanced budget.

   e. Decrease the budget deficit as a percent of GDP when facing a recessionary gap.

8. Using a graph like Figure 33-4, show how a monetarist can argue that a contractionary fiscal policy need not lead to a fall in real GDP given a fixed money supply. Explain.

WORK IT OUT

For interactive, step-by-step help in solving the following problem, visit LaunchPad by using the URL on the back cover of this book.

9. Monetarists believed for a period of time that the velocity of money was stable within a country. However, with financial innovation, the velocity began shifting around erratically after 1980. As would be expected, the velocity of money is different across countries depending upon the sophistication of their financial systems—velocity of money tends to be higher in countries with developed financial systems. The accompanying table provides money supply and GDP information in 2013 for six countries.

Country	National currency	M1 (billions in national currency)	Nominal GDP (billions in national currency)
Egypt	Egyptian pounds	431	1,753
South Korea	Korean won	515,643	1,428,294
Thailand	Thai baht	1,608	11,898
United States	U.S. dollars	2,832	16,800
Kenya	Kenyan pounds	967	3,797
India	Indian rupees	19,118	113,550

Source: World Bank.

   a. Calculate the velocity of money for each of the countries. The accompanying table shows GDP per capita for each of these countries in 2013 in U.S. dollars.

Country	Nominal GDP per capita (U.S. dollars)
Egypt	$3,225
South Korea	24,328
Thailand	5,674
United States	53,101
Kenya	1,016
India	1,504

Source: IMF.

   b. Rank the countries in descending order of per capita income and velocity of money. Do wealthy countries or poor countries tend to "turn over" their money more times per year? Would you expect wealthy countries to have more sophisticated financial systems?

Open-Economy Macroeconomics

> ## What You Will Learn in This Chapter

- The meaning of the **balance of payments accounts**

- The determinants of international capital flows

- The role of the **foreign exchange market** and the **exchange rate**

- The importance of **real exchange rates** and their role in the **current account**

- Considerations that lead countries to choose different **exchange rate regimes,** such as **fixed exchange rates** and **floating exchange rates**

- Why open-economy considerations affect macroeconomic policy under floating exchange rates

SWITZERLAND DOESN'T WANT YOUR MONEY

In 2011, the Swiss National Bank undertook extraordinary actions to protect itself from the consequences of being an open economy.

Parking your money in a Swiss bank is no way to get rich, given the low interest rates Swiss bankers offer. Recently, in fact, Swiss banks have paid negative interest on deposits, charging customers for the service of keeping their funds.

But for generations, Swiss bank accounts have been seen as a way to *stay* rich, a safe place to store your wealth. In the troubled years that followed the 2008 financial crisis, the Swiss reputation for safety became especially important. European investors, in particular, poured money into Switzerland.

And the Swiss hated it—the result of the inflow of foreign funds was a surge in the value of the Swiss franc that wreaked havoc with Swiss exports.

At the beginning of 2008, one Swiss franc traded for about 0.6 euro. By mid-2011, the franc was trading for around 0.9 euro, a 50% appreciation. That meant that Swiss exports, other things equal, had seen a 50% rise in their labor costs relative to competitors elsewhere in Europe. Thanks to its reputation for quality, Switzerland has

been remarkably successful over the years at selling goods to the world market, despite high labor costs. Nobody expects to get a bargain on Swiss watches or Swiss chocolate. But a 50% appreciation of the Swiss franc pushed Swiss exports to the breaking point.

So what was to be done? Starting in early 2009, the Swiss National Bank, Switzerland's equivalent of the Federal Reserve, began selling francs on the foreign exchange market in an attempt to hold down the franc's value. In return for these francs, it received other currencies, mainly dollars and euros, which it added to its reserves. We're talking about a *lot* of sales: over a period of 2½ years, the bank added $180 billion to its foreign exchange reserves, equal to a third of Switzerland's GDP—the equivalent for the United States of selling $5 trillion.

Yet even that wasn't enough to stop the franc's rise. In September 2011, as the franc seemed headed for a value of 1 euro or more, the Swiss National Bank announced that it would do whatever it took—sell an unlimited amount of francs—to keep the franc below a maximum of 0.833 euro per

franc (that is, 1.2 francs per euro, which was the way the target was stated). That announcement finally seemed to stop the franc's rise, at least at first.

What the extraordinary efforts of the Swiss National Bank illustrated was the importance of a dimension of macroeconomics that we haven't emphasized so far—the fact that modern national economies are *open economies* that trade goods, services, and assets with the rest of the world. Open-economy macroeconomics is a branch of macroeconomics that deals with the relationships between national economies. As the Swiss story illustrates, economic interactions with the rest of the world can have a profound impact on a domestic economy.

In this chapter we'll learn about some of the key issues in open-economy macroeconomics: the determinants of a country's *balance of payments,* the factors affecting *exchange rates,* the different forms of *exchange rate policy* adopted by various countries, and the relationship between exchange rates and macroeconomic policy.

Capital Flows and the Balance of Payments

In 2013 people living in the United States sold about $4.2 trillion worth of stuff to people living in other countries and bought about $4.2 trillion worth of stuff in return. What kind of stuff? All kinds. Residents of the United States (including firms operating in the United States) sold airplanes, bonds, wheat, and many other items to residents of other countries. Residents of the United States bought cars, stocks, oil, and many other items from residents of other countries.

How can we keep track of these transactions? In Chapter 22 we learned that economists keep track of the domestic economy using the national income and product accounts. Economists keep track of international transactions using a different but related set of numbers, the *balance of payments accounts*.

Balance of Payments Accounts

A country's **balance of payments accounts** are a summary of the country's transactions with other countries for a given year.

To understand the basic idea behind the balance of payments accounts, let's consider a small-scale example: not a country, but a family farm. Let's say that we know the following about how last year went financially for the Costas, who own a small artichoke farm in California:

- They made $100,000 by selling artichokes.

- They spent $70,000 on running the farm, including purchases of new farm machinery, and another $40,000 buying food, paying utility bills, replacing their worn-out car, and so on.

- They received $500 in interest on their bank account but paid $10,000 in interest on their mortgage.

- They took out a new $25,000 loan to help pay for farm improvements but didn't use all the money immediately. So they put the extra in the bank.

TABLE 34-1 The Costas' Financial Year

	Sources of cash	Uses of cash	Net
Purchases or sales of goods and services	Artichoke sales: $100,000	Farm operation and living expenses: $110,000	−$10,000
Interest payments	Interest received on bank account: $500	Interest paid on mortgage: $10,000	−$9,500
Loans and deposits	Funds received from new loan: $25,000	Funds deposited in bank: $5,500	+$19,500
Total	$125,500	$125,500	$0

How could we summarize the Costas' transactions for the year? One way would be with a table like Table 34-1, which shows sources of cash coming in and uses of cash going out, characterized under a few broad headings. The first row of Table 34-1 shows sales and purchases of goods and services: sales of artichokes; purchases of groceries, heating oil, that new car, and so on. The second row shows interest payments: the interest the Costas received from their bank account and the interest they paid on their mortgage. The third row shows loans and deposits: cash coming in from a loan and cash deposited in the bank.

In each row we show the net inflow of cash from that type of transaction. So the net in the first row is −$10,000, because the Costas spent $10,000 more than they earned. The net in the second row is −$9,500, the difference between the interest the Costas received on their bank account and the interest they paid on the mortgage. The net in the third row is $19,500: the Costas brought in $25,000 with their new loan but put only $5,500 of that sum in the bank.

The last row shows the sum of cash coming in from all sources and the sum of all cash used. These sums are equal, by definition: every dollar has a source, and every dollar received gets used somewhere. (What if the Costas hid money under the mattress? Then that would be counted as another "use" of cash.)

A country's balance of payments accounts is a table which summarizes the country's transactions with the rest of the world for a given year in a manner very similar to the way we just summarized the Costas' financial year.

Table 34-2 shows a simplified version of the U.S. balance of payments accounts for 2013. Where the Costa family's accounts show sources and uses of cash, a country's balance of payments accounts show payments from foreigners—sources of cash for the United States as a whole—and payments to foreigners—uses of cash for the United States as a whole.

Row 1 of Table 34-2 shows payments that arise from U.S. sales to foreigners and U.S. purchases from foreigners of goods and services in 2013. For example, the number in the second column of row 1, $2,280 billion, incorporates items such as the value of U.S. wheat exports and the fees foreigners pay to U.S. consulting companies in 2013. The number in the third column of row 1, $2,756 billion, incorporates items such as the value of U.S. oil imports and the fees U.S. companies pay to Indian call centers—the people who often answer your 1-800 calls—in 2013.

Row 2 shows U.S. *factor income* in 2013—the income that foreigners paid to American residents

TABLE 34-2	The U.S. Balance of Payments in 2013 (billions of dollars)		
	Payments from foreigners	**Payments to foreigners**	**Net**
1 Sales and purchases of goods and services	$2,280	$2,756	−$476
2 Factor income	780	580	199
3 Transfers	118	242	−124
Current account (1 + 2 + 3)			**−400**
4 Asset sales and purchases (financial account)	1,018	−645	373
Financial account (4)			**373**
Statistical discrepancy	—	—	**−27**

Source: Bureau of Labor Statistics.

for the use of American-owned factors of production, as well as income paid by Americans to foreigners for the use of foreign-owned factors of production. Factor income mostly consists of investment income, such as interest paid by Americans on loans from overseas, profits of American-owned corporations that operate overseas, and the like. For example, the profits earned by Disneyland Paris, which is owned by the U.S.-based Walt Disney Company, are included in the $780 billion figure in the second column of row 2. The profits earned by the U.S. operations of Japanese auto companies are included in the $580 billion figure shown in the third column of row 2. Factor income also includes some labor income. For example, the wages of an American engineer who works temporarily on a construction site in Dubai are counted in the $780 billion figure in the second column.

Row 3 shows *international transfers* for the U.S. in 2013—funds sent by American residents to residents of other countries and vice versa. The figure in the second column of row 3, $118 billion, includes payments sent home by skilled American workers who work abroad. The third column accounts for the major portion of international transfers. The figure there, $242 billion, is composed mainly of remittances that immigrants who reside in the United States, such as the millions of Mexican-born workers employed in the United States, send to their families in their country of origin. In addition there is also a lot of money sent home by U.S. skilled workers abroad.

Row 4 of the table contains payments accruing from sales and purchases of assets between American residents and foreigners in 2013. For example, in 2013 Shanghui, a Chinese food company, purchased Smithfield Foods, America's top pork packager, for $4.7 billion. As a payment to the American owners of Smithfield Foods for the purchase of their assets, that $4.7 billion is included in the figure $1,018 billion, found in the second column of row 4. Also in 2013, some major Wall Street firms were buying European debt, both private and public. As a payment by American residents to foreigners for the purchase of foreign assets, these purchases are included in the −$645 billion figure located in the third column of row 4.

In laying out Table 34-2, we have separated rows 1, 2, and 3 into one group, to distinguish them from row 4. This reflects a fundamental difference in how these two groups of transactions affect the future. When a U.S. resident sells a good such as wheat to a foreigner, that's the end of the transaction. But a financial asset, such as a bond, is different. Remember, a bond is a promise to pay interest and principal in the future. So when a U.S. resident sells a bond to a foreigner, that sale creates a liability: the U.S. resident will have to pay interest and repay principal in the future. The balance of payments accounts distinguish between transactions that don't create liabilities and those that do.

A country's **balance of payments on current account,** or **current account,** is its balance of payments on goods and services plus net international transfer payments and factor income.

A country's **balance of payments on goods and services** is the difference between its exports and its imports during a given period.

The **merchandise trade balance,** or **trade balance,** is the difference between a country's exports and imports of goods.

A country's **balance of payments on financial account,** or simply its **financial account,** is the difference between its sales of assets to foreigners and its purchases of assets from foreigners for a given period.

Transactions that don't create liabilities are considered part of the **balance of payments on current account,** often referred to simply as the **current account:** the balance of payments on goods and services plus net international transfer payments and factor income. This corresponds to rows 1, 2, and 3 in Table 34-2. In practice, row 1 of Table 34-2, amounting to –$476 billion in 2013, corresponds to the most important part of the current account: the **balance of payments on goods and services,** the difference between the value of exports and the value of imports during a given period.

If you read news reports on the economy, you may well see references to another measure, the **merchandise trade balance,** sometimes referred to as the **trade balance** for short. It is the difference between a country's exports and imports of goods alone—not including services. Economists sometimes focus on the merchandise trade balance, even though it's an incomplete measure, because data on international trade in services aren't as accurate as data on trade in physical goods, and they are also slower to arrive.

Transactions that involve the sale or purchase of assets, and therefore do create future liabilities, are considered part of the **balance of payments on financial account,** or the **financial account** for short, for a given period. This corresponds to row 4 in Table 34-2, which was $373 billion in 2013. (Until a few years ago, economists often referred to the financial account as the *capital account.* We'll use the modern term, but you may run across the older term.)

So how does it all add up? The shaded rows of Table 34-2 show the bottom lines: the overall U.S. current account and financial account for 2013. As you can see, in 2013 the United States ran a current account deficit: the amount it paid to foreigners for goods, services, factors, and transfers was more than the amount it received. Simultaneously, it ran a financial account surplus: the value of the assets it sold to foreigners was more than the value of the assets it bought from foreigners.

In the 2013 official data, the U.S. current account deficit and financial account surplus didn't exactly offset each other: the financial account surplus in 2013 was $27 billion smaller than the current account deficit. But that's just a statistical error, reflecting the imperfection of official data. (The discrepancy may have reflected foreign purchases of U.S. assets that official data somehow missed.)

FOR INQUIRING MINDS | GDP, GNP, and the Current Account

When we discussed national income accounting in Chapter 22, we derived the basic equation relating GDP to the components of spending:

$$Y = C + I + G + X - IM$$

where X and IM are exports and imports, respectively, of goods and services. But as we've learned, the balance of payments on goods and services is only one component of the current account balance. Why doesn't the national income equation use the current account as a whole?

The answer is that gross domestic product, Y, is the value of goods and services produced domestically. So it doesn't include international factor income and international transfers, two sources of income that are included in the calculation of the current account balance. The profits of Ford Motors U.K.

aren't included in the U.S. GDP, and the funds Latin American immigrants send home to their families aren't subtracted from GDP.

Shouldn't we have a broader measure that does include these sources of income? Actually, gross *national* product—GNP—does include international factor income. Estimates of U.S. GNP differ slightly from estimates of GDP because GNP adds in items such as the earnings of U.S. companies abroad and subtracts items such as the interest payments on bonds owned by residents of China and Japan. There isn't, however, any regularly calculated measure that includes transfer payments.

Why do economists use GDP rather than a broader measure? Two reasons. First, the original purpose of the national accounts was to track production rather than income. Second, data on

The funds of Latin American immigrants are included in GDP, even if they are sent abroad, because they were earned for services performed in the United States.

international factor income and transfer payments are generally considered somewhat unreliable. So if you're trying to keep track of movements in the economy, it makes sense to focus on GDP, which doesn't rely on these unreliable data. ∎

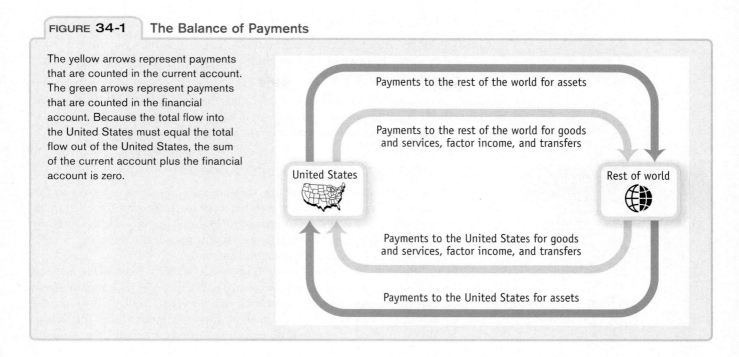

FIGURE 34-1   The Balance of Payments

The yellow arrows represent payments that are counted in the current account. The green arrows represent payments that are counted in the financial account. Because the total flow into the United States must equal the total flow out of the United States, the sum of the current account plus the financial account is zero.

Payments to the rest of the world for assets

Payments to the rest of the world for goods and services, factor income, and transfers

United States

Rest of world

Payments to the United States for goods and services, factor income, and transfers

Payments to the United States for assets

In fact, it's a basic rule of balance of payments accounting that the current account and the financial account must sum to zero:

(34-1) Current account (CA) + Financial account (FA) = 0

or

$$CA = -FA$$

Why must Equation 34-1 be true? We already saw the fundamental explanation in Table 34-1, which showed the accounts of the Costa family: in total, the sources of cash must equal the uses of cash. The same applies to balance of payments accounts. Figure 34-1, a variant on the circular-flow diagram we have found useful in discussing domestic macroeconomics, may help you visualize how this adding up works. Instead of showing the flow of money *within* a national economy, Figure 34-1 shows the flow of money *between* national economies.

Money flows into the United States from the rest of the world as payment for U.S. exports of goods and services, as payment for the use of U.S.-owned factors of production, and as transfer payments. These flows (indicated by the lower green arrow) are the positive components of the U.S. current account. Money also flows into the United States from foreigners who purchase U.S. assets (as shown by the lower green arrow)—the positive component of the U.S. financial account.

At the same time, money flows from the United States to the rest of the world as payment for U.S. imports of goods and services, as payment for the use of foreign-owned factors of production, and as transfer payments. These flows, indicated by the upper yellow arrow, are the negative components of the U.S. current account. Money also flows from the United States to purchase foreign assets, as shown by the upper green arrow—the negative component of the U.S. financial account. As in all circular-flow diagrams, the flow into a box and the flow out of a box are equal. This means that the sum of the yellow and green arrows going into the United States (the top two arrows) is equal to the sum of the yellow and green arrows going out of the United States (the bottom two arrows) That is,

(34-2) Positive entries on current account (lower yellow arrow) + Positive entries on financial account (lower green arrow) = Negative entries on current account (upper yellow arrow) + Negative entries on financial account (upper green arrow)

Equation 34-2 can be rearranged as follows:

(34-3) Positive entries on current account – Negative entries on current account + Positive entries on financial account – Negative entries on financial account = 0

Equation 34-3 is equivalent to Equation 34-1: the current account plus the financial account—both equal to positive entries minus negative entries—is equal to zero. But what determines the current account and the financial account?

-PLETCH-

BUILD IT AND, SOONER OR LATER, THEY WILL COME!

Modeling the Financial Account

A country's financial account measures its net sales of assets to foreigners. There is, however, another way to think about the financial account: it's a measure of *capital inflows*, of foreign savings that are available to finance domestic investment spending.

What determines these capital inflows?

Part of our explanation will have to wait for a little while because some international capital flows are carried out by governments and central banks, which sometimes act very differently from private investors. But we can gain insight into the motivations for capital flows that are the result of private decisions by using the *loanable funds model* we developed in Chapter 25. In using this model, we make two important simplifications:

- We simplify the reality of international capital flows by assuming that all flows are in the form of loans. In reality, capital flows take many forms, including purchases of shares of stock in foreign companies and foreign real estate as well as *direct foreign investment*, in which companies build factories or acquire other productive assets abroad.

- We also ignore the effects of expected changes in *exchange rates*, the relative values of different national currencies. We analyze the determination of exchange rates later in the chapter.

Figure 34-2 recaps the loanable funds model for a closed economy. Equilibrium corresponds to point E, at an interest rate of 4%, where the supply of loanable funds curve, S, intersects the demand

---

FIGURE **34-2** | **The Loanable Funds Model Revisited**

According to the loanable funds model of the interest rate, the equilibrium interest rate is determined by the intersection of the supply of loanable funds curve, *S,* and the demand for loanable funds curve, *D.* At point *E,* the equilibrium interest rate is 4%.

GLOBAL COMPARISION | Big Surpluses

As we've seen, the United States generally runs a large deficit in its current account. In fact, America leads the world in its current account deficit; other countries run bigger deficits as a share of GDP, but they have much smaller economies, so the U.S. deficit is much bigger in absolute terms.

For the world as a whole, however, deficits on the part of some countries must be matched with surpluses on the part of other countries. So who are the surplus nations offsetting U.S. deficits, and what if anything do they have in common?

The accompanying figure shows the average current account surplus of the six countries that ran the largest surpluses over the period from 2000 to 2013. You may not be surprised to learn that China tops the list. As we explain later in this chapter, China's surplus was largely due to its policy of keeping its currency weak relative to other currencies. But what about the others?

Japan and Germany run current account surpluses for more or less the same reasons: both are rich nations with high savings rates, giving them a lot of money to invest. Since some of that money goes abroad, the result is that they run deficits on the financial account and surpluses on current account.

Source: IMF World Economic Outlook, 2014.

The other three countries are all major oil exporters. (You may not think of Russia or Norway as "petro-economies," but Russia derives about two-thirds of its export revenue from oil, and Norway owns huge oil fields in the North Sea.) These countries are all deliberately building up assets abroad to help them sustain their spending when the oil runs out.

All in all, the surplus countries are a diverse group. If your picture of the world is simply one of American deficits versus Chinese surpluses, you're missing a large part of the story.

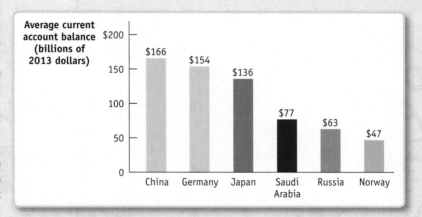

for loanable funds curve, *D.* But if international capital flows are possible, this diagram changes and *E* may no longer be the equilibrium. We can analyze the causes and effects of international capital flows using Figure 34-3, which places the loanable funds market diagrams for two countries side by side.

FIGURE 34-3 | Loanable Funds Markets in a Two-Country World

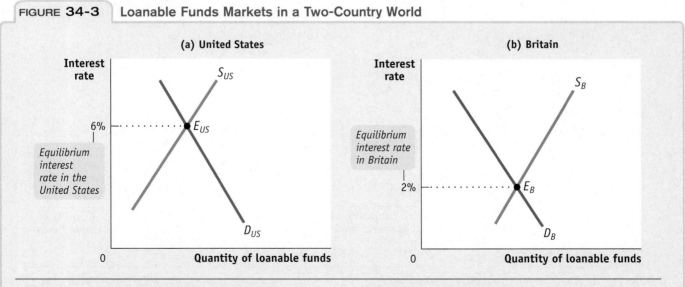

Here we show two countries, the United States and Britain, each with its own loanable funds market. The equilibrium interest rate is 6% in the U.S. market but only 2% in the British market.

This creates an incentive for capital to flow from Britain to the United States.

Figure 34-3 illustrates a world consisting of only two countries, the United States and Britain. Panel (a) shows the loanable funds market in the United States, where the equilibrium in the absence of international capital flows is at point E_{US} with an interest rate of 6%. Panel (b) shows the loanable funds market in Britain, where the equilibrium in the absence of international capital flows is at point E_B with an interest rate of 2%.

Will the actual interest rate in the United States remain at 6% and that in Britain at 2%? Not if it is easy for British residents to make loans to Americans. In that case, British lenders, attracted by high U.S. interest rates, will send some of their loanable funds to the United States. This capital inflow will increase the quantity of loanable funds supplied to American borrowers, pushing the U.S. interest rate down. At the same time, it will reduce the quantity of loanable funds supplied to British borrowers, pushing the British interest rate up. So international capital flows will narrow the gap between U.S. and British interest rates.

Let's further suppose that British lenders regard a loan to an American as being just as good as a loan to one of their own compatriots, and American borrowers regard a debt to a British lender as no more costly than a debt to an American lender. In that case, the flow of funds from Britain to the United States will continue until the gap between their interest rates is eliminated. In other words, when residents of the two countries believe that a foreign asset is as good as a domestic one and that a foreign liability is as good as a domestic one, then international capital flows will equalize the interest rates in the two countries.

Figure 34-4 shows an international equilibrium in the loanable funds markets where the equilibrium interest rate is 4% in both the United States and Britain. At this interest rate, the quantity of loanable funds demanded by American borrowers exceeds the quantity of loanable funds supplied by American lenders. This gap is filled by "imported" funds—a capital inflow from Britain. At the same time, the quantity of loanable funds supplied by British lenders is greater than the quantity of loanable funds demanded by British borrowers. This excess is "exported" in the form of a capital outflow to the United States. And the two markets are in equilibrium at a common interest rate of 4%—at that interest rate, the total quantity of

---

FIGURE 34-4 | **International Capital Flows in a Two-Country World**

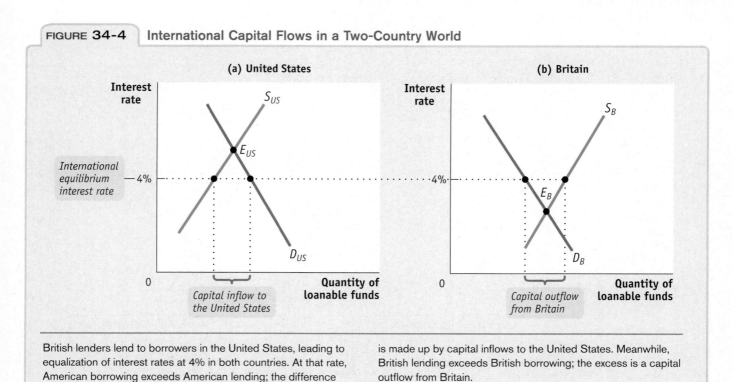

British lenders lend to borrowers in the United States, leading to equalization of interest rates at 4% in both countries. At that rate, American borrowing exceeds American lending; the difference is made up by capital inflows to the United States. Meanwhile, British lending exceeds British borrowing; the excess is a capital outflow from Britain.

loans demanded by borrowers across the two markets is equal to the total quantity of loans supplied by lenders across the two markets.

In short, international flows of capital are like international flows of goods and services. Capital moves from places where it would be cheap in the absence of international capital flows to places where it would be expensive in the absence of such flows.

Underlying Determinants of International Capital Flows

The open-economy version of the loanable funds model helps us understand international capital flows in terms of the supply and demand for funds. But what underlies differences across countries in the supply and demand for funds? Why, in the absence of international capital flows, would interest rates differ internationally, creating an incentive for international capital flows?

International differences in the demand for funds reflect underlying differences in investment opportunities. In particular, a country with a rapidly growing economy, other things equal, tends to offer more investment opportunities than a country with a slowly growing economy. So a rapidly growing economy typically—though not always—has a higher demand for capital and offers higher returns to investors than a slowly growing economy. As a result, capital tends to flow from slowly growing to rapidly growing economies.

The classic example, described in the upcoming Economics in Action, is the flow of capital from Britain to the United States, among other countries, between 1870 and 1914. During that era, the U.S. economy was growing rapidly as the population increased and spread westward and as the nation industrialized. This created a demand for investment spending on railroads, factories, and so on. Meanwhile, Britain had a much more slowly growing population, was already industrialized, and already had a railroad network covering the country. This left Britain with savings to spare, much of which were lent out to the United States and other New World economies.

International differences in the supply of funds reflect differences in savings across countries. These may be the result of differences in private savings rates, which vary widely among countries. For example, in 2010 gross private savings were 28.5% of Japan's GDP but only 19.2% of U.S. GDP. They may also reflect differences in savings by governments. In particular, government budget deficits, which reduce overall national savings, can lead to capital inflows.

FOR INQUIRING MINDS | A Global Savings Glut?

In the early years of the twenty-first century, the United States moved into massive deficit on current account, which meant that it became the recipient of huge capital inflows from the rest of the world (especially China, other Asian countries, and the Middle East). Why did that happen?

In an influential speech early in 2005, Ben Bernanke—who was at that time a governor of the Federal Reserve and who would soon become the Fed's chairman—offered a hypothesis: the United States wasn't responsible. The "principal causes of the U.S. current account deficit," he declared, lie "outside the country's borders." Specifically, he argued that special factors had

created a *global savings glut* that had pushed down interest rates worldwide and thereby led to an excess of investment spending over savings in the United States.

What caused this global savings glut? According to Bernanke, the main cause was the series of financial crises that began in Thailand in 1997; ricocheted across much of Asia; then hit Russia in 1998, Brazil in 1999, and Argentina in 2002. The ensuing fear and economic devastation led to a fall in investment spending and a rise in savings in a number of relatively poor countries. As a result, a number of these countries, which had previously been the recipients of capital inflows from advanced

countries like the United States, began experiencing large capital outflows. For the most part, the capital flowed to the United States, perhaps because "the depth and sophistication of the country's financial markets" made it an attractive destination.

When Bernanke gave his speech, it was viewed as reassuring: basically, he argued that the United States was responding in a sensible way to the availability of cheap money in world financial markets. Later, however, it would become clear that the cheap money from abroad helped fuel a housing bubble, which caused widespread financial and economic damage when it burst. ■

Two-Way Capital Flows

The loanable funds model helps us understand the direction of *net* capital flows—the excess of inflows into a country over outflows, or vice versa. The direction of net flows, other things equal, is determined by differences in interest rates between countries. As we saw in Table 34-2, however, *gross* flows take place in both directions: for example, the United States both sells assets to foreigners and buys assets from foreigners. Why does capital move in both directions?

The answer to this question is that in the real world, as opposed to the simple model we've just learned, there are other motives for international capital flows besides seeking a higher rate of interest.

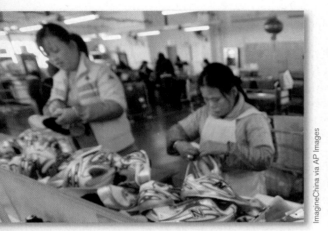

Many American companies have opened plants in China to access the growing Chinese market and to take advantage of low labor costs.

Individual investors often seek to diversify against risk by buying stocks in a number of countries. Stocks in Europe may do well when stocks in the United States do badly, or vice versa, so investors in Europe try to reduce their risk by buying some U.S. stocks, as investors in the United States try to reduce their risk by buying some European stocks. The result is capital flows in both directions.

Meanwhile, corporations often engage in international investment as part of their business strategy—for example, auto companies may find that they can compete better in a national market if they assemble some of their cars locally. Such business investments can also lead to two-way capital flows, as, say, European car makers build plants in the United States even as U.S. computer companies open facilities in Europe.

Finally, some countries, including the United States, are international banking centers: people from all over the world put money in U.S. financial institutions, which then invest many of those funds overseas.

The result of these two-way flows is that modern economies are typically both debtors (countries that owe money to the rest of the world) and creditors (countries to which the rest of the world owes money). Due to years of both capital inflows and outflows, at the end of 2013, the United States had accumulated foreign assets worth $23.7 trillion, and foreigners had accumulated assets in the United States worth $29.1 trillion.

ECONOMICS ▶ in Action

The Golden Age of Capital Flows

Technology, it's often said, shrinks the world. Jet planes have put most of the world's cities within a few hours of one another; modern telecommunications transmit information instantly around the globe. So you might think that international capital flows must now be larger than ever.

But if capital flows are measured as a share of world savings and investment, that belief turns out not to be true. The golden age of capital flows actually preceded World War I—from 1870 to 1914.

These capital flows went mainly from European countries, especially Britain, to what were then known as *zones of recent settlement,* countries that were attracting large numbers of European immigrants. Among the big recipients of capital inflows were Australia, Argentina, Canada, and the United States.

The large capital flows reflected differences in investment opportunities. Britain, a mature industrial economy with limited natural resources and a slowly growing population, offered relatively limited opportunities for new investment. The zones of recent settlement, with rapidly growing populations and abundant natural resources, offered investors a higher return and attracted capital inflows.

Estimates suggest that over this period Britain sent about 40% of its savings abroad, largely to finance railroads and other large projects. No country has matched that record in modern times.

Why can't we match the capital flows of our great-great-grandfathers? Economists aren't completely sure, but they have pointed to two causes: migration restrictions and political risks.

During the golden age of capital flows, capital movements were complementary to population movements: the big recipients of capital from Europe were also places to which large numbers of Europeans were moving. These large-scale population movements were possible before World War I because there were few legal restrictions on immigration. In today's world, by contrast, migration is limited by extensive legal barriers, as anyone considering a move to the United States or Europe can tell you.

The other factor that has changed is political risk. Modern governments often limit foreign investment because they fear it will diminish their national autonomy. And due to political or security concerns, governments sometimes seize foreign property, a risk that deters investors from sending more than a relatively modest share of their wealth abroad. In the nineteenth century such actions were rare, partly because some major destinations of investment were still European colonies, partly because in those days governments had a habit of sending troops and gunboats to enforce the claims of their investors.

Check Your Understanding   34-1

1. Which of the balance of payments accounts do the following events affect?
   a. Boeing, a U.S.-based company, sells a newly built airplane to China.
   b. Chinese investors buy stock in Boeing from Americans.
   c. A Chinese company buys a used airplane from American Airlines and ships it to China.
   d. A Chinese investor who owns property in the United States buys a corporate jet, which he will keep in the United States so he can travel around America.
2. What effect do you think the collapse of the U.S. housing bubble and the ensuing recession had on international capital flows into the United States?

Solutions appear at back of book.

The Role of the Exchange Rate

We've just seen how differences in the supply of loanable funds from savings and the demand for loanable funds for investment spending lead to international capital flows. We've also learned that a country's balance of payments on current account plus its balance of payments on financial account add to zero: a country that receives net capital inflows must run a matching current account deficit, and a country that generates net capital outflows must run a matching current account surplus.

The behavior of the financial account—reflecting inflows or outflows of capital—is best described by equilibrium in the international loanable funds market. At the same time, the balance of payments on goods and services, the main component of the current account, is determined by decisions in the international markets for goods and services. So given that the financial account reflects the movement of capital and the current account reflects the movement of goods and services, what ensures that the balance of payments really does balance? That is, what ensures that the two accounts actually offset each other?

Not surprisingly, a price is what makes these two accounts balance. Specifically, that price is the *exchange rate,* which is determined in the *foreign exchange market.*

Currencies are traded in the **foreign exchange market.**

The prices at which currencies trade are known as **exchange rates.**

When a currency becomes more valuable in terms of other currencies, it **appreciates.**

When a currency becomes less valuable in terms of other currencies, it **depreciates.**

TABLE **34-3**	Exchange Rates, November 21, 2014, 2 P.M.		
	U.S. dollars	**Yen**	**Euros**
One U.S. dollar exchanged for	1	117.76	0.8072
One yen exchanged for	0.0085	1	0.0069
One euro exchanged for	1.2388	145.88	1

PITFALLS

WHICH WAY IS UP?

Suppose someone says, "The U.S. exchange rate is up." What does that person mean?

It isn't clear. Sometimes the exchange rate is measured as the price of a dollar in terms of foreign currency, sometimes as the price of foreign currency in terms of dollars. So the statement could mean either that the dollar appreciated or that it depreciated!

You have to be particularly careful when using published statistics. Most countries other than the United States state their exchange rates in terms of the price of a dollar in their domestic currency—for example, Mexican officials will say that the exchange rate is 10, meaning 10 pesos per dollar. But Britain, for historical reasons, usually states its exchange rate the other way. On November 21, 2014, US$1 was worth £0.6362, and £1 was worth US$1.5718. More often than not, this number is reported as an exchange rate of 1.5718. In fact, on occasion, professional economists and consultants embarrass themselves by getting the direction in which the pound is moving wrong!

By the way, Americans generally follow other countries' lead: we usually say that the exchange rate against Mexico is 10 pesos per dollar but that the exchange rate against Britain is 1.57 dollars per pound. But this rule isn't reliable; exchange rates against the euro are often stated both ways.

So it's always important to check before using exchange rate data: which way is the exchange rate being measured?

Understanding Exchange Rates

In general, goods, services, and assets produced in a country must be paid for in that country's currency. American products must be paid for in dollars; European products must be paid for in euros; Japanese products must be paid for in yen. Occasionally, sellers will accept payment in foreign currency, but they will then exchange that currency for domestic money.

International transactions, then, require a market—the **foreign exchange market**—in which currencies can be exchanged for each other. This market determines **exchange rates,** the prices at which currencies trade. (The foreign exchange market is, in fact, not located in any one geographic spot. Rather, it is a global electronic market that traders around the world use to buy and sell currencies.)

Table 34-3 shows exchange rates among the world's three most important currencies as of 2 P.M., EDT, on Nov. 21, 2014. Each entry shows the price of the "row" currency in terms of the "column" currency. For example, at that time US$1 exchanged for €0.8072, so it took €0.8072 to buy US$1. Similarly, it took US$1.2388 to buy €1. These two numbers reflect the same rate of exchange between the euro and the U.S. dollar: 1/1.2388 = 0.8072.

There are two ways to write any given exchange rate. In this case, there were €0.8072 to US$1 and US$1.2388 to €1. Which is the correct way to write it? The answer is that there is no fixed rule. In most countries, people tend to express the exchange rate as the price of a dollar in domestic currency. However, this rule isn't universal, and the U.S. dollar–euro rate is commonly quoted both ways. The important thing is to be sure you know which one you are using! See the Pitfalls on this page.

When discussing movements in exchange rates, economists use specialized terms to avoid confusion. When a currency becomes more valuable in terms of other currencies, economists say that the currency **appreciates.** When a currency becomes less valuable in terms of other currencies, it **depreciates.** Suppose, for example, that the value of €1 went from $1 to $1.25, which means that the value of US$1 went from €1 to €0.80 (because 1/1.25 = 0.80). In this case, we would say that the euro appreciated and the U.S. dollar depreciated.

Movements in exchange rates, other things equal, affect the relative prices of goods, services, and assets in different countries. Suppose, for example, that the price of an American hotel room is US$100 and the price of a French hotel room is €100. If the exchange rate is €1 = US$1, these hotel rooms have the same price. If the exchange rate is €1.25 = US$1, the French hotel room is 20% cheaper than the American hotel room. If the exchange rate is €0.80 = US$1, the French hotel room is 25% more expensive than the American hotel room.

But what determines exchange rates? Supply and demand in the foreign exchange market.

The Equilibrium Exchange Rate

Imagine, for the sake of simplicity, that there are only two currencies in the world: U.S. dollars and euros. Europeans wanting to purchase American goods, services, and assets come to the foreign exchange market, wanting to exchange euros for U.S. dollars. That is, Europeans demand U.S. dollars from the foreign exchange market and, correspondingly, supply euros to that market. Americans wanting to buy European goods, services, and assets come to the foreign exchange market to exchange U.S. dollars for euros. That is,

FIGURE **34-5** The Foreign Exchange Market

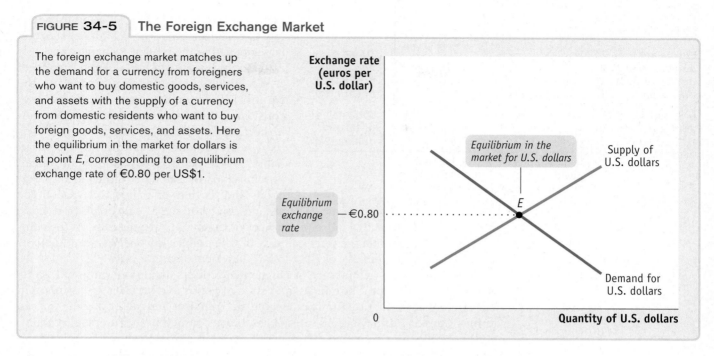

The foreign exchange market matches up the demand for a currency from foreigners who want to buy domestic goods, services, and assets with the supply of a currency from domestic residents who want to buy foreign goods, services, and assets. Here the equilibrium in the market for dollars is at point *E*, corresponding to an equilibrium exchange rate of €0.80 per US$1.

Americans supply U.S. dollars to the foreign exchange market and, correspondingly, demand euros from that market. (International transfers and payments of factor income also enter into the foreign exchange market, but to make things simple we'll ignore these.)

Figure 34-5 shows how the foreign exchange market works. The quantity of dollars demanded and supplied at any given euro–U.S. dollar exchange rate is shown on the horizontal axis, and the euro–U.S. dollar exchange rate is shown on the vertical axis. The exchange rate plays the same role as the price of a good or service in an ordinary supply and demand diagram.

The figure shows two curves, the demand curve for U.S. dollars and the supply curve for U.S. dollars. The key to understanding the slopes of these curves is that the level of the exchange rate affects exports and imports. When a country's currency appreciates (becomes more valuable), exports fall and imports rise. When a country's currency depreciates (becomes less valuable), exports rise and imports fall.

To understand why the demand curve for U.S. dollars slopes downward, recall that the exchange rate, other things equal, determines the prices of American goods, services, and assets relative to those of European goods, services, and assets. If the U.S. dollar rises against the euro (the dollar appreciates), American products will become more expensive to Europeans relative to European products. So Europeans will buy less from the United States and will acquire fewer dollars in the foreign exchange market: the quantity of U.S. dollars demanded falls as the number of euros needed to buy a U.S. dollar rises. If the U.S. dollar falls against the euro (the dollar depreciates), American products will become relatively cheaper for Europeans. Europeans will respond by buying more from the United States and acquiring more dollars in the foreign exchange market: the quantity of U.S. dollars demanded rises as the number of euros needed to buy a U.S. dollar falls.

A similar argument explains why the supply curve of U.S. dollars in Figure 34-5 slopes upward: the more euros required to buy a U.S. dollar, the more dollars Americans will supply. Again, the reason is the effect of the exchange rate on relative prices. If the U.S. dollar rises against the euro, European products look cheaper to Americans—who will demand more of them. This will require Americans to convert more dollars into euros.

The **equilibrium exchange rate** is the exchange rate at which the quantity of U.S. dollars demanded in the foreign exchange market is equal to the quantity of U.S. dollars supplied. In Figure 34-5, the equilibrium is at point *E*, and the equilibrium

The **equilibrium exchange rate** is the exchange rate at which the quantity of a currency demanded in the foreign exchange market is equal to the quantity supplied.

TABLE **34-4** A Hypothetical Equilibrium in the Foreign Exchange Market

European purchases of U.S. dollars (trillions of U.S. dollars)	To buy U.S. goods and services: 1.0	To buy U.S. assets: 1.0	Total purchases of U.S. dollars: 2.0
U.S. sales of U.S. dollars (trillions of U.S. dollars)	To buy European goods and services: 1.5	To buy European assets: 0.5	Total sales of U.S. dollars: 2.0
	U.S. balance of payments on current account: −0.5	U.S. balance of payments on financial account: +0.5	

exchange rate is 0.80. That is, at an exchange rate of €0.80 per US$1, the quantity of U.S. dollars supplied to the foreign exchange market is equal to the quantity of U.S. dollars demanded.

To understand the significance of the equilibrium exchange rate, it's helpful to consider a numerical example of what equilibrium in the foreign exchange market looks like. A hypothetical example is shown in Table 34-4. The first row shows European purchases of U.S. dollars, either to buy U.S. goods and services or to buy U.S. assets. The second row shows U.S. sales of U.S. dollars, either to buy European goods and services or to buy European assets. At the equilibrium exchange rate, the total quantity of U.S. dollars Europeans want to buy is equal to the total quantity of U.S. dollars Americans want to sell.

Remember that the balance of payments accounts divide international transactions into two types. Purchases and sales of goods and services are counted in the current account. (Again, we're leaving out transfers and factor income to keep things simple.) Purchases and sales of assets are counted in the financial account. At the equilibrium exchange rate, then, we have the situation shown in Table 34-4: the sum of the balance of payments on current account plus the balance of payments on financial account is zero.

Now let's briefly consider how a shift in the demand for U.S. dollars affects equilibrium in the foreign exchange market. Suppose that for some reason capital flows from Europe to the United States increase—say, due to a change in the preferences of European investors. The effects are shown in Figure 34-6. The demand for U.S. dollars in the foreign exchange market increases as European investors convert euros into dollars to fund their new investments in the United States. This is shown by the shift of the demand curve from D_1 to D_2. As a result, the U.S. dollar appreciates against the euro: the number of euros per U.S. dollar at the equilibrium exchange rate rises from XR_1 to XR_2.

What are the consequences of this increased capital inflow for the balance of payments? The total quantity of U.S. dollars supplied to the foreign exchange market still must equal the total quantity of U.S. dollars demanded. So the increased capital inflow to the United States—an increase in the balance of

FIGURE **34-6** An Increase in the Demand for U.S. Dollars

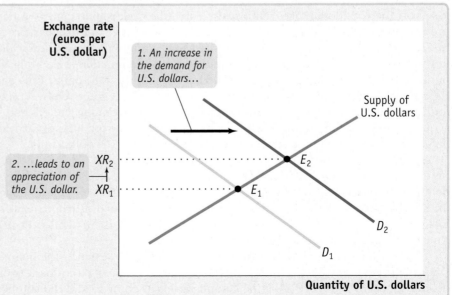

An increase in the demand for U.S. dollars might result from a change in the preferences of European investors. The demand curve for U.S. dollars shifts from D_1 to D_2. So the equilibrium number of euros per U.S. dollar rises— the dollar appreciates against the euro. As a result, the balance of payments on current account falls as the balance of payments on financial account rises.

payments on financial account—must be matched by a decline in the balance of payments on current account. What causes the balance of payments on current account to decline? The appreciation of the U.S. dollar. A rise in the number of euros per U.S. dollar leads Americans to buy more European goods and services and Europeans to buy fewer American goods and services.

Table 34-5 shows a hypothetical example of how this might work. Europeans are buying more U.S. assets, increasing the balance of payments on financial account from 0.5 to 1.0. This is offset by a reduction in European purchases of U.S. goods and services and a rise in U.S. purchases of European goods and services, both the result of the dollar's appreciation. *So any change in the U.S. balance of payments on financial account generates an equal and opposite reaction in the balance of payments on current account.* Movements in the exchange rate ensure that changes in the financial account and in the current account offset each other.

TABLE 34-5	A Hypothetical Example of Effects of Increased Capital Inflows		
European purchases of U.S. dollars (trillions of U.S. dollars)	To buy U.S. goods and services: 0.75 (down 0.25)	To buy U.S. assets: 1.5 (up 0.5)	**Total purchases of U.S. dollars: 2.25**
U.S. sales of U.S. dollars (trillions of U.S. dollars)	To buy European goods and services: 1.75 (up 0.25)	To buy European assets: 0.5 (no change)	**Total sales of U.S. dollars: 2.25**
	U.S. balance of payments on current account: −1.0 (down 0.5)	**U.S. balance of payments on financial account: +1.0 (up 0.5)**	

Let's briefly run this process in reverse. Suppose there is a reduction in capital flows from Europe to the United States—again due to a change in the preferences of European investors. The demand for U.S. dollars in the foreign exchange market falls, and the dollar depreciates: the number of euros per U.S. dollar at the equilibrium exchange rate falls. This leads Americans to buy fewer European products and Europeans to buy more American products. Ultimately, this generates an increase in the U.S. balance of payments on current account. So a fall in capital flows into the United States leads to a weaker dollar, which in turn generates an increase in U.S. net exports.

Inflation and Real Exchange Rates

In 1993 one U.S. dollar exchanged, on average, for 3.1 Mexican pesos. By 2013, the peso had fallen against the dollar by more than 75%, with an average exchange rate in 2013 of 12.8 pesos per dollar. Did Mexican products also become much cheaper relative to U.S. products over that 20-year period? Did the price of Mexican products expressed in terms of U.S. dollars also fall by 75%? The answer is no, because Mexico had much higher inflation than the United States over that period. In fact, the relative price of U.S. and Mexican products changed little between 1993 and 2013, although the exchange rate changed a lot.

To take account of the effects of differences in inflation rates, economists calculate **real exchange rates,** exchange rates adjusted for international differences in aggregate price levels. Suppose that the exchange rate we are looking at is the number of Mexican pesos per U.S. dollar. Let P_{US} and P_{Mex} be indexes of the aggregate price levels in the United States and Mexico, respectively. Then the real exchange rate between the Mexican peso and the U.S. dollar is defined as:

(34-4) Real exchange rate = Mexican pesos per U.S. dollar $\times \dfrac{P_{US}}{P_{Mex}}$

To distinguish it from the real exchange rate, the exchange rate unadjusted for aggregate price levels is sometimes called the *nominal* exchange rate.

To understand the significance of the difference between the real and nominal exchange rates, let's consider the following example. Suppose that the Mexican peso depreciates against the U.S. dollar, with the exchange rate going from 10 pesos per U.S. dollar to 15 pesos per U.S. dollar, a 50% change. But suppose that at the same time the price of everything in Mexico, measured in pesos,

Real exchange rates are exchange rates adjusted for international differences in aggregate price levels.

increases by 50%, so that the Mexican price index rises from 100 to 150. At the same time, suppose that there is no change in U.S. prices, so that the U.S. price index remains at 100. Then the initial real exchange rate is:

$$\text{Pesos per dollar before depreciation} \times \frac{P_{US}}{P_{Mex}} = 10 \times \frac{100}{100} = 10$$

After the peso depreciates and the Mexican price level increases, the real exchange rate is:

$$\text{Pesos per dollar after depreciation} \times \frac{P_{US}}{P_{Mex}} = 15 \times \frac{100}{150} = 10$$

In this example, the peso has depreciated substantially in terms of the U.S. dollar, but the *real* exchange rate between the peso and the U.S. dollar hasn't changed at all. And because the real peso–U.S. dollar exchange rate hasn't changed, the nominal depreciation of the peso against the U.S. dollar will have no effect either on the quantity of goods and services exported by Mexico to the United States or on the quantity of goods and services imported by Mexico from the United States.

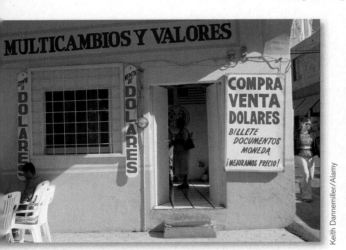

It's the real exchange rate, not the nominal exchange rate, that counts in decisions about buying and selling abroad.

To see why, consider again the example of a hotel room. Suppose that this room initially costs 1,000 pesos per night, which is $100 at an exchange rate of 10 pesos per dollar. After both Mexican prices and the number of pesos per dollar rise by 50%, the hotel room costs 1,500 pesos per night—but 1,500 pesos divided by 15 pesos per dollar is $100, so the Mexican hotel room still costs $100. As a result, a U.S. tourist considering a trip to Mexico will have no reason to change plans.

The same is true for all goods and services that enter into trade: *the current account responds only to changes in the real exchange rate, not the nominal exchange rate.* A country's products become cheaper to foreigners only when that country's currency depreciates in real terms, and those products become more expensive to foreigners only when the currency appreciates in real terms. As a consequence, economists who analyze movements in exports and imports of goods and services focus on the real exchange rate, not the nominal exchange rate.

Figure 34-7 illustrates just how important it can be to distinguish between nominal and real exchange rates. The line labeled "Nominal exchange rate"

FIGURE 34-7 Real Versus Nominal Exchange Rates, 1993–2013

Between November 1993 and December 2013, the price of a dollar in Mexican pesos increased dramatically. But because Mexico had higher inflation than the United States, the real exchange rate, which measures the relative price of Mexican goods and services, ended up roughly where it started.

Source: Federal Reserve Bank of St. Louis.

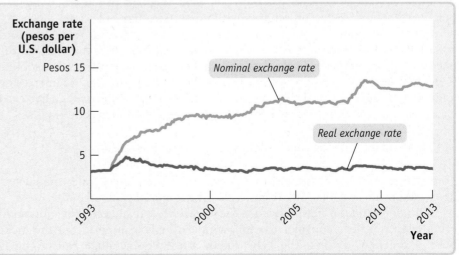

shows the number of pesos it took to buy a U.S. dollar from 1993 to 2013. As you can see, the peso depreciated massively over that period. But the line labeled "Real exchange rate" shows the real exchange rate: it was calculated using Equation 34-4, with price indexes for both Mexico and the United States set so that 1993 = 100. In real terms, the peso depreciated between 1994 and 1995, but not by nearly as much as the nominal depreciation. By 2013, the real peso–U.S. dollar exchange rate was just about back where it started.

Purchasing Power Parity

A useful tool for analyzing exchange rates, closely connected to the concept of the real exchange rate, is known as *purchasing power parity*. The **purchasing power parity** between two countries' currencies is the nominal exchange rate at which a given basket of goods and services would cost the same amount in each country. Suppose, for example, that a basket of goods and services that costs $100 in the United States costs 1,000 pesos in Mexico. Then the purchasing power parity is 10 pesos per U.S. dollar: at that exchange rate, 1,000 pesos = $100, so the market basket costs the same amount in both countries.

Calculations of purchasing power parities are usually made by estimating the cost of buying broad market baskets containing many goods and services—everything from automobiles and groceries to housing and telephone calls. But as the following For Inquiring Minds explains, once a year the magazine *The Economist* publishes a list of purchasing power parities based on the cost of buying a market basket that contains only one item—a McDonald's Big Mac.

Nominal exchange rates almost always differ from purchasing power parities. Some of these differences are systematic: in general, aggregate price levels are

The **purchasing power parity** between two countries' currencies is the nominal exchange rate at which a given basket of goods and services would cost the same amount in each country.

FOR INQUIRING MINDS | Burgernomics

For a number of years the British magazine *The Economist* has produced an annual comparison of the cost in different countries of one particular consumption item that is found around the world—a McDonald's Big Mac. The magazine finds the price of a Big Mac in local currency, then computes two numbers: the price of a Big Mac in U.S. dollars using the prevailing exchange rate and the exchange rate at which the price of a Big Mac would equal the U.S. price. If purchasing power parity held for Big Macs, the dollar price of a Big Mac would be the same everywhere. If purchasing power parity is a good theory for the long run, the exchange rate at which a Big Mac's price matches the U.S. price should offer some guidance about where the exchange rate will eventually end up.

Table 34-6 shows the *Economist* estimates for selected countries as of July 2014, ranked in increasing order of the dollar price of a Big Mac. The countries with the cheapest Big Macs, and therefore by this measure with the

most undervalued currencies, are India and China, both developing countries. But not all developing countries have low-priced Big Macs: the price of a Big Mac in Brazil, converted into dollars, is considerably higher than in the United States. This reflects a sharp appreciation of the *real*, Brazil's currency, in recent years as the country

has become a favorite of international investors.

And topping the list, with a Big Mac some 75% more expensive than in the United States, is Switzerland—the nation that, as we described in this chapter's opening story, took extraordinary action later in 2011 in an effort to depreciate its currency.

TABLE 34-6 Purchasing Power Parity and the Price of a Big Mac

Country	Big Mac price		Local currency per dollar	
	In local currency	In U.S. dollars	Implied PPP	Actual exchange rate
India	Rupee 105	1.75	21.90	60.09
China	Yuan 16.9	2.73	3.52	6.20
Mexico	Peso 42	3.25	8.76	12.93
Britain	£ 2.89	4.93	0.60	0.59
United States	$4.80	4.80	1.00	1.00
Japan	¥ 370	3.64	77.16	101.53
Euro area	€ 3.68	4.95	0.77	0.74
Brazil	Real 13	5.86	2.71	2.22
Switzerland	SFr 6.16	6.83	1.28	0.90

| FIGURE **34-8** | Purchasing Power Parity versus the Nominal Exchange Rate, 1990–2013 |

The purchasing power parity between the United States and Canada—the exchange rate at which a basket of goods and services would have cost the same amount in both countries—changed very little over the period shown, staying near C$1.20 per US$1. But the nominal exchange rate fluctuated widely.
Source: OECD.

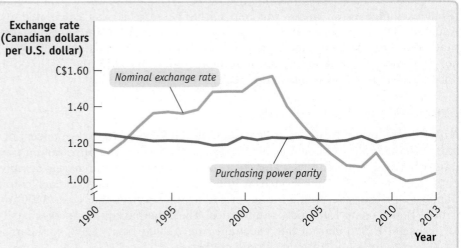

lower in poor countries than in rich countries because services tend to be cheaper in poor countries. But even among countries at roughly the same level of economic development, nominal exchange rates vary quite a lot from purchasing power parity. Figure 34-8 shows the nominal exchange rate between the Canadian dollar and the U.S. dollar, measured as the number of Canadian dollars per U.S. dollar, from 1990 to 2013, together with an estimate of the purchasing power parity exchange rate between the United States and Canada over the same period.

The purchasing power parity didn't change much over the whole period because the United States and Canada had about the same rate of inflation. But at the beginning of the period the nominal exchange rate was below purchasing power parity, so a given market basket was more expensive in Canada than in the United States. By 2002 the nominal exchange rate was far above the purchasing power parity, so a market basket was much cheaper in Canada than in the United States.

Over the long run, however, purchasing power parities are pretty good at predicting actual changes in nominal exchange rates. In particular, nominal exchange rates between countries at similar levels of economic development tend to fluctuate around levels that lead to similar costs for a given market basket. In fact, by July 2005 the nominal exchange rate between the United States and Canada was C$1.22 per US$1—just about the purchasing power parity. And by 2013 the cost of living was once again higher in Canada than in the United States.

ECONOMICS ▶ in Action

Low-Cost America

Does the exchange rate matter for business decisions? And how. Consider what European auto manufacturers were doing in 2008. One report from the University of Iowa summarized the situation as follows:

While luxury German carmakers BMW and Mercedes have maintained plants in the American South since the 1990s, BMW aims to expand U.S. manufacturing in South Carolina by 50% during the next 5 years. Volvo of Sweden is in negotiations to build a plant in New Mexico. Analysts at Italian carmaker Fiat determined that it needs to build a North American factory to profit from the upcoming relaunch of its Alfa Romeo model. Tennessee recently closed a deal with Volkswagen to build a $1 billion factory by offering $577 million in incentives.

Why were European automakers flocking to America? To some extent because they were being offered special incentives, as the case of Volkswagen in Tennessee illustrates. But the big factor was the exchange rate. In the early 2000s one euro was, on average, worth less than a dollar; by the summer of 2008 the exchange rate was around €1 = $1.50. This change in the exchange rate made it substantially cheaper for European car manufacturers to produce in the United States than at home—especially if the cars were intended for the U.S. market.

Automobile manufacturing wasn't the only U.S. industry benefiting from the weak dollar; across the board, U.S. exports surged after 2006 while import growth fell off. Figure 34-9 shows one measure of U.S. trade performance, real net exports of goods and services: exports minus imports, both measured in 2009 dollars. As you can see, this balance, after a long slide, turned sharply upward in 2006. There was a modest reversal in 2009–2010, as an economy recovering from the 2007–2009 recession pulled in more imports, but a major narrowing of the trade gap remained in place.

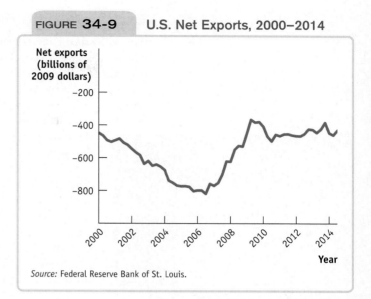

FIGURE **34-9**   U.S. Net Exports, 2000–2014

Source: Federal Reserve Bank of St. Louis.

Check Your Understanding 34-2

1. Mexico discovers huge reserves of oil and starts exporting oil to the United States. Describe how this would affect the following.
   a. The nominal peso–U.S. dollar exchange rate
   b. Mexican exports of other goods and services
   c. Mexican imports of goods and services

2. A basket of goods and services that costs $100 in the United States costs 800 pesos in Mexico, and the current nominal exchange rate is 10 pesos per U.S. dollar. Over the next five years, the cost of that market basket rises to $120 in the United States and to 1,200 pesos in Mexico, although the nominal exchange rate remains at 10 pesos per U.S. dollar. Calculate the following.
   a. The real exchange rate now and five years from now, if today's price index in both countries is 100
   b. Purchasing power parity today and five years from now

Solutions appear at back of book.

Exchange Rate Policy

The nominal exchange rate, like other prices, is determined by supply and demand. Unlike the price of wheat or oil, however, the exchange rate is the price of a country's money (in terms of another country's money). Money isn't a good or service produced by the private sector; it's an asset whose quantity is determined by government policy. As a result, governments have much more power to influence nominal exchange rates than they have to influence ordinary prices.

The nominal exchange rate is a very important price for many countries: the exchange rate determines the price of imports and the price of exports; in economies where exports and imports are large percentages of GDP, movements in the exchange rate can have major effects on aggregate output and the aggregate price level. What do governments do with their power to influence this important price?

The answer is, it depends. At different times and in different places, governments have adopted a variety of *exchange rate regimes*. Let's talk about these regimes, how they are enforced, and how governments choose a regime. (From now on, we'll adopt the convention that we mean the nominal exchange rate when we refer to the exchange rate.)

Exchange Rate Regimes

An **exchange rate regime** is a rule governing policy toward the exchange rate. There are two main kinds of exchange rate regimes. A country has a **fixed exchange rate** when the government keeps the exchange rate against some other currency at or near a particular target. For example, Hong Kong has an official policy of setting an exchange rate of HK$7.80 per US$1. In contrast, a country has a **floating exchange rate** when the government lets market forces determine the exchange rate. This is the policy followed by Britain, Canada, and the United States.

Fixed exchange rates and floating exchange rates aren't the only possibilities. At various times, countries have adopted compromise policies that lie somewhere between fixed and floating exchange rates. These include exchange rates that are fixed at any given time but are adjusted frequently, exchange rates that aren't fixed but are "managed" by the government to avoid wide swings, and exchange rates that float within a "target zone" but are prevented from leaving that zone. In this book, however, we'll focus on the two main exchange rate regimes.

The immediate dilemma posed by a fixed exchange rate is how a government can fix the exchange rate when the exchange rate is determined by supply and demand.

Exchange rates play a very important role in the global economy.

How Can an Exchange Rate Be Held Fixed?

To understand how it is possible for a country to fix its exchange rate, let's consider a hypothetical country, Genovia, which for some reason has decided to fix the value of its currency, the geno, at US$1.50.

The obvious problem is that $1.50 may not be the equilibrium exchange rate in the foreign exchange market: the equilibrium rate may be either higher or lower than the target exchange rate. Figure 34-10 shows the foreign exchange market for genos, with the quantities of genos supplied and demanded on the horizontal axis and the exchange rate of the geno, measured in U.S. dollars per geno, on the vertical axis. Panel (a) shows the case in which the equilibrium value of the geno is *below* the target exchange rate. Panel (b) shows the case in which the equilibrium value of the geno is *above* the target exchange rate.

Consider first the case in which the equilibrium value of the geno is below the target exchange rate. As panel (a) shows, at the target exchange rate of $1.50 per geno, there is a surplus of genos in the foreign exchange market, which would normally push the value of the geno down. How can the Genovian government support the value of the geno to keep the rate where it wants? There are three possible answers, all of which have been used by governments at some point.

One way the Genovian government can support the geno is to "soak up" the surplus of genos by buying its own currency in the foreign exchange market. A government purchase or sale of currency in the foreign exchange market is called an **exchange market intervention.** To buy genos in the foreign exchange market, of course, the Genovian government must have U.S. dollars to exchange for genos. In fact, most countries maintain **foreign exchange reserves,** stocks of foreign currency (usually U.S. dollars or euros) that they can use to buy their own currency to support its price.

We mentioned earlier in the chapter that an important part of international capital flows is the result of purchases and sales of foreign assets by governments and central banks. Now we can see why governments sell foreign assets: they are supporting their currency through exchange market intervention. As we'll see in a moment, governments that keep the value of their currency *down* through exchange market intervention must *buy* foreign assets. First, however, let's talk about the other ways governments fix exchange rates.

An **exchange rate regime** is a rule governing policy toward the exchange rate.

A country has a **fixed exchange rate** when the government keeps the exchange rate against some other currency at or near a particular target.

A country has a **floating exchange rate** when the government lets market forces determine the exchange rate.

A government purchase or sale of currency in the foreign exchange market is an **exchange market intervention.**

Foreign exchange reserves are stocks of foreign currency that governments maintain to buy their own currency on the foreign exchange market.

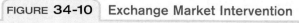

FIGURE **34-10**   Exchange Market Intervention

In both panels, the imaginary country of Genovia is trying to keep the exchange rate of the geno fixed at US$1.50 per geno. In panel (a), the equilibrium exchange rate is below $1.50, leading to a surplus of genos on the foreign exchange market. To keep the geno from falling below $1.50, the Genovian government can buy genos and sell U.S. dollars. In panel (b), the equilibrium exchange rate is above $1.50, leading to a shortage of genos on the foreign exchange market. To keep the geno from rising above $1.50, the Genovian government can sell genos and buy U.S. dollars.

A second way for the Genovian government to support the geno is to try to shift the supply and demand curves for the geno in the foreign exchange market. Governments usually do this by changing monetary policy. For example, to support the geno the Genovian central bank can raise the Genovian interest rate. This will increase capital flows into Genovia, increasing the demand for genos, at the same time that it reduces capital flows out of Genovia, reducing the supply of genos. So, other things equal, an increase in a country's interest rate will increase the value of its currency.

Third, the Genovian government can support the geno by reducing the supply of genos to the foreign exchange market. It can do this by requiring domestic residents who want to buy foreign currency to get a license and giving these licenses only to people engaging in approved transactions (such as the purchase of imported goods the Genovian government thinks are essential). Licensing systems that limit the right of individuals to buy foreign currency are called **foreign exchange controls.** Other things equal, foreign exchange controls increase the value of a country's currency.

So far we've been discussing a situation in which the government is trying to prevent a depreciation of the geno. Suppose, instead, that the situation is as shown in panel (b) of Figure 34-10, where the equilibrium value of the geno is *above* the target exchange rate of $1.50 per geno and there is a shortage of genos. To maintain the target exchange rate, the Genovian government can apply the same three basic options in the reverse direction. It can intervene in the foreign exchange market, in this case *selling* genos and acquiring U.S. dollars, which it can add to its foreign exchange reserves. It can *reduce* interest rates to increase the supply of genos and reduce the demand. Or it can impose foreign exchange controls that limit the ability of foreigners to buy genos. All of these actions, other things equal, will reduce the value of the geno.

As we said, all three techniques have been used to manage fixed exchange rates. But we haven't said whether fixing the exchange rate is a good idea. In fact, the choice of exchange rate regime poses a dilemma for policy makers, because fixed and floating exchange rates each have both advantages and disadvantages.

Foreign exchange controls are licensing systems that limit the right of individuals to buy foreign currency.

The Exchange Rate Regime Dilemma

Few questions in macroeconomics produce as many arguments as that of whether a country should adopt a fixed or a floating exchange rate. The reason there are so many arguments is that both sides have a case.

To understand the case for a fixed exchange rate, consider for a moment how easy it is to conduct business across state lines in the United States. There are a number of things that make interstate commerce trouble-free, but one of them is the absence of any uncertainty about the value of money: a dollar is a dollar, in both New York City and Los Angeles.

By contrast, a dollar isn't a dollar in transactions between New York City and Toronto. The exchange rate between the Canadian dollar and the U.S. dollar fluctuates, sometimes widely. If a U.S. firm promises to pay a Canadian firm a given number of U.S. dollars a year from now, the value of that promise in Canadian

FOR INQUIRING MINDS | From Bretton Woods to the Euro

In 1944, while World War II was still raging, representatives of Allied nations met in Bretton Woods, New Hampshire, to establish a postwar international monetary system of fixed exchange rates among major currencies. The system was highly successful at first, but it broke down in 1971. After a confusing interval during which policy makers tried unsuccessfully to establish a new fixed exchange rate system, by 1973 most economically advanced countries had moved to floating exchange rates.

In Europe, however, many policy makers were unhappy with floating exchange rates, which they believed created too much uncertainty for business. From the late 1970s onward they tried several times to create a system of more or less fixed exchange rates in Europe, culminating in an arrangement known as the Exchange Rate Mechanism. (The Exchange Rate Mechanism was, strictly speaking, a "target zone" system—European exchange rates were free to move within a narrow band, but not outside it.) And in 1991 they agreed to move to the ultimate in fixed exchange rates: a common European currency, the euro. To the surprise of many analysts, they pulled it off: today most of Europe has abandoned national currencies for the euro.

Figure 34-11 illustrates the history of European exchange rate arrangements. It shows the exchange rate between the French franc and the German mark, measured as francs per mark, from 1971 until their replacement by the euro. The exchange rate fluctuated widely at first. The plateaus you can see in the data—eras when the exchange rate

fluctuated only modestly—are periods when attempts to restore fixed exchange rates were in process. The Exchange Rate Mechanism, after a couple of false starts, became effective in 1987, stabilizing the exchange rate at about 3.4 francs per mark. (The wobbles in the early 1990s reflect two *currency crises*—episodes in which widespread expectations of imminent devaluations led to large but temporary capital flows.)

In 1999 the exchange rate was *locked*—no further fluctuations were allowed as the countries prepared to switch from francs and marks to the euro. At the end of 2001, the franc and the mark ceased to exist.

The transition to the euro has not been without costs. Countries that adopted the euro sacrificed some important policy tools: they could no longer tailor monetary policy to their specific economic circumstances, and they could no longer lower their costs relative to other European nations simply by letting their currencies depreciate.

At the time this book went to press, the euro area was under serious stress, with several nations—including Greece, Spain, and Italy, three big economies—facing widespread skepticism about their ability to make needed economic adjustments without defaulting on their debts and abandoning the euro.

FIGURE **34-11** The Road to the Euro

Source: Federal Reserve Bank of St. Louis.

currency can vary by 10% or more. This uncertainty has the effect of deterring trade between the two countries. So one benefit of a fixed exchange rate is certainty about the future value of a currency.

There is also, in some cases, an additional benefit to adopting a fixed exchange rate: by committing itself to a fixed rate, a country is also committing itself not to engage in inflationary policies. For example, in 1991 Argentina, which has a long history of irresponsible policies leading to severe inflation, adopted a fixed exchange rate of US$1 per Argentine peso in an attempt to commit itself to non-inflationary policies in the future. (Argentina's fixed exchange rate regime collapsed disastrously in late 2001. But that's another story.)

The point is that there is some economic value in having a stable exchange rate. Indeed, as the previous For Inquiring Minds explains, the presumed benefits of stable exchange rates motivated the international system of fixed exchange rates created after World War II. It was also a major reason for the creation of the euro.

However, there are also costs to fixing the exchange rate. To stabilize an exchange rate through intervention, a country must keep large quantities of foreign currency on hand—usually a low-return investment. Furthermore, even large reserves can be quickly exhausted when there are large capital flows out of a country. If a country chooses to stabilize an exchange rate by adjusting monetary policy rather than through intervention, it must divert monetary policy from other goals, notably stabilizing the economy and managing the inflation rate. Finally, foreign exchange controls, like import quotas and tariffs, distort incentives for importing and exporting goods and services. They can also create substantial costs in terms of red tape and corruption.

So there's a dilemma. Should a country let its currency float, which leaves monetary policy available for macroeconomic stabilization but creates uncertainty for business? Or should it fix the exchange rate, which eliminates the uncertainty but means giving up monetary policy, adopting exchange controls, or both? Different countries reach different conclusions at different times. Most European countries, except for Britain, have long believed that exchange rates among major European economies, which do most of their international trade with each other, should be fixed. But Canada seems happy with a floating exchange rate with the United States, even though the United States accounts for most of Canada's trade.

Fortunately we don't have to resolve this dilemma. For the rest of the chapter, we'll take exchange rate regimes as given and ask how they affect macroeconomic policy.

ECONOMICS ▶ *in Action*

China Pegs the Yuan

In the early years of the twenty-first century, China provided a striking example of the lengths to which countries sometimes go to maintain a fixed exchange rate. Here's the background: China's spectacular success as an exporter led to a rising surplus on current account. At the same time, non-Chinese private investors became increasingly eager to shift funds into China, to invest in its growing domestic economy. These capital flows were somewhat limited by foreign exchange controls—but kept coming in anyway. As a result of the current account surplus and private capital inflows, China found itself in the position described by panel (b) of Figure 34-10: at the target exchange rate, the demand for yuan exceeded the supply. Yet the Chinese government was determined to keep the exchange rate fixed at a value below its equilibrium level.

China provides a striking example of the lengths to which countries sometimes go to maintain a fixed exchange rate.

AFP/Getty Images

To keep the rate fixed, China had to engage in large-scale exchange market intervention, selling yuan, buying up other countries' currencies (mainly U.S. dollars) on the foreign exchange market, and adding them to its reserves. In 2010, China added $450 billion to its foreign exchange reserves, and by the summer of 2011, those reserves had risen to $3.2 trillion.

To get a sense of how big these totals are, in 2010 China's GDP was approximately $5.9 trillion. This means that in 2010 China bought U.S. dollars and other currencies equal to about 7.5% of its GDP, making its accumulated reserves equal to more than half its GDP. That's as if the U.S. government had bought well over $1 trillion worth of yen and euros in a single year, even though it was already sitting on an $8 trillion pile of foreign currencies. Not surprisingly, China's exchange rate policy led to some friction with its trading partners, who felt that it had the effect of subsidizing Chinese exports.

Over the next few years, however, China's current account surplus dwindled. Partly this reflected rising Chinese wages, which made China less competitive, and partly it reflected the rise of new competitors, like Vietnam. At the time of writing, friction over China's exchange rate policy was greatly diminished.

Check Your Understanding 34-3

1. Draw a diagram, similar to Figure 34-10, representing the foreign exchange situation of China when it kept the exchange rate fixed. (*Hint:* Express the exchange rate as U.S. dollars per yuan.) Then show with a diagram how each of the following policy changes might eliminate the disequilibrium in the market.
   a. An appreciation of the yuan
   b. Placing restrictions on foreigners who want to invest in China
   c. Removing restrictions on Chinese who want to invest abroad
   d. Imposing taxes on Chinese exports, such as shipments of clothing, that are causing a political backlash in the importing countries

Solutions appear at back of book.

Exchange Rates and Macroeconomic Policy

When the euro was created in 1999, there were celebrations across the nations of Europe—with a few notable exceptions. You see, some countries chose not to adopt the new currency. The most important of these was Britain, but other European countries, such as Sweden, also decided that the euro was not for them.

Why did Britain say no? Part of the answer was national pride: if Britain gave up the pound, it would also have to give up currency that bears the portrait of the queen. But there were also serious economic concerns about giving up the pound in favor of the euro. British economists who favored adoption of the euro argued that if Britain used the same currency as its neighbors, the country's international trade would expand and its economy would become more productive. But other economists pointed out that adopting the euro would take away Britain's ability to have an independent monetary policy and might lead to macroeconomic problems.

As this discussion suggests, the fact that modern economies are open to international trade and capital flows adds a new level of complication to our analysis of macroeconomic policy. Let's look at three policy issues raised by open-economy macroeconomics.

1. Devaluation and Revaluation of Fixed Exchange Rates

Historically, fixed exchange rates haven't been permanent commitments. Sometimes countries with a fixed exchange rate switch to a floating rate. In other cases, they retain a fixed rate but change the target exchange rate. Such adjustments in the target were common during the Bretton Woods era described in the preceding For Inquiring Minds. For example, in 1967 Britain changed the exchange rate of the pound against the U.S. dollar from US$2.80 per £1 to US$2.40 per £1. A modern example is Argentina, which maintained a fixed exchange rate against the dollar from 1991 to 2001 but switched to a floating exchange rate at the end of 2001.

A reduction in the value of a currency that is set under a fixed exchange rate regime is called a **devaluation.** As we've already learned, a *depreciation* is a downward move in a currency. A devaluation is a depreciation that is due to a revision in a fixed exchange rate target. An increase in the value of a currency that is set under a fixed exchange rate regime is called a **revaluation.**

A devaluation, like any depreciation, makes domestic goods cheaper in terms of foreign currency, which leads to higher exports. At the same time, it makes foreign goods more expensive in terms of domestic currency, which reduces imports. The effect is to increase the balance of payments on current account. Similarly, a revaluation makes domestic goods more expensive in terms of foreign currency, which reduces exports, and makes foreign goods cheaper in domestic currency, which increases imports. So a revaluation reduces the balance of payments on current account.

Devaluations and revaluations serve two purposes under fixed exchange rates. First, they can be used to eliminate shortages or surpluses in the foreign exchange market. For example, in 2010 some economists and politicians were urging China to revalue the yuan because they believed that China's exchange rate policy unfairly aided Chinese exports.

Second, devaluation and revaluation can be used as tools of macroeconomic policy. A devaluation, by increasing exports and reducing imports, increases aggregate demand. So a devaluation can be used to reduce or eliminate a recessionary gap. A revaluation has the opposite effect, reducing aggregate demand. So a revaluation can be used to reduce or eliminate an inflationary gap.

> A **devaluation** is a reduction in the value of a currency that is set under a fixed exchange rate regime.
>
> A **revaluation** is an increase in the value of a currency that is set under a fixed exchange rate regime.

2. Monetary Policy Under Floating Exchange Rates

Under a floating exchange rate regime, a country's central bank retains its ability to pursue independent monetary policy: it can increase aggregate demand by cutting the interest rate or decrease aggregate demand by raising the interest rate. But the exchange rate adds another dimension to the effects of monetary policy. To see why, let's return to the hypothetical country of Genovia and ask what happens if the central bank cuts the interest rate.

Just as in a closed economy, a lower interest rate leads to higher investment spending and higher consumer spending. But the decline in the interest rate also affects the foreign exchange market. Foreigners have less incentive to move funds into Genovia because they will receive a lower interest rate on their loans. As a result, they have less need to exchange U.S. dollars for genos, so the demand for genos falls. At the same time, Genovians have *more* incentive to move funds abroad because the interest rate on loans at home has fallen, making investments outside the country more attractive. As a result, they need to exchange more genos for U.S. dollars, so the supply of genos rises.

Figure 34-12 shows the effect of an interest rate reduction on the foreign exchange market. The demand curve for genos shifts leftward, from D_1 to D_2, and the supply curve shifts rightward, from S_1 to S_2. The equilibrium exchange rate, as measured in U.S. dollars per geno, falls from XR_1 to XR_2. That is, a reduction in the Genovian interest rate causes the geno to *depreciate.*

The depreciation of the geno, in turn, affects aggregate demand. We've already seen that a devaluation—a depreciation that is the result of a change in a fixed exchange rate—increases exports and reduces imports, thereby increasing aggregate demand. A depreciation that results from an interest rate cut has the same effect: it increases exports and reduces imports, increasing aggregate demand.

FIGURE 34-12 Monetary Policy and the Exchange Rate

Here we show what happens in the foreign exchange market if Genovia cuts its interest rate. Residents of Genovia have a reduced incentive to keep their funds at home, so they invest more abroad. As a result, the supply of genos shifts rightward, from S_1 to S_2. Meanwhile, foreigners have less incentive to put funds into Genovia, so the demand for genos shifts leftward, from D_1 to D_2. The geno depreciates: the equilibrium exchange rate falls from XR_1 to XR_2.

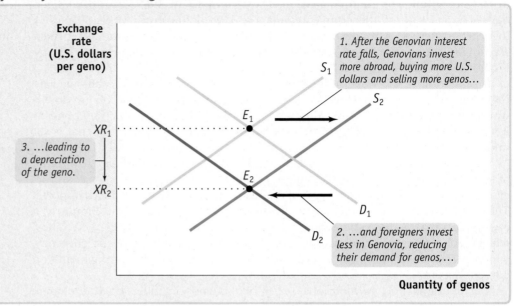

1. After the Genovian interest rate falls, Genovians invest more abroad, buying more U.S. dollars and selling more genos...

2. ...and foreigners invest less in Genovia, reducing their demand for genos,...

3. ...leading to a depreciation of the geno.

In other words, monetary policy under floating rates has effects beyond those we've described in looking at closed economies. In a closed economy, a reduction in the interest rate leads to a rise in aggregate demand because it leads to more investment spending and consumer spending. In an open economy with a floating exchange rate, the interest rate reduction leads to increased investment spending and consumer spending, but it also increases aggregate demand in another way: it leads to a currency depreciation, which increases exports and reduces imports, and further increases aggregate demand.

3. International Business Cycles

Up to this point, we have discussed macroeconomics, even in an open economy, as if all demand shocks originate from the domestic economy. In reality, however, economies sometimes face shocks coming from abroad. For example, recessions in the United States have historically led to recessions in Mexico.

The key point is that changes in aggregate demand affect the demand for goods and services produced abroad as well as at home: other things equal, a recession leads to a fall in imports and an expansion leads to a rise in imports. And one country's imports are another country's exports. This link between aggregate demand in different national economies is one reason business cycles in different countries sometimes—but not always—seem to be synchronized. The prime example is the Great Depression, which affected countries around the world.

The extent of this link depends, however, on the exchange rate regime. To see why, think about what happens if a recession abroad reduces the demand for Genovia's exports. A reduction in foreign demand for Genovian goods and services is also a reduction in demand for genos in the foreign exchange market. If Genovia has a fixed exchange rate, it responds to this decline with exchange market intervention. But if Genovia has a floating exchange rate, the geno depreciates. Because Genovian goods and services become cheaper to foreigners when the demand for exports falls, the quantity of goods and services exported doesn't fall by as much as it would under a fixed rate. At the same time, the fall in the geno makes imports more expensive to Genovians, leading to a fall in imports. Both effects limit the decline in Genovia's aggregate demand compared to what it would have been under a fixed exchange rate.

One of the virtues of a floating exchange rate, according to advocates of such exchange rates, is that they help insulate countries from recessions originating abroad. This theory looked pretty good in the early 2000s: Britain, with a floating exchange rate, managed to stay out of a recession that affected the rest of Europe, and Canada, which also has a floating rate, suffered a less severe recession than the United States.

In 2008, however, a financial crisis that began in the United States led to a recession in virtually every country. In this case, it appears that the international linkages among financial markets were much stronger than any insulation from overseas disturbances provided by floating exchange rates.

ECONOMICS ▶ *in Action*

The Little Currency That Could

In 2008 Iceland—population around 325,000—was a tiny country with a very big economic problem. Between 2003 and 2007 the country's main banks expanded very aggressively, mainly with money borrowed from banks in other countries, and the banking boom led in turn to a booming local economy. But then the boom went bust, as did the banks, and Iceland needed to go back to more mundane ways of making a living, like fishing and tourism. To do this it needed to reduce costs, mainly by cutting wages. It wasn't the only country in this position; other nations that had borrowed a lot of money, like Greece, also needed to make big adjustments.

But there was one big difference between Iceland and Greece (aside from the weather): Greece no longer had its own currency, because it had adopted the euro, whereas Iceland, tiny though it was, still had its own currency, the krona (plural kronur)—and Icelandic wages are set in kronur, not euros or dollars.

This meant that the process of cutting wages was very different in Iceland than it was in euro-using countries. In Greece, employers actually had to tell workers that they would be paid less—something companies are reluctant to do, because at best it creates bad feelings and at worst leads to strikes. Iceland, however, could gain competitiveness without wage cuts, simply by letting the krona fall.

Figure 34-13 shows how the different options played out. One line shows average wages in the euro area as a whole, with 2007 = 100, while another line shows Greek wages over the same period. As you can see, Greece did manage to cut wages gradually over time while wages in other European nations rose, so the Greek economy gradually became more competitive. It was, however, a slow and extremely painful process.

The other two lines show Iceland's story. One line shows wages in kronur—that is, in Iceland's own currency. These continued to rise; there were no nominal wage cuts. The other shows Icelandic wages in euros, which fell dramatically thanks to the depreciation of the krona. It would be wrong to say that this process was painless—Icelandic workers saw the prices of imported goods rise, reducing their purchasing power. But it wasn't nearly as painful as Greece's adjustment. In Greece, unemployment rose year after year, peaking at 28% in late 2013 before it began inching down. In Iceland, by contrast, the jobs crisis only lasted about two years, and by late 2014 the unemployment rate was under 5%.

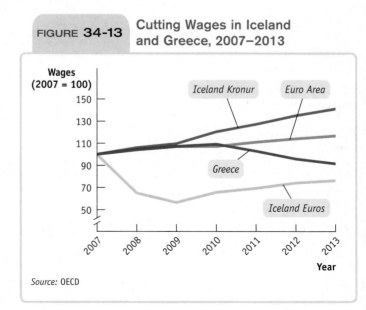

FIGURE 34-13 Cutting Wages in Iceland and Greece, 2007–2013

Source: OECD

● Countries can change fixed exchange rates. **Devaluation** or **revaluation** can help reduce surpluses or shortages in the foreign exchange market and can increase or reduce aggregate demand.

● In an open economy with a floating exchange rate, interest rates also affect the exchange rate, and so monetary policy affects aggregate demand through the effects of the exchange rate on imports and exports.

● Because one country's imports are another country's exports, business cycles are sometimes synchronized across countries. However, floating exchange rates may reduce this link.

Overall, Iceland's experience was an object lesson in the advantages of having your own currency—even, in some cases, when your country is no bigger than a medium-sized American town.

Check Your Understanding   34-4

1. Look at the data in Figure 34-11. Where do you see devaluations and revaluations of the franc against the mark?

2. In the late 1980s Canadian economists argued that the high interest rate policies of the Bank of Canada weren't just causing high unemployment—they were also making it hard for Canadian manufacturers to compete with the United States. Explain this complaint, using our analysis of how monetary policy works under floating exchange rates.

Solutions appear at back of book.

A Yen for Japanese Cars

At the end of 2012 Shinzo Abe, a veteran politician, became prime minister of Japan. He surprised most observers by seeking radical changes in Japan's economic policy. With Japanese inflation running at a slightly negative rate, he oversaw a dramatic easing of monetary policy. The Bank of Japan greatly increased the monetary base and assured investors that it would do whatever it took to raise inflation to 2%. Two years later, the overall results of this policy were still uncertain, but one effect was a much weaker yen. For most of 2012 the yen traded at around 80 per dollar, but by late 2014 the exchange rate was around 115 yen per dollar, a 44% depreciation.

The weaker yen, in turn, made some Japanese businesses happy—especially Japanese auto companies, who sell many of their vehicles in overseas markets. There were many headlines like these: "Weak yen fuels Japan Inc." in the *Financial Times* (reporting on Toyota), or "Subaru profit soaring as weaker yen benefits exports." "Abenomics" had definitely helped Japan's car industry.

However, the benefits weren't equally spread: while Toyota was doing fairly well, Subaru was really taking off. Why? Well, over the years Toyota has moved the majority of its production out of Japan, operating numerous plants in the United States, Mexico, Canada, and various other countries. Subaru, which is a smaller company with a more limited product range, still mainly produces in Japan.

Kazuhiro Nogi/AFP/Getty Images

So while you can argue that what's good for Japan is good for Japanese auto companies—assuming, that is, that Abenomics actually works—it's better for some Japanese auto companies than others.

QUESTIONS FOR THOUGHT

1. Why would Abenomics lead to a weaker yen?
2. Why is a weaker yen good for the profits of Japanese auto companies?
3. Why does Subaru gain more than Toyota?

SUMMARY

1. A country's **balance of payments accounts** summarize its transactions with the rest of the world. The **balance of payments on current account,** or **current account,** includes the **balance of payments on goods and services** together with balances on factor income and transfers. The **merchandise trade balance,** or **trade balance,** is a frequently cited component of the balance of payments on goods and services. The **balance of payments on financial account,** or **financial account,** measures capital flows. By definition, the balance of payments on current account plus the balance of payments on financial account is zero.

2. Capital flows respond to international differences in interest rates and other rates of return; they can be usefully analyzed using an international version of the loanable funds model, which shows how a country where the interest rate would be low in the absence of capital flows sends funds to a country where the interest rate would be high in the absence of capital flows. The underlying determinants of capital flows are international differences in savings and opportunities for investment spending.

3. Currencies are traded in the **foreign exchange market;** the prices at which they are traded are **exchange rates.** When a currency rises against another currency, it **appreciates;** when it falls, it **depreciates.** The **equilibrium exchange rate** matches the quantity of that currency supplied to the foreign exchange market to the quantity demanded.

4. To correct for international differences in inflation rates, economists calculate **real exchange rates,** which multiply the exchange rate between two countries' currencies by the ratio of the countries' price levels. The current account responds only to changes in the real exchange rate, not the nominal exchange rate. **Purchasing power parity** is the exchange rate that makes the cost of a basket of goods and services equal in two countries. While purchasing power parity and the nominal exchange rate almost always differ, purchasing power parity is a good predictor of actual changes in the nominal exchange rate.

5. Countries adopt different **exchange rate regimes,** rules governing exchange rate policy. The main types are **fixed exchange rates,** where the government takes action to keep the exchange rate at a target level, and **floating exchange rates,** where the exchange rate is free to fluctuate. Countries can fix exchange rates using **exchange market intervention,** which requires them to hold **foreign exchange reserves** that they use to buy any surplus of their currency. Alternatively, they can change domestic policies, especially monetary policy, to shift the demand and supply curves in the foreign exchange market. Finally, they can use **foreign exchange controls.**

6. Exchange rate policy poses a dilemma: there are economic payoffs to stable exchange rates, but the policies used to fix the exchange rate have costs. Exchange market intervention requires large reserves, and exchange controls distort incentives. If monetary policy is used to help fix the exchange rate, it isn't available to use for domestic policy.

7. Fixed exchange rates aren't always permanent commitments: countries with a fixed exchange rate sometimes engage in **devaluations,** reductions in the target value of the currency, or **revaluations,** increases in the target value of the currency. In addition to helping eliminate a surplus of domestic currency on the foreign exchange market, a devaluation increases aggregate demand. Similarly, a revaluation reduces shortages of domestic currency and reduces aggregate demand.

8. Under floating exchange rates, expansionary monetary policy works in part through the exchange rate: cutting domestic interest rates leads to a depreciation, and through that to higher exports and lower imports, which increases aggregate demand. Contractionary monetary policy has the reverse effect.

9. The fact that one country's imports are another country's exports creates a link between the business cycle in different countries. Floating exchange rates, however, may reduce the strength of that link.

KEY TERMS

Balance of payments accounts, p. 998
Balance of payments on current account (current account), p. 1000
Balance of payments on goods and services, p. 1000
Merchandise trade balance (trade balance), p. 1000
Balance of payments on financial account (financial account), p. 1000

Foreign exchange market, p. 1008
Exchange rates, p. 1008
Appreciation, p. 1008
Depreciation, p. 1008
Equilibrium exchange rate, p. 1009
Real exchange rate, p. 1011
Purchasing power parity, p. 1013
Exchange rate regime, p. 1016

Fixed exchange rate, p. 1016
Floating exchange rate, p. 1016
Exchange market intervention, p. 1016
Foreign exchange reserves, p. 1016
Foreign exchange controls, p. 1017
Devaluation, p. 1021
Revaluation, p. 1021

PROBLEMS

1. How would the following transactions be categorized in the U.S. balance of payments accounts? Would they be entered in the current account (as a payment to or from a foreigner) or the financial account (as a sale of assets to or purchase of assets from a foreigner)? How will the balance of payments on the current and financial accounts change?

   a. A French importer buys a case of California wine for $500.

   b. An American who works for a French company deposits her paycheck, drawn on a Paris bank, into her San Francisco bank.

   c. An American buys a bond from a Japanese company for $10,000.

   d. An American charity sends $100,000 to Africa to help local residents buy food after a harvest shortfall.

2. The accompanying diagram shows foreign-owned assets in the United States and U.S.-owned assets abroad, both as a percentage of foreign GDP. As you can see from the diagram, both increased around fivefold from 1980 to 2013.

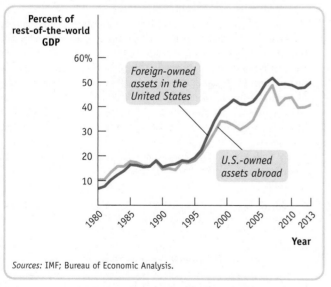

Sources: IMF; Bureau of Economic Analysis.

   a. As U.S.-owned assets abroad increased as a percentage of foreign GDP, does this mean that the United States, over the period, experienced net capital outflows?

   b. Does this diagram indicate that world economies were more tightly linked in 2013 than they were in 1980?

3. In the economy of Scottopia in 2014, exports equaled $400 billion of goods and $300 billion of services, imports equaled $500 billion of goods and $350 billion of services, and the rest of the world purchased $250 billion of Scottopia's assets. What was the merchandise trade balance for Scottopia? What was the balance of payments on current account in Scottopia? What was the balance of payments on financial account? What was the value of Scottopia's purchases of assets from the rest of the world?

4. In the economy of Popania in 2014, total Popanian purchases of assets in the rest of the world equaled $300 billion, purchases of Popanian assets by the rest of the world equaled $400 billion, and Popania exported goods and services equal to $350 billion. What was Popania's balance of payments on financial account in 2014? What was its balance of payments on current account? What was the value of its imports?

5. Suppose that Northlandia and Southlandia are the only two trading countries in the world, that each nation runs a balance of payments on both current and financial accounts equal to zero, and that each nation sees the other's assets as identical to its own. Using the accompanying diagrams, explain how the demand and supply of loanable funds, the interest rate, and the balance of payments on current and financial accounts will change in each country if international capital flows are possible.

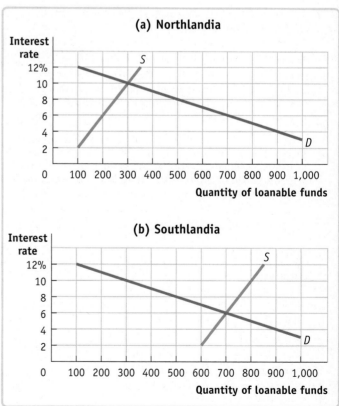

6. Based on the exchange rates for the first trading days of 2013 and 2014 shown in the accompanying table, did the U.S. dollar appreciate or depreciate during 2014? Did the movement in the value of the U.S. dollar make American goods and services more or less attractive to foreigners?

October 1, 2013	October 1, 2014
US$1.62 to buy 1 British pound sterling	US$1.62 to buy 1 British pound sterling
29.51 Taiwan dollars to buy US$1	30.43 Taiwan dollars to buy US$1
US$0.97 to buy 1 Canadian dollar	US$0.89 to buy 1 Canadian dollar
98.04 Japanese yen to buy US$1	109.31 Japanese yen to buy US$1
US$1.35 to buy 1 euro	US$1.26 to buy 1 euro
0.91 Swiss franc to buy US$1	0.96 Swiss franc to buy US$1

7. Go to http://fx.sauder.ubc.ca. Using the table labeled "The Most Recent Cross-Rates of Major Currencies," determine whether the British pound (GBP), the Canadian dollar (CAD), the Japanese yen (JPY), the euro (EUR), and the Swiss franc (CHF) have appreciated or depreciated against the U.S. dollar (USD) since October 1, 2014. The exchange rates on October 1, 2014, are listed in the table in Problem 6.

8. From January 1, 2001, to June 2003, the U.S. federal funds rate decreased from 6.5% to 1%. During the same period, the marginal lending facility rate at the European Central Bank decreased from 5.75% to 3%.

    a. Considering the change in interest rates over the period and using the loanable funds model, would you have expected funds to flow from the United States to Europe or from Europe to the United States over this period?

    b. The accompanying diagram shows the exchange rate between the euro and the U.S. dollar from January 1, 2001, through September 2008. Is the movement of the exchange rate over the period January 2001 to June 2003 consistent with the movement in funds predicted in part a?

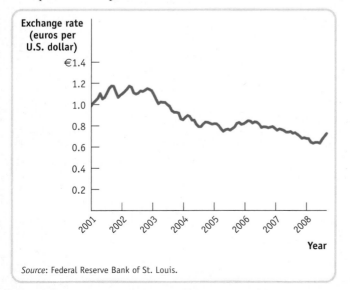

Source: Federal Reserve Bank of St. Louis.

9. In each of the following scenarios, suppose that the two nations are the only trading nations in the world. Given inflation and the change in the nominal exchange rate, which nation's goods become more attractive?

    a. Inflation is 10% in the United States and 5% in Japan; the U.S. dollar–Japanese yen exchange rate remains the same.

    b. Inflation is 3% in the United States and 8% in Mexico; the price of the U.S. dollar falls from 12.50 to 10.25 Mexican pesos.

    c. Inflation is 5% in the United States and 3% in the euro area; the price of the euro falls from $1.30 to $1.20.

    d. Inflation is 8% in the United States and 4% in Canada; the price of the Canadian dollar rises from US$0.60 to US$0.75.

10. Starting from a position of equilibrium in the foreign exchange market under a fixed exchange rate regime, how must a government react to an increase in the demand for the nation's goods and services by the rest of the world to keep the exchange rate at its fixed value?

11. Suppose that Albernia's central bank has fixed the value of its currency, the bern, to the U.S. dollar (at a rate of US$1.50 to 1 bern) and is committed to that exchange rate. Initially, the foreign exchange market for the bern is also in equilibrium, as shown in the accompanying diagram. However, both Albernians and Americans begin to believe that there are big risks in holding Albernian assets; as a result, they become unwilling to hold Albernian assets unless they receive a higher rate of return on them than they do on U.S. assets. How would this affect the diagram? If the Albernian central bank tries to keep the exchange rate fixed using monetary policy, how will this affect the Albernian economy?

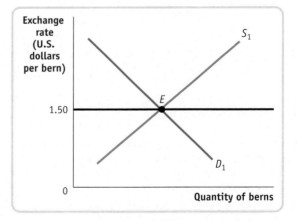

12. Your study partner asks you, "If central banks lose the ability to use discretionary monetary policy under fixed exchange rates, why would nations agree to a fixed exchange rate system?" How do you respond?

WORK IT OUT

For interactive, step-by-step help in solving the following problem, visit LaunchPad by using the URL on the back cover of this book.

13. Suppose the United States and Japan are the only two trading countries in the world. What will happen to the value of the U.S. dollar if the following occur, other things equal?

a. Japan relaxes some of its import restrictions.

b. The United States imposes some import tariffs on Japanese goods.

c. Interest rates in the United States rise dramatically.

d. A report indicates that Japanese cars last much longer than previously thought, especially compared with American cars.

Macroeconomic Data Tables

Table 1   MACROECONOMIC DATA FOR THE UNITED STATES 1929–2014
Table 2   MACROECONOMIC DATA FOR SELECT COUNTRIES
GDP (Billions of U.S. Dollars)
Table 3   MACROECONOMIC DATA FOR SELECT COUNTRIES
GDP PER PERSON (U.S. Dollars)

Table 1
MACROECONOMIC DATA FOR THE UNITED STATES 1929–2014[1]

	1929	1933	1939	1945	1950	1955	1960	1965
Nominal GDP and Its Components								
1. + Consumer spending (C)	77.4	45.9	67.2	120.0	192.2	258.7	331.6	443.6
2. + Investment spending (I)	17.2	2.3	10.2	12.4	56.5	73.8	86.5	129.6
3. + Government purchases of goods and services (G)	9.6	8.9	15.2	96.6	50.7	93.3	121.0	164.9
4. + Exports (X)	5.9	2.0	4.0	6.8	12.4	17.7	27.0	37.1
5. – Imports (IM)	5.6	1.9	3.1	7.5	11.6	17.2	22.8	31.5
6. = Gross Domestic Product (GDP)	**104.6**	**57.2**	**93.5**	**228.2**	**300.2**	**426.2**	**543.3**	**743.7**
7. + Income from abroad earned by Americans	1.1	0.4	0.7	0.8	2.2	3.5	4.9	7.9
8. – Income paid to foreigners	0.4	0.1	0.3	0.5	0.7	1.1	1.8	2.6
9. = Gross National Product (GNP)	**105.3**	**57.5**	**93.8**	**228.4**	**301.6**	**428.6**	**546.4**	**749.0**
10. National income	94.2	49.0	82.5	201.4	267.0	377.6	479.9	660.3
11. Government transfers	1.2	1.7	2.5	5.6	14.0	15.7	25.7	36.2
12. Taxes	1.7	0.8	1.5	19.4	18.9	32.9	46.1	57.7
13. Disposable income	83.5	46.4	72.1	156.3	215.0	291.7	376.5	513.2
14. Private savings	3.9	–0.4	3.9	35.2	20.0	28.2	37.8	58.3
Real GDP and Growth Measures								
15. Real GDP (billions of 2009 dollars)	1,056.6	778.3	1,163.6	2,217.8	2,184.0	2,739.0	3,108.7	3,976.7
16. Real GDP growth (percent change from previous year)	–	–1.3%	8.0%	–1.0%	8.7%	7.1%	2.6%	6.5%
17. Real GDP per capita (2009 dollars)	8,669	6,192	8,881	15,850	14,398	16,572	17,198	20,462
18. Real GDP per capita growth (percent change from previous year)	–	–1.8%	7.1%	–2.0%	6.9%	5.3%	0.5%	5.2%
Prices and Inflation								
19. Consumer Price Index (1982 – 1984 = 100)	17.2	12.9	13.9	18.0	24.1	26.8	29.6	31.5
20. CPI inflation rate	–	–5.2%	–1.3%	2.3%	1.1%	–0.3%	1.5%	1.6%
21. Producer Price Index (all commodities, 1982 = 100)	16.4	11.4	13.3	18.2	27.3	29.4	31.7	32.3
22. PPI inflation rate	–	1.8%	–2.2%	1.7%	3.8%	0.3%	0.0%	2.2%
23. GDP deflator (2009 = 100)	9.9	7.3	8.0	10.3	13.7	15.6	17.5	18.7
24. GDP deflator inflation rate	–	–2.8%	–0.9%	2.6%	1.2%	1.7%	1.4%	1.8%
Population and Employment								
25. Population (thousands)	121,878	125,690	131,028	139,928	151,684	165,275	180,760	194,347
26. Labor force (thousands)[2]	49,180	51,590	55,230	53,860	62,122	64,964	69,659	74,424
27. Unemployed (thousands)[2]	1,550	12,830	9,480	1,040	3,230	2,834	3,874	3,354
28. Unemployment rate	3.2%	24.9%	17.2%	1.9%	5.2%	4.4%	5.5%	4.5%
Government Finance and Money								
29. Federal budget balance	0.7	–2.6	–3.4	–48.7	–4.7	–4.1	0.5	–1.6
30. Budget balance (percent of GDP)	0.7%	–4.5%	–3.6%	–21.3%	–1.6%	–1.0%	0.1%	–0.2%
31. M1	–	–	–	–	–	–	140.3	163.4
32. M2	–	–	–	–	–	–	304.3	442.5
33. Federal funds (yearly average)	–	–	–	–	–	1.8%	3.2%	4.1%
International Trade								
34. Current account balance	–	–	–	–	–1.9	0.4	3.2	6.2

Sources: Bureau of Economic Analysis; Federal Bank of St. Louis; Office of Management and Budget.

1. Data in billions of current dollars unless otherwise stated. Only select dates shown for 1929 through 1965; annual data supplied for 1965 through 2014.
2. Until 1947, includes workers 14 years and older; 1948 and after, includes workers 16 years and older.

1966	1967	1968	1969	1970	1971	1972	1973	1974	1975	1976
480.6	507.4	557.4	604.5	647.7	701.0	769.4	851.1	932.0	1,032.8	1,150.2
144.2	142.7	156.9	173.6	170.1	196.8	228.1	266.9	274.5	257.3	323.2
186.4	208.1	226.8	240.4	254.2	269.3	288.2	306.4	343.1	382.9	405.8
40.9	43.5	47.9	51.9	59.7	63.0	70.8	95.3	126.7	138.7	149.5
37.1	39.9	46.6	50.5	55.8	62.3	74.2	91.2	127.5	122.7	151.1
815.0	**861.7**	**942.5**	**1,019.9**	**1,075.9**	**1,167.8**	**1,282.4**	**1,428.5**	**1,548.8**	**1,688.9**	**1,877.6**
8.1	8.7	10.1	11.8	12.8	14.0	16.3	23.5	29.8	28.0	32.4
3.0	3.3	4.0	5.7	6.4	6.4	7.7	10.9	14.3	15.0	15.5
820.1	**867.1**	**948.6**	**1,026.0**	**1,082.3**	**1,175.4**	**1,291.0**	**1,441.2**	**1,564.3**	**1,701.9**	**1,894.4**
719.7	760.2	832.1	899.5	940.1	1,017.0	1,123.0	1,257.0	1,350.8	1,451.1	1,614.8
39.6	48.0	56.1	62.3	74.7	88.1	97.9	112.6	133.3	170.0	184.0
66.4	73.0	87.0	104.5	103.1	101.7	123.6	132.4	151.0	147.6	172.3
554.2	592.8	643.8	695.8	761.5	830.4	899.9	1,006.1	1,098.3	1,219.3	1,325.8
61.4	72.2	72.1	75.0	96.1	110.1	109.2	131.8	141.7	159.0	147.3
4,238.9	4,355.2	4,569.0	4,712.5	4,722.0	4,877.6	5,134.3	5,424.1	5,396.0	5,385.4	5,675.4
6.6%	2.7%	4.9%	3.1%	0.2%	3.3%	5.3%	5.6%	−0.5%	−0.2%	5.4%
21,561	21,913	22,760	23,245	23,024	23,485	24,458	25,593	25,227	24,935	26,024
5.4%	1.6%	3.9%	2.1%	−0.9%	2.0%	4.1%	4.6%	−1.4%	−1.2%	4.4%
32.5	33.4	34.8	36.7	38.8	40.5	41.8	44.4	49.3	53.8	56.9
3.0%	2.8%	4.3%	5.5%	5.8%	4.3%	3.3%	6.2%	11.1%	9.1%	5.7%
33.3	33.4	34.2	35.6	36.9	38.1	39.8	45	53.5	58.4	61.1
3.1%	0.3%	2.4%	4.1%	3.7%	3.3%	4.5%	13.1%	18.9%	9.2%	4.6%
19.2	19.8	20.6	21.6	22.8	23.9	25.0	26.3	28.7	31.4	33.1
2.8%	2.9%	4.3%	4.9%	5.3%	5.1%	4.3%	5.4%	9.0%	9.3%	5.5%
196,599	198,752	200,745	202,736	205,089	207,692	209,924	211,939	213,898	215,981	218,086
75,745	77,348	78,710	80,705	82,796	84,376	87,011	89,411	91,976	93,770	96,151
2,867	2,972	2,797	2,830	4,127	5,022	4,876	4,359	5,173	7,940	7,398
3.8%	3.8%	3.6%	3.5%	5.0%	6.0%	5.6%	4.9%	5.6%	8.5%	7.7%
−3.1	−12.6	−27.7	−0.5	−8.7	−26.1	−26.1	−15.2	−7.2	−54.1	−69.4
−0.4%	−1.5%	−2.9%	0.0%	−0.8%	−2.2%	−2.0%	−1.1%	−0.5%	−3.2%	−3.7%
171.0	177.7	190.1	201.4	209.1	223.1	239.0	256.3	269.1	281.3	297.2
471.4	503.6	545.3	578.7	601.5	674.4	758.2	831.8	880.6	963.5	1,086.5
5.1%	4.2%	5.7%	8.2%	7.2%	4.7%	4.4%	8.7%	10.5%	5.8%	5.1%
3.8	3.5	1.6	1.6	3.7	0.3	−4.1	8.9	6	19.9	7.1

(continued on next page)

	1977	1978	1979	1980	1981	1982	1983	1984
Nominal GDP and Its Components								
1. + Consumer spending (C)	1,276.7	1,426.2	1,589.5	1,754.6	1,937.5	2,073.9	2,286.5	2,498.2
2. + Investment spending (I)	396.6	478.4	539.7	530.1	631.2	581.0	637.5	820.1
3. + Government purchases of goods and services (G)	435.8	477.4	525.5	590.8	654.7	710.0	765.7	825.2
4. + Exports (X)	159.4	186.9	230.1	280.8	305.2	283.2	277.0	302.4
5. − Imports (IM)	182.4	212.3	252.7	293.8	317.8	303.2	328.6	405.1
6. = Gross Domestic Product (GDP)	**2,086.0**	**2,356.6**	**2,632.1**	**2,862.5**	**3,211.0**	**3,345.0**	**3,638.1**	**4,040.7**
7. + Income from abroad earned by Americans	37.2	46.3	68.3	79.1	92.0	101.0	101.9	121.9
8. − Income paid to foreigners	16.9	24.7	36.4	44.9	59.1	64.5	64.8	85.6
9. = Gross National Product (GNP)	**2,106.2**	**2,378.2**	**2,664.1**	**2,896.7**	**3,243.9**	**3,381.5**	**3,675.2**	**4,077.0**
10. National income	1,798.7	2,029.9	2,248.2	2,426.8	2,722.1	2,840.4	3,060.5	3,444.0
11. Government transfers	194.2	209.6	235.3	279.5	318.4	354.8	383.7	400.1
12. Taxes	197.5	229.4	268.7	298.9	345.2	354.1	352.3	377.4
13. Disposable income	1,456.7	1,630.1	1,809.3	2,018.0	2,250.7	2,424.7	2,617.4	2,903.9
14. Private savings	148.2	166.6	177.5	213.2	252.5	277.7	247.0	312.1
Real GDP and Growth Measures								
15. Real GDP (billions of 2009 dollars)	5,937.0	6,267.2	6,466.2	6,450.4	6,617.7	6,491.3	6,792.0	7,285.0
16. Real GDP growth (percent change from previous year)	4.6%	5.6%	3.2%	−0.2%	2.6%	−1.9%	4.6%	7.3%
17. Real GDP per capita (2009 dollars)	26,951	28,151	28,725	28,325	28,772	27,953	28,984	30,817
18. Real GDP per capita growth (percent change from previous year)	3.6%	4.5%	2.0%	−1.4%	1.6%	−2.8%	3.7%	6.3%
Prices and Inflation								
19. Consumer Price Index (1982 – 1984 = 100)	60.6	65.2	72.6	82.4	90.9	96.5	99.6	103.9
20. CPI inflation rate	6.5%	7.6%	11.3%	13.5%	10.3%	6.1%	3.2%	4.3%
21. Producer Price Index (all commodities, 1982 = 100)	64.9	69.9	78.7	89.8	98	100	101.3	103.7
22. PPI inflation rate	6.2%	7.7%	12.6%	14.1%	9.1%	2.0%	1.3%	2.4%
23. GDP deflator (2009 = 100)	35.1	37.6	40.7	44.4	48.5	51.5	53.6	55.5
24. GDP deflator inflation rate	6.2%	7.0%	8.3%	9.0%	9.3%	6.2%	3.9%	3.5%
Population and Employment								
25. Population (thousands)	220,289	222,629	225,106	227,726	230,008	232,218	234,333	236,394
26. Labor force (thousands)[2]	98,984	102,233	104,961	106,974	108,676	110,244	111,515	113,532
27. Unemployed (thousands)[2]	6,967	6,187	6,135	7,671	8,276	10,715	10,694	8,529
28. Unemployment rate	7.1%	6.1%	5.9%	7.2%	7.6%	9.7%	9.6%	7.5%
Government Finance and Money								
29. Federal budget balance	−49.9	−55.4	−39.6	−73.1	−73.9	−120.6	−207.7	−185.3
30. Budget balance (percent of GDP)	−2.4%	−2.4%	−1.5%	−2.6%	−2.3%	−3.6%	−5.7%	−4.6%
31. M1	319.9	346.2	372.6	395.7	425.0	453.0	503.2	538.6
32. M2	1,221.2	1,322.2	1,425.7	1,540.2	1,679.3	1,831.1	2,054.8	2,219.3
33. Federal funds (yearly average)	5.5%	7.9%	11.2%	13.4%	16.4%	12.3%	9.1%	10.2%
International Trade								
34. Current account balance	−10.9	−12.7	−1.2	8.5	3.4	−3.3	−35.1	−90.1

Sources: Bureau of Economic Analysis; Federal Bank of St. Louis; Office of Management and Budget.

1. Data in billions of current dollars unless otherwise stated. Only select dates shown for 1929 through 1965; annual data supplied for 1965 through 2014.
2. Until 1947, includes workers 14 years and older; 1948 and after, includes workers 16 years and older.

1985	1986	1987	1988	1989	1990	1991	1992	1993	1994	1995
2,722.7	2,898.4	3,092.1	3,346.9	3,592.8	3,825.6	3,960.2	4,215.7	4,471.0	4,741.0	4,984.2
829.6	849.1	892.2	937.0	999.7	993.5	944.3	1,013.0	1,106.8	1,256.5	1,317.5
908.4	974.5	1,030.8	1,078.2	1,151.9	1,238.4	1,298.2	1,345.4	1,366.1	1,403.7	1,452.2
303.2	321.0	363.9	444.6	504.3	551.9	594.9	633.1	654.8	720.9	812.8
417.2	452.9	508.7	554.0	591.0	629.7	623.5	667.8	720.0	813.4	902.6
4,346.7	**4,590.2**	**4,870.2**	**5,252.6**	**5,657.7**	**5,979.6**	**6,174.0**	**6,539.3**	**6,878.7**	**7,308.8**	**7,664.1**
112.7	111.3	123.3	152.1	177.7	188.8	168.4	152.1	155.6	184.5	229.8
87.3	94.4	105.8	129.5	152.9	154.2	136.8	121.0	123.6	160.7	201.1
4,372.1	**4,607.1**	**4,887.7**	**5,275.3**	**5,682.5**	**6,014.3**	**6,205.6**	**6,570.4**	**6,910.7**	**7,332.6**	**7,692.8**
3,684.2	3,848.2	4,119.2	4,493.4	4,782.2	5,036.1	5,186.1	5,499.7	5,754.8	6,140.2	6,479.5
424.9	451.0	467.6	496.5	542.6	594.9	665.9	745.8	790.8	826.4	878.9
417.3	437.2	489.1	504.9	566.1	592.7	586.6	610.5	646.5	690.5	743.9
3,098.5	3,287.9	3,466.3	3,770.4	4,052.1	4,311.8	4,484.5	4,800.3	5,000.2	5,244.2	5,532.6
265.1	269.4	252.1	294.7	316.5	335.4	365.9	426.0	367.6	331.4	352.9
7,593.8	7,860.5	8,132.6	8,474.5	8,786.4	8,955.0	8,948.4	9,266.6	9,521.0	9,905.4	10,174.8
4.2%	3.5%	3.5%	4.2%	3.7%	1.9%	−0.1%	3.6%	2.7%	4.0%	2.7%
31,839	32,659	33,489	34,581	35,517	35,794	35,295	36,068	36,580	37,598	38,167
3.3%	2.6%	2.5%	3.3%	2.7%	0.8%	−1.4%	2.2%	1.4%	2.8%	1.5%
107.6	109.6	113.6	118.3	124.0	130.7	136.2	140.3	144.5	148.2	152.4
3.5%	1.9%	3.7%	4.1%	4.8%	5.4%	4.2%	3.0%	3.0%	2.6%	2.8%
103.2	100.2	102.8	106.9	112.2	116.3	116.5	117.2	118.9	120.5	124.8
−0.5%	−2.9%	2.6%	4.0%	5.0%	3.7%	0.2%	0.6%	1.5%	1.3%	3.6%
57.2	58.4	59.9	62.0	64.4	66.8	69.0	70.6	72.2	73.8	75.3
3.2%	2.0%	2.6%	3.5%	3.9%	3.7%	3.3%	2.3%	2.4%	2.1%	2.1%
238,506	240,683	242,843	245,061	247,387	250,181	253,530	256,922	260,282	263,455	266,588
115,467	117,846	119,853	121,671	123,851	125,857	126,352	128,099	129,185	131,047	132,315
8,313	8,245	7,414	6,697	6,524	7,061	8,640	9,611	8,927	7,976	7,407
7.2%	7.0%	6.2%	5.5%	5.3%	5.6%	6.9%	7.5%	6.9%	6.1%	5.6%
−221.5	−237.9	−168.4	−192.3	−205.4	−277.6	−321.4	−340.4	−300.4	−258.8	−226.4
−5.1%	−5.2%	−3.5%	−3.7%	−3.6%	−4.6%	−5.2%	−5.2%	−4.4%	−3.5%	−3.0%
587.0	666.3	743.6	774.8	782.2	810.6	859.0	965.9	1,078.4	1,145.2	1,143.0
2,416.9	2,613.6	2,783.9	2,933.5	3,056.3	3,223.6	3,342.0	3,403.4	3,437.8	3,482.2	3,553.0
8.1%	6.8%	6.7%	7.6%	9.2%	8.1%	5.7%	3.5%	3.0%	4.2%	5.8%
−114.3	−142.7	−154.1	−115.8	−92.4	−74.9	7.9	−45.6	−78.5	−114.7	−105.1

(continued on next page)

MACROECONOMIC DATA FOR THE UNITED STATES 1929–2014[1]

	1996	1997	1998	1999	2000	2001	2002	2003
Nominal GDP and Its Components								
1. + Consumer spending (C)	5,268.1	5,560.7	5,903.0	6,307.0	6,792.4	7,103.1	7,384.1	7,765.5
2. + Investment spending (I)	1,432.1	1,595.6	1,735.3	1,884.2	2,033.8	1,928.6	1,925.0	2,027.9
3. + Government purchases of goods and services (G)	1,496.4	1,554.2	1,613.5	1,726.0	1,834.4	1,958.8	2,094.9	2,220.8
4. + Exports (X)	867.6	953.8	953.0	992.0	1,096.8	1,026.7	1,002.5	1,040.3
5. – Imports (IM)	964.0	1,055.8	1,115.7	1,248.6	1,472.6	1,395.4	1,429.0	1,543.9
6. = Gross Domestic Product (GDP)	**8,100.2**	**8,608.5**	**9,089.2**	**9,660.6**	**10,284.8**	**10,621.8**	**10,977.5**	**11,510.7**
7. + Income from abroad earned by Americans	246.4	280.1	286.8	321.4	382.7	325.3	315.8	356.1
8. – Income paid to foreigners	214.6	256.0	268.5	294.3	345.7	273.5	267.2	289.0
9. = Gross National Product (GNP)	**8,132.0**	**8,632.6**	**9,107.4**	**9,687.8**	**10,321.8**	**10,673.6**	**11,026.1**	**11,577.8**
10. National income	6,899.4	7,380.4	7,857.3	8,324.4	8,907.0	9,184.6	9,436.8	9,864.2
11. Government transfers	924.1	949.2	977.9	1,021.6	1,083.0	1,188.1	1,280.3	1,342.9
12. Taxes	832.0	926.2	1,026.4	1,107.5	1,232.3	1,234.8	1,050.3	1,000.9
13. Disposable income	5,829.9	6,148.9	6,561.3	6,876.3	7,400.5	7,752.3	8,099.2	8,485.8
14. Private savings	345.2	352.2	405.3	302.9	307.2	335.0	405.1	408.7
Real GDP and Growth Measures								
15. Real GDP (billions of 2009 dollars)	10,561.0	11,034.9	11,525.9	12,065.9	12,559.7	12,682.2	12,908.8	13,271.1
16. Real GDP growth (percent change from previous year)	3.8%	4.5%	4.4%	4.7%	4.1%	1.0%	1.8%	2.8%
17. Real GDP per capita (2009 dollars)	39,156	40,427	41,737	43,196	44,475	44,464	44,829	45,664
18. Real GDP per capita growth (percent change from previous year)	2.6%	3.2%	3.2%	3.5%	3.0%	0.0%	0.8%	1.9%
Prices and Inflation								
19. Consumer Price Index (1982 – 1984 = 100)	156.9	160.5	163.0	166.6	172.2	177.1	179.9	184.0
20. CPI inflation rate	2.9%	2.3%	1.6%	2.2%	3.4%	2.8%	1.6%	2.3%
21. Producer Price Index (all commodities, 1982 = 100)	127.7	127.6	124.4	125.5	132.7	134.2	131.1	138.1
22. PPI inflation rate	2.3%	–0.1%	–2.5%	0.9%	5.7%	1.1%	–2.3%	5.3%
23. GDP deflator (2009 = 100)	76.7	78.0	78.9	80.1	81.9	83.8	85.0	86.7
24. GDP deflator inflation rate	1.8%	1.7%	1.1%	1.5%	2.3%	2.3%	1.5%	2.0%
Population and Employment								
25. Population (thousands)	269,714	272,958	276,154	279,328	282,398	285,225	287,955	290,626
26. Labor force (thousands)[2]	133,951	136,301	137,680	139,380	142,586	143,769	144,856	146,500
27. Unemployed (thousands)[2]	7,231	6,729	6,204	5,879	5,685	6,830	8,375	8,770
28. Unemployment rate	5.4%	4.9%	4.5%	4.2%	4.0%	4.7%	5.8%	6.0%
Government Finance and Money								
29. Federal budget balance	–174.0	–103.2	–29.9	1.9	86.4	–32.4	–317.4	–538.4
30. Budget balance (percent of GDP)	–2.1%	–1.2%	–0.3%	0.0%	0.8%	–0.3%	–2.9%	–4.7%
31. M1	1,106.8	1,070.2	1,080.6	1,102.3	1,103.7	1,140.2	1,196.7	1,273.8
32. M2	3,723.5	3,910.4	4,189.5	4,497.2	4,769.2	5,178.9	5,561.8	5,949.9
33. Federal funds (yearly average)	5.3%	5.5%	5.4%	5.0%	6.2%	3.9%	1.7%	1.1%
International Trade								
34. Current account balance	–114.1	–129.3	–204.5	–287.1	–404.2	–389	–450.9	–516.6

Sources: Bureau of Economic Analysis; Federal Bank of St. Louis; Office of Management and Budget.

1. Data in billions of current dollars unless otherwise stated. Only select dates shown for 1929 through 1965; annual data supplied for 1965 through 2014.
2. Until 1947, includes workers 14 years and older; 1948 and after, includes workers 16 years and older.

2004	2005	2006	2007	2008	2009	2010	2011	2012	2013	2014
8,260.0	8,794.1	9,304.0	9,750.5	10,013.6	9,847.0	10,202.2	10,689.3	11,083.1	11,484.3	11,928.4
2,276.7	2,527.1	2,680.6	2,643.7	2,424.8	1,878.1	2,100.8	2,239.9	2,479.2	2,648.0	2,855.8
2,357.4	2,493.7	2,642.2	2,801.9	3,003.2	3,089.1	3,174.0	3,168.7	3,169.2	3,143.9	3,174.5
1,181.5	1,308.9	1,476.3	1,664.6	1,841.9	1,587.7	1,852.3	2,106.4	2,194.2	2,262.2	2,334.2
1,800.7	2,030.1	2,247.3	2,383.2	2,565.0	1,983.2	2,365.0	2,686.4	2,762.5	2,770.4	2,872.3
12,274.9	**13,093.7**	**13,855.9**	**14,477.6**	**14,718.6**	**14,418.7**	**14,964.4**	**15,517.9**	**16,163.2**	**16,768.1**	**17,420.7**
451.4	575.8	724.2	875.7	856.9	648.9	720.0	792.6	793.8	810.4	NA
362.3	483.2	656.6	750.1	684.9	497.8	514.1	546.0	566.5	586.1	NA
12,364.1	**13,186.3**	**13,923.5**	**14,603.2**	**14,890.6**	**14,569.8**	**15,170.3**	**15,764.6**	**16,390.5**	**16,992.4**	**NA**
10,540.9	11,239.8	12,004.8	12,321.4	12,427.8	12,126.1	12,739.5	13,352.3	14,069.5	14,577.1	NA
1,416.7	1,512.0	1,609.6	1,722.8	1,884.0	2,140.2	2,276.9	2,307.9	2,350.7	2,414.5	2,523.5
1,046.0	1,208.5	1,352.1	1,487.9	1,435.2	1,144.9	1,191.5	1,400.6	1,503.7	1,661.8	1,735.7
9,002.3	9,400.8	10,036.9	10,507.0	10,994.4	10,942.5	11,237.9	11,801.4	12,384.0	12,505.1	12,980.9
410.0	237.9	329.5	310.3	542.2	672.0	628.0	711.1	896.2	608.1	625.1
13,773.5	14,234.2	14,613.8	14,873.7	14,830.4	14,418.7	14,783.8	15,020.6	15,369.2	15,710.3	16,089.8
3.8%	3.3%	2.7%	1.8%	−0.3%	−2.8%	2.5%	1.6%	2.3%	2.2%	2.4%
46,967	48,090	48,905	49,300	48,697	46,930	47,724	48,138	48,908	49,643	50,487
2.9%	2.4%	1.7%	0.8%	−1.2%	−3.6%	1.7%	0.9%	1.6%	1.5%	1.7%
188.9	195.3	201.6	207.3	215.3	214.5	218.1	224.9	229.6	233.0	236.7
2.7%	3.4%	3.2%	2.9%	3.8%	−0.4%	1.6%	3.2%	2.1%	1.5%	1.6%
146.7	157.4	164.8	172.7	189.6	172.9	184.7	201.1	202.2	203.4	205.4
6.2%	7.3%	4.7%	4.8%	9.8%	−8.8%	6.8%	8.9%	0.5%	0.6%	1.0%
89.1	92.0	94.8	97.3	99.2	100.0	101.2	103.3	105.2	106.7	108.3
2.7%	3.2%	3.1%	2.7%	2.0%	0.8%	1.2%	2.1%	1.8%	1.5%	1.4%
293,262	295,993	298,818	301,696	304,543	307,240	309,776	312,034	314,246	316,465	318,688
147,380	149,289	151,409	153,123	154,322	154,189	153,886	153,615	154,962	155,379	155,899
8,140	7,579	6,991	7,073	8,948	14,295	14,810	13,736	12,496	11,449	9,596
5.5%	5.1%	4.6%	4.6%	5.8%	9.3%	9.6%	8.9%	8.1%	7.4%	6.2%
−568.0	−493.6	−434.5	−342.2	−641.8	−1549.7	−1371.4	−1366.8	−1148.9	−719.0	−514.1
−4.6%	−3.8%	−3.1%	−2.4%	−4.4%	−10.7%	−9.2%	−8.8%	−7.1%	−4.3%	−2.8%
1,344.3	1,371.8	1,374.8	1,372.6	1,434.3	1,637.6	1,741.9	2,009.6	2,311.4	2,544.7	2,806.2
6,236.3	6,505.6	6,848.0	7,269.9	7,766.2	8,392.3	8,601.2	9,229.4	10,019.2	10,691.8	11,349.0
1.4%	3.2%	5.0%	5.0%	1.9%	0.2%	0.2%	0.1%	0.1%	0.1%	0.1%
−626.4	−742.9	−804	−717.6	−686.1	−377.3	−447.9	−480.5	−482.2	−422.2	NA

Table 2
MACROECONOMIC DATA FOR SELECT COUNTRIES
GDP (Billions of U.S. Dollars)

Country	1985	1986	1987	1988	1989	1990	1991	1992	1993
Argentina	88.19	106.05	108.73	127.36	81.71	141.35	189.61	228.79	236.52
Australia	175.24	182.37	214.15	272.44	308.27	323.44	324.18	317.65	309.02
Austria	67.93	96.39	120.54	132.22	131.89	165.17	172.62	193.49	188.53
Belgium	83.44	115.64	143.64	156.17	157.87	197.71	202.87	225.95	216.06
Brazil	231.76	268.85	292.63	326.90	448.77	465.01	407.73	390.59	438.30
Bulgaria	28.05	24.83	28.78	47.03	47.90	21.12	2.07	8.40	4.56
Canada	362.96	376.39	430.12	508.32	566.84	594.61	610.39	591.33	575.16
Chile	17.16	18.45	21.76	25.65	29.55	32.85	37.81	46.07	49.29
China	307.02	297.59	323.97	404.15	451.31	390.28	409.17	488.22	613.22
Colombia	48.46	48.53	50.51	54.46	54.91	55.93	57.27	68.44	77.49
Cyprus	2.40	3.05	3.66	4.22	4.51	5.52	5.70	6.83	6.53
Czech Republic	n/a	n/a	n/a	n/a	n/a	n/a	n/a	n/a	n/a
Denmark	61.20	86.37	107.37	113.23	110.06	135.84	136.70	150.20	140.63
Dominican Republic	6.49	7.88	8.30	7.60	8.58	7.99	9.79	11.49	12.90
Ecuador	19.06	13.99	13.07	12.43	12.20	12.39	13.90	15.20	17.75
Egypt	46.45	51.43	73.57	88.00	109.71	91.38	46.06	42.01	47.10
Estonia	n/a	n/a	n/a	n/a	n/a	n/a	n/a	n/a	1.73
Finland	55.29	72.39	90.19	107.35	116.83	139.23	125.76	110.81	87.46
France	547.83	759.86	918.82	1,003.15	1,007.96	1,247.35	1,249.64	1,375.83	1,298.40
Germany	639.70	913.64	1,136.93	1,225.73	1,216.80	1,547.03	1,815.06	2,068.96	2,008.55
Ghana	8.05	6.74	6.71	7.23	7.41	8.84	11.12	11.26	8.89
Greece	45.13	53.10	61.79	71.95	74.57	92.20	99.42	109.56	102.61
Guatemala	10.39	5.62	6.50	7.04	8.12	7.07	8.70	9.60	10.46
Hungary	21.04	24.24	26.64	29.15	29.76	33.73	34.11	38.01	39.38
Iceland	2.94	3.93	5.44	6.01	5.58	6.36	6.80	6.97	6.12
India	237.62	252.75	283.75	299.65	300.19	326.61	274.84	293.26	284.19
Ireland	20.76	27.84	33.00	36.15	37.29	47.25	47.89	53.84	49.89
Israel	26.66	32.82	39.20	48.56	49.41	58.30	66.13	73.90	74.27
Italy	446.03	631.72	792.88	878.45	913.63	1,140.24	1,204.45	1,278.10	1,027.75
Jamaica	1.99	2.37	2.67	3.18	3.69	4.66	4.29	4.33	5.52
Japan	1,384.53	2,051.06	2,485.24	3,015.39	3,017.05	3,103.70	3,536.80	3,852.79	4,414.96
Kenya	8.68	10.31	11.30	11.71	11.61	12.08	11.41	11.24	7.81
Korea	98.50	113.74	143.38	192.11	236.23	270.41	315.58	338.17	372.21
Latvia	n/a	n/a	n/a	n/a	n/a	n/a	n/a	1.56	2.48
Lithuania	n/a	n/a	n/a	n/a	n/a	n/a	n/a	n/a	n/a
Luxembourg	4.57	6.65	8.26	9.36	9.96	12.70	13.76	15.42	15.81
Malaysia	31.30	27.82	31.70	34.75	38.27	43.37	49.13	59.15	66.89
Mexico	223.42	154.69	169.64	207.53	252.91	298.46	357.80	414.93	504.07
Netherlands	133.17	185.60	227.33	243.12	239.55	295.57	304.44	336.95	327.68
New Zealand	22.38	27.23	36.67	45.15	43.63	45.29	43.17	41.16	44.35
Nigeria	25.97	20.56	21.91	24.31	23.49	31.48	28.34	25.52	15.79
Norway	64.26	77.20	92.45	100.06	100.77	117.62	119.66	128.30	118.17
Paraguay	4.21	5.03	4.22	5.58	3.82	4.96	7.06	7.18	7.25
Peru	17.21	25.81	42.63	33.73	41.62	28.97	34.54	36.15	34.93
Philippines	33.91	33.09	36.78	41.98	47.17	48.97	50.22	58.70	60.24
Poland	70.78	73.68	63.71	68.61	66.90	62.08	80.45	88.71	90.37
Portugal	26.82	37.30	46.67	54.60	58.90	78.24	88.55	106.49	93.70
Romania	47.80	51.77	57.89	59.93	53.69	38.24	28.85	19.58	26.36
Russia	n/a	n/a	n/a	n/a	n/a	n/a	n/a	85.59	183.82
Saudi Arabia	103.68	86.71	85.41	87.96	95.02	116.69	131.84	136.67	137.41
Singapore	18.46	18.73	21.55	26.48	31.41	38.84	45.19	52.01	60.47
South Africa	57.27	65.42	85.79	92.24	95.98	112.00	120.24	130.53	130.45
Spain	176.59	244.34	309.57	363.71	401.16	520.42	560.48	612.67	514.66
Sweden	105.68	139.88	170.41	192.54	202.99	242.88	256.26	265.31	202.04
Switzerland	101.90	146.07	182.94	197.91	191.08	244.03	246.91	257.02	249.96
Thailand	38.90	43.10	50.54	61.67	72.25	85.64	96.19	109.43	121.80
Turkey	90.58	100.48	115.90	121.90	144.09	202.25	203.49	213.78	242.47
Ukraine	n/a	n/a	n/a	n/a	n/a	n/a	n/a	21.46	33.87
United Arab Emirates	37.31	29.57	32.47	33.00	38.09	49.09	49.82	52.21	53.44
United Kingdom	468.96	570.88	704.09	855.78	865.96	1,024.56	1,069.91	1,112.86	998.35
United States	4,346.75	4,590.13	4,870.20	5,252.63	5,657.65	5,979.55	6,174.03	6,539.28	6,878.70
Vietnam	15.00	33.87	42.05	23.23	6.29	6.47	7.64	9.87	13.18

Source: International Monetary Fund, World Economic Outlook Database, April 2014.

1994	1995	1996	1997	1998	1999	2000	2001	2002	2003	2004
257.36	258.22	272.08	292.76	298.93	283.66	284.41	268.96	97.40	127.55	151.82
353.16	379.72	425.18	426.76	380.56	411.30	399.47	376.85	423.80	540.75	657.79
201.89	238.80	234.77	208.08	213.62	212.58	192.63	191.84	208.27	254.43	291.81
235.72	284.79	275.88	250.08	255.94	254.84	233.35	232.69	253.69	312.29	362.16
546.49	769.74	840.05	871.52	844.13	586.92	644.73	554.19	506.04	552.38	663.73
8.01	13.42	10.14	10.62	13.16	13.29	12.94	13.88	16.03	20.71	25.32
575.98	602.00	626.97	650.99	631.45	674.31	739.45	732.74	752.52	887.78	1,018.39
56.86	73.27	77.68	84.84	81.54	75.24	77.98	71.29	70.10	76.10	99.27
559.22	727.95	856.08	952.65	1,019.48	1,083.28	1,198.48	1,324.81	1,453.83	1,640.96	1,931.65
97.42	110.30	119.44	112.18	108.62	96.44	99.88	98.21	97.96	94.64	117.08
7.36	9.14	9.23	8.79	9.43	9.66	9.20	9.61	10.48	13.18	15.66
n/a	57.79	64.90	59.46	63.86	62.17	58.80	64.38	78.43	95.29	113.98
153.59	181.99	184.44	170.44	173.65	173.94	160.08	160.48	173.88	212.62	244.73
14.09	15.51	17.01	19.23	20.44	21.71	24.00	24.90	26.46	21.15	21.86
21.41	23.25	24.33	27.34	27.81	19.98	18.54	24.61	28.55	32.43	36.59
51.88	60.16	67.63	75.87	84.82	90.39	99.62	97.27	85.84	80.99	78.80
2.42	3.78	4.73	5.06	5.60	5.72	5.70	6.25	7.35	9.86	12.04
101.07	130.95	128.38	123.17	129.94	130.49	122.15	124.75	135.66	164.57	189.31
1,370.63	1,573.08	1,573.13	1,423.13	1,470.90	1,458.34	1,330.22	1,339.45	1,457.17	1,795.64	2,058.38
2,152.74	2,525.02	2,437.81	2,159.87	2,181.16	2,133.84	1,891.93	1,882.51	2,013.69	2,428.45	2,729.92
7.86	8.40	9.18	10.61	11.92	12.67	7.36	7.44	9.48	11.19	14.56
109.83	131.82	139.31	136.07	136.77	140.84	127.61	131.14	147.91	194.99	230.34
11.84	13.32	14.20	16.09	17.31	16.49	17.19	18.70	20.78	21.92	23.97
42.35	45.57	45.93	46.53	47.95	48.26	46.39	52.72	66.39	83.54	101.93
6.29	7.01	7.31	7.42	8.27	8.73	8.68	7.90	8.91	10.97	13.25
333.01	366.60	399.79	423.19	428.77	466.84	476.64	493.93	523.77	618.37	721.59
54.75	67.92	74.39	81.38	88.29	96.71	97.62	105.26	123.45	159.03	186.53
84.78	100.72	110.38	113.65	114.77	115.33	129.38	127.26	117.33	123.25	131.33
1,060.06	1,132.36	1,266.70	1,199.96	1,226.17	1,209.77	1,107.25	1,124.67	1,229.52	1,517.40	1,737.80
5.53	6.54	7.39	8.40	8.79	8.89	9.07	9.20	9.72	9.43	10.17
4,850.35	5,333.93	4,706.19	4,324.28	3,914.58	4,432.60	4,731.20	4,159.86	3,980.82	4,302.94	4,655.82
9.35	11.85	11.95	13.18	13.66	12.78	12.60	12.98	13.15	14.91	16.09
435.59	531.14	573.00	532.24	357.51	461.81	533.39	504.58	575.93	643.76	721.98
4.16	4.97	5.67	6.28	6.92	7.33	7.78	8.22	9.23	11.15	13.74
n/a	6.73	8.43	10.13	11.25	10.97	11.50	12.22	14.24	18.70	22.66
17.59	20.69	20.59	18.54	19.38	21.21	20.33	20.22	22.65	29.20	34.12
74.48	88.83	100.85	100.17	72.18	79.15	93.79	92.78	100.85	110.20	124.75
527.29	343.78	397.29	480.39	501.96	579.35	683.54	724.71	741.53	713.28	770.04
351.98	419.35	418.11	387.01	403.20	412.00	386.20	401.00	439.36	539.34	610.69
52.30	61.64	68.40	68.23	56.15	58.28	53.44	52.55	61.40	81.65	100.70
18.09	36.95	46.02	35.39	32.75	35.87	46.39	44.14	59.12	67.66	87.85
124.52	148.92	160.16	158.22	151.14	159.05	168.29	170.92	191.93	224.88	260.03
7.86	9.06	9.79	9.97	9.03	8.39	8.20	7.66	6.33	6.59	8.00
44.98	53.76	55.97	59.21	56.83	51.58	53.36	53.96	56.78	61.36	69.70
71.00	82.12	91.79	91.23	72.21	83.00	81.02	76.26	81.36	83.91	91.37
103.68	139.10	156.66	157.08	172.00	167.79	171.26	190.42	198.21	216.81	253.02
98.19	116.40	121.18	115.85	123.04	126.59	117.64	120.44	132.75	162.24	185.64
30.07	35.48	35.32	35.29	42.12	35.59	37.33	40.59	45.99	59.47	75.80
276.90	313.45	391.78	404.95	271.04	195.91	259.70	306.58	345.13	430.29	591.18
139.65	147.94	163.43	170.88	151.96	167.05	194.81	189.36	194.88	221.47	258.74
73.24	87.06	95.18	99.30	85.01	84.88	94.31	87.70	90.64	95.96	112.70
135.82	151.12	143.83	148.84	134.22	133.11	132.97	118.56	111.36	168.22	219.42
516.43	596.94	622.30	573.05	601.29	618.34	582.05	609.38	688.73	885.53	1,045.98
217.55	253.68	276.46	253.18	254.72	258.81	247.26	227.36	250.96	314.71	362.09
276.72	323.98	312.03	272.27	278.90	273.56	256.04	262.65	286.66	334.59	374.23
144.31	168.02	181.95	150.89	111.86	122.63	122.73	115.54	126.88	142.64	161.34
174.99	227.81	244.39	255.65	269.53	250.33	266.67	196.06	232.45	303.12	392.23
36.76	37.01	44.56	50.15	41.88	31.58	31.26	38.01	42.39	50.13	64.89
57.45	63.64	70.99	76.20	73.39	82.87	103.89	103.31	109.82	124.35	147.82
1,080.84	1,181.01	1,243.17	1,384.54	1,477.97	1,518.51	1,496.61	1,485.66	1,623.56	1,877.12	2,221.92
7,308.70	7,664.05	8,100.15	8,608.48	9,089.13	9,665.70	10,289.73	10,625.28	10,980.20	11,512.28	12,277.03
16.31	20.80	24.69	26.89	27.23	28.70	31.18	32.52	35.10	39.56	49.52

(continued on next page)

MACROECONOMIC DATA FOR SELECT COUNTRIES
GDP (Billions of U.S. Dollars)

Country	2005	2006	2007	2008	2009	2010	2011	2012	2013
Argentina	181.36	212.51	260.07	324.41	305.77	367.56	444.61	475.21	488.21
Australia	733.04	781.55	948.92	1,054.64	997.58	1,249.25	1,498.53	1,555.29	1,505.28
Austria	305.51	325.26	375.58	416.12	384.73	378.38	416.37	394.68	415.37
Belgium	378.01	400.34	460.28	509.77	474.48	472.03	513.79	483.22	506.56
Brazil	882.04	1,089.26	1,366.85	1,653.54	1,622.31	2,142.91	2,474.64	2,247.75	2,242.85
Bulgaria	28.97	33.25	42.18	52.14	48.65	47.84	53.58	51.33	53.05
Canada	1,164.18	1,310.80	1,457.87	1,542.56	1,370.84	1,614.07	1,778.63	1,821.45	1,825.10
Chile	123.06	154.72	173.09	179.58	172.13	217.31	250.79	266.27	276.98
China	2,256.92	2,712.92	3,494.24	4,519.95	4,990.53	5,930.39	7,321.99	8,229.38	9,181.38
Colombia	146.57	162.59	207.42	243.98	233.82	287.02	336.35	369.79	381.82
Cyprus	16.92	18.42	21.77	25.25	23.47	23.10	25.02	23.00	21.83
Czech Republic	130.07	148.37	180.48	225.43	197.19	198.49	216.06	196.45	198.31
Denmark	257.68	274.38	311.42	343.88	310.55	312.95	333.74	315.16	330.96
Dominican Republic	33.84	35.84	41.22	45.73	46.73	51.61	55.58	58.98	60.77
Ecuador	41.51	46.80	51.01	61.76	62.52	69.56	79.78	87.50	94.14
Egypt	89.52	107.38	130.35	162.44	188.61	218.76	235.58	262.26	271.43
Estonia	13.93	16.82	22.02	23.87	19.47	19.08	22.56	22.39	24.48
Finland	196.12	208.14	246.48	273.25	240.00	237.15	262.62	247.28	256.92
France	2,140.27	2,257.80	2,586.10	2,845.11	2,626.49	2,569.82	2,784.76	2,612.67	2,737.36
Germany	2,771.06	2,905.45	3,328.59	3,640.73	3,306.78	3,310.60	3,631.44	3,427.85	3,635.96
Ghana	17.41	20.41	24.76	28.53	25.80	32.19	38.75	40.44	44.22
Greece	240.49	261.96	305.87	343.20	321.85	294.77	290.15	248.56	241.80
Guatemala	27.21	30.23	34.11	39.14	37.73	41.34	47.69	50.24	54.38
Hungary	110.32	112.53	136.09	154.22	126.65	127.50	137.72	124.59	132.43
Iceland	16.32	16.73	20.43	16.83	12.12	12.57	14.04	13.58	14.66
India	834.22	949.12	1,238.48	1,223.21	1,365.34	1,708.54	1,880.10	1,858.75	1,870.65
Ireland	202.93	222.97	259.95	265.28	226.03	209.78	226.24	210.75	217.88
Israel	138.57	150.99	174.97	213.13	205.79	231.68	258.21	257.62	291.50
Italy	1,789.38	1,874.72	2,130.24	2,318.16	2,116.63	2,059.19	2,198.35	2,014.38	2,071.96
Jamaica	11.23	11.94	12.88	13.74	12.11	13.20	14.40	14.75	14.29
Japan	4,571.87	4,356.75	4,356.35	4,849.19	5,035.14	5,495.39	5,905.63	5,937.77	4,901.53
Kenya	18.74	22.50	27.24	30.47	30.60	32.23	34.33	40.70	45.08
Korea	844.87	951.77	1,049.24	931.41	834.06	1,014.89	1,114.47	1,129.60	1,221.80
Latvia	15.94	19.85	28.65	33.45	25.85	24.10	28.48	28.38	30.95
Lithuania	26.10	30.24	39.32	47.48	37.05	36.71	43.08	42.34	47.56
Luxembourg	37.71	42.58	51.40	55.00	49.55	52.15	58.06	55.17	59.84
Malaysia	143.54	162.75	193.61	231.07	202.28	247.54	289.05	304.73	312.43
Mexico	865.85	966.25	1,042.65	1,100.70	894.54	1,050.85	1,169.23	1,183.51	1,258.54
Netherlands	639.58	678.32	783.69	874.91	798.40	778.61	833.52	770.49	800.01
New Zealand	112.32	108.58	132.91	132.74	119.46	142.30	162.68	170.41	181.33
Nigeria	112.25	145.43	168.68	209.20	170.65	231.60	248.19	264.20	286.47
Norway	304.06	340.04	393.48	453.89	378.85	420.95	490.81	500.03	511.25
Paraguay	8.74	10.65	13.80	18.50	15.93	20.67	24.14	24.94	28.33
Peru	79.39	92.32	107.25	126.87	126.95	153.81	176.55	199.59	206.54
Philippines	103.07	122.21	149.36	173.60	168.49	199.59	224.10	250.18	272.02
Poland	303.98	341.67	425.32	529.43	431.46	469.80	515.67	489.78	516.13
Portugal	192.18	201.98	232.08	253.11	234.73	229.37	238.11	212.26	219.97
Romania	99.17	122.70	170.76	205.79	164.95	164.78	183.56	169.18	189.66
Russia	763.70	989.93	1,299.70	1,660.85	1,222.65	1,524.92	1,893.79	2,004.25	2,118.01
Saudi Arabia	328.46	376.90	415.96	519.80	429.10	526.81	669.51	733.96	745.27
Singapore	125.43	146.01	178.26	190.32	190.16	233.29	272.32	284.30	295.74
South Africa	246.95	261.18	285.81	273.45	285.42	365.17	404.34	382.34	350.78
Spain	1,132.76	1,237.50	1,443.50	1,600.91	1,458.11	1,387.43	1,455.87	1,323.21	1,358.69
Sweden	370.58	399.08	462.51	486.16	405.78	463.06	536.00	523.94	557.94
Switzerland	384.76	405.18	450.53	524.29	509.47	549.11	658.87	631.18	650.81
Thailand	176.35	207.09	246.98	272.58	263.71	318.91	345.67	365.97	387.16
Turkey	482.74	529.28	646.43	730.63	614.39	731.54	774.73	788.04	827.21
Ukraine	86.18	107.75	142.72	180.12	117.23	136.42	163.42	176.24	177.83
United Arab Emirates	180.62	221.97	257.92	315.48	254.80	287.42	348.60	383.80	396.24
United Kingdom	2,324.18	2,486.60	2,858.18	2,709.57	2,217.43	2,296.93	2,464.64	2,484.45	2,535.76
United States	13,095.43	13,857.90	14,480.35	14,720.25	14,417.95	14,958.30	15,533.83	16,244.58	16,799.70
Vietnam	57.65	66.39	77.52	98.27	101.63	112.77	134.60	155.57	170.57

Source: International Monetary Fund, World Economic Outlook Database, April 2014.

Table 3
MACROECONOMIC DATA FOR SELECT COUNTRIES
GDP PER PERSON (U.S. Dollars)

Country	1985	1986	1987	1988	1989	1990	1991	1992	1993
Argentina	2,928.87	3,477.26	3,525.01	4,079.01	2,584.99	4,379.50	5,796.41	6,900.12	7,028.62
Australia	11,021.04	11,300.02	13,062.01	16,326.18	18,200.98	18,837.97	18,653.26	18,092.08	17,439.83
Austria	8,988.26	12,740.75	15,911.50	17,431.46	17,309.05	21,511.83	22,259.58	24,678.01	23,847.20
Belgium	8,464.36	11,729.28	14,561.04	15,813.79	15,902.22	19,875.05	20,313.44	22,545.24	21,459.22
Brazil	1,742.55	1,979.52	2,111.51	2,313.33	3,116.50	3,172.10	2,734.71	2,577.34	2,846.37
Bulgaria	3,130.66	2,777.16	3,232.53	5,313.22	5,449.79	2,422.34	239.51	981.87	538.52
Canada	14,060.69	14,438.27	16,291.17	19,001.44	20,828.27	21,518.68	21,809.72	20,877.26	20,074.52
Chile	1,418.04	1,497.75	1,736.13	2,012.07	2,279.28	2,492.74	2,817.17	3,370.94	3,543.52
China	290.05	276.81	296.41	364.01	400.44	341.35	353.27	416.68	517.41
Colombia	1,573.62	1,543.74	1,573.96	1,662.06	1,641.85	1,638.97	1,644.09	1,926.10	2,140.21
Cyprus	4,390.66	5,512.95	6,541.58	7,466.26	7,858.91	9,428.03	9,476.93	11,064.83	10,322.07
Czech Republic	n/a	n/a	n/a	n/a	n/a	n/a	n/a	n/a	n/a
Denmark	11,974.67	16,880.56	20,950.32	22,075.41	21,454.88	26,451.46	26,560.90	29,095.51	27,144.62
Dominican Republic	1,061.73	1,258.73	1,292.91	1,292.91	1,277.82	1,166.21	1,404.34	1,611.67	1,768.14
Ecuador	2,039.63	1,458.57	1,329.10	1,231.84	1,179.82	1,170.44	1,283.67	1,372.56	1,569.24
Egypt	997.96	1,077.02	1,507.61	1,767.07	2,155.49	1,779.26	878.62	785.04	862.41
Estonia	n/a	n/a	n/a	n/a	n/a	n/a	n/a	n/a	1,145.29
Finland	11,259.11	14,696.74	18,262.52	21,666.93	23,486.11	27,854.86	25,006.32	21,920.30	17,223.04
France	9,932.14	13,713.16	16,501.33	17,924.31	17,912.96	22,046.99	21,984.99	24,090.71	22,632.31
Germany	8,358.02	11,929.09	14,841.80	15,904.15	15,632.06	19,500.58	22,586.06	25,550.75	24,693.86
Ghana	638.02	521.19	506.05	531.59	531.46	617.60	757.76	748.15	575.87
Greece	4,543.24	5,325.20	6,174.13	7,163.58	7,387.05	9,073.88	9,702.81	10,585.18	9,807.41
Guatemala	1,431.50	754.67	852.19	900.11	1,012.37	860.29	1,034.15	1,112.25	1,181.10
Hungary	1,985.30	2,295.26	2,534.76	2,785.72	2,855.53	3,250.63	3,287.86	3,663.94	3,799.05
Iceland	12,211.18	16,228.24	22,274.72	24,289.84	22,154.55	25,077.03	26,568.62	26,825.10	23,336.04
India	313.07	326.03	358.16	370.28	363.31	385.41	318.01	332.54	315.42
Ireland	5,863.83	7,861.61	9,304.87	10,239.26	10,624.69	13,478.01	13,583.60	15,147.74	13,959.02
Israel	6,529.38	7,910.34	9,297.91	11,316.35	11,271.15	12,957.64	14,247.65	15,373.02	14,897.07
Italy	7,882.06	11,161.62	14,009.86	15,517.72	16,127.82	20,111.95	21,226.03	22,512.31	18,087.21
Jamaica	879.43	1,036.04	1,160.02	1,374.42	1,590.50	1,974.11	1,800.91	1,803.94	2,279.03
Japan	11,464.24	16,890.81	20,367.18	24,604.40	24,522.43	25,139.58	28,541.69	30,972.98	35,376.66
Kenya	420.09	481.65	509.93	510.91	489.89	493.59	452.13	432.75	292.71
Korea	2,413.94	2,759.70	3,444.79	4,570.73	5,565.10	6,307.66	7,288.84	7,729.98	8,422.05
Latvia	n/a	n/a	n/a	n/a	n/a	n/a	n/a	582.08	928.28
Lithuania	n/a	n/a	n/a	n/a	n/a	n/a	n/a	n/a	n/a
Luxembourg	12,442.97	18,021.25	22,237.43	24,974.22	26,331.00	33,198.13	35,486.78	39,216.06	39,639.77
Malaysia	1,978.11	1,711.46	1,900.58	2,032.66	2,185.66	2,374.17	2,649.14	3,102.25	3,412.71
Mexico	2,960.57	2,008.52	2,159.17	2,590.36	3,096.75	3,586.12	4,219.65	4,804.19	5,731.04
Netherlands	9,189.30	12,736.41	15,501.24	16,471.39	16,132.50	19,767.94	20,201.82	22,191.00	21,430.99
New Zealand	6,891.89	8,310.97	11,093.14	13,532.61	12,943.73	13,278.32	12,331.48	11,635.06	12,389.85
Nigeria	331.05	254.85	263.86	284.38	266.90	347.63	304.17	266.62	160.53
Norway	15,449.40	18,495.98	22,020.51	23,706.38	23,805.28	27,677.12	27,996.21	29,842.34	27,323.22
Paraguay	1,167.85	1,351.62	1,097.58	1,408.95	934.28	1,213.14	1,621.53	1,610.22	1,587.11
Peru	881.63	1,293.11	2,088.09	1,616.27	1,952.82	1,331.72	1,557.49	1,599.87	1,542.74
Philippines	620.25	590.90	640.73	715.08	784.88	796.27	797.08	911.42	914.07
Poland	1,896.08	1,961.68	1,687.80	1,815.82	1,768.61	1,625.84	2,101.35	2,311.09	2,347.12
Portugal	2,673.64	3,713.01	4,644.18	5,438.18	5,873.55	7,815.79	8,868.11	10,670.29	9,380.59
Romania	2,083.00	2,243.90	2,495.19	2,569.62	2,293.82	1,631.94	1,233.00	839.92	1,137.13
Russia	n/a	n/a	n/a	n/a	n/a	n/a	n/a	575.99	1,238.65
Saudi Arabia	8,714.81	6,940.77	6,510.77	6,385.68	6,569.77	7,683.59	8,267.14	8,063.88	7,953.12
Singapore	6,748.29	6,853.03	7,767.00	9,303.40	10,715.16	12,745.06	14,412.55	16,099.09	18,250.52
South Africa	1,768.86	1,974.65	2,532.63	2,664.42	2,713.23	3,097.65	3,253.18	3,454.77	3,379.14
Spain	4,597.63	6,343.29	8,017.90	9,400.08	10,347.53	13,400.00	14,393.42	15,681.85	13,132.26
Sweden	12,643.39	16,689.33	20,253.00	22,761.72	23,805.06	28,273.05	29,645.84	30,523.05	23,102.87
Switzerland	15,783.83	22,524.91	28,045.15	30,136.76	28,863.83	36,564.25	36,540.67	37,559.37	36,184.71
Thailand	750.97	813.60	938.09	1,122.03	1,306.77	1,521.05	1,688.66	1,893.55	2,087.83
Turkey	1,842.02	1,998.71	2,256.13	2,412.47	2,811.28	3,857.05	3,804.24	3,919.23	4,372.37
Ukraine	n/a	n/a	n/a	n/a	n/a	n/a	n/a	415.01	652.90
United Arab Emirates	27,036.00	20,533.02	21,644.07	18,435.20	20,478.53	26,621.51	25,847.41	25,960.97	25,654.37
United Kingdom	8,292.22	10,071.35	12,395.15	15,035.78	15,172.00	17,900.27	18,626.80	19,325.51	17,298.21
United States	18,231.83	19,078.41	20,062.55	21,442.13	22,878.98	23,913.66	24,365.53	25,466.73	26,441.65
Vietnam	251.20	556.02	674.88	365.89	97.16	98.03	113.65	144.15	189.26

Source: International Monetary Fund, World Economic Outlook Database, April 2014.

1994	1995	1996	1997	1998	1999	2000	2001	2002	2003	2004
7,576.83	7,531.45	7,862.15	8,381.06	8,478.20	7,970.20	7,917.15	7,417.62	2,656.23	3,439.37	4,048.33
19,736.85	20,956.45	23,195.59	23,055.48	20,344.65	21,739.81	20,869.98	19,438.58	21,616.19	27,273.31	32,813.77
25,439.40	30,043.89	29,497.01	26,113.72	26,780.11	26,598.11	24,044.50	23,854.31	25,769.47	31,340.72	35,720.10
23,336.92	28,112.09	27,199.28	24,589.11	25,111.41	24,950.55	22,790.54	22,671.37	24,606.76	30,155.42	34,834.91
3,493.49	4,844.95	5,207.27	5,321.31	5,077.39	3,477.97	3,764.21	3,188.49	2,870.29	3,090.41	3,664.89
956.59	1,617.77	1,232.72	1,300.58	1,622.98	1,647.47	1,588.36	1,758.26	2,042.62	2,654.17	3,261.89
19,888.86	20,572.16	21,202.83	21,795.99	20,961.72	22,205.35	24,127.69	23,658.37	24,035.69	28,092.96	31,925.39
4,017.86	5,090.12	5,321.97	5,733.65	5,437.33	4,950.72	5,064.47	4,577.87	4,452.26	4,780.25	6,168.39
466.60	601.01	699.48	770.59	817.15	861.21	945.60	1,038.04	1,131.80	1,269.83	1,486.02
2,642.68	2,942.08	3,134.98	2,906.21	2,770.85	2,429.31	2,479.40	2,406.78	2,370.41	2,261.58	2,763.47
11,398.57	14,011.84	13,922.15	13,056.25	13,829.80	13,996.55	13,185.64	13,615.20	14,676.48	18,226.81	21,360.39
n/a	5,592.28	6,287.48	5,768.12	6,200.85	6,041.60	5,721.18	6,291.60	7,687.87	9,349.14	11,179.28
29,556.47	34,891.59	35,123.93	32,309.50	32,796.45	32,735.71	30,033.99	29,999.90	32,389.91	39,495.21	45,339.84
1,898.15	2,052.67	2,210.62	2,455.39	2,564.03	2,674.48	2,904.12	2,959.81	3,090.17	2,426.77	2,463.43
1,854.07	1,975.84	2,032.46	2,248.07	2,252.69	1,595.11	1,458.49	1,906.82	2,180.39	2,434.98	2,700.12
930.63	1,057.35	1,162.07	1,277.18	1,397.39	1,457.85	1,573.84	1,503.34	1,300.65	1,203.48	1,148.67
1,641.19	2,609.58	3,317.06	3,596.63	4,021.33	4,147.08	4,151.15	4,568.35	5,397.58	7,273.07	8,914.16
19,822.50	25,592.36	25,013.86	23,928.37	25,184.63	25,234.25	23,576.21	24,013.85	26,057.31	31,528.53	36,151.81
23,810.08	27,238.24	27,152.86	24,487.66	25,230.31	24,930.36	22,600.49	22,600.48	24,413.99	29,876.70	34,019.75
26,401.49	30,861.58	29,725.01	26,321.44	26,587.54	25,970.71	22,999.57	22,834.83	24,397.52	29,424.49	33,089.64
496.58	517.76	551.55	621.73	680.68	705.42	399.84	393.73	489.64	563.21	714.67
10,387.83	12,352.02	12,949.18	12,664.05	12,654.18	12,966.90	11,702.85	11,993.06	13,484.89	17,728.19	20,868.54
1,301.69	1,425.39	1,480.48	1,633.57	1,711.32	1,588.07	1,530.34	1,625.48	1,761.78	1,812.72	1,933.15
4,091.42	4,408.84	4,450.22	4,517.35	4,664.55	4,706.43	4,537.82	5,168.72	6,524.77	8,236.87	10,074.70
23,729.08	26,255.31	27,280.43	27,479.36	30,355.48	31,678.60	31,094.08	27,879.06	31,106.72	38,026.10	45,602.99
362.37	391.25	418.60	434.74	432.23	462.13	463.12	471.31	492.23	572.30	657.52
15,266.86	18,860.13	20,516.34	22,209.16	23,841.08	25,847.66	25,759.86	27,359.37	31,515.30	39,959.31	46,110.44
16,418.21	18,890.55	20,120.06	20,186.90	19,911.59	19,576.84	21,514.03	20,761.78	18,806.43	19,413.38	20,302.71
18,648.74	19,919.85	22,282.90	21,096.53	21,547.92	21,257.87	19,451.50	19,744.64	21,575.16	26,560.28	30,224.76
2,262.90	2,655.30	2,975.14	3,347.37	3,467.54	3,473.44	3,510.58	3,529.72	3,700.06	3,562.46	3,816.38
38,758.66	42,516.46	37,424.79	34,307.37	30,981.06	35,014.33	37,303.81	32,711.10	31,241.17	33,717.88	36,444.19
341.85	423.47	417.50	450.13	457.02	418.08	402.88	404.14	398.41	439.60	461.92
9,757.50	11,778.76	12,586.61	11,582.11	7,723.84	9,906.50	11,346.66	10,654.82	12,093.73	13,451.10	15,028.82
1,584.66	1,988.82	2,293.81	2,568.52	2,858.36	3,056.42	3,264.81	3,493.18	3,974.67	4,847.76	6,033.31
n/a	n/a	n/a	n/a	n/a	3,113.15	3,286.36	3,510.15	4,104.12	5,413.15	6,594.32
43,478.77	50,532.67	49,663.68	44,157.70	45,572.41	49,184.31	46,514.02	45,744.89	50,712.31	64,559.68	74,420.36
3,697.94	4,295.15	4,752.05	4,601.40	3,231.71	3,454.84	3,991.91	3,846.24	4,078.35	4,352.36	4,815.65
5,888.49	3,771.74	4,291.74	5,114.55	5,269.86	5,998.35	6,977.30	7,266.61	7,347.67	6,992.48	7,475.73
22,881.25	27,126.46	26,922.47	24,791.02	25,670.20	26,055.94	24,249.91	24,990.55	27,206.45	33,241.45	37,507.13
14,415.37	16,737.11	18,285.63	18,012.92	14,702.99	15,175.99	13,832.93	13,501.87	15,503.65	20,226.14	24,589.36
178.95	355.76	431.26	322.73	290.68	309.86	389.95	361.11	470.70	524.26	662.47
28,635.64	34,078.34	36,459.94	35,851.38	34,036.02	35,554.23	37,390.55	37,819.98	42,206.93	49,176.47	56,537.85
1,681.00	1,894.88	2,002.74	2,038.92	1,846.46	1,717.14	1,533.11	1,404.44	1,136.19	1,160.49	1,382.75
1,956.72	2,302.93	2,361.12	2,459.80	2,324.91	2,078.00	2,116.95	2,107.94	2,184.22	2,324.51	2,600.53
1,051.68	1,200.43	1,311.13	1,273.33	960.71	1,080.95	1,055.12	970.38	1,014.94	1,024.77	1,093.48
2,687.41	3,605.31	4,057.58	4,065.33	4,448.94	4,339.24	4,475.91	4,977.81	5,182.89	5,672.93	6,625.21
9,813.71	11,602.56	12,048.19	11,480.79	12,146.47	12,444.99	11,504.54	11,700.72	12,803.71	15,538.79	17,676.77
1,305.21	1,548.97	1,550.50	1,557.48	1,868.29	1,586.44	1,671.53	1,817.91	2,061.24	2,742.19	3,502.87
1,864.66	2,113.63	2,641.77	2,739.83	1,837.54	1,333.61	1,775.13	2,095.58	2,376.90	2,967.51	4,096.86
7,889.53	8,157.46	8,795.62	8,976.16	7,790.87	8,359.73	9,515.06	9,027.49	9,067.84	10,057.69	11,467.10
21,419.97	24,702.00	25,929.64	26,158.10	21,647.26	21,441.38	23,413.77	21,194.09	21,705.06	23,319.87	27,047.14
3,447.02	3,755.40	3,505.11	3,562.00	3,159.42	3,087.07	3,043.70	2,637.63	2,442.79	3,642.33	4,666.61
13,141.98	15,155.43	15,762.74	14,477.10	15,137.31	15,486.72	14,455.73	14,964.58	16,626.43	20,986.01	24,405.15
24,675.35	28,705.08	31,257.62	28,615.37	28,768.35	29,206.66	27,835.73	25,519.75	28,069.13	35,062.93	40,181.34
39,707.59	46,157.59	44,184.21	38,450.51	39,304.07	38,399.27	35,739.32	36,488.58	39,506.19	45,746.13	50,818.23
2,441.95	2,825.72	3,026.60	2,481.11	1,819.86	1,988.75	1,983.32	1,835.78	1,999.30	2,228.26	2,479.03
3,103.68	3,965.18	4,175.16	4,287.91	4,314.94	3,950.73	4,150.39	3,010.11	3,521.55	4,532.82	5,791.72
710.71	721.41	875.87	995.07	838.10	637.42	636.50	781.06	878.77	1,048.30	1,367.74
25,762.53	26,394.42	29,058.86	29,535.55	25,897.65	27,321.04	34,688.98	32,621.29	32,790.71	35,017.31	39,304.51
18,679.62	20,353.45	21,373.49	23,742.84	25,275.21	25,876.12	25,415.32	25,132.49	27,369.96	31,520.64	37,129.69
27,755.48	28,762.68	30,047.22	31,553.44	32,928.95	34,619.90	36,450.14	37,253.44	38,123.18	39,597.37	41,845.61
230.31	288.87	337.52	361.91	360.93	374.72	401.57	413.34	440.21	489.03	603.67

(continued on next page)

Table 3, continued
MACROECONOMIC DATA FOR SELECT COUNTRIES
GDP PER PERSON (U.S. Dollars)

Country	2005	2006	2007	2008	2009	2010	2011	2012	2013
Argentina	4,781.86	5,540.64	6,705.04	8,270.21	7,707.99	9,162.21	10,958.90	11,582.48	11,766.48
Australia	36,089.91	37,888.68	45,151.85	49,108.55	45,623.13	56,342.54	66,541.40	67,855.88	64,863.17
Austria	37,143.21	39,339.41	45,245.56	49,915.00	46,003.57	45,111.55	49,444.29	46,620.24	48,956.92
Belgium	36,187.16	38,086.18	43,486.09	47,789.59	44,125.30	43,545.52	46,705.46	43,553.78	45,384.00
Brazil	4,809.85	5,869.97	7,284.37	8,720.60	8,472.44	11,088.60	12,693.89	11,437.39	11,310.88
Bulgaria	3,753.28	4,329.16	5,520.39	6,854.99	6,432.50	6,374.12	7,311.80	7,048.62	7,328.49
Canada	36,151.54	40,296.67	44,382.83	46,464.70	40,821.77	47,530.60	51,850.32	52,488.73	51,989.51
Chile	7,564.85	9,415.56	10,428.22	10,712.39	10,167.64	12,712.18	14,540.05	15,300.35	15,775.93
China	1,726.05	2,063.87	2,644.56	3,403.53	3,739.62	4,422.66	5,434.36	6,077.65	6,747.23
Colombia	3,417.37	3,745.85	4,721.95	5,488.89	5,198.61	6,306.50	7,303.68	7,935.72	8,097.84
Cyprus	22,742.03	24,305.48	28,038.83	31,685.72	28,657.18	27,501.69	29,021.50	26,376.76	24,761.31
Czech Republic	12,753.04	14,512.93	17,600.40	21,794.22	18,913.42	18,972.65	20,603.29	18,699.47	18,857.91
Denmark	47,617.12	50,553.49	57,171.43	62,800.30	56,345.41	56,542.77	60,019.04	56,475.85	59,190.75
Dominican Republic	3,746.55	3,897.88	4,403.46	4,798.60	4,816.97	5,226.86	5,529.79	5,765.01	5,834.40
Ecuador	3,025.01	3,351.48	3,588.31	4,267.47	4,241.94	4,633.25	5,225.83	5,637.69	5,968.03
Egypt	1,278.85	1,505.96	1,771.00	2,160.04	2,452.63	2,779.71	2,930.12	3,178.95	3,225.52
Estonia	10,333.63	12,510.63	16,404.50	17,800.95	14,522.88	14,237.77	16,836.09	17,295.23	19,031.94
Finland	37,316.14	39,443.69	46,501.68	51,302.50	44,848.61	44,118.26	48,621.90	45,567.52	47,129.30
France	35,107.47	36,772.17	41,849.57	45,789.29	42,046.84	40,943.40	44,153.25	41,223.21	42,999.97
Germany	33,613.84	35,296.70	40,484.99	44,397.84	40,424.06	40,495.85	45,207.64	42,569.47	44,999.50
Ghana	833.40	952.74	1,126.86	1,266.11	1,116.42	1,358.13	1,594.44	1,622.26	1,729.96
Greece	21,717.43	23,573.94	27,447.71	30,691.61	28,760.54	26,357.68	26,084.90	22,346.58	21,857.28
Guatemala	2,140.94	2,320.30	2,554.52	2,859.65	2,690.09	2,875.31	3,236.13	3,325.85	3,512.53
Hungary	10,925.11	11,166.95	13,519.92	15,352.90	12,625.81	12,732.45	13,791.08	12,543.96	13,404.83
Iceland	55,590.44	55,786.89	66,390.20	53,354.20	37,935.14	39,557.68	44,074.89	42,482.30	45,535.58
India	748.85	839.93	1,080.70	1,052.67	1,158.91	1,430.19	1,552.55	1,514.63	1,504.54
Ireland	49,090.31	52,675.44	59,405.71	59,146.02	49,858.39	46,056.37	49,452.99	45,961.96	45,620.71
Israel	20,984.22	22,339.21	25,330.42	30,190.17	28,523.42	31,420.31	34,264.73	33,450.93	37,035.26
Italy	30,918.10	32,287.05	36,587.14	39,523.42	35,874.68	34,789.38	37,031.28	33,915.46	34,714.70
Jamaica	4,186.20	4,429.58	4,754.77	5,053.91	4,436.94	4,816.10	5,228.36	5,328.13	5,133.66
Japan	35,780.57	34,076.75	34,038.35	37,865.07	39,321.22	42,916.74	46,175.36	46,530.38	38,491.35
Kenya	523.65	612.24	721.46	785.78	768.37	787.86	816.84	942.54	1,016.49
Korea	17,550.88	19,676.11	21,590.17	19,028.07	16,958.65	20,540.18	22,388.40	22,590.16	24,328.98
Latvia	7,084.34	8,911.82	12,971.07	15,262.65	11,953.72	11,364.95	13,728.02	13,899.26	15,205.42
Lithuania	7,644.31	8,909.56	12,168.04	14,846.68	11,713.80	11,851.95	14,227.76	14,170.84	16,003.20
Luxembourg	80,971.40	90,049.03	106,916.14	112,429.42	99,456.13	102,759.38	111,788.65	103,806.62	110,423.84
Malaysia	5,421.34	6,065.61	7,144.42	8,372.19	7,203.34	8,658.68	9,979.41	10,387.16	10,547.97
Mexico	8,183.98	9,010.18	9,565.44	9,934.74	7,943.43	9,194.43	10,107.03	10,110.69	10,629.88
Netherlands	39,189.91	41,497.70	47,838.63	53,198.73	48,300.07	46,861.68	49,932.22	45,988.60	47,633.62
New Zealand	27,117.93	25,900.99	31,376.19	31,042.42	27,621.12	32,518.40	36,879.13	38,384.91	40,481.37
Nigeria	823.82	1,038.76	1,172.54	1,415.31	1,123.63	1,484.11	1,547.86	1,603.60	1,692.26
Norway	65,646.21	72,784.95	83,335.71	94,815.85	78,231.37	85,764.69	98,693.79	99,249.00	100,318.32
Paraguay	1,481.61	1,771.72	2,254.08	2,970.05	2,512.81	3,204.84	3,678.75	3,734.48	4,169.72
Peru	2,916.68	3,340.24	3,800.44	4,427.11	4,362.46	5,204.83	5,883.15	6,549.64	6,674.34
Philippines	1,208.93	1,405.21	1,683.69	1,918.26	1,851.48	2,155.41	2,378.93	2,611.50	2,790.37
Poland	7,962.95	8,954.31	11,155.83	13,890.16	11,313.67	12,308.93	13,383.56	12,708.96	13,394.34
Portugal	18,217.21	19,082.70	21,876.67	23,827.93	22,076.41	21,562.35	22,355.83	20,019.90	20,727.59
Romania	4,589.36	5,686.89	7,923.16	9,564.29	7,677.59	7,683.24	8,584.00	7,929.14	8,910.47
Russia	5,310.88	6,912.93	9,101.56	11,630.58	8,567.94	10,671.21	13,252.56	14,015.75	14,818.64
Saudi Arabia	14,079.15	15,624.82	16,677.72	20,157.28	16,094.68	19,112.70	23,593.82	25,139.00	24,847.16
Singapore	29,403.39	33,174.49	38,848.26	39,326.78	38,127.43	45,953.53	52,533.15	53,516.04	54,775.53
South Africa	5,183.69	5,410.73	5,843.48	5,517.50	5,682.97	7,174.74	7,839.13	7,314.01	6,620.72
Spain	25,943.54	27,896.44	31,910.42	34,815.20	31,446.80	29,797.10	31,150.71	28,294.11	29,150.35
Sweden	40,958.21	43,790.68	50,366.61	52,521.66	43,442.55	49,180.46	56,523.12	54,829.11	57,909.29
Switzerland	51,888.75	54,321.34	59,998.62	69,049.02	66,155.87	70,524.65	83,718.85	79,344.25	81,323.96
Thailand	2,707.51	3,172.30	3,756.87	4,110.00	3,943.07	4,740.33	5,114.73	5,390.41	5,674.39
Turkey	7,040.48	7,627.03	9,206.37	10,276.78	8,527.26	10,020.67	10,476.39	10,523.36	10,815.46
Ukraine	1,829.76	2,304.92	3,071.49	3,899.27	2,550.45	2,979.67	3,583.97	3,877.28	3,919.41
United Arab Emirates	43,988.56	44,283.30	41,472.29	39,074.84	31,073.63	34,778.05	40,951.45	43,773.84	43,875.93
United Kingdom	38,585.28	41,043.81	46,866.10	44,131.29	35,885.34	36,891.36	38,945.08	38,999.21	39,567.41
United States	44,224.13	46,358.36	47,963.56	48,307.78	46,906.90	48,294.15	49,797.25	51,708.98	53,101.01
Vietnam	699.68	796.93	920.46	1,154.49	1,181.45	1,297.23	1,532.31	1,752.62	1,901.70

Source: International Monetary Fund, World Economic Outlook Database, April 2014.

Solutions to Check Your Understanding Questions

This section offers suggested answers to the "Check Your Understanding" questions found within chapters.

Chapter One

1-1 Check Your Understanding

1. a. This illustrates the concept of opportunity cost. Given that a person can only eat so much at one sitting, having a slice of chocolate cake requires that you forgo eating something else, such as a slice of coconut cream pie.

b. This illustrates the concept that resources are scarce. Even if there were more resources in the world, the total amount of those resources would be limited. As a result, scarcity would still arise. For there to be no scarcity, there would have to be unlimited amounts of everything (including unlimited time in a human life), which is clearly impossible.

c. This illustrates the concept that people usually exploit opportunities to make themselves better off. Students will seek to make themselves better off by signing up for the tutorials of teaching assistants with good reputations and avoiding those teaching assistants with poor reputations. It also illustrates the concept that resources are scarce. If there were unlimited spaces in tutorials with good teaching assistants, they would not fill up.

d. This illustrates the concept of marginal analysis. Your decision about allocating your time is a "how much" decision: how much time spent exercising versus how much time spent studying. You make your decision by comparing the benefit of an additional hour of exercising to its cost, the effect on your grades of one fewer hour spent studying.

2. a. Yes. The increased time spent commuting is a cost you will incur if you accept the new job. That additional time spent commuting—or equivalently, the benefit you would get from spending that time doing something else—is an opportunity cost of the new job.

b. Yes. One of the benefits of the new job is that you will be making $50,000. But if you take the new job, you will have to give up your current job; that is, you have to give up your current salary of $45,000. So $45,000 is one of the opportunity costs of taking the new job.

c. No. A more spacious office is an additional benefit of your new job and does not involve forgoing something else. So it is not an opportunity cost.

1-2 Check Your Understanding

1. a. This illustrates the concept that markets usually lead to efficiency. Any seller who wants to sell a book for at least $30 does indeed sell to someone who is willing to buy a book for $30. As a result, there is no way to change how used textbooks are distributed among buyers and sellers in a way that would make one person better off without making someone else worse off.

b. This illustrates the concept that there are gains from trade. Students trade tutoring services based on their different abilities in academic subjects.

c. This illustrates the concept that when markets don't achieve efficiency, government intervention can improve society's welfare. In this case the market, left alone, will permit bars and nightclubs to impose costs on their neighbors in the form of loud music, costs that the bars and nightclubs have no incentive to take into account. This is an inefficient outcome because society as a whole can be made better off if bars and nightclubs are induced to reduce their noise.

d. This illustrates the concept that resources should be used as efficiently as possible to achieve society's goals. By closing neighborhood clinics and shifting funds to the main hospital, better health care can be provided at a lower cost.

e. This illustrates the concept that markets move toward equilibrium. Here, because books with the same amount of wear and tear sell for about the same price, no buyer or seller can be made better off by engaging in a different trade than he or she undertook. This means that the market for used textbooks has moved to an equilibrium.

2. a. This does not describe an equilibrium situation. Many students should want to change their behavior and switch to eating at the restaurants. Therefore, the situation described is not an equilibrium. An equilibrium will be established when students are equally as well off eating at the restaurants as eating at the dining hall—which would happen if, say, prices at the dining hall were higher than at the restaurants.

b. This does describe an equilibrium situation. By changing your behavior and riding the bus, you would not be made better off. Therefore, you have no incentive to change your behavior.

1-3 Check Your Understanding

1. a. This illustrates the principle that government policies can change spending. The tax cut would increase people's after-tax incomes, leading to higher consumer spending.

b. This illustrates the principle that one person's spending is another person's income. As oil companies increase their spending on labor by hiring more workers, or pay existing workers higher wages, those workers' incomes rise. In turn, these workers increase their consumer spending, which becomes income to restaurants and other consumer businesses.

c. This illustrates the principle that overall spending sometimes gets out of line with the economy's productive capacity. In this case, spending on housing was too high relative to the economy's capacity to create new housing. This first led to a rise in house prices, and then—as a result—to a rise in overall prices, or *inflation*.

Chapter Two

2-1 Check Your Understanding

1. a. False. An increase in the resources available to Boeing for use in producing Dreamliners and small jets changes the production possibility frontier by shifting it outward. This is because Boeing can now produce more small jets and Dreamliners than before. In the accompanying figure, the line labeled "Boeing's original *PPF*" represents Boeing's original production possibility frontier, and the line labeled "Boeing's new *PPF*" represents the new production possibility frontier that results from an increase in resources available to Boeing.

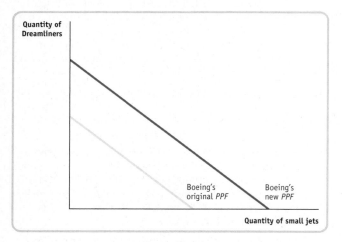

b. True. A technological change that allows Boeing to build more small jets for any amount of Dreamliners built results in a change in its production possibility frontier. This is illustrated in the accompanying figure: the new production possibility frontier is represented by the line labeled "Boeing's new *PPF*," and the original production frontier is represented by the line labeled "Boeing's original *PPF*." Since the maximum quantity of Dreamliners that Boeing can build is the same as before, the new production possibility frontier intersects the vertical axis at the same point as the original frontier. But since the maximum possible quantity of small jets is now greater than before, the new frontier intersects the horizontal axis to the right of the original frontier.

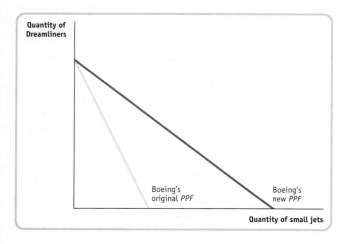

c. False. The production possibility frontier illustrates how much of one good an economy must give up to get more of another good only when resources are used efficiently in production. If an economy is producing inefficiently—that is, inside the frontier—then it does not have to give up a unit of one good in order to get another unit of the other good. Instead, by becoming more efficient in production, this economy can have more of both goods.

2. a. The United States has an absolute advantage in automobile production because it takes fewer Americans (6) to produce a car in one day than Italians (8). The United States also has an absolute advantage in washing machine production because it takes fewer Americans (2) to produce a washing machine in one day than Italians (3).

b. In Italy the opportunity cost of a washing machine in terms of an automobile is $3/8$: $3/8$ of a car can be produced with the same number of workers and in the same time it takes to produce 1 washing machine. In the United States the opportunity cost of a washing machine in terms of an automobile is $2/6 = 1/3$: $1/3$ of a car can be produced with the same number of workers and in the same time it takes to produce 1 washing machine. Since $1/3 < 3/8$, the United States has a comparative advantage in the production of washing machines: to produce a washing machine, only $1/3$ of a car must be given up in the United States but $3/8$ of a car must be given up in Italy. This means that Italy has a comparative advantage in automobiles. This can be checked as follows. The opportunity cost of an automobile in terms of a washing machine in Italy is $8/3$, equal to $2 2/3$: $2 2/3$ washing machines can be produced with the same number of workers and in the time it takes to produce 1 car in Italy. And the opportunity cost of an automobile in terms of a washing machine in the United States is $6/2$, equal to 3: 3 washing machines can be produced with the same number of workers and in the time it takes to produce 1 car in the United States. Since $2 2/3 < 3$, Italy has a comparative advantage in producing automobiles.

c. The greatest gains are realized when each country specializes in producing the good for which it has a comparative advantage. Therefore, the United States should specialize in washing machines and Italy should specialize in automobiles.

3. At a trade of 10 U.S. large jets for 15 Brazilian small jets, Brazil gives up less for a large jet than it would if it were building large jets itself. Without trade, Brazil gives up 3 small jets for each large jet it produces. With trade, Brazil gives up only 1.5 small jets for each large jet from the United States. Likewise, the United States gives up less for a small jet than it would if it were producing small jets itself. Without trade, the United States gives up $3/4$ of a large jet for each small jet. With trade, the United States gives up only $2/3$ of a large jet for each small jet from Brazil.

4. An increase in the amount of money spent by households results in an increase in the flow of goods to households. This, in turn, generates an increase in demand for factors of production by firms. So, there is an increase in the number of jobs in the economy.

2-2 Check Your Understanding

1. a. This is a normative statement because it stipulates what should be done. In addition, it may have no "right" answer. That is, should people be prevented from all dangerous personal behavior if they enjoy that behavior—like skydiving? Your answer will depend on your point of view.

b. This is a positive statement because it is a description of fact.

2. a. True. Economists often have different value judgments about the desirability of a particular social goal. But despite those differences in value judgments, they will tend to agree that society, once it has decided to pursue a given social goal, should adopt the most efficient policy to achieve that goal. Therefore economists are likely to agree on adopting policy choice B.

b. False. Disagreements between economists are more likely to arise because they base their conclusions on different models or because they have different value judgments about the desirability of the policy.

c. False. Deciding which goals a society should try to achieve is a matter of value judgments, not a question of economic analysis.

Chapter Three

3-1 Check Your Understanding

1. a. The quantity of umbrellas demanded is higher at any given price on a rainy day than on a dry day. This is a rightward *shift of* the demand curve, since at any given price the quantity demanded rises. This implies that any specific quantity can now be sold at a higher price.

b. The quantity of summer Caribbean cruises demanded rises in response to a price reduction. This is a *movement along* the demand curve for summer Caribbean cruises.

c. The demand for roses increases the week of Valentine's Day. This is a rightward *shift of* the demand curve.

d. The quantity of gasoline demanded falls in response to a rise in price. This is a *movement along* the demand curve.

3-2 Check Your Understanding

1. a. The quantity of houses supplied rises as a result of an increase in prices. This is a *movement along* the supply curve.

b. The quantity of strawberries supplied is higher at any given price. This is a rightward *shift of* the supply curve.

c. The quantity of labor supplied is lower at any given wage. This is a leftward *shift of* the supply curve compared to the supply curve during school vacation. So, in order to attract workers, fast-food chains have to offer higher wages.

d. The quantity of labor supplied rises in response to a rise in wages. This is a *movement along* the supply curve.

e. The quantity of cabins supplied is higher at any given price. This is a rightward *shift of* the supply curve.

3-3 Check Your Understanding

1. a. The supply curve shifts rightward. At the original equilibrium price of the year before, the quantity of grapes supplied exceeds the quantity demanded. This is a case of surplus. The price of grapes will fall.

b. The demand curve shifts leftward. At the original equilibrium price, the quantity of hotel rooms supplied exceeds the quantity demanded. This is a case of surplus. The rates for hotel rooms will fall.

c. The demand curve for second-hand snowblowers shifts rightward. At the original equilibrium price, the quantity of second-hand snowblowers demanded exceeds the quantity supplied. This is a case of shortage. The equilibrium price of second-hand snowblowers will rise.

3-4 Check Your Understanding

1. a. The market for large cars: this is a rightward shift in demand caused by a decrease in the price of a complement, gasoline. As a result of the shift, the equilibrium price of large cars will rise and the equilibrium quantity of large cars bought and sold will also rise.

b. The market for fresh paper made from recycled stock: this is a rightward shift in supply due to a technological innovation. As a result of this shift, the equilibrium price of fresh paper made from recycled stock will fall and the equilibrium quantity bought and sold will rise.

c. The market for movies at a local movie theater: this is a leftward shift in demand caused by a fall in the price of a substitute, on-demand films. As a result of this shift, the equilibrium price of movie tickets will fall and the equilibrium number of people who go to the movies will also fall.

2. Upon the announcement of the new chip, the demand curve for computers using the earlier chip shifts leftward, as demand decreases, and the supply curve for these computers shifts rightward, as supply increases.

a. If demand decreases relatively more than supply increases, then the equilibrium quantity falls, as shown here:

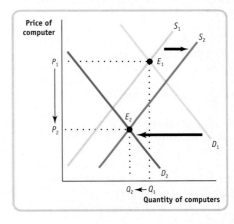

b. If supply increases relatively more than demand decreases, then the equilibrium quantity rises, as shown here:

c. In both cases, the equilibrium price falls.

Chapter Four

4-1 Check Your Understanding

1. A consumer buys each pepper if the price is less than (or just equal to) the consumer's willingness to pay for that pepper. The demand schedule is constructed by asking how many peppers will be demanded at any given price. The accompanying table illustrates the demand schedule.

Price of pepper	Quantity of peppers demanded	Quantity of peppers demanded by Casey	Quantity of peppers demanded by Josey
$0.90	1	1	0
0.80	2	1	1
0.70	3	2	1
0.60	4	2	2
0.50	5	3	2
0.40	6	3	3
0.30	8	4	4
0.20	8	4	4
0.10	8	4	4
0.00	8	4	4

When the price is $0.40, Casey's consumer surplus from the first pepper is $0.50, from his second pepper $0.30, from his third pepper $0.10, and he does not buy any more peppers. Casey's individual consumer surplus is therefore $0.90. Josey's consumer surplus from her first pepper is $0.40, from her second pepper $0.20, from her third pepper $0.00 (since the price is exactly equal to her willingness to pay, she buys the third pepper but receives no consumer surplus from it), and she does not buy any more peppers. Josey's individual consumer surplus is therefore $0.60. Total consumer surplus at a price of $0.40 is therefore $0.90 + $0.60 = $1.50.

4-2 Check Your Understanding

1. **a.** A producer supplies each pepper if the price is greater than (or just equal to) the producer's cost of producing that pepper. The supply schedule is constructed by asking how many peppers will be supplied at any price. The accompanying table illustrates the supply schedule.

   b. When the price is $0.70, Cara's producer surplus from the first pepper is $0.60, from her second pepper $0.60, from her third pepper $0.30, from her fourth pepper $0.10, and she does not supply any more peppers. Cara's individual producer surplus is therefore $1.60. Jamie's producer surplus from his first pepper is $0.40, from his second pepper $0.20, from his third pepper $0.00 (since the price is exactly equal to his cost, he sells the third pepper but receives no producer surplus from it), and he does not supply any more peppers. Jamie's individual producer surplus is therefore $0.60. Total producer surplus at a price of $0.70 is therefore $1.60 + $0.60 = $2.20.

Price of pepper	Quantity of peppers supplied	Quantity of peppers supplied by Cara	Quantity of peppers supplied by Jamie
$0.90	8	4	4
0.80	7	4	3
0.70	7	4	3
0.60	6	4	2
0.50	5	3	2
0.40	4	3	1
0.30	3	2	1
0.20	2	2	0
0.10	2	2	0
0.00	0	0	0

4-3 Check Your Understanding

1. The quantity demanded equals the quantity supplied at a price of $0.50, the equilibrium price. At that price, a total quantity of five peppers will be bought and sold. Casey will buy three peppers and receive consumer surplus of $0.40 on his first, $0.20 on his second, and $0.00 on his third pepper. Josey will buy two peppers and receive consumer surplus of $0.30 on her first and $0.10 on her second pepper. Total consumer surplus is therefore $1.00. Cara will supply three peppers and receive producer surplus of $0.40 on her first, $0.40 on her second, and $0.10 on her third pepper. Jamie will supply two peppers and receive producer surplus of $0.20 on his first and $0.00 on his second pepper. Total producer surplus is therefore $1.10. Total surplus in this market is therefore $1.00 + $1.10 = $2.10.

2. **a.** If Josey consumes one fewer pepper, she loses $0.60 (her willingness to pay for her second pepper); if Casey consumes one more pepper, he gains $0.30 (his willingness to pay for his fourth pepper). This results in an overall loss of consumer surplus of $0.60 − $0.30 = $0.30.

b. Cara's cost of the last pepper she supplied (the third pepper) is $0.40, and Jamie's cost of producing one more (his third pepper) is $0.70. Total producer surplus therefore falls by $0.70 – $0.40 = $0.30.

c. Josey's willingness to pay for her second pepper is $0.60; this is what she would lose if she were to consume one fewer pepper. Cara's cost of producing her third pepper is $0.40; this is what she would save if she were to produce one fewer pepper. If we therefore reduced quantity by one pepper, we would lose $0.60 – $0.40 = $0.20 of total surplus.

3. The new guideline is likely to reduce the total life span of kidney recipients because older recipients (those with small children) are more likely to get a kidney compared to the original guideline. As a result, total surplus is likely to fall. However, this new policy can be justified as an acceptable sacrifice of efficiency for fairness because it's a desirable goal to reduce the chance of a small child losing a parent.

4-4 Check Your Understanding

1. When these rights are separated, someone who owns both the above-ground and the mineral rights can sell each of these separately in the market for above-ground rights and the market for mineral rights. And each of these markets will achieve efficiency: If the market price for above-ground rights is higher than the seller's cost, the seller will sell that right and total surplus increases. If the market price for mineral rights is higher than the seller's cost, the seller will sell that right and total surplus increases. If the two rights, however, cannot be sold separately, a seller can only sell both rights or none at all. Imagine a situation in which the seller values the mineral right highly (that is, has a high cost of selling it) but values the above-ground right much less. If the two rights are separate, the owner may sell the above-ground right (increasing total surplus) but not the mineral right. If, however, the two rights cannot be sold separately, and the owner values the mineral right sufficiently highly, she may not sell either of the two rights. In this case, surplus could have been created through the sale of the above-ground right but goes unrealized because the two rights could not be sold separately.

2. There will be many sellers willing to sell their books but only a few buyers who want to buy books at that price. As a result, only a few transactions will actually occur, and many transactions that would have been mutually beneficial will not take place. This, of course, is inefficient.

3. Markets, alas, do not always lead to efficiency. When there is market failure, the market outcome may be inefficient. This can occur for three main reasons. Markets can fail when, in an attempt to capture more surplus, one party—a monopolist, for instance—prevents mutually beneficial trades from occurring. Markets can also fail when one individual's actions have side effects—externalities—on the welfare of others. Finally, markets can fail when the goods themselves—such as goods about which some relevant information is private—are unsuited for efficient management by markets. And when markets don't achieve efficiency, government intervention can improve society's welfare.

Chapter Five

5-1 Check Your Understanding

1. a. Fewer homeowners are willing to rent out their driveways because the price ceiling has reduced the payment they receive. This is an example of a fall in price leading to a fall in the quantity supplied. It is shown in the accompanying diagram by the movement from point E to point A along the supply curve, a reduction in quantity of 400 parking spaces.

b. The quantity demanded increases by 400 spaces as the price decreases. At a lower price, more fans are willing to drive and rent a parking space. It is shown in the diagram by the movement from point E to point B along the demand curve.

c. Under a price ceiling, the quantity demanded exceeds the quantity supplied; as a result, shortages arise. In this case, there will be a shortage of 800 parking spaces. It is shown by the horizontal distance between points A and B.

d. Price ceilings result in wasted resources. The additional time fans spend to guarantee a parking space is wasted time.

e. Price ceilings lead to inefficient allocation of a good— here, the parking spaces—to consumers.

f. Price ceilings lead to black markets.

2. a. False. By lowering the price that producers receive, a price ceiling leads to a decrease in the quantity supplied.

b. True. A price ceiling leads to a lower quantity supplied than in an efficient, unregulated market. As a result, some people who would have been willing to pay the market price, and so would have gotten the good in an unregulated market, are unable to obtain it when a price ceiling is imposed.

c. True. Those producers who still sell the product now receive less for it and are therefore worse off. Other producers will no longer find it worthwhile to sell the product at all and so will also be made worse off.

3. a. Since the apartment is rented quickly at the same price, there is no change (either gain or loss) in producer surplus. So any change in total surplus comes from changes in consumer surplus. When you are evicted, the amount of consumer surplus you lose is equal to the difference between your willingness to pay for the apartment and the rent-controlled price. When the apartment is rented to someone else at the same price, the amount of consumer surplus the new renter gains is equal to the difference between his or her willingness to pay and the rent-controlled price. So this will be a pure transfer of surplus from one person to another only if both your willingness to pay and the new renter's willingness to pay are the same. Since under rent control apartments are not always allocated to those who have the highest willingness to pay, the new renter's willingness to pay may be either equal to, lower than, or higher than your willingness to pay. If the new renter's willingness to pay is lower than yours, this will create additional deadweight loss: there is some additional consumer surplus that is lost. However, if the new renter's willingness to pay is higher than yours, this will create an increase in total surplus, as the new renter gains more consumer surplus than you lost.

b. This creates deadweight loss: if you were able to give the ticket away, someone else would be able to obtain consumer surplus, equal to his or her willingness to pay for the ticket. You neither gain nor lose any surplus, since you cannot go to the concert whether or not you give the ticket away. If you were able to sell the ticket, the buyer would obtain consumer surplus equal to the difference between his or her willingness to pay for the ticket and the price at which you sell the ticket. In addition, you would obtain producer surplus equal to the difference between the price at which you sell the ticket and your cost of selling the ticket (which, since you won the ticket, is presumably zero). Since the restriction to neither sell nor give away the ticket means that this surplus cannot be obtained by anybody, it creates deadweight loss. If you could give the ticket away, as described above, there would be consumer surplus that accrues to the recipient of the ticket; and if you give the ticket to the person with the highest willingness to pay, there would be no deadweight loss.

c. This creates deadweight loss. If students buy ice cream on campus, they obtain consumer surplus: their willingness to pay must be higher than the price of the ice cream. Your college obtains producer surplus: the price is higher than your college's cost of selling the ice cream. Prohibiting the sale of ice cream on campus means that these two sources of total surplus are lost: there is deadweight loss.

d. Given that your dog values ice cream equally as much as you do, this is a pure transfer of surplus. As you lose consumer surplus, your dog gains equally as much consumer surplus.

5-2 Check Your Understanding

1. a. Some gas station owners will benefit from getting a higher price. Q_F indicates the sales made by these owners. But some will lose; there are those who make sales at the market equilibrium price of P_E but do not make sales at the regulated price of P_F. These missed sales are indicated on the graph by the fall in the quantity demanded along the demand curve, from point E to point A.

b. Those who buy gas at the higher price of P_F will probably receive better service; this is an example of *inefficiently high quality* caused by a price floor as gas station owners compete on quality rather than price. But opponents are correct to claim that consumers are generally worse off—those who buy at P_F would have been happy to buy at P_E, and many who were willing to buy at a price between P_E and P_F are now unwilling to buy. This is indicated on the graph by the fall in the quantity demanded along the demand curve, from point E to point A.

c. Proponents are wrong because consumers and some gas station owners are hurt by the price floor, which creates "missed opportunities"—desirable transactions between consumers and station owners that never take place. The deadweight loss, the amount of total surplus lost because of missed opportunities, is indicated by the shaded area in the accompanying figure. Moreover, the inefficiency of wasted resources arises as consumers spend time and money driving to other states. The price floor also tempts people to engage in black market activity. With the price floor, only Q_F units are sold. But at prices between P_E and P_F, there are drivers who cumulatively want to buy more than Q_F and owners who are willing to sell to them, a situation likely to lead to illegal activity.

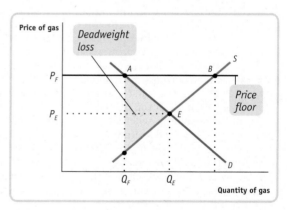

5-3 Check Your Understanding

1. a. The price of a ride is $7 since the quantity demanded at this price is 6 million: $7 is the *demand price* of 6 million rides. This is represented by point A in the accompanying figure.

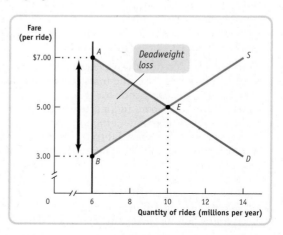

b. At 6 million rides, the supply price is $3 per ride, represented by point B in the figure. The wedge between the demand price of $7 per ride and the supply price of $3 per ride is the quota rent per ride, $4. This is represented in the figure above by the vertical distance between points A and B.

c. The quota discourages 4 million mutually beneficial transactions. The shaded triangle in the figure represents the deadweight loss.

d. At 9 million rides, the demand price is $5.50 per ride, indicated by point C in the accompanying figure, and the supply price is $4.50 per ride, indicated by point D. The quota rent is the difference between the demand price and the supply price: $1. The deadweight loss is represented by the shaded triangle in the figure. As you can see, the deadweight loss is smaller when the quota is set at 9 million rides than when it is set at 6 million rides.

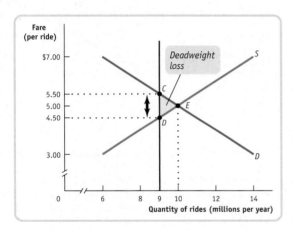

2. The accompanying figure shows a decrease in demand by 4 million rides, represented by a leftward shift of the demand curve from D_1 to D_2: at any given price, the quantity demanded falls by 4 million rides. (For example, at a price of $5, the quantity demanded falls from 10 million to 6 million rides per year.) This eliminates the effect of a quota limit of 8 million rides. At point E_2, the new market equilibrium, the equilibrium quantity is equal to the quota limit; as a result, the quota has no effect on the market.

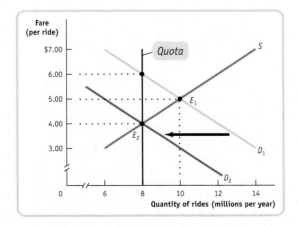

Chapter Six

6-1 Check Your Understanding

1. By the midpoint method, the percent change in the price of strawberries is

$$\frac{\$1.00 - \$1.50}{(\$1.50 + \$1.00)/2} \times 100 = \frac{-\$0.50}{\$1.25} \times 100 = -40\%$$

Similarly, the percent change in the quantity of strawberries demanded is

$$\frac{200,000 - 100,000}{(100,000 + 200,000)/2} \times 100 = \frac{100,000}{150,000} \times 100 = 67\%$$

Dropping the minus sign, the price elasticity of demand using the midpoint method is 67%/40% = 1.7.

2. By the midpoint method, the percent change in the quantity of movie tickets demanded in going from 4,000 tickets to 5,000 tickets is

$$\frac{5,000 - 4,000}{(4,000 + 5,000)/2} \times 100 = \frac{1,000}{4,500} \times 100 = 22\%$$

Since the price elasticity of demand is 1 at the current consumption level, it will take a 22% reduction in the price of movie tickets to generate a 22% increase in quantity demanded.

3. Since price rises, we know that quantity demanded must fall. Given the current price of $0.50, a $0.05 increase in price represents a 10% change, using the method in Equation 6-2. So the price elasticity of demand is

$$\frac{\text{change in quantity demanded}}{10\%} = 1.2$$

so that the percent change in quantity demanded is 12%. A 12% decrease in quantity demanded represents $100,000 \times 0.12$, or 12,000 sandwiches.

6-2 Check Your Understanding

1. a. Elastic demand. Consumers are highly responsive to changes in price. For a rise in price, the quantity effect (which tends to reduce total revenue) outweighs the price effect (which tends to increase total revenue). Overall, this leads to a fall in total revenue.

b. Unit-elastic demand. Here the revenue lost to the fall in price is exactly equal to the revenue gained from higher sales. The quantity effect exactly offsets the price effect.

c. Inelastic demand. Consumers are relatively unresponsive to changes in price. For consumers to purchase a given percent increase in output, the price must fall by an even greater percent. The price effect of a fall in price (which tends to reduce total revenue) outweighs the quantity effect (which tends to increase total revenue). As a result, total revenue decreases.

d. Inelastic demand. Consumers are relatively unresponsive to price, so the percent fall in output is smaller than the percent rise in price. The price effect of a rise in price (which tends to increase total revenue) outweighs the quantity effect (which tends to reduce total revenue). As a result, total revenue increases.

2. a. The demand of an accident victim for a blood transfusion is very likely to be perfectly inelastic because there is no substitute and it is necessary for survival. The demand curve will be vertical, at a quantity equal to the needed transfusion quantity.

b. Students' demand for green erasers is likely to be perfectly elastic because there are easily available substitutes: nongreen erasers. The demand curve will be horizontal, at a price equal to that of nongreen erasers.

6-3 Check Your Understanding

1. By the midpoint method, the percent increase in Chelsea's income is

$$\frac{\$18{,}000 - \$12{,}000}{(\$12{,}000 + \$18{,}000)/2} \times 100 = \frac{\$6{,}000}{\$15{,}000} \times 100 = 40\%$$

Similarly, the percent increase in her consumption of albums is

$$\frac{40 - 10}{(10 + 40)/2} \times 100 = \frac{30}{25} \times 100 = 120\%$$

So Chelsea's income elasticity of demand for albums is 120%/40% = 3.

2. Sanjay's consumption of expensive restaurant meals will fall more than 10% because a given percent change in income (a fall of 10% here) induces a larger percent change in consumption of an income-elastic good.

3. The cross-price elasticity of demand is 5%/20% = 0.25. Since the cross-price elasticity of demand is positive, the two goods are substitutes.

6-4 Check Your Understanding

1. By the midpoint method, the percent change in the number of hours of web-design services contracted is

$$\frac{500{,}000 - 300{,}000}{(300{,}000 + 500{,}000)/2} \times 100 = \frac{200{,}000}{400{,}000} \times 100 = 50\%$$

Similarly, the percent change in the price of web-design services is:

$$\frac{\$150 - \$100}{(\$100 + \$150)/2} \times 100 = \frac{\$50}{\$125} \times 100 = 40\%$$

The price elasticity of supply is 50%/40% = 1.25. So supply is elastic.

2. True. An increase in demand raises price. If the price elasticity of supply of milk is low, then relatively little additional quantity supplied will be forthcoming as the price rises. As a result, the price of milk will rise substantially to satisfy the increased demand for milk. If the price elasticity of supply is high, then there will be a relatively large increase in quantity supplied when the price rises. As a result, the price of milk will rise only by a little to satisfy the higher demand for milk.

3. False. It is true that long-run price elasticities of supply are generally larger than short-run elasticities of supply. But this means that the short-run supply curves are generally steeper, not flatter, than the long-run supply curves.

4. True. When supply is perfectly elastic, the supply curve is a horizontal line. So a change in demand has no effect on price; it affects only the quantity bought and sold.

Chapter Seven

7-1 Check Your Understanding

1. The following figure shows that, after introduction of the excise tax, the price paid by consumers rises to $1.20; the price received by producers falls to $0.90. Consumers bear $0.20 of the $0.30 tax per pound of butter; producers bear $0.10 of the $0.30 tax per pound of butter. The tax drives a wedge of $0.30 between the price paid by consumers and the price received by producers. As a result, the quantity of butter bought and sold is now 9 million pounds.

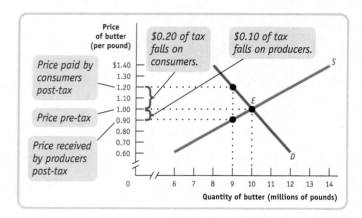

2. The fact that demand is very inelastic means that consumers will reduce their demand for textbooks very little in response to an increase in the price caused by the tax. The fact that supply is somewhat elastic means that suppliers will respond to the fall in the price by reducing supply. As a result, the incidence of the tax will fall heavily on consumers of economics textbooks and very little on publishers, as shown in the accompanying figure.

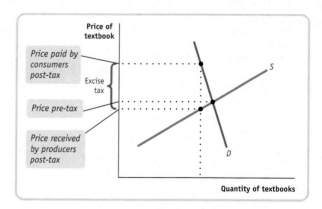

3. True. When a substitute is readily available, demand is elastic. This implies that producers cannot easily pass on the cost of the tax to consumers because consumers will respond to an increased price by switching to the substitute. Furthermore, when producers have difficulty adjusting the amount of the good produced, supply is inelastic. That is, producers cannot easily reduce output in response to a lower price net of tax. So the tax burden will fall more heavily on producers than consumers.

4. The fact that supply is very inelastic means that producers will reduce their supply of bottled water very little in response to the fall in price caused by the tax. Demand, on the other hand, will fall in response to an increase in price because demand is somewhat elastic. As a result, the incidence of the tax will fall heavily on producers of bottled spring water and very little on consumers, as shown in the accompanying figure.

5. True. The lower the elasticity of supply, the more the burden of a tax will fall on producers rather than consumers, other things equal.

7-2 Check Your Understanding

1. a. Without the excise tax, Zhang, Yves, Xavier, and Walter sell, and Ana, Bernice, Chizuko, and Dagmar buy one can of soda each, at $0.40 per can. So the quantity bought and sold is 4.

b. At a price to consumers of $0.60, only Ana and Bernice are willing to buy a can of soda. At a price paid to producers of only $0.20, only Zhang and Yves are willing to sell. So the quantity bought and sold is 2.

c. Without the excise tax, Ana's individual consumer surplus is $0.70 − $0.40 = $0.30, Bernice's is $0.60 − $0.40 = $0.20, Chizuko's is $0.50 − $0.40 = $0.10, and Dagmar's is $0.40 − $0.40 = $0.00. Total consumer surplus is $0.30 + $0.20 + $0.10 + $0.00 = $0.60. With the tax, Ana's individual consumer surplus is $0.70 − $0.60 = $0.10 and Bernice's is $0.60 − $0.60 = $0.00. Total consumer surplus post-tax is $0.10 + $0.00 = $0.10. So the total consumer surplus lost because of the tax is $0.60 − $0.10 = $0.50.

d. Without the excise tax, Zhang's individual producer surplus is $0.40 − $0.10 = $0.30, Yves's is $0.40 − $0.20 = $0.20, Xavier's is $0.40 − $0.30 = $0.10, and Walter's is $0.40 − $0.40 = $0.00. Total producer surplus is $0.30 + $0.20 + $0.10 + $0.00 = $0.60. With the tax, Zhang's individual producer surplus is $0.20 − $0.10 = $0.10 and Yves's is $0.20 − $0.20 = $0.00. Total producer surplus post-tax is $0.10 + $0.00 = $0.10. So the total producer surplus lost because of the tax is $0.60 − $0.10 = $0.50.

e. With the tax, two cans of soda are sold, so the government tax revenue from this excise tax is 2 × $0.40 = $0.80.

f. Total surplus without the tax is $0.60 + $0.60 = $1.20. With the tax, total surplus is $0.10 + $0.10 = $0.20, and government tax revenue is $0.80. So deadweight loss from this excise tax is $1.20 − ($0.20 + $0.80) = $0.20.

2. a. The demand for gasoline is inelastic because there is no close substitute for gasoline itself and it is difficult for drivers to arrange substitutes for driving, such as taking public transportation. As a result, the deadweight loss from a tax on gasoline would be relatively small, as shown in the accompanying diagram.

b. The demand for milk chocolate bars is elastic because there are close substitutes: dark chocolate bars, milk chocolate kisses, and so on. As a result, the deadweight loss from a tax on milk chocolate bars would be relatively large, as shown in the accompanying diagram.

7-3 Check Your Understanding

1. a. Since drivers are the beneficiaries of highway safety programs, this tax performs well according to the benefits principle. But since the level of the tax does not depend on ability to pay the tax, it does not perform well according to the ability-to-pay principle. Since higher-income car purchasers are likely to spend more on a new car, a tax assessed as a percentage of the purchase price of the car would perform better on the ability-to-pay principle. A $500-per-car tax will cause people to buy fewer new cars, but a percentage-based tax will cause people to buy fewer cars and less expensive cars.

b. This tax does not perform well according to the benefits principle because the payers are nonresidents of the local area, but the beneficiaries are local residents who will enjoy greater government services. But to the extent that people who stay in hotels have higher income compared to those who don't, the tax performs well according to the ability-to-pay principle. It will distort the action of staying in a hotel room in this area, resulting in fewer nights of hotel room stays.

c. This tax performs well according to the benefits principle because local homeowners are the users of local schools. It also performs well according to the ability-to-pay principle because it is assessed as a percentage of home value: higher-income residents, who own more expensive homes, will pay higher taxes. It will distort the action of buying a house in this area versus another area with a lower property tax rate or the action of making changes to a house that increase its assessed value.

d. This tax performs well according to the benefits principle because food consumers are the beneficiaries of government food safety programs. It does not perform well according to the ability-to-pay principle because food is a necessity, and lower-income people will pay approximately as much as higher-income people. This tax will distort the action of buying food, leading people to purchase cheaper varieties of food.

7-4 Check Your Understanding

1. a. The marginal tax rate for someone with income of $5,000 is 1%: for each additional $1 in income, $0.01 or 1%, is taxed away. This person pays total tax of $5,000 × 1% = $50, which is ($50/$5,000) × 100 = 1% of his or her income.

b. The marginal tax rate for someone with income of $20,000 is 2%: for each additional $1 in income, $0.02 or 2%, is taxed away. This person pays total tax of $10,000 × 1% + $10,000 × 2% = $300, which is ($300/$20,000) × 100 = 1.5% of his or her income.

c. Since the high-income taxpayer pays a larger percentage of his or her income than the low-income taxpayer, this tax is progressive.

2. A 1% tax on consumption spending means that a family earning $15,000 and spending $10,000 will pay a tax of 1% × $10,000 = $100, equivalent to 0.67% of its income; ($100/$15,000) × 100 = 0.67%. But a family earning $10,000 and spending $8,000 will pay a tax of 1% × $8,000 = $80, equivalent to 0.80% of its income; ($80/$10,000) × 100 = 0.80%. So the tax is regressive, since the lower-income family pays a higher percentage of its income in tax than the higher-income family.

3. a. False. Recall that a seller always bears some burden of a tax as long as his or her supply of the good is not perfectly elastic. Since the supply of labor a worker offers is not perfectly elastic, some of the payroll tax will be borne by the worker, and therefore the tax will affect the person's incentive to take a job.

b. False. Under a proportional tax, the percentage of the tax base is the same for everyone. Under a lump-sum tax, the total tax paid is the same for everyone, regardless of their income.

Chapter Eight

8-1 Check Your Understanding

1. a. To determine comparative advantage, we must compare the two countries' opportunity costs for a given good. Take the opportunity cost of 1 ton of corn in

terms of bicycles. In China, the opportunity cost of 1 bicycle is 0.01 ton of corn; so the opportunity cost of 1 ton of corn is 1/0.01 bicycles = 100 bicycles. The United States has the comparative advantage in corn since its opportunity cost in terms of bicycles is 50, a smaller number. Similarly, the opportunity cost in the United States of 1 bicycle in terms of corn is 1/50 ton of corn = 0.02 ton of corn. This is greater than 0.01, the Chinese opportunity cost of 1 bicycle in terms of corn, implying that China has a comparative advantage in bicycles.

b. Given that the United States can produce 200,000 bicycles if no corn is produced, it can produce 200,000 bicycles × 0.02 ton of corn/bicycle = 4,000 tons of corn when no bicycles are produced. Likewise, if China can produce 3,000 tons of corn if no bicycles are produced, it can produce 3,000 tons of corn × 100 bicycles/ton of corn = 300,000 bicycles if no corn is produced. These points determine the vertical and horizontal intercepts of the U.S. and Chinese production possibility frontiers, as shown in the accompanying diagram.

(a) U.S. Production Possibility Frontier

Quantity of corn (tons)

U.S. production with trade

Slope = −0.02

U.S. consumption with trade

U.S. PPF

4,000

1,000

0   200,000   *Quantity of bicycles*

(b) Chinese Production Possibility Frontier

Quantity of corn (tons)

Chinese consumption with trade

Slope = −0.01

Chinese production with trade

China PPF

3,000

0   100,000   300,000   *Quantity of bicycles*

c. The diagram shows the production and consumption points of the two countries. Each country is clearly better off with international trade because each now consumes a bundle of the two goods that lies outside its own production possibility frontier, indicating that these bundles were unattainable in autarky.

2. a. According to the Heckscher–Ohlin model, this pattern of trade occurs because the United States has a relatively larger endowment of factors of production, such as human capital and physical capital, that are suited to the production of movies, but France has a relatively larger endowment of factors of production suited to wine-making, such as vineyards and the human capital of vintners.

b. According to the Heckscher–Ohlin model, this pattern of trade occurs because the United States has a relatively larger endowment of factors of production, such as human and physical capital, that are suited to making machinery, but Brazil has a relatively larger endowment of factors of production suited to shoe-making, such as unskilled labor and leather.

8-2 Check Your Understanding

1. In the accompanying diagram, P_A is the U.S. price of grapes in autarky and P_W is the world price of grapes under international trade. With trade, U.S. consumers pay a price of P_W for grapes and consume quantity Q_D, U.S. grape producers produce quantity Q_S, and the difference, $Q_D - Q_S$, represents imports of Mexican grapes. As a consequence of the strike by truckers, imports are halted, the price paid by American consumers rises to the autarky price, P_A, and U.S. consumption falls to the autarky quantity, Q_A.

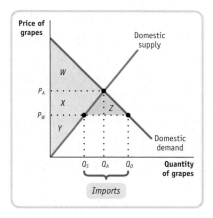

a. Before the strike, U.S. consumers enjoyed consumer surplus equal to areas $W + X + Z$. After the strike, their consumer surplus shrinks to W. So consumers are worse off, losing consumer surplus represented by $X + Z$.

b. Before the strike, U.S. producers had producer surplus equal to the area Y. After the strike, their producer surplus increases to $Y + X$. So U.S. producers are better off, gaining producer surplus represented by X.

c. U.S. total surplus falls as a result of the strike by an amount represented by area Z, the loss in consumer surplus that does not accrue to producers.

2. Mexican grape producers are worse off because they lose sales of exported grapes to the United States, and Mexican grape pickers are worse off because they lose the wages that were associated with the lost sales. The lower demand for Mexican grapes caused by the strike implies that the price Mexican

consumers pay for grapes falls, making them better off. U.S. grape pickers are better off because their wages increase as a result of the increase of $Q_A - Q_S$ in U.S. sales.

8-3 Check Your Understanding

1. a. If the tariff is $0.50, the price paid by domestic consumers for a pound of imported butter is $0.50 + $0.50 = $1.00, the same price as a pound of domestic butter. Imported butter will no longer have a price advantage over domestic butter, imports will cease, and domestic producers will capture all the feasible sales to domestic consumers, selling amount Q_A in the accompanying figure. If the tariff is $0.25, the price paid by domestic consumers for a pound of imported butter is $0.50 + $0.25 = $0.75, $0.25 cheaper than a pound of domestic butter. American butter producers will gain sales in the amount of $Q_2 - Q_1$ as a result of the $0.25 tariff. But this is smaller than the amount they would have gained under the $0.50 tariff, the amount $Q_A - Q_1$.

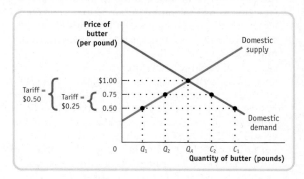

b. As long as the tariff is at least $0.50, increasing it more has no effect. At a tariff of $0.50, all imports are effectively blocked.

2. All imports are effectively blocked at a tariff of $0.50. So such a tariff corresponds to an import quota of 0.

8-4 Check Your Understanding

1. There are many fewer businesses that use steel as an input than there are consumers who buy sugar or clothing. So it will be easier for such businesses to communicate and coordinate among themselves to lobby against tariffs than it will be for consumers. In addition, each business will perceive that the cost of a steel tariff is quite costly to its profits, but an individual consumer is either unaware of or perceives little loss from tariffs on sugar or clothing. The tariffs were indeed lifted at the end of 2003.

2. Countries are often tempted to protect domestic industries by claiming that an import poses a quality, health, or environmental danger to domestic consumers. A WTO official should examine whether domestic producers are subject to the same stringency in the application of quality, health, or environmental regulations as foreign producers. If they are, then it is more likely that the regulations are for legitimate, non–trade protection purposes; if they are not, then it is more likely that the regulations are intended as trade protection measures.

Chapter Nine

9-1 Check Your Understanding

1. a. Supplies are an explicit cost because they require an outlay of money.

b. If the basement could be used in some other way that generates money, such as renting it to a student, then the implicit cost is that money forgone. Otherwise, the implicit cost is zero.

c. Wages are an explicit cost.

d. By using the van for their business, Karma and Don forgo the money they could have gained by selling it. So use of the van is an implicit cost.

e. Karma's forgone wages from her job are an implicit cost.

2. We need only compare the choice of becoming a machinist to the choice of taking a job in advertising in order to make the right choice. We can discard the choice of acquiring a teaching degree because we already know that taking a job in advertising is always superior to it. Now let's compare the remaining two alternatives: becoming a skilled machinist versus immediately taking a job in advertising. As an apprentice machinist, Ashley will earn only $30,000 over the first two years, versus $57,000 in advertising. So she has an implicit cost of $30,000 − $57,000 = − $27,000 by becoming a machinist instead of immediately working in advertising. However, two years from now the value of her lifetime earnings as a machinist is $725,000 versus $600,000 in advertising, giving her an accounting profit of $125,000 by choosing to be a machinist. Summing, her economic profit from choosing a career as a machinist over a career in advertising is $125,000 − $27,000 = $98,000. In contrast, her economic profit from choosing the alternative, a career in advertising over a career as a machinist, is −$125,000 + $27,000 = −$98,000. By the principle of "either–or" decision making, Ashley should choose to be a machinist because that career has a positive economic profit.

3. You can discard alternative A because both B and C are superior to it. But you must now compare B versus C. You should then choose the alternative—B or C—that carries a positive economic profit.

9-2 Check Your Understanding

1. a. The marginal cost of doing your laundry is any monetary outlays plus the opportunity cost of your time spent doing laundry today—that is, the value you would place on spending time today on your next best alternative activity, like seeing a movie. The marginal benefit is having more clean clothes today to choose from.

b. The marginal cost of changing your oil is the opportunity cost of time spent changing your oil now as well as the explicit cost of the oil change. The marginal benefit is the improvement in your car's performance.

c. The marginal cost is the unpleasant feeling of a burning mouth that you receive from it plus any explicit cost of the jalapeno. The marginal benefit of another jalapeno on your nachos is the pleasant taste that you receive from it.

d. The marginal benefit of hiring another worker in your company is the value of the output that worker produces. The marginal cost is the wage you must pay that worker.

e. The marginal cost is the value lost due to the increased side effects from this additional dose. The marginal benefit of another dose of the drug is the value of the reduction in the patient's disease.

f. The marginal cost is the opportunity cost of your time—what you would have gotten from the next best use of your time. The marginal benefit is the probable increase in your grade.

2. The accompanying table shows Alex's new marginal cost and his new profit. It also reproduces Alex's marginal benefit from Table 9-5.

Years of schooling	Total cost	Marginal cost	Marginal benefit	Profit
0	$0			
		$90,000	$300,000	$210,000
1	90,000			
		30,000	150,000	120,000
2	120,000			
		50,000	90,000	40,000
3	170,000			
		80,000	60,000	−20,000
4	250,000			
		120,000	50,000	−80,000
5	370,000			

Alex's marginal cost is decreasing until he has completed two years of schooling, after which marginal cost increases because of the value of his forgone income. The optimal amount of schooling is still three years. For less than three years of schooling, marginal benefit exceeds marginal cost; for more than three years, marginal cost exceeds marginal benefit.

9-3 Check Your Understanding

1. a. Your sunk cost is $8,000 because none of the $8,000 spent on the truck is recoverable.

b. Your sunk cost is $4,000 because 50% of the $8,000 spent on the truck is recoverable.

2. a. This is an invalid argument because the time and money already spent are a sunk cost at this point.

b. This is also an invalid argument because what you should have done two years ago is irrelevant to what you should do now.

c. This is a valid argument because it recognizes that sunk costs are irrelevant to what you should do now.

d. This is a valid argument given that you are concerned about disappointing your parents. But your parents' views are irrational because they do not recognize that the time already spent is a sunk cost.

9-4 Check Your Understanding

1. a. Jenny is exhibiting loss aversion. She has an oversensitivity to loss, leading to an unwillingness to recognize a loss and move on.

b. Dan is doing mental accounting. Dollars from his unexpected overtime earnings are worth less—spent on a weekend getaway—than the dollars earned from his regular hours that he uses to pay down his student loan.

c. Carol may have unrealistic expectations of future behavior. Even if she does not want to participate in the plan now, she should find a way to commit to participating at a later date.

d. Jeremy is showing signs of status quo bias. He is avoiding making a decision altogether; in other words, he is sticking with the status quo.

2. You would determine whether a decision was rational or irrational by first accurately accounting for all the costs and benefits of the decision. In particular, you must accurately measure all opportunity costs. Then calculate the economic payoff of the decision relative to the next best alternative. If you would still make the same choice after this comparison, then you have made a rational choice. If not, then the choice was irrational.

Chapter Ten

10-1 Check Your Understanding

1. Consuming a unit that generates negative marginal utility leaves the consumer with lower total utility than not consuming that unit at all. A rational consumer, a consumer who maximizes utility, would not do that. For example, from Figure 10-1 you can see that Cassie receives 64 utils if she consumes 8 clams; but if she consumes the 9th clam, she loses a util, netting her a total utility of only 63 utils. So whenever consuming a unit generates negative marginal utility, the consumer is made better off by not consuming that unit, even when that unit is free.

2. Since Marta has diminishing marginal utility of coffee, her first cup of coffee of the day generates the greatest increase in total utility. Her third and last cup of the day generates the least.

3. a. Mabel does not have diminishing marginal utility of exercising since each additional unit consumed brings more additional enjoyment than the previous unit.

b. Mei does not have diminishing marginal utility of albums because each additional unit generates the same additional enjoyment as the previous unit.

c. Dexter has diminishing marginal utility of restaurant meals since the additional utility generated by a good restaurant meal is less when he consumes lots of them than when he consumed few of them.

10-2 Check Your Understanding

1. a. The accompanying table shows the consumer's consumption possibilities, *A* through *C*. These consumption possibilities are plotted in the accompanying diagram, along with the consumer's budget line, *BL*.

Consumption bundle	Quantity of popcorn (buckets)	Quantity of movie tickets
A	0	2
B	2	1
C	4	0

b. The accompanying table shows the consumer's consumption possibilities, *A* through *D*. These consumption possibilities are plotted in the accompanying diagram, along with the consumer's budget line, *BL*.

Consumption bundle	Quantity of underwear (pairs)	Quantity of socks (pairs)
A	0	6
B	1	4
C	2	2
D	3	0

10-3 Check Your Understanding

1. From Table 10-3 you can see that Sammy's marginal utility per dollar from increasing his consumption of clams from 3 pounds to 4 pounds and his marginal utility per dollar from increasing his consumption of potatoes from 9 to 10 pounds are the same, 0.75 utils. But a consumption bundle consisting of 4 pounds of clams and 10 pounds of potatoes is not Sammy's optimal consumption bundle because it is not affordable given his income of $20; 4 pounds of clams and 10 pounds of potatoes costs $4 × 4 + $2 × 10 = $36, $16 more than Sammy's income. This can be illustrated with Sammy's budget line from panel (a) of Figure 10-3: a bundle of 4 pounds of clams and 10 pounds of potatoes is represented by point *X* in the accompanying diagram, a point that lies outside Sammy's budget line. If you look at the horizontal axis of panel (a) of Figure 10-3, it is quite clear that there is no such thing in Sammy's consumption possibilities as a bundle consisting of 4 pounds of clams and 10 pounds of potatoes.

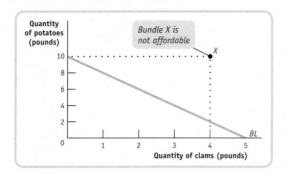

2. Sammy's maximum utility per dollar is generated when he goes from consuming 0 to 1 pound of clams (3.75 utils) and as he goes from 0 to 1 pound of potatoes (5.75 utils). But this bundle consisting of 1 pound of clams and 1 pound of potatoes generates only 26.5 utils for him. Instead, Sammy should choose the consumption bundle that satisfies his budget constraint and for which the marginal utility per dollar for both goods is equal.

10-4 Check Your Understanding

1. a. Since spending on orange juice is a small share of Clare's spending, the income effect from a rise in the price of orange juice is insignificant. Only the substitution effect, represented by the substitution of lemonade in place of orange juice, is significant.

   b. Since rent is a large share of Delia's expenditures, the increase in rent generates a significant income effect, making Delia feel poorer. Since housing is a normal good for Delia, the income and substitution effects move in the same direction, leading her to reduce her consumption of housing by moving to a smaller apartment.

   c. Since a meal ticket is a significant share of the students' living costs, an increase in its price will generate a significant income effect. Because cafeteria meals are an inferior good, the substitution effect (which would induce students to substitute restaurant meals in place of cafeteria meals) and the income effect (which would induce them to eat in the cafeteria more often because they are poorer) move in opposite directions.

2. In order to determine whether any good is a Giffen good, you must first establish whether it is an inferior good. In other words, if students' incomes decrease, other things equal, does the quantity of cafeteria meals demanded increase? Once you have established that the good is an inferior good, you must then establish that the income effect outweighs the substitution effect. That is, as the price of cafeteria meals rises, other things equal, does the quantity of cafeteria meals demanded increase? Be careful that, in fact, all other things remain equal. But if the quantity of cafeteria meals demanded truly increases in response to a price rise, you really have found a Giffen good.

Chapter Eleven

11-1 Check Your Understanding

1. a. The fixed input is the 10-ton machine, and the variable input is electricity.

   b. As you can see from the declining numbers in the third column of the accompanying table, electricity does indeed exhibit diminishing returns: the marginal product of each additional kilowatt of electricity is less than that of the previous kilowatt.

Quantity of electricity (kilowatts)	Quantity of ice (pounds)	Marginal product of electricity (pounds per kilowatt)
0	0	
		1,000
1	1,000	
		800
2	1,800	
		600
3	2,400	
		400
4	2,800	

   c. A 50% increase in the size of the fixed input means that Bernie now has a 15-ton machine. So the fixed input is now the 15-ton machine. Since it generates a 100% increase in output for any given amount of electricity, the quantity of output and marginal product are now as shown in the accompanying table.

Quantity of electricity (kilowatts)	Quantity of ice (pounds)	Marginal product of electricity (pounds per kilowatt)
0	0	
		2,000
1	2,000	
		1,600
2	3,600	
		1,200
3	4,800	
		800
4	5,600	

11-2 Check Your Understanding

1. a. As shown in the accompanying table, the marginal cost for each pie is found by multiplying the marginal cost of the previous pie by 1.5. Variable cost for each output level is found by summing the marginal cost for all the pies produced to reach that output level. So, for example, the variable cost of three pies is $1.00 + $1.50 + $2.25 = $4.75. Average fixed cost for Q pies is calculated as $9.00/$Q$ since fixed cost is $9.00. Average variable cost for Q pies is equal to variable cost for the Q pies divided by Q; for example, the average variable cost of five pies is $13.19/5, or approximately $2.64. Finally, average total cost can be calculated in two equivalent ways: as TC/Q or as $AVC + AFC$.

Quantity of pies	Marginal cost of pie	Variable cost	Average fixed cost of pie	Average variable cost of pie	Average total cost of pie
0		$0.00	—	—	—
	$1.00				
1		1.00	$9.00	$1.00	$10.00
	1.50				
2		2.50	4.50	1.25	5.75
	2.25				
3		4.75	3.00	1.58	4.58
	3.38				
4		8.13	2.25	2.03	4.28
	5.06				
5		13.19	1.80	2.64	4.44
	7.59				
6		20.78	1.50	3.46	4.96

b. The spreading effect dominates the diminishing returns effect when average total cost is falling: the fall in *AFC* dominates the rise in *AVC* for pies 1 to 4. The diminishing returns effect dominates when average total cost is rising: the rise in *AVC* dominates the fall in *AFC* for pies 5 and 6.

c. Alicia's minimum-cost output is 4 pies; this generates the lowest average total cost, $4.28. When output is less than 4, the marginal cost of a pie is less than the average total cost of the pies already produced. So making an additional pie lowers average total cost. For example, the marginal cost of pie 3 is $2.25, whereas the average total cost of pies 1 and 2 is $5.75. So making pie 3 lowers average total cost to $4.58, equal to (2 × $5.75 + $2.25)/3. When output is more than 4, the marginal cost of a pie is greater than the average total cost of the pies already produced. Consequently, making an additional pie raises average total cost. So, although the marginal cost of pie 6 is $7.59, the average total cost of pies 1 through 5 is $4.44. Making pie 6 raises average total cost to $4.96, equal to (5 × $4.44 + $7.59)/6.

11-3 Check Your Understanding

1. a. The accompanying table shows the average total cost of producing 12,000, 22,000, and 30,000 units for each of the three choices of fixed cost. For example, if the firm makes choice 1, the total cost of producing 12,000

units of output is $8,000 + 12,000 × $1.00 = $20,000. The average total cost of producing 12,000 units of output is therefore $20,000/12,000 = $1.67. The other average total costs are calculated similarly.

	12,000 units	22,000 units	30,000 units
Average total cost from choice 1	$1.67	$1.36	$1.27
Average total cost from choice 2	1.75	1.30	1.15
Average total cost from choice 3	2.25	1.34	1.05

So if the firm wanted to produce 12,000 units, it would make choice 1 because this gives it the lowest average total cost. If it wanted to produce 22,000 units, it would make choice 2. If it wanted to produce 30,000 units, it would make choice 3.

b. Having historically produced 12,000 units, the firm would have adopted choice 1. When producing 12,000 units, the firm would have had an average total cost of $1.67. When output jumps to 22,000 units, the firm cannot alter its choice of fixed cost in the short run, so its average total cost in the short run will be $1.36. In the long run, however, it will adopt choice 2, making its average total cost fall to $1.30.

c. If the firm believes that the increase in demand is temporary, it should not alter its fixed cost from choice 1 because choice 2 generates higher average total cost as soon as output falls back to its original quantity of 12,000 units: $1.75 versus $1.67.

2. a. This firm is likely to experience constant returns to scale. To increase output, the firm must hire more workers, purchase more computers, and pay additional telephone charges. Because these inputs are easily available, their long-run average total cost is unlikely to change as output increases.

b. This firm is likely to experience decreasing returns to scale. As the firm takes on more projects, the costs of communication and coordination required to implement the expertise of the firm's owner are likely to increase. As a result, the firm's long-run average total cost will increase as output increases.

c. This firm is likely to experience increasing returns to scale. Because diamond mining requires a large initial set-up cost for excavation equipment, long-run average total cost will fall as output increases.

3. The accompanying diagram shows the long-run average total cost curve (*LRATC*) and the short-run average total cost curve corresponding to a long-run output choice of 5 cases of salsa (ATC_5). The curve ATC_5 shows the short-run average total cost for which the level of fixed cost minimizes average total cost at an output of 5 cases of salsa. This is confirmed by the fact that at 5 cases per day, ATC_5 touches *LRATC*, the long-run average total cost curve.

If Selena expects to produce only 4 cases of salsa for a long time, she should change her fixed cost. If she does *not* change her fixed cost and produces 4 cases of salsa, her average total cost in the short run is indicated by point *B* on ATC_5; it is no longer on the *LRATC*. If she changes her fixed cost, though, her average total cost could be lower, at point *A*.

Chapter Twelve

12-1 Check Your Understanding

1. a. With only two producers in the world, each producer will represent a sizable share of the market. So the industry will not be perfectly competitive.

b. Because each producer of natural gas from the North Sea has only a small market share of total world supply of natural gas, and since natural gas is a standardized product, the natural gas industry will be perfectly competitive.

c. Because each designer has a distinctive style, high-fashion clothes are not a standardized product. So the industry will not be perfectly competitive.

d. The market described here is the market in each city for tickets to baseball games. Since there are only one or two teams in each major city, each team will represent a sizable share of the market. So the industry will not be perfectly competitive.

12-2 Check Your Understanding

1. a. The firm should shut down immediately when price is less than minimum average variable cost, the shut-down price. In the accompanying diagram, this is optimal for prices in the range 0 to P_1.

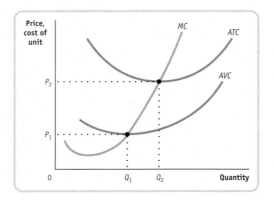

b. When price is greater than minimum average variable cost (the shut-down price) but less than minimum average total cost (the break-even price), the firm should continue to operate in the short run even though it is making a loss. This is optimal for prices in the range P_1 to P_2 and for quantities Q_1 to Q_2.

c. When price exceeds minimum average total cost (the break-even price), the firm makes a profit. This happens for prices in excess of P_2 and results in quantities greater than Q_2.

2. This is an example of a temporary shut-down by a firm when the market price lies below the shut-down price, the minimum average variable cost. In this case, the market price is the price of a lobster meal and variable cost is the variable cost of serving such a meal, such as the cost of the lobster, employee wages, and so on. In this example, however, it is the average variable cost curve rather than the market price that shifts over time, due to seasonal changes in the cost of lobsters. Maine lobster shacks have relatively low average variable cost during the summer, when cheap Maine lobsters are available. During the rest of the year, their average variable cost is relatively high due to the high cost of imported lobsters. So the lobster shacks are open for business during the summer, when their minimum average variable cost lies below price. But they close during the rest of the year, when price lies below their minimum average variable cost.

12-3 Check Your Understanding

1. a. A fall in the fixed cost of production generates a fall in the average total cost of production and, in the short run, an increase in each firm's profit at the current output level. So in the long run new firms will enter the industry. The increase in supply drives down price and profits. Once profits are driven back to zero, entry will cease.

b. An increase in wages generates an increase in the average variable and the average total cost of production at every output level. In the short run, firms incur losses at the current output level, and so in the long run some firms will exit the industry. (If the average variable cost rises sufficiently, some firms may even shut down in the short run.) As firms exit, supply decreases, price rises, and losses are reduced. Exit will cease once losses return to zero.

c. Price will rise as a result of the increased demand, leading to a short-run increase in profits at the current output level. In the long run, firms will enter the industry, generating an increase in supply, a fall in price, and a fall in profits. Once profits are driven back to zero, entry will cease.

d. The shortage of a key input causes that input's price to increase, resulting in an increase in average variable and average total costs for producers. Firms incur losses in the short run, and some firms will exit the industry in the long run. The fall in supply generates an increase in price and decreased losses. Exit will cease when losses have returned to zero.

2. In the following diagram, point X_{MKT} in panel (b), the intersection of S_1 and D_1, represents the long-run industry equilibrium before the change in consumer tastes. When tastes change, demand falls and the industry moves in the short run to point Y_{MKT} in panel (b), at the intersection of the new demand curve D_2 and S_1, the short-run supply curve representing the same number of egg producers as in the original equilibrium at point X_{MKT}. As the market price falls, an individual firm reacts by producing less— as shown in panel (a)—as long as the market price remains above the minimum average variable cost. If market price falls below minimum average variable cost, the firm would shut down immediately. At point Y_{MKT} the price of eggs is below minimum average total cost, creating losses for producers. This leads some firms to exit, which shifts the short-run industry supply curve leftward to S_2. A new long-run equilibrium is established at point Z_{MKT}. As this occurs, the market price rises again, and, as shown in panel (c), each remaining producer reacts by increasing output (here, from point Y to point Z). All remaining producers again make zero profits. The decrease in the quantity of eggs supplied in the industry comes entirely from the exit of some producers from the industry. The long-run industry supply curve is the curve labeled *LRS* in panel (b).

Chapter Thirteen

13-1 Check Your Understanding

1. a. This does not support the conclusion. Texas Tea has a limited amount of oil, and the price has risen in order to equalize supply and demand.

b. This supports the conclusion because the market for home heating oil has become monopolized, and a monopolist will reduce the quantity supplied and raise price to generate profit.

c. This does not support the conclusion. Texas Tea has raised its price to consumers because the price of its input, home heating oil, has increased.

d. This supports the conclusion. The fact that other firms have begun to supply heating oil at a lower price implies that Texas Tea must have earned sufficient profits to attract the others to Frigid.

e. This supports the conclusion. It indicates that Texas Tea enjoys a barrier to entry because it controls access to the only Alaskan heating oil pipeline.

2. a. Extending the length of a patent increases the length of time during which the inventor can reduce the quantity supplied and increase the market price. Since this increases the period of time during which the inventor can earn economic profits from the invention, it increases the incentive to invent new products.

b. Extending the length of a patent also increases the period of time during which consumers have to pay higher prices. So determining the appropriate length of a patent involves making a trade-off between the desirable incentive for invention and the undesirable high price to consumers.

3. a. When a large number of other people use Passport credit cards, then any one merchant is more likely to accept the card. So the larger the customer base, the more likely a Passport card will be accepted for payment.

b. When a large number of people own a car with a new type of engine, it will be easier to find a knowledgeable mechanic who can repair it.

c. When a large number of people use such a website, the more likely it is that you will be able to find a buyer for something you want to sell or a seller for something you want to buy.

13-2 Check Your Understanding

1. a. The price at each output level is found by dividing the total revenue by the number of emeralds produced; for example, the price when 3 emeralds are produced is $252/3 = \$84$. The price at the various output levels is then used to construct the demand schedule in the accompanying table.

b. The marginal revenue schedule is found by calculating the change in total revenue as output increases by one unit. For example, the marginal revenue generated by increasing output from 2 to 3 emeralds is ($252 - \$186) = \$66$.

c. The quantity effect component of marginal revenue is the additional revenue generated by selling one more unit of the good at the market price. For example, as shown in the accompanying table, at 3 emeralds, the market price is $84; so when going from 2 to 3 emeralds, the quantity effect is equal to \$84.

d. The price effect component of marginal revenue is the decline in total revenue caused by the fall in price when one more unit is sold. For example, as shown in the table, when only 2 emeralds are sold, each emerald sells at a price of $93. However, when Emerald, Inc. sells an additional emerald, the price must fall by $9 to \$84. So the price effect component in going from 2 to 3 emeralds is $(-\$9) \times 2 = -\$18$. That's because 2 emeralds can only be sold at a price of $84 when 3 emeralds in total are sold, although they could have been sold at a price of \$93 when only 2 in total were sold.

Quantity of emeralds demanded	Price of emerald	Marginal revenue	Quantity effect component	Price effect component
1	$100			
		$86	$93	–$7
2	93			
		66	84	–18
3	84			
		28	70	–42
4	70			
		–30	50	–80
5	50			

e. In order to determine Emerald, Inc.'s profit-maximizing output level, you must know its marginal cost at each output level. Its profit-maximizing output level is the one at which marginal revenue is equal to marginal cost.

2. As the accompanying diagram shows, the marginal cost curve shifts upward to $400. The profit-maximizing price rises and quantity falls. Profit falls from $3,200 to $300 × 6 = $1,800. Competitive industry profits, though, are unchanged at zero.

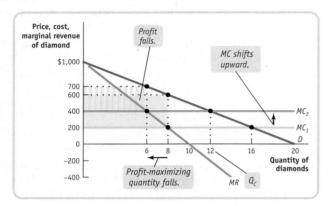

13-3 Check Your Understanding

1. a. Cable Internet service is a natural monopoly. So the government should intervene only if it believes that price exceeds average total cost, where average total cost is based on the cost of laying the cable. In this case it should impose a price ceiling equal to average total cost. Otherwise, it should do nothing.

   b. The government should approve the merger only if it fosters competition by transferring some of the company's landing slots to another, competing airline.

2. a. False. As can be seen from Figure 13-8, panel (b), the inefficiency arises from the fact that some of the consumer surplus is transformed into deadweight loss (the yellow area), not that it is transformed into profit (the green area).

   b. True. If a monopolist sold to all customers who have a valuation greater than or equal to marginal cost, all mutually beneficial transactions would occur and there would be no deadweight loss.

3. As shown in the accompanying diagram, a profit-maximizing monopolist produces Q_M, the output level at which $MR = MC$. A monopolist who mistakenly believes that $P = MR$ produces the output level at which $P = MC$ (when, in fact, $P > MR$, and at the true profit-maximizing level of output, $P > MR = MC$). This misguided monopolist will produce the output level Q_C, where the demand curve crosses the marginal cost curve—the same output level produced if the industry were perfectly competitive. It will charge the price P_C, which is equal to marginal cost, and make zero profit. The entire shaded area is equal to the consumer surplus, which is also equal to total surplus in this case (since the monopolist receives zero producer surplus). There is no deadweight loss since every consumer who is willing to pay as much as or more than marginal cost gets the good. A smart monopolist, however, will produce the output level Q_M and charge the price P_M. Profit equals the green area, consumer surplus corresponds to the blue area, and total surplus is equal to the sum of

the green and blue areas. The yellow area is the deadweight loss generated by the monopolist.

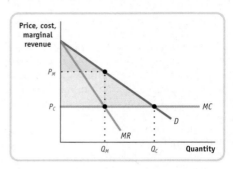

13-4 Check Your Understanding

1. a. False. A price-discriminating monopolist will sell to some customers that a single-price monopolist will refuse to—namely, customers with a high price elasticity of demand who are willing to pay only a relatively low price for the good.

   b. False. Although a price-discriminating monopolist does indeed capture more of the consumer surplus, inefficiency is lower: more mutually beneficial transactions occur because the monopolist makes more sales to customers with a low willingness to pay for the good.

   c. True. Under price discrimination consumers are charged prices that depend on their price elasticity of demand. A consumer with highly elastic demand will pay a lower price than a consumer with inelastic demand.

2. a. This is not a case of price discrimination because all consumers, regardless of their price elasticities of demand, value the damaged merchandise less than undamaged merchandise. So the price must be lowered to sell the merchandise.

   b. This is a case of price discrimination. Senior citizens have a higher price elasticity of demand for restaurant meals (their demand for restaurant meals is more responsive to price changes) than other patrons. Restaurants lower the price to high-elasticity consumers (senior citizens). Consumers with low price elasticity of demand will pay the full price.

   c. This is a case of price discrimination. Consumers with a high price elasticity of demand will pay a lower price by collecting and using discount coupons. Consumers with a low price elasticity of demand will not use coupons.

   d. This is not a case of price discrimination; it is simply a case of supply and demand.

Chapter Fourteen

14-1 Check Your Understanding

1. a. The world oil industry is an oligopoly because a few countries control a necessary resource for production, oil reserves.

   b. The microprocessor industry is an oligopoly because two firms possess superior technology and so dominate industry production.

c. The wide-body passenger jet industry is an oligopoly because there are increasing returns to scale in production.

2. a. The HHI in this industry is $67^2 + 18^2 + 11^2 + 3^2 + 1^2 = 4944$.

   b. If Yahoo! and Bing were to merge, making their combined market $11\% + 18\% = 29\%$, the HHI in this industry would be $67^2 + 29^2 + 3^2 + 1^2 = 5340$.

14-2 Check Your Understanding

1. a. The firm is likely to act noncooperatively and raise output, which will generate a negative price effect. But because the firm's current market share is small, the negative price effect will fall much more heavily on its rivals' revenues than on its own. At the same time, the firm will benefit from a positive quantity effect.

   b. The firm is likely to act noncooperatively and raise output, which will generate a fall in price. Because its rivals have higher costs, they will lose money at the lower price while the firm continues to make profits. So the firm may be able to drive its rivals out of business by increasing its output.

   c. The firm is likely to collude. Because it is costly for consumers to switch products, the firm would have to lower its price quite substantially (by increasing quantity a lot) to induce consumers to switch to its product. So increasing output is likely to be unprofitable given the large negative price effect.

   d. The firm is likely to act uncooperatively because it knows its rivals cannot increase their output in retaliation.

14-3 Check Your Understanding

1. When Margaret builds a missile, Nikita's payoff from building a missile as well is −10; it is −20 if he does not. The same set of payoffs holds for Margaret when Nikita builds a missile: her payoff is −10 if she builds one as well, −20 if she does not. So it is a Nash (or noncooperative) equilibrium for both Margaret and Nikita to build missiles, and their total payoff is (−10) + (−10) = −20. But their total payoff is greatest when neither builds a missile: their total payoff is 0 + 0 = 0. But this outcome—the cooperative outcome—is unlikely. If Margaret builds a missile but Nikita does not, Margaret gets a payoff of +8, rather than the 0 she gets if she doesn't build a missile. So Margaret is better off if she builds a missile but Nikita doesn't. Similarly, Nikita is better off if he builds a missile but Margaret doesn't: he gets a payoff of +8, rather than the 0 he gets if he doesn't build a missile. So both players have an incentive to build a missile. Both will build a missile, and each gets a payoff of −10. So unless Nikita and Margaret are able to communicate in some way to enforce cooperation, they will act in their own individual interests and each will build a missile.

2. a. Future entry by several new firms will increase competition and drive down industry profits. As a result, there is less future profit to protect by behaving cooperatively today. So each oligopolist is more likely to behave non-cooperatively today.

   b. When it is very difficult for a firm to detect if another firm has raised output, then it is very difficult to enforce cooperation by playing tit for tat. So it is more likely that a firm will behave noncooperatively.

   c. When firms have coexisted while maintaining high prices for a long time, each expects cooperation to continue. So the value of behaving cooperatively today is high, and it is likely that firms will engage in tacit collusion.

14-4 Check Your Understanding

1. a. This is likely to be interpreted as evidence of tacit collusion. Firms in the industry are able to tacitly collude by setting their prices according to the published "suggested" price of the largest firm in the industry. This is a form of price leadership.

   b. This is not likely to be interpreted as evidence of tacit collusion. Considerable variation in market shares indicates that firms have been competing to capture one anothers' business.

   c. This is not likely to be interpreted as evidence of tacit collusion. These features make it more unlikely that consumers will switch products in response to lower prices. So this is a way for firms to avoid any temptation to gain market share by lowering price. This is a form of product differentiation used to avoid direct competition.

   d. This is likely to be interpreted as evidence of tacit collusion. In the guise of discussing sales targets, firms can create a cartel by designating quantities to be produced by each firm.

   e. This is likely to be interpreted as evidence of tacit collusion. By raising prices together, each firm in the industry is refusing to undercut its rivals by leaving its price unchanged or lowering it. Because it could gain market share by doing so, refusing to do it is evidence of tacit collusion.

Chapter Fifteen

15-1 Check Your Understanding

1. a. Ladders are not differentiated as a result of monopolistic competition. A ladder producer makes different ladders (tall ladders versus short ladders) to satisfy different consumer needs, not to avoid competition with rivals. So two tall ladders made by two different producers will be indistinguishable by consumers.

   b. Soft drinks are an example of product differentiation as a result of monopolistic competition. For example, several producers make colas; each is differentiated in terms of taste, which fast-food chains sell it, and so on.

   c. Department stores are an example of product differentiation as a result of monopolistic competition. They serve different clienteles that have different price sensitivities and different tastes. They also offer different levels of customer service and are situated in different locations.

   d. Steel is not differentiated as a result of monopolistic competition. Different types of steel (beams versus sheets) are made for different purposes, not to distinguish one steel manufacturer's products from another's.

2. a. Perfectly competitive industries and monopolistically competitive industries both have many sellers. So it may be hard to distinguish between them solely in terms of number of firms. And in both market structures, there is free entry into and exit from the industry in the long run. But in a perfectly competitive industry, one standardized product is sold; in a monopolistically competitive industry, products are differentiated. So you should ask whether products are differentiated in the industry.

b. In a monopoly there is only one firm, but a monopolistically competitive industry contains many firms. So you should ask whether or not there is a single firm in the industry.

15-2 Check Your Understanding

1. a. An increase in fixed cost raises average total cost and shifts the average total cost curve upward. In the short run, firms incur losses. In the long run, some will exit the industry, resulting in a rightward shift of the demand curves for those firms that remain in the industry, since each one now serves a larger share of the market. Long-run equilibrium is reestablished when the demand curve for each remaining firm has shifted rightward to the point where it is tangent to the firm's new, higher average total cost curve. At this point each firm's price just equals its average total cost, and each firm makes zero profit.

b. A decrease in marginal cost lowers average total cost and shifts the average total cost curve and the marginal cost curve downward. Because existing firms now make profits, in the long run new entrants are attracted into the industry. In the long run, this results in a leftward shift of each existing firm's demand curve since each firm now has a smaller share of the market. Long-run equilibrium is reestablished when each firm's demand curve has shifted leftward to the point where it is tangent to the new, lower average total cost curve. At this point each firm's price just equals average total cost, and each firm makes zero profit.

2. If all the existing firms in the industry joined together to create a monopoly, they would achieve monopoly profits. But this would induce new firms to create new, differentiated products and then enter the industry and capture some of the monopoly profits. So in the long run it would be impossible to maintain a monopoly. The problem arises from the fact that because new firms can create new products, there is no barrier to entry that can maintain a monopoly.

15-3 Check Your Understanding

1. a. False. As can be seen from panel (b) of Figure 15-4, a monopolistically competitive firm produces at a point where price exceeds marginal cost—unlike a perfectly competitive firm, which produces where price equals marginal cost (at the point of minimum average total cost). A monopolistically competitive firm will refuse to

sell at marginal cost. This would be below average total cost and the firm would incur a loss.

b. True. Firms in a monopolistically competitive industry could achieve higher profits (monopoly profits) if they all joined together and produced a single product. In addition, since the industry possesses excess capacity, producing a larger quantity of output would lower the firm's average total cost. The effect on consumers, however, is ambiguous. They would experience less choice. But if consolidation substantially reduces industry-wide average total cost and therefore substantially increases industry-wide output, consumers may experience lower prices under monopoly.

c. True. Fads and fashions are created and promulgated by advertising, which is found in oligopolies and monopolistically competitive industries but not in monopolies or perfectly competitive industries.

15-4 Check Your Understanding

1. a. This is economically useful because such advertisements are likely to focus on the medical benefits of aspirin.

b. This is economically wasteful because such advertisements are likely to focus on promoting Bayer aspirin versus a rival's aspirin product. The two products are medically indistinguishable.

c. This is economically useful because such advertisements are likely to focus on the health and enjoyment benefits of orange juice.

d. This is economically wasteful because such advertisements are likely to focus on promoting Tropicana orange juice versus a rival's product. The two are likely to be indistinguishable by consumers.

e. This is economically useful because the longevity of a business gives a potential customer information about its quality.

2. A successful brand name indicates a desirable attribute, such as quality, to a potential buyer. So, other things equal—such as price—a firm with a successful brand name will achieve higher sales than a rival with a comparable product but without a successful brand name. This is likely to deter new firms from entering an industry in which an existing firm has a successful brand name.

Chapter Sixteen

16-1 Check Your Understanding

1. a. The external cost is the pollution caused by the wastewater runoff, an uncompensated cost imposed by the poultry farms on their neighbors.

b. Since poultry farmers do not take the external cost of their actions into account when making decisions about how much wastewater to generate, they will create more runoff than is socially optimal in the absence of government intervention or a private deal. They will produce runoff up to the point at which the marginal social benefit of an additional unit of runoff is zero; however, their neighbors experience a high, positive level of marginal social cost of runoff from this output level. So the quantity of wastewater runoff is inefficient: reducing runoff by one unit would reduce total social benefit by less than it would reduce total social cost.

   c. At the socially optimal quantity of wastewater runoff, the marginal social benefit is equal to the marginal social cost. This quantity is lower than the quantity of wastewater runoff that would be created in the absence of government intervention or a private deal.

2. Yasmin's reasoning is not correct: allowing some late returns of books is likely to be socially optimal. Although you impose a marginal social cost on others every day that you are late in returning a book, there is some positive marginal social benefit to you of returning a book late—for example, you get a longer period to use it in working on a term paper.

   The socially optimal number of days that a book is returned late is the number at which the marginal social benefit equals the marginal social cost. A fine so stiff that it prevents any late returns is likely to result in a situation in which people return books although the marginal social benefit of keeping them another day is greater than the marginal social cost—an inefficient outcome. In that case, allowing an overdue patron another day would increase total social benefit more than it would increase total social cost. So charging a moderate fine that reduces the number of days that books are returned late to the socially optimal number of days is appropriate.

16-2 Check Your Understanding

1. This is a misguided argument. Allowing polluters to sell emissions permits makes polluters face a cost of polluting: the opportunity cost of the permit. If a polluter chooses not to reduce its emissions, it cannot sell its emissions permits. As a result, it forgoes the opportunity of making money from the sale of the permits. So despite the fact that the polluter receives a monetary benefit from selling the permits, the scheme has the desired effect: to make polluters internalize the externality of their actions.

2. a. If the emissions tax is smaller than the marginal social cost at Q_{OPT}, a polluter will face a marginal cost of polluting (equal to the amount of the tax) that is less than the marginal social cost at the socially optimal quantity of pollution. Since a polluter will produce emissions up to the point where the marginal social benefit is equal to its marginal cost, the resulting amount of pollution will be larger than the socially optimal quantity. As a result, there is inefficiency: if the amount of pollution is larger than the socially optimal quantity, the marginal social cost exceeds the marginal social benefit, and society could gain from a reduction in emissions levels.

   If the emissions tax is greater than the marginal social cost at Q_{OPT}, a polluter will face a marginal cost of polluting (equal to the amount of the tax) that is greater than the marginal social cost at the socially

optimal quantity of pollution. This will lead the polluter to reduce emissions below the socially optimal quantity. This also is inefficient: whenever the marginal social benefit is greater than the marginal social cost, society could benefit from an increase in emissions levels.

   b. If the total amount of allowable pollution is set too high, the supply of emissions permits will be high and so the equilibrium price at which permits trade will be low. That is, polluters will face a marginal cost of polluting (the price of a permit) that is "too low"—lower than the marginal social cost at the socially optimal quantity of pollution. As a result, pollution will be greater than the socially optimal quantity. This is inefficient and lowers total surplus.

   If the total level of allowable pollution is set too low, the supply of emissions permits will be low and so the equilibrium price at which permits trade will be high. That is, polluters will face a marginal cost of polluting (the price of a permit) that is "too high"—higher than the marginal social cost at the socially optimal quantity of pollution. As a result, pollution will be lower than the socially optimal quantity. This also is inefficient and lowers total surplus.

16-3 Check Your Understanding

1. College education provides external benefits through the creation of knowledge. And student aid acts like a Pigouvian subsidy on higher education. If the marginal social benefit of higher education is indeed $36 billion, then student aid is an optimal policy.

2. a. Planting trees generates an external benefit: the marginal social benefit of planting trees is higher than the marginal benefit to individual tree planters, since many people (not just those who plant the trees) can benefit from the increased air quality and lower summer temperatures. A Pigouvian subsidy could be placed on each tree planted in urban areas in order to increase the marginal benefit to individual tree planters to the same level as the marginal social benefit.

   b. Water-saving toilets impose an external benefit: the marginal benefit to individual homeowners from replacing a traditional toilet with a water-saving toilet is zero, since water is virtually costless. But the marginal social benefit is large, since fewer rivers and aquifers need to be pumped. A Pigouvian subsidy on installing water-saving toilets could bring the marginal benefit to individual homeowners in line with the marginal social benefit.

   c. Disposing of old computer monitors imposes an external cost: the marginal cost to those disposing of old computer monitors is lower than the marginal social cost, since environmental pollution is borne by people other than the person disposing of the monitor. The difference between the marginal social cost and the marginal cost to those disposing of old computer monitors is the marginal external cost. A Pigouvian tax on disposing of computer monitors, or a system of tradable permits for their disposal, could raise the marginal cost to those disposing of old computer monitors sufficiently to make it equal to the marginal social cost.

16-4 Check Your Understanding

1. a. The voltage of an appliance must be consistent with the voltage of the electrical outlet it is plugged into. Consumers will want to have 110-volt appliances when houses are wired for 110-volt outlets, and builders will want to install 110-volt outlets when most prospective homeowners use 110-volt appliances. So a network externality arises because a consumer will want to use appliances that operate with the same voltage as the appliances used by most other consumers.

b. Printers, copy machines, fax machines, and so on are designed for specific paper sizes. Consumers will want to purchase paper of a size that can be used in these machines, and machine manufacturers will want to manufacture their machines for the size of paper that most consumers use. So a network externality arises because a consumer will want to use the size of paper used by most other consumers—namely, 8½-by-11-inch paper rather than 8-by-12½-inch paper.

2. Of the two competing companies, the company able to achieve the higher number of sales is likely to dominate the market. In a market with a network externality, new consumers will base their buying decisions on the number of existing consumers of a specific product. In other words, the more consumers a company can attract initially, the more consumers will choose to buy that company's product; therefore, the good exhibits *positive feedback*. So it is important for a company to make a large number of sales early on. It can do this by pricing its good cheaply and taking a loss on each unit sold. The company that can best afford to subsidize a large number of sales early on is likely to be the winner of this competition.

Chapter Seventeen

17-1 Check Your Understanding

1. a. Use of a public park is nonexcludable, but it may or may not be rival in consumption, depending on the circumstances. For example, if both you and I use the park for jogging, then your use will not prevent my use—use of the park is nonrival in consumption. In this case the public park is a public good. But use of the park is rival in consumption if there are many people trying to use the jogging path at the same time or when my use of the public tennis court prevents your use of the same court. In this case the public park is a common resource.

b. A cheese burrito is both excludable and rival in consumption. Hence it is a private good.

c. Information from a password-protected website is excludable but nonrival in consumption. So it is an artificially scarce good.

d. Publicly announced information on the path of an incoming hurricane is nonexcludable and nonrival in consumption. So it is a public good.

2. A private producer will supply only a good that is excludable; otherwise, the producer won't be able to charge a price for it that covers the costs of production. So a private producer would be willing to supply a cheese burrito and information from a password-protected website but unwilling to supply a public park or publicly announced information about an incoming hurricane.

17-2 Check Your Understanding

1. a. With 10 Homebodies and 6 Revelers, the marginal social benefit schedule of money spent on the party is as shown in the accompanying table.

Money spent on party	Marginal social benefit
$0	
	$(10 \times \$0.05) + (6 \times \$0.13) = \$1.28$
1	
	$(10 \times \$0.04) + (6 \times \$0.11) = \$1.06$
2	
	$(10 \times \$0.03) + (6 \times \$0.09) = \$0.84$
3	
	$(10 \times \$0.02) + (6 \times \$0.07) = \$0.62$
4	

The efficient spending level is $2, the highest level for which the marginal social benefit is greater than the marginal cost ($1).

b. With 6 Homebodies and 10 Revelers, the marginal social benefit schedule of money spent on the party is as shown in the accompanying table.

Money spent on party	Marginal social benefit
$0	
	$(6 \times \$0.05) + (10 \times \$0.13) = \$1.60$
1	
	$(6 \times \$0.04) + (10 \times \$0.11) = \$1.34$
2	
	$(6 \times \$0.03) + (10 \times \$0.09) = \$1.08$
3	
	$(6 \times \$0.02) + (10 \times \$0.07) = \$0.82$
4	

The efficient spending level is now $3, the highest level for which the marginal social benefit is greater than the marginal cost ($1). The efficient level of spending has increased from that in part a because with relatively more Revelers than Homebodies, an additional dollar spent on the party generates a higher level of social benefit compared to when there are relatively more Homebodies than Revelers.

c. When the numbers of Homebodies and Revelers are unknown but residents are asked their preferences, Homebodies will pretend to be Revelers to induce a higher level of spending on the public party. That's because a Homebody still receives a positive individual marginal benefit from an additional $1 spent, despite the fact that his or her individual marginal benefit is lower than that of a Reveler for every additional $1. In this case the "reported" marginal social benefit schedule of money spent on the party will be as shown in the accompanying table.

Money spent on party	Marginal social benefit
$0	
	16 × $0.13 = $2.08
1	
	16 × $0.11 = $1.76
2	
	16 × $0.09 = $1.44
3	
	16 × $0.07 = $1.12
4	

As a result, $4 will be spent on the party, the highest level for which the "reported" marginal social benefit is greater than the marginal cost ($1). Regardless of whether there are 10 Homebodies and 6 Revelers (part a) or 6 Homebodies and 10 Revelers (part b), spending $4 in total on the party is clearly inefficient because marginal cost exceeds marginal social benefit at this spending level.

As a further exercise, consider how much Homebodies gain by this misrepresentation. In part a, the efficient level of spending is $2. So by misrepresenting their preferences, the 10 Homebodies gain, in total, 10 × ($0.03 + $0.02) = $0.50—that is, they gain the marginal individual benefit in going from a spending level of $2 to $4. The 6 Revelers also gain from the misrepresentations of the Homebodies; they gain 6 × ($0.09 + $0.07) = $0.96 in total. This outcome is clearly inefficient—when $4 in total is spent, the marginal cost is $1 but the marginal social benefit is only $0.62, indicating that too much money is being spent on the party.

In part b, the efficient level of spending is actually $3. The misrepresentation by the 6 Homebodies gains them, in total, 6 × $0.02 = $0.12, but the 10 Revelers gain 10 × $0.07 = $0.70 in total. This outcome is also clearly inefficient—when $4 is spent, marginal social benefit is only $0.12 + $0.70 = $0.82 but marginal cost is $1.

17-3 Check Your Understanding

1. When individuals are allowed to harvest freely, the government-owned forest becomes a common resource, and individuals will overuse it—they will harvest more trees than is efficient. In economic terms, the marginal social cost of harvesting a tree is greater than a private logger's individual marginal cost.

2. The three methods consistent with economic theory are (i) Pigouvian taxes, (ii) a system of tradable licenses, and (iii) allocation of property rights.

   i. *Pigouvian taxes.* You would enforce a tax on loggers that equals the difference between the marginal social cost and the individual marginal cost of logging a tree at the socially efficient harvest amount. In order to do this, you must know the marginal social cost schedule and the individual marginal cost schedule.

   ii. *System of tradable licenses.* You would issue tradable licenses, setting the total number of trees harvested equal to the socially efficient harvest number. The market that arises in these licenses will allocate the right to log efficiently when loggers differ in

their costs of logging: licenses will be purchased by those who have a relatively lower cost of logging. The market price of a license will be equal to the difference between the marginal social cost and the individual marginal cost of logging a tree at the socially efficient harvest amount. In order to implement this level, you need to know the socially efficient harvest amount.

   iii. *Allocation of property rights.* Here you would sell or give the forest to a private party. This party will have the right to exclude others from harvesting trees. Harvesting is now a private good—it is excludable and rival in consumption. As a result, there is no longer any divergence between social and private costs, and the private party will harvest the efficient level of trees. You need no additional information to use this method.

17-4 Check Your Understanding

1. a. The efficient price to a consumer is $0, since the marginal cost of allowing a consumer to download it is $0.

   b. Xenoid will not produce the software unless it can charge a price that allows it at least to make back the $300,000 cost of producing it. So the lowest price at which Xenoid is willing to produce it is $150. At this price, it makes a total revenue of $150 × 2,000 = $300,000; at any lower price, Xenoid will not cover its cost. The shaded area in the accompanying diagram shows the deadweight loss when Xenoid charges a price of $150.

Chapter Eighteen

18-1 Check Your Understanding

1. a. A pension guarantee program is a social insurance program. The possibility of an employer declaring bankruptcy and defaulting on its obligation to pay employee pensions creates insecurity. By providing pension income to those employees, such a program alleviates this source of economic insecurity.

   b. The SCHIP program is a poverty program. By providing health care to children in low-income households, it targets its spending specifically to the poor.

   c. The Section 8 housing program is a poverty program. By targeting its support to low-income households, it specifically helps the poor.

d. The federal flood program is a social insurance program. For many people, the majority of their wealth is tied up in the home they own. The potential for a loss of that wealth creates economic insecurity. By providing assistance to those hit by a major flood, the program alleviates this source of insecurity.

2. The poverty threshold is an absolute measure of poverty. It defines individuals as poor if their incomes fall below a level that is considered adequate to purchase the necessities of life, irrespective of how well other people are doing. And that measure is fixed: in 2014, for instance, it took $11,670 for an individual living alone to purchase the necessities of life, regardless of how well-off other Americans were. In particular, the poverty threshold is not adjusted for an increase in living standards: even if other Americans are becoming increasingly well-off over time, in real terms (that is, how many goods an individual at the poverty threshold can buy) the poverty threshold remains the same.

3. a. To determine mean (or average) income, we take the total income of all individuals in this economy and divide it by the number of individuals. Mean income is ($39,000 + $17,500 + $900,000 + $15,000 + $28,000)/5 = $999,500/5 = $199,900. To determine median income, look at the accompanying table, which ranks the five individuals in order of their income.

	Income
Vijay	$15,000
Kelly	17,500
Oskar	28,000
Sephora	39,000
Raul	900,000

The median income is the income of the individual in the exact middle of the income distribution: Oskar, with an income of $28,000. So the median income is $28,000.

Median income is more representative of the income of individuals in this economy: almost everyone earns income between $15,000 and $39,000, close to the median income of $28,000. Only Raul is the exception: it is his income that raises the mean income to $199,900, which is not representative of most incomes in this economy.

b. The first quintile is made up of the 20% (or one-fifth) of individuals with the lowest incomes in the economy. Vijay makes up the 20% of individuals with the lowest incomes. His income is $15,000, so that is the average income of the first quintile. Oskar makes up the 20% of individuals with the third-lowest incomes. His income is $28,000, so that is the average income of the third quintile.

4. As the Economics in Action pointed out, much of the rise in inequality reflects growing differences among highly educated workers. That is, workers with similar levels of education earn very dissimilar incomes. As a result, the principal source of rising inequality in the United States today is reflected by statement b: the rise in the bank CEO's salary relative to that of the branch manager.

18-2 Check Your Understanding

1. The Earned Income Tax Credit (EITC), a negative income tax, applies only to those workers who earn income; over a certain range of incomes, the more a worker earns, the higher the amount of EITC received. A person who earns no income receives no income tax credit. By contrast, poverty programs that pay individuals based solely on low income still make those payments even if the individual does not work at all; once the individual earns a certain amount of income, these programs discontinue payments. As a result, such programs contain an incentive not to work and earn income, since earning more than a certain amount makes individuals ineligible for their benefits. The negative income tax, however, provides an incentive to work and earn income because its payments increase the more an individual works.

2. The second column of Table 18-4 gives the percentage reduction in the overall poverty rate by government programs. So the reduction in the overall poverty rate by the U.S. welfare state is given by adding up the numbers in that second column, which gives a 16.7% reduction in the overall poverty rate. For those aged 65 or over, the welfare state cuts the poverty rate by 43.6%, the amount given by adding up the numbers in the last column of Table 18-4.

18-3 Check Your Understanding

1. a. The program benefits you and your parents because the pool of all college students contains a representative mix of healthy and less healthy people, rather than a selected group of people who want insurance because they expect to pay high medical bills. In that respect, this insurance is like *employment-based health insurance.* Because no student can opt out, the school can offer health insurance based on the health care costs of its average student. If each student had to buy his or her own health insurance, some students would not be able to obtain any insurance and many would pay more than they do to the school's insurance program.

b. Since all students are required to enroll in its health insurance program, even the healthiest students cannot leave the program in an effort to obtain cheaper insurance tailored specifically to healthy people. If this were to happen, the school's insurance program would be left with an adverse selection of less healthy students and so would have to raise premiums, beginning the adverse selection death spiral. But since no student can leave the insurance program, the school's program can continue to base its premiums on the average student's probability of requiring health care, avoiding the adverse selection death spiral.

2. According to critics, part of the reason the U.S. health care system is so much more expensive than those of other countries is its fragmented nature. Since each of the many insurance companies has significant administrative (overhead) costs—in part because each insurance company incurs marketing costs and exerts significant effort in weeding out high-risk insureds—the system tends to be more expensive than one in which there is only a single medical insurer. Another part of the explanation is that U.S. medical care includes many more expensive treatments than found in other wealthy countries, pays higher physician salaries, and has higher drug prices.

18-4 Check Your Understanding

1. a. Recall one of the principles from Chapter 1: one person's spending is another person's income. A high sales tax on consumer items is the same as a high marginal tax rate on income. As a result, the incentive to earn income by working or by investing in risky projects is reduced, since the payoff, after taxes, is lower.

   b. If you lose a housing subsidy as soon as your income rises above $25,000, your incentive to earn more than $25,000 is reduced. If you earn exactly $25,000, you obtain the housing subsidy; however, as soon as you earn $25,001, you lose the entire subsidy, making you worse off than if you had not earned the additional dollar. The complete withdrawal of the housing subsidy as income rises above $25,000 is what economists refer to as a *notch*.

2. Over the past 40 years, polarization in Congress has increased. Forty years ago, some Republicans were to the left of some Democrats. Today, the rightmost Democrats appear to be to the left of the leftmost Republicans.

Chapter Nineteen

19-1 Check Your Understanding

1. Many college professors will depart for other lines of work if the government imposes a wage that is lower than the market wage. Fewer professors will result in fewer courses taught and therefore fewer college degrees produced. It will adversely affect sectors of the economy that depend directly on colleges, such as the local shopkeepers who sell goods and services to students and faculty, college textbook publishers, and so on. It will also adversely affect firms that use the "output" produced by colleges: new college graduates. Firms that need to hire new employees with college degrees will be hurt as a smaller supply results in a higher market wage for college graduates. Ultimately, the reduced supply of college-educated workers will result in a lower level of human capital in the entire economy relative to what it would have been without the policy. And this will hurt all sectors of the economy that depend on human capital. The sectors of the economy that might benefit are firms that compete with colleges in the hiring of would-be college professors. For example, accounting firms will find it easier to hire people who would otherwise have been professors of accounting, and publishers will find it easier to hire people who would otherwise have been professors of English (easier in the sense that the firms can recruit would-be professors with a lower wage than before). In addition, workers who already have college degrees will benefit; they will command higher wages as the supply of college-educated workers falls.

19-2 Check Your Understanding

1. a. As the demand for services increases, the price of services will rise. And as the price of the output produced by the industries increases, this shifts the *VMPL* curve upward—that is, the demand for labor rises. This results in an increase in both the equilibrium wage rate and the quantity of labor employed.

   b. The fall in the catch per day means that the marginal product of labor in the industry declines. The *VMPL* curve shifts downward, generating a fall in the equilibrium wage rate and the equilibrium quantity of labor employed.

2. When firms from different industries compete for the same workers, then each worker in the various industries will be paid the same equilibrium wage rate, *W*. And since, by the marginal productivity theory of income distribution, $VMPL = P \times MPL = W$ for the last worker hired in equilibrium, the last worker hired in each of these different industries will have the same value of the marginal product of labor.

19-3 Check Your Understanding

1. a. False. Income disparities associated with gender, race, or ethnicity can be explained by the marginal productivity theory of income distribution provided that differences in marginal productivity across people are correlated with gender, race, or ethnicity. One possible source for such correlation is past discrimination. Such discrimination can lower individuals' marginal productivity by, for example, preventing them from acquiring the human capital that would raise their productivity. Another possible source of the correlation is differences in work experience that are associated with gender, race, or ethnicity. For example, in jobs where work experience or length of tenure is important, women may earn lower wages because on average more women than men take child-care-related absences from work.

   b. True. Companies that discriminate when their competitors do not are likely to hire less able workers because they discriminate against more able workers who are considered to be of the wrong gender, race, ethnicity, or other characteristic. And with less able workers, such companies are likely to earn lower profits than their competitors that don't discriminate.

   c. Ambiguous. In general, workers who are paid less because they have less experience may or may not be the victims of discrimination. The answer depends on the reason for the lack of experience. If workers have less experience because they are young or have chosen to do something else rather than gain experience, then they are not victims of discrimination if they are paid less. But if workers lack experience because previous job discrimination prevented them from gaining experience, then they are indeed victims of discrimination when they are paid less.

19-4 Check Your Understanding

1. a. Clive is made worse off if, before the new law, he had preferred to work more than 35 hours per week. As a result of the law, he can no longer choose his preferred time allocation; he now consumes fewer goods and more leisure than he would like.

b. Clive's utility is unaffected by the law if, before the law, he had preferred to work 35 or fewer hours per week. The law has not changed his preferred time allocation.

c. Clive can never be made better off by a law that restricts the number of hours he can work. He can only be made worse off (case a) or equally as well off (case b).

2. The substitution effect would induce Clive to work fewer hours and consume more leisure after his wage rate falls—the fall in the wage rate means the price of an hour of leisure falls, leading Clive to consume more leisure. But a fall in his wage rate also generates a fall in Clive's income. The income effect of this is to induce Clive to consume less leisure and therefore work more hours, since he is now poorer and leisure is a normal good. If the income effect dominates the substitution effect, Clive will in the end work more hours than before.

Chapter Twenty

20-1 Check Your Understanding

1. The family with the lower income is likely to be more risk-averse. In general, higher income or wealth results in lower degrees of risk aversion, due to diminishing marginal utility. Both families may be willing to buy an "unfair" insurance policy. Most insurance policies are "unfair" in that the expected claim is less than the premium. The degree to which a family is willing to pay more than an expected claim for insurance depends on the family's degree of risk aversion.

2. a. Karma's expected income is the weighted average of all possible values of her income, weighted by the probabilities with which she earns each possible value of her income. Since she makes $22,000 with a probability of 0.6 and $35,000 with a probability of 0.4, her expected income is $(0.6 \times \$22,000) + (0.4 \times \$35,000) = \$13,200 + \$14,000 = \$27,200$. Her expected utility is simply the expected value of the total utilities she will experience. Since with a probability of 0.6 she will experience a total utility of 850 utils (the utility to her from making $22,000), and with a probability of 0.4 she will experience a total utility of 1,260 utils (the utility to her from making $35,000), her expected utility is $(0.6 \times 850 \text{ utils}) + (0.4 \times 1,260 \text{ utils}) = 510 \text{ utils} + 504 \text{ utils} = 1,014 \text{ utils}$.

b. If Karma makes $25,000 for certain, she experiences a utility level of 1,014 utils. From the answer to part a, we know that this leaves her equally as well off as when she has a risky expected income of $27,200. Since Karma is indifferent between a risky expected income of $27,200 and a certain income of $25,000, you can conclude that she would prefer a certain income of $27,200 to a risky expected income of $27,200. That is, she would

definitely be willing to reduce the risk she faces when this reduction in risk leaves her expected income unchanged. In other words, Karma is risk-averse.

c. Yes. Karma experiences a utility level of 1,056 utils when she has a certain income of $26,000. This is higher than the expected utility level of 1,014 utils generated by a risky expected income of $27,200. So Karma is willing to pay a premium to guarantee a certain income of $26,000.

20-2 Check Your Understanding

1. a. An increase in the number of ships implies an increase in the quantity of insurance demanded at any given premium. This is a rightward shift of the demand curve, resulting in a rise in both the equilibrium premium and the equilibrium quantity of insurance bought and sold.

b. An increase in the number of trading routes means that investors can diversify more. In other words, they can reduce risk further. At any given premium, there are now more investors willing to supply insurance. This is a rightward shift of the supply curve for insurance, leading to a fall in the equilibrium premium and a rise in the equilibrium quantity of insurance bought and sold.

c. If shipowners in the market become even more risk-averse, they will be willing to pay even higher premiums for insurance. That is, at any given premium, there are now more people willing to buy insurance. This is a rightward shift of the demand curve for insurance, leading to a rise in both the equilibrium premium and the equilibrium quantity of insurance bought and sold.

d. If investors in the market become more risk-averse, they will be less willing to accept risk at any given premium. This is a leftward shift of the supply curve for insurance, leading to a rise in the equilibrium premium and a fall in the equilibrium quantity of insurance bought and sold.

e. As the overall level of risk increases, those willing to buy insurance will be more willing to buy insurance at any given premium; the demand curve for insurance shifts to the right. But since overall risk cannot be diversified away, those ordinarily willing to take on risk will be less willing to do so, leading to a leftward shift in the supply curve for insurance. As a result, the equilibrium premium will rise; the effect on the equilibrium quantity of insurance is uncertain.

f. If the wealth levels of investors fall, investors will become more risk-averse and so less willing to supply insurance at any given premium. This is a leftward shift of the supply curve for insurance, leading to a rise in the equilibrium premium and a fall in the equilibrium quantity of insurance bought and sold.

20-3 Check Your Understanding

1. The inefficiency caused by adverse selection is that an insurance policy with a premium based on the average risk of all drivers will attract only an adverse selection of bad drivers. Good (that is, safe) drivers will find this insurance premium too expensive and so will remain uninsured. This is inefficient. However, safe drivers are also those drivers who have had fewer moving violations for several years. Lowering premiums for only those drivers allows the insurance company to screen its customers and sell insurance to safe drivers, too. This means that at least some of the good drivers now are also insured, which decreases the inefficiency that arises from adverse selection. In a way, having no moving violations for several years is building a reputation for being a safe driver.

2. The moral hazard problem in home construction arises from private information about what the contractor does: whether she takes care to reduce the cost of construction or allows costs to increase. The homeowner cannot, or can only imperfectly, observe the cost-reduction effort of the contractor. If the contractor were fully reimbursed for all costs incurred during construction, she would have no incentive to reduce costs. Making the contractor responsible for any additional costs above the original estimate means that she now has an incentive to keep costs low. However, this imposes risk on the contractor. For instance, if the weather is bad, home construction will take longer, and will be more costly, than if the weather had been good. Since the contractor pays for any additional costs (such as weather-induced delays) above the original estimate, she now faces risk that she cannot control.

3. **a.** True. Drivers with higher deductibles have more incentive to take care in their driving, to avoid paying the deductible. This is a moral hazard phenomenon.

   b. True. Suppose you know that you are a safe driver. You have a choice of a policy with a high premium but a low deductible or one with a lower premium but a higher deductible. In this case, you would be more likely to choose the cheap policy with the high deductible because you know that you will be unlikely to have to pay the deductible. When there is adverse selection, insurance companies use screening devices such as this to make inferences about people's private information about how skillful they are as drivers.

   c. True. The wealthier you are, the less risk-averse you are. If you are less risk-averse, you are more willing to bear risk yourself. Having an insurance policy with a high deductible means that you are exposed to more risk: you have to pay more of any insurance claim yourself. This is an implication of how risk aversion changes with a person's income or wealth.

Chapter Twenty-One

21-1 Check Your Understanding

1. **a.** This is a microeconomic question because it addresses decisions made by consumers about a particular product.

   b. This is a macroeconomic question because it addresses consumer spending in the overall economy.

   c. This is a macroeconomic question because it addresses changes in the overall economy.

   d. This is a microeconomic question because it addresses changes in a particular market, in this case the market for geologists.

   e. This is a microeconomic question because it addresses choices made by consumers and producers about which mode of transportation to use.

   f. This is a microeconomic question because it addresses changes in a particular market.

   g. This is a macroeconomic question because it addresses changes in a measure of the economy's overall price level.

2. **a.** When people can't get credit to finance their purchases, they will be unable to spend money. This will weaken the economy, and as others see the economy weaken, they will also cut back on their spending in order to save for future bad times. As a result, the credit shortfall will spark a compounding effect through the economy as people cut back their spending, making the economy worse, leading to more cutbacks in spending, and so on.

   b. If you believe the economy is self-regulating, then you would advocate doing nothing in response to the slump.

   c. If you believe in Keynesian economics, you would advocate that policy makers undertake monetary and fiscal policies to stimulate spending in the economy.

21-2 Check Your Understanding

1. We talk about business cycles for the economy as a whole because recessions and expansions are not confined to a few industries—they reflect downturns and upturns for the economy as a whole. In downturns, almost every sector of the economy reduces output and the number of people employed. Moreover, business cycles are an international phenomenon, sometimes moving in rough synchrony across countries.

2. Recessions cause a great deal of pain across the entire society. They cause large numbers of workers to lose their jobs and make it hard to find new jobs. Recessions hurt the standard of living of many families and are usually associated with a rise in the number of people living below the poverty line, an increase in the number of people who lose their houses because they can't afford their mortgage payments, and a fall in the percentage of Americans with health insurance. Recessions also hurt the profits of firms.

21-3 Check Your Understanding

1. Countries with high rates of population growth will have to maintain higher growth rates of overall output than countries with low rates of population growth in order to achieve an increased standard of living per person because aggregate output will have to be divided among a larger number of people.

2. No, Argentina is not poorer than it was in the past. Both Argentina and Canada have experienced long-run growth. However, after World War II, Argentina did not make as much progress as Canada, perhaps because of political instability and bad macroeconomic policies. Canada's economy grew much faster than Argentina's. Although Canada is now about three times as rich as Argentina, Argentina still had long-run growth of its economy.

21-4 Check Your Understanding

1. a. As some prices have risen but other prices have fallen, there may be overall inflation or deflation. The answer is ambiguous.

b. As all prices have risen significantly, this sounds like inflation.

c. As most prices have fallen and others have not changed, this sounds like deflation.

21-5 Check Your Understanding

1. a. This situation reflects comparative advantage. Canada's comparative advantage results from the development of oil—Canada now has an abundance of oil.

b. This situation reflects comparative advantage. China's comparative advantage results from an abundance of labor; China is good at labor-intensive activities such as assembly.

c. This situation reflects macroeconomic forces. Germany has been running a huge trade surplus because of underlying decisions regarding savings and investment spending with its savings in excess of its investment spending.

d. This situation reflects macroeconomic forces. The United States was able to begin running a large trade deficit because the technology boom made the United States an attractive place to invest, with investment spending outstripping U.S. savings.

Chapter Twenty-Two

22-1 Check Your Understanding

1. Let's start by considering the relationship between the total value added of all domestically produced final goods and services and aggregate spending on domestically produced final goods and services. These two quantities are equal because every final good and service produced in the economy is either purchased by someone or added to inventories. And additions to inventories are counted as spending by firms. Next, consider the relationship between aggregate spending on domestically produced final goods and services and total factor income. These two quantities are equal because all spending that is channeled to firms to pay for purchases of domestically produced final goods and services is revenue for firms. Those revenues must be paid out by firms to their factors of production in the form of wages, profit, interest, and rent. Taken together, this means that all three methods of calculating GDP are equivalent.

2. Firms make sales to other firms, households, the government, and the rest of the world. Households are linked to firms through the sale of factors of production to firms, through purchases from firms of final goods and services, and through lending funds to firms in the financial markets. Households are linked to the government through their payment of taxes, their receipt of transfers, and their lending of funds to the government via the financial markets. Finally, households are linked to the rest of the world through their purchases of imports and transactions with foreigners in financial markets.

3. You would be counting the value of the steel twice—once as it was sold by American Steel to American Motors and once as part of the car sold by American Motors.

22-2 Check Your Understanding

1. a. In 2013 nominal GDP was $(1,000,000 \times \$0.40) + (800,000 \times \$0.60) = \$400,000 + \$480,000 = \$880,000$. A 25% rise in the price of french fries from 2013 to 2014 means that the 2014 price of french fries was $1.25 \times \$0.40 = \$0.50$. A 10% fall in servings means that $1,000,000 \times 0.9 = 900,000$ servings were sold in 2014. As a result, the total value of sales of french fries in 2014 was $900,000 \times \$0.50 = \$450,000$. A 15% fall in the price of onion rings from 2013 to 2014 means that the 2014 price of onion rings was $0.85 \times \$0.60 = \$0.51$. A 5% rise in servings sold means that $800,000 \times 1.05 = 840,000$ servings were sold in 2014. As a result, the total value of sales of onion rings in 2014 was $840,000 \times \$0.51 = \$428,400$. Nominal GDP in 2014 was $\$450,000 + \$428,400 = \$878,400$. To find real GDP in 2014, we must calculate the value of sales in 2014 using 2013 prices: $(900,000$ french fries $\times \$0.40) + (840,000$ onion rings $\times \$0.60) = \$360,000 + \$504,000 = \$864,000$.

b. The change in nominal GDP from 2013 to 2014 was $(($878,400 - \$880,000)/\$880,000) \times 100 = -0.18\%$, a decline. But a comparison using real GDP shows a decline of $((\$864,000 - \$880,000)/\$880,000) \times 100 = -1.8\%$. That is, a calculation based on real GDP shows a drop 10 times larger (1.8%) than a calculation based on nominal GDP (0.18%). In this case, the calculation based on nominal GDP underestimates the true magnitude of the change.

2. A price index based on 2005 prices will contain a relatively high price of electronics and a relatively low price of housing compared to a price index based on 2010 prices. This means that a 2005 price index used to calculate real GDP in 2013 will magnify the value of electronics production in the economy, but a 2010 price index will magnify the value of housing production in the economy.

22-3 Check Your Understanding

1. This market basket costs, pre-frost, $(100 \times \$0.20) + (50 \times \$0.60) + (200 \times \$0.25) = \$20 + \$30 + \$50 = \$100$. The same market basket, post-frost, costs $(100 \times \$0.40) + (50 \times \$1.00) + (200 \times \$0.45) = \$40 + \$50 + \$90 = \$180$. So the price index is $(\$100/\$100) \times 100 = 100$ before the frost and $(\$180/\$100) \times 100 = 180$ after the frost, implying a rise in the price index of 80%. This increase in the price index is less than the 84.2% increase calculated in the text. The reason for this difference is that the new market basket of 100 oranges, 50 grapefruit, and 200 lemons contains proportionately more of the items that have experienced relatively lower price increases (the lemons, whose price has increased by 80%) and proportionately fewer of the items that have experienced relatively large price increases (the oranges, whose price has increased by 100%). This shows that the price index can be very sensitive to the composition of the market basket. If the market basket contains a large proportion of goods whose prices have risen faster than the prices of other goods, it will lead to a higher estimate of the increase in the price level. If it contains a large proportion of goods whose prices have risen more slowly than the prices of other goods, it will lead to a lower estimate of the increase in the price level.

2. a. A market basket determined 10 years ago will contain fewer cars than at present. Given that the average price of a car has grown faster than the average prices of other goods, this basket will underestimate the true increase in the cost of living because it contains relatively too few cars.

b. A market basket determined 10 years ago will not contain broadband internet access. So it cannot track the fall in prices of internet access over the past few years. As a result, it will overestimate the true increase in the cost of living.

3. Using Equation 22-3, the inflation rate from 2012 to 2013 is ((229.324 − 226.229)/226.229) × 100 = 1.4%.

Chapter Twenty-Three

23-1 Check Your Understanding

1. The advent of websites that enable job-seekers to find jobs more quickly will reduce the unemployment rate over time. However, websites that induce discouraged workers to begin actively looking for work again will lead to an increase in the unemployment rate over time.

2. a. Rosa is not counted as unemployed because she is not actively looking for work, but she is counted in broader measures of labor underutilization as a discouraged worker.

b. Anthony is not counted as unemployed; he is considered employed because he has a job.

c. Grace is unemployed; she is not working and is actively looking for work.

d. Sergio is not unemployed, but underemployed; he is working part time for economic reasons. He is counted in broader measures of labor underutilization.

e. Natasha is not unemployed, but she is a marginally attached worker. She is counted in broader measures of labor underutilization.

3. Both parts a and b are consistent with the relationship, illustrated in Figure 23-5, between above-average or below-average growth in real GDP and changes in the unemployment rate: during years of above-average growth, the unemployment rate falls, and during years of below-average growth, the unemployment rate rises. However, part c is not consistent: it implies that a recession is associated with a fall in the unemployment rate, which is correct.

23-2 Check Your Understanding

1. a. When the pace of technological advance quickens, there will be higher rates of job creation and destruction as old industries disappear and new ones emerge. As a result, frictional unemployment will be higher as workers leave jobs in declining industries in search of jobs in expanding industries.

b. When the pace of technological advance quickens, there will be greater mismatch between the skills employees have and the skills employers are looking for, leading to higher structural unemployment.

c. When the unemployment rate is low, frictional unemployment will account for a larger share of total unemployment because other sources of unemployment will be diminished. So the share of total unemployment composed of the frictionally unemployed will rise.

2. A binding minimum wage represents a price floor below which wages cannot fall. As a result, actual wages cannot move toward equilibrium. So a minimum wage causes the quantity of labor supplied to exceed the quantity of labor demanded. Because this surplus of labor reflects unemployed workers, it affects the unemployment rate. Collective bargaining has a similar effect—unions are able to raise the wage above the equilibrium level to a level like W_U in the accompanying diagram. This will act like a minimum wage by causing the number of job-seekers to be larger than the number of workers firms are willing to hire. Collective bargaining causes the unemployment rate to be higher than it otherwise would be, as shown in the accompanying diagram.

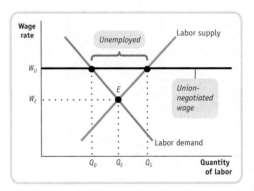

3. An increase in unemployment benefits at the peak of the business cycle reduces the cost to individuals of being unemployed, causing them to spend more time searching for new jobs. So the natural rate of unemployment would increase.

23-3 Check Your Understanding

1. Shoe-leather costs as a result of inflation will be lower because it is now less costly for individuals to manage their assets in order to economize on their money holdings. This reduction in the costs associated with converting other assets into money translates into lower shoe-leather costs.

2. If inflation came to an unexpected and complete stop over the next 15 or 20 years, the inflation rate would be zero, which of course is less than the expected inflation rate of 2% to 3%. Because the real interest rate is the nominal interest rate minus the inflation rate, the real interest rate on a loan would be higher than expected, and lenders would gain at the expense of borrowers. Borrowers would have to repay their loans with funds that have a higher real value than had been expected.

Chapter Twenty-Four

24-1 Check Your Understanding

1. Economic progress raises the living standards of the average resident of a country. An increase in overall real GDP does not accurately reflect an increase in an average resident's living standard because it does not account for growth in the number of residents. If, for example, real GDP rises by 10% but population grows by 20%, the living standard of the average resident falls: after the change, the average resident has only $(110/120) \times 100 = 91.6\%$ as much real income as before the change. Similarly, an increase in nominal GDP per capita does not accurately reflect an increase in living standards because it does not account for any change in prices. For example, a 5% increase in nominal GDP per capita generated by a 5% increase in prices implies that there has been no change in living standards. Real GDP per capita is the only measure that accounts for both changes in the population and changes in prices.

2. Using the Rule of 70, the amount of time it will take for China to double its real GDP per capita is $(70/7.6) = 9$ years; India, $(70/4.3) = 16$ years; Ireland, $(70/3.1) = 23$ years; the United States, $(70/1.7) = 41$ years; France, $(70/1.2) = 58$ years; and Argentina $(70/0.88) = 80$ years. Since the Rule of 70 can only be applied to a positive growth rate, we cannot apply it to the case of Zimbabwe, which experienced negative growth. If India continues to have a higher growth rate of real GDP per capita than the United States, then India's real GDP per capita will eventually surpass that of the United States.

3. The United States began growing rapidly over a century ago, but China and India have begun growing rapidly only recently. As a result, the living standard of the typical Chinese or Indian household has not yet caught up with that of the typical American household.

24-2 Check Your Understanding

1. a. Significant technological progress will result in a positive growth rate of productivity even though physical capital per worker and human capital per worker are unchanged.

   b. The growth rate of productivity will fall but remain positive due to diminishing returns to physical capital.

2. a. If output has grown 3% per year and the labor force has grown 1% per year, then productivity—output per person—has grown at approximately 3% − 1% = 2% per year.

   b. If physical capital has grown 4% per year and the labor force has grown 1% per year, then physical capital per worker has grown at approximately 4% − 1% = 3% per year.

   c. According to estimates, each 1% rise in physical capital, other things equal, increases productivity by 0.3%. So,

as physical capital per worker has increased by 3%, productivity growth that can be attributed to an increase in physical capital per worker is $0.3 \times 3\% = 0.9\%$. As a percentage of total productivity growth, this is $0.9\%/2\% \times 100\% = 45\%$.

   d. If the rest of productivity growth is due to technological progress, then technological progress has contributed 2% − 0.9% = 1.1% to productivity growth. As a percentage of total productivity growth, this is $1.1\%/2\% \times 100\% = 55\%$.

3. It will take a period of time for workers to learn how to use the new computer system and to adjust their routines. And because there are often setbacks in learning a new system, such as accidentally erasing your computer files, productivity at Multinomics may decrease for a period of time.

24-3 Check Your Understanding

1. A country that has high domestic savings is able to achieve a high rate of investment spending as a percent of GDP. This, in turn, allows the country to achieve a high growth rate.

2. It is likely that the United States will experience a greater pace of creation and development of new drugs because closer links between private companies and academic research centers will lead to work more directly focused on producing new drugs rather than on pure research.

3. It is likely that these events resulted in a fall in the country's growth rate because the lack of property rights would have dissuaded people from making investments in productive capacity.

24-4 Check Your Understanding

1. The conditional version of the convergence hypothesis says that countries grow faster, other things equal, when they start from relatively low GDP per capita. From this we can infer that they grow more slowly, other things equal, when their real GDP per capita is relatively higher. This points to lower future Asian growth. However, other things might not be equal: if Asian economies continue investing in human capital, if savings rates continue to be high, if governments invest in infrastructure, and so on, growth might continue at an accelerated pace.

2. The regions of East Asia, Western Europe, and the United States support the convergence hypothesis because a comparison among them shows that the growth rate of real GDP per capita falls as real GDP per capita rises. Eastern Europe, West Asia, Latin America, and Africa do not support the hypothesis because they all have much lower real GDP per capita than the United States but have either approximately the same growth rate (West Asia and Eastern Europe) or a lower growth rate (Africa and Latin America).

3. The evidence suggests that both sets of factors matter: better infrastructure is important for growth, but so is political and financial stability. Policies should try to address both areas.

24-5 Check Your Understanding

1. Economists are typically more concerned about environmental degradation than resource scarcity. The reason is that in modern economies the price response tends to alleviate the limits imposed by resource scarcity through conservation and the development of alternatives. However, because environmental degradation involves a negative externality—a cost imposed by individuals or firms on others without the requirement to pay compensation—effective government intervention is required to address it. As a result, economists are more concerned about the limits to growth imposed by environmental degradation because a market response would be inadequate.

2. Growth increases a country's greenhouse gas emissions. The current best estimates are that a large reduction in emissions will result in only a modest reduction in growth. The international burden sharing of greenhouse gas emissions reduction is contentious because rich countries are reluctant to pay the costs of reducing their emissions only to see newly emerging countries like China rapidly increase their emissions. Yet most of the current accumulation of gases is due to the past actions of rich countries. Poorer countries like China are equally reluctant to sacrifice their growth to pay for the past actions of rich countries.

Chapter Twenty-Five

25-1 Check Your Understanding

1. a. As there is a net capital inflow into the economy, the supply of loanable funds increases. This is illustrated by the shift of the supply curve from S_1 to S_2 in the accompanying diagram. As the equilibrium moves from E_1 to E_2, the equilibrium interest rate falls from r_1 to r_2, and the equilibrium quantity of loanable funds increases from Q_1 to Q_2.

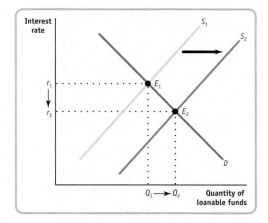

b. Savings fall due to the higher proportion of retired people, and the supply of loanable funds decreases. This is illustrated by the leftward shift of the supply curve from S_1 to S_2 in the accompanying diagram. The equilibrium moves from E_1 to E_2, the equilibrium interest rate rises

from r_1 to r_2, and the equilibrium quantity of loanable funds falls from Q_1 to Q_2.

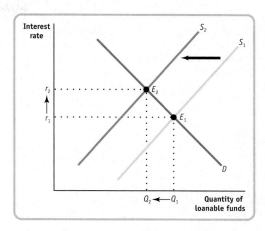

2. We know from the loanable funds market that as the interest rate rises, households want to save more and consume less. But at the same time, an increase in the interest rate lowers the number of investment spending projects with returns at least as high as the interest rate. The statement "households will want to save more money than businesses will want to invest" cannot represent an equilibrium in the loanable funds market because it says that the quantity of loanable funds offered exceeds the quantity of loanable funds demanded. If that were to occur, the interest rate must fall to make the quantity of loanable funds offered equal to the quantity of loanable funds demanded.

3. a. The real interest rate will not change. According to the Fisher effect, an increase in expected inflation drives up the nominal interest rate, leaving the real interest rate unchanged.

b. The nominal interest rate will rise by 3%. Each additional percentage point of expected inflation drives up the nominal interest rate by 1 percentage point.

c. As we saw in Figure 25-7, as long as inflation is expected, it does not affect the equilibrium quantity of loanable funds. Both the supply and demand curves for loanable funds are pushed upward, leaving the equilibrium quantity of loanable funds unchanged.

25-2 Check Your Understanding

1. The transaction costs for (a) a bank deposit and (b) a share of a mutual fund are approximately equal because each can typically be accomplished by making a phone call, going online, or visiting a branch office. Transaction costs are highest for (c) a share of a family business, since finding a buyer for the share consumes time and resources. The level of risk is lowest for (a) a bank deposit, since these deposits are insured by the Federal Deposit Insurance Corporation (FDIC) up to $250,000; somewhat higher for (b) a share of a mutual fund, since despite diversification, there is still risk associated with holding mutual funds; and highest for (c) a share of a family business, since this investment

is not diversified. The level of liquidity is highest for (a) a bank deposit, since withdrawals can usually be made immediately; somewhat lower for (b) a share of a mutual fund, since it may take a few days between selling your shares and the payment being processed; and lowest for (c) a share of a family business, since it can only be sold with the unanimous agreement of other members and it will take some time to find a buyer.

2. Economic development and growth are the result of, among other factors, investment spending on physical capital. Since investment spending is equal to savings, the greater the amount saved, the higher investment spending will be, and so the higher growth and economic development will be. So the existence of institutions that facilitate savings will help a country's growth and economic development. As a result, a country with a financial system that provides low transaction costs, opportunities for diversification of risk, and high liquidity to its savers will experience faster growth and economic development than a country that doesn't.

25-3 Check Your Understanding

1. a. Today's stock prices reflect the market's expectation of future stock prices, and according to the efficient markets hypothesis, stock prices always take account of all available information. The fact that this year's profits are low is not new information, so it is already built into the share price. However, when it becomes known that the company's profits will be high next year, the price of a share of its stock will rise today, reflecting this new information.

b. The expectations of investors about high profits were already built into the stock price. Since profits will be lower than expected, the market's expectations about the company's future stock price will be revised downward. This new information will lower the stock price.

c. When other companies in the same industry announce that sales are unexpectedly slow this year, investors are likely to conclude that sales will also be unexpectedly slow for this company. As a result, investors will revise downward their expectations of future profits and of the future stock price. This new information will result in a lower stock price today.

d. This announcement will either have no effect on the company's stock price or will increase it only slightly. It does not add any new information, beyond removing some uncertainty about whether the profit forecast was correct. It should therefore result in either no increase or only a small increase in the stock price.

2. The efficient markets hypothesis states that all available information is immediately taken into account in stock prices. So if investors consistently bought stocks the day after the Dow rose by 1%, a smart investor would *sell* on that day because demand—and so stock prices—would be high. If a profit can be made that way, eventually many investors would be selling, and it would no longer be true that investors always bought stocks the day after the Dow rose by 1%.

Chapter Twenty-Six

26-1 Check Your Understanding

1. A decline in investment spending, like a rise in investment spending, has a multiplier effect on real GDP—the only difference in this case is that real GDP falls instead of rises. The fall in I leads to an initial fall in real GDP, which leads to a fall in disposable income, which leads to lower consumer spending, which leads to another fall in real GDP, and so on. So consumer spending falls as an indirect result of the fall in investment spending.

2. When the MPC is 0.5, the multiplier is equal to $1/(1 - 0.5) = 1/0.5 = 2$. When the MPC is 0.8, the multiplier is equal to $1/(1 - 0.8) = 1/0.2 = 5$.

3. The greater the share of GDP that is saved rather than spent, the lower the MPC. Disposable income that goes to savings is like a "leak" in the system, reducing the amount of spending that fuels a further expansion. So it is likely that Amerigo will have the larger multiplier.

26-2 Check Your Understanding

1. a. Angelina's autonomous consumer spending is $8,000. When her current disposable income rises by $10,000, her consumer spending rises by $12,000 – $8,000 = $4,000. So her MPC is $4,000/$10,000 = 0.4 and her consumption function is $c = \$8,000 + 0.4 \times yd$. Felicia's autonomous consumer spending is $6,500. When her current disposable income rises by $10,000, her consumer spending rises by $14,500 – $6,500 = $8,000. So her MPC is $8,000/$10,000 = 0.8 and her consumption function is $c = \$6,500 + 0.8 \times yd$. Marina's autonomous consumer spending is $7,250. When her current disposable income rises by $10,000, her consumer spending rises by $14,250 – $7,250 = $7,000. So her MPC is $7,000/$10,000 = 0.7 and her consumption function is $c = \$7,250 + 0.7 \times yd$.

b. The aggregate autonomous consumer spending in this economy is $8,000 + $6,500 + $7,250 = $21,750. A $30,000 increase in disposable income (3 × $10,000) leads to a $4,000 + $8,000 + $7,000 = $19,000 increase in consumer spending. So the economy-wide MPC is $19,000/$30,000 = 0.63 and the aggregate consumption function is $C = \$21,750 + 0.63 \times YD$.

2. If you expect your future disposable income to fall, you would like to save some of today's disposable income to tide you over in the future. But you cannot do this if you cannot save. If you expect your future disposable income to rise, you would like to spend some of tomorrow's higher income today. But you cannot do this if you cannot borrow. If you cannot save or borrow, your expected future disposable income will have no effect on your consumer spending today. In fact, your MPC must always equal 1: you must consume all your current disposable income today, and you will be unable to smooth your consumption over time.

26-3 Check Your Understanding

1. a. An unexpected increase in consumer spending will result in a reduction in inventories as producers sell items from their inventories to satisfy this short-term increase in demand. This is negative unplanned inventory investment: it reduces the value of producers' inventories.

b. A rise in the cost of borrowing is equivalent to a rise in the interest rate: fewer investment spending projects are now profitable to producers, whether they are financed through borrowing or retained earnings. As a result, producers will reduce the amount of planned investment spending.

c. A sharp increase in the rate of real GDP growth leads to a higher level of planned investment spending by producers, according to the accelerator principle, as they increase production capacity to meet higher demand.

d. As sales fall, producers sell less, and their inventories grow. This leads to positive unplanned inventory investment.

2. Since the marginal propensity to consume is less than 1—because consumers normally spend part but not all of an additional dollar of disposable income—consumer spending does not fully respond to fluctuations in current disposable income. This behavior diminishes the effect of fluctuations in the economy on consumer spending. In contrast, by the accelerator principle, investment spending is directly related to the expected future growth rate of GDP. As a result, investment spending will magnify fluctuations in the economy: a higher expected future growth rate of real GDP leads to higher planned investment spending; a lower expected future growth rate of real GDP leads to lower planned investment spending.

3. When consumer spending is sluggish, firms with excess production capacity will cut back on planned investment spending because they think their existing capacities are sufficient for expected future sales. Similarly, when consumer spending is sluggish and firms have a large amount of unplanned inventory investment, they are likely to cut back their production of output because they think their existing inventories are sufficient for expected future sales. So an inventory overhang is likely to depress current economic activity as firms cut back on their planned investment spending and on their output.

26-4 Check Your Understanding

1. A slump in planned investment spending will lead to a fall in real GDP in response to an unanticipated increase in inventories. The fall in real GDP will translate into a fall in households' disposable income, and households will respond by reducing consumer spending. The decrease in consumer spending leads producers to further decrease output, further lowering disposable income and leading to further reductions in consumer spending. So although the slump originated in investment spending, it will cause a reduction in consumer spending.

2. a. After an autonomous fall in planned aggregate spending, the economy is no longer in equilibrium: real GDP is greater than planned aggregate spending. The accompanying figure shows this autonomous fall in planned aggregate spending by the shift of the aggregate spending curve from AE_1 to AE_2. The difference between the

two results in positive unplanned inventory investment: there is an unanticipated increase in inventories. Firms will respond by reducing production. This will eventually move the economy to a new equilibrium. In the accompanying figure, this is illustrated by the movement from the initial income–expenditure equilibrium at E_1 to the new income–expenditure equilibrium at E_2. As the economy moves to its new equilibrium, real GDP falls from its initial income–expenditure equilibrium level at Y_1^* to its new lower level, Y_2^*.

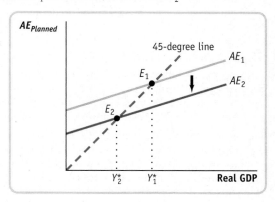

b. We know that the change in income–expenditure equilibrium GDP is given by Equation 26-17: $\Delta Y^* =$ Multiplier $\times \Delta AAE_{Planned}$. Here, the multiplier = $1/(1 - 0.5) = 1/0.5 = 2$. So a $300 million autonomous reduction in planned aggregate spending will lead to a $2 \times 300 million = $600 million ($0.6 billion) fall in income–expenditure equilibrium GDP. The new Y^* will be $500 billion − $0.6 billion = $499.4 billion.

Chapter Twenty-Seven

27-1 Check Your Understanding

1. a. This is a shift of the aggregate demand curve. A decrease in the quantity of money raises the interest rate, since people now want to borrow more and lend less. A higher interest rate reduces investment and consumer spending at any given aggregate price level. So the aggregate demand curve shifts to the left.

b. This is a movement up along the aggregate demand curve. As the aggregate price level rises, the real value of money holdings falls. This is the interest rate effect of a change in the aggregate price level: as the value of money falls, people want to hold more money. They do so by borrowing more and lending less. This leads to a rise in the interest rate and a reduction in consumer and investment spending. So it is a movement along the aggregate demand curve.

c. This is a shift of the aggregate demand curve. Expectations of a poor job market, and so lower average disposable incomes, will reduce people's consumer spending today at any given aggregate price level. So the aggregate demand curve shifts to the left.

d. This is a shift of the aggregate demand curve. A fall in tax rates raises people's disposable income. At any given aggregate price level, consumer spending is now higher. So the aggregate demand curve shifts to the right.

e. This is a movement down along the aggregate demand curve. As the aggregate price level falls, the real value of assets rises. This is the wealth effect of a change in the aggregate price level: as the value of assets rises, people will increase their consumption plans. This leads to higher consumer spending. So it is a movement along the aggregate demand curve.

f. This is a shift of the aggregate demand curve. A rise in the real value of assets in the economy due to a surge in real estate values raises consumer spending at any given aggregate price level. So the aggregate demand curve shifts to the right.

27-2 Check Your Understanding

1. a. This represents a movement along the *SRAS* curve because the CPI—like the GDP deflator—is a measure of the aggregate price level, the overall price level of final goods and services in the economy.

b. This represents a shift of the *SRAS* curve because oil is a commodity. The *SRAS* curve will shift to the right because production costs are now lower, leading to a higher quantity of aggregate output supplied at any given aggregate price level.

c. This represents a shift of the *SRAS* curve because it involves a change in nominal wages. An increase in legally mandated benefits to workers is equivalent to an increase in nominal wages. As a result, the *SRAS* curve will shift leftward because production costs are now higher, leading to a lower quantity of aggregate output supplied at any given aggregate price level.

2. You would need to know what happened to the aggregate price level. If the increase in the quantity of aggregate output supplied was due to a movement along the *SRAS* curve, the aggregate price level would have increased at the same time as the quantity of aggregate output supplied increased. If the increase in the quantity of aggregate output supplied was due to a rightward shift of the *LRAS* curve, the aggregate price level might not rise. Alternatively, you could make the determination by observing what happened to aggregate output in the long run. If it fell back to its initial level in the long run, then the temporary increase in aggregate output was due to a movement along the *SRAS* curve. If it stayed at the higher level in the long run, the increase in aggregate output was due to a rightward shift of the *LRAS* curve.

27-3 Check Your Understanding

1. a. An increase in the minimum wage raises the nominal wage and, as a result, shifts the short-run aggregate supply curve to the left. As a result of this negative supply shock, the aggregate price level rises and aggregate output falls.

b. Increased investment spending shifts the aggregate demand curve to the right. As a result of this positive demand shock, both the aggregate price level and aggregate output rise.

c. An increase in taxes and a reduction in government spending both result in negative demand shocks, shifting the aggregate demand curve to the left. As a

result, both the aggregate price level and aggregate output fall.

d. This is a negative supply shock, shifting the short-run aggregate supply curve to the left. As a result, the aggregate price level rises and aggregate output falls.

2. As the rise in productivity increases potential output, the long-run aggregate supply curve shifts to the right. If, in the short run, there is now a recessionary gap (aggregate output is less than potential output), nominal wages will fall, shifting the short-run aggregate supply curve to the right. This results in a fall in the aggregate price level and a rise in aggregate output. As prices fall, we move along the aggregate demand curve due to the wealth and interest rate effects of a change in the aggregate price level. Eventually, as long-run macroeconomic equilibrium is reestablished, aggregate output will rise to be equal to potential output.

27-4 Check Your Understanding

1. a. An economy is overstimulated when an inflationary gap is present. This will arise if an expansionary monetary or fiscal policy is implemented when the economy is currently in long-run macroeconomic equilibrium. This shifts the aggregate demand curve to the right, in the short run raising the aggregate price level and aggregate output and creating an inflationary gap. Eventually nominal wages will rise and shift the short-run aggregate supply curve to the left, and aggregate output will fall back to potential output. This is the scenario envisaged by the speaker.

b. No, this is not a valid argument. When the economy is not currently in long-run macroeconomic equilibrium, an expansionary monetary or fiscal policy does not lead to the outcome described above. Suppose a negative demand shock has shifted the aggregate demand curve to the left, resulting in a recessionary gap. An expansionary monetary or fiscal policy can shift the aggregate demand curve back to its original position in long-run macroeconomic equilibrium. In this way, the short-run fall in aggregate output and deflation caused by the original negative demand shock can be avoided. So, if used in response to demand shocks, fiscal or monetary policy is an effective policy tool.

2. Those within the Fed who advocated lowering interest rates were focused on boosting aggregate demand in order to counteract the negative demand shock caused by the collapse of the housing bubble. Lowering interest rates will result in a rightward shift of the aggregate demand curve, increasing aggregate output but raising the aggregate price level. Those within the Fed who advocated holding interest rates steady were focused on the fact that fighting the slump in aggregate demand in the face of a negative supply shock could result in a rise in inflation. Holding interest rates steady relies on the ability of the economy to self-correct in the long run, with the aggregate price level and aggregate output only gradually returning to their levels before the negative supply shock.

Chapter Twenty-Eight

28-1 Check Your Understanding

1. a. This is a contractionary fiscal policy because it is a reduction in government purchases of goods and services.

  b. This is an expansionary fiscal policy because it is an increase in government transfers that will increase disposable income.

  c. This is a contractionary fiscal policy because it is an increase in taxes that will reduce disposable income.

2. Federal disaster relief that is quickly disbursed is more effective than legislated aid because there is very little time lag between the time of the disaster and the time it is received by victims. So it will stabilize the economy after a disaster. In contrast, legislated aid is likely to entail a time lag in its disbursement, potentially destabilizing the economy.

3. This statement implies that expansionary fiscal policy will result in crowding out of the private sector, and that the opposite, contractionary fiscal policy, will lead the private sector to grow. Whether this statement is true or not depends upon whether the economy is at full employment; it is only then that we should expect expansionary fiscal policy to lead to crowding out. If, instead, the economy has a recessionary gap, then we should expect instead that the private sector grows along with the fiscal expansion, and contracts along with a fiscal contraction.

28-2 Check Your Understanding

1. A $500 million increase in government purchases of goods and services directly increases aggregate spending by $500 million, which then starts the multiplier in motion. It will increase real GDP by $500 million × $1/(1 - MPC)$. A $500 million increase in government transfers increases aggregate spending only to the extent that it leads to an increase in consumer spending. Consumer spending rises by $MPC × \$1$ for every $1 increase in disposable income, where MPC is less than 1. So a $500 million increase in government transfers will cause a rise in real GDP only MPC times as much as a $500 million increase in government purchases of goods and services. It will increase real GDP by $500 million × $MPC/(1 - MPC)$.

2. This is the same issue as in Problem 1, but in reverse. If government purchases of goods and services fall by $500 million, the initial fall in aggregate spending is $500 million. If there is a $500 million reduction in government transfers, the initial fall in aggregate spending is $MPC × \$500$ million, which is less than $500 million.

3. Boldovia will experience greater variation in its real GDP than Moldovia because Moldovia has automatic stabilizers while Boldovia does not. In Moldovia the effects of slumps will be lessened by unemployment insurance benefits that will support residents' incomes, while the effects of booms will be diminished because tax revenues will go up. In contrast, incomes will not be supported in Boldovia during slumps because there

is no unemployment insurance. In addition, because Boldovia has lump-sum taxes, its booms will not be diminished by increases in tax revenue.

28-3 Check Your Understanding

1. The actual budget balance takes into account the effects of the business cycle on the budget deficit. During recessionary gaps, it incorporates the effect of lower tax revenues and higher transfers on the budget balance; during inflationary gaps, it incorporates the effect of higher tax revenues and reduced transfers. In contrast, the cyclically adjusted budget balance factors out the effects of the business cycle and assumes that real GDP is at potential output. Since, in the long run, real GDP tends to potential output, the cyclically adjusted budget balance is a better measure of the long-run sustainability of government policies.

2. In recessions, real GDP falls. This implies that consumers' incomes, consumer spending, and producers' profits also fall. So in recessions, states' tax revenue (which depends in large part on consumers' incomes, consumer spending, and producers' profits) falls. In order to balance the state budget, states have to cut spending or raise taxes. But that deepens the recession. Without a balanced-budget requirement, states could use expansionary fiscal policy during a recession to lessen the fall in real GDP.

28-4 Check Your Understanding

1. a. A higher growth rate of real GDP implies that tax revenue will increase. If government spending remains constant and the government runs a budget surplus, the size of the public debt will be less than it would otherwise have been.

  b. If retirees live longer, the average age of the population increases. As a result, the implicit liabilities of the government increase because spending on programs for older Americans, such as Social Security and Medicare, will rise.

  c. A decrease in tax revenue without offsetting reductions in government spending will cause the public debt to increase.

  d. Public debt will increase as a result of government borrowing to pay interest on its current public debt.

2. In order to stimulate the economy in the short run, the government can use fiscal policy to increase real GDP. This entails borrowing, increasing the size of the public debt further and leading to undesirable consequences: in extreme cases, governments can be forced to default on their debts. Even in less extreme cases, a large public debt is undesirable because government borrowing crowds out borrowing for private investment spending. This reduces the amount of investment spending, reducing the long-run growth of the economy.

3. Fiscal austerity is the same as a contractionary fiscal policy. It reduces government spending, which in turn reduces income and reduces tax revenue. With less tax revenue, the government is less able to pay its debts. Also, a failing economy causes lenders to have less confidence that a government is able to pay its debts and leads them to raise interest rates on the debt. Higher interest rates on the debt make it even less likely the government can repay.

Chapter Twenty-Nine

29-1 Check Your Understanding

1. The defining characteristic of money is its liquidity: how easily it can be used to purchase goods and services. Although a gift card can easily be used to purchase a very defined set of goods or services (the goods or services available at the store issuing the gift card), it cannot be used to purchase any other goods or services. A gift card is therefore not money, since it cannot easily be used to purchase all goods and services.

2. Again, the important characteristic of money is its liquidity: how easily it can be used to purchase goods and services. M1, the narrowest definition of the money supply, contains only currency in circulation, traveler's checks, and checkable bank deposits. CDs aren't checkable—and they can't be made checkable without incurring a cost because there's a penalty for early withdrawal. This makes them less liquid than the assets counted in M1.

3. Commodity-backed money uses resources more efficiently than simple commodity money, like gold and silver coins, because commodity-backed money ties up fewer valuable resources. Although a bank must keep some of the commodity—generally gold and silver—on hand, it only has to keep enough to satisfy demand for redemptions. It can then lend out the remaining gold and silver, which allows society to use these resources for other purposes, with no loss in the ability to achieve gains from trade.

29-2 Check Your Understanding

1. Even though you know that the rumor about the bank is not true, you are concerned about other depositors pulling their money out of the bank. And you know that if enough other depositors pull their money out, the bank will fail. In that case, it is rational for you to pull your money out before the bank fails. All depositors will think like this, so even if they all know that the rumor is false, they may still rationally pull their money out, leading to a bank run. Deposit insurance leads depositors to worry less about the possibility of a bank run. Even if a bank fails, the FDIC will currently pay each depositor up to $250,000 per account. This will make you much less likely to pull your money out in response to a rumor. Since other depositors will think the same, there will be no bank run.

2. The aspects of modern bank regulation that would frustrate this scheme are *capital requirements* and *reserve requirements*. Capital requirements mean that a bank has to have a certain amount of capital—the difference between its assets (loans plus reserves) and its liabilities (deposits). So the con artist could not open a bank without putting any of his own wealth in because the bank needs a certain amount of capital—that is, it needs to hold more assets (loans plus reserves) than deposits. So

the con artist would be at risk of losing his own wealth if his loans turn out badly.

29-3 Check Your Understanding

1. Since they only have to hold $100 in reserves, instead of $200, banks now lend out $100 of their reserves. Whoever borrows the $100 will deposit it in a bank, which will lend out $100 \times (1 - rr) = $100 \times 0.9 = $90. Whoever borrows the $90 will put it into a bank, which will lend out $90 \times 0.9 = $81, and so on. Overall, deposits will increase by $100/0.1 = $1,000.

2. Silas puts $1,000 in the bank, of which the bank lends out $1,000 \times (1 - rr) = $1,000 \times 0.9 = $900. Whoever borrows the $900 will keep $450 in cash and deposit $450 in a bank. The bank will lend out $450 \times 0.9 = $405. Whoever borrows the $405 will keep $202.50 in cash and deposit $202.50 in a bank. The bank will lend out $202.50 \times 0.9 = $182.25, and so on. Overall, this leads to an increase in deposits of $1,000 + $450 + $202.50 + . . . But it decreases the amount of currency in circulation: the amount of cash is reduced by the $1,000 Silas puts into the bank. This is offset, but not fully, by the amount of cash held by each borrower. The amount of currency in circulation therefore changes by −$1,000 + $450 + $202.50 + . . . The money supply therefore increases by the sum of the increase in deposits and the change in currency in circulation, which is $1,000 − $1,000 + $450 + $450 + $202.50 + $202.50 + . . . and so on.

29-4 Check Your Understanding

1. An open-market purchase of $100 million by the Fed increases banks' reserves by $100 million as the Fed credits their accounts with additional reserves. In other words, this open-market purchase increases the monetary base (currency in circulation plus bank reserves) by $100 million. Banks lend out the additional $100 million. Whoever borrows the money puts it back into the banking system in the form of deposits. Of these deposits, banks lend out $100 million \times (1 - rr) = $100 million \times 0.9 = $90 million. Whoever borrows the money deposits it back into the banking system. And banks lend out $90 million \times 0.9 = $81 million, and so on. As a result, bank deposits increase by $100 million + $90 million + $81 million + . . . = $100 million/rr = $100 million/0.1 = $1,000 million = $1 billion. Since in this simplified example all money lent out is deposited back into the banking system, there is no increase of currency in circulation, so the increase in bank deposits is equal to the increase in the money supply. In other words, the money supply increases by $1 billion. This is greater than the increase in the monetary base by a factor of 10: in this simplified model in which deposits are the only component of the money supply and in which banks hold no excess reserves, the money multiplier is $1/rr = 10$.

29-5 Check Your Understanding

1. The Panic of 1907, the S&L crisis, and the crisis of 2008 all involved losses by financial institutions that were less regulated than banks. In the crises of 1907 and

2008, there was a widespread loss of confidence in the financial sector and collapse of credit markets. Like the crisis of 1907 and the S&L crisis, the crisis of 2008 exerted a powerful negative effect on the economy.

2. The creation of the Federal Reserve failed to prevent bank runs because it did not eradicate the fears of depositors that a bank collapse would cause them to lose their money. The bank runs eventually stopped after federal deposit insurance was instituted and the public came to understand that their deposits were now protected.

3. The balance sheet effect occurs when asset sales cause declines in asset prices, which then reduce the value of other firms' net worth as the value of the assets on their balance sheets declines. In the vicious cycle of deleveraging, the balance sheet effect on firms forces their creditors to call in their loan contracts, forcing the firms to sell assets to pay back their loans, leading to further asset sales and price declines. Because the vicious cycle of deleveraging occurs across different firms and no single firm can stop it, it is necessary for the government to step in to stop it.

Chapter Thirty

30-1 Check Your Understanding

1. a. By increasing the opportunity cost of holding money, a high interest rate reduces the quantity of money demanded. This is a movement up and to the left along the money demand curve.

b. A 10% fall in prices reduces the quantity of money demanded at any given interest rate, shifting the money demand curve leftward.

c. This technological change reduces the quantity of money demanded at any given interest rate. So it shifts the money demand curve leftward.

d. This will increase the demand for money at any given interest rate. With more of the economy's assets in overseas bank accounts that are difficult to access, people will want to hold more cash to finance purchases.

2. a. A 1% processing fee on debit/credit card transactions for purchases less than $50 reduces the opportunity cost of holding cash because consumers will save money by paying with cash.

b. An increase in the interest paid on six-month CDs raises the opportunity cost of holding cash because holding cash requires forgoing the higher interest paid.

c. This reduces the opportunity cost of holding cash because it can now be used to fund purchases at very low prices, compensating its owner for any interest forgone by holding cash.

d. Because many purchases of food are made in cash, a significant increase in the cost of food reduces the opportunity cost of holding cash.

30-2 Check Your Understanding

1. In the accompanying diagram, the increase in the demand for money is shown as a rightward shift of the money demand curve, from MD_1 to MD_2. This raises the equilibrium interest rate from r_1 to r_2.

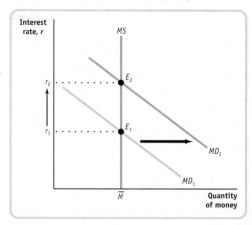

2. In order to prevent the interest rate from rising, the Federal Reserve must make an open-market purchase of Treasury bills, shifting the money supply curve rightward. This is shown in the accompanying diagram as the move from MS_1 to MS_2.

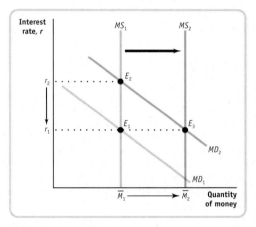

3. a. Frannie is better off buying a one-year bond today and a one-year bond next year because this allows her to get the higher interest rate one year from now.

b. Frannie is better off buying a two-year bond today because it gives her a higher interest rate in the second year than if she bought two one-year bonds.

30-3 Check Your Understanding

1. a. The money supply curve shifts to the right.

b. The equilibrium interest rate falls.

c. Investment spending rises, due to the fall in the interest rate.

d. Consumer spending rises, due to the multiplier process.

e. Aggregate output rises because of the rightward shift of the aggregate demand curve.

2. The central bank that uses a Taylor rule is likely to respond more directly to a financial crisis than one that uses inflation targeting because with a Taylor rule the central bank does not have to set policy to meet a pre-specified inflation target.

30-4 Check Your Understanding

1. a. Aggregate output rises in the short run, then falls back to equal potential output in the long run.

   b. The aggregate price level rises in the short run, but by less than 25%. It rises further in the long run, for a total increase of 25%.

   c. The interest rate falls in the short run, then rises back to its original level in the long run.

2. In the short run, a change in the interest rate alters the economy because it affects investment spending, which in turn affects aggregate demand and real GDP through the multiplier process. However, in the long run, changes in consumer spending and investment spending will eventually result in changes in nominal wages and the nominal prices of other factors of production. For example, an expansionary monetary policy will eventually cause a rise in factor prices; a contractionary policy will eventually cause a fall in factor prices. In response, the short-run aggregate supply curve will shift to move the economy back to long-run equilibrium. So in the long run monetary policy has no effect on the economy.

Chapter Thirty-One

31-1 Check Your Understanding

1. The inflation rate is more likely to quickly reflect changes in the money supply when the economy has had an extended period of high inflation. That's because an extended period of high inflation sensitizes workers and firms to raise nominal wages and prices of intermediate goods when the aggregate price level rises. As a result, there will be little or no increase in real output in the short run after an increase in the money supply, and the increase in the money supply will simply be reflected in an equal-sized percent increase in prices. In an economy where people are not sensitized to high inflation because of low inflation in the past, an increase in the money supply will lead to an increase in real output in the short run. This illustrates the fact that the classical model of the price level best applies to economies with *persistently* high inflation, not those with little or no history of high inflation even though they may currently have high inflation.

2. Yes, there can still be an inflation tax because the tax is levied on people who hold money. As long as people hold money, regardless of whether prices are indexed or not, the government is able to use seignorage to capture real resources from the public.

31-2 Check Your Understanding

1. When real GDP equals potential output, cyclical unemployment is zero and the unemployment rate is equal to the natural rate. This is given by point E_1 in Figure 31-7.

Assuming a 0% expected inflation rate, this also corresponds to a 6% unemployment rate on curve $SRPC_0$ in Figure 31-9. Any unemployment in excess of this 6% rate, or less than the 6% rate, represents cyclical unemployment. An increase in aggregate demand leads to a fall in the unemployment rate below the natural rate (negative cyclical unemployment) and an increase in the inflation rate. This is given by the movement from E_1 to E_2 in Figure 31-7 and traces a movement upward along the short-run Phillips curve. A reduction in aggregate demand leads to a rise in the unemployment rate above the natural rate (positive cyclical unemployment) and a fall in the inflation rate. This would be represented by a movement down along the short-run Phillips curve from point E_1. So for a given expected inflation rate, the short-run Phillips curve illustrates the relationship between cyclical unemployment and the actual inflation rate.

2. A fall in commodities prices leads to a positive supply shock, which lowers the aggregate price level and reduces inflation. As a result, any given level of unemployment can be sustained with a lower inflation rate now—meaning that the short-run Phillips curve has shifted downward. In contrast, a surge in commodities prices leads to a negative supply shock, which raises the aggregate price level and increases inflation. Any given level of unemployment can be sustained only with a higher inflation rate—meaning that the short-run Phillips curve has shifted upward.

31-3 Check Your Understanding

1. There is no long-run trade-off between inflation and unemployment because once expectations of inflation adjust, wages will also adjust, returning employment and the unemployment rate to their equilibrium (natural) levels. This implies that once expectations of inflation fully adjust to any change in actual inflation, the unemployment rate will return to the natural rate of unemployment, or NAIRU. This also implies that the long-run Phillips curve is vertical.

2. There are two possible explanations for this. First, negative supply shocks (for example, increases in the price of oil) will cause an increase in unemployment and an increase in inflation. Second, it is possible that British policy makers attempted to peg the unemployment rate below the natural rate of unemployment. Any attempt to peg unemployment below the natural rate will result in an increase in inflation.

3. Disinflation is costly because to reduce the inflation rate, aggregate output in the short run must typically fall below potential output. This, in turn, results in an increase in the unemployment rate above the natural rate. In general, we would observe a reduction in real GDP. The costs of disinflation can be reduced by not allowing inflation to increase in the first place. Second, the costs of any disinflation will be lower if the central bank is credible and it announces in advance its policy to reduce inflation. In this situation, the adjustment to the disinflationary policy will be more rapid, resulting in a smaller loss of aggregate output.

31-4 Check Your Understanding

1. If the nominal interest rate is negative, an individual is better off simply holding cash, which has a 0% nominal rate of return. If the options facing an individual are to lend and receive a negative nominal interest rate or to hold cash and receive a 0% nominal interest rate, the individual will hold cash. Such a scenario creates the possibility of a liquidity trap, in which monetary policy is ineffective because the nominal interest rate cannot fall below zero. Once the nominal interest rate falls to zero, further increases in the money supply will lead firms and individuals to simply hold the additional cash.

Chapter Thirty-Two

32-1 Check Your Understanding

1. **a.** This is not an example of maturity transformation because no short-term liabilities are being turned into long-term assets. So it is not subject to a bank run.

   b. This is an example of maturity transformation: Dana incurs a short-term liability, credit card debt, to fund the acquisition of a long-term asset, better job skills. It can result in a bank-run-like phenomenon if her credit card lender becomes fearful of her ability to repay and stops lending to her. If this happens, she will not be able to finish her course and, as a result, will not be able to get the better job that would allow her to pay off her credit card loans.

   c. This is not an example of maturity transformation because there are no short-term liabilities. The partnership itself has no obligation to repay an individual partner's investment and so has no liabilities, short term or long term.

   d. This is an example of maturity transformation: the checking accounts are short-term liabilities of the student union savings bank, and the student loans are long-term assets.

32-2 Check Your Understanding

1. **a.** The asset bubble occurred in Irish real estate.

   b. The channel of the financial contagion was the short-term lending that Irish banks depended on from the wholesale interbank lending market. When lenders began to worry about the soundness of the Irish banks, they refused to lend any more money, leading to a type of bank run and putting the Irish banks at great risk of failure.

2. Because the bank run started with fears among lenders to Irish banks, the Irish government sought to eliminate those fears by guaranteeing the lenders that they would be repaid in full. It was a questionable strategy, though, because it put the Irish taxpayers on the hook for potentially very large losses, so large that they threatened the solvency of the Irish government.

32-3 Check Your Understanding

1. The Federal Reserve was able to prevent a replay of the Great Depression because, unlike in the 1930s, it acted as a lender of last resort to stabilize the banking sector and halt the contagion. But it was unable to significantly reduce the surge in unemployment because the United States experienced a credit crunch and a vicious circle of deleveraging, leaving monetary policy relatively ineffective.

2. In the aftermath of a severe banking crisis, businesses and households have high debt and reduced assets. They cut back on spending to try to reduce their debt. So they are unwilling to borrow regardless of how low the interest rate is.

32-4 Check Your Understanding

1. According to standard macroeconomics, a government should adopt expansionary policies to increase aggregate demand to address an economic slump. France, however, did just the opposite, responding to a weaker economy with a contractionary fiscal policy that would make the economy even weaker. This shows that the French government had adopted the austerity view, believing that it was more important to try to assure markets of its solvency than to support the economy.

32-5 Check Your Understanding

1. Because shadow banks like Lehman relied on short-term borrowing to fund their operations, fears about their soundness could quickly lead lenders to immediately cut off their credit and force them into failure. And without membership in the lender-of-last-resort system, shadow banks like Lehman could not borrow from the Federal Reserve to make up for the short-term loans it had lost.

2. If there had been only a formal depository banking sector, several factors would have mitigated the potential and scope of a banking crisis. First, there would have been no repo financing; the only short-term liabilities would have been customers' deposits, and these would have been largely covered by deposit insurance. Second, capital requirements would have reduced banks' willingness to take on excessive risk, such as holding onto subprime mortgages. Also, direct oversight by the Federal Reserve would have prevented so much concentration of risk within the banking sector. Finally, depository banks are within the lender-of-last-resort system; as a result, depository banks had another layer of protection against the fear of depositors and other creditors that they couldn't meet their obligations. All of these factors would have reduced the potential and scope of a banking crisis.

3. Because the shadow banking sector had become such a critical part of the U.S. economy, the crisis of 2008 made it clear that in the event of another crisis the government would find it necessary to guarantee a wide range of financial institution debts, including those of shadow banks as well as depository banks. This created an incentive problem because it would induce shadow banks to take more risk, knowing that the government would bail them out in the event of a meltdown. To counteract this, the Dodd-Frank bill gave the government the power to regulate "systemically important" shadow banks (those likely to require bailing out) in order to reduce their risk taking. It also gave the government the power

to seize control of failing shadow banks in a way that was fair to taxpayers and didn't unfairly enrich the owners of the banks.

Chapter Thirty-Three

33-1 Check Your Understanding

1. A classical economist would have said that although expansionary monetary policy would probably have some effect in the short run, the short run was unimportant. Instead, a classical economist would have stressed the long run, claiming expansionary monetary policy would result only in an increase in the aggregate price level without affecting aggregate output.

33-2 Check Your Understanding

1. The statement would seem very familiar to a Keynesian economist. According to Keynes, business confidence (which he called "animal spirits") is mainly responsible for recessions. If business confidence is low, a Keynesian economist would think of this as a case for macroeconomic policy activism: that the government should use expansionary monetary and fiscal policy to help the economy recover.

33-3 Check Your Understanding

1. **a.** According to the velocity equation, $M \times V = P \times Y$, where M is the money supply, V the velocity of money, P the aggregate price level, and Y real GDP. If the Federal Reserve had pursued a monetary policy rule of constant money supply growth, the collapse in the velocity of money beginning in 2008 and visible in Figure 33-5 would have resulted in a dramatic decline in aggregate output.

   b. Although monetarists generally believe that monetary policy is not only effective but, in fact, more effective than fiscal policy, they also generally do not favor macroeconomic policy activism. Instead, monetarists generally advocate monetary policy rules, such as a low but constant rate of money supply growth. In addition, the natural rate hypothesis states that although monetary policy may be effective in helping return unemployment to its natural rate, it cannot permanently reduce unemployment below the natural rate.

2. Fiscal policy is limited by time lags in recognizing economic problems, forming a response, passing legislation, and implementing the policies. Monetary policy is also limited by time lags, but these lags are not as severe as those for fiscal policy because the Federal Reserve tends to act more quickly than Congress. Attempts to reduce unemployment below the natural rate via both fiscal and monetary policy are limited by predictions of the natural rate hypothesis: that these attempts will result in accelerating inflation. Also, both fiscal and monetary policy are limited by concerns about the political business cycle: that they will be used to satisfy political ends and will end up destabilizing the economy.

33-4 Check Your Understanding

1. **a.** Rational expectations theorists would argue that only unexpected changes in the money supply would have any short-run effect on economic activity. They would also argue that expected changes in the money supply would affect only the aggregate price level, with no short-run effect on aggregate output. So such theorists would give credit to the Fed for limiting the severity of the Great Recession only if the Fed's monetary policy had been more aggressive than individuals expected during this period.

   b. Real business cycle theorists would argue that the Fed's policy had no effect on ending the Great Recession because they believe that fluctuations in aggregate output are caused largely by changes in total factor productivity.

33-5 Check Your Understanding

1. The liquidity trap brought on by the Great Recession greatly diminished the Great Moderation consensus because it considered monetary policy to be the main policy tool and monetary policy was now largely ineffective. The continuing disagreements over fiscal policy were now brought to the forefront as fiscal policy was used by policy makers to support their deeply depressed economies. A new consensus is unlikely to emerge anytime soon because results of the various policies have been unclear or disappointing: fiscal stimulus has failed to bring down unemployment substantially (although some say the stimulus was too small); conventional monetary policy does not work; and the Fed's unconventional monetary policy seemed to have relatively little effect.

Chapter Thirty-Four

34-1 Check Your Understanding

1. **a.** The sale of the new airplane to China represents an export of a good to China and so enters the current account.

   b. The sale of Boeing stock to Chinese investors is a sale of a U.S. asset and so enters the financial account.

   c. Even though the plane already exists, when it is shipped to China it is an export of a good from the United States. So the sale of the plane enters the current account.

   d. Because the plane stays in the United States, the Chinese investor is buying a U.S. asset. So this is identical to the answer to part b: the sale of the jet enters the financial account.

2. The collapse of the U.S. housing bubble and the ensuing recession led to a dramatic fall in interest rates in the United States because of the deeply depressed economy. Consequently, capital inflows into the United States dried up.

34-2 Check Your Understanding

1. **a.** The increased purchase of Mexican oil will cause U.S. individuals (and firms) to increase their demand for the peso. To purchase pesos, individuals will increase their supply of U.S. dollars to the foreign exchange market, causing a rightward shift in the supply curve of U.S. dollars. This will cause the peso price of the dollar to fall (the amount of pesos per dollar will

fall). The peso has appreciated and the U.S. dollar has depreciated as a result.

b. This appreciation of the peso means it will take more U.S. dollars to obtain the same quantity of Mexican pesos. If we assume that the price level (measured in Mexican pesos) of other Mexican goods and services does not change, other Mexican goods and services become more expensive to U.S. households and firms. The dollar cost of other Mexican goods and services will rise as the peso appreciates. So Mexican exports of goods and services other than oil will fall.

c. U.S. goods and services become cheaper in terms of pesos, so Mexican imports of goods and services will rise.

2. a. The real exchange rate equals

$$\text{Pesos per U.S. dollar} \times \frac{\text{Aggregate price level in the U.S.}}{\text{Aggregate price level in Mexico}}$$

Today, the aggregate price levels in both countries are both equal to 100. The real exchange rate today is $10 \times (100/100) = 10$. The aggregate price level in five years in the U.S. will be $100 \times (120/100) = 120$, and in Mexico it will be $100 \times (1,200/800) = 150$. The real exchange rate in five years, assuming the nominal exchange rate does not change, will be $10 \times (120/150) = 8$.

b. Today, a basket of goods and services that costs $100 costs 800 pesos, so the purchasing power parity is 8 pesos per U.S. dollar. In five years, a basket that costs $120 will cost 1,200 pesos, so the purchasing power parity will be 10 pesos per U.S. dollar.

34-3 Check Your Understanding

1. The accompanying diagram shows the supply of and demand for the yuan, with the U.S. dollar price of the yuan on the vertical axis. In 2005, prior to the revaluation, the exchange rate was pegged at 8.28 yuan per U.S. dollar or, equivalently, 0.121 U.S. dollars per yuan ($0.121). At the target exchange rate of $0.121, the quantity of yuan demanded exceeded the quantity of yuan supplied, creating the shortage depicted in the diagram. Without any intervention by the Chinese government, the U.S. dollar price of the yuan would be bid up, causing an appreciation of the yuan. The Chinese government, however, intervened to prevent this appreciation.

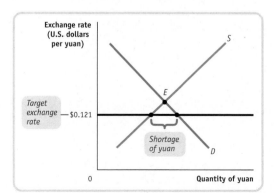

a. If the exchange rate were allowed to move freely, the U.S. dollar price of the exchange rate would move toward the equilibrium exchange rate (labeled XR^* in the accompanying diagram). This would occur

as a result of the shortage, when buyers of the yuan would bid up its U.S. dollar price. As the exchange rate increases, the quantity of yuan demanded would fall and the quantity of yuan supplied would increase. If the exchange rate were to increase to XR^*, the disequilibrium would be entirely eliminated.

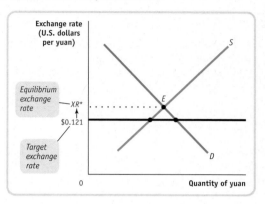

b. Placing restrictions on foreigners who want to invest in China would reduce the demand for the yuan, causing the demand curve to shift in the accompanying diagram from D_1 to something like D_2. This would cause a reduction in the shortage of the yuan. If demand fell to D_3, the disequilibrium would be completely eliminated.

c. Removing restrictions on Chinese who wish to invest abroad would cause an increase in the supply of the yuan and a rightward shift in the supply curve. This increase in supply would also cause a reduction in the size of the shortage. If, for example, supply increased from S_1 to S_2, the disequilibrium would be eliminated completely in the accompanying diagram.

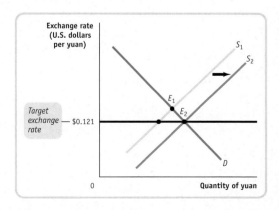

d. Imposing a tax on exports (Chinese goods sold to foreigners) would raise the price of these goods and decrease the amount of Chinese goods purchased. This would also decrease the demand for the yuan. The graphical analysis here is virtually identical to that found in the figure accompanying part b.

34-4 Check Your Understanding

1. The devaluations and revaluations most likely occurred in those periods when there was a sudden change in the franc–mark exchange rate: 1974, 1976, the early 1980s, 1986, and 1993–1994.

2. The high Canadian interest rates would likely have caused an increase in capital inflows to Canada. To obtain these assets (which yielded a relatively higher interest rate) in Canada, investors would first have had to obtain Canadian dollars. The increase in the demand for the Canadian dollar would have caused the Canadian dollar to appreciate. This appreciation of the Canadian currency would have raised the price of Canadian goods to foreigners (measured in terms of the foreign currency). This would have made it more difficult for Canadian firms to compete in other markets.

GLOSSARY

A

ability-to-pay principle the principle of tax fairness by which those with greater ability to pay a tax should pay more tax.

absolute advantage the advantage conferred on an individual or country in an activity if the individual or country can do it better than others. A country with an absolute advantage can produce more output per worker than other countries.

absolute value the value of a number without regard to a plus or minus sign.

accelerator principle the proposition that a higher rate of growth in real GDP results in a higher level of planned investment spending, and a lower growth rate in real GDP leads to lower planned investment spending.

accounting profit revenue minus explicit cost.

actual investment spending the sum of planned investment spending and unplanned inventory investment.

AD–AS model the basic model used to understand fluctuations in aggregate output and the aggregate price level. It uses the aggregate supply curve and the aggregate demand curve together to analyze the behavior of the economy in response to shocks or government policy.

administrative costs (of a tax) the resources used (which is a cost) by government to collect the tax, and by taxpayers to pay it, over and above the amount of the tax, as well as to evade it.

adverse selection the case in which an individual knows more about the way things are than other people do. Adverse selection problems can lead to market problems: private information leads buyers to expect hidden problems in items offered for sale, leading to low prices and the best items being kept off the market.

aggregate consumption function the relationship for the economy as a whole between aggregate current disposable income and aggregate consumer spending.

aggregate demand curve a graphical representation that shows the relationship between the aggregate price level and the quantity of aggregate output demanded by households, firms, the government, and the rest of the world. The aggregate demand curve has a negative slope due to the wealth effect of a change in the aggregate price level and the interest rate effect of a change in the aggregate price level.

aggregate output the total quantity of final goods and services the economy produces for a given time period, usually a year. Real GDP is the numerical measure of aggregate output typically used by economists.

aggregate price level a single number that represents the overall price level for final goods and services in the economy.

aggregate production function a hypothetical function that shows how productivity (real GDP per worker) depends on the quantities of physical capital per worker and human capital per worker as well as the state of technology.

aggregate spending the total flow of funds into markets for domestically produced final goods and services; the sum of consumer spending, investment spending, government purchases of goods and services, and exports minus imports.

aggregate supply curve a graphical representation that shows the relationship between the aggregate price level and the total quantity of aggregate output supplied.

antitrust policy legislative and regulatory efforts undertaken by the government to prevent oligopolistic industries from becoming or behaving like monopolies.

appreciation a rise in the value of one currency in terms of other currencies.

artificially scarce good a good that is excludable but nonrival in consumption.

asset bubble the price of an asset pushed to an unreasonably high level because of expectations of further price gains.

autarky a situation in which a country does not trade with other countries.

automatic stabilizers government spending and taxation rules that cause fiscal policy to be automatically expansionary when the economy contracts and automatically contractionary when the economy expands without requiring any deliberate actions by policy makers. Taxes that depend on disposable income are the most important example of automatic stabilizers.

autonomous change in aggregate spending an initial rise or fall in aggregate spending at a given level of real GDP.

average cost an alternative term for average total cost; the total cost divided by the quantity of output produced.

average fixed cost the fixed cost per unit of output.

average total cost total cost divided by quantity of output produced. Also referred to as average cost.

average variable cost the variable cost per unit of output.

B

backward-bending individual labor supply curve an individual labor supply curve that slopes upward at low to moderate wage rates and slopes downward at higher wage rates.

balance of payments accounts a summary of a country's transactions with other countries, including two main elements: the balance of payments on current account and the balance of payments on financial account.

balance of payments on current account (current account) transactions that don't create liabilities; a country's balance of payments on goods and services plus net international transfer payments and factor income.

balance of payments on financial account (financial account) international transactions that involve the sale or purchase of assets, and therefore create future liabilities.

balance of payments on goods and services the difference between the value of exports and the value of imports during a given period.

balance sheet effects the reduction in a firm's net worth from falling asset prices.

bank a financial intermediary that provides liquid assets in the form of bank deposits to lenders and uses those funds to finance the illiquid investments or investment spending needs of borrowers.

bank deposit a claim on a bank that obliges the bank to give the depositor his or her cash when demanded.

bank reserves currency held by banks in their vaults plus their deposits at the Federal Reserve.

bank run a phenomenon in which many of a bank's depositors try to withdraw their funds because of fears of a bank failure.

banking crisis an episode in which a large part of the depository banking sector or the shadow banking sector fails or threatens to fail.

bar graph a graph that uses bars of varying heights or lengths to show the comparative sizes of different observations of a variable.

barrier to entry something that prevents other firms from entering an industry. Crucial in protecting the profits of a monopolist. There are five types of barriers to entry: control over scarce resources or inputs, increasing returns to scale, technological superiority, network externalities, and government-created barriers.

barter the direct exchange of goods or services for other goods or services without the use of money.

benefits principle the principle of tax fairness by which those who benefit from public spending should bear the burden of the tax that pays for that spending.

black market a market in which goods or services are bought and sold illegally, either because it is illegal to sell them at all or because the prices charged are legally prohibited by a price ceiling.

bond a legal document based on borrowing in the form of an IOU that pays interest.

bounded rationality a basis for decision making that leads to a choice that is close to but not exactly the one that leads to the best possible economic outcome; the "good enough" method of decision making.

brand name a name owned by a particular firm that distinguishes its products from those of other firms.

break-even price the market price at which a firm earns zero profits.

budget balance the difference between tax revenue and government spending. A positive budget balance is referred to as a budget surplus; a negative budget balance is referred to as a budget deficit.

budget constraint the limitation that the cost of a consumer's consumption bundle cannot exceed the consumer's income.

budget deficit the difference between tax revenue and government spending when government spending exceeds tax revenue; dissaving by the government in the form of a budget deficit is a negative contribution to national savings.

budget line all the consumption bundles available to a consumer who spends all of his or her income.

budget surplus the difference between tax revenue and government spending when tax revenue exceeds government spending; saving by the government in the form of a budget surplus is a positive contribution to national savings.

business cycle the short-run alternation between economic downturns, known as recessions, and economic upturns, known as expansions.

business-cycle peak the point in time at which the economy shifts from expansion to recession.

business-cycle trough the point in time at which the economy shifts from recession to expansion.

C

capital the total value of assets owned by an individual or firm—physical assets plus financial assets.

capital at risk funds that an insurer places at risk when providing insurance.

cartel an agreement among several producers to obey output restrictions in order to increase their joint profits.

causal relationship the relationship between two variables in which the value taken by one variable directly influences or determines the value taken by the other variable.

central bank an institution that oversees and regulates the banking system and controls the monetary base.

chained dollars method of calculating real GDP that splits the difference between growth rates calculated using early base years and the growth rate calculated using a late base year.

checkable bank deposits bank accounts on which people can write checks.

circular-flow diagram a diagram that represents the transactions in an economy by two kinds of flows around a circle: flows of physical things such as goods or labor in one direction and flows of money to pay for these physical things in the opposite direction.

classical model of the price level a simplified financial model of the price level in which the real quantity of money, M/P, is always at its long-run equilibrium level. This model ignores the distinction between the short run and the long run but is useful for analyzing the case of high inflation.

Coase theorem the proposition that even in the presence of externalities an economy can always reach an efficient solution as long as transaction costs are sufficiently low.

collusion cooperation among producers to limit production and raise prices so as to raise one another's profits.

commercial bank a bank that accepts deposits and is covered by deposit insurance.

commodity output of different producers regarded by consumers as the same good; also referred to as a standardized product.

commodity-backed money a medium of exchange that has no intrinsic value whose ultimate value is guaranteed by a promise that it can be converted into valuable goods on demand.

commodity money a medium of exchange that is a good, normally gold or silver, that has intrinsic value in other uses.

common resource a resource that is nonexcludable and rival in consumption.

comparative advantage the advantage conferred on an individual or country in producing a good or service if the opportunity cost of producing the good or service is lower for that individual or country than for other producers.

compensating differentials wage differences across jobs that reflect the fact that some jobs are less pleasant or more dangerous than others.

competitive market a market in which there are many buyers and sellers of the same good or service, none of whom can influence the price at which the good or service is sold.

complements pairs of goods for which a rise in the price of one good leads to a decrease in the demand for the other good.

constant marginal cost each additional unit costs the same to produce as the previous one.

constant returns to scale long-run average total cost is constant as output increases.

consumer price index (CPI) a measure of prices; calculated by surveying market prices for a market basket intended to represent the consumption of a typical urban American family of four. The CPI is the most commonly used measure of prices in the United States.

consumer spending household spending on goods and services from domestic and foreign firms.

consumer surplus a term often used to refer both to individual consumer surplus and to total consumer surplus.

consumption bundle (of an individual) the collection of all the goods and services consumed by a given individual.

consumption function an equation showing how an individual household's consumer spending varies with the household's current disposable income.

consumption possibilities the set of all consumption bundles that can be consumed given a consumer's income and prevailing prices.

contractionary fiscal policy fiscal policy that reduces aggregate demand by decreasing government purchases, increasing taxes, or decreasing transfers.

contractionary monetary policy monetary policy that, through the raising of the interest rate, reduces aggregate demand and therefore output.

convergence hypothesis a principle of economic growth that holds that international differences in real GDP per capita tend to narrow over time because countries that start with lower real GDP per capita tend to have higher growth rates.

copyright the exclusive legal right of the creator of a literary or artistic work to profit from that work; like a patent, it is a temporary monopoly.

cost (of seller) the lowest price at which a seller is willing to sell a good.

cost-benefit analysis an estimate of the costs and benefits of providing a good. When governments use cost-benefit analysis, they estimate the social costs and social benefits of providing a public good.

credit crunch a reduction in the availability of credit in which potential borrowers can't get credit at all or must pay very high interest rates.

cross-price elasticity of demand a measure of the effect of the change in the price of one good on the quantity demanded of the other; it is equal to the percent change in the quantity demanded of one good divided by the percent change in the price of another good.

crowding out the negative effect of budget deficits on private investment, which occurs because government borrowing drives up interest rates.

currency in circulation actual cash held by the public.

current account (balance of payments on current account) transactions that don't create liabilities; a country's balance of payments on goods and services plus net international transfer payments and factor income.

curve a line on a graph, which may be curved or straight, that depicts a relationship between two variables.

cyclical unemployment the difference between the actual rate of unemployment and the natural rate of unemployment due to downturns in the business cycle.

cyclically adjusted budget balance an estimate of what the budget balance would be if real GDP were exactly equal to potential output.

D

deadweight loss the loss in total surplus that occurs whenever an action or a policy reduces the quantity transacted below the efficient market equilibrium quantity.

debt deflation the reduction in aggregate demand arising from the increase in the real burden of outstanding debt caused by deflation; occurs because borrowers, whose real debt rises as a result of deflation, are likely to cut spending sharply, and lenders, whose real assets are now more valuable, are less likely to increase spending.

debt overhang high debt but diminished assets, resulting from a vicious cycle of deleveraging.

debt–GDP ratio government debt as a percentage of GDP, frequently used as a measure of a government's ability to pay its debts.

decreasing marginal benefit each additional unit of an activity yields less benefit than the previous unit.

decreasing marginal cost each additional unit costs less to produce than the previous one.

decreasing returns to scale long-run average total cost increases as output increases (also known as diseconomies of scale).

deductible a sum specified in an insurance policy that the insured individual must pay before being compensated for a claim; deductibles reduce moral hazard.

default the failure of a bond issuer to make payments as specified by the bond contract.

deflation a fall in the overall level of prices.

demand curve a graphical representation of the demand schedule, showing the relationship between quantity demanded and price.

demand price the price of a given quantity at which consumers will demand that quantity.

demand schedule a list or table showing how much of a good or service consumers will want to buy at different prices.

demand shock an event that shifts the aggregate demand curve. A positive demand shock is associated with higher demand for aggregate output at any price level and shifts the curve to the right. A negative demand shock is associated with lower demand for aggregate output at any price level and shifts the curve to the left.

dependent variable the determined variable in a causal relationship.

deposit insurance a guarantee that a bank's depositors will be paid even if the bank can't come up with the funds, up to a maximum amount per account.

depreciation a fall in the value of one currency in terms of other currencies.

devaluation a reduction in the value of a currency that is set under a fixed exchange rate regime.

diminishing marginal rate of substitution the principle that the more of one good that is consumed in proportion to another, the less of the second good the consumer is willing to substitute for another unit of the first good.

diminishing returns to an input the effect observed when an increase in the quantity of an input, while holding the levels of all other inputs fixed, leads to a decline in the marginal product of that input.

diminishing returns to physical capital in an aggregate production function when the amount of human capital per worker and the state of technology are held fixed, each successive increase in the amount of physical capital per worker leads to a smaller increase in productivity.

discount rate the rate of interest the Federal Reserve charges on loans to banks that fall short of reserve requirements.

discount window a protection against bank runs in which the Federal Reserve stands ready to lend money to banks in trouble.

discouraged workers individuals who want to work but who have stated to government researchers that they aren't currently searching for a job because they see little prospect of finding one given the state of the job market.

discretionary fiscal policy fiscal policy that is the direct result of deliberate actions by policy makers rather than automatic adjustments or rules.

discretionary monetary policy policy actions, either changes in interest rates or changes in the money supply, undertaken by the central bank based on its assessment of the state of the economy.

disinflation the process of bringing down inflation that has become embedded in expectations.

disposable income income plus government transfers minus taxes; the total amount of household income available to spend on consumption and to save.

diversification investment in several different assets with unrelated, or independent, risks, so that the possible losses are independent events.

domestic demand curve a demand curve that shows how the quantity of a good demanded by domestic consumers depends on the price of that good.

domestic supply curve a supply curve that shows how the quantity of a good supplied by domestic producers depends on the price of that good.

dominant strategy in game theory, an action that is a player's best action regardless of the action taken by the other player.

duopolist one of the two firms in a duopoly.

duopoly an oligopoly consisting of only two firms.

E

economic growth the growing ability of the economy to produce goods and services.

economic profit revenue minus the opportunity cost of resources used; usually less than the accounting profit.

economic signal any piece of information that helps people make better economic decisions.

economics the social science that studies the production, distribution, and consumption of goods and services.

economy a system for coordinating society's productive activities.

efficiency wages wages that employers set above the equilibrium wage rate as an incentive for workers to deliver better performance.

efficiency-wage model a model in which some employers pay an above-equilibrium wage as an incentive for better performance.

efficient description of a market or economy that takes all opportunities to make some people better off without making other people worse off.

efficient allocation of risk an allocation of risk in which those most willing to bear risk are those who end up bearing it.

efficient markets hypothesis a principle of asset price determination that holds that asset prices embody all publicly available information. The hypothesis implies that stock prices should be unpredictable, or follow a random walk, since changes should occur only in response to new information about fundamentals.

elastic demand the case in which the price elasticity of demand is greater than 1.

emissions tax a tax that depends on the amount of pollution a firm produces.

employment the total number of people currently employed for pay in the economy, either full time or part time.

environmental standards rules established by a government to protect the environment by specifying actions by producers and consumers.

equilibrium an economic situation in which no individual would be better off doing something different.

equilibrium exchange rate the exchange rate at which the quantity of a currency demanded in the foreign exchange market is equal to the quantity supplied.

equilibrium interest rate a situation where the interest rate at which the quantity of loanable funds supplied equals the quantity of loanable funds demanded.

equilibrium price the price at which the market is in equilibrium, that is, the quantity of a good or service demanded equals the quantity of that good or service supplied; also referred to as the market-clearing price.

equilibrium quantity the quantity of a good or service bought and sold at the equilibrium (or market-clearing) price.

equilibrium value of the marginal product the additional value produced by the last unit of a factor employed in the factor market as a whole.

equity fairness; everyone gets his or her fair share. Since people can disagree about what is "fair," equity is not as well defined a concept as efficiency.

European Union (EU) a customs union among 28 European nations.

excess capacity the failure to produce enough to minimize average total cost; characteristic of monopolistically competitive firms.

excess reserves a bank's reserves over and above the reserves required by law or regulation.

exchange market intervention government purchases or sales of currency in the foreign exchange market.

exchange rate the price at which currencies trade, determined by the foreign exchange market.

exchange rate regime a rule governing policy toward the exchange rate.

excise tax a tax on sales of a good or service.

excludable referring to a good, describes the case in which the supplier can prevent those who do not pay from consuming the good.

expansion period of economic upturn in which output and employment are rising; most economic numbers are following their normal upward trend; also referred to as a recovery.

expansionary fiscal policy fiscal policy that increases aggregate demand by increasing government purchases, decreasing taxes, or increasing transfers.

expansionary monetary policy monetary policy that, through the lowering of the interest rate, increases aggregate demand and therefore output.

expected utility the expected value of an individual's total utility given uncertainty about future outcomes.

expected value in reference to a random variable, the weighted average of all possible values, where the weights on each possible value correspond to the probability of that value occurring.

explicit cost a cost that requires an outlay of money.

exporting industries industries that produce goods and services that are sold abroad.

exports goods and services sold to other countries.

external benefit an uncompensated benefit that an individual or firm confers on others; also known as positive externality.

external cost an uncompensated cost that an individual or firm imposes on others; also known as negative externality.

externalities external benefits and external costs.

F

factor distribution of income the division of total income among labor, land, and capital.

factor intensity the difference in the ratio of factors used to produce a good in various industries. For example, oil refining is capital-intensive compared to auto seat production because oil refiners use a higher ratio of capital to labor than do producers of auto seats.

factor markets markets in which firms buy the resources they need to produce goods and services.

factors of production the resources used to produce goods and services. Labor and capital are examples of factors.

fair insurance policy an insurance policy for which the premium is equal to the expected value of the claim.

federal funds market a financial market that allows banks that fall short of reserve requirements to borrow funds from banks with excess reserves.

federal funds rate the interest rate at which funds are borrowed and lent in the federal funds market.

fiat money a medium of exchange whose value derives entirely from its official status as a means of payment.

final goods and services goods and services sold to the final, or end, user.

financial account (balance of payments on financial account) international transactions that involve the sale or purchase of assets, and therefore create future liabilities.

financial asset a paper claim that entitles the buyer to future income from the seller. Loans, stocks, bonds, and bank deposits are types of financial assets.

financial contagion a vicious downward spiral among depository banks or shadow banks: each bank's failure worsens fears and increases the likelihood that another bank will fail.

financial intermediary an institution, such as a mutual fund, pension fund, life insurance company, or bank, that transforms the funds it gathers from many individuals into financial assets.

financial markets the banking, stock, and bond markets, which channel private savings and foreign lending into investment spending, government borrowing, and foreign borrowing.

financial panic a sudden and widespread disruption of the financial markets that occurs when people suddenly lose faith in the liquidity of financial institutions and markets.

financial risk uncertainty about future outcomes that involve financial losses or gains.

firm an organization that produces goods and services for sale.

fiscal austerity contractionary fiscal measures such as spending cuts and tax increases aimed at reducing budget deficits.

fiscal policy changes in government spending and taxes designed to affect overall spending.

fiscal year the time period used for much of government accounting, running from October 1 to September 30 in the United States. Fiscal years are labeled by the calendar year in which they end.

Fisher effect the principle by which an increase in expected future inflation drives up the nominal interest rate, leaving the expected real interest rate unchanged.

fixed cost a cost that does not depend on the quantity of output produced; the cost of a fixed input.

fixed exchange rate an exchange rate regime in which the government keeps the exchange rate against some other currency at or near a particular target.

fixed input an input whose quantity is fixed for a period of time and cannot be varied (for example, land).

floating exchange rate an exchange rate regime in which the government lets market forces determine the exchange rate.

forecast a simple prediction of the future.

foreign exchange controls licensing systems that limit the right of individuals to buy foreign currency.

foreign exchange market the market in which currencies can be exchanged for each other.

foreign exchange reserves stocks of foreign currency that governments can use to buy their own currency on the foreign exchange market.

free entry and exit describes an industry that potential producers can easily enter or current producers can leave.

free trade trade that is unregulated by government tariffs or other artificial barriers; the levels of exports and imports occur naturally, as a result of supply and demand.

free-rider problem problem that results when individuals who have no incentive to pay for their own consumption of a good take a "free ride" on anyone who does pay; a problem with goods that are nonexcludable.

frictional unemployment unemployment due to time workers spend in job search.

G

gains from trade gains achieved by dividing tasks and trading; in this way people can get more of what they want through trade than they could if they tried to be self-sufficient.

game theory the study of behavior in situations of interdependence. Used to explain the behavior of an oligopoly.

GDP deflator a price measure for a given year that is equal to 100 times the ratio of nominal GDP to real GDP in that year.

GDP per capita GDP divided by the size of the population; equivalent to the average GDP per person.

Giffen good the hypothetical inferior good for which the income effect outweighs the substitution effect and the demand curve slopes upward.

Gini coefficient a number that summarizes a country's level of income inequality based on how unequally income is distributed across quintiles.

globalization the phenomenon of growing economic linkages among countries.

government borrowing the total amount of funds borrowed by federal, state, and local governments in financial markets to buy goods and services.

government purchases of goods and services total purchases by federal, state, and local governments of goods and services.

government transfers payments by the government to individuals for which no good or service is provided in return.

Great Moderation the period from 1985 to 2007 when the U.S. economy experienced small fluctuations and low inflation.

Great Moderation consensus a belief in monetary policy as the main tool of stabilization combined with skepticism toward the use of fiscal policy and an acknowledgment of the policy constraints imposed by the natural rate of unemployment and the political business cycle.

gross domestic product (GDP) the total value of all final goods and services produced in the economy during a given period, usually a year.

growth accounting accounting that estimates the contribution of each of the major factors (physical and human capital, labor, and technology) in the aggregate production function.

H

Heckscher–Ohlin model a model of international trade in which a country has a comparative advantage in a good whose production is intensive in the factors that are abundantly available in that country.

horizontal axis the horizontal number line of a graph along which values of the x-variable are measured; also referred to as the x-axis.

horizontal intercept the point at which a curve hits the horizontal axis; it indicates the value of the x-variable when the value of the y-variable is zero.

household a person or a group of people that share their income.

human capital the improvement in labor created by education and knowledge that is embodied in the workforce.

I

illiquid describes an asset that cannot be quickly converted into cash with relatively little loss of value.

imperfect competition a market structure in which no firm is a monopolist, but producers nonetheless have market power they can use to affect market prices.

implicit cost a cost that does not require the outlay of money; it is measured by the value, in dollar terms, of forgone benefits.

implicit cost of capital the opportunity cost of the use of one's own capital—the income earned if the capital had been employed in its next best alternative use.

implicit liabilities spending promises made by governments that are effectively a debt despite the fact that they are not included in the usual debt statistics. In the United States, the largest implicit liabilities arise from Social Security and Medicare, which promise transfer payments to current and future retirees (Social Security) and to the elderly (Medicare).

import quota a legal limit on the quantity of a good that can be imported.

import-competing industries industries that produce goods and services that are also imported.

imports goods and services purchased from other countries.

incentive anything that offers rewards to people who change their behavior.

incidence (of a tax) a measure of who really pays a tax.

income distribution the way in which total income is divided among the owners of the various factors of production.

income effect the change in the quantity of a good consumed that results from the change in a consumer's purchasing power due to the change in the price of the good.

income elasticity of demand the percent change in the quantity of a good demanded when a consumer's income changes divided by the percent change in the consumer's income.

income tax a tax on the income of an individual or family.

income-elastic demand the case in which the income elasticity of demand for a good is greater than 1.

income–expenditure equilibrium a situation in which aggregate output, measured by real GDP, is equal to planned aggregate spending and firms have no incentive to change output.

income–expenditure equilibrium GDP the level of real GDP at which real GDP equals planned aggregate spending.

income-inelastic demand the case in which the income elasticity of demand for a good is positive but less than 1.

increasing marginal cost each additional unit costs more to produce than the previous one.

increasing returns to scale long-run average total cost declines as output increases (also referred to as economies of scale).

independent events events for which the occurrence of one does not affect the likelihood of occurrence of any of the others.

independent variable the determining variable in a causal relationship.

indifference curve a contour line showing all consumption bundles that yield the same amount of total utility for an individual.

indifference curve map a collection of indifference curves for a given individual that represents the individual's entire utility function; each curve corresponds to a different total utility level.

individual choice the decision by an individual of what to do, which necessarily involves a decision of what not to do.

individual consumer surplus the net gain to an individual buyer from the purchase of a good; equal to the difference between the buyer's willingness to pay and the price paid.

individual demand curve a graphical representation of the relationship between quantity demanded and price for an individual consumer.

individual labor supply curve a graphical representation showing how the quantity of labor supplied by an individual depends on that individual's wage rate.

individual producer surplus the net gain to an individual seller from selling a good; equal to the difference between the price received and the seller's cost.

individual supply curve a graphical representation of the relationship between quantity supplied and price for an individual producer.

industry supply curve a graphical representation that shows the relationship between the price of a good and the total output of the industry for that good.

inefficient describes a market or economy in which there are missed opportunities: some people could be made better off without making other people worse off.

inefficient allocation of sales among sellers a form of inefficiency in which sellers who would be willing to sell a good at the lowest price are not always those who actually manage to sell it; often the result of a price floor.

inefficient allocation to consumers a form of inefficiency in which people who want a good badly and are willing to pay a high price don't get it, and those who care relatively little about the good and are only willing to pay a low price do get it; often a result of a price ceiling.

inefficiently high quality a form of inefficiency in which sellers offer high-quality goods at a high price even though buyers would prefer a lower quality at a lower price; often the result of a price floor.

inefficiently low quality a form of inefficiency in which sellers offer low-quality goods at a low price even though buyers would prefer a higher quality at a higher price; often a result of a price ceiling.

inelastic demand the case in which the price elasticity of demand is less than 1.

inferior good a good for which a rise in income decreases the demand for the good.

inflation a rise in the overall level of prices.

inflation rate the annual percent change in a price index—typically the consumer price index. The inflation rate is positive when the aggregate price level is rising (inflation) and negative when the aggregate price level is falling (deflation).

inflation targeting an approach to monetary policy that requires that the central bank try to keep the inflation rate near a predetermined target rate.

inflation tax the reduction in the value of money held by the public caused by inflation.

inflationary gap the gap that exists when aggregate output is above potential output.

infrastructure physical capital, such as roads, power lines, ports, information networks, and other parts of an economy, that provides the underpinnings, or foundation, for economic activity.

in-kind benefit a benefit given in the form of goods or services.

input a good or service used to produce another good or service.

interaction (of choices) my choices affect your choices, and vice versa; a feature of most economic situations. The results of this interaction are often quite different from what the individuals intend.

interdependence a relationship among firms in which their decisions significantly affect one another's profits; characteristic of oligopolies.

interest rate the price, calculated as a percentage of the amount borrowed, that a lender charges a borrower for the use of their savings for one year.

interest rate effect of a change in the aggregate price level the effect on consumer spending and investment spending caused by a change in the purchasing power of consumers' money holdings when the aggregate price level changes. A rise (fall) in the aggregate price level decreases (increases) the purchasing power of consumers' money holdings. In response, consumers try to increase (decrease) their money holdings, which drives up (down) interest rates, thereby decreasing (increasing) consumption and investment.

intermediate goods and services goods and services—bought from one firm by another firm—that are inputs for production of final goods and services.

internalize the externality take into account external costs and external benefits.

international trade agreements treaties by which countries agree to lower trade protections against one another.

inventories stocks of goods and raw materials held to facilitate business operations.

inventory investment the value of the change in total inventories held in the economy during a given period. Unlike other types of investment spending, inventory investment can be negative, if inventories fall.

investment bank a bank that trades in financial assets and is not covered by deposit insurance.

investment spending spending on productive physical capital—such as machinery and construction of buildings—and on changes to inventories.

invisible hand a phrase used by Adam Smith to refer to the way in which an individual's pursuit of self-interest can lead, without the individual intending it, to good results for society as a whole.

irrational describes a decision maker who chooses an option that leaves him or her worse off than choosing another available option.

J

job search when workers spend time looking for employment.

jobless recovery a period in which real GDP growth rate is positive but the unemployment rate is still rising.

K

Keynesian cross a diagram that identifies income–expenditure equilibrium as the point where the planned aggregate spending line crosses the 45-degree line.

Keynesian economics a school of thought emerging out of the works of John Maynard Keynes; according to Keynesian economics, a depressed economy is the result of inadequate spending and government intervention can help a depressed economy through monetary policy and fiscal policy.

L

labor force the sum of employment and unemployment; that is, the number of people who are currently working plus the number of people who are currently looking for work.

labor force participation rate the percentage of the population age 16 or older that is in the labor force.

labor productivity output per worker; also referred to as simply productivity. Increases in labor productivity are the only source of long-run economic growth.

law of demand the principle that a higher price for a good or service, other things equal, leads people to demand a smaller quantity of that good or service.

leisure the time available for purposes other than earning money to buy marketed goods.

lender of last resort an institution, usually a country's central bank, that provides funds to financial institutions when they are unable to borrow from private credit markets.

leverage the degree to which a financial institution is financing its investments with borrowed funds.

liability a requirement to pay income in the future.

license the right, conferred by the government or an owner, to supply a good.

life insurance company a financial intermediary that sells policies guaranteeing a payment to a policyholder's beneficiaries when the policyholder dies.

linear relationship the relationship between two variables in which the slope is constant and therefore is depicted on a graph by a curve that is a straight line.

liquid describes an asset that can be quickly converted into cash with relatively little loss of value.

liquidity preference model of the interest rate a model of the market for money in which the interest rate is determined by the supply and demand for money.

liquidity trap the economy is in a liquidity trap when monetary policy is ineffective because nominal interest rates are up against the zero bound.

loan a lending agreement between an individual lender and an individual borrower. Loans are usually tailored to the individual borrower's needs and ability to pay but carry relatively high transaction costs.

loanable funds market a hypothetical market that brings together those who want to lend money (savers) and those who want to borrow (firms with investment spending projects).

loan-backed securities assets created by pooling individual loans and selling shares in that pool.

long run the time period in which all inputs can be varied.

long-run aggregate supply curve a graphical representation that shows the relationship between the aggregate price level and the quantity of aggregate output supplied that would exist if all prices, including nominal wages, were fully flexible. The long-run aggregate supply curve is vertical because the aggregate price level has no effect on aggregate output in the long run; in the long run, aggregate output is determined by the economy's potential output.

long-run average total cost curve a graphical representation showing the relationship between output and average total cost when fixed cost has been chosen to minimize average total cost for each level of output.

long-run economic growth the sustained rise in the quantity of goods and services the economy produces.

long-run industry supply curve a graphical representation that shows how quantity supplied responds to price once producers have had time to enter or exit the industry.

long-run macroeconomic equilibrium the point at which the short-run macroeconomic equilibrium is on the long-run aggregate supply curve; so short-run equilibrium aggregate output is equal to potential output.

long-run market equilibrium an economic balance in which, given sufficient time for producers to enter or exit an industry, the quantity supplied equals the quantity demanded.

long-run Phillips curve a graphical representation of the relationship between unemployment and inflation in the long run after expectations of inflation have had time to adjust to experience.

long-term interest rate the interest rate on financial assets that mature a number of years into the future.

loss aversion oversensitivity to loss, leading to unwillingness to recognize a loss and move on.

lump-sum tax a tax that is the same for everyone, regardless of any actions people take.

M

macroeconomic policy activism the use of monetary policy and fiscal policy to smooth out the business cycle.

macroeconomics the branch of economics that is concerned with the overall ups and downs in the economy.

marginal analysis the study of marginal decisions.

marginal benefit the additional benefit derived from producing one more unit of a good or service.

marginal benefit curve a graphical representation showing how the benefit from producing one more unit depends on the quantity that has already been produced.

marginal cost the additional cost incurred by producing one more unit of a good or service.

marginal cost curve a graphical representation showing how the cost of producing one more unit depends on the quantity that has already been produced.

marginal decision a decision made at the "margin" of an activity to do a bit more or a bit less of that activity.

marginal product the additional quantity of output produced by using one more unit of a given input.

marginal productivity theory of income distribution the proposition that every factor of production is paid its equilibrium value of the marginal product.

marginal propensity to consume (*MPC*) the increase in consumer spending when disposable income rises by $1. Because consumers normally spend part but not all of an additional dollar of disposable income, *MPC* is between 0 and 1.

marginal propensity to save (*MPS*) the fraction of an additional dollar of disposable income that is saved; *MPS* is equal to $1 - MPC$.

marginal rate of substitution (*MRS*) the ratio of the marginal utility of one good to the marginal utility of another.

marginal revenue the change in total revenue generated by an additional unit of output.

marginal revenue curve a graphical representation showing how marginal revenue varies as output varies.

marginal social benefit of pollution the additional gain to society as a whole from an additional unit of pollution.

marginal social cost of pollution the additional cost imposed on society as a whole by an additional unit of pollution.

marginal tax rate the percentage of an increase in income that is taxed away.

marginal utility the change in total utility generated by consuming one additional unit of a good or service.

marginal utility curve a graphical representation showing how marginal utility depends on the quantity of the good or service consumed.

marginal utility per dollar the additional utility gained from spending one more dollar on a good or service.

marginally attached workers nonworking individuals who say they would like a job and have looked for work in the recent past but are not currently looking for work.

market basket a hypothetical consumption bundle of consumer purchases of goods and services, used to measure changes in overall price level.

market economy an economy in which decisions about production and consumption are made by individual producers and consumers.

market failure the failure of a market to be efficient.

market power the ability of a producer to raise prices.

market share the fraction of the total industry output accounted for by a given producer's output.

market-clearing price the price at which the market is in equilibrium, that is, the quantity of a good or service demanded equals the quantity of that good or service supplied; also referred to as the equilibrium price.

markets for goods and services markets in which firms sell goods and services that they produce to households.

maturity transformation the conversion of short-term liabilities into long-term assets.

maximum the highest point on a nonlinear curve, where the slope changes from positive to negative.

mean household income the average income across all households.

means-tested describes a program in which benefits are available only to individuals or families whose incomes fall below a certain level.

median household income the income of the household lying at the exact middle of the income distribution.

medium of exchange an asset that individuals acquire for the purpose of trading for goods and services rather than for their own consumption.

mental accounting the habit of mentally assigning dollars to different accounts so that some dollars are worth more than others.

menu cost the real cost of changing a listed price.

merchandise trade balance (trade balance) the difference between a country's exports and imports of goods alone—not including services.

microeconomics the branch of economics that studies how people make decisions and how those decisions interact.

midpoint method a technique for calculating the percent change in which changes in a variable are compared with the average, or midpoint, of the starting and final values.

minimum the lowest point on a nonlinear curve, where the slope changes from negative to positive.

minimum wage a legal floor on the wage rate. The wage rate is the market price of labor.

minimum-cost output the quantity of output at which the average total cost is lowest—the bottom of the U-shaped average total cost curve.

model a simplified representation of a real situation that is used to better understand real-life situations.

monetarism a theory of business cycles, associated primarily with Milton Friedman, that asserts that GDP will grow steadily if the money supply grows steadily.

monetary aggregate an overall measure of the money supply. The most common monetary aggregates in the United States are M1, which includes currency in circulation, traveler's checks, and checkable bank deposits, and M2, which includes M1 as well as near-moneys.

monetary base the sum of currency in circulation and bank reserves.

monetary neutrality the concept that changes in the money supply have no real effects on the economy in the long run and only result in a proportional change in the price level.

monetary policy changes in the quantity of money in circulation designed to alter interest rates and affect the level of overall spending.

monetary policy rule a formula that determines the central bank's actions.

money any asset that can easily be used to purchase goods and services.

money demand curve a graphical representation of the relationship between the interest rate and the quantity of money demanded. The money demand curve slopes downward because, other things equal, a higher interest rate increases the opportunity cost of holding money.

money multiplier the ratio of the money supply to the monetary base.

money supply the total value of financial assets in the economy that are considered money.

money supply curve a graphical representation of the relationship between the quantity of money supplied by the Federal Reserve and the interest rate.

monopolist a firm that is the only producer of a good that has no close substitutes.

monopolistic competition a market structure in which there are many competing producers in an industry, each producer sells a differentiated product, and there is free entry and exit into and from the industry in the long run.

monopoly an industry controlled by a monopolist.

monopsonist a firm that is the sole buyer in a market.

monopsony a market in which there is only one buyer but many sellers.

moral hazard the situation that can exist when an individual knows more about his or her own actions than other people do. This leads to a distortion of incentives to take care or to expend effort when someone else bears the costs of the lack of care or effort.

movement along the demand curve a change in the quantity demanded of a good that results from a change in the price of that good.

movement along the supply curve a change in the quantity supplied of a good that results from a change in the price of that good.

multiplier the ratio of total change in real GDP caused by an autonomous change in aggregate spending to the size of that autonomous change.

mutual fund a financial intermediary that creates a stock portfolio by buying and holding shares in companies and then selling shares of this portfolio to individual investors.

N

Nash equilibrium in game theory, the equilibrium that results when all players choose the action that maximizes their payoffs given the actions of other players, ignoring the effect of that action on the payoffs of other players; also known as noncooperative equilibrium.

national income and product accounts (national accounts) method of calculating and keeping track of consumer spending, sales of producers, business investment spending, government purchases, and a variety of other flows of money between different sectors of the economy; also referred to as national accounts.

national savings the sum of private savings and the government's budget balance; the total amount of savings generated within the economy.

natural monopoly a monopoly that exists when increasing returns to scale provide a large cost advantage to having all output produced by a single firm.

natural rate hypothesis the hypothesis that because inflation is eventually embedded into expectations, to avoid accelerating inflation over time the unemployment rate must be high enough that the actual inflation rate equals the expected inflation rate.

natural rate of unemployment the normal unemployment rate around which the actual unemployment rate fluctuates; the unemployment rate that arises from the effects of frictional and structural unemployment.

near-moneys financial assets that can't be directly used as a medium of exchange but can be readily converted into cash or checkable bank deposits.

negative externalities external costs.

negative income tax a government program that supplements the income of low-income working families.

negative relationship a relationship between two variables in which an increase in the value of one variable is associated with a decrease in the value of the other variable. It is illustrated by a curve that slopes downward from left to right.

net capital inflow the total inflow of funds into a country minus the total outflow of funds out of a country.

net exports the difference between the value of exports and the value of imports. A positive value for net exports indicates that a country is a net exporter of goods and services; a negative value indicates that a country is a net importer of goods and services.

network externality the increase in the value of a good or service to an individual is greater when a large number of others own or use the same good or service.

new classical macroeconomics an approach to the business cycle that returns to the classical view that shifts in the aggregate demand curve affect only the aggregate price level, not aggregate output.

new Keynesian economics a theory that argues that market imperfections can lead to price stickiness for the economy as a whole.

nominal GDP the value of all final goods and services produced in the economy during a given year, calculated using the prices current in the year in which the output is produced.

nominal interest rate the interest rate in dollar terms.

nominal wage the dollar amount of any given wage paid.

nonaccelerating inflation rate of unemployment (NAIRU) the unemployment rate at which, other things equal, inflation does not change over time.

noncooperative behavior actions by firms that ignore the effects of those actions on the profits of other firms.

noncooperative equilibrium in game theory, the equilibrium that results when all players choose the action that maximizes their payoffs given the actions of other players, ignoring the effect of that action on the payoffs of other players; also known as Nash equilibrium.

nonexcludable referring to a good, describes the case in which the supplier cannot prevent those who do not pay from consuming the good.

nonlinear curve a curve in which the slope is not the same between every pair of points.

nonlinear relationship the relationship between two variables in which the slope is not constant and therefore is depicted on a graph by a curve that is not a straight line.

nonprice competition competition in areas other than price to increase sales, such as new product features and advertising; especially engaged in by firms that have a tacit understanding not to compete on price.

nonrival in consumption referring to a good, describes the case in which the same unit can be consumed by more than one person at the same time.

normal good a good for which a rise in income increases the demand for that good—the "normal" case.

normative economics the branch of economic analysis that makes prescriptions about the way the economy should work.

North American Free Trade Agreement (NAFTA) a trade agreement among the United States, Canada, and Mexico.

O

offshore outsourcing the practice in which businesses hire people in another country to perform various tasks.

Okun's law the negative relationship between the output gap and the unemployment rate, whereby each additional percentage point of output gap reduces the unemployment rate by about ½ of a percentage point.

oligopolist a firm in an industry with only a small number of producers.

oligopoly an industry with only a small number of producers.

omitted variable an unobserved variable that, through its influence on other variables, creates the erroneous appearance of a direct causal relationship among those variables.

open economy an economy that trades goods and services with other countries.

open-market operation a purchase or sale of U.S. Treasury bills by the Federal Reserve, normally through a transaction with a commercial bank.

opportunity cost the real cost of an item: what you must give up in order to get it.

optimal consumption bundle the consumption bundle that maximizes a consumer's total utility given that consumer's budget constraint.

optimal output rule the principle that profit is maximized by producing the quantity of output at which the marginal revenue of the last unit produced is equal to its marginal cost.

optimal quantity the quantity that generates the highest possible total net gain.

optimal time allocation rule the principle that an individual should allocate time so that the marginal utility gained from the income earned from an additional hour worked is equal to the marginal utility of an additional hour of leisure.

ordinary goods in a consumer's utility function, those for which additional units of one good are required to compensate for fewer units of another, and vice versa; and for which the consumer experiences a diminishing marginal rate of substitution when substituting one good in place of another.

origin the point where the axes of a two-variable graph meet.

other things equal assumption in the development of a model, the assumption that all relevant factors except the one under study remain unchanged.

output gap the percentage difference between actual aggregate output and potential output.

overuse the depletion of a common resource that occurs when individuals ignore the fact that their use depletes the amount of the resource remaining for others.

P

patent a temporary monopoly given by the government to an inventor for the use or sale of an invention.

payoff in game theory, the reward received by a player (for example, the profit earned by an oligopolist).

payoff matrix in game theory, a diagram that shows how the payoffs to each of the participants in a two-player game depend on the actions of both; a tool in analyzing interdependence.

payroll tax a tax on the earnings an employer pays to an employee.

pension fund a type of mutual fund that holds assets in order to provide retirement income to its members.

perfect complements goods a consumer wants to consume in the same ratio, regardless of their relative price.

perfect price discrimination the price discrimination that results when a monopolist charges each consumer the maximum that the consumer is willing to pay.

perfect substitutes goods for which the indifference curves are straight lines; the marginal rate of substitution of one good in place of another good is constant, regardless of how much of each an individual consumes.

perfectly competitive industry an industry in which all producers are price-takers.

perfectly competitive market a market in which all participants are price-takers.

perfectly elastic demand the case in which any price increase will cause the quantity demanded to drop to zero; the demand curve is a horizontal line.

perfectly elastic supply the case in which even a tiny increase or reduction in the price will lead to very large changes in the quantity supplied, so that the price elasticity of supply is infinite; the perfectly elastic supply curve is a horizontal line.

perfectly inelastic demand the case in which the quantity demanded does not respond at all to changes in the price; the demand curve is a vertical line.

perfectly inelastic supply the case in which the price elasticity of supply is zero, so that changes in the price of the good have no effect on the quantity supplied; the perfectly inelastic supply curve is a vertical line.

physical asset a claim on a tangible object that can be used to generate future income.

physical capital manufactured resources, such as buildings and machines.

pie chart a circular graph that shows how some total is divided among its components, usually expressed in percentages.

Pigouvian subsidy a payment designed to encourage activities that yield external benefits.

Pigouvian taxes taxes designed to reduce external costs.

planned aggregate spending the total amount of planned spending in the economy; includes consumer spending and planned investment spending.

planned investment spending the investment spending that firms intend to undertake during a given period. Planned investment spending may differ from actual investment spending due to unplanned inventory investment.

political business cycle a business cycle that results from the use of macro-economic policy to serve political ends.

pooling a strong form of diversification in which an investor takes a small share of the risk in many independent events, so the payoff has very little total overall risk.

positive economics the branch of economic analysis that describes the way the economy actually works.

positive externalities external benefits.

positive feedback put simply, success breeds success, failure breeds failure; the effect is seen with goods that are subject to network externalities.

positive relationship a relationship between two variables in which an increase in the value of one variable is associated with an increase in the value of the other variable. It is illustrated by a curve that slopes upward from left to right.

positively correlated describes a relationship between events such that each event is more likely to occur if the other event also occurs.

potential output the level of real GDP the economy would produce if all prices, including nominal wages, were fully flexible.

poverty program a government program designed to aid the poor.

poverty rate the percentage of the population with incomes below the poverty threshold.

poverty threshold the annual income below which a family is officially considered poor.

premium a payment to an insurance company in return for the promise to pay a claim in certain states of the world.

present value (of X) the amount of money needed today in order to receive X at a future date given the interest rate.

price ceiling a maximum price sellers are allowed to charge for a good or service; a form of price control.

price controls legal restrictions on how high or low a market price may go.

price discrimination charging different prices to different consumers for the same good.

price elasticity of demand the ratio of the percent change in the quantity demanded to the percent change in the price as we move along the demand curve.

price elasticity of supply a measure of the responsiveness of the quantity of a good supplied to the price of that good; the ratio of the percent change in the quantity supplied to the percent change in the price as we move along the supply curve.

price floor a minimum price buyers are required to pay for a good or service; a form of price control.

price index a measure of the cost of purchasing a given market basket in a given year, where that cost is normalized so that it is equal to 100 in the selected base year; a measure of overall price level.

price leadership a pattern of behavior in which one firm sets its price and other firms in the industry follow.

price regulation a limitation on the price a monopolist is allowed to charge.

price stability a situation in which the overall cost of living is changing slowly or not at all.

price war a collapse of prices when tacit collusion breaks down.

price-taking consumer a consumer whose actions have no effect on the market price of the good or service he or she buys.

price-taking firm's optimal output rule the principle that the profit of a price-taking firm is maximized by producing the quantity of output at which the market price is equal to the marginal cost of the last unit produced.

price-taking producer a producer whose actions have no effect on the market price of the good or service it sells.

principle of diminishing marginal utility the proposition that each successive unit of a good or service consumed adds less to total utility than did the previous unit.

principle of "either–or" decision making the principle that, in a decision between two activities, the one with the positive economic profit should be chosen.

prisoner's dilemma a game based on two premises: (1) each player has an incentive to choose an action that benefits itself at the other player's expense; and (2) both players are then worse off than if they had acted cooperatively.

private good a good that is both excludable and rival in consumption.

private health insurance a program in which each member of a large pool of individuals pays a fixed amount to a private company that agrees to pay most of the medical expenses of the pool's members.

private information information that some people have, but others do not.

private savings disposable income minus consumer spending; disposable income that is not spent on consumption but rather goes into financial markets.

producer price index (PPI) a measure of the cost of a typical basket of goods and services purchased by producers. Because these commodity prices respond quickly to changes in demand, the PPI is often regarded as a leading indicator of changes in the inflation rate.

producer surplus a term often used to refer both to individual producer surplus and to total producer surplus.

product differentiation the attempt by firms to convince buyers that their products are different from those of other firms in the industry. If firms can so convince buyers, they can charge a higher price.

production function the relationship between the quantity of inputs a firm uses and the quantity of output it produces.

production possibility frontier a model that illustrates the trade-offs facing an economy that produces only two goods. It shows the maximum quantity of one good that can be produced for any given quantity produced of the other.

productivity output per worker; a shortened form of the term labor productivity.

profit-maximizing principle of marginal analysis the proposition that in a profit-maximizing "how much" decision the optimal quantity is the largest quantity at which marginal benefit is greater than or equal to marginal cost.

profits tax a tax on the profits of a firm.

progressive tax a tax that takes a larger share of the income of high-income taxpayers than of low-income taxpayers.

property rights the rights of owners of valuable items, whether resources or goods, to dispose of those items as they choose.

property tax a tax on the value of property, such as the value of a home.

proportional tax a tax that is the same percentage of the tax base regardless of the taxpayer's income or wealth.

protection an alternative term for trade protection; policies that limit imports.

public debt government debt held by individuals and institutions outside the government.

public good a good that is both nonexcludable and nonrival in consumption.

public ownership the case in which goods are supplied by the government or by a firm owned by the government to protect the interests of the consumer in response to natural monopoly.

purchasing power parity (between two countries' currencies) the nominal exchange rate at which a given basket of goods and services would cost the same amount in each country.

Q

quantity control an upper limit, set by the government, on the quantity of some good that can be bought or sold; also referred to as a quota.

quantity demanded the actual amount of a good or service consumers are willing to buy at some specific price.

quantity supplied the actual amount of a good or service producers are willing to sell at some specific price.

quota an upper limit, set by the government, on the quantity of some good that can be bought or sold; also referred to as a quantity control.

quota limit the total amount of a good under a quota or quantity control that can be legally transacted.

quota rent the difference between the demand price and the supply price at the quota limit; this difference, the earnings that accrue to the license-holder, is equal to the market price of the license when the license is traded.

R

random variable a variable with an uncertain future value.

random walk the movement over time of an unpredictable variable.

rational describes a decision maker who chooses the available option that leads to the outcome he or she most prefers.

rational expectations a theory of expectation formation that holds that individuals and firms make decisions optimally, using all available information.

rational expectations model a model of the economy in which expected changes in monetary policy have no effect on unemployment and output and only affect the price level.

real business cycle theory a theory of business cycles that asserts that fluctuations in the growth rate of total factor productivity cause the business cycle.

real exchange rate the exchange rate adjusted for international differences in aggregate price levels.

real GDP the total value of all final goods and services produced in the economy during a given year, calculated using the prices of a selected base year.

real income income divided by the price level.

real interest rate the nominal interest rate minus the inflation rate.

real wage the wage rate divided by the price level.

recession a downturn in the economy when output and employment are falling; also referred to as a contraction.

recessionary gap the gap that exists when aggregate output is below potential output.

regressive tax a tax that takes a smaller share of the income of high-income taxpayers than of low-income taxpayers.

relative price the ratio of the price of one good to the price of another.

relative price rule at the optimal consumption bundle, the marginal rate of substitution of one good in place of another is equal to the relative price.

rental rate the cost, implicit or explicit, of using a unit of land or capital for a given period of time.

reputation a long-term standing in the public regard that serves to reassure others that private information is not being concealed; a valuable asset in the face of adverse selection.

research and development (R&D) spending to create new technologies and prepare them for practical use.

reserve ratio the fraction of bank deposits that a bank holds as reserves. In the United States, the minimum required reserve ratio is set by the Federal Reserve.

reserve requirements rules set by the Federal Reserve that set the minimum reserve ratio for banks. For checkable bank deposits in the United States, the minimum reserve ratio is set at 10%.

resource anything, such as land, labor, and capital, that can be used to produce something else; includes natural resources (from the physical environment) and human resources (labor, skill, intelligence).

revaluation an increase in the value of a currency that is set under a fixed exchange rate regime.

reverse causality the error committed when the true direction of causality between two variables is reversed, and the independent variable and the dependent variable are incorrectly identified.

Ricardian model of international trade a model that analyzes international trade under the assumption that opportunity costs are constant.

risk uncertainty about future outcomes.

risk-averse describes individuals who choose to reduce risk when that reduction leaves the expected value of their income or wealth unchanged.

risk-aversion the willingness to sacrifice some economic payoff in order to avoid a potential loss.

risk-neutral describes individuals who are completely insensitive to risk.

rival in consumption referring to a good, describes the case in which one unit cannot be consumed by more than one person at the same time.

Rule of 70 a mathematical formula that states that the time it takes real GDP per capita, or any other variable that grows gradually over time, to double is approximately 70 divided by that variable's annual growth rate.

S

sales tax a tax on the value of goods sold.

savings and loans (thrifts) deposit-taking banks, usually specialized in issuing home loans.

savings–investment spending identity an accounting fact that states that savings and investment spending are always equal for the economy as a whole.

scarce in short supply; a resource is scarce when there is not enough of the resource available to satisfy all the various ways a society wants to use it.

scatter diagram a graph that shows points that correspond to actual observations of the x- and y-variables; a curve is usually fitted to the scatter of points to indicate the trend in the data.

screening using observable information about people to make inferences about their private information; a way to reduce adverse selection.

securitization the pooling of loans and mortgages made by a financial institution and the sale of shares in such a pool to other investors.

self-correcting describes an economy in which shocks to aggregate demand affect aggregate output in the short run but not in the long run.

self-regulating describes an economy in which problems such as unemployment are resolved without government intervention, through the working of the invisible hand, and in which government attempts to improve the economy's performance would be ineffective at best, and would probably make things worse.

shadow bank a nondepository financial institution that engages in maturity transformation.

share a partial ownership of a company.

shift of the demand curve a change in the quantity demanded at any given price, represented graphically by the change of the original demand curve to a new position, denoted by a new demand curve.

shift of the supply curve a change in the quantity supplied of a good or service at any given price, represented graphically by the change of the original supply curve to a new position, denoted by a new supply curve.

shoe-leather costs (of inflation) the increased costs of transactions caused by inflation.

short run the time period in which at least one input is fixed.

shortage the insufficiency of a good or service that occurs when the quantity demanded exceeds the quantity supplied; shortages occur when the price is below the equilibrium price.

short-run aggregate supply curve a graphical representation that shows the positive relationship between the aggregate price level and the quantity of aggregate output supplied that exists in the short run, the time period when many production costs, particularly nominal wages, can be taken as fixed. The short-run aggregate supply curve has a positive slope because a rise in the aggregate price level leads to a rise in profits, and therefore output, when production costs are fixed.

short-run equilibrium aggregate output the quantity of aggregate output produced in short-run macroeconomic equilibrium.

short-run equilibrium aggregate price level the aggregate price level in short-run macroeconomic equilibrium.

short-run individual supply curve a graphical representation that shows how an individual producer's profit-maximizing output quantity depends on the market price, taking fixed cost as given.

short-run industry supply curve a graphical representation that shows how the quantity supplied by an industry depends on the market price given a fixed number of producers.

short-run macroeconomic equilibrium the point at which the quantity of aggregate output supplied is equal to the quantity demanded.

short-run market equilibrium an economic balance that results when the quantity supplied equals the quantity demanded, taking the number of producers as given.

short-run Phillips curve a graphical representation of the negative short-run relationship between the unemployment rate and the inflation rate.

short-term interest rate the interest rate on financial assets that mature within less than a year.

shut-down price the price at which a firm ceases production in the short run because the market price has fallen below the minimum average variable cost.

signaling taking some action to establish credibility despite possessing private information; a way to reduce adverse selection.

single-payer system a health care system in which the government is the principal payer of medical bills funded through taxes.

single-price monopolist a monopolist that offers its product to all consumers at the same price.

slope a measure of how steep a line or curve is. The slope of a line is measured by "rise over run"—the change in the y-variable between two points on the line divided by the change in the x-variable between those same two points.

social insurance government programs—like Social Security, Medicare, unemployment insurance, and food stamps—intended to protect families against economic hardship.

social insurance program a government program designed to provide protection against unpredictable financial distress.

socially optimal quantity of pollution the quantity of pollution that society would choose if all the costs and benefits of pollution were fully accounted for.

specialization the situation in which each person specializes in the task that he or she is good at performing.

stabilization policy the use of government policy to reduce the severity of recessions and to rein in excessively strong expansions. There are two main tools of stabilization policy: monetary policy and fiscal policy.

stagflation the combination of inflation and falling aggregate output.

standardized product output of different producers regarded by consumers as the same good; also referred to as a commodity.

state of the world a possible future event.

status quo bias the tendency to avoid making a decision.

sticky wages nominal wages that are slow to fall even in the face of high unemployment and slow to rise even in the face of labor shortages.

stock a share in the ownership of a company held by a shareholder.

store of value an asset that is a means of holding purchasing power over time.

strategic behavior actions taken by a firm that attempt to influence the future behavior of other firms.

structural unemployment unemployment that results when there are more people seeking jobs in a particular labor market than there are jobs available at the current wage rate, even when the economy is at the peak of the business cycle.

subprime lending lending to home-buyers who don't meet the usual criteria for borrowing.

substitutes pairs of goods for which a rise in the price of one of the goods leads to an increase in the demand for the other good.

substitution effect the change in the quantity of a good consumed as the consumer substitutes other goods that are now relatively cheaper in place of the good that has become relatively more expensive.

sunk cost a cost that has already been incurred and is not recoverable.

supply and demand model a model of how a competitive market behaves.

supply curve a graphical representation of the supply schedule, showing the relationship between quantity supplied and price.

supply price the price of a given quantity at which producers will supply that quantity.

supply schedule a list or table showing how much of a good or service producers will supply at different prices.

supply shock an event that shifts the short-run aggregate supply curve. A negative supply shock raises production costs and reduces the quantity supplied at any aggregate price level, shifting the curve leftward. A positive supply shock decreases production costs and increases the quantity supplied at any aggregate price level, shifting the curve rightward.

surplus the excess of a good or service that occurs when the quantity supplied exceeds the quantity demanded; surpluses occur when the price is above the equilibrium price.

sustainable long-run economic growth long-run growth that can continue in the face of the limited supply of natural resources and the impact of growth on the environment.

T

T-account a simple tool that summarizes a business's financial position by showing, in a single table, the business's assets and liabilities, with assets on the left and liabilities on the right.

tacit collusion cooperation among producers, without a formal agreement, to limit production and raise prices so as to raise one another's profits.

tangency condition on a graph of a consumer's budget line and available indifference curves of available consumption bundles, the point at which an indifference curve and the budget line just touch. When the indifference curves have the typical convex shape, this point determines the optimal consumption bundle.

tangent line a straight line that just touches a nonlinear curve at a particular point; the slope of the tangent line is equal to the slope of the nonlinear curve at that point.

target federal funds rate the Federal Reserve's desired level for the federal funds rate. The Federal Reserve adjusts the money supply through the purchase and sale of Treasury bills until the actual rate equals the desired rate.

tariff a tax levied on imports.

tax base the measure or value, such as income or property value, that determines how much tax an individual pays.

tax rate the amount of tax people are required to pay per unit of whatever is being taxed.

tax structure specifies how a tax depends on the tax base; usually expressed in percentage terms.

Taylor rule for monetary policy a rule that sets the federal funds rate according to the level of the inflation rate and either the output gap or the unemployment rate.

technological progress an advance in the technical means of production of goods and services.

technology the technical means for producing goods and services.

technology spillover an external benefit that results when knowledge spreads among individuals and firms.

time allocation the decision about how many hours to spend on different activities, which leads to a decision about how much labor to supply.

time allocation budget line an individual's possible trade-off between consumption of leisure and the income that allows consumption of marketed goods.

time-series graph a two-variable graph that has dates on the horizontal axis and values of a variable that occurred on those dates on the vertical axis.

tit for tat in game theory, a strategy that involves playing cooperatively at first, then doing whatever the other player did in the previous period.

total consumer surplus the sum of the individual consumer surpluses of all the buyers of a good in a market.

total cost the sum of the fixed cost and the variable cost of producing a given quantity of output.

total cost curve a graphical representation of the total cost, showing how total cost depends on the quantity of output.

total factor productivity the amount of output that can be produced with a given amount of factor inputs.

total producer surplus the sum of the individual producer surpluses of all the sellers of a good in a market.

total product curve a graphical representation of the production function, showing how the quantity of output depends on the quantity of the variable input for a given quantity of the fixed input.

total revenue the total value of sales of a good or service (the price of the good or service multiplied by the quantity sold).

total surplus the total net gain to consumers and producers from trading in a market; the sum of the consumer surplus and the producer surplus.

tradable emissions permits licenses to emit limited quantities of pollutants that can be bought and sold by polluters.

trade the practice, in a market economy, in which individuals provide goods and services to others and receive goods and services in return.

trade balance (merchandise trade balance) the difference between a country's exports and imports of goods alone—not including services.

trade deficit the deficit that results when the value of the goods and services bought from foreigners is more than the value of the goods and services sold to consumers abroad.

trade protection policies that limit imports; also known simply as protection.

trade surplus the surplus that results when the value of goods and services bought from foreigners is less than the value of the goods and services sold to them.

trade-off a comparison of costs and benefits of doing something.

trade-off between equity and efficiency the dynamic whereby a well-designed tax system can be made more efficient only by making it less fair, and vice versa.

transaction costs the expenses of negotiating and executing a deal.

truncated cut; in a truncated axis, some of the range of values are omitted, usually to save space.

U

underemployment the number of people who work part time because they cannot find full-time jobs.

unemployment the total number of people who are actively looking for work but aren't currently employed.

unemployment rate the percentage of the total number of people in the labor force who are unemployed, calculated as unemployment/(unemployment + employment).

unions organizations of workers that try to raise wages and improve working conditions for their members by bargaining collectively.

unit of account a measure used to set prices and make economic calculations.

unit-elastic demand the case in which the price elasticity of demand is exactly 1.

unit-of-account costs (of inflation) costs arising from the way inflation makes money a less reliable unit of measurement.

unplanned inventory investment unplanned changes in inventories, which occur when actual sales are more or less than businesses expected.

U-shaped average total cost curve a distinctive graphical representation of the relationship between output and average total cost; the average total cost curve at first falls when output is low and then rises as output increases.

util a unit of utility.

utility (of a consumer) a measure of the satisfaction derived from consumption of goods and services.

utility function (of an individual) the total utility generated by an individual's consumption bundle.

utility-maximizing principle of marginal analysis the principle that the marginal utility per dollar spent must be the same for all goods and services in the optimal consumption bundle.

V

value added (of a producer) the value of a producer's sales minus the value of its purchases of intermediate goods and services.

value of the marginal product the value of the additional output generated by employing one more unit of a given factor, such as labor.

value of the marginal product curve a graphical representation showing how the value of the marginal product of a factor depends on the quantity of the factor employed.

variable a quantity that can take on more than one value.

variable cost a cost that depends on the quantity of output produced; the cost of a variable input.

variable input an input whose quantity the firm can vary at any time (for example, labor).

velocity of money the ratio of nominal GDP to the money supply.

vertical axis the vertical number line of a graph along which values of the y-variable are measured; also referred to as the y-axis.

vertical intercept the point at which a curve hits the vertical axis; it shows the value of the y-variable when the value of the x-variable is zero.

vicious cycle of deleveraging describes the sequence of events that takes place when a firm's asset sales to cover losses produce negative balance sheet effects on other firms and force creditors to call in their loans, forcing sales of more assets and causing further declines in asset prices.

W

wasted resources a form of inefficiency in which people expend money, effort, and time to cope with the shortages caused by a price ceiling.

wealth (of a household) the value of accumulated savings.

wealth effect of a change in the aggregate price level the effect on consumer spending caused by the change in the purchasing power of consumers' assets when the aggregate price level changes. A rise in the aggregate price level decreases the purchasing power of consumers' assets, so consumers decrease their consumption; a fall in the aggregate price level increases the purchasing power of consumers' assets, so consumers increase their consumption.

wealth tax a tax on the wealth of an individual.

wedge the difference between the demand price of the quantity transacted and the supply price of the quantity transacted for a good when the supply of the good is legally restricted. Often created by a quantity control, or quota.

welfare state the collection of government programs designed to alleviate economic hardship.

willingness to pay the maximum price a consumer is prepared to pay for a good.

world price the price at which a good can be bought or sold abroad.

World Trade Organization (WTO) an international organization of member countries that oversees international trade agreements and rules on disputes between countries over those agreements.

X

x-axis the horizontal number line of a graph along which values of the x-variable are measured; also referred to as the horizontal axis.

Y

y-axis the vertical number line of a graph along which values of the y-variable are measured; also referred to as the vertical axis.

Z

zero bound the lower bound of zero on the nominal interest rate.

zero lower bound for interest rates statement of the fact that interest rates cannot fall below zero.

zero-profit equilibrium an economic balance in which each firm makes zero profit at its profit-maximizing quantity.

Note: Key terms appear in **bold-face** type.

A

Abengoa, 845
ability-to-pay principle, 203, 204, 512–513, 534
absolute advantage, 36, 222–224
absolute value, 56
   of price elasticity of demand, 163
ACA. *See* Affordable Care Act (ACA)
academic performance, monetary incentives to improve, 10
accelerator principle, 763
account
   money as unit of, 856
accountability
   inflation targeting and, 904
accounting, mental, 268
accounting profit, 250, 251–252, 364
acid rain, 467, 472, 477, 478
actual inventory spending, 764
AD-AS model, 802–810
   long-run macroeconomic equilibrium and, 806–809
   short-run effects of shifts of aggregate demand and, 803–806
   short-run macroeconomic equilibrium and, 802–803
   short-run Phillips curve and, 930
ADM. *See* Archer Daniels Midland (ADM)
administrative costs, 200
Advanced Micro Devices (AMD), 390, 421
advance purchase restrictions, 411
adverse selection, 597–598
   adverse selection death spiral and, 526, 527, 598
   health insurance and, 526, 527
advertising, product differentiation and, 457–458
AFC. *See* average fixed cost (AFC)
AFDC. *See* Aid to Families with Dependent Children (AFDC)
Affordable Care Act (ACA), 511, 521–522, 530–533
   cost control and, 532
   launch of, 532–533
   uninsured people and, 531–532
Africa
   economic growth in, 701–702, 703–704, 705
aggregate consumption function, 758–760
aggregate demand, 784–792
   interest rate effect and, 786
   monetary policy and, 901–906
   wealth effect and, 786

aggregate demand curve, 784–790. *See also* AD-AS model
   downward slope of, 785–786
   income-expenditure model and, 786–788
   movement along, 789, 792
   shifts of, 788–791, 822
aggregate output, 640. *See also* real GDP
   equilibrium, short-run, 803
aggregate price level, 644
   changes in, shifts of money demand curve and, 893–894
   equilibrium, short-run, 803
   interest rate effect of a change in, 786
   normalization of measure of, 644
   wealth effect of a change in, 786
aggregate production function, 689–693
aggregate spending, 633
   autonomous change in, 754
aggregate supply curve. *See also AD-AS* model; long-run aggregate supply curve; short-run aggregate supply curve
   short-run, 792
   short-run Phillips curve and, 930
aggregate wealth
   changes in, aggregate consumption function and, 760
agriculture
   corn production and, 371–372
   decline of, in United States, 176
   development and, 254–255
   European farm surpluses and, 180
   falling prices and, 12
   income elasticity of demand and, 176
   preserved farmland and, 479–480
   price floors and, 141–143
   price of farmland and, 115–116, 254–255
   subsidies and, 240, 478, 480
   trade, wages, and land prices in the 19th century and, 233–234
   yield per acre and, 329
Aid to Families with Dependent Children (AFDC), 522
AIG. *See* American International Group (AIG)
Airbnb, 121–122
Airbus, 421, 712
airline industry
   British, rivalry in, 440
   fuel costs and, 79, 81
   niche members of, 421
   price discrimination in, 407–409, 413

price elasticity of demand and, 182
   price floors and, 145
air pollution
   economic growth and, 707–708
   greenhouse gas emissions and, 710–711
   pollution in China, 683
Ajinomoto, 419, 420, 423
Alaskan crab fishing, 152–153, 359
Alaskan halibut fishers, 502–503
Alcoa, 96
Allegis Group, 678
Allen, Paul, 735
allocation
   to consumers, inefficient, 136–137
   efficiency in, 29
   reallocation of consumption among consumers and, 118
   of risk, efficient, 590–591
   of sales among sellers, inefficient, 144
   of time, 564, 575–576
Alrosa, 421
Amazon, 103, 211, 351, 379, 414, 421, 438, 717
ambulance rides, price of, 161–162
AMD. *See* Advanced Micro Devices (AMD)
American Economic Association, 5
American International Group (AIG), 602
American Recovery and Reinvestment Act, 42, 819, 822, 825, 826–827, 845
Amtrak, 403
Anarchy, State, and Utopia (Nozick), 513
anchoring, 266
antitrust case, against Microsoft, 483–484
antitrust policy, 387, 402, 419, 421, 434
Apple, 217, 390, 420, 421, 482
Applebee's, 75
appreciation, 1008
apprentice system, German, 561
Archer Daniels Midland (ADM), 419, 420, 423
arc method of calculating slope, 56–58
area, below or above a curve, calculating, 59–60
Argentina
   default by, 839
   drug prices in, 391
   education level in, 695, 696, 699
   long-run economic growth in, 618–619
   real GDP per capita in, 701–702, 703
Armenia
   hyperinflation in, 919

arms races, 429
Army Corps of Engineers, 498
artificially scarce goods, 124, 503–505
asbestos, lawsuits related to, 596
asset bubble, 953
asset prices
   expectations for, 741–743
   macroeconomics and, 743–744
assets
   of Federal Reserve System (Fed), 871–873, 874–875
   financial. *See* financial assets
   illiquid, 734
   liquid, 734
   physical, 263, 731
asymmetric information. *See* private information
ATC. *See* average total cost (ATC)
ATMs, 890
AT&T, 421, 422
at the margin, 284, 329
Austen, Jane, 545
austerity
   multiplier and, 830–831
Australia
   cap and trade system in, 477
   cotton production in, 95
   entrepreneurship in, 538
   income inequality in, 515
   individual transferable quotas in, 502
   minimum wage in, 145
   net public debt of, 838
   per capita greenhouse gas emissions in, 473
   unemployment in, 668
   voter turnout in, 496
   work hours in, 567
Austria
   GDP per capita and well-being in, 642
   unemployment and inflation in, 934
autarky, 220, 222
Authors United, 414
automatic stabilizers, 830
automobile industry
   American, 45
   Japanese, 225
   product differentiation in, 437
autonomous change in aggregate spending, 754
autonomous consumer spending, 756
Autor, David, 543
AVC. *See* average variable cost (AVC)
average cost, 337, 339–341, 349
average fixed cost (AFC), 340–342, 349
average total cost (ATC), 339–341, 349
   long-run, 347–348
   marginal cost vs., 258
   minimum, 342, 367
   monopolistic competition vs. perfect competition and, 456

average total cost curve, 341–342
short- vs. long-run, 345–348
U-shaped, 340
average variable cost (AVC), 340–342, 349
axes, of a graph, 52

B

babysitting cooperative, 20
backward-bending individual labor supply curve, 578
balance of payments accounts, 998
balance of payments on current account (current account), 1000
balance of payments on goods and services, 1000
balance sheet effect, 879
banana trade, 239, 420
bandwagon effect, 482
Banerjee, Abhijit, 42
Bangladesh
clothing production of, 37, 39, 225
comparative advantage and, 39
bank, 738
bank deposits, 732, 737–738
checkable, 854
bank failures
money multiplier and, 868–869
bank holiday
declared by Franklin Roosevelt, 877
banking crisis, 952
banking system, United States Federal Reserve System and. See Federal Reserve System (Fed)
banking system, U.S., 875–882
crisis in, in early twentieth century, 875–878
evolution of, 875
financial crisis of 2008 and, 878–882
S&L crisis of 1980s and, 878
Bank of England, 873
inflation targeting and, 904
Bank of Japan, 940
bank reserves, 860
excess, 866–867
bank runs, 860
causes of, 861–862
deposit insurance and, 863–864
in 1930s, 877
banks, 737–738, 860–864
central. See central banks; European Central Bank (ECB); Federal Reserve System (Fed)
commercial. See commercial banks
commercial, open-market operations and, 871–873
functions of, 860–861
investment, 877
money creation by, 864–866
regulation of, 862–863
runs on. See bank runs
bank's capital, 862–863
bar graphs, 62

BarnesandNoble.com, 211
barriers to entry, 389–393
barter, 37
Battle of Trenton, 2
Bazalgette, Joseph, 489
Bear Stearns, 874, 875, 881
behavioral economics, 249, 265–270, 742
irrationality and, 266–269
rationality and, 265–266
behavioral finance, 742
Belgium
entrepreneurship in, 538
GDP per capita and well-being in, 642
international trade of, 218
minimum wage in, 144
net public debt of, 838
unemployment and inflation in, 934
unemployment in, 668
voter turnout in, 496
Bell Telephone, 434
benefit(s). See also marginal benefit; marginal social benefit entries; social benefit
external, 466. See also positive externalities
benefits principle, 203–204
Bernanke, Ben, 812, 869, 904, 908–909
Bertrand, Marianne, 562
Best Buy, 379, 438
bias, status quo, 268–269
biotech industry, sunk costs and, 264–265
black labor, 145–146
black markets, 139
black rhinos, legalized hunting of, 506
BMW, 561
Board of Governors, 655
Boatbound, 122
Boehner, John, 819
Boeing, 25, 39, 45, 421, 712
bonds, 630, 734
Booth School of Business, 42
borrowing
government, 632
bounded rationality, 266
brand names, 458–459
Brazil
economy of, 125
hyperinflation in, 673
U.S. subsidies to cotton farmers and, 240
breakage, 883
break-even price, 367
breakfast cereal industry, 359, 420
Britain. See United Kingdom
British Airways, 403, 440
British Telecom, 403
Brooks, Frederick P., Jr., 336
Bryan, William Jennings, 675
Brynjolfsson, Eric, 695
budget balance, 719, 831–836
cyclically adjusted, 832–834
as measure of fiscal policy, 832
value of, 835
budget constraints, 281, 285–286, 288
budget deficits, 719

consumer spending and, 825
debt versus, 838
European, 835–836
fiscal policy and, 836–838
in practice, 840–841
unemployment and, 833
budget line, 286–287
change in income and, 320–323
income and substitution effects and, 323–325
slope of, 312–313
time allocation, 575–576
budget surplus, 719
Buick, 449
Bureau of Consumer Financial Protection, 881
Bureau of Economic Analysis GDP estimates of, 649
Bureau of Labor Statistics (BLS)
data collection by, 648
income and spending figures provided by, 755
labor underutilization measures calculated by, 658
Burger King, 298, 445
business cycle, 611–616
charting, 612–613
cyclically adjusted budget balance and, 832–834
depressions and. See depressions; Great Depression
as international phenomenon, 615
Montgomery Ward's decline and, 624
recessions and. See Great Recession; recessions
taming, 615
business-cycle peaks, 613
business cycles, correlation with risks, 595
business-cycle troughs, 613
business opportunities
perceived changes in, shifts of demand for loanable funds and, 726
business world. See also industries; specific industries
corporate bailouts and, 602
economists in, 43–44
entrepreneurs and, 121, 254
firms in, 38

C

cable providers, as monopsonists, 405
Cadbury Canada, 425
Cadillac, 449
Cambodia, clothing exports of, 37
Camp, Garrett, 97
Canada
auto industry of, 226
drug prices in, 391
entrepreneurship in, 538
forest product exports of, 224
gasoline consumption in, 71
GDP per capita and well-being in, 642
government size in, 820
health care in, 529–530
high-speed Internet access in, 407
income inequality in, 515

international trade of, 218
long-run economic growth in, 618–619
minimum wage in, 145
money and inflation in, 909
net public debt of, 838
per capita greenhouse gas emissions in, 473
taxes in, 209
unemployment in, 668
voter turnout in, 496
work hours in, 567
cap and trade systems, 477–478
capital, 252
bank's, 862–863
changes in inflows of, shifts of supply of loanable funds and, 727–728
financial. See financial capital
foreign, economic growth and, 696
human. See human capital
implicit cost of, 253
market for, 553–554
physical. See physical capital
capital at risk, 589–590
capital market, 38
carbon trading, 477–478
Cardpool.com, 883
Carl Jr.'s, 298
cartels, 423, 433, 435
Cassano, Joseph, 602
catch-share schemes, 502–503
causality, reverse, 64
causal relationships, 52–53
cell phones. See also smartphone industry
use while driving, 466
central banks, 869, 873. See also European Central Bank (ECB); Federal Reserve System (Fed)
in eurozone, 874
inflation targeting and, 904
monetary policy and. See monetary policy
centrally planned economies, 2, 125
certificate of deposit (CD), 890
chained dollars, 641
chained dollars, 641
Champagne, 360
Chanel, 460
Chavez, Hugo, 140
checkable bank deposits, 854
Chevalier, Judith, 122
Chevrolet, 449
chicken, diminishing marginal utility and, 284–285
children, poverty among, 516–517
Chile
grape exports of, 224
unemployment in, 668
China
air pollution in, 683
clothing exports of, 37
clothing production in, 225
cotton production in, 95
demand for cotton clothing in, 95
"disappearing girls" in, 10–11
economic growth in, 683, 684, 696
economy of, 125

education level in, 696, 697, 699
food consumption in, 116
increasing demand for food of, 176
international trade of, 218
per capita greenhouse gas emissions in, 473
pollution control in, 477
quantity of currency in circulation in, 855
size of economy of, 629, 640
smartphone production and, 217, 219–223
supply shocks of twenty-first century and, 806
trade surplus of, 621
U.S. tire import tariffs and, 240
wages in, 241
chocolate industry, price-fixing in, 425
choice. See consumer choice; individual choice
Christmas tree farming, 357
Chrysler, 45, 421
Churchill, Winston, 496
cigarettes, excise taxes on, 203
circular-flow diagram, 27, 37–39
national accounts and, 630–633
Citizens' Bank of Louisiana, 859
classical model of the price level, 920–922
Clean Air Act of 1970, 472–473
Clean Air Act of 1990, 472, 710
climate, comparative advantage and, 224
closed economies
savings-investment spending identity in, 718–719
clothing industry
Chinese, 37, 95, 225
comparative advantage in, 37, 39, 225
in Hong Kong, 226–227
U.S. import quotas on clothing and, 237
The Club of Rome, 706
Coase, Ronald, 470
Coase theorem, 470
Coca-Cola, 68, 420
Cold War, 437
collective bargaining, 666
college. See higher education
collusion, 423–424, 431–432
tacit, 429–431, 435–436
Comcast, 405, 407
command economies, 2, 125
commercial banks, 877
open-market operations and, 871–873
commodities, 359
commodity-backed money, 856–857, 859
commodity money, 856
commodity prices
changes in, shifts of the short-run aggregate supply curve and, 796, 797
common carriage rules, 407
common resources, 124, 489, 499–503
efficient use and maintenance of, 501–502
overuse of, 499–501

comparative advantage, 27, 33–37, 39, 218–227
absolute advantage vs., 36, 222–224
factor intensity and, 222–224
gains from, 36, 221–222
Heckscher-Ohlin model and, 224–225, 232–233
production possibilities and, 219–221
in real world, 36–37
sources of, 224–227
compensating differentials, 558
competition
collusion and, 423–424
imperfect, 420. See also monopolistic competition; oligopoly
nonprice, 437
product differentiation and, 448
competitive markets, 66
supply and demand model of. See demand curve; demand schedule; supply and demand model; supply curve; supply schedule
complements, 74
changes in prices of, shifts of the demand curve and, 82
perfect, 318
in production, 82
computer operating systems, 482, 483–484
concert tickets, market for, 89–90
condiments, variety of, 289–290
conditional convergence, 705
congestion pricing, 78
Congressional Budget Office (CBO), 927
unemployment rate and, 669
Conner, Christopher, 425
Connolly, Marie, 126
constant costs
across industry, 376
marginal, 257
constant marginal cost, 257
constant returns to scale, 349
consumer(s)
excise tax paid mainly by, price elasticities and, 191–192
inefficient allocation to, 136–137
preferences of, consumer choice and, 315–316
price-taking, 358. See also perfect competition
rational. See marginal utility; rational consumer; utility
reallocation of consumption among, 118
consumer choice, 307–316
income and, 320–323
income and substitution effects and, 323–325
marginal rate of substitution and, 308–311, 313–314
preferences and, 315–316
price increases and, 319–320
slope of budget line and, 312–313

tangency condition and, 311–312
consumer price index (CPI), 645–646
"core," 937–938
payments indexed to, 647–648
consumer spending, 630, 755–761
autonomous, 756
budget deficits and, 825
crowding out of, by government spending, 824
current disposable income and, 755–758
fiscal policy and, 821–822
income and, 18–19, 822
shifts of aggregate consumption function and, 758–760
consumer surplus, 103
demand curve and, 104–111
export effects on, 230–231
gains from trade and, 116–117
import effects on, 229–230
individual, 105, 112
price changes and, 107–110
price controls and, 136
tariffs and, 235
total, 106
willingness to pay and, 104–107
consumption
inefficiently low, 492
marginal analysis and, 262–263
marginal propensity to consume and, 752–753, 754, 756–757
nonrival in, 490
reallocation among consumers, 118
rival in, 490
taxing, taxing income vs., 209
utility and, 282
consumption bundle, 282, 288, 644
consumption function, 756–760
aggregate, 758–760
consumption possibilities, 286
container-shipping industry, 814
contractionary fiscal policy, 823–824
contractionary monetary policy, 901–902
Convention on International Trade in Endangered Species (CITES), 506
convergence hypothesis, 703, 704–706
copyrights, 391–392
core inflation rate, 938
corn production, 371–372
corporate bailouts, 602
cost(s), 111
administrative, of a tax, 200
average. See average entries
of capital, implicit, 253
constant. See constant costs
explicit vs. implicit, 250–251
external, 466. See also negative externalities; pollution
of extreme weather events, 581
fixed. See fixed costs
of human life, 263

increasing. See increasing costs
marginal. See marginal cost(s)
menu, of inflation, 673–674, 677
opportunity. See opportunity cost
present value of projects with, 279
producer surplus and, 111–114
of production, efficiency in long-run equilibrium and, 377
of quantity controls, 151–152
shoe-leather, of inflation, 673, 677
short- vs. long-run, 345–350
of taxation, 198–200
total. See total cost
transaction, 732
unit-of-account, of inflation, 674
variable, 334, 349
of welfare state, 534–535
cost-benefit analysis, 497–498
Costco, 271, 421, 569
cost curves, 329, 330. See also average total cost curve
production function and, 334–336
cost-of-living allowances (COLAs)
indexing of, to CPI, 648
nominal wage and, 797
cotton
prices of, 95
U.S. subsidies to cotton farmers and, 240
Council of Economic Advisers, 43
counterfeiting, 853, 942
Coupons.com, 379
crab fishing, in Alaska, quota-share system and, 152–153, 359
CrateandBarrel.com, 351
credit card overuse, 268
credit crunch, 958
credit-default swaps (CDSs), 602
credit markets
changes in, shifts of money demand curve and, 894
cross-price elasticity of demand, 174–175, 181
crowding out, 726–727
expansionary fiscal policy and, 824
currencies. See also dollar
government borrowing and, 843
quantity in circulation, global comparison of, 855
reasons for holding, 858
currency in circulation, 854
current account (balance of payments on current account), 1000
curves, 53–54. See also specific curves
calculating area below or above, 59–60
horizontal, 55–56
maximum and minimum points, 58–59
nonlinear, 56–58

slope of, 54–59
vertical, 55–56
customers, changes in number of, shift of demand curve and, 75–77
cycle of poverty, 480–481
cyclically adjusted budget balance, 832–834
cyclical unemployment, 667
output gap and, 927–928
Czech Republic
unemployment in, 670

D

Dalmo, Wiggo, 538
Daly, Mary, 801–802
deadweight loss, 135
monopoly and, 401–402
quantity controls and, 151
from a tax, elasticity and, 200–203
deadweight-loss triangle, 135
De Beers, 385, 387, 392–393, 402, 421
debt
government. See government debt
monetization of, 922
public, 838
debt deflation, 938–939
debt-GDP ratio, 840–841
debt overhang, 959
decision making, 249–275
behavioral economics and. See behavioral economics
costs, benefits, and profits and, 250–255
marginal analysis and. See marginal analysis
sunk costs and, 263–265
when time is a factor, present value and, 277–279
decreasing marginal benefit, 258
decreasing marginal cost, 257
decreasing returns to scale, 348, 349
dedicated taxes, 842
deductibles, 599–600
default, 734
on government debt, 839
deficit
budget, 719
deflation, 676, 938–941
causes of, 619–620
debt, 938–939
expected, effects of, 939–940
negative demand shocks and, 809
pain of, 620
De Grauwe, Paul, 843
De La Rue, 942
Delta, 420
demand
changes in, 90–96
for cotton clothing, 95
derived, 544
elastic, 167, 170
elasticity of. See cross-price elasticity of demand; elasticity of demand; price elasticity of demand
for housing, 741

for housing, mortgage rates and, 296–297
income-elastic, 176
income-inelastic, 176
inelastic, 163, 167, 170
law of, 70, 163, 294–295, 785
for loanable funds, 722–724
for natural gas, 67
perfectly elastic, 167
perfectly inelastic, 166
quantity demanded vs., 72
seasonal, shut down and, 369–370
for stocks, 739–741
unit-elastic, 167, 170
demand curve, 69–78
consumer surplus and, 104–111
demand schedule and, 69–70
domestic, 228
for factors, shifts of, 550–551
individual, 75–77
for labor, 552–553
market, 76
for money. See money demand curve
of monopolist, 393–397
movements along, 72, 80–81
price elasticity along, 171–172
shifts of, 70–78, 91–92
simultaneous shift of demand curve and supply curve and, 93–94
demand price, 148–150
demand schedule, 69–70, 104
demand shocks, 784, 803–804, 806, 807
stabilization policy and, 811–812
supply shocks versus, 809–810
Denmark
entrepreneurship in, 538
GDP per capita and well-being in, 642
income inequality in, 515
Depardieu, Gerard, 197
dependent variable, 52–53
deposit insurance, 862
depositors, 737
depreciation, 1008
depressions
preventing, 610–611
derived demand, 544
Desktime, 122
devaluation, 1021
diamonds, De Beers monopoly in, 392–393
diminishing marginal rate of substitution, 310–311
diminishing marginal utility, 283–285
risk aversion and, 583
diminishing returns effect, 341
diminishing returns to an input, 332–333, 336–337
diminishing returns to physical capital, 690
Dior, 460
disappeared daughters, 11
discount rate, 870–871
discount window, 863
discouraged workers, 658
discretionary fiscal policy, 830
discretionary monetary policy, 980

discrimination, employment, 561–562
diseconomies of scale, 348, 349
disinflation, 919
costs of, 936–937
of 1980s, 937–938
disposable income, 630, 631, 822
consumer spending and, 755–758
expected, changes in, aggregate consumption function and, 759–760
distracted driving, cell phone use and, 466
diversification, 581, 589, 592–594, 733
diversified portfolio of stocks, 736
diversity, value in, product differentiation and, 448
dividends, 630
"dixies," 859
Dodd-Frank Act, 881
dollar
breaking of link to gold, 859
as fiat money, 857, 859
history of, 859
marginal, 290–295
unit-of-account role of, 674
Dollar Shave Club (DSC), 461
domestic demand curve, 228
domestic supply curve, 228
dominant strategy, 427–428
double coincidence of wants, 854–855
double-dip recessions, 809
drinking water
in London, 489
pollution by fracking, 465
Duffie, Darrell, 26
duopolists, 422
duopoly, 422–423

E

early-childhood intervention programs, 480–481
Earned Income Tax Credit (EITC), 205, 521, 522–523
earnings
retained, 763
East Asia
economic growth in, 701–703, 705
Eastern European countries, economies of, 125
East Germany
structural unemployment in, 670–671
eBay, 90, 482
econometrics
failures of, 760–761
origin of, 760
Economic Experts Panel of Chicago Booth's Initiative on Global Markets, 42
economic fluctuations, 3–4
economic growth, 4
long-run. See long-run economic growth
production possibilities frontier and, 31–33
economic inequality, 517–521
alleviating, 512

economic insecurity, 519
alleviating, 500
economic interaction. See interaction
economic loss, 252
economic models. See models; specific models
economic policy, 19–20
economic profit, 250, 251–252, 253, 364, 367, 377
economic questions, 1
economics, 2
behavioral, 742
economic signals, 123–124
The Economics of Welfare (Pigou), 474
economies
convergence of, 703, 704–706
self-correcting, 808, 809, 810
economies of scale, 348, 349
economists
in business world and government, 43–44
disagreement among, 41–43
economy, 2
command (planned), 2, 125
market. See market economies
self-regulating, 610
Edison, Thomas, 697
education. See also higher education
choice between work and, 249, 250–252
economic growth and, 696
government subsidies to, 699
human capital and, 448–449, 544
poverty and, 516
wage inequality and, 543, 558–559
efficiency, 15–17, 121. See also inefficiency
in allocation, 29
in long-run equilibrium, costs of production and, 377
of markets, consumer surplus and producer surplus and, 117–122
in production, 29
production possibilities frontier and, 29
progressive taxation and, 207
supply of private goods by markets and, 491–492
trade-off between equity and, 203–206
efficiency-wage model, 560–561
efficiency wages, 560–561
structural unemployment and, 667
efficient allocation of risk, 590–591
efficient markets hypothesis, 741–743
Eichengreen, Barry, 610
Eisenhower, Dwight D., 75
EITC. See Earned Income Tax Credit (EITC)
"either-or" decision making, 252–253
Elance-oDesk, 670, 678
elastic demand, 167, 170
elasticity, 161–186
deadweight loss from a tax and, 200–203

of demand. *See* cross-price elasticity of demand; elasticity of demand; price elasticity of demand
estimating, 165
midpoint method for calculating, 164–165
price discrimination and, 409–410
of supply. *See* elasticity of supply; price elasticity of supply
table of, 181
as unit-free measure, 175
elasticity of demand
income, 162, 174, 175–176
perfectly elastic demand and, 167
perfectly inelastic demand and, 166
price. *See* cross-price elasticity of demand; price elasticity of demand
unit-elastic demand and, 167, 170
elasticity of supply
perfectly elastic supply and, 179, 376
perfectly inelastic supply and, 179
price. *See* price elasticity of supply
electricity
carbon emissions and production of, 471–472
deregulation of, 399–400, 406
public ownership of power companies and, 403
SMART Grid technologies and, 344–345
U.S. electrical equipment conspiracy of the 1950s and, 436
El Salvador, comparative advantage and, 39
embedded inflation, 906
Embraer, 33, 39
emissions taxes, 473–474
emotion, investing and, 594
employee/employer mismatches structural unemployment and, 667
employment, 656. *See also* labor *entries*; wage(s)
employee decisions about investing in 401(k) funds and, 268–269
poverty and, 516
temporary, 670, 678
tradeoff between work and leisure and, 563–564, 575–576
youth, decline of summer jobs and, 568
employment-based health insurance, 526–527, 528
employment discrimination, 561–562
English language proficiency, poverty and, 516
entrepreneurs, 121–122, 254
entry
barriers to, 389–393
free, 359–360, 370, 461–463

monopolistic competition in long run and, 461–463
Environmental Protection Agency (EPA), 472
emitted by electric plants and, 471
greenhouse gas emissions and, 710
environmental standards, 472–473
comparison of, 475–477
EPA. *See* Environmental Protection Agency (EPA)
equilibrium, 13–15
on freeways, 17–18
income-expenditure, 768–770, 786, 787
macroeconomic. *See* macroeconomic equilibrium
market. *See* market equilibrium
Nash, 428
noncooperative, 428
zero-profit, 452–453
equilibrium exchange rate, 1009
equilibrium interest rate, 895–897
loanable funds market and, 725–726
equilibrium price, 69, 86
concert ticket market and, 89–90
market price above, 88
market price below, 88–89
equilibrium quantity, 69, 86
equilibrium value of the marginal product, 553
equity, 15–16, 120, 121
progressive taxation and, 207
rationality and, 266
trade-off between efficiency and, 203–206
welfare state and, 501
An Essay on the Principle of Population (Malthus), 693–694
estate tax, 208
estimation, of elasticity of demand, 165
ethanol
in gasoline, 115–116, 371
U.S. tariff on, 237
Ethiopia, wheat yield of, 332
EU. *See* European Union (EU)
euro
France's switch to, 671
government borrowing and, 843
Spain's adoption of, 622
Europe. *See also* Eastern European countries; European Union (EU); *specific countries*
income inequality in, 515
move from mayhem to Renaissance, 492–493
stability pact of, 835–836
unemployment in, 667
European Central Bank (ECB), 835, 843–844, 873–874
deflation and, 940–941
European Union (EU), 239, 419, 434
antitrust regulation in, 434

cap and trade system in, 477, 478
farm surpluses in, 180
tariff on banana imports of, 239
Eurosclerosis, 667
eurozone
central banks in, 874
quantity of currency in circulation in, 855
unemployment and inflation in, 934
excess capacity, 456
excess demand. *See* shortages
excess reserves, 866–867
excess supply. *See* consumer surplus; producer surplus; surpluses
exchange
money as medium of, 855
exchange market intervention, 1016
exchange rate, 1008
exchange rate regime, 1016
excise taxes, 188, 191–193
on cigarettes, 203
paid mainly by consumers, 191–192
paid mainly by producers, 192–193
quantities and prices and, 188–191
revenue from, 194–195
excludable, 490
free, 359–360, 370
monopolistic competition in long run and, 461–463
expansionary fiscal policy, 822–823, 824–825
expansionary monetary policy, 901
expansions, 613
definition of, 614
unemployment during, 660
expectations
for asset prices, 741–743
changes in, shifts of aggregate demand curve and, 789, 790
changes in, shifts of demand curve and, 75
changes in, shifts of supply curve and, 82–83
for inflation, short-run Phillips curve and, 931–933
risk and, 582–583
unrealistic, about future behavior, 268
expected deflation
effects of, 939–940
expected utility, 583
expected value, 582
explicit costs, 250–251
export(s), 218, 632
effects on international trade, 230–231
net, 638
exporters, 93
exporting industries, 232
external benefits, 466. *See also* positive externalities
external costs, 466. *See also* negative externalities; pollution

externalities, 124, 465–488
internalizing, 470
negative. *See* negative externalities; pollution
network. *See* network externalities
positive. *See* positive externalities
private solutions to, 469–470
Exxon, 402, 434
ExxonMobil, 68, 402

F

Facebook, 717
factor abundance, comparative advantage and, 224–225
factor demand, value of the marginal product of labor and, 548–550
factor demand curve, shifts of, 550–551
factor distribution of income, 545–546
in United States, 545–546
factor income
earned from firms, gross domestic product as, 637
income distribution and, 544–546
factor intensity, 224–225
factor markets, 38, 543
factor prices, wages as, 232, 543
factors of production, 32, 224, 544–546
changes in supply of, shifts of factor demand curve and, 550–551
comparative advantage and, 224–225
Heckscher-Ohlin model and, 224–225
movement between industries, 232
prices of, wages as, 232, 543
fair insurance policies, 583–585
fairness. *See* equity
Fannie Mae, 878, 881
FAO Schwartz, 438
farming. *See* agriculture
fashion models, market for, 94
fast-food restaurants
healthier food at, 298
product differentiation and, 445
risk and, 600–601
Fed. *See* Federal Reserve System (Fed)
Federal Deposit Insurance Corporation (FDIC), 738, 862
federal funds market, 870
federal funds rate, 870
target, 895, 898–899, 900
Taylor rule and, 903
Federal Insurance Contribution Act (FICA) tax
incidence of, 193–194
structure of, 205
Federalist Party, 187
Federal Open Market Committee (FOMC), 783, 870
response to financial crisis in 2008, 783, 784
target federal funds rate and, 900

Federal Reserve System (Fed), 791, 853, 868–874
assets and liabilities of, 871–875
balance sheet of, 874–875
creation of, 876–878
discount rate and, 870–871
interest on assets of, 873
open-market operations and, 869, 871–873
reserve requirements and, 870–871
structure of, 869–870
Federal Trade Commission, 421
feedback, positive, 482
female-headed families, poverty among, 515
fiat money, 857, 859
FICA tax. *See* Federal Insurance Contribution Act (FICA) tax
final goods and services, 633
domestically produced, GDP as spending on, 635–636
GDP as value of production of, 634–635
finance
behavioral, 742
financial account (balance of payments on financial account), 1000
financial assets, 263, 731
types of, 734–735
financial capital
definition of, 720
financial contagion, 953
financial crises
economic problems caused by, 783, 784
of 2008, 26, 878–882
financial crisis of 2007–2009. *See* Great Recession, 2007–2009
financial intermediaries, 735–738, 860. *See also* banks
financial markets, 631, 722
financial panic, 953
financial risk, 582–583, 732–733
financial system, 717, 731–739
economic growth and, 699–700
financial intermediaries and, 735–738
fluctuations in, 739–745
tasks of, 732–734
types of financial assets and, 734–735
Finkelstein, Amy, 42
Finland
GDP per capita and well-being in, 642
unemployment and inflation in, 934
unemployment in, 668
firms, 38, 330. *See also* producer(s)
gross domestic product as factor income earned from, 637
price-taking, optimal output rule for, 362–364, 547
recessions and, 614
fiscal austerity, 965
fiscal policy, 610, 819–850

budget balance as measure of, 832
contractionary, 823–824
discretionary, 830
expansionary, 822–823, 824–825
government budget and total spending and, 821–822
government spending and, 821
government transfers and, 821
lags in, 825–826
long-run implications of, 836–844
multiplier and, 827–831
shifts of the aggregate demand curve and, 790, 791
taxes and, 820–821
fiscal years, 837–838
Fisher, Irving, 729, 938–939
Fisher effect, 729–730, 938–939
fishing
as common resource, 499, 500
for crab, in Alaska, quota-share system and, 152–153, 359
fixed costs, 334, 349
average, 340–341, 349
changing, 370
short-run production decision and, 367–368
fixed exchange rate, 1016
fixed inputs, 330
flat taxes, 206
floating exchange rate, 1016
food
healthier, at fast-food restaurants, 298
income elasticity of demand for, 176
share of income spent on food consumed at home and, 177
shortages of, in Venezuela, 140
food stamps, 521, 522
football games, blackout of, 504–505
Ford, 45, 421
Ford, Henry, 449
forecasts, 41
401(k) funds, employee decisions about investing in, 268–269
foreign exchange controls, 1017
foreign exchange market, 1008
foreign exchange reserves, 1016
Fox Searchlight Pictures, 147
fracking, 67, 68, 465
Williston, North Dakota population and, 544
France
currency conversion in, 671
drug prices in, 391
gasoline consumption in, 71
GDP per capita and well-being in, 642
government size in, 820
health care in, 529–530
international trade of, 218
minimum wage in, 145
net public debt of, 838
stability pact and, 835
taxes in, 209

unemployment and inflation in, 934
welfare state in, 535, 536–537
wheat yield of, 332
work hours in, 567
franchises, risk of, 600–601
Freddie Mac, 878, 881
free entry and exit, 359–360, 370, 461–463
free-rider problem, 491
free trade, 234
free-trade agreements, between United States and South Korea, 242–243
freeways, equilibrium on, 17–18
"French Paradox," 261
frictional unemployment, 663–664, 670
Friedman, Milton, 615, 759–760, 931
Fryer, Roland, Jr., 10
fuel prices, airline industry and, 81
fundamentals, 741–742
Fung, Victor, 244

G

gains from trade, 12
international, 221–222, 224
money's role in generating, 854
total surplus and, 116–117
gambling, risk aversion and, 587
game theory, 426–432
prisoners' dilemma, 426–429
repeated interaction and, 429–431
tacit collusion and, 429–431
Gap, 351, 883
gasoline
consumption of, international comparison of, 71
ethanol in, 115–116, 371
seasonal demand for, 81
shortage of, price controls and, 132
Gates, Bill, 735
GDP. *See* gross domestic product (GDP)
GDP deflator, 646, 647
GDP per capita, 641–642
well-being and, 642
Gebbia, Joe, 121
gender discrimination, poverty and, 516
gender-wage gap, 559
Genentech, 264
General Electric, 436
General Mills, 359, 420
General Motors (GM), 45, 421, 449, 663, 775
The General Theory of Employment, Interest, and Money (Keynes), 610, 615
generic drugs, 360–361
genetically modified seed industry, price-fixing case and, 424
Germany
budget deficit in, 837
gasoline consumption in, 71
GDP per capita and well-being in, 642

hyperinflation in, 855, 919, 923
income inequality in, 515
inflation in, 673
international trade of, 218
invasion of France, 253
manufacture in, 561
Nazi takeover of, economic causes of, 610, 808
net public debt of, 838
Normandy invasion and, 253
productivity in, 698
real GDP of, 693
savings-investment spending identity in, 720–721
stability pact and, 835
supply shocks of twenty-first century and, 806
trade surplus of, 621
unemployment and inflation in, 934
unemployment in, 668
unions in, 561
work hours in, 567
Getaround, 122
Giffen goods, 296, 325
gift cards, 883
Gilded Age, 520
Gillette, 461
Gini coefficient, 518–519
global comparison of, 515
Glass-Steagall Act, 877, 878
global comparisons
of antitrust regulation, 434
of comparative advantage in clothing manufacturing, 37, 39
of corporate bonds, 737
of disinflation, 936
of drug prices, 391
of gasoline consumption, 71
of health care, 529–530
of imports and exports as percentage of gross domestic product, 218
of income inequality, 515
of inflation targets, 904
of minimum wages, 145
of per capita greenhouse gas emissions, 473
of portion sizes, 261
of productivity and wages, 223
of quantity of currency in circulation, 855
of real GDP per capita, 2013, 685
recessions and, 615
of share of income spent on food, 176
of supply shocks of twenty-first century, 806
of taxes as share of gross domestic product, 209
of technological progress and productivity, 698
of unemployment, 668
of voting as public good, 496
of wheat yields, 332
of work hours, 567
globalization, 218. *See also* export *entries;* import *entries;* international trade; trade
challenges to, 240–242

comparative advantage and. *See* comparative advantage
Great Recession and, 607–608
hyperglobalization and, 217
offshore outsourcing and, 240, 241
of price fixing, 434
GM. *See* General Motors (GM)
Goldin, Claudia, 520
Goldman Sachs, 43, 602
goods
artificially scarce, 124, 503–505
changes in prices of, shifts in factor demand curve and, 550
complements. *See* complements
final. *See* final goods and services
Giffen, 296, 325
government purchases of, 632
inferior, 74–75, 175, 296, 321–323
as inputs. *See* inputs
markets for, 38
necessary vs. luxury, price elasticity of demand and, 172
nonrival in consumption, 490
private. *See* private goods
public. *See* public goods
rival in consumption, 490
share of income spent on, price elasticity of demand and, 172
substitutes. *See* marginal rate of substitution (MRS); substitutes
goods and services
final, 633
government purchases of, multiplier effects of, 827–828
intermediate, 633
Google, 717
Gordon, Robert, 694–695
Gourville, John T., 271
governance
economic growth and, 700
government. *See also* Federal *entries*
antitrust policy and, 387, 402, 419, 421, 434
barriers to entry created by, 391–392
in circular-flow diagram, 632
economists in, 43
health insurance provided by, 511, 521, 533–534. *See also* Affordable Care Act (ACA)
macroeconomic policy and, 19–20
taxes and. *See* excise taxes; Federal Insurance Contribution Act (FICA) tax; tax(es)
welfare state and. *See* welfare state
government borrowing, 632
changes in, shifts of demand for loanable funds and, 726

crowding out of private investment by, 824
currencies and, 843
government budget
budget balance and. *See* budget balance
fiscal policy and, 821–822
government debt, 836–837
budget deficits versus, 838
debt-GDP ratio and, 840–841
default on, 839
in practice, 840–841
problems posed by, 839–840
from World War II, 841
government intervention, 16–17
government policies. *See also* fiscal policy; monetary policy
aggregate demand and, 791
economic growth and, 698–700
spending and, 19–20
unemployment and, 667, 670
government purchases of goods and services, 632
multiplier effects of, 827–828
government spending
crowding out of private spending by, 824
fiscal policy and, 821
government transfers, 512, 630, 631. *See also* **welfare state**
changes in, multiplier effects of, 828–829
fiscal policy and, 821
implicit liabilities due to, 841–843
Grameen America, 746
Grameen Bank, 746
graphs, 51–66
bar, 62
calculating area above or below curve and, 59–60
curves on, 53–54
numerical, 60–64
pie charts, 62
scatter diagrams, 61–62
slope of curve and, 54–59
time-series, 60–61
two-variable, 51–53
variables and, 51
Great American Housing Bust, 270
Great Compression, 520
Great Depression, 19
causes of, 803–804, 881
deflation during, 676
econometrics and, 760
end of, causes of, 803–804
Great Recession compared with, 607, 608, 610
money multiplier and, 868–869
national accounts and, 639
Nazi takeover of Germany and, 610
origin of macroeconomics and, 608, 615
policy focus of macroeconomics and, 609–610
price indexes during, 647
Great Leap Forward, 125
Great Moderation consensus, 988

Great Plains, ground water in, 501
Great Recession, 2007–2009
causes of, 919
decline of summer jobs and, 568
global effects of, 607–608
Great Depression compared with, 607, 608, 610
mortgage-backed securities and, 26
oil prices and, 810
Phillips curve in, 933–934
preventing depression following, 610–611
recession of 2001 compared with, 616
sticky wages in, 801–802
unemployment following, 664
U.S. programs and poverty in, 524–525
Great Stink, 489
Greece
budget deficit in, 835–837
fiscal crisis in, 843
government debt of, 839
net public debt of, 838
unemployment and inflation in, 934
unemployment in, 668
Green Acres Program, 478
greenbacks, 859
greenhouse gas emissions. *See also* acid rain; pollution
carbon trading and, 477
electricity generation and, 471–472
global comparisons of, 473
reducing, 710–711
Greenspan, Alan, 745, 843, 869
Gross, Bill, 911
gross domestic product (GDP), 629, 633–639
calculating, 633–638
change in level versus rate of change in, 686
components of, 636, 637–638
gross national product versus, 638
imputed value in, 635
income-expenditure equilibrium, 769
nominal. *See* nominal GDP
per capita, in United States, 60–61
real. *See* real GDP
taxes as share of, global comparison of, 209
uses of, 639
wages and, global comparison of, 223
gross national product (GNP), 638
ground water, in Great Plains, 501
growth accounting, 689, 691
growth recessions, 661

H

Hachette, 414
Half.com, 103
Hamill Manufacturing, 555–556
Hamilton, Alexander, 187
H&R Block, 200
hats, demand curve for, 75

health care
Affordable Care Act and. *See* Affordable Care Act (ACA)
economics of, 525–534
health maintenance organizations and, 560
in other countries, 529–530
providing access to, 513
social benefit of access to, 513
Veterans Health Administration and, 528
health insurance, 511
adverse selection and, 526, 527
employment-based, 526–527, 528
government, 511, 521, 533–534. *See also* Affordable Care Act (ACA)
need for, 525–527
private, 525–526
uninsured people and, 528–529
health maintenance organizations (HMOs), 560
Heckscher-Ohlin model, 224–225, 232–233
herd mentality, 742
Herfindahl-Hirschman Index (HHI), 421
Herriot, James, 85
Hershey Canada, 425
HHI. *See* Herfindahl-Hirschman Index (HHI)
higher education
opportunity cost of attending college and, 8
raising tuition and, effect of, 173–174
unemployment rate among new graduates and, 661–662
value of, 543
high-speed Internet access, regulation of, 406–407
HMOs. *See* health maintenance organizations (HMOs)
Hobijn, Bart, 801–802
Hollande, Francois, 197
Honda, 421
Honduras, clothing exports of, 37
Hong Kong
clothing production of, 226–227
economic growth in, 244, 702
GDP per capita and well-being in, 642
Hoover, Herbert, 284
horizontal axis, 52
horizontal curves, 55–56
horizontal intercept, 54
household(s), 38
in circular-flow diagram, 630–633
income, mean and median, 517–518
housing. *See also* mortgage *entries*
demand for, 741
demand for, mortgage rates and, 296–297
shortage of, in New York City, 131

taxes on house sales and, 193
U.S. housing bubble and, 744–745, 751, 754–755, 765–766
housing bubble
subprime lending and, 879–880
housing market crash, 602
jingle mail and, 269–270
real estate commissions and, 454
"how much" decisions. *See* marginal analysis
Hoynes, Hilary, 42
human capital, 544, 718. *See also* **education; higher education**
definition of, 720
growth in productivity and, 689
wage inequality and, 558–559
human life, marginal benefit of saving, 263
Hurricane Irene, 581
Hurricane Isaac, 581
Hurricane Katrina, 67, 498–499
Hurricane Sandy, 581
price controls following, 132
hydraulic fracturing, 67, 68
hyperglobalization, 217
hyperinflation, 620
in Armenia, 919
in Brazil, 673
in Germany, 673, 855, 919, 923
logic of, 923–925
in Nicaragua, 919
in Zimbabwe, 919, 925

IBM, 336, 480
Iceland
individual transferable quotas in, 502
money and inflation in, 909
illegal activity, price floors and, 145–146
illiquid assets, 734
IMF. *See* International Monetary Fund (IMF)
imperfect competition, 420. *See also* monopolistic competition; oligopoly
imperfectly competitive markets prices in, 793
imperfect substitutes, 447
implicit cost(s), 250–251
implicit cost of capital, 253
implicit liabilities, 841–843
import(s), 218, 632
effects on international trade, 228–230
import-competing industries, 232
import quotas, 236–237
imputed value
in gross domestic product, 635
incentives, 9–10
incidence, 190–194
income. *See also* wage(s)
changes in, shift of demand curve and, 74–75
consumption and, 320–323
disposable. *See* disposable income

expected changes in, change in demand and, 75
factor, earned from firms, gross domestic product as, 637
household, mean and median, 517–518
limited, 6
real, 672
risk aversion and, 587
share spent on a good, price elasticity of demand and, 172
share spent on food consumed at home, 177
spending and, 18–19, 822
taxing, taxing consumption vs., 209
income distribution, 38. *See also* factor distribution of income
factor incomes and, 544–546
marginal productivity theory of. *See* marginal productivity theory of income distribution
in United States, 517–518
income effect, 295–296, 297
consumer choice and, 323–325
labor supply and, 564–566, 568
wages and labor supply and, 568, 576–578
income-elastic demand, 175, 176
income elasticity of demand, 162, 174, 175–176, 181
income-expenditure equilibrium, 768–770, 786, 787
income-expenditure equilibrium GDP, 769
income-expenditure model, 766–774
aggregate demand curve and, 786–788
equilibrium and, 768–770
multiplier process and inventory adjustment and, 770–774
planned aggregate spending and real GDP and, 767–768
income-inelastic demand, 175, 176
income inequality. *See also* poverty
economic insecurity and, 519
Gini coefficient and, 518–519
global comparisons of, 515
globalization and, 241
rationales for welfare state and, 512–513
in United States, 517–518, 519–521
welfare state effects on, 523–524
income support programs, 511. *See also* poverty; Social Security; welfare state
income taxes, 200, 206. *See also* tax(es)
consumption taxes vs., 209
cuts in, 197, 208, 210
Earned Income Tax Credit and, 205, 521, 522–523

fiscal policy and, 821
indexing of brackets, to CPI, 648
negative, 522–523
increasing costs
across industry, 376
marginal, 256, 258
increasing marginal cost, 256, 258
increasing returns to scale, 348, 389
international trade and, 226
oligopoly and, 420
specialization and, 349
independent events, 592
independent variable, 52–53
index funds, 594
India
arms race with Pakistan, 429
cotton exports of, 95
disappearing girls in, 11
economic growth in, 684
economy of, 125
money and inflation in, 909
per capita greenhouse gas emissions in, 473
real GDP per capita in, 687–688
voter turnout in, 496
indifference curve(s), 303–319
consumer choice and. *See* consumer choice
less than perfect substitutes and, 319
marginal rate of substitution and, 308–311
perfect complements and, 318
perfect substitutes and, 316–318
properties of, 306–307
utility function and, 282, 303–307
indifference curve analysis, of labor supply, 575–580
indifference curve maps, 305
individual choice, 5, 6–11
incentives and, 9–10
opportunity cost and, 7–8
resource scarcity and, 6–7
trade-offs and, 8–9
individual consumer surplus, 105
individual demand curve, 75–77
individual labor supply curve, 565
backward-bending, 578
individual mandate, 532
individual marginal costs, of common resources, 500
individual producer surplus, 112
individual supply curve, 83, 372
short-run, 369
individual transferable quotas (ITQs), oceans and, 502–503
Industrial Revolution, 618
factor distribution of income and social change in, 545
industries. *See also specific industries*
concentration of, 421, 435
factor movement between, 232
perfectly competitive, 358–359

industry supply curve, 357, 372–378
cost of production and efficiency in long-run equilibrium and, 377
long-run, 373–377
short-run, 372–373
IndyMac, 863–864
inefficiency, 124. *See also* efficiency
caused by natural monopoly, 402–403
caused by price ceilings, 134–138
of monopolistic competition, 456–457
of planned economies, 125
price floors causing, 143–145
resource use and, 15
inefficient allocation of sales among sellers, 144
inefficient allocation to consumers, 136–137
inefficiently high quality, 145
inefficiently low consumption, 492
inefficiently low production, 491
inefficiently low quality, 138–139
inefficiently low quantity, 143
inelastic demand, 163, 167, 170
inequality. *See* income inequality
infant industry argument for trade protection, 238
inferior goods, 74–75, 175, 296, 321–323
inflation, 19, 919–938. *See also* deflation; hyperinflation
causes of, 619–620
classical model of money and prices and, 920–922
costs of disinflation and, 936–938
disinflation and, 676
embedded, 906
expectations for, short-run Phillips curve and, 931–933
Fisher effect and, 729–730, 938–939
inflation tax and, 922–923
loanable funds market and, 728–731
long-run Phillips curve and, 934–936
McDonald's hamburger costs and, 620
menu costs of, 673–674, 677
nonaccelerating inflation rate of unemployment and, 936
Okun's law and, 928
output gap and unemployment rate and, 926–927
pain of, 620
price level and, 671–672
shoe-leather costs of, 673, 677
short-run Phillips curve and, 928–933
supply shocks and, 784
in United States, 919
unit-of-account costs of, 674
in Venezuela, 643
winners and losers from, 675–676

inflationary gaps, 808–809
inflation rate, 672–674
 price indexes and, 645
inflation targeting, 903–904
inflation tax, 922–923
infrastructure
 government subsidies to, 698–699
in-kind benefits, 522
inputs, 81
 availability of, price elasticity of supply and, 179
 changes in prices of, shifts of the supply curve and, 81–82
 diminishing returns to, 332–333, 336–337
 fixed, 330
 increasing, average total cost and, 341
 production function and, 330–337
 scarce, monopoly and, 389
 variable, 330
Institute for Supply Management (ISM), 649
institutions
 changes in, shifts of money demand curve and, 894
insurance
 adverse selection and, 598
 deductibles and, 599–600
 fair insurance policies and, 583–585
 health. See health insurance
 Lloyd's of London and, 588–589, 594, 595, 596
 moral hazard and, 599–600
 premiums for, 525–526, 531, 583, 587–588
 social, 512–513
 trading risk and, 589–591
 uncertainty and, 587
 unemployment, 523
insurance companies, as monopsonists, 405
Intel, 389–390, 421
intellectual property rights
 economic growth and, 700
interaction, 5, 12–18
 economy-wide, 18–20
 efficiency and, 15–16
 equilibrium and, 13–15
 gains from trade and, 12–13
 government intervention and, 16–17
interdependence, 426
interest
 on Treasury bills, 873
interest rate effect of a change in the aggregate price level, 786
interest rates, 277, 895–900
 discount, 870–871
 equilibrium, 895–897
 equilibrium, loanable funds market and, 725–726
 federal funds. See federal funds rate
 Fisher effect and, 729–730, 938–939
 holding money and, 890–891
 inflation and, 675
 investment spending and, 762–763

liquidity preference model of, 896
 loanable funds market and, 728–730
 loanable funds model of, 897
 in long run, changes in money supply and, 908–909
 long-term, 899–900
 models of, 897
 monetary policy and, 897–899, 900
 on mortgages, housing demand and, 296–297
 nominal. See nominal interest rate
 present value and, 277–279
 prime, 792
 real. See real interest rate
 short-term, 891–892
 zero lower bound for, 905
interest rate effect of a change in the aggregate price level, 786
intermediate goods and services, 633
internalizing the externality, 470
Internal Revenue Service, 200. See also income taxes
international comparisons. See global comparisons
International Monetary Fund (IMF), 43–44
International Panel on Climate Change (IPCC), 710
international trade, 217–248
 comparative advantage and, 218–227
 export effects and, 230–231
 import effects and, 228–230
 increasing returns to scale and, 226
 Ricardian model of, 219–223
 trade protection and. See trade protection
 unbalanced, 621–623
 wages and, 232–234
 wages and land prices in the 19th century and, 233–234
international trade agreements, 239–240
International Union for the Conservation of Nature, 506
internet
 finding realtors on, 454
 high-speed, access to, regulation of, 406–407
 web browsers and, 482, 483–484
internships, unpaid, 146–147
inventories, 632
 multiplier process and, 770–773
 unplanned investment spending and, 764–765
inventory investment, 764
 unplanned, 764
inventory spending
 actual, 764
investing, emotion and, 594
investment
 inventory, 764

investment spending versus, 718
investment banks, 877
investment spending, 761–766
 circular-flow diagram and, 632
 economic growth and, 696
 expected future real GDP and production capacity and, 763–764
 interest rate and, 762–763
 investment versus, 718
 planned, 762
 recessions and, 773–774
 savings-investment spending identity and, 718–721
 unplanned, inventories and, 764–765
invisible hand, 2–3
iPhones, 217. See also smartphone industry
Ireland
 budget deficit in, 835–836
 entrepreneurship in, 538
 GDP per capita and well-being in, 642
 government debt of, 839
 infrastructure in, 698–699
 minimum wage in, 145
 net public debt of, 838
 price of potatoes during 19th century in, 296
 unemployment and inflation in, 934
 unemployment in, 668
irrationality, 249, 265, 266–269
Israel
 GDP per capita and well-being in, 642
 inflation in, 673–674, 677
 money and inflation in, 909
 share of income spent on food, 176
 taxes in, 209
Italy
 budget deficit in, 835–836
 disinflation in, 936
 GDP per capita and well-being in, 642
 government debt of, 839
 net public debt of, 838
 productivity in, 698
 unemployment and inflation in, 934
 unemployment in, 668
Italy, gasoline consumption in, 71
ITQs. See individual transferable quotas (ITQs)

J

Jack in the Box, 298
James, LeBron, 8
Japan
 automobile exports of, 225
 cash society in, 894–895
 deflation in, 940
 economic growth in, 696, 705
 gasoline consumption in, 71
 GDP per capita and well-being in, 642
 government size in, 820
 high-speed Internet access in, 407
 international trade of, 218

natural resources of, 693
 net public debt of, 838
 productivity and wages in, 223
 quantity of currency in circulation in, 855
 real GDP per capita in, 695
 size of economy of, 629, 640
 unemployment in, 668
 wheat yield of, 332
 work hours in, 567
J.C. Penney, 271
Jefferson, Thomas, 187
jingle mail, 269–270
job creation argument for trade protection, 238
jobless recovery, 661
job search, 663
Johnson, Lyndon, 513
Johnson, Ron, 271
justice, welfare state and, 513
just-in-time production, 45

K

Kahneman, Daniel, 265, 269
Kaiser Family Foundation, 528
Kalanick, Travis, 97
KB Toys, 438
Kellogg's, 359, 420
Kennedy, John F., 671
Kenya, wildlife hunting in, 506
Keynes, John Maynard, 770, 811, 920
 The General Theory of Employment, Interest, and Money and, 610, 615
Keynesian cross, 770
Keynesian economics, 610
KFC, 75
kidney transplants, UNOS guidelines for, 110
kimchi, 360
Kiva Systems, 351
Knickerbocker Trust, 876
Korea. See South Korea
Kraft, 290
Krueger, Alan, 126
Kuwait
 real GDP of, 693
Kuznets, Simon, 639

L

labor
 "black," 145–146
 comparative advantage and, 223–224
 diminishing returns to, 332
 marginal product of. See marginal product of labor (MPL)
 units of, 333
labor demand curve, market, 552–553
labor force, 657
 changes in, 669
 participation rate, 657
labor force participation rate, 657
labor market
 flows in, 663–664
labor productivity. See productivity
labor strikes, 666
labor supply
 indifference curve analysis of, 575–580

wages and, 576–578
work vs. leisure and, 575–576
labor supply curve
 individual, 565, 578
 shifts of, 566–568
labor turnover, 569
labor unions
 structural unemployment and, 666–667
Laffer, Arthur, 197
Laffer curve, 197
land, market for, 553–554
Latin America
 economic growth in, 701–702, 703, 705
law of demand, 70, 163, 785
 substitution effect and, 294–295
lean manufacturing, 45
legal monopoly, 360
Lehman Brothers, 783, 881
leisure, 564
 tradeoff between work and, 563–564, 575–576
Lemann, Nicholas, 908–909
lemons problem. See adverse selection
lender of last resort, 960
lending
 subprime, housing bubble and, 879–880
leverage, 878–879
Levinson, Arthur, 264
Levi's, 244
Levitt, Steve, 10
liabilities, 732
 of Federal Reserve System (Fed), 871–872, 874–875
 implicit, 841–843
Libya
 printing of banknotes for, 942
licenses, 148
life insurance companies, 737
Li & Fung, 244
linear relationships, 53
Lipitor, 391
liquid assets, 734
liquidity
 financial system and, 733–734
liquidity preference model of the interest rate, 896
liquidity trap, 938–939
Lloyd's of London, 588–589, 594, 595, 596
loanable funds market, 722–731
 demand for loanable funds and, 722–724
 equilibrium interest rate and, 725–726
 inflation and interest rates and, 728–731
 shifts of demand for loanable funds and, 726–727
 shifts of supply of loanable funds and, 727–728
 supply of loanable funds and, 724–725
loan-backed securities, 734–735
loans, 734
location, product differentiation by, 448
The Logic of Collective Action (Olson), 496
London, England
 air pollution in, 707–708

congestion pricing in, 78
 sewer system in, 489
long run, 330
 definition of, 800
 monopolistic competition in, 451–453
long-run aggregate supply curve, 798–800
 movement from short-run aggregate supply curve to, 800–801
long-run average total cost curve (LRATC), 347–348, 349
long-run costs, short-run costs vs., 345–350
long-run economic growth, 616–619, 683–716
 aggregate production function and, 689–693
 beginning of, 618
 differences in, 701–706
 end of, 694–695
 government's role in promoting, 698–701
 natural resources and, 693–694, 706–707
 productivity and, 688–689
 rates of, 686–687, 695–701
 real GDP per capita and, 684–686
 sustainable, 706
long-run equilibrium, efficiency in, costs of production and, 377
long-run industry supply curve, 373–377
long-run macroeconomic equilibrium, 806–809
long-run market equilibrium, 374–375
long-run Phillips curve, 934–936
Long-Term Capital Management (LTCM), 878–879, 882
long-term interest rates, 891, 899–900
Los Angeles, congestion pricing in, 78
loss aversion, 268, 742
lowflation, 940–941
LRATC. See long-run average total cost curve (LRATC)
lump-sum taxes, 205, 829
luxuries, price elasticity of demand and, 172
lysine market, 419, 420

M

Macroeconomic Advisers, 43, 649
macroeconomic equilibrium
 long-run, 806–809
 short-run, 802–803
macroeconomic policy activism, 978
macroeconomic policy, 19–20
 development of focus on, 609–610
 inflation and. See inflation
 stabilization, 810–813
 unemployment and. See unemployment
macroeconomic questions, 608–609
macroeconomics, 3–4, 607

asset prices and, 743–744
business cycle and. See business cycle
inflation and deflation and. See deflation; hyperinflation; inflation
international imbalances and, 621–623
long-run economic growth and. See long-run economic growth
origins of, 608, 615
Maddison, Angus, 618, 695
Maduro, Nicolas, 140
Maersk, 814
Malthus, Thomas, 336, 693–694, 706
M1 and M2 monetary aggregates, 857–858, 890, 893–894
manufacturing, German, 561
Mao Zedong, 125
Marcellus gas fields, 465
marginal analysis, 9, 255–263
 marginal benefit and. See marginal benefit entries
 marginal cost and. See marginal cost(s)
 profit-maximizing principle of, 261
 profit-maximizing quantity of output and, 362–364
 uses of, 262–263
 utility-maximizing principle of, 293–294, 576
marginal benefit, 258–259, 292
 decreasing, 258
 environmental policies and, 475–477
marginal benefit curve, 258
 pollution and, 475–476
marginal cost(s), 256–258, 292, 337–339, 349
 constant, 257
 decreasing, 257, 258
 goods nonrival in consumption and, 491
 increasing, 256, 258
 monopolistic competition vs. perfect competition and, 455
 social and individual, of common resources, 500
 total cost vs., 258
marginal cost curve, 341–342
 slope of, 343–344
marginal decisions, 9
marginal dollar, 290–294
marginally attached workers, 658
marginal product, 331–333
marginal productivity theory of income distribution, 543, 551–553, 555–563
 discrimination and, 561–562
 efficiency wages and, 560–561
 market power and, 559–560
 markets for land and capital and, 553–554
 wage disparities in practice and, 557
 wage inequality and, 558–559, 562–563
marginal product of labor (MPL), 331–333

equilibrium value of, 553
value of, 546–550
marginal propensity to consume (MPC), 752–753, 754, 756–757
marginal propensity to save (MPS), 752
marginal rate of substitution (MRS), 308–311
 constant, 317
 diminishing, 310–311
 prices and, 313–314
 undefined, 318
marginal revenue, 362
 monopoly and, 393–397
marginal revenue curve, 363
marginal social benefit (MSB), 494–496
 of preserved farmland, 479–480
marginal social benefit of pollution, 467
marginal social cost (MSC), 456, 479
marginal social cost of common resources, 500
marginal social cost of pollution, 467
marginal tax rates, 207, 210
marginal utility, 282, 283, 309
 diminishing, 283–285
 substitution effect and, 294–295
marginal utility curve, 283
marginal utility per dollar, 290–295
 optimal consumption and, 292–293
Margo, Robert, 520
market(s)
 black, price ceilings and, 139
 capital, 38
 competitive. See competitive markets
 for concert tickets, 89–90
 efficiency and. See efficiency
 entry and exit. See entry; exit
 factor, 38
 for fashion models, 94
 financial. See financial markets
 for goods and services, 38
 housing. See housing
 inefficient, 124
 interrelatedness of, 122
 for land and capital, 553–554
 for loanable funds. See loanable funds market
 monopsonist, 405
 perfectly competitive, 358
 for secondhand textbooks, 103
market basket, 644
 price indexes and, 644–645
market-clearing price, 86
market demand curve, 76
market economy, 2, 5, 122–125
 amount of pollution produced in, 468–469
 economic signals and, 123–124
 property rights and, 123
market equilibrium, 69, 86
 long-run, 374–375
 shift of demand curve and, 91–92

short-run, 373–374, 375–376
market failure, 3, 16, 121, 124
 side effects and, 465
market labor demand curve,
 552–553
market power, 420
 advertising and, 457
 marginal productivity theory
 of income distribution
 and, 559–560
market price, 87–89
 above equilibrium price, 88
 below equilibrium price,
 88–89
 short-run production decision
 and, 369
markets
 federal funds, 870
 financial, 631
**markets for goods and ser-
 vices,** 38
market share, 359, 421
market structures, 385, 386–387.
 See also monopolistic
 competition; monopoly;
 oligopoly; perfect com-
 petition
 Herfindahl-Hirschman Index
 and, 421
market supply curve, 83–84
market timing, 743
Mars Canada, 425
Marshall, Alfred, 1, 4, 284
maturity transformation, 950
maximum, 58–59
MBSs. *See* mortgage-backed
 securities (MBSs)
McAfee, Andrew, 695
McDonald's, 75, 177, 298, 445,
 459, 600
 hamburger prices and inflation and. *See* deflation;
 inflation
mean household income,
 517–518
means-tested programs, 522–
 523, 528, 535
Medallion Financial, 154
median household income,
 517–518
Medicaid, 511, 521, 527–528,
 533–534, 821, 830
medical care. *See* Affordable
 Care Act (ACA); health
 care; health insurance
Medicare, 205, 210, 511, 521,
 527–528, 821
 implicit liabilities due to, 841,
 842
Medici family, 492
medium of exchange, 855
Mendelsohn, Robert, 471
mental accounting, 268
menu costs, 673
 of inflation, 673–674, 677
**merchandise trade balance
 (trade balance),** 1000
Merck, 391
Mexico
 clothing exports of, 37
 international trade of, 218
 money and inflation in, 909
 oil market and, 432
 real GDP per capita in, 695
 unemployment in, 668

microeconomic questions, 608
 theory and policy and,
 609–610
 whole as greater than sum of
 its parts and, 609
microeconomics, 3, 607
Microsoft, 390, 482, 483–484,
 721, 735
middlemen, 86
midpoint method, 164–165
Milan, congestion pricing in, 78
minimum, 58–59
minimum average total cost,
 342, 367
minimum-cost output, 342,
 364–365, 456
minimum wage, 141, 144, 145
 structural unemployment and,
 665–666
 unpaid internships and,
 146–147
Mississippi River, public projects
 and, 498–499
MLS. *See* Multiple Listing
 Service (MLS)
Mobil, 402, 434
mobile coupons, 379
models, 25–49
 circular-flow diagram as,
 37–39
 comparative advantage as,
 33–37
 economists' disagreements
 and, 41–43
 economists in business world
 and government and,
 43–44
 efficiency-wage, 560–561
 financial crisis of 2008–2009
 and, 26
 Heckscher-Ohlin model, 224–
 225, 232–233
 illustrating with graphs, 51.
 See also graphs
 positive vs. normative economics and, 40–41
 of price ceilings, 133–134
 production possibilities frontier as, 27–33
 of rational consumer. *See*
 marginal utility;
 rational consumer;
 utility
 Ricardian, of international
 trade, 219–223
 supply and demand. *See*
 demand curve; demand
 schedule; supply and
 demand model; supply
 curve; supply schedule
 tax, 26
Momek, 538
monetarism, 980
monetary aggregates, 857–858,
 890, 893–894
monetary base, 867–868
monetary incentives, to improve
 academic performance,
 10
monetary neutrality, 908,
 909–910
monetary policy, 610, 655,
 889–914
 aggregate demand and,
 901–906

changes in interest rate and,
 in long run, 908–909
 contractionary, 901–902
 demand for money and,
 890–895
 effectiveness of, 905–906
 expansionary, 901
 increase in, short- and long-
 run effects of, 906–908
 interest rates and, 895–900
 monetary neutrality and, 908,
 909–910
 shifts of the aggregate
 demand curve and, 790,
 791
 Taylor rule for, 903
monetary policy rule, 982
monetization
 of debt, 922
money, 854–859
 classical model of the price
 level and, 920–922
 commodity, 856
 commodity-backed, 856–857,
 859
 counterfeiting of, 842, 853
 definition of, 854–855
 fiat. *See* fiat money
 opportunity cost of holding,
 890–892
 printing of, 942
 roles of, 855–856
 supply of. *See* money supply
money demand curve, 892–894
 shifts of, 893–894
money multiplier, 866
 in reality, 867–869
 reserves and bank deposits
 and, 866–867
money supply, 620, 854, 864–
 869
 bank creation of money and,
 864–866
 changes in, interest rate in
 long run and, 908–909
 components of, 857
 increase in, short- and long-
 run effects of, 906–908
 measuring, 857–858
 money multiplier in reality
 and, 867–869
 reserves, bank deposits, and
 money multiplier and,
 866–867
money supply curve, 896
monopolist(s), 124, 385, 387
 demand curve of, 393–397
 profit-maximizing output and
 price and, 397–398
 profit of, 398–399
 single-price, 407
monopolistic competition, 386,
 420, 445–447, 449–457
 differentiated products in. *See*
 product differentiation
 free exit and entry under, 447
 inefficiency of, 456–457
 in long run, 451–453
 number of producers in, 446
 perfect competition vs.,
 455–457
 in short run, 450–451
 monopolization, 482
monopoly, 376, 385, 386,
 387–406

antitrust policies and, 402
 effects of, 387–388
 lack of supply curve for, 398
 legal, 360
 natural. *See* natural
 monopoly
 perfect competition vs., 398
 price discrimination and. *See*
 price discrimination
 profit maximization under,
 393–400
 public policy and, 400–407
 reasons for, 389–393
 welfare effects of, 401–402
monopsonists, 405
monopsony, 405
Monsanto, 424
Montgomery Ward
 business cycle and, 624
moral hazard, 597, 599–600
Morgan, J. P., 876
Morgan Stanley, 43, 911
mortgage-backed securities
 (MBSs), 602
 financial crisis of 2008–2009
 and, 26
mortgages
 defaulting on, 269–270
 inflation and, 675
 rates, consumer demand and,
 296–297
Moscow, congestion pricing
 in, 78
**movement along the demand
 curve,** 72
**movement along the supply
 curve,** 80–81, 91
movie industry, zero-profit equilibrium and, 453
MPL. *See* marginal product of
 labor (MPL)
MRS. *See* marginal rate of substitution (MRS)
MSB. *See* marginal social benefit
 (MSB)
MSC. See marginal social cost
 (MSC)
M3 monetary aggregate, 857,
 894
Mugabe, Robert, 925
Mullainathan, Sendhil, 562
Muller, Nicholas Z., 471
Multiple Listing Service (MLS),
 454
multiplier, 751, 752–755,
 827–831
 algebraic derivation of, 781
 austerity and, 830–831
 changes in government
 transfers and taxes and,
 828–829
 increase in government purchases of goods and ser-
 vices and, 827–828
 money. *See* money multiplier
 tax effects on, 829–830
 taxes and, 851–852
multiyear projects, present value
 of, calculating, 278–279
Mumbai, India, rent control in,
 138
Murstein, Andrew, 154
mutual funds, 735–736
The Mythical Man-Month
 (Brooks), 336–337

N

NAFTA. *See* North American Free Trade Agreement (NAFTA)
Nash, John, 428
Nash equilibrium, 428
Nasonex, 391
national accounts, 630–639
circular-flow diagram and, 630–633
creating, 639
gross domestic product and, 633–639
National Association of Realtors, 454
National Bureau of Economic Research (NBER), 613, 614
National Football League, 504–505
National Income, 1929–35, 639
national income and product accounts, 630. *See also* national accounts
national savings, 719
national security argument for trade protection, 238
natural gas industry, 389
boom and, 67–68
change in price and, 69, 73, 77–78
Hurricane Katrina and, 67, 92
natural monopoly, 389, 402–407, 503
inefficiency caused by, 402–403
public ownership as solution to, 403
regulation as solution to, 403–407
natural rate hypothesis, 983
natural rate of unemployment, 662–671
changes in, 668–670
cyclical unemployment and, 667
frictional unemployment and, 663–664, 670
job creation and job destruction and, 662–663
long-run Phillips curve and, 936
structural unemployment and, 665–667, 670–671
natural resources
long-run economic growth and, 693–694, 706–707
NBC News, 147
near moneys, 857–858
necessities, price elasticity of demand and, 172
negative demand shocks, 809
negative externalities, 465, 709
pollution as. *See* pollution
private solutions to, 469–470
negative income tax, 522–523
negative relationships, 54
negative supply shocks, 804, 805, 810
Nestlé Canada, 425
net capital inflow, 719–720
net exports, 638
Netflix, 491–492, 503

Netherlands
GDP per capita and well-being in, 642
unemployment and inflation in, 934
unemployment in, 668
network externalities, 349, 390, 481–484
external benefits of, 481–483
Microsoft Windows and, 483–484
new classical macroeconomics, 985
New Growth Theory, 699–700
new Keynesian economics, 985
New Mexico Airlines, 421
News Corporation, 485
New York City
rent control in, 131, 132–133, 136
taxi medallions in, 131, 147–148, 151–152, 154
New York Clearinghouse, 876
New Zealand
apple exports of, 224
cap and trade system in, 477
entrepreneurship in, 538
individual transferable quotas in, 502
inflation targeting in, 904
unemployment in, 668
Nexium, 391
Nicaragua
hyperinflation in, 919
Nigeria
natural resources of, 693
real GDP per capita in, 701–702, 703–704
Nintendo, 421
Nissan, 421
nominal GDP, 641
real GDP versus, in Venezuela, 643
nominal interest rate, 675
long-term, 891
real interest rate versus, 728
nominal wages, 793
average, 794
changes in, shifts of the short-run aggregate supply curve and, 796–797
nonaccelerating inflation rate of unemployment (NAIRU), 935
long-run Phillips curve and, 935–936
noncooperative behavior, 424
noncooperative equilibrium, 428
nonexcludable goods, 490
nonlinear curves, 56–58
nonlinear relationships, 53
nonprice competition, 437
nonrival in consumption, 490
marginal cost and, 491
Nordhaus, William, 471
normal goods, 74–75, 175, 296, 321
normalization
of measure of aggregate price level, 644
normative economics, 40–41
North American Free Trade Agreement (NAFTA), 239

Northern Rock, 864
Norway
congestion pricing in, 78
entrepreneurship in, 538
income inequality in, 515
net public debt of, 838
unemployment in, 668
notches, 535
Nozick, Robert, 513
numerical graphs, 60–64
interpreting, 62–64
types of, 60–62

O

Obama, Barack, 67, 68, 569, 819, 877
Obamacare. *See* Affordable Care Act (ACA)
Obama stimulus. *See* American Recovery and Reconstruction Act of 2009
Occupy Wall Street movement, 536
oceans, individual transferable quotas and, 502–503
offshore outsourcing, 240, 241
Ogallala Aquifer, 501
oil
Norway's exports of, 838
price controls on, 132
real price of, 706, 707
as source of wealth, 693
U.S. consumption of, economic growth and, 707–708
oil prices
container-shipping industry and, 814
economic problems caused by rises in, 783, 784
nominal wage in 1970s and, 796–797
recessions caused by rise in, 809–810
short-run Phillips curve and, 933
Okun, Arthur, 928
Okun's law, 928
Old River Control Structure, 498
oligopolists, 388, 420
oligopoly, 376, 386, 419–444
airline industry as, 407
collusion and competition and, 423–424
duopoly example of, 422–423
importance of, 437–438
increasing returns to scale and, 420
legal framework of, 433–435
prevalence of, 420–422
price leadership and, 437
price wars and, 435–436, 438–439
prisoner's dilemma and, 426–431
product differentiation and, 436–437
repeated interaction and, 429–431
tacit collusion and, 429–431, 435–436
Olive Garden, 75
Olson, Mancur, 496
omitted variables, 63–64
one-child policy, 10–11

one-price strategy, at J.C. Penney, 271
one-year projects, present value of, calculating, 277–278
OPEC. *See* Organization of Petroleum Exporting Countries (OPEC)
open economy, 621
savings-investment spending identity in, 719–721
open-market operations, 869, 871–873
opportunities, changes in, shifts of labor supply curve and, 567
opportunity cost, 7–8, 111–112, 250, 285, 377
choice of education vs. work and, 249, 250–252
constant, 30
of holding money, 890–892
increasing, 30
misperceptions of, 267
production possibilities frontier and, 30–31
of reducing pollution, 467
of taxi medallions, 151
optimal consumption, marginal utility per dollar and, 292–293
optimal consumption bundle, 287–289, 312
optimal consumption rule, 307, 314, 564
optimal output rule, 362–364
of price-taking firms, 362–364, 547
optimal quantity, 260
optimal time allocation rule, 576
order fulfillment technology, 351
ordinary goods, 307, 311
organ(s), for transplant, supply of, 110, 117–118
Organization for Economic Cooperation and Development (OECD)
natural unemployment around, 668
Organization of Petroleum Exporting Countries (OPEC), 423
rise and fall of, 431–432
origin, 52
O'Rourke, Kevin, 610
Oslo, Norway, congestion pricing in, 78
other things equal assumption, 27, 70, 74, 296
outlet stores, 412
output
aggregate. *See also* real GDP
minimum-cost, 342, 364–365
potential, 799
production function and, 330–337
output gap, 809
unemployment rate and, 926–928. *See* Phillips curve; short-run Phillips curve
outsourcing, offshore, 240, 241
overconfidence, 267–268, 742
overfishing, individual transferable quotas and, 502–503
overuse, 499–501

OXFAM, 332
oysters, diminishing marginal utility and, 284–285

P

PacAdvantage, 527
Pacific Investment Management Company (PIMCO), 911
pajama republics, 37
Pakistan
    arms race with India, 429
    cotton production in, 95
    share of income spent on food, 176
    voter turnout in, 496
panic buying, 95
Panic of 1907, 876, 877
paradox of thrift, 609, 772–773
ParkAtMyHouse, 122
patents, 391–392, 700
Patient Protection and Affordable Care Act. *See* Affordable Care Act (ACA)
Paulson, John, 742
pauper labor fallacy, 223, 224
payoff, 426–427
payoff matrix, 426–427
payroll taxes, 206. *See also* Federal Insurance Contribution Act (FICA) tax
pay-to-delay tactic, 360–361
Penny Pinchin' Mom, 271
pension funds, 736
Pepsi, 68, 420
perfect competition, 357–380, 386
    definition of, 358
    free entry and exit under, 359–360, 370
    monopolistic competition vs., 455–457
    monopoly vs., 398
    necessary conditions for, 358–359
    optimal output rule and, 362–364
    profitability and production conditions under, 361–372
perfect complements, 318
    industry supply curve and, 372–378
perfectly competitive industries, 358
perfectly competitive markets, 358
    prices in, 793
perfectly elastic demand, 167, 394
perfectly elastic supply, 179, 376
perfectly inelastic demand, 166
perfectly inelastic supply, 179
perfect price discrimination, 410–412
perfect substitutes, 316–318
perfume industry, advertising and, 459–460
Pfizer, 468, 480
pharmaceutical industry
    global price differences and, 391
    monopoly and, 391

"pay-to-delay" tactic in, 360–361
Phelps, Edmund, 931
Phillips, A. W. H., 928
Phillips curve
    in Great Recession, 933–934
    long-run, 934–936
physical assets, 263, 731
physical capital, 544, 718
    definition of, 720
    diminishing returns to, 690–691, 692
    growth in productivity and, 689
    size of stock of, shifts of the aggregate demand curve and, 789–790
pie charts, 62
Pigou, A. C., 474
Pigouvian subsidies, 480
Pigouvian taxes, 474, 501–502
Pioneer Hi-Bred International, 424
Pizza Hut, 601
planned aggregate spending, 767
    income-expenditure model and, 767–768
planned economies, 2, 125
planned investment spending, 762
poaching, 556
point method of calculating slope, 58
Poland
    unemployment in, 668
political business cycle, 983
political stability
    economic growth and, 700, 704
politics
    correlation of political events with risks and, 595
    of trade protection, 238–239
    of welfare state, 535–536
pollution, 467–469
    amount produced in a market economy, 468–469
    emissions taxes and, 473–474
    environmental policies compared and, 475–477
    environmental standards and, 472–473
    external costs and, 466, 471
    fracking and, 465
    marginal social benefit of, 467
    marginal social cost of, 467
    socially optimal quantity of, 467–468
    tradable emissions permits and, 474–475, 477–478
pooling, 594
population, changes in, shifts of labor supply curve and, 566–567
population growth
    standard of living and, 693–694, 706
portion sizes
    global comparison of, 261
    of snack foods, 294
Portugal
    budget deficit in, 835–836
    GDP per capita and well-being in, 642

government debt of, 839
net public debt of, 838
unemployment and inflation in, 934
positive economics, 40–41
positive externalities, 466, 478–481, 497
    preserved farmland as, 479–480
    in today's economy, 480
positive feedback, 482
positively correlated events, 595
positive relationships, 54
positive supply shocks, 804, 805
Post Foods, 359, 420
potential output, 799
poverty, 514–517
    causes of, 516
    consequences of, 516–517
    cycle of, 480–481
    health insurance and, 528–529
    incidence of, 515–516
    reducing, 513
    social benefit of alleviating, 513
    trends in, 514–515
    war on, 513
    welfare state effects on, 523–524
poverty programs, 512
poverty rate, 514–515
poverty threshold, 514
PPF. *See* production possibility frontier (PPF)
preferences
    changes in, shifts of labor supply curve and, 566
    consumer choice and, 315–316
    risk aversion and, 587
premiums, 525–526, 531, 583, 587–588
present value, 277–279, 723
    of multiyear projects, calculating, 278–279
    of one-year project, calculating, 277–278
    of projects with revenues and costs, 279
price(s)
    of ambulance rides, 161–162
    of assets. *See* asset prices
    break-even, 367
    brick-and-mortar retailer survival and, 379
    buying vs. selling, 86
    changes in. *See* price changes
    commodity, changes in, shifts of the short-run aggregate supply curve and, 796, 797
    congestion pricing and, 78
    demand, 148–150
    equilibrium. *See* equilibrium price
    excise taxes and, 188–191
    expected changes in, change in demand and, 75
    factor, wage rate as, 232, 543
    imperfectly versus imperfectly competitive markets, 793
    of land, world trade in agriculture in 19th century and, 233–234
    marginal rate of substitution and, 313–314

market. *See* market price
market-clearing, 86
monopolistic competition vs. perfect competition and, 455–456
monopoly and, 397–398
received vs. paid, 86
relative, 222, 313
shut-down, 368–370
single-price monopolists and, 407
supply, 148–150
unresponsive, 161–162
willingness to pay and, 104–107
world, 228–229
price ceilings, 131, 132–141
    inefficiency caused by, 134–139
    modeling, 133–134
    on monopolists, 403
    quantities and, 143
    reasons for, 139
price changes
    consumer surplus and, 107–110
    expected, change in demand and, 75
    of goods, shifts of factor demand curve and, 550
    increases, consumer choice and, 319–320
    producer surplus and, 114–116
    shift of demand curve and, 74
    shift of supply curve and, 81–82
    time elapsed since, price elasticity of demand and, 172–173
price controls, 132. *See also* price ceilings; price floors
    consumer surplus and producer surplus and, 136
    inefficient allocation and, 136–137
price discrimination, 391, 392, 407–413
    elasticity and, 409–410
    perfect, 410–412
price effect, monopoly and, 395, 396, 424
price elasticity of demand, 162–163, 181
    along demand curve, 171–172
    calculating, 162–165
    classifying, 166–174
    estimating, 165
    factors determining, 172–173
    tax incidence and, 191–193
price elasticity of supply, 162, 177–180, 181
    factors determining, 179–180
    measuring, 178–179
    tax incidence and, 191–193
price fixing, 419
    globalization and, 434
price floors, 131, 132, 141–147
    European farm surpluses and, 180
    inefficiency caused by, 143–145
    quantities and, 143
    reasons for, 146

price indexes, 629, 643–648
  CPI, 645–646
  market baskets and, 644–645
  PPI, 646
price leadership, 437
price levels. *See also* inflation
  rate
  aggregate. *See* aggregate price
    level
  inflation and, 671–672. *See
    also* deflation; inflation
Priceline.com, 21
price regulation, 403–405
price stability, 620, 811–812, 902
price-taking consumers, 358.
    See also perfect competi-
    tion
**price-taking firm's optimal
  output rule,** 362–364,
  547
price-taking producers,
  358. *See also* perfect
  competition
price wars, 436, 438–439
prime rate, 792
**principle of diminishing mar-
  ginal utility,** 283–285
**principle of "either-or" deci-
  sion making,** 252–253
prisoners' dilemma, 426–429
private goods, 489, 490–493
  characteristics of, 490–491
  efficient supply of, 491–492
private health insurance,
  525–526
private information, 124, 581,
  591, 596–601
  adverse selection and, 597–598
  moral hazard and, 599–600
private investment
  crowding out of, by govern-
    ment borrowing, 824
private savings, 631
  changes in, shifts of supply
    of loanable funds and,
    727–728
producer(s)
  changes in number of, shifts
    of the supply curve and,
    83–84
  excise tax paid mainly by,
    price elasticities and,
    192–193
  number of, market structure
    and, 386
  price-taking, 358. *See also* per-
    fect competition
producer price index (PPI),
  646
producer surplus, 103, 111–116
  cost and, 111–114
  export effects on, 230–231
  gains from trade and, 116–117
  import effects on, 229–230
  individual, 112
  price changes and, 114–116
  price controls and, 136
  tariffs and, 235
  total, 112–113
product(s). *See also* goods
  standardized, 359, 360
product differentiation, 386,
  445, 446, 447–449,
  457–460
  advertising and, 457–458

brand names and, 458–459
  by location, 448
  oligopoly and, 436–437
  by quality, 448
  by style or type, 447–448
production
  complements in, 82
  costs of, efficiency in long-run
    equilibrium and, 377
  efficiency in, 29
  inefficiently low, 491
  just-in-time, 45
  profitability of, 364–367
  substitutes in, 82, 85
production capacity
  investment spending and,
    763–764
production decision, short-run,
  367–370
production function, 329,
  330–337
  aggregate, 689–693
  cost curves and, 334–336
  inputs and outputs and,
    330–333
**production possibility frontier
  (PPF),** 27–33
  comparative advantage and,
    219–221
  economic growth and, 31–33
  efficiency and, 29
  opportunity cost and, 30–31
productivity, 688
  changes in, shifts of the short-
    run aggregate supply
    curve and, 797
  international comparison of,
    223
  long-run economic growth
    and, 688–689
  total factor, 693
profit
  accounting, 250, 251–252, 364
  in competitive markets, 96
  economic, 250, 251–252, 253,
    364, 365, 367
  of monopolists, 398–399
  during recessions, 614
  profitability, of production,
    364–367
**profit-maximizing principle of
  marginal analysis,** 261,
  362–364
profit-maximizing quantity of
  output
  marginal analysis to choose,
    362–364
  for monopoly, 397–398
profits taxes, 206
progressive taxes, 207
Propecia, 391
property rights, 123, 502
  economic growth and, 700,
    704
property taxes, 206
proportional taxes, 206
protection, 234. *See also* trade
  protection.
public debt, 838
public goods, 124, 204, 489,
  493–499
  amount to be provided,
    494–497
  cost-benefit analysis of provid-
    ing, 497–498

European move from mayhem
  to Renaissance and,
  492–493
  funding of public projects
    and, 498–499
  provision of, 493–494
  voting as, 496
public ownership, 403
public policy, monopoly and,
  400–407
Puerto Rico, entrepreneurship
  in, 538
purchases
  government, of goods and ser-
    vices, 632
purchasing power
  inflation and. *See* inflation
purchasing power parity, 1013

Q

Quaker Oats Company, 359, 420
Qualcomm, 468
quality
  inefficiently high, price floors
    and, 144–145
  inefficiently low, price floors
    and, 138–139
  product differentiation by,
    448
quantitative easing, 940–941
quantity
  excise taxes and, 188–191
  inefficiently low, price floors
    and, 135
  optimal, 260
  price ceilings and price floors
    and, 143
quantity controls, 147–153
  anatomy of, 148–151
  costs of, 151–152
quantity demanded, 69
  demand vs., 72
quantity effect, monopoly and,
  395, 396, 424
quantity supplied, 79
quantity traded, changing, gains
  from trade and, 119–121
quota(s), 148. *See also* quantity
  controls
  for crab, 152–153
  import, 236–237
quota limits, 148
quota rent, 150–151
quota share, 153

R

Race Against the Machine
  (Brynjolfsson and
  McAfee), 695
racial discrimination, poverty
  and, 516
railroads, 433
random variables, 582
random walk, 743
rational, 265
rational consumer, 281–302
  budget constraints and budget
    lines and, 285–287
  default on mortgages and,
    269–270
  income effect and, 295–297
  optimal consumption choice
    and, 287–290
  utility and. *See* marginal util-
    ity; utility

rational decision makers,
  265–266
rational expectations, 985
rational expectations model,
  985
rationality, bounded, 266
rationing, during World War II,
  110–111
Rawls, John, 513
Reagan, Ronald, 197, 210
real business cycle theory,
  986
real estate commissions, housing
  bust and, 454
real exchange rates, 1011
real GDP, 640–643
  calculating, 640–641
  changes in, shifts of money
    demand curve and, 894
  future, expected, investment
    spending and, 763–764
  income-expenditure model
    and, 767–768
  nominal GDP versus, in
    Venezuela, 643
  per capita, 684–686. *See also*
    economic growth; GDP
    per capita; long-run eco-
    nomic growth
real GDP per capita
  growth rates of, 686–687
real incomes, 672
real interest rate, 675
  nominal interest rate versus,
    728
real wage, 672
recessionary gaps, 807–808
recessions, 3–4, 19, 20
  babysitting cooperative in, 20
  definition of, 614
  double-dip, 809
  "growth," 661
  investment spending and,
    773–774
  of 1979–1980 and 1981–1982,
    809
  pain of, 613–614
  of 2001 and 2007–2009, com-
    pared, 616
  of 2007–2009. *See* Great
    Recession, 2007–2009
  unemployment during,
    659–660
recessionary gap, 806
Reconstruction Finance
  Corporation (RFC), 877
recoveries. *See* expansions
Recovery Act. *See* American
  Recovery and
  Reinvestment Act
Redfin.com, 454
regressive taxes, 207
regulation
  antitrust, global comparison
    of, 434
  of banks, 862–863
  deregulation of electricity and,
    399–400
  of high-speed Internet access,
    406–407
  price, 403–405
  as solution to natural monop-
    oly, 403–407
Regulation Q, 877, 878
regulatory capture, 406

related goods. See complements; substitutes
relative price(s), 313, 314, 320
gains from trade and, 222
relative price rule, 313–314
Relay-Rides, 122
relevant range, 284
rent, quota, 150–151
rental rate, 554
rent control, 131
in Mumbai, India, 138
in New York City, 132–133, 136, 139
repeated interaction, 429–431
Republican Party, 187
reputation, 598
research and development (R&D), 697
economic growth and, 696–697
government subsidies to, 699
research clusters, 480
Research Triangle (North Carolina), 480
reserve ratio, 861
reserve requirements, 863
resources, 6
common. See common resources
efficient use of, 15–16
scarce. See scarce resources
wasted. See wasted resources
retained earnings, 763
retirement, employee decisions about investing in 401(k) funds and, 268–269
returns to scale, 348–349
increasing, 389
revaluation, 1021
revenue
from excise taxes, 194–195
marginal. See marginal revenue
present value of projects with, 279
tax rates and, 195–197
total, price elasticity of demand and, 167–170
reverse causality, 64
rhinos, legalized hunting of, 506
Rhodes, Cecil, 387, 392, 393
Ricardian equivalence, 825
Ricardian model of international trade, 219–223
Ricardo, David, 234, 825
Rio Tinto, 421
risk, 581, 582–596
capital at risk and, 589–590
diversification and, 581, 589, 592–595
efficient allocation of, 590–591
financial, 582–583, 732–733
of franchises, 600–601
insurance and, 596
pooling of risks and, 594
positively correlated, 595
trading, 589–591
warranties and, 588
risk-averse people, 584–586
risk aversion, 266, 582–588, 733
diminishing marginal utility and, 583
expectations and uncertainty and, 582–583
gambling and, 587

logic of, 583–587
paying to avoid risk and, 587–588
risk-neutral, 586
risk-neutral people, 586
rival in consumption, 490
robots, order fulfillment using, 351
rock concert promotion, 126
Rockefeller, John D., 402, 433, 876
Romer, Christina, 905, 906
Romer, David, 905, 906
Romer, Paul, 699–700
Roosevelt, Franklin Delano, 210, 523, 859, 863
bank holiday declared by, 877
Rule of 70, 686, 693
rule of the road, 14
Russia
economy of, 125
wheat yield of, 332

S
Sachs, Jeffrey, 704
Saez, Emmanuel, 42
safeguard mechanism, 240
Saks Fifth Avenue, 351
sales
inefficient allocation among sellers, 144
price discrimination and, 412
reallocation among sellers, 119
SaleSorter (app), 379
sales taxes, 206, 208, 211
Samoa, rule of the road in, 14
Samsung, 420, 421
San Francisco 49ers, 504–505
satiety, 287
Saudi Arabia
oil exports of, 225
oil market and, 432
trade surplus of, 621
savings
economic growth and, 696
marginal propensity to save and, 752
private, 631
savings and loans, 878
savings-investment spending identity, 718–721
actual versus desired investment spending and, 721
in closed economy, 718–719
in open economy, 719–721
scale, returns to, 348–349
scarce resources, 6–7
artificially scarce goods and, 124, 503–505
monopoly and, 389
opportunity cost and. See opportunity cost
scatter diagrams, 61–62
SCC. See social cost of carbon (SCC)
Schick, 461
SCHIP, 516
Schumpeter, Joseph, 611
screening, 598
Sears, Roebuck and Co., 624
seasonal demand, shut down and, 369–370
Second Industrial Revolution, 694

Secret Service, 853
securities, 26, 602
loan-backed, 734–735
securitization, 734, 880
seignorage, 923, 924, 942
self-correcting economy, 808, 809, 810
self-regulating economy, 610
sellers
competition among, product differentiation and, 448
inefficient allocation of sales among, 144
Sen, Amartya, 11
server farms, 717
services
final. See final goods and services
government purchases of, 632
as inputs. See inputs
markets for, 38
severe weather. See also Hurricane entries
correlation with other risks, 595
sewer systems
in London, 489
as public good, 493
shadow bank, 950
shares, 593
sharing economy, 121–122
Sherman Antitrust Act of 1890, 434
shifts of aggregate demand
short-run effects of, 803–804
shifts of demand
for loanable funds, 726–727
shifts of supply
of loanable funds, 727–728
shifts of the aggregate demand curve, 788–790, 822
shifts of the demand curve, 70–78, 91–92
shifts of the money demand curve, 893–894
shifts of the short-run aggregate supply curve, 795–797, 804–806
shifts of the supply curve, 80–85, 92–93
Shiller, Robert, 742
Shindell, Robert, 146
shoe-leather costs of inflation, 673, 677
shopping apps, 379
shortages, 86–87
of housing in New York City, 131
market price and, 88–89
in wine market, 378
short run, 330
monopolistic competition in, 450–451
short-run aggregate supply curve, 792, 793–797
movement to long-run aggregate supply curve from, 800–801
shifts of, 795–797
short-run costs, long-run costs vs., 345–354
short-run equilibrium aggregate output, 803
short-run equilibrium aggregate price level, 803

short-run individual supply curve, 369
short-run industry supply curve, 372–373
short-run macroeconomic equilibrium, 802–803
short-run market equilibrium, 373–374, 375–376
short-run Phillips curve, 928–933
aggregate supply curve and, 930
inflation expectations and, 931–933
supply shocks and, 929, 931, 933
short-run production decision, 367–370
short-term interest rate, 891–892
showrooming, 379
shrimp
Thai production of, 219, 222, 224, 240
Vietnamese production of, 219, 222, 224, 240
shut-down price, 368–370
side effects, market failure and, 465
signaling, 598
Singapore
congestion pricing in, 78
economic growth in, 702
GDP per capita and well-being in, 642
voter turnout in, 496
single-payer system, 529
single-price monopolists, 407
Skype, 482
Sloan, Alfred P., 449
slope, 54–59
arc method of calculating, 56–58
constant, 30
negative, increasing and decreasing, 56, 57
point method of calculating, 58
positive, increasing and decreasing, 56, 57
Slovak Republic
high-speed Internet access in, 407
unemployment in, 668
Slovenia, high-speed Internet access in, 407
SMART Grid technologies, 344–345
smartphone industry, 217, 219–223, 420
Smith, Adam, 2, 3, 12–13, 856, 857
smog
in Los Angeles, 709
SNAP. See Supplemental Nutrition Assistance Program (SNAP)
Snapchat, 485
SnapGoods, 122
snowclearing equipment, 350
social benefit
marginal. See marginal social benefit
of poverty reduction and access to health care, 513

social cost(s), marginal, of common resources, 500
social cost of carbon (SCC), 471
social insurance, 821
social insurance programs, 512–513
social insurance taxes, 820
socially optimal quantity of pollution, 467–468
social media, 485
social norms, changes in, shifts of labor supply curve and, 566
Social Security, 205, 210, 511, 521, 523, 821
  implicit liabilities due to, 841–843
  indexing of, to CPI, 647–648
  trust fund, 842–843
society
  loss to, 135
  marginal benefit to, of saving a human life, 263
Solana, 845
solar power, 845
Solow, Robert, 701
South Africa
  drug prices in, 391
  money and inflation in, 909
  voter turnout in, 496
South America's Club, 412, 421
South Korea
  economic growth in, 738–739
  free-trade agreement with United States, 242–243
  gasoline consumption in, 71
  high-speed Internet access in, 407
  money and inflation in, 909
  real GDP per capita in, 701–703
  smartphone production and, 217
  taxes in, 209
  unemployment in, 668
Soviet Union, former
  arms race with United States and, 429
  command economy of, 2
  De Beers agreement with, 392
Sozzi, Brian, 438
Spain
  budget deficit in, 835–836
  economic growth in, 705
  GDP per capita and well-being in, 642
  government debt of, 839
  Great Recession and, 607
  net public debt of, 838
  trade surplus of, 622
  unemployment and inflation in, 934
  unemployment in, 668
Spain, drug prices in, 391
specialization, 12–13
  increasing returns to scale and, 349
spending
  aggregate. See aggregate spending
  consumer, 630. See consumer spending
  government policies and, 19–20
  income and, 18–19

income elasticity of demand and, 177
  inflation and, 19
  investment. See investment spending
spreading effect, 341
Sprint, 421
Sri Lanka
  clothing exports of, 37
  comparative advantage and, 39
stabilization policy, 810–813
stagflation, 784, 805, 933
standardized products, 359, 360
standard of living
  population growth and, 693–694, 706
  recessions and, 614
Standard Oil Company, 402, 433, 434
Standard Oil of New Jersey, 434
Standard Oil of New York, 434
Staples, 351
state of the world, 582
status quo bias, 268–269
sticky wages, 793, 794
  in Great Recession, 801–802
Stiglitz, Joseph, 819
stimulus package. See American Recovery and Reinvestment Act
Stockholm, congestion pricing in, 78
stock market, 593
stocks, 630, 735
  demand for, 739–741
  diversified portfolio of, 736
  market timing and, 743
Stokey, Nancy, 545
store of value, 856
strategic behavior, 429–431
structural unemployment, 665–667, 669, 670–671
StubHub, 90, 126
style, product differentiation by, 447–448
subprime lending, 879–880
subsidies
  agricultural, 240, 478, 480
  government, productivity and, 698–699
  Pigouvian, 480
substitutes, 74. See also marginal rate of substitution (MRS)
  changes in prices of, shifts of the demand curve and, 82
  imperfect, 447
  less than perfect, 319
  perfect, 316–318
  price elasticity of demand and, 172
  in production, 82, 85
substitution effect, 294–295, 297
  consumer choice and, 323–325
  labor supply and, 564–566, 568, 576–578
  wages and labor supply and, 568, 576–578
sugar industry, trade protection for, 238–239
sulfur dioxide, acid rain and, 467, 477, 478

summer jobs, decline of, 568
Sundararajan, Arun, 122
sunk costs, 263–265, 269–270
Supervalu, 425
Supplemental Nutrition Assistance Program (SNAP), 522
Supplemental Poverty Measure, 523–524
Supplemental Security Income program, 522
supply
  changes in, 90–96
  excess. See surpluses
  of labor. See labor supply; labor supply curve
  of loanable funds, 724–725
  of money. See money supply
  of natural gas, 67
  of organs for transplant, 110, 117–118
  of other factors, changes in, shifts of factor demand curve and, 550–551
  perfectly elastic, 179, 376
  perfectly inelastic, 179
  price elasticity of. See price elasticity of supply
supply and demand model, 67–97. See also demand; demand curve; demand schedule; supply; supply curve; supply schedule
  changes in supply and demand and, 90–96
  competitive markets and, 68, 96
  equilibrium and, 86–90
  key elements of, 68–69
supply curve, 79–90
  domestic, 228
  individual, 83, 369, 372
  industry. See industry supply curve
  for labor, shifts of, 566–568
  lack of, for monopoly, 398
  market, 83–84
  for money, 896
  movements along, 80–81, 91
  shifts of, 80–85, 92–93
  simultaneous shift of demand curve and, 93–94
  supply schedule and, 79–80
supply price, 148–150
supply schedule, 79–80
supply shocks, 784, 804–806
  demand shocks versus, 809–810
  macroeconomic policy and, 812
  negative, 804, 805, 810
  short-run Phillips curve and, 929, 931, 933
  of twenty-first century, 806
surge pricing, 97, 566
surpluses, 86
  budget, 719
  consumer. See consumer surplus
  market price and, 88
  producer. See producer surplus
  total, 117
  transfer of, 135
  in wine market, 378

Survey of Current Business, 639
sustainable long-run economic growth, 706
Sveriges Riksbank, 873
sweatshop labor fallacy, 223–224
Sweden
  entrepreneurship in, 538
  GDP per capita and well-being in, 642
  income inequality in, 515
  taxes in, 209
  unemployment in, 668
  work hours in, 567
Switzerland
  drug prices in, 391
  income inequality in, 515
  money and inflation in, 909
  unemployment in, 668
  watch production of, 225

T

T-accounts, 860–861
tacit collusion, 429–431, 435–436
Taco Bell, 600
Taiwan
  economic growth in, 702
TANF. See Temporary Assistance for Needy Families (TANF)
tangency condition, 311–312
tangent line, 58
Target, 379, 438
target federal funds rate, 895, 898–899, 900
tariffs, 234–236
  on tire imports to United States, 240
tastes, changes in, shift of demand curve and, 75
tax(es), 187–215
  changes in, multiplier effects of, 828–829
  consumption vs. income, 209
  costs of taxation and, 198–200
  deadweight loss of, 200–203
  dedicated, 842
  effect on multiplier, 829–830
  emissions, 473–474
  equity vs. efficiency trade-off and, 204–205
  estate, 208
  excise. See excise taxes
  fairness of, 203–204
  federal, principle underlying, 205–206
  FICA. See Federal Insurance Contribution Act (FICA) tax
  fiscal policy and, 820–821
  flat, 206
  incidence of, 190–194
  income. See income taxes
  inflation, 922–923
  international comparison of, 209
  lump-sum, 205, 829
  multiplier and, 851–852
  payroll, 206
  Pigouvian, 474, 501–502
  profits, 206
  progressive, 207, 209
  proportional, 206
  regressive, 207, 209–210
  sales, 206, 208, 211

social insurance, 820
value-added, 42, 209
wealth, 206
welfare state and, 534–535
tax base, 206
tax competition, 209
tax models, 26
tax rates
French, Laffer curve and, 197
marginal, 207, 210
revenue and, 195–197
in United States, 208
tax structure, 206–207
of income tax, 205–206
taxis
medallions in New York City, 131, 147–148, 154
rainy days and, 566
Uber as alternative to, 97, 566
Taylor, John, 903
Taylor rule for monetary policy, 903
technological change
in banking, shifts of money demand curve and, 894
natural rate of unemployment and, 670
technological progress, 689
economic growth and, 712
exogenous versus endogenous sources of, 699–700
productivity growth and, 689, 692–693
technology, 32
cell phone. See cell phones; iPhone; smartphone industry
changes in, shifts of factor demand curve and, 551
changes in, shifts of supply curve and, 82
comparative advantage and, 224, 225–226
Internet and. See Internet
monopoly and, 389–390
order fulfillment, 351
SMART Grid, 344–345
technology spillovers, 480
TEC/TVC ratio, 471
TED spread, 881
Temporary Assistance for Needy Families (TANF), 521, 522
temporary employment, 670, 678
textbooks, secondhand, market in, 103
textiles, U.S. import quotas on, 237
Thailand, shrimp production of, 219, 222, 224, 240
TheFind (app), 379
A Theory of Justice (Rawls), 513
A Theory of the Consumption Function (Friedman), 759–760
Thoma, Mark, 44
Ticketmaster, 126
TicketsNow, 126
time. *See also* long run; short run
decision making when time is a factor, present value and, 277–279
elapsed since a price change, price elasticity of demand and, 172–173

limited, 6
price elasticity of supply and, 179–180
time allocation, 564
time allocation budget line, 575–576
time lags
in fiscal policy, 825–826
time-series graphs, 60–61
Time Warner Cable, 405, 407
tires, U.S. import tariffs on, 240
tit for tat strategy, 430–431
T-Mobile, 421, 422
Tognum, 561
total catch quota system, 152
total consumer surplus, 106
total cost, 334–336, 339, 349. *See also* average total cost (ATC)
total cost curve, 335–336
total factor productivity, 693
total producer surplus, 112–113
total product curve, 330–331
change in levels of inputs and, 333–334
total revenue, 167–170
total surplus, 117
total utility, 282, 288
toy industry, price wars and, 438–439
Toyota, 421, 663
Toys "R" Us, 438
A Tract on Monetary Reform (Keynes), 811
tradable emissions permits, 474–475, 477–478
trade, 12. *See also* international trade
free, 234
gains from. *See* gains from trade
trade balance, 1000
trade deficits, 621
trade-off(s), 8–9
between tax fairness and tax efficiency, 203–206
between work and leisure, 563–564, 575–576
trade-off between equity and efficiency, 205–206
welfare state and, 534
trade protection, 234–243
arguments for, 238
challenges to globalization and, 240–242
import quotas as, 236–237
international trade agreements and World Trade Organization and, 239–240, 242–243
politics of, 238–239
tariffs as, 234–236
in United States, 237
trade surpluses, 621
traffic congestion
congestion pricing and, 78
as overuse of a common resource, 500
transaction costs, 470, 732
transfers, of surplus, 135
Transonic Wind Tunnel, 25
transparency
inflation targeting and, 904
travel industry, Priceline.com and, 21

Treasury bills
interest on, 873
truncation, 63
trusts, 433
tuition, raising, effect of, 173–174
Tumblr, 485
Turkey
inflation in, 920
money and inflation in, 909
trusts
Panic of 1907 and, 876
Tversky, Amos, 265, 269
Twitter, 485
two-part tariffs, 412
two-variable graphs, 51–53
type, product differentiation by, 447–448

U

U-6, 658
Uber, 97, 566
Uganda, wheat yield of, 332
uncertainty
insurance and, 587
risk and, 582–583
underemployment, 658
unemployment, 656–671
budget deficit and, 833
cyclical, 667. *See* cyclical unemployment
definition of, 656
duration of, 664
frictional, 663–664, 670
growth and, 659–661
measuring, 656–657
natural rate of. *See* natural rate of unemployment
among new graduates, 661–662
during recessions, 613–614
structural, 665–667, 670–671, 679
in United States, 1979–2014, 659–660
unemployment insurance, 523
unemployment rate, 657
natural. *See* natural rate of unemployment
output gap and, 926–928. *See* Phillips curve; short-run Phillips curve
significance of, 657–659
in United States, 1948–2014, 656
in United States, 1949–2013, 660–661
unions, 559–560
German, 561
structural unemployment and, 669
wage differences and, 559–560
unit(s), of labor, 333
unit of account, 856
United Kingdom
disinflation in, 936
drug prices in, 391
economic growth in, 700–701
gasoline consumption in, 71
GDP per capita and well-being in, 642
health care in, 529–530
high-speed Internet access in, 407
income inequality in, 515
minimum wage in, 145

net public debt of, 838
public ownership in, 403
taxes in, 209
television programming in, 494–495
unemployment in, 668
voter turnout in, 496
welfare state in, 535
work hours in, 567
United Network for Organ Sharing (UNOS), 110, 117–118
United States. *See also* Federal *entries*
antitrust regulation in, 434
arms race with Soviet Union and, 429
auto industry in, 45, 226
banking system in. *See* banking system, U.S.
budget deficits of, 840–841
cap and trade system in, 477
deflation in, 676
disinflation in, 936, 937–938
drug prices in, 391
economic growth in, 684, 705
economic inequality in, 517, 519–521
entrepreneurship in, 538
factor distribution of income in, 545–546
free-trade agreement with South Korea, 242–243
gasoline consumption in, 71
GDP per capita and well-being in, 60–61, 642
government debt of, 840–841
government size in, 820
government spending in, 821
Great Depression in. *See* Great Depression
Great Recession, 2007–2009 in. *See* Great Recession, 2007–2009
health care in, 529–530
high-speed Internet access in, 407
housing bubble in, 744–745, 751, 754–755, 765–766
income distribution in, 517–518, 519–521
inflation in, 674, 919
interest rates in, 730–731
international trade of, 218
litigation with De Beers, 392
long-run economic growth in, 617–618
market economy of. *See* market economies
medical device exports of, 225
minimum wage in, 145
money and inflation in, 909
negative income tax in, 522–523
net public debt of, 838
oil consumption and economic growth of, 707–708
as open economy, 621
per capita greenhouse gas emissions in, 473
poverty in, 514–515, 516
productivity and wages in, 223
productivity growth in, 693
productivity in, 698
public ownership in, 403

"quantitative easing" in, 940–941
quantity of currency in circulation in, 855
real GDP per capita in, 685
recessions in, 3–4, 524–525
regulation of natural monopolies in, 403
rule of the road in, 14
savings-investment spending identity in, 720–721
share of income spent on food, 176
smartphone production and, 217, 219–223, 222–223
supply shocks of twenty-first century and, 806
taxes in, 208, 209
trade deficit of, 621
trade protection in, 237
unemployment in, 668
unemployment rate in, 1948–2014, 656
unemployment rate in, 1949–2013, 660–661
unemployment rate in, 1979–2014, 659–660
voter turnout in, 496
welfare state in, 521–525, 535
wheat yield of, 332
work hours in, 567
U.S. Census Bureau
unemployed defined by, 656
U.S. International Trade Commission, 237
U.S. Justice Department, 421
U.S. Postal Service, 403
unit-elastic demand, 167, 170
unit-free measure, elasticity as, 175
unit of account
money as, 856
unit-of-account costs, 674
UNOS. See United Network for Organ Sharing (UNOS)
unpaid interns, 146–147
unplanned inventory investment, 764
US Airways, 420
U-shaped average total cost curve, 340
util(s), 282
utilities. See also electricity; natural gas industry
as natural monopolies, 389
utility, 281, 282–285
consumption and, 282
expected, 583
marginal. See marginal utility
total, 288
utility function, 282, 303–307. See also indifference curve(s)
utility-maximizing principle of marginal analysis, 293–294, 576
Uzbekistan, per capita greenhouse gas emissions in, 473

V

value
absolute. See absolute value
in diversity, product differentiation and, 448
expected, 582

imputed, in gross domestic product, 635
money as store of, 856
present. See present value
value added, 635
value-added taxes (VAT), 42, 209
value of the marginal product, 546–550
value of the marginal product curve, 548–550
factor demand and, 548–550
value plays, 461
variable(s), 51
dependent, 52–53
independent, 52–53
omitted, 63–64
random, 582
variable costs, 334, 349
average, 340–341, 349
short-run production decision and, 368–369
variable inputs, 330
VAT. See value-added taxes (VAT)
velocity of money, 982
Venezuela
price controls in, 140
real versus nominal GDP in, 643
Verizon, 421
vertical axis, 52
vertical curves, 55–56
vertical intercept, 54
Veterans Health Administration, 528
veterinary services, substitutes in production and, 85
vicious cycle of deleveraging, 879
Vietnam
clothing exports of, 37
shrimp production of, 219, 222, 224, 240
Vincent, Lou, 511
Virgin Atlantic, 440
volume discounts, 411
voting, as public good, 496

W

wage(s)
compensating differentials and, 558
efficiency, 560–561
efficiency, structural unemployment and, 667
as factor prices, 232, 543
gender-wage gap and, 559
higher education and, 543
international comparison of, 223
international inequality of, 241
international trade and, 232–233
marginal productivity theory of income distribution and. See marginal productivity theory of income distribution
minimum. See minimum wage
nominal. See nominal wages
real, 672
sticky. See sticky wages
unions and, 559–560, 561
world trade in agriculture in 19th century and, 233–234

wage rate
as factor price, 232
higher, effect of, 576–578
Walgreens, 351
Wall Street reform and Consumer Protection Act, 881
Walmart, 244, 271, 379, 438, 569, 624
war on poverty, 513
warranties, 588
Washington, George, 2, 187
wasted resources, 137
price controls and, 137–138
price floors and, 144
wasteful duplication, monopolistic competition and, 456
water pollution. See pollution
wealth, 731
aggregate, changes in, aggregate consumption function and, 760
changes in, shifts of aggregate demand curve and, 789, 790
changes in, shifts of labor supply curve and, 567
risk aversion and, 587
wealth effect of a change in the aggregate price level, 786, 789
Wealth of Nations, The (Smith), 2, 12–13, 856, 857
wealth taxes, 206
weather, severe. See also Hurricane entries
correlation with other risks, 595
web browsers, 482, 483–484
wedge, 150
Weight Watchers plan, 288
welfare effects of monopoly, 401–402, 404–405
welfare state, 511–541
cost of, 534–535
economic inequality and, 515, 517–521, 536
economic insecurity and, 519
effects on poverty and inequality, 523–524
French, 536–537
in Great Recession, 524–525
health care and. See health care
justice and, 513
logic of, 512–513
means-tested programs for, 522–523
Norwegian, 538
politics of, 535–536
poverty and. See poverty
problems with, 534–535
Social Security and, 523
in United States, 521–525
well-being
and GDP per capita, 642
Wendy's, 298, 445, 600
Western Europe. See also specific countries
income inequality in, 515
Whiskey Rebellion, 187, 204
white buffalo, legalized hunting of, 506
Whole Foods, 421, 883
wholesale price index, 646

wildlife hunting, legalized, 506
Wild Oats, 421
willingness to pay, 104–107
Williston, North Dakota, fracking and population of, 544
wine market, glut and shortage in, 378
Wolfe, Chris, 485
work. See employment; labor entries
Works Progress Administration (WPA), 830
World Bank, 43
world price, 228–229
World Trade Organization (WTO), 239, 241
World War I, German invasion of France and, 253
World War II
government debt from, 841
Normandy invasion and, 253
price ceilings during, 132
price indexes during, 647
rationing during, 110–111
Wright, Wilbur and Orville, 25
Wright Flyer, 25
WTO. See World Trade Organization (WTO)

X

x-axis, 52
Xoma, 264–265

Y

y-axis, 52
Yellen, Janet, 655, 908–909
Yost, Ashley, 501
youth employment, decline of summer jobs and, 568
Yunus, Mohammed, 746

Z

Zany Brainy, 438
zero bound, 938
zero interest rate policy (ZIRP), 940
zero lower bound for interest rates, 905
zero-profit equilibrium, 452–453
Zillow.com, 454
Zimbabwe
hyperinflation in, 674, 919, 925
Zuckerberg, Mark, 8

Applications in Economics

Continued from inside front cover

CHAPTER	CHAPTER-OPENING STORIES	GLOBAL COMPARISONS
21: Macroeconomics: The Big Picture, 607	**21:** NEW: The Pain in Spain, 607	**21:** NEW: Slumps Across the Atlantic, 615
22: GDP and the CPI: Tracking the Macroeconomy, 629	**22:** The New #2, 629	**22:** GDP and the Meaning of Life, 642
23: Unemployment and Inflation, 655	**23:** NEW: Hitting the Braking Point, 655	**23:** Natural Unemployment Around the OECD, 668
24: Long-Run Economic Growth, 683	**24:** NEW: Airpocalypse Now, 683	**24:** NEW: What's the Matter with Italy? 698
25: Savings, Investment Spending, and the Financial System, 717	**25:** Funds for Facebook, 717	**25:** NEW: Bonds Versus Banks, 737
26: Income and Expenditure, 751	**26:** From Boom to Bust, 751	
27: Aggregate Demand and Aggregate Supply, 783	**27:** NEW: What Kind of Shock?, 783	**27:** Supply Shocks of the Twenty-first Century, 806
28: Fiscal Policy, 819	**28:** How Big Is Big Enough?, 819	**28:** The American Way of Debt, 838
29: Money, Banking, and the Federal Reserve System, 853	**29:** NEW: Funny Money, 853	**29:** The Big Moneys, 855
30: Monetary Policy, 889	**30:** NEW: The Most Powerful Person in Government, 889	**30:** Inflation Targets, 904
31: Inflation, Disinflation, and Deflation, 919	**31:** Bringing a Suitcase to the Bank, 919	**31:** Disinflation Around the World, 936
32: Crises and Consequences, 947	**32:** From Purveyor of Dry Goods to Destroyer of Worlds, 947	
33: Macroeconomics: Events and Ideas, 973	**33:** A Tale of Two Slumps, 973	
34: Open-Economy Macroeconomics, 997	**34:** Switzerland Doesn't Want Your Money, 997	**34:** Big Surpluses, 1003

WORLD VIEW